Connect™ Accountin...

Instructors...

Q Want to **streamline** lesson planning, student progress reporting, and assignment grading? (Less time planning means more time teaching...)

Need to **collect data and generate reports** required by accreditation organizations, such as AACSB and AICPA? (Say goodbye to manually tracking student learning outcomes...)

Want an **instant view** of student or class performance relative to learning objectives? (No more wondering if students understand...)

A With **McGraw-Hill Connect™ Accounting,**

INSTRUCTORS GET

- The ability to **post assignments** and other communication between students and instructors.

- Simple **assignment management**, allowing you to spend more time teaching.

- **Auto-graded homework.**

- **Customized course gradebook** where grades are automatically posted.

- **Online testing capability**.

- A **progress-tracking** function that allows you to easily assign materials that conform to AACSB and AICPA standards.

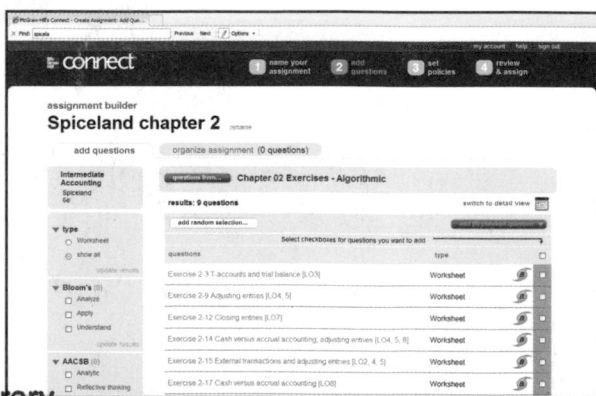

Want an online, **searchable version** of your textbook?

Wish your textbook could be available online while you're doing your homework?

Connect™ Plus Accounting eBook

If your instructor has chosen to use *Connect™ Plus Accounting*, you have an affordable and searchable online version of your book integrated with your other online homework tools.

Connect™ Plus Accounting eBook offers features like:

- topic search
- adjustable text size
- jump to page number
- print by section

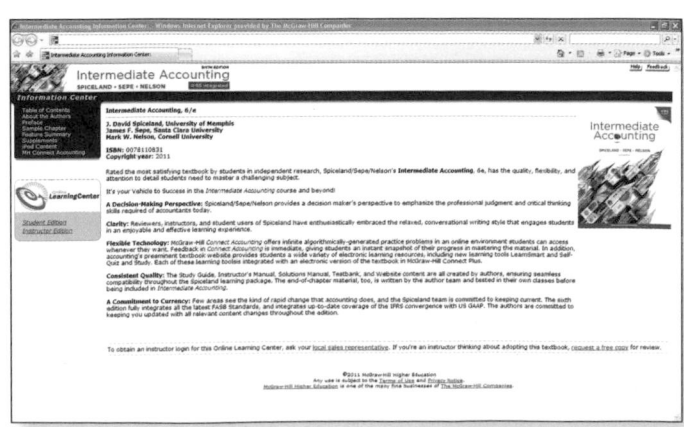

Want to get more **value** from your textbook purchase?

Think learning accounting should be a little bit more **interesting**?

Check out the companion website for this textbook www.mhhe.com/spiceland6e

We put it there for you. Go online for test tips and practice problems whenever you study. The companion website for this book includes **quizzes, PowerPoints, and Internet activities** to help you study. Get more from your textbook—use the Online Learning Center.

Intermediate Accounting

Intermediate Accounting

SIXTH EDITION

J. DAVID SPICELAND
University of Memphis

JAMES F. SEPE
Santa Clara University

MARK W. NELSON
Cornell University

McGraw-Hill Irwin

INTERMEDIATE ACCOUNTING

Published by McGraw-Hill/Irwin, a business unit of The McGraw-Hill Companies, Inc., 1221 Avenue of the Americas, New York, NY, 10020. Copyright 2011, 2009, 2007, 2004, 2001, 1998 by The McGraw-Hill Companies, Inc. All rights reserved. No part of this publication may be reproduced or distributed in any form or by any means, or stored in a database or retrieval system, without the prior written consent of The McGraw-Hill Companies, Inc., including, but not limited to, in any network or other electronic storage or transmission, or broadcast for distance learning.

Some ancillaries, including electronic and print components, may not be available to customers outside the United States.

This book is printed on acid-free paper.

1 2 3 4 5 6 7 8 9 0 DOW/DOW 1 0 9 8 7 6 5 4 3 2 1 0

ISBN-13: 978-0-07-811083-2 (combined edition)
ISBN-10: 0-07-811083-1 (combined edition)
ISBN-13: 978-0-07-732891-7 (volume 1)
ISBN-10: 0-07-732891-4 (volume 1)
ISBN-13: 978-0-07-732890-0 (volume 2)
ISBN-10: 0-07-732890-6 (volume 2)

Vice president and editor-in-chief: *Brent Gordon*
Editorial director: *Stewart Mattson*
Publisher: *Tim Vertovec*
Senior sponsoring editor: *Dana L. Woo*
Director of development: *Ann Torbert*
Senior development editor: *Daryl Horrocks*
Vice president and director of marketing: *Robin J. Zwettler*
Marketing director: *Sankha Basu*
Marketing manager: *Michelle Heaster*
Vice president of editing, design, and production: *Sesha Bolisetty*
Lead project manager: *Pat Frederickson*
Senior production supervisor: *Debra R. Sylvester*
Design manager: *Laurie Entringer*
Senior photo research coordinator: *Jeremy Cheshareck*
Photo researcher: *Allison Grimes*
Lead media project manager: *Kerry Bowler*
Cover designer: *Heidi Baughman*
Cover photo credit: © *Ian McKinnell Getty Images*
Typeface: *10.5/12 Times Lt Std-Roman*
Compositor: *Laserwords Private Limited*
Printer: *R. R. Donnelley*

Library of Congress Cataloging-in-Publication Data

Spiceland, J. David, 1949-
    Intermediate accounting/J. David Spiceland, James F. Sepe, Mark Nelson.—6th ed.
      p. cm.
    Includes index.
    ISBN-13: 978-0-07-811083-2 (combined edition: alk. paper)
    ISBN-10: 0-07-811083-1 (combined edition: alk. paper)
    ISBN-13: 978-0-07-732891-7 (volume 1: alk. paper)
    ISBN-10: 0-07-732891-4 (volume 1: alk. paper)
    [etc.]
    1. Accounting. I. Sepe, James F. II. Nelson, Mark (Mark W.) III. Title.
HF5636.S773 2011
657'.044—dc22
                                                        2010000003

www.mhhe.com

Dedicated to:

David's wife Charlene, daughters Denise and Jessica, and sons Michael David, Michael, and David
Jim's wife Barbara, children Kristina, Matt, and Dave, son-in-law Bob and daughter-in-law Donna, and granddaughters Kaitlyn and Meghan
Mark's wife Cathy, daughters Lizzie and Clara, and parents Mary and Richard H. Nelson

About the Authors

DAVID SPICELAND

David Spiceland is professor of accounting at the University of Memphis, where he teaches intermediate accounting and other financial accounting courses at the undergraduate and master's levels. He received his BS degree in finance from the University of Tennessee, his MBA from Southern Illinois University, and his PhD in accounting from the University of Arkansas. Professor Spiceland's primary research interests are in earnings management and educational research. He has published articles in a variety of journals including *The Accounting Review, Accounting and Business Research, Journal of Financial Research,* and *Journal of Accounting Education.* David has received university and college awards and recognition for his teaching, research, and technological innovations in the classroom.

JIM SEPE

Jim Sepe is an associate professor of accounting at Santa Clara University where he teaches primarily intermediate accounting in both the undergraduate and graduate programs. He previously taught at California Poly State University–San Luis Obispo and the University of Washington and has visited at Stanford University and the Rome campus of Loyola University of Chicago.

Professor Sepe received his BS from Santa Clara University, MBA from the University of California–Berkeley, and PhD from the University of Washington. His research interests concern financial reporting issues and the use of financial information by capital markets. He has published in *The Accounting Review,* the *Journal of Business Finance and Accounting, Financial Management,* the *Journal of Forensic Accounting,* the *Journal of Applied Business Research,* and the *Journal of Accounting Education.* He is a past recipient of the American Accounting Association's Competitive Manuscript Award and has served as a member of the editorial board of *The Accounting Review.*

Jim has received numerous awards for his teaching excellence and innovations in the classroom, including Santa Clara University's Brutocao Award for Excellence in Curriculum Innovation.

MARK NELSON

Mark Nelson is the Eleanora and George Landew Professor of Accounting at Cornell University's Johnson Graduate School of Management, where he teaches intermediate accounting at the MBA level. He received his BBA degree from Iowa State University and his MA and PhD degrees from Ohio State University. Professor Nelson has won teaching awards at Ohio State and Cornell, including three of the Johnson School's Apple Award for Teaching Excellence.

Professor Nelson's research is focused on decision making in financial accounting and auditing. His research has been published in *The Accounting Review,* the *Journal of Accounting Research, Contemporary Accounting Research, Accounting Organizations and Society, Auditing: A Journal of Practice and Theory,* and several other journals. He has won the American Accounting Association's Notable Contribution to Accounting Literature Award, and also the AAA's Wildman Medal for work judged to make the most significant contribution to the advancement of the public practice of accountancy. He has served three times as an editor or associate editor of *The Accounting Review,* and serves on the editorial boards of several journals. Professor Nelson also served for four years on the FASB's Financial Accounting Standards Advisory Council.

Thank You

The authors and McGraw-Hill's *Intermediate Accounting* team thank Larry Tomassini for his many contributions to the book over the last few editions. Larry is an innovator in the use of technology to tutor students, most notably through his creation of Coach. We wish him the best of luck in his future endeavors!

Your Vehicle to Success

As your students embark on their professional careers, they will be challenged to think critically and make good decisions. This new edition of *Intermediate Accounting* has been designed to ensure that your students' careers soar to the greatest heights—to be their vehicle to success!

Intermediate Accounting is the work not just of its talented authors but of the more than 175 faculty reviewers who shared their insights, experience, and opinions with us. Our reviewers helped us to build *Intermediate Accounting* into the vehicle that can propel your students to success in their accounting course.

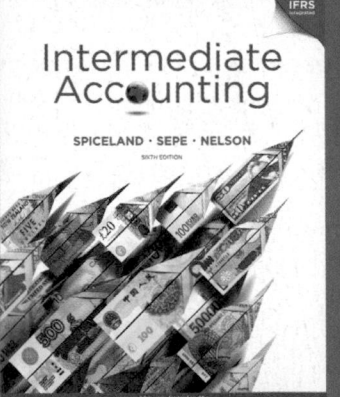

Our development process began in the summer of 2008, when we received the first of what would become more than 175 in-depth reviews of *Intermediate Accounting*. A blend of Spiceland users and non-users, these reviewers explained how they use textbooks in their teaching, and many answered detailed questions about every one of Spiceland's 21 chapters. And the work of improving *Intermediate Accounting* is ongoing—even now, we're scheduling new symposia and reviewers' conferences to collect even more opinions from faculty.

Intermediate Accounting was designed from the start to be not simply a textbook, but a complete learning system, encompassing the textbook, key ancillaries, and online content, all of which are written by authors Spiceland, Sepe, and Nelson. The *Intermediate Accounting* learning system is built around five key attributes:

in Intermediate Accounting

① **Clarity:** Reviewers, instructors, and students all have hailed *Intermediate Accounting*'s ability to explain both simple and complex topics in language that is clear and approachable. Its highly acclaimed conversational writing style establishes a friendly dialogue between the text and each individual student. So readable is Spiceland that we've even received letters from students who bought the book themselves—despite their instructors using competing books in the course!

② **A Decision-Making Perspective:** Recent events have focused public attention on the key role of accounting in providing information useful to decision makers. The CPA exam, too, is redirecting its focus to emphasize the professional skills needed to critically evaluate accounting method alternatives. *Intermediate Accounting* provides a decision maker's perspective to emphasize the professional judgment and critical thinking skills required of accountants today.

③ **Flexible Technology:** Today's accounting students have come of age in a digital world, and Spiceland's Learning System reflects that trend through its comprehensive technology package. The sixth edition contains even more technology features than the previous editions of Spiceland's Learning System, featuring: McGraw-Hill *Connect Accounting*, Self-Quiz and Study, LearnSmart self-study technology, and Tegrity Campus. See pages xii, xiii and xvii for more details!

④ **Consistent Quality:** The *Intermediate Accounting* author team ensures seamless compatibility throughout the Spiceland learning package by writing every major supplement themselves: Study Guide, Instructor's Resource Manual, Solutions Manual, Testbank, and website content are all created by authors Spiceland, Sepe, and Nelson. The end-of-chapter material, too, is written by the author team and tested in their classrooms before being included in *Intermediate Accounting*.

⑤ **A Commitment to Currency:** Few disciplines see the rapid change that accounting experiences, and the Spiceland team is committed to keeping your course up to date. The sixth edition fully integrates the latest FASB standards, including SFAS No. 168, "*The FASB Accounting Standards Codification*™ *and the Hierarchy of Generally Accepted Accounting Principles—a replacement of FASB Statement No. 162*"; SFAS No. 166, "Accounting for Transfers of Financial Assets—an Amendment of FASB Statement No. 140"; SFAS No. 165, "Subsequent Events"; and FSP No.'s 115-2 and 124-2, "Recognition and Presentation of Other-Than-Temporary Impairments."

"The best available text for the intermediate accounting courses at both the graduate and undergraduate level."

—Gerard M. Engeholm,
Pace University

"An excellent textbook that covers accounting procedures thoroughly from a real-world perspective. It is very current and is accompanied by a great variety of learning aids to help students succeed."

—Kathy Hsiao Yu Hsu,
University of Louisiana–Lafayette

"When someone other than the authors prepares the [end-of-chapter material] they generally do not mirror the material that is presented in the chapters and they contain quite a few errors."

—Gloria Worthy, Southwest
Tennessee Community College

"Overall, I find the Spiceland end-of-chapter material far superior to that in Kieso in terms of quantity, especially as it relates to the diversity of the problem material."

—Chula King,
University of West Florida

What Stands Out in the Sixth Edition?

The United States is moving rapidly toward converging U.S. GAAP with the **International Financial Reporting Standards (IFRS)** that are followed by most of the rest of the world. Therefore, a premier intermediate text must not only offer thorough coverage of U.S. GAAP, but also provide clear coverage of key differences between U.S. GAAP and IFRS with end-of-chapter assignment material to test student understanding of those differences. In light of this need, we have made the following changes for the sixth edition:

(1) Updated our overview of the background and current status of the convergence process in Chapter 1.

(2) Expanded our IFRS coverage significantly. This coverage is integrated with text content by including boxes at appropriate points in each chapter, allowing instructors to identify key differences between U.S. GAAP and IFRS as they so choose and discuss those differences in the context of the chapter topics. Many of these "IFRS boxes" now include numerical illustrations demonstrating the differences from U.S. GAAP, providing comparative illustrations, and showing real world examples.

> **"Provides up to date material on many topics, for example IFRS. Students will find it easy to follow and to find examples in working homework."**
>
> —*Terry G. Elliott,*
> *Morehead State University*

(3) Expanded and revised end-of-chapter assignment materials to provide extensively more opportunities for students to apply their knowledge of IFRS and the differences between IFRS and U.S. GAAP. IFRS assignments are included in end-of-chapter questions, brief exercises, exercises, problems and cases. The Testbank also contains many new IFRS items for most chapters.

(4) To provide students the experience of considering a set of IFRS-based financial statements from an all-inclusive perspective, we added the **Comprehensive British Airways Case.** That case has questions appearing as Broaden Your Perspective cases in most of the text's chapters, allowing instructors to discuss IFRS and U.S. GAAP differences in the context of a single IFRS-based financial reporting setting. For instructors who prefer to cover IFRS on fewer days in a more concentrated fashion, the British Airways Case questions are repeated in Appendix C but divided into six broad topical classifications to permit coverage in logical groupings during the course.

BRITISH AIRWAYS

Revising a book as successful as **Intermediate Accounting** takes careful consideration and a strong vision of what a textbook should be. New features aren't piled on for their own sake; the Spiceland team only implements changes that constitute real improvements that have been identified through extensive research with users. The result is a book that never loses its original strengths as it gains in usefulness and flexibility with each revision.

WHERE WE'RE HEADED

● LO12

The FASB and IASB are working together on a standard that would have a dramatic impact on the format of financial statements.

The FASB and IASB are working together on a project, Financial Statement Presentation, to establish a common standard for presenting information in the financial statements, including classifying and displaying line items and aggregating line items into subtotals and totals. This standard will have a dramatic impact on the format of financial statements. An important part of the proposal involves the organization of elements of the balance sheet (statement of financial position), statement of comprehensive income (including the income statement), and statement of cash flows (SCF) into a common set of classifications.

The FASB and IASB (International Accounting Standards Board) have set a June 2011 target date for the completion of 11 major joint projects that are intended to improve the standards of both Boards while further aligning U.S. GAAP and IFRS. We have placed **Where We're Headed** boxes throughout the text to describe the potential financial reporting effects of many of these projects or of other pronouncements by the Boards. Because an unprecedented concentration of major changes is scheduled to occur in an unusually short time frame, not only do we feel that these carefully delineated descriptions of not-yet-GAAP potentialities are warranted, but that it would be a disservice to students to ignore them.

If your school has paid for a site license of the Academic Accounting Access Program, faculty and students will have free access to the FASB Codification. Check with your accounting department to determine if your school has registered for this program. All of the features available with the Professional View version (http://asc.fasb.org) are included with the Academic Accounting Access Program.

"Very well written in a streamlined 21 chapter approach with IFRS incorporated throughout and excellent end of chapter materials."

—Michael Slaubaugh, Indiana University/Purdue University

The **FASB Codification** became effective on July 1, 2009 and now represents the single source of authoritative nongovernmental U.S. GAAP, except for rules and interpretive releases of the SEC which remain also as sources of authoritative GAAP. All other literature is now nonauthoritative. Throughout the sixth edition, we use the new Accounting Standards Codification System (ASC) in footnotes when referencing generally accepted accounting principles (FASB ASC followed by the appropriate number). For ease of transition, each citation also includes a reference to the original accounting standard that is codified in ASC. End-of-chapter exercises and cases have been added that provide students with practice in researching the FASB's Accounting Standards Codification.

The **financial statements** and **disclosure notes** of Dell are included in Appendix B of the text. The statements and notes also are available through a link provided at the text website. These replace the Google statements packaged with the fifth edition. The Dell statements and notes are the basis for text references and cases in most chapters.

Market-Leading Technology

McGraw-Hill *Connect Accounting*

Less Managing. More Teaching. Greater Learning.

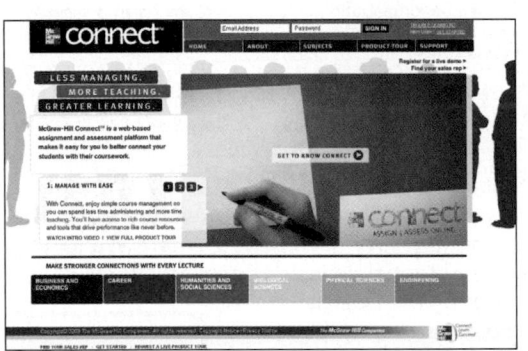

McGraw-Hill *Connect Accounting* is an online assignment and assessment solution that connects students with the tools and resources they'll need to achieve success.

McGraw-Hill *Connect Accounting* helps prepare students for their future by enabling faster learning, more efficient studying, and higher retention of knowledge.

McGraw-Hill *Connect Accounting* Features

Connect Accounting offers a number of powerful tools and features to make managing assignments easier, so faculty can spend more time teaching. With *Connect Accounting*, students can engage with their coursework anytime and anywhere, making the learning process more accessible and efficient. *Connect Accounting* offers you the features described on the next page.

Student Study Center

The *Connect Accounting* Student Study Center is the place for students to access additional resources. The Student Study Center:

- Offers students quick access to lectures, practice materials, eBooks, and more.
- Provides instant practice material and study questions, easily accessible on the go.
- Gives students access to the Self-Quiz and Study resource described on page xvii.

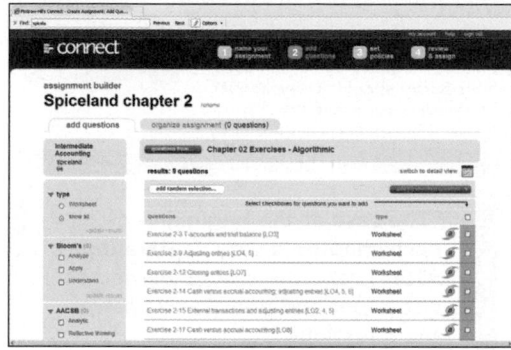

Simple Assignment Management

With *Connect Accounting,* creating assignments is easier than ever, so you can spend more time teaching and less time managing. The assignment management function enables you to:

- Create and deliver assignments easily with selectable end-of-chapter questions and test bank items.
- Streamline lesson planning, student progress reporting, and assignment grading to make classroom management more efficient than ever.
- Go paperless with the eBook and online submission and grading of student assignments.

Smart Grading

When it comes to studying, time is precious. *Connect Accounting* helps students learn more efficiently by providing feedback and practice material when they need it, where they need it. When it comes to teaching, your time also is precious. The grading function enables you to:

- Have assignments scored automatically, giving students immediate feedback on their work and side-by-side comparisons with correct answers.
- Access and review each response; manually change grades or leave comments for students to review.
- Reinforce classroom concepts with practice tests and instant quizzes.

Instructor Library

The *Connect Accounting* Instructor Library is your repository for additional resources to improve student engagement in and out of class. You can select and use any asset that enhances your lecture. The *Connect Accounting* Instructor Library includes:

- eBook
- PowerPoints

What Keeps Spiceland Users Coming Back?

Financial Reporting Cases

Each chapter opens with a Financial Reporting Case that places the student in the role of the decision maker, engaging the student in an interesting situation related to the accounting issues to come. Then, the cases pose questions of the student in the role of decision maker. Marginal notations throughout the chapter point out locations where each question is addressed. Finally, the questions are answered at the end of the chapter.

FINANCIAL REPORTING CASE SOLUTION

1. **How would you explain restructuring costs and its negative amount in 2009 to Becky? Are restructuring costs something Becky should worry about?** *(p. 177)* Restructuring costs include employee severance and termination benefits plus other costs associated with the shutdown or relocation of facilities or downsizing of operations. Certain restructuring costs must be estimated. The negative number in 2009 is a consequence of overestimating restructuring costs are not necessarily bad. In fact, the objective The costs are incurred now in hopes of better ear

2. **In addition to discontinued operations,** reported separately in the income

> "The case at the beginning of each chapter is very captivating. After I read the case, I wanted to get paper and pencil and answer the questions."
>
> —Carol Shaver,
> Louisiana Tech University

Decision Makers' Perspective

These sections appear throughout the text to illustrate how accounting information is put to work in today's firms. With the CPA exam placing greater focus on application of skills in realistic work settings, these discussions help your students gain an edge that will remain with them as they enter the workplace.

DECISION MAKERS' PERSPECTIVE

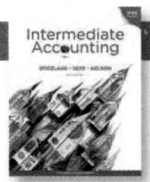

Cash often is referred to as a *nonearning* asset because it earns no interest. For this reason, managers invest idle cash in either cash equivalents or short-term investments, both of which provide a return. Management's goal is to hold the minimum amount of cash necessary to conduct normal business operations, meet its obligations, and take advantage of opportunities. Too much cash reduces profits through lost returns, while too little cash increases risk. This trade-off between risk and return is an ongoing choice made by management (internal decision makers). Whether the choice made is appropriate is an o by investors and creditors (external decision makers).

A company must have cash available for the compensating bala previous section as well as for planned disbursements related to n ing, and financing cash flows. However, because cash inflows and planned amounts, a company needs an additional cash cushion as

> "This is an excellent feature of the book. It is so important to know why and how information is used and not just memorizing the "right" answers."
>
> —Jeff Mankin, Lipscomb University

Star Problems

Star problems were a new feature in the fifth edition. These are problems (more than one-third new) in each chapter that are designated by a ★ to indicate that they are particularly challenging, requiring students to combine multiple concepts or requiring judgment beyond explicit explanation in chapter discussions.

> "The Star Problems are challenging—a good way to illustrate the more difficult concepts and calculations."
>
> —Kenneth R. Henry,
> Florida International University

In talking to so many intermediate accounting faculty, we heard more than how to improve the book—there was much, much more that both users and nonusers insisted we keep exactly as it was. Here are some of the features that have made Spiceland such a phenomenal success in its previous editions.

ADDITIONAL CONSIDERATION

We discuss in significant depth in Chapter 7 the problem of accounting for bad debts. However, bad debts related to receivables on s create a unique problem. The reason a comp reliably estimate bad debts. Therefore, the expense or create an allowance for uncollecti bad debts are dealt with implicitly by deferrin never is collected, the related deferred gros illustrate, assume that in the example describ collected the first payment but the customer Typically, the seller would repossess the item

> **"This is a good technique that I actually use in my class and it's good to see it in a book!"**
>
> —*Ramesh Narasimhan, Montclair State University*

Repossessed inventory		
Deferred gross profit		
Installment receivable		600,000

This entry removes the receivable and the remaining deferred gross profit and records the repossessed land in an inventory account. This example assumes that the repossessed land's current fair value is equal to the net receivable of $420,000. If the land's fair value at the date of repossession is less than $420,000, a loss on repossession is recorded (debited).

ETHICAL DILEMMA

The Precision Parts Corporation manufacture a profit every year since the company's ince accomplishment and believes one important plan that rewards top management a bonus *the operating income goal for the year is a* and prospects for attaining the income goal

Tony Smith, the company's chief financ December sales by an amount sufficient to year and earn bonuses for all top manageme parts to be shipped on January 15, 2012. To can get that order ready by December 31 e overtime. We can then just leave the order o wrong with recognizing the sale in 2011, si we do have a firm order from a reputable to ship goods f.o.b. destination and to recog the parts.

> **"Having ethical dilemma boxes in every chapter is much more significant than having a separate chapter devoted to ethics. Students can relate to the importance of being ethical in every aspect of business dealings."**
>
> —*Gloria Worthy, Southwest Tennessee Community College*

BROADEN YOUR PERSPECTIVE

Apply your critical-thinking ability to the knowledge you've gained. These cases will provide you an opportunity to develop your research, analysis, judgment, and communication skills. You also will work with other students, integrate what you've learned, apply it in real world situations, and consider its global and ethical ramifications. This practice will broaden your knowledge and further develop your decision-making abilities.

Ethics Case 6–1
Rate of return
● LO1

The Damon Investment Company manages a mutual fund composed mostly of speculative stocks. You recently saw an ad claiming that investments in the funds have been earning a rate of return of 21%. This rate seemed quite high so you called a friend who works for o figure was determined by dividing the two-ment. In other words, $100 invested in the f

Required:
Discuss the ethics of the 21% return claim

Analysis Case 6–2
Bonus alternatives:

Sally Hamilton has performed well as the earned a bonus. She has a choice among the

> **"I think students would benefit tremendously from the cases."**
>
> —*Joyce Njoroge, Drake University*

Additional Consideration Boxes

These are "on the spot" considerations of important, but incidental or infrequent aspects of the primary topics to which they relate. Their parenthetical nature, highlighted by enclosure in Additional Consideration boxes, helps maintain an appropriate level of rigor of topic coverage without sacrificing clarity of explanation.

Ethical Dilemmas

Because ethical ramifications of business decisions impact so many individuals as well as the core of our economy, Ethical Dilemmas are incorporated within the context of accounting issues as they are discussed. These features lend themselves very well to impromptu class discussions and debates.

Broaden Your Perspective Cases

Finish each chapter with these powerful and effective cases, a great way to reinforce and expand concepts learned in the chapter.

How Does Spiceland Help My Students

Online Learning Center (OLC)

www.mhhe.com/spiceland6e

Today's students are every bit as comfortable using a web browser as they are reading a printed book. That's why we offer an Online Learning Center (OLC) that follows **Intermediate Accounting** chapter by chapter. It doesn't require any building or maintenance on your part, and is ready to go the moment you and your students type in the URL.

As your students study, they can refer to the OLC website for such benefits as:

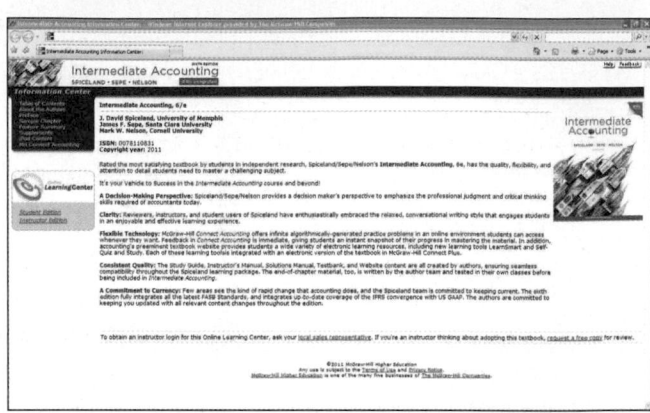

iPod content
Self-grading quizzes
Electronic flash cards
Audio narrated PowerPoints
Alternate exercises and problems

Check figures
Practice exams
FASB pronouncements, summaries and updates
Text updates

A secured Instructor Resource Center stores your essential course materials to save you prep time before class. The Instructor's Resource Manual, Solutions Manual, PowerPoint, and sample syllabi are now just a couple of clicks away. You will also find useful packaging information and transition notes.

CPA and CMA Review Questions

A **CPA and CMA Review Questions** section includes multiple choice questions used in the Kaplan CPA Review Course and focus on the key topics within each chapter, permitting quick and efficient reinforcement of those topics as well as conveying a sense of the way the topics are covered in the CPA exam. The CMA questions are adapted from questions that previously appeared on Certified Management Accountant (CMA) exams.

CPA AND CMA REVIEW QUESTIONS

CPA Exam Questions

The following questions are used in the Kaplan CPA Review Course to study current liabilities while preparing for the CPA examination. Determine the response that best completes the state[ments or] questions.

● LO3   1. On March 1, 2010, Fine Co. borrowed $10,000 and signed a two-year note bearing interest [...] compounded annually. Inte[rest is] payable in f[ull at] maturity on February 28, 2012. What a[...]

> **"Intermediate Accounting** is current, complete, well written, and highly detailed. It belongs in the library of anyone who is preparing for the CPA exam."
>
> —Barbara K. Parks, American Intercontinental University—Online

iPod Content

Harness the power of one of the most popular technology tools students use today—the Apple iPod®. Our innovative approach allows students to download audio and video presentations right into their iPod and take learning materials with them wherever they go.

Students just need to visit the Online Learning Center at **www.mhhe.com/spiceland6e** to download our iPod content. For each chapter of the book, they will be able to download audio narrated lecture presentations, slideshows and even self-quizzes designed for use on various versions of iPods.

Improve Their Performance?

CPA Simulations

Kaplan CPA Exam Simulations allow students to practice intermediate accounting concepts in a web-based environment similar to that used in the actual CPA exam. There will be no hesitation or confusion when your students sit for the real exam: they'll know exactly what they need to do.

Self-Quiz and Study

Self-Quiz and Study (SQS) resource in *Connect Accounting* connects each student to the learning resources needed for success in the course. For each chapter, students:

- Take a practice test to initiate the Self-Quiz and Study.
- Immediately upon completing the practice test, see how their performance compares to chapter learning objectives or content by sections within chapters.
- Receive a Self-Quiz and Study resource that recommends specific readings from the text, supplemental study material, and practice work that will improve their understanding and mastery of each learning objective.

Diagnostic and Adaptive Learning of Concepts: LearnSmart

Students want to make the best use of their study time. The LearnSmart adaptive self-study technology within *Connect Accounting* provides students with a seamless combination of practice, assessment, and remediation for every concept in the textbook. LearnSmart's intelligent software adapts to every student response and automatically delivers concepts that advance the student's understanding while reducing time devoted to the concepts already mastered. The result for every student is the fastest path to mastery of the chapter concepts. LearnSmart:

- Applies an intelligent concept engine to identify the relationships between concepts and to serve new concepts to each student only when he or she is ready.
- Adapts automatically to each student, so students spend less time on the topics they understand and practice more those they have yet to master.
- Provides continual reinforcement and remediation, but gives only as much guidance as students need.
- Integrates diagnostics as part of the learning experience.
- Enables you to assess which concepts students have efficiently learned on their own, thus freeing class time for more applications and discussion.

Student Progress Tracking

Connect Accounting keeps instructors informed about how each student, section, and class is performing, allowing for more productive use of lecture and office hours. The progress-tracking function enables you to:

- View scored work immediately and track individual or group performance with assignment and grade reports.
- Access an instant view of student or class performance relative to learning objectives.

home   library   reports

reports

section performance

81.79%* overall section average for 3 assignment(s)
⚠ 0 student(s) have an overall average between 0-59%

assignments
*As of 06/23/2008 10:45 AM CDT

report types

assignment results
See student scores in high, medium and low ranges.

student performance
Quickly review an individual student's performance.

assignment statistics
Mean, highest, lowest scores on each assignment.

item analysis
How your students scored on each assignment item.

category analysis
Performance based on item category criteria you choose.

Try a New e-Book Option!

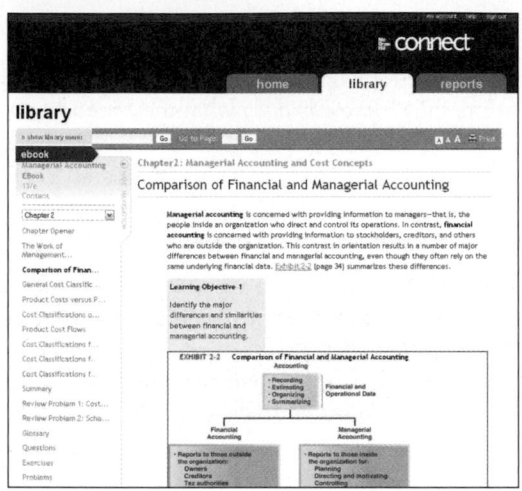

McGraw-Hill *Connect Plus Accounting*

McGraw-Hill reinvents the textbook learning experience for the modern student with *Connect Plus Accounting.* A seamless integration of an eBook and *Connect Accounting, Connect Plus Accounting* provides all of the *Connect Accounting* features plus the following:

- An integrated eBook, allowing for anytime, anywhere access to the textbook.
- Dynamic links between the problems or questions you assign to your students and the location in the eBook where that problem or question is covered.
- A powerful search function to pinpoint and connect key concepts in a snap.

In short, *Connect Accounting* offers you and your students powerful tools and features that optimize your time and energies, enabling you to focus on course content, teaching, and student learning. *Connect Accounting* also offers a wealth of content resources for both instructors and students. This state-of-the-art, thoroughly tested system supports you in preparing students for the world that awaits.

For more information about *Connect Plus Accounting,* go to **www.mcgrawhillconnect.com,** or contact your local McGraw-Hill sales representative.

CourseSmart

CourseSmart is a new way to find and buy eTextbooks. At CouseSmart you can can save up to 50 percent off the cost of a printed textbook, reduce your impact on the environment, and gain access to powerful Web tools for learning. CourseSmart has the largest selection of eTextbooks available anywhere, offering thousands of the most commonly adopted textbooks from a wide variety of higher education publishers. CourseSmart eTextbooks are available in one standard online reader with full text search, notes and highlighting, and email tools for sharing notes between classmates.

From innovative self-guided assessment and guidance to complete online course solutions, McGraw-Hill/Irwin lets you take full advantage of everything the digital age has to offer.

Flexible Online Course Content

No matter what platform you use, McGraw-Hill is committed to making your online course a success. We provide free, WebCT- and Blackboard-compatible course cartridges containing all the content you need.

> "The course I will use this text for is a 'blended' course . . . partially online and partially on campus. This will be very useful."
>
> —Kathy Simons, Bryant College

Tegrity Campus: Lectures 24/7

Tegrity Campus is a service that makes class time available 24/7 by automatically capturing every lecture in a search-able format for students to review when they study and complete assignments. With a simple one-click start-and-stop process, you capture all computer screens and correspond-ing audio. Students can replay any part of any class with easy-to-use browser-based view-ing on a PC or Mac.

Educators know that the more students can see, hear, and experience class resources, the better they learn. In fact, studies prove it. With Tegrity Campus, students quickly recall key moments by using Tegrity Campus's unique search feature. This search helps students effi-ciently find what they need, when they need it, across an entire semester of class recordings. Help turn all your students' study time into learning moments immediately supported by your lecture.

To learn more about Tegrity watch a 2-minute Flash demo at:
http://tegritycampus.mhhe.com

McGraw-Hill Customer Care Contact Information

At McGraw-Hill, we understand that getting the most from new technology can be challeng-ing. That's why our services don't stop after you purchase our products. You can e-mail our Product Specialists 24 hours a day to get product-training online. Or you can search our knowl-edge bank of Frequently Asked Questions on our support website. For Customer Support, call **800-331-5094**, e-mail **hmsupport@mcgraw-hill.com**, or visit **www.mhhe.com/support**. One of our Technical Support Analysts will be able to assist you in a timely fashion.

A GREAT LEARNING SYSTEM DOESN'T STOP WITH THE BOOK.

INSTRUCTOR SUPPLEMENTS

> "Very readable, impressive web-based supplements, excellent topic coverage."
>
> —Karen Foust, Tulane University

ASSURANCE OF LEARNING READY

Many educational institutions today are focused on the notion of *assurance of learning,* an important element of some accreditation standards. *Intermediate Accounting* is designed specifically to support your assurance of learning initiatives with a simple, yet powerful solution.

Each test bank question for *Intermediate Accounting* maps to a specific chapter learning objective listed in the text. You can use our test bank software, EZ Test and EZ Test Online, or *Connect Accounting* to easily query for learning objectives that directly relate to the learning objectives for your course. You can then use the reporting features of EZ Test to aggregate student results in similar fashion, making the collection and presentation of assurance of learning data simple and easy.

AACSB STATEMENT

The McGraw-Hill Companies is a proud corporate member of AACSB International. Understanding the importance and value of AACSB accreditation, *McGraw-Hill's Accounting series* recognizes the curricula guidelines detailed in the AACSB standards for business accreditation by connecting selected questions in the text and the test bank to the six general knowledge and skill guidelines in the AACSB standards.

The statements contained in *Intermediate Accounting* are provided only as a guide for the users of this textbook. The AACSB leaves content coverage and assessment within the purview of individual schools, the mission of the school, and the faculty. While *Intermediate Accounting* and the teaching package make no claim of any specific AACSB qualification or evaluation, we have within *Intermediate Accounting* labeled selected questions according to the six general knowledge and skills areas.

INSTRUCTOR'S RESOURCE MANUAL

This manual provides for each chapter: (a) a chapter overview; (b) a comprehensive lecture outline; (c) extensive teaching transparency masters that can be modified to suit an instructor's particular needs or preferences; (d) a variety of suggested class activities (real world, ethics,

Dell, professional development activities including research, analysis, communication and judgment, and others); and (e) an assignment chart indicating topic, learning objective, and estimated completion time for every question, exercise, problem, and case.

SOLUTIONS MANUAL

The Solutions Manual includes detailed solutions for every question, exercise, problem, and case in the text.

INSTRUCTOR'S CD-ROM

ISBN-13: 9780077328832 (ISBN-10: 0077328833)

This all-in-one resource contains the Instructor's Resource Manual, Solutions Manual, Testbank Word files, Computerized, Testbank, and PowerPoint® slides.

TESTBANK

The **Testbank** is a key component of our Learning System. For the sixth edition, an extensive review process was undertaken to ensure the most complete, accurate, rigorous, and flexible Testbank available. Greater variety was added at each level of rigor. It has been revised for all changes and additions to the text, most notably the extensive expansion of IFRS coverage. Over 120 additional IFRS items were added to the sixth edition Testbank, which now includes nearly 4,000 items. In addition, new IFRS materials were added to the Instructor Resource Manual, Online Quizzes, and the Study Guide.

AUDIO POWERPOINT SLIDES

The Audio PowerPoint slides are created by Jon Booker and Charles Caldwell of Tennessee Technological University, Susan Galbreath of David Lipscomb University, and Cynthia J. Rooney, University of New Mexico, Los Alamos. The slides include an accompanying audio lecture with notes and are available on the Online Learning Center (OLC).

Online Learning Center (OLC): www.mhhe.com/spiceland6e

Intermediate Accounting authors Spiceland, Sepe, and Nelson know from their years of teaching experience what separates a great textbook from a merely adequate one. Every component of the learning package must be imbued with the same style and approach, and that's why the **Intermediate Accounting** authors write every major ancillary themselves, whether printed or online. It's one more thing that sets **Intermediate Accounting** far above the competition.

STUDENT SUPPLEMENTS

STUDY GUIDE

Volume 1: ISBN-13: 9780077328870 (ISBN-10: 0077328876)
Volume 2: ISBN-13: 9780077328887 (ISBN-10: 0077328884)

The Study Guide, written by the text authors, provides chapter summaries, detailed illustrations, and a wide variety of self-study questions, exercises, and multiple-choice problems (with solutions).

WORKING PAPERS

ISBN-13: 9780077328894 (ISBN-10: 0077328892)

Working Papers provide students with formatted templates to aid them in doing homework assignments.

EXCEL TEMPLATES

Selected end-of-chapter exercises and problems, marked in the text with an icon, can be solved using these Microsoft Excel templates, located on the OLC.

UNDERSTANDING CORPORATE ANNUAL REPORTS

Seventh Edition, by William R. Pasewark

ISBN-13: 9780073526935 (ISBN-10: 0073526932)

This project provides students with instruction for obtaining an annual report from a publicly traded corporation and for making an industry or competitor comparison.

> "This is a well-written text, with good integration. It has a full range of computerized and other support materials; and the authors personally write and check the practice questions, examples, and text items."
>
> —*Elaine Henry, University of Miami*

ALTERNATE EXERCISES AND PROBLEMS

This online manual includes additional exercises and problems for each chapter in the text. Available on the OLC.

PRACTICE SETS

ISBN-13: 9780077328771 (ISBN-10: 0077328779)

Grady Wholesale Practice Set: Review of the Accounting Cycle

> "The quality of the material presented is second to none. Chapters can be rearranged as we constantly improve our accounting curriculum. Most important, students will read this book! The end-of-chapter material is outstanding."
>
> —*Barbara Reider, University of Montana*

What's New in the Sixth Edition?

Chapter
1
ENVIRONMENT AND THEORETICAL STRUCTURE OF FINANCIAL ACCOUNTING

- Revised the section on our global market-place to reflect the most recent developments in the move toward global accounting standards.
- Revised the Conceptual Framework material to reflect the completed Phase A of the joint FASB and IASB conceptual framework project. End-of-chapter assignment materials have been revised accordingly.
- Included information describing the FASB Accounting Standards Codification.
- Updated the material on fair value and the fair value option.
- Added a "Where We're Headed" box providing more information on the joint FASB/IASB conceptual framework project.

Chapter
2
REVIEW OF THE ACCOUNTING PROCESS

- Enhanced the sections on reversing entries and the conversion of cash basis to accrual basis and added additional assignment material on these topics.

Chapter
3
THE BALANCE SHEET AND FINANCIAL DISCLOSURES

- Revised the section on subsequent event disclosures to reflect new GAAP.
- Added assignment material on the topics of financial disclosures and liquidity and financing ratios.
- Added an IFRS box describing the differences in balance sheets prepared according to U.S. GAAP and those prepared applying IFRS as well as assignment material on those differences.
- The FASB/IASB joint project on Financial Statement Presentation potentially will dramatically alter the appearance and content of our major financial statements. We added a "Where We're Headed" box describing the proposed new look for the financials and specifically the statement of financial position (balance sheet).
- Added a British Airways case related to reporting the balance sheet using IFRS.

Chapter
4
THE INCOME STATEMENT AND STATEMENT OF CASH FLOWS

- A proposed FASB staff position is slated to change the definition of what constitutes a discontinued operation. We revised the section on discontinued operations to reflect the change.
- Enhanced the coverage of the balance sheet presentation of assets and liabilities of components considered "held-for-sale."
- Added an IFRS box describing the differences in income statements prepared according to U.S. GAAP and those prepared applying IFRS as well as assignment material on those differences.
- Expanded the IFRS boxes on comprehensive income and the statement of cash flows and added assignment material on both topics.
- Added a British Airways case related to reporting the income statement and statement of cash flows using IFRS.

Chapter
5
INCOME MEASUREMENT AND PROFITABILITY ANALYSIS

- Revised Graphics 5-2 and 5-3 to better relate to each other and to add clarity to the chapter discussions.
- Expanded and enhanced the discussion of revenue recognition at delivery of products and services
- Revised discussion of revenue recognition with respect to software and other multiple-deliverable contracts.
- Provided a new profitability analysis illustration, based on a comparison of Target and Walmart.
- Expanded the IFRS boxes on long-term construction contracts and multiple-deliverable contracts and enhanced assignment material related to both topics
- Added an IFRS box comparing revenue recognition concepts between U.S. GAAP and IFRS.,.
- Added a "Where We're Headed" box describing the joint FASB/IASB revenue recognition project.
- Added a British Airways case related to accounting for revenue under IFRS.

Chapter
6
TIME VALUE OF MONEY CONCEPTS

- Expanded the discussion, illustration, and assignment material on the valuation of long-term bonds to include the calculation of interest expense.

Chapter
7
CASH AND RECEIVABLES

- Extensively revised the section describing financing with receivables to reflect new GAAP.
- Revised the discussion of earning quality with respect to receivables.
- Revised the former Appendix 12B ("Impairment of a Receivable Due to a Troubled Debt Restructuring") and moved it to be Appendix 7B.
- Added IFRS boxes concerning cash and cash equivalents, accounts receivable, transfers of receivables, and accounting for impairments and added related assignment material.
- Added a Where We're Headed box describing FASB and IASB projects concerning asset derecognition (relevant to transfers of receivables).
- Added a British Airways case related to accounting for cash and receivables using IFRS.

Chapter
8
INVENTORIES: MEASUREMENT

- Revised the illustration describing the flow of costs for a manufacturing company for greater clarity.
- Revised the section on supplemental LIFO disclosures to enhance the coverage of LIFO reserves and added related assignment material.
- Expanded the IFRS box describing the prohibition on the use of LIFO under IFRS.
- Added a British Airways case related to the measurement of inventories using IFRS.

Chapter
9
INVENTORIES: ADDITIONAL ISSUES

- Enhanced the section on inventory write-downs related to the income statement presentation of the write-down.

We received an incredible amount of feedback prior to writing the sixth edition of **Intermediate Accounting.** The following list of changes and improvements is a testament to our users and their commitment to making **Intermediate Accounting** the best book of its kind.

- Added end-of-chapter material on inventory errors.
- Expanded the IFRS box on the differences between U.S. GAAP and IFRS in the application of the lower-of-cost-or-market rule including a comparative illustration and new assignment material.
- Added a British Airways case related to accounting for inventories using IFRS.

Chapter
10
PROPERTY, PLANT, AND EQUIPMENT AND INTANGIBLE ASSETS: ACQUISITION AND DISPOSITION

- Expanded the IFRS box on the differences between U.S. GAAP and IFRS in accounting for research and development including a comparative illustration and new assignment material.
- Added an IFRS box and new assignment material on the differences in accounting for software development costs using U.S. GAAP and IFRS.
- Added a British Airways case related to accounting for the acquisition and disposition of property, plant, and equipment and intangible assets using IFRS.

Chapter
11
PROPERTY, PLANT, AND EQUIPMENT AND INTANGIBLE ASSETS: UTILIZATION AND IMPAIRMENT

- Revised Graphics 11-1A, B and C for greater clarity.
- Added new assignment material on asset impairment.
- Enhanced the IFRS boxes on the subsequent valuation of property, plant, and equipment, the subsequent valuation of intangible assets, the measurement of impairment of value for property, plant, and equipment and finite-life intangible assets, and the impairment of value of goodwill, by expanding the discussions and by adding illustrations. Added new assignment material on these topics.
- Added IFRS boxes on the calculation of depreciation, biological assets, and the impairment of value for indefinite-life intangible assets other than goodwill including new assignment material. Added a "Where We're Headed" box on the status of the joint FASB/IASB impairment project.
- Added a British Airways case related to accounting for the utilization and impairment

of property, plant, and equipment and intangible assets using IFRS.

Chapter
12
INVESTMENTS

- Revised the discussion of impairments to reflect new GAAP.
- Added Appendix 12B on impairments to provide a comprehensive discussion of other-than-temporary impairments and new GAAP.
- Revised IFRS boxes concerning the fair value option and the equity method and related assignment material.
- Added IFRS boxes related to investments (including both IFRS No. 9 and IAS No. 39), transfers between investment categories, the cost method, and accounting for other-than-temporary impairments, and also added related assignment material.
- Added "Where We're Headed" boxes describing the FASB and IASB projects concerning a comprehensive overhaul of accounting for investments and other financial instruments, as well as an IASB project likely to require use of the equity method (rather than proportionate consolidation) to account for joint ventures.
- Added a British Airways case related to accounting for investments using IFRS.

Chapter
13
CURRENT LIABILITIES AND CONTINGENCIES

- Added new discussion of accounting for gift cards and other unearned revenue.
- Revised IFRS boxes related to classification of liabilities to be refinanced and accounting for contingencies and added new assignment material.
- Added "Where We're Headed" boxes describing FASB and IASB projects concerning performance reporting and accounting for contingencies.
- Added a British Airways case related to accounting for current liabilities and contingencies using IFRS.

Chapter
14
BONDS AND LONG-TERM NOTES

- FASB ASC 825–10–25–1: "Financial Instruments–Overall–Recognition–Fair Value

Option" provides companies the option to value some or all of their financial assets and liabilities at fair value. Discussion of how the fair value option is applied to liabilities has been relocated from Part A (Bonds) of the chapter to a new Part D (Option to Report Liabilities at Fair Value) to provided added flexibility of coverage and to emphasize its applicability to debt in general and not just to bonds.
- Enhanced coverage of accounting for convertible debt and added new assignment material for convertibles and bonds with detachable warrants.
- Expanded IFRS coverage of accounting for transaction costs (called debt issue costs under U.S. GAAP) including a comparative illustration and added assignment material.
- Added a "Where We're Headed" box describing the likely change in how we account for convertible debt based on an ongoing joint project of the IASB and FASB, a recent FASB Staff Position, and current treatment under IFRS.
- Expanded IFRS coverage of accounting for convertible debt including a comparative illustration and added assignment material.
- Added a new comparison of the fair value option between IFRS and U.S. GAAP.
- Added a British Airways case related to accounting for bonds and long-term notes using IFRS.

Chapter
15
LEASES

- Re-ordered the discussions of bargain purchase options and the effects of residual values to make each more meaningful to students.
- Expanded IFRS coverage of lease classification including a comparative illustration and added assignment material.
- Added a "Where We're Headed" box describing the "right-of-use" model that is the focus of the ongoing joint project of the IASB and FASB.
- Enhanced the Comprehensive Summary of Lease Terms and Concepts.
- Added discussion of the effect of operating lease commitments on company survival during the recent economic crisis.
- Expanded IFRS coverage of accounting for sale-leaseback transactions including a comparative illustration and added assignment material.
- Added a British Airways case related to accounting for leases using IFRS.

Chapter

16

ACCOUNTING FOR INCOME TAXES

- Revised and enhanced the discussion and illustration of "Coping with Uncertainty in Income Taxes."
- Expanded coverage of the effect of non-tax differences between U.S. GAAP and IFRS on reported amounts for deferred taxes including a comparative example.
- Added discussion of intraperiod tax allocation within the statement of comprehensive income.
- Added an IFRS box indicating the effect of the IFRS prohibition of extraordinary items on intraperiod tax allocation.
- Omitted a no-longer-timely section dealing with criticisms of deferred tax accounting.
- Added a British Airways case related to accounting for income taxes using IFRS.

Chapter

17

PENSIONS AND OTHER POSTRETIREMENT BENEFIT PLANS

- Added discussion of the effect of the recent economic crisis on the funded status of pension plans.
- Expanded the integrated IFRS coverage of accounting for actuarial gains and losses including a comparative illustration and added assignment material.
- Added integrated coverage of differences between U.S. GAAP and IFRS in accounting for prior service cost (called past service cost under IFRS) including a comparative illustration and added assignment material.
- Added new discussion and T-Account visuals enhance student understanding of the way we record changes in the PBO and Plan Assets.
- Added a "Where We're Headed" box describing the direction of International Financial Reporting Standards for pensions and other postretirement plans based on a recent Exposure Draft proposing that we report in net income *all* changes in the obligation and the value of plan assets.
- Added a British Airways case related to accounting for postretirement benefit plans using IFRS.

Chapter

18

SHAREHOLDERS' EQUITY

- Added a new learning objective and combined two others to better reflect the core competencies within the chapter.
- Added integrated coverage of differences between U.S. GAAP and IFRS in reporting comprehensive income including a com-

parative illustration and added assignment material.
- Added coverage of the use of the term "reserves" and other terminology differences between U.S. GAAP and IFRS including a comparative illustration and added assignment material.
- Added a new illustration demonstrating the distribution of dividends to preferred shareholders.
- Revised the integrated coverage of distinguishing between debt and equity under U'S. GAAP and IFRS.
- Added a "Where We're Headed" box describing the FASB/IASB joint project on Financial Statement Presentation and its effect on the presentation of equity in each of the financial statements.
- Added a British Airways case related to accounting for shareholders' equity using IFRS.

Chapter

19

SHARE-BASED COMPENSATION AND EARNINGS PER SHARE

- Added integrated coverage of differences between U.S. GAAP and IFRS in the recognition of deferred tax asset for stock options including a comparative illustration and added assignment material.
- Frequently stock option awards specify that recipients gradually become eligible to exercise their options rather than all at once. This is called "graded vesting." We added a section on accounting for such plans including an illustration and an IFRS box and added related assignment material.
- Revised the integrated IFRS coverage of earnings per share.
- Restricted stock awards are quickly replacing stock options as the share-based compensation plan of choice. The discussion of the effect of these stock award plans on EPS calculations is expanded and is presented in a way that allows flexibility in the extent to which it is included in lesson plans and assignments.
- Added a "Where We're Headed" box describing the FASB/IASB joint project on earnings per share.
- Added a British Airways case related to accounting for share-based compensation and earnings per share using IFRS.

Chapter

20

ACCOUNTING CHANGES AND ERRORS

- LIFO is not a permissible method for accounting for inventory under IFRS. An IFRS box is added to point out that the

changes to and from the LIFO method we discuss in this chapter would not occur if International standards were being applied.
- U.S. GAAP and International standards are largely converged regarding accounting changes and error corrections, but one difference concerns error corrections. An IFRS box is added to indicate that when correcting errors in previously issued financial statements, IFRS permits the effect of the error to be reported in the current period if it's not considered practicable to report it retrospectively as is required by U.S. GAAP. Related assignment material was added.

Chapter

21

STATEMENT OF CASH FLOWS REVISITED

- At the heart of the collapse of Bear Stearns, Lehman Brothers, AIG, Citigroup, Fannie Mae, Freddie Mac and many other stalwart companies and the subsequent worldwide economic decline was a shortage of cash flows. Discussion was added of how describing how each of these meltdowns involved a lack of measuring and monitoring the ebb and flow of cash.
- At the heart of the FASB/IASB joint project on Financial Statement Presentation is the classification of activities in a common fashion within each of the financial statements, perhaps following the current classification within the statement of cash flows. We added a "Where We're Headed" box describing the proposed new look for the financials and the possible elimination of the indirect method of reporting operating activities.
- Added integrated coverage of differences between U.S. GAAP and IFRS in the classification of cash flows including a comparative illustration and added assignment material.
- Added a British Airways case related to reporting a statement of cash flows using IFRS.

Acknowledgments

Sixth Edition Reviewers

Peter Aghimien, *Indiana University–South Bend*

Pervaiz Alam, *Kent State University*

Dave Alldredge, *Salt Lake Community College*

Matthew J. Anderson, *Michigan State University–East Lansing*

Marie Archambault, *Marshall University*

Debbie Archambeault, *University of Tennessee–Chattanooga*

Paul Ashcroft, *Missouri State University*

Florence Atiase, *University of Texas–Austin*

Steven Balsam, *Temple University*

James Bannister, *University of Hartford*

Charles P. Baril, *James Madison University*

Cheryl Bartlett, *Central New Mexico Community College*

Homer Bates, *University of North Florida*

Ira Bates, *Florida A & M University*

Deborah F. Beard, *Southeast Missouri State University*

Yoel Beniluz, *Rutgers University–New Brunswick*

Rick Berschback, *Walsh College*

Mark Bezik, *Idaho State University*

Bruce Branson, *NC State University–Raleigh*

Phil Buchanan, *George Mason University*

Jay Buchanon, *Burlington Community College*

Charles A. Carslaw, *University of Nevada–Reno*

Dennis Chambers, *Kennesaw State University*

Kimberly Charland, *Kansas State University*

Linda Chase, *Baldwin-Wallace College*

Agnes Cheng, *Louisiana State University–Baton Rouge*

Cal Christian, *East Carolina University*

Stan Chu, *Borough of Manhattan Community College*

Karen Collins, *Lehigh University*

Elizabeth Conner, *University of Colorado–Denver*

Teresa Conover, *University of North Texas*

Paul Copley, *James Madison University*

John Dallmus, *Arizona State University–West*

Li Dang, *California Polytechnic State University*

Charles Davis, *California State University–Sacramento*

Denise de la Rosa, *Grand Valley State University*

Keren Deal, *Auburn University–Montgomery*

Robert Depasquale, *Saint Vincent College*

Patricia Derrick, *Salisbury University*

Robert Derstine, *Villanova University*

Doug DeVidal, *University of Texas–Austin*

Victoria Dickinson, *University of Florida–Gainesville*

Jan Duffy, *Iowa State University*

Barbara Durham, *University of Central Florida*

Terry G. Elliott, *Morehead State University*

James Emig, *Villanova University*

Denise English, *Boise State University*

Kathryn Epps, *Kennesaw State University*

Ed Etter, *Eastern Michigan University*

Larry Farmer, *Middle Tennessee State University*

Anita Feller, *University of Illinois–Champaign*

Pat Fort, *University of Alaska–Anchorage*

Karen Foust, *Tulane University*

Gail Fraser, *Kean University*

Ann Gabriel, *Ohio University–Athens*

Clyde Galbraith, *West Chester University of PA*

Aloke Ghosh, *Bernard M. Baruch College*

Daniel Gibbons, *Columbia College–Christian County*

John Giles, *NC State University–Raleigh*

Lisa Gillespie, *Loyola University–Chicago*

Dan Givoly, *Penn State University–University Park*

Ronald Gray, *University of West Florida*

Daryl Max Guffey, *Clemson University*

Ronald Halsac, *Community College of Allegheny County*

Coby Harmon, *University of California–Santa Barbara*

Carolyn Hartwell, *Wright State University–Dayton*

Daniel He, *Monmouth University*

John Hoffer, *Stark State College of Technology*

Harry Howe, *State University College–Geneseo*

Kathy Hsiao Yu Hsu, *University of Louisiana–Lafayette*

Patricia Hughes, *University of Pittsburgh*

Evelyn Hwang, *Eastern Michigan University*

Raghavan J. Iyengar, *North Carolina Central University*

Christopher Jones, *California State University–Northridge*

Lisa Koonce, *University of Texas–Austin*

Jerry Kreuze, *Western Michigan University–Kalamazoo*

Timothy Krumwiede, *Bryant University*

Steven Lafave, *Augsburg College*

Sheldon Langsam, *Western Michigan University–Kalamazoo*

Doug Laufer, *Metro State College of Denver*

As you know if you've read this far, **Intermediate Accounting** would not be what it is without the passionate feedback of our colleagues. Through your time and effort, we were able to create a learning system that truly responds to the needs of the market, and for that, we sincerely thank each of you.

Janice Lawrence, *University of Nebraska–Lincoln*

Charles Leflar, *University of Arkansas–Fayetteville*

Tim Lindquist, *University of Northern Iowa*

Joseph Lipari, *Montclair State University*

Danny Litt, *University of California–Los Angeles*

Chao-Shin Liu, *University of Notre Dame*

Heidemarie Lundblad, *California State University–Northridge*

Susan A. Lynn, *University of Baltimore*

Jeff Mankin, *Lipscomb University*

Josephine Mathias, *Mercer County Community College*

Florence McGovern, *Bergen Community College*

Tammy Metzke, *Milwaukee Area Technical College*

John Mills, *University of Nevada–Reno*

Birendra Mishra, *University of California–Riverside*

Richard Monbrod, *DeVry University–Chicago*

Louella Moore, *Arkansas State University–State University*

Tommy Moores, *University of Nevada–Las Vegas*

Lisa Murawa, *Mott Community College*

Brian Nagle, *Duquesne University*

Albert Nagy, *John Carroll University*

Ramesh Narasimhan, *Montclair State University*

Siva Nathan, *Georgia State University*

Linda Nichols, *Texas Tech University*

Michelle Nickla, *Ivy Tech Community College of Indiana*

Sewon O, *Texas Southern University*

Emeke Ofobike, *University of Akron*

Lori Olsen, *North Dakota State University–Fargo*

Don Pagach, *NC State University–Raleigh*

Hong S. Pak, *California State Polytechnic University–Pomona*

Susan Pallas, *Southeast Community College*

Patricia Parker, *Columbus State Community College*

Simon Pearlman, *California State University–Long Beach*

Ray Pfeiffer, *University of Massachusetts–Amherst*

Catherine Plante, *University of New Hampshire*

John Plouffe, *California State University–Los Angeles*

Grace Pownall, *Emory University*

Dale Prondzinski, *Davenport University*

Monsur Rahman, *Indiana University of PA–Indiana*

Kenneth C. Rakow, *Louisiana State University–Baton Rouge*

Barbara Reider, *University of Montana*

Raymond Reisig, *Pace University*

Jeri Ricketts, *University of Cincinnati*

Carol Rogers, *Central New Mexico Community College*

Eric Rothenburg, *Kingsborough Community College*

Huldah A. Ryan, *Iona College–New Rochelle*

Maria Sanchez, *Rider University*

Lisa Sandifer, *Delta State University*

Alexander Sannella, *Rutgers University–Newark*

William Schwartz, *University of Arizona*

Michael Serif, *Dowling College*

Kathy Sevigny, *Bridgewater State College*

Andreas Simon, *California Polytechnic State University*

Kathleen Simons, *Bryant University*

Debra Sinclair, *Georgia Southern University*

Mike Slaubaugh, *Indiana University/Purdue University–Ft. Wayne*

Cynthia Sneed, *Jacksonville State University*

Nancy Snow, *University of Toledo*

Victor Stanton, *University of California–Berkeley*

Lorraine Stern, *York College*

Benjamin Tai, *California State University–Fresno*

Pavani Tallapally, *Slippery Rock University of PA*

Karen Teitel, *College of the Holy Cross*

Forrest Thompson, *Florida A & M University*

Samuel Tiras, *Louisiana State University–Baton Rouge*

Terry Tranter, *University of Minnesota–Minneapolis*

Mike Vasilou, *Devry University–Chicago*

Marcia Veit, *University of Central Florida*

Kenton Walker, *University of Wyoming–Laramie*

Bruce Wampler, *Louisiana State University–Shreveport*

Jane Wells, *University of Kentucky–Lexington*

Michael Yampuler, *University of Houston*

Linda Zucca, *Kent State University*

Fifth Edition Reviewers

The Spiceland team also extends sincere thanks to the reviewers of our previous edition, without whose input we could not have made *Intermediate Accounting* the extraordinary success it has been.

Matilda Abavana, *Essex County College*

Habib Abo-El-Yazeed, *Minnesota State University–Mankato*

Noel D. Addy, Jr., *Mississippi State University*

Pervaiz Alam, *Kent State University*

Matthew Anderson, *Michigan State University*

Acknowledgments

Joseph W. Antenucci, *Youngstown State University*

Marie Archambault, *Marshall University*

Jack Aschkenazi, *American Intercontinental University*

Florence Atiase, *University of Texas*

Joyce Barden, *DeVry University–Phoenix*

Yoel Beniluz, *Rutgers University*

Lila Bergman, *Hunter College*

John Bildersee, *New York University*

Robert Bloom, *John Carroll University*

William J. Bradberry, *Bluefield State College*

Russell Briner, *University of Texas*

Nat R. Briscoe, *Northwestern State University*

R. Eugene Bryson, *University of Alabama–Huntsville*

Gary Burkette, *East Tennessee State University*

Al Case, *Southern Oregon University*

Jack M. Cathey, *University of North Carolina–Charlotte*

Lanny Chasteen, *Oklahoma State University*

C.S. Agnes Cheng, *University of Houston*

Stanley Chu, *Bernard M. Baruch College*

Kwang Chung, *Pace University*

Edwin Cohen, *DePaul University*

Teresa Conover, *University of North Texas*

Cheryl Corke, *Genesee Community College*

John Corless, *California State University–Sacramento*

Charles D'Alessandro, *SUNY–Suffolk*

Bobbie W. Daniels, *Jackson State University*

Mark Dawkins, *University of Georgia*

Denise de la Rosa, *Grand Valley State University*

Susan A. Dehner, *Delaware Tech Community College–Dover*

Larry A. Deppe, *Weber State University*

Wendy Duffy, *Illinois State University*

Gerard M. Engeholm, *Pace University*

Kathryn K. Epps, *Kennesaw State University*

Patricia A. Fedje, *Minot State University*

Anita Feller, *University of Illinois–Champaign*

Ehsan H. Feroz, *University of Washington–Tacoma*

Karen Foust, *Tulane University*

Gail E. Fraser, *Kean University*

Jeanne Gerard, *Franklin Pierce College*

Aloke Ghosh, *Bernard M. Baruch College*

Lori Grady, *Bucks County Community College*

Julia Grant, *Case Western Reserve University*

Mary Halford, *Prince Georges Community College*

John M. Hassell, *Indiana University/Purdue University –Indianapolis*

Frank Heflin, *Florida State University–Tallahassee*

Kenneth Henry, *Florida International University–Miami*

Paula Irwin, *Muhlenberg College*

Marianne James, *California State University–Los Angeles*

Agatha Jeffers, *Montclair State University*

Cynthia Jeffrey, *Iowa State University*

Keith Jones, *George Mason University*

Khondkar Karim, *Rochester Institute of Technology*

Ronald Kilgore, *University of Tennessee–Martin*

Gordon Klein, *University of California–Los Angeles*

Lisa Koonce, *University of Texas–Austin*

Cynthia L. Krom, *Marist College*

Joan Lacher, *Nassau Community College*

Janice Lawrence, *University of Nebraska–Lincoln*

Philip Lee, *Nashville State Tech Community College*

Kevin Lightner, *San Diego State University*

Tim M. Lindquist, *University of Northern Iowa*

Danny S. Litt, *University of California–Los Angeles*

Patty Lobingier, *Virginia Polytechnic Institute*

Susan Logorda, *Lehigh Carbon Community College*

Heidemarie Lundblad, *California State University–Northridge*

Jeff Mankin, *Lipscomb University*

Josephine Mathias, *Mercer County Community College*

Robert W. McGee, *Barry University*

Mike Metzcar, *Indiana Wesleyan University*

Charles Miller, *California Polytechnic State University*

Anita Morgan, *CTU Online*

Barbara Muller, *Arizona State University*

Ramesh Narasimhan, *Montclair University*

Sia Nassiripour, *William Paterson University*

Siva Nathan, *Georgia State University*

Joyce Njoroge, *Drake University*

George Nogler, *University of Massachusetts Lowell*

Emeka Ofobike, *University of Akron*

Derek Oler, *Indiana University*

William A. Padley, *Madison Area Technical College–Truax*

Hong S. Pak, *California State Poly University–Pomona*

Barbara K. Parks, *American Intercontinental University*

Keith Patterson, *Brigham Young University*

Simon Pearlman, *California State University–Long Beach*

Rachel Pernia, *Essex County College*

Anthony R. Piltz, *Rocky Mountain College*

Joann Pinto, *Montclair State University*

Terence Pitre, *University of South Carolina*

David Plumlee, *University of Utah*

Grace Pownall, *Emory University*

Frederick M. Richardson, *Virginia Polytechnic Institute*

Michael Riordan, *James Madison University*

Byung Ro, *Purdue University–West Lafayette*

Pamela Roush, *University of Central Florida*

Huldah A. Ryan, *Iona College*

Anwar Salimi, *California State Poly University– Pomona*

Angela Sandberg, *Jacksonville State University*

Alex Sannella, *Rutgers University*

Gerald Savage, *Essex County College*

Gary Schader, *Kean University*

Paul Schloemer, *Ashland University*

Kathy Sevigny, *Bridgewater State College*

Carol Shaver, *Louisiana Tech University*

Ronald Singleton, *Western Washington University*

Kenneth Smith, *Salisbury University*

Nancy Snow, *University of Toledo*

Paulette Tandy, *University of Nevada–Las Vegas*

Katherene P. Terrell, *University of Central Oklahoma*

Robert Terrell, *University of Central Oklahoma*

Karen Turner, *University of Northern Colorado*

Michael Tyler, *Barry University*

Michael G. Welker, *Drexel University*

Michael L. Werner, *University of Miami– Coral Gables*

Gloria Worthy, *Southwest Tennessee University*

Jing-Wen Yang, *California State University– East Bay*

We Are Grateful

We would like to acknowledge Ilene Persoff, CW Post Campus/Long Island University, for her detailed accuracy check of the Testbank. Special thanks are also due to Vic Stanton of the University of California–Berkeley and Stanford University for his contributions to the accuracy and quality of the PowerPoints. Anita Feller of the University of Illinois–Champaign made many valuable contributions to our codification exercises and cases. Bill Padley of Madison Area Technical College contributed greatly to the production of the Working Papers. In addition, we thank Jon A. Booker and Charles W. Caldwell of Tennessee Technological University, Cynthia J. Rooney of University of New Mexico, and Susan C. Galbreath of David Lipscomb University for crafting the PowerPoint Slides; and Jack E. Terry, ComSource Associates, for developing the Excel Templates. Anita Feller of the University of Illinois–Champaign, Lawrence Tomassini of the Ohio State University, Andreas Simon of California Polytechnic State University, Barbara Muller of Arizona State University, and Mark McCarthy of East Carolina University contributed new content and accuracy checks of our new LearnSmart and Self-Quiz and Study products. We greatly appreciate everyone's hard work on these products!

Ilene Persoff, CW Post Campus/Long Island University, and Mark McCarthy, East Carolina University, made significant contributions to the accuracy of the text, end-of-chapter material, and solutions manual. In addition, we appreciate the help and guidance received from Teresa Conover from North Texas University, for her insights regarding the International Financial Reporting Standards. A big thank you to Jerry Kreuze of Western Michigan University for his detailed analysis of the end-of-chapter material. We appreciate the assistance of James Lynch at KPMG, who provided us with valuable feedback on various difficult issues.

We are most grateful for the talented assistance and support from the many people at McGraw-Hill/Irwin. We would particularly like to thank Brent Gordon, editor in chief; Stewart Mattson, editorial director; Tim Vertovec, publisher; Dana Woo, senior sponsoring editor, Daryl Horrocks, senior developmental editor; Michelle Heaster, marketing manager; Greg Patterson, regional sales manager; Pat Frederickson, lead project manager; Debra Sylvester, senior production supervisor; Laurie Entringer, designer; Jeremy Cheshareck, senior photo research coordinator; and Kerry Bowler, media project manager.

Finally, we extend our thanks to Kaplan CPA Review for their assistance developing simulations for our inclusion in the end-of-chapter material, as well as Dell and British Airways for allowing us to use their Annual Reports throughout the text. We also acknowledge permission from the AICPA to adapt material from the Uniform CPA Examination, the IMA for permission to adapt material from the CMA Examination, and Dow Jones & Co., Inc., for permission to excerpt material from *The Wall Street Journal*.

David Spiceland
Jim Sepe
Mark Nelson

Contents in Brief

The Role of Accounting as an Information System

1 Environment and Theoretical Structure of Financial Accounting, 2
2 Review of the Accounting Process, 50
3 The Balance Sheet and Financial Disclosures, 112
4 The Income Statement and Statement of Cash Flows, 168
5 Income Measurement and Profitability Analysis, 232
6 Time Value of Money Concepts, 298

SECTION 1

Economic Resources

7 Cash and Receivables, 336
8 Inventories: Measurement, 394
9 Inventories: Additional Issues, 446
10 Property, Plant, and Equipment and Intangible Assets: Acquisition and Disposition, 500
11 Property, Plant, and Equipment and Intangible Assets: Utilization and Impairment, 556

SECTION 2

Financial Instruments and Liabilities

12 Investments, 618
13 Current Liabilities and Contingencies, 690
14 Bonds and Long-Term Notes, 746
15 Leases, 806
16 Accounting for Income Taxes, 872
17 Pensions and Other Postretirement Benefits, 934
18 Shareholders' Equity, 1006

SECTION 3

Additional Financial Reporting Issues

19 Share-Based Compensation and Earnings Per Share, 1068
20 Accounting Changes and Error Corrections, 1136
21 The Statement of Cash Flows Revisited, 1182

SECTION 4

Appendix A: Derivatives, A–0
Appendix B: Dell Annual Report, B–1
Appendix C: IFRS Comprehensive Case, C–0
Glossary, G–0
Photo Credits, Cr–1
Index, I–0
Present and Future Value Tables, P–1

Contents

1 SECTION

The Role of Accounting as an Information System

1 CHAPTER
Environment and Theoretical Structure of Financial Accounting, 2

Part A: Financial Accounting Environment, 4
The Economic Environment and Financial Reporting, 5
   The Investment-Credit Decision—A Cash Flow Perspective, 6
   Cash versus Accrual Accounting, 7
The Development of Financial Accounting and Reporting Standards, 9
   Historical Perspective and Standards, 9
   The Establishment of Accounting Standards—A Political Process, 12
   Our Global Marketplace, 13
   The Role of the Auditor, 16
   Financial Reporting Reform, 16
   A Move Away from Rules-Based Standards, 18
Ethics in Accounting, 19
   Ethics and Professionalism, 19
   Analytical Model for Ethical Decisions, 19

Part B: The Conceptual Framework, 20
Objective of Financial Reporting, 21
Qualitative Characteristics of Financial Reporting Information, 22
   Fundamental Qualitative Characteristics, 23
   Enhancing Qualitative Characteristics, 24
Practical Boundaries (Constraints) to Achieving Desired Qualitative Characteristics, 25
   Cost Effectiveness, 25
   Materiality, 25
   Conservatism, 26
Elements of Financial Statements, 26
Recognition and Measurement Concepts, 27
   Recognition, 27
   Measurement, 28
   Underlying Assumptions, 28
   Broad Accounting Principles, 29
Evolution of Accounting Principles, 33
   The Asset/Liability Approach, 33
   The Move toward Fair Value, 34
Questions for Review of Key Topics, 38

Brief Exercises, 38
Exercises, 39
CPA and CMA Review Questions, 43
Broaden Your Perspective, 45

2 CHAPTER
Review of the Accounting Process, 50

The Basic Model, 52
   The Accounting Equation, 52
   Account Relationships, 53
The Accounting Processing Cycle, 55
Concept Review Exercise: Journal Entries for External Transactions, 64
Adjusting Entries, 66
   Prepayments, 67
   Accruals, 70
   Estimates, 72
Concept Review Exercise: Adjusting Entries, 74
Preparing the Financial Statements, 76
   The Income Statement, 76
   The Balance Sheet, 77
   The Statement of Cash Flows, 78
   The Statement of Shareholders' Equity, 79
The Closing Process, 79
Concept Review Exercise: Financial Statement Preparation and Closing, 81
Conversion from Cash Basis to Accrual Basis, 83
Appendix 2A: Use of a Worksheet, 87
Appendix 2B: Reversing Entries, 88
Appendix 2C: Subsidiary Ledgers and Special Journals, 90
Questions for Review of Key Topics, 93
Brief Exercises, 93
Exercises, 94
CPA Review Questions, 101
Problems, 102
Broaden Your Perspective, 109

3 CHAPTER
The Balance Sheet and Financial Disclosures, 112

Part A: The Balance Sheet, 115
Usefulness and Limitations, 115
Classifications, 116
  Assets, 116
  Liabilities, 120
  Shareholders' Equity, 121
Concept Review Exercise: Balance Sheet Classification, 123
Part B: Financial Disclosures, 124
Disclosure Notes, 125
  Summary of Significant Accounting Policies, 125
  Subsequent Events, 125
  Noteworthy Events and Transactions, 126
Management Discussion and Analysis, 128
Management's Responsibilities, 128
Auditors' Report, 129
Compensation of Directors and Top Executives, 131
Part C: Risk Analysis, 132
Using Financial Statement Information, 132
Liquidity Ratios, 133
  Financing Ratios, 135
Appendix 3: Reporting Segment Information, 140
Questions for Review of Key Topics, 143
Brief Exercises, 144
Exercises, 145
CPA and CMA Review Questions, 153
Problems, 154
Broaden Your Perspective, 160

4 CHAPTER
The Income Statement and Statement of Cash Flows, 168

Part A: The Income Statement and Comprehensive Income, 170
Income from Continuing Operations, 170
  Revenues, Expenses, Gains, and Losses, 170
  Income Tax Expense, 172
  Operating versus Nonoperating Income, 172
  Income Statement Formats, 172
Earnings Quality, 175
  Manipulating Income and Income Smoothing, 175
  Operating Income and Earnings Quality, 176
  Nonoperating Income and Earnings Quality, 179
Separately Reported Items, 180
  Intraperiod Income Tax Allocation, 180
  Discontinued Operations, 182
  Extraordinary Items, 186
  Unusual or Infrequent Items, 187
Accounting Changes, 188

  Change in Accounting Principle, 188
  Change in Depreciation, Amortization, or Depletion Method, 189
  Change in Accounting Estimate, 190
  Change in Reporting Entity, 191
Correction of Accounting Errors, 192
  Prior Period Adjustments, 192
Earnings per Share Disclosures, 192
Comprehensive Income, 194
  Other Comprehensive Income, 194
  Flexibility in Reporting, 194
  Accumulated Other Comprehensive Income, 196
Concept Review Exercise: Income Statement Presentation, 197
Part B: The Statement of Cash Flows, 198
Usefulness of the Statement of Cash Flows, 198
Classifying Cash Flows, 199
  Operating Activities, 199
  Investing Activities, 203
  Financing Activities, 203
  Noncash Investing and Financing Activities, 204
Concept Review Exercise: Statement of Cash Flows, 205
Questions for Review of Key Topics, 209
Brief Exercises, 209
Exercises, 211
CPA and CMA Review Questions, 218
Problems, 219
Broaden Your Perspective, 225
British Airways Case, 230
CPA Simulation 4–1, 231

5 CHAPTER
Income Measurement and Profitability Analysis, 232

Part A: Revenue Recognition, 234
Revenue Recognition at Delivery, 238
  Product Revenue, 238
  Service Revenue, 238
Revenue Recognition after Delivery, 239
  Installment Sales, 239
Concept Review Exercise: Installment Sales, 243
  Right of Return, 243
  Consignment Sales, 245
Revenue Recognition Prior to Delivery, 245
  A Comparison of the Completed Contract and Percentage-of-Completion Methods, 251
Concept Review Exercise: Long-Term Construction Contracts, 257
Industry-Specific Revenue Issues, 258
  Software and Other Multiple-Deliverable Arrangements, 259
  Franchise Sales, 260
Part B: Profitability Analysis, 263
  Activity Ratios, 263
  Profitability Ratios, 265
Profitability Analysis—An Illustration, 267
Appendix 5: Interim Reporting, 271

Questions for Review of Key Topics, 273
Brief Exercises, 273
Exercises, 275
CPA and CMA Review Questions, 282
Problems, 284
Broaden Your Perspective, 291
British Airways Case, 297
CPA Simulation 5–1, 297

6 CHAPTER
Time Value of Money Concepts, 298

Part A: Basic Concepts, 300
Time Value of Money, 300
    Simple versus Compound Interest, 300
Valuing a Single Cash Flow Amount, 301
    Future Value of a Single Amount, 301
    Present Value of a Single Amount, 302
    Solving for Other Values When FV and PV are Known, 304
Concept Review Exercise: Valuing a Single Cash Flow Amount, 305
Preview of Accounting Applications of Present Value Techniques—Single Cash Amount, 306

Expected Cash Flow Approach, 308
Part B: Basic Annuities, 309
Future Value of an Annuity, 310
    Future Value of an Ordinary Annuity, 310
    Future Value of an Annuity Due, 311
Present Value of an Annuity, 312
    Present Value of an Ordinary Annuity, 312
    Present Value of an Annuity Due, 313
    Present Value of a Deferred Annuity, 314
Financial Calculators and Excel, 316
Solving for Unknown Values in Present Value Situations, 316
Concept Review Exercise: Annuities, 319
Preview of Accounting Applications of Present Value Techniques—Annuities, 320
    Valuation of Long-Term Bonds, 320
    Valuation of Long-Term Leases, 321
    Valuation of Pension Obligations, 321
Summary of Time Value of Money Concepts, 322
Questions for Review of Key Topics, 324
Brief Exercises, 325
Exercises, 326
CPA and CMA Review Questions, 329
Problems, 331
Broaden Your Perspective, 334

2 SECTION
Economic Resources

7 CHAPTER
Cash and Receivables, 336

Part A: Cash and Cash Equivalents, 338
Internal Control, 338
    Internal Control Procedures—Cash Receipts, 339
    Internal Control Procedures—Cash Disbursements, 339
Restricted Cash and Compensating Balances, 340
Decision Makers' Perspective, 341
Part B: Current Receivables, 342
Accounts Receivable, 342
    Initial Valuation of Accounts Receivable, 342
    Subsequent Valuation of Accounts Receivable, 344
Concept Review Exercise: Uncollectible Accounts Receivable, 351
Notes Receivable, 352
    Interest-Bearing Notes, 352
    Noninterest-Bearing Notes, 353
    Subsequent Valuation of Notes Receivable, 355

Financing with Receivables, 356
    Secured Borrowing, 356
    Sale of Receivables, 358
    Transfers of Notes Receivable, 361
    Deciding Whether to Account for a Transfer as a Sale or a Secured Borrowing, 361
    Disclosures, 362
Concept Review Exercise: Financing with Receivables, 365
Decision Makers' Perspective, 365
Appendix 7A: Cash Controls, 369
Appendix 7B: Impairment of a Receivable Due to a Troubled Debt Restructuring, 372
Questions for Review of Key Topics, 374
Brief Exercises, 375
Exercises, 376
CPA and CMA Review Questions, 382
Problems, 384
Broaden Your Perspective, 390
British Airways Case, 393

8 CHAPTER
Inventories: Measurement, 394

Part A: Recording and Measuring Inventory, 396

Types of Inventory, 396
   Merchandising Inventory, 396
   Manufacturing Inventories, 396

Perpetual Inventory System, 397

Periodic Inventory System, 398

A Comparison of the Perpetual and Periodic Inventory Systems, 399

What is Included in Inventory?, 400
   Physical Quantities Included in Inventory, 400
   Expenditures Included in Inventory, 401

Inventory Cost Flow Assumptions, 404
   Specific Identification, 405
   Average Cost, 405
   First-In, First-Out (FIFO), 407
   Last-In, First-Out (LIFO), 408
   Comparison of Cost Flow Methods, 410

Decision Makers' Perspective—Factors Influencing Method Choice, 411

Concept Review Exercise: Inventory Cost Flow Methods, 414

Decision Makers' Perspective, 417

Part B: Methods of Simplifying LIFO, 420

LIFO Inventory Pools, 420

Dollar-Value LIFO, 421
   Advantages of DVL, 422
   Cost Indexes, 422
   The DVL Inventory Estimation Technique, 422

Concept Review Exercise: Dollar-Value LIFO, 423

Questions for Review of Key Topics, 425
Brief Exercises, 426
Exercises, 427
CPA and CMA Review Questions, 433
Problems, 435
Broaden Your Perspective, 441
British Airways Case, 445

9 CHAPTER
Inventories: Additional Issues, 446

Part A: Reporting—Lower of Cost or Market, 448

Determining Market Value, 449
   Applying Lower of Cost or Market, 451
   Adjusting Cost to Market, 452

Concept Review Exercise: Lower of Cost or Market, 454

Part B: Inventory Estimation Techniques, 455

The Gross Profit Method, 456
   A Word of Caution, 457

The Retail Inventory Method, 458
   Retail Terminology, 459
   Cost Flow Methods, 460

   Other Issues Pertaining to the Retail Method, 462

Concept Review Exercise: Retail Inventory Method, 463

Part C: Dollar-Value LIFO Retail, 465

Concept Review Exercise: Dollar-Value LIFO Retail Method, 468

Part D: Change in Inventory Method and Inventory Errors, 469

Change in Inventory Method, 469
   Most Inventory Changes, 469
   Change to the LIFO Method, 471

Inventory Errors, 472
   When the Inventory Error is Discovered the Following Year, 473
   When the Inventory Error is Discovered Subsequent to the Following Year, 473

Concept Review Exercise: Inventory Errors, 474

Earnings Quality, 474

Appendix 9: Purchase Commitments, 476
Questions for Review of Key Topics, 478
Brief Exercises, 479
Exercises, 480
CPA and CMA Review Questions, 487
Problems, 489
Broaden Your Perspective, 494
British Airways Case, 497
CPA Simulation 9–1, 498
CPA Simulation 9–2, 498

10 CHAPTER
Property, Plant, and Equipment and Intangible Assets: Acquisition and Disposition, 500

Part A: Valuation at Acquisition, 502

Types of Assets, 502

Costs to Be Capitalized, 504
   Property, Plant, and Equipment, 504
   Intangible Assets, 509

Lump-Sum Purchases, 512

Noncash Acquisitions, 512
   Deferred Payments, 513
   Issuance of Equity Securities, 515
   Donated Assets, 515

Decision Makers' Perspective, 516

Part B: Dispositions and Exchanges, 517

Dispositions, 517

Exchanges, 518
   Fair Value Not Determinable, 519
   Exchange Lacks Commercial Substance, 519

Concept Review Exercise: Exchanges, 521

Part C: Self-Constructed Assets and Research and Development, 521

Self-Constructed Assets, 521
   Overhead Allocation, 522
   Interest Capitalization, 522
   Research and Development (R & D), 526

Appendix 10: Oil and Gas Accounting, 534

Questions for Review of Key Topics, 535
Brief Exercises, 536
Exercises, 537
CPA and CMA Review Questions, 543
Problems, 546
Broaden Your Perspective, 550
British Airways Case, 554

11 CHAPTER
Property, Plant, and Equipment and Intangible Assets: Utilization and Impairment, 556

Part A: Depreciation, Depletion, and Amortization, 558
Cost Allocation—An Overview, 558
Measuring Cost Allocation, 559
    Service Life, 559
    Allocation Base, 559
    Allocation Method, 560
Depreciation, 560
    Time-Based Depreciation Methods, 560
    Activity-Based Depreciation Methods, 562
Decision Makers' Perspective—Selecting a Depreciation Method, 563
Concept Review Exercise: Depreciation Methods, 565
Group and Composite Depreciation Methods, 566
Depletion of Natural Resources, 569
Amortization of Intangible Assets, 571
    Intangible Assets Subject to Amortization, 571
    Intangible Assets Not Subject to Amortization, 572
Concept Review Exercise: Depletion and Amortization, 573
Part B: Additional Issues, 575
Partial Periods, 575
Changes in Estimates, 576
Change in Depreciation, Amortization, or Depletion Method, 577
Error Correction, 578
Impairment of Value, 580
    Assets to Be Held and Used, 580
Assets to Be Sold, 587
    Impairment Losses and Earnings Quality, 588
Part C: Subsequent Expenditures, 589
    Expenditures Subsequent to Acquisition, 589
    Repairs and Maintenance, 589
    Additions, 590
    Improvements, 590
    Rearrangements, 590
    Costs of Defending Intangible Rights, 591
Appendix 11A: Comparison with MACRS (Tax Depreciation), 594
Appendix 11B: Retirement and Replacement Methods of Depreciation, 594
Questions for Review of Key Topics, 596
Brief Exercises, 596
Exercises, 598
CPA and CMA Review Questions, 605
Problems, 607
Broaden Your Perspective, 612
British Airways Case, 616
CPA Simulation 11–1, 617

3 SECTION
Financial Instruments and Liabilities

12 CHAPTER
Investments, 618

Part A: Investor Lacks Significant Influence, 620
Securities to Be Held to Maturity, 622
Trading Securities, 625
Securities Available-for-Sale, 629
    Comparison of HTM, TS, and AFS Approaches, 635
Transfers between Reporting Categories, 637
    Fair Value Option, 637
Impairment of Investments, 639
Concept Review Exercise: Various Investment Securities, 640
Financial Statement Presentation and Disclosure, 642
Part B: Investor Has Significant Influence, 644
How the Equity Method Relates to Consolidated Financial Statements, 644
What Is Significant Influence?, 645
A Single Entity Concept, 645
Further Adjustments, 647
Reporting the Investment, 649
What If Conditions Change?, 651
    If an Equity Method Investment Is Sold, 652

Comparison of Fair Value and Equity Methods, 652
Fair Value Option, 653

Concept Review Exercise: The Equity Method, 654

Decision Makers' Perspective, 656

Financial Instruments and Investment Derivatives, 657

Appendix 12A: Other Investments (Special Purpose Funds, Investments in Life Insurance Policies), 659

Appendix 12B: Impairment of Investments, 660

Questions for Review of Key Topics, 666

Brief Exercises, 668

Exercises, 669

CPA and CMA Review Questions, 676

Problems, 678

Broaden Your Perspective, 685

British Airways Case, 688

CPA Simulation 12–1, 689

13 CHAPTER
Current Liabilities and Contingencies, 690

Part A: Current Liabilities, 692

Characteristics of Liabilities, 692

What Is a Current Liability?, 693

Open Accounts and Notes, 693
Accounts Payable and Trade Notes Payable, 694
Short-Term Notes Payable, 694
Commercial Paper, 697

Accrued Liabilities, 697
Accrued Interest Payable, 698
Salaries, Commissions, and Bonuses, 698

Liabilities from Advance Collections, 700
Deposits and Advances from Customers, 700
Gift Cards, 701
Collections for Third Parties, 702

A Closer Look at the Current and Noncurrent Classification, 702
Current Maturities of Long-Term Debt, 702
Obligations Callable by the Creditor, 702
When Short-Term Obligations Are Expected to Be Refinanced, 703

Concept Review Exercise: Current Liabilities, 704

Part B: Contingencies, 705

Loss Contingencies, 706
Product Warranties and Guarantees, 708
Premiums, 710
Litigation Claims, 711
Subsequent Events, 713
Unasserted Claims and Assessments, 715

Gain Contingencies, 716

Concept Review Exercise: Contingencies, 717

Decision Makers' Perspective, 719

Appendix 13: Payroll-Related Liabilities, 721

Questions for Review of Key Topics, 723

Brief Exercises, 724

Exercises, 725

CPA and CMA Review Questions, 731

Problems, 733

Broaden Your Perspective, 738

British Airways Case, 744

14 CHAPTER
Bonds and Long-Term Notes, 746

The Nature of Long-Term Debt, 747

Part A: Bonds, 748

The Bond Indenture, 748

Recording Bonds at Issuance, 749
Determining the Selling Price, 750

Determining Interest—Effective Interest Method, 752
Zero-Coupon Bonds, 753
Bonds Sold at a Premium, 754
When Financial Statements Are Prepared between Interest Dates, 756

The Straight-Line Method—A Practical Expediency, 756

Concept Review Exercise: Issuing Bonds and Recording Interest, 757

Debt Issuance Costs, 758

Part B: Long-Term Notes, 759

Note Issued for Cash, 760

Note Exchanged for Assets or Services, 760

Installment Notes, 762

Financial Statement Disclosures, 763

Decision Makers' Perspective, 765

Concept Review Exercise: Note with an Unrealistic Interest Rate, 767

Part C: Debt Retired Early, Convertible into Stock, or Providing an Option to Buy Stock, 769

Early Extinguishment of Debt, 769

Convertible Bonds, 769
When the Conversion Option Is Exercised, 771
Induced Conversion, 772

Bonds with Detachable Warrants, 772

Concept Review Exercise: Issuance and Early Extinguishment of Debt, 774

Part D: Option to Report Liabilities at Fair Value, 775

Determining Fair Value, 775
Reporting Changes in Fair Value, 775
Mix and Match, 777

Appendix 14A: Bonds Issued between Interest Dates, 779

Appendix 14B: Troubled Debt Restructuring, 780

Questions for Review of Key Topics, 784

Brief Exercises, 785

Exercises, 786

CPA and CMA Review Questions, 792

Problems, 794

Broaden Your Perspective, 800

British Airways Case, 804

CPA Simulation 14–1, 805

15 CHAPTER
Leases, 806

Part A: Accounting by the Lessor and Lessee, 808
Decision Makers' Perspective—Advantages of Leasing, 808

Capital Leases and Installment Notes Compared, 809

Lease Classification, 810
  Classification Criteria, 811
  Additional Lessor Conditions, 813

Operating Leases, 815
  Advance Payments, 815
  Leasehold Improvements, 816

Capital Leases—Lessee and Lessor, 817
  Depreciation, 819
  Accrued Interest, 820

Concept Review Exercise: Direct Financing Lease, 821

Sales-Type Leases, 822

Part B: Bargain Purchase Options and Residual Value, 824
Bargain Purchase Options, 824
  When a BPO Is Exercisable Before the End of the Lease Term, 827

Residual Value, 827
  Effect on the Lessee of a Residual Value, 828
  Effect on the Lessor of a Residual Value, 828

Part C: Other Lease Accounting Issues, 832
Executory Costs, 832

Discount Rate, 832
  When the Lessee's Incremental Borrowing Rate is Less Than the Lessor's Implicit Rate, 833
  When the Lessor's Implicit Rate is Unknown, 833
  Lessor's Initial Direct Costs, 834

Contingent Rentals, 835

A Brief Summary, 835

Lease Disclosures, 835

Decision Makers' Perspective—Financial Statement Impact, 838
  Balance Sheet and Income Statement, 838
  Statement of Cash Flow Impact, 839

Concept Review Exercise: Various Lease Accounting Issues, 840

Part D: Special Leasing Arrangements, 842
Sale-Leaseback Arrangements, 842
  Capital Leases, 843
  Operating Leases, 844
  Losses on Sale-Leasebacks, 845

Real Estate Leases, 846
  Leases of Land Only, 846
  Leases of Land and Building, 846
  Leases of Only Part of a Building, 846

Leveraged Leases, 846
Questions for Review of Key Topics, 848
Brief Exercises, 849
Exercises, 850
CPA and CMA Review Questions, 857

Problems, 859
Broaden Your Perspective, 866
British Airways Case, 869
CPA Simulation 15–1, 870

16 CHAPTER
Accounting for Income Taxes, 872

Part A: Deferred Tax Assets and Deferred Tax Liabilities, 874
Conceptual Underpinning, 874

Temporary Differences, 875

Deferred Tax Liabilities, 875
  The FASB's Balance Sheet Approach, 877
  Types of Temporary Differences, 878

Deferred Tax Assets, 882

Valuation Allowance, 885

Permanent Differences, 886

Concept Review Exercise: Temporary and Permanent Differences, 889

Part B: Other Tax Accounting Issues, 890
Tax Rate Considerations, 890
  When Enacted Tax Rates Differ, 890
  Changes in Tax Laws or Rates, 891

Multiple Temporary Differences, 892

Net Operating Losses, 894
  Operating Loss Carryforward, 895
  Operating Loss Carryback, 896

Financial Statement Presentation, 897
  Balance Sheet Classification, 897
  Disclosure Notes, 898

Coping with Uncertainty in Income Taxes, 900

Intraperiod Tax Allocation, 902

Decision Makers' Perspective, 904

Concept Review Exercise: Multiple Differences and Operating Loss, 905
Questions for Review of Key Topics, 908
Brief Exercises, 909
Exercises, 911
CPA and CMA Review Questions, 918
Problems, 920
Broaden Your Perspective, 926
British Airways Case, 931
CPA Simulation 16–1, 932

17 CHAPTER
Pensions and Other Postretirement Benefits, 934

Part A: The Nature of Pension Plans, 936
Defined Contribution Pension Plans, 938
Defined Benefit Pension Plans, 939

Pension Expense—An Overview, 940

Part B: The Pension Obligation and Plan Assets, 941

The Pension Obligation, 941
    Accumulated Benefit Obligation, 941
    Vested Benefit Obligation, 941
    Projected Benefit Obligation, 942
    Illustration Expanded to Consider the Entire Employee Pool, 947

Pension Plan Assets, 947
    Reporting the Funded Status of the Pension Plan, 949

Part C: Determining Pension Expense, 949

The Relationship between Pension Expense and Changes in the PBO and Plan Assets, 949
    Components of Pension Expense, 951
    Income Smoothing, 953

Part D: Reporting Issues, 955

Recording Gains and Losses, 955

Recording the Pension Expense, 956

Recording the Funding of Plan Assets, 958

Comprehensive Income, 960

Income Tax Considerations, 961

Putting the Pieces Together, 962

Decision Makers' Perspective, 963

Settlement or Curtailment of Pension Plans, 963

Concept Review Exercise: Pension Plans, 964

Part E: Postretirement Benefits Other Than Pensions, 966

What Is a Postretirement Benefit Plan?, 967
    Postretirement Health Benefits and Pension Benefits Compared, 967
    Determining the Net Cost of Benefits, 968

Postretirement Benefit Obligation, 969
    Measuring the Obligation, 969
    Attribution, 969

Accounting for Postretirement Benefit Plans Other Than Pensions, 970
    A Comprehensive Illustration, 972

Decision Makers' Perspective, 973

Concept Review Exercise: Other Postretirement Benefits, 974

Appendix 17: Service Method of Allocating Prior Service Cost, 977
Questions for Review of Key Topics, 978
Brief Exercises, 979
Exercises, 980
CPA and CMA Review Questions, 989
Problems, 990
Broaden Your Perspective, 998
British Airways Case, 1003
CPA Simulation 17–1, 1004

18 CHAPTER Shareholders' Equity, 1006

Part A: The Nature of Shareholders' Equity, 1008
Financial Reporting Overview, 1008
    Paid-in Capital, 1009
    Retained Earnings, 1010

    Treasury Stock, 1010
    Accumulated Other Comprehensive Income, 1010
    Reporting Shareholders' Equity, 1012

The Corporate Organization, 1015
    Limited Liability, 1015
    Ease of Raising Capital, 1015
    Disadvantages, 1015
    Types of Corporations, 1016
    Hybrid Organizations, 1016
    The Model Business Corporation Act, 1016

Part B: Paid-In Capital, 1017
Fundamental Share Rights, 1017

Distinguishing Classes of Shares, 1017
    Typical Rights of Preferred Shares, 1018
    Is It Equity or Is It Debt?, 1019

The Concept of Par Value, 1020

Accounting for the Issuance of Shares, 1020
    Shares Issued For Cash, 1020
    Shares Issued for Noncash Consideration, 1021
    More Than One Security Issued for a Single Price, 1021
    Share Issue Costs, 1022

Concept Review Exercise: Expansion of Corporate Capital, 1023

Share Buybacks, 1024

Decision Makers' Perspective, 1024
    Shares Formally Retired or Viewed as Treasury Stock, 1025
    Accounting for Retired Shares, 1026
    Accounting for Treasury Stock, 1027
    Resale of Shares, 1028

Concept Review Exercise: Treasury Stock, 1028

Part C: Retained Earnings, 1031
Characteristics of Retained Earnings, 1031

Dividends, 1031
    Liquidating Dividend, 1031
    Retained Earnings Restrictions, 1032
    Cash Dividends, 1032
    Property Dividends, 1033

Stock Dividends and Splits, 1033
    Stock Dividends, 1033
    Stock Splits, 1035
    Stock Splits Effected in the Form of Stock Dividends (Large Stock Dividends), 1035

Decision Makers' Perspective, 1037

Concept Review Exercise: Changes in Retained Earnings, 1038

Appendix 18: Quasi Reorganizations, 1042
Questions for Review of Key Topics, 1044
Brief Exercises, 1044
Exercises, 1046
CPA and CMA Review Questions, 1053
Problems, 1054
Broaden Your Perspective, 1060
British Airways Case, 1066
CPA Simulation 18–1, 1066

4
SECTION

Additional Financial Reporting Issues

19 CHAPTER
Share-Based Compensation and Earnings Per Share, 1068

Part A: Share-Based Compensation, 1070
Stock Award Plans, 1070
Stock Option Plans, 1071
  Expense—The Great Debate, 1072
  Recognizing the Fair Value of Options, 1073
  When Options are Exercised, 1075
  When Unexercised Options Expire, 1075
  Plans with Graded Vesting, 1077
  Plans with Performance or Market Conditions, 1079
Employee Share Purchase Plans, 1080
Decision Makers' Perspective, 1080
Concept Review Exercise: Share-Based
Compensation Plans, 1081
Part B: Earnings Per Share, 1082
Basic Earnings Per Share, 1083
  Issuance of New Shares, 1083
  Stock Dividends and Stock Splits, 1084
  Reacquired Shares, 1085
  Earnings Available to Common Shareholders, 1086
Diluted Earnings Per Share, 1087
  Potential Common Shares, 1087
  Options, Rights, and Warrants, 1087
  Convertible Securities, 1088
Antidilutive Securities, 1092
  Options, Warrants, Rights, 1092
  Convertible Securities, 1093
  Order of Entry for Multiple Convertible Securities, 1093
Concept Review Exercise: Basic and Diluted EPS, 1095
Additional EPS Issues, 1096
  Components of the "Proceeds" in the Treasury Stock
  Method, 1096
  Contingently Issuable Shares, 1097
  Summary of the Effect of Potential Common Shares on
  Earnings Per Share, 1098
  Actual Conversions, 1099
  Financial Statement Presentation of Earnings Per Share
  Data, 1100
Decision Makers' Perspective, 1102
Concept Review Exercise: Additional EPS Issues, 1104
Appendix 19A: Option-Pricing Theory, 1107

Appendix 19B: Stock Appreciation Rights, 1108
Questions for Review of Key Topics, 1111
Brief Exercises, 1112
Exercises, 1113
CPA and CMA Review Questions, 1119
Problems, 1121
Broaden Your Perspective, 1127
British Airways Case, 1134
CPA Simulation 19–1, 1134

20 CHAPTER
Accounting Changes and Error Corrections, 1136

Part A: Accounting Changes, 1138
Change in Accounting Principle, 1139
Decision Makers' Perspective—Motivation for Accounting
Choices, 1139
  The Retrospective Approach: Most Changes in Accounting
  Principle, 1141
  The Prospective Approach, 1144
Change in Accounting Estimate, 1146
  Changing Depreciation, Amortization, and Depletion
  Methods, 1147
Change in Reporting Entity, 1148
Error Correction, 1149
Concept Review Exercise: Accounting Changes, 1150
Part B: Correction of Accounting Errors, 1152
Prior Period Adjustments, 1152
Error Correction Illustrated, 1153
  Error Discovered in the Same Reporting Period That It
  Occurred, 1153
  Error Affecting Previous Financial Statements, but Not Net
  Income, 1154
  Error Affecting a Prior Year's Net Income, 1154
Concept Review Exercise: Correction of Errors, 1159
Questions for Review of Key Topics, 1161
Brief Exercises, 1161
Exercises, 1162
CPA and CMA Review Questions, 1168
Problems, 1170
Broaden Your Perspective, 1177

21 CHAPTER
The Statement of Cash Flows Revisited, 1182

Part A: The Content and Value of the Statement of Cash Flows, 1184

Decision Makers' Perspective—Usefulness of Cash Flow Information, 1184

Cash Inflows and Outflows, 1184

Role of the Statement of Cash Flows, 1185

    The Importance of Cash Flows in an Economic Decline, 1187

    Cash and Cash Equivalents, 1187

    Primary Elements of the Statement of Cash Flows, 1188

Preparation of the Statement of Cash Flows, 1194

Part B: Preparing an SCF: The Direct Method of Reporting Cash Flows from Operating Activities, 1197

Using a Spreadsheet, 1197

    Income Statement Accounts, 1199

    Balance Sheet Accounts, 1207

Concept Review Exercise: Comprehensive Review, 1214

Part C: Preparing an SCF: The Indirect Method of Reporting Cash Flows from Operating Activities, 1218

Getting There through the Back Door, 1218

Components of Net Income That Do Not Increase or Decrease Cash, 1219

Components of Net Income That Do Increase or Decrease Cash, 1219

Comparison with the Direct Method, 1220

Reconciliation of Net Income to Cash Flows from Operating Activities, 1221

Decision Makers' Perspective—Cash Flow Ratios, 1223

Appendix 21A: Spreadsheet for the Indirect Method, 1225

Appendix 21B: The T-Account Method of Preparing the Statement of Cash Flows, 1229

Questions for Review of Key Topics, 1231

Brief Exercises, 1232

Exercises, 1233

CPA and CMA Review Questions, 1242

Problems, 1244

Broaden Your Perspective, 1256

British Airways Case, 1263

CPA Simulation 21–1, 1263

Appendix A: Derivatives, A–0
Appendix B: Dell Annual Report, B–1
Appendix C: IFRS Comprehensive Case, C–0
Glossary, G–0
Photo Credits, Cr–1
Index, I–0
Present and Future Value Tables, P–1

1

Environment and Theoretical Structure of Financial Accounting

/// OVERVIEW

The primary function of financial accounting is to provide useful financial information to users external to the business enterprise. The focus of financial accounting is on the information needs of investors and creditors. These users make critical resource allocation decisions that affect the nation's economy. The primary means of conveying financial information to external users is through financial statements and related notes.

In this chapter you explore important topics such as the FASB's conceptual framework that serve as a foundation for a more detailed study of financial statements, the way the statement elements are measured, and the concepts underlying these measurements and related disclosures.

/// LEARNING OBJECTIVES

After studying this chapter, you should be able to:

- LO1 Describe the function and primary focus of financial accounting. (page 4)
- LO2 Explain the difference between cash and accrual accounting. (page 7)
- LO3 Define generally accepted accounting principles (GAAP) and discuss the historical development of accounting standards. (page 9)
- LO4 Explain why the establishment of accounting standards is characterized as a political process. (page 12)
- LO5 Explain the purpose of the FASB's conceptual framework. (page 20)
- LO6 Identify the objective of financial reporting, the qualitative characteristics of financial reporting information, and the elements of financial statements. (page 21)
- LO7 Describe the four basic assumptions underlying GAAP. (page 28)
- LO8 Describe the four broad accounting principles that guide accounting practice. (page 29)

Misguided Marketing Major

During a class break in your investments class, a marketing major tells the following story to you and some friends:

The chief financial officer (CFO) of a large company is interviewing three candidates for the top accounting position with his firm. He asks each the same question:

CFO:	What is two plus two?
First candidate:	Four.
CFO:	What is two plus two?
Second candidate:	Four.
CFO:	What is two plus two?
Third candidate:	What would you like it to be?
CFO:	You're hired.

After you take some good-natured ribbing from the nonaccounting majors, your friend says, "Seriously, though, there must be ways the accounting profession prevents that kind of behavior. Aren't there some laws, or rules, or something? Are they based on some sort of theory, or are they just arbitrary?"

By the time you finish this chapter, you should be able to respond appropriately to the questions posed in this case. Compare your response to the solution provided at the end of the chapter.

QUESTIONS ///

1. What should you tell your friend about the presence of accounting standards in the United States? Who has the authority for standard setting? Who has the responsibility? (page 9)

2. What is the economic and political environment in which standard setting occurs? (page 12)

3. What is the relationship among management, auditors, investors, and creditors that tends to preclude the "What would you like it to be?" attitude? (page 16)

4. In general, what is the conceptual framework that underlies accounting principles? (page 20)

PART **A**

FINANCIAL ACCOUNTING ENVIRONMENT

In 1984 an undergraduate student at the University of Texas used $1,000 of his own funds to found a company called PC's Limited. The student's vision was to capitalize on the emerging personal computer (PC) business by selling directly to customers rather than through traditional retail outlets. The customer's PC would not be manufactured until it was ordered. This just-in-time (JIT) approach to production combined with the direct sales model would allow the company to better understand customer needs and more efficiently provide the most effective computing solutions.

In 1985, the first full year of company operations, the student's family contributed $300,000 in expansion capital, and revenue topped $73 million.[1] These were the humble beginnings for a visionary student named Michael Dell and a company eventually renamed **Dell Inc.,** that has become the world's largest PC manufacturer. Company profits for the year ended January 30, 2009, exceeded $2.4 billion and revenue topped $61 billion.

Many factors have contributed to the success of Dell Inc. The company's founder was visionary in terms of his approach to marketing and production. Importantly, too, the ability to raise external capital from investors and creditors at various times in the company's history was critical to its growth. Funding began with Michael Dell's initial $1,000 outlay and his family's $300,000 investment. In 1988, an initial public offering of the company's stock provided $30 million in equity financing.

> "Michael S. Dell built the multibillion-dollar company that bears his name not by inventing new products or services, but by constantly looking for ways to sell technology 'better, faster, cheaper,' as the company's mantra goes."[2]

Investors and creditors use information to assess risk and return.

Investors and creditors use many different kinds of information before supplying capital to business enterprises like Dell. The information is used to assess the future risk and return of their potential investments in the enterprise.[3] For example, information about the enterprise's products and its management is of vital importance to this assessment. In addition, various kinds of financial information are extremely important to investors and creditors.

● **LO1**

The primary focus of financial accounting is on the information needs of investors and creditors.

You might think of accounting as a special "language" used to communicate financial information about a business to those who wish to use the information to make decisions. Financial accounting, in particular, is concerned with providing relevant financial information to various *external* users. The chart in Graphic 1–1 illustrates a number of financial information supplier groups as well as several external user groups. Of these groups, the primary focus of financial accounting is on the financial information provided by *profit-oriented companies to their present and potential investors and creditors.* The reason for this focus is discussed in a later section of this chapter. One external user group, often referred to as *financial intermediaries,* includes financial analysts, stockbrokers, mutual fund managers, and credit rating organizations. These users provide advice to investors and creditors and/or make investment-credit decisions on their behalf. The collapse of **Enron Corporation** in 2001 and other high profile accounting failures made immensely clear the importance of reporting reliable financial information.

On the other hand, managerial accounting deals with the concepts and methods used to provide information to an organization's *internal* users, that is, its managers. You study managerial accounting elsewhere in your curriculum.

Financial statements convey financial information to external users.

The primary means of conveying financial information to investors, creditors, and other external users is through financial statements and related disclosure notes. The financial statements most frequently provided are (1) the balance sheet or statement of financial position, (2) the income statement or statement of operations, (3) the statement of cash flows, and (4) the statement of shareholders' equity. As you progress through this text, you will review and expand your knowledge of the information in these financial statements, the way the elements in these statements are measured, and the concepts underlying these measurements and

---

[1]"Dell, Inc.—Company History," **www.fundinguniverse.com**.
[2]Elizabeth Schwinn, "A Focus on Efficiency," *The Chronicle of Philanthropy* (April 6, 2006).
[3]Risk refers to the variability of possible outcomes from an investment. Return is the amount received over and above the investment and usually is expressed as a percentage.

PROVIDERS OF FINANCIAL INFORMATION	EXTERNAL USER GROUPS
• Profit-oriented companies	• Investors
	• Creditors (banks, bondholders, other lenders)
	• Employees
	• Labor unions
• Not-for-profit entities (e.g., government entities, charitable organizations, schools)	• Customers
	• Suppliers
	• Government regulatory agencies (e.g., Internal Revenue Service, Securities and Exchange Commission)
• Households	• Financial intermediaries (e.g., financial analysts, stockbrokers, mutual fund managers, credit-rating organizations)

GRAPHIC 1–1

Financial Information Supplier Groups and External User Groups

related disclosures. We use the term **financial reporting** to refer to the process of providing this information to external users. Keep in mind, though, that external users receive important financial information in a variety of other formats as well, including news releases and management forecasts, prospectuses, and reports filed with regulatory agencies.

Dell Inc.'s 2009 financial statements and related disclosure notes are provided in Appendix B located at the back of the text. You also can locate the 2009 statements and notes online at **www.dell.com**. To provide context for our discussions throughout the text, we occasionally refer to these statements and notes. Also, as new topics are introduced in later chapters, you might want to refer to the information to see how Dell reported the items being discussed.

The Economic Environment and Financial Reporting

In the United States, we have a highly developed free-enterprise economy with the majority of productive resources privately owned rather than government owned. It's important in this type of system that a mechanism exists to allocate the scarce resources of our society, both natural resources and labor, in an efficient manner. Resources should be allocated to private enterprises that will use them best to provide goods and services desired by society and not to enterprises that will waste them. The mechanisms that foster this efficient allocation of resources are the **capital markets.** We can think of the capital markets simply as a composite of all investors and creditors.

The three primary forms of business organization are the sole proprietorship, the partnership, and the corporation. In the United States, sole proprietorships and partnerships outnumber corporations. However, the dominant form of business organization, in terms of the ownership of productive resources, is the **corporation.** The corporate form makes it easier for an enterprise to acquire resources through the capital markets. Investors provide resources, usually cash, to a corporation in exchange for evidence of ownership interest, that is, shares of stock. Creditors such as banks lend cash to the corporation. Also, creditors can lend the corporation cash through the medium of bonds. Stocks and bonds usually are traded on organized security markets such as the New York Stock Exchange and the NASDAQ. The advantages and disadvantages of the corporate form are discussed at greater length in Chapter 18.

The capital markets provide a mechanism to help our economy allocate resources efficiently.

Corporations acquire capital from investors in exchange for ownership interest and from creditors by borrowing.

Secondary market transactions provide for the transfer of stocks and bonds among individuals and institutions.

The transfers of these stocks and bonds among individuals and institutions are referred to as **secondary market transactions.** Corporations receive no new cash from secondary market transactions. New cash is provided in *primary* market transactions in which the shares or bonds are sold by the corporation to the initial owners. Nevertheless, secondary market transactions are extremely important to the efficient allocation of resources in our economy. These transactions help establish market prices for additional shares and for bonds that corporations may wish to issue in the future to acquire additional capital. Also, many shareholders and bondholders might be unwilling to initially provide resources to corporations if there were no available mechanism for the future sale of their stocks and bonds to others.

What information do investors and creditors need to decide which companies will be provided capital? We explore that question next.

The Investment-Credit Decision—A Cash Flow Perspective

Investors and creditors both are interested in earning a fair return on the resources provided.

While the decisions made by investors and by creditors are somewhat different, they are similar in at least one important way. They both are concerned with providing resources to companies, usually cash, with the expectation of receiving more cash in return at some time in the future. A corporation's shareholders will receive cash from their investment through the ultimate sale of the ownership shares of stock. In addition, many corporations distribute cash to their shareholders in the form of periodic dividends. For example, if an investor provides a company with $10,000 cash (that is, purchases ownership shares) at the end of 2010, receives $400 in dividends from the company during 2011, and sells the ownership interest (shares) at the end of 2011 for $10,600 ($600 share price appreciation), the investment would have generated a **rate of return** of 10% for 2011, calculated as follows:

$$\frac{\$400 \text{ dividends} + \$600 \text{ share price appreciation}}{\$10,000 \text{ initial investment}} = 10\%$$

The expected *rate of return* and uncertainty, or risk, of that return are key variables in the investment decision.

Investors always are faced with more than one investment opportunity. There are many factors to consider before one of these opportunities is chosen. Two extremely important variables are the *expected rate of return* from each investment option, and the *uncertainty,* or *risk,* of that expected return. For example, consider the following two investment options:

1. Invest $10,000 in a savings account insured by the U.S. government that will generate a 5% rate of return.
2. Invest $10,000 in a profit-oriented company.

While the rate of return from option 1 is known with virtual certainty, the return from option 2 is uncertain. The amount and timing of the cash to be received in the future from option 2 are unknown. Investors require information about the company that will help them estimate the unknown return.

A company will be able to provide a return to investors and creditors only if it can generate a profit from selling its products or services.

In the long run, a company will be able to provide investors with a return only if it can generate a profit. That is, it must be able to use the resources provided by investors and creditors to generate cash receipts from selling a product or service that exceed the cash disbursements necessary to provide that product or service. If this excess can be generated, the marketplace is implicitly saying that society's resources have been efficiently allocated. The marketplace is assigning a value to the product or service that exceeds the value assigned to the resources used to produce that product or service.

The objective of financial accounting is to provide investors and creditors with useful information for decision making.

In summary, the primary objective of financial accounting is to provide investors and creditors with information that will help them make investment and credit decisions. More specifically, the information should help investors and creditors evaluate the *amounts, timing,* and *uncertainty* of the enterprise's future cash receipts and disbursements. The better this information is, the more efficient will be investor and creditor resource allocation decisions. Financial accounting, in providing key elements of the information set used by capital market participants, plays a vital societal role in the resource allocation process. The importance of this role to society explains why the primary focus of financial accounting is on the information needs of investors and creditors.

The Financial Accounting Standards Board, the current private sector body responsible for setting accounting standards in the United States, has published a conceptual framework for financial reporting (discussed later in this chapter) that is currently being revised. The first phase of the revised framework describes the specific objective of external financial reporting. This objective affirms the importance of the cash flow information needs of investors and creditors.

Throughout this text, you will be reminded of this cash flow perspective. For example, Chapter 4 describes certain events that are reported separately in the income statement due to the fact that these historical events have implications for future cash flows that are different from the normal operating activities. Separation of these events from normal operating activities provides financial statement users with information to more easily predict an enterprise's future cash flows.

Cash versus Accrual Accounting

Even though predicting future cash flows is the primary objective, the model best able to achieve that objective is the accrual accounting model. A competing model is cash basis accounting. Each model produces a periodic measure of performance that could be used by investors and creditors for predicting future cash flows.

● LO2

CASH BASIS ACCOUNTING. Cash basis accounting produces a measure called net operating cash flow. This measure is the difference between cash receipts and cash disbursements during a reporting period from transactions related to providing goods and services to customers.

Net operating cash flow is very easy to understand and all information required to measure it is factual. Also, it certainly relates to a variable of critical interest to investors and creditors. What could be better in helping to predict future cash flows from selling products and services than current cash flows from these activities? Remember, a company will be able to provide a return to investors and creditors only if it can use the capital provided to generate a positive net operating cash flow. However, there is a major drawback to using the current period's operating cash flow to predict future operating cash flows. Over the life of the company, net operating cash flow definitely is the variable of concern. However, over short periods of time, *operating cash flows may not be indicative of the company's long-run cash-generating ability* (that is, its ability to generate positive net operating cash flows in the future).

To demonstrate this, consider the following example. In Illustration 1–1 net operating cash flows are determined for the Carter Company during its first three years of operations.

Over the three-year period, Carter generated a positive net operating cash flow of $60,000. At the end of this three-year period, Carter has no outstanding debts. Because total sales and cash receipts over the three-year period were each $300,000, nothing is owed to Carter by customers. Also, at the beginning of the first year, Carter prepaid $60,000 for three years' rent on the facilities. There are no uncompleted transactions at the end of the three-year period. In that sense, we can view this three-year period as a micro version of the entire life of a company.

Net operating cash flow is the difference between cash receipts and cash disbursements from providing goods and services.

	Year 1	Year 2	Year 3	Total
Sales (on credit)	$100,000	$100,000	$100,000	$300,000
Net Operating Cash Flows				
Cash receipts from customers	$ 50,000	$125,000	$125,000	$300,000
Cash disbursements:				
Prepayment of three years' rent	(60,000)	–0–	–0–	(60,000)
Salaries to employees	(50,000)	(50,000)	(50,000)	(150,000)
Utilities	(5,000)	(15,000)	(10,000)	(30,000)
Net operating cash flow	$ (65,000)	$ 60,000	$ 65,000	$ 60,000

ILLUSTRATION 1–1

Cash Basis Accounting

The company incurred utility costs of $10,000 per year over the period. However, during the first year only $5,000 actually was paid, with the remainder being paid the second year. Employee salary costs of $50,000 were paid in full each year.

Is net operating cash flow for year 1 (negative $65,000) an accurate indicator of future cash-generating ability?[4] Obviously, it is not a good predictor of the positive net cash flows that occur in the next two years. Is the three-year pattern of net operating cash flows indicative of the company's year-by-year performance? No. But, if we measure the same activities by the accrual accounting model, we get a more accurate prediction of future operating cash flows and a more reasonable portrayal of the balanced operating performance of the company over the three years.

Over short periods of time, operating cash flow may not be an accurate predictor of future operating cash flows.

Net income is the difference between revenues and expenses.

ACCRUAL ACCOUNTING.   The accrual accounting model measures the entity's accomplishments and resource sacrifices during the period, regardless of when cash is received or paid. The accrual accounting model's measure of periodic accomplishments is called *revenues,* and the periodic measure of resource sacrifices is called *expenses.* The difference between revenues and expenses is *net income,* or net loss if expenses are greater than revenues.[5]

How would we measure revenues and expenses in this very simplistic situation? Illustration 1–2 offers a possible solution.

ILLUSTRATION 1–2	CARTER COMPANY Income Statements			
Accrual Accounting		Year 1	Year 2	Year 3	Total
	Revenues	$100,000	$100,000	$100,000	$300,000
	Expenses:				
	Rent	20,000	20,000	20,000	60,000
	Salaries	50,000	50,000	50,000	150,000
	Utilities	10,000	10,000	10,000	30,000
	Total expenses	80,000	80,000	80,000	240,000
	Net Income	$ 20,000	$ 20,000	$ 20,000	$ 60,000

The accrual accounting model provides a measure of periodic performance called *net income,* the difference between revenues and expenses.

Net income is considered a better indicator of future operating cash flows than is current net operating cash flow.

Net income of $20,000 for year 1 appears to be a reasonable predictor of the company's cash-generating ability as total net operating cash flow for the three-year period is a positive $60,000. Also, compare the three-year pattern of net operating cash flows in Illustration 1–1 to the three-year pattern of net income in Illustration 1–2. The net income pattern is more representative of the steady operating performance over the three-year period.[6]

While this example is somewhat simplistic, it allows us to see the motivation for using the accrual accounting model. Accrual income attempts to measure the accomplishments and sacrifices that occurred during the year, which may not correspond to cash inflows and outflows. For example, revenue for year 1 is the $100,000 in sales. This is a better measure of the company's accomplishments during year 1 than the $50,000 cash collected from customers.

Does this mean that information about cash flows from operating activities is not useful? No. Indeed, when combined with information about cash flows from investing and financing activities, this information provides valuable input into decisions made by investors and creditors. In fact, collectively, this cash flow information constitutes the statement of cash flows—one of the basic financial statements.[7]

---

[4]A negative cash flow is possible only if invested capital (i.e., owners contributed cash to the company in exchange for ownership interest) is sufficient to cover the cash deficiency. Otherwise, the company would have to either raise additional external funds or go bankrupt.

[5]Net income also includes gains and losses, which are discussed later in the chapter.

[6]Empirical evidence that accrual accounting provides a better measure of short-term performance than cash flows is provided by Patricia DeChow, "Accounting Earnings and Cash Flows as Measures of Firm Performance: The Role of Accrual Accounting," *Journal of Accounting and Economics* 18 (1994), pp. 3–42.

[7]The statement of cash flows is discussed in detail in Chapters 4 and 21.

The Development of Financial Accounting and Reporting Standards

Accrual accounting is the financial reporting model used by the majority of profit-oriented companies and by many not-for-profit companies. The fact that companies use the same model is important to financial statement users. Investors and creditors use financial information to make their resource allocation decisions. It's critical that they be able to *compare* financial information among companies. To facilitate these comparisons, financial accounting employs a body of standards known as generally accepted accounting principles, often abbreviated as GAAP (and pronounced *gap*). GAAP is a dynamic set of both broad and specific guidelines that companies should follow when measuring and reporting the information in their financial statements and related notes. The more important broad principles underlying GAAP are discussed in a subsequent section of this chapter and revisited throughout the text in the context of accounting applications for which they provide conceptual support.[8] Specific standards, such as how to measure and report a lease transaction, receive more focused attention in subsequent chapters.

● LO3

FINANCIAL Reporting Case

Q1, p. 3

Historical Perspective and Standards

Pressures on the accounting profession to establish uniform accounting standards began to surface after the stock market crash of 1929. Some feel that insufficient and misleading financial statement information led to inflated stock prices and that this contributed to the stock market crash and the subsequent depression.

The 1933 Securities Act and the 1934 Securities Exchange Act were designed to restore investor confidence. The 1933 act sets forth accounting and disclosure requirements for initial offerings of securities (stocks and bonds). The 1934 act applies to secondary market transactions and mandates reporting requirements for companies whose securities are publicly traded on either organized stock exchanges or in over-the-counter markets.[9] The 1934 act also created the Securities and Exchange Commission (SEC).

The Securities and Exchange Commission (SEC) was created by Congress with the 1934 Securities Exchange Act.

In the 1934 act, *Congress gave the SEC the authority to set accounting and reporting standards for companies whose securities are publicly traded.* However, the SEC, a government appointed body, has delegated the task of setting accounting standards to the private sector. It is important to understand that the power still lies with the SEC. If the SEC does not agree with a particular standard issued by the private sector, it can force a change in the standard. In fact, it has done so in the past.

The SEC has the authority to set accounting standards for companies, but has delegated the task to the private sector.

The SEC does issue its own accounting standards in the form of *Financial Reporting Releases (FRRs),* which regulate what information companies must report to it. The SEC also issues *Staff Accounting Bulletins* as authoritative supplements for reporting issues. These standards usually agree with those previously issued by the private sector. To learn more about the SEC, consult its Internet site at **www.sec.gov**.[10]

EARLY STANDARD SETTING.   The first private sector body to assume the task of setting accounting standards was the Committee on Accounting Procedure (CAP). The CAP was a committee of the American Institute of Accountants (AIA). The AIA, which was renamed the American Institute of Certified Public Accountants (AICPA) in 1957, is the national professional organization for certified professional public accountants. From 1938 to 1959, the CAP issued 51 *Accounting Research Bulletins (ARBs)* which dealt with specific accounting and reporting problems. No theoretical framework for financial accounting was established. This approach of dealing with individual issues without a framework led to stern criticism of the accounting profession.

In 1959 the Accounting Principles Board (APB) replaced the CAP. Members of the APB also belonged to the AICPA. The APB operated from 1959 through 1973 and issued

The Accounting Principles Board (APB) followed the CAP.

---

[8]The terms *standards* and *principles* sometimes are used interchangeably.

[9]Reporting requirements for SEC registrants include Form 10-K, the annual report form, and Form 10-Q, the report that must be filed for the first three quarters of each fiscal year.

[10]In 2000, the SEC issued regulation FD (Fair Disclosure) which redefined how companies interact with analysts and the public in disclosing material information. Prior to regulation FD, companies often disclosed important information to a select group of analysts before disseminating the information to the general public. Now, this type of selective disclosure is prohibited. The initial disclosure of market-sensitive information must be made available to the general public.

31 *Accounting Principles Board Opinions (APBOs)*, various *Interpretations*, and four *Statements*. The *Opinions* also dealt with specific accounting and reporting problems. Many *ARBs* and *APBOs* have not been superseded and still represent authoritative GAAP.

The APB's main effort to establish a theoretical framework for financial accounting and reporting was *APB Statement No. 4*, "Basic Concepts and Accounting Principles Underlying Financial Statements of Business Enterprises." Unfortunately, the effort was not successful.

The APB was composed of members of the accounting profession and was supported by their professional organization. Members participated in the activities of the board on a voluntary, part-time basis. The APB was criticized by industry and government for its inability to establish an underlying framework for financial accounting and reporting and for its inability to act quickly enough to keep up with financial reporting issues as they developed. Perhaps the most important flaw of the APB was a perceived lack of independence. Composed almost entirely of certified public accountants, the board was subject to the criticism that the clients of the represented public accounting firms were exerting self-interested pressure on the board and influencing decisions. Another complaint was the absence of varied interest groups in the standard-setting process.

CURRENT STANDARD SETTING. Criticism of the APB led to the creation in 1973 of the **Financial Accounting Standards Board (FASB)** and its supporting structure. The FASB differs from its predecessor in many ways. There are five full-time members of the FASB, compared to 18–21 part-time members of the APB. While all of the APB members belonged to the AICPA, FASB members represent various constituencies concerned with accounting standards. Members have included representatives from the accounting profession, profit-oriented companies, accounting educators, and government. The APB was supported financially by the AICPA, while the FASB is supported by its parent organization, the **Financial Accounting Foundation (FAF)**. The FAF is responsible for selecting the members of the FASB and its Advisory Council, ensuring adequate funding of FASB activities, and exercising general oversight of the FASB's activities.[11] The FASB is, therefore, an independent, private sector body whose members represent a broad constituency of interest groups.[12]

In 1984, the FASB's **Emerging Issues Task Force (EITF)** was formed to provide more timely responses to emerging financial reporting issues. The EITF membership includes 15 individuals from public accounting and private industry, along with a representative from the FASB and an SEC observer. The membership of the task force is designed to include individuals who are in a position to be aware of emerging financial reporting issues. The task force considers these emerging issues and attempts to reach a consensus on how to account for them. If consensus can be reached, generally no FASB action is required. The task force disseminates its rulings in the form of *EITF Issues*. These pronouncements are considered part of generally accepted accounting principles.

If a consensus can't be reached, FASB involvement may be necessary. The EITF plays an important role in the standard-setting process by identifying potential problem areas and then acting as a filter for the FASB. This speeds up the standard-setting process and allows the FASB to focus on pervasive long-term problems.

One of the FASB's most important activities has been the formulation of a conceptual framework. The conceptual framework, discussed in more depth later in this chapter, deals with theoretical and conceptual issues and provides an underlying structure for current and future accounting and reporting standards. The Board also has issued over 160 specific accounting standards, called *Statements of Financial Accounting Standards (SFASs)*, as well as numerous FASB *Interpretations, Staff Positions* and *Technical Bulletins*.[13]

The FASB currently sets accounting standards.

The Emerging Issues Task Force (EITF) identifies financial reporting issues and attempts to resolve them without involving the FASB.

In addition to issuing specific accounting standards, the FASB has formulated a conceptual framework to provide an underlying theoretical and conceptual structure for accounting standards.

---

[11]The FAF's primary sources of funding are contributions and the sales of the FASB's publications. The FAF is governed by trustees, the majority of whom are appointed from the membership of eight sponsoring organizations. These organizations represent important constituencies involved with the financial reporting process. For example, one of the founding organizations is the Association of Investment Management and Research (formerly known as the Financial Analysts Federation) which represents financial information *users,* and another is the Financial Executives International which represents financial information *preparers.* The FAF also raises funds to support the activities of the Government Accounting Standards Board (GASB).

[12]The FASB organization also includes the Financial Accounting Standards Advisory Council (FASAC). The major responsibility of the FASAC is to advise the FASB on the priorities of its projects, including the suitability of new projects that might be added to its agenda.

[13]For more information, go to the FASB's Internet site at **www.fasb.org**.

HIERARCHY OF STANDARD-SETTING AUTHORITY

```
        Congress
           │
          SEC
           │
      Private Sector
           │
   ┌───────┼───────┐
  CAP     APB    FASB
1938–1959  1959–1973  1973–Present
```

Graphic 1–2 summarizes this discussion on accounting standards. The graphic shows the hierarchy of accounting standard setting in order of authority. Congress gave the SEC the authority to set accounting standards, specifically for companies whose securities are publicly traded. However, the SEC has delegated the task to various private sector bodies (currently the FASB) while retaining its legislated authority.

> The Codification does not change GAAP; instead it reorganizes the thousands of U.S. GAAP pronouncements into roughly 90 accounting topics, and displays all topics using a consistent structure.[14]

From the above discussion, we can see that multiple sources comprise the body of literature referred to as GAAP, including pronouncements and interpretations of the SEC, CAP, APB, and FASB, as well as AICPA industry guides, bulletins, and interpretations. Determining the appropriate accounting treatment for a particular event or transaction might require an accountant to research several of these sources. To simplify the task of researching an accounting topic, in 2007 the FASB launched its *FASB Accounting Standards Codification* project. The objective of the project was to integrate and topically organize all relevant accounting pronouncements comprising GAAP in a searchable, online database.

The codification became effective on July 1, 2009, and now represents the single source of authoritative nongovernmental U.S. GAAP, except for rules and interpretive releases of the SEC, which remain also as sources of authoritative GAAP. All other literature is now nonauthoritative. The codification is organized into nine main topics and approximately 90 subtopics. The main topics and related numbering system are illustrated in Graphic 1–3.[15] The Codification can be located at **www.fasb.org**.

> The *FASB Accounting Standards Codification* is now the only source of authoritative U.S. GAAP. Exceptions are rules and interpretive releases of the SEC, which remain as sources of authoritative GAAP.

FASB Accounting Standards Codification Topics	
Topic	Numbered
General Principles	100–199
Presentation	200–299
Assets	300–399
Liabilities	400–499
Equity	500–599
Revenues	600–699
Expenses	700–799
Broad Transactions	800–899
Industry	900–999

---

[14]"FASB Accounting Standards Codification™ Expected to Officially Launch on July 1, 2009," *FASB News Release* (Norwalk, Conn.: FASB, December 4, 2008).

[15]FASB ASC 105–10: Generally Accepted Accounting Principles—Overall (previously "The FASB Accounting Standards Codification™ and the Hierarchy of Generally Accepted Accounting Principles—a replacement of FASB Statement No. 162," *Statement of Financial Accounting Standards No. 168* (Norwalk, Conn.: FASB: 2009)).

Throughout the text, we use the new Accounting Standards Codification System (ASC) in footnotes when referencing generally accepted accounting principles (FASB ASC followed by the appropriate number). Each footnote also includes a reference to the original accounting standard that is codified in ASC. Your instructor may assign end-of-chapter exercises and cases that ask you to research the FASB's Accounting Standards Codification.

ADDITIONAL CONSIDERATION

Accounting standards and the standard-setting process discussed above relate to standards governing the measurement and reporting of information for profit-oriented organizations and nongovernmental not-for-profit entities. In 1984, the Government Accounting Standards Board (GASB) was created to develop accounting standards for governmental units such as states and cities. The GASB operates under the oversight of the Financial Accounting Foundation and the Governmental Accounting Standards Advisory Council.

The Establishment of Accounting Standards—A Political Process

● **LO4**

FINANCIAL Reporting Case

Q2, p. 3

The FASB must consider potential economic consequences of a change in an accounting standard or the introduction of a new standard.

The setting of accounting and reporting standards often has been characterized as a *political process*. Standards, particularly changes in standards, can have significant differential effects on companies, investors and creditors, and other interest groups. A change in an accounting standard or the introduction of a new standard by the issuance of an accounting standards update can result in a substantial redistribution of wealth within our economy.

The role of the FASB in setting accounting standards is a complex one. Sound accounting principles can provide significant guidance in determining the appropriate method to measure and report an economic transaction. However, the FASB must gauge the potential economic consequences of a change in a standard to the various interest groups as well as to society as a whole. One obvious desired consequence is that the new standard will provide a better set of information to external users and thus improve the resource allocation process.

An example of the effect of economic consequences on standard setting was the highly controversial debate surrounding accounting for employee stock options. Employees often are given the option to buy shares in the future at a preset price as an integral part of their total compensation package. The accounting objective for any form of compensation is to report compensation expense during the period of service for which the compensation is given. At issue is the amount of compensation to be recognized as expense for stock options.

Historically, options were measured at their intrinsic value, which is the simple difference between the market price of the shares and the option price at which they could be acquired. For instance, an option that permits an employee to buy $60 stock for $42 has an intrinsic value of $18. The problem is that options for which the exercise price equals the market value of the underlying stock at the date of grant (which describes most plans) have no intrinsic value and thus result in zero compensation when measured this way, even though the fair value of the options can be quite substantial. To the FASB and many others, it seemed counterintuitive to not record any compensation expense for arrangements that routinely provide a large part of the total compensation of executives and a potentially significant amount for other employees receiving options.

Public pressure sometimes prevails over conceptual merit in the standard-setting arena.

In 1995, after lengthy debate, the FASB bowed to public pressure and consented to encourage, rather than require, companies to expense the fair value of employee stock options. Nearly a decade later, the contentious issue resurfaced, and the FASB issued a standard requiring companies to measure options at their fair values and to expense that amount over an appropriate service period. This issue is discussed at greater length in Chapter 19.

Another example is the heated debate that occurred on the issue of accounting for business combinations. Back in 1996, the FASB added to its agenda a project to consider a possible revision in the practice of allowing two separate and distinct methods of accounting for business combinations, the pooling of interests method and the purchase method. A thorough explanation of the differences between these methods is beyond the scope of this text. For our discussion here, just note that a key issue in the debate related to goodwill, an intangible asset that arises only in business combinations accounted for using the purchase method. Under the then-existing standards, goodwill, like any other intangible asset, was amortized (expensed) over its estimated useful life thus reducing reported net income for several years following the acquisition. It was that negative impact on earnings that motivated many companies involved in a business combination to take whatever steps necessary to structure the transaction as a pooling of interests, thereby avoiding goodwill, its amortization to expense, and the resulting reduction in earnings.

> **DENNIS POWELL—CISCO SYSTEMS, INC. VP**
> Clearly the FASB listened and responded to extensive comments from the public and the financial community to make the purchase method of accounting more effective and realistic.[16]

As you might guess, when the FASB initially proposed eliminating the pooling method, many companies that were actively engaged in business acquisitions vigorously opposed the elimination of this means of avoiding goodwill. To support their opposition these companies argued that if they were required to use purchase accounting, many business combinations important to economic growth would prove unattractive due to the negative impact on earnings caused by goodwill amortization and would not be undertaken.

To satisfy opposition to its proposal, the FASB suggested several modifications over the years, but it wasn't until the year 2000 that a satisfactory compromise was reached. Specifically, under the accounting standards issued in 2001,[17] only the purchase method, now called the acquisition method, is acceptable, but to soften the impact, the resulting goodwill is *not* amortized. We discuss goodwill and its measurement in Chapters 10 and 11.

The most recent example of the political process at work in standard setting is the controversy surrounding the implementation of the fair value accounting standard issued in 2007. As we discuss later in this chapter and in subsequent chapters, many financial assets and liabilities are reported at fair value in the balance sheet, and many types of fair value changes are included in net income. A key issue concerns the appropriate valuation of financial assets in illiquid markets such as those we've witnessed during the recent economic slowdown. Many have argued that accounting standards were applied in a manner that exacerbated the financial crisis of 2008–2009 by forcing financial institutions to take larger than necessary write-downs of financial assets. Pressure from lobbyists and politicians influenced the FASB to revise its guidance on measuring fair value in these situations, and ongoing pressure remains for the FASB and international standard setters to reduce the extent to which fair value changes are reported in net income.

The FASB's dilemma is to balance accounting considerations and political considerations resulting from perceived possible adverse economic consequences. To help solve this dilemma, the board undertakes a series of elaborate information-gathering steps before issuing an accounting standards update involving alternative accounting treatments for an economic transaction. These steps include open hearings, deliberations, and requests for written comments from interested parties. Graphic 1–4 outlines the FASB's standard-setting process.

> *The FASB undertakes a series of information-gathering steps before issuing an accounting standards update.*

These steps are the FASB's attempt to acquire consensus as to the preferred method of accounting, as well as to anticipate adverse economic consequences. The board's process is similar to that of an elected political representative, a U.S. congresswoman for example, trying to determine consensus among her constituency before voting on a bill on the floor of the House of Representatives. For this reason, accounting standard setting is a political process.

Our Global Marketplace

Advances in communication and transportation systems continue to expand the marketplace in which companies operate. The world economy is more integrated than ever, and many of the larger U.S. corporations are truly multinational in nature. These multinational corporations have their home in the United States but operate and perhaps raise capital in other countries. For example, **Coca-Cola**, **IBM**, **Colgate-Palmolive**, **Intel**, and many other companies generate more than 50% of their revenue from foreign sales. It is not uncommon for even relatively small companies to transact business in many different countries. Of course, many

> *Many U.S. and foreign companies operate and raise capital in more than one country.*

---

[16]Jonathan Weil, "FASB Backs Down on Goodwill-Accounting Rules," *The Wall Street Journal* (December 7, 2000).

[17]FASB ASC 805: Business Combinations (previously "Business Combinations," *Statement of Financial Accounting Standards No. 141 (revised)* (Norwalk, Conn.: FASB, 2007)), and FASB ASC 350: Intangibles—Goodwill and Other (previously "Goodwill and Other Intangible Assets," *Statement of Financial Accounting Standards No. 142* (Norwalk, Conn.: FASB, 2001)).

GRAPHIC 1–4

The FASB's Standard-Setting Process

Step	Explanation
1.	The Board receives requests/recommendations for possible projects and reconsideration of existing standards from various sources.
2.	The FASB Chairman decides whether to add a project to the technical agenda, subject to oversight by the Foundation's Board of Trustees and after appropriate consultation with FASB Members and others.
3.	The Board deliberates at one or more public meetings the various issues identified and analyzed by the staff.
4.	The Board issues an Exposure Draft. (In some projects, a Discussion Paper may be issued to obtain input at an early stage that is used to develop an Exposure Draft.)
5.	The Board holds a public roundtable meeting on the Exposure Draft, if necessary.
6.	The staff analyzes comment letters, public roundtable discussion, and any other information. The Board redeliberates the proposed provisions at public meetings.
7.	The Board issues an Accounting Standards Update describing amendments to the Accounting Standards Codification.

foreign corporations operate in the United States as well. In fact, companies such as **Bridgestone Americas Holding** are owned by companies that reside in other countries.

The financial marketplace also has taken on a global dimension, with many companies crossing geographic boundaries to raise capital. For example, over 400 foreign companies are listed on the New York Stock Exchange and the London Stock Exchange. This expanded marketplace requires that company management understand the laws, customs, regulations, *and* accounting and reporting standards of many different countries.

TOWARD GLOBAL ACCOUNTING STANDARDS.   Most industrialized countries have organizations responsible for determining accounting and reporting standards. In some countries, the United Kingdom, for instance, the responsible organization is a private sector body similar to the FASB in the United States. In other countries, such as France, the organization is a governmental body.

Accounting standards prescribed by these various groups are not the same. Standards differ from country to country for many reasons, including different legal systems, levels of inflation, culture, degrees of sophistication and use of capital markets, and political and economic ties with other countries. These differences can cause problems for multinational corporations. A company doing business in more than one country may find it difficult to comply with more than one set of accounting standards if there are important differences among the sets. These differences also cause problems for investors who must struggle to compare companies whose financial statements are prepared under different standards. It has been argued that different national accounting standards impair the ability of companies to raise capital in international markets.

The *International Accounting Standards Board (IASB)* is dedicated to developing a single set of global accounting standards.

In response to this problem, the International Accounting Standards Committee (IASC) was formed in 1973 to develop global accounting standards. The IASC reorganized itself in 2001 and created a new standard-setting body called the International Accounting Standards Board (IASB). The IASC now acts as an umbrella organization similar to the Financial Accounting Foundation (FAF) in the United States. The IASB's main objective is to develop a single set of high-quality, understandable, and enforceable global accounting standards to help participants in the world's capital markets and other users make economic decisions.[18]

---

[18]www.iasb.org.

The IASC issued 41 International Accounting Standards (IASs). The IASB endorsed these standards when it was formed in 2001. Since then, the IASB has revised many of them and has issued nine standards of its own, called International Financial Reporting Standards (IFRSs). Compliance with these standards is voluntary, since the IASB has no enforcement authority. However, more and more countries are basing their national accounting standards on IFRS. The International Organization of Securities Commissions (IOSCO) approved a resolution permitting its members to use these standards to prepare their financial statements for cross-border offerings and listings. By late 2009, 117 jurisdictions, including Hong Kong, Egypt, Australia, and the countries in the European Union (EU), either require or permit the use of IFRS or a local variant of IFRS.[19] EU companies affected number between 7,000 and 8,000. Canada and India plan to adopt IFRS in 2011. In 2007, China began requiring its 1,400 listed companies to report under IFRS-aligned standards.

International Financial Reporting Standards are gaining support around the globe.

In the United States, the move toward convergence of accounting standards began in earnest with the cooperation of the FASB and the IASC in 1994 that led to a common EPS standard for both IFRS and U.S. GAAP. Chapter 19 describes this standard.

ROBERT HERZ—FASB CHAIRMAN

We believe now is the appropriate time to develop a plan for moving all U.S. public companies to an improved version of IFRS and to consider any actions needed to strengthen the IASB as the global accounting standard setter. (From his testimony before Congress, October 2007.)

In 2002, the FASB and IASB signed the so-called Norwalk Agreement, formalizing their commitment to convergence of U.S. GAAP and IFRS. Under this agreement, the boards pledged to remove existing differences between their standards and to coordinate their future standard-setting agendas so that major issues are worked on together. Recent standards issued by the FASB that you will encounter in our later discussions on share-based compensation, nonmonetary exchanges, inventory costs, and the fair value option are examples of this commitment to convergence. In 2007 the SEC eliminated the requirement for foreign companies that issue stock in the United States to include in their financial statements a reconciliation of IFRS to U.S. GAAP. In the spring of 2008, the FASB and IASB outlined their plan to accelerate the convergence of U.S. GAAP and IFRS to enable U.S. companies to move to international standards. "It is a new world and we're going to have to figure out how to play in that," said Robert Herz, chairman of the FASB.[20] In the "new world" to which Herz refers, the financial statements in all major capital markets are based on a single set of standards.

The commitment to narrowing differences between U.S. GAAP and international standards has influenced many FASB Standards.

In November 2008, the SEC proposed a *Roadmap* for the potential use of financial statements prepared in accordance with IFRS. The Roadmap sets forth several milestones that, if achieved, could lead to the required use of IFRS by publicly traded U.S. companies in 2014. The first milestone, "Improvements in accounting standards," refers to a Memorandum of Understanding between the Boards. This agreement sets a June 2011 target date for the completion of 11 major joint projects that are intended to improve the standards of both Boards while further aligning U.S. GAAP and IFRS. You will read **Where We're Headed** boxes throughout the text that describe many of these projects. At the time this textbook is being written, the Roadmap had not yet been finalized. It may be that convergence will take the form of a required whole-scale adoption of IFRS by U.S. companies. On the other hand, convergence already is gradually occurring through cooperation between the FASB and IASB and may be nearly complete when IFRS is adopted in the U.S., depending on when the SEC mandates the switch.

The SEC Roadmap proposes that IFRS be required by U.S. companies in 2014.

Although many argue that a single set of global standards will improve comparability of financial reporting and facilitate access to capital, others argue that U.S. standards should remain customized to fit the stringent legal and regulatory requirements of the U.S. business environment. There also is concern that differences in implementation and enforcement from country to country will make accounting appear more uniform than actually is the case. Another argument is that competition between alternative standard-setting regimes is healthy and can lead to improved standards.

---

[19]See **www.iasplus.com/country/useias.htm**.
[20]"FASB, IASB Speed Up Plan for Convergence," *Reuters*, May 1, 2008.

International Financial Reporting Standards boxes are included throughout the text that describe the important differences that still remain between U.S. GAAP and IFRS. In addition, your instructor may assign end-of-chapter IFRS questions, exercises, problems, and cases that explore these differences.

The Role of the Auditor

It is the responsibility of management to apply accounting standards when communicating with investors and creditors through financial statements. Another group, auditors, serves as an independent intermediary to help ensure that management has in fact appropriately applied GAAP in preparing the company's financial statements. Auditors examine (audit) financial statements to express a professional, independent opinion. The opinion reflects the auditors' assessment of the statements' "fairness," which is determined by the extent to which they are prepared in compliance with GAAP.

The report of the independent auditors of **Dell Inc.**'s financial statements is in the annual report information in Appendix B located at the back of the text. The first paragraph provides the auditors' opinion and explains the scope of the audit. After conducting its audit, the accounting firm of **PricewaterhouseCoopers LLP** stated that "In our opinion, the consolidated financial statements listed in the accompanying index present fairly . . . , in conformity with accounting principles generally accepted in the United States of America." This is known as a clean opinion. Had there been any material departures from GAAP or other problems that caused the auditors to question the fairness of the statements, the report would have been modified to inform readers. The report also provides the auditors' opinion on the effectiveness of the company's internal control over financial reporting. We discuss this second opinion in the next section.

The auditor adds credibility to the financial statements, increasing the confidence of capital market participants who rely on the information. Auditors, therefore, play an important role in the resource allocation process.

In most states, only individuals licensed as certified public accountants (CPAs) in the state can represent that the financial statements have been audited in accordance with generally accepted auditing standards. Requirements to be licensed as a CPA vary from state to state, but all states specify education, testing, and experience requirements. The testing requirement is to pass the Uniform CPA Examination.

Financial Reporting Reform

The dramatic collapse of **Enron** in 2001 and the dismantling of the international public accounting firm of **Arthur Andersen** in 2002 severely shook U.S. capital markets. The credibility of the accounting profession itself as well as of corporate America was called into question. Public outrage over accounting scandals at high-profile companies like **WorldCom**, **Xerox**, **Merck**, **Adelphia Communications**, and others increased the pressure on lawmakers to pass measures that would restore credibility and investor confidence in the financial reporting process.

> **PAUL SARBANES—U.S. SENATOR**
> We confront an increasing crisis of confidence with the public's trust in our markets. If this continues, I think it poses a real threat to our economic health.[21]

Driven by these pressures, Congress acted swiftly and passed the *Public Company Accounting Reform and Investor Protection Act of 2002,* commonly referred to as the *Sarbanes-Oxley Act* for the two congressmen who sponsored the bill. The legislation is comprehensive in its inclusion of the key players in the financial reporting process. The law provides for the regulation of auditors of public securities-issuing entities and the types of services they furnish to clients, increases accountability of corporate executives, addresses conflicts of interest for securities analysts, and provides for stiff criminal penalties for violators. Graphic 1–5 outlines the key provisions of the act.

The changes imposed by the legislation are dramatic in scope and pose a significant challenge for the public accounting profession. At the same time, many maintain the changes

---

[21]James Kuhnhenn, "Bush Vows to Punish Corporate Lawbreakers," *San Jose Mercury News* (July 9, 2002), p. 8A.

GRAPHIC 1–5

Public Company
Accounting Reform
and Investor Protection
Act of 2002
(Sarbanes-Oxley)

Key Provisions of the Act:

- **Oversight board.** The five-member (two accountants) Public Company Accounting Oversight Board has the authority to establish standards dealing with auditing, quality control, ethics, independence and other activities relating to the preparation of audit reports, or can choose to delegate these responsibilities to the AICPA. Prior to the act, the AICPA set auditing standards. The SEC has oversight and enforcement authority.
- **Corporate executive accountability.** Corporate executives must personally certify the financial statements and company disclosures with severe financial penalties and the possibility of imprisonment for fraudulent misstatement.
- **Nonaudit services.** The law makes it unlawful for the auditors of public companies to perform a variety of nonaudit services for audit clients. Prohibited services include bookkeeping, internal audit outsourcing, appraisal or valuation services, and various other consulting services. Other nonaudit services, including tax services, require pre-approval by the audit committee of the company being audited.
- **Retention of work papers.** Auditors of public companies must retain all audit or review work papers for seven years or face the threat of a prison term for willful violations.
- **Auditor rotation.** Lead audit partners are required to rotate every five years. Mandatory rotation of audit firms came under consideration.
- **Conflicts of interest.** Audit firms are not allowed to audit public companies whose chief executives worked for the audit firm and participated in that company's audit during the preceding year.
- **Hiring of auditor.** Audit firms are hired by the audit committee of the board of directors of the company, not by company management.
- **Internal control.** Section 404 of the act requires that company management document and assess the effectiveness of all internal control processes that could affect financial reporting. The PCAOB's *Auditing Standard No. 2* (since replaced by *Auditing Standard No. 5*) requires that the company auditors express an opinion on whether the company has maintained effective internal control over financial reporting.

were necessary to lessen the likelihood of corporate and accounting fraud and to restore investor confidence in the U.S. capital markets.

Section 404 is perhaps the most controversial provision of the 2002 act. No one argues the importance of adequate internal controls. However, the costs of implementing this section of the act have been substantial. Companies are required to document internal controls and assess their adequacy. The Public Company Accounting Oversight Board's (PCAOB) *Auditing Standard No. 2* added an additional requirement that auditors express an opinion on whether the company has maintained effective internal control over financial reporting.[22]

Are the benefits of Section 404 greater than the compliance costs? The benefits of 404 are difficult to assess. How many business failures like Enron are avoided as a result of the added attention given to the implementation and maintenance of adequate internal controls? The costs of compliance, on the other hand, are easier to see. For example, the four large, international public accounting firms employed a consulting company to survey a sample of the firms' Fortune 1,000 clients to determine the costs for the first two years of Section 404 compliance. The survey determined that the average cost of compliance for firms with a market capitalization of over $700 million, including internal costs and auditor fees, was approximately $8.5 million and $4.77 million in years 1 and 2, respectively.[23] The costs dropped significantly in year 2 as expected, but they still were substantial.

WILLIAM J. MCDONOUGH—PCAOB CHAIRMAN

This standard (*Auditing Standard No. 2*) is one of the most important and far-reaching auditing standards the board will ever adopt. In the past, internal controls were merely considered by auditors; now they will have to be tested and examined in detail. (As quoted in *PCAOBUS.org*, June 18, 2004.)

Complying with Section 404 of SOX costs companies millions of dollars annually.

[22]"An Audit of Internal Control over Financial Reporting Performed in Conjunction with an Audit of Financial Statements," *Auditing Standard No. 2* (Washington, D.C.: PCAOB, 2004).
[23]"Sarbanes-Oxley 404 Costs and Implementation Issues: Spring 2006 Survey Update," CRA International (April 17, 2006).

In response to the high cost of 404 compliance, the PCAOB issued *Auditing Standard No. 5* to replace its *Auditing Standard No. 2*.[24] The new standard emphasizes audit efficiency with a more focused, risk-based testing approach for material areas. These guidelines should reduce the total costs of 404 compliance.

We revisit Section 404 in Chapter 7 in the context of an introduction to internal controls.

A Move Away from Rules-Based Standards?

A principles-based, or objectives-oriented, approach to standard setting stresses professional judgment, as opposed to following a list of rules.

The accounting scandals at Enron and other companies also rekindled the debate over **principles-based,** or more recently termed **objectives-oriented,** versus **rules-based** accounting standards. In fact, a provision of the Sarbanes-Oxley Act required the SEC to study the issue and provide a report to Congress on its findings. That report, issued in July 2003, recommended that accounting standards be developed using an objectives-oriented approach.[25] The FASB also issued a proposal addressing this issue.[26]

An objectives-oriented approach to standard setting stresses using professional judgment, as opposed to following a list of rules when choosing the appropriate accounting treatment for a transaction. Lease accounting provides a useful example for comparing the two approaches. In Chapter 15 you will learn that a company records a long-term lease of an asset as either a *capital lease* or an *operating lease*. If a leasing arrangement is "in substance" the purchase of an asset with the lease payments effectively serving as payments for that purchase, we should account for the transaction that way. A capital lease requires that the property being leased be recorded as an asset and a liability to pay for the asset. No asset or liability is recorded for an operating lease. Therein lies the problem. Because company managers are aware that analysts view debt as indicative of financial risk, those managers often try to avoid reporting more debt than absolutely necessary. As a result, firms frequently stretch the limits of the rules to structure lease agreements so that they technically sidestep the FASB's detailed rules, principally four criteria for identifying capital leases that require recording a liability.

ROBERT HERZ—FASB CHAIRMAN
Under a principles-based approach, one starts with laying out the key objectives of good reporting in the subject area and then provides guidance explaining the objective and relating it to some common examples. While rules are sometimes unavoidable, the intent is not to try to provide specific guidance or rules for every possible situation. Rather, if in doubt, the reader is directed back to the principles. (From his presentation to the FEI in 2002.)

In contrast, the IASB employs an objectives-oriented approach to lease accounting in its *IAS 17*. In that standard, the focus is on professional judgment rather than specific rules to determine whether the leasing arrangement effectively transfers the "risk and rewards" of ownership. Professional judgment is then applied to determine if the risk and rewards have been transferred.

Which approach is more likely to capture the economic substance of the lease, rather than its form? The FASB's criteria were designed to aid the accountant in determining whether the risk and rewards of ownership have been transferred. Many would argue, though, that the result has been the opposite. Rather than use the criteria to enhance judgment, management and its accountants can use the rules as an excuse to avoid using professional judgment altogether and instead focus on the rules alone. Proponents of an objectives-oriented approach argue that its focus is squarely on professional judgment, there are few rules to sidestep, and we more likely will arrive at an appropriate accounting treatment. Detractors, on the other hand, argue that the absence of detailed rules opens the door to even more abuse. Even in the absence of intentional misuse, reliance on professional judgment could result in different interpretations for similar transactions, raising concerns about comparability.

The FASB is actively considering whether to move toward objectives-oriented standard setting. That the IASB primarily follows an objectives-oriented approach, coupled with the FASB's recent moves toward convergence of U.S. and international standards, hints at a leaning in that direction. Opposition, though, is ardent. The debate has by no means ended.

---

[24]"An Audit of Internal Control Over Financial Reporting That Is Integrated with an Audit of Financial Statements," *Auditing Standard No. 5* (Washington, D.C.: PCAOB, 2007).

[25]"Study Pursuant to Section 108 (d) of the Sarbanes-Oxley Act of 2002 on the Adoption by the United States Financial Reporting System of a Principles-Based Accounting System," Securities and Exchange Commission (July 2003).

[26]"Principles-Based Approach to U.S. Standard Setting," *A Financial Accounting Standards Board Proposal* (Norwalk, Conn.: FASB, 2002).

In a previous section we covered the financial reporting reform in the United States that followed high-profile frauds such as **Enron** and **WorldCom**. The ethical values of key executives in these corporations were tested and found lacking. We now turn to a discussion of ethics in the accounting profession.

Ethics in Accounting

Ethics is a term that refers to a code or moral system that provides criteria for evaluating right and wrong. An ethical dilemma is a situation in which an individual or group is faced with a decision that tests this code. Many of these dilemmas are simple to recognize and resolve. For example, have you ever been tempted to call your professor and ask for an extension on the due date of an assignment by claiming a fictitious illness? Temptation like this will test your personal ethics.

Ethics deals with the ability to distinguish right from wrong.

Accountants, like others operating in the business world, are faced with many ethical dilemmas, some of which are complex and difficult to resolve. For instance, the capital markets' focus on periodic profits may tempt a company's management to bend or even break accounting rules to inflate reported net income. In these situations, technical competence is not enough to resolve the dilemma.

Ethics and Professionalism

One of the elements that many believe distinguishes a profession from other occupations is the acceptance by its members of a responsibility for the interests of those it serves. A high standard of ethical behavior is expected of those engaged in a profession. These standards often are articulated in a code of ethics. For example, law and medicine are professions that have their own codes of professional ethics. These codes provide guidance and rules to members in the performance of their professional responsibilities.

Public accounting has achieved widespread recognition as a profession. The AICPA, the national organization of certified public accountants, has its own Code of Professional Conduct which prescribes the ethical conduct members should strive to achieve. Similarly, the Institute of Management Accountants (IMA)—the primary national organization of accountants working in industry and government—has its own code of ethics, as does the Institute of Internal Auditors—the national organization of accountants providing internal auditing services for their own organizations.

Analytical Model for Ethical Decisions

Ethical codes are informative and helpful. However, the motivation to behave ethically must come from within oneself and not just from the fear of penalties for violating professional codes. Presented below is a sequence of steps that provide a framework for analyzing ethical issues. These steps can help you apply your own sense of right and wrong to ethical dilemmas:[27]

Step 1. Determine the facts of the situation. This involves determining the who, what, where, when, and how.

Step 2. Identify the ethical issue and the stakeholders. Stakeholders may include shareholders, creditors, management, employees, and the community.

Step 3. Identify the values related to the situation. For example, in some situations confidentiality may be an important value that may conflict with the right to know.

Step 4. Specify the alternative courses of action.

Step 5. Evaluate the courses of action specified in step 4 in terms of their consistency with the values identified in step 3. This step may or may not lead to a suggested course of action.

---

[27]Adapted from Harold Q. Langenderfer and Joanne W. Rockness, "Integrating Ethics into the Accounting Curriculum: Issues, Problems, and Solutions," *Issues in Accounting Education* (Spring 1989). These steps are consistent with those provided by the American Accounting Association's Advisory Committee on Professionalism and Ethics in their publication *Ethics in the Accounting Curriculum: Cases and Readings, 1990.*

Step 6. Identify the consequences of each possible course of action. If step 5 does not provide a course of action, assess the consequences of each possible course of action for all of the stakeholders involved.

Step 7. Make your decision and take any indicated action.

Ethical dilemmas are presented throughout the text. These dilemmas are designed to raise your consciousness on accounting issues with ethical ramifications. The analytical steps outlined above provide a framework with which to evaluate these situations. In addition, your instructor may assign end-of-chapter ethics cases for further discussion and application.

 ETHICAL DILEMMA

You have recently been employed by a large retail chain that sells sporting goods. One of your tasks is to help prepare periodic financial statements for external distribution. The chain's largest creditor, National Savings & Loan, requires quarterly financial statements, and you are currently working on the statements for the three-month period ending June 30, 2011.

During the months of May and June, the company spent $1,200,000 on a large radio and TV advertising campaign. The $1,200,000 included the costs of producing the commercials as well as the radio and TV time purchased to run the commercials. All of the costs were charged to advertising expense. The company's chief financial officer (CFO) has asked you to prepare a June 30 adjusting entry to remove the costs from advertising expense and to set up an asset called *prepaid advertising* that will be expensed in July. The CFO explained that "This advertising campaign has produced significant sales in May and June and I think it will continue to bring in customers through the month of July. By recording the ad costs as an asset, we can match the cost of the advertising with the additional July sales. Besides, if we expense the advertising in May and June, we will show an operating loss on our income statement for the quarter. The bank requires that we continue to show quarterly profits in order to maintain our loan in good standing."

PART B

THE CONCEPTUAL FRAMEWORK

The increasing complexity of our business world creates growing pressure on the FASB to delicately balance the many constituents of the accounting standard-setting process and to develop a set of accounting standards that are consistent with each other. The task of the FASB is made less complex if there exists a set of cohesive objectives and fundamental concepts on which financial accounting and reporting can be based. A number of years after coming into existence in 1973, the FASB's efforts resulted in the establishment of these objectives and concepts.

The **conceptual framework** has been described as a constitution, a coherent system of interrelated objectives and fundamentals that can lead to consistent standards and that prescribe the nature, function, and limits of financial accounting and reporting. The fundamentals are the underlying concepts of accounting, concepts that guide the selection of events to be accounted for, the measurement of those events, and the means of summarizing and communicating them to interested parties.[28]

The FASB disseminated this framework through seven Statements of Financial Accounting Concepts *(SFACs)*. *SFAC 1* and *SFAC 2* deal with the Objectives and Qualitative Characteristics of financial information, respectively. *SFAC 3,* describing the elements of financial statements, was superseded by *SFAC 6*. The objectives of financial reporting for nonprofit organizations are the subject of *SFAC 4* and are not covered in this text. Concept Statements 5 and 7 deal with recognition and measurement. It's important to realize that

FINANCIAL Reporting Case

Q4, p. 3

● LO5

The conceptual framework does not prescribe GAAP. It provides an underlying foundation for accounting standards.

---

[28]"Conceptual Framework for Financial Accounting and Reporting: Elements of Financial Statements and Their Measurement," *Discussion Memorandum* (Stamford, Conn.: FASB, 1976), p. 2.

FASB

A common goal of the Boards—a goal shared by their constituents—is for their standards to be clearly based on consistent principles. To be consistent, principles must be rooted in fundamental concepts rather than a collection of conventions.[29]

the conceptual framework provides structure and direction to financial accounting and reporting and does not directly prescribe GAAP.

Earlier in the chapter we discussed the ongoing efforts of standard setters to converge U.S. GAAP and International Financial Reporting Standards. As part of that process, the FASB and the IASB are working together to develop a common and improved conceptual framework that will provide the foundation for developing principles-based, common standards.

The joint conceptual framework project consists of eight phases:

A. Objective and Qualitative Characteristics
B. Elements and Recognition
C. Measurement
D. Reporting Entity
E. Presentation and Disclosure
F. Framework for a GAAP Hierarchy
G. Applicability to the Not-For-Profit Sector
H. Remaining Issues

When formulated, this framework will replace the Statements of Financial Accounting Concepts. The Boards currently are working on the first four phases of the project and only Phase A is complete. This phase replaces *SFAC 1* and *SFAC 2*. It likely will take several years before the project is completed.

In the remainder of this section we discuss the components of the conceptual framework that influence financial statements as depicted in Graphic 1–6 on the next page. The financial statements and their elements are most informative when they possess specific qualitative characteristics, subject to certain constraints. Proper recognition and measurement of financial information rely on several assumptions and principles that underlie the financial reporting process.

Our discussions of the objective and qualitative characteristics of financial reporting information are based on the completed first phase of the joint FASB and IASB project (indicated as Phase A in Graphic 1–6 on the next page), while the remainder of our conceptual framework coverage relies on the relevant FASB Concept Statement still in effect. We discuss and illustrate the financial statements themselves in subsequent chapters.

Objective of Financial Reporting

In specifying the overriding objective of financial reporting, the boards stated that their mandate is to assist in the efficient functioning of economies and the efficient allocation of resources in capital markets. The objective would be quite different in a socialist economy where the majority of productive resources are government owned.

● LO6

We previously discussed the importance to our economy of providing capital market participants with information, including the specific cash flow information needs of investors and creditors. The importance of investor and creditor needs is reflected in the objective of general purpose financial reporting.

The objective of general purpose financial reporting is to provide financial information about the reporting entity that is useful to present and potential equity investors, lenders, and other creditors in making decisions in their capacity as capital providers. Information that is decision useful to capital providers may also be useful to other users of financial reporting information who are not capital providers.[30]

[29]"Conceptual Framework for Financial Reporting: The Objective of Financial Reporting and Qualitative Characteristics and Constraints of Decision-Useful Financial Reporting Information," *FASB Exposure Draft* (Norwalk, Conn.: FASB, 2008).
[30]Ibid., par. OB2.

GRAPHIC 1–6
The Conceptual
Framework

The primary objective
of financial reporting
is to provide useful
information to capital
providers.

Notice that the objective specifies a focus on investors and creditors. However, the information needs of those key users also is likely to have general utility to other groups of external users who are interested in essentially the same financial aspects of a business.

Both equity investors and lenders are directly interested in the amount, timing, and uncertainty of an entity's future cash flows. Information about a company's economic resources (assets) and claims to those resources (liabilities) also is important. Not only does this information about resources and claims provide insight into future cash flows, it also helps decision makers identify the company's financial strengths and weaknesses and assess liquidity and solvency.

Qualitative Characteristics of Financial Reporting Information

● LO6

To be useful,
information must make
a difference in the
decision process.

Given the stated objective of financial reporting, what characteristics should information have to best meet the objective? Graphic 1–7 indicates the desirable qualitative characteristics of financial reporting information, presented in the form of a hierarchy of their perceived importance. Notice that the main focus is on **decision usefulness**—the ability to be useful in decision making.

GRAPHIC 1–7   Hierarchy of Qualitative Characteristics of Financial Information

Fundamental Qualitative Characteristics

For financial information to be useful, it should possess the fundamental decision-specific qualities of **relevance** and **faithful representation.** Both are critical. No matter how relevant, if information does not faithfully represent the appropriate economic phenomenon, it is useless. Conversely, information is of little value if it is not relevant. Let's look closer at each of these two qualitative characteristics, including the components that make those characteristics desirable. We also consider other characteristics that enhance usefulness.

> To be useful for decision making, information should possess the qualities of *relevance* and *faithful representation.*

RELEVANCE.   Obviously, to make a difference in the decision process, information must be relevant to the decision. Relevance in the context of financial reporting means that the information must possess **predictive value** and/or **confirmatory value,** typically both. For example, if net income and its components confirm investor expectations about a company's future cash-generating ability, then net income has confirmatory value for investors. This confirmation also can be useful in predicting the company's future cash-generating ability as expectations are revised.

This predictive ability is central to the concept of "earnings quality," the ability of reported earnings (income) to predict a company's future earnings. This is a concept we revisit frequently throughout this textbook in order to explore the impact on earnings quality of various topics under discussion. For instance, in Chapter 4 we discuss the contents of the income statement and certain classifications used in the statement from the perspective of helping analysts separate a company's transitory earnings from its permanent earnings. This separation is critical to a meaningful prediction of future earnings. In later chapters, we look at how various financial reporting decisions affect earnings quality.

FAITHFUL REPRESENTATION.   Faithful representation exists when there is agreement between a measure or description and the phenomenon it purports to represent. For example, assume that the term *inventory* in the balance sheet of a retail company is understood by external users to represent items that are intended for sale in the ordinary course of business. If inventory includes, say, machines used to produce inventory, then it lacks faithful representation.

> *Faithful representation means agreement between a measure and a real-world phenomenon that the measure is supposed to represent.*

To break it down further, faithful representation requires that information be *complete, neutral,* and *free from material error.* A depiction of an economic phenomenon is **complete** if it includes all information that is necessary for faithful representation of the economic phenomena that it purports to represent. Omitting a portion of that information can cause the depiction to be false or misleading and thus not helpful to the users of the information.[31]

Faithful representation also assumes the information being relied on is free from bias. Financial information should not influence decision making to achieve a predetermined result. In that regard, neutrality is highly related to the establishment of accounting standards. You learned earlier that changes in accounting standards can lead to adverse economic consequences for certain companies, their investors and creditors, and other interest groups. Accounting standards should be established with overall societal goals and specific objectives in mind and should try not to achieve particular social outcomes or favor particular groups or companies.

The FASB faces a difficult task in balancing neutrality and the consideration of economic consequences. A new accounting standard may favor one group of companies over others, but the FASB must convince the financial community that this is a consequence of the standard and not an objective used to set the standard.

Uncertainty is a fact of life when we measure many items of financial information included in financial statements. Estimates are common. We would not expect all measurements to be error-free. However, the information should be free from material error if it is to be useful.

Enhancing Qualitative Characteristics

Accounting information should be comparable across different companies and over different time periods.

Graphic 1–7 identifies four *enhancing* qualitative characteristics, *comparability (including consistency), verifiability, timeliness,* and *understandability.* Comparability helps users see similarities and differences between events and conditions. We already have discussed the importance of investors and creditors being able to compare information among companies to make their resource allocation decisions. Closely related to comparability is the notion that consistency of accounting practices over time permits valid comparisons among different reporting periods. The predictive and confirmatory value of information is enhanced if users can compare the performance of a company over time.[32] In the **Dell** financial statements and disclosure notes, notice that disclosure Note 1 includes a summary of significant accounting policies. If Dell were to change one of these policies, new numbers might not be comparable to numbers measured under a previous policy. To be sure readers are aware of the change, Dell would need to provide a full disclosure in the notes to the financial statements.

Verifiability implies a consensus among different measurers. For example, the historical cost of a piece of land to be reported in a company's balance sheet usually is highly verifiable. The cost can be traced to an exchange transaction, the purchase of the land. However, the fair value of that land is much more difficult to verify. Appraisers could differ in their assessment of fair value. The term *objectivity* often is linked to verifiability. The historical cost of the land is objective and easy to verify, but the land's fair value is subjective, influenced by the measurer's past experience and prejudices. A measurement that is subjective is difficult to verify, which makes it less reliable to users.

Information is timely if it is available to users before a decision is made.

Timeliness also is important for information to be decision useful. Information is timely when it is available to users early enough to allow them to use it in their decision process. The need for timely information requires that companies provide information to external users on a periodic basis. To enhance timeliness, the SEC requires its registrants to submit financial statement information on a quarterly as well as on an annual basis for each fiscal year.

Understandability means that users must understand the information within the context of the decision being made. This is a user-specific quality because users will differ in their ability to comprehend any set of information. The overriding objective of financial reporting is to provide comprehensible information to those who have a *reasonable understanding* of business and economic activities and are willing to study the information.

---

[31]Ibid., par. QC9.

[32]Companies occasionally do change their accounting practices, which makes it difficult for users to make comparisons among different reporting periods. Chapter 4 and Chapter 20 describe the disclosures that a company makes in this situation to restore consistency among periods.

Practical Boundaries (Constraints) to Achieving Desired Qualitative Characteristics

Most of us learn early in life that we can't get everything we want. The latest electronic gadget may have all the qualitative characteristics that current technology can provide, but limited resources may lead us to purchase a functional model with fewer bells and whistles. Cost effectiveness constrains the accounting choices we make. Specifically, it's important that the benefits of endowing financial information with all the qualitative characteristics we've discussed exceed the costs of doing so.

A related constraint on the type of information we provide is the concept of materiality. Assume that for an additional $50 you can add the latest enhancement to that electronic gadget you're considering. However, despite the higher specs, if you feel it will provide no discernible improvement in the performance of the product as you will use it, why pay the extra $50? In an accounting context, if a more costly way of providing information is not expected to have a material effect on decisions made by those using the information, the less costly method may be acceptable.

Cost effectiveness and materiality impart practical constraints on each of the qualitative characteristics of financial information. Both suggest that a particular accounting treatment might be different from that dictated solely by consideration of the desired qualities of information.

Cost Effectiveness

The costs of providing financial information include those of gathering, processing, and disseminating information. There also are costs to users when interpreting information. In addition, costs include possible adverse economic consequences of implementing accounting standards. These costs in particular are difficult, if not impossible, to quantify.

For example, consider the requirement that companies operating in more than one operating segment must disclose certain disaggregated financial information.[33] In addition to the costs of information gathering, processing, and communicating that information, many companies feel that this reporting requirement imposes what could be called *competitive disadvantage costs*. These companies are concerned that their competitors will gain some advantage from having access to the disaggregated data.

The perceived benefit from this or any accounting standard is increased *decision usefulness* of the information provided, which, hopefully, improves the resource allocation process. It is inherently impossible to quantify this benefit. The elaborate information-gathering process undertaken by the FASB in setting accounting standards is an attempt to assess both costs and benefits of a proposed accounting standard, even if in a subjective, nonquantifiable manner. In the case of reporting disaggregated information, the FASB decided that the perceived benefits of disclosing this information exceeded the costs of providing it.

> The costs of providing financial information include any possible adverse economic consequences of accounting standards.

> Information is *cost effective* only if the perceived benefit of increased *decision usefulness* exceeds the anticipated costs of providing that information.

Materiality

Materiality is another pervasive constraint. Information is material if it can have an effect on a decision made by users. One consequence of considering materiality is that GAAP need not be followed if an item is immaterial. For example, GAAP requires that receivables be measured at their net realizable value. If bad debts are anticipated, they should be estimated and subtracted from the face amount of receivables for balance sheet measurement. This is called the *allowance method* of accounting for bad debts. However, if the amount of anticipated bad debts is not considered to be large enough to affect decisions made by users, the *direct write-off method* of accounting for bad debts can be used even though it is not a generally accepted technique. This method does not require estimating bad debts for existing receivables.

The threshold for materiality will depend principally on the *relative* dollar amount of the transaction. For example, $10,000 in total anticipated bad debts for a multibillion dollar company like **Dell** would not be considered material. The method used to account for these anticipated bad debts will not affect the decisions made by Dell's financial statement users.

> Information is *material* if it has an effect on decisions.

---

[33]FASB ASC 280: Segment Reporting (previously "Disclosures about Segments of an Enterprise and Related Information," *Statement of Financial Accounting Standards No. 131* (Norwalk, Conn.: FASB, 1997)).

This same $10,000 amount, however, might easily be material for a neighborhood pizza parlor. The FASB has been reluctant to establish any quantitative materiality guidelines. The threshold for materiality has been left to the subjective judgment of the company preparing the financial statements and its auditors.

Materiality is concerned not only with the dollar amount of an item but with the nature of the item as well. In 1999, the SEC issued *Staff Accounting Bulletin No. 99.*[34] The bulletin expresses the SEC's view that exclusive reliance on quantitative benchmarks (numbers) to assess materiality in preparing financial statements is inappropriate. Many other factors, including whether the item in question involves an unlawful transaction, should also be considered when determining materiality. For example, an activity such as the illegal payment of $10,000 to an official of a foreign government to secure a valuable contract would probably be considered material even if the amount is small relative to the size of the company. Similarly, a small dollar amount that changes a net loss to a net income for the reporting period could be viewed as material to financial statement users for qualitative reasons.

> Professional judgment determines what amount is material in each situation.

Conservatism

> *Conservatism* is a justification for some accounting practices, *not* a desired qualitative characteristic of financial information.

Conservatism is a practice followed in an attempt to ensure that uncertainties and risks inherent in business situations are adequately considered. It is a frequently cited characteristic of financial information. Conservatism is not, however, a desired qualitative characteristic but a practical justification for some accounting choices. In that sense, conservatism is considered by some to be a third constraint on the achievement of various qualitative characteristics.[35]

The need for conservatism often is discussed in conjunction with the estimates required to comply with GAAP. For example, assume that a company estimates that its anticipated bad debts on existing receivables could be any number between $20,000 and $30,000, with the most likely amount being $25,000, and that these amounts are material. A conservative estimate would be $30,000, thus showing the lowest amount (of a range of possible values) in the balance sheet for net receivables and the highest expense (and therefore the lowest net income) in the income statement.

However, financial information users could just as easily be misled by a conservative estimate as by an optimistic one. If $25,000 is the best estimate of anticipated bad debts, then that is the number that should be used. Conservatism is *not* a desirable characteristic nor is it an accounting principle. Nevertheless, some accounting practices, such as the lower-of-cost-or-market method for measuring inventory (Chapter 9), appear to be generated by a desire to be conservative. However, these practices are motivated by other accounting principles such as the realization principle as discussed later in this chapter. They also are influenced by practical realities of our legal system. Investors and creditors who lose money from stock purchases or loans are less likely to sue when bad news is exaggerated and good news is underestimated. Also, they may be protected more effectively from poor management decision making if conservative accounting triggers debt covenants and other aspects of contracts that allow changes in contracts to occur.

Now that we've discussed the qualities that the elements of financial statements should possess, let's look more closely at the elements themselves.

Elements of Financial Statements

> ● LO6
>
> The 10 elements of financial statements defined in *SFAC 6* describe financial position and periodic performance.

SFAC 6 defines 10 elements of financial statements. These elements are "the building blocks with which financial statements are constructed—the classes of items that financial statements comprise."[36] They focus directly on items related to measuring performance and to reporting financial position. The *accrual accounting* model actually is embodied in the element definitions. The FASB recognized that accrual accounting produces information that is more successful in predicting future cash flows than is cash flow accounting.

---

[34]FASB ASC 250–10–S99–1, SAB Topic 1.M: Assessing Materiality (originally "Materiality," *Staff Accounting Bulletin No. 99* (Washington, D.C.: SEC, August 1999)).

[35]The hierarchy of qualitative characteristics does not specifically identify conservatism as a constraint. Most theorists include conservatism as one of the underlying accounting principles that guide accounting practice. Our classification recognizes its very real role in accounting choices as well as the practical motivation for those choices.

[36]"Elements of Financial Statements," *Statement of Financial Accounting Concepts No. 6* (Stamford, Conn.: FASB, 1985), par. 5.

For now, we list and define the elements in Graphic 1–8. You will learn much more about these in subsequent chapters.

GRAPHIC 1–8

Elements of Financial Statements

Elements of Financial Statements	
Assets	Probable future economic benefits obtained or controlled by a particular entity as a result of past transactions or events.
Liabilities	Probable future sacrifices of economic benefits arising from present obligations of a particular entity to transfer assets or provide services to other entities in the future as a result of past transactions or events.
Equity (or net assets)	Called shareholders' equity or stockholders' equity for a corporation, it is the residual interest in the assets of an entity that remains after deducting its liabilities.
Investments by owners	Increases in equity of a particular business enterprise resulting from transfers to it from other entities of something of value to obtain or increase ownership interests in it.
Distributions to owners	Decreases in equity of a particular enterprise resulting from transfers to owners.
Comprehensive income	The change in equity of a business enterprise during a period from transactions and other events and circumstances from nonowner sources. It includes all changes in equity during a period except those resulting from investments by owners and distributions to owners.
Revenues	Inflows or other enhancements of assets of an entity or settlements of its liabilities during a period from delivering or producing goods, rendering services, or other activities that constitute the entity's ongoing major or central operations.
Expenses	Outflows or other using up of assets or incurrences of liabilities during a period from delivering or producing goods, rendering services, or other activities that constitute the entity's ongoing major or central operations.
Gains	Increases in equity from peripheral or incidental transactions of an entity.
Losses	Represent decreases in equity arising from peripheral or incidental transactions of an entity.

Recognition and Measurement Concepts

Now that the various elements of financial statements have been identified, we discuss when they should be recognized (recorded) and how they should be measured. *SFAC 5* addresses these issues. **Recognition** refers to the process of admitting information into the basic financial statements. **Measurement** is the process of associating numerical amounts to the elements. For example, a revenue was previously defined as an inflow of assets from selling a good or providing a service. But *when* should the revenue event be recorded, and at *what* amount?

Recognition

According to *SFAC 5,* an item should be recognized in the basic financial statements when it meets the following four criteria, subject to a cost effectiveness constraint and materiality threshold:

1. *Definition.* The item meets the definition of an element of financial statements.
2. *Measurability.* The item has a relevant attribute measurable with sufficient reliability.
3. *Relevance.* The information about it is capable of making a difference in user decisions.
4. *Reliability.* The information is representationally faithful, verifiable, and neutral.[37]

Recognition criteria.

---

[37]"Recognition and Measurement in Financial Statements," *Statement of Financial Accounting Concepts No. 5* (Stamford, Conn.: FASB, 1984), par. 63. Phase A of the joint FASB and IASB conceptual framework project has replaced reliability with faithful representation as the second primary qualitative characteristic of financial information. See Graphic 1–7.

These obviously are very general guidelines. The concept statement does not address *specific* recognition issues.

Measurement

The question of measurement involves two choices: (1) the choice of a unit of measurement, and (2) the choice of an attribute to be measured. *SFAC 5* essentially confirmed existing practice in both of these areas. The monetary unit or measurement scale used in financial statements is nominal units of money without any adjustment for changes in purchasing power. In addition, the board acknowledged that different attributes such as historical cost, net realizable value, and present value of future cash flows are presently used to measure different financial statement elements, and that they expect that practice to continue. For example, property, plant, and equipment are measured at historical cost; accounts receivable are measured at their net realizable value; and most long-term liabilities, such as bonds, are measured at the present value of future cash payments.

> *SFAC No. 7 provides a framework for using future cash flows in accounting measurements.*

Present value measurements have long been associated with accounting valuation. However, because of its increased prominence, present value is the focus of an FASB concept statement that provides a framework for using future cash flows as the basis for accounting measurement and also asserts that the objective in valuing an asset or liability using present value is to approximate the fair value of that asset or liability.[38] We explore this objective in more depth in Chapter 6.

Answers to the recognition and measurement questions are imbedded in generally accepted accounting principles. *SFAC 5* confirmed some of the more important of these principles used in present practice. GAAP consist of broad principles and specific standards. The accrual accounting model is an example of a broad principle. Before addressing additional key broad principles, we look at some important assumptions that underlie those fundamental principles.

Underlying Assumptions

> ● **LO7**

The four basic assumptions underlying GAAP are (1) the economic entity assumption, (2) the going concern assumption, (3) the periodicity assumption, and (4) the monetary unit assumption.

> *The economic entity assumption presumes that economic events can be identified specifically with an economic entity.*

ECONOMIC ENTITY ASSUMPTION.   An essential assumption is that all economic events can be identified with a particular economic entity. Investors desire information about an economic entity that corresponds to their ownership interest. For example, if you were considering buying some ownership stock in **Google**, you would want information on the various operating units that constitute Google. You would need information not only about its United States operations but also about its European and other international operations. Also, you would not want the information about Google combined with that of **Yahoo! Inc.**, another Internet information provider. These would be two separate *economic entities*. The financial information for the various companies (subsidiaries) in which Google owns a controlling interest (greater than 50% ownership of voting stock) should be combined with that of Google (the parent). The parent and its subsidiaries are separate *legal* entities but one *accounting* entity.

Another key aspect of this assumption is the distinction between the economic activities of owners and those of the company. For example, the economic activities of a sole proprietorship, Uncle Jim's Restaurant, should be separated from the activities of its owner, Uncle Jim. Uncle Jim's personal residence, for instance, is not an asset of the business.

> *Financial statements of a company presume the business is a going concern.*

GOING CONCERN ASSUMPTION.   Another necessary assumption is that, in the absence of information to the contrary, it is anticipated that a business entity will continue to operate indefinitely. Accountants realize that the going concern assumption does not always hold since there certainly are many business failures. However, companies are begun with the hope of a long life, and many achieve that goal.

---

[38]"Using Cash Flow Information and Present Value in Accounting Measurements," *Statement of Financial Accounting Concepts No. 7* (Norwalk, Conn.: FASB, 2000).

This assumption is critical to many broad and specific accounting principles. For example, the assumption provides justification for measuring many assets based on their historical costs. If it were known that an enterprise was going to cease operations in the near future, assets and liabilities would not be measured at their historical costs but at their current liquidation values. Similarly, depreciation of a building over an estimated life of 40 years presumes the business will operate that long.

PERIODICITY ASSUMPTION. The periodicity assumption relates to the qualitative characteristic of *timeliness*. External users need *periodic* information to make decisions. This need for periodic information requires that the economic life of an enterprise (presumed to be indefinite) be divided into artificial time periods for financial reporting. Corporations whose securities are publicly traded are required to provide financial information to the SEC on a quarterly and annual basis.[39] Financial statements often are prepared on a monthly basis for banks and others that might need more timely information.

For many companies, the annual time period (the fiscal year) used to report to external users is the calendar year. However, other companies have chosen a fiscal year that does not correspond to the calendar year. The accounting profession and the Securities and Exchange Commission advocate that companies adopt a fiscal year that corresponds to their natural business year. A natural business year is the 12-month period that ends when the business activities of a company reach their lowest point in the annual cycle. For example, many retailers, **Walmart** for example, have adopted a fiscal year ending on January 31. Business activity in January generally is quite slow following the very busy Christmas period. We can see from the Dell financial statements that the company's fiscal year ends at the end of January. The **Campbell Soup Company**'s fiscal year ends in July; **Clorox**'s in June; and **Monsanto**'s in August.

> The *periodicity assumption* allows the life of a company to be divided into artificial time periods to provide timely information.

MONETARY UNIT ASSUMPTION. Recall that to *measure* financial statement elements, a unit or scale of measurement must be chosen. Information would be difficult to use if, for example, assets were listed as "three machines, two trucks, and a building." A common denominator is needed to measure all elements. The dollar in the United States is the most appropriate common denominator to express information about financial statement elements and changes in those elements.

> The *monetary unit assumption* states that financial statement elements should be measured in terms of the United States dollar.

One problem with this assumption is that the monetary unit is presumed to be stable over time. That is, the value of the dollar, in terms of its ability to purchase certain goods and services, is constant over time. This obviously does not strictly hold. The U.S. economy has experienced periods of rapidly changing prices. To the extent that prices are unstable, and those machines, trucks and building were purchased at different times, the monetary unit used to measure them is not the same. The effect of changing prices on financial information generally is discussed elsewhere in your accounting curriculum, often in an advanced accounting course.

Broad Accounting Principles

There are four important broad accounting principles that provide significant guidance for accounting practice: (1) the historical cost principle, (2) the realization principle (also known as the *revenue recognition principle*), (3) the matching principle, and (4) the full-disclosure principle. These principles deal with the critical issues of recognition and measurement. The accrual accounting model is embodied in each of the principles.

● LO8

HISTORICAL COST PRINCIPLE. The FASB recognized in *SFAC 5* that elements in financial statements currently are measured by different attributes. In general, however, GAAP measure assets and liabilities based on their *original transaction value*, that is, their historical costs. For an asset, this is the fair value of what is given in exchange (usually cash) for the asset at its initial acquisition. For liabilities, it is the current cash equivalent received in exchange for assuming the liability. For example, if a company borrowed $1 million cash and signed an interest-bearing note promising to repay the cash in the future, the liability would be valued at $1 million, the cash received in exchange.[40]

> The *historical cost principle* states that asset and liability measurements should be based on the amount given or received in the exchange transaction.

---

[39]The report that must be filed for the first three quarters of each fiscal year is Form 10-Q and the annual report is Form 10-K.
[40]This current cash equivalent for many liabilities also will equal the present value of future cash payments. This is illustrated in a subsequent chapter.

Historical cost measurement provides relevant cash flow information and also is highly verifiable.

Why base measurement on historical costs? After all, the current value of a company's manufacturing plant might seem more relevant than its original cost. First, historical cost provides important cash flow information as it represents the cash or cash equivalent paid for an asset or received in exchange for the assumption of a liability. Second, because historical cost valuation is the result of an exchange transaction between two independent parties, the agreed on exchange value is objective and highly *verifiable*. Alternatives such as measuring an asset at its current fair value involve *estimating* a selling price. An example given earlier in the chapter concerned the valuation of a parcel of land. Appraisers could easily differ in their assessment of current fair value.

A departure from historical cost valuation sometimes is appropriate.

There are occasions where a departure from measuring an asset based on its historical cost is warranted. Some assets, for instance, are measured at their *net realizable value*. For example, if customers purchased goods or services on account for $10,000, the asset, accounts receivable, would initially be valued at $10,000, the original transaction value. Subsequently, if $2,000 in bad debts were anticipated, net receivables should be valued at $8,000, the net realizable value. Departures from historical cost measurement such as this provide more appropriate information in terms of the overall objective of providing information to aid in the prediction of future cash flows.

REALIZATION PRINCIPLE. Determining accounting income by the accrual accounting model is a challenging task. When to recognize revenue is critical to this determination. Revenues are inflows of assets resulting from providing a product or service to a customer. At what point is this event recognized by an increase in assets? The **realization principle** requires that two criteria be satisfied before revenue can be recognized:

Revenue should be recognized when the earnings process is virtually complete and collection is reasonably assured.

1. The earnings process is judged to be complete or virtually complete.
2. There is reasonable certainty as to the collectibility of the asset to be received (usually cash).

These criteria help ensure that a revenue event is not recorded until an enterprise has performed all or most of its earnings activities for a financially capable buyer. The primary earnings activity that triggers the recognition of revenue is known as the *critical event*. The critical event for many businesses occurs at the **point-of-sale.** This usually takes place when the goods or services sold to the buyer are *delivered* (i.e., title is transferred).

Both revenue recognition criteria usually are met at the *point-of-sale*.

The *timing* of revenue recognition is a key element of earnings measurement. An income statement should report the results of all operating activities for the time period specified in the financial statements. A one-year income statement should report the company's accomplishments only for that one-year period. Revenue recognition criteria help ensure that a proper cut-off is made each reporting period and that exactly one year's activity is reported in that income statement. Not adhering to revenue recognition criteria could result in overstating revenue and hence net income in one reporting period and, consequently, understating revenue and net income in a subsequent period. Notice that revenue recognition criteria allow for the implementation of the accrual accounting model. Revenue should be recognized in the period it is earned, *not necessarily in the period in which cash is received.*

Revenue is recognized when *earned*, regardless of when cash actually is received.

Some revenue-producing activities call for revenue recognition over time, rather than at one particular point in time. For example, revenue recognition could take place *during* the earnings process for long-term construction contracts. We discuss revenue recognition in considerable depth in Chapter 5. That chapter also describes in more detail the concept of an earnings process and how it relates to performance measurement.

Expenses are recognized in the same reporting period as the related revenues.

MATCHING PRINCIPLE. Expenses were defined earlier in the chapter as "outflows or other using up of assets or incurrences of liabilities." When are expenses recognized? In practice, expense recognition often is motivated by a matching process. The **matching principle** states that expenses are recognized in the same period as the related revenues.[41] There is a cause-and-effect relationship between revenue and expense recognition implicit

---

[41]Matching appears in the concepts statements underlying both U.S. GAAP and IFRS. For example, *SFAC. 6* states that "recognition of revenues, expenses, gains, and losses and the related increments or decrements in assets and liabilities—including matching of costs and revenues, allocation, and amortization—is the essence of using accrual accounting to measure performance of entities" (par. 145). However, the IASB also notes that applying matching should not result in recognizing items in the balance sheet that do not meet the definitions of assets and liabilities (IASC, 1989, par. 95).

in this definition. In a given period, revenue is recognized according to the realization principle. The matching principle then requires that all expenses incurred in generating that same revenue also be recognized. The net result is a measure—net income—that matches current period accomplishments and sacrifices. This accrual-based measure provides a good indicator of future cash-generating ability.

Although the concept is straightforward, its implementation can be difficult. The difficulty arises in trying to identify cause-and-effect relationships. Many expenses are not incurred *directly* because of a revenue event. Instead, the expense is incurred to generate the revenue, but the association is indirect.

The matching principle is implemented by one of four different approaches, depending on the nature of the specific expense. Only the first approach involves an actual cause-and-effect relationship between revenue and expense. In the other three approaches, the relationship is indirect.

An expense can be recognized:

1. Based on an exact cause-and-effect relationship between a revenue and expense event.
2. By associating an expense with the revenues recognized in a specific time period.
3. By a systematic and rational allocation to specific time periods.
4. In the period incurred, without regard to related revenues.

The first approach is appropriate for *cost of goods sold.* There is a definite cause-and-effect relationship between **Dell Inc.**'s revenue from the sale of personal computers and the costs to produce those computers. Commissions paid to salespersons for obtaining revenues also is an example of an expense recognized based on this approach.

> There is a direct relationship between some expenses and revenues.

Unfortunately, for most expenses there is no obvious cause-and-effect relationship between a revenue and expense event. In other words, the revenue event does not directly *cause* expenses to be incurred. Many expenses, however, can be related to periods of time during which revenue is earned. For example, the monthly salary paid to an office worker is not directly related to any specific revenue event. The employee provides services during the month. The asset used to pay the employee, cash, provides benefits to the company only for that one month and *indirectly* relates to the revenue recognized in that same period.

> Some expenses are associated indirectly with revenues of a particular period.

Some costs are incurred to acquire assets that provide benefits to the company for more than one reporting period. Refer again to the Carter Company example in Illustration 1–1 on page 7. At the beginning of year 1, $60,000 in rent was paid covering a three-year period. This asset, prepaid rent, helps generate revenues for more than one reporting period. In that example, we chose to "systematically and rationally" allocate rent expense equally to each of the three one-year periods rather than to charge the expense to year 1.

> Some expenses are allocated to specific time periods.

The fourth approach to expense recognition is called for in situations when costs are incurred but it is impossible to determine in which period or periods, if any, revenues will occur. For example, consider the cost of advertising. Advertising expenditures are made with the presumption that incurring that expense will generate incremental revenues. Let's say Google spends $1 million for a series of television commercials. It's difficult to determine when, how much, or even whether additional revenues occur as a result of that particular series of ads. Because of this difficulty, advertising expenditures are recognized as expense in the period incurred, with no attempt made to match them with revenues.

> Some expenses are recognized in the period incurred, without regard to related revenues.

THE FULL-DISCLOSURE PRINCIPLE.   Remember, the purpose of accounting is to provide information that is useful to decision makers. So, naturally, if there is accounting information not included in the primary financial statements that would benefit users, that information should be provided too. The full-disclosure principle means that the financial reports should include any information that could affect the decisions made by external users. Of course, the benefits of that information, as noted earlier, should exceed the costs of providing the information. Supplemental information is disclosed in a variety of ways, including:

> Any information useful to decision makers should be provided in the financial statements, subject to the cost effectiveness constraint.

1. **Parenthetical comments** or **modifying comments** placed on the face of the financial statements.
2. **Disclosure notes** conveying additional insights about company operations, accounting principles, contractual agreements, and pending litigation.
3. **Supplemental financial statements** that report more detailed information than is shown in the primary financial statements.

We find examples of these disclosures in the **Dell Inc.** financial statements in Appendix B located at the back of the text. A parenthetical or modifying comment is provided in the stockholders' equity section of the balance sheet with disclosure of the number of shares of stock authorized, issued, and outstanding, and the statements include several notes. We discuss and illustrate disclosure requirements as they relate to specific financial statement elements in later chapters as those elements are discussed.

Graphic 1–9 provides a summary of the accounting assumptions and principles that guide the recognition and measurement of accounting information.

GRAPHIC 1–9

Summary of Recognition and Measurement Concepts

Assumptions	Description
Economic entity	All economic events can be identified with a particular economic entity.
Going concern	In the absence of information to the contrary, it is anticipated that a business entity will continue to operate indefinitely.
Periodicity	The life of a company can be divided into artificial time periods to provide timely information to external users.
Monetary unit	In the United States, financial statement elements should be measured in terms of the U.S. dollar.
Principles	
Historical cost	Asset and liability measurements should be based on the amount given or received in an exchange transaction.
Realization	Revenue should be recognized only after the earnings process is virtually complete and there is reasonable certainty of collecting the asset to be received from the customer.
Matching	Expenses should be recognized in the same reporting period as the related revenues.
Full disclosure	Any information that could change the decisions made by external users should be provided in the financial statements, subject to the cost effectiveness constraint.

WHERE WE'RE HEADED

Earlier in the chapter you learned that the FASB and IASB are working together to develop a common and improved conceptual framework. The project has eight phases, and the Boards currently are working on the first four. Phase A, "Objective and Qualitative Characteristics," has been completed and that material is incorporated in this and subsequent chapters where applicable. Phase D, "Reporting Entity," is scheduled to be completed in 2010, after this text has been published. There is no timetable for the completion of the remaining phases. However, the Boards have reached some tentative conclusions highlighted below.

Phase B: Elements and Recognition. The Boards have tentatively adopted working definitions for assets and liabilities that differ from those contained in *SFAC 6*.

	SFAC 6	Phase B
Assets	Probable future economic benefits obtained or controlled by a particular entity as a result of past transactions or events.	A present economic resource to which an entity has a right or other access that others do not have.
Liabilities	Probable future sacrifices of economic benefits arising from present obligations of a particular entity to transfer assets or provide services to other entities in the future as a result of past transactions or events.	A present economic obligation for which the entity is the obligor.

(continued)

(concluded)

SFAC 6 identifies more elements than does the IASB's framework, and the two frameworks define common elements differently. The Boards are working toward a common set of elements and definitions.

Phase C: Measurement. The objective of Phase C is to provide guidance for selecting measurement bases that satisfy the objective and qualitative characteristics of financial reporting. No tentative conclusions have been reached on this issue.

Phase D: Reporting Entity. The objective of Phase D is to determine what constitutes a reporting entity for the purposes of financial reporting. The Board's preliminary view is that *control* is a key aspect in determining what constitutes a reporting entity. The Board defines "control" as the ability to direct the financing and operating policies of an entity.

Evolution of Accounting Principles

Earlier in the chapter you learned that the convergence of accounting standards with international standards is having a profound effect on financial reporting in the United States. An approach to recognizing revenues and expenses that has become known as the "asset/liability" approach and an apparent progression toward fair value accounting have influenced several recent IASB and FASB standards and signify fundamental changes in accounting principles. We discuss these two concepts next.

The Asset/Liability Approach

You know from introductory accounting that the balance sheet and income statement are intertwined and must reconcile with each other. For example, the revenues listed in the income statement depict inflows of assets whose balances at a particular point in time are shown in the balance sheet. But which comes first, identifying revenues and expenses, or identifying assets and liabilities?

The realization and matching principles sometimes are described as "income-statement focused," because they focus on determining when we recognize revenues and expenses in the income statement. From this perspective, sometimes referred to as the **revenue/expense approach,** principles for recognizing revenues and expenses are emphasized, with assets and liabilities recognized as necessary to make the balance sheet reconcile with the income statement. For example, when accounting for a sales transaction our focus would be on whether revenue has been earned, and if we determined that it has, we would record an asset (accounts receivable) that is associated with the revenue. In subsequent chapters you will see that much of our accounting for revenues and expenses follows this revenue/expense approach.

Under the alternative **asset/liability approach** we first measure the assets and liabilities that exist at a balance sheet date and then recognize the revenues, expenses, gains and losses needed to account for the changes in these assets and liabilities from the previous measurement date. Under this approach, principles for asset and liability measurement are emphasized, and revenues, expenses, gains and losses are recognized as necessary to make the balance sheet reconcile with the income statement. For example, when accounting for a sales transaction, our focus would be on whether a potential accounts receivable meets the definition of an asset, and if it does, we would record that asset and recognize whatever amount of revenue is implied by the inflow of that asset. In subsequent chapters you will see that recent standards involving accounting for investments and income taxes follow this asset/liability approach.

It may seem like it shouldn't matter whether standard setters use the revenue/expense or asset/liability approach, given that both approaches affect both the income statement and balance sheet. However, the particular approach used by a standard setter can affect the amounts and timing of recognition on both statements. In particular, the asset/liability approach encourages standard setters to focus on accurately measuring assets and liabilities. It perhaps is not surprising, then, that a focus on assets and liabilities has led standard setters to lean more and more toward fair value measurement, our next topic.

With the *asset/liability approach*, the measurement of assets and liabilities drives revenue and expense recognition.

The Move toward Fair Value

In your study of accounting you've learned that the historical cost principle is the basis of measurement for most assets and liabilities. Often overlooked, though, is that there are over 40 instances in GAAP in which assets or liabilities are required or permitted to be measured at fair value. The FASB has provided a framework for measuring fair value whenever fair value is called for in applying generally accepted accounting principles.[42] Also, GAAP gives a company the option to report some or all of its *financial* assets and liabilities at fair value.[43] Let's look closer at the fair value measurement framework and the fair value option.

FAIR VALUE DEFINED.   The FASB's framework for measuring fair value doesn't change the number of situations in which fair value is used, but defines fair value and provides improved guidance about how to measure it. Fair value is defined as:

Fair value definition

The price that would be received to sell assets or paid to transfer a liability in an orderly transaction between market participants at the measurement date.

GAAP provides improved guidance to companies when measuring fair value.

A key aspect of this definition is its focus on the perspective of *market participants.* For instance, if a company buys a competitor's patent, not intending to use it but merely to keep the competitor from using it, the company still will have to assign a value to the asset because a market participant would find value in using the patent.

Fair value can be measured using:
1. *Market approaches*
2. *Income approaches*
3. *Cost approaches*

There are three types of valuation techniques that can be used to measure fair value. *Market approaches* base valuation on market information. For example, the value of a share of a company's stock that's not traded actively could be estimated by multiplying the earnings of that company by the P/E (price of shares/earnings) multiples of similar companies. *Income approaches* estimate value by first estimating future amounts (for example, earnings or cash flows) and then mathematically converting those amounts to a single present value. You will see how to apply such techniques in Chapter 6 when you study time value of money concepts. *Cost approaches* determine value by estimating the amount that would be required to buy or construct an asset of similar quality and condition. The firm can use one or more of these valuation approaches, depending on availability of the data, and should try to use them consistently unless changes in circumstances require a change in approach.

To increase consistency and comparability in applying this definition, the FASB provides a hierarchy that prioritizes the inputs companies should use when determining fair value. The priority is based on three broad preference levels. The higher the level (Level 1 is the highest), the more preferable the input. The FASB encourages companies to strive to obtain the highest level input available for each situation. Graphic 1–10 describes the type of inputs and provides an example for each level.

The framework also expands the amount of information companies must disclose about the use of fair value to measure assets and liabilities. The additional disclosures include a description of the inputs used to measure fair value. For recurring fair value measurements that rely on significant *unobservable* inputs (within Level 3 of the fair value hierarchy), companies should disclose the effect of the measurements on earnings (or changes in net assets) for the period.

You are not yet familiar with some of the examples mentioned in Graphic 1–10, but as you progress through the book, you will encounter many instances in which we use fair value for valuation purposes. Refer back frequently to this discussion and speculate on the level of input that would be available to a company in these situations. When a company has the option to measure financial assets or liabilities at fair value (discussed next), we address the choices available to the company in those situations.

---

[42]FASB ASC 820: Fair Value Measurements and Disclosures (previously "Fair Value Measurements," *Statement of Financial Accounting Standards No. 157* (Norwalk, Conn.: FASB, 2006)).

[43]FASB ASC 825–10–25–1: Financial Instruments—Overall—Recognition—Fair Value Option (previously "The Fair Value Option for Financial Assets and Financial Liabilities," *Statement of Financial Accounting Standards No. 159* (Norwalk, Conn.: FASB, 2007)). .

GRAPHIC 1–10   Fair Value Hierarchy

	Fair Value Hierarchy	
Level	**Inputs**	**Example**
1 **Most Desirable**	Quoted market prices in active markets for identical assets or liabilities.	In Chapter 12 you will learn that certain investments in marketable securities are reported at their *fair values*. Fair value in this case would be measured using the quoted market price from the NYSE, NASDAQ, or other exchange on which the security is traded.
2	Inputs other than quoted prices that are *observable* for the asset or liability. These inputs include quoted prices for *similar* assets or liabilities in active or inactive markets and inputs that are derived principally from or corroborated by observable related market data.	In Chapter 10 we discuss how companies sometimes acquire assets with consideration other than cash. In any noncash transaction, the controlling valuation principle is that each element of the transaction is recorded at its *fair value*. If one of the assets in the exchange is a building, for instance, then quoted market prices for similar buildings recently sold could be used to value the building or, if there were no similar buildings recently exchanged from which to obtain a comparable market price, valuation could be based on the price per square foot derived from observable market data.
3 **Least Desirable**	*Unobservable* inputs that reflect the entity's own assumptions about the assumptions market participants would use in pricing the asset or liability developed based on the best information available in the circumstances.	Asset retirement obligations (AROs), discussed in Chapter 10, are measured at *fair value*. Neither Level 1 nor Level 2 inputs would be possible in most ARO valuation situations. Fair value would be estimated using Level 3 inputs to include the expected cash flows estimated using the entity's own data if there is no information that indicates that market participants would use different assumptions. This Level 3 input would be used in a present value calculation together with other inputs such as the credit-adjusted risk-free interest rate.

FAIR VALUE OPTION.   GAAP gives a company the *option* to value some or all of its financial assets and liabilities at fair value. If a company chooses to value a financial asset or financial liability at fair value, then future changes in fair value are reported as gains and losses in the income statement.

What differentiates financial assets and liabilities from, say, buildings or land? Financial assets and liabilities are cash and other assets and liabilities that convert directly into known amounts of cash. Included are investments in stocks and bonds of other entities, notes receivable and payable, bonds payable, and derivative securities.[44] Some of these financial assets and liabilities currently are *required* under GAAP to be reported at fair value. For example, in Chapter 12 you will learn that investments in the stock of other corporations that are designated as either "trading securities" or "securities available for sale" must be valued at fair value.

A company can *choose* to report its other financial instruments at fair value as well. If the fair value option is chosen, changes in fair value of the instrument would be reported as gains and losses in the income statement. Liabilities, too, can be reported at fair value. For instance, a company can choose to report bonds payable at fair value rather than at amortized original issue price as described in Chapter 14.

If a company elects the fair value option, it's not necessary that the company elect the option to report all of its financial instruments at fair value or even all instruments of a particular type at fair value. Companies can "mix and match" on an instrument-by-instrument basis. However, a company is not allowed to switch methods once a method is chosen.

The FASB's objective for allowing the fair value option is to improve financial reporting by providing companies a way to reduce volatility in reported earnings without having to comply with complex hedge accounting standards. It also helps in the convergence with

GAAP gives a company the option to value financial assets and liabilities at fair value rather than at historical cost.

---

[44]The fair value option does not apply to certain specified financial instruments, including pension obligations and assets or liabilities arising from leases.

international accounting standards we discussed earlier in the chapter as the IASB also has adopted a fair value option for financial instruments.

It is not expected that many companies will employ the fair value option. In a 2008 survey of CFOs and controllers, only about one-third said they plan to make use of the option.[46] However, many believe that the fair value option is just the first step in a broader fair value agenda by the FASB that could lead to future standards requiring fair value measurement not only for financial assets and liabilities, but for some nonfinancial assets as well.

> There is a strong contingent who believe that fair value is the best measure to use in financial reporting. The FASB and IASB have agreed to long-term objectives for accounting for financial instruments that include a requirement that they be measured at fair value. The recent run of elective fair value standards will provide investors with an important training ground for understanding how fair value accounting is going to change the results we see.[45]

The move toward fair value is controversial. Proponents of fair value cite its relevance, and are convinced that historical cost information may not be useful for many types of decisions. Opponents of fair value counter that estimates of fair value are not sufficiently reliable, particularly when based on inputs from Level 3 in the fair value hierarchy (see Graphic 1–10), and that managers might be tempted to exploit the unverifiability of such inputs to bias earnings. They argue that accounting should emphasize verifiability recognizing only those gains and other increases in fair value that actually have been realized in transactions or are virtually certain to exist.[47]

The financial crisis of 2008–2009 provided additional ammunition for fair value opponents. As we discussed earlier in the chapter, many claimed that inappropriate valuations of financial assets in illiquid markets exacerbated the crisis by forcing financial institutions to report larger than necessary losses.

We will revisit the fair value option in subsequent chapters that address the key financial assets and liabilities that now can be measured at fair value. You'll find it easier to understand the concepts introduced in this chapter in the context of the financial assets and liabilities affected: investments (Chapter 12), and bonds payable (Chapter 14).

FINANCIAL REPORTING CASE SOLUTION

1. **What should you tell your friend about the presence of accounting standards in the United States? Who has the authority for standard setting? Who has the responsibility?** *(p. 9)* In the United States we have a set of standards known as generally accepted accounting principles (GAAP). GAAP is a dynamic set of both broad and specific guidelines that companies should follow when measuring and reporting the information in their financial statements and related notes. The Securities and Exchange Commission has the authority to set accounting standards for companies whose securities are publicly traded but always has delegated the primary responsibility to the accounting profession. At present, the Financial Accounting Standards Board is the private sector body responsible for standard setting.

2. **What is the economic and political environment in which standard setting occurs?** *(p. 12)* The setting of accounting and reporting standards often has been characterized as a *political process*. Standards, particularly changes in standards, can have significant differential effects on companies, investors and creditors, and other interest groups. A change in an accounting standard or the introduction of a new standard

---

[45]"FAS No. 159 Adoptions Raise Concerns—The Fair Value Option," Bear Stearns (May 8, 2007).

[46]"Fair Uptake on the Fair Value Option," Treasury and **Risk.com** (October 2008).

[47]Watts, R. L., "Conservatism in Accounting Part I: Explanations and Implications," *Accounting Horizons* (September 2003), pp. 207–21.

can result in a substantial redistribution of wealth within our economy. The FASB must consider potential economic consequences of a change in an accounting standard or the introduction of a new standard.

3. **What is the relationship among management, auditors, investors, and creditors that tends to preclude the "What would you like it to be?" attitude?** *(p. 16)* It is the responsibility of management to apply accounting standards when communicating with investors and creditors through financial statements. Auditors serve as independent intermediaries to help ensure that the management-prepared statements are presented fairly in accordance with GAAP. In providing this assurance, the auditor precludes the "What would you like it to be?" attitude.

4. **In general, what is the conceptual framework that underlies accounting principles?** *(p. 20)* The conceptual framework is a coherent system of interrelated objectives and fundamentals that can lead to consistent standards and that prescribe the nature, function, and limits of financial accounting and reporting. The fundamentals are the underlying concepts of accounting, concepts that guide the selection of events to be accounted for, the measurement of those events, and the means of summarizing and communicating them to interested parties. ●

THE BOTTOM LINE

● **LO1**   Financial accounting is concerned with providing relevant financial information to various external users. However, the primary focus is on the financial information provided by profit-oriented companies to their present and potential investors and creditors. (p. 4)

● **LO2**   Cash basis accounting provides a measure of periodic performance called *net operating cash flow,* which is the difference between cash receipts and cash disbursements from transactions related to providing goods and services to customers. Accrual accounting provides a measure of performance called *net income,* which is the difference between revenues and expenses. Periodic net income is considered a better indicator of future operating cash flows than is current net operating cash flows. (p. 7)

● **LO3**   Generally accepted accounting principles (GAAP) comprise a dynamic set of both broad and specific guidelines that companies follow when measuring and reporting the information in their financial statements and related notes. The Securities and Exchange Commission (SEC) has the authority to set accounting standards in the United States. However, the SEC has always delegated the task to a private sector body, at this time the Financial Accounting Standards Board (FASB). The International Accounting Standards Board (IASB) sets global accounting standards and works with national accounting standard-setters to achieve convergence in accounting standards around the world. (p. 9)

● **LO4**   Accounting standards can have significant differential effects on companies, investors, creditors, and other interest groups. For this reason, the setting of accounting standards often has been characterized as a political process. (p. 12)

● **LO5**   The FASB's conceptual framework is a set of cohesive objectives and fundamental concepts on which financial accounting and reporting standards can be based. (p. 20)

● **LO6**   The objective of financial reporting is to provide useful financial information to capital providers. The primary decision-specific qualities that make financial information useful are relevance and faithful representation. To be relevant, information must possess predictive value and/or confirmatory value. Completeness, neutrality, and free from material error are the components of faithful representation. The 10 elements of financial statements are assets, liabilities, equity, investments by owners, distributions to owners, revenues, expenses, gains, losses, and comprehensive income. (p. 21)

● **LO7**   The four basic assumptions underlying GAAP are (1) the economic entity assumption, (2) the going concern assumption, (3) the periodicity assumption, and (4) the monetary unit assumption. (p. 28)

● **LO8**   The four broad accounting principles that guide accounting practice are (1) the historical cost principle, (2) the realization principle, (3) the matching principle, and (4) the full-disclosure principle. (p. 29) ●

QUESTIONS FOR REVIEW OF KEY TOPICS

Q 1–1   What is the function and primary focus of financial accounting?

Q 1–2   What is meant by the phrase *efficient allocation of resources?* What mechanism fosters the efficient allocation of resources in the United States?

Q 1–3   Identify two important variables to be considered when making an investment decision.

Q 1–4   What must a company do in the long run to be able to provide a return to investors and creditors?

Q 1–5   What is the primary objective of financial accounting?

Q 1–6   Define net operating cash flows. Briefly explain why periodic net operating cash flows may not be a good indicator of future operating cash flows.

Q 1–7   What is meant by GAAP? Why should all companies follow GAAP in reporting to external users?

Q 1–8   Explain the roles of the SEC and the FASB in the setting of accounting standards.

Q 1–9   Explain the role of the auditor in the financial reporting process.

Q 1–10   List three key provisions of the Sarbanes-Oxley Act of 2002. Order your list from most important to least important in terms of the likely long-term impact on the accounting profession and financial reporting.

Q 1–11   Explain what is meant by *adverse economic consequences* of new or changed accounting standards.

Q 1–12   Why does the FASB undertake a series of elaborate information-gathering steps before issuing a substantive accounting standard?

Q 1–13   What is the purpose of the FASB's conceptual framework project?

Q 1–14   Discuss the terms *relevance* and *faithful representation* as they relate to financial accounting information.

Q 1–15   What are the components of relevant information? What are the components of faithful representation?

Q 1–16   Explain what is meant by: The benefits of accounting information must exceed the costs.

Q 1–17   What is meant by the term *materiality* in financial reporting?

Q 1–18   Briefly define the financial accounting elements: (1) assets, (2) liabilities, (3) equity, (4) investments by owners, (5) distributions to owners, (6) revenues, (7) expenses, (8) gains, (9) losses, and (10) comprehensive income.

Q 1–19   What are the four basic assumptions underlying GAAP?

Q 1–20   What is the going concern assumption?

Q 1–21   Explain the periodicity assumption.

Q 1–22   What are the four key broad accounting principles that guide accounting practice?

Q 1–23   What are two important reasons to base the valuation of assets and liabilities on their historical cost?

Q 1–24   Describe the two criteria that must be satisfied before revenue can be recognized.

Q 1–25   What are the four different approaches to implementing the matching principle? Give an example of an expense that is recognized under each approach.

Q 1–26   In addition to the financial statement elements arrayed in the basic financial statements, what are some other ways to disclose financial information to external users?

Q 1–27   Briefly describe the inputs that companies should use when determining fair value. Organize your answer according to preference levels, from highest to lowest priority.

BRIEF EXERCISES

BE 1–1
Accrual accounting
● LO2

Cash flows during the first year of operations for the Harman-Kardon Consulting Company were as follows: Cash collected from customers, $340,000; Cash paid for rent, $40,000; Cash paid to employees for services rendered during the year, $120,000; Cash paid for utilities, $50,000.

In addition, you determine that customers owed the company $60,000 at the end of the year and no bad debts were anticipated. Also, the company owed the gas and electric company $2,000 at year-end, and the rent payment was for a two-year period. Calculate accrual net income for the year.

BE 1–2
Financial statement elements
● LO6

For each of the following items, identify the appropriate financial statement element or elements: (1) probable future sacrifices of economic benefits; (2) probable future economic benefits owned by the company; (3) inflows of assets from ongoing, major activities; (4) decrease in equity from peripheral or incidental transactions.

BE 1–3
Basic assumptions and principles
● LO6 through LO8

Listed below are several statements that relate to financial accounting and reporting. Identify the basic assumption, broad accounting principle, or pervasive constraint that applies to each statement.
1. **Sirius Satellite Radio Inc.** files its annual and quarterly financial statements with the SEC.
2. The president of **Applebee's International, Inc.** travels on the corporate jet for business purposes only and does not use the jet for personal use.

3. Jackson Manufacturing does not recognize revenue for unshipped merchandise even though the merchandise has been manufactured according to customer specifications.
4. Lady Jane Cosmetics depreciates the cost of equipment over their useful lives.

BE 1–4
Basic assumptions and principles
● LO6 through LO8

Identify the basic assumption or broad accounting principle that was violated in each of the following situations.
1. Astro Turf Company recognizes an expense, cost of goods sold, in the period the product is manufactured.
2. McCloud Drug Company owns a patent that it purchased three years ago for $2 million. The controller recently revalued the patent to its approximate market value of $8 million.
3. Philips Company pays the monthly mortgage on the home of its president, Larry Crosswhite, and charges the expenditure to miscellaneous expense.

BE 1–5
Basic assumptions and principles
● LO6 through LO8

For each of the following situations, (1) indicate whether you agree or disagree with the financial reporting practice employed and (2) state the basic assumption, pervasive constraint, or accounting principle that is applied (if you agree), or violated (if you disagree).
1. Winderl Corporation did not disclose that it was the defendant in a material lawsuit because the trial was still in progress.
2. Alliant Semiconductor Corporation files quarterly and annual financial statements with the SEC.
3. Reliant Pharmaceutical paid rent on its office building for the next two years and charged the entire expenditure to rent expense.
4. Rockville Engineering records revenue only after products have been shipped, even though customers pay Rockville 50% of the sales price in advance.

EXERCISES

An alternate exercise and problem set is available on the text website: www.mhhe.com/spiceland6e

E 1–1
Accrual accounting
● LO2

Listed below are several transactions that took place during the first two years of operations for the law firm of Pete, Pete, and Roy.

	Year 1	Year 2
Amounts billed to customers for services rendered	$170,000	$220,000
Cash collected from customers	160,000	190,000
Cash disbursements:		
Salaries paid to employees for services rendered during the year	90,000	100,000
Utilities	30,000	40,000
Purchase of insurance policy	60,000	–0–

In addition, you learn that the company incurred utility costs of $35,000 in year one, that there were no liabilities at the end of year two, no anticipated bad debts on receivables, and that the insurance policy covers a three-year period.

Required:
1. Calculate the net operating cash flow for years 1 and 2.
2. Prepare an income statement for each year similar to Illustration 1–2 on page 8 according to the accrual accounting model.
3. Determine the amount of receivables from customers that the company would show in its year 1 and year 2 balance sheets prepared according to the accrual accounting model.

E 1–2
Accrual accounting
● LO2

Listed below are several transactions that took place during the second two years of operations for RPG Consulting.

	Year 2	Year 3
Amounts billed to customers for services rendered	$350,000	$450,000
Cash collected from credit customers	260,000	400,000
Cash disbursements:		
Payment of rent	80,000	–0–
Salaries paid to employees for services rendered during the year	140,000	160,000
Travel and entertainment	30,000	40,000
Advertising	15,000	35,000

In addition, you learn that the company incurred advertising costs of $25,000 in year 2, owed the advertising agency $5,000 at the end of year 1, and there were no liabilities at the end of year 3. Also, there were no anticipated bad debts on receivables, and the rent payment was for a two-year period, year 2 and year 3.

Required:

1. Calculate accrual net income for both years.

2. Determine the amount due the advertising agency that would be shown as a liability on the RPG's balance sheet at the end of year 2.

E 1–3
FASB codification research
● LO3

The *FASB Accounting Standards Codification* represents the single source of authoritative U.S. generally accepted accounting principles.

Required:

1. Obtain the relevant authoritative literature on fair value measurements using the FASB's Codification Research System at the FASB website (**www.fasb.org**). Identify the Codification topic number that provides guidance on fair value measurements.

2. What is the specific citation that lists the disclosures required in the notes to the financial statements for each major category of assets and liabilities measured at fair value?

3. List the disclosure requirements.

E 1–4
FASB codification research
● LO3

Access the FASB's Codification Research System at the FASB website (**www.fasb.org**). Determine the specific citation for each of the following items:

1. The topic number for business combinations.

2. The topic number for related party disclosures.

3. The topic, subtopic, and section number for the initial measurement of internal-use software.

4. The topic, subtopic and section number for the subsequent measurement of asset retirement obligations.

5. The topic, subtopic, and section number for the recognition of stock compensation.

E 1–5
Participants in establishing GAAP
● LO3

Three groups that participate in the process of establishing GAAP are users, preparers, and auditors. These groups are represented by various organizations. For each organization listed below, indicate which of these groups it primarily represents.

1. Securities and Exchange Commission

2. Financial Executives International

3. American Institute of Certified Public Accountants

4. Institute of Management Accountants

5. Association of Investment Management and Research

E 1–6
Financial statement elements
● LO6

For each of the items listed below, identify the appropriate financial statement element or elements.

1. Obligation to transfer cash or other resources as a result of a past transaction.

2. Dividends paid by a corporation to its shareholders.

3. Inflow of an asset from providing a good or service.

4. The financial position of a company.

5. Increase in equity during a period from nonowner transactions.

6. Increase in equity from peripheral or incidental transaction.

7. Sale of an asset used in the operations of a business for less than the asset's book value.

8. The owners' residual interest in the assets of a company.

9. An item owned by the company representing probable future benefits.

10. Revenues plus gains less expenses and losses.

11. An owner's contribution of cash to a corporation in exchange for ownership shares of stock.

12. Outflow of an asset related to the production of revenue.

E 1–7
Concepts; terminology; conceptual framework
● LO6

Listed below are several terms and phrases associated with the FASB's conceptual framework. Pair each item from List A (by letter) with the item from List B that is most appropriately associated with it.

List A	List B
_____ 1. Predictive value	a. Decreases in equity resulting from transfers to owners.
_____ 2. Relevance	b. Requires consideration of the costs and value of information.
_____ 3. Timeliness	c. Important for making interfirm comparisons.
_____ 4. Distribution to owners	d. Applying the same accounting practices over time.
_____ 5. Confirmatory value	e. Users understand the information in the context of the decision being made.
_____ 6. Understandability	f. Agreement between a measure and the phenomenon it purports to represent.
_____ 7. Gain	g. Information is available prior to the decision.
_____ 8. Faithful representation	h. Pertinent to the decision at hand. (continued)

(concluded)

List A	List B
_____ 9. Comprehensive income	i. Implies consensus among different measurers.
_____10. Materiality	j. Information confirms expectations.
_____11. Comparability	k. The change in equity from nonowner transactions.
_____12. Neutrality	l. The process of admitting information into financial statements.
_____13. Recognition	m. The absence of bias.
_____14. Consistency	n. Results if an asset is sold for more than its book value.
_____15. Cost effectiveness	o. Information is useful in predicting the future.
_____16. Verifiability	p. Concerns the relative size of an item and its effect on decisions.

E 1–8
Qualitative
characteristics
● **LO6**

Phase A of the joint FASB and IASB conceptual framework project stipulates the desired fundamental and enhancing qualitative characteristics of accounting information. Several constraints impede achieving these desired characteristics. Answer each of the following questions related to these characteristics and constraints.

1. Which constraint would allow a company to record the purchase of a $120 printer as an expense rather than capitalizing the printer as an asset?

2. Donald Kirk, former chairman of the FASB, once noted that " . . . there must be public confidence that the standard-setting system is credible, that selection of board members is based on merit and not the influence of special interests . . ." Which characteristic is implicit in Mr. Kirk's statement?

3. Allied Appliances, Inc., changed its revenue recognition policies. Which characteristic is jeopardized by this change?

4. National Bancorp, a publicly traded company, files quarterly and annual financial statements with the SEC. Which characteristic is relevant to the timing of these periodic filings?

5. In general, relevant information possesses which qualities?

6. When there is agreement between a measure or description and the phenomenon it purports to represent, information possesses which characteristic?

7. Jeff Brown is evaluating two companies for future investment potential. Jeff's task is made easier because both companies use the same accounting methods when preparing their financial statements. Which characteristic does the information Jeff will be using possess?

8. A company should disclose information only if the perceived benefits of the disclosure exceed the costs of providing the information. Which constraint does this statement describe?

E 1–9
Basic assumptions,
principles, and
constraints
● **LO6 through
LO8**

Listed below are several terms and phrases associated with basic assumptions, broad accounting principles, and constraints. Pair each item from List A (by letter) with the item from List B that is most appropriately associated with it.

List A	List B
_____ 1. Matching principle	a. The enterprise is separate from its owners and other entities.
_____ 2. Periodicity	b. A common denominator is the dollar.
_____ 3. Historical cost principle	c. The entity will continue indefinitely.
_____ 4. Materiality	d. Record expenses in the period the related revenue is recognized.
_____ 5. Realization principle	e. The original transaction value upon acquisition.
_____ 6. Going concern assumption	f. All information that could affect decisions should be reported.
_____ 7. Monetary unit assumption	g. The life of an enterprise can be divided into artificial time periods.
_____ 8. Economic entity assumption	h. Criteria usually satisfied at point of sale.
_____ 9. Full-disclosure principle	i. Concerns the relative size of an item and its effect on decisions.

E 1–10
Basic assumptions
and principles
● **LO6 through
LO8**

Listed below are several statements that relate to financial accounting and reporting. Identify the basic assumption, broad accounting principle, or constraint that applies to each statement.

1. Jim Marley is the sole owner of Marley's Appliances. Jim borrowed $100,000 to buy a new home to be used as his personal residence. This liability was not recorded in the records of Marley's Appliances.

2. **Apple Computer, Inc.**, distributes an annual report to its shareholders.

3. **Hewlett-Packard Corporation** depreciates machinery and equipment over their useful lives.

4. Crosby Company lists land on its balance sheet at $120,000, its original purchase price, even though the land has a current fair value of $200,000.

5. **Honeywell Corporation** records revenue when products are delivered to customers, even though the cash has not yet been received.

6. Liquidation values are not normally reported in financial statements even though many companies do go out of business.

7. **IBM Corporation**, a multibillion dollar company, purchased some small tools at a cost of $800. Even though the tools will be used for a number of years, the company recorded the purchase as an expense.

E 1–11
Basic assumptions and principles
● LO7 LO8

Identify the basic assumption or broad accounting principle that was violated in each of the following situations.

1. Pastel Paint Company purchased land two years ago at a price of $250,000. Because the value of the land has appreciated to $400,000, the company has valued the land at $400,000 in its most recent balance sheet.

2. Atwell Corporation has not prepared financial statements for external users for over three years.

3. The Klingon Company sells farm machinery. Revenue from a large order of machinery from a new buyer was recorded the day the order was received.

4. Don Smith is the sole owner of a company called Hardware City. The company recently paid a $150 utility bill for Smith's personal residence and recorded a $150 expense.

5. Golden Book Company purchased a large printing machine for $1,000,000 (a material amount) and recorded the purchase as an expense.

6. Ace Appliance Company is involved in a major lawsuit involving injuries sustained by some of its employees in the manufacturing plant. The company is being sued for $2,000,000, a material amount, and is not insured. The suit was not disclosed in the most recent financial statements because no settlement had been reached.

E 1–12
Basic assumptions and principles
● LO6 through LO8

For each of the following situations, indicate whether you agree or disagree with the financial reporting practice employed and state the basic assumption, constraint, or accounting principle that is applied (if you agree) or violated (if you disagree).

1. Wagner Corporation adjusted the valuation of all assets and liabilities to reflect changes in the purchasing power of the dollar.

2. Spooner Oil Company changed its method of accounting for oil and gas exploration costs from successful efforts to full cost. No mention of the change was included in the financial statements. The change had a material effect on Spooner's financial statements.

3. Cypress Manufacturing Company purchased machinery having a five-year life. The cost of the machinery is being expensed over the life of the machinery.

4. Rudeen Corporation purchased equipment for $180,000 at a liquidation sale of a competitor. Because the equipment was worth $230,000, Rudeen valued the equipment in its subsequent balance sheet at $230,000.

5. Davis Bicycle Company received a large order for the sale of 1,000 bicycles at $100 each. The customer paid Davis the entire amount of $100,000 on March 15. However, Davis did not record any revenue until April 17, the date the bicycles were delivered to the customer.

6. Gigantic Corporation purchased two small calculators at a cost of $32.00. The cost of the calculators was expensed even though they had a three-year estimated useful life.

7. Esquire Company provides financial statements to external users every three years.

E 1–13
Basic assumptions, principles, and constraints
● LO6 through LO8

For each of the following situations, state whether you agree or disagree with the financial reporting practice employed, and briefly explain the reason for your answer.

1. The controller of the Dumars Corporation increased the carrying value of land from its original cost of $2 million to its recently appraised value of $3.5 million.

2. The president of Vosburgh Industries asked the company controller to charge miscellaneous expense for the purchase of an automobile to be used solely for personal use.

3. At the end of its 2011 fiscal year, Dower, Inc., received an order from a customer for $45,350. The merchandise will ship early in 2012. Because the sale was made to a long-time customer, the controller recorded the sale in 2011.

4. At the beginning of its 2011 fiscal year, Rossi Imports paid $48,000 for a two-year lease on warehouse space. Rossi recorded the expenditure as an asset to be expensed equally over the two-year period of the lease.

5. The Reliable Tire Company included a note in its financial statements that described a pending lawsuit against the company.

6. The Hughes Corporation, a company whose securities are publicly traded, prepares monthly, quarterly, and annual financial statement for internal use but disseminates to external users only the annual financial statements.

E 1–14
Basic assumptions, principles, and constraints
● LO6 through LO8

Listed below are the basic assumptions, broad accounting principles, and constraints discussed in this chapter.

a. Economic entity assumption	g. Matching principle
b. Going concern assumption	h. Full-disclosure principle
c. Periodicity assumption	i. Cost effectiveness
d. Monetary unit assumption	j. Materiality
e. Historical cost principle	k. Conservatism
f. Realization principle	

Identify by letter the assumption, principle, or constraint that relates to each statement or phrase below.

_____ 1. Revenue is recognized only after certain criteria are satisfied.

_____ 2. Information that could affect decision making should be reported.

_____ 3. Cause-and-effect relationship between revenues and expenses.

_____ 4. The basis for measurement of many assets and liabilities.

_____ 5. Relates to the qualitative characteristic of timeliness.

_____ 6. All economic events can be identified with a particular entity.

_____ 7. The benefits of providing accounting information should exceed the cost of doing so.

_____ 8. A consequence is that GAAP need not be followed in all situations.

_____ 9. Not a qualitative characteristic, but a practical justification for some accounting choices.

_____10. Assumes the entity will continue indefinitely.

_____11. Inflation causes a violation of this assumption.

E 1–15
Multiple choice;
concept statements,
basic assumptions,
principles
● **LO5 through
   LO8**

Determine the response that best completes the following statements or questions.

1. The primary objective of financial reporting is to provide information
   a. About a firm's management team.
   b. Useful to capital providers.
   c. Concerning the changes in financial position resulting from the income-producing efforts of the entity.
   d. About a firm's financing and investing activities.

2. *Statements of Financial Accounting Concepts* issued by the FASB
   a. Represent GAAP.
   b. Have been superseded by *SFAS*s.
   c. Are subject to approval of the SEC.
   d. Identify the conceptual framework within which accounting standards are developed.

3. In general, revenue is recognized as earned when the earning process is virtually complete and
   a. The sales price has been collected.
   b. A purchase order has been received.
   c. There is reasonable certainty as to the collectibility of the asset to be received.
   d. A contract has been signed.

4. In depreciating the cost of an asset, accountants are most concerned with
   a. Conservatism.
   b. The realization principle.
   c. Full disclosure.
   d. The matching principle.

5. The primary objective of the matching principle is to
   a. Provide full disclosure.
   b. Record expenses in the period that related revenues are recognized.
   c. Provide timely information to decision makers.
   d. Promote comparability between financial statements of different periods.

6. The separate entity assumption states that, in the absence of contrary evidence, all entities will survive indefinitely.
   a. True
   b. False

CPA AND CMA REVIEW QUESTIONS

CPA Exam
Questions

The following questions are used in the Kaplan CPA Review Course to study the environment and theoretical structure of financial accounting while preparing for the CPA examination. Determine the response that best completes the statements or questions.

● **LO6**

1. Which of the following is *not* a qualitative characteristic of accounting information according to the FASB's conceptual framework?
   a. Auditor independence.
   b. Neutrality.
   c. Timeliness.
   d. Predictive value.

● LO6   2. According to the conceptual framework, neutrality is a characteristic of
a. Understandability.
b. Faithful representation.
c. Relevance.
d. Both relevance and faithful representation.

● LO3   3. The Financial Accounting Standards Board (FASB)
a. Is a division of the Securities and Exchange Commission (SEC).
b. Is a private body that helps set accounting standards in the United States.
c. Is responsible for setting auditing standards that all auditors must follow.
d. Consists entirely of members of the American Institute of Certified Public Accountants.

● LO6   4. Confirmatory value is an ingredient of the primary quality of

	Relevance	Faithful Representation
a.	Yes	No
b.	No	Yes
c.	Yes	Yes
d.	No	No

● LO6   5. Predictive value is an ingredient of

	Faithful Representation	Relevance
a.	Yes	No
b.	No	No
c.	Yes	Yes
d.	No	Yes

● LO6   6. Completeness is an ingredient of the primary quality of
a. Verifiability.
b. Faithful representation.
c. Relevance.
d. Understandability.

● LO6   7. The objective of financial reporting for business enterprises is based on
a. Generally accepted accounting principles.
b. The needs of the users of the information.
c. The need for conservatism.
d. None of above.

● LO6   8. According to the FASB's conceptual framework, comprehensive income includes which of the following?

	Operating Income	Investments by Owners
a.	No	Yes
b.	No	No
c.	Yes	Yes
d.	Yes	No

CMA Exam Questions

The following questions dealing with the environment and theoretical structure of financial accounting are adapted from questions that previously appeared on Certified Management Accountant (CMA) examinations. The CMA designation sponsored by the Institute of Management Accountants (**www.imanet.org**) provides members with an objective measure of knowledge and competence in the field of management accounting. Determine the response that best completes the statements or questions.

● LO3   1. Accounting standard setting in the United States is
a. Done primarily by the Securities and Exchange Commission.
b. Done primarily by the private sector.
c. The responsibility of the public sector.
d. Done primarily by the International Accounting Standards Committee.

● LO6   2. Verifiability as used in accounting includes
a. Determining the revenue first, then determining the costs incurred in earning that revenue.
b. The entity's giving the same treatment to comparable transactions from period to period.
c. Similar results being obtained by both the accountant and an independent party using the same measurement methods.
d. The disclosure of all facts that may influence the judgment of an informed reader.

● LO6

3. Recognition is the process of formally recording and reporting an item in the financial statements. In order for a revenue item to be recognized, it must be all of the following except
a. Measurable.
b. Relevant.
c. Material.
d. Realized or realizable.

BROADEN YOUR PERSPECTIVE

Apply your critical-thinking ability to the knowledge you've gained. These cases will provide you an opportunity to develop your research, analysis, judgment, and communication skills. You will also work with other students, integrate what you've learned, apply it in real-world situations, and consider its global and ethical ramifications. This practice will broaden your knowledge and further develop your decision-making abilities.

**Judgment
Case 1–1**
The development
of accounting
standards
● LO3

In 1934, Congress created the Securities and Exchange Commission (SEC) and gave the commission both the power and responsibility for setting accounting and reporting standards in the United States.

Required:

1. Explain the relationship between the SEC and the various private sector standard-setting bodies that have, over time, been delegated the responsibility for setting accounting standards.

2. Can you think of any reasons why the SEC has delegated this responsibility rather than set standards directly?

**Research
Case 1–2**
Accessing SEC
information
through the Internet
● LO3

Internet access to the World Wide Web has provided a wealth of information accessible with our personal computers. Many chapters in this text contain Real World Cases that require you to access the web to research an accounting issue. The purpose of this case is to introduce you to the Internet home page of the Securities and Exchange Commission (SEC) and its EDGAR database.

Required:

1. Access the SEC home page on the Internet. The web address is **www.sec.gov**.

2. Choose the subaddress "About the SEC." What are the two basic objectives of the 1933 Securities Act?

3. Return to the SEC home page and access EDGAR. Describe the contents of the database.

**Research
Case 1–3**
Accessing FASB
information
through the Internet
● LO4

The purpose of this case is to introduce you to the information available on the website of the Financial Accounting Standards Board (FASB).

Required:

Access the FASB home page on the Internet. The web address is **www.fasb.org**. Answer the following questions.

1. Describe the mission of the FASB.

2. Who are the current Board members? Briefly describe their backgrounds.

3. How are topics added to the FASB's technical agenda?

**Research
Case 1–4**
Accessing IASB
information
through the Internet
● LO3

The purpose of this case is to introduce you to the information available on the website of the International Accounting Standards Board (IASB).

Required:

Access the IASB home page on the Internet. The web address is **www.iasb.org**. Answer the following questions.

1. Describe the mission of the IASB.

2. The IASB has how many board members?

3. Who is the current chairman of the IASB?

4. Where is the IASB located?

**Research
Case 1–5**
Accounting
standards in China
● LO3 LO4

Economic reforms in the People's Republic of China are moving that nation toward a market-driven economy. China's accounting practices must also change to accommodate the needs of potential investors. In an article entitled "Institutional Factors Influencing China's Accounting Reforms and Standards," Professor Bing Xiang analyzes the changes in the accounting environment of China during the recent economic reforms and their implications for the development of accounting reforms.

Required:

1. In your library or from some other source, locate the indicated article in *Accounting Horizons,* June 1998.
2. Briefly describe the economic reforms that led to the need for increased external financial reporting in China.
3. Conformity with International Accounting Standards was specified as an overriding objective in formulating China's accounting standards. What is the author's opinion of this objective?

Communication Case 1–6
Relevance and faithful representation
● LO6

Some theorists contend that companies that create pollution should report the social cost of that pollution in income statements. They argue that such companies are indirectly subsidized as the cost of pollution is borne by society while only production costs (and perhaps minimal pollution fines) are shown in the income statement. Thus, the product sells for less than would be necessary if all costs were included.

Assume that the FASB is considering a standard to include the social costs of pollution in the income statement. The process would require considering both relevance and faithful representation of the information produced by the new standard. Your instructor will divide the class into two to six groups depending on the size of the class. The mission of your group is to explain how the concepts of relevance and faithful representation relate to this issue.

Required:

Each group member should consider the question independently and draft a tentative answer prior to the class session for which the case is assigned.

In class, each group will meet for 10 to 15 minutes in different areas of the classroom. During that meeting, group members will take turns sharing their suggestions for the purpose of arriving at a single group treatment.

After the allotted time, a spokesperson for each group (selected during the group meetings) will share the group's solution with the class. The goal of the class is to incorporate the views of each group into a consensus answer to the question.

Communication Case 1–7
Accounting standard setting
● LO4

One of your friends is a financial analyst for a major stock brokerage firm. Recently she indicated to you that she had read an article in a weekly business magazine that alluded to the political process of establishing accounting standards. She had always assumed that accounting standards were established by determining the approach that conceptually best reflected the economics of a transaction.

Required:

Write a one to two-page article for a business journal explaining what is meant by the political process for establishing accounting standards. Be sure to include in your article a discussion of the need for the FASB to balance accounting considerations and economic consequences.

Ethics Case 1–8
The auditors' responsibility
● LO4

It is the responsibility of management to apply accounting standards when communicating with investors and creditors through financial statements. Another group, auditors, serves as an independent intermediary to help ensure that management has in fact appropriately applied GAAP in preparing the company's financial statements. Auditors examine (audit) financial statements to express a professional, independent opinion. The opinion reflects the auditors' assessment of the statements' fairness, which is determined by the extent to which they are prepared in compliance with GAAP.

Some feel that it is impossible for an auditor to give an independent opinion on a company's financial statements because the auditors' fees for performing the audit are paid by the company. In addition to the audit fee, quite often the auditor performs other services for the company such as preparing the company's income tax returns.

Required:

How might an auditor's ethics be challenged while performing an audit?

Judgment Case 1–9
Qualitative characteristics
● LO6

Generally accepted accounting principles do not require companies to disclose forecasts of any financial variables to external users. A friend, who is a finance major, is puzzled by this and asks you to explain why such relevant information is not provided to investors and creditors to help them predict future cash flows.

Required:

Explain to your friend why this information is not routinely provided to investors and creditors.

Judgment Case 1–10
GAAP, comparability, and the role of the auditor
● LO4 LO6

Mary McQuire is trying to decide how to invest her money. A friend recommended that she buy the stock of one of two corporations and suggested that she should compare the financial statements of the two companies before making a decision.

Required:

1. Do you agree that Mary will be able to compare the financial statements of the two companies?
2. What role does the auditor play in ensuring comparability of financial statements between companies?

Judgment Case 1–11

Cost effectiveness

● LO6

Phase A of the joint FASB and IASB conceptual framework project includes a discussion of the constraint cost effectiveness. Assume that the FASB is considering revising an important accounting standard.

Required:

1. What is the desired benefit from revising an accounting standard?
2. What are some of the possible costs that could result from a revision of an accounting standard?
3. What does the FASB do in order to assess possible benefits and costs of a proposed revision of an accounting standard?

Judgment Case 1–12

The realization principle

● LO8

A new client, the Wolf Company, asks your advice concerning the point in time that the company should recognize revenue from the rental of its office buildings. Renters usually pay rent on a quarterly basis at the beginning of the quarter. The owners contend that the critical event that motivates revenue recognition should be the date the cash is received from renters. After all, the money is in hand and is very seldom returned.

Required:

1. Describe the two criteria that must be satisfied before revenue can be recognized.
2. Do you agree or disagree with the position of the owners of Wolf Company? Support your answer.

Analysis Case 1–13

The matching principle

● LO8

Revenues measure the accomplishments of a company during the period. Expenses are then matched with revenues to produce a periodic measure of performance called *net income.*

Required:

1. Explain what is meant by the phrase *matched with revenues.*
2. Describe the four approaches used to implement the matching principle and label them 1 through 4.
3. For each of the following, identify which matching approach should be used to recognize the cost as expense.
   a. The cost of producing a product.
   b. The cost of advertising.
   c. The cost of monthly rent on the office building.
   d. The salary of an office employee.
   e. Depreciation on an office building.

Judgment Case 1–14

Capitalize or expense?

● LO8

When a company makes an expenditure that is neither a payment to a creditor nor a distribution to an owner, management must decide if the expenditure should be capitalized (recorded as an increase in an asset) or expensed (recorded as an expense thereby decreasing owners' equity).

Required:

1. Which factor or factors should the company consider when making this decision?
2. Which key accounting principle is involved?
3. Are there any constraints that could cause the company to alter its decision?

Real World Case 1–15

Elements; disclosures; The GAP

● LO6 LO8

Selected financial statements from a recent annual report of **The GAP, Inc.** follow. Use these statements to answer the following questions.

Required:

1. What amounts did The GAP report for the following items for the fiscal year ended January 31, 2009?
   a. Total net revenues
   b. Total operating expenses
   c. Net income (earnings)
   d. Total assets
   e. Total stockholders' equity

Real World Financials

2. How many shares of common stock did the company have issued on January 31, 2009?
3. Why do you think The GAP reports more than one year of data in its financial statements?

THE GAP, INC.
Consolidated Balance Sheets

($ and shares in millions except par value)	January 31, 2009	February 2, 2008
Assets		
Current assets:		
Cash and cash equivalents	$ 1,715	$ 1,724
Short-term investments	—	177
Restricted cash	41	38
Merchandise inventory	1,506	1,575
Other current assets	743	572
Total current assets	4,005	4,086
Property and equipment, net	2,933	3,267
Other long-term assets	626	485
Total assets	$ 7,564	$ 7,838
Liabilities and Stockholders' Equity		
Current liabilities:		
Current maturities of long-term debt	$ 50	$ 138
Accounts payable	975	1,006
Accrued expenses and other current liabilities	1,076	1,259
Income taxes payable	57	30
Total current liabilities	2,158	2,433
Long-term liabilities:		
Long-term debt	—	50
Lease incentives and other long-term liabilities	1,019	1,081
Total long-term liabilities	1,019	1,131
Commitments and contingencies (see Notes 11 and 15)		
Stockholders' equity:		
Common stock $0.05 par value		
Authorized 2,300 shares; Issued 1,105 and 1,100 shares;		
Outstanding 694 and 734 shares	55	55
Additional paid-in capital	2,895	2,783
Retained earnings	9,947	9,223
Accumulated other comprehensive earnings	123	125
Treasury stock, at cost (411 and 366 shares)	(8,633)	(7,912)
Total stockholders' equity	4,387	4,274
Total liabilities and stockholders' equity	$ 7,564	$ 7,838

THE GAP, INC.
Consolidated Statements of Earnings

($ and shares in millions except per share amounts)	Fiscal Year Ended		
	January 31, 2009	February 2, 2008	February 3, 2007
Net sales	$14,526	$15,763	$15,923
Cost of goods sold and occupancy expenses	9,079	10,071	10,266
Gross profit	5,447	5,692	5,657
Operating expenses	3,899	4,377	4,432
Operating income	1,548	1,315	1,225
Interest expense	1	26	41
Interest income	(37)	(117)	(131)
Earnings from continuing operations before income taxes	1,584	1,406	1,315
Income taxes	617	539	506
Earnings from continuing operations, net of income taxes	967	867	809
Loss from discontinued operation, net of income tax benefit	—	(34)	(31)
Net earnings	$ 967	$ 833	$ 778
Weighted-average number of shares—basic	716	791	831
Weighted-average number of shares—diluted	719	794	836
Basic earnings per share:			
Earnings from continuing operations, net of income taxes	$ 1.35	$ 1.10	$ 0.97
Loss from discontinued operation, net of income tax benefit	—	(0.05)	(0.03)
Net earnings per share	$ 1.35	$ 1.05	$ 0.94
Diluted earnings per share:			
Earnings from continuing operations, net of income taxes	$ 1.34	$ 1.09	$ 0.97
Loss from discontinued operation, net of income tax benefit	—	(0.04)	(0.04)
Net earnings per share	$ 1.34	$ 1.05	$ 0.93

CHAPTER

2

Review of the Accounting Process

||| || || || || || || || || || || || || || || || || || || || || || ||

/// OVERVIEW

Chapter 1 explained that the primary means of conveying financial information to investors, creditors, and other external users is through financial statements and related notes. The purpose of this chapter is to review the fundamental accounting process used to produce the financial statements. This review establishes a framework for the study of the concepts covered in intermediate accounting.

Actual accounting systems differ significantly from company to company. This chapter focuses on the many features that tend to be common to any accounting system.

/// LEARNING OBJECTIVES

After studying this chapter, you should be able to:

● **LO1** Analyze routine economic events—transactions—and record their effects on a company's financial position using the accounting equation format. (page 52)

● **LO2** Record transactions using the general journal format. (page 56)

● **LO3** Post the effects of journal entries to general ledger accounts and prepare an unadjusted trial balance. (page 63)

● **LO4** Identify and describe the different types of adjusting journal entries. (page 66)

● **LO5** Record adjusting journal entries in general journal format, post entries, and prepare an adjusted trial balance. (page 67)

● **LO6** Describe the four basic financial statements. (page 76)

● **LO7** Explain the closing process. (page 79)

● **LO8** Convert from cash basis net income to accrual basis net income. (page 83)

Engineering Profits

After graduating from college last year, two of your engineering-major friends started an Internet consulting practice. They began operations on July 1 and felt they did quite well during their first year. Now they would like to borrow $20,000 from a local bank to buy new computing equipment and office furniture. To support their loan application, the friends presented the bank with the following income statement for their first year of operations ending June 30:

Consulting revenue		$96,000
Operating expenses:		
Salaries	$32,000	
Rent	9,000	
Supplies	4,800	
Utilities	3,000	
Advertising	1,200	(50,000)
Net income		$46,000

The bank officer noticed that there was no depreciation expense in the income statement and has asked your friends to revise the statement after making year-end adjustments. After agreeing to help, you discover the following information:

a. The friends paid $80,000 for equipment when they began operations. They think the equipment will be useful for five years.

b. They pay $500 a month to rent office space. In January, they paid a full year's rent in advance. This is included in the $9,000 rent expense.

c. Included in consulting revenue is $13,000 they received from a customer in June as a deposit for work to be performed in August.

By the time you finish this chapter, you should be able to respond appropriately to the questions posed in this case. Compare your response to the solution provided at the end of the chapter.

QUESTIONS ///

1. What purpose do adjusting entries serve? (page 67)

2. What year-end adjustments are needed to revise the income statement? Did your friends do as well their first year as they thought? (page 67)

A solid foundation is vital to a sound understanding of intermediate accounting. So, we review the fundamental accounting process here to serve as a framework for the new concepts you will learn in this course.

Chapter 1 introduced the theoretical structure of financial accounting and the environment within which it operates. The primary function of financial accounting—to provide relevant and reliable financial information to external users—is accomplished by periodically disseminating financial statements and related notes. In this chapter we review the *process* used to identify, analyze, record, summarize, and then report the economic events affecting a company's financial position.

Keep in mind as you study this chapter that the accounting information systems businesses actually use are quite different from company to company. Larger companies generally use more complex systems than smaller companies use. The types of economic events affecting companies also cause differences in systems. We focus on the many features that tend to be common to all accounting systems.

It is important to understand that this chapter and its appendixes are not intended to describe actual accounting systems. In most business enterprises, the sheer volume of data that must be processed precludes a manual accounting system. Fortunately, the computer provides a solution. *We describe and illustrate a manual accounting information system to provide an overview of the basic model that underlies the computer software programs actually used to process accounting information.*

Electronic data processing is fast, accurate, and affordable. Many large and medium-sized companies own or rent their own mainframe computers and company-specific data processing systems. Smaller companies can take advantage of technology with relatively inexpensive micro- and minicomputers and generalized data software packages such as QuickBooks and Peachtree Accounting Software. Enterprise Resource Planning (ERP) systems are now being installed in companies of all sizes. The objective of ERP is to create a customized software program that integrates all departments and functions across a company onto a single computer system that can serve the information needs of those different departments, including the accounting department.

Computers are used to process accounting information. In this chapter we provide an overview of the basic model that underlies computer software programs.

The Basic Model

Economic events cause changes in the financial position of the company.

The first objective of any accounting system is to identify the **economic events** that can be expressed in financial terms by the system.[1] An economic event is any event that *directly* affects the financial position of the company. Recall from Chapter 1 that financial position comprises assets, liabilities, and owners' equity. Broad and specific accounting principles determine which events should be recorded, when the events should be recorded, and the dollar amount at which they should be measured.

External events involve an exchange between the company and another entity.

Economic events can be classified as either external events or internal events. **External events** involve an exchange between the company and a separate economic entity. Examples are purchasing merchandise inventory for cash, borrowing cash from a bank, and paying salaries to employees. In each instance, the company receives something (merchandise, cash, and services) in exchange for something else (cash, assumption of a liability, and cash).

Internal events do not involve an exchange transaction but do affect the company's financial position.

On the other hand, **internal events** directly affect the financial position of the company but don't involve an exchange transaction with another entity. Examples are the depreciation of machinery and the use of supplies. As we will see later in the chapter, these events must be recorded to properly reflect a company's financial position and results of operations in accordance with the accrual accounting model.

The Accounting Equation

● LO1

The **accounting equation** underlies the process used to capture the effect of economic events.

$$\text{Assets} = \text{Liabilities} + \text{Owners' Equity}$$

The elements of the equation were defined in Chapter 1.

This general expression portrays the equality between the total economic resources of an entity (its assets)—shown on the left side of the equation—and the total claims to those

---

[1]There are many economic events that affect a company *indirectly* and are not recorded. For example, when the Federal Reserve changes its discount rate, it is an important economic event that can affect the company in many ways, but it is not recorded by the company.

resources (liabilities and equity)—shown on the right side. In other words, the resources of an enterprise are provided by creditors or owners.

The equation also implies that each economic event affecting this equation will have a dual effect because resources always must equal claims to those resources. For illustration, consider the events (we refer to these throughout the text as transactions) in Illustration 2–1.

---

1. An attorney invested $50,000 to open a law office.
An investment by the owner causes both assets and owners' equity to increase.

Assets	=	Liabilities	+	Owners' Equity
+$50,000 (cash)				+$50,000 (investment by owner)

2. $40,000 was borrowed from a bank and a note payable was signed.
This transaction causes assets and liabilities to increase. A bank loan increases cash and creates an obligation to repay it.

Assets	=	Liabilities	+	Owners' Equity
+$40,000 (cash)		+$40,000 (note payable)		

3. Supplies costing $3,000 were purchased on account.
Buying supplies on credit also increases both assets and liabilities.

Assets	=	Liabilities	+	Owners' Equity
+$3,000 (supplies)		+$3,000 (accounts payable)		

4. Services were performed on account for $10,000.
Transactions 4, 5, and 6 are revenue and expense transactions. Revenues and expenses (and gains and losses) are events that cause owners' equity to change. Revenues and gains describe inflows of assets, causing owners' equity to increase. Expenses and losses describe outflows of assets (or increases in liabilities), causing owners' equity to decrease.

Assets	=	Liabilities	+	Owners' Equity
+$10,000 (receivables)				+$10,000 (revenue)

5. Salaries of $5,000 were paid to employees.

Assets	=	Liabilities	+	Owners' Equity
−$5,000 (cash)				−$5,000 (expense)

6. $500 of supplies were used.

Assets	=	Liabilities	+	Owners' Equity
−$500 (supplies)				−$500 (expense)

7. $1,000 was paid on account to the supplies vendor.
This transaction causes assets and liabilities to decrease.

Assets	=	Liabilities	+	Owners' Equity
−$1,000 (cash)		−$1,000 (accounts payable)		

ILLUSTRATION 2–1
Transaction Analysis

Each transaction is analyzed to determine its effect on the equation and on the specific financial position elements.

The accounting equation can be expanded to include a column for each type of asset and liability and for each type of change in owners' equity.

As discussed in Chapter 1, owners of a corporation are its shareholders, so owners' equity for a corporation is referred to as shareholders' equity. Shareholders' equity for a corporation arises primarily from two sources: (1) amounts *invested* by shareholders in the corporation and (2) amounts *earned* by the corporation (on behalf of its shareholders). These are reported as (1) **paid-in capital** and (2) **retained earnings.** Retained earnings equals net income less distributions to shareholders (primarily dividends) since the inception of the corporation. Graphic 2–1 shows the basic accounting equation for a corporation with shareholders' equity expanded to highlight its composition. We use the corporate format throughout the remainder of the chapter.

Each event, or transaction, has a dual effect on the accounting equation.

Owners' equity for a corporation, called shareholders' equity, is classified by source as either paid-in capital or retained earnings.

Account Relationships

All transactions could be recorded in columnar fashion as increases or decreases to elements of the accounting equation. However, even for a very small company with few transactions, this would become cumbersome. So, most companies use a process called the **double-entry system.** The term *double-entry* refers to the dual effect that each transaction has on the accounting equation.

The double-entry system is used to process transactions.

GRAPHIC 2–1

Accounting Equation for a Corporation

A *general ledger* is a collection of storage areas, called *accounts*, used to keep track of increases and decreases in financial position elements.

In the double-entry system, *debit* means *left* side of an account and *credit* means *right* side of an account.

Asset *increases* are entered on the *debit* side of accounts and *decreases* are entered on the *credit* side. Liability and equity account *increases* are *credits* and *decreases* are *debits*.

Elements of the accounting equation are represented by accounts which are contained in a general ledger. Increases and decreases in each element of a company's financial position are recorded in these accounts. A separate account is maintained for individual assets and liabilities, retained earnings, and paid-in capital. Also, to accumulate information needed for the income statement, we use separate accounts to keep track of the changes in retained earnings caused by revenues, expenses, gains, and losses. The number of accounts depends on the complexity of the company's operations.

An account includes the account title, an account number to aid the processing task, and columns or fields for increases, decreases, the cumulative balance, and the date. For instructional purposes we use T-accounts instead of formal ledger accounts. A T-account has space at the top for the account title and two sides for recording increases and decreases.

Account Title

For centuries, accountants have effectively used a system of debits and credits to increase and decrease account balances in the ledger. Debits merely represent the *left* side of the account and credits the *right* side, as shown below.

Account Title

debit side	credit side

Whether a debit or a credit represents an increase or a decrease depends on the type of account. Accounts on the left side of the accounting equation (assets) are *increased* (+) by *debit* entries and *decreased* (−) by *credit* entries. Accounts on the right side of the accounting equation (liabilities and shareholders' equity) are *increased* (+) by *credit* entries and *decreased* (−) by *debit* entries. This arbitrary, but effective, procedure ensures that for each transaction the net impact on the left sides of accounts always equals the net impact on the right sides of accounts.

For example, consider the bank loan in our earlier illustration. An asset, cash, increased by $40,000. Increases in assets are *debits*. Liabilities also increased by $40,000. Increases in liabilities are *credits*.

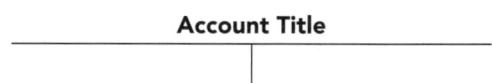

Assets		=	Liabilities		+	Owners' Equity
Cash			**Note Payable**			
debit	credit		debit	credit		
+ 40,000				40,000 +		

The debits equal the credits in every transaction (dual effect), so both before and after a transaction the accounting equation is in balance.

Prior exposure to the terms debit and credit probably comes from your experience with a bank account. For example, when a bank debits your checking account for service charges, it decreases your account balance. When you make a deposit, the bank credits your account, increasing your account balance. You must remember that from the bank's perspective, your bank account balance is a liability—it represents the amount that the bank owes you. Therefore, when the bank debits your account, it is decreasing its liability. When the bank credits your account, its liability increases.

Graphic 2–2 illustrates the relationship among the accounting equation, debits and credits, and the increases and decreases in financial position elements.

Notice that increases and decreases in retained earnings are recorded *indirectly*. For example, an expense represents a decrease in retained earnings, which requires a debit. That debit, however, is recorded in an appropriate expense account rather than in retained earnings

GRAPHIC 2–2 Accounting Equation, Debits and Credits, Increases and Decreases

itself. This allows the company to maintain a separate record of expenses incurred during an accounting period. The debit to retained earnings for the expense is recorded in a closing entry (reviewed later) at the end of the period, only after the expense total is reflected in the income statement. Similarly, an increase in retained earnings due to a revenue is recorded indirectly with a credit to a revenue account, which is later reflected as a credit to retained earnings.

The general ledger accounts serve as control accounts. Subsidiary accounts associated with a particular general ledger control account are maintained in separate subsidiary ledgers. For example, a subsidiary ledger for accounts receivable contains individual account receivable accounts for each of the company's credit customers and the total of all subsidiary accounts would equal the amount in the control account. Subsidiary ledgers are discussed in more detail in Appendix 2C.

Each general ledger account can be classified as either *permanent* or *temporary*. **Permanent accounts** represent assets, liabilities, and shareholders' equity at a point in time. **Temporary accounts** represent changes in the retained earnings component of shareholders' equity for a corporation caused by revenue, expense, gain, and loss transactions. It would be cumbersome to record each revenue/expense, gain/loss transaction directly into the retained earnings account. The different types of events affecting retained earnings should be kept separate to facilitate the preparation of the financial statements. The balances in these temporary accounts are periodically, usually once a year, closed (zeroed out), and the net effect is recorded in the permanent retained earnings account. The temporary accounts need to be zeroed out to measure income on an annual basis. This closing process is discussed in a later section of this chapter.

Permanent accounts represent the basic financial position elements of the accounting equation.

Temporary accounts keep track of the changes in the retained earnings component of shareholders' equity.

The Accounting Processing Cycle

Now that we've reviewed the basics of the double-entry system, let's look closer at the process used to identify, analyze, record, and summarize transactions and prepare financial statements. This section deals only with *external transactions,* those that involve an exchange transaction with another entity. Internal transactions are discussed in a later section.

The 10 steps in the accounting processing cycle are listed in Graphic 2–3. Steps 1–4 take place during the accounting period while steps 5–8 occur at the end of the accounting period. Steps 9 and 10 are required only at the end of the year.

We now discuss these steps in order.

The first step in the process is to *identify* external transactions affecting the accounting equation. An accountant usually does not directly witness business transactions. A mechanism is needed to relay the essential information about each transaction to the accountant. **Source documents** such as sales invoices, bills from suppliers, and cash register tapes serve this need.

STEP 1

Obtain information about transactions from *source documents.*

GRAPHIC 2–3

The Accounting
Processing Cycle

The Steps of the Accounting Processing Cycle

These source documents usually identify the date and nature of each transaction, the participating parties, and the monetary terms. For example, a sales invoice identifies the date of sale, the customer, the specific goods sold, the dollar amount of the sale, and the payment terms. With this information, the second step in the processing cycle, **transaction analysis,** can be accomplished. Transaction analysis is the process of reviewing the source documents to determine the dual effect on the accounting equation and the specific elements involved.

STEP 2

Analyze the transaction.

This process is summarized in Illustration 2–2 for the seven transactions described previously in Illustration 2–1. The item in each T-account is numbered to show the related transaction.

STEP 3

Record the transaction
in a *journal.*

The third step in the process is to record the transaction in a **journal.** Journals provide a chronological record of all economic events affecting a firm. Each journal entry is expressed in terms of equal debits and credits to accounts affected by the transaction being recorded. Debits and credits represent increases or decreases to specific accounts, depending on the type of account, as explained earlier. For example, for credit sales, a debit to accounts receivable and a credit to sales revenue is recorded in a sales journal.

A sales journal is an example of a **special journal** used to record a repetitive type of transaction. Appendix 2C discusses the use of special journals in more depth. In this chapter and throughout the text, we use the **general journal** format to record all transactions.

● **LO2**

Any type of transaction can be recorded in a general journal. It has a place for the date of the transaction, a place for account titles, account numbers, and supporting explanations, as well as a place for debit entries, and a place for credit entries. A simplified journal entry is used throughout the text that lists the account titles to be debited and credited and the dollar amounts. A common convention is to list the debited accounts first, indent the credited accounts, and use the first of two columns for the debit amounts and the second column for the credit amounts. For example, the **journal entry** for the bank loan in Illustration 2–1, which requires a debit to cash and a credit to note payable, is recorded as follows:

To record the
**borrowing of cash and
the signing of a note
payable.**

Cash	40,000	
Note payable		40,000

STEP 4

Post from the journal
to the general ledger
accounts.

Step 4 is to periodically transfer or *post* the debit and credit information from the journal to individual ledger accounts. Recall that a ledger is simply a collection of all of the company's various accounts. Each account provides a summary of the effects of all events and transactions on that individual account. This process is called **posting.** Posting involves transferring debits and credits recorded in individual journal entries to the specific accounts affected. As discussed earlier in the chapter, most accounting systems today are computerized, with the

ILLUSTRATION 2–2 Transaction Analysis, the Accounting Equation, and Debits and Credits

Accounting Equation

Transaction	Transaction Analysis	Assets	=	Liabilities	+	Owners' Equity	Account Entry
1. An attorney invested $50,000 to open a law office.	Assets (cash) and owners' equity each increased by $50,000.	+50,000	=		+	+50,000	**Cash** — 1. 50,000 **Owners' Equity** — 50,000 1.
	Cumulative balances	50,000	=		+	50,000	
2. $40,000 was borrowed from a bank and a note payable was signed.	Assets (cash) and liabilities (note payable) each increased by $40,000.	+40,000	=	+40,000	+		**Cash** — 1. 50,000 / 2. 40,000 **Note Payable** — 40,000 2.
	Cumulative balances	90,000	=	40,000	+	50,000	
3. Supplies costing $3,000 were purchased on account.	Assets (supplies) and liabilities (accounts payable) each increased by $3,000.	+3,000	=	+3,000	+		**Supplies** — 3. 3,000 **Accounts Payable** — 3,000 3.
	Cumulative balances	93,000	=	43,000	+	50,000	
4. Services were performed on account for $10,000.	Assets (accounts receivable) and owners' equity (revenue) each increased by $10,000.	+10,000	=		+	+10,000	**Accounts Receivable** — 4. 10,000 **Owners' Equity (Revenue)** — 10,000 4.
	Cumulative balances	103,000	=	43,000	+	60,000	
5. Salaries of $5,000 were paid to employees.	Assets (cash) decreased and owners' equity decreased (salaries expense increased) by $5,000.	−5,000	=		+	−5,000	**Cash** — 1. 50,000 / 2. 40,000	5,000 5. **Owners' Equity (Salaries Expense)** — 5. 5,000
	Cumulative balances	98,000	=	43,000	+	55,000	
6. $500 of supplies were used.	Assets (supplies) decreased and owners' equity decreased (supplies expense increased) by $500.	−500	=		+	−500	**Supplies** — 3. 3,000	500 6. **Owners' Equity (Supplies Expense)** — 6. 500
	Cumulative balances	97,500	=	43,000	+	54,500	
7. $1,000 was paid on account to the supplies vendor.	Assets (cash) and liabilities (accounts payable) each decreased by $1,000.	−1,000	=	−1,000	+		**Cash** — 1. 50,000 / 2. 40,000	5,000 5. / 1,000 7. **Accounts Payable** — 7. 1,000	3,000 3.
	Cumulative balances	96,500	=	42,000	+	54,500	

journal and ledger kept on disk. For these systems, the journal input information is automatically and instantly posted to the ledger accounts.

These first four steps in the processing cycle are illustrated using the external transactions in Illustration 2–3 which occurred during the month of July 2011, the first month of operations for Dress Right Clothing Corporation. The company operates a retail store that sells men's and women's clothing. Dress Right is organized as a corporation so owners' equity is classified by source as either paid-in capital or retained earnings.

ILLUSTRATION 2–3 External Transactions for July 2011	July	1	Two individuals each invested $30,000 in the corporation. Each investor was issued 3,000 shares of common stock.
		1	Borrowed $40,000 from a local bank and signed two notes. The first note for $10,000 requires payment of principal and 10% interest in six months. The second note for $30,000 requires the payment of principal in two years. Interest at 10% is payable each year on July 1, 2012, and July 1, 2013.
		1	Paid $24,000 in advance for one year's rent on the store building.
		1	Purchased furniture and fixtures from Acme Furniture for $12,000 cash.
		3	Purchased $60,000 of clothing inventory on account from the Birdwell Wholesale Clothing Company.
		6	Purchased $2,000 of supplies for cash.
		4–31	During the month sold merchandise costing $20,000 for $35,000 cash.
		9	Sold clothing on account to St. Jude's School for Girls for $3,500. The clothing cost $2,000.
		16	Subleased a portion of the building to a jewelry store. Received $1,000 in advance for the first two months' rent beginning on July 16.
		20	Paid Birdwell Wholesale Clothing $25,000 on account.
		20	Paid salaries to employees for the first half of the month, $5,000.
		25	Received $1,500 on account from St. Jude's.
		30	The corporation paid its shareholders a cash dividend of $1,000.

The local bank requires that Dress Right furnish financial statements on a monthly basis. The transactions listed in the illustration are used to demonstrate the accounting processing cycle for the month of July 2011.

For each transaction, a source document provides the necessary information to complete steps two and three in the processing cycle, transaction analysis and recording the appropriate journal entry. Each transaction listed in Illustration 2–3 is analyzed below, preceded by the necessary journal entry.

To record the issuance of common stock.

July 1
| Cash | 60,000 | |
| Common stock | | 60,000 |

This first transaction is an investment by owners that increases an asset, cash, and also increases shareholders' equity. Increases in assets are recorded as debits and increases in shareholders' equity are recorded as credits. We use the paid-in capital account called common stock because stock was issued in exchange for cash paid in.[2]

To record the borrowing of cash and the signing of notes payable.

July 1
| Cash | 40,000 | |
| Notes payable | | 40,000 |

This transaction causes increases in both cash and the liability, notes payable. Increases in assets are debits and increases in liabilities are credits. The notes require payment of $40,000 in principal and $6,500 ([$10,000 × 10% × $\frac{6}{12}$ = $500] + [$30,000 × 10% × 2 years = $6,000])

---
[2]The different types of stock are discussed in Chapter 18.

in interest. However, at this point we are concerned only with the external transaction that occurs when the cash is borrowed and the notes are signed. Later we discuss how the interest is recorded.

July 1		
Prepaid rent	24,000	
Cash		24,000

To record the payment of one year's rent in advance.

This transaction increased an asset called prepaid rent, which is debited, and decreased the asset cash (a credit). Dress Right acquired the right to use the building for one full year. This is an asset because it represents a future benefit to the company. As we will see later, this asset expires over the one-year rental period.

July 1		
Furniture and fixtures	12,000	
Cash		12,000

To record the purchase of furniture and fixtures.

This transaction increases one asset, furniture and fixtures, and decreases another, cash.

July 3		
Inventory	60,000	
Accounts payable		60,000

To record the purchase of merchandise inventory.

This purchase of merchandise on account is recorded by a debit to inventory, an asset, and a credit to accounts payable, a liability. Increases in assets are debits, and increases in liabilities are credits.

The Dress Right Clothing Company uses the *perpetual inventory system* to keep track of its merchandise inventory. This system requires that the cost of merchandise purchased be recorded in inventory, an asset account. When inventory is sold, the inventory account is decreased by the cost of the item sold. The alternative method, the periodic system, is briefly discussed on the next page, and Chapters 8 and 9 cover the topic of inventory in depth.

July 6		
Supplies	2,000	
Cash		2,000

To record the purchase of supplies.

The acquisition of supplies is recorded as a debit to the asset account supplies (an increase) and a credit to the asset cash (a decrease). Supplies are recorded as an asset because they represent future benefits.

July 4–31		
Cash	35,000	
Sales revenue		35,000
Cost of goods sold (expense)..	20,000	
Inventory		20,000

To record the month's cash sales and the cost of those sales.

During the month of July, cash sales to customers totaled $35,000. The company's assets (cash) increase by this amount as does shareholders' equity. This increase in equity is recorded by a credit to the temporary account sales revenue.

At the same time, an asset, inventory, decreases and retained earnings decreases. Recall that expenses are outflows or using up of assets from providing goods and services. Dress Right incurred an expense equal to the cost of the inventory sold. The temporary account cost of goods sold increases. However, this increase in an expense represents a *decrease* in shareholders' equity—retained earnings—and accordingly the account is debited. Both of these transactions are *summary* transactions. Each sale made during the month requires a separate and similar entry.

To record a credit sale and the cost of that sale.

July 9		
Accounts receivable	3,500	
Sales revenue		3,500
Cost of goods sold	2,000	
Inventory		2,000

This transaction is similar to the cash sale above. The only difference is that the asset acquired in exchange for merchandise is accounts receivable rather than cash.

ADDITIONAL CONSIDERATION

Periodic Inventory System

The principal alternative to the perpetual inventory system is the periodic system. This system requires that the cost of merchandise purchased be recorded in a temporary account called *purchases*. When inventory is sold, the inventory account is not decreased and cost of goods sold is not recorded. Cost of goods sold for a period is determined and the inventory account is adjusted only at the end of a reporting period.

For example, the purchase of $60,000 of merchandise on account by Dress Right Clothing is recorded as follows:

Purchases	60,000	
Accounts payable		60,000

No cost of goods sold entry is recorded when sales are made in the periodic system.

At the end of July, the amount of ending inventory is determined (either by means of a physical count of goods on hand or by estimation) to be $38,000 and cost of goods sold for the month is determined as follows:

Beginning inventory	–0–
Plus: Purchases	60,000
Less: Ending inventory	(38,000)
Cost of goods sold	22,000

The following journal entry records cost of goods sold for the period and adjusts the inventory account to the actual amount on hand (in this case from zero to $38,000):

Cost of goods sold..	22,000	
Inventory...	38,000	
Purchases...		60,000

Inventory is discussed in depth in Chapters 8 and 9.

To record the receipt of rent in advance.

July 16		
Cash	1,000	
Unearned rent revenue (liability)		1,000

Cash increases by $1,000 so the cash account is debited. At this point, Dress Right does not recognize revenue even though cash has been received. Recall that the first criterion required for revenue recognition as stated in the realization principle is that the "earnings process is judged to be complete or virtually complete." Dress Right does not earn the revenue until it has provided the jewelry store with the use of facilities; that is, the revenue is earned as the rental period expires. On receipt of the cash, a liability called *unearned rent revenue* increases and is credited. This liability represents Dress Right's obligation to provide the use of facilities to the jewelry store.

July 20		
Accounts payable	25,000	
Cash		25,000

To record the payment of accounts payable.

This transaction decreases both an asset (cash) and a liability (accounts payable). A debit decreases, the liability and a credit decreases the asset.

July 20		
Salaries expense	5,000	
Cash		5,000

To record the payment of salaries for the first half of the month.

Employees were paid for services rendered during the first half of the month. The cash expenditure did not create an asset since no future benefits result. Cash decreases and is credited; shareholders' equity decreases and is debited. The debit is recorded in the temporary account salaries expense.

July 25		
Cash	1,500	
Accounts receivable		1,500

To record receipt of cash on account.

This transaction is an exchange of one asset, accounts receivable, for another asset, cash.

July 30		
Retained earnings	1,000	
Cash		1,000

To record the payment of a cash dividend.

The payment of a cash dividend is a distribution to owners that reduces both cash and retained earnings.

ADDITIONAL CONSIDERATION

An alternative method of recording a cash dividend is to debit a temporary account called dividends. In that case, the dividends account is later closed (transferred) to retained earnings along with the other temporary accounts at the end of the fiscal year. The journal entry to record the dividend using this approach is

Dividends	1,000	
Cash		1,000

We discuss and illustrate the closing process later in the chapter.

Illustration 2–4 summarizes each of the transactions just discussed as they would appear in a general journal. In addition to the date, account titles, debit and credit columns, the journal also has a column titled Post Ref. (Posting Reference). This usually is a number assigned to the general ledger account that is being debited or credited. For purposes of this illustration, all asset accounts have been assigned numbers in the 100s, all liabilities are 200s, permanent shareholders' equity accounts are 300s, revenues are 400s, and expenses are 500s.

ILLUSTRATION 2–4

The General Journal

	General Journal			Page 1
Date 2011	Account Title and Explanation	Post Ref.	Debit	Credit
July 1	Cash	100	60,000	
	Common stock	300		60,000
	To record the issuance of common stock.			
1	Cash	100	40,000	
	Notes payable	220		40,000
	To record the borrowing of cash and the signing of notes payable.			
1	Prepaid rent	130	24,000	
	Cash	100		24,000
	To record the payment of one year's rent in advance.			
1	Furniture and fixtures	150	12,000	
	Cash	100		12,000
	To record the purchase of furniture and fixtures.			
3	Inventory	140	60,000	
	Accounts payable	210		60,000
	To record the purchase of merchandise inventory.			
6	Supplies	125	2,000	
	Cash	100		2,000
	To record the purchase of supplies.			
4–31	Cash	100	35,000	
	Sales revenue	400		35,000
	To record cash sales for the month.			
4–31	Cost of goods sold	500	20,000	
	Inventory	140		20,000
	To record the cost of cash sales.			
9	Accounts receivable	110	3,500	
	Sales revenue	400		3,500
	To record credit sale.			
9	Cost of goods sold	500	2,000	
	Inventory	140		2,000
	To record the cost of a credit sale.			
16	Cash	100	1,000	
	Unearned rent revenue	230		1,000
	To record the receipt of rent in advance.			
20	Accounts payable	210	25,000	
	Cash	100		25,000
	To record the payment of accounts payable.			
20	Salaries expense	510	5,000	
	Cash	100		5,000
	To record the payment of salaries for the first half of the month.			
25	Cash	100	1,500	
	Accounts receivable	110		1,500
	To record the receipt of cash on account.			
30	Retained earnings	310	1,000	
	Cash	100		1,000
	To record the payment of a cash dividend.			

The ledger accounts also contain a posting reference, usually the page number of the journal in which the journal entry was recorded. This allows for easy cross-referencing between the journal and the ledger. Page 1 is used for Illustration 2–4.

Step 4 in the processing cycle is to transfer (post) the debit/credit information from the journal to the general ledger accounts. Illustration 2–5 contains the ledger accounts (in T-account form) for Dress Right *after* all the general journal transactions have been posted. The reference GJ1 next to each of the posted amounts indicates that the source of the entry is page 1 of the general journal.

Balance Sheet Accounts

ILLUSTRATION

General Ledger Accounts

Cash — 100

July 1 GJ1	60,000	24,000	July 1 GJ1
1 GJ1	40,000	12,000	1 GJ1
4–31GJ1	35,000	2,000	6 GJ1
16 GJ1	1,000	25,000	20 GJ1
25 GJ1	1,500	5,000	20 GJ1
		1,000	30 GJ1
July 31 Bal.	68,500		

Prepaid rent — 130

July 1 GJ1	24,000		
July 31 Bal.	24,000		

Accounts receivable — 110

July 9 GJ1	3,500	1,500	July 25 GJ1
July 31 Bal.	2,000		

Inventory — 140

July 3 GJ1	60,000	20,000	July 4–31
		2,000	9 GJ1
July 31 Bal.	38,000		

Supplies — 125

July 6 GJ1	2,000		
July 31 Bal.	2,000		

Furniture and fixtures — 150

July 1 GJ1	12,000		
July 31 Bal.	12,000		

Accounts payable — 210

July 20 GJ1	25,000	60,000	July 3 GJ1
		35,000	July 31 Bal.

Notes payable — 220

		40,000	July 1 GJ1
		40,000	July 31 Bal.

Unearned rent revenue — 230

		1,000	July 16 GJ1
		1,000	July 31 Bal.

Common stock — 300

		60,000	July 1 GJ1
		60,000	July 31 Bal.

Retained earnings — 310

July 30 GJ1	1,000		
July 31 Bal.	1,000		

Income Statement Accounts

Sales revenue — 400

		35,000	July 4–31 GJ1
		3,500	9 GJ1
		38,500	July 31 Bal.

Cost of goods sold — 500

July 4–31 GJ1	20,000		
July 9 GJ1	2,000		
July 31 Bal.	22,000		

Salaries expense — 510

July 20 GJ1	5,000		
July 31 Bal.	5,000		

5

are an *unadjusted*
balance.

Before financial statements are prepared and before adjusting entries (internal transactions) are recorded at the end of an accounting period, an **unadjusted trial balance** usually is prepared—step 5. A trial balance is simply a list of the general ledger accounts, listed in the order that they appear in the ledger, along with their balances at a particular date. Its purpose is to allow us to check for completeness and to prove that the sum of the accounts with debit balances equals the sum of the accounts with credit balances, that is, the accounting equation is in balance. The fact that the debits and credits are equal, though, does not necessarily ensure that the equal balances are correct. The trial balance could contain offsetting errors. As we will see later in the chapter, this trial balance also facilitates the preparation of adjusting entries.

The unadjusted trial balance at July 31, 2011, for the Dress Right Clothing Corporation appears in Illustration 2–6. Notice that retained earnings has a debit balance of $1,000. This reflects the payment of the cash dividend to shareholders. The increases and decreases in retained earnings from revenue, expense, gain and loss transactions are recorded indirectly in temporary accounts. Before the start of the next year, these increases and decreases are transferred to the retained earnings account.

ILLUSTRATION 2–6	DRESS RIGHT CLOTHING CORPORATION		
Unadjusted Trial Balance	Unadjusted Trial Balance		
	July 31, 2011		
	Account Title	**Debits**	**Credits**
	Cash	68,500	
	Accounts receivable	2,000	
	Supplies	2,000	
	Prepaid rent	24,000	
	Inventory	38,000	
	Furniture and fixtures	12,000	
	Accounts payable		35,000
	Notes payable		40,000
	Unearned rent revenue		1,000
	Common stock		60,000
	Retained earnings	1,000	
	Sales revenue		38,500
At any time, the total	Cost of goods sold	22,000	
of all debit balances	Salaries expense	5,000	
should equal the total	Totals	174,500	174,500
of all credit balances.			

CONCEPT REVIEW EXERCISE

JOURNAL ENTRIES FOR EXTERNAL TRANSACTIONS

The Wyndham Wholesale Company began operations on August 1, 2011. The following transactions occur during the month of August.

a. Owners invest $50,000 cash in the corporation in exchange for 5,000 shares of common stock.
b. Equipment is purchased for $20,000 cash.
c. On the first day of August, $6,000 rent on a building is paid for the months of August and September.
d. Merchandise inventory costing $38,000 is purchased on account. The company uses the perpetual inventory system.
e. $30,000 is borrowed from a local bank, and a note payable is signed.
f. Credit sales for the month are $40,000. The cost of merchandise sold is $22,000.
g. $15,000 is collected on account from customers.
h. $20,000 is paid on account to suppliers of merchandise.
i. Salaries of $7,000 are paid to employees for August.

j. A bill for $2,000 is received from the local utility company for the month of August.
k. $20,000 cash is loaned to another company, evidenced by a note receivable.
l. The corporation pays its shareholders a cash dividend of $1,000.

Required:
1. Prepare a journal entry for each transaction.
2. Prepare an unadjusted trial balance as of August 31, 2011.

1. Prepare a journal entry for each transaction.   **SOLUTION**

  a. The issuance of common stock for cash increases both cash and shareholders' equity
     (common stock).

Cash	50,000	
Common Stock		50,000

  b. The purchase of equipment increases equipment and decreases cash.

Equipment	20,000	
Cash		20,000

  c. The payment of rent in advance increases prepaid rent and decreases cash.

Prepaid rent	6,000	
Cash		6,000

  d. The purchase of merchandise on account increases both inventory and accounts payable.

Inventory	38,000	
Accounts payable		38,000

  e. Borrowing cash and signing a note increases both cash and note payable.

Cash	30,000	
Note payable		30,000

  f. The sale of merchandise on account increases both accounts receivable and sales
     revenue. Also, cost of goods sold increases and inventory decreases.

Accounts receivable	40,000	
Sales revenue		40,000
Cost of goods sold	22,000	
Inventory		22,000

  g. The collection of cash on account increases cash and decreases accounts receivable.

Cash	15,000	
Accounts receivable		15,000

  h. The payment of suppliers on account decreases both accounts payable and cash.

Accounts payable	20,000	
Cash		20,000

i. The payment of salaries for the period increases salaries expense (decreases retained earnings) and decreases cash.

Salaries expense	7,000	
Cash		7,000

j. The receipt of a bill for services rendered increases both an expense (utilities expense) and accounts payable. The expense decreases retained earnings.

Utilities expense	2,000	
Accounts payable		2,000

k. The lending of cash to another entity and the signing of a note increases note receivable and decreases cash.

Note receivable	20,000	
Cash		20,000

l. Cash dividends paid to shareholders reduce both retained earnings and cash.

Retained earnings[3]	1,000	
Cash		1,000

2. Prepare an unadjusted trial balance as of August 31, 2011.

Account Title	Debits	Credits
Cash	21,000	
Accounts receivable	25,000	
Prepaid rent	6,000	
Inventory	16,000	
Note receivable	20,000	
Equipment	20,000	
Accounts payable		20,000
Note payable		30,000
Common stock		50,000
Retained earnings	1,000	
Sales revenue		40,000
Cost of goods sold	22,000	
Salaries expense	7,000	
Utilities expense	2,000	
Totals	140,000	140,000

● LO4

STEP 6

Record *adjusting entries* and post to the ledger accounts.

Adjusting Entries

Step 6 in the processing cycle is to record in the general journal and post to the ledger accounts the effect of *internal events* on the accounting equation. These transactions do not involve an exchange transaction with another entity and, therefore, are not initiated by a source document. They are recorded *at the end of any period when financial statements are prepared.* These transactions are commonly referred to as **adjusting entries.**

Even when all transactions and events are analyzed, corrected, journalized, and posted to appropriate ledger accounts, some account balances will require updating. Adjusting entries

---

[3]An alternative is to debit a temporary account—dividends—that is closed to retained earnings at the end of the fiscal year along with the other temporary accounts.

are required to implement the *accrual accounting model.* More specifically, these entries are required to satisfy the *realization principle* and the *matching principle.* Adjusting entries help ensure that all revenues earned in a period are recognized in that period, regardless of when the cash is received. Also, they enable a company to recognize all expenses incurred during a period, regardless of when cash payment is made. As a result, a period's income statement provides a more complete measure of a company's operating performance and a better measure for predicting future operating cash flows. The balance sheet also provides a more complete assessment of assets and liabilities as sources of future cash receipts and disbursements. You might think of adjusting entries as a method of bringing the company's financial information up to date before preparing the financial statements.

Adjusting entries are necessary for three situations:

1. **Prepayments,** sometimes referred to as *deferrals.*
2. **Accruals.**
3. **Estimates.**

Prepayments

Prepayments occur when the cash flow *precedes* either expense or revenue recognition. For example, a company may buy supplies in one period but use them in a later period. The cash outflow creates an asset (supplies) which then must be expensed in a future period as the asset is used up. Similarly, a company may receive cash from a customer in one period but provide the customer with a good or service in a future period. For instance, magazine publishers usually receive cash in advance for magazine subscriptions. The cash inflow creates a liability (unearned revenue) that is recognized as revenue in a future period when it is earned.

PREPAID EXPENSES.   **Prepaid expenses** are the costs of assets acquired in one period and expensed in a future period. Whenever cash is paid, and it is not to (1) satisfy a liability or (2) pay a dividend or return capital to owners, it must be determined whether or not the payment creates future benefits or whether the payment benefits only the current period. The purchase of machinery, equipment, or supplies or the payment of rent in advance are examples of payments that create future benefits and should be recorded as assets. The benefits provided by these assets expire in future periods and their cost is expensed in future periods as related revenues are recognized.

To illustrate this concept, assume that a company paid a radio station $2,000 in July for advertising. If that $2,000 were for advertising provided by the radio station during the month of July, the entire $2,000 would be expensed in the same period as the cash disbursement. If, however, the $2,000 was a payment for advertising to be provided in a future period, say the month of August, then the cash disbursement creates an asset called *prepaid advertising.* An adjusting entry is required at the end of August to increase advertising expense (decrease shareholders' equity) and to decrease the asset prepaid advertising by $2,000. Assuming that the cash disbursement records a debit to an asset, as in this example, the adjusting entry for a prepaid expense is, therefore, a *debit to an expense* and a *credit to an asset.*

The unadjusted trial balance can provide a starting point for determining which adjusting entries are required for a period, particularly for prepayments. Review the July 31, 2011, unadjusted trial balance for the Dress Right Clothing Corporation in Illustration 2–6 on page 64 and try to anticipate the required adjusting entries for prepaid expenses.

The first asset that requires adjustment is supplies, $2,000 of which were purchased during July. This transaction created an asset as the supplies will be used in future periods. The company could either track the supplies used or simply count the supplies at the end of the period and determine the dollar amount of supplies remaining. Assume that Dress Right determines that at the end of July, $1,200 of supplies remain. The following adjusting journal entry is required.

FINANCIAL
Reporting Case

Q1, p. 51

FINANCIAL
Reporting Case

Q2, p. 51

Prepayments are transactions in which the cash flow *precedes* expense or revenue recognition.

Prepaid expenses represent assets recorded when a cash disbursement creates benefits beyond the current reporting period.

The adjusting entry required for a prepaid expense is a *debit to an expense* and a *credit to an asset.*

● **LO5**

July 31		
Supplies expense	800	
Supplies		800

To record the cost of supplies used during the month of July.

Supplies

Beg. bal.	0		
	2,000	800	
End bal.	1,200		

Supplies Expense

Beg. bal.	0	
	800	
End bal.	800	

After this entry is recorded and posted to the ledger accounts, the supplies (asset) account is reduced to a $1,200 debit balance, and the supplies expense account will have an $800 debit balance.

The next prepaid expense requiring adjustment is rent. Recall that at the beginning of July, the company paid $24,000 to its landlord representing one year's rent in advance. As it is reasonable to assume that the rent services provided each period are equal, the monthly rent is $2,000. At the end of July 2011, one month's prepaid rent has expired and must be recognized as expense.

To record the cost of expired rent for the month of July.

July 31

Rent expense ($24,000 ÷ 12)	2,000	
Prepaid rent		2,000

Prepaid Rent

Beg. bal.	0		
	24,000	2,000	
End bal.	22,000		

Rent Expense

Beg. bal.	0	
	2,000	
End bal.	2,000	

After this entry is recorded and posted to the ledger accounts, the prepaid rent account will have a debit balance of $22,000, representing 11 remaining months at $2,000 per month, and the rent expense account will have a $2,000 debit balance.

The final prepayment involves the asset represented by furniture and fixtures that was purchased for $12,000. This asset has a long life but nevertheless will expire over time. For the previous two adjusting entries, it was fairly straightforward to determine the amount of the asset that expired during the period.

However, it is difficult, if not impossible, to determine how much of the benefits from using the furniture and fixtures expired during any particular period. Recall from Chapter 1 that one approach to implementing the matching principle is to "recognize an expense by a systematic and rational allocation to specific time periods."

Assume that the furniture and fixtures have a useful life of five years (60 months) and will be worthless at the end of that period, and that we choose to allocate the cost equally over the period of use. The amount of monthly expense, called *depreciation expense,* is $200 ($12,000 ÷ 60 months = $200), and the following adjusting entry is recorded.

To record depreciation of furniture and fixtures for the month of July.

July 31

Depreciation expense	200	
Accumulated depreciation—furniture and fixtures		200

The entry reduces an asset, furniture and fixtures, by $200. However, the asset account is not reduced directly. Instead, the credit is to an account called *accumulated depreciation.* This is a contra account to furniture and fixtures. The normal balance in a contra asset account will be a credit, that is, "contra," or opposite, to the normal debit balance in an asset account. The purpose of the contra account is to keep the original cost of the asset intact while reducing it indirectly. In the balance sheet, furniture and fixtures is reported net of accumulated depreciation. This topic is covered in depth in Chapter 11.

After this entry is recorded and posted to the ledger accounts, the accumulated depreciation account will have a credit balance of $200 and the depreciation expense account will have a $200 debit balance. If a required adjusting entry for a prepaid expense is not recorded, net income, assets, and shareholders' equity (retained earnings) will be overstated.

Unearned revenues represent liabilities recorded when cash is received from customers in advance of providing a good or service.

UNEARNED REVENUES.   Unearned revenues are created when a company receives cash from a customer in one period for goods or services that are to be provided in a future period. The cash receipt, an external transaction, is recorded as a debit to cash and a credit to a liability. This liability reflects the company's obligation to provide goods or services in the future.

To illustrate an unearned revenue transaction, assume that during the month of June a magazine publisher received $24 in cash for a 24-month subscription to a monthly magazine. The subscription begins in July. On receipt of the cash, the publisher records a liability, unearned subscription revenue, of $24. Subsequently, revenue of $1 is earned as each monthly magazine is published and mailed to the customer. An adjusting entry is required each month to increase shareholders' equity (revenue) to recognize the $1 in revenue earned and to decrease the liability. Assuming that the cash receipt entry included a credit to a liability, the adjusting entry for unearned revenues, therefore, is a *debit to a liability,* in this case unearned subscription revenue, and a *credit to revenue.*

> The adjusting entry required when unearned revenues are earned is a *debit to a liability* and a *credit to revenue.*

Once again, the unadjusted trial balance provides information concerning unearned revenues. For Dress Right Clothing Corporation, the only unearned revenue in the trial balance is unearned rent revenue. Recall that the company subleased a portion of its building to a jewelry store for $500 per month. On July 16, the jewelry store paid Dress Right $1,000 in advance for the first two months' rent. The transaction was recorded as a debit to cash and a credit to unearned rent revenue.

At the end of July, how much of the $1,000 has been earned? Approximately one-half of one month's rent has been earned, or $250, requiring the following adjusting journal entry.

July 31		
Unearned rent revenue	250	
Rent revenue		250

> To record previously unearned rent revenue earned during July.

After this entry is recorded and posted to the ledger accounts, the unearned rent revenue account is reduced to a credit balance of $750 for the remaining one and one-half months' rent, and the rent revenue account will have a $250 credit balance. If this entry is not recorded, net income and shareholders' equity (retained earnings) will be understated, and liabilities will be overstated.

Unearned Rent Revenue

	0	Beg. bal.
250	1,000	
	750	End bal.

Rent Revenue

	0	Beg. bal.
	250	
	250	End bal.

ALTERNATIVE APPROACH TO RECORD PREPAYMENTS.

The same end result can be achieved for prepayments by recording the external transaction directly into an expense or revenue account. In fact, many companies prefer this approach. For simplicity, bookkeeping instructions may require all cash payments for expenses to be debited to the appropriate expense account and all cash receipts for revenues to be credited to the appropriate revenue account. The adjusting entry then records the *unexpired* prepaid expense (asset) or *unearned* revenue (liability) as of the end of the period.

For example, on July 1, 2011, Dress Right paid $24,000 in cash for one year's rent on its building. The entry included a debit to prepaid rent. The company could have debited rent expense instead.

Alternative Approach

July 1		
Rent expense	24,000	
Cash		24,000

Rent Expense

Beg. bal.	0	
	24,000	22,000
End bal.	2,000	

The adjusting entry then records the amount of prepaid rent as of the end of July, $22,000, and reduces rent expense to $2,000, the cost of rent for the month of July.

Alternative Approach

July 31		
Prepaid rent	22,000	
Rent expense		22,000

Prepaid Rent

Beg. bal.	0	
	22,000	
End bal.	22,000	

The net effect of handling the transactions in this manner is the same as the previous treatment. Either way, the prepaid rent account will have a debit balance at the end of July of $22,000, and the rent expense account will have a debit balance of $2,000. What's important is that an adjusting entry is recorded to ensure the appropriate amounts are reflected in both the expense and asset *before financial statements are prepared.*

Similarly, the July 16 cash receipt from the jewelry store representing an advance for two months' rent could have been recorded by Dress Right as a credit to rent revenue instead of unearned rent revenue (a liability).

Rent Revenue

	0 Beg. bal.
750	1,000
	250 End bal.

Alternative Approach

July 16

Cash	1,000	
Rent revenue		1,000

If Dress Right records the entire $1,000 as rent revenue in this way, it would then use the adjusting entry to record the amount of unearned revenue as of the end of July, $750, and reduce rent revenue to $250, the amount of revenue earned during the month of July.

Unearned Rent Revenue

	0 Beg. bal.
	750
	750 End bal.

Alternative Approach

July 31

Rent revenue	750	
Unearned rent revenue		750

Accruals

Accruals involve transactions where the cash outflow or inflow takes place in a period subsequent to expense or revenue recognition.

Accruals occur when the cash flow comes *after* either expense or revenue recognition. For example, a company often uses the services of another entity in one period and pays for them in a subsequent period. An expense must be recognized in the period incurred and an accrued liability recorded. Also, goods and services often are provided to customers on credit. In such instances, a revenue is recognized in the period earned and an asset, a receivable, is recorded.

Many accruals involve external transactions that automatically are recorded from a source document. For example, a sales invoice for a credit sale provides all the information necessary to record the debit to accounts receivable and the credit to sales revenue. However, there are some accruals that involve internal transactions and thus require adjusting entries. Because accruals involve recognition of expense or revenue before cash flow, the unadjusted trial balance will not be as helpful in identifying required adjusting entries as with prepayments.

Accrued liabilities represent liabilities recorded when an expense has been incurred prior to cash payment.

The adjusting entry required to record an accrued liability is a debit to an expense and a credit to a liability.

To record accrued salaries at the end of July.

ACCRUED LIABILITIES. For accrued liabilities, we are concerned with expenses incurred but not yet paid. Dress Right Clothing Corporation requires two adjusting entries for accrued liabilities at July 31, 2011.

The first entry is for employee salaries for the second half of July. Recall that on July 20 the company paid employees $5,000 for salaries for the first half of the month. Salaries for the second half of July will probably be paid in early August. Nevertheless, the company incurred an expense in July for services provided to it by its employees. Also, there exists an obligation at the end of July to pay the salaries earned by employees. An adjusting entry is required to increase salaries expense (decrease shareholders' equity) and to increase liabilities for the salaries payable. The adjusting entry for an accrued liability always includes a *debit to an expense,* and a *credit to a liability.* Assuming that salaries for the second half of July are $5,500, the following adjusting entry is recorded.

July 31

Salaries expense...	5,500	
Salaries payable..		5,500

Salaries Payable

	0 Beg. bal.
	5,500
	5,500 End bal.

After this entry is recorded and posted to the general ledger, the salaries expense account will have a debit balance of $10,500 ($5,000 + 5,500), and the salaries payable account will have a credit balance of $5,500.

The unadjusted trial balance does provide information about the second required accrued liability entry. In the trial balance we can see a balance in the notes payable account of $40,000. The company borrowed this amount on July 1, 2011, evidenced by two notes, each requiring the payment of 10% interest. Whenever the trial balance reveals interest-bearing debt, and interest is not paid on the last day of the period, an adjusting entry is required for the amount of interest that has built up (accrued) since the last payment date or the last date interest was accrued. In this case, we calculate interest as follows:

Salaries Expense		
Beg. bal.	0	
July 20	5,000	
	5,500	
End bal.	10,500	

$$\text{Principal} \times \text{Interest rate} \times \text{Time} = \text{Interest}$$
$$\$40{,}000 \times \quad 10\% \quad \times \quad \tfrac{1}{12} \ = \$333 \ (\text{rounded})$$

Interest rates always are stated as the annual rate. Therefore, the above calculation uses this annual rate multiplied by the principal amount multiplied by the amount of time outstanding, in this case one month or one-twelfth of a year.

To accrue interest expense for July on notes payable.

July 31
Interest expense 333
　　Interest payable 333

After this entry is recorded and posted to the ledger accounts, the interest expense account will have a debit balance of $333, and the interest payable account will have a credit balance of $333. Failure to record a required adjusting entry for an accrued liability will cause net income and shareholders' equity (retained earnings) to be overstated, and liabilities to be understated.[4]

ACCRUED RECEIVABLES.   Accrued receivables involve the recognition of revenue earned *before* cash is received. An example of an internal accrued revenue event is the recognition of interest earned on a loan to another entity. For example, assume that Dress Right loaned another corporation $30,000 at the beginning of August, evidenced by a note receivable. Terms of the note call for the payment of principal, $30,000, and interest at 8% in three months. An external transaction records the cash disbursement—a debit to note receivable and a credit to cash of $30,000.

Accrued receivables involve situations when the revenue is earned in a period prior to the cash receipt.

What adjusting entry would be required at the end of August? Dress Right needs to record the interest revenue earned but not yet received and the corresponding receivable. Interest receivable increases and interest revenue (shareholders' equity) also increases. The adjusting entry for accrued receivables always includes a *debit to an asset,* a receivable, and a *credit to revenue.* In this case, at the end of August Dress Right recognizes $200 in interest revenue ($30,000 \times 8\% \times \tfrac{1}{12}$) and makes the following adjusting entry. If this entry is not recorded, net income, assets, and shareholders' equity (retained earnings) will be understated.

The adjusting entry required to record an accrued revenue is a debit to an asset, a receivable, and a credit to revenue.

August 31
Interest receivable 200
　　Interest revenue 200

To accrue interest revenue earned in August on note receivable.

There are no accrued revenue adjusting entries required for Dress Right at the end of July.

The required adjusting entries for prepayments and accruals are recapped with the aid of T-accounts in Graphic 2–4. In each case an expense or revenue is recognized in a period that differs from the period in which cash was paid or received. These adjusting entries are necessary to properly measure operating performance and financial position on an accrual basis.

---

[4]Dress Right Clothing is a corporation. Corporations are income-tax-paying entities. Income taxes—federal, state, and local—are assessed on an annual basis and payments are made throughout the year. An additional adjusting entry would be required for Dress Right to accrue the amount of estimated income taxes payable that are applicable to the month of July. Accounting for income taxes is introduced in Chapter 4 and covered in depth in Chapter 16.

GRAPHIC 2–4

Adjusting Entries

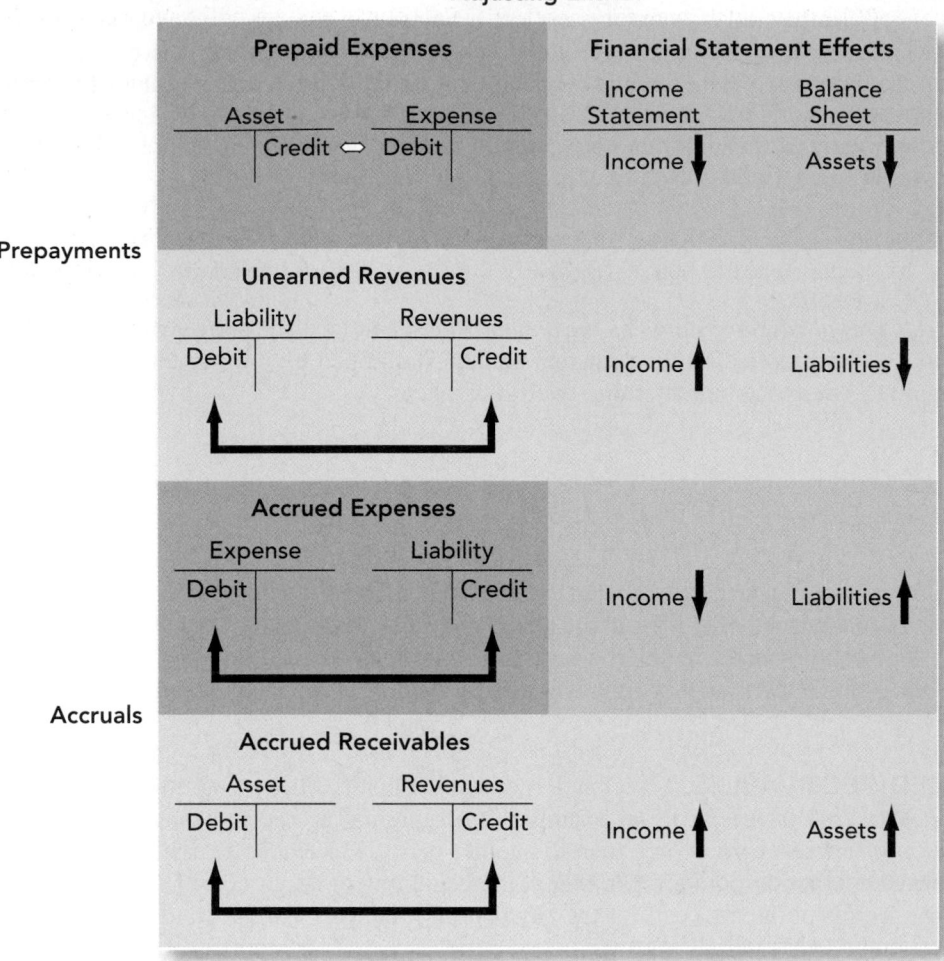

Estimates

Accountants often must make *estimates* in order to comply with the accrual accounting model.

A third classification of adjusting entries is **estimates.** Accountants often must make estimates of future events to comply with the accrual accounting model. For example, the calculation of depreciation expense requires an estimate of expected useful life of the asset being depreciated as well as its expected residual value. We discussed the adjusting entries for depreciation expense in the context of its being a prepayment, but it also could be thought of as an estimate.

One situation involving an estimate that does not fit neatly into either the prepayment or accrual classification is **bad debt expense.** This expense is neither a prepayment nor an accrual because it does not involve the payment of cash either before or after an expense is incurred. In Chapter 1 we looked briefly at the allowance method of accounting for bad debts. For this method we need an estimate of the amount of accounts receivable that ultimately will prove to be uncollectible. This estimate is needed to properly match the bad debt expense with the revenue it helps generate, as well as to reflect the collectible portion of the receivable in the balance sheet. Here's an example.

The July 31, 2011, unadjusted trial balance for Dress Right shows a balance in accounts receivable of $2,000. Assume that the company's management felt that, of this amount, only $1,500 ultimately would be collected. An adjusting entry is required to decrease accounts receivable and increase bad debt expense (decrease shareholders' equity) by $500. The adjusting entry is:

To record bad debt expense for July.

July 31		
Bad debt expense	500	
Allowance for uncollectible accounts		500

Notice that we don't reduce the accounts receivable account directly. Instead we credit a contra account, called *allowance for uncollectible accounts,* to reduce it indirectly. After this entry is recorded and posted to the ledger accounts, bad debt expense will have a debit balance of $500 and the allowance for uncollectible accounts account will have a credit balance of $500.[5]

The contra account is used to keep intact in the accounts receivable account the total amount of receivables that are still outstanding. The allowance account will always have a credit balance equal to estimated bad debts on existing accounts receivable. Only when a specific customer's account is actually written off as uncollectible would accounts receivable be reduced. At this point, the $500 is just an estimate. In the balance sheet, accounts receivable is shown net of the allowance account, in this case $1,500. The focus of this adjustment approach is to value accounts receivable, net of the allowance, at an amount that reflects the company's best estimate of what it thinks will actually be collected from customers.

We explore accounts receivable and bad debts in more depth in Chapter 7.

Illustration 2–7 recaps the July 31, 2011, adjusting entries for Dress Right Clothing Corporation as they would appear in a general journal. The journal entries are numbered (1) to (7) corresponding to the number used in the worksheet illustrated in Appendix 2A.

		DRESS RIGHT CLOTHING CORPORATION				
		General Journal			**Page 2**	
Date 2011		**Account Title and Explanation**	**Post. Ref.**	**Debit**	**Credit**	
July (1)	31	Supplies expense	520	800		
		Supplies	125		800	
		To record the cost of supplies used during the month of July.				
(2)	31	Rent expense	530	2,000		
		Prepaid rent	130		2,000	
		To record the cost of expired rent for the month of July.				
(3)	31	Depreciation expense	540	200		
		Accumulated depreciation—furniture and fixtures	155		200	
		To record depreciation of furniture and fixtures for the month of July.				
(4)	31	Unearned rent revenue	230	250		
		Rent revenue	410		250	
		To record previously unearned rent revenue earned during July.				
(5)	31	Salaries expense	510	5,500		
		Salaries payable	230		5,500	
		To record accrued salaries at the end of July.				
(6)	31	Interest expense	550	333		
		Interest payable	240		333	
		To accrue interest expense for July on notes payable.				
(7)	31	Bad debt expense	560	500		
		Allowance for uncollectible accounts	115		500	
		To record bad debt expense for July.				

ILLUSTRATION 2–7

The General Journal—Adjusting Entries

After the adjusting entries are posted to the general ledger accounts, the next step—step 7—in the processing cycle is to prepare an **adjusted trial balance.** The term adjusted refers to the fact that adjusting entries have now been posted to the accounts. Recall that the column titled Post Ref. (Posting Reference) is the number assigned to the general ledger account that is being debited or credited. Illustration 2–8 shows the July 31, 2011, adjusted trial balance for Dress Right Clothing Corporation.

---

[5]If the allowance for uncollectible accounts had a credit balance before the adjusting entry, say $150, the adjusting entry would have required only a $350 debit to bad debt expense and credit to the allowance account.

ILLUSTRATION 2–8

Adjusted Trial Balance

STEP 7

Prepare an *adjusted trial balance.*

DRESS RIGHT CLOTHING CORPORATION
Adjusted Trial Balance
July 31, 2011

Account Title	Debits	Credits
Cash	68,500	
Accounts receivable	2,000	
Allowance for uncollectible accounts		500
Supplies	1,200	
Prepaid rent	22,000	
Inventory	38,000	
Furniture and fixtures	12,000	
Accumulated depreciation—furniture and fixtures		200
Accounts payable		35,000
Notes payable		40,000
Unearned rent revenue		750
Salaries payable		5,500
Interest payable		333
Common stock		60,000
Retained earnings	1,000	
Sales revenue		38,500
Rent revenue		250
Cost of goods sold	22,000	
Salaries expense	10,500	
Supplies expense	800	
Rent expense	2,000	
Depreciation expense	200	
Interest expense	333	
Bad debt expense	500	
Totals	181,033	181,033

CONCEPT REVIEW EXERCISE

ADJUSTING ENTRIES

The Wyndham Wholesale Company needs to prepare financial statements at the end of August 2011 for presentation to its bank. An unadjusted trial balance as of August 31, 2011, was presented in a previous concept review exercise on page 66.

The following information also is available:

a. The company anticipates that of the $25,000 in accounts receivable from customers, $2,500 will *not* be collected.
b. The note payable requires the entire $30,000 in principal plus interest at 10% to be paid on July 31, 2012. The date of the loan is August 1, 2011.
c. Depreciation on the equipment for the month of August is $500.
d. The note receivable is dated August 16, 2011. The note requires the entire $20,000 in principal plus interest at 12% to be repaid in four months (the loan was outstanding for one-half month during August).
e. The prepaid rent of $6,000 represents rent for the months of August and September.

Required:
1. Prepare any necessary adjusting entries at August 31, 2011.
2. Prepare an adjusted trial balance as of August 31, 2011.
3. What is the total net effect on income (overstated or understated) if the adjusting entries are not made?

SOLUTION

1. Prepare any necessary adjusting entries at August 31, 2011.

a. An adjusting entry is required to adjust allowance for uncollectible accounts to $2,500. Because there is no balance in the allowance account before adjustment, the adjusting entry must record a bad debt expense of $2,500.

| Bad debt expense .... | 2,500 | |
| Allowance for uncollectible accounts .... | | 2,500 |

b. An adjusting entry is required to accrue the interest expense on the note payable for the month of August. Accrued interest is calculated as follows:

$$\$30,000 \times 10\% \times \tfrac{1}{12} = \$250$$

| Interest expense .... | 250 | |
| Interest payable .... | | 250 |

c. Depreciation expense on the equipment must be recorded.

| Depreciation expense .... | 500 | |
| Accumulated depreciation—equipment .... | | 500 |

d. An adjusting entry is required for the one-half month of accrued interest revenue earned on the note receivable. Accrued interest is calculated as follows:

$$\$20,000 \times 12\% \times \tfrac{1}{12} \times \tfrac{1}{2} = \$100$$

| Interest receivable .... | 100 | |
| Interest revenue .... | | 100 |

e. An adjusting entry is required to recognize the amount of prepaid rent that expired during August.

| Rent expense .... | 3,000 | |
| Prepaid rent .... | | 3,000 |

2. Prepare an adjusted trial balance as of August 31, 2011.

Account Title	Debits	Credits
Cash	21,000	
Accounts receivable	25,000	
Allowance for uncollectible accounts		2,500
Prepaid rent	3,000	
Inventory	16,000	
Interest receivable	100	
Note receivable	20,000	
Equipment	20,000	
Accumulated depreciation—equipment		500
Accounts payable		20,000
Interest payable		250
Note payable		30,000
Common stock		50,000
Retained earnings	1,000	
Sales revenue		40,000
Interest revenue		100
Cost of goods sold	22,000	
Salaries expense	7,000	
Utilities expense	2,000	
Bad debt expense	2,500	
Interest expense	250	
Depreciation expense	500	
Rent expense	3,000	
Totals	143,350	143,350

3. What is the effect on income (overstated or understated), if the adjusting entries are not made?

Adjusting Entry	Income overstated (understated)
Bad debt expense	$2,500
Interest expense	250
Depreciation expense	500
Interest revenue	(100)
Rent expense	3,000
Net effect, income overstated by	$6,150

We now turn our attention to the preparation of financial statements.

Preparing the Financial Statements

● LO6

STEP 8

Preparation of *financial statements.*

The purpose of each of the steps in the processing cycle to this point is to provide information for step 8—preparation of the **financial statements.** The adjusted trial balance contains the necessary information. After all, the financial statements are the primary means of communicating financial information to external parties.

The Income Statement

The *income statement* is a *change* statement that summarizes the profit-generating transactions that caused shareholders' equity (retained earnings) to change during the period.

The purpose of the **income statement** is to summarize the profit-generating activities of a company that occurred during a particular period of time. It is a *change* statement in that it reports the changes in shareholders' equity (retained earnings) that occurred during the period as a result of revenues, expenses, gains, and losses. Illustration 2–9 shows the income statement for Dress Right Clothing Corporation for the month of July 2011.

The income statement indicates a profit for the month of July of $2,417. During the month, the company was able to increase its net assets (equity) from activities related to selling its product. Dress Right is a corporation and subject to the payment of income tax on its profits. We ignore this required accrual here and address income taxes in a later chapter.

The components of the income statement usually are classified, that is, grouped according to common characteristics. A common classification scheme is to separate operating items from nonoperating items, as we do in Dress Right's income statement. Operating items include revenues and expenses directly related to the principal revenue-generating activities

ILLUSTRATION 2–9 Income Statement	DRESS RIGHT CLOTHING CORPORATION Income Statement For the Month of July 2011		
	Sales revenue		$38,500
	Cost of goods sold		22,000
	Gross profit		16,500
	Operating expenses:		
	Salaries	$10,500	
	Supplies	800	
	Rent	2,000	
	Depreciation	200	
	Bad debt	500	
	Total operating expenses		14,000
	Operating income		2,500
	Other income (expense):		
	Rent revenue	250	
	Interest expense	(333)	(83)
	Net income		$ 2,417

of the company. For example, operating items for a manufacturing company include sales revenues from the sale of products and all expenses related to this activity. Companies that sell products like Dress Right often report a subtotal within operating income, sales less cost of goods sold, called *gross profit.* Nonoperating items include gains and losses and revenues and expenses from peripheral activities. For Dress Right Clothing, rent revenue and interest expense are nonoperating items because they do not relate to the principal revenue-generating activity of the company, selling clothes. In Chapter 4 we discuss the format and content of the income statement in more depth.

The Balance Sheet

The purpose of the **balance sheet** is to present the financial position of the company on a particular date. Unlike the income statement, which is a change statement reporting events that occurred *during a period of time,* the balance sheet is a statement that presents an organized list of assets, liabilities, and shareholders' equity *at a point in time.* To provide a quick overview, Illustration 2–10 shows the balance sheet for Dress Right at July 31, 2011.

The *balance sheet* is a position statement that presents an organized list of assets, liabilities and equity at a particular point in time.

ILLUSTRATION 2–10
Balance Sheet

DRESS RIGHT CLOTHING CORPORATION
Balance Sheet
At July 31, 2011
Assets

Current assets:
Cash		$ 68,500
Accounts receivable	$ 2,000	
Less: Allowance for uncollectible accounts	500	1,500
Supplies		1,200
Inventory		38,000
Prepaid rent		22,000
Total current assets		131,200
Property and equipment:		
Furniture and fixtures	12,000	
Less: Accumulated depreciation	200	11,800
Total assets		$143,000

Liabilities and Shareholders' Equity

Current liabilities:		
Accounts payable		$ 35,000
Salaries payable		5,500
Unearned rent revenue		750
Interest payable		333
Note payable		10,000
Total current liabilities		51,583
Long-term liabilities:		
Note payable		30,000
Shareholders' equity:		
Common stock, 6,000 shares issued and outstanding	$60,000	
Retained earnings	1,417*	
Total shareholders' equity		61,417
Total liabilities and shareholders' equity		$143,000

*Beginning retained earnings + Net income – Dividends
   0   + $2,417 – 1,000   = $1,417

As we do in the income statement, we group the balance sheet elements into meaningful categories. For example, most balance sheets include the classifications of **current assets** and **current liabilities.** Current assets are those assets that are cash, will be converted into cash, or will be used up within one year or the operating cycle, whichever is longer. Current liabilities are those liabilities that will be satisfied within one year or the operating cycle, whichever is longer. For a manufacturing company, the operating cycle refers to the period

Balance sheet items usually are classified (grouped) according to common characteristics.

of time necessary to convert cash to raw materials, raw materials to a finished product, the finished product to receivables, and then finally receivables back to cash. For most companies, this period is less than a year.

Examples of assets not classified as current include property and equipment and long-term receivables and investments. The only noncurrent asset that Dress Right has at July 31, 2011, is furniture and fixtures, which is classified under the property and equipment category.

All liabilities not classified as current are listed as long term. Dress Right's liabilities at July 31, 2011, include the $30,000 note payable due to be paid in 23 months. This liability is classified as long term.

Shareholders' equity lists the *paid-in capital* portion of equity—common stock—and *retained earnings*. Notice that the income statement we looked at in Illustration 2–9 ties in to the balance sheet through retained earnings. Specifically, the revenue, expense, gain, and loss transactions that make up net income in the income statement ($2,417) become the major components of retained earnings. Later in the chapter we discuss the closing process we use to transfer, or close, these *temporary* income statement accounts to the *permanent* retained earnings account.

During the month, retained earnings, which increased by the amount of net income, also decreased by the amount of the cash dividend paid to shareholders, $1,000. The net effect of these two changes is an increase in retained earnings from zero at the beginning of the period to $1,417 ($2,417 − 1,000) at the end of the period and also is reported in the statement of shareholders' equity in Illustration 2–12 on page 79.

The Statement of Cash Flows

The purpose of the *statement of cash flows* is to summarize the transactions that caused cash to change during the period.

Similar to the income statement, the statement of cash flows also is a change statement, disclosing the events that caused cash to change during the period. The statement classifies all transactions affecting cash into one of three categories: (1) operating activities, (2) investing activities, and (3) financing activities. Operating activities are inflows and outflows of cash related to transactions entering into the determination of net income. Investing activities involve the acquisition and sale of (1) long-term assets used in the business and (2) nonoperating investment assets. Financing activities involve cash inflows and outflows from transactions with creditors and owners.

The statement of cash flows for Dress Right for the month of July 2011 is shown in Illustration 2–11. As this is the first period of operations for Dress Right, the cash balance at the

ILLUSTRATION 2–11	
Statement of Cash Flows	**DRESS RIGHT CLOTHING CORPORATION** **Statement of Cash Flows** **For the Month of July 2011**

DRESS RIGHT CLOTHING CORPORATION
Statement of Cash Flows
For the Month of July 2011

Cash Flows from Operating Activities		
Cash inflows:		
From customers	$36,500	
From rent	1,000	
Cash outflows:		
For rent	(24,000)	
For supplies	(2,000)	
To suppliers of merchandise	(25,000)	
To employees	(5,000)	
Net cash flows from operating activities		$(18,500)
Cash Flows from Investing Activities		
Purchase of furniture and fixtures		(12,000)
Cash Flows from Financing Activities		
Issue of common stock	$60,000	
Increase in notes payable	40,000	
Payment of cash dividend	(1,000)	
Net cash flows from financing activities		99,000
Net increase in cash		$ 68,500

beginning of the period is zero. The net increase in cash of $68,500, therefore, equals the ending balance of cash disclosed in the balance sheet.

There are two generally accepted formats that can be used to report operating activities, the direct method and the indirect method. In Illustration 2–11 we use the direct method. These two methods are discussed and illustrated in subsequent chapters.

The Statement of Shareholders' Equity

The final statement, the statement of shareholders' equity, also is a change statement. It discloses the sources of the changes in the various permanent shareholders' equity accounts that occurred during the period. Illustration 2–12 shows the statement of shareholders' equity for Dress Right for the month of July 2011.[6]

The individual profit-generating transactions causing retained earnings to change are summarized in the income statement. Therefore, the statement of shareholders' equity only shows the net effect of these transactions on retained earnings, in this case an increase of $2,417. In addition, the company paid its shareholders a cash dividend that reduced retained earnings.

The *statement of shareholders' equity* discloses the sources of changes in the permanent shareholders' equity accounts.

DRESS RIGHT CLOTHING CORPORATION Statement of Shareholders' Equity For the Month of July 2011			
	Common Stock	Retained Earnings	Total Shareholders' Equity
Balance at July 1, 2011	$ –0–	$ –0–	$ –0–
Issue of common stock	60,000		60,000
Net income for July 2011		2,417	2,417
Less: Dividends		(1,000)	(1,000)
Balance at July 31, 2011	$60,000	$1,417	$61,417

ILLUSTRATION 2–12

Statement of Shareholders' Equity

The Closing Process

At the end of any interim reporting period, the accounting processing cycle is now complete. An interim reporting period is any period when financial statements are produced other than at the end of the fiscal year. However, at the end of the fiscal year, two final steps are necessary, closing the temporary accounts—step 9—and preparing a post-closing trial balance—step 10.

The closing process serves a *dual purpose:* (1) the temporary accounts (revenues, expenses, gains and losses) are reduced to *zero balances,* ready to measure activity in the upcoming accounting period, and (2) these temporary account balances are *closed (transferred) to retained earnings* to reflect the changes that have occurred in that account during the period. Often, an intermediate step is to close revenues and expenses to income summary, then income summary is closed to retained earnings. The use of the income summary account is just a bookkeeping convenience that provides a check that all temporary accounts have been properly closed (that is, the balance equals net income or loss).

To illustrate the closing process, assume that the fiscal year-end for Dress Right Clothing Corporation is July 31. Using the adjusted trial balance in Illustration 2–8, we can prepare the following general journal entries.

STEP 9

Close the temporary accounts to retained earnings (at year-end only).

● LO7

July 31		
Sales revenue	38,500	
Rent revenue	250	
Income summary		38,750

To close the revenue accounts to income summary.

---
[6]Some companies choose to disclose the changes in the retained earnings component of shareholders' equity in a separate statement or in a combined statement of income and retained earnings.

The first closing entry transfers the revenue account balances to income summary. Because revenue accounts have credit balances, they are debited to bring them to zero. After this entry is posted to the accounts, both revenue accounts have a zero balance.

To close the expense accounts to income summary.

July 31		
Income summary	36,333	
Cost of goods sold		22,000
Salaries expense		10,500
Supplies expense		800
Rent expense		2,000
Depreciation expense		200
Interest expense		333
Bad debt expense		500

The second closing entry transfers the expense account balances to income summary. As expense accounts have debit balances, they are credited to bring them to zero. After this entry is posted to the accounts, the expense accounts have a zero balance and the income summary account has a credit balance equal to net income for the period, in this case $2,417.

Income Summary

Expenses	36,333	38,750	Revenues
		2,417	Net income

To close the income summary account to retained earnings.

July 31		
Income summary	2,417	
Retained earnings		2,417

After this entry is posted to the accounts, the temporary accounts have zero balances and retained earnings has increased by the amount of the net income. It is important to remember that the temporary accounts are closed only at year-end and not at the end of any interim period. Closing the temporary accounts during the year would make it difficult to prepare the annual income statement.

ADDITIONAL CONSIDERATION

A previous additional consideration indicated that an alternative method of recording a cash dividend is to debit a temporary account called dividends, rather than debiting retained earnings. If this approach is used, an additional closing entry is required to close the dividend account to retained earnings, as follows:

Retained earnings	1,000	
Dividends		1,000

As you can see, the net result of a cash dividend is the same—a reduction in retained earnings and a reduction in cash.

STEP 10

Prepare a *post-closing trial balance* (at year-end only).

After the closing entries are posted to the ledger accounts, a **post-closing trial balance** is prepared. The purpose of this trial balance is to verify that the closing entries were prepared and posted correctly and that the accounts are now ready for next year's transactions. Illustration 2–13 shows the post-closing trial balance for Dress Right at July 31, 2011, assuming a July 31 fiscal year-end.

DRESS RIGHT CLOTHING CORPORATION
Post-Closing Trial Balance
July 31, 2011

Account Title	Debits	Credits
Cash	68,500	
Accounts receivable	2,000	
Allowance for uncollectible accounts		500
Supplies	1,200	
Prepaid rent	22,000	
Inventory	38,000	
Furniture and fixtures	12,000	
Accumulated depreciation—furniture and fixtures		200
Accounts payable		35,000
Notes payable		40,000
Unearned rent revenue		750
Salaries payable		5,500
Interest payable		333
Common stock		60,000
Retained earnings		1,417
Totals	143,700	143,700

ILLUSTRATION 2–13

Post-Closing Trial Balance

CONCEPT REVIEW EXERCISE

Refer to the August 31, 2011, adjusted trial balance of the Wyndham Wholesale Company presented in a previous concept review exercise on page 75.

Required:
1. Prepare an income statement and a statement of shareholders' equity for the month ended August 31, 2011, and a classified balance sheet as of August 31, 2011.
2. Assume that August 31 is the company's fiscal year-end. Prepare the necessary closing entries and a post-closing trial balance.

FINANCIAL STATEMENT PREPARATION AND CLOSING

1. Prepare an income statement and a statement of shareholders' equity for the month ended August 31, 2011, and a classified balance sheet as of August 31, 2011.

SOLUTION

WYNDHAM WHOLESALE COMPANY
Income Statement
For the Month of August 2011

Sales revenue		$40,000
Cost of goods sold		22,000
Gross profit		18,000
Operating expenses:		
Salaries	$7,000	
Utilities	2,000	
Bad debt	2,500	
Depreciation	500	
Rent	3,000	
Total operating expenses		15,000
Operating income		3,000
Other income (expense):		
Interest revenue	100	
Interest expense	(250)	(150)
Net income		$ 2,850

WYNDHAM WHOLESALE COMPANY
Statement of Shareholders' Equity
For the Month of August 2011

	Common Stock	Retained Earnings	Total Shareholders' Equity
Balance at August 1, 2011	$ –0–	$ –0–	$ –0–
Issue of common stock	50,000		50,000
Net income for August 2011		2,850	2,850
Less: Dividends		(1,000)	(1,000)
Balance at August 31, 2011	$50,000	$1,850	$51,850

WYNDHAM WHOLESALE COMPANY
Balance Sheet
At August 31, 2011
Assets

Current assets:		
Cash		$ 21,000
Accounts receivable	$25,000	
Less: Allowance for uncollectible accounts	2,500	22,500
Inventory		16,000
Interest receivable		100
Note receivable		20,000
Prepaid rent		3,000
Total current assets		82,600
Property and equipment:		
Equipment	20,000	
Less: Accumulated depreciation	500	19,500
Total assets		$102,100

Liabilities and Shareholders' Equity

Current liabilities:		
Accounts payable		$ 20,000
Interest payable		250
Note payable		30,000
Total current liabilities		50,250
Shareholders' equity:		
Common stock, 5,000 shares issued and outstanding	$50,000	
Retained earnings	1,850	
Total shareholders' equity		51,850
Total liabilities and shareholders' equity		$102,100

2. Assume that August 31 is the company's fiscal year-end. Prepare the necessary closing entries and a post-closing trial balance.

To close the revenue accounts to income summary.	**August 31**		
	Sales revenue	40,000	
	Interest revenue	100	
	Income summary		40,100
To close the expense accounts to income summary.	**August 31**		
	Income summary	37,250	
	Cost of goods sold		22,000
	Salaries expense		7,000
	Utilities expense		2,000
	Bad debt expense		2,500
	Depreciation expense		500
	Rent expense		3,000
	Interest expense		250

(continued)

(concluded)

August 31

Income summary	2,850	
Retained earnings		2,850

To close the income summary account to retained earnings.

Post-Closing Trial Balance

Account Title	Debits	Credits
Cash	21,000	
Accounts receivable	25,000	
Allowance for uncollectible accounts		2,500
Prepaid rent	3,000	
Inventory	16,000	
Interest receivable	100	
Note receivable	20,000	
Equipment	20,000	
Accumulated depreciation—equipment		500
Accounts payable		20,000
Interest payable		250
Note payable		30,000
Common stock		50,000
Retained earnings		1,850
Totals	105,100	105,100

Conversion from Cash Basis to Accrual Basis

In Chapter 1, we discussed and illustrated the differences between cash and accrual accounting. Cash basis accounting produces a measure called *net operating cash flow*. This measure is the difference between cash receipts and cash disbursements during a reporting period from transactions related to providing goods and services to customers. On the other hand, the accrual accounting model measures an entity's accomplishments and resource sacrifices during the period, regardless of when cash is received or paid. At this point, you might wish to review the material in Chapter 1 on pages 7 and 8 to reinforce your understanding of the motivation for using the accrual accounting model.

● LO8

Adjusting entries, for the most part, are conversions from cash basis to accrual basis. Prepayments and accruals occur when cash flow precedes or follows expense or revenue recognition.

Accountants sometimes are called upon to convert cash basis financial statements to accrual basis financial statements, particularly for small businesses. You now have all of the tools you need to make this conversion. For example, if a company paid $20,000 cash for insurance during the fiscal year and you determine that there was $5,000 in prepaid insurance at the beginning of the year and $3,000 at the end of the year, then you can determine (accrual basis) *insurance expense* for the year. Prepaid insurance decreased by $2,000 during the year, so insurance expense must be $22,000 ($20,000 in cash paid *plus* the decrease in prepaid insurance). You can visualize as follows:

Prepaid Insurance	
Balance, beginning of year	$ 5,000
Plus: Cash paid	20,000
Less: Insurance expense	?
Balance, end of year	$ 3,000

Insurance expense of $22,000 completes the explanation of the change in the balance of prepaid insurance. Prepaid insurance of $3,000 is reported as an asset in an accrual basis balance sheet.

Suppose a company paid $150,000 for salaries to employees during the year and you determine that there were $12,000 and $18,000 in salaries payable at the beginning and end of the year, respectively. What was salaries expense for the year?

Salaries Payable	
Balance, beginning of year	$ 12,000
Plus: Salaries expense	?
Less: Cash paid	150,000
Balance, end of year	$ 18,000

Salaries payable increased by $6,000 during the year, so *salaries expense* must be $156,000 ($150,000 in cash paid *plus* the increase in salaries payable). Salaries payable of $18,000 is reported as a liability in an accrual basis balance sheet.

Using T-accounts is a convenient approach for converting from cash to accrual accounting.

Salaries Payable			Salaries Expense	
	12,000 Beg. balance			
Cash paid 150,000				
	? Salaries expense		?	
	18,000 End balance			

The debit to salaries expense and credit to salaries payable must have been $156,000 to balance the salaries payable account.

For another example using T-accounts, assume that the amount of cash collected from customers during the year was $220,000, and you know that accounts receivable at the beginning of the year was $45,000 and $33,000 at the end of the year. You can use T-accounts to determine that *sales revenue* for the year must have been $208,000, the necessary debit to accounts receivable and credit to sales revenue to balance the accounts receivable account.

Accounts Receivable			Sales Revenue	
Beg. balance 45,000				
Credit sales ?			? Credit sales	
	220,000 Cash collections			
End balance 33,000				

Now suppose that, on occasion, customers pay in advance of receiving a product or service. Recall from our previous discussion of adjusting entries that this event creates a liability called unearned revenue. Assume the same facts in the previous example except you also determine that unearned revenues were $10,000 and $7,000 at the beginning and end of the year, respectively. A $3,000 decrease in unearned revenues means that the company earned an additional $3,000 in sales revenue for which the cash had been collected in a previous year. So, *sales revenue* for the year must have been $211,000, the $208,000 determined in the previous example *plus* the $3,000 decrease in unearned revenue.

Illustration 2–14 provides another example of converting from cash basis net income to accrual basis net income.

Notice a pattern in the adjustments to cash net income. When converting from cash to accrual income, we add increases and deduct decreases in assets. For example, an increase in accounts receivable means that the company earned more revenue than cash collected, requiring the addition to cash basis income. Conversely, we add decreases and deduct increases in accrued liabilities. For example, a decrease in interest payable means that the company incurred less interest expense than the cash interest it paid, requiring the addition to cash basis income. These adjustments are summarized in Graphic 2–5.

Most companies keep their books on an accrual basis.[7] A more important conversion for these companies is from the accrual basis to the cash basis. This conversion, essential for

Most companies must convert from an accrual basis to a cash basis when preparing the statement of cash flows.

[7]Generally accepted accounting principles require the use of the accrual basis. Some small, nonpublic companies might use the cash basis in preparing their financial statements if they are not concerned with complying with GAAP.

The Krinard Cleaning Services Company maintains its records on the cash basis, with one exception. The company reports equipment as an asset and records depreciation expense on the equipment. During 2011, Krinard collected $165,000 from customers, paid $92,000 in operating expenses, and recorded $10,000 in depreciation expense, resulting in net income of $63,000. The owner has asked you to convert this $63,000 in net income to full accrual net income. You are able to determine the following information about accounts receivable, prepaid expenses, accrued liabilities, and unearned revenues:

ILLUSTRATION 2–14

Cash to Accrual

	January 1, 2011	**December 31, 2011**
Accounts receivable	$16,000	$25,000
Prepaid expenses	7,000	4,000
Accrued liabilities (for operating expenses)	2,100	1,400
Unearned revenues	3,000	4,200

Accrual net income is $68,500, determined as follows:

Cash basis net income		$63,000
Add:	Increase in accounts receivable	9,000
Deduct:	Decrease in prepaid expenses	(3,000)
Add:	Decrease in accrued liabilities	700
Deduct:	Increase in unearned revenues	(1,200)
Accrual basis net income		$68,500

GRAPHIC 2–5

Converting Cash Basis to Accrual Basis Income

Converting Cash Basis Income to Accrual Basis Income		
	Increases	**Decreases**
Assets	Add	Deduct
Liabilities	Deduct	Add

the preparation of the statement of cash flows, is discussed and illustrated in Chapters 4 and 21. The lessons learned here, though, will help you with that conversion. For example, if sales revenue for the period is $120,000 and beginning and ending accounts receivable are $20,000 and $24,000, respectively, how much cash did the company collect from its customers during the period? The answer is $116,000. An increase in accounts receivable of $4,000 means that the company collected $4,000 less from customers than accrual sales revenue, and cash basis income is $4,000 less than accrual basis income.

FINANCIAL REPORTING CASE SOLUTION

1. **What purpose do adjusting entries serve?** *(p. 67)* Adjusting entries help ensure that only revenues actually earned in a period are recognized in that period, regardless of when cash is received. In this instance, for example, $13,000 cash has been received for services that haven't yet been performed. Also, adjusting entries enable a company to recognize all expenses incurred during a period, regardless of when cash is paid. Without depreciation, the friends' cost of using the equipment is not taken into account. Conversely, without adjustment, the cost of rent is overstated by $3,000 paid in advance for part of next year's rent.

With adjustments, we get an accrual income statement that provides a more complete measure of a company's operating performance and a better measure for predicting future operating cash flows. Similarly, the balance sheet provides a more complete assessment of assets and liabilities as sources of future cash receipts and disbursements.

2. **What year-end adjustments are needed to revise the income statement? Did your friends do as well their first year as they thought?** *(p. 67)* Three year-end adjusting entries are needed:

1. Depreciation expense ($80,000 ÷ 5 years)	16,000	
Accumulated depreciation—equipment		16,000
2. Prepaid rent ($500 × 6 months [July–Dec.])	3,000	
Rent expense		3,000
3. Consulting revenue	13,000	
Unearned consulting revenue		13,000

No, your friends did not fare as well as their cash based statement would have indicated. With appropriate adjustments, their net income is actually only $20,000:

Consulting revenue ($96,000 − 13,000)		$83,000
Operating expenses:		
Salaries	$32,000	
Rent ($9,000 − 3,000)	6,000	
Supplies	4,800	
Utilities	3,000	
Advertising	1,200	
Depreciation	16,000	63,000
Net income		$20,000

THE BOTTOM LINE

● **LO1** The accounting equation underlies the process used to capture the effect of economic events. The equation (Assets = Liabilities + Owners' Equity) implies an equality between the total economic resources of an entity (its assets) and the total claims to those resources (liabilities and equity). It also implies that each economic event affecting this equation will have a dual effect because resources always must equal claims to those resources. (p. 52)

● **LO2** After determining the dual effect of external events on the accounting equation, the transaction is recorded in a journal. A journal is a chronological list of transactions in debit/credit form. (p. 56)

● **LO3** The next step in the processing cycle is to periodically transfer, or *post,* the debit and credit information from the journal to individual general ledger accounts. A general ledger is simply a collection of all of the company's various accounts. Each account provides a summary of the effects of all events and transactions on that individual account. This process is called *posting.* An unadjusted trial balance is then prepared. (p. 63)

● **LO4** The next step in the processing cycle is to record the effect of *internal events* on the accounting equation. These transactions are commonly referred to as *adjusting entries.* Adjusting entries can be classified into three types: (1) prepayments, (2) accruals, and (3) estimates. Prepayments are transactions in which the cash flow *precedes* expense or revenue recognition. Accruals involve transactions where the cash outflow or inflow takes place in a period *subsequent* to expense or revenue recognition. Estimates for items such as future bad debts on receivables often are required to comply with the accrual accounting model. (p. 66)

● **LO5** Adjusting entries are recorded in the general journal and posted to the ledger accounts at the end of any period when financial statements must be prepared for external use. After these entries are posted to the general ledger accounts, an adjusted trial balance is prepared. (p. 67)

● **LO6** The adjusted trial balance is used to prepare the financial statements. The four basic financial statements are: (1) the income statement, (2) the balance sheet, (3) the statement of cash flows, and (4) the statement of shareholders' equity. The purpose of the income statement is to summarize the profit-generating activities of the company that occurred during a particular period of time. The balance sheet presents the financial position of the company on a particular date. The statement of cash flows discloses the events that caused cash to change during the reporting period. The statement of shareholders' equity discloses the sources of the changes in the various permanent shareholders' equity accounts that occurred during the period. (p. 76)

● **LO7**   At the end of the fiscal year, a final step in the accounting processing cycle, closing, is required. The closing process serves a *dual purpose:* (1) the temporary accounts (revenues and expenses) are reduced to *zero balances,* ready to measure activity in the upcoming accounting period, and (2) these temporary account balances are *closed (transferred) to retained earnings* to reflect the changes that have occurred in that account during the period. Often, an intermediate step is to close revenues and expenses to *income summary;* then *income summary* is closed to *retained earnings.* (p. 79)

● **LO8**   Cash basis accounting produces a measure called *net operating cash flow.* This measure is the difference between cash receipts and cash disbursements during a reporting period from transactions related to providing goods and services to customers. On the other hand, the accrual accounting model measures an entity's accomplishments and resource sacrifices during the period, regardless of when cash is received or paid. Accountants sometimes are called upon to convert cash basis financial statements to accrual basis financial statements, particularly for small businesses. (p. 83) ●

USE OF A WORKSHEET

APPENDIX 2A

A worksheet can be used as a tool to facilitate the preparation of adjusting and closing entries and the financial statements.

A worksheet often is used to organize the accounting information needed to prepare adjusting and closing entries and the financial statements. It is an informal tool only and is not part of the accounting system. There are many different ways to design and use worksheets. We will illustrate a representative method using the financial information for the Dress Right Clothing Corporation presented in the chapter. Computerized programs such as Lotus 1-2-3 and Excel facilitate the use of worksheets.

Illustration 2A–1 presents the completed worksheet. The worksheet is utilized in conjunction with step 5 in the processing cycle, preparation of an unadjusted trial balance.

ILLUSTRATION 2A–1   Worksheet, Dress Right Clothing Corporation, July 31, 2011

Worksheet, Dress Right Clothing Corporation, July 31, 2011

Account Title	Unadjusted Trial Balance Dr.	Unadjusted Trial Balance Cr.	Adjusting Entries Dr.		Adjusting Entries Cr.		Adjusted Trial Balance Dr.	Adjusted Trial Balance Cr.	Income Statement Dr.	Income Statement Cr.	Balance Sheet Dr.	Balance Sheet Cr.
Cash	68,500						68,500				68,500	
Accounts receivable	2,000						2,000				2,000	
Allowance for uncollectible accounts		0			(7)	500		500				500
Supplies	2,000				(1)	800	1,200				1,200	
Prepaid rent	24,000				(2)	2,000	22,000				22,000	
Inventory	38,000						38,000				38,000	
Furniture & fixtures	12,000						12,000				12,000	
Accumulated depreciation- furniture & fixtures		0			(3)	200		200				200
Accounts payable		35,000						35,000				35,000
Note payable		40,000						40,000				40,000
Unearned rent revenue		1,000	(4)	250				750				750
Salaries payable		0			(5)	5,500		5,500				5,500
Interest payable		0			(6)	333		333				333
Common stock		60,000						60,000				60,000
Retained earnings	1,000						1,000				1,000	
Sales revenue		38,500						38,500		38,500		
Rent revenue		0			(4)	250		250		250		
Cost of goods sold	22,000						22,000		22,000			
Salaries expense	5,000		(5)	5,500			10,500		10,500			
Supplies expense	0		(1)	800			800		800			
Rent expense	0		(2)	2,000			2,000		2,000			
Depreciation expense	0		(3)	200			200		200			
Interest expense	0		(6)	333			333		333			
Bad debt expense	0		(7)	500			500		500			
Totals	174,500	174,500	9,583		9,583		181,033	181,033				
Net Income									2,417			2,417
Totals									38,750	38,750	144,700	144,700

The first step is to enter account titles in column A and the unadjusted account balances in columns B and C.

Step 1. The account titles as they appear in the general ledger are entered in column A and the balances of these accounts are copied onto columns B and C, entitled Unadjusted Trial Balance. The accounts are copied in the same order as they appear in the general ledger, which usually is assets, liabilities, shareholders' equity permanent accounts, revenues, and expenses. The debit and credit columns are totaled to make sure that they balance. This procedure is repeated for each set of columns in the worksheet to check for accuracy.

The second step is to determine end-of-period adjusting entries and enter them in columns E and G.

Step 2. The end-of-period adjusting entries are determined and entered directly on the worksheet in columns E and G, entitled Adjusting Entries. The adjusting entries for Dress Right Clothing Corporation were discussed in detail in the chapter and exhibited in general journal form in Illustration 2–7 on page 73. You should refer back to this illustration and trace each of the entries to the worksheet. For worksheet purposes, the entries have been numbered from (1) to (7) for easy referencing.

For example, entry (1) records the cost of supplies used during the month of July with a debit to supplies expense and a credit to supplies for $800. A (1) is placed next to the $800 in the debit column in the supplies expense row as well as next to the $800 in the credit column in the supplies row. This allows us to more easily reconstruct the entry for general journal purposes and locate errors if the debit and credit columns do not balance.

The third step adds or deducts the effects of the adjusting entries on the account balances.

Step 3. The effects of the adjusting entries are added to or deducted from the account balances listed in the Unadjusted Trial Balance columns and copied across to columns H and I, entitled Adjusted Trial Balance. For example, supplies had an unadjusted balance of $2,000. Adjusting entry (1) credited this account by $800, reducing the balance to $1,200.

The fourth step is to transfer the temporary retained earnings account balances to columns J and K.

Step 4. The balances in the temporary retained earnings accounts, revenues and expenses, are transferred to columns J and K, entitled Income Statement. The difference between the total debits and credits in these columns is equal to net income or net loss. In this case, because credits (revenues) exceed debits (expenses), a net income of $2,417 results. To balance the debits and credits in this set of columns, a $2,417 debit entry is made in the line labeled Net income.

The fifth step is to transfer the balances in the permanent accounts to columns L and M.

Step 5. The balances in the permanent accounts are transferred to columns L and M, entitled Balance Sheet. To keep the debits and credits equal in the worksheet, a $2,417 credit must be recorded to offset the $2,417 debit recorded in step 4 and labeled as net income. This credit represents the fact that when the temporary accounts are closed out to retained earnings, a $2,417 credit to retained earnings will result. The credit in column M, therefore, represents an increase in retained earnings for the period, that is, net income.

After the worksheet is completed, the financial statements can be prepared directly from columns J–M. The financial statements for Dress Right Clothing Corporation are shown in Illustrations 2–9 through 2–12. The accountant must remember to then record the adjusting entries in the general journal and post them to the general ledger accounts. An adjusted trial balance should then be prepared which should be identical to the one in the worksheet. At fiscal year-end, the income statement columns can then be used to prepare closing entries. ●

APPENDIX 2B REVERSING ENTRIES

Accountants sometimes use **reversing entries** at the beginning of a reporting period. These optional entries remove the effects of some of the adjusting entries made at the end of the previous reporting period for the sole purpose of simplifying journal entries made during the new period. If the accountant does use reversing entries, these entries are recorded in the general journal and posted to the general ledger accounts on the first day of the new period.

Reversing entries are used most often with accruals. For example, the following adjusting entry for accrued salaries was recorded at the end of July 2011 for the Dress Right Clothing Corporation in the chapter:

To record accrued salaries at the end of July.

July 31		
Salaries expense	5,500	
Salaries payable		5,500

If reversing entries are not used, when the salaries actually are paid in August, the accountant needs to remember to debit salaries payable and not salaries expense.

The account balances before and after salary payment can be seen below with the use of T-accounts.

Salaries Expense		Salaries Payable	
Bal. July 31 10,500		5,500	Bal. July 31
	(Cash Payment) 5,500		
		–0–	Balance

If the accountant for Dress Right employs reversing entries, the following entry is made on August 1, 2011:

August 1
Salaries payable 5,500
   Salaries expense 5,500

To reverse accrued salaries expense recorded at the end of July.

This entry reduces the salaries payable account to zero and reduces the salary expense account by $5,500. When salaries actually are paid in August, the debit is to salaries expense, thus increasing the account by $5,500.

Salaries Expense		Salaries Payable	
Bal. July 31 10,500		5,500	Bal. July 31
	5,500 (Reversing entry) 5,500		
(Cash payment) 5,500			
Balance 10,500		–0–	Balance

We can see that balances in the accounts after cash payment is made are identical. The use of reversing entries for accruals, which is optional, simply allows cash payments or cash receipts to be entered directly into the temporary expense or revenue accounts without regard to the accruals made at the end of the previous period.

Reversing entries also can be used with prepayments and unearned revenues. For example, earlier in the chapter Dress Right Clothing Corporation used the following entry to record the purchase of supplies on July 6:

July 6
Supplies 2,000
   Cash 2,000

To record the purchase of supplies.

If reversing entries are not used, an adjusting entry is needed at the end of July to record the amount of supplies consumed during the period. In the illustration, Dress Right recorded this adjusting entry at the end of July:

July 31
Supplies expense 800
   Supplies 800

To record the cost of supplies used during the month of July.

T-accounts help us visualize the account balances before and after the adjusting entry.

Supplies		Supplies Expense	
(Cash payment) 2,000			
	800 (Adjusting entry) 800		
Bal. July 31 1,200		Bal. July 31 800	

If the accountant for Dress Right employs reversing entries, the purchase of supplies is recorded as follows:

To record the purchase of supplies.

July 6		
Supplies expense	2,000	
Cash		2,000

The adjusting entry then is used to establish the balance in the supplies account at $1,200 (amount of supplies still on hand at the end of the month) and reduce the supplies expense account from the amount purchased to the amount used.

To record the cost of supplies on hand at the end of July.

July 31		
Supplies (balance on hand)	1,200	
Supplies expense ($2,000 – 800)		1,200

T-accounts make the process easier to see before and after the adjusting entry:

Supplies		Supplies Expense	
		(Cash payment) 2,000	
1,200		(Adjusting entry)	1,200
Bal. July 31 1,200		Bal. July 31 800	

Notice that the ending balances in both accounts are the same as when reversing entries are not used. Up to this point, this approach is the alternate approach to recording prepayments discussed on page 69. The next step is an optional expediency.

On August 1, the following reversing entry can be recorded:

To reverse the July adjusting entry for supplies on hand.

August 1		
Supplies expense	1,200	
Supplies		1,200

This entry reduces the supplies account to zero and increases the supplies expense account to $2,000. Subsequent purchases would then be entered into the supplies expense account and future adjusting entries would record the amount of supplies still on hand at the end of the period. At the end of the fiscal year, the supplies expense account, along with all other temporary accounts, is closed to retained earnings.

Using reversing entries for prepayments, which is optional, simply allows cash payments to be entered directly into the temporary expense accounts without regard to whether only the current, or both the current and future periods, are benefitted by the expenditure. Adjustments are then made at the end of the period to reflect the amount of the unexpired benefit (asset). ●

APPENDIX 2C

SUBSIDIARY LEDGERS AND SPECIAL JOURNALS
Subsidiary Ledgers

Accounting systems employ a *subsidiary ledger* which contains a group of subsidiary accounts associated with particular general ledger control accounts.

The general ledger contains what are referred to as *control accounts.* In addition to the general ledger, a subsidiary ledger contains a group of subsidiary accounts associated with a particular general ledger control account. For example, there will be a subsidiary ledger for accounts receivable that keeps track of the increases and decreases in the account receivable balance for each of the company's customers purchasing goods or services on credit. After all of the postings are made from the appropriate journals, the balance in the accounts receivable control account should equal the sum of the balances in the accounts receivable subsidiary ledger accounts. Subsidiary ledgers also are used for accounts payable, property and equipment, investments, and other accounts.

Special Journals

An actual accounting system employs many different types of journals. The purpose of each journal is to record, in chronological order, the dual effect of a transaction in debit/credit form. The chapter used the general journal format to record each transaction. However, even for small companies with relatively few transactions, the general journal is used to record only a few types of transactions.[8]

The majority of transactions are recorded in special journals. These journals capture the dual effect of *repetitive* types of transactions. For example, cash receipts are recorded in a cash receipts journal, cash disbursements in a cash disbursements journal, credit sales in a sales journal, and the purchase of merchandise on account in a purchases journal.

> For most external transactions, *special journals* are used to capture the dual effect of the transaction in debit/credit form.

Special journals simplify the recording process in the following ways:

1. Journalizing the effects of a particular transaction is made more efficient through the use of specifically designed formats.
2. Individual transactions are not posted to the general ledger accounts but are accumulated in the special journals and a summary posting is made on a periodic basis.
3. The responsibility for recording journal entries for the repetitive types of transactions is placed on individuals who have specialized training in handling them.

The concepts of subsidiary ledgers and special journals are illustrated using the *sales journal* and the *cash receipts journal*.

Sales Journal

The purpose of the sales journal is to record all credit sales. Cash sales are recorded in the cash receipts journal. Every entry in the sales journal has exactly the same effect on the accounts; the sales revenue account is credited and the accounts receivable control account is debited. Therefore, there is only one column needed to record the debit/credit effect of these transactions. Other columns are needed to capture information for updating the accounts receivable subsidiary ledger. Illustration 2C–1 presents the sales journal for Dress Right Clothing Corporation for the month of August 2011.

> All credit sales are recorded in the *sales journal.*

				Page 1
Date	Accounts Receivable Subsidiary Account No.	Customer Name	Sales Invoice No.	Cr. Sales Revenue (400) Dr. Accounts Receivable (110)
2011				
Aug. 5	801	Leland High School	10-221	1,500
9	812	Mr. John Smith	10-222	200
18	813	Greystone School	10-223	825
22	803	Ms. Barbara Jones	10-224	120
29	805	Hart Middle School	10-225	650
				3,295

ILLUSTRATION 2C–1

Sales Journal, Dress Right Clothing Corporation, August 2011

During the month of August, the company made five credit sales, totaling $3,295. This amount is posted as a debit to the accounts receivable control account, account number 110, and a credit to the sales revenue account, account number 400. The T-accounts for accounts receivable and sales revenue appear below. The reference SJ1 refers to page 1 of the sales journal.

General Ledger

Accounts Receivable	110		Sales Revenue	400
July 31 Balance 2,000				
Aug. 31 SJ1 3,295			3,295 Aug. 31 SJ1	

[8]For example, end of period adjusting entries would be recorded in the general journal.

In a computerized accounting system, as each transaction is recorded in the sales journal, the subsidiary ledger accounts for the customer involved will automatically be updated. For example, the first credit sale of the month is to Leland High School for $1,500. The sales invoice number for this sale is 10-221 and the customer's subsidiary account number is 801. As this transaction is entered, the subsidiary account 801 for Leland High School is debited for $1,500.

Accounts Receivable Subsidiary Ledger

Leland High School		801
August 5 SJ1	1,500	

As cash is collected from this customer, the cash receipts journal records the transaction with a credit to the accounts receivable control account and a debit to cash. At the same time, the accounts receivable subsidiary ledger account number 801 also is credited. After the postings are made from the special journals, the balance in the accounts receivable control account should equal the sum of the balances in the accounts receivable subsidiary ledger accounts.

Cash Receipts Journal

All cash receipts are recorded in the cash receipts journal.

The purpose of the **cash receipts journal** is to record all cash receipts, regardless of the source. Every transaction recorded in this journal produces a debit entry to the cash account with the credit to various other accounts. Illustration 2C–2 shows a cash receipts journal using transactions of the Dress Right Clothing Corporation for the month of August 2011.

Because every transaction results in a debit to the cash account, No. 100, a column is provided for that account. At the end of August, an $11,750 debit is posted to the general ledger cash account with the source labeled CR1, cash receipts journal, page 1.

ILLUSTRATION 2C–2

Cash Receipts Journal, Dress Right Clothing Corporation, August 2011

Page 1

Date	Explanation or Account Name	Dr. Cash (100)	Cr. Accounts Receivable (110)	Cr. Sales Revenue (400)	Cr. Other	Other Accounts
2011						
Aug. 7	Cash sale	500		500		
11	Borrowed cash	10,000			10,000	Note payable (220)
17	Leland High School	750	750			
20	Cash sale	300		300		
25	Mr. John Smith	200	200			
		11,750	950	800	10,000	

Because cash and credit sales are common, separate columns are provided for these accounts. At the end of August, a $950 credit is posted to the accounts receivable general ledger account, No. 110, and an $800 credit is posted to the sales revenue account, No. 400. Two additional credit columns are provided for uncommon cash receipt transactions, one for the credit amount and one for the account being credited. We can see that in August, Dress Right borrowed $10,000 requiring a credit to the note payable account, No. 220.

In addition to the postings to the general ledger control accounts, each time an entry is recorded in the accounts receivable column, a credit is posted to the accounts receivable subsidiary ledger account for the customer making the payment. For example, on August 17, Leland High School paid $750 on account. The subsidiary ledger account for Leland High School is credited for $750.

Accounts Receivable Subsidiary Ledger

Leland High School			801
August 5 SJ1	1,500		
		750	August 17 CR1

QUESTIONS FOR REVIEW OF KEY TOPICS

Q 2–1   Explain the difference between external events and internal events. Give an example of each type of event.

Q 2–2   Each economic event or transaction will have a dual effect on financial position. Explain what is meant by this dual effect.

Q 2–3   What is the purpose of a journal? What is the purpose of a general ledger?

Q 2–4   Explain the difference between permanent accounts and temporary accounts. Why does an accounting system include both types of accounts?

Q 2–5   Describe how debits and credits affect assets, liabilities, and permanent owners' equity accounts.

Q 2–6   Describe how debits and credits affect temporary owners' equity accounts.

Q 2–7   What is the first step in the accounting processing cycle? What role do source documents fulfill in this step?

Q 2–8   Describe what is meant by transaction analysis.

Q 2–9   Describe what is meant by posting, the fourth step in the processing cycle.

Q 2–10   Describe the events that correspond to the following two journal entries:

1. Inventory	20,000	
Accounts payable		20,000
2. Accounts receivable	30,000	
Sales revenue		30,000
Cost of goods sold	18,000	
Inventory		18,000

Q 2–11   What is an unadjusted trial balance? An adjusted trial balance?

Q 2–12   Define adjusting entries and discuss their purpose.

Q 2–13   Define closing entries and their purpose.

Q 2–14   Define prepaid expenses and provide at least two examples.

Q 2–15   Unearned revenues represent liabilities recorded when cash is received from customers in advance of providing a good or service. What adjusting journal entry is required at the end of a period to recognize the amount of unearned revenues that were earned during the period?

Q 2–16   Define accrued liabilities. What adjusting journal entry is required to record accrued liabilities?

Q 2–17   Describe the purpose of each of the four primary financial statements.

Q 2–18   [Based on Appendix A] What is the purpose of a worksheet? In a columnar worksheet similar to Illustration 2A–1, what would be the result of incorrectly transferring the balance in a liability account to column K, the credit column under income statement?

Q 2–19   [Based on Appendix B] Define reversing entries and discuss their purpose.

Q 2–20   [Based on Appendix C] What is the purpose of special journals? In what ways do they simplify the recording process?

Q 2–21   [Based on Appendix C] Explain the difference between the general ledger and a subsidiary ledger.

BRIEF EXERCISES

BE 2–1
Transaction analysis
● LO1

The Marchetti Soup Company entered into the following transactions during the month of June: (1) purchased inventory on account for $165,000 (assume Marchetti uses a perpetual inventory system); (2) paid $40,000 in salaries to employees for work performed during the month; (3) sold merchandise that cost $120,000 to credit customers for $200,000; (4) collected $180,000 in cash from credit customers; and (5) paid suppliers of inventory $145,000. Analyze each transaction and show the effect of each on the accounting equation for a corporation.

BE 2–2
Journal entries
● LO2

Prepare journal entries for each of the transactions listed in BE 2–1.

BE 2–3
T-accounts
● LO3

Post the journal entries prepared in BE 2–2 to T-accounts. Assume that the opening balances in each of the accounts is zero except for cash, accounts receivable, and accounts payable that had opening balances of $65,000, $43,000, and $22,000 respectively.

BE 2–4
Journal entries
● LO2

Prepare journal entries for each of the following transactions for a company that has a fiscal year-end of December 31: (1) on October 1, $12,000 was paid for a one-year fire insurance policy; (2) on June 30 the company lent its chief financial officer $10,000; principal and interest at 6% are due in one year; and (3) equipment costing $60,000 was purchased at the beginning of the year for cash.

BE 2–5
Adjusting entries
● LO4 LO5

Prepare the necessary adjusting entries at December 31 for each of the items listed in BE 2–4. Depreciation on the equipment is $12,000 per year.

BE 2–6
Adjusting entries; income determination
● LO5

If the adjusting journal entries prepared in BE 2–5 were not made, would net income be higher or lower and by how much?

BE 2–7
Adjusting entries
● LO4 LO5

Prepare the necessary adjusting entries at its year-end of December 31, 2011, for the Jamesway Corporation for each of the following situations. No adjusting entries were made during the year.
1. On December 20, 2011, Jamesway received a $4,000 payment from a customer for services to be rendered early in 2012. Service revenue was credited.
2. On December 1, 2011, the company paid a local radio station $2,000 for 40 radio ads that were to be aired, 20 per month, throughout December and January. Prepaid advertising was debited.
3. Employee salaries for the month of December totaling $16,000 will be paid on January 7, 2012.
4. On August 31, 2011, Jamesway borrowed $60,000 from a local bank. A note was signed with principal and 8% interest to be paid on August 31, 2012.

BE 2–8
Income determination
● LO5

If none of the adjusting journal entries prepared in BE 2–7 were made, would assets, liabilities, and shareholders' equity on the 12/31/11 balance sheet be higher or lower and by how much?

BE 2–9
Financial statements
● LO6

The following account balances were taken from the 2011 adjusted trial balance of the Bowler Corporation: sales revenue, $325,000; cost of goods sold, $168,000; salaries expense; $45,000; rent expense, $20,000; depreciation expense, $30,000; and miscellaneous expense, $12,000. Prepare an income statement for 2011.

BE 2–10
Financial statements
● LO6

The following account balances were taken from the 2011 post-closing trial balance of the Bowler Corporation: cash, $5,000; accounts receivable, $10,000; inventory, $16,000; machinery and equipment, $100,000; accumulated depreciation—machinery and equipment, $40,000; accounts payable, $20,000; salaries payable, $12,000; retained earnings, $9,000; and common stock, $50,000. Prepare a 12/31/11 balance sheet.

BE 2–11
Closing entries
● LO7

The year-end adjusted trial balance of the Timmons Tool and Die Corporation included the following account balances: retained earnings, $220,000; sales revenue, $850,000; cost of goods sold, $580,000; salaries expense, $180,000; rent expense, $40,000; and interest expense, $15,000. Prepare the necessary closing entries.

BE 2–12
Cash versus accrual accounting
● LO8

Newman Consulting Company maintains its records on a cash basis. During 2011 the following cash flows were recorded: cash received from customers, $420,000; and cash paid for salaries, utilities, and advertising, $240,000, $35,000, and $12,000, respectively. You also determine that customers owed the company $52,000 and $60,000 at the beginning and end of the year, respectively, and that the company owed the utility company $6,000 and $4,000 at the beginning and end of the year, respectively. Determine accrual net income for the year.

EXERCISES

An alternate exercise and problem set is available on the text website: www.mhhe.com/spiceland6e

E 2–1
Transaction analysis
● LO1

The following transactions occurred during March 2011 for the Wainwright Corporation. The company owns and operates a wholesale warehouse.
1. Issued 30,000 shares of common stock in exchange for $300,000 in cash.
2. Purchased equipment at a cost of $40,000. $10,000 cash was paid and a note payable was signed for the balance owed.
3. Purchased inventory on account at a cost of $90,000. The company uses the perpetual inventory system.
4. Credit sales for the month totaled $120,000. The cost of the goods sold was $70,000.
5. Paid $5,000 in rent on the warehouse building for the month of March.

6. Paid $6,000 to an insurance company for fire and liability insurance for a one-year period beginning April 1, 2011.
7. Paid $70,000 on account for the merchandise purchased in 3.
8. Collected $55,000 from customers on account.
9. Recorded depreciation expense of $1,000 for the month on the equipment.

Required:

Analyze each transaction and show the effect of each on the accounting equation for a corporation.
Example:

Assets   = Liabilities + Paid-In Capital + Retained Earnings
1.   +300,000 (cash)   + 300,000 (common stock)

E 2–2
Journal entries
● LO2

Prepare journal entries to record each of the transactions listed in Exercise 2–1.

E 2–3
T-accounts and trial balance
● LO3

Post the journal entries prepared in Exercise 2–2 to T-accounts. Assume that the opening balances in each of the accounts is zero. Prepare a trial balance from the ending account balances.

E 2–4
Journal entries
● LO2

The following transactions occurred during the month of June 2011 for the Stridewell Corporation. The company owns and operates a retail shoe store.

1. Issued 100,000 shares of common stock in exchange for $500,000 cash.
2. Purchased furniture and fixtures at a cost of $100,000. $40,000 was paid in cash and a note payable was signed for the balance owed.
3. Purchased inventory on account at a cost of $200,000. The company uses the perpetual inventory system.
4. Credit sales for the month totaled $280,000. The cost of the goods sold was $140,000.
5. Paid $6,000 in rent on the store building for the month of June.
6. Paid $3,000 to an insurance company for fire and liability insurance for a one-year period beginning June 1, 2011.
7. Paid $120,000 on account for the merchandise purchased in 3.
8. Collected $55,000 from customers on account.
9. Paid shareholders a cash dividend of $5,000.
10. Recorded depreciation expense of $2,000 for the month on the furniture and fixtures.
11. Recorded the amount of prepaid insurance that expired for the month.

Required:

Prepare journal entries to record each of the transactions and events listed above.

E 2–5
The accounting processing cycle
● LO2 through LO7

Listed below are several terms and phrases associated with the accounting processing cycle. Pair each item from List A (by letter) with the item from List B that is most appropriately associated with it.

List A	List B
_____ 1. Source documents	a. Record of the dual effect of a transaction in debit/credit form.
_____ 2. Transaction analysis	b. Internal events recorded at the end of a reporting period.
_____ 3. Journal	c. Primary means of disseminating information to external decision makers.
_____ 4. Posting	d. To zero out the owners' equity temporary accounts.
_____ 5. Unadjusted trial balance	e. Determine the dual effect on the accounting equation.
_____ 6. Adjusting entries	f. List of accounts and their balances before recording adjusting entries.
_____ 7. Adjusted trial balance	g. List of accounts and their balances after recording closing entries.
_____ 8. Financial statements	h. List of accounts and their balances after recording adjusting entries.
_____ 9. Closing entries	i. A means of organizing information: not part of the formal accounting system.
_____ 10. Post-closing trial balance	j. Transferring balances from the journal to the ledger.
_____ 11. Worksheet	k. Used to identify and process external transactions.

E 2–6
Debits and credits
● LO2

Indicate whether a debit will increase (I) or decrease (D) each of the following accounts listed in items 1 through 16:

Increase (I) or Decrease (D)	Account
1. ____	Inventory
2. ____	Depreciation expense
3. ____	Accounts payable
4. ____	Prepaid rent
5. ____	Sales revenue
6. ____	Common stock
7. ____	Wages payable
8. ____	Cost of goods sold
9. ____	Utility expense
10. ____	Equipment
11. ____	Accounts receivable
12. ____	Allowance for uncollectible accounts
13. ____	Bad debt expense
14. ____	Interest expense
15. ____	Interest revenue
16. ____	Gain on sale of equipment

E 2–7
Transaction analysis; debits and credits
● LO2

Some of the ledger accounts for the Sanderson Hardware Company are numbered and listed below. For each of the October 2011 transactions numbered 1 through 12 below, indicate by account number which accounts should be debited and which should be credited. The company uses the perpetual inventory system. Assume that appropriate adjusting entries were made at the end of September.

(1) Accounts payable	(2) Equipment	(3) Inventory
(4) Accounts receivable	(5) Cash	(6) Supplies
(7) Supplies expense	(8) Prepaid rent	(9) Sales revenue
(10) Retained earnings	(11) Note payable	(12) Common stock
(13) Unearned revenue	(14) Rent expense	(15) Wages payable
(16) Cost of goods sold	(17) Wage expense	(18) Interest expense

	Account(s) Debited	Account(s) Credited
Example: Purchased inventory for cash	3	5

1. Paid a cash dividend.
2. Paid rent for the next three months.
3. Sold goods to customers on account.
4. Purchased inventory on account.
5. Purchased supplies for cash.
6. Paid employees wages for September.
7. Issued common stock in exchange for cash.
8. Collected cash from customers for goods sold in 3.
9. Borrowed cash from a bank and signed a note.
10. At the end of October, recorded the amount of supplies that had been used during the month.
11. Received cash for advance payment from customer.
12. Accrued employee wages for October.

E 2–8
Adjusting entries
● LO4 LO5

Prepare the necessary adjusting entries at December 31, 2011, for the Falwell Company for each of the following situations. Assume that no financial statements were prepared during the year and no adjusting entries were recorded.

1. A three-year fire insurance policy was purchased on July 1, 2011, for $12,000. The company debited insurance expense for the entire amount.
2. Depreciation on equipment totaled $15,000 for the year.
3. The company determined that accounts receivable in the amount of $6,500 will probably not be collected. The allowance for uncollectible accounts account has a credit balance of $2,000 before any adjustment.
4. Employee salaries of $18,000 for the month of December will be paid in early January 2012.
5. On November 1, 2011, the company borrowed $200,000 from a bank. The note requires principal and interest at 12% to be paid on April 30, 2012.
6. On December 1, 2011, the company received $3,000 in cash from another company that is renting office space in Falwell's building. The payment, representing rent for December and January, was credited to unearned rent revenue.

E 2–9
Adjusting entries
● LO4 LO5

Prepare the necessary adjusting entries at December 31, 2011, for the Microchip Company for each of the following situations. Assume that no financial statements were prepared during the year and no adjusting entries were recorded.

1. On October 1, 2011, Microchip lent $90,000 to another company. A note was signed with principal and 8% interest to be paid on September 30, 2012.

2. On November 1, 2011, the company paid its landlord $6,000 representing rent for the months of November through January. Prepaid rent was debited.

3. On August 1, 2011, collected $12,000 in advance rent from another company that is renting a portion of Microchip's factory. The $12,000 represents one year's rent and the entire amount was credited to rent revenue.

4. Depreciation on machinery is $4,500 for the year.

5. Vacation pay for the year that had been earned by employees but not paid to them or recorded is $8,000.

6. Microchip began the year with $2,000 in its asset account, supplies. During the year, $6,500 in supplies were purchased and debited to supplies. At year-end, supplies costing $3,250 remain on hand.

E 2–10
Adjusting entries;
solving for unknowns
● LO4 LO5

The Eldorado Corporation's controller prepares adjusting entries only at the end of the fiscal year. The following adjusting entries were prepared on December 31, 2011:

	Debit	Credit
Interest expense	7,200	
Interest payable		7,200
Rent expense	35,000	
Prepaid rent		35,000
Interest receivable	500	
Interest revenue		500

Additional information:

1. The company borrowed $120,000 on March 31, 2011. Principal and interest are due on March 31, 2012. This note is the company's only interest-bearing debt.

2. Rent for the year on the company's office space is $60,000. The rent is paid in advance.

3. On October 31, 2011, Eldorado lent money to a customer. The customer signed a note with principal and interest at 6% due in one year.

Required:

Determine the following:

1. What is the interest rate on the company's note payable?

2. The 2011 rent payment was made at the beginning of which month?

3. How much did Eldorado lend its customer on October 31?

E 2–11
Financial statements
and closing entries
● LO6 LO7

The December 31, 2011, adjusted trial balance for the Blueboy Cheese Corporation is presented below.

Account Title	Debits	Credits
Cash	21,000	
Accounts receivable	300,000	
Allowance for uncollectible accounts		20,000
Prepaid rent	10,000	
Inventory	50,000	
Equipment	600,000	
Accumulated depreciation—equipment		250,000
Accounts payable		40,000
Note payable (due in six months)		60,000
Salaries payable		8,000
Interest payable		2,000
Common stock		400,000
Retained earnings		100,000
Sales revenue		800,000
Cost of goods sold	480,000	
Salaries expense	120,000	
Rent expense	30,000	
Depreciation expense	60,000	
Interest expense	4,000	
Bad debt expense	5,000	
Totals	1,680,000	1,680,000

Required:

1. Prepare an income statement for the year ended December 31, 2011, and a classified balance sheet as of December 31, 2011.

2. Prepare the necessary closing entries at December 31, 2011.

E 2–12
Closing entries
● LO7

American Chip Corporation's fiscal year-end is December 31. The following is a partial adjusted trial balance as of December 31, 2011.

Account Title	Debits	Credits
Retained earnings		80,000
Sales revenue		750,000
Interest revenue		3,000
Cost of goods sold	420,000	
Salaries expense	100,000	
Rent expense	15,000	
Depreciation expense	30,000	
Interest expense	5,000	
Insurance expense	6,000	

Required:
Prepare the necessary closing entries at December 31, 2011.

E 2–13
Closing entries
● LO7

Presented below is income statement information of the Schefter Corporation for the year ended December 31, 2011.

Sales revenue	$492,000	Cost of goods sold	$284,000
Salaries expense	80,000	Insurance expense	12,000
Interest revenue	6,000	Interest expense	4,000
Advertising expense	10,000	Income tax expense	30,000
Gain on sale of investments	8,000	Depreciation expense	20,000

Required:
Prepare the necessary closing entries at December 31, 2011.

E 2–14
Cash versus accrual accounting; adjusting entries
● LO4 LO5 LO8

The Righter Shoe Store Company prepares monthly financial statements for its bank. The November 30 and December 31, 2011, trial balances contained the following account information:

	Nov. 30		Dec. 31	
	Dr.	Cr.	Dr.	Cr.
Supplies	1,500		3,000	
Prepaid insurance	6,000		4,500	
Wages payable		10,000		15,000
Unearned rent revenue		2,000		1,000

The following information also is known:
a. The December income statement reported $2,000 in supplies expense.
b. No insurance payments were made in December.
c. $10,000 was paid to employees during December for wages.
d. On November 1, 2011, a tenant paid Righter $3,000 in advance rent for the period November through January. Unearned rent revenue was credited.

Required:
1. What was the cost of supplies purchased during December?
2. What was the adjusting entry recorded at the end of December for prepaid insurance?
3. What was the adjusting entry recorded at the end of December for accrued wages?
4. What was the amount of rent revenue earned in December? What adjusting entry was recorded at the end of December for unearned rent?

E 2–15
External transactions and adjusting entries
● LO2 LO4 LO5

The following transactions occurred during 2011 for the Beehive Honey Corporation:

Feb. 1 Borrowed $12,000 from a bank and signed a note. Principal and interest at 10% will be paid on January 31, 2012.

Apr. 1 Paid $3,600 to an insurance company for a two-year fire insurance policy.

July 17 Purchased supplies costing $2,800 on account. The company records supplies purchased in an asset account. At the December 31, 2011, year-end, supplies costing $1,250 remained on hand.

Nov. 1 A customer borrowed $6,000 and signed a note requiring the customer to pay principal and 8% interest on April 30, 2012.

Required:
1. Record each transaction in general journal form. Omit explanations.
2. Prepare any necessary adjusting entries at the December 31, 2011, year-end. No adjusting entries were made during the year for any item.

E 2–16
Accrual accounting
income
determination
● **LO4 LO8**

During the course of your examination of the financial statements of the Hales Corporation for the year ended December 31, 2011, you discover the following:

a. An insurance policy covering three years was purchased on January 1, 2011, for $6,000. The entire amount was debited to insurance expense and no adjusting entry was made for this item.

b. During 2011, the company received a $1,000 cash advance from a customer for merchandise to be manu-factured and shipped in 2012. The $1,000 was credited to sales revenue. No entry was made for the cost of merchandise.

c. There were no supplies listed in the balance sheet under assets. However, you discover that supplies costing $750 were on hand at December 31.

d. Hales borrowed $20,000 from a local bank on October 1, 2011. Principal and interest at 12% will be paid on September 30, 2012. No accrual was made for interest.

e. Net income reported in the 2011 income statement is $30,000 before reflecting any of the above items.

Required:
Determine the proper amount of net income for 2011.

E 2–17
Cash versus accrual
accounting
● **LO8**

Stanley and Jones Lawn Service Company (S&J) maintains its books on a cash basis. However, the company recently borrowed $100,000 from a local bank and the bank requires S&J to provide annual financial statements prepared on an accrual basis. During 2011, the following cash flows were recorded:

Cash collected from customers		$320,000
Cash paid for:		
Salaries	$180,000	
Supplies	25,000	
Rent	12,000	
Insurance	6,000	
Miscellaneous	20,000	243,000
Net operating cash flow		$ 77,000

You are able to determine the following information about accounts receivable, prepaid expenses, and accrued liabilities:

	January 1, 2011	December 31, 2011
Accounts receivable	$32,000	$27,000
Prepaid insurance	–0–	2,000
Supplies	1,000	1,500
Accrued liabilities		
(for miscellaneous expenses)	2,400	3,400

In addition, you learn that the bank loan was dated September 30, 2011, with principal and interest at 6% due in one year. Depreciation on the company's equipment is $10,000 for the year.

Required:
Prepare an accrual basis income statement for 2011. (Ignore income taxes)

E 2–18
Cash versus accrual
accounting
● **LO8**

Haskins and Jones, Attorneys-at-Law, maintains its books on a cash basis. During 2011, the company collected $545,000 in fees from its clients and paid out $412,000 in expenses. You are able to determine the following information about accounts receivable, prepaid expenses, unearned fee revenue, and accrued liabilities:

	January 1, 2011	December 31, 2011
Accounts receivable	$62,000	$55,000
Prepaid insurance	4,500	6,000
Prepaid rent	9,200	8,200
Unearned fee revenue	9,200	11,000
Accrued liabilities		
(for various expenses)	12,200	15,600

In addition, 2011 depreciation expense on furniture and fixtures is $22,000.

Required:
Determine accrual basis net income for 2011.

E 2–19
Worksheet
● **Appendix A**

The December 31, 2011, unadjusted trial balance for the Wolkstein Drug Company is presented below. December 31 is the company's fiscal year-end.

Account Title	Debits	Credits
Cash	20,000	
Accounts receivable	35,000	
Allowance for uncollectible accounts		2,000
Prepaid rent	5,000	
Inventory	50,000	
Equipment	100,000	
Accumulated depreciation—equipment		30,000
Accounts payable		23,000
Wages payable		–0–
Common stock		100,000
Retained earnings		29,000
Sales revenue		323,000
Cost of goods sold	180,000	
Wage expense	71,000	
Rent expense	30,000	
Depreciation expense	–0–	
Utility expense	12,000	
Bad debt expense	4,000	
Totals	507,000	507,000

The following year-end adjusting entries are required:

a. Depreciation expense for the year on the equipment is $10,000.

b. The company has determined that the allowance for uncollectible accounts should be $5,000.

c. Accrued wages payable at year-end should be $4,000.

Required:

1. Prepare and complete a worksheet similar to Illustration 2A–1.

2. Prepare an income statement for 2011 and a balance sheet as of December 31, 2011.

E 2–20

Reversing entries

● **Appendix B**

The employees of Xitrex, Inc., are paid each Friday. The company's fiscal year-end is June 30, which falls on a Wednesday for the current year. Wages are earned evenly throughout the five-day workweek, and $10,000 will be paid on Friday, July 2.

Required:

1. Prepare an adjusting entry to record the accrued wages as of June 30, a reversing entry on July 1, and an entry to record the payment of wages on July 2.

2. Prepare journal entries to record the accrued wages as of June 30 and the payment of wages on July 2 assuming a reversing entry is not made.

E 2–21

Reversing entries

● **Appendix B**

Refer to Exercise 2–9 and respond to the following requirements.

Required:

1. If Microchip's accountant employed reversing entries for accruals, which adjusting entries would she likely reverse at the beginning of the following year?

2. Prepare the adjusting entries at the end of 2011 for the adjustments you identified in requirement 1.

3. Prepare the appropriate reversing entries at the beginning of 2012.

E 2–22

Reversing entries

● **Appendix B**

Refer to Exercise 2–9 and respond to the following requirements.

Required:

1. If Microchip's accountant employed reversing entries for prepayments, which transactions would be affected?

2. Prepare the original transactions creating the prepayments and the adjusting entries at the end of 2011 for the transactions you identified in requirement 1.

3. Prepare the appropriate reversing entries at the beginning of 2012.

E 2–23

Special journals

● **Appendix C**

The White Company's accounting system consists of a general journal (GJ), a cash receipts journal (CR), a cash disbursements journal (CD), a sales journal (SJ), and a purchases journal (PJ). For each of the following, indicate which journal should be used to record the transaction.

Transaction	Journal
1. Purchased merchandise on account.	_____
2. Collected an account receivable.	_____
3. Borrowed $20,000 and signed a note.	_____

(continued)

(concluded)

4. Recorded depreciation expense.   _____
5. Purchased equipment for cash.   _____
6. Sold merchandise for cash (the sale only, not the cost of the merchandise).   _____
7. Sold merchandise on credit (the sale only, not the cost of the merchandise).   _____
8. Recorded accrued wages payable.   _____
9. Paid employee wages.   _____
10. Sold equipment for cash.   _____
11. Sold equipment on credit.   _____
12. Paid a cash dividend to shareholders.   _____
13. Issued common stock in exchange for cash.   _____
14. Paid accounts payable.   _____

E 2–24
Special journals
● **Appendix C**

The accounting system of K and M Manufacturing consists of a general journal (GJ), a cash receipts journal (CR), a cash disbursements journal (CD), a sales journal (SJ), and a purchases journal (PJ). For each of the following, indicate which journal should be used to record the transaction.

Transaction	Journal
1. Paid interest on a loan.	_____
2. Recorded depreciation expense.	_____
3. Purchased furniture for cash.	_____
4. Purchased merchandise on account.	_____
5. Sold merchandise on credit (the sale only, not the cost of the merchandise).	_____
6. Sold merchandise for cash (the sale only, not the cost of the merchandise).	_____
7. Paid rent.	_____
8. Recorded accrued interest payable.	_____
9. Paid advertising bill.	_____
10. Recorded bad debt expense.	_____
11. Sold machinery on credit.	_____
12. Collected cash from customers on account.	_____
13. Paid employees wages.	_____
14. Collected interest on a note receivable.	_____

CPA REVIEW QUESTIONS

CPA Exam Questions

The following questions are used in the Kaplan CPA Review Course to study the accounting processing cycle while preparing for the CPA examination. Determine the response that best completes the statements or questions.

● **LO1**

1. JME Corporation bills its customers when services are rendered and recognizes revenue at the same time. This event causes an
   a. Increase in assets.
   b. Increase in net income.
   c. Increase in retained earnings.
   d. All of the above.

● **LO5**

2. Fay Corp. pays its outside salespersons fixed monthly salaries as well as commissions on net sales. Sales commissions are paid in the month following the month of sale, while the fixed salaries are expensed but considered advances against commissions. However, if salespersons' fixed salaries exceed their sales commissions earned for a month, such excess is not returned to the company. Pertinent data for the month of March for the three salespersons are as follows:

Salesperson	Fixed Salary	Net Sales	Commission Rate
A	$10,000	$ 200,000	4%
B	14,000	400,000	6%
C	18,000	600,000	6%
Totals	$42,000	$1,200,000	

What amount should Fay accrue as a debit to sales commissions expense and a credit to sales commissions payable at March 31?

a. $26,000
b. $28,000
c. $68,000
d. $70,000

● LO8

3. Compared to the accrual basis of accounting, the cash basis of accounting produces a lower amount of income by the net decrease during the accounting period of

	Accounts Receivable	Accrued Liabilities
a.	Yes	No
b.	No	Yes
c.	Yes	Yes
d.	No	No

● LO8

4. On April 1 Ivy Corp. began operating a service company with an initial cash investment by shareholders of $1,000,000. The company provided $3,200,000 of services in April and received full payment in May. Ivy also incurred expenses of $1,500,000 in April that were paid in June. During May, Ivy paid its shareholders cash dividends of $500,000. What was the company's income before income taxes for the two months ended May 31 under the following methods of accounting?

	Cash Basis	Accrual Basis
a.	$3,200,000	$1,700,000
b.	$2,700,000	$1,200,000
c.	$1,700,000	$1,700,000
d.	$3,200,000	$1,200,000

● LO8

5. Under East Co.'s accounting system, all insurance premiums paid are debited to prepaid insurance. During the year, East records monthly estimated charges to insurance expense with credits to prepaid insurance. Additional information for the year ended December 31 is as follows:

Prepaid insurance at January 1	$105,000
Insurance expense recognized during the year	437,500
Prepaid insurance at December 31	122,500

What was the total amount of cash paid by East for insurance premiums during the year?

a. $332,500
b. $420,000
c. $437,500
d. $455,000

PROBLEMS

An alternate exercise and problem set is available on the text website: www.mhhe.com/spiceland6e

P 2–1
Accounting cycle through unadjusted trial balance

● LO2 LO3

Halogen Laminated Products Company began business on January 1, 2011. During January, the following transactions occurred:

Jan. 1   Issued common stock in exchange for $100,000 cash.
2   Purchased inventory on account for $35,000 (the perpetual inventory system is used).
4   Paid an insurance company $2,400 for a one-year insurance policy.
10   Sold merchandise on account for $12,000. The cost of the merchandise was $7,000.
15   Borrowed $30,000 from a local bank and signed a note. Principal and interest at 10% is to be repaid in six months.
20   Paid employees $6,000 wages for the first half of the month.
22   Sold merchandise for $10,000 cash. The cost of the merchandise was $6,000.
24   Paid $15,000 to suppliers for the merchandise purchased on January 2.
26   Collected $6,000 on account from customers.
28   Paid $1,000 to the local utility company for January gas and electricity.
30   Paid $4,000 rent for the building. $2,000 was for January rent, and $2,000 for February rent.

Required:
1. Prepare general journal entries to record each transaction. Omit explanations.
2. Post the entries to T-accounts.
3. Prepare an unadjusted trial balance as of January 30, 2011.

P 2–2
Accounting cycle
through unadjusted
trial balance
● LO2 LO3

The following is the post-closing trial balance for the Whitlow Manufacturing Corporation as of December 31, 2010.

Account Title	Debits	Credits
Cash	5,000	
Accounts receivable	2,000	
Inventory	5,000	
Equipment	11,000	
Accumulated depreciation—equipment		3,500
Accounts payable		3,000
Common stock		10,000
Retained earnings		6,500
Sales revenue		–0–
Cost of goods sold	–0–	
Wage expense	–0–	
Rent expense	–0–	
Advertising expense	–0–	
Totals	23,000	23,000

The following transactions occurred during January 2011:

Jan.	1	Sold merchandise for cash, $3,500. The cost of the merchandise was $2,000. The company uses the perpetual inventory system.
	2	Purchased equipment on account for $5,500 from the Strong Company.
	4	Received a $150 bill from the local newspaper for an advertisement that appeared in the paper on January 2.
	8	Sold merchandise on account for $5,000. The cost of the merchandise was $2,800.
	10	Purchased merchandise on account for $9,500.
	13	Purchased equipment for cash, $800.
	16	Paid the entire amount due to the Strong Company.
	18	Received $4,000 from customers on account.
	20	Paid $800 to the owner of the building for January's rent.
	30	Paid employees $3,000 for salaries for the month of January.
	31	Paid a cash dividend of $1,000 to shareholders.

Required:
1. Set up T-accounts and enter the beginning balances as of January 1, 2011.
2. Prepare general journal entries to record each transaction. Omit explanations.
3. Post the entries to T-accounts.
4. Prepare an unadjusted trial balance as of January 31, 2011.

P 2–3
Adjusting entries
● LO4 LO5

Pastina Company manufactures and sells various types of pasta to grocery chains as private label brands. The company's fiscal year-end is December 31. The unadjusted trial balance as of December 31, 2011, appears below.

Account Title	Debits	Credits
Cash	30,000	
Accounts receivable	40,000	
Allowance for uncollectible accounts		3,000
Supplies	1,500	
Inventory	60,000	
Note receivable	20,000	

(continued)

(concluded)

Interest receivable	–0–	
Prepaid rent	2,000	
Prepaid insurance	–0–	
Equipment	80,000	
Accumulated depreciation—equipment		30,000
Accounts payable		28,000
Wages payable		–0–
Note payable		50,000
Interest payable		–0–
Unearned revenue		–0–
Common stock		60,000
Retained earnings		24,500
Sales revenue		148,000
Interest revenue		–0–
Cost of goods sold	70,000	
Wage expense	18,900	
Rent expense	11,000	
Depreciation expense	–0–	
Interest expense	–0–	
Supplies expense	1,100	
Insurance expense	6,000	
Bad debt expense	3,000	
Totals	343,500	343,500

Information necessary to prepare the year-end adjusting entries appears below.

1. Depreciation on the equipment for the year is $10,000.
2. The company estimates that of the $40,000 in accounts receivable outstanding at year-end, $5,500 probably will not be collected.
3. Employee wages are paid twice a month, on the 22nd for wages earned from the 1st through the 15th, and on the 7th of the following month for wages earned from the 16th through the end of the month. Wages earned from December 16 through December 31, 2011, were $1,500.
4. On October 1, 2011, Pastina borrowed $50,000 from a local bank and signed a note. The note requires interest to be paid annually on September 30 at 12%. The principal is due in 10 years.
5. On March 1, 2011, the company lent a supplier $20,000 and a note was signed requiring principal and interest at 8% to be paid on February 28, 2012.
6. On April 1, 2011, the company paid an insurance company $6,000 for a two-year fire insurance policy. The entire $6,000 was debited to insurance expense.
7. $800 of supplies remained on hand at December 31, 2011.
8. A customer paid Pastina $2,000 in December for 1,500 pounds of spaghetti to be manufactured and delivered in January 2012. Pastina credited sales revenue.
9. On December 1, 2011, $2,000 rent was paid to the owner of the building. The payment represented rent for December and January 2012, at $1,000 per month.

Required:
Prepare the necessary December 31, 2011, adjusting journal entries.

P 2–4
Accounting cycle; adjusting entries through post-closing trial balance

● LO3 LO5 through LO7

Refer to Problem 2–3 and complete the following steps:
1. Enter the unadjusted balances from the trial balance into T-accounts.
2. Post the adjusting entries prepared in Problem 2–3 to the accounts.
3. Prepare an adjusted trial balance.
4. Prepare an income statement and a statement of shareholders' equity for the year ended December 31, 2011, and a classified balance sheet as of December 31, 2011. Assume that no common stock was issued during the year and that $4,000 in cash dividends were paid to shareholders during the year.
5. Prepare closing entries and post to the accounts.
6. Prepare a post-closing trial balance.

P 2–5
Adjusting entries
● LO5

Howarth Company's fiscal year-end is December 31. Below are the unadjusted and adjusted trial balances for December 31, 2011.

Account Title	Unadjusted Debits	Unadjusted Credits	Adjusted Debits	Adjusted Credits
Cash	50,000		50,000	
Accounts receivable	35,000		35,000	
Allowance for uncollectible accounts		2,000		3,500
Prepaid rent	2,000		1,200	
Supplies	1,500		800	
Inventory	60,000		60,000	
Note receivable	30,000		30,000	
Interest receivable	–0–		1,500	
Equipment	45,000		45,000	
Accumulated depreciation—equipment		15,000		20,000
Accounts payable		32,000		32,000
Wages payable		–0–		6,200
Note payable		50,000		50,000
Interest payable		–0–		2,500
Unearned rent revenue		–0–		2,000
Common stock		46,000		46,000
Retained earnings		20,000		20,000
Sales revenue		244,000		244,000
Rent revenue		6,000		4,000
Interest revenue		–0–		1,500
Cost of goods sold	126,000		126,000	
Wage expense	45,000		51,200	
Rent expense	11,000		11,800	
Depreciation expense	–0–		5,000	
Supplies expense	1,100		1,800	
Interest expense	5,400		7,900	
Bad debt expense	3,000		4,500	
Totals	415,000	415,000	431,700	431,700

Required:
Prepare the adjusting journal entries that were made at December 31, 2011.

P 2–6
Accounting cycle
● LO2 through LO7

The general ledger of the Karlin Company, a consulting company, at January 1, 2011, contained the following account balances:

Account Title	Debits	Credits
Cash	30,000	
Accounts receivable	15,000	
Allowance for uncollectible accounts		500
Equipment	20,000	
Accumulated depreciation		6,000
Salaries payable		9,000
Common stock		40,000
Retained earnings		9,500
Total	65,000	65,000

The following is a summary of the transactions for the year:
a. Sales of services, $100,000, of which $30,000 was on credit.
b. Collected on accounts receivable, $27,300.
c. Issued shares of common stock in exchange for $10,000 in cash.
d. Paid salaries, $50,000 (of which $9,000 was for salaries payable).
e. Paid miscellaneous expenses, $24,000.
f. Purchased equipment for $15,000 in cash.
g. Paid $2,500 in cash dividends to shareholders.

Required:
1. Set up the necessary T-accounts and enter the beginning balances from the trial balance.
2. Prepare a general journal entry for each of the summary transactions listed above.
3. Post the journal entries to the accounts.
4. Prepare an unadjusted trial balance.
5. Prepare and post adjusting journal entries. Accrued salaries at year-end amounted to $1,000. Depreciation for the year on the equipment is $2,000. The allowance for uncollectible accounts is estimated to be $1,500.
6. Prepare an adjusted trial balance.
7. Prepare an income statement for 2011 and a balance sheet as of December 31, 2011.
8. Prepare and post closing entries.
9. Prepare a post-closing trial balance.

P 2–7
Adjusting entries and income effects
● LO4 LO5

The information necessary for preparing the 2011 year-end adjusting entries for Vito's Pizza Parlor appears below. Vito's fiscal year-end is December 31.
a. On July 1, 2011, purchased $10,000 of **IBM Corporation** bonds at face value. The bonds pay interest twice a year on January 1 and July 1. The annual interest rate is 12%.
b. Vito's depreciable equipment has a cost of $30,000, a five-year life, and no salvage value. The equipment was purchased in 2009. The straight-line depreciation method is used.
c. On November 1, 2011, the bar area was leased to Jack Donaldson for one year. Vito's received $6,000 representing the first six months' rent and credited unearned rent revenue.
d. On April 1, 2011, the company paid $2,400 for a two-year fire and liability insurance policy and debited insurance expense.
e. On October 1, 2011, the company borrowed $20,000 from a local bank and signed a note. Principal and interest at 12% will be paid on September 30, 2012.
f. At year-end there is a $1,800 debit balance in the supplies (asset) account. Only $700 of supplies remain on hand.

Required:
1. Prepare the necessary adjusting journal entries at December 31, 2011.
2. Determine the amount by which net income would be misstated if Vito's failed to make these adjusting entries. (Ignore income tax expense.)

P 2–8
Adjusting entries
● LO4 LO5

Excalibur Corporation manufactures and sells video games for personal computers. The unadjusted trial balance as of December 31, 2011, appears below. December 31 is the company's fiscal year-end. The company uses the perpetual inventory system.

Account Title	Debits	Credits
Cash	23,300	
Accounts receivable	32,500	
Allowance for uncollectible accounts		100
Supplies	–0–	
Prepaid rent	–0–	
Inventory	65,000	
Equipment	75,000	
Accumulated depreciation—equipment		10,000
Accounts payable		26,000
Wages payable		3,000
Note payable		30,000
Common stock		80,000
Retained earnings		16,050
Sales revenue		180,000
Cost of goods sold	95,000	
Interest expense	–0–	
Wage expense	32,350	
Rent expense	14,000	
Supplies expense	2,000	
Utility expense	6,000	
Bad debt expense	–0–	
Totals	345,150	345,150

Information necessary to prepare the year-end adjusting entries appears below.
1. The equipment was purchased in 2009 and is being depreciated using the straight-line method over an eight-year useful life with no salvage value.
2. Accrued wages at year-end should be $4,500.

3. The company estimates that 2% of all year-end accounts receivable will probably not be collected.

4. The company borrowed $30,000 on September 1, 2011. The principal is due to be repaid in 10 years. Interest is payable twice a year on each August 31 and February 28 at an annual rate of 10%.

5. The company debits supplies expense when supplies are purchased. Supplies on hand at year-end cost $500.

6. Prepaid rent at year-end should be $1,000.

Required:
Prepare the necessary December 31, 2011, adjusting entries.

P 2–9
Accounting cycle;
unadjusted trial
balance through
closing

● LO3 LO4 LO5
LO7

e**X**cel

The unadjusted trial balance as of December 31, 2011, for the Bagley Consulting Company appears below. December 31 is the company's fiscal year-end.

Account Title	Debits	Credits
Cash	8,000	
Accounts receivable	9,000	
Allowance for uncollectible accounts		50
Prepaid insurance	3,000	
Land	200,000	
Buildings	50,000	
Accumulated depreciation—buildings		20,000
Equipment	100,000	
Accumulated depreciation—equipment		40,000
Accounts payable		35,000
Salaries payable		–0–
Unearned rent revenue		–0–
Common stock		200,000
Retained earnings		56,450
Sales revenue		90,000
Interest revenue		3,000
Rent revenue		7,500
Salaries expense	37,000	
Bad debt expense	–0–	
Depreciation expense	–0–	
Insurance expense	–0–	
Utility expense	30,000	
Maintenance expense	15,000	
Totals	452,000	452,000

Required:
1. Enter the account balances in T-accounts.
2. From the trial balance and information given, prepare adjusting entries and post to the accounts.
   a. The buildings have an estimated useful life of 50 years with no salvage value. The company uses the straight-line depreciation method.
   b. The equipment is depreciated at 10 percent of original cost per year.
   c. Prepaid insurance expired during the year, $1,500.
   d. It is estimated that 10% of the accounts receivable balance will be uncollectible.
   e. Accrued salaries at year-end, $1,500.
   f. Unearned rent revenue at year-end should be $1,200.
3. Prepare an adjusted trial balance.
4. Prepare closing entries.
5. Prepare a post-closing trial balance.

P 2–10
Accrual
accounting;
financial statements

● LO4 LO6 LO8

McGuire Corporation began operations in 2011. The company purchases computer equipment from manufacturers and then sells to retail stores. During 2011, the bookkeeper used a check register to record all cash receipts and cash disbursements. No other journals were used. The following is a recap of the cash receipts and disbursements made during the year.

Cash receipts:	
Sale of common stock	$ 50,000
Collections from customers	320,000
Borrowed from local bank on April 1, note signed requiring principal and interest at 12% to be paid on March 31, 2012	40,000
Total cash receipts	$410,000

(continued)

(concluded)

Cash disbursements:	
Purchase of merchandise	$220,000
Payment of salaries	80,000
Purchase of equipment	30,000
Payment of rent on building	14,000
Miscellaneous expenses	10,000
Total cash disbursements	$354,000

You are called in to prepare financial statements at December 31, 2011. The following additional information was provided to you:

1. Customers owed the company $22,000 at year-end. Of this amount, it was anticipated that $3,000 would probably not be collected. There were no actual bad debt write-offs in 2011.

2. At year-end, $30,000 was still due to suppliers of merchandise purchased on credit.

3. At year-end, merchandise inventory costing $50,000 still remained on hand.

4. Salaries owed to employees at year-end amounted to $5,000.

5. On December 1, $3,000 in rent was paid to the owner of the building used by McGuire. This represented rent for the months of December through February.

6. The equipment, which has a 10-year life and no salvage value, was purchased on January 1, 2011. Straight-line depreciation is used.

Required:
Prepare an income statement for 2011 and a balance sheet as of December 31, 2011.

P 2–11
Cash versus accrual accounting
● LO8

Selected balance sheet information for the Wolf Company at November 30, and December 31, 2011, is presented below. The company uses the perpetual inventory system and all sales to customers are made on credit.

	Nov. 30		Dec. 31	
	Dr.	Cr.	Dr.	Cr.
Accounts receivable	10,000		3,000	
Prepaid insurance	5,000		7,500	
Inventory	7,000		6,000	
Accounts payable		12,000		15,000
Wages payable		5,000		3,000

The following cash flow information also is available:

a. Cash collected from credit customers—$80,000.

b. Cash paid for insurance—$5,000.

c. Cash paid to suppliers of inventory—$60,000 (the entire accounts payable amounts relate to inventory purchases).

d. Cash paid to employees for wages—$10,000.

Required:
1. Determine the following for the month of December:
   a. Sales revenue
   b. Cost of goods sold
   c. Insurance expense
   d. Wage expense
2. Prepare a summary journal entry to record the month's sales and cost of those sales.

P 2–12
Cash versus accrual accounting
● LO8

Zambrano Wholesale Corporation maintains its records on a cash basis. At the end of each year the company's accountant obtains the necessary information to prepare accrual basis financial statements. The following cash flows occurred during the year ended December 31, 2011:

Cash receipts:	
From customers	$675,000
Interest on note	4,000
Loan from a local bank	100,000
Total cash receipts	$779,000
Cash disbursements:	
Purchase of merchandise	$390,000
Annual insurance payment	6,000
Payment of salaries	210,000
Dividends paid to shareholders	10,000
Annual rent payment	24,000
Total cash disbursements	$640,000

Selected balance sheet information:

	12/31/10	12/31/11
Cash	$25,000	$164,000
Accounts receivable	62,000	92,000
Inventory	80,000	62,000
Prepaid insurance	2,500	?
Prepaid rent	11,000	?
Interest receivable	3,000	?
Note receivable	50,000	50,000
Equipment	100,000	100,000
Accumulated depreciation—equipment	(40,000)	(50,000)
Accounts payable (for merchandise)	110,000	122,000
Salaries payable	20,000	24,000
Note payable	–0–	100,000
Interest payable	–0–	?

Additional information:

1. On March 31, 2010, Zambrano lent a customer $50,000. Interest at 8% is payable annually on each March 31. Principal is due in 2014.

2. The annual insurance payment is made in advance on April 30.

3. On October 31, 2011, Zambrano borrowed $100,000 from a local bank. Principal and interest at 6% are due on October 31, 2012.

4. Annual rent on the company's facilities is paid in advance on June 30.

Required:

1. Prepare an accrual basis income statement for 2011 (ignore income taxes).

2. Determine the following balance sheet amounts on December 31, 2011:

    a. Prepaid insurance

    b. Prepaid rent

    c. Interest receivable

    d. Interest payable

P 2–13
Worksheet
● Appendix A

Using the information from Problem 2–8, prepare and complete a worksheet similar to Illustration 2A–1. Use the information in the worksheet to prepare an income statement and a statement of shareholders' equity for 2011 and a balance sheet as of December 31, 2011. Cash dividends paid to shareholders during the year amounted to $6,000. Also prepare the necessary closing entries assuming that adjusting entries have been correctly posted to the accounts.

BROADEN YOUR PERSPECTIVE

Apply your critical-thinking ability to the knowledge you've gained. These cases will provide you an opportunity to develop your research, analysis, judgment, and communication skills. You also will work with other students, integrate what you've learned, apply it in real world situations, and consider its global and ethical ramifications. This practice will broaden your knowledge and further develop your decision-making abilities.

Judgment
Case 2–1
Cash versus
accrual accounting;
adjusting entries;
Chapters 1 and 2
● LO4 LO8

You have recently been hired by Davis & Company, a small public accounting firm. One of the firm's partners, Alice Davis, has asked you to deal with a disgruntled client, Mr. Sean Pitt, owner of the city's largest hardware store. Mr. Pitt is applying to a local bank for a substantial loan to remodel his store. The bank requires accrual based financial statements but Mr. Pitt has always kept the company's records on a cash basis. He does not see the purpose of accrual based statements. His most recent outburst went something like this: "After all, I collect cash from customers, pay my bills in cash, and I am going to pay the bank loan with cash. And, I already show my building and equipment as assets and depreciate them. I just don't understand the problem."

Required:

1. Explain the difference between a cash basis and an accrual basis measure of performance.

2. Why, in most cases, does accrual basis net income provide a better measure of performance than net operating cash flow?

3. Explain the purpose of adjusting entries as they relate to the difference between cash and accrual accounting.

Judgment Case 2–2

Cash versus accrual accounting

● LO8

Refer to Case 2–1 above. Mr. Pitt has relented and agrees to provide you with the information necessary to convert his cash basis financial statements to accrual basis statements. He provides you with the following transaction information for the fiscal year ending December 31, 2011:

1. A comprehensive insurance policy requires a payment every year for the upcoming year. The last payment of $12,000 was made on September 1, 2011.

2. Mr. Pitt allows customers to pay using a credit card. At the end of the current year, various credit card companies owed Mr. Pitt $6,500. At the end of last year, customer credit card charges outstanding were $5,000.

3. Employees are paid once a month, on the 10th of the month following the work period. Cash disbursements to employees were $8,200 and $7,200 for January 10, 2012, and January 10, 2011, respectively.

4. Utility bills outstanding totaled $1,200 at the end of 2011 and $900 at the end of 2010.

5. A physical count of inventory is always taken at the end of the fiscal year. The merchandise on hand at the end of 2011 cost $35,000. At the end of 2010, inventory on hand cost $32,000.

6. At the end of 2010, Mr. Pitt did not have any bills outstanding to suppliers of merchandise. However, at the end of 2011, he owed suppliers $4,000.

Required:

1. Mr. Pitt's 2011 cash basis net income (including depreciation expense) is $26,000. Determine net income applying the accrual accounting model.

2. Explain the effect on Mr. Pitt's balance sheet of converting from cash to accrual. That is, would assets, liabilities, and owner's equity be higher or lower and by what amounts?

Communication Case 2–3

Adjusting entries

● LO4

"I don't understand," complained Chris, who responded to your bulletin board posting in your responsibilities as a tutor. The complaint was in response to your statements that recording adjusting entries is a critical step in the accounting processing cycle, and the two major classifications of adjusting entries are prepayments and accruals.

Required:

Respond to Chris.

1. When do prepayments occur? Accruals?

2. Describe the appropriate adjusting entry for prepaid expenses and for unearned revenues. What is the effect on net income, assets, liabilities, and shareholders' equity of not recording a required adjusting entry for prepayments?

3. Describe the required adjusting entry for accrued liabilities and for accrued receivables. What is the effect on net income, assets, liabilities, and shareholders' equity of not recording a required adjusting entry for accruals?

3

The Balance Sheet and Financial Disclosures

|||||||||||||||||||||||||||||||||||||||||||||||||||||||||||||||

/// OVERVIEW

Chapter 1 stressed the importance of the financial statements in helping investors and creditors predict future cash flows. The balance sheet, along with accompanying disclosures, provides relevant information useful in helping investors and creditors not only to predict future cash flows, but also to make the related assessments of liquidity and long-term solvency.

The purpose of this chapter is to provide an overview of the balance sheet and financial disclosures and to explore how this information is used by decision makers.

/// LEARNING OBJECTIVES

After studying this chapter, you should be able to:

- **LO1** Describe the purpose of the balance sheet and understand its usefulness and limitations. (page 115)
- **LO2** Distinguish among current and noncurrent assets and liabilities. (page 116)
- **LO3** Identify and describe the various balance sheet asset classifications. (page 117)
- **LO4** Identify and describe the two balance sheet liability classifications. (page 120)
- **LO5** Explain the purpose of financial statement disclosures. (page 124)
- **LO6** Explain the purpose of the management discussion and analysis disclosure. (page 128)
- **LO7** Explain the purpose of an audit and describe the content of the audit report. (page 129)
- **LO8** Describe the techniques used by financial analysts to transform financial information into forms more useful for analysis. (page 132)
- **LO9** Identify and calculate the common liquidity and financing ratios used to assess risk. (page 133)
- **LO10** Discuss the primary differences between U.S. GAAP and IFRS with respect to the balance sheet, financial disclosures, and segment reporting. (pages 122 and 141)

FINANCIAL REPORTING CASE

What's It Worth?

"I can't believe it. Why don't you accountants prepare financial statements that are relevant?" Your friend Jerry is a finance major and is constantly badgering you about what he perceives to be a lack of relevance of financial statements prepared according to generally accepted accounting principles. "For example, take a look at this balance sheet for **Electronic Arts** that I just downloaded off the Internet. Electronic Arts is the company in California that produces all those cool video games like Battlefield 2, NBA Live, and Madden NFL. Anyway, the shareholders' equity of the company according to the 2009 balance sheet is about $3 billion. But if you multiply the number of outstanding shares by the most recent stock price per share, the company's market value is four times that amount. I thought financial statements were supposed to help investors and creditors value a company." You decide to look at the company's balance sheet and try to set Jerry straight.

By the time you finish this chapter, you should be able to respond appropriately to the questions posed in this case. Compare your response to the solution provided at the end of the chapter.

QUESTIONS ///

1. Respond to Jerry's criticism that shareholders' equity does not represent the market value of the company. What information does the balance sheet provide? (page 115)

2. The usefulness of the balance sheet is enhanced by classifying assets and liabilities according to common characteristics. What are the classifications used in Electronic Arts' balance sheets and what elements do those categories include? (page 116)

ELECTRONIC ARTS INC.
AND SUBSIDIARIES
Consolidated Balance Sheets
(In millions, except par value data)

Assets	March 31, 2009	March 31, 2008
Current assets:		
Cash and cash equivalents	$1,621	$1,553
Short-term investments	534	734
Marketable equity securities	365	729
Receivables, net of allowances of $217 and $238, respectively	116	306
Inventories	217	168
Deferred income taxes, net	51	145
Other current assets	216	290
Total current assets	3,120	3,925
Property and equipment, net	354	396
Goodwill	807	1,152
Other intangibles, net	221	265
Deferred income taxes, net	61	164
Other assets	115	157
Total Assets	$4,678	$6,059
Liabilities and Stockholders' Equity		
Current liabilities:		
Accounts payable	$ 152	$ 182
Accrued and other current liabilities	723	730
Deferred net revenue (packaged goods and digital content)	261	387
Total current liabilities	1,136	1,299
Income tax obligations	268	319
Deferred income taxes, net	42	5
Other liabilities	98	97
Total liabilities	1,544	1,720
Commitments and contingencies (See Note 10)		
Stockholders' equity:		
Preferred stock, $0.01 par value. 10 shares authorized	—	—
Common stock, $0.01 par value. 1,000 shares authorized; 323 and 318 shares issued and outstanding, respectively	3	3
Paid-in capital	2,142	1,864
Retained earnings	800	1,888
Accumulated other comprehensive income	189	584
Total stockholders' equity	3,134	4,339
Total Liabilities and Stockholders' Equity	$4,678	$6,059

The balance sheet, along with accompanying disclosures, provides a wealth of information to external decision makers. The information provided is useful not only in the prediction of future cash flows but also in the related assessments of liquidity and long-term solvency.

This chapter begins our discussion of the financial statements by providing an overview of the balance sheet and the financial disclosures that accompany the financial statements. The first part of the chapter describes the usefulness and limitations of the balance sheet and illustrates the content of the statement. The second part illustrates financial statement disclosures presented to external users in addition to the basic financial statements. In the third part we discuss how this information can be used by decision makers to assess business risk. That discussion introduces some common financial ratios used to assess liquidity and long-term solvency.

Chapter 4 continues this discussion of the financial statements with its coverage of the income statement and the statement of cash flows.

THE BALANCE SHEET

The purpose of the balance sheet, sometimes referred to as the statement of financial position, is to report a company's financial position on a particular date. Unlike the income statement, which is a change statement reporting events that occurred *during a period of time,* the balance sheet presents an organized array of assets, liabilities, and shareholders' equity *at a point in time.* It is a freeze frame or snapshot of financial position at the end of a particular day marking the end of an accounting period.

● LO1

Usefulness and Limitations

An important limitation of the balance sheet is that *it does not portray the market value of the entity* as a going concern, nor its liquidation value. Many assets, like land and buildings for example, are measured at their historical costs rather than their fair values. Relatedly, many company resources including its trained employees, its experienced management team, and its reputation are not recorded as assets at all. Also, many items and amounts reported in the balance sheet are heavily reliant on estimates rather than determinable amounts. For example, companies estimate the amount of receivables they will be able to actually collect and the amount of warranty costs they will eventually incur for products already sold. For these and other reasons, a company's book value, its assets minus its liabilities as shown in the balance sheet, usually will not directly measure the company's market value (number of shares of common stock outstanding multiplied by the price per share).

> **FINANCIAL Reporting Case**
>
> Q1, p. 113
>
> **Assets minus liabilities, measured according to GAAP, is not likely to be representative of the market value of the entity.**

Consider for example that early in 2009, the 30 companies constituting the Dow Jones Industrial Average had an average ratio of market value to book value of approximately 2.5. The ratio for **IBM**, one of the world's largest technology companies, was approximately 9.0. Can you think of a reason why IBM's market value would be nine times higher than its book value? A significant reason is the way we account for research and development costs. IBM invests considerable amounts, over $6 billion in 2008 alone, on research and development of new products. Quite a few of these products that the company has developed over the years have been market successes, and yet the costs to discover and develop them are not represented in the balance sheet. We expense research and development costs in the period incurred rather than capitalize them as assets for the balance sheet.

During the financial crisis of 2008–2009 we saw stock prices plummet resulting in historic declines in the market to book ratio for most companies. For example, in 2007 the average ratio of market to book for the 30 Dow Jones Industrial Average companies was 4.46, almost twice the early 2009 average. Particularly hard hit were financial services companies. Early in 2009, both **Bank of America** and **Citigroup** had market to book ratios significantly less than 1.0. Later in 2009, Citigroup was replaced and is no longer one of the Dow Jones Industrial 30 companies.

Despite these limitations, the balance sheet does have significant value. An important feature of the statement is that it describes many of the resources a company has available for generating future cash flows. Another way the statement's content is informative is in combination with income statement items. For example, the relation between net income and assets provides a measure of return that is useful in predicting future profitability. In fact, many of the amounts reported in either of the two statements are more informative when viewed relative to an amount from the other statement.[1]

> **The balance sheet provides information useful for assessing future cash flows, liquidity, and long-term solvency.**

The balance sheet does not simply list assets and liabilities. Instead, assets and liabilities are classified (grouped) according to common characteristics. These classifications, which we explore in the next section, along with related disclosure notes, help the balance sheet to provide additional important information about liquidity and long-term solvency. Liquidity refers to the period of time before an asset is converted to cash or until a liability is paid. This information is useful in assessing a company's ability to pay its *current* obligations.

---

[1]We explore some of these relationships in Chapter 5.

Long-term solvency refers to the riskiness of a company with regard to the amount of liabilities in its capital structure. Other things being equal, the risk to an investor or creditor increases as the percentage of liabilities, relative to equity, increases.

Solvency also provides information about *financial flexibility*—the ability of a company to alter cash flows in order to take advantage of unexpected investment opportunities and needs. For example, the higher the percentage of a company's liabilities to its equity, the more difficult it typically will be to borrow additional funds either to take advantage of a promising investment opportunity or to meet obligations. In general, the less financial flexibility, the more risk there is that an enterprise will fail. In a subsequent section of this chapter, we introduce some common ratios used to assess liquidity and long-term solvency.

In summary, even though the balance sheet does not *directly measure* the market value of the entity, it provides valuable information that can be used to help *judge* market value.

Classifications

FINANCIAL Reporting Case

Q2, p. 113

The key classification of assets and liabilities in the balance sheet is the current versus noncurrent distinction.

The usefulness of the balance sheet is enhanced when assets and liabilities are grouped according to common characteristics. *The broad distinction made in the balance sheet is the current versus noncurrent classification of both assets and liabilities.* The remainder of Part A provides an overview of the balance sheet. We discuss each of the three primary elements of the balance sheet (assets, liabilities, and shareholders' equity) in the order they are reported in the statement as well as the classifications typically made within the elements. The balance sheet elements were defined in Chapter 1 as follows:

Assets are probable future economic benefits obtained or controlled by a particular entity as a result of past transactions or events.

GRAPHIC 3–1 Classification of Elements within a Balance Sheet

Assets
Current assets
Investments
Property, plant, and equipment
Intangible assets
Other assets
Liabilities
Current liabilities
Long-term liabilities
Shareholders' Equity
Paid-in capital
Retained earnings

● LO2

Current assets include cash and all other assets expected to become cash or be consumed within one year or the *operating cycle,* whichever is longer.

Liabilities are probable future sacrifices of economic benefits arising from present obligations of a particular entity to transfer assets or provide services to other entities in the future as a result of past transactions or events.

Equity (or net assets), called **shareholders' equity** or **stockholders' equity** for a corporation, is the residual interest in the assets of an entity that remains after deducting liabilities.

Graphic 3–1 lists the balance sheet elements along with their subclassifications.

We intentionally avoid detailed discussion of the question of valuation in order to focus on an overview of the balance sheet. In later chapters we look closer at the nature and valuation of the specific assets and liabilities.

Assets

CURRENT ASSETS. Current assets include cash and other assets that are reasonably expected to be converted to cash or consumed within the coming year, or within the normal operating cycle of the business if that's longer than one year. The **operating cycle** for a typical manufacturing company refers to the period of time necessary to convert cash to raw materials, raw materials to a finished product, the finished product to receivables, and then finally receivables back to cash. This concept is illustrated in Graphic 3–2.

In some businesses, such as shipbuilding or distilleries, the operating cycle extends far beyond one year. For example, if it takes two years to build an oil-carrying supertanker, then the shipbuilder will classify as current those assets that will be converted to cash or consumed within two years. But for most businesses the operating cycle will be shorter than one year. In these situations the one-year convention is used to classify both assets and liabilities. Where a company has no clearly defined operating cycle, the one-year convention is used.

Graphic 3–3 presents the current asset sections of **Dell Inc.**'s 2009 and 2008 balance sheets (statements of financial position) that also can be located in the company's financial statements in Appendix B at the back of the text. In keeping with common practice, the individual current assets are listed in the order of their liquidity (nearness to cash).

Cash and Cash Equivalents.   The most liquid asset, cash, is listed first. Cash includes cash on hand and in banks that is available for use in the operations of the business and such items as bank drafts, cashier's checks, and money orders. Cash equivalents frequently include certain negotiable items such as commercial paper, money market funds, and U.S. treasury bills. These are highly liquid investments that can be quickly converted into cash. Most companies draw a distinction between investments classified as cash equivalents and the next category of current assets, short-term investments, according to the scheduled maturity of the investment. It is common practice to classify investments that have a maturity date of three months or less from the date of purchase as cash equivalents. **Dell Inc.**'s policy follows this practice and is disclosed in the summary of significant accounting policies disclosure note. The portion of the note from the company's 2009 financial statements is shown in Graphic 3–4.

● LO3

GRAPHIC 3–2   Operating Cycle of a Typical Manufacturing Company

GRAPHIC 3–3
Current Assets—
Dell Inc.

Real World Financials

(In millions)	January 30, 2009	February 1, 2008
Assets		
Current assets:		
Cash and cash equivalents	$ 8,352	$ 7,764
Short-term investments	740	208
Accounts receivable, net	4,731	5,961
Financing receivables, net	1,712	1,732
Inventories, net	867	1,180
Other current assets	3,749	3,035
Total current assets	20,151	19,880

GRAPHIC 3–4
Disclosure of Cash Equivalents—Dell Inc.

Real World Financials

Note 1—Description of Business and Summary of Significant Accounting Policies
Cash and Cash Equivalents
All highly liquid investments, including credit card receivables, due from banks, with original maturities of three months or less at date of purchase are carried at cost and are considered to be cash equivalents. All other investments not considered to be cash equivalents are separately categorized as investments.

Cash that is restricted for a special purpose and not available for current operations should not be classified as a current asset. For example, if cash is being accumulated to repay a debt due in five years, the cash is classified as investments, a noncurrent asset.[2]

Short-Term Investments.   Liquid investments not classified as cash equivalents are reported as either short-term investments, sometimes called *temporary investments* or *short-term marketable securities.* Investments in stock and debt securities of other corporations are included as short-term investments *if* the company has the ability and intent to sell those securities within the next 12 months or operating cycle, whichever is longer.

Investments are classified as current if management has the ability and intent to liquidate the investment in the near term.

---
[2]If the debt is due in the next year and classified as a current liability, then the cash also would be classified as current.

If, for example, a company owns 1,000 shares of **IBM Corporation** stock and intends to hold those shares for several years, the stock is a long-term investment and should be classified as a noncurrent asset, investments.

For reporting purposes, investments in debt and equity securities are classified in one of three categories: (1) held to maturity, (2) trading securities, or (3) securities available for sale. We discuss these different categories and their accounting treatment in Chapter 12.

Accounts Receivable. Accounts receivable result from the sale of goods or services on credit. Notice in Graphic 3–3 that Dell's accounts receivable and financing receivables (discussed in Chapter 7) are valued net, that is, less the amount not expected to be collected. Accounts receivable often are referred to as *trade receivables* because they arise in the course of a company's normal trade. *Nontrade receivables* result from loans or advances by the company to individuals and other entities. When receivables are supported by a formal agreement or note that specifies payment terms they are called notes receivable.

Accounts receivable usually are due in 30 to 60 days, depending on the terms offered to customers and are, therefore, classified as current assets. Any receivable, regardless of the source, not expected to be collected within one year or the operating cycle, whichever is longer, is classified as a noncurrent asset, investments.

Inventories. Inventories include goods awaiting sale (finished goods), goods in the course of production (work in process), and goods to be consumed directly or indirectly in production (raw materials). Inventory for a wholesale or retail company consists only of finished goods, but the inventory of a manufacturer will include all three types of goods. Occasionally, a manufacturing company will report all three types of inventory directly in the balance sheet. More often, only the total amount of inventories is shown in the balance sheet and the balances of each type are shown in a disclosure note. For example, the note shown in Graphic 3–5 lists the components of inventory in the 2009 financial statements of **Dell Inc.**

Inventories consist of assets that a retail or wholesale company acquires for resale or goods that manufacturers produce for sale.

GRAPHIC 3–5

Inventories Disclosure—Dell Inc.

Real World Financials

Note 12—Supplemental Consolidated Financial Information (in part)		
	January 30, 2009	February 1, 2008
Inventories, net:		
Production materials	$454	$ 714
Work-in-process	150	144
Finished goods	263	322
Total	$867	$1,180

Inventories are reported as current assets because they normally are sold within the operating cycle.

Prepaid Expenses. Recall from Chapter 2 that a prepaid expense represents an asset recorded when an expense is paid in advance, creating benefits beyond the current period. Examples are prepaid rent and prepaid insurance. Even though these assets are not converted to cash, they would involve an outlay of cash if not prepaid.

Whether a prepaid expense is current or noncurrent depends on when its benefits will be realized. For example, if rent on an office building were prepaid for one year, then the entire prepayment is classified as a current asset. However, if rent were prepaid for a period extending beyond the coming year, a portion of the prepayment is classified as an other asset, a noncurrent asset.[3] **Dell Inc.** includes prepaid expenses in the other current assets category. Other current assets also include assets—such as nontrade receivables—that, because their amounts are not material, did not warrant separate disclosure.

When assets are expected to provide economic benefits beyond the next year, or operating cycle, they are reported as *noncurrent assets*. Typical classifications of noncurrent assets are (1) investments, (2) property, plant, and equipment, and (3) intangible assets.

---

[3]Companies often include prepayments for benefits extending beyond one year as current assets when the amounts are not material.

INVESTMENTS.   Most companies occasionally acquire assets that are not used directly in the operations of the business. These assets include investments in equity and debt securities of other corporations, land held for speculation, noncurrent receivables, and cash set aside for special purposes (such as for future plant expansion). These assets are classified as noncurrent because management does not intend to convert the assets into cash in the next year (or the operating cycle if that's longer).

Investments **are assets not used directly in operations.**

PROPERTY, PLANT, AND EQUIPMENT.   Virtually all companies own assets classified as **property, plant, and equipment.** The common characteristics these assets share are that they are *tangible, long-lived,* and *used in the operations of the business.* Property, plant, and equipment, along with intangible assets, often are the primary revenue-generating assets of the business.

Tangible, long-lived assets used in the operations of the business are classified as *property, plant, and equipment.*

Property, plant, and equipment includes land, buildings, equipment, machinery, and furniture, as well as natural resources, such as mineral mines, timber tracts, and oil wells. These various assets usually are reported as a single amount in the balance sheet, with details provided in a note. They are reported at original cost less accumulated depreciation (or depletion for natural resources) to date. Quite often, a company will present only the net amount of property, plant, and equipment in the balance sheet and provide details in a disclosure note. Land often is listed as a separate item in this classification because it has an unlimited useful life and thus is not depreciated.

INTANGIBLE ASSETS.   Some assets used in the operations of a business have no physical substance. These are appropriately called **intangible assets.** Generally, these represent the ownership of an exclusive right to something such as a product, a process, or a name. This right can be a valuable resource in generating future revenues. Patents, copyrights, and franchises are examples. They are reported in the balance sheet net of accumulated amortization. Some companies include intangible assets as part of property, plant, and equipment, while others report them either in a separate intangible asset classification or as other noncurrent assets.

Intangible assets **generally represent exclusive rights that a company can use to generate future revenues.**

Quite often, much of the value of intangibles is not reported in the balance sheet. For example, it would not be unusual for the historical cost of a patent to be significantly lower than its market value. As we discuss in Chapter 10, for internally developed intangibles, the costs that are included as part of historical cost are limited. Specifically, none of the research and development costs incurred in developing the intangible are included in cost.

OTHER ASSETS.   Balance sheets often include a catch-all classification of noncurrent assets called **other assets.** This classification includes long-term prepaid expenses, called *deferred charges,* and any noncurrent asset not falling in one of the other classifications. For instance, if a company's noncurrent investments are not material in amount, they might be reported in the other asset classification rather than in a separate investments category.

Graphic 3–6 reproduces the noncurrent asset section of **Dell Inc.**'s 2009 and 2008 balance sheets. For Dell, noncurrent assets include property, plant, and equipment, investments, long-term financing receivables, goodwill (an intangible asset), purchased intangible assets, and other noncurrent assets.

	January 30, 2009	February 1, 2008
(In millions)		
Assets		
Property, plant, and equipment, net	2,277	2,668
Investments	454	1,560
Long-term financing receivables, net	500	407
Goodwill	1,737	1,648
Purchased intangible assets, net	724	780
Other noncurrent assets	657	618

GRAPHIC 3–6

Noncurrent Assets— Dell Inc.

Real World Financials

We've seen how assets are grouped into current and noncurrent categories and that noncurrent assets always are subclassified further. Let's now turn our attention to liabilities. These, too, are separated into current and noncurrent (long-term) categories.

Liabilities

● LO4

Liabilities represent obligations to other entities. The information value of reporting these amounts is enhanced by classifying them as current liabilities and long-term liabilities. Graphic 3–7 shows the liability section of Dell Inc.'s 2009 and 2008 balance sheets.

GRAPHIC 3–7

Liabilities—Dell Inc.

Real World Financials

(In millions)	January 30, 2009	February 1, 2008
Liabilities		
Current liabilities:		
Short-term debt	$ 113	$ 225
Accounts payable	8,309	11,492
Accrued and other	3,788	4,323
Short-term deferred service revenue	2,649	2,486
Total current liabilities	14,859	18,526
Long-term debt	1,898	362
Long-term deferred service revenue	3,000	2,774
Other noncurrent liabilities	2,472	2,070
Total liabilities	22,229	23,732

Current liabilities are expected to be satisfied within one year or the operating cycle, whichever is longer.

CURRENT LIABILITIES.   Current liabilities are those obligations that are expected to be satisfied through the use of current assets or the creation of other current liabilities. So, this classification includes all liabilities that are expected to be satisfied within one year or the operating cycle, whichever is longer. An exception is a liability that management intends to refinance on a long-term basis. For example, if management intends to refinance a six-month note payable by substituting a two-year note payable and has the ability to do so, then the liability would not be classified as current even though it's due within the coming year. This exception is discussed in more detail in Chapter 13.

Current liabilities usually include *accounts* and *notes payable, unearned revenues, accrued liabilities,* and the *current maturities of long-term debt.*

The most common current liabilities are accounts payable, notes payable (short-term borrowings), unearned revenues, accrued liabilities, and the currently maturing portion of long-term debt. **Accounts payable** are obligations to suppliers of merchandise or of services purchased on open account, with payment usually due in 30 to 60 days. **Notes payable** are written promises to pay cash at some future date (I.O.U.s). Unlike accounts payable, notes usually require the payment of explicit interest in addition to the original obligation amount. Notes maturing in the next year or operating cycle, whichever is longer, will be classified as current liabilities. **Unearned revenues,** sometimes called deferred revenues as in Dell's balance sheet, represent cash received from a customer for goods or services to be provided in a future period.

Accrued liabilities represent obligations created when expenses have been incurred but will not be paid until a subsequent reporting period. Examples are accrued salaries payable, accrued interest payable, and accrued taxes payable. **Dell Inc.**'s accrued liabilities include accrued warranty liabilities, accrued income taxes, accrued compensation, and other.

Current liabilities include the *current maturities of long-term debt.*

Long-term notes, loans, mortgages, and bonds payable usually are reclassified and reported as current liabilities as they become payable within the next year (or operating cycle if that's longer).[4] Likewise, when long-term debt is payable in installments, the installment payable currently is reported as a current liability. For example, a $1,000,000 note payable requiring $100,000 in principal payments to be made in each of the next 10 years is classified as a $100,000 current liability—**current maturities of long-term debt**—and a $900,000 long-term liability.

Chapter 13 provides a more detailed analysis of current liabilities.

---

[4]Payment can be with current assets or the creation of other current liabilities.

LONG-TERM LIABILITIES.   Long-term liabilities are obligations that will *not* be satisfied in the next year or operating cycle, whichever is longer. They do not require the use of current assets or the creation of current liabilities for payment. Examples are long-term notes, bonds, pension obligations, and lease obligations.

> Noncurrent, or long-term liabilities, usually are those payable beyond the current year.

But simply classifying a liability as long-term doesn't provide complete information to external users. For instance, long-term could mean anything from 2 to 20, 30, or 40 years. Payment terms, interest rates, and other details needed to assess the impact of these obligations on future cash flows and long-term solvency are reported in a disclosure note.

Dell Inc. reports long-term debt, long-term deferred service revenue, and other non-current liabilities at the end of its 2009 fiscal year. A disclosure note indicates that other noncurrent liabilities include warranty liabilities, income taxes payable, and other. Long-term liabilities are discussed in subsequent chapters.

Shareholders' Equity

Recall from our discussions in Chapters 1 and 2 that owners' equity is simply a residual amount derived by subtracting liabilities from assets. For that reason, it's sometimes referred to as net assets. Also recall that owners of a corporation are its shareholders, so owners' equity for a corporation is referred to as shareholders' equity or stockholders' equity. Shareholders' equity for a corporation arises primarily from two sources: (1) amounts *invested* by shareholders in the corporation, and (2) amounts *earned* by the corporation (on behalf of its shareholders). These are reported as (1) **paid-in capital** and (2) **retained earnings.** Retained earnings represents the accumulated net income earned since the inception of the corporation and not (yet) paid to shareholders as dividends.

> Shareholders' equity is composed of *paid-in capital* (invested capital) and *retained earnings* (earned capital).

Graphic 3–8 presents the shareholders' equity section of **Dell Inc.**'s 2009 and 2008 fiscal year-end balance sheets.

	January 30, 2009	February 1, 2008
(In millions)		
Stockholders' equity:		
Preferred stock and capital in excess of $.01 par value; shares authorized: 5,000; shares issued and outstanding: none	—	—
Common stock and capital in excess of $.01 par value; shares authorized: 7,000; shares issued: 3,338 and 3,320, respectively; shares outstanding; 1,944 and 2,060, respectively	11,189	10,589
Treasury stock, at cost: 919 and 785 shares, respectively	(27,904)	(25,037)
Retained earnings	20,677	18,199
Accumulated other comprehensive income (loss)	309	(16)
Total stockholders' equity	4,271	3,735

GRAPHIC 3–8

Shareholders' Equity—Dell Inc.

Real World Financials

From the inception of the corporation through January 30, 2009, Dell has accumulated net income, less dividends, of $20,677 million which is reported as *retained earnings.* The company's *paid-in capital* is represented by common stock and additional paid-in capital which collectively represent cash invested by shareholders in exchange for ownership interests. Information about the number of shares the company has authorized and how many shares have been issued also must be disclosed.

In addition to paid-in capital and retained earnings, shareholders' equity may include a few other equity components. For example, Dell reports accumulated other comprehensive income (loss). Accumulated other comprehensive income is discussed in Chapters 4, 12, and 18. Other equity components are addressed in later chapters, Chapter 18 in particular. We also discuss the concept of par value in Chapter 18.

● LO10

Real World Financials

INTERNATIONAL FINANCIAL REPORTING STANDARDS

Balance Sheet Presentation. There are more similarities than differences in balance sheets prepared according to U.S. GAAP and those prepared applying IFRS. Some of the differences are:

- International standards specify a minimum list of items to be presented in the balance sheet. U.S. GAAP has no minimum requirements.
- *IAS No.1, revised,*[5] changed the title of the balance sheet to *statement of financial position,* although companies are not required to use that title. Some U.S. companies use the statement of financial position title as well.
- Under U.S. GAAP, we present current assets and liabilities before noncurrent assets and liabilities. *IAS No. 1* doesn't prescribe the format of the balance sheet, but balance sheets prepared using IFRS often report noncurrent items first. For example, the balance sheet of **Sanofi-Aventis**, a French pharmaceutical company, included in a recent half-year report, presented assets, liabilities, and equity in the following order:

Sanofi-Aventis
Balance Sheet (condensed)
At June 30

(€ in millions)	2009
Noncurrent assets (including property, plant, and equipment)	€58,233
Current assets	18,525
Total assets	€76,758
Shareholders' equity	€44,784
Noncurrent liabilities	21,187
Current liabilities	10,787
Total liabilities and equity	€76,758

WHERE WE'RE HEADED

● LO10

The FASB and IASB are working together on a standard that would have a dramatic impact on the format of financial statements.

Demonstrating the cohesiveness among the financial statements is a key objective of the Financial Statement Presentation project.

The FASB and IASB are working together on a project, Financial Statement Presentation, to establish a common standard for presenting information in the financial statements, including classifying and displaying line items and aggregating line items into subtotals and totals. This standard will have a dramatic impact on the format of financial statements. An important part of the proposal involves the organization of elements of the balance sheet (statement of financial position), statement of comprehensive income (including the income statement), and statement of cash flows into a common set of classifications.

Each of the financial statements will include classifications by operating, investing, and financing activities, providing a "cohesive" financial picture that stresses the relationships among the financial statements. Recall from your previous accounting education and from our brief discussion in Chapter 2, that this is the way we currently classify activities in the statement of cash flows.

(continued)

---

[5]"Financial Statement Presentation," *International Accounting Standard No. 1* (IASCF), as amended effective January 1, 2009.

(concluded)

For each statement, though, operating and investing activities will be included within a new category, "business" activities. Each statement also will include three additional groupings: discontinued operations, income taxes, and equity (if needed). The new look for the balance sheet (statement of financial position) will be:

Statement of Financial Position

Business
- Operating assets and liabilities
- Investing assets and liabilities

Financing
- Financing assets
- Financing liabilities

Income Taxes

Discontinued Operations

Equity

The project has multiple phases and is not scheduled for completion until 2011.

CONCEPT REVIEW EXERCISE

The following is a post-closing trial balance for the Sepia Paint Corporation at December 31, 2011, the end of the company's fiscal year:

BALANCE SHEET CLASSIFICATION

Account Title	Debits	Credits
Cash	80,000	
Accounts receivable	200,000	
Allowance for uncollectible accounts		20,000
Inventories	300,000	
Prepaid expenses	30,000	
Note receivable (due in one month)	60,000	
Investments	50,000	
Land	120,000	
Buildings	550,000	
Machinery	500,000	
Accumulated depreciation—buildings and machinery		450,000
Patent (net of amortization)	50,000	
Accounts payable		170,000
Salaries payable		40,000
Interest payable		10,000
Note payable		100,000
Bonds payable (due in 10 years)		500,000
Common stock, no par		400,000
Retained earnings		250,000
Totals	1,940,000	1,940,000

The $50,000 balance in the investment account consists of marketable equity securities of other corporations. The company's intention is to hold the securities for at least three years. The $100,000 note payable is an installment loan. $10,000 of the principal, plus interest, is due on each July 1 for the next 10 years. At the end of the year, 100,000 shares of common stock were issued and outstanding. The company has 500,000 shares of common stock authorized.

Required:
Prepare a classified balance sheet for the Sepia Paint Corporation at December 31, 2011.

SOLUTION

SEPIA PAINT CORPORATION
Balance Sheet
At December 31, 2011

Assets

Current assets:		
Cash		$ 80,000
Accounts receivable	$ 200,000	
Less: Allowance for uncollectible amounts	(20,000)	180,000
Note receivable		60,000
Inventories		300,000
Prepaid expenses		30,000
Total current assets		650,000
Investments		50,000
Property, plant, and equipment:		
Land	120,000	
Buildings	550,000	
Machinery	500,000	
	1,170,000	
Less: Accumulated depreciation	(450,000)	
Net property, plant, and equipment		720,000
Intangible assets:		
Patent		50,000
Total assets		$1,470,000

Liabilities and Shareholders' Equity

Current liabilities:		
Accounts payable		$ 170,000
Salaries payable		40,000
Interest payable		10,000
Current maturities of long-term debt		10,000
Total current liabilities		230,000
Long-term liabilities:		
Note payable	$ 90,000	
Bonds payable	500,000	
Total long-term liabilities		590,000
Shareholders' equity:		
Common stock, no par, 500,000 shares authorized, 100,000 shares issued and outstanding	400,000	
Retained earnings	250,000	
Total shareholders' equity		650,000
Total liabilities and shareholders' equity		$1,470,000

The usefulness of the balance sheet, as well as the other financial statements, is significantly enhanced by financial statement disclosures. We now turn our attention to these disclosures.

PART B

FINANCIAL DISCLOSURES

● LO5

Financial statements are included in the annual report a company mails to its shareholders. They are, though, only part of the information provided. Critical to understanding the financial statements and to evaluating a firm's performance and financial health are additional disclosures included in the annual report.

Financial statement disclosures are provided (1) by including additional information, often parenthetically, on the face of the statement following a financial statement item and (2) in disclosure notes that often include supporting schedules. Common examples of disclosures included on the face of the balance sheet are the allowance for uncollectible accounts and information about common stock. Disclosure notes, discussed and illustrated in the next section, are the most common means of providing these additional disclosures. The specific format of disclosure is not important, only that the information is, in fact, disclosed.

> **The full-disclosure principle requires that financial statements provide all material relevant information concerning the reporting entity.**

Disclosure Notes

Disclosure notes typically span several pages and either explain or elaborate upon the data presented in the financial statements themselves, or provide information not directly related to any specific item in the statements. Throughout this text you will encounter examples of items that usually are disclosed this way. For instance, the fair values of financial instruments and "off-balance-sheet" risk associated with financial instruments are disclosed in notes. Information providing details of many financial statement items is provided using disclosure notes. Some examples include:

- Pension plans
- Leases
- Long-term debt
- Investments
- Income taxes
- Property, plant and equipment
- Employee benefit plans

Disclosure notes must include certain specific notes such as a summary of significant accounting policies, descriptions of subsequent events, and related third-party transactions, but many notes are fashioned to suit the disclosure needs of the particular reporting enterprise. Actually, any explanation that contributes to investors' and creditors' understanding of the results of operations, financial position, or cash flows of the company should be included. Let's take a look at just a few disclosure notes.

Summary of Significant Accounting Policies

There are many areas where management chooses from among equally acceptable alternative accounting methods. For example, management chooses whether to use accelerated or straight-line depreciation, whether to use FIFO, LIFO, or average cost to measure inventories, and whether the completed contract or percentage-of-completion method best reflects the performance of construction operations. The company also defines which securities it considers to be cash equivalents and its policies regarding the timing of recognizing revenues. Typically, the first disclosure note consists of a summary of significant accounting policies that discloses the choices the company makes.[6] Graphic 3–9 shows you a portion of a typical summary note from a recent annual report of the **Starbucks Corporation**.

> **The *summary of significant accounting policies* conveys valuable information about the company's choices from among various alternative accounting methods.**

Studying this note is an essential step in analyzing financial statements. Obviously, knowing which methods were used to derive certain accounting numbers is critical to assessing the adequacy of those amounts.

Subsequent Events

When an event that has a material effect on the company's financial position occurs after the fiscal year-end but before the financial statements are issued or "available to be issued," the

---

[6]FASB ASC 235–10–50: Notes to Financial Statements—Overall—Disclosure (previously "Disclosure of Accounting Policies," *Accounting Principles Board Opinion No. 22* (New York: AICPA, 1972)).

GRAPHIC 3–9 Summary of Significant Accounting Policies—Starbucks Corporation

Note 1: Summary of Accounting Policies (in part)

Principles of Consolidation

The consolidated financial statements reflect the financial position and operating results of Starbucks, which includes wholly owned subsidiaries and investees controlled by the Company.

Cash Equivalents

The Company considers all highly liquid instruments with a maturity of three months or less at the time of purchase to be cash equivalents.

Inventories

Inventories are stated at the lower of cost (primarily moving average cost) or market. The Company records inventory reserves for obsolete and slow-moving items and for estimated shrinkage between physical inventory counts.

Property, Plant, and Equipment

Property, plant, and equipment are carried at cost less accumulated depreciation. Depreciation of property, plant, and equipment which includes assets under capital leases, is provided on the straight-line method over estimated useful lives, generally ranging from two to seven years for equipment and 30 to 40 years for buildings. Leasehold improvements are amortized over the shorter of their estimated useful lives or the related lease life, generally 10 years.

Revenue Recognition

Company-operated retail store revenues are recognized when payment is tendered at the point of sale. Revenues from the Company's store value cards, such as the Starbucks Card, are recognized when tendered for payment, or upon redemption. Outstanding customer balances are included in Deferred revenue on the consolidated balance sheets.

Real World Financials

A *subsequent event* is a significant development that occurs after a company's fiscal year-end but before the financial statements are issued or available to be issued.

event is described in a **subsequent event** disclosure note.[7] Examples include the issuance of debt or equity securities, a business combination or the sale of a business, the sale of assets, an event that sheds light on the outcome of a loss contingency, or any other event having a material effect on operations. Graphic 3–10 illustrates the required disclosure by showing a note that **Walmart Stores, Inc.**, included in its January 31, 2009, financial statements, announcing both an increase in the company's annual dividend and the issuance of notes payable.

We cover subsequent events in more depth in Chapter 13.

GRAPHIC 3–10

Subsequent Event— Walmart Stores, Inc.

Real World Financials

14 Subsequent Events (in part)

On March 5, 2009, the Company's Board of Directors approved an increase in the annual dividends for fiscal 2010 to $1.09 per share. The annual dividend will be paid in four quarterly installments on April 6, 2009, June 1, 2009, September 8, 2009, and January 4, 2010, to holders of record on March 13, May 15, August 14, and December 11, 2009, respectively.

On March 27, 2009, the Company issued and sold $1.0 billion of 5.625% Notes Due 2034 at an issue price equal to 98.981% of the notes' aggregate principal amount.

Noteworthy Events and Transactions

Some transactions and events occur only occasionally, but when they do occur are potentially important to evaluating a company's financial statements. In this category are related-party transactions, errors and irregularities, and illegal acts. The more frequent of these is related-party transactions.

Sometimes a company will engage in transactions with owners, management, families of owners or management, affiliated companies, and other parties that can significantly influence

---

[7]Financial statements are viewed as issued if they have been widely distributed to financial statement users in a format consistent with GAAP. Some entities (for example, private companies) don't widely distribute their financial statements to users. For those entities, the key date for subsequent events is not the date of issuance but rather the date upon which the financial statements are "available to be issued," which occurs when the financial statements are complete, in a format consistent with GAAP, and have obtained the necessary approvals for issuance. Companies must disclose the date through which subsequent events have been evaluated. (FASB ASC 855: Subsequent Events (previously "Subsequent Events," *Statement of Financial Accounting Standards No. 165* (Stamford, Conn.: FASB, 2009))).

or be influenced by the company. The potential problem with **related-party transactions** is that their economic substance may differ from their legal form. For instance, borrowing or lending money at an interest rate that differs significantly from the market interest rate is an example of a transaction that could result from a related-party involvement. As a result of the potential for misrepresentation, financial statement users are particularly interested in more details about these transactions.

When related-party transactions occur, companies must disclose the nature of the relationship, provide a description of the transactions, and report the dollar amounts of transactions and any amounts due from or to related parties.[8] Graphic 3–11 shows a disclosure note from a recent annual report of **Williams-Sonoma, Inc.** The note describes a lease arrangement with a company owned by Howard Lester, Williams-Sonoma's chief executive officer and chairman of the board of directors.

> The economic substance of *related-party* transactions should be disclosed, including dollar amounts involved.

Note M: Related Party Transactions (in part)

On May 16, 2008, we completed two transactions relating to our corporate aircraft. First, we sold our Bombardier Global Express airplane for approximately $46,787,000 in cash (a net after-tax cash benefit of approximately $29,000,000) to an unrelated third party. This resulted in a gain on sale of asset of approximately $16,000,000 in the second quarter of fiscal 2008. Second, we entered into an Aircraft Lease Agreement (the "Lease Agreement") with a limited liability company (the "LLC") owned by W. Howard Lester, our Chief Executive Officer and Chairman of the Board of Directors, for use of a Bombardier Global 5000 owned by the LLC. These transactions were approved by our Board of Directors.

GRAPHIC 3–11

Related-Party Transactions Disclosure—Williams-Sonoma, Inc.

Real World Financials

More infrequent are errors, irregularities, and illegal acts; however, when they do occur, their disclosure is important. The distinction between errors and **irregularities** is that errors are unintentional while irregularities are *intentional* distortions of financial statements.[9] Obviously, management fraud might cause a user to approach financial analysis from an entirely different and more cautious viewpoint.

Closely related to irregularities are **illegal acts** such as bribes, kickbacks, illegal contributions to political candidates, and other violations of the law. Accounting for illegal practices has been influenced by the Foreign Corrupt Practices Act passed by Congress in 1977. The Act is intended to discourage illegal business practices through tighter controls and also encourage better disclosure of those practices when encountered. The nature of such disclosures should be influenced by the materiality of the impact of illegal acts on amounts disclosed in the financial statements.[10] However, the SEC issued guidance expressing its view that exclusive reliance on quantitative benchmarks to assess materiality in preparing financial statements is inappropriate.[11] A number of other factors, including whether the item in question involves an unlawful transaction, should also be considered when determining materiality.

As you might expect, any disclosures of related-party transactions, irregularities, and illegal acts can be quite sensitive. Although auditors must be considerate of the privacy of the parties involved, that consideration cannot be subordinate to users' needs for full disclosure.

We've discussed only a few of the disclosure notes most frequently included in annual reports. Other common disclosures include details concerning earnings per share calculations, income taxes, property and equipment, contingencies, long-term debt, leases, pensions, stock options, changes in accounting methods, fair values of financial instruments, and exposure to market risk and credit risk. We discuss and illustrate these in later chapters in the context of related financial statement elements.

> Disclosure notes for some financial statement elements are required. Others are provided when required by specific situations in the interest of full disclosure.

---

[8]FASB ASC 850–10–50: Related Party Disclosures—Overall—Disclosure (previously "Related Party Disclosures," *Statement of Financial Accounting Standards No. 57* (Stamford, Conn.: FASB, 1982)).

[9]"The Auditor's Responsibility to Detect and Report Errors and Irregularities," *Statement on Auditing Standards No. 53* (New York: AICPA, 1988).

[10]"Illegal Acts by Clients," *Statement on Auditing Standards No. 54* (New York: AICPA, 1988).

[11]FASB ASC 250–10–S99–1, SAB Topic 1.M: Assessing Materiality (originally "Materiality," *Staff Accounting Bulletin No. 99* (Washington, D.C.: SEC, August 1999)).

Management Discussion and Analysis

● LO6

The management discussion and analysis provides a biased but informed perspective of a company's (a) operations, (b) liquidity, and (c) capital resources.

Each annual report of a public company requires a fairly lengthy discussion and analysis provided by the company's management. In this section, management provides its views on significant events, trends, and uncertainties pertaining to the company's (a) operations, (b) liquidity, and (c) capital resources. Although the management discussion and analysis (MD&A) section may embody management's biased perspective, it can offer an informed insight that might not be available elsewhere. Graphic 3–12 contains part of the liquidity and capital resources portion of **PetSmart, Inc.**'s MDA that followed a discussion of operations in its annual report for the fiscal year ended February 1, 2009.

GRAPHIC 3–12

Management Discussion and Analysis—PetSmart, Inc.

Real World Financials

Management Discussion and Analysis of Financial Condition and Results of Operations
(In part: Liquidity and Capital Resources only)

Cash Flow

Global capital and credit markets have recently experienced increased volatility and disruption. Despite this volatility and disruption, we have continued to have full access to our credit facility and to generate operating cash flow sufficient to meet our financing needs. We believe that our operating cash flow and cash on hand will be adequate to meet our operating, investing and financing needs in the foreseeable future.

Common Stock Purchase Program

During 2008, we purchased 2.3 million shares of our common stock for $50.0 million. As of February 1, 2009, $25.0 million remained available under the $300.0 million program.

Common Stock Dividends

We presently believe our ability to generate cash allows us to invest in the growth of the business and, at the same time, distribute a quarterly dividend. Our credit facility and letter of credit facility permit us to pay dividends, so long as we are not in default and the payment of dividends would not result in default. During each of 2008, 2007, and 2006, we paid aggregate dividends of $0.12 per share.

Operating Capital and Capital Expenditure Requirements

Substantially all our stores are leased facilities. We opened 112 new stores and closed 8 stores in 2008. Generally, each new store requires capital expenditures of approximately $0.7 million for fixtures, equipment and leasehold improvements, approximately $0.3 million for inventory and approximately $0.1 million for preopening costs. We expect total capital spending to be approximately $115.0 to $125.0 million for 2009, based on our plan to open approximately 40 net new stores and 20 new PetsHotels, continuing our investment in the development of our information systems, adding to our services capacity with the expansion of certain grooming salons, remodeling or replacing certain store assets and continuing our store refresh program.

Management's Responsibilities

Management prepares and is responsible for the financial statements and other information in the annual report. To enhance the awareness of the users of financial statements concerning the relative roles of management and the auditor, annual reports of public companies include a management's responsibilities section that asserts the responsibility of management for the information contained in the annual report as well as an assessment of the company's internal control procedures.

Graphic 3–13 contains the statement of responsibility disclosure for **Home Depot, Inc.** included with the company's financial statements for the year ended February 1, 2009. Recall from our discussion of financial reporting reform in Chapter 1, that the *Sarbanes-Oxley Act of 2002* requires corporate executives to personally certify the financial statements. Submission of false statements carries a penalty of up to 20 years in jail. The graphic also contains Management's Report on Internal Control Over Financial Reporting. Francis S. Blake, Home Depot's chairman and chief executive officer, and Carol B. Tomé, the company's chief financial officer, signed the required certifications as well as these statements of responsibility.

Management's Responsibility for Financial Statements

The financial statements presented in this Annual Report have been prepared with integrity and objectivity and are the responsibility of the management of The Home Depot, Inc. These financial statements have been prepared in conformity with U.S. generally accepted accounting principles and properly reflect certain estimates and judgments based upon the best available information.

The financial statements of the Company have been audited by KPMG LLP, an independent registered public accounting firm. Their accompanying report is based upon an audit conducted in accordance with the standards of the Public Company Accounting Oversight Board (United States).

The Audit Committee of the Board of Directors, consisting solely of outside directors, meets five times a year with the independent registered public accounting firm, the internal auditors and representatives of management to discuss auditing and financial reporting matters. In addition, a telephonic meeting is held prior to each quarterly earnings release. The Audit Committee retains the independent registered public accounting firm and regularly reviews the internal accounting controls, the activities of the independent registered public accounting firm and internal auditors and the financial condition of the Company. Both the Company's independent registered public accounting firm and the internal auditors have free access to the Audit Committee.

Management's Report on Internal Control over Financial Reporting

Our management is responsible for establishing and maintaining adequate internal control over financial reporting, as such term is defined in Rules 13a–15(f) promulgated under the Securities Exchange Act of 1934, as amended. Under the supervision and with the participation of our management, including our chief executive officer and chief financial officer, we conducted an evaluation of the effectiveness of our internal control over financial reporting as of February 1, 2009 based on the framework in *Internal Control—Integrated Framework* issued by the Committee of Sponsoring Organizations of the Treadway Commission (COSO). Based on our evaluation, our management concluded that our internal control over financial reporting was effective as of February 1, 2009, in providing reasonable assurance regarding the reliability of financial reporting and the preparation of financial statements for external purposes in accordance with generally accepted accounting principles. The effectiveness of our internal control over financial reporting as of February 1, 2009, has been audited by KPMG LLP, an independent registered public accounting firm, as stated in their report which is included on page 26 in this Form 10-K.

Francis S. Blake
Chairman & Chief Executive Officer

Carol B. Tomé
Chief Financial Officer

GRAPHIC 3–13

Management's Responsibilities— Home Depot, Inc.

Real World Financials

The *management's responsibilities* section avows the responsibility of management for the company's *financial statements and internal control system.*

Auditors' Report

Auditors examine financial statements and the internal control procedures designed to support the content of those statements. Their role is to attest to the fairness of the financial statements based on that examination. The auditors' attest function results in an opinion stated in the **auditors' report.**

One step in financial analysis should be an examination of the auditors' report, which is issued by the CPAs who audit the financial statements and inform users of the audit findings. Every audit report of a public company looks similar to the one prepared by **Deloitte & Touche LLP** for the financial statements of **Microsoft Corporation**, as shown in Graphic 3–14 (on the next page).

The reason for the similarities is that auditors' reports of public companies must be in compliance with the specifications of the PCAOB.[12] In most cases, including the report for Microsoft, the auditors will be satisfied that the financial statements "present fairly" the financial position, results of operations, and cash flows and are "in conformity with accounting principles generally accepted in the United States of America." These situations prompt an unqualified opinion. Notice that the last paragraph in Microsoft's report references the

● LO7

The auditors' report provides the analyst with an independent and professional opinion about the fairness of the representations in the financial statements and about the effectiveness of internal controls.

---

[12]"An Audit of Internal Control over Financial Reporting That Is Integrated with An Audit of Financial Statements," *Auditing Standard No. 5* (Washington, D.C., PCAOB, 2007).

Report of Independent Registered Public Accounting Firm

To the Board of Directors and Stockholders of Microsoft Corporation:

We have audited the accompanying consolidated balance sheets of Microsoft Corporation and subsidiaries (the "Company") as of June 30, 2009 and 2008, and the related consolidated statements of income, cash flows, and stockholders' equity for each of the three years in the period ended June 30, 2009. These financial statements are the responsibility of the Company's management. Our responsibility is to express an opinion on these financial statements based on our audits.

We conducted our audits in accordance with the standards of the Public Company Accounting Oversight Board (United States). Those standards require that we plan and perform the audit to obtain reasonable assurance about whether the financial statements are free of material misstatement. An audit includes examining, on a test basis, evidence supporting the amounts and disclosures in the financial statements. An audit also includes assessing the accounting principles used and significant estimates made by management, as well as evaluating the overall financial statement presentation. We believe that our audits provide a reasonable basis for our opinion.

In our opinion, such consolidated financial statements present fairly, in all material respects, the financial position of Microsoft Corporation and subsidiaries as of June 30, 2009 and 2008, and the results of their operations and their cash flows for each of the three years in the period ended June 30, 2009, in conformity with accounting principles generally accepted in the United States of America.

As discussed in Note 18 to the financial statements, on July 1, 2007, the Company adopted the provisions of Financial Accounting Standards Board Interpretation No. 48, *Accounting for Uncertainty in Income Taxes—an interpretation of FASB Statement No. 109*, and Emerging Issues Task Force Issue No. 06-2, *Accounting for Sabbatical Leave and Other Similar Benefits Pursuant to FASB Statement No. 43*.

We have also audited, in accordance with the standards of the Public Company Accounting Oversight Board (United States), the Company's internal control over financial reporting as of June 30, 2009, based on the criteria established in *Internal Control— Integrated Framework* issued by the Committee of Sponsoring Organizations of the Treadway Commission and our report dated July 29, 2009, expressed an unqualified opinion on the Company's internal control over financial reporting.

Deloitte & Touche LLP
Seattle, Washington
July 29, 2009

auditors' separate report on the effectiveness of the company's internal control over financial reporting.

Sometimes, as with the Microsoft report, circumstances cause the auditors' report to include an explanatory paragraph in addition to the standard wording, even though the report is unqualified. Most notably, these include:

- *Lack of consistency* due to a change in accounting principle such that comparability is affected even though the auditor concurs with the desirability of the change.
- *Uncertainty* as to the ultimate resolution of a contingency for which a loss is material in amount but not necessarily probable or probable but not estimable.
- *Emphasis* of a matter concerning the financial statements that does not affect the existence of an unqualified opinion but relates to a significant event such as a related-party transaction.

Some audits result in the need to issue other than an unqualified opinion due to exceptions such as (a) nonconformity with generally accepted accounting principles, (b) inadequate disclosures, and (c) a limitation or restriction of the scope of the examination. In these situations the auditor will issue a (an):

- *Qualified opinion* This contains an exception to the standard unqualified opinion but not of sufficient seriousness to invalidate the financial statements as a whole.
- *Adverse opinion* This is necessary when the exceptions (a) and (b) above are so serious that a qualified opinion is not justified. Adverse opinions are rare because

auditors usually are able to persuade management to rectify problems to avoid this undesirable report.

• *Disclaimer* An auditor will disclaim an opinion for item (c) above such that insufficient information has been gathered to express an opinion.

During the course of each audit, the auditor is required to evaluate the company's ability to continue for a reasonable time as a going concern. If the auditor determines there is significant doubt, an explanation of the potential problem must be included in the auditors' report.[13]

Obviously, the auditors' report is most informative when any of these deviations from the standard unqualified opinion are present. These departures from the norm should raise a red flag to a financial analyst and prompt additional search for information.

The auditors' report of **General Motors Corporation** exhibited in Graphic 3–15, included a fourth paragraph after the standard first three paragraphs.

> The auditor should assess the firm's ability to continue as a going concern.

The accompanying consolidated financial statements for the year ended December 31, 2008, have been prepared assuming that the Corporation will continue as a going concern. As discussed in Note 2 to the consolidated financial statements, the Corporation's recurring losses from operations, stockholders' deficit, and inability to generate sufficient cash flow to meet its obligations and sustain its operations raise substantial doubt about its ability to continue as a going concern. Management's plans concerning these matters are also discussed in Note 2 to the consolidated financial statements. The consolidated financial statements do not include any adjustments that might result from the outcome of this uncertainty.

GRAPHIC 3–15

Going Concern Paragraph—General Motors Corporation

Real World Financials

Compensation of Directors and Top Executives

In the early 1990s, the compensation large U.S. corporations paid their top executives became an issue of considerable public debate and controversy. Shareholders, employees, politicians, and the public in general began to question the huge pay packages received by company officials at the same time that more and more rank and file employees were being laid off as a result of company cutbacks. Contributing to the debate was the realization that the compensation gap between executives and lower level employees was much wider than in Japan and most other industrial countries. During this time, it also became apparent that discovering exactly how much compensation corporations paid their top people was nearly impossible.

Part of the problem stemmed from the fact that disclosures of these amounts were meager; but a large part of the problem was that a substantial portion of executive pay often is in the form of stock options. Executive stock options give their holders the right to buy stock at a specified price, usually equal to the market price when the options are granted. When stock prices rise, executives can exercise their options and realize a profit. In some cases, options have made executive compensation seem extremely high. Stock options are discussed in depth in Chapter 19.

To help shareholders and others sort out the content of executive pay packages and better understand the commitments of the company in this regard, SEC requirements provide for more disclosures on compensation to directors and executives, and in particular, concerning stock options. The proxy statement that must be sent each year to all shareholders, usually in the same mailing with the annual report, invites shareholders to the meeting to elect board members and to vote on issues before the shareholders or to vote using an enclosed proxy card. The proxy statement also includes compensation and stock option information for directors and top executives. Graphic 3–16 shows a portion of **Best Buy Co. Inc.**'s 2009 summary compensation table included in a recent proxy statement.

> The *proxy statement* contains disclosures on compensation to directors and executives.

---

[13]"The Auditor's Consideration of an Entity's Ability to Continue as a Going Concern," *Statement on Auditing Standards No. 59* (New York: AICPA, 1988).

GRAPHIC 3–16   Summary Compensation Table—Best Buy Co. Inc.

Summary Compensation Table (in part)

Name and Position	Fiscal Year	Salary[1]	Stock Awards[2]	Option Awards[2]	All Other Compensation[3]	Total
Bradbury H. Anderson Chief Executive Officer	2009	$1,247,311	$635,268	—	$15,869	$1,898,448
James L. Muehlbauer Executive Vice President Chief Financial Officer	2009	551,878	501,507	$493,487	16,541	1,563,413
Brian J. Dunn President and Chief Operating Officer	2009	876,926	571,745	1,910,536	15,140	3,374,347
Robert A. Willett Chief Executive Officer—Best Buy International	2009	821,157	1,412,092	1,191,190	44,047	3,468,486
Shari L Ballard Executive Vice President—Retail Channel Management	2009	630,770	585,741	870,011	12,329	2,098,851
David J. Morrish Executive Vice President—Connected Digital Solutions	2009	470,301	170,863	236,862	1,827,122	2,705,148

[1]These amounts are before any deferrals under the Deferred Compensation Plan.
[2]These amounts reflect the expense recognized for financial statement reporting purposes for fiscal 2009.
[3]Including retirement plan contributions, life and disability insurance premiums, and other.

Real World Financials

PART C   RISK ANALYSIS

Using Financial Statement Information

● LO8

The overriding objective of financial reporting is providing information that investors and creditors can use to make decisions. Nevertheless, it's sometimes easy to lose sight of that objective while dealing with the intricacies that specific concepts and procedures can involve. In this part of the chapter we provide an overview of financial statement analysis and then demonstrate the use of ratios, a popular financial statement analysis technique, to analyze risk.

Investors, creditors, and others use information that companies provide in corporate financial reports to make decisions. Although the financial reports focus primarily on the past performance and the present financial condition of the reporting company, information users are most interested in the outlook for the future. Trying to gain a glimpse of the future from past and present data entails using various tools and techniques to formulate predictions. This is the goal of financial statement analysis.

Comparative financial statements allow financial statement users to compare year-to-year financial position, results of operations, and cash flows.

Financial statements are not presented in isolation. Every financial statement issued is accompanied by the corresponding financial statement of the preceding year, and often the previous two years. These are called **comparative financial statements.** They enable investors, creditors, and other users to compare year-to-year financial position, results of operations, and cash flows. These comparative data help an analyst detect and predict trends. Because operations often expand and contract in a cyclical fashion, analysis of any one year's data may not provide an accurate picture of a company.

Some analysts enhance their comparison by expressing each item as a percentage of that same item in the financial statements of another year (base amount) in order to more easily see year-to-year changes. This is referred to as **horizontal analysis.** Similarly, **vertical analysis** involves expressing each item in the financial statements as a percentage of an appropriate corresponding total, or base amount, but within the same year. For example, cash, inventory, and other assets can be restated as a percentage of total assets; net income and each expense can be restated as a percentage of revenues.

Regardless of the specific technique used, the essential point is that accounting numbers are virtually meaningless in isolation. Their value derives from comparison with other numbers. The most common way of comparing accounting numbers to evaluate the performance and risk of a firm is ratio analysis.

We use ratios every day. Batting averages indicate how well our favorite baseball players are performing. We evaluate basketball players by field goal percentage and rebounds per game. Speedometers measure the speed of our cars in terms of miles per hour. We compare grocery costs on the basis of price per pound or ounce. In each of these cases, the ratio is more meaningful than a single number by itself. Do 45 hits indicate satisfactory performance? It depends on the number of at-bats. Is $2 a good price for cheese? It depends on how many ounces the $2 buys. Ratios make these measurements meaningful.

> No accounting numbers are meaningful in and of themselves.

Likewise, we can use ratios to help evaluate a firm's performance and financial position. Is net income of $4 million a cause for shareholders to celebrate? Probably not if shareholders' equity is $10 billion. But if shareholders equity is $10 million, that's a 40% return on equity! Although ratios provide more meaningful information than absolute numbers alone, the ratios are most useful when analyzed relative to some standard of comparison. That standard of comparison may be previous performance of the same company, the performance of a competitor company, or an industry average for the particular ratio.

> Evaluating information in ratio form allows analysts to control for size differences over time and among firms.

Accountants should be conversant with ratio analysis for at least three reasons. First, when preparing financial statements, accountants should be familiar with the ways users will use the information provided to make better decisions concerning what and how to report. Second, when accountants participate in company decisions concerning operating and financing alternatives, they may find ratio analysis helpful in evaluating available choices. Third, during the planning stages of an audit, independent auditors often use ratio analysis. This analysis assists in identifying potential audit problems and determining the specific audit procedures that should be performed.

We introduce ratios related to risk analysis in this chapter and ratios related to profitability analysis in Chapter 5. You will also employ ratios in Decision Makers' Perspective sections of many of the chapters in this text. Analysis cases that benefit from ratio analysis are included in many of these chapters as well.

Investors and creditors use financial information to assess the future risk and return of their investments in business enterprises. The balance sheet provides information useful to this assessment. A key element of risk analysis is investigating a company's ability to pay its obligations when they come due. This type of risk often is referred to as default risk. Another aspect of risk is operational risk which relates more to how adept a company is at withstanding various events and circumstances that might impair its ability to earn profits. Obviously, these two types of risk are not completely independent of one another. Inability to earn profits certainly increases a company's chances of defaulting on its obligations. Conversely, regardless of a company's long-run prospects for generating profits, if it can't meet its obligations, the company's operations are at risk.

Assessing risk necessarily involves consideration of a variety of economywide risk factors such as inflation, interest rates, and the general business climate. Industrywide influences including competition, labor conditions, and technological forces also affect a company's risk profile. Still other risk factors are specific to the company itself. Financial ratios often are used in risk analysis to investigate a company's liquidity and long-term solvency. As we discuss some of the more common ratios in the following paragraphs, keep in mind the inherent relationship between risk and return and thus between our risk analysis in this chapter and our profitability analysis in Chapter 5.

Liquidity Ratios

Liquidity refers to the readiness of assets to be converted to cash. By comparing a company's liquid assets with its short-term obligations, we can obtain a general idea of the firm's ability to pay its short-term debts as they come due. Usually, current assets are thought of as the most liquid of a company's assets. Obviously, though, some are more liquid than others, so

● LO9

it's important also to evaluate the specific makeup of current assets. Two common measures of liquidity are (1) the current ratio and (2) the acid-test ratio (or quick ratio) calculated as follows:

$$\text{Current ratio} = \frac{\text{Current assets}}{\text{Current liabilities}}$$

$$\text{Acid-test ratio (or quick ratio)} = \frac{\text{Quick assets}}{\text{Current liabilities}}$$

Working capital, **the difference between current assets and current liabilities, is a popular measure of a company's ability to satisfy its short-term obligations.**

CURRENT RATIO. Implicit in the definition of a current liability is the relationship between current assets and current liabilities. The difference between current assets and current liabilities is called **working capital.** By comparing a company's obligations that will shortly become due with the company's cash and other assets that, by definition, are expected to shortly be converted to cash, the analysis offers some indication as to ability to pay those debts. Although used in a variety of decisions, it is particularly useful to those considering whether to extend short-term credit. The **current ratio** is computed by dividing current assets by current liabilities. A current ratio of 2 indicates that the company has twice as many current assets available as current liabilities.

Dell Inc.'s working capital (in millions) at the end of its January 30, 2009, fiscal year is $5,292, consisting of current assets of $20,151 (Graphic 3–3 on page 117) minus current liabilities of $14,859 (Graphic 3–7 on page 120). The current ratio can be computed as follows:

$$\text{Current ratio} = \frac{\$20,151}{\$14,859} = 1.36$$

Working capital may not present an accurate or complete picture of a company's liquidity.

Care should be taken, however, in assessing liquidity based solely on working capital. Liabilities usually are paid with cash, not other components of working capital. A company could have difficulty paying its liabilities even with a current ratio significantly greater than 1.0. For example, if a significant portion of current assets consisted of inventories, and inventories usually are not converted to cash for several months, there could be a problem in paying accounts payable due in 30 days. On the other hand, a current ratio of less than 1.0 doesn't necessarily mean the company will have difficulty meeting its current obligations. A line of credit, for instance, which the company can use to borrow funds, provides financial flexibility. That also must be considered in assessing liquidity.

ETHICAL DILEMMA

The Raintree Cosmetic Company has several loans outstanding with a local bank. The debt agreements all contain a covenant stipulating that Raintree must maintain a current ratio of at least .9. Jackson Phillips, company controller, estimates that the 2011 year-end current assets and current liabilities will be $2,100,000 and $2,400,000, respectively. These estimates provide a current ratio of only .875. Violation of the debt agreement will increase Raintree's borrowing costs as the loans are renegotiated at higher rates.

Jackson proposes to the company president that Raintree purchase inventory of $600,000 on credit before year-end. This will cause both current assets and current liabilities to increase by the same amount, but the current ratio will increase to .9. The extra $600,000 in inventory will be used over the later part of 2012. However, the purchase will cause warehousing costs and financing costs to increase.

Jackson is concerned about the ethics of his proposal. What do you think?

The *acid-test ratio* provides a more stringent indication of a company's ability to pay its current obligations.

ACID-TEST RATIO (OR QUICK RATIO). Some analysts like to modify the current ratio to consider only current assets that are readily available to pay current liabilities. One such variation in common use is the **acid-test ratio.** This ratio excludes inventories and prepaid items from current assets before dividing by current liabilities. The numerator, then, consists of cash, short-term investments, and accounts receivable, the "quick assets." By eliminating current assets less readily convertible into cash, the acid-test ratio provides a more rigorous indication of liquidity than does the current ratio.

Dell Inc.'s quick assets at the end of its January 30, 2009, fiscal year (in millions) total $15,535 ($8,352 + 740 + 4,731 + 1,712). The acid-test ratio can be computed as follows:

$$\text{Acid-test ratio} = \frac{\$15,535}{\$14,859} = 1.05$$

Are these liquidity ratios adequate? It's generally difficult to say without some point of comparison. As indicated previously, common standards for such comparisons are industry averages for similar ratios or ratios of the same company in prior years. Industry averages for the above two ratios are as follows:

Industry Average
Current ratio = 2.21
Acid-test ratio = 1.81

Dell's ratios are lower than the industry average. Does this indicate a liquidity problem? Not necessarily, but it raises a red flag that calls for caution in analyzing other areas. Remember that each ratio is but one piece of the entire puzzle. For instance, profitability is perhaps the best indication of liquidity in the long run. We discuss ratios that measure profitability in Chapter 5.

Also, management may be very efficient in managing current assets so that, let's say, receivables are collected faster than normal or inventory is sold faster than normal, making those assets more liquid than they otherwise would be. Higher turnover ratios, relative to those of a competitor or the industry, generally indicate a more liquid position for a given level of the current ratio. In Dell's case, its inventory turnover ratio is 49 compared with an industry average of 11. This means that Dell turns over its inventory nearly five times faster than the industry average. We discuss these turnover ratios in Chapter 5.

> Liquidity ratios should be assessed in the context of both profitability and efficiency of managing assets.

Financing Ratios

Investors and creditors, particularly long-term creditors, are vitally interested in a company's long-term solvency and stability. Financing ratios provide some indication of the riskiness of a company with regard to its ability to pay its long-term debts. Two common financing ratios are (1) the debt to equity ratio and (2) the times interest earned ratio. These ratios are calculated as follows:

> ● LO9

$$\text{Debt to equity ratio} = \frac{\text{Total liabilities}}{\text{Shareholders' equity}}$$

$$\text{Times interest earned ratio} = \frac{\text{Net income} + \text{Interest expense} + \text{Taxes}}{\text{Interest expense}}$$

DEBT TO EQUITY RATIO.   The debt to equity ratio compares resources provided by creditors with resources provided by owners. It is calculated by dividing total liabilities (current and noncurrent) by total shareholders' equity (including retained earnings).[14]

The ratio provides a measure of creditors' protection in the event of insolvency. Other things being equal, the higher the ratio, the higher the risk. The higher the ratio, the greater the creditor claims on assets, so the higher the likelihood an individual creditor would not be paid in full if the company is unable to meet its obligations. Relatedly, a high ratio indicates not only more fixed interest obligations, but probably a higher *rate* of interest as well because lenders tend to charge higher rates as the level of debt increases.

> The *debt to equity ratio* indicates the extent of reliance on creditors, rather than owners, in providing resources.

Dell Inc.'s liabilities at the end of its January 30, 2009, fiscal year (in millions) total $22,229 (Graphic 3–7 on page 120), and stockholders' equity totals $4,271 (Graphic 3–8 on page 121). The debt to equity ratio can be computed as follows:

$$\text{Debt to equity ratio} = \frac{\$22,229}{\$\,4,271} = 5.2$$

---

[14]A commonly used variation of the debt to equity ratio is found by dividing total liabilities by *total assets* (or total equities), rather than by shareholders' equity only. Of course, in this configuration the ratio measures precisely the same attribute of the firm's capital structure but can be interpreted as the percentage of a company's total assets provided by funds from creditors, rather than by owners.

As with all ratios, the debt to equity ratio is more meaningful if compared to some standard such as an industry average or a competitor. For example, the debt to equity ratio for **Hewlett-Packard (HP)**, a major competitor, is 2.9, significantly lower than Dell's ratio, indicating that Dell has more liabilities in its capital structure than does HP. Does this mean that Dell's default risk is more than that of HP? Other things equal—yes. Is that good? Not necessarily. As discussed in the next section, it may be that debt is being underutilized by Hewlett-Packard. More debt might increase the potential for return to shareholders, but the price would be higher risk. This is a fundamental trade-off faced by virtually all firms when trying to settle on the optimal capital structure.

The makeup of liabilities also is important. For example, Dell's liabilities include $5,649 million of unearned revenues, representing 25% of total liabilities. Recall that unearned revenues are liabilities recorded when cash is received from customers in advance of providing a good or service. Dell will satisfy these liabilities not by paying cash, but by providing a service to its customers.

> The debt to equity ratio indicates the extent of trading on the equity by using *financial leverage*.

Relationship Between Risk and Profitability.   The proportion of debt in the capital structure also is of interest to shareholders. After all, shareholders receive no return on their investments until after all creditor claims are paid. Therefore, the higher the debt to equity ratio, the higher the risk to shareholders. On the other hand, by earning a return on borrowed funds that exceeds the cost of borrowing the funds, a company can provide its shareholders with a total return higher than it could achieve by employing equity funds alone. This is referred to as favorable **financial leverage.**

For illustration, consider a newly formed corporation attempting to determine the appropriate mix of debt and equity. The initial capitalization goal is $50 million. The capitalization mix alternatives have been narrowed to two: (1) $10 million in debt and $40 million in equity and (2) $30 million in debt and $20 million in equity.

Also assume that regardless of the capitalization mix chosen, the corporation will be able to generate a 16% annual return, *before payment of interest and income taxes,* on the $50 million in assets acquired. In other words, income before interest and taxes will be $8 million (16% × $50 million). If the interest rate on debt is 8% and the income tax rate is 40%, comparative net income for the first year of operations for the two capitalization alternatives can be calculated as follows:

	Alternative 1	Alternative 2
Income before interest and taxes	$8,000,000	$8,000,000
Less: Interest expense	(800,000)[a]	(2,400,000)[b]
Income before taxes	$7,200,000	$5,600,000
Less: Income tax expense (40%)	(2,880,000)	(2,240,000)
Net income	$4,320,000	$3,360,000

[a]8% × $10,000,000
[b]8% × $30,000,000

Choose Alternative 1? Probably not. Although alternative 1 provides a higher net income, the return on the shareholders' equity (net income divided by shareholders' equity) is higher for alternative 2. Here's why:

> Favorable financial leverage means earning a return on borrowed funds that exceeds the cost of borrowing the funds.

	Alternative 1	Alternative 2
Return on shareholders' equity[15] =	$\dfrac{\$4,320,000}{\$40,000,000}$	$\dfrac{\$3,360,000}{\$20,000,000}$
=	10.8%	16.8%

[15]If return is calculated on *average* shareholders' equity, we're technically assuming that all income is paid to shareholders in cash dividends, so that beginning, ending, and average shareholders' equity are the same. If we assume *no* dividends are paid, rates of return would be:

	Alternative 1	Alternative 2
Return on shareholders' equity =	$\dfrac{\$4,320,000}{(\$44,320,000 + 40,000,000)/2}$	$\dfrac{\$3,360,000}{(\$20,000,000 + 23,360,000)/2}$
=	10.25%	15.50%

In any case our conclusions are the same.

Alternative 2 generated a higher return for each dollar invested by shareholders. This is because the company leveraged its $20 million equity investment with additional debt. Because the cost of the additional debt (8%) is less than the return on assets invested (16%), the return to shareholders is higher. This is the essence of favorable financial leverage.

Be aware, though, leverage is not always favorable; the cost of borrowing the funds might exceed the returns they provide. If the return on assets invested turned out to be less than expected, the additional debt could result in a lower return on equity for alternative 2. If, for example, the return on assets invested (before interest and taxes) had been 6%, rather than 16%, alternative 1 would have provided the better return on equity:

	Alternative 1	Alternative 2
Income before interest and taxes	$3,000,000	$3,000,000
Less: Interest expense	(800,000)[a]	(2,400,000)[b]
Income before taxes	$2,200,000	$ 600,000
Less: Income tax expense (40%)	(880,000)	(240,000)
Net income	$1,320,000	$ 360,000

[a]8% × $10,000,000
[b]8% × $30,000,000

$$\text{Return on shareholders' equity}^{16} = \frac{\$1,320,000}{\$40,000,000} \qquad \frac{\$360,000}{\$20,000,000}$$

$$= \qquad 3.3\% \qquad\qquad 1.8\%$$

So, shareholders typically are faced with a trade-off between the risk that high debt denotes and the potential for a higher return from having the higher debt. In any event, the debt to equity ratio offers a basis for making the choice.

TIMES INTEREST EARNED RATIO.   Another way to gauge the ability of a company to satisfy its fixed debt obligations is by comparing interest charges with the income available to pay those charges. The **times interest earned ratio** is designed to do this. It is calculated by dividing income before subtracting interest expense and income taxes by interest expense.

> The *times interest earned ratio* indicates the margin of safety provided to creditors.

Bondholders, noteholders, and other creditors can measure the margin of safety they are accorded by a company's earnings. If income is many times greater than interest expense, creditors' interests are more protected than if income just barely covers this expense. For this purpose, income should be the amount available to pay interest which is income before subtracting interest and income taxes, calculated by adding back to net income the interest and taxes that were deducted.

As an example, **Dell Inc.**'s financial statements for the fiscal year ended January 30, 2009, report the following:

	($ in millions)
Net income	$2,478
Interest expense	93
Income taxes	846
Income before interest and taxes	$3,417

The times interest earned ratio can be computed as follows:

$$\text{Times interest earned ratio} = \frac{\$3,417}{\$93} = 37 \text{ times}$$

---

[16]If we assume *no* dividends are paid, rates of return would be:

	Alternative 1	Alternative 2
Return on shareholders' equity =	$\dfrac{\$1,320,000}{(\$41,320,000 + 40,000,000)/2}$	$\dfrac{\$360,000}{(\$20,000,000 + 20,360,000)/2}$
=	3.25%	1.78%

In any case our conclusions are the same.

The ratio of 37 times indicates a considerable margin of safety for creditors. Income could decrease many times and the company would still be able to meet its interest payment obligations.[17] Dell is a highly profitable company with very little interest-bearing debt. In comparison, the average times interest earned ratio for the S&P 500 companies is approximately 31 times.

Especially when viewed alongside the debt-equity ratio, the coverage ratio seems to indicate a comfortable safety cushion for creditors. It also indicates a degree of financial mobility if the company were to decide to raise new debt funds to "trade on the equity" and attempt to increase the return to shareholders through favorable financial leverage.

FINANCIAL REPORTING CASE SOLUTION

1. **Respond to Jerry's criticism that shareholders' equity does not represent the market value of the company. What information does the balance sheet provide?** *(p. 115)* Jerry is correct. The financial statements are supposed to help investors and creditors value a company. However, the balance sheet is not intended to portray the market value of the entity. The assets of a company minus its liabilities as shown in the balance sheet (shareholders' equity) usually will not equal the company's market value for several reasons. For example, many assets are measured at their historical costs rather than their fair values. Also, many company resources including its trained employees, its experienced management team, and its reputation are not recorded as assets at all. The balance sheet must be used in conjunction with other financial statements, disclosure notes, and other publicly available information.

   The balance sheet does, however, provide valuable information that can be used by investors and creditors to help determine market value. After all, it is the balance sheet that describes many of the resources a company has available for generating future cash flows. The balance sheet also provides important information about liquidity and long-term solvency.

2. **The usefulness of the balance sheet is enhanced by classifying assets and liabilities according to common characteristics. What are the classifications used in Electronic Arts' balance sheets and what elements do those categories include?** *(p. 116)*

   Electronic Arts' balance sheets contain the following classifications:

   Assets:
   - *Current assets* include cash and several other assets that are reasonably expected to be converted to cash or consumed within the coming year, or within the normal operating cycle of the business if that's longer than one year.
   - *Property and equipment* are the tangible long-lived assets used in the operations of the business. This category includes land, buildings, equipment, machinery, and furniture, as well as natural resources.
   - *Goodwill* is a unique intangible asset in that its cost can't be directly associated with any specifically identifiable right and is not separable from the company as a whole. It represents the unique value of the company as a whole over and above all identifiable tangible and intangible assets.
   - *Other intangibles* are assets that represent exclusive rights to something such as a product, a process, or a name. Patents, copyrights, and franchises are examples.
   - *Deferred income taxes* result from temporary differences between taxable income and accounting income.
   - *Other assets* is a "catch-all" classification of noncurrent assets and could include long-term prepaid expenses and any noncurrent asset not included in one of the other categories.

   Liabilities:
   - *Current liabilities* are those obligations that are expected to be satisfied through the use of current assets or the creation of other current liabilities. Usually, this means

---

[17]Of course, interest is paid with cash, not with "income." The times interest earned ratio often is calculated by using cash flow from operations before subtracting either interest payments or tax payments as the numerator and interest payments as the denominator.

liabilities that are expected to be paid within one year, or the operating cycle if that's longer than one year.

* *Long-term liabilities* are payable further in the future and include bonds, deferred income taxes, and pension obligations. Electronic Arts lists *income tax obligations, deferred income taxes,* and *other liabilities* as its long-term liabilities.

Shareholders' equity:

* *Common stock* and *paid-in capital* collectively equal the amounts invested by shareholders in the corporation.
* *Retained earnings* represents the accumulated net income earned since inception of the corporation and not yet paid out to shareholders as dividends.
* *Accumulated other comprehensive income* is the cumulative amount of other comprehensive income items. This topic is addressed in subsequent chapters. ●

THE BOTTOM LINE

● **LO1**   The balance sheet is a position statement that presents an organized array of assets, liabilities, and shareholders' equity at a particular point in time. The statement does not portray the market value of the entity. However, the information in the statement can be useful in assessing market value, as well as in providing important information about liquidity and long-term solvency. (p. 115)

● **LO2**   Current assets include cash and other assets that are reasonably expected to be converted to cash or consumed during one year, or within the normal operating cycle of the business if the operating cycle is longer than one year. All other assets are classified as various types of noncurrent assets. Current liabilities are those obligations that are expected to be satisfied through the use of current assets or the creation of other current liabilities. All other liabilities are classified as long term. (p. 116)

● **LO3**   In addition to cash and cash equivalents, current assets include short-term investments, accounts receivable, inventories, and prepaid expenses. Other asset classifications include investments; property, plant, and equipment; intangible assets; and other assets. (p. 117)

● **LO4**   Current liabilities include notes and accounts payable, unearned revenues, accrued liabilities, and the current maturities of long-term debt. Long-term liabilities include long-term notes, loans, mortgages, bonds, pension and lease obligations, as well as deferred income taxes. (p. 120)

● **LO5**   Financial disclosures are used to convey additional information about the account balances in the basic financial statements as well as to provide supplemental information. This information is disclosed, often parenthetically in the basic financial statements, or in disclosure notes that often include supporting schedules. (p. 124)

● **LO6**   Annual financial statements of public companies will include management's discussion and analysis of key aspects of the company's business. The purpose of this disclosure is to provide external parties with management's insight into certain transactions, events, and circumstances that affect the enterprise, including their financial impact. (p. 128)

● **LO7**   The purpose of an audit is to provide a professional, independent opinion as to whether or not the financial statements are prepared in conformity with generally accepted accounting principles. The standard audit report of a public company contains four paragraphs; the first two deal with the scope of the audit and the third paragraph states the auditors' opinion regarding the financial statements. The fourth paragraph provides the auditors' opinion on the effectiveness of the company's internal control. (p. 129)

● **LO8**   Financial analysts use various techniques to transform financial information into forms more useful for analysis. Horizontal analysis and vertical analysis provide a useful way of analyzing year-to-year changes. Ratio analysis allows analysts to control for size differences over time and among firms while investigating important relationships among financial variables. (p. 132)

● **LO9**   The balance sheet provides information that can be useful in assessing risk. A key element of risk analysis is investigating a company's ability to pay its obligations when they come due. Liquidity ratios and financing ratios provide information about a company's ability to pay its obligations. (p. 133)

● **LO10**   There are more similarities than differences in balance sheets and financial disclosures prepared according to U.S. GAAP and those prepared applying IFRS. Balance sheet presentation is one important difference. Under U.S. GAAP, we present current assets and liabilities before noncurrent assets and liabilities. IFRS doesn't prescribe the format of the balance sheet, but balance sheets prepared using IFRS often report noncurrent items first. Reportable segment disclosures also are similar. However, IFRS requires an additional disclosure, the amount of segment liabilities (Appendix 3). (pp. 122 and 141) ●

REPORTING SEGMENT INFORMATION

Financial analysis of diversified companies is especially difficult. Consider, for example, a company that operates in several distinct business segments including computer peripherals, home health care systems, textiles, and consumer food products. The results of these distinctly different activities will be aggregated into a single set of financial statements, making difficult an informed projection of future performance. It may well be that the five-year outlook differs greatly among the areas of the economy represented by the different segments. To make matters worse for an analyst, the integrated financial statements do not reveal the relative investments in each of the business segments nor the success the company has had within each area. Given the fact that so many companies these days have chosen to balance their operating risks through diversification, aggregated financial statements pose a widespread problem for analysts, lending and credit officers, and other financial forecasters.

Many companies operate in several business segments as a strategy to achieve growth and to reduce operating risk through diversification.

Reporting by Operating Segment

Segment reporting facilitates the financial statement analysis of diversified companies.

To address the problem, the accounting profession requires companies engaged in more than one significant business to provide supplemental information concerning individual operating segments. The supplemental disaggregated data do not include complete financial statements for each reportable segment, only certain specified items.

WHAT IS A REPORTABLE OPERATING SEGMENT?

According to FASB guidelines, a *management approach* is used in determining which segments of a company are reportable. This approach is based on the way that management organizes the segments within the enterprise for making operating decisions and assessing performance. The segments are, therefore, evident from the structure of the enterprise's internal organization.

More formally, the following characteristics define an **operating segment:**[18]
An operating segment is a component of an enterprise:

- That engages in business activities from which it may earn revenues and incur expenses (including revenues and expenses relating to transactions with other components of the same enterprise).
- Whose operating results are regularly reviewed by the enterprise's chief operating decision maker to make decisions about resources to be allocated to the segment and assess its performance.
- For which discrete financial information is available.

The FASB hopes that this approach provides insights into the risk and opportunities management sees in the various areas of company operations. Also, reporting information based on the enterprise's internal organization should reduce the incremental cost to companies of providing the data. In addition, there are quantitative thresholds for the definition of an operating segment to limit the number of reportable segments. Only segments of certain size (10% or more of total company revenues, assets, or net income) must be disclosed. However, a company must account for at least 75% of consolidated revenue through segment disclosures.

WHAT AMOUNTS ARE REPORTED BY AN OPERATING SEGMENT?

For areas determined to be reportable operating segments, the following disclosures are required:

a. General information about the operating segment.
b. Information about reported segment profit or loss, including certain revenues and expenses included in reported segment profit or loss, segment assets, and the basis of measurement.

---

[18]FASB ASC 280–10–50–1: Segment Reporting—Overall—Disclosure (previously "Disclosures about Segments of an Enterprise and Related Information," *Statement of Financial Accounting Standards No. 131* (Norwalk, Conn.: FASB, 1997), par. 10).

c. Reconciliations of the totals of segment revenues, reported profit or loss, assets, and other significant items to corresponding enterprise amounts.

d. Interim period information.[19]

Graphic 3A–1 shows the business segment information reported by **3M Co.** in its 2008 annual report.

GRAPHIC 3A–1

Business Segment Information Disclosure—3M Co.

Real World Financials

Business Segment Information
($ in millions)

		Net Sales	Operating Income	Assets	Depr. and Amort.	Capital Expendit.
Industrial and Transportation	2008	$ 7,818	$ 1,477	$ 6,202	$ 312	$ 395
	2007	7,266	1,497	5,872	294	396
	2006	6,632	1,338	5,180	287	284
Health Care	2008	4,293	1,173	3,096	161	210
	2007	3,968	1,882	2,909	138	213
	2006	4,011	1,845	2,477	162	159
Safety, Security, and Protection Services	2008	3,642	736	3,326	170	180
	2007	3,070	611	2,344	161	205
	2006	2,663	549	2,601	120	151
Consumer and Office	2008	3,448	663	1,786	86	107
	2007	3,411	692	1,720	82	101
	2006	3,172	633	1,577	77	103
Display and Graphics	2008	3,255	580	3,479	243	379
	2007	3,904	1,163	3,199	222	341
	2006	3,747	1,045	3,035	232	323
Electro and Communications	2008	2,791	531	2,186	141	177
	2007	2,763	492	2,063	146	136
	2006	2,654	410	2,003	173	117
Corporate and Unallocated	2008	22	58	5,472	40	23
	2007	80	(144)	6,587	29	30
	2006	44	(124)	4,961	28	31
Total Company	2008	$25,269	$ 5,218	$25,547	$1,153	$1,471
	2007	24,462	6,193	24,694	1,072	1,422
	2006	22,923	5,696	21,294	1,079	1,168

● LO10

INTERNATIONAL FINANCIAL REPORTING STANDARDS

Segment Reporting. U.S. GAAP requires companies to report information about reported segment profit or loss, including certain revenues and expenses included in reported segment profit or loss, segment assets, and the basis of measurement. The international standard on segment reporting, *IFRS No. 8*,[20] requires that companies also disclose total *liabilities* of its reportable segments.

[19]FASB ASC 280–10–50–20 through 26 and 280–10–50–32: Segment Reporting—Overall—Disclosure (previously "Disclosures about Segments of an Enterprise and Related Information," *Statement of Financial Accounting Standards No. 131* (Norwalk, Conn.: FASB, 1997), par. 25).

[20]"Operating Segments," *International Financial Reporting Standard No. 8* (IASCF), as amended effective January 1, 2009.

REPORTING BY GEOGRAPHIC AREA

In today's global economy it is sometimes difficult to distinguish domestic and foreign companies. Most large U.S. firms conduct significant operations in other countries in addition to having substantial export sales from this country. Differing political and economic environments from country to country means risks and associated rewards sometimes vary greatly among the various operations of a single company. For instance, manufacturing facilities in a South American country embroiled in political unrest pose different risks from having a plant in Vermont, or even Canada. Without disaggregated financial information, these differences cause problems for analysts.

GAAP requires an enterprise to report certain geographic information unless it is impracticable to do so. This information includes:

a. Revenues from external customers (1) attributed to the enterprise's country of domicile and (2) attributed to all foreign countries in total from which the enterprise derives revenues, and

b. Long-lived assets other than financial instruments, long-term customer relationships of a financial institution, mortgage and other servicing rights, deferred policy acquisition costs, and deferred tax assets (1) located in the enterprise's country of domicile and (2) located in all foreign countries in total in which the enterprise holds assets.[21]

3M reported its geographic area information separately in a table reproduced in Graphic 3A–2. Notice that both the business segment (Graphic 3A–1) and geographic information disclosures include a reconciliation to company totals. For example, in both graphics, year 2008 net sales of both the segments and the geographic areas are reconciled to the company's total net sales of $25,269 ($ in millions).

GRAPHIC 3A–2   Geographic Area Information Disclosure—3M Company

Geographic Areas
($ in millions)

		United States	Asia Pacific	Europe, Middle East, and Africa	Latin America and Canada	Other Unallocated	Total Company
Net sales to customers	2008	$9,179	$6,423	$6,941	$2,723	$ 3	$25,269
	2007	8,987	6,601	6,503	2,365	6	24,462
	2006	8,853	6,251	5,726	2,080	13	22,923
Operating income	2008	1,578	1,662	1,294	693	(9)	5,218
	2007	1,894	2,062	1,626	616	(5)	6,193
	2006	2,117	2,013	1,012	585	(31)	5,696
Property, plant, and equipment	2008	3,901	1,304	1,263	418	—	6,886
	2007	3,668	1,116	1,308	490	—	6,582
	2006	3,382	959	1,162	404	—	5,907

Real World Financials

For another example of both business segment and geographic area disclosures, see the **Dell Inc.** segment information reported in the financial statements in Appendix B at the back of the text.

INFORMATION ABOUT MAJOR CUSTOMERS

Revenues from major customers must be disclosed.

Some companies in the defense industry derive substantial portions of their revenues from contracts with the Defense Department. When cutbacks occur in national defense or in specific defense systems, the impact on a company's operations can be considerable. Obviously, financial analysts are extremely interested in information concerning the extent to

---

[21]FASB ASC 280–10–50–41: Segment Reporting—Overall—Disclosure (previously "Disclosures about Segments of an Enterprise and Related Information," *Statement of Financial Accounting Standards No. 131* (Norwalk, Conn.: FASB, 1997), par. 38).

GRAPHIC 3A–3

Major Customer Disclosure—Procter & Gamble Company

Real World Financials

Note 12. Segment Information (in part)

Our largest customer, Walmart Stores, Inc. and its affiliates, accounted for 15% of consolidated net sales in 2009, 2008, and 2007.

which a company's prosperity depends on one or more major customers such as in the situation described here. For this reason, if 10% or more of the revenue of an enterprise is derived from transactions with a single customer, the enterprise must disclose that fact, the total amount of revenue from each such customer, and the identity of the operating segment or segments earning the revenue. The identity of the major customer or customers need not be disclosed, although companies routinely provide that information. In its 2008 annual report, 3M did not report any major customer information. As an example of this type of disclosure, **Procter & Gamble Company**'s business segment disclosure included information on its largest customer, **Walmart**, as shown in Graphic 3A–3 (above). ●

QUESTIONS FOR REVIEW OF KEY TOPICS

Q 3–1	Describe the purpose of the balance sheet.
Q 3–2	Explain why the balance sheet does not portray the market value of the entity.
Q 3–3	Define current assets and list the typical asset categories included in this classification.
Q 3–4	Define current liabilities and list the typical liability categories included in this classification.
Q 3–5	Describe what is meant by an operating cycle for a typical manufacturing company.
Q 3–6	Explain the difference(s) between investments in equity securities classified as current assets versus those classified as noncurrent assets.
Q 3–7	Describe the common characteristics of assets classified as property, plant, and equipment and identify some assets included in this classification.
Q 3–8	Distinguish between property, plant, and equipment and intangible assets.
Q 3–9	Explain how each of the following liabilities would be classified in the balance sheet:

- A note payable of $100,000 due in five years.
- A note payable of $100,000 payable in annual installments of $20,000 each, with the first installment due next year.

Q 3–10	Define the terms *paid-in-capital* and *retained earnings*.
Q 3–11	Disclosure notes are an integral part of the information provided in financial statements. In what ways are the notes critical to understanding the financial statements and to evaluating the firm's performance and financial health?
Q 3–12	A summary of the company's significant accounting policies is a required disclosure. Why is this disclosure important to external financial statement users?
Q 3–13	Define a subsequent event.
Q 3–14	Every annual report of a public company includes an extensive discussion and analysis provided by the company's management. Specifically, which aspects of the company must this discussion address? Isn't management's perspective too biased to be of use to investors and creditors?
Q 3–15	The auditors' report provides the analyst with an independent and professional opinion about the fairness of the representations in the financial statements. What are the four main types of opinion an auditor might issue? Describe each.
Q 3–16	What is a proxy statement? What information does it provide?
Q 3–17	Define the terms *working capital, current ratio,* and *acid-test ratio* (or *quick ratio*).
Q 3–18	Show the calculation of the following financing ratios: (1) the debt to equity ratio, and (2) the times interest earned ratio.
⊕ IFRS Q 3–19	Where can we find authoritative guidance for balance sheet presentation under IFRS?
⊕ IFRS Q 3–20	Describe at least two differences between U.S. GAAP and IFRS in balance sheet presentation.
Q 3–21	(Based on Appendix 3) Segment reporting facilitates the financial statement analysis of diversified companies. What determines whether an operating segment is a reportable segment for this purpose?
Q 3–22	(Based on Appendix 3) For segment reporting purposes, what amounts are reported by each operating segment?
⊕ IFRS Q 3–23	(Based on Appendix 3) Describe any differences in segment disclosure requirements between U.S. GAAP and IFRS.

BRIEF EXERCISES

BE 3–1
Current versus
noncurrent
classification
● LO2

Indicate whether each of the following assets and liabilities should be classified as current or noncurrent: (a) accounts receivable; (b) prepaid rent for the next six months; (c) note receivable due in two years; (d) note payable due in 90 days; (e) note payable due in five years; and (f) patent.

BE 3–2
Balance sheet
classification
● LO3 LO4

The trial balance for K and J Nursery, Inc. listed the following account balances at December, 31, 2011, the end of its fiscal year: cash, $16,000; accounts receivable, $11,000; inventories, $25,000; equipment (net), $80,000; accounts payable, $14,000; wages payable, $9,000; interest payable, $1,000; note payable (due in 18 months), $30,000; common stock, $50,000. Calculate total current assets and total current liabilities that would appear in the company's year-end balance sheet.

BE 3–3
Balance sheet
classification
● LO3 LO4

Refer to the situation described in BE 3–2. Determine the year-end balance in retained earnings for K and J Nursery, Inc.

BE 3–4
Balance sheet
preparation
● LO2 through
LO4

Refer to the situation described in BE 3–2. Prepare a classified balance sheet for K and J Nursery, Inc. The equipment originally cost $140,000.

BE 3–5
Balance sheet
preparation
● LO2 through
LO4

The following is a December 31, 2011, post-closing trial balance for Culver City Lighting, Inc. Prepare a classified balance sheet for the company.

Account Title	Debits	Credits
Cash	55,000	
Accounts receivable	39,000	
Inventories	45,000	
Prepaid insurance	15,000	
Equipment	100,000	
Accumulated depreciation—equipment		34,000
Patent, net	40,000	
Accounts payable		12,000
Interest payable		2,000
Note payable (due in 10, equal annual installments)		100,000
Common stock		70,000
Retained earnings		76,000
Totals	294,000	294,000

BE 3–6
Balance sheet
classification
● LO2 through
LO4

You have been asked to review the December 31, 2011, balance sheet for Champion Cleaning. After completing your review, you list the following three items for discussion with your superior:

1. An investment of $30,000 is included in current assets. Management has indicated that it has no intention of liquidating the investment in 2012.

2. A $100,000 note payable is listed as a long-term liability, but you have determined that the note is due in 10, equal annual installments with the first installment due on March 31, 2012.

3. Unearned revenue of $60,000 is included as a current liability even though only two-thirds will be earned in 2012.

Determine the appropriate classification of each of these items.

BE 3–7
Balance sheet
preparation;
missing elements
● LO2 through LO4

The following information is taken from the balance sheet of Raineer Plumbing: cash and cash equivalents, $40,000; accounts receivable, $120,000; inventories, ?; total current assets, $235,000; property, plant, and equipment (net), ?; total assets, $400,000; accounts payable, $32,000; note payable (due in two years), $50,000; common stock, $100,000; and retained earnings, ?. Determine the missing amounts.

BE 3–8
Financial
disclosures
● LO5

For each of the following note disclosures, indicate whether the disclosure would likely appear in (A) the summary of significant accounts policies or (B) a separate note: (1) depreciation method; (2) contingency information; (3) significant issuance of common stock after the fiscal year-end; (4) cash equivalent designation; (5) long-term debt information; and (6) inventory costing method.

BE 3–9
Calculating ratios
● LO9

Refer to the trial balance information in BE 3–5. Calculate the (a) current ratio, (b) acid-test ratio, and (c) debt to equity ratio.

BE 3–10
Effect of decisions on ratios
● LO9

At the end of 2011, Barker Corporation's preliminary trial balance indicated a current ratio of 1.2. Management is contemplating paying some of its accounts payable balance before the end of the fiscal year. Explain the effect this transaction would have on the current ratio. Would your answer be the same if the preliminary trial balance indicated a current ratio of .8?

BE 3–11
Calculating ratios; solving for unknowns
● LO9

The current asset section of Stibbe Pharmaceutical Company's balance sheet included cash of $20,000 and accounts receivable of $40,000. The only other current asset is inventories. The company's current ratio is 2.0 and its acid-test ratio is 1.5. Determine the ending balance in inventories and total current liabilities.

EXERCISES

An alternate exercise and problem set is available on the text website: www.mhhe.com/spiceland6e

E 3–1
Balance sheet; missing elements
● LO3 LO4 LO8

The following December 31, 2011, fiscal year-end account balance information is available for the Stonebridge Corporation:

Cash and cash equivalents	$ 5,000
Accounts receivable (net)	20,000
Inventories	60,000
Property, plant, and equipment (net)	120,000
Accounts payable	44,000
Wages payable	15,000
Paid-in-capital	100,000

The only asset not listed is short-term investments. The only liabilities not listed are a $30,000 note payable due in two years and related accrued interest of $1,000 due in four months. The current ratio at year-end is 1.5:1.

Required:
Determine the following at December 31, 2011:
1. Total current assets
2. Short-term investments
3. Retained earnings

E 3–2
Balance sheet classification
● LO3 LO4

The following are the typical classifications used in a balance sheet:
a. Current assets
b. Investments and funds
c. Property, plant, and equipment
d. Intangible assets
e. Other assets

f. Current liabilities
g. Long-term liabilities
h. Paid-in-capital
i. Retained earnings

Required:
For each of the following balance sheet items, use the letters above to indicate the appropriate classification category. If the item is a contra account, place a minus sign before the chosen letter.

1. _____ Equipment
2. _____ Accounts payable
3. _____ Allowance for uncollectible accounts
4. _____ Land, held for investment
5. _____ Note payable, due in 5 years
6. _____ Unearned rent revenue
7. _____ Note payable, due in 6 months
8. _____ Income less dividends, accumulated
9. _____ Investment in XYZ Corp., long-term

10. _____ Inventories
11. _____ Patent
12. _____ Land, in use
13. _____ Accrued liabilities
14. _____ Prepaid rent
15. _____ Common stock
16. _____ Building, in use
17. _____ Cash
18. _____ Taxes payable

E 3–3
Balance sheet
classification
● LO3 LO4

The following are the typical classifications used in a balance sheet:
a. Current assets
b. Investments and funds
c. Property, plant, and equipment
d. Intangible assets
e. Other assets
f. Current liabilities
g. Long-term liabilities
h. Paid-in-capital
i. Retained earnings

Required:

For each of the following 2011 balance sheet items, use the letters above to indicate the appropriate classification category. If the item is a contra account, place a minus sign before the chosen letter.

1. ____ Accrued interest payable
2. ____ Franchise
3. ____ Accumulated depreciation
4. ____ Prepaid insurance, for 2013
5. ____ Bonds payable, due in 10 years
6. ____ Current maturities of long-term debt
7. ____ Note payable, due in three months
8. ____ Long-term receivables
9. ____ Bond sinking fund, will be used to retire bonds in 10 years
10. ____ Supplies
11. ____ Machinery
12. ____ Land, in use
13. ____ Unearned revenue
14. ____ Copyrights
15. ____ Preferred stock
16. ____ Land, held for speculation
17. ____ Cash equivalents
18. ____ Wages payable

E 3–4
Balance sheet
preparation
● LO2 through
  LO4

The following is a December 31, 2011, post-closing trial balance for the Jackson Corporation.

Account Title	Debits	Credits
Cash	40,000	
Accounts receivable	34,000	
Inventories	75,000	
Prepaid rent	16,000	
Marketable securities (short term)	10,000	
Machinery	145,000	
Accumulated depreciation—machinery		11,000
Patent (net of amortization)	83,000	
Accounts payable		8,000
Wages payable		4,000
Taxes payable		32,000
Bonds payable (due in 10 years)		200,000
Common stock		100,000
Retained earnings		48,000
Totals	403,000	403,000

Required:
Prepare a classified balance sheet for Jackson Corporation at December 31, 2011.

E 3–5
Balance sheet
preparation
● LO2 through
  LO4

The following is a December 31, 2011, post-closing trial balance for the Valley Pump Corporation.

Account Title	Debits	Credits
Cash	25,000	
Accounts receivable	56,000	
Inventories	81,000	
Interest payable		10,000
Marketable securities	44,000	
Land	120,000	
Buildings	300,000	
Accumulated depreciation—buildings		100,000
Equipment	75,000	
Accumulated depreciation—equipment		25,000
Copyright (net of amortization)	12,000	
Prepaid expenses	32,000	
Accounts payable		65,000
Unearned revenues		20,000
Notes payable		250,000
Allowance for uncollectible accounts		5,000
Common stock		200,000
Retained earnings		70,000
Totals	745,000	745,000

Additional information:

1. The $120,000 balance in the land account consists of $100,000 for the cost of land where the plant and office buildings are located. The remaining $20,000 represents the cost of land being held for speculation.

2. The $44,000 in the marketable securities account represents an investment in the common stock of another corporation. Valley intends to sell one-half of the stock within the next year.

3. The notes payable account consists of a $100,000 note due in six months and a $150,000 note due in three annual installments of $50,000 each, with the first payment due in August of 2012.

Required:

Prepare a classified balance sheet for the Valley Pump Corporation at December 31, 2011.

E 3–6
Balance sheet;
current versus
noncurrent
classification
● LO2 through
LO4

Presented below is a partial trial balance for the Kansas Instruments Corporation at December 31, 2011.

Account Title	Debits	Credits
Cash	20,000	
Accounts receivable	130,000	
Raw materials	24,000	
Note receivable	100,000	
Interest receivable	3,000	
Interest payable		5,000
Marketable securities	32,000	
Land	50,000	
Buildings	1,300,000	
Accumulated depreciation—buildings		620,000
Work in process	42,000	
Finished goods	89,000	
Equipment	300,000	
Accumulated depreciation—equipment		130,000
Patent (net of amortization)	120,000	
Prepaid rent (for the next two years)	60,000	
Unearned revenue		36,000
Accounts payable		180,000
Note payable		400,000
Cash restricted for payment of note payable	80,000	
Allowance for uncollectible accounts		13,000
Sales revenue		800,000
Cost of goods sold	450,000	
Rent expense	28,000	

Additional information:

1. The note receivable, along with any accrued interest, is due on November 22, 2012.

2. The note payable is due in 2015. Interest is payable annually.

3. The marketable securities consist of treasury bills, all of which mature in the next year.

4. Unearned revenue will be earned equally over the next two years.

Required:

Determine the company's working capital (current assets minus current liabilities) at December 31, 2011.

E 3–7
Balance sheet
preparation; errors
● LO2 through
LO4

The following balance sheet for the Los Gatos Corporation was prepared by a recently hired accountant. In reviewing the statement you notice several errors.

LOS GATOS CORPORATION
Balance Sheet
At December 31, 2011
Assets

Cash	$ 40,000
Accounts receivable	80,000
Inventories	55,000
Machinery (net)	120,000
Franchise (net)	30,000
Total assets	$325,000

Liabilities and Shareholders' Equity

Accounts payable	$ 50,000
Allowance for uncollectible accounts	5,000
Note payable	55,000
Bonds payable	110,000
Shareholders' equity	105,000
Total liabilities and shareholders' equity	$325,000

Additional information:

1. Cash includes a $20,000 bond sinking fund to be used for repayment of the bonds payable in 2015.
2. The cost of the machinery is $190,000.
3. Accounts receivable includes a $20,000 note receivable from a customer due in 2014.
4. The note payable includes accrued interest of $5,000. Principal and interest are both due on February 1, 2012.
5. The company began operations in 2006. Income less dividends since inception of the company totals $35,000.
6. 50,000 shares of no par common stock were issued in 2006. 100,000 shares are authorized.

Required:

Prepare a corrected, classified balance sheet.

E 3–8
Balance sheet; current versus noncurrent classification
● LO2 through LO4

Cone Corporation is in the process of preparing its December 31, 2011, balance sheet. There are some questions as to the proper classification of the following items:

a. $50,000 in cash set aside in a savings account to pay bonds payable. The bonds mature in 2015.
b. Prepaid rent of $24,000, covering the period January 1, 2012, through December 31, 2013.
c. Note payable of $200,000. The note is payable in annual installments of $20,000 each, with the first installment payable on March 1, 2012.
d. Accrued interest payable of $12,000 related to the note payable.
e. Investment in marketable securities of other corporations, $80,000. Cone intends to sell one-half of the securities in 2012.

Required:

Prepare a partial classified balance sheet to show how each of the above items should be reported.

E 3–9
Balance sheet preparation; cash versus accrual accounting; Chapters 2 and 3
● LO2 through LO4

The following is the balance sheet of Korver Supply Company at December 31, 2010.

KORVER SUPPLY COMPANY
Balance Sheet
At December 31, 2010

Assets

Cash	$120,000
Accounts receivable	300,000
Inventories	200,000
Furniture and fixtures, net	150,000
Total assets	$770,000

Liabilities and Shareholders' Equity

Accounts payable (for merchandise)	$190,000
Note payable	200,000
Interest payable	6,000
Common stock	100,000
Retained earnings	274,000
Total liabilities and shareholders' equity	$770,000

Transactions during 2011 were as follows:

1. Sales to customers on account	$800,000
2. Cash collected from customers	780,000
3. Purchase of merchandise on account	550,000
4. Cash payment to suppliers	560,000
5. Cost of merchandise sold	500,000
6. Cash paid for operating expenses	160,000
7. Cash paid for interest on note	12,000

The note payable is dated June 30, 2010 and is due on June 30, 2012. Interest at 6% is payable annually on June 30. Depreciation on the furniture and fixtures for the year is $20,000. The furniture and fixtures originally cost $300,000.

Required:

Prepare a classified balance sheet at December 21, 2011 (ignore income taxes).

E 3–10
Financial
disclosures

● LO5

The following are typical disclosures that would appear in the notes accompanying financial statements. For each of the items listed, indicate where the disclosure would likely appear—either in (A) the significant accounting policies note or (B) a separate note.

1. Inventory costing method   A
2. Information on related party transactions   ___
3. Composition of property, plant, and equipment   ___
4. Depreciation method   ___
5. Subsequent event information   ___
6. Basis of revenue recognition on long-term contracts ___
7. Important merger occurring after year-end   ___
8. Composition of receivables   ___

E 3–11
Disclosure notes

● LO5

Hallergan Company produces car and truck batteries that it sells primarily to auto manufacturers. Dorothy Hawkins, the company's controller, is preparing the financial statements for the year ended December 31, 2011. Hawkins asks for your advice concerning the following information that has not yet been included in the statements. The statements will be issued on February 28, 2012.

1. Hallergan leases its facilities from the brother of the chief executive officer.

2. On January 8, 2012, Hallergan entered into an agreement to sell a tract of land that it had been holding as an investment. The sale, which resulted in a material gain, was completed on February 2, 2012.

3. Hallergan uses the straight-line method to determine depreciation on all of the company's depreciable assets.

4. On February 8, 2012, Hallergan completed negotiations with its bank for a $10,000,000 line of credit.

5. Hallergan uses the first-in, first-out (FIFO) method to value inventory.

Required:

For each of the above items, discuss any additional disclosures that Hawkins should include in Hallergan's financial statements.

E 3–12
Financial
disclosures

● LO5

Parkman Sporting Goods is preparing its annual report for its 2011 fiscal year. The company's controller has asked for your help in determining how best to disclose information about the following items:

1. A related-party transaction.

2. Depreciation method.

3. Allowance for uncollectible accounts.

4. Composition of investments.

5. Composition of long-term debt.

6. Inventory costing method.

7. Number of shares of common stock authorized, issued, and outstanding.

8. Employee benefit plans.

Required:

Indicate whether the above items should be disclosed (A) in the summary of significant accounting policies note, (B) in a separate disclosure note, or (C) on the face of the balance sheet.

E 3–13
FASB codification
research

● LO5

The *FASB Accounting Standards Codification* represents the single source of authoritative U.S. generally accepted accounting principles.

Required:

1. Obtain the relevant authoritative literature on the disclosure of accounting policies using the FASB's Codification Research System at the FASB website (**www.fasb.org**). Identify the topic number that provides guidance on information contained in the notes to the financial statements.

2. What is the specific citation that requires a company to identify and describe in the notes to the financial statements the accounting principles and methods used to prepare the financial statements?

3. Describe the disclosure requirements.

E 3–14
FASB codification
research

● LO5

Access the FASB's Codification Research System at the FASB website (**www.fasb.org**). Determine the specific citation for each of the following items:

1. What is the balance sheet classification for a note payable due in six months which was used to purchase a building?

2. Which assets may be excluded from current assets?

3. Should a note receivable from a related party be included in the balance sheet with notes receivable or accounts receivable from customers?

4. What items are nonrecognized subsequent events that require a disclosure in the notes to the financial statements?

E 3–15
Concepts; terminology
● LO2 through LO5 LO7

Listed below are several terms and phrases associated with the balance sheet and financial disclosures. Pair each item from List A (by letter) with the item from List B that is most appropriately associated with it.

List A	List B
___ 1. Balance sheet	a. Will be satisfied through the use of current assets.
___ 2. Liquidity	b. Items expected to be converted to cash or consumed within one year or the operating cycle, whichever is longer.
___ 3. Current assets	
___ 4. Operating cycle	c. The statements are presented fairly in conformity with GAAP.
___ 5. Current liabilities	d. An organized array of assets, liabilities, and equity.
___ 6. Cash equivalent	e. Important to a user in comparing financial information across companies.
___ 7. Intangible asset	
___ 8. Working capital	f. Scope limitation or a departure from GAAP.
___ 9. Accrued liabilities	g. Recorded when an expense is incurred but not yet paid.
___ 10. Summary of significant accounting policies	h. Relates to the amount of time before an asset is converted to cash or a liability is paid.
___ 11. Subsequent events	i. Occurs after the fiscal year-end but before the statements are issued.
___ 12. Unqualified opinion	j. Cash to cash.
___ 13. Qualified opinion	k. One-month U.S. Treasury bill.
	l. Current assets minus current liabilities.
	m. Lacks physical substance.

E 3–16
Calculating ratios
● LO9

The 2011 balance sheet for Hallbrook Industries, Inc. is shown below.

HALLBROOK INDUSTRIES, INC.
Balance Sheet
December 31, 2011
($ in 000s)

Assets

Cash	$ 200
Short-term investments	150
Accounts receivable	200
Inventories	350
Property, plant, and equipment (net)	1,000
Total assets	$1,900

Liabilities and Shareholders' Equity

Current liabilities	$ 400
Long-term liabilities	350
Paid-in capital	750
Retained earnings	400
Total liabilities and shareholders' equity	$1,900

The company's 2011 income statement reported the following amounts ($ in 000s):

Net sales	$4,600
Interest expense	40
Income tax expense	100
Net income	160

Required:
Determine the following ratios for 2011:

1. Current ratio
2. Acid-test ratio
3. Debt to equity ratio
4. Times interest earned ratio

E 3–17
Calculating ratios;
Best Buy

● LO9

Real World Financials

Best Buy Co, Inc., is a leading retailer specializing in consumer electronics. A condensed income statement and balance sheet for the fiscal year ended February 28, 2009, are shown below.

Best Buy Co., Inc.
Balance Sheet
At February 28, 2009
($ in millions)

Assets

Current assets:	
Cash and cash equivalents	$ 498
Short-term investments	11
Accounts receivable, net	1,868
Merchandise inventories	4,753
Other current assets	1,062
Total current assets	8,192
Noncurrent assets	7,634
Total assets	$15,826

Liabilities and Shareholders' Equity

Current liabilities:	
Accounts payable	$ 4,997
Other current liabilities	3,438
Total current liabilities	8,435
Long-term liabilities	2,748
Shareholders' equity	4,643
Total liabilities and shareholders' equity	$15,826

Best Buy Co., Inc.
Income Statement
For the Year Ended February 28, 2009
($ in millions)

Revenues	$45,015
Costs and expenses	43,145
Operating income	1,870
Investment loss, net*	(193)
Income before income taxes	1,677
Income tax expense	674
Net income	$ 1,003

*Includes $94 of interest expense.

Liquidity and financing ratios for the industry are as follows:

	Industry Average
Current ratio	1.2
Acid-test ratio	.6
Debt to equity	.43
Times interest earned	.8 times

Required:

1. Determine the following ratios for Best Buy for its fiscal year ended February, 28, 2009:
   1. Current ratio
   2. Acid-test ratio
   3. Debt to equity ratio
   4. Times interest earned ratio
2. Using the ratios from requirement 1, assess Best Buy's liquidity and solvency relative to its industry.

E 3–18
Calculating ratios;
solve for unknowns
● LO9

The current asset section of the Excalibur Tire Company's balance sheet consists of cash, marketable securities, accounts receivable, and inventories. The December 31, 2011, balance sheet revealed the following:

Inventories	$ 840,000
Total assets	$2,800,000
Current ratio	2.25
Acid-test ratio	1.2
Debt to equity ratio	1.8

Required:
Determine the following 2011 balance sheet items:
1. Current assets
2. Shareholders' equity
3. Noncurrent assets
4. Long-term liabilities

E 3–19
Calculating ratios;
solve for unknowns
● LO9

The current asset section of Guardian Consultant's balance sheet consists of cash, accounts receivable, and prepaid expenses. The 2011 balance sheet reported the following: cash, $1,300,000; prepaid expenses, $360,000; noncurrent assets, $2,400,000; and shareholders' equity, $2,500,000. The current ratio at the end of the year was 2.0 and the debt to equity ratio was 1.4.

Required:
Determine the following 2011 amounts and ratios:
1. Current liabilities.
2. Long-term liabilities.
3. Accounts receivable.
4. The acid-test ratio.

E 3–20
Effect of
management
decisions on ratios
● LO9

Most decisions made by management impact the ratios analysts use to evaluate performance. Indicate (by letter) whether each of the actions listed below will immediately increase (I), decrease (D), or have no effect (N) on the ratios shown. Assume each ratio is less than 1.0 before the action is taken.

Action	Current Ratio	Acid-Test Ratio	Debt to Equity Ratio
1. Issuance of long-term bonds	_____	_____	_____
2. Issuance of short-term notes	_____	_____	_____
3. Payment of accounts payable	_____	_____	_____
4. Purchase of inventory on account	_____	_____	_____
5. Purchase of inventory for cash	_____	_____	_____
6. Purchase of equipment with a 4-year note	_____	_____	_____
7. Retirement of bonds	_____	_____	_____
8. Sale of common stock	_____	_____	_____
9. Write-off of obsolete inventory	_____	_____	_____
10. Purchase of short-term investment for cash	_____	_____	_____
11. Decision to refinance on a long-term basis some currently maturing debt	_____	_____	_____

E 3–21
Segment reporting
● Appendix

The Canton Corporation operates in four distinct business segments. The segments, along with 2011 information on revenues, assets and net income, are listed below ($ in millions):

Segment	Revenues	Assets	Net Income
Pharmaceuticals	$2,000	$1,000	$200
Plastics	3,000	1,500	270
Farm equipment	2,500	1,250	320
Electronics	500	250	40
Total company	$8,000	$4,000	$830

Required:
1. For which segments must Canton report supplementary information according to U.S. GAAP?
2. What amounts must be reported for the segments you identified in requirement 1?

E 3–22
Segment reporting
● Appendix LO10

Refer to Exercise 3–21.

Required:

How might your answers differ if Canton Corporation prepares its segment disclosure according to International Financial Reporting Standards?

CPA AND CMA EXAM QUESTIONS

The following questions are used in the Kaplan CPA Review Course to study balance sheet presentation, financial disclosures, and liquidity ratios while preparing for the CPA examination. Determine the response that best completes the statements or questions.

● LO2

1. In Merf's April 30, 2011, balance sheet, a note receivable was reported as a noncurrent asset and the related accrued interest for eight months was reported as a current asset. Which of the following descriptions would fit Merf's receivable classification?
   a. Both principal and interest amounts are due on August 31, 2011, and August 31, 2012.
   b. Principal is due August 31, 2012, and interest is due August 31, 2011, and August 31, 2012.
   c. Principal and interest are due December 31, 2011.
   d. Both principal and interest amounts are due on December 31, 2011, and December 31, 2012.

● LO2

2. Mill Co.'s trial balance included the following account balances at December 31, 2011:

Accounts payable	$15,000
Bond payable, due 2012	22,000
Dividends payable 1/31/12	8,000
Notes payable, due 2013	20,000

   What amount should be included in the current liability section of Mill's December 31, 2011, balance sheet?
   a. $45,000
   b. $51,000
   c. $65,000
   d. $78,000

● LO5

3. Which of the following would be disclosed in the summary of significant accounting policies disclosure note?

	Composition of Plant Assets	Inventory Pricing
a.	No	Yes
b.	Yes	No
c.	Yes	Yes
d.	No	No

● LO7

4. How are management's responsibility and the auditor's report represented in the standard auditor's report?

	Management's Responsibility	Auditor's Responsibility
a.	Implicitly	Explicitly
b.	Implicitly	Implicitly
c.	Explicitly	Explicitly
d.	Explicitly	Implicitly

● LO9

5. At December 30, Vida Co. had cash of $200,000, a current ratio of 1.5:1, and a quick ratio of .5:1. On December 31, all the cash was used to reduce accounts payable. How did this cash payment affect the ratios?

	Current Ratio	Quick Ratio
a.	Increased	No effect
b.	Increased	Decreased
c.	Decreased	Increased
d.	Decreased	No effect

● LO9

6. Zenk Co. wrote off obsolete inventory of $100,000 during 2011. What was the effect of this write-off on Zenk's ratio analysis?
   a. Decrease in the current ratio but not the quick ratio.
   b. Decrease in the quick ratio but not in the current ratio.
   c. Increase in the current ratio but not in the quick ratio.
   d. Increase in the quick ratio but not in the current ratio.

The following questions dealing with balance sheet presentation, financial disclosures, and liquidity ratios are adapted from questions that previously appeared on Certified Management Accountant (CMA) examinations. The CMA designation sponsored by the Institute of Management Accountants (**www.imanet.org**) provides members with an objective measure of knowledge and competence in the field of management accounting. Determine the response that best completes the statements or questions.

● LO5

1. The Financial Accounting Standards Board has provided guidance on disclosures of transactions between related parties, for example, transactions between subsidiaries of a common parent. GAAP regarding related-party transactions requires all of the following disclosures except
   a. The nature of the relationship involved.
   b. A description of the transactions for each period an income statement is presented.
   c. The dollar amounts of transactions for each period an income statement is presented.
   d. The effect on the cash flow statement for each period a cash flow statement is presented.

● LO6

2. The Management's Discussion and Analysis (MD&A) section of an annual report
   a. Includes the company president's letter.
   b. Covers three financial aspects of a firm's business: liquidity, capital resources, and results of operations.
   c. Is a technical analysis of past results and a defense of those results by management.
   d. Covers marketing and product line issues.

● LO9

3. Windham Company has current assets of $400,000 and current liabilities of $500,000. Windham Company's current ratio would be increased by
   a. The purchase of $100,000 of inventory on account.
   b. The payment of $100,000 of accounts payable.
   c. The collection of $100,000 of accounts receivable.
   d. Refinancing a $100,000 long-term loan with short-term debt.

PROBLEMS

An alternate exercise and problem set is available on the text website: www.mhhe.com/spiceland6e

P 3–1
Balance sheet
preparation

● LO2 through
LO4

Presented below is a list of balance sheet accounts in alphabetical order.

Accounts payable	Inventories
Accounts receivable	Land (in use)
Accumulated depreciation—buildings	Long-term investments
Accumulated depreciation—equipment	Notes payable (due in 6 months)
Allowance for uncollectible accounts	Notes receivable (due in 2 years)
Bond sinking fund	Patent
Bonds payable (due in 10 years)	Preferred stock
Buildings	Prepaid expenses
Cash	Rent payable (current)
Common stock	Retained earnings
Copyright	Short-term investments
Equipment	Taxes payable
Interest receivable (due in three months)	Wages payable

Required:
Prepare a classified balance sheet ignoring monetary amounts.

P 3–2
Balance sheet
preparation;
missing elements

● LO2 through
LO4

The data listed below are taken from a balance sheet of Trident Corporation. Some amounts, indicated by question marks, have been intentionally omitted.

	($ in 000s)
Cash and cash equivalents	$ 239,186
Short-term investments	353,700
Accounts receivable (net of allowance)	504,944
Inventories	?
Prepaid expenses (current)	83,259
Total current assets	1,594,927
Long-term receivables	110,800
Property and equipment (net)	?
Total assets	?
Notes payable and short-term debt	31,116
Accounts payable	?
Accrued liabilities	421,772
Other current liabilities	181,604
Total current liabilities	693,564
Long-term debt and deferred taxes	?
Total liabilities	956,140
Shareholders' equity	1,370,627

Required:
1. Determine the missing amounts.
2. Prepare Trident's classified balance sheet.

P 3–3
Balance sheet preparation

● LO2 through LO4

e**X**cel

The following is a December 31, 2011, post-closing trial balance for Almway Corporation.

Account Title	Debits	Credits
Cash	45,000	
Investments	110,000	
Accounts receivable	60,000	
Inventories	200,000	
Prepaid insurance	9,000	
Land	90,000	
Buildings	420,000	
Accumulated depreciation—buildings		100,000
Equipment	110,000	
Accumulated depreciation—equipment		60,000
Patents (net of amortization)	10,000	
Accounts payable		75,000
Notes payable		130,000
Interest payable		20,000
Bonds payable		240,000
Common stock		300,000
Retained earnings		129,000
Totals	1,054,000	1,054,000

Additional information:
1. The investment account includes an investment in common stock of another corporation of $30,000 which management intends to hold for at least three years. The balance of these investments are intended to be sold in the coming year.
2. The land account includes land which cost $25,000 that the company has not used and is currently listed for sale.
3. The cash account includes $15,000 set aside in a fund to pay bonds payable that mature in 2014 and $23,000 set aside in a three-month Treasury bill.
4. The notes payable account consists of the following:
   a. a $30,000 note due in six months.
   b. a $50,000 note due in six years.
   c. a $50,000 note due in five annual installments of $10,000 each, with the next installment due February 15, 2012.
5. The $60,000 balance in accounts receivable is net of an allowance for uncollectible accounts of $8,000.
6. The common stock account represents 100,000 shares of no par value common stock issued and outstanding. The corporation has 500,000 shares authorized.

Required:
Prepare a classified balance sheet for the Almway Corporation at December 31, 2011.

P 3–4
Balance sheet preparation

● LO2 through LO4

e**X**cel

The following is a December 31, 2011, post-closing trial balance for the Weismuller Publishing Company.

Account Title	Debits	Credits
Cash	65,000	
Accounts receivable	160,000	
Inventories	285,000	
Prepaid expenses	148,000	
Machinery and equipment	320,000	
Accumulated depreciation—equipment		110,000
Investments	140,000	
Accounts payable		60,000
Interest payable		20,000
Unearned revenue		80,000
Taxes payable		30,000
Notes payable		200,000
Allowance for uncollectible accounts		16,000
Common stock		400,000
Retained earnings		202,000
Totals	1,118,000	1,118,000

Additional information:

1. Prepaid expenses include $120,000 paid on December 31, 2011, for a two-year lease on the building that houses both the administrative offices and the manufacturing facility.

2. Investments include $30,000 in Treasury bills purchased on November 30, 2011. The bills mature on January 30, 2012. The remaining $110,000 includes investments in marketable equity securities that the company intends to sell in the next year.

3. Unearned revenue represents customer prepayments for magazine subscriptions. Subscriptions are for periods of one year or less.

4. The notes payable account consists of the following:

   a. a $40,000 note due in six months.

   b. a $100,000 note due in six years.

   c. a $60,000 note due in three annual installments of $20,000 each, with the next installment due August 31, 2012.

5. The common stock account represents 400,000 shares of no par value common stock issued and outstanding. The corporation has 800,000 shares authorized.

Required:

Prepare a classified balanced sheet for the Weismuller Publishing Company at December 31, 2011.

P 3–5

Balance sheet preparation

● LO2 through LO4

The following is a June 30, 2011, post-closing trial balance for Excell Company.

Account Title	Debits	Credits
Cash	83,000	
Short-term investments	65,000	
Accounts receivable	280,000	
Prepaid expenses	32,000	
Land	75,000	
Buildings	320,000	
Accumulated depreciation—buildings		160,000
Equipment	265,000	
Accumulated depreciation—equipment		120,000
Accounts payable		173,000
Accrued expenses		45,000
Notes payable		100,000
Mortgage payable		250,000
Common stock		100,000
Retained earnings		172,000
Totals	1,120,000	1,120,000

Additional information:

1. The short-term investments account includes $18,000 in U.S. treasury bills purchased in May. The bills mature in July.

2. The accounts receivable account consists of the following:

a. Amounts owed by customers	$225,000
b. Allowance for uncollectible accounts—trade customers	(15,000)
c. Nontrade note receivable (due in three years)	65,000
d. Interest receivable on note (due in four months)	5,000
Total	$280,000

3. The notes payable account consists of two notes of $50,000 each. One note is due on September 30, 2011, and the other is due on November 30, 2012.

4. The mortgage payable is payable in *semiannual* installments of $5,000 each plus interest. The next payment is due on October 31, 2011. Interest has been properly accrued and is included in accrued expenses.

5. Five hundred thousand shares of no par common stock are authorized, of which 200,000 shares have been issued and are outstanding.

6. The land account includes $50,000 representing the cost of the land on which the company's office building resides. The remaining $25,000 is the cost of land that the company is holding for investment purposes.

Required:

Prepare a classified balance sheet for the Excell Company at June 30, 2011.

P 3–6

Balance sheet
preparation;
disclosures

● **LO2 through
LO5**

The following is a December 31, 2011, post-closing trial balance for the Vosburgh Electronics Corporation.

Account Title	Debits	Credits
Cash	67,000	
Short-term investments	182,000	
Accounts receivable	123,000	
Long-term investments	35,000	
Inventories	215,000	
Loans to employees	40,000	
Prepaid expenses (for 2012)	16,000	
Land	280,000	
Building	1,550,000	
Machinery and equipment	637,000	
Patent	152,000	
Franchise	40,000	
Note receivable	250,000	
Interest receivable	12,000	
Accumulated depreciation — building		620,000
Accumulated depreciation — equipment		210,000
Accounts payable		189,000
Dividends payable (payable on 1/16/12)		10,000
Interest payable		16,000
Taxes payable		40,000
Unearned revenue		60,000
Notes payable		300,000
Allowance for uncollectible accounts		8,000
Common stock		2,000,000
Retained earnings		146,000
Totals	3,599,000	3,599,000

Additional information:

1. The common stock represents 1 million shares of no par stock authorized, 500,000 shares issued and outstanding.

2. The loans to employees are due on June 30, 2012.

3. The note receivable is due in installments of $50,000, payable on each September 30. Interest is payable annually.

4. Short-term investments consist of marketable equity securities that the company plans to sell in 2012 and $50,000 in treasury bills purchased on December 15 of the current year that mature on February 15, 2012. Long-term investments consist of marketable equity securities that the company does not plan to sell in the next year.

5. Unearned revenue represents customer payments for extended service contracts. Eighty percent of these contracts expire in 2012, the remainder in 2013.

6. Notes payable consists of two notes, one for $100,000 due on January 15, 2013, and another for $200,000 due on June 30, 2014.

Required:

1. Prepare a classified balance sheet for Vosburgh at December 31, 2011.

2. Identify the items that would require additional disclosure, either on the face of the balance sheet or in a disclosure note.

P 3–7

Balance sheet
preparation; errors

● **LO2 through
LO4**

The following balance sheet for the Hubbard Corporation was prepared by the company:

HUBBARD CORPORATION
Balance Sheet
At December 31, 2011

Assets

Buildings	$ 750,000
Land	250,000
Cash	60,000
Accounts receivable (net)	120,000
Inventories	240,000
Machinery	280,000
Patent (net)	100,000
Investment in marketable equity securities	60,000
Total assets	$1,860,000

(continued)

(concluded)

Liabilities and Shareholders' Equity

Accounts payable	$ 215,000
Accumulated depreciation	255,000
Notes payable	500,000
Appreciation of inventories	80,000
Common stock, authorized and issued 100,000 shares of no par stock	430,000
Retained earnings	380,000
Total liabilities and shareholders' equity	$1,860,000

Additional information:

1. The buildings, land, and machinery are all stated at cost except for a parcel of land that the company is holding for future sale. The land originally cost $50,000 but, due to a significant increase in market value, is listed at $120,000. The increase in the land account was credited to retained earnings.

2. Marketable equity securities consist of stocks of other corporations and are recorded at cost, $20,000 of which will be sold in the coming year. The remainder will be held indefinitely.

3. Notes payable are all long-term. However, a $100,000 note requires an installment payment of $25,000 due in the coming year.

4. Inventories are recorded at current resale value. The original cost of the inventories is $160,000.

Required:

Prepare a corrected classified balance sheet for the Hubbard Corporation at December 31, 2011.

P 3–8
Balance sheet;
errors; missing
amounts

● LO2 through
LO4

The following incomplete balance sheet for the Sanderson Manufacturing Company was prepared by the company's controller. As accounting manager for Sanderson, you are attempting to reconstruct and revise the balance sheet.

Sanderson Manufacturing Company
Balance Sheet
At December 31, 2011
($ in 000s)

Assets

Current assets:		
Cash	$ 1,250	
Accounts receivable	3,500	
Allowance for uncollectible accounts	(400)	
Finished goods inventory	6,000	
Prepaid expenses	1,200	
Total current assets	11,550	
Noncurrent assets:		
Investments	3,000	
Raw materials and work in process inventory	2,250	
Equipment	15,000	
Accumulated depreciation—equipment	(4,200)	
Patent	?	
Total assets	$?	

Liabilities and Shareholders' Equity

Current liabilities:		
Accounts payable	$ 5,200	
Note payable	4,000	
Interest payable—note	100	
Unearned revenue	3,000	
Total current liabilities	12,300	
Long-term liabilities:		
Bonds payable	5,500	
Interest payable—bonds	200	
Shareholders' equity:		
Common stock	$?	
Retained earnings	?	?
Total liabilities and shareholders' equity		?

Additional information ($ in 000s):

1. Certain records that included the account balances for the patent and shareholders' equity items were lost. However, the controller told you that a complete, preliminary balance sheet prepared before the records were lost showed a debt to equity ratio of 1.2. That is, total liabilities are 120% of total shareholders' equity. Retained earnings at the beginning of the year was $4,000. Net income for 2011 was $1,560 and $560 in cash dividends were declared and paid to shareholders.

2. Management intends to sell the investments in the next six months.

3. Interest on both the note and the bonds is payable annually.

4. The note payable is due in annual installments of $1,000 each.

5. Unearned revenue will be earned equally over the next two fiscal years.

6. The common stock represents 400,000 shares of no par stock authorized, 250,000 shares issued and outstanding.

Required:
Prepare a complete, corrected, classified balance sheet.

P 3–9

Balance sheet preparation

● LO2 through LO4

Presented below is the balance sheet for HHD, Inc., at December 31, 2011.

Current assets	$ 600,000	Current liabilities	$ 400,000
Investments	500,000	Long-term liabilities	1,100,000
Property, plant, and equipment	2,000,000	Shareholders' equity	1,800,000
Intangible assets	200,000		
Total assets	$3,300,000	Total liabilities and shareholders' equity	$3,300,000

The captions shown in the summarized statement above include the following:

a. Current assets: cash, $150,000; accounts receivable, $200,000; inventories, $225,000; and prepaid insurance, $25,000.

b. Investments: investments in common stock, short term, $90,000, and long term, $160,000; and bond sinking fund, $250,000.

c. Property, plant, and equipment: buildings, $1,500,000 less accumulated depreciation, $600,000; equipment, $500,000 less accumulated depreciation, $200,000; and land, $800,000.

d. Intangible assets: patent, $110,000; and copyright, $90,000.

e. Current liabilities: accounts payable, $100,000; notes payable, short term, $150,000, and long term, $90,000; and taxes payable, $60,000.

f. Long-term liabilities: bonds payable due 2016.

g. Shareholders' equity: common stock, $1,000,000; retained earnings, $800,000. Five hundred thousand shares of no par common stock are authorized, of which 200,000 shares were issued and are outstanding.

Required:
Prepare a corrected classified balance sheet for HHD, Inc., at December 31, 2011.

P 3–10

Balance sheet preparation

● LO2 through LO4

Melody Lane Music Company was started by John Ross early in 2011. Initial capital was acquired by issuing shares of common stock to various investors and by obtaining a bank loan. The company operates a retail store that sells records, tapes, and compact discs. Business was so good during the first year of operations that John is considering opening a second store on the other side of town. The funds necessary for expansion will come from a new bank loan. In order to approve the loan, the bank requires financial statements.

John asks for your help in preparing the balance sheet and presents you with the following information for the year ending December 31, 2011:

a. Cash receipts consisted of the following:

From customers	$360,000
From issue of common stock	100,000
From bank loan	100,000

b. Cash disbursements were as follows:

Purchase of inventory	$300,000
Rent	15,000
Salaries	30,000
Utilities	5,000
Insurance	3,000
Purchase of equipment and furniture	40,000

c. The bank loan was made on March 31, 2011. A note was signed requiring payment of interest and principal on March 31, 2012. The interest rate is 12%.

d. The equipment and furniture were purchased on January 3, 2011, and have an estimated useful life of 10 years with no anticipated salvage value. Depreciation per year is $4,000.

e. Inventories on hand at the end of the year cost $100,000.

f. Amounts owed at December 31, 2011, were as follows:

To suppliers of inventory	$20,000
To the utility company	1,000

g. Rent on the store building is $1,000 per month. On December 1, 2011, four months' rent was paid in advance.

h. Net income for the year was $76,000. Assume that the company is not subject to federal, state, or local income tax.

i. One hundred thousand shares of no par common stock are authorized, of which 20,000 shares were issued and are outstanding.

Required:
Prepare a balance sheet at December 31, 2011.

BROADEN YOUR PERSPECTIVE

Apply your critical-thinking ability to the knowledge you've gained. These cases will provide you an opportunity to develop your research, analysis, judgment, and communication skills. You also will work with other students, integrate what you've learned, apply it in real world situations, and consider its global and ethical ramifications. This practice will broaden your knowledge and further develop your decision-making abilities.

Communication Case 3–1
Current versus noncurrent classification
● LO2

A first-year accounting student is confused by a statement made in a recent class. Her instructor stated that the assets listed in the balance sheet of the **IBM Corporation** include computers that are classified as current assets as well as computers that are classified as noncurrent assets. In addition, the instructor stated that investments in marketable securities of other corporations could be classified in the balance sheet as either current or noncurrent assets.

Required:
Explain to the student the distinction between current and noncurrent assets pertaining to the IBM computers and the investments in marketable securities.

Analysis Case 3–2
Current versus noncurrent classification
● LO2

The usefulness of the balance sheet is enhanced when assets and liabilities are grouped according to common characteristics. The broad distinction made in the balance sheet is the current versus noncurrent classification of both assets and liabilities.

Required:
1. Discuss the factors that determine whether an asset or liability should be classified as current or noncurrent in a balance sheet.

2. Identify six items that under different circumstances could be classified as either current or noncurrent. Indicate the factors that would determine the correct classification.

Communication Case 3–3
FASB codification research; inventory or property, plant, and equipment
● LO2 LO3

The Red Hen Company produces, processes, and sells fresh eggs. The company is in the process of preparing financial statements at the end of its first year of operations and has asked for your help in determining the appropriate treatment of the cost of its egg-laying flock. The estimated life of a laying hen is approximately two years, after which they are sold to soup companies.

The controller considers the company's operating cycle to be two years and wants to present the cost of the egg-producing flock as inventory in the current asset section of the balance sheet. He feels that the hens are "goods awaiting sale." The chief financial officer does not agree with this treatment. He thinks that the cost of the flock should be classified as property, plant, and equipment because the hens are used in the production of product—the eggs.

The focus of this case is the balance sheet presentation of the cost of the egg-producing flock. Your instructor will divide the class into two to six groups depending on the size of the class. The mission of your group is to reach consensus on the appropriate presentation.

Required:
1. Each group member should deliberate the situation independently and draft a tentative argument prior to the class session for which the case is assigned.

2. In class, each group will meet for 10 to 15 minutes in different areas of the classroom. During that meeting, group members will take turns sharing their suggestions for the purpose of arriving at a single group treatment.

3. After the allotted time, a spokesperson for each group (selected during the group meetings) will share the group's solution with the class. The goal of the class is to incorporate the views of each group into a consensus approach to the situation.

IFRS Case 3–4
Balance sheet
presentation;
Vodafone Group,
Plc.

● **LO2 through
LO4 LO10**

Real World Financials

Vodafone Group, Plc., a U.K. company, is the largest mobile telecommunications network company in the world. The company prepares its financial statements in accordance with International Financial Reporting Standards. Below are partial company balance sheets included in a recent annual report:

Vodafone Group, Plc. Consolidated Balance Sheets At March 31	2009	2008
	£m	£m
Noncurrent assets		
Goodwill	53,958	51,336
Other intangible assets	20,980	18,995
Property, plant, and equipment	19,250	16,735
Investments	41,775	29,912
Deferred tax assets	630	436
Other	3,077	1,132
	139,670	118,546
Current assets		
Inventory	412	417
Trade and other receivables	7,739	6,608
Cash and cash equivalents	4,878	1,699
	13,029	8,724
Total assets	152,699	127,270
Equity (details provided in complete statement)	84,777	76,471
Noncurrent liabilities		
Long-term borrowings	31,749	22,662
Deferred tax liabilities	6,642	5,109
Postemployment benefits	240	104
Provisions	533	306
Other	811	645
	39,975	28,826
Current liabilities		
Short-term borrowings	9,624	4,532
Current taxation liabilities	4,552	5,123
Provisions	373	356
Trade and other payables	13,398	11,962
	27,947	21,973
Total equity and liabilities	152,699	127,270

Required:

1. Describe the differences between Vodafone's balance sheet and a typical U.S. company balance sheet.
2. What type of liabilities do you think are included in the *provisions* category in Vodafone's balance sheet?

**Judgment
Case 3–5**
Balance sheet;
errors

● **LO2 through
LO5**

You recently joined the internal auditing department of Marcus Clothing Corporation. As one of your first assignments, you are examining a balance sheet prepared by a staff accountant.

MARCUS CLOTHING CORPORATION Balance Sheet At December 31, 2011	
Assets	
Current assets:	
Cash	$ 137,000
Accounts receivable, net	80,000
Note receivable	53,000
Inventories	240,000
Investments	66,000
Total current assets	576,000

(continued)

(concluded)	Other assets:		
	Land	$200,000	
	Equipment, net	320,000	
	Prepaid expenses	27,000	
	Patent	22,000	
	Total other assets		569,000
	Total assets		$1,145,000

Liabilities and Shareholders' Equity

Current liabilities:			
Accounts payable		$ 125,000	
Salaries payable		32,000	
Total current liabilities		157,000	
Long-term liabilities:			
Note payable	$100,000		
Bonds payable	300,000		
Interest payable	20,000		
Total long-term liabilities		420,000	
Shareholders' equity:			
Common stock	500,000		
Retained earnings	68,000		
Total shareholders' equity		568,000	
Total liabilities and shareholders' equity		$1,145,000	

In the course of your examination you uncover the following information pertaining to the balance sheet:

1. The company rents its facilities. The land that appears in the statement is being held for future sale.

2. The note receivable is due in 2013. The balance of $53,000 includes $3,000 of accrued interest. The next interest payment is due in July 2012.

3. The note payable is due in installments of $20,000 per year. Interest on both the notes and bonds is payable annually.

4. The company's investments consist of marketable equity securities of other corporations. Management does not intend to liquidate any investments in the coming year.

Required:

Identify and explain the deficiencies in the statement prepared by the company's accountant. Include in your answer items that require additional disclosure, either on the face of the statement or in a note.

Judgment Case 3–6
Financial disclosures
● LO5

You recently joined the auditing staff of Best, Best, and Krug, CPAs. You have been assigned to the audit of Clearview, Inc., and have been asked by the audit senior to examine the balance sheet prepared by Clearview's accountant.

CLEARVIEW, INC.
Balance Sheet
At December 31, 2011
($ in millions)

Assets

Current assets:	
Cash	$ 10.5
Accounts receivable	112.1
Inventories	220.6
Prepaid expenses	5.5
Total current assets	348.7
Investments	22.0
Property, plant, and equipment, net	486.9
Total assets	$857.6

(continued)

(concluded)	**Liabilities and Shareholders' Equity**		
Current liabilities:			
Accounts payable			$ 83.5
Accrued taxes and interest			25.5
Current maturities of long-term debt			20.0
Total current liabilities			129.0
Long-term liabilities:			420.0
Total liabilities			549.0
Shareholders' equity:			
Common stock		$100.0	
Retained earnings		208.6	
Total shareholders' equity			308.6
Total liabilities and shareholders' equity			$857.6

Required:

Identify the items in the statement that most likely would require further disclosure either on the face of the statement or in a note. Further identify those items that would require disclosure in the significant accounting policies note.

Real World Case 3–7
Balance sheet and significant accounting policies disclosure; Walmart Stores

● **LO3 through LO5 LO9**

Real World Financials

The balance sheet and disclosure of significant accounting policies taken from the 2009 annual report of **Walmart Stores, Inc.**, appear below. Use this information to answer the following questions:

1. What are the asset classifications contained in Walmart's balance sheet?
2. What amounts did Walmart report for the following items for 2009:
    a. Total assets
    b. Current assets
    c. Current liabilities
    d. Total shareholders' equity
    e. Retained earnings
    f. Inventories
3. What is the par value of Walmart's common stock? How many shares of common stock are authorized, issued, and outstanding at the end of 2009?
4. Compute Walmart's current ratio for 2009.
5. Identify the following items:
    a. The company's inventory valuation method.
    b. The company's depreciation method.
    c. The definition of cash equivalents.

WALMART STORES, INC.
Consolidated Balance Sheets
(Amounts in millions except per share data)

January 31,	2009	2008
Assets		
Current assets:		
Cash and cash equivalents	$7,275	$5,492
Receivables	3,905	3,642
Inventories	34,511	35,159
Prepaid expenses and other	3,063	2,760
Current assets of discontinued operations	195	967
Total current assets	48,949	48,020
Property and equipment, at cost:		
Land	19,852	19,879
Buildings and improvements	73,810	72,141
Fixtures and equipment	29,851	28,026
Transportation equipment	2,307	2,210
Property and equipment, at cost	125,820	122,256
Less accumulated depreciation	(32,964)	(28,531)
Property and equipment, net	92,856	93,725

(continued)

(concluded)

Property under capital lease:		
Property under capital lease	5,341	5,736
Less accumulated amortization	(2,544)	(2,594)
Property under capital lease, net	2,797	3,142
Goodwill	15,260	15,879
Other assets and deferred charges	3,567	2,748
Total assets	$163,429	$163,514

Liabilities and Shareholders' Equity

Current liabilities:		
Commercial paper	$1,506	$5,040
Accounts payable	28,849	30,344
Accrued liabilities	18,112	15,725
Accrued income taxes	677	1,000
Long-term debt due within one year	5,848	5,913
Obligations under capital leases due within one year	315	316
Current liabilities of discontinued operations	83	140
Total current liabilities	55,390	58,478
Long-term debt	31,349	29,799
Long-term obligations under capital leases	3,200	3,603
Deferred income taxes and other	6,014	5,087
Minority interest	2,191	1,939
Commitments and contingencies		
Shareholders' equity:		
Preferred stock ($0.10 par value; 100 shares authorized, none issued)	—	—
Common stock ($0.10 par value; 11,000 shares authorized, 3,925	393	397
and 3,973 issued and outstanding at January 31, 2009 and		
January 31, 2008, respectively)		
Capital in excess of par value	3,920	3,028
Retained earnings	63,660	57,319
Accumulated other comprehensive (loss) income	(2,688)	3,864
Total shareholders' equity	65,285	64,608
Total liabilities and shareholders' equity	$163,429	$163,514

NOTES TO CONSOLIDATED FINANCIAL STATEMENTS
WALMART STORES, INC.

1 Summary of Significant Accounting Policies (in part)

Cash and Cash Equivalents
The Company considers investments with a maturity of three months or less when purchased to be cash equivalents.

Inventories
The Company values inventories at the lower of cost or market as determined primarily by the retail method of accounting, using the last-in, first-out ("LIFO") method for substantially all of the Walmart U.S. segment's merchandise inventories. Inventories of foreign operations are primarily valued by the retail method of accounting, using the first-in, first-out ("FIFO") method. At January 31, 2009 and 2008, our inventories valued at LIFO approximate those inventories as if they were valued at FIFO.

Revenue Recognition
The Company recognizes sales revenue net of sales taxes and estimated sales returns at the time it sells merchandise to the customer. Customer purchases of shopping cards are not recognized as revenue until the card is redeemed and the customer purchases merchandise by using the shopping card. The Company also recognizes revenue from service transactions at the time the service is performed. Generally, revenue from services is classified as net sales.

Depreciation and Amortization
Depreciation and amortization for financial statement purposes are provided on the straight-line method over the estimated useful lives of the various assets.

Judgment Case 3–8
Post fiscal year-end events
● LO5

The fiscal year-end for the Northwest Distribution Corporation is December 31. The company's 2011 financial statements were issued on March 15, 2012. The following events occurred between December 31, 2011, and March 15, 2012.

1. On January 22, 2012, the company negotiated a major merger with Blandon Industries. The merger will be completed by the middle of 2012.

2. On February 3, 2012, Northwest negotiated a $10 million long-term note with the Credit Bank of Ohio. The amount of the note is material.

3. On February 25, 2012, a flood destroyed one of the company's manufacturing plants causing $600,000 of uninsured damage.

Required:

Determine the appropriate treatment of each of these events in the 2011 financial statements of Northwest Distribution Corporation.

Research Case 3–9
FASB codification; locate and extract relevant information and cite authoritative support for a financial reporting issue; related-party disclosures; Enron Corporation
● LO5

Real World Financials

Enron Corporation was a darling in the energy-provider arena, and in January 2001 its stock price rose above $100 per share. A collapse of investor confidence in 2001 and revelations of accounting irregularities led to one of the largest bankruptcies in U.S. history. By the end of the year, Enron's stock price had plummeted to less than $1 per share. Investigations and lawsuits followed. One problem area concerned transactions with related parties that were not adequately disclosed in the company's financial statements. Critics stated that the lack of information about these transactions made it difficult for analysts following Enron to identify problems the company was experiencing.

Required:

1. Obtain the relevant authoritative literature on related-party transactions using the FASB's Codification Research System. You might gain access at the FASB website (**www.fasb.org**). What is the specific citation that outlines the required information on related-party disclosures that must be included in the notes to the financial statements?

2. Describe the disclosures required for related-party transactions.

3. Use EDGAR (**www.sec.gov**) or another method to locate the December 31, 2000, financial statements of Enron. Search for the related-party disclosure. Briefly describe the relationship central to the various transactions described.

4. Why is it important that companies disclose related-party transactions? Use the Enron disclosure of the sale of dark fiber inventory in your answer.

Real World Case 3–10
Disclosures; proxy statement; Borders
● LO5 LO7

Real World Financials

EDGAR, the Electronic Data Gathering, Analysis, and Retrieval system, performs automated collection, validation, indexing, and forwarding of submissions by companies and others who are required by law to file forms with the SEC. All publicly traded domestic companies use EDGAR to make the majority of their filings. (Some foreign companies file voluntarily.) Form 10-K, which includes the annual report, is required to be filed on EDGAR. The SEC makes this information available on the Internet.

Required:

1. Access EDGAR on the Internet. The web address is **www.sec.gov**.

2. Search for **Borders Group, Inc.**, a leading bookstore chain. Access the 10-K for the fiscal year ended January 31, 2009. Search or scroll to find the disclosure notes and audit report.

3. Answer the following questions:
   a. Describe the subsequent events disclosed by the company.
   b. Which firm is the company's auditor? What type of audit opinion did the auditor render?

4. Access the proxy statement filed with the SEC on April 23, 2009 (the proxy statement designation is Def 14A) and answer the following questions:
   a. What is the principal position of Ron Marshall?
   b. What was the annual salary paid to Mr. Marshall?

Judgment Case 3–11
Debt versus equity
● LO8

A common problem facing any business entity is the debt versus equity decision. When funds are required to obtain assets, should debt or equity financing be used? This decision also is faced when a company is initially formed. What will be the mix of debt versus equity in the initial capital structure? The characteristics of debt are very different from those of equity as are the financial implications of using one method of financing as opposed to the other.

Cherokee Plastics Corporation is formed by a group of investors to manufacture household plastic products. Their initial capitalization goal is $50,000,000. That is, the incorporators have decided to raise $50,000,000 to acquire the initial assets of the company. They have narrowed down the financing mix alternatives to two:

1. All equity financing.
2. $20,000,000 in debt financing and $30,000,000 in equity financing.

No matter which financing alternative is chosen, the corporation expects to be able to generate a 10% annual return, before payment of interest and income taxes, on the $50,000,000 in assets acquired. The interest rate on debt would be 8%. The effective income tax rate will be approximately 50%.

Alternative 2 will require specified interest and principal payments to be made to the creditors at specific dates. The interest portion of these payments (interest expense) will reduce the taxable income of the corporation and hence the amount of income tax the corporation will pay. The all-equity alternative requires no specified payments to be made to suppliers of capital. The corporation is not legally liable to make distributions to its owners. If the board of directors does decide to make a distribution, it is not an expense of the corporation and does not reduce taxable income and hence the taxes the corporation pays.

Required:

1. Prepare abbreviated income statements that compare first-year profitability for each of the two alternatives.
2. Which alternative would be expected to achieve the highest first-year profits? Why?
3. Which alternative would provide the highest rate of return on shareholders' equity? Why?
4. What other related implications of the decision should be considered?

Analysis Case 3–12
Obtain and critically evaluate an actual annual report
● LO5 LO7 through LO9

Real World Financials

Financial reports are the primary means by which corporations report their performance and financial condition. Financial statements are one component of the annual report mailed to their shareholders and to interested others.

Required:

Obtain an annual report from a corporation with which you are familiar. Using techniques you learned in this chapter and any analysis you consider useful, respond to the following questions:

1. Do the firm's auditors provide a clean opinion on the financial statements?
2. Has the company made changes in any accounting methods it uses?
3. Have there been any subsequent events, errors and irregularities, illegal acts, or related-party transactions that have a material effect on the company's financial position?
4. What are two trends in the company's operations or capital resources that management considers significant to the company's future?
5. Is the company engaged in more than one significant line of business? If so, compare the relative profitability of the different segments.
6. How stable are the company's operations?
7. Has the company's situation deteriorated or improved with respect to liquidity, solvency, asset management, and profitability?

Note: You can obtain a copy of an annual report from a local company, from a friend who is a shareholder, from the investor relations department of the corporation, from a friendly stockbroker, or from EDGAR (Electronic Data Gathering, Analysis, and Retrieval) on the Internet (**www.sec.gov**).

Analysis Case 3–13
Obtain and compare annual reports from companies in the same industry
● LO5 LO8 LO9

Real World Financials

Insight concerning the performance and financial condition of a company often comes from evaluating its financial data in comparison with other firms in the same industry.

Required:

Obtain annual reports from three corporations in the same primary industry. Using techniques you learned in this chapter and any analysis you consider useful, respond to the following questions:

1. Are there differences in accounting methods that should be taken into account when making comparisons?
2. How do earnings trends compare in terms of both the direction and stability of income?
3. Which of the three firms had the greatest earnings relative to resources available?
4. Which corporation has made most effective use of financial leverage?
5. Of the three firms, which seems riskiest in terms of its ability to pay short-term obligations? Long-term obligations?

Note: You can obtain copies of annual reports from friends who are shareholders, from the investor relations department of the corporations, from a friendly stockbroker, or from EDGAR (Electronic Data Gathering, Analysis, and Retrieval) on the Internet (**www.sec.gov**).

**Analysis
Case 3–14**
Balance sheet
information
● LO3 through
   LO5

Refer to the financial statements and related disclosure notes of **Dell Inc.** in Appendix B located at the back of the text.

Required:

1. What categories does the company use to classify its assets? Its liabilities?
2. Why are investments shown as a current asset?
3. Explain the current liability "deferred service revenue."
4. What purpose do the disclosure notes serve?
5. What method does the company use to depreciate its property and equipment?
6. Does the company report any subsequent events or related party transactions in its disclosure notes?

**Analysis
Case 3–15**
Segment reporting
concepts
● Appendix LO10

Levens Co. operates in several distinct business segments. The company does not have any reportable foreign operations or major customers.

Required:

1. What is the purpose of operating segment disclosures?
2. Define an operating segment.
3. List the amounts to be reported by operating segment.
4. How would your answer to requirement 3 differ if Levens Co. prepares its segment disclosure according to International Financial Reporting Standards?

Ethics Case 3–16
Segment reporting
● Appendix

You are in your third year as an accountant with McCarver-Lynn Industries, a multidivisional company involved in the manufacturing, marketing, and sales of surgical prosthetic devices. After the fiscal year-end, you are working with the controller of the firm to prepare supplemental business segment disclosures. Yesterday you presented her with the following summary information:

		($ in millions)				
	Domestic	Union of South Africa	Egypt	France	Denmark	Total
Revenues	$ 845	$222	$265	$343	$311	$1,986
Capital expenditures	145	76	88	21	42	372
Assets	1,005	301	290	38	285	1,919

Upon returning to your office after lunch, you find the following memo:

Nice work. Let's combine the data this way:

	($ in millions)			
	Domestic	Africa	Europe	Total
Revenues	$ 845	$487	$654	$1,986
Capital expenditures	145	164	63	372
Assets	1,005	591	323	1,919

Some of our shareholders might react unfavorably to our recent focus on South African operations.

Required:

Do you perceive an ethical dilemma? What would be the likely impact of following the controller's suggestions? Who would benefit? Who would be injured?

BRITISH AIRWAYS CASE

BRITISH AIRWAYS

● LO10

British Airways, Plc. (BA), a U.K. company, prepares its financial statements according to International Financial Reporting Standards. BA's annual report for the year ended March 31, 2009, which includes financial statements and disclosure notes, is included with all new textbooks and can be found at **www.britishairways.com**. When answering questions, focus on BA's "Group" financial information (which is equivalent to "Consolidated" under U.S. GAAP).

Required:

Describe the apparent differences in the order of presentation of the components of the balance sheet between IFRS as applied by British Airways (BA) and a typical balance sheet prepared in accordance with U.S. GAAP.

The Income Statement and Statement of Cash Flows

/// **OVERVIEW**

The purpose of the income statement is to summarize the profit-generating activities that occurred during a particular reporting period. The purpose of the statement of cash flows is to provide information about the cash receipts and cash disbursements of an enterprise that occurred during the period.

This chapter has a twofold purpose: (1) to consider important issues dealing with income statement content, presentation, and disclosure and (2) to provide an *overview* of the statement of cash flows, which is covered in depth in Chapter 21.

/// **LEARNING OBJECTIVES**

After studying this chapter, you should be able to:

● **LO1** Discuss the importance of income from continuing operations and describe its components. (page 170)
● **LO2** Describe earnings quality and how it is impacted by management practices to manipulate earnings. (page 175)
● **LO3** Discuss the components of operating and nonoperating income and their relationship to earnings quality. (page 176)
● **LO4** Define what constitutes discontinued operations and describe the appropriate income statement presentation for these transactions. (page 182)
● **LO5** Define extraordinary items and describe the appropriate income statement presentation for these transactions. (page 186)
● **LO6** Describe the measurement and reporting requirements for a change in accounting principle. (page 188)
● **LO7** Explain the accounting treatments of changes in estimates and correction of errors. (page 190)
● **LO8** Define earnings per share (EPS) and explain required disclosures of EPS for certain income statement components. (page 192)
● **LO9** Explain the difference between net income and comprehensive income and how we report components of the difference. (page 194)
● **LO10** Describe the purpose of the statement of cash flows. (page 198)
● **LO11** Identify and describe the various classifications of cash flows presented in a statement of cash flows. (page 199)
● **LO12** Discuss the primary differences between U.S. GAAP and IFRS with respect to the income statement and statement of cash flows. (pages 174, 182, 187, 195, 199, and 204)

FINANCIAL REPORTING CASE

Alberto-Culver Company

Your friend, Becky Morgan, just received a generous gift from her grandfather. Accompanying a warm letter were 200 shares of stock of the **Alberto-Culver Company**, a global manufacturer of beauty and health care products, along with the most recent quarterly financial statements of the company. Becky knows that you are an accounting major and pleads with you to explain some items in the company's income statement. "I remember studying the income statement in my introductory accounting course," says Becky, "but I am still confused. What is this item *discontinued operations?* How about *restructuring costs?* These don't sound good. Are they something I should worry about? And the negative number in 2009 makes no sense at all. We studied earnings per share briefly, but what does *diluted earnings per share* mean?" You agree to try to help.

ALBERTO-CULVER COMPANY
Income Statements
Three Months Ended March 31
($ in thousands, except per share data)

	2009	2008
Sales	$344,332	$349,369
Cost of products sold	170,966	163,309
Gross profit	173,366	186,060
Marketing, selling and administrative expenses	131,447	147,713
Restructuring costs	(21)	2,070
Operating income	41,940	36,277
Interest income, net of interest expense	659	2,298
Income from continuing operations before income taxes	42,599	38,575
Provision for income taxes	14,769	11,938
Income from continuing operations	27,830	26,637
Income from discontinued operations, net of income taxes	248	2,390
Net income	$ 28,078	$ 29,027
Basic earnings per share:		
Continuing operations	$ .29	$ .27
Discontinued operations	—	.02
Net income	$ .29	$ .29
Diluted earnings per share:		
Continuing operations	$ .28	$ .26
Discontinued operations	—	.02
Net income	$ .28	$ .28

By the time you finish this chapter, you should be able to respond appropriately to the questions posed in this case. Compare your response to the solution provided at the end of the chapter. **QUESTIONS ///**

1. How would you explain restructuring costs and the negative amount for that item in 2009 to Becky? Are restructuring costs something Becky should worry about? (page 177)

2. In addition to discontinued operations, what other events sometimes are reported separately in the income statement that you might tell Becky about? Why are these items reported separately? (page 180)

3. Explain to Becky what is meant by discontinued operations and describe to her how that item is reported in an income statement. (page 182)

4. Describe to Becky the difference between basic and diluted earnings per share. (page 193)

In Chapter 1 we discussed the critical role of financial accounting information in allocating resources within our economy. Ideally, resources should be allocated to private enterprises that will (1) provide the goods and services our society desires and (2) at the same time provide a fair rate of return to those who supply the resources. A company will be able to achieve these goals only if it can use the resources society provides to generate revenues from selling products and services that exceed the expenses necessary to provide those products and services (that is, generate a profit).

The income statement displays a company's operating performance, that is, its net profit or loss, during the reporting period.

The purpose of the **income statement,** sometimes called the statement of operations or statement of earnings, is to summarize the profit-generating activities that occurred during a particular reporting period. Many investors and creditors perceive it as the statement most useful for predicting future profitability (future cash-generating ability).

The purpose of the statement of cash flows is to provide information about the cash receipts and cash disbursements of an enterprise that occurred during a period. In describing cash flows, the statement provides valuable information about the operating, investing, and financing activities that occurred during the period.

The *income statement* and *statement of cash flows* report changes that occurred during a particular reporting period.

Unlike the balance sheet, which is a position statement, the income statement and the statement of cash flows are *change* statements. The income statement reports the changes in shareholders' equity (retained earnings) that occurred during the reporting period as a result of revenues, expenses, gains, and losses. The statement of cash flows also is a change statement, disclosing the events that caused cash to change during the period.

This chapter is divided into two parts. The first part describes the content and presentation of the income statement and related disclosure issues. The second part provides an overview of the statement of cash flows.

PART A — THE INCOME STATEMENT AND COMPREHENSIVE INCOME

Before we discuss the specific components of an income statement in much depth, let's take a quick look at the general makeup of the statement. Graphic 4–1 offers a statement for a hypothetical manufacturing company that you can refer to as we proceed through the chapter. At this point, our objective is only to gain a general perspective on the items reported and classifications contained in corporate income statements.

Let's first look closer at the components of net income. At the end of this part, we'll see how net income fits within the concept of comprehensive income.

Income from Continuing Operations

● LO1

Income from continuing operations includes the revenues, expenses, gains and losses that will probably continue in future periods.

The need to provide information to help analysts predict future cash flows emphasizes the importance of properly reporting the amount of income from the entity's continuing operations. Clearly, it is the operating transactions that probably will continue into the future that are the best predictors of future cash flows. The components of income from continuing operations are revenues, expenses (including income taxes), gains, and losses, excluding those related to discontinued operations and extraordinary items.[1]

Revenues, Expenses, Gains, and Losses

Revenues are inflows of resources resulting from providing goods or services to customers. For merchandising companies like **Walmart**, the main source of revenue is sales revenue derived from selling merchandise. Service firms such as **FedEx** and **State Farm Insurance** generate revenue by providing services.

Expenses are outflows of resources incurred while generating revenue. They represent the costs of providing goods and services. The *matching principle* is a key player in the way we measure expenses. We attempt to establish a causal relationship between revenues and expenses. If causality can be determined, expenses are reported in the same period that the related revenue is recognized. If a causal relationship cannot be established, we either relate the expense to a particular period, allocate it over several periods, or expense it as incurred.

[1]These two separately reported items are addressed in a subsequent section.

Income Statements
(In millions, except earnings per share)

	Years Ended June 30	
	2011	**2010**
Sales revenue	$1,450.6	$1,380.0
Cost of goods sold	832.6	800.4
Gross profit	618.0	579.6
Operating expenses:		
Selling	123.5	110.5
General and administrative	147.8	139.1
Research and development	55.0	65.0
Restructuring costs	125.0	—
Total operating expenses	451.3	314.6
Operating income	166.7	265.0
Other income (expense):		
Interest income	12.4	11.1
Interest expense	(25.9)	(24.8)
Gain on sale of investments	18.0	19.0
Income from continuing operations before income taxes and extraordinary item	171.2	270.3
Income tax expense	59.9	94.6
Income from continuing operations before extraordinary item	111.3	175.7
Discontinued operations:		
Loss from operations of discontinued component (including gain on disposal in 2011 of $47)	(7.6)	(45.7)
Income tax benefit	2.0	13.0
Loss on discontinued operations	(5.6)	(32.7)
Income before extraordinary item	105.7	143.0
Extraordinary gain, net of $11 in tax expense	—	22.0
Net income	$ 105.7	$ 165.0
Earnings per common share—basic:		
Income from continuing operations before extraordinary item	$ 2.14	$ 3.38
Discontinued operations	(.11)	(.62)
Extraordinary gain	—	.42
Net income	$ 2.03	$ 3.18
Earnings per common share—diluted:		
Income from continuing operations before extraordinary item	$ 2.06	$ 3.25
Discontinued operations	(.11)	(.62)
Extraordinary gain	—	.42
Net income	$ 1.95	$ 3.05

Left margin labels: Income from Continuing Operations; Separately Reported Items; Earnings per Share

Gains and losses are increases or decreases in equity from peripheral or incidental transactions of an entity. In general, these gains and losses are those changes in equity that do not result directly from operations but nonetheless are related to those activities. For example, gains and losses from the routine sale of equipment, buildings, or other operating assets and from the sale of investment assets normally would be included in income from continuing operations. Later in the chapter we discuss certain gains and losses that are excluded from continuing operations.

Income Tax Expense

Income taxes represent a major expense to a corporation, and accordingly, income tax expense is given special treatment in the income statement. Income taxes are levied on tax-payers in proportion to the amount of taxable income that is reported to taxing authorities. Like individuals, corporations are income-tax-paying entities.[2] Because of the importance and size of income tax expense (sometimes called *provision for income taxes*), it always is reported as a separate expense in corporate income statements.

Federal, state, and sometimes local taxes are assessed annually and usually are determined by first applying a designated percentage (or percentages), the tax rate (or rates), to taxable income. Taxable income comprises revenues, expenses, gains, and losses as measured according to the regulations of the appropriate taxing authority.

Many of the components of taxable income and income reported in the income statement coincide. But sometimes tax rules and GAAP differ with respect to when and even whether a particular revenue or expense is included in income. When tax rules and GAAP differ regarding the timing of revenue or expense recognition, the actual payment of taxes may occur in a period different from when income tax expense is reported in the income statement. A common example is when a corporation takes advantage of tax laws by legally deducting more depreciation in the early years of an asset's life on its federal income tax return than it reports in its income statement. The amount of tax actually paid in the early years is less than the amount that is found by applying the tax rate to the reported GAAP income before taxes. We discuss this and other issues related to accounting for income taxes in Chapter 16. At this point, consider income tax expense to be simply a percentage of income before taxes.

Operating versus Nonoperating Income

Many corporate income statements distinguish between operating income and nonoperating income. Operating income includes revenues and expenses directly related to the primary revenue-generating activities of the company. For example, operating income for a manufacturing company includes sales revenues from selling the products it manufactures as well as all expenses related to this activity. Similarly, operating income might also include gains and losses from selling equipment and other assets used in the manufacturing process.[3]

Nonoperating income relates to peripheral or incidental activities of the company. For example, a manufacturer would include interest and dividend revenue, gains and losses from selling investments, and interest expense in nonoperating income. *Other income (expense)* often is the classification heading companies use in the income statement for nonoperating items. On the other hand, a financial institution like a bank would consider those items to be a part of operating income because they relate to the principal revenue-generating activities for that type of business.

Graphic 4–2 presents the 2009, 2008, and 2007 income statements for **Dell Inc.** Notice that Dell distinguishes between operating income and nonoperating income (labeled Investment and other income, net). Nonoperating revenues, expenses, gains and losses, and income tax expense (called Income tax provision) are added to or subtracted from operating income to arrive at net income. As Dell has no separately reported items, *income from continuing operations equals net income.*[4]

Now let's consider the formats used to report the components of net income.

Income Statement Formats

No specific standards dictate how income from continuing operations must be displayed, so companies have considerable latitude in how they present the components of income from continuing operations. This flexibility has resulted in a variety of income statement presentations. However, we can identify two general approaches, the single-step and the multiple-step

---

[2]Partnerships are not tax-paying entities. Their taxable income or loss is included in the taxable income of the individual partners.
[3]FASB ASC 360–10–45–5: Property, plant, and equipment—Overall—Other Presentation Matters (previously "Accounting for the Impairment of Long-Lived Assets and for Long-Lived Assets to Be Disposed Of," *Statement of Financial Accounting Standards No. 144* (Norwalk, Conn.: FASB, 2001)).
[4]In a later section we discuss items that are reported separately from continuing operations.

GRAPHIC 4–2

Income Statements—
Dell Inc.

Consolidated Statements of Income

(In millions, except per share amounts)

	Fiscal Year Ended		
	January 30, 2009	February 1, 2008	February 2, 2007
Net revenue	$61,101	$61,133	$57,420
Cost of net revenue	50,144	49,462	47,904
Gross margin	10,957	11,671	9,516
Operating expenses:			
Selling, general, and administrative	7,102	7,538	5,948
In-process research and development	2	83	—
Research, development, and engineering	663	610	498
Total operating expenses	7,767	8,231	6,446
Operating income	3,190	3,440	3,070
Investment and other income, net	134	387	275
Income before income taxes	3,324	3,827	3,345
Income tax provision	846	880	762
Net income	$ 2,478	$ 2,947	$ 2,583
Earnings per common share:			
Basic	$ 1.25	$ 1.33	$ 1.15
Diluted	$ 1.25	$ 1.31	$ 1.14

Real World Financials

formats, that might be considered the two extremes, with the income statements of most companies falling somewhere in between.

The **single-step** format first lists all the revenues and gains included in income from continuing operations. Then, expenses and losses are grouped, subtotaled, and subtracted—in a single step—from revenues and gains to derive income from continuing operations. Operating and nonoperating items are not separately classified. Illustration 4–1 shows an example of a single-step income statement for a hypothetical manufacturing company, Maxwell Gear Corporation.

A *single-step* income statement format groups all revenues and gains together and all expenses and losses together.

MAXWELL GEAR CORPORATION
Income Statement
For the Year Ended December 31, 2011

Revenues and gains:		
Sales		$573,522
Interest and dividends		26,400
Gain on sale of investments		5,500
Total revenues and gains		605,422
Expenses and losses:		
Cost of goods sold	$302,371	
Selling	47,341	
General and administrative	24,888	
Research and development	16,300	
Interest	14,522	
Income taxes	80,000	
Total expenses and losses		485,422
Net income		$120,000

ILLUSTRATION 4–1

Single-Step Income Statement

The **multiple-step** format reports a series of intermediate subtotals such as gross profit, operating income, and income before taxes. The overview income statements presented in Graphic 4–1 and the **Dell Inc.** income statements in Graphic 4–2 are variations of the multiple-step format. Illustration 4–2 presents a multiple-step income statement for the Maxwell Gear Corporation.

A *multiple-step* income statement format includes a number of intermediate subtotals before arriving at income from continuing operations.

ILLUSTRATION 4–2

Multiple-Step
Income Statement

MAXWELL GEAR CORPORATION
Income Statement
For the Year Ended December 31, 2011

Sales revenue		$573,522
Cost of goods sold		302,371
Gross profit		271,151
Operating expenses:		
Selling	$47,341	
General and administrative	24,888	
Research and development	16,300	
Total operating expenses		88,529
Operating income		182,622
Other income (expense):		
Interest and dividend revenue	26,400	
Gain on sale of investments	5,500	
Interest expense	(14,522)	
Total other income, net		17,378
Income before income taxes		200,000
Income tax expense		80,000
Net income		$120,000

In addition to net income, the components of the income statement and their presentation also are important to financial statement users in their assessment of earnings quality.

An advantage of the single-step format is its simplicity. Revenues and expenses are not classified or prioritized. A primary advantage of the multiple-step format is that, by separately classifying operating and nonoperating items, it provides information that might be useful in analyzing trends. Similarly, the classification of expenses by function also provides useful information. For example, reporting gross profit for merchandising companies highlights the important relationship between sales revenue and cost of goods sold. It is important to note that this issue is one of presentation. The bottom line, net income, is the same regardless of the format used. A recent survey of income statements of 500 large public companies indicates that the multiple-step format is used more than five times as often as the single-step format.[5] We use the multiple-step format for illustration purposes throughout the remainder of this chapter.

Before we investigate separately reported items, let's take a closer look at the components of both operating and nonoperating income and their relationship to earnings quality.

● **LO12**

INTERNATIONAL FINANCIAL REPORTING STANDARDS

Income Statement Presentation. There are more similarities than differences between income statements prepared according to U.S. GAAP and those prepared applying international standards. Some of the differences are:

- International standards require certain minimum information to be reported on the face of the income statement. U.S. GAAP has no minimum requirements.

- International standards allow expenses to be classified either by function (e.g., cost of goods sold, general and administrative, etc.), or by natural description (e.g., salaries, rent, etc.). SEC regulations require that expenses be classified by function.

- In the United States, the "bottom line" of the income statement usually is called either *net income* or *net loss*. The descriptive term for the bottom line of the income statement prepared according to international standards is either *profit* or *loss*.

- As we discuss later in the chapter, we report "extraordinary items" separately in an income statement prepared according to U.S. GAAP. International standards prohibit reporting "extraordinary items."

[5]*Accounting Trends and Techniques—2009* (New York: AICPA, 2009), p. 321.

Earnings Quality

Financial analysts are concerned with more than just the bottom line of the income statement—net income. The presentation of the components of net income and the related supplemental disclosures provide clues to the user of the statement in an assessment of *earnings quality*. Earnings quality is used as a framework for more in-depth discussions of operating and nonoperating income.

● LO2

Earnings quality refers to the ability of reported earnings (income) to predict a company's future earnings.

The term **earnings quality** refers to the ability of reported earnings (income) to predict a company's future earnings. After all, an income statement simply reports on events that already have occurred. The relevance of any historical-based financial statement hinges on its predictive value. To enhance predictive value, analysts try to separate a company's *transitory earnings* effects from its *permanent earnings*. Transitory earnings effects result from transactions or events that are not likely to occur again in the foreseeable future, or that are likely to have a different impact on earnings in the future. Later in the chapter we address two items that, because of their transitory nature, are required to be reported separately at the bottom of the income statement. Analysts begin their assessment of permanent earnings with income before these two items, that is, income from continuing operations.

It would be a mistake, though, to assume income from continuing operations reflects permanent earnings entirely. In other words, there may be transitory earnings effects included in income from continuing operations. In a sense, the phrase *continuing* may be misleading.

Manipulating Income and Income Smoothing

KEN SCHAPIRO—CONDOR CAPITAL MANAGEMENT
IBM has run out of easy things to do to generate earnings growth. Now they have to do the hard stuff.[6]

ARTHUR LEVITT, JR.
While the problem of earnings management is not new, it has swelled in a market that is unforgiving of companies that miss their estimates. I recently read of one major U.S. company that failed to meet its so-called numbers by one penny and lost more than six percent of its stock value in one day.[9]

A *Fortune* magazine article "Hocus-Pocus: How IBM Grew 27% a Year" contained a subtitle "Do you want to believe in the IBM miracle? Then don't look too closely at the numbers."[7] The article is highly critical of IBM's earnings management practices that allowed the company to report earnings per share growth of 27% per year from 1994 through 1999 with only minimal growth in revenues. The article's author attributes the increase in earnings per share to share buybacks, the sale of assets, and gains in pension fund assets, not a growth in permanent earnings.

An often-debated contention is that, within GAAP, managers have the power, to a limited degree, to manipulate reported company income. And the manipulation is not always in the direction of higher income. One author states that "Most executives prefer to report earnings that follow a smooth, regular, upward path. They hate to report declines, but they also want to avoid increases that vary wildly from year to year; it's better to have two years of 15% earnings increases than a 30% gain one year and none the next. As a result, some companies 'bank' earnings by understating them in particularly good years and use the banked profits to polish results in bad years."[8]

Many believe that manipulating income reduces earnings quality because it can mask permanent earnings. A 1998 *BusinessWeek* issue was devoted entirely to the topic of earnings management. The issue, entitled "Corporate Earnings: Who Can You Trust," contains articles that are highly critical of corporate America's earnings manipulation practices. Arthur Levitt, Jr., former Chairman of the Securities and Exchange Commission, has been outspoken in his criticism of corporate earnings management practices and their effect on earnings quality. In an article appearing in the *CPA Journal,* he states,

Many believe that corporate earnings management practices reduce the quality of reported earnings.

---

[6]Bethany McLean, "Hocus-Pocus: How IBM Grew 27% a Year," *Fortune,* June 26, 2000, p. 168.
[7]Ibid.
[8]Ford S. Worthy, "Manipulating Profits: How It's Done," *Fortune,* June 25, 1984, p. 50.
[9]Arthur Levitt, Jr., "The Numbers Game," *The CPA Journal,* December 1998, p. 16.

Increasingly, I have become concerned that the motivation to meet Wall Street earnings expectations may be overriding commonsense business practices. Too many corporate managers, auditors, and analysts are participants in a game of nods and winks. In the zeal to satisfy consensus earnings estimates and project a smooth earnings path, wishful thinking may be winning the day over faithful representation. As a result, I fear that we are witnessing an erosion in the *quality of earnings,* and therefore, the quality of financial reporting. Managing may be giving way to manipulation; integrity may be losing out to illusion. (emphasis added)[10]

How do managers manipulate income? Two major methods are (1) income shifting and (2) income statement classification. Income shifting is achieved by accelerating or delaying the recognition of revenues or expenses. For example, a practice called "channel stuffing" accelerates revenue recognition by persuading distributors to purchase more of your product than necessary near the end of a reporting period. The most common income statement classification manipulation involves the inclusion of recurring operating expenses in "special charge" categories such as restructuring costs (discussed below). This practice sometimes is referred to as "big bath" accounting, a reference to cleaning up company balance sheets. Asset reductions, or the incurrence of liabilities, for these restructuring costs result in large reductions in income that might otherwise appear as normal operating expenses either in the current or future years.

Mr. Levitt called for changes by standard setters to improve the transparency of financial statements. He did not want to eliminate necessary flexibility in financial reporting, but wanted to make it easier for financial statement users to "see through the numbers" to the future. A key to a meaningful assessment of a company's future profitability is to understand the events reported in the income statement and their relationship with future earnings. Let's now revisit the components of operating income.

Operating Income and Earnings Quality

● LO3

Should all items of revenue and expense included in operating income be considered indicative of a company's permanent earnings? No, not necessarily. Sometimes, for example, operating expenses include some unusual items that may or may not continue in the future. Look closely at the 2009 and 2008 partial income statements of **JDS Uniphase Corporation**, a leading provider of optical products for telecommunications service providers, presented in Graphic 4–3. What items appear unusual? Certainly "Impairment of goodwill," "Impairment of long-lived assets," and "Restructuring costs," require further investigation. We discuss restructuring costs first.

GRAPHIC 4–3

Partial Income Statements—JDS Uniphase Corporation

Real World Financials

Income Statements (in part) ($ in millions)	**Years Ended**	
	June 27, 2009	**June 28, 2008**
Net revenue	$1,294.4	$1,530.1
Cost of sales	802.3	938.8
Gross profit	492.1	591.3
Operating expenses:		
Research and development	170.1	188.1
Selling, general and administrative	404.6	455.8
Amortization of intangibles	27.0	30.0
Impairment of goodwill	741.7	37.0
Impairment of long-lived assets	13.2	6.7
Restructuring costs	38.7	6.7
Total operating expenses	1,395.3	724.3
Operating loss	(903.2)	(133.0)

---

[10]Ibid., p. 14.

RESTRUCTURING COSTS.   It's not unusual for a company to reorganize its operations to attain greater efficiency. When this happens, the company often incurs significant associated **restructuring costs.** Facility closings and related employee layoffs translate into costs incurred for severance pay and relocation costs. Restructuring costs are incurred in connection with:

A program that is planned and controlled by management, and materially changes either the scope of a business undertaken by an entity, or the manner in which that business is conducted.[11]

Restructuring costs appear frequently in corporate income statements. In fact, a recent survey reports that in 2008, of the 500 companies surveyed, 45% included restructuring costs in their income statements.[12] For instance, consider again our JDS Uniphase Corporation example. A disclosure note accompanying the company's financial statements indicates 2009 workforce reductions in North American, Asian, and European locations. Graphic 4–4 reports a portion of the disclosure note related to the restructuring costs incurred during the second quarter of 2009.

Restructuring costs include costs associated with shutdown or relocation of facilities or downsizing of operations.

Restructuring Costs (in part)

During the second quarter of fiscal 2009, the Company recorded $6.6 million in restructuring costs which included $4.6 million for severance and benefits, $1.0 million for manufacturing transfer cost, and $1.0 million to adjust accruals on previously restructured leases. One hundred and five employees were notified for termination.

GRAPHIC 4–4

Disclosure of Restructuring Costs—JDS Uniphase Corporation

Real World Financials

Restructuring costs are recognized in the period the **exit or disposal cost obligation** actually is incurred. As an example, suppose terminated employees are to receive termination benefits, but only after they remain with the employer beyond a minimum retention period. In that case, a liability for termination benefits, and corresponding expense, should be accrued in the period(s) the employees render their service. On the other hand, if future service beyond a minimum retention period is not required, the liability and corresponding expense for benefits are recognized at the time the company communicates the arrangement to employees. In both cases, the liability and expense are recorded at the point they are deemed incurred. Similarly, costs associated with closing facilities and relocating employees are recognized when goods or services associated with those activities are received.

GAAP requires that restructuring costs be recognized only in the period incurred.

GAAP also establishes that fair value is the objective for initial measurement of the liability, and that a liability's fair value often will be measured by determining the present value of future estimated cash outflows. We discuss such present value calculations at length in later chapters, particularly in Chapters 6 and 14. Because some restructuring costs require estimation, actual costs could differ. Also, the costs might not occur until a subsequent reporting period. As we discuss later in this chapter and throughout the text, when an estimate is changed, the company should record the effect of the change in the period the estimate is changed rather than by restating prior years' financial statements to correct the estimate. On occasion, this process has resulted in a negative expense amount for restructuring costs due to the overestimation of costs in a prior reporting period.

Fair value is the objective for the initial measurement of a liability associated with restructuring costs.

Now that we understand the nature of restructuring costs, we can address the important question: Should investors attempting to forecast future earnings consider these costs to be part of a company's permanent earnings stream, or are they transitory in nature? There is no easy answer. For example, JDS Uniphase incurred restructuring costs in both 2009 and 2008. Will the company incur these costs again in the near future? Consider the following facts. During the 10-year period from 1999 through 2008, the Dow Jones Industrial 30 companies reported 113 restructuring charges in their collective income statements. That's an average of approximately 3.77 per company. But the average is deceiving. Three of the

Should restructuring costs be considered part of a company's permanent earnings stream?

---

[11]FASB ASC 420–10–20: Exit or Disposal Cost Obligations—Overall—Glossary (previously "Accounting for Costs Associated with Exit or Disposal Activities," *Statement of Financial Accounting Standards No. 146* (Norwalk, Conn.: FASB, 2002)).
[12]*Accounting Trends and Techniques—2009* (New York: AICPA, 2009), p. 340.

30 companies reported no restructuring charges during that period. However, **Pfizer** incurred restructuring charges in 8 of the 10 years. The inference: an analyst must interpret restructuring charges in light of a company's past history. In general, the more frequently these sorts of unusual charges occur, the more appropriate it is that the analyst include them in the company's permanent earnings stream. Information in disclosure notes describing the restructuring and management plans related to the business involved also can be helpful.

Two other expenses in JDS Uniphase's income statements that warrant additional scrutiny are *impairment of goodwill* and *impairment of long-lived assets*. These expenses involve what is referred to as asset impairment losses or charges. Any long-lived asset, whether tangible or intangible, should have its balance reduced if there has been a significant impairment of value. We explore property, plant, and equipment and intangible assets in Chapters 10 and 11. After discussing this topic in more depth in those chapters, we revisit the concept of earnings quality as it relates to asset impairment.

> **ARTHUR LEVITT, JR.**
> When a company decides to restructure, management and employees, investors and creditors, customers and suppliers all want to understand the expected effects. We need, of course, to ensure that financial reporting provides this information. But this should not lead to flushing all the associated costs—and maybe a little extra—through the financial statements.[13]

Is it possible that financial analysts might look favorably at a company in the year it incurs a substantial restructuring charge or other unusual expense such as an asset impairment loss? Perhaps so, if they view management as creating higher profits in future years through operating efficiencies. Would analysts then reward that company again in future years when those operating efficiencies materialize? Certainly this double halo effect might provide an attractive temptation to the management of some companies.

Unusual or infrequent items included in operating income require investigation to determine their permanent or transitory nature.

These aren't the only components of operating expenses that call into question this issue of earnings quality. For example, in Chapter 9 we discuss the write-down of inventory to comply with the lower-of-cost-or-market rule. Earnings quality also is influenced by the way companies record income from investments (Chapter 12) and account for their pension plans (Chapter 17).

Earnings quality is affected by revenue issues as well. As an example, suppose that toward the end of its fiscal year, a company loses a major customer that can't be replaced. That would mean the current year's revenue numbers include a transitory component equal to the revenue generated from sales to the lost customer. Of course, in addition to its effect on revenues, losing the customer would have implications for the transitory/permanent nature of expenses and net income.

Another revenue issue affecting earnings quality is the timing of revenue recognition. Companies face continual pressure to meet their earnings expectations. That pressure often has led to premature revenue recognition, reducing the quality of reported earnings.

Real World Financials

Accelerating revenue recognition has caused problems for many companies. For example, **Lucent Technologies'** revenue recognition practices attracted the attention of the SEC. Nine current and former employees were charged with securities fraud for improperly recognizing sales of $1.15 billion in fiscal 2000. The SEC accused the former employees of falsely inflating revenues through aggressive sales practices, including the filing of false documents on sales to **Winstar Communications**, which later went bankrupt.[14] In 2008, **International Rectifier Corporation**, a manufacturer of power management products, was named defendant in a federal class action suit related to numerous irregularities including premature revenue recognition. The company admitted shipping products and recording sales with no obligation by customers to receive and pay for the products.

We explore these issues in Chapter 5, when we discuss revenue recognition in considerable depth, and in Chapter 13, when we discuss liabilities that companies must record when they receive payment prior to having actually earned the related revenue. Now, though, let's discuss earnings quality issues related to *nonoperating* items.

---

[13]Arthur Levitt, Jr. "The Numbers Game," *The CPA Journal,* December 1998, p. 16.
[14]Jeffrey Marshall, "The Perils of Revenue Recognition," *Financial Executive,* July–August 2004.

Nonoperating Income and Earnings Quality

Most of the components of earnings in an income statement relate directly to the ordinary, continuing operations of the company. Some, though, such as interest and gains or losses are only tangentially related to normal operations. These we refer to as nonoperating items. Some nonoperating items have generated considerable discussion with respect to earnings quality, notably gains and losses generated from the sale of investments. For example, as the stock market boom reached its height late in the year 2000, many companies recorded large gains from sale of investments that had appreciated significantly in value. How should those gains be interpreted in terms of their relationship to future earnings? Are they transitory or permanent? Let's consider an example.

Intel Corporation is the world's largest manufacturer of semiconductors. Graphic 4–5 shows the nonoperating section of Intel's income statements for the 2000 and 1999 fiscal years. In 2000, income before taxes increased by approximately 35% from the prior year. But notice that the *gains on investments, net* (net means net of losses) increased from $883 million to over $3.7 billion, accounting for a large portion of the increase in income. Some analysts questioned the quality of Intel's 2000 earnings because of these large gains.

> **Gains and losses from the sale of investments often can significantly inflate or deflate current earnings.**

> **GRAPHIC 4–5**
>
> Income Statements (in part)—Intel Corporation
>
> Real World Financials

Income Statements (in part)
(in millions)

| | Years Ended December 30 | |
	2000	1999
Operating income	10,395	9,767
Gains on investments, net	3,759	883
Interest and other, net	987	578
Income before taxes	15,141	11,228

Consider **Hecla Mining**, a precious metals company. In a recent fiscal year, the company reported income before income taxes of $61.8 million. Included in this amount was a $36.4 million gain on the sale of investments, representing 59% of total before-tax income. Can Hecla sustain these gains? Should they be considered part of permanent earnings or are they transitory? There are no easy answers to these questions. It's interesting to note that in the prior two years Hecla reported no investment gains.

Companies often voluntarily provide a pro forma earnings number when they announce annual or quarterly earnings. Supposedly, these pro forma earnings numbers are management's view of "permanent earnings," in the sense of being a better long-run performance measure. For example, in January of 2009, **Google Inc.** announced that its income for the fourth quarter was $382 million or 1.21 per share. At the same time, the company announced that its *pro forma net income* (for which Google excluded stock-based compensation, impairment charges, and costs related to the settlement of a copyright infringement lawsuit) for the quarter was $1.62 billion or $5.10 per share. These pro forma earnings numbers are controversial because determining which items to exclude is at the discretion of management. Therefore, management could mislead investors. Nevertheless, these disclosures do represent management's perception of what its permanent earnings are and provides additional information to the financial community.

> **Many companies voluntarily provide** *pro forma earnings*—**management's assessment of permanent earnings.**
>
> Real World Financials

The Sarbanes-Oxley Act addressed pro forma earnings in its Section 401. One of the act's important provisions requires that if pro forma earnings are included in any periodic or other report filed with the SEC or in any public disclosure or press release, the company also must provide a reconciliation with earnings determined according to generally accepted accounting principles.[15]

> **The Sarbanes-Oxley Act requires a reconciliation between pro forma earnings and earnings determined according to GAAP.**

We now turn our attention to two income statement items—discontinued operations and extraordinary items—that, because of their nature, are more obviously not part of a company's permanent earnings and, appropriately, are excluded from continuing operations.

---

[15]The Congress of the United States of America, *The Sarbanes-Oxley Act of 2002*, Section 401 (b) (2), Washington, D.C., 2004.

Separately Reported Items

The information in the income statement is useful if it can help users predict the future. Toward this end, users should be made aware of events reported in the income statement that are not likely to occur again in the foreseeable future.

There are two types of events that, if they have a material effect[16] on the income statement, require separate reporting below income from continuing operations as well as separate disclosure: (1) discontinued operations, and (2) extraordinary items.[17] Although a company has considerable flexibility in reporting income from *continuing operations,* the presentation order of these items is mandated as follows:[18]

Income from continuing operations before income taxes and extraordinary items	$xxx
Income tax expense	xx
Income from continuing operations before extraordinary items	xxx
Discontinued operations, net of $xx in tax	xx
Extraordinary items, net of $xx in tax[19]	xx
Net income	**$xxx**

The objective is to separately report all of the income effects of these items. That's why we include the income tax effect of each item in this separate presentation rather than report them as part of income tax expense. The process of associating income tax effects with the income statement components that create them is referred to as *intraperiod tax allocation.* We address this process in the next section.

A third separately reported item, the *cumulative effect of a change in accounting principle,* might be included for certain mandated changes in accounting principles. Before 2005, most voluntary changes in accounting principles also were treated this way, by including the cumulative effect on the income of previous years from having used the old method rather than the new method in the income statement of the year of change as a separately reported item below extraordinary items. Now, most voluntary changes in accounting principles require retrospective treatment. We no longer report the entire effect in the year of the change. Instead, we retrospectively recast prior years' financial statements when we report those statements again (in comparative statements, for example) so that they appear as if the newly adopted accounting method had been used in those years presented. We discuss the retrospective approach later in this chapter and in subsequent chapters. A subsequent section in this chapter also addresses the distinction between voluntary and mandated changes in accounting principles.

Intraperiod Income Tax Allocation

Intraperiod tax allocation associates (allocates) income tax expense (or income tax benefit if there is a loss) with each major component of income that causes it.[20] More specifically, income tax is allocated to income from continuing operations and each of the two separately reported items. For example, assume a company experienced an extraordinary gain during the year.[21] The amount of income tax expense deducted from income from continuing operations is the amount of income tax expense that the company would have incurred *if there were no extraordinary gain.* The effect on income taxes caused by the extraordinary item is

---

[16]The concept of materiality was discussed in Chapter 1. If the effect on the income statement is not material, these items are included in income from continuing operations.

[17]FASB ASC 225–20–45: Income Statement—Extraordinary Items—Other Presentation Matters, and FASB ASC 205–20–45: Presentation of Financial Statement—Discontinued Operations—Other Presentation Matters (previously "Reporting Results of Operations," *Accounting Principles Board Opinion No. 30* (New York: AICPA, 1973)).

[18]The presentation of these separately reported items is the same for single-step and multiple-step income statement formats. The single-step versus multiple-step distinction applies to items included in income from continuing operations.

[19]Companies that report discontinued operations and one of the other separately reported items often show a subtotal after discontinued operations. This is not required. However, due to its frequency of use, we use this convention in examples and illustrations in the remainder of this chapter.

[20]*Intraperiod* tax allocation concerns the association of income tax with income statement components. *Interperiod* tax allocation, covered in Chapter 16, addresses the problem created when taxable income does not equal income before taxes as determined by GAAP because of differences in the timing of revenue or expense recognition.

[21]The criteria for classifying gains and losses as extraordinary are discussed in a later section of this chapter.

deducted from the extraordinary gain in the income statement. Illustration 4–3 demonstrates this concept.

The Maxwell Gear Corporation had income from continuing operations before income tax expense of $200,000 and an extraordinary gain of $60,000 in 2011. The income tax rate is 40% on all items of income or loss. Therefore, the company's total income tax expense is $104,000 (40% × $260,000).	**ILLUSTRATION 4–3** Intraperiod Tax Allocation

How should the company allocate the tax expense between income from continuing operations and the extraordinary gain? A partial income statement, beginning with income from continuing operations before income tax expense, *ignoring* intraperiod tax allocation, is shown in Illustration 4–3A.

Incorrect Presentation		**ILLUSTRATION 4–3A**
Income before income taxes and extraordinary item	$200,000	Income Statement
Income tax expense	(104,000)	Presented
		Incorrectly—No
Income before extraordinary item	96,000	Intraperiod
Extraordinary gain (gross)	60,000	Tax Allocation
		(extraordinary gain)
Net income	$156,000	

The deficiency of this presentation is that the apparent contribution to net income of (a) income before the extraordinary gain (that is, income from continuing operations) and (b) the extraordinary gain, is misleading. If the extraordinary gain had not occurred, income tax expense would not have been $104,000 but rather $80,000 (40% × $200,000). Similarly, the net benefit of the extraordinary gain is not $60,000, but rather $36,000 ($60,000 minus 40% × $60,000). The total tax expense of $104,000 must be *allocated,* $80,000 to continuing operations and $24,000 (40% × $60,000) to the extraordinary gain. The appropriate income statement presentation appears in Illustration 4–3B.

Correct Presentation		**ILLUSTRATION 4–3B**
Income before income taxes and extraordinary item	$200,000	Income Statement
Income tax expense	(80,000)	Presented
		Correctly—
Income before extraordinary item	120,000	Intraperiod
Extraordinary gain, net of $24,000 tax expense	36,000	Tax Allocation
		(extraordinary gain)
Net income	$156,000	

Net income is $156,000 either way. Intraperiod tax allocation is not an issue of measurement but an issue of presentation. The $120,000 income before extraordinary gain properly reflects income from continuing operations *including* the appropriate tax effects. Also, notice that income tax expense represents taxes that relate to the total of all of the revenue, expense, gain, and loss items included in continuing operations. Each of the items following continuing operations (discontinued operations and extraordinary items) are presented *net of their tax effect.* No individual items included in the computation of income from continuing operations are reported net of tax.

In the illustration, the extraordinary gain caused additional income tax expense to be incurred. What if the company had experienced an extraordinary loss of $60,000 instead of an extraordinary gain? In that case, rather than creating additional tax, the loss actually decreases tax due to its reducing taxable income by $60,000. The company's total income tax expense would be $56,000 [40% × ($200,000 − 60,000)].

The extraordinary loss *decreased* the amount of tax the company otherwise would have had to pay by $24,000. This is commonly referred to as a *tax benefit.* A partial income statement, beginning with income from continuing operations before income tax expense, *ignoring* intraperiod tax allocation is shown in Illustration 4–3C.

The two items reported separately below income from continuing operations are presented net of the related income tax effect.

ILLUSTRATION 4–3C	**Incorrect Presentation**	
Income Statement Presented *Incorrectly*—No Intraperiod Tax Allocation (extraordinary loss)	Income before income taxes and extraordinary item	$200,000
	Income tax expense	(56,000)
	Income before extraordinary item	144,000
	Extraordinary loss (gross)	(60,000)
	Net income	$ 84,000

Once again, income before the extraordinary loss (that is, income from continuing operations) is misleading. If the extraordinary loss had not occurred, income tax expense would not have been $56,000 but rather $80,000 (40% × $200,000). The total tax expense of $56,000 must be *allocated,* $80,000 tax expense to continuing operations and $24,000 tax benefit to the extraordinary loss. The appropriate income statement presentation appears in Illustration 4–3D.

ILLUSTRATION 4–3D	**Correct Presentation**	
Income Statement Presented *Correctly*— Intraperiod Tax Allocation (extraordinary loss)	Income before income taxes and extraordinary item	$200,000
	Income tax expense	(80,000)
	Income before extraordinary item	120,000
	Extraordinary loss, net of $24,000 tax benefit	(36,000)
	Net income	$ 84,000

Now that we have seen how to report items net of their related tax effects, let's look closer at the two items reported net of tax below income from continuing operations: discontinued operations and extraordinary items.

Discontinued Operations

● **LO4**

Q3, p. 169

H&R Block, Inc., is perhaps best known for providing a variety of financial services to customers, principally income tax preparation and consulting services. Prior to 2008, the company also operated a mortgage services business that specialized in mortgage loans. But the company sold the mortgage services segment in 2008. **Time Warner, Inc.,** is a leading media and entertainment company. Prior to 2009, the company operated the following business segments: AOL, cable, filmed entertainment, networks, and publishing. In 2009, the company sold its cable business. H&R Block's sale of its mortgage services business and Time Warner's sale of its cable business are examples of **discontinued operations.**

WHAT CONSTITUTES AN OPERATION? For purposes of reporting discontinued operations, in 2001 the FASB issued a standard that defined an operation as a *component of an entity* whose operations and cash flows can be clearly distinguished, operationally and for financial reporting purposes, from the rest of the entity. International standards also defined a discontinued operation as a discontinued component of an entity. However, what constitutes a "component" of an entity differed significantly between U.S. GAAP and *IFRS No. 5.*[23]

As part of the continuing process to converge U.S. GAAP and international standards, the FASB and IASB worked together to develop a common definition of discontinued operations and a common set of disclosures for disposals of components of an entity. The FASB issued an exposure draft (ED) that

> **COMPONENT OF AN ENTITY**
>
> . . . a component of an entity that is either an *operating segment* that has either been disposed of or held for sale; or a *business* that meets the criteria to be classified as held for sale on acquisition.[22]

---

[22]"Amending the Criteria for Reporting a Discontinued Operation," *Proposed FASB Staff Position No. 144-d* (Stamford, Conn.: FASB, 2009).
[23]"Non-current Assets Held for Sale and Discontinued Operations," *International Financial Reporting Standard No. 5* (IASCF), as amended effective January 1, 2009.

outlined the Boards' preliminary position. At the time this text was published, a final pronouncement had not been issued.

The ED defines a "component" of an entity for this purpose as either:

a. An *operating segment* (defined below) that has either been disposed of or is classified as "held for sale"; or
b. A *business* (defined below) that meets the criteria to be classified as held for sale on acquisition.

An **operating segment** that might be considered discontinued is defined the same as an operating segment for segment reporting purposes. As discussed further in the appendix to Chapter 3, an operating segment is a part of an enterprise:

• That may earn revenues and incur expenses.
• Whose operating results are regularly reviewed to make decisions about resources to be allocated to the segment and assess its performance.
• For which discrete financial information is available.[24]

A **business** that might be considered discontinued is defined the same as when accounting for business combinations, specifically:

• An integrated set of activities and assets.
• Capable of being conducted and managed to provide a return in the form of dividends, lower costs, or other economic benefits.[25]

Many were critical of prior U.S. GAAP for its broad definition of a component of the entity. In addition to achieving convergence with international standards, the new guidance, if finalized as outlined in the exposure draft, is expected to reduce the number of business segments that are considered to be components of the entity requiring separate income statement presentation.

REPORTING DISCONTINUED OPERATIONS. By definition, the income or loss stream from a discontinued operation no longer will continue. An analyst concerned with H&R Block's and Time Warner's future profitability is more interested in the results of their operations that will continue. It is informative, then, for companies to separate the effects of the discontinued operations from the results of operations that will continue. This information might have a significant impact on the analyst's assessment of future profitability.

For this reason, the revenues, expenses, gains, losses, and income tax related to a *discontinued* operation must be removed from *continuing* operations and reported separately for all years presented.[26] A key for assessing profitability is comparing the company's performance from *continuing* operations from year to year and from company to company.

Sometimes a discontinued component actually has been sold by the end of a reporting period. Often, though, the component is being held for sale, but the disposal transaction has not yet been completed as of the end of the reporting period. We consider these two possibilities next.

The net-of-tax income effects of a discontinued operation are reported separately in the income statement, below income from continuing operations.

When the component has been sold.   When the discontinued component is sold before the end of the reporting period, the reported income effects of a discontinued operation will include two elements:

1. Operating income or loss (revenues, expenses, gains, and losses) of the component from the beginning of the reporting period to the disposal date.
2. Gain or loss on disposal of the component's assets.

---

[24]FASB ASC 280–10–50–1: Segment Reporting—Overall—Disclosure (previously "Disclosures about Segments of an Enterprise and Related Information," *Statement of Financial Accounting Standards No. 131* (Norwalk, Conn.: FASB, 1997), par. 10).

[25]FASB ASC 805–10–20: Business Combinations–Overall–Glossary (previously "Business Combinations," *Statement of Financial Accounting Standards No. 141 (revised)* (Norwalk, Conn.: FASB, 2007)).

[26]For example, even though Time Warner did not sell its cable business until 2009, it's important for comparative purposes to separate the effects for any prior years presented. This allows an apples-to-apples comparison of income from *continuing* operations. So, in its 2009 three-year comparative income statements, the 2008 and 2007 income statements would be reclassified and the income from discontinued operations presented as a separately reported item.

These two elements can be combined or reported separately, net of their tax effects. If combined, the gain or loss component must be indicated. In our illustrations to follow, we combine the income effects. Illustration 4–4 describes a situation in which the discontinued component is sold before the end of the reporting period.

ILLUSTRATION 4–4 Discontinued Operations—Gain on Disposal	The Duluth Holding Company has several operating divisions. In October 2011, management decided to sell one of its divisions that qualifies as a separate component according to generally accepted accounting principles. The division was sold on December 18, 2011, for a net selling price of $14,000,000. On that date, the assets of the division had a book value of $12,000,000. For the period January 1 through disposal, the division reported a pretax operating loss of $4,200,000. The company's income tax rate is 40% on all items of income or loss. Duluth generated after-tax profits of $22,350,000 from its continuing operations. 　Duluth's income statement for the year 2011, beginning with income from continuing operations, would be reported as follows:

Income from continuing operations		$22,350,000
Discontinued operations:		
Loss from operations of discontinued component		
(including gain on disposal of $2,000,000*)	$(2,200,000)[†]	
Income tax benefit	880,000[‡]	
Loss on discontinued operations		(1,320,000)
Net income		$21,030,000

*Net selling price of $14 million less book value of $12 million
[†]Operating loss of $4.2 million less gain on disposal of $2 million
[‡]$2,200,000 × 40%

Notice that a tax *benefit* occurs because a *loss* reduces taxable income, saving the company $880,000. On the other hand, had there been *income* from operations of $2,200,000, the $880,000 income tax effect would have represented additional income tax expense.

For comparison purposes, the net of tax operating income or loss of the discontinued component for any prior years included in the comparative income statements also are separately reported as discontinued operations.

When the component is considered held for sale. What if a company has decided to discontinue a component but, when the reporting period ends, the component has not yet been sold? If the situation indicates that the component is likely to be sold within a year, the component is considered "held for sale."[27] In that case, the income effects of the discontinued operation still are reported, but the two components of the reported amount are modified as follows:

If a component to be discontinued has not yet been sold, its income effects, including any impairment loss, usually still are reported separately as discontinued operations.

1. Operating income or loss (revenues, expenses, gains and losses) of the component from the beginning of the reporting period *to the end of the reporting period.*
2. An "impairment loss" if the carrying value (book value) of the assets of the component is more than fair value minus cost to sell.

The two income elements can be combined or reported separately, net of their tax effects. In addition, if the amounts are combined and there is an impairment loss, the loss must be disclosed, either parenthetically on the face of the statement or in a disclosure note. Consider the example in Illustration 4–5.

A disclosure note would provide additional details about the discontinued component, including the identity of the component, the major classes of assets and liabilities of the component, the reason for the discontinuance, and the expected manner of disposition. Also, the net-of-tax operating income or loss of the component being discontinued is also reported separate from continuing operations for any prior year that is presented for comparison purposes along with the 2011 income statement.

---

[27]Six criteria are used to determine whether the component is likely to be sold and therefore considered "held for sale." You can find these criteria in FASB ASC 360–10–45–9: Property, Plant, and Equipment—Overall—Other Presentation Matters—Long-Lived Assets Classified as Held for Sale (previously "Accounting for the Impairment or Disposal of Long-Lived Assets," *Statement of Financial Accounting Standards No. 144* (Norwalk, Conn.: FASB, 2001), par. 30).

The Duluth Holding Company has several operating divisions. In October 2011, management decided to sell one of its divisions that qualifies as a separate component according to generally accepted accounting principles. On December 31, 2011, the end of the company's fiscal year, the division had not yet been sold. On that date, the assets of the division had a book value of $12,000,000 and a fair value, minus anticipated costs to sell, of $9,000,000. For the year, the division reported a pre-tax operating loss of $4,200,000. The company's income tax rate is 40% on all items of income or loss. Duluth generated after-tax profits of $22,350,000 from its continuing operations.

Duluth's income statement for 2011, beginning with income from continuing operations, would be reported as follows:

Income from continuing operations		$22,350,000
Discontinued operations:		
Loss from operations of discontinued component (including impairment loss of $3,000,000)	$(7,200,000)*	
Income tax benefit	2,880,000†	
Loss on discontinued operations		(4,320,000)
Net income		$18,030,000

ILLUSTRATION 4–5

Discontinued Operations— Impairment Loss

*Operating loss of $4.2 million plus impairment loss of $3 million
†$7,200,000 × 40%

In Illustration 4–5, if the fair value of the division's assets minus cost to sell exceeded the book value of $12,000,000, there is no impairment loss and the income effects of the discontinued operation would include only the operating loss of $4,200,000, less the income tax benefit.[28]

The balance sheet is affected, too. The assets and liabilities of the component considered held for sale are reported at the lower of their carrying amount (book value) or fair value minus cost to sell. And, because it's not in use, an asset classified as held for sale is no longer reported as part of property, plant, and equipment or intangible assets and is not depreciated or amortized.

As an example, **Talbots, Inc.,** is a specialty retailer of women's apparel. Late in its fiscal year ended January 31, 2009, the company adopted a plan to sell its **J. Jill** business and at year-end J. Jill was considered held for sale. The current asset and current liability sections of the year-end balance sheet reported $109,966 thousand in "Assets held for sale," and $94,190 thousand in "Liabilities held for sale," respectively. Information about the discontinued operation was included in the disclosure note shown in Graphic 4–6.

4. Discontinued Operations (in part)

Presented below is a summarized balance sheet for the J. Jill assets and liabilities held for sale. Since the Company expects to complete the sale of the J. Jill business within one year, all assets and liabilities held for sale are classified as current within the Company's consolidated balance sheet as of January 31, 2009.

($ in thousands)	January 31, 2009
Merchandise inventories	$ 50,250
Other current assets	9,217
Property and equipment, net	15,899
Trademarks	30,200
Other intangible assets, net	4,400
Total assets held for sale	$109,966
Current liabilities	$ 57,152
Other liabilities	37,038
Total liabilities held for sale	$ 94,190

GRAPHIC 4–6

Discontinued Operations Disclosure— Talbots, Inc.

Real World Financials

[28]In the following year when the component is sold, the income effects must also be reported as a discontinued operation.

Notice that the assets and liabilities held for sale are classified as *current* because "the Company expects to complete the sale of the J. Jill business within one year." In the February 2, 2008, balance sheet presented for comparison purposes with the January 31, 2009, balance sheet, the assets and liabilities of the J. Jill business were appropriately reclassified as held for sale and included with noncurrent assets and liabilities.

Interim reporting.   Remember that companies whose ownership shares are publicly traded in the United States must file quarterly reports with the Securities and Exchange Commission. If a component of an entity is considered held for sale at the end of a quarter, the income effects of the discontinued component must be separately reported in the quarterly income statement. These effects would include the operating income or loss for the quarter as well as an impairment loss if the component's assets have a book value more than fair value minus cost to sell. If the assets are impaired and written down, any gain or loss on disposal in a subsequent quarter is determined relative to the new, written-down book value.

Let's now turn our attention to the second separately reported item, extraordinary gains and losses.

Extraordinary Items

● LO5

Occasionally, an unusual event may occur that materially affects the current year's income but is highly unlikely to occur again in the foreseeable future. If such an item is allowed to simply alter net income without pointing out its extraordinary nature, earnings quality is seriously compromised and investors and creditors may be misled into basing predictions of future income on current income that includes the nonrecurring event. For that reason, extraordinary items are "red flagged" in an income statement by being reported separately, net of tax, and appropriately labeled. Extraordinary items are material events and transactions that are both:

1. Unusual in nature
2. Infrequent in occurrence[29]

Extraordinary items are material gains and losses that are both unusual in nature and infrequent in occurrence.

These criteria must be considered in light of the environment in which the entity operates. There obviously is a considerable degree of subjectivity involved in the determination. The concepts of unusual and infrequent require judgment. In making these judgments, an accountant should keep in mind the overall objective of the income statement. The key question is how the event relates to a firm's future profitability. If it is judged that the event, because of its unusual nature and infrequency of occurrence, *is not likely to occur again,* separate reporting is warranted.

Companies often experience *unexpected* events that are not considered extraordinary items. The loss of a major customer or the death of the company president are unexpected events that likely will affect a company's future but are both normal risks of operating a business that could recur in the future. Other gains and losses from unexpected events that are *not* considered extraordinary include the effects of a strike, including those against competitors and major suppliers, and the adjustment of accruals on long-term contracts.[30]

The determination of whether an item is unusual and infrequent should consider the environment in which the company operates.

A key point in the definition of an extraordinary item is that determining whether an event satisfies *both* criteria depends on the environment in which the firm operates. The environment includes factors such as the type of products or services sold and the geographical location of the firm's operations. What is extraordinary for one firm may not be extraordinary for another firm. For example, a loss caused by a hurricane in Florida may not be judged to be extraordinary. However, hurricane damage in New York may indeed be unusual and infrequent.

Companies frequently sell subsidiary companies or their partial ownership interest in companies. Generally, the gain or loss is reported as a nonoperating item in the income statement or as a discontinued operation if the subsidiary is considered a component of the

---

[29]FASB ASC 225–20–45–2: Income Statement—Extraordinary and Unusual Items—Other Presentation Matters (previously "Reporting Results of Operations," *Accounting Principles Board Opinion No. 30* (New York: AICPA, 1973), par. 20).

[30]FASB ASC 225–20–45–4: Income Statement—Extraordinary and Unusual Items—Other Presentation Matters (previously "Reporting Results of Operations," *Accounting Principles Board Opinion No. 30* (New York: AICPA, 1973), par. 23).

entity according to generally accepted accounting principles. In contrast, though, consider the disclosure note from a recent quarterly financial statement of **Verizon Communications, Inc.**, shown in Graphic 4–7.

Extraordinary Item (in part)

In January of the current year, the Bolivarian Republic of Venezuela declared its intent to nationalize certain companies, including CANTV. In February, we entered into a Memorandum of Understanding (MOU) with the Republic. The MOU provides that the Republic will offer to purchase all of the equity securities of CANTV, including our 28.5% interest . . . at a price equivalent to $17.85 . . . Based upon the terms of the MOU and our current investment balance in CANTV, we recorded an extraordinary loss on our investment of $131 million, net of tax, or $.05 per diluted shares, in the first quarter.

GRAPHIC 4–7

Extraordinary Loss Disclosure—Verizon Communications, Inc.

Real World Financials

Why was the loss on sale of the company's 28.5% interest in a Venezuelan company considered an extraordinary item? The unusual nature of the forced sale, the nationalization (expropriation) of CANTV by a foreign government, resulted in the conclusion by Verizon that such a loss was unlikely to occur again in the foreseeable future.

Logic and reasoning must be applied to the determination of whether or not an event is extraordinary. Keep in mind that the income statement should be a guide to predicting the future. If it is extremely unlikely that a material gain or loss will occur again in the future, the quality of earnings is improved and the usefulness of the income statement in predicting the future is enhanced if the income effects of that gain or loss are reported separately.

As shown previously on page 180, the net-of-tax effects of extraordinary gains and losses are presented in the income statement below discontinued operations. In addition, a disclosure note is necessary to describe the nature of the event and the tax effects, if they are not indicated on the face of the income statement.[31]

Extraordinary gains and losses are presented, net of tax, in the income statement below discontinued operations.

INTERNATIONAL FINANCIAL REPORTING STANDARDS

● LO12

Extraordinary Items. U.S. GAAP provides for the separate reporting, as an extraordinary item, of a material gain or loss that is unusual in nature and infrequent in occurrence. In 2003, the IASB revised *IAS No. 1*.[32] The revision states that neither the income statement nor any notes may contain any items called "extraordinary."

A recent survey of 500 large public companies reported that only two of the companies disclosed an extraordinary gain or loss in their 2008 income statements.[33] Losses from two 21st century "extraordinary" events, the September 11, 2001, terrorist attacks and Hurricane Katrina in 2005, did not qualify for extraordinary treatment. The treatment of these two events, the scarcity of extraordinary gains and losses reported in corporate income statements, and the desire to converge U.S. and international accounting standards could guide the FASB to the elimination of the extraordinary item classification.[34]

Very few extraordinary gains and losses are reported in corporate income statements.

The extraordinary item classification could soon be eliminated.

Unusual or Infrequent Items

If the income effect of an event is material and the event is either unusual or infrequent—but not both—the item should be *included in continuing operations* but reported as a separate income statement component. Recall the JDS Uniphase Corporation example in

The income effect of an event that is either unusual or infrequent should be reported as a separate component of continuing operations.

---

[31]For several years the FASB required companies to report material gains and losses from the early extinguishment of debt as extraordinary items. This is no longer the case and now these gains and losses are subject to the same criteria as other gains and losses for such treatment; namely, that they be both (a) unusual in nature and (b) infrequent in occurrence.

[32]"Financial Statement Presentation," *International Accounting Standard No. 1* (IASCF), as amended effective January 1, 2009.

[33]*Accounting Trends and Techniques—2009* (New York: AICPA, 2009), p. 441.

[34]For a thorough discussion of this topic, see Massoud, Raiborn and Humphrey, "Extraordinary Items: Time to Eliminate the Classification," *The CPA Journal* (February 2007).

Graphic 4–3 on page 176. Restructuring costs and the impairment of goodwill and long-lived assets included in that company's continuing operations are examples of this type of event. The events may be unusual or infrequent, but, by their nature, they could occur again in the foreseeable future. However, rather than include these items with other gains and losses or with other expenses, they are reported as a separate line item in the income statement.[35] This method of reporting, including note disclosure, enhances earnings quality by providing information to the statement user to help assess the events' relationship with future profitability.

As we discussed earlier, the cumulative effect of a voluntary change in accounting principle no longer is reported as a separate item in the income statement. A recent standard requires that we retrospectively adjust prior financial statements instead. As a result, the income statement and other financial statements are affected by these changes differently than before. In the next section, we explore the way various types of accounting changes are reported.

Accounting Changes

Accounting changes fall into one of three categories: (1) a change in an accounting principle, (2) a change in estimate, or (3) a change in reporting entity. The correction of an error is another adjustment that is accounted for in the same way as certain accounting changes. A brief overview of each is provided here. We cover accounting changes in detail in Chapter 20.

Change in Accounting Principle

● LO6

A change in accounting principle refers to a change from one acceptable accounting method to another. There are many situations that allow alternative treatments for similar transactions. Common examples of these situations include the choice among FIFO, LIFO, and average cost for the measurement of inventory and among alternative revenue recognition methods. New standards issued by the FASB also require companies to change their accounting methods.

VOLUNTARY CHANGES IN ACCOUNTING PRINCIPLES. Occasionally, a company will change from one generally accepted treatment to another. When these changes in accounting principles occur, information lacks consistency, hampering the ability of external users to compare financial information among reporting periods. If, for example, inventory and cost of goods sold are measured in one reporting period using LIFO and using the FIFO method in a subsequent period, inventory, cost of goods sold, and hence net income for the two periods are not comparable. Difficulties created by inconsistency and lack of comparability are alleviated by the way we report voluntary accounting changes.

Voluntary changes in accounting principles are accounted for retrospectively by revising prior years' financial statements.

GAAP requires that voluntary accounting changes be accounted for retrospectively.[36] Prior to this standard, the cumulative effect on the income of previous years from having used the old method rather than the new method was included in the income statement of the year of change as a separately reported item. We no longer report the cumulative effect in the year of the change. Instead, we retrospectively recast prior years' financial statements when we report those statements again (in comparative statements, for example). For each year in the comparative statements reported, we revise the balance of each account affected to make those statements appear as if the newly adopted accounting method had been applied all along. Then, a journal entry is created to adjust all account balances affected to what those amounts would have been. An adjustment is made to the beginning balance of retained earnings for the earliest period reported in the comparative statements of shareholders' equity to

---

[35]These items are *not* reported net of tax. Only the two separately reported items—discontinued operations and extraordinary items—are reported net of tax.

[36]FASB ASC 250–10–45–5: Accounting Changes and Error Corrections—Overall—Other Presentation Matters (previously "Accounting Changes and Error Corrections—a replacement of APB Opinion No. 20 and FASB Statement No. 3," *Statement of Financial Accounting Standard No. 154* (Norwalk, Conn.: FASB, 2005)).

account for the cumulative income effect of changing to the new principle in periods prior to those reported.[37]

Let's suppose that in 2011 the Dearborn Corporation switched from the LIFO inventory method to FIFO. In addition to the 2011 statements, Dearborn presents two additional years of income statements and statements of shareholders' equity (2010 and 2009) as well as a 2010 balance sheet for comparative purposes. Here are the steps Dearborn would follow to account for the change.

1. The comparative financial statements are revised. For all three years—2009, 2010, and 2011—income statements will appear as if FIFO had been applied all along. Dearborn uses its new method, FIFO, to determine cost of goods sold, income tax expense, and net income in 2011 and recalculates the 2009 and 2010 numbers using FIFO rather than LIFO. Similarly, inventory and retained earnings in each year's balance sheet are reported using the newly adopted FIFO method. In its statements of shareholders' equity, Dearborn reports retained earnings each year as if it had used FIFO all along, and because 2009 is the earliest year reported, beginning retained earnings that year is revised to reflect the cumulative income effect of the difference in inventory methods for all years prior to 2009.
2. The appropriate accounts are adjusted. Dearborn will create a journal entry to adjust the book balances from their current LIFO amounts to what those balances would have been using FIFO. Since differences in cost of goods sold and income are reflected in retained earnings, as are the income tax effects, the journal entry updates these accounts.
3. A disclosure note provides additional information. Dearborn must provide clear justification that the change to FIFO is appropriate in a disclosure note. The note also indicates the effects of the change on items not reported on the face of the primary statements, as well as any per share amounts affected for the current period and all prior periods presented. In addition, the note discloses the cumulative effect of the change on retained earnings or other components of equity as of the beginning of the earliest period presented.

We will see these steps demonstrated in Chapter 9 in the context of our discussion of inventory methods. Later, we'll revisit accounting changes in depth in Chapter 20.

MANDATED CHANGES IN ACCOUNTING PRINCIPLES.   When a new FASB standard mandates a change in accounting principle, the board often allows companies to choose among multiple ways of accounting for the changes. One approach generally allowed is to account for the change retrospectively, exactly as we account for voluntary changes in principles. A second approach is to allow companies to report the cumulative effect on the income of previous years from having used the old method rather than the new method in the income statement of the year of change as a separately reported item below extraordinary items.

As an example of accounting for a mandated change with a cumulative adjustment, consider **Marvell Technology Group LTD.**, a leading global semiconductor provider. Marvell adopted newly revised GAAP regarding share-based payments for its fiscal year ended January 27, 2007. The revision in GAAP, which we discuss in detail in Chapter 19, requires all companies to expense the estimated cost of employee stock options. Marvell accounted for the adoption of the new standard by including the $8.8 million, net of tax, cumulative effect of the change in its 2007 income statement as a separately reported item. Graphic 4–8 shows a portion of the disclosure note that explained the change.

Change in Depreciation, Amortization, or Depletion Method

A change in depreciation, amortization, or depletion method is considered to be a change in accounting estimate that is achieved by a change in accounting principle. We account for these changes prospectively, exactly as we would any other change in estimate. We discuss and illustrate this approach in the next section.

> Changes in depreciation, amortization, or depletion methods are accounted for the same way as a change in an accounting estimate.

---

[37]Sometimes a lack of information makes it impracticable to report a change retrospectively so the new method is simply applied prospectively, that is, we simply use the new method from now on. Also, if a new standard specifically requires prospective accounting, that requirement is followed.

GRAPHIC 4–8

Disclosure of Change in Accounting Principle— Marvell Technology Group LTD.

Real World Financials

> **14. Stock-Based Incentive Plans (in part)**
>
> The adoption of *SFAS No. 123R* [FASB ASC 718 and 505] resulted in a cumulative benefit from the change in accounting principle of $8.8 million, net of tax, as of the year ended January 27, 2007, reflecting the net cumulative impact of estimated forfeitures that were previously not included in the determination of historic stock-based compensation expense in periods prior to January 28, 2006.

Change in Accounting Estimate

● **LO7**

A change in accounting estimate is reflected in the financial statements of the current period and future periods.

Estimates are a necessary aspect of accounting. A few of the more common accounting estimates are the amount of future bad debts on existing accounts receivable, the useful life and residual value of a depreciable asset, and future warranty expenses.

Because estimates require the prediction of future events, it's not unusual for them to turn out to be wrong. When an estimate is modified as new information comes to light, accounting for the change in estimate is quite straightforward. We do not revise prior years' financial statements to reflect the new estimate. Instead, we merely incorporate the new estimate in any related accounting determinations from that point on, that is, prospectively.[38]

Consider the example in Illustration 4–6.

ILLUSTRATION 4–6

Change in Accounting Estimate

The Maxwell Gear Corporation purchased machinery in 2008 for $2 million. The useful life of the machinery was estimated to be 10 years with no residual value. The straight-line depreciation method was used in 2008 through 2010, with a full year of depreciation taken in 2008. In 2011, the company revised the useful life of the machinery to eight years.

Neither depreciation expense nor accumulated depreciation reported in prior years is restated. No account balances are adjusted. Rather, in 2011 and later years, the adjusting entry to record depreciation expense simply will reflect the new useful life. In 2011, the entry is:

Depreciation expense (below) 280,000
 Accumulated depreciation 280,000

	$2,000,000	Cost
$200,000		Previous annual depreciation ($2,000,000 ÷ 10 years)
× 3 years	600,000	Depreciation to date (2008–2010)
	$1,400,000	Book value as of 1/1/11
	÷ 5 yrs.	Estimated remaining life (8 years − 3 years)
	$ 280,000	New annual depreciation

When a company makes a change in an estimate that affects several future periods, such as revising its estimate of an asset's useful life, the company reports in a disclosure note the effect of that change on the current year's income before extraordinary items, net income, and earnings per share. That disclosure isn't necessary for more routine changes such as revising estimates regarding uncollectible accounts, unless the effect of the change is material.

A recent quarterly report of **Saga, Inc.,** provides us an example. The company operates radio and television stations in 26 markets throughout the United States. Graphic 4–9 reproduces the disclosure note that described a change in the useful life of its television analog equipment.

As we discussed in a previous section, a change in depreciation, amortization, or depletion method is considered a change in estimate resulting from a change in principle. For that reason, we account for such a change prospectively, similar to the way we account for other changes in estimate. One difference is that most changes in estimate do not require a company to justify the change. However, this change in estimate is a result of changing an

---

[38]If the original estimate had been based on erroneous information or calculations or had not been made in good faith, the revision of that estimate would constitute the correction of an error.

Change in Accounting Estimate

In the second quarter of 2008, the Company reviewed the estimated useful lives of its television analog equipment. This review was performed because of the Federal Communications Commission's ("FCC") mandatory requirement that all television stations convert from analog to digital spectrum by February 2009. As a result of this review, the Company's depreciation rate of its analog equipment was increased to reflect the estimated period during which these assets will remain in service. In accordance with FASB 154, *"Accounting Changes and Error Corrections,"* [FASB ASC 250–10–45–17] this change of estimated useful lives is deemed as a change in accounting estimate and has been accounted for prospectively, effective April 1, 2008. The effect of this change in estimate was to decrease net income approximately $347,000 and decrease basic and diluted earnings per share by $.07 for the year ended December 31, 2008.

accounting principle and therefore requires a clear justification as to why the new method is preferable. Illustration 4–7 provides an example.

ILLUSTRATION 4–7

Change in Depreciation Method

The Maxwell Gear Corporation uses the double-declining balance (DDB) depreciation method for most of its equipment. In 2011, for consistency with other firms in the industry, the company switched from the DDB method to straight-line depreciation for a large group of equipment purchased at the beginning of 2009. Maxwell purchased this equipment at a cost of $50 million. The machinery has an expected useful life of five years and no estimated residual value.

When the change occurs, the company does not revise either depreciation expense or accumulated depreciation reported in prior years. No account balances are adjusted. Rather, in 2011 and later years, its adjusting entry to record depreciation expense simply will reflect the new depreciation method (straight-line). In 2011, the adjusting entry is ($ in millions):

Depreciation expense (below)	6	
Accumulated depreciation		6

DDB depreciation:

2009	$20 ($50 × 40%*)
2010	12 ([$50 − 20] × 40%*)
Total	$32

*Double the straight-line rate for five years [(1/5 = 20%) × 2 = 40%]

$50	Cost
32	Depreciation to date, DDB (2009–2010)
$18	Undepreciated cost as of 1/1/11
÷ 3 yrs.	Remaining life (5 years − 2 years)
$ 6	New annual depreciation

A disclosure note reports the effect on net income and earnings per share along with clear justification for changing depreciation methods.

Change in Reporting Entity

A third type of change—the **change in reporting entity**—involves the preparation of financial statements for an accounting entity other than the entity that existed in the previous period.[39]

Some changes in reporting entity are a result of changes in accounting rules. For example, GAAP requires companies like Ford, General Motors and General Electric to consolidate their manufacturing operations with their financial subsidiaries, creating a new entity

[39]In Chapter 20 we discuss the different types of situations that result in a change in accounting entity.

that includes them both.[40] For those changes in entity, the prior-period financial statements that are presented for comparative purposes should be restated to appear as if the new entity existed in those periods.

However, the more frequent change in entity occurs when one company acquires another one. In those circumstances, the financial statements of the acquirer include the acquiree as of the date of acquisition, and the acquirer's prior-period financial statements that are presented for comparative purposes are *not* restated. This makes it difficult to make year-to-year comparisons for a company that frequently acquires other companies. Acquiring companies are required to provide a disclosure note that presents key financial statement information as if the acquisition had occurred before the beginning of the previous year. At a minimum, the supplemental pro forma information should display revenue, income before extraordinary items, net income, and earnings per share.

Correction of Accounting Errors

Errors occur when transactions are either recorded incorrectly or not recorded at all. We briefly discuss the correction of errors here as an overview and in later chapters in the context of the effect of errors on specific chapter topics. In addition, Chapter 20 provides comprehensive coverage of the correction of errors.

Accountants employ various control mechanisms to ensure that transactions are accounted for correctly. In spite of this, errors occur. When errors do occur, they can affect any one or several of the financial statement elements on any of the financial statements a company prepares. In fact, many kinds of errors simultaneously affect more than one financial statement. When errors are discovered, they should be corrected.

Most errors are discovered in the same year that they are made. These errors are simple to correct. The original erroneous journal entry is reversed and the appropriate entry is recorded. If an error is discovered in a year subsequent to the year the error is made, accounting treatment depends on whether or not the error is material with respect to its effect on the financial statements. In practice, the vast majority of errors are not material and are, therefore, simply corrected in the year discovered.

Prior Period Adjustments

After its financial statements are published and distributed to shareholders, Roush Distribution Company discovers a material error in the statements. What does it do? The correction of material errors is considered to be a **prior period adjustment**.[41] A prior period adjustment refers to an addition to or reduction in the beginning retained earnings balance in a statement of shareholders' equity (or statement of retained earnings if that's presented instead).

When it's discovered that the ending balance of retained earnings in the period prior to the discovery of an error was incorrect as a result of that error, the balance is corrected. However, simply reporting a corrected amount might cause misunderstanding for someone familiar with the previously reported amount. Explicitly reporting a prior period adjustment on the statement of shareholders' equity (or statement of retained earnings) avoids this confusion.

In addition to reporting the prior period adjustment to retained earnings, previous years' financial statements that are incorrect as a result of the error are retrospectively restated to reflect the correction. Also, a disclosure note communicates the impact of the error on income.

Earnings per Share Disclosures

● **LO8**

As we discussed in Chapter 3, financial statement users often use summary indicators, called *ratios,* to more efficiently make comparisons among different companies and over time for the same company. Besides highlighting important relationships among financial statement variables, ratios also accommodate differences in company size.

---

[40]The issuance of *SFAS No. 94,* "Consolidation of All Majority-Owned Subsidiaries," [codified in FASB ASC 810 and 840] resulted in hundreds of entities consolidating previously unconsolidated finance subsidiaries.
[41]FASB ASC 250–10–45–23: Accounting Changes and Error Corrections—Overall—Other Presentation Matters (previously "Prior Period Adjustments," *Statement of Financial Accounting Standards No. 16* (Norwalk, Conn.: FASB, 1977)).

One of the most widely used ratios is **earnings per share (EPS),** which shows the amount of income earned by a company expressed on a per share basis. Public companies report basic EPS and, if there are certain potentially dilutive securities, **diluted** EPS, generally on the face of the income statement. Basic EPS is computed by dividing income available to common shareholders (net income less any preferred stock dividends) by the weighted-average number of common shares outstanding (weighted by time outstanding) for the period. For example, suppose the Fetzer Corporation reported net income of $600,000 for its fiscal year ended December 31, 2011. Preferred stock dividends of $75,000 were declared during the year. Fetzer had one million shares of common stock outstanding at the beginning of the year and issued an additional one million shares on March 31, 2011. Basic EPS of $.30 per share for 2011 is computed as follows:

$$\frac{\$600,000 - 75,000}{\underset{\substack{\text{Shares} \\ \text{at Jan. 1}}}{1,000,000} + \underset{\text{New shares}}{1,000,000 \ (9/12)}} = \frac{\$525,000}{1,750,000} = \$0.30$$

Diluted EPS reflects the potential dilution that could occur for companies that have certain securities outstanding that are convertible into common shares or stock options that could create additional common shares if the options were exercised. These items could cause EPS to decrease (become diluted). Because of the complexity of the calculation and the importance of EPS to investors, we devote a substantial portion of Chapter 19 to this topic. At this point, we focus on the financial statement presentation of EPS. In Graphic 4–2 on page 173, **Dell Inc.** discloses both basic and diluted EPS in its income statements for all years presented.

When the income statement includes one or more of the separately reported items, we report per-share amounts for both income (loss) from continuing operations and net income (loss), as well as for each separately reported item. We see this demonstrated in income statements of **Charming Shoppes, Inc.,** a specialty retailer of plus-size women's apparel that includes the Lane Bryant brand, partially reproduced in Graphic 4–10.

FINANCIAL Reporting Case

Q4, p. 169

All corporations whose common stock is publicly traded must disclose EPS.

Companies must disclose per share amounts for (1) income (loss) before any separately reported items, (2) each separately reported item, and (3) net income (loss).

GRAPHIC 4–10
EPS Disclosures—
Charming Shoppes,
Inc.

Real World Financials

CHARMING SHOPPES, INC. Consolidated Statements of Operations (in part)		
	Year Ended	
($ in thousands, except per share data)	**January 31, 2009**	**February 2, 2008**
Income (loss) from continuing operations before extraordinary item	$(169,289)	$ 714
Loss from discontinued operations, net of tax	(74,922)	(85,039)
Extraordinary item, net of tax	—	912
Net loss	$(244,211)	$(83,413)
Basic earnings (loss) per share:		
Income (loss) from continuing operations before extraordinary item	$ (1.48)	$ .01
Loss from discontinued operations	(.65)	(.70)
Extraordinary item	—	.01
Net loss	$ (2.13)	$ (.68)
Diluted earnings (loss) per share:		
Income (loss) from continuing operations before extraordinary item	$ (1.48)	$ .01
Loss from discontinued operations	(.65)	(.69)
Extraordinary gain	—	.01
Net loss	$ (2.13)	$ (.67)

Comprehensive Income

● LO9

Accounting professionals have engaged in an ongoing debate concerning which transactions should be included as components of periodic income. For instance, some argue that certain changes in shareholders' equity besides those attributable to traditional net income should be included in the determination of income. In what might be viewed as a compromise, the FASB decided to maintain the traditional view of net income, but to require companies also to report an expanded version of income called **comprehensive income** to include four types of gains and losses that traditionally hadn't been included in income statements. Let's consider what that means.

Other Comprehensive Income

Comprehensive income is the total change in equity for a reporting period other than from transactions with owners.

The calculation of net income omits certain types of gains and losses that are included in comprehensive income. As one example, in Chapter 12 you will learn that certain investments are reported in the balance sheet at their fair values, but that the gains and losses resulting from adjusting those investments to fair value might not be included in net income. Instead, they are reported as a separate component of shareholders' equity, **other comprehensive income (OCI) (loss).**

Companies must report both net income and comprehensive income and reconcile the difference between the two.[42] Be sure to remember that net income actually is a part of comprehensive income. The reconciliation simply extends net income to include other comprehensive income items, reported net of tax, as shown in Illustration 4–8.

ILLUSTRATION 4–8 Comprehensive Income		($ in millions)
Net income		$xxx
Other comprehensive income:		
Net unrealized holding gains (losses) on investments (net of tax)*	$x	
Gains (losses) from and amendments to postretirement benefit plans (net of tax)†	(x)	
Deferred gains (losses) from derivatives (net of tax)‡	(x)	
Gains (losses) from foreign currency translation (net of tax)§	x	xx
Comprehensive income		$xxx

*Changes in the market value of securities available for sale (described in Chapter 12).[43]
†Gains and losses due to revising assumptions or market returns differing from expectations and prior service cost from amending the plan (described in Chapter 17).
‡When a derivative designated as a cash flow hedge is adjusted to fair value, the gain or loss is deferred as a component of comprehensive income and included in earnings later, at the same time as earnings are affected by the hedged transaction (described in the Derivatives Appendix to the text).
§Gains or losses from changes in foreign currency exchange rates. The amount could be an addition to or reduction in shareholders' equity. (This item is discussed elsewhere in your accounting curriculum.)

Comprehensive income includes net income as well as other gains and losses that change shareholders' equity but are not included in traditional net income.

The actual terminology used by companies for the four other comprehensive income items varies considerably. For instance, deferred gains (losses) from derivatives are sometimes called *derivative mark-to-market adjustments* or *changes in fair value of derivatives,* and gains (losses) from foreign currency translation are often identified as *foreign currency translation adjustments.*

Flexibility in Reporting

The presentation shown in Illustration 4–8 can be (a) included as an extension to the income statement, (b) reported (exactly the same way) as a separate statement of comprehensive income, usually as part of a disclosure note, or (c) included in the statement of changes in

---

[42]FASB ASC 220–10–45: Comprehensive Income–Overall–Other Presentation Matters (previously "Reporting Comprehensive Income," *Statement of Financial Accounting Standards No. 130* (Norwalk, Conn.: FASB, 1997)).
[43]An unrealized loss also might occur from recording an impairment of a held-to-maturity (HTM) investment. As described in Chapter 12, if the fair value of an HTM investment falls below its amortized cost, and that decline if viewed as other than temporary, the current period credit loss is included in net income, but any amount that exceeds the current period credit loss is recorded as a loss in Other Comprehensive Income.

shareholders' equity (Chapter 18). Each component of other comprehensive income can be displayed net of tax, as in Illustration 4–8, or alternatively, before tax with one amount shown for the aggregate income tax expense (or benefit).[44] A recent survey of reporting practices of 500 large public companies indicates that, of those companies that had other comprehensive income items, 84% chose to include the presentation of comprehensive income in their statements of changes in shareholders' equity.[45]

Many companies, though, such as **McAfee, Inc.**, and **The Standard Register Company**, choose to present comprehensive income as an extension to their income statements. The **Dell Inc.** statements of stockholders' equity in the company's annual report (in Appendix B at the back of the text) provides an example of a presentation of comprehensive income in that statement. Chapter 18 also illustrates the presentation of comprehensive income in the statement of changes in shareholders' equity. On the other hand, in its 2009 financial statements, **Astro-Med Inc.**, a manufacturer of a broad range of specialty technology products, chose to use the separate statement approach, as shown in Graphic 4–11.

ASTRO-MED INC. Consolidated Statements of Comprehensive Income For the Year Ended January 31,			
($ in thousands)	**2009**	**2008**	**2007**
Net income	$2,964	$4,310	$6,059
Other comprehensive income (loss):			
Foreign currency translation adjustments, net of tax	(627)	285	132
Unrealized gain (loss) on securities available for sale, net of tax	(21)	78	7
Other comprehensive income (loss)	(648)	363	139
Comprehensive income	$2,316	$4,673	$6,198

INTERNATIONAL FINANCIAL REPORTING STANDARDS

Comprehensive Income. As part of a joint project with the FASB, the International Accounting Standards Board (IASB) in 2007 issued a new version of *IAS No. 1*[46] that revised the standard to bring international reporting of comprehensive income largely in line with U.S. standards. It provides the option of presenting revenue and expense items and components of OCI either in (a) a single statement of comprehensive income or (b) in a separate income statement followed by a statement of comprehensive income. U.S. GAAP also allows the reporting of other comprehensive income in the statement of shareholders' equity.

Illustration 4–8 lists four possible OCI items according to U.S. GAAP. There is an additional possible item, *changes in revaluation surplus*, under IFRS. In Chapter 10 you will learn that *IAS No. 16*[47] permits companies to value property, plant, and equipment at (1) cost less accumulated depreciation or (2) fair value (revaluation). *IAS No. 38*[48] provides a similar option for the valuation of intangible assets. U.S. GAAP prohibits revaluation.

If the revaluation option is chosen and fair value is higher than book value, the difference, changes in revaluation surplus, is reported as *other comprehensive income* and then accumulates in a revaluation surplus account in equity.

Reporting comprehensive income can be accomplished with a separate statement or by including the information in either the income statement or the statement of changes in shareholders' equity.

GRAPHIC 4–11
Comprehensive Income Presented as a Separate Statement— Astro-Med Inc.

Real World Financials

● LO12

International standards do not allow the reporting of other comprehensive income in the statement of shareholders' equity.

---

[44]GAAP does not require the reporting of comprehensive earnings per share.
[45]*Accounting Trends and Techniques—2009* (New York: AICPA, 2009), p. 447.
[46]"Financial Statement Presentation," *International Accounting Standard No. 1* (IASCF), as amended effective January 1, 2009.
[47]"Property, Plant and Equipment," *International Accounting Standard No. 16* (IASCF), as amended effective January 1, 2009
[48]"Intangible Assets," *International Accounting Standard No. 38* (IASCF), as amended effective January 1, 2009.

The cumulative total of OCI (or comprehensive loss) is reported as accumulated other comprehensive income *(AOCI)*, an additional component of shareholders' equity that is displayed separately.

Accumulated Other Comprehensive Income

In addition to reporting OCI that occurs in the current reporting period, we must also report these amounts on a cumulative basis in the balance sheet. This is consistent with the way we report net income that occurs in the current reporting period in the income statement and also report accumulated net income (that hasn't been distributed as dividends) in the balance sheet as retained earnings. Similarly, we report OCI as it occurs in the current reporting period and also report accumulated other comprehensive income (AOCI) in the balance sheet. This is demonstrated in Graphic 4–11A for Astro-Med Inc.

GRAPHIC 4–11A

Shareholders' Equity— Astro-Med Inc.

Real World Financials

ASTRO-MED INC. Consolidated Balance Sheets (in part) Years ended January 31		
($ in thousands)	2009	2008
Shareholders' equity:		
Common stock	410	402
Additional paid-in capital	33,741	32,363
Retained earnings	25,350	24,064
Accumulated other comprehensive income	1	649
Treasury stock	(8,030)	(8,123)
Total shareholders' equity	$51,472	$49,355

Referring to the numbers reported in Graphic 4–11, we can reconcile the changes in both retained earnings and AOCI:

AOCI decreased by **$648** thousand, from **$649** thousand to **$1** thousand.

($ in thousands)	Retained Earnings	Accumulated Other Comprehensive Income
Balance, 1/31/08	$24,064	$ 649
Add: Net income	2,964	
Deduct: Dividends	(1,678)	
Other comprehensive income (loss)		(648)
Balance, 1/31/09	$25,350	$ 1

To further understand the relationship between net income and other comprehensive income, consider another example. Suppose Philips Corporation began 2011 with retained earnings of $600 million and accumulated other comprehensive income of $34 million. Let's also assume that net income for 2011, before considering the gain discussed below, is $100 million, of which $40 million was distributed to shareholders as dividends. Now assume that Philips purchased shares of IBM stock for $90 million during the year and sold them at year-end for $100 million. In that case, Philips would include the realized gain of $10 million in determining net income, If the income tax rate is 40%, net income includes a $6 million net-of-tax gain from the sale. This means that shareholders' equity, specifically retained earnings, also will include the $6 million.

($ in millions)	Retained Earnings	Accumulated Other Comprehensive Income
Balance, 12/31/10	$600	$34
Net income ($100 + 6)	106	
Dividends	(40)	
Other comprehensive income		–0–
Balance, 12/31/11	$666	$34

On the other hand, what if the shares are not sold before the end of the fiscal year but the year-end fair value is $100 million and Philips accounts for the shares as securities available-for-sale? In that case, the *unrealized* gain of $10 million is not included in net income. Instead, $6 million net-of-tax gain is considered a component of *other comprehensive income (loss)* for 2011 and results in an increase in *accumulated other comprehensive income (loss),* rather than retained earnings, in the 2011 balance sheet. The total of retained earnings and accumulated other comprehensive income is $700 million either way, as demonstrated below.

($ in millions)	Retained Earnings	Accumulated Other Comprehensive Income
Balance, 12/31/10	$600	$34
Net income	100	
Dividends	(40)	
Other comprehensive income		6
Balance, 12/31/11	$660	$40

If the shares are not sold, the *unrealized* gain is part of other comprehensive income.

Net income and comprehensive income are identical for an enterprise that has no other comprehensive income items. Components of other comprehensive income are described in subsequent chapters.

CONCEPT REVIEW EXERCISE

The Barrington Construction Company builds office buildings. It also owns and operates a chain of motels throughout the Northwest. On September 30, 2011, the company decided to sell the entire motel business for $40 million. The sale was completed on December 15, 2011. Income statement information for 2011 is provided below for the two components of the company.

INCOME STATEMENT PRESENTATION

	($ in millions)	
	Construction Component	Motel Component
Sales revenue	$450.0	$200.0
Operating expenses	226.0	210.0
Other income (loss)*	16.0	(30.0)
Income (loss) before income taxes	$240.0	$ (40.0)
Income tax expense (benefit)†	96.0	(16.0)
Net income (loss)	$144.0	$ (24.0)

*For the motel component, the entire Other income (loss) amount represents the loss on sale of assets of the component for $40 million when their book value was $70 million.
†A 40% tax rate applies to all items of income or loss.

In addition to the revenues and expenses of the construction and motel components, Barrington experienced a before-tax loss of $20 million to its construction business from damage to buildings and equipment caused by volcanic activity at Mount St. Helens. The event was considered unusual and infrequent.

Required:
Prepare a 2011 income statement for the Barrington Construction Company including EPS disclosures. There were 100 million shares of common stock outstanding throughout 2011. The company had no potential common shares outstanding.

BARRINGTON CONSTRUCTION COMPANY
Income Statement
For the Year Ended December 31, 2011
($ in millions, except per share amounts)

Sales revenue		$450.0
Operating expenses		226.0
Operating income		224.0
Other income		16.0
Income from continuing operations before income taxes and extraordinary item		240.0
Income tax expense		96.0
Income from continuing operations before extraordinary item		144.0
Discontinued operations:		
Loss from operations of discontinued motel component (including loss on disposal of $30)	$(40)	
Income tax benefit	16	
Loss on discontinued operations		(24.0)
Income before extraordinary item		120.0
Extraordinary loss from volcano damage, net of $8.0 tax benefit		(12.0)
Net income		$108.0
Earnings per share:		
Income from continuing operations before extraordinary item		$ 1.44
Discontinued operations		(.24)
Extraordinary loss		(.12)
Net income		$ 1.08

Now that we have discussed the presentation and content of the income statement, we turn our attention to the statement of cash flows.

PART B

● LO10

A statement of cash flows is presented for each period for which results of operations are provided.

THE STATEMENT OF CASH FLOWS

In addition to the income statement and the balance sheet, a statement of cash flows (SCF) is an essential component within the set of basic financial statements.[49] Specifically, when a balance sheet and an income statement are presented, a statement of cash flows is required for each income statement period. The purpose of the SCF is to provide information about the cash receipts and cash disbursements of an enterprise that occurred during a period. Similar to the income statement, it is a *change* statement, summarizing the transactions that caused cash to change during a reporting period. The term *cash* refers to *cash plus cash equivalents.* Cash equivalents, discussed in Chapter 3, include highly liquid (easily converted to cash) investments such as Treasury bills. Chapter 21 is devoted exclusively to the SCF. A brief overview is provided here.

Usefulness of the Statement of Cash Flows

We discussed the difference between cash and accrual accounting in Chapter 1. It was pointed out and illustrated that over short periods of time, operating cash flows may not be indicative of the company's long-run cash-generating ability, and that accrual-based net income provides a more accurate prediction of future operating cash flows. Nevertheless, information about cash flows from operating activities, when combined with information about cash flows from other activities, can provide information helpful in assessing future

---

[49]FASB ASC 230–10–45: Statement of Cash Flows—Overall—Other Presentation Matters (previously "Statement of Cash Flows," *Statement of Financial Accounting Standards No. 95* (Norwalk, Conn.: FASB, 1987)).

profitability, liquidity, and long-term solvency. After all, a company must pay its debts with cash, not with income.

Of particular importance is the amount of cash generated from operating activities. In the long run, a company must be able to generate positive cash flow from activities related to selling its product or service. These activities must provide the necessary cash to pay debts, provide dividends to shareholders, and provide for future growth.

Classifying Cash Flows

● LO11

A list of cash flows is more meaningful to investors and creditors if they can determine the type of transaction that gave rise to each cash flow. Toward this end, the statement of cash flows classifies all transactions affecting cash into one of three categories: (1) operating activities, (2) investing activities, and (3) financing activities.

Operating Activities

The inflows and outflows of cash that result from activities reported in the income statement are classified as cash flows from operating activities. In other words, this classification of cash flows includes the elements of net income reported on a cash basis rather than an accrual basis.[50]

Operating activities are inflows and outflows of cash related to the transactions entering into the determination of net operating income.

Cash inflows include cash received from:

1. Customers from the sale of goods or services.
2. Interest and dividends from investments.

These amounts may differ from sales and investment income reported in the income statement. For example, sales revenue measured on the accrual basis reflects revenue earned during the period, not necessarily the cash actually collected. Revenue will not equal cash collected from customers if receivables from customers or unearned revenue changed during the period.

Cash outflows include cash paid for:

1. The purchase of inventory.
2. Salaries, wages, and other operating expenses.
3. Interest on debt.
4. Income taxes.

Likewise, these amounts may differ from the corresponding accrual expenses reported in the income statement. Expenses are reported when incurred, not necessarily when cash is actually paid for those expenses. Also, some revenues and expenses, like depreciation expense, don't affect cash at all and aren't included as cash outflows from operating activities.

The difference between the inflows and outflows is called *net cash flows from operating activities.* This is equivalent to net income if the income statement had been prepared on a cash basis rather than an accrual basis.

INTERNATIONAL FINANCIAL REPORTING STANDARDS

Classification of Cash Flows. Like U.S. GAAP, international standards also require a statement of cash flows. Consistent with U.S. GAAP, cash flows are classified as operating, investing, or financing. However, the U.S. standard designates cash outflows for interest payments and cash inflows from interest and dividends received as operating cash flows. Dividends paid to shareholders are classified as financing cash flows.

● LO12

(continued)

---

[50]Cash flows related to gains and losses from the sale of assets shown in the income statement are reported as investing activities in the SCF.

(concluded)

IAS No. 7,[51] on the other hand, allows more flexibility. Companies can report interest and dividends paid as either operating or financing cash flows and interest and dividends received as either operating or investing cash flows. Interest and dividend payments usually are reported as financing activities. Interest and dividends received normally are classified as investing activities.

Typical Classification of Cash Flows from Interest and Dividends

U.S. GAAP	IFRS
Operating Activities	*Operating Activities*
Dividends received	
Interest received	
Interest paid	
Investing Activities	*Investing Activities*
	Dividends received
	Interest received
Financing Activities	*Financing Activities*
Dividends paid	Dividends paid
	Interest paid

Siemens AG, a German company, prepares its financial statements according to IFRS. In the statement of cash flows for nine months ended June 30, 2009, the company reported interest and dividends received as operating cash flows, as would a U.S. company. However, Siemens classified interest paid as a financing cash flow.

SIEMENS AG
Statement of Cash Flows (partial)
For the Nine Months Ended June 2009

(€ in millions)

Cash flows from financing activities:	
Proceeds from re-issuance of treasury stock	134
Proceeds from issuance of long-term debt	3,973
Repayment of long-term debt	(500)
Change in short-term debt and other	296
Interest paid	(639)
Dividends paid	(1,380)
Dividends paid to minority shareholders	(110)
Net cash provided by financing activities	1,774

DIRECT AND INDIRECT METHODS OF REPORTING. Two generally accepted formats can be used to report operating activities, the direct method and the indirect method. Under the **direct method,** the cash effect of each operating activity is reported directly in the statement. For example, *cash received from customers* is reported as the cash effect of sales activities. Income statement transactions that have no cash flow effect, such as depreciation, are simply not reported.

By the **indirect method,** on the other hand, we arrive at net cash flow from operating activities indirectly by starting with reported net income and working backwards to convert that amount to a cash basis. Two types of adjustments to net income are needed. First, components of net income that do not affect cash are reversed. That means that noncash revenues and gains are subtracted, while noncash expenses and losses are added. For example, depreciation expense does not reduce cash, but it is subtracted in the income statement. To reverse this, then, we add back depreciation expense to net income to arrive at the amount that we would have had if depreciation had not been subtracted.

---

[51]"Statement of Cash Flows," *International Accounting Standard No. 7* (IASCF), as amended effective January 1, 2009.

Real World Financials

By the *direct method,* the cash effect of each operating activity is reported directly in the SCF.

By the *indirect method,* cash flow from operating activities is derived indirectly by starting with reported net income and adding or subtracting items to convert that amount to a cash basis.

Second, we make adjustments for changes in operating assets and liabilities during the period that indicate that amounts included as components of net income are not the same as cash flows for those components. For instance, suppose accounts receivable increases during the period because cash collected from customers is less than sales revenue. This increase in accounts receivable would then be subtracted from net income to arrive at *cash flow from operating activities*. In the indirect method, positive adjustments to net income are made for decreases in related assets and increases in related liabilities, while negative adjustments are made for increases in those assets and decreases in those liabilities.

To contrast the direct and indirect methods further, consider the example in Illustration 4–9.

Arlington Lawn Care (ALC) began operations at the beginning of 2011. ALC's 2011 income statement and its year-end balance sheet are shown below ($ in thousands).

ARLINGTON LAWN CARE
Income Statement
For the Year Ended December 31, 2011

Service revenue		$90
Operating expenses:		
General and administrative	$32*	
Depreciation	8	
Total operating expenses		40
Income before income taxes		50
Income tax expense		15
Net income		$35

*Includes $6 in insurance expense

ARLINGTON LAWN CARE
Balance Sheet
At December 31, 2011

Assets			Liabilities and Shareholders' Equity		
Current assets:			Current liabilities:		
Cash	$ 54		Accounts payable**	$ 7	
Accounts receivable	12		Income taxes payable	15	
Prepaid insurance	4		Total current liabilities	22	
Total current assets	70		Shareholders' equity:		
Equipment	40		Common stock	50	
Less: Accumulated depreciation	(8)		Retained earnings	30***	
Total assets	$102		Total liabilities and shareholders' equity	$102	

**For general and administrative expenses
***Net income of $35 less $5 in cash dividends paid

ILLUSTRATION 4–9

Contrasting the Direct and Indirect Methods of Presenting Cash Flows from Operating Activities

Net income is $35,000, but cash flow from these same activities is not necessarily the same amount.

Changes in assets and liabilities can indicate that cash inflows are different from revenues and cash outflows are different from expenses.

DIRECT METHOD. Let's begin with the direct method of presentation. We illustrated this method previously in Chapter 2. In that chapter, specific cash transactions were provided and we simply included them in the appropriate cash flow category in the SCF. Here, we start with account balances, so the direct method requires a bit more reasoning.

From the income statement, we see that ALC's net income has four components. Three of those—service revenue, general and administrative expenses, and income tax expense—affect cash flows, but not by the accrual amounts reported in the income statement. One component—depreciation—reduces net income but not cash; it's simply an allocation over time of a prior year's expenditure for a depreciable asset. So, to report these operating activities on a cash basis, rather than an accrual basis, we take the three items that affect cash and adjust the amounts to reflect cash inflow rather than revenue earned and cash outflows rather than expenses incurred. Let's start with service revenue.

Accounts receivable

Beg. bal.	0		
Revenue	90		
		78	Cash
End bal.	12		

Service revenue is $90,000, but ALC did not collect that much cash from its customers. We know that because accounts receivable increased from $0 to $12,000, so ALC must have collected to date only $78,000 of the amount earned.

Similarly, general and administrative expenses of $32,000 were incurred, but $7,000 of that hasn't yet been paid. We know that because accounts payable increased by $7,000. Also, prepaid insurance increased by $4,000 so ALC must have paid $4,000 more cash for insurance coverage than the amount that expired and was reported as insurance expense. That means cash paid thus far for general and administrative expenses was only $29,000 ($32,000 less the $7,000 increase in accounts payable plus the $4,000 increase in prepaid insurance). The other expense, income tax, was $15,000, but that's the amount by which income taxes payable increased so no cash has yet been paid for income taxes.

We can report ALC's cash flows from operating activities using the direct method as shown in Illustration 4–9A.

ILLUSTRATION 4–9A

Direct Method of Presenting Cash Flows from Operating Activities

By the direct method, we report the components of net income on a cash basis.

ARLINGTON LAWN CARE
Statement of Cash Flows
For the Year Ended December 31, 2011

($ in thousands)

Cash Flows from Operating Activities

Cash received from customers*	$78
Cash paid for general and administrative expenses**	(29)
Net cash flows from operating activities	$49

*Service revenue of $90 thousand, less increase of $12 thousand in accounts receivable.

**General and administrative expenses of $32 thousand, less increase of $7 thousand in accounts payable, plus increase of $4 thousand in prepaid insurance.

Depreciation expense does not reduce cash, but is subtracted in the income statement. So, we add back depreciation expense to net income to eliminate it.

INDIRECT METHOD. To report operating cash flows using the indirect method, we take a different approach. We start with ALC's net income but realize that the $35,000 includes both cash and noncash components. We need to adjust net income, then, to eliminate the noncash effects so that we're left with only the cash flows. We start by eliminating the only noncash component of net income in our illustration—depreciation expense. Depreciation of $8,000 was subtracted in the income statement, so we simply add it back in to eliminate it.

We make adjustments for changes in assets and liabilities that indicate that components of net income are not the same as cash flows.

That leaves us with the three components that do affect cash but not by the amounts reported. For those, we need to make adjustments to net income to cause it to reflect cash flows rather than accrual amounts. For instance, we saw earlier that only $78,000 cash was received from customers even though $90,000 in revenue is reflected in net income. That means we need to include an adjustment to reduce net income by $12,000, the increase in accounts receivable. In a similar manner, we include adjustments for the changes in accounts payable, income taxes payable, and prepaid insurance to cause net income to reflect cash payments rather than expenses incurred. For accounts payable and taxes payable, because more was subtracted in the income statement than cash paid for the expenses related to these two liabilities, we need to add back the differences. Note that if these liabilities had decreased, we would have subtracted, rather than added, the changes. For prepaid insurance, because less was subtracted in the income statement than cash paid, we need to subtract the difference—the increase in prepaid insurance. If this asset had decreased, we would have added, rather than subtracted, the change.

Cash flows from operating activities using the indirect method are shown in Illustration 4–9B.

Both the direct and the indirect methods produce the same net cash flows from operating activities ($49 thousand in our illustration); they are merely alternative approaches to reporting the cash flows. The FASB, in promulgating GAAP for the statement of cash flows, stated its preference for the direct method. However, while both methods are used in practice, the direct method is infrequently used.

The choice of presentation method for cash flow from operating activities has no effect on how investing activities and financing activities are reported. We now look at how cash flows are classified into those two categories.

ARLINGTON LAWN CARE Statement of Cash Flows For the Year Ended December 31, 2011			**ILLUSTRATION 4–9B** Indirect Method of Presenting Cash Flows from Operating Activities
		($ in thousands)	
Cash Flows from Operating Activities			
Net income		$35	
Adjustments for noncash effects:			**By the indirect method, we start with net income and work backwards to convert that amount to a cash basis.**
Depreciation expense	$ 8		
Changes in operating assets and liabilities:			
Increase in prepaid insurance	(4)		
Increase in accounts receivable	(12)		
Increase in accounts payable	7		
Increase in income taxes payable	15	14	
Net cash flows from operating activities		$49	

Investing Activities

Cash flows from **investing activities** include inflows and outflows of cash related to the acquisition and disposition of long-lived assets used in the operations of the business (such as property, plant, and equipment) and investment assets (except those classified as cash equivalents and trading securities). The purchase and sale of inventories are not considered investing activities. Inventories are purchased for the purpose of being sold as part of the company's operations, so their purchase and sale are included with operating activities rather than investing activities.

Investing activities involve the acquisition and sale of (1) long-term assets used in the business and (2) nonoperating investment assets.

Cash outflows from investing activities include cash paid for:

1. The purchase of long-lived assets used in the business.
2. The purchase of investment securities like stocks and bonds of other entities (other than those classified as cash equivalents and trading securities).
3. Loans to other entities.

Later, when the assets are disposed of, cash inflow from the sale of the assets (or collection of loans and notes) also is reported as cash flows from investing activities. As a result, cash inflows from these transactions are considered investing activities:

1. The sale of long-lived assets used in the business.
2. The sale of investment securities (other than cash equivalents and trading securities).
3. The collection of a nontrade receivable (excluding the collection of interest, which is an operating activity).

Net cash flows from investing activities represents the difference between the inflows and outflows. The only investing activity indicated in Illustration 4–9 is ALC's investment of $40,000 cash for equipment.

Financing Activities

Financing activities relate to the external financing of the company. Cash inflows occur when cash is borrowed from creditors or invested by owners. Cash outflows occur when cash is paid back to creditors or distributed to owners. The payment of interest to a creditor, however, is classified as an operating activity.

Financing activities involve cash inflows and outflows from transactions with creditors (excluding trade creditors) and owners.

Cash inflows include cash received from:

1. Owners when shares are sold to them.
2. Creditors when cash is borrowed through notes, loans, mortgages, and bonds.

Cash outflows include cash paid to:

1. Owners in the form of dividends or other distributions.
2. Owners for the reacquisition of shares previously sold.
3. Creditors as repayment of the principal amounts of debt (excluding trade payables that relate to operating activities).

Net cash flows from financing activities is the difference between the inflows and outflows. The only financing activities indicated in Illustration 4–9 are ALC's receipt of $50,000 cash from issuing common stock and the payment of $5,000 in cash dividends.

Noncash Investing and Financing Activities

Significant investing and financing transactions not involving cash also are reported.

As we just discussed, the statement of cash flows provides useful information about the investing and financing activities in which a company is engaged. Even though these primarily result in cash inflows and cash outflows, there may be significant investing and financing activities occurring during the period that do not involve cash flows at all. In order to provide complete information about these activities, any significant *noncash* investing and financing activities (that is, noncash exchanges) are reported either on the face of the SCF or in a disclosure note. An example of a significant noncash investing and financing activity is the acquisition of equipment (an investing activity) by issuing either a long-term note payable or equity securities (a financing activity).

The 2011 statement of cash flows for ALC, beginning with net cash flows from operating activities, is shown in Illustration 4–10.

ILLUSTRATION 4–10

Statement of Cash Flows (beginning with net cash flows from operating activities)

ARLINGTON LAWN CARE
Statement of Cash Flows (in part)
For the Year Ended December 31, 2011

		($ in thousands)
Net cash flows from operating activities		$49
Cash flows from investing activities:		
Purchase of equipment		(40)
Cash flows from financing activities:		
Sale of common stock	$50	
Payment of cash dividends	(5)	
Net cash flows from financing activities		45
Net increase in cash		54
Cash balance, January 1		0
Cash balance, December 31		$54

We know $40 thousand was paid to buy equipment because that balance sheet account increased from no balance to $40 thousand. Likewise, because common stock increased from zero to $50 thousand, we include that amount as a cash inflow from financing activities. Finally, Illustration 4–9 told us that $5 thousand was paid as a cash dividend, also a financing activity.

WHERE WE'RE HEADED

● LO12

The FASB and IASB are working together on a standard that would have a dramatic impact on the format of financial statements.

The FASB and IASB are working together on a project, Financial Statement Presentation, to establish a common standard for presenting information in the financial statements, including classifying and displaying line items and aggregating line items into subtotals and totals. This standard will have a dramatic impact on the format of financial statements. An important part of the proposal involves the organization of elements of the balance sheet (statement of financial position), statement of comprehensive income (including the income statement), and statement of cash flows (SCF) into a common set of classifications.

(continued)

(concluded)

The income statement (statement of comprehensive income) and the statement of cash flows are slated to change in several ways. First, though, we should note that the SCF retains the three major classifications of cash flows. The income statement (and balance sheet as well) also will include classifications by operating, investing, and financing activities, providing a "cohesive" financial picture that stresses the relationships among the financial statements.

For each statement, though, operating and investing activities will be included within a new category, "business" activities. Each statement also will include three additional groupings: discontinued operations, income taxes, and equity (if needed). The new look for the statement of comprehensive income and the statement of cash flows will be:

Statement of Comprehensive Income	Statement of Cash Flows
Business • Operating income and expenses • Investing income and expenses	**Business** • Operating cash flows • Investing cash flows
Financing • Financing asset income • Financing liability expense	**Financing** • Financing asset cash flows • Financing liability cash flows
Income Taxes	**Income Taxes**
Discontinued Operations (net of tax)	**Discontinued Operations**
Other Comprehensive Income (net of tax)	**Equity**

One change planned for the statement of cash flows is to no longer permit a choice between the direct method and the indirect method, but to require the direct method, reasoning that it provides more useful information to investors. Another change is to eliminate the concept of cash equivalents in favor of cash only. Also, while we still will have operating, investing, and financing activities, some cash flows will switch categories. Under the new "management approach," cash flows will be classified based on how related assets and liabilities are used by management. For instance, expenditures for property, plant, and equipment likely would be classified as operating, because those assets are used in the "core" business. Investing activities would be limited primarily to investments in stock, bonds, and other securities.

CONCEPT REVIEW EXERCISE

Dublin Enterprises, Inc. (DEI) owns a chain of retail electronics stores located in shopping malls. The following are the company's 2011 income statement and comparative balance sheets ($ in millions):

STATEMENT OF CASH FLOWS

Income Statement
For the Year Ended December 31, 2011

Revenue		$2,100
Cost of goods sold		1,400
Gross profit		700
Operating expenses:		
Selling and administrative	$ 355	
Depreciation	85	
Total operating expenses		440
Income before income taxes		260
Income tax expense		78
Net income		$ 182

(continued)

(concluded)

Comparative Balance Sheets	12/31/11	12/31/10
Assets:		
Cash	$ 300	$ 220
Accounts receivable (net)	227	240
Inventory	160	120
Property, plant & equipment	960	800
Less: Accumulated depreciation	(405)	(320)
Total assets	$1,242	$1,060
Liabilities and shareholders' equity:		
Accounts payable	$ 145	$ 130
Payables for selling and admin. expenses	147	170
Income taxes payable	95	50
Long-term debt	–0–	100
Common stock	463	400
Retained earnings	392	210
Total liabilities and shareholders' equity	$1,242	$1,060

Required:

1. Prepare DEI's 2011 statement of cash flows using the direct method.
2. Prepare the cash flows from operating activities section of DEI's 2011 statement of cash flows using the indirect method.

SOLUTION   1. Prepare DEI's 2011 statement of cash flows using the direct method.

DUBLIN ENTERPRISES, INC.
Statement of Cash Flows
For the Year Ended December 31, 2011
($ in millions)

Cash Flows from Operating Activities		
Collections from customers[1]	$2,113	
Purchase of inventory[2]	(1,425)	
Payment of selling and administrative expenses[3]	(378)	
Payment of income taxes[4]	(33)	
Net cash flows from operating activities		$277
Cash Flows from Investing Activities		
Purchase of property, plant, and equipment		(160)
Cash Flows from Financing Activities		
Issuance of common stock	63	
Payment on long-term debt	(100)	
Net cash flows from financing activities		(37)
Net increase in cash		80
Cash, January 1		220
Cash, December 31		$300

[1]Sales revenue of $2,100 million, plus $13 million decrease in accounts receivable (net).
[2]Cost of goods sold of $1,400 million, plus $40 million increase in inventory, less $15 million increase in accounts payable.
[3]Selling and administrative expenses of $355 million, plus $23 million decrease in payables for selling and administrative expenses.
[4]Income tax expense of $78 million, less $45 million increase in income taxes payable.

2. Prepare the cash flows from operating activities section of DEI's 2011 statement of cash flows using the indirect method.

DUBLIN ENTERPRISES, INC.
Statement of Cash Flows
For the Year Ended December 31, 2011
($ in millions)

Cash Flows from Operating Activities

Net Income	$182	
Adjustments for noncash effects:		
Depreciation expense	85	
Changes in operating assets and liabilities:		
Decrease in accounts receivable (net)	13	
Increase in inventory	(40)	
Increase in accounts payable	15	
Increase in income taxes payable	45	
Decrease in payables for selling and administrative expenses	(23)	
Net cash flows from operating activities		$277

FINANCIAL REPORTING CASE SOLUTION

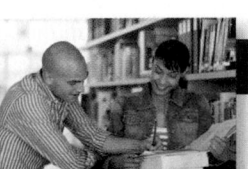

1. **How would you explain restructuring costs and its negative amount in 2009 to Becky? Are restructuring costs something Becky should worry about?** *(p. 177)* Restructuring costs include employee severance and termination benefits plus other costs associated with the shutdown or relocation of facilities or downsizing of operations. Certain restructuring costs must be estimated. The negative number in 2009 is a consequence of overestimating restructuring costs in the prior year. Restructuring costs are not necessarily bad. In fact, the objective is to make operations more efficient. The costs are incurred now in hopes of better earnings later.

2. **In addition to discontinued operations, what other events sometimes are reported separately in the income statement that you might tell Becky about? Why are these items reported separately?** *(p. 180)* In addition to discontinued operations, extraordinary items also are reported separately in the income statement when they are present. The predictive ability of an income statement is significantly enhanced if normal and recurrent transactions are separated from unusual and nonrecurrent items. The income statement is a historical report, summarizing the most recent profit-generating activities of a company. The information in the statement is useful if it can help users predict the future. Toward this end, users should be made aware of events reported in the income statement that are not likely to occur again in the foreseeable future.

3. **Explain to Becky what is meant by discontinued operations and describe to her how that item is reported in an income statement.** *(p. 182)* A discontinued operation occurs when a company decides to discontinue a separate component. The net-of-tax effect of discontinued operations is separately reported below income from continuing operations. If the component has been disposed of by the end of the reporting period, the income effects include: (1) income or loss from operations of the discontinued component from the beginning of the reporting period through the disposal date and (2) gain or loss on disposal of the component's assets. If the component has not been disposed of by the end of the reporting period, the income effects include: (1) income or loss from operations of the discontinued component from the beginning of the reporting period through the end of the reporting period, and (2) an impairment loss if the fair value minus cost to sell of the component's assets is less than their carrying amount (book value).

4. Describe to Becky the difference between basic and diluted earnings per share. *(p. 193)*   Basic earnings per share is computed by dividing income available to common shareholders (net income less any preferred stock dividends) by the weighted-average number of common shares outstanding for the period. Diluted earnings per share reflects the potential dilution that could occur for companies that have certain securities outstanding that are convertible into common shares or stock options that could create additional common shares if the options were exercised. These items could cause earnings per share to decrease (become diluted). Because of the complexity of the calculation and the importance of earnings per share to investors, the text devotes a substantial portion of Chapter 19 to this topic. ●

THE BOTTOM LINE

● **LO1**   The components of income from continuing operations are revenues, expenses (including income taxes), gains, and losses, excluding those related to discontinued operations and extraordinary items. Companies often distinguish between operating and nonoperating income within continuing operations. (p. 170)

● **LO2**   The term *earnings quality* refers to the ability of reported earnings (income) to predict a company's future earnings. The relevance of any historical-based financial statement hinges on its predictive value. To enhance predictive value, analysts try to separate a company's *transitory earnings* effects from its *permanent earnings.* Many believe that manipulating income reduces earnings quality because it can mask permanent earnings. Two major methods used by managers to manipulate earnings are (1) income shifting and (2) income statement classification. (p. 175)

● **LO3**   Analysts begin their assessment of permanent earnings with income from continuing operations. It would be a mistake to assume income from continuing operations reflects permanent earnings entirely. In other words, there may be transitory earnings effects included in both operating and nonoperating income. (p. 176)

● **LO4**   A discontinued operation refers to the disposal or planned disposal of a component of the entity. The net-of-tax effect of discontinued operations is separately reported below income from continuing operations. (p. 182)

● **LO5**   Extraordinary items are material gains and losses that are both unusual in nature and infrequent in occurrence. The net-of-tax effects of extraordinary items are presented in the income statement below discontinued operations, if any. (p. 186)

● **LO6**   Most voluntary changes in accounting principles are reported retrospectively. This means revising all previous periods' financial statements to appear as if the newly adopted accounting method had been applied all along. Some changes are reported prospectively. These include: (a) changes in the method of depreciation, amortization, or depletion, (b) some changes in principle for which retrospective application is impracticable, and (c) a few changes for which an authoritative pronouncement requires or allows prospective application. (p. 188)

● **LO7**   A change in accounting estimate is treated currently and prospectively, rather than by recasting prior years' financial statements to correct the estimate. In other words, the new estimate merely is used from that point on. Most errors are discovered in the same year that they are made. These errors are simple to correct. However, material errors discovered in a year subsequent to the year the error was made are considered prior period adjustments. The correction of the error is accounted for by restating prior years' financial statements, causing an adjustment to retained earnings at the beginning of the period. (p. 190)

● **LO8**   Earnings per share (EPS) is the amount of income achieved during a period expressed per share of common stock outstanding. The EPS must be disclosed for income from continuing operations and for each item below continuing operations. (p. 192)

● **LO9**   The FASB's Concept Statement 6 defines the term *comprehensive income* as the change in equity from nonowner transactions. The calculation of net income, however, excludes certain transactions that are included in comprehensive income. To convey the relationship between the two measures, companies must report both net income and comprehensive income and reconcile the difference between the two. The presentation can be (a) included as an extension to the income statement, (b) reported (exactly the same way) as a separate statement of comprehensive income, or (c) included in the statement of changes in shareholders' equity. (p. 194)

● **LO10**   When a company provides a set of financial statements that reports both financial position and results of operations, a statement of cash flows is reported for each period for which results of operations are provided. The purpose of the statement is to provide information about the cash receipts and cash disbursements that occurred during the period. (p. 198)

● **LO11**   To enhance the usefulness of the information, the statement of cash flows classifies all transactions affecting cash into one of three categories: (1) operating activities, (2) investing activities, or (3) financing activities. (p. 199)

● **LO12**   There are more similarities than differences between income statements and statements of cash flows prepared according to U.S. GAAP and those prepared applying international standards. However, we report extraordinary items separately in an income statement prepared according to U.S. GAAP, but international standards prohibit reporting extraordinary items. In a statement of cash flows, some differences are possible in the classifications of interest and divided revenue, interest expense, and dividends paid. (pp. 174, 182, 187, 195, 199, and 204) ●

QUESTIONS FOR REVIEW OF KEY TOPICS

Q 4–1   The income statement is a change statement. Explain what is meant by this.

Q 4–2   What transactions are included in income from continuing operations? Briefly explain why it is important to segregate income from continuing operations from other transactions affecting net income.

Q 4–3   Distinguish between operating and nonoperating income in relation to the income statement.

Q 4–4   Briefly explain the difference between the single-step and multiple-step income statement formats.

Q 4–5   Explain what is meant by the term earnings quality.

Q 4–6   What are restructuring costs and where are they reported in the income statement?

Q 4–7   Define intraperiod tax allocation. Why is the process necessary?

Q 4–8   How are discontinued operations reported in the income statement?

Q 4–9   Define extraordinary items.

Q 4–10   How should extraordinary gains and losses be reported in the income statement?

Q 4–11   What is meant by a change in accounting principle? Describe the accounting treatment for a voluntary change in accounting principle.

Q 4–12   Accountants very often are required to make estimates, and very often those estimates prove incorrect. In what period(s) is the effect of a change in an accounting estimate reported?

Q 4–13   The correction of a material error discovered in a year subsequent to the year the error was made is considered a prior period adjustment. Briefly describe the accounting treatment for prior period adjustments.

Q 4–14   Define earnings per share (EPS). For which income statement items must EPS be disclosed?

Q 4–15   Define comprehensive income. What are the three ways companies can present the reconciliation between net income and comprehensive income?

Q 4–16   Describe the purpose of the statement of cash flows.

Q 4–17   Identify and briefly describe the three categories of cash flows reported in the statement of cash flows.

Q 4–18   Explain what is meant by noncash investing and financing activities pertaining to the statement of cash flows. Give an example of one of these activities.

Q 4–19   Distinguish between the direct method and the indirect method for reporting the results of operating activities in the statement of cash flows.

⊕ IFRS   Q 4–20   Identify any differences between U.S. GAAP and International Financial Reporting Standards (IFRS) in the number of possible separately reported items that could appear in income statements.

⊕ IFRS   Q 4–21   Describe the difference between U.S. GAAP and IFRS in the allowable options for presenting the components of other comprehensive income.

⊕ IFRS   Q 4–22   Describe the potential statement of cash flows classification differences between U.S. GAAP and IFRS.

BRIEF EXERCISES

BE 4–1
Single-step income statement
● LO1

The adjusted trial balance of Pacific Scientific Corporation on December 31, 2011, the end of the company's fiscal year, contained the following income statement items ($ in millions): sales revenue, $2,106; cost of goods sold, $1,240; selling expenses, $126; general and administrative expenses, $105; interest expense, $35; and gain on sale of investments, $45. Income tax expense has not yet been accrued. The income tax rate is 40%. Prepare a single-step income statement for 2011. Ignore EPS disclosures.

BE 4–2
Multiple-step income statement
● LO1 LO3

Refer to the situation described in BE 4–1. If the company's accountant prepared a multiple-step income statement, what amount would appear in that statement for (a) operating income and (b) nonoperating income?

BE 4–3
Multiple-step income statement
● LO1 LO3

Refer to the situation described in BE 4–1. Prepare a multiple-step income statement for 2011. Ignore EPS disclosures.

BE 4–4
Multiple-step income statement
● LO1 LO3

The following is a partial year-end adjusted trial balance.

Account Title	Debits	Credits
Sales revenue		300,000
Loss on sale of investments	22,000	
Interest revenue		4,000
Loss from flood damage (unusual and infrequent)	50,000	
Cost of goods sold	160,000	
General and administrative expenses	40,000	
Restructuring costs	50,000	
Selling expenses	25,000	
Income tax expense	0	

Income tax expense has not yet been accrued. The income tax rate is 40%. Determine the following: (a) operating income (loss), (b) income (loss) before any separately reported items, and (c) net income (loss).

BE 4–5
Extraordinary item
● LO5

Memorax Company earned before-tax income of $790,000 for its 2011 fiscal year. During the year the company experienced a $520,000 loss from earthquake damage that it considered to be an extraordinary item. This loss is not included in the $790,000 before-tax income figure. The company's income tax rate is 40%. Prepare the lower portion of the 2011 income statement beginning with $790,000.

BE 4–6
Separately reported items
● LO3 LO5 LO8

The following are partial income statement account balances taken from the December 31, 2011, year-end trial balance of White and Sons, Inc.: restructuring costs, $300,000; interest revenue, $40,000; loss from earthquake (unusual and infrequent), $400,000; and loss on sale of investments, $50,000. Income tax expense has not yet been accrued. The income tax rate is 40%. Prepare the lower portion of the 2011 income statement beginning with $850,000 income before income taxes and extraordinary item. Include appropriate basic EPS disclosures. The company had 100,000 shares of common stock outstanding throughout the year.

BE 4–7
Discontinued operations
● LO4

On December 31, 2011, the end of the fiscal year, California Microtech Corporation completed the sale of its semiconductor business for $10 million. The business segment qualifies as a component of the entity according to GAAP. The book value of the assets of the segment was $8 million. The operating loss of the segment during 2011 was $3.6 million. Pretax income from continuing operations for the year totaled $5.8 million. The income tax rate is 30%. Prepare the lower portion of the 2011 income statement beginning with pretax income from continuing operations. Ignore EPS disclosures.

BE 4–8
Discontinued operations
● LO4

Refer to the situation described in BE 4–7. Assume that the semiconductor segment was not sold during 2011 but was held for sale at year-end. The estimated fair value of the segment's assets, less costs to sell, on December 31 was $10 million. Prepare the lower portion of the 2011 income statement beginning with pretax income from continuing operations. Ignore EPS disclosures.

BE 4–9
Discontinued operations
● LO4

Refer to the situation described in BE 4–8. Assume instead that the estimated fair value of the segment's assets, less costs to sell, on December 31 was $7 million rather than $10 million. Prepare the lower portion of the 2011 income statement beginning with pretax income from continuing operations. Ignore EPS disclosures.

BE 4–10
Accounting change
● LO6

The Korver Company decided to change its inventory costing method from average to FIFO. The depreciation method also was changed from double-declining balance to straight line. Identify the type of accounting change for these two changes and briefly describe the difference in accounting treatment between the two, if any.

BE 4–11
Accounting change
● LO7

Powell Manufacturing purchased machinery for $300,000 at the beginning of 2009. A six-year life was estimated and no residual value was anticipated. Straight-line depreciation is used. At the beginning of 2011, the estimated useful life was revised to 10 years in total. What type of accounting change is this? Determine depreciation for 2011.

BE 4–12
Comprehensive income
● LO9

O'Reilly Beverage Company reported net income of $650,000 for 2011. In addition, the company deferred a $60,000 pretax loss on derivatives and had pretax net unrealized holding gains on investment securities of $40,000. Prepare a statement of comprehensive income for 2011. The company's income tax rate is 40%.

BE 4–13
Statement of cash flows; direct method
● LO11

The following are summary cash transactions that occurred during the year for Hilliard Healthcare Co. (HHC):

Cash received from:	
Customers	$660,000
Interest on note receivable	12,000
Collection of note receivable	100,000
Sale of land	40,000
Issuance of common stock	200,000
Cash paid for:	
Interest on note payable	18,000
Purchase of equipment	120,000
Operating expenses	440,000
Dividends to shareholders	30,000

Prepare the cash flows from operating activities section of HHC's statement of cash flows using the direct method.

BE 4–14
Statement of cash flows; investing and financing activities
● LO11

Refer to the situation described in BE 4–13. Prepare the cash flows from investing and financing activities sections of HHC's statement of cash flows.

BE 4–15
Statement of cash flows; indirect method
● LO11

Net income of Mansfield Company was $45,000. The accounting records reveal depreciation expense of $80,000 as well as increases in prepaid rent, salaries payable, and income taxes payable of $60,000, $15,000, and $12,000, respectively. Prepare the cash flows from operating activities section of Mansfield's statement of cash flows using the indirect method.

BE 4–16
IFRS; Statement of cash flows
● LO11
LO12

Refer to the situation described in BE 4–13 and BE 4–14. How might your solution to those brief exercises differ if Hilliard Healthcare Co. prepares its statement of cash flows according to International Financial Reporting Standards?

EXERCISES

An alternate exercise and problem set is available on the text website: www.mhhe.com/spiceland6e

E 4–1
Income statement format; single step and multiple step
● LO1 LO8

The following is a partial trial balance for the Green Star Corporation as of December 31, 2011:

Account Title	Debits	Credits
Sales revenue		1,300,000
Interest revenue		30,000
Gain on sale of investments		50,000
Cost of goods sold	720,000	
Salaries expense	160,000	
Depreciation expense	50,000	
Interest expense	40,000	
Rent expense	25,000	
Income tax expense	130,000	

100,000 shares of common stock were outstanding throughout 2011.

Required:

1. Prepare a single-step income statement for 2011, including EPS disclosures.
2. Prepare a multiple-step income statement for 2011, including EPS disclosures.

E 4–2
Income statement
format; single step
and multiple step

● LO1 LO3 LO5
  LO8

The following is a partial trial balance for General Lighting Corporation as of December 31, 2011:

Account Title	Debits	Credits
Sales revenue		2,350,000
Rental revenue		80,000
Loss on sale of investments	22,500	
Loss from flood damage (event is both unusual and infrequent)	120,000	
Cost of goods sold	1,200,300	
Loss from write-down of inventory due to obsolescence	200,000	
Salaries expense	300,000	
Depreciation expense	100,000	
Interest expense	90,000	
Rent expense	50,000	

300,000 shares of common stock were outstanding throughout 2011. Income tax expense has not yet been accrued. The income tax rate is 40%.

Required:

1. Prepare a single-step income statement for 2011, including EPS disclosures.
2. Prepare a multiple-step income statement for 2011, including EPS disclosures.

E 4–3
Multiple-step
statement of
income and
comprehensive
income

● LO1 LO5 LO8
  LO9

The trial balance for Lindor Corporation, a manufacturing company, for the year ended December 31, 2011, included the following income accounts:

Account Title	Debits	Credits
Sales revenue		2,300,000
Gain on litigation settlement (unusual and infrequent)		400,000
Cost of goods sold	1,400,000	
Selling and administrative expenses	420,000	
Interest expense	40,000	
Unrealized holding gains on investment securities		80,000

The trial balance does not include the accrual for income taxes. Lindor's income tax rate is 30%. One million shares of common stock were outstanding throughout 2011.

Required:

Prepare a combined multiple-step statement of income and comprehensive income for 2011, including appropriate EPS disclosures.

E 4–4
Income statement
presentation;
intraperiod tax
allocation

● LO1 LO5 L08

The following *incorrect* income statement was prepared by the accountant of the Axel Corporation:

AXEL CORPORATION
Income Statement
For the Year Ended December 31, 2011

Revenues and gains:		
Sales		$592,000
Interest and dividends		32,000
Gain from litigation settlement		86,000
Total revenues and gains		710,000
Expenses and losses:		
Cost of goods sold	$325,000	
Selling expenses	67,000	
Administrative expenses	87,000	
Interest	26,000	
Restructuring costs	55,000	
Income taxes	60,000	
Total expenses and losses		620,000
Net Income		$ 90,000
Earnings per share		$ 0.90

Required:

Prepare a multiple-step income statement for 2011 applying generally accepted accounting principles. The income tax rate is 40%. The gain from litigation settlement is considered an unusual and infrequent event.

E 4–5
Discontinued
operations
● LO4 LO8

Chance Company had two operating divisions, one manufacturing farm equipment and the other office supplies. Both divisions are considered separate components as defined by generally accepted accounting principles. The farm equipment component had been unprofitable, and on September 1, 2011, the company adopted a plan to sell the assets of the division. The actual sale was effected on December 15, 2011, at a price of $600,000. The book value of the division's assets was $1,000,000, resulting in a before-tax loss of $400,000 on the sale.

The division incurred before-tax operating losses of $130,000 from the beginning of the year through December 15. The income tax rate is 40%. Chance's after-tax income from its continuing operations is $350,000.

Required:

Prepare an income statement for 2011 beginning with income from continuing operations. Include appropriate EPS disclosures assuming that 100,000 shares of common stock were outstanding throughout the year.

E 4–6
Income statement
presentation;
discontinued
operations;
restructuring
charges
● LO1 LO3 LO4

Esquire Comic Book Company had income before tax of $1,000,000 in 2011 *before* considering the following material items:

1. Esquire sold one of its operating divisions, which qualified as a separate component according to generally accepted accounting principles. The before-tax loss on disposal was $350,000. The division generated before-tax operating income from the beginning of the year through disposal of $500,000. Neither the loss on disposal nor the operating income is included in the $1,000,000 before-tax income the company generated from its other divisions.

2. The company incurred restructuring costs of $80,000 during the year.

Required:

Prepare a 2011 income statement for Esquire beginning with income from continuing operations. Assume an income tax rate of 40%. Ignore EPS disclosures.

E 4–7
Discontinued
operations; disposal
in subsequent year
● LO4

Kandon Enterprises, Inc., has two operating divisions; one manufactures machinery and the other breeds and sells horses. Both divisions are considered separate components as defined by generally accepted accounting principles. The horse division has been unprofitable, and on November 15, 2011, Kandon adopted a formal plan to sell the division. The sale was completed on April 30, 2012. At December 31, 2011, the component was considered held for sale.

On December 31, 2011, the company's fiscal year-end, the book value of the assets of the horse division was $250,000. On that date, the fair value of the assets, less costs to sell, was $200,000. The before-tax operating loss of the division for the year was $140,000. The company's effective tax rate is 40%. The after-tax income from continuing operations for 2011 was $400,000.

Required:

1. Prepare a partial income statement for 2011 beginning with income from continuing operations. Ignore EPS disclosures.

2. Repeat requirement 1 assuming that the estimated net sales price of the horse division's assets was $400,000, instead of $200,000.

E 4–8
Discontinued
operations; disposal
in subsequent
year; solving for
unknown
● LO4

On September 17, 2011, Ziltech, Inc. entered into an agreement to sell one of its divisions that qualifies as a component of the entity according to generally accepted accounting principles. By December 31, 2011, the company's fiscal year-end, the division had not yet been sold, but was being held for sale. The net fair value (fair value minus costs to sell) of the division's assets at the end of the year was $11 million. The pretax operating income of the division during 2011 was $4 million. Pretax income from continuing operations for the year totaled $14 million. The income tax rate is 40%. Ziltech reported net income for the year of $7.2 million.

Required:

Determine the book value of the division's assets on December 31, 2011.

E 4–9
Accounting change
● LO6

Canliss Milling Company purchased machinery on January 2, 2009, for $800,000. A five-year life was estimated and no residual value was anticipated. Canliss decided to use the double-declining balance method and recorded depreciation of $320,000 in 2009 and $192,000 in 2010. Early in 2011, the company changed its depreciation method to the straight-line method.

Required:

1. Briefly describe the way Canliss should report this accounting change in the 2010–2011 comparative financial statements.

2. Prepare any 2011 journal entry related to the change.

E 4–10
Accounting change
● LO7

[This is a variation of the previous exercise]
Canliss Milling Company purchased machinery on January 2, 2009, for $800,000. A five-year life was estimated and no residual value was anticipated. Canliss decided to use the straight-line depreciation method and recorded $160,000 in depreciation in 2009 and 2010. Early in 2011, the company revised the *total* estimated life of the machinery to eight years.

Required:

1. What type of accounting change is this?
2. Briefly describe the accounting treatment for this change.
3. Determine depreciation for 2011.

E 4–11
Accounting change
● LO7

On July 1, 2009, Horrocks Engineering purchased a patent for $2,400,000. A 10-year useful life was estimated with no residual value. The straight-line amortization method is used. Early in 2012, the company determined that the patent would be useful for only five more years (2012–2016).

Required:

1. What type of accounting change is this?
2. Determine amortization expense for 2012.

E 4–12
Earnings per share
● LO8

The Esposito Import Company had 1 million shares of common stock outstanding during 2011. Its income statement reported the following items: income from continuing operations, $5 million; loss from discontinued operations, $1.6 million; extraordinary gain, $2.2 million. All of these amounts are net of tax.

Required:

Prepare the 2011 EPS presentation for the Esposito Import Company.

E 4–13
Comprehensive income
● LO9

The Massoud Consulting Group reported net income of $1,354,000 for its fiscal year ended December 31, 2011. In addition, during the year the company experienced a foreign currency translation adjustment gain of $240,000 and had unrealized losses on investment securities of $80,000. The company's effective tax rate on all items affecting comprehensive income is 30%. Each component of other comprehensive income is displayed net of tax.

Required:

1. Prepare a combined statement of income and comprehensive income for 2011, beginning with net income.
2. Prepare a separate statement of comprehensive income for 2011.

E 4–14
IFRS; reporting comprehensive income
● LO9 LO12

Exercise 4–13 requires the presentation of other comprehensive income items in (1) a combined statement of income and comprehensive income and (2) in a separate statement of comprehensive income.

Required:

1. What other option(s) are available for the presentation of other comprehensive income items according to U.S. GAAP?
2. What options for the presentation of other comprehensive income items are available to companies complying with International Financial Reporting Standards?

E 4–15
Statement of cash flows; classifications
● LO11

The statement of cash flows classifies all cash inflows and outflows into one of the three categories shown below and lettered from a through c. In addition, certain transactions that do not involve cash are reported in the statement as noncash investing and financing activities, labeled d.
a. Operating activities
b. Investing activities
c. Financing activities
d. Noncash investing and financing activities

Required:

For each of the following transactions, use the letters above to indicate the appropriate classification category.
1. _____ Purchase of equipment for cash.
2. _____ Payment of employee salaries.
3. _____ Collection of cash from customers.
4. _____ Cash proceeds from a note payable.
5. _____ Purchase of common stock of another corporation for cash.
6. _____ Issuance of common stock for cash.
7. _____ Sale of machinery for cash.
8. _____ Payment of interest on note payable.
9. _____ Issuance of bonds payable in exchange for land and building.
10. _____ Payment of cash dividends to shareholders.
11. _____ Payment of principal on note payable.

E 4–16

Statement of cash flows preparation

● LO11

The following summary transactions occurred during 2011 for Bluebonnet Bakers:

Cash Received from:	
Customers	$380,000
Interest on note receivable	6,000
Principal on note receivable	50,000
Sale of investments	30,000
Proceeds from note payable	100,000
Cash Paid for:	
Purchase of inventory	160,000
Interest on note payable	5,000
Purchase of equipment	85,000
Salaries to employees	90,000
Principal on note payable	25,000
Payment of dividends to shareholders	20,000

The balance of cash and cash equivalents at the beginning of 2011 was $17,000.

Required:

Prepare a statement of cash flows for 2011 for Bluebonnet Bakers. Use the direct method for reporting operating activities.

E 4–17

IFRS; statement of cash flows

● LO11 LO12

Refer to the situation described in Exercise 4–16.

Required:

How might your solution differ if Bluebonnet Bakers prepares the statement of cash flows according to International Financial Reporting Standards?

E 4–18

Indirect method; reconciliation of net income to net cash flows from operating activities

● LO11

The accounting records of Hampton Company provided the data below ($ in 000s).

Net income	$17,300
Depreciation expense	7,800
Increase in accounts receivable	4,000
Decrease in inventory	5,500
Decrease in prepaid insurance	1,200
Decrease in salaries payable	2,700
Increase in interest payable	800

Required:

Prepare a reconciliation of net income to net cash flows from operating activities.

E 4–19

Statement of cash flows directly from transactions

● LO11

The following transactions occurred during March 2011 for the Wainwright Corporation. The company owns and operates a wholesale warehouse. [These are the same transactions analyzed in Exercise 2–1, when we determined their effect on elements of the accounting equation.]

1. Issued 30,000 shares of capital stock in exchange for $300,000 in cash.
2. Purchased equipment at a cost of $40,000. $10,000 cash was paid and a note payable was signed for the balance owed.
3. Purchased inventory on account at a cost of $90,000. The company uses the perpetual inventory system.
4. Credit sales for the month totaled $120,000. The cost of the goods sold was $70,000.
5. Paid $5,000 in rent on the warehouse building for the month of March.
6. Paid $6,000 to an insurance company for fire and liability insurance for a one-year period beginning April 1, 2011.
7. Paid $70,000 on account for the merchandise purchased in 3.
8. Collected $55,000 from customers on account.
9. Recorded depreciation expense of $1,000 for the month on the equipment.

Required:

1. Analyze each transaction and classify each as a financing, investing and/or operating activity (a transaction can represent more than one type of activity). In doing so, also indicate the cash effect of each, if any. If there is no cash effect, simply place a check mark (√) in the appropriate column(s).

   Example:

Financing	Investing	Operating
1. $300,000		

2. Prepare a statement of cash flows, using the direct method to present cash flows from operating activities. Assume the cash balance at the beginning of the month was $40,000.

E 4–20
Statement of cash flows, indirect method
● **LO11**

Cemptex Corporation prepares its statement of cash flows using the indirect method to report operating activities. Net income for the 2011 fiscal year was $624,000. Depreciation and amortization expense of $87,000 was included with operating expenses in the income statement. The following information describes the changes in current assets and liabilities other than cash:

Decrease in accounts receivable	$22,000
Increase in inventories	9,200
Increase prepaid expenses	8,500
Increase in salaries payable	10,000
Decrease in income taxes payable	14,000

Required:
Prepare the operating activities section of the 2011 statement of cash flows.

E 4–21
IFRS; statement of cash flows
● **LO11 LO12**

The statement of cash flows for the year ended December 31, 2011, for Bronco Metals is presented below.

BRONCO METALS
Statement of Cash Flows
For the Year Ended December 31, 2011

Cash flows from operating activities:		
Collections from customers	$ 353,000	
Interest on note receivable	4,000	
Dividends received from investments	2,400	
Purchase of inventory	(186,000)	
Payment of operating expenses	(67,000)	
Payment of interest on note payable	(8,000)	
Net cash flows from operating activities		$ 98,400
Cash flows from investing activities:		
Collection of note receivable	100,000	
Purchase of equipment	(154,000)	
Net cash flows from investing activities		(54,000)
Cash flows from financing activities:		
Proceeds from issuance of common stock	200,000	
Dividends paid	(40,000)	
Net cash flows from financing activities		160,000
Net increase in cash		204,400
Cash and cash equivalents, January 1		28,600
Cash and cash equivalents, December 31		$233,000

Required:
Prepare the statement of cash flows assuming that Bronco prepares its financial statements according to International Financial Reporting Standards. Where IFRS allows flexibility, use the classification used most often in IFRS financial statements.

E 4–22
Statement of cash flows; indirect method
● **LO11**

Presented below is the 2011 income statement and comparative balance sheet information for Tiger Enterprises.

TIGER ENTERPRISES
Income Statement
For the Year Ended December 31, 2011

($ in thousands)		
Sales revenue		$7,000
Operating expenses:		
Cost of goods sold	$3,360	
Depreciation	240	
Insurance	100	
Administrative and other	1,800	
Total operating expenses		5,500
Income before income taxes		1,500
Income tax expense		600
Net income		$ 900

(continued)

(concluded)

Balance Sheet Information ($ in thousands)	Dec. 31, 2011	Dec. 31, 2010
Assets:		
Cash	$ 300	$ 200
Accounts receivable	750	830
Inventory	640	600
Prepaid insurance	50	20
Plant and equipment	2,100	1,800
Less: Accumulated depreciation	(840)	(600)
Total assets	$3,000	$2,850
Liabilities and Shareholders' Equity:		
Accounts payable	$ 300	$ 360
Payables for administrative and other expenses	300	400
Income taxes payable	200	150
Note payable (due 12/31/2012)	800	600
Common stock	900	800
Retained earnings	500	540
Total liabilities and shareholders' equity	$3,000	$2,850

Required:

Prepare Tiger's statement of cash flows, using the indirect method to present cash flows from operating activities. (Hint: You will have to calculate dividend payments.)

E 4–23
Statement of cash flows; direct method
● LO11

Refer to the situation described in Exercise 4–22.

Required:

Prepare the cash flows from operating activities section of Tiger's 2011 statement of cash flows using the direct method. Assume that all purchases and sales of inventory are on account, and that there are no anticipated bad debts for accounts receivable. (Hint: Use T-accounts for the pertinent items to isolate the information needed for the statement.)

E 4–24
FASB codification research
● LO8

The *FASB Accounting Standards Codification* represents the single source of authoritative U.S. generally accepted accounting principles.

Required:

1. Obtain the relevant authoritative literature on earnings per share using the FASB's Codification Research System at the FASB website (**www.fasb.org**). Identify the Codification topic number that provides the accounting for earnings per share.
2. What is the specific citation that describes the additional information for earnings per share that must be included in the notes to the financial statements?
3. Describe the required disclosures.

E 4–25
FASB codification research
● LO5 LO8 LO9 LO11

Access the FASB's Codification Research System at the FASB website (**www.fasb.org**). Determine the specific citation for each of the following items:
1. The criteria for determining if a gain or loss should be reported as an extraordinary item.
2. The calculation of the weighted average number of shares for basic earnings per share purposes.
3. The alternative formats permissible for reporting comprehensive income.
4. The classifications of cash flows required in the statement of cash flows.

E 4–26
Concepts; terminology
● LO1 through LO11

Listed below are several terms and phrases associated with income statement presentation and the statement of cash flows. Pair each item from List A (by letter) with the item from List B that is most appropriately associated with it.

List A	List B
____ 1. Intraperiod tax allocation	a. Unusual, infrequent, and material gains and losses.
____ 2. Comprehensive income	b. Starts with net income and works backwards to convert to cash.
____ 3. Extraordinary items	c. Reports the cash effects of each operating activity directly on the statement.
____ 4. Operating income	d. Correction of a material error of a prior period.
____ 5. A discontinued operation	e. Related to the external financing of the company.
____ 6. Earnings per share	f. Associates tax with income statement item.
____ 7. Prior period adjustment	g. Total nonowner change in equity.
____ 8. Financing activities	h. Related to the transactions entering into the determination of net income.
____ 9. Operating activities (SCF)	i. Related to the acquisition and disposition of long-term assets.
____ 10. Investing activities	j. Required disclosure for publicly traded corporation.
____ 11. Direct method	k. A component of an entity.
____ 12. Indirect method	l. Directly related to principal revenue-generating activities.

CPA AND CMA REVIEW QUESTIONS

**CPA Exam
Questions**

The following questions are used in the Kaplan CPA Review Course to study the income statement and statement of cash flows while preparing for the CPA examination. Determine the response that best completes the statements or questions.

● LO4

1. Roco Company manufactures both industrial and consumer electronics. Due to a change in its strategic focus, the company decided to exit the consumer electronics business, and in 2011 sold the division to Sunny Corporation. The consumer electronics division qualifies as a component of the entity according to GAAP. How should Roco report the sale in its 2011 income statement?
   a. Include in income from continuing operations as a nonoperating gain or loss.
   b. As an extraordinary item.
   c. As a discontinued operation, reported below income from continuing operations.
   d. None of the above.

● LO3 LO4 LO5
LO7

2. Bridge Company's results for the year ended December 31, 2011, include the following material items:

Sales revenue	$5,000,000
Cost of goods sold	3,000,000
Administrative expenses	1,000,000
Gain on sale of equipment	200,000
Loss on discontinued operations	400,000
Loss from earthquake damage (unusual and infrequent event)	500,000
Understatement of depreciation expense in 2010 caused by mathematical error	250,000

Bridge Company's income from continuing operations before income taxes for 2011 is:
   a. $700,000
   b. $950,000
   c. $1,000,000
   d. $1,200,000

● LO4 LO5

3. In Baer Food Co.'s 2011 single-step income statement, the section titled "Revenues" consisted of the following:

Net sales revenue	$187,000
Income on discontinued operations including gain on disposal of $21,000 and net taxes of $6,000	12,000
Interest revenue	10,200
Gain on sale of equipment	4,700
Extraordinary gain net of $750 tax effect	1,500
Total revenues	$215,400

In the revenues section of the 2011 income statement, Baer Food should have reported total revenues of
   a. $201,900
   b. $203,700
   c. $215,400
   d. $216,300

● LO4

4. On November 30, 2011, Pearman Company committed to a plan to sell a division that qualified as a component of the entity according to GAAP, and was properly classified as held for sale on December 31, 2011, the end of the company's fiscal year. The division was tested for impairment and a $400,000 loss was indicated. The division's loss from operations for 2011 was $1,000,000. The final sale was expected to occur on February 15, 2012. What before-tax amount(s) should Pearman report as loss on discontinued operations in its 2011 income statement?
   a. $1,400,000 loss.
   b. $400,000 loss.
   c. None.
   d. $400,000 impairment loss included in continuing operations and a $1,000,000 loss from discontinued operations.

● LO7

5. For 2010, Pac Co. estimated its two-year equipment warranty costs based on $100 per unit sold. Experience during 2011 indicated that the estimate should have been based on $110 per unit. The effect of this $10 difference from the change in estimate is reported

a. As an accounting change below 2011 income from continuing operations.
b. As an accounting change requiring the 2011 financial statements to be restated.
c. As a correction of an error requiring 2011 financial statements to be restated.
d. In 2011 income from continuing operations.

● LO11

6. Which of the following items is *not* considered an operating cash flow in the statement of cash flows?
a. Dividends paid to stockholders.
b. Cash received from customers.
c. Interest paid to creditors.
d. Cash paid for salaries.

● LO11

7. Which of the following items is *not* considered an investing cash flow in the statement of cash flows?
a. Purchase of equipment.
b. Purchase of securities.
c. Issuing common stock for cash.
d. Sale of land.

CMA Exam Questions

The following questions dealing with the income statement are adapted from questions that previously appeared on Certified Management Accountant (CMA) examinations. The CMA designation sponsored by the Institute of Management Accountants (**www.imanet.org**) provides members with an objective measure of knowledge and competence in the field of management accounting. Determine the response that best completes the statements or questions.

● LO1

1. Which one of the following items is included in the determination of income from continuing operations?
a. Discontinued operations.
b. Extraordinary loss.
c. Cumulative effect of a change in an accounting principle.
d. Unusual loss from a write-down of inventory.

● LO3

2. In a multiple-step income statement for a retail company, all of the following are included in the operating section except
a. Sales.
b. Cost of goods sold.
c. Dividend revenue.
d. Administrative and selling expenses.

● LO5

3. When reporting extraordinary items,
a. Each item (net of tax) is presented on the face of the income statement separately as a component of net income for the period.
b. Each item is presented exclusive of any related income tax.
c. Each item is presented as an unusual item within income from continuing operations.
d. All extraordinary gains or losses that occur in a period are summarized as total gains and total losses, then offset to present the net extraordinary gain or loss.

PROBLEMS

An alternate exercise and problem set is available on the text website: www.mhhe.com/spiceland6e

P 4–1
Comparative income statements; multiple-step format

● LO1 LO3 through LO5 LO8

Selected information about income statement accounts for the Reed Company are presented below (the company's fiscal year ends on December 31):

	2011	2010
Sales	$4,400,000	$3,500,000
Cost of goods sold	2,860,000	2,000,000
Administrative expenses	800,000	675,000
Selling expenses	360,000	312,000
Interest revenue	150,000	140,000
Interest expense	200,000	200,000
Loss on sale of assets of discontinued component	50,000	—

On July 1, 2011, the company adopted a plan to discontinue a division that qualifies as a component of an entity as defined by GAAP. The assets of the component were sold on September 30, 2011, for $50,000 less than their book value. Results of operations for the component (*included* in the above account balances) were as follows:

	1/1/11–9/30/11	2010
Sales	$400,000	$500,000
Cost of goods sold	(290,000)	(320,000)
Administrative expenses	(50,000)	(40,000)
Selling expenses	(20,000)	(30,000)
Operating income before taxes	$ 40,000	$110,000

In addition to the account balances above, several events occurred during 2011 that have *not* yet been reflected in the above accounts:

1. A fire caused $50,000 in uninsured damages to the main office building. The fire was considered to be an infrequent but not unusual event.

2. An earthquake caused $100,000 in property damage to one of Reed's factories. The amount of the loss is material and the event is considered unusual and infrequent.

3. Inventory that had cost $40,000 had become obsolete because a competitor introduced a better product. The inventory was sold as scrap for $5,000.

4. Income taxes have not yet been accrued.

Required:
Prepare a multiple-step income statement for the Reed Company for 2011, showing 2010 information in comparative format, including income taxes computed at 40% and EPS disclosures assuming 300,000 shares of common stock.

P 4–2
Discontinued
operations
● LO4

The following condensed income statements of the Jackson Holding Company are presented for the two years ended December 31, 2011 and 2010:

	2011	2010
Sales	$15,000,000	$9,600,000
Cost of goods sold	9,200,000	6,000,000
Gross profit	5,800,000	3,600,000
Operating expenses	3,200,000	2,600,000
Operating income	2,600,000	1,000,000
Gain on sale of division	600,000	—
	3,200,000	1,000,000
Income tax expense	1,280,000	400,000
Net income	$ 1,920,000	$ 600,000

On October 15, 2011, Jackson entered into a tentative agreement to sell the assets of one of its divisions. The division comprises operations and cash flows that can be clearly distinguished, operationally and for financial reporting purposes, from the rest of the company. The division was sold on December 31, 2011, for $5,000,000. Book value of the division's assets was $4,400,000. The division's contribution to Jackson's operating income before-tax for each year was as follows:

2011	$400,000 loss
2010	$300,000 loss

Assume an income tax rate of 40%.

Required:
1. Prepare revised income statements according to generally accepted accounting principles, beginning with income from continuing operations before income taxes. Ignore EPS disclosures.

2. Assume that by December 31, 2011, the division had not yet been sold but was considered held for sale. The fair value of the division's assets on December 31 was $5,000,000. How would the presentation of discontinued operations be different from your answer to requirement 1?

3. Assume that by December 31, 2011, the division had not yet been sold but was considered held for sale. The fair value of the division's assets on December 31 was $3,900,000. How would the presentation of discontinued operations be different from your answer to requirement 1?

P 4–3
Income statement
presentation
● LO4 LO5 LO7

For the year ending December 31, 2011, Micron Corporation had income from continuing operations before taxes of $1,200,000 before considering the following transactions and events. All of the items described below are before taxes and the amounts should be considered material.

1. During 2011, one of Micron's factories was damaged in an earthquake. As a result, the firm recognized a loss of $800,000. The event is considered unusual and infrequent.

2. In November of 2011, Micron sold its Waffle House restaurant chain that qualified as a component of an entity. The company had adopted a plan to sell the chain in May of 2011. The operating income of the chain from January 1, 2011, through November was $160,000 and the loss on sale of the chain's assets was $300,000.

3. In 2011, Micron sold one of its six factories for $1,200,000. At the time of the sale, the factory had a carrying value of $1,100,000. The factory was not considered a component of the entity.

4. In 2009, Micron's accountant omitted the annual adjustment for patent amortization expense of $120,000. The error was not discovered until December 2011.

Required:

1. Prepare Micron's income statement, beginning with income from continuing operations before taxes, for the year ended December 31, 2011. Assume an income tax rate of 30%. Ignore EPS disclosures.

2. Briefly explain the motivation for segregating certain income statement events from income from continuing operations.

P 4–4
Income statement presentation; unusual items
● LO3 LO5 LO7

The preliminary 2011 income statement of Alexian Systems, Inc., is presented below:

ALEXIAN SYSTEMS, INC.
Income Statement
For the Year Ended December 31, 2011
($ in millions, except earnings per share)

Revenues and gains:	
Net sales	$ 425
Interest	3
Other income	126
Total revenues and gains	554
Expenses:	
Cost of goods sold	270
Selling and administrative	154
Income taxes	52
Total expenses	476
Net Income	$ 78
Earnings per share	$3.90

Additional information:

1. Selling and administrative expenses include $26 million in restructuring costs.

2. Included in other income is an extraordinary gain of $120 million. The remaining $6 million is from the gain on sale of investments.

3. Cost of goods sold was increased by $5 million to correct an error in the calculation of 2010's ending inventory. The amount is material.

Required:
For each of the three additional facts listed above, discuss the appropriate presentation of the item described. Do not prepare a revised statement.

P 4–5
Income statement presentation; unusual items
● LO1 LO3 LO5 LO7 LO8

[This is a variation of the previous problem focusing on income statement presentation.]

Required:
Refer to the information presented in Problem 4–4. Prepare a revised income statement for 2011 reflecting the additional facts. Use a multiple-step format. Assume that an income tax rate of 40% applies to all income statement items, and that 20 million shares of common stock were outstanding throughout the year.

P 4–6
Income statement presentation
● LO1 LO3 through LO5 LO8

Rembrandt Paint Company had the following income statement items for the year ended December 31, 2011 ($ in 000s):

Net sales	$18,000	Cost of goods sold	$10,500
Interest income	200	Selling and administrative expenses	2,500
Interest expense	350	Restructuring costs	800
Extraordinary gain	3,000		

In addition, during the year the company completed the disposal of its plastics business and incurred a loss from operations of $1.6 million and a gain on disposal of the component's assets of $2 million. 500,000 shares of common stock were outstanding throughout 2011. Income tax expense has not yet been accrued. The income tax rate is 30% on all items of income (loss).

Required:
Prepare a multiple-step income statement for 2011, including EPS disclosures.

P 4–7
Income statement presentation; unusual items
● LO1 LO3 LO4 LO5 LO7 LO8 LO9

The following income statement items appeared on the adjusted trial balance of Schembri Manufacturing Corporation for the year ended December 31, 2011 ($ in 000s): sales revenue, $15,300; cost of goods sold, $6,200; selling expenses, $1,300; general and administrative expenses, $800; interest revenue, $85; interest expense, $180. Income taxes have not yet been accrued. The company's income tax rate is 40% on all items of income or loss. These revenue and expense items appear in the company's income statement every year. The company's controller, however, has asked for your help in determining the appropriate treatment of the following nonrecurring transactions that also occurred during 2011 ($ in 000s). All transactions are material in amount.

1. Investments were sold during the year at a loss of $220. Schembri also had unrealized gains of $320 for the year on investments accounted for as securities available for sale.
2. One of the company's factories was closed during the year. Restructuring costs incurred were $1,200.
3. An earthquake destroyed a warehouse causing $2,000 in damages. The event is considered to be unusual and infrequent.
4. During the year, Schembri completed the sale of one of its operating divisions that qualifies as a component of the entity according to GAAP. The division had incurred an operating loss of $560 in 2011 prior to the sale, and its assets were sold at a gain of $1,400.
5. In 2011, the company's accountant discovered that depreciation expense in 2010 for the office building was understated by $200.
6. Foreign currency translation losses for the year totaled $240.

Required:
Prepare Schembri's combined statement of income and comprehensive income for 2011, including basic earnings per share disclosures. One million shares of common stock were outstanding at the beginning of the year and an additional 400,000 shares were issued on July 1, 2011.

P 4–8
Multiple-step statement of income and comprehensive income
● LO1 LO3 LO5 LO7 LO9

Duke Company's records show the following account balances at December 31, 2011:

Sales	$15,000,000
Cost of goods sold	9,000,000
General and administrative expenses	1,000,000
Selling expenses	500,000
Interest expense	700,000

Income tax expense has not yet been determined. The following events also occurred during 2011. All transactions are material in amount.

1. $300,000 in restructuring costs were incurred in connection with plant closings.
2. The company operates a factory in South America. During the year, the foreign government took over (expropriated) the factory and paid Duke $1,000,000, which was one-fourth of the book value of the assets involved.
3. Inventory costing $400,000 was written off as obsolete. Material losses of this type are not considered to be unusual.
4. It was discovered that depreciation expense for 2010 was understated by $50,000 due to a mathematical error.
5. The company experienced a foreign currency translation adjustment loss of $200,000 and had unrealized gains on securities available for sale of $180,000.

Required:
Prepare a combined multiple-step statement of income and comprehensive income for 2011. The company's effective tax rate on all items affecting comprehensive income is 40%. Each component of other comprehensive income should be displayed net of tax. Ignore EPS disclosures.

P 4–9
Statement of cash flows
● LO11

The Diversified Portfolio Corporation provides investment advice to customers. A condensed income statement for the year ended December 31, 2011, appears below:

Service revenue	$900,000
Operating expenses	700,000
Income before income taxes	200,000
Income tax expense	80,000
Net income	$120,000

The following balance sheet information also is available:

	12/31/11	12/31/10
Cash	$275,000	$ 70,000
Accounts receivable	120,000	100,000
Accounts payable (operating expenses)	70,000	60,000
Income taxes payable	10,000	15,000

In addition, the following transactions took place during the year:

1. Common stock was issued for $100,000 in cash.
2. Long-term investments were sold for $50,000 in cash. The original cost of the investments also was $50,000.
3. $80,000 in cash dividends was paid to shareholders.
4. The company has no outstanding debt, other than those payables listed above.
5. Operating expenses include $30,000 in depreciation expense.

Required:

1. Prepare a statement of cash flows for 2011 for the Diversified Portfolio Corporation. Use the direct method for reporting operating activities.
2. Prepare the cash flows from operating activities section of Diversified's 2011 statement of cash flows using the indirect method.

P 4–10
Integration
of financial
statements;
Chapters 3 and 4
● LO11

The chief accountant for Grandview Corporation provides you with the company's 2011 statement of cash flows and income statement. The accountant has asked for your help with some missing figures in the company's comparative balance sheets. These financial statements are shown next ($ in millions).

GRANDVIEW CORPORATION
Statement of Cash Flows
For the Year Ended December 31, 2011

Cash Flows from Operating Activities:		
Collections from customers	$71	
Payment to suppliers	(30)	
Payment of general & administrative expenses	(18)	
Payment of income taxes	(9)	
Net cash flows from operating activities		$14
Cash Flows from Investing Activities:		
Sale of investments		65
Cash Flows from Financing Activities:		
Issuance of common stock	10	
Payment of dividends	(3)	
Net cash flows from financing activities		7
Net increase in cash		$86

GRANDVIEW CORPORATION
Income Statement
For the Year Ended December 31, 2011

Sales revenue		$80
Cost of goods sold		32
Gross profit		48
Operating expenses:		
General and administrative	$18	
Depreciation	10	
Total operating expenses		28
Operating income		20
Other income:		
Gain on sale of investments		15
Income before income taxes		35
Income tax expense		7
Net income		$28

GRANDVIEW CORPORATION
Balance Sheets
At December 31

	2011	2010
Assets:		
Cash	$145	$?
Accounts receivable	?	84
Investments	—	50
Inventory	60	?
Property, plant & equipment	150	150
Less: Accumulated depreciation	(65)	?
Total assets	?	?
Liabilities and Shareholders' Equity:		
Accounts payable to suppliers	$ 40	$30
Payables for selling & admin. expenses	9	9
Income taxes payable	22	?
Common stock	240	230
Retained earnings	?	47
Total liabilities and shareholders' equity	?	?

Required:

1. Calculate the missing amounts.
2. Prepare the operating activities section of Grandview's 2011 statement of cash flows using the indirect method.

P 4–11
Statement of cash flows; indirect method
● LO11

Presented below are the 2011 income statement and comparative balance sheets for Santana Industries.

SANTANA INDUSTRIES
Income Statement
For the Year Ended December 31, 2011
($ in thousands)

Sales revenue	$14,250	
Service revenue	3,400	
Total revenue		$17,650
Operating expenses:		
Cost of goods sold	7,200	
Selling	2,400	
General and administrative	1,500	
Total operating expenses		11,100
Operating income		6,550
Interest expense		200
Income before income taxes		6,350
Income tax expense		2,500
Net income		$ 3,850

Balance Sheet Information ($ in thousands)	Dec. 31, 2011	Dec. 31, 2010
Assets:		
Cash	$ 7,350	$ 2,200
Accounts receivable	2,500	2,200
Inventory	4,000	3,000
Prepaid rent	150	300
Plant and equipment	14,500	12,000
Less: Accumulated depreciation	(5,100)	(4,500)
Total assets	$23,400	$15,200
Liabilities and Shareholders' Equity:		
Accounts payable	$ 1,400	$ 1,100
Interest payable	100	0
Unearned service revenue	800	600
Income taxes payable	550	800
Loan payable (due 12/31/2014)	5,000	0
Common stock	10,000	10,000
Retained earnings	5,550	2,700
Total liabilities and shareholders' equity	$23,400	$15,200

Additional information for the 2011 fiscal year ($ in thousands):

1. Cash dividends of $1,000 were declared and paid.
2. Equipment costing $4,000 was purchased with cash.
3. Equipment with a book value of $500 (cost of $1,500 less accumulated depreciation of $1,000) was sold for $500.
4. Depreciation of $1,600 is included in operating expenses.

Required:
Prepare Santana Industries' 2011 statement of cash flows, using the indirect method to present cash flows from operating activities.

BROADEN YOUR PERSPECTIVE

Apply your critical-thinking ability to the knowledge you've gained. These cases will provide you an opportunity to develop your research, analysis, judgment, and communication skills. You also will work with other students, integrate what you've learned, apply it in real world situations, and consider its global and ethical ramifications. This practice will broaden your knowledge and further develop your decision-making abilities.

Judgment Case 4–1
Earnings quality
● LO2 LO3

The financial community in the United States has become increasingly concerned with the quality of reported company earnings.

Required:
1. Define the term *earnings quality*.
2. Explain the distinction between permanent and transitory earnings as it relates to the concept of earnings quality.
3. How do earnings management practices affect the quality of earnings?
4. Assume that a manufacturing company's annual income statement included a large gain from the sale of investment securities. What factors would you consider in determining whether or not this gain should be included in an assessment of the company's permanent earnings?

Judgment Case 4–2
Restructuring costs
● LO3

The appearance of restructuring costs in corporate income statements increased significantly in the 1980s and 1990s.

Required:
1. What types of costs are included in restructuring costs?
2. When are restructuring costs recognized?
3. How would you classify restructuring costs in a multi-step income statement?
4. What factors would you consider in determining whether or not restructuring costs should be included in an assessment of a company's permanent earnings?

Judgment Case 4–3
Earnings management
● LO2 LO3

Companies often are under pressure to meet or beat Wall Street earnings projections in order to increase stock prices and also to increase the value of stock options. Some resort to earnings management practices to artificially create desired results.

Required:
Is *earnings management* always intended to produce higher income? Explain.

Real World Case 4–4
Earnings quality and pro forma earnings; Cisco
● LO3

Real World Financials

[The solution to this case requires access to company data via the Internet.]
   Cisco Systems, Inc., the world's largest networking products company, announced on May 8, 2001, that its *pro forma earnings* for the quarter ended April 28, 2001, were $230 million. The company also disclosed that actual earnings for the quarter, determined according to generally accepted accounting principles, were a *loss* of $2.69 billion.

Required:
1. What is meant by the term *pro forma earnings* in this context?
2. How do pro forma earnings relate to the concept of earnings quality?
3. Access the company's 10-Q (quarterly report) for the quarter ended April 28, 2001. You can go to the company's Internet site, or EDGAR (**www.sec.gov**). Using the company's income statement for the quarter and disclosure notes, reconcile the GAAP loss of $2.69 billion to the pro forma earnings figure of $230 million. Remember that both of these earnings (loss) figures are net of tax.

Communication Case 4–5
Income statement presentation of gain
● LO5

McMinville Corporation manufactures paper products. In 2007, the company purchased several large tracts of timber for $22 million with the intention of harvesting the timber rather than buying this critical raw material from outside suppliers. However, in 2011, McMinville abandoned the idea and all of the timber tracts were sold for $31 million. Net income for 2011, before considering this event, is $17.5 million and the company's effective tax rate is 30%.

The focus of this case is the income statement presentation of the gain on the sale of the timber tracts. Your instructor will divide the class into two to six groups depending on the size of the class. The mission of your group is to reach consensus on the appropriate income statement presentation of the gain.

Required:

Each group member should deliberate the situation independently and draft a tentative argument prior to the class session for which the case is assigned.

In class, each group will meet for 10 to 15 minutes in different areas of the classroom. During that meeting, group members will take turns sharing their suggestions for the purpose of arriving at a single group treatment.

After the allotted time, a spokesperson for each group (selected during the group meetings) will share the group's solution with the class. The goal of the class is to incorporate the views of each group into a consensus approach to the situation.

Communication Case 4–6
Income statement presentation
● LO5

Carter Hawley Hale Stores (CHHS), Inc. was one of the largest department store retailers in the United States. At the end of fiscal 1989, the company operated 113 stores in the sunbelt regions of the country. The company's divisions included The Broadway, with 43 stores in Southern California and 11 stores in the southwest, and Emporium, with 22 stores in the greater San Francisco Bay Area.

On October 17, 1989, a 7.1 Richter scale earthquake caused significant amounts of monetary damage to the San Francisco Bay Area. This was the largest earthquake to hit the Bay Area since the quake of 1906 destroyed much of San Francisco. California is lined with many active earthquake faults. Hundreds of small earthquakes occur each year throughout the state.

The Emporium division of CHHS suffered extensive damage as a result of the October 17 earthquake. Twelve of the twenty-two stores were closed for varying periods of time, with the Oakland store hardest hit. In total, uninsured damage was $27.5 million ($16.5 million after tax benefits).

For the fiscal year ending August 4, 1990, CHHS reported an after-tax loss of $9.47 million *before* considering the earthquake loss. Total revenues for the year were $2.857 billion.

Required:

Assume that you are the CHHS controller. The chief financial officer of CHHS has asked you to prepare a short report (1–2 pages) in memo form giving your recommendation as to the proper reporting of the earthquake damage costs in the income statement for the year ending August 4, 1990. Explain why your recommendation is appropriate. Be sure to include in your report any references to authoritative pronouncements that support your recommendation.

Ethics Case 4–7
Income statement presentation of unusual loss
● LO3

After a decade of consistent income growth, the Cranor Corporation sustained a before-tax loss of $8.4 million in 2011. The loss was primarily due to $10 million in expenses related to a product recall. Cranor manufactures medical equipment, including x-ray machines. The recall was attributable to a design flaw in the manufacture of the company's new line of machines.

The company controller, Jim Dietz, has suggested that the loss should be included in the 2011 income statement as an extraordinary item. "If we report it as an extraordinary item, our income from continuing operations will actually show an increase from the prior year. The stock market will appreciate the continued growth in ongoing profitability and will discount the one-time loss. And our bonuses are tied to income from continuing operations, not net income."

The chief executive officer asked Jim to justify this treatment. "I know we have had product recalls before and, of course, they do occur in our industry," Jim replied, "but we have never had a recall of this magnitude, and we fixed the design flaw and upgraded our quality control procedures."

Required:

Discuss the ethical dilemma faced by Jim Dietz and the company's chief executive officer.

Research Case 4–8
FASB codification; locate and extract relevant information and cite authoritative support for a financial reporting issue; restructuring costs; exit or disposal cost obligations
● LO2 LO3

The accrual of restructuring costs creates obligations (liabilities) referred to as *exit or disposal cost obligations.*

Required:

1. Obtain the relevant authoritative literature on exit or disposal cost obligations using the FASB's Codification Research System. You might gain access at the FASB website (**www.fasb.org**). What is the Codification topic number that addresses this issue?
2. What is the specific citation that addresses the initial measurement of these obligations?
3. How are these obligations and related costs to be measured?
4. What is the specific citation that describes the disclosure requirements in the notes to the financial statements for exit or disposal obligations?
5. List the required disclosures.

**Judgment
Case 4–9**

Income statement
presentation

● LO3 through
LO6

Each of the following situations occurred during 2011 for one of your audit clients:

1. The write-off of inventory due to obsolescence.
2. Discovery that depreciation expenses were omitted by accident from 2010's income statement.
3. The useful lives of all machinery were changed from eight to five years.
4. The depreciation method used for all equipment was changed from the declining-balance to the straight-line method.
5. Ten million dollars face value of bonds payable were repurchased (paid off) prior to maturity resulting in a material loss of $500,000. The company considers the event unusual and infrequent.
6. Restructuring costs were incurred.
7. The Stridewell Company, a manufacturer of shoes, sold all of its retail outlets. It will continue to manufacture and sell its shoes to other retailers. A loss was incurred in the disposition of the retail stores. The retail stores are considered components of the entity.
8. The inventory costing method was changed from FIFO to average cost.

Required:

1. For each situation, identify the appropriate reporting treatment from the list below (consider each event to be material):
    a. As an extraordinary item.
    b. As an unusual or infrequent gain or loss.
    c. As a prior period adjustment.
    d. As a change in accounting principle.
    e. As a discontinued operation.
    f. As a change in accounting estimate.
    g. As a change in accounting estimate achieved by a change in accounting principle.
2. Indicate whether each situation would be included in the income statement in continuing operations (CO) or below continuing operations (BC), or if it would appear as an adjustment to retained earnings (RE). Use the format shown below to answer requirements 1 and 2.

Situation	Treatment (a–g)	Financial Statement Presentation (CO, BC, or RE)
1.		
2.		
3.		
4.		
5.		
6.		
7.		
8.		

**Judgment
Case 4–10**

Income statement
presentation

● LO3 through
LO7

The following events occurred during 2011 for various audit clients of your firm. Consider each event to be independent and the effect of each event to be material.

1. A manufacturing company recognized a loss on the sale of investments.
2. An automobile manufacturer sold all of the assets related to its financing component. The operations of the financing business can be clearly distinguished from the rest of the entity.
3. A company changed its depreciation method from the double-declining-balance method to the straight-line method.
4. Due to obsolescence, a company engaged in the manufacture of high-technology products incurred a loss on the write-down of inventory.
5. One of your clients discovered that 2010's depreciation expense was overstated. The error occurred because of a miscalculation of depreciation for the office building.
6. A cosmetics company decided to discontinue the manufacture of a line of women's lipstick. Other cosmetic lines will be continued. A loss was incurred on the sale of assets related to the lipstick product line. The operations of the discontinued line cannot be distinguished from the rest of the cosmetics business.

Required:

Discuss the 2011 financial statement presentation of each of the above events. Do not consider earnings per share disclosures.

IFRS Case 4–11
Comprehensive income; statement of cash flows; GlaxoSmithKline Plc.

● LO9 LO11 LO12

Real World Financials

GlaxoSmithKline Plc. (GSK) is a global pharmaceutical and consumer health-related products company located in the United Kingdom. The company prepares its financial statements in accordance with International Financial Reporting Standards. Below is a portion of the company's statements of cash flows included in recent financial statements:

GLAXOSMITHKLINE PLC.
Consolidated Statements of Cash Flows (in part)
For the Years Ended December 31

	Notes	2008 £m	2007 £m	2006 £m
Cash flow from investing activities				
Purchase of property, plant and equipment		(1,437)	(1,516)	(1,366)
Proceeds from sale of property, plant and equipment		20	35	43
Purchase of intangible assets		(632)	(627)	(224)
Proceeds from sale of intangible assets		171	9	175
Purchase of equity investments		(87)	(186)	(57)
Proceeds from sale of equity investments		42	45	32
Share transactions with minority shareholders	38	—	—	(157)
Purchase of businesses, net of cash acquired	38	(454)	(1,027)	(273)
Disposal of businesses and interest in associates	38	—	—	5
Investments in associates and joint ventures	38	(9)	(1)	(13)
Decrease/(increase) in liquid investments		905	(39)	(55)
Interest received		320	247	299
Dividends from associates and joint ventures		12	12	15
Net cash outflow from investing activities		(1,149)	(3,048)	(1,576)
Cash flow from financing activities				
Proceeds from own shares for employee share options		9	116	151
Shares acquired by ESOP Trusts		(19)	(26)	—
Issue of share capital	33	62	417	316
Purchase of own shares for cancellation		(3,706)	(213)	—
Purchase of Treasury shares		—	(3,538)	(1,348)
Increase in long-term loans		5,523	3,483	—
Repayment of long-term loans		—	(207)	—
Net (repayment of)/increase in short-term loans		(3,059)	1,632	(739)
Net repayment of obligations under finance leases		(48)	(39)	(34)
Interest paid		(730)	(378)	(414)
Dividends paid to shareholders		(2,929)	(2,793)	(2,598)
Dividends paid to minority interests		(79)	(77)	(87)
Other financing cash flows		68	(79)	16
Net cash outflow from financing activities		(4,908)	(1,702)	(4,737)
Increase/(decrease) in cash and bank overdrafts	37	1,148	1,411	(1,956)

Required:

1. Identify the items in the above statements that would be reported differently if GlaxoSmithKline prepared its financial statements according to U.S. GAAP rather than IFRS.

2. GSK's financial statements included income statements and separate statements of comprehensive income that reported its other comprehensive income items for the periods. What other options did the company have for reporting its other comprehensive income items? What options do companies have for the presentation of other comprehensive income items using U.S. GAAP?

Judgment Case 4–12
Income statement presentation; unusual items; comprehensive income

● LO3 through LO5 LO7 LO9

Norse Manufacturing, Inc., prepares an annual combined statement of income and comprehensive income. The following situations occurred during the company's 2011 fiscal year:

1. Restructuring costs were incurred due to the closing of a factory.

2. Investments were sold, and a loss was recognized.

3. Gains from foreign currency translation were recognized.

4. Interest expense was incurred.

5. A division was sold that qualifies as a separate component according to GAAP.

6. Obsolete inventory was written off.

7. The controller discovered an error in the calculation of 2010's patent amortization expense.

8. A volcano destroyed a storage facility on a South Sea island. The event is considered to be unusual and infrequent in occurrence.

Required:

1. For each situation, identify the appropriate reporting treatment from the list below (consider each event to be material).

      a. As a component of operating income.

      b. As a nonoperating income item (other income or expense).

      c. As a separately reported item.

      d. As an other comprehensive income item.

      e. As an adjustment to retained earnings.

  2. Identify the situations that would be reported net-of-tax.

Judgment Case 4–13
Management incentives for change
● LO2 LO6

It has been suggested that not all accounting choices are made by management in the best interest of fair and con-sistent financial reporting.

Required:

What motivations can you think of for management's choice of accounting methods?

Research Case 4–14
Pro forma earnings
● LO3

Companies often voluntarily provide a pro forma earnings number when they announce annual or quarterly earn-ings. These pro forma earnings numbers are controversial as they represent management's view of permanent earnings. The Sarbanes-Oxley Act (SOX), issued in 2002, requires that if pro forma earnings are included in any periodic or other report filed with the SEC or in any public disclosure or press release, the company also must provide a reconciliation with earnings determined according to GAAP.

    Professors Entwistle, Feltham, and Mbagwu, in "Financial Reporting Regulation and the Reporting of Pro Forma Earnings," examine whether firms changed their reporting practice in response to the pro forma regulations included in SOX.

Required:

  1. In your library or from some other source, locate the indicated article in *Accounting Horizons,* March 2006.

  2. What sample of firms did the authors use in their examination?

  3. What percent of firms reported pro forma earnings in 2001? In 2003?

  4. What percent of firms had pro forma earnings greater than GAAP earnings in 2001? In 2003?

  5. What was the most frequently reported adjusting item in 2001? In 2003?

  6. What are the authors' main conclusions of the impact of SOX on pro forma reporting?

Integrating Case 4–15
Balance sheet and income statement; Chapters 3 and 4
● LO3 LO5

Rice Corporation is negotiating a loan for expansion purposes and the bank requires financial statements. Before closing the accounting records for the year ended December 31, 2011, Rice's controller prepared the following financial statements:

RICE CORPORATION
Balance Sheet
At December 31, 2011
($ in 000s)

Assets	
Cash	$ 275
Marketable securities	78
Accounts receivable	487
Inventories	425
Allowance for uncollectible accounts	(50)
Property and equipment, net	160
Total assets	$1,375

Liabilities and Shareholders' Equity	
Accounts payable and accrued liabilities	$ 420
Notes payable	200
Common stock	260
Retained earnings	495
Total liabilities and shareholders' equity	$1,375

RICE CORPORATION
Income Statement
For the Year Ended December 31, 2011
($ in 000s)

Net sales		$1,580
Expenses:		
Cost of goods sold	$755	
Selling and administrative	385	
Miscellaneous	129	
Income taxes	100	
Total expenses		1,369
Net income		$ 211

Additional information:

1. The company's common stock is traded on an organized stock exchange.

2. The investment portfolio consists of short-term investments valued at $57,000. The remaining investments will not be sold until the year 2013.

3. Miscellaneous expense represents the before-tax loss from damages caused by an earthquake. The event is considered to be both unusual and infrequent.

4. Notes payable consist of two notes:

   Note 1: $80,000 face value dated September 30, 2011. Principal and interest at 10% are due on September 30, 2012.

   Note 2: $120,000 face value dated April 30, 2011. Principal is due in two equal installments of $60,000 plus interest on the unpaid balance. The two payments are scheduled for April 30, 2012, and April 30, 2013.

   Interest on both loans has been correctly accrued and is included in accrued liabilities on the balance sheet and selling and administrative expenses on the income statement.

5. Selling and administrative expenses include a $90,000 charge incurred by the company in restructuring some of its operations. The amount of the charge is material.

Required:

Identify and explain the deficiencies in the presentation of the statements prepared by the company's controller. Do not prepare corrected statements. Include in your answer a list of items which require additional disclosure, either on the face of the statement or in a note.

Analysis Case 4–16
Income statement information
● LO1

Refer to the income statements of **Dell Inc.** included in the company's financial statements in Appendix B at the back of the text.

Required:

1. What was the percentage increase or decrease in the company's net income from 2008 to 2009? From 2007 to 2008?

2. Using 2009 data, what is the company's approximate income tax rate?

3. Using 2009 data, what is the percentage of net income relative to revenue dollars?

Real World Case 4–17
Income statement information
● LO1 LO3 through LO5

Real World Financials

EDGAR, the Electronic Data Gathering, Analysis, and Retrieval system, performs automated collection, validation, indexing, and forwarding of submissions by companies and others who are required by law to file forms with the U.S. Securities and Exchange Commission (SEC). All publicly traded domestic companies use EDGAR to make the majority of their filings. (Some foreign companies file voluntarily.) Form 10-K, which includes the annual report, is required to be filed on EDGAR. The SEC makes this information available on the Internet.

Required:

1. Access EDGAR on the Internet. The web address is **www.sec.gov**.

2. Search for a public company with which you are familiar. Access the most recent 10-K filing. Search or scroll to find the financial statements and related notes.

3. Answer the following questions related to the company's income statement:

   a. Does the company use the single-step or multiple-step format, or a variation?

   b. Does the income statement contain any separately reported items in any year presented (discontinued operation or extraordinary item)? If it does, describe the event that caused the item. (Hint: there should be a related disclosure note.)

   c. Describe the trend in net income over the years presented.

4. Repeat requirements 2 and 3 for two additional companies.

BRITISH AIRWAYS CASE

BRITISH AIRWAYS
● LO12

British Airways, Plc. (BA), a U.K. company, prepares its financial statements according to International Financial Reporting Standards. BA's annual report for the year ended March 31, 2009, which includes financial statements and disclosure notes, is included with all new textbooks and can be found at **www.britishairways.com**. When answering questions, focus on BA's "Group" financial information (which is equivalent to "Consolidated" under U.S. GAAP).

Required:

1. How does BA classify operating expenses in its income statement? How are these expenses typically classified in a U.S. company income statement?

2. How does BA classify interest paid, interest received, and dividends received in its statement of cash flows? What other alternatives, if any, does the company have for the classification of these items? How are these items classified under U.S. GAAP?

CPA SIMULATION 4–1

Best Consultants
Financial
Statements

CPA Review

Test your knowledge of the concepts discussed in this chapter, practice critical professional skills necessary for career success, and prepare for the computer-based CPA exam by accessing our CPA simulations at the text website: **www.mhhe.com/spiceland6e**.

The Best Consultants simulation tests your knowledge of (a) the content and structure of the income statement, (b) the reporting of discontinued operations and comprehensive income, (c) the difference between cash and accrual income statement items addressed in Chapters 1 and 2, and (d) the transactions that cause a change in retained earnings discussed in Chapters 2 and 18.

As on the CPA exam itself, you will be asked to use tools including a spreadsheet, a calculator, and generally accepted accounting principles to conduct research, derive solutions, and communicate conclusions related to these issues in a simulated environment.

Specific tasks in the simulation include:

- Converting income statement items from a cash to accrual basis.
- Demonstrating your knowledge of the content and structure of the income statement.
- Understanding the transactions that affect retained earnings.
- Communicating various aspects of the reporting requirements for discontinued operations.
- Researching the disclosure requirements for the presentation of comprehensive income.

5

Income Measurement and Profitability Analysis

||||||||||||||||||||||||||||||||||||||||||||||||||

/// OVERVIEW

The focus of this chapter is revenue recognition. We first discuss the general circumstance in which revenue is recognized when a good or service is delivered. Then we discuss circumstances in which revenue should be deferred to a point after delivery or should be recognized at a point prior to delivery.

/// LEARNING OBJECTIVES

After studying this chapter, you should be able to:

- **LO1** Discuss the general objective of the timing of revenue recognition, list the two general criteria that must be satisfied before revenue can be recognized, and explain why these criteria usually are satisfied at a specific point in time. (page 234)

- **LO2** Describe the installment sales and cost recovery methods of recognizing revenue for some types of installment sales and explain the unusual conditions under which these methods might be used. (page 239)

- **LO3** Discuss the implications for revenue recognition of allowing customers the right of return. (page 244)

- **LO4** Identify situations that call for the recognition of revenue over time and distinguish between the percentage-of-completion and completed contract methods of recognizing revenue for long-term contracts. (page 245)

- **LO5** Discuss the revenue recognition issues involving multiple-deliverable contracts, software, and franchise sales. (pages 258 and 260)

- **LO6** Identify and calculate the common ratios used to assess profitability. (page 265)

- **LO7** Discuss the primary differences between U.S. GAAP and IFRS with respect to revenue recognition. (pages 237, 256, 260, and 262)

FINANCIAL REPORTING CASE

You Don't Have to Be a Rocket Scientist

"Good news! I got the job," she said, closing the door behind her.

Your sister, an aerospace engineer, goes on to explain that she accepted a position at **Lockheed Martin Corporation**, a world leader in the design, development, manufacture, and servicing of aircraft, spacecraft and launch vehicles, missiles, electronics, and information and telecommunication systems. She will supervise a long-term government contract beginning Tuesday.

"I got the salary I was asking for too," she continued. "Mr. Watson, my supervisor, also said I'll be getting a bonus tied to the gross profit on the project. It didn't hit me until I left his office, though, that this project will take two and a half years to complete. I hope I don't have to wait that long to get my bonus." Pointing to a page where she's circled part of a disclosure note, your sister hands you Lockheed's annual report. "I can't believe they wait that long to record income on all these multiyear projects. You're the accountant in the family; is that what this note is telling us?"

Sales and earnings (in part)
We record sales and anticipated profits under long-term fixed-price design, development, and production contracts on a percentage of completion basis . . .

By the time you finish this chapter, you should be able to respond appropriately to the questions posed in this case. Compare your response to the solution provided at the end of the chapter.

QUESTIONS ///

1. Does your sister have to wait two and a half years to get her bonus? Explain. (page 246)

2. How are gross profits recognized using the percentage-of-completion method? (page 249)

3. Are there other situations in which revenue is recognized at times other than when a product is delivered? (page 239)

PART A   REVENUE RECOGNITION

In Chapter 4 we discussed the *nature of income* and its presentation in the income statement. In this chapter we turn our attention to the *measurement* of periodic accounting income. Of primary interest here is the timing of revenue recognition. This is an important issue not only in its own right but also because, according to the matching principle, expenses should be recognized in the period in which the related revenues are recognized, so the timing of revenue recognition affects the timing of some expense recognition.

What is revenue? According to the FASB, "Revenues are inflows or other enhancements of assets of an entity or settlements of its liabilities (or a combination of both) from delivering or producing goods, rendering services, or other activities that constitute the entity's ongoing major or central operations."[1] In other words, revenue tracks the inflow of net assets that occurs when a business provides goods or services to its customers.

Why is the timing of revenue recognition so important? An income statement should report the results of operations only for the time period specified in the report. That is, a one-year income statement should report the company's accomplishments and sacrifices (revenues and expenses) only for that one-year period.[2] Revenue recognition criteria help ensure that a proper cutoff is made each period and that no more than one year's activity is reported in the annual income statement. Revenues reflect positive inflows from activities that eventually generate cash flows. By comparing these activity levels period to period, a user can better assess future activities and thus future cash flows.

Our objective, then, is to recognize revenue in the period or periods that the revenue-generating activities of the company are performed. But we also must consider that recognizing revenue presumes that an asset (usually cash) has been received or will be received in exchange for the goods or services sold. Our judgment as to the collectibility of the cash from the sale of a product or service will, therefore, affect the timing of revenue recognition. These two concepts of performance and collectibility are captured by the general guidelines for revenue recognition in the realization principle.

The **realization principle** requires that two criteria be satisfied before revenue can be recognized (recorded):[3]

1. The earnings process is judged to be complete or virtually complete (the earnings process refers to the activity or activities performed by the company to generate revenue).
2. There is reasonable certainty as to the collectibility of the asset to be received (usually cash).

Even with these guidelines, revenue recognition continues to be a controversial issue. Premature revenue recognition reduces the quality of reported earnings, particularly if those revenues never materialize. Many sad stories have surfaced involving companies forced to revise earnings numbers downward due to a restatement of revenues. The case of **Krispy Kreme Doughnuts** offers a prime example. In January 2005, the company announced that it would be restating its earnings for the last three quarters of fiscal 2004. Investors were already alarmed by the recent filing of a lawsuit that alleged the company routinely padded sales by doubling shipments to wholesale customers at the end of the quarter. In the two-day period following the announced restatement, the company's stock price dropped over 20% in value!

ARTHUR LEVITT, JR.
Lastly, companies try to boost earnings by manipulating the recognition of revenue. Think about a bottle of fine wine. You wouldn't pop the cork on that bottle before it was ready. But some companies are doing this with their revenue . . .[4]

> Revenue recognition criteria help ensure that an income statement reflects the actual accomplishments of a company for the period.

● LO1

[1]"Elements of Financial Statements," *Statement of Financial Concepts No. 6* (Stamford, Conn.: FASB, 1985, par. 78).
[2]In addition to reporting on an annual basis, companies often provide information quarterly and, on occasion, monthly. The SEC requires its registrants to provide information on a quarterly and annual basis. This information, referred to as *interim financial statements,* pertains to any financial report covering a period of less than one year. The key accounting issues related to the presentation of interim statements are discussed in Appendix 5.
[3]These criteria are addressed in SFAC 5, "Recognition and Measurement in Financial Statements," *Statement of Financial Accounting Concepts No. 5* (Stamford, Conn.: FASB, 1984).
[4]Arthur Levitt, Jr., "The Numbers Game," *The CPA Journal,* December 1998, p. 18.

As part of its crackdown on earnings management, the SEC issued *Staff Accounting Bulletin (SAB) No. 101*,[5] summarizing the SEC's views on revenue. The Bulletin provides additional criteria for judging whether or not the realization principle is satisfied:

1. Persuasive evidence of an arrangement exists.
2. Delivery has occurred or services have been rendered.
3. The seller's price to the buyer is fixed or determinable.
4. Collectibility is reasonably assured.

In addition to these four criteria, *SAB 101* also poses a number of revenue recognition questions relating to each of the criteria. The questions provide the facts of the scenario and then the SEC offers its interpretive response. These responses and supporting explanations provide guidance to companies with similar revenue recognition issues. For example, the following question relates to the delivery and performance criteria necessary to recognize revenue on a transaction commonly referred to as a "Bill and Hold" sale:

Facts: Company A receives purchase orders for products it manufactures. At the end of its fiscal quarters, customers may not yet be ready to take delivery of the products for various reasons. These reasons may include, but are not limited to, a lack of available space for inventory, having more than sufficient inventory in their distribution channel, or delays in customers' production schedules.

Questions: May Company A recognize revenue for the sale of its products once it has completed manufacturing if it segregates the inventory of the products in its own warehouse from its own products? May Company A recognize revenue for the sale if it ships the products to a third-party warehouse but (1) Company A retains title to the product and (2) payment by the customer is dependent upon ultimate delivery to a customer-specified site?

How would you answer these questions? The SEC's response is generally, no. It believes that delivery generally is not considered to have occurred unless the customer has taken title and assumes the risk and rewards of ownership of the specific products in the customer's purchase order or sales agreement. Typically this occurs when a product is delivered to the customer's delivery site and accepted by the customer.[6]

Soon after *SAB No. 101* was issued, many companies changed their revenue recognition methods. In most cases, the changes resulted in a deferral of revenue recognition. As a case in point, consider the change made by **Brown & Sharpe Manufacturing Company**, a multinational manufacturer of metrology products, described in a disclosure note, displayed in Graphic 5–1.

---

2. Accounting Change (in part)

In 2000, the Company adopted *SEC Staff Accounting Bulletin No. 101 (SAB 101)*. As a result of adopting *SAB 101*, the Company changed the way it recognizes revenue for machines sold to customers. Prior to the adoption of *SAB 101*, the Company recognized revenue when the machines were shipped and title passed to the customer. Effective as of January 1, 2001, the Company recognizes revenue for machines sold to customers once the performance of machines is accepted by the customers.

GRAPHIC 5–1

Disclosure of Change in Revenue Recognition Policy—Brown & Sharpe Manufacturing Company

Real World Financials

In requiring customer acceptance as part of the agreement, revenue recognition is delayed until this part of the earnings process is completed. Although the Brown and Sharpe example relates to product delivery, many of the changes in revenue recognition companies made in response to *SAB No. 101* are related to service revenue. We discuss some of these later in the chapter.

---

[5]FASB ASC 605–10–S99: Revenue Recognition–Overall–SEC Materials (originally "Revenue Recognition in Financial Statements," *Staff Accounting Bulletin No. 101* (Washington, D.C.: SEC, December 1999) and *Staff Accounting Bulletin No. 104* (Washington, D.C.: SEC, December 2003)).

[6]Ibid., p. 5.

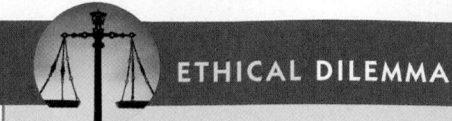

ETHICAL DILEMMA

The Precision Parts Corporation manufactures automobile parts. The company has reported a profit every year since the company's inception in 1980. Management prides itself on this accomplishment and believes one important contributing factor is the company's incentive plan that rewards top management a bonus equal to a percentage of operating income *if the operating income goal for the year is achieved*. However, 2011 has been a tough year, and prospects for attaining the income goal for the year are bleak.

Tony Smith, the company's chief financial officer, has determined a way to increase December sales by an amount sufficient to boost operating income over the goal for the year and earn bonuses for all top management. A reputable customer ordered $120,000 of parts to be shipped on January 15, 2012. Tony told the rest of top management "I know we can get that order ready by December 31 even though it will require some production line overtime. We can then just leave the order on the loading dock until shipment. I see nothing wrong with recognizing the sale in 2011, since the parts will have been manufactured and we do have a firm order from a reputable customer." The company's normal procedure is to ship goods f.o.b. destination and to recognize sales revenue when the customer receives the parts.

Graphic 5–2 relates various revenue-recognition methods to critical steps in the earnings process, and Graphic 5–3 provides a more detailed overview of the methods used in current practice.[7] Recall that the realization principle indicates that the central issues for recognizing revenue are (a) judging when the earnings process is substantially complete and (b) whether there is reasonable certainty as to the collectibility of the cash to be received. Often this decision is straightforward and tied to delivery of the product from the seller to the buyer. At delivery, the earnings process is virtually complete and the seller receives either cash or a receivable. At other times, though, recognizing revenue upon delivery may be inappropriate. It may be that revenue should be deferred to a point *after* delivery because the seller is unable to estimate whether the buyer will return the product or pay the receivable. Or, sometimes revenue should be recognized at a point *prior* to delivery because the earnings process occurs over multiple reporting periods and the company can better inform financial statement users by making reliable estimates of revenue and cost prior to delivery.

GRAPHIC 5–2

Relation between Earnings Process and Revenue Recognition Methods

Now let's consider specific revenue recognition methods in more detail. We start with revenue recognition at delivery, then discuss circumstances where revenue recognition must be postponed until after delivery, and then discuss circumstances that allow revenue recognition prior to delivery.

[7]As described in more detail on pp. 262–263, the FASB is partnering with the International Accounting Standards Board to develop a comprehensive statement on revenue recognition that could change some aspects of current practice. At the time this text was published, no new pronouncements had yet resulted from the project. Updates are available at the FASB website (see **http://www.fasb.org/revenue_recognition.shtml**).

Nature of the Revenue	Usually Recognize Revenue for:	
	Sale of a Product	**Sale of a Service**
Revenue Recognition Prior to Delivery, Because:		
Dependable estimates of progress are available.	Each period during the earnings process (e.g., long-term construction contract) in proportion to its percentage of completion (percentage-of-completion method)	Not applicable
Dependable estimates of progress are *not* available.	At the completion of the project (completed contract method)	Not applicable
Revenue Recognition at Delivery	When product is delivered and title transfers	When the service is provided or the key activity is performed
Revenue Recognition After Delivery, Because:		
• Payments are significantly uncertain	When cash is collected (installment sales or cost recovery method)	When cash is collected
• Reliable estimates of product returns are unavailable	When critical event occurs that reduces product return uncertainty	Not applicable
• The product sold is out on consignment	When the consignee sells the product to the ultimate consumer	Not applicable

GRAPHIC 5–3

Revenue Recognition Methods

When revenue is being earned in a multi-period contract, sometimes it is more meaningful to recognize revenue over time and prior to completion in proportion to the percentage of work completed.

We usually recognize revenue at or near the completion of the earnings process.

If collectibility is an issue, we defer revenue recognition until we can reasonably estimate the amount to be received.

INTERNATIONAL FINANCIAL REPORTING STANDARDS

Revenue Recognition Concepts. *IAS No. 18* governs most revenue recognition under IFRS. Similar to U.S. GAAP, it defines revenue as "the gross inflow of economic benefits during the period arising in the course of the ordinary activities of an entity when those inflows result in increases in equity, other than increases relating to contributions from equity participants."[8] IFRS allows revenue to be recognized when the following conditions have been satisfied:

● LO7

(a) The amount of revenue and costs associated with the transaction can be measured reliably,

(b) It is probable that the economic benefits associated with the transaction will flow to the seller,

(c) (for sales of goods) the seller has transferred to the buyer the risks and rewards of ownership, and doesn't effectively manage or control the goods,

(d) (for sales of services) the stage of completion can be measured reliably.

These general conditions typically will lead to revenue recognition at the same time and in the same amount as would occur under U.S. GAAP, but there are exceptions. For example, later in this chapter we discuss differences between IFRS and U.S. GAAP that may affect the timing of revenue recognition with respect to multiple-deliverable contracts. More generally, IFRS has much less industry-specific guidance that does U.S. GAAP, leading to fewer exceptions to applying these revenue recognition conditions.

---

[8]"Revenue," *International Accounting Standard No. 18* (IASCF), as amended effective January 1, 2009, par. 7.

Revenue Recognition at Delivery

Product Revenue

While revenue usually is earned during a period of time, it often is recognized at one specific point in time when both revenue recognition criteria are satisfied.

Consider the timing of revenue recognition for a typical manufacturing company that sells its products on credit. Graphic 5–2 shows three alternative points in time during the earnings process that could be considered the critical event for revenue recognition. It should be pointed out that revenue actually is earned *throughout* the earnings process. The critical event is the point in time when the realization principle is satisfied.[9]

Let's first consider the date production ends. At that point, it might be said that the earnings process is virtually complete. After all, the majority of the costs that must be expended to generate revenue have been incurred. The product has been produced and the remaining tasks are to sell the product and collect the asset to be exchanged for the product, which is usually cash.

Revenue from the sale of products usually is recognized at the point of product delivery.

However, at this point there usually exists significant uncertainties. We don't know if the product will be sold, the selling price, the buyer, or the collectibility of the asset to be received. Because of these uncertainties, revenue recognition usually is delayed until the point of sale, at product delivery. The product delivery date occurs when legal title to the goods passes from seller to buyer. This occurs either on the date the product is shipped from the seller's facility or when the goods actually are received by the buyer, depending on the terms of the sales agreement. If the goods are shipped *f.o.b. (free on board) shipping point,* then legal title to the goods changes hands at the point of shipment, when the seller delivers the goods to the common carrier (for example, a trucking company), and the purchaser is responsible for shipping costs and transit insurance. On the other hand, if the goods are shipped *f.o.b. destination,* the seller is responsible for shipping, and legal title does not pass until the goods arrive at the customer's location.[10]

The point of delivery refers to the date legal title to the product passes from seller to buyer.

The basic journal entries to record revenue upon delivery should look familiar. As an example, assume that Taft Company sells a supercomputer for $5,000,000 that cost $4,100,000 to produce. The journal entries to record the sale, assuming that Taft uses the perpetual inventory method, would be

Accounts receivable...	5,000,000	
Revenue...		5,000,000
Cost of goods sold...	4,100,000	
Inventory..		4,100,000

This sale yields gross profit of $900,000 ($5,000,000 – 4,100,000).

At the product delivery date we know the product has been sold, the price, and the buyer. However, usually the buyer is given a length of time, say 30 days, to pay for the goods after they have been delivered. Therefore, the only remaining uncertainty at the time of delivery involves the ultimate cash collection, which usually can be accounted for by estimating and recording allowances for possible return of the product and for uncollectibility of the cash, that is, bad debts. Both of these estimates are discussed in Chapter 7. As we discuss later in this chapter, significant uncertainty at point of product delivery related to either collectibility or product return causes a delay in revenue recognition.

Service Revenue

Service revenue, too, often is recognized at a point in time if there is one final activity that is deemed critical to the earnings process. In this case, all revenue is deferred until this final activity has been performed. For example, a moving company will pack, load, transport, and deliver household goods for a fixed fee. Although packing, loading, and transporting all are important to the earning process, delivery is the culminating event of the earnings

---

[9]As you will learn later in this chapter when we discuss the percentage-of-completion method, revenue can be recognized during the earnings process rather than at one particular point in time as long as particular criteria have been met.
[10]We discuss this aspect of title transfer in Chapter 7.

process. So, the entire service fee is recognized as revenue after the goods have been delivered. **FedEx** recognizes revenue in this manner. The Company's Summary of Significant Accounting Policies disclosure note indicates that "Revenue is recognized upon delivery of shipments." As with the sale of product, estimates of uncollectible amounts must be made for service revenue provided to customers on a credit basis.

However, in many instances, service revenue activities occur over extended periods, so recognizing revenue at any single date within one period would be inappropriate. Instead, it's more meaningful to recognize revenue over time as the service is performed.

> Service revenue often is recognized over time, in proportion to the amount of service performed.

As an example, consider the revenue a property owner earns when renting office space. If a landlord charges a tenant $12,000 in rent for the upcoming year, it would seem logical to recognize $1,000 of rent revenue each month over the one-year period (i.e., straight-line method) since similar services are performed throughout the period. The landlord recognizes rent revenue in proportion to the passage of time. Likewise, **Gold's Gym** will recognize revenue from a two-year membership ratably over the 24-month membership period. If the customer pays in advance in such cases, the seller debits cash and credits a liability (unearned revenue) because the seller is holding the customer's cash and has the obligation to provide the service. The seller only reduces that liability when the service has been provided and therefore revenue has been earned. We discuss unearned revenue liabilities and customer advances more in Chapter 13.

A similar situation occurs if you buy a season pass to Disney World. When would **Walt Disney Co.** recognize revenue for the cash it collects for the sale of a 365-day pass? Rationalizing that a pass can be used any number of times during the season, thus making it difficult to determine when service is provided, many companies once recognized all revenue from the sale of season passes on the date of sale. However, the SEC's *Staff Accounting Bulletin No. 101*, discussed earlier in the chapter, motivated most of these companies to change to recognizing revenue throughout the service period. For example, Graphic 5–4 provides a disclosure note **Walt Disney Co.** included in a recent annual report. Notice that the company now recognizes revenue *over time*, based on the anticipated usage of the season pass over the operating season.

Revenue Recognition (in part)

Revenues from advance theme park ticket sales are recognized when the tickets are used. For nonexpiring, multi-day tickets, we recognize revenue over a three-year time period based on estimated usage patterns that are derived from historical usage patterns. Revenues from corporate sponsors at the theme parks are generally recognized over the period of the applicable agreements commencing with the opening of the related attraction.

GRAPHIC 5–4

Disclosure of Revenue Recognition Policy— Walt Disney Co.

Real World Financials

Revenue Recognition after Delivery

Recognizing revenue when goods and services are delivered as described in the previous section assumes we are able to make reasonable estimates of amounts due from customers that potentially might be uncollectible. For product sales, this also includes amounts not collectible due to customers returning the products they purchased. Otherwise, we would violate one of the requirements of the revenue realization principle we discussed earlier—that there must be reasonable certainty as to the collectibility of cash from the customer. In this section we address a few situations in which uncertainties are so severe that they could cause a delay in recognizing revenue from a sale of a product or service. For each of these situations, notice that the accounting is essentially the same—*deferring* recognition of the gross profit arising from a sale of a product or service until uncertainties have been resolved.

> **FINANCIAL Reporting Case**
>
> Q3, p. 233

Installment Sales

● LO2

Customers sometimes are allowed to pay for purchases in installments over a long period of time. Many large retail stores, such as **Sears** and **J.C. Penney**, sell products on an installment plan. Increasing the length of time allowed for payment usually increases the uncertainty about whether the store actually will collect a receivable. Is the uncertainty sufficient in an installment sale to cause these companies to delay recognizing revenue and related expenses beyond the point of sale? Usually, it's not.

In most situations, the increased uncertainty concerning the collection of cash from installment sales can be accommodated satisfactorily by estimating uncollectible amounts. If, however, the installment sale creates significant uncertainty concerning cash collection, making impossible a reasonable assessment of future bad debts, then revenue and expense recognition should be delayed. For example, real estate sales often are made on an installment basis with relatively small down payments and long payment periods, perhaps 25 years or more. These payment characteristics, combined with the general speculative nature of many of these transactions, may translate into extreme uncertainty concerning the collectibility of the installment receivable.[11] In fact, GAAP requires that the installment sales method (discussed below) be applied to a retail land sale that meets certain criteria.[12]

When extreme uncertainty exists regarding the ultimate collectibility of cash, we delay recognizing revenue and related expenses using one of two accounting techniques, the installment sales method or the cost recovery method. *We emphasize that these methods should be used only in situations involving exceptional uncertainty.* As an example, **Rouse Company** acquires, develops, and manages income-producing properties throughout the United States and develops and sells land for residential, commercial, and other uses. Graphic 5–5 shows the company's revenue recognition disclosure note included with recent annual financial statements. The note indicates that the preferred method is to recognize revenue upon delivery (full accrual method), but that in certain circumstances, one of these two alternative methods could be used.

GRAPHIC 5–5

Disclosure of Revenue Recognition Policy— Rouse Company

Real World Financials

Revenue Recognition and Related Matters (in part)

Revenues from land sales are recognized using the full accrual method provided that various criteria relating to the terms of the transactions and any subsequent involvement by us with the land sold are met. Revenues relating to transactions that do not meet the established criteria are deferred and recognized when the criteria are met or using the installment or cost recovery methods, as appropriate in the circumstances.

INSTALLMENT SALES METHOD.   To deal with the uncertainty of collection, the installment sales method recognizes revenue and costs only when cash payments are received. Each payment is assumed to be composed of two components: (1) a partial recovery of the cost of the item sold and (2) a gross profit component. These components are determined by the gross profit percentage applicable to the sale. For example, if the gross profit percentage (gross profit ÷ sales price) is 40%, then 60% of each dollar collected represents cost recovery and the remaining 40% is gross profit. Consider the example in Illustration 5–1.

ILLUSTRATION 5–1

Installment Sales Method

On November 1, 2011, the Belmont Corporation, a real estate developer, sold a tract of land for $800,000. The sales agreement requires the customer to make four equal annual payments of $200,000 plus interest on each November 1, beginning November 1, 2011. The land cost $560,000 to develop. The company's fiscal year ends on December 31.

The gross profit of $240,000 ($800,000 − 560,000) represents 30% of the sales price ($240,000 ÷ $800,000). The collection of cash and the recognition of gross profit under the installment method are summarized below. In this example, we ignore the collection of interest charges and the recognition of interest revenue to concentrate on the collection of the $800,000 sales price and the recognition of gross profit on the sale.

---

[11]For income tax purposes, the installment sales method applies only to gains from the sale of certain types of properties. The tax law requires the use of the installment sales method for these transactions unless a taxpayer elects not to use the method.

[12]FASB ASC 360–20: Property, Plant, and Equipment—Real Estate Sales (previously "Accounting for Sales of Real Estate," *Statement of Financial Accounting Standards No. 66* (Stamford, Conn.: FASB, 1982)).

Date	Cash Collected	Amount Allocated to:	
		Cost (70%)	Gross Profit (30%)
Nov. 1, 2011	$200,000	$140,000	$ 60,000
Nov. 1, 2012	200,000	140,000	60,000
Nov. 1, 2013	200,000	140,000	60,000
Nov. 1, 2014	200,000	140,000	60,000
Totals	$800,000	$560,000	$240,000

The gross profit recognized in a period will be equal to the gross profit percentage multiplied by the period's cash collection. The following journal entries are recorded (interest charges ignored):

Make Installment Sale:		
November 1, 2011		
Installment receivables..	800,000	
Inventory...		560,000
Deferred gross profit...		240,000
To record installment sale.		

> Inventory is credited for the portion of the receivable that represents the cost of the land sold. The difference is deferred gross profit.

The first entry records the installment receivable and the reduction of inventory. The difference between the $800,000 selling price and the $560,000 cost of sales represents the gross profit on the sale of $240,000. As it will be recognized in net income only as collections are made, it is recorded in an account called *deferred gross profit*. This is a contra account to the installment receivable. It will be reduced to zero as the payments are received.[13]

Collect Cash:		
November 1, 2011		
Cash...	200,000	
Installment receivables		200,000
To record cash collection from installment sale.		
Deferred gross profit..	60,000	
Realized gross profit..		60,000
To recognize gross profit from installment sale.		

> When payments are received, gross profit is recognized, and is calculated by applying the gross profit percentage to the cash collected (30% × $200,000).

The second set of entries records the collection of the first installment and recognizes the gross profit component of the payment, $60,000. Realized gross profit gets closed to income summary as part of the normal year-end closing process and is included in net income in the income statement. Journal entries to record the remaining three payments on November 1, 2012, 2013, and 2014, are identical.

At the end of 2011, the balance sheet would report the following:

Installment receivables ($800,000 − $200,000)	$600,000
Less: Deferred gross profit ($240,000 − $60,000)	(180,000)
Installment receivables (net)	$420,000

---

[13]Accountants sometimes record installment sales in the following manner:

Installment receivables...	800,000	
Installment sales...		800,000
To record installment sales.		

Cost of installment sales...	560,000	
Inventory..		560,000
To record the cost of installment sales.		

Then at the end of the period, the following adjusting/closing entry is recorded:

Installment sales...	800,000	
Cost of installment sales.......................................		560,000
Deferred gross profit on installment sales..............		240,000

The text entries concentrate on the effect of the transactions and avoid this unnecessary procedural complexity.

The net amount of the receivable reflects the portion of the remaining payments that represents cost recovery (70% × $600,000). The installment receivables are classified as current assets if they will be collected within one year (or within the company's operating cycle, if longer); otherwise, they are classified as noncurrent assets.

The income statement for 2011 would report gross profit from installment sales of $60,000. Sales and cost of goods sold usually are not reported in the income statement under the installment method, just the resulting gross profit. However, if those amounts aren't included in the income statement in the period in which the installment sale is made, they need to be included in the notes to the financial statements, along with the amount of gross profit that has not yet been recognized.

ADDITIONAL CONSIDERATION

We discuss in significant depth in Chapter 7 the problem of accounting for bad debts. However, bad debts related to receivables on sales accounted for using the installment method create a unique problem. The reason a company uses the installment method is that it can't reliably estimate bad debts. Therefore, the company doesn't explicitly recognize bad debt expense or create an allowance for uncollectible accounts in the installment method. Rather, bad debts are dealt with implicitly by deferring gross profit until cash is collected. If the cash never is collected, the related deferred gross profit never gets included in net income. To illustrate, assume that in the example described in Illustration 5–1, the Belmont Corporation collected the first payment but the customer was unable to make the remaining payments. Typically, the seller would repossess the item sold and make the following journal entry:

Repossessed inventory...	420,000	
Deferred gross profit..	180,000	
Installment receivable...		600,000

This entry removes the receivable and the remaining deferred gross profit and records the repossessed land in an inventory account. This example assumes that the repossessed land's current fair value is equal to the net receivable of $420,000. If the land's fair value at the date of repossession is less than $420,000, a loss on repossession is recorded (debited).

COST RECOVERY METHOD. In situations where there is an extremely high degree of uncertainty regarding the ultimate cash collection on an installment sale, an even more conservative approach, the cost recovery method, can be used. This method defers all gross profit recognition until the cost of the item sold has been recovered. The gross profit recognition pattern applying the cost recovery method to the Belmont Corporation situation used in Illustration 5–1 is shown below.

> The *cost recovery method* defers all gross profit recognition until cash equal to the cost of the item sold has been received.

Date	Cash Collected	Cost Recovery	Gross Profit Recognized
Nov. 1, 2011	$200,000	$200,000	$ –0–
Nov. 1, 2012	200,000	200,000	–0–
Nov. 1, 2013	200,000	160,000	40,000
Nov. 1, 2014	200,000	–0–	200,000
Totals	$800,000	$560,000	$240,000

The journal entries using this method are similar to those for the installment sales method except that $40,000 in gross profit is recognized in 2013 and $200,000 in 2014.

> The cost recovery method's initial journal entry is identical to the installment sales method.

Make Installment Sale:
November 1, 2011

Installment receivables...	800,000	
Inventory...		560,000
Deferred gross profit		240,000
To record installment sale.		

Collect Cash:
November 1, 2011, 2012, 2013, and 2014

Cash...	200,000	
Installment receivables...		200,000

To record cash collection from installment sale.

November 1, 2011 and 2012
No entry for gross profit.

November 1, 2013

Deferred gross profit...	40,000	
Realized gross profit...		40,000

To recognize gross profit from installment sale.

November 1, 2014

Deferred gross profit...	200,000	
Realized gross profit...		200,000

To recognize gross profit from installment sale.

> **When payments are received, gross profit is recognized only after cost has been fully recovered.**

Why not use the installment sales method or cost recovery method for all installment sales? Because doing so would violate the realization principle and be inconsistent with accrual accounting. If bad debts can be reasonably estimated, there is no reason to delay revenue recognition.

CONCEPT REVIEW EXERCISE

INSTALLMENT SALES

Boatwright Implements, Inc., manufactures and sells farm machinery. For most of its sales, revenue and cost of sales are recognized at the delivery date. In 2011 Boatwright sold a cotton baler to a new customer for $100,000. The cost of the machinery was $60,000. Payment will be made in five annual installments of $20,000 each, with the first payment due in 2011. Boatwright usually does not allow its customers to pay in installments. Due to the unusual nature of the payment terms and the uncertainty of collection of the installment payments, Boatwright is considering alternative methods of recognizing profit on this sale.

Required:
Ignoring interest charges, prepare a table showing the gross profit to be recognized from 2011 through 2015 on the cotton-baler sale using the following three methods:

1. Point of delivery revenue recognition.
2. The installment sales method.
3. The cost recovery method.

SOLUTION

	Point of Delivery	Installment Sales Method (40% × cash collection)	Cost Recovery Method
2011	$40,000	$ 8,000	$ –0–
2012	–0–	8,000	–0–
2013	–0–	8,000	–0–
2014	–0–	8,000	20,000
2015	–0–	8,000	20,000
Totals	$40,000	$40,000	$40,000

Right of Return

Retailers usually give their customers the right to return merchandise if they are not satisfied. In most situations, even though the right to return merchandise exists, revenues and expenses can be appropriately recognized at point of delivery. Based on past experience, a company usually can estimate the returns that will result for a given volume of sales. These estimates are used to reduce both sales and cost of goods sold in anticipation of returns. The purpose of the estimates is to avoid overstating gross profit in the period of sale and understating gross profit in the period of return. The specific accounting treatment for sales returns is illustrated in Chapter 7 in conjunction with discussing the valuation of accounts receivable.

● LO3

Because the return of merchandise can negate the benefits of having made a sale, the seller must meet certain criteria before revenue is recognized in situations when the **right of return** exists. The most critical of these criteria is that the seller must be able to make reliable estimates of future returns.[14] In certain situations, these criteria are not satisfied at the point of delivery of the product. For example, manufacturers of semiconductors like **Intel Corporation** and **Motorola Corporation** usually sell their products through independent distributor companies. Economic factors, competition among manufacturers, and rapid obsolescence of the product motivate these manufacturers to grant the distributors the right of return if they are unable to sell the semiconductors. So, revenue recognition often is deferred beyond the delivery point to the date the products actually are sold by the distributor to an end user. The disclosure note shown in Graphic 5–6 appeared in a recent annual report of Intel Corporation.

GRAPHIC 5–6

Disclosure of Revenue Recognition Policy— Intel Corporation

Real World Financials

Revenue Recognition

The company recognizes net revenue when the earnings process is complete, as evidenced by an agreement with the customer, transfer of title and acceptance, if applicable, as well as fixed pricing and probable collectibility. . . . Because of frequent sales price reductions and rapid technology obsolescence in the industry, sales made to distributors under agreements allowing price protection and/or right of return are deferred until the distributors sell the merchandise.

For Intel, the event critical to revenue recognition is *not* the delivery of the product to a distributor but the ultimate sale of the product by the distributor to an end user.

Alternatively, the right of return could be specified contractually as expiring on some future date, and revenue recognition could be deferred to that date. Regardless, the accounting treatment in these situations would be similar to that used for the installment sales and cost recovery methods. The difference is that the journal entries we use to move deferred gross profit to realized gross profit would be recorded in whatever period that returns can be estimated reliably or the right of return no longer exists.

Similarly, sometimes, a sales agreement requires additional, important performance steps to be performed by the seller. In this case, the earnings process is not virtually complete until those steps are performed, but as in the case of significant uncertainty about cash collection, revenue recognition must be deferred. Graphic 5–1 on page 235 illustrates a situation where the seller, Brown & Sharpe, delays revenue recognition beyond delivery of machines until the performance of the machines has been accepted by the buyer. Customer acceptance is an important part of the agreement between buyer and seller.

Any time a company recognizes revenue at a point other than the point of delivery, the revenue recognition method used is disclosed in the summary of significant accounting policies. Intel's disclosure note is an example. As another example, Graphic 5–7 shows a disclosure note included with the 2009 financial statements of **Helicos Biosciences Corporation**, a producer of genetic analysis instrumentation for research, pharmaceutical and medical applications.

GRAPHIC 5–7

Disclosure of Revenue Recognition Policy— Helicos Biosciences Corporation

Real World Financials

2. Summary of Significant Accounting Policies: Revenue Recognition (in part)

The Company recognizes revenue in accordance with Staff Accounting Bulletin No. 104, "Revenue Recognition in Financial Statements." . . . SAB No. 104 requires that persuasive evidence of a sales arrangement exists; delivery of goods occurs through transfer of title and risk and rewards of ownership, the selling price is fixed or determinable and collectibility is reasonably assured. . . .

In instances where the Company sells an instrument with specified acceptance criteria, the Company will defer revenue recognition until such acceptance has been obtained.

---

[14]Other, less critical criteria are listed in FASB ASC 605–15–25: Revenue Recognition–Products–Recognition (previously "Revenue Recognition When Right of Return Exists," *Statement of Financial Accounting Standards No. 48* (Stamford, Conn.: FASB, 1981)).

As the note indicates, some of Helicos's revenue is delayed beyond the point of product delivery. Until the product has been installed and meets customer acceptance criteria, there is a high degree of uncertainty concerning the possibility the product might be returned, so Helicos has not completed its obligation to its customer until acceptance has occurred.

Consignment Sales

Sometimes a company arranges for another company to sell its product under consignment. The "consignor" physically transfers the goods to the other company (the consignee), but the consignor retains legal title. If the consignee can't find a buyer within an agreed-upon time, the consignee returns the goods to the consignor. However, if a buyer is found, the consignee remits the selling price (less commission and approved expenses) to the consignor.

Because the consignor retains the risks and rewards of ownership of the product and title does not pass to the consignee, the consignor does not record a sale (revenue and related expenses) until the consignee sells the goods and title passes to the eventual customer. Of course, that means goods on consignment still are part of the consignor's inventory. As an example, **Sonic Solutions** earns revenue primarily from licensing, developing, maintaining, and supporting its software. Some of the company's product is sold using consignment arrangements. Graphic 5–8 shows a portion of the revenue recognition disclosure note that Sonic Solutions included in its 2009 annual report.

> **Note 1: Business and Summary of Significant Accounting Policies: *Revenue Recognition* (in part)**
>
> Except in the case of consignment arrangements, the Company recognizes revenue from the sale of its packaged software products when title transfers to the distributor or retailer. When the Company sells packaged software products to distributors and retailers on a consignment basis, it recognizes revenue upon sell through to an end customer.

Consigned inventory stays in the balance sheet of the consignor until an arms-length transaction transfers title to a buyer.

GRAPHIC 5–8

Disclosure of Revenue Recognition Policy— Sonic Solutions

Real World Financials

Up until now, we've focused on revenue-generating activities in which some specific event (e.g., delivery, collection, product performance, and resale) indicates that the earnings process is substantially completed and significant uncertainties have been alleviated, prompting us to recognize revenue and related expenses. We now turn our attention to situations in which it's desirable to recognize revenue over more than one reporting period— before a specific event indicates the earnings process is substantially completed.

Revenue Recognition Prior to Delivery

Revenue recognition when an earnings process is virtually complete is inappropriate for certain types of long-term contracts. The types of companies that make use of long-term contracts are many and varied. A recent survey of reporting practices of 500 large public companies indicates that approximately one in every five companies engages in long-term contracts.[15] And they are not just construction companies. In fact, even services such as research, installation, and consulting often are contracted for on a long-term basis. Graphic 5–9 lists just a sampling of companies that use long-term contracts, many of which you might recognize.

The general revenue recognition criteria described in the realization principle suggest that revenue should be recognized when a long-term project is finished (that is, when the earnings process is virtually complete). This is known as the completed contract method of revenue recognition. The problem with this method is that all revenues, expenses, and resulting income from the project are recognized in the period in which the project is completed; no revenues or expenses are reported in the income statements of earlier reporting periods in which much of the work may have been performed. Net income should provide a measure of periodic accomplishment to help predict future accomplishments. Clearly, income statements prepared using the completed contract method do not fairly report each period's accomplishments when a project spans more than one reporting period. Much of the earnings process is far removed from the point of delivery.

● LO4

The *completed contract method* recognizes revenue at a point in time when the earnings process is complete.

---

[15]*Accounting Trends and Techniques—2009* (New York: AICPA, 2009), p. 428.

GRAPHIC 5–9

Companies Engaged in Long-Term Contracts

Company	Type of Industry or Product
Oracle Corp.	Computer software, license and consulting fees
Lockheed Martin Corporation	Aircraft, missiles, and spacecraft
EDS	Information technology and outsourcing
Northrop Grumman Newport News	Shipbuilding
Nortel Networks Corp.	Networking solutions and services to support the Internet
SBA Communications Corp.	Telecommunications
Layne Christensen Company	Water supply services and geotechnical construction
Kaufman & Broad Home Corp.	Commercial and residential construction
Raytheon Company	Defense electronics
Foster Wheeler Corp.	Construction, petroleum and chemical facilities
Halliburton	Construction, energy services
Allied Construction Products Corp.	Large metal stamping presses

FINANCIAL Reporting Case

Q1, p. 233

Using the *percentage-of-completion method* we allocate a share of a project's revenues and expenses to each reporting period during construction.

The **percentage-of-completion method** of revenue recognition for long-term construction and other projects is designed to help address this problem. By this approach, we recognize revenues (and expenses) over time by allocating a share of the project's expected revenues and expenses to each period in which the earnings process occurs, that is, the contract period. Although the contract usually specifies total revenues, the project's expenses are not known until completion. Consequently, it's necessary for a company to estimate the project's future costs at the end of each reporting period in order to estimate total gross profit to be earned on the project.

Because the percentage-of-completion method does a better job of recognizing revenue in the periods in which revenue is earned, U.S. and International GAAP require the use of that method unless it's not possible to make reliable estimates of revenues, expenses, and progress toward completion.[16] Companies prefer the percentage-of-completion method as well because it allows earlier revenue and profit recognition than does the completed contract method. For both reasons, the percentage-of-completion method is more prevalent in practice. However, much of the accounting is the same under either method, so we start by discussing the similarities between the two methods, and then the differences. You'll see that we recognize the same total amounts or revenue and profit over the life of the contract under either method. Only the timing of recognition differs.

Illustration 5–2 provides information to compare accounting for long-term contracts using the completed contract and percentage-of-completion methods.

ILLUSTRATION 5–2

Completed Contract and Percentage-of-Completion Methods Compared

At the beginning of 2011, the Harding Construction Company received a contract to build an office building for $5 million. The project is estimated to take three years to complete. According to the contract, Harding will bill the buyer in installments over the construction period according to a prearranged schedule. Information related to the contract is as follows:

	2011	2012	2013
Actual construction costs incurred during the year	$1,500,000	$1,000,000	$1,600,000
Actual construction costs incurred in prior years	–0–	1,500,000	2,500,000
Cumulative actual construction costs	1,500,000	2,500,000	4,100,000
Estimated costs to complete at end of year	2,250,000	1,500,000	–0–
Total construction costs (actual + estimated)	$3,750,000	$4,000,000	$4,100,000
Billings made during the year	$1,200,000	$2,000,000	$1,800,000
Cash collections during year	1,000,000	1,400,000	2,600,000

[16]Specifically, U.S. GAAP requires that the percentage-of-completion method be used whenever (1) reasonable estimates can be made of revenues and costs, (2) the contract specifies the parties' rights, consideration to be paid, and payment terms, and (3) both the purchaser and seller have the ability and expectation to fulfill their obligations under the contract [FASB ASC 605–35-25: Revenue Recognition–Construction–Type and Production–Type Contracts–Recognition (previously "Accounting for Performance of Construction-Type and Certain Production-Type Contracts," *Statement of Position 81-1* (New York: AICPA, 1981))]. Similar criteria are included in IAS No. 11, "Construction Contracts" (IASCF, as amended, effective January 1, 2009, paragraph 23).

Construction costs include the labor, materials, and overhead costs directly related to the construction of the building. Notice how the total of estimated and actual construction costs changes from period to period. Cost revisions are typical in long-term contracts in which costs are estimated over long periods of time.

ACCOUNTING FOR THE COST OF CONSTRUCTION AND ACCOUNTS RECEIVABLE.
Summary journal entries for both the percentage-of-completion and completed contract methods are shown in Illustration 5–2A for construction costs, billings, and cash receipts.

ILLUSTRATION 5–2A   Journal Entries—Costs, Billings, and Cash Receipts

	2011		2012		2013	
Construction in progress	1,500,000		1,000,000		1,600,000	
Cash, materials, etc.		1,500,000		1,000,000		1,600,000
To record construction costs.						
Accounts receivable..............................	1,200,000		2,000,000		1,800,000	
Billings on construction contract		1,200,000		2,000,000		1,800,000
To record progress billings.						
Cash...	1,000,000		1,400,000		2,600,000	
Accounts receivable		1,000,000		1,400,000		2,600,000
To record cash collections.						

With both the completed contract and percentage-of-completion methods, all costs of construction are recorded in an asset account called **construction in progress.** This account is equivalent to the asset work-in-process inventory in a manufacturing company. This is logical since the construction project is essentially an inventory item in process for the contractor.

Notice that periodic billings are credited to **billings on construction contract.** This account is a contra account to the construction in progress asset. At the end of each period, the balances in these two accounts are compared. If the net amount is a debit, it is reported in the balance sheet as an asset. Conversely, if the net amount is a credit, it is reported as a liability.[17]

To understand why we use the billings on construction contract account, consider a key difference between accounting for a long-term contract and accounting for a typical sale in which revenue is recognized upon delivery. Recall our earlier example in which Taft Company gives up its physical asset (inventory; in this instance a supercomputer) and recognizes cost of goods sold at the same time it gets a financial asset (an account receivable) and recognizes revenue. So, first a physical asset is in the balance sheet, and then a financial asset, but the two are not in the balance sheet at the same time.

Now consider our Harding Construction example. Harding is creating a physical asset (construction in progress) in the same periods it recognizes a financial asset (first recognizing accounts receivable when the customer is billed and then recognizing cash when the receivable is collected). Having both the physical asset and the financial asset in the balance sheet at the same time constitutes double counting the same arrangement. The billings on construction contract account solves this problem. Whenever an account receivable is recognized, the other side of the journal entry increases the billings on construction contract account, which is contra to (and thus reduces) construction in progress. As a result, the financial asset (accounts receivable) increases and the physical asset (the net of construction in progress and billings) decreases, and no double counting occurs.

GROSS PROFIT RECOGNITION—GENERAL APPROACH.
Now let's consider recognition of gross profit. The top portion of Illustration 5–2B shows the journal entry to

> Accounting for costs, billings, and cash receipts are the same for both the percentage-of-completion and completed contract methods.

> *Construction in progress* is the contractor's work-in-process inventory.

> The billings on construction contract account prevents "double counting" assets by reducing construction in progress whenever an accounts receivable is recognized.

---

[17]If the company is engaged in more than one long-term contract, all contracts for which construction in progress exceeds billings are grouped together and all contracts for which billings exceed construction in progress also are grouped together. This would result in the presentation of both an asset and a liability in the balance sheet.

recognize revenue, cost of construction (think of this as cost of goods sold), and gross profit under the completed contract method, while the bottom portion shows the journal entries that achieve this for the percentage-of-completion method.

ILLUSTRATION 5–2B Journal Entries—Profit Recognition

	2011	2012	2013
Completed Contract			
Construction in progress (gross profit)			900,000
Cost of construction			4,100,000
Revenue from long-term contracts			5,000,000
To record gross profit.			
Percentage-of-Completion			
Construction in progress (gross profit)	500,000	125,000	275,000
Cost of construction	1,500,000	1,000,000	1,600,000
Revenue from long-term contracts	2,000,000	1,125,000	1,875,000
To record gross profit.			

The same total amount of profit or loss is recognized under both the completed contract and the percentage-of-completion methods, but the timing of recognition differs.

It's important to understand two key aspects of Illustration 5–2B. First, the same amounts of revenue, cost, and gross profit are recognized under both the completed contract and percentage-of-completion methods. The only difference is timing. To check this, sum all of the revenue recognized for both methods over the three years:

	Percentage-of-Completion	Completed Contract
Revenue recognized:		
2011	$2,000,000	–0–
2012	1,125,000	–0–
2013	1,875,000	$5,000,000
Total revenue	$5,000,000	$5,000,000

Construction in progress includes profits and losses on the contract that have been recognized to date.

Second, notice that in both methods we add gross profit (the difference between revenue and cost) to the construction in progress asset. That seems odd—why add *profit* to what is essentially an *inventory* account? The key here is that, when Harding recognizes gross profit, Harding is acting like it has sold some portion of the asset to the customer, but Harding keeps the asset in Harding's own balance sheet (in the construction in progress account) until delivery to the customer. Putting recognized gross profit into the construction in progress account just updates that account to reflect the total value (cost + gross profit = sales price) of the customer's asset. However, don't forget that the billings on construction contract account is contra to the construction in progress account. Over the life of the construction project, Harding will bill the customer for the entire sales price of the asset. Therefore, at the end of the contract, the construction in progress account (containing total cost and gross profit) and the billings on construction contract account (containing all amounts billed to the customer) will have equal balances that exactly offset to create a net value of zero.

The same journal entry is recorded to close out the billings and construction in progress accounts under the completed contract and percentage-of-completion methods.

When title officially passes to the customer, Harding will prepare a journal entry that removes the contract from its balance sheet by debiting billings on construction contract and crediting construction in progress for the entire value of the contract. As shown in Illustration 5–2C, the same journal entry is recorded to close out the billings on construction contract and construction in progress accounts under the completed contract and percentage-of-completion methods.

ILLUSTRATION 5–2C

Journal Entry to Close Billings and Construction in Progress Accounts

	2011	2012	2013
Billings on construction contract			5,000,000
Construction in progress			5,000,000
To close accounts.			

Now that we've seen how gross profit is recognized for long-term contracts, let's consider how the timing of that recognition differs between the completed contract and percentage-of-completion methods.

TIMING OF GROSS PROFIT RECOGNITION UNDER THE COMPLETED CONTRACT METHOD.

The timing of gross profit recognition under the completed contract method is simple. As the name implies, all revenues and expenses related to the project are recognized when the contract is completed. As shown in Illustration 5–2B and in the T-accounts below, completion occurs in 2013 for our Harding example. Prior to then, construction in progress includes only costs, showing a balance of $1,500,000 and $2,500,000 of cost at the end of 2011 and 2012, respectively, and including $4,100,000 of cost when the project is completed in 2013. Harding includes an additional $900,000 of gross profit in construction in progress when the project is completed in 2013 because the asset is viewed as "sold" on that date. The company records revenue of $5,000,000, cost of construction (similar to cost of goods sold) of $4,100,000, and the resulting $900,000 gross profit on that date.

> Under the completed contract method, profit is not recognized until the project is completed.

> **FINANCIAL**
> **Reporting Case**
>
> Q2, p. 233
>
> Under the completed contract method, construction in progress is updated to include gross profit at the end of the life of the contract.

Completed Contract

	Construction in Progress		Billings on Construction Contract	
2011 construction costs	1,500,000		1,200,000	2011 billings
End balance, 2011	1,500,000		2,000,000	2012 billings
2012 construction costs	1,000,000		1,800,000	2013 billings
End balance, 2012	2,500,000		5,000,000	Balance, before closing
2013 construction costs	1,600,000			
2013 gross profit	900,000			
Balance, before closing	5,000,000			

TIMING OF GROSS PROFIT RECOGNITION UNDER THE PERCENTAGE-OF-COMPLETION METHOD.

Using the percentage-of-completion method we recognize a portion of the estimated gross profit each period based on progress to date. How should progress to date be estimated?

One approach is to use *output* measures like units of production. For example, with a multi-year contract to deliver airplanes we might recognize progress according to the number of planes delivered. Another example of an output measure is recognizing portions of revenue associated with achieving particular milestones specified in a sales contract. Accounting guidance[18] states a preference for output measures when they can be established, arguing that they are more directly and reliably related to assessing progress than are input measures.

Another approach is to use an *input* measure like the "cost-to-cost ratio," by which progress to date is estimated by calculating the percentage of estimated total cost that has been incurred to date. Similar input measures might be used instead, like the number of labor hours incurred to date compared to estimated total hours. One advantage of input measures is that they capture progress on long-term contracts that may not translate easily into simple output measures. For example, a natural output measure for highway construction might be finished miles of road, but that measure could be deceptive if not all miles of road require the same effort. A highway contract for the state of Arizona would likely pay the contractor more for miles of road blasted through the mountains than for miles paved across flat dessert, and a cost-to-cost approach reflects that difference. Recent research suggests that the cost-to-cost input measure is most common in practice.[19]

> Under the percentage-of-completion method, profit is recognized over the life of the project as the project is completed.

> Progress to date can be estimated as the proportion of the project's cost incurred to date divided by total estimated costs, or by relying on an engineer's or architect's estimate.

---

[18]FASB ASC 605–35–25–71: Revenue Recognition–Construction–Type and Production-Type Contracts–Recognition–Input and Output Measures (previously "Accounting for Performance of Construction-Type and Certain Production-Type Contracts," *Statement of Position No. 81-1* (New York: AICPA, 1981)).

[19]R. K. Larson and K. L. Brown, 2004, "Where Are We with Long-Term Contract Accounting?" *Accounting Horizons*, September, pp. 207–219.

Regardless of the specific approach used to estimate progress to date, under the percentage-of-completion method we determine the amount of gross profit recognized in each period using the following logic:

$$\begin{pmatrix} \text{Gross profit} \\ \text{recognized this} \\ \text{period} \end{pmatrix} = \begin{pmatrix} \text{Total estimated} \\ \text{gross profit} \end{pmatrix} \times \begin{pmatrix} \text{Percentage completed} \\ \text{to date} \end{pmatrix} - \begin{pmatrix} \text{Gross profit} \\ \text{recognized in} \\ \text{prior periods} \end{pmatrix}$$

where total estimated gross profit = total estimated revenue – total estimated cost.

Illustration 5–2D shows the calculation of gross profit for each of the years for our Harding Construction Company example, with progress to date estimated using the cost-to-cost ratio. Refer to the bottom part of Illustration 5–2B to see the journal entries used to recognize gross profit in each period, and the T-accounts below Illustration 5–2D to see that the gross profit recognized in each period is added to the construction in progress account.

ILLUSTRATION 5–2D		2011	2012	2013
Percentage-of-Completion Method—Allocation of Gross Profit to Each Period	**Contract price**	$5,000,000	$5,000,000	$5,000,000
	Construction costs:			
	Actual costs incurred during the year	$1,500,000	$1,000,000	$1,600,000
	Actual costs incurred in prior years	–0–	1,500,000	2,500,000
	Cumulative actual costs incurred to date	$1,500,000	$2,500,000	$4,100,000
	Estimated remaining costs to complete	2,250,000	1,500,000	–0–
	Total costs (actual + estimated)	$3,750,000	$4,000,000	$4,100,000
	Total gross profit (contract price – total costs)	$1,250,000	$1,000,000	$ 900,000
	Multiplied by:	×	×	×
	Percentage-of-completion: Actual costs to date divided by the estimated total project cost	$\left(\dfrac{\$1,500,000}{\$3,750,000}\right)$ = 40%	$\left(\dfrac{\$2,500,000}{\$4,000,000}\right)$ = 62.5%	$\left(\dfrac{\$4,100,000}{\$4,100,000}\right)$ = 100%
	Equals:			
	Gross profit earned to date	$ 500,000	$ 625,000	$ 900,000
	Less:			
	Gross profit recognized in prior periods	–0–	(500,000)	(625,000)
	Equals:			
	Gross profit recognized currently	$ 500,000	$ 125,000	$ 275,000

Percentage-of-Completion

Under the percentage-of-completion method, construction in progress is updated each period to include gross profit.

	Construction in Progress		Billings on Construction Contract	
2011 construction costs	1,500,000		1,200,000	2011 billings
2011 gross profit	500,000		2,000,000	2012 billings
End balance, 2011	2,000,000		1,800,000	2013 billings
2012 construction costs	1,000,000		5,000,000	Balance, before closing
2012 gross profit	125,000			
End balance, 2012	3,125,000			
2013 construction costs	1,600,000			
2013 gross profit	275,000			
Balance, before closing	5,000,000			

In the income statement, we separate the gross profit into its two components: revenue and cost of construction.

Income statements are more informative if the sales revenue and cost components of gross profit are reported rather than the net figure alone. So, the income statement for each year will report the appropriate revenue and cost of construction amounts. For example, in 2011, the gross profit of $500,000 consists of revenue of $2,000,000 (40% of the $5,000,000 contract price) less the $1,500,000 cost of construction. In subsequent periods, we calculate revenue by multiplying the percentage of completion by the contract price and then subtracting revenue recognized in prior periods, similar to the way we calculate gross profit each period. The cost of construction, then, is the difference between revenue and gross profit. In most cases, cost of construction also equals the construction costs incurred during the period.[20] The table in Illustration 5–2E shows the revenue and cost of construction recognized in each of the three years of our example. Of course, as you can see in this illustration, we could have initially determined the gross profit by first calculating revenue and then subtracting cost of construction.[21]

		ILLUSTRATION 5–2E
2011		Percentage-of-Completion Method—Allocation of Revenue and Cost of Construction to Each Period
Revenue recognized ($5,000,000 × 40%)	$2,000,000	
Cost of construction	(1,500,000)	
Gross profit	$ 500,000	
2012		
Revenue recognized to date ($5,000,000 × 62.5%)	$3,125,000	
Less: revenue recognized in 2011	2,000,000	
Revenue recognized	$1,125,000	
Cost of construction	(1,000,000)	
Gross profit	$ 125,000	
2013		
Revenue recognized to date ($5,000,000 × 100%)	$5,000,000	
Less: revenue recognized in 2011 and 2012	3,125,000	
Revenue recognized	$1,875,000	
Cost of construction	(1,600,000)	
Gross profit	$ 275,000	

A Comparison of the Completed Contract and Percentage-of-Completion Methods

INCOME RECOGNITION. Illustration 5–2B shows journal entries that would determine the amount of revenue, cost, and therefore gross profit that would appear in the income statement under the percentage-of-completion and completed contract methods. Comparing the gross profit patterns produced by each method of revenue recognition demonstrates the essential difference between them:

	Percentage-of-Completion	Completed Contract
Gross profit recognized:		
2011	$500,000	–0–
2012	125,000	–0–
2013	275,000	$900,000
Total gross profit	**$900,000**	**$900,000**

The same total amount of profit or loss is recognized under both the completed contract and the percentage-of-completion methods, but the timing of recognition differs.

The percentage-of-completion method provides a more realistic measure of a project's periodic profitability and almost always is used for long-term construction contracts.

Although both methods yield identical gross profit of $900,000 for the entire 3-year period, the timing differs. The completed contract method defers all gross profit to 2013, when the

---

[20]Cost of construction does not equal the construction costs incurred during the year when a loss is projected on the entire project. This situation is illustrated later in the chapter.

[21]As a practical matter, if the percentage of completion figure is rounded we may calculate different amounts of revenue by (a) directly calculating revenue using the percentage of completion, and (b) indirectly calculating revenue by first calculating gross profit using the percentage of completion and then calculating revenue by adding gross profit to cost of construction. In that case, given that gross profit is defined as revenue minus cost, it is best to use approach (a) and first calculate revenue directly, solving for gross profit by subtracting cost of construction from revenue.

project is completed. Obviously, the percentage-of-completion method provides a better measure of the company's economic activity and progress over the three-year period. That's why the percentage-of-completion method is preferred, and, as mentioned previously, the completed contract method should be used only when the company is unable to make dependable estimates of future costs necessary to apply the percentage-of-completion method.[22]

BALANCE SHEET RECOGNITION. The balance sheet presentation for the construction-related accounts by both methods is shown in Illustration 5–2F. The balance in the construction in progress account differs between methods because of the earlier gross profit recognition that occurs under the percentage-of-completion method.

ILLUSTRATION 5–2F Balance Sheet Presentation	Balance Sheet (End of Year)		
		2011	**2012**
Percentage-of-Completion:			
Current assets:			
Accounts receivable		$200,000	$800,000
Costs and profit ($2,000,000) in excess of billings ($1,200,000)		800,000	
Current liabilities:			
Billings ($3,200,000) in excess of costs and profit ($3,125,000)			$75,000
Completed Contract:			
Current assets:			
Accounts receivable		$200,000	$800,000
Costs ($1,500,000) in excess of billings ($1,200,000)		$300,000	
Current liabilities:			
Billings ($3,200,000) in excess of costs ($2,500,000)			$700,000

Billings on construction contract are subtracted from construction in progress to determine balance sheet presentation.

In the balance sheet, the construction in progress (CIP) account (containing costs and profit) is offset against the billings on construction contract account, with CIP > Billings shown as an asset and Billings > CIP shown as a liability. Because a company may have some contracts that have a net asset position and others that have a net liability position, we usually will see both net assets and net liabilities shown in a balance sheet at the same time.

Construction in progress in excess of billings essentially represents an unbilled receivable. Sometimes companies include it as a component of accounts receivable in their balance sheets, or as part of inventory. The construction company is incurring construction costs (and recognizing gross profit using the percentage-of-completion method) for which it will be paid by the buyer. If the construction company bills the buyer an amount exactly equal to these costs (and profits recognized) then the accounts receivable balance properly reflects the claims of the construction company. If, however, the amount billed is less than the costs incurred (plus profits recognized) the difference represents the remaining claim to cash—an asset.

Disclosure of the method used to account for long-term contracts will appear in the summary of significant accounting policies.

On the other hand, *Billings in excess of construction in progress* essentially indicates that the overbilled accounts receivable overstates the amount of the claim to cash earned to that date and must be reported as a liability. This is similar to the unearned revenue liability that is recorded when a customer pays for a product or service in advance. The advance is properly shown as a liability representing the obligation to provide the good or service in the future.

The first disclosure note to any set of financial statements usually is a summary of significant accounting policies. This note discloses the method the company uses to account for its long-term contracts. As an example of this, Graphic 5–10 shows the disclosure note that appeared in a recent annual report of **Fluor Corporation**.

---

[22]For income tax purposes, the completed contract method may be used for home construction contracts and certain other real estate construction contracts. All other contracts must use the percentage-of-completion method.

GRAPHIC 5–10

Disclosure of Revenue Recognition Policy for Construction Contracts—Fluor Corporation

Real World Financials

Notes: Engineering and Construction Contracts (in part)

The company recognizes engineering and construction contract revenues using the percentage-of-completion method, based primarily on contract costs incurred to date compared with total estimated contract costs. . . . Changes to total estimated contract costs or losses, if any, are recognized in the period in which they are determined. Revenue recognized in excess of amounts billed is classified as current assets under contract work in progress. Amounts billed to clients in excess of revenues recognized to date are classified as current liabilities under advance billings on contracts.

LONG-TERM CONTRACT LOSSES. The Harding Construction Company example above involves a situation in which a profit was realized on the construction contract. Unfortunately, losses sometimes occur on long-term contracts. As a prelude to the following discussion, notice in Graphic 5–10 that Fluor Corporation recognizes losses "in the period in which they are determined."

Periodic Loss Occurs for Profitable Project. When using the percentage-of-completion method, a loss sometimes must be recognized in at least one period over the life of the project even though the project as a whole is expected to be profitable. We determine the loss in precisely the same way we determined the profit in profitable years. For example, assume the same $5 million contract for Harding Construction Company described in Illustration 5–2 but with the following cost information:

	2011	2012	2013
Actual costs incurred during the year	$1,500,000	$1,260,000	$1,840,000
Actual costs incurred in prior years	–0–	1,500,000	2,760,000
Cumulative actual costs incurred to date	1,500,000	2,760,000	4,600,000
Estimated costs to complete at end of year	2,250,000	1,840,000	–0–
Total costs (actual + estimated)	$3,750,000	$4,600,000	$4,600,000

At the end of 2011, gross profit of $500,000 (revenue of $2,000,000 less cost of construction of $1,500,000) is recognized as previously determined.

At the end of 2012, the company now forecasts a total profit of $400,000 ($5,000,000 − $4,600,000) on the project and, at that time, the project is estimated to be 60% complete ($2,760,000 ÷ $4,600,000). Applying this percentage to the anticipated gross profit of $400,000 results in a gross profit *to date* of $240,000. But remember, a gross profit of $500,000 was recognized in 2011.

This situation is treated as a *change in accounting estimate* because it resulted from a change in the estimation of costs to complete at the end of 2011. Costs to complete—$4,600,000—were much higher than the 2011 year-end estimate of $3,750,000. Recall from our discussion of changes in accounting estimates in Chapter 4 that we don't go back and restate the prior year's gross profit. Instead, the 2012 income statement would report *a loss of $260,000* ($500,000 − 240,000) so that the cumulative amount recognized to date totals $240,000 of gross profit. The loss consists of revenue of $1,000,000 ($5,000,000 × 60% = $3,000,000 less 2011 revenue of $2,000,000) less cost of construction of $1,260,000 (cost incurred in 2012). The following journal entry records the loss:

Cost of construction	1,260,000	
Revenue from long-term contracts (below)		1,000,000
Construction in progress (loss)		260,000

Recognized losses on long-term contracts reduce the construction in progress account.

The 2013 income statement would report a gross profit of $160,000 determined as follows:

Project gross profit	$400,000
Less: Gross profit recognized in prior periods ($500,000 − 260,000)	(240,000)
2013 gross profit	$160,000

The 2013 gross profit comprises $2,000,000 in revenue ($5,000,000 less revenue of $3,000,000 recognized in 2008 and 2009) and $1,840,000 in cost of construction (cost incurred in 2013).

Of course, when using the completed contract method, no profit or loss is recorded in 2011 or 2012. Instead, a $400,000 gross profit (revenue of $5,000,000 and cost of construction of $4,600,000) is recognized in 2013.

Loss Is Projected on the Entire Project. When using either the percentage-of-completion or completed contract methods, a more conservative approach is indicated when an overall loss is projected on the entire contract. Again consider the Harding Construction Company example but with the following cost information:

	2011	2012	2013
Actual costs incurred during the year	$1,500,000	$1,260,000	$2,440,000
Actual costs incurred in prior years	–0–	1,500,000	2,760,000
Cumulative actual costs incurred to date	1,500,000	2,760,000	5,200,000
Estimated costs to complete at end of year	2,250,000	2,340,000	–0–
Total costs (actual + estimated)	$3,750,000	$5,100,000	$5,200,000

An estimated loss on a long-term contract is fully recognized in the first period the loss is anticipated, regardless of the revenue recognition method used.

At the end of 2012, revised costs indicate a loss of $100,000 for the entire project ($5,000,000 − 5,100,000). In this situation, the *total* anticipated loss must be recognized in 2012 for both the percentage-of-completion method and the completed contract method. As a gross profit of $500,000 was recognized in 2011 using the percentage-of-completion method, *a $600,000 loss is recognized in 2012* so that the cumulative amount recognized to date totals a $100,000 loss. Once again, this situation is treated as a change in accounting estimate, with no restatement of 2011 income. If the completed contract method is used, because no gross profit is recognized in 2011, the $100,000 loss for the project is recognized in 2012 by debiting loss from long-term contracts and crediting construction in progress for $100,000.

Why recognize the estimated overall loss of $100,000 in 2012, rather than at the end of the contract? If the loss was not recognized in 2012, construction in progress would be valued at an amount greater than the company expects to realize from the contract. To avoid that problem, the construction in progress account is reduced to $2,660,000 ($2,760,000 in costs to date less $100,000 estimated total loss). This amount combined with the estimated costs to complete of $2,340,000 equals the realizable contract price of $5,000,000. Recognizing losses on long-term projects in the period the losses become known is equivalent to measuring inventory at the lower of cost or market.

The pattern of gross profit (loss) over the contract period for the two methods is summarized in the following table. Notice that an unanticipated increase in costs of $100,000 causes a further loss of $100,000 to be recognized in 2013.

	Percentage-of-Completion	Completed Contract
Gross profit (loss) recognized:		
2011	$ 500,000	–0–
2012	(600,000)	$(100,000)
2013	(100,000)	(100,000)
Total project loss	$(200,000)	$(200,000)

The table in Illustration 5–2G shows the revenue and cost of construction recognized in each of the three years using the percentage-of-completion method.

Revenue is recognized in the usual way by multiplying a percentage of completion by the total contract price. In situations where a loss is expected on the entire project, cost of construction for the period will no longer be equal to cost incurred during the period. The easiest way to compute cost of construction is to add the amount of the recognized loss to the amount of revenue recognized. For example, in 2012 revenue

2011		
Revenue recognized ($5,000,000 × 40%)		$2,000,000
Costs of construction		(1,500,000)
Gross profit		$ 500,000
2012		
Revenue recognized to date ($5,000,000 × 54.12%)*	$2,706,000	
Less: Revenue recognized in 2011	(2,000,000)	
Revenue recognized		$ 706,000
Cost of construction†		(1,306,000)
Loss		$ (600,000)
2013		
Revenue recognized to date ($5,000,000 × 100%)	$5,000,000	
Less: Revenue recognized in 2011 and 2012	(2,706,000)	
Revenue recognized		$2,294,000
Cost of construction†		(2,394,000)
Loss		$ (100,000)

ILLUSTRATION 5–2G

Percentage-of-Completion Method: Allocation of Revenue and Cost of Construction to Each Period—Loss on Entire Project

*$2,760,000 ÷ $5,100,000 = 54.12%
†The difference between revenue and loss

recognized of $706,000 is added to the loss of $600,000 to arrive at the cost of construction of $1,306,000.[23]

The journal entries to record the losses in 2012 and 2013 are as follows:

2012		
Cost of construction	1,306,000	
Revenue from long-term contracts		706,000
Construction in progress (loss)		600,000
2013		
Cost of construction	2,394,000	
Revenue from long-term contracts		2,294,000
Construction in progress (loss)		100,000

Recognized losses on long-term contracts reduce the construction in progress account.

Using the completed contract method, no revenue or cost of construction is recognized until the contract is complete. In 2012, a loss on long-term contracts (an income statement account) of $100,000 is recognized. In 2013, the income statement will report revenue of $5,000,000 and cost of construction of $5,100,000, thus reporting the additional loss of $100,000. The journal entries to record the losses in 2012 and 2013 are as follows:

2012		
Loss on long-term contracts	100,000	
Construction in progress (loss)		100,000
2013		
Cost of construction	5,100,000	
Revenue from long-term contracts		5,000,000
Construction in progress (loss)		100,000

[23]The cost of construction also can be determined as follows:

Loss to date (100% recognized)		$ 100,000
Add:		
Remaining total project cost, not including the loss		
($5,100,000 − 100,000)	$5,000,000	
Multiplied by the percentage of completion	× .5412*	2,706,000
Total		2,806,000
Less: Cost of construction recognized in 2011		(1,500,000)
Cost of construction recognized in 2012		$1,306,000

*$2,760,000 ÷ $5,100,000

You can see from this example that use of the percentage-of-completion method in this case produces a large overstatement of income in 2011 and a large understatement in 2012 caused by a change in the estimation of future costs. These estimate revisions happen occasionally. However, recall that if management believes they are unable to make dependable forecasts of future costs, the completed contract method should be used.

● LO7

IFRS ILLUSTRATION

INTERNATIONAL FINANCIAL REPORTING STANDARDS

Long-Term Construction Contracts. *IAS No. 11* governs revenue recognition for long-term construction contracts.[24] Like U.S. GAAP, that standard requires the use of the percentage-of-completion method when reliable estimates can be made. However, unlike U.S. GAAP, *IAS No. 11* requires the use of the cost recovery method rather than the completed contract method when reliable estimates can't be made.[25] Under the cost recovery method, contract costs are expensed as incurred, and an offsetting amount of contract revenue is recognized to the extent that it is probable that costs will be recoverable from the customer. No gross profit is recognized until all costs have been recovered, which is why this method is also sometimes called the "zero-profit method." Note that under both the completed contract and cost recovery methods no gross profit is recognized until the contract is essentially completed, but revenue and construction costs will be recognized earlier under the cost recovery method than under the completed contract method. Also, under both methods an expected loss is recognized immediately.

To see this difference between the completed contract and cost recovery methods, here is a version of Illustration 5–2B that compares revenue, cost and gross profit recognition under the two methods:

	2011	2012	2013
Completed Contract			
Construction in progress (gross profit).................			900,000
Cost of construction.........			4,100,000
Revenue from long-term contracts...			5,000,000
To record gross profit.			
Cost Recovery			
Construction in progress (gross profit).................			900,000
Cost of construction.........	1,500,000	1,000,000	1,600,000
Revenue from long-term contracts...	1,500,000	1,000,000	2,500,000
To record gross profit.			

Revenue recognition occurs earlier under the cost recovery method than under the completed contract method, but gross profit recognition occurs at the end of the contract for both methods. As a result, gross profit as a percentage of revenue differs between the two methods at various points in the life of the contract.

---

[24]"Construction Contracts," *International Accounting Standard No. 11* (IASCF), as amended, effective January 1, 2009.

[25]Earlier in this chapter we referred to the "cost recovery method" in a different circumstance—when a company had already delivered a product to a customer but had to delay gross profit recognition until a point after delivery because of an inability to make reliable estimates of uncollectible accounts. In that case, gross profit only could be recognized after costs had been recovered (and cash collections exceeded cost of goods sold). IFRS' use of "cost recovery method" is similar, in that gross profit recognition is delayed until after cost has been recovered, but note that in this case the product is being constructed for the customer and therefore has not yet been delivered.

CONCEPT REVIEW EXERCISE

During 2011, the Samuelson Construction Company began construction on an office building for the City of Gernon. The contract price is $8,000,000 and the building will take approximately 18 months to complete. Completion is scheduled for early in 2013. The company's fiscal year ends on December 31.

The following is a year-by-year recap of construction costs incurred and the estimated costs to complete the project as of the end of each year. Progress billings and cash collections also are indicated.

	2011	2012	2013
Actual costs incurred during the year	$1,500,000	$4,500,000	$1,550,000
Actual costs incurred in prior years	–0–	1,500,000	6,000,000
Cumulative actual costs incurred to date	1,500,000	6,000,000	7,550,000
Estimated costs to complete at end of year	4,500,000	1,500,000	–0–
Total costs (actual + estimated)	$6,000,000	$7,500,000	$7,550,000
Billings made during the year	$1,400,000	$5,200,000	$1,400,000
Cash collections during year	1,000,000	4,000,000	3,000,000

Required:

1. Determine the amount of gross profit or loss to be recognized in each of the three years applying both the percentage-of-completion and completed contract methods.
2. Prepare the necessary summary journal entries for each of the three years to account for construction costs incurred, recognized revenue and cost of construction, contract billings, and cash collections and to close the construction accounts in 2013 using the percentage-of-completion method only.
3. Prepare a partial balance sheet for 2011 and 2012 to include all construction-related accounts using the percentage-of-completion method.

1. Determine the amount of gross profit or loss to be recognized in each of the three years applying both the percentage-of-completion and completed contract methods.

	Percentage-of-Completion Method		
	2011	2012	2013
Contract price	$8,000,000	$8,000,000	$8,000,000
Less: total cost*	6,000,000	$7,500,000	7,550,000
Total estimated gross profit to date	2,000,000	500,000	450,000
Multiplied by % of completion**	25%	80%	100%
Gross profit recognized to date	500,000	400,000	450,000
Less gross profit recognized in prior years	–0–	(500,000)	(400,000)
Gross profit (loss) recognized	$ 500,000	$ (100,000)	$ 50,000

*Estimated in 2011 & 2012; Actual in 2013.
**Estimates of percentage-of-completion:

2011	2012	2013
$\frac{1,500,000}{6,000,000} = 25\%$	$\frac{6,000,000}{7,500,000} = 80\%$	Project complete

	Completed Contract Method		
	2011	2012	2013
Gross profit recognized	–0–	–0–	$450,000

2. Prepare the necessary summary journal entries for each of the three years to account for construction costs incurred, recognized revenue and cost of construction, contract billings, and cash collections and to close the construction accounts in 2013 using the percentage-of-completion method only.

	2011		2012		2013	
Construction in progress	1,500,000		4,500,000		1,550,000	
Cash, materials, etc.		1,500,000		4,500,000		1,550,000
To record construction costs.						
Construction in progress (gross profit)	500,000				50,000	
Cost of construction	1,500,000				1,550,000	
Revenue from long-term						
contracts (below)		2,000,000				1,600,000
To record gross profit.						
Cost of construction			4,500,000			
Revenue from long-term						
contracts (below)				4,400,000		
Construction in progress (loss)				100,000		
To record loss.						
Accounts receivable	1,400,000		5,200,000		1,400,000	
Billings on construction contract		1,400,000		5,200,000		1,400,000
To record progress billings.						
Cash	1,000,000		4,000,000		3,000,000	
Accounts receivable		1,000,000		4,000,000		3,000,000
To record cash collections.						
Billings on construction contract					8,000,000	
Construction in progress						8,000,000
To close accounts.						

Revenue recognized:

2011:	$8,000,000 \times 25\%$ =	$2,000,000
2012:	$8,000,000 \times 80\%$ =	$6,400,000
	Less: Revenue recognized in 2011	(2,000,000)
	Revenue recognized in 2012	$4,400,000
2013:	$8,000,000 \times 100\%$ =	$8,000,000
	Less: Revenue recognized in 2011 and 2012	(6,400,000)
	Revenue recognized in 2013	$1,600,000

3. Prepare a partial balance sheet for 2011 and 2012 to include all construction related accounts using the percentage-of-completion method.

Balance Sheet
(End of Year)

	2011	2012
Current assets:		
Accounts receivable	$400,000	$1,600,000
Costs and profit ($2,000,000) in		
excess of billings ($1,400,000)	600,000	
Current liabilities:		
Billings ($6,600,000) in excess of costs and		
profit ($6,400,000)		200,000

Industry-Specific Revenue Issues

● LO5

The previous sections addressed situations when revenue is recognized either at a point in time after the earnings process is virtually complete or over time during the earnings process. We now look at situations that require revenue recognition using a combination of the two approaches.

Software and Other Multiple-Deliverable Arrangements

The software industry is a key economic component of our economy. **Microsoft** alone reported revenues in excess of $58 billion for its 2009 fiscal year. Yet, the recognition of software revenues has been a controversial accounting issue. The controversy stems from the way software vendors typically package their products. It is not unusual for these companies to sell multiple software deliverables in a bundle for a lump-sum contract price. The bundle often includes product, upgrades, postcontract customer support, and other services. The critical accounting question concerns the timing of revenue recognition.

The American Institute of Certified Public Accountants (AICPA) issued authoritative guidance in this area. The AICPA position indicates that if a software arrangement includes multiple elements, the revenue from the arrangement should be allocated to the various elements based on "vendor-specific objective evidence" ("VSOE") of fair values of the individual elements. It doesn't matter what separate prices are indicated in the multiple-element contract. Rather, the VSOE of fair values are the sales prices of the elements when sold separately by that vendor. If VSOE doesn't exist, revenue recognition is deferred until VSOE is available or until all elements of the arrangement are delivered.[26]

For example, suppose that a vendor sold software to a customer for $90,000. As part of the contract, the vendor promises to provide "free" technical support over the next six months. However, the vendor sells the same software without technical support for $80,000, and the vendor sells a stand-alone six-month technical support contract for $20,000, so those products would sell for $100,000 if sold separately. Based on that VSOE, the software comprises 80% of the total fair values, and the technical support 20%. Prior to the AICPA guidance, some vendors were recognizing the entire $90,000 as revenue when the initial software was delivered. Now, the $90,000 contract price must be allocated based on VSOE. Therefore, the seller would recognize $72,000 ($90,000 × 80%) in revenue up front when the software is delivered, and defer the remaining $18,000 ($90,000 × 20%) and recognize it ratably over the next six months as the technical support service is provided. If VSOE was not available, the vendor couldn't recognize any revenue initially, and instead would recognize the entire $90,000 ratably over the six-month period.

> Generally, a portion of the proceeds received from the sale of software is deferred and recognized as revenue in future periods.

These revenue deferrals can be material. For example, in its 2009 balance sheet, Microsoft reported a liability for unearned (deferred) software revenue in excess of $14 billion.

More recently, the FASB's Emerging Issues Task Force (EITF) issued guidance to broaden the application of this basic perspective to other arrangements that involve "multiple deliverables."[27] Examples of such arrangements include products that contain both hardware and software that are essential to the functioning of the product, such as computers and PDAs that are always sold with an operating system. Also included are other multiple-deliverable contracts such as sales of appliances with maintenance contracts, cellular phone contracts that come with a "free phone," and even painting services that include sales of paint as well as labor. A concern motivating the EITF was that companies were recognizing revenue too early for some parts of these arrangements. Now, as with software, sellers allocate total revenue from a multiple-deliverable arrangement to the parts of the arrangement that have stand-alone value to the customer on the basis of the relative stand-alone selling prices of the parts. Sellers must defer revenue recognition for parts that don't have stand-alone value, or whose value is contingent upon other undelivered parts. However, unlike with software, starting in fiscal years beginning after June 15, 2010, sellers will be able to *estimate* selling prices when they lack VSOE from stand-alone sales prices. This should allow earlier revenue recognition than would be the case if sellers had to have VSOE in order to recognize revenue.

As an example, consider the disclosure by **Affiliated Computer Services** in their 2009 annual report shown in Graphic 5–11.

---

[26]FASB ASC 985–605–25: Software–Revenue Recognition–Recognition (previously "Software Revenue Recognition," *Statement of Position 97-2* (New York: AICPA, 1997), p. 14).

[27]FASB ASC 605–25–25: Revenue Recognition–Multiple-Element Arrangements–Recognition (previously *EITF 08-1: Revenue Arrangements with Multiple Deliverables* (Stamford, Conn.: FASB, 2009), and *EITF 09-3: Applicability of AICPA Statement of Position 97-2 to Certain Arrangements That Include Software Elements* (Stamford, Conn.: FASB, 2009)).

GRAPHIC 5–11

Disclosure of Revenue Recognition Policy for Multiple Deliverables— Affiliated Computer Services

Real World Financials

Critical Accounting Policies (in part)

At times, we may contract with a client to provide more than one service; for instance, we may contract for an implementation or development project and also provide services or operate the system over a period of time. In these situations, we follow the guidance of Emerging Issues Task Force Issue No. 00-21, "Revenue Arrangements with Multiple Deliverables" ("EITF 00-21") [FASB ASC 605-25]. EITF 00-21 provides the methodology for separating the contract elements and allocating total arrangement consideration to the contract elements but does not stipulate the revenue recognition methodology that should be applied to these separate elements. Once the contract has been separated under the guidance of EITF 00-21 and arrangement consideration allocated, revenue recognition for each of the segments follows the applicable revenue recognition method, as described above. In certain instances where revenue cannot be allocated to a contract element delivered earlier than other elements, costs of delivery are deferred and recognized as the subsequent elements are delivered.

● LO7

INTERNATIONAL FINANCIAL REPORTING STANDARDS

Multiple-Deliverable Arrangements. IFRS contains very little guidance about multiple-deliverable arrangements. *IAS No. 18* simply states that: ". . . in certain circumstances, it is necessary to apply the recognition criteria to the separately identifiable components of a single transaction in order to reflect the substance of the transaction" and gives a couple of examples.[28] Allocations of total revenue to individual components are based on fair value, with no requirements to focus on VSOE. Also, IFRS tends to encourage focus on the underlying economics of revenue transactions, so particular contractual characteristics like contingencies may matter less under IFRS than they do under U.S. GAAP.

Franchise Sales

● LO5

The use of franchise arrangements has become increasingly popular in the United States over the past 30 years. Many retail outlets for fast food, restaurants, motels, and auto rental agencies are operated as franchises. In the franchise arrangements, the **franchisor,** for example **McDonald's Corporation**, grants to the **franchisee,** quite often an individual, the right to sell the franchisor's products and use its name for a specified period of time. The restaurant where you ate your last Big Mac was probably owned and operated by an individual under a franchise agreement, not by McDonald's Corporation.

The fees to be paid by the franchisee to the franchisor usually comprise (1) the *initial franchise fee* and (2) *continuing franchise fees.* The services to be performed by the franchisor in exchange for the initial franchise fee, in addition to the right to use its name and sell its products, might include assistance in finding a location, constructing the facilities, and training employees. The initial franchise fee usually is a fixed amount, but it may be payable in installments.

The continuing franchise fees are paid to the franchisor for continuing rights as well as for advertising and promotion and other services provided over the life of the franchise agreement. These fees sometimes are a fixed annual or monthly amount, a percentage of the volume of business done by the franchise, or a combination of both.

The continuing franchise fees usually do not present any accounting difficulty and are recognized by the franchisor as

> **FASB**
> Franchise fee revenue from an individual franchise sale ordinarily shall be recognized, with an appropriate provision for estimated uncollectible amounts, when all material services or conditions relating to the sale have been substantially performed or satisfied by the franchisor.[29]

---

[28]"Revenue" *International Accounting Standard No. 18* (IASCF,), as amended effective January 1, 2009, par. 13.
[29]FASB ASC 952–605–25: Franchisors–Revenue Recognition–Recognition (previously "Accounting for Franchise Fee Revenue," *Statement of Financial Accounting Standards No. 45* (Stamford, Conn.: FASB, 1981)).

revenue *over time* in the periods the services are performed by the franchisor, which generally corresponds to the periods they are received. The challenging revenue recognition issue pertains to the initial franchise fee. In the early 1960s and 1970s, many franchisors recognized the entire initial franchise fee as revenue in the period in which the contract was signed. In many cases, there were significant services to be performed and the fee was collectible in installments over an extended period of time creating uncertainty as to cash collection.

Specific guidelines for revenue recognition of the initial franchise fee are provided by GAAP. You should notice the similarity of these specific guidelines with those of the general revenue recognition guidelines we've discussed previously. A key to these conditions is the concept of *substantial performance*. It requires that substantially all of the initial services of the franchisor required by the franchise agreement be performed before the initial franchise fee can be recognized as revenue. The term *substantial* requires professional judgment on the part of the accountant. In situations when the initial franchise fee is collectible in installments, even after substantial performance has occurred, the installment sales or cost recovery methods should be used for profit recognition, if a reasonable estimate of uncollectibility cannot be made.

Consider the example in Illustration 5–3.

On March 31, 2011, the Red Hot Chicken Wing Corporation entered into a franchise agreement with Thomas Keller. In exchange for an initial franchise fee of $50,000, Red Hot will provide initial services to include the selection of a location, construction of the building, training of employees, and consulting services over several years. $10,000 is payable on March 31, 2011, with the remaining $40,000 payable in annual installments which include interest at an appropriate rate. In addition, the franchisee will pay continuing franchise fees of $1,000 per month for advertising and promotion provided by Red Hot, beginning immediately after the franchise begins operations. Thomas Keller opened his Red Hot franchise for business on September 30, 2011.	**ILLUSTRATION 5–3** Franchise Sales

INITIAL FRANCHISE FEE.   Assuming that the initial services to be performed by Red Hot subsequent to the contract signing are substantial but that collectibility of the installment receivable is reasonably certain, the following journal entry is recorded:

March 31, 2011
Cash	10,000	
Note receivable	40,000	
Unearned franchise fee revenue		50,000
To record franchise agreement and down payment.		

Unearned franchise fee revenue is a liability. It would be reduced to zero and revenue would be recognized when the initial services have been performed. This could occur in increments or at one point in time, depending on the circumstances.[30] For example, in our illustration, if substantial performance was deemed to have occurred when the franchise began operations, the following entry would be recorded:

Sept. 30, 2011
Unearned franchise fee revenue	50,000	
Franchise fee revenue		50,000
To recognize franchise fee revenue.		

If collectibility of the installment receivable is uncertain and there is no basis for estimating uncollectible amounts, the initial entry would record a credit to deferred franchise fee revenue which is then recognized as being earned using either the installment sales or cost recovery methods.

[30]Franchise agreements sometimes require that any payments made to the franchisor will be refunded if the franchise fails to open. If this condition is present, it would be an important factor in deciding whether to recognize revenue before the franchise opens.

CONTINUING FRANCHISE FEES. Continuing franchise fee revenue is recognized on a monthly basis as follows:

Cash (or accounts receivable)	1,000	
Service revenue		1,000
To recognize continuing franchise fee revenue.		

Expenses incurred by the franchisor in providing these continuing franchise services should be recognized in the same periods as the service revenue.

Other unique industry-specific revenue recognition situations exist besides those we have discussed. The FASB and AICPA have issued detailed revenue recognition guidance for such industries as insurance, record and music, cable television, and motion pictures.[31] These industry standards are beyond the scope of this text. However, in each case, the objective is the same: to recognize revenue in the period or periods that the revenue-generating activities of the company are performed.

ADDITIONAL CONSIDERATION

In certain circumstances, revenue is recognized at the completion of the production process (before delivery). This approach generally is used by companies that deal in precious metals, and ". . . agricultural, mineral, and other products, units of which are interchangeable and have an immediate marketability at quoted prices. . . ."[32] This is called the *production basis* of recognizing revenue and is accomplished by writing inventory up from cost to market value.

Recall that in a typical manufacturing situation, revenue is not recognized at the completion of the production process due to significant uncertainty as to the collectibility of the asset to be received. We don't know if the product will be sold, nor the selling price, nor the buyer if eventually sold. These uncertainties are not significant when there is immediate marketability at quoted market prices for products like precious metals.

In cases when the production basis of recognizing revenue is used, full disclosure of the fact is required.

WHERE WE'RE HEADED

The FASB and IASB are working together on a comprehensive revenue-recognition standard.

● LO7

The FASB and IASB are currently working on a new, comprehensive approach to revenue recognition.[33] Why? Currently, the FASB has over 100 revenue-related standards that sometimes contradict each other and that treat similar economic events differently. The IASB has two primary standards (*IAS No. 11* and *IAS No. 18*) that also sometimes contradict each other and that don't offer guidance in some important areas (like multiple deliverables).[34] And, although both the FASB and IASB define revenue in terms of flows of assets and liabilities, the FASB guidance typically bases revenue recognition on the earnings process, while the IASB standards base it on the transfer of the risks and rewards of ownership, which can lead to different outcomes. So, the accounting guidance on revenue recognition could use some improvement.

---

[31]FASB ASC 944: Financial Services–Insurance (previously "Accounting and Reporting by Insurance Enterprises," *Statement of Financial Accounting Standards No. 60* (Stamford, Conn.: FASB, 1982)); FASB ASC 928—Entertainment–Music (previously "Financial Reporting in the Record and Music Industry," *Statement of Financial Accounting Standards No. 50* (Stamford, Conn.: FASB, 1981)); FASB ASC 922: Entertainment—Cable Television (previously "Financial Reporting by Cable Television Companies," *Statement of Financial Accounting Standards No. 51* (Stamford, Conn.: FASB, 1981)); FASB ASC 928: Entertainment–Films (previously "Accounting by Producers or Distributors of Films," *Statement of Position 00-2* (New York: AICPA, 2000)).
[32]FASB ASC 330–10–35–16 : Inventory–Overall–Subsequent Measurement–Stating Inventories Above Cost (previously "Restatement and Revision of Accounting Research Bulletins," *Accounting Research Bulletin No. 43* (New York: AICPA, 1953), Chapter 4, par. 16).
[33]For a complete description of this project, see **http://www.fasb.org/revenue_recognition.shtml**.
[34]"Construction Contracts," *International Accounting Standard No. 11* (IASCF), as amended effective January 1, 2009, and "Revenue," *International Accounting Standard No. 18* (IASCF), as amended effective January 1, 2009.

The Boards are working on a new approach that defines revenue as resulting from inflows and outflows of assets and liabilities that underlie the "performance obligations" inherent in a contract between a company (the "seller") and its customer. Revenue is *recognized* when the seller satisfies a performance obligation by transferring a promised asset (a good or a service) to the customer, with "transfer" having occurred when the customer controls the asset (a service is viewed as an asset that is consumed immediately by the customer, so it typically doesn't appear in the customer's balance sheet as an asset). Revenue is *measured* at the transaction price (the amount of consideration that the customer promises when the contract is made). If a contract requires that the seller provide multiple goods and services, the seller estimates the stand-alone selling price of each of those goods and services and allocates the transaction price to each good and service on that basis.

For many types of sales arrangements, adopting this new approach would not change current practice much, but in some areas it would change practice considerably. For example, because revenue is recognized only when the seller transfers control of the asset to the buyer, percentage-of-completion accounting would not be allowed unless the customer controls the asset being constructed. On the other hand, some performance obligations that now are ignored from a revenue recognition standpoint (like a warranty that is not sold separately, which we will discuss in Chapter 13) would now be viewed as producing revenue, with estimation necessary to allocate part of the transaction price to each performance obligation.

It is likely that this comprehensive revenue standard will be controversial, and it could change or even be abandoned before implementation. However, the Boards appear committed to improving accounting in this area.

PROFITABILITY ANALYSIS

PART B

Chapter 3 provided an overview of financial statement analysis and introduced some of the common ratios used in risk analysis to investigate a company's liquidity and long-term solvency. We now introduce ratios related to profitability analysis.

Activity Ratios

One key to profitability is how well a company manages and utilizes its assets. Some ratios are designed to evaluate a company's effectiveness in managing assets. Of particular interest are the activity, or turnover ratios, of certain assets. The greater the number of times an asset turns over—the higher the ratio—the fewer assets are required to maintain a given level of activity (revenue). Given that a company incurs costs to finance its assets with debt (paying interest) or equity (paying dividends), high turnovers are usually attractive.

Activity ratios measure a company's efficiency in managing its assets.

Although, in concept, the activity or turnover can be measured for any asset, activity ratios are most frequently calculated for total assets, accounts receivable, and inventory. These ratios are calculated as follows:

$$\text{Asset turnover ratio} = \frac{\text{Net sales}}{\text{Average total assets}}$$

$$\text{Receivables turnover ratio} = \frac{\text{Net sales}}{\text{Average accounts receivable (net)}}$$

$$\text{Inventory turnover ratio} = \frac{\text{Cost of goods sold}}{\text{Average inventory}}$$

ASSET TURNOVER.   A broad measure of asset efficiency is the **asset turnover ratio.** The ratio is computed by dividing a company's net sales or revenues by the average total assets available for use during a period. The denominator, average assets, is determined by adding beginning and ending total assets and dividing by two. The asset turnover ratio provides an indication of how efficiently a company utilizes all of its assets to generate revenue.

The *asset turnover ratio* measures a company's efficiency in using assets to generate revenue.

The *receivables turnover ratio* offers an indication of how quickly a company is able to collect its accounts receivable.

RECEIVABLES TURNOVER.   The receivables turnover ratio is calculated by dividing a period's net credit sales by the average net accounts receivable. Because income statements seldom distinguish between cash sales and credit sales, this ratio usually is computed using total net sales as the numerator. The denominator, average accounts receivable, is determined by adding beginning and ending net accounts receivable (gross accounts receivable less allowance for uncollectible accounts) and dividing by two.[35]

The receivables turnover ratio provides an indication of a company's efficiency in collecting receivables. The ratio shows the number of times during a period that the average accounts receivable balance is collected. The higher the ratio, the shorter the average time between credit sales and cash collection.

The *average collection period* indicates the average age of accounts receivable.

A convenient extension is the average collection period. This measure is computed simply by dividing 365 days by the receivables turnover ratio. The result is an approximation of the number of days the average accounts receivable balance is outstanding.

$$\text{Average collection period} = \frac{365}{\text{Receivables turnover ratio}}$$

Monitoring the receivables turnover ratio (and average collection period) over time can provide useful information about a company's future prospects. For example, a decline in the receivables turnover ratio (an increase in the average collection period) could be an indication that sales are declining because of customer dissatisfaction with the company's products. Another possible explanation is that the company has changed its credit policy and is granting extended credit terms in order to maintain customers. Either explanation could signal a future increase in bad debts. Ratio analysis does not explain what is wrong. It does provide information that highlights areas for further investigation.

INVENTORY TURNOVER.   An important activity measure for a merchandising company (a retail, wholesale, or manufacturing company) is the inventory turnover ratio. The ratio shows the number of times the average inventory balance is sold during a reporting period. It indicates how quickly inventory is sold. The more frequently a business is able to sell, or turn over, its inventory, the lower its investment in inventory must be for a given level of sales. The ratio is computed by dividing the period's cost of goods sold by the average inventory balance. The denominator, average inventory, is determined by adding beginning and ending inventory and dividing by two.[36]

The *inventory turnover ratio* measures a company's efficiency in managing its investment in inventory.

A relatively high ratio, say compared to a competitor, usually is desirable. A high ratio indicates comparative strength, perhaps caused by a company's superior sales force or maybe a successful advertising campaign. However, it might also be caused by a relatively low inventory level, which could mean either very efficient inventory management or stockouts and lost sales in the future.

On the other hand, a relatively low ratio, or a decrease in the ratio over time, usually is perceived to be unfavorable. Too much capital may be tied up in inventory. A relatively low ratio may result from overstocking, the presence of obsolete items, or poor marketing and sales efforts.

Similar to the receivables turnover, we can divide the inventory turnover ratio into 365 days to compute the average days in inventory. This measure indicates the number of days it normally takes to sell inventory.

$$\text{Average days in inventory} = \frac{365}{\text{Inventory turnover ratio}}$$

---

[35]Although *net* accounts receivable typically is used in practice for the denominator of receivables turnover, some prefer to use *gross* accounts receivable. Why? As the allowance for bad debts increases, net accounts receivable decreases, so if net accounts receivable is in the denominator, more bad debts have the effect of decreasing the denominator and therefore increasing receivables turnover. All else equal, an analyst would rather see receivables turnover improve because of more sales or less gross receivables, and not because of an increase in the allowance for bad debts.

[36]Notice the consistency in the measure used for the numerator and denominator of the two turnover ratios. For the receivables turnover ratio, both numerator and denominator are based on sales dollars, whereas they are both based on cost for the inventory turnover ratio.

Profitability Ratios

A fundamental element of an analyst's task is to develop an understanding of a firm's profitability. Profitability ratios attempt to measure a company's ability to earn an adequate return relative to sales or resources devoted to operations. Resources devoted to operations can be defined as total assets or only those assets provided by owners, depending on the evaluation objective.

Profitability ratios assist in evaluating various aspects of a company's profit-making activities.

Three common profitability measures are (1) the profit margin on sales, (2) the return on assets, and (3) the return on shareholders' equity. These ratios are calculated as follows:

$$\text{Profit margin on sales} = \frac{\text{Net income}}{\text{Net sales}}$$

$$\text{Return on assets} = \frac{\text{Net income}}{\text{Average total assets}}$$

$$\text{Return on shareholder's equity} = \frac{\text{Net income}}{\text{Average shareholders' equity}}$$

Notice that for all of the profitability ratios, our numerator is net income. Recall our discussion in Chapter 4 on earnings quality. The relevance of any historical-based financial statement hinges on its predictive value. To enhance predictive value, analysts often adjust net income in these ratios to separate a company's *transitory earnings* effects from its *permanent earnings.* Analysts begin their assessment of permanent earnings with income from continuing operations. Then, adjustments are made for any unusual, one-time gains or losses included in income from continuing operations. It is this adjusted number that they use as the numerator in these ratios.

When calculating profitability ratios, analysts often adjust net income for any transitory income effects.

PROFIT MARGIN ON SALES.   The profit margin on sales is simply net income divided by net sales. The ratio measures an important dimension of a company's profitability. It indicates the portion of each dollar of revenue that is available to cover expenses. It offers a measure of the company's ability to withstand either higher expenses or lower revenues.

The profit margin on sales measures the amount of net income achieved per sales dollar.

What is considered to be a desirable profit margin is highly sensitive to the nature of the business activity. For instance, you would expect a specialty shop to have a higher profit margin than, say, **Walmart**. A low profit margin can be compensated for by a high asset turnover rate, and vice versa, which brings us to considering the trade-offs inherent in generating return on assets.

RETURN ON ASSETS.   The return on assets (ROA) ratio expresses income as a percentage of the average total assets available to generate that income. Because total assets are partially financed with debt and partially by equity funds, this is an inclusive way of measuring earning power that ignores specific sources of financing.

Profit margin and asset turnover combine to yield return on assets, which measures the return generated by a company's assets.

A company's return on assets is related to both profit margin and asset turnover. Specifically, profitability can be achieved by either a high profit margin, high turnover, or a combination of the two. In fact, the return on assets can be calculated by multiplying the profit margin and the asset turnover.

$$\text{Return on assets} = \text{Profit margin} \times \text{Asset turnover}$$

$$\frac{\text{Net income}}{\text{Average total assets}} = \frac{\text{Net income}}{\text{Net sales}} \times \frac{\text{Net sales}}{\text{Average total assets}}$$

Industry standards are particularly important when evaluating asset turnover and profit margin. Some industries are characterized by low turnover but typically make up for it with higher profit margins. Others have low profit margins but compensate with high turnover. Grocery stores typically have relatively low profit margins but relatively high asset turnover. In comparison, a manufacturer of specialized equipment will have a higher profit margin but a lower asset turnover ratio.

RETURN ON SHAREHOLDERS' EQUITY.   Equity investors typically are concerned about the amount of profit that management can generate from the resources that owners

The return on shareholders' equity measures the return to suppliers of equity capital.

provide. A closely watched measure that captures this concern is **return on equity (ROE)**, calculated by dividing net income by average shareholders' equity.

ADDITIONAL CONSIDERATION

The return on assets ratio often is computed as follows:

$$\text{Return on assets} = \frac{\text{Net income} + \text{Interest expense} (1 - \text{Tax rate})}{\text{Average total assets}}$$

The reason for adding back interest expense (net of tax) is that interest represents a return to suppliers of debt capital and should not be deducted in the computation of net income when computing the return on total assets. In other words, the numerator is the total amount of income available to both debt and equity capital.

The DuPont framework shows that return on equity depends on profitability, activity, and financial leverage.

In addition to monitoring return on equity, investors want to understand how that return can be improved. The **DuPont framework** provides a convenient basis for analysis that breaks return on equity into three key components: [37]

- **Profitability,** measured by the profit margin (Net income ÷ Sales). As discussed already, a higher profit margin indicates that a company is generating more profit from each dollar of sales.
- **Activity,** measured by asset turnover (Sales ÷ Average total assets). As discussed already, higher asset turnover indicates that a company is using its assets efficiently to generate more sales from each dollar of assets.
- **Financial Leverage,** measured by the equity multiplier (Average total assets ÷ Average total equity). A high equity multiplier indicates that relatively more of the company's assets have been financed with debt. As indicated in Chapter 3, leverage can provide additional return to the company's equity holders.

In equation form, the DuPont framework looks like this:

Return on equity = Profit margin × Asset turnover × Equity multiplier

$$\frac{\text{Net income}}{\text{Avg. total equity}} = \frac{\text{Net income}}{\text{Total sales}} \times \frac{\text{Total sales}}{\text{Avg. total assets}} \times \frac{\text{Avg. total assets}}{\text{Avg. total equity}}$$

Notice that total sales and average total assets appear in the numerator of one ratio and the denominator of another, so they cancel to yield net income ÷ average total equity, or ROE.

We have already seen that ROA is determined by profit margin and asset turnover, so another way to compute ROE is by multiplying ROA by the equity multiplier:

Because profit margin and asset turnover combine to create return on assets, the DuPont framework can also be viewed as indicating that return on equity depends on return on assets and financial leverage.

Return on equity = Return on assets × Equity multiplier

$$\frac{\text{Net income}}{\text{Avg. total equity}} = \frac{\text{Net income}}{\text{Avg. total assets}} \times \frac{\text{Avg. total assets}}{\text{Avg. total equity}}$$

We can see from this equation that an equity multiplier of greater than 1 will produce a return on equity that is higher than the return on assets. However, as with all ratio analysis, there are trade-offs. If leverage is too high, creditors become concerned about the potential for default on the company's debt and require higher interest rates. Because interest is recognized as an expense, net income is reduced, so at some point the benefits of a higher equity multiplier are offset by a lower profit margin. Part of the challenge of managing a company is to identify the combination of profitability, activity, and leverage that produces the highest return for equity holders.

---

[37]DuPont analysis is so named because the basic model was developed by F. Donaldson Brown, an electrical engineer who worked for DuPont in the early part of the 20th century.

ADDITIONAL CONSIDERATION

Sometimes when return on equity is calculated, shareholders' equity is viewed more narrowly to include only common shareholders. In that case, preferred stock is excluded from the denominator, and preferred dividends are deducted from net income in the numerator. The resulting rate of return on common shareholders' equity focuses on profits generated on resources provided by common shareholders.

Graphic 5–12 provides a recap of the ratios we have discussed.

GRAPHIC 5–12

Summary of Profitability Analysis Ratios

Activity ratios

$$\text{Asset turnover} = \frac{\text{Net sales}}{\text{Average total assets}}$$

$$\text{Receivables turnover} = \frac{\text{Net sales}}{\text{Average accounts receivable (net)}}$$

$$\text{Average collection period} = \frac{365}{\text{Receivables turnover ratio}}$$

$$\text{Inventory turnover} = \frac{\text{Cost of goods sold}}{\text{Average inventory}}$$

$$\text{Average days in inventory} = \frac{365}{\text{Inventory turnover ratio}}$$

Profitability ratios

$$\text{Profit margin on sales} = \frac{\text{Net income}}{\text{Net sales}}$$

$$\text{Return on assets} = \frac{\text{Net income}}{\text{Average total assets}}$$

$$\text{Return on shareholders' equity} = \frac{\text{Net income}}{\text{Average shareholders' equity}}$$

Leverage ratio

$$\text{Equity multiplier} = \frac{\text{Average total assets}}{\text{Average total equity}}$$

Profitability Analysis—An Illustration

To illustrate the application of the DuPont framework and the computation of the activity and profitability ratios, we analyze the 2009 financial statements of two well-known retailers, **Target Corporation** and **Walmart Stores, Inc.** The operations of these two companies are similar in terms of their focus on operating large general-merchandising and food discount stores. Illustration 5–4A presents selected financial statement information for the two companies.

On the surface it appears that Walmart is far more profitable than Target. As shown in Illustration 5–4A, Walmart's 2009 net income was $13.254 billion, compared to Target's $2.214 billion.[38] But that's not the whole story. Even though both are very large companies, Walmart is almost four times the size of Target in terms of total assets, so how can they be compared? Focusing on financial ratios helps adjust for size differences, and the DuPont framework helps identify the determinants of profitability from the perspective of shareholders.

[38]Consistent with financial statement analysis being concerned with prediction, our illustration analyzes continuing operations. For Target this focus required no adjustment, but for Walmart we excluded its Gazeley Limited business, which was sold during fiscal 2009 and therefore treated as a discontinued operation in Walmart's 2009 financial statements.

ILLUSTRATION 5–4A

Selected Financial Information for Target Corporation and Walmart Stores

Real World Financials

	Target		Walmart	
	2009	**2008**	**2009**	**2008**
Accounts receivable (net)	$ 8,084	$ 8,054	$ 3,905	$ 3,642
Inventories	$ 6,705	$ 6,780	$ 34,511	$ 35,159
Total assets	$44,106	$44,560	$163,429	$163,514
Total liabilities	$30,394	$29,253	$ 98,144	$ 98,906
Total shareholders' equity	$13,712	$15,307	$ 65,285	$ 64,608
Two-year averages:				
Accounts receivable (net)		$ 8,069		$ 3,774
Inventories		$ 6,743		$ 34,835
Total assets		$44,333		$163,472
Total shareholders' equity		$14,510		$ 64,947
Income Statement—2009				
Net sales		$64,948		$405,607
Cost of goods sold		$44,157		$306,158
Net Income (income from continuing operations for Walmart)		$ 2,214		$ 13,254

Illustration 5–4B includes the DuPont analysis for Walmart and Target, as well as some additional activity ratios that we have discussed. Walmart's return on assets (ROA) is higher than Target's (8.11% for Walmart compared to 4.99% for Target). Why? Remember that both profitability and activity combine to determine return on assets. Target's profit margin

ILLUSTRATION 5–4B

DuPont Framework and Activity Ratios—Target Corporation and Walmart Stores

	Target		Walmart		Industry Average*
DuPont analysis:					
Profit margin on sales	$= \dfrac{\$2,214}{\$64,948} =$	3.41%	$\dfrac{\$13,254}{\$405,607} =$	3.27%	2.38%
	×		×		×
Asset turnover	$= \dfrac{\$64,948}{\$44,333} =$	1.47	$\dfrac{\$405,607}{\$163,472} =$	2.48	2.68
	=		=		=
Return on assets	$= \dfrac{\$2,214}{\$44,333} =$	4.99%	$\dfrac{\$13,254}{\$163,472} =$	8.11%	6.38%
	×		×		×
Equity Multiplier	$= \dfrac{\$44,333}{\$14,510} =$	3.06	$\dfrac{\$163,472}{\$64,947} =$	2.52	2.04
	=		=		=
Return on shareholders' equity	$= \dfrac{\$2,214}{\$14,510} =$	15.33%	$\dfrac{\$13,254}{\$64,947} =$	20.41%	13.01%
Other activity ratios:					
Receivables turnover	$= \dfrac{\$64,948}{\$8,069} =$	8.05	$\dfrac{\$405,607}{\$3,774} =$	107.5	179.2
Average collection period	$= \dfrac{365}{8.05} =$	45.3 days	$\dfrac{365}{107.5} =$	3.4 days	2.04days
Inventory turnover	$= \dfrac{\$44,157}{\$6,743} =$	6.55	$\dfrac{\$306,158}{\$34,835} =$	8.79	8.61
Average days in inventory	$= \dfrac{365}{6.55} =$	55.7 days	$\dfrac{365}{8.79} =$	41.5 days	42 days

*Industry average based on sample of twelve discount retail companies

actually is a bit higher than Walmart's (3.41% compared to 3.27%), but Walmart's asset turnover is much higher than Target's (2.48 compared to 1.47). So, even though Target makes more profit on each sale, Walmart makes significantly more sales with their assets, and Walmart ends up coming out ahead on return on assets.

The average days in inventory provides insight into Walmart's higher asset turnover. Inventory takes only 41.5 days on average before being sold by Walmart, compared with 55.7 days for Target. Walmart also turns over its accounts receivable faster than Target does, but accounts receivable are small and don't matter much for Walmart (Target offers a charge card and so maintains a higher receivable balance, on which it earns interest revenue).

What matters most to the shareholders of these companies is not return on assets, but the return on equity (ROE). Walmart also wins on this measure, with an ROE of 20.4% compared to Target's 15.3%. Target's equity multiplier is higher than Walmart's (3.06 for Target compared to 2.52 for Walmart), but that difference in leverage is not enough to make up for Walmart's much higher ROA.

A Target shareholder looking at these numbers might wonder how best to increase ROE. Should Target attempt to increase operational efficiency in hopes of approaching Walmart on the asset turnover dimension? Or, should Target attempt to increase profit margin? Given competitive pressures on retail pricing, can Target earn a much higher profit margin with its current product mix by including more upscale items in their inventory? Or, should Target attempt to increase leverage, such that debtholders are financing a greater percentage of assets?

The essential point of our discussion here, and in Part C of Chapter 3, is that raw accounting numbers alone mean little to decision makers. The numbers gain value when viewed in relation to other numbers. Similarly, the financial ratios formed by those relationships provide even greater perspective when compared with similar ratios of other companies, or relatedly, with averages for several companies in the same industry. Accounting information is useful in making decisions. Financial analysis that includes comparisons of financial ratios enhances the value of that information.

FINANCIAL REPORTING CASE SOLUTION

1. **Does your sister have to wait two and a half years to get her bonus? Explain.** *(p. 246)* No. The *general* revenue recognition criteria would suggest that revenue and costs should be recognized when a project is finished. The difficulty this would create is that all revenues, expenses, and resulting profit from the project are recognized when the project is completed; no revenues or expenses would be reported in the income statements of earlier reporting periods in which much of the work may have been performed. The percentage-of-completion method of revenue recognition for long-term projects addresses this problem. A share of the project's profit is allocated to each period in which the earnings process occurs. This is two and a half years in this instance.

2. **How are gross profits recognized using the percentage-of-completion method?** *(p. 249)* The percentage-of-completion method recognizes part of the estimated gross profit each period. The amount recognized is based on progress to date which is estimated as the fraction of the project's cost incurred to date divided by total estimated costs. The estimated percentage of completion is multiplied by the revised project gross profit estimate. This yields the estimated gross profit earned from the beginning of the project. The gross profit recognized is calculated by subtracting from this amount the gross profit recognized in previous periods.

3. **Are there other situations in which revenue is recognized at times other than when a product is delivered?** *(p. 239)* Yes, revenue recognition sometimes is delayed until after the product is delivered. These situations involve either the possibility of product returns or bad debts. In most cases, product returns and bad debt are estimated and revenues are recognized when a product is delivered. However, in situations involving an abnormal degree of uncertainty about cash collection caused by potential returns or bad debts, revenue recognition *after* delivery sometimes is appropriate. ●

THE BOTTOM LINE

● **LO1**   The objective of revenue recognition is to recognize revenue in the period or periods that the revenue-generating activities of the company are performed. Also, judgment as to the collectibility of the cash from the sale of a product or service will impact the timing of revenue recognition. These two concepts of performance and collectibility are captured by the general guidelines for revenue recognition in the realization principle which requires that revenue should be recognized only after (1) the earnings process is virtually complete and (2) there is reasonable certainty of collecting the asset to be received (usually cash) from the customer. For the sale of product, these criteria usually are satisfied at the point of product delivery. At that point, the majority of the productive activities have taken place and any remaining uncertainty concerning asset collection can be accounted for by estimating possible returns and bad debts. Also, service revenue often is recognized at a point in time if there is one final activity that is deemed critical to the earnings process. (p. 234)

● **LO2**   The installment sales method recognizes gross profit in collection periods by applying the gross profit percentage on the sale to the amount of cash actually received. The cost recovery method defers all gross profit recognition until cash has been received equal to the cost of the item sold. These methods of recognizing revenue should only be used in situations where there is an unusually high degree of uncertainty regarding the ultimate cash collection on an installment sale. (p. 239)

● **LO3**   In most situations, even though the right to return merchandise exists, revenues and expenses can be appropriately recognized at point of delivery. Based on past experience, a company usually can estimate the returns that will result for a given volume of sales. These estimates reduce both sales and cost of goods sold in anticipation of returns. Revenue cannot be recognized at the point of delivery unless the seller is able to make reliable estimates of future returns. Otherwise, revenue recognition is deferred beyond the delivery point. (p. 244)

● **LO4**   Revenue recognition at a single point in time when the earnings process is virtually complete is inappropriate for certain types of service revenue activities and also, usually, for long-term contracts. The completed contract method recognizes revenues and expenses on long-term construction and other long-term contracts at a point in time when the project is complete. This method is only used in unusual situations. The preferable method for recognizing revenues and expenses for long-term contracts is the percentage-of-completion method, which recognizes revenues over time by assigning a share of the project's revenues and costs to each reporting period during the project. (p. 245)

● **LO5**   Industry guidelines require that the lump-sum contract price for software be allocated to the various elements of the package based on the relative fair values of the individual elements. Generally, this results in a deferral of a portion of the proceeds that are then recognized as revenue in future periods. Other multiple-deliverable arrangements are accounted for in a similar manner. The use of franchise arrangements has become increasingly popular. The fees to be paid by the franchisee to the franchisor usually are composed of (1) the initial franchise fee and (2) continuing franchise fees. GAAP requires that the franchisor has substantially performed the services promised in the franchise agreement and that the collectibility of the initial franchise fee is reasonably assured before the initial fee can be recognized as revenue. The continuing franchise fees are recognized by the franchisor as revenue over time in the periods the services are performed by the franchisor. (pp. 258 and 260)

● **LO6**   Activity and profitability ratios provide information about a company's profitability. Activity ratios include the receivables turnover ratio, the inventory turnover ratio, and the asset turnover ratio. Profitability ratios include the profit margin on sales, the return on assets, and the return on shareholders' equity. DuPont analysis explains return on stockholders' equity as determined by profit margin, asset turnover, and the extent to which assets are financed with equity versus debt. (p. 265)

● **LO7**   For the most part, revenue recognition requirements are similar under U.S. GAAP and IFRS. U.S. GAAP is much more detailed, though, especially with respect to industry-specific guidance and multi-deliverable arrangements. In addition, when the percentage-of-completion method is not used to account for a long-term contract, U.S. GAAP requires the use of the completed contract method (in which revenue, cost, and gross profit are all typically recognized at the end of the contract), while IFRS requires the cost recovery method (in which revenue and cost are recognized over the life of the contract, but gross profit is recognized only after all costs have been recovered, which is typically at the end of the contract). (pp. 237, 256, 260, and 262) ●

INTERIM REPORTING

Financial statements covering periods of less than a year are called *interim reports*. Companies registered with the SEC, which includes most public companies, must submit quarterly reports, and you will see excerpts from these reports throughout this book.[39] Though there is no requirement to do so, most also send quarterly reports to their shareholders and typically include abbreviated, unaudited interim reports as supplemental information within their annual reports. For instance, Graphic 5A–1 shows the quarterly information disclosed in the 2009 annual report of **Dell, Inc.**

Interim reports are issued for periods of less than a year, typically as quarterly financial statements.

For accounting information to be useful to decision makers, it must be available on a timely basis. One of the objectives of interim reporting is to enhance the timeliness of financial information. In addition, quarterly reports provide investors and creditors with additional insight on the seasonality of business operations that might otherwise get lost in annual reports.

GRAPHIC 5A–1   Interim Data in Annual Report—Dell, Inc.

	Fiscal Year 2009			
	First Quarter	Second Quarter	Third Quarter	Fourth Quarter
	(in millions, except per share data)			
Net revenue	$16,077	$16,434	$15,162	$13,428
Gross margin	2,965	2,827	2,853	2,312
Net income	784	616	727	351
Earnings per common share:				
Basic	0.39	0.31	0.37	0.18
Diluted	0.38	0.31	0.37	0.18
Weighted-average shares outstanding:				
Basic	2,036	1,991	1,953	1,944
Diluted	2,040	1,999	1,957	1,948
Stock sales price per share:				
High	21.18	25.26	26.04	13.32
Low	18.13	18.66	10.59	8.72

Real World Financials

However, the downside to these benefits is the relative unreliability of interim reporting. With a shorter reporting period, questions associated with estimation and allocation are magnified. For example, certain expenses often benefit an entire year's operations and yet are incurred primarily within a single interim period. Similarly, should smaller companies use lower tax rates in the earlier quarters and higher rates in later quarters as higher tax brackets are reached? Another result of shorter reporting periods is the intensified effect of major events such as discontinued operations or extraordinary items. A second quarter casualty loss, for instance, that would reduce annual profits by 10% might reduce second quarter profits by 40% or more. Is it more realistic to allocate such a loss over the entire year? These and similar questions tend to hinge on the way we view an interim period in relation to the fiscal year. More specifically, should each interim period be viewed as a *discrete* reporting period or as an *integral part* of the annual period?

The fundamental debate regarding interim reporting centers on the choice between the discrete and integral part approaches.

Reporting Revenues and Expenses

Existing practice and current reporting requirements for interim reporting generally follow the viewpoint that interim reports are an integral part of annual statements, although the discrete approach is applied to some items. Most revenues and expenses are recognized

---

[39]Quarterly reports are filed with the SEC on form 10-Q. Annual reports to the SEC are on form 10-K.

using the same accounting principles applicable to annual reporting. Some modifications are necessary to help cause interim statements to relate better to annual statements. This is most evident in the way costs and expenses are recognized. Most are recognized in interim periods as incurred. But when an expenditure clearly benefits more than just the period in which it is incurred, the expense should be allocated among the periods benefited on an allocation basis consistent with the company's annual allocation procedures. For example, annual repair expenses, property tax expense, and advertising expenses incurred in the first quarter that clearly benefit later quarters are assigned to each quarter through the use of accruals and deferrals. Costs and expenses subject to year-end adjustments, such as depreciation and bad debt expense, are estimated and allocated to interim periods in a systematic way. Similarly, income tax expense at each interim date should be based on estimates of the effective tax rate for the whole year. This would mean, for example, that if the estimated effective rate has changed since the previous interim period(s), the tax expense that period would be determined as the new rate times the cumulative pretax income to date, less the total tax expense reported in previous interim periods.

Reporting Unusual Items

On the other hand, major events such as discontinued operations or extraordinary items should be reported separately in the interim period in which they occur. That is, these amounts should not be allocated among individual quarters within the fiscal year. The same is true for items that are unusual or infrequent but not both. Treatment of these items is more consistent with the discrete view than the integral part view.

Earnings Per Share

A second item that is treated in a manner consistent with the discrete view is earnings per share. EPS calculations for interim reports follow the same procedures as annual calculations that you will study in Chapter 19. The calculations are based on conditions actually existing during the particular interim period rather than on conditions estimated to exist at the end of the fiscal year.

Reporting Accounting Changes

Recall from Chapter 4 that we account for a change in accounting principle retrospectively, meaning we recast prior years' financial statements when we report those statements again in comparative form. In other words, we make those statements appear as if the newly adopted accounting method had been used in those prior years. It's the same with interim reporting. We retrospectively report a change made during an interim period in similar fashion. Then in financial reports of subsequent interim periods of the same fiscal year, we disclose how that change affected (a) income from continuing operations, (b) net income, and (c) related per share amounts for the postchange interim period.

Minimum Disclosures

Complete financial statements are not required for interim period reporting, but certain minimum disclosures are required as follows:[40]

- Sales, income taxes, extraordinary items, and net income.
- Earnings per share.
- Seasonal revenues, costs, and expenses.
- Significant changes in estimates for income taxes.
- Discontinued operations, extraordinary items, and unusual or infrequent items.
- Contingencies.
- Changes in accounting principles or estimates.

[40]FASB ASC 270–10–50: Interim Reporting–Overall–Disclosure (previously "Interim Financial Reporting," *Accounting Principles Board Opinion No 28* (New York: AICPA, 1973)).

- Information about fair value of financial instruments and the methods and assumptions used to estimate fair values.
- Significant changes in financial position.

When fourth quarter results are not separately reported, material fourth quarter events, including year-end adjustments, should be reported in disclosure notes to annual statements. ●

QUESTIONS FOR REVIEW OF KEY TOPICS

Q 5–1 What are the two general criteria that must be satisfied before a company can recognize revenue?

Q 5–2 Explain why, in most cases, a seller recognizes revenue when it delivers its product rather than when it produces the product.

Q 5–3 Revenue recognition for most installment sales occurs at the point of delivery of the product or service. Under what circumstances would a seller delay revenue recognition for installment sales beyond the delivery date?

Q 5–4 Distinguish between the installment sales method and the cost recovery method of accounting for installment sales.

Q 5–5 How does a company report deferred gross profit resulting from the use of the installment sales method in its balance sheet?

Q 5–6 Revenue recognition for most product sales that allow the right of return occurs at the point of product delivery. Under what circumstances would revenue recognition be delayed?

Q 5–7 Describe a consignment sale. When does a consignor recognize revenue for a consignment sale?

Q 5–8 Service revenue is recognized either at one point in time or over extended periods. Explain the rationale for recognizing revenue using these two approaches.

Q 5–9 Distinguish between the percentage-of-completion and completed contract methods of accounting for long-term contracts with respect to income recognition. Under what circumstances should a company use the completed contract method?

🌐 **IFRS** Q 5–10 When percentage-of-completion accounting is not appropriate, U.S. GAAP requires the use of the completed contract method, while IFRS requires the use of the cost recovery method. Explain how the two methods affect recognition of revenue, cost of construction, and gross profit over the life of a profitable contract.

Q 5–11 Periodic billings to the customer for a long-term construction contract are recorded as billings on construction contract. How is this account reported in the balance sheet?

Q 5–12 When is an estimated loss on a long-term contract recognized using the percentage-of-completion method? The completed contract method?

Q 5–13 Briefly describe the guidelines for recognizing revenue from the sale of software and other multiple-deliverable arrangements.

🌐 **IFRS** Q 5–14 Briefly describe how IFRS guidelines for recognizing revenue from multiple-deliverable arrangements differ from U.S. GAAP guidelines.

Q 5–15 Briefly describe the guidelines provided by GAAP for the recognition of revenue by a franchisor for an initial franchise fee.

Q 5–16 Show the calculation of the following activity ratios: (1) the receivables turnover ratio, (2) the inventory turnover ratio, and (3) the asset turnover ratio. What information about a company do these ratios offer?

Q 5–17 Show the calculation of the following profitability ratios: (1) the profit margin on sales, (2) the return on assets, and (3) the return on shareholders' equity. What information about a company do these ratios offer?

Q 5–18 Show the DuPont framework's calculation of the three components of return on shareholders' equity. What information about a company do these ratios offer?

Q 5–19 [Based on Appendix 5] Interim reports are issued for periods of less than a year, typically as quarterly financial statements. Should these interim periods be viewed as separate periods or integral parts of the annual period?

BRIEF EXERCISES

BE 5–1
Point of delivery recognition
● LO1

On July 1, 2011, Apache Company sold a parcel of undeveloped land to a construction company for $3,000,000. The book value of the land on Apache's books was $1,200,000. Terms of the sale required a down payment of $150,000 and 19 annual payments of $150,000 plus interest at an appropriate interest rate due on each July 1 beginning in 2012. Apache has no significant obligations to perform services after the sale. How much gross profit will Apache recognize in both 2011 and 2012 assuming point of delivery profit recognition?

BE 5–2
Installment sales method
● LO2

Refer to the situation described in BE 5–1. How much gross profit will Apache recognize in both 2011 and 2012 applying the installment sales method?

BE 5–3
Cost recovery method
● LO2

Refer to the situation described in BE 5–1. How much gross profit will Apache recognize in both 2011 and 2012 applying the cost recovery method?

BE 5–4
Installment sales method
● LO2

Refer to the situation described in BE 5–1. What should be the balance in the deferred gross profit account at the end of 2012 applying the installment sales method?

BE 5–5
Right of return
● LO3

Meyer Furniture sells office furniture mainly to corporate clients. Customers who return merchandise within 90 days for any reason receive a full refund. Discuss the issues Meyer must consider in determining its revenue recognition policy.

BE 5–6
Percentage-of-completion method; profit recognition
● LO4

A construction company entered into a fixed-price contract to build an office building for $20 million. Construction costs incurred during the first year were $6 million and estimated costs to complete at the end of the year were $9 million. How much gross profit will the company recognize in the first year using the percentage-of-completion method? How much revenue will appear in the company's income statement?

BE 5–7
Percentage-of-completion method; balance sheet
● LO4

Refer to the situation described in BE 5–6. During the first year the company billed its customer $7 million of which $5 million was collected before year-end. What would appear in the year-end balance sheet related to this contract?

BE 5–8
Completed contract method
● LO4

Refer to the situation described in BE 5–6. The building was completed during the second year. Construction costs incurred during the second year were $10 million. How much gross profit will the company recognize in the first year and in the second year applying the completed contract method?

BE 5–9
IFRS; cost recovery method
● LO4
  LO7

Refer to the situation described in BE 5–8. How much revenue, cost, and gross profit will the company recognize in the first and second year of the contract applying the cost recovery method that is required by IFRS?

BE 5–10
Percentage-of-completion and completed contract methods; loss on entire project
● LO4

Franklin Construction entered into a fixed-price contract to build a freeway-connecting ramp for $30 million. Construction costs incurred in the first year were $16 million and estimated costs to complete at the end of the year were $17 million. How much gross profit or loss will Franklin recognize the first year applying the percentage-of-completion method? Applying the completed contract method?

BE 5–11
Revenue recognition; software contracts
● LO5

Orange, Inc., sells a LearnIt-Plus software package that consists of their normal LearnIt math tutorial program along with a one-year subscription to the on-line LearnIt Office Hours virtual classroom. LearnIt-Plus retails for $200. When sold separately, the LearnIt math tutorial sells for $150, and access to the LearnIt Office Hours sells for $100 per year. When should Orange recognize revenue for the parts of this arrangement? Would your answer change if Orange did not sell the LearnIt Office Hours separately, but believed it would price it at $100 per year if they ever decided to do so?

BE 5–12
Revenue recognition; software contracts under IFRS
● LO5
  LO7

Refer to the situation described in BE 5–11. How would your answer change if Orange reported under IFRS?

BE 5–13
Revenue
recognition;
franchise sales
● LO5

Collins, Inc., entered into a 10-year franchise agreement with an individual. For an initial franchise fee of $40,000, Collins agrees to assist in design and construction of the franchise location and in all other necessary start-up activities. Also, in exchange for advertising and promotional services, the franchisee agrees to pay continuing franchise fees equal to 5% of revenue generated by the franchise. When should Collins recognize revenue for the initial and continuing franchise fees?

BE 5–14
Receivables and
inventory turnover
ratios
● LO6

Universal Calendar Company began the year with accounts receivable and inventory balances of $100,000 and $80,000, respectively. Year-end balances for these accounts were $120,000 and $60,000, respectively. Sales for the year of $600,000 generated a gross profit of $200,000. Calculate the receivables and inventory turnover ratios for the year.

BE 5–15
Profitability ratios
● LO6

The 2011 income statement for Anderson TV and Appliance reported sales revenue of $420,000 and net income of $65,000. Average total assets for 2011 was $800,000. Shareholders' equity at the beginning of the year was $500,000 and $20,000 was paid to shareholders as dividends. There were no other shareholders' equity transactions that occurred during the year. Calculate the profit margin on sales, return on assets, and return on shareholders' equity for 2011.

BE 5–16
Profitability ratios
● LO6

Refer to the facts described in BE 5–15. Show the DuPont framework's calculation of the three components of the 2011 return on shareholders' equity for Anderson TV and Appliance.

BE 5–17
Inventory turnover
ratio
● LO6

During 2011, Rogue Corporation reported sales revenue of $600,000. Inventory at both the beginning and end of the year totaled $75,000. The inventory turnover ratio for the year was 6.0. What amount of gross profit did the company report in its income statement for 2011?

EXERCISES

An alternate exercise and problem set is available on the text website: www.mhhe.com/spiceland6e

E 5–1
Service revenue
● LO1

Alpine West, Inc., operates a downhill ski area near Lake Tahoe, California. An all-day, adult ticket can be purchased for $55. Adult customers also can purchase a season pass that entitles the pass holder to ski any day during the season, which typically runs from December 1 through April 30. The season pass is nontransferable, and the $450 price is nonrefundable. Alpine expects its season pass holders to use their passes equally throughout the season. The company's fiscal year ends on December 31.

On November 6, 2011, Jake Lawson purchased a season ticket.

Required:
1. When should Alpine West recognize revenue from the sale of its season passes?
2. Prepare the appropriate journal entries that Alpine would record on November 6 and December 31.
3. What will be included in the 2011 income statement and 2011 balance sheet related to the sale of the season pass to Jake Lawson?

E 5–2
Installment sales
method
● LO2

Charter Corporation, which began business in 2011, appropriately uses the installment sales method of accounting for its installment sales. The following data were obtained for sales made during 2011 and 2012:

	2011	2012
Installment sales	$360,000	$350,000
Cost of installment sales	234,000	245,000
Cash collections on installment sales during:		
2011	150,000	100,000
2012	—	120,000

Required:
1. How much gross profit should Charter recognize in 2011 and 2012 from installment sales?
2. What should be the balance in the deferred gross profit account at the end of 2011 and 2012?

E 5–3
Installment sales
method; journal
entries
● LO2

[This is a variation of Exercise 5–2 focusing on journal entries.]

Charter Corporation, which began business in 2011, appropriately uses the installment sales method of accounting for its installment sales. The following data were obtained for sales during 2011 and 2012:

	2011	2012
Installment sales	$360,000	$350,000
Cost of installment sales	234,000	245,000
Cash collections on installment sales during:		
2011	150,000	100,000
2012	—	120,000

Required:

Prepare summary journal entries for 2011 and 2012 to account for the installment sales and cash collections. The company uses the perpetual inventory system.

E 5–4

Installment sales; alternative recognition methods

● LO2

On July 1, 2011, the Foster Company sold inventory to the Slate Corporation for $300,000. Terms of the sale called for a down payment of $75,000 and three annual installments of $75,000 due on each July 1, beginning July 1, 2012. Each installment also will include interest on the unpaid balance applying an appropriate interest rate. The inventory cost Foster $120,000. The company uses the perpetual inventory system.

Required:

1. Compute the amount of gross profit to be recognized from the installment sale in 2011, 2012, 2013, and 2014 using point of delivery revenue recognition. Ignore interest charges.
2. Repeat requirement 1 applying the installment sales method.
3. Repeat requirement 1 applying the cost recovery method.

E 5–5

Journal entries; point of delivery, installment sales, and cost recovery methods

● LO1 LO2

[This is a variation of Exercise 5–4 focusing on journal entries.]

On July 1, 2011, the Foster Company sold inventory to the Slate Corporation for $300,000. Terms of the sale called for a down payment of $75,000 and three annual installments of $75,000 due on each July 1, beginning July 1, 2012. Each installment also will include interest on the unpaid balance applying an appropriate interest rate. The inventory cost Foster $120,000. The company uses the perpetual inventory system.

Required:

1. Prepare the necessary journal entries for 2011 and 2012 using point of delivery revenue recognition. Ignore interest charges.
2. Repeat requirement 1 applying the installment sales method.
3. Repeat requirement 1 applying the cost recovery method.

E 5–6

Installment sales and cost recovery methods; solve for unknowns

● LO2

Wolf Computer Company began operations in 2011. The company allows customers to pay in installments for many of its products. Installment sales for 2011 were $1,000,000. If revenue is recognized at the point of delivery, $600,000 in gross profit would be recognized in 2011. If the company instead uses the cost recovery method, $100,000 in gross profit would be recognized in 2011.

Required:

1. What was the amount of cash collected on installment sales in 2011?
2. What amount of gross profit would be recognized if the company uses the installment sales method?

E 5–7

Installment sales; default and repossession

● LO2

Sanchez Development Company uses the installment sales method to account for some of its installment sales. On October 1, 2011, Sanchez sold a parcel of land to the Kreuze Corporation for $4 million. This amount was not considered significant relative to Sanchez's other sales during 2011. The land had cost Sanchez $1.8 million to acquire and develop. Terms of the sale required a down payment of $800,000 and four annual payments of $800,000 plus interest at an appropriate interest rate, with payments due on each October 1 beginning in 2012. Kreuze paid the down payment, but on October 1, 2012, defaulted on the remainder of the contract. Sanchez repossessed the land. On the date of repossession the land had a fair value of $1.3 million.

Required:

Prepare the necessary entries for Sanchez to record the sale, receipt of the down payment, and the default and repossession applying the installment sales method. Ignore interest charges.

E 5–8

Real estate sales; gain recognition

● LO1 LO2

On April 1, 2011, the Apex Corporation sold a parcel of underdeveloped land to the Applegate Construction Company for $2,400,000. The book value of the land on Apex's books was $480,000. Terms of the sale required a down payment of $120,000 and 19 annual payments of $120,000 plus interest at an appropriate interest rate due on each April 1 beginning in 2012. Apex has no significant obligations to perform services after the sale.

Required:

1. Prepare the necessary entries for Apex to record the sale, receipt of the down payment, and receipt of the first installment assuming that Apex is able to make a reliable estimate of possible uncollectible amounts (that is, point of delivery profit recognition is used). Ignore interest charges.

2. Repeat requirement 1 assuming that Apex cannot make a reliable estimate of possible uncollectible amounts and decides to use the installment sales method for profit recognition.

E 5–9
Long-term contract; percentage-of-completion and completed contract methods
● **LO4**

Assume **Nortel Networks** contracted to provide a customer with Internet infrastructure for $2,000,000. The project began in 2011 and was completed in 2012. Data relating to the contract are summarized below:

	2011	2012
Costs incurred during the year	$ 300,000	$1,575,000
Estimated costs to complete as of 12/31	1,200,000	–0–
Billings during the year	380,000	1,620,000
Cash collections during the year	250,000	1,750,000

Required:

1. Compute the amount of gross profit or loss to be recognized in 2011 and 2012 using the percentage-of-completion method.
2. Compute the amount of gross profit or loss to be recognized in 2011 and 2012 using the completed contract method.
3. Prepare a partial balance sheet to show how the information related to this contract would be presented at the end of 2011 using the percentage-of-completion method.
4. Prepare a partial balance sheet to show how the information related to this contract would be presented at the end of 2011 using the completed contract method.

E 5–10
Long-term contract; percentage of completion, completed contract and cost recovery methods
● **LO4 LO7**

On June 15, 2011, Sanderson Construction entered into a long-term construction contract to build a baseball stadium in Washington D.C. for $220 million. The expected completion date is April 1 of 2013, just in time for the 2013 baseball season. Costs incurred and estimated costs to complete at year-end for the life of the contract are as follows ($ in millions):

	2011	2012	2013
Costs incurred during the year	$ 40	$80	$50
Estimated costs to complete as of 12/31	120	60	—

Required:

1. Determine the amount of gross profit or loss to be recognized in each of the three years using the percentage-of-completion method.
2. How much revenue will Sanderson report in its 2011 and 2012 income statements related to this contract using the percentage-of-completion method?
3. Determine the amount of gross profit or loss to be recognized in each of the three years using the completed contract method.
4. Determine the amount of revenue, cost, and gross profit or loss to be recognized in each of the three years under IFRS, assuming that using the percentage-of-completion method is not appropriate.
5. Suppose the estimated costs to complete at the end of 2012 are $80 million instead of $60 million. Determine the amount of gross profit or loss to be recognized in 2012 using the percentage-of-completion method.

E 5–11
Percentage-of-completion method; loss projected on entire project
● **LO4**

On February 1, 2011, Arrow Construction Company entered into a three-year construction contract to build a bridge for a price of $8,000,000. During 2011, costs of $2,000,000 were incurred with estimated costs of $4,000,000 yet to be incurred. Billings of $2,500,000 were sent and cash collected was $2,250,000.

In 2012, costs incurred were $2,500,000 with remaining costs estimated to be $3,600,000. 2012 billings were $2,750,000 and $2,475,000 cash was collected. The project was completed in 2013 after additional costs of $3,800,000 were incurred. The company's fiscal year-end is December 31. Arrow uses the *percentage-of-completion* method.

Required:

1. Calculate the amount of gross profit or loss to be recognized in each of the three years.
2. Prepare journal entries for 2011 and 2012 to record the transactions described (credit various accounts for construction costs incurred).
3. Prepare a partial balance sheet to show the presentation of the project as of December 31, 2011 and 2012.

E 5–12
Completed contract method; loss projected on entire project
● **LO4**

[This is a variation of Exercise 5–11 focusing on the completed contract method.]

On February 1, 2011, Arrow Construction Company entered into a three-year construction contract to build a bridge for a price of $8,000,000. During 2011, costs of $2,000,000 were incurred with estimated costs of $4,000,000 yet to be incurred. Billings of $2,500,000 were sent and cash collected was $2,250,000.

In 2012, costs incurred were $2,500,000 with remaining costs estimated to be $3,600,000. 2012 billings were $2,750,000 and $2,475,000 cash was collected. The project was completed in 2013 after additional costs of $3,800,000 were incurred. The company's fiscal year-end is December 31. Arrow uses the *completed contract* method.

Required:

1. Calculate the amount of gross profit or loss to be recognized in each of the three years.
2. Prepare journal entries for 2011 and 2012 to record the transactions described (credit various accounts for construction costs incurred).
3. Prepare a partial balance sheet to show the presentation of the project as of December 31, 2011 and 2012.

E 5–13
Income (loss) recognition; percentage-of-completion and completed contract methods compared
● LO4

Brady Construction Company contracted to build an apartment complex for a price of $5,000,000. Construction began in 2011 and was completed in 2013. The following are a series of independent situations, numbered 1 through 6, involving differing costs for the project. All costs are stated in thousands of dollars.

	Costs Incurred During Year			Estimated Costs to Complete (As of the End of the Year)		
Situation	2011	2012	2013	2011	2012	2013
1	1,500	2,100	900	3,000	900	—
2	1,500	900	2,400	3,000	2,400	—
3	1,500	2,100	1,600	3,000	1,500	—
4	500	3,000	1,000	3,500	875	—
5	500	3,000	1,300	3,500	1,500	—
6	500	3,000	1,800	4,600	1,700	—

Required:

Copy and complete the following table.

	Gross Profit (Loss) Recognized					
	Percentage-of-Completion			Completed Contract		
Situation	2011	2012	2013	2011	2012	2013
1						
2						
3						
4						
5						
6						

E 5–14
Percentage-of-completion method; solve for unknowns
● LO4

In 2011, Long Construction Corporation began construction work under a three-year contract. The contract price is $1,600,000. Long uses the percentage-of-completion method for financial reporting purposes. The financial statement presentation relating to this contract at December 31, 2011, is as follows:

Balance Sheet

Accounts receivable (from construction progress billings)		$30,000
Construction in progress	$100,000	
Less: Billings on construction contract	(94,000)	
Cost of uncompleted contracts in excess of billings		6,000

Income Statement

Income (before tax) on the contract recognized in 2011	$20,000

Required:

1. What was the cost of construction actually incurred in 2011?
2. How much cash was collected in 2011 on this contract?
3. What was the estimated cost to complete as of the end of 2011?
4. What was the estimated percentage of completion used to calculate income in 2011?

(AICPA adapted)

E 5–15
Revenue recognition; software
● LO5

Easywrite Software Company shipped software to a customer on July 1, 2011. The arrangement with the customer also requires the company to provide technical support over the next 12 months and to ship an expected software upgrade on January 1, 2012. The total contract price is $243,000, and Easywrite estimates that the individual fair values of the components of the arrangement if sold separately would be:

Software	$210,000
Technical support	30,000
Upgrade	30,000

Required:

1. Determine the timing of revenue recognition for the $243,000.

2. Assume that the $243,000 contract price was paid in advance on July 1, 2011. Prepare a journal entry to record the cash receipt. Do not worry about the cost of the items sold.

E 5–16
Multiple-deliverable arrangements
● LO5

Richardson Systems sells integrated bottling manufacturing systems that involve a conveyer, a labeler, a filler, and a capper. All of this equipment is sold separately by other vendors, and the fair values of the separate equipment are as follows:

Conveyer	$20,000
Labeler	10,000
Filler	15,000
Capper	5,000
Total	$50,000

Richardson sells the integrated system for $45,000. Each of the components is shipped separately to the customer for the customer to install.

Required:

1. Assume that each of the components can be used independently, even though Richardson sells them as an integrated system. How much revenue should be allocated to each component?

2. Now assume that the labeler, filler, and capper can't be used in production without the conveyer, and that the conveyer is the last component installed. How much revenue should be recognized at the time the conveyer is installed?

E 5–17
Multiple-deliverable arrangements under IFRS
● LO5 LO7

Assume the same facts as in E5–16, but that Richardson Systems reports under IFRS. How would your answers change? (Assume for requirement 2 that separate shipment is part of the normal course of Richardson's operations, and successful customer installation is highly probable.)

E 5–18
Revenue recognition; franchise sales
● LO5

On October 1, 2011, the Submarine Sandwich Company entered into a franchise agreement with an individual. In exchange for an initial franchise fee of $300,000, Submarine will provide initial services to the franchisee to include assistance in design and construction of the building, help in training employees, and help in obtaining financing. 10% of the initial franchise fee is payable on October 1, 2011, with the remaining $270,000 payable in nine equal annual installments beginning on October 1, 2012. These installments will include interest at an appropriate rate. The franchise opened for business on January 15, 2012.

Required:

Assume that the initial services to be performed by Submarine Sandwich subsequent to October 1, 2011, are substantial and that collectibility of the installment receivable is reasonably certain. Substantial performance of the initial services is deemed to have occurred when the franchise opened. Prepare the necessary journal entries for the following dates (ignoring interest charges):

1. October 1, 2011

2. January 15, 2012

E 5–19
Concepts; terminology
● LO2 through LO6

Listed below are several terms and phrases associated with revenue recognition and profitability analysis. Pair each item from List A (by letter) with the item from List B that is most appropriately associated with it.

List A	List B
_____ 1. Inventory turnover	a. Net income divided by net sales.
_____ 2. Return on assets	b. Defers recognition until cash collected equals cost.
_____ 3. Return on shareholders' equity	c. Defers recognition until project is complete.
_____ 4. Profit margin on sales	d. Net income divided by assets.
_____ 5. Cost recovery method	e. Risks and rewards of ownership retained by seller.
_____ 6. Percentage-of-completion method	f. Contra account to construction in progress.
_____ 7. Completed contract method	g. Net income divided by shareholders' equity.
_____ 8. Asset turnover	h. Cost of goods sold divided by inventory.
_____ 9. Receivables turnover	i. Recognition is in proportion to work completed.
_____ 10. Right of return	j. Recognition is in proportion to cash received.
_____ 11. Billings on construction contract	k. Net sales divided by assets.
_____ 12. Installment sales method	l. Net sales divided by accounts receivable.
_____ 13. Consignment sales	m. Could cause the deferral of revenue recognition beyond delivery point.

E 5–20
Inventory turnover;
calculation and
evaluation
● LO6

The following is a portion of the condensed income statement for Rowan, Inc., a manufacturer of plastic containers:

Net sales		$2,460,000
Less: Cost of goods sold:		
Inventory, January 1	$ 630,000	
Net purchases	1,900,000	
Inventory, December 31	(690,000)	1,840,000
Gross profit		$ 620,000

Required:

1. Determine Rowan's inventory turnover.
2. What information does this ratio provide?

E 5–21
Evaluating
efficiency of asset
management
● LO6

The 2011 income statement of Anderson Medical Supply Company reported net sales of $8 million, cost of goods sold of $4.8 million, and net income of $800,000. The following table shows the company's comparative balance sheets for 2011 and 2010:

	($ in 000s)	
	2011	**2010**
Assets		
Cash	$ 300	$ 380
Accounts receivable	700	500
Inventory	900	700
Property, plant, and equipment (net)	2,400	2,120
Total assets	$4,300	$3,700
Liabilities and Shareholders' Equity		
Current liabilities	$ 960	$ 830
Bonds payable	1,200	1,200
Paid-in capital	1,000	1,000
Retained earnings	1,140	670
Total liabilities and shareholders' equity	$4,300	$3,700

Some industry averages for Anderson's line of business are

Inventory turnover	5 times
Average collection period	25 days
Asset turnover	1.8 times

Required:

Assess Anderson's asset management relative to its industry.

E 5–22
Profitability ratios
● LO6

The following condensed information was reported by Peabody Toys, Inc., for 2011 and 2010:

	($ in 000s)	
	2011	**2010**
Income statement information		
Net sales	$5,200	$4,200
Net income	180	124
Balance sheet information		
Current assets	$ 800	$ 750
Property, plant, and equipment (net)	1,100	950
Total assets	$1,900	$1,700
Current liabilities	$ 600	$ 450
Long-term liabilities	750	750
Paid-in capital	400	400
Retained earnings	150	100
Liabilities and shareholders' equity	$1,900	$1,700

Required:

1. Determine the following ratios for 2011:

    a. Profit margin on sales

    b. Return on assets

    c. Return on shareholders' equity

2. Determine the amount of dividends paid to shareholders during 2011.

E 5–23
DuPont analysis
● **LO6**

This exercise is based on the Peabody Toys, Inc., data from Exercise 5–22.

Required:

1. Determine the following components of the DuPont framework for 2011:

    a. Profit margin on sales.

    b. Asset turnover.

    c. Equity multiplier.

    d. Return on shareholders' equity.

2. Write an equation that relates these components in calculating ROE. Use the Peabody Toys data to show that the equation is correct.

E 5–24
Interim financial statements; income tax expense [Based on Appendix 5]
● **LO1**

Joplin Laminating Corporation reported income before income taxes during the first three quarters and management's estimates of the annual effective tax rate at the end of each quarter as shown below:

	Quarter		
	First	**Second**	**Third**
Income before income taxes	$50,000	$40,000	$100,000
Estimated annual effective tax rate	34%	30%	36%

Required:

Determine the income tax expense to be reported in the income statement in each of the three quarterly reports.

E 5–25
Interim reporting; recognizing expenses [Based on Appendix 5]
● **LO1**

Security-Rand Corporation determines executive incentive compensation at the end of its fiscal year. At the end of the first quarter, management estimated that the amount will be $300 million. Depreciation expense for the year is expected to be $60 million. Also during the quarter, the company realized a gain of $23 million from selling two of its manufacturing plants.

Required:

What amounts for these items should be reported in the first quarter's income statement?

E 5–26
Interim financial statements; reporting expenses [Based on Appendix 5]
● **LO1**

Shields Company is preparing its interim report for the second quarter ending June 30. The following payments were made during the first two quarters:

Required:

Expenditure	Date	Amount
Annual advertising	January	$800,000
Property tax for the fiscal year	February	350,000
Annual equipment repairs	March	260,000
Extraordinary casualty loss	April	185,000
Research and development	May	96,000

For each expenditure indicate the amount that would be reported in the quarterly income statements for the periods ending March 31, June 30, September 30, and December 31.

E 5–27
FASB codification research
● **LO4**

The *FASB Accounting Standards Codification* represents the single source of authoritative U.S. generally accepted accounting principles.

Required:

1. Obtain the relevant authoritative literature on the percentage-of-completion method using the FASB's Codification Research System at the FASB website (**www.fasb.org**). What is the specific citation that describes the circumstances and conditions under which it is preferable to use the percentage-of-completion method?

2. List the circumstances and conditions.

E 5–28
FASB codification research
● **LO2 LO3 LO4**

Access the *FASB's Codification Research System* at the FASB website (**www.fasb.org**).

Required:

Determine the specific citation for accounting for each of the following items:

1. When a provision for loss is recognized for a percentage-of-completion contract.

2. Circumstances indicating when the installment method or cost recovery method is appropriate for revenue recognition.

3. Criteria determining when a seller can recognize revenue at the time of sale from a sales transaction in which the buyer has the right to return the product.

CPA AND CMA REVIEW QUESTIONS

CPA Exam Questions

The following questions are used in the Kaplan CPA Review Course to study revenue recognition while preparing for the CPA examination. Determine the response that best completes the statements or questions.

KAPLAN

● LO1

1. On October 1, 2011, Acme Fuel Co. sold 100,000 gallons of heating oil to Karn Co. at $3 per gallon. Fifty thousand gallons were delivered on December 15, 2011, and the remaining 50,000 gallons were delivered on January 15, 2012. Payment terms were 50% due on October 1, 2011, 25% due on first delivery, and the remaining 25% due on second delivery. What amount of revenue should Acme recognize from this sale during 2012?
   a. $ 75,000
   b. $150,000
   c. $225,000
   d. $300,000

● LO2

2. Since there is no reasonable basis for estimating the degree of collectibility, Astor Co. uses the installment sales method of revenue recognition for the following sales:

	2011	2012
Sales	$600,000	$900,000
Collections from:		
2011 sales	200,000	100,000
2012 sales	—	300,000
Accounts written off:		
2011 sales	50,000	150,000
2012 sales	—	50,000
Gross profit percentage	30%	40%

What amount should Astor report as deferred gross profit in its December 31, 2012, balance sheet for the 2011 and 2012 sales?
   a. $225,000
   b. $150,000
   c. $160,000
   d. $250,000

● LO2

3. Dolce Co., which began operations on January 1, 2011, appropriately uses the installment sales method of accounting to record revenues. The following information is available for the years ended December 31, 2011 and 2012:

	2011	2012
Sales	$1,000,000	$2,000,000
Gross profit realized on sales made in:		
2011	150,000	90,000
2012	—	200,000
Gross profit percentages	30%	40%

What amount of installment accounts receivable should Dolce report in its December 31, 2012, balance sheet?
   a. $1,700,000
   b. $1,225,000
   c. $1,300,000
   d. $1,775,000

● LO4   4. Which of the following statements regarding the percentage-of-completion method of accounting is FALSE? The construction-in-progress account:

    a. is shown net of advance billings as a liability if the amount is less than the amount of advance billings.

    b. is an asset.

    c. is shown net of advance billings on the balance sheet.

    d. does not include the cumulative effect of gross profit recognition.

● LO4   5. The following data relates to a construction job started by Syl Co. during 2011:

Total contract price	$100,000
Actual costs during 2011	20,000
Estimated remaining costs	40,000
Billed to customer during 2011	30,000
Received from customer during 2011	10,000

Under the percentage-of-completion method, how much should Syl recognize as gross profit for 2011?

    a. $26,667

    b. $0

    c. $13,333

    d. $33,333

● LO4   6. Hansen Construction, Inc., has consistently used the percentage-of-completion method of recognizing income. During 2011, Hansen started work on a $3,000,000 fixed-price construction contract. The accounting records disclosed the following data for the year ended December 31, 2011:

Costs incurred	$ 930,000
Estimated cost to complete	2,170,000
Progress billings	1,100,000
Collections	700,000

How much loss should Hansen have recognized in 2011?

    a. $180,000

    b. $230,000

    c. $30,000

    d. $100,000

CMA Exam Questions

The following questions dealing with income measurement are adapted from questions that previously appeared on Certified Management Accountant (CMA) examinations. The CMA designation sponsored by the Institute of Management Accountants (**www.imanet.org**) provides members with an objective measure of knowledge and competence in the field of management accounting. Determine the response that best completes the statements or questions.

● LO1   1. On May 28, Markal Company purchased a tooling machine from Arens and Associates for $1,000,000 payable as follows: 50 percent at the transaction closing date and 50 percent due June 28. The cost of the machine to Arens is $800,000. Markal paid Arens $500,000 at the transaction closing date and took possession of the machine. On June 10, Arens determined that a change in the business environment has created a great deal of uncertainty regarding the collection of the balance due from Markal, and the amount is probably uncollectible. Arens and Markal have a fiscal year-end of May 31. The revenue recognized by Arens and Associates on May 28 is

    a. $200,000.

    b. $800,000.

    c. $1,000,000.

    d. $0.

● LO4   2. The percentage-of-completion method of accounting for long-term construction contracts is an exception to the

    a. Matching principle.

    b. Going-concern assumption.

    c. Economic-entity assumption.

    d. Revenue recognition principle.

● LO4   3. Roebling Construction signed a $24 million contract on August 1, 2010, with the city of Candu to construct a bridge over the Vine River. Roebling's estimated cost of the bridge on that date was $18 million. The bridge was to be completed by April 2013. Roebling uses the percentage-of-completion method for income recognition. Roebling's fiscal year ends May 31. Data regarding the bridge contract are presented in the schedule below.

	At May 31 ($000 omitted)	
	2011	**2012**
Actual costs to date	$ 6,000	$15,000
Estimated costs to complete	12,000	5,000
Progress billings to date	5,000	14,000
Cash collected to date	4,000	12,000

The gross profit or loss recognized in the fiscal year ended May 31, 2011, from this bridge contract is
a. $6,000,000 gross profit.
b. $2,000,000 gross profit.
c. $3,000,000 gross profit.
d. $1,000,000 gross profit.

PROBLEMS

|ACCOUNTING

An alternate exercise and problem set is available on the text website: www.mhhe.com/spiceland6e

P 5–1
Income statement presentation; installment sales method (Chapters 4 and 5)
● LO2

Reagan Corporation computed income from continuing operations before income taxes of $4,200,000 for 2011. The following material items have not yet been considered in the computation of income:

1. The company sold equipment and recognized a gain of $50,000. The equipment had been used in the manufacturing process and was replaced by new equipment.

2. In December, the company received a settlement of $1,000,000 for a lawsuit it had filed based on antitrust violations of a competitor. The settlement was considered to be an unusual and infrequent event.

3. Inventory costing $400,000 was written off as obsolete. Material losses of this type were incurred twice in the last eight years.

4. It was discovered that depreciation expense on the office building of $50,000 per year was not recorded in either 2010 or 2011.

In addition, you learn that *included* in revenues is $400,000 from installment sales made during the year. The cost of these sales is $240,000. At year-end, $100,000 in cash had been collected on the related installment receivables. Because of considerable uncertainty regarding the collectibility of receivables from these sales, the company's accountant should have used the installment sales method to recognize revenue and gross profit on these sales.

Also, the company's income tax rate is 40% and there were 1 million shares of common stock outstanding throughout the year.

Required:
Prepare an income statement for 2011 beginning with income from continuing operations before income taxes. Include appropriate EPS disclosures.

P 5–2
Installment sales and cost recovery methods
● LO2

Ajax Company appropriately accounts for certain sales using the installment sales method. The perpetual inventory system is used. Information related to installment sales for 2011 and 2012 is as follows:

	2011	**2012**
Sales	$300,000	$400,000
Cost of sales	180,000	280,000
Customer collections on:		
2011 sales	120,000	100,000
2012 sales		150,000

Required:
1. Calculate the amount of gross profit that would be recognized each year from installment sales.
2. Prepare all necessary journal entries for each year.
3. Repeat requirements 1 and 2 assuming that Ajax uses the cost recovery method to account for its installment sales.

P 5–3
Installment
sales; alternative
recognition
methods
● LO2

On August 31, 2011, the Silva Company sold merchandise to the Bendix Corporation for $500,000. Terms of the sale called for a down payment of $100,000 and four annual installments of $100,000 due on each August 31, beginning August 31, 2012. Each installment also will include interest on the unpaid balance applying an appropriate interest rate. The book value of the merchandise on Silva's books on the date of sale was $300,000. The perpetual inventory system is used. The company's fiscal year-end is December 31.

Required:
1. Prepare a table showing the amount of gross profit to be recognized in each of the five years of the installment sale applying each of the following methods:
   a. Point of delivery revenue recognition.
   b. Installment sales method.
   c. Cost recovery method.
2. Prepare journal entries for each of the five years applying the three revenue recognition methods listed in requirement 1. Ignore interest charges.
3. Prepare a partial balance sheet as of the end of 2011 and 2012 listing the items related to the installment sale applying each of the three methods listed in requirement 1.

P 5–4
Installment sales
and cost recovery
methods
● LO2

Mulcahey Builders (MB) remodels office buildings in low-income urban areas that are undergoing economic revitalization. MB typically accepts a 25% down payment when they complete a job and a note which requires that the remainder be paid in three equal installments over the next three years, plus interest. Because of the inherent uncertainty associated with receiving these payments, MB has historically used the cost recovery method to recognize revenue.

As of January 1, 2011, MB's outstanding gross installment accounts receivable (not net of deferred gross profit) consist of the following:

1. $400,000 due from the Bluebird Motel. MB completed the Bluebird job in 2009, and estimated gross profit on that job is 25%.
2. $150,000 due from the PitStop Gas and MiniMart. MB completed the PitStop job in 2008, and estimated gross profit on that job is 35%.

Dan Mulcahey has been considering switching from the cost recovery method to the installment sales method, because he wants to show the highest possible gross profit in 2011 and he understands that the installment sales method recognizes gross profit sooner than does the cost recovery method.

Required:
1. Calculate how much gross profit is expected to be earned on these jobs in 2011 under the cost recovery method, and how much would be earned if MB instead used the installment sales method. Ignore interest.
2. If Dan is primarily concerned about 2011, do you think he would be happy with a switch to the installment sales method? Explain.

P 5–5
Percentage-of-
completion method
● LO4

In 2011, the Westgate Construction Company entered into a contract to construct a road for Santa Clara County for $10,000,000. The road was completed in 2013. Information related to the contract is as follows:

	2011	2012	2013
Cost incurred during the year	$2,400,000	$3,600,000	$2,200,000
Estimated costs to complete as of year-end	5,600,000	2,000,000	–0–
Billings during the year	2,000,000	4,000,000	4,000,000
Cash collections during the year	1,800,000	3,600,000	4,600,000

Westgate uses the percentage-of-completion method of accounting for long-term construction contracts.

Required:
1. Calculate the amount of gross profit to be recognized in each of the three years.
2. Prepare all necessary journal entries for each of the years (credit *various accounts* for construction costs incurred).
3. Prepare a partial balance sheet for 2011 and 2012 showing any items related to the contract.
4. Calculate the amount of gross profit to be recognized in each of the three years assuming the following costs incurred and costs to complete information:

	2011	2012	2013
Costs incurred during the year	$2,400,000	$3,800,000	$3,200,000
Estimated costs to complete as of year-end	5,600,000	3,100,000	–0–

5. Calculate the amount of gross profit to be recognized in each of the three years assuming the following costs incurred and costs to complete information:

	2011	2012	2013
Costs incurred during the year	$2,400,000	$3,800,000	$3,900,000
Estimated costs to complete as of year-end	5,600,000	4,100,000	–0–

P 5–6
Completed contract method
● LO4

[This is a variation of Problem 5–5 modified to focus on the completed contract method.]

Required:
Complete the requirements of Problem 5–5 assuming that Westgate Construction uses the completed contract method.

P 5–7
Construction accounting under IFRS
● LO4 LO7

[This is a variation of the Problem 5–5 modified to focus on IFRS.]

Required:
Complete the requirements of Problem 5–5 assuming that Westgate Construction reports under IFRS and concludes that the percentage-of-completion method is not appropriate.

P 5–8
Construction accounting; loss projected on entire project
● LO4

Curtiss Construction Company, Inc., entered into a fixed-price contract with Axelrod Associates on July 1, 2011, to construct a four-story office building. At that time, Curtiss estimated that it would take between two and three years to complete the project. The total contract price for construction of the building is $4,000,000. Curtiss appropriately accounts for this contract under the completed contract method in its financial statements. The building was completed on December 31, 2013. Estimated percentage of completion, *accumulated* contract costs incurred, estimated costs to complete the contract, and *accumulated* billings to Axelrod under the contract were as follows:

	At 12-31-11	At 12-31-12	At 12-31-13
Percentage of completion	10%	60%	100%
Costs incurred to date	$ 350,000	$2,500,000	$4,250,000
Estimated costs to complete	3,150,000	1,700,000	–0–
Billings to Axelrod, to date	720,000	2,170,000	3,600,000

Required:
1. Prepare schedules to compute gross profit or loss to be recognized as a result of this contract for each of the three years.
2. Assuming Curtiss uses the percentage-of-completion method of accounting for long-term construction contracts, compute gross profit or loss to be recognized in each of the three years.
3. Assuming the percentage-of-completion method, compute the amount to be shown in the balance sheet at the end of 2011 and 2012 as either cost in excess of billings or billings in excess of costs.

(AICPA adapted)

P 5–9
Long-term contract; percentage-of-completion and completed contract methods
● LO1 LO4

Citation Builders, Inc., builds office buildings and single-family homes. The office buildings are constructed under contract with reputable buyers. The homes are constructed in developments ranging from 10–20 homes and are typically sold during construction or soon after. To secure the home upon completion, buyers must pay a deposit of 10% of the price of the home with the remaining balance due upon completion of the house and transfer of title. Failure to pay the full amount results in forfeiture of the down payment. Occasionally, homes remain unsold for as long as three months after construction. In these situations, sales price reductions are used to promote the sale.

During 2011, Citation began construction of an office building for Altamont Corporation. The total contract price is $20 million. Costs incurred, estimated costs to complete at year-end, billings, and cash collections for the life of the contract are as follows:

	2011	2012	2013
Costs incurred during the year	$ 4,000,000	$ 9,500,000	$4,500,000
Estimated costs to complete as of year-end	12,000,000	4,500,000	—
Billings during the year	2,000,000	10,000,000	8,000,000
Cash collections during the year	1,800,000	8,600,000	9,600,000

Also during 2011, Citation began a development consisting of 12 identical homes. Citation estimated that each home will sell for $600,000, but individual sales prices are negotiated with buyers. Deposits were received for eight of the homes, three of which were completed during 2011 and paid for in full for $600,000 each by the buyers. The completed homes cost $450,000 each to construct. The construction costs incurred during 2011 for the nine uncompleted homes totaled $2,700,000.

Required:

1. Briefly explain the difference between the percentage-of-completion and the completed contract methods of accounting for long-term construction contracts.

2. Answer the following questions assuming that Citation uses the completed contract method for its office building contracts:

   a. What is the amount of gross profit or loss to be recognized for the Altamont contract during 2011 and 2012?

   b. How much revenue related to this contract will Citation report in its 2011 and 2012 income statements?

   c. What will Citation report in its December 31, 2011, balance sheet related to this contract (ignore cash)?

3. Answer requirements 2a–2c assuming that Citation uses the percentage-of-completion method for its office building contracts.

4. Assume that as of year end 2012 the estimated cost to complete the office building is $9,000,000 and that Citation uses the percentage-of-completion method.

   a. What is the amount of gross profit or loss to be recognized for the Altamont contract during 2012?

   b. How much revenue related to this contract will Citation report in the 2012 income statement?

   c. What will Citation report in its 2012 balance sheet related to this contract (ignore cash)?

5. When should Citation recognize revenue for the sale of its single-family homes?

6. What will Citation report in its 2011 income statement and 2011 balance sheet related to the single-family home business (ignore cash in the balance sheet)?

P 5–10
Franchise sales;
installment sales
method
● **LO2 LO5**

Olive Branch Restaurant Corporation sells franchises throughout the western states. On January 30, 2011, the company entered into the following franchise agreement with Jim and Tammy Masters:

1. The initial franchise fee is $1.2 million. $200,000 is payable immediately and the remainder is due in 10, $100,000 installments plus 10% interest on the unpaid balance each January 30, beginning January 30, 2012. The 10% interest rate is an appropriate market rate.

2. In addition to allowing the franchisee to use the franchise name for the 10-year term of the agreement, in exchange for the initial fee Olive Branch agrees to assist the franchisee in selecting a location, obtaining financing, designing and constructing the restaurant building, and training employees.

3. All of the initial down payment of $200,000 is to be refunded by Olive Branch and the remaining obligation canceled if, for any reason, the franchisee fails to open the franchise.

4. In addition to the initial franchise fee, the franchisee is required to pay a monthly fee of 3% of franchise sales for advertising, promotion, menu planning, and other continuing services to be provided by Olive Branch over the life of the agreement. This fee is payable on the 10th of the following month.

Substantial performance of the initial services provided by Olive Branch, which are significant, is deemed to have occurred when the franchise opened on September 1, 2011. Franchise sales for the month of September 2011 were $40,000.

Required:

1. Assuming that collectibility of the installment receivable is reasonably certain, prepare the necessary journal entries for Olive Branch on the following dates (ignore interest charges on the installment receivable and the costs of providing franchise services):

   a. January 30, 2011

   b. September 1, 2011

   c. September 30, 2011

   d. January 30, 2012

2. Assume that significant uncertainty exists as to the collection of the installment receivable and that Olive Branch elects to recognize initial franchise fee revenue using the installment sales method. Prepare the necessary journal entries for the dates listed in requirement 1 (ignore interest charges on the installment receivable and the costs of providing franchise services).

3. Examine your answer to requirement 2a of this problem (the January 30, 2011, journal entry under the installment sales method). What is the effect of that journal entry on Olive Branch's balance sheet? (Ignore cash.) Briefly explain your answer.

P 5–11
Calculating activity
and profitability
ratios

● LO6

Financial statements for Askew Industries for 2011 are shown below:

2011 Income Statement

	($ in 000s)
Sales	$ 9,000
Cost of goods sold	(6,300)
Gross profit	2,700
Operating expenses	(2,000)
Interest expense	(200)
Tax expense	(200)
Net income	$ 300

Comparative Balance Sheets

	Dec. 31	
	2011	**2010**
Assets		
Cash	$ 600	$ 500
Accounts receivable	600	400
Inventory	800	600
Property, plant, and equipment (net)	2,000	2,100
	$4,000	$3,600
Liabilities and Shareholders' Equity		
Current liabilities	$1,100	$ 850
Bonds payable	1,400	1,400
Paid-in capital	600	600
Retained earnings	900	750
	$4,000	$3,600

Required:
Calculate the following ratios for 2011.

1. Inventory turnover ratio
2. Average days in inventory
3. Receivables turnover ratio
4. Average collection period
5. Asset turnover ratio
6. Profit margin on sales
7. Return on assets
8. Return on shareholders' equity
9. Equity multiplier
10. Return on shareholders' equity (using the DuPont framework)

P 5–12
Use of ratios to
compare two
companies in the
same industry

● LO6

Presented below are condensed financial statements adapted from those of two actual companies competing in the pharmaceutical industry—**Johnson and Johnson (J&J)** and **Pfizer, Inc.** ($ in millions, except per share amounts).

Required:
Evaluate and compare the two companies by responding to the following questions.

   Note: Because two-year comparative statements are not provided, you should use year-end balances in place of average balances as appropriate.

1. Which of the two companies appears more efficient in collecting its accounts receivable and managing its inventory?
2. Which of the two firms had greater earnings relative to resources available?
3. Have the two companies achieved their respective rates of return on assets with similar combinations of profit margin and turnover?
4. From the perspective of a common shareholder, which of the two firms provided a greater rate of return?
5. From the perspective of a common shareholder, which of the two firms appears to be using leverage more effectively to provide a return to shareholders above the rate of return on assets?

Balance Sheets
($ in millions, except per share data)

	J&J	Pfizer
Assets:		
Cash	$ 5,377	$ 1,520
Short-term investments	4,146	10,432
Accounts receivable (net)	6,574	8,775
Inventories	3,588	5,837
Other current assets	3,310	3,177
Current assets	22,995	29,741
Property, plant, and equipment (net)	9,846	18,287
Intangibles and other assets	15,422	68,747
Total assets	$48,263	$116,775
Liabilities and Shareholders' Equity:		
Accounts payable	$ 4,966	$ 2,601
Short-term notes	1,139	8,818
Other current liabilities	7,343	12,238
Current liabilities	13,448	23,657
Long-term debt	2,955	5,755
Other long-term liabilities	4,991	21,986
Total liabilities	21,394	51,398
Capital stock (par and additional paid-in capital)	3,120	67,050
Retained earnings	30,503	29,382
Accumulated other comprehensive income (loss)	(590)	195
Less: treasury stock and other equity adjustments	(6,164)	(31,250)
Total shareholders' equity	26,869	65,377
Total liabilities and shareholders' equity	$48,263	$116,775

Income Statements

	J&J	Pfizer
Net sales	$41,862	$ 45,188
Cost of goods sold	12,176	9,832
Gross profit	29,686	35,356
Operating expenses	19,763	28,486
Other (income) expense—net	(385)	3,610
Income before taxes	10,308	3,260
Tax expense	3,111	1,621
Net income	$ 7,197	$ 1,639*
Basic net income per share	$ 2.42	$ .22

* This is before income from discontinued operations.

P 5–13
Creating a balance sheet from ratios;
Chapters 3 and 5
● LO6

Cadux Candy Company's income statement for the year ended December 31, 2011, reported interest expense of $2 million and income tax expense of $12 million. Current assets listed in its balance sheet include cash, accounts receivable, and inventories. Property, plant, and equipment is the company's only noncurrent asset. Financial ratios for 2011 are listed below. Profitability and turnover ratios with balance sheet items in the denominator were calculated using year-end balances rather than averages.

Debt to equity ratio	1.0
Current ratio	2.0
Acid-test ratio	1.0
Times interest earned ratio	17 times
Return on assets	10%
Return on shareholders' equity	20%
Profit margin on sales	5%
Gross profit margin (gross profit divided by net sales)	40%
Inventory turnover	8 times
Receivables turnover	20 times

Required:
Prepare a December 31, 2011, balance sheet for the Cadux Candy Company.

P 5–14
Compare two
companies in the
same industry;
Chapters 3 and 5
● LO6

Presented below are condensed financial statements adapted from those of two actual companies competing as the primary players in a specialty area of the food manufacturing and distribution industry. ($ in millions, except per share amounts.)

Balance Sheets

Assets	Metropolitan	Republic
Cash	$ 179.3	$ 37.1
Accounts receivable (net)	422.7	325.0
Short-term investments	—	4.7
Inventories	466.4	635.2
Prepaid expenses and other current assets	134.6	476.7
Current assets	$1,203.0	$1,478.7
Property, plant, and equipment (net)	2,608.2	2,064.6
Intangibles and other assets	210.3	464.7
Total assets	$4,021.5	$4,008.0

Liabilities and Shareholders' Equity	Metropolitan	Republic
Accounts payable	$ 467.9	$ 691.2
Short-term notes	227.1	557.4
Accruals and other current liabilities	585.2	538.5
Current liabilities	$1,280.2	$1,787.1
Long-term debt	535.6	542.3
Deferred tax liability	384.6	610.7
Other long-term liabilities	104.0	95.1
Total liabilities	$2,304.4	$3,035.2
Common stock (par and additional paid-in capital)	144.9	335.0
Retained earnings	2,476.9	1,601.9
Less: treasury stock	(904.7)	(964.1)
Total liabilities and shareholders' equity	$4,021.5	$4,008.0

Income Statements

	Metropolitan	Republic
Net sales	$5,698.0	$7,768.2
Cost of goods sold	(2,909.0)	(4,481.7)
Gross profit	$2,789.0	$3,286.5
Operating expenses	(1,743.7)	(2,539.2)
Interest expense	(56.8)	(46.6)
Income before taxes	$ 988.5	$ 700.7
Tax expense	(394.7)	(276.1)
Net income	$ 593.8	$ 424.6
Net income per share	$ 2.40	$ 6.50

Required:
Evaluate and compare the two companies by responding to the following questions.
Note: Because comparative statements are not provided you should use year-end balances in place of average balances as appropriate.
1. Which of the two firms had greater earnings relative to resources available?
2. Have the two companies achieved their respective rates of return on assets with similar combinations of profit margin and turnover?
3. From the perspective of a common shareholder, which of the two firms provided a greater rate of return?
4. Which company is most highly leveraged and which has made most effective use of financial leverage?
5. Of the two companies, which appears riskier in terms of its ability to pay short-term obligations?
6. How efficiently are current assets managed?
7. From the perspective of a creditor, which company offers the most comfortable margin of safety in terms of its ability to pay fixed interest charges?

P 5–15
Interim financial reporting (Based on Appendix 5)
● LO1

Branson Electronics Company is a small, publicly traded company preparing its first quarter interim report to be mailed to shareholders. The following information for the quarter has been compiled:

Revenues		$180,000
Cost of goods sold		35,000
Operating expenses:		
Fixed	$59,000	
Variable	48,000	107,000

Fixed operating expenses include payments of $50,000 to an advertising firm to promote the firm through various media throughout the year. The income tax rate for the firm's level of operations in the first quarter is 30%, but management estimates the effective rate for the entire year will be 36%.

Required:
Prepare the income statement to be included in Branson's first quarter interim report.

BROADEN YOUR PERSPECTIVE

Apply your critical-thinking ability to the knowledge you've gained. These cases will provide you an opportunity to develop your research, analysis, judgment, and communication skills. You also will work with other students, integrate what you've learned, apply it in real world situations, and consider its global and ethical ramifications. This practice will broaden your knowledge and further develop your decision-making abilities.

**Real World
Case 5–1**
Chainsaw Al; revenue recognition and earnings management
● LO1

In May 2001, the Securities and Exchange Commission sued the former top executives at Sunbeam, charging the group with financial reporting fraud that allegedly cost investors billions in losses. **Sunbeam Corporation** is a recognized designer, manufacturer, and marketer of household and leisure products, including Coleman, Eastpak, First Alert, Grillmaster, Mixmaster, Mr. Coffee, Oster, Powermate, and Campingaz. In the mid-1990s, Sunbeam needed help: its profits had declined by over 80% percent, and in 1996, its stock price was down over 50% from its high. To the rescue: Albert Dunlap, also known as "Chainsaw Al" based on his reputation as a ruthless executive known for his ability to restructure and turn around troubled companies, largely by eliminating jobs.

The strategy appeared to work. In 1997, Sunbeam's revenues had risen by 18 percent. However, in April 1998, the brokerage firm of **Paine Webber** downgraded Sunbeam's stock recommendation. Why the downgrade? Paine Webber had noticed unusually high accounts receivable, massive increases in sales of electric blankets in the third quarter 1997, which usually sell best in the fourth quarter, as well as unusually high sales of barbeque grills for the fourth quarter. Soon after, Sunbeam announced a first quarter loss of $44.6 million, and Sunbeam's stock price fell 25 percent.

It eventually came to light that Dunlap and Sunbeam had been using a "bill and hold" strategy with retail buyers. This involved selling products at large discounts to retailers before they normally would buy and then holding the products in third-party warehouses, with delivery at a later date.

Many felt Sunbeam had deceived shareholders by artificially inflating earnings and the company's stock price. A class-action lawsuit followed, alleging that Sunbeam and Dunlap violated federal securities laws, suggesting the motivation to inflate the earnings and stock price was to allow Sunbeam to complete hundreds of millions of dollars of debt financing in order to complete some ongoing mergers. Shareholders alleged damages when Sunbeam's subsequent earnings decline caused a huge drop in the stock price.

Required:

1. How might Sunbeam's 1997 "bill and hold" strategy have contributed to artificially high earnings in 1997?

2. How would the strategy have led to the unusually high accounts receivable Paine Webber noticed?

3. How might Sunbeam's 1997 "bill and hold" strategy have contributed to a 1998 earnings decline?

4. How does earnings management of this type affect earnings quality?

**Judgment
Case 5–2**
Revenue recognition
● LO1

Revenue earned by a business enterprise is recognized for accounting purposes at different times, according to the circumstances. In some situations revenue is recognized approximately as it is earned in the economic sense. In other situations revenue is recognized at point of delivery.

Required:

1. Explain and justify why revenue often is recognized as earned at point of delivery.

2. Explain in what situations it would be useful to recognize revenue as the productive activity takes place.

3. At what times, other than those included in (1) and (2) above, may it be appropriate to recognize revenue?

**Judgment
Case 5–3**
Service revenue
● LO1

Mega Fitness, Inc., operates fitness centers throughout the Western states. Members pay a nonrefundable, initial fee of $100, as well as a monthly fee of $40. As an option, a member could reduce the monthly fee to $30 by increasing the initial fee to $300. The monthly fee is billed to the member near the end of each month and is due by the 15th of the following month. The only cost incurred by Mega when a new member joins a center is the cost of issuing a laminated identification card with the member's picture. The card costs $3 to produce.

Required:

When should Mega Fitness recognize revenue for the initial fee and for the monthly fee?

Judgment Case 5–4
Revenue recognition; trade-ins
● LO1

Apex Computer Company manufactures and sells large, mainframe computers. The computers range in price from $1 to $3 million and gross profit averages 40% of sales price. The company has a liberal trade-in policy. Customers are allowed to trade in their computers for a new generation machine anytime within three years of sale. The trade-in allowance granted will vary depending on the number of years between original sale and trade-in. However, in all cases, the allowance is expected to be approximately 25% higher than the prevailing market price of the computer.

As an example, in 2011 a customer who purchased a computer in 2009 for $2 million (the computer cost Apex $1,200,000 to manufacture) decided to trade it in for a new computer. The sales price of the new computer was $2.5 million and a trade-in allowance of $600,000 was granted on the old machine. As a result of the trade-in allowance, the customer had to pay only $1.9 million ($2.5 million less $600,000) for the new computer. The old computer taken back by Apex had a resale value of $480,000. The new computer cost $1.5 million to manufacture. The company accounted for the trade-in by recognizing revenue of $2,380,000 ($1.9 million received in cash + $480,000 value of old computer).

Required:

Does the company's revenue recognition policy for trade-ins seem appropriate? If not, describe the problem created by the liberal trade-in policy.

Communication Case 5–5
Revenue recognition
● LO1

Jerry's Ice Cream Parlor is considering a marketing plan to increase sales of ice cream cones. The plan will give customers a free ice cream cone if they buy 10 ice cream cones at regular prices. Customers will be issued a card that will be punched each time an ice cream cone is purchased. After 10 punches, the card can be turned in for a free cone.

Jerry Donovan, the company's owner, is not sure how the new plan will affect accounting procedures. He realizes that the company will be incurring costs each time a free ice cream cone is awarded, but there will be no corresponding revenue or cash inflow.

The focus of this case is the matching of revenues and expenses related to the free ice cream cones that will be awarded if the new plan is adopted. Your instructor will divide the class into two to six groups depending on the size of the class. The mission of your group is to reach consensus on the appropriate accounting treatment for the new plan.

Required:

1. Each group member should deliberate the situation independently and draft a tentative argument prior to the class session for which the case is assigned.

2. In class, each group will meet for 10–15 minutes in different areas of the classroom. During that meeting, group members will take turns sharing their suggestions for the purpose of arriving at a single group treatment.

3. After the allotted time, a spokesperson for each group (selected during the group meetings) will share the group's solution with the class. The goal of the class is to incorporate the views of each group into a consensus approach to the situation.

Research Case 5–6
Long-term contract accounting
● LO4

An article published in *Accounting Horizons* describes the current accounting practices and disclosures for long-term contracts for the Fortune 500 companies.

Required:

In your library or from some other source, locate the indicated article in *Accounting Horizons,* September 2004, and answer the following questions:

1. How many firms reported the use of one of the two long-term contract accounting methods?

2. Approximately half of the firms are in which industry?

3. How many firms reported the use of the percentage-of-completion method? The completed contract method?

4. What is the most frequently used approach to estimating a percentage-of-completion?

Research Case 5–7
Earnings management with respect to revenues
● LO1

An article published in *Accounting Horizons* describes various techniques that companies use to manage their earnings.

Required:

In your library or from some other source, locate the article "How Are Earnings Managed? Evidence from Auditors" in *Accounting Horizons,* 2003 (Supplement) and answer the following questions:

1. What are the four most common revenue-recognition abuses identified by auditors in that article? From the examples provided in the article, briefly explain each abuse.

2. What is the revenue-recognition abuse identified in the article related to the percentage-of-completion method?

3. Did revenue-recognition abuses tend to increase or decrease net income in the year they occurred?

4. Did auditors tend to require their clients to make adjustments that reduced the revenue-recognition abuses they detected?

Ethics Case 5–8
Revenue
recognition
● LO1

Horizon Corporation manufactures personal computers. The company began operations in 2002 and reported profits for the years 2004 through 2009. Due primarily to increased competition and price slashing in the industry, 2010's income statement reported a loss of $20 million. Just before the end of the 2011 fiscal year, a memo from the company's chief financial officer to Jim Fielding, the company controller, included the following comments:

If we don't do something about the large amount of unsold computers already manufactured, our auditors will require us to write them off. The resulting loss for 2011 will cause a violation of our debt covenants and force the company into bankruptcy. I suggest that you ship half of our inventory to J.B. Sales, Inc., in Oklahoma City. I know the company's president and he will accept the merchandise and acknowledge the shipment as a purchase. We can record the sale in 2011 which will boost profits to an acceptable level. Then J.B. Sales will simply return the merchandise in 2012 after the financial statements have been issued.

Required:

Discuss the ethical dilemma faced by Jim Fielding.

Judgment Case 5–9
Revenue
recognition;
installment sale
● LO1 LO2

On October 1, 2011, the Marshall Company sold a large piece of machinery to the Hammond Construction Company for $80,000. The cost of the machine was $40,000. Hammond made a down payment of $10,000 and agreed to pay the remaining balance in seven equal monthly installments of $10,000, plus interest at 12% on the unpaid balance, beginning November 1.

Required:

1. Identify three alternative methods for recognizing revenue and costs for the situation described and compute the amount of gross profit that would be recognized in 2011 using each method.

2. Discuss the circumstances under which each of the three methods would be used.

Judgment Case 5–10
Revenue
recognition;
SAB 101 questions;
FASB codification
● LO1

As part of its crackdown on earnings management, the SEC issued *Staff Accounting Bulletin No. 101* to provide additional guidance on when revenue should be recognized. Consider the following situations posed by the SEC and, for each, discuss whether or not you believe it is appropriate to recognize revenue. You might gain access to this literature through the FASB Codification Research System via the FASB website (**www.fasb.org**), the SEC (**www.sec.gov**), your school library, or some other source.

1. **Facts:** Company M is a discount retailer. It generates revenue from annual membership fees it charges customers to shop at its stores and from the sale of products at a discount price to those customers. The membership arrangements with retail customers require the customer to pay the entire membership fee (e.g., $35) at the outset of the arrangement. However, the customer has the unilateral right to cancel the arrangement at any time during its term and receive a full refund of the initial fee. Based on historical data collected over time for a large number of homogeneous transactions, Company M estimates that approximately 40% of the customers will request a refund before the end of the membership contract term. Company M's data for the past five years indicates that significant variations between actual and estimated cancellations have not occurred, and Company M does not expect significant variations to occur in the foreseeable future.

   Question: May Company M recognize revenue for the membership fees and accrue the costs to provide membership services at the outset of the arrangement?

2. **Facts:** Company Z enters into an arrangement with Customer A to deliver Company Z's products to Customer A on a consignment basis. Pursuant to the terms of the arrangement, Customer A is a consignee, and title to the products does not pass from Company Z to Customer A until Customer A consumes the products in its operations. Company Z delivers product to Customer A under the terms of their arrangement.

   Question: May Company Z recognize revenue upon delivery of its product to Customer A?

3. **Facts:** Company R is a retailer that offers "layaway" sales to its customers. Company R retains the merchandise, sets it aside in its inventory, and collects a cash deposit from the customer. Although Company R may set a time period within which the customer must finalize the purchase, Company R does not require the customer to enter into an installment note or other fixed payment commitment or agreement when the initial deposit is received. The merchandise generally is not released to the customer until the customer pays the full purchase price. In the event that the customer fails to pay the remaining purchase price, the customer forfeits its cash deposit. In the event the merchandise is lost, damaged, or destroyed, Company R either must refund the cash deposit to the customer or provide replacement merchandise.

   Question: When may Company R recognize revenue for merchandise sold under its layaway program?

Research Case 5–11
Locate and extract relevant information and authoritative support for a financial reporting issue; revenue recognition; right of return; FASB codification

● LO3

Many companies sell products allowing their customers the right to return merchandise if they are not satisfied. Because the return of merchandise can retroactively negate the benefits of having made a sale, the seller must meet certain criteria before revenue is recognized in situations when the right of return exists. Generally accepted accounting principles list the criteria, the most critical of which is that the seller must be able to make reliable estimates of future returns.

Required:

1. Obtain the relevant authoritative literature on accounting for the right to return merchandise using the FASB's Codification Research System. You might gain access at the FASB website (**www.fasb.org**), from your school library, or some other source.
2. What factors do generally accepted accounting principles discuss that may impair the ability to make a reasonable estimate of returns? Cite the reference location regarding these factors.
3. List the criteria that must be met before revenue can be recognized when the right of return exists.
4. Using EDGAR (**www.sec.gov**) access the 10-K reports for the most recent fiscal year for **Hewlett-Packard Company** and for **Advanced Micro Devices, Inc.** Search for the revenue recognition policy to determine when these two companies recognize revenue for product sales allowing customers the right of return.
5. Using your answers to requirements 2 and 3, speculate as to why the two revenue recognition policies differ.

Research Case 5–12
FASB codification; locate and extract relevant information and authoritative support for a financial reporting issue; reporting revenue as a principal or as an agent

● LO1

Real World Financials

The birth of the Internet in the 1990s led to the creation of a new industry of online retailers such as **Amazon, Overstock.com**, and **PC Mall, Inc.** Many of these companies often act as intermediaries between the manufacturer and the customer without ever taking possession of the merchandise sold. Revenue recognition for this type of transaction has been controversial.

Assume that **Overstock.com** sold you a product for $200 that cost $150. The company's profit on the transaction clearly is $50. Should Overstock recognize $200 in revenue and $150 in cost of goods sold (the gross method), or should it recognize only the $50 in gross profit (the net method) as commission revenue?

Required:

1. Obtain the relevant authoritative literature on reporting revenue at gross versus net using the FASB's Codification Research System. You might gain access at the FASB website (**www.fasb.org**), from your school library, or some other source. *Hint:* this guidance was originally issued in the Emerging Issues Task Force document EITF 99-19, and you can use the codification's "Cross Reference" function to identify where that EITF appears in the codification.
2. What factors does the authoritative literature discuss that will influence the choice of reporting method used by these companies? Cite the reference location and the specific titles pertaining to this reference location.
3. Using EDGAR (**www.sec.gov**), access **Google, Inc.**'s 2008 10-K. Locate the disclosure note that discusses the company's revenue recognition policy.
4. Does Google discuss determining whether they should report revenue on a gross versus net basis with respect to any of their products or services? What is the reason Google provides for its choices? Do you agree with Google's reasoning?

Judgment Case 5–13
Revenue recognition; service sales

● LO1 LO4

Each of the following situations concerns revenue recognition for services.

1. **Delta Airlines** books a reservation for a roundtrip flight to Orlando for Ming Tsai on April 12. Delta charges the $425 to Tsai's Visa card on April 13 and receives the cash from Visa on May 1. The roundtrip flight commences on May 15. The ticket is nonrefundable.
2. Highlife Ski Resort in Colorado sells a season pass to Larry Werner on October 15. Highlife usually opens its season just after Thanksgiving and stays open until approximately April 30.
3. Dixon Management requires tenants to sign a three-year lease and charges $5,000 per month for one floor in its midtown high-rise. In addition to the monthly fee, payable at the beginning of each month, tenants pay a nonrefundable fee of $12,000 to secure the lease.
4. Janora Hawkins, attorney, agrees to accept an accident victim's case. Hawkins will be paid on a contingency basis. That is, if she wins the case, she will receive 30% of the total settlement. The case commences on July 15 and is settled successfully on August 28. On September 15, Hawkins receives her contingency payment of $60,000.

Required:

For each of the above situations, determine the appropriate timing of revenue recognition.

Judgment Case 5–14
Revenue recognition; long-term construction contracts

● LO4

Two accounting students were discussing the alternative methods of accounting for long-term construction contracts. The discussion focused on which method was most like the typical revenue recognition method of recognizing revenue at point of product delivery. Bill argued that the completed contract method was preferable because it was analogous to recognizing revenue at the point of delivery. John disagreed and supported the percentage-of-completion method, stating that it was analogous to accruing revenue during the earnings process, that is, as the work was performed.

Required:

Discuss the arguments made by both students. Which argument do you support? Why?

Communication Case 5–15
Percentage-of-completion and completed contract methods
● LO4

Willingham Construction is in the business of building high-priced, custom, single-family homes. The company, headquartered in Anaheim, California, operates throughout the Southern California area. The construction period for the average home built by Willingham is six months, although some homes have taken as long as nine months.

You have just been hired by Willingham as the assistant controller and one of your first tasks is to evaluate the company's revenue recognition policy. The company presently uses the completed contract method for all of its projects and management is now considering a switch to the percentage-of-completion method.

Required:

Write a 1- to 2-page memo to Virginia Reynolds, company controller, describing the differences between the percentage-of-completion and completed contract methods. Be sure to include references to GAAP as they pertain to the choice of method. Do not address the differential effects on income taxes nor the effect on the financial statements of switching between methods.

IFRS Case 5–16
Comparison of revenue recognition in Sweden and the United States
● LO1 LO7

Vodafone Group, Plc, headquartered in the United Kingdom, is one of the world's largest telecommunications companies. Excerpts from the revenue recognition disclosure included in its 2009 annual report are reproduced below.

Note 2: Significant accounting policies

Revenue

Revenue is recognised to the extent the Group has delivered goods or rendered services under an agreement, the amount of revenue can be measured reliably and it is probable that the economic benefits associated with the transaction will flow to the Group. Revenue is measured at the fair value of the consideration received, exclusive of sales taxes and discounts.

The Group principally obtains revenue from providing the following telecommunication services: access charges, airtime usage, messaging, interconnect fees, data services and information provision, connection fees and equipment sales. Products and services may be sold separately or in bundled packages.

Revenue for access charges, airtime usage and messaging by contract customers is recognised as revenue as services are performed, with unbilled revenue resulting from services already provided accrued at the end of each period and unearned revenue from services to be provided in future periods deferred. Revenue from the sale of prepaid credit is deferred until such time as the customer uses the airtime, or the credit expires.

Revenue from interconnect fees is recognised at the time the services are performed.

Revenue from data services and information provision is recognised when the Group has performed the related service and, depending on the nature of the service, is recognised either at the gross amount billed to the customer or the amount receivable by the Group as commission for facilitating the service. . . .

Revenue for device sales is recognised when the device is delivered to the end customer and the sale is considered complete. For device sales made to intermediaries, revenue is recognised if the significant risks associated with the device are transferred to the intermediary and the intermediary has no general right of return. If the significant risks are not transferred, revenue recognition is deferred until sale of the device to an end customer by the intermediary or the expiry of the right of return.

Required:

On the basis of the information the disclosures provide, compare revenue recognition under IFRS (as applied by Vodafone) with that in the United States.

IFRS Case 5–17
Comparison of revenue recognition for construction contracts
● LO4 LO7

ThyssenKrupp AG, headquartered in Germany, is one of the world's biggest technology companies, with more than 199,000 employees worldwide and primary segments in steel, technology, and capital goods and services.

Required:

1. Access ThyssenKrupp's most recent annual report using the Internet. Find the footnote describing significant accounting policies. Indicate the methods that ThyssenKrupp uses to account for long-term construction contracts when they can and cannot make an accurate estimate of the income on a construction contract.
2. If ThyssenKrupp was a U.S company, how would you expect its accounting for these contracts to differ?

Trueblood Accounting Case 5–18
Revenue recognition; license agreement
● LO1

The following Trueblood case is recommended for use with this chapter. The case provides an excellent opportunity for class discussion, group projects, and writing assignments. The case, along with Professor's Discussion Material, can be obtained from the Deloitte Foundation at its website: **www.deloitte.com/us/truebloodcases**.

Case 04-7: *Lighthouse*

This case concerns the appropriate timing of revenue recognition for a bundled product and service.

Trueblood Accounting Case 5–19
Revenue recognition for multiple-deliverable contracts
● LO5

The following Trueblood case is recommended for use with this chapter. The case provides an excellent opportunity for class discussion, group projects, and writing assignments. The case, along with Professor's Discussion Material, can be obtained from the Deloitte Foundation at its website **www.deloitte.com/us/truebloodcases**.

Case 07-3 Part 1: *Columbia On-Line Networks*

This case concerns recognizing revenue of arrangements that have multiple elements.

Real World Case 5–20
Revenue recognition; franchise sales
● LO5

EDGAR, the Electronic Data Gathering, Analysis, and Retrieval system, performs automated collection, validation, indexing, and forwarding of submissions by companies and others who are required by law to file forms with the U.S. Securities and Exchange Commission (SEC). All publicly traded domestic companies use EDGAR to make the majority of their filings. (Some foreign companies file voluntarily.) Form 10-K or 10-KSB, which include the annual report, is required to be filed on EDGAR. The SEC makes this information available on the Internet.

Required:

1. Access EDGAR on the Internet. The web address is **www.sec.gov**.
2. Search for **Jack in the Box, Inc.** Access the most recent 10-K filing. Search or scroll to find the financial statements and related notes.
3. Answer the following questions related to the company's revenue recognition policies:
   a. When does the company recognize initial franchise license fee revenue?
   b. How are continuing fees determined?
4. Repeat requirements 2 and 3 for two additional companies that you suspect also earn revenues through the sale of franchise rights. Compare their revenue recognition policies with the policies of Jack in the Box.

Analysis Case 5–21
Evaluating profitability and asset management; obtain and compare annual reports from companies in the same industry
● LO6

Performance and profitability of a company often are evaluated using the financial information provided by a firm's annual report in comparison with other firms in the same industry. Ratios are useful in this assessment.

Required:

Obtain annual reports from two corporations in the same primary industry. Using techniques you learned in this chapter and any analysis you consider useful, respond to the following questions:

1. How do earnings trends compare in terms of both the direction and stability of income?
2. Which of the two firms had greater earnings relative to resources available?
3. How efficiently are current assets managed?
4. Has each of the companies achieved its respective rate of return on assets with similar combinations of profit margin and turnover?
5. Are there differences in accounting methods that should be taken into account when making comparisons?

Note: You can obtain copies of annual reports from friends who are shareholders, the investor relations department of the corporations, from a friendly stockbroker, or from EDGAR (Electronic Data Gathering, Analysis, and Retrieval) on the Internet (**www.sec.gov**).

Judgment Case 5–22
Relationships among ratios; Chapters 3 and 5
● LO6

You are a part-time financial advisor. A client is considering an investment in common stock of a waste recycling firm. One motivation is a rumor the client heard that the company made huge investments in a new fuel creation process. Unable to confirm the rumor, your client asks you to determine whether the firm's assets had recently increased significantly.

Because the firm is small, information is sparse. Last quarter's interim report showed total assets of $324 million, approximately the same as last year's annual report. The only information more current than that is a press release last week in which the company's management reported "record net income for the year of $21 million, representing a 14.0% return on shareholders' equity. Performance was enhanced by the Company's judicious use of financial leverage on a debt/equity ratio of 2 to 1."

Required:

Use the information available to provide your client with an opinion as to whether the waste recycling firm invested in the new fuel creation process during the last quarter of the year.

Integrating Case 5–23
Using ratios to test reasonableness of data; Chapters 3 and 5
● LO6

You are a new staff accountant with a large regional CPA firm, participating in your first audit. You recall from your auditing class that CPAs often use ratios to test the reasonableness of accounting numbers provided by the client. Since ratios reflect the relationships among various account balances, if it is assumed that prior relationships still hold, prior years' ratios can be used to estimate what current balances should approximate. However, you never actually performed this kind of analysis until now. The CPA in charge of the audit of Covington Pike Corporation brings you the list of ratios shown below and tells you these reflect the relationships maintained by Covington Pike in recent years.

Profit margin on sales = 5%
Return on assets = 7.5%
Gross profit margin = 40%
Inventory turnover ratio = 6 times
Receivables turnover ratio = 25
Acid-test ratio = .9
Current ratio = 2 to 1
Return on shareholders' equity = 10%
Debt to equity ratio = 1/3
Times interest earned ratio = 12 times

Jotted in the margins are the following notes:

- Net income $15,000
- Only one short-term note ($5,000); all other current liabilities are trade accounts
- Property, plant, and equipment are the only noncurrent assets
- Bonds payable are the only noncurrent liabilities
- The effective interest rate on short-term notes and bonds is 8%
- No investment securities
- Cash balance totals $15,000

Required:

You are requested to approximate the current year's balances in the form of a balance sheet and income statement, to the extent the information allows. Accompany those financial statements with the calculations you use to estimate each amount reported.

BRITISH AIRWAYS CASE

British Airways, Plc. (BA), a U.K. company, prepares its financial statements according to International Financial Reporting Standards. BA's annual report for the year ended March 31, 2009, which includes financial statements and disclosure notes, is included with all new textbooks and can be found at **www.britishairways.com**. When answering questions, focus on BA's "Group" financial information (which is equivalent to "Consolidated" under U.S. GAAP).

Required:

BA changed how it accounts for BA miles that are earned by members of their "Executive Club." How does BA account for that revenue? Is this accounting approach consistent with how U.S. GAAP accounts for multiple-deliverable contracts? Explain. Based on your reading of their footnotes, how important an amount do you think this is for BA?

CPA SIMULATION 5–1

Leonard Brothers
Revenue Recognition

CPA Review

Test your knowledge of the concepts discussed in this chapter, practice critical professional skills necessary for career success, and prepare for the computer-based CPA exam by accessing our CPA simulations at the text website: **www.mhhe.com/spiceland6e**.

The Leonard Brothers simulation tests your knowledge of various revenue recognition issues and methods, including (a) the installment sales method, (b) revenue recognition for long-term contracts, and (c) accounting for franchise sales.

As on the CPA exam itself, you will be asked to use tools including a spreadsheet, a calculator, and generally accepted accounting principles, to conduct research, derive solutions, and communicate conclusions related to these issues in a simulated environment.

Specific tasks in the simulation address:

- Applying judgment in determining the revenue recognition method appropriate in various situations.
- Demonstrating an understanding of the installment sales method.
- Determining the appropriate journal entries for a long-term contract accounted for using the percentage-of-completion method.
- Analyzing the effect on the income statement and balance sheet of applying the percentage-of-completion method.
- Communicating the financial statement effects of using the percentage-of-completion method.
- Researching the accounting treatment and disclosure requirements for franchise sales.

6

Time Value of Money Concepts

|||||||||||||||||||||||||||||||||||||||||||||||||||||||||||||

/// OVERVIEW

Time value of money concepts, specifically future value and present value, are essential in a variety of accounting situations. These concepts and the related computational procedures are the subjects of this chapter. Present values and future values of *single amounts* and present values and future values of *annuities* (series of equal periodic payments) are described separately but shown to be interrelated.

/// LEARNING OBJECTIVES

After studying this chapter, you should be able to:

- **LO1** Explain the difference between simple and compound interest. (page 300)
- **LO2** Compute the future value of a single amount. (page 301)
- **LO3** Compute the present value of a single amount. (page 302)
- **LO4** Solve for either the interest rate or the number of compounding periods when present value and future value of a single amount are known. (page 304)
- **LO5** Explain the difference between an ordinary annuity and an annuity due situation. (page 309)
- **LO6** Compute the future value of both an ordinary annuity and an annuity due. (page 310)
- **LO7** Compute the present value of an ordinary annuity, an annuity due, and a deferred annuity. (page 312)
- **LO8** Solve for unknown values in annuity situations involving present value. (page 316)
- **LO9** Briefly describe how the concept of the time value of money is incorporated into the valuation of bonds, long-term leases, and pension obligations. (page 320)

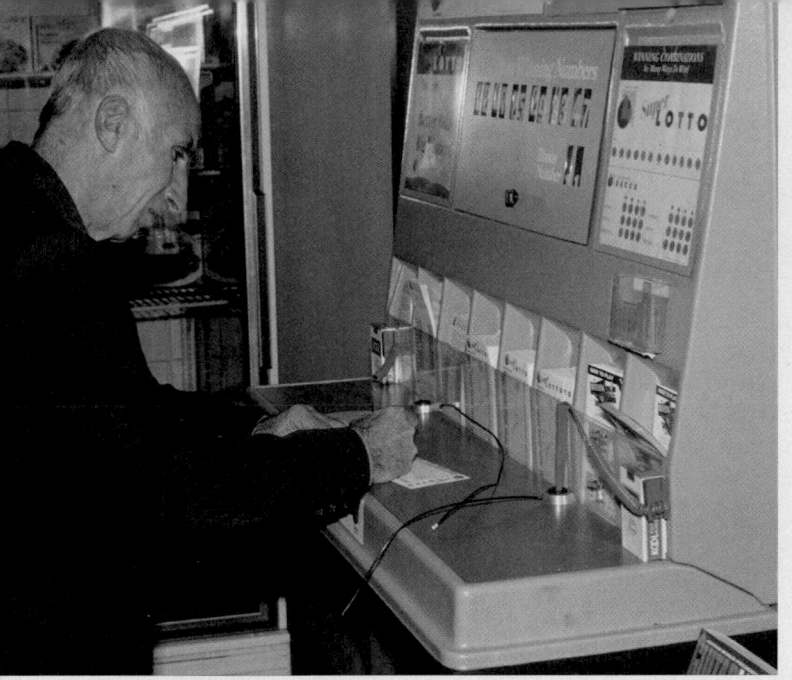

The Winning Ticket

Al Castellano had been buying California State lottery tickets for 15 years at his neighborhood grocery store. On Sunday, June 24, 2010, his world changed. When he awoke, opened the local newspaper, and compared his lottery ticket numbers with Saturday night's winning numbers, he couldn't believe his eyes. All of the numbers on his ticket matched the winning numbers. He went outside for a walk, came back into the kitchen and checked the numbers again. He woke his wife Carmen, told her what had happened, and they danced through their apartment. Al, a 66-year-old retired supermarket clerk, and Carmen, a 62-year-old semiretired secretary, had won the richest lottery in California's history, $141 million!

On Monday when Al and Carmen claimed their prize, their ecstasy waned slightly when they were informed that they would soon be receiving a check for approximately $43 million. When the Castellanos purchased the lottery ticket, they indicated that they would like to receive any lottery winnings in one lump payment rather than in 26 equal annual installments beginning now. They knew beforehand that the State of California is required to withhold 31% of lottery winnings for federal income tax purposes, but this reduction was way more than 31%.

Source: This case is adapted from an actual situation.

By the time you finish this chapter, you should be able to respond appropriately to the questions posed in this case. Compare your response to the solution provided at the end of the chapter.

QUESTIONS ///

1. Why were the Castellanos to receive $43 million rather than the $141 million lottery prize? (page 312)

2. What interest rate did the State of California use to calculate the $43 million lump-sum payment? (page 318)

3. What are some of the accounting applications that incorporate the time value of money into valuation? (page 320)

BASIC CONCEPTS
Time Value of Money

The *time value of money* means that money can be invested today to earn interest and grow to a larger dollar amount in the future.

The key to solving the problem described in the financial reporting case is an understanding of the concept commonly referred to as the **time value of money.** This concept means that money invested today will grow to a larger dollar amount in the future. For example, $100 invested in a savings account at your local bank yielding 6% annually will grow to $106 in one year. The difference between the $100 invested now—the present value of the investment—and its $106 future value represents the time value of money.

This concept has nothing to do with the worth or buying power of those dollars. Prices in our economy can change. If the inflation rate were higher than 6%, then the $106 you would have in the savings account actually would be worth less than the $100 you had a year earlier. The time value of money concept concerns only the growth in the dollar amounts of money.

Time value of money concepts are useful in valuing several assets and liabilities.

The concepts you will learn in this chapter are useful in solving many business decisions such as, for example, the determination of the lottery award presented in the financial reporting case at the beginning of this chapter. More important, the concepts also are necessary when valuing assets and liabilities for financial reporting purposes. As you will see in this and subsequent chapters, most accounting applications that incorporate the time value of money involve the concept of present value. The valuation of leases, bonds, pension obligations, and certain notes receivable and payable are a few prominent examples. It is important that you master the concepts and tools we review here. This knowledge is essential to the remainder of your accounting education.

Simple versus Compound Interest

● **LO1**

Interest is the amount of money paid or received in excess of the amount borrowed or lent.

Interest is the "rent" paid for the use of money for some period of time. In dollar terms, it is the amount of money paid or received in excess of the amount of money borrowed or lent. If you lent the bank $100 today and "received" $106 a year from now, your interest earned would be $6. Interest also can be expressed as a rate at which money will grow. In this case, that rate is 6%. It is this interest that gives money its time value.

Simple interest is computed by multiplying an initial investment times both the applicable interest rate and the period of time for which the money is used. For example, simple interest earned each year on a $1,000 investment paying 10% is $100 ($1,000 × 10%).

Compound interest includes interest not only on the initial investment but also on the accumulated interest in previous periods.

Compound interest results in increasingly larger interest amounts for each period of the investment. The reason is that interest is now being earned not only on the initial investment amount but also on the accumulated interest earned in previous periods.

For example, Cindy Johnson invested $1,000 in a savings account paying 10% interest *compounded* annually. How much interest will she earn each year, and what will be her investment balance after three years?

Date	Interest (Interest rate × Outstanding balance = Interest)	Balance
Initial deposit		$1,000
End of year 1	10% × $1,000 = $100	$1,100
End of year 2	10% × $1,100 = $110	$1,210
End of year 3	10% × $1,210 = $121	$1,331

With compound interest at 10% annually, the $1,000 investment would grow to $1,331 at the end of the three-year period. Of course, if Cindy withdrew the interest earned each year, she would earn only $100 in interest each year, that is, the amount of simple interest. If the investment period had been 20 years, 20 individual calculations would be needed. However, calculators, computer programs, and compound interest tables make these calculations much easier.

Most banks compound interest more frequently than once a year. Daily compounding is common for savings accounts. More rapid compounding has the effect of increasing the actual rate, which is called the **effective rate,** at which money grows per year. It is important to note that interest is typically stated as an annual rate regardless of the length of the compounding period involved. In situations when the compounding period is less than a year, the interest rate per compounding period is determined by dividing the annual rate by the number of periods. Assuming an annual rate of 12%:

Compounded	Interest Rate Per Compounding Period
Semiannually	12% ÷ 2 = 6%
Quarterly	12% ÷ 4 = 3%
Monthly	12% ÷ 12 = 1%

Interest rates are typically stated as annual rates.

As an example, now let's assume Cindy Johnson invested $1,000 in a savings account paying 10% interest *compounded* twice a year. There are two six-month periods paying interest at 5% (the annual rate divided by two periods). How much interest will she earn the first year, and what will be her investment balance at the end of the year?

Date	Interest (Interest rate × Outstanding balance = Interest)	Balance
Initial deposit		$1,000.00
After six months	5% × $1,000 = $50.00	$1,050.00
End of year 1	5% × $1,050 = $52.50	$1,102.50

The $1,000 would grow by $102.50, the interest earned, to $1,102.50, $2.50 more than if interest were compounded only once a year. The effective annual interest rate, often referred to as the annual *yield,* is 10.25% ($102.50 ÷ $1,000).

The *effective interest rate* is the rate at which money actually will grow during a full year.

Valuing a Single Cash Flow Amount

Future Value of a Single Amount

In the first Cindy example, in which $1,000 was invested for three years at 10% compounded annually, the $1,331 is referred to as the **future value (FV).** A time diagram is a useful way to visualize this relationship, with 0 indicating the date of the initial investment.

● LO2

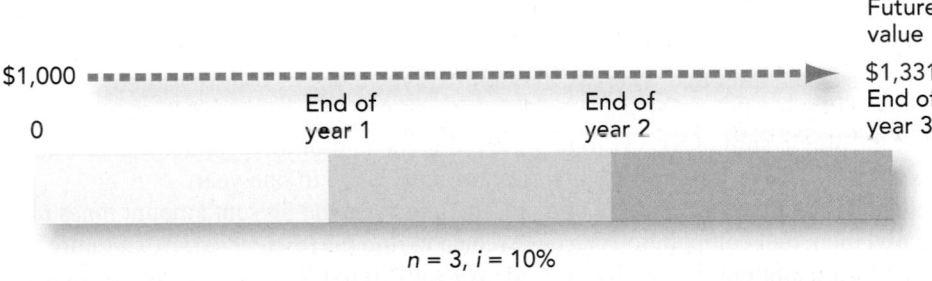

$n = 3, i = 10\%$

Future value of a single amount.

The future value after one year can be calculated as $1,000 × 1.10 (1.00 + .10) = $1,100. After three years, the future value is $1,000 × 1.10 × 1.10 × 1.10 = $1,331. In fact, the future value of any invested amount can be determined as follows:

$$FV = I\,(1 + i)^n$$

where: FV = Future value of the invested amount
          I = Amount invested at the beginning of the period
          i = Interest rate
          n = Number of compounding periods

The *future value* of a single amount is the amount of money that a dollar will grow to at some point in the future.

The future value can be determined by using Table 1, Future Value of $1, located at the end of this textbook. The table contains the future value of $1 invested for various periods of time, *n,* and at various rates, *i.*

With this table, it's easy to determine the future value of any invested amount simply by multiplying it by the table value at the *intersection* of the column for the desired rate and the row for the number of compounding periods. Graphic 6–1 contains an excerpt from Table 1.

GRAPHIC 6–1

Future Value of $1 (excerpt from Table 1 located at the end of this textbook)

Periods (n)	Interest Rates (i)					
	7%	8%	9%	10%	11%	12%
1	1.07000	1.08000	1.09000	1.10000	1.11000	1.12000
2	1.14490	1.16640	1.18810	1.21000	1.23210	1.25440
3	1.22504	1.25971	1.29503	1.33100	1.36763	1.40493
4	1.31080	1.36049	1.41158	1.46410	1.51807	1.57352
5	1.40255	1.46933	1.53862	1.61051	1.68506	1.76234
6	1.50073	1.58687	1.67710	1.77156	1.87041	1.97382
7	1.60578	1.71382	1.82804	1.94872	2.07616	2.21068
8	1.71819	1.85093	1.99256	2.14359	2.30454	2.47596

The table shows various values of $(1 + i)^n$ for different combinations of i and n. From the table you can find the future value factor for three periods at 10% to be 1.331. This means that $1 invested at 10% compounded annually will grow to approximately $1.33 in three years. So, the future value of $1,000 invested for three years at 10% is $1,331:

$$FV = I \times FV\ factor$$
$$FV = \$1,000 \times 1.331^* = \$1,331$$
*Future value of $1; n = 3, i = 10%

The future value function in *financial calculators* or *in computer spreadsheet programs* calculates future values in the same way. Determining future values (and present values) electronically avoids the need for tables such as those in the chapter appendix. It's important to remember that the n in the future value formula refers to the number of compounding periods, not necessarily the number of years. For example, suppose you wanted to know the future value *two* years from today of $1,000 invested at 12% with *quarterly* compounding. The number of periods is therefore eight and the compounding rate is 3% (12% annual rate divided by four, the number of quarters in a year). The future value factor from Table 1 is 1.26677, so the future value is $1,266.77 ($1,000 × 1.26677).[1]

Present Value of a Single Amount

● LO3

The *present value* of a single amount is today's equivalent to a particular amount in the future.

The example used to illustrate future value reveals that $1,000 invested today is equivalent to $1,100 received after one year, $1,210 after two years, or $1,331 after three years, assuming 10% interest compounded annually. Thus, the $1,000 investment (I) is the **present value (PV)** of the single sum of $1,331 to be received at the end of three years. It is also the present value of $1,210 to be received in two years and $1,100 in one year.

Remember that the future value of a present amount is the present amount *times* $(1 + i)^n$. Logically, then, that computation can be reversed to find the *present value* of a future amount to be the future amount *divided* by $(1 + i)^n$. We substitute PV for I (invested amount) in the future value formula above.

$$FV = PV\ (1 + i)^n$$

$$PV = \frac{FV}{(1 + i)^n}$$

---

[1]When interest is compounded more frequently than once a year, the effective annual interest rate, or yield, can be determined using the following equation:

$$Yield = (1 + \frac{i}{p})^p - 1$$

with i being the annual interest rate and p the number of compounding periods per year. In this example, the annual yield would be 12.55%, calculated as follows:

$$Yield = (1 + \frac{.12}{4})^4 - 1 = 1.1255 - 1 = .1255$$

Determining the yield is useful when comparing returns on investment instruments with different compounding period length.

In our example,

$$PV = \frac{\$1,331}{(1 + .10)^3} = \frac{\$1,331}{1.331} = \$1,000$$

Of course, dividing by $(1 + i)^n$ is the same as multiplying by its reciprocal, $1/(1 + i)^n$.

$$PV = \$1,331 \times \frac{1}{(1 + .10)^3} = \$1,331 \times .75131 = \$1,000$$

As with future value, these computations are simplified by using calculators, computer programs, or present value tables. Table 2, Present Value of $1, located at the end of this textbook provides the solutions of $1/(1 + i)^n$ for various interest rates (i) and compounding periods (n). These amounts represent the present value of $1 to be received at the *end* of the different periods. The table can be used to find the present value of any single amount to be received in the future by *multiplying* that amount by the value in the table that lies at the *intersection* of the column for the appropriate rate and the row for the number of compounding periods.[2] Graphic 6–2 contains an excerpt from Table 2.

		Interest Rates (*i*)				
Periods (*n*)	**7%**	**8%**	**9%**	**10%**	**11%**	**12%**
1	.93458	.92593	.91743	.90909	.90090	.89286
2	.87344	.85734	.84168	.82645	.81162	.79719
3	.81630	.79383	.77218	.75131	.73119	.71178
4	.76290	.73503	.70843	.68301	.65873	.63552
5	.71299	.68058	.64993	.62092	.59345	.56743
6	.66634	.63017	.59627	.56447	.53464	.50663
7	.62275	.58349	.54703	.51316	.48166	.45235
8	.58201	.54027	.50187	.46651	.43393	.40388

GRAPHIC 6–2

Present Value of $1 (excerpt from Table 2 located at the end of this textbook)

Notice that the farther into the future the $1 is to be received, the less valuable it is now. This is the essence of the concept of the time value of money. Given a choice between $1,000 now and $1,000 three years from now, you would choose to have the money now. If you have it now, you could put it to use. But the choice between, say, $740 now and $1,000 three years from now would depend on your time value of money. If your time value of money is 10%, you would choose the $1,000 in three years, because the $740 invested at 10% for three years would grow to only $984.94 [$740 × 1.331 (FV of $1, i = 10%, n = 3)]. On the other hand, if your time value of money is 11% or higher, you would prefer the $740 now. Presumably, you would invest the $740 now and have it grow to $1,012.05 ($740 × 1.36763) in three years.

Using the present value table above, the present value of $1,000 to be received in three years assuming a time value of money of 10% is $751.31 [$1,000 × .75131 (PV of $1, i = 10% and n = 3)]. Because the present value of the future amount, $1,000, is higher than $740 we could have today, we again determine that with a time value of money of 10%, the $1,000 in three years is preferred to the $740 now.

In our earlier example, $1,000 now is equivalent to $1,331 in three years, assuming the time value of money is 10%. Graphically, the relation between the present value and the future value can be viewed this way:

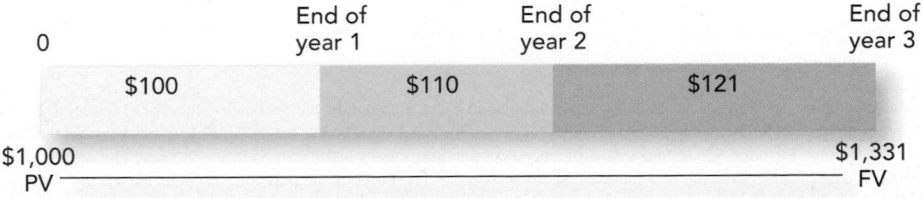

0	End of year 1	End of year 2	End of year 3
$100	$110	$121	

$1,000
PV ——————————————————————————————— FV $1,331

---

[2]The factors in Table 2 are the reciprocals of those in Table 1. For example, the future value factor for 10%, three periods is 1.331, while the present value factor is .75131. $1 ÷ 1.331 = $.75131, and $1 ÷ .75131 = $1.331.

The calculation of future value requires the addition of interest, while the calculation of present value requires the removal of interest.

While the calculation of future value of a single sum invested today requires the *inclusion* of compound interest, present value problems require the *removal* of compound interest. The process of computing present value *removes* the $331 of interest earned over the three-year period from the future value of $1,331, just as the process of computing future value *adds* $331 of interest to the present value of $1,000 to arrive at the future value of $1,331.

Accountants use PV calculations much more frequently than FV.

As we demonstrate later in this chapter and in subsequent chapters, present value calculations are incorporated into accounting valuation much more frequently than future value.

Solving for Other Values When FV and PV are Known

● LO4

There are four variables in the process of adjusting single cash flow amounts for the time value of money: the present value (PV), the future value (FV), the number of compounding periods (n), and the interest rate (i). If you know any three of these, the fourth can be determined. Illustration 6–1 solves for an unknown interest rate and Illustration 6–2 determines an unknown number of periods.

DETERMINING THE UNKNOWN INTEREST RATE

ILLUSTRATION 6–1 Determining i When PV, FV, and n are Known	Suppose a friend asks to borrow $500 today and promises to repay you $605 two years from now. What is the annual interest rate you would be agreeing to?

The following time diagram illustrates the situation:

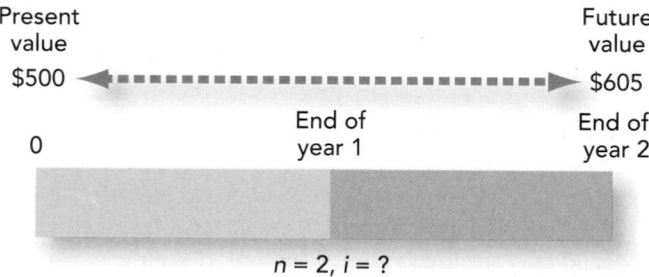

$$n = 2, i = ?$$

The interest rate is the discount rate that will provide a present value of $500 when discounting (determining present value) the $605 to be received in two years:

$$\$500 \text{ (present value)} = \$605 \text{ (future value)} \times ?*$$
*Present value of $1: $n = 2$, $i = ?$

The unknown variable is the interest rate.

Rearranging algebraically, we find that the present value table factor is .82645.

$$\$500 \text{ (present value)} \div \$605 \text{ (future value)} = .82645*$$
*Present value of $1: $n = 2$, $i = ?$

When you consult the present value table, Table 2, you search row two ($n = 2$) for this value and find it in the 10% column. So the effective interest rate is 10%. Notice that the computed factor value exactly equals the table factor value.[3]

---

[3]If the calculated factor lies between two table factors, interpolation is useful in finding the unknown value. For example, if the future value in our example is $600, instead of $605, the calculated PV factor is .83333 ($500 ÷ $600). This factor lies between the 9% factor of .84168 and the 10% factor of .82645. The total difference between these factors is .01523 (.84168 − .82645). The difference between the calculated factor of .83333 and the 10% factor of .82645 is .00688. This is 45% of the difference between the 9% and 10% factors:

$$\frac{.00688}{.01523} = .45$$

Therefore, the interpolated interest rate is 9.55% (10 − .45).

DETERMINING THE UNKNOWN NUMBER OF PERIODS

You want to invest $10,000 today to accumulate $16,000 for graduate school. If you can invest at an interest rate of 10% compounded annually, how many years will it take to accumulate the required amount?	**ILLUSTRATION 6–2** Determining *n* When PV, FV, and *i* are Known

The following time diagram illustrates the situation:

The number of years is the value of *n* that will provide a present value of $10,000 when discounting $16,000 at a rate of 10%:

$$\$10,000 \text{ (present value)} = \$16,000 \text{ (future value)} \times \text{?*}$$
*Present value of $1; n = ?, i = 10%

The unknown variable is the number of periods.

Rearranging algebraically, we find that the present value table factor is .625.

$$\$10,000 \text{ (present value)} \div \$16,000 \text{ (future value)} = .625\text{*}$$
*Present value of $1: n = ?, i = 10%

When you consult the present value table, Table 2, you search the 10% column ($i = 10\%$) for this value and find .62092 in row five. So it would take approximately five years to accumulate $16,000 in the situation described.

ADDITIONAL CONSIDERATION

Solving for the unknown factor in either of these examples could just as easily be done using the future value tables. The number of years is the value of *n* that will provide a present value of $10,000 when discounting $16,000 at a discount rate of 10%.

$$\$16,000 \text{ (future value)} = \$10,000 \text{ (present value)} \times \text{?*}$$
*Future value of $1: n = ?, i = 10%

Rearranging algebraically, the future value table factor is 1.6.

$$\$16,000 \text{ (future value)} \div \$10,000 \text{ (present value)} = 1.6\text{*}$$
*Future value of $1: n = ?, i = 10%

When you consult the future value table, Table 1, you search the 10% column ($i = 10\%$) for this value and find 1.61051 in row five. So it would take approximately five years to accumulate $16,000 in the situation described.

CONCEPT REVIEW EXERCISE

Using the appropriate table, answer each of the following independent questions.

VALUING A SINGLE CASH FLOW AMOUNT

1. What is the future value of $5,000 at the end of six periods at 8% compound interest?
2. What is the present value of $8,000 to be received eight periods from today assuming a compound interest rate of 12%?
3. What is the present value of $10,000 to be received two *years* from today assuming an annual interest rate of 24% and *monthly* compounding?

4. If an investment of $2,000 grew to $2,520 in three periods, what is the interest rate at which the investment grew? Solve using both present and future value tables.

5. Approximately how many years would it take for an investment of $5,250 to accumulate to $15,000, assuming interest is compounded at 10% annually? Solve using both present and future value tables.

SOLUTION

1. $FV = \$5,000 \times 1.58687^* = \$7,934$
   *Future value of $1: $n = 6$, $i = 8\%$ (from Table 1)

2. $FV = \$8,000 \times .40388^* = \$3,231$
   *Present value of $1: $n = 8$, $i = 12\%$ (from Table 2)

3. $FV = \$10,000 \times .62172^* = \$6,217$
   *Present value of $1: $n = 24$, $i = 2\%$ (from Table 2)

4. Using present value table,
   $$\frac{\$2,000}{\$2,520} = .7937^*$$
   *Present value of $1: $n = 3$, $i = ?$ (from Table 2, i approximately **8%**)

   Using future value table,
   $$\frac{\$2,520}{\$2,000} = 1.260^*$$
   *Future value of $1: $n = 3$, $i = ?$ (from Table 1, i approximately **8%**)

5. Using present value table,
   $$\frac{\$5,250}{\$15,000} = .35^*$$
   *Present value of $1: $n = ?$, $i = 10\%$ (from Table 2, n approximately **11 years**)

   Using future value table,
   $$\frac{\$15,000}{\$5,250} = 2.857^*$$
   *Future value of $1: $n = ?$. $i = 10\%$ (from Table 1, n approximately **11 years**)

Preview of Accounting Applications of Present Value Techniques—Single Cash Amount

Kile Petersen switched off his television set immediately after watching the Super Bowl game and swore to himself that this would be the last year he would watch the game on his 10-year-old 20-inch TV set. "Next year, a big screen TV," he promised himself. Soon after, he saw an advertisement in the local newspaper from Slim Jim's TV and Appliance offering a Philips 60-inch large screen television on sale for $1,800. And the best part of the deal was that Kile could take delivery immediately but would not have to pay the $1,800 for one whole year! "In a year, I can easily save the $1,800," he thought.

In the above scenario, the seller, Slim Jim's TV and Appliance, records a sale when the TV is delivered to Kile. How should the company value its receivable and corresponding sales revenue? We provide a solution to this question at the end of this section on page 308. The following discussion will help you to understand that solution.

Most monetary assets and monetary liabilities are valued at the present value of future cash flows.

Many assets and most liabilities are monetary in nature. Monetary assets include money and claims to receive money, the amount of which is fixed or determinable. Examples include cash and most receivables. Monetary liabilities are obligations to pay amounts of cash, the amount of which is fixed or determinable. Most liabilities are monetary. For example, if you borrow money from a bank and sign a note payable, the amount of cash to be repaid to the bank is fixed. Monetary receivables and payables are valued based on the fixed amount of cash to be received or paid in the future with proper reflection of the time value of money. In other words, we value most receivables and payables at the present value of future cash flows, reflecting an appropriate time value of money.[4]

The example in Illustration 6–3 demonstrates this concept.

---

[4]FASB ASC 835–30: Interest—Imputation of Interest (previously "Interest on Receivables and Payables," *Accounting Principles Board Opinion No. 21* (New York: AICPA, 1971)). As you will learn in Chapter 7, normal trade accounts receivable and accounts payable are valued at the amount expected to be received or paid, not the present value of those amounts. The difference between the amount expected to be received or paid and present values often is immaterial.

Explicit Interest	**ILLUSTRATION 6–3**
The Stridewell Wholesale Shoe Company manufactures athletic shoes for sale to retailers. The company recently sold a large order of shoes to Harmon Sporting Goods for $50,000. Stridewell agreed to accept a note in payment for the shoes requiring payment of $50,000 in one year plus interest at 10%.	Valuing a Note: One Payment, Explicit Interest

How should Stridewell value the note receivable and corresponding sales revenue earned? How should Harmon value the note payable and corresponding inventory purchased? As long as the interest rate explicitly stated in the agreement properly reflects the time value of money, the answer is $50,000, the face value of the note. It's important to realize that this amount also equals the present value of future cash flows at 10%. Future cash flows equal $55,000, $50,000 in note principal plus $5,000 in interest ($50,000 × 10%). Using a time diagram:

In equation form, we can solve for present value as follows:

$55,000 (future value) × .90909* = $50,000 (present value)

*Present value of $1: n = 1, i = 10%

By calculating the present value of $55,000 to be received in one year, the interest of $5,000 is removed from the future value, resulting in a proper note receivable/sales revenue value of $50,000 for Stridewell and a $50,000 note payable/inventory value for Harmon.

While most notes, loans, and mortgages explicitly state an interest rate that will properly reflect the time value of money, there can be exceptions. Consider the example in Illustration 6–4.

No Explicit Interest	**ILLUSTRATION 6–4**
The Stridewell Wholesale Shoe Company recently sold a large order of shoes to Harmon Sporting Goods. Terms of the sale require Harmon to sign a noninterest-bearing note of $60,500 with payment due in two years.	Valuing a Note: One Payment, No Explicit Interest

How should Stridewell and Harmon value the note receivable/payable and corresponding sales revenue/inventory? Even though the agreement states a noninterest-bearing note, the $60,500 does, in fact, include interest for the two-year period of the loan. We need to remove the interest portion of the $60,500 to determine the portion that represents the sales price of the shoes. We do this by computing the present value. The following time diagram illustrates the situation assuming that a rate of 10% reflects the appropriate interest rate for a loan of this type:

Present value ? ◄---- $60,500 Future value
0   End of year 1   End of year 2

n = 2, i = 10%

Again, using the present value of $1 table,

$$\$60,500 \text{ (future value)} \times .82645^* = \$50,000 \text{ (present value)}$$

*Present value of $1: $n = 2$, $i = 10\%$

Both the note receivable for Stridewell and the note payable for Harmon initially will be valued at $50,000. The difference of $10,500 ($60,500 − 50,000) represents interest revenue/expense to be recognized over the life of the note. The appropriate journal entries are illustrated in later chapters.

Now can you answer the question posed in the scenario at the beginning of this section? Assuming that a rate of 10% reflects the appropriate interest rate in this situation, Slim Jim's TV and Appliance records a receivable and sales revenue of $1,636 which is the present value of the $1,800 to be received from Kile Petersen one year from the date of sale.

$$\$1,800 \text{ (future value)} \times .90909^* = \$1,636 \text{ (present value)}$$

*Present value of $1: $n = 1$, $i = 10\%$ (from Table 2)

Expected Cash Flow Approach

SFAC No. 7

SFAC No. 7 provides
a framework for
using future cash
flows in accounting
measurements.

Present value measurement has long been integrated with accounting valuation and is specifically addressed in several accounting standards. Because of its increased importance, the FASB in 2000 issued *Statement of Financial Accounting Concepts No. 7,* "Using Cash Flow Information and Present Value in Accounting Measurements."[5] This statement provides a framework for using future cash flows as the basis for accounting measurement and asserts that the objective in valuing an asset or liability using present value is to approximate the fair value of that asset or liability. Key to that objective is determining the present value of future cash flows associated with the asset or liability, *taking into account any uncertainty concerning the amounts and timing of the cash flows.* Although future cash flows in many instances are contractual and certain, the amounts and timing of cash flows are less certain in other situations.

For example, lease payments are provided in the contract between lessor and lessee. On the other hand, the future cash flows to be paid to settle a pending lawsuit may be highly uncertain. Traditionally, the way uncertainty has been considered in present value calculations has been by discounting the "best estimate" of future cash flows applying a discount rate that has been adjusted to reflect the uncertainty or risk of those cash flows. With the approach described by *SFAC No. 7,* though, the adjustment for uncertainty or risk of cash flows is applied to the cash flows, not the discount rate. This new *expected cash flow approach* incorporates specific probabilities of cash flows into the analysis. Consider Illustration 6–5.

Compare the approach described in Illustration 6–5 to the traditional approach that uses the present value of the most likely estimate of $200 million and ignores information about cash flow probabilities.

The discount rate used to determine present value when applying the expected cash flow approach should be the company's *credit-adjusted risk-free rate of interest.* Other elements of uncertainty are incorporated into the determination of the probability-weighted expected cash flows. In the traditional approach, elements of uncertainty are incorporated into a risk-adjusted discount rate.

> **SFAC NO. 7**
> "While many accountants do not routinely use the expected cash flow approach, expected cash flows are inherent in the techniques used in some accounting measurements, like pensions, other postretirement benefits, and some insurance obligations."[6]

The company's credit-adjusted risk-free rate of interest is used when applying the expected cash flow approach to the calculation of present value.

The FASB expects that the traditional approach to calculating present value will continue to be used in many situations, particularly those where future cash flows are contractual. The Board also believes that the expected cash flow approach is more appropriate in more complex situations. In fact, the board has incorporated

---

[5]"Using Cash Flow Information and Present Value in Accounting Measurements," *Statement of Financial Accounting Concepts No. 7* (Norwalk, Conn.: FASB, 2000). Recall that Concept Statements do not directly prescribe GAAP, but instead provide structure and direction to financial accounting.
[6]Ibid., para. 48.

LDD Corporation faces the likelihood of having to pay an uncertain amount in five years in connection with an environmental cleanup. The future cash flow estimate is in the range of $100 million to $300 million with the following estimated probabilities:

ILLUSTRATION 6–5

Expected Cash Flow Approach

Loss Amount	Probability
$100 million	10%
$200 million	60%
$300 million	30%

The expected cash flow, then, is $220 million:

$$
\begin{aligned}
\$100 \times 10\% &= \$\ 10 \text{ million} \\
200 \times 60\% &= \ 120 \text{ million} \\
300 \times 30\% &= \ \underline{\ \ 90} \text{ million} \\
&\ \ \ \ \$220 \text{ million}
\end{aligned}
$$

If the company's credit-adjusted risk-free rate of interest is 5%, LDD will report a liability of $172,376,600, the present value of the expected cash outflow:

$$
\begin{aligned}
\$220,&000,000 \\
\times\ &.78353^* \\
\hline
\$172,&376,600
\end{aligned}
$$

*Present value of $1, n = 5, i = 5% (from Table 2)

the concepts developed in *SFAC No. 7* into recent standards on asset retirement obligations, impairment losses, and business combinations. In Chapter 10 we illustrate the use of the expected cash flow approach as it would be applied to the measurement of an asset retirement obligation. In Chapter 13, we use the approach to measure the liability associated with a loss contingency.

BASIC ANNUITIES

The previous examples involved the receipt or payment of a single future amount. Financial instruments frequently involve multiple receipts or payments of cash. If the same amount is to be received or paid each period, the series of cash flows is referred to as an **annuity.** A common annuity encountered in practice is a loan on which periodic interest is paid in equal amounts. For example, bonds typically pay interest semiannually in an amount determined by multiplying a stated rate by a fixed principal amount. Some loans and most leases are paid in equal installments during a specified period of time.

● LO5

An agreement that creates an annuity can produce either an **ordinary annuity** or an **annuity due** (sometimes referred to as an annuity in advance) situation. The first cash flow (receipt or payment) of an ordinary annuity is made one compounding period *after* the date on which the agreement begins. The final cash flow takes place on the *last* day covered by the agreement. For example, an installment note payable dated December 31, 2011, might require the debtor to make three equal annual payments, with the first payment due on December 31, 2012, and the last one on December 31, 2014. The following time diagram illustrates an ordinary annuity:

In an *ordinary annuity* cash flows occur at the end of each period.

Ordinary annuity.

12/31/11	12/31/12	12/31/13	12/31/14
	1st payment	2nd payment	3rd payment

The first payment of an annuity due is made on the *first* day of the agreement, and the last payment is made one period *before* the end of the agreement. For example, a three-year

In an *annuity due* cash flows occur at the beginning of each period.

lease of a building that begins on December 31, 2011, and ends on December 31, 2014, may require the first year's lease payment in advance on December 31, 2011. The third and last payment would take place on December 31, 2013, the beginning of the third year of the lease. The following time diagram illustrates this situation:

Annuity due.

Future Value of an Annuity
Future Value of an Ordinary Annuity

Let's first consider the future value of an ordinary annuity in Illustration 6–6.

ILLUSTRATION 6–6 Future Value of an Ordinary Annuity	Sally Rogers wants to accumulate a sum of money to pay for graduate school. Rather than investing a single amount today that will grow to a future value, she decides to invest $10,000 a year over the next three years in a savings account paying 10% interest compounded annually. She decides to make the first payment to the bank one year from today.

The following time diagram illustrates this ordinary annuity situation. Time 0 is the start of the first period.

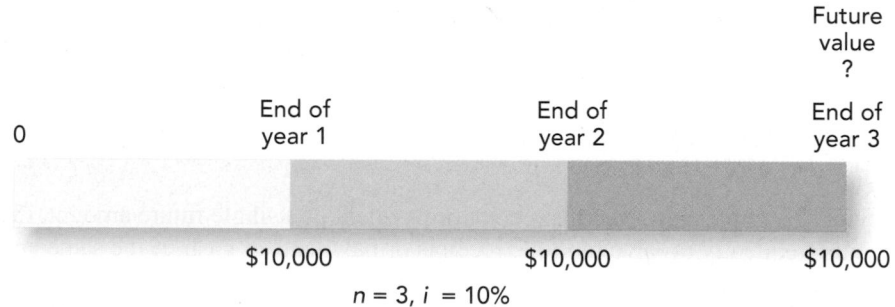

Using the FV of $1 factors from Table 1, we can calculate the future value of this annuity by calculating the future value of each of the individual payments as follows:

	Payment		FV of $1 i = 10%		Future Value (at the end of year 3)	n
First payment	$10,000	×	1.21	=	$12,100	2
Second payment	10,000	×	1.10	=	11,000	1
Third payment	10,000	×	1.00	=	10,000	0
Total			3.31		$33,100	

In the future value of an ordinary annuity, the last cash payment will not earn any interest.

● LO6

From the time diagram, we can see that the first payment has two compounding periods to earn interest. The factor used, 1.21, is the FV of $1 invested for two periods at 10%. The second payment has one compounding period and the last payment does not earn any interest because it is invested on the last day of the three-year annuity period. Therefore, the factor used is 1.00.

This illustration shows that it's possible to calculate the future value of the annuity by separately calculating the FV of each payment and then adding these amounts together. Fortunately, that's not necessary. Table 3, Future Value of an Ordinary Annuity of $1, located

GRAPHIC 6–3

Future Value of an
Ordinary Annuity of $1
(excerpt from Table 3
located at the end of
this textbook)

	Interest Rates (i)					
Periods (n)	7%	8%	9%	10%	11%	12%
1	1.0000	1.0000	1.0000	1.0000	1.0000	1.0000
2	2.0700	2.0800	2.0900	2.1000	2.1100	2.1200
3	3.2149	3.2464	3.2781	3.3100	3.3421	3.3744
4	4.4399	4.5061	4.5731	4.6410	4.7097	4.7793
5	5.7507	5.8666	5.9847	6.1051	6.2278	6.3528
6	7.1533	7.3359	7.5233	7.7156	7.9129	8.1152
7	8.6540	8.9228	9.2004	9.4872	9.7833	10.0890
8	10.2598	10.6366	11.0285	11.4359	11.8594	12.2997

at the end of this textbook simplifies the computation by summing the individual FV of $1
factors for various factors of n and i. Graphic 6–3 contains an excerpt from Table 3.

The future value of $1 at the end of each of three periods invested at 10% is shown in
Table 3 to be $3.31. We can simply multiply this factor by $10,000 to derive the FV of our
ordinary annuity (FVA):

$$\text{FVA} = \$10,000 \text{ (annuity amount)} \times 3.31^* = \$33,100$$

*Future value of an ordinary annuity of $1: $n = 3$, $i = 10\%$

Future Value of an Annuity Due

Let's modify the previous illustration to create an annuity due in Illustration 6–7.

Sally Rogers wants to accumulate a sum of money to pay for graduate school. Rather than investing a single amount today that will grow to a future value, she decides to invest $10,000 a year over the next three years in a savings account paying 10% interest compounded annually. She decides to make the first payment to the bank immediately. How much will Sally have available in her account at the end of three years?	**ILLUSTRATION 6–7** Future Value of an Annuity Due

The following time diagram depicts the situation. Again, note that 0 is the start of the first
period.

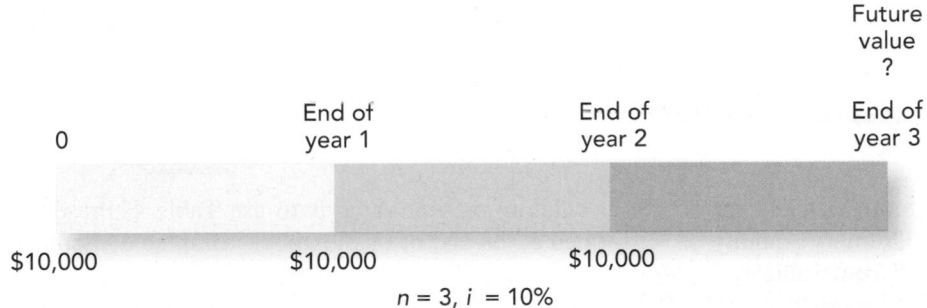

The future value can be found by separately calculating the FV of each of the three payments and then summing those individual future values:

	Payment		FV of $1 $i = 10\%$		Future Value (at the end of year 3)	n
First payment	$10,000	×	1.331	=	$13,310	3
Second payment	10,000	×	1.210	=	12,100	2
Third payment	10,000	×	1.100	=	11,000	1
Total			3.641		$36,410	

In the future value of
an annuity due, the last
cash payment will earn
interest.

And, again, this same future value can be found by using the future value of an annuity due (FVAD) factor from Table 5, Future Value of an Annuity Due of $1, located at the end of this textbook, as follows:

$$\text{FVAD} = \$10,000 \text{ (annuity amount)} \times 3.641^* = \$36,410$$

*Future value of an annuity due of $1: $n = 3$, $i = 10\%$

Of course, if *unequal* amounts are invested each year, we can't solve the problem by using the annuity tables. The future value of each payment would have to be calculated separately.

Present Value of an Annuity

Present Value of an Ordinary Annuity

● LO7

You will learn in later chapters that liabilities and receivables, with the exception of certain trade receivables and payables, are reported in financial statements at their present values. Most of these financial instruments specify equal periodic interest payments or installment payments. As a result, the most common accounting applications of the time value of money involve determining present value of annuities. As in the future value applications we discussed above, an annuity can be either an ordinary annuity or an annuity due. Let's look at an ordinary annuity first.

In Illustration 6–6 on page 310, we determined that Sally Rogers could accumulate $33,100 for graduate school by investing $10,000 at the end of each of three years at 10%. The $33,100 is the future value of the ordinary annuity described. Another alternative is to invest one single amount at the beginning of the three-year period. (See Illustration 6–8.) This single amount will equal the present value at the beginning of the three-year period of the $33,100 future value. It will also equal the present value of the $10,000 three-year annuity.

ILLUSTRATION 6–8	Sally Rogers wants to accumulate a sum of money to pay for graduate school. She wants to invest a single amount today in a savings account earning 10% interest compounded annually that is equivalent to investing $10,000 at the end of each of the next three years.
Present Value of an Ordinary Annuity	

The present value can be found by separately calculating the PV of each of the three payments and then summing those individual present values:

	Payment		PV of $1 $i = 10\%$		Present Value (at the beginning of year 1)	n
First payment	$10,000	×	.90909	=	$ 9,091	1
Second payment	10,000	×	.82645	=	8,264	2
Third payment	10,000	×	.75131	=	7,513	3
Total			2.48685		$24,868	

A more efficient method of calculating present value is to use Table 4, Present Value of an Ordinary Annuity of $1, located at the end of this textbook. Graphic 6–4 contains an excerpt from Table 4.

GRAPHIC 6–4

Present Value of an Ordinary Annuity of $1 (excerpt from Table 4 located at the end of this textbook)

	Interest Rates (i)					
Periods (n)	7%	8%	9%	10%	11%	12%
1	0.93458	0.92593	0.91743	0.90909	0.90090	0.89286
2	1.80802	1.78326	1.75911	1.73554	1.71252	1.69005
3	2.62432	2.57710	2.53129	2.48685	2.44371	2.40183
4	3.38721	3.31213	3.23972	3.16987	3.10245	3.03735
5	4.10020	3.99271	3.88965	3.79079	3.69590	3.60478
6	4.76654	4.62288	4.48592	4.35526	4.23054	4.11141
7	5.38929	5.20637	5.03295	4.86842	4.71220	4.56376
8	5.97130	5.74664	5.53482	5.33493	5.14612	4.96764

Using Table 4, we calculate the PV of the ordinary annuity (PVA) as follows:

$$PVA = \$10,000 \text{ (annuity amount)} \times 2.48685^* = \$24,868$$
*Present value of an ordinary annuity of $1: $n = 3$, $i = 10\%$

The relationship between the present value and the future value of the annuity can be depicted graphically as follows:

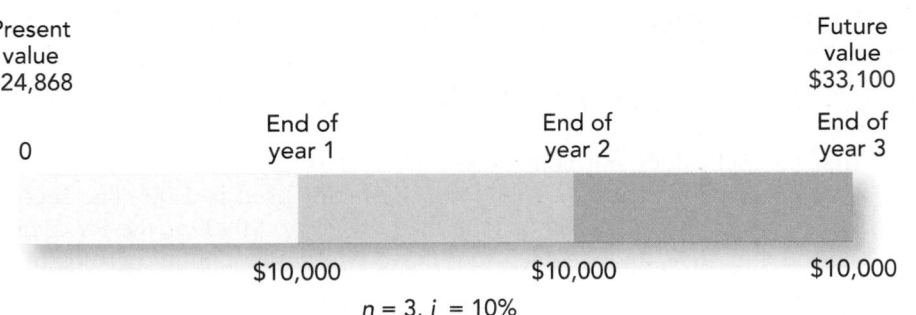

This can be interpreted in several ways:

1. $10,000 invested at 10% at the end of each of the next three years will accumulate to $33,100 at the end of the third year.
2. $24,868 invested at 10% now will grow to $33,100 after three years.
3. Someone whose time value of money is 10% would be willing to pay $24,868 now to receive $10,000 at the end of each of the next three years.
4. If your time value of money is 10%, you should be indifferent with respect to paying/receiving (a) $24,868 now, (b) $33,100 three years from now, or (c) $10,000 at the end of each of the next three years.

ADDITIONAL CONSIDERATION

We also can verify that these are the present value and future value of the same annuity by calculating the present value of a single cash amount of $33,100 three years hence:

$$PV = \$33,100 \text{ (future value)} \times .75131^* = \$24,868$$
*Present value of $1: $n = 3$, $i = 10\%$

Present Value of an Annuity Due

In the previous illustration, suppose that the three equal payments of $10,000 are to be made at the *beginning* of each of the three years. Recall from Illustration 6–7 on page 311 that the future value of this annuity is $36,410. What is the present value?

ILLUSTRATION 6–9
Present Value of an Annuity Due

The following time diagram depicts this situation:

Present value of an annuity due.

Present value ?
0 | End of year 1 | End of year 2 | End of year 3
$10,000 | $10,000 | $10,000
$n = 3$, $i = 10\%$

Once again, using individual PV factors of $1 from Table 2, the PV of the annuity due can be calculated as follows:

	Payment		PV of $1 $i = 10\%$		Present Value (at the beginning of year 1)	n
First payment	$10,000	×	1.00000	=	$10,000	0
Second payment	10,000	×	.90909	=	9,091	1
Third payment	10,000	×	.82645	=	8,264	2
Total			2.73554		$27,355	

In the present value of an annuity due, no interest needs to be removed from the first cash payment.

The first payment does not contain any interest since it is made on the first day of the three-year annuity period. Therefore, the factor used is 1.00. The second payment has one compounding period and the factor used of .90909 is the PV factor of $1 for one period and 10%, and we need to remove two compounding periods of interest from the third payment. The factor used of .82645 is the PV factor of $1 for two periods and 10%.

Relationship between present value and future value—annuity due.

The relationship between the present value and the future value of the annuity can be depicted graphically as follows:

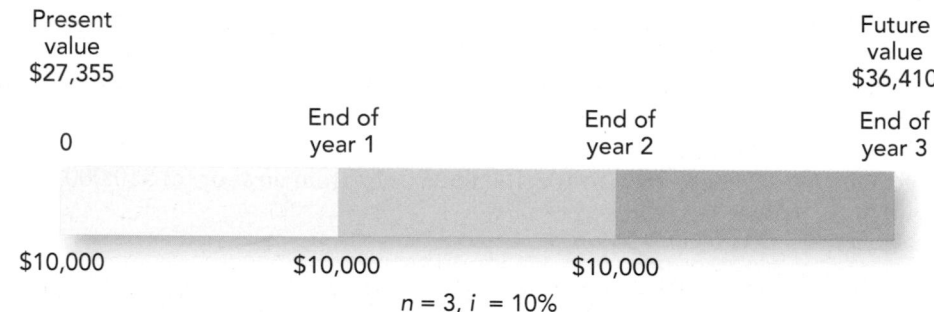

Using Table 6, Present Value of an Annuity Due, located at the end of this book, we can more efficiently calculate the PV of the annuity due (PVAD):

$$\text{PVAD} = \$10,000 \text{ (annuity amount)} \times 2.73554* = \$27,355$$
*Present value of an annuity due of $1: $n = 3, i = 10\%$

To better understand the relationship between Tables 4 and 6, notice that the PVAD factor for three periods, 10%, from Table 6 is 2.73554. This is simply the PVA factor for two periods, 10%, of 1.73554, plus 1.0. The addition of 1.0 reflects the fact that the first payment does not require the removal of any interest.

Present Value of a Deferred Annuity

A *deferred annuity* exists when the first cash flow occurs more than one period after the date the agreement begins.

Accounting valuations often involve the present value of annuities in which the first cash flow is expected to occur more than one time period after the date of the agreement. As the inception of the annuity is deferred beyond a single period, this type of annuity is referred to as a **deferred annuity**.[7]

---

[7]The future value of a deferred annuity is the same as the future amount of an annuity not deferred. That is because there are no interest compounding periods prior to the beginning of the annuity period.

At January 1, 2011, you are considering acquiring an investment that will provide three equal payments of $10,000 each to be received at the end of three consecutive years. However, the first payment is not expected until *December 31, 2013*. The time value of money is 10%. How much would you be willing to pay for this investment?	**ILLUSTRATION 6–10** Deferred Annuity

The following time diagram depicts this situation:

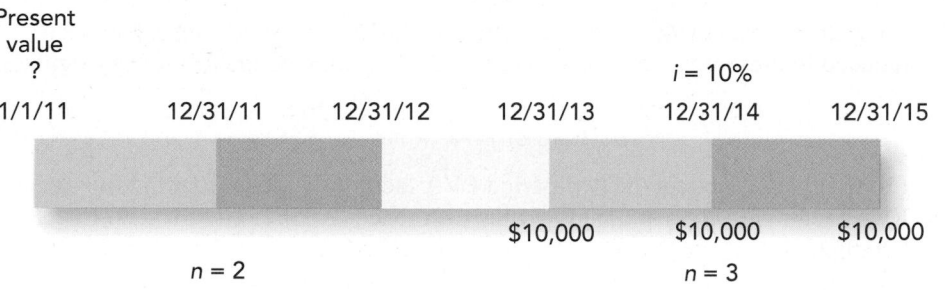

Cash flows for a deferred annuity.

The present value of the deferred annuity can be calculated by summing the present values of the three individual cash flows, each discounted to today's PV:

	Payment		PV of $1 $i = 10\%$		Present Value	n
First payment	$10,000	×	.75131	=	$ 7,513	3
Second payment	10,000	×	.68301	=	6,830	4
Third payment	10,000	×	.62092	=	6,209	5
					$20,552	

A more efficient way of calculating the present value of a deferred annuity involves a two-step process:

1. Calculate the PV of the annuity as of the beginning of the annuity period.
2. Discount the single amount calculated in (1) to its present value *as of today*.

In this case, we compute the present value of the annuity as of December 31, 2012, by multiplying the annuity amount by the three-period ordinary annuity factor:

$$PVA = \$10,000 \text{ (annuity amount)} \times 2.48685^* = \$24,868$$
*Present value of an ordinary annuity of $1: $n = 3$, $i = 10\%$

This is the present value as of December 31, 2012. This single amount is then reduced to present value as of January 1, 2011, by making the following calculation:

$$PV = \$24,868 \text{ (future amount)} \times .82645^* = \$20,552$$
*Present value of $1: $n = 2$, $i = 10\%$

The following time diagram illustrates this two-step process:

Present value of a deferred annuity— two-step process.

Present value: $20,552

Present value (at beginning of the annuity period): $24,868

1/1/11   12/31/11   12/31/12   12/31/13   12/31/14   12/31/15

$i = 10\%$

$10,000 $10,000 $10,000

$n = 2$ $n = 3$

If you recall the concepts you learned in this chapter, you might think of other ways the present value of a deferred annuity can be determined. Among them:

1. Calculate the PV of an annuity due, rather than an ordinary annuity, and then discount that amount three periods rather than two:

$$\text{PVAD} = \$10,000 \text{ (annuity amount)} \times 2.73554^* = \$27,355$$
*Present value of an annuity due of $1: $n = 3$, $i = 10\%$

This is the present value as of December 31, 2013. This single amount is then reduced to present value as of January 1, 2011 by making the following calculation:

$$\text{PV} = \$27,355 \times .75131^* = \$20,552$$
*Present value of $1: $n = 3$, $i = 10\%$

2. From Table 4, subtract the two-period PVA factor (1.73554) from the five-period PVA factor (3.79079) and multiply the difference (2.05525) by $10,000 to get $20,552.

Financial Calculators and Excel

As previously mentioned, financial calculators can be used to solve future and present value problems. For example, a Texas Instruments model BA-35 has the following pertinent keys:

$$\boxed{\text{N}} \quad \boxed{\%\text{I}} \quad \boxed{\text{PV}} \quad \boxed{\text{FV}} \quad \boxed{\text{PMT}} \quad \boxed{\text{CPT}}$$

These keys are defined as follows:

N = number of periods
$\%I$ = interest rate
PV = present value
FV = future value
PMT = annuity payments
CPT = compute button

Using a calculator:
Enter: $\boxed{\text{N}}$ 10 $\boxed{\text{I}}$ 10
$\boxed{\text{PMT}}$ -200
Output: $\boxed{\text{PV}}$ 1,229

Using Excel, enter:
= PV(.10,10,200)
Output: 1,229

To illustrate its use, assume that you need to determine the present value of a 10-period ordinary annuity of $200 using a 10% interest rate. You would enter $\boxed{\text{N}}$ 10, $\boxed{\%\text{I}}$ 10, $\boxed{\text{PMT}}$ −200, then press $\boxed{\text{CPT}}$ and $\boxed{\text{PV}}$ to obtain the answer of $1,229.

Many professionals choose to use spreadsheet software, such as Excel, to solve time value of money problems. These spreadsheets can be used in a variety of ways. A template can be created using the formulas shown in Graphic 6–5 on page 323. An alternative is to use the software's built-in financial functions. For example, Excel has a function called PV that calculates the present value of an ordinary annuity. To use the function, you would select the pull-down menu for "Insert," click on "Function" and choose the category called "Financial." Scroll down to PV and double-click. You will then be asked to input the necessary variables—interest rate, the number of periods, and the payment amount.

In subsequent chapters we illustrate the use of both a calculator and Excel in addition to present value tables to solve present value calculations for selected examples and illustrations.

Solving for Unknown Values in Present Value Situations

● LO8

In present value problems involving annuities, there are four variables: (1) present value of an ordinary annuity (PVA) or present value of an annuity due (PVAD), (2) the amount of each annuity payment, (3) the number of periods, n, and (4) the interest rate, i. If you know any three of these, the fourth can be determined.

Assume that you borrow $700 from a friend and intend to repay the amount in four equal annual installments beginning one year from today. Your friend wishes to be reimbursed for the time value of money at an 8% annual rate. What is the required annual payment that must be made (the annuity amount), to repay the loan in four years?	**ILLUSTRATION 6–11** Determining the Annuity Amount When Other Variables Are Known

The following time diagram illustrates the situation:

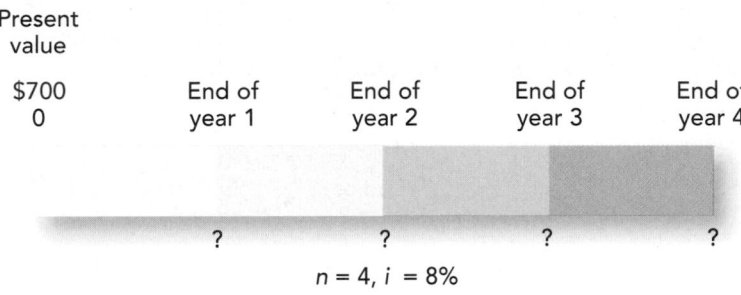

Determining the unknown annuity amount—ordinary annuity.

The required payment is the annuity amount that will provide a present value of $700 when discounting that amount at a discount rate of 8%:

$$\$700 \text{ (present value)} = 3.31213^* \times \text{annuity amount}$$

The unknown variable is the annuity amount.

Rearranging algebraically, we find that the annuity amount is $211.34.

$$\$700 \text{ (present value)} \div 3.31213^* = \$211.34 \text{ (annuity amount)}$$
*Present value of an ordinary annuity of $1: $n = 4$, $i = 8\%$

You would have to make four annual payments of $211.34 to repay the loan. Total payments of $845.36 (4 × $211.34) would include $145.36 in interest ($845.36 − 700.00).

Assume that you borrow $700 from a friend and intend to repay the amount in equal installments of $100 per year over a period of years. The payments will be made at the end of each year beginning one year from now. Your friend wishes to be reimbursed for the time value of money at a 7% annual rate. How many years would it take before you repaid the loan?	**ILLUSTRATION 6–12** Determining n When Other Variables Are Known

Once again, this is an ordinary annuity situation because the first payment takes place one year from now. The following time diagram illustrates the situation:

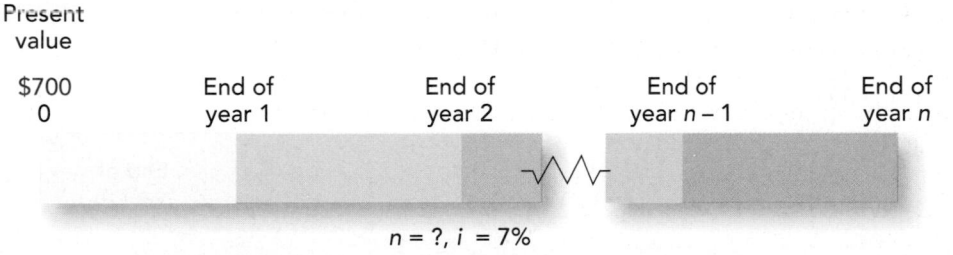

Determining the unknown number of periods—ordinary annuity.

The number of years is the value of n that will provide a present value of $700 when discounting $100 at a discount rate of 7%:

$$\$700 \text{ (present value)} = \$100 \text{ (annuity amount)} \times ?^*$$
*Present value of an ordinary annuity of $1: $n = ?$, $i = 7\%$

The unknown variable is the number of periods.

Rearranging algebraically, we find that the PVA table factor is 7.0.

$$\$700 \text{ (present value)} \div \$100 \text{ (annuity amount)} = 7.0^*$$
*Present value of an ordinary annuity of $1: $n = ?$, $i = 7\%$

When you consult the PVA table, Table 4, you search the 7% column ($i = 7\%$) for this value and find 7.02358 in row 10. So it would take approximately 10 years to repay the loan in the situation described.

ILLUSTRATION 6–13 Determining i When Other Variables Are Known	Suppose that a friend asked to borrow $331 today (present value) and promised to repay you $100 (the annuity amount) at the end of each of the next four years. What is the annual interest rate implicit in this agreement?

FINANCIAL Reporting Case

Q2, p. 299

Determining the unknown interest rate—ordinary annuity.

First of all, we are dealing with an ordinary annuity situation as the payments are at the end of each period. The following time diagram illustrates the situation:

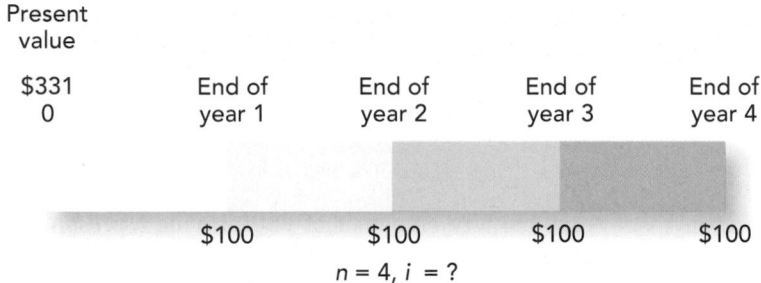

The interest rate is the discount rate that will provide a present value of $331 when discounting the $100 four-year ordinary annuity:

The unknown variable is the interest rate.

$$\$331 \text{ (present value)} = \$100 \text{ (annuity amount)} \times ?*$$
*Present value of an ordinary annuity of $1: $n = 4$, $i = ?$

Rearranging algebraically, we find that the PVA table factor is 3.31.

$$\$331 \text{ (present value)} \div \$100 \text{ (annuity amount)} = 3.31*$$
*Present value of an ordinary annuity of $1: $n = 4$, $i = ?$

When you consult the PVA table, Table 4, you search row four ($n = 4$) for this value and find it in the 8% column. So the effective interest rate is 8%.

ILLUSTRATION 6–14 Determining i When Other Variables Are Known—Unequal Cash Flows	Suppose that you borrowed $400 from a friend and promised to repay the loan by making three annual payments of $100 at the end of each of the next three years plus a final payment of $200 at the end of year four. What is the interest rate implicit in this agreement?

The following time diagram illustrates the situation:

Determining the unknown interest rate—unequal cash flow.

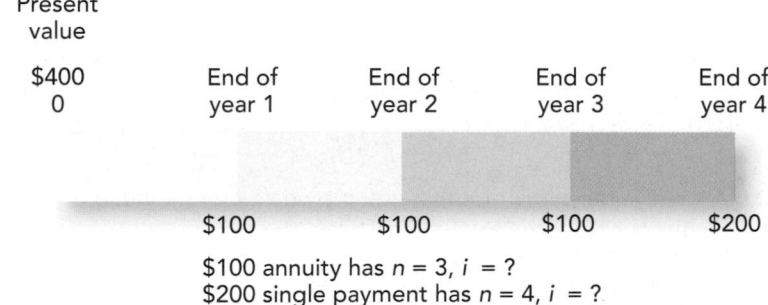

The interest rate is the discount rate that will provide a present value of $400 when discounting the $100 three-year ordinary annuity plus the $200 to be received in four years:

The unknown variable is the interest rate.

$$\$400 \text{ (present value)} = \$100 \text{ (annuity amount)} \times ?* + \$200 \text{ (single payment)} \times ?†$$
*Present value of an ordinary annuity of $1: $n = 3$, $i = ?$
†Present value of $1: $n = 4$, $i = ?$

This equation involves two unknowns and is not as easily solved as the two previous examples. One way to solve the problem is to trial-and-error the answer. For example, if we assumed i to be 9%, the total PV of the payments would be calculated as follows:

$$PV = \$100 \, (2.53129^*) + \$200 \, (.70843^\dagger) = \$395$$
*Present value of an ordinary annuity of $1: $n = 3$, $i = 9\%$
$\dagger$Present value of $1: $n = 4$, $i = 9\%$

Because the present value computed is less than the $400 borrowed, using 9% removes too much interest. Recalculating PV with $i = 8\%$ results in a PV of $405. This indicates that the interest rate implicit in the agreement is between 8% and 9%.

CONCEPT REVIEW EXERCISE

Using the appropriate table, answer each of the following independent questions.

ANNUITIES

1. What is the future value of an annuity of $2,000 invested at the *end* of each of the next six periods at 8% interest?
2. What is the future value of an annuity of $2,000 invested at the *beginning* of each of the next six periods at 8% interest?
3. What is the present value of an annuity of $6,000 to be received at the *end* of each of the next eight periods assuming an interest rate of 10%?
4. What is the present value of an annuity of $6,000 to be received at the *beginning* of each of the next eight periods assuming an interest rate of 10%?
5. Jane bought a $3,000 audio system and agreed to pay for the purchase in 10 equal annual installments of $408 beginning one year from today. What is the interest rate implicit in this agreement?
6. Jane bought a $3,000 audio system and agreed to pay for the purchase in 10 equal annual installments beginning one year from today. The interest rate is 12%. What is the amount of the annual installment?
7. Jane bought a $3,000 audio system and agreed to pay for the purchase by making nine equal annual installments beginning one year from today plus a lump-sum payment of $1,000 at the end of 10 periods. The interest rate is 10%. What is the required annual installment?
8. Jane bought an audio system and agreed to pay for the purchase by making four equal annual installments of $800 beginning one year from today plus a lump-sum payment of $1,000 at the end of five years. The interest rate is 12%. What was the cost of the audio system? (Hint: What is the present value of the cash payments?)
9. Jane bought an audio system and agreed to pay for the purchase by making five equal annual installments of $1,100 beginning four years from today. The interest rate is 12%. What was the cost of the audio system? (Hint: What is the present value of the cash payments?)

SOLUTION

1. FVA = $2,000 × 7.3359* = $14,672
   *Future value of an ordinary annuity of $1: $n = 6$, $i = 8\%$ (from Table 3)

2. FVAD = $2,000 × 7.9228* = $15,846
   *Future value of an annuity due of $1: $n = 6$, $i = 8\%$ (from Table 5)

3. PVA = $6,000 × 5.33493* = $32,010
   *Present value of ordinary annuity of $1: $n = 8$, $i = 10\%$ (from Table 4)

4. PVAD = $6,000 × 5.86842* = $35,211
   *Present value of an annuity due of $1: $n = 8$, $i = 10\%$ (from Table 6)

5. $\dfrac{\$3,000}{\$408} = 7.35^*$

   *Present value of an ordinary annuity of $1: $n = 10$, $i = ?$ (from Table 4, i approximately 6%)

6. Each annuity payment $= \dfrac{\$3,000}{5.65022^*} = \$531$

   *Present value of an ordinary annuity of $1: $n = 10$, $i = 12\%$ (from Table 4)

7. Each annuity payment $= \dfrac{\$3{,}000 - [\text{PV of } \$1{,}000 \ (n = 10, \ i = 10\%)]}{5.75902^*}$

Each annuity payment $= \dfrac{\$3{,}000 - (\$1{,}000 \times .38554^{\dagger})}{5.75902^*}$

Each annuity payment $= \dfrac{\$2{,}614}{5.75902^*} = \$454$

*Present value of an ordinary annuity of $1: $n = 9$, $i = 10\%$ (from Table 4)
†Present value of $1: $n = 10$, $i = 10\%$ (from Table 2)

8. $\text{PV} = (\$800 \times 3.03735^*) + (\$1{,}000 \times .56743^{\dagger}) = \$2{,}997$

*Present value of an ordinary annuity of $1: $n = 4$, $i = 12\%$ (from Table 4)
†Present value of $1: $n = 5$, $i = 12\%$ (from Table 2)

9. $\text{PVA} = \$1{,}100 \times 3.60478^* = \$3{,}965$

*Present value of an ordinary annuity of $1: $n = 5$, $i = 12\%$ (from Table 4)

This is the present value three years from today (the beginning of the five-year ordinary annuity). This single amount is then reduced to present value as of today by making the following calculation:

$\text{PV} = \$3{,}965 \times .71178^{\dagger} = \$2{,}822$

†Present value of $1: $n = 3$, $i = 12\%$, (from Table 2)

Preview of Accounting Applications of Present Value Techniques—Annuities

● LO9

The time value of money has many applications in accounting. Most of these applications involve the concept of present value. Because financial instruments typically specify equal periodic payments, these applications quite often involve annuity situations. For example, let's consider one accounting situation using both an ordinary annuity and the present value of a single amount (long-term bonds), one using an annuity due (long-term leases), and a third using a deferred annuity (pension obligations).

Valuation of Long-Term Bonds

FINANCIAL Reporting Case

Q3, p. 299

You will learn in Chapter 14 that a long-term bond usually requires the issuing (borrowing) company to repay a specified amount at maturity and make periodic stated interest payments over the life of the bond. The *stated* interest payments are equal to the contractual stated rate multiplied by the face value of the bonds. At the date the bonds are issued (sold), the marketplace will determine the price of the bonds based on the *market* rate of interest for investments with similar characteristics. The market rate at date of issuance may not equal the bonds' stated rate in which case the price of the bonds (the amount the issuing company actually is borrowing) will not equal the bonds' face value. Bonds issued at more than face value are said to be issued at a premium, while bonds issued at less than face value are said to be issued at a discount. Consider the example in Illustration 6–15.

ILLUSTRATION 6–15 Valuing a Long-term Bond Liability	On June 30, 2011, Fumatsu Electric issued 10% stated rate bonds with a face amount of $200 million. The bonds mature on June 30, 2031 (20 years). The market rate of interest for similar issues was 12%. Interest is paid semiannually (5%) on June 30 and December 31, beginning December 31, 2011. The interest payment is $10 million (5% × $200 million). What was the price of the bond issue? What amount of interest expense will Fumatsu record for the bonds in 2011?

To determine the price of the bonds, we calculate the present value of the 40-period annuity (40 semiannual interest payments of $10 million) and the lump-sum payment of $200 million paid at maturity using the semiannual market rate of interest of 6%. In equation form,

$$PVA = \$10 \text{ million (annuity amount)} \times 15.04630^* = \$150,463,000$$
$$PV = \$200 \text{ million (lump-sum)} \times .09722^{**} = \underline{\quad 19,444,000}$$
$$\text{Price of the bond issue} = \underline{\underline{\$169,907,000}}$$

* Present value of an ordinary annuity of $1: $n = 40$, $i = 6\%$
**Present value of $1: $n = 40$, $i = 6\%$

The bonds will sell for $169,907,000, which represents a discount of $30,093,000 ($200,000,000 − 169,907,000). The discount results from the difference between the semiannual stated rate of 5% and the market rate of 6%. Fumatsu records a $169,907,000 increase in cash and a corresponding liability for bonds payable.

Interest expense for the first six months is determined by multiplying the carrying value (book value) of the bonds ($169,907,000) by the semiannual effective rate (6%) as follows:

$$\$169,907,000 \times 6\% = \$10,194,420$$

The difference between interest expense ($10,194,420) and interest paid ($10,000,000) increases the carrying value of the bond liability. Interest for the second six months of the bond's life is determined by multiplying the new carrying value by the 6% semiannual effective rate.

We discuss the specific accounts used to record these transactions in Chapter 14.

Valuation of Long-Term Leases

Companies frequently acquire the use of assets by leasing rather than purchasing them. Leases usually require the payment of fixed amounts at regular intervals over the life of the lease. You will learn in Chapter 15 that certain long-term, noncancelable leases are treated in a manner similar to an installment sale by the lessor and an installment purchase by the lessee. In other words, the lessor records a receivable and the lessee records a liability for the several installment payments. For the lessee, this requires that the leased asset and corresponding lease liability be valued at the present value of the lease payments. Consider the example in Illustration 6–16.

ILLUSTRATION 6–16
Valuing a Long-Term Lease Liability

On January 1, 2011, the Stridewell Wholesale Shoe Company signed a 25-year non-cancelable lease agreement for an office building. Terms of the lease call for Stridewell to make annual lease payments of $10,000 at the beginning of each year, with the first payment due on January 1, 2011. Assuming an interest rate of 10% properly reflects the time value of money in this situation, how should Stridewell value the asset acquired and the corresponding lease liability if it is to be treated in a manner similar to an installment purchase?

Once again, by computing the present value of the lease payments, we remove the portion of the payments that represents interest, leaving the portion that represents payment for the asset itself. Because the first payment is due immediately, as is common for leases, this is an annuity due situation. In equation form:

$$PVAD = \$10,000 \text{ (annuity amount)} \times 9.98474^* = \$99,847$$
*Present value of an annuity due of $1: $n = 25$, $i = 10\%$

Certain long-term leases require the recording of an asset and corresponding liability at the present value of future lease payments.

Stridewell initially will value the leased asset and corresponding lease liability at $99,847.

| Leased office building | 99,847 | |
| Lease payable | | 99,847 |

Journal entry at the inception of a lease.

The difference between this amount and total future cash payments of $250,000 ($10,000 × 25) represents the interest that is implicit in this agreement. That difference is recorded as interest over the life of the lease.

Valuation of Pension Obligations

Pension plans are important compensation vehicles used by many U.S. companies. These plans are essentially forms of deferred compensation as the pension benefits are paid to employees after they retire. You will learn in Chapter 17 that some pension plans create obligations during employees' service periods that must be paid during their retirement periods. These obligations are funded during the employment period. This means companies contribute cash to pension funds annually with the intention of accumulating sufficient funds to pay employees the retirement benefits they have earned. The amounts contributed are determined using estimates of retirement benefits. The actual amounts paid to employees during retirement depend on many factors including future compensation levels and length of life. Consider Illustration 6–17.

ILLUSTRATION 6–17 Valuing a Pension Obligation	On January 1, 2011, the Stridewell Wholesale Shoe Company hired Sammy Sossa. Sammy is expected to work for 25 years before retirement on December 31, 2035. Annual retirement payments will be paid at the end of each year during his retirement period, expected to be 20 years. The first payment will be on December 31, 2036. During 2011 Sammy earned an annual retirement benefit estimated to be $2,000 per year. The company plans to contribute cash to a pension fund that will accumulate to an amount sufficient to pay Sammy this benefit. Assuming that Stridewell anticipates earning 6% on all funds invested in the pension plan, how much would the company have to contribute at the end of 2011 to pay for pension benefits earned in 2011?

To determine the required contribution, we calculate the present value on December 31, 2011, of the deferred annuity of $2,000 that begins on December 31, 2036, and is expected to end on December 31, 2055.

The following time diagram depicts this situation:

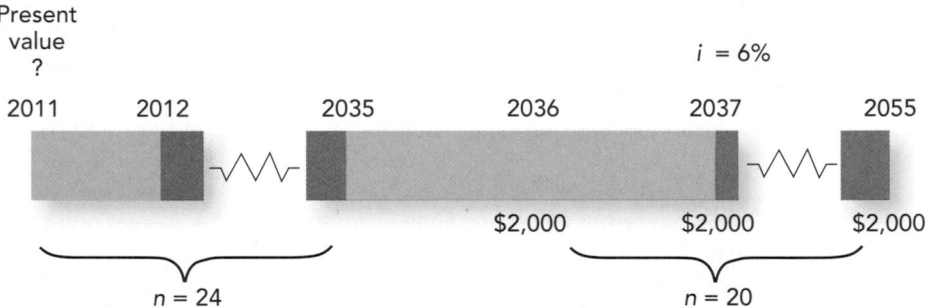

We can calculate the present value of the annuity using a two-step process. The first step computes the present value of the annuity as of December 31, 2035, by multiplying the annuity amount by the 20-period ordinary annuity factor:

$$PVA = \$2,000 \text{ (annuity amount)} \times 11.46992^* = \$22,940$$
*Present value of an ordinary annuity of $1: n = 20, i = 6%

This is the present value as of December 31, 2035. This single amount is then reduced to present value as of December 31, 2011, by a second calculation:

$$PV = \$22,940 \text{ (future amount)} \times .24698^* = \$5,666$$
*Present value of $1: n = 24, i = 6%

Stridewell would have to contribute $5,666 at the end of 2011 to fund the estimated pension benefits earned by its employee in 2011. Viewed in reverse, $5,666 invested now at 6% will accumulate a fund balance of $22,940 at December 31, 2035. If the fund balance remains invested at 6%, $2,000 can be withdrawn each year for 20 years before the fund is depleted.

Among the other situations you'll encounter using present value techniques are valuing notes (Chapters 10 and 14) and other postretirement benefits (Chapter 17).

Summary of Time Value of Money Concepts

Graphic 6–5 summarizes the time value of money concepts discussed in this chapter.

Concept	Summary	Formula	Table
Future value (FV) of $1	The amount of money that a dollar will grow to at some point in the future.	$FV = \$1\,(1 + i)^n$	1
Present value (PV) of $1	The amount of money today that is equivalent to a given amount to be received or paid in the future.	$PV = \dfrac{\$1}{(1 + i)^n}$	2
Future value of an ordinary annuity (FVA) of $1	The future value of a series of equal-sized cash flows with the first payment taking place at the end of the first compounding period.	$FVA = \dfrac{(1 + i)^n - 1}{i}$	3
Present value of an ordinary annuity (PVA) of $1	The present value of a series of equal-sized cash flows with the first payment taking place at the end of the first compounding period.	$PVA = \dfrac{1 - \dfrac{1}{(1 + i)^n}}{i}$	4
Future value of an annuity due (FVAD) of $1	The future value of a series of equal-sized cash flows with the first payment taking place at the beginning of the annuity period.	$FVAD = \left[\dfrac{(1 + i)^n - 1}{i}\right] \times (1 + i)$	5
Present value of an annuity due (PVAD) of $1	The present value of a series of equal-sized cash flows with the first payment taking place at the beginning of the annuity period.	$PVAD = \left[\dfrac{1 - \dfrac{1}{(1 + i)^n}}{i}\right] \times (1 + i)$	6

FINANCIAL REPORTING CASE SOLUTION

1. **Why were the Castellanos to receive $43 million rather than the $141 million lottery prize?** *(p. 312)*   The Castellanos chose to receive their lottery winnings in one lump payment immediately rather than in 26 equal annual installments beginning immediately. The state calculates the present value of the 26 equal payments, withholds the necessary federal income tax, and pays the Castellanos the remainder.

2. **What interest rate did the State of California use to calculate the $43 million lump-sum payment?** *(p. 318)*   The equal payment is determined by dividing $141 million by 26 periods:

$141 million ÷ 26 =	$5,423,077
Less: 31% federal income tax	(1,681,154)
Net-of-tax payment	$3,741,923

Since the first payment is made immediately, this is an annuity due situation. We must find the interest rate that provides a present value of $43 million. There is no 26 period row in Table 6. We can subtract the first payment from the $43 million since it is paid immediately and solve using the 25-period ordinary annuity table (that is, the 25 remaining annual payments beginning in one year):

$$PVA \text{ factor} = \frac{\$43,000,000 - 3,741,923}{\$3,741,923} = 10.4914^*$$

*Present value of an ordinary annuity of $1: $n = 25$, $i = ?$ (from Table 4, i = approximately 8%)

So, the interest rate used by the state was approximately 8%.

3. **What are some of the accounting applications that incorporate the time value of money into valuation?** *(p. 320)* Accounting applications that incorporate the time value of money techniques into valuation include the valuation of long-term notes receivable and various long-term liabilities that include bonds, notes, leases, pension obligations, and postretirement benefits other than pensions. We study these in detail in later chapters. ●

THE BOTTOM LINE

● **LO1** A dollar today is worth more than a dollar to be received in the future. The difference between the present value of cash flows and their future value represents the time value of money. Interest is the rent paid for the use of money over time. (p. 300)

● **LO2** The future value of a single amount is the amount of money that a dollar will grow to at some point in the future. It is computed by *multiplying* the single amount by $(1 + i)^n$, where i is the interest rate and n the number of compounding periods. The Future Value of $1 table allows for the calculation of future value for any single amount by providing the factors for various combinations of i and n. (p. 301)

● **LO3** The present value of a single amount is the amount of money today that is equivalent to a given amount to be received or paid in the future. It is computed by *dividing* the future amount by $(1 + i)^n$. The Present Value of $1 table simplifies the calculation of the present value of any future amount. (p. 302)

● **LO4** There are four variables in the process of adjusting single cash flow amounts for the time value of money: present value (PV), future value (FV), i and n. If you know any three of these, the fourth can be computed easily. (p. 304)

● **LO5** An annuity is a series of equal-sized cash flows occurring over equal intervals of time. An ordinary annuity exists when the cash flows occur at the end of each period. An annuity due exists when the cash flows occur at the beginning of each period. (p. 309)

● **LO6** The future value of an ordinary annuity (FVA) is the future value of a series of equalsized cash flows with the first payment taking place at the end of the first compounding period. The last payment will not earn any interest since it is made at the end of the annuity period. The future value of an annuity due (FVAD) is the future value of a series of equal-sized cash flows with the first payment taking place at the beginning of the annuity period (the beginning of the first compounding period). (p. 310)

● **LO7** The present value of an ordinary annuity (PVA) is the present value of a series of equal-sized cash flows with the first payment taking place at the end of the first compounding period. The present value of an annuity due (PVAD) is the present value of a series of equal-sized cash flows with the first payment taking place at the beginning of the annuity period. The present value of a deferred annuity is the present value of a series of equal-sized cash flows with the first payment taking place more than one time period after the date of the agreement. (p. 312)

● **LO8** In present value problems involving annuities, there are four variables: PVA or PVAD, the annuity amount, the number of compounding periods (n) and the interest rate (i). If you know any three of these, you can determine the fourth. (p. 316)

● **LO9** Most accounting applications of the time value of money involve the present values of annuities. The initial valuation of long-term bonds is determined by calculating the present value of the periodic stated interest payments and the present value of the lump-sum payment made at maturity. Certain long-term leases require the lessee to compute the present value of future lease payments to value the leased asset and corresponding lease obligation. Also, pension plans require the payment of deferred annuities to retirees. (p. 320) ●

QUESTIONS FOR REVIEW OF KEY TOPICS

Q 6–1 Define interest.

Q 6–2 Explain compound interest.

Q 6–3 What would cause the annual interest rate to be different from the annual effective rate or yield?

Q 6–4 Identify the three items of information necessary to calculate the future value of a single amount.

Q 6–5 Define the present value of a single amount.

Q 6–6   Explain the difference between monetary and nonmonetary assets and liabilities.

Q 6–7   What is an annuity?

Q 6–8   Explain the difference between an ordinary annuity and an annuity due.

Q 6–9   Explain the relationship between Table 2, Present Value of $1, and Table 4, Present Value of an Ordinary Annuity of $1.

Q 6–10   Prepare a time diagram for the present value of a four-year ordinary annuity of $200. Assume an interest rate of 10% per year.

Q 6–11   Prepare a time diagram for the present value of a four-year annuity due of $200. Assume an interest rate of 10% per year.

Q 6–12   What is a deferred annuity?

Q 6–13   Assume that you borrowed $500 from a friend and promised to repay the loan in five equal annual installments beginning one year from today. Your friend wants to be reimbursed for the time value of money at an 8% annual rate. Explain how you would compute the required annual payment.

Q 6–14   Compute the required annual payment in Question 6–13.

Q 6–15   Explain how the time value of money concept is incorporated into the valuation of long-term leases.

BRIEF EXERCISES

BE 6–1
Simple versus
compound interest
● LO1

Fran Smith has two investment opportunities. The interest rate for both investments is 8%. Interest on the first investment will compound annually while interest on the second will compound quarterly. Which investment opportunity should Fran choose? Why?

BE 6–2
Future value; single
amount
● LO2

Bill O'Brien would like to take his wife, Mary, on a trip three years from now to Europe to celebrate their 40th anniversary. He has just received a $20,000 inheritance from an uncle and intends to invest it for the trip. Bill estimates the trip will cost $23,500 and he believes he can earn 5% interest, compounded annually, on his investment. Will he be able to pay for the trip with the accumulated investment amount?

BE 6–3
Future value; solving
for unknown; single
amount
● LO4

Refer to the situation described in BE 6–2. Assume that the trip will cost $26,600. What interest rate, compounded annually, must Bill earn to accumulate enough to pay for the trip?

BE 6–4
Present value;
single amount
● LO3

John has an investment opportunity that promises to pay him $16,000 in four years. He could earn a 6% annual return investing his money elsewhere. What is the maximum amount he would be willing to invest in this opportunity?

BE 6–5
Present value;
solving for
unknown; single
amount
● LO4

Refer to the situation described in BE 6–4. Suppose the opportunity requires John to invest $13,200 today. What is the interest rate John would earn on this investment?

BE 6–6
Future value;
ordinary annuity
● LO6

Leslie McCormack is in the spring quarter of her freshman year of college. She and her friends already are planning a trip to Europe after graduation in a little over three years. Mary would like to contribute to a savings account over the next three years in order to accumulate enough money to take the trip. Assuming an interest rate of 4%, compounded quarterly, how much will she accumulate in three years by depositing $500 at the *end* of each of the next 12 quarters, beginning three months from now?

BE 6–7
Future value;
annuity due
● LO6

Refer to the situation described in BE 6–6. How much will Leslie accumulate in three years by depositing $500 at the *beginning* of each of the next 12 quarters?

BE 6–8
Present value;
ordinary annuity
● LO7

Canliss Mining Company borrowed money from a local bank. The note the company signed requires five annual installment payments of $10,000 beginning one year from today. The interest rate on the note is 7%. What amount did Canliss borrow?

BE 6–9
Present value; annuity due
● LO7

Refer to the situation described in BE 6–8. What amount did Canliss borrow assuming that the first $10,000 payment was due immediately?

BE 6–10
Deferred annuity
● LO7

Refer to the situation described in BE 6–8. What amount did Canliss borrow assuming that the first of the five annual $10,000 payments was not due for three years?

BE 6–11
Solve for unknown; annuity
● LO8

Kingsley Toyota borrowed $100,000 from a local bank. The loan requires Kingsley to pay 10 equal annual installments beginning one year from today. Assuming an interest rate of 8%, what is the amount of each annual installment payment?

BE 6–12
Price of a bond
● LO9

On December 31, 2011, Interlink Communications issued 6% stated rate bonds with a face amount of $100 million. The bonds mature on December 31, 2041. Interest is payable annually on each December 31, beginning in 2012. Determine the price of the bonds on December 31, 2011, assuming that the market rate of interest for similar bonds was 7%.

BE 6–13
Lease payment
● LO9

On September 30, 2011, Ferguson Imports leased a warehouse. Terms of the lease require Ferguson to make 10 annual lease payments of $55,000 with the first payment due immediately. Accounting standards require the company to record a lease liability when recording this type of lease. Assuming an 8% interest rate, at what amount should Ferguson record the lease liability on September 30, 2011, before the first payment is made?

EXERCISES

An alternate exercise and problem set is available on the text website: www.mhhe.com/spiceland6e

E 6–1
Future value; single amount
● LO2

Determine the future value of the following single amounts:

	Invested Amount	Interest Rate	No. of Periods
1.	$15,000	6%	12
2.	20,000	8	10
3.	30,000	12	20
4.	50,000	4	12

E 6–2
Future value; single amounts
● LO2

Determine the future value of $10,000 under each of the following sets of assumptions:

	Annual Rate	Period Invested	Interest Compounded
1.	10%	10 years	Semiannually
2.	12	5 years	Quarterly
3.	24	30 months	Monthly

E 6–3
Present value; single amount
● LO3

Determine the present value of the following single amounts:

	Future Amount	Interest Rate	No. of Periods
1.	$20,000	7%	10
2.	14,000	8	12
3.	25,000	12	20
4.	40,000	10	8

E 6–4
Present value; multiple, unequal amounts
● LO3

Determine the combined present value as of December 31, 2011, of the following four payments to be received at the end of each of the designated years, assuming an annual interest rate of 8%.

Payment	Year Received
$5,000	2012
6,000	2013
8,000	2015
9,000	2017

E 6–5
Noninterest-bearing note; single payment
● LO3

The Field Detergent Company sold merchandise to the Abel Company on June 30, 2011. Payment was made in the form of a noninterest-bearing note requiring Abel to pay $85,000 on June 30, 2013. Assume that a 10% interest rate properly reflects the time value of money in this situation.

Required:
Calculate the amount at which Field should record the note receivable and corresponding sales revenue on June 30, 2011.

E 6–6
Solving for
unknowns; single
amounts
● LO4

For each of the following situations involving single amounts, solve for the unknown (?). Assume that interest is compounded annually. (i = interest rate, and n = number of years)

	Present Value	Future Value	i	n
1.	?	$ 40,000	10%	5
2.	$36,289	65,000	?	10
3.	15,884	40,000	8	?
4.	46,651	100,000	?	8
5.	15,376	?	7	20

E 6–7
Future value;
annuities
● LO6

Wiseman Video plans to make four annual deposits of $2,000 each to a special building fund. The fund's assets will be invested in mortgage instruments expected to pay interest at 12% on the fund's balance. Using the appropriate annuity table, determine how much will be accumulated in the fund on December 31, 2014, under each of the following situations:
1. The first deposit is made on December 31, 2011, and interest is compounded annually.
2. The first deposit is made on December 31, 2010, and interest is compounded annually.
3. The first deposit is made on December 31, 2010, and interest is compounded quarterly.
4. The first deposit is made on December 31, 2010, interest is compounded annually, *and* interest earned is withdrawn at the end of each year.

E 6–8
Present value;
annuities
● LO7

Using the appropriate present value table and assuming a 12% annual interest rate, determine the present value on December 31, 2011, of a five-period annual annuity of $5,000 under each of the following situations:
1. The first payment is received on December 31, 2012, and interest is compounded annually.
2. The first payment is received on December 31, 2011, and interest is compounded annually.
3. The first payment is received on December 31, 2012, and interest is compounded quarterly.

E 6–9
Solving for
unknowns;
annuities
● LO8

For each of the following situations involving annuities, solve for the unknown (?). Assume that interest is compounded annually and that all annuity amounts are received at the *end* of each period. (i = interest rate, and n = number of years)

	Present Value	Annuity Amount	i	n
1.	?	$ 3,000	8%	5
2.	$242,980	75,000	?	4
3.	161,214	20,000	9	?
4.	500,000	80,518	?	8
5.	250,000	?	10	4

E 6–10
Future value;
solving for annuities
and single amount
● LO4 LO8

John Rider wants to accumulate $100,000 to be used for his daughter's college education. He would like to have the amount available on December 31, 2016. Assume that the funds will accumulate in a certificate of deposit paying 8% interest compounded annually.

Required:
Answer each of the following independent questions.
1. If John were to deposit a single amount, how much would he have to invest on December 31, 2011?
2. If John were to make five equal deposits on each December 31, beginning on December 31, 2012, what is the required deposit?
3. If John were to make five equal deposits on each December 31, beginning on December 31, 2011, what is the required deposit?

E 6–11
Future and present
value
● LO3 LO6 LO7

Answer each of the following independent questions.
1. Alex Meir recently won a lottery and has the option of receiving one of the following three prizes: (1) $64,000 cash immediately, (2) $20,000 cash immediately and a six-period annuity of $8,000 beginning one year from today, or (3) a six-period annuity of $13,000 beginning one year from today. Assuming an interest rate of 6%, which option should Alex choose?
2. The Weimer Corporation wants to accumulate a sum of money to repay certain debts due on December 31, 2020. Weimer will make annual deposits of $100,000 into a special bank account at the end of each of 10 years beginning December 31, 2011. Assuming that the bank account pays 7% interest compounded annually, what will be the fund balance after the last payment is made on December 31, 2020?

E 6–12
Deferred annuities
● LO7

Lincoln Company purchased merchandise from Grandville Corp. on September 30, 2011. Payment was made in the form of a noninterest-bearing note requiring Lincoln to make six annual payments of $5,000 on each September 30, beginning on September 30, 2014.

Required:
Calculate the amount at which Lincoln should record the note payable and corresponding purchases on September 30, 2011, assuming that an interest rate of 10% properly reflects the time value of money in this situation.

E 6–13
Solving for unknown annuity payment
● LO8

Don James purchased a new automobile for $20,000. Don made a cash down payment of $5,000 and agreed to pay the remaining balance in 30 monthly installments, beginning one month from the date of purchase. Financing is available at a 24% *annual* interest rate.

Required:
Calculate the amount of the required monthly payment.

E 6–14
Solving for unknown interest rate
● LO8

Lang Warehouses borrowed $100,000 from a bank and signed a note requiring 20 annual payments of $13,388 beginning one year from the date of the agreement.

Required:
Determine the interest rate implicit in this agreement.

E 6–15
Solving for unknown annuity amount
● LO8

Sandy Kupchack just graduated from State University with a bachelors degree in history. During her four years at the U, Sandy accumulated $12,000 in student loans. She asks for your help in determining the amount of the *quarterly* loan payment. She tells you that the loan must be paid back in five years and that the annual interest rate is 8%. Payments begin in three months.

Required:
Determine Sandy's quarterly loan payment.

E 6–16
Deferred annuities; solving for annuity amount
● LO7 LO8

On April 1, 2011, John Vaughn purchased appliances from the Acme Appliance Company for $1,200. In order to increase sales, Acme allows customers to pay in installments and will defer any payments for six months. John will make 18 equal monthly payments, beginning October 1, 2011. The annual interest rate implicit in this agreement is 24%.

Required:
Calculate the monthly payment necessary for John to pay for his purchases.

E 6–17
Price of a bond
● LO9

On September 30, 2011, the San Fillipo Corporation issued 8% stated rate bonds with a face amount of $300 million. The bonds mature on September 30, 2031 (20 years). The market rate of interest for similar bonds was 10%. Interest is paid semiannually on March 31 and September 30.

Required:
Determine the price of the bonds on September 30, 2011.

E 6–18
Price of a bond; interest expense
● LO9

On June 30, 2011, Singleton Computers issued 6% stated rate bonds with a face amount of $200 million. The bonds mature on June 30, 2026 (15 years). The market rate of interest for similar bond issues was 5% (2.5% semiannual rate). Interest is paid semiannually (3%) on June 30 and December 31, beginning on December 31, 2011.

Required:
1. Determine the price of the bonds on June 30, 2011.
2. Calculate the interest expense Singleton reports in 2011 for these bonds.

E 6–19
Lease payments
● LO9

On June 30, 2011, Fly-By-Night Airlines leased a jumbo jet from **Boeing Corporation**. The terms of the lease require Fly-By-Night to make 20 annual payments of $400,000 on each June 30. Generally accepted accounting principles require this lease to be recorded as a liability for the present value of scheduled payments. Assume that a 7% interest rate properly reflects the time value of money in this situation.

Required:
1. At what amount should Fly-By-Night record the lease liability on June 30, 2011, assuming that the first payment will be made on June 30, 2012?
2. At what amount should Fly-By-Night record the lease liability on June 30, 2011, *before* any payments are made, assuming that the first payment will be made on June 30, 2011?

E 6–20
Lease payments; solve for unknown interest rate
● LO8 LO9

On March 31, 2011, Southwest Gas leased equipment from a supplier and agreed to pay $200,000 annually for 20 years beginning March 31, 2012. Generally accepted accounting principles require that a liability be recorded for this lease agreement for the present value of scheduled payments. Accordingly, at inception of the lease, Southwest recorded a $2,293,984 lease liability.

Required:
Determine the interest rate implicit in the lease agreement.

E 6–21
Concepts;
terminology

● **LO1 through**
LO3 LO5

Listed below are several terms and phrases associated with concepts discussed in the chapter. Pair each item from List A with the item from List B (by letter) that is most appropriately associated with it.

List A	List B
____ 1. Interest	a. First cash flow occurs one period after agreement begins.
____ 2. Monetary asset	b. The rate at which money will actually grow during a year.
____ 3. Compound interest	c. First cash flow occurs on the first day of the agreement.
____ 4. Simple interest	d. The amount of money that a dollar will grow to.
____ 5. Annuity	e. Amount of money paid/received in excess of amount borrowed/lent.
____ 6. Present value of a single amount	
____ 7. Annuity due	f. Obligation to pay a sum of cash, the amount of which is fixed.
____ 8. Future value of a single amount	g. Money can be invested today and grow to a larger amount.
____ 9. Ordinary annuity	h. No fixed dollar amount attached.
____ 10. Effective rate or yield	i. Computed by multiplying an invested amount by the interest rate.
____ 11. Nonmonetary asset	j. Interest calculated on invested amount plus accumulated interest.
____ 12. Time value of money	k. A series of equal-sized cash flows.
____ 13. Monetary liability	l. Amount of money required today that is equivalent to a given future amount.
	m. Claim to receive a fixed amount of money.

CPA AND CMA REVIEW QUESTIONS

CPA Exam
Questions

The following questions are used in the Kaplan CPA Review Course to study the time value of money while preparing for the CPA examination. Determine the response that best completes the statements or questions.

● **LO3**

1. An investment product promises to pay $25,458 at the end of nine years. If an investor feels this investment should produce a rate of return of 14 percent, compounded annually, what's the most the investor should be willing to pay for the investment?

n	PV of $1 @ 14%
8	0.3506
9	0.3075
10	0.2697

   a. $6,866
   b. $7,828
   c. $8,926
   d. $9,426

● **LO7**

2. On January 1, 2011, Ott Company sold goods to Fox Company. Fox signed a noninterest-bearing note requiring payment of $60,000 annually for seven years. The first payment was made on January 1, 2011. The prevailing rate of interest for this type of note at date of issuance was 10%. Information on present value factors is as follows:

Periods	Present Value of 1 at 10%	Present Value of Ordinary Annuity of 1 at 10%
6	.56	4.36
7	.51	4.87

   Ott should record sales revenue in January 2011 of
   a. $214,200
   b. $261,600
   c. $292,600
   d. $321,600

● **LO7**

3. An annuity will pay eight annual payments of $100, with the first payment to be received one year from now. If the interest rate is 12 percent per year, what is the present value of this annuity? Use the appropriate table located at the end of the textbook to solve this problem.
   a. $497
   b. $556
   c. $801
   d. $897

● LO7

4. An annuity will pay four annual payments of $100, with the first payment to be received three years from now. If the interest rate is 12 percent per year, what is the present value of this annuity? Use the appropriate table located at the end of the textbook to solve this problem.
   a. $181
   b. $242
   c. $304
   d. $400

● LO7

5. Justin Banks just won the lottery and is trying to decide between the annual cash flow payment option of $100,000 per year for 15 years beginning today, or the lump-sum option. Justin can earn 8 percent investing his money. At what lump-sum payment amount would he be indifferent between the two alternatives? Use the appropriate table located at the end of the textbook to solve this problem.
   a. $824,424
   b. $855,948
   c. $890,378
   d. $924,424

● LO3 LO7 LO9

6. An investor purchases a 10-year, $1,000 par value bond that pays *annual* interest of $100. If the market rate of interest is 12 percent, what is the current market value of the bond?
   a. $ 887
   b. $ 950
   c. $1,000
   d. $1,100

● LO8

7. You borrow $15,000 to buy a car. The loan is to be paid off in monthly installments over five years at 12 percent interest annually. The first payment is due one month from today. If the present value of an ordinary annuity of $1 for 5 years @12% with monthly compounding is $44.955, what is the amount of each monthly payment?
   a. $334
   b. $456
   c. $546
   d. $680

CMA Exam Questions

The following questions dealing with the time value of money are adapted from questions that previously appeared on Certified Management Accountant (CMA) examinations. The CMA designation sponsored by the Institute of Management Accountants (**www.imanet.org**) provides members with an objective measure of knowledge and competence in the field of management accounting. Determine the response that best completes the statements or questions.

● LO2

1. Janet Taylor Casual Wear has $75,000 in a bank account as of December 31, 2009. If the company plans on depositing $4,000 in the account at the end of each of the next 3 years (2010, 2011, and 2012) and all amounts in the account earn 8% per year, what will the account balance be at December 31, 2012? Ignore the effect of income taxes.

| | **8% Interest Rate Factors** | |
Period	**Future Value of an Amount of $1**	**Future Value of an Ordinary Annuity of $1**
1	1.08	1.00
2	1.17	2.08
3	1.26	3.25
4	1.36	4.51

   a. $ 87,000
   b. $ 88,000
   c. $ 96,070
   d. $107,500

● LO7 LO9

2. Essex Corporation is evaluating a lease that takes effect on March 1. The company must make eight equal payments, with the first payment due on March 1. The concept most relevant to the evaluation of the lease is
   a. The present value of an annuity due.
   b. The present value of an ordinary annuity.
   c. The future value of an annuity due.
   d. The future value of an ordinary annuity.

PROBLEMS

An alternate exercise and problem set is available on the text website: www.mhhe.com/spiceland6e

P 6–1
Analysis of
alternatives
● LO3 LO7

Esquire Company needs to acquire a molding machine to be used in its manufacturing process. Two types of machines that would be appropriate are presently on the market. The company has determined the following:

Machine A could be purchased for $48,000. It will last 10 years with annual maintenance costs of $1,000 per year. After 10 years the machine can be sold for $5,000.

Machine B could be purchased for $40,000. It also will last 10 years and will require maintenance costs of $4,000 in year three, $5,000 in year six, and $6,000 in year eight. After 10 years, the machine will have no salvage value.

Required:
Determine which machine Esquire should purchase. Assume an interest rate of 8% properly reflects the time value of money in this situation and that maintenance costs are paid at the end of each year. Ignore income tax considerations.

P 6–2
Present and future
value
● LO6 LO7 LO9

Johnstone Company is facing several decisions regarding investing and financing activities. Address each decision independently.

1. On June 30, 2011, the Johnstone Company purchased equipment from Genovese Corp. Johnstone agreed to pay Genovese $10,000 on the purchase date and the balance in five annual installments of $8,000 on each June 30 beginning June 30, 2012. Assuming that an interest rate of 10% properly reflects the time value of money in this situation, at what amount should Johnstone value the equipment?

2. Johnstone needs to accumulate sufficient funds to pay a $400,000 debt that comes due on December 31, 2016. The company will accumulate the funds by making five equal annual deposits to an account paying 6% interest compounded annually. Determine the required annual deposit if the first deposit is made on December 31, 2011.

3. On January 1, 2011, Johnstone leased an office building. Terms of the lease require Johnstonc to make 20 annual lease payments of $120,000 beginning on January 1, 2011. A 10% interest rate is implicit in the lease agreement. At what amount should Johnstone record the lease liability on January 1, 2011, *before* any lease payments are made?

P 6–3
Analysis of
alternatives
● LO3 LO7

Harding Company is in the process of purchasing several large pieces of equipment from Danning Machine Corporation. Several financing alternatives have been offered by Danning:

1. Pay $1,000,000 in cash immediately.
2. Pay $420,000 immediately and the remainder in 10 annual installments of $80,000, with the first installment due in one year.
3. Make 10 annual installments of $135,000 with the first payment due immediately.
4. Make one lump-sum payment of $1,500,000 five years from date of purchase.

Required:
Determine the best alternative for Harding, assuming that Harding can borrow funds at an 8% interest rate.

P 6–4
Investment analysis
● LO3 LO7

John Wiggins is contemplating the purchase of a small restaurant. The purchase price listed by the seller is $800,000. John has used past financial information to estimate that the net cash flows (cash inflows less cash outflows) generated by the restaurant would be as follows:

Years	Amount
1–6	$80,000
7	70,000
8	60,000
9	50,000
10	40,000

If purchased, the restaurant would be held for 10 years and then sold for an estimated $700,000.

Required:
Assuming that John desires a 10% rate of return on this investment, should the restaurant be purchased? (Assume that all cash flows occur at the end of the year.)

P 6–5
Investment decision;
varying rates
● LO3 LO7

John and Sally Claussen are contemplating the purchase of a hardware store from John Duggan. The Claussens anticipate that the store will generate cash flows of $70,000 per year for 20 years. At the end of 20 years, they intend to sell the store for an estimated $400,000. The Claussens will finance the investment with a variable rate mortgage. Interest rates will increase twice during the 20-year life of the mortgage. Accordingly, the Claussens' desired rate of return on this investment varies as follows:

Years 1–5	8%
Years 6–10	10%
Years 11–20	12%

Required:
What is the maximum amount the Claussens should pay John Duggan for the hardware store? (Assume that all cash flows occur at the end of the year.)

P 6–6
Solving for
unknowns
● LO8

The following situations should be considered independently.

1. John Jamison wants to accumulate $60,000 for a down payment on a small business. He will invest $30,000 today in a bank account paying 8% interest compounded annually. Approximately how long will it take John to reach his goal?

2. The Jasmine Tea Company purchased merchandise from a supplier for $28,700. Payment was a noninterest-bearing note requiring Jasmine to make five annual payments of $7,000 beginning one year from the date of purchase. What is the interest rate implicit in this agreement?

3. Sam Robinson borrowed $10,000 from a friend and promised to pay the loan in 10 equal annual installments beginning one year from the date of the loan. Sam's friend would like to be reimbursed for the time value of money at a 9% annual rate. What is the annual payment Sam must make to pay back his friend?

P 6–7
Solving for
unknowns
● LO8

Lowlife Company defaulted on a $250,000 loan that was due on December 31, 2011. The bank has agreed to allow Lowlife to repay the $250,000 by making a series of equal annual payments beginning on December 31, 2012.

Required:
1. Calculate the required annual payment if the bank's interest rate is 10% and four payments are to be made.
2. Calculate the required annual payment if the bank's interest rate is 8% and five payments are to be made.
3. If the bank's interest rate is 10%, how many annual payments of $51,351 would be required to repay the debt?
4. If three payments of $104,087 are to be made, what interest rate is the bank charging Lowlife?

P 6–8
Deferred annuities
● LO7

On January 1, 2011, the Montgomery company agreed to purchase a building by making six payments. The first three are to be $25,000 each, and will be paid on December 31, 2011, 2012, and 2013. The last three are to be $40,000 each and will be paid on December 31, 2014, 2015, and 2016. Montgomery borrowed other money at a 10% annual rate.

Required:
1. At what amount should Montgomery record the note payable and corresponding cost of the building on January 1, 2011?
2. How much interest expense on this note will Montgomery recognize in 2011?

P 6–9
Deferred annuities
● LO7

John Roberts is 55 years old and has been asked to accept early retirement from his company. The company has offered John three alternative compensation packages to induce John to retire:

1. $180,000 cash payment to be paid immediately.
2. A 20-year annuity of $16,000 beginning immediately.
3. A 10-year annuity of $50,000 beginning at age 65.

Required:
Which alternative should John choose assuming that he is able to invest funds at a 7% rate?

P 6–10
Noninterest-bearing
note; annuity and
lump-sum payment
● LO3 LO7

On January 1, 2011, The Barrett Company purchased merchandise from a supplier. Payment was a noninterest-bearing note requiring five annual payments of $20,000 on each December 31 beginning on December 31, 2011, and a lump-sum payment of $100,000 on December 31, 2015. A 10% interest rate properly reflects the time value of money in this situation.

Required:
Calculate the amount at which Barrett should record the note payable and corresponding merchandise purchased on January 1, 2011.

P 6–11
Solving for
unknown lease
payment
● LO8 LO9

Benning Manufacturing Company is negotiating with a customer for the lease of a large machine manufactured by Benning. The machine has a cash price of $800,000. Benning wants to be reimbursed for financing the machine at an 8% annual interest rate.

Required:
1. Determine the required lease payment if the lease agreement calls for 10 equal annual payments beginning immediately.

2. Determine the required lease payment if the first of 10 annual payments will be made one year from the date of the agreement.

3. Determine the required lease payment if the first of 10 annual payments will be made immediately and Benning will be able to sell the machine to another customer for $50,000 at the end of the 10-year lease.

P 6–12
Solving for
unknown lease
payment;
compounding
periods of varying
length
● LO9

(This is a variation of the previous problem focusing on compounding periods of varying length.)

Benning Manufacturing Company is negotiating with a customer for the lease of a large machine manufactured by Benning. The machine has a cash price of $800,000. Benning wants to be reimbursed for financing the machine at a 12% annual interest rate over the five-year lease term.

Required:

1. Determine the required lease payment if the lease agreement calls for 10 equal semiannual payments beginning six months from the date of the agreement.

2. Determine the required lease payment if the lease agreement calls for 20 equal quarterly payments beginning immediately.

3. Determine the required lease payment if the lease agreement calls for 60 equal monthly payments beginning one month from the date of the agreement. The present value of an ordinary annuity factor for $n = 60$ and $i = 1\%$ is 44.9550.

P 6–13
Lease vs. buy
alternatives
● LO3 LO7 LO9

Kiddy Toy Corporation needs to acquire the use of a machine to be used in its manufacturing process. The machine needed is manufactured by Lollie Corp. The machine can be used for 10 years and then sold for $10,000 at the end of its useful life. Lollie has presented Kiddy with the following options:

1. *Buy machine.* The machine could be purchased for $160,000 in cash. All maintenance and insurance costs, which approximate $5,000 per year, would be paid by Kiddy.

2. *Lease machine.* The machine could be leased for a 10-year period for an annual lease payment of $25,000 with the first payment due immediately. All maintenance and insurance costs will be paid for by the Lollie Corp. and the machine will revert back to Lollie at the end of the 10-year period.

Required:
Assuming that a 12% interest rate properly reflects the time value of money in this situation and that all maintenance and insurance costs are paid at the end of each year, determine which option Kiddy should choose. Ignore income tax considerations.

P 6–14
Deferred annuities;
pension obligation
● LO7 LO9

Three employees of the Horizon Distributing Company will receive annual pension payments from the company when they retire. The employees will receive their annual payments for as long as they live. Life expectancy for each employee is 15 years beyond retirement. Their names, the amount of their annual pension payments, and the date they will receive their first payment are shown below:

Employee	Annual Payment	Date of First Payment
Tinkers	$20,000	12/31/14
Evers	25,000	12/31/15
Chance	30,000	12/31/16

Required:

1. Compute the present value of the pension obligation to these three employees as of December 31, 2011. Assume an 11% interest rate.

2. The company wants to have enough cash invested at December 31, 2014, to provide for all three employees. To accumulate enough cash, they will make three equal annual contributions to a fund that will earn 11% interest compounded annually. The first contribution will be made on December 31, 2011. Compute the amount of this required annual contribution.

P 6–15
Bonds and leases;
deferred annuities
● LO3 LO7 LO9

On the last day of its fiscal year ending December 31, 2011, the Sedgwick & Reams (S&R) Glass Company completed two financing arrangements. The funds provided by these initiatives will allow the company to expand its operations.

1. S&R issued 8% stated rate bonds with a face amount of $100 million. The bonds mature on December 31, 2031 (20 years). The market rate of interest for similar bond issues was 9% (4.5% semiannual rate). Interest is paid semiannually (4%) on June 30 and December 31, beginning on June 30, 2012.

2. The company leased two manufacturing facilities. Lease A requires 20 annual lease payments of $200,000 beginning on January 1, 2012. Lease B also is for 20 years, beginning January 1, 2012. Terms of the lease require 17 annual lease payments of $220,000 beginning on January 1, 2015. Generally accepted accounting principles require both leases to be recorded as liabilities for the present value of the scheduled payments. Assume that a 10% interest rate properly reflects the time value of money for the lease obligations.

Required:
What amounts will appear in S&R's December 31, 2011, balance sheet for the bonds and for the leases?

BROADEN YOUR PERSPECTIVE

Apply your critical-thinking ability to the knowledge you've gained. These cases will provide you an opportunity to develop your research, analysis, judgment, and communication skills. You also will work with other students, integrate what you've learned, apply it in real world situations, and consider its global and ethical ramifications. This practice will broaden your knowledge and further develop your decision-making abilities.

Ethics Case 6–1
Rate of return
● LO1

The Damon Investment Company manages a mutual fund composed mostly of speculative stocks. You recently saw an ad claiming that investments in the funds have been earning a rate of return of 21%. This rate seemed quite high so you called a friend who works for one of Damon's competitors. The friend told you that the 21% return figure was determined by dividing the two-year appreciation on investments in the fund by the average investment. In other words, $100 invested in the fund two years ago would have grown to $121 ($21 ÷ $100 = 21%).

Required:

Discuss the ethics of the 21% return claim made by the Damon Investment Company.

Analysis Case 6–2
Bonus alternatives; present value analysis
● LO3 LO7

Sally Hamilton has performed well as the chief financial officer of the Maxtech Computer Company and has earned a bonus. She has a choice among the following three bonus plans:
1. A $50,000 cash bonus paid now.
2. A $10,000 annual cash bonus to be paid each year over the next six years, with the first $10,000 paid now.
3. A three-year $22,000 annual cash bonus with the first payment due three years from now.

Required:

Evaluate the three alternative bonus plans. Sally can earn a 6% annual return on her investments.

Communication Case 6–3
Present value of annuities
● LO7

Harvey Alexander, an all-league professional football player, has just declared free agency. Two teams, the San Francisco 49ers and the Dallas Cowboys, have made Harvey the following offers to obtain his services:

49ers: $1 million signing bonus payable immediately and an annual salary of $1.5 million for the five-year term of the contract.

Cowboys: $2.5 million signing bonus payable immediately and an annual salary of $1 million for the five-year term of the contract.

With both contracts, the annual salary will be paid in one lump sum at the end of the football season.

Required:

You have been hired as a consultant to Harvey's agent, Phil Marks, to evaluate the two contracts. Write a short letter to Phil with your recommendation including the method you used to reach your conclusion. Assume that Harvey has no preference between the two teams and that the decision will be based entirely on monetary considerations. Also assume that Harvey can invest his money and earn an 8% annual return.

Analysis Case 6–4
Present value of an annuity
● LO7

On a rainy afternoon two years ago, John Smiley left work early to attend a family birthday party. Eleven minutes later, a careening truck slammed into his SUV on the freeway causing John to spend two months in a coma. Now he can't hold a job or make everyday decisions and is in need of constant care. Last week, the 40-year-old Smiley won an out-of-court settlement from the truck driver's company. He was awarded payment for all medical costs and attorney fees, plus a lump-sum settlement of $2,330,716. At the time of the accident, John was president of his family's business and earned approximately $200,000 per year. He had anticipated working 25 more years before retirement.[8]

John's sister, an acquaintance of yours from college, has asked you to explain to her how the attorneys came up with the settlement amount. "They said it was based on his lost future income and a 7% rate of some kind," she explained. "But it was all 'legal-speak' to me."

Required:

How was the amount of the lump-sum settlement determined? Create a calculation that might help John's sister understand.

Judgment Case 6–5
Replacement decision
● LO3 LO7

Hughes Corporation is considering replacing a machine used in the manufacturing process with a new, more efficient model. The purchase price of the new machine is $150,000 and the old machine can be sold for $100,000. Output for the two machines is identical; they will both be used to produce the same amount of product for five years. However, the annual operating costs of the old machine are $18,000 compared to $10,000 for the new machine. Also, the new machine has a salvage value of $25,000, but the old machine will be worthless at the end of the five years.

Required:

Should the company sell the old machine and purchase the new model? Assume that an 8% rate properly reflects the time value of money in this situation and that all operating costs are paid at the end of the year. Ignore the effect of the decision on income taxes.

---

[8]This case is based on actual events.

Real World Case 6–6
Zero-coupon bonds; Johnson & Johnson
● LO3 LO9

Real World Financials

Johnson & Johnson is one of the world's largest manufacturers of health care products. The company's 2009 financial statements included the following information in the long-term debt disclosure note:

	($ in millions) 2009
Zero-coupon convertible subordinated debentures, due 2020	$189

The disclosure note stated that the debenture bonds were issued early in 2000 and have a maturity value of $272.5 million. The maturity value indicates the amount that Johnson & Johnson will pay bondholders in 2020. Each individual bond has a maturity value (face amount) of $1,000. Zero-coupon bonds pay no cash interest during the term to maturity. The company is "accreting" (gradually increasing) the issue price to maturity value using the bonds' effective interest rate computed on a semiannual basis.

Required:

1. Determine the effective interest rate on the bonds.
2. Determine the issue price in early 2000 of a single, $1,000 maturity-value bond.

Real World Case 6–7
Leases; Southwest Airlines
● LO3 LO9

Real World Financials

Southwest Airlines provides scheduled air transportation services in the United States. Like many airlines, Southwest leases many of its planes from **Boeing Company**. In its long-term debt disclosure note included in the financial statements for the year ended December 31, 2008, the company listed $39 million in lease obligations. The note also disclosed that existing leases had a three-year remaining life and that future lease payments averaged approximately $14 million per year.

Required:

1. Determine the effective interest rate the company used to determine the lease liability assuming that lease payments are made at the end of each fiscal year.
2. Repeat requirement 1 assuming that lease payments are made at the beginning of each fiscal year.

Cash and Receivables

/// **OVERVIEW**

We begin our study of assets by looking at cash and receivables—the two assets typically listed first in a balance sheet. For cash, the key issues are internal control and classification in the balance sheet. For receivables, the key issues are valuation and the related income statement effects of transactions involving accounts receivable and notes receivable.

/// **LEARNING OBJECTIVES**

After studying this chapter, you should be able to:

● **LO1** Define what is meant by internal control and describe some key elements of an internal control system for cash receipts and disbursements. (page 338)

● **LO2** Explain the possible restrictions on cash and their implications for classification in the balance sheet. (page 340)

● **LO3** Distinguish between the gross and net methods of accounting for cash discounts. (page 343)

● **LO4** Describe the accounting treatment for merchandise returns. (page 344)

● **LO5** Describe the accounting treatment of anticipated uncollectible accounts receivable. (page 347)

● **LO6** Describe the two approaches to estimating bad debts. (page 347)

● **LO7** Describe the accounting treatment of short-term notes receivable. (page 352)

● **LO8** Differentiate between the use of receivables in financing arrangements accounted for as a secured borrowing and those accounted for as a sale. (page 356)

● **LO9** Describe the variables that influence a company's investment in receivables and calculate the key ratios used by analysts to monitor that investment. (page 365)

● **LO10** Discuss the primary differences between U.S. GAAP and IFRS with respect to cash and receivables. (pages 341, 356, 364, and 374)

FINANCIAL REPORTING CASE

What Does It All Mean?

Your roommate, Todd Buckley, was surfing the net looking for information about his future employer, **Cisco Systems**. Todd, an engineering major, recently accepted a position with Cisco, the world's largest provider of hardware, software, and services that drive the Internet. He noticed an article on TheStreet.com entitled "Cisco Triples Bad-Account Provision." "This doesn't look good," Todd grumbled. "The article says that my new employer's deadbeat account column has more than tripled in the span of a year. I guess all those dot-com companies are not paying their bills. But this sentence is confusing. 'For the fiscal first quarter Cisco moved $275 million from operating cash to cover potential nonpayments from failed customers.' Did they actually move cash and if so, where did they move it and why?"

You studied accounting for bad debts in your intermediate accounting class and are confident you can help. After reading the article, you comfort Todd. "First of all, the term *provision* just means expense, and no, Cisco didn't move any cash. The company uses what is called the *allowance method* to account for its bad debts, and it looks like it simply recorded $275 million in expense for the quarter and increased the allowance for uncollectible accounts." Todd was not happy with your answer. "Provisions! Allowance method! Uncollectible accounts! I want you to help me understand, not make things worse." "Okay," you offer, "let's start at the beginning."

By the time you finish this chapter, you should be able to respond appropriately to the questions posed in this case. Compare your response to the solution provided at the end of the chapter.

QUESTIONS ///

1. Explain the allowance method of accounting for bad debts. (page 347)
2. What approaches might Cisco have used to arrive at the $275 million bad debt provision? (page 348)
3. Are there any alternatives to the allowance method? (page 350)

In the earlier chapters of this text, we studied the underlying measurement and reporting concepts for the basic financial statements presented to external decision makers. Now we turn our attention to the elements of those financial statements. Specifically, we further explore the elements of the balance sheet, and also consider the income statement effects of transactions involving these elements. We first address assets, then liabilities, and finally shareholders' equity. This chapter focuses on the current assets **cash and cash equivalents** and **receivables.**

PART A

CASH AND CASH EQUIVALENTS

Cash includes currency and coins, balances in checking accounts, and items acceptable for deposit in these accounts, such as checks and money orders received from customers. These forms of cash represent amounts readily available to pay off debt or to use in operations, without any legal or contractual restriction.

Managers typically invest temporarily idle cash to earn interest on those funds rather than keep an unnecessarily large checking account. These amounts are essentially equivalent to cash because they can quickly become available for use as cash. So, short-term, highly liquid investments that can be readily converted to cash with little risk of loss are viewed as cash equivalents. For financial reporting we make no distinction between cash in the form of currency or bank account balances and amounts held in cash equivalent investments.

Cash equivalents include money market funds, treasury bills, and commercial paper. To be classified as cash equivalents, these investments must have a maturity date no longer than three months *from the date of purchase*. Companies are permitted flexibility in designating cash equivalents and must establish individual policies regarding which short-term, highly liquid investments are classified as cash equivalents. A company's policy should be consistent with the usual motivation for acquiring these investments. The policy should be disclosed in the notes to the financial statements. Graphic 7–1 shows a note from a 2009 quarterly report of **Mannatech Incorporated**, a manufacturer of dietary supplements and other wellness products, that provides a description of the company's cash equivalents.

> A company's policy concerning which short-term, highly liquid investments it classifies as cash equivalents should be described in a disclosure note.

GRAPHIC 7–1

Disclosure of Cash Equivalents—Mannatech Incorporated

Real World Financials

Note 1: Organization and Summary of Significant Accounting Policies (in part)
Cash and Cash Equivalents

The Company considers all highly liquid investments with original maturities of three months or less to be cash equivalents. The Company includes in its cash and cash equivalents credit card receivables due from its credit card processor, as the cash proceeds from credit card receivables are generally received within 24 to 72 hours.

Notice in the disclosure note that Mannatech includes credit card receivables as cash equivalents. These receivables typically are converted to cash within a few business days.

The measurement and reporting of cash and cash equivalents are largely straightforward because cash generally presents no measurement problems. It is the standard medium of exchange and the basis for measuring assets and liabilities. Cash and cash equivalents usually are combined and reported as a single amount in the balance sheet. However, cash that is not available for use in current operations because it is restricted for a special purpose usually is classified in one of the noncurrent asset categories. Restricted cash is discussed later in this chapter.

> Credit and debit card receivables often are included in cash equivalents.

All assets must be safeguarded against possible misuse. However, cash is the most liquid asset and the asset most easily expropriated. As a result, a system of internal control of cash is a key accounting issue.

Internal Control

> ● LO1

The success of any business enterprise depends on an effective system of internal control. Internal control refers to a company's plan to (a) encourage adherence to company policies and procedures, (b) promote operational efficiency, (c) minimize errors and theft, and (d) enhance the reliability and accuracy of accounting data. From a financial accounting perspective, the focus is on controls intended to improve the accuracy and reliability of accounting information and to safeguard the company's assets.

> The Sarbanes-Oxley Act requires a company to document and assess its internal controls. Auditors express an opinion on management's assessment.

Recall from our discussion in Chapter 1 that Section 404 of the *Sarbanes-Oxley Act of 2002* requires that companies document their internal controls and assess their adequacy. The Public Company Accounting Oversight Board's *Auditing Standard No. 5* further requires the auditor to express its own opinion on whether the company has maintained effective internal control over financial reporting.

Many companies have incurred significant costs in an effort to comply with the requirements of Section 404.[1] A cottage industry of consulting firms and software products has arisen to help these companies. A framework for designing an internal control system is provided by the **Committee of Sponsoring Organizations (COSO)** of the Treadway Commission.[2] Formed in 1985, the organization is dedicated to improving the quality of financial reporting through, among other things, effective internal controls.

COSO defines internal control as a process, undertaken by an entity's board of directors, management and other personnel, designed to provide reasonable assurance regarding the achievement of objectives in the following categories:

- Effectiveness and efficiency of operations.
- Reliability of financial reporting.
- Compliance with applicable laws and regulations.[3]

A critical aspect of an internal control system is the *separation of duties.* Individuals that have physical responsibility for assets should not also have access to accounting records. For example, if the same individual has control of both the supplies inventory and the accounting records, the theft of supplies could be concealed by a reduction of the supplies account.

Employees involved in recordkeeping should not also have physical access to the assets.

Internal Control Procedures—Cash Receipts

As cash is the most liquid of all assets, a well-designed and functioning system of internal control must surround all cash transactions. Separation of duties is critical. Ideally, those who handle cash should not be involved in or have access to accounting records nor be involved in the reconciliation of cash book balances to bank balances.

Consider the cash receipt process. Most nonretail businesses receive payment for goods by checks received through the mail. An approach to internal control over cash receipts might include the following steps:

1. Employee A opens the mail each day and prepares a multicopy listing of all checks including the amount and payor's name.
2. Employee B takes the checks, along with one copy of the listing, to the person responsible for depositing the checks in the company's bank account.
3. A second copy of the check listing is sent to the accounting department where the receipts are entered into the records.

The amount received should equal the amount deposited as verified by comparison with the bank-generated deposit slip and the amount recorded in the accounting records. This helps ensure accuracy as well as safeguard cash against theft.

Internal Control Procedures—Cash Disbursements

Proper controls for cash disbursements should be designed to prevent any unauthorized payments and ensure that disbursements are recorded in the proper general ledger and subsidiary ledger accounts. Important elements of a cash disbursement control system include:

1. All disbursements, other than very small disbursements from petty cash, should be made by check. This provides a permanent record of all disbursements.
2. All expenditures should be *authorized* before a check is prepared. For example, a vendor invoice for the purchase of inventory should be compared with the purchase order and receiving report to ensure the accuracy of quantity, price, part numbers, and so on. This process should include verification of the proper ledger accounts to be debited.
3. Checks should be signed only by authorized individuals.

---

[1]In response to the high cost of 404 compliance, the PCAOB issued a second standard, *Auditing Standard No. 5,* to replace its Standard No. 2. The new standard emphasizes audit efficiency with a more focused, risk-based testing approach for material areas. These guidelines should reduce the total costs of 404 compliance.

[2]The sponsoring organizations include the AICPA, the Financial Executives International, the Institute of Internal Auditors, the American Accounting Association, and the Institute of Management Accountants.

[3]**www.coso.org**.

Responsibilities for check signing, check writing, check mailing, cash disbursement documentation, and recordkeeping ideally should be separated whenever possible.

An important part of any system of internal control of cash is the periodic reconciliation of book balances and bank balances to the correct balance. In addition, a petty cash system is employed by many business enterprises. We cover these two topics in Appendix 7A beginning on page 369.

Restricted Cash and Compensating Balances

● LO2

We discussed the classification of assets and liabilities in Chapter 3. You should recall that only cash available for current operations or to satisfy current liabilities is classified as a current asset. Cash that is restricted in some way and not available for current use usually is reported as a noncurrent asset such as *investments and funds* or *other assets*.

Restrictions on cash can be informal, arising from management's intent to use a certain amount of cash for a specific purpose. For example, a company may set aside funds for future plant expansion. This cash, if material, should be classified as investments and funds or other assets. Sometimes restrictions are contractually imposed. Debt instruments, for instance, frequently require the borrower to set aside funds (often referred to as a sinking fund) for the future payment of a debt. In these instances, the restricted cash is classified as noncurrent investments and funds or other assets if the debt is classified as noncurrent. On the other hand, if the liability is current, the restricted cash also is classified as current. Disclosure notes should describe any material restrictions of cash.

The effect of a *compensating balance* is a higher effective interest rate on the debt.

Banks frequently require cash restrictions in connection with loans or loan commitments (lines of credit). Typically, the borrower is asked to maintain a specified balance in a low interest or noninterest-bearing account at the bank (creditor). The required balance usually is some percentage of the committed amount (say 2% to 5%). These are known as compensating balances because they compensate the bank for granting the loan or extending the line of credit.

A compensating balance results in the borrower's paying an effective interest rate higher than the stated rate on the debt. For example, suppose that a company borrows $10,000,000 from a bank at an interest rate of 12%. If the bank requires a compensating balance of $2,000,000 to be held in a noninterest-bearing checking account, the company really is borrowing only $8,000,000 (the loan less the compensating balance). This means an effective interest rate of 15% ($1,200,000 interest divided by $8,000,000 cash available for use).

A material compensating balance must be disclosed regardless of the classification of the cash.

The classification and disclosure of a compensating balance depends on the nature of the restriction and the classification of the related debt.[4] If the restriction is legally binding, the cash is classified as either current or noncurrent (investments and funds or other assets) depending on the classification of the related debt. In either case, note disclosure is appropriate.

If the compensating balance arrangement is informal with no contractual agreement that restricts the use of cash, the compensating balance can be reported as part of cash and cash equivalents, with note disclosure of the arrangement. Graphic 7–2 provides an example of a note disclosure of a compensating balance for **CNB Financial Services, Inc.**, a bank holding company incorporated in West Virginia.

GRAPHIC 7–2

Disclosure of Compensating Balances—CNB Financial Services, Inc.

Real World Financials

> **Note 10—Lines of Credit (in part)**
>
> The Bank entered into an open-ended unsecured line of credit with Mercantile Safe Deposit and Trust Company for $3,000,000 for federal fund purchases. Funds issued under this agreement are at the Mercantile Safe Deposit and Trust Company federal funds rate effective at the time of borrowing. The line . . . has a compensating balance requirement of $250,000.

---

[4]FASB ASC *210–10–S99–2: SAB Topic 6.H–Balance Sheet—Overall—SEC* Materials, *Accounting Series Release 148* (originally "Amendments to Regulations S-X and Related Interpretations and Guidelines Regarding the Disclosure of Compensating Balances and Short-Term Borrowing Arrangements," *Accounting Series Release No. 148,* Securities and Exchange Commission (November 13, 1973)).

INTERNATIONAL FINANCIAL REPORTING STANDARDS

Cash and Cash Equivalents. In general, cash and cash equivalents are treated similarly under IFRS and U.S. GAAP. One difference relates to bank overdrafts, which occur when withdrawals from a bank account exceed the available balance. U.S. GAAP requires that overdrafts typically be treated as liabilities. In contrast, *IAS No. 7* allows bank overdrafts to be offset against other cash accounts when overdrafts are payable on demand and fluctuate between positive and negative amounts as part of the normal cash management program that a company uses to minimize their cash balance.[5]

● LO10

IFRS ILLUSTRATION

For example, imagine LaDonia Company has two cash accounts with the following balances as of December 31, 2011:

National Bank: $300,000
Central Bank: (15,000)

Under U.S. GAAP, LaDonia's 12/31/11 balance sheet would report a cash asset of $300,000 and an overdraft current liability of $15,000. Under IFRS, LaDonia would report a cash asset of $285,000.

DECISION MAKERS' PERSPECTIVE

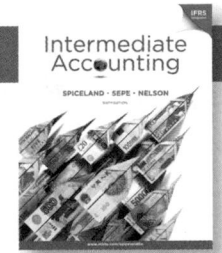

Cash often is referred to as a *nonearning* asset because it earns no interest. For this reason, managers invest idle cash in either cash equivalents or short-term investments, both of which provide a return. Management's goal is to hold the minimum amount of cash necessary to conduct normal business operations, meet its obligations, and take advantage of opportunities. Too much cash reduces profits through lost returns, while too little cash increases risk. This trade-off between risk and return is an ongoing choice made by management (internal decision makers). Whether the choice made is appropriate is an ongoing assessment made by investors and creditors (external decision makers).

A company must have cash available for the compensating balances we discussed in the previous section as well as for planned disbursements related to normal operating, investing, and financing cash flows. However, because cash inflows and outflows can vary from planned amounts, a company needs an additional cash cushion as a precaution against that contingency. The size of the cushion depends on the company's ability to convert cash equivalents and short-term investments into cash quickly, along with its short-term borrowing capacity.

Companies hold cash to pay for planned and unplanned transactions and to satisfy compensating balance requirements.

Liquidity is a measure of a company's cash position and overall ability to obtain cash in the normal course of business. A company is assumed to be liquid if it has sufficient cash or is capable of converting its other assets to cash in a relatively short period of time so that current needs can be met. Frequently, liquidity is measured with respect to the ability to pay currently maturing debt. The current ratio is one of the most common ways of measuring liquidity and is calculated by dividing current assets by current liabilities. By comparing liabilities that must be satisfied in the near term with assets that either are cash or will be converted to cash in the near term we have a base measure of a company's liquidity. We can refine the measure by adjusting for the implicit assumption of the current ratio that all current assets are equally liquid. In the acid-test or quick ratio, the numerator consists of "quick assets," which include only cash and cash equivalents, short-term investments, and accounts receivable. By eliminating inventories and prepaid expenses, the current assets that are less readily convertible into cash, we get a more precise indication of a company's short-term solvency than with the current ratio. We discussed and illustrated these liquidity ratios in Chapter 3.

We should evaluate the adequacy of any ratio in the context of the industry in which the company operates and other specific circumstances. Bear in mind, though, that industry

---

[5]"Statement of Cash Flows," *International Accounting Standard No. 7* (IASCF), as amended, effective January 1, 2009, par. 8.

averages are only one indication of acceptability and any ratio is but one indication of liquidity. Profitability, for instance, is perhaps the best long-run indication of liquidity. And a company may be very efficient in managing its current assets so that, say, receivables are more liquid than they otherwise would be. The receivables turnover ratio we discuss in Part B of this chapter offers a measure of management's efficiency in this regard.

There are many techniques that a company can use to manage cash balances. A discussion of these techniques is beyond the scope of this text. However, it is sufficient here to understand that management must make important decisions related to cash that have a direct impact on a company's profitability and risk. Because the lack of prudent cash management can lead to the failure of an otherwise sound company, it is essential that managers as well as outside investors and creditors maintain close vigil over this facet of a company's health. ●

> A manager should actively monitor the company's cash position.

CURRENT RECEIVABLES

Receivables represent a company's claims to the future collection of cash, other assets, or services. Receivables resulting from the sale of goods or services on account are called accounts receivable and often are referred to as *trade receivables*. *Nontrade receivables* are those other than trade receivables and include tax refund claims, interest receivable, and loans by the company to other entities including stockholders and employees. When a receivable, trade or nontrade, is accompanied by a formal promissory note, it is referred to as a note receivable. We consider notes receivable after first discussing accounts receivable.

> An account receivable and an account payable are two sides of the same coin.

As you study receivables, realize that one company's claim to the future collection of cash corresponds to another company's (or individual's) obligation to pay cash. One company's account receivable will be the mirror image of another company's account payable. Chapter 13 addresses accounts payable and other current liabilities.

Accounts Receivable

> Accounts receivable are current assets because, by definition, they will be converted to cash within the normal operating cycle.

Most businesses provide credit to their customers, either because it's not practical to require immediate cash payment or to encourage customers to purchase the company's product or service. Accounts receivable are *informal* credit arrangements supported by an invoice and normally are due in 30 to 60 days after the sale. They almost always are classified as *current* assets because their normal collection period, even if longer than a year, is part of, and therefore less than, the operating cycle.

> Typically, revenue and related accounts receivable are recognized at the point of delivery of the product or service.

The point at which accounts receivable are recognized depends on the earnings process of the company. We discussed the realization principle in Chapter 5 and the criteria that must be met before revenue can be recognized. Recall that revenue can be recognized only after the earnings process is *virtually complete* and *collection* from the customer is *reasonably assured*. For the typical credit sale, these criteria are satisfied at the point of delivery of the product or service, so revenue and the related receivable are recognized at that time.

Initial Valuation of Accounts Receivable

> The typical account receivable is valued at the amount expected to be received, not the present value of that amount.

We know from prior discussions that receivables should be recorded at the present value of future cash receipts using a realistic interest rate. So, a $10,000 sale on credit due in 30 days should result in a receivable valued at the present value of the $10,000. In other words, the interest portion of the $10,000 due in 30 days should be removed and recognized as interest revenue over the 30-day period, not as sales revenue at date of delivery of the product. If the monthly interest rate is 2%, the receivable would be valued at $9,804, calculated by multiplying the future cash payment of $10,000 by the present value of $1 factor for one period at 2% (.98039).

However, because the difference between the future and present values of accounts receivable often is immaterial, GAAP specifically excludes accounts receivable from the general rule that receivables be recorded at present value.[6] Therefore, accounts receivable

---

[6]FASB ASC 835–30–15–3: Interest—Imputation of Interest—Scope and Scope Exceptions (previously "Interest on Receivables and Payables," *Accounting Principles Board Opinion No. 21* (New York: AICPA, 1971)).

initially are valued at the exchange price agreed on by the buyer and seller. In our example, both the account receivable and sales revenue would be recorded at $10,000. Let's discuss two aspects of accounts receivable related to their initial valuation—trade discounts and cash discounts.

TRADE DISCOUNTS. Companies frequently offer trade discounts to customers, usually a percentage reduction from the list price. Trade discounts can be a way to change prices without publishing a new catalog or to disguise real prices from competitors. They also are used to give quantity discounts to large customers. For example, a manufacturer might list a machine part at $2,500 but sell it to a customer at list less a 10% discount. The trade discount of $250 is not recognized directly when recording the transaction. The discount is recognized indirectly by recording the sale at the net of discount price of $2,250, not at the list price.

CASH DISCOUNTS. Be careful to distinguish a *trade* discount from a *cash* discount. Cash discounts, often called *sales discounts,* represent reductions not in the selling price of a good or service but in the amount to be paid by a credit customer if paid within a specified period of time. It is a discount intended to provide incentive for quick payment.

Cash discounts reduce the amount to be paid if remittance is made within a specified short period of time.

The amount of the discount and the time period within which it's available usually are conveyed by terms like 2/10, n/30 (meaning a 2% discount if paid within 10 days, otherwise full payment within 30 days). There are two ways to record cash discounts, the gross method and the net method. Conceptually, the gross method views a discount not taken by the customer as part of sales of revenue. On the other hand, the net method considers sales revenue to be the net amount, after discount, and any discounts not taken by the customer as interest revenue. The discounts are viewed as compensation to the seller for providing financing to the customer. With both methods, discounts *taken* reduce sales revenue. Consider the example in Illustration 7–1.

● LO3

The *gross method* views cash discounts *not* taken as part of sales revenue.

The Hawthorne Manufacturing Company offers credit customers a 2% cash discount if the sales price is paid within 10 days. Any amounts not paid within 10 days are due in 30 days. These repayment terms are stated as 2/10, n/30. On October 5, 2011, Hawthorne sold merchandise at a price of $20,000. The customer paid $13,720 ($14,000 less the 2% cash discount) on October 14 and the remaining balance of $6,000 on November 4.	**ILLUSTRATION 7–1** Cash Discounts

The appropriate journal entries to record the sale and cash collection, comparing the gross and net methods are as follows:

Gross Method			**Net Method**		
October 5, 2011					
Accounts receivable	20,000		Accounts receivable	19,600	
Sales revenue		20,000	Sales revenue		19,600
October 14, 2011					
Cash	13,720		Cash	13,720	
Sales discounts	280		Accounts receivable		13,720
Accounts receivable		14,000			
November 4, 2011					
Cash	6,000		Cash	6,000	
Accounts receivable		6,000	Accounts receivable		5,880
			Interest revenue		120

By either method, net sales is reduced by discounts *taken.*

Discounts *not* taken are included in sales revenue using the gross method and interest revenue using the net method.

Notice that by using the gross method, we record the revenue and related receivable at the full $20,000 price. On remittance within the discount period, the $280 discount is recorded as a debit to an account called *sales discounts.* This is a contra account to sales revenue and is deducted from sales revenue to derive the net sales reported in the income statement. For payments made after the discount period, cash is simply increased and accounts receivable decreased by the gross amount originally recorded.

The *net method* considers cash discounts *not* taken as interest revenue.

Under the net method, we record revenue and the related accounts receivable at the agreed-on price *less* the 2% discount applied to the entire price. Payments made within the discount period are recorded as debits to cash and credits to accounts receivable for the amount received. If a customer loses a discount by failing to pay within the discount period, the discount not taken is recorded as interest revenue. In this case, $120 in cash (2% × $6,000) is interest.

Total revenue in the 2011 income statement would be the same by either method:

Revenue comparison of the gross method and the net method.

	Gross Method	**Net Method**
Sales	$20,000	$19,600
Less: Sales discounts	(280)	–0–
Net sales revenue	19,720	19,600
Interest revenue	0	120
Total revenue	$19,720	$19,720

Which is correct? Conceptually, the net method usually reflects the reality of the situation—the real price is $19,600 and $120 is an interest penalty for not paying promptly. The net price usually is the price expected by the seller because the discount usually reflects a hefty interest cost that prudent buyers are unwilling to bear. Consider Illustration 7–1. Although the discount rate is stated as 2%, the effective rate really is 37.23%. In order to save $2, the buyer must pay $98 twenty days earlier than otherwise due, effectively "investing" $98 to "earn" $2, a rate of return of 2.04% ($2/$98) for a 20-day period. To convert this 20-day rate to an annual rate, we multiply by 365/20:

$$2.04\% \times 365/20 = 37.23\% \text{ effective rate}$$

Understandably, most buyers try to take the discount if at all possible.

The difference between the two methods, in terms of the effect of the transactions on income, is in the timing of the recognition of any discounts not taken. The gross method recognizes discounts not taken as revenue when the sale is made. The net method recognizes them as revenue after the discount period has passed and the cash is collected. These two measurement dates could be in different reporting periods.

From a practical standpoint, the effect on the financial statements of the difference between the two methods usually is immaterial. As a result, most companies use the gross method because it's easier and doesn't require adjusting entries for discounts not taken.

Subsequent Valuation of Accounts Receivable

Following the initial valuation of an account receivable, two situations possibly could cause the cash ultimately collected to be less than the initial valuation of the receivable: (1) the customer could return the product, or (2) the customer could default and not pay the agreed-upon sales price. When accounting for sales and accounts receivable, we anticipate these possibilities.

● LO4

Recognizing *sales returns* when they occur could result in an overstatement of income in the period of the related sale.

SALES RETURNS.   Customers frequently are given the right to return the merchandise they purchase if they are not satisfied. We discussed how this policy affects revenue recognition in Chapter 5. We now discuss it from the perspective of asset valuation.

When merchandise is returned for a refund or for credit to be applied to other purchases, the situation is called a **sales return.** When practical, a dissatisfied customer might be given a special price reduction as an incentive to keep the merchandise purchased.[7] Returns are common and often substantial in some industries such as food products, publishing, and retailing. In these cases, recognizing returns and allowances only as they occur could cause profit to be overstated in the period of the sale and understated in the return period. For

---

[7]Price reductions sometimes are referred to as *sales allowances* and are distinguished from situations when the products actually are returned for a refund or credit (sales returns).

example, assume merchandise is sold to a customer for $10,000 in December 2011, the last month in the selling company's fiscal year, and that the merchandise cost $6,000. If all of the merchandise is returned in 2012 after financial statements for 2011 are issued, gross profit will be overstated in 2011 and understated in 2012 by $4,000. Assets at the end of 2011 also will be overstated by $4,000 because a $10,000 receivable would be recorded instead of $6,000 in inventory.

To avoid misstating the financial statements, sales revenue and accounts receivable should be reduced by the amount of returns in the period of sale if the amount of returns is anticipated to be material. We must account for all returns, including those that occur in the period of sale and those that are estimated to occur in future periods. The returns that occur in the period of sale are easy to account for, but the returns estimated for future periods are more difficult. We reduce sales revenue and accounts receivable for estimated returns by debiting a sales returns account (which is a contra account to sales revenue) and crediting an "allowance for sales returns" account (which is a contra account to accounts receivable). When returns actually occur in a following reporting period, the allowance for sales returns is debited and accounts receivable is credited. In this way, income is not reduced in the return period but in the period of the sales revenue.[8]

For an example, refer to Illustration 7–2. The perpetual inventory system records increases (debits) and decreases (credits) in the inventory account as they occur. The inventory of $78,000 in the first set of entries represents merchandise actually returned and on hand, while the inventory of $42,000 in the second set of entries represents an estimate of the cost of merchandise expected to be returned. This later amount is included in the period-end inventory in the company's balance sheet even though the actual merchandise belongs to other entities, because ownership of the goods is expected to revert back to the company.

ILLUSTRATION 7–2
Sales Returns

During 2011, its first year of operations, the Hawthorne Manufacturing Company sold merchandise on account for $2,000,000. This merchandise cost $1,200,000 (60% of the selling price). Industry experience indicates that 10% of all sales will be returned. Customers returned $130,000 in sales during 2011, prior to making payment.

The entries to record sales and merchandise returned during the year, *assuming that a perpetual inventory system is used,* are as follows:

Sales

Accounts receivable	2,000,000	
Sales revenue		2,000,000
Cost of goods sold (60% × $2,000,000)	1,200,000	
Inventory		1,200,000

Actual Returns

Sales returns (actual returns)	130,000	
Accounts receivable		130,000
Inventory	78,000	
Cost of goods sold (60% × $130,000)		78,000

At the end of 2011, the company would anticipate the remaining estimated returns using the following adjusting entries:

Adjusting Entries

Sales returns ([10% × $2,000,000] – $130,000 actual returns)	70,000	
Allowance for sales returns		70,000
Inventory—estimated returns	42,000	
Cost of goods sold (60% × $70,000)		42,000

If sales returns are material, they should be estimated and recorded in the same period as the related sales.

---

[8]Of course, if the allowance for sales returns is estimated incorrectly, income in both the period of the sale and the return will be misstated.

Assuming that the estimates of future returns are correct, the following (summary) journal entry would be recorded in 2012:

Allowance for sales returns	70,000	
Accounts receivable		70,000[9]

Quite often, a customer will return merchandise because it has been damaged during shipment or is defective. This possibility must be anticipated in a company's estimate of returns. As you will study in Chapter 9, inventory is valued at the lower-of-cost-or-market. Therefore, damaged or defective merchandise returned from a customer must be written down to market value.

What happens if the estimate of future returns turns out to be more or less than $70,000? Remember from previous discussions that when an estimate turns out to be wrong, we don't revise prior years' financial statements to reflect the new estimate. Instead, we merely incorporate the new estimate in any related accounting determinations from that point on. Suppose in our illustration that in 2012 actual returns from 2011 sales are $60,000, instead of $70,000. If that happens, the allowance account will have a $10,000 balance and the inventory account will have a $6,000 balance ($10,000 × 60%) representing inventory that was not returned as anticipated. These balances can be used to offset actual returns in 2012 from 2012 sales. As a result, the 2012 adjusting entry to record estimated returns would be $10,000 ($6,000 in cost of goods sold/inventory) less than if the 2011 estimate had been correct. Similarly, if actual returns are $80,000, the 2012 adjusting entry will be $10,000 ($6,000) higher than if the 2011 estimate had been correct.

How do companies estimate returns? Principally they rely on past history, taking into account any changes that might affect future experience. For example, changes in customer base, payment terms offered to customers, and overall economic conditions might suggest that future returns will differ from past returns. The task of estimating returns is made easier for many large retail companies whose fiscal year-end is the end of January. Since retail companies generate a large portion of their annual sales during the Christmas season, most returns from these sales would already have been accounted for by the end of January.

AVX Corporation is a leading manufacturer of electronic components. Graphic 7–3, drawn from AVX's 2009 annual report, describes the company's approach to estimating returns.

GRAPHIC 7–3

Disclosure of Sales Returns Policy—AVX Corporation

Real World Financials

Summary of Significant Accounting Policies (in part)
Returns

Sales revenue and cost of sales reported in the income statement are reduced to reflect estimated returns. We record an estimated sales allowance for returns at the time of sale based on using historical trends, current pricing and volume information, other market specific information and input from sales, marketing and other key management. The amount accrued reflects the return of value of the customer's inventory. These procedures require the exercise of significant judgments. We believe that these procedures enable us to make reliable estimates of future returns. Our actual results approximate our estimates. When the product is returned and verified, the customer is given credit against their accounts receivable.

In some industries, returns typically are small and infrequent. Companies in these industries usually simply record returns in the period they occur because the effect on income measurement and asset valuation is immaterial. In a few situations, significant uncertainty as to future collection is created by the right of return, because returns cannot be estimated reliably. In those cases, revenue recognition is deferred until the uncertainty is resolved. We discussed this possibility in Chapter 5.

---

[9]Another way to record these journal entries would be to set up an allowance for the entire amount of estimated returns when we record 2011 sales revenue, and then reduce the allowance when any actual returns occur in this or future periods. Under that approach, when we record sales revenue and cost of goods sold, we also debit sales returns and credit the allowance for sales returns for the entire amount of estimated returns (10% × $2,000,000 = $200,000), and debit inventory and credit cost of goods sold for 60% of that amount ($120,000). Then, when actual returns occurred, we would debit allowance for sales returns and credit accounts receivable, for a total of $130,000 in 2011 and $70,000 in 2012. Note that this approach takes us to the same outcomes in 2011 and 2012.

UNCOLLECTIBLE ACCOUNTS RECEIVABLE. Companies that extend credit to customers know that it's unlikely that all customers will fully pay their accounts. **Bad debt expense** is an inherent cost of granting credit. It's an operating expense incurred to make sales. As a result, even when specific customer accounts haven't been proven uncollectible by the end of the reporting period, the expense should be matched with sales revenue in the income statement for that period. Likewise, as it's not expected that all accounts receivable will be collected, the balance sheet should report only the expected **net realizable value** of the asset, that is, the amount of cash the company expects to actually collect from customers.

Companies account for bad debts by recording an adjusting entry that debits bad debt expense and reduces accounts receivable indirectly by crediting a contra account (allowance for uncollectible accounts) to accounts receivable for an estimate of the amount that eventually will prove uncollectible. This approach to accounting for bad debts is known as the **allowance method.** Quite often, companies report the allowance for uncollectible accounts (often called *allowance for doubtful accounts*) parenthetically or alongside the accounts receivable account title separated by a dash or a comma. Other times they will simply show the net balance in the balance sheet, and then describe the allowance in a footnote. For example, **Dell Inc.** reported the following under current assets in its comparative balance sheets for 2009 and 2008:

● LO5

FINANCIAL Reporting Case

Q1, p. 337

The use of the *allowance method* is an attempt to satisfy the matching principle in accounting for bad debts and to record accounts receivable at net realizable value.

($ in millions)	January 30, 2009	February 1, 2008
Accounts receivable, net	$4,731	$5,961

The company then included the following in Note 12 to its financial statements:

NOTE 12—SUPPLEMENTAL CONSOLIDATED FINANCIAL INFORMATION

Supplemental Consolidated Statements of Financial Position Information:	January 30, 2009	February 1, 2008
	(in millions)	
Accounts receivable, net		
Gross accounts receivable	$4,843	$6,064
Allowance for doubtful accounts	(112)	(103)
Total	$4,731	$5,961

The $4,731 million figure at the end of 2009 is the company's estimate of the net realizable value of accounts receivable. Actual (gross) accounts receivable at the end of 2009 were $4,843 million ($4,731 + $112).

There are two ways commonly used to arrive at this estimate of future bad debts—the income statement approach and the balance sheet approach. Illustration 7–3 is used to demonstrate both approaches. As you proceed through the illustration, remember that the two approaches represent alternative ways to estimate the *amount* of future bad debts. Except for the amounts, the accounting entries are identical.

● LO6

The Hawthorne Manufacturing Company sells its products offering 30 days' credit to its customers. During 2011, its first year of operations, the following events occurred:

Sales on credit	$1,200,000
Cash collections from credit customers	(895,000)
Accounts receivable, end of year	$ 305,000

There were no specific accounts determined to be uncollectible in 2011. The company anticipates that 2% of all credit sales will ultimately become uncollectible.

ILLUSTRATION 7–3
Bad Debts

Income statement approach. Using the income statement approach, we estimate bad debt expense as a percentage of each period's net credit sales. This percentage usually is determined by reviewing the company's recent history of the relationship between credit

**FINANCIAL
Reporting Case**

Q2, p. 337

sales and actual bad debts. For a relatively new company, this percentage may be obtained by referring to other sources such as industry averages.

Under the income statement approach, the Hawthorne Manufacturing Company would make the following adjusting journal entry at the end of 2011:

Bad debt expense (2% × $1,200,000)	24,000	
Allowance for uncollectible accounts		24,000

In the current asset section of the 2011 balance sheet, accounts receivable would be reported *net* of the allowance, as follows:

Accounts receivable	$305,000
Less: Allowance for uncollectible accounts	(24,000)
Net accounts receivable	$281,000

Using the *income statement approach*, the balance sheet amount is an incidental result of estimating bad debt expense as a percentage of net credit sales.

It's important to notice that the income statement approach focuses on the current year's credit sales. The effect on the balance sheet—the allowance for uncollectible accounts and hence net accounts receivable—is an incidental result of estimating the expense. An alternative is to focus on the balance sheet amounts instead. We look at this approach next.

Using the *balance sheet approach*, bad debt expense is an incidental result of estimating the net realizable value of accounts receivable.

Balance sheet approach.   Using the balance sheet approach to estimate future bad debts, we determine bad debt expense by estimating the net realizable value of accounts receivable to be reported in the balance sheet. In other words, the allowance for uncollectible accounts is determined. Bad debt expense is an incidental result of adjusting the allowance account to the desired balance.

For the Hawthorne Manufacturing Company example in Illustration 7–3, the company would estimate the amount of uncollectible accounts that will result from the $305,000 in accounts receivable outstanding at the end of 2011. This could be done by analyzing each customer account, by applying a percentage to the entire outstanding receivable balance, or by applying different percentages to accounts receivable balances depending on the length of time outstanding. This latter approach normally employs an accounts receivable aging schedule. For example, the aging schedule for Hawthorne's 2011 year-end accounts receivable is shown in Illustration 7–3A.

ILLUSTRATION 7–3A
Accounts Receivable
Aging Schedule

Customer	Accounts Receivable 12/31/11	0–60 Days	61–90 Days	91–120 Days	Over 120 Days
Axel Manufacturing Co.	$ 20,000	$ 14,000	$ 6,000		
Banner Corporation	33,000		20,000	$10,000	$ 3,000
Dando Company	60,000	50,000	10,000		
＼＼＼＼	＼＼	＼＼	＼＼	＼＼	＼＼
＼＼＼＼	＼＼	＼＼	＼＼	＼＼	＼＼
Xicon Company	18,000	10,000	4,000	3,000	1,000
Totals	$305,000	$220,000	$50,000	$25,000	$10,000

The schedule assumes older accounts are more likely to prove uncollectible.

Higher estimated default percentages are applied to groups of older receivables.

	Summary		
Age Group	Amount	Estimated Percent Uncollectible	Estimated Allowance
0–60 days	$220,000	5%	$11,000
61–90 days	50,000	10%	5,000
91–120 days	25,000	20%	5,000
Over 120 days	10,000	45%	4,500
Allowance for uncollectible accounts			$25,500

The schedule classifies the year-end receivable balances according to their length of time outstanding. Presumably, the longer an account has been outstanding the more likely it will prove uncollectible. Based on past experience or other sources of information, a percentage is applied to age group totals.

The 2011 entry to record bad debts adjusts the balance in the allowance for uncollectible accounts to this required amount of $25,500. Because it is the first year of operations for Hawthorne and the beginning balance in the allowance account is zero, the adjusting entry would *debit* bad debt expense and *credit* allowance for uncollectible accounts for $25,500.

To illustrate the concept further, let's suppose that this was not the first year of operations and the allowance account prior to the adjusting entry had a *credit* balance of $4,000. Then the amount of the entry would be $21,500—the amount necessary to adjust a credit balance of $4,000 to a credit balance of $25,500. Similarly, if the allowance account prior to the adjusting entry had a *debit* balance[10] of $4,000, then the amount of the entry would be $29,500.

Allowance	
Beg. bal.	4,000
Adj. entry	21,500
Bal.	25,500

Some companies use a combination of approaches in estimating bad debts. For example, Hawthorne could decide to accrue bad debts on a monthly basis using the income statement approach and then employ the balance sheet approach at the end of the year based on an aging of receivables. Each month an adjusting entry would record a debit to bad debt expense and a credit to allowance for uncollectible accounts equal to 2% of credit sales. In our illustration, the monthly accruals for 2011 would result in the following account balances at the end of 2011:

Accounts Receivable		Bad Debt Expense	
305,000		24,000	

Allowance for Uncollectible Accounts	
	24,000

At the end of the year, if the aging revealed a required allowance of $25,500, the following adjusting entry would be recorded:

Bad debt expense	1,500	
Allowance for uncollectible accounts		1,500

This entry adjusts the allowance account to the required amount.

In the 2011 balance sheet, accounts receivable would be reported net of the allowance, as follows:

Accounts receivable	$305,000
Less: Allowance for uncollectible accounts	(25,500)
Net accounts receivable	$279,500

When accounts are deemed uncollectible.   The actual write-off of a receivable occurs when it is determined that all or a portion of the amount due will not be collected. Using the allowance method, the write-off is recorded as a debit to allowance for uncollectible accounts and a credit to accounts receivable. In our illustration, assume that actual bad debts in 2012 were $25,000. These write-offs would be recorded (in a summary journal entry) as follows:

Allowance for uncollectible accounts	25,000	
Accounts receivable		25,000

---

[10]A debit balance could result if the amount of receivables actually written off (discussed below) during the period exceeds the beginning credit balance in the allowance account.

The write-off of an account receivable reduces both receivables and the allowance, thus having no effect on income or financial position.

Net realizable value is not affected directly by the write-offs.

Accounts receivable	$280,000
Less: Allowance for uncollectible accounts	(500)
Net accounts receivable	$279,500

Of course, actual bad debts will tend to differ from estimates. However, the year in which the estimate is made, 2011 in this case, is unaffected by the incorrect estimate. If the prior year's estimate of bad debts is too low, then, using the balance sheet approach, bad debt expense in the subsequent year will be increased. If the estimate is too high, then bad debt expense in the subsequent year will be decreased. For example, in our illustration, the allowance at the end of 2011 is $25,500. Actual bad debts related to 2011 receivables are $25,000. 2011's financial information cannot be changed. Instead, the $500 credit balance in allowance for uncollectible accounts will cause 2012's bad debt expense to be less than if 2011's estimate of bad debts had been correct.

ETHICAL DILEMMA

The management of the Auto Parts Division of the Santana Corporation receives a bonus if the division's income achieves a specific target. For 2011 the target will be achieved by a wide margin. Mary Beth Williams, the controller of the division, has been asked by Philip Stanton, the head of the division's management team, to try to reduce this year's income and "bank" some of the profits for future years. Mary Beth suggests that the division's bad debt expense as a percentage of net credit sales for 2011 be increased from 3% to 5%. She believes that 3% is the more accurate estimate but knows that both the corporation's internal auditors as well as the external auditors allow some flexibility when estimates are involved. Does Mary Beth's proposal present an ethical dilemma?

Recoveries of accounts receivable previously written off require the reinstatement of both the receivable and the allowance.

When previously written-off accounts are collected. Occasionally, a receivable that has been written off will be collected in part or in full. When this happens, the receivable and the allowance should be reinstated. In other words, the entry to write off the account simply is reversed. The collection is then recorded the usual way as a debit to cash and a credit to accounts receivable. This process ensures that the company will have a complete record of the payment history of the customer. For example, assume that in our illustration, $1,200 that was previously written off is collected. The following journal entries record the event:

To reinstate the receivable previously written off.

Accounts receivable	1,200	
Allowance for uncollectible accounts		1,200
To reinstate the receivable previously written off.		

To record the cash collection.

Cash	1,200	
Accounts receivable		1,200
To record the cash collection.		

FINANCIAL Reporting Case

Q3, p. 337

Direct write-off of uncollectible accounts. If uncollectible accounts are not anticipated or are immaterial, or if it's not possible to reliably estimate uncollectible accounts, an allowance for uncollectible accounts is not appropriate. In these few cases, adjusting entries are not recorded and any bad debts that do arise simply are written off as bad debt expense. A $750 uncollectible account would be recorded as follows:

Bad debt expense	750	
Accounts receivable		750

This approach is known as the **direct write-off method**. Of course, if the sale that generated this receivable occurred in a previous reporting period, the matching principle is violated. Operating expenses would have been understated and assets overstated in that period. This is why the direct write-off method of accounting for uncollectible accounts is not permitted by GAAP except in limited circumstances. Specifically, the allowance method must be used if it is probable that a material amount of receivables will not be collected and the amount can be reasonably estimated.[11] For federal income tax purposes, however, the direct write-off method is the required method for most companies and the allowance method is not permitted.

Graphic 7–4 summarizes the key issues involving measuring and reporting accounts receivable.

> The *direct write-off method* is used only rarely for financial reporting, but it is the required method for income tax purposes.

Recognition	Depends on the earnings process; for most credit sales, revenue and the related receivables are recognized at the point of delivery.
Initial valuation	Initially recorded at the exchange price agreed upon by the buyer and seller.
Subsequent valuation	Initial valuation reduced to net realizable value by: 1. Allowance for sales returns 2. Allowance for uncollectible accounts: —The income statement approach —The balance sheet approach
Classification	Almost always classified as a current asset.

GRAPHIC 7–4

Measuring and Reporting Accounts Receivable

CONCEPT REVIEW EXERCISE

The Hawthorne Manufacturing Company sells its products, offering 30 days' credit to its customers. Uncollectible amounts are estimated by accruing a monthly charge to bad debt expense equal to 2% of credit sales. At the end of the year, the allowance for uncollectible accounts is adjusted based on an aging of accounts receivable. The company began 2012 with the following balances in its accounts:

UNCOLLECTIBLE ACCOUNTS RECEIVABLE

Accounts receivable	$305,000
Allowance for uncollectible accounts	(25,500)

During 2012, sales on credit were $1,300,000, cash collections from customers were $1,250,000, and actual write-offs of accounts were $25,000. An aging of accounts receivable at the end of 2012 indicates a required allowance of $30,000.

Required:
1. Determine the balances in accounts receivable and allowance for uncollectible accounts at the end of 2012.
2. Determine bad debt expense for 2012.
3. Prepare journal entries for the accrual of bad debts (in summary form, with one entry covering all twelve months of the year), the write-off of receivables, and the year-end adjusting entry for bad debts.

1. Determine the balances in accounts receivable and allowance for uncollectible accounts at the end of 2012.

SOLUTION

Accounts receivable	
Beginning balance	$ 305,000
Add: Credit sales	1,300,000
Less: Cash collections	(1,250,000)
Write-offs	(25,000)
Ending balance	$ 330,000

[11]FASB ASC 450–20–25–2: Contingencies—Loss Contingencies—Recognition (previously "Accounting for Contingencies," *Statement of Financial Accounting Standards No. 5* (Stamford, Conn.: FASB, 1975), par. 8).

Allowance for uncollectible accounts:		
Beginning balance	$	25,500
Add: Bad debt expense (2% × $1,300,000)		26,000
Less: Write-offs		(25,000)
Balance before year-end adjustment		26,500
Year-end adjustment		3,500*
Ending balance	$	30,000

*Required allowance of $30,000 less $26,500 already in allowance account.

2. Determine bad debt expense for 2012.

   Bad debt expense would be $29,500 (accrual of $26,000 plus year-end adjustment of an additional $3,500).

3. Prepare journal entries for the accrual of bad debts (in summary form), the write-off of receivables, and the year-end adjusting entry for bad debts.

Bad debt expense (2% × $1,300,000)	26,000	
Allowance for uncollectible accounts		26,000
Accrual of 2% of credit sales—summary entry (actually prepared monthly).		
Allowance for uncollectible accounts	25,000	
Accounts receivable		25,000
Write-off of accounts receivable as they are determined uncollectible.		
Bad debt expense	3,500	
Allowance for uncollectible accounts		3,500
Year-end adjusting entry for bad debts.		

Notes Receivable

● LO7

Notes receivable are formal credit arrangements between a creditor (lender) and a debtor (borrower). Notes arise from loans to other entities including affiliated companies and to stockholders and employees, from the extension of the credit period to trade customers, and occasionally from the sale of merchandise, other assets, or services. Notes receivable are classified as either current or noncurrent depending on the expected collection date(s).

Our examples below illustrate short-term notes. When the term of a note is longer than a year, it is reported as a long-term note. Long-term notes receivable are discussed in conjunction with long-term notes payable in Chapter 14.

Interest-Bearing Notes

The typical note receivable requires payment of a specified face amount, also called *principal,* at a specified maturity date or dates. In addition, interest is paid at a stated percentage of the face amount. Interest on notes is calculated as:

Face amount × Annual rate × Fraction of the annual period

For an example, consider Illustration 7–4.

ILLUSTRATION 7–4	The Stridewell Wholesale Shoe Company manufactures athletic shoes that it sells to retailers.
Note Receivable	On May 1, 2011, the company sold shoes to Harmon Sporting Goods. Stridewell agreed to accept a $700,000, 6-month, 12% note in payment for the shoes. Interest is payable at maturity. Stridewell would account for the note as follows:*

May 1, 2011

Note receivable	700,000	
Sales revenue		700,000
To record the sale of goods in exchange for a note receivable.		

(continued)

November 1, 2011			ILLUSTRATION 7–4
Cash ($700,000 + $42,000)	742,000		(concluded)
Interest revenue ($700,000 × 12% × $\frac{6}{12}$)		42,000	
Note receivable		700,000	
To record the collection of the note at maturity.			

*To focus on recording the note we intentionally omit the entry required for the cost of the goods sold if the perpetual inventory system is used.

If the sale in the illustration occurs on August 1, 2011, and the company's fiscal year-end is December 31, a year-end adjusting entry accrues interest earned.

December 31, 2011		
Interest receivable	35,000	
Interest revenue ($700,000 × 12% × $\frac{5}{12}$)		35,000

The February 1 collection is then recorded as follows:

February 1, 2012		
Cash ($700,000 + [$700,000 × 12% × $\frac{6}{12}$])	742,000	
Interest revenue ($700,000 × 12% × $\frac{1}{12}$)		7,000
Interest receivable (accrued at December 31)		35,000
Note receivable		700,000

Noninterest-Bearing Notes

Sometimes a receivable assumes the form of a so-called noninterest-bearing note. The name is a misnomer, though. Noninterest-bearing notes actually do bear interest, but the interest is deducted (or discounted) from the face amount to determine the cash proceeds made available to the borrower at the outset. For example, the preceding note could be packaged as a $700,000 noninterest-bearing note, with a 12% discount rate. In that case, the $42,000 interest would be discounted at the outset rather than explicitly stated. As a result, the selling price of the shoes would have been only $658,000. Assuming a May 1, 2011 sale, the transaction is recorded as follows:[12]

May 1, 2011			
Note receivable (face amount)	700,000		The discount becomes interest revenue in a noninterest-bearing note.
Discount on note receivable ($700,000 × 12% × $\frac{6}{12}$)		42,000	
Sales revenue (difference)		658,000	
November 1, 2011			
Discount on note receivable	42,000		
Interest revenue		42,000	
Cash	700,000		
Note receivable (face amount)		700,000	

---

[12]The entries shown assume the note is recorded by the gross method. By the net method, the interest component is netted against the face amount of the note as follows:

May 1, 2011		
Note receivable	658,000	
Sales revenue		658,000
November 1, 2011		
Cash	700,000	
Note receivable		658,000
Interest revenue ($700,000 × 12% × $\frac{6}{12}$)		42,000

When interest is discounted from the face amount of a note, the effective interest rate is higher than the stated discount rate.

The discount on note receivable is a contra account to the note receivable account. That is, the note receivable would be reported in the balance sheet net (less) any remaining discount. The discount represents future interest revenue that will be recognized as it is earned over time. The sales revenue under this arrangement is only $658,000, but the interest is calculated as the discount rate times the $700,000 face amount. This causes the *effective* interest rate to be higher than the 12% stated rate.

$ 42,000	Interest for 6 months
÷ $658,000	Sales price
= 6.383%	Rate for 6 months
× 2*	To annualize the rate
= 12.766%	Effective interest rate

*Two 6-month periods

Using a calculator:
Enter: N 1 I .06383
PMT − 700000
Output: PV 658,000

Using Excel, enter:
= PV(.06383,1,700000)
Output: 658,000

As we discussed earlier in the chapter, receivables, other than normal trade receivables, should be valued at the present value of future cash receipts. The present value of $700,000 to be received in six months using an effective interest rate of 6.383% is $658,000 ($700,000 ÷ 1.06383 = $658,000). The use of present value techniques for valuation purposes was introduced in Chapter 6, and we'll use these techniques extensively in subsequent chapters to value various long-term liabilities.

In the illustration, if the sale occurs on August 1, the December 31, 2011, adjusting entry and the entry to record the cash collection on February 1, 2012, are recorded as follows:

December 31, 2011		
Discount on note receivable	35,000	
Interest revenue ($700,000 × 12% × 5/12)		35,000
February 1, 2012		
Discount on note receivable	7,000	
Interest revenue ($700,000 × 12% × 1/12)		7,000
Cash	700,000	
Note receivable (face amount)		700,000

In the December 31, 2011 balance sheet, the note receivable is shown at $693,000, face amount ($700,000) less remaining discount ($7,000).

Choice Hotels, Inc., accepts noninterest-bearing notes from franchisees who open new hotels. The 2009 disclosure note shown in Graphic 7–5 describes the company's revenue recognition policy for these notes.

GRAPHIC 7–5

Disclosure of Revenue Recognition for License Agreements—Choice Hotels, Inc.

Real World Financials

Note 2: Notes Receivable (in part)

The Company has provided financing to franchisees in support of the development of Cambria Suites properties. These notes include noninterest-bearing receivables as well as notes bearing market interest and are due upon maturity. Noninterest-bearing notes receivable at December 31, 2008, were recorded net of their unamortized discounts totaling $0.02 million. Interest income associated with these notes receivable is reflected in the accompanying consolidated statements of income under the caption interest and other investment (income) loss.

When a noninterest-bearing note is received solely in exchange for cash, the amount of cash exchanged is the basis for valuing the note.

NOTES RECEIVED SOLELY FOR CASH. If a note with an unrealistic interest rate— even a noninterest-bearing note—is received *solely* in exchange for cash, the cash paid to the issuer is considered to be its present value.[13] Even if this means recording interest at a

---

[13]This assumes that no other present or future considerations are included in the agreement. For example, a noninterest-bearing note might be given to a vendor in exchange for cash *and* a promise to provide future inventories at prices lower than anticipated market prices. The issuer values the note at the present value of cash payments using a realistic interest rate, and the difference between present value and cash payments is recognized as interest revenue over the life of the note. This difference also increases future inventory purchases to realistic market prices.

ridiculously low or zero rate, the amount of cash exchanged is the basis for valuing the note. When a non-cash asset is exchanged for a note with a low stated rate, we can argue that its real value is less than it's purported to be, but we can't argue that the present value of a sum of cash currently exchanged is less than that sum. If the noninterest-bearing note in the previous example had been received solely in exchange for $700,000 cash, the transaction would be recorded as follows:

Note receivable (face amount)	700,000	
Cash (given)		700,000

Subsequent Valuation of Notes Receivable

Similar to accounts receivable, if a company anticipates bad debts on short-term notes receivable, it uses an allowance account to reduce the receivable to net realizable value. The process of recording bad debt expense is the same as with accounts receivable.

Long-term notes present a more significant measurement problem. The longer the duration of the note, the more likely are bad debts. One of the more difficult measurement problems facing banks and other lending institutions is the estimation of bad debts on their long-term notes (loans). As an example, **Wells Fargo & Company**, a large bank holding company, reported the following in the asset section of its March 31, 2009, quarter-end balance sheet:

(in millions)	3/31/2009	12/31/2008
Loans	$843,579	$864,830
Allowance for loan losses	(22,281)	(21,013)
Net loans	$821,298	$843,817

A disclosure note, reproduced in Graphic 7–6, describes Wells Fargo's loan loss policy.

Allowance for Credit Losses

The allowance for credit losses, which consists of the allowance for loan losses and the reserve for unfunded credit commitments, is management's estimate of credit losses inherent in the loan portfolio at the balance sheet date and excludes loans carried at fair value. The process for determining the adequacy of the allowance for credit losses is critical to our financial results. It requires difficult, subjective and complex judgments, as a result of the need to make estimates about the effect of matters that are uncertain.

GRAPHIC 7–6

Disclosure of Allowance for Loan Losses—Wells Fargo & Company

Real World Financials

GAAP requires that companies disclose the fair value of their notes receivable in the disclosure notes (they don't have to disclose the fair value of accounts receivable when the carrying value of the receivables approximates their fair value).[14] Also, GAAP recently changed to allow companies to choose to carry receivables at fair value in their balance sheets, with changes in fair value recognized as gains or losses in the income statements.[15] This "fair value option" is discussed in Chapter 12.

When it becomes probable that a creditor will be unable to collect all amounts due according to the contractual terms of a note, the receivable is considered impaired. When a creditor's investment in a note receivable becomes impaired for any reason, the receivable is remeasured as the discounted present value of currently expected cash flows at the loan's original effective rate. Impairments of receivables are discussed in Appendix 7B.

---

[14]FASB ASC 825–10–50–10: Financial Instruments—Overall—Disclosure—Fair Value of Financial Instruments (previously "Disclosures about Fair Value of Financial Instruments" *Statement of Financial Accounting Standards No. 107* (Norwalk, Conn.: FASB, 1991)).
[15]FASB ASC 825–10–25: Financial Instruments—Overall—Recognition Fair Value Option (previously "The Fair Value Option for Financial Assets and Financial Liabilities" *Statement of Financial Accounting Standards No. 159* (Norwalk, Conn.: FASB, 2007)).

● LO10

● LO8

Financing with Receivables

Financial institutions have developed a wide variety of ways for companies to use their receivables to obtain immediate cash. Companies can find this attractive because it shortens their operating cycles by providing cash immediately rather than having to wait until credit customers pay the amounts due. Also, many companies avoid the difficulties of servicing (billing and collecting) receivables by having financial institutions take on that role. Of course, financial institutions require compensation for providing these services, usually interest and/or a finance charge.

The various approaches used to finance with receivables differ with respect to which rights and risks are retained by the *transferor* (the company who was the original holder of the receivables) and which are passed on to the *transferee* (the new holder, the financial institution). Despite this diversity, any of these approaches can be described as either:

1. *A secured borrowing.* Under this approach, the transferor (borrower) simply acts like it borrowed money from the transferee (lender), with the receivables remaining in the transferor's balance sheet and serving as collateral for the loan. On the other side of the transaction, the transferee recognizes a note receivable.
2. *A sale of receivables.* Under this approach, the transferor (seller) "derecognizes" (removes) the receivables from its balance sheet, acting like it sold them to the transferee (buyer). On the other side of the transaction, the transferee recognizes the receivables that it obtained and measures them at their fair value.

Let's discuss each of these approaches in more detail as they apply to accounts receivable and notes receivable. Then we'll discuss the circumstances under which GAAP requires each approach.

Secured Borrowing

As indicated in the previous section, companies sometimes use receivables as collateral for loans. You already may be familiar with the concept of assigning or pledging receivables as collateral if you or someone you know has a mortgage on a home. The bank or other

---

[16]"Financial Instruments: Recognition and Measurement," *International Accounting Standard No. 39* (IASCF), as amended effective January 1, 2009.

[17]"Financial Instruments," *International Financial Reporting Standard No. 9* (IASCF), November 12, 2009.

financial institution holding the mortgage will require that, if the homeowner defaults on the mortgage payments, the home be sold and the proceeds used to pay off the mortgage debt. Similarly, in the case of an assignment of receivables, nonpayment of a debt will require the proceeds from collecting the assigned receivables to go directly toward repayment of the debt.

In these arrangements, the lender typically lends an amount of money that is less than the amount of receivables assigned by the borrower. The difference provides some protection for the lender to allow for possible uncollectible accounts. Also, the lender (sometimes called an *assignee*) usually charges the borrower (sometimes called an *assignor*) an up-front finance charge in addition to stated interest on the loan. The receivables might be collected either by the lender or the borrower, depending on the details of the arrangement. Illustration 7–5 provides an example.

On December 1, 2011, the Santa Teresa Glass Company borrowed $500,000 from Finance Bank and signed a promissory note. Interest at 12% is payable monthly. The company assigned $620,000 of its receivables as collateral for the loan. Finance Bank charges a finance fee equal to 1.5% of the accounts receivable assigned.

Santa Teresa Glass records the borrowing as follows:

Cash (difference)	490,700	
Finance charge expense* (1.5% × $620,000)	9,300	
Liability—financing arrangement		500,000

Santa Teresa will continue to collect the receivables, and will record any discounts, sales returns, and bad debt write-offs, but will remit the cash to Finance Bank, usually on a monthly basis. When $400,000 of the receivables assigned are collected in December, Santa Teresa Glass records the following entries:

Cash	400,000	
Accounts receivable		400,000
Interest expense ($500,000 × 12% × $\frac{1}{12}$)	5,000	
Liability—financing arrangement	400,000	
Cash		405,000

ILLUSTRATION 7–5
Assignment of Accounts Receivable

*In theory, this fee should be allocated over the entire period of the loan rather than recorded as an expense in the initial period. However, amounts usually are small and the loan period usually is short. For expediency, then, we expense the entire fee immediately.

In Santa Teresa's December 31, 2011, balance sheet, the company would report the receivables and note payable together as follows:

Current assets:

Accounts receivable assigned ($620,000 − 400,000)	$220,000
Less: Liability—financing arrangement ($500,000 − 400,000)	(100,000)
Equity in accounts receivable assigned	$120,000

Netting a liability against a related asset, also called offsetting, usually is not allowed by GAAP. However, in this case, we deduct the note payable from the accounts receivable assigned because, by contractual agreement, the note will be paid with cash collected from the receivables. In Santa Teresa's financial statements, the arrangement also is described in a disclosure note.

A variation of assigning specific receivables occurs when trade receivables in general rather than specific receivables are pledged as collateral. The responsibility for collection of the receivables remains solely with the company. This variation is referred to as a **pledging** of accounts receivable. No special accounting treatment is needed and the arrangement is simply described in a disclosure note. For example, Graphic 7–7 shows a portion of the long-term debt disclosure note included in the July 31, 2009, quarter-end financial statements of **Virco Mfg. Corporation**, a manufacturer of office furniture.

GRAPHIC 7–7

Disclosure of
Receivables Used as
Collateral—Virco Mfg.
Corporation

Real World Financials

Note 5: Debt (in part)

The Revolving Credit facility is secured by certain of the Company's and its subsidiaries' accounts receivable, inventories, equipment and real property.

Sale of Receivables

Accounts and notes receivable, like any other assets, can be sold at a gain or a loss. The basic accounting treatment for the sale of receivables is similar to accounting for the sale of other assets. The seller (transferor) (a) removes from the accounts the receivables (and any allowance for bad debts associated with them), (b) recognizes at fair value any assets acquired or liabilities assumed by the seller in the transaction, and (c) records the difference as a gain or loss.

The sale of accounts receivable became an increasingly popular method of financing over the past couple of decades. Traditionally a technique used by companies in a few industries or with poor credit ratings, the sale of receivables is now a common occurrence for many different types of companies. For example, **Harley-Davidson**, **Toyota**, **Whirlpool**, and **Raytheon** all sell receivables. The two most common types of selling arrangements are **factoring** and **securitization.** We'll now discuss each type.

A *factor* is a financial institution that buys receivables for cash, handles the billing and collection of the receivables, and charges a fee for this service. Actually, credit cards like VISA and Mastercard are forms of factoring arrangements. The seller relinquishes all rights to the future cash receipts in exchange for cash from the buyer (the *factor*).

As an example, Graphic 7–8 shows an excerpt from a recent advertisement of **Bankers Mutual Capital Corporation**, a financial institution that offers factoring as one of its services.

GRAPHIC 7–8

Advertisement of
Factoring Service—
Bankers Mutual Capital
Corporation

Accounts Receivable Factoring

Accounts receivable factoring is the selling of your invoices (accounts receivable) for cash versus waiting 30–60 days to be paid by your customer. Factoring will get you the working capital you need now and improve your cash flow. Bankers will advance 65%–80% against the invoice you generate and pay you the balance less our fee (typically 3%–6%) when the invoice is paid.

Notice that the factor, Bankers Mutual, advances only between 65%–80% of the factored receivables. The remaining balance is retained as security until all of the receivables are collected and then remitted to the transferor, net of the factor's fee. The fee charged by this factor ranges from 3%–6%. The range depends on, among other things, the quality of the receivables and the length of time before payment is required.

Another popular arrangement used to sell receivables has been securitization. In a typical accounts receivable securitization, the company creates a "special purpose entity" (SPE), usually a trust or a subsidiary. The SPE buys a pool of trade receivables, credit card receivables, or loans from the company, and then sells related securities, typically debt such as bonds or commercial paper, that are backed (collateralized) by the receivables. Securitizing receivables using an SPE can provide significant economic advantages, allowing companies to reach a large pool of investors and to obtain more favorable financing terms.[18]

As an example of a securitization, Graphic 7–9 shows a portion of the disclosure note included in the 2009 annual report of **Flextronics International Limited**, a worldwide

The text in the left margin reads:

Two popular
arrangements used for
the sale of receivables
are *factoring* and
securitization.

---

[18]Because the SPE is a separate legal entity, it typically is viewed as "bankruptcy remote," meaning that the transferor's creditors can't access the receivables if the transferor goes bankrupt. This increases the safety of the SPE's assets and typically allows it to obtain more favorable financing terms than could the transferor.

leader in design, manufacturing and logistics services, describing the securitization of its trade accounts receivable.

GRAPHIC 7–9

Description of Securitization Program—Flextronics International Limited

Real World Financials

> **Note 6: TRADE RECEIVABLES SECURITIZATION (in part)**
>
> The Company continuously sells a designated pool of trade receivables to a third-party qualified special purpose entity. . . . The securitization agreement allows the operating subsidiaries participating in the securitization program to receive a cash payment for sold receivables, less a deferred purchase price receivable. The Company continues to service, administer and collect the receivables on behalf of the special purpose entity and receives a servicing fee of 1.00% of serviced receivables per annum.

ADDITIONAL CONSIDERATION

Dropping the Q. What if a company had to consolidate its securitization SPE? In that case, it would eliminate any transactions between the SPE and the company, such that, after consolidation, it no longer would appear as if the company had sold its receivables to an outside entity. Instead, the company would appear to have kept its receivables and engaged in a secured borrowing with whoever loaned money to the SPE. Until recently, companies that securitized their receivables could avoid some consolidation rules by setting up a particular type of SPE, called a "qualifying SPE" ("QSPE"), which operated solely to facilitate securitization transactions. The company would sell its receivables to its QSPE, often recognizing a gain on the sale, and the QSPE (not the company) would hold the receivables and related debt in the QSPE's balance sheet. Effective in 2010, the FASB eliminated the QSPE concept, leaving these SPEs vulnerable to consolidation requirements.[19] The FASB also tightened consolidation requirements with respect to these sorts of entities.[20] As a consequence, securitizations are much less likely to qualify for sales treatment after 2009 than they were previously.

The specifics of sale accounting vary depending on the particular arrangement between the seller and buyer (transferee).[21] One key feature is whether the receivables are transferred **without recourse** or **with recourse.**

SALE WITHOUT RECOURSE.

If a factoring arrangement is made without recourse, the buyer can't ask the seller for more money if customers don't pay the receivables. Therefore, the buyer assumes the risk of bad debts. Illustration 7–6 on the next page provides an example of receivables factored without recourse.

Note that, in Illustration 7–6, the fair value ($50,000) of the last 10% of the receivables to be collected is less than 10% of the total book value of the receivables (10% × $600,000 = $60,000). That is typical, because the last receivables to be collected are likely to be reduced by sales returns and allowances, and therefore have a lower fair value.

The buyer assumes the risk of uncollectibility when accounts receivable are sold without recourse.

SALE WITH RECOURSE.

When a company sells accounts receivable with recourse, the seller retains all of the risk of bad debts. In effect, the seller guarantees that the buyer will be paid even if some receivables prove to be uncollectible. In Illustration 7–6, even if the receivables were sold with recourse, Santa Teresa Glass still could account for the transfer as a sale so long as the conditions for sale treatment are met. The only difference would be the additional requirement that Santa Teresa record the estimated fair value of its recourse obligation as a liability. The recourse obligation is the estimated amount that Santa Teresa will have to pay Factor Bank as a reimbursement for uncollectible receivables. Illustration 7–7 on the next page, under Illustration 7–6, provides an example of receivables factored with recourse.

The seller retains the risk of uncollectibility when accounts receivable are sold with recourse.

---

[19]FASB ASC 860: Transfers and Servicing (previously "Accounting for Transfers of Financial Assets, an amendment of FASB Statement No. 140," *Statement of Financial Accounting Standards No. 166* (Norwalk, Conn.: FASB, 2009)).

[20]FASB ASC 810: Consolidation (previously "Amendments to FASB Interpretation No. 46R," *Statement of Financial Accounting Standards No. 167* (Norwalk, Conn.: FASB, 2009)).

[21]FASB ASC 860: Transfers and Servicing (previously "Accounting for Transfers of Financial Assets, an amendment of FASB Statement No. 140," *Statement of Financial Accounting Standards No. 166* (Norwalk, Conn.: FASB, 2009)).

ILLUSTRATION 7–6 Accounts Receivable Factored without Recourse	In December 2011, the Santa Teresa Glass Company factored accounts receivable that had a book value of $600,000 to Factor Bank. The transfer was made without recourse. Under this arrangement, Santa Teresa transfers the $600,000 of receivables to Factor, and Factor immediately remits to Santa Teresa cash equal to 90% of the factored amount (90% × $600,000 = $540,000). Factor retains the remaining 10% to cover its factoring fee (equal to 4% of the total factored amount; 4% × $600,000 = $24,000) and to provide a cushion against potential sales returns and allowances. After Factor has collected cash equal to the amount advanced to Santa Teresa plus their factoring fee, Factor remits the excess to Santa Teresa. Therefore, under this arrangement Factor provides Santa Teresa with cash up front and a "beneficial interest" in the transferred receivables equal to the fair value of the last 10% of the receivables to be collected (which management estimates to equal $50,000), less the 4% factoring fee.[22]

Santa Teresa Glass records the transfer as follows:

Cash (90% × $600,000)	540,000	
Loss on sale of receivables (to balance)	34,000	
Receivable from factor ($50,000 − 24,000 fee)	26,000	
Accounts receivable (book value sold)		600,000

ILLUSTRATION 7–7 Accounts Receivable Factored with Recourse	Assume the same facts as in Illustration 7–6, except that Santa Teresa sold the receivables to Factor *with recourse* and estimates the fair value of the recourse obligation to be $5,000. Santa Teresa records the transfer as follows:

Cash (90% × $600,000)	540,000	
Loss on sale of receivables (to balance)	39,000	
Receivable from factor ($50,000 − 24,000 fee)	26,000	
Recourse liability		5,000
Accounts receivable (book value sold)		600,000

Notice that the estimated recourse liability increases the loss on sale. If the factor collects all of the receivables, Santa Teresa eliminates the recourse liability and increases income (reduces the loss).

ADDITIONAL CONSIDERATION

Gain-on-Sale Accounting. When applying the sales approach to accounting for a transfer of receivables, what if a transferor estimates a relatively high fair value associated with its beneficial interest? The higher valuation will result in a higher debit associated with that "beneficial interest" (in Illustrations 7–6 and 7–7, the "receivable from factor"). The offsetting credit produces a lower loss or higher gain. In the years leading up to the financial crisis of 2008/2009, high valuations of beneficial interests on securitized receivables were so prevalent that the sales approach was known on Wall Street as "gain-on-sale" accounting, because a gain usually was recognized in the transaction. This accounting approach likely contributed to the financial crisis by encouraging mortgage lenders to make loans (and record gains upon securitization of those loans) that were of low quality. As discussed elsewhere in this chapter, recent changes in GAAP make it harder to qualify for the sales approach, and therefore are likely to decrease the prevalence of "gain-on-sale" accounting.

---

[22]Consistent with Graphic 7–8, Illustration 7–6 depicts an arrangement in which the factor's fee is paid out of the 10% of receivables retained by the factor. Alternatively, a factoring arrangement could be structured to have the factor's fee withheld from the cash advanced to the company at the start of the arrangement. In that case, in Illustration 7–6 the journal entry recorded by Santa Teresa would be:

Cash ([90% × $600,000] − $24,000 fee)	516,000	
Loss on sale of receivables (to balance)	34,000	
Receivable from factor	50,000	
Accounts receivable (book value sold)		600,000

Transfers of Notes Receivable

We handle transfers of notes receivable in the same manner as transfers of accounts receivable. A note receivable can be used to obtain immediate cash from a financial institution either by pledging the note as collateral for a loan or by selling the note. Notes also can be securitized.

The transfer of a note to a financial institution is referred to as discounting. The financial institution accepts the note and gives the seller cash equal to the maturity value of the note reduced by a discount. The discount is computed by applying a discount rate to the maturity value and represents the financing fee the financial institution charges for the transaction. Illustration 7–8 provides an example of the calculation of the proceeds received by the transferor.

> The transfer of a note receivable to a financial institution is called *discounting*.

On December 31, 2011, the Stridewell Wholesale Shoe Company sold land in exchange for a nine-month, 10% note. The note requires the payment of $200,000 plus interest on September 30, 2012. The company's fiscal year-end is December 31. The 10% rate properly reflects the time value of money for this type of note. On March 31, 2012, Stridewell discounted the note at the Bank of the East. The bank's discount rate is 12%. Because the note had been outstanding for three months before it's discounted at the bank, Stridewell first records the interest that has accrued prior to being discounted:

March 31, 2012

Interest receivable	5,000	
Interest revenue ($200,000 $\times$ 10% $\times$ $\frac{3}{12}$)		5,000

Next, the value of the note if held to maturity is calculated. Then the discount for the time remaining to maturity is deducted to determine the cash proceeds from discounting the note:

$200,000	Face amount
15,000	Interest to maturity ($200,000 $\times$ 10% $\times$ $\frac{9}{12}$)
215,000	Maturity value
(12,900)	Discount ($215,000 $\times$ 12% $\times$ $\frac{6}{12}$)
$202,100	Cash proceeds

ILLUSTRATION 7–8

Discounting a Note Receivable

STEP 1: Accrue interest earned on the note receivable prior to its being discounted.

STEP 2: Add interest to maturity to calculate maturity value.

STEP 3: Deduct discount to calculate cash proceeds.

Similar to accounts receivable, Stridewell potentially could account for the transfer as a sale or a secured borrowing. For example, Illustration 7–9 shows the appropriate journal entries to account for the transfer as a sale.

Cash (proceeds determined above)	202,100	
Loss on sale of note receivable (to balance)	2,900	
Note receivable (face amount)		200,000
Interest receivable (accrued interest determined above)		5,000

ILLUSTRATION 7–9

Discounted Note Treated as a Sale

Deciding Whether to Account for a Transfer as a Sale or a Secured Borrowing

Transferors usually prefer to use the sale approach rather than the secured borrowing approach to account for the transfer of a receivable, because the sale approach makes the transferor seem less leveraged, more liquid, and perhaps more profitable than does the secured borrowing approach. Graphic 7–10 explains why by describing particular effects on key accounting metrics.

So, when is a company allowed to account for the transfer of receivables as a sale? The most critical element is the extent to which the company (the transferor) *surrenders control over the assets transferred.* For some arrangements, surrender of control is clear (e.g., when a receivable is sold without recourse and without any other rights, continuing servicing, or other involvement by the transferor). However, for other arrangements this distinction is not obvious. Indeed, some companies appear to structure transactions in ways that qualify for sale treatment but retain enough involvement to have control. This led the FASB to provide

GRAPHIC 7–10

Why Do Transferors of Receivables Generally Want to Account for the Transfer as a Sale?

Does the Accounting Approach:	Transfer of Receivables Accounted for as a:		Why Sales Approach is Preferred by the Transferor:
	Sale	Secured Borrowing	
Derecognize A/R, reducing assets?	Yes	No	Sale approach produces lower total assets and higher return on assets (ROA)
Recognize liability for cash received?	No	Yes	Sale approach produces lower liabilities and less leverage (debt/equity)
Where is cash received shown in the statement of cash flows?	May be in operating or financing sections	Always in financing section	Sale approach can produce higher cash flow from operations at time of transfer
Recognize gain on transfer?	More likely	Less likely	Sale approach can produce higher income at time of transfer.

guidelines designed to constrain inappropriate use of the sale approach. Specifically, the transferor (defined to include the company, its consolidated affiliates, and people acting on behalf of the company) is determined to have surrendered control over the receivables if and only if all of the following conditions are met:[23]

If the transferor is deemed to have surrendered control over the transferred receivables, the arrangement is accounted for as a sale; otherwise as a secured borrowing.

a. The transferred assets have been isolated from the transferor—beyond the reach of the transferor and its creditors.
b. Each transferee has the right to pledge or exchange the assets it received.
c. The transferor does not maintain *effective control* over the transferred assets. Effective control would exist, for example, if the transfer is structured such that the assets are likely to end up returned to the transferor.

If all of these conditions are met, the transferor accounts for the transfer as a sale. If any of the above conditions are *not* met, the transferor treats the transaction as a secured borrowing.

Graphic 7–11 provides a disclosure note from **United Components Inc. (UCI)** in which UCI accounts for the factoring of its trade accounts receivable as a sale, indicating that the conditions for sale treatment have been met.

GRAPHIC 7–11

Disclosure of Factoring Arrangement—United Components Inc.

Real World Financials

Note C: Sales of Receivables

UCI has agreements to sell undivided interests in certain of its receivables with factoring companies, which in turn have the right to sell an undivided interest to a financial institution or other third party. . . . UCI retained no rights or interest, and has no obligations, with respect to the sold receivables. UCI does not service the receivables after the sales. The sales of receivables were accounted for as a sale. . . . The sold receivables were removed from the balance sheet at the time of the sales.

Graphic 7–12 summarizes the decision process that is used to determine whether a transfer of a receivable is accounted for as a secured borrowing or a sale.

Disclosures

The amount of disclosures relevant to asset transfers increased dramatically in response to the 2008/2009 financial crisis. In particular, much disclosure is required when the transferor has continuing involvement in the transferred assets but accounts for the transfer as a sale. Why? Those are the circumstances under which it's most likely that the transferor may still

[23]FASB ASC 860–10–40: Transfers and Servicing—Overall—Derecognition (previously "Accounting for Transfers and Servicing of Financial Assets and Extinguishments of Liabilities," *Statement of Financial Accounting Standards No. 140* (Norwalk, Conn.: FASB, 2000), as amended by *SFAS No. 166*).

bear significant risk associated with the arrangement, so those are the arrangements that financial statement users may want to instead view as a secured borrowing. As a result, transferors must provide qualitative and quantitative information about the transfer at a level that allows financial statement users to fully understand (a) the transfer, (b) any continuing involvement with the transferred assets, and (c) any ongoing risks to the transferor.

The company also has to provide information about the quality of the transferred assets. For example, for transferred receivables, the company needs to disclose the amount of receivables that are past due and any credit losses occurring during the period. Among the other information the company must disclose are:

- How fair values were estimated when recording the transaction.
- Any cash flows occurring between the transferor and the transferee.
- How any continuing involvement in the transferred assets will be accounted for on an ongoing basis.[25]

ADDITIONAL CONSIDERATION

Participating Interests. What if, rather than transferring all of a particular receivable, a company transfers only part of it? For example, what if a company transfers the right to receive future interest payments on a note, but retains the right to receive the loan principal? Recent changes in U.S. GAAP require that a partial transfer be treated as a secured borrowing unless the amount transferred qualifies as a "**participating interest**" as well as meeting the "surrender of control" requirements described above. Participating interests are defined as sharing proportionally in the cash flows of the receivable and having equal and substantial rights with respect to the receivable. Many common financing arrangements do not qualify as participating interests, so this change in GAAP makes it harder for partial transfers to qualify for the sale approach. However, GAAP also emphasizes that the particular legal form of a transfer determines its accounting,[24] so anticipate the financial services industry working creatively to structure transfers in a manner that achieves the accounting that its customers desire.

---

[24]FASB ASC 860–10–40: Transfers and Servicing—Overall—Derecognition (previously "Accounting for Transfers of Financial Assets, an amendment of FASB Statement No. 140," *Statement of Financial Accounting Standards No. 166* (Norwalk, Conn.: FASB, 2009), par. 26C).
[25]FASB ASC 860–10–40: Transfers and Servicing—Overall—Derecognition (previously "Accounting for Transfers of Financial Assets, an amendment of FASB Statement No. 140," *Statement of Financial Accounting Standards No. 166* (Norwalk, Conn.: FASB, 2009), par. 17).

● LO10

INTERNATIONAL FINANCIAL REPORTING STANDARDS

Transfers of Receivables. *IAS No. 39*[26] and FASB ASC 860 [27] cover financing with receivables under IFRS and U.S. GAAP, respectively. The international and U.S. guidance often lead to similar accounting treatments. Both seek to determine whether an arrangement should be treated as a secured borrowing or a sale, and, having concluded which approach is appropriate, both account for the approaches in a similar fashion. Also, the recent change in U.S. GAAP that eliminated the concept of QSPEs is a step toward convergence with IFRS, and is likely to reduce the proportion of U.S. securitizations that qualify for sale accounting.

Where IFRS and U.S. GAAP most differ is in the conceptual basis for their choice of accounting approaches and in the decision process they require to determine which approach to use. As you have seen in this chapter, U.S. GAAP focuses on whether control of assets has shifted from the transferor to the transferee. In contrast, IFRS requires a more complex decision process. The company has to have transferred the rights to receive the cash flows from the receivable, and then considers whether the company has transferred "substantially all of the risks and rewards of ownership," as well as whether the company has transferred control. Under IFRS:

1. If the company *transfers* substantially all of the risks and rewards of ownership, the transfer is treated as a sale.
2. If the company *retains* substantially all of the risks and rewards of ownership, the transfer is treated as a secured borrowing.
3. If neither conditions 1 or 2 hold, the company accounts for the transaction as a sale if it has transferred control, and as a secured borrowing if it has retained control.

Whether risks and rewards have been transferred is evaluated by comparing how variability in the amounts and timing of the cash flows of the transferred asset affect the company before and after the transfer.

This is a broad overview of the IFRS guidance. Application of the detailed rules is complex, and depending on the specifics of an arrangement, a company could have different accounting under IFRS and U.S. GAAP.

WHERE WE'RE HEADED

The FASB and IASB both have projects under way relevant to transfers of receivables.

● LO10

As indicated previously in this chapter, the FASB recently modified accounting for transfers of receivables. However, the Board also indicated that those changes were a short-term solution and that it intended to work with the IASB to produce a standard that comprehensively addressed derecognition of assets and liabilities (which would include determining when transfers of receivables can be accounted for as sales). At the time this book was written, the IASB had issued an exposure draft of a proposed standard, and the IASB and FASB intended to consider the comments the IASB receives before going forward.[28] The IASB's proposed standard focuses on transfers of control rather than transfers of risks and rewards of ownership, and in that sense moves IFRS closer to the approach used currently in U.S. GAAP, but many differences between current IFRS and U.S. GAAP remain to be resolved before full convergence is achieved in this area.

---

[26]"Financial Instruments: Recognition and Measurement," *International Accounting Standard No. 39* (IASCF), as amended effective January 1, 2009.
[27]FASB ASC 860: Transfers and Servicing (previously "Accounting for Transfers of Financial Assets, an amendment of FASB Statement No. 140," *Statement of Financial Accounting Standards No. 166* (Norwalk, Conn.: FASB, 2009)).
[28]*Exposure Draft: Derecognition, Proposed Amendments to IAS 39 and IFRS 7* (IASCF), April 2009.

CONCEPT REVIEW EXERCISE

The Hollywood Lumber Company obtains financing from the Midwest Finance Company by factoring (or discounting) its receivables. During June 2011, the company factored $1,000,000 of accounts receivable to Midwest. The transfer was made *without* recourse. The factor, Midwest Finance, remits 80% of the factored receivables and retains 20%. When the receivables are collected by Midwest, the retained amount, less a 3% fee (3% of the total factored amount), will be remitted to Hollywood Lumber. Hollywood estimates that the fair value of the amount retained by Midwest is $180,000.

In addition, on June 30, 2011, Hollywood discounted a note receivable without recourse. The note, which originated on March 31, 2011, requires the payment of $150,000 *plus* interest at 8% on March 31, 2012. Midwest's discount rate is 10%. The company's fiscal year-end is December 31.

Required:

Prepare journal entries for Hollywood Lumber for the factoring of accounts receivable and the note receivable discounted on June 30. Assume that the required criteria are met and the transfers are accounted for as sales.

The Factoring of Receivables		
Cash (80% × $1,000,000)	800,000	
Loss on sale of receivables (to balance)	50,000	
Receivable from factor ($180,000 − 30,000 fee)	150,000	
Accounts receivable (balance sold)		1,000,000

The Note Receivable Discounted		
Interest receivable	3,000	
Interest revenue ($150,000 × 8% × 3/12)		3,000
Cash (proceeds determined below)	149,850	
Loss on sale of note receivable (difference)	3,150	
Note receivable (face amount)		150,000
Interest receivable (accrued interest determined above)		3,000

Add interest to maturity to calculate maturity value.

Deduct discount to calculate cash proceeds.

$150,000	Face amount
12,000	Interest to maturity ($150,000 × 8%)
162,000	Maturity value
(12,150)	Discount ($162,000 × 10% × 9/12)
$149,850	Cash proceeds

DECISION MAKERS' PERSPECTIVE

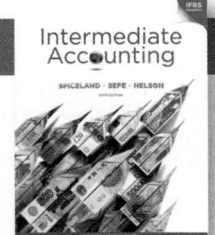

RECEIVABLES MANAGEMENT   A company's investment in receivables is influenced by several variables, including the level of sales, the nature of the product or service sold, and credit and collection policies. These variables are, of course, related. For example, a change in credit policies could affect sales. In fact, more liberal credit policies—allowing customers a longer time to pay or offering cash discounts for early payment—often are initiated with the specific objective of increasing sales volume.

● LO9

Management must evaluate the costs and benefits of any change in credit and collection policies.

Management's choice of credit and collection policies often involves trade-offs. For example, offering cash discounts may increase sales volume, accelerate customer payment, and reduce bad debts. These benefits are not without cost. The cash discounts reduce the amount of cash collected from customers who take advantage of the discounts. Extending payment terms also may increase sales volume. However, this creates an increase in the required investment in receivables and may increase bad debts.

The ability to use receivables as a method of financing also offers management alternatives. Assigning, factoring, and discounting receivables are alternative methods of financing operations that must be evaluated relative to other financing methods such as lines of credit or other types of short-term borrowing.

Investors, creditors, and financial analysts can gain important insights by monitoring a company's investment in receivables. Chapter 5 introduced the receivables turnover ratio and the related average collection period, ratios designed to monitor receivables. Recall that these ratios are calculated as follows:

$$\text{Receivables turnover ratio} = \frac{\text{Net sales}}{\text{Average accounts receivable (net)}}$$

$$\text{Average collection period} = \frac{365 \text{ days}}{\text{Receivables turnover ratio}}$$

The turnover ratio shows the number of times during a period that the average accounts receivable balance is collected, and the average collection period is an approximation of the number of days the average accounts receivable balance is outstanding.

As a company's sales grow, receivables also will increase. If the percentage increase in receivables is greater than the percentage increase in sales, the receivables turnover ratio will decline (the average collection period will increase). This could indicate customer dissatisfaction with the product or that the company has extended too generous payment terms in order to attract new customers, which, in turn, could increase sales returns and bad debts.

These ratios also can be used to compare the relative effectiveness of companies in managing the investment in receivables. Of course, it would be meaningless to compare the receivables turnover ratio of a computer products company such as **IBM** with that of, say, a food products company like **Hershey**. A company selling high-priced, low-volume products like mainframe computers generally will grant customers longer payment terms than a company selling lower priced, higher volume food products. Graphic 7–13 lists the 2009 receivables turnover ratio for some well-known companies. The differences are as expected, given the nature of the companies' products and operations. In particular, companies designing expensive products for medical and business applications turn over their receivables less frequently than do consumer-goods manufacturers and wholesalers.

GRAPHIC 7–13
Receivables Turnover Ratios

Company	2009 Receivables Turnover Ratio
Medtronic (medical technology)	3.88
Autodesk (design software)	5.56
General Mills (wholesale consumer foods)	13.10

To illustrate receivables analysis in more detail, let's compute the 2009 receivables turnover ratio and the average collection period for two companies in the software industry, **Symantec Corp.** and **CA, Inc.** (formerly Computer Associates, Inc.).

Balance sheet and income statement information—Symantec Corp. and CA, Inc.

($ in millions)	Symantec Corp.		CA, Inc.	
	2009	2008	2009	2008
Accounts receivable (net)	$837	$758	$839	$970
Two-year averages	$797.5		$904.5	
Net sales—2009	$6,150		$4,271	

Receivables turnover and average collection period—Symantec Corp. and CA, Inc.

	Symantec Corp.	CA, Inc.	Industry Average
Receivables Turnover	$= \dfrac{\$6,150}{\$797.5} = 7.71$	$\dfrac{\$4,271}{\$904.5} = 4.72$	6.3
Average Collection Period	$= \dfrac{365}{7.71} = 47 \text{ days}$	$\dfrac{365}{4.72} = 77 \text{ days}$	58 days

On average, Symantec collects its receivables 30 days sooner than does CA, and 11 days faster than the industry average. A major portion of Symantec's sales of products like Norton antivirus software are made directly to consumers online who pay immediately with credit cards, significantly accelerating payment. CA, on the other hand, sells primarily to businesses, who take longer to pay.

Academic research has shown receivables information to be useful in financial statement analysis. Professors Lev and Thiagarajan empirically demonstrated the importance of a set of 12 fundamental variables in valuing companies' common stock. The set of variables included accounts receivable (change in accounts receivable minus change in sales) and allowance for uncollectible accounts (change in accounts receivable minus change in the allowance). Motivation for the receivables variable was that disproportionate increases in accounts receivable (relative to sales increases) can indicate difficulties in selling products, reflected in more lenient credit policies. The allowance variable was expected to indicate inadequate bad debt provisions. Both were found to be significant indicators of stock returns during high inflation years.[29]

> **ARTHUR LEVITT, JR.**
> A third illusion played by some companies is using unrealistic assumptions to estimate . . . such items as sales returns, loan losses or warranty costs. In doing so, they stash accruals in cookie jars during good times and reach into them when needed in the bad times.[30]

EARNINGS QUALITY. Recall our discussion in Chapter 4 concerning earnings quality. We learned that managers have the ability, to a limited degree, to manipulate reported income and that many observers believe this practice diminishes earnings quality because it can mask "permanent" earnings. Former SEC Chairman Arthur Levitt listed discretionary accruals, which he called "Miscellaneous Cookie Jar Reserves," as one of the most popular methods companies use to manipulate income.

> Bad debt expense is one of a variety of discretionary accruals that provide management with the opportunity to manipulate income.

Dell Inc. provides an example of a company that engaged in this sort of behavior. Dell had to restate four years of financial statements (from 2003 to 2007) after it discovered that executives had been using a variety of accounting techniques to achieve quarterly earnings targets. For example, revenue associated with software licenses and product warranties was being recognized too quickly, and extra warranty reserves were maintained that could be adjusted to compensate for earnings shortfalls.

Sometimes financial statement users can examine accounts receivable, the allowance for bad debts, and other accounts to detect low earnings quality. For example, in April 1998, **PaineWebber Inc.** downgraded its stock recommendation for **Sunbeam, Inc.**, after noticing unusually high accounts receivable and unexpected increases in sales of certain products. Also, Sunbeam's allowance for uncollectible accounts had shown large increases in prior periods. It eventually came to light that Sunbeam had been manipulating its income by using a "bill and hold" strategy with retail buyers. This involved selling products at large discounts to retailers before they normally would buy and then holding the products in third-party warehouses, with delivery at a later date.

Often times, though, financial statement users must rely on the company's internal control system to prevent fraud and preserve earnings quality, because the effects of poor accounting quality can be difficult for outsiders to detect. Dell's accounting problems were identified by an internal investigation that followed an SEC inquiry on another matter. Dell acknowledged that poor internal controls contributed to its problems. Dell's income manipulation was never extreme enough to be detected by outsiders, but strong internal controls could have prevented it from occurring at all.

Another area for accounting-quality concern is the sale method used to account for transfers of receivables. Recent research suggests that some companies manage earnings by distorting the fair value estimates that are made as part of recording securitizations.[31]

---

[29]B. Lev and S. R. Thiagarajan, "Fundamental Information Analysis," *Journal of Accounting Research* 31, No. 2 (Autumn 1993). The main conclusion of the study was that fundamental variables, not just earnings, are useful in firm valuation, particularly when examined in the context of macroeconomic conditions such as inflation.

[30]Arthur Levitt, Jr., "The Numbers Game," *The CPA Journal,* December 1998, p. 16.

[31]P. M. Dechow, L. A. Myers, and C. Shakespeare, "Fair Value Accounting and Gains from Asset Securitizations: A Convenient Earnings Management Tool with Compensation Side-Benefits," Working paper, February 11, 2009.

Also, some firms classify cash flows associated with selling their accounts receivable in the operating section of the statement of cash flows, such that changes in the extent to which accounts receivable are sold can be used to manipulate cash flow from operations. In fact, evidence suggests that sophisticated investors and bond-rating agencies undo sales accounting to treat transfers of receivables as secured borrowings before assessing the riskiness of a company's debt.[32] As noted earlier in this chapter, recent changes in GAAP have made it more difficult for transfers to qualify for sales accounting, but Wall Street is very good at identifying clever ways to structure transactions around accounting standards, so it is important to be vigilant regarding the accounting for these transactions. ●

FINANCIAL REPORTING CASE SOLUTION

1. **Explain the allowance method of accounting for bad debts.** *(p. 347)* The allowance method estimates future bad debts in order to (1) match bad debt expense with related revenues and (2) report accounts receivable in the balance sheet at net realizable value. In an adjusting entry, we record bad debt expense and reduce accounts receivable indirectly by crediting a contra account to accounts receivable for an estimate of the amount that eventually will prove uncollectible.

2. **What approaches might Cisco have used to arrive at the $275 million bad debt provision?** *(p. 348)* There are two ways commonly used to arrive at an estimate of future bad debts: the income statement approach and the balance sheet approach. Using the income statement approach, we estimate bad debt expense as a percentage of each period's net credit sales. The balance sheet approach determines bad debt expense by estimating the net realizable value of accounts receivable. In other words, the allowance for uncollectible accounts is determined and bad debt expense is an indirect outcome of adjusting the allowance account to the desired balance.

3. **Are there any alternatives to the allowance method?** *(p. 350)* An alternative to the allowance method is the direct write-off method. Using this method, adjusting entries are not recorded and any bad debt that does arise simply is written off as bad debt expense. Of course, if the sale that generated this receivable occurred in a previous reporting period, this violates the matching principle. Operating expenses would have been understated and assets overstated that period. This is why the direct write-off method is not permitted by GAAP except in limited circumstances. ●

THE BOTTOM LINE

● **LO1** Internal control refers to the plan designed to encourage adherence to company policies and procedures; promote operational efficiency; minimize irregularities, errors, thefts or fraud; and maximize the reliability and accuracy of accounting data. Key elements of an internal control system for cash receipts and disbursements include separation of record keeping from control of cash duties and the periodic preparation of a bank reconciliation. (p. 338)

● **LO2** Cash can be informally restricted by management for a particular purpose. Restrictions also can be contractually imposed. If restricted cash is available for current operations or to pay current liabilities, it's classified as a current asset; otherwise, it's classified as investments and funds or other assets. (p. 340)

● **LO3** The gross method of accounting for cash discounts considers a discount not taken as part of sales revenue. The net method considers a discount not taken as interest revenue. (p. 343)

● **LO4** When merchandise returns are anticipated, an allowance for sales returns should be recorded as a contra account to accounts receivable and sales revenue also should be reduced by the anticipated sales returns. (p. 344)

---

[32]Other recent research provides evidence that investors treat securitizations as loans rather than asset sales, suggesting that they are unconvinced that a sale has truly taken place. For example, see W. R. Landsman, K. Peasnell, and C. Shakespeare, "Are Asset Securitizations Sales or Loans?" *The Accounting Review* 83, no. 5 (2008), pp. 1251–72.

● **LO5** Uncollectible accounts receivable should be anticipated in order to match bad debt expense with revenues generated. Likewise, accounts receivable should be reduced by an allowance for uncollectible accounts to report accounts receivable at net realizable value. (p. 347)

● **LO6** There are two approaches to estimating future bad debts. The income statement approach estimates bad debt expense based on the notion that a certain percentage of each period's credit sales will prove to be uncollectible. The balance sheet approach to estimating future bad debts indirectly determines bad debt expense by directly estimating the net realizable value of accounts receivable at the end of the period. (p. 347)

● **LO7** Notes receivable are formal credit arrangements between a creditor (lender) and a debtor (borrower). The typical note receivable requires the payment of a specified face amount, also called principal, at a specified maturity date or dates. In addition, interest is paid at a stated percentage of the face amount. Interest on notes is calculated by multiplying the face amount by the annual rate by the fraction of the annual period. (p. 352)

● **LO8** A wide variety of methods exists for companies to use their receivables to obtain immediate cash. These methods can be described as either:

   a.   A secured borrowing

   b.   A sale of receivables

   If three conditions indicating surrender of control are met, the transferor accounts for the transfer of receivables as a sale; otherwise as a secured borrowing. (p. 356)

● **LO9** A company's investment in receivables is influenced by several related variables, to include the level of sales, the nature of the product or service, and credit and collection policies. Investors, creditors, and financial analysts can gain important insights by monitoring a company's investment in receivables. The receivables turnover and average collection period ratios are designed to monitor receivables. (p. 365)

● **LO10** Accounting for cash and accounts receivable are similar under U.S. GAAP and IFRS. Other than some differences in terminology and balance sheet classifications, the most important differences involve accounting for transfers of receivables. Both IFRS and U.S. GAAP seek to distinguish between determining whether a sales treatment or secured borrowing treatment is appropriate, but they use different conceptual frameworks to guide that choice. U.S. GAAP focuses on whether control of the receivables is transferred, while IFRS use a more complex decision process that also considers whether substantially all of the risks and rewards of ownership have been transferred. Convergence efforts in this area currently are under way. (pp. 341, 356, 364, and 374) ●

CASH CONTROLS

Bank Reconciliation

One of the most important tools used in the control of cash is the bank reconciliation. Since all cash receipts are deposited into the bank account and cash disbursements are made by check, the bank account provides a separate record of cash. It's desirable to periodically compare the bank balance with the balance in the company's own records and reconcile any differences.

From your own personal experience, you know that the ending balance in your checking account reported on the monthly bank statement you receive rarely equals the balance you have recorded in your checkbook. Differences arise from two types of items: timing differences and errors.

Timing differences occur when the company and the bank record transactions at different times. At any point in time the company may have adjusted the cash balance for items of which the bank is not yet aware. Likewise, the bank may have adjusted its record of that balance by items of which the company is not yet aware. For example, checks written and cash deposits are not all processed by the bank in the same month that they are recorded by the company. Also, the bank may adjust the company's account for items such as service charges that the company is not aware of until the bank statement is received.

Errors can be made either by the company or the bank. For example, a check might be written for $210 but recorded on the company's books as a $120 disbursement; a deposit of $500 might be processed incorrectly by the bank as a $50 deposit. In addition to serving

Differences between the cash book and bank balance occur due to differences in the timing of recognition of certain transactions and errors.

STEP 1: Adjust the bank balance to the corrected cash balance.

as a safeguard of cash, the bank reconciliation also uncovers errors such as these and helps ensure that the proper cash balance is reported in the balance sheet.

Bank reconciliations include adjustments to the balance per bank for timing differences involving transactions already reflected in the company's accounting records that have not yet been processed by the bank. These adjustments usually include *checks outstanding* and *deposits outstanding* (also called *deposits in transit*). In addition, the balance per bank would be adjusted for any bank errors discovered. These adjustments produce an adjusted bank balance that represents the corrected cash balance.

STEP 2: Adjust the book balance to the corrected cash balance.

The balance per books is similarly adjusted for timing differences involving transactions already reflected by the bank of which the company is unaware until the bank statement is received. These would include service charges, charges for NSF (nonsufficient funds) checks, and collections made by the bank on the company's behalf. In addition, the balance per books is adjusted for any company errors discovered, resulting in an adjusted book balance that will also represent the corrected cash balance. *Each of these adjustments requires a journal entry to correct the book balance.* Only adjustments to the book balance require journal entries. Graphic 7A–1 recaps these reconciling items.

GRAPHIC 7A–1

Bank Reconciliation— Reconciling Items

Bank balance
+ Deposits outstanding
− Checks outstanding
± Errors

Corrected balance

Book balance
+ Collections by bank
− Service charges
− NSF checks
± Errors

Corrected balance

The two corrected balances must equal.

Step 1: Adjustments to Bank Balance:

1. *Add deposits outstanding.* These represent cash amounts received by the company and debited to cash that have not been deposited in the bank by the bank statement cutoff date and cash receipts deposited in the bank near the end of the period that are not recorded by the bank until after the cutoff date.
2. *Deduct checks outstanding.* These represent checks written and recorded by the company as credits to cash that have not yet been processed by the bank before the cutoff date.
3. *Bank errors.* These will either be increases or decreases depending on the nature of the error.

Step 2: Adjustments to Book Balance:

1. *Add collections made by the bank* on the company's behalf and other increases in cash that the company is unaware of until the bank statement is received.
2. *Deduct service and other charges* made by the bank that the company is unaware of until the bank statement is received.
3. *Deduct NSF (nonsufficient funds) checks.* These are checks previously deposited for which the payors do not have sufficient funds in their accounts to cover the amount of the checks. The checks are returned to the company whose responsibility it is to seek payment from payors.
4. *Company errors.* These will either be increases or decreases depending on the nature of the error.

To demonstrate the bank reconciliation process, consider Illustration 7A–1.

ILLUSTRATION 7A–1

Bank Reconciliation

The Hawthorne Manufacturing Company maintains a general checking account at the First Pacific Bank. First Pacific provides a bank statement and canceled checks once a month. The cutoff date is the last day of the month. The bank statement for the month of May is summarized as follows:

Balance, May 1, 2011	$32,120
Deposits	82,140
Checks processed	(78,433)
Service charges	(80)
NSF checks	(2,187)
Note payment collected by bank (includes $120 interest)	1,120
Balance, May 31, 2011	$34,680

(continued)

The company's general ledger cash account has a balance of $35,276 at the end of May. A review of the company records and the bank statement reveals the following:	**ILLUSTRATION 7A–1** (concluded)

1. Cash receipts not yet deposited totaled $2,965.
2. A deposit of $1,020 was made on May 31 that was not credited to the company's account until June.
3. All checks written in April have been processed by the bank. Checks written in May that had not been processed by the bank total $5,536.
4. A check written for $1,790 was incorrectly recorded by the company as a $790 disbursement. The check was for payment to a supplier of raw materials.

The bank reconciliation prepared by the company appears as follows:

Step 1: Bank Balance to Corrected Balance

Balance per bank statement	$34,680
Add: Deposits outstanding	3,985*
Deduct: Checks outstanding	(5,536)
Corrected cash balance	$33,129

Step 2: Book Balance to Corrected Balance

Balance per books	$35,276
Add: Note collected by bank	1,120
Deduct:	
Service charges	(80)
NSF checks	(2,187)
Error—understatement of check	(1,000)
Corrected cash balance	$33,129

*$2,965 + 1,020 = $3,985

The next step is to prepare adjusting journal entries to reflect each of the adjustments to the balance per books. These represent amounts the company was not previously aware of until receipt of the bank statement. No adjusting entries are needed for the adjustments to the balance per bank because the company has already recorded these items. However, the bank needs to be notified of any errors discovered.

Cash	1,120	
Notes receivable		1,000
Interest revenue		120

To record the receipt of principal and interest on note collected directly by the bank.

Miscellaneous expense (bank service charges)	80	
Accounts receivable (NSF checks)	2,187	
Accounts payable (error in check to supplier)	1,000	
Cash		3,267

To record credits to cash revealed by the bank reconciliation.

After these entries are posted, the general ledger cash account will equal the corrected balance of $33,129.

Petty Cash

Most companies keep a small amount of cash on hand to pay for low-cost items such as postage, office supplies, delivery charges, and entertainment expenses. It would be inconvenient, time consuming, and costly to process a check each time these small payments are made. A petty cash fund provides a more efficient way to handle these payments.

A petty cash fund is established by transferring a specified amount of cash from the company's general checking account to an employee designated as the petty cash custodian. The amount of the fund should approximate the expenditures made from the fund during a relatively short period of time (say a week or a month). The custodian disburses cash from the fund when the appropriate documentation is presented, such as a receipt for the purchase of office supplies. At any point in time, the custodian should be in possession of cash and appropriate

The petty cash fund always should have cash and receipts that together equal the amount of the fund.

receipts that sum to the amount of the fund. The receipts serve as the basis for recording appropriate expenses each time the fund is replenished. Consider the example in Illustration 7A–2.

ILLUSTRATION 7A–2 Petty Cash Fund	On May 1, 2011, the Hawthorne Manufacturing Company established a $200 petty cash fund. John Ringo is designated as the petty cash custodian. The fund will be replenished at the end of each month. On May 1, 2011, a check is written for $200 made out to John Ringo, petty cash custodian. During the month of May, John paid bills totaling $160 summarized as follows:

Postage	$ 40
Office supplies	35
Delivery charges	55
Entertainment	30
Total	$160

In journal entry form, the transaction to establish the fund would be recorded as follows:

A petty cash fund is established by writing a check to the custodian.

May 1, 2011
Petty Cash	200	
Cash (checking account)		200

No entries are recorded at the time the actual expenditures are made from the fund. The expenditures are recorded when reimbursement is requested at the end of the month. At that time, a check is written to John Ringo, petty cash custodian, for the total of the fund receipts, $160 in this case. John cashes the check and replenishes the fund to $200. In journal entry form, replenishing the fund would be recorded as follows:

The appropriate expense accounts are debited when the petty cash fund is reimbursed.

May 31, 2011
Postage expense	40	
Office supplies expense	35	
Delivery expense	55	
Entertainment expense	30	
Cash (checking account)		160

The petty cash account is not debited when replenishing the fund. If, however, the size of the fund is increased at time of replenishment, the account is debited for the increase. Similarly, petty cash would be credited if the size of the fund is decreased.

To maintain the control objective of separation of duties, the petty cash custodian should not be involved in the process of writing or approving checks, nor in recordkeeping. In addition, management should arrange for surprise counts of the fund. ●

APPENDIX 7B IMPAIRMENT OF A RECEIVABLE DUE TO A TROUBLED DEBT RESTRUCTURING

When a company holds a receivable from another company, there is some potential that the receivable will eventually be impaired.[33] Earlier in this chapter you learned about accounting for bad debts, which is how impairments of ordinary receivables are handled. For longer-term notes and loans receivable, present values come into play.

Impairment of a loan receivable occurs if the company believes it is probable that it will not receive all of the cash flows (principal and any interest payments) associated with the receivable. In that case, the receivable is remeasured based on the discounted present value of

---

[33]This appendix discusses accounting for the impairment of individual accounts and notes receivable, as specified in ASC 310–10–35: Receivables—Overall—Subsequent Measurement (previously "Accounting by Creditors for Impairment of a Loan–An amendment of FASB Statements No. 5 and 15," *Statement of Financial Accounting Standards No. 114* (Norwalk, Conn.: FASB, 1993)). When a receivable has been securitized, or when a company has elected to account for a receivable under the fair value option, the receivable is viewed as an investment and different GAAP applies, as described in Appendix 12B.

currently expected cash flows at the loan's original effective rate. The adjustment necessary to record the impaired receivable should seem familiar—a loss is included in current income, typically as part of bad debt expense, by debiting bad debt expense and crediting the allowance for uncollectible accounts. If additional information indicates that conditions have changed, bad debts expense and the allowance for uncollectible accounts are increased or decreased as necessary to reflect the change, as with short-term receivables.

Often the original terms of a debt agreement are changed as a result of financial difficulties experienced by the debtor (borrower). In that case, the new arrangement is referred to as a **troubled debt restructuring.** We discuss troubled debt restructurings in much more detail in Chapter 14. The essential point here is that such an arrangement involves some concessions on the part of the creditor (lender), resulting in the impairment of the creditor's asset: the receivable.

When the Receivable Is Continued, but with Modified Terms

In a troubled debt restructuring, it is likely that the bank allows the receivable to continue but with the terms of the debt agreement modified to make it easier for the debtor to comply. The lender might agree to reduce or delay the scheduled interest payments. Or, it may agree to reduce or delay the maturity amount. Often a troubled debt restructuring will call for some combination of these concessions.

Illustration 7B–1 shows one of many possibilities. Suppose the bank agrees to (1) forgive the interest accrued from last year, (2) reduce the two remaining interest payments from $3 million each to $2 million each, and (3) reduce the face amount from $30 million to $25 million. Clearly, the bank's investment in the receivable has been impaired. The extent of impairment is the difference between the $33 million carrying amount of the receivable (the present value of the receivable's cash flows prior to the restructuring) and the present value of the revised cash flows discounted at the loan's original effective rate (10%).

After restructuring, the lender still records interest annually at the 10% effective rate.

Brillard Properties owes First Prudent Bank $30 million under a 10% note with two years remaining to maturity. Due to financial difficulties of the developer, the previous year's interest ($3 million) was not paid. First Prudent Bank agrees to:
1. Forgive the interest accrued from last year.
2. Reduce the remaining two interest payments to $2 million each.
3. Reduce the principal to $25 million.

ILLUSTRATION 7B–1
Receivable Impaired by Troubled Debt Restructuring—Terms Modified

Analysis

Previous Value

Accrued interest	(10% × $30,000,000) $ 3,000,000	
Principal	30,000,000	
Carrying amount of the receivable		$ 33,000,000

The discounted present value of the cash flows prior to the restructuring is the same as the receivable's carrying amount.

New Value

Present value of future interest	$ 2 million × 1.73554* = $ 3,471,080	
Present value of principal	$25 million × 0.82645† = 20,661,250	
Present value of the receivable		(24,132,330)
Loss		$ 8,867,670

The discounted present value of the cash flows after the restructuring is less.

*Present value of an ordinary annuity of $1: n = 2, i = 10%
†Present value of $1: n = 2, i = 10%

Journal Entry

Loss on troubled debt restructuring (to balance)	8,867,670	
Accrued interest receivable (10% × $30,000,000).............		3,000,000
Allowance for uncollectible accounts		
($30,000,000 − 24,132,330)		5,867,670

The difference is a loss.

● LO10

INTERNATIONAL FINANCIAL REPORTING STANDARDS

Impairments. IFRS and U.S. GAAP generally have similar treatments of impairments of accounts and notes receivable. In particular, both allow reversals of impairments if circumstances change to indicate that the amount of the impairment has decreased. Reversals increase the carrying amount of the receivable and increase income (for example, by debiting the allowance for uncollectible accounts and crediting bad debts expense in the period of reversal). The amount of reversal is limited to the amount of the original impairment.

When the Receivable Is Settled Outright

Sometimes a receivable in a troubled debt restructuring is actually settled at the time of the restructuring with the receipt of cash (or a noncash asset), or even shares of the debtor's stock. In that case, the creditor simply records a loss for the difference between the carrying amount of the receivable and the fair value of the asset(s) or equity securities received. Illustration 7B–2 provides an example.

ILLUSTRATION 7B–2 Debt Settled at the Time of a Restructuring	First Prudent Bank is owed $30 million by Brillard Properties under a 10% note with two years remaining to maturity. Due to financial difficulties of the developer, the previous year's interest ($3 million) was not received. The bank agrees to settle the receivable (and accrued interest receivable) in exchange for property having a fair value of $20 million.

	($ in millions)	
Land (fair value)	20	
Loss on troubled debt restructuring (to balance)	13	
Accrued interest receivable (10% × $30 million)		3
Note receivable (balance)		30

The carrying amount of the receivable is $33 million.

For most active lenders, a troubled debt restructuring unfortunately is not both unusual and infrequent; so the loss is not reported as an extraordinary loss. ●

QUESTIONS FOR REVIEW OF KEY TOPICS

	Q 7–1	Define cash equivalents.
	Q 7–2	Explain the primary functions of internal controls procedures in the accounting area. What is meant by separation of duties?
	Q 7–3	What are the responsibilities of management described in Section 404 of the Sarbanes-Oxley Act? What are the responsibilities of the company's auditor?
	Q 7–4	Define a compensating balance. How are compensating balances reported in financial statements?
● IFRS	Q 7–5	Do U.S. GAAP and IFRS differ in how bank overdrafts are treated? Explain.
	Q 7–6	Explain the difference between a trade discount and a cash discount.
	Q 7–7	Distinguish between the gross and net methods of accounting for cash discounts.
	Q 7–8	Briefly explain the accounting treatment for sales returns.
	Q 7–9	Explain the typical way companies account for uncollectible accounts receivable (bad debts). When is it permissible to record bad debt expense only at the time when receivables actually prove uncollectible?
	Q 7–10	Briefly explain the difference between the income statement approach and the balance sheet approach to estimating bad debts.
● IFRS	Q 7–11	If a company has accounts receivable from ordinary customers and from related parties, can they combine those receivables in their financial statements under U.S. GAAP? Under IFRS?
	Q 7–12	Is any special accounting treatment required for the assigning of accounts receivable in general as collateral for debt?

Q 7–13   Explain any possible differences between accounting for an account receivable factored with recourse compared with one factored without recourse.

IFRS   Q 7–14   Do U.S. GAAP and IFRS differ in the criteria they use to determine whether a transfer of receivables is treated as a sale? Explain.

Q 7–15   What is meant by the discounting of a note receivable? Describe the four-step process used to account for discounted notes.

Q 7–16   What are the key variables that influence a company's investment in receivables? Describe the two ratios used by financial analysts to monitor a company's investment in receivables.

Q 7–17   (Based on Appendix 7A) In a two-step bank reconciliation, identify the items that might be necessary to adjust the bank balance to the corrected cash balance. Identify the items that might be necessary to adjust the book balance to the corrected cash balance.

Q 7–18   (Based on Appendix 7A) How is a petty cash fund established? How is the fund replenished?

Q 7–19   (Based on Appendix 7B) Marshall Companies, Inc., holds a note receivable from a former subsidiary. Due to financial difficulties, the former subsidiary has been unable to pay the previous year's interest on the note. Marshall agreed to restructure the debt by both delaying and reducing remaining cash payments. The concessions impair the creditor's investment in the receivable. How is this impairment recorded?

IFRS   Q 7–20   (Based on Appendix 7B) Do U.S. GAAP and IFRS differ in the ability of a company to recognize in net income the recovery of impairment losses of accounts and notes receivable?

BRIEF EXERCISES

BE 7–1
Internal control
● LO1

Janice Dodds opens the mail for the Ajax Plumbing Company. She lists all customer checks on a spreadsheet that includes the name of the customer and the check amount. The checks, along with the spreadsheet, are then sent to Jim Seymour in the accounting department who records the checks and deposits them daily in the company's checking account. How could the company improve its internal control procedure for the handling of its cash receipts?

BE 7–2
Bank overdrafts
● LO2 LO10

Cutler Company has a cash account with a balance of $250,000 with Wright Bank and a cash account with an overdraft of $5,000 at Lowe Bank. What would the current assets section of Cutler's balance sheet include for "cash" under IFRS? Under U.S. GAAP?

BE 7–3
Cash and cash equivalents
● LO2

The following items appeared on the year-end trial balance of Consolidated Freight Corporation: cash in a checking account, U.S. Treasury bills that mature in six months, undeposited customer checks, cash in a savings account, and currency and coins. Which of these items would be included in the company's balance sheet as cash and cash equivalents?

BE 7–4
Cash discounts;
gross method
● LO3

On December 28, 2011, Tristar Communications sold 10 units of its new satellite uplink system to various customers for $25,000 each. The terms of each sale were 1/10, n/30. Tristar uses the gross method to account for sales discounts. In what year will income before tax be affected by discounts, assuming that all customers paid the net-of-discount amount on January 6, 2012? By how much?

BE 7–5
Cash discounts; net method
● LO3

Refer to the situation described in BE 7–4. Answer the questions assuming that Tristar uses the net method to account for sales discounts.

BE 7–6
Sales returns
● LO4

During 2011, its first year of operations, Hollis Industries recorded sales of $10,600,000 and experienced returns of $720,000. Cost of goods sold totaled $6,360,000 (60% of sales). The company estimates that 8% of all sales will be returned. Prepare the year-end adjusting journal entries to account for anticipated sales returns.

BE 7–7
Accounts receivable classification
● LO5 LO10

Singletary Associates has accounts receivable due from normal credit customers, and also has an account receivable due from a director of the company. Singletary would like to combine both of those receivables on one line in the current assets section of their balance sheet and in the footnotes. Is that permissible under U.S. GAAP? Under IFRS? Explain.

BE 7–8
Uncollectible
accounts; income
statement approach
● LO5 LO6

The following information relates to a company's accounts receivable: accounts receivable balance at the beginning of the year, $300,000; allowance for uncollectible accounts at the beginning of the year, $25,000 (credit balance); credit sales during the year, $1,500,000; accounts receivable written off during the year, $16,000; cash collections from customers, $1,450,000. Assuming the company estimates bad debts at an amount equal to 2% of credit sales, calculate (1) bad debt expense for the year and (2) the year-end balance in the allowance for uncollectible accounts.

BE 7–9
Uncollectible
accounts; balance
sheet approach
● LO5 LO6

Refer to the situation described in BE 7–8. Answer the two questions assuming the company estimates that future bad debts will equal 10% of the year-end balance in accounts receivable.

BE 7–10
Uncollectible
accounts; solving
for unknown
● LO5 LO6

A company's year-end balance in accounts receivable is $2,000,000. The allowance for uncollectible accounts had a beginning-of-year credit balance of $30,000. An aging of accounts receivable at the end of the year indicates a required allowance of $38,000. If bad debt expense for the year was $40,000, what was the amount of bad debts written off during the year?

BE 7–11
Uncollectible
accounts; solving
for unknown
● LO5 LO6

Refer to the situation described in BE 7–10. If credit sales for the year were $8,200,000 and $7,950,000 was collected from credit customers, what was the beginning-of-year balance in accounts receivable?

BE 7–12
Note receivable
● LO7

On December 1, 2011, Davenport Company sold merchandise to a customer for $20,000. In payment for the merchandise, the customer signed a 6% note requiring the payment of interest and principal on March 1, 2012. How much interest revenue will the company recognize during 2011? In 2012?

BE 7–13
Factoring of
accounts receivable
● LO8

Logitech Corporation transferred $100,000 of accounts receivable to a local bank. The transfer was made without recourse. The local bank remits 85% of the factored amount to Logitech and retains the remaining 15%. When the bank collects the receivables, it will remit to Logitech the retained amount less a fee equal to 3% of the total amount factored. Logitech estimates a fair value of its 15% interest in the receivables of $11,000 (not including the 3% fee). What is the effect of this transaction on the company's assets, liabilities, and income before income taxes?

BE 7–14
Factoring of
accounts receivable
● LO8

Refer to the situation described in BE 7–13. Assuming that the sale criteria are not met, describe how Logitech would account for the transfer.

BE 7–15
Transfers of
accounts receivable
● LO8 LO10

Huling Associates plans to transfer $300,000 of accounts receivable to Mitchell Inc. in exchange for cash. Huling has structured the arrangement so that they retain substantially all the risks and rewards of ownership but shift control over the receivables to Mitchell. Assuming all other criteria are met for recognizing the transfer as a sale, how would Huling account for this transaction under IFRS? Under U.S. GAAP?

BE 7–16
Discounting a note
● LO8

On March 31, Dower Publishing discounted a $30,000 note at a local bank. The note was dated February 28 and required the payment of the principal amount and interest at 6% on May 31. The bank's discount rate is 8%. How much cash will Dower receive from the bank on March 31?

BE 7–17
Receivables turnover
● LO8

Camden Hardware's credit sales for the year were $320,000. Accounts receivable at the beginning and end of the year were $50,000 and $70,000, respectively. Calculate the accounts receivable turnover ratio and the average collection period for the year.

EXERCISES

An alternate exercise and problem set is available on the text website: www.mhhe.com/spiceland6e

E 7–1
Cash and cash
equivalents;
restricted cash
● LO2

The controller of the Red Wing Corporation is in the process of preparing the company's 2011 financial statements. She is trying to determine the correct balance of cash and cash equivalents to be reported as a current asset in the balance sheet. The following items are being considered:

a. Balances in the company's accounts at the First National Bank; checking $13,500, savings $22,100.
b. Undeposited customer checks of $5,200.

c. Currency and coins on hand of $580.

d. Savings account at the East Bay Bank with a balance of $400,000. This account is being used to accumulate cash for future plant expansion (in 2013).

e. $20,000 in a checking account at the East Bay Bank. The balance in the account represents a 20% compensating balance for a $100,000 loan with the bank. Red Wing may not withdraw the funds until the loan is due in 2014.

f. U.S. Treasury bills; 2-month maturity bills totaling $15,000, and 7-month bills totaling $20,000.

Required:

1. Determine the correct balance of cash and cash equivalents to be reported in the current asset section of the 2011 balance sheet.

2. For each of the items not included in your answer to requirement 1, explain the correct classification of the item.

E 7–2
Cash and cash equivalents
● **LO2**

Delta Automotive Corporation has the following assets listed in its 12/31/11 trial balance:

Cash in bank—checking account	$22,500
U.S. Treasury bills (mature in 60 days)*	5,000
Cash on hand (currency and coins)	1,350
U.S. Treasury bills (mature in six months)*	10,000
Undeposited customer checks	1,840

*Purchased on 11/30/11

Required:

1. Determine the correct balance of cash and cash equivalents to be reported in the current asset section of the 2011 balance sheet.

2. For each of the items not included in your answer to requirement 1, explain the correct classification of the item.

E 7–3
Bank overdrafts
● **LO2 LO10**

Parker Inc. has the following cash balances:

First Bank:	$150,000
Second Bank:	(10,000)
Third Bank:	25,000
Fourth Bank:	(5,000)

Required:

1. Prepare the current assets and current liabilities section of Parker's 2011 balance sheet, assuming Parker reports under U.S. GAAP.

2. Prepare the current assets and current liabilities section of Parker's 2011 balance sheet, assuming Parker reports under IFRS.

E 7–4
Trade and cash discounts; the gross method and the net method compared
● **LO3**

Tracy Company, a manufacturer of air conditioners, sold 100 units to Thomas Company on November 17, 2011. The units have a list price of $600 each, but Thomas was given a 30% trade discount. The terms of the sale were 2/10, n/30.

Required:

1. Prepare the journal entries to record the sale on November 17 (ignore cost of goods) and collection on November 26, 2011, assuming that the gross method of accounting for cash discounts is used.

2. Prepare the journal entries to record the sale on November 17 (ignore cost of goods) and collection on December 15, 2011, assuming that the gross method of accounting for cash discounts is used.

3. Repeat requirements 1 and 2 assuming that the net method of accounting for cash discounts is used.

E 7–5
Cash discounts; the gross method
● **LO3**

Harwell Company manufactures automobile tires. On July 15, 2011, the company sold 1,000 tires to the Nixon Car Company for $50 each. The terms of the sale were 2/10, n/30. Harwell uses the gross method of accounting for cash discounts.

Required:

1. Prepare the journal entries to record the sale on July 15 (ignore cost of goods) and collection on July 23, 2011.

2. Prepare the journal entries to record the sale on July 15 (ignore cost of goods) and collection on August 15, 2011.

E 7–6
Cash discounts; the net method
● **LO3**

[This is a variation of Exercise 7–5 modified to focus on the net method of accounting for cash discounts.]

Harwell Company manufactures automobile tires. On July 15, 2011, the company sold 1,000 tires to the Nixon Car Company for $50 each. The terms of the sale were 2/10, n/30. Harwell uses the net method of accounting for cash discounts.

Required:

1. Prepare the journal entries to record the sale on July 15 (ignore cost of goods) and payment on July 23, 2011.

2. Prepare the journal entries to record the sale on July 15 (ignore cost of goods) and payment on August 15, 2011.

E 7–7
Sales returns
● LO4

Halifax Manufacturing allows its customers to return merchandise for any reason up to 90 days after delivery and receive a credit to their accounts. The company began 2011 with an allowance for sales returns of $300,000. During 2011, Halifax sold merchandise on account for $11,500,000. This merchandise cost Halifax $7,475,000 (65% of selling prices). Also during the year, customers returned $450,000 in sales for credit. Sales returns, estimated to be 4% of sales, are recorded as an adjusting entry at the end of the year.

Required:

1. Prepare the entry to record the merchandise returns and the year-end adjusting entry for estimated returns.
2. What is the amount of the year-end allowance for sales returns after the adjusting entry is recorded?

E 7–8
Uncollectible accounts; allowance method vs. direct write-off method
● LO5 LO6

Johnson Company uses the allowance method to account for uncollectible accounts receivable. Bad debt expense is established as a percentage of credit sales. For 2011, net credit sales totaled $4,500,000, and the estimated bad debt percentage is 1.5%. The allowance for uncollectible accounts had a credit balance of $42,000 at the beginning of 2011 and $40,000, after adjusting entries, at the end of 2011.

Required:

1. What is bad debt expense for 2011?
2. Determine the amount of accounts receivable written off during 2011.
3. If the company uses the direct write-off method, what would bad debt expense be for 2011?

E 7–9
Uncollectible accounts; allowance method; balance sheet approach
● LO5 LO6

Colorado Rocky Cookie Company offers credit terms to its customers. At the end of 2011, accounts receivable totaled $625,000. The allowance method is used to account for uncollectible accounts. The allowance for uncollectible accounts had a credit balance of $32,000 at the beginning of 2011 and $21,000 in receivables were written off during the year as uncollectible. Also, $1,200 in cash was received in December from a customer whose account previously had been written off. The company estimates bad debts by applying a percentage of 10% to accounts receivable at the end of the year.

Required:

1. Prepare journal entries to record the write-off of receivables, the collection of $1,200 for previously written off receivables, and the year-end adjusting entry for bad debt expense.
2. How would accounts receivable be shown in the 2011 year-end balance sheet?

E 7–10
Uncollectible accounts; allowance method and direct write-off method compared; solving for unknown
● LO6

Castle Company provides estimates for its uncollectible accounts. The allowance for uncollectible accounts had a credit balance of $17,280 at the beginning of 2011 and a $22,410 credit balance at the end of 2011 (after adjusting entries). If the direct write-off method had been used to account for uncollectible accounts (bad debt expense equals actual write-offs), the income statement for 2011 would have included bad debt expense of $17,100 and revenue of $2,200 from the collection of previously written off bad debts.

Required:

Determine bad debt expense for 2011 according to the allowance method.

E 7–11
Uncollectible accounts; allowance method; solving for unknowns
● LO5 LO6

Real World Financials

General Mills reported the following information in its 2009 financial statements ($ in millions):

	2009	2008
Balance Sheet:		
Accounts receivable, net	$ 953	$1,084
2009 Income statement:		
Sales revenue	$4,271	

A note disclosed that the allowance for uncollectible accounts had a balance of $18 million and $16 million at the end of 2009 and 2008, respectively. Bad debt expense for 2009 was $14 million.

Required:

Determine the amount of cash collected from customers during 2009.

E 7–12
Note receivable
● LO7

On June 30, 2011, the Esquire Company sold some merchandise to a customer for $30,000. In payment, Esquire agreed to accept a 6% note requiring the payment of interest and principal on March 31, 2012. The 6% rate is appropriate in this situation.

Required:

1. Prepare journal entries to record the sale of merchandise (omit any entry that might be required for the cost of the goods sold), the December 31, 2011 interest accrual, and the March 31, 2012 collection.
2. If the December 31 adjusting entry for the interest accrual is not prepared, by how much will income before income taxes be over- or understated in 2011 and 2012?

E 7–13
Noninterest-bearing note receivable
● LO7

[This is a variation of Exercise 7–12 modified to focus on a noninterest-bearing note.]

On June 30, 2011, the Esquire Company sold some merchandise to a customer for $30,000 and agreed to accept as payment a noninterest-bearing note with an 8% discount rate requiring the payment of $30,000 on March 31, 2012. The 8% rate is appropriate in this situation.

Required:

1. Prepare journal entries to record the sale of merchandise (omit any entry that might be required for the cost of the goods sold), the December 31, 2011 interest accrual, and the March 31, 2012 collection.
2. What is the *effective* interest rate on the note?

E 7–14
Interest-bearing note receivable; solving for unknown rate
● LO7

On January 1, 2011, the Apex Company exchanged some shares of common stock it had been holding as an investment for a note receivable. The note principal plus interest is due on January 1, 2012. The 2011 income statement reported $2,200 in interest revenue from this note and a $6,000 gain on sale of investment in stock. The stock's book value was $16,000. The company's fiscal year ends on December 31.

Required:

1. What is the note's effective interest rate?
2. Reconstruct the journal entries to record the sale of the stock on January 1, 2011, and the adjusting entry to record interest revenue at the end of 2011. The company records adjusting entries only at year-end.

E 7–15
Assigning of specific accounts receivable
● LO8

On June 30, 2011, the High Five Surfboard Company had outstanding accounts receivable of $600,000. On July 1, 2011, the company borrowed $450,000 from the Equitable Finance Corporation and signed a promissory note. Interest at 10% is payable monthly. The company assigned specific receivables totaling $600,000 as collateral for the loan. Equitable Finance charges a finance fee equal to 1.8% of the accounts receivable assigned.

Required:

Prepare the journal entry to record the borrowing on the books of High Five Surfboard.

E 7–16
Factoring of accounts receivable without recourse
● LO8

Mountain High Ice Cream Company transferred $60,000 of accounts receivable to the Prudential Bank. The transfer was made *without recourse.* Prudential remits 90% of the factored amount to Mountain High and retains 10%. When the bank collects the receivables, it will remit to Mountain High the retained amount (which Mountain estimates has a fair value of $5,000) less a 2% fee (2% of the total factored amount).

Required:

Prepare the journal entry to record the transfer on the books of Mountain High assuming that the sale criteria are met.

E 7–17
Factoring of accounts receivable with recourse
● LO8

[This is a variation of Exercise 7–16 modified to focus on factoring with recourse.]

Mountain High Ice Cream Company transferred $60,000 of accounts receivable to the Prudential Bank. The transfer was made *with recourse.* Prudential remits 90% of the factored amount to Mountain High and retains 10% to cover sales returns and allowances. When the bank collects the receivables, it will remit to Mountain High the retained amount (which Mountain estimates has a fair value of $5,000). Mountain High anticipates a $3,000 recourse obligation. The bank charges a 2% fee (2% of $60,000), and requires that amount to be paid at the start of the factoring arrangement.

Required:

Prepare the journal entry to record the transfer on the books of Mountain High assuming that the sale criteria are met.

E 7–18
Factoring of accounts receivable with recourse under IFRS
● LO8 LO10

[This is a variation of Exercise 7–17 modified to focus on factoring with recourse under IFRS.]

Mountain High Ice Cream Company reports under IFRS. Mountain High transferred $60,000 of accounts receivable to the Prudential Bank. The transfer was made *with recourse.* Prudential remits 90% of the factored amount to Mountain High and retains 10% to cover sales returns and allowances. When the bank collects the receivables, it will remit to Mountain High the retained amount (which Mountain estimates has a fair value of $5,000). Mountain High anticipates a $3,000 recourse obligation. The bank charges a 2% fee (2% of $60,000), and requires that amount to be paid at the start of the factoring arrangement. Mountain High has transferred control over the receivables, but determines that it still retains substantially all risks and rewards associated with them.

Required:

Prepare the journal entry to record the transfer on the books of Mountain High, considering whether the sale criteria under IFRS have been met.

E 7–19
Discounting a note receivable
● LO8

Selkirk Company obtained a $15,000 note receivable from a customer on January 1, 2011. The note, along with interest at 10%, is due on July 1, 2011. On February 28, 2011, Selkirk discounted the note at Unionville Bank. The bank's discount rate is 12%.

Required:

Prepare the journal entries required on February 28, 2011, to accrue interest and to record the discounting (round all calculations to the nearest dollar) for Selkirk. Assume that the discounting is accounted for as a sale.

E 7–20
Concepts;
terminology
● LO1 through
LO8

Listed below are several terms and phrases associated with cash and receivables. Pair each item from List A (by letter) with the item from List B that is most appropriately associated with it.

List A	List B
____ 1. Internal control	a. Restriction on cash.
____ 2. Trade discount	b. Cash discount not taken is sales revenue.
____ 3. Cash equivalents	c. Includes separation of duties.
____ 4. Allowance for uncollectibles	d. Bad debt expense as % of credit sales.
____ 5. Cash discount	e. Recognizes bad debts as they occur.
____ 6. Balance sheet approach	f. Sale of receivables to as financial institution.
____ 7. Income statement approach	g. Include highly liquid investments.
____ 8. Net method	h. Estimate of bad debts.
____ 9. Compensating balance	i. Reduction in amount paid by credit customer.
____ 10. Discounting	j. Reduction below list price.
____ 11. Gross method	k. Cash discount not taken is interest revenue.
____ 12. Direct write-off method	l. Bad debt expense determined by estimating realizable value.
____ 13. Factoring	m. Sale of note receivable to a financial institution.

E 7–21
Receivables;
transaction analysis
● LO3 LO5
through LO8

Weldon Corporation's fiscal year ends December 31. The following is a list of transactions involving receivables that occurred during 2011:

Mar. 17	Accounts receivable of $1,700 were written off as uncollectible. The company uses the allowance method.
30	Loaned an officer of the company $20,000 and received a note requiring principal and interest at 7% to be paid on March 30, 2012.
May 30	Discounted the $20,000 note at a local bank. The bank's discount rate is 8%. The note was discounted without recourse and the sale criteria are met.
June 30	Sold merchandise to the Blankenship Company for $12,000. Terms of the sale are 2/10, n/30. Weldon uses the gross method to account for cash discounts.
July 8	The Blankenship Company paid its account in full.
Aug. 31	Sold stock in a nonpublic company with a book value of $5,000 and accepted a $6,000 non-interest-bearing note with a discount rate of 8%. The $6,000 payment is due on February 28, 2012. The stock has no ready market value.
Dec. 31	Bad debt expense is estimated to be 2% of credit sales for the year. Credit sales for 2011 were $700,000.

Required:

1. Prepare journal entries for each of the above transactions (round all calculations to the nearest dollar).
2. Prepare any additional year-end adjusting entries indicated.

E 7–22
Ratio analysis
● LO9

Real World Financials

Microsoft Corporation reported the following information in its financial statements for three successive quarters during the 2009 fiscal year ($ in millions):

	Three Months Ended		
	3/31/09 (Q3)	12/31/09 (Q2)	9/30/09 (Q1)
Balance sheets:			
Accounts receivable, net	$ 9,182	$10,953	$ 9,535
Income statements:			
Sales revenue	$13,648	$16,629	$15,061

Required:

Compute the receivables turnover ratio and the average collection period for the second and third quarters. Assume that each quarter consists of 91 days.

E 7–23
Ratio analysis;
solve for unknown
● LO9

The current asset section of the Moorcroft Outboard Motor Company's balance sheet reported the following amounts:

	12/31/11	12/31/10
Accounts receivable, net	$400,000	$300,000

The average collection period for 2011 is 50 days.

Required:

Determine net sales for 2011.

E 7–24
Petty cash
● Appendix 7A

Loucks Company established a $200 petty cash fund on October 2, 2011. The fund is replenished at the end of each month. At the end of October 2011, the fund contained $37 in cash and the following receipts:

Office supplies	$76
Lunch with client	48
Postage	20
Miscellaneous	19

Required:

Prepare the necessary general journal entries to establish the petty cash fund on October 2 and to replenish the fund on October 31.

E 7–25
Petty cash
● Appendix 7A

The petty cash fund of Ricco's Automotive contained the following items at the end of September 2011:

Currency and coins		$ 58
Receipts for the following expenditures:		
Delivery charges	$16	
Printer paper	11	
Paper clips and rubber bands	8	35
An I.O.U. from an employee		25
Postage		32
Total		$150

The petty cash fund was established at the beginning of September with a transfer of $150 from cash to the petty cash account.

Required:

Prepare the journal entry to replenish the fund at the end of September.

E 7–26
Bank reconciliation
● Appendix 7A

Jansen Company's general ledger showed a checking account balance of $23,820 at the end of May 2011. The May 31 cash receipts of $2,340, included in the general ledger balance, were placed in the night depository at the bank on May 31 and were processed by the bank on June 1. The bank statement dated May 31, 2011, showed bank service charges of $38. All checks written by the company had been processed by the bank by May 31 and were listed on the bank statement except for checks totaling $1,890.

Required:

Prepare a bank reconciliation as of May 31, 2011. [*Hint:* You will need to compute the balance that would appear on the bank statement.]

E 7–27
Bank reconciliation and adjusting entries
● Appendix 7A

Harrison Company maintains a checking account at the First National City Bank. The bank provides a bank statement along with canceled checks on the last day of each month. The July 2011 bank statement included the following information:

Balance, July 1, 2011	$ 55,678
Deposits	179,500
Checks processed	(192,610)
Service charges	(30)
NSF checks	(1,200)
Monthly loan payment deducted directly by bank from account	
(includes $320 in interest)	(3,320)
Balance, July 31, 2011	$ 38,018

The company's general ledger account had a balance of $38,918 at the end of July. Deposits outstanding totaled $6,300 and all checks written by the company were processed by the bank except for those totaling $8,420. In addition, a $2,000 July deposit from a credit customer was recorded as a $200 debit to cash and credit to accounts receivable, and a check correctly recorded by the company as a $30 disbursement was incorrectly processed by the bank as a $300 disbursement.

Required:

1. Prepare a bank reconciliation for the month of July.
2. Prepare the necessary journal entries at the end of July to adjust the general ledger cash account.

E 7–28
Impairment of securities available-for-sale; troubled debt restructuring
● Appendix 7B

At January 1, 2011, Clayton Hoists Inc. owed Third BancCorp $12 million, under a 10% note due December 31, 2012. Interest was paid last on December 31, 2009. Clayton was experiencing severe financial difficulties and asked Third BancCorp to modify the terms of the debt agreement. After negotiation Third BancCorp agreed to:
• Forgive the interest accrued for the year just ended.
• Reduce the remaining two years' interest payments to $1 million each.
• Reduce the principal amount to $11 million.

Required:

Prepare the journal entries by Third BancCorp necessitated by the restructuring of the debt at
1. January 1, 2011.
2. December 31, 2011.
3. December 31, 2012.

E 7–29
Impairment of
securities available-
for-sale; troubled
debt restructuring
● **Appendix 7B**

At January 1, 2011, NCI Industries, Inc. was indebted to First Federal Bank under a $240,000, 10% unsecured note. The note was signed January 1, 2009, and was due December 31, 2012. Annual interest was last paid on December 31, 2009. NCI was experiencing severe financial difficulties and negotiated a restructuring of the terms of the debt agreement. First Federal agreed to reduce last year's interest and the remaining two years' interest payments to $11,555 each and delay all payments until December 31, 2012, the maturity date.

Required:

Prepare the journal entries by First Federal Bank necessitated by the restructuring of the debt at
1. January 1, 2011.
2. December 31, 2011.
3. December 31, 2012.

E 7–30
FASB codification
research
● **LO1**

The *FASB Accounting Standards Codification* represents the single source of authoritative U.S. generally accepted accounting principles.

Required:

1. Obtain the relevant authoritative literature on accounting for accounts receivable using the FASB's Codification Research System at the FASB website (**www.fasb.org**). What is the specific citation that describes disclosure of accounting policies for credit losses and doubtful accounts?
2. List the disclosure requirements.

E 7–31
FASB codification
research
● **LO2 LO6 LO7**

Access the *FASB's Codification Research System* at the FASB website (**www.fasb.org**).

Required:

Determine the specific citation for accounting for each of the following items:
1. Accounts receivables from related parties should be shown separately from trade receivables.
2. The definition of cash equivalents.
3. Notes exchanged for cash are valued at the cash proceeds.
4. The two conditions that must be met to accrue a loss on an accounts receivable.

CPA AND CMA REVIEW QUESTIONS

**CPA Exam
Questions**

The following questions are used in the Kaplan CPA Review Course to study receivables while preparing for the CPA examination. Determine the response that best completes the statements or questions.

● **LO5**

1. At January 1, 2011, Simpson Co. had a credit balance of $260,000 in its allowance for uncollectible accounts. Based on past experience, 2 percent of Simpson's credit sales have been uncollectible. During 2011, Simpson wrote off $325,000 of accounts receivable. Credit sales for 2011 were $9,000,000. In its December 31, 2011, balance sheet, what amount should Simpson report as allowance for uncollectible accounts?
   a. $115,000
   b. $180,000
   c. $245,000
   d. $440,000

● **LO5 LO6**

2. The balance in accounts receivable at the beginning of 2011 was $600. During 2011, $3,200 of credit sales were recorded. If the ending balance in accounts receivable was $500 and $200 in accounts receivable were written off during the year, the amount of cash collected from customers was
   a. $3,100
   b. $3,200
   c. $3,300
   d. $3,800

● LO5

3. A company uses the allowance method to account for bad debts. What is the effect on each of the following accounts of the collection of an account previously written off?

	Allowance for Uncollectible Accounts	**Bad Debt Expense**
a.	Increase	Decrease
b.	No effect	Decrease
c.	Increase	No effect
d.	No effect	No effect

● LO4 LO5

4. The following information relates to Jay Co.'s accounts receivable for 2011:

Accounts receivable balance, 1/1/11	$650,000
Credit sales for 2011	2,700,000
Sales returns during 2011	75,000
Accounts receivable written off during 2011	40,000
Collections from customers during 2011	2,150,000
Allowance for uncollectible accounts balance, 12/31/11	110,000

What amount should Jay report for accounts receivable, before allowances, at December 31, 2011?
a. $ 925,000
b. $1,085,000
c. $1,125,000
d. $1,200,000

● LO8

5. Gar Co. factored its receivables without recourse with Ross Bank. Gar received cash as a result of this transaction, which is best described as a
a. Loan from Ross collateralized by Gar's accounts receivable.
b. Loan from Ross to be repaid by the proceeds from Gar's accounts receivables.
c. Sale of Gar's accounts receivable to Ross, with the risk of uncollectible accounts transferred to Ross.
d. Sale of Gar's accounts receivable to Ross, with the risk of uncollectible accounts retained by Gar.

● LO5 LO6

6. The following information pertains to Tara Co.'s accounts receivable at December 31, 2011:

Days Outstanding	Amount	Estimated % Uncollectible
0–60	$120,000	1%
61–120	90,000	2%
Over 120	100,000	6%
	$310,000	

During 2011, Tara wrote off $7,000 in receivables and recovered $4,000 that had been written off in prior years. Tara's December 31, 2010, allowance for uncollectible accounts was $22,000. Under the aging method, what amount of allowance for uncollectible accounts should Tara report at December 31, 2011?
a. $ 9,000
b. $10,000
c. $13,000
d. $19,000

● LO5 LO6

7. West Company had the following account balances at December 31, 2011, before recording bad debt expense for the year:

Accounts receivable	$ 900,000
Allowance for uncollectible accounts (credit balance)	16,000
Credit sales for 2011	1,750,000

West is considering the following methods of estimating bad debts for 2011:
• Based on 2% of credit sales
• Based on 5% of year-end accounts receivable
What amount should West charge to bad debt expense at the end of 2011 under each method?

	Percentage of Credit Sales	**Percentage of Accounts Receivable**
a.	$35,000	$29,000
b.	$35,000	$45,000
c.	$51,000	$29,000
d.	$51,000	$45,000

CMA Exam
Questions

The following questions dealing with receivables are adapted from questions that previously appeared on Certified Management Accountant (CMA) examinations. The CMA designation sponsored by the Institute of Management Accountants (**www.imanet.org**) provides members with an objective measure of knowledge and competence in the field of management accounting. Determine the response that best completes the statements or questions.

● LO5 LO6

1. Bad debt expense must be estimated in order to satisfy the matching principle when expenses are recorded in the same periods as the related revenues. In estimating bad debt expense for a period, companies generally accrue
   a. Either an amount based on a percentage of total sales or an amount based on a percentage of accounts receivable after adjusting for any balance in the allowance for doubtful accounts.
   b. A percentage of total sales.
   c. Either an amount based on a percentage of credit sales or an amount based on a percentage of accounts receivable after adjusting for any balance in the allowance for doubtful accounts.
   d. An amount equal to last year's bad debt expense.

Questions 2 and 3 are based on the following information:

Madison Corporation uses the allowance method to value its accounts receivable and is making the annual adjustments at fiscal year-end, November 30. The proportion of uncollectible accounts is estimated based on past experience, which indicates 1.5% of net credit sales will be uncollectible. Total sales for the year were $2,000,000, of which $200,000 were cash transactions. Madison has determined that the Norris Corporation accounts receivable balance of $10,000 is uncollectible and will write off this account before year-end adjustments are made. Listed below are Madison's account balances at November 30 prior to any adjustments and the $10,000 write-off.

Sales	$2,000,000
Accounts receivable	750,000
Sales discounts	125,000
Allowance for doubtful accounts	16,500
Sales returns and allowances	175,000
Bad debt expense	0

● LO5

2. The entry to write off Norris Corporation's accounts receivable balance of $10,000 will
   a. Increase total assets and decrease net income.
   b. Decrease total assets and net income.
   c. Have no effect on total assets and decrease net income.
   d. Have no effect on total assets and net income.

● LO5

3. As a result of the November 30 adjusting entry to provide for bad debts, the allowance for doubtful accounts will
   a. Increase by $30,000.
   b. Increase by $25,500.
   c. Increase by $22,500.
   d. Decrease by $22,500.

PROBLEMS

An alternate exercise and problem set is available on the text website: www.mhhe.com/spiceland6e

P 7–1
Uncollectible
accounts;
allowance method;
income statement
and balance sheet
approach

● LO5 LO6

eXcel

Swathmore Clothing Corporation grants its customers 30 days' credit. The company uses the allowance method for its uncollectible accounts receivable. During the year, a monthly bad debt accrual is made by multiplying 3% times the amount of credit sales for the month. At the fiscal year-end of December 31, an aging of accounts receivable schedule is prepared and the allowance for uncollectible accounts is adjusted accordingly.

At the end of 2010, accounts receivable were $574,000 and the allowance account had a credit balance of $54,000. Accounts receivable activity for 2011 was as follows:

Beginning balance	$ 574,000
Credit sales	2,620,000
Collections	(2,483,000)
Write-offs	(68,000)
Ending balance	$ 643,000

The company's controller prepared the following aging summary of year-end accounts receivable:

	Summary	
Age Group	Amount	Percent Uncollectible
0–60 days	$430,000	4%
61–90 days	98,000	15
91–120 days	60,000	25
Over 120 days	55,000	40
Total	$643,000	

Required:
1. Prepare a summary journal entry to record the monthly bad debt accrual and the write-offs during the year.
2. Prepare the necessary year-end adjusting entry for bad debt expense.
3. What is total bad debt expense for 2011? How would accounts receivable appear in the 2011 balance sheet?

P 7–2
Uncollectible accounts
● LO5

Real World Financials

Amdahl Corporation manufactures large-scale, high performance computer systems. In a recent annual report, the balance sheet included the following information (dollars in thousands):

	Current Year	Previous Year
Current assets:		
Receivables, net of allowances of $5,042 and $6,590 in the previous year	$504,944	$580,640

In addition, the income statement reported sales revenue of $2,158,755 ($ in thousands) for the current year. All sales are made on a credit basis. The statement of cash flows indicates that cash collected from customers during the current year was $2,230,065 ($ in thousands). There were no recoveries of accounts receivable previously written off.

Required:
1. Compute the following (dollar amounts in thousands):
    a. The amount of uncollectibles written off by Amdahl during the current year.
    b. The amount of bad debt expense that Amdahl would include in its income statement for the current year.
    c. The approximate percentage that Amdahl used to estimate uncollectibles for the current year, assuming that it uses the income statement approach.
2. Suppose that Amdahl had used the direct write-off method to account for uncollectibles. Compute the following (dollars in thousands):
    a. The accounts receivable information that would be included in the year-end balance sheet.
    b. The amount of bad debt expense that Amdahl would include in its income statement for the current year.

P 7–3
Bad debts
● LO5

Real World Financials

Cirrus Logic, Inc., is a leading designer and manufacturer of advanced integrated circuits that integrate algorithms and mixed-signal processing for mass storage, communications, consumer electronics, and industrial markets. The company's 2009 financial statements contained the following information:

	($ in thousands)	
Balance sheets	2009	2008
Current assets:		
Accounts receivable, net	$ 13,306	$ 22,652
Income statements	2009	2008
Net sales	$174,642	$181,885

In addition, the statement of cash flows disclosed that accounts receivable decreased during 2009 by $9,346 (in thousands). This indicates that cash received from customers was $9,346 (in thousands) more than accrual sales revenue. Also, a disclosure note reported that the allowance for uncollectible accounts (in thousands) was $451 and $404 at the end of 2009 and 2008, respectively.

Required:
1. What is the amount of accounts receivable due from customers at the end of 2009 and 2008?
2. Assuming that all sales are made on a credit basis, determine the amount of bad debt expense for 2009 and the amount of actual bad debt write-offs made in 2009.

P 7–4
Uncollectible
accounts

● LO5 LO6

Raintree Cosmetic Company sells its products to customers on a credit basis. An adjusting entry for bad debt expense is recorded only at December 31, the company's fiscal year-end. The 2010 balance sheet disclosed the following:

Current assets:
    Receivables, net of allowance for uncollectible accounts of $30,000 $432,000

During 2011, credit sales were $1,750,000, cash collections from customers $1,830,000, and $35,000 in accounts receivable were written off. In addition, $3,000 was collected from a customer whose account was written off in 2010. An aging of accounts receivable at December 31, 2011, reveals the following:

Age Group	Percentage of Year-End Receivables in Group	Percent Uncollectible
0–60 days	65%	4%
61–90 days	20	15
91–120 days	10	25
Over 120 days	5	40

Required:
1. Prepare summary journal entries to account for the 2011 write-offs and the collection of the receivable previously written off.
2. Prepare the year-end adjusting entry for bad debts according to each of the following situations:
   a. Bad debt expense is estimated to be 3% of credit sales for the year.
   b. Bad debt expense is estimated by computing net realizable value of the receivables. The allowance for uncollectible accounts is estimated to be 10% of the year-end balance in accounts receivable.
   c. Bad debt expense is estimated by computing net realizable value of the receivables. The allowance for uncollectible accounts is determined by an aging of accounts receivable.
3. For situations (a)–(c) in requirement 2 above, what would be the net amount of accounts receivable reported in the 2011 balance sheet?

P 7–5
Receivables; bad
debts and returns

● LO4 LO5

Real World Financials

Symantec Corp., located in Cupertino, California, is one of the world's largest producers of security and systems management software. The company's consolidated balance sheets for the 2009 and 2008 fiscal years included the following ($ in thousands):

	2009	2008
Current assets:		
Receivables, less allowances of $20,991 in 2009 and $23,314 in 2008	$837,010	$758,200

A disclosure note accompanying the financial statements reported the following ($ in thousands):

	Year Ended	
	2009	2008
	(In thousands)	
Trade accounts receivable, net:		
Receivables	$858,001	$781,514
Less: allowance for doubtful accounts	(8,863)	(8,915)
Less: reserve for product returns	(12,128)	(14,399)
Trade accounts receivable, net:	$837,010	$758,200

Assume that the company reported bad debt expense in 2009 of $1,500 and had products returned for credit totaling $3,155 (sales price). Net sales for 2009 were $6,149,800 (all numbers in thousands).

Required:
1. What is the amount of accounts receivable due from customers at the end of 2009 and 2008?
2. What amount of accounts receivable did Symantec write off during 2009?
3. What is the amount of Symantec's gross sales for the 2009 fiscal year?
4. Assuming that all sales are made on a credit basis, what is the amount of cash Symantec collected from customers during the 2009 fiscal year?

P 7–6

Notes receivable; solving for unknowns

● LO7

Cypress Oil Company's December 31, 2011, balance sheet listed $645,000 of notes receivable and $16,000 of interest receivable included in current assets. The following notes make up the notes receivable balance:

Note 1	Dated 8/31/11, principal of $300,000 and interest at 10% due on 2/28/12.
Note 2	Dated 6/30/11, principal of $150,000 and interest due 3/31/12.
Note 3	$200,000 face value noninterest-bearing note dated 9/30/11, due 3/31/12. Note was issued in exchange for merchandise.

The company records adjusting entries only at year-end. There were no other notes receivable outstanding during 2011.

Required:

1. Determine the rate used to discount the noninterest-bearing note.

2. Determine the explicit interest rate on Note 2.

3. What is the amount of interest revenue that appears in the company's 2011 income statement related to these notes?

P 7–7

Factoring versus assigning of accounts receivable

● LO8

Lonergan Company occasionally uses its accounts receivable to obtain immediate cash. At the end of June 2011, the company had accounts receivable of $780,000. Lonergan needs approximately $500,000 to capitalize on a unique investment opportunity. On July 1, 2011, a local bank offers Lonergan the following two alternatives:

a. Borrow $500,000, sign a note payable, and assign the entire receivable balance as collateral. At the end of each month, a remittance will be made to the bank that equals the amount of receivables collected plus 12% interest on the unpaid balance of the note at the beginning of the period.

b. Transfer $550,000 of specific receivables to the bank without recourse. The bank will charge a 2% finance charge on the amount of receivables transferred. The bank will collect the receivables directly from customers. The sale criteria are met.

Required:

1. Prepare the journal entries that would be recorded on July 1 for each of the alternatives.

2. Assuming that 80% of all June 30 receivables are collected during July, prepare the necessary journal entries to record the collection and the remittance to the bank.

3. For each alternative, explain any required note disclosures that would be included in the July 31, 2011, financial statements.

P 7–8

Factoring of accounts receivable; without recourse

● LO8

Samson Wholesale Beverage Company regularly factors its accounts receivable with the Milpitas Finance Company. On April 30, 2011, the company transferred $800,000 of accounts receivable to Milpitas. The transfer was made without recourse. Milpitas remits 90% of the factored amount and retains 10%. When Milpitas collects the receivables, it remits to Samson the retained amount less a 4% fee (4% of the total factored amount). Samson estimates the fair value of the last 10% of its receivables to be $60,000.

Required:

Prepare journal entries for Samson Wholesale Beverage for the transfer of accounts receivable on April 30 assuming the sale criteria are met.

P 7–9

Cash and accounts receivable under IFRS

● LO2 LO5 LO8 LO10

The following facts apply to Walken Company during December 2011:

a. Walken began December with an accounts receivable balance (net of bad debts) of €25,000.

b. Walken had credit sales of €85,000.

c. Walken had cash collections of €30,000.

d. Walken factored €20,000 of net accounts receivable with Reliable Factor Company, transferring all risks and rewards associated with the receivable, and otherwise meeting all criteria necessary to qualify for treating the transfer of receivables as a sale.

e. Walken factored €15,000 of net accounts receivable with Dependable Factor Company, retaining all risks and rewards associated with the receivable, and otherwise meeting all criteria necessary to qualify for treating the transfer of receivables as a sale.

f. Walken did not recognize any additional bad debts expense, and had no write-offs of bad debts during the month.

g. At December 31, 2011, Walken had a balance of €40,000 of cash at M&V Bank and an overdraft of (€5000) at First National Bank. (That cash balance includes any effects on cash of the other transactions described in this problem.)

Required:

Prepare the cash and accounts receivable lines of the current assets section of Walken's balance sheet, as of December 31, 2011.

P 7–10
Miscellaneous
receivable
transactions

● LO3 LO4 LO7
LO8

Evergreen Company sells lawn and garden products to wholesalers. The company's fiscal year-end is December 31. During 2011, the following transactions related to receivables occurred:

Feb. 28	Sold merchandise to Lennox, Inc. for $10,000 and accepted a 10%, 7-month note. 10% is an appropriate rate for this type of note.
Mar. 31	Sold merchandise to Maddox Co. and accepted a noninterest-bearing note with a discount rate of 10%. The $8,000 payment is due on March 31, 2012.
Apr. 3	Sold merchandise to Carr Co. for $7,000 with terms 2/10, n/30. Evergreen uses the gross method to account for cash discounts.
11	Collected the entire amount due from Carr Co.
17	A customer returned merchandise costing $3,200. Evergreen reduced the customer's receivable balance by $5,000, the sales price of the merchandise. Sales returns are recorded by the company as they occur.
30	Transferred receivables of $50,000 to a factor without recourse. The factor charged Evergreen a 1% finance charge on the receivables transferred. The sale criteria are met.
June 30	Discounted the Lennox, Inc., note at the bank. The bank's discount rate is 12%. The note was discounted without recourse.
Aug. 31	Lennox, Inc., paid the note amount plus interest to the bank.

Required:
1. Prepare the necessary journal entries for Evergreen for each of the above dates. For transactions involving the sale of merchandise, ignore the entry for the cost of goods sold (round all calculations to the nearest dollar).
2. Prepare any necessary adjusting entries at December 31, 2011. Adjusting entries are only recorded at year-end (round all calculations to the nearest dollar).
3. Prepare a schedule showing the effect of the journal entries in requirements 1 and 2 on 2011 income before taxes.

P 7–11
Discounting a note
receivable

● LO7

Descriptors are provided below for six situations involving notes receivable being discounted at a bank. In each case, the maturity date of the note is December 31, 2011, and the principal and interest are due at maturity. For each, determine the proceeds received from the bank on discounting the note.

Note	Note Face Value	Date of Note	Interest Rate	Date Discounted	Discount Rate
1	$50,000	3/31/11	8%	6/30/11	10%
2	50,000	3/31/11	8	9/30/11	10
3	50,000	3/31/11	8	9/30/11	12
4	80,000	6/30/11	6	10/31/11	10
5	80,000	6/30/11	6	10/31/11	12
6	80,000	6/30/11	6	11/30/11	10

P 7–12
Accounts and
notes receivable;
discounting a
note receivable;
receivables
turnover ratio

● LO5 LO6 LO7
LO8 LO9

Chamberlain Enterprises Inc. reported the following receivables in its December 31, 2011, year-end balance sheet:

Current assets:
Accounts receivable, net of $24,000 in allowance for uncollectible accounts	$218,000
Interest receivable	6,800
Notes receivable	260,000

Additional information:
1. The notes receivable account consists of two notes, a $60,000 note and a $200,000 note. The $60,000 note is dated October 31, 2011, with principal and interest payable on October 31, 2012. The $200,000 note is dated June 30, 2011, with principal and 6% interest payable on June 30, 2012.
2. During 2012, sales revenue totaled $1,340,000, $1,280,000 cash was collected from customers, and $22,000 in accounts receivable were written off. All sales are made on a credit basis. Bad debt expense is recorded at year-end by adjusting the allowance account to an amount equal to 10% of year-end accounts receivable.
3. On March 31, 2012, the $200,000 note receivable was discounted at the Bank of Commerce. The bank's discount rate is 8%. Chamberlain accounts for the discounting as a sale.

Required:
1. In addition to sales revenue, what revenue and expense amounts related to receivables will appear in Chamberlain's 2012 income statement?
2. What amounts will appear in the 2012 year-end balance sheet for accounts receivable?
3. Calculate the receivables turnover ratio for 2012.

P 7–13
Bank reconciliation
and adjusting
entries; cash and
cash equivalents

● Appendix 7A

The bank statement for the checking account of Management Systems Inc. (MSI) showed a December 31, 2011, balance of $14,632.12. Information that might be useful in preparing a bank reconciliation is as follows:

a. Outstanding checks were $1,320.25.

b. The December 31, 2011, cash receipts of $575 were not deposited in the bank until January 2, 2012.

c. One check written in payment of rent for $246 was correctly recorded by the bank but was recorded by MSI as a $264 disbursement.

d. In accordance with prior authorization, the bank withdrew $450 directly from the checking account as payment on a mortgage note payable. The interest portion of that payment was $350. MSI has made no entry to record the automatic payment.

e. Bank service charges of $14 were listed on the bank statement.

f. A deposit of $875 was recorded by the bank on December 13, but it did not belong to MSI. The deposit should have been made to the checking account of MIS, Inc.

g. The bank statement included a charge of $85 for an NSF check. The check was returned with the bank statement and the company will seek payment from the customer.

h. MSI maintains a $200 petty cash fund that was appropriately reimbursed at the end of December.

i. According to instructions from MSI on December 30, the bank withdrew $10,000 from the account and purchased U.S. Treasury bills for MSI. MSI recorded the transaction in its books on December 31 when it received notice from the bank. Half of the Treasury bills mature in two months and the other half in six months.

Required:

1. Prepare a bank reconciliation for the MSI checking account at December 31, 2011. You will have to compute the balance per books.

2. Prepare any necessary adjusting journal entries indicated.

3. What amount would MSI report as cash and cash equivalents in the current asset section of the December 31, 2011, balance sheet?

P 7–14
Bank reconciliation
and adjusting
entries

● Appendix 7A

El Gato Painting Company maintains a checking account at American Bank. Bank statements are prepared at the end of each month. The November 30, 2011, reconciliation of the bank balance is as follows:

Balance per bank, November 30		$3,231
Add: Deposits outstanding		1,200
Less: Checks outstanding		
#363	$123	
#365	201	
#380	56	
#381	86	
#382	340	(806)
Adjusted balance per bank, November 30		$3,625

The company's general ledger checking account showed the following for December:

Balance, December 1	$ 3,625
Receipts	42,650
Disbursements	(41,853)
Balance, December 31	$ 4,422

The December bank statement contained the following information:

Balance, December 1	$ 3,231
Deposits	43,000
Checks processed	(41,918)
Service charges	(22)
NSF checks	(440)
Balance, December 31	$ 3,851

The checks that were processed by the bank in December include all of the outstanding checks at the end of November except for check #365. In addition, there are some December checks that had not been processed by the bank by the end of the month. Also, you discover that check #411 for $320 was correctly recorded by the bank but was incorrectly recorded on the books as a $230 disbursement for advertising expense. Included in the bank's deposits is a $1,300 deposit incorrectly credited to the company's account. The deposit should have been posted to the credit of the Los Gatos Company. The NSF checks have not been redeposited and the company will seek payment from the customers involved.

Required:
1. Prepare a bank reconciliation for the El Gato checking account at December 31, 2011.
2. Prepare any necessary adjusting journal entries indicated.

P 7–15
Impairment of securities available-for-sale; troubled debt restructuring

● Appendix 7B

Rothschild Chair Company, Inc., was indebted to First Lincoln Bank under a $20 million, 10% unsecured note. The note was signed January 1, 2005, and was due December 31, 2014. Annual interest was last paid on December 31, 2009. At January 1, 2011, Rothschild Chair Company was experiencing severe financial difficulties and negotiated a restructuring of the terms of the debt agreement.

Required:
Prepare all journal entries by First Lincoln Bank to record the restructuring and any remaining transactions, for current and future years, relating to the debt under each of the independent circumstances below:
1. First Lincoln Bank agreed to settle the debt in exchange for land having a fair value of $16 million but carried on Rothschild Chair Company's books at $13 million.
2. First Lincoln Bank agreed to (a) forgive the interest accrued from last year, (b) reduce the remaining four interest payments to $1 million each, and (c) reduce the principal to $15 million.
3. First Lincoln Bank agreed to defer all payments (including accrued interest) until the maturity date and accept $27,775,000 at that time in settlement of the debt.

BROADEN YOUR PERSPECTIVE

Apply your critical-thinking ability to the knowledge you've gained. These cases will provide you an opportunity to develop your research, analysis, judgment, and communication skills. You also will work with other students, integrate what you've learned, apply it in real world situations, and consider its global and ethical ramifications. This practice will broaden your knowledge and further develop your decision-making abilities.

**Judgment
Case 7–1**
Accounts and notes receivable

● LO5 LO6 LO8

Magrath Company has an operating cycle of less than one year and provides credit terms for all of its customers. On April 1, 2011, the company factored, without recourse, some of its accounts receivable. Magrath transferred the receivables to a financial institution, and will have no further association with the receivables.

Magrath uses the allowance method to account for uncollectible accounts. During 2011, some accounts were written off as uncollectible and other accounts previously written off as uncollectible were collected.

Required:
1. How should Magrath account for and report the accounts receivable factored on April 1, 2011? Why is this accounting treatment appropriate?
2. How should Magrath account for the collection of the accounts previously written off as uncollectible?
3. What are the two basic approaches to estimating uncollectible accounts under the allowance method? What is the rationale for each approach?

(AICPA adapted)

**Communication
Case 7–2**
Uncollectible accounts

● LO5

You have been hired as a consultant by a parts manufacturing firm to provide advice as to the proper accounting methods the company should use in some key areas. In the area of receivables, the company president does not understand your recommendation to use the allowance method for uncollectible accounts. She stated, "Financial statements should be based on objective data rather than the guesswork required for the allowance method. Besides, since my uncollectibles are fairly constant from period to period, with significant variations occurring infrequently, the direct write-off method is just as good as the allowance method."

Required:
Draft a one-page response in the form of a memo to the president in support of your recommendation for the company to use the allowance method.

**Judgment
Case 7–3**
Accounts receivable

● LO3 LO7 LO8

Hogan Company uses the net method of accounting for sales discounts. Hogan offers trade discounts to various groups of buyers.

On August 1, 2011, Hogan factored some accounts receivable on a without recourse basis. Hogan incurred a finance charge.

Hogan also has some notes receivable bearing an appropriate rate of interest. The principal and total interest are due at maturity. The notes were received on October 1, 2011, and mature on September 30, 2012. Hogan's operating cycle is less than one year.

Required:

1. a. Using the net method, how should Hogan account for the sales discounts at the date of sale? What is the rationale for the amount recorded as sales under the net method?

   b. Using the net method, what is the effect on Hogan's sales revenues and net income when customers do not take the sales discounts?

2. What is the effect of trade discounts on sales revenues and accounts receivable? Why?

3. How should Hogan account for the accounts receivable factored on August 1, 2011? Why?

4. How should Hogan report the effects of the interest-bearing notes receivable in its December 31, 2011, balance sheet and its income statement for the year ended December 31, 2011? Why?

(AICPA adapted)

Ethics Case 7–4
Uncollectible
accounts
● LO5

You have recently been hired as the assistant controller for Stanton Industries, a large, publicly held manufacturing company. Your immediate superior is the controller who, in turn, is responsible to the vice president of finance.

The controller has assigned you the task of preparing the year-end adjusting entries. In the receivables area, you have prepared an aging of accounts receivable and have applied historical percentages to the balances of each of the age categories. The analysis indicates that an appropriate balance for the allowance for uncollectible accounts is $180,000. The existing balance in the allowance account prior to any adjusting entry is a $20,000 credit balance.

After showing your analysis to the controller, he tells you to change the aging category of a large account from over 120 days to current status and to prepare a new invoice to the customer with a revised date that agrees with the new aging category. This will change the required allowance for uncollectible accounts from $180,000 to $135,000. Tactfully, you ask the controller for an explanation for the change and he tells you "We need the extra income, the bottom line is too low."

Required:

1. What is the effect on income before taxes of the change requested by the controller?

2. Discuss the ethical dilemma you face. Consider your options and responsibilities along with the possible consequences of any action you might take.

**Judgment
Case 7–5**
Internal control
● LO1

For each of the following independent situations, indicate the apparent internal control weaknesses and suggest alternative procedures to eliminate the weaknesses.

1. John Smith is the petty cash custodian. John approves all requests for payment out of the $200 fund, which is replenished at the end of each month. At the end of each month, John submits a list of all accounts and amounts to be charged and a check is written to him for the total amount. John is the only person ever to tally the fund.

2. All of the company's cash disbursements are made by check. Each check must be supported by an approved voucher, which is in turn supported by the appropriate invoice and, for purchases, a receiving document. The vouchers are approved by Dean Leiser, the chief accountant, after reviewing the supporting documentation. Betty Hanson prepares the checks for Leiser's signature. Leiser also maintains the company's check register (the cash disbursements journal) and reconciles the bank account at the end of each month.

3. Fran Jones opens the company's mail and makes a listing of all checks and cash received from customers. A copy of the list is sent to Jerry McDonald who maintains the general ledger accounts. Fran prepares and makes the daily deposit at the bank. Fran also maintains the subsidiary ledger for accounts receivable, which is used to generate monthly statements to customers.

**Real World
Case 7–6**
Receivables; bad
debts
● LO5

Real World Financials

EDGAR, the Electronic Data Gathering, Analysis, and Retrieval system, performs automated collection, validation, indexing, and forwarding of submissions by companies and others who are required by law to file forms with the U.S. Securities and Exchange Commission (SEC). All publicly traded domestic companies use EDGAR to make the majority of their filings. (Some foreign companies file voluntarily.) Form 10-K or 10-KSB, which include the annual report, is required to be filed on EDGAR. The SEC makes this information available on the Internet.

Required:

1. Access EDGAR on the Internet. The web address is **www.sec.gov**.

2. Search for **Avon Products, Inc.** Access the 10-K filing for the most recent fiscal year. Search or scroll to find the financial statements.

3. Answer the following questions related to the company's accounts receivable and bad debts:

   a. What is the amount of gross trade accounts receivable at the end of the year?

   b. What is the amount of bad debt expense for the year? (*Hint:* check the statement of cash flows.)

   c. Determine the amount of actual bad debt write-offs made during the year. Assume that all bad debts relate only to trade accounts receivable.

   d. Using only information from the balance sheets, income statements, and your answer to requirement 3(c), determine the amount of cash collected from customers during the year. Assume that all sales are made on a credit basis, that the company provides no allowances for sales returns, that no previously written-off receivables were collected, and that all sales relate to trade accounts receivable.

Integrating Case 7–7

Change in estimate of bad debts

● LO5

McLaughlin Corporation uses the allowance method to account for bad debts. At the end of the company's fiscal year, accounts receivable are analyzed and the allowance for uncollectible accounts is adjusted. At the end of 2011, the company reported the following amounts:

Accounts receivable	$10,850,000
Less: Allowance for uncollectible accounts	(450,000)
Accounts receivable, net	$10,400,000

In 2012, it was determined that $1,825,000 of year-end 2011 receivables had to be written off as uncollectible. This was due in part to the fact that Hughes Corporation, a long-standing customer that had always paid its bills, unexpectedly declared bankruptcy in 2012. Hughes owed McLaughlin $1,400,000. At the end of 2011, none of the Hughes receivable was considered uncollectible.

Required:

Describe the appropriate accounting treatment and required disclosures for McLaughlin's underestimation of bad debts at the end of 2011.

Analysis Case 7–8

Financing with receivables

● LO8

Financial institutions have developed a wide variety of methods for companies to use their receivables to obtain immediate cash. The methods differ with respect to which rights and risks are retained by the transferor (the original holder of the receivable) and those passed on to the transferee (the new holder, usually a financial institution).

Required:

1. Describe the alternative methods available for companies to use their receivables to obtain immediate cash.
2. Discuss the alternative accounting treatments for these methods.

Real World Case 7–9

Financing with receivables

● LO5 LO8 LO10

Search on the Internet for the 2008 annual report for **Sanofi-Aventis**. Find the accounts receivable footnote.

Required:

1. Sanofi-Aventis subtracts "impairment" from the gross value of accounts receivable to obtain the net value. Interpret the impairment of (€88) in 2008 in terms of how that amount would typically be described in U.S. GAAP.
2. To what extent does Sanofi-Aventis factor or securitize accounts receivable? How do you know?
3. Assume that Sanofi-Aventis decided to increase the extent to which it securitizes its accounts receivable, changing to a policy of securitizing accounts receivable immediately upon making a sale and treating the securitization as a sale of accounts receivable. Indicate the likely effect of that change in policy on:
   a. Accounts receivable in the period of the change.
   b. Cash flow from operations in the period of the change.
   c. Accounts receivable in subsequent periods.
   d. Cash flow from operations in subsequent periods.
4. Given your answers to requirement 3, could a company change the extent to which it factors or securitizes receivables to create one-time changes in its cash flow? Explain.

Research Case 7–10

Locate and extract relevant information and authoritative support for a financial reporting issue; financing with receivables

● LO8

You are spending the summer working for a local wholesale furniture company, Samson Furniture, Inc. The company is considering a proposal from a local financial institution, Old Reliant Financial, to factor Samson's receivables. The company controller is unfamiliar with the prevailing GAAP that deals with accounting for the transfer of financial assets and has asked you to do some research. The controller wants to make sure the arrangement with the financial institution is structured in such a way as to allow the factoring to be accounted for as a sale.

Old Reliant has offered to factor all of the company's receivables on a "without recourse" basis. Old Reliant will remit to Samson 90% of the factored amount, collect the receivables from Samson's customers, and retain the remaining 10% until all of the receivables have been collected. When Old Reliant collects all of the receivables, it will remit to Samson the retained amount, less a 4% fee (4% of the total factored amount).

Required:

1. Explain the meaning of the term *without recourse.*
2. Access the relevant authoritative literature on accounting for the transfer of financial assets using the FASB's Codification Research System. You might gain access at the FASB website (**www.fasb.org**), from your school library, or some other source. What conditions must be met for a transfer of receivables to be accounted for as a sale (or in accounting terms, "derecognized")? What is the specific citation that Samson would rely on in applying that accounting treatment?
3. Assuming that the conditions for treatment as a sale are met, prepare Samson's journal entry to record the factoring of $400,000 of receivables. Assume that the fair value of the last 10% of Samson's receivables is equal to $25,000.

4. An agreement that both entitles and obligates the transferor, Samson, to repurchase or redeem transferred assets from the transferee, Old Reliant, maintains the transferor's effective control over those assets and the transfer is accounted for as a secured borrowing, not a sale, if and only if what conditions are met?

Analysis Case 7–11
Compare receivables management using ratios
● LO9

Real World Financials

The table below contains selected financial information included in the 2009 financial statements of **Del Monte Foods Co.** and **Smithfield Foods Inc.**

| | ($ in millions) | | | |
| | Del Monte | | Smithfield | |
	2009	**2008**	**2009**	**2008**
Balance sheet:				
Accounts receivable, net	$ 189	$ 277	$ 595	$ 738
Income statement:				
Net sales	3,627	3,180	12,488	11,351

Required:

1. Calculate the 2009 receivables turnover ratio and average collection period for both companies. Evaluate the management of each company's investment in receivables.

2. Obtain annual reports from three corporations in the same primary industry and compare the management of each company's investment in receivables.
   Note: You can obtain copies of annual reports from your library, from friends who are shareholders, from the investor relations department of the corporations, from a friendly stockbroker, or from EDGAR (Electronic Data Gathering, Analysis, and Retrieval) on the Internet (**www.sec.gov**).

Analysis Case 7–12
Reporting cash and receivables
● LO2 LO5

Refer to the financial statements and related disclosure notes of **Dell Inc.** included with all new copies of the text.

Required:

1. What is Dell's policy for designating investments as cash equivalents?

2. At the end of the 2009 fiscal year, how much cash was included in cash and cash equivalents?

3. Determine the gross amount of accounts receivable outstanding at January 30, 2009, and February 1, 2008.

BRITISH AIRWAYS CASE

British Airways, Plc. (BA), a U.K. company, prepares its financial statements according to International Financial Reporting Standards. BA's annual report for the year ended March 31, 2009, which includes financial statements and disclosure notes, is included with all new textbooks and can be found at **www.britishairways.com**. When answering questions, focus on BA's "Group" financial information (which is equivalent to "Consolidated" under U.S. GAAP).

Required:

Examine BA's note 23, dealing with trade receivables. Do any aspects of that note appear unusual to you from the perspective of U.S. GAAP? Explain.

Inventories: Measurement

| | | | | | | | | | | | | | | | | | | | | | | | | | | | | | | | | | | | | | | | | | | | | | | | | | | |

The next two chapters continue our study of assets by investigating the measurement and reporting issues involving inventories and the related expense—cost of goods sold. Inventory refers to the assets a company (1) intends to sell in the normal course of business, (2) has in production for future sale, or (3) uses currently in the production of goods to be sold.

After studying this chapter, you should be able to:

- **LO1** Explain the difference between a perpetual inventory system and a periodic inventory system. (page 399)
- **LO2** Explain which physical quantities of goods should be included in inventory. (page 400)
- **LO3** Determine the expenditures that should be included in the cost of inventory. (page 401)
- **LO4** Differentiate between the specific identification, FIFO, LIFO, and average cost methods used to determine the cost of ending inventory and cost of goods sold. (page 404)
- **LO5** Discuss the factors affecting a company's choice of inventory method. (page 411)
- **LO6** Understand supplemental LIFO disclosures and the effect of LIFO liquidations on net income. (page 413)
- **LO7** Calculate the key ratios used by analysts to monitor a company's investment in inventories. (page 419)
- **LO8** Determine ending inventory using the dollar-value LIFO inventory method. (page 421)
- **LO9** Discuss the primary difference between U.S. GAAP and IFRS with respect to determining the cost of inventory. (page 411)

FINANCIAL REPORTING CASE

Inventory Measurement at ConocoPhillips

A recent article in the financial section of your local newspaper reported record profits generated by U.S. oil companies. When you showed the article to a friend, he laughed, "I'll bet U.S. oil companies use LIFO to value their inventories. That way they can report lower profits than they would if using another inventory method. If the profits are too high it could cause the government to jump in and impose an excess profits tax as it did in the 1980s." Curiosity aroused, you downloaded from the Internet a recent quarterly report of ConocoPhillips, one of the large U.S. oil companies. The report included the following disclosure:

Note 4—Inventories (in part)

Inventories consisted of the following ($ in millions):

	March 31 2009	December 31 2008
Crude oil and petroleum products	$5,573	$4,232
Materials, supplies, and other	907	863
Total inventories	$6,480	$5,095

Inventories valued on a LIFO basis totaled $5,378 million and $3,939 million at March 31, 2009, and December 31, 2008, respectively. The remaining inventories were valued under various methods, including FIFO and weighted average. The excess of current replacement cost over LIFO cost of inventories amounted to $2,400 million and $1,959 million at March 31, 2009, and December 31, 2008, respectively. The replacement cost of inventories approximates FIFO cost.

By the time you finish this chapter, you should be able to respond appropriately to the questions posed in this case. Compare your response to the solution provided at the end of the chapter.

QUESTIONS ///

1. What inventory methods does ConocoPhillips use to value its inventories? Is this permissible according to GAAP? (page 410)

2. What is the purpose of disclosing the difference between the reported LIFO inventory amounts and the replacement cost, which is equivalent to a FIFO basis? (page 412)

3. Is your friend correct in his assertion that, by using LIFO, ConocoPhillips was able to report lower profits for the first quarter of 2009? (page 418)

RECORDING AND MEASURING INVENTORY

Inventory refers to the assets a company (1) intends to sell in the normal course of business, (2) has in production for future sale (work in process), or (3) uses currently in the production of goods to be sold (raw materials). The computers produced by **Apple Inc.** that are intended for sale to customers are inventory, as are partially completed components in the assembly lines of Apple's Cupertino facility, and the computer chips and memory modules that will go into computers produced later. The computers *used* by Apple to maintain its accounting system, however, are classified and accounted for as plant and equipment. Similarly, the stocks and bonds a securities dealer holds for sale are inventory, whereas Apple would classify the securities it holds as investments.

Proper accounting for inventories is essential for manufacturing, wholesale, and retail companies (enterprises that earn revenue by selling goods). Inventory usually is one of the most valuable assets listed in the balance sheet for these firms. Cost of goods sold—the expense recorded when inventory is sold—typically is the largest expense in the income statement. For example, a recent balance sheet for **Sara Lee Corporation** reported inventories of $1,028 million, which represented 11% of total assets. The company's income statement reported cost of goods sold of $8,098 million representing 66% of operating expenses.

In this and the following chapter we discuss the measurement and reporting issues involving inventory, an asset, and the related expense, cost of goods sold. Inventory represents *quantities* of goods acquired, manufactured, or in the process of being manufactured. The inventory amount in the balance sheet at the end of an accounting period represents the cost of the inventory still on hand, and cost of goods sold in the income statement represents the cost of the inventory sold during the period. The historical cost principle and matching principle offer guidance for measuring inventory and cost of goods sold, but as we will see in this and the next chapter, it's usually difficult to measure inventory (cost of goods sold) at the exact cost of the actual physical quantities on hand (sold). Fortunately, accountants can use one of several techniques to approximate the desired result and satisfy our measurement objectives.

Types of Inventory

Merchandising Inventory

Wholesale and retail companies purchase goods that are primarily in finished form. These companies are intermediaries in the process of moving goods from the manufacturer to the end-user. They often are referred to as merchandising companies and their inventory as merchandise inventory. *The cost of merchandise inventory includes the purchase price plus any other costs necessary to get the goods in condition and location for sale.* We discuss the concept of condition and location and the types of costs that typically constitute inventory later in this chapter.

Manufacturing Inventories

Unlike merchandising companies, manufacturing companies actually produce the goods they sell to wholesalers, retailers, or other manufacturers. Inventory for a manufacturer consists of (1) raw materials, (2) work in process, and (3) finished goods. **Raw materials** represent the cost of components purchased from other manufacturers that will become part of the finished product. For example, Apple's raw materials inventory includes semiconductors, circuit boards, plastic, and glass that go into the production of personal computers.

Work-in-process inventory refers to the products that are not yet complete. The cost of work in process includes the cost of raw materials used in production, the cost of labor that can be directly traced to the goods in process, and an allocated portion of other manufacturing costs, called *manufacturing overhead.* Overhead costs include electricity and other utility costs to operate the manufacturing facility, depreciation of manufacturing equipment, and many other manufacturing costs that cannot be directly linked to the production of specific goods. Once the manufacturing process is completed, these costs that have accumulated in work in process are transferred to **finished goods.**

Manufacturing companies generally disclose, either in a note or directly in the balance sheet, the dollar amount of each inventory category. For example, **Dell Inc.**'s note disclosure of inventory categories was shown on page 118. **Sara Lee Corporation** reports inventory categories directly in the balance sheet, as illustrated in Graphic 8–1.

GRAPHIC 8–1

Inventories
Disclosure—Sara Lee
Corporation

Real World Financials

Balance Sheet		
	($ in millions)	
	2009	**2008**
Current assets:		
Inventories		
Finished goods	$ 660	$ 775
Work in process	38	43
Materials and supplies	330	402
Total	$1,028	$1,220

The inventory accounts and the cost flows for a typical manufacturing company are shown using T-accounts in Graphic 8–2. The costs of raw materials used, direct labor applied, and manufacturing overhead applied flow into work in process and then to finished goods. When the goods are sold, the cost of those goods flows to cost of goods sold.

GRAPHIC 8–2

Inventory Components
and Cost Flow for
a Manufacturing
Company

**The costs of inventory
units follow their
physical movement
from one stage of
activity to another.**

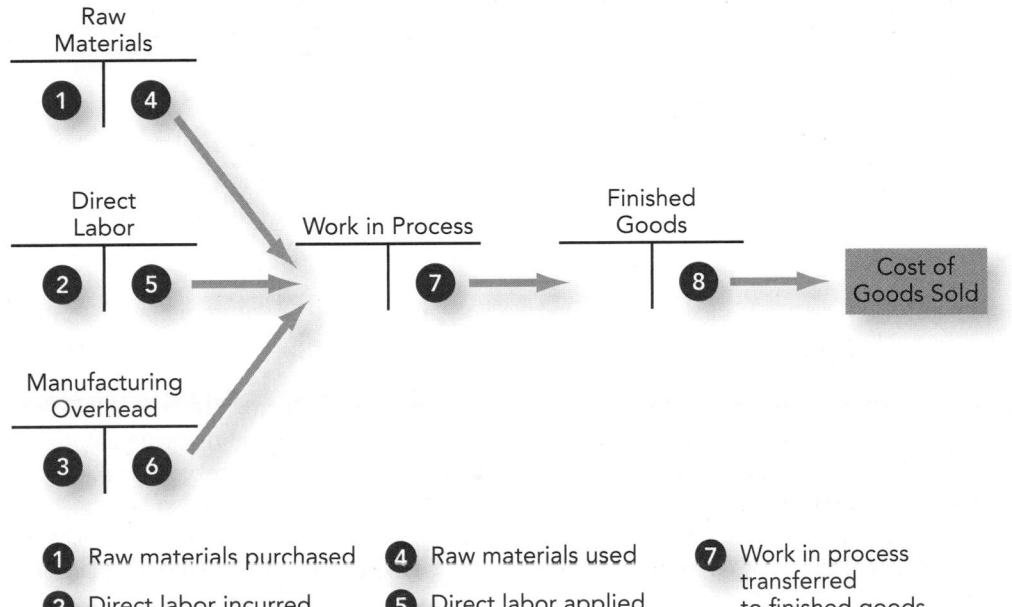

1 Raw materials purchased   **4** Raw materials used   **7** Work in process transferred to finished goods

2 Direct labor incurred   **5** Direct labor applied

3 Manufacturing overhead incurred   **6** Manufacturing overhead applied   **8** Finished goods sold

We focus in this text primarily on merchandising companies (wholesalers and retailers). Still, most of the accounting principles and procedures discussed here also apply to manufacturing companies. The unique problems involved with accumulating the direct costs of raw materials and labor and with allocating manufacturing overhead are addressed in managerial and cost accounting textbooks.

Perpetual Inventory System

Two accounting systems are used to record transactions involving inventory: the **perpetual inventory system** and the **periodic inventory system.** The perpetual system was introduced in Chapter 2. The system is aptly termed perpetual because the account *inventory* is continually adjusted for each change in inventory, whether it's caused by a purchase, a sale,

*A perpetual inventory
system continuously
records both changes
in inventory quantity
and inventory cost.*

or a return of merchandise by the company to its supplier (a *purchase return* for the buyer, a *sales return* for the seller).[1] The cost of goods sold account, along with the inventory account, is adjusted each time goods are sold or are returned by a customer. This concept is applied to the Lothridge Wholesale Beverage Company for which inventory information is provided in Illustration 8–1. This hypothetical company also will be used in the next several illustrations.

ILLUSTRATION 8–1 Perpetual Inventory System	The Lothridge Wholesale Beverage Company purchases soft drinks from producers and then sells them to retailers. The company begins 2011 with merchandise inventory of $120,000 on hand. During 2011 additional merchandise is purchased on account at a cost of $600,000. Sales for the year, all on account, totaled $820,000. The cost of the soft drinks sold is $540,000. Lothridge uses the perpetual inventory system to keep track of both inventory quantities and inventory costs.

The following summary journal entries record the inventory transactions for the Lothridge Company:

2011

Inventory	600,000	
Accounts payable		600,000
To record the purchase of merchandise inventory.		

2011

Accounts receivable	820,000	
Sales revenue		820,000
To record sales on account.		
Cost of goods sold	540,000	
Inventory		540,000
To record the cost of sales.		

An important feature of a perpetual system is that it is designed to track inventory quantities from their acquisition to their sale. If the system is accurate, it allows management to determine how many goods are on hand on any date without having to take a physical count. However, physical counts of inventory usually are made anyway, either at the end of the fiscal year or on a sample basis throughout the year, to verify that the perpetual system is correctly tracking quantities. Differences between the quantity of inventory determined by the physical count and the quantity of inventory according to the perpetual system could be caused by system errors, theft, breakage, or spoilage. In addition to keeping up with inventory, a perpetual system also directly determines how many items are sold during a period.

You are probably familiar with the scanning mechanisms used at grocery store checkout counters. The scanners not only record the sale on the cash register but also can be used to track the sale of merchandise for inventory management purposes. For a company to use the perpetual inventory system to record inventory and cost of goods sold transactions, merchandise cost data also must be included on the system. That is, when merchandise is purchased/sold, the system must be able to record not only the addition/reduction in inventory quantity but also the addition/reduction in the *cost* of inventory.

> **A perpetual inventory system tracks both inventory quantities and inventory costs.**

Periodic Inventory System

> **A *periodic inventory system* adjusts inventory and records cost of goods sold only at the end of each reporting period.**

A **periodic inventory system** is not designed to track either the quantity or cost of merchandise. The merchandise inventory account balance is not adjusted as purchases and sales are made but only periodically at the end of a reporting period. A physical count of the period's ending inventory is made and costs are assigned to the quantities determined. Merchandise purchases, purchase returns, purchase discounts, and freight-in (purchases plus freight-in less returns and discounts equals net purchases) are recorded in temporary accounts and the period's cost of goods sold is determined at the end of the period by combining the temporary accounts with the inventory account:

> **Cost of goods sold equation**

Beginning inventory + Net purchases − Ending inventory = Cost of goods sold

---

[1]We discussed accounting for sales returns in Chapter 7.

The cost of goods sold equation assumes that all inventory quantities not on hand at the end of the period were sold. This may not be the case if inventory items were either damaged or stolen. If damaged and stolen inventory are identified, they must be removed from beginning inventory or purchases before calculating cost of goods sold and then classified as a separate expense item.

Illustration 8–2 looks at the periodic system using the Lothridge Wholesale Beverage Company example.

The Lothridge Wholesale Beverage Company purchases soft drinks from producers and then sells them to retailers. The company began 2011 with merchandise inventory of $120,000 on hand. During 2011 additional merchandise was purchased on account at a cost of $600,000. Sales for the year, all on account, totaled $820,000. Lothridge uses a periodic inventory system. A physical count determined the cost of inventory at the end of the year to be $180,000.	**ILLUSTRATION 8–2** Periodic Inventory System

The following journal entries summarize the inventory transactions for 2011. Of course, each individual transaction would actually be recorded as incurred:

2011
Purchases	600,000	
Accounts payable		600,000
To record the purchase of merchandise inventory.		

2011
Accounts receivable	820,000	
Sales revenue		820,000
To record sales on account.		
No entry is recorded for the cost of inventory sold.		

Because cost of goods sold isn't determined automatically and continually by the periodic system, it must be determined indirectly after a physical inventory count. Cost of goods sold for 2011 is determined as follows:

Beginning inventory	$120,000
Plus: Purchases	600,000
Cost of goods available for sale	720,000
Less: Ending inventory (per physical count)	(180,000)
Cost of goods sold	$540,000

The following journal entry combines the components of cost of goods sold into a single expense account and updates the balance in the inventory account:

December 31, 2011
Cost of goods sold	540,000	
Inventory (ending)...	180,000	
Inventory (beginning)..		120,000
Purchases		600,000
To adjust inventory, close the purchases account, and record cost of goods sold.		

This entry adjusts the inventory account to the correct period-end amount, closes the temporary purchases account, and records the residual as cost of goods sold. Now let's compare the two inventory accounting systems.

A Comparison of the Perpetual and Periodic Inventory Systems

Beginning inventory plus net purchases during the period is the cost of goods available for sale. The main difference between a perpetual and a periodic system is that the periodic system allocates cost of goods available for sale between ending inventory and cost of goods

● LO1

sold (periodically) *at the end of the period.* In contrast, the perpetual system performs this allocation by decreasing inventory and increasing cost of goods sold (perpetually) *each time goods are sold.*

The impact on the financial statements of choosing one system over the other generally is not significant. The choice between the two approaches usually is motivated by management control considerations as well as the comparative costs of implementation. Perpetual systems can provide more information about the dollar amounts of inventory levels on a continuous basis. They also facilitate the preparation of interim financial statements by providing fairly accurate information without the necessity of a physical count of inventory.

On the other hand, a perpetual system may be more expensive to implement than a periodic system. This is particularly true for inventories consisting of large numbers of low-cost items. Perpetual systems are more workable with inventories of high-cost items such as construction equipment or automobiles. However, with the help of computers and electronic sales devices such as cash register scanners, the perpetual inventory system is now available to many small businesses that previously could not afford them and is economically feasible for a broader range of inventory items than before.

The periodic system is less costly to implement during the period but requires a physical count before ending inventory and cost of goods sold can be determined. This makes the preparation of interim financial statements more costly unless an inventory estimation technique is used.[2] And, perhaps most importantly, the inventory monitoring features provided by a perpetual system are not available. However, it is important to remember that a perpetual system involves the tracking of both inventory quantities *and* costs. Many companies that determine costs only periodically employ systems to constantly monitor inventory quantities.

What is Included in Inventory?

Physical Quantities Included in Inventory

● LO2

Regardless of the system used, the measurement of inventory and cost of goods sold starts with determining the physical quantities of goods. Typically, determining the physical quantity that should be included in inventory is a simple matter because it consists of items in the possession of the company. However, in some situations the identification of items that should be included in inventory is more difficult. Consider, for example, goods in transit, goods on consignment, and sales returns.

GOODS IN TRANSIT. At the end of a reporting period, it's important to ensure a proper inventory cutoff. This means determining the ownership of goods that are in transit between the company and its customers as well as between the company and its suppliers. For example, in December 2011, the Lothridge Wholesale Beverage Company sold goods to the Jabbar Company. The goods were shipped on December 29, 2011, and arrived at Jabbar's warehouse on January 3, 2012. The fiscal year-end for both companies is December 31.

Should the merchandise shipped to Jabbar be recorded as a sale by Lothridge and a purchase by Jabbar in 2011 and thus included in Jabbar's 2011 ending inventory? Should recording the sale/purchase be delayed until 2012 and the merchandise be included in Lothridge's 2011 ending inventory? The answer depends on who owns the goods at December 31. Ownership depends on the terms of the agreement between the two companies. If the goods are shipped **f.o.b. (free on board) shipping point,** then legal title to the goods changes hands at the point of shipment when the seller delivers the goods to the common carrier (for example, a trucking company), and the purchaser is responsible for shipping costs and transit insurance. In that case, Lothridge records the sale and inventory reduction in 2011 and Jabbar records a 2011 purchase and includes the goods in 2011 ending inventory even though the company is not in physical possession of the goods on the last day of the fiscal year.

---

[2]In Chapter 9 we discuss inventory estimation techniques that avoid the necessity of a physical count to determine ending inventory and cost of goods sold.

On the other hand, if the goods are shipped **f.o.b. destination,** the seller is responsible for shipping and legal title does not pass until the goods arrive at their destination (the customer's location). In our example, if the goods are shipped f.o.b. destination, Lothridge includes the merchandise in its 2011 ending inventory and the sale is recorded in 2012. Jabbar records the purchase in 2012.

GOODS ON CONSIGNMENT. Sometimes a company arranges for another company to sell its product under **consignment.** The goods are physically transferred to the other company (the consignee), but the transferor (consignor) retains legal title. If the consignee can't find a buyer, the goods are returned to the consignor. If a buyer is found, the consignee remits the selling price (less commission and approved expenses) to the consignor.

As we discussed in Chapter 5, because risk is retained by the consignor, the sale is not complete (revenue is not recognized) until an eventual sale to a third party occurs. As a result, goods held on consignment generally are not included in the consignee's inventory. While in stock, they belong to the consignor and should be included in inventory of the consignor even though not in the company's physical possession. A sale is recorded by the consignor only when the goods are sold by the consignee and title passes to the customer.

SALES RETURNS. Recall from our discussions in Chapters 5 and 7 that when the right of return exists, a seller must be able to estimate those returns before revenue can be recognized. The adjusting entry for estimated sales returns reduces sales revenue and accounts receivable. At the same time, cost of goods sold is reduced and inventory is increased (see Illustration 7–2 on page 345). As a result, a company includes in inventory the cost of merchandise it anticipates will be returned.

Now that we've considered which goods are part of inventory, let's examine the types of costs that should be associated with those inventory quantities.

Expenditures Included in Inventory

As mentioned earlier, the cost of inventory includes all necessary expenditures to acquire the inventory and bring it to its desired *condition* and *location* for sale or for use in the manufacturing process. Obviously, the cost includes the purchase price of the goods. But usually the cost of acquiring inventory also includes freight charges on incoming goods borne by the buyer; insurance costs incurred by the buyer while the goods are in transit (if shipped f.o.b. shipping point); and the costs of unloading, unpacking, and preparing merchandise inventory for sale or raw materials inventory for use.[3] The costs included in inventory are called **product costs.** They are associated with products and *expensed as cost of goods sold only when the related products are sold.*[4]

Shipping charges on outgoing goods (freight-out) are reported in the income statement either as part of cost of goods sold or as an operating expense, usually among selling expenses. If a company adopts a policy of not including shipping charges in cost of goods sold, both the amounts incurred during the period as well as the income statement classification of the expense must be disclosed.[5]

FREIGHT-IN ON PURCHASES. Freight-in on purchases is commonly included in the cost of inventory. These costs clearly are necessary to get the inventory in location for sale or use and can generally be associated with particular goods. Freight costs are added to the inventory account in a perpetual system. In a periodic system, freight costs generally are added to a temporary account called **freight-in** or **transportation-in,** which is added to purchases in determining net purchases. The account is closed to cost of goods sold along

[3]Generally accepted accounting principles require that abnormal amounts of certain costs be recognized as current period expenses rather than being included in the cost of inventory, specifically idle facility costs, freight, handling costs, and waste materials (spoilage). FASB ASC 330–10–30: Inventory–Overall–Initial Measurement (previously "Inventory Costs—An Amendment of *ARB No. 43, Chapter 4,*" *Statement of Financial Accounting Standards No. 151* (Norwalk, Conn.: FASB, 2004)).

[4]For practical reasons, though, some of these expenditures often are not included in inventory cost and are treated as **period costs.** They often are immaterial or it is impractical to associate the expenditures with particular units of inventory (for example, unloading and unpacking costs). Period costs are not associated with products and are expensed in the *period* incurred.

[5]FASB ASC 605–45–50–2: Revenue Recognition–Principal Agent Considerations–Disclosure–Shipping and Handling Fees and Costs (previously "Accounting for Shipping and Handling Fees and Costs," *EITF Issue No. 00–10* (Norwalk, Conn.: FASB, 2000) par. 6).

with purchases and other components of cost of goods sold at the end of the reporting period. (See Illustration 8–4 on page 403.) From an accounting system perspective, freight-in also could be added to the purchases account. From a control perspective, by recording freight-in as a separate item, management can more easily track its freight costs. The same perspectives pertain to purchases returns and purchase discounts, which are discussed next.

PURCHASE RETURNS.   In Chapter 7 we discussed merchandise returns from the perspective of the selling company. We now address returns from the buyer's point of view. You may recall that the seller views a return as a reduction of net sales. Likewise, a buyer views a return as a reduction of net purchases. When the buyer returns goods to the seller, a **purchase return** is recorded. In a perpetual inventory system, this means a reduction in both inventory and accounts payable (if the account has not yet been paid) at the time of the return. In a periodic system an account called *purchase returns* temporarily accumulates these amounts. Purchase returns are subtracted from purchases when determining net purchases. The account is closed to cost of goods sold at the end of the reporting period.

> A *purchase return* represents a reduction of net purchases.

PURCHASE DISCOUNTS.   Cash discounts also were discussed from the seller's perspective in Chapter 7. These discounts really are quick-payment discounts because they represent reductions in the amount to be paid by the buyer in the event payment is made within a specified period of time. The amount of the discount and the time period within which it's available are conveyed by terms like 2/10, n/30 (meaning a 2% discount if paid within 10 days, otherwise full payment within 30 days). As with the seller, the purchaser can record these **purchase discounts** using either the **gross method** or the **net method**. Consider Illustration 8–3 which is similar to the cash discount illustration in Chapter 7.

> *Purchase discounts* represent reductions in the amount to be paid if remittance is made within a designated period of time.

ILLUSTRATION 8–3	On October 5, 2011, the Lothridge Wholesale Beverage Company purchased merchandise at a price of $20,000. The repayment terms are stated as 2/10, n/30. Lothridge paid $13,720 ($14,000 less the 2% cash discount) on October 14 and the remaining balance of $6,000 on November 4. Lothridge employs a periodic inventory system.
Purchase Discounts	The gross and net methods of recording the purchase and cash payment are compared as follows:

	Gross Method			**Net Method**		
	October 5, 2011					
By either method, net purchases is reduced by discounts taken.	Purchases*.......................	20,000		Purchases*......................	19,600	
	Accounts payable		20,000	Accounts payable.......		19,600
	October 14, 2011					
	Accounts payable	14,000		Accounts payable...........	13,720	
	Purchase discounts*.....		280	Cash...........................		13,720
Discounts not taken are included as purchases using the gross method and as interest expense using the net method.	Cash		13,720			
	November 4, 2011					
	Accounts payable	6,000		Accounts payable...........	5,880	
	Cash		6,000	Interest expense.............	120	
				Cash		6,000

*The inventory account is used in a perpetual system.

> The *gross method* views discounts not taken as part of inventory cost.
>
> The *net method* considers discounts not taken as interest expense.

Conceptually, the gross method views a discount not taken as part of the cost of inventory. The net method considers the cost of inventory to include the net, after-discount amount, and any discounts not taken are reported as *interest expense.*[6] The discount is viewed as compensation to the seller for providing financing to the buyer.

Purchase discounts recorded under the gross method are subtracted from purchases when determining net purchases. The account is a temporary account that is closed to cost of goods sold at the end of the reporting period. Under the perpetual inventory system, purchase discounts are treated as a reduction in the inventory account.

---

[6]An alternative treatment is to debit an expense account called *purchase discounts lost* rather than interest expense. This enables a company to more easily identify the forgone discounts.

The effect on the financial statements of the difference between the two methods usually is immaterial. Net income over time will be the same using either method. There will, however, be a difference in gross profit between the two methods equal to the amount of discounts not taken. In the preceding illustration, $120 in discounts not taken is included as interest expense using the net method and cost of goods sold using the gross method.

Illustration 8–4 compares the perpetual and periodic inventory systems, using the net method.

The Lothridge Wholesale Beverage Company purchases soft drinks from producers and then sells them to retailers. The company began 2011 with merchandise inventory of $120,000 on hand. During 2011 additional merchandise is purchased on account at a cost of $600,000. Lothridge's suppliers offer credit terms of 2/10, n/30. All discounts were taken. Lothridge uses the net method to record purchase discounts. All purchases are made f.o.b. shipping point. Freight charges paid by Lothridge totaled $16,000. Merchandise with a net of discount cost of $20,000 was returned to suppliers for credit. Sales for the year, all on account, totaled $830,000. The cost of the soft drinks sold is $550,000. $154,000 of inventory remained on hand at the end of 2011.

The above transactions are recorded in summary form according to both the perpetual and periodic inventory systems as follows:

($ in 000s)

Perpetual System		Periodic System	
Purchases			
Inventory ($600 × 98%) ... 588		Purchases ($600 × 98%) 588	
Accounts payable	588	Accounts payable	588
Freight			
Inventory 16		Freight-in 16	
Cash	16	Cash	16
Returns			
Accounts payable 20		Accounts payable 20	
Inventory	20	*Purchase returns*	20
Sales			
Accounts receivable 830		Accounts receivable 830	
Sales revenue	830	Sales revenue	830
Cost of goods sold 550		No entry	
Inventory	550		
End of period			
No Entry		Cost of goods sold (below) 550	
		Inventory (ending) 154	
		Purchase returns 20	
		Inventory (beginning)	120
		Purchases	588
		Freight-in	16

Supporting Schedule:

Cost of goods sold:		
Beginning inventory		$120
Purchases	$588	
Less: Returns	(20)	
Plus: Freight-in	16	
Net purchases		584
Cost of goods available		704
Less: Ending inventory		(154)
Cost of goods sold		$550

ILLUSTRATION 8–4

Inventory Transactions— Perpetual and Periodic Systems

Inventory Cost Flow Assumptions

● LO4

Regardless of whether the perpetual or periodic system is used, it's necessary to assign dollar amounts to the physical quantities of goods sold and goods remaining in ending inventory. Unless each item of inventory is specifically identified and traced through the system, assigning dollars is accomplished by making an assumption regarding how units of goods (and their associated costs) flow through the system. We examine the common cost flow assumptions next. In previous illustrations, dollar amounts of the cost of goods sold and the cost of ending inventory were assumed known. However, if various portions of inventory are acquired at different costs, we need a way to decide which units were sold and which remain in inventory. Illustration 8–5 will help explain.

ILLUSTRATION 8–5
Cost Flow

Goods available for sale include beginning inventory plus purchases.

The Browning Company began 2011 with $22,000 of inventory. The cost of beginning inventory (Beg. inv.) is composed of 4,000 units purchased for $5.50 each. Merchandise transactions during 2011 were as follows:

Purchases

Date of Purchase	Units	Unit Cost*	Total Cost
Jan. 17	1,000	$6.00	$ 6,000
Mar. 22	3,000	7.00	21,000
Oct. 15	3,000	7.50	22,500
Totals	7,000		$49,500

Sales

Date of Sale	Units
Jan. 10	2,000
Apr. 15	1,500
Nov. 20	3,000
Total	6,500

*Includes purchase price and cost of freight.

As the data show, 7,000 units were purchased during 2011 at various prices and 6,500 units were sold. What is the cost of the 6,500 units sold? If all units, including beginning inventory, were purchased at the same price, then the answer would be simple. However, that rarely is the case.

The year started with 4,000 units, 7,000 units were purchased, and 6,500 units were sold. This means 4,500 units remain in ending inventory. This allocation of units available for sale is depicted in Graphic 8–3.

GRAPHIC 8–3

Allocation of Units
Available

If a periodic system is used, what is the cost of the 4,500 units in ending inventory? In other words, which of the 11,000 (4,000 + 7,000) units available for sale were sold? Are they the more expensive ones bought toward the end of the year, or the less costly ones acquired before prices increased? Using the numbers given, let's consider the question as follows:

Beginning inventory (4,000 units @ $5.50)	$22,000
Plus: Purchases (7,000 units @ various prices)	49,500
Cost of goods available for sale (11,000 units)	$71,500
Less: Ending inventory (4,500 units @ ?)	?
Cost of goods sold (6,500 units @ ?)	?

The $71,500 in cost of goods available for sale must be allocated to ending inventory and cost of goods sold. The allocation decision is depicted in Graphic 8–4.

GRAPHIC 8–4

Allocation of Cost of Goods Available

Let's turn our attention now to the various inventory methods that can be used to achieve this allocation.

Specific Identification

It's sometimes possible for each unit sold during the period or each unit on hand at the end of the period to be matched with its actual cost. Actual costs can be determined by reference to the invoice representing the purchase of the item. This method is used frequently by companies selling unique, expensive products with low sales volume which makes it relatively easy and economically feasible to associate each item with its actual cost. For example, automobiles have unique serial numbers that can be used to match a specific auto with the invoice identifying the actual purchase price.

The specific identification method, however, is not feasible for many types of products either because items are not uniquely identifiable or because it is too costly to match a specific purchase price with each item sold or each item remaining in ending inventory. Most companies use cost flow methods to determine cost of goods sold and ending inventory. Cost flow methods are based on assumptions about how inventory might flow in and out of a company. However, it's important to note that the actual flow of a company's inventory does not have to correspond to the cost flow assumed. The various motivating factors that influence management's choice among alternative methods are discussed later in this chapter. We now explore the three most common cost flow methods: average cost, first-in, first-out (FIFO) and last-in, first-out (LIFO).

Average Cost

The average cost method assumes that cost of goods sold and ending inventory consist of a mixture of all the goods available for sale. The average unit cost applied to goods sold or to ending inventory is not simply an average of the various unit costs of purchases during the period but an average unit cost *weighted* by the number of units acquired at the various unit costs.

The *average cost method* assumes that items sold and items in ending inventory come from a mixture of all the goods available for sale.

In a perpetual inventory system, the average cost method is applied by computing a moving-average unit cost each time additional inventory is purchased.

PERIODIC AVERAGE COST.   In a periodic inventory system, this weighted average is calculated at the end of the period as follows:

$$\text{Weighted-average unit cost} = \frac{\text{Cost of goods available for sale}}{\text{Quantity available for sale}}$$

The calculation of average cost is demonstrated in Illustration 8–5A using data from Illustration 8–5.

ILLUSTRATION 8–5A		
Average Cost—Periodic Inventory System	Beginning inventory (4,000 units @ $5.50)	$22,000
	Plus: Purchases (7,000 units @ various prices)	49,500
	Cost of goods available for sale (11,000 units)	71,500
	Less: Ending inventory (determined below)	(29,250)
	Cost of goods sold (6,500 units)	$42,250

Cost of Ending Inventory:

$$\text{Weighted-average unit cost} = \frac{\$71,500}{11,000 \text{ units}} = \$6.50$$

4,500 units × $6.50 = $29,250

Cost of goods sold also could be determined directly by multiplying the weighted-average unit cost of $6.50 by the number of units sold ($6.50 × 6,500 = $42,250).

PERPETUAL AVERAGE COST.   The weighted-average unit cost in a perpetual inventory system becomes a moving-average unit cost. A new weighted-average unit cost is calculated each time additional units are *purchased*. The new average is determined after each purchase by (1) summing the cost of the previous inventory balance and the cost of the new purchase, and (2) dividing this new total cost (cost of goods available for sale) by the number of units on hand (the inventory units that are available for sale). This average is then used to cost any units sold before the next purchase is made. The moving-average concept is applied in Illustration 8–5B.

ILLUSTRATION 8–5B   Average Cost—Perpetual Inventory System

Date	Purchased	Sold	Balance
Beginning inventory	4,000 @ $5.50 = $22,000		4,000 @ $5.50 = $22,000
Jan. 10		2,000 @ $5.50 = $ 11,000	2,000 @ $5.50 = $11,000
Jan. 17	1,000 @ $6.00 = $6,000		$11,000 + $6,000 = $17,000
			2,000 + 1,000 = 3,000 units
	$\left[\dfrac{\$17,000}{3,000 \text{ units}}\right] = \$5.667/\text{unit}$		
Mar. 22	3,000 @ $7.00 = $21,000		$17,000 + $21,000 = $38,000
	$\left[\dfrac{\$38,000}{6,000 \text{ units}}\right] = \$6.333/\text{unit}$		3,000 + 3,000 = 6,000 units
Apr. 15		1,500 @ $6.333 = $ 9,500	4,500 @ $6.333 = $28,500
Oct. 15	3,000 @ $7.50 = $22,500		$28,500 + $22,500 = $51,000
	$\left[\dfrac{\$51,000}{7,500 \text{ units}}\right] = \$6.80/\text{unit}$		4,500 + 3,000 = 7,500 units
Nov. 20		3,000 @ $6.80 = $ 20,400	4,500 @ $6.80 = **$30,600**
	Total cost of goods sold	= **$40,900**	

On January 17 the new average of $5.667 (rounded) is calculated by dividing the $17,000 cost of goods available ($11,000 from beginning inventory + $6,000 purchased on

January 17) by the 3,000 units available (2,000 units from beginning inventory + 1,000 units acquired on January 17). The average is updated to $6.333 (rounded) with the March 22 purchase. The 1,500 units sold on April 15 are then costed at the average cost of $6.333.

Periodic average cost and perpetual average cost generally produce different allocations to cost of goods sold and ending inventory.

First-In, First-Out (FIFO)

The **first-in, first-out (FIFO) method** assumes that units sold are the first units acquired. Beginning inventory is sold first, followed by purchases during the period in the chronological order of their acquisition. In our illustration, 6,500 units were sold during 2011. Applying FIFO, these would be the 4,000 units in beginning inventory, the 1,000 units purchased on January 17, and 1,500 of the 3,000 units from the March 22 purchase. By default, ending inventory consists of the most recently acquired units. In this case, the 4,500 units in ending inventory consist of the 3,000 units purchased on October 15, and 1,500 of the 3,000 units purchased on March 22. Graphically, the flow is as follows:

The *first-in, first-out (FIFO) method* assumes that items sold are those that were acquired first.

Ending inventory applying FIFO consists of the most recently acquired items.

FIFO flow

Units Available

Beg. inv.	4,000	
Jan. 17	1,000	} 6,500 units sold
Mar. 22	1,500	
Mar. 22	1,500	
		} 4,500 units in ending inventory
Oct. 15	3,000	
Total	11,000	

PERIODIC FIFO.   Recall that we determine physical quantities on hand in a periodic inventory system by taking a physical count. Costing the 4,500 units in ending inventory this way automatically gives us the cost of goods sold as well. Using the numbers from our illustration, we determine cost of goods sold to be $38,500 by subtracting the $33,000 ending inventory from $71,500 cost of goods available for sale as shown in Illustration 8–5C.

Beginning inventory (4,000 units @ $5.50)		$22,000
Plus: Purchases (7,000 units @ various prices)		49,500
Cost of goods available for sale (11,000 units)		71,500
Less: Ending inventory (determined below)		(33,000)
Cost of goods sold (6,500 units)		$38,500

Cost of Ending Inventory:

Date of Purchase	Units	Unit Cost	Total Cost
Mar. 22	1,500	$7.00	$10,500
Oct. 15	3,000	7.50	22,500
Total	4,500		$33,000

ILLUSTRATION 8–5C

FIFO—Periodic Inventory System

Of course, the 6,500 units sold could be costed directly as follows:

Date of Purchase	Units	Unit Cost	Total Cost
Beg. inv.	4,000	$5.50	$22,000
Jan. 17	1,000	6.00	6,000
Mar. 22	1,500	7.00	10,500
Total	6,500		$38,500

PERPETUAL FIFO. The same ending inventory and cost of goods sold amounts are always produced in a perpetual inventory system as in a periodic inventory system when FIFO is used. This is because the same units and costs are first in and first out whether cost of goods sold is determined as each sale is made or at the end of the period as a residual amount. The application of FIFO in a perpetual system is shown in Illustration 8–5D.

ILLUSTRATION 8–5D	Date	Purchased	Sold	Balance
FIFO—Perpetual Inventory System	Beginning inventory	4,000 @ $5.50 = $22,000		4,000 @ $5.50 = $22,000
	Jan. 10		2,000 @ $5.50 = $11,000	2,000 @ $5.50 = $11,000
	Jan. 17	1,000 @ $6.00 = $6,000		2,000 @ $5.50 } $17,000 1,000 @ $6.00
	Mar. 22	3,000 @ $7.00 = $21,000		2,000 @ $5.50 1,000 @ $6.00 } $38,000 3,000 @ $7.00
	Apr. 15		1,500 @ $5.50 = $8,250	500 @ $5.50 1,000 @ $6.00 } $29,750 3,000 @ $7.00
	Oct. 15	3,000 @ $7.50 = $22,500		500 @ $5.50 1,000 @ $6.00 3,000 @ $7.00 } $52,250 3,000 @ $7.50
	Nov. 20		500 @ $5.50 + 1,000 @ $6.00 +	1,500 @ $7.00 } **$33,000** 3,000 @ $7.50
			1,500 @ $7.00 = $19,250	
		Total cost of goods sold	= **$38,500**	

Last-In, First-Out (LIFO)

The last-in, first-out (LIFO) method assumes that items sold are those that were most recently acquired.

The **last-in, first-out (LIFO) method** assumes that the units sold are the most recent units purchased. In our illustration, the 6,500 units assumed sold would be the 6,500 units acquired most recently: the 3,000 units acquired on October 15, the 3,000 units acquired on March 22, and 500 of the 1,000 units purchased on January 17. Ending inventory, then, consists of the units acquired first; in this case, the 4,000 units from beginning inventory and 500 of the 1,000 units purchased on January 17. Graphically, the flow is as follows:

Ending inventory applying LIFO consists of the items acquired first.

Units Available

Beg. inv.	4,000 } 4,500 units in ending inventory
Jan. 17	500
Jan. 17	500 } 6,500 units sold
Mar. 22	3,000
Oct. 15	3,000
Total	11,000

LIFO flow

PERIODIC LIFO. The cost of ending inventory determined to be $25,000 (calculated below) by the LIFO assumption and using a periodic system is subtracted from cost of goods available for sale to arrive at the cost of goods sold of $46,500 as shown in Illustration 8–5E.

Beginning inventory (4,000 units @ $5.50)			$22,000
Plus: Purchases (7,000 units @ various prices)			49,500
Cost of goods available for sale (11,000 units)			71,500
Less: Ending inventory (determined below)			(25,000)
Cost of goods sold (6,500 units)			$46,500

Cost of Ending Inventory:

Date of Purchase	Units	Unit Cost	Total Cost
Beginning inventory	4,000	$5.50	$22,000
Jan. 17	500	6.00	3,000
Total	4,500		$25,000

ILLUSTRATION 8–5E

LIFO—Periodic Inventory System

The 6,500 sold could be costed directly as follows:

Date of Purchase	Units	Unit Cost	Total Cost
Jan. 17	500	$6.00	$ 3,000
Mar. 22	3,000	7.00	21,000
Oct. 15	3,000	7.50	22,500
Total	6,500		$46,500

PERPETUAL LIFO. The application of LIFO in a perpetual system is shown in Illustration 8–5F. Each time inventory is purchased or sold, the LIFO layers are adjusted. For example, after the March 22 purchase, we have three layers of inventory at different unit costs listed in the chronological order of their purchase. When 1,500 units are sold on April 15, we assume they come from the most recent layer of 3,000 units purchased at $7.00.

Date	Purchased	Sold	Balance
Beginning inventory	4,000 @ $5.50 = $22,000		4,000 @ $5.50 = $22,000
Jan. 10		2,000 @ $5.50 = $11,000	2,000 @ $5.50 = $11,000
Jan. 17	1,000 @ $6.00 = $6,000		2,000 @ $5.50 } 1,000 @ $6.00 } $17,000
Mar. 22	3,000 @ $7.00 = $21,000		2,000 @ $5.50] 1,000 @ $6.00 } $38,000 3,000 @ $7.00]
Apr. 15		1,500 @ $7.00 = $10,500	2,000 @ $5.50] 1,000 @ $6.00 } $27,500 1,500 @ $7.00]
Oct. 15	3,000 @ $7.50 = $22,500		2,000 @ $5.50] 1,000 @ $6.00] 1,500 @ $7.00 } $50,000 3,000 @ $7.50]
Nov. 20		3,000 @ $7.50 = $22,500	2,000 @ $5.50] 1,000 @ $6.00 } $27,500 1,500 @ $7.00]
	Total cost of goods sold	= $44,000	

ILLUSTRATION 8–5F

LIFO—Perpetual Inventory System

Notice that $44,000 of the cost of goods available for sale is allocated to cost of goods sold by perpetual LIFO and $27,500 to ending inventory (the balance after the last transaction), which is different from the periodic LIFO result of $46,500 and $25,000. Unlike FIFO, applying LIFO in a perpetual inventory system will generally result in an ending inventory and cost of goods sold different from the allocation arrived at applying LIFO in a periodic system. Periodic LIFO applies the last-in, first-out concept to total sales and total purchases only at the conclusion of the reporting period. Perpetual LIFO applies the same concept, but several times during the period—every time a sale is made.

For example, when 2,000 units are sold on January 10, perpetual LIFO costs those units at $5.50, the beginning inventory unit cost. Periodic LIFO, by contrast, would be applied at year-end. By the end of the year, enough purchases have been made that the beginning inventory would be assumed to remain intact, and the January 10 units sold would be costed at a more recent price.

Comparison of Cost Flow Methods

The three cost flow methods are compared below assuming a periodic inventory system.

	Average	FIFO	LIFO
Cost of goods sold	$42,250	$38,500	$46,500
Ending inventory	29,250	33,000	25,000
Total	$71,500	$71,500	$71,500

Notice that the average cost method in this example produces amounts that fall in between the FIFO and LIFO amounts for both cost of goods sold and ending inventory. This will usually be the case. Whether it will be FIFO or LIFO that produces the highest or lowest value of cost of goods sold and ending inventory depends on the pattern of the actual unit cost changes during the period.

During periods of generally rising costs, as in our example, FIFO results in a lower cost of goods sold than LIFO because the lower costs of the earliest purchases are assumed sold. LIFO cost of goods sold will include the more recent higher cost purchases. On the other hand, FIFO ending inventory includes the most recent higher cost purchases which results in a higher ending inventory than LIFO. LIFO ending inventory includes the lower costs of the earliest purchases. Conversely, if costs are declining, then FIFO will result in a higher cost of goods sold and lower ending inventory than LIFO.[7]

Each of the three methods is permissible according to generally accepted accounting principles and frequently is used. Also, a company need not use the same method for all of its inventory. For example, **International Paper Company** uses LIFO for its raw materials and finished pulp and paper products, and both the FIFO and average cost methods for other inventories. Because of the importance of inventories and the possible differential effects of different methods on the financial statements, a company must identify in a disclosure note the method(s) it uses. The chapter's opening case included an example of this disclosure for **ConocoPhillips**, and you will encounter additional examples later in the chapter.

Graphic 8–5 shows the results of a survey of inventory methods used by 500 large public companies in 2008 and 600 companies in 1973.[8] FIFO is the most popular method in both

	2008		1973	
	# of Companies	**% of Companies**	**# of Companies**	**% of Companies**
FIFO	323	49%	394	43%
LIFO	179	27	150	16
Average	146	22	235	25
Other*	17	2	148	16
Total	665	100%	927	100%

*"Other" includes the specific identification method and miscellaneous less popular methods.

---

[7]The differences between the various methods also hold when a perpetual inventory system is used.
[8]*Accounting Trends and Techniques—2009* and *1974* (New York, New York: AICPA, 2009 and 1974), p. 195.

periods, but there has been a significant increase in the use of LIFO since the earlier period. Notice that the column total for the number of companies is greater than 500 (600 in 1973), indicating that many companies included in this sample do use multiple methods.

INTERNATIONAL FINANCIAL REPORTING STANDARDS

Inventory Cost Flow Assumptions.   *IAS No. 2*[9] does not permit the use of LIFO. Because of this restriction, many U.S. multinational companies use LIFO only for their domestic inventories and FIFO or average cost for their foreign subsidiaries. A disclosure note included in a recent annual report of **General Mills** provides an example:

● LO9

Inventories (in part)

All inventories in the United States other than grain are valued at the lower of cost, using the last-in, first-out (LIFO) method, or market. . . . Inventories outside of the United States are valued at the lower of cost, using the first-in, first-out (FIFO) method, or market.

Real World Financials

This difference could prove to be a significant impediment to U.S. convergence to international standards. Unless the U.S. Congress repeals the LIFO conformity rule (see page 412), convergence would cause many corporations to lose a valuable tax shelter, the use of LIFO for tax purposes. If these companies were immediately taxed on the difference between LIFO inventories and inventories valued using another method, it would cost companies billions of dollars. Some industries would be particularly hard hit. Most oil companies and auto manufacturers, for instance, use LIFO. As an example, it would cost **ExxonMobil** over $4 billion. The companies affected most certainly will lobby heavily to retain the use of LIFO for tax purposes.

DECISION MAKERS' PERSPECTIVE—Factors Influencing Method Choice

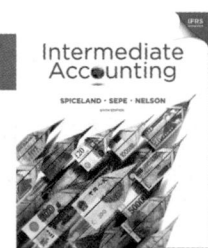

What factors motivate companies to choose one method over another? What factors have caused the increased popularity of LIFO? Choosing among alternative accounting methods is a complex issue. Often such choices are not made in isolation but in such a way that the combination of inventory cost flow assumptions, depreciation methods, pension assumptions, and other choices meet a particular objective. Also, many believe managers sometimes make these choices to maximize their own personal benefits rather than those of the company or its external constituents. But regardless of the motive, the impact on reported numbers is an important consideration in each choice of method. The inventory choice determines (a) how closely reported costs reflect the actual physical flow of inventory, (b) the timing of reported income and income tax expense, and (c) how well costs are matched with associated revenues.

● LO5

PHYSICAL FLOW.   If a company wanted to choose a method that most closely approximates specific identification, then the actual physical flow of inventory in and out of the company would motivate the choice of method.

For example, companies often attempt to sell the oldest goods in inventory first for some of their products. This certainly is the case with perishable goods such as many grocery items. The FIFO method best mirrors the physical flow in these situations. The average cost method might be used for liquids such as chemicals where items sold are taken from a mixture of inventory acquired at different times and different prices. There are very few inventories that actually flow in a LIFO manner. It is important for you to understand that there is no requirement that companies choose an inventory method that approximates actual physical flow and few companies make the choice on this basis. In fact, as we discuss next, the effect of inventory method on income and income taxes is the primary motivation that influences method choice.

A company is not required to choose an inventory method that approximates actual physical flow.

---

[9]"Inventories," *International Accounting Standard No. 2* (IASCF), as amended effective January 1, 2009.

INCOME TAXES AND NET INCOME. If the unit cost of inventory changes during a period, the inventory method chosen can have a significant effect on the amount of income reported by the company to external parties and also on the amount of income taxes paid to the Internal Revenue Service (IRS) and state and local taxing authorities. Over the entire life of a company, cost of goods sold for all years will equal actual costs of items sold regardless of the inventory method used. However, as we have discussed, different inventory methods can produce significantly different results in each particular year.

When prices rise and inventory quantities are not decreasing, LIFO produces a higher cost of goods sold and therefore lower net income than the other methods. The company's income tax returns will report a lower taxable income using LIFO and lower taxes will be paid currently. Taxes are not reduced permanently, only deferred. The reduced amount will be paid to the taxing authorities when either the unit cost of inventory or the quantity of inventory subsequently declines. However, we know from our discussion of the time value of money that it is advantageous to save a dollar today even if it must be paid back in the future. Recall from the recent survey results exhibited earlier that the popularity of LIFO increased significantly between 1973 and 2008. The main reason for this increased popularity is attributable to high inflation (increasing prices) during the 1970s which motivated many companies to switch to LIFO in order to gain this tax benefit.

A corporation's taxable income comprises revenues, expenses (including cost of goods sold), gains, and losses measured according to the regulations of the appropriate taxing authority. Income before tax as reported in the income statement does not always equal taxable income. In some cases, differences are caused by the use of different measurement methods.[10] However, IRS regulations, which determine federal taxable income, require that if a company uses LIFO to measure taxable income, the company also must use LIFO for external financial reporting. This is known as the **LIFO conformity rule** with respect to inventory methods.

Because of the LIFO conformity rule, to obtain the tax advantages of using LIFO in periods of rising prices, lower net income is reported to shareholders, creditors, and other external parties. The income tax motivation for using LIFO may be offset by a desire to report higher net income. Reported net income could have an effect on a corporation's share price,[11] on bonuses paid to management, or on debt agreements with lenders. For example, research has indicated that the managers of companies with bonus plans tied to income measures are more likely to choose accounting methods that maximize their bonuses (often those that increase net income).[12]

In 1981, the LIFO conformity rule was liberalized to permit LIFO users to report non-LIFO inventory valuations in a supplemental disclosure note, but not on the face of the income statement. For example, Graphic 8–6 shows the note provided in a recent annual report of **The Great Atlantic & Pacific Tea Company, Inc.**, a large supermarket chain, disclosing its use of LIFO for part of its inventories.[13]

LIFO RESERVES. Many companies use LIFO for external reporting and income tax purposes but maintain their internal records using FIFO or average cost. There is a variety of reasons, including: (1) the high recordkeeping costs for LIFO, (2) contractual agreements such as bonus or profit sharing plans that calculate net income with a method other than LIFO, and (3) using FIFO or average cost information for pricing decisions.

---

[10] For example, a corporation can take advantage of incentives offered by Congress by deducting more depreciation in the early years of an asset's life in its federal income tax return than it reports in its income statement.

[11] The concept of capital market efficiency has been debated for many years. In an efficient capital market, the market is not fooled by differences in accounting method choice that do not translate into real cash flow differences. The only apparent cash flow difference caused by different inventory methods is the amount of income taxes paid currently. In an efficient market, we would expect the share price of a company that switched its method to LIFO and saved tax dollars to increase even though it reported lower net income than if LIFO had not been adopted. Research on this issue is mixed. For example, see William E. Ricks, "Market's Response to the 1974 LIFO Adoptions," *Journal of Accounting Research* (Autumn 1982), and Robert Moren Brown, "Short-Range Market Reaction to Changes to LIFO Using Preliminary Earnings Announcement Dates," *Journal of Accounting Research* (Spring 1980).

[12] For example, see P. M. Healy, "The Effect of Bonus Schemes on Accounting Decisions," *Journal of Accounting and Economics* (April 1985), and D. Dhaliwal, G. Salamon, and E. Smith, "The Effect of Owner Versus Management Control on the Choice of Accounting Methods," *Journal of Accounting and Economics* (July 1982).

[13] The Great Atlantic and Pacific Tea Company uses both the FIFO and LIFO cost methods. Earlier in the chapter we noted that a company need not use the same inventory method for all of its inventories.

Many companies choose LIFO in order to reduce income taxes in periods when prices are rising.

If a company uses LIFO to measure its taxable income, IRS regulations require that LIFO also be used to measure income reported to investors and creditors (the *LIFO conformity rule*).

FINANCIAL Reporting Case

Q2, p. 395

Summary of Significant Accounting Policies (in part)
Inventories
Store inventories are stated principally at the lower of cost or market. As of February 28, 2009, and February 28, 2008, cost of 61.0% and 61.1% of our inventories, respectively, was determined using the first-in, first-out ("FIFO") method and the cost of 39.0% and 38.9% of our inventories was determined using the last-in, first-out ("LIFO") method. At February 28, 2009, and February 23, 2008, if valued on a FIFO basis, the LIFO inventory carrying values would have been approximately $10 million and $2 million higher, respectively.

GRAPHIC 8–6

Inventories Disclosure—The Great Atlantic & Pacific Tea Company, Inc.

Real World Financials

● LO6

Generally, the conversion to LIFO from the internal records occurs at the end of the reporting period without actually entering the adjustment into the company's records. Some companies, though, enter the conversion adjustment—the difference between the internal method and LIFO—directly into the records as a "contra account" to inventory. This contra account is called either the **LIFO reserve** or the **LIFO allowance.**

For illustration, let's say that the Doubletree Corporation began 2011 with a balance of $475,000 in its LIFO reserve account, the difference between inventory valued internally using FIFO and inventory valued using LIFO. At the end of 2011, assume this difference increased to $535,000. The entry to record the increase in the reserve is:

Cost of goods sold ($535,000 – 475,000)	60,000	
LIFO reserve		60,000

If the difference between inventory valued internally using FIFO and inventory valued using LIFO had decreased, this entry would be reversed. Companies such as Doubletree often use a disclosure note to show the difference between ending inventory valued using the internal method and the LIFO inventory amount reported in the balance sheet. As an example, Graphic 8–7 shows the disclosure note from a recent annual report of **Winnebago Industries, Inc.,** that indicated the composition of the company's inventories:

Note 5: Inventories
Inventories are valued at the lower of cost or market, with cost being determined under the last-in, first-out (LIFO) method.
Inventories consist of the following:

($ in thousands)	2009	2008
Finished goods	$ 18,709	$ 41,716
Work-in-process	24,982	31,187
Raw materials	33,305	75,010
	77,196	147,913
LIFO reserve	(30,346)	(37,317)
Total inventories	$ 46,850	$ 110,596

GRAPHIC 8–7

Inventories Disclosure— Winnebago Industries, Inc.

Real World Financials

LIFO LIQUIDATIONS.   Earlier in the text, we demonstrated the importance of matching revenues and expenses in creating an income statement that is useful in predicting future cash flows. If prices change during a period, then LIFO generally will provide a better match of revenues and expenses. Sales reflect the most recent selling prices, and cost of goods sold includes the costs of the most recent purchases.

For the same reason, though, inventory costs in the balance sheet with LIFO generally are out of date because they reflect old purchase transactions. It is not uncommon for a company's LIFO inventory balance to be based on unit costs actually incurred several years earlier.

This distortion sometimes carries over to the income statement as well. When inventory quantities decline during a period, then these out-of-date inventory layers are liquidated and cost of goods sold will partially match noncurrent costs with current selling prices. If costs

Proponents of LIFO argue that it results in a better match of revenues and expenses.

have been increasing (decreasing), LIFO liquidations produce higher (lower) net income than would have resulted if the liquidated inventory were included in cost of goods sold at current costs. The paper profits (losses) caused by including out of date, low (high) costs in cost of goods sold is referred to as the effect on income of liquidations of LIFO inventory.

To illustrate this problem, consider the example in Illustration 8–6.

ILLUSTRATION 8–6 LIFO Liquidation	National Distributors, Inc., uses the LIFO inventory method. The company began 2011 with inventory of 10,000 units that cost $20 per unit. During 2011, 30,000 units were purchased for $25 each and 35,000 units were sold. National's LIFO cost of goods sold for 2011 consists of:

$$
\begin{array}{rl}
30,000 \text{ units @ \$25 per unit} & = \$750,000 \\
\underline{5,000} \text{ units @ \$20 per unit} & = \underline{\$100,000} \\
35,000 & \underline{\$850,000}
\end{array}
$$

Included in cost of goods sold are 5,000 units from beginning inventory that have now been liquidated. If the company had purchased at least 35,000 units, no liquidation would have occurred. Then cost of goods sold would have been $875,000 (35,000 units × $25 per unit) instead of $850,000. The difference between these two cost of goods sold figures is $25,000 ($875,000 – 850,000). This is the before tax income effect of the LIFO liquidation. Assuming a 40% income tax rate, the net effect of the liquidation is to increase net income by $15,000 [$25,000 × (1 – .40)]. The lower the costs of the units liquidated, the more severe the effect on income.

A material effect on net income of LIFO layer liquidation must be disclosed in a note.

A company must disclose in a note any material effect of **LIFO liquidation** on net income. For example, Graphic 8–8 shows the disclosure note included with recent financial statements of **SuperValue Inc.**, one of the largest grocery chains in the United States.

GRAPHIC 8–8

LIFO Liquidation Disclosure—SuperValue Inc.

Real World Financials

> **Summary of Significant Accounting Policies (in part)**
> **Inventories**
> During fiscal 2009, 2008, and 2007, inventory quantities in certain LIFO layers were reduced. These reductions resulted in a liquidation of LIFO inventory quantities carried at lower costs prevailing in prior years as compared with the cost of fiscal 2009, 2008, and 2007 purchases. As a result, cost of goods sold decreased by $10, $5, and $6 million in fiscal 2009, 2008, and 2007, respectively, and net income increased by approximately $6, $3, and $3.6 million, respectively.

In our illustration, National Distributors, Inc. would disclose that LIFO liquidations increased income by $15,000 in 2011, assuming that this effect on income is considered material.

We've discussed several factors that influence companies in their choice of inventory method. A company could be influenced by the actual physical flow of its inventory, by the effect of inventory method on reported net income and the amount of income taxes payable currently, or by a desire to provide a better match of expenses with revenues. You've seen that the direction of the change in unit costs determines the effect of using different methods on net income and income taxes. While the United States has experienced persistent inflation for many years (increases in the general price-level), the prices of many goods and services have experienced periods of declining prices (for example, personal computers). ●

CONCEPT REVIEW EXERCISE

INVENTORY COST FLOW METHODS

The Rogers Company began 2011 with an inventory of 10 million units of its principal product. These units cost $5 each. The following inventory transactions occurred during the first six months of 2011.

Date	Transaction
Feb. 15	Purchased, on account, 5 million units at a cost of $6.50 each.
Mar. 20	Sold, on account, 8 million units at a selling price of $12 each.
Apr. 30	Purchased, on account, 5 million units at a cost of $7 each.

On June 30, 2011, 12 million units were on hand.

Required:

1. Prepare journal entries to record the above transactions. The company uses a periodic inventory system.
2. Prepare the required adjusting entry on June 30, 2011, applying each of the following inventory methods:

   a. Average
   b. FIFO
   c. LIFO

3. Repeat requirement 1 assuming that the company uses a perpetual inventory system.

1. Prepare journal entries to record the above transactions. The company uses a periodic inventory system.   **SOLUTION**

February 15	($ in millions)	
Purchases (5 million × $6.50)	32.5	
Accounts payable		32.5
To record the purchase of inventory.		
March 20		
Accounts receivable (8 million × $12)	96	
Sales revenue		96
To record sales on account.		
No entry is recorded for the cost of inventory sold.		
April 30		
Purchases (5 million × $7)	35	
Accounts payable		35
To record the purchase of inventory.		

2. Prepare the required adjusting entry on June 30, 2011, applying each method.

		($ in millions)			
Date	Journal entry	Average	FIFO	LIFO	
June 30	Cost of goods sold (determined below)	47.0	40.0	54.5	
	Inventory (ending—determined below)	70.5	77.5	63.0	
	Inventory (beginning − [10 million @ $5])	50.0	50.0	50.0	
	Purchases ($32.5 million + 35 million)	67.5	67.5	67.5	

Calculation of Ending Inventory and Cost of Goods Sold:

a. Average:

	($ in millions)
Beginning inventory (10 million units @ $5.00)	$ 50.0
Plus: Purchases (10 million units @ various prices)	67.5
Cost of goods available for sale (20 million units)	117.5
Less: Ending inventory (determined below)	(70.5)
Cost of goods sold	$ 47.0

Cost of ending inventory:

$$\text{Weighted-average unit cost} = \frac{\$117.5}{20 \text{ million units}} = \$5.875$$

$$12 \text{ million units} \times \$5.875 = \$70.5 \text{ million}$$

b. FIFO:

Cost of goods available for sale (20 million units)	$117.5
Less: Ending inventory (determined below)	(77.5)
Cost of goods sold	$ 40.0

Cost of ending inventory:

Date of Purchase	Units	Unit Cost	Total Cost
Beg. inv.	2 million	$5.00	10.0
Feb. 15	5 million	6.50	32.5
April 30	5 million	7.00	35.0
Total	12 million		$77.5

c. LIFO:

Cost of goods available for sale (20 million units)	$117.5
Less: Ending inventory (determined below)	(63.0)
Cost of goods sold	$ 54.5

Cost of ending inventory:

Date of Purchase	Units	Unit Cost	Total Cost
Beg. inv.	10 million	$5.00	$50.0
Feb. 15	2 million	6.50	13.0
Total	12 million		$63.0

3. Repeat requirement 1 assuming that the company uses a perpetual inventory system.

February 15	**($ in millions)**	
Inventory (5 million units × $6.50)	32.5	
Accounts payable		32.5
To record the purchase of inventory.		
April 30		
Inventory (5 million units × $7.00)	35.0	
Accounts payable		35.0
To record the purchase of inventory.		

	($ in millions)		
Journal Entries—March 20	**Average**	**FIFO**	**LIFO**
Accounts receivable (8 million × $12)	96.0	96.0	96.0
Sales revenue	96.0	96.0	96.0
To record sales on account.			
Cost of goods sold (determined below)	44.0	40.0	47.5
Inventory (determined below)	44.0	40.0	47.5
To record cost of goods sold.			

Calculation of Cost of Goods Sold:

a. Average:

Cost of goods sold:

($, except unit costs, in millions)		
Date	**Purchased**	**Sold**	**Balance**
Beg. inv.	10 million @ $5.00 = $50.0		10 million @ $5.00 = $50.0
Feb. 15	5 million @ $6.50 = $32.5		$50 + $32.5 = $82.5
	$\dfrac{\$82.5}{15 \text{ million units}} = \$5.50/\text{unit}$		
Mar. 20		8 million @ $5.50 = $44.0	

b. FIFO:

Cost of goods sold:

Units Sold	Cost of Units Sold	Total Cost
8 million (from Beg. inv.)	$5.00	$40.0

c. LIFO:

Cost of goods sold:

Units Sold	Cost of Units Sold	Total Cost
5 million (from Feb. 15 purchase)	$6.50	$32.5
3 million (from Beg. inv.)	5.00	15.0
8 million		$47.5

DECISION MAKERS' PERSPECTIVE

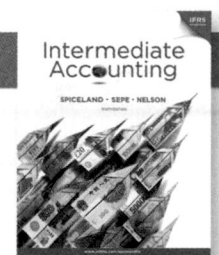

INVENTORY MANAGEMENT.   Managers closely monitor inventory levels to (1) ensure that the inventories needed to sustain operations are available, and (2) hold the cost of ordering and carrying inventories to the lowest possible level.[14] Unfortunately, these objectives often conflict with one another. Companies must maintain sufficient quantities of inventory to meet customer demand. However, maintaining inventory is costly. Fortunately, a variety of tools are available, including computerized inventory control systems and the outsourcing of inventory component production, to help balance these conflicting objectives.[15]

A **just-in-time (JIT) system** is another valuable technique that many companies have adopted to assist them with inventory management. JIT is a system used by a manufacturer to coordinate production with suppliers so that raw materials or components arrive just as they are needed in the production process. Have you ever ordered a personal computer from **Dell Inc.**? If so, the PC you received was not manufactured until you placed your order, and many of the components used in the production of your PC were not even acquired by Dell until then as well. This system enables Dell to maintain relatively low inventory balances. At the same time, the company's efficient production techniques, along with its excellent relationships with suppliers ensuring prompt delivery of components, enables Dell to quickly meet customer demand. In its January 30, 2009, fiscal year-end financial

> A company should maintain sufficient inventory quantities to meet customer demand while at the same time minimizing inventory ordering and carrying costs.

---

[14]The cost of carrying inventory includes the possible loss from the write-down of obsolete inventory. We discuss inventory write-downs in Chapter 9. There are analytical models available to determine the appropriate amount of inventory a company should maintain. A discussion of these models is beyond the scope of this text.

[15]Eugene Brigham and Joel Houston, *Fundamentals of Financial Management*, 12th ed. (Florence, Kentucky: South-Western, 2010).

statements, Dell reported an inventory balance of $867 million. With this relatively low investment in inventory, Dell was able to generate over $61 billion in sales revenue. To appreciate the advantage this provides, compare these numbers with **Hewlett Packard (HP)**, a company that includes PCs among its wide variety of technology products. For its fiscal year ended October 31, 2008, HP reported product revenue of $91 billion. However, to achieve this level of sales, HP's investment in inventory was nearly $8 billion.

It is important for a financial analyst to evaluate a company's effectiveness in managing its inventory. As we discussed in Chapter 5, one key to profitability is how well a company utilizes its assets. This evaluation is influenced by the company's inventory method choice. The choice of inventory method is an important and complex management decision. The many factors affecting this decision were discussed in a previous section. The inventory method also affects the analysis of a company's liquidity and profitability by investors, creditors, and financial analysts. Analysts must make adjustments when evaluating companies that use different inventory methods. During periods of rising prices, we would expect a company using FIFO to report higher income than a LIFO or average cost company. If one of the companies being analyzed uses LIFO, precise adjustments can often be made using the supplemental disclosures provided by many LIFO companies. Recall that the LIFO conformity rule was liberalized to permit LIFO users to report in a note the effect of using a method other than LIFO for inventory valuation.

For example, the disclosure note shown in Graphic 8–6 on page 413 reveals that **The Great Atlantic & Pacific Tea Company, Inc.** (GAPT) uses both the LIFO and FIFO methods, with 39% of its inventories valued using LIFO. Additional information from the company's recent financial statements is provided below.

FINANCIAL Reporting Case

Q3, p. 395

Real World Financials

	For the Year Ended	
($ in millions)	February 28, 2009	February 23, 2008
Balance sheets:		
Inventories	$ 474	$ 505
Income statements:		
Net sales	9,516	6,401
Cost of goods sold	6,613	4,431

Supplemental LIFO disclosures can be used to convert LIFO inventories and cost of goods sold amounts.

Suppose an analyst wanted to compare GAPT with a competitor that used all FIFO, or that used both LIFO and FIFO but with different percentages of LIFO and FIFO. To compare apples with apples, we can convert GAPT's inventories and cost of goods sold (and the competitor's if necessary) to a 100% FIFO basis before comparing the two companies by using the information provided in Graphic 8–6. Inventories recorded at LIFO were lower by approximately $10 million at February 28, 2009, and $2 million at February 23, 2008, than if they had been valued at FIFO:

	2009	2008
Inventories (as reported)	$474	$505
Add: conversion to FIFO	10	2
Inventories (100% FIFO)	$484	$507

If GAPT had used FIFO instead of LIFO, beginning inventory would have been $2 million higher, and ending inventory would have been higher by $10 million. As a result, cost of goods sold for the 2009 fiscal year would have been $8 million lower. This is because an increase in beginning inventory causes an *increase* in cost of goods sold, but an increase in ending inventory causes a *decrease* in cost of goods sold. Purchases for 2009 are the same regardless of the inventory valuation method used. Cost of goods sold, then, would have been $6,605 million ($6,613 − 8) if FIFO had been used for all inventories.

We can now use the 100% FIFO amounts to compare the two companies. Since cost of goods sold is lower by $8 million, income taxes and net income require similar adjustments before calculating a profitability ratio. Also, the converted inventory amounts can be used to compute liquidity ratios.

One useful profitability indicator that involves cost of goods sold is **gross profit** or **gross margin,** which highlights the important relationship between net sales revenue and cost of goods sold. The **gross profit ratio** is computed as follows:

$$\text{Gross profit ratio} = \frac{\text{Gross profit}}{\text{Net sales}}$$

● **LO7**

The *gross profit ratio* indicates the percentage of each sales dollar available to cover other expenses and provide a profit.

The higher the ratio, the higher is the markup a company is able to achieve on its products. For example, a product that costs $100 and sells for $150 provides a gross profit of $50 ($150 − 100) and the gross profit ratio is 33% ($50 ÷ $150). If that same product can be sold for $200, the gross profit increases to $100 and the gross profit ratio increases to 50% ($100 ÷ $200), so more dollars are available to cover expenses other than cost of goods sold.

The 2009 gross profit ($ in millions), for GAPT, using the 100% FIFO amounts, is $2,911 ($9,516 − 6,605), and the gross profit ratio is 30.6% ($2,911 ÷ $9,516). The same ratio for the grocery industry is 20%, indicating that GAPT is able to sell its products at significantly higher markups than the average for its competitors. GAPT's percentage of each sales dollar available to cover other expenses and to provide a profit is 50% higher than the industry average.

Monitoring this ratio over time can provide valuable insights. For example, a declining ratio might indicate that the company is unable to offset rising costs with corresponding increases in selling price, or perhaps that sales prices are declining without a commensurate reduction in costs. In either case, the decline in the ratio has important implications for future profitability.

In Chapter 5 we were introduced to an important ratio, the **inventory turnover ratio,** which is designed to evaluate a company's effectiveness in managing its investment in inventory. The ratio shows the number of times the average inventory balance is sold during a reporting period. The more frequently a business is able to sell or turn over its inventory, the lower its investment in inventory must be for a given level of sales. Usually, the higher the ratio the more profitable a company will be. Monitoring the inventory turnover ratio over time can highlight potential problems. A declining ratio generally is unfavorable and could be caused by the presence of obsolete or slow-moving products, or poor marketing and sales efforts.

Recall that the ratio is computed as follows:

$$\text{Inventory turnover ratio} = \frac{\text{Cost of goods sold}}{\text{Average inventory}}$$

If the analysis is prepared for the fiscal year reporting period, we can divide the inventory turnover ratio into 365 days to calculate the **average days in inventory,** which indicates the average number of days it normally takes the company to sell its inventory.

For GAPT, the inventory turnover ratio for the 2009 fiscal year, using the 100% FIFO amounts, is 13.33 ($6,605 ÷ [($484 + 507) ÷ 2]) and the average days in inventory is 27 days (365 ÷ 13.33). This compares to an industry average of 23 days. GAPT's products command a higher markup (higher gross profit ratio) but take longer to sell (higher average days in inventory) than the industry average.

Inventory increases that outrun increases in cost of goods sold might indicate difficulties in generating sales. These inventory buildups may also indicate that a company has obsolete or slow-moving inventory. This proposition was tested in an important academic research study. Professors Lev and Thiagarajan empirically demonstrated the importance of a set of 12 fundamental variables in valuing companies' common stock. The set of variables included inventory (change in inventory minus change in sales). The inventory variable was found to be a significant indicator of returns on investments in common stock, particularly during high and medium inflation years.[16]

[16]B. Lev and S. R. Thiagarajan, "Fundamental Information Analysis," *Journal of Accounting Research* (Autumn 1993). The main conclusion of the study was that fundamental variables, not just earnings, are useful in firm valuation, particularly when examined in the context of macroeconomic conditions such as inflation.

EARNINGS QUALITY. Changes in the ratios we discussed above often provide information about the quality of a company's current period earnings. For example, a slowing turnover ratio combined with higher than normal inventory levels may indicate the potential for decreased production, obsolete inventory, or a need to decrease prices to sell inventory (which will then decrease gross profit ratios and net income).

The choice of which inventory method to use also affects earnings quality, particularly in times of rapidly changing prices. Earlier in this chapter we discussed the effect of a LIFO liquidation on company profits. A LIFO liquidation profit (or loss) reduces the quality of current period earnings. Fortunately for analysts, companies must disclose these profits or losses, if material. In addition, LIFO cost of goods sold determined using a periodic inventory system is more susceptible to manipulation than is FIFO. Year-end purchases can have a dramatic effect on LIFO cost of goods sold in rapid cost-change environments. Recall again our discussion in Chapter 4 concerning earnings quality. Many believe that manipulating income reduces earnings quality because it can mask permanent earnings. Inventory write-downs and changes in inventory method are two additional inventory-related techniques a company could use to manipulate earnings. We discuss these issues in the next chapter. ●

PART B   METHODS OF SIMPLIFYING LIFO

The LIFO method described and illustrated to this point is called *unit LIFO*[17] because the last-in, first-out concept is applied to individual units of inventory. One problem with unit LIFO is that it can be very costly to implement. It requires records of each unit of inventory. The costs of maintaining these records can be significant, particularly when a company has numerous individual units of inventory and when unit costs change often during a period.

The recordkeeping costs of unit LIFO can be significant.

In the previous section, a second disadvantage of unit LIFO was identified—the possibility that LIFO layers will be liquidated if the quantity of a particular inventory unit declines below its beginning balance. Even if a company's total inventory quantity is stable or increasing, if the quantity of any particular inventory unit declines, unit LIFO will liquidate all or a portion of a LIFO layer of inventory. When inventory quantity declines in a period of rising costs, noncurrent lower costs will be included in cost of goods sold and matched with current selling prices, resulting in LIFO liquidation profit.

Another disadvantage of unit LIFO is the possibility of LIFO liquidation.

This part of the chapter discusses techniques that can be used to significantly reduce the recordkeeping costs of LIFO and to minimize the probability of LIFO inventory layers being liquidated. Specifically, we discuss the use of inventory pools and the dollar-value LIFO method.

LIFO Inventory Pools

The objectives of using **LIFO inventory pools** are to simplify recordkeeping by grouping inventory units into pools based on physical similarities of the individual units and to reduce the risk of LIFO layer liquidation. For example, a glass company might group its various grades of window glass into a single window pool. Other pools might be auto glass and sliding door glass. A lumber company might pool its inventory into hardwood, framing lumber, paneling, and so on.

A pool consists of inventory units grouped according to natural physical similarities.

This allows a company to account for a few inventory pools rather than every specific type of inventory separately. Within pools, all purchases during a period are considered to have been made at the same time and at the same cost. Individual unit costs are converted to an average cost for the pool. If the quantity of ending inventory for the pool increases, then ending inventory will consist of the beginning inventory plus a single layer added during the period at the average acquisition cost for that pool.

The average cost for all of the pool purchases during the period is applied to the current year's LIFO layer.

---

[17]Unit LIFO sometimes is called *specific goods LIFO*.

Here's an example. Let's say Diamond Lumber Company has a rough-cut lumber inventory pool that includes three types: oak, pine, and maple. The beginning inventory consisted of the following:

	Quantity (Board Feet)	Cost (Per Foot)	Total Cost
Oak	16,000	$2.20	$35,200
Pine	10,000	3.00	30,000
Maple	14,000	2.40	33,600
	40,000		$98,800

The average cost for this pool is $2.47 per board foot ($98,800 ÷ 40,000 board feet). Now assume that during the next reporting period Diamond sold 46,000 board feet of lumber and purchased 50,000 board feet as follows:

	Quantity (Board Feet)	Cost (Per Foot)	Total Cost
Oak	20,000	$2.25	$ 45,000
Pine	14,000	3.00	42,000
Maple	16,000	2.50	40,000
	50,000		$127,000

The average cost for this pool is $2.54 per board foot ($127,000 ÷ 50,000 board feet). Because the quantity of inventory for the pool increased by 4,000 board feet (50,000 purchased less 46,000 sold), ending inventory will include the beginning inventory and a LIFO layer consisting of the 4,000 board feet increase. We would add this LIFO layer at the average cost of purchases made during the period, $2.54. The ending inventory of $108,960 now consists of two layers:

	Quantity (Board Feet)	Cost (Per Foot)	Total Cost
Beginning inventory	40,000	$2.47	$ 98,800
LIFO layer added	4,000	2.54	10,160
Ending inventory	44,000		$108,960

Despite the advantages of LIFO inventory pools, it's easy to imagine situations in which its benefits are not achieved. Suppose, for instance, that a company discontinues a certain product included in one of its pools. The old costs that existed in prior layers of inventory would be recognized as cost of goods sold and produce LIFO liquidation profit. Even if the product is replaced with another product, the replacement may not be similar enough to be included in the same inventory pool. In fact, the process itself of having to periodically redefine pools as changes in product mix occur can be expensive and time consuming. The dollar-value LIFO approach helps overcome these problems.

Dollar-Value LIFO

Dollar-value LIFO (DVL) gained such widespread popularity during the 1960s and 1970s that most LIFO applications are now based on this approach. DVL extends the concept of inventory pools by allowing a company to combine a large variety of goods into one pool. Physical units are not used in calculating ending inventory. Instead, the inventory is viewed as a quantity of value instead of a physical quantity of goods. Instead of layers of units from different purchases, the DVL inventory pool is viewed as comprising layers of dollar value from different years.

Because the physical characteristics of inventory items are not relevant to DVL, an inventory pool is identified in terms of economic similarity rather than physical similarity.

● LO8

A DVL pool is made up of items that are likely to face the same cost change pressures.

Specifically, a pool should consist of those goods that are likely to be subject to the same cost change pressures.

Advantages of DVL

The DVL method has important advantages. First, it simplifies the recordkeeping procedures compared to unit LIFO because no information is needed about unit flows. Second, it minimizes the probability of the liquidation of LIFO inventory layers, even more so than the use of pools alone, through the aggregation of many types of inventory into larger pools. In addition, the method can be used by firms that do not replace units sold with new units of the same kind. For firms whose products are subject to annual model changes, for example, the items in one year's inventory are not the same as the prior year's. Under pooled LIFO, the new replacement items must be substantially identical to previous models to be included in the same pool. Under DVL, no distinction is drawn between the old and new merchandise on the basis of their physical characteristics, so a much broader range of goods can be included in the pool. That is, the acquisition of the new items is viewed as replacement of the dollar value of the old items. Because the old layers are maintained, this approach retains the benefits of LIFO by matching the most recent acquisition cost of goods with sales measured at current selling prices.

Cost Indexes

In either the unit LIFO approach or the pooled LIFO approach, we determine whether a new LIFO layer was added by comparing the ending quantity with the beginning quantity. The focus is on *units* of inventory. Under DVL, we determine whether a new LIFO layer was added by comparing the ending dollar amount with the beginning dollar amount. The focus is on inventory *value*, not units. However, if the price level has changed, we need a way to determine whether an observed increase is a real increase (an increase in the quantity of inventory) or one caused by an increase in prices. So before we compare the beginning and ending inventory amounts, we need to deflate inventory amounts by any increase in prices so that both the beginning and ending amounts are measured in terms of the same price level. We accomplish this by using cost indexes. A cost index for a particular layer year is determined as follows:

$$\text{Cost index in layer year} = \frac{\text{Cost in layer year}}{\text{Cost in base year}}$$

The cost index for the base year (the year DVL is initially adopted) is set at 1.00.

The base year is the year in which the DVL method is adopted and the layer year is any subsequent year in which an inventory layer is created. The cost index for the base year is set at 1.00. Subsequent years' indexes reflect cost changes relative to the base year. For example, if a "basket" of inventory items cost $120 at the end of the current year, and $100 at the end of the base year, the cost index for the current year would be: $120 ÷ $100 = 120%, or 1.20. This index simply tells us that costs in the layer year are 120% of what they were in the base year (i.e., costs increased by 20%).

There are several techniques that can be used to determine an index for a DVL pool. An external index like the Consumer Price Index or the Producer Price Index can be used. However, in most cases these indexes would not properly reflect cost changes for any individual DVL pool. Instead, most companies use an internally generated index. These indexes can be calculated using one of several techniques such as the *double-extension method* or the *link-chain method*. A discussion of these methods is beyond the scope of this text. In our examples and illustrations, we assume cost indexes are given.

The DVL Inventory Estimation Technique

The starting point in DVL is determining the current year's ending inventory valued at year-end costs.

DVL estimation begins with the determination of the current year's ending inventory valued in terms of year-end costs. It's not necessary for a company using DVL to track the item-by-item cost of purchases during the year. All that's needed is to take the physical quantities of goods on hand at the end of the year and apply year-end costs. Let's say the Hanes Company adopted the dollar-value LIFO method on January 1, 2011, when the inventory value was $400,000. The 2011 ending inventory valued at year-end costs is $441,000, and the cost index for the year is 1.05 (105%).

What is the 2011 ending inventory valued at DVL cost? The first step is to convert the ending inventory from year-end costs to base year costs so we can see if there was a real increase in inventory rather than an illusory one caused by price increases. We divide the ending inventory by the year's cost index to get an amount that can be compared directly with beginning inventory.

$$\text{Ending inventory at } base\ year \text{ cost} = \frac{\$441,000}{1.05} = \$420,000$$

The $420,000 reflects the 2011 ending inventory deflated to base year cost.

Next we compare the $420,000 ending inventory at base year cost to the beginning inventory, also at base year cost, of $400,000. The $20,000 increase in base-year dollars signifies a real increase in inventory quantity during the year. Applying the LIFO concept, ending inventory at base year cost consists of the beginning inventory layer of $400,000 plus a $20,000 2011 layer. These are the hypothetical costs of the layers as if each was acquired at base year prices.

Once the layers are identified, each is restated to prices existing when the layers were acquired. Each layer is multiplied by the cost index for the year it was acquired. The costs are totaled to obtain ending inventory at DVL cost.[18]

Date	Ending Inventory at Base Year Cost	×	Cost Index	=	Ending Inventory at DVL Cost
1/1/11	$400,000		1.00		$400,000
2011 layer	20,000		1.05		21,000
Totals	$420,000				$421,000

STEP 1: Convert ending inventory valued at year-end cost to base year cost.

STEP 2: Identify the layers of ending inventory and the years they were created.

STEP 3: Convert each layer's base year cost to layer year cost using the cost index for the year it was acquired.

If we determined that inventory quantity had decreased during the year, then there would have been no 2011 layer added. The most recently added layer, in this case the beginning inventory layer, would be decreased to the inventory valuation determined in step 1. Once a layer of inventory or a portion of a layer is used (that is, sold) it cannot be replaced. In our example, if the base year layer is reduced to $380,000, it will never be increased. Future increases in inventory quantity will result in new layers being added. This situation is illustrated in the concept review exercise that follows.

CONCEPT REVIEW EXERCISE

DOLLAR-VALUE LIFO

On January 1, 2011, the Johnson Company adopted the dollar-value LIFO method. The inventory value on this date was $500,000. Inventory data for 2011 through 2014 are as follows:

Date	Ending Inventory at Year-End Costs	Cost Index
12/31/11	$556,500	1.05
12/31/12	596,200	1.10
12/31/13	615,250	1.15
12/31/14	720,000	1.25

Required:
Calculate Johnson's ending inventory for the years 2011 through 2014.

---

[18]It is important to note that the costs of the year's layer are only an approximation of actual acquisition cost. DVL assumes that all inventory quantities added during a particular year were acquired at a single cost.

		JOHNSON COMPANY		SOLUTION	
		Step 1	Step 2	Step 3	
Date	Ending Inventory at Year-End Cost	Ending Inventory at Base Year Cost	Inventory Layers at Base Year Cost	Inventory Layers Converted to Acquisition Year Cost	Ending Inventory At DVL Cost
1/1/11	$500,000 (base year)	$\frac{\$500,000}{1.00} = \$500,000$	$500,000 (base)	$500,000 × 1.00 = $500,000	**$500,000**
12/31/11	556,500	$\frac{\$556,500}{1.05} = \$530,000$	$500,000 (base) 30,000 (2011)	$500,000 × 1.00 = $500,000 30,000 × 1.05 = 31,500	**531,500**
12/31/12	596,200	$\frac{\$596,200}{1.10} = \$542,000$	$500,000 (base) 30,000 (2011) 12,000 (2012)	$500,000 × 1.00 = $500,000 30,000 × 1.05 = 31,500 12,000 × 1.10 = 13,200	**544,700**
12/31/13	615,250	$\frac{\$615,250}{1.15} = \$535,000^*$	$500,000 (base) 30,000 (2011) 5,000 (2012)	$500,000 × 1.00 = $500,000 30,000 × 1.05 = 31,500 5,000 × 1.10 = 5,500	**537,000**
12/31/14	720,000	$\frac{\$720,000}{1.25} = \$576,000$	$500,000 (base) 30,000 (2011) 5,000 (2012) 41,000 (2014)	$500,000 × 1.00 = $500,000 30,000 × 1.05 = 31,500 5,000 × 1.10 = 5,500 41,000 × 1.25 = 51,250	**588,250**

*Since inventory declined during 2013 (from $542,000 to $535,000 at base year costs), no new layer is added. Instead the most recently acquired layer, 2012, is reduced to arrive at the $535,000 ending inventory at base year cost.

FINANCIAL REPORTING CASE SOLUTION

1. **What inventory methods does ConocoPhillips use to value its inventories? Is this permissible according to GAAP?** *(p. 410)*   ConocoPhillips uses the LIFO inventory method to value the majority of its inventories. The cost of the remaining inventories is determined using various other methods, including FIFO and weighted average. Yes, each of these methods is permissible according to generally accepted accounting principles. A company need not use the same method for all of its inventories.

2. **What is the purpose of disclosing the difference between the reported LIFO inventory amounts and the replacement cost, which is equivalent to a FIFO basis?** *(p. 412)*   The LIFO conformity rule requires that if a company uses LIFO to measure taxable income, it also must use LIFO for external financial reporting. ConocoPhillips does this. However, in 1981, the LIFO conformity rule was liberalized to allow LIFO users to report non-LIFO inventory valuations in a supplemental disclosure note, but not on the face of the income statement. The company's disclosure note offers this additional information.

3. **Is your friend correct in his assertion that, by using LIFO, ConocoPhillips was able to report lower profits for the first quarter of 2009?** *(p. 418)*   Yes. If ConocoPhillips had used FIFO instead of LIFO for its LIFO inventories, income before taxes for all prior years, including the first quarter of 2009, would have been higher by $2,400 million (the increase in March 31, 2009, ending inventory). For the first quarter of 2009 alone, income before taxes would have been *higher* by $441 million. Here's why. The increase in ending inventory of $2,400 million *decreases* cost of goods sold, but the increase in beginning inventory of $1,959 million *increases* cost of goods sold, resulting in a net decrease in cost of goods sold of $441 million. FIFO provides a lower cost of goods sold when costs are rising. During the first quarter of 2009, the price of crude oil rose from approximately $30 to $40 per barrel. ●

THE BOTTOM LINE

● **LO1**   In a perpetual inventory system, inventory is continually adjusted for each change in inventory. Cost of goods sold is adjusted each time goods are sold or returned by a customer. A periodic inventory system adjusts inventory and records cost of goods sold only at the end of a reporting period. (p. 399)

● **LO2**   Generally, determining the physical quantity that should be included in inventory is a simple matter, because it consists of items in the possession of the company. However, at the end of a reporting period it's important to determine the ownership of goods that are in transit between the company and its customers as well as between the company and its suppliers. Also, goods on consignment should be included in inventory of the consignor even though the company doesn't have physical possession of the goods. In addition, a company anticipating sales returns includes in inventory the cost of merchandise it estimates will be returned. (p. 400)

● **LO3**   The cost of inventory includes all expenditures necessary to acquire the inventory and bring it to its desired condition and location for sale or use. Generally, these expenditures include the purchase price of the goods reduced by any returns and purchase discounts, plus freight-in charges. (p. 401)

● **LO4**   Once costs are determined, the cost of goods available for sale must be allocated between cost of goods sold and ending inventory. Unless each item is specifically identified and traced through the system, the allocation requires an assumption regarding the flow of costs. First-in, first-out (FIFO) assumes that units sold are the first units acquired. Last-in, first-out (LIFO) assumes that the units sold are the most recent units purchased. The average cost method assumes that cost of goods sold and ending inventory consist of a mixture of all the goods available for sale. (p. 404)

● **LO5**   A company's choice of inventory method will be influenced by (a) how closely cost flow reflects the actual physical flow of its inventory, (b) the timing of income tax expenses, and (c) how costs are matched with revenues. (p. 411)

● **LO6**   The LIFO conformity rule requires that if a company uses LIFO to measure taxable income, it also must use LIFO for external financial reporting. LIFO users often provide supplemental disclosures describing the effect on inventories of using another method on inventory valuation rather than LIFO. If a company uses LIFO and inventory quantities decline during a period, then out of date inventory layers are liquidated and the cost of goods sold will partially match noncurrent costs with current selling prices. If costs have been increasing (decreasing), LIFO liquidations produce higher (lower) net income than would have resulted if the liquidated inventory were included in cost of goods sold at current costs. The paper profits (losses) caused by including out of date, low (high) costs in cost of goods sold is referred to as the effect on income of liquidations of LIFO inventory. (p. 413)

● **LO7**   Investors, creditors, and financial analysts can gain important insights by monitoring a company's investment in inventories. The gross profit ratio, inventory turnover ratio, and average days in inventory are designed to monitor inventories. (p. 419)

● **LO8**   The dollar-value LIFO method converts ending inventory at year-end cost to base year cost using a cost index. After identifying the layers in ending inventory with the years they were created, each year's base year cost measurement is converted to layer year cost measurement using the layer year's cost index. The layers are then summed to obtain total ending inventory at cost. (p. 421)

● **LO9**   The primary difference between U.S. GAAP and IFRS with respect to determining the cost of inventory is that IFRS does not allow the use of the LIFO method to value inventory. (p. 411) ●

QUESTIONS FOR REVIEW OF KEY TOPICS

Q 8–1   Describe the three types of inventory of a manufacturing company.

Q 8–2   What is the main difference between a perpetual inventory system and a periodic inventory system?

Q 8–3   The Cloud Company employs a perpetual inventory system and the McKenzie Corporation uses a periodic system. Describe the differences between the two systems in accounting for the following events: (1) purchase of merchandise, (2) sale of merchandise, (3) return of merchandise to supplier, and (4) payment of freight charge on merchandise purchased. Indicate which accounts would be debited and credited for each event.

Q 8–4   The Bockner Company shipped merchandise to Laetner Corporation on December 28, 2011. Laetner received the shipment on January 3, 2012. December 31 is the fiscal year-end for both companies. The merchandise was shipped f.o.b. shipping point. Explain the difference in the accounting treatment of the merchandise if the shipment had instead been designated f.o.b. destination.

Q 8–5   What is a consignment arrangement? Explain the accounting treatment of goods held on consignment.

Q 8–6   Distinguish between the gross and net methods of accounting for purchase discounts.

Q 8–7   The Esquire Company employs a periodic inventory system. Indicate the effect (increase or decrease) of the following items on cost of goods sold:

1. Beginning inventory
2. Purchases
3. Ending inventory
4. Purchase returns
5. Freight-in

Q 8–8   Identify four methods of assigning cost to ending inventory and cost of goods sold and briefly explain the difference in the methods.

Q 8–9   It's common in the electronics industry for unit costs of raw materials inventories to decline over time. In this environment, explain the difference between LIFO and FIFO, in terms of the effect on income and financial position. Assume that inventory quantities remain the same for the period.

Q 8–10   Explain why proponents of LIFO argue that it provides a better match of revenue and expenses. In what situation would it not provide a better match?

Q 8–11   Explain what is meant by the Internal Revenue Service conformity rule with respect to the inventory method choice.

Q 8–12   Describe the ratios used by financial analysts to monitor a company's investment in inventories.

Q 8–13   What is a LIFO inventory pool? How is the cost of ending inventory determined when pools are used?

Q 8–14   Identify two advantages of dollar-value LIFO compared with unit LIFO.

Q 8–15   The Austin Company uses the dollar-value LIFO inventory method with internally developed price indexes. Assume that ending inventory at year-end cost has been determined. Outline the remaining steps used in the dollar-value LIFO computations.

🌐 IFRS   Q 8–16   Identify any differences between U.S. GAAP and International Financial Reporting Standards in the methods allowed to value inventory.

BRIEF EXERCISES

BE 8–1
Determining ending inventory; periodic system
● LO1

A company began its fiscal year with inventory of $186,000. Purchases and cost of goods sold for the year were $945,000 and $982,000, respectively. What was the amount of ending inventory?

BE 8–2
Perpetual system; journal entries
● LO1

Litton Industries uses a perpetual inventory system. The company began its fiscal year with inventory of $267,000. Purchases of merchandise on account during the year totaled $845,000. Merchandise costing $902,000 was sold on account for $1,420,000. Prepare the journal entries to record these transactions.

BE 8–3
Goods in transit
● LO2

Kelly Corporation shipped goods to a customer f.o.b. destination on December 29, 2011. The goods arrived at the customer's location in January. In addition, one of Kelly's major suppliers shipped goods to Kelly f.o.b. shipping point on December 30. The merchandise arrived at Kelly's location in January. Which shipments should be included in Kelly's December 31 inventory?

BE 8–4
Purchase discounts; gross method
● LO3

On December 28, 2011, Videotech Corporation (VTC) purchased 10 units of a new satellite uplink system from Tristar Communications for $25,000 each. The terms of each sale were 1/10, n/30. VTC uses the gross method to account for purchase discounts and a perpetual inventory system. VTC paid the net-of-discount amount on January 6, 2012. Prepare the journal entries on December 28 and January 6 to record the purchase and payment.

BE 8–5
Purchase discounts; net method
● LO3

Refer to the situation described in BE 8–4. Prepare the necessary journal entries assuming that VTC uses the net method to account for purchase discounts.

BE 8–6
Inventory cost flow
methods; periodic
system
● LO4

Samuelson and Messenger (S&M) began 2011 with 200 units of its one product. These units were purchased near the end of 2010 for $25 each. During the month of January, 100 units were purchased on January 8 for $28 each and another 200 units were purchased on January 19 for $30 each. Sales of 125 units and 100 units were made on January 10 and January 25, respectively. There were 275 units on hand at the end of the month. S&M uses a *periodic* inventory system. Calculate ending inventory and cost of goods sold for January using (1) FIFO, and (2) average cost.

BE 8–7
Inventory cost flow
methods; perpetual
system
● LO4

Refer to the situation described in BE 8–6. S&M uses a *perpetual* inventory system. Calculate ending inventory and cost of goods sold for January using (1) FIFO, and (2) average cost.

BE 8–8
LIFO method
● LO4

Esquire Inc. uses the LIFO method to value its inventory. Inventory at January 1, 2011, was $500,000 (20,000 units at $25 each). During 2011, 80,000 units were purchased, all at the same price of $30 per unit. 85,000 units were sold during 2011. Esquire uses a periodic inventory system. Calculate the December 31, 2011, ending inventory and cost of goods sold for 2011.

BE 8–9
LIFO method
● LO4

AAA Hardware uses the LIFO method to value its inventory. Inventory at the beginning of the year consisted of 10,000 units of the company's one product. These units cost $15 each. During the year, 60,000 units were purchased at a cost of $18 each and 64,000 units were sold. Near the end of the fiscal year, management is considering the purchase of an additional 5,000 units at $18. What would be the effect of this purchase on income before income taxes? Would your answer be the same if the company used FIFO instead of LIFO?

BE 8–10
LIFO liquidation
● LO6

Refer to the situation described in BE 8–8. Assuming an income tax rate of 40%, what is LIFO liquidation profit or loss that the company would report in a disclosure note accompanying its financial statements?

BE 8–11
Supplemental
LIFO disclosures;
SuperValue
● LO6

Real World Financials

SuperValue Inc., one of the largest grocery chains in the United States, reported inventories of $2,709 million and $2,776 million in its February 28, 2009, and February 23, 2008, balance sheets, respectively. Cost of goods sold for the fiscal year ended February 28, 2009, was $34,451 million. The company uses primarily the LIFO inventory method. A disclosure note reported that if FIFO had been used instead of LIFO, inventory would have been higher by $258 million and $180 million at the end of the February 28, 2009, and February 23, 2008, fiscal years, respectively. Calculate cost of goods sold for the February 28, 2009, fiscal year assuming SuperValue used FIFO instead of LIFO.

BE 8–12
Ratio analysis
● LO7

Selected financial statement data for Schmitzer Inc. is shown below:

	2011	2010
Balance sheet:		
Inventories	60,000	48,000
Ratios:		
Gross profit ratio for 2011	40%	
Inventory turnover ratio for 2011	5	

What was the amount of net sales for 2011?

BE 8–13
Dollar-value LIFO
● LO8

At the beginning of 2011, a company adopts the dollar-value LIFO inventory method for its one inventory pool. The pool's value on that date was $1,400,000. The 2011 ending inventory valued at year-end costs was $1,664,000 and the year-end cost index was 1.04. Calculate the inventory value at the end of 2011 using the dollar-value LIFO method.

EXERCISES

An alternate exercise and problem set is available on the text website: www.mhhe.com/spiceland6e

E 8–1
Perpetual inventory
system; journal
entries
● LO1

John's Specialty Store uses a perpetual inventory system. The following are some inventory transactions for the month of May 2011:
1. John's purchased merchandise on account for $5,000. Freight charges of $300 were paid in cash.
2. John's returned some of the merchandise purchased in (1). The cost of the merchandise was $600 and John's account was credited by the supplier.
3. Merchandise costing $2,800 was sold for $5,200 in cash.

Required:
Prepare the necessary journal entries to record these transactions.

E 8–2
Periodic inventory system; journal entries
● LO1

[This is a variation of the previous exercise modified to focus on the periodic inventory system.]

John's Specialty Store uses a periodic inventory system. The following are some inventory transactions for the month of May 2011:
1. John's purchased merchandise on account for $5,000. Freight charges of $300 were paid in cash.
2. John's returned some of the merchandise purchased in (1). The cost of the merchandise was $600 and John's account was credited by the supplier.
3. Merchandise costing $2,800 was sold for $5,200 in cash.

Required:
Prepare the necessary journal entries to record these transactions.

E 8–3
Determining cost of goods sold; periodic inventory system
● LO1

Askew Company uses a periodic inventory system. The June 30, 2011, year-end trial balance for the company contained the following information:

Account	Debit	Credit
Merchandise inventory, 7/1/10	32,000	
Sales		380,000
Sales returns	12,000	
Purchases	240,000	
Purchase discounts		6,000
Purchase returns		10,000
Freight-in	17,000	

In addition, you determine that the June 30, 2011, inventory balance is $40,000.

Required:
1. Calculate the cost of goods sold for the Askew Company for the year ending June 30, 2011.
2. Prepare the year-end adjusting entry to record cost of goods sold.

E 8–4
Perpetual and periodic inventory systems compared
● LO1

The following information is available for the Johnson Corporation for 2011:

Beginning inventory	$ 25,000
Merchandise purchases (on account)	155,000
Freight charges on purchases (paid in cash)	10,000
Merchandise returned to supplier (for credit)	12,000
Ending inventory	30,000
Sales (on account)	250,000
Cost of merchandise sold	148,000

Required:
Applying both a perpetual and a periodic inventory system, prepare the journal entries that summarize the transactions that created these balances. Include all end-of-period adjusting entries indicated.

E 8–5
Periodic inventory system; missing data
● LO1

The Playa Company uses a periodic inventory system. The following information is taken from Playa's records. Certain data have been intentionally omitted. ($ in thousands)

	2011	2012	2013
Beginning inventory	?	?	225
Cost of goods sold	627	621	?
Ending inventory	?	225	216
Cost of goods available for sale	876	?	800
Purchases (gross)	630	?	585
Purchase discounts	18	15	?
Purchase returns	24	30	14
Freight-in	13	32	16

Required:
Determine the missing numbers. Show computations where appropriate.

E 8–6
Goods in transit
● LO2

The Kwok Company's inventory balance on December 31, 2011, was $165,000 (based on a 12/31/11 physical count) *before* considering the following transactions:
1. Goods shipped to Kwok f.o.b. destination on December 20, 2011, were received on January 4, 2012. The invoice cost was $30,000.
2. Goods shipped to Kwok f.o.b. shipping point on December 28, 2011, were received on January 5, 2012. The invoice cost was $17,000.
3. Goods shipped from Kwok to a customer f.o.b. destination on December 27, 2011, were received by the customer on January 3, 2012. The sales price was $40,000 and the merchandise cost $22,000.
4. Goods shipped from Kwok to a customer f.o.b. destination on December 26, 2011, were received by the customer on December 30, 2011. The sales price was $20,000 and the merchandise cost $13,000.
5. Goods shipped from Kwok to a customer f.o.b. shipping point on December 28, 2011, were received by the customer on January 4, 2012. The sales price was $25,000 and the merchandise cost $12,000.

Required:
Determine the correct inventory amount to be reported in Kwok's 2011 balance sheet.

E 8–7
Goods in transit;
consignment
● LO2

The December 31, 2011, year-end inventory balance of the Raymond Corporation is $210,000. You have been asked to review the following transactions to determine if they have been correctly recorded.
1. Goods shipped to Raymond f.o.b. destination on December 26, 2011, were received on January 2, 2012. The invoice cost of $30,000 *is* included in the preliminary inventory balance.
2. At year-end, Raymond held $14,000 of merchandise on consignment from the Harrison Company. This merchandise *is* included in the preliminary inventory balance.
3. On December 29, merchandise costing $6,000 was shipped to a customer f.o.b. shipping point and arrived at the customer's location on January 3, 2012. The merchandise is *not* included in the preliminary inventory balance.
4. At year-end, Raymond had merchandise costing $15,000 on consignment with the Joclyn Corporation. The merchandise is *not* included in the preliminary inventory balance.

Required:
Determine the correct inventory amount to be reported in Raymond's 2011 balance sheet.

E 8–8
Physical quantities
and costs included
in inventory
● LO2

The Phoenix Corporation's fiscal year ends on December 31. Phoenix determines inventory quantity by a physical count of inventory on hand at the close of business on December 31. The company's controller has asked for your help in deciding if the following items should be included in the year-end inventory count.
1. Merchandise held on consignment for Trout Creek Clothing.
2. Goods shipped f.o.b. destination on December 28 that arrived at the customer's location on January 4.
3. Goods purchased from a vendor shipped f.o.b. shipping point on December 26 that arrived on January 3.
4. Goods shipped f.o.b. shipping point on December 28 that arrived at the customer's location on January 5.
5. Phoenix had merchandise on consignment at Lisa's Markets, Inc.
6. Goods purchased from a vendor shipped f.o.b. destination on December 27 that arrived on January 3.
7. Goods sold to a customer sitting on the loading dock on December 31 waiting to be picked up by the customer.
8. Freight charges on goods purchased in 3.

Required:
Determine if each of the items above should be included or excluded from the company's year-end inventory.

E 8–9
Purchase discounts;
the gross method
● LO3

On July 15, 2011, the Nixon Car Company purchased 1,000 tires from the Harwell Company for $50 each. The terms of the sale were 2/10, n/30. Nixon uses a periodic inventory system and the *gross* method of accounting for purchase discounts.

Required:
1. Prepare the journal entries to record the purchase on July 15 and payment on July 23, 2011.
2. Prepare the journal entry to record the payment on August 15, 2011.
3. If Nixon instead uses a perpetual inventory system, explain any changes to the journal entries created in requirements 1 and 2.

E 8–10
Purchase discounts;
the net method
● LO3

[This is a variation Exercise 8–9 modified to focus on the net method of accounting for purchase discounts.]

On July 15, 2011, the Nixon Car Company purchased 1,000 tires from the Harwell Company for $50 each. The terms of the sale were 2/10, n/30. Nixon uses a periodic inventory system and the *net* method of accounting for purchase discounts.

Required:

1. Prepare the journal entries to record the purchase on July 15 and payment on July 23, 2011.
2. Prepare the journal entry to record the payment on August 15, 2011.
3. If Nixon instead uses a perpetual inventory system, explain any changes to the journal entries created in requirements 1 and 2.

E 8–11
Trade and purchase discounts; the gross method and the net method compared
● LO3

Tracy Company, a manufacturer of air conditioners, sold 100 units to Thomas Company on November 17, 2011. The units have a list price of $500 each, but Thomas was given a 30% trade discount. The terms of the sale were 2/10, n/30. Thomas uses a periodic inventory system.

Required:

1. Prepare the journal entries to record the purchase by Thomas on November 17 and payment on November 26, 2011, using the gross method of accounting for purchase discounts.
2. Prepare the journal entry to record the payment on December 15, 2011, using the gross method of accounting for purchase discounts.
3. Repeat requirements 1 and 2 using the net method of accounting for purchase discounts.

E 8–12
FASB codification research
● LO2 LO3

Access the FASB's Codification Research System at the FASB website (**www.fasb.org**). Determine the specific citation for each of the following items:

1. Define the meaning of cost as it applies to the initial measurement of inventory.
2. Indicate the circumstances when it is appropriate to initially measure agricultural inventory at fair value.
3. What is a major objective of accounting for inventory?
4. Are abnormal freight charges included in the cost of inventory?

E 8–13
Inventory cost flow methods; periodic system
● LO1 LO4

Altira Corporation uses a periodic inventory system. The following information related to its merchandise inventory during the month of August 2011 is available:

Aug. 1	Inventory on hand—2,000 units; cost $6.10 each.
8	Purchased 10,000 units for $5.50 each.
14	Sold 8,000 units for $12.00 each.
18	Purchased 6,000 units for $5.00 each.
25	Sold 7,000 units for $11.00 each.
31	Inventory on hand—3,000 units.

Required:

Determine the inventory balance Altira would report in its August 31, 2011, balance sheet and the cost of goods sold it would report in its August 2011 income statement using each of the following cost flow methods:

1. First-in, first-out (FIFO)
2. Last-in, first-out (LIFO)
3. Average cost

E 8–14
Inventory cost flow methods; perpetual system
● LO1 LO4

[This is a variation of Exercise 8–13 modified to focus on the perpetual inventory system and alternative cost flow methods.]

Altira Corporation uses a perpetual inventory system. The following transactions affected its merchandise inventory during the month of August 2011:

Aug. 1	Inventory on hand—2,000 units; cost $6.10 each.
8	Purchased 10,000 units for $5.50 each.
14	Sold 8,000 units for $12.00 each.
18	Purchased 6,000 units for $5.00 each.
25	Sold 7,000 units for $11.00 each.
31	Inventory on hand—3,000 units.

Required:

Determine the inventory balance Altira would report in its August 31, 2011, balance sheet and the cost of goods sold it would report in its August 2011 income statement using each of the following cost flow methods:

1. First-in, first-out (FIFO)
2. Last-in, first-out (LIFO)
3. Average cost

E 8–15
Comparison of
FIFO and LIFO;
periodic system
● LO1 LO4

Alta Ski Company's inventory records contained the following information regarding its latest ski model. The company uses a periodic inventory system.

Beginning inventory, January 1, 2011	600 units @ $80 each
Purchases:	
January 15	1,000 units @ $95 each
January 21	800 units @ $100 each
Sales:	
January 5	400 units @ $120 each
January 22	800 units @ $130 each
January 29	400 units @ $135 each
Ending inventory, January 31, 2011	800 units

Required:

1. Which method, FIFO or LIFO, will result in the highest cost of goods sold figure for January 2011? Why? Which method will result in the highest ending inventory balance? Why?
2. Compute cost of goods sold for January and the ending inventory using both the FIFO and LIFO methods.

E 8–16
Average cost
method; periodic
and perpetual
systems
● LO1 LO4

The following information is taken from the inventory records of the CNB Company:

Beginning inventory, 9/1/11	5,000 units @ $10.00
Purchases:	
9/7	3,000 units @ $10.40
9/25	8,000 units @ $10.75
Sales:	
9/10	4,000 units
9/29	5,000 units

7,000 units were on hand at the end of September.

Required:

1. Assuming that CNB uses a periodic inventory system and employs the average cost method, determine cost of goods sold for September and September's ending inventory.
2. Repeat requirement 1 assuming that the company uses a perpetual inventory system.

E 8–17
FIFO, LIFO,
and average cost
methods
● LO1 LO4

Causwell Company began 2011 with 10,000 units of inventory on hand. The cost of each unit was $5.00. During 2011 an additional 30,000 units were purchased at a single unit cost, and 20,000 units remained on hand at the end of 2011 (20,000 units therefore were sold during 2011). Causwell uses a periodic inventory system. Cost of goods sold for 2011, applying the average cost method, is $115,000. The company is interested in determining what cost of goods sold would have been if the FIFO or LIFO methods were used.

Required:

1. Determine the cost of goods sold for 2011 using the FIFO method. [*Hint:* Determine the cost per unit of 2011 purchases.]
2. Determine the cost of goods sold for 2011 using the LIFO method.

E 8–18
Supplemental LIFO
disclosures; LIFO
reserve; Steelcase
● LO6

Real World Financials

Steelcase Inc. is the global leader in providing furniture for office environments. The company uses the LIFO inventory method for external reporting and for income tax purposes but maintains its internal records using FIFO. The following disclosure note was included in a recent annual report:

5. Inventories ($ in millions):

	February 27, 2009	February 29, 2008
Raw materials	$ 61.3	$ 67.5
Work-in-process	15.9	20.9
Finished goods	79.9	87.9
	157.1	176.3
LIFO reserve	(27.2)	(29.6)
	$ 129.9	$ 146.7

The company's income statement reported cost of goods sold of $2,236.7 million for the fiscal year ended February 27, 2009.

Required:

1. Steelcase adjusts the LIFO reserve at the end of its fiscal year. Prepare the February 27, 2009, adjusting entry to make the cost of goods sold adjustment.
2. If Steelcase had used FIFO to value its inventories, what would cost of goods sold have been for the 2009 fiscal year?

E 8–19
LIFO liquidation
● **LO1 LO6**

The Reuschel Company began 2011 with inventory of 10,000 units at a cost of $7 per unit. During 2011, 50,000 units were purchased for $8.50 each. Sales for the year totaled 54,000 units leaving 6,000 units on hand at the end of 2011. Reuschel uses a periodic inventory system and the LIFO inventory cost method.

Required:

1. Calculate cost of goods sold for 2011.
2. From a financial reporting perspective, what problem is created by the use of LIFO in this situation? Describe the disclosure required to report the effects of this problem.

E 8–20
FASB codification research
● **LO6**

The *FASB Accounting Standards Codification* represents the single source of authoritative U.S. generally accepted accounting principles.

Required:

1. Obtain the relevant authoritative literature on the disclosure of accounting policies using the FASB's Codification Research System at the FASB website (**www.fasb.org**).
2. What is the specific citation that describes the disclosure requirements that must be made by publicly traded companies for a LIFO liquidation?
3. Describe the disclosure requirements.

E 8–21
Ratio analysis; Home Depot and Lowe's
● **LO7**

Real World Financials

The table below contains selected information from recent financial statements of **The Home Depot, Inc.,** and **Lowe's Companies, Inc.,** two companies in the home improvement retail industry ($ in millions):

	Home Depot		**Lowe's**	
	2/1/09	**2/3/08**	**1/30/09**	**2/21/08**
Net sales	$71,288	$77,349	$48,230	$48,283
Cost of goods sold	47,298	51,352	31,729	31,556
Year-end inventory	10,673	11,731	8,209	7,611

Industry averages:	
Gross profit ratio	33%
Inventory turnover ratio	4
Average days in inventory	91

Required:

Calculate the gross profit ratio, the inventory turnover ratio, and the average days in inventory for the two companies using the most recent fiscal year data. Compare your calculations for the two companies, taking into account the industry averages.

E 8–22
Dollar-value LIFO
● **LO8**

On January 1, 2011, the Haskins Company adopted the dollar-value LIFO method for its one inventory pool. The pool's value on this date was $660,000. The 2011 and 2012 ending inventory valued at year-end costs were $690,000 and $760,000, respectively. The appropriate cost indexes are 1.04 for 2011 and 1.08 for 2012.

Required:

Calculate the inventory value at the end of 2011 and 2012 using the dollar-value LIFO method.

E 8–23
Dollar-value LIFO
● **LO8**

Mercury Company has only one inventory pool. On December 31, 2011, Mercury adopted the dollar-value LIFO inventory method. The inventory on that date using the dollar-value LIFO method was $200,000. Inventory data are as follows:

Year	Ending Inventory at Year-End Costs	Ending Inventory at Base Year Costs
2012	$231,000	$220,000
2013	299,000	260,000
2014	300,000	250,000

Required:

Compute the inventory at December 31, 2012, 2013, and 2014, using the dollar-value LIFO method.

(AICPA adapted)

E 8–24
Concepts;
terminology
● LO1 through
  LO5

Listed below are several terms and phrases associated with inventory measurement. Pair each item from List A with the item from List B (by letter) that is most appropriately associated with it.

List A	List B
_____ 1. Perpetual inventory system	a. Legal title passes when goods are delivered to common carrier.
_____ 2. Periodic inventory system	b. Goods are transferred to another company but title remains with transferor.
_____ 3. F.o.b. shipping point	c. Purchase discounts not taken are included in inventory cost.
_____ 4. Gross method	d. If LIFO is used for taxes, it must be used for financial reporting.
_____ 5. Net method	e. Items sold are those acquired first.
_____ 6. Cost index	f. Items sold are those acquired last.
_____ 7. F.o.b. destination	g. Purchase discounts not taken are considered interest expense.
_____ 8. FIFO	h. Used to convert ending inventory at year-end cost to base year cost.
_____ 9. LIFO	i. Continuously records changes in inventory.
_____ 10. Consignment	j. Items sold come from a mixture of goods acquired during the period.
_____ 11. Average cost	k. Legal title passes when goods arrive at location.
_____ 12. IRS conformity rule	l. Adjusts inventory at the end of the period.

CPA AND CMA REVIEW QUESTIONS

CPA Exam
Questions

The following questions are used in the Kaplan CPA Review Course to study inventory while preparing for the CPA examination. Determine the response that best completes the statements or questions.

● LO2

1. Herc Co.'s inventory at December 31, 2011, was $1,500,000 based on a physical count priced at cost, and before any necessary adjustment for the following:
   - Merchandise costing $90,000, shipped f.o.b shipping point from a vendor on December 30, 2011, was received and recorded on January 5, 2012.
   - Goods in the shipping area were excluded from inventory although shipment was not made until January 4, 2012. The goods, billed to the customer f.o.b. shipping point on December 30, 2011, had a cost of $120,000.

   What amount should Herc report as inventory in its December 31, 2011, balance sheet?
   a. $1,500,000
   b. $1,590,000
   c. $1,700,000
   d. $1,710,000

● LO3

2. Dixon Menswear Shop regularly buys shirts from Colt Company. Dixon purchased shirts from Colt on May 27, and received an invoice with a list price amount of $3,600 and payment terms of 2/10, n/30. Dixon uses the net method to record purchases. Dixon should record the purchase at
   a. $3,430
   b. $3,500
   c. $3,528
   d. $3,600

● LO4

Questions 3 through 5 are based on the following information. Esquire Corp. uses the periodic inventory system. During its first year of operations, Esquire made the following purchases (list in chronological order of acquisition):
   - 20 units at $50
   - 35 units at $40
   - 85 units at $30

Sales for the year totaled 135 units, leaving 5 units on hand at the end of the year.

3. Ending inventory using the average cost method is
   a. $ 150
   b. $ 177
   c. $ 250
   d. $1,540

4. Ending inventory using the FIFO method is
   a. $ 150
   b. $ 177
   c. $ 250
   d. $1,540

5. Ending inventory using the LIFO method is
   a. $ 150
   b. $ 177
   c. $ 250
   d. $1,540

● LO4 LO5

6. Jamison Corporation's inventory cost in its balance sheet is lower using the first-in, first-out method than it would have been had it used the last-in, first-out method. Assuming no beginning inventory, what direction did the cost of purchases move during the period?
   a. Up.
   b. Down.
   c. Unchanged.
   d. Can't be determined.

● LO8

7. Dalton Company adopted the dollar-value LIFO inventory method on January 1, 2011. In applying the LIFO method, Dalton uses internal price indexes and the multiple-pools approach. The following data were available for Inventory Pool No. 1 for the two years following the adoption of LIFO:

	Ending Inventory		
	At Current Year Cost	At Base Year Cost	Cost Index
1/1/11	$100,000	$100,000	1.00
12/31/11	126,000	120,000	1.05
12/31/12	140,800	128,000	1.10

Under the dollar-value LIFO method the inventory at December 31, 2012, should be
a. $128,000
b. $129,800
c. $130,800
d. $140,800

CMA Exam Questions

The following questions dealing with inventory are adapted from questions that previously appeared on Certified Management Accountant (CMA) examinations. The CMA designation sponsored by the Institute of Management Accountants (**www.imanet.org**) provides members with an objective measure of knowledge and competence in the field of management accounting. Determine the response that best completes the statements or questions.

● LO1 LO4

Questions 1 through 3 are based on the following information. Thomas Engine Company is a wholesaler of marine engine parts. The activity of carburetor 2642J during the month of March is presented below.

Date	Balance or Transaction	Units	Unit Cost	Unit Sales Price
Mar 1	Inventory	3,200	$64.30	$86.50
4	Purchase	3,400	64.75	87.00
14	Sales	3,600		87.25
25	Purchase	3,500	66.00	87.25
28	Sales	3,450		88.00

1. If Thomas uses a first-in, first-out perpetual inventory system, the total cost of the inventory for carburetor 2642J at March 31 is
   a. $196,115
   b. $197,488

c. $201,300
d. $263,825

2. If Thomas uses a last-in, first-out periodic inventory system, the total cost of the inventory for carburetor 2642J at March 31 is
   a. $196,115
   b. $197,488
   c. $201,300
   d. $268,400

3. If Thomas uses a last-in, first-out perpetual inventory system, the total cost of the inventory for carburetor 2642J at March 31 is
   a. $196,200
   b. $197,488
   c. $263,863
   d. $268,400

PROBLEMS

An alternate exercise and problem set is available on the text website: www.mhhe.com/spiceland6e

P 8–1
Various inventory transactions; journal entries
● LO1 through LO3

James Company began the month of October with inventory of $15,000. The following inventory transactions occurred during the month:
a. The company purchased merchandise on account for $22,000 on October 12, 2011. Terms of the purchase were 2/10, n/30. James uses the net method to record purchases. The merchandise was shipped f.o.b. shipping point and freight charges of $500 were paid in cash.
b. On October 18 the company returned merchandise costing $3,000. The return reduced the amount owed to the supplier. The merchandise returned came from beginning inventory, not from the October 12 purchase.
c. On October 31, James paid for the merchandise purchased on October 12.
d. During October merchandise costing $18,000 was sold on account for $28,000.
e. It was determined that inventory on hand at the end of October cost $16,060.

Required:
1. Assuming that the James Company uses a periodic inventory system, prepare journal entries for the above transactions including the adjusting entry at the end of October to record cost of goods sold.
2. Assuming that the James Company uses a perpetual inventory system, prepare journal entries for the above transactions.

P 8–2
Items to be included in inventory
● LO2

The following inventory transactions took place near December 31, 2011, the end of the Rasul Company's fiscal year-end:
1. On December 27, 2011, merchandise costing $2,000 was shipped to the Myers Company on consignment. The shipment arrived at Myers's location on December 29, but none of the merchandise was sold by the end of the year. The merchandise was *not* included in the 2011 ending inventory.
2. On January 5, 2012, merchandise costing $8,000 was received from a supplier and recorded as a purchase on that date and *not* included in the 2011 ending inventory. The invoice revealed that the shipment was made f.o.b. shipping point on December 28, 2011.
3. On December 29, 2011, the company shipped merchandise costing $12,000 to a customer f.o.b. destination. The goods, which arrived at the customer's location on January 4, 2012, were *not* included in Rasul's 2011 ending inventory. The sale was recorded in 2011.
4. Merchandise costing $4,000 was received on December 28, 2011, on consignment from the Aborn Company. A purchase was *not* recorded and the merchandise was *not* included in 2011 ending inventory.
5. Merchandise costing $6,000 was received and recorded as a purchase on January 8, 2012. The invoice revealed that the merchandise was shipped from the supplier on December 28, 2011, f.o.b. destination. The merchandise was *not* included in 2011 ending inventory.

Required:
State whether Rasul correctly accounted for each of the above transactions. Give the reason for your answer.

P 8–3
Costs included in
inventory
● LO2 LO3

Reagan Corporation is a wholesale distributor of truck replacement parts. Initial amounts taken from Reagan's records are as follows:

Inventory at December 31 (based on a physical count
of goods in Reagan's warehouse on December 31) $1,250,000
Accounts payable at December 31:

Vendor	Terms	Amount
Baker Company	2%, 10 days, net 30	$ 265,000
Charlie Company	Net 30	210,000
Dolly Company	Net 30	300,000
Eagler Company	Net 30	225,000
Full Company	Net 30	—
Greg Company	Net 30	—
Accounts payable, December 31		$1,000,000
Sales for the year		$9,000,000

Additional information:

1. Parts held by Reagan on consignment from Charlie, amounting to $155,000, were included in the physical count of goods in Reagan's warehouse and in accounts payable at December 31.

2. Parts totaling $22,000, which were purchased from Full and paid for in December, were sold in the last week of the year and appropriately recorded as sales of $28,000. The parts were included in the physical count of goods in Reagan's warehouse on December 31 because the parts were on the loading dock waiting to be picked up by customers.

3. Parts in transit on December 31 to customers, shipped f.o.b. shipping point on December 28, amounted to $34,000. The customers received the parts on January 6 of the following year. Sales of $40,000 to the customers for the parts were recorded by Reagan on January 2.

4. Retailers were holding goods on consignment from Reagan, which had a cost of $210,000 and a retail value of $250,000.

5. Goods were in transit from Greg to Reagan on December 31. The cost of the goods was $25,000, and they were shipped f.o.b. shipping point on December 29.

6. A freight bill in the amount of $2,000 specifically relating to merchandise purchased in December, all of which was still in the inventory at December 31, was received on January 3. The freight bill was not included in either the inventory or in accounts payable at December 31.

7. All the purchases from Baker occurred during the last seven days of the year. These items have been recorded in accounts payable and accounted for in the physical inventory at cost before discount. Reagan's policy is to pay invoices in time to take advantage of all discounts, adjust inventory accordingly, and record accounts payable net of discounts.

Required:

Prepare a schedule of adjustments to the initial amounts using the format shown below. Show the effect, if any, of each of the transactions separately and if the transactions would have no effect on the amount shown, state *none*.

	Inventory	Accounts Payable	Sales
Initial amounts	$1,250,000	$1,000,000	$ 9,000,000
Adjustments—increase (decrease):			
1.			
2.			
3.			
4.			
5.			
6.			
7.			
Total adjustments			
Adjusted amounts	$	$	$

(AICPA adapted)

P 8–4

Various inventory transactions; determining inventory and cost of goods

● LO1 through LO4

Johnson Corporation began 2011 with inventory of 10,000 units of its only product. The units cost $8 each. The company uses a periodic inventory system and the LIFO cost method. The following transactions occurred during 2011:

a. Purchased 50,000 additional units at a cost of $10 per unit. Terms of the purchases were 2/10, n/30, and 100% of the purchases were paid for within the 10-day discount period. The company uses the gross method to record purchase discounts. The merchandise was purchased f.o.b. shipping point and freight charges of $.50 per unit were paid by Johnson.

b. 1,000 units purchased during the year were returned to suppliers for credit. Johnson was also given credit for the freight charges of $.50 per unit it had paid on the original purchase. The units were defective and were returned two days after they were received.

c. Sales for the year totaled 45,000 units at $18 per unit.

d. On December 28, 2011, Johnson purchased 5,000 additional units at $10 each. The goods were shipped f.o.b. destination and arrived at Johnson's warehouse on January 4, 2012.

e. 14,000 units were on hand at the end of 2011.

Required:

1. Determine ending inventory and cost of goods sold for 2011.

2. Assuming that operating expenses other than those indicated in the above transactions amounted to $150,000, determine income before income taxes for 2011.

P 8–5

Various inventory costing methods

● LO1 LO4

Ferris Company began 2011 with 6,000 units of its principal product. The cost of each unit is $8. Merchandise transactions for the month of January 2011 are as follows:

	Purchases		
Date of Purchase	Units	Unit Cost*	Total Cost
Jan. 10	5,000	$ 9	$ 45,000
Jan. 18	6,000	10	60,000
Totals	11,000		$105,000

*Includes purchase price and cost of freight.

Sales	
Date of Sale	Units
Jan. 5	3,000
Jan. 12	2,000
Jan. 20	4,000
Total	9,000

8,000 units were on hand at the end of the month.

Required:

Calculate January's ending inventory and cost of goods sold for the month using each of the following alternatives:

1. FIFO, periodic system

2. LIFO, periodic system

3. LIFO, perpetual system

4. Average cost, periodic system

5. Average cost, perpetual system

P 8–6

Various inventory costing methods; gross profit ratio

● LO1 LO4 LO7

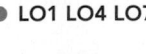

Topanga Group began operations early in 2011. Inventory purchase information for the quarter ended March 31, 2011, for Topanga's only product is provided below. The unit costs include the cost of freight. The company uses a periodic inventory system.

Date of Purchase	Units	Unit Cost	Total Cost
Jan. 7	5,000	$4.00	$ 20,000
Feb. 16	12,000	4.50	54,000
March 22	17,000	5.00	85,000
Totals	34,000		$159,000

Sales for the quarter, all at $7.00 per unit, totaled 20,000 units leaving 14,000 units on hand at the end of the quarter.

Required:

1. Calculate the Topanga's gross profit ratio for the first quarter using:

    a. FIFO

    b. LIFO

    c. Average cost

2. Comment on the relative effect of each of the three inventory methods on the gross profit ratio.

P 8–7
Various inventory
costing methods
● LO1 LO4

Carlson Auto Dealers Inc. sells a handmade automobile as its only product. Each automobile is identical; however, they can be distinguished by their unique ID number. At the beginning of 2011, Carlson had three cars in inventory, as follows:

Car ID	Cost
203	$60,000
207	60,000
210	63,000

During 2011, each of the three autos sold for $90,000. Additional purchases (listed in chronological order) and sales for the year were as follows:

Car ID	Cost	Selling Price
211	$63,000	$ 90,000
212	63,000	93,000
213	64,500	not sold
214	66,000	96,000
215	69,000	100,500
216	70,500	not sold
217	72,000	105,000
218	72,300	106,500
219	75,000	not sold

Required:

1. Calculate 2011 ending inventory and cost of goods sold assuming the company uses the specific identification inventory method.

2. Calculate ending inventory and cost of goods sold assuming FIFO and a periodic inventory system.

3. Calculate ending inventory and cost of goods sold assuming LIFO and a periodic inventory system.

4. Calculate ending inventory and cost of goods sold assuming the average cost method and a periodic inventory system.

P 8–8
Supplemental
LIFO disclosures;
Caterpillar
● LO4 LO6

Real World Financials

Caterpillar, Inc., is one of the world's largest manufacturers of construction, mining, and forestry machinery. The following disclosure note is included in the company's 2008 financial statements:

D. Inventories ($ in millions)

Inventories are stated at the lower of cost or market. Cost is principally determined using the last-in, first-out, (LIFO) method. The value of inventories on the LIFO basis represented about 70% of total inventories at December 31, 2008, and about 75% of total inventories at December 31, 2007, and 2006.

If the FIFO (first-in, first-out) method had been in use, inventories would have been $3,183 million, $2,617 million, and $2,403 million higher than reported at December 31, 2008, 2007, and 2006, respectively.

If inventories valued at LIFO cost had been valued at FIFO cost, net income would have been $447 million higher in 2008 and $169 million higher in 2007.

Required:

1. Approximate the company's effective income tax rate for the year ended December 31, 2008.

2. Why might the information contained in the disclosure note be useful to a financial analyst?

3. Using the income tax rate calculated in 1, how much higher (lower) would retained earnings have been at the end of 2008 if Caterpillar had used the FIFO inventory method for all of its inventory?

P 8–9
LIFO liquidation
● LO4 LO6

Taylor Corporation has used a periodic inventory system and the LIFO cost method since its inception in 2004. The company began 2011 with the following inventory layers (listed in chronological order of acquisition):

10,000 units @ $15	$150,000
15,000 units @ $20	300,000
Beginning inventory	$450,000

During 2011, 30,000 units were purchased for $25 per unit. Due to unexpected demand for the company's product, 2011 sales totaled 40,000 units at various prices, leaving 15,000 units in ending inventory.

Required:
1. Calculate cost of goods sold for 2011.
2. Determine the amount of LIFO liquidation profit that the company must report in a disclosure note to its 2011 financial statements. Assume an income tax rate of 40%.
3. If the company decided to purchase an additional 10,000 units at $25 per unit at the end of the year, how much income tax currently payable would be saved?

P 8–10
LIFO liquidation
● LO4 LO6

Cansela Corporation uses a periodic inventory system and the LIFO method to value its inventory. The company began 2011 with inventory of 4,500 units of its only product. The beginning inventory balance of $64,000 consisted of the following layers:

2,000 units at $12 per unit	=	$24,000
2,500 units at $16 per unit	=	40,000
		$64,000

During the three years 2011–2013 the cost of inventory remained constant at $18 per unit. Unit purchases and sales during these years were as follows:

	Purchases	Sales
2011	10,000	11,000
2012	13,000	14,500
2013	12,000	13,000

Required:
1. Calculate cost of goods sold for 2011, 2012, and 2013.
2. Disregarding income tax, determine the LIFO liquidation profit or loss, if any, for each of the three years.
3. Prepare the company's LIFO liquidation disclosure note that would be included in the 2013 financial statements to report the effects of any liquidation on cost of goods sold and net income. Assume any liquidation effects are material and that Cansela's effective income tax rate is 40%. Cansela's 2013 financial statements include income statements for two prior years for comparative purposes.

P 8–11
Inventory cost flow methods: LIFO liquidation; ratios
● LO4 LO6 LO7

Cast Iron Grills, Inc., manufactures premium gas barbecue grills. The company uses a periodic inventory system and the LIFO cost method for its grill inventory. Cast Iron's December 31, 2011, fiscal year-end inventory consisted of the following (listed in chronological order of acquisition):

Units	Unit Cost
5,000	$700
4,000	800
6,000	900

The replacement cost of the grills throughout 2012 was $1,000. Cast Iron sold 27,000 grills during 2012. The company's selling price is set at 200% of the current replacement cost.

Required:
1. Compute the gross profit (sales minus cost of goods sold) and the gross profit ratio for 2012 assuming that Cast Iron purchased 28,000 units during the year.
2. Repeat requirement 1 assuming that Cast Iron purchased only 15,000 units.
3. Why does the number of units purchased affect your answers to the above requirements?
4. Repeat requirements 1 and 2 assuming that Cast Iron uses the FIFO inventory cost method rather than the LIFO method.
5. Why does the number of units purchased have no effect on your answers to requirements 1 and 2 when the FIFO method is used?

P 8–12
Integrating problem; inventories and accounts receivable; Chapters 7 and 8
● **LO4 LO6 LO7**

Inverness Steel Corporation is a producer of flat-rolled carbon, stainless and electrical steels, and tubular products. The company's income statement for the 2011 fiscal year reported the following information ($ in millions):

Sales	$6,255
Cost of goods sold	5,190

The company's balance sheets for 2011 and 2010 included the following information ($ in millions):

	2011	2010
Current assets:		
Accounts receivable, net	$703	$583
Inventories	880	808

The statement of cash flows reported bad debt expense for 2011 of $8 million. The summary of significant accounting policies included the following notes ($ in millions):

Accounts Receivable (in part)

The allowance for uncollectible accounts was $10 and $7 at December 31, 2011 and 2010, respectively. All sales are on credit.

Inventories

Inventories are valued at the lower of cost or market. The cost of the majority of inventories is measured using the last in, first out (LIFO) method. Other inventories are measured principally at average cost and consist mostly of foreign inventories and certain raw materials. If the entire inventory had been valued on an average cost basis, inventory would have been higher by $480 and $350 at the end of 2011 and 2010, respectively.

During 2011, 2010, and 2009, liquidation of LIFO layers generated income of $6, $7, and $25, respectively.

Required:
Using the information provided:
1. Determine the amount of accounts receivable Inverness wrote off during 2011.
2. Calculate the amount of cash collected from customers during 2011.
3. Calculate what cost of goods sold would have been for 2011 if the company had used average cost to value its entire inventory.
4. Calculate the following ratios for 2011:
   a. Receivables turnover ratio
   b. Inventory turnover ratio
   c. Gross profit ratio
5. Explain briefly what caused the income generated by the liquidation of LIFO layers. Assuming an income tax rate of 35%, what was the effect of the liquidation of LIFO layers on cost of goods sold in 2011?

P 8–13
Dollar-value LIFO
● **LO8**

On January 1, 2011, the Taylor Company adopted the dollar-value LIFO method. The inventory value for its one inventory pool on this date was $400,000. Inventory data for 2011 through 2013 are as follows:

Date	Ending Inventory at Year-End Costs	Cost Index
12/31/11	$441,000	1.05
12/31/12	487,200	1.12
12/31/13	510,000	1.20

Required:
Calculate Taylor's ending inventory for 2011, 2012, and 2013.

P 8–14
Dollar-value LIFO
● **LO8**

Kingston Company uses the dollar-value LIFO method of computing inventory. An external price index is used to convert ending inventory to base year. The company began operations on January 1, 2011, with an inventory of $150,000. Year-end inventories at year-end costs and cost indexes for its one inventory pool were as follows:

Year Ended December 31	Ending Inventory at Year-End Costs	Cost Index (Relative to Base Year)
2011	$200,000	1.08
2012	245,700	1.17
2013	235,980	1.14
2014	228,800	1.10

Required:
Calculate inventory amounts at the end of each year.

P 8–15
Dollar-value LIFO
● LO8

On January 1, 2011, Avondale Lumber adopted the dollar-value LIFO inventory method. The inventory value for its one inventory pool on this date was $260,000. An internally generated cost index is used to convert ending inventory to base year. Year-end inventories at year-end costs and cost indexes for its one inventory pool were as follows:

Year Ended December 31	Inventory Year-End Costs	Cost Index (Relative to Base Year)
2011	$340,000	1.02
2012	350,000	1.06
2013	400,000	1.07
2014	430,000	1.10

Required:
Calculate inventory amounts at the end of each year.

P 8–16
Dollar-value
LIFO; solving for
unknowns
● LO8

At the beginning of 2011, Quentin and Kopps (Q&K) adopted the dollar-value LIFO (DVL) inventory method. On that date the value of its one inventory pool was $84,000. The company uses an internally generated cost index to convert ending inventory to base year. Inventory data for 2011 through 2014 are as follows:

Year Ended December 31	Ending Inventory at Year-End Costs	Ending Inventory at Base-Year Costs	Cost Index	Ending Inventory At DVL cost
2011	$100,800	$ 96,000	1.05	?
2012	136,800	?	1.14	?
2013	150,000	125,000	?	?
2014	?	?	1.25	$133,710

Required:
Determine the missing amounts.

BROADEN YOUR PERSPECTIVE

Apply your critical-thinking ability to the knowledge you've gained. These cases will provide you an opportunity to develop your research, analysis, judgment, and communication skills. You also will work with other students, integrate what you've learned, apply it in real world situations, and consider its global and ethical ramifications. This practice will broaden your knowledge and further develop your decision-making abilities.

**Judgment
Case 8–1**
Riding the Merry-
Go-Round
● LO7

Real World Financials

Merry-Go-Round Enterprises, the clothing retailer for dedicated followers of young men's and women's fashion, was looking natty as a company. It was March 1993, and the Joppa, Maryland-based outfit had just announced the acquisition of Chess King, a rival clothing chain, a move that would give it the biggest share of the young men's clothing market. Merry-Go-Round told brokerage firm analysts that the purchase would add $13 million, or 15 cents a share, to profits for the year. So some Wall Street analysts raised their earnings estimates for Merry-Go-Round. The company's stock rose $2.25, or 15 percent, to $17 on the day of the Chess King news. Merry-Go-Round was hot—$100 of its stock in January 1988 was worth $804 five years later. In 1993 the chain owned 1,460 stores in 44 states, mostly under the Cignal, Chess King, and Merry-Go-Round names.

Merry-Go-Round's annual report for the fiscal year ended January 30, 1993, reported a 15% sales growth, to $877.5 million from $761.2 million. A portion of the company's balance sheet is reproduced below:

	Jan. 30, 1993	Feb. 1, 1992
Assets		
Cash and cash equivalents	$40,115,000	$29,781,000
Marketable securities	—	9,703
Receivables	6,466,000	6,195
Merchandise inventories	82,197,000	59,971,000

But Merry-Go-Round spun out. The company lost $544,000 in the first six months of 1993, compared with earnings of $13.5 million in the first half of 1992. In the fall of 1992, Leonard "Boogie" Weinglass, Merry-Go-Round's flamboyant founder and chairman who had started the company in 1968, boarded up his

Merry-Go-Ranch in Aspen, Colorado, and returned to management after a 12-year hiatus. But the pony-tailed, shirtsleeved entrepreneur—the inspiration for the character Boogie in the movie *Diner*—couldn't save his company from bankruptcy. In January 1994, the company filed for Chapter 11 protection in Baltimore. Shares crumbled below $3.

Required:

In retrospect, can you identify any advance warning at the date of the financial statements of the company's impending bankruptcy?
[Adapted from Jonathan Burton, "Due Diligence," *Worth,* June 1994, pp. 89–96.]

Real World Case 8–2
Physical quantities and costs included in inventory; Sport Chalet
● LO2

Real World Financials

Determining the physical quantity that should be included in inventory normally is a simple matter because that amount consists of items in the possession of the company. The cost of inventory includes all necessary expenditures to acquire the inventory and bring it to its desired *condition* and *location* for sale or for use in the manufacturing process.

Required:

1. Identify and describe the situations in which physical quantity included in inventory is more difficult than simply determining items in the possession of the company.

2. In addition to the direct acquisition costs such as the price paid and transportation costs to obtain inventory, what other expenditures might be necessary to bring the inventory to its desired condition and location?

3. Access EDGAR on the Internet. The web address is **www.sec.gov**. Search for **Sport Chalet Inc.,** a leading operator of full-service, specialty sporting goods stores in California and Nevada. Access the 10-K filing for the most recent fiscal year. Search or scroll to find the disclosure notes (footnotes). What costs does Sport Chalet include in its inventory?

Judgment Case 8–3
The specific identification inventory method; inventoriable costs
● LO3 LO4

Happlia Co. imports household appliances. Each model has many variations and each unit has an identification number. Happlia pays all costs for getting the goods from the port to its central warehouse in Des Moines. After repackaging, the goods are consigned to retailers. A retailer makes a sale, simultaneously buys the appliance from Happlia, and pays the balance due within one week.

To alleviate the overstocking of refrigerators at a Minneapolis retailer, some were reshipped to a Kansas City retailer where they were still held in inventory at December 31, 2011. Happlia paid the costs of this reshipment. Happlia uses the specific identification inventory costing method.

Required:

1. In regard to the specific identification inventory costing method:
   a. Describe its key elements.
   b. Discuss why it is appropriate for Happlia to use this method.
2. a. What general criteria should Happlia use to determine inventory carrying amounts at December 31, 2011?
   b. Give four examples of costs included in these inventory carrying amounts.
3. What costs should be reported in Happlia's 2011 income statement? Ignore lower of cost or market considerations.

(AICPA adapted)

Communication Case 8–4
LIFO versus FIFO
● LO4 LO5

You have just been hired as a consultant to Tangier Industries, a newly formed company. The company president, John Meeks, is seeking your advice as to the appropriate inventory method Tangier should use to value its inventory and cost of goods sold. Mr. Meeks has narrowed the choice to LIFO and FIFO. He has heard that LIFO might be better for tax purposes, but FIFO has certain advantages for financial reporting to investors and creditors. You have been told that the company will be profitable in its first year and for the foreseeable future.

Required:

Prepare a report for the president describing the factors that should be considered by Tangier in choosing between LIFO and FIFO.

Communication Case 8–5
LIFO versus FIFO
● LO4 LO5

An accounting intern for a local CPA firm was reviewing the financial statements of a client in the electronics industry. The intern noticed that the client used the FIFO method of determining ending inventory and cost of goods sold. When she asked a colleague why the firm used FIFO instead of LIFO, she was told that the client used FIFO to minimize its income tax liability. This response puzzled the intern because she thought that LIFO would minimize income tax liability.

Required:

What would you tell the intern to resolve the confusion?

**Judgment
Case 8–6**
Goods in transit
● LO2

At the end of 2011, the Biggie Company performed its annual physical inventory count. John Lawrence, the manager in charge of the physical count, was told that an additional $22,000 in inventory that had been sold and was in transit to the customer should be included in the ending inventory balance. John was of the opinion that the merchandise shipped should be excluded from the ending inventory since Biggie was not in physical possession of the merchandise.

Required:
Discuss the situation and indicate why John's opinion might be incorrect.

Ethics Case 8–7
Profit manipulation
● LO4

In 2010 the Moncrief Company purchased from Jim Lester the right to be the sole distributor in the western states of a product called Zelenex. In payment, Moncrief agreed to pay Lester 20% of the gross profit recognized from the sale of Zelenex in 2011.

Moncrief uses a periodic inventory system and the LIFO inventory method. Late in 2011, the following information is available concerning the inventory of Zelenex:

Beginning inventory, 1/1/11 (10,000 units @ $30)	$ 300,000
Purchases (40,000 units @ $30)	1,200,000
Sales (35,000 units @ $60)	$2,100,000

By the end of the year, the purchase price of Zelenex had risen to $40 per unit. On December 28, 2011, three days before year-end, Moncrief is in a position to purchase 20,000 additional units of Zelenex at the $40 per unit price. Due to the increase in purchase price, Moncrief will increase the selling price in 2012 to $80 per unit. Inventory on hand before the purchase, 15,000 units, is sufficient to meet the next six months' sales and the company does not anticipate any significant changes in purchase price during 2012.

Required:
1. Determine the effect of the purchase of the additional 20,000 units on the 2011 gross profit from the sale of Zelenex and the payment due to Jim Lester.
2. Discuss the ethical dilemma Moncrief faces in determining whether or not the additional units should be purchased.

**Real World
Case 8–8**
Effects of inventory valuation methods; supplemental LIFO disclosures; The Kroger Company
● LO4 LO6

Real World Financials

Income statement and balance sheet information abstracted from a recent annual report of **The Kroger Company**, one of the world's largest retailers, appears below:

Balance Sheets
($ in millions)

	January 31, 2009	February 2, 2008
Current assets:		
Inventories	$4,859	$4,849

Income Statements
($ in millions)

For the Year Ended		
	January 31, 2009	February 2, 2008
Net sales	$76,000	$70,235
Cost of goods sold	58,564	53,779
Gross profit	$17,436	$16,456

The significant accounting policies note disclosure contained the following:

Inventories (in part)
Inventories are stated at the lower of cost (principally on a LIFO basis) or market. In total, approximately 98% of inventories were valued using the LIFO method. Cost for the balance of the inventories was determined using the first-in, first-out ("FIFO") method. Replacement cost was higher than the carrying amount by $800 million at January 31, 2009, and by $604 million at February 2, 2008.

Required:

1. Why is Kroger disclosing the replacement cost of its LIFO inventory?

2. Assuming that year-end replacement cost figures approximate FIFO inventory values, estimate what the beginning and ending inventory balances for the fiscal year ended 1/31/09 would have been if Kroger had used FIFO for all of its inventories.

3. Estimate the effect on cost of goods sold (that is, would it have been greater or less and by how much?) for the fiscal year ended 1/31/09 if Kroger had used FIFO for all of its inventories.

Real World Case 8–9

Effects of inventory valuation methods; Whole Foods Market

● LO4 LO5 LO7

Real World Financials

EDGAR, the Electronic Data Gathering, Analysis, and Retrieval system, performs automated collection, validation, indexing, and forwarding of submission by companies and others who are required by law to file forms with the U.S. Securities and Exchange Commission (SEC). All publicly traded domestic companies use EDGAR to make the majority of their filings. (Some foreign companies file voluntarily.) Form 10-K, which includes the annual report, is required to be filed on EDGAR. The SEC makes this information available on the Internet.

Required:

1. Access EDGAR on the Internet. The web address is **www.sec.gov**.

2. Search for **Whole Foods Market, Inc.** Access the 10-K filing for the most recent fiscal year. Search or scroll to find the financial statements and related notes.

3. Answer the following questions related to the company's inventories:
   a. What method(s) does the company use to value its inventories?
   b. Calculate what cost of sales would have been for the year if the company had used FIFO to value its inventories.
   c. Calculate inventory turnover for the year using the reported numbers.

Communication Case 8–10

Dollar-value LIFO method

● LO8

Maxi Corporation uses the unit LIFO inventory method. The costs of the company's products have been steadily rising since the company began operations in 2001 and cost increases are expected to continue. The chief financial officer of the company would like to continue using LIFO because of its tax advantages. However, the controller, Sally Hamel, would like to reduce the recordkeeping costs of LIFO that have steadily increased over the years as new products have been added to the company's product line. Sally suggested the use of the dollar-value LIFO method. The chief financial officer has asked Sally to describe the dollar-value LIFO procedure.

Required:

Describe the dollar-value LIFO procedure.

Research Case 8–11

FASB codification; locate and extract relevant information and authoritative support for a financial reporting issue; product financing arrangement

● LO2 LO3

You were recently hired to work in the controller's office of the Balboa Lumber Company. Your boss, Alfred Eagleton, took you to lunch during your first week and asked a favor. "Things have been a little slow lately, and we need to borrow a little cash to tide us over. Our inventory has been building up and the CFO wants to pledge the inventory as collateral for a short-term loan. But I have a better idea." Mr. Eagleton went on to describe his plan. "On July 1, 2011, the first day of the company's third quarter, we will sell $100,000 of inventory to the Harbaugh Corporation for $160,000. Harbaugh will pay us immediately and then we will agree to repurchase the merchandise in two months for $164,000. The $4,000 is Harbaugh's fee for holding the inventory and for providing financing. I already checked with Harbaugh's controller and he has agreed to the arrangement. Not only will we obtain the financing we need, but the third quarter's before-tax profits will be increased by $56,000, the gross profit on the sale less the $4,000 fee. Go research the issue and make sure we would not be violating any specific accounting standards related to product financing arrangements."

Required:

1. Obtain the relevant authoritative literature on product financing arrangements using the FASB's Codification Research System. You might gain access at the FASB website (**www.fasb.org**). What is the specific citation that provides guidance for determining whether an arrangement involving the sale of inventory is "in substance" a financing arrangement?

2. What is the specific citation that addresses the recognition of a product financing arrangement?

3. Determine the appropriate treatment of product financing arrangements like the one proposed by Mr. Eagleton.

4. Prepare the journal entry for Balboa Lumber to record the "sale" of the inventory and subsequent repurchase.

Analysis Case 8–12

Compare inventory management using ratios; Saks and Dillards

● LO7

The table below contains selected financial information included in the 2009 financial statements of **Saks, Inc.**, and **Dillards, Inc.**, two companies in the department store industry.

Real World Financials

	($ in millions)			
	Saks, Inc.		Dillards, Inc.	
	2009	**2008**	**2009**	**2008**
Balance sheet:				
Inventories	$ 729	$857	$1,374	$1,779
Income statement:				
Net sales	$3,030		$6,831	
Cost of goods sold	2,062		4,828	

Required:

1. Calculate the 2009 gross profit ratio, inventory turnover ratio, and average days in inventory for both companies. Evaluate the management of each company's investment in inventory. Industry averages for these ratios are as follows:

Gross profit	25%
Inventory turnover	2.73
Average days in inventory	134

2. Obtain annual reports from three corporations in an industry other than autos and compare the management of each company's investment in inventory.

Note: You can obtain copies of annual reports from your library, from friends who are shareholders, from the investor relations department of the corporations, from a friendly stockbroker, or from EDGAR (Electronic Data Gathering, Analysis, and Retrieval) on the Internet (**www.sec.gov**).

BRITISH AIRWAYS CASE

BRITISH AIRWAYS

● LO9

British Airways, Plc. (BA), a U.K. company, prepares its financial statements according to International Financial Reporting Standards. BA's annual report for the year ended March 31, 2009, which includes financial statements and disclosure notes, is included with all new textbooks and can be found at **www.britishairways.com**. When answering questions, focus on BA's "Group" financial information (which is equivalent to "Consolidated" under U.S. GAAP).

Required:

What method does the company use to value its inventory? What other alternatives are available under IFRS? Under U.S. GAAP?

CHAPTER 9

Inventories: Additional Issues

/// OVERVIEW

We covered most of the principal measurement and reporting issues involving the asset inventory and the corresponding expense cost of goods sold in the previous chapter. In this chapter we complete our discussion of inventory measurement by explaining the lower-of-cost-or-market rule used to value inventories. In addition, we investigate inventory estimation techniques, methods of simplifying LIFO, changes in inventory method, and inventory errors.

/// LEARNING OBJECTIVES

After studying this chapter, you should be able to:

● **LO1** Understand and apply the lower-of-cost-or-market rule used to value inventories. (page 448)

● **LO2** Estimate ending inventory and cost of goods sold using the gross profit method. (page 456)

● **LO3** Estimate ending inventory and cost of goods sold using the retail inventory method, applying the various cost flow methods. (page 458)

● **LO4** Explain how the retail inventory method can be made to approximate the lower-of-cost-or-market rule. (page 461)

● **LO5** Determine ending inventory using the dollar-value LIFO retail inventory method. (page 465)

● **LO6** Explain the appropriate accounting treatment required when a change in inventory method is made. (page 469)

● **LO7** Explain the appropriate accounting treatment required when an inventory error is discovered. (page 472)

● **LO8** Discuss the primary differences between U.S. GAAP and IFRS with respect to the lower-of-cost-or-market rule for valuing inventory. (page 453)

FINANCIAL REPORTING CASE

Does It Count?

Today you drove over to Sears to pick up a few items. Yesterday, your accounting professor had discussed inventory measurement issues and the different methods (FIFO, LIFO, and average) used by companies to determine ending inventory and cost of goods sold. You can't imagine actually counting the inventory in all of the Sears stores around the country. "There must be some way they can avoid counting all of that inventory every time they want to produce financial statements," you tell your dog when you get home. "I think I'll go check their financial statements on the Internet to see what kind of inventory method they use." You find the following in the summary of significant accounting policies included in Sears's most recent financial statements:

Merchandise Inventories (in part):

Merchandise inventories are valued at the lower of cost or market. For Kmart and Sears Domestic, cost is primarily determined using the retail inventory method. Approximately 50% of consolidated merchandise inventories are valued using LIFO. To estimate the effects of inflation on inventories, we utilize external price indices determined by an outside source, the Bureau of Labor Statistics.

By the time you finish this chapter, you should be able to respond appropriately to the questions posed in this case. Compare your response to the solution provided at the end of the chapter.

QUESTIONS ///

1. Sears values its inventory at the lower of cost or market. What does that mean? Under what circumstances might Sears be justified in reporting its inventory at less than cost? (page 448)

2. How does Sears avoid counting all its inventory every time it produces financial statements? What are external price indices used for? (page 465)

REPORTING—LOWER OF COST OR MARKET

In the previous chapter you learned that there are several methods a company could use to determine the cost of inventory at the end of a period and the corresponding cost of goods sold for the period. You also learned that it is important for a company to disclose the inventory method that it uses. Otherwise, investors and creditors would be unable to meaningfully compare accounting information from company to company. This disclosure typically is made in the summary of significant accounting policies accompanying the financial statements. **Coca-Cola Company**'s inventory method disclosure is shown in Graphic 9–1.

GRAPHIC 9–1

Disclosure of Inventory Method—Coca-Cola Company

Real World Financials

Inventories

Inventories consists primarily of raw materials and packaging (which includes ingredients and supplies) and finished goods (which includes concentrates and syrups in our concentrate and foodservice operations, and finished beverages in our bottling and canning operations). Inventories are valued at the lower of cost or market. We determine cost on the basis of the average cost or first-in, first-out methods.

● **LO1**

FINANCIAL Reporting Case

Q1, p. 447

The LCM approach to valuing inventory is required by GAAP.

Real World Financials

The disclosure indicates that Coca-Cola uses both the average cost and FIFO methods to determine the cost of its inventories. Notice that inventories actually are valued at the *lower of cost or market.* Assets are initially valued at their historical costs, but a departure from cost is warranted when the utility of an asset (its probable future economic benefits) is no longer as great as its cost. Accounts receivable, for example, are valued at net realizable value by reducing initial valuation with an allowance for uncollectible accounts.

The utility, or benefits, a company receives from inventory result from the ultimate sale of the goods. So deterioration, obsolescence, changes in price levels, or any situation that might compromise the inventory's salability impairs that utility. The lower-of-cost-or-market (LCM) approach to valuing inventory was developed to avoid reporting inventory at an amount greater than the benefits it can provide. Reporting inventories at LCM causes losses to be recognized in the period the value of inventory declines below its cost rather than in the period in which the goods ultimately are sold. LCM is not an optional approach to valuing inventory; it is required by GAAP.

The tremendous growth of the Internet that took place during the decade of the 90s allowed companies that produced products that support the Internet to become extremely profitable. **Cisco Systems, Inc.**, the world's largest networking products company, is one of those companies. In 1993, Cisco reported $649 million in sales revenue. By 2000, sales had reached nearly $19 billion! Growth rates of 50% year-to-year were commonplace. The company's market capitalization (price per share of common stock multiplied by the number of common shares outstanding) soared to over $500 billion. To keep pace with this growth in sales, inventories swelled from $71 million in 1993 to over $2.5 billion in 2000.

At the end of 2000, corporate spending on Internet infrastructure took a drastic downturn. Many dot-com companies went bankrupt, and companies like Cisco saw their fantastic growth rates nosedive. Early in 2001, the company reported its first-ever quarterly loss and, due to declining demand for its products, recorded an inventory write-down in excess of $2 billion. The company's once lofty market capitalization dropped to just over $100 billion.

CISCO POSTS $5BN LOSS ON HUGE WRITE-DOWNS
Technology giant Cisco Systems posted on Tuesday a third-quarter net loss of $2.69 billion, its first ever, following a write-down of inventory, restructuring costs and a sharp drop-off in corporate spending.

. . . and a write-down of over $2 billion for excess inventory.

Cisco said 80 percent of the inventory charge relates to raw materials, such as semiconductor memories, optical components, . . .

"Most of the excess inventory cannot be sold as it is custom built for Cisco," chief financial officer Mr. Larry Carter said in a conference call.[1]

---

[1]Fiona Buffini, "Cisco Posts $5bn Loss on Huge Writedowns," *Financial Review,* May 9, 2001.

Determining Market Value

From the preceding discussion, you might interpret the term *market* to mean the amount that could be realized if the inventory were sold. However, generally accepted accounting principles define market for LCM purposes as the inventory's current replacement cost (by purchase or reproduction) except that market should not:

    a. Exceed the net realizable value (that is, estimated selling price in the ordinary course of business less reasonably predictable costs of completion and disposal).

    b. Be less than net realizable value reduced by an allowance for an approximately normal profit margin.

In effect, we have a ceiling and a floor between which market (that is, replacement cost) must fall. **Net realizable value (NRV)** represents the upper limit and **net realizable value less a normal profit margin (NRV − NP)** provides the lower limit. If **replacement cost (RC)** is within the range, it represents market; if it is above the ceiling or below the floor, the ceiling or the floor becomes market. As a result, the designated market value is the number that falls in the middle of the three possibilities: replacement cost, net realizable value, and net realizable value less a normal profit margin. The designated market value is compared with cost, and the lower of the two is used to value inventory.

Graphic 9–2 portrays the lower-of-cost-or-market approach to inventory valuation.

Replacement cost (RC) generally means the cost to replace the item by purchase or manufacture.

The ceiling of *net realizable value (NRV)* and the floor of *net realizable value less a normal profit margin (NRV − NP)* establish a range within which the market must fall.

Lower-of-cost-or-market Approach to Valuing Inventory

GRAPHIC 9–2

Lower-of-Cost-or-Market Approach to Valuing Inventory

Let's see how the LCM rule is applied in Illustration 9–1 and then we will discuss its theoretical merit.

Notice that the designated market value is the middle amount of the three market possibilities. This number is then compared to cost and the lower of the two is the final inventory value. For item A, cost is lower than market. For each of the other items, the designated market is lower than cost, requiring an adjustment to the carrying value of inventory. We discuss the adjustment procedure later in the chapter. First though, let's consider the conceptual justification of the LCM rule.

THEORETICAL MERITS.   What is the logic for designating replacement cost as the principal meaning of market value in the LCM rule? First, a change in replacement cost usually is a good indicator of the direction of change in selling price. If replacement cost declines, selling price usually will decline, or already has declined. Another reason is that if previously

ILLUSTRATION 9–1

Lower of Cost or Market

The Collins Company has five inventory items on hand at the end of 2011. The year-end unit costs (determined by applying the average cost method), current unit selling prices, and estimated disposal (selling) costs for each of the items are presented below. The gross profit ratio for each of the products is 20% of selling price.

Item	Cost	Replacement Cost	Selling Price	Estimated Disposal Costs
A	$ 50	$55	$100	$15
B	100	90	120	20
C	80	70	85	20
D	90	37	100	24
E	95	92	110	24

The determination of inventory value is a two-step process: first, determine the designated market value and second, compare the designated market value to cost. The lower of the two is the LCM inventory value.

Inventory is valued at the lower of cost or the designated market value.

	(1)	(2)	(3)	(4)		(5)
Item	RC	NRV (The Ceiling)	NRV − NP (The Floor)	Designated Market Value [Middle Value of (1), (2) and (3)]	Cost	Inventory Value [Lower of (4) and (5)]
A	$55	$ 85	$65	$65	$ 50	$50
B	90	100	76	90	100	90
C	70	65	48	65	80	65
D	37	76	56	56	90	56
E	92	86	64	86	95	86

RC = Current replacement cost.
NRV = Estimated selling price less estimated disposal costs.
NRV − NP = NRV less a normal profit margin.

Example for item B:

Selling price	$120
Less: Disposal costs	(20)
NRV	100
Less: Normal profit	(24) ($120 selling price × 20%)
NRV − NP	$ 76

acquired inventory is revalued at its replacement cost, then the profit margin realized on its sale will likely approximate the profit margin realizable on the sale of newly acquired items.

The upper limit placed on replacement cost prevents inventory from being valued at an amount above what can be realized from its sale. The lower limit prevents inventory from being valued at an amount below what can be realized from its sale after considering normal profit margin. For example, consider item D in our illustration. If item D is valued at its replacement cost of $37 without considering the ceiling or floor, a loss of $53 ($90 cost less $37) would be recognized. If the item is subsequently sold at its current selling price less usual disposal costs (NRV = $76), then a gross profit of $39 ($76 less $37) would be recognized. This is much higher than its normal profit of $20 (20% × $100) and causes a shifting of income from the period the inventory loss is recognized to the period the item is sold. The ceiling and floor prohibit this kind of profit distortion.

Some accountants complain that LCM promotes conservatism at the expense of consistency.

On the other hand, critics of LCM contend that the method causes losses to be recognized that haven't actually occurred. Others maintain that it introduces needless inconsistency in order to be conservative. Inconsistency is created because LCM recognizes decreases in market value as they occur, but not increases.

The practice of recognizing decreases but not increases is not simply an application motivated by conservatism. Recall our discussions in previous chapters on revenue recognition and the realization principle. Recognizing increases in the value of inventory prior to sale would, in most cases, violate the realization principle. Assume that merchandise costing $100 has a net realizable value of $150. Recognizing the increase in value would increase pretax income by $50. This is equivalent to recognizing revenue of $150, cost of goods sold of $100, and gross profit of $50. Either way, pretax income is increased in a period prior to sale of the product. Prior to sale, there usually exists significant uncertainty as to the collectibility of the asset to be received. We don't know if the product will be sold, nor the selling price, or the buyer if eventually sold.

The LCM rules are intended as a guide rather than a literal rule. In practice, companies frequently define market as net realizable value. This is a number that often is easier to estimate than replacement cost. Also, assuming the NRV does not change, when the item is sold, there will be neither gross profit nor additional loss. The entire effect on income is recognized in the period the realizable value drops below cost.

ETHICAL DILEMMA

The Hartley Paper Company, owned and operated by Bill Hartley, manufactures and sells different types of computer paper. The company has reported profits in the majority of years since the company's inception in 1967 and is projecting a profit in 2011 of $65,000, down from $96,000 in 2010.

Near the end of 2011, the company is in the process of applying for a bank loan. The loan proceeds will be used to replace manufacturing equipment necessary to modernize the manufacturing operation. In preparing the financial statements for the year, the chief accountant, Don Davis, mentioned to Bill Hartley that approximately $40,000 of paper inventory has become obsolete and should be written off as a loss in 2011. Bill is worried that the write-down would lower 2011 income to a level that might cause the bank to refuse the loan. Without the loan, it would be difficult for the company to compete. This could cause decreased future business and employees might have to be laid off. Bill is considering waiting until 2012 to write down the inventory. Don Davis is contemplating his responsibilities in this situation.

LCM APPLICATION
The most common practice is to apply the *lower of cost or market rule* separately to each item of the inventory. However, if there is only one end-product category the cost utility of the total stock—the inventory in its entirety—may have the greatest significance for accounting purposes.

Similarly, where more than one major product or operational category exists, the application of the *lower of cost or market, whichever is lower* rule to the total of items included in such major categories may result in the most useful determination of income.[2]

Applying Lower of Cost or Market

Lower of cost or market can be applied to individual inventory items, to logical categories of inventory, or to the entire inventory. A major product line can be considered a logical category of inventory. For income tax purposes, the lower-of-cost-or-market rule must be applied on an individual item basis.

Let's return to our illustration and assume the unit amounts pertain to 1,000 units of each inventory item. Also, let's say items A–B and items C–E are two collections of similar items that can be considered logical categories of inventory. Illustration 9–1A compares the LCM valuation accounting to each of three possible applications.

The final LCM inventory value is different for each of the three applications. The inventory value is $347,000 if LCM is applied to each item, $357,000 if it is applied to product line categories, and $362,000 if applied to the entire inventory. Applying LCM to groups of inventory items will usually cause a higher inventory valuation than if applied on an item-by-item basis because group application permits decreases in the market value of some items to be offset by increases in others. Each approach is acceptable but should be applied consistently from one period to another.

> The LCM rule can be applied to individual inventory items, logical inventory categories, or the entire inventory.

---

[2]FASB ASC 330–10–35–9 and 10: Inventory—Overall—Subsequent Measurement (previously "Restatement and Revision of Accounting Research Bulletins," *Accounting Research Bulletin No. 43* (New York: AICPA, 1953), Ch. 4, par. 11).

ILLUSTRATION 9–1A

LCM Determination— Application at Different Levels of Aggregation

Item	Cost	Designated Market Value	Lower-of-Cost-or-Market By Individual Items	By Product Line	By Total Inventory
A	$ 50,000	$ 65,000	$ 50,000		
B	100,000	90,000	90,000		
Total A + B	$150,000	$155,000		$150,000	
C	$ 80,000	$ 65,000	65,000		
D	90,000	56,000	56,000		
E	95,000	86,000	86,000		
Total C, D, & E	$265,000	$207,000		207,000	
Total	$415,000	$362,000	$347,000	$357,000	$362,000

Adjusting Cost to Market

When a company applies the LCM rule and a material write-down of inventory is required, the company has two choices of how to report the reduction. One way found in practice is to report the loss as a separate item in the income statement. An alternative is to include the loss as part of the cost of goods sold.

Loss on write-down of inventory ... xx		Cost of goods sold xx
Inventory* xx	or	Inventory* xx

*Or, inventory can be reduced indirectly with a credit to an allowance account.

If inventory write-downs are commonplace for a company, it usually will include the losses as part of cost of goods sold. However, a write-down loss that is substantial and unusual should be reported as a separate item among operating expenses. Including these losses in cost of goods sold would distort the relationship between sales and cost of goods sold. Conceptually, cost of goods sold should include only the cost of goods actually sold during the period.

Recall from our introductory discussion to this chapter that **Cisco Systems, Inc.**, recorded an inventory write-down in excess of $2 billion. To understand how the relationship between sales and cost of goods sold can be distorted, let's consider the top part of the company's income statements for the first quarter of 2001 and 2000 shown in Graphic 9–3.

RECORDING INVENTORY WRITE-DOWNS

When substantial and unusual losses result from the application of cost or market, it will frequently be desirable to disclose the amount of the loss in the income statement as a separate charge separately identified from the consumed inventory costs described as cost of goods sold.[3]

GRAPHIC 9–3

Partial Income Statements—Cisco Systems, Inc.

Real World Financials

INCOME STATEMENTS (IN PART)
For the Three Months Ended,
($ in millions)

	April 28, 2001	April 29, 2000
Net sales	$4,728	$4,933
Cost of sales	4,400	1,761
Gross profit	328	3,172

Using the information in the statements, the gross profit ratio dropped from 64% ($3,172 ÷ $4,933) in 2000 to 7% ($328 ÷ $4,728) in 2001. An analyst might conclude that

[3]FASB ASC 330–10–50–2: Inventory—Overall—Disclosure—Losses from Application of Lower of Cost or Market (previously "Restatement and Revision of Accounting Research Bulletins," *Accounting Research Bulletin No. 43* (New York: AICPA, 1953), Ch. 4, par. 14).

there was a significant deterioration in the markup the company was able to achieve on its products. However, this assessment is premature. A disclosure note included in the financial statements for the first quarter of 2001 reported that during the quarter Cisco recorded "an excess inventory charge of $2.25 billion classified as cost of sales." We get a more accurate portrayal of the company's gross profit ratio if we reduce the cost of goods sold by the inventory charge (write-down):

Sales	$4,728
Adjusted cost of sales ($4,400 − 2,250)	2,150
Adjusted gross profit	2,578
Adjusted gross profit ratio	55%

> Reporting a substantial and unusual loss from an inventory write-down as part of cost of goods sold distorts the relationship between sales and cost of goods sold.

Cisco's gross profit ratio did decline from the prior year, but not nearly as drastically as the reported financial statement information would lead us to believe.

Regardless of which approach we use to report the write-down, the reduced inventory value becomes the new cost basis for subsequent reporting, and if the inventory value later recovers prior to its sale, we do not write it back up.[4]

INTERNATIONAL FINANCIAL REPORTING STANDARDS

Lower of cost or market. International standards also require inventory to be valued at the lower of cost or market. You just learned that in the United States, market is defined as replacement cost with a ceiling of net realizable value (NRV) and a floor of NRV less a normal profit margin. However, the designated market value according to *IAS No. 2*[5] always is net realizable value.

● LO8

IAS No. 2 also specifies that if circumstances indicate that an inventory write-down is no longer appropriate, it must be reversed. Reversals are not permitted under U.S. GAAP.

Under U.S. GAAP, the LCM rule can be applied to individual items, logical inventory categories, or the entire inventory. Using the international standard, the LCM assessment usually is applied to individual items, although using logical inventory categories is allowed under certain circumstances.

Consider the following illustration:

Biddle and White, LTD, prepares its financial statements according to IFRS. Using the data in Illustrations 9–1 and 9–1A, the company would determine the inventory carrying value at year-end, assuming the LCM rule is applied to individual items, as $377,000.

IFRS ILLUSTRATION

Item	Cost	NRV	LCM
A	$ 50,000	$ 85,000	$ 50,000
B	100,000	100,000	100,000
C	80,000	65,000	65,000
D	90,000	76,000	76,000
E	95,000	86,000	86,000
Totals	$415,000		$377,000

Notice that the carrying value of $377,000 is larger than the $347,000 determined using U.S. GAAP. This normally will be the case because replacement cost usually is less than NRV.

The entry to record the write-down is as follows:

Inventory write-down expense ($415,000 − 377,000)	38,000	
Inventory valuation allowance		38,000

(continued)

> To record the write-down of inventory to market value.

[4]The SEC, in *Staff Accounting Bulletin No. 100,* "Restructuring and Impairment Charges" (Washington, D.C.: SEC, November, 1999), paragraph B.B., [FASB ASC 330–10–S35–1: SAB Topic 5.BB], reaffirmed the provisions of GAAP literature on this issue. For interim reporting purposes, however, recoveries of losses on the same inventory in subsequent interim periods of the same fiscal year through market price recoveries should be recognized as gains in the later interim period, not to exceed the previously recognized losses.

[5]"Inventories," *International Accounting Standard No. 2* (IASCF), as amended effective January 1, 2009.

Real World Financials

(concluded)

Because IFRS allows companies to reverse write-downs later if NRV increases, it's convenient to use an inventory valuation account in the above entry rather than reducing inventory directly. Reversals, then, are recorded by debiting the allowance account. IFRS does not require the write-down to be recorded in any specific income statement account.

Cadbury Schweppes, Plc., a U.K. company, prepares its financial statements according to IFRS. The following disclosure note illustrates the designation of market as net realizable value.

Inventories (in part)

Inventories are recorded at the lower of average cost and estimated net realizable value.

ADDITIONAL CONSIDERATION

In very limited circumstances, businesses are allowed under GAAP to carry inventory at a market value above cost. This approach is restricted generally to companies that deal in precious metals, and ". . . agricultural, mineral, and other products, units of which are interchangeable and have an immediate marketability at quoted prices . . ."[6] Writing inventory up to market value means recognizing revenue for the increase. This is called the *production basis* of recognizing revenue. In rare cases when the method is appropriate, full disclosure of the fact that inventory is valued at market is required.

CONCEPT REVIEW EXERCISE

LOWER OF COST OR MARKET

The Strand Company sells four products that can be grouped into two major categories. Information necessary to apply the LCM rule at the end of 2011 for each of the four products is presented below. The normal profit margin for each of the products is 25% of selling price. The company records any losses from adjusting cost to market as separate income statement items and reduces inventory directly.

Product	Cost	Replacement Cost	Selling Price	Disposal Costs
101	$ 80,000	$ 85,000	$160,000	$30,000
102	175,000	160,000	200,000	25,000
201	160,000	140,000	180,000	50,000
202	45,000	20,000	60,000	22,000

Products 101 and 102 are in category A and products 201 and 202 are in category B.

Required:

1. Determine the designated market value for each of the four products according to the LCM rule.
2. Determine the amount of the loss from write-down of inventory that would be required, applying the LCM rule to:
   a. Individual items
   b. Major categories
   c. The entire inventory

SOLUTION

1. Determine the designated market value for each of the four products according to the LCM rule.

---

[6]FASB ASC 330–10–35–16: Inventory—Overall—Subsequent Measurement (previously "Restatement and Revision of Accounting Research Bulletins," *Accounting Research Bulletin No. 43* (New York: AICPA, 1953), Ch. 4, par. 16).

Product	(1) RC	(2) NRV (Selling Price Less Disposal Costs)	(3) NRV − NP	(4) Designated Market Value [Middle Value of (1), (2) & (3)]
101	$ 85,000	$130,000	$ 90,000	$ 90,000
102	160,000	175,000	125,000	160,000
201	140,000	130,000	85,000	130,000
202	20,000	38,000	23,000	23,000

Calculation of NRV − NP:

Product	NRV	NP	NRV − NP
101	$ 130,000	$40,000 (25% × $160,000)	$ 90,000
102	175,000	50,000 (25% × $200,000)	125,000
201	130,000	45,000 (25% × $180,000)	85,000
202	38,000	15,000 (25% × $60,000)	23,000

2. Determine the amount of the loss from write-down of inventory that would be required.

Product	Cost	Designated Market Value	Lower-of-Cost-or-Market By Individual Products	By Category	By Total Inventory
101	$ 80,000	$ 90,000	$ 80,000		
102	175,000	160,000	160,000		
Total 101 + 102	$255,000	$250,000		$250,000	
201	$160,000	$130,000	130,000		
202	45,000	23,000	23,000		
Total 201 + 202	$205,000	$153,000		153,000	
Total	$460,000	$403,000	$393,000	$403,000	$403,000

The LCM value for both the category application and the entire inventory application are identical because, in this particular case, market is below cost for both of the categories.

Amount of loss from write-down using individual items:

$460,000 − 393,000 = **$67,000**

Amount of loss from write-down using categories or the entire inventory:

$460,000 − 403,000 = **$57,000**

INVENTORY ESTIMATION TECHNIQUES   PART B

The Southern Wholesale Company distributes approximately 100 products throughout the state of Mississippi. Southern uses a periodic inventory system and takes a physical count of inventory once a year at the end of the year. A recent fire destroyed the entire inventory in one of Southern's warehouses. How can the company determine the dollar amount of inventory destroyed when submitting an insurance claim to obtain reimbursement for the loss?

Home Improvement Stores, Inc., sells over 1,000 different products to customers in each of its 17 retail stores. The company uses a periodic inventory system and takes a physical count of inventory once a year at its fiscal year-end. Home Improvement's bank has asked for monthly financial statements as a condition attached to a recent loan. Can the company avoid the costly procedure of counting inventory at the end of each month to determine ending inventory and cost of goods sold?

These are just two examples of situations when it is either impossible or infeasible to determine the dollar amount of ending inventory by taking a count of the physical quantity of inventory on hand at the end of a period. Fortunately, companies can estimate inventory in these situations by either the gross profit method or the retail inventory method.

The Gross Profit Method

● LO2

The **gross profit method,** also known as the **gross margin method,** is useful in situations where estimates of inventory are desirable. The technique is valuable in a variety of situations:

1. In determining the cost of inventory that has been lost, destroyed, or stolen.
2. In estimating inventory and cost of goods sold for interim reports, avoiding the expense of a physical inventory count.
3. In auditors' testing of the overall reasonableness of inventory amounts reported by clients.
4. In budgeting and forecasting.

The *gross profit method* is not acceptable for the preparation of annual financial statements.

However, the gross profit method provides only an approximation of inventory and is not acceptable according to generally accepted accounting principles for annual financial statements.

The technique relies on a relationship you learned in the previous chapter—ending inventory and cost of goods sold always equal the cost of goods available for sale. Even when inventory is unknown, we can estimate it because accounting records usually indicate the cost of goods available for sale (beginning inventory plus net purchases), and the cost of goods sold can be estimated from available information. So by subtracting the cost of goods sold estimate from the cost of goods available for sale, we obtain an estimate of ending inventory. Let's compare that with the way inventory and cost of goods sold normally are determined.

Usually, in a periodic inventory system, ending inventory is known from a physical count and cost of goods sold is *derived* as follows:

Beginning inventory	(from the accounting records)
Plus: Net purchases	(from the accounting records)
Goods available for sale	
Less: Ending inventory	(from a physical count)
Cost of goods sold	

However, when using the gross profit method, the ending inventory is *not* known. Instead, the amount of sales is known—from which we can estimate the cost of goods sold—and ending inventory is the amount calculated.

Beginning inventory	(from the accounting records)
Plus: Net purchases	(from the accounting records)
Goods available for sale	
Less: Cost of goods sold	(estimated)
Ending inventory	(estimated)

So, a first step in estimating inventory is to estimate cost of goods sold. This estimate relies on the historical relationship among (a) net sales, (b) cost of goods sold, and (c) gross profit. Gross profit, you will recall, is simply net sales minus cost of goods sold. So, if we know what net sales are, and if we know what percentage of net sales the gross profit is, we can fairly accurately estimate cost of goods sold. Companies often sell products that have similar gross profit ratios. As a result, accounting records usually provide the information necessary to estimate the cost of ending inventory, even when a physical count is impractical. Let's use the gross profit method to solve the problem of Southern Wholesale Company introduced earlier in the chapter. Suppose the company began 2011 with inventory of $600,000, and on March 17 a warehouse fire destroyed the entire inventory. Company records indicate net purchases of $1,500,000 and net sales of $2,000,000 prior to the fire. The gross profit ratio in each of the previous three years has been very close to 40%. Illustration 9–2 shows how Southern can estimate the cost of the inventory destroyed for its insurance claim.

Beginning inventory (from records)		$ 600,000	**ILLUSTRATION 9–2**
Plus: Net purchases (from records)		1,500,000	Gross Profit Method
Goods available for sale		2,100,000	
Less: Cost of goods sold:			
Net sales	$2,000,000		
Less: Estimated gross profit of 40%	(800,000)		
Estimated cost of goods sold*		(1,200,000)	
Estimated ending inventory		$ 900,000	

*Alternatively, cost of goods sold can be calculated as $2,000,000 × (1 − .40) = $1,200,000.

A Word of Caution

The gross profit method provides only an estimate. The key to obtaining good estimates is the reliability of the gross profit ratio. The ratio usually is estimated from relationships between sales and cost of goods sold. However, the current relationship may differ from the past. In that case, all available information should be used to make necessary adjustments. For example, the company may have made changes in the markup percentage of some of its products. Very often different products have different markups. In these situations, a blanket ratio should not be applied across the board. The accuracy of the estimate can be improved by grouping inventory into pools of products that have similar gross profit relationships rather than using one gross profit ratio for the entire inventory.

> The key to obtaining good estimates is the reliability of the gross profit ratio.

The company's cost flow assumption should be implicitly considered when estimating the gross profit ratio. For example, if LIFO is used and the relationship between cost and selling price has changed for recent acquisitions, this would suggest a ratio different from one where the average cost method was used. Another difficulty with the gross profit method is that it does not explicitly consider possible theft or spoilage of inventory. The method assumes that if the inventory was not sold, then it must be on hand at the end of the period. Suspected theft or spoilage would require an adjustment to estimates obtained using the gross profit method.

ADDITIONAL CONSIDERATION

The gross profit ratio is, by definition, a percentage of sales. Sometimes, though, the gross profit is stated as a percentage of cost instead. In that case, it is referred to as the **markup on cost.** For instance, a 66⅔% markup on cost is equivalent to a gross profit ratio of 40%. Here's why:

A gross profit ratio of 40% can be formulated as:

$$\text{Sales} = \text{Cost} + \text{Gross profit}$$
$$100\% = 60\% + 40\%$$

Now, expressing gross profit as a percentage of cost we get:

$$\text{Gross profit \%} \div \text{Cost \%} = \text{Gross profit as a \% of cost}$$
$$40\% \div 60\% = 66\tfrac{2}{3}\%$$

Conversely, gross profit as a percentage of cost can be converted to gross profit as a percentage of sales (the gross profit ratio) as follows:

$$\text{Gross profit as a \% of sales} = \frac{\text{Gross profit as a \% of cost}}{1 + \text{Gross profit as a \% of cost}}$$

$$\frac{66\tfrac{2}{3}\%}{1 + 66\tfrac{2}{3}\%} = 40\%$$

Be careful to note which way the percentage is being stated. If stated as a markup on cost, it can be converted to the gross profit ratio, and the gross profit method can be applied the usual way.

The Retail Inventory Method

● LO3

The retail inventory method is similar to the gross profit method in that it relies on the relationship between cost and selling price to estimate ending inventory and cost of goods sold.

As the name implies, the method is used by many retail companies such as **Target**, **Walmart**, **Sears Holding Corporation**, **Saks**, **J.C. Penney**, and **Macy's**. Certain retailers like auto dealers and jewelry stores, whose inventory consists of few, high-priced items, can economically use the specific identification inventory method. However, high-volume retailers selling many different items at low unit prices find the retail inventory method ideal, although with the advent of bar coding on more and more retail merchandise, use of the method is declining. Similar to the gross profit method, its principal benefit is that a physical count of inventory is not required to estimate ending inventory and cost of goods sold.

The retail inventory method uses the cost-to-retail percentage based on a current relationship between cost and selling price.

The retail method tends to provide a more accurate estimate than the gross profit method because it's based on the current cost-to-retail percentage rather than on a historical gross profit ratio.

The increased reliability in the estimate of the cost percentage is achieved by comparing cost of goods available for sale with goods available for sale *at current selling prices*. So, to use the technique, a company must maintain records of inventory and purchases not only at cost, but also at current selling price. We refer to this as *retail information*. In its simplest form, the retail inventory method estimates the amount of ending inventory (at retail) by subtracting sales (at retail) from goods available for sale (at retail). This estimated ending inventory at retail is then converted to cost by multiplying it by the cost-to-retail percentage. This ratio is found by dividing goods available for sale at *cost* by goods available for sale at *retail*.

Let's use the retail inventory method to solve the problem of the Home Improvement Store introduced earlier in the chapter. Suppose the company's bank has asked for monthly financial statements as a condition attached to a loan dated May 31, 2011. To avoid a physical count of inventory, the company intends to use the retail inventory method to estimate ending inventory and cost of goods sold for the month of June. Using data available in its accounting records, Illustration 9–3 shows how Home Improvement can estimate ending inventory and cost of goods sold for June.

ILLUSTRATION 9–3
Retail Method

Goods available for sale (at retail) minus net sales equals estimated ending inventory (at retail).

	Cost	Retail
Beginning inventory	$ 60,000	$100,000
Plus: Net purchases	287,200	460,000
Goods available for sale	$347,200	$560,000
Cost-to-retail percentage: $\frac{\$347,200}{\$560,000} = 62\%$		
Less: Net sales		(400,000)
Estimated ending inventory at retail		$160,000
Estimated ending inventory at cost (62% × $160,000)	(99,200)	
Estimated cost of goods sold—goods available for sale (at cost) minus ending inventory (at cost) equals cost of goods sold	$248,000	

The retail inventory method can be used for financial reporting and income tax purposes.

Unlike the gross profit method, the retail inventory method is acceptable for external financial reporting if the results of applying the method are sufficiently close to what would have been achieved using a more rigorous determination of the cost of ending inventory. Also, it's allowed by the Internal Revenue Service as a method that can be used to determine cost of goods sold for income tax purposes.[7] Another advantage of the method is that different cost

---

[7] The retail method is acceptable for external reporting and for tax purposes because it tends to provide a better estimate than the gross profit method. The retail method uses a current cost-to-retail percentage rather than a historical gross profit ratio.

flow methods can be explicitly incorporated into the estimation technique. In other words, we can modify the application of the method to estimate ending inventory and cost of goods sold to approximate average cost, lower-of-average-cost-or-market (conventional method) and LIFO. (The FIFO retail method is possible but used less frequently in practice.) We illustrate these variations later in the chapter.

Like the gross profit method, the retail inventory method also can be used to estimate the cost of inventory lost, stolen, or destroyed; for testing the overall reasonableness of physical counts; in budgeting and forecasting as well as in generating information for interim financial statements. Even though the retail method provides fairly accurate estimates, a physical count of inventory usually is performed at least once a year to verify accuracy and detect spoilage, theft, and other irregularities.[8]

Retail Terminology

Our example above is simplified in that we implicitly assumed that the selling prices of beginning inventory and of merchandise purchased did not change from date of acquisition to the end of the period. This frequently is an unrealistic assumption. The terms in Graphic 9–4 are associated with changing retail prices of merchandise inventory.

Changes in the selling prices must be included in the determination of ending inventory at retail.

GRAPHIC 9–4

Terminology Used in Applying the Retail Method

Initial markup	Original amount of markup from cost to selling price.
Additional markup	Increase in selling price subsequent to initial markup.
Markup cancellation	Elimination of an additional markup.
Markdown	Reduction in selling price below the original selling price.
Markdown cancellation	Elimination of a markdown.

To illustrate, assume that a product purchased for $6 is initially marked up $4, from $6 to $10, the original selling price. If the selling price is subsequently increased to $12, the additional markup is $2. If the selling price is then subsequently decreased to $10.50, the markup cancellation is $1.50. We refer to the net effect of the additional changes ($2.00 − 1.50 = $.50) as the **net markup.** Graphic 9–5A depicts these events.

GRAPHIC 9–5A

Retail Inventory Method Terminology

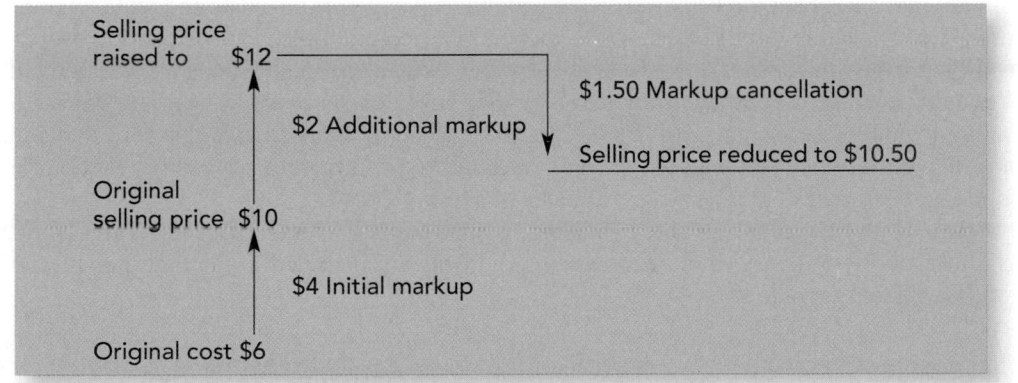

Now let's say the selling price of the product purchased for $6 and initially marked up to $10, is reduced to $7. The markdown is $3. If the selling price is later increased to $8, the markdown cancellation is $1. The net effect of the change ($3 − 1 = $2) is the **net markdown.** Graphic 9–5B depicts this possibility.

When applying the retail inventory method, *net markups and net markdowns must be included in the determination of ending inventory at retail.* We now continue our illustration of the retail inventory method, but expand it to incorporate markups and markdowns as well as to approximate cost by each of the alternative inventory cost flow methods.

Net markups and net markdowns are included in the retail column to determine ending inventory at retail.

---

[8]The retail inventory method also is allowable under IFRS. "Inventories," *International Accounting Standard No. 2* (IASCF), as amended effective January 1, 2009, par. 22.

GRAPHIC 9–5B

Retail Inventory
Method Terminology

Cost Flow Methods

Let's continue the Home Improvement Stores example into July with Illustration 9–4 and see how the retail inventory method can be used to approximate different cost flow assumptions. We'll also use the same illustration to see how the retail method can be modified to approximate lower of cost or market.

ILLUSTRATION 9–4

The Retail Inventory
Method—Various
Cost Flow Methods

Home Improvement Stores, Inc., uses a periodic inventory system and the retail inventory method to estimate ending inventory and cost of goods sold. The following data are available from the company's records for the month of July 2011:

	Cost	Retail
Beginning inventory	$ 99,200	$160,000
Net purchases	305,280[1]	470,000[2]
Net markups		10,000
Net markdowns		8,000
Net sales		434,000[3]

[1]Purchases at cost less returns, plus freight-in.
[2]Original selling price of purchased goods less returns at retail.
[3]Gross sales less returns.

To approximate average cost, the cost-to-retail percentage is determined for *all* goods available for sale.

APPROXIMATING AVERAGE COST. Recall that the average cost method assumes that cost of goods sold and ending inventory each consist of a *mixture* of all the goods available for sale. So when we use the retail method to approximate average cost, the cost-to-retail percentage should be based on the weighted averages of the costs and retail amounts for *all* goods available for sale. This is achieved by calculating the cost-to-retail percentage by dividing the total cost of goods available for sale by total goods available for sale at retail. When this average percentage is applied to ending inventory at retail, we get an estimate of ending inventory at average cost. If you look back to our simplified example for the month of June, you'll notice that we used this approach there. So, our ending inventory and cost of goods sold estimates for June were estimates of average cost.[9]

Now, we use the retail inventory method to approximate average costs for July. Notice in Illustration 9–5 that both markups and markdowns are included in the determination of goods available for sale at retail.

ILLUSTRATION 9–5

Retail Method—
Average Cost

	Cost	Retail
Beginning inventory	$ 99,200	$160,000
Plus: Net purchases	305,280	470,000
Net markups		10,000
Less: Net markdowns		(8,000)
Goods available for sale	404,480	632,000
Cost-to-retail percentage: $\frac{\$404,480}{\$632,000} = 64\%$		
Less: Net sales		(434,000)
Estimated ending inventory at retail		$198,000
Estimated ending inventory at cost (64% × $198,000)	(126,720)	
Estimated cost of goods sold	$277,760	

[9]We also implicitly assumed no net markups or markdowns.

APPROXIMATING AVERAGE LCM—THE CONVENTIONAL RETAIL METHOD.   ● LO4

Recall from our discussion earlier in the chapter that, however costs are determined, inventory should be reported in the balance sheet at LCM. Fortunately, we can apply the retail inventory method in such a way that LCM is approximated. This method often is referred to as the **conventional retail method.** We apply the method by *excluding markdowns from the calculation of the cost-to-retail percentage.* Markdowns still are subtracted in the retail column but only after the percentage is calculated. To approximate lower of average cost or market, the retail method is modified as shown in Illustration 9–6.

To approximate LCM, markdowns are not included in the calculation of the cost-to-retail percentage.

	Cost	Retail	
Beginning inventory	$ 99,200	$160,000	**ILLUSTRATION 9–6**
Plus: Net purchases	305,280	470,000	Retail Method—
Net markups		10,000	Average Cost, LCM
		640,000	
Cost-to-retail percentage: $\frac{\$404,480}{\$640,000} = 63.2\%$			
Less: Net markdowns		(8,000)	
Goods available for sale	404,480	632,000	
Less: Net sales		(434,000)	
Estimated ending inventory at retail		$198,000	
Estimated ending inventory at cost (63.2% × $198,000)	(125,136)		
Estimated cost of goods sold	$279,344		

Notice that by not subtracting net markdowns from the denominator, the cost-to-retail percentage is lower than it was previously (63.2% versus 64%). This always will be the case when markdowns exist. As a result, the cost approximation of ending inventory always will be less when markdowns exist. To understand why this lower amount approximates LCM, we need to realize that markdowns usually occur when obsolescence, spoilage, overstocking, price declines, or competition has lessened the utility of the merchandise. To recognize this decline in utility in the period it occurs, as LCM does, we exclude net markdowns from the calculation of the cost-to-retail (market) percentage. It should be emphasized that this approach provides only an *approximation* of what ending inventory might be as opposed to applying the LCM rule in the more exact way described earlier in the chapter.

The logic for using this approximation is that a markdown is evidence of a reduction in the utility of inventory.

Also notice that the ending inventory at retail is the same using both approaches ($198,000). This will be the case regardless of the cost flow method used because in all approaches this amount reflects the ending inventory at current retail prices.

The LCM variation is not generally used in combination with LIFO. This does not mean that a company using LIFO ignores the LCM rule. Any obsolete or slow-moving inventory that has not been marked down by year-end can be written down to market after the estimation of inventory using the retail method. This is usually not a significant problem. If prices are rising, LIFO ending inventory includes old lower priced items whose costs are likely to be lower than current market. The LCM variation could be applied to the FIFO method.

THE LIFO RETAIL METHOD.
The last-in, first-out (LIFO) method assumes that units sold are those most recently acquired. When there's a net increase in inventory quantity during a period, the use of LIFO results in ending inventory that includes the beginning inventory as well as one or more additional layers added during the period. When there's a net decrease in inventory quantity, LIFO layer(s) are liquidated. In applying LIFO to the retail method in the simplest way, we assume that the retail prices of goods remained stable during the period. This assumption, which is relaxed later in the chapter, allows us to look at the beginning and ending inventory in dollars to determine if inventory quantity has increased or decreased.

We'll use the numbers from our previous example to illustrate using the retail method to approximate LIFO so we can compare the results with those of the conventional retail method. Recall that beginning inventory at retail is $160,000 and ending inventory at retail is $198,000. If we assume stable retail prices, inventory quantity must have increased during

If inventory at retail increases during the year, a new layer is added.

the year. This means ending inventory includes the beginning inventory layer of $160,000 ($99,200 at cost) as well as some additional merchandise purchased during the period. To estimate total ending inventory at LIFO cost, we also need to determine the inventory layer added during the period. When using the LIFO retail method, we assume no more than one inventory layer is added per year if inventory increases.[10] Each layer will carry its own cost-to-retail percentage.

Illustration 9–7 shows how Home Improvement Stores would estimate total ending inventory and cost of goods sold for the period using the LIFO retail method. The beginning inventory layer carries a cost-to-retail percentage of 62% ($99,200 ÷ $160,000). The layer of inventory added during the period is $38,000 at retail, which is determined by subtracting beginning inventory at retail from ending inventory at retail ($198,000 − 160,000). This layer will be converted to cost by multiplying it by its own cost-to-retail percentage reflecting the *current* period's ratio of cost to retail amounts, in this case 64.68%.

ILLUSTRATION 9–7
LIFO Retail Method

Beginning inventory is excluded from the calculation of the cost-to-retail percentage.

	Cost	Retail
Beginning inventory	$ 99,200	$160,000
Plus: Net purchases	305,280	470,000
Net markups		10,000
Less: Net markdowns		(8,000)
Goods available for sale (excluding beginning inventory)	305,280	472,000
Goods available for sale (including beginning inventory)	404,480	632,000

Beginning inventory cost-to-retail percentage: $\dfrac{\$99{,}200}{\$160{,}000} = 62\%$

July cost-to-retail percentage: $\dfrac{\$305{,}280}{\$472{,}000} = 64.68\%$

	Cost	Retail
Less: Net sales		(434,000)
Estimated ending inventory at retail		$198,000

Estimated ending inventory at cost:

	Retail	Cost	
Beginning inventory	$160,000 × 62.00% =	$ 99,200	
Current period's layer	38,000 × 64.68% =	24,578	
Total	$198,000	$123,778	(123,778)
Estimated cost of goods sold			$280,702

Each layer has its own cost-to-retail percentage.

The next period's (August's) beginning inventory will include the two distinct layers (June and July), each of which carries its own unique cost-to-retail percentage. Notice in the illustration that both net markups and net markdowns are included in the calculation of the current period's cost-to-retail percentage.

Other Issues Pertaining to the Retail Method

To focus on the key elements of the retail method, we've so far ignored some of the details of the retail process. Fundamental elements such as returns and allowances, discounts, freight, spoilage, and shortages can complicate the retail method.

Recall that net purchases is found by adding freight-in to purchases and subtracting both purchase returns and purchase discounts. When these components are considered separately in the retail method, purchase returns are deducted from purchases on both the cost and retail side (at different amounts) and freight-in is added only to the cost side in determining net purchases. If the gross method is used to record purchases, purchase discounts taken also are deducted in determining the cost of net purchases.

---

[10]Of course, any number of layers at different costs can actually be added through the years. When using the regular LIFO method, rather than LIFO retail, we would keep track of each of those layers.

Likewise, net sales is found by subtracting sales returns from sales. However, sales discounts are *not* subtracted because to do so would cause the inventory to be overstated. Sales discounts do not represent an adjustment in selling price but a financial incentive for customers to pay early. On the other hand, when sales are recorded net of employee discounts, the discounts are *added* to net sales before sales are deducted in the retail column.

For example, suppose an item of merchandise purchased for $6 is initially marked up to $10. Original selling price is therefore $10. When the item is sold, we deduct sales of $10 from the retail column. But if the item is sold to an employee for $7 (a $3 employee discount) and recorded as a $7 sale, the $3 employee discount must be added back to sales so the full $10 is deducted from goods available at retail to arrive at ending inventory at retail.

We also need to consider spoilage, breakage, and theft. So far we've assumed that by subtracting goods sold from goods available for sale, we find ending inventory. It's possible, though, that some of the goods available for sale were lost to such shortages and therefore do not remain in ending inventory.

To take these shortages into account when using the retail method, we deduct the retail value of inventory lost due to spoilage, breakage, or theft in the retail column. These losses are expected for most retail ventures so they are referred to as *normal shortages* (spoilage, breakage, etc.), and are deducted in the retail column *after* the calculation of the cost-to-retail percentage. Because these losses are anticipated, they are included implicitly in the determination of selling prices. Including normal spoilage in the calculation of the percentage would distort the normal relationship between cost and retail. *Abnormal shortages* should be deducted in both the cost and retail columns *before* the calculation of the cost-to-retail percentage. These losses are not anticipated and are not included in the determination of selling prices.

We recap the treatment of special elements in the application of the retail method in Graphic 9–6 and illustrate the use of some of them in the concept review exercise that follows.

> If sales are recorded net of employee discounts, the discounts are added to sales.

> Normal shortages are deducted in the retail column *after* the calculation of the cost-to-retail percentage.

> Abnormal shortages are deducted in both the cost and retail columns *before* the calculation of the cost-to-retail percentage.

GRAPHIC 9–6 Recap of Other Retail Method Elements

Element	Treatment
Before calculating the cost-to-retail percentage:	
Freight-in	*Added* in the cost column.
Purchase returns	*Deducted* in both the cost and retail columns.
Purchase discounts taken (if gross method used to record purchases)	*Deducted* in the cost column.
Abnormal shortages (spoilage, breakage, theft)	*Deducted* in both the cost and retail columns.
After calculating the cost-to-retail percentage:	
Normal shortages (spoilage, breakage, theft)	*Deducted* in the retail column.
Employee discounts (if sales recorded net of discounts)	*Added* to net sales.

CONCEPT REVIEW EXERCISE

The Henderson Company uses the retail inventory method to estimate ending inventory and cost of goods sold. The following data for 2011 are available in Henderson's accounting records:

RETAIL INVENTORY METHOD

	Cost	Retail
Beginning inventory	$ 8,000	$12,000
Purchases	68,000	98,000
Freight-in	3,200	
Purchase returns	3,000	4,200
Net markups		6,000
Net markdowns		2,400
Normal spoilage		1,800
Net sales		92,000

The company records sales net of employee discounts. These discounts for 2011 totaled $2,300.

Required:

1. Estimate Henderson's ending inventory and cost of goods sold for the year using the average cost method.
2. Estimate Henderson's ending inventory and cost of goods sold for the year using the conventional retail method (LCM, average cost).
3. Estimate Henderson's ending inventory and cost of goods sold for the year using the LIFO retail method.

SOLUTION

1. Estimate Henderson's ending inventory and cost of goods sold for the year using the average cost method.

		Cost	Retail
Beginning inventory		$ 8,000	$ 12,000
Plus: Purchases		68,000	98,000
Freight-in		3,200	
Less: Purchase returns		(3,000)	(4,200)
Plus: Net markups			6,000
Less: Net markdowns			(2,400)
Goods available for sale		$76,200	$109,400
Cost-to-retail percentage: $\frac{\$76,200}{\$109,400} = 69.65\%$			
Less: Normal spoilage			(1,800)
Sales:			
Net sales			(92,000)
Employee discounts			(2,300)
Estimated ending inventory at retail			$ 13,300
Estimated ending inventory at cost (69.65% × $13,300)		(9,263)	
Estimated cost of goods sold		$66,937	

2. Estimate Henderson's ending inventory and cost of goods sold for the year using the conventional retail method (LCM, average cost).

		Cost	Retail
Beginning inventory		$ 8,000	$ 12,000
Plus: Purchases		68,000	98,000
Freight-in		3,200	
Less: Purchase returns		(3,000)	(4,200)
Plus: Net markups			6,000
			111,800
Cost-to-retail percentage: $\frac{\$76,200}{\$111,800} = 68.16\%$			
Less: Net markdowns			(2,400)
Goods available for sale		76,200	109,400
Less: Normal spoilage			(1,800)
Sales:			
Net sales			(92,000)
Employee discounts			(2,300)
Estimated ending inventory at retail			$ 13,300
Estimated ending inventory at cost (68.16% × $13,300)		(9,065)	
Estimated cost of goods sold		$67,135	

3. Estimate Henderson's ending inventory and cost of goods sold for the year using the LIFO retail method.

	Cost	Retail
Beginning inventory	$ 8,000	$ 12,000
Plus: Purchases	68,000	98,000
Freight-in	3,200	
Less: Purchase returns	(3,000)	(4,200)
Plus: Net markups		6,000
Less: Net markdowns		(2,400)
Goods available for sale (excluding beginning inventory)	68,200	97,400
Goods available for sale (including beginning inventory)	76,200	109,400

Cost-to-retail percentage: $\dfrac{\$68,200}{\$97,400} = 70.02\%$

		Retail
Less: Normal spoilage		(1,800)
Sales:		
Net sales		(92,000)
Employee discounts		(2,300)
Estimated ending inventory at retail		$ 13,300

Estimated ending inventory at cost:

	Retail	Cost	
Beginning inventory	$12,000 × 66.67%* =	$8,000	
Current period's layer	1,300 × 70.02% =	910	
Total	$13,300	$8,910	(8,910)
Estimated cost of goods sold			$67,290

*$8,000 ÷ $12,000 = 66.67%

DOLLAR-VALUE LIFO RETAIL

PART C

● LO5

FINANCIAL
Reporting Case

Q2, p. 447

Using the retail method
to approximate LIFO
is referred to as the
*dollar-value LIFO retail
method.*

In our earlier illustration of the LIFO retail method, we assumed that the retail prices of the inventory remained stable during the period. If you recall, we compared the ending inventory (at retail) with the beginning inventory (at retail) to see if inventory had increased. If the dollar amount of ending inventory exceeded the beginning amount, we assumed a new LIFO layer had been added. But this isn't necessarily true. It may be that the dollar amount of ending inventory exceeded the beginning amount simply because prices increased, without an actual change in the quantity of goods. So, to see if there's been a "real" increase in quantity, we need a way to eliminate the effect of any price changes before we compare the ending inventory with the beginning inventory. Fortunately, we can accomplish this by combining two methods we've already discussed—the LIFO retail method (Part B of this chapter) and dollar-value LIFO (previous chapter). The combination is called the **dollar-value LIFO retail method.**

To illustrate, we return to the Home Improvement Stores situation (Illustration 9–7) in which we applied LIFO retail. We keep the same inventory data, but change the illustration from the month of July to the fiscal year 2011. This allows us to build into Illustration 9–7A a significant change in retail prices over the year of 10% (an increase in the retail price index from 1 to 1.10). We follow the LIFO retail procedure up to the point of comparing the ending inventory with the beginning inventory. However, because prices have risen, the apparent increase in inventory is only partly due to an additional layer of inventory and partly due to the increase in retail prices. The real increase is found by

ILLUSTRATION 9–7A

The Dollar-Value
LIFO Retail Method

	Cost	Retail
Beginning inventory	$ 99,200	$160,000
Plus: Net purchases	305,280	470,000
Net markups		10,000
Less: Net markdowns		(8,000)
Goods available for sale (excluding beginning inventory)	305,280	472,000
Goods available for sale (including beginning inventory)	404,480	632,000

Base layer cost-to-retail percentage: $\dfrac{\$99{,}200}{\$160{,}000} = 62\%$

2011 layer cost-to-retail percentage: $\dfrac{\$305{,}280}{\$472{,}000} = 64.68\%$

	Cost	Retail
Less: Net sales		(434,000)
Ending inventory at current year retail prices		$198,000
Estimated ending inventory at cost (calculated below)	(113,430)	
Estimated cost of goods sold	$291,050	

Base year retail amounts are converted to layer year retail and then to cost.

Ending Inventory at Year-End Retail Prices	Step 1 Ending Inventory at Base Year Retail Prices	Step 2 Inventory Layers at Base Year Retail Prices	Step 3 Inventory Layers Converted to Cost
$198,000 (determined above)	$\dfrac{\$198{,}000}{1.10} = \$180{,}000$ →	$180,000	

$$\underline{160{,}000\ (\text{base}) \times 1.00 \times .62\ } = \$\ 99{,}200$$
$$\underline{\$\ 20{,}000\ (2011) \times 1.10 \times .6468} =\ \ \ 14{,}230$$

| Total ending inventory at dollar-value LIFO retail cost | | | $113,430 |

deflating the ending inventory amount to beginning of the year prices before comparing beginning and ending amounts. We did this with the dollar-value LIFO technique discussed in the previous chapter.[11]

In this illustration, a $20,000 year 2011 layer is added to the base layer. Two adjustments are needed to convert this amount to LIFO cost. Multiplying by the 2011 price index (1.10) converts it from its base year retail to 2011 retail. Multiplying by the 2011 cost-to-retail percentage (.6468) converts it from its 2011 retail to 2011 cost. The two steps are combined in our illustration. The base year inventory also is converted to cost. The two layers are added to derive ending inventory at dollar-value LIFO retail cost.

Each layer year carries its unique retail price index and its unique cost-to-retail percentage.

When additional layers are added in subsequent years, their LIFO amounts are determined the same way. For illustration, let's assume ending inventory in 2012 is $226,200 at current retail prices and the price level has risen to 1.16. Also assume that the cost-to-retail percentage for 2012 net purchases is 63%. In Illustration 9–7B, the ending inventory is converted to base year retail (step 1). This amount is apportioned into layers, each at base year retail (step 2). Layers then are converted to layer year costs (step 3).

Now, let's assume that ending inventory in 2012 is $204,160 at current retail prices (instead of $226,200) and the price level has risen to 1.16. Also assume that the cost-to-retail percentage for 2012 net purchases is 63%. Step 1 converts the ending inventory to a base year price of $176,000 ($204,160 ÷ 1.16). A comparison to the beginning

---

[11]The index used here is analogous to the cost index used in regular DVL except that it reflects the change in retail prices rather than in acquisition costs.

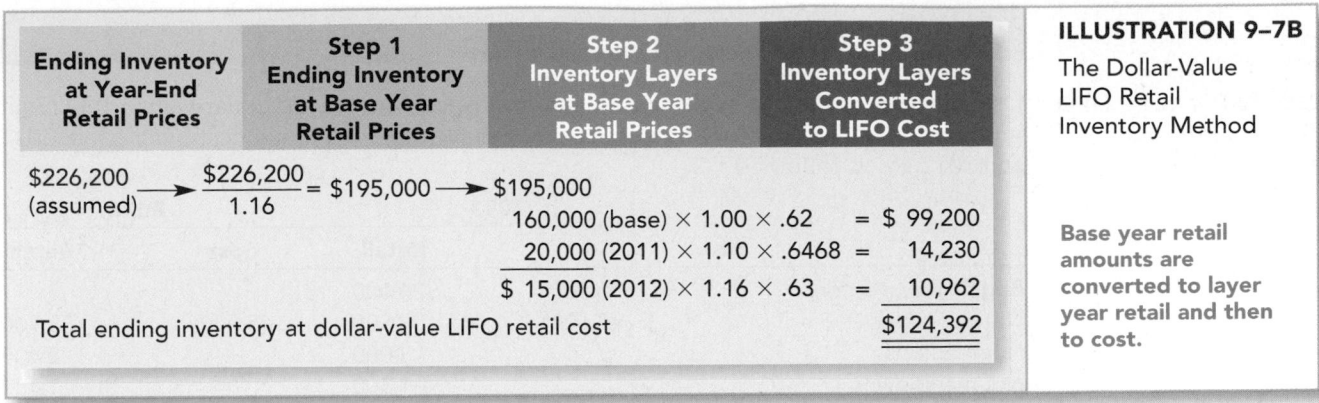

ILLUSTRATION 9–7B

The Dollar-Value LIFO Retail Inventory Method

Base year retail amounts are converted to layer year retail and then to cost.

inventory at base year prices of $180,000 ($160,000 base year layer + $20,000 2011 layer) indicates that inventory *decreased* during 2012. In this case, no 2012 layer is added and 2012 ending inventory at dollar-value LIFO retail of $110,584 is determined in Illustration 9–7C.

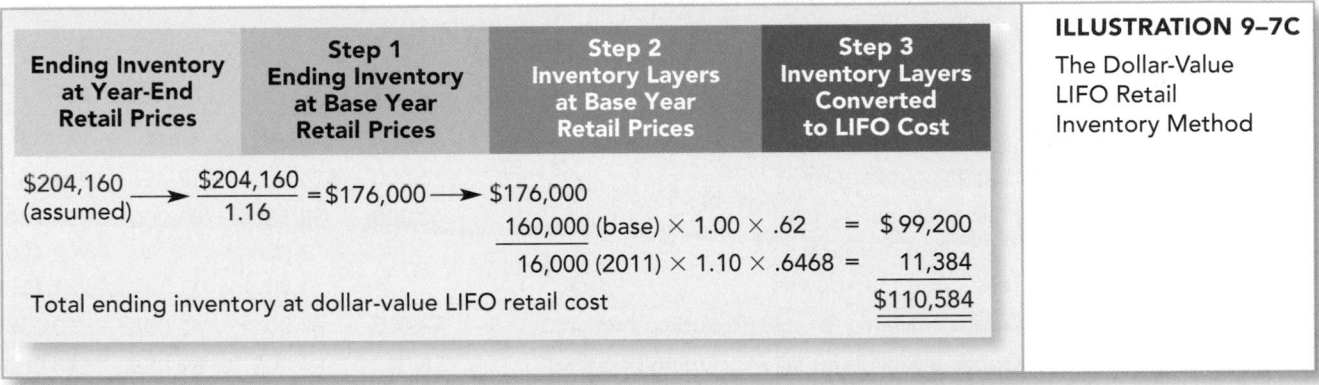

ILLUSTRATION 9–7C

The Dollar-Value LIFO Retail Inventory Method

A portion of the 2011 inventory layer has been liquidated—reduced from $20,000 to $16,000 at base year prices—to reduce total inventory at base year prices to $176,000.

As we mentioned earlier in this section, many high-volume retailers selling many different items use the retail method. **J.C. Penney Company, Inc.**, for example, uses the dollar-value LIFO variation of the retail method. Graphic 9–7 shows the inventory disclosure note included in the company's recent financial statements.

Summary of Significant Accounting Policies (in part) Merchandise Inventories

Inventories are valued primarily at the lower of cost (using the last-in, first-out, or "LIFO" method) or market, determined by the retail method for department stores, regional warehouses, and store distribution centers, and standard cost, representing average vendor cost, for Direct. The lower of cost or market is determined on an aggregate basis for similar types of merchandise. To estimate the effects of inflation/deflation on ending inventory, an internal index measuring price changes from the beginning to the end of the year is calculated using merchandise cost data at the item level.

GRAPHIC 9–7

Disclosure of Inventory Method—J.C. Penney Company, Inc.

Real World Financials

Notice that J.C. Penney uses an internal index to adjust for changing prices and that the lower-of-cost-or-market rule is determined on an aggregate basis for similar types of merchandise.

CONCEPT REVIEW EXERCISE

DOLLAR-VALUE LIFO RETAIL METHOD

On January 1, 2011, the Nicholson Department Store adopted the dollar-value LIFO retail inventory method. Inventory transactions at both cost and retail and cost indexes for 2011 and 2012 are as follows:

	2011		2012	
	Cost	**Retail**	**Cost**	**Retail**
Beginning inventory	$16,000	$24,000		
Net purchases	42,000	58,500	45,000	58,700
Net markups		3,000		2,400
Net markdowns		1,500		1,100
Net sales		56,000		57,000
Price index:				
January 1, 2011		1.00		
December 31, 2011		1.08		
December 31, 2012		1.15		

Required:

Estimate the 2011 and 2012 ending inventory and cost of goods sold using the dollar-value LIFO retail inventory method.

SOLUTION

	2011		2012	
	Cost	**Retail**	**Cost**	**Retail**
Beginning inventory	$16,000	$24,000	$17,456	$28,000
Plus: Net purchases	42,000	58,500	45,000	58,700
Net markups		3,000		2,400
Less: Net markdowns		(1,500)		(1,100)
Goods available for sale (excluding beg. inv.)	42,000	60,000	45,000	60,000
Goods available for sale (including beg. inv.)	58,000	84,000	62,456	88,000

Base layer

Cost-to-retail percentage: $\dfrac{\$16,000}{\$24,000} = 66.67\%$

2011

Cost-to-retail percentage: $\dfrac{\$42,000}{\$60,000} = 70\%$

2012

Cost-to-retail percentage: $\dfrac{\$45,000}{\$60,000} = 75\%$

	2011	2012
Less: Net sales	(56,000)	(57,000)
Estimated ending inv. at current year retail prices	$28,000	$31,000
Less: Estimated ending inventory at cost (below)	(17,456)	(18,345)
Estimated cost of goods sold	$40,544	$44,111

2011

Ending Inventory at Year-End Retail Prices	Step 1 Ending Inventory at Base Year Retail Prices	Step 2 Inventory Layers at Base Year Retail Prices	Step 3 Inventory Layers Converted to Cost
$28,000 (above)	$\dfrac{\$28,000}{1.08} = 25,926$	$24,000 (base) × 1.00 × 66.67% =	$16,000
		1,926 (2011) × 1.08 × 70.00% =	1,456
Total ending inventory at dollar-value LIFO retail cost			$17,456

2012

Ending Inventory at Year-End Retail Prices	Step 1 Ending Inventory at Base Year Retail Prices	Step 2 Inventory Layers at Base Year Retail Prices	Step 3 Inventory Layers Converted to Cost
$31,000 (above)	$\dfrac{\$31,000}{1.15} = \$26,957$	$24,000 (base) × 1.00 × 66.67% = 1,926 (2011) × 1.08 × 70.00% = 1,031 (2012) × 1.15 × 75.00% =	$16,000 1,456 889
	Total ending inventory at dollar-value LIFO retail cost		$18,345

CHANGE IN INVENTORY METHOD AND INVENTORY ERRORS

Change in Inventory Method

● LO6

Accounting principles should be applied consistently from period to period to allow for comparability of operating results. However, changes within a company as well as changes in the external economic environment may require a company to change an accounting method. As we mentioned in Chapter 8, high inflation in the 1970s motivated many companies to switch to the LIFO inventory method.

Specific accounting treatment and disclosures are prescribed for companies that change accounting principles. Chapter 4 introduced the subject of accounting changes and Chapter 20 provides in-depth coverage of the topic. Here we provide an overview of how changes in inventory methods are reported.

Most Inventory Changes

Recall from our discussion in Chapter 4 that most voluntary changes in accounting principles are reported retrospectively. This means reporting all previous periods' financial statements as if the new method had been used in all prior periods. Changes in inventory methods, other than a change to LIFO, are treated this way. We discuss the *to LIFO* exception in the next section. In Chapter 4 we outlined the steps a company undertakes to account for a change in inventory method. We demonstrate those steps using a real world example in Illustrations 9–8 and 9–8A.

Changes in inventory methods, other than a change to LIFO, are accounted for retrospectively.

McKesson Corporation is a Fortune 100 company producing products and services in the healthcare industry. In a note accompanying its 2009 financial statements, the company disclosed that it uses the LIFO inventory method for 88% of its inventories and FIFO for the remainder. The company's balance sheets reported inventories of $8,527 million and $9,000 million at the end of 2009 and 2008, respectively. The inventory disclosure note reports that if the FIFO method had been used to value the entire inventory, instead of just 12% of it, inventories would have been $8,612 million and $9,077 million at the end of 2009 and 2008, respectively. Partial income statements for 2009 and 2008 are as follows:

ILLUSTRATION 9–8

Change in Inventory Method—McKesson Corporation

Real World Financials

McKESSON CORPORATION
Partial Income Statements
For the Years Ended March 31,

($ in millions)

	2009	2008
Sales revenue	$106,632	$101,703
Cost of goods sold	101,254	96,694
Gross profit	5,378	5,009
Operating expenses	4,182	3,531
Operating income	$ 1,196	$ 1,478

Let's suppose that in 2009 McKesson decided to value all of its inventories using the FIFO method.

ILLUSTRATION 9–8A
Income statements—
100% FIFO

McKESSON CORPORATION
Partial Income Statements
For the Years Ended March 31,

($ in millions)

	2009	2008
Sales revenue	$106,632	$101,703
Cost of goods sold	101,246	96,708
Gross profit	5,386	4,995
Operating expenses	4,182	3,531
Operating income	1,204	1,464

McKesson would report 2009 cost of goods sold by its newly adopted method, 100% FIFO.

McKesson would increase the amount it reported last year for its cost of goods sold as if 100% FIFO had been used.

The cost of goods sold of $101,246 million in 2009 is $8 million lower on a 100% FIFO basis. Here's why. McKesson's note reported that beginning inventory is $77 million higher ($9,077 − 9,000), and ending inventory also is higher by $85 million ($8,612 − 8,527). An increase in beginning inventory causes an *increase* in cost of goods sold, but an increase in ending inventory causes a *decrease* in cost of goods sold. The net effect of the two adjustments ($85 − 77) is the $8 million decrease in cost of goods sold.

In a similar manner, the 2008 cost of goods sold would be adjusted to $96,708 million. A note included in McKesson's 2008 financial statements reports that 2007 ending inventory of $8,153 million would have been $8,244 million on an all FIFO basis. 2008's beginning inventory would have been $91 higher ($8,244 − 8,153) and ending inventory for 2008 would be $77 million higher ($9,077 − 9,000). The net effect of the two adjustments ($91 − 77) is that cost of goods sold would be $14 million higher.

Step 1: Revise Comparative Financial Statements

The first step is to revise prior years' financial statements. That is, for each year reported in the comparative statements, McKesson makes those statements appear as if the newly adopted accounting method (100% FIFO) had been applied all along. In its balance sheets, McKesson would report 2009 inventory by its newly adopted method, 100% FIFO, and also would revise the amounts it reported last year for its 2008 inventory. In its income statements, cost of goods sold also would reflect the new method in both 2009 and 2008 as shown in Illustration 9–8A.

In its statements of shareholders' equity, McKesson would report retained earnings each year as if it had used FIFO all along, and for the earliest year reported, it would revise beginning retained earnings that year to reflect the cumulative income effect of the difference in inventory methods for all prior years. We see this step illustrated in Chapter 20 after you have studied the statement of shareholders' equity in more depth.

Step 2: The appropriate accounts are adjusted.

McKesson also would create a journal entry to adjust the book balances from their current amounts to what those balances would have been using 100% FIFO. Since differences in cost of goods sold and income are reflected in retained earnings, as are the income tax effects, the journal entry updates inventory, retained earnings, and the appropriate income tax account. We ignore the income tax effects here and include those effects in an illustration in Chapter 20. The journal entry below, *ignoring income taxes,* adjusts the 2009 beginning inventory to the 100% FIFO basis amount of $9,077 million.

Inventory at the beginning of 2009 would be $77 million higher if FIFO is used to value the entire inventory.

	($ in millions)	
Inventory ($9,077 − 9,000)	77	
Retained earnings		77

Step 3: A disclosure note provides additional information.

McKesson must provide in a disclosure note clear justification that the change to 100% FIFO is appropriate. The note also would indicate the effects of the change on (a) items not reported on the face of the primary statements, (b) any per share amounts affected for the current period and all prior periods, and (c) the cumulative effect of the change on retained earnings or other components of equity as of the beginning of the earliest period presented.

We see an example of such a note in a recent annual report of **Chromcraft Revington, Inc.,** a residential and commercial furniture company, when it changed its inventory method from LIFO to FIFO. Graphic 9–8 shows the disclosure note that described the change.

GRAPHIC 9–8

Disclosure of Change in Inventory Method—Chromcraft Revington, Inc.

Real World Financials

Change in Accounting Method (in part)

In 2008, the Company changed its method of accounting for inventory from the last-in, first-out ("LIFO") method to the first-in, first-out ("FIFO") method. Prior to the change in accounting method, the percentage of inventory accounted for under the LIFO method represented approximately 60% of total inventories at December 31, 2007.

The Company's management believes the new method of accounting for inventory is preferable because the FIFO method better reflects the current value of inventories on the Consolidated Balance Sheet; provides better matching of revenue and expense under the Company's business model; and provides uniformity across the Company's operations with respect to the method of inventory accounting for both financial reporting and income tax purposes.

All prior periods presented have been retrospectively adjusted to apply the new method of accounting. The cumulative effect of the change in accounting principle on periods prior to those presented has been reflected as an adjustment to the opening balance of retained earnings as of January 1, 2007. Accordingly, retained earnings as of January 1, 2007 was increased by $2,054,000, which is net of the related income tax expense of $1,369,000.

Chromcraft Revington's note also disclosed the effect of the change on various financial statement items, including net income and earnings per share.

Change to the LIFO Method

When a company changes *to the LIFO inventory method* from any other method, it usually is impossible to calculate the income effect on prior years. To do so would require assumptions as to when specific LIFO inventory layers were created in years prior to the change. As a result, a company changing to LIFO usually does not report the change retrospectively. Instead, the LIFO method simply is used from that point on. The base year inventory for all future LIFO determinations is the beginning inventory in the year the LIFO method is adopted.[12]

A disclosure note is needed to explain (a) the nature of and justification for the change, (b) the effect of the change on current year's income and earnings per share, and (c) why retrospective application was impracticable. When **Seneca Foods Corporation** adopted the LIFO inventory method, it reported the change in the note shown in Graphic 9–9.

GRAPHIC 9–9

Change in Inventory Method Disclosure—Seneca Foods Corporation

Real World Financials

10. Inventories (in part)

The Company decided to change its inventory valuation method from the lower of cost; determined under the FIFO method; or market, to the lower of cost; determined under the LIFO method or market. In the high inflation environment that the Company is experiencing, the Company believes that the LIFO inventory method is preferable over the FIFO method because it better compares the cost of current production to current revenue. Selling prices are established to reflect current market activity, which recognizes the increasing costs. Under FIFO, revenue and costs are not aligned. Under LIFO, the current cost of sales is matched to the current revenue.

The Company determined that retrospective application of LIFO for periods prior to fiscal 2009 was impracticable because the period-specific information necessary to analyze inventories, including inventories acquired as part of the fiscal 2008 Signature acquisition, were not readily available and could not be precisely determined at the appropriate level of detail, including the commodity, size and item code information necessary to perform the detailed calculations required to retrospectively compute the internal LIFO indices applicable to fiscal 2008 and prior years. The effect of this change was to reduce net earnings by $37,917,000 and $18,307,000 in 2009 and 2008, respectively, below that which would have been reported using the Company's previous inventory method. The reduction in earnings per share was $3.12 ($3.09 diluted) and $1.50 per share ($1.49 diluted) in 2009 and 2008, respectively.

[12]A change to LIFO is handled the same way for income tax purposes.

Accounting records usually are inadequate for a company changing to *LIFO* to report the change retrospectively.

As we discussed in Chapter 8, an important motivation for using LIFO in periods of rising costs is that it produces higher cost of goods sold and lowers income and income taxes. Notice in the Seneca Foods disclosure note that the switch to LIFO did cause a decrease in income and therefore income taxes in the year of the switch indicating an environment of increasing costs.

ADDITIONAL CONSIDERATION

When changing from one generally accepted accounting principle to another, a company must justify that the change results in financial information that more properly portrays operating results and financial position. For income tax purposes, a company generally must obtain consent from the Internal Revenue Service before changing an accounting method. A special form also must be filed with the IRS when a company intends to adopt the LIFO inventory method. When a company changes from LIFO for tax purposes, it can't change back to LIFO until five tax returns have been filed using the non-LIFO method.

● LO7

Inventory Errors

Accounting errors must be corrected when they are discovered. In Chapter 4 we briefly discussed the correction of accounting errors and Chapter 20 provides in-depth coverage. Here we provide an overview of the accounting treatment and disclosures in the context of inventory errors. Inventory errors include the over- or understatement of ending inventory due to a mistake in physical count or a mistake in pricing inventory quantities. Also, errors include the over- or understatement of purchases which could be caused by the cutoff errors described in Chapter 8.

If an inventory error is discovered in the same accounting period it occurred, the original erroneous entry should simply be reversed and the appropriate entry recorded. This situation presents no particular reporting problem.

For material errors, previous years' financial statements are retrospectively restated.

Incorrect balances are corrected.

A correction of retained earnings is reported as a prior period adjustment.

If a *material* inventory error is discovered in an accounting period subsequent to the period in which the error was made, any previous years' financial statements that were incorrect as a result of the error are retrospectively restated to reflect the correction.[13] And, of course, any account balances that are incorrect as a result of the error are corrected by journal entry. If, due to an error affecting net income, retained earnings is one of the incorrect accounts, the correction is reported as a prior period adjustment to the beginning balance on the statement of shareholders' equity.[14] In addition, a disclosure note is needed to describe the nature of the error and the impact of its correction on net income, income before extraordinary items, and earnings per share.

When analyzing inventory errors, it's helpful to visualize the way cost of goods sold, net income, and retained earnings are determined (see Graphic 9–10). Beginning inventory

GRAPHIC 9–10

Visualizing the Effect of Inventory Errors

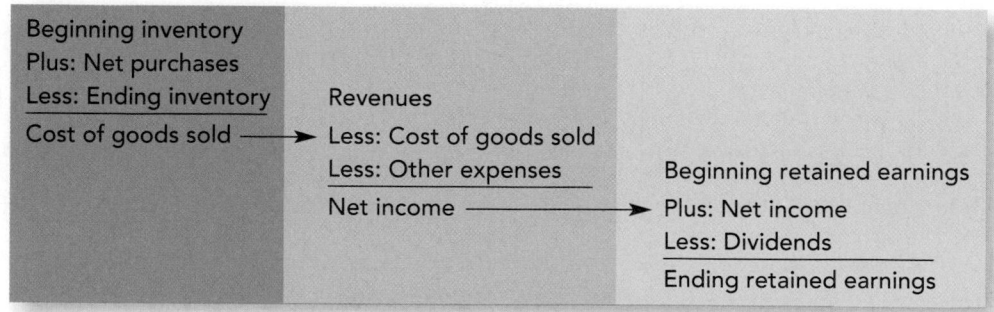

---

[13]If the effect of the error is not material, it is simply corrected in the year of discovery.

[14]The prior period adjustment is applied to beginning retained earnings for the year following the error, or for the earliest year being reported in the comparative financial statements when the error occurs prior to the earliest year presented. The retained earnings balances in years after the first year also are adjusted to what those balances would be if the error had not occurred, but a company may choose not to explicitly report those adjustments as separate line items.

and net purchases are *added* in the calculation of cost of goods sold. If either of these is overstated (understated) then cost of goods sold would be overstated (understated). On the other hand, ending inventory is *deducted* in the calculation of cost of goods sold, so if ending inventory is overstated (understated) then cost of goods sold is understated (overstated). Of course, errors that affect income also will affect income taxes. In the illustration that follows, we ignore the tax effects of the errors and focus on the errors themselves rather than their tax aspects.

Let's look at an example in Illustration 9–9.

A disclosure note describes the nature and the impact of the error.

The Barton Company uses a periodic inventory system. At the end of 2010, a mathematical error caused an $800,000 overstatement of ending inventory. Ending inventories for 2011 and 2012 are correctly determined.

    The way we correct this error depends on when the error is discovered. Assuming that the error is not discovered until after 2011, the 2010 and 2011 effects of the error, ignoring income tax effects, are shown below. The overstated and understated amounts are $800,000 in each instance.

Analysis: **U = Understated**   **O = Overstated**

2010		2011	
Beginning inventory		Beginning inventory	O - 800,000
Plus: Net purchases		Plus: Net purchases	
Less: Ending inventory	O - 800,000	Less: Ending inventory	
Cost of goods sold	U - 800,000	Cost of goods sold	O - 800,000
Revenues		Revenues	
Less: Cost of goods sold	U - 800,000	Less: Cost of goods sold	O - 800,000
Less: Other expenses		Less: Other expenses	
Net income	O - 800,000	Net income	U - 800,000
↓		↓	
Retained earnings	O - 800,000	Retained earnings	*corrected*

ILLUSTRATION 9–9

Inventory Error Correction

When the Inventory Error is Discovered the Following Year

First, let's assume the error is discovered in 2011. The 2010 financial statements that were incorrect as a result of the error are retrospectively restated to reflect the correct inventory amount, cost of goods sold, net income, and retained earnings when those statements are reported again for comparative purposes in the 2011 annual report. The following journal entry, ignoring income taxes, corrects the error.

Previous years' financial statements are retrospectively restated.

Retained earnings	800,000	
Inventory		800,000

A journal entry corrects any incorrect account balance.

    Because retained earnings is one of the accounts that is incorrect, when the error is discovered in 2011, the correction to that account is reported as a prior period adjustment to the 2011 beginning retained earnings balance in Barton's statement of shareholders' equity (or statement of retained earnings). Prior period adjustments do not flow through the income statement but directly adjust retained earnings. This adjustment is illustrated in Chapter 20.

When retained earnings requires correction, a prior period adjustment is made on the statement of shareholders' equity.

When the Inventory Error is Discovered Subsequent to the Following Year

If the error isn't discovered until 2012, the 2011 financial statements also are retrospectively restated to reflect the correct cost of goods sold and net income even though no correcting entry would be needed at that point. Inventory and retained earnings would not require adjustment. The error has self-corrected and no prior period adjustment is needed.

A disclosure note describes the nature of the error and the impact of the correction on income.

Also, a disclosure note in Barton's annual report should describe the nature of the error and the impact of its correction on each year's net income (overstated by $800,000 in 2010; understated by $800,000 in 2011), income before extraordinary items (same as net income in this case), and earnings per share.

CONCEPT REVIEW EXERCISE

INVENTORY ERRORS

In 2011, the controller of the Fleischman Wholesale Beverage Company discovered the following material errors related to the 2009 and 2010 financial statements:

a. Inventory at the end of 2009 was understated by $50,000.
b. Late in 2010, a $3,000 purchase was incorrectly recorded as a $33,000 purchase. The invoice has not yet been paid.
c. Inventory at the end of 2010 was overstated by $20,000.

The company uses a periodic inventory system.

Required:

1. Assuming that the errors were discovered after the 2010 financial statements were issued, analyze the effect of the errors on 2009 and 2010 cost of goods sold, net income, and retained earnings. Ignore income taxes.

SOLUTION

2. Prepare a journal entry to correct the errors.

1. **Analysis: U = Understated   O = Overstated**

2009		2010	
Beginning inventory		Beginning inventory	U - 50,000
Plus: Net purchases		Plus: Net purchases	O - 30,000
Less: Ending inventory	U - 50,000	Less: Ending inventory	O - 20,000
Cost of goods sold	O - 50,000	Cost of goods sold	U - 40,000
Revenues		Revenues	
Less: Cost of goods sold	O - 50,000	Less: Cost of goods sold	U - 40,000
Less: Other expenses		Less: Other expenses	
Net income	U - 50,000	Net income	O - 40,000
↓		↓	
Retained earnings	U - 50,000	Retained earnings	U - 10,000

2. Prepare a journal entry to correct the errors.

Accounts payable	30,000	
Inventory		20,000
Retained earnings		10,000

Earnings Quality

A change in the accounting method a company uses to value inventory is one way managers can artificially manipulate income. However, this method of income manipulation is transparent. As we learned in a previous section, the effect on income of switching from one inventory method to another must be disclosed. That disclosure restores comparability between periods and enhances earnings quality.

Inventory write-downs often are cited as a method used to shift income between periods.

On the other hand, inventory write-downs are included in the broader category of "big bath" accounting techniques some companies use to manipulate earnings. By overstating

> **WILLIAM SCHAFF—BAY ISLE FINANCIAL**
>
> I have nothing on which to base these theories other than the fact that writing off a whole quarter's inventory seems a bit much to just shrug off. It's very disturbing.[15]

[15]William Schaff, "What Is the Definition of an Earnings Bath," *Information Week Online*, April 24, 2001.

the write-down, profits are increased in future periods as the inventory is used or sold. When the demand for many high technology products decreased significantly in late 2000 and early 2001, several companies, including **Sycamore Networks**, **Lucent Technologies**, and **JDS Uniphase**, recorded large inventory write-offs, some in the billions of dollars. In the introduction to this chapter, we discussed the over $2 billion inventory write-off recorded by **Cisco Systems**. Certainly these write-offs reflected the existing economic environment. However, some analysts questioned the size of some of the write-offs. For example, William Schaff, an investment officer at Bay Isle Financial noted that Cisco's write-off was approximately equal to the balance of inventory on hand at the end of the previous quarter and about equal to the cost of goods actually sold during the quarter.

A financial analyst must carefully consider the effect of any significant asset write-down on the assessment of a company's permanent earnings.

FINANCIAL REPORTING CASE SOLUTION

1. **Sears values its inventory at the lower of cost or market. What does that mean? Under what circumstances might Sears be justified in reporting its inventory at less than cost?** *(p. 448)*   A departure from historical cost is warranted when the probable benefits to be received from any asset drop below the asset's cost. The benefits from inventory result from the ultimate sale of the goods. Deterioration, obsolescence, and changes in price levels are situations that might cause the benefits to be received from sale to drop below cost. The lower-of-cost-or-market approach recognizes losses in the period when the value of the inventory declines below its cost rather than in the period in which the goods ultimately are sold.

2. **How does Sears avoid counting all its inventory every time it produces financial statements? What are external price indices used for?** *(p. 465)*   Sears uses the dollar-value LIFO retail inventory method. The retail inventory estimation technique avoids the counting of ending inventory by keeping track of goods available for sale not only at cost but also at retail prices. Each period's sales, at sales prices, are deducted from the retail amount of goods available for sale to arrive at ending inventory at retail. This amount is then converted to cost using a cost-to-retail percentage.

   The dollar-value LIFO retail method uses a price index to first convert ending inventory at retail to base year prices. Yearly LIFO layers are then determined and each layer is converted to that year's current year retail prices using the year's price index and then to cost using the layer's cost-to-retail percentage. For the price index, Sears uses an external index rather than an internally generated price index. ●

THE BOTTOM LINE

● **LO1**   Inventory is valued at the lower of cost or market (LCM). The designated market value in the LCM rule is the middle number of replacement cost (RC), net realizable value (NRV), and net realizable value less a normal profit margin (NRV – NP). (p. 448)

● **LO2**   The gross profit method estimates cost of goods sold which is then subtracted from cost of goods available for sale to estimate ending inventory. The estimate of cost of goods sold is determined by subtracting an estimate of gross profit from net sales. The estimate of gross profit is determined by multiplying the historical gross profit ratio times net sales. (p. 456)

● **LO3**   The retail inventory method determines the amount of ending inventory at retail by subtracting sales for the period from goods available for sale at retail. Ending inventory at retail is then converted to *cost* by multiplying it by the cost-to-retail percentage, which is based on a current relationship between cost and selling price. (p. 458)

● **LO4**   By the conventional retail method, we estimate average cost at lower of cost or market. Average cost is estimated by including beginning inventory in the calculation of the cost-to-retail percentage. LCM is estimated by excluding markdowns from the calculation. Markdowns are subtracted in the retail column after the percentage is calculated. (p. 461)

● LO5   By the LIFO retail method, ending inventory includes the beginning inventory plus the current year's layer. To determine layers, we compare ending inventory at retail to beginning inventory at retail and assume that no more than one inventory layer is added if inventory increases. Each layer carries its own cost-to-retail percentage which is used to convert each layer from retail to cost. The dollar-value LIFO retail inventory method combines the LIFO retail method and the dollar-value LIFO method (Chapter 8) to estimate LIFO from retail prices when the price level has changed. (p. 465)

● LO6   Most changes in inventory methods are reported retrospectively. This means revising all previous periods' financial statements to appear as if the newly adopted inventory method had been applied all along. An exception is a change to the LIFO method. In this case, it usually is impossible to calculate the income effect on prior years. To do so would require assumptions as to when specific LIFO inventory layers were created in years prior to the change. As a result, a company changing to LIFO usually does not report the change retrospectively. Instead, the LIFO method simply is used from that point on. (p. 469)

● LO7   If a material inventory error is discovered in an accounting period subsequent to the period in which the error is made, previous years' financial statements that were incorrect as a result of the error are retrospectively restated to reflect the correction. Account balances are corrected by journal entry. A correction of retained earnings is reported as a prior period adjustment to the beginning balance in the statement of shareholders' equity. In addition, a disclosure note is needed to describe the nature of the error and the impact of its correction on income. (p. 472)

● LO8   When applying the lower-of-cost-or-market rule for valuing inventory according to U.S. GAAP, market is defined as replacement cost with a ceiling of net realizable value (NRV) and a floor of NRV less a normal profit margin. However, the designated market value according to *IAS No. 2* always is net realizable value. *IAS No. 2* also specifies that if circumstances reveal that an inventory write-down is no longer appropriate, it must be reversed. Reversals are not permitted under U.S. GAAP. Under U.S. GAAP, the LCM rule can be applied to individual items, logical inventory categories, or the entire inventory. Using the international standard, the LCM assessment usually is applied to individual items, although using logical inventory categories is allowed under certain circumstances. (p. 453) ●

APPENDIX 9 PURCHASE COMMITMENTS

Purchase commitments protect the buyer against price increases and provide a supply of product.

Purchase commitments are contracts that obligate a company to purchase a specified amount of merchandise or raw materials at specified prices on or before specified dates. Companies enter into these agreements to make sure they will be able to obtain important inventory as well as to protect against increases in purchase price. However, if the purchase price decreases before the agreement is exercised, the commitment has the disadvantage of requiring the company to purchase inventory at a higher than market price. If this happens, a loss on the purchase commitment is recorded.

Purchases made pursuant to a purchase commitment are recorded at the lower of contract price or market price on the date the contract is executed.

Because purchase commitments create the possibility of this kind of loss, the loss occurs when the market price falls below the commitment price rather than when the inventory eventually is sold. This means recording the loss when the product is purchased or, if the commitment is still outstanding, at the end of the reporting period. In other words, purchases are recorded at market price when that price is lower than the contract price, and a loss is recognized for the difference. Also, losses are recognized for any purchase commitments outstanding at the end of a reporting period when market price is less than contract price. In effect, the LCM rule is applied to purchase commitments. This is best understood by the example in Illustration 9A–1.

ILLUSTRATION 9A–1 Purchase Commitments	In July 2011, the Lassiter Company signed two purchase commitments. The first requires Lassiter to purchase inventory for $500,000 by November 15, 2011. The second requires the company to purchase inventory for $600,000 by February 15, 2012. Lassiter's fiscal year-end is December 31. The company uses a perpetual inventory system.

Contract Period within Fiscal Year

The contract period for the first commitment is contained within a single fiscal year. Lassiter would record the purchase at the contract price if the market price at date of acquisition is at least *equal to* the contract price of $500,000.[16]

Inventory (contract price)	500,000	
Cash (or accounts payable)		500,000

If market price is equal to or greater than the contract price, the purchase is recorded at the contract price.

If the market price at acquisition is *less* than the contract price, inventory is recorded at the market price and a loss is recognized.[17] For example, if the market price is $425,000, the following entry records the purchase:

Inventory (market price)	425,000	
Loss on purchase commitment	75,000	
Cash (or accounts payable)		500,000

If market price is less than the contract price, the purchase is recorded at the market price.

The objective of this treatment is to associate the loss with the period in which the price declines rather than with the period in which the company eventually sells the inventory. This is the same objective as the LCM rule you studied in the chapter.

Contract Period Extends beyond Fiscal Year

Now let's consider Lassiter's second purchase commitment that is outstanding at the end of the fiscal year 2011 (that is, the purchases have not yet been made). If the market price at the end of the year is at least *equal* to the contract price of $600,000, no entry is recorded. However, if the market price at year-end is *less* than the contract price, a loss must be recognized to satisfy the LCM objective of associating the loss with the period in which the price declines rather than with the period in which the company eventually sells the inventory. Let's say the year-end market price of the inventory for Lassiter's second purchase commitment is $540,000. The following adjusting entry is recorded:

December 31, 2011		
Estimated loss on purchase commitment ($600,000 − 540,000)	60,000	
Estimated liability on purchase commitment		60,000

If the market price at year-end is less than the contract price a loss is recorded for the difference.

At this point, the loss is an *estimated* loss. The actual loss, if any, will not be known until the inventory actually is purchased. The best estimate of the market price on date of purchase is the current market price, in this case $540,000. Because no inventory has been acquired, we can't credit inventory for the LCM loss. Instead, a liability is credited because, in a sense, the loss represents an obligation to the seller of the inventory to purchase inventory above market price.

A liability is credited for estimated losses on purchase commitments.

The entry to record the actual purchase on or before February 15, 2012, will vary depending on the market price of the inventory at date of purchase. If the market price is unchanged or has increased from the year-end price, the following entry is made:

If market price on purchase date has not declined from year-end price, the purchase is recorded at the year-end market price.

Inventory (accounting cost)	540,000	
Estimated liability on purchase commitment	60,000	
Cash (or accounts payable)		600,000

---

[16]In each of the following situations, if a periodic inventory system is used *purchases* is debited instead of *inventory*.
[17]Recall from the LCM discussion in the chapter that the preferred method of recording losses from inventory write-downs is to recognize the loss as a separate item in the income statement, rather than as an increase in cost of goods sold.

Even if the market price of the inventory increases, there is no recovery of the $60,000 loss recognized in 2011. Remember that when the LCM rule is applied, the reduced inventory value, in this case the reduced value of purchases, is considered to be the new cost and any recovery of value is ignored.

If market price on purchase date declines from year-end price, the purchase is recorded at the market price.

If the market price declines even further from year-end levels, an additional loss is recognized. For example, if the market price of the inventory covered by the commitment declines to $510,000, the following entry is recorded:

Inventory (market price)	510,000	
Loss on purchase commitment ($540,000 − 510,000)	30,000	
Estimated liability on purchase commitment	60,000	
Cash (or accounts payable)		600,000

The total loss on this purchase commitment of $90,000 is thus allocated between 2011 and 2012 according to when the decline in value of the inventory covered by the commitment occurred.

If there are material amounts of purchase commitments outstanding at the end of a reporting period, the contract details are disclosed in a note. This disclosure is required even if no loss estimate has been recorded. ●

QUESTIONS FOR REVIEW OF KEY TOPICS

Q 9–1   Explain the lower-of-cost-or-market approach to valuing inventory.

Q 9–2   What is the meaning of market in the lower-of-cost-or-market rule?

Q 9–3   What are the various ways the LCM determination can be made?

Q 9–4   Describe the preferred method of adjusting from cost to market for material inventory write-downs.

Q 9–5   Explain the gross profit method of estimating ending inventory.

Q 9–6   The Rider Company uses the gross profit method to estimate ending inventory and cost of goods sold. The cost percentage is determined based on historical data. What factors could cause the estimate of ending inventory to be overstated?

Q 9–7   Explain the retail inventory method of estimating ending inventory.

Q 9–8   Both the gross profit method and the retail inventory method provide a way to estimate ending inventory. What is the main difference between the two estimation techniques?

Q 9–9   Define each of the following retail terms: initial markup, additional markup, markup cancellation, markdown, markdown cancellation.

Q 9–10   Explain how to estimate the average cost of inventory when using the retail inventory method.

Q 9–11   What is the conventional retail method?

Q 9–12   Explain the LIFO retail inventory method.

Q 9–13   Discuss the treatment of freight-in, net markups, normal spoilage, and employee discounts in the application of the retail inventory method.

Q 9–14   Explain the difference between the retail inventory method using LIFO and the dollar-value LIFO retail method.

Q 9–15   Describe the accounting treatment for a change in inventory method other than to LIFO.

Q 9–16   When a company changes its inventory method to LIFO, an exception is made for the way accounting changes usually are reported. Explain the difference in the accounting treatment of a change *to* the LIFO inventory method from other inventory method changes.

Q 9–17   Explain the accounting treatment of material inventory errors discovered in an accounting period subsequent to the period in which the error is made.

Q 9–18   It is discovered in 2011 that ending inventory in 2009 was understated. What is the effect of the understatement on the following:

2009:	Cost of goods sold
	Net income
	Ending retained earnings
2010:	Net purchases
	Cost of goods sold
	Net income
	Ending retained earnings

IFRS   Q 9–19   Identify any differences between U.S. GAAP and IFRS when applying the lower-of-cost-or-market rule to inventory valuation.

Q 9–20   (Based on Appendix 9) Define purchase commitments. What is the advantage(s) of these agreements to buyers?

Q 9–21   (Based on Appendix 9) Explain how the lower-of-cost-or-market rule is applied to purchase commitments.

BRIEF EXERCISES

BE 9–1
Lower of cost or market
● LO1

Ross Electronics has one product in its ending inventory. Per unit data consist of the following: cost, $20; replacement cost, $18; selling price, $30; disposal costs, $4. The normal profit margin is 30% of selling price. What unit value should Ross use when applying the LCM rule to ending inventory?

BE 9–2
Lower of cost or market
● LO1

SLR Corporation has 1,000 units of each of its two products in its year-end inventory. Per unit data for each of the products are as follows:

	Product 1	Product 2
Cost	$50	$30
Replacement cost	48	26
Selling price	70	36
Disposal costs	6	4
Normal profit margin	10	8

Determine the balance sheet carrying value of SLR's inventory assuming that the LCM rule is applied to individual products. What is the before-tax income effect of the LCM adjustment?

BE 9–3
IFRS; lower of cost or market
● LO1
  LO8

Refer to the situation described in BE 9–2. Determine the balance sheet carrying value of SLR's inventory assuming that the LCM rule is applied to individual products and that SLR prepares its financial statements according to IFRS. What is the before-tax income effect of the LCM adjustment?

BE 9–4
Gross profit method
● LO2

On February 26 a hurricane destroyed the entire inventory stored in a warehouse owned by the Rockford Corporation. The following information is available from the records of the company's periodic inventory system: beginning inventory, $220,000; purchases and net sales from the beginning of the year through February 26, $400,000 and $600,000, respectively; gross profit ratio, 30%. Estimate the cost of the inventory destroyed by the hurricane using the gross profit method.

BE 9–5
Gross profit method; solving for unknown
● LO2

Adams Corporation estimates that it lost $75,000 in inventory from a recent flood. The following information is available from the records of the company's periodic inventory system: beginning inventory, $150,000; purchases and net sales from the beginning of the year through the date of the flood, $450,000 and $700,000, respectively. What is the company's gross profit ratio?

BE 9–6
Retail inventory method; average cost
● LO3

Kiddie World uses a periodic inventory system and the retail inventory method to estimate ending inventory and cost of goods sold. The following data are available for the quarter ending September 30, 2011:

	Cost	Retail
Beginning inventory	$300,000	$ 450,000
Net purchases	861,000	1,210,000
Freight-in	22,000	
Net markups		48,000
Net markdowns		18,000
Net sales		1,200,000

Estimate ending inventory and cost of goods sold (average cost).

BE 9–7
Retail inventory method; LIFO
● LO3

Refer to the situation described in BE 9–6. Estimate ending inventory and cost of goods sold (LIFO).

BE 9–8
Conventional retail method
● LO4

Refer to the situation described in BE 9–6. Estimate ending inventory and cost of goods sold using the conventional method (average cost and the LCM approximation).

BE 9–9
Conventional retail method
● LO4

Roberson Corporation uses a periodic inventory system and the retail inventory method. Accounting records provided the following information for the 2011 fiscal year:

	Cost	Retail
Beginning inventory	$220,000	$ 400,000
Net purchases	640,000	1,180,000
Freight-in	17,800	
Net markups		16,000
Net markdowns		6,000
Normal spoilage		3,000
Net sales		1,300,000

The company records sales to employees net of discounts. These discounts totaled $15,000 for the year. Estimate ending inventory and cost of goods sold using the conventional method (average cost and the LCM approximation).

BE 9–10
Dollar-value LIFO retail
● LO5

On January 1, 2011, Sanderson Variety Store adopted the dollar-value LIFO retail inventory method. Accounting records provided the following information:

	Cost	Retail
Beginning inventory	$ 40,800	$ 68,000
Net purchases	155,440	270,000
Net markups		6,000
Net markdowns		8,000
Net sales		250,000
Retail price index, end of year		1.02

Calculate the inventory value at the end of the year using the dollar-value LIFO retail method.

BE 9–11
Dollar-value LIFO retail
● LO5

This exercise is a continuation of BE 9–10. During 2012, purchases at cost and retail were $168,000 and $301,000, respectively. Net markups, net markdowns, and net sales for the year were $3,000, $4,000, and $280,000, respectively. The retail price index at the end of 2012 was 1.06. Calculate the inventory value at the end of 2012 using the dollar-value LIFO retail method.

BE 9–12
Change in inventory costing methods
● LO6

In 2011, Hopyard Lumber changed its inventory method from LIFO to FIFO. Inventory at the end of 2010 of $127,000 would have been $145,000 if FIFO had been used. Inventory at the end of 2011 is $162,000 using the new FIFO method but would have been $151,000 if the company had continued to use LIFO. Describe the steps Hopyard should take to report this change. What is the effect of the change on 2011 cost of goods sold?

BE 9–13
Change in inventory costing methods
● LO6

In 2011, Wade Window and Glass changed its inventory method from FIFO to LIFO. Inventory at the end of 2010 is $150,000. Describe the steps Wade Window and Glass should take to report this change.

BE 9–14
Inventory error
● LO7

In 2011, Winslow International, Inc.'s controller discovered that ending inventories for 2009 and 2010 were overstated by $200,000 and $500,000, respectively. Determine the effect of the errors on retained earnings at January 1, 2011. (Ignore income taxes.)

BE 9–15
Inventory error
● LO7

Refer to the situation described in BE 9–14. What steps would be taken to report the error in the 2011 financial statements?

EXERCISES

An alternate exercise and problem set is available on the text website: www.mhhe.com/spiceland6e

E 9–1
Lower of cost or market
● LO1

Herman Company has three products in its ending inventory. Specific per unit data for each of the products are as follows:

	Product 1	Product 2	Product 3
Cost	$20	$ 90	$50
Replacement cost	18	85	40
Selling price	40	120	70
Disposal costs	6	40	10
Normal profit margin	5	30	12

Required:
What unit values should Herman use for each of its products when applying the LCM rule to ending inventory?

E 9–2
IFRS; Lower of
cost or market
● LO1 LO8

Refer to the situation described in Exercise 9–1.

Required:

How might your solution differ if Herman Company prepares its financial statements according to International Financial Reporting Standards?

E 9–3
Lower of cost or
market
● LO1

Tatum Company has four products in its inventory. Information about the December 31, 2011, inventory is as follows:

Product	Total Cost	Total Replacement Cost	Total Net Realizable Value
101	$120,000	$110,000	$100,000
102	90,000	85,000	110,000
103	60,000	40,000	50,000
104	30,000	28,000	50,000

The normal gross profit percentage is 25% of *cost*.

Required:

1. Determine the balance sheet inventory carrying value at December 31, 2011, assuming the LCM rule is applied to individual products.
2. Assuming that Tatum recognizes an inventory write-down as a separate income statement item, determine the amount of the loss.

E 9–4
IFRS; lower of cost
or market
● LO1 LO8

Refer to the situation described in Exercise 9–3. Assume that Tatum Company prepares its financial statements according to IFRS.

Required:

1. Determine the balance sheet inventory carrying value at December 31, 2011, assuming Tatum applies the LCM rule to individual products.
2. Prepare a journal entry to record the inventory write-down, if necessary.

E 9–5
Lower of cost or
market
● LO1

The inventory of Royal Decking consisted of five products. Information about the December 31, 2011, inventory is as follows:

Product	Per Unit Cost	Replacement Cost	Selling Price
A	$ 40	$35	$ 60
B	80	70	100
C	40	55	80
D	100	70	130
E	20	28	30

Disposal costs consist only of a sales commission equal to 10% of selling price and shipping costs equal to 5% of cost. The normal gross profit percentage is 30% of selling price.

Required:

What unit value should Royal Decking use for each of its products when applying the LCM rule to units of inventory?

E 9–6
FASB codification
research
● LO1

The *FASB Accounting Standards Codification* represents the single source of authoritative U.S. generally accepted accounting principles.

Required:

1. Obtain the relevant authoritative literature on the lower-of-cost-or-market rule for valuing inventory using the FASB's Codification Research System at the FASB website (**www.fasb.org**). Identify the circumstances in which inventory is stated at the lower of cost or market.
2. What are the specific citations that discuss the level of aggregation that should be used in applying the LCM rule?
3. Summarize the discussion.

E 9–7
FASB codification
research
● LO1 LO3
   LO6 LO7

Access the FASB's Codification Research System at the FASB website (**www.fasb.org**). Determine the specific citation for each of the following items:

1. The income statement presentation of losses from the write-down of inventory.
2. The determination of market value for applying LCM to inventory.
3. The accounting treatment required for a correction of an inventory error in previously issued financial statements.
4. The use of the retail method to value inventory.

E 9–8
Gross profit
method
● LO2

On September 22, 2011, a flood destroyed the entire merchandise inventory on hand in a warehouse owned by the Rocklin Sporting Goods Company. The following information is available from the records of the company's periodic inventory system:

Inventory, January 1, 2011	$140,000
Net purchases, January 1 through September 22	370,000
Net sales, January 1 through September 22	550,000
Gross profit ratio	25%

Required:
Estimate the cost of inventory destroyed in the flood using the gross profit method.

E 9–9
Gross profit
method
● LO2

On November 21, 2011, a fire at Hodge Company's warehouse caused severe damage to its entire inventory of Product Tex. Hodge estimates that all usable damaged goods can be sold for $12,000. The following information was available from the records of Hodge's periodic inventory system:

Inventory, November 1	$100,000
Net purchases from November 1, to the date of the fire	140,000
Net sales from November 1, to the date of the fire	220,000

Based on recent history, Hodge's gross profit ratio on Product Tex is 35% of net sales.

Required:
Calculate the estimated loss on the inventory from the fire, using the gross profit method.

(AICPA adapted)

E 9–10
Gross profit
method
● LO2

A fire destroyed a warehouse of the Goren Group, Inc., on May 4, 2011. Accounting records on that date indicated the following:

Merchandise inventory, January 1, 2011	$1,900,000
Purchases to date	5,800,000
Freight-in	400,000
Sales to date	8,200,000

The gross profit ratio has averaged 20% of sales for the past four years.

Required:
Use the gross profit method to estimate the cost of the inventory destroyed in the fire.

E 9–11
Gross profit
method
● LO2

Royal Gorge Company uses the gross profit method to estimate ending inventory and cost of goods sold when preparing monthly financial statements required by its bank. Inventory on hand at the end of October was $58,500. The following information for the month of November was available from company records:

Purchases	$110,000
Freight-in	3,000
Sales	180,000
Sales returns	5,000
Purchases returns	4,000

In addition, the controller is aware of $8,000 of inventory that was stolen during November from one of the company's warehouses.

Required:
1. Calculate the estimated inventory at the end of November, assuming a gross profit ratio of 40%.
2. Calculate the estimated inventory at the end of November, assuming a markup on cost of 100%.

E 9–12
Gross profit
method; solving
for unknown cost
percentage
● LO2

National Distributing Company uses a periodic inventory system to track its merchandise inventory and the gross profit method to estimate ending inventory and cost of goods sold for interim periods. Net purchases for the month of August were $31,000. The July 31 and August 31, 2011, financial statements contained the following information:

Income Statements
For the Months Ending

	August 31, 2011	July 31, 2011
Net sales	$50,000	$40,000

Balance Sheets
At

	August 31, 2011	July 31, 2011
Assets:		
Merchandise inventory	$28,000	$27,000

Required:
Determine the company's cost percentage.

E 9–13
Retail inventory
method; average
cost
● LO3

San Lorenzo General Store uses a periodic inventory system and the retail inventory method to estimate ending inventory and cost of goods sold. The following data are available for the month of October 2011:

	Cost	Retail
Beginning inventory	$35,000	$50,000
Net purchases	19,120	31,600
Net markups		1,200
Net markdowns		800
Net sales		32,000

Required:
Estimate the average cost of ending inventory and cost of goods sold for October. Do not approximate LCM.

E 9–14
Conventional retail
method
● LO4

Campbell Corporation uses the retail method to value its inventory. The following information is available for the year 2011:

	Cost	Retail
Merchandise inventory, January 1, 2011	$190,000	$280,000
Purchases	600,000	840,000
Freight-in	8,000	
Net markups		20,000
Net markdowns		4,000
Net sales		800,000

Required:
Determine the December 31, 2011, inventory that approximates average cost, lower of cost or market.

E 9–15
Retail inventory
method; LIFO
● LO3

Crosby Company owns a chain of hardware stores throughout the state. The company uses a periodic inventory system and the retail inventory method to estimate ending inventory and cost of goods sold. The following data are available for the three months ending March 31, 2011:

	Cost	Retail
Beginning inventory	$160,000	$280,000
Net purchases	607,760	840,000
Net markups		20,000
Net markdowns		4,000
Net sales		800,000

Required:
Estimate the LIFO cost of ending inventory and cost of goods sold for the three months ending March 31, 2011. Assume stable retail prices during the period.

E 9–16
Conventional retail method; normal spoilage
● LO4

Almaden Valley Variety Store uses the retail inventory method to estimate ending inventory and cost of goods sold. Data for 2011 are as follows:

	Cost	Retail
Beginning inventory	$ 12,000	$ 20,000
Purchases	102,600	165,000
Freight-in	3,480	
Purchase returns	4,000	7,000
Net markups		6,000
Net markdowns		3,000
Normal spoilage		4,200
Net sales		152,000

Required:
Estimate the ending inventory and cost of goods sold for 2011, applying the conventional retail method (average, LCM).

E 9–17
Conventional retail method; employee discounts
● LO3 LO4

LeMay Department Store uses the retail inventory method to estimate ending inventory for its monthly financial statements. The following data pertain to one of its largest departments for the month of March 2011:

	Cost	Retail
Beginning inventory	$ 40,000	$ 60,000
Purchases	207,000	400,000
Freight-in	14,488	
Purchase returns	4,000	6,000
Net markups		5,800
Net markdowns		3,500
Normal breakage		6,000
Net sales		280,000
Employee discounts		1,800

Sales are recorded net of employee discounts.

Required:
1. Compute estimated ending inventory and cost of goods sold for March applying the conventional retail method (average, LCM).
2. Recompute the cost-to-retail percentage using the average cost method and ignoring LCM considerations.

E 9–18
Retail inventory method; solving for unknowns
● LO3

Adams Corporation uses a periodic inventory system and the retail inventory method to estimate ending inventory and cost of goods sold. The following data are available for the month of September 2011:

	Cost	Retail
Beginning inventory	$21,000	$35,000
Net purchases	10,500	?
Net markups		4,000
Net markdowns		1,000
Net sales		?

The company used the average cost flow method and estimated inventory at the end of September to be $17,437.50. If the company had used the LIFO cost flow method, the cost-to-retail percentage would have been 50%.

Required:
Compute net purchases at retail and net sales for the month of September.

E 9–19
Dollar-value LIFO retail
● LO5

On January 1, 2011, the Brunswick Hat Company adopted the dollar-value LIFO retail method. The following data are available for 2011:

	Cost	Retail
Beginning inventory	$ 71,280	$132,000
Net purchases	112,500	255,000
Net markups		6,000
Net markdowns		11,000
Net sales		232,000
Retail price index, 12/31/11		1.04

Required:
Calculate the estimated ending inventory and cost of goods sold for 2011.

E 9–20
Dollar-value LIFO retail
● **LO5**

Canova Corporation adopted the dollar-value LIFO retail method on January 1, 2011. On that date, the cost of the inventory on hand was $15,000 and its retail value was $18,750. Information for 2011 and 2012 is as follows:

Date	Ending Inventory at Retail	Retail Price Index	Cost-to-Retail Percentage
12/31/11	$25,000	1.25	82%
12/31/12	28,600	1.30	85

Required:

1. What is the cost-to-retail percentage for the inventory on hand at 1/1/11?
2. Calculate the inventory value at the end of 2011 and 2012 using the dollar-value LIFO retail method.

E 9–21
Dollar-value LIFO retail
● **LO5**

Lance-Hefner Specialty Shoppes decided to use the dollar-value LIFO retail method to value its inventory. Accounting records provide the following information:

	Cost	Retail
Merchandise inventory, January 1, 2011	$160,000	$250,000
Net purchases	350,200	510,000
Net markups		7,000
Net markdowns		2,000
Net sales		380,000

Pertinent retail price indexes are as follows:

January 1, 2011	1.00
December 31, 2011	1.10

Required:
Determine ending inventory and cost of goods sold.

E 9–22
Dollar-value LIFO retail; solving for unknowns
● **LO5**

Bosco Company adopted the dollar-value LIFO retail method at the beginning of 2011. Information for 2011 and 2012 is as follows, with certain data intentionally omitted:

	Inventory		Retail	Cost-to-Retail
Date	Cost	Retail	Price Index	Percentage
Inventory, 1/1/11	$21,000	$28,000	1.00	?
Inventory, 12/31/11	22,792	33,600	1.12	?
2012 net purchases	60,000	88,400		
2012 net sales		80,000		
Inventory, 12/31/12	?	?	1.20	

Required:
Determine the missing data.

E 9–23
Change in inventory costing methods
● **LO6**

In 2011, CPS Company changed its method of valuing inventory from the FIFO method to the average cost method. At December 31, 2010, CPS's inventories were $32 million (FIFO). CPS's records indicated that the inventories would have totaled $23.8 million at December 31, 2010, if determined on an average cost basis.

Required:

1. Prepare the journal entry to record the adjustment. (Ignore income taxes.)
2. Briefly describe other steps CPS should take to report the change.

E 9–24
Change in inventory costing methods
● **LO6**

Goddard Company has used the FIFO method of inventory valuation since it began operations in 2008. Goddard decided to change to the average cost method for determining inventory costs at the beginning of 2011. The following schedule shows year-end inventory balances under the FIFO and average cost methods:

Year	FIFO	Average Cost
2008	$45,000	$54,000
2009	78,000	71,000
2010	83,000	78,000

Required:

1. Ignoring income taxes, prepare the 2011 journal entry to adjust the accounts to reflect the average cost method.
2. How much higher or lower would cost of goods sold be in the 2010 revised income statement?

E 9–25
Error correction;
inventory error
● LO7

During 2011, WMC Corporation discovered that its ending inventories reported in its financial statements were misstated by the following material amounts:

| 2009 | understated by | $120,000 |
| 2010 | overstated by | 150,000 |

WMC uses a periodic inventory system and the FIFO cost method.

Required:

1. Determine the effect of these errors on retained earnings at January 1, 2011, before any adjustments. Explain your answer. (Ignore income taxes.)
2. Prepare a journal entry to correct the errors.
3. What other step(s) would be taken in connection with the correction of the errors?

E 9–26
Inventory errors
● LO7

For each of the following inventory errors occurring in 2011, determine the effect of the error on 2011's cost of goods sold, net income, and retained earnings. Assume that the error is not discovered until 2012 and that a periodic inventory system is used. Ignore income taxes.

U = understated   O = overstated   NE = no effect

	Cost of Goods Sold	Net Income	Retained Earnings
1. Overstatement of ending inventory	U	O	O
2. Overstatement of purchases			
3. Understatement of beginning inventory			
4. Freight-in charges are understated			
5. Understatement of ending inventory			
6. Understatement of purchases			
7. Overstatement of beginning inventory			
8. Understatement of purchases plus understatement of ending inventory by the same amount			

E 9–27
Inventory error
● LO7

In 2011, the internal auditors of Development Technologies, Inc. discovered that a $4 million purchase of merchandise in 2011 was recorded in 2010 instead. The physical inventory count at the end of 2010 was correct.

Required:

Prepare the journal entry needed in 2011 to correct the error. Also, briefly describe any other measures Development Technologies would take in connection with correcting the error. (Ignore income taxes.)

E 9–28
Inventory errors
● LO7

In 2011, the controller of Sytec Corporation discovered that $42,000 of inventory purchases were incorrectly charged to advertising expense in 2010. In addition, the 2010 year-end inventory count failed to include $30,000 of company merchandise held on consignment by Erin Brothers. Sytec uses a periodic inventory system. Other than the omission of the merchandise on consignment, the year-end inventory count was correct. The amounts of the errors are deemed to be material.

Required:

1. Determine the effect of the errors on retained earnings at January 1, 2011. Explain your answer. (Ignore income taxes.)
2. Prepare a journal entry to correct the errors.
3. What other step(s) would be taken in connection with the correction of the errors?

E 9–29
Concepts;
terminology
● LO1 through LO7

Listed below are several terms and phrases associated with inventory measurement. Pair each item from List A with the item from List B (by letter) that is most appropriately associated with it.

List A	List B
_____ 1. Gross profit ratio	a. Reduction in selling price below the original selling price.
_____ 2. Cost-to-retail percentage	b. Beginning inventory is not included in the calculation of the cost-to-retail percentage.
_____ 3. Additional markup	c. Deducted in the retail column after the calculation of the cost-to-retail percentage.
_____ 4. Markdown	d. Requires base year retail to be converted to layer year retail and then to cost.
_____ 5. Net markup	e. Gross profit divided by net sales.
_____ 6. Retail method, FIFO and LIFO	f. Material inventory error discovered in a subsequent year.
_____ 7. Conventional retail method	g. Must be deducted with retail column if sales are recorded net of discounts.
_____ 8. Change from LIFO	h. Deducted in the retail column to arrive at goods available for sale at retail.
_____ 9. Dollar-value LIFO retail	i. Divide cost of goods available for sale by goods available at retail.
_____ 10. Normal spoilage	j. Average cost, LCM.
_____ 11. Requires retrospective restatement	k. Added to the retail column to arrive at goods available for sale.
_____ 12. Employee discounts	l. Increase in selling price subsequent to initial markup.
_____ 13. Net markdowns	m. Ceiling in the determination of market.
_____ 14. Net realizable value	n. Accounting change requiring retrospective treatment.

E 9–30
Purchase
commitments
● Appendix

On October 6, 2011, the Elgin Corporation signed a purchase commitment to purchase inventory for $60,000 on or before March 31, 2012. The company's fiscal year-end is December 31. The contract was exercised on March 21, 2012, and the inventory was purchased for cash at the contract price. On the purchase date of March 21, the market price of the inventory was $54,000. The market price of the inventory on December 31, 2011, was $56,000. The company uses a perpetual inventory system.

Required:
1. Prepare the necessary adjusting journal entry (if any is required) on December 31, 2011.
2. Prepare the journal entry to record the purchase on March 21, 2012.

E 9–31
Purchase
commitments
● Appendix

In March 2011, the Phillips Tool Company signed two purchase commitments. The first commitment requires Phillips to purchase inventory for $100,000 by June 15, 2011. The second commitment requires the company to purchase inventory for $150,000 by August 20, 2011. The company's fiscal year-end is June 30. Phillips uses a periodic inventory system.

   The first commitment is exercised on June 15, 2011, when the market price of the inventory purchased was $85,000. The second commitment was exercised on August 20, 2011, when the market price of the inventory purchased was $120,000.

Required:
Prepare the journal entries required on June 15, June 30, and August 20, 2011, to account for the two purchase commitments. Assume that the market price of the inventory related to the outstanding purchase commitment was $140,000 at June 30.

CPA AND CMA REVIEW QUESTIONS

**CPA Exam
Questions**

The following questions are used in the Kaplan CPA Review Course to study inventory while preparing for the CPA examination. Determine the response that best completes the statements or questions.

● LO1

1. Kahn Co., in applying the lower of cost or market method, reports its inventory at replacement cost. Which of the following statements are correct?

	Cost is greater than replacement cost	NRV, less a normal profit margin, is greater than replacement cost
a.	Yes	Yes
b.	No	No
c.	Yes	No
d.	No	Yes

● LO1

2. Moss Co. has determined its year-end inventory on a FIFO basis to be $400,000. Information pertaining to that inventory is as follows:

Estimated selling price	$408,000
Estimated cost of disposal	20,000
Normal profit margin	60,000
Current replacement cost	360,000

What should be the carrying value of Moss's inventory?
a. $328,000
b. $360,000
c. $388,000
d. $400,000

● LO2

3. On May 2, a fire destroyed the entire merchandise inventory on hand of Sanchez Wholesale Corporation. The following information is available:

Sales, January 1 through May 2	$360,000
Inventory, January 1	80,000
Merchandise purchases, January 1 through May 2 (including $40,000 of goods in transit on May 2, shipped f.o.b. shipping point)	330,000
Markup percentage on cost	20%

What is the estimated inventory on May 2 immediately prior to the fire?
a. $ 70,000
b. $ 82,000
c. $110,000
d. $122,000

● LO4

4. Hutch, Inc., uses the conventional retail inventory method to account for inventory. The following information relates to current year's operations:

	Average	
	Cost	Retail
Beginning inventory and purchases	$600,000	$920,000
Net markups		40,000
Net markdowns		60,000
Sales		780,000

What amount should be reported as cost of sales for the year?
a. $480,000
b. $487,500
c. $500,000
d. $525,000

● LO7

5. Bren Co.'s beginning inventory on January 1 was understated by $26,000, and its ending inventory on December 31 was overstated by $52,000. As a result, Bren's cost of goods sold for the year was
a. Understated by $26,000.
b. Overstated by $78,000.
c. Understated by $78,000.
d. Overstated by $26,000.

CMA Exam Questions

The following questions dealing with inventory are adapted from questions that previously appeared on Certified Management Accountant (CMA) examinations. The CMA designation sponsored by the Institute of Management Accountants (**www.imanet.org**) provides members with an objective measure of knowledge and competence in the field of management accounting. Determine the response that best completes the statements or questions.

● LO4

1. The following FCL Corporation inventory information is available for the year ended December 31:

	Cost	Retail
Beginning inventory at 1/1	$35,000	$100,000
Net purchases	55,000	110,000
Net markups		15,000
Net markdowns		25,000
Net sales		150,000

The December 31 ending inventory at cost using the conventional (lower of average cost or market) retail inventory method equals
a. $17,500
b. $20,000
c. $27,500
d. $50,000

● LO7

2. All sales and purchases for the year at Ross Corporation are credit transactions. Ross uses a perpetual inventory system. During the year, it shipped certain goods that were correctly excluded from ending inventory although the sale was not recorded. Which one of the following statements is correct?
a. Accounts receivable was not affected, inventory was not affected, sales were understated, and cost of goods sold was understated.
b. Accounts receivable was understated, inventory was not affected, sales were understated, and cost of goods sold was understated.
c. Accounts receivable was understated, inventory was overstated, sales were understated, and cost of goods sold was overstated.
d. Accounts receivable was understated, inventory was not affected, sales were understated, and cost of goods sold was not affected.

● LO7

3. During the year 1 year-end physical inventory count at Tequesta Corporation, $40,000 worth of inventory was counted twice. Assuming that the year 2 year-end inventory was correct, the result of the year 1 error was that
a. Year 1 retained earnings was understated, and year 2 ending inventory was correct.
b. Year 1 cost of goods sold was overstated, and year 2 income was understated.
c. Year 1 income was overstated, and year 2 ending inventory was overstated.
d. Year 1 cost of goods sold was understated, and year 2 retained earnings was correct.

PROBLEMS

An alternate exercise and problem set is available on the text website: www.mhhe.com/spiceland6e

P 9–1
Lower of cost or market

● LO1

Decker Company has five products in its inventory. Information about the December 31, 2011, inventory follows.

Product	Quantity	Unit Cost	Unit Replacement Cost	Unit Selling Price
A	1,000	$10	$12	$16
B	800	15	11	18
C	600	3	2	8
D	200	7	4	6
E	600	14	12	13

The selling cost for each product consists of a 15 percent sales commission. The normal profit percentage for each product is 40 percent of the selling price.

Required:
1. Determine the balance sheet inventory carrying value at December 31, 2011, assuming the LCM rule is applied to individual products.
2. Determine the balance sheet inventory carrying value at December 31, 2011, assuming the LCM rule is applied to the entire inventory. Also, assuming that Decker recognizes an inventory write-down as a separate income statement item, determine the amount of the loss.

P 9–2
Lower of cost or market

● LO1

Almaden Hardware Store sells two distinct types of products, tools and paint products. Information pertaining to its 2011 year-end inventory is as follows:

Inventory, by Product Type	Quantity	Per Unit Cost	Designated Market
Tools:			
Hammers	100	$ 5.00	$5.50
Saws	200	10.00	9.00
Screwdrivers	300	2.00	2.60
Paint products:			
1-gallon cans	500	6.00	5.00
Paint brushes	100	4.00	4.50

Required:
1. Determine the balance sheet inventory carrying value at year-end, assuming the LCM rule is applied to (a) individual products, (b) product type, and (c) total inventory.
2. Assuming that the company recognizes an inventory write-down as a separate income statement item, for each of the LCM applications determine the amount of the loss.

P 9–3
Gross profit method

● LO2

Smith Distributors, Inc., supplies ice cream shops with various toppings for making sundaes. On November 17, 2011, a fire resulted in the loss of all of the toppings stored in one section of the warehouse. The company must provide its insurance company with an estimate of the amount of inventory lost. The following information is available from the company's accounting records:

	Fruit Toppings	Marshmallow Toppings	Chocolate Toppings
Inventory, January 1, 2011	$ 20,000	$ 7,000	$ 3,000
Net purchases through Nov. 17	150,000	36,000	12,000
Net sales through Nov. 17	200,000	55,000	20,000
Historical gross profit ratio	20%	30%	35%

Required:
1. Calculate the estimated cost of each of the toppings lost in the fire.
2. What factors could cause the estimates to be over-or understated?

P 9–4
Retail inventory method; various cost methods

● LO3 LO4

Sparrow Company uses the retail inventory method to estimate ending inventory and cost of goods sold. Data for 2011 are as follows:

	Cost	Retail
Beginning inventory	$ 90,000	$180,000
Purchases	355,000	580,000
Freight-in	9,000	
Purchase returns	7,000	11,000

(continued)

(concluded)

Net markups		16,000
Net markdowns		12,000
Normal spoilage		3,000
Abnormal spoilage	4,800	8,000
Sales		540,000
Sales returns		10,000

The company records sales net of employee discounts. Discounts for 2011 totaled $4,000.

Required:
Estimate Sparrow's ending inventory and cost of goods sold for the year using the retail inventory method and the following applications:

1. Average cost
2. Conventional (average, LCM)

P 9–5
Retail inventory method; conventional and LIFO

● LO3 LO4

Alquist Company uses the retail method to estimate its ending inventory. Selected information about its year 2011 operations is as follows:

a. January 1, 2011, beginning inventory had a cost of $100,000 and a retail value of $150,000.
b. Purchases during 2011 cost $1,387,500 with an original retail value of $2,000,000.
c. Freight costs were $10,000 for incoming merchandise.
d. Net additional markups were $300,000 and net markdowns were $150,000.
e. Based on prior experience, shrinkage due to shoplifting was estimated to be $15,000 of retail value.
f. Merchandise is sold to employees at a 20% of selling price discount. Employee sales are recorded in a separate account at the net selling price. The balance in this account at the end of 2011 is $250,000.
g. Sales to customers totaled $1,750,000 for the year.

Required:
1. Estimate ending inventory and cost of goods sold using the conventional retail method (average, LCM).
2. Estimate ending inventory and cost of goods sold using the LIFO retail method. (Assume stable prices.)

P 9–6
Retail inventory method; conventional

● LO4

Grand Department Store, Inc., uses the retail inventory method to estimate ending inventory for its monthly financial statements. The following data pertain to a single department for the month of October 2011:

Inventory, October 1, 2011:	
At cost	$ 20,000
At retail	30,000
Purchases (exclusive of freight and returns):	
At cost	100,151
At retail	146,495
Freight-in	5,100
Purchase returns:	
At cost	2,100
At retail	2,800
Additional markups	2,500
Markup cancellations	265
Markdowns (net)	800
Normal spoilage and breakage	4,500
Sales	135,730

Required:
1. Using the conventional retail method, prepare a schedule computing estimated lower-of-cost-or-market inventory for October 31, 2011.
2. A department store using the conventional retail inventory method estimates the cost of its ending inventory as $29,000. An accurate physical count reveals only $22,000 of inventory at lower of cost or market. List the factors that may have caused the difference between computed inventory and the physical count.

(AICPA adapted)

P 9–7
Retail method—average cost and LCM

● LO3 LO4

Smith-Kline Company maintains inventory records at selling prices as well as at cost. For 2011, the records indicate the following data:

	($ in 000s)	
	Cost	**Retail**
Beginning inventory	$ 80	$ 125
Purchases	671	1,006
Freight-in on purchases	30	
Purchase returns	1	2
Net markups		4
Net markdowns		8
Net sales		916

Required:
Use the retail method to approximate cost of ending inventory in each of the following ways:
1. Average cost
2. Average (LCM) cost

P 9–8
Dollar-value LIFO retail method
● LO5

[This is a variation of the previous problem, modified to focus on the dollar-value LIFO retail method.] Smith-Kline Company maintains inventory records at selling prices as well as at cost. For 2011, the records indicate the following data:

	($ in 000s)	
	Cost	Retail
Beginning inventory	$ 80	$ 125
Purchases	671	1,006
Freight-in on purchases	30	
Purchase returns	1	2
Net markups		4
Net markdowns		8
Net sales		916

Required:
Assuming the price level increased from 1.00 at January 1 to 1.10 at December 31, 2011, use the dollar-value LIFO retail method to approximate cost of ending inventory and cost of goods sold.

P 9–9
Dollar-value LIFO retail
● LO5

On January 1, 2011, HGC Camera Store adopted the dollar-value LIFO retail inventory method. Inventory transactions at both cost and retail, and cost indexes for 2011 and 2012 are as follows:

	2011		2012	
	Cost	Retail	Cost	Retail
Beginning inventory	$28,000	$ 40,000		
Net purchases	85,000	108,000	90,000	114,000
Freight-in	2,000		2,500	
Net markups		10,000		8,000
Net markdowns		2,000		2,200
Net sales to customers		100,000		104,000
Sales to employees (net of 20% discount)		2,400		4,000
Price Index:				
January 1, 2011				1.00
December 31, 2011				1.06
December 31, 2012				1.10

Required:
Estimate the 2011 and 2012 ending inventory and cost of goods sold using the dollar-value LIFO retail inventory method.

P 9–10
Retail inventory method; various applications
● LO3 through LO5

Raleigh Department Store converted from the conventional retail method to the LIFO retail method on January 1, 2009, and is now considering converting to the dollar-value LIFO retail inventory method. Management requested, during your examination of the financial statements for the year ended December 31, 2011, that you furnish a summary showing certain computations of inventory costs for the past three years. Available information follows:

a. The inventory at January 1, 2009, had a retail value of $45,000 and a cost of $27,500 based on the conventional retail method.

b. Transactions during 2009 were as follows:

	Cost	Retail
Gross purchases	$282,000	$490,000
Purchase returns	6,500	10,000
Purchase discounts	5,000	
Gross sales		492,000
Sales returns		5,000
Employee discounts		3,000
Freight-in	26,500	
Net markups		25,000
Net markdowns		10,000

Sales to employees are recorded net of discounts.

c. The retail value of the December 31, 2010, inventory was $56,100, the cost-to-retail percentage for 2010 under the LIFO retail method was 62%, and the appropriate price index was 102% of the January 1, 2010, price level.

d. The retail value of the December 31, 2011, inventory was $48,300, the cost-to-retail percentage for 2011 under the LIFO retail method was 61%, and the appropriate price index was 105% of the January 1, 2010, price level.

Required:

1. Prepare a schedule showing the computation of the cost of inventory at December 31, 2009, based on the conventional retail method.

2. Prepare a similar schedule as in requirement 1 based on the LIFO retail method.

3. Same requirement as (1) for December 31, 2010 and 2011, based on the dollar-value LIFO retail method.

(AICPA adapted)

P 9–11
Retail inventory method; various applications
● LO3 through LO5

On January 1, 2011, Pet Friendly Stores adopted the retail inventory method. Inventory transactions at both cost and retail, and cost indexes for 2011 and 2012 are as follows:

	2011		2012	
	Cost	Retail	Cost	Retail
Beginning inventory	$ 90,000	$150,000		
Purchases	478,000	730,000	511,000	760,000
Purchase returns	2,500	3,500	2,200	4,000
Freight-in	6,960		8,000	
Net markups		8,500		10,000
Net markdowns		4,000		6,000
Net sales to customers		650,000		680,000
Sales to employees (net of 30% discount)		14,000		17,500
Normal spoilage		5,000		6,600
Price Index:				
January 1, 2011	1.00			
December 31, 2011	1.03			
December 31, 2012	1.06			

Required:

1. Estimate the 2011 and 2012 ending inventory and cost of goods sold using the dollar-value LIFO retail method.

2. Estimate the 2011 ending inventory and cost of goods sold using the average cost method.

3. Estimate the 2011 ending inventory and cost of goods sold using the conventional retail method (average, LCM).

P 9–12
Change in methods
● LO6

Rockwell Corporation uses a periodic inventory system and has used the FIFO cost method since inception of the company in 1976. In 2011, the company decided to switch to the average cost method. Data for 2011 are as follows:

Beginning inventory, FIFO (5,000 units @ $30)		$150,000
Purchases:		
5,000 units @ $36	$180,000	
5,000 units @ $40	200,000	380,000
Cost of goods available for sale		$530,000
Sales for 2011 (8,000 units @ $70)		$560,000

Additional Information:

a. The company's effective income tax rate is 40% for all years.

b. If the company had used the average cost method prior to 2011, ending inventory for 2010 would have been $130,000.

c. 7,000 units remained in inventory at the end of 2011.

Required:

1. Ignoring income taxes, prepare the 2011 journal entry to adjust the accounts to reflect the average cost method.

2. What is the effect of the change in methods on 2011 net income?

P 9–13
Inventory errors
● LO7

You have been hired as the new controller for the Ralston Company. Shortly after joining the company in 2011, you discover the following errors related to the 2009 and 2010 financial statements:

a. Inventory at 12/31/09 was understated by $6,000.

b. Inventory at 12/31/10 was overstated by $9,000.

c. On 12/31/10, inventory was purchased for $3,000. The company did not record the purchase until the inventory was paid for early in 2011. At that time, the purchase was recorded by a debit to purchases and a credit to cash.

The company uses a periodic inventory system.

Required:
1. Assuming that the errors were discovered after the 2010 financial statements were issued, analyze the effect of the errors on 2010 and 2009 cost of goods sold, net income, and retained earnings. (Ignore income taxes.)
2. Prepare a journal entry to correct the errors.
3. What other step(s) would be taken in connection with the errors?

P 9–14
Inventory errors
● LO7

The December 31, 2011, inventory of Tog Company, based on a physical count, was determined to be $450,000. Included in that count was a shipment of goods that cost $50,000 received from a supplier at the end of the month. The purchase was recorded and paid for in 2012. Another supplier shipment costing $20,000 was correctly recorded as a purchase in 2011. However, the merchandise, shipped FOB shipping point, was not received until 2012 and was incorrectly omitted from the physical count. A third purchase, shipped from a supplier FOB shipping point on December 28, 2011, did not arrive until January 3, 2012. The merchandise, which cost $80,000, was not included in the physical count and the purchase has not yet been recorded.
The company uses a periodic inventory system.

Required:
1. Determine the correct December 31, 2011, inventory balance and, assuming that the errors were discovered after the 2011 financial statements were issued, analyze the effect of the errors on 2011 cost of goods sold, net income, and retained earnings. (Ignore income taxes.)
2. Prepare a journal entry to correct the errors.

P 9–15
Integrating problem; Chapters 8 and 9; inventory errors
● LO7

Capwell Corporation uses a periodic inventory system. The company's ending inventory on December 31, 2011, its fiscal-year end, based on a physical count, was determined to be $326,000. Capwell's unadjusted trial balance also showed the following account balances: Purchases, $620,000; Accounts payable; $210,000; Accounts receivable, $225,000; Sales revenue, $840,000.
The internal audit department discovered the following items:
1. Goods valued at $32,000 held on consignment from Dix Company were included in the physical count but not recorded as a purchase.
2. Purchases from Xavier Corporation were incorrectly recorded at $41,000 instead of the correct amount of $14,000. The correct amount was included in the ending inventory.
3. Goods that cost $25,000 were shipped from a vendor on December 28, 2011, terms f.o.b. destination. The merchandise arrived on January 3, 2012. The purchase and related accounts payable were recorded in 2011.
4. One inventory item was incorrectly included in ending inventory as 100 units, instead of the correct amount of 1,000 units. This item cost $40 per unit.
5. The 2010 balance sheet reported inventory of $352,000. The internal auditors discovered that a mathematical error caused this inventory to be understated by $62,000. This amount is considered to be material.
6. Goods shipped to a customer f.o.b. destination on December 25, 2011, were received by the customer on January 4, 2012. The sales price was $40,000 and the merchandise cost $22,000. The sale and corresponding accounts receivable were recorded in 2011.
7. Goods shipped from a vendor f.o.b. shipping point on December 27, 2011, were received on January 3, 2012. The merchandise cost $18,000. The purchase was not recorded until 2012.

Required:
1. Determine the correct amounts for 2011 ending inventory, purchases, accounts payable, sales revenue, and accounts receivable.
2. Calculate cost of goods sold for 2011.
3. Describe the steps Capwell would undertake to correct the error in the 2010 ending inventory. What was the effect of the error on 2010 before-tax income?

P 9–16
Purchase commitments
● Appendix

In November 2011, the Brunswick Company signed two purchase commitments. The first commitment requires Brunswick to purchase 10,000 units of inventory at $10 per unit by December 15, 2011. The second commitment requires the company to purchase 20,000 units of inventory at $11 per unit by March 15, 2012. Brunswick's fiscal year-end is December 31. The company uses a periodic inventory system. Both contracts were exercised on their expiration date.

Required:
1. Prepare the journal entry to record the December 15 purchase for cash assuming the following alternative unit market prices on that date:
   a. $10.50
   b. $ 9.50

2. Prepare any necessary adjusting entry at December 31, 2011, for the second purchase commitment assuming the following alternative unit market prices on that date:

   a. $12.50

   b. $10.30

3. Assuming that the unit market price on December 31 was $10.30, prepare the journal entry to record the purchase on March 15, 2010, assuming the following alternative unit market prices on that date:

   a. $11.50

   b. $10.00

BROADEN YOUR PERSPECTIVE

Apply your critical-thinking ability to the knowledge you've gained. These cases will provide you an opportunity to develop your research, analysis, judgment, and communication skills. You also will work with other students, integrate what you've learned, apply it in real world situations, and consider its global and ethical ramifications. This practice will broaden your knowledge and further develop your decision-making abilities.

Judgment Case 9–1

Inventoriable costs; lower of cost or market; retail inventory method

● LO1 LO3 LO4

Hudson Company, which is both a wholesaler and a retailer, purchases its inventories from various suppliers. Additional facts for Hudson's wholesale operations are as follows:

a. Hudson incurs substantial warehousing costs.

b. Hudson uses the lower-of-cost-or-market method. The replacement cost of the inventories is below the net realizable value and above the net realizable value less the normal profit margin. The original cost of the inventories is above replacement cost and below the net realizable value.

Additional facts for Hudson's retail operations are as follows:

a. Hudson determines the estimated cost of its ending inventories held for sale at retail using the conventional retail inventory method, which approximates lower of average cost or market.

b. Hudson incurs substantial freight-in costs.

c. Hudson has net markups and net markdowns.

Required:

1. Theoretically, how should Hudson account for the warehousing costs related to its wholesale inventories? Why?

2. a. In general, why is the lower-of-cost-or-market method used to value inventory?

   b. At which amount should Hudson's wholesale inventories be reported in the balance sheet? Explain the application of the lower-of-cost-or-market method in this situation.

3. In the calculation of the cost-to-retail percentage used to determine the estimated cost of its ending retail inventories, how should Hudson treat

   a. Freight-in costs?

   b. Net markups?

   c. Net markdowns?

4. Why does Hudson's retail inventory method approximate lower of average cost or market?

(AICPA adapted)

Communication Case 9–2

Lower of cost or market

● LO1

The lower-of-cost-or-market approach to valuing inventory is a departure from the accounting principle of reporting assets at their historical costs. There are those who believe that inventory, as well as other assets, should be valued at market, regardless of whether market is above or below cost.

The focus of this case is the justification for the lower-of-cost-or-market rule for valuing inventories. Your instructor will divide the class into two to six groups depending on the size of the class. The mission of your group is to defend the lower-of-cost-or-market approach against the alternatives of valuing inventory at either historical cost or market value.

Required:

1. Each group member should consider the situation independently and draft a tentative argument prior to the class session for which the case is assigned.

2. In class, each group will meet for 10 to 15 minutes in different areas of the classroom. During that meeting, group members will take turns sharing their suggestions for the purpose of arriving at a single group argument.

3. After the allotted time, a spokesperson for each group (selected during the group meetings) will share the group's solution with the class. The goal of the class is to incorporate the views of each group into a consensus approach to the situation.

**Integrating
Case 9–3**
Unit LIFO and
LCM
● LO1

York Co. sells one product, which it purchases from various suppliers. York's trial balance at December 31, 2011, included the following accounts:

Sales (33,000 units @ $16)	$528,000
Sales discounts	7,500
Purchases	368,900
Purchase discounts	18,000
Freight-in	5,000

York Co.'s inventory purchases during 2011 were as follows:

	Units	Cost per Unit	Total Cost
Beginning inventory	8,000	$8.20	$ 65,600
Purchases, quarter ended March 31	12,000	8.25	99,000
Purchases, quarter ended June 30	15,000	7.90	118,500
Purchases, quarter ended September 30	13,000	7.50	97,500
Purchases, quarter ended December 31	7,000	7.70	53,900
	55,000		$434,500

Additional Information:

a. York's accounting policy is to report inventory in its financial statements at the lower of cost or market, applied to total inventory. Cost is determined under the last-in, first-out (LIFO) method.

b. York has determined that, at December 31, 2011, the replacement cost of its inventory was $8 per unit and the net realizable value was $8.80 per unit. York's normal profit margin is $1.05 per unit.

Required:

1. Prepare York's schedule of cost of goods sold, with a supporting schedule of ending inventory. York uses the direct method of reporting losses from market decline of inventory.

2. Explain the rule of lower of cost or market and its application in this situation.

(AICPA adapted)

**Judgment
Case 9–4**
The dollar-value
LIFO method; the
retail inventory
method
● LO3 LO4

Huddell Company, which is both a wholesaler and retailer, purchases merchandise from various suppliers. The dollar-value LIFO method is used for the wholesale inventories.

Huddell determines the estimated cost of its retail ending inventories using the conventional retail inventory method, which approximates lower of average cost or market.

Required:

1. a. What are the advantages of using the dollar-value LIFO method as opposed to the traditional LIFO method?

   b. How does the application of the dollar-value LIFO method differ from the application of the traditional LIFO method?

2. a. In the calculation of the cost-to-retail percentage used to determine the estimated cost of its ending inventories, how should Huddell use

   • Net markups?
   • Net markdowns?

   b. Why does Huddell's retail inventory method approximate lower of average cost or market?

(AICPA adapted)

**Communication
Case 9–5**
Retail inventory
method
● LO3 LO4

The Brenly Paint Company, your client, manufactures paint. The company's president, Mr. Brenly, decided to open a retail store to sell paint as well as wallpaper and other items that would be purchased from other suppliers. He has asked you for information about the retail method of estimating inventories at the retail store.

Required:

Prepare a report to the president explaining the retail method of estimating inventories.

**Analysis
Case 9–6**
Change in
inventory method
● LO6

Generally accepted accounting principles should be applied consistently from period to period. However, changes within a company, as well as changes in the external economic environment, may force a company to change an accounting method. The specific reporting requirements when a company changes from one generally accepted inventory method to another depend on the methods involved.

Required:

Explain the accounting treatment for a change in inventory method (a) not involving LIFO, (b) from the LIFO method, and (c) to the LIFO method. Explain the logic underlying those treatments. Also, describe how disclosure requirements are designed to address the departure from consistency and comparability of changes in accounting principle.

Real World Case 9–7

Change in inventory method; W.R. Grace

● LO6

Real World Financials

W.R. Grace & Co. is a global specialty chemicals company. The following disclosure note was included in recent financial statements:

Change in Accounting Principle

In the third quarter of 2008, Grace changed its method of accounting for the cost of its U.S. inventories from the last-in/first-out method, or LIFO, to the first-in/first-out method, or FIFO. Grace decided to make this change in order to achieve a consistent inventory costing method for both U.S. and non-U.S. inventories. Grace has retrospectively restated prior periods' financial statements for all periods presented herein to account for all inventories using FIFO in compliance with generally accepted accounting principles.

Required:

Why does GAAP require W.R. Grace to retrospectively adjust prior periods' financial statement for this type of accounting change?

Real World Case 9–8

Various inventory issues; Chapters 8 and 9; J.C. Penney

● LO1 LO5 LO6

Real World Financials

J.C. Penney is one the major retailers in the United States. Access the company's 10-K for the fiscal year ended January 31, 2009. You can find the 10-K at the company's website, **www.jcpenney.com**, or by using EDGAR at **www.sec.gov**. Answer the following questions.

Required:

1. What inventory methods does J.C. Penney use to value its inventory?
2. How does the company estimate the effects of changing prices on ending inventory?
3. How does J.C. Penney apply the lower-of-cost-or-market rule?
4. A company that uses LIFO is allowed to provide supplemental disclosures reporting the effect of using another inventory method rather than LIFO. Using J.C. Penney's supplemental LIFO disclosures, determine the income effect of using LIFO versus another method for the current fiscal year.
5. Calculate the company's inventory turnover ratio for the fiscal year ended January 31, 2009.
6. Assume that in the next fiscal year the company decides to switch to the average cost method. Describe the accounting treatment required for the switch.

Communication Case 9–9

Change in inventory method; disclosure note

● LO6

Mayfair Department Stores, Inc., operates over 30 retail stores in the Pacific Northwest. Prior to 2011, the company used the FIFO method to value its inventory. In 2011, Mayfair decided to switch to the dollar value LIFO retail inventory method. One of your responsibilities as assistant controller is to prepare the disclosure note describing the change in method that will be included in the company's 2011 financial statements. Kenneth Meier, the controller, provided the following information:

a. Internally developed retail price indexes are used to adjust for the effects of changing prices.
b. If the change had not been made, cost of goods sold for the year would have been $22 million lower. The company's income tax rate is 40% and there were 100 million shares of common stock outstanding during 2011.
c. The cumulative effect of the change on prior years' income is not determinable.
d. The reasons for the change were (a) to provide a more consistent matching of merchandise costs with sales revenue, and (b) the new method provides a more comparable basis of accounting with competitors that also use the LIFO method.

Required:

1. Prepare for Kenneth Meier the disclosure note that will be included in the 2011 financial statements.
2. Explain why the "cumulative effect of the change on prior years' income is not determinable."

Judgment Case 9–10

Inventory errors

● LO7

Some inventory errors are said to be self-correcting in that the error has the opposite financial statement effect in the period following the error, thereby correcting the original account balance errors.

Required:

Despite this self-correcting feature, discuss why these errors should not be ignored and describe the steps required to account for the error correction.

Ethics Case 9–11
Overstatement of ending inventory
● **LO7**

Danville Bottlers is a wholesale beverage company. Danville uses the FIFO inventory method to determine the cost of its ending inventory. Ending inventory quantities are determined by a physical count. For the fiscal year-end June 30, 2011, ending inventory was originally determined to be $3,265,000. However, on July 17, 2011, John Howard, the company's controller, discovered an error in the ending inventory count. He determined that the correct ending inventory amount should be $2,600,000.

Danville is a privately owned corporation with significant financing provided by a local bank. The bank requires annual audited financial statements as a condition of the loan. By July 17, the auditors had completed their review of the financial statements which are scheduled to be issued on July 25. They did not discover the inventory error.

John's first reaction was to communicate his finding to the auditors and to revise the financial statements before they are issued. However, he knows that his and his fellow workers' profit-sharing plans are based on annual pretax earnings and that if he revises the statements, everyone's profit-sharing bonus will be significantly reduced.

Required:

1. Why will bonuses be negatively affected? What is the effect on pretax earnings?
2. If the error is not corrected in the current year and is discovered by the auditors during the following year's audit, how will it be reported in the company's financial statements?
3. Discuss the ethical dilemma John Howard faces.

Analysis Case 9–12
Purchase commitments
● **Appendix**

The management of the Esquire Oil Company believes that the wholesale price of heating oil that they sell to homeowners will increase again as the result of increased political problems in the Middle East. The company is currently paying $.80 a gallon. If they are willing to enter an agreement in November 2011 to purchase a million gallons of heating oil during the winter of 2012, their supplier will guarantee the price at $.80 per gallon. However, if the winter is a mild one, Esquire would not be able to sell a million gallons unless they reduced their retail price and thereby increase the risk of a loss for the year. On the other hand, if the wholesale price did increase substantially, they would be in a favorable position with respect to their competitors. The company's fiscal year-end is December 31.

Required:

Discuss the accounting issues related to the purchase commitment that Esquire is considering.

BRITISH AIRWAYS CASE

● **LO8**

British Airways, Plc. (BA), a U.K. company, prepares its financial statements according to International Financial Reporting Standards. BA's annual report for the year ended March 31, 2009, which includes financial statements and disclosure notes, is included with all new textbooks and can be found at **www.britishairways.com**. When answering questions, focus on BA's "Group" financial information (which is equivalent to "Consolidated" under U.S. GAAP).

Required:

BA's inventories are valued at the lower of cost and net realizable value. How does this approach differ from U.S. GAAP?

CPA SIMULATION 9–1

Central Engines
Inventory Costing Methods

CPA Review

Test your knowledge of the concepts discussed in this chapter, practice critical professional skills necessary for career success, and prepare for the computer-based CPA exam by accessing our CPA simulations at the text website: **www.mhhe.com/spiceland6e**.

The Central Engines simulation tests your knowledge of (a) the differential effects on financial statements of the various inventory costing methods, the difference between the gross and net method of accounting for purchase discounts, and LIFO liquidations that you studied in Chapter 8 and (b) the lower-of-cost or market approach to valuing inventory covered in this chapter.

As on the CPA exam itself, you will be asked to use tools including a spreadsheet, a calculator, and generally accepted accounting principles to conduct research, derive solutions, and communicate conclusions related to these issues in a simulated environment.

Specific tasks in the simulation address:

- Demonstrating your knowledge of the effect on inventory and cost of goods sold of using different cost flow assumptions.
- Understanding the implications of using LIFO versus FIFO to value inventory.
- Analyzing the effects of differing cost flow assumptions on numerous financial statement elements.
- Understanding the differences between the gross and net method of accounting for purchase discounts.
- Communicating the effect of a LIFO liquidation on financial statements.
- Researching the application of the lower-of-cost-or market approach to valuing inventory.

CPA SIMULATION 9–2

Ohio Valley Pet Company

Inventory

CPA Review

Test your knowledge of the concepts discussed in this chapter, practice critical professional skills necessary for career success, and prepare for the computer-based CPA exam by accessing our CPA simulations at the text website: **www.mhhe.com/spiceland6e**.

The Ohio Valley Pet Company simulation tests your knowledge of (a) the costs to be included in inventory and the inventory turnover ratio addressed in Chapter 8, (b) the application of the lower-of-cost-or-market approach to valuing inventory, inventory estimation techniques, and inventory errors covered in this chapter, and (c) accounting for purchase commitments covered in the Appendix to this chapter.

As on the CPA exam itself, you will be asked to use tools including a spreadsheet, a calculator, and generally accepted accounting principles, to conduct research, derive solutions, and communicate conclusions related to these issues in a simulated environment.

Specific tasks in the simulation address:

- Determining whether or not certain costs should be included in inventory.
- Analyzing the effect of various transactions on the inventory turnover ratio.
- Applying the lower-of-cost-or-market approach to valuing inventory.
- Understanding the retail inventory method and the gross profit method used for estimating ending inventory.
- Communicating the effects of inventory errors on financial statement elements.
- Researching how to report an unrealized loss on an outstanding purchase commitment.

10 Property, Plant, and Equipment and Intangible Assets: Acquisition and Disposition

| | | | | | | | | | | | | | | | | | | | | | | | | | | | | | | | | | | |

/// **OVERVIEW**

This chapter and the one that follows address the measurement and reporting issues involving property, plant, and equipment and intangible assets, the tangible and intangible long-lived assets that are used in the production of goods and services. This chapter covers the valuation at date of acquisition and the disposition of these assets. In Chapter 11 we discuss the allocation of the cost of property, plant, and equipment and intangible assets to the periods benefited by their use, the treatment of expenditures made over the life of these assets to maintain and improve them, and impairment.

/// **LEARNING OBJECTIVES**

After studying this chapter, you should be able to:

● **LO1** Identify the various costs included in the initial cost of property, plant, and equipment, natural resources, and intangible assets. (page 504)

● **LO2** Determine the initial cost of individual property, plant, and equipment and intangible assets acquired as a group for a lump-sum purchase price. (page 512)

● **LO3** Determine the initial cost of property, plant, and equipment and intangible assets acquired in exchange for a deferred payment contract. (page 513)

● **LO4** Determine the initial cost of property, plant, and equipment and intangible assets acquired in exchange for equity securities or through donation. (page 515)

● **LO5** Calculate the fixed-asset turnover ratio used by analysts to measure how effectively managers use property, plant, and equipment. (page 516)

● **LO6** Explain how to account for dispositions and exchanges for other nonmonetary assets. (page 517)

● **LO7** Identify the items included in the cost of a self-constructed asset and determine the amount of capitalized interest. (page 521)

● **LO8** Explain the difference in the accounting treatment of costs incurred to purchase intangible assets versus the costs incurred to internally develop intangible assets. (page 526)

● **LO9** Discuss the primary differences between U.S. GAAP and IFRS with respect to the acquisition and disposition of property, plant, and equipment and intangible assets. (page 532)

FINANCIAL REPORTING CASE

A Disney Adventure

"Now I'm really confused," confessed Stan, your study partner, staring blankly at the Walt Disney Company balance sheet that your professor handed out last week. "I thought that interest is always expensed in the income statement. Now I see that Disney is capitalizing interest. I'm not even sure what *capitalize* means! And what about this other account called *goodwill?* What's that all about?" "If you hadn't missed class today, we wouldn't be having this conversation. Let's take a look at the Disney financial statements and the disclosure note on capitalized interest and I'll try to explain it all to you."

Borrowings (in part):
The Company capitalizes interest on assets constructed for its theme parks, resort and other property, and on theatrical and television productions in process. In 2009, 2008, and 2007, total interest capitalized was $57 million, $62 million, and $37 million, respectively.

By the time you finish this chapter, you should be able to respond appropriately to the questions posed in this case. Compare your response to the solution provided at the end of the chapter.

QUESTIONS ///

1. Describe to Stan what it means to capitalize an expenditure. What is the general rule for determining which costs are capitalized when property, plant, and equipment or an intangible asset is acquired? (page 504)

2. Which costs might be included in the initial cost of equipment? (page 504)

3. In what situations is interest capitalized rather than expensed? (page 522)

4. What is the three-step process used to determine the amount of interest capitalized? (page 523)

5. What is goodwill and how is it measured? (page 510)

General Motors Corporation has significant investments in the production facilities it uses to manufacture the automobiles it sells. On the other hand, the principal revenue-producing assets of **Microsoft Corporation** are the copyrights on its computer software that permit it the exclusive rights to earn profits from those products. Timber reserves provide major revenues to **International Paper**. From a reporting perspective, we classify GM's production facilities as property, plant, and equipment;[1] Microsoft's copyrights as intangible assets; and International Paper's timber reserves as natural resources. Together, these three noncurrent assets constitute the *long-lived, revenue-producing assets* of a company. Unlike manufacturers, many service firms and merchandising companies rely primarily on people or investments in inventories rather than on property, plant, and equipment and intangible assets to generate revenues. Even nonmanufacturing firms, though, typically have at least modest investments in buildings and equipment.

---

[1]These are sometimes called *plant assets* or *fixed assets*.

The measurement and reporting issues pertaining to this group of assets include valuation at date of acquisition, disposition, the treatment of expenditures made over the life of these assets to maintain and improve them, the allocation of cost to reporting periods that benefit from their use, and impairment. The allocation of asset cost over time is called *depreciation* for plant and equipment, *amortization* for intangible assets, and *depletion* for natural resources. We focus on initial valuation and disposition in this chapter, and subsequent expenditures, cost allocation, and impairment in the next chapter.

PART A

VALUATION AT ACQUISITION

Types of Assets

For financial reporting purposes, long-lived, revenue-producing assets typically are classified in two categories:

1. **Property, plant, and equipment.** Assets in this category include land, buildings, equipment, machinery, autos, and trucks. **Natural resources** such as oil and gas deposits, timber tracts, and mineral deposits also are included.
2. **Intangible assets.** Unlike property, plant, and equipment and natural resources, these lack physical substance and the extent and timing of their future benefits typically are highly uncertain. They include patents, copyrights, trademarks, franchises, and goodwill.

Of course, every company maintains its own unique mix of these assets. The way these assets are classified and combined for reporting purposes also varies from company to company. As an example, a recent **Tyson Foods, Inc.**, balance sheet reported net property, plant, and equipment of $3,576 million and $3,519 million at the end of fiscal 2009 and 2008, respectively. A disclosure note, shown in Graphic 10–1, provided the details.

GRAPHIC 10–1

Property, Plant, and Equipment—Tyson Foods, Inc.

Real World Financials

Property, Plant, and Equipment and Depreciation (in part):
The major categories of property, plant, and equipment and accumulated depreciation, at cost, at September 26, 2009, and September 27, 2008, are as follows:

	($ in millions)	
	2009	**2008**
Land	$ 96	$ 89
Buildings and leasehold improvements	2,570	2,440
Machinery and equipment	4,640	4,382
Land improvements and other	227	210
Buildings and equipment under construction	297	352
	7,830	7,473
Less: accumulated depreciation	4,254	3,954
Net property, plant, and equipment	$3,576	$3,519

In practice, some companies report intangibles as part of property, plant, and equipment. Some include intangible assets in the other asset category in the balance sheet, and others show intangibles as a separate balance sheet category.

For example, **Layne Christensen Company**, a leading construction and exploration company, reported goodwill of $90,029 thousand and other intangible assets of $25,475 thousand in a recent balance sheet. A disclosure note, shown in Graphic 10–2, provided the details of the other intangible assets. We discuss goodwill, tradenames, patents, and other traditional intangible assets later in this part of the chapter. Technology and capitalized software are addressed in Part C of the chapter.

Before we examine in detail specific assets, you should find it helpful to study the overview provided by Graphic 10–3 on page 503.

GRAPHIC 10–2

Intangible Assets—
Layne Christensen
Company

Real World Financials

(5) Goodwill and Other Intangible Assets

Goodwill and other intangible assets consisted of the following as of January 31:

(in thousands)	2009		2008	
	Gross Carrying Amount	Accumulated Amortization	Gross Carrying Amount	Accumulated Amortization
Goodwill	$90,029	$ —	$85,706	$ —
Amortizable intangible assets:				
Tradenames	$18,962	$(2,275)	$18,962	$(1,464)
Customer-related	332	(332)	332	(340)
Patents	3,152	(569)	2,902	(307)
Noncompetition agreements	439	(387)	379	(273)
Other	2,590	(910)	1,292	(553)
Total amortizable intangible assets	$25,475	$(4,473)	$23,867	$(2,937)

GRAPHIC 10–3   Property, Plant, and Equipment and Intangible Assets and Their Acquisition Costs

Asset	Description	Typical Acquisition Costs
Property, plant, and equipment	Productive assets that derive their value from long-term use in operations rather than from resale.	All expenditures necessary to get the asset in condition and location for its intended use.
Equipment	Broad term that includes machinery, computers and other office equipment, vehicles, furniture, and fixtures.	Purchase price (less discounts), taxes, transportation, installation, testing, trial runs, reconditioning.
Land	Real property used in operations (land held for speculative investment or future use is reported as investments or other assets).	Purchase price, attorney's fees, title, recording fees, commissions, back taxes, mortgages, liens, clearing, filling, draining, removing old buildings.
Land improvements	Enhancements to property such as parking lots, driveways, private roads, fences, landscaping, and sprinkler systems.	Separately identifiable costs.
Buildings	Structures that include warehouses, plant facilities, and office buildings.	Purchase price, attorney's fees, commissions, reconditioning.
Natural resources	Productive assets that are physically consumed in operations such as timber, mineral deposits, and oil and gas reserves.	Acquisition, exploration, development, and restoration costs.
Intangible Assets	Productive assets that lack physical substance and have long-term but typically uncertain benefits.	All expenditures necessary to get the asset in condition and location for its intended use.
Patents	Exclusive 20-year right to manufacture a product or use a process.	Purchase price, legal fees, filing fees, not including internal R&D.
Copyrights	Exclusive right to benefit from a creative work such as a song, film, painting, photograph, or book.	Purchase price, legal fees, filing fees, not including internal R&D.
Trademarks (tradenames)	Exclusive right to display a word, a slogan, a symbol, or an emblem that distinctively identifies a company, product, or a service.	Purchase price, legal fees, filing fees, not including internal R&D.
Franchises	A contractual arrangement under which a franchisor grants the franchisee the exclusive right to use the franchisor's trademark or tradename and certain product rights.	Franchise fee plus any legal fees.
Goodwill	The unique value of the company as a whole over and above all identifiable assets.	Excess of the fair value of the consideration exchanged for the company over the fair value of the net assets acquired.

Costs to Be Capitalized

● LO1

FINANCIAL
Reporting Case

Q1, p. 501

The initial cost of
property, plant,
and equipment
and intangible
assets includes the
purchase price and all
expenditures necessary
to bring the asset to its
desired condition and
location for use.

Property, plant, and equipment and intangible assets can be acquired through purchase, exchange, lease, donation, self-construction, or a business combination. We address acquisitions through leasing in Chapter 15 and acquisitions through business combinations later in this chapter and in Chapter 12.

The initial valuation of property, plant, and equipment and intangible assets usually is quite simple. We know from prior study that assets are valued on the basis of their original costs. In Chapter 8 we introduced the concept of condition and location in determining the cost of inventory. For example, if Thompson Company purchased inventory for $42,000 and incurred $1,000 in freight costs to have the inventory shipped to its location, the initial cost of the inventory is $43,000. This concept applies to the valuation of property, plant, and equipment and intangible assets as well. The initial cost of these assets includes the purchase price and all expenditures necessary to bring the asset to its desired condition and location for use. We discuss these additional expenditures in the next section.

Our objective in identifying the costs of an asset is to distinguish the expenditures that produce future benefits from those that produce benefits only in the current period. The costs in the second group are recorded as expenses, but those in the first group are *capitalized;* that is, they are recorded as an asset and expensed in future periods.[2] For example, the cost of a major improvement to a delivery truck that extends its useful life generally would be capitalized. On the other hand, the cost of an engine tune-up for the delivery truck simply allows the truck to continue its productive activity but does not increase future benefits. These maintenance costs would be expensed. Subsequent expenditures for these assets are discussed in Chapter 11.

The distinction is not trivial. This point was unmistakably emphasized in the summer of 2002 when **WorldCom, Inc.**, disclosed that it had improperly capitalized nearly $4 billion in expenditures related to the company's telecom network. This massive fraud resulted in one of the largest financial statement restatements in history and triggered the collapse of the once powerful corporation. Capitalizing rather than expensing these expenditures caused a substantial overstatement of reported income for 2001 and the first quarter of 2002, in fact, producing impressive profits where losses should have been reported. If the deception had not been discovered, not only would income for 2001 and 2002 have been overstated, but income for many years into the future would have been understated as the fraudulent capitalized assets were depreciated. Of course, the balance sheet also would have overstated the assets and equity of the company.

Property, Plant, and Equipment

FINANCIAL
Reporting Case

Q2, p. 501

COST OF EQUIPMENT.   Equipment is a broad term that encompasses machinery used in manufacturing, computers and other office equipment, vehicles, furniture, and fixtures. The cost of equipment includes the purchase price plus any sales tax (less any discounts received from the seller), transportation costs paid by the buyer to transport the asset to the location in which it will be used, expenditures for installation, testing, legal fees to establish title, and any other costs of bringing the asset to its condition and location for use. To the extent that these costs can be identified and measured, they should be included in the asset's initial valuation rather than expensed currently.

Although most costs can be identified easily, others are more difficult. For example, the costs of training personnel to operate machinery could be considered a cost necessary to make the asset ready for use. However, because it is difficult to measure the amount of training costs associated with specific assets, these costs usually are expensed. Consider Illustration 10–1.

COST OF LAND.   The cost of land also should include each expenditure needed to get the land ready for its intended use. These include the purchase price plus closing costs such

---

[2]Exceptions are land and certain intangible assets that have indefinite useful lives. Costs to acquire these assets also produce future benefits and therefore are capitalized, but unlike other property, plant, and equipment and intangible assets, their costs are not systematically expensed in future periods as depreciation or amortization.

ILLUSTRATION 10–1

Initial Cost of Equipment

Central Machine Tools purchased an industrial lathe to be used in its manufacturing process. The purchase price was $62,000. Central paid a freight company $1,000 to transport the machine to its plant location plus $300 shipping insurance. In addition, the machine had to be installed and mounted on a special platform built specifically for the machine at a cost of $1,200. After installation, several trial runs were made to ensure proper operation. The cost of these trials including wasted materials was $600. At what amount should Central capitalize the lathe?

Purchase price	$62,000
Freight and handling	1,000
Insurance during shipping	300
Special foundation	1,200
Trial runs	600
	$65,100

Each of the expenditures described was necessary to bring the machine to its condition and location for use and should be capitalized and then expensed in the future periods in which the asset is used.

as fees for the attorney, real estate agent commissions, title and title search, and recording. If the property is subject to back taxes, liens, mortgages, or other obligations, these amounts are included also. In addition, any expenditures such as clearing, filling, draining, and even removing (razing) old buildings that are needed to prepare the land for its intended use are part of the land's cost. Proceeds from the sale of salvaged materials from old buildings torn down after purchase reduce the cost of land. Illustration 10–2 provides an example.

ILLUSTRATION 10–2

Initial Cost of Land

The Byers Structural Metal Company purchased a six-acre tract of land and an existing building for $500,000. The company plans to raze the old building and construct a new office building on the site. In addition to the purchase price, the company made the following expenditures at closing of the purchase:

Title insurance	$ 3,000
Commissions	16,000
Property taxes	6,000

Shortly after closing, the company paid a contractor $10,000 to tear down the old building and remove it from the site. An additional $5,000 was paid to grade the land. The $6,000 in property taxes included $4,000 of delinquent taxes paid by Byers on behalf of the seller and $2,000 attributable to the portion of the current fiscal year after the purchase date. What should be the capitalized cost of the land?

Capitalized cost of land:	
Purchase price of land (and building to be razed)	$500,000
Title insurance	3,000
Commissions	16,000
Delinquent property taxes	4,000
Cost of removing old building	10,000
Cost of grading	5,000
Total cost of land	$538,000

Two thousand dollars of the property taxes relate only to the current period and should be expensed. Other costs were necessary to acquire the land and are capitalized.

LAND IMPROVEMENTS. It's important to distinguish between the cost of land and the cost of land improvements because land has an indefinite life and land improvements usually do not. Examples of land improvements include the cost of parking lots, driveways, and private roads and the costs of fences and lawn and garden sprinkler systems. Costs of these assets are separately identified and capitalized. We depreciate their cost over periods benefited by their use.

The costs of *land improvements* are capitalized and depreciated.

COST OF BUILDINGS. The cost of acquiring a building usually includes realtor commissions and legal fees in addition to the purchase price. Quite often a building must be refurbished, remodeled, or otherwise modified to suit the needs of the new owner. These reconditioning costs are part of the building's acquisition cost. When a building is constructed rather than purchased, unique accounting issues are raised. We discuss these in the "Self-Constructed Assets" section of this chapter.

COST OF NATURAL RESOURCES. Natural resources that provide long-term benefits are reported as property, plant, and equipment. These include timber tracts, mineral deposits, and oil and gas deposits. They can be distinguished from other assets by the fact that their benefits are derived from their physical consumption. For example, mineral deposits are physically diminishing as the minerals are extracted from the ground and either sold or used in the production process.[3] On the contrary, equipment, land, and buildings produce benefits for a company through their *use* in the production of goods and services. Unlike those of natural resources, their physical characteristics usually remain unchanged during their useful lives.

Sometimes a company buys natural resources from another company. In that case, initial valuation is simply the purchase price plus any other costs necessary to bring the asset to condition and location for use. More frequently, though, the company will develop these assets. In this situation, the initial valuation can include (a) acquisition costs, (b) exploration costs, (c) development costs, and (d) restoration costs. Acquisition costs are the amounts paid to acquire the rights to explore for undiscovered natural resources or to extract proven natural resources. Exploration costs are expenditures such as drilling a well, or excavating a mine, or any other costs of searching for natural resources. Development costs are incurred after the resource has been discovered but before production begins. They include a variety of costs such as expenditures for tunnels, wells, and shafts. It is not unusual for the cost of a natural resource, either purchased or developed, also to include estimated restoration costs. These are costs to restore land or other property to its original condition after extraction of the natural resource ends. Because restoration expenditures occur later—after production begins—they initially represent an obligation incurred in conjunction with an asset retirement. Restoration costs are one example of *asset retirement obligations,* the topic of the next subsection.

On the other hand, the costs of heavy equipment and other assets a company uses during drilling or excavation usually are not considered part of the cost of the natural resource itself. Instead, they are considered depreciable plant and equipment. However, if an asset used in the development of a natural resource cannot be moved and has no alternative use, its depreciable life is limited by the useful life of the natural resource.

ASSET RETIREMENT OBLIGATIONS. Sometimes a company incurs obligations associated with the disposition of property, plant, and equipment and natural resources, often as a result of acquiring those assets. For example, an oil and gas exploration company might be required to restore land to its original condition after extraction is completed. Before 2001, there was considerable diversity in the ways companies accounted for these obligations. Some companies recognized these asset retirement obligations (AROs) gradually over the life of the asset while others did not recognize the obligations until the asset was retired or sold.

Generally accepted accounting principles now require that an existing legal obligation associated with the retirement of a tangible, long-lived asset be recognized as a liability and measured at fair value, if value can be reasonably estimated. When the liability is credited, the offsetting debit is to the related asset.[4] These retirement obligations could arise in connection with several types of assets. We introduce the topic here because it often arises with natural resources. Let's consider some of the provisions of the standard that addresses these obligations.

> The cost of a natural resource includes the *acquisition costs* for the use of land, the *exploration* and *development costs* incurred before production begins, and *restoration costs* incurred during or at the end of extraction.

> An asset retirement obligation (ARO) is measured at fair value and is recognized as a liability and corresponding increase in asset valuation.

---

[3]Because of this characteristic, natural resources sometimes are called *wasting assets.*

[4]FASB ASC 410–20–25: Asset Retirement and Environmental Obligations–Asset Retirement Obligations–Recognition (previously "Accounting for Asset Retirement Obligations," *Statement of Financial Accounting Standards No. 143* (Norwalk, Conn.: FASB, 2001)).

Scope.   AROs arise only from *legal* obligations associated with the retirement of a tangible long-lived asset that result from the acquisition, construction, or development and (or) normal operation of a long-lived asset.

Recognition.   A retirement obligation might arise at the inception of an asset's life or during its operating life. For instance, an offshore oil-and-gas production facility typically incurs its removal obligation when it begins operating. On the other hand, a landfill or a mining operation might incur a reclamation obligation gradually over the life of the asset as space is consumed with waste or as the mine is excavated.

Measurement.   A company recognizes the fair value of an ARO in the period it's incurred. The liability increases the valuation of the related asset. Usually, the fair value is estimated by calculating the present value of estimated future cash outflows.

Present Value Calculations.   Traditionally, the way uncertainty has been considered in present value calculations has been by discounting the "best estimate" of future cash flows applying a discount rate that has been adjusted to reflect the uncertainty or risk of those cash flows. That's not the approach we take here. Instead, we follow the approach described in the FASB's Concept Statement No. 7[5] which is to adjust the cash flows, not the discount rate, for the uncertainty or risk of those cash flows. This expected cash flow approach incorporates specific probabilities of cash flows into the analysis. We use a discount rate equal to the *credit-adjusted risk free rate.* The higher a company's credit risk, the higher will be the discount rate. All other uncertainties or risks are incorporated into the cash flow probabilities. We first considered an illustration of this approach in Chapter 6. Illustration 10–3 demonstrates the approach in connection with the acquisition of a natural resource.

As we discuss in Chapter 11, the cost of the coal mine is allocated to future periods as *depletion* using a depletion rate based on the estimated amount of coal discovered. The $600,000 cost of the excavation equipment, less any anticipated residual value, is allocated to future periods as *depreciation.*

The difference between the asset retirement liability of $468,360 and the probability weighted expected cash outflow of $590,000 is recognized as accretion expense, an additional expense that accrues as an operating expense, over the three-year excavation period. This process increases the liability to $590,000 by the end of the excavation period.

Year	Accretion Expense	Increase in Balance	Asset Retirement Obligation
			468,360
1	8% (468,360) = 37,469	37,469	505,829
2	8% (505,829) = 40,466	40,466	546,295
3	8% (546,295) = 43,705*	43,705	590,000

*rounded

If the actual restoration costs are more (less) than the $590,000, a loss (gain) on retirement of the obligation is recognized for the difference.

St. Mary Land & Exploration Company is engaged in the exploration, development, acquisition, and production of natural gas and crude oil. For the six months ended June 30, 2009, St. Mary reported $123 million in asset retirement obligations in its balance sheet. Graphic 10–4 describes the company's policy and provides a summary of disclosure requirements.

It is important to understand that asset retirement obligations could result from the acquisition of many different types of tangible assets, not just natural resources. For example, **Dow Chemical Company** reported a $106 million asset retirement liability in its 2008 balance sheet related to anticipated demolition and remediation activities at its manufacturing sites in the United States, Canada, Europe, Italy, and Brazil.

Asset retirement obligations could result from the acquisition of many different types of tangible assets, not just natural resources.

[5]"Using Cash Flow Information and Present Value in Accounting Measurements," *Statement of Financial Accounting Concepts No. 7* (Norwalk, Conn.: FASB, 2000).

ILLUSTRATION 10–3
Cost of Natural
Resources

The Jackson Mining Company paid $1,000,000 for the right to explore for a coal deposit on 500 acres of land in Pennsylvania. Costs of exploring for the coal deposit totaled $800,000 and intangible development costs incurred in digging and erecting the mine shaft were $500,000. In addition, Jackson purchased new excavation equipment for the project at a cost of $600,000. After the coal is removed from the site, the equipment will be sold.

Jackson is required by its contract to restore the land to a condition suitable for recreational use after it extracts the coal. The company has provided the following three cash flow possibilities (A, B and C) for the restoration costs to be paid in three years, after extraction is completed:

	Cash Outflow	Probability
A	$500,000	30%
B	600,000	50%
C	700,000	20%

The company's credit-adjusted risk free interest rate is 8%.
Total capitalized cost for the coal deposit is:

Purchase of rights to explore	$1,000,000
Exploration costs	800,000
Development costs	500,000
Restoration costs	468,360*
Total cost of coal deposit	$2,768,360

*Present value of expected cash outflow for restoration costs (asset retirement obligation):
$500,000 × 30% = $150,000
600,000 × 50% = 300,000
700,000 × 20% = 140,000
$590,000 × .79383 = $468,360
(.79383 is the present value of $1, $n = 3$, $i = 8\%$)

Journal Entries:

Coal mine (determined above)	2,768,360	
Cash ($1,000,000 + 800,000 + 500,000)		2,300,000
Asset retirement liability (determined above)		468,360
Excavation equipment	600,000	
Cash (cost)		600,000

GRAPHIC 10–4

Disclosure of
Asset Retirement
Obligations—St. Mary
Land & Exploration
Company

Real World Financials

Note 9—Asset Retirement Obligations (in part)

The Company recognizes an estimated liability for future costs associated with the abandonment of its oil and gas properties. A liability for the fair value of an asset retirement obligation and a corresponding increase to the carrying value of the related long-lived asset are recorded at the time a well is completed or acquired. The increase in carrying value is included in proved oil and gas properties in the consolidated balance sheets. The Company depletes the amount added to proved oil and gas property costs and recognizes accretion expense in connection with the discounted liability over the remaining estimated economic lives of the respective oil and gas properties. Cash paid to settle asset retirement obligations is included in the operating section of the Company's consolidated statement of cash flows.

The Company's estimated asset retirement obligation liability is based on historical experience in abandoning wells, estimated economic lives, estimates as to the cost to abandon the wells in the future and federal, and state regulatory requirements. The liability is discounted using a credit-adjusted risk-free rate estimated at the time the liability is incurred or revised. The credit-adjusted risk-free rates used to discount the Company's abandonment liabilities range from 6.5 percent to 12.0 percent. Revisions to the liability could occur due to changes in estimated abandonment costs or well economic lives, or if federal or state regulators enact new requirements regarding the abandonment of wells.

Sometimes, after exploration or development, it becomes apparent that continuing the project is economically infeasible. If that happens, any costs incurred are expensed rather than capitalized. An exception is in the oil and gas industry, where we have two generally accepted accounting alternatives for accounting for projects that prove unsuccessful. We discuss these alternatives in Appendix 10.

Intangible Assets

Intangible assets include such items as patents, copyrights, trademarks, franchises, and goodwill. Despite their lack of physical substance, these assets can be extremely valuable resources for a company. For example, **Interbrand Sampson**, the world's leading branding consulting company, estimated the value of the **Coca-Cola** trademark to be $69 billion.[6] In general, intangible assets refer to the ownership of exclusive rights that provide benefits to the owner in the production of goods and services.

Intangible assets generally represent exclusive rights that provide benefits to the owner.

The issues involved in accounting for intangible assets are similar to those of property, plant, and equipment. One key difference, though, is that the future benefits that we attribute to intangible assets usually are much less certain than those attributed to tangible assets. For example, will the new toy for which a company acquires a patent be accepted by the market? If so, will it be a blockbuster like Beanie Babies or Rubik's Cube, or will it be only a moderate success? Will it have lasting appeal like Barbie dolls, or will it be a short-term fad? In short, it's often very difficult to anticipate the timing, and even the existence, of future benefits attributable to many intangible assets. In fact, this uncertainty is a discriminating characteristic of intangible assets that perhaps better distinguishes them from tangible assets than their lack of physical substance. After all, other assets, too, do not exist physically but are not considered intangible assets. Accounts receivable and prepaid expenses, for example, have no physical substance and yet are reported among tangible assets.

Companies can either (1) *purchase* intangible assets from other entities (existing patent, copyright, trademark, or franchise rights) or (2) *develop* intangible assets internally (say, develop a new product or process that is then patented). In either case, we amortize its cost, unless it has an indefinite useful life.[7] Also, just like property, plant, and equipment, intangibles are subject to asset impairment rules. We discuss amortization and impairment in Chapter 11. In this chapter, we consider the acquisition cost of intangible assets.

Intangible assets with finite useful lives are amortized; intangible assets with indefinite useful lives are not amortized.

The initial valuation of purchased intangible assets usually is quite simple. We value a purchased intangible at its original cost, which includes its purchase price and all other costs necessary to bring it to condition and location for intended use. For example, if a company purchases a patent from another entity, it might pay legal fees and filing fees in addition to the purchase price. We value intangible assets acquired in exchange for stock, or for other nonmonetary assets, or with deferred payment contracts exactly as we do property, plant, and equipment. Let's look briefly at the costs of purchasing some of the more common intangible assets.

Purchased intangible assets are valued at their original cost.

PATENTS.   A patent is an exclusive right to manufacture a product or to use a process. This right is granted by the U.S. Patent Office for a period of 20 years. In essence, the holder of a patent has a monopoly on the use, manufacture, or sale of the product or process. If a patent is purchased from an inventor or another individual or company, the amount paid is its initial valuation. The cost might also include such other costs as legal and filing fees to secure the patent. Holders of patents often need to defend a patent in court against infringement. Any attorney fees and other costs of successfully defending a patent are added to the patent account.

When a patent is *developed internally,* the research and development costs of doing so are expensed as incurred. We discuss research and development in more detail in a later section. We capitalize legal and filing fees to secure the patent, even if internally developed.

---

[6]This $69 billion represents an estimate of the fair value to the company at the time the estimate was made, not the historical cost valuation that appears in the balance sheet of Coca-Cola.
[7]FASB ASC 350–30–35–1: Intangibles–Goodwill and Other–General Intangibles Other Than Goodwill–Subsequent Measurement, and FASB ASC 350–20–35–1: Intangibles–Goodwill and Other–Goodwill–Subsequent Measurement (previously "Goodwill and Other Intangible Assets," *Statement of Financial Accounting Standards No. 142* (Norwalk, Conn.: FASB, 2001)).

COPYRIGHTS. A copyright is an exclusive right of protection given to a creator of a published work, such as a song, film, painting, photograph, or book. Copyrights are protected by law and give the creator the exclusive right to reproduce and sell the artistic or published work for the life of the creator plus 70 years. Accounting for the costs of copyrights is virtually identical to that of patents.

Trademarks or tradenames often are considered to have indefinite useful lives.

TRADEMARKS. A trademark, also called tradename, is an exclusive right to display a word, a slogan, a symbol, or an emblem that distinctively identifies a company, a product, or a service. The trademark can be registered with the U.S. Patent Office which protects the trademark from use by others for a period of 10 years. The registration can be renewed for an indefinite number of 10-year periods, so a trademark is an example of an intangible asset whose useful life could be indefinite.

Trademarks or tradenames often are acquired through a business combination. As an example, in 2002, **Hewlett-Packard Company (HP)** acquired all of the outstanding stock of **Compaq Computer Corporation** for $24 billion. Of that amount, $1.4 billion was assigned to the Compaq tradename. HP stated in a disclosure note that this ". . . intangible asset will not be amortized because it has an indefinite remaining useful life based on many factors and considerations, including the length of time that the Compaq name has been in use, the Compaq brand awareness and market position and the plans for continued use of the Compaq brand within a portion of HP's overall product portfolio."

Trademarks can be very valuable. The estimated value of $69 billion for the Coca-Cola trademark mentioned previously is a good example. Note that the cost of the trademark reported in the balance sheet is far less than the estimate of its worth to the company. The Coca-Cola Company's 2008 balance sheet disclosed trademarks at a cost of only $6 billion.

Franchise operations are among the most common ways of doing business.

FRANCHISES. A franchise is a contractual arrangement under which the franchisor grants the franchisee the exclusive right to use the franchisor's trademark or tradename and may include product and formula rights, within a geographical area, usually for a specified period of time. Many popular retail businesses such as fast food outlets, automobile dealerships, and motels are franchises. For example, the last time you ordered a hamburger at McDonald's, you were probably dealing with a franchise.

The owner of that McDonald's outlet paid **McDonald's Corporation** a fee in exchange for the exclusive right to use the McDonald's name and to sell its products within a specified geographical area. In addition, many franchisors provide other benefits to the franchisee, such as participating in the construction of the retail outlet, training of employees, and national advertising.

Payments to the franchisor usually include an initial payment plus periodic payments over the life of the franchise agreement. The franchisee capitalizes as an intangible asset the initial franchise fee plus any legal costs associated with the contract agreement. The franchise asset is then amortized over the life of the franchise agreement. The periodic payments usually relate to services provided by the franchisor on a continuing basis and are expensed as incurred.

Most purchased intangibles are *specifically identifiable*. That is, cost can be directly associated with a specific intangible right. An exception is goodwill, which we discuss next.

Goodwill can only be purchased through the acquisition of another company.

GOODWILL. Goodwill is a unique intangible asset in that its cost can't be directly associated with any specifically identifiable right and it is not separable from the company itself. It represents the unique value of a company as a whole over and above its identifiable tangible and intangible assets. Goodwill can emerge from a company's clientele and reputation, its trained employees and management team, its favorable business location, and any other unique features of the company that can't be associated with a specific asset.

FINANCIAL
Reporting Case

Q5, p. 501

Because goodwill can't be separated from a company, it's not possible for a buyer to acquire it without also acquiring the whole company or a portion of it. Goodwill will appear as an asset in a balance sheet only when it was purchased in connection with the acquisition of control over another company. In that case, the capitalized cost of goodwill equals the fair value of the consideration exchanged (purchase price) for the company less the fair value of the net assets acquired. The fair value of the net assets equals the fair value of all identifiable tangible and intangible assets less the fair value of any liabilities of the selling company assumed by the buyer. Goodwill is a residual asset; it's the amount left after other assets are identified and valued. Consider Illustration 10–4.

Goodwill **is the excess of the fair value of the consideration exchanged over the fair value of the net assets acquired.**

				ILLUSTRATION 10–4
The Smithson Corporation acquired all of the outstanding common stock of the Rider Corporation in exchange for $18 million cash.* Smithson assumed all of Rider's long-term debts which have a fair value of $12 million at the date of acquisition. The fair values of all identifiable assets of Rider are as follows ($ in millions):				Goodwill

Receivables		$ 5
Inventory		7
Property, plant, and equipment		9
Patent		4
Total		$25

The cost of the goodwill resulting from the acquisition is $5 million:

Fair value of consideration exchanged		$18
Less: Fair value of net assets acquired		
Assets	$25	
Less: Fair value of liabilities assumed	(12)	(13)
Goodwill		$ 5

The Smithson Corporation records the acquisition as follows:

Receivables (fair value)	5	
Inventory (fair value)	7	
Property, plant, and equipment (fair value)	9	
Patent (fair value)	4	
Goodwill (difference)	5	
Liabilities (fair value)		12
Cash (purchase price)		18

*Determining the amount a purchaser is willing to pay for a company in excess of the identifiable net assets is a question of determining the value of a company as a whole. This question is addressed in most introductory and advanced finance textbooks.

Of course, a company can develop its own goodwill through advertising, training, and other efforts. In fact, most do. However, a company must expense all such costs incurred in the internal generation of goodwill. By not capitalizing these items, accountants realize that the matching principle is violated because many of these expenditures do result in significant future benefits. Also, it's difficult to compare two companies when one has purchased goodwill and the other has not. But imagine how difficult it would be to associate these expenditures with any objective measure of goodwill. In essence, we have a situation where the characteristic of faithful representation overshadows relevance.

As we discussed in Chapter 1, accounting standards have significantly changed the way we account for business combinations. Before the current standard regarding accounting for goodwill, we amortized (expensed over time) goodwill just like any other intangible asset. Now, just like for other intangible assets that have indefinite useful lives, *we do not amortize goodwill*. This makes it imperative that companies make every effort to identify specific intangibles other than goodwill that they acquire in a business combination since goodwill is the amount left after other assets are identified.

Goodwill, along with other intangible assets with indefinite useful lives, is not amortized.

> ## ADDITIONAL CONSIDERATION
>
> It's possible for the fair value of net assets to exceed the fair value of the consideration exchanged for those net assets. A "bargain purchase" situation could result from an acquisition involving a "forced sale" in which the seller is acting under duress. The FASB previously required this excess, deemed negative goodwill, to be allocated as a pro rata reduction of the amounts that otherwise would have been assigned to particular assets acquired. This resulted in assets acquired being recorded at amounts less than their fair values. However, current GAAP effective for acquisitions made during fiscal years beginning on or after December 15, 2008, makes it mandatory that assets and liabilities acquired in a business combination be valued at their fair values.[8] Any negative goodwill is reported as a gain in the year of the combination.

In a business combination, an intangible asset must be recognized as an asset apart from goodwill if it arises from contractual or other legal rights or is separable.

In keeping with that goal, GAAP provides guidelines for determining which intangibles should be separately recognized and valued. Specifically, an intangible should be recognized as an asset apart from goodwill if it arises from contractual or other legal rights or is capable of being separated from the acquired entity. Possibilities are patents, trademarks, copyrights, and franchise agreements, and such items as customer lists, license agreements, order backlogs, employment contracts, and noncompetition agreements.[9] In past years, some of these intangibles, if present in a business combination, often were included in the cost of goodwill.[10]

Lump-Sum Purchases

● LO2

It's not unusual for a group of assets to be acquired for a single sum. If these assets are indistinguishable, for example 10 identical delivery trucks purchased for a lump-sum price of $150,000, valuation is obvious. Each of the trucks would be valued at $15,000 ($150,000 ÷ 10). However, if the lump-sum purchase involves different assets, it's necessary to allocate the lump-sum acquisition price among the separate items. The assets acquired may have different characteristics and different useful lives. For example, the acquisition of a factory may include assets that are significantly different such as land, building, and equipment.

The allocation is made in proportion to the individual assets' relative fair values. This process is best explained by an example in Illustration 10–5.

The relative fair value percentages are multiplied by the lump-sum purchase price to determine the initial valuation of each of the separate assets. Notice that the lump-sum purchase includes inventories. The procedure used here to allocate the purchase price in a lump-sum acquisition pertains to any type of asset mix, not just to property, plant, and equipment and intangible assets.

Noncash Acquisitions

Assets acquired in noncash transactions are valued at the fair value of the assets given or the fair value of the assets received, whichever is more clearly evident.

Companies sometimes acquire assets without paying cash but instead by issuing debt or equity securities, receiving donated assets, or exchanging other assets. *The controlling principle in each of these situations is that in any noncash transaction (not just those dealing with property, plant, and equipment and intangible assets), the components of the transaction are recorded at their fair values.* The first indicator of fair value is the fair value of the assets, debt, or equity securities given. Sometimes the fair value of the assets received is used when their fair value is more clearly evident than the fair value of the assets given.

---

[8]FASB ASC 805: Business Combinations (previously "Business Combinations," *Statement of Financial Accounting Standards No. 141 (revised)* (Norwalk, Conn.: FASB, 2007)).

[9]Ibid.

[10]An assembled workforce is an example of an intangible asset that is not recognized as a separate asset. A workforce does not represent a contractual or legal right, nor is it separable from the company as a whole.

The Smyrna Hand & Edge Tools Company purchased an existing factory for a single sum of $2,000,000. The price included title to the land, the factory building, and the manufacturing equipment in the building, a patent on a process the equipment uses, and inventories of raw materials. An independent appraisal estimated the fair values of the assets (if purchased separately) at $330,000 for the land, $550,000 for the building, $660,000 for the equipment, $440,000 for the patent and $220,000 for the inventories. The lump-sum purchase price of $2,000,000 is allocated to the separate assets as follows:

ILLUSTRATION 10–5

Lump-Sum Purchase

	Fair Values	
Land	$ 330,000	15%
Building	550,000	25
Equipment	660,000	30
Patent	440,000	20
Inventories	220,000	10
Total	$2,200,000	100%

Land	(15% × $2,000,000)..	300,000
Building	(25% × $2,000,000)..	500,000
Equipment	(30% × $2,000,000)..	600,000
Patent	(20% × $2,000,000)..	400,000
Inventories	(10% × $2,000,000)..	200,000
Cash	....	2,000,000

The total purchase price is allocated in proportion to the relative fair values of the assets acquired.

ETHICAL DILEMMA

Grandma's Cookie Company purchased a factory building. The company controller, Don Nelson, is in the process of allocating the lump-sum purchase price between land and building. Don suggests to the company's chief financial officer, Judith Prince, that they fudge a little by allocating a disproportionately higher share of the price to land. Don reasons that this will reduce depreciation expense, boost income, increase their profit-sharing bonus, and hopefully, increase the price of the company's stock. Judith has some reservations about this because the higher reported income will also cause income taxes to be higher than they would be if a correct allocation of the purchase price is made.

What are the ethical issues? What stakeholders' interests are in conflict?

Deferred Payments

● LO3

A company can acquire an asset by giving the seller a promise to pay cash in the future and thus creating a liability, usually a note payable. The initial valuation of the asset is, again, quite simple as long as the note payable explicitly requires the payment of interest at a realistic interest rate. For example, suppose a machine is acquired for $15,000 and the buyer signs a note requiring the payment of $15,000 sometime in the future *plus* interest in the meantime at a realistic interest rate. The machine would be valued at $15,000 and the transaction recorded as follows:

Machine	15,000	
Note payable		15,000

We know from our discussion of the time value of money in Chapter 6 that most liabilities are valued at the present value of future cash payments, reflecting an appropriate time value of money. As long as the note payable explicitly contains a realistic interest rate, the present value will equal the face value of the note, $15,000 in our previous example. This also should be equal to the fair value of the machine purchased. On the other hand, when an interest rate is not specified or is unrealistic, determining the cost of the asset is less straight-forward. In that case, the accountant should look beyond the form of the transaction and record its substance. Consider Illustration 10–6.

ILLUSTRATION 10–6 Asset Acquired with Debt—Present Value of Note Indicative of Fair Value	On January 2, 2011, the Midwestern Steam Gas Corporation purchased an industrial furnace. In payment, Midwestern signed a noninterest-bearing note requiring $50,000 to be paid on December 31, 2012. If Midwestern had borrowed cash to buy the furnace, the bank would have required an interest rate of 10%.

Some portion of the payment(s) required by a noninterest-bearing note in reality is interest.

On the surface, it might appear that Midwestern is paying $50,000 for the furnace, the eventual cash payment. However, when you recognize that the agreement specifies no interest even though the payment won't be made for two years, it becomes obvious that a portion of the $50,000 payment is not actually payment for the furnace, but instead is interest on the note. At what amount should Midwestern value the furnace and the related note payable?

Noncash transactions are recorded at the fair value of the items exchanged.

The answer is fair value, as it is for any noncash transaction. This might be the fair value of the furnace or the fair value of the note. Let's say, in this situation, that the furnace is custom-built, so its cash price is unavailable. But Midwestern can determine the fair value of the note payable by computing the present value of the cash payments at the appropriate interest rate of 10%. The amount actually paid for the machine, then, is the present value of the cash flows called for by the loan agreement, discounted at the market rate—10% in this case.

$$PV = \$50,000 \, (.82645^*) = \$41,323$$
*Present value of $1: $n = 2$, $i = 10\%$ (from Table 2)

So the furnace should be recorded at its *real* cost, $41,323, as follows:[11]

The economic essence of a transaction should prevail over its outward appearance.

Furnace (determined above)	41,323	
Discount on note payable (difference)	8,677	
Note payable (face amount)		50,000

Notice that the note also is recorded at $41,323, its present value, but this is accomplished by using a contra account, called *discount on note payable,* for the difference between the face amount of the note ($50,000) and its present value ($41,323). The difference of $8,677 is the portion of the eventual $50,000 payment that represents interest and is recognized as interest expense over the life of the note.

Assuming that Midwestern's fiscal year-end is December 31 and that adjusting entries are recorded only at the end of each year, the company would record the following entries at the end of 2011 and 2012 to accrue interest and the payment of the note:

December 31, 2011

Interest expense ($41,323 × 10%)	4,132	
Discount on note payable		4,132

Note payable

Jan. 1, 2011	50,000
	50,000 Dec. 31, 2012
Bal. 12/31/12	0

December 31, 2012

Interest expense ([$41,323 + 4,132]* × 10%)	4,545	
Discount on note payable		4,545
Note payable (face amount)	50,000	
Cash		50,000

Discount on note payable

8,677	Jan. 1, 2011
Dec. 31, 2011 4,132	
Dec. 31, 2012 4,545	
0	Bal. 12/31/12

*The 2011 unpaid interest increases the amount owed by $4,132.

---

[11]The entry shown assumes the note is recorded using the gross method. By the net method, a discount account is not used and the note is simply recorded at present value.

Machine	41,323	
Note payable		41,323

Sometimes, the fair value of an asset acquired in a noncash transaction is readily available from price lists, previous purchases, or otherwise. In that case, this fair value may be more clearly evident than the fair value of the note and it would serve as the best evidence of the exchange value of the transaction. As an example, let's consider Illustration 10–7.

On January 2, 2011, Dennison, Inc., purchased a machine and signed a noninterest-bearing note in payment. The note requires the company to pay $100,000 on December 31, 2013. Dennison is not sure what interest rate appropriately reflects the time value of money. However, price lists indicate the machine could have been purchased for cash at a price of $79,383.

Dennison records both the asset and liability at $79,383 on January 2:

Machine (cash price)	79,383	
Discount on note payable (difference)	20,617	
Note payable (face amount)		100,000

ILLUSTRATION 10–7
Noninterest-Bearing Note—Fair Value of Asset Is Known

In this situation, we infer the present value of the note from the fair value of the asset. Again, the difference between the note's $79,383 present value and the cash payment of $100,000 represents interest. We can determine the interest rate that is implicit in the agreement as follows:

$79,383 (present value) = $100,000 (face amount) × PV factor
$79,383 ÷ $100,000 = .79383*
*Present value of $1: n = 3, i = ? (from Table 2, i = 8%)

We refer to the 8% rate as the *implicit rate of interest.* Dennison records interest each year at 8% in the same manner as demonstrated in Illustration 10–6 and discussed in greater depth in Chapter 14.

We now turn our attention to the acquisition of assets acquired in exchange for equity securities or through donation.

Issuance of Equity Securities

● LO4

The most common situation in which equity securities are issued for property, plant, and equipment and intangible assets occurs when small companies incorporate and the owner or owners contribute assets to the new corporation in exchange for ownership securities, usually common stock. Because the common shares are not publicly traded, it's difficult to determine their fair value. In that case, the fair value of the assets received by the corporation is probably the better indicator of the transaction's exchange value. In other situations, particularly those involving corporations whose stock is actively traded, the market value of the shares is the best indication of fair value. Consider Illustration 10–8.

On March 31, 2011, the Elcorn Company issued 10,000 shares of its nopar common stock in exchange for land. On the date of the transaction, the fair value of the common stock, evidenced by its market price, was $20 per share. The journal entry to record this transaction is:

Land	200,000	
Common stock (10,000 shares × $20)		200,000

ILLUSTRATION 10–8
Asset Acquired by Issuing Equity Securities

If the fair value of the common stock had not been reliably determinable, the value of the land as determined through an independent appraisal would be used as the cost of the land and the value of the common stock.

Donated Assets

Assets acquired by issuing common stock are valued at the fair value of the securities or the fair value of the assets, whichever is more clearly evident.

On occasion, companies acquire assets through donation. The donation usually is an enticement to do something that benefits the donor. For example, the developer of an industrial park might pay some of the costs of building a manufacturing facility to entice a company to locate in its park. Companies record assets donated by unrelated parties at their fair values

Donated assets are recorded at their fair values.

based on either an available market price or an appraisal value. This should not be considered a departure from historical cost valuation. Instead, it is equivalent to the donor contributing cash to the company and the company using the cash to acquire the asset.

As the recipient records the asset at its fair value, what account receives the offsetting credit? Over the years, there has been disagreement over this question. Should the recipient increase its paid-in capital—the part of shareholders' equity representing investments in the firm? Or, should the donated asset be considered revenue? *GAAP* requires that donated assets be recorded as *revenue*.[12] Recall that revenues generally are inflows of assets from delivering or producing goods, rendering services, or from other activities that constitute the entity's ongoing major or central operations. The rationale is that the company receiving the donation is performing a service for the donor in exchange for the asset donated.

Revenue is credited for the amount paid by an unrelated party.

Corporations occasionally receive donations from governmental units. A local governmental unit might provide land or pay all or some of the cost of a new office building or manufacturing plant to entice a company to locate within its geographical boundaries. For example, the city of San Jose, California, paid a significant portion of the cost of a new office building for **IBM Corporation**. The new office building, located in downtown San Jose, brought jobs to a revitalized downtown area and increased revenues to the city. The City of San Jose did not receive an equity interest in IBM through its donation, but significantly benefited nevertheless.

Illustration 10–9 provides an example.

ILLUSTRATION 10–9 Asset Donation	Elcorn Enterprises decided to relocate its office headquarters to the city of Westmont. The city agreed to pay 20% of the $20 million cost of building the headquarters in order to entice Elcorn to relocate. The building was completed on May 3, 2011. Elcorn paid its portion of the cost of the building in cash. Elcorn records the transaction as follows:	
	Building	20,000,000	
	Cash		16,000,000
	Revenue—donation of asset (20% × $20 million)		4,000,000

Property, plant, and equipment and intangible assets also can be acquired in an exchange. Because an exchange transaction inherently involves a disposition of one asset as it is given up in exchange for another, we cover these transactions in Part B, Dispositions and Exchanges.

DECISION MAKERS' PERSPECTIVE

The property, plant, and equipment and intangible asset acquisition decision is among the most significant decisions that management must make. A decision to acquire a new fleet of airplanes or to build or purchase a new office building or manufacturing plant could influence a company's performance for many years.

These decisions, often referred to as **capital budgeting** decisions, require management to forecast all future net cash flows (cash inflows minus cash outflows) generated by the asset(s). These cash flows are then used in a model to determine if the future cash flows are sufficient to warrant the capital expenditure. One such model, the net present value model, compares the present value of future net cash flows with the required initial acquisition cost of the asset(s). If the present value is higher than the acquisition cost, the asset is acquired. You have studied or will study capital budgeting in considerable depth in a financial management course. The introduction to the time value of money concept in Chapter 6 provided you with important tools necessary to evaluate capital budgeting decisions.

● LO5

A key to profitability is how well a company manages and utilizes its assets. Financial analysts often use activity, or turnover, ratios to evaluate a company's effectiveness in

---

[12]FASB ASC 958–605–15–2 and FASB ASC 958–605–15–4: Not-for-Profit Entities–Revenue Recognition–Scope and Scope Exceptions–Contributions Received (previously "Accounting for Contributions Received and Contributions Made," *Statement of Financial Accounting Standards No. 116* (Norwalk, Conn.: FASB, 1993)).

managing assets. This concept was illustrated with receivables and inventory in previous chapters. Property, plant, and equipment (PP&E) usually are a company's primary revenue-generating assets. Their efficient use is critical to generating a satisfactory return to owners. One ratio analysts often use to measure how effectively managers use PP&E is the **fixed-asset turnover ratio.** This ratio is calculated as follows:

$$\text{Fixed-asset turnover ratio} = \frac{\text{Net sales}}{\text{Average fixed assets}}$$

The ratio indicates the level of sales generated by the company's investment in fixed assets. The denominator usually is the book value (cost less accumulated depreciation and depletion) of property, plant, and equipment.[13]

As with other turnover ratios, we can compare a company's fixed-asset turnover with that of its competitors, with an industry average, or with the same company's ratio over time. Let's compare the fixed-asset turnover ratios for **The GAP, Inc.,** and **The Gymboree Corporation,** two companies in the retail apparel industry.

The fixed-asset turnover ratio measures a company's effectiveness in managing property, plant, and equipment.

| | ($ in millions) | | | |
| | **GAP** | | **Gymboree** | |
	2009	**2008**	**2009**	**2008**
Property, plant, and equipment (net)	$2,933	$3,267	$204	$186
Net sales—2009	$14,526		$1,001	

Real World Financials

The 2009 fixed-asset turnover for GAP is 4.69 ($14,526 ÷ [($2,933 + 3,267) ÷ 2]) compared to Gymboree's turnover of 5.13 ($1,001 ÷ [($204 ÷ 186) ÷ 2]). Gymboree is able to generate $.44 more in sales dollars than GAP for each dollar invested in fixed assets. ●

DISPOSITIONS AND EXCHANGES

PART B

● LO6

After using property, plant, and equipment and intangible assets, companies will sell, retire, or exchange those assets. Accounting for exchanges differs somewhat from accounting for sales and retirements because they involve both an acquisition and a disposition. So let's look first at sales and retirements and then we'll address accounting for exchanges. Be sure to note that in each case, the companies should record depreciation, depletion, or amortization up to the date of disposition or exchange.

Dispositions

When selling property, plant, and equipment and intangible assets for monetary consideration (cash or a receivable), the seller recognizes a gain or loss for the difference between the consideration received and the book value of the asset sold. Illustration 10–10 provides an example.

The Robosport Company sold for $6,000 machinery that originally cost $20,000. Depreciation of $12,000 had been recorded up to the date of sale. Since the $8,000 book value of the asset ($20,000 − 12,000) exceeds the $6,000 consideration Robosport received, the company recognizes a $2,000 loss. The sale is recorded as follows:

Cash (selling price)	6,000	
Accumulated depreciation (account balance)	12,000	
Loss on disposal of machinery (difference)	2,000	
Machinery (account balance)		20,000

ILLUSTRATION 10–10

Sale of Property, Plant, and Equipment

A gain or loss is recognized for the difference between the consideration received and the asset's book value.

---

[13]If intangible assets are significant, their book value could be added to the denominator to produce a turnover that reflects all long-lived, revenue-producing assets. The use of book value provides an approximation of the company's current investment in these assets.

Property, plant, and equipment and intangible assets to be disposed of by sale are classified as held for sale and measured at the lower of book value or fair value less cost to sell.

Retirements (or abandonments) are treated similarly. The only difference is that there will be no monetary consideration received. A loss is recorded for the remaining book value of the asset.

When property, plant, and equipment or an intangible asset is to be disposed of by *sale*, we classify it as "held for sale" and report it at the lower of its book value or fair value less any cost to sell.[14] If the fair value less cost to sell is below book value, we recognize an impairment loss. Assets classified as held for sale are not depreciated or amortized. Recall from your study of discontinued operations in Chapter 4 that this treatment is the same one we employed in accounting for a component of an entity that is held for sale. We cover this topic in more depth in the impairment section of Chapter 11.

ADDITIONAL CONSIDERATION

Involuntary Conversions

Occasionally companies dispose of property, plant, and equipment and intangible assets unintentionally. These so-called involuntary conversions include destruction by fire, earthquake, flood, or other catastrophe and expropriation by a governmental body.

Usually, the company receives a cash settlement from an insurance company for destroyed assets or from the governmental body for expropriated assets. The company often immediately reinvests this cash in similar assets. Nevertheless, involuntary conversions are treated precisely the same as voluntary conversions. That is, the proceeds are recorded, the book value of the lost assets are removed, and a gain or loss is recognized for the difference.

Exchanges

Sometimes a company will acquire an asset in exchange for an asset other than cash. This frequently involves a trade-in by which a new asset is acquired in exchange for an old asset, and cash is given to equalize the fair values of the assets exchanged. The basic principle followed in these nonmonetary asset[15] exchanges is to value the asset received at fair value. This can be the fair value of the asset(s) given up or the fair value of the asset(s) received plus (or minus) any cash exchanged. We first look to the fair value of the asset given up. However, in a trade-in, quite often the fair value of the new asset is more clearly evident than the second-hand value of the asset traded in. We recognize a gain or loss for the difference between the fair value of the asset given up and its book value. See the example in Illustration 10–11A.

Let's modify the illustration slightly by assuming that the fair value of the old equipment is $75,000 instead of $150,000. Illustration 10–11B shows the journal entry to record the transaction.

Gain or loss is the difference between fair value and book value of the asset given.

It's important to understand that the gain or loss recognized in these transactions is the difference between the fair value and book value of the asset given. *The amount of cash given or received has no effect on the amount of gain or loss recognized.* The cash given or received simply serves to equalize the fair value of the assets exchanged.

Until 2005, the accounting treatment of nonmonetary asset exchanges depended on a number of factors including (1) whether the assets exchanged were similar or dissimilar, (2) whether a gain or loss was indicated in the exchange, and (3) whether cash was given or received. A new accounting standard[16] simplified accounting for exchanges by requiring the use of fair value except in rare situations in which the fair value can't be determined or the exchange lacks commercial substance.[17]

Let's discuss each of these situations.

---

[14]FASB ASC 360–10–35–15: Property, Plant, and Equipment–Overall–Subsequent Measurement–Impairment or Disposal of Long-Lived Assets (previously "Accounting for the Impairment or Disposal of Long-lived Assets," *Statement of Financial Accounting Standards No. 144* (Norwalk, Conn.: FASB, 2001)).

[15]Monetary items are assets and liabilities whose *amounts are fixed,* by contract or otherwise, in terms of a specific number of dollars. Others are considered nonmonetary.

[16]FASB ASC 845: Nonmonetary Transactions (previously "Exchanges of Nonmonetary Assets an amendment of APB Opinion No. 29," *Statement of Financial Accounting Standards No. 153* (Norwalk, Conn.: FASB, 2004)).

[17]There is a third situation which precludes the use of fair value in a nonmonetary exchange. The transaction is an exchange of inventories to facilitate sales to customers other than the parties to the exchange.

The Elcorn Company traded its laser equipment for the newer air-cooled ion lasers manufactured by American Laser Corporation. The old equipment had a book value of $100,000 (cost of $500,000 less accumulated depreciation of $400,000) and a fair value of $150,000. To equalize the fair values of the assets exchanged, in addition to the old machinery, Elcorn paid American Laser $430,000 in cash. This means that the fair value of the new laser equipment is $580,000. We know this because American Laser was willing to trade the new lasers in exchange for old lasers worth $150,000 plus $430,000 cash. The following journal entry records the transaction:

Laser equipment—new (fair value: $150,000 + 430,000) ...	580,000	
Accumulated depreciation (account balance)	400,000	
Laser equipment—old (account balance)		500,000
Cash (amount paid)...		430,000
Gain (to balance; also: $150,000 − 100,000)......................		50,000

The new laser equipment is recorded at $580,000, the fair value of the old equipment, $150,000, plus the cash given of $430,000. This also equals the fair value of the new lasers. Elcorn recognizes a gain of $50,000, which is simply the difference between the old equipment's fair value of $150,000 and its $100,000 book value as well as the amount needed to allow the debits to equal credits in the journal entry.

ILLUSTRATION 10–11A

Nonmonetary Asset Exchange

An asset received in an exchange of nonmonetary assets generally is valued at fair value.

A gain is recognized when the fair value of an asset given is more than its book value.

The Elcorn Company traded its laser equipment for the newer air-cooled ion lasers manufactured by American Laser Corporation. The old equipment had a book value of $100,000 (cost of $500,000 less accumulated depreciation of $400,000) and a fair value of $75,000. To equalize the fair values of the assets exchanged, in addition to the old machinery, Elcorn paid American Laser $430,000 in cash. This means that the fair value of the new laser equipment is $505,000. We know this because American Laser was willing to trade the new lasers in exchange for old lasers worth $75,000 plus $430,000 in cash. The following journal entry records the transaction:

Laser equipment—new (fair value: $75,000 + 430,000)	505,000	
Accumulated depreciation (account balance)	400,000	
Loss (to balance; also: $100,000 − 75,000)	25,000	
Laser equipment—old (account balance)		500,000
Cash (amount paid)		430,000

The $25,000 difference between the equipment's fair value of $75,000 and its book value of $100,000 is recognized as a loss. The new equipment is valued at $505,000, the fair value of the old equipment of $75,000 plus the $430,000 cash given.

ILLUSTRATION 10–11B

Nonmonetary Asset Exchange

A loss is recognized when the fair value of an asset given is less than its book value.

Fair Value Not Determinable

It would be unusual for a company to be unable to reasonably determine fair value of either asset in an exchange. Nevertheless, if the situation does occur, the company would simply use the book value of the asset given up, plus (minus) any cash given (received) to value the asset acquired. For example, if fair value had not been determinable in Illustration 10–11A, Elcorn would have recorded the exchange as follows:

Equipment—new (book value + cash: $100,000 + 430,000)	530,000	
Accumulated depreciation (account balance)	400,000	
Equipment—old (account balance)		500,000
Cash (amount paid)		430,000

If we can't determine the fair value of either asset in the exchange, the asset received is valued at the book value of the asset given.

The new equipment is valued at the book value of the old equipment ($100,000) plus the cash given ($430,000). No gain or loss is recognized.

Exchange Lacks Commercial Substance

If we record an exchange at fair value, we recognize a gain or loss for the difference between the fair value and book value of the asset(s) given up. To preclude the possibility of a company exchanging appreciated assets solely to recognize a gain, fair value can be used only in gain situations that have "commercial substance."

Commercial substance is present when future cash flows change as a result of the exchange.

A nonmonetary exchange is considered to have commercial substance if future cash flows will change as a result of the exchange. Most exchanges are for legitimate business reasons and would not be transacted if there were no anticipated change in future cash flows. The exchange of old laser equipment for the *newer* model in Illustration 10–11A is an example of an exchange transacted for legitimate business reasons.

GAIN SITUATION.   Suppose a company owned a tract of land that had a book value of $1 million and a fair value of $5 million. The only ways to recognize the $4 million appreciation are to either sell the land or to exchange the land for another nonmonetary asset for a legitimate business purpose. For example, if the land were exchanged for a different type of asset, say a building, then future cash flows most likely will change, the exchange has commercial substance, fair value is used and the $4 million gain can be recognized. On the other hand, if the land were exchanged for a tract of land that has the identical characteristics as the land given, then it is unlikely that future cash flows would change. In this case, the exchange lacks commercial substance and the new land is valued at the book value of the old land. Illustration 10–12 provides an example.

ILLUSTRATION 10–12 Nonmonetary Asset Exchange— Exchange Lacks Commercial Substance	The Elcorn Company traded a tract of land to Sanchez Development for a similar tract of land. The old land had a book value of $2,500,000 and a fair value of $4,500,000. To equalize the fair values of the assets exchanged, in addition to the land, Elcorn paid Sanchez $500,000 in cash. This means that the fair value of the land acquired is $5,000,000. The following journal entry records the transaction, *assuming that the exchange lacks commercial substance:*

Land—new (book value + cash paid: $2,500,000 + 500,000) ...   3,000,000
  Land—old (account balance)   2,500,000
  Cash (amount paid)   500,000

The new land is recorded at $3,000,000, the book value of the old land, $2,500,000, plus the cash given of $500,000. No gain is recognized.

When the fair value of the asset given is less than its book value, we always use fair value to record the exchange.

LOSS SITUATION.   In Illustration 10–12, what if the fair value of the land given was less than its book value? It's unlikely that a company would enter into this type of transaction unless there was a legitimate business reason. The FASB's intent in including the commercial substance requirement for the use of fair value was to avoid companies' trading *appreciated* property for no legitimate reason other than to recognize the gain. This means that when a loss is indicated in a nonmonetary exchange, it's okay to record the loss and we use fair value to value the asset acquired.

ADDITIONAL CONSIDERATION

In Illustration 10–12, cash was given to equalize the fair values of the assets exchanged. What if cash was received? Suppose that $500,000 cash was *received* instead of given and that the fair value of the old land was $5,000,000. This means that the fair value of the land received is $4,500,000. In that case, part of the transaction is considered monetary and we would recognize a portion of the $2,500,000 gain ($5,000,000 − 2,500,000). The amount of gain recognized is equal to the proportion of cash received relative to total received:[18]

$$\frac{\$500,000}{\$500,000 + 4,500,000} = 10\%$$

Elcorn would recognize a $250,000 gain (10% × $2,500,000) and would value the land received at $2,250,000, the book value of the land given ($2,500,000), plus the gain recognized ($250,000), less the cash received ($500,000). The following journal entry records the transaction:

Land—new ($2,500,000 + 250,000 − 500,000)   2,250,000
Cash   500,000
  Land—old   2,500,000
  Gain   250,000

---

[18]If the amount of monetary consideration received is deemed significant, the transaction is considered to be monetary and the entire gain is recognized. In other words, the transaction is accounted for as if it had commercial substance. GAAP defines "significance" in this situation as 25% or more of the fair value of the exchange. FASB ASC 845–10–25–6: Nonmonetary transactions–Overall–Recognition (previously "Interpretations of *APB Opinion No. 29*," *EITF Abstracts No. 01–02* (Norwalk, Conn.: FASB, 2002)).

CONCEPT REVIEW EXERCISE

The MD Corporation recently acquired new equipment to be used in its production process. **EXCHANGES** In exchange, the company traded in an existing asset that had an original cost of $60,000 and accumulated depreciation on the date of the exchange of $45,000. In addition, MD paid $40,000 cash to the equipment manufacturer. The fair value of the old equipment is $17,000.

Required:

1. Prepare the journal entry MD would use to record the exchange transaction assuming that the transaction has commercial substance.
2. Prepare the journal entry MD would use to record the exchange transaction assuming that the transaction does *not* have commercial substance.

1. Prepare the journal entry MD would use to record the exchange transaction assuming **SOLUTION** that the transaction has commercial substance.

Equipment—new ($17,000 + 40,000)	57,000	
Accumulated depreciation (account balance)	45,000	
Cash (amount paid)		40,000
Equipment—old (account balance)		60,000
Gain ($17,000 fair value – $15,000 book value)		2,000

2. Prepare the journal entry MD would use to record the exchange transaction assuming that the transaction does *not* have commercial substance.

Equipment—new ($15,000 + 40,000)	55,000	
Accumulated depreciation (account balance)	45,000	
Cash (amount paid)		40,000
Equipment—old (account balance)		60,000

SELF-CONSTRUCTED ASSETS AND RESEARCH AND DEVELOPMENT

PART C

Two types of expenditures relating to property, plant, and equipment and intangible assets whose accounting treatment has generated considerable controversy are interest costs pertaining to self-constructed assets and amounts spent for research and development. We now consider those expenditures and why those controversies have developed.

Self-Constructed Assets

A company might decide to construct an asset for its own use rather than buy an existing ● LO7 one. For example, a retailer like **Nordstrom** might decide to build its own store rather than purchase an existing building. A manufacturing company like **Intel** could construct its own manufacturing facility. In fact, Nordstrom and Intel are just two of the many companies that self-construct assets. Other recognizable examples include **Walt Disney**, **Sears**, and **Caterpillar**. Quite often these companies act as the main contractor and then subcontract most of the actual construction work.

The critical accounting issue in these instances is identifying the cost of the self-constructed asset. The task is more difficult than for purchased assets because there is no external transaction to establish an exchange price. Actually, two difficulties arise in connection with assigning costs to self-constructed assets: (1) determining the amount of the company's indirect manufacturing costs (overhead) to be allocated to the construction and (2) deciding on the proper treatment of interest (actual or implicit) incurred during construction.

Overhead Allocation

One difficulty of associating costs with self-constructed assets is the same difficulty encountered when determining cost of goods manufactured for sale. The costs of material and direct labor usually are easily identified with a particular construction project and are included in cost. However, the treatment of manufacturing overhead cost and its allocation between construction projects and normal production is a controversial issue.

Some accountants advocate the inclusion of only the *incremental* overhead costs in the total cost of construction. That is, the asset's cost would include only those additional costs that are incurred because of the decision to construct the asset. This would exclude such indirect costs as depreciation and the salaries of supervisors that would be incurred whether or not the construction project is undertaken. If, however, a new construction supervisor was hired specifically to work on the project, then that salary would be included in asset cost.

Others advocate assigning overhead on the same basis that is used for a regular manufacturing process. That is, all overhead costs are allocated both to production and to self-constructed assets based on the relative amount of a chosen cost driver (for example, labor hours) incurred. This is known as the *full-cost approach* and is the generally accepted method used to determine the cost of a self-constructed asset.

Interest Capitalization

To reiterate, the cost of an asset includes all costs necessary to get the asset ready for its intended use. Unlike one purchased from another company, a self-constructed asset requires time to create it. During this construction period, the project must be financed in some way. This suggests the question as to whether interest costs during the construction period are one of the costs of acquiring the asset itself or simply costs of financing the asset. On the one hand, we might point to interest charges to finance inventories during their period of manufacture or to finance the purchase of plant assets from others and argue that construction period interest charges are merely costs of financing the asset that should be expensed as incurred like all other interest costs. On the other hand, we might argue that self-constructed assets are different in that during the construction period, they are not yet ready for their intended use for producing revenues. And, so, in keeping with both the historical cost principle and the matching concept, all costs during this period, including interest, should be capitalized and then allocated as depreciation during later periods when the assets are providing benefits.

QUALIFYING ASSETS. Generally accepted accounting principles are consistent with the second argument. Specifically, interest is capitalized during the construction period for (a) assets built for a company's own use as well as for (b) assets constructed *as discrete projects* for sale or lease (a ship or a real estate development, for example). This excludes from interest capitalization consideration inventories that are routinely manufactured in large quantities on a repetitive basis and assets that already are in use or are ready for their intended use.[19] Interest costs incurred during the productive life of the asset are expensed as incurred.

PERIOD OF CAPITALIZATION. The capitalization period for a self-constructed asset starts with the first expenditure (materials, labor, or overhead) and ends either when the asset is substantially complete and ready for use or when interest costs no longer are being incurred. Interest costs incurred can pertain to borrowings other than those obtained specifically for the construction project. However, interest costs can't be imputed; actual interest costs must be incurred.

AVERAGE ACCUMULATED EXPENDITURES. Because we consider interest to be a necessary cost of getting a self-constructed asset ready for use, the amount capitalized is only that portion of interest cost incurred during the construction period that *could have*

---

[19]FASB ASC 835–20–25: Interest–Capitalization of Interest–Recognition (previously "Capitalization of Interest Costs," *Statement of Financial Accounting Standards No. 34* (Stamford, Conn.: FASB, 1979)).

been avoided if expenditures for the asset had not been made. In other words, if construction had not been undertaken, debt incurred for the project would not have been necessary and/or other interest-bearing debt could have been liquidated or employed elsewhere.

As a result, interest should be determined for only the construction expenditures actually incurred during the capitalization period. And unless all expenditures are made at the outset of the period, it's necessary to determine the *average* amount outstanding during the period. This is the amount of debt that would be required to finance the expenditures and thus the amount on which interest would accrue. For instance, if a company accumulated $1,500,000 of construction expenditures fairly evenly throughout the construction period, the average expenditures would be:

Average accumulated expenditures approximates the average debt necessary for construction.

Total accumulated expenditures incurred evenly throughout the period	$1,500,000
	÷2
Average accumulated expenditures	$ 750,000

At the beginning of the period, no expenditures have accumulated, so no interest has accrued (on the equivalent amount of debt). But, by the end of the period interest is accruing on the total amount, $1,500,000. On average, then, interest accrues on half the total or $750,000.

Average accumulated expenditures is determined by time-weighting individual expenditures made during the construction period.

If expenditures are not incurred evenly throughout the period, a simple average is insufficient. In that case, a weighted average is determined by time-weighting individual expenditures or groups of expenditures by the number of months from their incurrence to the end of the construction period. This is demonstrated in Illustration 10–13.

On January 1, 2011, the Mills Conveying Equipment Company began construction of a building to be used as its office headquarters. The building was completed on June 30, 2012. Expenditures on the project, mainly payments to subcontractors, were as follows:

ILLUSTRATION 10–13

Interest Capitalization

January 3, 2011	$ 500,000
March 31, 2011	400,000
September 30, 2011	600,000
Accumulated expenditures at December 31, 2011 (before interest capitalization)	$1,500,000
January 31, 2012	600,000
April 30, 2012	300,000

On January 2, 2011, the company obtained a $1 million construction loan with an 8% interest rate. The loan was outstanding during the entire construction period. The company's other interest-bearing debt included two long-term notes of $2,000,000 and $4,000,000 with interest rates of 6% and 12%, respectively. Both notes were outstanding during the entire construction period.

The weighted-average accumulated expenditures by the end of 2011 are:

January 3, 2011	$500,000 × $^{12}/_{12}$ =	$500,000
March 31, 2011	400,000 × $^9/_{12}$ =	300,000
September 30, 2011	600,000 × $^3/_{12}$ =	150,000
Average accumulated expenditures for 2011	=	$950,000

FINANCIAL Reporting Case

Q4, p. 501

Again notice that the average accumulated expenditures are less than the total accumulated expenditures of $1,500,000. If Mills had borrowed exactly the amount necessary to finance the project, it would not have incurred interest on a loan of $1,500,000 for the whole year but only on an average loan of $950,000. The next step is to determine the interest to be capitalized for the average accumulated expenditures.

STEP 1: Determine the average accumulated expenditures.

INTEREST RATES. In this situation, debt financing was obtained specifically for the construction project, and the amount borrowed is sufficient to cover the average accumulated expenditures. To determine the interest capitalized, then, we simply multiply the construction loan rate of 8% by the average accumulated expenditures.

STEP 2: Calculate the amount of interest to be capitalized.

Interest capitalized for 2011 = $950,000 × 8% = $76,000

Notice that this is the same answer we would get by assuming separate 8% construction loans were made for each expenditure at the time each expenditure was made:

Loans		Annual Rate		Portion of Year Outstanding		Interest
$500,000	×	8%	×	$12/12$	=	$40,000
400,000	×	8%	×	$9/12$	=	24,000
600,000	×	8%	×	$3/12$	=	12,000
Interest capitalized for 2011						$76,000

The interest of $76,000 is added to the cost of the building, bringing accumulated expenditures at December 31, 2011, to $1,576,000 ($1,500,000 + 76,000). The remaining interest cost incurred but not capitalized is expensed.

It should be emphasized that interest capitalization does not require that funds actually be borrowed for this specific purpose, only that the company does have outstanding debt. The presumption is that even if the company doesn't borrow specifically for the project, funds from other borrowings must be diverted to finance the construction. Either way—directly or indirectly—interest costs are incurred. In our illustration, for instance, even without the construction loan, interest would be capitalized because other debt was outstanding. The capitalized interest would be the average accumulated expenditures multiplied by the weighted-average rate on these other loans. The weighted-average interest rate on all debt other than the construction loan would be 10%, calculated as follows:[20]

Loans		Rate		Interest
$2,000,000	×	6%	=	$120,000
4,000,000	×	12%	=	480,000
$6,000,000				$600,000

$$\text{Weighted-average rate: } \frac{\$600,000}{\$6,000,000} = 10\%$$

This is a weighted average because total interest is $600,000 on total debt of $6,000,000.

ADDITIONAL CONSIDERATION

The weighted-average rate isn't used for 2011 in our illustration because the specific construction loan is sufficient to cover the average accumulated expenditures. If the specific construction loan had been insufficient to cover the average accumulated expenditures, its 8% interest rate would be applied to the average accumulated expenditures up to the amount of the specific borrowing, and any remaining average accumulated expenditures in excess of specific borrowings would be multiplied by the weighted-average rate on all other outstanding interest-bearing debt. Suppose, for illustration, that the 8% construction loan had been only $500,000 rather than $1,000,000. We would calculate capitalized interest using both the specific rate and the weighted-average rate:

	Average Accumulated Expenditures		Rate		Interest
Total	$950,000				
Specific borrowing	500,000	×	8%	=	$40,000
Excess	$450,000	×	10%	=	45,000
Capitalized interest					$85,000

In our illustration, it's necessary to use this approach in 2012.

---

[20]The same result can be obtained simply by multiplying the individual debt interest rates by the relative amount of debt at each rate. In this case, one-third of total debt is at 6% and two-thirds of the total debt is at 12% (1/3 × 6% + 2/3 × 12% = 10%).

It's possible that the amount of interest calculated to be capitalized exceeds the amount of interest actually incurred. If that's the case, we limit the interest capitalized to the actual interest incurred. In our illustration, total interest cost incurred during 2011 far exceeds the $76,000 of capitalized interest calculated, so it's not necessary to limit the capitalized amount.

Interest capitalized is limited to interest incurred.

STEP 3: Compare calculated interest with actual interest incurred.

Loans		Annual Rate		Actual Interest	Calculated Interest
$1,000,000	×	8%	=	$ 80,000	
2,000,000	×	6%	=	120,000	
4,000,000	×	12%	=	480,000	
				$680,000	$76,000

Use lower amount

Continuing the example based on the information in Illustration 10–13, let's determine the amount of interest capitalized during 2012 for the building. The total accumulated expenditures by the end of the project are:

Accumulated expenditures at the beginning of 2012 (including interest capitalization)	$1,576,000
January 31, 2012	600,000
April 30, 2012	300,000
Accumulated expenditures at June 30, 2012 (before 2012 interest capitalization)	$2,476,000

The weighted-average accumulated expenditures by the end of the project are:

January 1, 2012	$1,576,000 × % =	$1,576,000
January 31, 2012	600,000 × % =	500,000
April 30, 2012	300,000 × % =	100,000
Average accumulated expenditures for 2012		$2,176,000

STEP 1: Determine the average accumulated expenditures.

Notice that the 2012 expenditures are weighted relative to the construction period of six months because the project was finished on June 30, 2012. Interest capitalized for 2012 would be $98,800, calculated as follows:

	Average Accumulated Expenditures		Annual Rate		Fraction of Year		
	$2,176,000						
Specific borrowing	1,000,000	×	8%	×	⁶⁄₁₂	=	$40,000
Excess	$1,176,000	×	10%	×	⁶⁄₁₂	=	58,800
Capitalized interest							$98,800

STEP 2: Calculate the amount of interest to be capitalized.

Multiplying by six-twelfths reflects the fact that the interest rates are annual rates (12-month rates) and the construction period is only 6 months.

Loans		Annual Rate		Actual Interest	Calculated Interest
$1,000,000	×	8% × ⁶⁄₁₂ =		$ 40,000	
2,000,000	×	6% × ⁶⁄₁₂ =		60,000	
4,000,000	×	12% × ⁶⁄₁₂ =		240,000	
				$340,000	$98,800

STEP 3: Compare calculated interest with actual interest incurred.

Use lower amount

ADDITIONAL CONSIDERATION

To illustrate how the actual interest limitation might come into play, let's assume the nonspecific borrowings in our illustration were $200,000 and $400,000 (instead of $2,000,000 and $4,000,000). Our comparison would change as follows:

Loans		Annual Rate	Actual Interest	Calculated Interest
$1,000,000	$\times$	8% $\times$ $\frac{6}{12}$ =	$40,000	
200,000	$\times$	6% $\times$ $\frac{6}{12}$ =	6,000	
400,000	$\times$	12% $\times$ $\frac{6}{12}$ =	24,000	
			$70,000	$98,800

↑
Use lower amount

For the first six months of 2012, $98,800 of interest would be capitalized, bringing the total capitalized cost of the building to $2,574,800 ($2,476,000 + 98,800), and $241,200 in interest would be expensed ($340,000 − 98,800).

The method of determining interest to capitalize that we've discussed is called the **specific interest method** because we use rates from specific construction loans to the extent of specific borrowings before using the average rate of other debt. Sometimes, though, it's difficult to associate specific borrowings with projects. In these situations, it's acceptable to just use the weighted-average rate on all interest-bearing debt, including all construction loans. This is known as the **weighted-average method.** In our illustration, for example, if the $1,000,000, 8% loan had not been specifically related to construction, we would calculate a single weighted-average rate as shown below.

Weighted-average method

Loans		Rate		Interest
$1,000,000	$\times$	8%	=	$ 80,000
2,000,000	$\times$	6%	=	120,000
4,000,000	$\times$	12%	=	480,000
$7,000,000				$680,000

$$\text{Weighted-average rate: } \frac{\$680,000}{\$7,000,000} = 9.7\%$$

If we were using the weighted-average method rather than the specific interest method, we would simply multiply this single rate times the average accumulated expenditures to determine capitalizable interest.

If material, the amount of interest capitalized during the period must be disclosed.

DISCLOSURE.   For an accounting period in which interest costs are capitalized, both the total amount of interest costs incurred and the amount that has been capitalized should be disclosed. Graphic 10–5 shows an interest capitalization disclosure note that was included in a recent annual report of **Walmart Stores, Inc.**, the world's largest retailer.

GRAPHIC 10–5

Capitalized Interest Disclosure—Walmart Stores, Inc.

Real World Financials

Capitalized Interest

Interest costs capitalized on construction projects were $88 million, $150 million, and $182 million in fiscal 2009, 2008, and 2007, respectively.

Research and Development (R&D)

● LO8

Prior to 1974, the practice was to allow companies to either expense or capitalize R&D costs, but GAAP now requires all research and development costs to be charged to expense when incurred.[21] This was a controversial change opposed by many companies that preferred delaying the recognition of these expenses until later years when presumably the expenditures bear fruit.

A company undertakes an R&D project because it believes the project will eventually provide benefits that exceed the current expenditures. Unfortunately, though, it's difficult to predict which individual research and development projects will ultimately provide benefits. In fact, only 1 in 10 actually reach commercial production. Moreover, even for those projects that pan out, a direct relationship between research and development costs and specific future revenue is difficult to establish. In other words, even if R&D costs do lead to future benefits, it's difficult to objectively determine the size of the benefits and in which periods the costs should be expensed if they are capitalized. These are the issues that prompted the FASB to require immediate expensing.

The FASB's approach is certain in most cases to understate assets and overstate current expense because at least some of the R&D expenditures will likely produce future benefits.

> *Most R&D costs are expensed in the periods incurred.*
>
> *R&D costs entail a high degree of uncertainty of future benefits and are difficult to match with future revenues.*

DETERMINING R&D COSTS. GAAP distinguishes research and development as follows:

Research is planned search or critical investigation aimed at discovery of new knowledge with the hope that such knowledge will be useful in developing a new product or service or a new process or technique or in bringing about a significant improvement to an existing product or process.

Development is the translation of research findings or other knowledge into a plan or design for a new product or process or for a significant improvement to an existing product or process whether intended for sale or use.[22]

R&D costs include salaries, wages, and other labor costs of personnel engaged in R&D activities, the costs of materials consumed, equipment, facilities, and intangibles used in R&D projects, the costs of services performed by others in connection with R&D activities, and a reasonable allocation of indirect costs related to those activities. General and administrative costs should not be included unless they are clearly related to the R&D activity.

If an asset is purchased specifically for a single R&D project, its cost is considered R&D and expensed immediately even though the asset's useful life extends beyond the current year. However, the cost of an asset that has an alternative future use beyond the current R&D project is *not* a current R&D expense. Instead, the depreciation or amortization of these alternative-use assets is included as R&D expenses in the current and future periods the assets are used for R&D activities.

> *R&D expense includes the depreciation and amortization of assets used in R&D activities.*

In general, R&D costs pertain to activities that occur prior to the start of commercial production, and costs of starting commercial production and beyond are not R&D costs. Graphic 10–6 captures this concept with a time line beginning with the start of an R&D project and ending with the ultimate sale of a developed product or the use of a developed process. The graphic also provides examples of activities typically included as R&D and examples of activities typically excluded from R&D.[23]

Costs incurred before the start of commercial production are all expensed as R&D. The costs incurred after commercial production begins would be either expensed or treated as manufacturing overhead and included in the cost of inventory. Let's look at an example in Illustration 10–14.

The salaries and wages, supplies consumed, and payments to others for R&D services are expensed in 2011 as R&D. The equipment is capitalized and the 2011 depreciation is expensed as R&D. Even though the costs to develop the patented product are expensed, the filing and legal costs for the patent are capitalized and amortized in future periods just as similar costs are capitalized for purchased intangibles. Amortization of the patent is discussed in Chapter 11.

> *Filing and legal costs for patents, copyrights, and other developed intangibles are capitalized and amortized in future periods.*

---

[21]FASB ASC 730–10–25–1: Research and Development–Overall–Recognition (previously "Accounting for Research and Development Costs," *Statement of Financial Accounting Standards No. 2* (Stamford, Conn.: FASB, 1974), par. 12).

[22]Ibid., section 730–10–20 (previously par. 8 of *SFAS No. 2*).

[23]Ibid., section 730–10–55 (previously par. 9 of *SFAS No. 2*).

GRAPHIC 10–6
Research and Development Expenditures

Start of R&D Activity	Start of Commercial Production	Sale of Product or Process

Costs incurred *before* the start of commercial production are all expensed as R&D.

Costs incurred *after* commercial production begins would be either expensed or included in the cost of inventory.

Examples of R&D Costs:

• Laboratory research aimed at discovery of new knowledge

• Searching for applications of new research findings or other knowledge

• Design, construction, and testing of preproduction prototypes and models

• Modification of the formulation or design of a product or process

Examples of Non-R&D Costs:

• Engineering follow-through in an early phase of commercial production

• Quality control during commercial production including routine testing of products

• Routine ongoing efforts to refine, enrich, or otherwise improve on the qualities of an existing product

• Adaptation of an existing capability to a particular requirement or customer's need as a part of a continuing commercial activity

ILLUSTRATION 10–14
Research and Development Costs

The Askew Company made the following cash expenditures during 2011 related to the development of a new industrial plastic:

R&D salaries and wages	$10,000,000
R&D supplies consumed during 2011	3,000,000
Purchase of R&D equipment	5,000,000
Patent filing and legal costs	100,000
Payments to others for services performed in connection with R&D activities	1,200,000
Total	$19,300,000

The project resulted in a new product to be manufactured in 2012. A patent was filed with the U.S. Patent Office. The equipment purchased will be employed in other projects. Depreciation on the equipment for 2011 was $500,000.

The various expenditures would be recorded as follows:

R&D expense ($10,000,000 + 3,000,000 + 1,200,000)	14,200,000	
Cash		14,200,000
To record R&D expenses.		
Equipment	5,000,000	
Cash		5,000,000
To record the purchase of equipment.		
R&D expense	500,000	
Accumulated depreciation—equipment		500,000
To record R&D depreciation.		
Patent	100,000	
Cash		100,000
To capitalize the patent filing and legal costs.		

Expenditures reconciliation:

Recorded as R&D	$14,200,000
Capitalized as equipment	5,000,000
Capitalized as patent	100,000
Total expenditures	$19,300,000

GAAP requires that total R&D expense incurred must be disclosed either as a line item in the income statement or in a disclosure note. For example, **Microsoft** reported $9,010 million of R&D expense on the face of its 2009 income statement. In our illustration, total R&D expense disclosed in 2011 would be $14,700,000 ($14,200,000 in expenditures and $500,000 in depreciation). Note that if Askew later sells this patent to another company for, say, $15 million, the buyer would capitalize the entire purchase price rather than only the filing and legal costs. Once again, the reason for the apparent inconsistency in accounting treatment of internally generated intangibles and externally purchased intangibles is the difficulty of associating costs and benefits.

GAAP requires disclosure of total R&D expense incurred during the period.

R&D PERFORMED FOR OTHERS.

The principle requiring the immediate expensing of R&D does not apply to companies that perform R&D for other companies under contract. In these situations, the R&D costs are capitalized as inventory and carried forward into future years until the project is completed. Of course, justification is that the benefits of these expenditures are the contract fees that are determinable and are earned over the term of the project. Income from these contracts can be recognized using either the percentage-of-completion or completed contract method. We discussed these alternatives in Chapter 5.

Another exception pertains to a company that develops computer software. Expenditures made after the software is determined to be technologically feasible but before it is ready for commercial production are capitalized. Costs incurred before technological feasibility is established are expensed as incurred. We discuss software development costs below.

START-UP COSTS.

For the fiscal year ended January 31, 2009, **Barnes & Noble Inc.**, opened 35 new stores. The company incurred a variety of one-time preopening costs for salaries of employees supervising construction, training, travel, and relocation of employees totaling $12.8 million. In fact, whenever a company introduces a new product or service, or commences business in a new territory or with a new customer, it incurs similar start-up costs. As with R&D expenditures, a company must expense all the costs related to a company's start-up activities in the period incurred, rather than capitalize those costs as an asset. Start-up costs also include organization costs related to organizing a new entity, such as legal fees and state filing fees to incorporate.[24]

Start-up costs are expensed in the period incurred.

ADDITIONAL CONSIDERATION

Development Stage Enterprises

A development stage enterprise is a new business that has either not commenced its principal operations or has begun its principal operations but has not generated significant revenues. Prior to 1975, many of these companies recorded an asset for the normal operating costs incurred during the development stage. This asset was then expensed over a period of time beginning with the commencement of operations.

GAAP now requires that these enterprises comply with the same generally accepted accounting principles that apply to established operating companies in determining whether a cost is to be charged to expense when incurred or capitalized and expensed in future periods.[25] Therefore, normal operating costs incurred during the development stage are expensed, not capitalized. Development stage enterprises are allowed to provide items of supplemental information to help financial statement readers more readily assess their future cash flows.

---

[24]FASB ASC 720–15–25–1: Other Expenses–Start-Up Costs–Recognition (previously "Reporting on the Costs of Start-Up Activities," *Statement of Position 98-5* (New York: AICPA, 1998)).

[25]FASB ASC 915: Development Stage Entities (previously "Accounting and Reporting by Development Stage Enterprises," *Statement of Financial Accounting Standards No. 7* (Stamford, Conn.: FASB, 1975)).

SOFTWARE DEVELOPMENT COSTS. The computer software industry has become a large and important U.S. business over the last two decades. Relative newcomers such as **Microsoft** and **Adobe Systems**, as well as traditional hardware companies like **IBM**, are leaders in this multibillion dollar industry. A significant expenditure for these companies is the cost of developing software. Prior to 1985, some companies were capitalizing software development costs and expensing them in future periods and others were expensing these costs in the period incurred.

Now GAAP requires that companies record R&D as an expense, until technological feasibility of the software has been established, for costs they incur to develop or purchase computer software to be sold, leased, or otherwise marketed.[26] We account for the costs incurred to develop computer software *to be used internally* in a similar manner. Costs incurred during the preliminary project stage are expensed as R&D. After the application development stage is reached (for example, at the coding stage or installation stage), we capitalize any further costs.[27] We generally capitalize the costs of computer software *purchased* for internal use.

Technological feasibility is established "when the enterprise has completed all planning, designing, coding, and testing activities that are necessary to establish that the product can be produced to meet its design specifications including functions, features, and technical performance requirements."[28] Costs incurred after technological feasibility but before the software is available for general release to customers are capitalized as an intangible asset. These costs include coding and testing costs and the production of product masters. Costs incurred after the software release date usually are not R&D expenditures. Graphic 10–7 shows the R&D time line introduced earlier in the chapter modified to include the point at which technological feasibility is established. Only the costs incurred between technological feasibility and the software release date are capitalized.

GRAPHIC 10–7

Research and Development Expenditures— Computer Software

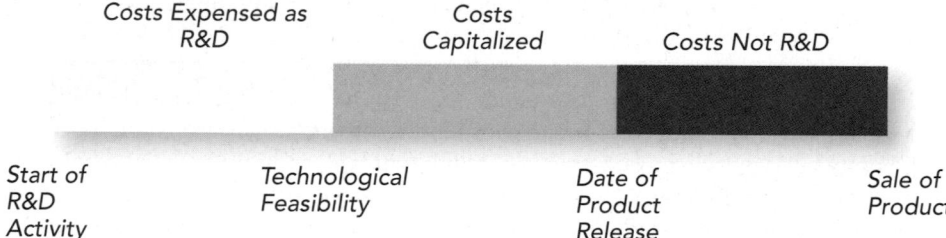

The amortization of capitalized computer software development costs begins when the product is available for general release to customers. The periodic amortization percentage is the greater of (1) the ratio of current revenues to current and anticipated revenues (percentage-of-revenue method) or (2) the straight-line percentage over the useful life of the asset, as shown in Illustration 10–15.

Graphic 10–8 shows the software disclosure included in a recent annual report of **CA, Inc.** The note provides a good summary of the accounting treatment of software development costs.

Why do generally accepted accounting principles allow this exception to the general rule of expensing all R&D? We could attribute it to the political process. Software is a very important industry to our economy and perhaps its lobbying efforts resulted in the standard allowing software companies to capitalize certain R&D costs.

We could also attribute the exception to the nature of the software business. Recall that R&D costs in general are expensed in the period incurred for two reasons: (1) they entail a high degree of uncertainty of future benefits, and (2) they are difficult to match with future benefits. With software, there is an important identifiable engineering milestone, technological

---

[26]FASB ASC 985–20–25–1: Software–Costs of Software to be Sold, Leased, or Marketed–Recognition (previously "Accounting for the Costs of Computer Software to be Sold, Leased, or Otherwise Marketed," *Statement of Financial Accounting Standards No. 86* (Stamford, Conn.: FASB, 1985)).

[27]FASB ASC 350–40–25: Intangibles–Goodwill and Other–Internal-Use Software–Recognition (previously "Accounting for the Costs of Computer Software Developed or Obtained for Internal Use," *Statement of Position 98-1* (New York: AICPA, 1998)).

[28]FASB ASC 985–20–25–2: Software–Costs of Software to be Sold, Leased, or Marketed–Recognition (previously "Accounting for the Costs of Computer Software to be Sold, Leased, or Otherwise Marketed," *Statement of Financial Accounting Standards No. 86* (Stamford, Conn.: FASB, 1985), par. 4).

ILLUSTRATION 10–15

Software
Development Costs

The Astro Corporation develops computer software graphics programs for sale. A new development project begun in 2010 reached technological feasibility at the end of June 2011, and the product was available for release to customers early in 2012. Development costs incurred in 2011 prior to June 30 were $1,200,000 and costs incurred from June 30 to the product availability date were $800,000. 2012 revenues from the sale of the new product were $3,000,000 and the company anticipates an additional $7,000,000 in revenues. The economic life of the software is estimated at four years.

Astro Corporation would expense the $1,200,000 in costs incurred prior to the establishment of technological feasibility and capitalize the $800,000 in costs incurred between technological feasibility and the product availability date. 2012 amortization of the intangible asset, software development costs, is calculated as follows:

1. Percentage-of-revenue method:

$$\frac{\$3,000,000}{\$3,000,000 + 7,000,000} = 30\% \times \$800,000 = \$240,000$$

2. Straight-line method:

$$\text{¼ or } 25\% \times \$800,000 = \$200,000.$$

The percentage-of-revenue method is used because it produces the greater amortization, $240,000.

GRAPHIC 10–8

Software
Disclosure—CA, Inc.

Real World Financials

Capitalized Software Costs and Other Identified Intangible Assets (in part)
In accordance with *SFAS No. 86*, "Accounting for the Costs of Computer Software to be Sold, Leased, or Otherwise Marketed," [FASB ASC 985–20], internally generated software development costs associated with new products and significant enhancements to existing software products are expensed as incurred until technological feasibility has been established. Internally generated software development costs of approximately $135 million, $112 million, and $85 million were capitalized during fiscal years 2009, 2008, and 2007, respectively.

Annual amortization of capitalized software costs is the greater of the amount computed using the ratio that current gross revenues for a product bear to the total of current and anticipated future gross revenues for that product or the straight-line method over the remaining estimated economic life of the software product, generally estimated to be five years from the date the product became available for general release to customers.

feasibility. When this milestone is attained, the probability of the software product's success increases significantly. And because the useful life of software is fairly short (one to four years in most cases), it is much easier to determine the periods of increased revenues than for R&D projects in other industries. Compare this situation with, say, the development of a new drug. Even after the drug has been developed, it must go through extensive testing to meet FDA (Food and Drug Administration) approval, which may never be attained. If attained, the useful life of the drug could be anywhere from a few months to many years.

PURCHASED RESEARCH AND DEVELOPMENT.   It's not unusual for one company to buy another company in order to obtain technology that the acquired company has developed or is in the process of developing. Any time a company buys another, it values the tangible and intangible assets acquired at fair value. When technology is involved, we distinguish between *developed technology* and *in-process research and development.* To do that, we borrow a criterion used in accounting for software development costs, and determine whether *technological feasibility* has been achieved. If so, the value of that technology is considered "developed," and we capitalize its fair value (record it as an asset) and amortize that amount over its useful life just like any other finite-life intangible asset.

We treat in-process R&D differently. Before 2009, we expensed the amount allocated to in-process R&D in the period of the acquisition. A new standard now requires the capitalization of the fair value of in-process R&D. But, unlike developed technology, we view

For business acquisitions made during fiscal years beginning on or after December 15, 2008, the fair value of in-process research and development is capitalized as an indefinite-life intangible asset.

● LO9

IFRS requires companies to capitalize development expenditures that meet specified criteria.

Real World Financials

INTERNATIONAL FINANCIAL REPORTING STANDARDS

Research and Development Expenditures. Except for software development costs incurred after technological feasibility has been established, U.S. GAAP requires all research and development expenditures to be expensed in the period incurred. *IAS No. 38*[29] draws a distinction between research activities and development activities. Research expenditures are expensed in the period incurred. However, development expenditures that meet specified criteria are capitalized as an intangible asset. Under both U.S. GAAP and IFRS, any direct costs to secure a patent, such as legal and filing fees, are capitalized.

Heineken, a company based in Amsterdam, prepares its financial statements according to IFRS. The following disclosure note describes the company's adherence to *IAS No. 38*. The note also describes the criteria for capitalizing development expenditures as well as the types of expenditures capitalized.

Software, Research and Development and Other Intangible Assets (in part)

Expenditures on research activities, undertaken with the prospect of gaining new technical knowledge and understanding, is recognized in the income statement when incurred. Development activities involve a plan or design for the production of new or substantially improved products and processes. Development expenditures are capitalized only if development costs can be measured reliably, the product or process is technically and commercially feasible, future economic benefits are probable, and Heineken intends to and has sufficient resources to complete development and to use or sell the asset. The expenditures capitalized include the cost of materials, direct labor and overhead costs that are directly attributable to preparing the asset for its intended use.

Amortization of capitalized development costs begins when development is complete and the asset is available for use. Heineken disclosed that it amortizes its capitalized development costs using the straight-line method over an estimated 3-year useful life.

it as an *indefinite-life* intangible asset.[30] As you will learn in Chapter 11, we don't amortize indefinite-life intangibles. Instead, we test them for impairment at least annually. If the R&D project is completed successfully, we switch to the way we account for developed technology and amortize the capitalized amount over the estimated period the product or process developed will provide benefits. If the project instead is abandoned, we expense the entire balance immediately. Research and development costs incurred after the acquisition to complete the project are expensed as incurred, consistent with the treatment of any other R&D expenditure not acquired in an acquisition.

Real World Financials

As an example, during its fiscal year ended July 25, 2009, **Cisco Systems, Inc.**, acquired 100% of the shares of **PostPath, Inc.**, an e-mail and calendaring company, for $215 million. The fair values assigned included $52 million for finite-life life intangible assets (including developed technology), $152 million for goodwill, and $3 million for in-process research and development.

Cisco immediately expensed the $3 million of in-process R&D. For acquisitions that occur in the company's subsequent fiscal year, that $3 million would instead be capitalized as an indefinite-life intangible asset and accounted for subsequently as discussed above.

● LO9

INTERNATIONAL FINANCIAL REPORTING STANDARDS

Software Development Costs. The percentage we use to amortize computer software development costs under U.S. GAAP is the greater of (1) the ratio of current revenues to current and anticipated revenues or (2) the straight-line percentage over the useful life of the software. This approach is allowed under IFRS, but not required.

---

[29]"Intangible Assets," *International Accounting Standard No. 38* (IASCF), as amended effective January 1, 2009.
[30]FASB ASC 805: Business Combinations (previously "Business Combinations," *Statement of Financial Accounting Standards No. 141 (revised)* (Norwalk, Conn.: FASB, 2007)).

FINANCIAL REPORTING CASE SOLUTION

1. **Describe to Stan what it means to capitalize an expenditure. What is the general rule for determining which costs are capitalized when property, plant, and equipment or an intangible asset is acquired?** *(p. 504)*   To capitalize an expenditure simply means to record it as an asset. All expenditures other than payments to shareholders and debt repayments are either expensed as incurred or capitalized. In general, the choice is determined by whether the expenditure benefits more than just the current period. Exceptions to this general principle are discussed in the chapter. The initial cost of an asset includes all expenditures necessary to bring the asset to its desired condition and location for use.

2. **Which costs might be included in the initial cost of equipment?** *(p. 504)*   In addition to the purchase price, the cost of equipment might include the cost of transportation, installation, testing, and legal fees to establish title.

3. **In what situations is interest capitalized rather than expensed?** *(p. 522)*   Interest is capitalized only for assets constructed for a company's own use or for assets constructed as discrete products for sale or lease. For example, **Walt Disney** capitalizes interest on assets constructed for its theme parks, resorts and other property, and on theatrical and television productions in process. During the construction period, interest is considered a cost necessary to get the asset ready for its intended use.

4. **What is the three-step process used to determine the amount of interest capitalized?** *(p. 523)*   The first step is to determine the average accumulated expenditures for the period. The second step is to multiply the average accumulated expenditures by an appropriate interest rate or rates to determine the amount of interest capitalized. A final step compares the interest determined in step two with actual interest incurred. Interest capitalized is limited to the amount of interest incurred.

5. **What is goodwill and how is it measured?** *(p. 510)*   Goodwill represents the unique value of a company as a whole over and above its identifiable tangible and intangible assets. Because goodwill can't be separated from a company, it's not possible for a buyer to acquire it without also acquiring the whole company or a controlling portion of it. Goodwill will appear as an asset in a balance sheet only when it was purchased in connection with the acquisition of another company. In that case, the capitalized cost of goodwill equals the fair value of the consideration exchanged for the company less the fair value of the net assets acquired. Goodwill is a residual asset; it's the amount left after other assets are identified and valued. Prior to the current standard for accounting for goodwill, we amortized (expensed over time) goodwill just like any other intangible asset. Now, just like for other intangible assets that have indefinite useful lives, we do not amortize goodwill. ●

THE BOTTOM LINE

● **LO1**   The initial cost of property, plant, and equipment and intangible assets acquired in an exchange transaction includes the purchase price and all expenditures necessary to bring the asset to its desired condition and location for use. The cost of a natural resource includes the acquisition costs for the use of land, the exploration and development costs incurred before production begins, and restoration costs incurred during or at the end of extraction. Purchased intangible assets are valued at their original cost to include the purchase price and legal and filing fees. (p. 504)

● **LO2**   If a lump-sum purchase involves different assets, it is necessary to allocate the lump-sum acquisition price among the separate items according to some logical allocation method. A widely used allocation method is to divide the lump-sum purchase price according to the individual assets' relative fair values. (p. 512)

● **LO3**   Assets acquired in exchange for deferred payment contracts are valued at their fair value or the present value of payments using a realistic interest rate. (p. 513)

● **LO4**   Assets acquired through the issuance of equity securities are valued at the fair value of the securities if known; if not known, the fair value of the assets received is used. Donated assets are valued at their fair value. (p. 515)

● **LO5** A key to profitability is how well a company manages and utilizes its assets. Financial analysts often use activity, or turnover, ratios to evaluate a company's effectiveness in managing its assets. Property, plant, and equipment (PP&E) usually are a company's primary revenue-generating assets. Their efficient use is critical to generating a satisfactory return to owners. One ratio that analysts often use to measure how effectively managers use PP&E is the fixed-asset turnover ratio. This ratio is calculated by dividing net sales by average fixed assets. (p. 516)

● **LO6** When an item of property, plant, and equipment or an intangible asset is sold, a gain or loss is recognized for the difference between the consideration received and the asset's book value. The basic principle used for nonmonetary exchanges is to value the asset(s) received based on the fair value of the asset(s) given up. In certain situations, the valuation of the asset(s) received is based on the book value of the asset(s) given up. (p. 517)

● **LO7** The cost of a self-constructed asset includes identifiable materials and labor and a portion of the company's manufacturing overhead costs. In addition, GAAP provide for the capitalization of interest incurred during construction. The amount of interest capitalized is equal to the average accumulated expenditures for the period multiplied by the appropriate interest rates, not to exceed actual interest incurred. (p. 521)

● **LO8** Research and development costs incurred to internally develop an intangible asset are expensed in the period incurred. Filing and legal costs for developed intangibles are capitalized. (p. 526)

● **LO9** Other than software development costs incurred after technological feasibility has been established, U.S. GAAP requires all research and development expenditures to be expensed in the period incurred. *IAS No. 38* draws a distinction between research activities and development activities. Research expenditures are expensed in the period incurred. However, development expenditures that meet specified criteria are capitalized as an intangible asset. (p. 532) ●

APPENDIX 10 OIL AND GAS ACCOUNTING

Chapter 1 characterized the establishment of accounting and reporting standards as a political process. Standards, particularly changes in standards, can have significant differential effects on companies, investors and creditors, and other interest groups. The FASB must consider potential economic consequences of a change in an accounting standard or the introduction of a new standard. The history of oil and gas accounting provides a good example of this political process and the effect of possible adverse economic consequences on the standard-setting process.

There are two generally accepted methods that companies can use to account for oil and gas exploration costs. The **successful efforts method** requires that exploration costs that are known *not* to have resulted in the discovery of oil or gas (sometimes referred to as *dry holes*) be included as expenses in the period the expenditures are made. The alternative, the **full-cost method,** allows costs incurred in searching for oil and gas within a large geographical area to be capitalized as assets and expensed in the future as oil and gas from the successful wells are removed from that area. Both of these methods are widely used. Illustration 10A–1 compares the two alternatives.

ILLUSTRATION 10A–1 Oil and Gas Accounting	The Shannon Oil Company incurred $2,000,000 in exploration costs for each of 10 oil wells drilled in 2011 in west Texas. Eight of the 10 wells were dry holes. The accounting treatment of the $20 million in total exploration costs will vary significantly depending on the accounting method used. The summary journal entries using each of the alternative methods are as follows:

	Successful Efforts			**Full Cost**		
Oil deposit	4,000,000		Oil deposit	20,000,000	
Exploration expense	16,000,000		Cash		20,000,000
Cash		20,000,000			

Using the full-cost method, Shannon would capitalize the entire $20 million which is expensed as oil from the two successful wells is depleted. On the other hand, using the successful efforts method, the cost of the unsuccessful wells is expensed in 2011, and only the $4 million cost related to the successful wells is capitalized and expensed in future periods as the oil is depleted.

In 1977 the FASB attempted to establish uniformity in the accounting treatment of oil and gas exploration costs. A standard was issued requiring all companies to use the successful efforts method.[31]

This Standard met with criticism from the oil and gas companies that were required to switch from full cost to successful efforts accounting. These companies felt that the switch would seriously depress their reported income over time. As a result, they argued, their ability to raise capital in the securities markets would be inhibited, which would result in a cutback of new exploration. The fear that the standard would cause domestic companies to significantly reduce oil and gas exploration and thus increase our dependence on foreign oil was compelling to the U.S. Congress, the SEC, and the Department of Energy.

Extensive pressure from Congress, the SEC, and affected companies forced the FASB to rescind the Standard. Presently, oil and gas companies can use either the successful efforts or full-cost method to account for oil and gas exploration costs. Of course, the method used must be disclosed. For example, Graphic 10A–1 shows how **Chevron Corp.** disclosed its use of the successful efforts method in a note to recent financial statements. ●

> Many feared that the requirement to switch to successful efforts accounting would cause a significant cutback in the exploration for new oil and gas in the United States.

Properties, Plant and Equipment
The successful efforts method is used for crude oil and gas exploration and production activities.

GRAPHIC 10A–1

Oil and Gas Accounting Disclosure—Chevron Corp.

Real World Financials

QUESTIONS FOR REVIEW OF KEY TOPICS

Q 10–1   Explain the difference between tangible and intangible long-lived, revenue-producing assets.

Q 10–2   What is included in the original cost of property, plant, and equipment and intangible assets acquired in an exchange transaction?

Q 10–3   Identify the costs associated with the initial valuation of a developed natural resource.

Q 10–4   Briefly summarize the accounting treatment for intangible assets, explaining the difference between purchased and internally developed intangible assets.

Q 10–5   What is goodwill and how is it measured?

Q 10–6   Explain the method generally used to allocate the cost of a lump-sum purchase to the individual assets acquired.

Q 10–7   When an asset is acquired and a note payable is assumed, explain how acquisition cost of the asset is determined when the interest rate for the note is less than the current market rate for similar notes.

Q 10–8   Explain how assets acquired in exchange for equity securities are valued.

Q 10–9   Explain how property, plant, and equipment and intangible assets acquired through donation are valued.

Q 10–10   When an item of property, plant, and equipment is disposed of, how is gain or loss on disposal computed?

Q 10–11   What is the basic principle for valuing property, plant, and equipment and intangible assets acquired in exchange for other nonmonetary assets?

Q 10–12   Identify the two exceptions to valuing property, plant, and equipment and intangible assets acquired in nonmonetary exchanges at the fair value of the asset(s) given up.

Q 10–13   In what situations is interest capitalized?

Q 10–14   Define average accumulated expenditures and explain how it is computed.

Q 10–15   Explain the difference between the specific interest method and the weighted-average method in determining the amount of interest to be capitalized.

Q 10–16   Define R&D according to U.S. GAAP.

Q 10–17   Explain the accounting treatment of equipment acquired for use in R&D projects.

Q 10–18   Explain the accounting treatment of costs incurred to develop computer software.

---

[31]The rescinded standard was "Financial Accounting and Reporting by Oil and Gas Producing Companies," *Statement of Financial Accounting Standards No. 19* (Stamford, Conn.: FASB, 1977). Authoritative guidance on this topic can now be found at FASB ASC 932: Extractive Activities–Oil and Gas.

Q 10–19 Explain the difference in the accounting treatment of the cost of developed technology and the cost of in-process R&D in an acquisition.

IFRS Q 10–20 Identify any differences between U.S. GAAP and International Financial Reporting Standards in the treatment of research and development expenditures.

IFRS Q 10–21 Identify any differences between U.S. GAAP and International Financial Reporting Standards in the treatment of software development costs.

Q 10–22 (Based on Appendix 10) Explain the difference between the successful efforts and the full-cost methods of accounting for oil and gas exploration costs.

BRIEF EXERCISES

BE 10–1
Acquisition cost; machine
● LO1

Beaverton Lumber purchased a milling machine for $35,000. In addition to the purchase price, Beaverton made the following expenditures: freight, $1,500; installation, $3,000; testing, $2,000; personal property tax on the machine for the first year, $500. What is the initial cost of the machine?

BE 10–2
Acquisition cost; land and building
● LO1

Fullerton Waste Management purchased land and a warehouse for $600,000. In addition to the purchase price, Fullerton made the following expenditures related to the acquisition: broker's commission, $30,000; title insurance, $3,000; miscellaneous closing costs, $6,000. The warehouse was immediately demolished at a cost of $18,000 in anticipation of the building of a new warehouse. Determine the amounts Fullerton should capitalize as the cost of the land and the building.

BE 10–3
Lump-sum acquisition
● LO2

Refer to the situation described in BE 10–2. Assume that Fullerton decides to use the warehouse rather than demolish it. An independent appraisal estimates the fair values of the land and warehouse at $420,000 and $280,000, respectively. Determine the amounts Fullerton should capitalize as the cost of the land and the building.

BE 10–4
Cost of a natural resource
● LO1

Smithson Mining operates a silver mine in Nevada. Acquisition, exploration, and development costs totaled $5.6 million. After the silver is extracted in approximately five years, Smithson is obligated to restore the land to its original condition, including constructing a wildlife preserve. The company's controller has provided the following three cash flow possibilities for the restoration costs: (1) $500,000, 20% probability; (2) $550,000, 45% probability; and (3) $650,000, 35% probability. The company's credit-adjusted, risk-free rate of interest is 6%. What is the initial cost of the silver mine?

BE 10–5
Cost of a natural resource
● LO1

Refer to the situation described in BE 10–4. What is the carrying value of the asset retirement liability at the end of one year? Assuming that the actual restoration costs incurred after extraction is completed are $596,000, what amount of gain or loss will Smithson recognize on retirement of the liability?

BE 10–6
Goodwill
● LO1

Pro-tech Software acquired all of the outstanding stock of Reliable Software for $14 million. The book value of Reliable's net assets (assets minus liabilities) was $8.3 million. The fair values of Reliable's assets and liabilities equaled their book values with the exception of certain intangible assets whose fair values exceeded book values by $2.5 million. Calculate the amount paid for goodwill.

BE 10–7
Acquisition cost; noninterest-bearing note
● LO3

On June 30, 2011, Kimberly Farms purchased custom-made harvesting machinery from a local producer. In payment, Kimberly signed a noninterest-bearing note requiring the payment of $60,000 in two years. The fair value of the machinery is not known, but an 8% interest rate properly reflects the time value of money for this type of loan agreement. At what amount will Kimberly initially value the machinery? How much interest expense will Kimberly recognize in its income statement for this note for the year ended December 31, 2011?

BE 10–8
Acquisition cost; issuance of equity securities
● LO4

Shackelford Corporation acquired a patent from its founder, Jim Shackelford, in exchange for 50,000 shares of the company's nopar common stock. On the date of the exchange, the common stock had a fair value of $22 per share. Determine the cost of the patent.

BE 10–9
Fixed-asset turnover ratio; solve for unknown
● LO5

The balance sheets of Pinewood Resorts reported net fixed assets of $740,000 and $940,000 at the end of 2010 and 2011, respectively. The fixed-asset turnover ratio for 2011 was 3.25. Calculate Pinewood's net sales for 2011.

BE 10–10
Disposal of
property, plant, and
equipment
● LO6

Lawler Clothing sold manufacturing equipment for $16,000. Lawler originally purchased the equipment for $80,000, and depreciation through the date of sale totaled $71,000. What was the gain or loss on the sale of the equipment?

BE 10–11
Nonmonetary
exchange
● LO6

Calaveras Tire exchanged machinery for two pickup trucks. The book value and fair value of the machinery were $20,000 (original cost of $65,000 less accumulated depreciation of $45,000) and $17,000, respectively. To equalize fair values, Calaveras paid $8,000 in cash. At what amount will Calaveras value the pickup trucks? How much gain or loss will the company recognize on the exchange? Assume the exchange has commercial substance.

BE 10–12
Nonmonetary
exchange
● LO6

Refer to the situation described in BE 10–11. Answer the questions assuming that the fair value of the machinery was $24,000, instead of $17,000.

BE 10–13
Nonmonetary
exchange
● LO6

Refer to the situation described in BE 10–12. Answer the questions assuming that the exchange lacks commercial substance.

BE 10–14
Interest
capitalization
● LO7

A company constructs a building for its own use. Construction began on January 1 and ended on December 30. The expenditures for construction were as follows: January 1, $500,000; March 31, $600,000; June 30, $400,000; October 30, $600,000. To help finance construction, the company arranged a 7% construction loan on January 1 for $700,000. The company's other borrowings, outstanding for the whole year, consisted of a $3 million loan and a $5 million note with interest rates of 8% and 6%, respectively. Assuming the company uses the *specific interest method,* calculate the amount of interest capitalized for the year.

BE 10–15
Interest
capitalization
● LO7

Refer to the situation described in BE 10–14. Assuming the company uses the *weighted-average method,* calculate the amount of interest capitalized for the year.

BE 10–16
Research and
development
● LO8

Maxtor Technology incurred the following costs during the year related to the creation of a new type of personal computer monitor:

Salaries	$220,000
Depreciation on R&D facilities and equipment	125,000
Utilities and other direct costs incurred for the R&D facilities	66,000
Patent filing and related legal costs	22,000
Payment to another company for performing a portion of the development work	120,000
Costs of adapting the new monitor for the specific needs of a customer	80,000

What amount should Maxtor report as research and development expense in its income statement?

EXERCISES

An alternate exercise and problem set is available on the text website: www.mhhe.com/spiceland6e

E 10–1
Acquisition costs;
land and building
● LO1

On March 1, 2011, Beldon Corporation purchased land as a factory site for $60,000. An old building on the property was demolished, and construction began on a new building that was completed on December 15, 2011. Costs incurred during this period are listed below:

Demolition of old building	$ 4,000
Architect's fees (for new building)	12,000
Legal fees for title investigation of land	2,000
Property taxes on land (for period beginning March 1, 2011)	3,000
Construction costs	500,000
Interest on construction loan	5,000

Salvaged materials resulting from the demolition of the old building were sold for $2,000.

Required:

Determine the amounts that Beldon should capitalize as the cost of the land and the new building.

E 10–2
Acquisition cost; machinery
● LO1

Oaktree Company purchased a new machine and made the following expenditures:

Purchase price	$45,000
Sales tax	2,200
Freight charges for shipment of machine	700
Insurance on the machine for the first year	900
Installation of machine	1,000

The machine, including sales tax, was purchased on open account, with payment due in 30 days. The other expenditures listed above were paid in cash.

Required:

Prepare the necessary journal entries to record the above expenditures.

E 10–3
Acquisition costs; lump-sum acquisition
● LO1 LO2

Semtech Manufacturing purchased land and building for $4 million. In addition to the purchase price, Semtech made the following expenditures in connection with the purchase of the land and building:

Title insurance	$16,000
Legal fees for drawing the contract	5,000
Pro-rated property taxes for the period after acquisition	36,000
State transfer fees	4,000

An independent appraisal estimated the fair values of the land and building, if purchased separately, at $3.3 and $1.1 million, respectively. Shortly after acquisition, Semtech spent $82,000 to construct a parking lot and $40,000 for landscaping.

Required:

1. Determine the initial valuation of each asset Semtech acquired in these transactions.
2. Repeat requirement 1, assuming that immediately after acquisition, Semtech demolished the building. Demolition costs were $250,000 and the salvaged materials were sold for $6,000. In addition, Semtech spent $86,000 clearing and grading the land in preparation for the construction of a new building.

E 10–4
Cost of a natural resource
● LO1

Jackpot Mining Company operates a copper mine in central Montana. The company paid $1,000,000 in 2011 for the mining site and spent an additional $600,000 to prepare the mine for extraction of the copper. After the copper is extracted in approximately four years, the company is required to restore the land to its original condition, including repaving of roads and replacing a greenbelt. The company has provided the following three cash flow possibilities for the restoration costs:

	Cash Outflow	Probability
1	$300,000	25%
2	400,000	40%
3	600,000	35%

To aid extraction, Jackpot purchased some new equipment on July 1, 2011, for $120,000. After the copper is removed from this mine, the equipment will be sold. The credit-adjusted, risk-free rate of interest is 10%.

Required:

1. Determine the cost of the copper mine.
2. Prepare the journal entries to record the acquisition costs of the mine and the purchase of equipment.

E 10–5
Intangibles
● LO1

Freitas Corporation was organized early in 2011. The following expenditures were made during the first few months of the year:

Attorneys' fees in connection with the organization of the corporation	$ 12,000
State filing fees and other incorporation costs	3,000
Purchase of a patent	20,000
Legal and other fees for transfer of the patent	2,000
Purchase of furniture	30,000
Pre-opening salaries	40,000
Total	$107,000

Required:

Prepare a summary journal entry to record the $107,000 in cash expenditures.

E 10–6
Goodwill
● LO1

On March 31, 2011, Wolfson Corporation acquired all of the outstanding common stock of Barney Corporation for $17,000,000 in cash. The book values and fair values of Barney's assets and liabilities were as follows:

	Book Value	Fair Value
Current assets	$ 6,000,000	$ 7,500,000
Property, plant, and equipment	11,000,000	14,000,000
Other assets	1,000,000	1,500,000
Current liabilities	4,000,000	4,000,000
Long-term liabilities	6,000,000	5,500,000

Required:
Calculate the amount paid for goodwill.

E 10–7
Goodwill
● LO1

Johnson Corporation purchased all of the outstanding common stock of Smith Corporation for $11,000,000 in cash. The book value of Smith's net assets (assets minus liabilities) was $7,800,000. The fair values of all of Smith's assets and liabilities were equal to their book values with the following exceptions:

	Book Value	Fair Value
Receivables	$1,300,000	$1,100,000
Property, plant, and equipment	8,000,000	9,400,000
Intangible assets	200,000	1,200,000

Required:
Calculate the amount paid for goodwill.

E 10–8
Lump-sum
acquisition
● LO2

Pinewood Company purchased two buildings on four acres of land. The lump-sum purchase price was $900,000. According to independent appraisals, the fair values were $450,000 (building A) and $250,000 (building B) for the buildings and $300,000 for the land.

Required:
Determine the initial valuation of the buildings and the land.

E 10–9
Acquisition cost;
noninterest-bearing
note
● LO3

On January 1, 2011, Byner Company purchased a used tractor. Byner paid $5,000 down and signed a noninterest-bearing note requiring $25,000 to be paid on December 31, 2013. The fair value of the tractor is not determinable. An interest rate of 10% properly reflects the time value of money for this type of loan agreement. The company's fiscal year-end is December 31.

Required:
1. Prepare the journal entry to record the acquisition of the tractor. Round computations to the nearest dollar.
2. How much interest expense will the company include in its 2011 and 2012 income statements for this note?
3. What is the amount of the liability the company will report in its 2011 and 2012 balance sheets for this note?

E 10–10
Acquisition costs;
noninterest-bearing
note
● LO1 LO3

Teradene Corporation purchased land as a factory site and contracted with Maxtor Construction to construct a factory. Teradene made the following expenditures related to the acquisition of the land, building, and machinery to equip the factory:

Purchase price of the land	$1,200,000
Demolition and removal of old building	80,000
Clearing and grading the land before construction	150,000
Various closing costs in connection with acquiring the land	42,000
Architect's fee for the plans for the new building	50,000
Payments to Maxtor for building construction	3,250,000
Machinery purchased	860,000
Freight charges on machinery	32,000
Trees, plants, and other landscaping	45,000
Installation of a sprinkler system for the landscaping	5,000
Cost to build special platforms and install wiring for the machinery	12,000
Cost of trial runs to ensure proper installation of the machinery	7,000
Fire and theft insurance on the factory for the first year of use	24,000

In addition to the above expenditures, Teradene purchased four forklifts from **Caterpillar.** In payment, Teradene paid $16,000 cash and signed a noninterest-bearing note requiring the payment of $70,000 in one year. An interest rate of 7% properly reflects the time value of money for this type of loan.

Required:
Determine the initial valuation of each of the assets Teradene acquired in the above transactions.

E 10–11
Acquisition cost;
issuance of equity
securities and
donation
● LO4

On February 1, 2011, the Xilon Corporation issued 5,000 shares of its nopar common stock in exchange for five acres of land located in the city of Monrovia. On the date of the acquisition, Xilon's common stock had a fair value of $18 per share. An office building was constructed on the site by an independent contractor. The building was completed on November 2, 2011, at a cost of $600,000. Xilon paid $400,000 in cash and the remainder was paid by the city of Monrovia.

Required:
Prepare the journal entries to record the acquisition of the land and the building.

E 10–12
Fixed-asset
turnover ratio;
Cisco
● LO5

Real World Financials

Cisco Systems, Inc., reported the following information in its 2009 financial statements ($ in millions):

	2009	2008
Balance sheets		
Property, plant, and equipment (net)	$ 4,043	$4,151
Income statement		
Net sales for 2009	$36,117	

Required:
1. Calculate Cisco's 2009 fixed-asset turnover ratio.
2. How would you interpret this ratio?

E 10–13
Disposal of
property, plant, and
equipment
● LO6

Funseth Farms, Inc. purchased a tractor in 2008 at a cost of $30,000. The tractor was sold for $3,000 in 2011. Depreciation recorded through the disposal date totaled $26,000.

Required:
1. Prepare the journal entry to record the sale.
2. Assuming that the tractor was sold for $10,000, prepare the journal entry to record the sale.

E 10–14
Nonmonetary
exchange
● LO6

Cedric Company recently traded in an older model computer for a new model. The old model's book value was $180,000 (original cost of $400,000 less $220,000 in accumulated depreciation) and its fair value was $200,000. Cedric paid $60,000 to complete the exchange which has commercial substance.

Required:
Prepare the journal entry to record the exchange.

E 10–15
Nonmonetary
exchange
● LO6

[This is a variation of the previous exercise.]

Required:
Assume the same facts as in Exercise 10–14, except that the fair value of the old equipment is $170,000. Prepare the journal entry to record the exchange.

E 10–16
Nonmonetary
exchange
● LO6

The Bronco Corporation exchanged land for equipment. The land had a book value of $120,000 and a fair value of $150,000. Bronco paid the owner of the equipment $10,000 to complete the exchange which has commercial substance.

Required:
1. What is the fair value of the equipment?
2. Prepare the journal entry to record the exchange.

E 10–17
Nonmonetary
exchange
● LO6

[This is a variation of the previous exercise.]

Required:
Assume the same facts as in Exercise 10–16 except that Bronco *received* $10,000 from the owner of the equipment to complete the exchange.
1. What is the fair value of the equipment?
2. Prepare the journal entry to record the exchange.

E 10–18
Nonmonetary
exchange
● LO6

The Tinsley Company exchanged land that it had been holding for future plant expansion for a more suitable parcel located farther from residential areas. Tinsley carried the land at its original cost of $30,000. According to an independent appraisal, the land currently is worth $72,000. Tinsley gave $14,000 in cash to complete the transaction.

Required:
1. What is the fair value of the new parcel of land received by Tinsley?
2. Prepare the journal entry to record the exchange assuming the exchange has commercial substance.
3. Prepare the journal entry to record the exchange assuming the exchange lacks commercial substance.

E 10–19
Acquisition cost;
multiple methods
● **LO1 LO3 LO4
LO6**

Connors Corporation acquired manufacturing equipment for use in its assembly line. Below are four *independent* situations relating to the acquisition of the equipment.

1. The equipment was purchased on account for $25,000. Credit terms were 2/10, n/30. Payment was made within the discount period and the company records the purchases of equipment net of discounts.

2. Connors gave the seller a noninterest-bearing note. The note required payment of $27,000 one year from date of purchase. The fair value of the equipment is not determinable. An interest rate of 10% properly reflects the time value of money in this situation.

3. Connors traded in old equipment that had a book value of $6,000 (original cost of $14,000 and accumulated depreciation of $8,000) and paid cash of $22,000. The old equipment had a fair value of $2,500 on the date of the exchange. The exchange has commercial substance.

4. Connors issued 1,000 shares of its nopar common stock in exchange for the equipment. The market value of the common stock was not determinable. The equipment could have been purchased for $24,000 in cash.

Required:
For each of the above situations, prepare the journal entry required to record the acquisition of the equipment. Round computations to the nearest dollar.

E 10–20
FASB codification
research
● **LO6**

The *FASB Accounting Standards Codification* represents the single source of authoritative U.S. generally accepted accounting principles.

Required:
1. Obtain the relevant authoritative literature on nonmonetary exchanges using the FASB's Codification Research System at the FASB website (**www.fasb.org**). Identify the Codification topic number for nonmonetary transactions.
2. What are the specific citations that list the disclosure requirements for nonmonetary transactions?
3. Describe the disclosure requirements.

E 10–21
FASB codification
research
● **LO1 LO6 LO7
LO8**

Access the FASB's Codification Research System at the FASB website (**www.fasb.org**). Determine the specific citation for each of the following items:
1. The disclosure requirements in the notes to the financial statements for depreciation on property, plant, and equipment.
2. The criteria for determining commercial substance in a nonmonetary exchange.
3. The disclosure requirements for interest capitalization.
4. The elements of costs to be included as R&D activities.

E 10–22
Interest
capitalization
● **LO7**

On January 1, 2011, the Marjlee Company began construction of an office building to be used as its corporate headquarters. The building was completed early in 2012. Construction expenditures for 2011, which were incurred evenly throughout the year, totaled $6,000,000. Marjlee had the following debt obligations which were outstanding during all of 2011:

Construction loan, 10%	$1,500,000
Long-term note, 9%	2,000,000
Long-term note, 6%	4,000,000

Required:
Calculate the amount of interest capitalized in 2011 for the building using the specific interest method.

E 10–23
Interest
capitalization
● **LO7**

On January 1, 2011, the Shagri Company began construction on a new manufacturing facility for its own use. The building was completed in 2012. The only interest-bearing debt the company had outstanding during 2011 was long-term bonds with a book value of $10,000,000 and an effective interest rate of 8%. Construction expenditures incurred during 2011 were as follows:

January 1	$500,000
March 1	600,000
July 31	480,000
September 30	600,000
December 31	300,000

Required:
Calculate the amount of interest capitalized for 2011.

E 10–24
Interest
capitalization
● LO7

On January 2, 2011, the Highlands Company began construction on a new manufacturing facility for its own use. The building was completed in 2012. The company borrowed $1,500,000 at 8% on January 1 to help finance the construction. In addition to the construction loan, Highlands had the following debt outstanding throughout 2011:

$5,000,000, 12% bonds
$3,000,000, 8% long-term note

Construction expenditures incurred during 2011 were as follows:

January 1	$ 600,000
March 31	1,200,000
June 30	800,000
September 30	600,000
December 31	400,000

Required:
Calculate the amount of interest capitalized for 2011 using the specific interest method.

E 10–25
Research and
development
● LO8

In 2011, Space Technology Company modified its model Z2 satellite to incorporate a new communication device. The company made the following expenditures:

Basic research to develop the technology	$2,000,000
Engineering design work	680,000
Development of a prototype device	300,000
Acquisition of equipment	60,000
Testing and modification of the prototype	200,000
Legal and other fees for patent application on the new communication system	40,000
Legal fees for successful defense of the new patent	20,000
Total	$3,300,000

The equipment will be used on this and other research projects. Depreciation on the equipment for 2011 is $10,000.

During your year-end review of the accounts related to intangibles, you discover that the company has capitalized all of the above as costs of the patent. Management contends that the device simply represents an improvement of the existing communication system of the satellite and, therefore, should be capitalized.

Required:
Prepare correcting entries that reflect the appropriate treatment of the expenditures.

E 10–26
Research and
development
● LO8

Delaware Company incurred the following research and development costs during 2011:

Salaries and wages for lab research	$ 400,000
Materials used in R&D projects	200,000
Purchase of equipment	900,000
Fees paid to outsiders for R&D projects	320,000
Patent filing and legal costs for a developed product	65,000
Salaries, wages, and supplies for R&D work performed for another company under a contract	350,000
Total	$2,235,000

The equipment has a seven-year life and will be used for a number of research projects. Depreciation for 2011 is $120,000.

Required:
Calculate the amount of research and development expense that Delaware should report in its 2011 income statement.

E 10–27
IFRS; research and
development
● LO8 LO9

Janson Pharmaceuticals incurred the following costs in 2011 related to a new cancer drug:

Research for new formulas	$2,425,000
Development of a new formula	1,600,000
Legal and filing fees for a patent for the new formula	60,000
Total	$4,085,000

The development costs were incurred after technological and commercial feasibility was established and after the future economic benefits were deemed probable. The project was successfully completed and the new drug was patented before the end of the 2011 fiscal year.

Required:

1. Calculate the amount of research and development expense Janson should report in its 2011 income statement related to this project.

2. Repeat requirement 1 assuming that Janson prepares its financial statements according to International Financial Reporting Standards.

E 10–28
Concepts;
terminology

● LO1 LO4 LO6
LO7

Listed below are several terms and phrases associated with property, plant, and equipment and intangible assets. Pair each item from List A with the item from List B (by letter) that is most appropriately associated with it.

List A	List B
____ 1. Depreciation	a. Exclusive right to display a word, a symbol, or an emblem.
____ 2. Depletion	b. Exclusive right to benefit from a creative work.
____ 3. Amortization	c. Assets that represent rights.
____ 4. Average accumulated expenditures	d. The allocation of cost for natural resources.
	e. Purchase price less fair value of net identifiable assets.
____ 5. Revenue—donation of asset	f. The allocation of cost for plant and equipment.
____ 6. Nonmonetary exchange	g. Approximation of average amount of debt if all construction funds were borrowed.
____ 7. Natural resources	h. Account credited when assets are donated to a corporation.
____ 8. Intangible assets	i. The allocation of cost for intangible assets.
____ 9. Copyright	j. Basic principle is to value assets acquired using fair value of assets given.
____ 10. Trademark	k. Wasting assets.
____ 11. Goodwill	

E 10–29
Software
development costs

● LO8

Early in 2011, the Excalibur Company began developing a new software package to be marketed. The project was completed in December 2011 at a cost of $6 million. Of this amount, $4 million was spent before technological feasibility was established. Excalibur expects a useful life of five years for the new product with total revenues of $10 million. During 2012, revenue of $4 million was recognized.

Required:

1. Prepare a journal entry to record the 2011 development costs.

2. Calculate the required amortization for 2012.

3. At what amount should the computer software costs be reported in the December 31, 2012, balance sheet?

E 10–30
Full-cost and
successful efforts
methods compared

● Appendix

The Manguino Oil Company incurred exploration costs in 2011 searching and drilling for oil as follows:

Well 101	$ 50,000
Well 102	60,000
Well 103	80,000
Wells 104–108	260,000
Total	$450,000

It was determined that Wells 104–108 were dry holes and were abandoned. Wells 101, 102, and 103 were determined to have sufficient oil reserves to be commercially successful.

Required:

1. Prepare a summary journal entry to record the indicated costs assuming that the company uses the full-cost method of accounting for exploration costs. All of the exploration costs were paid in cash.

2. Prepare a summary journal entry to record the indicated costs assuming that the company uses the successful efforts method of accounting for exploration costs. All of the exploration costs were paid in cash.

CPA AND CMA REVIEW QUESTIONS

**CPA Exam
Questions**

● LO1

The following questions are used in the Kaplan CPA Review Course to study property, plant, and equipment and intangible assets while preparing for the CPA examination. Determine the response that best completes the statements or questions.

1. Simons Company purchased land to build a new factory. The following expenditures were made in conjunction with the land purchase:
   • Purchase price of the land, $150,000
   • Real estate commissions of 7% of the purchase price

- Land survey, $5,000
- Back taxes, $5,000

What is the initial value of the land?
a. $160,000
b. $160,500
c. $165,500
d. $170,500

LO1

2. During 2011, Burr Co. made the following expenditures related to the acquisition of land and the construction of a building:

Purchase price of land	$ 60,000
Legal fees for contracts to purchase land	2,000
Architects' fees	8,000
Demolition of old building on site	5,000
Sale of scrap from old building	3,000
Construction cost of new building (fully completed)	350,000

What amounts should be recorded as the initial values of the land and the building?

	Land	Building
a.	$60,000	$360,000
b.	$62,000	$360,000
c.	$64,000	$358,000
d.	$65,000	$362,000

LO3

3. On December 31, 2011, Bart Inc. purchased a machine from Fell Corp. in exchange for a noninterest-bearing note requiring eight payments of $20,000. The first payment was made on December 31, 2011, and the remaining seven payments are due annually on each December 31, beginning in 2012. At the date of the transaction, the prevailing rate of interest for this type of note was 11%. Present value factors are as follows:

Period	Present value of ordinary annuity of 1 at 11%	Present value of an annuity due of 1 at 11%
7	4.712	5.231
8	5.146	5.712

The initial value of the machine is
a. $ 94,240
b. $102,920
c. $104,620
d. $114,240

LO6

4. Amble Inc. exchanged a truck with a book value of $12,000 and a fair value of $20,000 for a truck and $5,000 cash. The exchange has commercial substance. At what amount should Amble record the truck received?
a. $12,000
b. $15,000
c. $20,000
d. $25,000

LO7

5. Dahl Corporation has just built a machine to produce car doors. Dahl had to build this machine because it couldn't purchase one that met its specifications. The following are the costs related to the machine's construction and the first month of operations:
- Construction materials, $20,000
- Labor, $9,000 (construction, $3,000; testing, $1,000; operations, $5,000)
- Engineering fees, $5,000
- Utilities, $4,000 (construction, $1,000; testing, $1,000; operations, $2,000)

What is the initial value of the machine?
a. $28,000
b. $29,000
c. $31,000
d. $38,000

LO7

6. Cole Co. began constructing a building for its own use in January 2011. During 2011, Cole incurred interest of $50,000 on specific construction debt, and $20,000 on other borrowings. Interest computed on the weighted-average amount of accumulated expenditures for the building during 2011 was $40,000. What amount of interest should Cole capitalize?

a. $20,000
b. $40,000
c. $50,000
d. $70,000

● LO8   7. On December 31, 2010, Bit Co. had capitalized costs for a new computer software product with an economic life of five years. Sales for 2011 were 30 percent of expected total sales of the software. At December 31, 2011, the software had a fair value equal to 90 percent of the capitalized cost. What percentage of the original capitalized cost should be reported as the net amount in Bit's December 31, 2011, balance sheet?
a. 70%
b. 72%
c. 80%
d. 90%

● LO8   8. During the current year, Orr Company incurred the following costs:

Research and development services performed by Key Corp. for Orr	$150,000
Design, construction, and testing of preproduction prototypes and models	200,000
Testing in search for new products or process alternatives	175,000

In its income statement for the current year, what amount should Orr report as research and development expense?
a. $150,000
b. $200,000
c. $350,000
d. $525,000

CMA Exam Questions

The following questions dealing with property, plant, and equipment and intangible assets are adapted from questions that previously appeared on Certified Management Accountant (CMA) examinations. The CMA designation sponsored by the Institute of Management Accountants (**www.imanet.org**) provides members with an objective measure of knowledge and competence in the field of management accounting. Determine the response that best completes the statements or questions.

● LO1   1. Pearl Corporation acquired manufacturing machinery on January 1 for $9,000. During the year, the machine produced 1,000 units, of which 600 were sold. There was no work-in-process inventory at the beginning or at the end of the year. Installation charges of $300 and delivery charges of $200 were also incurred. The machine is expected to have a useful life of five years with an estimated salvage value of $1,500. Pearl uses the straight-line depreciation method. The original cost of the machinery to be recorded in Pearl's books is
a. $9,500
b. $9,300
c. $9,200
d. $9,000

● LO6   Questions 2 and 3 are based on the following information. Harper is contemplating exchanging a machine used in its operations for a similar machine on May 31. Harper will exchange machines with either Austin Corporation or Lubin Company. The data relating to the machines are presented below. Assume that the exchanges would have commercial substance.

	Harper	Austin	Lubin
Original cost of the machine	$162,500	$180,000	$150,000
Accumulated depreciation thru May 31	98,500	70,000	65,000
Fair value at May 31	80,000	95,000	60,000

2. If Harper exchanges its used machine and $15,000 cash for Austin's used machine, the gain that Harper should recognize from this transaction for financial reporting purposes would be
a. $0
b. $2,526
c. $15,000
d. $16,000

3. If Harper exchanges its used machine for Lubin's used machine and also receives $20,000 cash, the gain that Harper should recognize from this transaction for financial reporting purposes would be
a. $0
b. $4,000
c. $16,000
d. $25,000

PROBLEMS

An alternate exercise and problem set is available on the text website: www.mhhe.com/spiceland6e

P 10–1
Acquisition costs
● LO1 through LO4

Tristar Production Company began operations on September 1, 2011. Listed below are a number of transactions that occurred during its first four months of operations.

1. On September 1, the company acquired five acres of land with a building that will be used as a warehouse. Tristar paid $100,000 in cash for the property. According to appraisals, the land had a fair value of $75,000 and the building had a fair value of $45,000.

2. On September 1, Tristar signed a $40,000 noninterest-bearing note to purchase equipment. The $40,000 payment is due on September 1, 2012. Assume that 8% is a reasonable interest rate.

3. On September 15, a truck was donated to the corporation. Similar trucks were selling for $2,500.

4. On September 18, the company paid its lawyer $3,000 for organizing the corporation.

5. On October 10, Tristar purchased machinery for cash. The purchase price was $15,000 and $500 in freight charges also were paid.

6. On December 2, Tristar acquired various items of office equipment. The company was short of cash and could not pay the $5,500 normal cash price. The supplier agreed to accept 200 shares of the company's nopar common stock in exchange for the equipment. The fair value of the stock is not readily determinable.

7. On December 10, the company acquired a tract of land at a cost of $20,000. It paid $2,000 down and signed a 10% note with both principal and interest due in one year. Ten percent is an appropriate rate of interest for this note.

Required:
Prepare journal entries to record each of the above transactions.

P 10–2
Acquisition costs; land and building
● LO1 LO2 LO7

On January 1, 2011, the Blackstone Corporation purchased a tract of land (site number 11) with a building for $600,000. Additionally, Blackstone paid a real estate broker's commission of $36,000, legal fees of $6,000, and title insurance of $18,000. The closing statement indicated that the land value was $500,000 and the building value was $100,000. Shortly after acquisition, the building was razed at a cost of $75,000.

Blackstone entered into a $3,000,000 fixed-price contract with Barnett Builders, Inc., on March 1, 2011, for the construction of an office building on land site 11. The building was completed and occupied on September 30, 2012. Additional construction costs were incurred as follows:

Plans, specifications, and blueprints	$12,000
Architects' fees for design and supervision	95,000

To finance the construction cost, Blackstone borrowed $3,000,000 on March 1, 2011. The loan is payable in 10 annual installments of $300,000 plus interest at the rate of 14%. Blackstone's average amounts of accumulated building construction expenditures were as follows:

For the period March 1 to December 31, 2011	$ 900,000
For the period January 1 to September 30, 2012	2,300,000

Required:
1. Prepare a schedule that discloses the individual costs making up the balance in the land account in respect of land site 11 as of September 30, 2012.

2. Prepare a schedule that discloses the individual costs that should be capitalized in the office building account as of September 30, 2012.

(AICPA adapted)

P 10–3
Acquisition costs
● LO1 LO4 LO6

The plant asset and accumulated depreciation accounts of Pell Corporation had the following balances at December 31, 2010:

	Plant Asset	Accumulated Depreciation
Land	$ 350,000	$ —
Land improvements	180,000	45,000
Building	1,500,000	350,000
Machinery and equipment	1,158,000	405,000
Automobiles	150,000	112,000

Transactions during 2011 were as follows:

a. On January 2, 2011, machinery and equipment were purchased at a total invoice cost of $260,000, which included a $5,500 charge for freight. Installation costs of $27,000 were incurred.

b. On March 31, 2011, a machine purchased for $58,000 in 2007 was sold for $36,500. Depreciation recorded through the date of sale totaled $24,650.

c. On May 1, 2011, expenditures of $50,000 were made to repave parking lots at Pell's plant location. The work was necessitated by damage caused by severe winter weather.

d. On November 1, 2011, Pell acquired a tract of land with an existing building in exchange for 10,000 shares of Pell's common stock that had a market price of $38 per share. Pell paid legal fees and title insurance totaling $23,000. Shortly after acquisition, the building was razed at a cost of $35,000 in anticipation of new building construction in 2012.

e. On December 31, 2011, Pell purchased a new automobile for $15,250 cash and trade-in of an old automobile purchased for $18,000 in 2007. Depreciation on the old automobile recorded through December 31, 2011, totaled $13,500. The fair value of the old automobile was $3,750.

Required:

1. Prepare a schedule analyzing the changes in each of the plant assets during 2011, with detailed supporting computations.

2. Prepare a schedule showing the gain or loss from each asset disposal that would be recognized in Pell's income statement for the year ended December 31, 2011.

(AICPA adapted)

P 10–4
Intangibles
● LO1 LO8

The Horstmeyer Corporation commenced operations early in 2011. A number of expenditures were made during 2011 that were debited to one account called *intangible asset.* A recap of the $644,000 balance in this account at the end of 2011 is as follows:

Date	Transaction	Amount
2/3/11	State incorporation fees and legal costs related to organizing the corporation	$ 7,000
3/1/11	Fire insurance premium for three-year period	6,000
3/15/11	Purchased a copyright	20,000
4/30/11	Research and development costs	40,000
6/15/11	Legal fees for filing a patent on a new product resulting from an R&D project	3,000
9/30/11	Legal fee for successful defense of patent developed above	12,000
10/13/11	Entered into a 10-year franchise agreement with franchisor	40,000
Various	Advertising costs	16,000
11/30/11	Purchase of all of the outstanding common stock of Stiltz Corp.	500,000
	Total	$644,000

The total purchase price of the Stiltz Corp. stock was debited to this account. The fair values of Stiltz Corp.'s assets and liabilities on the date of the purchase were as follows:

Receivables	$ 100,000
Equipment	350,000
Patent	150,000
Total assets	600,000
Note payable assumed	(220,000)
Fair value of net assets	$ 380,000

Required:

Prepare the necessary journal entries to clear the intangible asset account and to set up accounts for separate intangible assets, other types of assets, and expenses indicated by the transactions.

P 10–5
Acquisition costs;
journal entries
● LO1 LO3 LO6
LO8

Consider each of the transactions below. All of the expenditures were made in cash.

1. The Edison Company spent $12,000 during the year for experimental purposes in connection with the development of a new product.

2. In April, the Marshall Company lost a patent infringement suit and paid the plaintiff $7,500.

3. In March, the Cleanway Laundromat bought equipment. Cleanway paid $6,000 down and signed a noninterest-bearing note requiring the payment of $18,000 in nine months. The cash price for this equipment was $23,000.

4. On June 1, the Jamsen Corporation installed a sprinkler system throughout the building at a cost of $28,000.

5. The Mayer Company, plaintiff, paid $12,000 in legal fees in November, in connection with a successful infringement suit on its patent.

6. The Johnson Company traded its old machine with an original cost of $7,400 and a book value of $3,000 plus cash of $8,000 for a new one that had a fair value of $10,000. The exchange has commercial substance.

Required:
Prepare journal entries to record each of the above transactions.

P 10–6
Nonmonetary
exchange
● LO6

Southern Company owns a building that it leases. The building's fair value is $1,400,000 and its book value is $800,000 (original cost of $2,000,000 less accumulated depreciation of $1,200,000). Southern exchanges this for another building owned by the Eastern Company. The building's book value on Eastern's books is $950,000 (original cost of $1,600,000 less accumulated depreciation of $650,000). Eastern also gives Southern $140,000 to complete the exchange. The exchange has commercial substance for both companies.

Required:
Prepare the journal entries to record the exchange on the books of both Southern and Eastern.

P 10–7
Nonmonetary
exchange
● LO6

On September 3, 2011, the Robers Company exchanged equipment with Phifer Corporation. The facts of the exchange are as follows:

	Robers' Asset	Phifer's Asset
Original cost	$120,000	$140,000
Accumulated depreciation	55,000	63,000
Fair value	75,000	70,000

To equalize the exchange, Phifer paid Robers $5,000 in cash.

Required:
Record the exchange for both Robers and Phifer. The exchange has commercial substance for both companies.

P 10–8
Nonmonetary
exchange
● LO6

Case A. Kapono Farms exchanged an old tractor for a newer model. The old tractor had a book value of $12,000 (original cost of $28,000 less accumulated depreciation of $16,000) and a fair value of $9,000. Kapono paid $20,000 cash to complete the exchange. The exchange has commercial substance.

Required:
1. What is the amount of gain or loss that Kapono would recognize on the exchange? What is the initial value of the new tractor?
2. Repeat requirement 1 assuming that the fair value of the old tractor is $14,000 instead of $9,000.

Case B. Kapono Farms exchanged 100 acres of farmland for similar land. The farmland given had a book value of $500,000 and a fair value of $700,000. Kapono paid $50,000 cash to complete the exchange. The exchange has commercial substance.

Required:
1. What is the amount of gain or loss that Kapono would recognize on the exchange? What is the initial value of the new land?
2. Repeat requirement 1 assuming that the fair value of the farmland given is $400,000 instead of $700,000.
3. Repeat requirement 1 assuming that the exchange lacked commercial substance.

P 10–9
Interest
capitalization;
specific interest
method
● LO7

On January 1, 2011, the Mason Manufacturing Company began construction of a building to be used as its office headquarters. The building was completed on September 30, 2012.
    Expenditures on the project were as follows:

January 1, 2011	$1,000,000
March 1, 2011	600,000
June 30, 2011	800,000
October 1, 2011	600,000
January 31, 2012	270,000
April 30, 2012	585,000
August 31, 2012	900,000

On January 1, 2011, the company obtained a $3 million construction loan with a 10% interest rate. The loan was outstanding all of 2011 and 2012. The company's other interest-bearing debt included two long-term notes of $4,000,000 and $6,000,000 with interest rates of 6% and 8%, respectively. Both notes were outstanding during all of 2011 and 2012. Interest is paid annually on all debt. The company's fiscal year-end is December 31.

Required:
1. Calculate the amount of interest that Mason should capitalize in 2011 and 2012 using the specific interest method.
2. What is the total cost of the building?
3. Calculate the amount of interest expense that will appear in the 2011 and 2012 income statements.

P 10–10
Interest
capitalization;
weighted-average
method

● LO7

This is a variation of the previous problem, modified to focus on the weighted-average interest method.]

Required:
Refer to the facts in Problem 10–9 and answer the following questions:
1. Calculate the amount of interest that Mason should capitalize in 2011 and 2012 using the weighted-average method.
2. What is the total cost of the building?
3. Calculate the amount of interest expense that will appear in the 2011 and 2012 income statements.

P 10–11
Research and
development

● LO8

In 2011, Starsearch Corporation began work on three research and development projects. One of the projects was completed and commercial production of the developed product began in December. The company's fiscal year-end is December 31. All of the following 2011 expenditures were included in the R&D expense account:

Salaries and wages for:	
Lab research	$ 300,000
Design and construction of preproduction prototype	160,000
Quality control during commercial production	20,000
Materials and supplies consumed for:	
Lab research	60,000
Construction of preproduction prototype	30,000
Purchase of equipment	600,000
Patent filing and legal fees for completed project	40,000
Payments to others for research	120,000
Total	$1,330,000

$200,000 of equipment was purchased solely for use in one of the projects. After the project is completed, the equipment will be abandoned. The remaining $400,000 in equipment will be used on future R&D projects. The useful life of equipment is five years. Assume that all of the equipment was acquired at the beginning of the year.

Required:
Prepare journal entries, reclassifying amounts in R&D expense, to reflect the appropriate treatment of the expenditures.

P 10–12
Acquisition
costs; lump-sum
acquisition;
noninterest-bearing
note; interest
capitalization

● LO1 LO2
   LO3 LO7

Early in its fiscal year ending December 31, 2011, San Antonio Outfitters finalized plans to expand operations. The first stage was completed on March 28 with the purchase of a tract of land on the outskirts of the city. The land and existing building were purchased for $800,000. San Antonio paid $200,000 and signed a noninterest-bearing note requiring the company to pay the remaining $600,000 on March 28, 2013. An interest rate of 8% properly reflects the time value of money for this type of loan agreement. Title search, insurance, and other closing costs totaling $20,000 were paid at closing.

During April, the old building was demolished at a cost of $70,000, and an additional $50,000 was paid to clear and grade the land. Construction of a new building began on May 1 and was completed on October 29. Construction expenditures were as follows:

May 30	$1,200,000
July 30	1,500,000
September 1	900,000
October 1	1,800,000

San Antonio borrowed $3,000,000 at 8% on May 1 to help finance construction. This loan, plus interest, will be paid in 2012. The company also had the following debt outstanding throughout 2011:

$2,000,000, 9% long-term note payable
$4,000,000, 6% long-term bonds payable

In November, the company purchased 10 identical pieces of equipment and office furniture and fixtures for a lump-sum price of $600,000. The fair values of the equipment and the furniture and fixtures were $455,000 and $245,000, respectively. In December, San Antonio paid a contractor $285,000 for the construction of parking lots and for landscaping.

Required:
1. Determine the initial values of the various assets that San Antonio acquired or constructed during 2011. The company uses the specific interest method to determine the amount of interest capitalized on the building construction.
2. How much interest expense will San Antonio report in its 2011 income statement?

BROADEN YOUR PERSPECTIVE

Apply your critical-thinking ability to the knowledge you've gained. These cases will provide you an opportunity to develop your research, analysis, judgment, and communication skills. You also will work with other students, integrate what you've learned, apply it in real world situations, and consider its global and ethical ramifications. This practice will broaden your knowledge and further develop your decision-making abilities.

**Judgment
Case 10–1**
Acquisition costs
● LO1 LO3 LO6

A company may acquire property, plant, and equipment and intangible assets for cash, in exchange for a deferred payment contract, by exchanging other assets, or by a combination of these methods.

Required:

1. Identify six types of costs that should be capitalized as the cost of a parcel of land. For your answer, assume that the land has an existing building that is to be removed in the immediate future in order that a new building can be constructed on the site.
2. At what amount should a company record an asset acquired in exchange for a deferred payment contract?
3. In general, at what amount should assets received in exchange for other nonmonetary assets be valued? Specifically, at what amount should a company value a new machine acquired by exchanging an older, similar machine and paying cash?

(AICPA adapted)

**Research
Case 10–2**
FASB codification; locate and extract relevant information and cite authoritative support for a financial reporting issue; restoration costs; asset retirement obligation
● LO1

Your client, Hazelton Mining, recently entered into an agreement to obtain the rights to operate a coal mine in West Virginia for $15 million. Hazelton incurred development costs of $6 million in preparing the mine for extraction, which began on July 1, 2011. The contract requires Hazelton to restore the land and surrounding area to its original condition after extraction is complete in three years.

The company controller, Alice Cushing, is not sure how to account for the restoration costs and has asked your advice. Alice is aware of a recent accounting pronouncement addressing this issue, but is not sure of its provisions. She has narrowed down the possible cash outflows for the restoration costs to four possibilities:

Cash Outflow	Probability
$3 million	20%
4 million	30%
5 million	25%
6 million	25%

Alice also informs you that the company's credit-adjusted risk-free interest rate is 9%. Before responding to Alice, you need to research the issue.

Required:

1. Obtain the relevant authoritative literature on accounting for asset retirement obligations using the FASB's Codification Research System. You might gain access at the FASB website (**www.fasb.org**). Explain the basic treatment of asset retirement obligations. What are the specific citations that you would rely on to determine (a) the accounting treatment for an asset retirement obligation and (b) how to measure the obligation?
2. Determine the capitalized cost of the coal mine.
3. Prepare a summary journal entry to record the acquisition costs of the mine.
4. How much accretion expense will the company record in its income statement for the 2011 fiscal year, related to this transaction? What are the specific citations from the FASB's Codification Research System that address (a) the calculation of accretion expense and (b) the classification of accretion expense in the income statement?
5. Explain to Alice how Hazelton would account for the restoration if the restoration costs differed from the recorded liability in three years. By way of explanation, prepare the journal entry to record the payment of the retirement obligation in three years assuming that the actual restoration costs were $4.7 million.
6. Describe to Alice the necessary disclosure requirements for the obligation. What is the specific citation from the FASB's Codification Research System that contains these disclosure requirements?

**Judgment
Case 10–3**
Self-constructed assets
● LO7

Chilton Peripherals manufactures printers, scanners, and other computer peripheral equipment. In the past, the company purchased equipment used in manufacturing from an outside vendor. In March 2011, Chilton decided to design and build equipment to replace some obsolete equipment. A section of the manufacturing plant was set aside to develop and produce the equipment. Additional personnel were hired for the project. The equipment was completed and ready for use in September.

Required:

1. In general, what costs should be capitalized for a self-constructed asset?
2. Discuss two alternatives for the inclusion of overhead costs in the cost of the equipment constructed by Chilton. Which alternative is generally accepted for financial reporting purposes?
3. Under what circumstance(s) would interest be included in the cost of the equipment?

Judgment Case 10–4
Interest capitalization
● LO7

GAAP provides guidelines for the inclusion of interest in the initial cost of a self-constructed asset.

Required:

1. What assets qualify for interest capitalization? What assets do not qualify for interest capitalization?
2. Over what period should interest be capitalized?
3. Explain average accumulated expenditures.
4. Explain the two methods that could be used to determine the appropriate interest rate(s) to be used in capitalizing interest.
5. Describe the three steps used to determine the amount of interest capitalized during a reporting period.

Research Case 10–5
Goodwill
● LO1

Accounting for purchased goodwill has been a controversial issue for many years. In the United States, the amount of purchased goodwill is capitalized and not amortized. Globally, the treatment of goodwill varies significantly, with some countries not recognizing goodwill as an asset. Professors Johnson and Petrone, in "Is Goodwill an Asset?" discuss this issue.

Required:

1. In your library or from some other source, locate the indicated article in *Accounting Horizons,* September 1998.
2. Does goodwill meet the FASB's definition of an asset?
3. What are the key concerns of those that believe goodwill is not an asset?

Real World Case 10–6
Property, plant, and equipment; intangibles; Target
● LO1

Real World Financials

Target Corporation, a major U.S. retailer, reported the following amounts in the asset section of its balance sheets for the years ended January 31, 2009, and February 2, 2008:

	($ in millions)	
	January 31, 2009	**February 2, 2008**
Property and equipment, net	$25,756	$24,095

In addition, the statement of cash flows for the year ended January 31, 2009, included the following items ($ in millions):

Depreciation	$1,814
Additions to property and equipment	3,547
Proceeds from the sale of property and equipment	39

Required:

What was the gain or loss Target recognized in the year ended January 31, 2009, from the sale of property and equipment?

Judgment Case 10–7
Goodwill
● LO1

Athena Paper Corporation acquired for cash 100% of the outstanding common stock of Georgia, Inc., a supplier of wood pulp. The purchase price of $4,500,000 was significantly higher than the book value of Georgia's net assets (assets less liabilities) of $2,800,000. The Athena controller recorded the difference of $1,700,000 as an asset, goodwill.

Required:

1. Discuss the meaning of the term *goodwill.*
2. In what situation would the Athena controller be correct in her valuation of goodwill?

Judgment Case 10–8
Research and development
● LO8

Prior to 1974, accepted practice was for companies to either expense or capitalize R&D costs. In 1974, the FASB issued a Standard that requires all research and development costs to be charged to expense when incurred. This was a controversial standard, opposed by many companies who preferred delaying the recognition of these expenses until later years when presumably the expenditures bear fruit.

Several research studies have been conducted to determine if the standard had any impact on the behavior of companies. One interesting finding was that, prior to 1974, companies that expensed R&D costs were significantly larger than those companies that capitalized R&D costs.

Required:

1. Explain the FASB's logic in deciding to require all companies to expense R&D costs in the period incurred.
2. Identify possible reasons to explain why, prior to 1974, companies that expensed R&D costs were significantly larger than those companies that capitalized R&D costs.

**Judgment
Case 10–9**
Research and
development
● LO8

Clonal, Inc., a biotechnology company, developed and patented a diagnostic product called Trouver. Clonal purchased some research equipment to be used exclusively for Trouver and subsequent research projects. Clonal defeated a legal challenge to its Trouver patent, and began production and marketing operations for the project.

Corporate headquarters' costs were allocated to Clonal's research division as a percentage of the division's salaries.

Required:

1. How should the equipment purchased for Trouver be reported in Clonal's income statements and statements of financial position?
2. a. Describe the matching principle.
   b. Describe the accounting treatment of research and development costs and consider whether this is consistent with the matching principle. What is the justification for the accounting treatment of research and development costs?
3. How should corporate headquarters' costs allocated to the research division be classified in Clonal's income statements? Why?
4. How should the legal expenses incurred in defending Trouver's patent be reported in Clonal's financial statements?

(AICPA adapted)

**Communication
Case 10–10**
Research and
development
● LO8

The focus of this case is the situation described in Case 10–9. What is the appropriate accounting for R&D costs? Do you believe that (1) capitalization is the correct treatment of R&D costs, (2) expensing is the correct treatment of R&D costs, or (3) that companies should be allowed to choose between expensing and capitalizing R&D costs?

Required:

1. Develop a list of arguments in support of your view prior to the class session for which the case is assigned. Do not be influenced by the method required by the FASB. Base your opinion on the conceptual merit of the options.
2. In class, your instructor will pair you (and everyone else) with a classmate who also has independently developed a position.
   a. You will be given three minutes to argue your view to your partner. Your partner likewise will be given three minutes to argue his or her view to you. During these three-minute presentations, the listening partner is not permitted to speak.
   b. Then after each person has had a turn attempting to convince his or her partner, the two partners will have a three-minute discussion in which they will decide which alternative is more convincing and arguments will be merged into a single view for each pair.
3. After the allotted time, a spokesperson for each of the three alternatives will be selected by the instructor. Each spokesperson will field arguments from the class as to the appropriate alternative. The class will then discuss the merits of the alternatives and attempt to reach a consensus view, though a consensus is not necessary.

**Communication
Case 10–11**
Research and
development
● LO8

Thomas Plastics is in the process of developing a revolutionary new plastic valve. A new division of the company was formed to develop, manufacture, and market this new product. As of year-end (December 31, 2011), the new product has not been manufactured for sale; however, prototype units were built and are in operation.

Throughout 2011, the new division incurred a variety of costs. These costs included expenses (including salaries of administrative personnel) and market research costs. In addition, approximately $500,000 in equipment (estimated useful life of 10 years) was purchased for use in developing and manufacturing the new valve. Approximately $200,000 of this equipment was built specifically for developing the design of the new product; the remaining $300,000 of the equipment was used to manufacture the preproduction prototypes and will be used to manufacture the new product once it is in commercial production.

The president of the company, Sally Rogers, has been told that research and development costs must be expensed as incurred, but she does not understand this treatment. She believes the research will lead to a profitable product and to increased future revenues. Also, she wonders how to account for the $500,000 of equipment purchased by the new division. "I thought I understood accounting," she growled. "Explain to me why expenditures that benefit our future revenues are expensed rather than capitalized!"

Required:

Write a one-to two-page report to Sally Rogers explaining the generally accepted accounting principles relevant to this issue. The report should also address the treatment of the equipment purchases.

(AICPA adapted)

Ethics
Case 10–12
Research and
development
● LO8

Mayer Biotechnical, Inc., develops, manufactures, and sells pharmaceuticals. Significant research and development (R&D) expenditures are made for the development of new drugs and the improvement of existing drugs. During 2011, $220 million was spent on R&D. Of this amount, $30 million was spent on the purchase of equipment to be used in a research project involving the development of a new antibiotic.

The controller, Alice Cooper, is considering capitalizing the equipment and depreciating it over the five-year useful life of the equipment at $6 million per year, even though the equipment likely will be used on only one project. The company president has asked Alice to make every effort to increase 2011 earnings because in 2012 the company will be seeking significant new financing from both debt and equity sources. "I guess we might use the equipment in other projects later," Alice wondered to herself.

Required:

1. Assuming that the equipment was purchased at the beginning of 2011, by how much would Alice's treatment of the equipment increase before tax earnings as opposed to expensing the equipment cost?

2. Discuss the ethical dilemma Alice faces in determining the treatment of the $30 million equipment purchase.

IFRS Case 10–13
Research and
development;
comparison of
U.S. GAAP and
IFRS; Cadbury
Schweppes
● LO8 LO9

Cadbury Schweppes, Plc., a U.K. company, is an international confectionery and beverage business that sells its products in almost every country in the world. The company prepares its financial statements according to IFRS.

Required:

1. Use the Internet to locate Cadbury's most recent annual report. The address is **www.cadburyschweppes.com**. Locate the significant accounting policies disclosure note.

2. How does the company account for research and development expenditures? Does this policy differ from U.S. GAAP?

Analysis
Case 10–14
Fixed-asset
turnover ratio;
National
Semiconductor
● LO5

Real World Financials

National Semiconductor Corporation, headquartered in Santa Clara, California, is a global semiconductor manufacturer. The company's 2009 fixed-asset turnover ratio, using the average book value of property, plant, and equipment (PP&E) as the denominator, was approximately 2.87. Additional information taken from the company's 2009 annual report is as follows:

	($ in millions)
Book value of PP&E—beginning of 2009	$557
Purchases of PP&E during 2009	84
Depreciation of PP&E for 2009	175

Equipment having a book value of $4 million was sold during 2009.

Required:

1. How is the fixed-asset turnover ratio computed? How would you interpret National's ratio of 2.87?

2. Use the data to determine National's net sales for 2009.

3. Obtain annual reports from three corporations in the same primary industry as National Semiconductor (Intel Corporation and Advanced Micro Devices are two well-known competitors) and compare the management of each company's investment in property, plant, and equipment.

Note: You can obtain copies of annual reports from your library, from friends who are shareholders, from the investor relations department of the corporations, from a friendly stockbroker, or from EDGAR (Electronic Data Gathering, Analysis, and Retrieval) on the Internet (**www.sec.gov**).

Judgment
Case 10–15
Computer software
costs
● LO8

The Elegant Software Company recently completed the development and testing of a new software program that provides the ability to transfer data from among a variety of operating systems. The company believes this product will be quite successful and capitalized all of the costs of designing, developing, coding, and testing the software. These costs will be amortized over the expected useful life of the software on a straight-line basis.

Required:

1. Was Elegant correct in its treatment of the software development costs? Why?

2. Explain the appropriate method for determining the amount of periodic amortization for any capitalized software development costs.

Real World Case 10–16

Property, plant, and equipment; Home Depot

● LO1 LO7

Real World Financials

EDGAR, the Electronic Data Gathering, Analysis, and Retrieval system, performs automated collection, validation, indexing, and forwarding of submissions by companies and others who are required by law to file forms with the U.S. Securities and Exchange Commission (SEC). All publicly traded domestic companies use EDGAR to make the majority of their filings. (Some foreign companies file voluntarily.) Form 10-K, which includes the annual report, is required to be filed on EDGAR. The SEC makes this information available on the Internet.

Required:

1. Access EDGAR on the Internet. The web address is **www.sec.gov**.

2. Search for **Home Depot, Inc.** Access the 10-K filing for the most recent fiscal year. Search or scroll to find the financial statements and related notes.

3. Answer the following questions related to the company's property, plant, and equipment:
   a. Name the different types of assets the company lists in its balance sheet under property, plant, and equipment.
   b. How much cash was used for the acquisition of property, plant, and equipment during the year?
   c. What was the amount of interest capitalized during the year?
   d. Compute the fixed-asset turnover ratio for the fiscal year.

Analysis Case 10–17

Reporting property, plant, and equipment and intangible assets

● LO1 LO5

Refer to the financial statements and related disclosure notes of **Dell Inc.** in Appendix B located at the back of the text.

Required:

1. What categories of property, plant, and equipment and intangible assets does Dell report in its 2009 balance sheet?

2. How much cash was used in 2009 to purchase property and equipment? How does this compare with purchases in previous years?

3. The fixed-asset turnover ratio for **Hewlett-Packard Company**, a Dell competitor, is 9.84. How does this compare with Dell's ratio? What is the ratio intended to measure?

BRITISH AIRWAYS CASE

BRITISH AIRWAYS

● LO9

British Airways, Plc. (BA), a U.K. company, prepares its financial statements according to International Financial Reporting Standards. BA's annual report for the year ended March 31, 2009, which includes financial statements and disclosure notes, is included with all new textbooks and can be found at **www.britishairways.com**. When answering questions, focus on BA's "Group" financial information (which is equivalent to "Consolidated" under U.S. GAAP).

Required:

1. What method does British Airways use to amortize the cost of computer software development costs? How does this approach differ from U.S. GAAP?

2. BA does not report any research and development expenses in its income statement. If it did, its approach to accounting for research and development would be significantly different from U.S. GAAP. Describe the differences between IFRS and U.S. GAAP in accounting for research and development expenditures.

11 Property, Plant, and Equipment and Intangible Assets: Utilization and Impairment

| | | | | | | | | | | | | | | | | | | | | | | | | | | | | | | | | | | | | | | | | | | | | | | | | |

/// OVERVIEW

This chapter completes our discussion of accounting for property, plant, and equipment and intangible assets. We address the allocation of the cost of these assets to the periods benefited by their use.

The usefulness of most of these assets is consumed as the assets are applied to the production of goods or services. Cost allocation corresponding to this consumption of usefulness is known as *depreciation* for plant and equipment, *depletion* for natural resources, and *amortization* for intangibles.

We also consider impairment of these assets, and the treatment of expenditures incurred subsequent to acquisition.

/// LEARNING OBJECTIVES

After studying the chapter you should be able to:

● **LO1** Explain the concept of cost allocation as it pertains to property, plant, and equipment and intangible assets. (page 558)

● **LO2** Determine periodic depreciation using both time-based and activity-based methods. (page 560)

● **LO3** Calculate the periodic depletion of a natural resource. (page 569)

● **LO4** Calculate the periodic amortization of an intangible asset. (page 571)

● **LO5** Explain the appropriate accounting treatment required when a change is made in the service life or residual value of property, plant, and equipment and intangible assets. (page 576)

● **LO6** Explain the appropriate accounting treatment required when a change in depreciation, amortization, or depletion method is made. (page 577)

● **LO7** Explain the appropriate treatment required when an error in accounting for property, plant, and equipment and intangible assets is discovered. (page 578)

● **LO8** Identify situations that involve a significant impairment of the value of property, plant, and equipment and intangible assets and describe the required accounting procedures. (page 580)

● **LO9** Discuss the accounting treatment of repairs and maintenance, additions, improvements, and rearrangements to property, plant, and equipment and intangible assets. (page 589)

● **LO10** Discuss the primary differences between U.S. GAAP and IFRS with respect to the utilization and impairment of property, plant, and equipment and intangible assets. (pages 565, 568, 571, 573, 583, 584, 586, 589, and 592)

FINANCIAL REPORTING CASE

What's in a Name?

"I don't understand this at all," your friend Penny Lane moaned. "Depreciation, depletion, amortization; what's the difference? Aren't they all the same thing?" Penny and you are part of a class team working on a case involving **Weyerhaeuser Company,** a large forest products company. Part of the project involves comparing reporting methods over a three-year period. "Look at these disclosure notes from last year's annual report. Besides mentioning those three terms, they also talk about asset impairment. How is that different?" Penny showed you the disclosure notes.

Property and Equipment and Timber and Timberlands (in part)

Depreciation is calculated using a straight-line method at rates based on estimated service lives. Logging railroads and truck roads are generally amortized—as timber is harvested—at rates based on the volume of timber estimated to be removed. We carry timber and timberlands at cost less depletion. To determine depletion rates, we divide the net carrying value by the related volume of timber estimated to be available.

Impairment of Long-lived Assets (in part)

We review long-lived assets—including certain identifiable intangibles—for impairment whenever events or changes in circumstances indicate that the carrying amount of the assets may not be recoverable.

By the time you finish this chapter, you should be able to respond appropriately to the questions posed in this case. Compare your response to the solution provided at the end of the chapter.

QUESTIONS ///

1. Is Penny correct? Do the terms *depreciation, depletion,* and *amortization* all mean the same thing? (page 558)

2. Weyerhaeuser determines depletion based on the "volume of timber estimated to be available." Explain this approach. (page 562)

3. Explain how asset impairment differs from depreciation, depletion, and amortization. How do companies measure impairment losses for property, plant, and equipment and intangible assets with finite useful lives? (page 580)

PART A

DEPRECIATION, DEPLETION, AND AMORTIZATION

Cost Allocation—an Overview

● LO1

Property, plant, and equipment and intangible assets are purchased with the expectation that they will provide future benefits, usually for several years. Specifically, they are acquired to be used as part of the revenue-generating operations. Logically, then, the costs of acquiring the assets should be allocated to expense during the reporting periods benefited by their use. That is, their costs are matched with the revenues they help generate.

Let's suppose that a company purchases a used delivery truck for $8,200 to be used to deliver product to customers. The company estimates that five years from the acquisition date the truck will be sold for $2,200. It is estimated, then, that $6,000 ($8,200 − 2,200) of the truck's purchase price will be used up (consumed) during a five-year useful life. The situation is portrayed in Graphic 11–1.

GRAPHIC 11–1

Cost Allocation

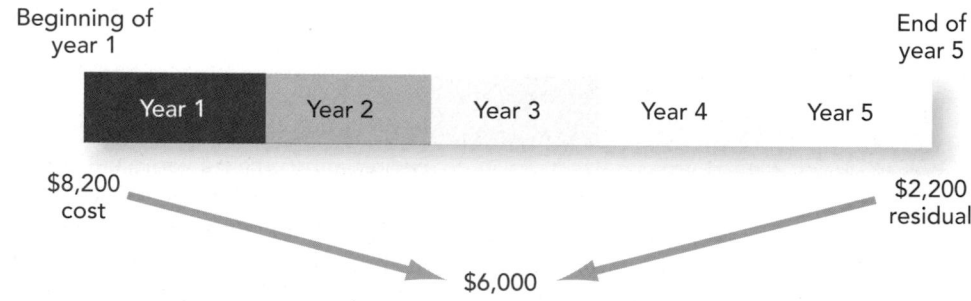

Theoretically, the matching principle requires that the $6,000 be allocated to the five individual years of asset use in direct proportion to the role the asset played in revenue production. However, very seldom is there a clear-cut relationship between the use of the asset and revenue production. In other words, we can't tell precisely the portion of the total benefits of the asset that was consumed in any particular period. As a consequence, we must resort to arbitrary allocation methods to approximate a matching of expense with revenue. Contrast this situation with the $24,000 prepayment of one year's rent on an office building at $2,000 per month. In that case, we know precisely that the benefits of the asset, prepaid rent, are consumed at a rate of $2,000 per month.

Cost allocation is known as **depreciation** for plant and equipment, **depletion** for natural resources, and **amortization** for intangibles. The process often is confused with measuring a decline in fair value of an asset. For example, let's say our delivery truck purchased for $8,200 can be sold for $5,000 at the end of one year but we intend to keep it for the full five-year estimated life. It has experienced a decline in value of $3,200 ($8,200 − 5,000). However, *depreciation is a process of cost allocation, not valuation.* We would not record depreciation expense of $3,200 for year one of the truck's life. Instead, we would distribute the cost of the asset, less any anticipated residual value, over the estimated useful life in a systematic and rational manner that attempts to match revenues with the *use* of the asset, not the decline in its value. After all, the truck is purchased to be used in operations, not to be sold.

The specific accounting treatment depends on the intended use of the asset. For assets used in the manufacture of a product, for example, depreciation, depletion, or amortization is considered a product cost to be included as part of the cost of inventory. Eventually, when the product is sold, it becomes part of the cost of goods sold. For assets *not* used in production, primarily plant and equipment and certain intangibles used in the selling and administrative functions of the company, periodic depreciation or amortization is reported as expense in the income statement. You might recognize this distinction as the difference between a product cost and a period cost. When a product cost is reported as an expense (cost of goods sold) depends on when the product is sold; when a period cost is reported as an expense depends on the reporting period in which it is incurred.

Measuring Cost Allocation

The process of cost allocation requires that three factors be established at the time the asset is put into use. These factors are:

1. **Service life**—the estimated use that the company expects to receive from the asset.
2. **Allocation base**—the value of the usefulness that is expected to be consumed.
3. **Allocation method**—the pattern in which the usefulness is expected to be consumed.

Let's consider these one at a time.

Service Life

The **service life**, or **useful life**, is the amount of use that the company expects to obtain from the asset before disposing of it. This use can be expressed in units of time, or in units of activity. For example, the estimated service life of a delivery truck could be expressed in terms of years or in terms of the number of miles that the company expects the truck to be driven before disposition. We use the terms service life and useful life interchangeably throughout the chapter.

The service life, or useful life, can be expressed in units of time or in units of activity.

Physical life provides the upper bound for service life of tangible, long-lived assets. Physical life will vary according to the purpose for which the asset is acquired and the environment in which it is operated. For example, a diesel powered electric generator may last for many years if it is used only as an emergency backup or for only a few years if it is used regularly.

Expected obsolescence can shorten service life below physical life.

The service life of a tangible asset may be less than physical life for a variety of reasons. For example, the expected rate of technological change may shorten service life. If suppliers are expected to develop new technologies that are more efficient, the company may keep an asset for a period of time much shorter than physical life. Likewise, if the company sells its product in a market that frequently demands new products, the machinery and equipment used to produce products may be useful only for as long as its output can be sold. Similarly, a mineral deposit might be projected to contain 4 million tons of a mineral, but it may be economically feasible with existing extraction methods to mine only 2 million tons. For intangible assets, legal or contractual life often is a limiting factor. For instance, a patent might be capable of providing enhanced profitability for 50 years, but the legal life of a patent is only 20 years.

Management intent also may shorten the period of an asset's usefulness below its physical, legal, or contractual life. For example, a company may have a policy of using its delivery trucks for a three-year period and then trading the trucks for new models.

Companies quite often disclose the range of service lives for different categories of assets. For example, Graphic 11–2 shows how **IBM Corporation** disclosed its service lives in a note accompanying recent financial statements.

Summary of Significant Accounting Policies (in part)
Depreciation and Amortization

The estimated useful lives of certain depreciable assets are as follows: buildings, 50 years; building equipment, 10 to 20 years; land improvements, 20 years; plant, laboratory and office equipment, 2 to 15 years; and computer equipment, 1.5 to 5 years.

GRAPHIC 11–2

Service Life Disclosure— International Business Machines Corporation

Real World Financials

Allocation Base

The total amount of cost to be allocated over an asset's service life is called its **allocation base**. The amount is the difference between the initial value of the asset at its acquisition (its cost) and its **residual value**. Residual or **salvage value** is the amount the company expects to receive for the asset at the end of its service life less any anticipated disposal costs. In our delivery truck example above, the allocation base is $6,000 ($8,200 cost less $2,200 anticipated residual value).

Allocation base is the difference between the cost of the asset and its anticipated residual value.

In certain situations, residual value can be estimated by referring to a company's prior experience or to publicly available information concerning resale values of various types of assets. For example, if a company intends to trade its delivery trucks in three years for the new model, approximations of the three-year residual value for that type of truck can be obtained from used truck values.

However, estimating residual value for many assets can be very difficult due to the uncertainty about the future. For this reason, along with the fact that residual values often are immaterial, many companies simply assume a residual value of zero. Companies usually do not disclose estimated residual values.

Allocation Method

The *allocation method* used should be systematic and rational and correspond to the pattern of asset use.

In determining how much cost to allocate to periods of an asset's use, a method should be selected that corresponds to the pattern of the loss of the asset's usefulness. Generally accepted accounting principles state that the chosen method should allocate the asset's cost "as equitably as possible to the periods during which services are obtained from [its] use." GAAP further specifies that the method should produce a cost allocation in a "systematic and rational manner."[1] The objective is to try to allocate cost to the period in an amount that is proportional to the amount of benefits generated by the asset during the period relative to the total benefits provided by the asset during its life.

In practice, there are two general approaches that attempt to obtain this systematic and rational allocation. The first approach allocates the cost base according to the *passage of time*. Methods following this approach are referred to as **time-based** methods. The second approach allocates an asset's cost base using a measure of the asset's *input* or *output*. This is an **activity-based** method. We compare these approaches first in the context of depreciation. Later we see that depletion of natural resources typically follows an activity-based approach and the amortization of intangibles typically follows a time-based approach.

Depreciation

● LO2

To demonstrate and compare the most common depreciation methods, we refer to the situation described in Illustration 11–1.

ILLUSTRATION 11–1
Depreciation Methods

The Hogan Manufacturing Company purchased a machine for $250,000. The company expects the service life of the machine to be five years. During that time, it is expected that the machine will produce 140,000 units. The anticipated residual value is $40,000. The machine was disposed of after five years of use. Actual production during the five years of the asset's life was:

Year	Units Produced
1	24,000
2	36,000
3	46,000
4	8,000
5	16,000
Total	130,000

Time-Based Depreciation Methods

The *straight-line depreciation method* allocates an equal amount of depreciable base to each year of the asset's service life.

STRAIGHT-LINE METHOD. By far the most easily understood and widely used depreciation method is straight line. By this approach, an equal amount of depreciable base is allocated to each year of the asset's service life. The depreciable base is simply divided by

[1]FASB ASC 360–10–35–4: Property, Plant, and Equipment—Overall—Subsequent Measurement (previously "Restatement and Revision of Accounting Research Bulletins," *Accounting Research Bulletin No. 43* (New York: AICPA, 1953), Ch. 9).

the number of years in the asset's life to determine annual depreciation. In our illustration, the straight-line annual depreciation is $42,000, calculated as follows:

$$\frac{\$250,000 - 40,000}{5 \text{ years}} = \$42,000 \text{ per year}$$

ACCELERATED METHODS.   Using the straight-line method implicitly assumes that the benefits derived from the use of the asset are the same each year. In some situations it might be more appropriate to assume that the asset will provide greater benefits in the early years of its life than in the later years. In these cases, a more appropriate matching of depreciation with revenues is achieved with a declining pattern of depreciation, with higher depreciation in the early years of the asset's life and lower depreciation in later years. An accelerated depreciation method also would be appropriate when benefits derived from the asset are approximately equal over the asset's life, but repair and maintenance costs increase significantly in later years. The early years incur higher depreciation and lower repairs and maintenance expense, while the later years have lower depreciation and higher repairs and maintenance. Two commonly used ways to achieve such a declining pattern are the sum-of-the-years'-digits method and declining balance methods.

Accelerated depreciation methods are appropriate when the asset is more useful in its earlier years.

Sum-of-the-Years'-Digits Method.   The **sum-of-the-years'-digits (SYD) method** has no logical foundation other than the fact that it accomplishes the objective of accelerating depreciation in a systematic manner. This is achieved by multiplying the depreciable base by a fraction that declines each year and results in depreciation that decreases by the same amount each year. The denominator of the fraction remains constant and is the sum of the digits from one to n, where n is the number of years in the asset's service life. For example, if there are five years in the service life, the denominator is the sum of 1, 2, 3, 4, and 5, which equals 15.[2] The numerator decreases each year; it begins with the value of n in the first year and decreases by one each year until it equals one in the final year of the asset's estimated service life. The annual fractions for an asset with a five-year life are: $\frac{5}{15}$, $\frac{4}{15}$, $\frac{3}{15}$, $\frac{2}{15}$, and $\frac{1}{15}$. We calculate depreciation for the five years of the machine's life using the sum-of-the-years'-digits method in Illustration 11–1A.

The SYD method multiplies depreciable base by a declining fraction.

ILLUSTRATION 11–1A   Sum-of-the-Years'-Digits Depreciation

Year	Depreciable Base ($250,000 − 40,000)	×	Depreciation Rate per Year	=	Depreciation	Accumulated Depreciation	Book Value End of Year ($250,000 less Accum. Depreciation)
1	$210,000		$\frac{5}{15}$*		$ 70,000	$ 70,000	$180,000
2	$210,000		$\frac{4}{15}$		56,000	126,000	124,000
3	$210,000		$\frac{3}{15}$		42,000	168,000	82,000
4	$210,000		$\frac{2}{15}$		28,000	196,000	54,000
5	$210,000		$\frac{1}{15}$		14,000	210,000	40,000
Totals			$\frac{15}{15}$		$210,000		

$$*\frac{n(n + 1)}{2} = \frac{5(5 + 1)}{2} = 15$$

Declining Balance Methods.   As an alternative, an accelerated depreciation pattern can be achieved by various declining balance methods. Rather than multiplying a constant balance by a declining fraction as we do in SYD depreciation, we multiply a constant fraction by a declining balance each year. Specifically, we multiply a constant percentage rate times the decreasing book value (cost less accumulated depreciation), also referred to as carrying value, of the asset (*not depreciable base*) at the beginning of the year. Because the rate remains constant while the book value declines, annual depreciation is less each year.

Declining balance depreciation methods multiply beginning-of-year book value, not depreciable base, by an annual rate that is a multiple of the straight-line rate.

[2]A formula useful when calculating the denominator is $n(n + 1)/2$.

The rates used are multiples of the straight-line rate. The straight-line rate is simply one, divided by the number of years in the asset's service life. For example, the straight-line rate for an asset with a five-year life is one-fifth, or 20%. Various multiples used in practice are 125%, 150%, or 200% of the straight-line rate. When 200% is used as the multiplier, the method is known as the **double-declining-balance (DDB) method** because the rate used is twice the straight-line rate.

In our illustration, the double-declining-balance rate would be 40% (two times the straight-line rate of 20%). Depreciation is calculated in Illustration 11–1B for the five years of the machine's life using the double-declining-balance method.

ILLUSTRATION 11–1B

Double-Declining-Balance Depreciation

Year	Book Value Beginning of Year	×	Depreciation Rate per Year	=	Depreciation	Accumulated Depreciation	Book Value End of Year ($250,000 less Accum. Depreciation)
1	$250,000		40%		$100,000	$100,000	$150,000
2	150,000		40%		60,000	160,000	90,000
3	90,000		40%		36,000	196,000	54,000
4	54,000				14,000*	210,000	40,000
5	40,000				—		40,000
Total					$210,000		

*Amount necessary to reduce book value to residual value.

Notice that in the fourth year depreciation expense is a plug amount that reduces book value to the expected residual value (book value beginning of year, $54,000, minus expected residual value, $40,000 = $14,000). There is no depreciation expense in year 5 since book value has already been reduced to the expected residual value. Declining balance methods often allocate the asset's depreciable base over fewer years than the expected service life.

It is not uncommon for a company to switch from accelerated to straight line approximately halfway through an asset's useful life as part of the company's planned depreciation approach.

SWITCH FROM ACCELERATED TO STRAIGHT LINE.   The result of applying the double-declining-balance method in our illustration produces an awkward result in the later years of the asset's life. By using the double-declining-balance method in our illustration, no depreciation expense is recorded in year 5 even though the asset is still producing benefits. In practice, many companies switch to the straight-line method approximately halfway through an asset's useful life.

In our illustration, the company would switch to straight line in either year 3 or year 4. Assuming the switch is made at the beginning of year 4, and the book value at the beginning of that year is $54,000, an additional $14,000 ($54,000 − 40,000 in residual value) of depreciation must be recorded. Applying the straight-line concept, $7,000 ($14,000 divided by two remaining years) in depreciation is recorded in both year 4 and year 5.

It should be noted that this switch to straight line is not a change in depreciation method. The switch is part of the company's planned depreciation approach. However, as you will learn later in the chapter, the accounting treatment is the same as a change in depreciation method.

Activity-Based Depreciation Methods

Activity-based depreciation methods estimate service life in terms of some measure of productivity.

The most logical way to allocate an asset's cost to periods of an asset's use is to measure the usefulness of the asset in terms of its productivity. For example, we could measure the service life of a machine in terms of its *output* (for example, the estimated number of units it will produce) or in terms of its *input* (for example, the number of hours it will operate). We have already mentioned that one way to measure the service life of a vehicle is to estimate the number of miles it will operate. The most common activity-based method is called the **units-of-production method.**

The measure of output used is the estimated number of units (pounds, items, barrels, etc.) to be produced by the machine. We could also use a measure of input such as the number of hours the machine is expected to operate. By the units-of-production method,

FINANCIAL
Reporting Case

Q2, p. 557

we first compute the average depreciation rate per unit by dividing the depreciable base by the number of units expected to be produced. This per unit rate is then multiplied by the number of units produced each period. In our illustration, the depreciation rate per unit is $1.50, computed as follows:

$$\frac{\$250,000 - 40,000}{140,000 \text{ units}} = \$1.50 \text{ per unit}$$

> The *units-of-production method* computes a depreciation rate per measure of activity and then multiplies this rate by actual activity to determine periodic depreciation.

Each unit produced will require $1.50 of depreciation to be recorded. As we are estimating service life based on units produced rather than in years, depreciation is not constrained by time. However, total depreciation is constrained by the asset's cost and the anticipated residual value. In our illustration, suppose the company intended to dispose of the asset at the end of five years. Depreciation for year five must be modified. Depreciation expense would be an amount necessary to bring the book value of the asset down to residual value. Depreciation for the five years is determined in Illustration 11–1C using the units-of-production method. Notice that the last year's depreciation expense is a plug amount that reduces book value to the expected residual value.

Year	Units Produced	×	Depreciation Rate per Unit	=	Depreciation	Accumulated Depreciation	Book Value End of Year ($250,000 less Accum. Depreciation)
1	24,000		$1.50		$ 36,000	$ 36,000	$214,000
2	36,000		1.50		54,000	90,000	160,000
3	46,000		1.50		69,000	159,000	91,000
4	8,000		1.50		12,000	171,000	79,000
5	16,000				39,000*	210,000	40,000
Totals	130,000				$210,000		

ILLUSTRATION 11–1C

Units-of-Production Depreciation

*Amount necessary to reduce book value to residual value.

DECISION MAKERS' PERSPECTIVE—Selecting a Depreciation Method

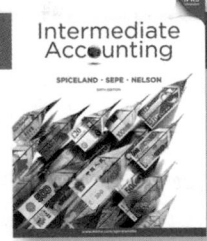

Illustration 11–1D compares periodic depreciation calculated using each of the alternatives we discussed and illustrated.

Year	Straight Line	Sum-of-the-Years' Digits	Double-Declining Balance	Units of Production
1	$ 42,000	$ 70,000	$100,000	$ 36,000
2	42,000	56,000	60,000	54,000
3	42,000	42,000	36,000	69,000
4	42,000	28,000	14,000	12,000
5	42,000	14,000	0	39,000
Total	$210,000	$210,000	$210,000	$210,000

ILLUSTRATION 11–1D

Comparison of Various Depreciation Methods

All methods provide the same total depreciation over an asset's life.

Theoretically, using an activity-based depreciation method provides a better matching of revenues and expenses. Clearly, the productivity of a plant asset is more closely associated with the benefits provided by that asset than the mere passage of time. Also, these methods allow for random patterns of depreciation to correspond with the random patterns of asset use.

Activity-based methods
are theoretically
superior to time-based
methods but often are
impractical to apply in
practice.

However, activity-based methods quite often are either infeasible or too costly to use. For example, buildings don't have an identifiable measure of productivity. Even for machinery, there may be an identifiable measure of productivity such as machine hours or units produced, but it frequently is more costly to determine each period than it is to simply measure the passage of time. For these reasons, most companies use time-based depreciation methods.

Graphic 11–3 shows the results of a recent survey of depreciation methods used by large public companies.[3]

GRAPHIC 11–3

Use of Various
Depreciation Methods

Depreciation Method	Number of Companies
Straight line	494
Declining balance	10
Sum-of-the-years'-digits	3
Accelerated method—not specified	21
Units of production	14
Group/composite	7

Why do so many companies use the straight-line method as opposed to other time-based methods? Many companies perhaps consider the benefits derived from the majority of plant assets to be realized approximately evenly over these assets' useful lives. Certainly a contributing factor is that straight-line is the easiest method to understand and apply.

Another motivation is the positive effect on reported income. Straight-line depreciation produces a higher net income than accelerated methods in the early years of an asset's life. In Chapter 8 we pointed out that reported net income can affect bonuses paid to management or debt agreements with lenders.

A company does not
have to use the same
depreciation method
for both financial
reporting and income
tax purposes.

Conflicting with the desire to report higher profits is the desire to reduce taxes by reducing taxable income. An accelerated method serves this objective by reducing taxable income more in the early years of an asset's life than straight line. You probably recall a similar discussion from Chapter 8 in which the benefits were described of using the LIFO inventory method during periods of increasing costs. However, remember that the LIFO conformity rule requires companies using LIFO for income tax reporting to also use LIFO for financial reporting. *No such conformity rule exists for depreciation methods.* Income tax regulations allow firms to use different approaches to computing depreciation in their tax returns and in their financial statements. The method used for tax purposes is therefore not a constraint in the choice of depreciation methods for financial reporting. As a result, most companies use the straight-line method for financial reporting and the Internal Revenue Service's prescribed accelerated method (discussed in Appendix 11A) for income tax purposes. For example, Graphic 11–4 shows **Merck & Co.**'s depreciation policy as reported in a disclosure note accompanying recent financial statements.

GRAPHIC 11–4

Depreciation Method
Disclosure—Merck &
Co.

Real World Financials

**Summary of Accounting Policies (in part):
Depreciation**

Depreciation is provided over the estimated useful lives of the assets, principally using the straight-line method. For tax purposes, accelerated methods are used.

It is not unusual for a company to use different depreciation methods for different classes of assets. For example, Graphic 11–5 illustrates the **International Paper Company** depreciation policy disclosure contained in a note accompanying recent financial statements.

GRAPHIC 11–5

Depreciation Method
Disclosure—
International Paper
Company

Real World Financials

**Summary of Accounting Policies (in part):
Plants, Properties, and Equipment**

Plants, properties, and equipment are stated at cost, less accumulated depreciation. The units-of-production method of depreciation is used for major pulp and paper mills and the straight-line method is used for other plants and equipment.

[3]*Accounting Trends and Techniques—2009* (New York: AICPA, 2009), p. 404.

INTERNATIONAL FINANCIAL REPORTING STANDARDS

Depreciation. *IAS No. 16* requires that each component of an item of property, plant, and equipment must be depreciated separately if its cost is significant in relation to the total cost of the item.[4] In the United States, component depreciation is allowed but is not often used in practice.

● LO10

Consider the following illustration:

Cavandish LTD. purchased a delivery truck for $62,000. The truck is expected to have a service life of six years and a residual value of $12,000. At the end of three years, the over-sized tires, which have a cost of $6,000 (included in the $62,000 purchase price), will be replaced.

IFRS ILLUSTRATION

Under U.S. GAAP, the typical accounting treatment is to depreciate the $50,000 ($62,000 − 12,000) depreciable base of the truck over its six-year useful life. Using IFRS, the depreciable base of the truck is $44,000 ($62,000 − 12,000 − 6,000) and is depreciated over the truck's six-year useful life, and the $6,000 cost of the tires is depreciated separately over a three-year useful life.

U.S. GAAP and IFRS determine depreciable base in the same way, by subtracting estimated residual value from cost. However, IFRS requires a review of residual values at least annually.

Sanofi-Aventis, a French pharmaceutical company, prepares its financial statements using IFRS. In its property, plant, and equipment note, the company discloses its use of the component-based approach to accounting for depreciation.

Real World Financials

Property, plant, and equipment (in part)

The component-based approach to accounting for property, plant, and equipment is applied. Under this approach, each component of an item of property, plant, and equipment with a cost which is significant in relation to the total cost of the item and which has a different useful life from the other components must be depreciated separately.

CONCEPT REVIEW EXERCISE

The Sprague Company purchased a fabricating machine on January 1, 2011, at a net cost of $130,000. At the end of its four-year useful life, the company estimates that the machine will be worth $30,000. Sprague also estimates that the machine will run for 25,000 hours during its four-year life. The company's fiscal year ends on December 31.

DEPRECIATION METHODS

Required:
Compute depreciation for 2011 through 2014 using each of the following methods:

1. Straight line.
2. Sum-of-the-years'-digits.
3. Double-declining balance.
4. Units of production (using machine hours). Actual production was as follows:

Year	Machine Hours
2011	6,000
2012	8,000
2013	5,000
2014	7,000

1. Straight line.

SOLUTION

$$\frac{\$130,000 - 30,000}{4 \text{ years}} = \$25,000 \text{ per year}$$

---

[4]"Property, Plant and Equipment," *International Accounting Standard No. 16* (IASCF), par. 42, as amended effective January 1, 2009.

2. Sum-of-the-years'-digits.

Year	Depreciable Base	×	Depreciation Rate per Year	=	Depreciation
2011	$100,000		4/10		$ 40,000
2012	100,000		3/10		30,000
2013	100,000		2/10		20,000
2014	100,000		1/10		10,000
Total					$100,000

3. Double-declining balance.

Year	Book Value Beginning of Year	×	Depreciation Rate per Year	=	Depreciation	Book Value End of Year
2011	$130,000		50%		$ 65,000	$65,000
2012	65,000		50		32,500	32,500
2013	32,500				2,500*	30,000
2014	30,000				—	30,000
Total					$100,000	

*Amount necessary to reduce book value to residual value.

4. Units of production (using machine hours).

Year	Machine Hours	×	Depreciation Rate per Hour	=	Depreciation	Book Value End of Year
2011	6,000		$4*		$ 24,000	$106,000
2012	8,000		4		32,000	74,000
2013	5,000		4		20,000	54,000
2014	7,000				24,000[†]	30,000
Total					$100,000	

*($130,000 − 30,000)/25,000 hours = $4 per hour.
[†]Amount necessary to reduce book value to residual value.

Group and Composite Depreciation Methods

Group and composite depreciation methods aggregate assets to reduce the recordkeeping costs of determining periodic depreciation.

As you might imagine, depreciation records could become quite cumbersome and costly if a company has hundreds, or maybe thousands, of depreciable assets. However, the burden can be lessened if the company uses the group or composite method to depreciate assets collectively rather than individually. The two methods are the same except for the way the collection of assets is aggregated for depreciation. The group depreciation method defines the collection as depreciable assets that share similar service lives and other attributes. For example, group depreciation could be used for fleets of vehicles or collections of machinery. The composite depreciation method is used when assets are physically dissimilar but are aggregated anyway to gain the convenience of a collective depreciation calculation. For instance, composite depreciation can be used for all of the depreciable assets in one manufacturing plant, even though individual assets in the composite may have widely diverse service lives.

Both approaches are similar in that they involve applying a single straight-line rate based on the average service lives of the assets in the group or composite.[5] The process is demonstrated using Illustration 11–2.

The depreciation rate is applied to the total cost of the group or composite for the period.

If there are no changes in the assets contained in the group, depreciation of $52,800 per year (16% × $330,000) will be recorded for 5.15 years. This means the depreciation in the sixth year will be $7,920 (.15 of a full year's depreciation = 15% × $52,800), which depreciates the cost of the group down to its estimated residual value. In other words, the group will be depreciated over the average service life of the assets in the group.

In practice, there very likely will be changes in the assets constituting the group as new assets are added and others are retired or sold. Additions are recorded by increasing the

---

[5]A declining balance method could also be used with either the group or composite method by applying a multiple (e.g., 200%) to the straight-line group or composite rate.

The Express Delivery Company began operations in 2011. It will depreciate its fleet of delivery vehicles using the group method. The cost of vehicles purchased early in 2011, along with residual values, estimated lives, and straight-line depreciation per year by type of vehicle, are as follows:

ILLUSTRATION 11–2
Group Depreciation

Asset	Cost	Residual Value	Depreciable Base	Estimated Life (yrs.)	Depreciation per Year (straight line)
Vans	$150,000	$30,000	$120,000	6	$20,000
Trucks	120,000	16,000	104,000	5	20,800
Wagons	60,000	12,000	48,000	4	12,000
Totals	$330,000	$58,000	$272,000		$52,800

The *group depreciation* rate is determined by dividing the depreciation per year by the total cost. The group's *average service* life is calculated by dividing the depreciable base by the depreciation per year:

$$\text{Group depreciation rate} = \frac{\$52,800}{\$330,000} = 16\%$$

$$\text{Average service life} = \frac{\$272,000}{\$52,800} = 5.15 \text{ years (rounded)}$$

group asset account for the cost of the addition. Depreciation is determined by multiplying the group rate by the total cost of assets in the group for that period. Once the group or composite rate and the average service life are determined, they normally are continued despite the addition and disposition of individual assets. This implicitly assumes that the service lives of new assets approximate those of individual assets they replace.

Because depreciation records are not kept on an individual asset basis, dispositions are recorded under the assumption that the book value of the disposed item exactly equals any proceeds received and no gain or loss is recorded. For example, if a delivery truck in the above illustration that cost $15,000 is sold for $3,000 in the year 2014, the following journal entry is recorded:

No gain or loss is recorded when a group or composite asset is retired or sold.

Cash	3,000	
Accumulated depreciation (difference)	12,000	
Vehicles		15,000

Any actual gain or loss is included in the accumulated depreciation account. This practice generally will not distort income as the unrecorded gains tend to offset unrecorded losses.

The group and composite methods simplify the recordkeeping of depreciable assets. This simplification justifies any immaterial errors in income determination. Graphic 11–6 shows a disclosure note accompanying recent financial statements of the **El Paso Natural Gas Company (EPNG)** describing the use of the group depreciation method for its regulated property.

GRAPHIC 11–6
Disclosure of Depreciation Method—El Paso Natural Gas Company

Real World Financials

Summary of Significant Accounting Policies (in part)
Property, Plant, and Equipment (in part)

We use the group method to depreciate property, plant, and equipment. Under this method, assets with similar lives and characteristics are grouped and depreciated as one asset. We apply the FERC-accepted depreciation rate to the total cost of the group until its net book value equals its salvage value. For certain general plant and rights-of-way, we depreciate the asset to zero. The majority of our property, plant, and equipment are on our EPNG system which has depreciation rates ranging from one to 20 percent and the depreciable lives ranging from five to 92 years.

When we retire property, plant, and equipment, we charge accumulated depreciation and amortization for the original cost of the assets in addition to the cost to remove, sell, or dispose of the assets, less their salvage value. We do not recognize a gain or loss unless we sell an entire operating unit.

Additional group-based depreciation methods, the retirement and replacement methods, are discussed in Appendix 11B.

● LO10

INTERNATIONAL FINANCIAL REPORTING STANDARDS

Valuation of Property, Plant, and Equipment. As we've discussed, under U.S. GAAP a company reports property, plant, and equipment (PP&E) in the balance sheet at cost less accumulated depreciation (book value). *IAS No. 16*[6] allows a company to report property, plant, and equipment at that amount or, alternatively, at its fair value (revaluation). If a company chooses revaluation, all assets within a class of PP&E must be revalued on a regular basis. U.S. GAAP prohibits revaluation.

If the revaluation option is chosen, the way the company reports the difference between fair value and book value depends on which amount is higher:

- If fair value is higher than book value, the difference is reported as *other comprehensive income (OCI)* which then accumulates in a "revaluation surplus" (sometimes called revaluation reserve) account in equity.

- If book value is higher than fair value, the difference is reported as an *expense in the income statement*. An exception is when a revaluation surplus account relating to the same asset has a balance from a previous *increase* in fair value, that balance is eliminated before debiting revaluation expense.

Consider the following illustration:

IFRS ILLUSTRATION

Candless Corporation prepares its financial statements according to IFRS. At the beginning of its 2011 fiscal year, the company purchased equipment for $100,000. The equipment is expected to have a five-year useful life with no residual value, so depreciation for 2011 is $20,000. At the end of the year, Candless chooses to revalue the equipment as permitted by *IAS No. 16*. Assuming that the fair value of the equipment at year-end is $84,000, Candless records depreciation and the revaluation using the following journal entries:

(a) Depreciation expense ($100,000 ÷ 5 years)   20,000
      Accumulated depreciation   20,000

After this entry, the book value of the equipment is $80,000; the fair value is $84,000. We use the ratio of the two amounts to adjust both the equipment and the accumulated depreciation accounts (and thus the book value) to fair value ($ in thousands):

December 31, 2011	Before Revaluation				After Revaluation
Equipment	$100	×	84/80	=	$105
Accumulated depreciation	20	×	84/80	=	21
Book value	$ 80	×	84/80	=	$ 84

The entries to revalue the equipment and the accumulated depreciation accounts (and thus the book value) are:

To record the revaluation of equipment to its fair value.

(b) Equipment ($105,000 − 100,000)   5,000
      Accumulated depreciation ($21,000 − 20,000)   1,000
      Revaluation surplus—OCI ($84,000 − 80,000)   4,000

The new basis for the equipment is its fair value of $84,000 ($105,000 − 21,000), and the following years' depreciation is based on that amount. Thus, 2012 depreciation would be $84,000 divided by the four remaining years, or $21,000:[7]

(a) Depreciation expense ($84,000 ÷ 4 years)   21,000
      Accumulated depreciation   21,000

(continued)

---

[6]"Property, Plant and Equipment," *International Accounting Standard No. 16* (IASCF), as amended effective January 1, 2009.
[7]*IAS No. 16* allows companies to choose between the method illustrated here and an alternative. The second method eliminates the entire accumulated depreciation account and adjusts the asset account (equipment in this illustration) to fair value. Using either method, the revaluation surplus (or expense) would be the same.

(concluded)

After this entry, the book value of the equipment is $63,000. Let's say the fair value now is $57,000. We use the ratio of the two amounts to adjust both the equipment and the accumulated depreciation accounts (and thus the book value) to fair value ($ in thousands):

December 31, 2012	Before Revaluation			After Revaluation
Equipment	$105	× 57/63	=	$95
Accumulated depreciation ($21 + 21)	42	× 57/63	=	38
Book value	$ 63	× 57/63	=	$57

The entries to revalue the equipment and the accumulated depreciation accounts (and thus the book value) are:

(b) Revaluation surplus—OCI ($57,000 − 63,000 = $6,000;
    limit: $4,000 balance) 4,000
    Revaluation expense (to balance) 2,000
    Accumulated depreciation ($38,000 − 42,000) 4,000
        Equipment ($95,000 − 105,000) 10,000

A decrease in fair value, as occurred in 2012, is expensed unless it reverses a revaluation surplus account relating to the same asset, as in this illustration. So, of the $6,000 decrease in value ($63,000 book value less $57,000 fair value), $4,000 is debited to the previously created revaluation surplus and the remaining $2,000 is recorded as revaluation expense in the income statement.

Real World Financials

Investcorp, a provider and manager of alternative investment products headquartered in London, prepares its financial statements according to IFRS. The following disclosure note included in a recent annual report discusses the company's decision to change its method of valuing its premises and equipment.

Change in Accounting Policy

During the current period, the Group changed its policy with respect of carrying value of premises and equipment. These assets have been revalued to their fair value in the current period and shall be carried at their revalued amount less any accumulated depreciation and cumulative impairment losses. The revaluation surplus has been recognized in other comprehensive income and included as separate component of equity as revaluation surplus.

Depletion of Natural Resources

Allocation of the cost of natural resources is called depletion. Because the usefulness of natural resources generally is directly related to the amount of the resources extracted, the activity-based units-of-production method is widely used to calculate periodic depletion. Service life is therefore the estimated amount of natural resource to be extracted (for example, tons of mineral or barrels of oil).

● LO3

Depletion base is cost less any anticipated residual value. Residual value could be significant if cost includes land that has a value after the natural resource has been extracted.

The example in Illustration 11–3 was first introduced in Chapter 10.

The Jackson Mining Company paid $1,000,000 for the right to explore for a coal deposit on 500 acres of land in Pennsylvania. Costs of exploring for the coal deposit totaled $800,000 and intangible development costs incurred in digging and erecting the mine shaft were $500,000. In addition, Jackson purchased new excavation equipment for the project at a cost of $600,000. After the coal is removed from the site, the equipment will be sold for an anticipated residual value of $60,000.

ILLUSTRATION 11–3
Depletion of Natural Resources

The company geologist estimates that 1 million tons of coal will be extracted over the three-year period. During 2011, 300,000 tons were extracted. Jackson is required by its contract to restore the land to a condition suitable for recreational use after it extracts the coal.

In Chapter 10 on page 508 we determined that the capitalized cost of the natural resource, coal mine, including the restoration costs, is $2,768,360. Since there is no residual value to the land, the depletion base equals cost and the depletion rate per ton is calculated as follows:

Depletion of the cost of natural resources usually is determined using the units-of-production method.

$$\text{Depletion per ton} = \frac{\text{Depletion base}}{\text{Estimated extractable tons}}$$

$$\text{Depletion per ton} = \frac{\$2,768,360}{1,000,000 \text{ tons}} = \$2.76836 \text{ per ton}$$

For each ton of coal extracted, $2.768360 in depletion is recorded. In 2011, the following journal entry records depletion.

Depletion ($2.76836 × 300,000 tons)	830,508	
Coal mine		830,508

Notice that the credit is to the asset, coal mine, rather than to a contra account, accumulated depletion. Although this approach is traditional, the use of a contra account is acceptable.

Depletion is a product cost and is included in the cost of the inventory of coal, just as the depreciation on manufacturing equipment is included in inventory cost. The depletion is then included in cost of goods sold in the income statement when the coal is sold.

What about depreciation on the $600,000 cost of excavation equipment? If the equipment can be moved from the site and used on future projects, the equipment's depreciable base should be allocated over its useful life. If the asset is not movable, as in our illustration, then it should be depreciated over its useful life or the life of the natural resource, whichever is shorter.

The units-of-production method often is used to determine depreciation and amortization on assets used in the extraction of natural resources.

Quite often, companies use the units-of-production method to calculate depreciation and amortization on assets used in the extraction of natural resources. The activity base used is the same as that used to calculate depletion, the estimated recoverable natural resource. In our illustration, the depreciation rate would be $.54 per ton, calculated as follows.

$$\text{Depreciation per ton} = \frac{\$600,000 - 60,000}{1,000,000 \text{ tons}} = \$.54 \text{ per ton}$$

In 2011, $162,000 in depreciation ($.54 × 300,000 tons) is recorded and also included as part of the cost of the coal inventory.

The summary of significant accounting policies disclosure accompanying recent financial statements of **ConocoPhilips** shown in Graphic 11–7 provides a good summary of depletion, amortization, and depreciation for natural resource properties.

GRAPHIC 11–7

Depletion Method Disclosure— ConocoPhilips

Real World Financials

Summary of Significant Accounting Policies (in part)

Depletion and Amortization—Leasehold costs of producing properties are depleted using the units-of-production method based on estimated proved oil and gas reserves. Amortization of intangible development costs is based on the units-of-production method using estimated proved developed oil and gas reserves.

Depreciation and Amortization—Depreciation and amortization of properties, plants and equipment on producing oil and gas properties, certain pipeline assets, and on Syncrude mining operations are determined by the units-of-production method.

ADDITIONAL CONSIDERATION

Percentage Depletion

Depletion of cost less residual value required by GAAP should not be confused with percentage depletion (also called *statutory depletion*) allowable for income tax purposes for oil, gas, and most mineral natural resources. Under these tax provisions, a producer is allowed to deduct the greater of cost-based depletion or a fixed percentage of gross income as depletion expense. Over the life of the asset, depletion could exceed the asset's cost. The percentage allowed for percentage-based depletion varies according to the type of natural resource.

Because percentage depletion usually differs from cost depletion, a difference between taxable income and financial reporting income before tax results. These differences are discussed in Chapter 16.

INTERNATIONAL FINANCIAL REPORTING STANDARDS

Biological Assets. Living animals and plants, including the trees in a timber tract or in a fruit orchard, are referred to as *biological assets*. Under U.S. GAAP, a timber tract is valued at cost less accumulated depletion and a fruit orchard at cost less accumulated depreciation. Under IFRS, biological assets are valued at their fair value less estimated costs to sell.[8]

● LO10

Amortization of Intangible Assets

Let's turn now to a third type of long-lived asset—intangible assets. As with other assets we have discussed, we allocate the cost of an intangible asset over its service or useful life. However, for the few intangible assets with indefinite useful lives, amortization is inappropriate.

● LO4

Intangible Assets Subject to Amortization

Allocating the cost of intangible assets is called **amortization.** For an intangible asset with a finite useful life, we allocate its capitalized cost less any estimated residual value to periods in which the asset is expected to contribute to the company's revenue-generating activities. This requires that we determine the asset's useful life, its amortization base (cost less estimated residual value), and the appropriate allocation method, similar to our depreciating tangible assets.

The cost of an intangible asset with a *finite* useful life is *amortized.*

USEFUL LIFE.   Legal, regulatory, or contractual provisions often limit the useful life of an intangible asset. On the other hand, useful life might sometimes be less than the asset's legal or contractual life. For example, the useful life of a patent would be considerably less than its legal life of 20 years if obsolescence were expected to limit the longevity of a protected product.

RESIDUAL VALUE.   We discussed the cost of intangible assets in Chapter 10. The expected residual value of an intangible asset usually is zero. This might not be the case, though, if at the end of its useful life to the reporting entity the asset will benefit another entity. For example, if Quadra Corp. has a commitment from another company to purchase one of Quadra's patents at the end of its useful life at a determinable price, we use that price as the patent's residual value.

ALLOCATION METHOD.   The method of amortization should reflect the pattern of use of the asset in generating benefits. Most companies use the straight-line method. We discussed and illustrated a unique approach to determining the periodic amortization of software development costs in Chapter 10. Recall that the periodic amortization percentage for software development costs is the *greater* of (1) the ratio of current revenues to current and anticipated revenues (percentage of revenue method), or (2) the straight-line percentage over the useful life of the asset.

Intel Corporation reported several intangible assets in a recent balance sheet. A note, shown in Graphic 11–8, disclosed the range of estimated useful lives and the use of the straight-line method of amortization.

Summary of Significant Accounting Policies (in part)
Identified Intangible Assets

Intellectual property assets primarily represent rights acquired under technology licenses and are generally amortized on a straight-line basis over periods of benefit, ranging from 3 to 17 years. We amortize acquisition-related developed technology on a straight-line basis over approximately 4 years. We amortize other intangible assets over 4 years. We classify all identified intangible assets within other long-term assets. In the quarter following the period in which identified intangible assets become fully amortized, the fully amortized balances are removed from the gross asset and accumulated amortization amounts.

GRAPHIC 11–8

Intangible Asset Useful Life Disclosure—Intel Corporation

Real World Financials

---

[8]"Agriculture," *International Accounting Standard No. 41* (IASCF), as amended effective January 1, 2009.

Like depletion, amortization expense traditionally is credited to the asset account itself rather than to accumulated amortization. However, the use of a contra account is acceptable. Notice in Graphic 11–8 that Intel uses an accumulated amortization contra account. Let's look at an example in Illustration 11–4.

ILLUSTRATION 11–4 Amortization of Intangibles	Hollins Corporation began operations in 2011. Early in January, the company purchased a franchise from Ajax Industries for $200,000. The franchise agreement is for a period of 10 years. In addition, Hollins purchased a patent for $50,000. The remaining legal life of the patent is 13 years. However, due to expected technological obsolescence, the company estimates that the useful life of the patent is only 8 years. Hollins uses the straight-line amortization method for all intangible assets. The company's fiscal year-end is December 31.

The journal entries to record a full year of amortization for these intangibles are as follows:

Amortization expense ($200,000 ÷ 10 years)	20,000	
Franchise		20,000
To record amortization of franchise.		
Amortization expense ($50,000 ÷ 8 years)	6,250	
Patent		6,250
To record amortization of patent.		

Similar to depreciation, amortization is either a product cost or a period cost depending on the use of the asset. For intangibles used in the manufacture of a product, amortization is a product cost and is included in the cost of inventory (and doesn't become an expense until the inventory is sold). For intangible assets not used in production, such as the franchise cost in our illustration, periodic amortization is expensed in the period incurred.

Intangible Assets Not Subject to Amortization

The cost of an intangible asset with an indefinite useful life is not amortized

An intangible asset that is determined to have an indefinite useful life is not subject to periodic amortization. Useful life is considered indefinite if there is no foreseeable limit on the period of time over which the asset is expected to contribute to the cash flows of the entity.[9]

Indefinite does not necessarily mean permanent. For example, suppose Collins Corporation acquired a trademark in conjunction with the acquisition of a tire company. Collins plans to continue to produce the line of tires marketed under the acquired company's trademark. Recall from our discussion in Chapter 10 that trademarks have a legal life of 10 years, but the registration can be renewed for an indefinite number of 10-year periods. The life of the purchased trademark is initially considered to be indefinite and the cost of the trademark is not amortized. However, if after several years management decides to phase out production of the tire line over the next three years, Collins would amortize the remaining book value over a three-year period.

Trademarks or tradenames often are considered to have indefinite useful lives.

Recall the **Hewlett-Packard Company (HP)** acquisition of **Compaq Computer Corporation** discussed in Chapter 10. HP allocated $1.4 million of the purchase price to Compaq's tradename, which is not being amortized. Graphic 11–9 provides another example in a disclosure made by **Eddie Bauer Holdings, Inc.**, in a recent annual report.

GRAPHIC 11–9

Indefinite-Life Intangibles Disclosure—Eddie Bauer Holdings, Inc.

Real World Financials

Summary of Significant Accounting Policies (in part)
Intangible Assets

Goodwill and trademarks were determined to have indefinite useful lives and are not amortized into results of operations, but instead are reviewed for impairment annually, or more often if impairment indicators arise.

Goodwill is the most common intangible asset with an indefinite useful life. Recall that goodwill is measured as the difference between the purchase price of a company and the

---

[9]FASB ASC 350–30–35–4: Intangibles–Goodwill and Other—General Intangibles Other than Goodwill—Subsequent Measurement (previously "Goodwill and Other Intangible Assets," *Statement of Financial Accounting Standards No. 142* (Norwalk, Conn.: FASB, 2001), par. B45).

fair value of all of the identifiable net assets (tangible and intangible assets minus the fair value of liabilities assumed). Does this mean that goodwill and other intangible assets with indefinite useful lives will remain in a company's balance sheet at their original capitalized values indefinitely? Not necessarily. Like other assets, intangibles are subject to the impairment of value rules we discuss in a subsequent section of this chapter. In fact, indefinite-life intangible assets must be tested for impairment annually, or more frequently if events or circumstances indicate that the asset might be impaired.

> Goodwill is an intangible asset whose cost is *not* expensed through periodic amortization.

INTERNATIONAL FINANCIAL REPORTING STANDARDS

Valuation of Intangible Assets. *IAS No. 38*[10] allows a company to value an intangible asset subsequent to initial valuation at (1) cost less accumulated amortization or (2) fair value, if fair value can be determined by reference to an active market. If revaluation is chosen, all assets within that class of intangibles must be revalued on a regular basis. Goodwill, however, cannot be revalued. U.S. GAAP prohibits revaluation of any intangible asset.

● LO10

    Notice that the revaluation option is possible only if fair value can be determined by reference to an active market, making the option relatively uncommon. However, the option possibly could be used for intangibles such as franchises and certain license agreements.

    If the revaluation option is chosen, the accounting treatment is similar to the way we applied the revaluation option for property, plant, and equipment earlier in this chapter. Recall that the way the company reports the difference between fair value and book value depends on which amount is higher. If fair value is higher than book value, the difference is reported as other comprehensive income (OCI) and then accumulates in a revaluation surplus account in equity. On the other hand, if book value is higher than fair value, the difference is expensed.

    Consider the following illustration:

Amershan LTD. prepares its financial statements according to IFRS. At the beginning of its 2011 fiscal year, the company purchased a franchise for $500,000. The franchise has a 10-year contractual life and no residual value, so amortization in 2011 is $50,000. The company does not use an accumulated amortization account and credits the franchise account directly when amortization is recorded. At the end of the year, Amershan chooses to revalue the franchise as permitted by *IAS No. 38*. Assuming that the fair value of the franchise, determined by reference to an active market, at year-end is $600,000, Amershan records amortization and the revaluation using the following journal entries:

IFRS ILLUSTRATION

Amortization expense ($500,000 ÷ 10 years)	50,000	
Franchise		50,000
Franchise ($600,000 − 450,000)	150,000	
Revaluation surplus—OCI		150,000

To record the revaluation of franchise to its fair value.

    With the second entry Amershan increases the book value of the franchise from $450,000 ($500,000 − 50,000) to its fair value of $600,000 and records a revaluation surplus for the difference. The new basis for the franchise is its fair value of $600,000, and the following years' amortization is based on that amount. Thus, 2012 amortization would be $600,000 divided by the nine remaining years, or $66,667.

CONCEPT REVIEW EXERCISE

Part A:

On March 29, 2011, the Horizon Energy Corporation purchased the mineral rights to a coal deposit in New Mexico for $2 million. Development costs and the present value of estimated land restoration costs totaled an additional $3.4 million. The company removed 200,000 tons of coal during 2011 and estimated that an additional 1,600,000 tons would be removed over the next 15 months.

DEPLETION AND AMORTIZATION

---

[10]"Intangible Assets," *International Accounting Standard No. 38* (IASCF), as amended effective January 1, 2009.

Required:
Compute depletion on the mine for 2011.

SOLUTION

Cost of Coal Mine:	($ in millions)
Purchase price of mineral rights	$2.0
Development and restoration costs	3.4
	$5.4

Depletion:

$$\text{Depletion per ton} = \frac{\$5.4 \text{ million}}{1.8 \text{ million tons*}} = \$3 \text{ per ton}$$

*200,000 + 1,600,000

$$2011 \text{ depletion} = \$3 \times 200,000 \text{ tons} = \$600,000$$

Part B:
On October 1, 2011, Advanced Micro Circuits, Inc., completed the purchase of Zotec Corporation for $200 million. Included in the allocation of the purchase price were the following identifiable intangible assets ($ in millions), along with the fair values and estimated useful lives:

Intangible Asset	Fair value	Useful Life (in years)
Patent	$10	5
Developed technology	50	4
Customer list	10	2

In addition, the fair value of acquired tangible assets was $100 million. Goodwill was valued at $30 million. Straight-line amortization is used for all purchased intangibles.

During 2011, Advanced finished work on a software development project. Development costs incurred after technological feasibility was achieved and before the product release date totaled $2 million. The software was available for release to the general public on September 29, 2011. During the last three months of the year, revenue from the sale of the software was $4 million. The company estimates that the software will generate an additional $36 million in revenue over the next 45 months.

Required:
Compute amortization for purchased intangibles and software development costs for 2011.

SOLUTION

Amortization of Purchased Intangibles:

Patent	$10 million / 5 = $2 million × 3/12 year = $.5 million
Developed technology	$50 million / 4 = $12.5 million × 3/12 year = $3.125 million
Customer list	$10 million / 2 = $5 million × 3/12 year = $1.25 million
Goodwill	The cost of goodwill is not amortized.

Amortization of Software Development Costs:

(1) Percentage-of-revenue method:

$$\frac{\$4 \text{ million}}{(\$4 \text{ million} + 36 \text{ million})} = 10\% \times \$2 \text{ million} = \$200,000$$

(2) Straight-line:

$$\frac{3 \text{ months}}{48 \text{ months}} \text{ or } 6.25\% \times \$2 \text{ million} = \$125,000$$

Advanced will use the percentage-of-revenue method since it produces the greater amortization, $200,000.

ADDITIONAL ISSUES

In this part of the chapter, we discuss the following issues related to cost allocation:

1. Partial periods
2. Changes in estimates
3. Change in depreciation method
4. Error correction
5. Impairment of value

Partial Periods

Only in textbooks are property, plant, and equipment and intangible assets purchased and disposed of at the very beginning or very end of a company's fiscal year. When acquisition and disposal occur at other times, a company theoretically must determine how much depreciation, depletion, and amortization to record for the part of the year that each asset actually is used.

Let's repeat the Hogan Manufacturing Company illustration used earlier in the chapter but modify it in Illustration 11–5 to assume that the asset was acquired *during* the company's fiscal year.

On April 1, 2011, the Hogan Manufacturing Company purchased a machine for $250,000. The company expects the service life of the machine to be five years and the anticipated residual value is $40,000. The machine was disposed of after five years of use. The company's fiscal year-end is December 31. Partial-year depreciation is recorded based on the number of months the asset is in service.	**ILLUSTRATION 11–5** Depreciation Methods—Partial Year

Notice that no information is provided on the estimated output of the machine. Partial-year depreciation presents a problem only when time-based depreciation methods are used. In an activity-based method, the rate per unit of output simply is multiplied by the actual output for the period, regardless of the length of that period.

Depreciation per year of the asset's life calculated earlier in the chapter for the various time-based depreciation methods is shown in Illustration 11–5A.

Year	Straight Line	Sum-of-the-Years'-Digits	Double-Declining Balance	
1	$ 42,000	$ 70,000	$100,000	**ILLUSTRATION 11–5A** Yearly Depreciation
2	42,000	56,000	60,000	
3	42,000	42,000	36,000	
4	42,000	28,000	14,000	
5	42,000	14,000	0	
Total	$210,000	$210,000	$210,000	

Illustration 11–5B shows how Hogan would depreciate the machinery by these three methods assuming an April 1 acquisition date.

Notice that 2011 depreciation is three-quarters of the full year's depreciation for the first year of the asset's life, because the asset was used nine months, or 3/4 of the year. The remaining one-quarter of the first year's depreciation is included in 2012's depreciation along with 3/4 of the depreciation for the second year of the asset's life. This calculation is not necessary for the straight-line method because a full year's depreciation is the same for each year of the asset's life.

Usually, the above procedure is impractical or at least cumbersome. As a result, most companies adopt a simplifying assumption, or convention, for computing partial year's

ILLUSTRATION 11–5B   Partial-Year Depreciation

Year	Straight Line		Sum-of-the-Years'-Digits		Double-Declining Balance	
2011	$42,000 × 3/4 =	**$ 31,500**	$70,000 × 3/4 =	**$ 52,500**	$100,000 × 3/4 =	**$ 75,000**
2012		**$ 42,000**	$70,000 × 1/4 = $	17,500	$100,000 × 1/4 = $	25,000
			+56,000 × 3/4 =	42,000	+60,000 × 3/4 =	45,000
				$ 59,500		**$ 70,000***
2013		**$ 42,000**	$56,000 × 1/4 = $	14,000	$60,000 × 1/4 = $	15,000
			+42,000 × 3/4 =	31,500	+36,000 × 3/4 =	27,000
				$ 45,500		**$ 42,000**
2014		**$ 42,000**	$42,000 × 1/4 = $	10,500	$36,000 × 1/4 = $	9,000
			+28,000 × 3/4 =	21,000	+14,000 × 3/4 =	10,500
				$ 31,500		**$ 19,500**
2015		**$ 42,000**	$28,000 × 1/4 = $	7,000	$14,000 × 1/4 = $	**3,500**
			+14,000 × 3/4 =	10,500		
				$ 17,500		
2016	$42,000 × 1/4 =	**$ 10,500**	$14,000 × 1/4 = $	**3,500**		
	Totals	**$210,000**		**$210,000**		**$210,000**

*Could also be determined by multiplying the book value at the beginning of the year by twice the straight-line rate: ($250,000 − 75,000) × 40% = $70,000.

depreciation and use it consistently. A common convention is to record one-half of a full year's depreciation in the year of acquisition and another half year in the year of disposal. This is known as the **half-year convention.**[11]

Changes in Estimates

● LO5

A change in estimate should be reflected in the financial statements of the current period and future periods.

The calculation of depreciation, depletion, or amortization requires estimates of both service life and residual value. It's inevitable that at least some estimates will prove incorrect. Chapter 4 introduced the topic of changes in estimates along with coverage of changes in accounting principles and the correction of errors. Here and in subsequent sections of this chapter, we provide overviews of the accounting treatment and disclosures required for these changes and errors when they involve property, plant, and equipment and intangible assets.

Changes in estimates are accounted for prospectively. When a company revises a previous estimate based on new information, prior financial statements are not restated. Instead, the company merely incorporates the new estimate in any related accounting determinations from then on. So, it usually will affect some aspects of both the balance sheet and the income statement in the current and future periods. A disclosure note should describe the effect of a change in estimate on income before extraordinary items, net income, and related pershare amounts for the current period.

Consider the example in Illustration 11–6.

The asset's book value is depreciated down to the anticipated residual value of $22,000 at the end of the revised eight-year service life. In addition, a note discloses the effect of the change in estimate on income, if material. The before-tax effect is an increase in income of $18,000 (depreciation of $42,000 if the change had not been made, less $24,000 depreciation after the change).

Con-way Inc. is a transportation, logistics, and supply-chain management services company. The company recently revised its estimates of the service lives of its tractors. Graphic 11–10 shows the note that disclosed the change.

---

[11]Another common method is the modified half-year convention. This method records a full year's depreciation when the asset is acquired in the first half of the year or sold in the second half. No depreciation is recorded if the asset is acquired in the second half of the year or sold in the first half. These half-year conventions are simple and, in most cases, will not result in material differences from a more precise calculation.

On January 1, 2009, the Hogan Manufacturing Company purchased a machine for $250,000. The company expects the service life of the machine to be five years and its anticipated residual value to be $40,000. The company's fiscal year-end is December 31 and the straight-line depreciation method is used for all depreciable assets. During 2011, the company revised its estimate of service life from five to eight years and also revised estimated residual value to $22,000.

For 2009 and 2010, depreciation is $42,000 per year [($250,000 – 40,000) ÷ 5 years] or $84,000 for the two years. However, with the revised estimate, depreciation for 2011 and subsequent years is determined by allocating the book value remaining at the beginning of 2011 less the revised residual value equally over the remaining service life of six years (8 – 2). The remaining book value at the beginning of 2011 is $166,000 ($250,000 – 84,000) and depreciation for 2011 and subsequent years is recorded as follows:

Depreciation expense (below)	24,000	
Accumulated depreciation		24,000

	$250,000	Cost
$42,000		Previous annual depreciation ($210,000 ÷ 5 years)
× 2 years	84,000	Depreciation to date (2009–2010)
	166,000	Book value as of 1/1/11
	22,000	Less revised residual value
	144,000	Revised depreciable base
	÷ 6	Estimated remaining life (8 years – 2 years)
	$ 24,000	New annual depreciation

ILLUSTRATION 11–6

Change in Accounting Estimate

Property, Plant, and Equipment (in part)

Con-way periodically evaluates whether changes to estimated useful lives or salvage values are necessary to ensure that these estimates accurately reflect the economic use of the assets. In January 2009, Con-way Freight increased the estimated useful life of most of its tractors to 8 years from 7 years. As a result of this change, net loss applicable to common shareholders in the first three months of 2009 decreased by $2.0 million ($0.04 per diluted share).

GRAPHIC 11–10

Change in Estimate Disclosure—Con-way Inc.

Real World Financials

Change in Depreciation, Amortization, or Depletion Method

Recall from our discussion in Chapter 4 that generally accepted accounting principles require that a change in depreciation, amortization, or depletion method be considered a change in accounting estimate that is achieved by a change in accounting principle. We account for these changes prospectively, exactly as we would any other change in estimate. One difference is that most changes in estimate do not require a company to justify the change. However, this change in estimate is a result of changing an accounting principle and therefore requires a clear justification as to why the new method is preferable. Consider the example in Illustration 11–7.

Graphic 11–11 provides an example of a disclosure describing a recent change in depreciation method by **Performed Line Products (PLP)**, a worldwide manufacturer of cable hardware and fiber optics connection devices.

Frequently, when a company changes depreciation method, the change will be effective only for assets placed in service after that date. Of course, that means depreciation schedules do not require revision because the change does not affect assets depreciated in prior periods. A disclosure note still is required to provide justification for the change and to report the effect of the change in the current year's income.

● LO6

Changes in depreciation, amortization, or depletion methods are accounted for the same way as a change in accounting estimate.

ILLUSTRATION 11–7

Change in Depreciation Method

On January 1, 2009, the Hogan Manufacturing Company purchased a machine for $250,000. The company expects the service life of the machine to be five years and its anticipated residual value to be $30,000. The company's fiscal year-end is December 31 and the double-declining-balance (DDB) depreciation method is used. During 2011, the company switched from the DDB to the straight-line method. In 2011, the adjusting entry is:

Depreciation expense (below) 20,000
    Accumulated depreciation 20,000

DDB depreciation:
2009	$100,000	($250,000 × 40%*)
2010	60,000	([$250,000 – 100,000] × 40%*)
Total	$160,000	

*Double the straight-line rate for 5 years ([1/5 = 20%] × 2 = 40%)

$250,000	Cost
160,000	Depreciation to date, DDB (2009–2010)
90,000	Undepreciated cost as of 1/1/11
30,000	Less residual value
60,000	Depreciable base
÷ 3 yrs.	Remaining life (5 years – 2 years)
$ 20,000	New annual depreciation

A disclosure note reports the effect of the change on net income and earnings per share along with clear justification for changing depreciation methods.

GRAPHIC 11–11

Change in Depreciation Method—Performed Line Products

Real World Financials

Property and Equipment—Net (in part)

Effective January 1, 2009, the Company changed its method of computing depreciation from accelerated methods to the straight-line method for the Company's PLP-USA assets. Based on Statement of Financial Accounting Standards (SFAS) No. 154, "Accounting Changes and Error Corrections" [FASB ASC 250], the Company determined that the change in depreciation method from an accelerated method to a straight-line method is a change in accounting estimate affected by a change in accounting principle. Per SFAS 154 [FASB ASC 250], a change in accounting estimate affected by a change in accounting principle is to be applied prospectively. The change is considered preferable because the straight-line method will more accurately reflect the pattern of usage and the expected benefits of such assets and provide greater consistency with the depreciation methods used by other companies in the Company's industry. The net book value of assets acquired prior to January 1, 2009 with useful lives remaining will be depreciated using the straight-line method prospectively. As a result of the change to the straight-line method of depreciating PLP-USA's assets, depreciation expense decreased $.1 million for the three month period ended March 31, 2009 and the decrease is expected to approximate such amount in each of the remaining quarters in 2009.

Error Correction

● LO7

Errors involving property, plant, and equipment and intangible assets include computational errors in the calculation of depreciation, depletion, or amortization and mistakes made in determining whether expenditures should be capitalized or expensed. These errors can affect many years. For example, let's say a major addition to equipment should be capitalized but incorrectly is expensed. Not only is income in the year of the error understated, but subsequent years' income is overstated because depreciation is omitted.

Recall from our discussion of inventory errors in Chapter 9 that if a material error is discovered in an accounting period subsequent to the period in which the error is made, any previous years' financial statements that were incorrect as a result of the error are retrospectively restated to reflect the correction. Any account balances that are incorrect as a result of the error are corrected by journal entry. If retained earnings is one of the incorrect accounts, the correction is reported as a *prior period adjustment* to the beginning balance in the statement of shareholders' equity.[12] In addition, a disclosure note is needed to describe the nature of the error and the impact of its correction on net income, income before extraordinary items, and earnings per share.

Here is a summary of the treatment of material errors occurring in a previous year:

- Previous years' financial statements are retrospectively restated.
- Account balances are corrected.
- If retained earnings requires correction, the correction is reported as a prior period adjustment.
- A note describes the nature of the error and the impact of the correction on income.

Consider Illustration 11–8. The 2009 and 2010 financial statements that were incorrect as a result of the error are *retrospectively restated* to report the addition to the patent and to reflect the correct amount of amortization expense, assuming both statements are reported again for comparative purposes in the 2011 annual report.

In 2011, the controller of the Hathaway Corporation discovered an error in recording $300,000 in legal fees to successfully defend a patent infringement suit in 2009. The $300,000 was charged to legal fee expense but should have been capitalized and amortized over the five-year remaining life of the patent. Straight-line amortization is used by Hathaway for all intangibles.

ILLUSTRATION 11–8
Error Correction

Analysis

($ in thousands)

		Correct (Should Have Been Recorded)			Incorrect (As Recorded)	
2009	Patent	300		Expense	300	
	Cash		300	Cash		300
2009	Expense	60		Amortization entry omitted		
	Patent		60			
2010	Expense	60		Amortization entry omitted		
	Patent		60			

During the two-year period, amortization expense was *understated* by $120 thousand, but other expenses were *overstated* by $300 thousand, so net income during the period was *understated* by $180 thousand (ignoring income taxes). This means retained earnings is currently *understated* by that amount.

Patent is understated by $180 thousand.

Sometimes, the analysis is easier if you re-create the entries actually recorded incorrectly and those that would have been recorded if the error hadn't occurred, and then compare them.

($ in thousands)

Patent	180	
Retained earnings		180

To correct incorrect accounts.

Because retained earnings is one of the accounts incorrect as a result of the error, a correction to that account of $180,000 is reported as a prior period adjustment to the 2011 beginning retained earnings balance in Hathaway's comparative statements of shareholders'

---

[12]The prior period adjustment is applied to beginning retained earnings for the year following the error, or for the earliest year being reported in the comparative financial statements when the error occurs prior to the earliest year presented. The retained earnings balances in years after the first year also are adjusted to what those balances would be if the error had not occurred, but a company may choose not to explicitly report those adjustments as separate line items.

equity. Assuming that 2010 is included with 2011 in the comparative statements, a correction would be made to the 2010 beginning retained earnings balance as well. That prior period adjustment, though, would be for the pre-2010 difference: $300,000 − 60,000 = $240,000.

Also, a disclosure note accompanying Hathaway's 2011 financial statements should describe the nature of the error and the impact of its correction on each year's net income (understated by $240,000 in 2009 and overstated by $60,000 in 2010), income before extraordinary items (same as net income), and earnings per share.

Chapter 20 provides in-depth coverage of changes in estimates and methods, and of accounting errors. We cover the tax effect of these changes and errors in that chapter.

Impairment of Value

● LO8

FINANCIAL Reporting Case

Q3, p. 557

Depreciation, depletion, and amortization reflect a gradual consumption of the benefits inherent in property, plant, and equipment and intangible assets. An implicit assumption in allocating the cost of an asset over its useful life is that there has been no significant reduction in the anticipated total benefits or service potential of the asset. Situations can arise, however, that cause a significant decline or impairment of those benefits or service potentials. An extreme case would be the destruction of a plant asset—say a building destroyed by fire—before the asset is fully depreciated. The remaining carrying value of the asset in that case should be written off as a loss. Sometimes, though, the impairment of future value is more subtle.

The way we recognize and measure an impairment loss differs depending on whether the assets are to be held and used or are being held to be sold. Accounting is different, too, for assets with finite lives and those with indefinite lives. We consider those differences now.

Assets to Be Held and Used

An increasingly common occurrence in practice is the partial write-down of property, plant, and equipment and intangible assets that remain in use. For example, in the second quarter of 2001, **American Airlines** reduced the carrying value (book value) of certain aircraft by $685 million. The write-down reflected the significant reduction in demand for air travel that occurred even before the September 11, 2001, terrorist attacks on the World Trade Center and the Pentagon.

An asset held for use should be written down if there has been a significant impairment of value.

Conceptually, there is considerable merit for a policy requiring the write-down of an asset when there has been a significant decline in value. A write-down can provide important information about the future cash flows that a company can generate from using the asset. However, in practice, this process is very subjective. Even if it appears certain that significant impairment of value has occurred, it often is difficult to measure the amount of the required write-down.

For example, let's say a company purchased $2,000,000 of equipment to be used in the production of a new type of laser printer. Depreciation is determined using the straight-line method over a useful life of six years and the residual value is estimated at $200,000. At the beginning of year 3, the machine's book value has been reduced by accumulated depreciation to $1,400,000 [$2,000,000 − ($300,000 × 2)]. At that time, new technology is developed causing a significant reduction in the selling price of the new laser printer as well as a reduction in anticipated demand for the product. Management estimates that the equipment will be useful for only two more years and will have no significant residual value.

This situation is not simply a matter of a change in the estimates of useful life and residual value. Management must decide if the events occurring in year 3 warrant a write-down of the asset below $1,400,000. A write-down would be appropriate if the company decided that it would be unable to fully recover this amount through future use.

For assets to be held and used, different guidelines apply to (1) property, plant, and equipment and intangible assets with finite useful lives (subject to depreciation, depletion, or amortization) and (2) intangible assets with indefinite useful lives (not subject to amortization).

PROPERTY, PLANT, AND EQUIPMENT AND FINITE-LIFE INTANGIBLE ASSETS.

Generally accepted accounting principles provide guidelines for when to recognize and how to measure impairment losses of long-lived tangible assets and intangible assets with finite useful lives.[13] For purposes of this recognition and measurement, assets are grouped at the lowest level for which identifiable cash flows are largely independent of the cash flows of other assets.

When to Test for Impairment. It would be impractical to test all assets or asset groups for impairment at the end of every reporting period. GAAP requires investigation of possible impairment only if events or changes in circumstances indicate that the book value of the asset or asset group may not be recoverable. This might happen from:

> Property, plant, and equipment and finite-life intangible assets are tested for impairment only when events or changes in circumstances indicate book value may not be recoverable.

  a. A significant decrease in market price.
  b. A significant adverse change in how the asset is being used or in its physical condition.
  c. A significant adverse change in legal factors or in the business climate.
  d. An accumulation of costs significantly higher than the amount originally expected for the acquisition or construction of an asset.
  e. A current-period loss combined with a history of losses or a projection of continuing losses associated with the asset.
  f. A realization that the asset will be disposed of significantly before the end of its estimated useful life.[14]

Measurement. Determining whether to record an impairment loss and actually recording the loss is a two-step process. The first step is a *recoverability* test—an impairment loss is required only when the undiscounted sum of estimated future cash flows from an asset is less than the asset's book value. The *measurement* of impairment loss—step 2—is the difference between the asset's book value and its fair value. If an impairment loss is recognized, the written-down book value becomes the new cost base for future cost allocation. Later recovery of an impairment loss is prohibited.

> STEP 1—An impairment loss is required only when the undiscounted sum of future cash flows is less than book value.

Let's look closer at the measurement process (step two). Fair value is the amount at which the asset could be bought or sold in a current transaction between willing parties. Quoted market prices could be used if they're available. If fair value is not determinable, it must be estimated.

> STEP 2—The impairment loss is the excess of book value over fair value.

The process is best described by an example. Consider Illustration 11–9.

In the entry in Illustration 11–9, we reduce accumulated depreciation to zero and decrease the cost of the assets to their fair value of $135 million ($300 − 165). This adjusted amount serves as the revised basis for subsequent depreciation over the remaining useful life of the assets, just as if the assets had been acquired on the impairment date for their fair values.

Because the fair value of the factory assets was not readily available to Dakota in Illustration 11–9, the $135 million had to be estimated. One method that can be used to estimate fair value is to compute the discounted present value of future cash flows expected from the asset. Keep in mind that we use *undiscounted* estimates of cash flows in step one to determine whether an impairment loss is indicated, but *discounted* estimates of cash flows to determine the amount of the loss. In calculating present value, either a traditional approach or an expected cash flow approach can be used. The traditional approach is to incorporate risk and uncertainty into the discount rate. Recall from discussions in previous chapters that the expected cash flow approach incorporates risk and uncertainty instead

> The present value of future cash flows often is used as a measure of fair value.

---

[13]FASB ASC 360–10–35–15 through 20: Property, Plant, and Equipment—Overall—Subsequent Measurement—Impairment or Disposal of Long-Lived Assets (previously "Accounting for the Impairment of Long-Lived Assets and for Long-Lived Assets to Be Disposed Of," *Statement of Financial Accounting Standards No. 144* (Norwalk, Conn.: FASB, 2001)).

[14]FASB ASC 360–10–35–21: Property, Plant, and Equipment—Overall—Subsequent Measurement—Impairment or Disposal of Long-Lived Assets (previously "Accounting for the Impairment of Long-Lived Assets and for Long-Lived Assets to Be Disposed Of," *Statement of Financial Accounting Standards No. 144* (Norwalk, Conn.: FASB, 2001), par. 8).

ILLUSTRATION 11–9

Impairment Loss—
Property, Plant, and
Equipment

The Dakota Corporation operates several factories that manufacture medical equipment. Near the end of the company's 2011 fiscal year, a change in business climate related to a competitor's innovative products indicated to management that the $170 million book value (original cost of $300 million less accumulated depreciation of $130 million) of the assets of one of Dakota's factories may not be recoverable.

Management is able to identify cash flows from this factory and estimates that future cash flows over the remaining useful life of the factory will be $150 million. The fair value of the factory's assets is not readily available but is estimated to be $135 million.

Change in circumstances. A change in the business climate related to a competitor's innovative products requires Dakota to investigate for possible impairment.

Step 1. Recoverability. Because the book value of $170 million exceeds the $150 million undiscounted future cash flows, an impairment loss is indicated.

Step 2. Measurement of impairment loss. The impairment loss is $35 million, determined as follows:

Book value	$170 million
Fair value	135 million
Impairment loss	$ 35 million

The entry to record the loss is ($ in millions):

Loss on impairment	35	
Accumulated depreciation	130	
Factory assets		165

The loss normally is reported in the income statement as a separate component of operating expenses.

into a determination of a probability-weighted cash flow expectation, and then discounts this expected cash flow using a risk-free interest rate. We discussed and illustrated the expected cash flow approach in previous chapters.

A disclosure note is needed to describe the impairment loss. The note should include a description of the impaired asset or asset group, the facts and circumstances leading to the impairment, the amount of the loss if not separately disclosed on the face of the income statement, and the method used to determine fair value.

Sport Chalet Inc. operates specialty sporting goods stores in four western states. Graphic 11–12 shows Sport Chalet's disclosure note describing recent impairment losses. The note provides a summary of the process used to identify and measure impairment losses for property, plant, and equipment and finite-life intangible assets.

GRAPHIC 11–12

Asset Impairment
Disclosure—Sport
Chalet Inc.

Real World Financials

Impairment of Long-Lived Asset (in part)

We account for long-lived assets in accordance with the provisions of Statement of Financial Accounting Standards ("SFAS") No. 144, "Accounting for the Impairment or Disposal of Long-Lived Assets." [FASB ASC 360] We review long-lived assets for impairment whenever events or changes in circumstances indicate that the carrying amount of an asset may not be recoverable. Recoverability of assets to be held and used is determined by a comparison of the carrying amount of an asset to future undiscounted net cash flows expected to be generated by the asset. If such assets are considered impaired, the impairment recognized is measured by comparing projected individual store discounted cash flow to the asset carrying values. Declines in projected store cash flow could result in the impairment of assets.

Using the impairment evaluation methodology described herein, we recorded long-lived asset impairment charges totaling $10.7 million and $2.1 million, in the aggregate, during fiscal 2009 and 2008, respectively. The carrying value of property and equipment was approximately $57.7 million as of March 29, 2009.

INTERNATIONAL FINANCIAL REPORTING STANDARDS

Impairment of Value: Property, Plant, and Equipment and Finite-Life Intangible Assets. Highlighted below are some important differences in accounting for impairment of value for property, plant, and equipment and finite-life intangible assets between U.S. GAAP and *IAS No. 36*.[15]

● LO10

	U.S. GAAP	IFRS
When to Test	When events or changes in circumstances indicate that book value may not be recoverable.	Assets must be assessed for indicators of impairment at the end of each reporting period. Indicators of impairment are similar to U.S. GAAP.
Recoverability	An impairment loss is required when an asset's book value exceeds the undiscounted sum of the asset's estimated future cash flows.	There is no equivalent recoverability test. An impairment loss is required when an asset's book value exceeds the higher of the asset's value-in-use (present value of estimated future cash flows) and fair value less costs to sell.
Measurement	The impairment loss is the difference between book value and fair value.	The impairment loss is the difference between book value and the "recoverable amount" (the higher of the asset's value-in-use and fair value less costs to sell).
Subsequent Reversal of Loss	Prohibited.	Required if the circumstances that caused the impairment are resolved.

Let's look at an illustration highlighting the important differences described above.

The Jasmine Tea Company has a factory that has significantly decreased in value due to technological innovations in the industry. Below are data related to the factory's assets:

IFRS ILLUSTRATION

	($ in millions)
Book value	$18.5
Undiscounted sum of estimated future cash flows	19.0
Present value of cash flows	16.0
Fair value less cost to sell (determined by appraisal)	15.5

What amount of impairment loss should Jasmine Tea recognize, if any, under U.S. GAAP? Under IFRS?

U.S. GAAP   There is no impairment loss. The sum of undiscounted estimated future cash flows exceeds the book value.

IFRS   Jasmine should recognize an impairment loss of $2.5 million. Indicators of impairment are present and book value exceeds both value-in-use (present value of cash flows) and fair value less costs to sell. The recoverable amount is $16 million, the higher of value-in-use ($16 million) and fair value less costs to sell ($15.5 million). The impairment loss is the difference between book value of $18.5 million and the $16 million recoverable amount.

Cadbury Schweppes, Plc., a U.K. company, prepares its financial statements according to IFRS. The following disclosure note describes the company's impairment policy:

Real World Financials

Impairment Review (in part)

The Group carries out an impairment review of its tangible assets when a change in circumstances or situation indicates that those assets may have suffered an impairment loss. . . . Impairment is measured by comparing the carrying amount of an asset . . . with the "recoverable amount," that is the higher of its fair value less costs to sell and its "value in use." Value in use is calculated by discounting the expected future cash flows. . . .

---

[15]"Impairment of Assets," *International Accounting Standard No. 36* (IASCF), as amended effective January 1, 2009.

INDEFINITE-LIFE INTANGIBLE ASSETS OTHER THAN GOODWILL.

Intangible assets with indefinite useful lives should be tested for impairment annually, or more frequently if events or changes in circumstances indicate that the asset may be impaired. The measurement of an impairment loss for indefinite-life intangible assets other than goodwill is a one-step process. We compare the fair value of the asset with its book value. If book value exceeds fair value, an impairment loss is recognized for the difference. Notice that we omit the recoverability test with these assets. Because we anticipate cash flows to continue indefinitely, recoverability is not a good indicator of impairment.

Similar to property, plant, and equipment and finite-life intangible assets, if an impairment loss is recognized, the written-down book value becomes the new cost base for future cost allocation. Recovery of the impairment loss is prohibited. Disclosure requirements also are similar.

INTERNATIONAL FINANCIAL REPORTING STANDARDS

Impairment of Value: Indefinite-Life Intangible Assets Other than Goodwill. Similar to U.S. GAAP, IFRS requires indefinite-life intangible assets other than goodwill to be tested for impairment at least annually. However, under U.S. GAAP, the impairment loss is measured as the difference between book value and fair value, while under IFRS the impairment loss is the difference between book value and the recoverable amount. The recoverable amount is the higher of the asset's value-in-use (present value of estimated future cash flows) and fair value less costs to sell.

IFRS requires the reversal of an impairment loss if the circumstances that caused the impairment are resolved. Reversals are prohibited under U.S. GAAP.

Also, indefinite-life intangible assets may not be combined with other indefinite-life intangible assets for the required annual impairment test. Under U.S. GAAP, though, if certain criteria are met, indefinite-life intangible assets should be combined for the required annual impairment test.

GOODWILL.

Recall that goodwill is a unique intangible asset. Unlike other assets, its cost (a) can't be directly associated with any specific identifiable right and (b) is not separable from the company as a whole. Because of these unique characteristics, we can't measure the impairment of goodwill the same way as we do other assets. GAAP provides guidelines for impairment, which while similar to general impairment guidelines, are specific to goodwill.[16] Let's compare the two-step process for measuring goodwill impairment with the two-step process for measuring impairment for property, plant, and equipment and finite-life intangible assets.

In Step 1, for all classifications of assets, we decide whether a write-down due to impairment is required by determining whether the value of an asset has fallen below its book value. However, in this comparison, the value of assets for property, plant, and equipment and finite-life intangible assets is considered to be value-in-use as measured by the sum of undiscounted cash flows expected from the asset. But due to its unique characteristics, the value of goodwill is not associated with any specific cash flows and must be measured in a unique way. By its very nature, goodwill is inseparable from a particular *reporting unit*. So, for this step, we compare the value of the reporting unit itself with its book value. If the fair value of the reporting unit is less than its book value, an impairment loss is indicated. A reporting unit is an operating segment of a company or a component of an operating segment for which discrete financial information is available and segment management regularly reviews the operating results of that component.

If goodwill is tested for impairment at the same time as other assets of the reporting unit, the other assets must be tested first and any impairment loss and asset write-down recorded prior to testing goodwill.

---

[16]FASB ASC 350–20–35: Intangibles—Goodwill and Other—Goodwill—Subsequent Measurement (previously "Goodwill and Other Intangible Assets," *Statement of Financial Accounting Standards No. 142* (Norwalk, Conn.: FASB, 2001)).

In Step 2, for all classifications of property, plant, and equipment and intangible assets, if impairment is indicated from step 1, we measure the amount of impairment as the excess of the book value of the asset over its fair value. However, unlike for most other assets, the fair value of goodwill cannot be measured directly (market value, present value of associated cash flows, etc.) and so must be "implied" from the fair value of the reporting unit that acquired the goodwill.

The implied fair value of goodwill is calculated in the same way that goodwill is determined in a business combination. That is, it's a residual amount measured by subtracting the fair value of all identifiable net assets from the purchase price using the unit's previously determined fair value as the purchase price.[17] An example is provided in Illustration 11–10.

> **STEP 2—A goodwill impairment loss is measured as the excess of the book value of the goodwill over its "implied" fair value.**

In 2010, the Upjane Corporation acquired Pharmacopia Corporation for $500 million. Upjane recorded $100 million in goodwill related to this acquisition because the fair value of the net assets of Pharmacopia was $400 million. After the acquisition, Pharmacopia continues to operate as a separate company and is considered a reporting unit.

Upjane performs a goodwill impairment test at the end of every fiscal year. At the end of 2011, the book value of Pharmacopia's net assets is $440 million, including the $100 million in goodwill. On that date, the fair value of Pharmacopia has dropped to $360 million and the fair value of all of its identifiable tangible and intangible assets, excluding goodwill, is $335 million.

Step 1. Recoverability. Because the book value of the net assets of $440 million exceeds the $360 million fair value of the reporting unit, an impairment loss is indicated.

Step 2. Measurement of impairment loss. The impairment loss is $75 million, determined as follows:

Determination of implied goodwill:

Fair value of Pharmacopia	$360 million
Fair value of Pharmacopia's net assets (excluding goodwill)	335 million
Implied value of goodwill	$ 25 million

Measurement of impairment loss:

Book value of goodwill	$100 million
Implied value of goodwill	25 million
Impairment loss	$ 75 million

The entry to record the loss is ($ in millions):

Loss on impairment of goodwill	75	
Goodwill		75

The loss normally is reported in the income statement as a separate component of operating expenses.

> **ILLUSTRATION 11–10**
>
> Impairment Loss—Goodwill
>
> The "implied" fair value of goodwill is a residual amount measured by subtracting the fair value of all identifiable net assets from the unit's fair value.

Similar to other intangible assets with indefinite useful lives, goodwill should be tested for impairment on an annual basis and in between annual test dates if events or circumstances indicate that the fair value of the reporting unit is below its book value.

The acquiring company in a business combination often pays for the acquisition using its own stock. In the late 1990s, the stock prices of many companies were unusually high. These often-inflated stock prices meant high purchase prices for many acquisitions and, in many cases, incredibly high values allocated to goodwill. When stock prices retreated in 2000 and 2001, it became obvious that the book value of goodwill for many companies would never be recovered. Some examples of multibillion dollar goodwill impairment losses are shown in Graphic 11–13.

Blockbuster Inc., the video store company, provides a more recent example. Graphic 11–14 shows the disclosure note that describes a $432.6 million impairment charge and also provides a useful summary of accounting for goodwill impairment.

> **Goodwill should be tested for impairment at least annually.**

GRAPHIC 11–13

Goodwill Impairment
Losses

Company	Goodwill Impairment Loss
AOL Time Warner	$99 billion
JDS Uniphase	50 billion
Nortel Networks	12 billion
Lucent Technologies	4 billion
Vivendi Universal SA	15 billion (Euro dollars)

GRAPHIC 11–14

Goodwill Impairment
Disclosure—
Blockbuster Inc.

Real World Financials

Goodwill and Intangible Assets

In accordance with SFAS No. 142, *Goodwill and Other Intangible Assets* ("SFAS 142")
[FASB ASC 350], we assess goodwill and intangible assets with indefinite lives for
impairment at the reporting unit level on an annual basis and between annual tests if events
occur or circumstances change that would more likely than not reduce the fair value below
its carrying amount. SFAS 142 requires that the impairment test be performed through
the application of a two-step fair value test. The first step of the test compares the book
values of our reporting units, domestic and international, to their estimated fair values at the
respective test dates. The estimated fair values of the reporting units are computed using
the present value of estimated future cash flows. If fair value does not exceed carrying value
then the second step must be performed to quantify the amount of the impairment. The
second step of the goodwill impairment test compares the implied fair value of goodwill to
the book value of goodwill. To determine the implied fair value of goodwill, our estimated
fair value is allocated to the estimated fair value of our existing tangible assets and liabilities
as well as existing identified intangible assets and previously unidentified intangible assets in
a manner similar to a purchase price allocation. The estimated implied fair value of goodwill
and the estimated fair value of identified intangibles are compared to their respective
carrying values and any excess carrying value is recorded as a charge to operating income.

Impairment of Goodwill and Other Long-Lived Assets (in part)

We performed our annual impairment test as of October 31, the end of our fiscal year. The
estimated fair value of our domestic reporting unit was less than its related book value
and we determined that its goodwill balance was impaired. Accordingly, step two of the
goodwill impairment test was completed for the domestic reporting unit which resulted in
an impairment charge totaling $432.6 million in the fourth quarter.

● **LO10**

INTERNATIONAL FINANCIAL REPORTING STANDARDS

Impairment of Value: Goodwill. Highlighted below are some important differences in
accounting for the impairment of goodwill between U.S. GAAP and *IAS No. 36.*[18]

	U.S. GAAP	**IFRS**
Level of Testing	*Reporting unit*—a segment or a component of an operating segment for which discrete financial information is available.	*Cash-generating unit* (CGU)—the smallest identifiable group of assets that generates cash flows that are largely independent of the cash flows from other assets. A CGU can't be lower than a segment.
Measurement	*A two-step process:* 1. Compare the fair value of the reporting unit with its book value. A loss is indicated if fair value is less than book value. 2. The impairment loss is the excess of book value over implied fair value.	*A one-step process:* Compare the recoverable amount of the CGU to book value. If the recoverable amount is less, reduce goodwill first, then other assets. The recoverable amount is the higher of fair value less costs to sell and value-in-use (present value of estimated future cash flows).

(continued)

[18]"Impairment of Assets," *International Accounting Standard No. 36* (IASCF), as amended effective January 1, 2009.

(concluded)

U.S. GAAP and *IAS No. 36* both require goodwill to be tested for impairment at least annually, and both prohibit the reversal of goodwill impairment losses.

Let's look at an illustration highlighting the differences described above.

Canterbury LTD. has $38 million of goodwill in its balance sheet from the 2009 acquisition of Denton, Inc. At the end of 2011, Canterbury's management provided the following information for the year-end goodwill impairment test ($ in millions):

Fair value of Denton (determined by appraisal)	$132
Fair value of Denton's net assets (excluding goodwill)	120
Book value of Denton's net assets (including goodwill)	150
Present value of Denton's estimated future cash flows	135

Assume that Denton is considered a reporting unit under U.S. GAAP and a cash-generating unit under IFRS, and that its fair value approximates fair value less costs to sell. What is the amount of goodwill impairment loss that Canterbury should recognize, if any, under U.S. GAAP? Under IFRS?

U.S. GAAP	Fair value of Denton	$132
	Fair value of Denton's net assets (excluding goodwill)	120
	Implied value of goodwill	$ 12
	Book value of goodwill	$38
	Implied value of goodwill	12
	Impairment loss	**$ 26**
IFRS	The recoverable amount is $135 million, the higher of the $135 million value-in-use (present value of estimated future cash flows) and the $132 million fair value less costs to sell.	
	Denton's book value	$150
	Recoverable amount	135
	Impairment loss	**$ 15**

Royal Philips Electronics of the Netherlands is a world leader in health care, lifestyle, and lighting. The company prepares its financial statements according to IFRS. The following disclosures describe the company's goodwill impairment policy and a $301 million EUR goodwill impairment loss.

Impairment of Goodwill (in part)

Goodwill is not amortized but tested for impairment annually and whenever impairment indicators require. In most cases the Company identified its cash-generating unit as one level below that of an operating sector. . . . A goodwill impairment loss is recognized in the statement of income whenever and to the extent that the carrying amount of a cash-generating unit exceeds the recoverable amount of that unit.

Goodwill (in part)

Due to deteriorating economic circumstances and the decline of the market capitalization of the company, impairment tests were performed in the latter half of the year using updated assumptions. The tests resulted in goodwill impairment charges of EUR 301 million. . . .

Assets to Be Sold

We have been discussing the recognition and measurement for the impairment of value of assets to be held and used. We also test for impairment of assets held for sale. These are assets management has actively committed to immediately sell in their present condition and for which sale is probable.

An asset or group of assets classified as held for sale is measured at the lower of its book value, or fair value less cost to sell. An impairment loss is recognized for any write-down to fair value less cost to sell.[19] Except for including the cost to sell, notice the similarity to impairment of assets to be held and used. We don't depreciate or amortize these assets while classified as held for sale and we report them separately in the balance sheet. Recall from our discussion of discontinued operations in Chapter 4 that similar rules apply for a component of an entity that is classified as held for sale.

Graphic 11–15 summarizes the guidelines for the recognition and measurement of impairment losses.

GRAPHIC 11–15

Summary of Asset Impairment Guidelines

Type of Asset	When to Test for Impairment	Impairment Test
To Be Held and Used		
Property, plant, and equipment and finite-life intangible assets	When events or circumstances indicate book value may not be recoverable	Step 1—An impairment loss is required only when book value is not recoverable (undiscounted sum of estimated future cash flows less than book value). Step 2—The impairment loss is the excess of book value over fair value.
Indefinite-life intangible assets (other than goodwill)	At least annually, or more frequently if indicated	If book value exceeds fair value, an impairment loss is recognized for the difference.
Goodwill	At least annually, or more frequently if indicated	Step 1—A loss is indicated when the fair value of the reporting unit is less than its book value. Step 2—An impairment loss is measured as the excess of book value over implied fair value.
To Be Sold	When considered held for sale	If book value exceeds fair value less cost to sell, an impairment loss is recognized for the difference.

Impairment Losses and Earnings Quality

What do losses from the write-down of inventory and restructuring costs have in common? The presence of these items in a corporate income statement presents a challenge to an analyst trying to determine a company's permanent earnings—those likely to continue in the future. We discussed these issues in prior chapters.

We now can add asset impairment losses to the list of "big bath" accounting techniques some companies use to manipulate earnings. By writing off large amounts of assets, companies significantly reduce earnings in the year of the write-off but are able to increase future earnings by lowering future depreciation, depletion, or amortization. Here's how. We measure the impairment loss as the difference between an asset's book value and its fair value. However, in most cases, fair value must be estimated, and the estimation process usually involves a forecast of future net cash flows the company expects to generate from the asset's use. If a company underestimates future net cash flows, fair value is understated. This has two effects: (1) current year's income is unrealistically low due to the impairment loss being overstated and (2) future income is unrealistically high because depreciation, depletion, and amortization are based on understated asset values.

---

[19]If the asset is unsold at the end of a subsequent reporting period, a gain is recognized for any increase in fair value less cost to sell, but not in excess of the loss previously recognized.

WHERE WE'RE HEADED

In their 2006 *Memorandum of Understanding*, the FASB and IASB included impairment as one of their short-term convergence projects. However, in 2008 the Boards agreed to defer work on impairment. Early in 2009, the Boards identified impairment as a topic for longer term convergence. When this text was published, no specific impairment project had been proposed.

● **LO10**

The FASB and IASB have identified impairment as a topic for longer-term convergence.

SUBSEQUENT EXPENDITURES

PART C

Now that we have acquired and measured assets, we can address accounting issues incurred subsequent to their acquisition. This part of the chapter deals with the treatment of expenditures made over the life of these assets to maintain and/or improve them.

Expenditures Subsequent to Acquisition

● **LO9**

Many long-lived assets require expenditures to repair, maintain, or improve them. These expenditures can present accounting problems if they are material. In general, a choice must be made between capitalizing the expenditures by either increasing the asset's book value or creating a new asset, or expensing them in the period in which they are incurred. Conceptually, we can refer to the matching principle that requires the capitalization of expenditures that are expected to produce benefits beyond the current fiscal year. Expenditures that simply maintain a given level of benefits are expensed in the period they are incurred.

Expenditures related to assets can increase future benefits in the following ways:

1. An extension of the *useful life* of the asset.
2. An increase in the *operating efficiency* of the asset resulting in either an increase in the quantity of goods or services produced or a decrease in future operating costs.
3. An increase in the *quality* of the goods or services produced by the asset.

Theoretically, expenditures that cause any of these results should be capitalized initially and then expensed in future periods through depreciation, depletion, or amortization. This permits the matching of the expenditure with the future benefits. Of course, materiality is an important factor in the practical application of this approach.

For expediency, many companies set materiality thresholds for the capitalization of any expenditure. For example, a company might decide to expense all expenditures under $200 regardless of whether or not future benefits are increased. Judgment is required to determine the appropriate materiality threshold as well as the appropriate treatment of expenditures over $200. There often are practical problems in capitalizing these expenditures. For example, even if future benefits are increased by the expenditure, it may be difficult to determine how long the benefits will last. It's important for a company to establish a policy for treating these expenditures and apply it consistently.

Many companies do not capitalize any expenditure unless it exceeds a predetermined amount that is considered material.

We classify subsequent expenditures as (1) repairs and maintenance, (2) additions, (3) improvements, or (4) rearrangements.

Repairs and Maintenance

These expenditures are made to *maintain* a given level of benefits provided by the asset and do not *increase* future benefits. For example, the cost of an engine tune-up or the repair of an engine part for a delivery truck allows the truck to continue its productive activity. If the maintenance is not performed, the truck will not provide the benefits originally anticipated. In that sense, future benefits are provided; without the repair, the truck will no longer operate. The key, though, is that future benefits are not provided *beyond those originally anticipated.* Expenditures for these activities should be expensed in the period incurred.

Expenditures for *repairs and maintenance* generally are expensed when incurred.

> ### ADDITIONAL CONSIDERATION
>
> If repairs and maintenance costs are seasonal, interim financial statements may be misstated. For example, suppose annual maintenance is performed on a company's fleet of delivery trucks. The annual income statement correctly includes one year's maintenance expense. However, for interim reporting purposes, if the entire expenditure is made in one quarter, should that quarter's income statement include as expense the entire cost of the annual maintenance? If these expenditures can be anticipated, they should be accrued evenly throughout the year by crediting an allowance account. The allowance account is then debited when the maintenance is performed.

Additions

The costs of *additions* usually are capitalized.

As the term implies, additions involve adding a new major component to an existing asset and should be capitalized because future benefits are increased. For example, adding a refrigeration unit to a delivery truck increases the capability of the truck, thus increasing its future benefits. Other examples include the construction of a new wing on a building and the addition of a security system to an existing building.

The capitalized cost includes all necessary expenditures to bring the addition to a condition and location for use. For a building addition, this might include the costs of tearing down and removing a wall of the existing building. The capitalized cost of additions are depreciated over the remaining useful life of the original asset or its own useful life, whichever is shorter.

Improvements

The costs of *improvements* usually are capitalized.

Expenditures classified as improvements involve the replacement of a major component of an asset. The replacement can be a new component with the same characteristics as the old component or a new component with enhanced operating capabilities. For example, an existing refrigeration unit in a delivery truck could be replaced with a new but similar unit or with a new and improved refrigeration unit. In either case, the cost of the improvement usually increases future benefits and should be capitalized by increasing the book value of the related asset (the delivery truck) and depreciated over the useful life of the improved asset. There are three methods used to record the cost of improvements.

1. *Substitution.* The improvement can be recorded as both (1) a disposition of the old component and (2) the acquisition of the new component. This approach is conceptually appealing but it is practical only if the original cost and accumulated depreciation of the old component can be separately identified.
2. *Capitalization of new cost.* Another way to record an improvement is to include the cost of the improvement (net of any consideration received from the disposition of the old component) as a debit to the related asset account, without removing the original cost and accumulated depreciation of the original component. This approach is acceptable only if the book value of the original component has been reduced to an immaterial amount through prior depreciation.
3. *Reduction of accumulated depreciation.* Another way to increase an asset's book value is to leave the asset account unaltered but decrease its related accumulated depreciation. The argument for this method is that many improvements extend the useful life of an asset and are equivalent to a partial recovery of previously recorded depreciation. This approach produces the same book value as the capitalization of cost to the asset account. However, cost and accumulated depreciation amounts will differ under the two methods.

The three methods are compared in Illustration 11–11.

Rearrangements

The costs of material *rearrangements* should be capitalized if they clearly increase future benefits.

Expenditures made to restructure an asset without addition, replacement, or improvement are termed rearrangements. The objective is to create a new capability for the asset and

The Palmer Corporation replaced the air conditioning system in one of its office buildings that it leases to tenants. The cost of the old air conditioning system, $200,000, is included in the cost of the building. However, the company has separately depreciated the air conditioning system. Depreciation recorded up to the date of replacement totaled $160,000. The old system was removed and the new system installed at a cost of $230,000, which was paid in cash. Parts from the old system were sold for $12,000.

Accounting for the improvement differs depending on the alternative chosen.

Cash	12,000	
Accumulated depreciation—buildings	160,000	
Loss on disposal (difference)	28,000	
Buildings		200,000
Buildings	230,000	
Cash		230,000
Buildings	218,000	
Cash ($230,000 − 12,000)		218,000
Accumulated depreciation—buildings	218,000	
Cash ($230,000 − 12,000)		218,000

ILLUSTRATION 11–11
Improvements

Substitution (1) Disposition of old component.

(2) Acquisition of new component.

Capitalization of new cost

Reduction of accumulated depreciation

not necessarily to extend its useful life. Examples include the rearrangement of machinery on the production line to increase operational efficiency and the relocation of a company's operating plant or office building. If these expenditures are material and they clearly increase future benefits, they should be capitalized and expensed in the future periods benefited. If the expenditures are not material or if it's not certain that future benefits have increased, they should be expensed in the period incurred.

Graphic 11–16 provides a summary of the accounting treatment for the various types of expenditures related to property, plant, and equipment.

GRAPHIC 11–16
Expenditures Subsequent to Acquisition

Type of Expenditure	Definition	Usual Accounting Treatment
Repairs and maintenance	Expenditures to maintain a given level of benefits	Expense in the period incurred
Additions	The addition of a new major component to an existing asset	Capitalize and depreciate over the remaining useful life of the original asset or its own useful life, whichever is shorter
Improvements	The replacement of a major component	Capitalize and depreciate over the useful life of the improved asset
Rearrangements	Expenditures to restructure an asset without addition, replacement, or improvement	If expenditures are material and clearly increase future benefits, capitalize and depreciate over the future periods benefited

Costs of Defending Intangible Rights

Repairs, additions, improvements, and rearrangements generally relate to property, plant, and equipment. A possible significant expenditure incurred subsequent to the acquisition of intangible assets is the cost of defending the right that gives the asset its value. If an intangible right is *successfully* defended, the litigation costs should be capitalized and amortized

The costs incurred to *successfully* defend an intangible right should be capitalized.

over the remaining useful life of the related intangible. This is the appropriate treatment of these expenditures even if the intangible asset was originally developed internally rather than purchased.

If the defense of an intangible right is *unsuccessful,* then the litigation costs should be expensed as incurred because they provide no future benefit. In addition, the book value of any intangible asset should be reduced to realizable value. For example, if a company is unsuccessful in defending a patent infringement suit, the patent's value may be eliminated. The book value of the patent should be written off as a loss.

The costs incurred to *unsuccessfully* **defend an intangible right should be expensed.**

● LO10

INTERNATIONAL FINANCIAL REPORTING STANDARDS

Costs of Defending Intangible Rights. Under U.S. GAAP, litigation costs to successfully defend an intangible right are capitalized and amortized over the remaining useful life of the related intangible. Under IFRS, these costs are expensed, except in rare situations when an expenditure increases future benefits.[20]

FINANCIAL REPORTING CASE SOLUTION

1. **Is Penny correct? Do the terms** *depreciation, depletion,* **and** *amortization* **all mean the same thing?** *(p. 558)*   Penny is correct. Each of these terms refers to the cost allocation of assets over their service lives. The term *depreciation* is used for plant and equipment, *depletion* for natural resources, and *amortization* for intangibles.

2. **Weyerhaeuser determines depletion based on the "volume of timber estimated to be available." Explain this approach.** *(p. 562)*   Weyerhaeuser is using the units-of-production method to determine depletion. The units-of-production method is an activity-based method that computes a depletion (or depreciation or amortization) rate per measure of activity and then multiplies this rate by actual activity to determine periodic cost allocation. The method is used by Weyerhaeuser to measure depletion of the cost of timber harvested and the amortization of logging railroads and truck roads. The costs of logging are intangible assets because the company does not own the roads.

3. **Explain how asset impairment differs from depreciation, depletion, and amortization. How do companies measure impairment losses for property, plant, and equipment and intangible assets with finite useful lives?** *(p. 580)*   Depreciation, depletion, and amortization reflect a gradual consumption of the benefits inherent in a long-lived asset. An implicit assumption in allocating the cost of an asset over its useful life is that there has been no significant reduction in the anticipated total benefits or service potential of the asset. Situations can arise, however, that cause a significant decline or *impairment* of those benefits or service potentials. Determining whether to record an impairment loss for an asset and actually recording the loss is a two-step process. The first step is a recoverability test—an impairment loss is required only when the undiscounted sum of estimated future cash flows from an asset is less than the asset's book value. The measurement of impairment loss—step 2—is the difference between the asset's book value and its fair value. If an impairment loss is recognized, the written-down book value becomes the new cost base for future cost allocation. ●

---

[20]"Intangible Assets," *International Accounting Standard No. 38* (IASCF), par. 20, as amended effective January 1, 2009.

THE BOTTOM LINE

● **LO1**   The use of property, plant, and equipment and intangible assets represents a consumption of benefits, or service potentials, inherent in the assets. The matching principle requires that the cost of these inherent benefits or service potentials that were consumed be recognized as an expense. As there very seldom is a direct relationship between the use of assets and revenue production, accounting resorts to arbitrary allocation methods to achieve a matching of expenses with revenues. (p. 558)

● **LO2**   The allocation process for plant and equipment is called *depreciation.* Time-based depreciation methods estimate service life in years and then allocate depreciable base, cost less estimated residual value, using either a straight-line or accelerated pattern. Activity-based depreciation methods allocate the depreciable base by estimating service life according to some measure of productivity. (p. 560)

● **LO3**   The allocation process for natural resources is called *depletion.* The activity-based method called units-of-production usually is used to determine periodic depletion. (p. 569)

● **LO4**   The allocation process for intangible assets is called *amortization.* For an intangible asset with a finite useful life, the capitalized cost less any estimated residual value must be allocated to periods in which the asset is expected to contribute to the company's revenue-generating activities. An intangible asset that is determined to have an indefinite useful life is not subject to periodic amortization. Goodwill is perhaps the most typical intangible asset with an indefinite useful life. (p. 571)

● **LO5**   A change in either the service life or residual value of property, plant, and equipment and intangible assets should be reflected in the financial statements of the current period and future periods by recalculating periodic depreciation, depletion, or amortization. (p. 576)

● **LO6**   A change in depreciation, depletion, or amortization method is considered a change in accounting estimate that is achieved by a change in accounting principle. We account for these changes prospectively, exactly as we would any other change in estimate. One difference is that most changes in estimate do not require a company to justify the change. However, this change in estimate is a result of changing an accounting principle and therefore requires a clear justification as to why the new method is preferable. (p. 577)

● **LO7**   A material error in accounting for property, plant, and equipment and intangible assets that is discovered in a year subsequent to the year of the error requires that previous years' financial statements that were incorrect as a result of the error are retrospectively restated to reflect the correction. Any account balances that are incorrect as a result of the error are corrected by journal entry. If retained earnings is one of the incorrect accounts, the correction is reported as a prior period adjustment to the beginning balance in the statement of shareholders' equity. In addition, a disclosure note is needed to describe the nature of the error and the impact of its correction on income. (p. 578)

● **LO8**   Conceptually, there is considerable merit for a policy requiring the write-down of an asset when there has been a *significant* decline in value below carrying value (book value). The write-down provides important information about the future cash flows to be generated from the use of the asset. However, in practice this policy is very subjective. GAAP [FASB ASC 360] establishes guidance for when to recognize and how to measure impairment losses of property, plant, and equipment and intangible assets that have finite useful lives. GAAP [FASB ASC 350] also provides guidance for the recognition and measurement of impairment for indefinite-life intangibles and goodwill. (p. 580)

● **LO9**   Expenditures for repairs and maintenance generally are expensed when incurred. The costs of additions and improvements usually are capitalized. The costs of material rearrangements should be capitalized if they clearly increase future benefits. (p. 589)

● **LO10**   Among the several differences between U.S. GAAP and IFRS with respect to the utilization and impairment of property, plant, and equipment and intangible assets pertains to reporting assets in the balance sheet. IFRS allows a company to value property, plant, and equipment (PP&E) and intangible assets subsequent to initial valuation at (1) cost less accumulated depreciation/amortization or (2) fair value (revaluation). U.S. GAAP prohibits revaluation. There also are significant differences in accounting for the impairment of property, plant, and equipment and intangible assets. (pp. 565, 568, 571, 573, 583, 584, 586, 589, and 592) ●

COMPARISON WITH MACRS (TAX DEPRECIATION)

Depreciation for financial reporting purposes is an attempt to distribute the cost of the asset, less any anticipated residual value, over the estimated useful life in a systematic and rational manner that attempts to match revenues with the use of the asset. Depreciation for income tax purposes is influenced by the revenue needs of government as well as the desire to influence economic behavior. For example, accelerated depreciation schedules currently allowed are intended to provide incentive for companies to expand and modernize their facilities thus stimulating economic growth.

The federal income tax code allows taxpayers to compute depreciation for their tax returns on assets acquired after 1986 using the modified accelerated cost recovery system (MACRS).[21] Key differences between the calculation of depreciation for financial reporting and the calculation using MACRS are:

1. Estimated useful lives and residual values are not used in MACRS.
2. Firms can't choose among various accelerated methods under MACRS.
3. A half-year convention is used in determining the MACRS depreciation amounts.

Under MACRS, each asset generally is placed within a recovery period category. The six categories for personal property are 3, 5, 7, 10, 15, and 20 years. For example, the 5-year category includes automobiles, light trucks, and computers.

Depending on the category, fixed percentage rates are applied to the original cost of the asset. The rates for the 5-year asset category are as follows:

Year	Rate
1	20.00%
2	32.00
3	19.20
4	11.52
5	11.52
6	5.76
Total	100.00%

These rates are equivalent to applying the double-declining-balance method with a switch to straight-line in the year straight-line yields an equal or higher deduction than DDB. In most cases, the half-year convention is used regardless of when the asset is placed in service.[22] The first-year rate of 20% for the five-year category is one-half of the DDB rate for an asset with a five-year life (2 × 20%). The sixth year rate of 5.76% is one-half of the straight-line rate established in year 4, the year straight-line depreciation exceeds DDB depreciation.

Companies have the option to use the straight-line method for the entire tax life of the asset, applying the half-year convention, rather than using MACRS depreciation schedules. Because of the differences discussed above, tax depreciation for a given year will likely be different from GAAP depreciation. ●

RETIREMENT AND REPLACEMENT METHODS OF DEPRECIATION

Retirement and replacement depreciation methods occasionally are used to depreciate relatively low-valued assets with short service lives. Under either approach, an aggregate asset account that represents a group of similar assets is increased at the time the initial collection is acquired.

---

[21]For assets acquired between 1981 and 1986, tax depreciation is calculated using the accelerated cost recovery system (ACRS), which is similar to MACRS. For assets acquired before 1981, tax depreciation can be calculated using any of the depreciation methods discussed in the chapter. Residual values are used in the calculation of depreciation for pre-1981 assets.

[22]In certain situations, mid-quarter and mid-month conventions are used.

Retirement Method

Using the **retirement depreciation method,** the asset account also is increased for the cost of subsequent expenditures. When an item is disposed of, the asset account is credited for its cost, and depreciation expense is recorded for the difference between cost and proceeds received, if any. No other entries are made for depreciation. As a consequence, one or more periods may pass without any expense recorded. For example, the following entry records the purchase of 100 handheld calculators at $50 acquisition cost each:

Calculators (100 × $50)	5,000	
Cash		5,000
To record the acquisition of calculators.		

If 20 new calculators are acquired at $45 each, the asset account is increased.

Calculators (20 × $45)	900	
Cash		900
To record additional calculator acquisitions.		

Thirty calculators are disposed of (retired) by selling them secondhand to a bookkeeping firm for $5 each. The following entry reflects the retirement method:

Cash (30 × $5)	150	
Depreciation expense (difference)	1,350	
Calculators (30 × $50)		1,500
To record the sale/depreciation of calculators.		

Notice that the retirement system assumes a FIFO cost flow approach in determining the cost of assets, $50 each, that were disposed.

The *retirement depreciation method records* depreciation when assets are disposed of and measures depreciation as the difference between the proceeds received and cost.

Replacement Method

By the **replacement depreciation method,** the initial acquisition of assets is recorded the same way as by the retirement method; that is, the aggregate cost is increased. However, depreciation expense is the amount paid for new or replacement assets. Any proceeds received from asset dispositions reduces depreciation expense. For our example, the acquisition of 20 new calculators at $45 each is recorded as depreciation as follows:

By the *replacement method, depreciation* is recorded when assets are replaced.

Depreciation expense (20 × $45)	900	
Cash		900
To record the replacement/depreciation of calculators.		

The sale of the old calculators is recorded as a reduction of depreciation:

Cash (30 × $5)	150	
Depreciation expense		150
To record the sale of calculators.		

The asset account balance remains the same throughout the life of the aggregate collection of assets.

Because these methods are likely to produce aggregate expense measurements that differ from individual calculations, retirement and replacement methods are acceptable only in situations where the distortion in depreciation expense does not have a material effect on income. These methods occasionally are encountered in regulated industries such as utilities. ●

QUESTIONS FOR REVIEW OF KEY TOPICS

Q 11–1   Explain the similarities in and differences among depreciation, depletion, and amortization.

Q 11–2   Depreciation is a process of cost allocation, not valuation. Explain this statement.

Q 11–3   Identify and define the three characteristics of an asset that must be established to determine periodic depreciation, depletion, or amortization.

Q 11–4   Discuss the factors that influence the estimation of service life for a depreciable asset.

Q 11–5   What is meant by depreciable base? How is it determined?

Q 11–6   Briefly differentiate between activity-based and time-based allocation methods.

Q 11–7   Briefly differentiate between the straight-line depreciation method and accelerated depreciation methods.

Q 11–8   Why are time-based depreciation methods used more frequently than activity-based methods?

Q 11–9   What are some factors that could explain the predominant use of the straight-line depreciation method?

Q 11–10 Briefly explain the differences and similarities between the group approach and composite approach to depreciating aggregate assets.

Q 11–11 Define depletion and compare it with depreciation.

Q 11–12 Compare and contrast amortization of intangible assets with depreciation and depletion.

Q 11–13 What are some of the simplifying conventions a company can use to calculate depreciation for partial years?

Q 11–14 Explain the accounting treatment required when a change is made to the estimated service life of a machine.

Q 11–15 Explain the accounting treatment and disclosures required when a change is made in depreciation method.

Q 11–16 Explain the steps required to correct an error in accounting for property, plant, and equipment and intangible assets that is discovered in a year subsequent to the year the error was made.

Q 11–17 Explain what is meant by the impairment value of property, plant, and equipment and intangible assets. How should these impairments be accounted for?

Q 11–18 Explain the differences in the accounting treatment of repairs and maintenance, additions, improvements, and rearrangements.

● IFRS   Q 11–19 Identify any differences between U.S. GAAP and International Financial Reporting Standards in the subsequent valuation of property, plant, and equipment and intangible assets.

● IFRS   Q 11–20 Briefly explain the difference between U.S. GAAP and IFRS in the *measurement* of an impairment loss for property, plant, and equipment and finite-life intangible assets.

● IFRS   Q 11–21 Briefly explain the differences between U.S. GAAP and IFRS in the measurement of an impairment loss for goodwill.

● IFRS   Q 11–22 Under U.S. GAAP, litigation costs to successfully defend an intangible right are capitalized and amortized over the remaining useful life of the related intangible. How are these costs typically accounted for under IFRS?

BRIEF EXERCISES

BE 11–1
Cost allocation
● LO1

At the beginning of its fiscal year, Koeplin Corporation purchased a machine for $50,000. At the end of the year, the machine had a fair value of $32,000. Koeplin's controller recorded depreciation expense of $18,000 for the year, the decline in the machine's value. Why is this an incorrect approach to measuring periodic depreciation?

BE 11–2
Depreciation methods
● LO2

On January 1, 2011, Canseco Plumbing Fixtures purchased equipment for $30,000. Residual value at the end of an estimated four-year service life is expected to be $2,000. The company expects the machine to operate for 10,000 hours. Calculate depreciation expense for 2011 and 2012 using each of the following depreciation methods: (a) straight line, (b) sum-of-the-years'-digits, (c) double-declining balance, and (d) units-of-production using machine hours. The machine operated for 2,200 and 3,000 hours in 2011 and 2012, respectively.

BE 11–3
Depreciation methods; partial years
● LO2

Refer to the situation described in BE 11–2. Assume the machine was purchased on March 31, 2011, instead of January 1. Calculate depreciation expense for 2011 and 2012 using each of the following depreciation methods: (a) straight line, (b) sum-of-the-years'-digits, and (c) double-declining balance.

BE 11–4
Group depreciation
● LO2

Mondale Winery depreciates its equipment using the group method. The cost of equipment purchased in 2011 totaled $425,000. The estimated residual value of the equipment was $40,000 and the group depreciation rate was determined to be 18%. What is the annual depreciation for the group? If equipment that cost $42,000 is sold in 2012 for $35,000, what amount of gain or loss will the company recognize for the sale?

BE 11–5
Depletion
● LO3

Fitzgerald Oil and Gas incurred costs of $8.25 million for the acquisition and development of a natural gas deposit. The company expects to extract 3 million cubic feet of natural gas during a four-year period. Natural gas extracted during year 1 and year 2 were 700,000 and 800,000 cubic feet, respectively. What was the depletion for year 1 and year 2?

BE 11–6
Amortization
● LO4

On June 28 Lexicon Corporation acquired 100% of the common stock of Gulf & Eastern. The purchase price allocation included the following items: $4 million, patent; $3 million, developed technology; $2 million, in-process research and development; $5 million, goodwill. Lexicon's policy is to amortize intangible assets using the straight-line method, no residual value, and a five-year useful life. What is the total amount of expenses (ignoring taxes) that would appear in Lexicon's income statement for the year ended December 31 related to these items?

BE 11–7
Change in estimate; useful life of equipment
● LO5

At the beginning of 2009, Robotics Inc. acquired a manufacturing facility for $12 million. $9 million of the purchase price was allocated to the building. Depreciation for 2009 and 2010 was calculated using the straight-line method, a 25-year useful life, and a $1 million residual value. In 2011, the estimates of useful life and residual value were changed to 20 years and $500,000, respectively. What is depreciation on the building for 2011?

BE 11–8
Change in principle; change in depreciation method
● LO6

Refer to the situation described in BE 11–7. Assume that instead of changing the useful life and residual value, in 2011 the company switched to the double-declining-balance depreciation method. How should Robotics account for the change? What is depreciation on the building for 2011?

BE 11–9
Error correction
● LO7

Refer to the situation described in BE 11–7. Assume that 2009 depreciation was incorrectly recorded as $32,000. This error was discovered in 2011. How should Robotics account for the error? What is depreciation on the building for 2011 assuming no change in estimate of useful life or residual value?

BE 11–10
Impairment; property, plant, and equipment
● LO8

Collison and Ryder Company (C&R) has been experiencing declining market conditions for its sportswear division. Management decided to test the assets of the division for possible impairment. The test revealed the following: book value of division's assets, $26.5 million; fair value of division's assets, $21 million; sum of estimated future cash flows generated from the division's assets, $28 million. What amount of impairment loss should C&R recognize?

BE 11–11
Impairment; property, plant, and equipment
● LO8

Refer to the situation described in BE 11–10. Assume that the sum of estimated future cash flows is $24 million instead of $28 million. What amount of impairment loss should C&R recognize?

BE 11–12
IFRS; impairment; property, plant, and equipment
● LO8 LO10

Refer to the situation described in BE 11–10. Assume that the present value of the estimated future cash flows generated from the division's assets is $22 million and that their fair value approximates fair value less costs to sell. What amount of impairment loss should C&R recognize if the company prepares its financial statements according to IFRS?

BE 11–13
Impairment; goodwill
● LO8

WebHelper Inc. acquired 100% of the outstanding stock of Silicon Chips Corporation (SCC) for $45 million, of which $15 million was allocated to goodwill. At the end of the current fiscal year, the annual impairment test revealed the following: fair value of SCC, $40 million; fair value of SCC's net assets (excluding goodwill), $31 million; book value of SCC's net assets (including goodwill), $42 million. What amount of impairment loss should WebHelper recognize?

BE 11–14
Impairment; goodwill
● LO8

Refer to the situation described in BE 11–13. Assume that the fair value of SCC is $44 million instead of $40 million. What amount of impairment loss should WebHelper recognize?

BE 11–15
IFRS; impairment;
goodwill

● LO8 LO10

Refer to the situation described in BE 11–13. Assume that SCC's fair value of $40 million approximates fair value less costs to sell and that the present value of SCC's estimated future cash flows is $41 million. If WebHelper prepares its financial statements according to IFRS and SCC is considered a cash-generating unit, what amount of impairment loss, if any, should WebHelper recognize?

BE 11–16
Subsequent
expenditures

● LO9

Demmert Manufacturing incurred the following expenditures during the current fiscal year: annual maintenance on its machinery, $5,400; remodeling of offices, $22,000; rearrangement of the shipping and receiving area resulting in an increase in productivity, $35,000; addition of a security system to the manufacturing facility, $25,000. How should Demmert account for each of these expenditures?

EXERCISES

An alternate exercise and problem set is available on the text website: www.mhhe.com/spiceland6e

E 11–1
Depreciation
methods

● LO2

On January 1, 2011, the Excel Delivery Company purchased a delivery van for $33,000. At the end of its five-year service life, it is estimated that the van will be worth $3,000. During the five-year period, the company expects to drive the van 100,000 miles.

Required:

Calculate annual depreciation for the five-year life of the van using each of the following methods. Round all computations to the nearest dollar.

1. Straight line.
2. Sum-of-the-years' digits.
3. Double-declining balance.
4. Units of production using miles driven as a measure of output, and the following actual mileage:

Year	Miles
2011	22,000
2012	24,000
2013	15,000
2014	20,000
2015	21,000

E 11–2
Depreciation
methods

● LO2

On January 1, 2011, the Allegheny Corporation purchased machinery for $115,000. The estimated service life of the machinery is 10 years and the estimated residual value is $5,000. The machine is expected to produce 220,000 units during its life.

Required:

Calculate depreciation for 2011 and 2012 using each of the following methods. Round all computations to the nearest dollar.

1. Straight line.
2. Sum-of-the-years' digits.
3. Double-declining balance.
4. One hundred fifty percent declining balance.
5. Units of production (units produced in 2011, 30,000; units produced in 2012, 25,000).

E 11–3
Depreciation
methods; partial
years

● LO2

[This is a variation of the previous exercise modified to focus on depreciation for partial years.]

On October 1, 2011, the Allegheny Corporation purchased machinery for $115,000. The estimated service life of the machinery is 10 years and the estimated residual value is $5,000. The machine is expected to produce 220,000 units during its life.

Required:

Calculate depreciation for 2011 and 2012 using each of the following methods. Partial-year depreciation is calculated based on the number of months the asset is in service. Round all computations to the nearest dollar.

1. Straight line.
2. Sum-of-the-years' digits.
3. Double-declining balance.
4. One hundred fifty percent declining balance.
5. Units of production (units produced in 2011, 10,000; units produced in 2012, 25,000).

E 11–4
Depreciation
methods; asset
addition
● LO2 LO9

Funseth Company purchased a five-story office building on January 1, 2009, at a cost of $5,000,000. The building has a residual value of $200,000 and a 30-year life. The straight-line depreciation method is used. On June 30, 2011, construction of a sixth floor was completed at a cost of $1,650,000.

Required:
Calculate the depreciation on the building and building addition for 2011 and 2012 assuming that the addition did not change the life or residual value of the building.

E 11–5
Depreciation
methods; solving
for unknowns
● LO2

For each of the following depreciable assets, determine the missing amount (?). Abbreviations for depreciation methods are SL for straight line, SYD for sum-of-the-years' digits, and DDB for double-declining balance.

Asset	Cost	Residual Value	Service Life (Years)	Depreciation Method	Depreciation (Year 2)
A	?	$ 20,000	5	DDB	$ 24,000
B	$ 40,000	?	8	SYD	7,000
C	65,000	5,000	?	SL	6,000
D	230,000	10,000	10	?	22,000
E	200,000	20,000	8	150%DB	?

E 11–6
Depreciation
methods
● LO2

On April 29, 2011, Quality Appliances purchased equipment for $260,000. The estimated service life of the equipment is six years and the estimated residual value is $20,000. Quality's fiscal year ends on December 31.

Required:
Calculate depreciation for 2011 and 2012 using each of the three methods listed. Quality calculates partial year depreciation based on the number of months the asset is in service. Round all computations to the nearest dollar.
1. Straight-line.
2. Sum-of-the-years' digits.
3. Double-declining balance.

E 11–7
IFRS; depreciation
● LO2 LO10

On June 30, 2011, Rosetta Granite purchased a machine for $120,000. The estimated useful life of the machine is eight years and no residual value is anticipated. An important component of the machine is a specialized high-speed drill that will need to be replaced in four years. The $20,000 cost of the drill is included in the $120,000 cost of the machine. Rosetta uses the straight-line depreciation method for all machinery.

Required:
1. Calculate depreciation for 2011 and 2012 applying the typical U.S. GAAP treatment.
2. Repeat requirement 1 applying IFRS.

E 11–8
IFRS; revaluation
of machinery;
depreciation
● LO2 LO10

Dower Corporation prepares its financial statements according to IFRS. On March 31, 2011, the company purchased equipment for $240,000. The equipment is expected to have a six-year useful life with no residual value. Dower uses the straight-line depreciation method for all equipment. On December 31, 2011, the end of the company's fiscal year, Dower chooses to revalue the equipment to its fair value of $220,000.

Required:
1. Calculate depreciation for 2011.
2. Prepare the journal entry to record the revaluation of the equipment. Round calculations to the nearest thousand.
3. Calculate depreciation for 2012.
4. Repeat requirement 2 assuming that the fair value of the equipment at the end of 2011 is $195,000.

E 11–9
Group depreciation
● LO2

Highsmith Rental Company purchased an apartment building early in 2011. There are 20 apartments in the building and each is furnished with major kitchen appliances. The company has decided to use the group depreciation method for the appliances. The following data are available:

Appliance	Cost	Residual Value	Service Life (in Years)
Stoves	$15,000	$3,000	6
Refrigerators	10,000	1,000	5
Dishwashers	8,000	500	4

In 2014, three new refrigerators costing $2,700 were purchased for cash. The old refrigerators, which originally cost $1,500, were sold for $200.

Required:
1. Calculate the group depreciation rate, group life, and depreciation for 2011.
2. Prepare the journal entries to record the purchase of the new refrigerators and the sale of the old refrigerators.

E 11–10
Double-declining-
balance method;
switch to straight
line
● LO2 LO6

On January 2, 2011, the Jackson Company purchased equipment to be used in its manufacturing process. The equipment has an estimated life of eight years and an estimated residual value of $30,625. The expenditures made to acquire the asset were as follows:

Purchase price	$154,000
Freight charges	2,000
Installation charges	4,000

Jackson's policy is to use the double-declining-balance (DDB) method of depreciation in the early years of the equipment's life and then switch to straight line halfway through the equipment's life.

Required:

1. Calculate depreciation for each year of the asset's eight-year life.
2. Discuss the accounting treatment of the depreciation on the equipment.

E 11–11
Depletion
● LO3

On April 17, 2011, the Loadstone Mining Company purchased the rights to a coal mine. The purchase price plus additional costs necessary to prepare the mine for extraction of the coal totaled $4,500,000. The company expects to extract 900,000 tons of coal during a four-year period. During 2011, 240,000 tons were extracted and sold immediately.

Required:

1. Calculate depletion for 2011.
2. Discuss the accounting treatment of the depletion calculated in requirement 1.

E 11–12
Depreciation and
depletion
● LO2 LO3

At the beginning of 2011, Terra Lumber Company purchased a timber tract from Boise Cantor for $3,200,000. After the timber is cleared, the land will have a residual value of $600,000. Roads to enable logging operations were constructed and completed on March 30, 2011. The cost of the roads, which have no residual value and no alternative use after the tract is cleared, was $240,000. During 2011, Terra logged 500,000 of the estimated five million board feet of timber.

Required:

Calculate the 2011 depletion of the timber tract and depreciation of the logging roads assuming the units-of-production method is used for both assets.

E 11–13
Cost of a natural
resource; depletion
and depreciation;
Chapters 10 and 11
● LO2 LO3

[This exercise is a continuation of Exercise 10–4 in Chapter 10 focusing on depletion and depreciation.] Jackpot Mining Company operates a copper mine in central Montana. The company paid $1,000,000 in 2011 for the mining site and spent an additional $600,000 to prepare the mine for extraction of the copper. After the copper is extracted in approximately four years, the company is required to restore the land to its original condition, including repaving of roads and replacing a greenbelt. The company has provided the following three cash flow possibilities for the restoration costs:

	Cash Outflow	Probability
1	$300,000	25%
2	400,000	40%
3	600,000	35%

To aid extraction, Jackpot purchased some new equipment on July 1, 2011, for $120,000. After the copper is removed from this mine, the equipment will be sold for an estimated residual amount of $20,000. There will be no residual value for the copper mine. The credit-adjusted risk-free rate of interest is 10%.

The company expects to extract 10 million pounds of copper from the mine. Actual production was 1.6 million pounds in 2011 and 3 million pounds in 2012.

Required:

1. Compute depletion and depreciation on the mine and mining equipment for 2011 and 2012. The units-of-production method is used to calculate depreciation.
2. Discuss the accounting treatment of the depletion and depreciation on the mine and mining equipment.

E 11–14
Amortization
● LO4 LO5

Janes Company provided the following information on intangible assets:

a. A patent was purchased from the Lou Company for $700,000 on January 1, 2009. Janes estimated the remaining useful life of the patent to be 10 years. The patent was carried on Lou's accounting records at a net book value of $350,000 when Lou sold it to Janes.

b. During 2011, a franchise was purchased from the Rink Company for $500,000. The contractual life of the franchise is 10 years and Janes records a full year of amortization in the year of purchase.

c. Janes incurred research and development costs in 2011 as follows:

Materials and supplies	$140,000
Personnel	180,000
Indirect costs	60,000
Total	$380,000

d. Effective January 1, 2011, based on new events that have occurred, Janes estimates that the remaining life of the patent purchased from Lou is only five more years.

Required:

1. Prepare the entries necessary in 2009 and 2011 to reflect the above information.
2. Prepare a schedule showing the intangible asset section of Janes's December 31, 2011, balance sheet.

E 11–15
Patent
amortization;
patent defense
● LO4 LO9

On January 2, 2011, David Corporation purchased a patent for $500,000. The remaining legal life is 12 years, but the company estimated that the patent will be useful only for eight years. In January 2013, the company incurred legal fees of $45,000 in successfully defending a patent infringement suit. The successful defense did not change the company's estimate of useful life.

Required:
Prepare journal entries related to the patent for 2011, 2012, and 2013.

E 11–16
Change in estimate;
useful life of patent
● LO4 LO5

Van Frank Telecommunications has a patent on a cellular transmission process. The company has amortized the patent on a straight-line basis since 2007, when it was acquired at a cost of $9 million at the beginning of that year. Due to rapid technological advances in the industry, management decided that the patent would benefit the company over a total of six years rather than the nine-year life being used to amortize its cost. The decision was made at the end of 2011 (before adjusting and closing entries).

Required:
Prepare the appropriate adjusting entry for patent amortization in 2011 to reflect the revised estimate.

E 11–17
IFRS; revaluation
of patent;
amortization
● LO4 LO10

Saint John Corporation prepares its financial statements according to IFRS. On June 30, 2011, the company purchased a franchise for $1,200,000. The franchise is expected to have a 10-year useful life with no residual value. Saint John uses the straight-line amortization method for all intangible assets. On December 31, 2011, the end of the company's fiscal year, Saint John chooses to revalue the franchise. There is an active market for this particular franchise and its fair value on December 31, 2011, is $1,180,000.

Required:

1. Calculate amortization for 2011.
2. Prepare the journal entry to record the revaluation of the patent.
3. Calculate amortization for 2012.

E 11–18
Change in estimate;
useful life and
residual value of
equipment
● LO2 LO5

Wardell Company purchased a minicomputer on January 1, 2009, at a cost of $40,000. The computer was depreciated using the straight-line method over an estimated five-year life with an estimated residual value of $4,000. On January 1, 2011, the estimate of useful life was changed to a total of 10 years, and the estimate of residual value was changed to $900.

Required:

1. Prepare the appropriate adjusting entry for depreciation in 2011 to reflect the revised estimate.
2. Repeat requirement 1 assuming that the company uses the sum-of-the-years'-digits method instead of the straight-line method.

E 11–19
Change in
principle; change
in depreciation
methods
● LO2 LO6

Alteran Corporation purchased a machine for $1.5 million in 2008. The machine is being depreciated over a 10-year life using the sum-of-the-years'-digits method. The residual value is expected to be $300,000. At the beginning of 2011, Alteran decided to change to the straight-line depreciation method for this machine.

Required:
Prepare the 2011 depreciation adjusting entry.

E 11–20
Change in principle; change in depreciation methods
● LO2 LO6

For financial reporting, Clinton Poultry Farms has used the declining-balance method of depreciation for conveyor equipment acquired at the beginning of 2008 for $2,560,000. Its useful life was estimated to be six years, with a $160,000 residual value. At the beginning of 2011, Clinton decides to change to the straight-line method. The effect of this change on depreciation for each year is as follows:

	($ in 000s)		
Year	Straight Line	Declining Balance	Difference
2008	$ 400	$ 853	$453
2009	400	569	169
2010	400	379	(21)
	$1,200	$1,801	$601

Required:

1. Briefly describe the way Clinton should report this accounting change in the 2010–2011 comparative financial statements.

2. Prepare any 2011 journal entry related to the change.

E 11–21
Error correction
● LO2 LO7

In 2011, internal auditors discovered that PKE Displays, Inc., had debited an expense account for the $350,000 cost of a machine purchased on January 1, 2008. The machine's life was expected to be five years with no residual value. Straight-line depreciation is used by PKE.

Required:

1. Prepare the appropriate correcting entry assuming the error was discovered in 2011 before the adjusting and closing entries. (Ignore income taxes.)

2. Assume the error was discovered in 2013 after the 2012 financial statements are issued. Prepare the appropriate correcting entry.

E 11–22
Impairment; property, plant, and equipment
● LO8

Chadwick Enterprises, Inc., operates several restaurants throughout the Midwest. Three of its restaurants located in the center of a large urban area have experienced declining profits due to declining population. The company's management has decided to test the assets of the restaurants for possible impairment. The relevant information for these assets is presented below.

Book value	$6.5 million
Estimated undiscounted sum of future cash flows	4.0 million
Fair value	3.5 million

Required:

1. Determine the amount of the impairment loss, if any.

2. Repeat requirement 1 assuming that the estimated undiscounted sum of future cash flows is $6.8 million and fair value is $5 million.

E 11–23
IFRS; impairment; property, plant, and equipment
● LO8 LO10

Refer to the situation described in Exercise 11–22.

Required:

How might your solution differ if Chadwick Enterprises, Inc., prepares its financial statements according to International Accounting Standards? Assume that the fair value amount given in the exercise equals both (a) the fair value less costs to sell and (b) the present value of estimated future cash flows.

E 11–24
Impairment; property, plant, and equipment
● LO8

General Optic Corporation operates a manufacturing plant in Arizona. Due to a significant decline in demand for the product manufactured at the Arizona site, an impairment test is deemed appropriate. Management has acquired the following information for the assets at the plant:

Cost	$32,500,000
Accumulated depreciation	14,200,000
General's estimate of the total cash flows to be generated by selling the products manufactured at its Arizona plant, not discounted to present value	15,000,000

The fair value of the Arizona plant is estimated to be $11,000,000.

Required:

1. Determine the amount of impairment loss, if any.

2. If a loss is indicated, where would it appear in General Optic's multiple-step income statement?

3. If a loss is indicated, prepare the entry to record the loss.

4. Repeat requirement 1 assuming that the estimated undiscounted sum of future cash flows is $12,000,000 instead of $15,000,000.

5. Repeat requirement 1 assuming that the estimated undiscounted sum of future cash flows is $19,000,000 instead of $15,000,000

E 11–25
Impairment;
goodwill
● **LO8**

In 2009, Alliant Corporation acquired Centerpoint Inc. for $300 million, of which $50 million was allocated to goodwill. Alliant tests for goodwill impairment at the end of each year. At the end of 2011, management has provided the following information:

Fair value of Centerpoint, Inc.	$220 million
Fair value of Centerpoint's net assets (excluding goodwill)	200 million
Book value of Centerpoint's net assets (including goodwill)	250 million

Required:

1. Determine the amount of the impairment loss.

2. Repeat requirement 1 assuming that the fair value of Centerpoint is $270 million.

E 11–26
IFRS; impairment;
goodwill
● **LO8 LO10**

Refer to the situation described in E 11–25. Alliant prepares its financial statements according to IFRS, and Centerpoint is considered a cash-generating unit. Assume that Centerpoint's fair value of $220 million approximates fair value less costs to sell and that the present value of Centerpoint's estimated future cash flows is $225 million.

Required:

Determine the amount of goodwill impairment loss Alliant should recognize.

E 11–27
Goodwill valuation
and impairment;
Chapters 10 and 11
● **LO8**

On May 28, 2011, Pesky Corporation acquired all of the outstanding common stock of Harman, Inc., for $420 million. The fair value of Harman's identifiable tangible and intangible assets totaled $512 million, and the fair value of liabilities assumed by Pesky was $150 million.

Pesky performed the required goodwill impairment test at the end of its fiscal year ended December 31, 2011. Management has provided the following information:

Fair value of Harman, Inc.	$400 million
Fair value of Harman's net assets (excluding goodwill)	370 million
Book value of Harman's net assets (including goodwill)	410 million

Required:

1. Determine the amount of goodwill that resulted from the Harman acquisition.

2. Determine the amount of goodwill impairment loss that Pesky should recognize at the end of 2011, if any.

3. If an impairment loss is required, prepare the journal entry to record the loss.

E 11–28
FASB codification
research
● **LO8**

The *FASB Accounting Standards Codification* represents the single source of authoritative U.S. generally accepted accounting principles.

Required:

1. Obtain the relevant authoritative literature on the impairment or disposal of long-lived assets using the FASB's Codification Research System at the FASB website (**www.fasb.org**). Indicate the Codification topic number that provides guidance on accounting for the impairment of long-lived assets.

2. What is the specific citation that discusses the disclosures required in the notes to the financial statements for the impairment of long-lived assets classified as held and used?

3. Describe the disclosure requirements.

E 11–29
FASB codification
research
● **LO2 LO4**
   LO6 LO8

Access the FASB's Codification Research System at the FASB website (**www.fasb.org**). Determine the specific citation for each of the following items:

1. Depreciation involves a systematic and rational allocation of cost rather than a process of valuation.

2. The calculation of an impairment loss for property, plant, and equipment.

3. Accounting for a change in depreciation method.

4. Goodwill should not be amortized.

E 11–30
Subsequent
expenditures

● LO9

Belltone Company made the following expenditures related to its 10-year-old manufacturing facility:

1. The heating system was replaced at a cost of $250,000. The cost of the old system was not known. The company accounts for improvements as reductions of accumulated depreciation.

2. A new wing was added at a cost of $750,000. The new wing substantially increases the productive capacity of the plant.

3. Annual building maintenance was performed at a cost of $14,000.

4. All of the machinery on the assembly line in the plant was rearranged at a cost of $50,000. The rearrangement clearly increases the productive capacity of the plant.

Required:

Prepare journal entries to record each of the above expenditures.

E 11–31
IFRS; amortization;
cost to defend a
patent

● LO4 LO9 LO10

On September 30, 2009, Leeds LTD. acquired at patent in conjunction with the purchase of another company. The patent, valued at $6 million, was estimated to have a 10-year life and no residual value. Leeds uses the straight-line method of amortization for intangible assets. At the beginning of January 2011, Leeds successfully defended its patent against infringement. Litigation costs totaled $500,000.

Required:

1. Calculate amortization of the patent for 2009 and 2010.

2. Prepare the journal entry to record the 2011 litigation costs.

3. Calculate amortization for 2011.

4. Repeat requirements 2 and 3 assuming that Leeds prepares its financial statements according to IFRS.

E 11–32
Depreciation
methods; disposal;
Chapters 10 and 11

● LO2

Howarth Manufacturing Company purchased a lathe on June 30, 2007, at a cost of $80,000. The residual value of the lathe was estimated to be $5,000 at the end of a five-year life. The lathe was sold on March 31, 2011, for $17,000. Howarth uses the straight-line depreciation method for all of its plant and equipment. Partial-year depreciation is calculated based on the number of months the asset is in service.

Required:

1. Prepare the journal entry to record the sale.

2. Assuming that Howarth had instead used the sum-of-the-years'-digits depreciation method, prepare the journal entry to record the sale.

E 11–33
Concepts;
terminology

● LO1 through
LO6 LO8

Listed below are several items and phrases associated with depreciation, depletion, and amortization. Pair each item from List A with the item from List B (by letter) that is most appropriately associated with it.

List A	List B
_____ 1. Depreciation	a. Cost allocation for natural resource.
_____ 2. Service life	b. Accounted for prospectively.
_____ 3. Depreciable base	c. When there has been a significant decline in value.
_____ 4. Activity-based methods	d. The amount of use expected from plant and equipment
_____ 5. Time-based methods	and finite-life intangible assets.
_____ 6. Double-declining balance	e. Estimates service life in units of output.
_____ 7. Group method	f. Cost less residual value.
_____ 8. Composite method	g. Cost allocation for plant and equipment.
_____ 9. Depletion	h. Does not subtract residual value from cost.
_____ 10. Amortization	i. Accounted for in the same way as a change in estimate.
_____ 11. Change in useful life	j. Aggregates assets that are similar.
_____ 12. Change in depreciation method	k. Aggregates assets that are physically unified.
_____ 13. Write-down of asset	l. Cost allocation for an intangible asset.
	m. Estimates service life in years.

E 11–34
Retirement and
replacement
depreciation

● Appendix B

Cadillac Construction Company uses the retirement method to determine depreciation on its small tools. During 2009, the first year of the company's operations, tools were purchased at a cost of $8,000. In 2011, tools originally costing $2,000 were sold for $250 and replaced with new tools costing $2,500.

Required:

1. Prepare journal entries to record each of the above transactions.

2. Repeat requirement 1 assuming that the company uses the replacement depreciation method instead of the retirement method.

CPA AND CMA REVIEW QUESTIONS

CPA Exam Questions

The following questions are used in the Kaplan CPA Review Course to study property, plant, and equipment and intangible assets while preparing for the CPA examination. Determine the response that best completes the statements or questions.

● LO2

1. Slovac Company purchased a machine that has an estimated useful life of eight years for $7,500. Its salvage value is estimated at $500. What is the depreciation for the second year of the asset's life, assuming Slovac uses the double-declining balance method of depreciation?
   a. $1,406
   b. $1,438
   c. $1,875
   d. $3,750

● LO2

2. Calculate depreciation for year 2 based on the following information:

   > Historical cost $40,000
   > Useful life 5 years
   > Salvage value $3,000
   > Year 1 depreciation $7,400

   a. $7,000
   b. $7,400
   c. $8,000
   d. $8,600

● LO3

3. A company pays $20,000 for the rights to a well with 5 million gallons of water. If the company extracts 250,000 gallons of water in the first year, what is the total depletion in year 1?
   a. $ 400
   b. $1,000
   c. $1,250
   d. $5,000

● LO4

4. Black, Inc., purchased another company for $5,000,000. The fair value of all identifiable tangible and intangible assets was $4,500,000. Black will amortize any goodwill over the maximum number of years allowed. What is the annual amortization of goodwill for this acquisition?
   a. $12,500
   b. $20,000
   c. $25,000
   d.   0

● LO4

5. On January 2, 2011, Rafa Company purchased a franchise with a useful life of 10 years for $50,000. An additional franchise fee of 3% of franchise operating revenues also must be paid each year to the franchisor. Revenues during 2011 totaled $400,000. In its December 31, 2011, balance sheet, what net amount should Rafa report as an intangible asset-franchise?
   a. $33,000
   b. $43,800
   c. $45,000
   d. $50,000

● LO5

6. JME acquired a depreciable asset on January 1, 2009, for $60,000 cash. At that time JME estimated the asset would last 10 years and have no salvage value. During 2011, JME estimated the remaining life of the asset to be only three more years with a salvage value of $3,000. If JME uses straight-line depreciation, what is the depreciation for 2011?
   a. $ 6,000
   b. $12,000
   c. $15,000
   d. $16,000

● LO8

7. The following information concerns Franklin Inc.'s stamping machine:

> Acquired: January 1, 2005
> Cost: $22 million
> Depreciation: straight-line method
> Estimated useful life: 12 years
> Salvage value: $4 million

As of December 31, 2011, the stamping machine is expected to generate $1,500,000 per year for five more years and will then be sold for $1,000,000. The stamping machine is

a. Impaired because expected salvage value has declined.
b. Not impaired because annual expected revenue exceeds annual depreciation.
c. Not impaired because it continues to produce revenue.
d. Impaired because its book value exceeds expected future cash flows.

● LO9

8. During 2010, Yvo Corp. installed a production assembly line to manufacture furniture. In 2011, Yvo purchased a new machine and rearranged the assembly line to install this machine. The rearrangement did not increase the estimated useful life of the assembly line, but it did result in significantly more efficient production. The following expenditures were incurred in connection with this project:

Machine	$75,000
Labor to install machine	14,000
Parts added in rearranging the assembly line to provide future benefits	40,000
Labor and overhead to rearrange the assembly line	18,000

What amount of the above expenditures should be capitalized in 2011?

a. $ 75,000
b. $ 89,000
c. $107,000
d. $147,000

CMA Exam Questions

The following questions dealing with property, plant, and equipment and intangible assets are adapted from questions that previously appeared on Certified Management Accountant (CMA) examinations. The CMA designation sponsored by the Institute of Management Accountants (**www.imanet.org**) provides members with an objective measure of knowledge and competence in the field of management accounting. Determine the response that best completes the statements or questions.

● LO3

1. WD Mining Company purchased a section of land for $600,000 in 2000 to develop a zinc mine. The mine began operating in 2002. At that time, management estimated that the mine would produce 200,000 tons of quality ore. A total of 100,000 tons of ore was mined and processed from 2002 through December 31, 2009. During January 2010, a very promising vein was discovered. The revised estimate of ore still to be mined was 250,000 tons. Estimated salvage value for the mine land was $100,000 in both 2002 and 2010. Assuming that 10,000 tons of ore was mined in 2010, the computation WD Mining Company should use to determine the amount of depletion to record in 2010 would be

a. (($600,000 − $100,000)/450,000 tons) × 10,000 tons.
b. (($600,000 − $100,000)/350,000 tons) × 10,000 tons.
c. (($600,000 − $100,000 − $250,000)/350,000 tons) × 10,000 tons.
d. (($600,000 − $100,000 − $250,000)/250,000 tons) × 10,000 tons.

● LO4

2. On September 1, year 1, for $4,000,000 cash and $2,000,000 notes payable, Norbend Corporation acquired the net assets of Crisholm Company, which had a fair value of $5,496,000 on that date. Norbend's management is of the opinion that the goodwill generated has an indefinite life. During the year-end audit for year 3 after all adjusting entries have been made, the goodwill is determined to be worthless. The amount of the write-off as of December 31, year 3 should be

a. $504,000.
b. $478,800.
c. $466,200.
d. $474,600.

● LO9

3. Costs that are capitalized with regard to a patent include

   a. Legal fees of obtaining the patent, incidental costs of obtaining the patent, and costs of successful patent infringement suits.
   b. Legal fees of obtaining the patent, incidental costs of obtaining the patent, and research and development costs incurred on the invention that is patented.
   c. Legal fees of obtaining the patent, costs of successful patent infringement suits, and research and development costs incurred on the invention that is patented.
   d. Incidental costs of obtaining the patent, costs of successful and unsuccessful patent infringement suits, and the value of any signed patent licensing agreement.

PROBLEMS

An alternate exercise and problem set is available on the text website: www.mhhe.com/spiceland6e

P 11–1
Depreciation
methods; change in
methods
● LO2 LO6

The fact that generally accepted accounting principles allow companies flexibility in choosing between certain allocation methods can make it difficult for a financial analyst to compare periodic performance from firm to firm.

Suppose you were a financial analyst trying to compare the performance of two companies. Company A uses the double-declining-balance depreciation method. Company B uses the straight-line method. You have the following information taken from the 12/31/11 year-end financial statements for Company B:

Income Statement

Depreciation expense	$ 10,000

Balance Sheet

Assets:	
Plant and equipment, at cost	$200,000
Less: Accumulated depreciation	(40,000)
Net	$160,000

You also determine that all of the assets constituting the plant and equipment of Company B were acquired at the same time, and that all of the $200,000 represents depreciable assets. Also, all of the depreciable assets have the same useful life and residual values are zero.

Required:

1. In order to compare performance with Company A, estimate what B's depreciation expense would have been for 2011 if the double-declining-balance depreciation method had been used by Company B since acquisition of the depreciable assets.
2. If Company B decided to switch depreciation methods in 2011 from the straight line to the double-declining-balance method, prepare the 2011 adjusting journal entry to record depreciation for the year.

P 11–2
Comprehensive
problem; Chapters
10 and 11
● LO2 LO4

At December 31, 2010, Cord Company's plant asset and accumulated depreciation and amortization accounts had balances as follows:

Category	Plant Asset	Accumulated Depreciation and Amortization
Land	$ 175,000	$ —
Buildings	1,500,000	328,900
Machinery and equipment	1,125,000	317,500
Automobiles and trucks	172,000	100,325
Leasehold improvements	216,000	108,000
Land improvements	—	—

Depreciation methods and useful lives:
Buildings—150% declining balance; 25 years.
Machinery and equipment—Straight line; 10 years.
Automobiles and trucks—150% declining balance; 5 years, all acquired after 2007.
Leasehold improvements—Straight line.
Land improvements—Straight line.

Depreciation is computed to the nearest month and residual values are immaterial. *Transactions during 2011 and other information:*

a. On January 6, 2011, a plant facility consisting of land and building was acquired from King Corp. in exchange for 25,000 shares of Cord's common stock. On this date, Cord's stock had a fair value of $50 a share. Current assessed values of land and building for property tax purposes are $187,500 and $562,500, respectively.

b. On March 25, 2011, new parking lots, streets, and sidewalks at the acquired plant facility were completed at a total cost of $192,000. These expenditures had an estimated useful life of 12 years.

c. The leasehold improvements were completed on December 31, 2007, and had an estimated useful life of eight years. The related lease, which would terminate on December 31, 2013, was renewable for an additional four-year term. On April 29, 2011, Cord exercised the renewal option.

d. On July 1, 2011, machinery and equipment were purchased at a total invoice cost of $325,000. Additional costs of $10,000 for delivery and $50,000 for installation were incurred.

e. On August 30, 2011, Cord purchased a new automobile for $12,500.

f. On September 30, 2011, a truck with a cost of $24,000 and a carrying amount of $9,100 on date of sale was sold for $11,500. Depreciation for the nine months ended September 30, 2011, was $2,650.

g. On December 20, 2011, a machine with a cost of $17,000 and a book value of $2,975 at date of disposition was scrapped without cash recovery.

Required:

1. Prepare a schedule analyzing the changes in each of the plant asset accounts during 2011. This schedule should include columns for beginning balance, increase, decrease, and ending balance for each of the plant asset accounts. Do not analyze changes in accumulated depreciation and amortization.

2. For each asset category, prepare a schedule showing depreciation or amortization expense for the year ended December 31, 2011. Round computations to the nearest whole dollar.

(AICPA adapted)

P 11–3
Depreciation methods
● LO2

[This problem is a continuation of Problem 10–3 in Chapter 10 focusing on depreciation.]

Required:
For each asset classification, prepare a schedule showing depreciation expense for the year ended December 31, 2011, using the following depreciation methods and useful lives:

> Land improvements—Straight line; 15 years.
> Building—150% declining balance; 20 years.
> Machinery and equipment—Straight line; 10 years.
> Automobiles—150% declining balance; 3 years.

Depreciation is computed to the nearest month and no residual values are used.

(AICPA adapted)

P 11–4
Partial-year depreciation; asset addition; increase in useful life
● LO2 LO5 LO9

On April 1, 2009, the KB Toy Company purchased equipment to be used in its manufacturing process. The equipment cost $48,000, has an eight-year useful life, and has no residual value. The company uses the straight-line depreciation method for all manufacturing equipment.

On January 4, 2011, $12,350 was spent to repair the equipment and to add a feature that increased its operating efficiency. Of the total expenditure, $2,000 represented ordinary repairs and annual maintenance and $10,350 represented the cost of the new feature. In addition to increasing operating efficiency, the total useful life of the equipment was extended to 10 years.

Required:
Prepare journal entries for the following:
1. Depreciation for 2009 and 2010.
2. The 2011 expenditure.
3. Depreciation for 2011.

P 11–5
Property, plant, and equipment and intangible assets; comprehensive
● LO2

The Thompson Corporation, a manufacturer of steel products, began operations on October 1, 2009. The accounting department of Thompson has started the fixed-asset and depreciation schedule presented below. You have been asked to assist in completing this schedule. In addition to ascertaining that the data already on the schedule are correct, you have obtained the following information from the company's records and personnel:

a. Depreciation is computed from the first of the month of acquisition to the first of the month of disposition.

b. Land A and Building A were acquired from a predecessor corporation. Thompson paid $812,500 for the land and building together. At the time of acquisition, the land had a fair value of $72,000 and the building had a fair value of $828,000.

c. Land B was acquired on October 2, 2009, in exchange for 3,000 newly issued shares of Thompson's common stock. At the date of acquisition, the stock had a par value of $5 per share and a fair value of $25 per share. During October 2009, Thompson paid $10,400 to demolish an existing building on this land so it could construct a new building.

d. Construction of Building B on the newly acquired land began on October 1, 2010. By September 30, 2011, Thompson had paid $210,000 of the estimated total construction costs of $300,000. Estimated completion and occupancy are July 2012.

e. Certain equipment was donated to the corporation by the city. An independent appraisal of the equipment when donated placed the fair value at $16,000 and the residual value at $2,000.

f. Machine A's total cost of $110,000 includes installation charges of $550 and normal repairs and maintenance of $11,000. Residual value is estimated at $5,500. Machine A was sold on February 1, 2011.

g. On October 1, 2010, Machine B was acquired with a down payment of $4,000 and the remaining payments to be made in 10 annual installments of $4,000 each beginning October 1, 2011. The prevailing interest rate was 8%.

THOMPSON CORPORATION
Fixed Asset and Depreciation Schedule
For Fiscal Years Ended September 30, 2010, and September 30, 2011

Assets	Acquisition Date	Cost	Residual	Depreciation Method	Estimated Life in Years	Depreciation for Year Ended 9/30 2010	2011
Land A	10/1/09	$(1)	N/A	N/A	N/A	N/A	N/A
Building A	10/1/09	(2)	$47,500	SL	(3)	$14,000	$(4)
Land B	10/2/09	(5)	N/A	N/A	N/A	N/A	N/A
Building B	Under construction	210,000 to date	—	SL	30	—	(6)
Donated Equipment	10/2/09	(7)	2,000	150% Declining balance	10	(8)	(9)
Machine A	10/2/09	(10)	5,500	Sum-of-the-years'-digits	10	(11)	(12)
Machine B	10/1/10	(13)	—	SL	15	—	(14)

N/A = not applicable

Required:

Supply the correct amount for each numbered item on the schedule. Round each answer to the nearest dollar.

(AICPA adapted)

P 11–6
Depreciation methods; partial-year depreciation; sale of assets
● LO2

On March 31, 2011, the Herzog Company purchased a factory complete with machinery and equipment. The allocation of the total purchase price of $1,000,000 to the various types of assets along with estimated useful lives and residual values are as follows:

Asset	Cost	Estimated Residual Value	Estimated Useful Life in Years
Land	$ 100,000	N/A	N/A
Building	500,000	none	25
Machinery	240,000	10% of cost	8
Equipment	160,000	$13,000	6
Total	$1,000,000		

On June 29, 2012, machinery included in the March 31, 2011, purchase that cost $100,000 was sold for $80,000. Herzog uses the straight-line depreciation method for buildings and machinery and the sum-of-the-years'-digits method for equipment. Partial-year depreciation is calculated based on the number of months an asset is in service.

Required:

1. Compute depreciation expense on the building, machinery, and equipment for 2011.
2. Prepare the journal entries to record (1) depreciation on the machinery sold on June 29, 2012, and (2) the sale of machinery.
3. Compute depreciation expense on the building, remaining machinery, and equipment for 2012.

P 11–7
Depletion; change
in estimate

● LO3 LO5

In 2011, the Marion Company purchased land containing a mineral mine for $1,600,000. Additional costs of $600,000 were incurred to develop the mine. Geologists estimated that 400,000 tons of ore would be extracted. After the ore is removed, the land will have a resale value of $100,000.

To aid in the extraction, Marion built various structures and small storage buildings on the site at a cost of $150,000. These structures have a useful life of 10 years. The structures cannot be moved after the ore has been removed and will be left at the site. In addition, new equipment costing $80,000 was purchased and installed at the site. Marion does not plan to move the equipment to another site, but estimates that it can be sold at auction for $4,000 after the mining project is completed.

In 2011, 50,000 tons of ore were extracted and sold. In 2012, the estimate of total tons of ore in the mine was revised from 400,000 to 487,500. During 2012, 80,000 tons were extracted, of which 60,000 tons were sold.

Required:
1. Compute depletion and depreciation of the mine and the mining facilities and equipment for 2011 and 2012. Marion uses the units-of-production method to determine depreciation on mining facilities and equipment.
2. Compute the book value of the mineral mine, structures, and equipment as of December 31, 2012.
3. Discuss the accounting treatment of the depletion and depreciation on the mine and mining facilities and equipment.

P 11–8
Amortization

● LO4

The following information concerns the intangible assets of Epstein Corporation:
a. On June 30, 2011, Epstein completed the purchase of the Johnstone Corporation for $2,000,000 in cash. The fair value of the net identifiable assets of Johnstone was $1,700,000.
b. Included in the assets purchased from Johnstone was a patent that was valued at $80,000. The remaining legal life of the patent was 13 years, but Epstein believes that the patent will only be useful for another eight years.
c. Epstein acquired a franchise on October 1, 2011, by paying an initial franchise fee of $200,000. The contractual life of the franchise is 10 years.

Required:
1. Prepare year-end adjusting journal entries to record amortization expense on the intangibles at December 31, 2011.
2. Prepare the intangible asset section of the December 31, 2011, balance sheet.

P 11–9
Straight-line
depreciation;
change in useful
life and residual
value

● LO2 LO5

The property, plant, and equipment section of the Jasper Company's December 31, 2010, balance sheet contained the following:

Property, plant, and equipment:		
Land		$120,000
Building	$ 840,000	
Less: Accumulated depreciation	(200,000)	640,000
Equipment	180,000	
Less: Accumulated depreciation	?	?
Total property, plant, and equipment		?

The land and building were purchased at the beginning of 2006. Straight-line depreciation is used and a residual value of $40,000 for the building is anticipated.

The equipment is comprised of the following three machines:

Machine	Cost	Date Acquired	Residual Value	Life in Years
101	$70,000	1/1/08	$7,000	10
102	80,000	6/30/09	8,000	8
103	30,000	9/1/10	3,000	9

The straight-line method is used to determine depreciation on the equipment. On March 31, 2011, Machine 102 was sold for $52,500. Early in 2011, the useful life of machine 101 was revised to seven years in total, and the residual value was revised to zero.

Required:
1. Calculate the accumulated depreciation on the equipment at December 31, 2010.
2. Prepare the journal entry to record the sale of machine 102. Also prepare the journal entry to record 2011 depreciation on machine 102 up to the date of sale.
3. Prepare the 2011 year-end adjusting journal entries to record depreciation on the building and equipment.

P 11–10
Accounting
changes; three
accounting
situations

● **LO2 LO5 LO6**

Described below are three independent and unrelated situations involving accounting changes. Each change occurs during 2011 before any adjusting entries or closing entries are prepared.

a. On December 30, 2007, Rival Industries acquired its office building at a cost of $10,000,000. It has been depreciated on a straight-line basis assuming a useful life of 40 years and no residual value. Early in 2011, the estimate of useful life was revised to 28 years in total with no change in residual value.

b. At the beginning of 2007, the Hoffman Group purchased office equipment at a cost of $330,000. Its useful life was estimated to be 10 years with no residual value. The equipment has been depreciated by the sum-of-the-years'-digits method. On January 1, 2011, the company changed to the straight-line method.

c. At the beginning of 2011, Jantzen Specialties, which uses the sum-of-the-years'-digits method, changed to the straight-line method for newly acquired buildings and equipment. The change increased current year net income by $445,000.

Required:
For each situation:
1. Identify the type of change.
2. Prepare any journal entry necessary as a direct result of the change as well as any adjusting entry for 2011 related to the situation described. (Ignore income tax effects.)
3. Briefly describe any other steps that should be taken to appropriately report the situation.

P 11–11
Error correction;
change in
depreciation
method

● **LO2 LO6 LO7**

Collins Corporation purchased office equipment at the beginning of 2009 and capitalized a cost of $2,000,000. This cost figure included the following expenditures:

Purchase price	$1,850,000
Freight charges	30,000
Installation charges	20,000
Annual maintenance charge	100,000
Total	$2,000,000

The company estimated an eight-year useful life for the equipment. No residual value is anticipated. The double-declining-balance method was used to determine depreciation expense for 2009 and 2010.

In 2011, after the 2010 financial statements were issued, the company decided to switch to the straight-line depreciation method for this equipment. At that time, the company's controller discovered that the original cost of the equipment incorrectly included one year of annual maintenance charges for the equipment.

Required:
1. Ignoring income taxes, prepare the appropriate correcting entry for the equipment capitalization error discovered in 2011.
2. Ignoring income taxes, prepare any 2011 journal entry(s) related to the change in depreciation methods.

P 11–12
Depreciation and
amortization;
impairment

● **LO2 LO4 LO8**

At the beginning of 2009, Metatec Inc. acquired Ellison Technology Corporation for $600 million. In addition to cash, receivables, and inventory, the following assets and their fair values were also acquired:

Plant and equipment (depreciable assets)	$150 million
Patent	40 million
Goodwill	100 million

The plant and equipment are depreciated over a 10-year useful life on a straight-line basis. There is no estimated residual value. The patent is estimated to have a 5-year useful life, no residual value, and is amortized using the straight-line method.

At the end of 2011, a change in business climate indicated to management that the assets of Ellison might be impaired. The following amounts have been determined:

Plant and equipment:	
Undiscounted sum of future cash flows	$ 80 million
Fair value	60 million
Patent:	
Undiscounted sum of future cash flows	$ 20 million
Fair value	13 million
Goodwill:	
Fair value of Ellison Technology	$450 million
Fair value of Ellison's net assets (excluding goodwill)	390 million
Book value of Ellison's net assets (including goodwill)	470 million*

*After first recording any impairment losses on plant and equipment and the patent.

Required:

1. Compute the book value of the plant and equipment and patent at the end of 2011.

2. When should the plant and equipment and the patent be tested for impairment?

3. When should goodwill be tested for impairment?

4. Determine the amount of any impairment loss to be recorded, if any, for the three assets.

P 11–13
Chapters 10 and 11;
depreciation and
depletion; change
in useful life;
asset retirement
obligation

● LO2 LO3 LO5

On May 1, 2011, Hecala Mining entered into an agreement with the state of New Mexico to obtain the rights to operate a mineral mine in New Mexico for $10 million. Additional costs and purchases included the following:

Development costs in preparing the mine	$3,200,000
Mining machinery	140,000
Construction of various structures on site	68,000

After the minerals are removed from the mine, the machinery will be sold for an estimated residual value of $10,000. The structures will be torn down.

Geologists estimate that 800,000 tons of ore can be extracted from the mine. After the ore is removed the land will revert back to the state of New Mexico.

The contract with the state requires Hecala to restore the land to its original condition after mining operations are completed in approximately four years. Management has provided the following possible outflows for the restoration costs:

Cash Outflow	Probability
$600,000	30%
700,000	30%
800,000	40%

Hecala's credit-adjusted risk-free interest rate is 8%. During 2011, Hecala extracted 120,000 tons of ore from the mine.

Required:

1. Determine the amount at which Hecala will record the mine.

2. Calculate the depletion of the mine and the depreciation of the mining facilities and equipment for 2011, assuming that Hecala uses the units-of-production method for both depreciation and depletion. Round depletion and depreciation rates to four decimals.

3. Are depletion of the mine and depreciation of the mining facilities and equipment reported as separate expenses in the income statement? Discuss the accounting treatment of these items in the income statement and balance sheet.

4. During 2012, Hecala changed its estimate of the total amount of ore originally in the mine from 800,000 to 1,000,000 tons. Briefly describe the accounting treatment the company will employ to account for the change *and* calculate the depletion of the mine and depreciation of the mining facilities and equipment for 2012 assuming Hecala extracted 150,000 tons of ore in 2012.

BROADEN YOUR PERSPECTIVE

Apply your critical-thinking ability to the knowledge you've gained. These cases will provide you an opportunity to develop your research, analysis, judgment, and communication skills. You also will work with other students, integrate what you've learned, apply it in real world situations, and consider its global and ethical ramifications. This practice will broaden your knowledge and further develop your decision-making abilities.

**Analysis
Case 11–1**
Depreciation,
depletion, and
amortization

● LO1

The terms depreciation, depletion, and amortization all refer to the process of allocating the cost of an asset to the periods the asset is used.

Required:

Discuss the differences between depreciation, depletion, and amortization as the terms are used in accounting for property, plant, and equipment and intangible assets.

**Communication
Case 11–2**
Depreciation

● LO1

At a recent luncheon, you were seated next to Mr. Hopkins, the president of a local company that manufactures bicycle parts. He heard that you were a CPA and made the following comments to you:

Why is it that I am forced to recognize depreciation expense in my company's income statement when I know that I could sell many of my assets for more than I paid for them? I thought that the purpose of the balance sheet was to reflect the value of my business and that the purpose of the income statement was to report the net change in value or wealth of a company. It just doesn't make sense to penalize my profits when there hasn't been any loss in value from using the assets.

At the conclusion of the luncheon, you promised to send him a short explanation of the rationale for current depreciation practices.

Required:

Prepare a letter to Mr. Hopkins. Explain the accounting concept of depreciation and include a brief example in your explanation showing that over the life of the asset the change in value approach to depreciation and the allocation of cost approach will result in the same total effect on income.

Judgment Case 11–3
Straight-line method; composite depreciation
● LO1 LO2

Portland Co. uses the straight-line depreciation method for depreciable assets. All assets are depreciated individually except manufacturing machinery, which is depreciated by the composite method.

Required:

1. What factors should have influenced Portland's selection of the straight-line depreciation method?
2. a. What benefits should derive from using the composite method rather than the individual basis for manufacturing machinery?
   b. How should Portland have calculated the manufacturing machinery's annual depreciation in its first year of operation?

(AICPA adapted)

Judgment Case 11–4
Depreciation
● LO1 LO2

At the beginning of the year, Patrick Company acquired a computer to be used in its operations. The computer was delivered by the supplier, installed by Patrick, and placed into operation. The estimated useful life of the computer is five years, and its estimated residual value is significant.

Required:

1. a. What costs should Patrick capitalize for the computer?
   b. What is the objective of depreciation accounting?
2. What is the rationale for using accelerated depreciation methods?

(AICPA adapted)

Judgment Case 11–5
Capitalize or expense; materiality
● LO9

Redline Publishers, Inc., produces various manuals ranging from computer software instructional booklets to manuals explaining the installation and use of large pieces of industrial equipment. At the end of 2011, the company's balance sheet reported total assets of $62 million and total liabilities of $40 million. The income statement for 2011 reported net income of $1.1 million, which represents an approximate 3% increase from the prior year. The company's effective income tax rate is 30%.

Near the end of 2011, a variety of expenditures were made to overhaul the company's manufacturing equipment. None of these expenditures exceeded $750, the materiality threshold the company has set for the capitalization of any such expenditure. Even though the overhauls extended the service life of the equipment, the expenditures were expensed, not capitalized.

John Henderson, the company's controller, is worried about the treatment of the overhaul expenditures. Even though no individual expenditure exceeded the $750 materiality threshold, total expenditures were $70,000.

Required:

Should the overhaul expenditures be capitalized or expensed?

Communication Case 11–6
Capitalize or expense; materiality
● LO9

The focus of the case is the situation described in the previous case. Your instructor will divide the class into two to six groups depending on the size of the class. The mission of your group is to determine the treatment of the overhaul expenditures.

Required:

1. Each group member should deliberate the situation independently and draft a tentative argument prior to the class session for which the case is assigned.
2. In class, each group will meet for 10 to 15 minutes in different areas of the classroom. During the meeting, group members will take turns sharing their suggestions for the purpose of arriving at a single group treatment.
3. After the allotted time, a spokesperson for each group (selected during the group meetings) will share the group's solution with the class. The goal of the class is to incorporate the views of each group into a consensus approach to the situation.

Integrating Case 11–7
Errors; change in estimate; change in principle; inventory, patent, and equipment
● LO5 through LO7

Whaley Distributors is a wholesale distributor of electronic components. Financial statements for the year ended December 31, 2011, reported the following amounts and subtotals ($ in millions):

	Assets	Liabilities	Shareholders' Equity	Net Income	Expenses
2010	$640	$330	$310	$210	$150
2011	$820	$400	$420	$230	$175

In 2012 the following situations occurred or came to light:

a. Internal auditors discovered that ending inventories reported in the financial statements the two previous years were misstated due to faulty internal controls. The errors were in the following amounts:

2010 inventory	Overstated by $12 million
2011 inventory	Understated by $10 million

b. A patent costing $18 million at the beginning of 2010, expected to benefit operations for a total of six years, has not been amortized since acquired.

c. Whaley's conveyer equipment has been depreciated by the sum-of-the-years'-digits (SYD) method since constructed at the beginning of 2010 at a cost of $30 million. It has an expected useful life of five years and no expected residual value. At the beginning of 2012, Whaley decided to switch to straight-line depreciation.

Required:

For each situation:

1. Prepare any journal entry necessary as a direct result of the change or error correction as well as any adjusting entry for 2012 related to the situation described. (Ignore tax effects.)

2. Determine the amounts to be reported for each of the items shown above from the 2010 and 2011 financial statements when those amounts are reported again in the 2012, 2011, and 2010 comparative financial statements.

**Judgment
Case 11–8**
Accounting changes
● LO5 LO6

There are various types of accounting changes, each of which is required to be reported differently.

Required:

1. What type of accounting change is a change from the sum-of-the-years'-digits method of depreciation to the straight-line method for previously recorded assets? Under what circumstances does this type of accounting change occur?

2. What type of accounting change is a change in the expected service life of an asset arising because of more experience with the asset? Under what circumstances does this type of accounting change occur?

(AICPA adapted)

**Research
Case 11–9**
FASB codification; locate and extract relevant information and cite authoritative support for a financial reporting issue; impairment of property, plant, and equipment and intangible assets
● LO8

The company controller, Barry Melrose, has asked for your help in interpreting the authoritative accounting literature that addresses the recognition and measurement of impairment losses for property, plant, and equipment and intangible assets. "We have a significant amount of goodwill on our books from last year's acquisition of Churchill Corporation. Also, I think we may have a problem with the assets of some of our factories out West. And one of our divisions is currently considering disposing of a large group of depreciable assets."

Your task as assistant controller is to research the issue.

Required:

1. Obtain the relevant authoritative literature on accounting for the impairment of property, plant, and equipment and intangible assets using the FASB's Codification Research System. You might gain access at the FASB website (**www.fasb.org**). Cite the reference locations regarding impairment of property, plant, and equipment and intangible assets.

2. When should property, plant, and equipment and intangible assets be tested for impairment?

3. Explain the process for measuring an impairment loss for property, plant, and equipment and intangible assets to be held and used.

4. What are the specific criteria that must be met for an asset or asset group to be classified as held-for-sale? What is the specific citation reference from the FASB's Codification Research System that contains these criteria?

5. Explain the process for measuring an impairment loss for property, plant, and equipment and intangible assets classified as held-for-sale.

**Ethics
Case 11–10**
Asset impairment
● LO8

At the beginning of 2009, the Healthy Life Food Company purchased equipment for $42 million to be used in the manufacture of a new line of gourmet frozen foods. The equipment was estimated to have a 10-year service life and no residual value. The straight-line depreciation method was used to measure depreciation for 2009 and 2010.

Late in 2011, it became apparent that sales of the new frozen food line were significantly below expectations. The company decided to continue production for two more years (2012 and 2013) and then discontinue the line. At that time, the equipment will be sold for minimal scrap values.

The controller, Heather Meyer, was asked by Harvey Dent, the company's chief executive officer (CEO), to determine the appropriate treatment of the change in service life of the equipment. Heather determined that there has been an impairment of value requiring an immediate write-down of the equipment of $12,900,000. The remaining book value would then be depreciated over the equipment's revised service life.

The CEO does not like Heather's conclusion because of the effect it would have on 2011 income. "Looks like a simple revision in service life from 10 years to 5 years to me," Dent concluded. "Let's go with it that way, Heather."

Required:

1. What is the difference in before-tax income between the CEO's and Heather's treatment of the situation?
2. Discuss Heather Meyer's ethical dilemma.

Judgment Case 11–11
Earnings management and accounting changes; impairment
● LO5 LO6 LO8

Companies often are under pressure to meet or beat Wall Street earnings projections in order to increase stock prices and also to increase the value of stock options. Some resort to earnings management practices to artificially create desired results.

Required:

1. How can a company manage earnings by changing its depreciation method? Is this an effective technique to manage earnings?
2. How can a company manage earnings by changing the estimated useful lives of depreciable assets? Is this an effective technique to manage earnings?
3. Using a fictitious example and numbers you make up, describe in your own words how asset impairment losses could be used to manage earnings. How might that benefit the company?

Judgment Case 11–12
Subsequent expenditures
● LO9

The Cummings Company charged various expenditures made during 2011 to an account called repairs and maintenance expense. You have been asked by your supervisor in the company's internal audit department to review the expenditures to determine if they were appropriately recorded. The amount of each of the transactions included in the account is considered material.

1. Engine tune-up and oil change on the company's 12 delivery trucks—$1,300.
2. Rearrangement of machinery on the main production line—$5,500. It is not evident that the rearrangement will increase operational efficiency.
3. Installation of aluminum siding on the manufacturing plant—$32,000.
4. Replacement of the old air conditioning system in the manufacturing plant with a new system— $120,000.
5. Replacement of broken parts on three machines—$1,500.
6. Annual painting of the manufacturing plant—$11,000.
7. Purchase of new forklift to move finished product to the loading dock—$6,000.
8. Patching leaks in the roof of the manufacturing plant—$6,500. The repair work did not extend the useful life of the roof.

Required:

For each of the transactions listed above, indicate whether the expenditure is appropriately charged to the repair and maintenance expense account, and if not, indicate the proper account to be charged.

Real World Case 11–13
Disposition and depreciation; Chapters 10 and 11; Caterpillar
● LO1

Real World Financials

Caterpillar Inc. (CAT) is a world leader in the manufacture of construction and mining equipment, diesel and natural gas engines, and industrial gas turbines. CAT reported the following in a disclosure note accompanying its 2008 financial statements:

	2008	2007
($ in millions)		
Property, plant and equipment	$23,487	$19,208
Less: Accumulated depreciation	10,963	9,211
Property, plant and equipment - Net	$12,524	$ 9,997

Also, Note 10 disclosed that the total cost of property, plant, and equipment included $575 and $189 (dollars in millions) in land at the end of 2008 and 2007, respectively. In addition, the statement of cash flows for the year ended December 31, 2008, reported the following as cash flows from investing activities:

($ in millions)	
Payments for property, plant and equipment	$(4,597)
Proceeds from disposition of property, plant and equipment	982

The statement of cash flows also reported 2008 depreciation and amortization of $1,980 million (depreciation of $1,919 and amortization of $61).

Required:

1. Assume that all property, plant, and equipment acquired during 2008 were purchased for cash. Determine the amount of gain or loss from dispositions of property, plant, and equipment that Caterpillar recognized during 2008.

2. Assume that Caterpillar uses the straight-line method to depreciate plant and equipment. What is the approximate average service life of CAT's depreciable assets?

Real World Case 11–14

Depreciation and depletion method; asset impairment; subsequent expenditures; Chevron

● LO2 LO3
  LO8 LO9

Real World Financials

EDGAR, the Electronic Data Gathering, Analysis, and Retrieval system, performs automated collection, validation, indexing, and forwarding of submissions by companies and others who are required by law to file forms with the U.S. Securities and Exchange Commission (SEC). All publicly traded domestic companies use EDGAR to make the majority of their filings. (Some foreign companies file voluntarily.) Form 10-K, which includes the annual report, is required to be filed on EDGAR. The SEC makes this information available on the Internet.

Required:

1. Access EDGAR on the Internet. The web address is **www.sec.gov**.

2. Search for **Chevron Corporation**. Access the 10-K filing for most recent fiscal year. Search or scroll to find the financial statements and related notes.

3. Answer the following questions related to the company's property, plant, and equipment and intangible assets:

   a. Describe the company's depreciation and depletion policies.

   b. Describe the company's policy for subsequent expenditures made for plant and equipment.

IFRS Case 11–15

Subsequent valuation of property, plant, and equipment; comparison of U.S. GAAP and IFRS; Cadbury Schweppes

● LO10

Real World Financials

Cadbury Schweppes, Plc., a U.K. company, is an international confectionery and beverage business that sells its products in almost every country in the world. The company prepares its financial statements according to IFRS.

Required:

1. Use the Internet to locate Cadbury's most recent annual report. The address is **www.cadburyinvestors.com**. Locate the significant accounting policies disclosure note.

2. How does Cadbury value its property, plant, and equipment? Does the company have any other options under IFRS for valuing these assets? How do these options differ from U.S. GAAP?

Analysis Case 11–16

Depreciation and amortization

● LO2 LO4

Refer to the financial statements and related disclosure notes of **Dell** in Appendix B located at the back of the text.

Required:

1. What amount of depreciation and amortization did the company report in the fiscal year ended January 30, 2009?

2. What depreciation method is used for financial reporting purposes and what are the service lives of depreciable assets?

BRITISH AIRWAYS CASE

BRITISH AIRWAYS ➤

● LO10

British Airways, Plc. (BA), a U.K. company, prepares its financial statements according to International Financial Reporting Standards. BA's annual report for the year ended March 31, 2009, which includes financial statements and disclosure notes, is included with all new textbooks and can be found at **www.britishairways.com**. When answering questions, focus on BA's "Group" financial information (which is equivalent to "Consolidated" under U.S. GAAP).

Required:

1. BA's property, plant, and equipment is reported at cost. The group has a policy of not revaluing property, plant, and equipment. Suppose BA decided to revalue its equipment on March 31, 2009, and that the fair value of the equipment on that date was $280 million. Prepare the journal entry to record the revaluation assuming that the journal entry to record annual depreciation had already been recorded. (*Hint:* you will need

to locate the original cost and accumulated depreciation of the equipment at the end of the year in the appropriate disclosure note.)

2. Under U.S. GAAP, what alternatives do companies have to value their property, plant, and equipment?

3. BA calculates depreciation of plant and equipment on a straight-line basis, over the useful life of the asset. Describe any differences between IFRS and U.S. GAAP in the calculation of depreciation.

4. How often does BA review the residual values of its depreciable assets? How does this approach differ from U.S. GAAP?

5. When does BA test for the possible impairment of goodwill and for other nonfinancial assets? How do these approaches differ from U.S. GAAP?

6. Describe the approach BA uses to determine goodwill impairment losses. (*Hint:* see Note 19.) How does this approach differ from U.S. GAAP?

7. The following is included in BA's summary of significant accounting policies disclosure note: "Intangible assets are held at cost and are either amortised on a straight-line basis over their economic life, or they are deemed to have an indefinite economic life and are not amortised, but tested annually for impairment." Assume that on March 31, 2009, BA decided to revalue its landing rights intangible assets and that the fair value on that date was determined to be $190 million. Amortization expense for the year already has been recorded. Prepare the journal entry to record the revaluation.

CPA SIMULATION 11–1

Yamashita Kyle
Property, Plant, and Equipment and Intangible Assets

CPA Review

Test your knowledge of the concepts discussed in this chapter, practice critical professional skills necessary for career success, and prepare for the computer-based CPA exam by accessing our CPA simulations at the text website: **www.mhhe.com/spiceland6e**.

The Yamashita Kyle simulation tests your knowledge of (a) depreciation methods including group depreciation, and the measurement of impairment of value for property, plant, and equipment and intangible assets covered in this chapter, and (b) accounting for the disposal of property, plant, and equipment and intangible assets, the capitalization of interest, and research and development expenditures discussed in Chapter 10.

As on the CPA exam itself, you will be asked to use tools including a spreadsheet, a calculator, and generally accepted accounting principles, to conduct research, derive solutions, and communicate conclusions related to these issues in a simulated environment.

Specific tasks in the simulation address:

- Testing your knowledge of various aspects of accounting for interest capitalization.
- Calculating the appropriate amount of depreciation, applying several depreciation methods.
- Understanding the appropriate steps involved in determining the amount of impairment loss to recognize for property, plant, and equipment.
- Determining the appropriate income statement effect of the disposal of property, plant, and equipment and intangible assets.
- Communicating your understanding of (1) the treatment of expenditures subsequent to the acquisition of property, plant, and equipment and intangible assets and (2) the situations that require the capitalization of interest.
- Researching various items related to the measurement and reporting of property, plant, and equipment and intangible assets, including useful lives, group depreciation, and research and development expenditures.

12

Investments

/// OVERVIEW

In this chapter you will learn about various approaches used to account for investments that companies make in the debt and equity of other companies. An investing company always has the option to account for these investments at fair value, with changes in fair values reported on the income statement. However, depending on the nature of an investment, investors can use alternative accounting approaches that ignore most fair value changes (e.g., *held-to-maturity* investments) or that include fair value changes only in other comprehensive income (e.g., *available-for-sale* investments). And, when an equity investor can significantly influence an investee but does not control it, the investor can use the *equity method* of accounting, which ignores fair value changes but includes the investee's income when reporting the investor's income. In appendices to this chapter, you will learn about other types of investments, and also about how to deal with an investment whose value has been "other-than-temporarily impaired."

/// LEARNING OBJECTIVES

After studying this chapter, you should be able to:

● **LO1** Demonstrate how to identify and account for investments classified for reporting purposes as held-to-maturity. (page 622)

● **LO2** Demonstrate how to identify and account for investments classified for reporting purposes as trading securities. (page 625)

● **LO3** Demonstrate how to identify and account for investments classified for reporting purposes as available-for-sale securities. (page 629)

● **LO4** Explain what constitutes significant influence by the investor over the operating and financial policies of the investee. (page 645)

● **LO5** Demonstrate how to identify and account for investments accounted for under the equity method. (page 645)

● **LO6** Explain the adjustments made in the equity method when the fair value of the net assets underlying an investment exceeds their book value at acquisition. (page 647)

● **LO7** Explain how electing the fair value option affects accounting for investments. (page 637 and 653)

● **LO8** Discuss the primary differences between U.S. GAAP and IFRS with respect to investments. (pages 638, 639, 640, 644, 653, and 665)

FINANCIAL REPORTING CASE

A Case of Coke

You are the lone accounting major in your five-member group in your Business Policy class. A part of the case your group is working on is the analysis of the financial statements of the **Coca-Cola Company**.

The marketing major in the group is confused by the following disclosure note from Coca-Cola's 2008 annual report:

Note 10: Financial Instruments (in part)
Certain Debt and Marketable Equity Securities

Investments in debt and marketable equity securities, other than investments accounted for by the equity method, are categorized as trading, available-for-sale or held-to-maturity. Our marketable equity investments are categorized as trading or available-for-sale with their cost basis determined by the specific identification method. Realized and unrealized gains and losses on trading securities and realized gains and losses on available-for-sale securities are included in net income. Unrealized gains and losses, net of deferred taxes, on available-for-sale securities are included in our consolidated balance sheets as a component of AOCI. Debt securities categorized as held-to-maturity are stated at amortized cost.

As of December 31, 2008, trading, available-for-sale, and held-to-maturity securities consisted of the following (in millions):

	Cost	Gross Unrealized Gains	Gross Unrealized Losses	Estimated Fair Value
2008				
Trading securities:				
Equity securities	$ 74	$ —	$ (30)	$ 44
Other securities	7	—	(2)	5
	$ 81	$ —	$ (32)	$ 49
Available-for-sale securities:				
Equity securities	$329	$193	$ (7)	$515
Other securities	12	—	(5)	7
	$341	$193	$ (12)	$522
Held-to-maturity securities:				
Bank and corporate debt	$ 74	$ —	$ —	$ 74

"They say unrealized gains and losses are reported as part of AOCI. What's that? I don't see these gains and losses on the income statement," he complained. "And held-to-maturity securities—why are they treated differently? And what about equity method investments? On the balance sheet they have over $5 *billion* of investments accounted for under the equity method. They lost almost $900 million on those investments in 2008 but made almost $700 million in 2007, which is a swing of over $1.5 billion!"

To finance its operations, and often the expansion of those operations, a corporation raises funds by selling equity securities (common and preferred stock) and debt securities (bonds and notes). These securities are purchased as investments by individual investors, mutual funds, and also by other corporations. In later chapters we discuss equity and debt securities from the perspective of the issuing company. Our focus in this chapter is on the corporations that invest in debt and equity securities issued by other corporations as well as debt securities issued by governmental units (bonds, Treasury bills, and Treasury bonds).

Most companies invest in financial instruments issued by other companies. For some investors, these investments represent ongoing affiliations with the companies whose securities are acquired. For instance, in 2009 **Pfizer** acquired **Wyeth** in a deal valued at $68 billion, creating the world's largest pharmaceutical company, and in 2008 the Belgian company **InBev** acquired **Anheuser-Busch** in a deal valued at $52 billion, creating the global leader in beer. Some investments, though, are made not to obtain a favorable business relationship with another firm but simply to earn a return from the dividends or interest the securities pay or from increases in the market prices of the securities—the same reasons that might motivate you to buy stocks, bonds, or other investment securities.

With such diversity in investment objectives, it's not surprising that there is diversity in the approaches used to account for investments. As you'll discover when reading this chapter, investments are accounted for in five primary ways, depending on the nature of the investment relationship and the preferences of the investor. Before we discuss the approaches in detail, see the quick overview in Graphic 12–1.

In Part A of this chapter we discuss accounting for investments when the investor lacks significant influence over the operating and financial policies of the investee. In Part B we discuss accounting for "significant influence" investments. In both Parts A and B, we first discuss specific reporting methods and then discuss how the reporting changes if the investor elects the fair value option.

PART A   INVESTOR LACKS SIGNIFICANT INFLUENCE

The reporting approaches we use for investments differ according to how the approaches account for one or more of the four critical events that an investor experiences in the life of an investment:

1. Purchasing the investment.
2. Recognizing investment revenue (interest in the case of debt, dividends in the case of equity).
3. Holding the investment during periods in which the investment's fair value changes (and thus incurring *unrealized holding* gains and losses, since the security has not yet been sold).
4. Selling the investment (and thus incurring *realized* gains and losses, since the security has been sold and the gains or losses actually incurred).

Control Characteristics of the Investment	Reporting Method Used by the Investor
The investor *lacks significant influence* over the operating and financial policies of the investee:	
Investments in debt securities for which the investor has the "positive intent and ability" to hold to maturity	**Held-to-maturity ("HTM")**—investment reported at amortized cost*
Investments held in an active trading account	**Trading securities ("TS")**—investment reported at fair value (with unrealized holding gains and losses included in net income)
Other	**Securities available-for-sale ("AFS")**—investment reported at fair value (with unrealized holding gains and losses excluded from net income and reported in other comprehensive income)*
The investor *has significant influence* over the operating and financial policies of the investee:	
Typically the investor owns between 20% and 50% of the voting stock of the investee	**Equity method**—investment cost adjusted for subsequent earnings and dividends of the investee*
The investor *controls* the investee:	
The investor owns more than 50% of the investee	**Consolidation**—the financial statements of the investor and investee are combined as if they are a single company

*If the investor elects the *fair value option*, this type of investment also can be accounted for using the same approach that's used for trading securities, with the investment reported at fair value and unrealized holding gains and losses included in net income.

As shown in Graphic 12–1, when the investor lacks significant influence over the investee, the investment is classified in one of three categories: held-to-maturity securities (HTM), trading securities (TS), and available-for-sale securities (AFS). Each type of investment has its own reporting method. However, regardless of the investment type, investors can elect the "fair value option" that we discuss later in the chapter and classify HTM and AFS securities as TS. The key difference among the reporting approaches is how we account for unrealized holding gains and losses (critical event number 3 above), as shown in Graphic 12–2.

Reporting Approach	Treatment of Unrealized Holding Gains and Losses	Investment Reported in the Balance Sheet at
Held-to-maturity (HTM): used for debt that is planned to be held for its entire life	Not recognized	Amortized Cost*
Trading (TS): used for debt or equity that is held in an active trading account for immediate resale. Also used if the fair value option has been elected.	Recognized in net income, and therefore in retained earnings as part of shareholders' equity	Fair Value
Available-for-sale (AFS): used for debt or equity that does not qualify as held-to-maturity or trading	Recognized in other comprehensive income, and therefore in accumulated other comprehensive income in shareholders' equity	Fair Value

*Amortized cost is the original cost of the investment, less any accumulated amortization of premium or discount (which can be important for debt investments). GAAP sometimes refers to this as "amortized initial measurement." We use that terminology in Chapter 14 when discussing the fair value option with respect to liabilities.

Graphic 12–3 provides a description from a recent annual report of how the **Bank of America** accounts for its debt investments in each of the three reporting categories.

GRAPHIC 12–3
Disclosure about Investments—Bank of America

Real World Financials

Note 1 (in part): Securities
Debt Securities which management has the intent and ability to hold to maturity are classified as held-to-maturity and reported at amortized cost. Debt Securities that are bought and held principally for the purpose of resale in the near term are classified as Trading Account Assets and are stated at fair value with unrealized gains and losses included in Trading Account Profits. All other Debt Securities that management has the intent and ability to hold to recovery unless there is a significant deterioration in credit quality in any individual security are classified as available-for-sale (AFS) and carried at fair value with net unrealized gains and losses included in Accumulated OCI on an after-tax basis.

FINANCIAL
Reporting Case

Q1, p. 620

Why treat unrealized gains and losses differently depending on the type of investment? As you know, the primary purpose of accounting is to provide information useful for making decisions. What's most relevant for that purpose is not necessarily the same for each investment a company might make. For example, a company might invest in corporate bonds to provide a steady return until the bonds mature, in which case day-to-day changes in market value may not be viewed as very relevant, so the held-to-maturity approach is preferable. On the other hand, a company might invest in the same bonds because it plans to sell them at a profit in the near future, in which case the day-to-day changes in market value could be viewed as very relevant, and the trading security or available-for-sale approach is preferable.

Let's examine the three reporting classifications, one by one.

Securities to Be Held to Maturity

● LO1

Unlike a share of stock, a bond or other debt security has a specified date on which it matures. On its maturity date, the principal (also called the "face amount") is paid to investors. In the meantime, interest equal to a specified percentage of the principal is paid to investors on specified interest dates. Think of the principal and interest payments of the bond as a stream of cash flows that an investor will receive in exchange for purchasing the bond. The investor values that stream of cash flows using the prevailing market interest rate for debt of similar risk and maturity. If the interest rate paid by the bond (the "stated rate") is higher than the market rate, the bond can be sold for more than its maturity value (so it is "sold at a premium"). If the stated rate is lower than the market rate, the bond must be sold for less than its maturity value (so it is "sold at a discount"). For an example of valuing a bond, see Illustration 12–1.

The market value of a fixed-rate investment moves in the opposite direction of market rates of interest.

The fair value of a bond changes when market interest rates change. If market rates of interest *rise* after a fixed-rate security is purchased, the value of the fixed-interest payments declines. So, the fair value of the investment falls. Conversely, if market rates of interest *fall* after a fixed-rate security is purchased, the fixed interest payments become relatively more attractive, so the fair value of the investment rises.

Increases and decreases in fair value between the day a debt security is acquired and the day it matures to a prearranged maturity value are less important if sale before maturity isn't an alternative. For this reason, if an investor has the "positive intent and ability" to hold the securities to maturity, investments in debt securities can be classified as **held-to-maturity (HTM)** and reported at their *amortized cost* in the balance sheet.[1] A debt security cannot be classified as held-to-maturity if the investor might sell it before maturity in response to changes in market prices or interest rates, to meet the investor's liquidity needs, or similar factors.

Changes in market value are less relevant to an investor who will hold a security to its maturity regardless of those changes.

Let's use the bond from Illustration 12–1 to see how we account for an investment in held-to-maturity debt securities.

---

[1]FASB ASC 320–10–25–1: Investments–Debt and Equity Securities–Overall–Recognition (previously "Accounting for Certain Investments in Debt and Equity Securities," *Statement of Financial Accounting Standards No. 115* (Norwalk, Conn.: FASB, 1993)).

On July 1, 2011, Masterwear Industries issued $700,000 of 12% bonds, dated July 1. Interest of $42,000 is payable semiannually on June 30 and December 31. The bonds mature in three years, on June 30, 2014. The market interest rate for bonds of similar risk and maturity is 14%. The entire bond issue was purchased by United Intergroup, Inc.*

Calculation of the Price of the Bonds

		Present Values
Interest	$ 42,000 × 4.76654** =	$200,195
Principal (face amount)	$700,000 × 0.66634† =	466,438
Present value (price) of the bonds		$666,633

ILLUSTRATION 12–1

Bonds Purchased at a Discount

Because interest is paid semiannually, the present value calculations use:

a. one-half the stated rate (6%),

b. one-half the market rate (7%), and

c. 6 (=3 × 2) semiannual periods.

* The numbers in this illustration are the same as those in Illustration 14–2 in Chapter 14 (except for some differences in dates between the two chapters). This helps us to better appreciate in Chapter 14 how Masterwear's accounting for its bond liability to United compares to United's accounting for its investment in Masterwear bonds. You can find an explanation of why we calculate the bond price this way on pages 750 and 751.
** Present value of an ordinary annuity of $1: n = 6, i = 7% (Table 4, at the back of the book).
† Present value of $1: n = 6, i = 7% (Table 2, at the back of the book).
Note: Present value tables are provided at the end of this textbook. If you need to review the concept of the time value of money, refer to the discussions in Chapter 6.

PURCHASE OF INVESTMENT. The journal entry to record the *purchase* of the HTM investments is:

All investment securities are initially recorded at cost.

July 1
Investment in bonds (face amount)	700,000	
Discount on bond investment (difference)		33,367
Cash (price paid for the bonds)		666,633

Discount on bond investment is a contra-asset to the investment in bonds asset account that serves to reduce the carrying value of the bond asset to its cost at the date of purchase.

RECOGNIZE INVESTMENT REVENUE. The Masterwear bonds pay cash interest at a rate of 12%, but were issued at a time when the market rate of interest was 14%. As a result, the bonds were sold at a discount that was large enough to provide bond purchasers with the same effective rate of return on their investment (14%) that they could get elsewhere in the market. Think of it this way: a little piece of that initial discount serves each period to make up the difference between the relatively low rate of interest that the bond pays (12%) and the higher rate of interest that the market demands (14%). Recording interest each period as the *effective market rate of interest multiplied by the outstanding balance of the investment* is referred to as the effective interest method. This simply is an application of the accrual concept, consistent with accruing all revenues as they are earned, regardless of when cash is received.

The effective interest on debt is the market rate of interest multiplied by the outstanding balance of the debt.

Continuing our example, the initial investment is $666,633. Since the effective interest rate is 14%, interest recorded as revenue to the investor for the first six-month interest period is $46,664:

$666,633	×	[14% ÷ 2]	=	$46,664
Outstanding balance		Effective rate		Effective interest

However, the bond calls for semiannual interest payments of only $42,000—the *stated* rate (6%) times the *face amount* ($700,000). As always, when only a portion of revenue is received, the remainder becomes an asset—in this case an addition to the existing investment. So the difference, $4,664, increases the investment by reducing the discount to $28,703 ($33,367 − 4,664). The journal entry to record the interest received for the first six months as investment revenue is:

December 31
Cash (stated rate × face amount)	42,000	
Discount on bond investment (difference)	4,664	
Investment revenue (market rate × outstanding balance)		46,664

The amortized cost of the investment now is $700,000 − $28,703 = $671,297.

Graphic 12–4 demonstrates interest being recorded at the effective rate over the life of this investment. As you can see, the amortization of discount gradually increases the carrying value of the investment, until the investment reaches its face amount of $700,000 at the time when the debt matures.

We discuss accounting for discounts and premiums in much greater detail in Chapter 14.

GRAPHIC 12–4

Amortization Schedule—Discount

If a bond is purchased at a discount, less cash is received each period than the effective interest, so the unpaid difference increases the outstanding balance of the investment.

Date	Cash Interest	Effective Interest	Increase in Balance	Outstanding Balance
	(6% × Face amount)	(7% × Outstanding balance)	(Discount reduction)	
7/1/11				666,633
12/31/11	42,000	.07 (666,633) = 46,664	4,664	671,297
6/30/12	42,000	.07 (671,297) = 46,991	4,991	676,288
12/31/12	42,000	.07 (676,288) = 47,340	5,340	681,628
6/30/13	42,000	.07 (681,628) = 47,714	5,714	687,342
12/31/13	42,000	.07 (687,342) = 48,114	6,114	693,456
6/30/14	42,000	.07 (693,456) = 48,544*	6,544	700,000
	252,000	285,367	33,367	

*Rounded.

DO NOT RECOGNIZE UNREALIZED HOLDING GAINS AND LOSSES FOR HTM INVESTMENTS. Suppose that, as of the end of the first reporting period, the market interest rate for similar securities has fallen to 11%. A market participant valuing the Masterwear bonds at that time would do so at the current market interest rate (11%) because that's the rate of return she or he could get from similar bonds. Calculating the present value of the bonds using a lower discount rate results in a higher present value. Let's say that checking market prices in *The Wall Street Journal* indicates that the fair value of the Masterwear bonds on that date is $714,943. How will United account for this increase in fair value? If United views the bonds as HTM investments, that change in fair value will be ignored so long as it is viewed as temporary.[2] The investment simply will be recorded at amortized cost (the amounts in the right-hand column of the amortization schedule in

Using Excel, enter:
=PV(.055,5,42000,700000)
Output: 714,946

Using a calculator:
enter: N 5 I 5.5
PMT −42000 FM −700000
Output: = PV 714,946

ADDITIONAL CONSIDERATION

Suppose the bonds are not traded on an active exchange. How would you determine the fair value of the Masterwear bonds on December 31, 2011? Recall from Chapter 1 that GAAP identifies different ways that a firm can determine fair value. If the Masterwear bonds are publicly traded, United can find the fair value by looking up the current market price (this way of obtaining fair value is consistent with "level one" of the fair value hierarchy). On the other hand, if the bonds are not publicly traded, United can calculate the fair value by using the present value techniques shown in Illustration 12–1 (this way of obtaining fair value is consistent with "level two" of the fair value hierarchy). With five interest periods remaining, and a current market rate of 11% (5.5% semi-annually), the present value would be $714,943:

			Present Values
Interest	$ 42,000 × 4.27028*	=	$179,352
Principal	$700,000 × 0.76513†	=	535,591
	Present value of the bonds		$714,943

*Present value of an ordinary annuity of $1: n = 5, i = 5.5%. (Table 4)
†Present value of $1: n = 5, i = 5.5%. (Table 2)

---

[2]If an unrealized loss from holding an HTM investment is not viewed as temporary, an "other-than-temporary impairment" (OTT impairment) may have to be recorded. We discuss OTT impairments in more detail in Appendix 12B.

Graphic 12–4). United will *disclose* the fair value of its HTM investments in a footnote, but will not recognize any fair value changes in the income statement or balance sheet.[3]

SELL HTM INVESTMENTS.   Typically, held-to-maturity investments are—you guessed it—held to maturity. However, suppose that due to unforeseen circumstances the company decided to sell its debt investment for $725,000 on January 15, 2012.[4] United would record the sale as follows (for simplicity we ignore any interest earned during 2012):

January 15, 2012		
Cash...	725,000	
Discount on bond investment...	28,703	
Investment in Masterwear bonds		700,000
Gain on sale of investments (to balance)............................		53,703

In other words, United would record this sale just like any other asset sale, with a gain or loss determined by comparing the cash received with the carrying value (in this case, the amortized cost) of the asset given up.

We will revisit our discussion of investments in debt securities to be "held to maturity" in Chapter 14, "Bonds and Long-Term Notes." This way we can more readily see that accounting by the company that issues bonds and by the company that invests in those bonds is opposite but parallel; that is, each side of the transaction is the mirror image of the other.

Obviously, not all investments are intended to be held to maturity. When an investment is acquired to be held for an *unspecified period of time,* we classify the investment as either (a) "trading securities" or (b) "securities available-for-sale." These include investments in *debt* securities that are not classified as held-to-maturity and *equity* securities that have *readily determinable fair values.* You'll notice that, unlike held-to-maturity securities, we report investments in the other two categories at their fair values.

Trading Securities

● **LO2**

Some companies—primarily financial institutions—actively and frequently buy and sell securities, expecting to earn profits on short-term differences in price. Investments in debt or equity securities acquired principally for the purpose of selling them in the near term are classified as trading securities. The holding period for trading securities generally is measured in hours and days rather than months or years. These investments typically are reported among the investor's current assets. Relatively few investments are classified this way, because usually only banks and other financial operations invest in securities in the manner and for the purpose necessary to be categorized as trading securities. However, the FASB's decision to allow the fair value option could increase the prevalence of this classification.

Trading securities are actively managed in a trading account for the purpose of profiting from short-term price changes.

Just like other investments, trading securities initially are recorded at cost—that is, the total amount paid for the securities, including any brokerage fees. However, when a balance sheet is prepared in subsequent periods, this type of investment is written up or down to its fair value, or "marked to market."

Be sure to notice that fair value accounting is a departure from historical costs, which is the way most assets are reported in balance sheets. Why the difference? For these investments, fair value information is more relevant than for other assets intended primarily to be used in company operations, like buildings, land and equipment, or for investments to be *held to maturity.*[5]

---

[3]If United had chosen the fair value option for this investment, it would classify the investment as a trading security rather than as an HTM security. We'll illustrate the fair value option when we discuss trading securities.

[4]GAAP [FASB ASC 320–10–25–6: Investments–Debt and Equity Securities–Overall–Recognition, previously *SFAS No. 115*] lists major unforeseen events that could justify sale of an HTM investment. Sale for other reasons could call into question whether the company actually had the intent and ability to hold the investment to maturity. In that case, the company's HTM classification is viewed as "tainted," and the company can be required to reclassify all of its HTM investments as AFS investments and avoid using the HTM classification for two years. Similar provisions exist under IFRS for public companies.

[5]Investments to be held to maturity, of course, include only debt securities.

Unrealized holding gains and losses for trading securities are included in net income in the period in which fair value changes.

For instance, consider an investment in debt. As interest rates rise or fall, the fair value of the investment will decrease or increase. Movements in fair values are less relevant if the investment is to be held to maturity; the investor receives the same contracted interest payments and principal at maturity, regardless of changes in fair value.

However, if the debt investment is held for active trading, changes in market values, and thus market returns, provide an indication of management's success in deciding when to acquire the investment, when to sell it, whether to invest in fixed-rate or variable-rate securities, and whether to invest in long-term or short-term securities. For that reason, it makes sense to report unrealized holding gains and losses on trading securities in net income during a period that fair values change, even though those gains and losses haven't yet been realized through the sale of the securities.

FINANCIAL
Reporting Case

Q2, p. 620

To see how we account for trading securities, let's modify the example we used for HTM securities. We'll assume that those debt investments are held in an active trading portfolio, with United intending to profit from short-term changes in price. In addition, let's add a couple of equity (stock) investments to highlight that, while the HTM approach applies only to debt securities, the TS approach applies to both debt and equity securities. The relevant facts are included in Illustration 12–2. Assuming all investments are classified as trading securities, the accounting would be as follows.

ILLUSTRATION 12–2	United Intergroup, Inc., buys and sells both debt and equity securities of other companies
Accounting for Trading Securities and Securities Available-for-Sale	as investments. United's fiscal year-end is December 31. The following events during 2011 and 2012 pertain to the investment portfolio.

Purchase Investments July 1, 2011	Purchased Masterwear Industries' 12%, 3-year bonds for $666,633 to yield an effective interest rate of 14%. Purchased $1,500,000 of Arjent, Inc., common stock. Purchased $1,000,000 of Bendac common stock.
Receive Investment Revenue December 31, 2011	Received a semi-annual cash interest payment of $42,000 from Masterwear. Received a cash dividend of $75,000 from Arjent. (Bendac does not pay dividends)
Adjust Investments to Fair Value December 31, 2011	Valued the Masterwear bonds at $714,943. Valued the Arjent stock at $1,450,000. Valued the Bendac stock at $990,000.
Sell Investments January 15, 2012	Sold the Masterwear bonds for $725,000. Sold the Arjent stock for $1,446,000.
Adjust Remaining Investments to Fair Value December 31, 2012	Valued the Bendac stock at $985,000.

PURCHASE INVESTMENTS. The journal entry to record the purchase of the bond investment is the same as it is for HTM securities. The journal entries to record the equity investments are even simpler, just exchanging one asset (cash) for another (investment):

All investment securities are recorded initially at cost.

July 1, 2011		
Investment in Masterwear bonds...	700,000	
Discount on bond investment..		33,367
Cash..		666,633
Investment in Arjent stock	1,500,000	
Cash..		1,500,000
Investment in Bendac stock	1,000,000	
Cash..		1,000,000

RECOGNIZE INVESTMENT REVENUE. The journal entry to record the receipt of bond interest is the same as it is for HTM securities, with the carrying value of the investment increasing due to amortization of $4,664 of discount. The journal entry to record the receipt of dividends related to the Arjent equity investment is straightforward. There is no entry for the Bendac equity investment, because Bendac doesn't pay dividends.

December 31, 2011		
Cash (6% × $700,000)...	42,000	
Discount on bond investment......................................	4,664	
Investment revenue (interest: 7% × $666,633).......................		46,664
Cash...	75,000	
Investment revenue (dividends received)		75,000

Dividend and interest income are included in net income.

ADJUST TRADING SECURITY INVESTMENTS TO FAIR VALUE (2011). Unlike HTM securities, trading securities are carried at fair value in the balance sheet, so their carrying value must be adjusted to fair value at the end of every reporting period. Rather than increasing or decreasing the investment account itself, we use a valuation allowance, *fair value adjustment,* to increase or decrease the carrying value of the investment. At the same time, we record an unrealized holding gain or loss that is included in net income in the period in which fair value changes (the gain or loss is *unrealized* because the securities haven't actually been sold). The next table summarizes the relevant facts for United's investments.

Trading securities are adjusted to their fair value at each reporting date.

December 31, 2011

Security	Amortized Cost	Fair Value	Fair Value Adjustment
Masterwear	$ 671,297	$ 714,943	$43,646
Arjent	1,500,000	1,450,000	(50,000)
Bendac	1,000,000	990,000	(10,000)
Total	$3,171,297	$3,154,943	$(16,354)
Existing balance in fair value adjustment:			–0–
Increase (decrease) needed in fair value adjustment:			($16,354)

United has an unrealized loss of $16,354. Note that, to determine the amount of unrealized holding gain or loss on the Masterwear bonds, United first identifies the bonds' *amortized cost* and then determines the amount necessary to adjust them to fair value:

Face amount of the bond	$700,000
Less: Discount on bond investment	
$33,367 initial discount	
(4,664) accumulated amortization	
$28,703 discount at 12/31/11	(28,703)
Amortized cost of the bonds	671,297
+/ − Fair value adjustment (to balance)	+ 43,646
Fair value of the bond at 12/31/11	$714,943

There is no discount to amortize for the equity investments, so for the Arjent and Bendac investments, their amortized cost is simply their initial cost. The journal entry to record the unrealized loss in United's fair value adjustment is

December 31, 2011[6]		
Net unrealized holding gains and losses—I/S[7]	16,354	
Fair value adjustment...		16,354

[6]Sometimes companies don't bother with a separate fair value adjustment account and simply adjust the investment account to fair value. Also, sometimes companies set up separate fair value adjustment accounts for each investment.
[7]We title this account "Net unrealized holding gains and losses—I/S" to highlight that, for trading securities, unrealized holding gains and losses are included in the income statement (I/S) in the period in which they occur.

SELL TRADING SECURITY INVESTMENTS. To record the gain or loss realized on the sale of the Masterwear and Arjent investments, United records the receipt of cash ($725,000 for Masterwear and $1,446,000 for Arjent), removes all balance sheet accounts that are directly associated with the investments, and calculates the difference to determine realized gain or loss.[10]

Realized gain or loss for the difference between carrying value and the cash received from selling an AFS security is included in net income.

January 15, 2012

Cash (amount received)	725,000	
Discount on bond investment (account balance)	28,703	
Investment in Masterwear bonds (account balance)		700,000
Gain on sale of investments (to balance)		53,703
Cash (amount received)	1,446,000	
Loss on sale of investments (to balance)	54,000	
Investment in Arjent stock (account balance)		1,500,000

When trading securities are sold, *unrealized* gains or losses that were recorded previously are removed from the fair value adjustment and net income at the end of the accounting period.

For the Masterwear bonds, this journal entry is identical to what United used when recording the sale of held-to-maturity investments. However, United isn't done yet. Now that those investments are sold, United needs to remove the fair value adjustment from the balance sheet. Also, because United has recognized in this period's net income the entire gain or loss *realized* on sale of the investments, it must back out of this period's net income any *unrealized* gains and losses that were included in net income in prior periods. That way, this period's net income includes only the fair value changes arising since the last period, and United avoids double counting gains and losses (once when unrealized, and again when realized). United can accomplish all of this when it adjusts its investment portfolio to fair value at the end of the reporting period.

ADJUST TRADING SECURITY INVESTMENTS TO FAIR VALUE (2012). The following table summarizes the situation at the end of 2012:

December 31, 2012

Security	Amortized Cost	Fair Value	Fair Value Adjustment
Masterwear	(sold)	–0–	–0–
Arjent	(sold)	–0–	–0–
Bendac	$1,000,000	$985,000	($15,000)
Total	$1,000,000	$985,000	($15,000)
	Existing balance in fair value adjustment:		($16,354)
	Increase (decrease) needed in fair value adjustment:		$ 1,354

---

[8]"Messenger, Shot," *The Economist,* April 8, 2009.

[9]Sarah Johnson, "The Fair Value Blame Game," CFO.com, March 19, 2008.

[10]For purposes of this example, we ignore any unpaid interest associated with the bonds. In practice, that amount would be added to the sales price of the bonds and included in investment revenue.

The journal entry necessary to show the appropriate balance in the fair value adjustment at the end of 2012 is

December 31, 2012

Fair value adjustment	1,354	
Net unrealized holding gains and losses—I/S		1,354

This journal entry serves two purposes: it (a) accounts for changes in the fair value of investments that have not been sold (in this case, Bendac), and (b) removes from the fair value adjustment and net income any unrealized holding gains or losses that were recognized in prior periods and that are associated with investments that now have been sold (in this case, Masterwear and Arjent). We discuss those purposes in more detail when we show later in this chapter how these investments would be accounted for as available-for-sale securities.

FINANCIAL STATEMENT PRESENTATION.   We present trading securities in the financial statements as follows:

> The Board concluded that fair value information is more relevant than amortized cost information, in part because it reflects the effects of a management decision to buy a financial asset at a specific time and then continue to hold it for an unspecified period of time.

- **Income Statement and Comprehensive Income Statement:** For trading securities, fair value changes are included on the income statement in the periods in which they occur, regardless of whether they are realized or unrealized. Investments in trading securities do not affect other comprehensive income.
- **Balance Sheet:** Investments in trading securities are reported at fair value, typically as current assets, and do not affect accumulated other comprehensive income in shareholders' equity.
- **Cash Flow Statement:** Cash flows from buying and selling trading securities typically are classified as operating activities, because the financial institutions that routinely hold trading securities consider them as part of their normal operations. However, as discussed in more detail later, it may be appropriate to classify cash flows from buying and selling some trading securities as investing activities if they are not held for sale in the near term (which is particularly likely when an investment is classified as a trading security as a result of electing the fair value option).[11]

United's 2011 and 2012 financial statements will include the amounts shown in Illustration 12–3.

Securities Available-for-Sale

When you or I buy stock in a corporation, say **Coca-Cola**, we hope the market value will rise before we sell it. We also may look forward to the cash dividends Coca-Cola pays its shareholders every three months. We may even have planned when we will sell the stock, or we may intend to wait and see what happens to market prices. In either case, we aren't planning to trade the investment actively, but our investment is available to sell given the right combination of market factors and our own cash situation. These same considerations apply to companies that invest in the securities of other corporations or governmental entities. When a company acquires an investment, not for an active trading account (as a financial institution might) or to be held to maturity (which of course couldn't be stock because it has no maturity date), the company classifies its investment as securities available-for-sale (AFS). Like trading securities, we report investments in AFS securities in the balance sheet at fair value. Unlike trading securities, though, unrealized holding gains and losses on AFS securities are *not* included in net income. Instead, they are reported in the statement of comprehensive income as other comprehensive income (OCI).

● **LO3**

Investments in available-for-sale securities are reported at their fair values.

Unrealized holding gains and losses on available-for-sale securities affect comprehensive income, but not net income.

---

[11]FASB ASC 320: Investments (previously "The Fair Value Option for Financial Assets and Financial Liabilities," *Statement of Financial Accounting Standards No. 159* (Norwalk, Conn.: FASB, 2007, par. A42)). The relevant paragraphs from the original standard are not codified in the FASB Research System as they primarily provide a basis for conclusions.

ILLUSTRATION 12–3	Income Statement	2011	2012
Reporting Trading Securities	Revenues	$ ◆	$ ◆
	Expenses	◆	◆
For trading securities, fair value changes affect net income in the period in which they occur.	Other income (expense):		
	Interest and dividend income	121,664[a]	–0–
	Realized and unrealized gains and losses on investments	(16,354)[b]	$1,057[c]
	Tax expense	◆	◆
	Net income	◆	◆
Trading securities are reported at fair value in the balance sheet.	**Balance Sheet**		
	Assets:		
	Trading securities	3,154,943	985,000
Cash flows from buying and selling trading securities are classified as operating activities.	**Statement of Cash Flows (direct method)**		
	Operating Activities:		
	Cash from investment revenue	117,000	–0–
	Purchase of trading securities	(3,166,633)	–0–
	Sale of trading securities	–0–	2,171,000

[a]$121,664 is the sum of $46,664 interest revenue from Masterwear and $75,000 dividends from Arjent.
[b]$16,354 is the net unrealized loss from the 2011 fair value adjustment.
[c]$1,057 is the $1,354 net unrealized gain from the 2012 fair value adjustment minus the $297 loss realized on sale of investments during 2012 (the $297 net realized loss results from the $54,000 loss realized on sale of the Arjent stock and the $53,703 gain realized on sale of the Masterwear bonds).

Comprehensive income includes not only net income, but also other changes in equity that don't arise from transactions with owners.

COMPREHENSIVE INCOME. You may recall from Chapter 4 that comprehensive income is a more all-encompassing view of changes in shareholders' equity, including not only net income but also all other changes in equity that do not arise from transactions with owners.[12] Comprehensive income therefore includes net income and *other comprehensive income (OCI)*. Both net income and OCI accumulate in shareholders' equity in the balance sheet, but in different accounts. While net income accumulates in retained earnings, OCI accumulates in *accumulated other comprehensive income (AOCI)*.

FINANCIAL Reporting Case

Q3, p. 620

RATIONALE FOR AFS TREATMENT OF UNREALIZED HOLDING GAINS AND LOSSES. Why use an approach for accounting for AFS securities that differs from that used for trading securities? The big concern is that including in net income unrealized holding gains and losses on AFS investments might make income appear more volatile than it really is. For example, many companies purchase AFS investments for the purpose of having the changes in fair value of those investments offset changes in the fair value of liabilities. This *hedging* insulates the company from risk and ensures that earnings are stable. However, if fair value changes for investments were to be recognized in income (as is the case with trading securities), but the offsetting fair value changes for liabilities were not recognized in income as well, we could end up with income appearing very volatile when in fact the underlying assets and liabilities are hedged effectively.[13]

More generally, because AFS securities are likely to be held for multiple reporting periods, one could argue that there is sufficient time for unrealized holding gains in some periods to balance out with unrealized holding losses in other periods, so including unrealized holding gains and losses in income would confuse investors by making income appear more volatile than it really is over the long run. Of course, one could counter-argue that these unrealized holding gains and losses still are relevant, given that each period an investor has discretion over whether or not to continue holding the security or sell that security to realize a gain or loss.

---

[12]Transactions with owners primarily include dividends and the sale or purchase of shares of the company's stock.
[13]The option to report in earnings changes in the fair value of liabilities was not permitted at the time the FASB wrote the initial standard (*SFAS No. 115*) that specified appropriate accounting for investments in debt and equity securities. As we will see in Chapter 14, that option now is allowed.

To consider accounting for AFS investments, refer to the facts shown in Illustration 12–2. Let's assume now that United classifies its investments as AFS rather than trading securities.

PURCHASE INVESTMENTS.
The journal entries to record the purchase of the investments are the same for AFS securities as they are for trading securities:

July 1, 2011		
Investment in Masterwear bonds	700,000	
Discount on bond investment		33,367
Cash		666,633
Investment in Arjent stock	1,500,000	
Cash		1,500,000
Investment in Bendac stock	1,000,000	
Cash		1,000,000

All investment securities are initially recorded at cost.

RECOGNIZE INVESTMENT REVENUE.
The journal entries to record the receipt of investment revenue also are the same for AFS securities as they are for trading securities.

December 31, 2011		
Cash (6% × $700,000)	42,000	
Discount on bond investment (difference)	4,664	
Investment revenue (interest: 7% × $666,633)		46,664
Cash	75,000	
Investment revenue (dividends)		75,000

Interest income and dividends on AFS investments are included in net income.

ADJUST AFS INVESTMENTS TO FAIR VALUE (2011).
Let's first recall the facts:

December 31, 2011

Security	Amortized Cost	Fair Value	Fair Value Adjustment
Masterwear	$ 671,297	$ 714,943	$ 43,646
Arjent	1,500,000	1,450,000	(50,000)
Bendac	1,000,000	990,000	(10,000)
Total	$3,171,297	$3,154,943	$(16,354)
	Existing balance in fair value adjustment:		–0–
	Increase (decrease) needed in fair value adjustment:		($ 16,354)

Like trading securities, AFS securities are adjusted to fair value at the end of each reporting period, which produces an unrealized holding gain or loss due to holding the securities while their fair values change. The journal entry to record United's unrealized holding loss is:

December 31, 2011		
Net unrealized holding gains and losses—OCI[14]	16,354	
Fair value adjustment.....		16,354

AFS securities are adjusted to their fair value at each reporting date.

Notice that the amount of unrealized holding loss is the same as with trading securities. What differs is that the net unrealized holding loss of $16,354 is included in net income for

For AFS securities, unrealized holding gains and losses from fair value changes are not included in net income, but instead are recorded as OCI.

---

[14]We title this account "Net unrealized holding gains and losses—OCI" to highlight that, for available-for-sale securities, unrealized holding gains and losses are included in other comprehensive income (OCI) in the period in which they occur.

trading securities and in OCI for AFS securities.[15] At the end of the reporting period the net unrealized holding loss ends up being closed to a shareholders' equity account for both approaches. What differs is that it gets closed to retained earnings for trading securities and to AOCI for AFS securities.

SELL AFS INVESTMENTS.   AFS investments require the same journal entry on the date of sale as is made to record the sale of trading securities. United simply records the receipt of cash, removes from the balance sheet any accounts that are directly associated with the investment, and calculates the difference to determine realized gain or loss.

Realized gain or loss for the difference between carrying value and the cash received from selling a trading security is included in net income.

January 15, 2012		
Cash (amount received)	725,000	
Discount on bond investment (account balance)	28,703	
Investment in Masterwear bonds (account balance)		700,000
Gain on sale of investments (to balance)		53,703
Cash (amount received)	1,446,000	
Loss on sale of investments (to balance)	54,000	
Investment in Arjent stock (account balance)		1,500,000

When AFS securities are sold, *unrealized* gains or losses that were recorded previously are removed from the fair value adjustment and OCI.

United also needs to adjust the fair value adjustment account and AOCI to remove any unrealized gains or losses previously recorded that relate to the sold investments. That is typically done at the end of the accounting period as part of the journal entry that adjusts the AFS investment portfolio to fair value, as we see below.

ADJUST AFS INVESTMENTS TO FAIR VALUE (2012).   The following table summarizes the situation at the end of 2012:

December 31, 2012

Security	Amortized Cost	Fair Value	Unrealized Gain (loss)
Masterwear	(sold)	–0–	–0–
Arjent	(sold)	–0–	–0–
Bendac	1,000,000	985,000	($15,000)
Total	1,000,000	985,000	($15,000)
	Existing balance in fair value adjustment:		($16,354)
	Increase (decrease) needed in fair value adjustment:		$ 1,354

This analysis indicates that United needs to increase the fair value adjustment by $1,354 and record an unrealized gain of the same amount in OCI.

December 31, 2012		
Fair value adjustment	1,354	
Net unrealized holding gains and losses—OCI		1,354

This journal entry serves two purposes: it (a) accounts for new changes during 2012 in the fair value of investments that haven't been sold, and (b) removes amounts associated with investments that were sold during 2012.

($5,000)	to add 2012 unrealized loss associated with investments not sold
6,354	to remove 2011 net unrealized loss that's no longer unrealized
$1,354	2012 adjustment to OCI

Let's consider the two purposes separately.

---

[15]As with trading securities, we could have not used a separate valuation allowance and simply adjusted the AFS investment account itself to fair value, and we also could set up separate valuation allowances and record separate journal entries for each AFS investment.

New Changes in the Fair Value of Investments Held. The first purpose of the journal entry is to record in OCI any new unrealized gains or losses associated with investments that have not been sold. For United, that's the Bendac stock. The new unrealized gain or loss equals whatever amount is necessary to report the Bendac investment at fair value as of the end of 2012.

$1,000,000	initial cost of Bendac stock
(985,000)	fair value at the end of 2012
$ 15,000	balance needed at end of 2012
(10,000)	balance at end of 2011
$ 5,000	new unrealized loss in 2012

If the 2012 journal entry had focused only on this first purpose, the journal entry would have been to recognize an unrealized holding loss of $5,000:

Net unrealized holding gains and losses-OCI.............................	5,000	
Fair value adjustment...		5,000

Reclassification Adjustment. The second purpose of the journal entry is to remove from OCI any amounts associated with *sold* investments. What amounts must United consider? Last year, in 2011, United recorded a net unrealized loss of $6,354 on the Arjent and Masterwear investments as part of the $16,354 fair value adjustment made at the end of that year.

$50,000	2011 unrealized loss for the Arjent stock
43,646	2011 unrealized gain for the Masterwear bonds
$ 6,354	net unrealized loss in 2011

If the *2011* fair value adjustment had only included the net unrealized loss on the Arjent and Masterwear investments, it would have been:

Net unrealized holding gains and losses—OCI	6,354	
Fair value adjustment...		6,354

> For AFS securities, *unrealized* gains and losses affect OCI and accumulate in AOCI until such time as the investment is sold.

Because those investments have now been sold, United must reverse this entry in 2012 to remove their effects from OCI and the fair value adjustment. If the 2012 journal entry had focused only on this second purpose, it would have been:

Fair value adjustment..	6,354	
Net unrealized holding gains and losses—OCI..................		6,354

See how the two purposes combine to create the single journal entry we use to increase the fair value adjustment by $1,354 and recognize a net unrealized holding gain of that amount in OCI?

Fair value adjustment ($6,354 – 5,000)..	1,354	
Net unrealized holding gains and losses—OCI.....................		1,354

Now, why is this often referred to as a "reclassification adjustment"? Remember that United included a $6,354 unrealized loss in 2011 OCI (and therefore in AOCI). Then, in 2012, it backed out that amount from OCI (and AOCI) as part of the fair value adjustment entry, and included the realized gain or loss in net income (and therefore retained earnings). From the perspective of shareholders' equity, the amount was basically reclassified from AOCI to retained earnings in the period of sale.[16]

---

[16]Reclassification also avoids double accounting with respect to comprehensive income and equity. If United didn't back out the 2011 unrealized loss from 2012 OCI, it would end up having included it in comprehensive income twice, once in OCI (2011) and once in net income (2012), thereby overstating total shareholders' equity.

Note that we don't separately *record* the reclassification. That happens automatically as part of the fair value adjustment entry at the end of the period. What we do is *report* the reclassification in the statement of comprehensive income, as you will see in the next section.

FINANCIAL STATEMENT PRESENTATION.   We present AFS securities in the financial statements as follows:

- **Income Statement and Comprehensive Income Statement:** *Realized* gains and losses are shown in net income in the period in which securities are sold. *Unrealized* gains and losses are shown in OCI in the periods in which changes in fair value occur, and reclassified out of OCI in the periods in which securities are sold.
- **Balance Sheet:** Investments in AFS securities are reported at fair value. *Unrealized* gains and losses affect AOCI in shareholders' equity, and are reclassified out of AOCI in the periods in which securities are sold.
- **Cash Flow Statement:** Cash flows from buying and selling AFS securities typically are classified as investing activities.

United's 2011 and 2012 financial statements will include the amounts shown in Illustration 12–4.

ILLUSTRATION 12–4		2011	2012
Reporting Available-for-Sale Securities	**Income Statement**		
	Revenues	$ ◆	$ ◆
Only *realized* gains and losses are included in net income.	Expenses	◆	◆
	Other income (expense):		
	Interest and dividend income	121,664[a]	–0–
Other comprehensive income includes *unrealized* holding gains and losses *that occur during the reporting period.*	Realized net loss on sale of investments	–0–	(297)[c]
	Tax Expense	◆	◆
	Net income	◆	◆
	Other comprehensive income (loss) items (OCI):[17]		
	Unrealized holding gains (losses) on investments	(16,354)[b]	(5,000)[d]
	Reclassification adjustment for net gains and losses included in net income	–0–	6,354[e]
AFS securities are reported at fair value.	Total	(16,354)	1,354
	Comprehensive income	◆	◆
AOCI (in shareholders' equity) includes net unrealized holding gains or losses *accumulated over the current and prior periods.*	**Balance Sheet**		
	Assets:		
	Available-for-sale securities	3,154,943	985,000
	Stockholders' equity:		
	Accumulated other comprehensive income (AOCI)	(16,354)	(15,000)
	Statement of Cash Flows (direct method)		
Cash flows from buying and selling AFS securities are classified as investing activities.	Operating Activities:		
	Cash from investment revenue	117,000	–0–
	Investing Activities:		
	Purchase of available-for-sale securities	(3,166,633)	–0–
	Sale of available-for-sale securities	–0–	2,171,000

[a]$121,664 is the sum of $46,664 interest revenue from Masterwear and $75,000 dividends from Arjent.
[b]$16,354 is the net unrealized loss from the 2011 fair value adjustment.
[c]$297 is the loss realized on sale of investments during 2012, resulting from the $54,000 loss realized on sale of the Arjent stock and the $53,703 gain realized on sale of the Masterwear bonds.
[d]$5,000 is the new net unrealized loss included in the 2012 fair value adjustment for Bendac.
[e]$6,354 is the reclassification adjustment included in the 2012 fair value adjustment to remove from AOCI amounts associated with investments that now have been sold.

---

[17]As we discuss in more detail in Chapter 18, the statement of comprehensive income can be reported as a continuation of the income statement as shown here, or alternatively either in a separate statement or in the statement of shareholders' equity.

Individual securities available for sale are classified as either current or noncurrent assets, depending on how long they're likely to be held. An example from the 2009 annual report of **Cisco Systems** is shown in Graphic 12–5.

Item 1A: Risk Factors (in part)
We maintain an investment portfolio of various holdings, types, and maturities. These securities are generally classified as available-for-sale and, consequently, are recorded on our Consolidated Balance Sheets at fair value with unrealized gains or losses reported as a component of accumulated other comprehensive income, net of tax.

Note 7: Investments (in part)
The following tables summarize the Company's investments (in millions):

July 25, 2009	Amortized Cost	Gross Unrealized Gains	Gross Unrealized Losses	Fair Value
Fixed income securities:				
Government securities	$ 10,266	$ 23	$ (5)	$10,284
Government agency securities (1)	16,029	116	(2)	16,143
Corporate debt securities	1,740	51	(86)	1,705
Asset-backed securities	252	5	(34)	223
Total fixed income securities	28,287	195	(127)	28,355
Publicly traded equity securities	824	193	(89)	928
Total	$ 29,111	$ 388	$ (216)	$29,283

GRAPHIC 12–5

Investments in Securities Available-for-Sale—Cisco Systems

Real World Financials

Comparison of HTM, TS, and AFS Approaches

Illustration 12–5 compares accounting for the Masterwear bonds under the three different approaches used when an investor lacks significant influence.

ILLUSTRATION 12–5 Comparison of HTM, TS, and AFS Approaches

	Held-to-Maturity (HTM)	Trading (TS)	Available-for-Sale (AFS)
Purchase bonds at a discount	Investments 700,000 Discount 33,367 Cash 666,633	Same as HTM	Same as HTM
Receive investment revenue	Cash 42,000 Discount 4,664 Invest. income 46,664	Same as HTM	Same as HTM
Adjust to fair value	No entry (unless impaired)	FV adjustment 43,646 Net unrealized gain/loss—I/S 43,646	FV adjustment 43,646 Net unrealized gain/loss—OCI 43,646
Sell bonds for a realized gain	Discount 28,703 Cash 725,000 Investments 700,000 Gain 53,703	Recognize gain or loss: Same as HTM Reverse out previously recorded unrealized gain or loss that's no longer unrealized (automatically part of next adjustment to fair value): Net unrealized gain/loss—I/S 43,646 FV adjustment 43,646	Recognize gain or loss: Same as HTM Reverse out previously recorded unrealized gain or loss that's no longer unrealized (automatically part of next adjustment to fair value): Net unrealized gain/loss—OCI 43,646* FV adjustment 43,646

*Reported as a reclassification adjustment in the statement of comprehensive income.

This side-by-side comparison highlights several aspects of these accounting approaches:

- To record the purchase of an investment and the receipt of investment revenue, we use identical entries in all three approaches.

- To record changes in fair value, the entries we use for TS and AFS securities have the same effect on the investment (via the fair value adjustment valuation allowance) and the same eventual effect on shareholders' equity. What differs is whether the unrealized gain or loss is recognized in the income statement and then in retained earnings (TS) or recognized in OCI and then in AOCI (AFS).

- To record the sale of the security, we use identical entries in all three approaches. For TS and AFS securities, the fair value adjustment and unrealized holding gains and losses associated with sold securities are dealt with automatically as part of the next adjustment to fair value.

- Regardless of approach, the cash flows are the same, and the same total amount of gain or loss is recognized in the income statement (TS: $43,646 in 2011 + [$53,703 − $43,646] in 2012 = $53,703 total; AFS and HTM: $53,703 in 2012). Thus, the question is not how much total net income is recognized, but *when* that net income is recognized.

ADDITIONAL CONSIDERATION

Available-for-Sale Investments and Income Taxes

When comparing accounting for TS and AFS securities, we saw that total shareholders' equity ends up being the same amount, regardless of whether unrealized gains and losses are included in net income and closed to retained earnings in shareholders' equity (for TS) or included only in OCI and shown in AOCI in shareholders' equity (for AFS securities). But what about taxes? Tax expense affects net income, so retained earnings includes after-tax amounts. For AOCI to be equivalent to retained earnings, it also should include only after-tax amounts. Therefore, adjustments must be made to OCI and AOCI that include tax effects. Typically these adjustments also give rise to deferred tax assets and liabilities, as unrealized holding gains and losses rarely affect the current period's taxes payable.

INTERNATIONAL FINANCIAL REPORTING STANDARDS

Accounting for Investments When Investor Lacks Significant Influence. Until recently, *IAS No. 39*[18] was the standard that specified appropriate accounting for investments under IFRS. The primary categories in *IAS No. 39* are similar to those in U.S. GAAP, consisting of "Fair Value through Profit & Loss" ("FVTPL," similar to TS), HTM, and AFS.

IFRS No. 9,[19] issued November 12, 2009, will be required after January 1, 2013, and earlier adoption is allowed, so in the time period between 2010 and 2012 either *IAS No. 39* or *IFRS No. 9* might be in effect for a particular company. *IFRS No. 9* eliminates the HTM and AFS classifications, replaced by new classifications that are more restrictive. This has the general effect of pushing more investments into being accounted for at FVTPL, and thus having unrealized gains and losses included in net income. Specifically, under *IFRS No. 9*:

- Investments in debt securities are classified as either "Amortized Cost" or FVTPL. Like the previous HTM classification, debt in the amortized cost classification is accounted for at (you guessed it) amortized cost. However, to be included in the amortized cost category, a debt investment has to meet both (a) the "cash flow characteristics" test (which requires that the debt instrument consist of only principal and interest payments) and (b) the "business model test" (which requires that the objective of the company's business model is to hold the investment to collect the contractual cash flows rather than to sell the investment at a gain). If debt isn't classified in "amortized cost," it is classified in FVTPL—there is no equivalent to AFS accounting for debt under *IFRS No. 9*.

(continued)

---

[18]"Financial Instruments: Recognition and Measurement," *International Accounting Standard No. 39* (IASCF), as amended effective January 1, 2009.
[19]"Financial Instruments," *International Financial Reporting Standard No. 9* (IASCF), November 12, 2009.

(concluded)

- Investments in equity securities are classified as either "FVTPL" or "FVTOCI" ("Fair Value through Other Comprehensive Income). If the equity is held for trading, it must be classified as FVTPL, but otherwise the company can irrevocably elect to classify it as FVTOCI. Like the previous AFS classification, equity in the FVTOCI category has *unrealized* gains and losses included in OCI. However, unlike AFS, *realized* gains and losses are not reclassified out of OCI and into net income when the investment is later sold. Rather, the accumulated gain or loss associated with a sold investment is just transferred from AOCI to retained earnings (both shareholders' equity accounts), without passing through the income statement.

One other difference between U.S. GAAP and IFRS is worth noting. U.S. GAAP allows specialized accounting (beyond the scope of this textbook) for particular industries like securities brokers/dealers, investment companies, and insurance companies. IFRS does not.

Transfers between Reporting Categories

At acquisition, an investor assigns debt and equity securities to one of the three reporting classifications—held-to-maturity, available-for-sale, or trading. At each reporting date, the appropriateness of the classification is reassessed. For instance, if the investor no longer has the ability to hold certain securities to maturity and will now hold them for resale, those securities would be reclassified from HTM to AFS. When a security is reclassified between two reporting categories, the security is transferred at its fair value on the date of transfer. Any unrealized holding gain or loss at reclassification should be accounted for *in a manner consistent with the classification into which the security is being transferred.* A summary is provided in Graphic 12–6.

A transfer of a security between reporting categories is accounted for at fair value and in accordance with the new reporting classification.

GRAPHIC 12–6
Transfer between Investment Categories

Transfer from:	To:	Unrealized Gain or Loss from Transfer at Fair Value
Either HTM or AFS	Trading	Include in current net income
Trading	Either HTM or AFS	There is none (already recognized in net income)
Held-to-maturity	Available-for-sale	Report as a separate component of shareholders' equity (in Other Comprehensive Income)
Available-for-sale	Held-to-maturity	Don't write off any existing unrealized holding gain or loss, but amortize it to net income over the remaining life of the security (fair value amount becomes the security's amortized cost basis).

Reclassifications are quite unusual, so when they occur, disclosure notes should describe the circumstances that resulted in the transfers. Other footnote disclosures are described in a later section.

Fair Value Option

You may recall from Chapter 1 that GAAP allows a fair value option that permits companies to elect to account for most "financial" assets and liabilities at fair value. Under the fair value option, unrealized gains and losses are recognized in net income in the period in which they occur. That accounting approach should sound familiar—it's the same approach we use to account for trading securities.

Here's how the fair value option works for these investments. When a security that qualifies for HTM or AFS treatment is purchased, the investor makes an irrevocable decision about whether to elect the fair value option. The company can elect the fair value option for some securities and not for identical others—it's entirely up to the company, but the company has to explain in the notes why it made a partial election. If the fair value option is elected for a security that would normally be accounted for as HTM or AFS, the company

● **LO7**

TS already are accounted for at fair value, so there is no need to choose the fair value option for them.

● LO8

IFRS ILLUSTRATION

Real World Financials

INTERNATIONAL FINANCIAL REPORTING STANDARDS

Transfers Between Investment Categories. Until recently, IFRS did not allow transfers out of the "fair value through P&L" (FVTPL) classification (which is roughly equivalent to the trading securities classification in U.S. GAAP). However, in October 2008 the IASB responded to the financial crisis by amending *IAS No. 39* to allow transfers of debt investments out of the FVTPL category into AFS or HTM in "rare circumstances," and indicated that the current financial crisis qualified as one of those circumstances.[20] The change was justified as increasing convergence to U.S. GAAP, which also allows transfers out of the trading security category, but in fact reclassifications in U.S. GAAP continue to be rarer events than occurred under IFRS with this change.

This change allowed banks in October 2008 to transfer investments out of the FVTPL category as of July 1, 2008, and thus avoid recognizing in earnings the losses they knew had already occurred during the third quarter of 2008. The effect on bank profits was substantial. A study by J. P. Morgan indicated that 32 of 43 West European banks it covered reclassified assets worth almost €620 billion, increasing pretax profits by almost €27 billion.[21]

Lloyds Banking Group of the United Kingdom wrote the following explanation:

> **Note 49 Financial Risk Management (in part)**
> Reclassification of Financial Assets
> In accordance with the amendment to IAS 39 as disclosed in note 2, the Group reviewed the categorisation of its assets classified as held for trading and available-for-sale financial assets. On the basis that there was no longer an active market for some of those assets, which are therefore more appropriately managed as loans, the Group reclassified £2,993 million of assets classified as held for trading (measured at fair value through profit or loss immediately prior to reclassification) to loans and receivables with effect from 1 July 2008 . . . If the assets had not been transferred and had been kept as held for trading, a loss of £347 million would have been recognised in the income statement for the six months to 31 December 2008 within net trading income.

Under IFRS No. 9 (discussed earlier in this chapter), transfers of debt investments between the FVTPL and the amortized cost categories can occur only if the company changes its business model with respect to the debt investment. No transfers of equity investments between the FVTPL and FVTOCI categories are allowed.

Choosing the fair value option for HTM and AFS investments just means reclassifying those investments as TS.

just classifies that security as a trading security, and that's how it appears in the financial statements.[22] The only difference is that, unlike most trading securities, purchases and sale of investments accounted for under the fair value option are likely to be classified as investing activities in the statement of cash flows, because those investments are not held for sale in the near term and therefore are not operational in nature. Also, note that electing the fair value option is irrevocable. If a company elects the fair value option and later believes that the fair value of an investment is likely to decline, it can't change the election and discontinue use of fair value accounting.

Why allow the fair value option? Recall that a primary reason for creating the AFS approach was to allow companies to avoid excess earnings volatility that would result from reporting in earnings the fair value changes of only part of a hedging arrangement. As described in Appendix A of the text, other accounting rules apply to hedging arrangements that involve derivatives, but those rules are very complex and don't cover all forms of hedging arrangements. The fair value option simplifies this process by allowing companies to choose whether to use fair value for most types of financial assets and liabilities. Thus, when a company enters into a hedging arrangement, it just has to make sure to elect the fair value option for each asset and liability in the hedging arrangement, and fair value changes of those assets and liabilities will be included in earnings.

---

[20]"Reclassification of Financial Assets" *Amendments to IAS 39 Financial Instruments: Recognition and Measurement and IFRS 7 Financial Instruments: Disclosures,* IASB, October 2008.

[21]J.P. Morgan, *IAS 39 Reclassification: Impact on Banks' FY 08 Results and Equity,* May 11, 2009.

[22]FASB ASC 825–10–25: Financial Instruments–Overall–Recognition (previously "The Fair Value Option for Financial Assets and Financial Liabilities," *Statement of Financial Accounting Standards No. 159* (Norwalk, Conn.: FASB, 2007, par. 29)).

INTERNATIONAL FINANCIAL REPORTING STANDARDS

Fair Value Option. International accounting standards are more restrictive than U.S. standards for determining when firms are allowed to elect the fair value option. Under both *IAS No. 39* and *IFRS No. 9*, companies can elect the fair value option only in specific circumstances. For example, a firm could elect the fair value option for an asset or liability in order to avoid the "accounting mismatch" that occurs when some parts of a fair value risk-hedging arrangement are accounted for at fair value and others are not. Although U.S. GAAP indicates that the intent of the fair value option is to address these sorts of circumstances, it does not require that those circumstances exist.

● LO8

Impairment of Investments

In this chapter we've seen that declines (as well as increases) in the fair value of some investments are reported in earnings. For instance, if the fair value of an investment in trading securities declines, we reduce the reported amount of that investment in the balance sheet and include the loss from the fair value decline in the income statement. Likewise, if the investor has elected the fair value option for HTM or AFS investments, those investments are accounted for as trading securities, so fair value changes always are recognized in earnings. Otherwise, fair value changes for HTM and AFS investment typically are not recognized in earnings.

However, there is an exception. If the fair value of an HTM or AFS investment declines below the amortized cost of the investment, and that decline is deemed to be *other-than-temporary (OTT),* the company recognizes an OTT impairment loss in earnings. The specific process for determining whether an investment has an OTT impairment differs between equity and debt investments.[23] For equity investments, the question is whether the company has the intent and ability to hold the investment until fair value recovers. If it doesn't, the company recognizes an OTT impairment loss in earnings and reduces the carrying value of the investment in the balance sheet by that amount. For debt investments, the process is more complicated than for equity investments, both in determining whether an impairment is OTT and in determining the amount of the impairment to include in earnings. For both equity and debt investments, after an OTT impairment is recognized, the ordinary treatment of unrealized gains and losses is resumed; that is, further changes in fair value are reported in OCI for AFS investments and not recognized for HTM investments.

An in-depth discussion of accounting for OTT impairments is provided in Appendix 12B.

> An "other-than-temporary" impairment loss is recognized in net income even though the security hasn't been sold.

ADDITIONAL CONSIDERATION

What if the Fair Value Isn't "Readily Determinable"?

According to GAAP, the fair value of an equity security is considered readily determinable only if its selling price is currently available on particular securities exchanges or over-the-counter markets.[24] If the fair value of an equity security is *not* readily determinable, we use the *cost method* (except when the equity method described in Part B of this chapter is appropriate). The cost method is so named because the investment is carried in the balance sheet at cost, and temporary unrealized holding gains and losses are not recognized in either net income or other comprehensive income. Any dividends received are reported as investment revenue, and any gain or loss realized upon selling the investment is included in income. However, fair values still matter under the cost method, because the investment still is subject to testing for other-than-temporary impairments. Therefore, even if the fair value of an equity investment isn't viewed as readily determinable, companies have to determine it if there are indications that the investment has been impaired.

---

[23]FASB ASC 320–10–35: Investments–Overall–Subsequent Measurement (previously "Recognition and Presentation of Other-Than-Temporary Impairments," *FASB Staff Position No. 115-2 and 124-2* (Norwalk, Conn.: FASB April 9, 2009)).

[24]FASB ASC 320–10–20: Investments–Overall–Glossary–Readily Determinable Fair Value (previously "Accounting for Certain Investments in Debt and Equity Securities (as amended)," *Statement of Financial Accounting Standards No. 115* (Norwalk, Conn.: FASB 2008), par. 3a).

● LO8

CONCEPT REVIEW EXERCISE

VARIOUS INVESTMENT SECURITIES

Diversified Services, Inc., offers a variety of business services, including financial services through its escrow division. Diversified entered into the following investment activities during the last month of 2011 and the first week of 2012. Diversified's fiscal year ends on December 31. The only securities held by Diversified at December 1 were 12 million common shares of Shelby Laminations, Inc., purchased in November for $50 million and classified as available-for-sale.

2011

Dec. 1   Purchased $30 million of 12% bonds of Vince-Gill Amusement Corporation and $24 million of 10% bonds of Eastern Waste Disposal Corporation, both at face value and both to be held until they mature. Interest on each bond issue is payable semiannually on November 30 and May 31.

    9   Sold one-half of the Shelby Laminations common shares for $26 million.

    29   Received cash dividends of $1.5 million from the Shelby Laminations common shares.

    30   Purchased U.S. Treasury bonds for $5.8 million as trading securities hoping to earn profits on short-term differences in prices.

    31   Recorded the necessary adjusting entry(s) relating to the investments.

The year-end market price of the Shelby Laminations common stock was $4.25 per share. The fair values of the bond investments were $32 million for Vince-Gill Amusement Corporation and $20 million for Eastern Waste Disposal Corporation. A sharp rise in short-term interest rates on the last day of the year caused the fair value of the Treasury bonds to fall to $5.7 million.

2012

Jan. 7   Sold the remaining Shelby Laminations common shares for $27 million.

Required:
Prepare the appropriate journal entry for each transaction or event and show the amounts that would be reported in the company's 2011 income statement relative to these investments. Determine the effects of the Shelby Laminations investment on net income, other comprehensive income, and comprehensive income for 2011, 2012, and combined over both years.

2011

Dec. 1   Purchased $30 million of 12% bonds of Vince-Gill Amusement Corporation and $24 million of 10% bonds of Eastern Waste Disposal Corporation, both at face value and both to be held until they mature. Interest on each bond issue is payable semiannually on November 30 and May 31.

	($ in millions)	
Investment in Vince-Gill Amusement bonds	30	
Investment in Eastern Waste Disposal bonds	24	
Cash		54

Dec. 9   Sold one-half of the Shelby Laminations common shares for $26 million.

Sale of one-half of the Shelby Laminations shares results in a $1 million gain ($26 million sales price − [$50 million cost ÷ 2]).

	($ in millions)	
Cash (selling price)	26	
Investment in Shelby Laminations common shares ($50 × ½)		25
Gain on sale of investments (difference)		1

Dec. 29   Received cash dividends of $1.5 million from the Shelby Laminations common shares.

	($ in millions)	
Cash	1.5	
Investment revenue		1.5

Dec. 30   Purchased U.S. Treasury bonds for $5.8 million as trading securities, hoping to earn profits on short-term differences in prices.

	($ in millions)	
Investment in U.S. Treasury bonds	5.8	
Cash		5.8

Dec. 31   Recorded the necessary adjusting entry(s) relating to the investments.

Accrued Interest (one month)	($ in millions)	
Investment revenue receivable—Vince-Gill Amusement ($30 million × 12% × ¹⁄₁₂)	0.3	
Investment revenue receivable—Eastern Waste Disposal ($24 million × 10% × ¹⁄₁₂)	0.2	
Investment revenue		0.5
Fair Value Adjustments		
Net unrealized holding gains and losses—I/S ($5.7 − 5.8)	0.1	
Fair value adjustment, TS investments		0.1
Fair value adjustment, AFS investments ([12 million shares × ½ × $4.25] − [$50 million × ½])	0.5	
Net unrealized holding gains and losses—OCI		0.5

Note: Securities held-to-maturity are not adjusted to fair value.

Reported in the 2011 Income Statement:	($ in millions)
Investment revenue ($1.5 dividends + 0.5 interest)	$2.0
Gain on sale of investments (Shelby)	1.0
Unrealized holding loss on investments (trading securities)	(0.1)

Note: The $0.5 million unrealized holding gain for the Shelby Laminations common shares is not included in income because it pertains to securities available-for-sale rather than trading securities, and so is reflected in OCI.

2012

Jan. 7   Sold the remaining Shelby Laminations common shares for $27 million.

The fair value of the Shelby shares at the time of sale is $27 million. Those shares were purchased for $25 million ($50 million × ½), so the gain realized on the sale is $2 million.

	($ in millions)	
Cash (selling price)	27	
Investment in Shelby Laminations common shares (cost: ½ × $50)		25
Gain on sale of investments (difference)		2

Given that the fair value adjustment for the Shelby shares has a $0.5 million balance (recorded on 12/31/11), we need to remove that amount and eliminate the corresponding unrecognized gain from AOCI. This happens automatically when we next adjust the portfolio to fair value. If we were to make the adjustment separately, the entry would be:

	($ in millions)	
Net unrealized holding gains and losses—OCI	0.5	
Fair value adjustment, AFS investments		0.5

The Shelby investment affected net income, other comprehensive income, and comprehensive income as follows ($ in millions):

2011

$1.0	realized gain on sale of investments (in net income)
0.5	unrealized gain on investments (in OCI)
$1.5	total 2011 effect in comprehensive income

2012

$2.0	realized gain on sale of investments (in net income)
(0.5)	reclassification out of OCI of previously recognized unrealized gain associated with sold investments
$1.5	total 2012 effect in comprehensive income
$3.0	grand total effect in comprehensive income ($1.5 + 1.5).
$3.0	grand total effect in net income ($1.0 + 2.0).
$0.0	grand total effect in other comprehensive income ($0.5 + (0.5)).

Note that the $3.0 grand total effect of the Shelby shares on comprehensive income and net income reconciles with the difference between their purchase price ($50) and their sales price ($53, which is equal to the sum of $26 for the half sold in 2011 and $27 for the half sold in 2012). The only difference between comprehensive income and net income is timing.

Financial Statement Presentation and Disclosure

Trading securities, held-to-maturity securities and available-for-sale securities are either current or noncurrent depending on when they are expected to mature or to be sold. However, it's not necessary that a company report individual amounts for the three categories of investments—held-to-maturity, available-for-sale, or trading—on the face of the balance sheet as long as that information is presented in the disclosure notes.[25]

On the statement of cash flows, inflows and outflows of cash from buying and selling trading securities typically are considered operating activities because, for companies that routinely transact in trading securities (financial institutions), trading in those

---

[25]FASB ASC 320–10–45–13: Investments–Debt and Equity Securities–Overall–Other Presentation Matters (previously *Statement of Financial Accounting Standards No. 115*, "Accounting for Certain Investments in Debt and Equity Securities," (Norwalk, Conn.: FASB, 1993), par. 18).

securities constitutes an appropriate part of the companies' normal operations. But because held-to-maturity and available-for-sale securities are not purchased and held principally to be sold in the near term, cash flows from the purchase, sale, and maturity of these securities are considered investing activities. Also, if an investment that normally would be HTM or AFS is classified as a trading security because the company chose the fair value option, cash flows may be classified as investing, because they are viewed as nonoperating in nature.

Investors should disclose the following in the disclosure notes for each year presented:

- Aggregate fair value.
- Gross realized and unrealized holding gains.
- Gross realized and unrealized holding losses.
- Change in net unrealized holding gains and losses.
- Amortized cost basis by major security type.

The notes also include disclosures designed to help financial statement users understand the quality of the inputs companies use when determining fair values and to identify parts of the financial statements that are affected by those fair value estimates. For example, the notes should include the level of the fair value hierarchy (levels 1, 2, or 3) in which all fair value measurements fall. For fair value measurements that use unobservable inputs (level 3), the notes need to provide information about the effect of fair value measurements on earnings, including a reconciliation of beginning and ending balances of the investment that identifies:

> *Extensive footnote disclosure is provided to help financial statement users assess the quality of fair value measurements and understand where they affect the financial statements.*

- Total gains or losses for the period (realized and unrealized), unrealized gains and losses associated with assets and liabilities still held at the reporting date, and where those amounts are included in earnings or shareholders' equity.
- Purchases, sales, issuances and settlements.
- Transfers in and out of level 3 of the fair value hierarchy (for example, because of changes in the observability of inputs used to determine fair values).
- For instruments accounted for under the fair value option, an estimate of the gains or losses included in earnings that are attributable to changes in instrument-specific credit risk.

For annual financial statements, the disclosures should also describe the valuation techniques used to measure fair value. Publicly traded companies must include some fair value disclosures in interim financial statements as well as annual financial statements.[26]

Information about maturities should be reported for debt securities by disclosing the fair value and cost for at least four maturity groupings: (a) within 1 year, (b) after 1 year through 5 years, (c) after 5 years through 10 years, and (d) after 10 years. A disclosure note from **Microsoft**'s 2009 annual report (Graphic 12–7) provides an example.

The maturities of debt securities, including fixed-maturity securities, at June 30, 2009, were as follows:		
(In millions)	Cost basis	Estimated fair value
Due in one year or less	$ 8,487	$ 6,750
Due after one year through five years	9,796	10,071
Due after five years through ten years	1,212	1,248
Due after ten years	2,759	2,819
Total	$22,254	$20,888

GRAPHIC 12–7

Disclosures of Investment Securities— Microsoft Corporation

Real World Financials

---

[26]FASB ASC 320–10–50: Investments–Overall–Disclosure (previously "Interim Disclosures about Fair Value of Financial Instruments," *FASB Staff Position No. 107-1 and 28-1* (Norwalk, Conn.: FASB April 9, 2009)).

● LO8

WHERE WE'RE HEADED

Both the FASB and the IASB are working on comprehensive overhauls of accounting for all financial instruments. As discussed already in this chapter, the IASB has issued the first section of IFRS No. 9, which deals with recognition and measurement. At the time this textbook is being written, the FASB has not yet issued a related new standard.

Under the FASB's proposed standard, most investments would be "FV through Net Income," similar to the FASB's current TS category and the IASB's FVTPL category. For debt investments intended to be held for the purposes of collecting contractual cash flows (interest and principal), the FASB would permit an irrevocable election to account for the investment as "Fair Value through OCI," similar to the FASB's current AFS category and the IASB's FVTOCI category. The FASB is proposing doing away with the HTM category altogether, and not having anything similar to accounting for debt investments at amortized cost.

Of course, both of these projects are multifaceted. Many details could change over the next few years, and perhaps the projects will converge.[27]

PART B   INVESTOR HAS SIGNIFICANT INFLUENCE

When a company invests in the equity securities (primarily common stock) of another company, the investing company can benefit either (a) *directly* through dividends and/or market price appreciation or (b) *indirectly* through the creation of desirable operating relationships with the investee. The way we report a company's investment in the stock of another company depends on the nature of the relationship between the investor and the investee.

For reporting purposes, we classify the investment relationship in one of three ways, and account for the investment differently depending on the classification, as shown in Graphic 12–8:

GRAPHIC 12–8

Reporting Classifications for Investment Relationships

Relationship: How much does the investor influence the operating and financial policies of the investee?	Reporting Method
Lacks significant influence (usually < 20% equity ownership)	Varies by type of investment (see Part A of this chapter)
Has significant influence (usually 20%–50% equity ownership)	Equity method
Has control (usually > 50% equity ownership)	Consolidation

The *equity method* can be used when an investor can't control, but can significantly influence, the investee.

We focused on situations in which the investor lacks significant influence in Part A of this chapter. In Part B of this chapter we focus on situations in which the investor has significant influence and discuss the equity method and fair value option that are used to account for those investments.

A detailed discussion of the third classification—consolidated financial statements—is beyond the scope of this book. That discussion often is a major focus of the advanced accounting course or is taught as a separate consolidations course. In this chapter, we'll briefly overview consolidation only to provide perspective to aspects of the equity method that purposely mimic some effects of consolidation. Let's do that now, before addressing the specifics of the equity method.

How the Equity Method Relates to Consolidated Financial Statements

If a company acquires more than 50% of the voting stock of another company, it's said to have a controlling interest, because by voting those shares, the investor actually can control

---
[27]For the current status of both of these projects, see "Accounting for Financial Instruments" under "Projects" at **FASB.org**.

the company acquired. The investor is referred to as the *parent;* the investee is termed the *subsidiary.* For reporting purposes (although not legally), the parent and subsidiary are considered to be a single reporting entity, and their financial statements are *consolidated.* Both companies continue to operate as separate legal entities and the subsidiary reports separate financial statements. However, because of the controlling interest, the parent company reports consolidated financial statements.

Consolidated financial statements combine the separate financial statements of the parent and the subsidiary each period into a single aggregate set of financial statements as if there were only one company. This entails an item-by-item combination of the parent and subsidiary statements (after first eliminating any amounts that are shared by the separate financial statements).[28] For instance, if the parent has $8 million cash and the subsidiary has $3 million cash, the consolidated balance sheet would report $11 million cash.

Two aspects of the consolidation process are of particular interest to us in understanding the equity method. First, in consolidated financial statements, the acquired company's assets are included in the financial statements at their fair values as of the date of the acquisition, rather than their book values on that date. Second, if the acquisition price is more than the sum of the separate fair values of the acquired net assets (assets less liabilities), that difference is recorded as an intangible asset—goodwill.[29] We'll return to the discussion of these two aspects when we reach the point in our discussion of the equity method where their influence is felt. As we'll see, the equity method is in many ways a partial consolidation.

We use the equity method when the investor can't control the investee but can exercise significant influence over the operating and financial policies of an investee.

What Is Significant Influence?

When effective control is absent, the investor still may be able to exercise significant influence over the operating and financial policies of the investee. This would be the case if the investor owns a large percentage of the outstanding shares relative to other shareholders. By voting those shares as a block, decisions often can be swayed in the direction the investor desires. When significant influence exists, the investment should be accounted for by the equity method. It should be presumed, in the absence of evidence to the contrary, that the investor exercises significant influence over the investee when it owns between 20% and 50% of the investee's voting shares.[30]

A Single Entity Concept

Much like consolidation, the equity method views the investor and investee collectively as a special type of single entity (as if the two companies were one company). However, using the equity method, the investor doesn't include separate financial statement items of the investee on an item-by-item basis as in consolidation. Instead, the investor reports its equity interest in the investee as a single investment account. For that reason, the equity method sometimes is referred to as a "one-line consolidation," because it essentially collapses the consolidation approach into single lines in the balance sheet and income statement, while having the same effect on total income and shareholders' equity.

Under the equity method, the investor recognizes investment income equal to its percentage share (based on stock ownership) of the net income earned by the investee rather than the portion of that net income received as cash dividends. The rationale for this approach is the presumption of the equity method that the fortunes of the investor and investee are

Consolidated financial statements combine the individual elements of the parent and subsidiary statements.

The acquired company's assets are included in consolidated financial statements at their fair values as of the date of the acquisition, and the difference between the acquisition price and the sum of the fair values of the acquired net assets is recorded as goodwill.

● LO4

Usually an investor can exercise significant influence over the investee when it owns between 20% and 50% of the investee's voting shares.

● LO5

The investor's ownership interest in individual assets and liabilities of the investee is represented by a single investment account.

[28]This avoids double counting those amounts in the consolidated statements. For example, amounts owed by one company to the other are represented by accounts payable in one set of financial statements and accounts receivable in the other. These amounts are not included in the statements of the consolidated entity because a company can't "owe itself."

[29]This is the usual case because most companies are worth more than the sum of the values of individual components of the company due to reputation, longevity, managerial expertise, customer loyalty, or a host of other possibilities. Accounting for goodwill in acquisitions is discussed in Chapter 10.

[30]Shareholders are the owners of the corporation. By voting their shares, it is they who determine the makeup of the board of directors—who, in turn, appoint officers—who, in turn, manage the company. Common stock usually is the class of shares that has voting privileges. However, a corporation can create classes of preferred shares that also have voting rights. This is discussed at greater length in Chapter 18.

ADDITIONAL CONSIDERATION

It's possible that a company owns more than 20% of the voting shares but still cannot exercise significant influence over the investee. If, for instance, another company or a small group of shareholders owns 51% or more of the shares, they control the investee regardless of how other investors vote their shares. GAAP provides this and other examples of indications that an investor may be unable to exercise significant influence:

- The investee challenges the investor's ability to exercise significant influence (through litigation or complaints to regulators).
- The investor surrenders significant shareholder rights in a signed agreement.
- The investor is unable to acquire sufficient information about the investee to apply the equity method.
- The investor tries and fails to obtain representation on the board of directors of the investee.[31]

In such cases, the equity method would not be appropriate, and the investment would likely be treated as AFS.

Conversely, it's also possible that a company owns less than 20% of the voting shares but is able to exercise significant influence over the investee. Ability to exercise significant influence with less than 20% ownership might be indicated, for example, by having an officer of the investor corporation on the board of directors of the investee corporation or by having, say, 18% of the voting shares while no other single investor owns more than 50%. In such cases the equity method would be appropriate.

sufficiently intertwined that as the investee prospers, the investor prospers proportionately. Stated differently, as the investee earns additional net assets, the investor's share of those net assets increases.

Initially, the investment is recorded at cost. The carrying amount of this investment subsequently is:

- Increased by the investor's percentage share of the investee's net income (or decreased by its share of a loss).
- Decreased by dividends paid.

FINANCIAL
Reporting Case

Q4, p. 620

To see how the equity method works, let's assume that United Intergroup purchased 30% of Arjent, Inc.'s, common stock for $1,500,000 cash. Illustration 12–6 highlights that buying 30% of Arjent can be viewed as buying 30% of all of Arjent's assets and liabilities. Those assets and liabilities likely have book values on Arjent's balance sheet that differ from their separate fair values. We can think of United as paying a price equal to 30% of the sum of the fair values of all of those assets and liabilities, plus an extra amount, goodwill, that captures 30% of the value of other attractive aspects of Arjent (e.g., loyal customers, well-trained workers) that GAAP doesn't capture as separate assets or liabilities. We will see that, under the equity method, all of those amounts are shown in a single investment account, but we still need to track their individual information to account for them correctly.

The cost principal governs the acquisition of assets.

PURCHASE OF INVESTMENT.   Recording United's purchase of 30% of Arjent is straightforward. In fact, it requires the same entry used to record the purchase of the Arjent investment in Part A of this chapter.

Investment in Arjent stock	1,500,000	
Cash		1,500,000

As the investee earns additional net assets, the investor's investment in those net assets increases.

RECORDING INVESTMENT REVENUE.   Under the equity method, the investor includes in net income its proportionate share of the investee's net income. The reasoning

---

[31]FASB ASC 323–10–15–10: Investments–Equity Method and Joint Ventures–Overall–Scope and Scope Exceptions (previously "Criteria for Applying the Equity Method of Accounting for Investments in Common Stock," *FASB Interpretation No. 35* (Stamford, Conn.: FASB, 1981)).

Account	Book Value on Arjent's Financial Statements	Fair Value at Time of United's Investment	ILLUSTRATION 12–6 Equity Method
Buildings (10-year remaining useful life, no salvage value)	$1,000,000	$ 2,000,000	
Land	500,000	1,000,000	
Other net assets*	600,000	600,000	
Net assets	2,100,000	3,600,000	
Goodwill		1,400,000 (to balance)	
Total fair value of Arjent		$ 5,000,000	
		× 30% purchased	
		$1,500,000 purchase price	

Other information:

Arjent's 2011 net income:	$500,000	
Arjent's 2011 dividends:	$250,000	

*Other net assets = other assets – liabilities

is that, as the investee earns additional net assets, the investor's equity interest in those net assets also increases, so the investor increases its investment by the amount of income recognized. United's entry would be:

Investment in Arjent stock	150,000	
Investment revenue (30% × $500,000)		150,000

As the investee prospers, the investor prospers proportionately.

Of course, if Argent had recorded a net loss rather than net income, United would *reduce* its investment in Arjent and recognize a *loss* on investment for its share of the loss. Note that you won't always see these amounts called "investment revenue" or "investment loss." Rather, United might call this line "equity in earnings (losses) of affiliate" or some other title that suggests it is using the equity method.

RECEIVING DIVIDENDS.   Because investment revenue is recognized as it is earned by the investee, it would be inappropriate to recognize revenue again when earnings are distributed as dividends. That would be double counting. Instead, we view the dividend distribution as a reduction of the investee's net assets. The rationale is that the investee is returning assets to its investors in the form of a cash payment, so each investor's equity interest in the remaining net assets declines proportionately.

Cash	75,000	
Investment in Arjent stock (30% × $250,000)		75,000

As the investee distributes net assets as dividends, the investor does not recognize revenue. Rather, the investor's investment in the investee's net assets is reduced.

Further Adjustments

When the investor's expenditure to acquire an investment exceeds the book value of the underlying net assets acquired, additional adjustments to both the investment account and investment revenue might be needed. The purpose is to approximate the effects of consolidation, without actually consolidating financial statements. More specifically, both the investment account and investment revenue are adjusted for differences between net income reported by the investee and what that amount would have been if consolidation procedures had been followed. This process is often referred to as "amortizing the differential," because it mimics the process of expensing some of the difference between the price paid for the investment and the book value of the investment. Let's look closer at what that means.

● LO6

As mentioned earlier, consolidated financial statements report (a) the acquired company's assets at their fair values on the date of acquisition rather than their book values and

(b) goodwill for the excess of the acquisition price over the fair value of the identifiable net assets acquired.

The first of these two consequences of the consolidation process usually has an effect on income, and it's the income effect that we're interested in when applying the equity method. Increasing asset balances to their fair values usually will result in higher expenses. For instance, if buildings, equipment, or other depreciable assets are written up to higher values, depreciation expense will be higher during their remaining useful lives. Likewise, if the recorded amount of inventory is increased, cost of goods sold will be higher when the inventory is sold.

However, if it's land that's increased, there is no income effect because we don't depreciate land. Also, recording goodwill will not result in higher expenses. Goodwill is an intangible asset, but one whose cost usually is not charged to earnings.[32] As a consequence, then, of increasing asset balances to fair value but not of recording goodwill, expenses will rise and income will fall. It is this negative effect on income that the equity method seeks to imitate.

In our example, United needs to make adjustments for the fact that, at the time it purchased its investment in Arjent, the fair values of Arjent's assets and liabilities were higher than the book values of those assets and liabilities in Arjent's balance sheet. Graphic 12–9 highlights the portions of United's investment that may require adjustment:

GRAPHIC 12–9

Source of Differences between the Investment and the Book Value of Net Assets Acquired

	Investee Net Assets	Net Assets Purchased	($ in thousands) Difference Attributed to:
Cost	$5,000 × 30% =	$1,500	Goodwill: $420
Fair value	$3,600 × 30% =	$1,080	
			Undervaluation of:
			Buildings $300
			Land $150
Book value	$2,100 × 30% =	$630	

Notice in Graphic 12–9 that United paid (in thousands) $1,500 for identifiable net assets that, sold separately, would be worth $1,080 and the $420 difference is attributable to goodwill. The identifiable net assets worth $1,080 have a book value of only $630, and we assumed the $450 difference is attributable to undervalued buildings ($300) and land ($150).

ADJUSTMENTS FOR ADDITIONAL DEPRECIATION. When Arjent determines its net income, it bases depreciation expense on the book value of its buildings, but United needs to depreciate its share of the *fair value* of those buildings at the time it made its investment. Therefore, United must adjust its investment revenue for additional depreciation expense. Over the life of the buildings, United will need to recognize its 30% share of a total of $1,000,000 of additional depreciation expense ($2,000,000 fair value less $1,000,000 book value), or $300,000. Assuming a 10-year life of the buildings and straight-line depreciation, United must recognize $30,000 of additional depreciation each year. Had Arjent recorded that additional depreciation, United's portion of Arjent's net income would have been lower by $30,000 (ignoring taxes). To act as if Arjent had recorded the additional depreciation,

The investor adjusts its share of the investee's net income to reflect revenues and expenses associated with differences between the fair value and book value of the investee's assets and liabilities that existed at the time the investment was made.

[32]Goodwill is not amortized periodically to expense. Only if the asset's value is subsequently judged to be impaired is all or a portion of the recorded amount charged against earnings. FASB ASC 350–20–35: Intangibles–Goodwill and Other–Goodwill–Subsequent Measurement (previously "Goodwill and Other Intangible Assets," *Statement of Financial Accounting Standards No. 141* (Norwalk, Conn.: FASB, 2001)). For review, see Chapter 11.

United adjusts the accounts to reduce investment revenue and reduce its investment in Arjent stock by $30,000.

Investment revenue	30,000	
Investment in Arjent stock (30% × [$2,000,000 − 1,000,000] ÷ 10 yrs.)		30,000

NO ADJUSTMENTS FOR LAND OR GOODWILL.   United makes no adjustments for land or goodwill. Land, unlike buildings, is not an asset that we depreciate. As a result, the difference between the fair value and book value of the land would not cause higher expenses, and we have no need to adjust investment revenue or the investment in Arjent stock for the land.

Recall from Chapter 11 that goodwill, unlike most other intangible assets, is not amortized. In that sense, goodwill resembles land. Thus, acquiring goodwill will not cause higher expenses, so we have no need to adjust investment revenue or the investment in Arjent stock for goodwill.

ADJUSTMENTS FOR OTHER ASSETS AND LIABILITIES.   Also, because in our example there was no difference between the book value and fair value of the remaining net assets, we don't need an adjustment for them either. However, that often will not be the case.

For example, Arjent's inventory could have had a fair value that exceeded its book value at the time United purchased its Arjent investment. To recognize expense associated with that higher fair value, United would need to identify the period in which that inventory is sold (usually the next year) and, in that period, reduce its investment revenue and its investment in Arjent stock by its 30% share of the difference between the fair value and book value of the inventory. If, for instance, the $300,000 difference between fair value and book value had been attributable to inventory rather than buildings, and that inventory was sold by Arjent in the year following United's investment, United would reduce investment revenue by the entire $300,000 in the year following the investment. By so doing, United would be making an adjustment that yielded the same net investment revenue as if Arjent had carried the inventory on its books at fair value at the time the Arjent investment was made and therefore recorded higher cost of goods sold ($300,000) when it was sold in the next year. More generally, an equity method investor needs to make these sorts of adjustments whenever there are revenues or expenses associated with an asset or liability that had a difference between book value and fair value at the time the investment was made.

> If the fair value of purchased inventory exceeds its book value, we usually assume the inventory is sold in the next year and reduce investment revenue in the next year by the entire difference.

> **ADDITIONAL CONSIDERATION**
>
> **Effect on Deferred Income Taxes**
>
> Investment revenue is recorded by the equity method when income is earned by the investee, but that revenue is not taxed until it's actually received as cash dividends. This creates a temporary difference between book income and taxable income. You will learn in Chapter 16 that the investor must report a deferred tax liability for the income tax that ultimately will be paid when the income eventually is received as dividends.

Reporting the Investment

The fair value of the investment shares at the end of the reporting period is not reported when using the equity method. The investment account is reported at its original cost, increased by the investor's share of the investee's net income (adjusted for additional expenses like depreciation), and decreased by the portion of those earnings actually received as dividends. In other words, the investment account represents the investor's share of the investee's net assets initially acquired, adjusted for the investor's share of the subsequent increase in the investee's net assets (net assets earned and not yet distributed as dividends).

> The carrying amount of the investment is its initial cost plus the investor's equity in the undistributed earnings of the investee.

The balance of United's 30% investment in Arjent at December 31, 2011, would be calculated as follows:

Investment in Arjent Stock

Cost	1,500,000		
Share of income	150,000		
		30,000	Depreciation adjustment
		75,000	Dividends
	1,545,000		

In the statement of cash flows, the purchase and sale of the investment are reported as outflows and inflows of cash in the investing section, and the receipt of dividends is reported as an inflow of cash in the operating section.[33]

WHEN THE INVESTEE REPORTS A NET LOSS. Our illustration assumed the investee earned net income. If the investee reports a *net loss* instead, the investment account would be *decreased* by the investor's share of the investee's net loss (adjusted for additional expenses).

ADDITIONAL CONSIDERATION

It's possible that the investor's proportionate share of investee losses could exceed the carrying amount of the investment. If this happens, the investor should discontinue applying the equity method until the investor's share of subsequent investee earnings has equaled losses not recognized during the time the equity method was discontinued. This avoids reducing the investment account below zero.

WHEN THE INVESTMENT IS ACQUIRED IN MID-YEAR. Obviously, we've simplified the illustration by assuming the investment was acquired at the beginning of 2011, entailing a full year's income, dividends, and adjustments to account for the income effects of any differences between book value and fair value on the date the investment was acquired. In the more likely event that an investment is acquired sometime after the beginning of the year, the application of the equity method is easily modified to include the appropriate fraction of each of those amounts. For example, if United's purchase of 30% of Arjent had occurred on October 1 rather than January 2, we would simply record income, dividends, and adjustments for three months ($3/12$) of the year. This would result in the following entries to the investment account:

Changes in the investment account the first year are adjusted for the fraction of the year the investor has owned the investment.

Investment in Arjent Stock

Cost	1,500,000		
Share of income ($3/12 \times \$150,000$)	37,500		
		7,500	Depreciation adjustment ($3/12 \times \$30,000$)
		18,750	Dividends ($3/12 \times \$75,000$)
	1,511,250		

---

[33]Some companies prepare a statement of cash flows using the indirect method of reporting operating activities. In that case, the operating section begins with net income and adjustments are made to back out the effects of accrual accounting and calculate cash from operations. For companies with equity method investments, net income will include investment revenue and gains or losses associated with sold investments, but cash from operations should include only cash dividends. As an example, because United's 2011 net income includes $120,000 of investment revenue from Arjent ($150,000 portion of income − $30,000 depreciation adjustment), but United received only $75,000 of dividends from Arjent, an indirect method statement of cash flows would include an adjustment, often titled "undistributed earnings of investee," that reduces net income by $45,000 ($75,000 − $120,000) when determining cash from operations.

AT&T reported its June 30, 2009, investments in affiliated companies for which it exercised significant influence using the equity method as shown in Graphic 12–10.

GRAPHIC 12–10

Equity Method
Investments on the
Balance Sheet—AT&T

Real World Financials

	June 30, 2009	Dec 31, 2008
Total current assets	26,940	22,556
Property, plant, and equipment—Net	98,229	99,088
Goodwill	71,691	71,829
Licenses	47,674	47,306
Customer lists and relationships—Net	8,682	10,582
Other intangible assets—net	5,773	5,824
Investments in equity affiliates	2,749	2,332
Other assets	6,180	5,728
Total assets	$267,918	$265,245

What If Conditions Change?

A CHANGE FROM THE EQUITY METHOD TO ANOTHER METHOD.   When the investor's level of influence changes, it may be necessary to change from the equity method to another method. This could happen, for instance, if a sale of shares causes the investor's ownership interest to fall from, say, 25% to 15%, resulting in the equity method no longer being appropriate.[34] Another example is provided by **Sprint**, which in February 2001 agreed to end its exclusive alliance with **EarthLink** and relinquished its seats on EarthLink's board of directors. As a result, Sprint discontinued using the equity method for its investment in EarthLink.

When this situation happens, *no adjustment* is made to the remaining carrying amount of the investment. Instead, the equity method is simply discontinued and the new method applied from then on. The balance in the investment account when the equity method is discontinued would serve as the new cost basis for writing the investment up or down to fair value on the next set of financial statements.

A CHANGE FROM ANOTHER METHOD TO THE EQUITY METHOD.   Sometimes companies change from another method to the equity method. For example, in 2007 the **Bank of Tokyo-Mitsubishi UFJ** converted its investment in the consumer credit company **Jaccs Co.** into an equity method affiliate by raising its ownership in that company from 4.7% to around 20%. When a change *to* the equity method is appropriate, the investment account should be retroactively adjusted to the balance that would have existed if the equity method always had been used. As income also would have been different, retained earnings would be adjusted as well. For example, assume it's determined that an investor's share of investee net income, reduced by dividends, was $4 million during a period when the equity method was not used, but additional purchases of shares cause the equity method to be appropriate now. The following journal entry would record the change (ignoring taxes):

> Both the investment
> and retained earnings
> would be increased by
> the investor's share
> of the undistributed
> earnings in years prior
> to a change to the
> equity method.

	($ in millions)	
Investment in equity securities	4	
Retained earnings (investment revenue from the equity method)		4

In addition to the adjustment of account balances, financial statements would be restated to the equity method for each year reported in the annual report for comparative purposes. Also, the income effect for years prior to those shown in the comparative statements is reported on the statement of retained earnings as an adjustment to beginning retained

---

[34]When a portion of an equity method investment is sold, the investor removes from the investment account the appropriate proportion of the carrying value and records a gain or loss for the difference between that amount and the selling price.

earnings of the earliest year reported. A disclosure note also should describe the change. Reporting accounting changes is described in more detail in Chapter 20.

If an Equity Method Investment Is Sold

When an investment reported by the equity method is sold, a gain or loss is recognized if the selling price is more or less than the carrying amount (book value) of the investment. For example, let's continue our illustration and assume United sells its investment in Arjent on January 1, 2012, for $1,446,000. A journal entry would record a loss as follows:

Cash	1,446,000	
Loss on sale of investments (to balance)	99,000	
Investment in Arjent stock (account balance)		1,545,000

Comparison of Fair Value and Equity Methods

Illustration 12–7 compares accounting for the Arjent investment at fair value (as trading securities or securities available for sale, discussed in Part A of this chapter) and under the equity method (covered in Part B of this chapter):

ILLUSTRATION 12–7 Comparison of Fair Value and Equity Methods

	Fair Value Method		Equity Method	
Purchase equity investment	Investment in Arjent	1,500,000	Same as Fair Value Method	
	Cash	1,500,000		
Recognize proportionate share of investee's net income and any related adjustments	No entry		Investment in Arjent 150,000	
			Investment revenue	150,000
			Investment revenue 30,000	
			Investment in Arjent	30,000
Adjust investment to reflect changes in fair value from $1,500,000 to $1,450,000	Net unrealized gain/loss*	50,000	No entry	
	FV adjustment	50,000		
Receive dividend	Cash	75,000	Cash	75,000
	Investment revenue	75,000	Investment in Arjent	75,000
Sell equity investment	Recognize gain or loss:		Cash	1,446,000
	Cash	1,446,000	Loss (to balance) 99,000	
	Loss (to balance)	54,000	Investment in Arjent	1,545,000
	Investment in Arjent	1,500,000		
	Reverse out previously recorded unrealized gain or loss that's no longer unrealized (automatically part of next adjustment to fair value):			
	FV adjustment	50,000		
	Net unrealized gain/loss*	50,000		

*Net unrealized holding gains and losses are reported in net income for trading securities and in other comprehensive income for available-for-sale securities.

This side-by-side comparison highlights several aspects of these accounting approaches:

- To record the purchase of an investment, we use identical entries for both approaches.
- The two approaches differ in whether we record investment revenue when dividends are received and whether we recognize unrealized holding gains and losses associated with changes in the fair value of the investment.
- The differences in how the two approaches account for unrealized holding gains and losses result in different book values for the investment at the time the investment is

sold, and therefore result in different realized gains or losses when the investment is sold.

- Regardless of approach, the same cash flows occur, and the same total amount of net income is recognized over the life of the investment. In the case of Arjent:

  - **Fair value method:** A total of $21,000 of net income is recognized over the life of the investment, equal to $75,000 of dividend revenue minus $54,000 realized loss on sale of investment.

  - **Equity method:** A total of $21,000 of net income is recognized over the life of the investment, equal to $150,000 of United's portion of Arjent's income minus $30,000 depreciation adjustment and minus $99,000 realized loss on sale of investment.

  - Thus, the question is not how much total net income is recognized, but *when* that net income is recognized.

Fair Value Option

We learned in Part A of this chapter that GAAP allows a fair value option with respect to investments that otherwise would be accounted for using the held-to-maturity or available-for-sale approaches. Electing the fair value option for those investments is simple—the investments are reclassified as trading securities and accounted for in that manner.

● LO7

If the fair value option is chosen for investments otherwise accounted for by the equity method, the amount that is reported at fair value is clearly indicated.

Companies also can choose the fair value option for "significant influence" investments that otherwise would be accounted for under the equity method. The company makes an irrevocable decision about whether to elect the fair value option, and can make that election for some investments and not for others. As shown for the fair value method in Illustration 12–7, the company carries the investment at fair value in the balance sheet and includes unrealized gains and losses in earnings.

However, investments that otherwise would be accounted for under the equity method but for which the fair value option has been elected are not reclassified as trading securities. Instead, these investments are shown on their own line in the balance sheet or are combined with equity method investments with the amount at fair value shown parenthetically. Still, they are reported at fair value with changes in fair value reported in earnings as if they were trading securities. Also, all of the disclosures that are required when reporting fair values as well as some of those that would be required under the equity method still must be provided.[35]

Exactly how a company does the bookkeeping necessary to comply with these broad requirements is up to the company. One alternative is to account for the investment using entries similar to those that would be used to account for trading securities. A second alternative is to record all of the accounting entries during the period under the equity method, and then record a fair value adjustment at the end of the period. Regardless of which alternative the company uses to account for the investment during the period, though, the same fair value is reported in the balance sheet at the end of the period, and the same total amount is shown on the income statement (the fair value adjustment amount plus the investment revenue recorded).

INTERNATIONAL FINANCIAL REPORTING STANDARDS

Equity Method. Like U.S. GAAP, international accounting standards require the equity method for use with significant influence investees (which they call "associates"), but there are a few important differences. *IAS No. 28* governs application of the equity method and requires that the accounting policies of investees be adjusted to correspond to those of the investor when applying the equity method.[36] U.S. GAAP has no such requirement.

● LO8

(continued)

[35]FASB ASC 825–10–50–28: Financial Instruments–Overall–Disclosure–Fair Value Option (previously "The Fair Value Option for Financial Assets and Financial Liabilities," *Statement of Financial Accounting Standards No. 159* (Norwalk, Conn.: FASB, 2007), paragraph 18.f).
[36]"Investments in Associates," *International Accounting Standard 28* (London, UK: IASCF, 2003).

IFRS ILLUSTRATION

(concluded)

IAS No. 31 governs accounting for joint ventures, in which two or more investors have joint control. That standard allows investors to account for a joint venture using either the equity method or a method called "proportionate consolidation," whereby the investor combines its proportionate share of the investee's accounts with its own accounts on an item-by-item basis.[37] U.S. GAAP generally requires that the equity method be used to account for joint ventures.

For a quick example, return to Illustration 12–6 but assume that United spends $2,500,000 to invest in a joint venture called Arjent. With its investment, United owns 50% of Argent. Recall that the journal entry to record the investment under the equity method was:

Investment in Arjent stock	2,500,000	
Cash...		2,500,000

If United instead accounted for its investment under proportionate consolidation, the effect of the purchase would be disaggregated and assigned to the appropriate accounts in United's balance sheet:

Buildings (50% × $2,000,000 fair value	1,000,000	
Land (50% × $1,000,000 fair value)	500,000	
Other net assets (50% × $600,000)	300,000	
Goodwill (50% × $1,400,000)	700,000	
Cash...		2,500,000

Note that the net effect under proportionate consolidation is the same as under the equity method, with United adding net assets of $2,500,000 in exchange for $2,500,000 of cash. However, under proportionate consolidation the effects are distributed across the balance sheet in the various asset and liability accounts, and in subsequent periods any income effects will appear on various lines in the income statement ("depreciation expense," for instance) rather than being aggregated and shown as part of investment revenue.

WHERE WE'RE HEADED

The IASB has issued an exposure draft that requires the use of the equity method for joint ventures and, therefore, would eliminate the option of using proportionate consolidation for those investments.[38]

CONCEPT REVIEW EXERCISE

THE EQUITY METHOD

Delta Apparatus bought 40% of Clay Crating Corp.'s outstanding common shares on January 2, 2011, for $540 million. The carrying amount of Clay Crating's net assets (shareholders' equity) at the purchase date totaled $900 million. Book values and fair values were the same for all financial statement items except for inventory and buildings, for which fair values exceeded book values by $25 million and $225 million, respectively. All inventory on hand at the acquisition date was sold during 2011. The buildings have average remaining useful lives of 18 years. During 2011, Clay Crating reported net income of $220 million and paid an $80 million cash dividend.

Required:
1. Prepare the appropriate journal entries during 2011 for the investment.

[37]"Interests in Joint Ventures," *International Accounting Standard 31* (London, UK: IASCF, 2003).
[38]"ED 9: Joint Arrangements" (London, UK: IASCF, 2007).

2. Determine the amounts relating to the investment that Delta Apparatus should report in the 2011 financial statements:

   a. As an investment in the balance sheet.

   b. As investment revenue in the income statement.

   c. As investing and/or operating activities in the statement of cash flows (direct method).

1. Prepare the appropriate journal entries during 2011 for the investment.   **SOLUTION**

	($ in millions)	
Purchase		
Investment in Clay Crating shares	540	
Cash		540
Net income		
Investment in Clay Crating shares (40% × $220 million)	88	
Investment revenue		88
Dividends		
Cash (40% × $80 million)	32	
Investment in Clay Crating shares		32
Inventory		
Investment revenue (higher cost of goods sold during 2011		
if beginning inventory had been adjusted to fair value)	10	
Investment in Clay Crating shares (40% × $25 million)		10
Buildings		
Investment revenue ([$225 million × 40%] ÷ 18 years)	5	
Investment in Clay Crating shares		5

	Investee Net Assets ↓	Net Assets Purchased ↓	Difference Attributed to ↓	
Cost		$540 ⎤		
		⎰	Goodwill:	$80 [difference]
Fair value	$1,150† × 40% =	$460 ⎱	Undervaluation of inventory	$10 [$25 × 40%]
Book value	$ 900 × 40% =	$360 ⎦	Undervaluation of buildings	$90 [$225 × 40%]

†($900 + 25 + 225)

2. Determine the amounts that Delta Apparatus should report in the 2011 financial statements:

   a. As an investment in the balance sheet:

Investment in Clay Crating Shares

($ in millions)

Cost	540		
Share of income	88		
		32	Dividends
		10	Cost of goods sold adjustment for inventory
		5	Depreciation adjustment for buildings
Balance	581		

b. As investment revenue in the income statement:

$$\underset{\text{(share of income)}}{\$88 \text{ million}} - \underset{\text{(adjustments)}}{[\$10 + 5] \text{ million}} = \underline{\underline{\$73 \text{ million}}}$$

c. In the statement of cash flows (direct method):
- Investing activities: $\underline{\$540 \text{ million cash outflow}}$
- Operating activities: $\underline{\$32 \text{ million cash inflow}}$

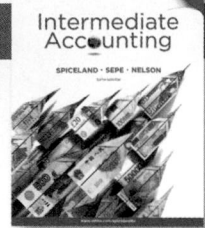

DECISION MAKERS' PERSPECTIVE

The various approaches used to account for investments can have very different effects on an investor's income statement and balance sheet. Consequently, it's critical that both managers and external decision makers clearly understand those effects and make decisions accordingly.

To highlight key considerations, suppose that, on January 1, 2011, BigCo spent $5,000,000 to purchase 20% of TechStart, a small start-up company that is developing products that apply an exciting new technology. The purchase price included $500,000 for BigCo's share of the difference between the fair value and book value of TechStart's inventory, all of which was then sold in 2011. TechStart paid a small dividend of $100,000 in 2011, so BigCo received 20% of it, or $20,000. TechStart incurs and expenses large amounts of research and development costs as it develops new technology, so it had a net loss in 2011 of $1,000,000. Yet, the future income-generating potential of the products that TechStart is developing has made TechStart a hot stock, and the fair value of BigCo's 20% investment increased to $5,500,000 by the end of 2011. Illustration 12–8 shows how BigCo's investment would be accounted for under three alternative approaches.

ILLUSTRATION 12–8	**Trading Security**	**Available-for-Sale**	**Equity Method**
Comparison of Methods Used to Account for Investments			
Share of investee net income[a]	–0–	–0–	($ 700,000)
Dividend income[b]	$ 20,000	$ 20,000	–0–
Increase in investee's fair value[c]	$ 500,000	–0–	–0–
Total 2011 effect on net income	$ 520,000	$ 20,000	($ 700,000)
12/31/11 investment book value[d]	$5,500,000	$5,500,000	$4,280,000

[a]Not recognized for trading securities or available-for-sale securities. Under the equity method, investment revenue (loss) is 20% × ($1,000,000 loss) + ($500,000) additional expense for fair value inventory adjustment = ($700,000).
[b]Not recognized for equity method investments. Instead, dividends reduce book value of the investment.
[c]Recognized in net income for trading securities, in other comprehensive income for available-for-sale securities, and not recognized for equity method investments.
[d]Equals fair value for trading securities and available-for-sale securities. Equals initial cost plus income (or minus loss) and minus dividends for equity method.

The way an investment is accounted for affects net income, investment book value, and the amount of gain or loss recognized in the future when the investment is sold.

The accounting method does not affect cash flows, but it has a big effect on net income in current and future periods. Also, because the accounting method affects the book value of the investment, it affects gain or loss on sale of that investment. In our example, if BigCo sold its TechStart investment at the beginning of 2012 for $5,000,000, it would recognize a $720,000 gain on sale if the investment was accounted for under the equity method, but a $500,000 loss if it was accounted for as a trading security or available-for-sale security. All of these income effects are predictable, but only if a user understands the relevant accounting methods and the fact that those methods all end up recognizing the same amount of total gain or loss over the life of an investment. Nevertheless, sometimes even experienced analysts get confused.[39]

---

[39]For example, in 2000, analysts were accustomed to including **Intel**'s investment gains as ordinary income, because those amounts were not particularly large and could be viewed as part of Intel's business. However, in the 2nd quarter of 2000, Intel recorded a net $2.1 billion gain from selling securities in its available-for-sale portfolio. Analysts were surprised and confused, with some eliminating the gain from their earnings estimates but others including them ("Intel Says Net Jumped 79%; Analysts Upset," *The Wall Street Journal,* July 19, 2000, p. A3).

One strength of the equity method is that it prevents the income manipulation that would be possible if a company recognized income when it received dividends and could significantly influence an investee to pay dividends whenever the company needed an income boost. Remember, under the equity method dividends aren't income, but rather reduce the book value of the investment. Nevertheless, users still need to realize that managers may choose and apply methods in ways that make their company appear most attractive. For example, research suggests that investments sometimes are structured to avoid crossing the 20 to 25 percent threshold that typically requires using the equity method,[40] presumably to avoid the negative effect on earnings that comes from having to recognize the investor's share of investee losses and other income adjustments. Also, a company might smooth income by timing the sale of available-for-sale or equity method investments to realize gains in otherwise poor periods and realize losses in otherwise good periods. While consistent with GAAP, mixing these sorts of one-time gains and losses with operating income could encourage users to think that operating income is less volatile than it really is.

> **Managers may structure investments to include only the amount of equity that qualifies for their preferred accounting approach.**

> **If investments are not accounted for at fair value, their sale can be timed to recognize gains or losses in particular accounting periods.**

Of particular concern is the potential for inaccurate fair value estimates. Even if management is trying to provide the most accurate fair value estimate possible, there is much potential for error, particularly when making estimates at level 3 of the fair value hierarchy. Also, a company conceivably could use the discretion inherent in fair value estimation to manage earnings with respect to trading securities or other investments for which they have elected the fair value option. Given this potential for error and bias, it's not surprising that investors are nervous about the accuracy of fair value estimates. To address these sorts of concerns, the FASB has required extensive footnote disclosure about the quality of inputs associated with estimates of fair value, but financial statement users need to know to look for those disclosures and still must understand that they cannot assess fully the accuracy of fair value estimates. ●

> **A concern with fair value accounting is that management has much discretion over fair values, and may not be able to estimate fair values accurately.**

Financial Instruments and Investment Derivatives

A **financial instrument** is defined as:

- Cash,
- Evidence of an *ownership interest* in an entity,[41]
- A contract that (a) imposes on one entity an obligation to *deliver* cash (say accounts payable) or another financial instrument and (b) conveys to the second entity a right to *receive* cash (say accounts receivable) or another financial instrument, or
- A contract that (a) imposes on one entity an obligation to *exchange* financial instruments on potentially unfavorable terms (say the issuer of a stock option) and (b) conveys to a second entity a right to *exchange* other financial instruments on potentially favorable terms (say the holder of a stock option).[42]

A complex class of financial instruments exists in financial markets in response to the desire of firms to manage risks. In fact, these financial instruments would not exist in their own right, but have been created solely to hedge against risks created by other financial instruments or by transactions that have yet to occur but are anticipated. Financial futures, interest rate swaps, forward contracts, and options have become commonplace. These financial instruments often are called derivatives because they "derive" their values or contractually required cash flows from some other security or index. For instance, an option to buy an asset in the future at a preset price has a value that is dependent on, or derived from, the value of the underlying asset. Their rapid acceptance as indispensable components of the corporate capital structure has left the accounting profession scrambling to keep pace.

> ***Derivatives* are financial instruments that "derive" their values from some other security or index.**

---

[40]E. E. Comiskey and C. W. Mulford, "Investment Decisions and the Equity Accounting Standard," *The Accounting Review* 61, no. 3 (July 1986), pp. 519–525.

[41]This category includes not just shares of stock, but also partnership agreements and stock options.

[42]FASB ASC Master Glossary. Financial Instrument (previously "Disclosure of Information about Financial Instruments with Off-Balance-Sheet Risk and Financial Instruments with Concentrations of Credit Risk," *Statement of Financial Accounting Standards No. 105* (Stamford, Conn.: FASB, 1990), par. 6).

The urgency to establish accounting standards for financial instruments has been accelerated by headline stories in the financial press reporting multimillion-dollar losses on exotic derivatives by **Enron Corporation**, **Procter & Gamble**, **Orange County** (California), **Piper Jaffrey**, and **Gibson Greetings**, to mention a few. The headlines have tended to focus attention on the misuse of these financial instruments rather than their legitimate use in managing risk.

> The FASB's ongoing financial instruments project is expected to lead to a consistent framework for accounting for all financial instruments.

The FASB has been involved since 1986 in a project to provide a consistent framework for resolving financial instrument accounting issues, including those related to derivatives and other "off-balance-sheet" instruments. The financial instruments project has three separate but related parts: disclosure, recognition and measurement, and distinguishing between liabilities and equities. Unfortunately, issues to be resolved are extremely complex and will likely require several more years to resolve. To help fill the disclosure gap in the meantime, the FASB has offered a series of temporary, "patchwork" solutions. These are primarily in the form of additional disclosures for financial instruments. More recently, the FASB has tackled the issues of recognition and measurement. We discuss these requirements in Appendix A after we've spent some time with the measurement issues necessary to understand accounting for derivatives.

FINANCIAL REPORTING CASE SOLUTION

1. **How should you respond? Why are held-to-maturity securities treated differently from other investment securities?** *(p. 622)*   You should explain that if an investor has the positive intent and ability to hold the securities to maturity, investments in debt securities are classified as held-to-maturity and reported at amortized cost in the balance sheet. Increases and decreases in fair value are not reported in the financial statements. The reasoning is that the changes are not as relevant to an investor who will hold a security to its maturity regardless of those changes. Changes in the fair value between the time a debt security is acquired and the day it matures to a prearranged maturity value aren't as important if sale before maturity isn't an alternative.[43]

2. **Why are unrealized gains and losses on trading securities reported in the income statement?** *(p. 626)*   Trading securities are acquired for the purpose of profiting from short-term market price changes, so gains and losses from holding these securities while prices change are often viewed as relevant performance measures that should be included in net income.

3. **Why are unrealized gains and losses on available-for-sale securities not reported in the income statement, but instead are in other comprehensive income, and then shown in accumulated other comprehensive income (AOCI) on the balance sheet?** *(p. 630)*   Available-for-sale securities are not acquired for the purpose of profiting from short-term market price changes, so gains and losses from holding these securities while prices change are viewed as insufficiently relevant performance measures to be included in net income. Instead, those amounts are shown in other comprehensive income (OCI) and accumulated in an owners' equity account (AOCI). It's likely that holding gains in some periods will be offset by holding losses in other periods. When the investment is sold, the net amount of gain or loss is removed from AOCI and recognized in net income.

4. **Explain why Coke accounts for some of its investments by the equity method and what that means.** *(p. 646)*   When an investor does not have "control," but still is able to exercise *significant influence* over the operating and financial policies of the investee, the investment should be accounted for by the equity method. Apparently Coke owns between 20% and 50% of the voting shares of some of the companies it invests in. By the equity method, Coke recognizes investment income in an amount equal to its percentage share of the net income earned by those companies, instead of the amount of that net income it receives as cash dividends. The rationale is that as the investee earns additional net assets, Coke's share of those net assets increases. ●

---

[43]Interest rate futures were traded for the first time in 1975 on the Chicago Board of Trade. Interest rate swaps were invented in the early 1980s. They now comprise over 70% of derivatives in use.

● **LO1** When an investor lacks significant influence over the operating and financial policies of the investee, its investment is classified for reporting purposes as held-to-maturity (HTM), available-for-sale (AFS), or trading securities (TS). If an investor has the positive intent and ability to hold the securities to maturity, investments in debt securities are classified as HTM and reported at amortized cost in the balance sheet. These investments are recorded at cost, and holding gains or losses from fair value changes are ignored. (p. 622)

● **LO2** Investments in debt or equity securities acquired principally for the purpose of selling them in the near term are classified as trading securities. They are reported at their fair values. Holding gains and losses for trading securities are included in earnings. (p. 625)

● **LO3** Investments in debt and equity securities that don't fit the definitions of the other reporting categories are classified as available-for-sale. They are reported at their fair values. Holding gains and losses from retaining securities during periods of price change are not included in the determination of income for the period; they are reported as a separate component of shareholders' equity. (p. 629)

● **LO4** When an investor is able to exercise significant influence over the operating and financial policies of the investee, the investment should be accounted for by the equity method. Usually an investor can exercise significant influence when it owns between 20% and 50% of the investee's voting shares. (p. 645)

● **LO5** By the equity method, the investor recognizes investment income equal to its percentage share (based on share ownership) of the net income earned by the investee, rather than the portion of that net income received as cash dividends. The investment account is adjusted for the investor's percentage share of net income or loss reported by the investee. When the investor actually receives dividends, the investment account is reduced accordingly. (p. 645)

● **LO6** When the cost of an investment exceeds the book value of the underlying net assets acquired, both the investment account and investment revenue are adjusted for differences between net income reported by the investee and what that amount would have been if consolidation procedures had been followed. (p. 647)

● **LO7** The fair value option allows companies to account for most financial assets and liabilities in the same way they account for trading securities, with unrealized holding gains and losses included in net income and the investment carried at fair value in the balance sheet. For HTM and AFS investments, this simply requires reclassifying those investments as trading securities. For equity method investments, this requires clearly identifying the portion of those investments classified in the significant-influence category that is being accounted for at fair value. In all cases, additional disclosures are required that indicate the quality of inputs used to calculate fair values. (pp. 637 and 653)

● **LO8** U.S. GAAP and IFRS are similar in most respects concerning how they account for investments, but accounting in this area is being overhauled by both the IASB and the FASB, and IFRS companies may report under two different standards (either *IAS No. 39* or *IFRS No. 9*) for 2009–2012 time period. IFRS allows proportionate consolidation as well as the equity method to account for joint ventures, although the option to use proportionate consolidation may be eliminated soon. IFRS is more restrictive in terms of the circumstances in which the fair-value option can be used. Finally, as discussed in Appendix 12B, IFRS recognizes different amounts of OTT impairment for HTM and AFS debt investments, and allows recovery of OTT impairments for debt investments (but not equity investments). (pp. 638, 639, 640, 644, 653, and 665) ●

OTHER INVESTMENTS (SPECIAL PURPOSE FUNDS, INVESTMENTS IN LIFE INSURANCE POLICIES)

APPENDIX 12A

Special Purpose Funds

It's often convenient for companies to set aside money to be used for specific purposes. You learned about one such special purpose fund in Chapter 7 when we discussed petty cash funds. Recall that a petty cash fund is money set aside to conveniently make small expenditures using currency rather than having to follow the time-consuming, formal procedures normally used to process checks. Similar funds sometimes are used to pay interest, payroll, or other short-term needs. Like petty cash, these short-term special purpose funds are reported as current assets.

Special purpose funds also are sometimes established to serve longer-term needs. It's common, for instance, to periodically set aside cash into a fund designated to repay bonds

Some special purpose funds—like petty cash—are current assets.

A special purpose fund can be established for virtually any purpose.

and other long-term debt. Such funds usually accumulate cash over the debt's term to maturity and are composed of the company's periodic contributions plus interest or dividends from investing the money in various return-generating investments. In fact, some debt contracts require the borrower to establish such a fund to repay the debt. In similar fashion, management might voluntarily choose to establish a fund to accumulate money to expand facilities, provide for unexpected losses, buy back shares of stock, or any other special purpose that might benefit from an accumulation of funds. Of course, funds that won't be used within the upcoming operating cycle are noncurrent assets. They typically are reported as part of investments. The same criteria for classifying securities into reporting categories that we discussed previously should be used to classify securities in which funds are invested. Any investment revenue from these funds is reported as such on the income statement.

Noncurrent special purpose funds are reported within the category investments and funds.

Investments in Life Insurance Policies

Certain life insurance policies can be surrendered while the insured is still alive in *exchange for its* cash surrender value.

Companies frequently buy life insurance policies on the lives of their key officers. Under normal circumstances, the company pays the premium for the policy and, as beneficiary, receives the proceeds when the officer dies. Of course, the objective is to compensate the company for the untimely loss of a valuable resource in the event the officer dies. However, some types of life insurance policies can be surrendered while the insured is still alive in exchange for a determinable amount of money, called the **cash surrender value.** In effect, a portion of each premium payment is not used by the insurance company to pay for life insurance coverage, but instead is invested on behalf of the insured company in a fixed-income investment. Accordingly, the cash surrender value increases each year by the portion of premiums invested plus interest on the previous amount invested. This is simply a characteristic of whole life insurance, unlike term insurance that has lower premiums and that provides death benefits only.

Part of each insurance premium represents an increase in the cash surrender value.

From an accounting standpoint, the periodic insurance premium should not be expensed in its entirety. Rather, part of each premium payment, the investment portion, is recorded as an asset. Illustration 12A–1 provides an example. ●

ILLUSTRATION 12A–1 Cash Surrender Value	Several years ago, American Capital acquired a $1 million insurance policy on the life of its chief executive officer, naming American Capital as beneficiary. Annual premiums are $18,000, payable at the beginning of each year. In 2011, the cash surrender value of the policy increased according to the contract from $5,000 to $7,000. The CEO died at the end of 2011.

Part of the annual premium represents a build-up in the cash surrender value.

Insurance expense (difference)	16,000	
Cash surrender value of life insurance ($7,000 – 5,000)	2,000	
Cash (2011 premium)		18,000

To record insurance expense and the increase in the investment.

The cash surrender value is considered to be a noncurrent investment and would be reported in the investments and funds section of the balance sheet. Of course when the insured officer dies, the corporation receives the death benefit of the insurance policy, and the cash surrender value ceases to exist because canceling the policy no longer is an option. The corporation recognizes a gain for the amount of the death benefit less the cash surrender value:

When the death benefit is paid, the cash surrender value becomes null and void.

Cash (death benefit)	1,000,000	
Cash surrender value of life insurance (balance)		7,000
Gain on life insurance settlement (difference)		993,000

To record the proceeds at death.

APPENDIX **12B** IMPAIRMENT OF INVESTMENTS

We saw in Chapter 11 that property, plant, and equipment, and intangible assets are subject to impairment losses if a decline in fair value indicates that the assets' value has been impaired. The same is true for investments. As indicated in Chapter 12, if the fair value of an investment declines to a level below cost, and that decline is not viewed as temporary, companies typically have to recognize an other-than-temporary (OTT) impairment loss in earnings. We don't need to worry about OTT impairments for trading securities or other investments for which a company has chosen the fair value option, because all changes in the fair values of those investments (whether temporary or OTT) always are recognized in earnings. However, that is not the case for HTM and AFS investments. Declines in fair value typically are ignored for HTM investments and recorded in OCI for AFS investments. Therefore, companies need to evaluate HTM and AFS investments to determine whether an OTT impairment loss has occurred.

We use a three-step process to determine whether an OTT impairment loss must be recognized and how that loss is to be measured and recorded: (1) determine if the investment is impaired, (2) determine whether any impairment is OTT, and (3) determine how to account for any OTT impairment.[44] Graphic 12B–1 summarizes those steps. As you can see, the specifics of accounting for OTT impairments depend on whether the investment is in equity or debt, so we'll discuss each in turn.

An "other-than-temporary" impairment loss is recognized in net income even though the security hasn't been sold.

	Investment in Equity Security	Investment in Debt Security
Is the investment impaired?	Yes, if the fair value is less than the investment's cost	**Same** (yes, if the fair value is less than the investment's amortized cost)
Is the impairment other-than-temporary?	Yes, if the investor cannot assert that it has the intent and ability to hold the investment until fair value recovers	Yes, if the investor (a) intends to sell the investment, (b) believes it is "more likely than not" that the investor will be required to sell the investment prior to recovering the amortized cost of the investment, less any current-period credit loss, or (c) has incurred credit losses
What is the amount of the other-than-temporary impairment loss?	Difference between the investment's amortized cost and its *fair value*	**Same,** but may need to be split into two components: **Credit loss** portion: Difference between the investment's amortized cost and the *PV of expected cash flows* **Noncredit loss** portion: The remainder of the impairment
Where is the other-than-temporary impairment loss reported?	In net income	In net income, if the investor intends to sell the security or "more likely than not" will be required to sell it before recovery of its amortized cost Otherwise: Credit-loss portion in net income; Noncredit portion in OCI

GRAPHIC 12B–1
Other-Than-Temporary Impairment of Equity Investments and Debt Investments Compared

[44]FASB ASC 320-10-35: Investments–Overall–Subsequent Measurement (originally "The Meaning of Other-Than-Temporary Impairment and Its Application to Certain Investments," *FASB Staff Position No. 115-1 and 124-1* (Norwalk, Conn.: FASB), November 3, 2005).

IMPAIRMENTS OF EQUITY INVESTMENTS

Recall that OTT impairments don't apply to trading securities and that equity investments cannot be classified as held-to-maturity. Therefore, when we consider OTT impairments of equity investments, we are looking at available-for-sale investments. Here are the three steps:

Equity impairments are OTT if the investor cannot assert it has the intent and ability to hold the investment until fair value recovers.

If an equity impairment is OTT:

- **Investment is written down to fair value**
- **All of the OTT impairment loss is included in net income**

1. *Is the investment impaired?* Impairment occurs when fair value has declined to a level below the investment's cost (which equals the investment's purchase price less previously recognized impairments and other adjustments).

2. *Is any impairment other-than-temporary (OTT)?* The impairment is temporary if the investing company can assert that it has the intent and ability to hold the investment until fair value recovers to a level that once again exceeds cost. That assertion is more difficult to defend if the expected recovery period is relatively long, the amount of impairment is large, or the financial condition of the investor or the issuer of the equity is weak.[45]

3. *How should the company account for the OTT impairment?* A *temporary* impairment of an equity investment is simply accounted for as an unrealized loss in OCI, as demonstrated previously for fair value declines in AFS securities in Illustration 12–2. However, if the impairment is viewed as OTT, the investor recognizes a loss in the income statement, just as if the loss had been realized by selling the investment. Also, because the equity investment is classified as AFS, recognizing an OTT impairment likely will involve reclassifying amounts out of OCI that were recorded previously as unrealized gains or losses.

For an example of an OTT impairment of an equity investment, we recall a portion of Illustration 12–2, and modify it as described in Illustration 12B–1:

ILLUSTRATION 12B–1 Other-Than-Temporary (OTT) Impairment of an Equity Investment	United Intergroup, Inc., buys and sells both debt and equity securities of other companies as investments. United's fiscal year-end is December 31. The following events during 2011 and 2012 pertain to the investment portfolio.

Purchase Investment

July 1, 2011	Purchased $1,000,000 of Bendac common stock.

Adjust Investment to Fair Value

December 31, 2011	Valued the Bendac stock at $990,000 and determined that the decline in FV should **not** be treated as an OTT impairment.
December 31, 2012	Valued the Bendac stock at $985,000 and determined that the decline in FV should be treated as an OTT impairment.

The journal entries to record the adjustments of the Bendac stock investment to fair value are:

December 31, 2011

Net unrealized holding gains and losses—OCI	10,000	
Fair value adjustment		10,000

December 31, 2012

Other-than-temporary impairment loss—I/S	15,000	
Investment in Bendac		15,000
Fair value adjustment	10,000	
Net unrealized holding gains and losses—OCI		10,000

The first 2012 journal entry in Illustration 12B–1 reduces the Bendac investment to reflect the OTT impairment and recognizes the entire $15,000 in 2012 earnings. United adjusts the Bendac investment directly rather than using a fair value adjustment account because the

---

[45]FASB ASC 320–10–S99: Investments–Overall–SEC Materials (previously "Other-Than-Temporary Impairment of Certain Investments in Equity Securities," *Staff Accounting Bulletin Topic 5.M*).

OTT impairment cannot be recovered. The second 2012 journal entry reclassifies any previously recognized unrealized losses associated with the investment, the same as if the investment had been sold. In 2011 United debited OCI and credited the fair value adjustment for $10,000 to reflect the decline in Bendac's fair value to $990,000, so the second 2012 journal entry reverses the 2011 entry to remove those amounts.

IMPAIRMENTS OF DEBT INVESTMENTS

As with equity investments, a three-step process is used to determine whether an impairment loss on debt investments must be recognized and how that loss is to be measured and recorded.[46] Debt investments can be classified either as HTM or AFS. We'll start with the assumption that the investment is AFS, and then indicate what is different if it is HTM.

1. ***Is the investment impaired?*** As with equity, impairment of a debt investment occurs when fair value has declined to a level below amortized cost. For debt investments, though, it also may be necessary to split the total amount of impairment into credit losses and noncredit losses. *Credit losses* reflect expected reductions in future cash flows from anticipated defaults on interest or principal payments. We calculate credit losses as the difference between the amortized cost of the debt and the *present value of the cash flows* expected to be collected, using a discount rate equal to the effective interest rate that existed at the date the investment was acquired. GAAP sometimes refers to "amortized cost less credit losses," which is just another way of referring to that present value. *Noncredit losses* capture other reductions in fair value such as those due to changes in general economic conditions.

2. ***Is any impairment other-than-temporary (OTT)?*** We view a debt impairment as OTT if one of three conditions holds:

   a. The investor intends to sell the investment, or
   b. The investor believes it is "more likely than not" that the investor will be required to sell the investment prior to recovering the amortized cost of the investment less any current-period credit losses, or
   c. The investor determines that a "credit loss" exists on the investment.

   The rationale for 2a and 2b is that an impairment is OTT if the investor is likely to sell the investment before fair value can recover. The rationale for 2c is that an impairment is OTT if the company believes the cash flows provided by the investment won't be enough to allow it to recover the amortized cost of the investment over the life of the investment.

3. ***How should the company account for the OTT impairment?*** If the debt impairment is considered OTT, the investor always writes the investment down to fair value in the balance sheet, but the amount included in net income or other comprehensive income depends on the reason the impairment is considered OTT:

   a. If the impairment is considered OTT due to reasons 2a or 2b above, the entire impairment loss is included in net income, because it is likely that the company will incur a loss equal to the entire difference between fair value and amortized cost.
   b. If the impairment is considered OTT due to reason 2c above, *only the credit loss* component reduces net income, as that amount of amortized cost is unlikely to be recovered. Any noncredit loss component reduces OCI, similar to how we normally account for unrealized gains and losses on AFS investments.

   Also, because the debt investment is classified as AFS, recognizing an OTT impairment may involve reclassifying amounts out of OCI that were recorded previously as unrealized gains or losses.

For an example of an OTT impairment for a debt investment, we modify our Bendac example again in Illustration 12B–2.

In both Cases 1 and 2 of Illustration 12B–2, the amortized cost of the investment is reduced by the amount of OTT impairment that is recognized in earnings. United achieves

Debt impairments can be divided into credit losses and noncredit losses.

Credit losses are due to anticipated reductions in cash flows from the debt investment; all others are *noncredit losses.*

Debt impairments are OTT if the investor:
a. intends to sell the investment, or
b. believes it is more likely than not that they will sell the investment prior to fair value recovery, or
c. has suffered a credit loss.

If a debt impairment is OTT:
- Investment is written down to fair value.
- If OTT because of (a) or (b), all of the OTT impairment loss is recognized in net income.
- If OTT because of (c), only the credit loss is recognized in net income; noncredit loss in OCI.

[46]FASB ASC 320–10–35: Investments–Overall–Subsequent Measurement (previously "Recognition and Presentation of Other-Than-Temporary Impairments," *FASB Staff Position No. 115-2 and 124-2* (Norwalk, Conn.: FASB April 9, 2009)).

ILLUSTRATION 12B–2 Other-than-temporary Impairment of Debt Investment	United Intergroup, Inc., buys and sells both debt and equity securities of other companies as investments, and classifies these investments as AFS. United's fiscal year-end is December 31. The following events occurred during 2012.

Purchase Investment

July 1, 2012 Purchased $1,000,000 of Bendac bonds, maturing on December 31, 2017.

Adjust Investment to Fair Value

December 31, 2012 Valued the Bendac bonds at $950,000. Of the $50,000 impairment, $30,000 is credit loss and $20,000 is noncredit loss.

We'll consider two cases:.

- **Case 1:** United either plans to sell the investment or believes it is more likely than not that it will have to sell the investment before fair value recovers (such that the impairment is viewed as OTT under 2a or 2b above).
- **Case 2:** United does *not* intend to sell the investment and does *not* believe it is more likely than not that it will have to sell the Bendac investment before fair value recovers, but estimates that $30,000 of credit losses have occurred (such that the impairment is viewed as OTT under 2c above).

	Case 1	Case 2
December 31, 2012		
OTT impairment loss—I/S	50,000	30,000
Discount on bond investment	50,000	30,000
OTT impairment loss—OCI		20,000
Fair value adjustment—Noncredit loss		20,000

Note: if United had included unrealized gains or losses for this investment in OCI in a prior period, it also would have to make a reclassification entry, as demonstrated for an equity OTT impairment in Illustration 12B–1.

this by crediting a contra-asset, discount on bond investment, which United amortizes over the remaining life of the debt the same way it would if it had initially purchased the debt at that discounted amount. In Case 2, the *noncredit-loss* component of the impairment is recognized in OCI, the same way it would be if it were viewed as an unrealized loss under normal accounting for fair value declines of AFS investments. In both cases the carrying value of the debt becomes $950,000, reduced by the entire amount of the OTT impairment. In Case 1 this occurs via the $50,000 discount, and in Case 2 via the combination of the $30,000 discount and $20,000 fair value adjustment.

GAAP requires that the entire OTT impairment be shown in the income statement, and then the portion attributed to noncredit losses backed out, such that only the credit loss portion reduces net income. That way, financial statement users are aware of the total amount as well as the amount included in net income. Continuing Illustration 12B–2, income statement presentation of the two cases would be as follows:

Income Statement Presentation, December 31, 2012	Case 1	Case 2
OTT impairment of AFS investments:		
Total OTT impairment loss	$50,000	$50,000
Less: portion recognized in OCI	-0-	20,000
Net impairment loss recognized in earnings	$50,000	$30,000

Graphic 12B–2 provides an example of OTT impairment recognition, obtained from **Wells Fargo**'s 10Q for the first quarter of 2009.

GRAPHIC 12B–2 Recognition of OTT Impairments— Wells Fargo & Company **Real World Financials**	Total OTTI on debt securities amounted to $603 million, which includes $263 million of credit-related OTTI and $6 million related to securities we intend to sell, both of which were recorded as part of gross realized losses (in net income), and $334 million recorded directly to other comprehensive income for non-credit-related impairment on securities.

What if a debt investment is classified as HTM rather than AFS? Most of the accounting is the same, but an important difference relates to the recognition of *noncredit* losses in OCI. HTM investments normally don't include unrealized gains and losses in OCI, so these won't routinely be adjusted up or down over time. Therefore, for HTM investments, GAAP requires that companies gradually reverse any amounts included in OCI over the remaining life of the investment, debiting the fair value adjustment and crediting OCI each period.

After an OTT impairment is recorded, the usual treatment of unrealized gains or losses is resumed. Changes in fair value are reported in OCI for AFS investments, and are ignored for HTM investments. ●

INTERNATIONAL FINANCIAL REPORTING STANDARDS

Accounting for OTT impairments. Under *IAS No. 39*, companies recognize OTT impairments if there exists objective evidence of impairment. Objective evidence must relate to one or more events occurring after initial recognition of the asset that affect the future cash flows that are going to be generated by the asset. Examples of objective evidence include significant financial difficulty of the issuer and default on interest or principal payments. For an equity security, a significant or prolonged decline in fair value below cost is viewed as objective evidence.

● LO8

(continued)

---

[47]Credit Suisse, *Focusing on Fair Value: An Update,* June 4, 2009.

(concluded)

Calculation of the amount of impairment differs depending on the classification of an investment. For an HTM investment, the impairment is calculated as the difference between the amortized cost of the asset and the present value of expected future cash flows, estimated at the asset's original effective rate. So, the impairment is essentially limited to the amount that would be considered a credit loss in U.S. GAAP. For an AFS investment (debt or equity), the impairment is calculated as the difference between amortized cost and fair value. Thus, under IFRS, an OTT impairment for a debt investment is likely to be larger if it is classified as AFS than if it is classified as HTM, because it includes the entire decline in fair value if classified as AFS but only the credit loss if classified as HTM. Under IFRS, all OTT impairments are recognized in earnings (there is no equivalent to recognizing in OCI any non-credit losses on debt investments). IFRS allows recoveries of impairments to be recognized in earnings for debt investments, but not for equity investments.

To illustrate, let's modify our Bendac debt example from Illustration 12B–2 to assume amortized cost of €1,000,000 and fair value of €950,000, with the €50,000 impairment consisting of €30,000 of credit losses and €20,000 of noncredit losses. If the investment was classified as AFS, IFRS would recognize a €50,000 OTT impairment:

IFRS ILLUSTRATION

Other-than-temporary impairment loss—I/S	50,000	
Investment in Bendac		50,000

On the other hand, if the investment had been classified as HTM, IFRS would recognize an OTT impairment of €30,000:

Other-than-temporary impairment loss—I/S	30,000	
Investment in Bendac		30,000

If in a subsequent period the fair value of the debt investment improved by €15,000, IFRS would allow *reversal* of that amount of impairment charge:

Investment in Bendac	15,000	
Reversal of other-than-temporary impairment loss—I/S		15,000

At the time this text was printed, the IASB had not yet finalized changes in impairment accounting with respect to IFRS No. 9.

QUESTIONS FOR REVIEW OF KEY TOPICS

Q 12–1 All investments in *debt* securities and investments in *equity* securities for which the investor lacks significant influence over the operation and financial policies of the investee are classified for reporting purposes in one of three categories, and can be accounted for differently depending on the classification. What are these three categories?

Q 12–2 When market rates of interest *rise* after a fixed-rate security is purchased, the value of the now-below-market, fixed-interest payments declines, so the market value of the investment falls. On the other hand, if market rates of interest *fall* after a fixed-rate security is purchased, the fixed-interest payments become relatively attractive, and the market value of the investment rises. Assuming these price changes are not viewed as giving rise to an other-than-temporary impairment, how are they reflected in the investment account for a security classified as held-to-maturity?

Q 12–3 Does GAAP distinguish between fair values that are readily determinable from a securities exchange versus those needing to be calculated based on the company's own assumptions? Explain how a user will know about the reliability of the inputs used to determine fair value.

Q 12–4 When an investment is acquired to be held for an unspecified period of time as opposed to being held to maturity, it is reported at the fair value of the investment securities on the reporting date. Why?

Q 12–5 Reporting an investment at its fair value means adjusting its carrying amount for changes in fair value after its acquisition (or since the last reporting date if it was held at that time). Such changes are called unrealized holding gains and losses because they haven't yet been realized through the sale of the security. If the security is classified as available-for-sale, how are unrealized holding gains and losses reported if they are not viewed as giving rise to an other-than-temporary impairment?

Q 12–6   What is "comprehensive income"? Its composition varies from company to company but may include which investment-related items that are not included in net income?

Q 12–7   Why are holding gains and losses treated differently for trading securities and securities available-for-sale?

Q 12–8   Western Die-Casting Company holds an investment in unsecured bonds of LGB Heating Equipment, Inc. When the investment was acquired, management's intention was to hold the bonds for resale. Now management has the positive intent and ability to hold the bonds to maturity. How should the reclassification of the investment be accounted for?

Q 12–9   Is it necessary for an investor to report individual amounts for the three categories of investments—held-to-maturity, available-for-sale, or trading—in the financial statements? What information should be disclosed about these investments?

IFRS Q 12–10   Are there circumstances in which the cost method is required under U.S. GAAP but not under IFRS? Explain.

Q 12–11   What is the effect of a company electing the fair value option with respect to a held-to-maturity investment or an available-for-sale investment?

IFRS Q 12–12   Do U.S. GAAP and IFRS differ in the amount of flexibility that companies have in electing the fair value option? Explain.

Q 12–13   Under what circumstances is the equity method used to account for an investment in stock?

Q 12–14   The equity method has been referred to as a *one-line consolidation*. What might prompt this description?

Q 12–15   In the application of the equity method, how should dividends from the investee be accounted for? Why?

Q 12–16   The fair value of depreciable assets of Penner Packaging Company exceeds their book value by $12 million. The assets' average remaining useful life is 10 years. They are being depreciated by the straight-line method. Finest Foods Industries buys 40% of Penner's common shares. When adjusting investment revenue and the investment by the equity method, how will the situation described affect those two accounts?

Q 12–17   Superior Company owns 40% of the outstanding stock of Bernard Company. During 2011, Bernard paid a $100,000 cash dividend on its common shares. What effect did this dividend have on Superior's 2011 financial statements?

Q 12–18   Sometimes an investor's level of influence changes, making it necessary to change from the equity method to another method. How should the investor account for this change in accounting method?

IFRS Q 12–19   How does IFRS differ from U.S. GAAP with respect to using the equity method?

Q 12–20   What is the effect of a company electing the fair value option with respect to an investment that otherwise would be accounted for using the equity method?

Q 12–21   Define a financial instrument. Provide three examples of current liabilities that represent financial instruments.

Q 12–22   Some financial instruments are called derivatives. Why?

Q 12–23   (Based on Appendix 12A) Northwest Carburetor Company established a fund in 2008 to accumulate money for a new plant scheduled for construction in 2011. How should this special purpose fund be reported in Northwest's balance sheet?

Q 12–24   (Based on Appendix 12A) Whole-life insurance policies typically can be surrendered while the insured is still alive in exchange for a determinable amount of money called the *cash surrender value*. When a company buys a life insurance policy on the life of a key officer to protect the company against the untimely loss of a valuable resource in the event the officer dies, how should the company account for the cash surrender value?

Q 12–25   (Based on Appendix 12B) When market rates of interest *rise* after a fixed-rate security is purchased, the value of the now-below-market, fixed-interest payments declines, so the market value of the investment falls. If that drop in fair value is viewed as giving rise to an other-than-temporary impairment, how would it be reflected in the investment account for a security classified as held-to-maturity?

Q 12–26   (Based on Appendix 12B) Reporting an investment at its fair value requires adjusting its carrying amount for changes in fair value after its acquisition (or since the last reporting date if it was held at that time). Such changes are called unrealized holding gains and losses because they haven't yet been realized through the sale of the security. If a security is classified as available-for-sale, and an unrealized holding loss is viewed as giving rise to an other-than-temporary (OTT) impairment, how is it reported in the financial statements?

Q 12–27   (Based on Appendix 12B) The market value of Helig Forestry and Mining Corporation common stock dropped 6 1/8 points when the federal government passed new legislation banning one of the company's primary techniques for extracting ore. Harris Corporation owns shares of Helig and classifies its investment as securities available-for-sale. How should the decline in market value be handled by Harris?

IFRS Q 12–28   (Based on Appendix 12B) Do U.S. GAAP and IFRS differ in how they account for other-than-temporary impairments? Explain.

BRIEF EXERCISES

BE 12–1
Securities held-to-maturity; bond investment; effective interest
● LO1

Lance Brothers Enterprises acquired $720,000 of 3% bonds, dated July 1, on July 1, 2011, as a long-term investment. Management has the positive intent and ability to hold the bonds until maturity. The market interest rate (yield) was 4% for bonds of similar risk and maturity. Lance Brothers paid $600,000 for the investment in bonds and will receive interest semiannually on June 30 and December 31. Prepare the journal entries (a) to record Lance Brothers' investment in the bonds on July 1, 2011, and (b) to record interest on December 31, 2011, at the effective (market) rate.

BE 12–2
Trading securities
● LO2

S&L Financial buys and sells securities expecting to earn profits on short-term differences in price. On December 27, 2011, S&L purchased **Coca-Cola** common shares for $875,000 and sold the shares on January 3, 2012, for $880,000. At December 31, the shares had a fair value of $873,000. What pretax amounts did S&L include in its 2011 and 2012 earnings as a result of this investment?

BE 12–3
Available-for-sale securities
● LO3

S&L Financial buys and sells securities which it classifies as available-for-sale. On December 27, 2011, S&L purchased **Coca-Cola** common shares for $875,000 and sold the shares on January 3, 2012, for $880,000. At December 31, the shares had a fair value of $873,000, and S&L has the intent and ability to hold the investment until fair value recovers. What pretax amounts did S&L include in its 2011 and 2012 earnings as a result of this investment?

BE 12–4
Securities available-for-sale; adjusting entry
● LO3

For several years Fister Links Products has held shares of **Microsoft** common stock, considered by the company to be securities available-for-sale. The shares were acquired at a cost of $500,000. Their fair value last year was $610,000 and is $670,000 this year. At what amount will the investment be reported in this year's balance sheet? What adjusting entry is required to accomplish this objective?

BE 12–5
Classification of securities; reporting
● LO3

Adams Industries holds 40,000 shares of **FedEx** common stock. On December 31, 2010, and December 31, 2011, the market value of the stock is $95 and $100 per share, respectively. What is the appropriate reporting category for this investment and at what amount will it be reported in the 2011 balance sheet?

BE 12–6
Fair value option; available-for-sale securities
● LO7

S&L Financial buys and sells securities that it typically classifies as available-for-sale. On December 27, 2011, S&L purchased **Coca-Cola** common shares for $875,000 and sold the shares on January 3, 2012, for $880,000. At December 31, the shares had a fair value of $873,000. When it purchased the Coca-Cola shares, S&L Financial decided to elect the fair value option for this investment. What pretax amounts did S&L include in its 2011 and 2012 earnings as a result of this investment?

BE 12–7
Trading securities, securities available-for-sale and dividends
● LO2 LO3

Turner Company owns 10% of the outstanding stock of ICA Company. During the current year, ICA paid a $5 million cash dividend on its common shares. What effect did this dividend have on Turner's 2011 financial statements? Explain the reasoning for this effect.

BE 12–8
Equity method and dividends

Turner Company owns 40% of the outstanding stock of ICA Company. During the current year, ICA paid a $5 million cash dividend on its common shares. What effect did this dividend have on Turner's 2011 financial statements? Explain the reasoning for this effect.

BE 12–9
Equity method
● LO6 LO7

The fair value of Wallis, Inc.'s depreciable assets exceeds their book value by $50 million. The assets have an average remaining useful life of 15 years and are being depreciated by the straight-line method. Park Industries buys 30% of Wallis's common shares. When Park adjusts its investment revenue and the investment by the equity method, how will the situation described affect those two accounts?

BE 12–10
Equity method investments
● LO6 LO8

Refer to the situation described in BE 12–9, but assume that Park Industries buys 50% of Wallis's common shares. Also assume that Park reports under International Financial Reporting Standards, and has elected the "proportionate consolidation" method to account for the Wallis investment. How would the situation described affect Park's depreciable asset accounts?

BE 12–11
Change in principle; change to the equity method
● LO5

At the beginning of 2011, Pioneer Products' ownership interest in the common stock of LLB Co. increased to the point that it became appropriate to begin using the equity method of accounting for the investment. The balance in the investment account was $44 million at the time of the change but would have been $56 million if Pioneer had used the equity method and the account had been adjusted for investee net income and dividends. How should Pioneer report the change? Would your answer be the same if Pioneer is changing *from* the equity method rather than *to* the equity method?

BE 12–12
Fair value option; equity method investments
● LO7

Turner Company purchased 40% of the outstanding stock of ICA Company for $10,000,000 on January 2, 2011. Turner elects the fair value option to account for the investment. During 2011, ICA earns $750,000 of income and on December 30 pays a dividend of $500,000. On December 31, 2011, the fair value of Turner's investment has increased to $11,500,000. What journal entries would Turner make to account for this investment during 2011, assuming Turner will account for the investment similar to how it would account for a trading security?

BE 12–13
Available-for-sale securities and impairment (Based on Appendix 12B)
● LO3

LED Corporation owns 100,000 shares of Branch Pharmaceuticals common stock and classifies its investment as securities available-for-sale. The market price of Branch's stock fell more than 30%, by $4.50 per share, due to concerns about one of the company's principal drugs. The concerns were justified when the FDA banned the drug. $1.00 per share of that decline in value already had been included in OCI as a temporary unrealized loss in a prior period. What journal entries should LED record to account for the decline in market value in the current period? How should the decline affect net income and comprehensive income?

BE 12–14
Available-for-sale securities and impairment (Based on Appendix 12B)
● LO3

LED Corporation owns $1,000,000 of Branch Pharmaceuticals bonds and classifies its investment as securities available-for-sale. The market price of Branch's bonds fell by $450,000, due to concerns about one of the company's principal drugs. The concerns were justified when the FDA banned the drug. $100,000 of that decline in value already had been included in OCI as a temporary unrealized loss in a prior period. LED views $200,000 of the $450,000 loss as related to *credit* losses, and the other $250,000 as *noncredit* losses. LED thinks it is more likely than not that it will have to sell the investment before fair value recovers. What journal entries should LED record to account for the decline in market value in the current period? How should the decline affect net income and comprehensive income?

BE 12–15
Available-for-sale securities and impairment (Based on Appendix 12B)
● LO3

LED Corporation owns $1,000,000 of Branch Pharmaceuticals bonds and classifies its investment as securities available-for-sale. The market price of Branch's bonds fell by $450,000, due to concerns about one of the company's principal drugs. The concerns were justified when the FDA banned the drug. $100,000 of that decline in value already had been included in OCI as a temporary unrealized loss in a prior period. LED views $200,000 of the $450,000 loss as related to *credit* losses, and the other $250,000 as *noncredit* losses. LED does not plan to sell the investment and does not think it is more likely than not that it will have to sell the investment before fair value recovers. What journal entries should LED record to account for the decline in market value in the current period? How should the decline affect net income and comprehensive income?

BE 12–16
Recovery of impairments under IFRS (Based on Appendix 12B)
● LO3 LO8

Wickum Corporation reports under IFRS, and recognized a $500,000 other-than-temporary impairment of an HTM debt investment in Right Corporation. Subsequently, the fair value of Wickum's investment in Right increased by $300,000. How would Wickum account for that increase in fair value?

EXERCISES

An alternate exercise and problem set is available on the text website: www.mhhe.com/spiceland6e

E 12–1
Securities held-to-maturity; bond investment; effective interest
● LO1

Tanner-UNF Corporation acquired as a long-term investment $240 million of 6% bonds, dated July 1, on July 1, 2011. Company management has the positive intent and ability to hold the bonds until maturity. The market interest rate (yield) was 8% for bonds of similar risk and maturity. Tanner-UNF paid $200 million for the bonds. The company will receive interest semiannually on June 30 and December 31. As a result of changing market conditions, the fair value of the bonds at December 31, 2011, was $210 million.

Required:
1. Prepare the journal entry to record Tanner-UNF's investment in the bonds on July 1, 2011.
2. Prepare the journal entries by Tanner-UNF to record interest on December 31, 2011, at the effective (market) rate.

3. At what amount will Tanner-UNF report its investment in the December 31, 2011, balance sheet? Why?

4. Suppose Moody's bond rating agency downgraded the risk rating of the bonds motivating Tanner-UNF to sell the investment on January 2, 2012, for $190 million. Prepare the journal entry to record the sale.

E 12–2
Securities
held-to-maturity
● LO1

FF&T Corporation is a confectionery wholesaler that frequently buys and sells securities to meet various investment objectives. The following selected transactions relate to FF&T's investment activities during the last two months of 2011. At November 1, FF&T held $48 million of 20-year, 10% bonds of Convenience, Inc., purchased May 1, 2011, at face value. Management has the positive intent and ability to hold the bonds until maturity. FF&T's fiscal year ends on December 31.

Nov. 1   Received semiannual interest of $2.4 million from the Convenience, Inc., bonds.
Dec. 1   Purchased 12% bonds of Facsimile Enterprises at their $30 million face value, to be held until they mature in 2024. Semiannual interest is payable May 31 and November 30.
    31   Purchased U.S. Treasury bills that mature in two months for $8.9 million.
    31   Recorded any necessary adjusting entry(s) relating to the investments.

The fair values of the investments at December 31 were:
Convenience bonds $44.7 million
Facsimile Enterprises bonds   30.9 million
U.S. Treasury bills   8.9 million

Required:
Prepare the appropriate journal entry for each transaction or event.

E 12–3
Purchase and sale
of investment
securities
● LO2 LO3

Shott Farm Supplies Corporation purchased 800 shares of **General Motors** stock at $50 per share and paid a brokerage fee of $1,200. Two months later, the shares were sold for $53 per share. The brokerage fee on the sale was $1,300.

Required:
Prepare entries for the purchase and the sale.

E 12–4
Various
transactions
relating to trading
securities
● LO2

Rantzow-Lear Company buys and sells securities expecting to earn profits on short-term differences in price. The company's fiscal year ends on December 31. The following selected transactions relating to Rantzow-Lear's trading account occurred during December 2011 and the first week of 2012.

2011
Dec. 17   Purchased 100,000 Grocers' Supply Corporation preferred shares for $350,000.
    28   Received cash dividends of $2,000 from the Grocers' Supply Corporation preferred shares.
    31   Recorded any necessary adjusting entry relating to the Grocers' Supply Corporation preferred shares. The market price of the stock was $4 per share.

2012
Jan. 5   Sold the Grocers' Supply Corporation preferred shares for $395,000.

Required:
1. Prepare the appropriate journal entry for each transaction.
2. Indicate any amounts that Rantzow-Lear Company would report in its 2011 balance sheet and income statement as a result of this investment.

E 12–5
Securities
available-for-sale;
adjusting entries
● LO3

Loreal-American Corporation purchased several marketable securities during 2011. At December 31, 2011, the company had the investments in common stock listed below. None was held at the last reporting date, December 31, 2010, and all are considered securities available-for-sale.

	Cost	Fair Value	Unrealized Holding Gain (Loss)
Short term:			
Blair, Inc.	$ 480,000	$ 405,000	$(75,000)
ANC Corporation	450,000	480,000	30,000
Totals	$ 930,000	$ 885,000	$(45,000)
Long term:			
Drake Corporation	$ 480,000	$ 560,000	$ 80,000
Aaron Industries	720,000	660,000	(60,000)
Totals	$1,200,000	$1,220,000	$ 20,000

Required:
1. Prepare appropriate adjusting entries at December 31, 2011.
2. What amounts would be reported in the income statement at December 31, 2011, as a result of these adjusting entries?

E 12–6
Classification of
securities; adjusting
entries
● LO3

On February 18, 2011, Union Corporation purchased 10,000 shares of **IBM** common stock as a long-term investment at $60 per share. On December 31, 2011, and December 31, 2012, the market value of IBM stock is $58 and $61 per share, respectively.

Required:

1. What is the appropriate reporting category for this investment? Why?
2. Prepare the adjusting entry for December 31, 2011.
3. Prepare the adjusting entry for December 31, 2012.

E 12–7
Various
transactions related
to securities
available-for-sale
● LO3

Construction Forms Corporation buys securities to be available for sale when circumstances warrant, not to profit from short-term differences in price and not necessarily to hold debt securities to maturity. The following selected transactions relate to investment activities of Construction Forms whose fiscal year ends on December 31. No investments were held by Construction Forms at the beginning of the year.

2011

Mar. 2	Purchased 1 million Platinum Gauges, Inc., common shares for $31 million, including brokerage fees and commissions.
Apr. 12	Purchased $20 million of 10% bonds at face value from Zenith Wholesale Corporation.
July 18	Received cash dividends of $2 million on the investment in Platinum Gauges, Inc., common shares.
Oct. 15	Received semiannual interest of $1 million on the investment in Zenith bonds.
16	Sold the Zenith bonds for $21 million.
Nov. 1	Purchased 500,000 LTD International preferred shares for $40 million, including brokerage fees and commissions.
Dec. 31	Recorded the necessary adjusting entry(s) relating to the investments. The market prices of the investments are $32 per share for Platinum Gauges, Inc., and $74 per share for LTD International preferred shares.

2012

Jan. 23	Sold half the Platinum Gauges, Inc., shares for $32 per share.
Mar. 1	Sold the LTD International preferred shares for $76 per share.

Required:

1. Prepare the appropriate journal entry for each transaction or event.
2. Show the amounts that would be reported in the company's 2011 income statement relative to these investments.

E 12–8
Securities
available-for-sale;
journal entries
● LO3

On January 2, 2011, Sanborn Tobacco Inc. bought 5% of Jackson Industry's capital stock for $90 million as a temporary investment. Sanborn classified the securities acquired as available-for-sale. Jackson Industry's net income for the year ended December 31, 2011, was $120 million. The fair value of the shares held by Sanborn was $98 million at December 31, 2011. During 2011, Jackson declared a dividend of $60 million.

Required:

1. Prepare all appropriate journal entries related to the investment during 2011.
2. Indicate the effect of this investment on 2011 income before taxes.

E 12–9
Various investment
securities
● LO1 LO2 LO3

At December 31, 2011, Hull-Meyers Corp. had the following investments that were purchased during 2011, its first year of operations:

	Cost	Fair Value
Trading Securities:		
Security A	$ 900,000	$ 910,000
Security B	105,000	100,000
Totals	$1,005,000	$1,010,000
Securities Available-for-Sale:		
Security C	$ 700,000	$ 780,000
Security D	900,000	915,000
Totals	$1,600,000	$1,695,000
Securities to Be Held-to-Maturity:		
Security E	$ 490,000	$ 500,000
Security F	615,000	610,000
Totals	$1,105,000	$1,110,000

No investments were sold during 2011. All securities except Security D and Security F are considered short-term investments. None of the fair value changes is considered permanent.

Required:
Determine the following amounts at December 31, 2011.
1. Investments reported as current assets.
2. Investments reported as noncurrent assets.
3. Unrealized gain (or loss) component of income before taxes.
4. Unrealized gain (or loss) component of accumulated other comprehensive income in shareholders' equity.

E 12–10
Securities
available-for-sale;
adjusting entries
● LO3

The accounting records of Jamaican Importers Inc. at January 1, 2011, included the following:

Assets:	
Investment in IBM common shares	$1,345,000
Less: Fair value adjustment	(145,000)
	$1,200,000
Shareholders' Equity:	
Accumulated unrealized holding gains and losses	$ 145,000

No changes occurred during 2011 in the investment portfolio.

Required:
Prepare appropriate adjusting entry(s) at December 31, 2011, assuming the fair value of the IBM common shares was:
1. $1,175,000
2. $1,275,000
3. $1,375,000

E 12–11
Securities
available-for-sale;
fair value
adjustment
● LO3

The investments of Harlon Enterprises included the following cost and fair value amounts:

($ in millions)		Fair Value, Dec. 31	
Securities Available-for-Sale	**Cost**	**2011**	**2012**
A Corporation shares	$ 20	$14	na
B Corporation bonds	35	35	$ 37
C Corporation shares	15	na	14
D Industries shares	45	46	50
Totals	$115	$95	$101

Harlon Enterprises sold its holdings of A Corporation shares on June 1, 2012, for $15 million. On September 12, it purchased the C Corporation shares.

Required:
1. What is the effect of the sale of the A Corporation shares and the purchase of the C Corporation shares on Harlon's 2012 pretax earnings?
2. At what amount should Harlon's securities available-for-sale portfolio be reported in its 2012 balance sheet? What adjusting entry is needed to accomplish this? What is the effect of the adjustment on Harlon's 2012 pretax earnings?

E 12–12
Investment
securities and
equity method
investments
compared
● LO3 LO4 LO5

As a long-term investment, Painters' Equipment Company purchased 20% of AMC Supplies Inc.'s 400,000 shares for $480,000 at the beginning of the fiscal year of both companies. On the purchase date, the fair value and book value of AMC's net assets were equal. During the year, AMC earned net income of $250,000 and distributed cash dividends of 25 cents per share. At year-end, the fair value of the shares is $505,000.

Required:
1. Assume no significant influence was acquired. Prepare the appropriate journal entries from the purchase through the end of the year.
2. Assume significant influence was acquired. Prepare the appropriate journal entries from the purchase through the end of the year.

E 12–13
Equity method;
purchase; investee
income; dividends
● LO4 LO5

As a long-term investment at the beginning of the fiscal year, Florists International purchased 30% of Nursery Supplies Inc.'s 8 million shares for $56 million. The fair value and book value of the shares were the same at that time. During the year, Nursery Supplies earned net income of $40 million and distributed cash dividends of $1.25 per share. At the end of the year, the fair value of the shares is $52 million.

Required:

Prepare the appropriate journal entries from the purchase through the end of the year.

E 12–14
Change in principle; change to the equity method
● LO5

The Trump Companies Inc. has ownership interests in several public companies. At the beginning of 2011, the company's ownership interest in the common stock of Milken Properties increased to the point that it became appropriate to begin using the equity method of accounting for the investment. The balance in the investment account was $31 million at the time of the change. Accountants working with company records determined that the balance would have been $48 million if the account had been adjusted for investee net income and dividends as prescribed by the equity method.

Required:

1. Prepare the journal entry to record the change in principle.
2. Briefly describe other steps Trump should take to report the change.
3. Suppose Trump is changing *from* the equity method rather than *to* the equity method. How would your answers to requirements 1 and 2 differ?

E 12–15
Error corrections; investment
● LO1 LO2 LO3

On December 12, 2011, an investment costing $80,000 was sold for $100,000. The total of the sale proceeds was credited to the investment account.

Required:

1. Prepare the journal entry to correct the error assuming it is discovered before the books are adjusted or closed in 2011. (Ignore income taxes.)
2. Prepare the journal entry to correct the error assuming it is not discovered until early 2012. (Ignore income taxes.)

E 12–16
Equity method; adjustment for depreciation
● LO5 LO6

Fizer Pharmaceutical paid $68 million on January 2, 2011, for 4 million shares of Carne Cosmetics common stock. The investment represents a 25% interest in the net assets of Carne and gave Fizer the ability to exercise significant influence over Carne's operations. Fizer received dividends of $1 per share on December 21, 2011, and Carne reported net income of $40 million for the year ended December 31, 2011. The fair value of Carne's common stock at December 31, 2011, was $18.50 per share.

• The book value of Carne's net assets was $192 million.
• The fair value of Carne's depreciable assets exceeded their book value by $32 million. These assets had an average remaining useful life of eight years.
• The remainder of the excess of the cost of the investment over the book value of net assets purchased was attributable to goodwill.

Required:

Prepare all appropriate journal entries related to the investment during 2011.

E 12–17
Equity method
● LO5 LO6

On January 1, 2011, Cameron Inc. bought 20% of the outstanding common stock of Lake Construction Company for $300 million cash. At the date of acquisition of the stock, Lake's net assets had a fair value of $900 million. Their book value was $800 million. The difference was attributable to the fair value of Lake's buildings and its land exceeding book value, each accounting for one-half of the difference. Lake's net income for the year ended December 31, 2011, was $150 million. During 2011, Lake declared and paid cash dividends of $30 million. The buildings have a remaining life of 10 years.

Required:

1. Prepare all appropriate journal entries related to the investment during 2011, assuming Cameron accounts for this investment by the equity method.
2. Determine the amounts to be reported by Cameron:
   a. As an investment in Cameron's 2011 balance sheet.
   b. As investment revenue in the income statement.
   c. Among investing activities in the statement of cash flows.

E 12–18
Proportionate consolidation of investments under IFRS
● LO6 LO8

[This is a variation of Exercise 12–17 focusing on using proportionate consolidation to account for joint ventures under IFRS.]

Refer to the situation described in Exercise 12–17, but assume that Cameron bought 50% of the outstanding stock of Lake for $750 million cash, that half of the book value and fair value of Lake's individual net assets is attributable to land and the other half to buildings, that Cameron reports under IFRS, and that Cameron has elected the proportionate consolidation method to account for its investment in Lake.

Required:

1. What would be the effect on January 1, 2011, of the Lake investment on the following accounts on Cameron's consolidated balance sheet?

    a. Buildings

    b. Land

    c. Goodwill

    d. Equity method investments

2. What would be the effect on December 31, 2011, of the Lake investment on the following accounts on Cameron's consolidated balance sheet?

    a. Buildings

    b. Land

    c. Goodwill

    d. Equity method investments

3. Would the effect on Cameron's December 31, 2011, retained earnings differ between an equity method and a proportionate consolidation treatment? Explain.

E 12–19
Fair value option; held-to-maturity investments
● LO1 LO2 LO7

[This is a variation of Exercise 12–1 focusing on the fair value option.]

    Tanner-UNF Corporation acquired as a long-term investment $240 million of 6% bonds, dated July 1, on July 1, 2011. Company management has the positive intent and ability to hold the bonds until maturity, but when the bonds were acquired Tanner-UNF decided to elect the fair value option for accounting for its investment. The market interest rate (yield) was 8% for bonds of similar risk and maturity. Tanner-UNF paid $200 million for the bonds. The company will receive interest semiannually on June 30 and December 31. As a result of changing market conditions, the fair value of the bonds at December 31, 2011, was $210 million.

Required:

1. Would this investment be classified on Tanner-UNF's balance sheet as held-to-maturity securities, trading securities, available-for-sale securities, significant-influence investments, or other? Explain.

2. Prepare the journal entry to record Tanner-UNF's investment in the bonds on July 1, 2011.

3. Prepare the journal entries by Tanner-UNF to record interest on December 31, 2011, at the effective (market) rate.

4. Prepare any journal entry necessary to recognize fair value changes as of December 31, 2011.

5. At what amount will Tanner-UNF report its investment in the December 31, 2011, balance sheet? Why?

6. Suppose Moody's bond rating agency downgraded the risk rating of the bonds motivating Tanner-UNF to sell the investment on January 2, 2012, for $190 million. Prepare the journal entry to record the sale.

E 12–20
Fair value option; available-for-sale investments
● LO2 LO3 LO7

[This is a variation of Exercise 12–7 focusing on the fair value option.]

    On January 2, 2011, Sanborn Tobacco, Inc., bought 5% of Jackson Industry's capital stock for $90 million as a temporary investment. Sanborn realized that these securities normally would be classified as available-for-sale, but elected the fair value option to account for the investment. Jackson Industry's net income for the year ended December 31, 2011, was $120 million. The fair value of the shares held by Sanborn was $98 million at December 31, 2011. During 2011, Jackson declared a dividend of $60 million.

Required:

1. Would this investment be classified on Sanborn's balance sheet as held-to-maturity securities, trading securities, available-for-sale securities, significant-influence investments, or other? Explain.

2. Prepare all appropriate journal entries related to the investment during 2011.

3. Indicate the effect of this investment on 2011 income before taxes.

E 12–21
Fair value option; equity method investments
● LO2 LO5 LO7

[This is a variation of Exercise 12–13 focusing on the fair value option.]

    As a long-term investment at the beginning of the fiscal year, Florists International purchased 30% of Nursery Supplies Inc.'s 8 million shares for $56 million. The fair value and book value of the shares were the same at that time. The company realizes that this investment typically would be accounted for under the equity method, but instead chooses the fair value option. During the year, Nursery Supplies earned net income of $40 million and distributed cash dividends of $1.25 per share. At the end of the year, the fair value of the shares is $52 million.

Required:

1. Would this investment be classified on Florists' balance sheet as held-to-maturity securities, trading securities, available-for-sale securities, significant-influence investments, or other? Explain.

2. Prepare all appropriate journal entries related to the investment during 2011.

3. Indicate the effect of this investment on 2011 income before taxes.

E 12–22
Life insurance policy (Based on Appendix 12A)

Edible Chemicals Corporation owns a $4 million whole life insurance policy on the life of its CEO, naming Edible Chemicals as beneficiary. The annual premiums are $70,000 and are payable at the beginning of each year. The cash surrender value of the policy was $21,000 at the beginning of 2011.

Required:

1. Prepare the appropriate 2011 journal entry to record insurance expense and the increase in the investment assuming the cash surrender value of the policy increased according to the contract to $27,000.

2. The CEO died at the end of 2011. Prepare the appropriate journal entry.

E 12–23
Life insurance policy (Based on Appendix 12A)

Below are two unrelated situations relating to life insurance.

Required:

Prepare the appropriate journal entry for each situation.

1. Ford Corporation owns a whole life insurance policy on the life of its president. Ford Corporation is the beneficiary. The insurance premium is $25,000. The cash surrender value increased during the year from $2,500 to $4,600.

2. Petroleum Corporation received a $250,000 life insurance settlement when its CEO died. At that time, the cash surrender value was $16,000.

E 12–24
Held-to-maturity securities; impairments (Based on Appendix 12B)
● LO1

Bloom Corporation purchased $1,000,000 of Taylor Company 5% bonds at par with the intent and ability to hold the bonds until they matured in 2020, so Bloom classifies their investment as HTM. Unfortunately, a combination of problems at Taylor Company and in the debt market caused the fair value of the Taylor investment to decline to $600,000 during 2011.

Required:

For each of the following scenarios, prepare appropriate entry(s) at December 31, 2011, and indicate how the scenario will affect the 2011 income statement (ignoring income taxes).

1. Bloom now believes it is more likely than not that it will have to sell the Taylor bonds before the bonds have a chance to recover their fair value. Of the $400,000 decline in fair value, Bloom attributes $250,000 to credit losses, and $150,000 to noncredit losses.

2. Bloom does not plan to sell the Taylor bonds prior to maturity, and does not believe it is more likely than not that it will have to sell the Taylor bonds before the bonds have a chance to recover their fair value. Of the $400,000 decline in fair value, Bloom attributes $250,000 to credit losses, and $150,000 to noncredit losses.

3. Bloom does not plan to sell the Taylor bonds prior to maturity, and does not believe it is more likely than not that it will have to sell the Taylor bonds before the bonds have a chance to recover their fair value. Bloom attributes the entire $400,000 decline in fair value to noncredit losses.

E 12–25
Available-for-sale debt securities; impairments (Based on Appendix 12B)
● LO3

(Note: This exercise is a variation of Exercise 12–24, modified to categorize the investment as securities available-for-sale.)

Assume all of the same facts and scenarios as E12–24, except that Bloom Corporation classifies their Taylor investment as AFS.

Required:

1. For each of the scenarios shown in E12–24, prepare the appropriate entry(s) at December 31, 2011. Indicate how the scenario will affect the 2011 income statement, OCI, and comprehensive income.

2. Repeat requirement 1, but now assume that, at the end of 2010, Bloom had recorded a temporary unrealized loss (not an OTT impairment) of $100,000 on the Taylor investment.

E 12–26
Available-for-sale equity securities; impairments (Based on Appendix 12B)
● LO3

In early December of 2011, Kettle Corp purchased $50,000 of Icalc Company common stock, which constitutes less than 1% of Icalc's outstanding shares. By December 31, 2011, the value of Icalc's investment had fallen to $40,000, and Kettle recorded an unrealized loss. By December 31, 2012, the value of the Icalc investment had fallen to $25,000, and Kettle determined that it can no longer assert that it has both the intent and ability to hold the shares long enough for their fair value to recover, so they recorded an OTT impairment. By December 31, 2013, fair value had recovered to $30,000.

Required:

Prepare appropriate entry(s) at December 31, 2011, 2012, and 2013, and for each year indicate how the scenario will affect net income, OCI, and comprehensive income.

E 12–27
Accounting for impairments under IFRS (Based on Appendix 12B)
● LO1 LO3 LO8

(Note: This exercise is a variation of E12–24 modified to consider accounting under IFRS.) Flower Corporation uses IFRS, and purchased €1,000,000 of James Company 5% bonds at face value during 2011. Unfortunately, a combination of problems at James Company and in the debt market caused the fair value of the James investment to decline to €600,000 by December 31, 2011. On December 31, 2011, Flower calculated the present value of the future cash flows expected to be collected from the James investment (using the interest rate effective when the investment was made) to equal €750,000. Flower recognized an OTT impairment. By December 31, 2012 the fair value of the investment increased to €875,000, and Flower calculated the present value of the future cash flows expected to be collected from the James investment (again using the interest rate effective when the investment was made) to equal €800,000.

Required:

1. Prepare appropriate entry(s) to account for the James investment at December 31, 2011, assuming Flower classifies its James investment as held to maturity.

2. Prepare appropriate entry(s) to account for the James investment at December 31, 2012, assuming Flower classifies its James investment as held to maturity.

3. Prepare appropriate entry(s) to account for the James investment at December 31, 2011, assuming Flower classifies its James investment as available for sale.

4. Prepare appropriate entry(s) to account for the James investment at December 31, 2012, assuming Flower classifies its James investment as available for sale.

5. How would your answer to requirement 4 change if the James investment was equity rather than debt?

E 12–28
FASB codification research
● LO1

The *FASB Accounting Standards Codification* represents the single source of authoritative U.S. generally accepted accounting principles.

Required:

1. Obtain the relevant authoritative literature on accounting for investments in held-to-maturity securities using the FASB's Codification Research System at the FASB website (**www.fasb.org**).

2. What is the specific citation that describes examples of circumstances under which an investment is available to be sold and therefore should not be classified as held-to-maturity?

3. List the circumstances and conditions.

E 12–29
FASB codification research
● LO2 LO3 LO5

Access the *FASB's Codification Research System* at the FASB website (**www.fasb.org**).

Required:

Determine the specific citation for accounting for each of the following items:

1. Unrealized holding gains for trading securities should be included in earnings.

2. Under the equity method, the investor accounts for its share of the earnings or losses of the investee in the periods they are reported by the investee in its financial statements.

3. Transfers of securities between categories shall be accounted for at fair value.

4. Disclosures for available-for-sale securities should include total losses for securities that have net losses included in accumulated other comprehensive income.

CPA AND CMA REVIEW QUESTIONS

CPA Exam Questions

The following questions are used in the Kaplan CPA Review Course to study investments while preparing for the CPA examination. Determine the response that best completes the statements or questions.

● LO2

1. During year 4, Wall Co. purchased 2,000 shares of Hemp Corp. common stock for $31,500 as a short-term investment. The investment was appropriately classified as a trading security. The market value of this investment was $29,500 at December 31, year 4. Wall sold all of the Hemp common stock for $14 per share on January 15, year 5, incurring $1,400 in brokerage commissions and taxes. On the sale, Wall should report a realized loss of:
   a. $1,500
   b. $2,900
   c. $3,500
   d. $4,900

● LO3

2. The following information pertains to Lark Corp.'s long-term marketable equity securities portfolio:

	December 31	
	2011	**2010**
Cost	$200,000	$200,000
Fair value	240,000	180,000

Differences between cost and market values are considered to be temporary. The decline in market value was properly accounted for at December 31, 2010. At December 31, 2011, what is the net unrealized holding gain or loss to be reported as:

	Other Comprehensive Income	Accumulated Other Comprehensive Income
a.	$60,000 gain	$40,000 gain
b.	$40,000 gain	$60,000 gain
c.	$20,000 loss	$20,000 loss
d.	–0–	–0–

● LO3

3. The following information was extracted from Gil Co.'s December 31, 2011, balance sheet:

Noncurrent assets:
Long-term investments in marketable
    equity securities (at fair value) $96,450
Stockholders' equity:
Accumulated other comprehensive
    income**   (25,000)

**Includes a net unrealized holding loss on long-term investments in marketable equity securities of $19,800.

The historical cost of the long-term investments in marketable equity securities was:
a. $ 63,595
b. $ 76,650
c. $ 96,450
d. $116,250

● LO3

4. On both December 31, 2010, and December 31, 2011, Kopp Co.'s only equity security investment had the same fair value, which was below its original cost. Kopp considered the decline in value to be temporary in 2010 but other-than-temporary in 2011. At the end of both years the security was classified as a noncurrent asset. Kopp could not exercise significant influence over the investee. What should be the effects of the determination that the decline was other-than-temporary on Kopp's 2011 net noncurrent assets and net income?
a. Decrease in both net noncurrent assets and net income.
b. No effect on both net noncurrent assets and net income.
c. Decrease in net noncurrent assets and no effect on net income.
d. No effect on net noncurrent assets and decrease in net income.

● LO5

5. When the equity method is used to account for investments in common stock, which of the following affect(s) the investor's reported investment income?

	A Change in Fair Value of Investee's Common Stock	Cash Dividends from Investee
a.	Yes	Yes
b.	No	Yes
c.	Yes	No
d.	No	No

● LO5

6. A corporation uses the equity method to account for its 40% ownership of another company. The investee earned $20,000 and paid $5,000 in dividends. The investor made the following entries:

Investment in affiliate	$8,000	
Equity in earnings of affiliate		$8,000
Cash	2,000	
Dividend revenue		2,000

What effect will these entries have on the investor's statement of financial position?
a. Investment in affiliate overstated, retained earnings understated.
b. Financial position will be fairly stated.
c. Investment in affiliate overstated, retained earnings overstated.
d. Investment in affiliate understated, retained earnings understated.

● LO6

7. Park Co. uses the equity method to account for its January 1, 2011, purchase of Tun Inc.'s common stock. On January 1, 2011, the fair values of Tun's FIFO inventory and land exceeded their carrying amounts. How do these excesses of fair values over carrying amounts affect Park's reported equity in Tun's 2011 earnings?

	Inventory Excess	Land Excess
a.	Decrease	Decrease
b.	Decrease	No effect
c.	Increase	No effect
d.	Increase	Increase

● LO4

8. On January 2, 2011, Well Co. purchased 10% of Rea Inc.'s outstanding common shares for $400,000. Well is the largest single shareholder in Rea, and Well's officers are a majority on Rea's board of directors. Rea reported net income of $500,000 for 2011, and paid dividends of $150,000. In its December 31, 2011, balance sheet, what amount should Well report as investment in Rea?
   a. $435,000
   b. $450,000
   c. $400,000
   d. $385,000

CMA Exam Questions

The following questions dealing with investments are adapted from questions that previously appeared on Certified Management Accountant (CMA) examinations. The CMA designation sponsored by the Institute of Management Accountants (**www.imanet.org**) provides members with an objective measure of knowledge and competence in the field of management accounting. Determine the response that best completes the statements or questions.

● LO3

1. An investment in available-for-sale securities is valued on the balance sheet at
   a. The cost to acquire the asset.
   b. Accumulated income minus accumulated dividends since acquisition.
   c. Fair value.
   d. The par or stated value of the securities.

Questions 2 and 3 are based on the following information concerning Monahan Company's portfolio of debt securities at May 31, year 2 and May 31, year 3. All of the debt securities were purchased by Monahan during June, year 1. Prior to June, year 1, Monahan had no investments in debt or equity securities.

As of May 31, Year 2	Amortized Cost	Fair Value
Cleary Company bonds	$164,526	$168,300
Beauchamp Industry bonds	204,964	205,200
Morrow Inc. bonds	305,785	285,200
Total	$675,275	$658,700

As of May 31, Year 3	Amortized Cost	Fair Value
Cleary Company bonds	$152,565	$147,600
Beauchamp Industry bonds	193,800	204,500
Morrow Inc. bonds	289,130	291,400
Total	$635,495	$643,500

● LO3

2. Assuming that the above securities are properly classified as available-for-sale securities under U.S. GAAP, the unrealized holding gain or loss as of May 31, year 3 would be
   a. recognized as an $8,005 unrealized holding gain on the income statement.
   b. recognized in accumulated other comprehensive income by a year-end credit of $8,005.
   c. recognized in accumulated other comprehensive income by a year-end debit of $8,005.
   d. not recognized.

● LO1

3. Assuming that the above securities are properly classified as held-to-maturity securities under U.S. GAAP, the unrealized holding gain or loss as of May 31, year 3 would be
   a. recognized as an $8,005 unrealized holding gain on the income statement.
   b. recognized in accumulated other comprehensive income by a year-end credit of $8,005.
   c. recognized in accumulated other comprehensive income by a year-end debit of $8,005.
   d. not recognized.

PROBLEMS

An alternate exercise and problem set is available on the text website: www.mhhe.com/spiceland6e

P 12–1
Securities held-to-maturity; bond investment; effective interest

● LO1

Fuzzy Monkey Technologies, Inc., purchased as a long-term investment $80 million of 8% bonds, dated January 1, on January 1, 2011. Management has the positive intent and ability to hold the bonds until maturity. For bonds of similar risk and maturity the market yield was 10%. The price paid for the bonds was $66 million. Interest is received semiannually on June 30 and December 31. Due to changing market conditions, the fair value of the bonds at December 31, 2011, was $70 million.

Required:

1. Prepare the journal entry to record Fuzzy Monkey's investment on January 1, 2011.
2. Prepare the journal entry by Fuzzy Monkey to record interest on June 30, 2011 (at the effective rate).
3. Prepare the journal entries by Fuzzy Monkey to record interest on December 31, 2011 (at the effective rate).
4. At what amount will Fuzzy Monkey report its investment in the December 31, 2011, balance sheet? Why?
5. How would Fuzzy Monkey's 2011 statement of cash flows be affected by this investment?

P 12–2
Trading securities;
bond investment;
effective interest
● **LO2**

[This problem is a variation of Problem 12–1, modified to categorize the investment as trading securities.]

Fuzzy Monkey Technologies, Inc., purchased as a short-term investment $80 million of 8% bonds, dated January 1, on January 1, 2011. Management intends to include the investment in a short-term, active trading portfolio. For bonds of similar risk and maturity the market yield was 10%. The price paid for the bonds was $66 million. Interest is received semiannually on June 30 and December 31. Due to changing market conditions, the fair value of the bonds at December 31, 2011, was $70 million.

Required:

1. Prepare the journal entry to record Fuzzy Monkey's investment on January 1, 2011.
2. Prepare the journal entry by Fuzzy Monkey to record interest on June 30, 2011 (at the effective rate).
3. Prepare the journal entries by Fuzzy Monkey to record interest on December 31, 2011 (at the effective rate).
4. At what amount will Fuzzy Monkey report its investment in the December 31, 2011, balance sheet? Why? Prepare any entry necessary to achieve this reporting objective.
5. How would Fuzzy Monkey's 2011 statement of cash flows be affected by this investment?

P 12–3
Securities
available-for-sale;
bond investment;
effective interest
● **LO3**

(Note: This problem is a variation of Problem 12–1, modified to categorize the investment as securities available-for-sale.)

Fuzzy Monkey Technologies, Inc., purchased as a long-term investment $80 million of 8% bonds, dated January 1, on January 1, 2011. Management intends to have the investment available for sale when circumstances warrant. For bonds of similar risk and maturity the market yield was 10%. The price paid for the bonds was $66 million. Interest is received semiannually on June 30 and December 31. Due to changing market conditions, the fair value of the bonds at December 31, 2011, was $70 million.

Required:

1. Prepare the journal entry to record Fuzzy Monkey's investment on January 1, 2011.
2. Prepare the journal entry by Fuzzy Monkey to record interest on June 30, 2011 (at the effective rate).
3. Prepare the journal entries by Fuzzy Monkey to record interest on December 31, 2011 (at the effective rate).
4. At what amount will Fuzzy Monkey report its investment in the December 31, 2011, balance sheet? Why? Prepare any entry necessary to achieve this reporting objective.
5. How would Fuzzy Monkey's 2011 statement of cash flows be affected by this investment?

P 12–4
Fair value option;
bond investment;
effective interest
● **LO1 LO2 LO3**
  LO7

[This problem is a variation of Problem 12–3, modified to cause the investment to be accounted for under the fair value option.]

Fuzzy Monkey Technologies, Inc., purchased as a long-term investment $80 million of 8% bonds, dated January 1, on January 1, 2011. Management intends to have the investment available for sale when circumstances warrant. When the company purchased the bonds, management elected to account for them under the fair value option. For bonds of similar risk and maturity the market yield was 10%. The price paid for the bonds was $66 million. Interest is received semiannually on June 30 and December 31. Due to changing market conditions, the fair value of the bonds at December 31, 2011, was $70 million.

Required:

1. Prepare the journal entry to record Fuzzy Monkey's investment on January 1, 2011.
2. Prepare the journal entry by Fuzzy Monkey to record interest on June 30, 2011 (at the effective rate).
3. Prepare the journal entries by Fuzzy Monkey to record interest on December 31, 2011 (at the effective rate).
4. At what amount will Fuzzy Monkey report its investment in the December 31, 2011, balance sheet? Why? Prepare any entry necessary to achieve this reporting objective.
5. How would Fuzzy Monkey's 2011 statement of cash flows be affected by this investment?
6. How would your answers to requirements 1–5 differ if management had the intent and ability to hold the investments until maturity?

P 12–5
Various
transactions related
to securities
available-for-sale
● **LO3**

The following selected transactions relate to investment activities of Ornamental Insulation Corporation. The company buys securities, *not* intending to profit from short-term differences in price and *not* necessarily to hold debt securities to maturity, but to have them available for sale when circumstances warrant. Ornamental's fiscal year ends on December 31. No investments were held by Ornamental on December 31, 2010.

2011

Feb. 21	Acquired Distribution Transformers Corporation common shares costing $400,000.
Mar. 18	Received cash dividends of $8,000 on the investment in Distribution Transformers common shares.
Sep. 1	Acquired $900,000 of American Instruments' 10% bonds at face value.
Oct. 20	Sold the Distribution Transformers shares for $425,000.
Nov. 1	Purchased M&D Corporation common shares costing $1,400,000.
Dec. 31	Recorded any necessary adjusting entry(s) relating to the investments. The market prices of the investments are:

American Instruments bonds	$ 850,000
M&D Corporation shares	$1,460,000

(Hint: Interest must be accrued for the American Instruments' bonds.)

2012

Jan. 20	Sold the M&D Corporation shares for $1,485,000.
Mar. 1	Received semiannual interest of $45,000 on the investment in American Instruments bonds.
Aug. 12	Acquired Vast Communication common shares costing $650,000.
Sept. 1	Received semiannual interest of $45,000 on the investment in American Instruments bonds.
Dec. 31	Recorded any necessary adjusting entry(s) relating to the investments. The market prices of the investments are:

Vast Communication shares	$670,000
American Instruments bonds	$830,000

Required:

1. Prepare the appropriate journal entry for each transaction or event during 2011.

2. Indicate any amounts that Ornamental Insulation would report in its 2011 balance sheet and income statement as a result of these investments.

3. Prepare the appropriate journal entry for each transaction or event during 2012.

4. Indicate any amounts that Ornamental Insulation would report in its 2012 balance sheet and income statement as a result of these investments.

P 12–6
Various transactions relating to trading securities
● LO2

American Surety and Fidelity buys and sells securities expecting to earn profits on short-term differences in price. For the first 11 months of 2011, gains from selling trading securities totaled $8 million, losses were $11 million, and the company had earned $5 million in investment revenue. The following selected transactions relate to American's trading account during December 2011, and the first week of 2012. The company's fiscal year ends on December 31. No trading securities were held by American on December 1, 2011.

2011

Dec. 12	Purchased FF&G Corporation bonds for $12 million.
13	Purchased 2 million Ferry Intercommunications common shares for $22 million.
15	Sold the FF&G Corporation bonds for $12.1 million.
22	Purchased U.S. Treasury bills for $56 million and Treasury bonds for $65 million.
23	Sold half the Ferry Intercommunications common shares for $10 million.
26	Sold the U.S. Treasury bills for $57 million.
27	Sold the Treasury bonds for $63 million.
28	Received cash dividends of $200,000 from the Ferry Intercommunications common shares.
31	Recorded any necessary adjusting entry(s) and closing entries relating to the investments. The market price of the Ferry Intercommunications stock was $10 per share.

2012

Jan. 2	Sold the remaining Ferry Intercommunications common shares for $10.2 million.
5	Purchased Warehouse Designs Corporation bonds for $34 million.

Required:

1. Prepare the appropriate journal entry for each transaction or event during 2011, including the closing entry to income summary for the year.

2. Indicate any amounts that American would report in its 2011 balance sheet and income statement as a result of these investments.

3. Prepare the appropriate journal entry for each transaction or event during 2012.

P 12–7
Securities held-to-maturity, securities available for sale, and trading securities

● LO1 LO2 LO3

Amalgamated General Corporation is a consulting firm that also offers financial services through its credit division. From time to time the company buys and sells securities intending to earn profits on short-term differences in price. The following selected transactions relate to Amalgamated's investment activities during the last quarter of 2011 and the first month of 2012. The only securities held by Amalgamated at October 1 were $30 million of 10% bonds of Kansas Abstractors, Inc., purchased on May 1 at face value. The company's fiscal year ends on December 31.

2011

Oct.	18	Purchased 2 million preferred shares of Millwork Ventures Company for $58 million as a speculative investment to be sold under suitable circumstances.
	31	Received semiannual interest of $1.5 million from the Kansas Abstractors bonds.
Nov.	1	Purchased 10% bonds of Holistic Entertainment Enterprises at their $18 million face value, to be held until they mature in 2018. Semiannual interest is payable April 30 and October 31.
	1	Sold the Kansas Abstractors bonds for $28 million because rising interest rates are expected to cause their fair value to continue to fall.
Dec.	1	Purchased 12% bonds of Household Plastics Corporation at their $60 million face value, to be held until they mature in 2028. Semiannual interest is payable May 31 and November 30.
	20	Purchased U. S. Treasury bonds for $5.6 million as trading securities, hoping to earn profits on short-term differences in prices.
	21	Purchased 4 million common shares of NXS Corporation for $44 million as trading securities, hoping to earn profits on short-term differences in prices.
	23	Sold the Treasury bonds for $5.7 million.
	29	Received cash dividends of $3 million from the Millwork Ventures Company preferred shares.
	31	Recorded any necessary adjusting entry(s) and closing entries relating to the investments. The market price of the Millwork Ventures Company preferred stock was $27.50 per share and $11.50 per share for the NXS Corporation common. The fair values of the bond investments were $58.7 million for Household Plastics Corporation and $16.7 million for Holistic Entertainment Enterprises.

2012

Jan.	7	Sold the NXS Corporation common shares for $43 million.

Required:
Prepare the appropriate journal entry for each transaction or event.

P 12–8
Securities available-for-sale; fair value adjustment; reclassification adjustment

● LO3

At December 31, 2011, the investments in securities available-for-sale of Beale Developments were reported at $78 million:

Securities available-for-sale	$74	
Plus: Fair value adjustment	4	$78

During 2012, Beale sold its investment in Schwab Pharmaceuticals, which had cost $25 million, for $28 million. Those shares had a fair value at December 31, 2011, of $27 million. No other investments were sold. At December 31, 2012, the investments in securities available-for-sale included the cost and fair value amounts shown below.

($ in millions) Securities Available-for-Sale	Cost	Fair Value	Unrealized Gain (Loss)
Daisy Theaters, Inc. shares	$40	$42	$2
Orpheum Entertainment bonds	9	12	3
Totals	$49	$54	$5

Required:
1. At what amount should Beale report its securities available-for-sale in its December 31, 2012, balance sheet?
2. What journal entry is needed to enable the investment to be reported at this amount?
3. What is the amount of the reclassification adjustment to 2012 other comprehensive income? Show how the reclassification adjustment should be reported.

P 12–9
Investment securities and equity method investments compared

● LO3 LO4 LO5 LO6

On January 4, 2011, Runyan Bakery paid $324 million for 10 million shares of Lavery Labeling Company common stock. The investment represents a 30% interest in the net assets of Lavery and gave Runyan the ability to exercise significant influence over Lavery's operations. Runyan received dividends of $2.00 per share on December 15, 2011, and Lavery reported net income of $160 million for the year ended December 31, 2011. The market value of Lavery's common stock at December 31, 2011, was $31 per share. On the purchase date, the book value of Lavery's net assets was $800 million and:

a. The fair value of Lavery's depreciable assets, with an average remaining useful life of six years, exceeded their book value by $80 million.

b. The remainder of the excess of the cost of the investment over the book value of net assets purchased was attributable to goodwill.

Required:

1. Prepare all appropriate journal entries related to the investment during 2011, assuming Runyan accounts for this investment by the equity method.

2. Prepare the journal entries required by Runyan, assuming that the 10 million shares represents a 10% interest in the net assets of Lavery rather than a 30% interest.

P 12–10

Fair value option; equity method investments

● LO2 LO4 LO7

[This problem is a variation of Problem 12–9 focusing on the fair value option.]

On January 4, 2011, Runyan Bakery paid $324 million for 10 million shares of Lavery Labeling Company common stock. The investment represents a 30% interest in the net assets of Lavery and gave Runyan the ability to exercise significant influence over Lavery's operations. Runyan chose the fair value option to account for this investment. Runyan received dividends of $2.00 per share on December 15, 2011, and Lavery reported net income of $160 million for the year ended December 31, 2011. The market value of Lavery's common stock at December 31, 2011, was $31 per share. On the purchase date, the book value of Lavery's net assets was $800 million and:

a. The fair value of Lavery's depreciable assets, with an average remaining useful life of six years, exceeded their book value by $80 million.

b. The remainder of the excess of the cost of the investment over the book value of net assets purchased was attributable to goodwill.

Required:

1. Prepare all appropriate journal entries related to the investment during 2011, assuming Runyan accounts for this investment under the fair value option and accounts for the Lavery investment in a manner similar to what they would use for trading securities.

2. What would be the effect of this investment on Runyan's 2011 net income?

P 12–11

Fair value option; equity method investments

● LO2 LO4 LO5 LO7

[This problem is an expanded version of Problem 12–10 that considers alternative ways in which a firm might apply the fair value option to account for significant-influence investments that would normally be accounted for under the equity method.]

Companies can choose the fair value option for investments that otherwise would be accounted for under the equity method. If the fair value option is chosen, the investment is shown at fair value in the balance sheet, and unrealized holding gains and losses are recognized in the income statement. However, exactly how a company complies with those broad requirements is up to the company. This problem requires you to consider alternative ways in which a company might apply the fair value option for investments that otherwise would be accounted for under the equity method.

On January 4, 2011, Runyan Bakery paid $324 million for 10 million shares of Lavery Labeling Company common stock. The investment represents a 30% interest in the net assets of Lavery and gave Runyan the ability to exercise significant influence over Lavery's operations. Runyan chose the fair value option to account for this investment. Runyan received dividends of $2.00 per share on December 15, 2011, and Lavery reported net income of $160 million for the year ended December 31, 2011. The market value of Lavery's common stock at December 31, 2011, was $31 per share. On the purchase date, the book value of Lavery's net assets was $800 million and:

a. The fair value of Lavery's depreciable assets, with an average remaining useful life of six years, exceeded their book value by $80 million.

b. The remainder of the excess of the cost of the investment over the book value of net assets purchased was attributable to goodwill.

Required:

1. Prepare all appropriate journal entries related to the investment during 2011, assuming Runyan accounts for this investment under the fair value option, and simply accounts for the Lavery investment in a manner similar to what it would use for trading securities. Indicate the effect of these journal entries on 2011 net income, and show the amount at which the investment is carried in the December 31, 2011, balance sheet.

2. Prepare all appropriate journal entries related to the investment during 2011, assuming Runyan accounts for this investment under the fair value option, but uses equity method accounting to account for Lavery's income and dividends, and then records a fair value adjustment at the end of the year that allows it to comply with GAAP. Indicate the effect of these journal entries on 2011 net income, and show the amount at which the investment is carried in the December 31, 2011, balance sheet. (Note: You should end up with the same total 2011 income effect and same carrying value on the balance sheet for requirements 1 and 2.)

P 12–12
Equity method
● LO5 LO6

Northwest Paperboard Company, a paper and allied products manufacturer, was seeking to gain a foothold in Canada. Toward that end, the company bought 40% of the outstanding common shares of Vancouver Timber and Milling, Inc., on January 2, 2011, for $400 million.

At the date of purchase, the book value of Vancouver's net assets was $775 million. The book values and fair values for all balance sheet items were the same except for inventory and plant facilities. The fair value exceeded book value by $5 million for the inventory and by $20 million for the plant facilities.

The estimated useful life of the plant facilities is 16 years. All inventory acquired was sold during 2011.

Vancouver reported net income of $140 million for the year ended December 31, 2011. Vancouver paid a cash dividend of $30 million.

Required:
1. Prepare all appropriate journal entries related to the investment during 2011.
2. What amount should Northwest report as its income from its investment in Vancouver for the year ended December 31, 2011?
3. What amount should Northwest report in its balance sheet as its investment in Vancouver?
4. What should Northwest report in its statement of cash flows regarding its investment in Vancouver?

P 12–13
Equity method
● LO5 LO6

On January 2, 2011, Miller Properties paid $19 million for 1 million shares of Marlon Company's 6 million outstanding common shares. Miller's CEO became a member of Marlon's board of directors during the first quarter of 2011.

The carrying amount of Marlon's net assets was $66 million. Miller estimated the fair value of those net assets to be the same except for a patent valued at $24 million above cost. The remaining amortization period for the patent is 10 years.

Marlon reported earnings of $12 million and paid dividends of $6 million during 2011. On December 31, 2011, Marlon's common stock was trading on the NYSE at $18.50 per share.

Required:
1. When considering whether to account for its investment in Marlon under the equity method, what criteria should Miller's management apply?
2. Assume Miller accounts for its investment in Marlon using the equity method. Ignoring income taxes, determine the amounts related to the investment to be reported in its 2011:
   a. Income statement.
   b. Balance sheet.
   c. Statement of cash flows.

P 12–14
Classifying investments
● LO1 through LO5

Indicate (by letter) the way each of the investments listed below most likely should be accounted for based on the information provided.

Item	Reporting Category
___ 1. 35% of the nonvoting preferred stock of American Aircraft Company.	T. Trading securities
___ 2. Treasury bills to be held to maturity.	M. Securities held-to-maturity
___ 3. Two-year note receivable from affiliate.	A. Securities available-for-sale
___ 4. Accounts receivable.	E. Equity method
___ 5. Treasury bond maturing in one week.	C. Consolidation
___ 6. Common stock held in trading account for immediate resale.	N. None of these
___ 7. Bonds acquired to profit from short-term differences in price.	
___ 8. 35% of the voting common stock of Computer Storage Devices Company.	
___ 9. 90% of the voting common stock of Affiliated Peripherals, Inc.	
___ 10. Corporate bonds of Primary Smelting Company to be sold if interest rates fall ½%.	
___ 11. 25% of the voting common stock of Smith Foundries Corporation: 51% family-owned by Smith family; fair value determinable.	
___ 12. 17% of the voting common stock of Shipping Barrels Corporation: Investor's CEO on the board of directors of Shipping Barrels Corporation.	

P 12–15
Fair value option; held-to-maturity investments
● LO1 LO7

On January 1, 2011, Ithaca Corp. purchases Cortland Inc. bonds that have a face value of $150,000. The Cortland bonds have a stated interest rate of 6%. Interest is paid semiannually on June 30 and December 31, and the bonds mature in 10 years. For bonds of similar risk and maturity, the market yield on particular dates is as follows:

January 1, 2011	7.0%
June 30, 2011	8.0%
December 31, 2011	9.0%

Required:

1. Calculate the price Ithaca would have paid for the Cortland bonds on January 1, 2011 (ignoring brokerage fees), and prepare a journal entry to record the purchase.

2. Prepare all appropriate journal entries related to the bond investment during 2011, assuming Ithaca accounts for the bonds as a held-to-maturity investment. Ithaca calculates interest revenue at the effective interest rate as of the date it purchased the bonds.

3. Prepare all appropriate journal entries related to the bond investment during 2011, assuming that Ithaca chose the fair value option when the bonds were purchased, and that Ithaca determines fair value of the bonds semiannually. Ithaca calculates interest revenue at the effective interest rate as of the date it purchased the bonds.

P 12–16

Accounting for other-than-temporary impairments (Based on Appendix 12B)

● LO1 LO2 LO3

Stewart Enterprises has the following investments, all purchased prior to 2011:

1. Bee Company 5% bonds, purchased at face value, with an amortized cost of $4,000,000, and classified as held to maturity. At December 31, 2011, the Bee investment had a fair value of $3,500,000, and Stewart calculated that $240,000 of the fair value decline is a credit loss and $260,000 is a noncredit loss. At December 31, 2012, the Bee investment had a fair value of $3,700,000, and Stewart calculated that $140,000 of the difference between fair value and amortized cost was a credit loss and $160,000 was a noncredit loss.

2. Oliver Corporation 4% bonds, purchased at face value, with an amortized cost of $2,500,000, classified as a trading security. Because of unrealized losses prior to 2011, the Oliver bonds have a fair value adjustment account with a credit balance of $200,000, such that the carrying value of the Oliver investment is $2,300,000 prior to making any adjusting entries in 2011. At December 31, 2011, the Oliver investment had a fair value of $2,200,000, and Stewart calculated that $120,000 of the difference between amortized cost and fair value is a credit loss and $180,000 is a noncredit loss. At December 31, 2012, the Oliver investment had a fair value of $2,700,000.

3. Jones Inc. 6% bonds, purchased at face value, with an amortized cost of $3,500,000, and classified as an available-for-sale investment. Because of unrealized losses prior to 2011, the Jones bonds have a fair value adjustment account with a credit balance of $400,000, such that the carrying value of the Jones investment is $3,100,000 prior to making any adjusting entries in 2011. At December 31, 2011, the Jones investment had a fair value of $2,700,000, and Stewart calculated that $225,000 of the difference between amortized cost and fair value is a credit loss and $575,000 is a noncredit loss. At December 31, 2012, the Jones investment had a fair value of $2,900,000, and Stewart calculated that $125,000 of the difference between amortized cost and fair value is a credit loss and $475,000 is a noncredit loss.

4. Helms Corp. equity, purchased for $1,000,000, classified as available for sale. Because of unrealized gains prior to 2011, the Helms shares have a fair value adjustment account with a debit balance of $120,000, such that the carrying value of the Helms investment is $1,120,000 prior to making any adjusting entries in 2011. At December 31, 2011 and 2012, the Helms investment had a fair value of $600,000 and $700,000, respectively.

Stewart does not intend to sell any of these investments and does not believe it is more likely than not that it will have to sell any of the bond investments before fair value recovers. However, Stewart cannot assert that it has the ability to hold the Helms equity investment before fair value recovers.

Required:

Prepare the appropriate adjusting journal entries to account for fair value changes during 2011 and 2012, assuming that each investment is viewed as qualifying as an other-than-temporary (OTT) impairment as of December 31, 2011, and then is accounted for normally during 2012 (with no additional OTT impairment in 2012).

P 12–17

Accounting for other-than-temporary impairments under IFRS (Based on Appendix 12B)

● LO1 LO2 LO3
  LO8

(Note: This problem is a variation of Problem 12–16, modified to consider accounting for impairments under IFRS.)

Required:

Consider the facts presented in P12–16, and assume that Stewart accounts for its investments under IFRS. Prepare the appropriate adjusting journal entries to account for fair value changes during 2011 and 2012, assuming that Stewart views each investment as meeting any criteria necessary for recognizing an other-than-temporary (OTT) impairment as of December 31, 2011, and then is accounted for normally during 2012 (with no additional OTT impairment in 2012).

BROADEN YOUR PERSPECTIVE

Apply your critical-thinking ability to the knowledge you've gained. These cases will provide you an opportunity to develop your research, analysis, judgment, and communication skills. You also will work with other students, integrate what you've learned, apply it in real world situations, and consider its global and ethical ramifications. This practice will broaden your knowledge and further develop your decision-making abilities.

**Real World
Case 12–1**
Intel's investments
● LO3

The following disclosure note appeared in the June 27, 2009, 10Q of the **Intel Corporation**.

Note 6: Available-for-Sale Investments (partial)

Table 1: Available-for-sale investments as of June 27, 2009, and December 27, 2008, were as follows:

(In millions)	June 27, 2009				December 27, 2008			
	Adjusted Cost	Gross Unrealized Gains	Gross Unrealized Losses	Fair Value	Adjusted Cost	Gross Unrealized Gains	Gross Unrealized Losses	Fair Value
Floating-rate notes	$ 6,576	$ 10	$ (49)	$ 6,537	$ 6,599	$ 3	$ (133)	$ 6,469
Commercial paper	3,658	2	—	3,660	3,244	4	—	3,248
Bank time deposits	582	3	—	585	606	2	—	608
Money market fund deposits	538	—	—	538	419	—	—	419
Marketable equity securities	398	115	—	513	393	2	(43)	352
Asset-backed securities	250	—	(60)	190	374	—	(43)	331
Corporate bonds	247	8	(19)	236	270	4	(6)	268
Total available-for-sale investments	**$ 12,249**	**$ 138**	**$ (128)**	**$12,259**	**$11,905**	**$ 15**	**$ (225)**	**$11,695**

Table 2: The before-tax net unrealized holding gains (losses) on available-for-sale investments that have been included in accumulated other comprehensive income (loss) were as follows:

(In millions)	Three Months Ended		Six Months Ended	
	June 27, 2009	June 28, 2008	June 27, 2009	June 28, 2008
Net unrealized holding gains (losses) included in accumulated other comprehensive income (loss)	$ 157	$ 100	$ 223	$ (359)

Required:

1. Looking only at Table 1, draw a T-account that shows the change between the December 27, 2008, and June 27, 2009, balances for the fair value adjustment associated with Intel's AFS investments for the first half of 2009. By how much did the fair value change during the first half of 2009?
2. Now look at Table 2, and prepare a journal entry that recognizes for the first six months of 2009 any net unrealized holding gains and losses. Ignore income taxes.
3. Using your journal entry from requirement 2, adjust your T-account from requirement 1. Have you accounted for the entire change in the fair value adjustment that occurred during the first half of 2009? If not, speculate as to what could be causing the difference.

**Real World
Case 12–2**
Reporting securities available-for-sale; obtain and critically evaluate an annual report
● LO3

Investments in common stocks potentially affect each of the various financial statements as well as the disclosure notes that accompany those statements.

Required:

1. Locate a recent annual report of a public company that includes a footnote that describes an investment in securities available-for-sale. You can use EDGAR at **www.sec.gov**.

2. Under what caption are the investments reported in the comparative balance sheets? Are they reported as current or noncurrent assets?

3. Are realized gains or losses reported in the comparative income statements?

4. Are unrealized gains or losses reported in the comparative statements and shareholders' equity?

5. Are unrealized gains or losses identifiable in the comparative balance sheets? If so, under what caption? Why are unrealized gains or losses reported here rather than in the income statements?

6. Are cash flow effects of these investments reflected in the company's comparative statements of cash flows? If so, what information is provided by this disclosure?

7. Does the footnote provide information not available in the financial statements?

Trueblood Accounting Case 12–3
Equity method
● LO3

The following Trueblood case is recommended for use with this chapter. The case provides an excellent opportunity for class discussion, group projects, and writing assignments. The case, along with Professor's Discussion Material, can be obtained from the Deloitte Foundation at its website: **www.deloitte.com/us/truebloodcases**.

Case: 03–10: Painless, Inc.

This case gives students an opportunity to discuss whether and how the equity method should ever be applied to preferred stock investments.

International Case 12–4
Comparison of equity method between IFRS and U.S. GAAP
● LO4 LO5
LO6 LO8

The following are excerpts from the 2008 financial statements of **Renault**, a large French automobile manufacturer.

Investment in Nissan: Renault holds 44.3% ownership in Nissan. Renault and Nissan have chosen to develop a unique type of alliance between two distinct companies with common interests, uniting forces to achieve optimum performance. The Alliance is organized so as to preserve individual brand identities and respect each company's corporate culture. Consequently:

- Renault does not hold the majority of Nissan voting rights;
- The terms of the Renault-Nissan agreements do not entitle Renault to appoint the majority of Nissan directors, nor to hold the majority of voting rights at meetings of Nissan's Board of Directors. . . .
- Renault can neither use nor influence the use of Nissan's assets in the same way as its own assets.
- Renault provides no guarantees in respect of Nissan's debt.

In view of this situation, Renault is considered to exercise significant influence in Nissan, and therefore uses the equity method to include its investment in Nissan in the consolidation. . . .

Nissan financial information under IFRS: (When accounting for its investment in Nissan, Renault makes restatements that) include adjustments for harmonization of accounting standards and the adjustments to fair value of assets and liabilities applied by Renault at the time of acquisitions in 1999 and 2002.

Required:

1. Go to Deloitte's IAS Plus website and examine the summary of the IASB's *IAS No. 28* (at **http://www.iasplus.com/standard/ias28.htm**), which governs application of the equity method. Focus on two areas: Identification of Associates and Applying the Equity Method of Accounting.

2. Evaluate Renault's decision to use the equity method to account for its investment in Nissan. Does Renault have insignificant influence, significant influence, or control?

3. Evaluate the fact that, when accounting for its investment in Nissan under the equity method, Renault makes adjustments that take into account the fair value of assets and liabilities at the time Renault invested in Nissan. Give an example of the sorts of adjustments that might be made. Are such adjustments consistent with IFRS? With U.S. GAAP? Explain.

4. Evaluate the fact that, when accounting for its investment in Nissan under the equity method, Renault makes adjustments for harmonization of accounting standards. Are such adjustments consistent with IFRS? With U.S. GAAP? Explain.

International Case 12–5
Comparison of equity method and proportionate consolidaton under IFRS
● LO5 LO8

Obtain the 2009 annual report of Vodafone (**www.vodafone.com**). Contrast the accounting approaches used in notes 13 for "investments in joint ventures" and 14 for "investments in associated undertakings." What are key similarities and differences?

Research Case 12–6
Researching the way investments are reported; retrieving information from the Internet
● LO1 LO2 LO3

All publicly traded domestic companies use EDGAR, the Electronic Data Gathering, Analysis, and Retrieval system, to make the majority of their filings with the SEC. You can access EDGAR at **www.sec.gov**.

Required:

1. Search for a public company with which you are familiar. Access its most recent 10-K filing. Search or scroll to find financial statements and related notes.

2. Answer the following questions. (If the chosen company does not report investments in the securities of other companies, choose another company.)

   a. What is the amount and classification of any investment securities reported in the balance sheet? Are unrealized gains or losses reported in the shareholders' equity section?

   b. Are any investments reported by the equity method?

   c. What amounts from these investments are reported in the comparative income statements? Has that income increased or decreased over the years reported?

   d. Are any acquisitions or disposals of investments reported in the statement of cash flows?

Real World Case 12–7
Merck's investments
● LO3 LO4 LO5

Corporations frequently invest in securities issued by other corporations. Some investments are acquired to secure a favorable business relationship with another company. On the other hand, others are intended only to earn an investment return from the dividends or interest the securities pay or from increases in the market prices of the securities—the same motivations that might cause you to invest in stocks, bonds, or other securities. This diversity in investment objectives means no single accounting method is adequate to report every investment.

Merck & Co., Inc. invests in securities of other companies. Access Merck's 2008 10-K (which includes financial statements) using EDGAR at **www.sec.gov**.

Required:

1. What is the amount and classification of any investment securities reported on the balance sheet? In which current and noncurrent asset categories are investments reported by Merck? What criteria are used to determine the classifications?

2. How are unrealized gains or losses reported? Realized gains and losses?

3. Are any investments reported by the equity method?

4. What amounts from equity method investments are reported in the comparative income statements?

5. Are cash flow effects of these investments reflected in the company's comparative statements of cash flows? If so, what information is provided by this disclosure?

Real World Case 12–8
Comprehensive income—Microsoft
● LO3

As required by GAAP [FASB ASC 320, previously *SFAS No. 115*], **Microsoft Corporation** reports its investments available-for-sale at the *fair value* of the investment securities. The *net* unrealized holding gain is not reported in the income statement. Instead, it's reported as part of Other comprehensive income and added to Accumulated other comprehensive income in shareholders' equity.

Comprehensive income is a broader view of the change in shareholders' equity than traditional net income, encompassing all changes in equity from nonowner transactions. Microsoft chose to report its Other comprehensive income as a separate statement in a disclosure note in its 2009 annual report.

NOTE 19 OTHER COMPREHENSIVE INCOME
The activity in other comprehensive income and related income tax effects were as follows:

(in millions)

Year Ended June 30	2009	2008	2007
Net unrealized gains on derivatives:			
Unrealized gains, net of tax effect of $472, $46, and $66	$ 876	$ 86	$ 123
Reclassification adjustment for gains included in net income, net of tax effect of $(309), $(36), and $(59)	(574)	(68)	(109)
Net unrealized gains on derivative	302	18	14
Net unrealized gains (losses) on investments:			
Unrealized gains (losses), net of tax effect of $(142), $(234), and $393	(263)	(435)	730
Reclassification adjustment for losses (gains) included in net income, net of tax effect of $16, $(117), and $(217)	30	(218)	(404)
Net unrealized gains (losses) on investments	(233)	(653)	326
Translation adjustments and other	(240)	121	85
Other comprehensive income (loss)	$(171)	$(514)	$ 425

The components of accumulated other comprehensive income were as follows:

(in millions)

Year Ended June 30	2009	2008	2007
Net unrealized gains on derivatives	$437	$ 135	$ 117
Net unrealized gains on investments	502	735	1,388
Translation adjustments and other	30	270	149
Accumulated other comprehensive income	$969	$1,140	$1,654

Required:

1. The note indicates Unrealized holding losses during 2009 in the amount of $(263) million. Is this the amount Microsoft would include as a separate component of shareholders' equity? Explain.

2. What does Microsoft mean by the term, "Reclassification adjustment for gains (losses) included in net income"?

Research Case 12–9
Changes in accounting for other-than-temporary impairments (Based on Appendix 12B)
● LO1 LO3

In Appendix 12B you learned that accounting for other-than-temporary impairments has changed recently. You also learned that these changes were controversial. In fact, two of the five members of the FASB voted against the changes and provided an explanation for their position when the standard that defined the changes was issued. That information isn't included in the FASB's Accounting Standards Codification, but you can find it in the original standard, "Recognition and Presentation of Other-Than-Temporary Impairments," FASB Staff Position (FSP) No. 115-2 and 124-2 (Norwalk, Conn.: FASB April 9, 2009), which is available under the "Standards" link at **www.FASB.org**.

Required:

Access the FSP and turn to p. 17, and read why FASB members Linsmeier and Siegel dissented. What were their major concerns with the new approach for accounting for OTT impairments? Do you find those concerns compelling?

BRITISH AIRWAYS CASE

BRITISH AIRWAYS

● LO8

British Airways, Plc. (BA), a U.K. company, prepares its financial statements according to International Financial Reporting Standards. BA's annual report for the year ended March 31, 2009, which includes financial statements and disclosure notes, is included with all new textbooks and can be found at **www.britishairways.com**. When answering questions, focus on BA's "Group" financial information (which is equivalent to "Consolidated" under U.S. GAAP).

Required:

1. How does BA account for "other current interest-bearing deposits"? Is that consistent with U.S. GAAP? What is the amount of those investments that are maturing after three months, as of March 31, 2009?

2. How does BA account for "available-for-sale assets"? Is that consistent with U.S. GAAP? What is the amount of those investments as of March 31, 2009?

3. How does BA account for its investments in associates? Is that accounting consistent with U.S. GAAP? Explain.

4. BA accounts for its investment in Iberia airline using the equity method, even though it only holds 13.15% of Iberia's equity. Is that approach consistent with U.S. GAAP? Explain.

5. (Appendix 12B) BA indicates that it sometimes recognizes impairments on held-to-maturity and available-for-sale investments. Describe how recognition of impairments could differ for IFRS and U.S. GAAP.

6. (Appendix 12B) BA recognized a £13 million impairment of their investment in Flybe for the year ended March 31, 2009. On what criteria did BA base their determination that the investment was impaired? Would that be handled similarly in U.S. GAAP?

CPA SIMULATION 12–1

Barbados Investments

Investments

CPA Review

Test your knowledge of the concepts discussed in this chapter, practice critical professional skills necessary for career success, and prepare for the computer-based CPA exam by accessing our CPA simulations at the text website: **www.mhhe.com/spiceland6e**.

The Barbados Investments simulation tests your knowledge of (a) the way we classify investment securities among the categories of trading securities, available-for-sale securities, and those held-to-maturity, (b) how we account for those investments, (c) the way accounting for investments affects comprehensive income, and (d) the appropriate use of the equity method.

As on the CPA exam itself, you will be asked to use tools including a spreadsheet, a calculator, and generally accepted accounting principles, to conduct research, derive solutions, and communicate conclusions related to these issues in a simulated environment.

Specific tasks in the simulation include:

- Analyzing various transactions involving investment securities and determining their appropriate balance sheet classification.
- Applying judgment in the application of the equity method.
- Determining the amount of interest revenue to be reported from a debt investment.
- Demonstrating an understanding of comprehensive income and how it is affected by investments in securities.
- Communicating the way we account for investments using the equity method.
- Researching the financial reporting ramifications of changing the classification of investment securities.

13 Current Liabilities and Contingencies

||||||||||||||||||||||||||||||||||||||||||||||||

/// **OVERVIEW**

With the discussion of investments in Chapter 12, we concluded our six-chapter coverage of assets that began in Chapter 7. Chapter 13 is the first of six chapters devoted to liabilities. Here we focus on short-term liabilities. Bonds and long-term notes are discussed in Chapter 14. Obligations relating to leases, income taxes, pensions, and other postretirement benefits are the subjects of the following four chapters. In Part A of this chapter, we discuss liabilities that are classified appropriately as current. In Part B we turn our attention to situations in which there is uncertainty as to whether an obligation really exists. These are designated as loss contingencies.

/// **LEARNING OBJECTIVES**

After studying this chapter, you should be able to:

● **LO1** Define liabilities and distinguish between current and long-term liabilities. (page 692)

● **LO2** Account for the issuance and payment of various forms of notes and record the interest on the notes. (page 695)

● **LO3** Characterize accrued liabilities and liabilities from advance collection and describe when and how they should be recorded. (page 697)

● **LO4** Determine when a liability can be classified as a noncurrent obligation. (page 702)

● **LO5** Identify situations that constitute contingencies and the circumstances under which they should be accrued. (page 706)

● **LO6** Demonstrate the appropriate accounting treatment for contingencies, including unasserted claims and assessments. (page 706)

● **LO7** Discuss the primary differences between U.S. GAAP and IFRS with respect to current liabilities and contingencies. (pages 704 and 716)

FINANCIAL REPORTING CASE

Dinstuhl's Dad

"My dad is confused," your friend Buzz Dinstuhl proclaimed at the office one morning. "You see, we're competing against each other in that investment game I told you about, and one of his hot investments is Syntel Microsystems. When he got the annual report yesterday afternoon, he started analyzing it, you know, really studying it closely. Then he asked me about this part here." Buzz pointed to the current liability section of the balance sheet and related disclosure note:

SYNTEL MICROSYSTEMS, INC.
Balance Sheet
December 31, 2011 and 2010
($ in millions)

Current Liabilities	2011	2010
Accounts payable	$233.5	$241.6
Short-term borrowings (Note 3)	187.0	176.8
Accrued liabilities	65.3	117.2
Accrued loss contingency	76.9	—
Other current liabilities	34.6	45.2
Current portion of long-term debt	44.1	40.3
Total current liabilities	$641.4	$621.1

Note 3: Short-Term Borrowings (in part)

The components of short-term borrowings and their respective weighted average interest rates at the end of the period are as follows:

$ in millions

	2011		2010	
	Amount	Average Interest Rate	Amount	Average Interest Rate
Commercial paper	$ 34.0	5.2%	$ 27.1	5.3%
Bank loans	218.0	5.5	227.7	5.6
Amount reclassified to long-term liabilities	(65.0)	—	(78.0)	—
Total short-term borrowings	$187.0		$176.8	

The Company maintains bank credit lines sufficient to cover outstanding short-term borrowings. As of December 31, 2011, the Company had $200.0 million fee-paid lines available.

At December 31, 2011 and 2010, the Company classified $65.0 million and $78.0 million, respectively, of commercial paper and bank notes as long-term debt. The Company has the intent and ability, through formal renewal agreements, to renew these obligations into future periods.

Note 6: Contingencies (in part)

Between 2009 and 2010, the Company manufactured cable leads that, the Company has learned, contribute to corrosion of linked components with which they are installed. At December 31, 2011, the Company accrued $132.0 million in anticipation of remediation and claims settlement deemed probable, of which $76.9 million is considered a current liability.

"So, what's the problem?" you asked.

"Well, he thinks I'm some sort of financial wizard because I'm in the business."

"And because you tell him so all the time," you interrupted.

"Maybe so, but he's been told that current liabilities are riskier than long-term liabilities, and now he's focusing on that. He can't see why some long-term debt is reported here in the current section. And it also looks like some is reported the other way around; some current liabilities reported as long term. Plus, the contingency amount seems like it's not even a contractual liability. Then he wants to know what some of those terms mean. Lucky for me, I had to leave before I had to admit I didn't know the answers. You're the accounting graduate; help me out."

By the time you finish this chapter, you should be able to respond appropriately to the questions posed in this case. Compare your response to the solution provided at the end of the chapter. **QUESTIONS ///**

1. What are accrued liabilities? What is commercial paper? (page 697)
2. Why did Syntel Microsystems include some long-term debt in the current liability section? (page 702)
3. Did they also report some current amounts as long-term debt? Explain. (page 703)
4. Must obligations be known contractual debts in order to be reported as liabilities? (page 706)
5. Is it true that current liabilities are riskier than long-term liabilities? (page 719)

PART A

CURRENT LIABILITIES

Liabilities and owners' equity accounts represent specific sources of a company's assets.

Before a business can invest in an asset it first must acquire the money to pay for it. This can happen in either of two ways—funds can be provided by owners or the funds must be borrowed. You may recognize this as a description of the basic accounting equation: liabilities and owners' equity on the right-hand side of the equation represent the two basic sources of the assets on the left-hand side. You studied assets in the chapters leading to this one and you will study owners' equity later. This chapter and the next four describe the various liabilities that constitute creditors' claims on a company's assets.

Characteristics of Liabilities

Most liabilities obligate the debtor to pay cash at specified times and result from legally enforceable agreements.

You already know what liabilities are. You encounter them every day. If you are paying for a car or a home with monthly payments, you have a personal liability. Similarly, when businesses issue notes and bonds, their creditors are the banks, individuals, and organizations that exchange cash for those securities. Each of these obligations represents the most common type of liability—one to be paid in cash and for which the amount and timing are specified by a legally enforceable contract.

Entities routinely incur most liabilities to acquire the funds, goods, and services they need to operate and just as routinely settle the liabilities they incur.[1]

Some liabilities are not contractual obligations and may not be payable in cash.

However, to be reported as a liability, an obligation need not be payable in cash. Instead, it may require the company to transfer other assets or to provide services. It also need not be represented by a written agreement nor be legally enforceable. Even the amount and timing of repayment need not be precisely known. From a financial reporting perspective, a liability has three essential characteristics. Liabilities:

● LO1

1. Are *probable, future* sacrifices of economic benefits.
2. Arise from *present* obligations (to transfer goods or provide services) to other entities.
3. Result from *past* transactions or events.[2]

---

[1]"Elements of Financial Statements," *Statement of Financial Accounting Concepts No. 6* (Stamford, Conn.: FASB, 1985), par. 38.
[2]Ibid.

Notice that the definition of a liability involves the present, the future, and the past. It is a present responsibility to sacrifice assets in the future because of a transaction or other event that already has happened.

Later in the chapter we'll discuss several liabilities that possess these characteristics but have elements of uncertainty regarding the amount and timing of payments and sometimes even their existence.

What Is a Current Liability?

In a classified balance sheet, we categorize liabilities as either current liabilities or long-term liabilities. We often characterize current liabilities as obligations payable within one year or within the firm's operating cycle, whichever is longer. This general definition usually applies. However, a more discriminating definition identifies current liabilities as those expected to be satisfied with *current assets* or by the creation of other *current liabilities*.[3]

Classifying liabilities as either current or long term helps investors and creditors assess the risk that the liabilities will require expenditure of cash or other assets in the near term. Is the due date years in the future, permitting resources to be used for other purposes without risking default or without compromising operating efficiency? Or, will payment require the use of current assets and reduce the amount of liquid funds available for other uses? If so, are sufficient liquid funds available to pay currently maturing obligations in addition to meeting current operating needs, or must additional funds be obtained by raising capital? The answers to these questions can have significant implications. For example, a major factor contributing to the collapse of the financial giant **Bear Stearns** in 2008 was the reliance on short-term debt that it couldn't refinance when lenders, clients, and trading partners grew concerned about the quality of Bear's investments.[4]

As you study the liabilities discussed in this chapter, you should be aware that a practical expediency usually affects the way current liabilities are reported on the balance sheet. Conceptually, liabilities should be recorded at their present values. In other words, the amount recorded is the present value of all anticipated future cash payments resulting from the debt (specifically, principal and interest payments). This is due to the time value of money.[5] However, in practice, liabilities payable within one year ordinarily are recorded instead at their maturity amounts.[6] The inconsistency usually is inconsequential because the relatively short-term maturity of current liabilities makes the interest or time value component immaterial.

The most common obligations reported as current liabilities are accounts payable, notes payable, commercial paper, income tax liability, dividends payable, and accrued liabilities. Liabilities related to income taxes are the subject of Chapter 16. We discuss the others here.

Before we examine specific current liabilities, let's use the current liability section of the balance sheet of **General Mills, Inc.,** and related disclosure notes to overview the chapter and to provide perspective on the liabilities we discuss (Graphic 13–1).

You may want to refer back to portions of Graphic 13–1 as corresponding liabilities are described later in the chapter. We discuss accounts payable and notes payable first.

Margin notes

Current liabilities are expected to require current assets and usually are payable within one year.

Classifying liabilities as either current or long term helps investors and creditors assess the relative risk of a business's liabilities.

Current liabilities ordinarily are reported at their maturity amounts.

Open Accounts and Notes

Many businesses buy merchandise or supplies on credit. Most also find it desirable to borrow cash from time to time to finance their activities. In this section we discuss the liabilities these borrowing activities create: namely, trade accounts and trade notes, bank loans, and commercial paper.

---

[3]FASB ASC Master Glossary (previously Committee on Accounting Procedure, American Institute of CPAs, *Accounting Research and Terminology Bulletin, Final Edition* (New York: AICPA, August 1961), p. 21).

[4]William D. Cohan, *House of Cards: A Tale of Hubris and Wretched Excess on Wall Street* (New York: Doubleday, 2009).

[5]The concepts of the time value of money and the mechanics of present value calculations are covered in Chapter 6.

[6]In fact, those arising in connection with suppliers in the normal course of business and due within a year are specifically exempted from present value reporting by FASB ASC 835–30–15–3: Interest—Imputation of Interest—Scope and Scope Exceptions (previously "Interest on Receivables and Payables," *Accounting Principles Board Opinion No. 21* (New York: AICPA, August 1971), par. 3).

GENERAL MILLS, INC.
Excerpt from Balance Sheet ($ in millions)
May 31, 2009 and May 25, 2008

Liabilities

Current Liabilities:	2009	2008
Accounts payable	$ 803	$ 937
Current portion of long-term debt	509	442
Notes payable	812	2,209
Deferred income taxes	—	28
Other current liabilities	1,482	1,240
Total current liabilities	$3,606	$4,856

8. Debt

Notes Payable The components of notes payable and their respective weighted average interest rates at the end of the period are as follows:

	2009		2008	
Dollars in millions:	**Note Payable**	**Weighted Average Interest Rate**	**Note Payable**	**Weighted Average Interest Rate**
U.S. commercial paper	$402	0.5%	$ 688	2.9%
Euro commercial paper	275	0.5	1,386	3.4
Financial institutions	135	12.9	135	9.6
Total notes payable	$812	2.6%	$2,209	3.6%

To ensure availability of funds, we maintain bank credit lines sufficient to cover our outstanding short-term borrowings. Commercial paper is a continuing source of short-term financing. We issue commercial paper in the United States, Canada, and Europe. Our commercial paper borrowings are supported by $2.9 billion of fee-paid committed credit lines, consisting of a $1.8 billion facility expiring in October 2012 and a $1.1 billion facility expiring in October 2010. We also have $401.9 million in uncommitted credit lines, which support our foreign operations. As of May 31, 2009, there were no amounts outstanding on the fee-paid committed credit lines and $134.7 million was drawn on the uncommitted lines.

Accounts Payable and Trade Notes Payable

Accounts payable are obligations to suppliers of merchandise or of services purchased on *open account.* Most trade credit is offered on open account. This means that the only formal credit instrument is the invoice. Because the time until payment usually is short (often 30, 45, or 60 days), these liabilities typically are noninterest-bearing and are reported at their face amounts. As shown in Graphic 13–1, General Mills's accounts payable in 2009 was $803 million. The key accounting considerations relating to accounts payable are determining their existence and ensuring that they are recorded in the appropriate accounting period. You studied these issues and learned how cash discounts are handled during your study of inventories in Chapter 8.

Trade notes payable differ from accounts payable in that they are formally recognized by a written promissory note. Often these are of a somewhat longer term than open accounts and bear interest.

Short-Term Notes Payable

The most common way for a corporation to obtain temporary financing is to arrange a short-term bank loan. When a company borrows cash from a bank and signs a promissory note (essentially an IOU), the firm's liability is reported as *notes payable* (sometimes *bank loans* or *short-term borrowings*). About two-thirds of bank loans are short term, but because many are routinely renewed, some tend to resemble long-term debt. In fact, in some cases we report them as long-term financing (as you'll see later in the chapter).

● LO2

Very often, smaller firms are unable to tap into the major sources of long-term financing to the extent necessary to provide for their capital needs. So they must rely heavily on short-term financing. Even large companies typically utilize short-term debt as a significant and indispensable component of their capital structure. One reason is that short-term funds usually offer lower interest rates than long-term debt. Perhaps most importantly, corporations desire flexibility. As a rule, managers want as many financing alternatives as possible.

CREDIT LINES. Usually short-term bank loans are arranged under an existing line of credit with a bank or group of banks. These can be noncommitted or committed lines of credit. A *noncommitted* line of credit is an informal agreement that permits a company to borrow up to a prearranged limit without having to follow formal loan procedures and paperwork. Banks sometimes require the company to maintain a compensating balance on deposit with the bank, say, 5% of the line of credit.[7] A *committed* line of credit is a more formal agreement that usually requires the firm to pay a commitment fee to the bank. A typical annual commitment fee is ¼% of the total committed funds, and may also require a compensating balance. A recent annual report of **IBM Corporation** illustrates a combination of committed and noncommitted lines of credit (Graphic 13–2).

A *line of credit* allows a company to borrow cash without having to follow formal loan procedures and paperwork.

GRAPHIC 13–2

Disclosure of Credit Lines—IBM Corporation

Real World Financials

K. Borrowings (in part)

LINES OF CREDIT: The company maintains a five-year, $10 billion Credit Agreement, which expires on June 28, 2012. The company's other lines of credit, most of which are uncommitted, totaled approximately $11,031 million and $9,992 million at December 31, 2008, and 2007, respectively. Interest rates and other terms of borrowing under these lines of credit vary from country to country, depending on local market conditions.

($ in millions)		
At December 31:	**2008**	**2007**
Unused lines:		
From the committed global credit facility	$ 9,888	$ 9,792
From other committed and uncommitted lines	8,376	7,895
TOTAL UNUSED LINES OF CREDIT	$18,264	$17,687

General Mills' disclosure notes that we looked at in Graphic 13–1 indicate that the company has both noncommitted and committed lines of credit.

INTEREST. When a company borrows money, it pays the lender interest in return for using the lender's money during the term of the loan. You might think of the interest as the "rent" paid for using money. Interest is stated in terms of a percentage rate to be applied to the face amount of the loan. Because the stated rate typically is an annual rate, when calculating interest for a short-term note we must adjust for the fraction of the annual period the loan spans. Interest on notes is calculated as:

$$\text{Face amount} \times \text{Annual rate} \times \text{Time to maturity}$$

This is demonstrated in Illustration 13–1.

---

[7]A compensating balance is a deposit kept by a company in a low-interest or noninterest-bearing account at the bank. The required deposit usually is some percentage of the committed amount or the amount used (say, 2% to 5%). The effect of the compensating balance is to increase the borrower's effective interest rate and the bank's effective rate of return.

ILLUSTRATION 13–1 Note Issued for Cash	On May 1, Affiliated Technologies, Inc., a consumer electronics firm borrowed $700,000 cash from First BancCorp under a noncommitted short-term line of credit arrangement and issued a six-month, 12% promissory note. Interest was payable at maturity.		
	May 1		
	Cash	700,000	
	Notes payable		700,000
Interest on notes is calculated as:	**November 1**		
Face amount $\times$ Annual rate $\times$ Time to maturity	Interest expense ($700,000 $\times$ 12% $\times$ 6/12)	42,000	
	Notes payable	700,000	
	Cash ($700,000 + 42,000)		742,000

Sometimes a bank loan assumes the form of a so-called noninterest-bearing note. Obviously, though, no bank will lend money without interest. Noninterest-bearing loans actually do bear interest, but the interest is deducted (or discounted) from the face amount to determine the cash proceeds made available to the borrower at the outset. For example, the preceding note could be packaged as a $700,000 noninterest-bearing note, with a 12% discount rate. In that case, the $42,000 interest would be discounted at the outset, rather than explicitly stated:[8]

The proceeds of the note are reduced by the interest in a noninterest-bearing note.	**May 1**	
	Cash (difference)	658,000	
	Discount on notes payable ($700,000 $\times$ 12% $\times$ 6/12)	42,000	
	Notes payable (face amount)		700,000
	November 1		
	Interest expense..	42,000	
	Discount on notes payable..		42,000
	Notes payable (face amount)	700,000	
	Cash		700,000

Notice that the amount borrowed under this arrangement is only $658,000, but the interest is calculated as the discount rate times the $700,000 face amount. This causes the *effective* interest rate to be higher than the 12% stated rate:

When interest is discounted from the face amount of a note, the effective interest rate is higher than the stated discount rate.

$$\frac{\$42{,}000 \text{ Interest for 6 months}}{\$658{,}000 \text{ Amount borrowed}} = 6.38\% \text{ Rate for 6 months}$$

To annualize:

$$6.38\% \times 12/6 = 12.76\% \text{ Effective interest rate}$$

We studied short-term notes from the perspective of the lender (note receivable) in Chapter 7.

Inventory or accounts receivable often are pledged as security for short-term loans.

SECURED LOANS. Sometimes short-term loans are *secured*, meaning a specified asset of the borrower is pledged as collateral or security for the loan. Although many kinds of assets can be pledged, the secured loans most frequently encountered in practice are secured by inventory or accounts receivable. For example, **Collins Industries, Inc.**, which sells vehicle chassis to major vehicle manufacturers, disclosed the secured notes described in Graphic 13–3.

---

[8]Be sure to understand that we are actually recording the note at 658,000, *not* 700,000, but are recording the interest portion separately in a contra-liability account, discount on notes payable. The entries shown reflect the gross method. By the net method, the interest component is netted against the face amount of the note as follows:

May 1		
Cash	658,000	
Notes payable		658,000
November 1		
Interest expense ($700,000 $\times$ 12% $\times$ 6/12)	42,000	
Notes payable	658,000	
Cash		700,000

GRAPHIC 13–3

Disclosure of Notes Secured by Inventory— Collins Industries, Inc.

Real World Financials

Note 4: Chassis Floorplan Notes Payable (in part)

Chassis floorplan notes are payable to a financing subsidiary of a chassis manufacturer. These notes are secured by the related chassis and are payable upon the earlier of the date the Company sells the chassis or 180 days from the date of the note.

When accounts receivable serve as collateral, we refer to the arrangement as *pledging* accounts receivable. Sometimes, the receivables actually are sold outright to a finance company as a means of short-term financing. This is called *factoring* receivables.[9]

Commercial Paper

Some large corporations obtain temporary financing by issuing commercial paper, often purchased by other companies as a short-term investment. Commercial paper refers to unsecured notes sold in minimum denominations of $25,000 with maturities ranging from 30 to 270 days (beyond 270 days the firm would be required to file a registration statement with the SEC). Interest often is discounted at the issuance of the note. Usually commercial paper is issued directly to the buyer (lender) and is backed by a line of credit with a bank. This allows the interest rate to be lower than in a bank loan. Commercial paper has become an increasingly popular way for large companies to raise funds, the total amount having expanded over fivefold in the last decade. In fact, large companies have become so dependent on obtaining financing through the commercial paper market that a freeze-up of that market contributed to a global economic crisis in 2008.[10]

A disclosure note in the March 31, 2009, 10Q of **GMAC Financial Services** describes the challenges it was facing from a combination of a tight commercial paper market and a poor credit rating, as shown in Graphic 13–4.

> Large, highly rated firms sometimes sell *commercial paper* to borrow funds at a lower rate than through a bank loan.

GRAPHIC 13–4

Disclosure of Commercial Paper Backed by a Line of Credit—GMAC Financial Services.

Real World Financials

12. Short-Term Debt (in part)

We obtain short-term funding from the sale of floating-rate demand notes under our Demand Notes program. These notes can be redeemed at any time at the option of the holder without restriction. Our domestic and international unsecured and secured commercial paper programs also provide short-term funding, as do short-term bank loans. Renewing our short-term debt maturities, particularly unsecured debt, including Demand Notes, continues to be challenging due to the heightened credit market turmoil and our credit-rating profile.

The name *commercial paper* refers to the fact that a paper certificate traditionally is issued to the lender to signify the obligation, although there is a trend toward total computerization of paper sold directly to the lender so that no paper is created. Since commercial paper is a form of notes payable, recording its issuance and payment is exactly the same as our earlier illustration.

In a statement of cash flows, the cash a company receives from using short-term notes to borrow funds as well as the cash it uses to repay the notes are reported among cash flows from financing activities. Most of the other liabilities we study in this chapter, such as accounts payable, interest payable, and bonuses payable, are integrally related to a company's primary operations and thus are part of operating activities. We discuss long-term notes in the next chapter.

> **FINANCIAL**
> **Reporting Case**
>
> Q1, p. 692

Accrued Liabilities

Accrued liabilities represent expenses already incurred but not yet paid (accrued expenses). These liabilities are recorded by adjusting entries at the end of the reporting period, prior to preparing financial statements. You learned how to record accrued liabilities in your study of

● LO3

---

[9]Both methods of accounts receivable financing are discussed in Chapter 7, "Cash and Receivables."
[10]Alan Greenspan, "Finance and Economics: Banks Need More Capital," *The Economist*, December 20, 2008, p. 122.

introductory accounting and you reinforced your understanding in Chapter 2. Common examples are salaries and wages payable, income taxes payable, and interest payable. Although recorded in separate liability accounts, accrued liabilities usually are combined and reported under a single caption or perhaps two accrued liability captions in the balance sheet. General Mills includes accrued liabilities in other liabilities (totaling $1,482 as of May 31, 2009).

Accrued Interest Payable

Liabilities accrue for expenses that are incurred but not yet paid.

Accrued interest payable arises in connection with notes like those discussed earlier in this chapter (as well as other forms of debt). For example, to continue Illustration 13–1, let's assume the fiscal period for Affiliated Technologies ends on June 30, two months after the six-month note is issued. The issuance of the note, intervening adjusting entry, and note payment would be recorded as shown in Illustration 13–1A.

ILLUSTRATION 13–1A

Note with Accrued Interest

At June 30, two months' interest has accrued and is recorded to avoid misstating expenses and liabilities on the June 30 financial statements.

Issuance of Note on May 1		
Cash	700,000	
Note payable		700,000
Accrual of Interest on June 30		
Interest expense ($700,000 × 12% × 2/12)	14,000	
Interest payable		14,000
Note Payment on November 1		
Interest expense ($700,000 × 12% × 4/12)	28,000	
Interest payable (from adjusting entry)	14,000	
Note payable	700,000	
Cash ($700,000 + 42,000)		742,000

Salaries, Commissions, and Bonuses

Compensation for employee services can be in the form of hourly wages, salary, commissions, bonuses, stock compensation plans, or pensions.[11] Accrued liabilities arise in connection with compensation expense when employee services have been performed as of a financial statement date, but employees have yet to be paid. These accrued expenses/accrued liabilities are recorded by adjusting entries at the end of the reporting period, prior to preparing financial statements.

VACATIONS, SICK DAYS, AND OTHER PAID FUTURE ABSENCES. Suppose a firm grants two weeks of paid vacation each year to nonsalaried employees. Some take their vacations during the year earned and are compensated then. Some wait. Is the compensation an expense during the year for only those who actually are paid that year for their absence? When you recall what you've learned about accrual accounting, you probably conclude otherwise.

An employer should accrue an expense and the related liability for employees' compensation for future absences (such as vacation pay) if the obligation meets *all* of the four conditions listed in Graphic 13–5.

GRAPHIC 13–5

Conditions for Accrual of Paid Future Absences

1. The obligation is attributable to employees' services already performed.
2. The paid absence can be taken in a later year—the benefit vests (will be compensated even if employment is terminated) or the benefit can be accumulated over time.
3. Payment is probable.
4. The amount can be reasonably estimated.

If these conditions look familiar, it's because they are simply the characteristics of a liability we discussed earlier, adapted to relate to a potential obligation for future absences of employees. Also, these conditions are consistent with the requirement that we accrue loss contingencies only when the obligation is both (a) probable and (b) can be reasonably estimated, as discussed in Part B of this chapter.

---

[11]We discuss pensions in Chapter 17 and share-based compensation plans in Chapter 19.

The liability for paid absences usually is accrued at the existing wage rate rather than at a rate estimated to be in effect when absences occur.[12] So, if wage rates have risen, the difference between the accrual and the amount paid increases compensation expense that year. This situation is demonstrated in Illustration 13–2, in which vacation time carried over from 2011 is taken in 2012 and the actual amount paid to employees is $5,700,000:

ILLUSTRATION 13–2
Paid Future Absences

Davidson-Getty Chemicals has 8,000 employees. Each employee earns two weeks of paid vacation per year. Vacation time not taken in the year earned can be carried over to subsequent years. During 2011, 2,500 employees took both weeks' vacation, but at the end of the year, 5,500 employees had vacation time carryovers as follows:

Employees	Vacation Weeks Earned but Not Taken	Total Carryover Weeks
2,500	0	0
2,000	1	2,000
3,500	2	7,000
8,000		9,000

During 2011, compensation averaged $600 a week per employee.

When Vacations Were Taken in 2011

Salaries and wages expense (2,500 × 2 wks. × $600) +		
(2,000 × 1 wk. × $600)	4,200,000	
Cash (or wages payable)		4,200,000

December 31, 2011 (adjusting entry)

Salaries and wages expense (9,000 carryover weeks × $600)	5,400,000	
Liability—compensated future absences		5,400,000

When the necessary conditions are met, compensated future absences are accrued in the year the compensation is earned.

When Year 2011 Vacations Are Taken in 2012

Liability—compensated future absences (account balance)	5,400,000	
Salaries and wages expense (difference)	300,000	
Cash (or salaries and wages payable) (given)		5,700,000

Company policy and actual practice should be considered when deciding whether the rights to payment for absences have been earned by services already rendered. Consider an illustrative situation. Suppose scientists in a private laboratory are eligible for paid sabbaticals every seven years. Should a liability be accrued at the end of a scientist's sixth year? No—if sabbatical leave is granted only to perform research beneficial to the employer. Yes—if past practice indicates that sabbatical leave is intended to provide unrestricted compensated absence for past service and other conditions are met.

Customary practice should be considered when deciding whether an obligation exists.

Custom and practice also influence whether unused rights to paid absences expire or can be carried forward. Obviously, if rights vest (payable even if employment is terminated) they haven't expired. But holiday time, military leave, maternity leave, and jury time typically do not accumulate if unused, so a liability for those benefits usually is not accrued. On the other hand, if it's customary that a particular paid absence, say holiday time, can be carried forward—if employees work on holidays, in this case—a liability is accrued if it's probable that employees will be compensated in a future year.

Interestingly, sick pay quite often meets the conditions for accrual, but accrual is not mandatory because future absence depends on future illness, which usually is not a certainty. Similar to other forms of paid absences, the decision of whether to accrue nonvesting sick pay should be based on actual policy and practice. If company policy or custom is that employees are paid sick pay even when their absences are not due to illness, it's appropriate to record a liability for unused sick pay. For example, some companies routinely allow unused sick pay benefits to be accumulated and paid at retirement (or to beneficiaries if

Accrual of sick pay is not required, but may be appropriate in some circumstances.

---

[12]Actually, FASB ASC 710–10–25: Compensation–General–Overall–Recognition (previously *SFAS 43*, "Accounting for Compensated Absences") is silent on how the liability should be measured. In practice, most companies accrue at the current rate because it avoids estimates and usually produces a lower expense and liability. Then, later, they remeasure periodically at updated rates.

death comes before retirement). If each condition is met except that the company finds it impractical to reasonably estimate the amount of compensation for future absences, a disclosure note should describe the situation.

ANNUAL BONUSES.   Sometimes compensation packages include annual bonuses tied to performance objectives designed to provide incentive to executives. The most common performance measures are earnings per share, net income, and operating income, each being used by about a quarter of firms having bonus plans. Nonfinancial performance measures, such as customer satisfaction and product or service quality, also are used.[13] In recent years, annual bonuses have been gaining in popularity, not just for executives, but for nonmanagerial personnel as well. Unfortunately for employees, bonuses often take the place of annual raises. This allows a company to increase employee pay without permanently locking in the increases in salaries. Bonuses are compensation expense of the period in which they are earned.

Liabilities from Advance Collections

Liabilities are created when amounts are received that will be returned or remitted to others. Deposits and advances from customers and collections for third parties are cases in point.

Deposits and Advances from Customers

Collecting cash from a customer as a refundable deposit or as an advance payment for products or services creates a liability to return the deposit or to supply the products or services.[14]

REFUNDABLE DEPOSITS.   In some businesses it's typical to require customers to pay cash as a deposit that will be refunded when a specified event occurs. You probably have encountered such situations. When apartments are rented, security or damage deposits often are collected. Utility companies frequently collect deposits when service is begun. Similarly, deposits sometimes are required on returnable containers, to be refunded when the containers are returned. The situation is demonstrated in Illustration 13–3.

ILLUSTRATION 13–3 Refundable Deposits	Rancor Chemical Company sells combustible chemicals in expensive, reusable containers. Customers are charged a deposit for each container delivered and receive a refund when the container is returned. Deposits collected on containers delivered during the year were $300,000. Deposits are forfeited if containers are not returned within one year. Ninety percent of the containers were returned within the allotted time. Deposits charged are twice the actual cost of containers. The inventory of containers remains on the company's books until deposits are forfeited.		

When Deposits Are Collected
Cash	300,000	
Liability—refundable deposits		300,000

When Containers Are Returned*
Liability—refundable deposits	270,000	
Cash		270,000

When Deposits Are Forfeited*
Liability—refundable deposits	30,000	
Revenue—sale of containers		30,000
Cost of goods sold	15,000	
Inventory of containers		15,000

*Of course, not all containers are returned at the same time, nor does the allotted return period expire at the same time for all containers not returned. These entries summarize the several individual returns and forfeitures.

---

[13]C. D. Ittner, D. F. Larker, and M. V. Rajan, "The Choice of Performance Measures in Annual Bonus Contracts," Working Paper, The Wharton School, University of Pennsylvania (August 1995).
[14]*SFAC 6* specifically identifies customer advances and deposits as liabilities under the definition provided in that statement. "Elements of Financial Statements," *Statement of Financial Accounting Concepts No. 6* (Stamford, Conn.: FASB, 1985), par. 197.

ADVANCES FROM CUSTOMERS.   At times, businesses require advance payments from customers that will be applied to the purchase price when goods are delivered or services provided. Gift certificates, magazine subscriptions, layaway deposits, special order deposits, and airline tickets are examples. These customer advances, also called *unearned revenue* or *deferred revenue,* represent liabilities until the related product or service is provided. For instance, one of the largest liabilities reported by **Readers Digest Association, Inc.,** is deferred revenue from the sale of magazine subscriptions ($379 million in 2008). Advances are demonstrated in Illustration 13–4.

Tomorrow Publications collects magazine subscriptions from customers at the time subscriptions are sold. Subscription revenue is recognized over the term of the subscription. Tomorrow collected $20 million in subscription sales during its first year of operations. At December 31, the average subscription was one-fourth expired.			**ILLUSTRATION 13–4** Customer Advance
		($ in millions)	
When Advance Is Collected			
Cash	20		A customer advance produces an obligation that is satisfied when the product or service is provided.
Unearned subscriptions revenue		20	
When Product Is Delivered			
Unearned subscriptions revenue	5		
Subscriptions revenue		5	

This illustration highlights that unearned revenue gets reduced when the revenue associated with the advance has been earned, either because the seller has delivered the goods or services as promised or because the buyer has forfeited the advance payment (for example, not redeeming a gift certificate before it expires). Less often, unearned revenue is reduced when an advance payment is returned by the seller to the buyer because the seller didn't deliver the goods or services as promised. This should sound familiar—recall from Chapter 5 that revenue recognition must be delayed if the seller hasn't delivered. When revenue recognition is delayed, but some advanced payment is received, the seller reports an unearned revenue liability until delivery has occurred.

Gift Cards

Gift cards or gift certificates are particularly common forms of advanced payments. When a company sells a gift card, it initially records the cash received as unearned revenue, and then recognizes revenue either when the gift card is redeemed or when the probability of redemption is viewed as remote (based on expiration or the company's experience). Graphic 13–6 provides an example from **Best Buy**'s 2009 Annual Report.

Note 1: Summary of Significant Accounting Policies (in part) **Gift Cards** We sell gift cards to our customers in our retail stores, through our Web sites, and through selected third parties. We do not charge administrative fees on unused gift cards, and our gift cards do not have an expiration date. We recognize revenue from gift cards when: (i) the gift card is redeemed by the customer, or (ii) the likelihood of the gift card being redeemed by the customer is remote ("gift card breakage"), and we determine that we do not have a legal obligation to remit the value of unredeemed gift cards to the relevant jurisdictions. We determine our gift card breakage rate based upon historical redemption patterns. Based on our historical information, the likelihood of a gift card remaining unredeemed can be determined 24 months after the gift card is issued. At that time, we recognize breakage income for those cards for which the likelihood of redemption is deemed remote and we do not have a legal obligation to remit the value of such unredeemed gift cards to the relevant jurisdictions. Gift card breakage income is included in revenue in our consolidated statements of earnings.	**GRAPHIC 13–6** Gift Cards—Best Buy, Inc. **Real World Financials**

Unearned revenue liability accounts produced by customer deposits and advances are classified as current or long-term liabilities depending on when the obligation is expected to be satisfied.

Collections for Third Parties

Companies often make collections for third parties from customers or from employees and periodically remit these amounts to the appropriate governmental (or other) units. Amounts collected this way represent liabilities until remitted.

An example is sales taxes. For illustration, assume a state sales tax rate of 4% and local sales tax rate of 3%. Adding the tax to a $100 sale creates a $7 liability until the tax is paid:

Cash (or accounts receivable)	107	
Sales revenue		100
Sales taxes payable ([4% + 3%] × $100)		7

Sales taxes collected from customers represent liabilities until remitted.

Amounts collected from employees in connection with payroll also represent liabilities until remitted.

Payroll-related deductions such as withholding taxes, Social Security taxes, employee insurance, employee contributions to retirement plans, and union dues also create current liabilities until the amounts collected are paid to appropriate parties. These payroll-related liabilities are discussed further in the appendix to this chapter.

A Closer Look at the Current and Noncurrent Classification

● **LO4**

Given a choice, do you suppose management would prefer to report an obligation as a current liability or as a noncurrent liability? Other things being equal, most would choose the noncurrent classification. The reason is that in most settings outsiders (like banks, bond-holders, and shareholders) consider debt that is payable currently to be riskier than debt that need not be paid for some time, because the current payable requires the company to be able to access the necessary cash relatively soon. Relatedly, the long-term classification enables the company to report higher working capital (current assets minus current liabilities) and a higher current ratio (current assets/current liabilities). Working capital and the current ratio often are explicitly restricted in loan contracts. As you study this section, you should view the classification choice from this perspective. That is, a manager might not so much ask the question "What amount should I report as a current liability?" but rather "What amount can I exclude from classification as a current liability?"

Current Maturities of Long-Term Debt

FINANCIAL **Reporting Case**

Q2, p. 692

The currently maturing portion of a long-term debt must be reported as a current liability.

Long-term obligations (bonds, notes, lease liabilities, deferred tax liabilities) usually are reclassified and reported as current liabilities when they become payable within the upcoming year (or operating cycle, if longer than a year). For example, a 20-year bond issue is reported as a long-term liability for 19 years but normally is reported as a current liability on the balance sheet prepared during the 20th year of its term to maturity.[15] General Mills reported $509 million of its long-term debt as a current liability in 2009 (see Graphic 13–1, page 694).

Obligations Callable by the Creditor

The requirement to classify currently maturing debt as a current liability includes debt that is *callable* (in other words, due on demand) *by the creditor* in the upcoming year (or operating cycle, if longer), even if the debt is not expected to be called. The current liability classification also is intended to include situations in which the creditor has the right to demand payment because an *existing violation* of a provision of the debt agreement makes it callable (say, working capital has fallen below a minimum specified by a debt agreement). This also includes situations in which debt is not yet callable but will be callable within the year if an

---

[15]Debt to be refinanced is an exception we discuss later.

existing violation is not corrected within a specified grace period (unless it's probable the violation will be corrected within the grace period or waived by the creditor).[16]

When Short-Term Obligations Are Expected to Be Refinanced

Reconsider the 20-year bond issue we discussed earlier. Normally we would reclassify it as a current liability on the balance sheet prepared during its 20th year. But suppose a second 20-year bond issue is sold specifically to refund the first issue when it matures. Do we have a long-term liability for 19 years, then a current liability in year 20, and then another long-term liability in years 21 and beyond? Or, do we have a single 40-year, long-term liability? If we look beyond the outward form of the transactions, the substance of the events obviously supports a single, continuing, noncurrent obligation. The concept of substance over form influences the classification of obligations expected to be refinanced.

Short-term obligations (including the callable obligations we discussed in the previous section) that are expected to be refinanced on a long-term basis can be reported as noncurrent, rather than current, liabilities only if two conditions are met:

(1)   the firm must intend to refinance on a long-term basis, and
(2)   the firm must actually have demonstrated the ability to refinance on a long-term basis.

Ability to refinance on a long-term basis can be demonstrated by either an existing refinancing agreement or by actual financing prior to the issuance of the financial statements.[17] An example will provide perspective (Illustration 13–5).

FINANCIAL Reporting Case

Q3, p. 692

Short-term obligations can be reported as noncurrent liabilities if the company (a) *intends* to refinance on a long-term basis and (b) demonstrates the *ability* to do so by a refinancing agreement or by actual financing.

Brahm Bros. Ice Cream had $12 million of notes that mature in May 2012 and also had $4 million of bonds issued in 1982 that mature in February 2012. On December 31, 2011, the company's fiscal year-end, management intended to refinance both on a long-term basis.

On February 7, 2012, the company issued $4 million of 20-year bonds, applying the proceeds to repay the bond issue that matured that month. In early March, prior to the actual issuance of the 2011 financial statements, Brahm Bros. negotiated a line of credit with a commercial bank for up to $7 million any time during 2012. Any borrowings will mature two years from the date of borrowing. Interest is at the prime London interbank borrowing rate.*

	December 31, 2011
Classification	($ in 000s)
Current Liabilities	
Notes payable	$5,000
Long-Term Liabilities	
Notes payable	$7,000
Bonds payable	4,000

Management's ability to refinance the bonds on a long-term basis was demonstrated by actual financing prior to the issuance of the financial statements. Ability to refinance $7 million of the notes is demonstrated by a refinancing agreement. The remaining $5 million must be reported as a current liability.

ILLUSTRATION 13–5
Short-Term Obligations that Are Expected to Be Refinanced on a Long-Term Basis

*This is a widely available rate often used as a basis for establishing interest rates on lines of credit and often abbreviated as LIBOR.

If shares of stock had been issued to refinance the bonds in the illustration, the bonds still would be excluded from classification as a current liability. The specific form of the long-term refinancing (bonds, bank loans, equity securities) is irrelevant when determining the appropriate classification. Requiring companies to actually demonstrate the ability to refinance on a long-term basis in addition to merely intending to do so avoids intentional or unintentional understatements of current liabilities.

---

[16]FASB ASC 470–10–45: Debt–Overall–Other Presentation Matters (previously "Classification of Obligations That Are Callable by the Creditor," *Statement of Financial Accounting Standards No. 78* (Stamford, Conn · FASB, 1983)).

[17]FASB ASC 470–10–45–14: Debt Overall–Other Presentation Matters (previously "Classification of Obligations Expected to Be Refinanced," *Statement of Financial Accounting Standards No. 6* (Stamford, Conn.: FASB, 1975)).

It's important to remember that several weeks usually pass between the end of a company's fiscal year and the date the financial statements for that year actually are issued. Events occurring during that period can be used to clarify the nature of financial statement elements at the reporting date. Here we consider refinancing agreements and actual securities transactions to support a company's ability to refinance on a long-term basis. Later in the chapter we use information that becomes available during this period to decide how loss contingencies are reported.

● LO7

INTERNATIONAL FINANCIAL REPORTING STANDARDS

Classification of Liabilities to be Refinanced. Under U.S. GAAP, liabilities payable within the coming year are classified as long-term liabilities if refinancing is completed before the date of issuance of the financial statements. Under IFRS, refinancing must be completed before the balance sheet date.[18]

WHERE WE'RE HEADED

As discussed more in Chapters 4 and 21, the FASB and IASB have a performance reporting project under way that could dramatically change the format of the financial statements.[19] Among the changes that may occur are the specific rules determining whether a liability is classified as short or long term. The Boards' *Preliminary Views* statement indicates that they are considering defining "short term" as one year, regardless of the length of a company's operating cycle.

CONCEPT REVIEW EXERCISE

**CURRENT
LIABILITIES**

The following selected transactions relate to liabilities of Southern Communications, Inc., for portions of 2011 and 2012. Southern's fiscal year ends on December 31.

Required:
Prepare the appropriate journal entries for these transactions.

2011

July 1   Arranged an uncommitted short-term line of credit with First City Bank amounting to $25,000,000 at the bank's prime rate (11.5% in July). The company will pay no commitment fees for this arrangement.

Aug. 9   Received a $30,000 refundable deposit from a major customer for copper-lined mailing containers used to transport communications equipment.

Oct. 7   Received most of the mailing containers covered by the refundable deposit and a letter stating that the customer will retain containers represented by $2,000 of the deposit and forfeits that amount. The cost of the forfeited containers was $1,500.

Nov. 1   Borrowed $7 million cash from First City Bank under the line of credit arranged in July and issued a nine-month promissory note. Interest at the prime rate of 12% was payable at maturity.

Dec. 31   Recorded appropriate adjusting entries for the liabilities described above.

[18]"Presentation of Financial Statements" *International Accounting Standard No. 1* (IASCF), as amended effective January 1, 2009.
[19]Discussion Paper, Preliminary Views on Financial Statement Presentation, FASB/IASB, October 16, 2008.

2012

Feb. 12   Using the unused portion of the credit line as support, issued $9 million of commercial paper and issued a six-month promissory note. Interest was discounted at issuance at a 10% discount rate.

Aug. 1   Paid the 12% note at maturity.

    12   Paid the commercial paper at maturity.

2011

July 1

No entry is made for a line of credit until a loan actually is made. The existence and terms of the line would be described in a disclosure note.

August 9

Cash	30,000	
Liability—refundable deposits		30,000

October 7

Liability—refundable deposits	30,000	
Cash		28,000
Revenue—sale of containers		2,000
Cost of goods sold	1,500	
Inventory of containers		1,500

November 1

Cash	7,000,000	
Notes payable		7,000,000

December 31

Interest expense ($7,000,000 × 12% × 2/12)	140,000	
Interest payable		140,000

2012

February 12

Cash ($9,000,000 − [$9,000,000 × 10% × 6/12])	8,550,000	
Discount on notes payable (difference)	450,000	
Note payable		9,000,000

Note that the effective interest rate is
[($9,000,000 × 10% × 6/12) ÷ $8,550,000] × 12/6 = $450,000 ÷ $8,550,000 × 2 = 10.53%

August 1

Interest expense ($7,000,000 × 12% × 7/12)	490,000	
Interest payable (from adjusting entry)	140,000	
Note payable (face amount)	7,000,000	
Cash ($7,000,000 + $630,000)		7,630,000

August 12

Interest expense ($9,000,000 × 10% × 6/12)	450,000	
Discount on notes payable		450,000
Note payable (face amount)	9,000,000	
Cash ($8,550,000 + $450,000)		9,000,000

CONTINGENCIES

PART B

The feature that distinguishes the loss contingencies we discuss in this part of the chapter from the liabilities we discussed previously is uncertainty as to whether an obligation really exists. The circumstance giving rise to the contingency already has occurred, but there is uncertainty about whether a liability exists that will be resolved only when some future event occurs (or doesn't occur). We also discuss gain contingencies because of their similarity to loss contingencies.

Loss Contingencies

Flextronics International Limited's 2009 financial statements indicated potential obligations from pending lawsuits (shown in Graphic 13–7).

> **Note 7: Commitments and Contingencies (in part)**
>
> The Company is subject to legal proceedings, claims, and litigation arising in the ordinary course of business. The Company defends itself vigorously against any such claims. Although the outcome of these matters is currently not determinable, management does not expect that the ultimate costs to resolve these matters will have a material adverse effect on its consolidated financial position, results of operations, or cash flows.

These "legal proceedings, claims, and litigation" all relate to situations that already have occurred (for example, selling an electronic component with an alleged defect). However, it is not clear that these situations have given rise to liabilities, because Flextronics doesn't know if the situation will result in future payments. Certainly the liabilities *may* exist on the date of the financial statements, given that very large expenditures could result from some outcomes. But how likely is an unfavorable outcome? Also, precise amounts of Flextronics' potential obligation are not known, but can they be estimated reliably? These are the key questions addressed by accounting standards for loss contingencies.

● **LO5**

A *loss contingency* involves an existing uncertainty as to whether a loss really exists, where the uncertainty will be resolved only when some future event occurs.

A loss contingency is an existing, uncertain situation involving potential loss depending on whether some future event occurs. Whether a contingency is accrued and reported as a liability depends on (a) the likelihood that the confirming event will occur and (b) what can be determined about the amount of loss. Consider an EPA investigation of possible violation of clean air laws, pending at year-end, and for which the outcome will not be known until after the financial statements are issued. The likelihood must be assessed that the company will pay penalties, and if so, what the payment amount will be.

Note that the event that gives rise to the potential liability must occur before the financial statement date. Otherwise, regardless of the likelihood of the eventual outcome, no liability could have existed at the statement date. Remember, one of the essential characteristics of a liability is that it results "from past transactions or events."

FINANCIAL
Reporting Case

Q4, p. 692

Likelihood That a Liability Exists

Generally accepted accounting principles require that the likelihood that the future event(s) will confirm the incurrence of the liability be (somewhat arbitrarily) categorized as probable, reasonably possible, or remote:[20]

Probable	Confirming event is likely to occur.
Reasonably possible	The chance the confirming event will occur is more than remote but less than likely.
Remote	The chance the confirming event will occur is slight.

● **LO6**

A loss contingency is accrued only if a loss is probable and the amount can reasonably be estimated.

Accrual of a Loss Contingency—Liability

Also key to reporting a contingent liability is its dollar amount. The amount of the potential loss is classified as either known, reasonably estimable, or not reasonably estimable.

A liability is accrued if it is both probable that the confirming event will occur and the amount can be at least reasonably estimated. A general depiction of the accrual of a loss contingency is:

Loss (or expense)	x,xxx	
Liability		x,xxx

---

[20]Because FASB ASC 740–10–25: Income Taxes–Overall–Recognition (previously "Accounting for Uncertainty in Income Taxes," *FASB Interpretation No. 48* (Norwalk, Conn.: FASB, 2006)) provides guidance on accounting for uncertainty in income taxes, FASB ASC 450–10: Contingencies–Loss Contingencies (previously *SFAS No. 5*) no longer applies to income taxes. GAAP regarding uncertainty in income taxes changes the threshold for recognition of tax positions from the most probable amount to the amount that has a "more likely than not" chance of being sustained upon examination. We discuss accounting for uncertainty in income taxes in Chapter 16.

If one amount within a range of possible loss appears better than other amounts within the range, that amount is accrued. When no amount within the range appears more likely than others, the minimum amount should be recorded and the possible additional loss should be disclosed.[21]

As an example of accruing a contingent loss, consider a March 31, 2009, 10Q filed by the **Alabama Gas Corporation (Alagasco)** (Graphic 13–8). Consistent with GAAP, Alagasco accrued the lower end of a range of possible values and disclosed the potential for other losses above that amount.

GRAPHIC 13–8

Accrual of Loss Contingency—Alabama Gas Corporation

Real World Financials

7. Commitments and Contingencies (in part)

In October 2008, Alagasco received a request from the United States Environmental Protection Agency (EPA) . . . in connection with a former manufactured gas plant site located in Huntsville, Alabama. The site, along with the Huntsville gas distribution system, was sold by Alagasco to the City of Huntsville in 1949. . . . Based on the limited information available at this time, Alagasco preliminarily estimates that it may incur costs associated with the site ranging from $2.9 million to $5.9 million. At the present time, the Company cannot conclude that any amount within this range is a better estimate than any other, and accordingly the Company has accrued a contingent liability of $2.9 million. The estimate assumes an action plan for surface soil. If it is determined that a greater scope of work is appropriate, then actual costs will likely exceed the preliminary estimate.

It is important to note that some loss contingencies don't involve liabilities at all. Some contingencies, when resolved, cause a noncash asset to be impaired, so accruing the contingency means reducing the related asset rather than recording a liability:

Loss (or expense)	x,xxx	
Asset (or valuation account)		x,xxx

Accrual of a Loss Contingency—Asset Impairment

The most common loss contingency of this type is an uncollectible receivable. You have recorded these before without knowing you were accruing a loss contingency (*Debit:* bad debt expense; *Credit:* allowance for uncollectible accounts).

If one or both criteria for accrual are not met, but there is at least a reasonable possibility that a loss will occur, a disclosure note should describe the contingency. It also should provide an estimate of the potential loss or range of loss, if possible. If an estimate cannot be made, a statement to that effect is needed.

As an example of only disclosing a contingent loss, consider a disclosure note accompanying recent financial statements issued by **Varian Medical Systems, Inc.,** which designs and manufactures cancer therapy systems. VMS felt that the loss contingency from an investment was only reasonably possible, and accordingly did not accrue a liability but provided the information noted in Graphic 13–9.

A loss contingency is disclosed in notes to the financial statements if there is at least a reasonable possibility that the loss will occur.

GRAPHIC 13–9

Disclosure of Loss Contingency—VMS, Inc.

Real World Financials

Note 9 (in part)

. . . we agreed to invest $5 million in a consortium to participate in the acquisition of a minority interest in dpiX LLC ("dpiX"), which supplies us with amorphous silicon based thin-film transistor arrays. Based on information provided by dpiX, management currently believes it is reasonably possible that we will recognize a loss of up to $5 million on this investment.

Graphic 13–10 highlights the appropriate accounting treatment for each possible combination of (a) the likelihood of an obligation's being confirmed and (b) the determinability of its dollar amount.

[21]FASB ASC 450 20 30: Contingencies–Loss Contingencies–Initial Measurement (previously "Reasonable Estimation of the Amount of the Loss," *FASB Interpretation No. 14* (Stamford, Conn.: FASB, 1976)).

	Dollar Amount of Potential Loss		
Likelihood	Known	Reasonably Estimable	Not Reasonably Estimable
Probable	Liability accrued and disclosure note	Liability accrued and disclosure note	Disclosure note only
Reasonably possible	Disclosure note only	Disclosure note only	Disclosure note only
Remote	No disclosure required*	No disclosure required*	No disclosure required*

*Except for certain guarantees and other specified off-balance-sheet risk situations discussed in chapter 14.

Product Warranties and Guarantees

MANUFACTURER'S ORIGINAL WARRANTY. Satisfaction guaranteed! Your money back if not satisfied! If anything goes wrong in the first five years or 100,000 miles . . . ! Three-year guarantee! These and similar promises accompany most consumer goods. The reason—to boost sales. It follows, then, that any costs of making good on such guarantees should be recorded as expenses in the same accounting period the products are sold (matching principle). Also, it is in the period of sale that the company becomes obligated to eventually make good on a guarantee, so it makes sense that it recognizes a liability in the period of sale. The challenge is that much of the cost of satisfying a guarantee usually occurs later, sometimes years later. This is a loss contingency. There may be a future sacrifice of economic benefits (cost of satisfying the guarantee) due to an existing circumstance (the guaranteed products have been sold) that depends on an uncertain future event (customer claim).

As you might expect, meeting the accrual criteria is more likely for some types of loss contingencies than for others. For instance, the outcome of pending litigation is particularly difficult to predict. On the other hand, the criteria for accrual almost always are met for product warranties (or product guarantees). While we usually can't predict the liability associated with an individual sale, reasonably accurate estimates of the *total* liability for a period usually are possible, because prior experience makes it possible to predict how many warrantees or guarantees (on average) will need to be satisfied. So the contingent liability for warranties and guarantees usually is accrued in the reporting period in which the product under warranty is sold. This is demonstrated in Illustration 13–6.

Estimates of warranty costs cannot be expected to be precise. However, if the estimating method is monitored and revised when necessary, overestimates and underestimates should cancel each other over time. The estimated liability may be classified as current or as part current and part long-term, depending on when costs are expected to be incurred.

Most consumer products are accompanied by a guarantee.

The contingent liability for product warranties almost always is accrued.

ILLUSTRATION 13–6
Product Warranty

The costs of satisfying guarantees should be recorded as expenses in the same accounting period the products are sold.

Caldor Health, a supplier of in-home health care products, introduced a new therapeutic chair carrying a two-year warranty against defects. Estimates based on industry experience indicate warranty costs of 3% of sales during the first 12 months following the sale and 4% the next 12 months, totaling 7% that should be accrued in the year of sale. During December 2011, its first month of availability, Caldor had $2 million of chair sales.

During December

Cash (and accounts receivable)	2,000,000	
Sales revenue		2,000,000

December 31, 2011 (adjusting entry)

Warranty expense ([3% + 4%] × $2,000,000)	140,000	
Estimated warranty liability		140,000

When customer claims are made and costs are incurred to satisfy those claims, the liability is reduced (let's say $61,000 in 2012):

Estimated warranty liability	61,000	
Cash, wages payable, parts and supplies, etc		61,000

EXPECTED CASH FLOW APPROACH. In Chapter 6, you learned of a framework for using future cash flows as the basis for measuring assets and liabilities, introduced by the FASB in 2000 with *Statement of Financial Accounting Concepts No. 7,* "Using Cash Flow Information and Present Value in Accounting Measurements."[22] The approach described in the Concept Statement offers a way to take into account *any uncertainty concerning the amounts and timing of the cash flows.* Although future cash flows in many instances are contractual and certain, the amounts and timing of cash flows are less certain in other situations, such as warranty obligations.

SFAC No. 7 provides a framework for using future cash flows in accounting measurements.

As demonstrated in Illustration 13–6, the traditional way of measuring a warranty obligation is to report the "best estimate" of future cash flows, ignoring the time value of money on the basis of immateriality. However, when the warranty obligation spans more than one year and we can associate probabilities with possible cash flow outcomes, the approach described by *SFAC No. 7* offers a more plausible estimate of the warranty obligation. This "expected cash flow approach" incorporates specific probabilities of cash flows into the analysis. In Chapter 6, we discussed the expected cash flow approach to determining present value. Illustration 13–7 provides an example.

ILLUSTRATION 13–7
Product Warranty

Caldor Health, a supplier of in-home health care products, introduced a new therapeutic chair carrying a two-year warranty against defects. During December of 2011, its first month of availability, Caldor had $2 million of chair sales. Industry experience indicates the following probability distribution for the potential warranty costs:

Warranty Costs	Probability
2012	
$50,000	20%
$60,000	50%
$70,000	30%
2013	
$70,000	20%
$80,000	50%
$90,000	30%

Probabilities are associated with possible cash outcomes.

An arrangement with a service firm requires that costs for the two-year warranty period be settled at the end of 2012 and 2013. The risk-free rate of interest is 5%. Applying the expected cash flow approach, at the end of the 2011 fiscal year, Caldor would record a warranty liability (and expense) of $131,564, calculated as follows:

$$\$50,000 \times 20\% = \$10,000$$
$$60,000 \times 50\% = 30,000$$
$$70,000 \times 30\% = 21,000$$
$$\$61,000$$
$$\times .95238^* = \$58,095$$

$$\$70,000 \times 20\% = \$14,000$$
$$80,000 \times 50\% = 40,000$$
$$90,000 \times 30\% = 27,000$$
$$\$81,000$$
$$\times .90703^† = 73,469$$
$$\$131,564$$

*Present value of $1, n = 1, i = 5% (from Table 2)
†Present value of $1, n = 2, i = 5% (from Table 2)

The probability-weighted cash outcomes provide the expected cash flows.

The present value of the expected cash flows is the estimated liability.

December 31, 2011 (adjusting entry)

Warranty expense	131,564	
Estimated warranty liability (calculated above)		131,564

---

[22]"Using Cash Flow Information and Present Value in Accounting Measurements," *Statement of Financial Accounting Concepts No. 7* (Norwalk, Conn.: FASB, 2000). Recall that Concept Statements do not directly prescribe GAAP, but instead provide structure and direction to financial accounting.

EXTENDED WARRANTY CONTRACTS. It's difficult these days to buy a CD player, a digital camera, a car, or almost any durable consumer product without being asked to buy an extended warranty agreement. An extended warranty provides warranty protection beyond the manufacturer's original warranty. Because an extended warranty is priced and sold separately from the warranteed product, it essentially constitutes a separate sales transaction. So, rather than only worrying about how to recognize the contingent liability associated with an extended warranty, we face another accounting question: "When should the revenue from the sale of an extended warranty be recognized?"

By the accrual concept, revenue is recognized when earned, not necessarily when cash is received. Because the earning process for an extended warranty continues over the entire warranty period, revenue should be recognized over the same period. However, cash typically is received up front, when the extended warranty is sold. So, revenue from separately priced extended warranty contracts is deferred as a liability at the time of sale and recognized on a straight-line basis over the contract period. Notice that this is similar to an advance payment for products or services that, as we discussed earlier, creates an "unearned revenue" liability to supply the products or services. We demonstrate accounting for extended warranties in Illustration 13–8.

ILLUSTRATION 13–8
Extended Warranty
 	
Revenue from the extended warranty is recognized during the three years of the contract period.
	Brand Name Appliances sells major appliances that carry a one-year manufacturer's warranty. Customers are offered the opportunity at the time of purchase to also buy a three-year extended warranty for an additional charge. On January 3, 2011, Brand Name sold a $60 extended warranty, covering years 2012, 2013, and 2014.
	
	January 3, 2011
	Cash (or accounts receivable) 60
	    Unearned revenue—extended warranties 60
	
	December 31, 2012, 2013, 2014 (adjusting entries)
	Unearned revenue—extended warranties 20
	    Revenue—extended warranties ($60 ÷ 3) 20

The costs incurred to satisfy customer claims under the extended warranties also will be recorded during the same three-year period, achieving a proper matching of revenues and expenses. If sufficient historical evidence indicates that the costs of satisfying customer claims will be incurred on other than a straight-line basis, revenue should be recognized by the same pattern (proportional to the costs).[23]

Premiums

Cash rebates have become commonplace. Cash register receipts, bar codes, rebate coupons, or other proofs of purchase often can be mailed to the manufacturer for cash rebates. Sometimes promotional offers promise premiums other than cash (like toys, dishes, and utensils) to buyers of certain products. Of course the purpose of these premium offers is to stimulate sales. So it follows that the estimated amount of the cash rebates or the cost of noncash premiums estimated to be given out represents both an expense and an estimated liability in the reporting period the product is sold. Like a manufacturer's warranty, this loss contingency almost always meets accrual criteria. As with warranties, even though it is difficult to predict whether a particular buyer will redeem a premium, it is much easier to predict the total number of premiums that will be redeemed based on experience with customer redemptions in similar circumstances. Premiums are illustrated in Illustration 13–9.

---

[23]FASB ASC 605–20–25: Revenue Recognition–Services–Recognition (previously "Accounting for Separately Priced Extended Warranty and Product Maintenance Contracts," *FASB Technical Bulletin 90-1*, 1990.)

ADDITIONAL CONSIDERATION

Accounting for contingencies is controversial. Many accountants dislike the idea of only recognizing a liability for a contingent loss when it is probable, and then reporting the liability at the best estimate of the future expenditure. The obvious alternative is fair value, which does not incorporate probability into determining whether to *recognize* a loss but rather considers probability when *measuring* the amount of loss. Recent changes in GAAP have adopted fair value approaches for some types of events that are contingent losses (or appear to be close relatives). Consider the following examples:

- Illustration 13–7 uses a discounted expected cash flow approach to measure the contingent liability associated with an extended warranty. That approach approximates fair value.

- Recall from Chapter 10 that asset retirement obligations are recorded at fair value when an asset is acquired. The offsetting liability is similar to a contingent liability because it is an uncertain future amount arising from the past purchase of the asset but is recorded at fair value.

- Sometimes a company provides a guarantee that may require it to make payment to the guaranteed party based on some future event. For example, a company might guarantee the debt of an affiliated company, thus making it easier for that affiliate to obtain financing. Recent GAAP views this sort of guarantee as having two parts: (1) a certain "stand ready obligation" to meet the terms of the guarantee, and (2) the uncertain contingent obligation to make future payments depending on future events (for example, the affiliate defaulting on their debt). The "stand ready obligation" is recorded initially at fair value, while the contingent obligation is handled as an ordinary contingent loss.[24]

CMX Corporation offered $2 cash rebates on a particular model of hand-held hair dryers. To receive the rebate, customers must mail in a rebate coupon enclosed in the package plus the cash register receipt. Previous experience indicates that 30% of coupons will be redeemed. One million hair dryers were sold in 2011 and total payments to customers were $225,000.			**ILLUSTRATION 13–9** Premiums
Promotional expense (30% × $2 × 1,000,000)	600,000		
Estimated premium liability		600,000	**The costs of promotional offers should be recorded as expenses in the same accounting period the products are sold.**
To record the estimated liability for premiums.			
Estimated premium liability	225,000		
Cash		225,000	
To record payments to customers for coupons.			

The remaining liability of $375,000 is reported in the 2011 balance sheet and is reduced as future rebates are paid. The liability should be classified as current or long term depending on when future rebates are expected to be paid.

Of course, if premiums actually are included in packages of products sold, no contingent liability is created. For example, the costs of toys in Cracker Jack boxes and cereal boxes, and phone cards and compact discs in drink cartons are simply expenses of the period the product is sold, for which the amount is readily determinable.

Litigation Claims

Pending litigation similar to that disclosed by **Flextronics** in Graphic 13–7 on page 706 is not unusual. In fact, the majority of medium and large corporations annually report loss contingencies due to litigation. By far the most common disclosure is nonspecific regarding the actual litigation but uses wording similar to this contingency disclosure from **Pfizer**'s 2008 annual report (Graphic 13–11).

---

[24]FASB ASC 460–10–25: Guarantees–Overall–Recognition (previously "Guarantor's Accounting and Disclosure Requirements for Guarantees, Including Indirect Guarantees of Indebtedness of Others," *FASB Interpretation No. 45* (Stamford, Conn.: FASB, 2002)).

ADDITIONAL CONSIDERATION

Cents-off coupons are a popular marketing tool. Coupons clipped from newspapers, from mail offers, or included in packages are redeemable for cash discounts at the time promoted items are purchased. Issuing the coupons creates a contingent liability to be recorded in the period the coupons are issued. However, because the hoped-for sales don't materialize until later, a question arises as to when the related expense should be recognized. Logically, since the purpose of coupon offers is to stimulate sales, the expense properly should be deferred as an asset until the coupons are redeemed (when the future sales occur).

Illustration

On December 18, 2011, Craft Foods distributed coupons in newspaper inserts offering 50 cents off the purchase price of one of its cereal brands when coupons are presented to retailers. Retailers are reimbursed by Craft for the face amount of coupons plus 10% for handling. Previous experience indicates that 20% of coupons will be redeemed. Coupons issued had a total face amount of $1,000,000 and total payments to retailers in 2011 were $50,000. Retailers were paid $170,000 in 2012.

Promotional expense (redeemed in 2011)	50,000	
Cash		50,000
To record payments to retailers for coupons in 2011.		
Deferred promotional expense (an asset)	170,000	
Estimated coupon liability ([20% × $1,000,000 × 1.10] − $50,000).......		170,000
To record the estimated liability for coupons at end of 2011.		
Estimated coupon liability	170,000	
Cash		170,000
Promotional expense (redeemed in 2012)	170,000	
Deferred promotional expense		170,000
To record payments to retailers for coupons in 2012.		

This situation, though prevalent, is not addressed by promulgated accounting standards. In practice, most firms either (a) recognize the entire expense with the liability in the period the coupons are issued, like we record premiums, or (b) recognize no liability in the period the coupons are issued, recording the expense when reimbursements are made. One reason is that the same coupons are reissued periodically, making it difficult to associate specific reimbursements with specific offers. Another reason is that the time lag between the time a merchant receives a coupon from customers and the time it's presented to the manufacturer for reimbursement prevents appropriate apportionment of the expense.

GRAPHIC 13–11

Disclosure of Litigation Contingencies—Pfizer.

Real World Financials

Note 19: Legal Proceedings and Contingencies (in part)
Legal Proceedings

We and certain of our subsidiaries are involved in various patent, product liability, consumer, commercial, securities, environmental and tax litigations and claims, government investigations, and other legal proceedings that arise from time to time in the ordinary course of our business. Litigation is inherently unpredictable, and excessive verdicts do occur. Although we believe we have substantial defenses in these matters, we could in the future incur judgments or enter into settlements of claims that could have a material adverse effect on our results of operations in any particular period.

In practice, accrual of a loss from pending or ongoing litigation is rare. Can you guess why? Suppose you are chief financial officer of Feinz Foods. Feinz is the defendant in a $44 million class action suit. The company's legal counsel informally advises you that the chance the company will win the lawsuit is quite doubtful. Counsel feels the company might lose $30 million. Now suppose you decide to accrue a $30 million loss in your financial statements. Later, in the courtroom, your disclosure that Feinz management feels it is probable that the company will lose $30 million would be welcome ammunition for the opposing legal counsel. Understanding this, most companies rely on the knowledge that in today's legal environment the outcome of litigation is highly uncertain, making likelihood predictions difficult. Companies may accrue estimated lawyer fees and other legal costs, but usually do not record a loss until after the ultimate settlement has been reached or negotiations for settlement are substantially completed. Instead, disclosure notes typically describe the specifics of the litigation along with whether management feels an adverse outcome would materially affect the financial position of the company. As you can see in Graphic 13–12, the **Las Vegas Sands Corporation**, in a recent quarterly report, disclosed but did not accrue damages from a lawsuit it lost, even after the award was affirmed by trial court, because the company was appealing the verdict.

GRAPHIC 13–12

Disclosure of a Lawsuit—Las Vegas Sands Corporation

Real World Financials

8: Commitments and Contingencies
Litigation Relating to Macao Operations (in part)

. . . ., On June 30, 2008, a judgment was entered in this matter in the amount of $58.6 million (including pre-judgment interest). . . . The Company intends to continue to vigorously pursue available appeals up to the Nevada Supreme Court. The Company believes that it has valid bases in law and fact to overturn or appeal the verdict. As a result, the Company believes that the likelihood that the amount of the judgment will be affirmed is not probable, and, accordingly, that the amount of any loss cannot be reasonably estimated at this time. Because the Company believes that this potential loss is not probable or estimable, it has not recorded any reserves or contingencies related to this legal matter. In the event that the Company's assumptions used to evaluate this matter as neither probable nor estimable change in future periods, it may be required to record a liability for an adverse outcome.

Subsequent Events

It's important to remember that several weeks usually pass between the end of a company's fiscal year and the date the financial statements for that year actually are issued or available to be issued.[25] Events occurring during this period can be used to clarify the nature of financial statement elements at the report date. This situation can be represented by the following time line:

For instance, if information becomes available that sheds light on a legal claim that existed when the fiscal year ended, that information should be used in determining the probability of a loss contingency materializing and in estimating the amount of the loss. The settlement of a lawsuit after the December 31 report date of **ADESA, Inc.**, apparently influenced its accrual of a loss contingency (Graphic 13–13).

> When the cause of a loss contingency occurs before the year-end, a clarifying event before financial statements are issued can be used to determine how the contingency is reported.

GRAPHIC 13–13

Accrual of Litigation Contingencies— ADESA, Inc.

Real World Financials

Note 21 Commitments and Contingencies (in part)

In January 2007, the settlement agreement was finalized and the federal district court formally dismissed the litigation. The Company recorded provisions totaling approximately $0.6 million in the third quarter of 2006. . . .

---

[25]Financial statements are viewed as *issued* if they have been widely distributed to financial statement users in a format consistent with GAAP. Some entities (for example, private companies) do not widely distribute their financial statements to users. For those entities, the key date for subsequent events is not the date of issuance but rather the date upon which the financial statements are *available to be issued,* which occurs when the financial statements are complete, in a format consistent with GAAP, and have obtained the necessary approvals for issuance. Entities must disclose the date through which subsequent events have been evaluated (FASB ASC 855: Subsequent Events (previously "Subsequent Events," *Statement of Financial Accounting Standards No. 165* (Stamford, Conn.: FASB, 2009)).

For a loss contingency to be accrued, the cause of the lawsuit must have occurred before the accounting period ended. It's not necessary that the lawsuit actually was filed during that reporting period.

Sometimes, the cause of a loss contingency occurs after the end of the year but before the financial statements are issued:

If an event giving rise to a contingency occurs after the year-end, a liability should not be accrued.

When a contingency comes into existence after the company's fiscal year-end, a liability cannot be accrued because it didn't exist at the end of the year. However, if the failure to disclose the possible loss would cause the financial statements to be misleading, the situation should be described in a disclosure note, including the effect of the possible loss on key accounting numbers affected.[26]

In fact, *any* event occurring after the fiscal year-end but before the financial statements are issued that has a material effect on the company's financial position must be disclosed in a subsequent events disclosure note. Examples are an issuance of debt or equity securities, a business combination, and discontinued operations.

A disclosure note of **Pfizer** from its 2008 annual report is shown in Graphic 13–14 and describes an event that occurred in the first quarter of 2009.

GRAPHIC 13–14

Subsequent Events—Pfizer

Real World Financials

> **21. Subsequent events (in part)**
>
> On January 26, 2009, we announced that we have entered into a definitive merger agreement under which we will acquire Wyeth in a cash-and-stock transaction valued on that date at $50.19 per share, or a total of $68 billion. We plan to finance this acquisition with a combination of cash (about $22.5 billion), debt financing (about $22.5 billion) and the issuance of common stock (about $23.0 billion, based on the price of our common stock on January 23, 2009, the last trading day prior to our announcement on January 26). We have received a commitment from a syndicate of banks for the debt financing related to this transaction.

> **ADDITIONAL CONSIDERATION**
>
> Contingent liabilities that a company acquires when it purchases another company are treated differently from those that arise during the normal course of business. GAAP for business combinations requires that accounting for an *acquired* contingency depends on whether the contingency is contractual (arising from a contract, such as a warranty agreement) or non-contractual (arising in some other way, such as litigation). Non-contractual contingencies are ignored if they are not viewed as "more likely than not." All other contingencies (whether contractual or non-contractual) are recognized at fair value as of the acquisition date. In the future, the contingent liability is shown in the balance sheet at the higher of acquisition-date fair value or the amount that would be recognized under FASB ASC 450—Contingencies (previously *SFAS No. 5*) if the contingent liability arose in the normal course of business. Any quarter-by-quarter changes are reported as gains or losses in the income statement.[27]

---

[26]FASB ASC 450–20–50v9: Contingencies—Loss Contingencies—Disclosure (previously "Accounting for Contingencies," *Statement of Financial Accounting Standards No. 5* (Stamford, Conn.: FASB, 1975), par. 11).

[27]FASB ASC 805-20-25: Business Combinations—Identifiable Assets and Liabilities, and Any Noncontrolling Interest—Recognition (previously "Business Combinations," *Statement of Financial Accounting Standards No. 141R* (Stamford, Conn.: FASB, 1975)).

Unasserted Claims and Assessments

Even if a claim has yet to be made when the financial statements are issued, a contingency may warrant accrual or disclosure. However, an unfiled lawsuit or an unasserted claim or assessment need not be disclosed unless it is *probable that the suit, claim, or assessment will occur*. If it is probable, then the likelihood of an unfavorable outcome and the feasibility of estimating a dollar amount should be considered in deciding whether and how to report the possible loss.

For example, suppose a trucking company frequently transports hazardous waste materials and is subject to environmental laws and regulations. Management has identified several sites at which it is or may be liable for remediation. For those sites for which no penalties have been asserted, management must assess the likelihood that a claim will be made, and if so, whether the company actually will be held liable. If management feels an assessment is probable, an estimated loss and contingent liability would be accrued only if an unfavorable outcome is probable and the amount can be reasonably estimated. However, a disclosure note alone would be appropriate if an unfavorable settlement is only reasonably possible or if the settlement is probable but cannot be reasonably estimated. No action is needed if chances of that outcome occurring are remote. Notice that when the claim or assessment is unasserted as yet, a two-step process is involved in deciding how it should be reported:

1. Is a claim or assessment probable? (If the answer to this question is no, no disclosure is needed; skip step 2.)
2. Only if a claim or assessment is probable should we evaluate (a) the likelihood of an unfavorable outcome and (b) whether the dollar amount can be estimated.

If the conclusion of step 1 is that the claim or assessment *is not* probable, no further action is required. If the conclusion of step 1 is that the claim or assessment *is* probable, the decision as to whether or not a liability is accrued or disclosed is precisely the same as when the claim or assessment already has been asserted.

As described in a March 31, 2009, disclosure note (see Graphic 13–15), **Union Pacific** felt that some unasserted claims met the criteria for accrual under this two-step decision process.

> It must be probable that an unasserted claim or assessment or an unfiled lawsuit will occur before considering whether and how to report the possible loss.

---

15. Commitments and Contingencies (in part)

Asserted and Unasserted Claims—Various claims and lawsuits are pending against us and certain of our subsidiaries. We cannot fully determine the effect of all asserted and unasserted claims on our consolidated results of operations, financial condition, or liquidity; however, to the extent possible, where asserted and unasserted claims are considered probable and where such claims can be reasonably estimated, we have recorded a liability.

GRAPHIC 13–15

Unasserted Claims—Union Pacific Corporation

Real World Financials

Notice that the treatment of contingent liabilities is consistent with the accepted definition of liabilities as (a) probable, future sacrifices of economic benefits (b) that arise from present obligations to other entities and (c) that result from past transactions or events.[28] The inherent uncertainty involved with contingent liabilities means additional care is required to determine whether future sacrifices of economic benefits are probable and whether the amount of the sacrifices can be quantified.

---

[28]"Elements of Financial Statements," *Statement of Financial Accounting Concepts No. 6* (Stamford, Conn.: FASB, 1985).

● **LO7**

INTERNATIONAL FINANCIAL REPORTING STANDARDS

Contingencies. Accounting for contingencies is part of a broader international standard, *IAS No. 37*, "Provisions, Contingent Liabilities and Contingent Assets." Overall, accounting for contingent losses currently is quite similar between IFRS and U.S. GAAP. A loss contingency is accrued under U.S. GAAP if it's both probable and can be reasonably estimated. IFRS is similar, but defines "probable" as "more likely than not," which is a lower threshold than typically associated with "probable" in U.S. GAAP. Also, IFRS refers to these accrued liabilities as "provisions," and refers to possible obligations that are not accrued as "contingent liabilities," while the term "contingent liabilities" is used for all of these obligations in U.S. GAAP. And, if there is a range of equally likely outcomes associated with a contingency, IFRS requires using the midpoint of the range, while U.S. GAAP requires use of the low end of the range.

Another difference in accounting relates to whether to report a long-term contingency at its expected future value or its present value. IFRS requires reporting present values of estimated cash flows when the effect of *time value of money is material.* U.S. GAAP allows using present values under some circumstances when the timing of cash flows is fixed or reliably determinable.[29]

IFRS ILLUSTRATION

Here's a portion of a footnote from the 2009 financial statements of **Vodafone**, which reports under IFRS:

Real World Financials

Note 2: Signifcant Accounting Policies (in part)

Provisions are recognised when the Group has a present obligation (legal or constructive) as a result of a past event, it is probable that the Group will be required to settle that obligation and a reliable estimate can be made of the amount of the obligation. Provisions are measured at the directors' best estimate of the expenditure required to settle the obligation at the balance sheet date and are discounted to present value where the effect is material.

WHERE WE'RE HEADED

The controversy over accounting for contingencies and mixture of approaches is likely to continue. The FASB recently removed from their agenda a project to reconsider the recognition and measurement of contingent losses, but may revisit the issue in the future. In the meantime, the FASB has a project ongoing that is intended to enhance footnote disclosures of contingent losses. The IASB has a project ongoing that is likely to move closer to fair-value recognition of contingencies. In particular, it is likely that the IASB will eliminate the requirement that an amount be "probable" to be recognized, such that amounts that now are currently only disclosed in the footnotes will be accrued and included as expenses and liabilities. Probability of loss will still matter, but only will be factored into measuring the expected value of the liability.[30]

Gain Contingencies

A gain contingency is an uncertain situation that might result in a gain. For example, in a pending lawsuit, one side—the defendant—faces a loss contingency; the other side—the plaintiff—has a gain contingency. As we discussed earlier, loss contingencies are accrued when the event confirming the obligation is probable and the amount can reasonably be estimated. However, gain contingencies are not accrued. The nonparallel treatment of gain

Gain contingencies are not accrued.

---

[29]FASB ASC 410–30–35–12: Asset Retirements and Environmental Obligations–Environmental Obligations–Subsequent Measurement.
[30]Exposure Draft of Proposed Amendments to IAS 37 Provisions, Contingent Liabilities and Contingent Assets and IAS 19 Employee Benefits, IASB, June 2005.

contingencies follows the same conservative reasoning that motivates reporting some assets at lower of cost or market. Specifically, it's desirable to anticipate losses, but recognizing gains should await their realization.

Though gain contingencies are not recorded in the accounts, material ones are disclosed in notes to the financial statements. Care should be taken that the disclosure note not give "misleading implications as to the likelihood of realization."[31]

CONCEPT REVIEW EXERCISE

Hanover Industries manufactures and sells food products and food processing machinery. While preparing the December 31, 2011, financial statements for Hanover, the following information was discovered relating to contingencies and possible adjustments to liabilities. Hanover's 2011 financial statements were issued on April 1, 2012.

CONTINGENCIES

a. On November 12, 2011, a former employee filed a lawsuit against Hanover alleging age discrimination and asking for damages of $750,000. At December 31, 2011, Hanover's attorney indicated that the likelihood of losing the lawsuit was possible but not probable. On March 5, 2012, Hanover agreed to pay the former employee $125,000 in return for withdrawing the lawsuit.
b. Hanover believes there is a possibility a service provider may claim that it has been undercharged for outsourcing a processing service based on verbal indications of the company's interpretation of a negotiated rate. The service provider has not yet made a claim for additional fees as of April 2012, but Hanover feels it will. Hanover's accountants and legal counsel believe the charges were appropriate but that if an assessment is made, there is a reasonable possibility that subsequent court action would result in an additional tax liability of $55,000.
c. Hanover grants a one-year warranty for each processing machine sold. Past experience indicates that the costs of satisfying warranties are approximately 2% of sales. During 2011, sales of processing machines totaled $21,300,000. 2011 expenditures for warranty repair costs were $178,000 related to 2011 sales and $220,000 related to 2010 sales. The January 1, 2011, balance of the warranty liability account was $250,000.
d. Hanover is the plaintiff in a $600,000 lawsuit filed in 2010 against Ansdale Farms for failing to deliver on contracts for produce. The suit is in final appeal. Legal counsel advises that it is probable that Hanover will prevail and will be awarded $300,000 (considered a material amount).
e. Included with certain food items sold in 2011 were coupons redeemable for a kitchen appliance at the rate of five coupons per appliance. During 2011, 30,000 coupons were issued and 5,000 coupons were redeemed. Although this is the first such promotion in years, past experience indicates that 60% of coupons are never redeemed. An inventory of kitchen appliances is maintained, and a count shows that 1,000 are on hand at December 31, 2011, with a normal retail value of $20,000 and a cost to Hanover of $8,000.

Required:

1. Determine the appropriate reporting for each situation. Briefly explain your reasoning.
2. Prepare any necessary journal entries and state whether a disclosure note is needed.

a. This is a loss contingency. Hanover can use the information occurring after the end of the year in determining appropriate disclosure. The cause for the suit existed at the end of the year. Hanover should accrue the $125,000 loss because an agreement has been reached confirming the loss and the amount is known.

SOLUTION

[31]FASB ASC 450–30–50: Contingencies–Gain Contingencies–Disclosure (previously "Accounting For Contingencies," *Statement of Financial Accounting Standards No. 5* (Stamford, Conn.: FASB, 1975), par. 17).

Loss—litigation	125,000	
Liability—litigation		125,000

A disclosure note also is appropriate.

b. At the time financial statements are issued, a claim is as yet unasserted. However, an assessment is probable. Thus, (a) the likelihood of an unfavorable outcome and (b) whether the dollar amount can be estimated are considered. No accrual is necessary because an unfavorable outcome is not probable. But because an unfavorable outcome is reasonably possible, a disclosure note is appropriate.

   Note: If the likelihood of a claim being asserted is not probable, disclosure is not required even if an unfavorable outcome is thought to be probable in the event of an assessment and the amount is estimable.

c. The contingency for warranties should be accrued because it is probable that expenditures will be made and the amount can be estimated from past experience. When customer claims are made and costs are incurred to satisfy those claims the liability is reduced.

Warranty expense (2% × $21,300,000)	426,000	
Estimated warranty liability		426,000
Estimated warranty liability ($178,000 + 220,000)	398,000	
Cash, wages payable, parts and supplies, etc.		398,000

The liability at December 31, 2011, would be reported as $278,000:

Warranty Liability
(in 000s)

		250	Balance, Jan. 1
		426	2011 expense
2011 expenditures	398		
		278	Balance, Dec. 31

A disclosure note also is appropriate.

d. This is a gain contingency. Gain contingencies cannot be accrued even if the gain is probable and reasonably estimable. The gain should be recognized only when realized. It can be disclosed, but care should be taken to avoid misleading language regarding the realizability of the gain.

e. The contingency for premiums should be accrued because it is probable that coupons will be redeemed and the amount can be estimated from past experience. When coupons are redeemed and appliances are issued, the liability is reduced.

Promotional expense (40% × [30,000 ÷ 5] × $8*)	19,200	
Estimated premium liability		19,200
Estimated premium liability ([5,000 ÷ 5] × $8*)	8,000	
Inventory of premiums		8,000

*$8,000 ÷ 1,000 = $8

The liability at December 31, 2011, would be reported as $11,200:

Premium Liability

		19,200	2011 expense
2011 expenditures	8,000		
		11,200	Balance, Dec. 31

DECISION MAKERS' PERSPECTIVE

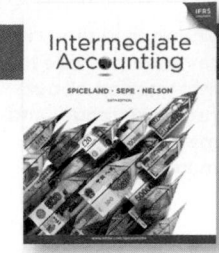

Current liabilities impact a company's liquidity. Liquidity refers to a company's cash position and overall ability to obtain cash in the normal course of business. A company is said to be liquid if it has sufficient cash (or other assets convertible to cash in a relatively short time) to pay currently maturing debts. Because the lack of liquidity can cause the demise of an otherwise healthy company, it is critical that managers as well as outside investors and creditors maintain close scrutiny of this aspect of a company's well-being.

> **A risk analyst should be concerned with a company's ability to meet its short-term obligations.**

FINANCIAL
Reporting Case

Q5, p. 692

Keeping track of the current ratio is one of the most common ways of doing this. The current ratio is intended as a measure of short-term solvency and is determined by dividing current assets by current liabilities.

When we compare liabilities that must be satisfied in the near term with assets that either are cash or will be converted to cash in the near term, we get a useful measure of a company's liquidity. A ratio of 1 to 1 or higher often is considered a rule-of-thumb standard, but like other ratios, acceptability should be evaluated in the context of the industry in which the company operates and other specific circumstances. Keep in mind, though, that industry averages are only one indication of adequacy and that the current ratio is but one indication of liquidity.

We can adjust for the implicit assumption of the current ratio that all current assets are equally liquid. The acid-test, or quick, ratio is similar to the current ratio but is based on a more conservative measure of assets available to pay current liabilities. Specifically, the numerator, quick assets, includes only cash and cash equivalents, short-term investments, and accounts receivable. By eliminating current assets such as inventories and prepaid expenses that are less readily convertible into cash, the acid-test ratio provides a more rigorous indication of a company's short-term solvency than does the current ratio.

> **A manager should actively monitor a company's liquidity.**

If either of these liquidity ratios is less than that of the industry as a whole, does that mean that liquidity is a problem? Perhaps. It does, though, raise a red flag that suggests caution when assessing other areas. It's important to remember that each ratio is but one piece of the puzzle. For example, profitability is probably the best long-run indication of liquidity. Also, management may be very efficient in managing current assets so that some current assets—receivables or inventory—are converted to cash more quickly than they otherwise would be and are more readily available to satisfy liabilities. The turnover ratios discussed in earlier chapters help measure the efficiency of asset management in this regard.

> **A liquidity ratio is but one indication of a company's liquidity.**

In fact, some companies view their accounts payable as a free loan from their suppliers, just as they view their accounts receivable as a free loan to their customers. These companies tend to pressure their customers to pay quickly, but try to obtain more extended terms with their suppliers. Although this would produce relatively low current assets and high current liabilities, and therefore a lower current ratio, it could be a very intelligent way to manage cash and decrease the overall amount of capital needed by the company to finance operations.

> **Some companies maintain relatively high current liabilities as part of a cash-management strategy**

Given the actual and perceived importance of a company's liquidity in the minds of analysts, it's not difficult to adopt a management perspective and imagine efforts to manipulate the ratios that measure liquidity. For instance, a company might use its economic muscle or persuasive powers to influence the timing of accounts payable recognition by asking suppliers to change their delivery schedules. Because accounts payable is included in the denominator in most measures of liquidity, such as the current ratio, the timing of their recognition could mean the difference between an unacceptable ratio and an acceptable one, or between violating a debt covenant and compliance. For example, suppose a company with a current ratio of 1.25 (current assets of $5 million and current liabilities of $4 million) is in violation of a debt covenant requiring a minimum current ratio of 1.3. By delaying the delivery of $1 million of inventory, the ratio would be 1.33 (current assets of $4 million and current liability of $3 million).

> **Analysts should be alert for efforts to manipulate measures of liquidity.**

It is important for creditors and analysts to be attentive for evidence of activities that would indicate timing strategies, such as unusual variations in accounts payable levels. You might notice that such timing strategies are similar to earnings management techniques we discussed previously—specifically, manipulating the timing of revenue and expense recognition in order to "smooth" income over time.

Finally, all financial statement users need to keep in mind the relation between the recognition of unearned revenue associated with advance payments and the later recognition of revenue. On the one hand, increases in unearned revenue can signal future revenue recognition because the unearned revenue likely will eventually be recognized as revenue. On the other hand, research suggests that some firms that report unearned revenue may manipulate the timing of revenue recognition to manage their earnings.[32]

In the next chapter, we continue our discussion of liabilities. Our focus will shift from current liabilities to long-term liabilities in the form of bonds and long-term notes. ●

Changes in unearned revenue provide information about future revenue, and may be used to manipulate it.

FINANCIAL REPORTING CASE SOLUTION

1. **What are accrued liabilities? What is commercial paper?** *(p. 697)* Accrued liabilities are reported for expenses already incurred but not yet paid (accrued expenses). These include salaries and wages payable, income taxes payable, and interest payable. Commercial paper is a form of notes payable sometimes used by large corporations to obtain temporary financing. It is sold to other companies as a short-term investment. It represents unsecured notes sold in minimum denominations of $25,000 with maturities ranging from 30 to 270 days. Typically, commercial paper is issued directly to the buyer (lender) and is backed by a line of credit with a bank.

2. **Why did Syntel Microsystems include some long-term debt in the current liability section?** *(p. 702)* Syntel Microsystems did include some long-term debt in the current liability section. The currently maturing portion of a long-term debt must be reported as a current liability. Amounts are reclassified and reported as current liabilities when they become payable within the upcoming year.

3. **Did they also report some current amounts as long-term debt? Explain.** *(p. 703)* Yes they did. It is permissible to report short-term obligations as noncurrent liabilities if the company (a) intends to refinance on a long-term basis and (b) demonstrates the ability to do so by a refinancing agreement or by actual financing. As the disclosure note explains, this is the case for a portion of Syntel's currently payable debt.

4. **Must obligations be known contractual debts in order to be reported as liabilities?** *(p. 706)* No. From an accounting perspective, it is not necessary that obligations be known, legally enforceable debts to be reported as liabilities. They must only be probable and the dollar amount reasonably estimable.

5. **Is it true that current liabilities are riskier than long-term liabilities?** *(p. 719)* Other things being equal, current liabilities generally are considered riskier than long-term liabilities. For that reason, management usually would rather report a debt as long term. Current debt, though, is not necessarily risky. The liquidity ratios we discussed in the chapter attempt to measure liquidity. Remember, any such measure must be assessed in the context of other factors: industry standards, profitability, turnover ratios, and risk management activities, to name a few. ●

THE BOTTOM LINE

● **LO1** Liabilities are present obligations to sacrifice assets in the future because of something that already has occurred. Current liabilities are expected to require current assets (or the creation of other current liabilities) and usually are payable within one year. (p. 692)

● **LO2** Short-term bank loans usually are arranged under an existing line of credit with a bank or group of banks. When interest is discounted from the face amount of a note (a type of noninterest-bearing note), the effective interest rate is higher than the stated discount rate. Large, highly rated firms sometimes sell commercial paper directly to the buyer (lender) to borrow funds at a lower rate than through a bank loan. (p. 695)

[32]Yuan Zhang, "An Empirical Analysis of Revenue Manipulation," Columbia Business School working paper, April 12, 2006.

● **LO3**   Accrued liabilities are recorded by adjusting entries for expenses already incurred, but for which cash has yet to be paid (accrued expenses). Familiar examples are salaries and wages payable, income taxes payable, and interest payable. (p. 697)

● **LO4**   Short-term obligations can be reported as noncurrent liabilities if the company (a) intends to refinance on a long-term basis and (b) demonstrates the ability to do so by actual financing or a formal agreement to do so. (p. 702)

● **LO5**   A loss contingency is an existing, uncertain situation involving potential loss depending on whether some future event occurs. Whether a contingency is accrued and reported as a liability depends on (a) the likelihood that the confirming event will occur and (b) what can be determined about the amount of loss. It is accrued if it is both probable that the confirming event will occur and the amount can be at least reasonably estimated. (p. 706)

● **LO6**   A clarifying event before financial statements are issued, but after the year-end, can be used to determine how the contingency is reported. An unasserted suit, claim, or assessment warrants accrual or disclosure if it is probable it will be asserted. A gain contingency is a contingency that might result in a gain. A gain contingency is not recognized until it actually is realized. (p. 706)

● **LO7**   IFRS and U.S. GAAP are relatively similar with respect to current liabilities and contingencies. Relatively minor differences relate to when financing must be in place for a liability expected to be refinanced to be classified as long term. Also, with respect to contingent losses, IFRS defines "probable" at a lower threshold, requires the accrual of the midpoint of a range of possible loss values, and requires the use of present values when measuring amounts to be accrued. (pp. 704 and 716) ●

PAYROLL-RELATED LIABILITIES

APPENDIX 13

All firms incur liabilities in connection with their payrolls. These arise primarily from legal requirements to withhold taxes from employees' paychecks and from payroll taxes on the firms themselves. Some payroll-related liabilities result from voluntary payroll deductions of amounts payable to third parties.

EMPLOYEES' WITHHOLDING TAXES

Employers are required by law to withhold federal (sometimes state) income taxes and Social Security taxes from employees' paychecks and remit these to the Internal Revenue Service. The amount withheld for federal income taxes is determined by a tax table furnished by the IRS and varies according to the amount earned and the number of exemptions claimed by the employee. Also, the Federal Insurance Contributions Act (FICA) requires employers to withhold a percentage of each employee's earnings up to a specified maximum. Both the percentage and the maximum are changed intermittently. As this text went to print, the deduction for Social Security was 6.2% of the first $106,800 an employee earns. Additionally, a deduction for Medicare tax was 1.45% with no limit on the base amount. The employer also must pay an equal (matching) amount on behalf of the employee. Self-employed persons must pay both the employer and employee portions (12.4% for Social Security and 2.9% for Medicare).

VOLUNTARY DEDUCTIONS

Besides the required deductions for income taxes and Social Security taxes, employees often authorize their employers to deduct other amounts from their paychecks. These deductions might include union dues, contributions to savings or retirement plans, and insurance premiums. Amounts deducted this way represent liabilities until paid to the appropriate organizations.

EMPLOYERS' PAYROLL TAXES

One payroll tax mentioned previously is the employer's matching amount of FICA taxes. The employer also must pay federal and state unemployment taxes on behalf of its employees. The Federal Unemployment Tax Act (FUTA) requires a tax of 6.2% of the first $7,000 earned by each employee. This amount is reduced by a 5.4% (maximum) credit for contributions to state unemployment programs, so the net federal rate often is .8%.[33] In many states the state rate is 5.4% but may be reduced if the employer maintains relatively low employee turnover.

---

[33]All states presently have unemployment tax programs.

FRINGE BENEFITS

In addition to salaries and wages, withholding taxes, and payroll taxes, many companies provide employees a variety of fringe benefits. Most commonly, employers pay all or part of employees' insurance premiums and/or contributions to retirement income plans.

Representative payroll-related liabilities are presented in Illustrations 13A–1.

ILLUSTRATION 13A–1 Payroll-Related Liabilities	Crescent Lighting and Fixtures' payroll for the second week in January was $100,000. The following deductions, fringe benefits, and taxes apply:	
	Federal income taxes to be withheld	$20,000
	State income taxes to be withheld	3,000
	Medical insurance premiums (Blue Cross)— 70% paid by employer	1,000
	Employee contribution to voluntary retirement plan (Fidelity Investments)—contributions matched by employer	4,000
	Union dues (Local No. 222)—paid by employees	100
	Life insurance premiums (Prudential Life)— 100% paid by employer	200
	Social Security tax rate	6.2%
Amounts withheld from paychecks represent liabilities until remitted to third parties.	Medicare tax rate	1.45%
	Federal unemployment tax rate (after state deduction)	0.80%
	State unemployment tax rate	5.40%
	Crescent's journal entries to record payroll:	
	Salaries and wages expense (total amount earned)	100,000
The employer's share of FICA and unemployment taxes constitute the employer's payroll tax expense.	Withholding taxes payable (federal income tax)	20,000
	Withholding taxes payable (state income tax)	3,000
	Social Security taxes payable (employees' portion, 6.2%)	6,200 ◄
	Medicare taxes payable (employees' portion, 1.45%)	1,450 ◄
	Payable to Blue Cross (employee's portion of insurance premiums—30%)	300 ◄
	Payable to Fidelity Investments (employees' investment)	4,000 ◄
Fringe benefits are part of salaries and wages expense and represent liabilities until remitted to third parties.	Payable to Local No. 222 (union dues)	100
	Salaries and wages payable (net pay)	64,950
	Payroll tax expense (total)	13,850
	Social Security taxes payable (employer's matching amount)	6,200 ◄
	Medicare taxes payable (employer's matching amount)	1,450 ◄
	FUTA payable (federal unemployment tax: .8%)	800
	State unemployment tax payable (5.4%)	5,400
	Salaries and wages expense (fringe benefits)	4,900
	Payable to Blue Cross (insurance premiums—70%)	700 ◄
	Payable to Fidelity Investments (employer's matching amount)	4,000 ◄
	Payable to Prudential life (insurance premiums)	200

As you study the illustration, you should note the similarity among all payroll-related liabilities. Amounts withheld from paychecks—voluntarily or involuntarily—are liabilities until turned over to appropriate third parties. Payroll taxes and expenses for fringe benefits are incurred as a result of services performed by employees and also are liabilities until paid to appropriate third parties. ●

QUESTIONS FOR REVIEW OF KEY TOPICS

Q 13–1   What are the essential characteristics of liabilities for purposes of financial reporting?

Q 13–2   What distinguishes current liabilities from long-term liabilities?

Q 13–3   Bronson Distributors owes a supplier $100,000 on open account. The amount is payable in three months. What is the theoretically correct way to measure the reportable amount for this liability? In practice, how will it likely be reported? Why?

Q 13–4   Bank loans often are arranged under existing lines of credit. What is a line of credit? How does a noncommitted line of credit differ from a committed line?

Q 13–5   Banks sometimes loan cash under noninterest-bearing notes. Is it true that banks lend money without interest?

Q 13–6   How does commercial paper differ from a bank loan? Why is the interest rate often less for commercial paper?

Q 13–7   Salaries of $5,000 have been earned by employees by the end of the period but will not be paid to employees until the following period. How should the expense and related liability be recorded? Why?

Q 13–8   Under what conditions should an employer accrue an expense and the related liability for employees' compensation for future absences? How do company custom and practice affect the accrual decision?

Q 13–9   How are refundable deposits and customer advances similar? How do they differ?

Q 13–10   How do companies account for gift cards?

Q 13–11   Amounts collected for third parties represent liabilities until remitted. Provide several examples of this kind of collection.

Q 13–12   Consider the following liabilities of Future Brands, Inc., at December 31, 2011, the company's fiscal year-end. Should they be reported as current liabilities or long-term liabilities?

1. $77 million of 8% notes are due on May 31, 2015. The notes are callable by the Company's bank, beginning March 1, 2012.
2. $102 million of 8% notes are due on May 31, 2016. A debt covenant requires Future to maintain a current ratio (ratio of current assets to current liabilities) of at least 2 to 1. Future is in violation of this requirement but has obtained a waiver from the bank until May 2012, since both companies feel Future will correct the situation during the first half of 2012.

Q 13–13   Long-term obligations usually are reclassified and reported as current liabilities when they become payable within the upcoming year (or operating cycle, if longer than a year). So, a 25-year bond issue is reported as a long-term liability for 24 years but normally is reported as a current liability on the balance sheet prepared during the 25th year of its term to maturity. Name a situation in which this would not be the case.

● IFRS   Q 13–14   How do IFRS and U.S. GAAP differ with respect to the classification of debt that is expected to be refinanced?

Q 13–15   Define a loss contingency. Provide three examples.

Q 13–16   List and briefly describe the three categories of likelihood that a future event(s) will confirm the incurrence of the liability for a loss contingency.

Q 13–17   Under what circumstances should a loss contingency be accrued?

● IFRS   Q 13–18   What is the difference between the use of the term *contingent liability* in U.S. GAAP and IFRS?

Q 13–19   Suppose the analysis of a loss contingency indicates that an obligation is not probable. What accounting treatment if any is warranted?

Q 13–20   Name two loss contingencies that almost always are accrued.

Q 13–21   Distinguish between the accounting treatment of a manufacturer's warranty and an extended warranty. Why the difference?

Q 13–22   At December 31, the end of the reporting period, the analysis of a loss contingency indicates that an obligation is only reasonably possible, though its dollar amount is readily estimable. During February, before the financial statements are issued, new information indicates the loss is probable. What accounting treatment is warranted?

Q 13–23   After the end of the reporting period, a contingency comes into existence. Under what circumstances, if any, should the contingency be reported in the financial statements for the period ended?

● IFRS   Q 13–24   How do U.S. GAAP and IFRS differ in their treatment of a range of equally likely losses?

Q 13–25   Suppose the Environmental Protection Agency is in the process of investigating Ozone Ruination Limited for possible environmental damage but has not proposed a penalty as of December 31, 2011, the company's fiscal year-end. Describe the two-step process involved in deciding how this unasserted assessment should be reported.

Q 13–26   You are the plaintiff in a lawsuit. Your legal counsel advises that your eventual victory is inevitable. "You will be awarded $12 million," your attorney confidently asserts. Describe the appropriate accounting treatment.

BRIEF EXERCISES

BE 13–1
Bank loan; accrued interest
● LO2

On October 1, Eder Fabrication borrowed $60 million and issued a nine-month, 12% promissory note. Interest was payable at maturity. Prepare the journal entry for the issuance of the note and the appropriate adjusting entry for the note at December 31, the end of the reporting period.

BE 13–2
Non-interest-bearing note; accrued interest
● LO2

On October 1, Eder Fabrication borrowed $60 million and issued a nine-month promissory note. Interest was discounted at issuance at a 12% discount rate. Prepare the journal entry for the issuance of the note and the appropriate adjusting entry for the note at December 31, the end of the reporting period.

BE 13–3
Determining accrued interest
● LO2

On July 1, Orcas Lab issued a $100,000, 12%, 8-month note. Interest is payable at maturity. What is the amount of interest expense that should be recorded in a year-end adjusting entry if the fiscal year-end is (a) December 31? (b) September 30?

BE 13–4
Commercial paper
● LO2

Branch Corporation issued $12 million of commercial paper on March 1 on a nine-month note. Interest was discounted at issuance at a 9% discount rate. Prepare the journal entry for the issuance of the commercial paper and its repayment at maturity.

BE 13–5
Non-interest-bearing note; effective interest rate
● LO2

Life.com issued $10 million of commercial paper on April 1 on a nine-month note. Interest was discounted at issuance at a 6% discount rate. What is the effective interest rate on the commercial paper?

BE 13–6
Advance collection
● LO3

On December 12, 2011, Pace Electronics received $24,000 from a customer toward a cash sale of $240,000 of diodes to be completed on January 16, 2012. What journal entries should Pace record on December 12 and January 16?

BE 13–7
Advance collection
● LO3

In Lizzie Shoes' experience, gift cards that have not been redeemed within 12 months are not likely to be redeemed. Lizzie Shoes sold gift cards for $18,000 during August of 2011. $4,000 of cards were redeemed in September of 2011, $3,000 in October, $2,500 in November, and $2,000 in December of 2011. In 2012 an additional $1,000 of cards were redeemed in January and $500 in February. How much gift card revenue associated with the August 2011 gift card sales would Lizzie get to recognize in 2011 and 2012?

BE 13–8
Sales tax
● LO3

During December, Rainey Equipment made a $600,000 credit sale. The state sales tax rate is 6% and the local sales tax rate is 1.5%. Prepare the appropriate journal entry.

BE 13–9
Refinancing debt
● LO4

Coulson Company is in the process of refinancing some long-term debt. Its fiscal year ends on December 31, 2011, and its financial statements will be issued on March 15, 2012. Under current U.S. GAAP, how would the debt be classified if the refinancing is completed on December 15, 2011? What if instead it is completed on January 15, 2012?

BE 13–10
Refinancing debt
● LO4 LO7

Fleener Company is in the process of refinancing some long-term debt. Its fiscal year ends on December 31, 2011, and its financial statements will be issued on March 15, 2012. Under current IFRS, how would the debt be classified if the refinancing is completed on December 15, 2011? What if instead it is completed on January 15, 2012?

BE 13–11
Warranties
● LO5 LO6

Right Medical introduced a new implant that carries a five-year warranty against manufacturer's defects. Based on industry experience with similar product introductions, warranty costs are expected to approximate 1% of sales. Sales were $15 million and actual warranty expenditures were $20,000 for the first year of selling the product. What amount (if any) should Right report as a liability at the end of the year?

BE 13–12
Product recall
● LO5 LO6

Consultants notified management of Goo Goo Baby Products that a crib toy poses a potential health hazard. Counsel indicated that a product recall is probable and is estimated to cost the company $5.5 million. How will this affect the company's income statement and balance sheet this period?

BE 13–13
Contingency
● LO5 LO6

Skill Hardware is the plaintiff in a $16 million lawsuit filed against a supplier. The litigation is in final appeal and legal counsel advises that it is virtually certain that Skill will win the lawsuit and be awarded $12 million. How should Skill account for this event?

BE 13–14
Contingency
● LO5 LO6

Bell International can estimate the amount of loss that will occur if a foreign government expropriates some company property. Expropriation is considered reasonably possible. How should Bell report the loss contingency?

BE 13–15
Contingencies
● LO5 LO6

Household Solutions manufactures kitchen storage products. During the year, the company became aware of potential costs due to (1) a possible product defect that is reasonably possible and can be reasonably estimated, (2) a safety hazard that is probable and cannot be reasonably estimated, and (3) a new product warranty that is probable and can be reasonably estimated. Which, if any, of these costs should be accrued?

BE 13–16
Contingencies
● LO5 LO6 LO7

Quandary Corporation has a major customer who is alleging a significant product defect. Quandary engineers and attorneys have analyzed the claim and have concluded that there is a 51% chance that the customer would be successful in court and that a successful claim would result in a range of damages from $10 million to $20 million, with each part of the range equally likely to occur. The damages would need to be paid soon enough that time-value-of-money considerations are not material. Would a liability be accrued under U.S. GAAP? Under IFRS? If a liability were accrued, what amount would be accrued under U.S. GAAP? Under IFRS?

BE 13–17
Unasserted
assessment
● LO5 LO6

At March 13, 2012, the Environmental Protection Agency is in the process of investigating a possible emissions leak last summer at a facility of Now Chemical. The EPA has not yet proposed a penalty assessment. Now's fiscal year ends on December 31, 2011, and its financial statements are published in March 2012. Management feels an assessment is *reasonably possible,* and if an assessment is made an unfavorable settlement of $13 million is *probable.* What, if any, action should Now take for its financial statements?

EXERCISES

An alternate exercise and problem set is available on the text website: www.mhhe.com/spiceland6e

E 13–1
Bank loan; accrued
interest
● LO2

On November 1, 2011, Quantum Technology, a geothermal energy supplier, borrowed $16 million cash to fund a geological survey. The loan was made by Nevada BancCorp under a noncommitted short-term line of credit arrangement. Quantum issued a nine-month, 12% promissory note. Interest was payable at maturity. Quantum's fiscal period is the calendar year.

Required:
1. Prepare the journal entry for the issuance of the note by Quantum Technology.
2. Prepare the appropriate adjusting entry for the note by Quantum on December 31, 2011.
3. Prepare the journal entry for the payment of the note at maturity.

E 13–2
Determining
accrued interest in
various situations
● LO2

On July 1, 2011, Ross-Livermore Industries issued nine-month notes in the amount of $400 million. Interest is payable at maturity.

Required:
Determine the amount of interest expense that should be recorded in a year-end adjusting entry under each of the following independent assumptions:

	Interest Rate	Fiscal Year-End
1.	12%	December 31
2.	10%	September 30
3.	9%	October 31
4.	6%	January 31

E 13–3
Short-term notes
● LO2

The following selected transactions relate to liabilities of United Insulation Corporation. United's fiscal year ends on December 31.

Required:
Prepare the appropriate journal entries through the maturity of each liability.

2011

Jan. 13   Negotiated a revolving credit agreement with Parish Bank that can be renewed annually upon bank approval. The amount available under the line of credit is $20 million at the bank's prime rate.

Feb. 1   Arranged a three-month bank loan of $5 million with Parish Bank under the line of credit agreement. Interest at the prime rate of 10% was payable at maturity.

May 1   Paid the 10% note at maturity.

Dec. 1   Supported by the credit line, issued $10 million of commercial paper on a nine-month note. Interest was discounted at issuance at a 9% discount rate.

31   Recorded any necessary adjusting entry(s).

2012

Sept. 1   Paid the commercial paper at maturity.

E 13–4
Paid future
absences
● LO3

JWS Transport Company's employees earn vacation time at the rate of 1 hour per 40-hour work period. The vacation pay vests immediately (that is, an employee is entitled to the pay even if employment terminates). During 2011, total wages paid to employees equaled $404,000, including $4,000 for vacations actually taken in 2011 but not including vacations related to 2011 that will be taken in 2012. All vacations earned before 2011 were taken before January 1, 2011. No accrual entries have been made for the vacations. No over-time premium and no bonuses were paid during the period.

Required:

Prepare the appropriate adjusting entry for vacations earned but not taken in 2011.

E 13–5
Paid future
absences
● LO3

On January 1, 2011, Poplar Fabricators Corporation agreed to grant its employees two weeks' vacation each year, with the stipulation that vacations earned each year can be taken the following year. For the year ended December 31, 2011, Poplar Fabricators' employees each earned an average of $900 per week. Seven hundred vacation weeks earned in 2011 were not taken during 2011.

Required:

1. Prepare the appropriate adjusting entry for vacations earned but not taken in 2011.
2. Suppose that, by the time vacations actually are taken in 2012, wage rates for employees have risen by an average of 5 percent from their 2011 level. Also, assume wages earned in 2012 (including vacations earned and taken in 2012) were $31 million. Prepare a journal entry that summarizes 2012 wages and the payment for 2011 vacations taken in 2012.

E 13–6
Customer
advances; sales
taxes
● LO3

Bavarian Bar and Grill opened for business in November 2011. During its first two months of operation, the restaurant sold gift certificates in various amounts totaling $5,200, mostly as Christmas presents. They are redeemable for meals within two years of the purchase date, although experience within the industry indicates that 80% of gift certificates are redeemed within one year. Certificates totaling $1,300 were presented for redemption during 2011 for meals having a total price of $2,100. The sales tax rate on restaurant sales is 4%, assessed at the time meals (not gift certificates) are purchased. Sales taxes will be remitted in January.

Required:

1. Prepare the appropriate journal entries (in summary form) for the gift certificates sold during 2011 (keeping in mind that, in actuality, each sale of a gift certificate or a meal would be recorded individually).
2. Determine the liability for gift certificates to be reported on the December 31, 2011, balance sheet.
3. What is the appropriate classification (current or noncurrent) of the liabilities at December 31, 2011? Why?

E 13–7
Customer deposits
● LO3

Diversified Semiconductors sells perishable electronic components. Some must be shipped and stored in reusable protective containers. Customers pay a deposit for each container received. The deposit is equal to the container's cost. They receive a refund when the container is returned. During 2011, deposits collected on containers shipped were $850,000.

Deposits are forfeited if containers are not returned within 18 months. Containers held by customers at January 1, 2011, represented deposits of $530,000. In 2011, $790,000 was refunded and deposits forfeited were $35,000.

Required:

1. Prepare the appropriate journal entries for the deposits received and returned during 2011.
2. Determine the liability for refundable deposits to be reported on the December 31, 2011, balance sheet.

E 13–8
Various
transactions
involving advance
collections
● LO3

The following selected transactions relate to liabilities of Interstate Farm Implements for December of 2011. Interstate's fiscal year ends on December 31.

Required:

Prepare the appropriate journal entries for these transactions.

1. On December 15, received $7,500 from Bradley Farms toward the purchase of a $98,000 tractor to be delivered on January 6, 2012.
2. During December, received $25,500 of refundable deposits relating to containers used to transport equipment parts.
3. During December, credit sales totaled $800,000. The state sales tax rate is 5% and the local sales tax rate is 2%. (This is a summary journal entry for the many individual sales transactions for the period.)

E 13–9
Gift Cards
● LO3

CircuitTown commenced a gift card program in January 2011 and sold $10,000 of gift cards in January, $15,000 in February, and $16,000 in March of 2011 before discontinuing further gift card sales. During 2011, gift card redemptions were $6,000 for the January gift cards sold, $4,500 for the February cards, and $4,000 for the March cards. CircuitTown considers gift cards to be "broken" (not redeemable) 10 months after sale. (For purposes of this question, assume that gift-card sales occur halfway through each month on average.)

Required:

1. How much revenue will CircuitTown recognize with respect to January gift card sales during 2011?
2. Prepare journal entries to record the sale of January gift cards, redemption of gift cards (ignore sales tax), and breakage (expiration) of gift cards.
3. How much revenue will CircuitTown recognize with respect to March gift card sales during 2011?
4. What liability for unearned revenue associated with gift card sales would CircuitTown show as of December 31, 2011?

E 13–10
Current–noncurrent classification of debt; Sprint Corporation
● LO1 LO4

An annual report of **Sprint Corporation** contained a rather lengthy narrative entitled "Review of Segmental Results of Operation." The narrative noted that short-term notes payable and commercial paper outstanding at the end of the year aggregated $756 million and that during the following year "This entire balance will be replaced by the issuance of long-term debt or will continue to be refinanced under existing long-term credit facilities."

Required:

How did Sprint report the debt in its balance sheet? Why?

E 13–11
Current–noncurrent classification of debt; Sprint Corporation
● LO1 LO4 LO7

Consider the information presented in E13-10.

Required:

1. How would Sprint report the debt in its balance sheet if it reported under IFRS? Why?
2. Would your answer to requirement 1 change if Sprint obtained its long-term credit facility after the balance sheet date? Why?

E 13–12
Current–noncurrent classification of debt
● LO1 LO4

At December 31, 2011, Newman Engineering's liabilities include the following:

1. $10 million of 9% bonds were issued for $10 million on May 31, 1988. The bonds mature on May 31, 2022, but bondholders have the option of calling (demanding payment on) the bonds on May 31, 2012. However, the option to call is not expected to be exercised, given prevailing market conditions.
2. $14 million of 8% notes are due on May 31, 2015. A debt covenant requires Newman to maintain current assets at least equal to 175% of its current liabilities. On December 31, 2011, Newman is in violation of this covenant. Newman obtained a waiver from National City Bank until June 2012, having convinced the bank that the company's normal 2 to 1 ratio of current assets to current liabilities will be reestablished during the first half of 2012.
3. $7 million of 11% bonds were issued for $7 million on August 31, 1978. The bonds mature on July 31, 2012. Sufficient cash is expected to be available to retire the bonds at maturity.

Required:

What portion of the debt can be excluded from classification as a current liability (that is, reported as a noncurrent liability)? Explain.

E 13–13
Warranties
● LO5 LO6

Cupola Awning Corporation introduced a new line of commercial awnings in 2011 that carry a two-year warranty against manufacturer's defects. Based on their experience with previous product introductions, warranty costs are expected to approximate 3% of sales. Sales and actual warranty expenditures for the first year of selling the product were:

Sales	Actual Warranty Expenditures
$5,000,000	$37,500

Required:

1. Does this situation represent a loss contingency? Why or why not? How should Cupola account for it?
2. Prepare journal entries that summarize sales of the awnings (assume all credit sales) and any aspects of the warranty that should be recorded during 2011.
3. What amount should Cupola report as a liability at December 31, 2011?

E 13–14
Extended warranties
● LO5 LO6

Carnes Electronics sells consumer electronics that carry a 90-day manufacturer's warranty. At the time of purchase, customers are offered the opportunity to also buy a two-year extended warranty for an additional charge. During the year, Carnes received $412,000 for these extended warranties (approximately evenly throughout the year).

Required:

1. Does this situation represent a loss contingency? Why or why not? How should it be accounted for?
2. Prepare journal entries that summarize sales of the extended warranties (assume all credit sales) and any aspects of the warranty that should be recorded during the year.

E 13–15
Contingency;
product recall
● LO5 LO6

Sound Audio manufactures and sells audio equipment for automobiles. Engineers notified management in December 2011 of a circuit flaw in an amplifier that poses a potential fire hazard. An intense investigation indicated that a product recall is virtually certain, estimated to cost the company $2 million. The fiscal year ends on December 31.

Required:
1. Should this loss contingency be accrued, disclosed only, or neither? Explain.
2. What loss, if any, should Sound Audio report in its 2011 income statement?
3. What liability, if any, should Sound Audio report in its 2011 balance sheet?
4. Prepare any journal entry needed.

E 13–16
Impairment of
accounts receivable
● LO5 LO6

The Manda Panda Company uses the allowance method to account for bad debts. At the beginning of 2011, the allowance account had a credit balance of $75,000. Credit sales for 2011 totaled $2,400,000 and the year-end accounts receivable balance was $490,000. During this year, $73,000 in receivables were determined to be uncollectible. Manda Panda anticipates that 3% of all credit sales will ultimately become uncollectible. The fiscal year ends on December 31.

Required:
1. Does this situation describe a loss contingency? Explain.
2. What is the bad debt expense that Manda Panda should report in its 2011 income statement?
3. Prepare the appropriate journal entry to record the contingency.
4. What is the net realizable value (book value) Manda Panda should report in its 2011 balance sheet?

E 13–17
Premiums
● LO5 LO6

Drew-Richards iMusic is a regional music media reseller. As a promotion, it offered $5 cash rebates on specific CDs. Customers must mail in a proof-of-purchase seal from the package plus the cash register receipt to receive the rebate. Experience suggests that 70% of the rebates will be claimed. Twenty thousand of the CDs were sold in 2011. Total rebates to customers in 2011 were $22,000 and were recorded as promotional expense when paid. The fiscal year ends on December 31.

Required:
1. What is the promotional expense that Drew-Richards should report in its 2011 income statement?
2. What is the premium liability that Drew-Richards should report in its 2011 balance sheet?
3. Prepare the appropriate journal entry to record the contingency.

E 13–18
Unasserted
assessment
● LO6

At April 1, 2012, the Environmental Protection Agency is in the process of investigating a possible chemical leak last June at a facility of Shu Lamination, Inc. The EPA has not yet proposed a penalty assessment. Shu's fiscal year ends on December 31, 2011. The company's financial statements are published in April 2012.

Required:
For each of the following scenarios, determine the appropriate way to report the situation. Explain your reasoning and prepare any necessary journal entry.
1. Management feels an assessment is *reasonably possible,* and if an assessment is made an unfavorable settlement of $13 million is *reasonably possible.*
2. Management feels an assessment is *reasonably possible,* and if an assessment is made an unfavorable settlement of $13 million is *probable.*
3. Management feels an assessment is *probable,* and if an assessment is made an unfavorable settlement of $13 million is *reasonably possible.*
4. Management feels an assessment is *probable,* and if an assessment is made an unfavorable settlement of $13 million is *probable.*

E 13–19
Various
transactions
involving
contingencies
● LO5 LO6

The following selected transactions relate to contingencies of Classical Tool Makers, Inc., which began operations in July 2011. Classical's fiscal year ends on December 31. Financial statements are published in April 2012.

Required:
Prepare the year-end entries for any amounts that should be recorded as a result of each of these contingencies and indicate whether a disclosure note is indicated.
1. Classical's products carry a one-year warranty against manufacturer's defects. Based on previous experience, warranty costs are expected to approximate 4% of sales. Sales were $2 million (all credit) for 2011. Actual warranty expenditures were $30,800 and were recorded as warranty expense when incurred.
2. Although no customer accounts have been shown to be uncollectible, Classical estimates that 2% of credit sales will eventually prove uncollectible.

3. In December 2011, the state of Tennessee filed suit against Classical, seeking penalties for violations of clean air laws. On January 23, 2012, Classical reached a settlement with state authorities to pay $1.5 million in penalties.

4. Classical is the plaintiff in a $4 million lawsuit filed against a supplier. The suit is in final appeal and attorneys advise that it is virtually certain that Classical will win the case and be awarded $2.5 million.

5. In November 2011, Classical became aware of a design flaw in an industrial saw that poses a potential electrical hazard. A product recall appears unavoidable. Such an action would likely cost the company $500,000.

6. Classical offered $25 cash rebates on a new model of jigsaw. Customers must mail in a proof-of-purchase seal from the package plus the cash register receipt to receive the rebate. Experience suggests that 60% of the rebates will be claimed. Ten thousand of the jigsaws were sold in 2011. Total rebates to customers in 2011 were $105,000 and were recorded as promotional expense when paid.

E 13–20
Various transactions involving contingencies
● LO5 LO6 LO7

The following selected circumstances relate to pending lawsuits for Erismus, Inc. Erismus's fiscal year ends on December 31. Financial statements are published in March 2012. Erismus prepares its financial statements according to International Financial Reporting Standards.

Required:
Indicate the amount of asset or liability that Erismus would record, and explain your answer.

1. Erismus is defending against a lawsuit. Erismus's management believes the company has a slightly worse than 50/50 chance of eventually prevailing in court, and that if it loses, the judgment will be $1,000,000.

2. Erismus is defending against a lawsuit. Erismus's management believes it is probable that the company will lose in court. If it loses, management believes that damages could fall anywhere in the range of $2,000,000 to $4,000,000, with any damage in that range equally likely.

3. Erismus is defending against a lawsuit. Erismus's management believes it is probable that the company will lose in court. If it loses, management believes that damages will eventually be $5,000,000, with a present value of $3,500,000.

4. Erismus is a plaintiff in a lawsuit. Erismus's management believes it is probable that the company eventually will prevail in court, and that if it prevails, the judgment will be $1,000,000.

E 13–21
Disclosures of liabilities
● LO1 through LO6

Indicate (by letter) the way each of the items listed below should be reported in a balance sheet at December 31, 2011.

Item	Reporting Method
_____ 1. Commercial paper.	N. Not reported
_____ 2. Noncommitted line of credit.	C. Current liability
_____ 3. Customer advances.	L. Long-term liability
_____ 4. Estimated warranty cost.	D. Disclosure note only
_____ 5. Accounts payable.	A. Asset
_____ 6. Long-term bonds that will be callable by the creditor in the upcoming year unless an existing violation is not corrected (there is a reasonable possibility the violation will be corrected within the grace period).	
_____ 7. Note due March 3, 2012.	
_____ 8. Interest accrued on note, Dec. 31, 2011.	
_____ 9. Short-term bank loan to be paid with proceeds of sale of common stock.	
_____ 10. A determinable gain that is contingent on a future event that appears extremely likely to occur in three months.	
_____ 11. Unasserted assessment of back taxes that probably will be asserted, in which case there would probably be a loss in six months.	
_____ 12. Unasserted assessment of back taxes with a reasonable possibility of being asserted, in which case there would probably be a loss in 13 months.	
_____ 13. A determinable loss from a past event that is contingent on a future event that appears extremely likely to occur in three months.	
_____ 14. Bond sinking fund.	
_____ 15. Long-term bonds callable by the creditor in the upcoming year that are not expected to be called.	

E 13–22
Warranty expense;
change in estimate
● LO5 LO6

Woodmier Lawn Products introduced a new line of commercial sprinklers in 2010 that carry a one-year warranty against manufacturer's defects. Because this was the first product for which the company offered a warranty, trade publications were consulted to determine the experience of others in the industry. Based on that experience, warranty costs were expected to approximate 2% of sales. Sales of the sprinklers in 2010 were $2.5 million. Accordingly, the following entries relating to the contingency for warranty costs were recorded during the first year of selling the product:

Accrued liability and expense		
Warranty expense (2% × $2,500,000)	50,000	
Estimated warranty liability		50,000
Actual expenditures (summary entry)		
Estimated warranty liability	23,000	
Cash, wages payable, parts and supplies, etc.		23,000

In late 2011, the company's claims experience was evaluated and it was determined that claims were far more than expected—3% of sales rather than 2%.

Required:

1. Assuming sales of the sprinklers in 2011 were $3.6 million and warranty expenditures in 2011 totaled $88,000, prepare any journal entries related to the warranty.

2. Assuming sales of the sprinklers were discontinued after 2010, prepare any journal entry(s) in 2011 related to the warranty.

E 13–23
Change in
accounting estimate
● LO3

The Commonwealth of Virginia filed suit in October 2009 against Northern Timber Corporation, seeking civil penalties and injunctive relief for violations of environmental laws regulating forest conservation. When the 2010 financial statements were issued in 2011, Northern had not reached a settlement with state authorities, but legal counsel advised Northern Timber that it was probable the ultimate settlement would be $1,000,000 in penalties. The following entry was recorded:

Loss—litigation	1,000,000	
Liability—litigation		1,000,000

Late in 2011, a settlement was reached with state authorities to pay a total of $600,000 to cover the cost of violations.

Required:

1. Prepare any journal entries related to the change.

2. Briefly describe other steps Northern should take to report the change.

E 13–24
Contingency; Dow
Chemical Company
disclosure
● LO5 LO6

Real World Financials

The **Dow Chemical Company** provides chemical, plastic, and agricultural products and services to various consumer markets. The following excerpt is taken from the disclosure notes of Dow's 2008 annual report:

At December 31, 2008, the Company had accrued obligations of $312 million for environmental remediation and restoration costs, including $22 million for the remediation of Superfund sites. This is management's best estimate of the costs for remediation and restoration with respect to environmental matters for which the Company has accrued liabilities, although the ultimate cost with respect to these particular matters could range up to approximately twice that amount. Inherent uncertainties exist in these estimates primarily due to unknown environmental conditions, changing governmental regulations and legal standards regarding liability, and emerging remediation technologies for handling site remediation and restoration.

Required:

Does the excerpt describe a loss contingency? Under what conditions would Dow accrue such a contingency? What journal entry would Dow use to record this amount of provision (loss)?

E 13–25
Payroll-related
liabilities
● Appendix

Lee Financial Services pays employees monthly. Payroll information is listed below for January 2011, the first month of Lee's fiscal year. Assume that none of the employees exceeded any relevant wage base.

Salaries	$500,000
Federal income taxes to be withheld	100,000
Federal unemployment tax rate	0.80%
State unemployment tax rate (after FUTA deduction)	5.40%
Social Security (FICA) tax rate	7.65%

Required:

Prepare the appropriate journal entries to record salaries and wages expense and payroll tax expense for the January 2011 pay period.

E 13–26
FASB codification research
● **LO5**

The *FASB Accounting Standards Codification* represents the single source of authoritative U.S. generally accepted accounting principles.

Required:

1. Obtain the relevant authoritative literature on recognition of contingent losses using the FASB's Codification Research System at the FASB website (**www.fasb.org**). What is the specific citation that describes the guidelines for determining when an expense and liability should be accrued for a contingent loss?
2. List the guidelines.

E 13–27
FASB codification research
● **LO3 LO4 LO5**

Access the FASB's Codification Research System at the FASB website (**www.fasb.org**).

Required:

Determine the specific citation for accounting for each of the following items:
1. If it is only reasonably possible that a contingent loss will occur, the contingent loss should be disclosed.
2. Criteria allowing short-term liabilities expected to be refinanced to be classified as long-term liabilities.
3. Accounting for the revenue from separately priced extended warranty contracts.
4. The criteria to determine if an employer must accrue a liability for vacation pay.

CPA AND CMA REVIEW QUESTIONS

CPA Exam Questions

The following questions are used in the Kaplan CPA Review Course to study current liabilities and contingencies while preparing for the CPA examination. Determine the response that best completes the statements or questions.

● **LO3**

1. On March 1, 2010, Fine Co. borrowed $10,000 and signed a two-year note bearing interest at 12% per annum compounded annually. Interest is payable in full at maturity on February 28, 2012. What amount should Fine report as a liability for accrued interest at December 31, 2011?
   a. $ 0
   b. $1,000
   c. $1,200
   d. $2,320

● **LO3**

2. North Corp. has an employee benefit plan for compensated absences that gives employees 10 paid vacation days and 10 paid sick days. Both vacation and sick days can be carried over indefinitely. Employees can elect to receive payment in lieu of vacation days; however, no payment is given for sick days not taken. At December 31, 2011, North's unadjusted balance of liability for compensated absences was $21,000. North estimated that there were 150 vacation days and 75 sick days available at December 31, 2011. North's employees earn an average of $100 per day. In its December 31, 2011, balance sheet, what amount of liability for compensated absences is North required to report?
   a. $15,000
   b. $21,000
   c. $22,500
   d. $36,000

● **LO4**

3. On December 31, 2011, Largo, Inc., had a $750,000 note payable outstanding, due July 31, 2012. Largo borrowed the money to finance construction of a new plant. Largo planned to refinance the note by issuing long-term bonds. Because Largo temporarily had excess cash, it prepaid $250,000 of the note on January 12, 2012. In February 2012, Largo completed a $1,500,000 bond offering. Largo will use the bond offering proceeds to repay the note payable at its maturity and to pay construction costs during 2012. On March 3, 2012, Largo issued its 2011 financial statements. What amount of the note payable should Largo include in the current liabilities section of its December 31, 2011, balance sheet?
   a. $250,000
   b. $750,000
   c. $500,000
   d. $ 0

● LO5

4. In May 2008, Caso Co. filed suit against Wayne, Inc., seeking $1,900,000 in damages for patent infringement. A court verdict in November 2011 awarded Caso $1,500,000 in damages, but Wayne's appeal is not expected to be decided before 2013. Caso's counsel believes it is probable that Caso will be successful against Wayne for an estimated amount in the range between $800,000 and $1,100,000, with $1,000,000 considered the most likely amount. What amount should Caso record as income from the lawsuit in the year ended December 31, 2011?
   a. $ 0
   b. $ 800,000
   c. $1,000,000
   d. $1,500,000

5. In December 2011, Mill Co. began including one coupon in each package of candy that it sells and offering a toy in exchange for 50 cents and five coupons. The toys cost Mill 80 cents each. Eventually 60% of the coupons will be redeemed. During December, Mill sold 110,000 packages of candy and no coupons were redeemed. In its December 31, 2011, balance sheet, what amount should Mill report as estimated liability for coupons?
   a. $ 3,960
   b. $10,560
   c. $19,800
   d. $52,800

● LO6

6. During 2011, Gum Co. introduced a new product carrying a two-year warranty against defects. The estimated warranty costs related to dollar sales are 2% within 12 months following the sale and 4% in the second 12 months following the sale. Sales and actual warranty expenditures for the years ended December 31, 2011, and 2012, are as follows:

	Sales	Actual Warranty Expenditures
2011	$150,000	$2,250
2012	250,000	7,500
	$400,000	$9,750

What amount should Gum report as estimated warranty liability in its December 31, 2012, balance sheet?
   a. $ 2,500
   b. $ 4,250
   c. $11,250
   d. $14,250

CMA Exam Questions

The following questions dealing with current liabilities and contingencies are adapted from questions that previously appeared on Certified Management Accountant (CMA) examinations. The CMA designation sponsored by the Institute of Management Accountants (**www.imanet.org**) provides members with an objective measure of knowledge and competence in the field of management accounting. Determine the response that best completes the statements or questions.

● LO4

1. Lister Company intends to refinance a portion of its short-term debt next year and is negotiating a long-term financing agreement with a local bank. This agreement will be noncancelable and will extend for 2 years. The amount of short-term debt that Lister Company can exclude from its statement of financial position at December 31
   a. May exceed the amount available for refinancing under the agreement.
   b. Depends on the demonstrated ability to consummate the refinancing.
   c. Must be adjusted by the difference between the present value and the market value of the short-term debt.
   d. Is reduced by the proportionate change in the working capital ratio.

● LO5

2. An employee has the right to receive compensation for future paid leave, and the payment of compensation is probable. If the obligation relates to rights that vest but the amount cannot be reasonably estimated, the employer should
   a. Accrue a liability with proper disclosure.
   b. Not accrue a liability nor disclose the situation.
   c. Accrue a liability; however, the additional disclosure is not required.
   d. Not accrue a liability; however, disclosure is required.

● LO5

3. The accrual of a contingent liability and the related loss should be recorded when the
   a. Loss resulting from a future event may be material in relation to income.
   b. Future event that gives rise to the liability is unusual in nature and nonrecurring.
   c. Amount of the loss resulting from the event is reasonably estimated and the occurrence of the loss is probable.
   d. Event that gives rise to the liability is unusual and its occurrence is probable.

● LO6

4. For the past 3 months, Kenton Inc. has been negotiating a labor contract with potentially significant wage increases. Before completing the year-end financial statements on November 30, Kenton determined that the contract was likely to be signed in the near future. Kenton has estimated that the effect of the new contract will cost the company either $100,000, $200,000, or $300,000. Also Kenton believes that each estimate has an equal chance of occurring and that the likelihood of the new contract being retroactive to the fiscal year ended November 30 is probable. According to GAAP regarding contingencies, Kenton should
   a. Do nothing because no loss will occur if the contract is never signed.
   b. Disclose each loss contingency amount in the notes to the November 30 financial statements.
   c. Accrue $100,000 in the income statement, and disclose the nature of the contingency and the additional loss exposure.
   d. Follow conservatism and accrue $300,000 in the income statement, and disclose the nature of the contingency.

PROBLEMS

An alternate exercise and problem set is available on the text website: www.mhhe.com/spiceland6e

P 13–1
Bank loan; accrued interest

● LO2

Blanton Plastics, a household plastic product manufacturer, borrowed $14 million cash on October 1, 2011, to provide working capital for year-end production. Blanton issued a four-month, 12% promissory note to L&T Bank under a prearranged short-term line of credit. Interest on the note was payable at maturity. Each firm's fiscal period is the calendar year.

Required:
1. Prepare the journal entries to record (a) the issuance of the note by Blanton Plastics and (b) L&T Bank's receivable on October 1, 2011.
2. Prepare the journal entries by both firms to record all subsequent events related to the note through January 31, 2012.
3. Suppose the face amount of the note was adjusted to include interest (a noninterest-bearing note) and 12% is the bank's stated discount rate. (a) Prepare the journal entries to record the issuance of the noninterest-bearing note by Blanton Plastics on October 1, 2011, the adjusting entry at December 31, and payment of the note at maturity. (b) What would be the effective interest rate?

P 13–2
Various transactions involving liabilities

● LO2 through LO4

Camden Biotechnology began operations in September 2011. The following selected transactions relate to liabilities of the company for September 2011 through March 2012. Camden's fiscal year ends on December 31. Its financial statements are issued in April.

2011
a. On September 5, opened checking accounts at Second Commercial Bank and negotiated a short-term line of credit of up to $15,000,000 at the bank's prime rate (10.5% at the time). The company will pay no commitment fees.
b. On October 1, borrowed $12 million cash from Second Commercial Bank under the line of credit and issued a five-month promissory note. Interest at the prime rate of 10% was payable at maturity. Management planned to issue 10-year bonds in February to repay the note.
c. Received $2,600 of refundable deposits in December for reusable containers used to transport and store chemical-based products.
d. For the September–December period, sales on account totaled $4,100,000. The state sales tax rate is 3% and the local sales tax rate is 3%. (This is a summary journal entry for the many individual sales transactions for the period.)
e. Recorded the adjusting entry for accrued interest.

2012
f. In February, issued $10 million of 10-year bonds at face value and paid the bank loan on the March 1 due date.
g. Half of the storage containers covered by refundable deposits were returned in March. The remaining containers are expected to be returned during the next six months.

Required:
1. Prepare the appropriate journal entries for these transactions.
2. Prepare the current and long-term liability sections of the December 31, 2011, balance sheet. Trade accounts payable on that date were $252,000.

P 13–3
Current–noncurrent classification of debt

● LO1 LO4

The balance sheet at December 31, 2011, for Nevada Harvester Corporation includes the liabilities listed below:

a. 11% bonds with a face amount of $40 million were issued for $40 million on October 31, 2000. The bonds mature on October 31, 2022. Bondholders have the option of calling (demanding payment on) the bonds on October 31, 2012, at a redemption price of $40 million. Market conditions are such that the call is not expected to be exercised.

b. Management intended to refinance $6 million of its 10% notes that mature in May 2012. In early March, prior to the actual issuance of the 2011 financial statements, Nevada Harvester negotiated a line of credit with a commercial bank for up to $5 million any time during 2012. Any borrowings will mature two years from the date of borrowing.

c. Noncallable 12% bonds with a face amount of $20 million were issued for $20 million on September 30, 1988. The bonds mature on September 30, 2012. Sufficient cash is expected to be available to retire the bonds at maturity.

d. A $12 million 9% bank loan is payable on October 31, 2017. The bank has the right to demand payment after any fiscal year-end in which Nevada Harvester's ratio of current assets to current liabilities falls below a contractual minimum of 1.7 to 1 and remains so for six months. That ratio was 1.45 on December 31, 2011, due primarily to an intentional temporary decline in inventory levels. Normal inventory levels will be reestablished during the first quarter of 2012.

Required:

1. Determine the amount that can be excluded from classification as a current liability (that is, reported as a noncurrent liability) for each. Explain the reasoning behind your classifications.

2. Prepare the liability section of a classified balance sheet and any necessary footnote disclosure for Nevada Harvester at December 31, 2011. Accounts payable and accruals are $22 million.

P 13–4
Various liabilities

● LO1 through LO4

The unadjusted trial balance of the Manufacturing Equitable at December 31, 2011, the end of its fiscal year, included the following account balances. Manufacturing's 2011 financial statements were issued on April 1, 2012.

Accounts receivable	$ 92,500
Accounts payable	35,000
Bank notes payable	600,000
Mortgage note payable	1,200,000

Other information:

a. The bank notes, issued August 1, 2011, are due on July 31, 2012, and pay interest at a rate of 10%, payable at maturity.

b. The mortgage note is due on March 1, 2012. Interest at 9% has been paid up to December 31 (assume 9% is a realistic rate). Manufacturing intended at December 31, 2011, to refinance the note on its due date with a new 10-year mortgage note. In fact, on March 1, Manufacturing paid $250,000 in cash on the principal balance and refinanced the remaining $950,000.

c. Included in the accounts receivable balance at December 31, 2011, were two subsidiary accounts that had been overpaid and had credit balances totaling $18,000. The accounts were of two major customers who were expected to order more merchandise from Manufacturing and apply the overpayments to those future purchases.

d. On November 1, 2011, Manufacturing rented a portion of its factory to a tenant for $30,000 per year, payable in advance. The payment for the 12 months ended October 31, 2012, was received as required and was credited to rent revenue.

Required:

1. Prepare any necessary adjusting journal entries at December 31, 2011, pertaining to each item of other information (a–d).

2. Prepare the current and long-term liability sections of the December 31, 2011, balance sheet.

P 13–5
Bonus compensation; algebra

● LO3

Sometimes compensation packages include bonuses designed to provide performance incentives to employees. The difficulty a bonus can cause accountants is not an accounting problem, but a math problem. The complication is that the bonus formula sometimes specifies that the calculation of the bonus is based in part on the bonus itself. This occurs anytime the bonus is a percentage of income because expenses are components of income, and the bonus is an expense.

Regalia Fashions has an incentive compensation plan through which a division manager receives a bonus equal to 10% of the division's net income. Division income in 2011 before the bonus and income tax was $150,000. The tax rate is 30%.

Required:

1. Express the bonus formula as one or more algebraic equation(s).*

2. Using these formulas calculate the amount of the bonus.

---

*Remember when you were studying algebra and you wondered if you would ever use it?

3. Prepare the adjusting entry to record the bonus compensation.
4. Bonus arrangements take many forms. Suppose the bonus specifies that the bonus is 10% of the division's income before tax, but after the bonus itself. Calculate the amount of the bonus.

P 13–6
Various contingencies
● **LO5 LO6**

Eastern Manufacturing is involved with several situations that possibly involve contingencies. Each is described below. Eastern's fiscal year ends December 31, and the 2011 financial statements are issued on March 15, 2012.

a. Eastern is involved in a lawsuit resulting from a dispute with a supplier. On February 3, 2012, judgment was rendered against Eastern in the amount of $107 million plus interest, a total of $122 million. Eastern plans to appeal the judgment and is unable to predict its outcome though it is not expected to have a material adverse effect on the company.

b. In November 2010, the State of Nevada filed suit against Eastern, seeking civil penalties and injunctive relief for violations of environmental laws regulating hazardous waste. On January 12, 2012, Eastern reached a settlement with state authorities. Based upon discussions with legal counsel, the Company feels it is probable that $140 million will be required to cover the cost of violations. Eastern believes that the ultimate settlement of this claim will not have a material adverse effect on the company.

c. Eastern is the plaintiff in a $200 million lawsuit filed against United Steel for damages due to lost profits from rejected contracts and for unpaid receivables. The case is in final appeal and legal counsel advises that it is probable that Eastern will prevail and be awarded $100 million.

d. At March 15, 2012, the Environmental Protection Agency is in the process of investigating possible soil contamination at various locations of several companies including Eastern. The EPA has not yet proposed a penalty assessment. Management feels an assessment is reasonably possible, and if an assessment is made an unfavorable settlement of up to $33 million is reasonably possible.

Required:
1. Determine the appropriate means of reporting each situation. Explain your reasoning.
2. Prepare any necessary journal entries and disclosure notes.

P 13–7
Various liabilities
● **LO4 LO5**
LO6 LO7

HolmesWatson (HW) is considering what the effect would be of reporting its liabilities under IFRS rather than U.S. GAAP. The following facts apply:

a. HW is defending against a lawsuit and believes it is virtually certain to lose in court. If it loses the lawsuit, management estimates it will need to pay a range of damages that falls between $5,000,000 and $10,000,000, with each amount in that range equally likely.

b. HW is defending against another lawsuit that is identical to item (a), but the relevant losses will only occur far into the future. The present values of the endpoints of the range are $3,000,000 and $8,000,000, with the timing of cash flow somewhat uncertain. HW considers these effects of the time value of money to be material.

c. HW is defending against another lawsuit for which management believes HW has a slightly worse than 50/50 chance of losing in court. If it loses the lawsuit, management estimates HW will need to pay a range of damages that falls between $3,000,000 and $9,000,000, with each amount in that range equally likely.

d. HW has $10,000,000 of short-term debt that it intends to refinance on a long-term basis. Soon after the balance sheet date, but before issuance of the financial statements, HW obtained the financing necessary to refinance the debt.

Required:
1. For each item, indicate how treatment of the amount would differ between U.S. GAAP and IFRS.
2. Consider the total effect of items a–d. If HW's goal is to show the lowest total liabilities, which set of standards, U.S. GAAP or IFRS, best helps it meet that goal?

P 13–8
Expected cash flow approach; product recall
● **LO6**

The Heinrich Tire Company recalled a tire in its subcompact line in December 2011. Costs associated with the recall were originally thought to approximate $50 million. Now, though, while management feels it is probable the company will incur substantial costs, all discussions indicate that $50 million is an excessive amount. Based on prior recalls in the industry, management has provided the following probability distribution for the potential loss:

Loss Amount	Probability
$40 million	20%
$30 million	50%
$20 million	30%

An arrangement with a consortium of distributors requires that all recall costs be settled at the end of 2012. The risk-free rate of interest is 5%.

Required:
1. Applying the expected cash flow approach of *SFAC No. 7*, estimate Heinrich's liability at the end of the 2011 fiscal year.
2. Prepare the journal entry to record the contingent liability (and loss).

3. Prepare the journal entry to accrue interest on the liability at the end of 2012.

4. Prepare the journal entry to pay the liability at the end of 2012, assuming the actual cost is $30 million. Heinrich records an additional loss if the actual costs are higher or a gain if the costs are lower.

5. By the traditional approach to measuring loss contingencies, what amount would Heinrich record at the end of 2011 for the loss and contingent liability?

P 13–9
Subsequent events
● LO6

Lincoln Chemicals became involved in investigations by the U.S. Environmental Protection Agency in regard to damages connected to waste disposal sites. Below are four possibilities regarding the timing of (A) the alleged damage caused by Lincoln, (B) an investigation by the EPA, (C) the EPA assessment of penalties, and (D) ultimate settlement. In each case, assume that Lincoln is unaware of any problem until an investigation is begun. Also assume that once the EPA investigation begins, it is probable that a damage assessment will ensue and that once an assessment is made by the EPA, it is reasonably possible that a determinable amount will be paid by Lincoln.

Required:
For each case, decide whether (a) a loss should be accrued in the financial statements with an explanatory note, (b) a disclosure note only should be provided, or (c) no disclosure is necessary.

P 13–10
Subsequent events;
classification
of debt; loss
contingency;
financial statement
effects

● LO4 LO5

Van Rushing Hunting Goods' fiscal year ends on December 31. At the end of the 2011 fiscal year, the company had notes payable of $12 million due on February 8, 2012. Rushing sold 2 million shares of its $0.25 par, common stock on February 3, 2012, for $9 million. The proceeds from that sale along with $3 million from the maturation of some 3-month CDs were used to pay the notes payable on February 8.

Through his attorney, one of Rushing's construction workers notified management on January 5, 2012, that he planned to sue the company for $1 million related to a work-site injury on December 20, 2011. As of December 31, 2011, management had been unaware of the injury, but reached an agreement on February 23, 2012, to settle the matter by paying the employee's medical bills of $75,000.

Rushing's financial statements were finalized on March 3, 2012.

Required:

1. What amount(s) if any, related to the situations described should Rushing report among current liabilities in its balance sheet at December 31, 2011? Why?

2. What amount(s) if any, related to the situations described should Rushing report among long-term liabilities in its balance sheet at December 31, 2011? Why?

3. How would your answers to requirements 1 and 2 differ if the settlement agreement had occurred on March 15, 2012, instead? Why?

4. How would your answers to requirements 1 and 2 differ if the work-site injury had occurred on January 3, 2012, instead? Why?

P 13–11
Concepts;
terminology

● LO1 through
LO4

Listed below are several terms and phrases associated with current liabilities. Pair each item from List A (by letter) with the item from List B that is most appropriately associated with it.

List A	List B
____ 1. Face amount × Interest rate × Time.	a. Informal agreement
____ 2. Payable with current assets.	b. Secured loan
____ 3. Short-term debt to be refinanced with common stock.	c. Refinancing prior to the issuance of the financial statements
____ 4. Present value of interest plus present value of principal.	d. Accounts payable
____ 5. Noninterest-bearing.	e. Accrued liabilities
____ 6. Noncommitted line of credit.	f. Commercial paper
____ 7. Pledged accounts receivable.	g. Current liabilities
____ 8. Reclassification of debt.	h. Long-term liability
____ 9. Purchased by other corporations.	i. Usual valuation of liabilities
____ 10. Expenses not yet paid.	j. Interest on debt
____ 11. Liability until refunded.	k. Customer advances
____ 12. Applied against purchase price.	l. Customer deposits

P 13–12
Various liabilities;
balance sheet
classification;
prepare liability
section of balance
sheet; write
footnotes

● LO4 LO5

Transit Airlines provides regional jet service in the Mid-South. The following is information on liabilities of Transit at December 31, 2011. Transit's fiscal year ends on December 31. Its annual financial statements are issued in April.

1. Transit has outstanding 6.5% bonds with a face amount of $90 million. The bonds mature on July 31, 2020. Bondholders have the option of calling (demanding payment on) the bonds on July 31, 2012, at a redemption price of $90 million. Market conditions are such that the call option is not expected to be exercised.

2. A $30 million 8% bank loan is payable on October 31, 2017. The bank has the right to demand payment after any fiscal year-end in which Transit's ratio of current assets to current liabilities falls below a contractual minimum of 1.9 to 1 and remains so for 6 months. That ratio was 1.75 on December 31, 2011, due primarily to an intentional temporary decline in parts inventories. Normal inventory levels will be reestablished during the sixth week of 2012.

3. Transit management intended to refinance $45 million of 7% notes that mature in May of 2012. In late February 2012, prior to the issuance of the 2011 financial statements, Transit negotiated a line of credit with a commercial bank for up to $40 million any time during 2012. Any borrowings will mature two years from the date of borrowing.

4. Transit is involved in a lawsuit resulting from a dispute with a food caterer. On February 13, 2012, judgment was rendered against Transit in the amount of $53 million plus interest, a total of $54 million. Transit plans to appeal the judgment and is unable to predict its outcome though it is not expected to have a material adverse effect on the company.

Required:

1. How should the 6.5% bonds be classified by Transit among liabilities in its balance sheet? Explain.

2. How should the 8% bank loan be classified by Transit among liabilities in its balance sheet? Explain.

3. How should the 7% notes be classified by Transit among liabilities in its balance sheet? Explain.

4. How should the lawsuit be reported by Transit? Explain.

5. Prepare the liability section of a classified balance sheet for Transit Airlines at December 31, 2011. Transit's accounts payable and accruals were $43 million.

6. Draft appropriate footnote disclosures for Transit's financial statements at December 31, 2011, for each of the five items described.

P 13–13
Payroll-related
liabilities

● Appendix

Alamar Petroleum Company offers its employees the option of contributing retirement funds up to 5% of their wages or salaries, with the contribution being matched by Alamar. The company also pays 80% of medical and life insurance premiums. Deductions relating to these plans and other payroll information for the first biweekly payroll period of February are listed as follows:

Wages and salaries	$2,000,000
Employee contribution to voluntary retirement plan	84,000
Medical insurance premiums	42,000
Life insurance premiums	9,000
Federal income taxes to be withheld	400,000
Local income taxes to be withheld	53,000
Payroll taxes:	
Federal unemployment tax rate	0.80%
State unemployment tax rate (after FUTA deduction)	5.40%
Social Security tax rate	6.2%
Medicare tax rate	1.45%

Required:
Prepare the appropriate journal entries to record salaries and wages expense and payroll tax expense for the biweekly pay period. Assume that no employee's cumulative wages exceed the relevant wage bases.

BROADEN YOUR PERSPECTIVE

Apply your critical-thinking ability to the knowledge you've gained. These cases will provide you an opportunity to develop your research, analysis, judgment, and communication skills. You also will work with other students, integrate what you've learned, apply it in real world situations, and consider its global and ethical ramifications. This practice will broaden your knowledge and further develop your decision-making abilities.

Research Case 13–1

Bank loan; accrued interest

● LO1 LO2

A fellow accountant has solicited your opinion regarding the classification of short-term obligations repaid prior to being replaced by a long-term security. Cheshire Foods, Inc., issued $5,000,000 of short-term commercial paper during 2010 to finance construction of a plant. At September 30, 2011, Cheshire's fiscal year-end, the company intends to refinance the commercial paper by issuing long-term bonds. However, because Cheshire temporarily has excess cash, in November 2011 it liquidates $2,000,000 of the commercial paper as the paper matures. In December 2011, the company completes a $10,000,000 long-term bond issue. Later during December, it issues its September 30, 2011, financial statements. The proceeds of the long-term bond issue are to be used to replenish $2,000,000 in working capital, to pay $3,000,000 of commercial paper as it matures in January 2012, and to pay $5,000,000 of construction costs expected to be incurred later that year to complete the plant.

You initially are hesitant because you don't recall encountering a situation in which short-term obligations were repaid prior to being replaced by a long-term security. However, you are encouraged by a vague memory that this general topic is covered by GAAP literature you came across when reading an Internet article.

Required:

Determine how the $5,000,000 of commercial paper should be classified by consulting the authoritative GAAP literature and citing the appropriate location in the FASB Codification. Before doing so, formulate your own opinion on the proper treatment.

Real World Case 13–2

Returnable containers

● LO1 LO3

Real World Financials

The **Zoo Doo Compost Company** processes a premium organic fertilizer made with the help of the animals at the Memphis Zoo. Zoo Doo is sold in a specially designed plastic pail that may be kept and used for household chores or returned to the seller. The fertilizer is sold for $12.50 per two-gallon pail (including the $1.76 cost of the pail). For each pail returned, Zoo Doo donates $1 to the Memphis Zoo and the pail is used again.[34]

Required:

The founder and president of this start-up firm has asked your opinion on how to account for the donations to be made when fertilizer pails are returned. (Ignore any tax implications.)

Research Case 13–3

Relationship of liabilities to assets and owners' equity

● LO1

SFAC No. 6, "Elements of Financial Statements," states that "an entity's assets, liabilities, and equity (net assets) all pertain to the same set of probable future economic benefits." Explain this statement.

Judgment Case 13–4

Paid future absences

● LO3

Cates Computing Systems develops and markets commercial software for personal computers and workstations. Three situations involving compensation for possible future absences of Cates's employees are described below.

a. Cates compensates employees at their regular pay rate for time absent for military leave, maternity leave, and jury time. Employees are allowed predetermined absence periods for each type of absence.

b. Members of the new product development team are eligible for three months' paid sabbatical leave every four years. Five members of the team have just completed their fourth year of participation.

c. Company policy permits employees four paid sick days each year. Unused sick days can accumulate and can be carried forward to future years.

Required:

1. What are the conditions that require accrual of an expense and related liability for employees' compensation for future absences?

2. For each of the three situations, indicate the circumstances under which accrual of an expense and related liability is warranted.

Ethics Case 13–5

Outdoors R Us

● LO1

Outdoors R Us owns several membership-based campground resorts throughout the Southwest. The company sells campground sites to new members, usually during a get-acquainted visit and tour. The campgrounds offer a wider array of on-site facilities than most. New members sign a multiyear contract, pay a down payment, and

---

[34]Case based on Kay McCullen, "Take The Zoo Home With You!" *Head Lions,* July 1991; and a conversation with the Zoo Doo Compost Company president, Pierce Ledbetter.

make monthly installment payments. Because no credit check is made and many memberships originate on a spur-of-the-moment basis, cancellations are not uncommon.

Business has been brisk during its first three years of operations, and since going public in 2000, the market value of its stock has tripled. The first sign of trouble came in 2011 when the new sales dipped sharply.

One afternoon, two weeks before the end of the fiscal year, Diane Rice, CEO, and Gene Sun, controller, were having an active discussion in Sun's office.

Sun: I've thought more about our discussion yesterday. Maybe something can be done about profits.

Rice: I hope so. Our bonuses and stock value are riding on this period's performance.

Sun: We've been recording unearned revenues when new members sign up. Rather than recording liabilities at the time memberships are sold, I think we can justify reporting sales revenue for all memberships sold.

Rice: What will be the effect on profits?

Sun: I haven't run the numbers yet, but let's just say very favorable.

Required:

1. Why do you think liabilities had been recorded previously?

2. Is the proposal ethical?

3. Who would be affected if the proposal is implemented?

**Trueblood
Case 13–6**
Contingencies;
research; GAAP

● LO5

The following Trueblood case is recommended for use with this chapter. The case provides an excellent opportunity for class discussion, group projects, and writing assignments. The case, along with Professor's Discussion Material, can be obtained from the Deloitte Foundation at its website: **www.deloitte.com/us/truebloodcases**.

Case 05–5: Guarantees-R-Us

This case gives students the opportunity to extend their knowledge beyond chapter coverage by researching FASB ASC 460–10: Guarantees–Overall (previously *FASB Interpretation No. 45,* "Guarantor's Accounting and Disclosure Requirements for Guarantees, Including Indirect Guarantees of Indebtedness of Others") and applying that GAAP to decide whether specific guarantees are loss contingencies. Cite the appropriate location in the FASB Codification.

**Communication
Case 13–7**
Exceptions
to the general
classification
guideline; group
interaction

● LO4

Domestic Transfer and Storage is a large trucking company headquartered in the Midwest. Rapid expansion in recent years has been financed in large part by debt in a variety of forms. In preparing the financial statements for 2012, questions have arisen regarding the way certain of the liabilities are to be classified in the company's classified balance sheet.

A meeting of several members of the accounting area is scheduled for tomorrow, April 8, 2012. You are confident that that meeting will include the topic of debt classification. You want to appear knowledgeable at the meeting, but realizing it's been a few years since you have dealt with classification issues, you have sought out information you think relevant. Questionable liabilities at the company's fiscal year-end (January 31, 2012) include the following:

a. $15 million of 9% commercial paper is due on July 31, 2012. Management intends to refinance the paper on a long-term basis. In early April 2012, Domestic negotiated a credit agreement with a commercial bank for up to $12 million any time during the next three years, any borrowings from which will mature two years from the date of borrowing.

b. $17 million of 11% notes were issued on June 30, 2009. The notes are due on November 30, 2012. The company has investments of $20 million classified as "available for sale."

c. $25 million of 10% notes were due on February 28, 2012. On February 21, 2012, the company issued 30-year, 9.4% bonds in a private placement to institutional investors.

d. Recently, company management has considered reducing debt in favor of a greater proportion of equity financing. $20 million of 12% bonds mature on July 31, 2012. Discussions with underwriters, which began on January 4, 2012, resulted in a contractual arrangement on March 15 under which new common shares will be sold in July for approximately $20 million.

In order to make notes to yourself in preparation for the meeting concerning the classification of these items, you decide to discuss them with a colleague. Specifically, you want to know what portion of the debt can be excluded from classification as a current liability (that is, reported as a noncurrent liability) and why.

Required:

1. What is the appropriate classification of each liability? Develop a list of arguments in support of your view prior to the class session for which the case is assigned.

2. In class, your instructor will pair you (and everyone else) with a classmate (who also has independently developed a position). You will be given three minutes to argue your view to your partner. Your partner likewise will be given three minutes to argue his or her view to you. During these three-minute presentations, the listening partner is not permitted to speak.

3. Then after each person has had a turn attempting to convince his or her partner, the two partners will have a three-minute discussion to decide which classifications are more convincing. Arguments will be merged into a single view for each pair.

4. After the allotted time, a spokesperson for each of the four liabilities will be selected by the instructor. Each spokesperson will field arguments from the class as to the appropriate classification. The class then will discuss the merits of the classification and attempt to reach a consensus view, though a consensus is not necessary.

Communication Case 13–8
Various contingencies
● LO5 LO6

"I see an all-nighter coming on," Gayle grumbled. "Why did Mitch just now give us this assignment?" Your client, Western Manufacturing, is involved with several situations that possibly involve contingencies. The assignment Gayle refers to is to draft appropriate accounting treatment for each situation described below in time for tomorrow's meeting of the audit group. Western's fiscal year is the calendar year 2011, and the 2011 financial statements are issued on March 15, 2012.

1. During 2011, Western experienced labor disputes at three of its plants. Management hopes an agreement will soon be reached. However negotiations between the Company and the unions have not produced an acceptable settlement and, as a result, strikes are ongoing at these facilities since March 1, 2012. It is virtually certain that material costs will be incurred but the amount of possible costs cannot be reasonably ascertained.

2. In accordance with a 2009 contractual agreement with A. J. Conner Company, Western is entitled to $37 million for certain fees and expense reimbursements. These were written off as bad debts in 2010. A. J. Conner has filed for bankruptcy. The bankruptcy court on February 4, 2012, ordered A. J. Conner to pay $23 million immediately upon consummation of a proposed merger with Garner Holding Group.

3. Western warrants most products it sells against defects in materials and workmanship for a period of a year. Based on their experience with previous product introductions, warranty costs are expected to approximate 2% of sales. A warranty liability of $39 million was reported at December 31, 2010. Sales of warranted products during 2011 were $2,100 million and actual warranty expenditures were $40 million. Expenditures in excess of the existing liability were debited to warranty expense.

4. Western is involved in a suit filed in January 2012 by Crump Holdings seeking $88 million, as an adjustment to the purchase price in connection with the Company's sale of its textile business in 2011. The suit alleges that Western misstated the assets and liabilities used to calculate the purchase price for the textile division. Legal counsel advises that it is reasonably possible that Western could end up losing an indeterminable amount not expected to have a material adverse effect on the Company's financial position.

Required:

1. Determine the appropriate means of reporting each situation.

2. In a memo to the audit manager, Mitch Riley, explain your reasoning. Include any necessary journal entries and drafts of appropriate disclosure notes.

Judgment Case 13–9
Loss contingency and full disclosure
● LO5 LO6

In the March 2012 meeting of Valleck Corporation's board of directors, a question arose as to the way a possible obligation should be disclosed in the forthcoming financial statements for the year ended December 31. A veteran board member brought to the meeting a draft of a disclosure note that had been prepared by the controller's office for inclusion in the annual report. Here is the note:

> On May 9, 2011, the United States Environmental Protection Agency (EPA) issued a Notice of Violation (NOV) to Valleck alleging violations of the Clean Air Act. Subsequently, in June 2011, the EPA commenced a civil action with respect to the foregoing violation seeking civil penalties of approximately $853,000. The EPA alleges that Valleck exceeded applicable volatile organic substance emission limits. The Company estimates that the cost to achieve compliance will be $190,000; in addition the Company expects to settle the EPA lawsuit for a civil penalty of $205,000 which will be paid in 2014.

"Where did we get the $205,000 figure?" he asked. On being informed that this is the amount negotiated last month by company attorneys with the EPA, the director inquires, "Aren't we supposed to report a liability for that in addition to the note?"

Required:

Explain whether Valleck should report a liability in addition to the note. Why or why not? For full disclosure, should anything be added to the disclosure note itself?

Communication Case 13–10
Change in loss contingency; write a memo
● LO5 LO6

Late in 2011, you and two other officers of Curbo Fabrications Corporation just returned from a meeting with officials of The City of Jackson. The meeting was unexpectedly favorable even though it culminated in a settlement with city authorities that required your company pay a total of $475,000 to cover the cost of violations of city construction codes. Jackson had filed suit in November 2009 against Curbo Fabrications Corporation, seeking civil penalties and injunctive relief for violations of city construction codes regulating earthquake damage standards. Alleged violations involved several construction projects completed during the previous three years. When the financial statements were issued in 2010, Curbo had not reached a settlement with state authorities, but legal counsel had advised the Company that it was probable the ultimate settlement would be $750,000 in penalties. The following entry had been recorded:

Loss—litigation	750,000	
Liability—litigation		750,000

The final settlement, therefore, was a pleasant surprise. While returning from the meeting, your conversation turned to reporting the settlement in the 2011 financial statements. You drew the short straw and were selected to write a memo to Janet Zeno, the financial vice president, advising the proper course of action.

Required:

Write the memo. Include descriptions of any journal entries related to the change in amounts. Briefly describe other steps Curbo should take to report the settlement.

Research Case 13–11
Researching the way contingencies are reported; retrieving information from the Internet
● LO5 LO6

EDGAR (Electronic Data Gathering, Analysis, and Retrieval system) performs automated collection, validation, indexing, acceptance, and forwarding of submissions by companies and others who are required by law to file forms with the U.S. Securities and Exchange Commission (SEC). All publicly traded domestic companies use EDGAR to make the majority of their filings. Form 10-K, which includes the annual report, is required to be filed on EDGAR. The SEC makes this information available on the Internet.

Required:

1. Access the FASB's Codification Research System at the FASB website (**www.fasb.org**). Identify the authoritative literature that provides guidance on accounting for contingent losses, and indicate the specific citations that describe the guidelines for determining when an expense and liability associated with a contingent loss should be accrued vs. only disclosed in the footnotes?

2. Access EDGAR on the Internet at: **www.sec.gov**.

3. Search for a public company with which you are familiar. Access its most recent 10-K filing. Search or scroll to find the financial statements and related notes.

4. Specifically, look for any contingency(s) reported in the disclosure notes. Identify the nature of the contingency(s) described and explain the reason(s) the loss or losses was or was not accrued.

5. Repeat requirements 2 and 3 for two additional companies.

Communication Case 13–12
Accounting changes
● LO5 LO6

Kevin Brantly is a new hire in the controller's office of Fleming Home Products. Two events occurred in late 2011 that the company had not previously encountered. The events appear to affect two of the company's liabilities, but there is some disagreement concerning whether they also affect financial statements of prior years. Each change occurred during 2011 before any adjusting entries or closing entries were prepared. The tax rate for Fleming is 40% in all years.

- Fleming Home Products introduced a new line of commercial awnings in 2010 that carry a one-year warranty against manufacturer's defects. Based on industry experience, warranty costs were expected to approximate 3% of sales. Sales of the awnings in 2010 were $3,500,000. Accordingly, warranty expense and a warranty liability of $105,000 were recorded in 2010. In late 2011, the company's claims experience was evaluated and it was determined that claims were far fewer than expected—2% of sales rather than 3%. Sales of the awnings in 2011 were $4,000,000 and warranty expenditures in 2011 totaled $91,000.

- In November 2009, the State of Minnesota filed suit against the company, seeking penalties for violations of clean air laws. When the financial statements were issued in 2010, Fleming had not reached a settlement with state authorities, but legal counsel advised Fleming that it was probable the company would have to pay $200,000 in penalties. Accordingly, the following entry was recorded:

Loss—litigation	200,000	
Liability—litigation		200,000

Late in 2011, a settlement was reached with state authorities to pay a total of $350,000 in penalties.

Required:

Kevin's supervisor, perhaps unsure of the answer, perhaps wanting to test Kevin's knowledge, e-mails the message, "Kevin, send me a memo on how we should handle our awning warranty and that clean air suit." Wanting to be accurate, Kevin consults his reference materials. What will he find? Prepare the memo requested.

Real World Case 13–13
Lawsuit settlement; SkillSoft
● LO5 LO6

Real World Financials

SkillSoft is a leading provider of content resources and complementary technologies for integrated enterprise learning. The company's fiscal year ends January 31, 2006, and it plans to file its financial statements with the SEC on April, 17, 2006. On April 13, the company issued the following press release (in part):

> NASHUA, N.H., April 13 /PRNewswire-FirstCall/—SkillSoft PLC (Nasdaq: SKIL), . . . has agreed . . . to settle a lawsuit filed against it and certain of its former and current officers and directors in late 2004 related to the 2002 securities class action lawsuit. This lawsuit included substantially the same claims as those set forth in the previously settled 2002 securities class action lawsuit. Under the terms of the settlement, SkillSoft will pay a total of $1.79 million to the plaintiffs prior to April 17, 2006.

Required:

1. From an accounting perspective, how should SkillSoft have treated the settlement?
2. Relying on the information provided by the press release, re-create the journal entry SkillSoft recorded for the settlement.
3. Suppose the settlement had occurred after April 17. How should SkillSoft have treated the settlement?

Ethics Case 13–14
Profits guaranteed
● LO5

This was Joel Craig's first visit to the controller's corner office since being recruited for the senior accountant position in May. Because he'd been directed to bring with him his preliminary report on year-end adjustments, Craig presumed he'd done something wrong in preparing the report. That he had not was Craig's first surprise. His second surprise was his boss's request to reconsider one of the estimated expenses.

S & G Fasteners was a new company, specializing in plastic industrial fasteners. All products carry a generous long-term warranty against manufacturer's defects. "Don't you think 4% of sales is a little high for our warranty expense estimate?" his boss wondered. "After all, we're new at this. We have little experience with product introductions. I just got off the phone with Blanchard (the company president). He thinks we'll have trouble renewing our credit line with the profits we're projecting. The pressure's on."

Required:

1. Should Craig follow his boss's suggestion?
2. Does revising the warranty estimate pose an ethical dilemma?
3. Who would be affected if the suggestion is followed?

IFRS Case 13–15
Current liabilities and contingencies; differences between U.S. GAAP and IFRS
● LO4 LO5 LO7

As a second-year financial analyst for A.J. Straub Investments, you are performing an initial analysis on Fizer Pharmaceuticals. A difficulty you've encountered in making comparisons with its chief rival is that Fizer uses U.S. GAAP and the competing company uses International Financial Reporting Standards. Some areas of concern are the following:

1. Fizer has been designated as a potentially responsible party by the United States Environmental Protection Agency with respect to certain waste sites. These claims are in various stages of administrative or judicial proceedings and include demands for recovery of past governmental costs and for future investigations or remedial actions. Fizer accrues costs associated with environmental matters when they become probable and reasonably estimable. Counsel has advised that the likelihood of payments of about $70 million is slightly more than 50%. Accordingly, payment is judged reasonably possible and the contingency was disclosed in a footnote.

2. Fizer had $10 million of bonds issued in 1985 that mature in February 2012. On December 31, 2011, the company's fiscal year-end, management intended to refinance the bonds on a long-term basis. On February 7, 2012, Fizer issued $10 million of 20-year bonds, applying the proceeds to repay the bond issue that matured that month. The bonds were reported in Fizer's balance sheet as long-term debt.

3. Fizer reported in its 2011 financial statements a long-term contingency at its face amount rather than its present value even though the difference was considered material. The reason the cash flows were not discounted is that their timing is uncertain.

Required:

If Fizer used IFRS as does its competitor, how would the items described be reported differently?

**Analysis
Case 13–16**
Analyzing financial
statements;
liquidity ratios
● LO1

IGF Foods Company is a large, primarily domestic, consumer foods company involved in the manufacture, distribution and sale of a variety of food products. Industry averages are derived from Troy's *The Almanac of Business and Industrial Financial Ratios*. Following are the 2011 and 2010 comparative balance sheets for IGF. (The financial data we use are from actual financial statements of a well-known corporation, but the company name used is fictitious and the numbers and dates have been modified slightly.)

IGF FOODS COMPANY
Comparative Balance Sheets
Years Ended December 31, 2011 and 2010
($ in millions)

	2011	2010
Assets		
Current assets:		
Cash	$ 48	$ 142
Accounts receivable	347	320
Marketable securities	358	—
Inventories	914	874
Prepaid expenses	212	154
Total current assets	$1,879	$1,490
Property, plant, and equipment (net)	2,592	2,291
Intangibles (net)	800	843
Other assets	74	60
Total assets	$5,345	$4,684
Liabilities and Shareholders' Equity		
Current liabilities:		
Accounts payables	$ 254	$ 276
Accrued liabilities	493	496
Notes payable	518	115
Current portion of long-term debt	208	54
Total current liabilities	$1,473	$ 941
Long-term debt	534	728
Deferred income taxes	407	344
Total liabilities	$2,414	$2,013
Shareholders' equity:		
Common stock	180	180
Additional paid-in capital	21	63
Retained earnings	2,730	2,428
Total shareholders' equity	$2,931	$2,671
Total liabilities and shareholders' equity	$5,345	$4,684

Liquidity refers to a company's cash position and overall ability to obtain cash in the normal course of business. A company is said to be liquid if it has sufficient cash or is capable of converting its other assets to cash in a relatively short period of time so that currently maturing debts can be paid.

Required:
1. Calculate the current ratio for IGF for 2011. The average ratio for the stocks listed on the New York Stock Exchange in a comparable time period was 1.5. What information does your calculation provide an investor?
2. Calculate IGF's acid-test or quick ratio for 2011. The ratio for the stocks listed on the New York Stock Exchange in a comparable time period was .80. What does your calculation indicate about IGF's liquidity?

**Analysis
Case 13–17**
Reporting current
liabilities; liquidity
● LO1

Refer to the financial statements and related disclosure notes of **Dell** located in the company's 2009 annual report included with all new copies of the text. They also can be found at **www.dell.com**. At the end of its 2009 fiscal year, Dell reported current liabilities of $14.9 billion in its balance sheet.

Required:

1. What are the four components of current liabilities?

2. Are current assets sufficient to cover current liabilities? What is the current ratio for 2009? How does the ratio compare with 2008?

3. Dell reported short-term deferred revenue among its current liabilities. That deferred revenue is associated with extended warranty and service contracts. Is that deferred revenue likely to require Dell to pay cash in order to reduce that liability? Explain.

**Real World
Case 13–18**
Contingencies
● **LO5**

Real World Financials

The following is an excerpt from *USAToday.com* in July 2007:

> Microsoft (MSFT) on Thursday extended the warranty on its Xbox 360 video game console and said it will take a charge of more than $1 billion to pay for "anticipated costs." Under the new warranty, Microsoft will pay for shipping and repairs for three years, worldwide, for consoles afflicted with what gamers call "the red ring of death." Previously, the warranty expired after a year for U.S. customers and two years for Europeans. The charge will be $1.05 billion to $1.15 billion for the quarter ended June 30. Microsoft reports its fourth-quarter results July 19.

Required:

1. Why must Microsoft report this charge of over $1 billion entirely in one quarter, the last quarter of the company's fiscal year ended June 30, 2007?

2. When the announcement was made, analyst Richard Doherty stated that either a high number of Xbox 360s will fail or the company is being overly conservative in its warranty estimate. From an accounting standpoint, what will Microsoft do in the future if the estimate of future repairs is overly conservative (too high)?

BRITISH AIRWAYS CASE

BRITISH AIRWAYS

British Airways, Plc. (BA), a U.K. company, prepares its financial statements according to International Financial Reporting Standards. BA's annual report for the year ended March 31, 2009, which includes financial statements and disclosure notes, is included with all new textbooks and can be found at **www.britishairways.com**. When answering questions, focus on BA's "Group" financial information (which is equivalent to "Consolidated" under U.S. GAAP).

Required:

1. BA has an account entitled "sales in advance of carriage." Explain the purpose of that account. Would transactions of this type be handled similarly under U.S. GAAP? What is the amount of "sales in advance of carriage" as of March 31, 2009?

2. Note 30 lists "provisions for liabilities and charges." Is the threshold for recognizing a liability associated with these items any different under IFRS than it is under U.S. GAAP? Explain. By how much has the total amount of the BA Group's "provisions for liabilities and charges" increased or decreased during fiscal 2009?

3. BA's note 37 lists contingent liabilities. Explain how the use of that term differs between IFRS and U.S. GAAP.

14

Bonds and Long-Term Notes

|||||| ||||||| ||||||| ||||||| ||||||| ||||||| ||||||| |||||

/// **OVERVIEW**

This chapter continues the presentation of liabilities. Specifically, the discussion focuses on the accounting treatment of long-term liabilities. Long-term notes and bonds are discussed, as well as the extinguishment of debt and debt convertible into stock.

/// **LEARNING OBJECTIVES**

After studying this chapter, you should be able to:

- **LO1** Identify the underlying characteristics of debt instruments and describe the basic approach to accounting for debt. (page 747)

- **LO2** Account for bonds issued at face value, at a discount, or at a premium, recording interest at the effective rate or by the straight-line method. (page 749)

- **LO3** Characterize the accounting treatment of notes, including installment notes, issued for cash or for noncash consideration. (page 759)

- **LO4** Describe the disclosures appropriate to long-term debt in its various forms and calculate related financial ratios. (page 763)

- **LO5** Record the early extinguishment of debt and its conversion into equity securities. (page 769)

- **LO6** Understand the option to report liabilities at their fair values. (page 775)

- **LO7** Discuss the primary differences between U.S. GAAP and IFRS with respect to accounting for bonds and long-term notes. (pages 751, 759, 771, and 777).

FINANCIAL REPORTING CASE

Service Leader, Inc.

The mood is both upbeat and focused on this cool October morning. Executives and board members of Service Leader, Inc., are meeting with underwriters and attorneys to discuss the company's first bond offering in its 20-year history. You are attending in the capacity of company controller and two-year member of the board of directors. The closely held corporation has been financed entirely by equity, internally generated funds, and short-term bank borrowings.

Bank rates of interest, though, have risen recently and the company's unexpectedly rapid, but welcome, growth has prompted the need to look elsewhere for new financing. Under consideration are 15-year, 6.25% first mortgage bonds with a principal amount of $70 million. The bonds would be callable at 103 any time after June 30, 2013, and convertible into Service Leader common stock at the rate of 45 shares per $1,000 bond.

Other financing vehicles have been discussed over the last two months, including the sale of additional stock, nonconvertible bonds, and unsecured notes. This morning *The Wall Street Journal* indicated that market rates of interest for debt similar to the bonds under consideration are about 6.5%.

By the time you finish this chapter, you should be able to respond appropriately to the questions posed in this case. Compare your response to the solution provided at the end of the chapter.

QUESTIONS ///

1. What does it mean that the bonds are "first mortgage" bonds? What effect does that have on financing? (page 749)

2. From Service Leader's perspective, why are the bonds callable? What does that mean? (page 749)

3. How will it be possible to sell bonds paying investors 6.25% when other, similar investments will provide the investors a return of 6.5%? (page 750)

4. Would accounting differ if the debt were designated as notes rather than bonds? (page 759)

5. Why might the company choose to make the bonds convertible into common stock? (page 769)

The Nature of Long-Term Debt

A company must raise funds to finance its operations and often the expansion of those operations. Presumably, at least some of the necessary funding can be provided by the company's own operations, though some funds must be provided by external sources. Ordinarily, external financing includes some combination of equity and debt funding. We explore debt financing first.

● LO1

In the present chapter, we focus on debt in the form of bonds and notes. The following three chapters deal with liabilities also, namely those arising in connection with leases (Chapter 15), deferred income taxes (Chapter 16), and pensions and employee benefits (Chapter 17). Some employee benefits create equity rather than debt, which are discussed in Chapter 19. In Chapter 18, we examine shareholders' interest arising from external *equity* financing. In Chapter 21, we see that cash flows from both debt and equity financing are reported together in a statement of cash flows as "cash flows from financing activities."

Liabilities signify *creditors'* **interest in a company's assets.**

As you read this chapter, you will find the focus to be on the liability side of the transactions we examine. Realize, though, that the mirror image of a liability is an asset (bonds payable/investment in bonds, note payable/note receivable, etc.). So as we discuss accounting for debts from the viewpoint of the issuers of the debt instruments (borrowers), we also will take the opportunity to see how the lender deals with the corresponding asset. Studying the two sides of the same transaction in tandem will emphasize their inherent similarities.

Accounting for a liability is a relatively straightforward concept. This is not to say that all debt instruments are unchallenging, "plain vanilla" loan agreements. Quite the contrary, the financial community continually devises increasingly exotic ways to flavor financial instruments in the attempt to satisfy the diverse and evolving tastes of both debtors and creditors.

Packaging aside, a liability requires the future payment of cash in specified (or estimated) amounts, at specified (or projected) dates. As time passes, interest accrues on debt. As a general rule, the periodic interest is the effective interest rate times the amount of the debt outstanding during the period. This same principle applies regardless of the specific form of the liability—note payable, bonds payable, lease liability, pension obligation, or other debt instruments. Also, as a general rule, long-term liabilities are reported at their present values. The present value of a liability is the present value of its related cash flows (principal and/or interest payments), discounted at the effective rate of interest at issuance.

We begin our study of long-term liabilities by examining accounting for bonds. We follow that section with a discussion of debt in the form of notes in Part B. It's important to note that, although particulars of the two forms of debt differ, the basic approach to accounting for each type is precisely the same. In Part C, we look at various ways bonds and notes are retired or converted into other securities. Finally, in Part D we discuss the option companies have to report liabilities at their fair values.

PART A   BONDS

A company can borrow cash from a bank or other financial institution by signing a promissory note. We discuss notes payable later in the chapter. Medium- and large-sized corporations often choose to borrow cash by issuing bonds. In fact, the most common form of corporate debt is bonds. A bond issue, in effect, breaks down a large debt (large corporations often borrow hundreds of millions of dollars at a time) into manageable parts—usually $1,000 or $5,000 units. This avoids the necessity of finding a single lender who is both willing and able to loan a large amount of money at a reasonable interest rate. So rather than signing a $400 million note to borrow cash from a financial institution, a company may find it more economical to sell 400,000 $1,000 bonds to many lenders—theoretically up to 400,000 lenders.

Bonds obligate the issuing corporation to repay a stated amount (variously referred to as the *principal, par value, face amount,* or *maturity value*) at a specified *maturity date.* Maturities for bonds typically range from 10 to 40 years. In return for the use of the money borrowed, the company also agrees to pay *interest* to bondholders between the issue date and maturity. The periodic interest is a stated percentage of face amount (variously referred to as the *stated rate, coupon rate,* or *nominal rate*). Ordinarily, interest is paid semiannually on designated interest dates beginning six months after the day the bonds are "dated."

The Bond Indenture

The specific promises made to bondholders are described in a document called a bond indenture. Because it would be impractical for the corporation to enter into a direct agreement with each of the many bondholders, the bond indenture is held by a trustee, usually a commercial bank or other financial institution, appointed by the issuing firm to represent the rights of the bondholders. If the company fails to live up to the terms of the bond indenture, the trustee may bring legal action against the company on behalf of the bondholders.

Most corporate bonds are debenture bonds. A debenture bond is secured only by the "full faith and credit" of the issuing corporation. No specific assets are pledged as security. Investors in debentures usually have the same standing as the firm's other general creditors.

[margin notes]

A note payable and a note receivable are two sides of the same coin.

Periodic interest is the effective interest rate times the amount of the debt outstanding during the interest period.

A bond issue divides a large liability into many smaller liabilities.

Corporations issuing bonds are obligated to repay a stated amount at a specified *maturity date* and periodic *interest* between the issue date and maturity.

A *bond indenture* describes the specific promises made to bondholders.

So in case of bankruptcy, debenture holders and other general creditors would be treated equally. An exception is the **subordinated debenture,** which is not entitled to receive any liquidation payments until the claims of other specified debt issues are satisfied.

A **mortgage bond,** on the other hand, is backed by a lien on specified real estate owned by the issuer. Because a mortgage bond is considered less risky than debentures, it typically will command a lower interest rate.

Today most corporate bonds are registered bonds. Interest checks are mailed directly to the owner of the bond, whose name is registered with the issuing company. Years ago, it was typical for bonds to be structured as **coupon bonds** (sometimes called *bearer bonds*). The name of the owner of a coupon bond was not registered. Instead, to collect interest on a coupon bond the holder actually clipped an attached coupon and redeemed it in accordance with instructions in the indenture. A carryover effect of this practice is that we still often see the term *coupon rate* in reference to the stated interest rate on bonds.

Most corporate bonds are **callable** (or redeemable). The call feature allows the issuing company to buy back, or call, outstanding bonds from bondholders before their scheduled maturity date. This feature affords the company some protection against being stuck with relatively high-cost debt in the event interest rates fall during the period before maturity. The call price must be pre-specified and often exceeds the bond's face amount (a call premium), sometimes declining as maturity is approached.

For example, financial statements of **Emhart Corporation** included this disclosure note:

> The Company's 9¼% (9.65% effective interest rate, after discount) sinking fund debentures are callable at prices decreasing from 105% of face amount currently to 100%.

"No call" provisions usually prohibit calls during the first few years of a bond's life. Very often, calls are mandatory. That is, the corporation may be required to redeem the bonds on a pre-specified, year-by-year basis. Bonds requiring such **sinking fund** redemptions often are labeled *sinking fund debentures.*

Serial bonds provide a more structured (and less popular) way to retire bonds on a piece-meal basis. Serial bonds are retired in installments during all or part of the life of the issue. Each bond has its own specified maturity date. So for a typical 30-year serial issue, 25 to 30 separate maturity dates might be assigned to specific portions of the bond issue.

Convertible bonds are retired as a consequence of bondholders choosing to convert them into shares of stock. We look closer at convertible bonds a little later in the chapter.

Recording Bonds at Issuance

Bonds represent a liability to the corporation that issues the bonds and an asset to a company that buys the bonds as an investment. Each side of the transaction is the mirror image of the other.[1] This is demonstrated in Illustration 14–1.

On January 1, 2011, Masterwear Industries issued $700,000 of 12% bonds. Interest of $42,000 is payable semiannually on June 30 and December 31. The bonds mature in three years (an unrealistically short maturity to shorten the illustration). The entire bond issue was sold in a private placement to United Intergroup, Inc., at the face amount.		
At Issuance (January 1)		
Masterwear (Issuer)		
Cash	700,000	
Bonds payable (face amount)		700,000
United (Investor)		
Investment in bonds (face amount)	700,000	
Cash		700,000

Side notes:

FINANCIAL
Reporting Case

Q1, p. 747

FINANCIAL
Reporting Case

Q2, p. 747

Real World Financials

Mandatory sinking fund redemptions retire a bond issue gradually over its term to maturity.

● LO2

ILLUSTRATION 14–1
Bonds Sold at Face Amount

---

[1]You should recall from Chapter 12 that investments in bonds that are to be held to maturity by the investor are reported at amortized cost, which is the method described here. However, also remember that investments in debt securities *not* to be held to maturity are reported at the fair value of the securities held, as described in Chapter 12, with the interest determined by the effective interest method.

Most bonds these days are issued on the day they are dated (date printed in the indenture contract). On rare occasions, there may be a delay in issuing bonds that causes them to be issued between interest dates, in which case the interest that has accrued since the day they are dated is added to the bonds' price. We discuss this infrequent event in an appendix to this chapter.

Determining the Selling Price

The price of a bond issue at any particular time is not necessarily equal to its face amount. The $700,000, 12% bond issue in the previous illustration, for example, may sell for more than face amount (at a **premium**) or less than face amount (at a **discount**), depending on how the 12% *stated* interest rate compares with the prevailing *market* or *effective rate* of interest (for securities of similar risk and maturity). For instance, if the 12% bonds are competing in a market in which similar bonds are providing a 14% return, the bonds could be sold only at a price less than $700,000. On the other hand, if the market rate is only 10%, the 12% stated rate would seem relatively attractive and the bonds would sell at a premium over face amount. The reason the stated rate often differs from the market rate, resulting in a *discount* or *premium*, is the inevitable delay between the date the terms of the issue are established and the date the issue comes to market.

Other things being equal, the lower the perceived riskiness of the corporation issuing bonds, the higher the price those bonds will command.

In addition to the characteristic terms of a bond agreement as specified in the indenture, the market rate for a specific bond issue is influenced by the creditworthiness of the company issuing the bonds. To evaluate the risk and quality of an individual bond issue, investors rely heavily on bond ratings provided by **Standard & Poor's Corporation** and by **Moody's Investors Service, Inc.** See the bond ratings in Graphic 14–1.

GRAPHIC 14–1

Bond Ratings*

	S&P	Moody's
Investment Grades:		
Highest	AAA	Aaa
High	AA	Aa
Medium	A	A
Minimum investment grade	BBB	Baa
"Junk" Ratings:		
Speculative	BB	Ba
Very speculative	B	B
Default or near default	CCC	Caa
	CC	Ca
	C	C
	D	

*Adapted from *Bond Record* (New York: Moody's Investors Service, monthly) and *Bond Guide* (New York: Standard & Poor's Corporation, monthly).

A bond issue will be priced by the marketplace to yield the market rate of interest for securities of similar risk and maturity.

Forces of supply and demand cause a bond issue to be *priced to yield the market rate.* In other words, an investor paying that price will earn an effective rate of return on the investment equal to the market rate. The price is calculated as the present value of all the cash flows required of the bonds, where the discount rate used in the present value calculation is the market rate. Specifically, the price will be the present value of the periodic cash interest payments (face amount × stated rate) plus the present value of the principal payable at maturity, both discounted at the market rate.

Bonds priced at a discount are described in Illustration 14–2.

On January 1, 2011, Masterwear Industries issued $700,000 of 12% bonds, dated January 1. Interest of $42,000 is payable semiannually on June 30 and December 31. The bonds mature in three years. The market yield for bonds of similar risk and maturity is 14%. The entire bond issue was purchased by United Intergroup, Inc.

Calculation of the Price of the Bonds

		Present Values
Interest	$ 42,000 × 4.76654* =	$200,195
Principal (face amount)	$700,000 × 0.66634† =	466,438
Present value (price) of the bonds		$666,633

*Present value of an ordinary annuity of $1: n = 6, i = 7% (Table 4).
†Present value of $1: n = 6, i = 7% (Table 2).
Because interest is paid semiannually, the present value calculations use: (a) one-half the stated rate (6%) to determine cash payments, (b) one-half the market rate (7%) as the discount rate, and (c) six (3 × 2) semiannual periods.
Note: Present value tables are provided at the end of this textbook. If you need to review the concept of the time value of money, refer to the discussions in Chapter 6.
Rounding: Because present value tables truncate decimal places, the solution may be slightly different if you use a calculator or Excel.

ILLUSTRATION 14–2

Bonds Sold at a Discount

Using a calculator:
Enter: N 6 I 7
PMT −42000 FV −700000
Output: PV 666,634

Using Excel, enter:
=PV(.07,6,42000,700000)

The calculation is illustrated in Graphic 14–2:

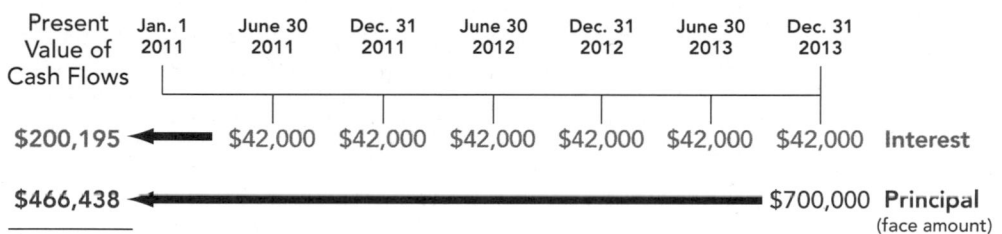

GRAPHIC 14–2

Cash Flows from a Bond Issue

$666,633 Present value of interest and principal

Although the cash flows total $952,000, the present value of those future cash flows as of January 1, 2011, is only $666,633. This is due to the time value of money. These bonds are issued at a discount because the present value of the cash flows is less than the face amount of the bonds.

Masterwear (Issuer)		
Cash (price calculated above)	666,633	
Discount on bonds payable (difference)	33,367	
Bonds payable (face amount)		700,000

United (Investor)		
Investment in bonds (face amount)	700,000	
Discount on bond investment (difference)		33,367
Cash (price calculated above)		666,633

Journal Entries at Issuance—Bonds Sold at a Discount

Note: A sometimes-used alternative way to record bonds is the "net method," shown next, in which the discount is included directly in the carrying amount.

Masterwear (Issuer)		
Cash	666,633	
Bonds payable		666,633

United (Investor)		
Investment in bonds	666,633	
Cash		666,633

The net method actually is the preferred method for companies that prepare financial statements according to International Financial Reporting Standards.

● LO7

When bond prices are quoted in financial media, they typically are stated in terms of a percentage of face amounts. Thus, a price quote of 98 means a $1,000 bond will sell for $980; a bond priced at 101 will sell for $1,010.

Determining Interest—Effective Interest Method

The effective interest on debt is the market rate of interest multiplied by the outstanding balance of the debt.

Interest accrues on an outstanding debt at a constant percentage of the debt each period. Of course, under the concept of accrual accounting, the periodic effective interest is not affected by the time at which the cash interest actually is paid. Recording interest each period as the *effective market rate of interest multiplied by the outstanding balance of the debt* (during the interest period) is referred to as the effective interest method. Although giving this a label—the effective interest method—implies some specialized procedure, this simply is an application of the accrual concept, consistent with accruing all expenses as they are incurred.

Continuing our example, we determined that the amount of debt when the bonds are issued is $666,633. Since the effective interest rate is 14%, interest recorded (as expense to the issuer and revenue to the investor) for the first six-month interest period is $46,664:

$$\underset{\text{Outstanding balance}}{\$666,633} \times \underset{\text{Effective rate}}{[14\% \div 2]} = \underset{\text{Effective interest}}{\$46,664}$$

However, the bond indenture calls for semiannual interest payments of only $42,000—the *stated* rate (6%) times the *face amount* ($700,000). The remainder, $4,664, increases the liability and is reflected as a reduction in the discount (a contra-liability account). This is illustrated in Graphic 14–3.

GRAPHIC 14–3

Change in Debt When Effective Interest Exceeds Cash Paid

The difference between the effective interest and the interest paid increases the existing liability.

	Outstanding Balance	Account Balances		
		Bonds Payable (face amount)		Discount on Bonds Payable
January 1	$666,633 =	$700,000	less	$33,367
Interest expense at 7%	46,664			
Interest paid	(42,000)			(4,664)
June 30	$671,297 =	$700,000	less	$28,703

Interest is calculated on the outstanding debt balance at the effective rate. Interest paid is the amount specified in the bond indenture—the stated rate times the face amount. These amounts and the change in the outstanding debt are recorded as follows:

Journal Entries—The Interest Method

The effective interest is calculated each period as the market rate times the amount of the debt outstanding during the interest period.

At the first Interest Date (June 30)		
Masterwear (Issuer)		
Interest expense (market rate × outstanding balance)	46,664	
Discount on bonds payable (difference)		4,664
Cash (stated rate × face amount)		42,000
United (Investor)		
Cash (stated rate × face amount)	42,000	
Discount on bond investment (difference)	4,664	
Interest revenue (market rate × outstanding balance)		46,664

Because the balance of the debt changes each period, the dollar amount of interest (balance × rate) also will change each period. To keep up with the changing amounts, it usually is convenient to prepare a schedule that reflects the changes in the debt over its term to maturity. An amortization schedule for the situation under discussion is shown in Graphic 14–4.

Amounts for the journal entries each interest date are found in the second, third, and fourth columns of the schedule. The essential point to remember is that the effective interest method is a straightforward application of the accrual concept, whereby interest expense (or revenue) is accrued periodically at the effective rate.

Determining interest in this manner has a convenient side effect. It results in reporting the liability at the present value of future cash payments—the appropriate valuation method for any liability. This is obvious at issuance; we actually calculated the present value to be

Date	Cash Interest	Effective Interest	Increase in Balance	Outstanding Balance
	(6% × Face amount)	(7% × Outstanding balance)	(Discount reduction)	
1/1/11				666,633
6/30/11	42,000	.07 (666,633) = 46,664	4,664	671,297
12/31/11	42,000	.07 (671,297) = 46,991	4,991	676,288
6/30/12	42,000	.07 (676,288) = 47,340	5,340	681,628
12/31/12	42,000	.07 (681,628) = 47,714	5,714	687,342
6/30/13	42,000	.07 (687,342) = 48,114	6,114	693,456
12/31/13	42,000	.07 (693,456) = 48,544*	6,544	700,000
	252,000	285,367	33,367	

*Rounded.

$666,633. What perhaps is not quite as obvious is that the outstanding amount of debt each subsequent period (shown in the right-hand column of the amortization schedule) is still the present value of the remaining cash flows, discounted at the original rate.

ADDITIONAL CONSIDERATION

Although the reported amount each period is the present value of the bonds, at any date after issuance this amount is not necessarily equal to the market value (fair value) of the bonds. This is because the market rate of interest will not necessarily remain the same as the rate implicit in the original issue price (the effective rate). Of course, for negotiable financial instruments, the issue price is the market price at any given time. Differences between market values and present values based on the original rate are holding gains and losses. If we were to use the market rate to revalue bonds on each reporting date—that is, recalculate the present value using the market rate—the reported amount always would be the market value. As we will see later, companies have the option to report their liabilities at fair value.

Zero-Coupon Bonds

A zero-coupon bond pays no interest. Instead, it offers a return in the form of a "deep discount" from the face amount. For illustration, let's look at the zero-coupon bonds issued by **General Mills, Inc.** Two billion, two hundred thirty million dollars face amount of the 20-year securities sold for one billion, five hundred one million dollars. As the amortization schedule in Graphic 14–5 (next page) demonstrates, they were priced to yield 2%.[2]

Zero-coupon bonds provide us with a convenient opportunity to reinforce a key concept we just learned: that we accrue the interest expense (or revenue) each period at the effective rate regardless of how much cash interest actually is paid (zero in this case). An advantage of issuing zero-coupon bonds or notes is that the corporation can deduct for tax purposes the annual interest expense (see schedule) but has no related cash outflow until the bonds mature. However, the reverse is true for investors in "zeros." Investors receive no periodic cash interest, even though annual interest revenue is reportable for tax purposes. So those who invest in zero-coupon bonds usually have tax-deferred or tax-exempt status, such as pension funds, individual retirement accounts (IRAs), and charitable organizations. Zero-coupon bonds and notes have popularity but still constitute a relatively small proportion of corporate debt.

---

[2]The present value of $2,230M, discounted at 2% for 20 years, is $1,501M.

GRAPHIC 14–5

Zero-Coupon Securities—General Mills, Inc.

Real World Financials

($ in millions)	Cash Interest	Effective Interest	Increase in Balance	Outstanding Balance*
	(0% × Face amount)	(2% × Outstanding debt)	(Discount reduction)	
				1,501
2002	0	.02 (1,501) = 30	30	1,531
2003	0	.02 (1,531) = 31	31	1,561
2004	0	.02 (1,561) = 31	31	1,593
◆	◆	◆	◆	◆
◆	◆	◆	◆	◆
◆	◆	◆	◆	◆
2021	0	.02 (2,143) = 43	43	2,186
2022	0	.02 (2,186) = 44	44	2,230
		729	729	

*Some numbers appear not to total because the underlying calculations are not rounded.

Bonds Sold at a Premium

In Illustration 14–2, Masterwear Industries sold the bonds at a price that would yield an effective rate higher than the stated rate. The result was a discount. On the other hand, if the 12% bonds had been issued when the market yield for bonds of similar risk and maturity was *lower* than the stated rate, say 10%, the issue would have been priced at a *premium*. Because the 12% rate would seem relatively attractive in a 10% market, the bonds would command an issue price of more than $700,000, calculated in Illustration 14–3.

ILLUSTRATION 14–3

Bonds Sold at a Premium

Because interest is paid *semiannually*, the present value calculations use:

a. **one-half the stated rate (6%),**
b. **one-half the market rate (5%), and**
c. **6 (3 × 2) semiannual periods.**

On January 1, 2011, Masterwear Industries issued $700,000 of 12% bonds, dated January 1. Interest of $42,000 is payable semiannually on June 30 and December 31. The bonds mature in three years. The market yield for bonds of similar risk and maturity is 10%. The entire bond issue was purchased by United Intergroup, Inc.

Calculation of the Price of the Bonds

	Present Values
Interest	$ 42,000 × 5.07569* = $213,179
Principal	$700,000 × 0.74622† = 522,354
Present value (price) of the bonds	$735,533

*Present value of an ordinary annuity of $1: $n = 6$, $i = 5\%$.
†Present value of $1: $n = 6$, $i = 5\%$.

Journal Entries at Issuance—Bonds Sold at Premium

Masterwear (Issuer)

Cash (price calculated above)	735,533	
Bonds payable (face amount)		700,000
Premium on bonds payable (difference)		35,533

United (Investor)

Investment in bonds (face amount)	700,000	
Premium on bond investment (difference)	35,533	
Cash (price calculated above)		735,533

Interest on bonds sold at a premium is determined in precisely the same manner as on bonds sold at a discount. Again, interest is the effective interest rate applied to the debt balance outstanding during each period (balance at the end of the previous interest period), and the cash paid is the stated rate times the face amount, as shown in Graphic 14–6.

Date	Cash Interest	Effective Interest	Decrease in Balance	Outstanding Balance
	(6% × Face amount)	(5% × Outstanding balance)	(Premium reduction)	
1/1/11				735,533
6/30/11	42,000	.05 (735,533) = 36,777	5,223	730,310
12/31/11	42,000	.05 (730,310) = 36,516	5,484	724,826
6/30/12	42,000	.05 (724,826) = 36,241	5,759	719,067
12/31/12	42,000	.05 (719,067) = 35,953	6,047	713,020
6/30/13	42,000	.05 (713,020) = 35,651	6,349	706,671
12/31/13	42,000	.05 (706,671) = 35,329*	6,671	700,000
	252,000	216,467	35,533	

GRAPHIC 14–6

Amortization Schedule—Premium

Since *more* cash is paid each period than the effective interest, the debt outstanding is reduced by the overpayment.

*Rounded.

Notice that the debt declines each period. As the premium is reduced by amortization, the carrying value of the bonds declines toward face value. This is because the effective interest each period is less than the cash interest paid. Remember, this is precisely the opposite of when debt is sold at a discount, when the effective interest each period is more than the cash paid. As the discount is reduced by amortization, the carrying value of the bonds increases toward face value. This is illustrated in Graphic 14–7:

GRAPHIC 14–7

Premium and Discount Amortization Compared

Whether bonds are issued at a premium or a discount, the outstanding balance becomes zero at maturity.

In practice, bonds rarely are issued at a premium. Because of the delay between the date the terms of the bonds are established and when the bonds are issued, it's difficult to set the stated rate equal to the ever-changing market rate. Knowing that, for marketing reasons, companies deliberately set the terms to more likely create a small discount rather than a premium at the issue date. Some investors are psychologically prone to prefer buying at a discount rather than a premium even if the yield is the same (the market rate).

ADDITIONAL CONSIDERATION

The preceding illustrations describe bonds sold at a discount and at a premium. The same concepts apply to bonds sold at face amount. But some of the procedures would be unnecessary. For instance, calculating the present value of the interest and the principal always will give us the face amount when the effective rate and the stated rate are the same:

Calculation of the Price of the Bonds

	Present Values		
Interest	$ 42,000 × 4.91732*	=	$206,528
Principal	$700,000 × 0.70496†	=	493,472
Present value (price) of the bonds			$700,000

*Present value of an ordinary annuity of $1: $n = 6$, $i = 6\%$.
†Present value of $1: $n = 6$, $i = 6\%$.

When Financial Statements Are Prepared between Interest Dates

Any interest that has accrued since the last interest date must be recorded by an adjusting entry prior to preparing financial statements.

When an accounting period ends between interest dates, it is necessary to record interest that has accrued since the last interest date. As an example, refer again to Illustration 14–2 on page 751. If the fiscal years of Masterwear and United end on October 31 and interest was last paid and recorded on June 30, four months' interest must be accrued in a year-end adjusting entry. Because interest is recorded for only a portion of a semiannual period, amounts recorded are simply the amounts shown in the amortization schedule (Graphic 14–4, p. 753) times the appropriate fraction of the semiannual period (in this case 4/6).

Adjusting Entries—To Accrue Interest

To avoid understating interest in the financial statements, four months' interest is recorded at the end of the reporting period.

At October 31		
Masterwear (Issuer)		
Interest expense (4/6 × 46,991)	31,327	
Discount on bonds payable (4/6 × 4,991)		3,327
Interest payable (4/6 × 42,000)		28,000
United (Investor)		
Interest receivable (4/6 × 42,000)	28,000	
Discount on bond investment (4/6 × 4,991)	3,327	
Interest revenue (4/6 × 46,991)		31,327

Two months later, when semiannual interest is paid next, the remainder of the interest is allocated to the first two months of the next fiscal year—November and December:

Of the six months' interest paid December 31, only the November and December interest is expensed in the new fiscal year.

At the December 31 Interest Date		
Masterwear (Issuer)		
Interest expense (2/6 × 46,991)	15,664	
Interest payable (from adjusting entry)	28,000	
Discount on bonds payable (2/6 × 4,991)		1,664
Cash (stated rate × face amount)		42,000
United (Investor)		
Cash (stated rate × face amount)	42,000	
Discount on bond investment (2/6 × 4,991)	1,664	
Interest receivable (from adjusting entry)		28,000
Interest revenue (2/6 × 46,991)		15,664

The Straight-Line Method—A Practical Expediency

In some circumstances the profession permits an exception to the conceptually appropriate method of determining interest for bond issues. A company is allowed to determine interest indirectly by allocating a discount or a premium equally to each period over the term to maturity—if doing so produces results that are not materially different from the usual (and preferable) interest method. The decision should be guided by whether the straight-line method would tend to mislead investors and creditors in the particular circumstance.

By the straight-line method, the discount in Illustration 14–2 and Graphic 14–4 would be allocated equally to the six semiannual periods (three years):

$$\$33,367 \div 6 \text{ periods} = \$5,561 \text{ per period}$$

At Each of the Six Interest Dates		
Masterwear (Issuer)		
Interest expense (to balance)	47,561	
Discount on bonds payable (discount ÷ 6 periods)		5,561
Cash (stated rate × face amount)		42,000
United (Investor)		
Cash (stated rate × face amount)	42,000	
Discount on bond investment (discount ÷ 6 periods)	5,561	
Interest revenue (to balance)		47,561

Journal Entries— Straight-Line Method

By the straight-line method, interest (expense and revenue) is a plug figure, resulting from calculating the amount of discount reduction.

Allocating the discount or premium equally over the life of the bonds by the straight-line method results in a constant dollar amount of interest each period. An amortization schedule, then, would serve little purpose. For example, if we prepared one for the straight-line method in this situation, it would provide the same amounts each period as shown in Graphic 14–8.

GRAPHIC 14–8

Amortization Schedule—Straight-Line Method

Date	Cash Interest	Recorded Interest	Increase in Balance	Outstanding Balance
	(6% × Face amount)	(Cash + Discount reduction)	($33,367 ÷ 6)	
1/1/11				666,633
6/30/11	42,000	(42,000 + 5,561) = 47,561	5,561	672,194
12/31/11	42,000	(42,000 + 5,561) = 47,561	5,561	677,755
6/30/12	42,000	(42,000 + 5,561) = 47,561	5,561	683,316
12/31/12	42,000	(42,000 + 5,561) = 47,561	5,561	688,877
6/30/13	42,000	(42,000 + 5,561) = 47,561	5,561	694,438
12/31/13	42,000	(42,000 + 5,561) = 47,561	5,561	700,000*
	252,000	285,366	33,366	

By the straight-line method, the amount of the discount to be reduced periodically is calculated, and the recorded interest is the plug figure.

*Rounded

Remember, constant dollar amounts are not produced when the effective interest method is used. By that method, the dollar amounts of interest vary over the term to maturity because the percentage rate of interest remains constant but is applied to a changing debt balance.

Also, be sure to realize that the straight-line method is not an alternative method of determining interest in a conceptual sense. Instead, it is an application of the materiality concept, by which an appropriate application of GAAP (e.g., the effective interest method) can be by-passed for reasons of practical expediency in situations when doing so has no material effect on the results. Based on the frequency with which the straight-line method is used in practice, we can infer that managers very frequently conclude that its use has no material impact on investors' decisions.

Determining interest by allocating the discount (or premium) on a straight-line basis is a practical expediency permitted in some situations by the materiality concept.

CONCEPT REVIEW EXERCISE

On January 1, 2011, the Meade Group issued $8,000,000 of 11% bonds, dated January 1. Interest is payable semiannually on June 30 and December 31. The bonds mature in four years. The market yield for bonds of similar risk and maturity is 10%.

ISSUING BONDS AND RECORDING INTEREST

Required:

1. Determine the price these bonds issued to yield the 10% market rate and record their issuance by the Meade Group.
2. Prepare an amortization schedule that determines interest at the effective rate and record interest on the first interest date, June 30, 2011.

SOLUTION

1. Determine the price these bonds sold for to yield the 10% market rate and record their issuance by the Meade Group.

Calculation of the Price of the Bonds

There are eight semiannual periods and one-half the market rate is 5%.

Interest	$ 440,000 × 6.46321* =	$2,843,812
Principal	$8,000,000 × 0.67684† =	5,414,720
Present value (price) of the bonds		$8,258,532

*Present value of an ordinary annuity of $1: $n = 8$, $i = 5\%$.
†Present value of $1: $n = 8$, $i = 5\%$.

Journal Entries at Issuance

Cash (price calculated above)	8,258,532	
Bonds payable (face amount)		8,000,000
Premium on bonds payable (difference)		258,532

2. Prepare an amortization schedule that determines interest at the effective rate and record interest on the first interest date, June 30, 2011.

Amortization Schedule

Date	Cash Interest	Effective Interest	Decrease in Balance	Outstanding Balance
	(5.5% × Face amount)	(5% × Outstanding balance)	(Premium reduction)	
1/1/11				8,258,532
6/30/11	440,000	.05 (8,258,532) = 412,927	27,073	8,231,459
12/31/11	440,000	.05 (8,231,459) = 411,573	28,427	8,203,032
6/30/12	440,000	.05 (8,203,032) = 410,152	29,848	8,173,184
12/31/12	440,000	.05 (8,173,184) = 408,659	31,341	8,141,843
6/30/13	440,000	.05 (8,141,843) = 407,092	32,908	8,108,935
12 /31/13	440,000	.05 (8,108,935) = 405,447	34,553	8,074,382
6/30/14	440.000	.05 (8,074,382) = 403,719	36,281	8,038,101
12/31/14	440,000	.05 (8,038,101) = 401,899*	38,101	8,000,000
	3,520,000	3,261,468	258,532	

More cash is paid each period than the effective interest, so the debt outstanding is reduced by the "overpayment."

*Rounded.

Interest expense (5% × $8,258,532)	412,927	
Premium on bonds payable (difference)	27,073	
Cash (5.5% × $8,000,000)		440,000
To record interest for six months.		

Debt Issue costs

Rather than sell bonds directly to the public, corporations usually sell an entire issue to an underwriter who then resells them to other security dealers and the public. By committing to purchase bonds at a set price, investment banks such as **JPMorgan Chase** and **Goldman Sachs** are said to underwrite any risks associated with a new issue. The underwriting fee is the spread between the price the underwriter pays and the resale price.

Alternatively, the issuing company may choose to sell the debt securities directly to a single investor (as we assumed in previous illustrations)—often a pension fund or an insurance company. This is referred to as *private placement*. Issue costs are less because privately placed securities are not subject to the costly and lengthy process of registering with the SEC that is required of public offerings. Underwriting fees also are avoided.[3]

With either publicly or privately sold debt, the issuing company will incur costs in connection with issuing bonds or notes, such as legal and accounting fees and printing costs, in addition to registration and underwriting fees. These **debt issue costs** are recorded *separately* and are amortized over the term of the related debt. GAAP requires a debit to an asset account—debt issue costs. The asset is allocated to expense, usually on a straight-line basis.

For example, let's assume issue costs in Illustration 14–3 had been $12,000. The entries for the issuance of the bonds would include a separate asset account for the issue costs:

> **Costs of issuing debt securities are recorded as a debit to an asset account, "debt issue costs," and amortized to expense over the term to maturity.**

Cash ($735,533 minus $12,000 issue costs)	723,533	
Debt issue costs	12,000	
Bonds payable (face amount)		700,000
Premium on bonds payable ($735,533 minus face amount)		35,533

Semiannual amortization of the asset would be:

Debt issue expense ($12,000 ÷ 6)	2,000	
Debt issue costs		2,000

> **The premium (or discount) is unaffected by debt issue costs because they are recorded in a separate account.**

INTERNATIONAL FINANCIAL REPORTING STANDARDS

Debt Issue costs. Under U.S. GAAP, these costs are recorded separately as an asset. A conceptually more appealing treatment, and the one prescribed by IFRS, is to reduce the recorded amount of the debt by the debt issue costs (called transaction costs under IFRS). The cost of these services reduces the net cash the issuing company receives from the sale of the financial instrument. A lower [net] amount is borrowed at the same cost, increasing the effective interest rate. However, unless the recorded amount of the debt is reduced by the transaction costs, the higher rate is not reflected in a higher recorded interest expense. The actual increase in the effective interest rate is reflected in the interest expense if the issue cost is allowed to reduce the carrying amount of the debt:

● LO7

Cash (price minus transaction costs).....	723,533	
Bonds payable ($735,533 – 12,000)...		723,533*

Also, this approach is consistent with the treatment of issue costs when equity securities are sold. You will see in Chapter 18 that the effect of share issue costs is to reduce the amount credited to stock accounts.

IFRS ILLUSTRATION

*Notice that the premium is combined with the face amount of the bonds. This is the "net method" that, as we saw earlier, is the preferred method under IFRS.

The corporate bond is the basic long-term debt instrument for most large companies. But for many firms, the debt instrument often used is a *note*. We discuss notes next.

LONG-TERM NOTES

PART B

When a company borrows cash from a bank and signs a promissory note (essentially an IOU), the firm's liability is reported as a *note payable*. Or a note might be issued in exchange for a noncash asset—perhaps to purchase equipment on credit. In concept, notes are accounted for in precisely the same way as bonds. In fact, we could properly substitute notes payable for bonds payable in each of our previous illustrations.

● LO3

FINANCIAL Reporting Case

Q4, p. 747

---

[3]Rule 144A of the Securities Act of 1933, as amended, allows for the private resale of unregistered securities to "qualified institutional buyers," which are generally large institutional investors with assets exceeding $100 million.

Note Issued for Cash

The interest rate stated in a note is likely to be equal to the market rate because the rate usually is negotiated at the time of the loan. So discounts and premiums are less likely for notes than on bonds. Accounting for a note issued for cash is demonstrated in Illustration 14–4.

ILLUSTRATION 14–4 Note Issued for Cash	On January 1, 2011, Skill Graphics, Inc., a product-labeling and graphics firm, borrowed $700,000 cash from First BancCorp and issued a three-year, $700,000 promissory note. Interest of $42,000 was payable semiannually on June 30 and December 31.

At Issuance

Skill Graphics (Borrower)

Cash	700,000	
Notes payable (face amount)		700,000

First BancCorp (Lender)

Notes receivable (face amount)	700,000	
Cash		700,000

At Each of the Six Interest Dates

Skill Graphics (Borrower)

Interest expense	42,000	
Cash (stated rate × face amount)		42,000

First BancCorp (Lender)

Cash (stated rate × face amount)	42,000	
Interest revenue		42,000

At Maturity

Skill Graphics (Borrower)

Notes payable	700,000	
Cash (face amount)		700,000

First BancCorp (Lender)

Cash (face amount)	700,000	
Notes receivable		700,000

Note Exchanged for Assets or Services

Occasionally the *stated* interest rate is not indicative of the *market* rate at the time a note is negotiated. The value of the asset (cash or noncash) or service exchanged for the note establishes the market rate.[4] For example, let's assume Skill Graphics purchased a package-labeling machine from Hughes–Barker Corporation by issuing a 12%, $700,000, three-year note that requires interest to be paid semiannually. Let's also assume that the machine could have been purchased at a cash price of $666,633. You probably recognize this numerical situation as the one used earlier to illustrate bonds sold at a discount (Illustration 14–2). Reference to the earlier example will confirm that exchanging this $700,000 note for a machine with a cash price of $666,633 implies an annual market rate of interest of 14%. That is, 7% is one-half the discount rate that yields a present value of $666,633 for the note's cash flows (interest plus principal):

			Present Values
Interest	$ 42,000 × 4.76654*	=	$200,195
Principal	$700,000 × 0.66634†	=	466,438
Present value of the note			$666,633

*Present value of an ordinary annuity of $1: $n = 6$, $i = 7\%$.
†Present value of $1: $n = 6$, $i = 7\%$.

---

[4]If the debt instrument is negotiable and a dependable exchange price is readily available, the market value of the debt may be better evidence of the value of the transaction than the value of a noncash asset, particularly if it has no established cash selling price. The value of the asset or the debt, whichever is considered more reliable, should be used to record the transaction.

This is referred to as the **implicit rate of interest**—the rate implicit in the agreement. It may be that the implicit rate is not apparent. Sometimes the value of the asset (or service) is not readily determinable, but the interest rate stated in the transaction is unrealistic relative to the rate that would be expected in a similar transaction under similar circumstances. Deciding what the appropriate rate should be is called *imputing* an interest rate.

For example, suppose the machine exchanged for the 12% note is custom-made for Skill Graphics so that no customary cash price is available with which to work backwards to find the implicit rate. In that case, the appropriate rate would have to be found externally. It might be determined, for instance, that a more realistic interest rate for a transaction of this type, at this time, would be 14%. Then it would be apparent that Skill Graphics actually paid less than $700,000 for the machine and that part of the face amount of the note in effect makes up for the lower than normal interest rate. You learned early in your study of accounting that the economic essence of a transaction should prevail over its outward appearance. In keeping with this basic precept, the accountant should look beyond the *form* of this transaction and record its *substance*. The amount actually paid for the machine is the present value of the cash flows called for by the loan agreement, discounted at the market rate—imputed in this case to be 14%. So both the asset acquired and the liability used to purchase it should be recorded at the real cost, $666,633.

A basic concept of accounting is *substance over form.*

ADDITIONAL CONSIDERATION

For another example, let's assume the more realistic interest rate for a transaction of this type is, say, 16%. In that case we would calculate the real cost of the machine by finding the present value of both the interest and the principal, discounted at half the 16% rate:

		Present Values
Interest	$ 42,000 × 4.62288* =	$194,161
Principal	$700,000 × 0.63017† =	441,119
Present value of the note		$635,280

*Present value of an ordinary annuity of $1: n = 6, i = 8%.
†Present value of $1: n = 6, i = 8%.

Both the asset acquired and the liability used to purchase the asset would be recorded at $635,280.

The accounting treatment is the same whether the amount is determined directly from the market value of the machine (and thus the note) or indirectly as the present value of the note (and thus the value of the asset):[5]

Skill Graphics (Buyer/Issuer)
Machinery (cash price)	666,633	
Discount on notes payable (difference)	33,367	
Notes payable (face amount)		700,000

Hughes–Barker (Seller/Lender)
Notes receivable (face amount)	700,000	
Discount on notes receivable (difference)		33,367
Sales revenue (cash price)		666,633

Journal Entries at Issuance—Note with Unrealistic Interest Rate

---

[5]The method shown is the *gross method.* Alternatively, the *net method* can be used as follows:

Skill Graphics (Buyer/Issuer)
Machinery (cash price)	666,633	
Notes payable		666,633

Hughes–Barker (Seller/Lender)
Notes receivable	666,633	
Sales revenue (cash price)		666,633

Under the net method, the note is recorded at the face amount reduced by the discount on notes payable, which is the difference between face value and present value. As cash interest is paid, the note balance increases by the difference between the cash interest payment and the interest revenue (and interest expense). After the last payment, the note account balance will be equal to the face amount of the note.

Likewise, whether the effective interest rate is determined as the rate implicit in the agreement, given the asset's market value, or whether the effective rate is imputed as the appropriate interest rate if the asset's value is unknown, both parties to the transaction should record periodic interest (interest expense to the borrower, interest revenue to the lender) at the effective rate, rather than the stated rate.

Journal Entries—The Interest Method

The effective interest (expense to the issuer; revenue to the investor) is calculated each period as the effective rate times the amount of the debt outstanding during the interest period.

At the first Interest Date (June 30)

Skill Graphics (Borrower)

Interest expense (effective rate × outstanding balance)	46,664	
Discount on notes payable (difference)		4,664
Cash (stated rate × face amount)		42,000
Hughes–Barker (Seller/Lender)		
Cash (stated rate × face amount)	42,000	
Discount on notes receivable (difference)......................................	4,664	
Interest revenue (effective rate × outstanding balance)		46,664

The interest expense (interest revenue for the lender) varies as the balance of the note changes over time. See the amortization schedule in Graphic 14–9.[6]

GRAPHIC 14–9

Amortization Schedule—Note

Since less cash is paid each period than the effective interest, the unpaid difference (the discount reduction) increases the outstanding balance (carrying value) of the note.

Date	Cash Interest	Effective Interest	Increase in Balance	Outstanding Balance
	(6% × Face amount)	(7% × Outstanding balance)	(Discount reduction)	
1/1/11				666,633
6/30/11	42,000	.07 (666,633) = 46,664	4,664	671,297
12/31/11	42,000	.07 (671,297) = 46,991	4,991	676,288
6/30/12	42,000	.07 (676,288) = 47,340	5,340	681,628
12/31/12	42,000	.07 (681,628) = 47,714	5,714	687,342
6/30/13	42,000	.07 (687,342) = 48,114	6,114	693,456
12/31/13	42,000	.07 (693,456) = 48,544*	6,544	700,000
	252,000	285,367	33,367	

*Rounded.

Installment Notes

You may have recently purchased a car, or maybe a house. If so, unless you paid cash, you signed a note promising to pay the purchase price over, say, four years for the car, or 30 years for the house. Car and house notes usually call for payment in monthly installments rather than by a single amount at maturity. Corporations, too, often borrow using installment notes. Typically, installment payments are equal amounts each period. Each payment includes both an amount that represents interest and an amount that represents a reduction of the outstanding balance (principal reduction). The periodic reduction of the balance is sufficient that at maturity the note is completely paid. This amount is easily calculated by dividing the amount of the loan by the appropriate discount factor for the present value of an annuity. The installment payment amount that would pay the note described in the previous section is:

$$\underset{\text{Amount of loan}}{\$666{,}633} \quad \div \quad \underset{\substack{\text{(from Table 4} \\ n = 6,\ i = 7.0\%)}}{4.76654} \quad \underset{\substack{\text{Installment} \\ \text{payment}}}{\$139{,}857}$$

---

[6]The creation of amortization schedules is simplified by an electronic spreadsheet such as Microsoft Excel.

Consider Graphic 14-10.

Date	Cash Payment	Effective Interest	Decrease in Debt	Outstanding Balance
		(7% × Outstanding balance)		
1/1/11				666,633
6/30/11	139,857	.07 (666,633) = 46,664	93,193	573,440
12/31/11	139,857	.07 (573,440) = 40,141	99,716	473,724
6/30/12	139,857	.07 (473,724) = 33,161	106,696	367,028
12/31/12	139,857	.07 (367,028) = 25,692	114,165	252,863
6/30/13	139,857	.07 (252,863) = 17,700	122,157	130,706
12/31/13	139,857	.07 (130,706) = 9,151*	130,706	0
	839,142		172,509	666,633

GRAPHIC 14–10

Amortization Schedule—Installment Note

Each installment payment includes interest on the outstanding debt at the effective rate. The remainder of each payment reduces the outstanding balance.

*Rounded.

   The procedure is the same as for a note whose principal is paid at maturity, but the periodic cash payments are larger and there is no lump-sum payment at maturity. We calculated the amount of the payments so that after covering the interest on the existing debt each period, the excess would exactly amortize the debt to zero at maturity (rather than to a designated maturity amount).
   For installment notes, the outstanding balance of the note does not eventually become its face amount as it does for notes with designated maturity amounts. Instead, at the maturity date the balance is zero. Consequently, the significance is lost of maintaining separate balances for the face amount (in a note account) and the discount (or premium). So an installment note typically is recorded at its net carrying amount in a single note payable (or receivable) account:

Skill Graphics (Buyer/Issuer)		
Machinery	666,633	
Note payable		666,633
Hughes–Barker (Seller/Lender)		
Note receivable	666,633	
Sales revenue		666,633

Journal Entries at Issuance—Installment Note

At the first Interest Date (June 30)		
Skill Graphics (Borrower)		
Interest expense (effective rate × outstanding balance)	46,664	
Notes payable (difference)	93,193	
Cash (installment payment calculated above)		139,857
Hughes–Barker (Seller/Lender)		
Cash (installment payment calculated above)	139,857	
Notes receivable (difference)		93,193
Interest revenue (effective rate × outstanding balance)		46,664

Each payment includes both an amount that represents interest and an amount that represents a reduction of principal.

Financial Statement Disclosures

In the balance sheet, long-term debt (liability for the debtor; asset for the creditor) typically is reported as a single amount, net of any discount or increased by any premium, rather than at its face amount accompanied by a separate valuation account for the discount or premium. Any portion of the debt to be paid (received) during the upcoming year, or operating cycle if longer, should be reported as a current amount.

● LO4

ADDITIONAL CONSIDERATION

You will learn in the next chapter that the liability associated with a capital lease is accounted for the same way as this installment note. In fact, if the asset described above had been leased rather than purchased, the cash payments would be designated lease payments rather than installment loan payments, and a virtually identical amortization schedule would apply.

The reason for the similarity is that we view a capital lease as being, in substance, equivalent to an installment purchase/sale. Naturally, then, accounting treatment of the two essentially identical transactions should be consistent. Be sure to notice the parallel treatment as you study leases in the next chapter.

Supplemental disclosure is required of the fair value of bonds, notes, and other financial instruments.

The fair value of financial instruments must be disclosed either in the body of the financial statements or in disclosure notes.[7] These fair values are available for bonds and other securities traded on market exchanges in the form of quoted market prices. On the other hand, financial instruments not traded on market exchanges require other evidence of market value. For example, the market value of a note payable might be approximated by the present value of principal and interest payments using a current discount rate commensurate with the risks involved.

The disclosure note for debt includes the nature of the company's liabilities, interest rates, maturity dates, call provisions, conversion options, restrictions imposed by creditors, and any assets pledged as collateral. For all long-term borrowings, disclosures also should include the aggregate amounts payable for each of the next five years. To comply, **Toys R Us, Inc.**'s annual report for the fiscal year ended January 31, 2009, included the disclosure shown in Graphic 14–11:

GRAPHIC 14–11

Debt Disclosures–
Toys R Us

Real World Financials

The total fair values of our Long-term debt, with carrying values of $5.5 billion at January 31, 2009, and $5.9 billion at February 2, 2008, were $2.9 billion and $5.1 billion, respectively. The fair values of our Long-term debt are estimated using the quoted market prices for the same or similar issues and other pertinent information available to management as of the end of the respective periods.

The annual maturities of our Long-term debt, including current portions, at January 31, 2009, are as follows:

(In millions)	Annual Maturities
2009	$ 98
2010	2,193
2011	560
2012	1,236
2013	990
2014 and subsequent	468
Total	$5,545

Borrowing is a financing activity; lending is an investing activity.

Paying or receiving interest is an operating activity.

In a statement of cash flows, issuing bonds or notes are reported as cash flows from financing activities by the issuer (borrower) and cash flows from investing activities by the investor (lender). Similarly, when the debt is repaid, the issuer (borrower) reports the cash outflow as a financing activity while the investor (lender) reports it as a cash inflow from investing activities. However, because both interest expense and interest revenue are components of the income statement, both parties to the transaction report cash payments for interest among operating activities.

---

[7]FASB ASC 825–10–50–10: Financial Instruments–Overall–Disclosure (previously "Disclosures About Fair Values of Financial Instruments," *Statement of Financial Accounting Standards No. 107* (Norwalk, Conn.: FASB, 1991)).

DECISION MAKERS' PERSPECTIVE

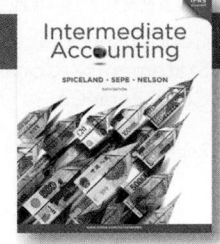

Business decisions involve risk. Failure to properly consider risk in those decisions is one of the most costly, yet one of the most common mistakes investors and creditors can make. Long-term debt is one of the first places decision makers should look when trying to get a handle on risk.

In general, debt increases risk. As an owner, debt would place you in a subordinate position relative to creditors because the claims of creditors must be satisfied first in case of liquidation. In addition, debt requires payment, usually on specific dates. Failure to pay debt interest and principal on a timely basis may result in default and perhaps even bankruptcy. The debt to equity ratio, total liabilities divided by shareholders' equity, often is calculated to measure the degree of risk. Other things being equal, the higher the debt to equity ratio, the higher the risk. The type of risk this ratio measures is called *default risk* because it presumably indicates the likelihood a company will default on its obligations.

Debt also can be an advantage. It can be used to enhance the return to shareholders. This concept, known as leverage, was described and illustrated in Chapter 3. If a company earns a return on borrowed funds in excess of the cost of borrowing the funds, shareholders are provided with a total return greater than what could have been earned with equity funds alone. This desirable situation is called *favorable financial leverage.* Unfortunately, leverage is not always favorable. Sometimes the cost of borrowing the funds exceeds the returns they generate. This illustrates the typical risk-return trade-off faced by shareholders.

Creditors demand interest payments as compensation for the use of their capital. Failure to pay interest as scheduled may cause several adverse consequences, including bankruptcy. Therefore, another way to measure a company's ability to pay its obligations is by comparing interest payments with income available to pay those charges. The times interest earned ratio does this by dividing income, before subtracting interest expense or income tax expense, by interest expense.

Two points about this ratio are important. First, because interest is deductible for income tax purposes, income before interest and taxes is a better indication of a company's ability to pay interest than is income after interest and taxes (i.e., net income). Second, income before interest and taxes is a rough approximation for cash flow generated from operations. The primary concern of decision makers is, of course, the cash available to make interest payments. In fact, this ratio often is computed by dividing cash flow generated from operations by interest payments.

For illustration, let's compare the ratios for **Coca-Cola** and **PepsiCo**. Graphic 14–12 on the next page provides condensed financial statements adapted from 2008 annual reports of those companies.

The debt to equity ratio is much higher for PepsiCo:

$$\text{Debt to equity ratio} = \frac{\text{Total liabilities}}{\text{Shareholders' equity}}$$

$$\text{Coca-Cola} = \frac{\$20{,}047}{\$20{,}472} = .98$$

$$\text{PepsiCo} = \frac{\$23{,}888}{\$12{,}106} = 1.97$$

Generally speaking, debt increases risk.

To evaluate a firm's risk, you might start by calculating its debt to equity ratio.

As a manager, you would try to create favorable financial leverage to earn a return on borrowed funds in excess of the cost of borrowing the funds.

As an external analyst or a manager, you are concerned with a company's ability to repay debt.

The debt to equity ratio indicates the extent of trading on the equity, or financial leverage.

GRAPHIC 14–12

Condensed Financial Statements—Coca-Cola, PepsiCo

Real World Financials

Balance Sheets		
	($ in millions)	
	Coca-Cola	**PepsiCo**
Assets		
Current assets	$12,176	$10,506
Property, plant, and equipment (net)	8,326	11,228
Intangibles and other assets	20,017	14,260
Total assets	$40,519	$35,994
Liabilities and Shareholders' Equity		
Current liabilities	$12,988	$ 8,787
Long-term liabilities	7,059	15,101
Total liabilities	$20,047	$23,888
Shareholders' equity	20,472	12,106
Total liabilities and shareholders' equity	$40,519	$35,994
Income Statements		
Net sales	$31,944	$43,251
Cost of goods sold	(11,374)	(20,351)
Gross profit	$20,570	$22,900
Operating and other expenses	(12,693)	(15,550)
Interest expense	(438)	(329)
Income before taxes	$ 7,439	$ 7,021
Tax expense	(1,632)	(1,879)
Net income	$ 5,807	$ 5,142

Remember, that's not necessarily a positive or a negative. Let's look closer. When the return on shareholders' equity is greater than the return on assets, management is using debt funds to enhance the earnings for shareholders. Both firms do this. We calculate return on assets as follows:

The rate of return on assets indicates profitability without regard to how resources are financed.

$$\text{Rate of return on assets}[8] = \frac{\text{Net income}}{\text{Total assets}}$$

$$\text{Coca-Cola} = \frac{\$5,807}{\$40,519} = 14.3\%$$

$$\text{PepsiCo} = \frac{\$5,142}{\$35,994} = 14.3\%$$

The return on assets indicates a company's overall profitability, ignoring specific sources of financing. In this regard, PepsiCo's profitability is virtually identical to Coca-Cola's. That advantage, though, swings to PepsiCo when we compare the return to shareholders:

The rate of return on shareholders' equity indicates the effectiveness of employing resources provided by owners.

$$\frac{\text{Rate of return on}}{\text{shareholders' equity}} = \frac{\text{Net income}}{\text{Shareholders' equity}}$$

---

[8] A more accurate way to calculate this ratio is:

$$\text{Rate of return on assets} = \frac{\text{Net income} + \text{Interest expense }(1 - \text{tax rate})}{\text{Average total assets}}$$

The reason for adding back interest expense (net of tax) is that interest represents a return to suppliers of debt capital and should not be deducted in the computation of net income when computing the return on total assets. In other words, the numerator is the total amount of income available to both debt and equity capital.

$$\text{Coca-Cola} = \frac{\$5,807}{\$20,472} = 28.4\%$$

$$\text{PepsiCo} = \frac{\$5,142}{\$12,106} = 42.5\%$$

PepsiCo's higher leverage has been used to provide a return to shareholders roughly 58% higher than Coca-Cola's. PepsiCo increased its return to shareholders 2.97 times (42.5%/14.3%) the return on assets. Coca-Cola increased its return to shareholders 2 times (28.4%/14.3%) the return on assets. Interpret this with caution, though. First, the difference is small. Second, PepsiCo's higher leverage means higher risk as well. In down times, PepsiCo's return to shareholders will suffer proportionally more than will Coca-Cola's.

From the perspective of a creditor, we might look at which company offers the most comfortable margin of safety in terms of its ability to pay fixed interest charges:

$$\frac{\text{Times interest}}{\text{earned ratio}} = \frac{\text{Net income plus interest plus taxes}}{\text{Interest}}$$

$$\text{Coca-Cola} = \frac{\$5,807 + 438 + 1,632}{\$438} = 18 \text{ times}$$

$$\text{PepsiCo} = \frac{\$5,142 + 329 + 1,879}{\$329} = 22.3 \text{ times}$$

> The times interest earned ratio indicates the margin of safety provided to creditors.

In this regard, Pepsi provides a greater margin of safety. Pepsi has more debt in its capital structure relative to Coca-Cola. However, it clearly is able to pay the cost of borrowing and return even more to its shareholders relative to Coca-Cola. Pepsi trades quite favorably on its leverage.

Liabilities also can have misleading effects on the income statement. Decision makers should look carefully at gains and losses produced by early extinguishment of debt. These have nothing to do with a company's normal operating activities. Unchecked, corporate management can be tempted to schedule debt buybacks to provide discretionary income in down years or even losses in up years to smooth income over time.

> Decision makers should be alert to gains and losses that have nothing to do with a company's normal operating activities.

Alert investors and lenders also look outside the financial statements for risks associated with "off-balance-sheet" financing and other commitments that don't show up on the face of financial statements but nevertheless expose a company to risk. Relatedly, most companies attempt to actively manage the risk associated with these and other obligations. It is important for top management to understand and closely monitor risk management strategies. Some of the financial losses that have grabbed headlines in recent years were permitted by a lack of oversight and scrutiny by senior management of companies involved. It is similarly important for investors and creditors to become informed about risks companies face and how well-equipped those companies are in managing that risk. The supplemental disclosures designed to communicate the degree of risk associated with the financial instruments we discuss in this chapter contribute to that understanding. We examine the significance of lease commitments in the next chapter. ●

> Outside analysts as well as managers should actively monitor risk management activities.

CONCEPT REVIEW EXERCISE

Cameron-Brown, Inc., constructed for Harmon Distributors a warehouse that was completed and ready for occupancy on January 2, 2011. Harmon paid for the warehouse by issuing a $900,000, four-year note that required 7% interest to be paid on December 31 of each year. The warehouse was custom-built for Harmon, so its cash price was not known. By comparison with similar transactions, it was determined that an appropriate interest rate was 10%.

> **NOTE WITH AN UNREALISTIC INTEREST RATE**

Required:

1. Prepare the journal entry for Harmon's purchase of the warehouse on January 2, 2011.
2. Prepare (a) an amortization schedule for the four-year term of the note and (b) the journal entry for Harmon's first interest payment on December 31, 2011.
3. Suppose Harmon's note had been an installment note to be paid in four equal payments. What would be the amount of each installment if payable (a) at the end of each year, beginning December 31, 2011? or (b) at the beginning of each year, beginning on January 2, 2011?

SOLUTION   1. Prepare the journal entry for Harmon's purchase of the warehouse on January 2, 2011.

	Present Values
Interest	$ 63,000 × 3.16987* = $199,702
Principal	$900,000 × 0.68301† = 614,709
Present value of the note	$814,411

*Present value of an ordinary annuity of $1: $n = 4$, $i = 10\%$.
†Present value of $1: $n = 4$, $i = 10\%$.

Warehouse (price determined above)	814,411	
Discount on notes payable (difference)	85,589	
Notes payable (face amount)		900,000

2. Prepare (a) an amortization schedule for the four-year term of the note and (b) the journal entry for Harmon's first interest payment on December 31, 2011.

a.

Dec. 31	Cash	Effective Interest	Increase in Balance	Outstanding Balance
	(7% × Face amount)	(10% × Outstanding balance)	(Discount reduction)	
				814,411
2011	63,000	.10 (814,411) = 81,441	18,441	832,852
2012	63,000	.10 (832,852) = 83,285	20,285	853,137
2013	63,000	.10 (853,137) = 85,314	22,314	875,451
2014	63,000	.10 (875,451) = 87,549*	24,549	900,000
	252,000	337,589	85,589	

*Rounded.

b.

Interest expense (effective rate × outstanding balance)	81,441	
Discount on notes payable (difference)		18,441
Cash (stated rate × face amount)		63,000

3. Suppose Harmon's note had been an installment note to be paid in four equal payments. What would be the amount of each installment if payable (a) at the end of each year, beginning December 31, 2011? or (b) at the beginning of each year, beginning on January 2, 2011?

a. $814,411   ÷   3.16987   = $256,923
    Amount of loan   (from Table 4
                           $n = 4$, $i = 10\%$)   Installment payment

b. $814,411   ÷   3.48685   = $233,566
    Amount of loan   (from Table 6
                           $n = 4$, $i = 10\%$)   Installment payment

DEBT RETIRED EARLY, CONVERTIBLE INTO STOCK, OR PROVIDING AN OPTION TO BUY STOCK

Early Extinguishment of Debt

● LO5

As we saw in the previous section, debt paid in installments is systematically retired over the term to maturity so that at the designated maturity date the outstanding balance is zero. On the other hand, when a maturity amount is specified as in our earlier illustrations, any discount or premium has been systematically reduced to zero as of the maturity date and the debt is retired simply by paying the maturity amount. Sometimes, though, companies choose to retire debt before its scheduled maturity. In that case, a gain or a loss may result.

Earlier we noted that a call feature accompanies most bonds to protect the issuer against declining interest rates. Even when bonds are not callable, the issuing company can retire bonds early by purchasing them on the open market. Regardless of the method, when debt of any type is retired prior to its scheduled maturity date, the transaction is referred to as **early extinguishment of debt.**

To record the extinguishment, the account balances pertinent to the debt obviously must be removed from the books. Of course cash is credited for the amount paid—the call price or market price. The difference between the carrying amount of the debt and the reacquisition price represents either a gain or a loss on the early extinguishment of debt. When the debt is retired for less than carrying value, the debtor is in a favorable position and records a gain. The opposite occurs for a loss. Let's continue an earlier example to illustrate the retirement of debt prior to its scheduled maturity (Illustration 14–5):

> **Any difference between the outstanding debt and the amount paid to retire that debt represents either a gain or a loss.**

On January 1, 2012, Masterwear Industries called its $700,000, 12% bonds when their carrying amount was $676,288. The indenture specified a call price of $685,000. The bonds were issued previously at a price to yield 14%.

Bonds payable (face amount)	700,000	
Loss on early extinguishment[9] ($685,000 − 676,288)	8,712	
Discount on bonds payable ($700,000 − 676,288)		23,712
Cash (call price)		685,000

> **ILLUSTRATION 14–5**
> Early Extinguishment of Debt

For instance, in its income statement for the second quarter of 2009, **Momentive Performance Materials Inc.**, a premier specialty metals company, reported a $179 million gain on the early extinguishment of debt.

Convertible Bonds

Sometimes corporations include a convertible feature as part of a bond offering. **Convertible bonds** can be converted into (that is, exchanged for) shares of stock at the option of the bondholder. Among the reasons for issuing convertible bonds rather than straight debt are (a) to sell the bonds at a higher price (which means a lower effective interest cost),[10] (b) to use as a medium of exchange in mergers and acquisitions, and (c) to enable smaller firms or debt-heavy companies to obtain access to the bond market. Sometimes convertible bonds serve as an indirect way to issue stock when there is shareholder resistance to direct issuance of additional equity.

Central to each of these reasons for issuing convertible debt is that the conversion feature is attractive to investors. This hybrid security has features of both debt and equity. The owner has a fixed-income security that can become common stock if and when the firm's prosperity makes that feasible. This increases the investor's upside potential while limiting the downside

> **FINANCIAL**
> **Reporting Case**
>
> Q5, p. 747
>
> **Convertible bonds can be exchanged for shares of stock at the option of the investor.**

---

[9]For several years the FASB required companies to report gains and losses from early extinguishment of debt as extraordinary items, but no longer. Now, these gains and losses are subject to the same criteria as other gains and losses for such treatment; namely, that they be both (a) unusual and (b) infrequent. FASB ASC 470–50–45: Debt–Modifications and Extinguishments–Other Presentation Matters (previously *Statement of Financial Accounting Standards No. 145*, "Rescission of FASB Statements No. 4, 44, and 64, Amendment of FASB Statement No. 13, and Technical Corrections" (Norwalk, Conn.: FASB, 2002)).

[10]Remember, there is an inverse relationship between bond prices and interest rates. When the price is higher, the rate (yield) is lower, and vice versa.

Convertible bonds have features of both debt and equity.

risk. The conversion feature has monetary value. Just how valuable it is depends on both the conversion terms and market conditions. But from an accounting perspective the question raised is how to account for its value. To evaluate the question, consider Illustration 14–6.

ILLUSTRATION 14–6 Convertible Bonds	On January 1, 2011, HTL Manufacturers issued $100 million of 8% convertible debentures due 2031 at 103 (103% of face value). The bonds are convertible at the option of the holder into no par common stock at a conversion ratio of 40 shares per $1,000 bond. HTL recently issued nonconvertible, 20-year, 8% debentures at 98.

Because of the inseparability of their debt and equity features, the entire issue price of convertible bonds is recorded as debt, as if they are nonconvertible bonds.

It would appear that the conversion feature is valued by the market at $5 million—the difference between the market value of the convertible bonds, $103 million, and the market value of the nonconvertible bonds, $98 million. Some accountants argue that we should record the value of the conversion option in a shareholders' equity account ($5 million in this case) and the debt value in the bond accounts ($100 million bonds payable less $2 million discount). However, counter to that intuitive argument, the currently accepted practice is to record the entire issue price as debt in precisely the same way as for nonconvertible bonds.[11] Treating the features as two inseparable parts of a single security avoids the practical difficulty of trying to measure the separate values of the debt and the conversion option.

Journal Entry at Issuance—Convertible Bonds

The value of the conversion feature is not separately recorded.

	($ in millions)	
Cash (103% × $100 million)	103	
Convertible bonds payable (face amount)		100
Premium on bonds payable (difference)		3

Since we make no provision for the separate value of the conversion option, all subsequent entries, including the periodic reduction of the premium, are exactly the same as if these were nonconvertible bonds. So the illustrations and examples of bond accounting we discussed earlier would pertain equally to nonconvertible or convertible bonds.

ADDITIONAL CONSIDERATION

While we normally don't separate the conversion option from the debt for convertible bonds, an exception is when the conversion option is deemed to be a "beneficial conversion feature." That's the case when the conversion option has a positive "intrinsic value" at the time the bonds are issued, meaning the fair value of the stock into which the bonds are convertible exceeds the face amount of the bonds.[12] Suppose, for instance, that HTL's stock in Illustration 14–6 has a fair value of $30 per share when the bonds are issued. This implies an intrinsic value of the conversion feature of $5 per share:

Price per share to convert: $1,000 ÷ 40 shares = $25 per share

Fair value of stock at issue date	$30
Conversion price for shares	25
Intrinsic value of beneficial conversion option per share	$ 5

Intrinsic value of beneficial conversion feature:

100,000 bonds × 40 shares = 4,000,000 shares × $5 per share = **$20,000,000**

The intrinsic value of the conversion option is recorded separately:

	($ in millions)	
Cash (103% × $100 million)	103	
Discount on bonds (to balance)	17	
Convertible bonds payable (face amount)		100
Equity—conversion option (intrinsic value)		20

---

[11]FASB ASC 470–20–25: Debt–Debt with Conversion Options–Recognition (previously "Accounting for Convertible Debt and Debt Issued with Stock Purchase Warrants," *Accounting Principles Board Opinion No. 14* (New York: APB, 1969)).

[12]FASB ASC 470–20–25–5: Debt–Debt with Conversion and Other Options–Recognition– Beneficial Conversion Features (previously "Accounting for Convertible Securities with Beneficial Conversion Features or Contingently Adjustable Conversion Ratios," *EITF Issue No. 98-5* (Norwalk, Conn.: FASB, 1998)).

Accounting for convertible debt is likely to change. In fact, the FASB plans to issue an exposure draft document in 2011 regarding convertible securities and similar instruments as a result of a joint project with the IASB regarding hybrid securities.[13] A recent FASB Staff Position (FSP 14-1) gives us a hint, perhaps, of the direction the project might take. For a limited subset of convertible securities not within the scope of current GAAP—those that could possibly be settled in cash rather than shares—companies must divide the proceeds from convertible securities into its two components and record the fair value of the debt as a liability and the conversion option in an equity account. Lending credence to that projection is the fact that international standards require that convertible debt be divided into its liability and equity elements, so moving in that direction would be a step closer to convergence of U.S. GAAP and IFRS.

● LO7

INTERNATIONAL FINANCIAL REPORTING STANDARDS

Convertible bonds. Under IFRS, unlike U.S. GAAP, convertible debt is divided into its liability and equity elements. In Illustration 14–6, if HTL prepared its financial statements in accordance with IFRS, it would record the convertible bonds as follows:

Journal Entry at Issuance—Convertible Bonds

IFRS ILLUSTRATION

	($ in millions)	
Cash (103% × $100 million)	103	
Convertible bonds payable (value of the debt only)		98*
Equity—conversion option (to balance)		5

*Notice that the discount is combined with the face amount of the bonds. This is the "net method" that we saw earlier and is the preferred method under IFRS.

In essence, HTL is selling two securities—(1) bonds and (2) an option to convert to stock—for one package price. The bonds represent a liability; the option is shareholders' equity. Compound instruments such as this one are separated into their liability and equity components in accordance with *IAS No. 32*.[14] Because the bonds have a separate fair value of $98 million, we record that amount as the liability and the remaining $5 million (the difference between the fair value of the convertible bonds, $103 million, and the $98 million) as equity. If the fair value of the bonds cannot be determined from an active trading market, that value can be calculated as the present value of the bonds' cash flows, using the market rate of interest.

The components of compound financial instruments such as convertible bonds are valued and reported separately under IFRS.

When the Conversion Option Is Exercised

If and when the bondholder exercises his or her option to convert the bonds into shares of stock, the bonds are removed from the accounting records and the new shares issued are recorded at the same amount (in other words, at the book value of the bonds). To illustrate, assume that half the convertible bonds issued by HTL Manufacturers are converted at a time when the remaining unamortized premium is $2 million:

Journal Entry at Conversion

	($ in millions)	
Convertible bonds payable (½ the account balance)	50	
Premium on bonds payable (½ the account balance)	1	
Common stock (to balance)		51

The 2 million shares issued are recorded at the $51 million book value of the bonds retired.

[13]This is a joint project of the FASB and IASB in which the Boards are developing a classification model that includes consideration of which financial instruments might be divided into separate components of liabilities and equity.
[14]"Financial Statements: Presentation," *International Accounting Standard (IAS) No. 32* (IASCF) as amended effective January 1, 2009.

ADDITIONAL CONSIDERATION

The method just described is referred to as the *book value method*, since the new shares are recorded at the book value of the redeemed bonds. It is by far the most popular method in practice. Another acceptable approach, the *market value method*, records the new shares at the market value of the shares themselves or of the bonds, whichever is more determinable. Because the market value most likely will differ from the book value of the bonds, a gain or loss on conversion will result. Assume for illustration that the market value of HTL's stock is $30 per share at the time of the conversion:

	($ in millions)	
Convertible bonds payable (½ the account balance)	50	
Premium on bonds payable (½ the account balance)	1	
Loss on conversion of bonds (to balance)	9	
Common stock [(50,000 bonds × 40 shares) × $30]		60

If the 50,000 convertible bonds were held by a single investor, that company would record the conversion as follows:

	($ in millions)	
Investment in common stock	51	
Investment in convertible bonds (account balance)		50
Premium on bond investment (account balance)		1

Induced Conversion

Investors often are reluctant to convert bonds to stock, even when share prices have risen significantly since the convertible bonds were purchased. This is because the market price of the convertible bonds will rise along with market prices of the stock. So companies sometimes try to induce conversion. The motivation might be to reduce debt and become a better risk to potential lenders or achieve a lower debt-to-equity ratio.

One way is through the call provision. As we noted earlier, most corporate bonds are callable by the issuing corporation. When the specified call price is less than the conversion value of the bonds (the market value of the shares), calling the convertible bonds provides bondholders with incentive to convert. Bondholders will choose the shares rather than the lower call price.

Any additional consideration provided to induce conversion of convertible debt is recorded as an expense of the period.

Occasionally, corporations may try to encourage voluntary conversion by offering an added inducement in the form of cash, stock warrants, or a more attractive conversion ratio. When additional consideration is provided to induce conversion, the fair value of that consideration is considered an expense incurred to bring about the conversion.[15]

Bonds with Detachable Warrants

Another (less common) way to sweeten a bond issue is to include detachable stock purchase warrants as part of the security issue. A stock warrant gives the investor an option to purchase a stated number of shares of common stock at a specified *option price*, often within a given period of time. Like a conversion feature, warrants usually mean a lower interest rate and often enable a company to issue debt when borrowing would not be feasible otherwise.

The issue price of bonds with detachable warrants is allocated between the two different securities on the basis of their market values.

However, unlike the conversion feature for convertible bonds, warrants can be separated from the bonds. This means they can be exercised independently or traded in the market separately from bonds, having their own market price. In essence, two different securities—

---

[15]FASB ASC 470–20–40: Debt–Debt with Conversion Options–Derecognition (previously "Induced Conversions of Convertible Debt," *Statement of Financial Accounting Standards No. 84* (Stamford, Conn.: FASB, 1985)).

the bonds and the warrants—are sold as a package for a single issue price. Accordingly, the issue price is allocated between the two different securities on the basis of their market values. If the independent market value of only one of the two securities is reliably determinable, that value establishes the allocation. This is demonstrated in Illustration 14–7.

	($ in millions)	
ILLUSTRATION 14–7		

On January 1, 2011, HTL Manufacturers issued $100 million of 8% debentures due 2018 at 103 (103% of face value). Accompanying each $1,000 bond were 20 warrants. Each warrant permitted the holder to buy one share of no par common stock at $25 per share. Shortly after issuance, the warrants were listed on the stock exchange at $3 per warrant.

ILLUSTRATION 14–7
Bonds with Detachable Warrants

	($ in millions)	
Cash (103% × $100 million)	103	
Discount on bonds payable (difference)	3	
Bonds payable (face amount)		100
Equity—stock warrants*		6

*Reported as part of shareholders' equity rather than as a liability.

ADDITIONAL CONSIDERATION

Market imperfections may cause the separate market values not to sum to the issue price of the package. In this event, allocation is achieved on the basis of the relative market values of the two securities. Let's say the bonds have a separate market price of $940 per bond (priced at 94):

Market Values	**Dollars**	**Percent**
Bonds (100,000 bonds × $940)	$ 94	94%
Warrants (100,000 bonds × 20 warrants × $3)	6	6
Total	$100	100%

Proportion of Issue Price Allocated to Bonds:

$103 million × 94% = $96,820,000

Proportion of Issue Price Allocated to Warrants:

$103 million × 6% = $6,180,000

	($ in millions)	
Cash (103% × $100 million)	103.00	
Discount on bonds payable ($100 million – $96.82 million)	3.18	
Bonds payable (face amount)		100.00
Equity—stock warrants (to balance)		6.18

Notice that this is the same approach we used in Chapter 10 to allocate a single purchase price to two or more assets bought for that single price. We also will allocate the total selling price of two equity securities sold for a single issue in proportion to their relative market values in Chapter 18.

If one-half of the warrants (1 million) in Illustration 14–7 are exercised when the market value of HTL's common stock is $30 per share, 1 million shares would be issued for one warrant each plus the exercise price of $25 per share.

	($ in millions)	
Cash (1,000,000 warrants × $25)	25	
Equity—stock warrants (1,000,000 warrants × $3)	3	
Common stock (to balance)		28

Journal Entry at Exercise of Detachable Warrants

The $30 market value at the date of exercise is not used in valuing the additional shares issued. The new shares are recorded at the total of the previously measured values of both the warrants and the shares.

CONCEPT REVIEW EXERCISE

ISSUANCE AND EARLY EXTINGUISHMENT OF DEBT

The disclosure notes to the 2011 financial statements of Olswanger Industries included the following:

Note 12: Bonds

On September 15, 2010, the Corporation sold bonds with an aggregate principal amount of $500,000,000 bearing a 14% interest rate. The bonds will mature on September 15, 2020, and are unsecured subordinated obligations of the Corporation. Interest is payable semiannually on March 15 and September 15. The Corporation may redeem the bonds at any time beginning September 15, 2010, as a whole or from time to time in part, through maturity, at specified redemption prices ranging from 112% of principal in declining percentages of principal amount through 2017 when the percentage is set at 100% of principal amount. The cost of issuing the bonds, totaling $11,000,000, and the discount of $5,000,000 are being amortized over the life of the bonds, using the straight-line method and the interest method, respectively. Amortization of these items for the year ended December 31, 2011, was $960,000 and $252,000, respectively.

During the year ended December 31, 2011, the Corporation repurchased, in open market transactions, $200,000,000 in face amount of the bonds for $219,333,000. The unamortized cost of issuing these bonds and the unamortized discount, $3,972,000 and $1,892,000, respectively, have been deducted in the current period.

From the information provided by Olswanger in Note 12, you should be able to recreate some of the journal entries the company recorded in connection with this bond issue.

Required:

1. Prepare the journal entry for the issuance of these bonds on September 15, 2010.
2. Prepare the journal entry for the repurchase of these bonds, assuming the date of repurchase was September 15, 2011. The cash paid to repurchase the bonds was $219,333,000.

SOLUTION

1. Prepare the journal entry for the issuance of these bonds on September 15, 2010.

	($ in 000s)	
Cash (to balance)	484,000	
Bond issue costs (given in note)	11,000	
Discount on bonds payable (given in note)	5,000	
Bonds payable (face amount—given in note)		500,000

2. Prepare the journal entry for the repurchase of these bonds, assuming the date of repurchase was September 15, 2011.

	($ in 000s)	
Bonds payable (face amount repurchased)	200,000	
Loss on early extinguishment (to balance)	25,197	
Discount on bonds payable (given in note)		1,892
Bond issue costs (given in note)		3,972
Cash (given in requirement 2)		219,333

Option to Report Liabilities at Fair Value

Companies are not required to, but have the option to, value some or all of their financial assets and liabilities at fair value.[16] In Chapter 12, we saw examples of the option applied to financial assets—specifically, companies reporting their investments in securities at fair value. Now, we see how liabilities, too, can be reported at fair value.

● LO6

A company has the option to value financial assets and liabilities at fair value.

How does a liability's fair value change? Remember that there are two sides to every investment. For example, if a company has an investment in **General Motors**' bonds, that investment is an asset to the investor, and the same bonds are a liability to General Motors. So, the same market forces that influence the fair value of an investment in debt securities (interest rates, economic conditions, risk, etc.) influence the fair value of liabilities. For bank loans or other debts that aren't traded on a market exchange, the mix of factors will differ, but in any case, changes in the current market rate of interest will be a major contributor to changes in fair value.

Determining Fair Value

For demonstration, we revisit the Masterwear Industries bonds that sold at a discount in Illustration 14–2 on page 751. Now, suppose it's six months later, the market rate of interest has fallen to 11%, and June 30 is the end of Masterwear's fiscal year. A decline in market interest rates means bond prices rise. Let's say that checking market prices in *The Wall Street Journal* indicates that the fair value of the Masterwear bonds on June 30, 2011, is $714,943. Referring to the amortization schedule on page 762, we see that on the same date, with 5 periods remaining to maturity, the present value of the bonds—their price—would have been $671,297 if the market rate still had been 14% (7% semiannually).

Changes in interest rates cause changes in the fair value of liabilities.

ADDITIONAL CONSIDERATION

If the bonds are not traded on a market exchange, their fair value would not be readily observable. In that case, the next most preferable way to determine fair value would be to calculate the fair value as the present value of the remaining cash flows discounted at the current interest rate. If the rate is 11% (5.5% semiannually), as we're assuming now, that present value would be $714,943:

	Present Values
Interest	$ 42,000 × 4.27028* = $179,352
Principal	$700,000 × 0.76513† = 535,591
Present value of the bonds	$714,943

*Present value of an ordinary annuity of $1: $n = 5$, $i = 5.5\%$.
†Present value of $1: $n = 5$, $i = 5.5\%$.

When the bonds were issued, Masterwear had a choice—report this liability (a) at its amortized initial measurement throughout the term to maturity or (b) at its current fair value on each reporting date. Had the company *not* elected the fair value option, on June 30 it would report the $671,297 we calculated earlier for the amortization schedule. On the other hand, if Masterwear had elected the fair value option, it would report the bonds at their current fair value, $714,943.

Reporting Changes in Fair Value

If a company chooses the option to report at fair value, then it must report *changes* in fair value in the income statement. In our example, Masterwear would report the increase in fair value from $666,633 to $714,943, or $48,310. Note, though, that part of the change is due to the unpaid interest we discussed earlier. Here's a recap.

---

[16]FASB ASC 825–10–25–1: Financial Instruments–Overall–Recognition–Fair Value Option (previously "The Fair Value Option for Financial Assets and Financial Liabilities," *Statement of Financial Accounting Standards No. 159* (Norwalk, Conn.: FASB, 2007)).

At June 30, 2011, the interest that accrued during the first six months was $46,664, but only $42,000 of that was paid in cash; so the debt balance increased by the $4,664 unpaid interest. We recorded the following entry:

Bonds payable
<u>**Less: Discount**</u>
Carrying value

Interest expense...	46,664	
Discount on bonds payable.......................................		4,664
Cash..		42,000

Amortizing the discount in this entry increased the book value of the liability by $4,664 to $671,297:

January 1 carrying value and fair value	$666,633
Increase from discount amortization	4,664
June 30 carrying value (amortized initial amount)	$671,297

FAIR VALUE RISES. Comparing that amount with the fair value of the bonds on that date provides the amount needed to adjust the bonds to their fair value.

When the fair value option is elected, we report changes in fair value in the income statement.

June 30 fair value	$714,943
June 30 carrying value (amortized initial amount)	671,297
Fair value adjustment needed	$ 43,646

Rather than increasing the bonds payable account itself, though, we instead adjust it *indirectly* with a credit to a valuation allowance (or contra) account:

Unrealized holding loss...	43,646	
Fair value adjustment ($714,943 – 671,297).............................		43,646

Masterwear must recognize the unrealized holding loss in the June 30, 2011, income statement. Notice that the effect on earnings is:

Electing the FVO means reporting unrealized holding gains and losses in earnings.

Interest expense	$46,664
Unrealized holding loss	43,646
Net decrease in earnings	$90,310

The new carrying value of the bonds is now the fair value:

The *credit* balance in the fair value adjustment *increases* the carrying value; the discount reduces it.

Bonds payable	$700,000
Less: Discount ($33,367 – 4,664)	(28,703)
Amortization table value	$671,297
Plus: Fair value adjustment	43,646
Carrying value, June 30	$714,943

FAIR VALUE FALLS. Suppose the fair value at June 30, 2011, had been $650,000 instead of $714,943. In that case, Masterwear would record a *reduction* in the liability from $671,297 to $650,000, or $21,297. The entry would be:

Fair value adjustment ($671,297 – 650,000)	21,297	
Unrealized holding gain		21,297

The effect on earnings in the second scenario is:

Interest expense	$46,664
Unrealized holding gain	(21,297)
Net decrease in earnings	$25,367

The new carrying value of the bonds is the fair value:

Bonds payable	$700,000
Less: Discount ($33,367 − 4,664)	(28,703)
Amortization table value	$671,297
Less: Fair value adjustment	(21,297)
Carrying value, June 30	$650,000

The *debit* balance in the fair value adjustment *reduces* the carrying value; as does the discount.

The outstanding balance in the last column of the amortization schedule at any date up to and including the balance at maturity will be the bonds payable less the discount (for instance $671,297 at June 30, 2011, on page 762). But the amount we report in the balance sheet at any reporting date, the fair value, will be that amortized initial amount from the amortization schedule plus or minus the fair value adjustment. That's the $714,943 or the $650,000 in the two scenarios above.

Mix and Match

Remember from our discussions in prior chapters that if a company elects the fair value option, it's not necessary that the company elect the option to report all of its financial instruments at fair value or even all instruments of a particular type at fair value. They can "mix and match" on an instrument-by-instrument basis. So Masterwear, for instance, might choose to report these bonds at fair value but all its other liabilities at their amortized initial measurement. However, the company must make the election when the item originates, in this case when the bonds are issued, and is not allowed to switch methods once a method is chosen.

Companies choose which financial instruments to report at fair value.

National Penn Bank Shares elected the option to report one of its liabilities (bonds) at fair value and accordingly reported the change in its fair value as a gain in its 2009 income statement. Graphic 14–13 presents an excerpt from a disclosure note describing that election.

GRAPHIC 14–13

Electing the Option to Report a Liability at Fair Value—National Penn Bank Shares

Real World Financials

> **11. FAIR VALUE MEASUREMENTS (in part)**
>
> The Company early adopted *SFAS No. 159* [FASB 825–10–25–1] as of January 1, 2007, and elected the fair value option for one discreet financial instrument. . . . Specifically, the fair value option was applied to the Company's only fixed rate subordinated debt liabilities with a cost basis of $65.2 million. This subordinated debt has a fixed rate of 7.85% and a maturity date of September 30, 2032, with a call provision after September 30, 2007. The Company believes that by electing the fair value option for this financial instrument, it will . . . provide more comparable accounting treatment for this long-term fixed rate debt with the Company's long-term fair valued assets for which the debt is a funding instrument, such as the long-term municipal bonds held in the Company's investment portfolio. . . . The Company recorded a gain of $151,000 in noninterest income for the change in fair value of the subordinated debt for the three months ended March 31, 2007.

INTERNATIONAL FINANCIAL REPORTING STANDARDS

● LO7

Fair Value Option. International accounting standards are more restrictive than U.S. standards for determining when firms are allowed to elect the fair value option for financial assets and liabilities. Under *IFRS No. 39*, companies can elect the fair value option only in specific circumstances.

To avoid misuse, the fair value option is limited to only those financial instruments falling into one of the following categories:

- A group of financial assets, financial liabilities, or both is managed and its performance is evaluated on a fair value basis, in accordance with a documented risk management or investment strategy,

(continued)

(concluded)

• The fair value option designation eliminates or significantly reduces an "accounting mismatch" that would otherwise arise if we measured the assets or liabilities or recognized gains and losses on them on different measurement bases.[17]

Although U.S. GAAP guidance indicates that the intent of the fair value option under U.S. GAAP is to address these sorts of circumstances, it does not require that those circumstances exist.

FINANCIAL REPORTING CASE SOLUTION

1. **What does it mean that the bonds are first mortgage bonds? What effect does that have on financing?** *(p. 749)*   A mortgage bond is backed by a lien on specified real estate owned by the issuer. This makes it less risky than unsecured debt, so Service Leader can expect to be able to sell the bonds at a higher price (lower interest rate).

2. **From Service Leader's perspective, why are the bonds callable? What does that mean?** *(p. 749)*   The call feature gives Service Leader some protection against being stuck with relatively high-cost debt in case interest rates fall during the 15 years to maturity. Service Leader can buy back, or call, the bonds from bondholders before the 15-year maturity date, after June 30, 2010. The call price is prespecified at 103 percent of the face value—$1,030 per $1,000 bond.

3. **How will it be possible to sell bonds paying investors 6.25% when other, similar investments will provide the investors a return of 6.5%?** *(p. 750)*   Service Leader will be able to sell its 6.25% bonds in a 6.5% market only by selling them at a discounted price, below face amount. Bonds are priced by the marketplace to yield the market rate of interest for securities of similar risk and maturity. The price will be the present value of all the periodic cash interest payments (face amount × stated rate) plus the present value of the principal payable at maturity, both discounted at the market rate.

4. **Would accounting differ if the debt were designated as notes rather than bonds?** *(p. 759)*   No. Other things being equal, whether they're called bonds, notes, or some other form of debt, the same accounting principles apply. They will be recorded at present value and interest will be recorded at the market rate over the term to maturity.

5. **Why might the company choose to make the bonds convertible into common stock?** *(p. 769)*   Convertible bonds can be converted at the option of the bondholders into shares of stock. Sometimes the motivation for issuing convertible bonds rather than straight debt is to use the bonds as a medium of exchange in mergers and acquisitions, as a way for smaller firms or debt-heavy companies to obtain access to the bond market, or as an indirect way to issue stock when there is shareholder resistance to direct issuance of additional equity. None of these seems pertinent to Service Leader. The most likely reason is to sell at a higher price. The conversion feature is attractive to investors. Investors have a fixed-income security that can become common stock if circumstances make that attractive. The investor has additional possibilities for higher returns, with downside risk limited by the underlying debt. ●

---

[17]A basic principle in *IAS 39* is that derivatives are carried at fair value. Gains and losses on many derivatives are reported immediately in the income statement. However, derivatives are commonly used to hedge assets and liabilities that, instead, are measured at cost, amortized cost, or at fair value with gains and losses recognized in equity. This creates a mismatch in the timing of gain and loss recognition.

THE BOTTOM LINE

- **LO1**   A liability requires the future payment of cash in specified amounts at specified dates. As time passes, interest accrues on debt at the effective interest rate times the amount of the debt outstanding during the period. This same principle applies regardless of the specific form of the liability. (p. 747)

- **LO2**   Forces of supply and demand cause a bond to be priced to yield the market rate, calculated as the present value of all the cash flows required, where the discount rate is the market rate. Interest expense is calculated as the effective market rate of interest multiplied by the outstanding balance (during the interest period). A company is permitted to allocate a discount or a premium equally to each period over the term to maturity if doing so produces results that are not materially different from the interest method. (p. 749)

- **LO3**   In concept, notes are accounted for in precisely the same way as bonds. When a note is issued with an unrealistic interest rate, the effective market rate is used both to determine the amount recorded in the transaction and to record periodic interest thereafter. (p. 759)

- **LO4**   In the balance sheet, disclosure should include, for all long-term borrowings, the aggregate amounts maturing and sinking fund requirements (if any) for each of the next five years. Supplemental disclosures are needed for (a) off-balance-sheet credit or market risk, (b) concentrations of credit risk, and (c) the fair value of financial instruments. (p. 763)

- **LO5**   A gain or loss on early extinguishment of debt should be recorded for the difference between the reacquisition price and the carrying amount of the debt. Convertible bonds are accounted for as straight debt, but the value of the equity feature is recorded separately for bonds issued with detachable warrants. (p. 769)

- **LO6**   Companies are not required to, but have the option to, value some or all of their liabilities at fair value. If the option is elected, an increase (or decrease) in fair value from one balance sheet to the next is reported as a loss (or gain) in the income statement. It's a one-time election for each liability when the liability is created. (p. 775)

- **LO7**   U.S. GAAP and IFRS are generally compatible with respect to accounting for bonds and long-term notes. Some differences exist in determining which securities are reported as debt, the way convertible securities and debt issuance costs are reported, and when the fair value option can be elected. (pp. 751, 759, 771, and 777). ●

BONDS ISSUED BETWEEN INTEREST DATES

APPENDIX 14A

In Part A of this chapter, we assumed that the bonds were issued on the day they were dated (date printed in the indenture contract). But suppose a weak market caused a delay in selling the bonds until two months after that date (four months before semiannual interest was to be paid). In that case, the buyer would be asked to pay the seller *accrued interest* for two months in addition to the price of the bonds. For illustration, assume that in Illustration 14–1 on page 749, Masterwear was unable to sell the bonds in the previous example until March 1—two months after they are dated. This variation is shown in Illustration 14A–1. United would pay the price of the bonds ($700,000) plus $14,000 accrued interest:

> All bonds sell at their price plus any interest that has accrued since the last interest date.

$700,000		12%		$\frac{2}{12}$		$14,000
Face amount	×	Annual rate	×	Fraction of the annual period	=	Accrued interest

At Issuance (March 1)			**ILLUSTRATION 14A–1**
Masterwear (Issuer)			Bonds Sold at Face Amount between Interest Dates
Cash (price plus accrued interest)	714,000		
Bonds payable (face amount)		700,000	
Interest payable (accrued interest determined above)		14,000	
United (Investor)			
Investment in bonds (face amount)	700,000		
Interest receivable (accrued interest determined above)	14,000		
Cash (price plus accrued interest)		714,000	

Since the investor will hold the bonds for only four months before receiving six months' interest, two months' accrued interest must be added to the price paid.

When Masterwear pays semiannual interest on June 30, a full six months' interest is paid. But having received two months' accrued interest in advance, Masterwear's net interest expense will be four months' interest, for the four months the bonds have been outstanding at that time. Likewise, when United receives six months' interest—after holding the bonds for only four months—United will net only the four months' interest to which it is entitled:

At the first Interest Date (June 30)		
Masterwear (Issuer)		
Interest expense (6 mo. – 2 mo. = 4 mo.)..	28,000	
Interest payable[18] (accrued interest determined above)...................	14,000	
Cash (stated rate × face amount)..		42,000
United (Investor)		
Cash (stated rate × face amount)	42,000	
Interest receivable (accrued interest determined above)..............		14,000
Interest revenue (6 mo. – 2 mo. = 4 mo.)		28,000

The issuer incurs interest expense, and the investor earns interest revenue, for only the four months the bonds are outstanding.

APPENDIX 14B

TROUBLED DEBT RESTRUCTURING

A sharp rise in debt restructurings accompanied the 2008/2009 economic crisis.

A respected real estate developer, Brillard Properties, was very successful developing and managing a number of properties in the southeastern United States. To finance these investments, the developer had borrowed hundreds of millions of dollars from several regional banks. For years, events occurred as planned. The investments prospered. Cash flow was high. Interest payments on the debt were timely and individual loans were repaid as they matured.

Almost suddenly, however, the real estate climate soured. Investments that had provided handsome profits now did not provide the cash flow necessary to service the debt. Bankers who had loaned substantial funds to Brillard now faced a dilemma. Because contractual interest payments were unpaid, the bankers had the legal right to demand payment, which would force the developer to liquidate all or a major part of the properties to raise the cash. Sound business practice? Not necessarily.

If creditors force liquidation, they then must share among themselves the cash raised from selling the properties—at forced sale prices. Believing the developer's financial difficulties were caused by temporary market forces, not by bad management, the bankers felt they could minimize their losses by *restructuring* the debt agreements, rather than by forcing liquidation.

When changing the original terms of a debt agreement is motivated by financial difficulties experienced by the debtor (borrower), the new arrangement is referred to as a **troubled debt restructuring.** By definition, a troubled debt restructuring involves some concessions on the part of the creditor (lender). In the first half of 2009, the economic crisis prompted nearly 40 companies to negotiate such deals with their creditors, a huge increase over the handful that normally would do so during a six-month period.[19] A troubled debt restructuring may be achieved in either of two ways:

1. The debt may be *settled* at the time of the restructuring.
2. The debt may be *continued,* but with *modified terms.*

---

[18]Some accountants prefer to credit interest expense, rather than interest payable, when the bonds are sold. When that is done, this entry would require simply a debit to interest expense and a credit to cash for $42,000. The interest expense account would then reflect the same *net* debit of four months' interest ($42,000 − $14,000).

Interest Expense	
	2 months
6 months	
4 months	

Similarly, the investor could debit interest revenue, rather than interest receivable when buying the bonds.

[19]David Henry, "The Time Bomb in Corporate Debt," *BusinessWeek,* July 15, 2009.

Debt Is Settled

In the situation described above, one choice the bankers had was to try to actually settle the debt outright at the time of the troubled debt restructuring. For instance, a bank holding a $30 million note from the developer might agree to accept a property valued at, let's say, $20 million as final settlement of the debt. In that case, the developer has a $10 million gain equal to the difference between the carrying amount of the debt and the fair value of the property transferred. The debtor may need to adjust the carrying amount of an asset to its fair value prior to recording its exchange for a debt. The developer in our example, for instance, would need to change the recorded amount for the property specified in the exchange agreement if it is carried at an amount other than its $20 million fair value. In such an instance, an ordinary gain or loss on disposition of assets should be recorded as shown in Illustration 14B–1.

> In all areas of accounting, a noncash transaction is recorded at fair value.

First Prudent Bank agrees to settle Brillard's $30 million debt in exchange for property having a fair value of $20 million. The carrying amount of the property on Brillard's books is $17 million:		
		($ in millions)
Land ($20 million minus $17 million)..	3	
Gain on disposition of assets		3
Note payable (carrying amount)..	30	
Gain on troubled debt restructuring...		10
Land (fair value)		20

ILLUSTRATION 14B–1

Debt Settled

An asset is adjusted to fair value prior to recording its exchange for a debt.

The payment to settle a debt in a troubled debt restructuring might be cash, or a non-cash asset (as in the example here), or even shares of the debtor's stock. An example of shares of stock given in exchange for debt forgiveness is the celebrated reorganization of TWA in 1992 (since acquired by American Airlines), when creditors received a 55% stake in the company's common shares in return for forgiving about $1 billion of the airline's $1.5 billion debt. In any case, the debtor's gain is the difference between the carrying amount of the debt and the fair value of the asset(s) or equity securities transferred.

Debt Is Continued, but with Modified Terms

We assumed in the previous example that First Prudent Bank agreed to accept property in full settlement of the debt. A more likely occurrence would be that the bank allows the debt to continue, but modifies the terms of the debt agreement to make it easier for the debtor to comply. The bank might agree to reduce or delay the scheduled *interest payments.* Or, it may agree to reduce or delay the *maturity amount.* Often a troubled debt restructuring will call for some combination of these concessions. Distressed by the 2008/2009 economic down-turn, amusement park operator **Six Flags** persuaded a group of creditors to trim its debt by 5%, or $130 million, a restructuring designed to give Six Flags a financial cushion going into its busy 2009 summer season and an opportunity to recover its interest-paying ability.

> The carrying amount of a debt is the current balance of the primary debt plus any accrued (unpaid) interest.

Let's say the stated interest rate on the note in question is 10% and annual interest payments of $3 million (10% × $30 million) are payable in December of each of two remaining years to maturity. Also assume that the developer was unable to pay the $3 million interest payment for the year just ended. This means that the amount owed—the carrying amount (or book value) of the debt—is $33 million ($30 million plus one year's accrued interest).

The way the debtor accounts for the restructuring depends on the extent of the reduction in cash payments called for by the restructured arrangement. More specifically, the accounting procedure depends on whether, under the new agreement, total cash payments (a) are *less than* the carrying amount of the debt or (b) still *exceed* the carrying amount of the debt.

> Two quite different situations are created when the terms of a debt are modified, depending on whether the cash payments are reduced to the extent that interest is eliminated.

WHEN TOTAL CASH PAYMENTS ARE LESS THAN THE CARRYING AMOUNT OF THE DEBT

By the original agreement, the debtor was to pay at maturity the $30 million loaned, plus enough periodic interest to provide a 10% effective rate of return. If the new agreement calls for less cash than the $33 million now owed, interest is presumed to have been eliminated.

As one of many possibilities, suppose the bank agrees to (1) forgive the interest accrued from last year, (2) reduce the two remaining interest payments from $3 million each to $2 million each, and (3) reduce the face amount from $30 million to $25 million. Clearly, the debtor will pay less by the new agreement than by the original one. In fact, if we add up the total payments called for by the new agreement, the total [($2 million × 2) plus $25 million] is less than the $33 million carrying amount. Because the $29 million does not exceed the amount owed, the restructured debt agreement no longer provides interest on the debt. Actually, the new payments are $4 million short of covering the debt itself. So, after the debt restructuring, no interest expense is recorded. All subsequent cash payments are considered to be payment of the debt itself. Consider Illustration 14B–2.

ILLUSTRATION 14B–2 Cash Payments Less than the Debt	Brillard Properties owes First Prudent Bank $30 million under a 10% note with two years remaining to maturity. Due to financial difficulties of the developer, the previous year's interest ($3 million) was not paid. First Prudent Bank agrees to:

1. Forgive the interest accrued from last year.
2. Reduce the remaining two interest payments to $2 million each.
3. Reduce the principal to $25 million.

Analysis:	Carrying amount		$30 million + $3 million =		$33 million
	Future payments		($2 million × 2) + $25 million =		29 million
	Gain				$ 4 million

Carrying Amount

Before Restr.	Adj.	After Restr.
$30	(1)	$29
3	(3)	0
$33	**(4)**	$29

	($ in millions)
Accrued interest payable (10% × $30 million)	3
Note payable ($30 million – $29 million)...	1
Gain on debt restructuring...	4

After restructuring, no interest expense is recorded. All cash payments are considered to be payment of the note itself.

When the total future cash payments are less than the carrying amount of the debt, the difference is recorded as a gain at the date of restructure. No interest should be recorded thereafter. That is, all subsequent cash payments result in reductions of principal.

At Each of the Two Interest Dates	($ in millions)	
Note payable..	2	
Cash (revised "interest" amount)...		2
At Maturity		
Note payable..	25	
Cash (revised principal amount)		25

The $25 million payment at maturity reduces the note to zero.

WHEN TOTAL CASH PAYMENTS EXCEED THE CARRYING AMOUNT OF THE DEBT

Let's modify the example in the previous section. Now suppose the bank agrees to delay the due date for all cash payments until maturity and accept $34,333,200 at that time in full settlement of the debt. Rather than just reducing the cash payments as in the previous illustration, the payments are delayed. It is not the nature of the change that creates the need to account differently for this situation, but the amount of the total cash payments under the agreement relative to the carrying amount of the debt. This situation is demonstrated in Illustration 14B–3.

As long as cash payments exceed the amount owed there will be interest—although at a lower effective rate.

Now the total payments called for by the new agreement, $34,333,200, exceed the $33 million carrying amount. Because the payments exceed the amount owed, the restructured debt agreement still provides interest on the debt—but less than before the agreement was revised. No longer is the effective rate 10%. The accounting objective now is to determine what the new effective rate is and *record interest for the remaining term of the loan at that new, lower rate,* as shown in Illustration 14B–3.

Unpaid interest is accrued at the effective rate times the carrying amount of the note.

Because the total future cash payments are not less than the carrying amount of the debt, no reduction of the existing debt is necessary and no entry is required at the time of the debt restructuring. Even though no cash is paid until maturity under the restructured debt agreement, interest expense still is recorded annually—but at the new rate.

Brillard Properties owes First Prudent Bank $30 million under a 10% note with two years remaining to maturity. Due to Brillard's financial difficulties, the previous year's interest ($3 million) was not paid. First Prudent Bank agrees to:
1. Delay the due date for all cash payments until maturity.
2. Accept $34,333,200 at that time in full settlement of the debt.

Analysis:	Future payments		$34,333,200
	Carrying amount	$30 million + $3 million =	33,000,000
	Interest		$ 1,333,200

Calculation of the New Effective Interest Rate
- $33,000,000 ÷ $34,333,200 = .9612, the Table 2 value for $n = 2$, $i = ?$
- In row 2 of Table 2, the number .9612 is in the 2% column. So, this is the new effective interest rate.

ILLUSTRATION 14B–3
Cash Payments More than the Debt

The discount rate that equates the present value on the debt ($33 million) and its future value ($34,333,200) is the effective rate of interest.

At the End of the First Year

Interest expense [2% × ($30,000,000 + 3,000,000)]..........................	660,000	
Accrued interest payable..		660,000

The carrying amount of the debt is increased by the unpaid interest from the previous year.

At the End of the Second Year

Interest expense [2% × ($30,000,000 + 3,660,000)]..........................	673,200	
Accrued interest payable..		673,200

At Maturity (End of the Second Year)

Note payable...	30,000,000	
Accrued interest payable ($3,000,000 + 660,000 + 673,200)	4,333,200	
Cash (required by new agreement)		34,333,200

The total of the accrued interest account plus the note account is equal to the amount scheduled to be paid at maturity.

ADDITIONAL CONSIDERATION

To keep up with the changing amounts, it may be convenient to prepare an amortization schedule for the debt.

Year	Cash Interest	Effective Interest	Increase in Balance	Outstanding Balance
		(2% × Outstanding balance)		
				33,000,000
1	0	.02 (33,000,000) = 660,000	660,000	33,660,000
2	0	.02 (33,660,000) = 673,200	673,200	34,333,200
	0	1,333,200	1,333,200	

An amortization schedule is particularly helpful if there are several years remaining to maturity.

In our example, the restructured debt agreement called for a single cash payment at maturity ($34,333,200). If more than one cash payment is required (as in the agreement in our earlier example), calculating the new effective rate is more difficult. The concept would remain straightforward: (1) determine the interest rate that provides a present value of all future cash payments that is equal to the current carrying amount and (2) record the interest at that rate thereafter. Mechanically, though, the computation by hand would be cumbersome, requiring a time-consuming trial-and-error calculation. Since our primary interest is understanding the concepts involved, we will avoid the mathematical complexities of such a situation.

You also should be aware that when a restructuring involves modification of terms, accounting for a liability by the debtor, as described in this section, and accounting for a receivable by the creditor, which was described in Chapter 12, are inconsistent. You may recall that when a creditor's investment in a receivable becomes impaired, due to a troubled debt restructuring or for any other reason, the receivable is remeasured based on the discounted present value of currently expected cash flows at the loan's original effective rate (regardless of the extent to which expected cash receipts have been reduced). For ease of comparison, the example in this chapter (Illustration 14B–3) describes the same situation as the example in Chapter 12 (Illustration 12B–2). There is no conceptual justification for the asymmetry between debtors' and creditors' accounting for troubled debt restructurings. The FASB will likely reconsider debtors' accounting in the future.[20] ●

QUESTIONS FOR REVIEW OF KEY TOPICS

Q 14–1 How is periodic interest determined for outstanding liabilities? For outstanding receivables? How does the approach compare from one form of debt instrument (say bonds payable) to another (say notes payable)?

Q 14–2 As a general rule, how should long-term liabilities be reported on the debtor's balance sheet?

Q 14–3 How are bonds and notes the same? How do they differ?

Q 14–4 What information is contained in a bond indenture? What purpose does it serve?

Q 14–5 On January 1, 2011, Brandon Electronics issued $85 million of 11.5% bonds, dated January 1. The market yield for bonds of maturity issued by similar firms in terms of riskiness is 12.25%. How can Brandon sell debt paying only 11.5% in a 12.25% market?

Q 14–6 How is the price determined for a bond (or bond issue)?

Q 14–7 A zero-coupon bond pays no interest. Explain.

Q 14–8 When bonds are issued at a premium the debt declines each period. Explain.

Q 14–9 Compare the two commonly used methods of determining interest on bonds.

Q 14–10 GAAP requires that debt issue costs be recorded separately and amortized over the term of the related debt. Describe a logical alternative to this accounting treatment.

Q 14–11 When a note's stated rate of interest is unrealistic relative to the market rate, the concept of substance over form should be employed. Explain.

Q 14–12 Mandatorily redeemable shares obligate the issuing company to buy back the shares in exchange for cash or other assets. Where in the balance sheet are these securities reported?

Q 14–13 How does an installment note differ from a note for which the principal is paid as a single amount at maturity?

Q 14–14 Long-term debt can be reported either (a) as a single amount, net of any discount or increased by any premium or (b) at its face amount accompanied by a separate valuation account for the discount or premium. Any portion of the debt to be paid during the upcoming year, or operating cycle if longer, should be reported as a current amount. Regarding amounts to be paid in the future, what additional disclosures should be made in connection with long-term debt?

Q 14–15 Early extinguishment of debt often produces a gain or a loss. How is the gain or loss determined?

Q 14–16 What criteria are used to classify a gain or loss on early extinguishment of debt as an extraordinary item in the income statement?

Q 14–17 Both convertible bonds and bonds issued with detachable warrants have features of both debt and equity. How does the accounting treatment differ for the two hybrid securities? Why is the accounting treatment different?

Q 14–18 At times, companies try to induce voluntary conversion by offering an added incentive—maybe cash, stock warrants, or a more favorable conversion ratio. How is such an inducement accounted for? How is it measured?

Q 14–19 Cordova Tools has bonds outstanding during a year in which the market rate of interest has risen. If Cordova has elected the fair value option for the bonds, will it report a gain or a loss on the bonds for the year? Explain.

🌐 **IFRS** Q 14–20 If a company prepares its financial statements according to International Financial Reporting Standards, how would it account for convertible bonds it issues for $12.5 million? What is the conceptual justification?

Q 14–21 (Based on Appendix A) Why will bonds always sell at their price plus any interest that has accrued since the last interest date?

[20]"Accounting by Creditors for Impairment of a Loan," *Statement of Financial Accounting Standards No. 114* (Norwalk, Conn.: FASB, 1993), par. 63.

Q 14–22   (Based on Appendix B) When the original terms of a debt agreement are changed because of financial difficulties experienced by the debtor (borrower), the new arrangement is referred to as a *troubled debt restructuring.* Such a restructuring can take a variety of forms. For accounting purposes, these possibilities are categorized. What are the accounting classifications of troubled debt restructurings?

Q 14–23   (Based on Appendix B) Pratt Industries owes First National Bank $5 million but, due to financial difficulties, is unable to comply with the original terms of the loan. The bank agrees to settle the debt in exchange for land having a fair value of $3 million. The carrying amount of the property on Pratt's books is $2 million. For the reporting period in which the debt is settled, what amount(s) will Pratt report on its income statement in connection with the troubled debt restructuring?

Q 14–24   (Based on Appendix B) The way a debtor accounts for the restructuring depends on the extent of the reduction in cash payments called for by the restructured arrangement. Describe, in general, the accounting procedure for the two basic cases: when, under the new agreement, total cash payments (a) are less than the carrying amount of the debt or (b) still exceed the carrying amount of the debt.

BRIEF EXERCISES

BE 14–1
Bond interest
● LO1

Holiday Brands issued $30 million of 6%, 30-year bonds for $27.5 million. What is the amount of interest that Holiday will pay semiannually to bondholders?

BE 14–2
Determining the price of bonds
● LO2

A company issued 5%, 20-year bonds with a face amount of $80 million. The market yield for bonds of similar risk and maturity is 6%. Interest is paid semiannually. At what price did the bonds sell?

BE 14–3
Determining the price of bonds
● LO2

A company issued 6%, 15-year bonds with a face amount of $75 million. The market yield for bonds of similar risk and maturity is 6%. Interest is paid semiannually. At what price did the bonds sell?

BE 14–4
Determining the price of bonds
● LO2

A company issued 5%, 20-year bonds with a face amount of $100 million. The market yield for bonds of similar risk and maturity is 4%. Interest is paid semiannually. At what price did the bonds sell?

BE 14–5
Effective interest on bonds
● LO2

On January 1, a company issued 7%, 15-year bonds with a face amount of $90 million for $82,218,585 to yield 8%. Interest is paid semiannually. What was interest expense at the effective interest rate on June 30, the first interest date?

BE 14–6
Effective interest on bonds
● LO2

On January 1, a company issued 3%, 20-year bonds with a face amount of $80 million for $69,033,776 to yield 4%. Interest is paid semiannually. What was the interest expense at the effective interest rate on the December 31 annual income statement?

BE 14–7
Straight-line interest on bonds
● LO2

On January 1, a company issued 3%, 20-year bonds with a face amount of $80 million for $69,033,776 to yield 4%. Interest is paid semiannually. What was the straight-line interest expense on the December 31 annual income statement?

BE 14–8
Investment in bonds
● LO2

On January 1, a company purchased 3%, 20-year corporate bonds for $69,033,776 as an investment. The bonds have a face amount of $80 million and are priced to yield 4%. Interest is paid semiannually. Prepare the journal entry to record revenue at the effective interest rate on December 31, the second interest payment date.

BE 14–9
Note with unrealistic interest rate
● LO3

Snipes Construction paid for earth-moving equipment by issuing a $300,000, 3-year note that specified 2% interest to be paid on December 31 of each year. The equipment's retail cash price was unknown, but it was determined that a reasonable interest rate was 5%. At what amount should Snipes record the equipment and the note? What journal entry should it record for the transaction?

BE 14–10
Installment note
● LO3

On January 1, a company borrowed cash by issuing a $300,000, 5%, installment note to be paid in three equal payments at the end of each year beginning December 31. What would be the amount of each installment? Prepare the journal entry for the second installment payment.

BE 14–11
Early extinguishment; effective interest
● LO5

A company retired $60 million of its 6% bonds at 102 ($61.2 million) before their scheduled maturity. At the time, the bonds had a remaining discount of $2 million. Prepare the journal entry to record the redemption of the bonds.

BE 14–12
Bonds with detachable warrants
● LO5

Hoffman Corporation issued $60 million of 5%, 20-year bonds at 102. Each of the 60,000 bonds was issued with 10 detachable stock warrants, each of which entitled the bondholder to purchase, for $20, one share of $1 par common stock. At the time of sale, the market value of the common stock was $25 per share and the market value of each warrant was $5. Prepare the journal entry to record the issuance of the bonds.

BE 14–13
Convertible bonds
● LO5

Hoffman Corporation issued $60 million of 5%, 20-year bonds at 102. Each of the 60,000 bonds was convertible into one share of $1 par common stock. Prepare the journal entry to record the issuance of the bonds.

BE 14–14
Reporting bonds at fair value
● LO6

AI Tool and Dye issued 8% bonds with a face amount of $160 million on January 1, 2011. The bonds sold for $150 million. For bonds of similar risk and maturity the market yield was 9%. Upon issuance, AI elected the option to report these bonds at their fair value. On June 30, 2011, the fair value of the bonds was $145 million as determined by their market value on the NASDAQ. Will AI report a gain or will it report a loss when adjusting the bonds to fair value? If the change in fair value is attributable to a change in the interest rate, did the rate increase or decrease?

EXERCISES

An alternate exercise and problem set is available on the text website: www.mhhe.com/spiceland6e

E 14–1
Bond valuation
● LO2

Your investment department has researched possible investments in corporate debt securities. Among the available investments are the following $100 million bond issues, each dated January 1, 2011. Prices were determined by underwriters at different times during the last few weeks.

	Company	Bond Price	Stated Rate
1.	BB Corp.	$109 million	11%
2.	DD Corp.	$100 million	10%
3.	GG Corp.	$ 91 million	9%

Each of the bond issues matures on December 31, 2030, and pays interest semiannually on June 30 and December 31. For bonds of similar risk and maturity, the market yield at January 1, 2011, is 10%.

Required:
Other things being equal, which of the bond issues offers the most attractive investment opportunity at the prices stated? the least attractive? Why?

E 14–2
Determine the price of bonds in various situations
● LO2

Determine the price of a $1 million bond issue under each of the following independent assumptions:

	Maturity	Interest Paid	Stated Rate	Effective (Market) Rate
1.	10 years	annually	10%	12%
2.	10 years	semiannually	10%	12%
3.	10 years	semiannually	12%	10%
4.	20 years	semiannually	12%	10%
5.	20 years	semiannually	12%	12%

E 14–3
Determine the price of bonds; issuance; effective interest
● LO2

The Bradford Company issued 10% bonds, dated January 1, with a face amount of $80 million on January 1, 2011. The bonds mature in 2020 (10 years). For bonds of similar risk and maturity, the market yield is 12%. Interest is paid semiannually on June 30 and December 31.

Required:

1. Determine the price of the bonds at January 1, 2011.

2. Prepare the journal entry to record their issuance by The Bradford Company on January 1, 2011.

3. Prepare the journal entry to record interest on June 30, 2011 (at the effective rate).

4. Prepare the journal entry to record interest on December 31, 2011 (at the effective rate).

E 14–4
Investor; effective interest
● LO2

(Note: This is a variation of the previous exercise modified to consider the investor's perspective.) The Bradford Company sold the entire bond issue described in the previous exercise to Saxton-Bose Corporation.

Required:

1. Prepare the journal entry to record the purchase of the bonds by Saxton-Bose on January 1, 2011.

2. Prepare the journal entry to record interest revenue on June 30, 2011 (at the effective rate).

3. Prepare the journal entry to record interest revenue on December 31, 2011 (at the effective rate).

E 14–5
Bonds; issuance; effective interest; financial statement effects
● LO2

Myriad Solutions, Inc., issued 10% bonds, dated January 1, with a face amount of $320 million on January 1, 2011 for $283,294,720. The bonds mature in 2021 (10 years). For bonds of similar risk and maturity the market yield is 12%. Interest is paid semiannually on June 30 and December 31.

Required:

1. What would be the net amount of the liability Myriad would report in its balance sheet at December 31, 2011?

2. What would be the amount related to the bonds that Myriad would report in its income statement for the year ended December 31, 2011?

3. What would be the amount(s) related to the bonds that Myriad would report in its statement of cash flows for the year ended December 31, 2011?

E 14–6
Bonds; issuance; effective interest
● LO2

The Gorman Group issued $900,000 of 13% bonds on June 30, 2011, for $967,707. The bonds were dated on June 30 and mature on June 30, 2031 (20 years). The market yield for bonds of similar risk and maturity is 12%. Interest is paid semiannually on December 31 and June 30.

Required:

1. Prepare the journal entry to record their issuance by The Gorman Group on June 30, 2011.

2. Prepare the journal entry to record interest on December 31, 2011 (at the effective rate).

3. Prepare the journal entry to record interest on June 30, 2012 (at the effective rate).

E 14–7
Determine the price of bonds; issuance; straight-line method
● LO2

Universal Foods issued 10% bonds, dated January 1, with a face amount of $150 million on January 1, 2011. The bonds mature on December 31, 2025 (15 years). The market rate of interest for similar issues was 12%. Interest is paid semiannually on June 30 and December 31. Universal uses the straight-line method.

Required:

1. Determine the price of the bonds at January 1, 2011.

2. Prepare the journal entry to record their issuance by Universal Foods on January 1, 2011.

3. Prepare the journal entry to record interest on June 30, 2011.

4. Prepare the journal entry to record interest on December 31, 2018.

E 14–8
Investor; straight-line method
● LO2

(Note: This is a variation of the previous exercise modified to consider the investor's perspective.) Universal Foods sold the entire bond issue described in the previous exercise to Wang Communications.

Required:

1. Prepare the journal entry to record the purchase of the bonds by Wang Communications on January 1, 2011.

2. Prepare the journal entry to record interest revenue on June 30, 2011.

3. Prepare the journal entry to record interest revenue on December 31, 2018.

E 14–9
Issuance of bonds; effective interest; amortization schedule; financial statement effects
● LO2

When Patey Pontoons issued 6% bonds on January 1, 2011, with a face amount of $600,000, the market yield for bonds of similar risk and maturity was 7%. The bonds mature December 31, 2014 (4 years). Interest is paid semiannually on June 30 and December 31.

Required:

1. Determine the price of the bonds at January 1, 2011.

2. Prepare the journal entry to record their issuance by Patey on January 1, 2011.

3. Prepare an amortization schedule that determines interest at the effective rate each period.

4. Prepare the journal entry to record interest on June 30, 2011.

5. What is the amount(s) related to the bonds that Patey will report in its balance sheet at December 31, 2011?

6. What is the amount(s) related to the bonds that Patey will report in its income statement for the year ended December 31, 2011? (Ignore income taxes.)

7. Prepare the appropriate journal entries at maturity on December 31, 2014.

E 14–10
Issuance of bonds; effective interest; amortization schedule
● LO2

National Orthopedics Co. issued 9% bonds, dated January 1, with a face amount of $500,000 on January 1, 2011. The bonds mature in 2014 (4 years). For bonds of similar risk and maturity the market yield was 10%. Interest is paid semiannually on June 30 and December 31.

Required:

1. Determine the price of the bonds at January 1, 2011.
2. Prepare the journal entry to record their issuance by National on January 1, 2011.
3. Prepare an amortization schedule that determines interest at the effective rate each period.
4. Prepare the journal entry to record interest on June 30, 2011.
5. Prepare the appropriate journal entries at maturity on December 31, 2014.

E 14–11
Bonds; effective interest; adjusting entry
● LO2

On February 1, 2011, Strauss-Lombardi issued 9% bonds, dated February 1, with a face amount of $800,000. The bonds sold for $731,364 and mature on January 31, 2031 (20 years). The market yield for bonds of similar risk and maturity was 10%. Interest is paid semiannually on July 31 and January 31. Strauss-Lombardi's fiscal year ends December 31.

Required:

1. Prepare the journal entry to record their issuance by Strauss-Lombardi on February 1, 2011.
2. Prepare the journal entry to record interest on July 31, 2011 (at the effective rate).
3. Prepare the adjusting entry to accrue interest on December 31, 2011.
4. Prepare the journal entry to record interest on January 31, 2012.

E 14–12
Bonds; straight-line method; adjusting entry
● LO2

On March 1, 2011, Stratford Lighting issued 14% bonds, dated March 1, with a face amount of $300,000. The bonds sold for $294,000 and mature on February 28, 2031 (20 years). Interest is paid semiannually on August 31 and February 28. Stratford uses the straight-line method and its fiscal year ends December 31.

Required:

1. Prepare the journal entry to record the issuance of the bonds by Stratford Lighting on March 1, 2011.
2. Prepare the journal entry to record interest on August 31, 2011.
3. Prepare the journal entry to accrue interest on December 31, 2011.
4. Prepare the journal entry to record interest on February 28, 2012.

E 14–13
Issuance of bonds; effective interest
● LO2

Federal Semiconductors issued 11% bonds, dated January 1, with a face amount of $800 million on January 1, 2011. The bonds sold for $739,814,813 and mature in 2030 (20 years). For bonds of similar risk and maturity the market yield was 12%. Interest is paid semiannually on June 30 and December 31.

Required:

1. Prepare the journal entry to record their issuance by Federal on January 1, 2011.
2. Prepare the journal entry to record interest on June 30, 2011 (at the effective rate).
3. Prepare the journal entry to record interest on December 31, 2011 (at the effective rate).
4. At what amount will Federal report the bonds among its liabilities in the December 31, 2011, balance sheet?

E 14–14
New debt issues; offerings announcements
● LO2

When companies offer new debt security issues, they publicize the offerings in the financial press and on Internet sites. Assume the following were among the debt offerings reported in December 2011:

New Securities Issues

Corporate

National Equipment Transfer Corporation—$200 million bonds via lead managers Second Tennessee Bank N.A. and Morgan, Dunavant & Co., according to a syndicate official. Terms: maturity, Dec. 15, 2017; coupon 7.46%; issue price, par; yield, 7.46%; noncallable, debt ratings: Ba-1 (Moody's Investors Service, Inc.), BBB + (Standard & Poor's).

IgWig Inc.—$350 million of notes via lead manager Stanley Brothers, Inc., according to a syndicate official. Terms: maturity, Dec. 1, 2019; coupon, 6.46%; Issue price, 99; yield, 6.56%; call date, NC; debt ratings: Baa-1 (Moody's Investors Service, Inc.), A (Standard & Poor's).

Required:

1. Prepare the appropriate journal entries to record the sale of both issues to underwriters. Ignore share issue costs and assume no accrued interest.
2. Prepare the appropriate journal entries to record the first semiannual interest payment for both issues.

E 14–15
Error correction;
accrued interest on
bonds
● LO2

At the end of 2010, Majors Furniture Company failed to accrue $61,000 of interest expense that accrued during the last five months of 2010 on bonds payable. The bonds mature in 2024. The discount on the bonds is amortized by the straight-line method. The following entry was recorded on February 1, 2011, when the semiannual interest was paid:

Interest expense	73,200	
Discount on bonds payable		1,200
Cash		72,000

Required:
Prepare any journal entry necessary to correct the error as of January 1, 2011, so that prior years' financial statements can be restated. Also, prepare any adjusting entry at February 28, 2011, related to the situation described. (Ignore income taxes.)

E 14–16
Error in
amortization
schedule
● LO3

Wilkins Food Products, Inc., acquired a packaging machine from Lawrence Specialists Corporation. Lawrence completed construction of the machine on January 1, 2009. In payment for the machine Wilkins issued a three-year installment note to be paid in three equal payments at the end of each year. The payments include interest at the rate of 10%.

    Lawrence made a conceptual error in preparing the amortization schedule, which Wilkins failed to discover until 2011. The error had caused Wilkins to understate interest expense by $45,000 in 2009 and $40,000 in 2010.

Required:
1. Determine which accounts are incorrect as a result of these errors at January 1, 2011, before any adjustments. Explain your answer. (Ignore income taxes.)
2. Prepare a journal entry to correct the error.
3. What other step(s) would be taken in connection with the error?

E 14–17
Note with
unrealistic interest
rate; amortization
schedule
● LO3

Amber Mining and Milling, Inc., contracted with Truax Corporation to have constructed a custom-made lathe. The machine was completed and ready for use on January 1, 2011. Amber paid for the lathe by issuing a $600,000, three-year note that specified 4% interest, payable annually on December 31 of each year. The cash market price of the lathe was unknown. It was determined by comparison with similar transactions that 12% was a reasonable rate of interest.

Required:
1. Prepare the journal entry on January 1, 2011, for Amber Mining and Milling's purchase of the lathe.
2. Prepare an amortization schedule for the three-year term of the note.
3. Prepare the journal entries to record (a) interest for each of the three years and (b) payment of the note at maturity.

E 14–18
Installment note;
amortization
schedule
● LO3

American Food Services, Inc., acquired a packaging machine from Barton and Barton Corporation. Barton and Barton completed construction of the machine on January 1, 2011. In payment for the $4 million machine, American Food Services issued a four-year installment note to be paid in four equal payments at the end of each year. The payments include interest at the rate of 10%.

Required:
1. Prepare the journal entry for American Food Services' purchase of the machine on January 1, 2011.
2. Prepare an amortization schedule for the four-year term of the installment note.
3. Prepare the journal entry for the first installment payment on December 31, 2011.
4. Prepare the journal entry for the third installment payment on December 31, 2013.

E 14–19
Installment note
● LO3

LCD Industries purchased a supply of electronic components from Entel Corporation on November 1, 2011. In payment for the $24 million purchase, LCD issued a 1-year installment note to be paid in equal monthly payments at the end of each month. The payments include interest at the rate of 12%.

Required:
1. Prepare the journal entry for LCD's purchase of the components on November 1, 2011.
2. Prepare the journal entry for the first installment payment on November 30, 2011.
3. What is the amount of interest expense that LCD will report in its income statement for the year ended December 31, 2011?

E 14–20
FASB codification research
● **LO2 LO3 LO4**

Access the FASB's Codification Research System at the FASB website (**www.fasb.org**). Determine the specific citation for accounting for each of the following items:

1. Disclosure requirements for maturities of long-term debt.
2. How to estimate the value of a note when a note having no ready market and no interest rate is exchanged for a noncash asset without a readily available fair value.
3. When the straight-line method can be used as an alternative to the interest method of determining interest.

E 14–21
Early extinguishment
● **LO5**

The balance sheet of Indian River Electronics Corporation as of December 31, 2010, included 12.25% bonds having a face amount of $90 million. The bonds had been issued in 2003 and had a remaining discount of $3 million at December 31, 2010. On January 1, 2011, Indian River Electronics called the bonds before their scheduled maturity at the call price of 102.

Required:

Prepare the journal entry by Indian River Electronics to record the redemption of the bonds at January 1, 2011.

E 14–22
Convertible bonds
● **LO5**

On January 1, 2011, Gless Textiles issued $12 million of 9%, 10-year convertible bonds at 101. The bonds pay interest on June 30 and December 31. Each $1,000 bond is convertible into 40 shares of Gless's no par common stock. Bonds that are similar in all respects, except that they are nonconvertible, currently are selling at 99 (that is, 99% of face amount). Century Services purchased 10% of the issue as an investment.

Required:

1. Prepare the journal entries for the issuance of the bonds by Gless and the purchase of the bond investment by Century.
2. Prepare the journal entries for the June 30, 2015, interest payment by both Gless and Century assuming both use the straight-line method.
3. On July 1, 2016, when Gless's common stock had a market price of $33 per share, Century converted the bonds it held. Prepare the journal entries by both Gless and Century for the conversion of the bonds (book value method).

E 14–23
IFRS; convertible bonds
● **LO5 LO7**

Refer to the situation described in the previous exercise.

Required:

How might your solution to requirement 1 for the issuer of the bonds differ if Gless Textiles prepares its financial statements according to International Financial Reporting Standards? Include any appropriate journal entry in your response.

E 14–24
Convertible bonds; induced conversion
● **LO5**

On January 1, 2011, Madison Products issued $40 million of 6%, 10-year convertible bonds at a net price of $40.8 million. Madison recently issued similar, but nonconvertible, bonds at 99 (that is, 99% of face amount). The bonds pay interest on June 30 and December 31. Each $1,000 bond is convertible into 30 shares of Madison's no par common stock. Madison records interest by the straight-line method.

On June 1, 2013, Madison notified bondholders of its intent to call the bonds at face value plus a 1% call premium on July 1, 2013. By June 30 all bondholders had chosen to convert their bonds into shares as of the interest payment date. On June 30, Madison paid the semiannual interest and issued the requisite number of shares for the bonds being converted.

Required:

1. Prepare the journal entry for the issuance of the bonds by Madison.
2. Prepare the journal entry for the June 30, 2011, interest payment.
3. Prepare the journal entries for the June 30, 2013, interest payment by Madison and the conversion of the bonds (book value method).

E 14–25
IFRS; convertible bonds
● **LO5 LO7**

Refer to the situation described in the previous exercise.

Required:

How might your solution for the issuer of the bonds differ if Madison Products prepares its financial statements according to International Financial Reporting Standards? Include any appropriate journal entries in your response.

E 14–26
Bonds with
detachable warrants
● LO5

On August 1, 2011, Limbaugh Communications issued $30 million of 10% nonconvertible bonds at 104. The bonds are due on July 31, 2031. Each $1,000 bond was issued with 20 detachable stock warrants, each of which entitled the bondholder to purchase, for $60, one share of Limbaugh Communications' no par common stock. Interstate Containers purchased 20% of the bond issue. On August 1, 2011, the market value of the common stock was $58 per share and the market value of each warrant was $8.

In February 2022, when Limbaugh's common stock had a market price of $72 per share and the unamortized discount balance was $1 million, Interstate Containers exercised the warrants it held.

Required:
1. Prepare the journal entries on August 1, 2011, to record (a) the issuance of the bonds by Limbaugh and (b) the investment by Interstate.
2. Prepare the journal entries for both Limbaugh and Interstate in February 2022, to record the exercise of the warrants.

E 14–27
Reporting bonds at
fair value
● LO6

(Note: This is a variation of E 14–13 modified to consider the fair value option for reporting liabilities.) Federal Semiconductors issued 11% bonds, dated January 1, with a face amount of $800 million on January 1, 2011. The bonds sold for $739,814,813 and mature in 2030 (20 years). For bonds of similar risk and maturity the market yield was 12%. Interest is paid semiannually on June 30 and December 31. Federal determines interest at the effective rate. Federal elected the option to report these bonds at their fair value. On December 31, 2011, the fair value of the bonds was $730 million as determined by their market value in the over-the-counter market.

Required:
1. Prepare the journal entry to adjust the bonds to their fair value for presentation in the December 31, 2011, balance sheet.
2. Assume the fair value of the bonds on December 31, 2012, had risen to $736 million. Prepare the journal entry to adjust the bonds to their fair value for presentation in the December 31, 2012, balance sheet.

E 14–28
Reporting bonds at
fair value
● LO6

On January 1, 2011, Rapid Airlines issued $200 million of its 8% bonds for $184 million. The bonds were priced to yield 10%. Interest is payable semiannually on June 30 and December 31. Rapid Airlines records interest at the effective rate and elected the option to report these bonds at their fair value. On December 31, 2011, the fair value of the bonds was $188 million as determined by their market value in the over-the-counter market.

Required:
1. Prepare the journal entry to record interest on June 30, 2011 (the first interest payment).
2. Prepare the journal entry to record interest on December 31, 2011 (the second interest payment).
3. Prepare the journal entry to adjust the bonds to their fair value for presentation in the December 31, 2011, balance sheet.

E 14–29
Reporting bonds at
fair value; calculate
fair value
● LO6

On January 1, 2011, Essence Communications issued $800,000 of its 10-year, 8% bonds for $700,302. The bonds were priced to yield 10%. Interest is payable semiannually on June 30 and December 31. Essence Communications records interest at the effective rate and elected the option to report these bonds at their fair value. On December 31, 2011, the market interest rate for bonds of similar risk and maturity was 9%. The bonds are not traded on an active exchange.

Required:
1. Using the information provided, estimate the fair value of the bonds at December 31, 2011.
2. Prepare the journal entry to record interest on June 30, 2011 (the first interest payment).
3. Prepare the journal entry to record interest on December 31, 2011 (the second interest payment).
4. Prepare the journal entry to adjust the bonds to their fair value for presentation in the December 31, 2011, balance sheet.

E 14–30
Accrued interest
● Appendix A

On March 1, 2011, Brown-Ferring Corporation issued $100 million of 12% bonds, dated January 1, 2011, for $99 million (plus accrued interest). The bonds mature on December 31, 2030, and pay interest semiannually on June 30 and December 31. Brown-Ferring's fiscal period is the calendar year.

Required:
1. Determine the amount of accrued interest that was included in the proceeds received from the bond sale.
2. Prepare the journal entry for the issuance of the bonds by Brown-Ferring.

E 14–31
Troubled debt
restructuring; debt
settled
● Appendix B

At January 1, 2011, Transit Developments owed First City Bank Group $600,000, under an 11% note with three years remaining to maturity. Due to financial difficulties, Transit was unable to pay the previous year's interest.

First City Bank Group agreed to settle Transit's debt in exchange for land having a fair value of $450,000. Transit purchased the land in 2007 for $325,000.

Required:
Prepare the journal entry(s) to record the restructuring of the debt by Transit Developments.

E 14–32
Troubled debt restructuring; modification of terms

● **Appendix B**

At January 1, 2011, Brainard Industries, Inc., owed Second BancCorp $12 million under a 10% note due December 31, 2013. Interest was paid last on December 31, 2009. Brainard was experiencing severe financial difficulties and asked Second BancCorp to modify the terms of the debt agreement. After negotiation Second BancCorp agreed to:

   a. Forgive the interest accrued for the year just ended.
   b. Reduce the remaining two years' interest payments to $1 million each and delay the first payment until December 31, 2012.
   c. Reduce the unpaid principal amount to $11 million.

Required:

Prepare the journal entries by Brainard Industries, Inc., necessitated by the restructuring of the debt at (1) January 1, 2011; (2) December 31, 2012; and (3) December 31, 2013.

E 14–33
Troubled debt restructuring; modification of terms; unknown effective rate

● **Appendix B**

At January 1, 2011, NCI Industries, Inc., was indebted to First Federal Bank under a $240,000, 10% unsecured note. The note was signed January 1, 2007, and was due December 31, 2012. Annual interest was last paid on December 31, 2009. NCI was experiencing severe financial difficulties and negotiated a restructuring of the terms of the debt agreement. First Federal agreed to reduce last year's interest and the remaining two years' interest payments to $11,555 each and delay all payments until December 31, 2012, the maturity date.

Required:

Prepare the journal entries by NCI Industries, Inc., necessitated by the restructuring of the debt at: (1) January 1, 2011; (2) December 31, 2011; and (3) December 31, 2012.

E 14–34
FASB codification research; legal fees in a troubled debt restructuring

● **Appendix B**

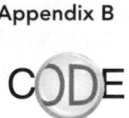

In negotiating and effecting a troubled debt restructuring, the creditor usually incurs various legal costs. The *FASB Accounting Standards Codification* represents the single source of authoritative U.S. generally accepted accounting principles.

Required:

1. Obtain the relevant authoritative literature on the accounting treatment of legal fees incurred by a creditor to effect a troubled debt restructuring using the FASB's Codification Research System at the FASB website (**www.fasb.org**).
2. What is the specific citation that describes the guidelines for reporting legal costs?
3. What is the appropriate accounting treatment?

CPA AND CMA REVIEW QUESTIONS

CPA Exam Questions

The following questions are used in the Kaplan CPA Review Course to study long-term liabilities while preparing for the CPA examination. Determine the response that best completes the statements or questions.

● **LO1**

1. The market price of a bond issued at a discount is the present value of its principal amount at the market (effective) rate of interest
   a. Less the present value of all future interest payments at the rate of interest stated on the bond.
   b. Plus the present value of all future interest payments at the rate of interest stated on the bond.
   c. Plus the present value of all future interest payments at the market (effective) rate of interest.
   d. Less the present value of all future interest payments at the market (effective) rate of interest.

● **LO2**

2. A bond issue on June 1, 2011, has interest payment dates of April 1 and October 1. Bond interest expense for the year ended December 31, 2011, is for a period of
   a. Three months
   b. Four months
   c. Six months
   d. Seven months

● **LO2**

3. On July 1, 2011, Pell Co. purchased Green Corp. 10-year, 8% bonds with a face amount of $500,000 for $420,000. The bonds mature on June 30, 2019, and pay interest semiannually on June 30 and December 31. Using the interest method, Pell recorded bond discount amortization of $1,800 for the six months ended December 31, 2011. From this long-term investment, Pell should report 2011 revenue of

    a. $16,800
    b. $18,200
    c. $20,000
    d. $21,800

● LO2

4. The following information pertains to Camp Corp.'s issuance of bonds on July 1, 2011:

Face amount	$800,000
Terms	10 years
Stated interest rate	6%
Interest payment dates	Annually on July 1
Yield	9%

	At 6%	At 9%
Present value of $1 for 10 periods	0.558	0.422
Future value of $1 for 10 periods	1.791	2.367
Present value of ordinary annuity of $1 for 10 periods	7.360	6.418

    What should be the issue price for each $1,000 bond?
    a. $ 700
    b. $ 807
    c. $ 864
    d. $1,000

● LO2

5. For a bond issue that sells for less than its face value, the market rate of interest is
    a. Higher than the rate stated on the bond.
    b. Dependent on the rate stated on the bond.
    c. Equal to the rate stated on the bond.
    d. Less than the rate stated on the bond.

● LO2

6. On January 31, 2011, Beau Corp. issued $300,000 maturity value, 12% bonds for $300,000 cash. The bonds are dated December 31, 2010, and mature on December 31, 2020. Interest will be paid semiannually on June 30 and December 31. What amount of accrued interest payable should Beau report in its September 30, 2011, balance sheet?
    a. $ 9,000
    b. $18,000
    c. $27,000
    d. $24,000

● LO5

7. On January 1, 2006, Fox Corp. issued 1,000 of its 10%, $1,000 bonds for $1,040,000. These bonds were to mature on January 1, 2016, but were callable at 101 any time after December 31, 2009. Interest was payable semiannually on July 1 and January 1. On July 1, 2011, Fox called all of the bonds and retired them. Bond premium was amortized on a straight-line basis. Before income taxes, Fox's gain or loss in 2011 on this early extinguishment of debt was
    a. $ 8,000 gain
    b. $10,000 loss
    c. $12,000 gain
    d. $30,000 gain

● LO5

8. On April 30, 2011, Witt Corp. had outstanding 8%, $1,000,000 face amount, convertible bonds maturing on April 30, 2019. Interest is payable on April 30 and October 31. On April 30, 2011, all these bonds were converted into 40,000 shares of $20 par common stock. On the date of conversion:
    • Unamortized bond discount was $30,000.
    • Each bond had a market price of $1,080.
    • Each share of stock had a market price of $28.

    Using the book value method, how much of a gain or loss should be recognized?
    a. $ 0
    b. $150,000
    c. $110,000
    d. $ 30,000

● LO5

9. On June 30, 2011, King Co. had outstanding 9%, $5,000,000 face value bonds maturing on June 30, 2016. Interest was payable semiannually every June 30 and December 31. On June 30, 2011, after amortization was recorded for the period, the unamortized bond premium and bond issuance costs were $30,000 and $50,000, respectively. On that date, King acquired all its outstanding bonds on the open market at 98 and retired them. At June 30, 2011, what amount should King recognize as gain before income taxes on redemption of bonds?

a. $ 20,000
b. $ 80,000
c. $120,000
d. $180,000

● LO5

10. Ray Corp. issued bonds with a face amount of $200,000. Each $1,000 bond contained detachable stock warrants for 100 shares of Ray's common stock. Total proceeds from the issue amounted to $240,000. The market value of each warrant was $2, and the market value of the bonds without the warrants was $196,000. The bonds were issued at a discount of (rounding the allocation percentage to two decimal places):
a. $ 0
b. $ 800
c. $ 4,000
d. $33,898

CMA Exam Questions

The following questions dealing with long-term liabilities are adapted from questions that previously appeared on Certified Management Accountant (CMA) examinations. The CMA designation sponsored by the Institute of Management Accountants (**www.imanet.org**) provides members with an objective measure of knowledge and competence in the field of management accounting. Determine the response that best completes the statements or questions.

Questions 1 and 2 are based on the following information. On January 1, Matthew Company issued 7% term bonds with a face amount of $1,000,000 due in 8 years. Interest is payable semiannually on January 1 and July 1. On the date of issue, investors were willing to accept an effective interest rate of 6%.

● LO1

1. The bonds were issued on January 1 at
a. a premium.
b. an amortized value.
c. book value.
d. a discount.

● LO2

2. Assume the bonds were issued on January 1 for $1,062,809. Using the effective interest amortization method, Matthew Company recorded interest expense for the 6 months ended June 30 in the amount of
a. $35,000
b. $70,000
c. $63,769
d. $31,884

● LO4

3. A bond issue sold at a premium is valued on the statement of financial position at the
a. maturity value.
b. maturity value plus the unamortized portion of the premium.
c. cost at the date of investment.
d. maturity value less the unamortized portion of the premium.

PROBLEMS

An alternate exercise and problem set is available on the text website: www.mhhe.com/spiceland6e

P 14–1
Determining the price of bonds; discount and premium; issuer and investor
● LO2

On January 1, 2011, Instaform, Inc., issued 10% bonds with a face amount of $50 million, dated January 1. The bonds mature in 2030 (20 years). The market yield for bonds of similar risk and maturity is 12%. Interest is paid semiannually.

Required:
1. Determine the price of the bonds at January 1, 2011, and prepare the journal entry to record their issuance by Instaform.
2. Assume the market rate was 9%. Determine the price of the bonds at January 1, 2011, and prepare the journal entry to record their issuance by Instaform.
3. Assume Broadcourt Electronics purchased the entire issue in a private placement of the bonds. Using the data in requirement 2, prepare the journal entry to record the purchase by Broadcourt.

P 14–2
Effective interest; financial statement effects
● LO2

On January 1, 2011, Baddour, Inc., issued 10% bonds with a face amount of $160 million. The bonds were priced at $140 million to yield 12%. Interest is paid semiannually on June 30 and December 31. Baddour's fiscal year ends September 30.

Required:
1. What amount(s) related to the bonds would Baddour report in its balance sheet at September 30, 2011?
2. What amount(s) related to the bonds would Baddour report in its income statement for the year ended September 30, 2011?
3. What amount(s) related to the bonds would Baddour report in its statement of cash flows for the year ended September 30, 2011? In which section(s) should the amount(s) appear?

P 14–3
Straight-line and effective interest compared
● LO2

eXcel

On January 1, 2011, Bradley Recreational Products issued $100,000, 9%, four-year bonds. Interest is paid semiannually on June 30 and December 31. The bonds were issued at $96,768 to yield an annual return of 10%.

Required:
1. Prepare an amortization schedule that determines interest at the effective interest rate.
2. Prepare an amortization schedule by the straight-line method.
3. Prepare the journal entries to record interest expense on June 30, 2013, by each of the two approaches.
4. Explain why the pattern of interest differs between the two methods.
5. Assuming the market rate is still 10%, what price would a second investor pay the first investor on June 30, 2013, for $10,000 of the bonds?

P 14–4
Bond amortization schedule
● LO2

On January 1, 2011, Tennessee Harvester Corporation issued debenture bonds that pay interest semiannually on June 30 and December 31. Portions of the bond amortization schedule appear below:

Payment	Cash Payment	Effective Interest	Increase in Balance	Outstanding Balance
				6,627,273
1	320,000	331,364	11,364	6,638,637
2	320,000	331,932	11,932	6,650,569
3	320,000	332,528	12,528	6,663,097
4	320,000	333,155	13,155	6,676,252
5	320,000	333,813	13,813	6,690,065
6	320,000	334,503	14,503	6,704,568
~	~	~	~	~
~	~	~	~	~
~	~	~	~	~
38	320,000	389,107	69,107	7,851,247
39	320,000	392,562	72,562	7,923,809
40	320,000	396,191	76,191	8,000,000

Required:
1. What is the face amount of the bonds?
2. What is the initial selling price of the bonds?
3. What is the term to maturity in years?
4. Interest is determined by what approach?
5. What is the stated annual interest rate?
6. What is the effective annual interest rate?
7. What is the total cash interest paid over the term to maturity?
8. What is the total effective interest expense recorded over the term to maturity?

P 14–5
Issuer and investor; effective interest; amortization schedule; adjusting entries
● LO2

eXcel

On February 1, 2011, Cromley Motor Products issued 9% bonds, dated February 1, with a face amount of $80 million. The bonds mature on January 31, 2015 (4 years). The market yield for bonds of similar risk and maturity was 10%. Interest is paid semiannually on July 31 and January 31. Barnwell Industries acquired $80,000 of the bonds as a long-term investment. The fiscal years of both firms end December 31.

Required:
1. Determine the price of the bonds issued on February 1, 2011.
2. Prepare amortization schedules that indicate (a) Cromley's effective interest expense and (b) Barnwell's effective interest revenue for each interest period during the term to maturity.
3. Prepare the journal entries to record (a) the issuance of the bonds by Cromley and (b) Barnwell's investment on February 1, 2011.
4. Prepare the journal entries by both firms to record all subsequent events related to the bonds through January 31, 2013.

P 14–6
Issuer and investor; straight-line method; adjusting entries

● LO2
  Appendix A

On April 1, 2011, Western Communications, Inc., issued 12% bonds, dated March 1, 2011, with face amount of $30 million. The bonds sold for $29.3 million and mature on February 28, 2014. Interest is paid semiannually on August 31 and February 28. Stillworth Corporation acquired $30,000 of the bonds as a long-term investment. The fiscal years of both firms end December 31, and both firms use the straight-line method.

Required:

1. Prepare the journal entries to record (a) issuance of the bonds by Western and (b) Stillworth's investment on April 1, 2011.

2. Prepare the journal entries by both firms to record all subsequent events related to the bonds through maturity.

P 14–7
Issuer and investor; effective interest

● LO2

McWherter Instruments sold $400 million of 8% bonds, dated January 1, on January 1, 2011. The bonds mature on December 31, 2030 (20 years). For bonds of similar risk and maturity, the market yield was 10%. Interest is paid semiannually on June 30 and December 31. Blanton Technologies, Inc., purchased $400,000 of the bonds as a long-term investment.

Required:

1. Determine the price of the bonds issued on January 1, 2011.

2. Prepare the journal entries to record (a) their issuance by McWherter and (b) Blanton's investment on January 1, 2011.

3. Prepare the journal entries by (a) McWherter and (b) Blanton to record interest on June 30, 2011 (at the effective rate).

4. Prepare the journal entries by (a) McWherter and (b) Blanton to record interest on December 31, 2011 (at the effective rate).

P 14–8
Bonds; effective interest; partial period interest; financial statement effects

● LO2

The fiscal year ends December 31 for Lake Hamilton Development. To provide funding for its Moonlight Bay project, LHD issued 5% bonds with a face amount of $500,000 on November 1, 2011. The bonds sold for $442,215, a price to yield the market rate of 6%. The bonds mature October 31, 2030 (20 years). Interest is paid semiannually on April 30 and October 31.

Required:

1. What amount of interest expense related to the bonds will LHD report in its income statement for the year ending December 31, 2011?

2. What amount(s) related to the bonds will LHD report in its balance sheet at December 31, 2011?

3. What amount of interest expense related to the bonds will LHD report in its income statement for the year ending December 31, 2012?

4. What amount(s) related to the bonds will LHD report in its balance sheet at December 31, 2012?

P 14–9
Zero-coupon bonds

● LO2

On January 1, 2011, Darnell Window and Pane issued $18 million of 10-year, zero-coupon bonds for $5,795,518.

Required:

1. Prepare the journal entry to record the bond issue.

2. Determine the effective rate of interest.

3. Prepare the journal entry to record annual interest expense at December 31, 2011.

4. Prepare the journal entry to record annual interest expense at December 31, 2012.

5. Prepare the journal entry to record the extinguishment at maturity.

P 14–10
Notes exchanged for assets; unknown effective rate

● LO3

At the beginning of the year, Lambert Motors issued the three notes described below. Interest is paid at year-end.

1. The company issued a two-year, 12%, $600,000 note in exchange for a tract of land. The current market rate of interest is 12%.

2. Lambert acquired some office equipment with a fair value of $94,643 by issuing a one-year, $100,000 note. The stated interest on the note is 6%.

3. The company purchased a building by issuing a three-year installment note. The note is to be repaid in equal installments of $1 million per year beginning one year hence. The current market rate of interest is 12%.

Required:
Prepare the journal entries to record each of the three transactions and the interest expense at the end of the first year for each.

P 14–11
Note with unrealistic interest rate

● LO3

At January 1, 2011, Brant Cargo acquired equipment by issuing a five-year, $150,000 (payable at maturity), 4% note. The market rate of interest for notes of similar risk is 10%.

Required:

1. Prepare the journal entry for Brant Cargo to record the purchase of the equipment.

2. Prepare the journal entry for Brant Cargo to record the interest at December 31, 2011.

3. Prepare the journal entry for Brant Cargo to record the interest at December 31, 2012.

P 14–12
Noninterest-bearing
installment note

● LO3

At the beginning of 2011, VHF Industries acquired a machine with a fair market value of $6,074,700 by issuing a four-year, noninterest-bearing note in the face amount of $8 million. The note is payable in four annual installments of $2 million at the end of each year.

Required:

1. What is the effective rate of interest implicit in the agreement?

2. Prepare the journal entry to record the purchase of the machine.

3. Prepare the journal entry to record the first installment payment at December 31, 2011.

4. Prepare the journal entry to record the second installment payment at December 31, 2012.

5. Suppose the market value of the machine was unknown at the time of purchase, but the market rate of interest for notes of similar risk was 11%. Prepare the journal entry to record the purchase of the machine.

P 14–13
Note and
installment note
with unrealistic
interest rate

● LO3

Braxton Technologies, Inc., constructed a conveyor for A&G Warehousers that was completed and ready for use on January 1, 2011. A&G paid for the conveyor by issuing a $100,000, four-year note that specified 5% interest to be paid on December 31 of each year, and the note is to be repaid at the end of four years. The conveyor was custom-built for A&G, so its cash price was unknown. By comparison with similar transactions it was determined that a reasonable interest rate was 10%.

Required:

1. Prepare the journal entry for A&G's purchase of the conveyor on January 1, 2011.

2. Prepare an amortization schedule for the four-year term of the note.

3. Prepare the journal entry for A&G's third interest payment on December 31, 2013.

4. If A&G's note had been an installment note to be paid in four equal payments at the end of each year beginning December 31, 2011, what would be the amount of each installment?

5. Prepare an amortization schedule for the four-year term of the installment note.

6. Prepare the journal entry for A&G's third installment payment on December 31, 2013.

P 14–14
Early
extinguishment of
debt

● LO5

Three years ago American Insulation Corporation issued 10 percent, $800,000, 10-year bonds for $770,000. Debt issue costs were $3,000. American Insulation exercised its call privilege and retired the bonds for $790,000. The corporation uses the straight-line method both to determine interest and to amortize debt issue costs.

Required:

Prepare the journal entry to record the call of the bonds.

P 14–15
Early
extinguishment;
effective interest

● LO5

The long-term liability section of Twin Digital Corporation's balance sheet as of December 31, 2010, included 12% bonds having a face amount of $20 million and a remaining discount of $1 million. Disclosure notes indicate the bonds were issued to yield 14%.

Interest expense is recorded at the effective interest rate and paid on January 1 and July 1 of each year. On July 1, 2011, Twin Digital retired the bonds at 102 ($20.4 million) before their scheduled maturity.

Required:

1. Prepare the journal entry by Twin Digital to record the semiannual interest on July 1, 2011.

2. Prepare the journal entry by Twin Digital to record the redemption of the bonds on July 1, 2011.

P 14–16
Debt issue
costs; issuance;
expensing; early
extinguishment;
straight-line interest

● LO2 LO5

Cupola Fan Corporation issued 10%, $400,000, 10-year bonds for $385,000 on June 30, 2011. Debt issue costs were $1,500. Interest is paid semiannually on December 31 and June 30. One year from the issue date (July 1, 2012), the corporation exercised its call privilege and retired the bonds for $395,000. The corporation uses the straight-line method both to determine interest expense and to amortize debt issue costs.

Required:

1. Prepare the journal entry to record the issuance of the bonds.

2. Prepare the journal entries to record the payment of interest and amortization of debt issue costs on December 31, 2011.

3. Prepare the journal entries to record the payment of interest and amortization of debt issue costs on June 30, 2012.

4. Prepare the journal entry to record the call of the bonds.

P 14–17
Early
extinguishment

● LO5

The long-term liability section of Eastern Post Corporation's balance sheet as of December 31, 2010, included 10% bonds having a face amount of $40 million and a remaining premium of $6 million. On January 1, 2011, Eastern Post retired some of the bonds before their scheduled maturity.

Required:

Prepare the journal entry by Eastern Post to record the redemption of the bonds under each of the independent circumstances below:

1. Eastern Post called half the bonds at the call price of 102 (102% of face amount).

2. Eastern Post repurchased $10 million of the bonds on the open market at their market price of $10.5 million.

P 14–18
Convertible
bonds; induced
conversion; bonds
with detachable
warrants
● LO5

Bradley-Link's December 31, 2011, balance sheet included the following items:

Long-Term Liabilities	($ in millions)
9.6% convertible bonds, callable at 101 beginning in 2012, due 2015 (net of unamortized discount of $2) [note 8]	$198
10.4% registered bonds callable at 104 beginning in 2021, due 2025 (net of unamortized discount of $1) [note 8]	49
Shareholders' Equity	
Equity—stock warrants	4

Note 8: Bonds (in part)

The 9.6% bonds were issued in 1998 at 97.5 to yield 10%. Interest is paid semiannually on June 30 and December 31. Each $1,000 bond is convertible into 40 shares of the Company's no par common stock.

The 10.4% bonds were issued in 2002 at 102 to yield 10%. Interest is paid semiannually on June 30 and December 31. Each $1,000 bond was issued with 40 detachable stock warrants, each of which entitles the holder to purchase one share of the Company's no par common stock for $25, beginning 2012.

On January 3, 2012, when Bradley-Link's common stock had a market price of $32 per share, Bradley-Link called the convertible bonds to force conversion. 90% were converted; the remainder were acquired at the call price. When the common stock price reached an all-time high of $37 in December of 2012, 40% of the warrants were exercised.

Required:

1. Prepare the journal entries that were recorded when each of the two bond issues was originally sold in 1998 and 2002.

2. Prepare the journal entry to record (book value method) the conversion of 90% of the convertible bonds in January 2012 and the retirement of the remainder.

3. Assume Bradley-Link induced conversion by offering $150 cash for each bond converted. Prepare the journal entry to record (book value method) the conversion of 90% of the convertible bonds in January 2012.

4. Assume Bradley-Link induced conversion by modifying the conversion ratio to exchange 45 shares for each bond rather than the 40 shares provided in the contract. Prepare the journal entry to record (book value method) the conversion of 90% of the convertible bonds in January 2012.

5. Prepare the journal entry to record the exercise of the warrants in December 2012.

P 14–19
Concepts;
terminology
● LO1 through
LO5

Listed below are several terms and phrases associated with long-term debt. Pair each item from List A with the item from List B (by letter) that is most appropriately associated with it.

List A	List B
_____ 1. Effective rate times balance	a. Straight-line method
_____ 2. Promises made to bondholders	b. Discount
_____ 3. Present value of interest plus present value of principal	c. Liquidation payments after other claims satisfied
	d. Name of owner not registered
_____ 4. Call feature	e. Premium
_____ 5. Debt issue costs	f. Checks are mailed directly
_____ 6. Market rate higher than stated rate	g. No specific assets pledged
_____ 7. Coupon bonds	h. Bond indenture
_____ 8. Convertible bonds	i. Backed by a lien
_____ 9. Market rate less than stated rate	j. Interest expense
_____ 10. Stated rate times face amount	k. May become stock
_____ 11. Registered bonds	l. Legal, accounting, printing
_____ 12. Debenture bond	m. Protection against falling rates
_____ 13. Mortgage bond	n. Periodic cash payments
_____ 14. Materiality concept	o. Bond price
_____ 15. Subordinated debenture	

P 14–20

Determine bond price; record interest; report bonds at fair value

● LO6

On January 1, 2011, NFB Visual Aids issued $800,000 of its 20-year, 8% bonds. The bonds were priced to yield 10%. Interest is payable semiannually on June 30 and December 31. NFB Visual Aids records interest expense at the effective rate and elected the option to report these bonds at their fair value. On December 31, 2011, the fair value of the bonds was $668,000 as determined by their market value in the over-the-counter market.

Required:

1. Determine the price of the bonds at January 1, 2011, and prepare the journal entry to record their issuance.

2. Prepare the journal entry to record interest on June 30, 2011 (the first interest payment).

3. Prepare the journal entry to record interest on December 31, 2011 (the second interest payment).

4. Prepare the journal entry to adjust the bonds to their fair value for presentation in the December 31, 2011, balance sheet.

P 14–21

Report bonds at fair value; quarterly reporting

● LO6

Appling Enterprises issued 8% bonds with a face amount of $400,000 on January 1, 2011. The bonds sold for $331,364 and mature in 2030 (20 years). For bonds of similar risk and maturity the market yield was 10%. Interest is paid semiannually on June 30 and December 31. Appling determines interest expense at the effective rate. Appling elected the option to report these bonds at their fair value. The fair values of the bonds at the end of each quarter during 2011 as determined by their market values in the over-the-counter market were the following:

March 31	$350,000
June 30	340,000
September 30	335,000
December 31	342,000

Required:

1. By how much will Appling's earnings be increased or decreased by the bonds (ignoring taxes) in the March 31 *quarterly* financial statements?

2. By how much will Appling's earnings be increased or decreased by the bonds (ignoring taxes) in the June 30 *quarterly* financial statements?

3. By how much will Appling's earnings be increased or decreased by the bonds (ignoring taxes) in the September 30 *quarterly* financial statements?

4. By how much will Appling's earnings be increased or decreased by the bonds (ignoring taxes) in the December 31 *annual* financial statements?

P 14–22

Investments in bonds; accrued interest; sale; straight-line interest

● LO2

● Appendix A

The following transactions relate to bond investments of Livermore Laboratories. The company's fiscal year ends on December 31. Livermore uses the straight-line method to determine interest.

2011

July	1	Purchased $16 million of Bracecourt Corporation 10% debentures, due in 20 years (June 30, 2031), for $15.7 million. Interest is payable on January 1 and July 1 of each year.
Oct.	1	Purchased $30 million of 12% Framm Pharmaceuticals debentures, due May 31, 2021, for $31,160,000 plus accrued interest. Interest is payable on June 1 and December 1 of each year.
Dec.	1	Received interest on the Framm bonds.
	31	Accrued interest.

2012

Jan.	1	Received interest on the Bracecourt bonds.
June	1	Received interest on the Framm bonds.
July	1	Received interest on the Bracecourt bonds.
Sept.	1	Sold $15 million of the Framm bonds at 101 plus accrued interest.
Dec.	1	Received interest on the remaining Framm bonds.
	31	Accrued interest.

2013

Jan.	1	Received interest on the Bracecourt bonds.
Feb.	28	Sold the remainder of the Framm bonds at 102 plus accrued interest.
Dec.	31	Accrued interest.

Required:

1. Prepare the appropriate journal entries for these long-term bond investments.

2. By how much will Livermore Labs' earnings increase in each of the three years as a result of these investments? (Ignore income taxes.)

P 14–23
Troubled debt
restructuring

● **Appendix B**

At January 1, 2011, Rothschild Chair Company, Inc., was indebted to First Lincoln Bank under a $20 million, 10% unsecured note. The note was signed January 1, 2008, and was due December 31, 2014. Annual interest was last paid on December 31, 2009. Rothschild Chair Company was experiencing severe financial difficulties and negotiated a restructuring of the terms of the debt agreement.

Required:

Prepare all journal entries by Rothschild Chair Company, Inc., to record the restructuring and any remaining transactions relating to the debt under each of the independent circumstances below:

1. First Lincoln Bank agreed to settle the debt in exchange for land having a fair value of $16 million but carried on Rothschild Chair Company's books at $13 million.
2. First Lincoln Bank agreed to (a) forgive the interest accrued from last year, (b) reduce the remaining four interest payments to $1 million each, and (c) reduce the principal to $15 million.
3. First Lincoln Bank agreed to defer all payments (including accrued interest) until the maturity date and accept $27,775,000 at that time in settlement of the debt.

BROADEN YOUR PERSPECTIVE

Apply your critical-thinking ability to the knowledge you've gained. These cases will provide you an opportunity to develop your research, analysis, judgment, and communication skills. You also will work with other students, integrate what you've learned, apply it in real world situations, and consider its global and ethical ramifications. This practice will broaden your knowledge and further develop your decision-making abilities.

**Communication
Case 14–1**
Convertible
securities and
warrants; concepts

● **LO5**

It is not unusual to issue long-term debt in conjunction with an arrangement under which lenders receive an option to buy common stock during all or a portion of the time the debt is outstanding. Sometimes the vehicle is convertible bonds; sometimes warrants to buy stock accompany the bonds and are separable. Interstate Chemical is considering these options in conjunction with a planned debt issue.

"You mean we have to report $7 million more in liabilities if we go with convertible bonds? Makes no sense to me," your CFO said. "Both ways seem pretty much the same transaction. Explain it to me, will you?"

Required:

Write a memo. Include in your explanation each of the following:
1. The differences in accounting for proceeds from the issuance of convertible bonds and of debt instruments with separate warrants to purchase common stock.
2. The underlying rationale for the differences.
3. Arguments that could be presented for the alternative accounting treatment.

**Real World
Case 14–2**
Zero-coupon debt;
Hewlett-Packard
Company

● **LO2**

The 2008 annual report of **Hewlett-Packard Company** reports zero-coupon notes issued at the end of its 1997 fiscal year. One billion, eight hundred million dollars face amount of 20-year debt sold for $968 million, a price to yield 3.149%. In fiscal 2002, HP repurchased $257 million in face value of the notes for a purchase price of $127 million, resulting in a gain on the early extinguishment of debt.

Required:

1. What journal entry did Hewlett-Packard use to record the sale in 1997?
2. Using an electronic spreadsheet, prepare an amortization schedule for the notes. Assume interest is calculated annually and use numbers expressed in millions of dollars; that is, the face amount is $1,800.
3. What was the effect on HP's earnings in 1998? Explain.
4. From the amortization schedule, determine the book value of the debt at the end of 2002.
5. What journal entry did Hewlett-Packard use to record the early extinguishment of debt in 2002, assuming the purchase was made at the end of the year?

**Communication
Case 14–3**
Is convertible debt
a liability or is
it shareholders'
equity? Group
Interaction

● **LO5**

Some financial instruments can be considered compound instruments in that they have features of both debt and shareholders' equity. The most common example encountered in practice is convertible debt—bonds or notes convertible by the investor into common stock. A topic of debate for several years has been whether:

View 1: Issuers should account for an instrument with both liability and equity characteristics entirely as a liability or entirely as an equity instrument depending on which characteristic governs.

View 2: Issuers should account for an instrument as consisting of a liability component and an equity component that should be accounted for separately.

In considering this question, you should disregard what you know about the current position of the FASB on the issue. Instead, focus on conceptual issues regarding the practicable and theoretically appropriate treatment, unconstrained by GAAP. Also, focus your deliberations on convertible bonds as the instrument with both liability and equity characteristics.

Required:

1. Which view do you favor? Develop a list of arguments in support of your view prior to the class session for which the case is assigned.

2. In class, your instructor will pair you (and everyone else) with a classmate (who also has independently developed an argument).

   a. You will be given three minutes to argue your view to your partner. Your partner likewise will be given three minutes to argue his or her view to you. During these three-minute presentations, the listening partner is not permitted to speak.

   b. After each person has had a turn attempting to convince his or her partner, the two partners will have a three-minute discussion in which they will decide which view is more convincing. Arguments will be merged into a single view for each pair.

3. After the allotted time, a spokesperson for each of the two views will be selected by the instructor. Each spokesperson will field arguments from the class in support of that view's position and list the arguments on the board. The class then will discuss the merits of the two lists of arguments and attempt to reach a consensus view, though a consensus is not necessary.

Analysis
Case 14–4
Issuance of bonds
● LO2

The following appeared in the October 15, 2011, issue of the *Financial World Journal:*

This announcement is not an offer of securities for sale or an offer to buy securities.
New Issue   October 15, 2011

$750,000,000
CRAFT FOODS, INC.
7.75% Debentures Due October 1, 2021
Price 99.57%
plus accrued interest if any from date of issuance

Copies of the prospectus and the related prospectus supplement may be obtained from such of the undersigned as may legally offer these securities under applicable securities laws.
Keegan Morgan & Co. Inc.
Coldwell Bros. & Co.
Robert Stacks & Co.
Sherwin-William & Co.

Required:

1. Explain what is being described by the announcement.
2. Can you think of a psychological reason for the securities to be priced as they are?
3. What are the accounting considerations for Craft Foods, Inc.? Describe how Craft recorded the sale.

Judgment
Case 14–5
Noninterest-bearing
debt
● LO3

While reading a recent issue of *Health & Fitness,* a trade journal, Brandon Wilde noticed an ad for equipment he had been seeking for use in his business. The ad offered oxygen therapy equipment under the following terms:

Model BL 44582
$204,000 zero interest loan
Quarterly payments of $17,000 for only 3 years

The ad captured Wilde's attention, in part because he recently had been concerned that the interest charges incurred by his business were getting out of line. The price, though, was somewhat higher than prices for this model he had seen elsewhere.

Required:

Advise Mr. Wilde on the purchase he is considering.

Judgment
Case 14–6
Noninterest-bearing
note exchanged
for cash and other
privileges
● LO3

The Jaecke Group, Inc., manufactures various kinds of hydraulic pumps. In June 2011, the company signed a four-year purchase agreement with one of its main parts suppliers, Hydraulics, Inc. Over the four-year period, Jaecke has agreed to purchase 100,000 units of a key component used in the manufacture of its pumps. The agreement allows Jaecke to purchase the component at a price lower than the prevailing market price at the time of purchase. As part of the agreement, Jaecke will lend Hydraulics $200,000 to be repaid after four years with no stated interest (the prevailing market rate of interest for a loan of this type is 10%).

Jaecke's chief accountant has proposed recording the note receivable at $200,000. The parts inventory purchase from Hydraulics over the next four years will then be recorded at the actual prices paid.

Required:

Do you agree with the accountant's valuation of the note and his intention to value the parts inventory acquired over the four-year period of the agreement at actual prices paid? If not, how would you account for the initial transaction and the subsequent inventory purchases?

Communication Case 14–7
Note receivable exchanged for cash and other services
● LO3

The Pastel Paint Company recently loaned $300,000 to KIX 96, a local radio station. The radio station signed a noninterest-bearing note requiring the $300,000 to be repaid in three years. As part of the agreement, the radio station will provide Pastel with a specified amount of free radio advertising over the three-year term of the note.

The focus of this case is the valuation of the note receivable by Pastel Paint Company and the treatment of the "free" advertising provided by the radio station. Your instructor will divide the class into two to six groups depending on the size of the class. The mission of your group is to reach consensus on the appropriate note valuation and accounting treatment of the free advertising.

Required:

1. Each group member should deliberate the situation independently and draft a tentative argument prior to the class session for which the case is assigned.

2. In class, each group will meet for 10 to 15 minutes in different areas of the classroom. During that meeting, group members will take turns sharing their suggestions for the purpose of arriving at a single group treatment.

3. After the allotted time, a spokesperson for each group (selected during the group meetings) will share the group's solution with the class. The goal of the class is to incorporate the views of each group into a consensus approach to the situation.

Ethics Case 14–8
Debt for equity swaps; have your cake and eat it too
● LO5

The cloudy afternoon mirrored the mood of the conference of division managers. Claude Meyer, assistant to the controller for Hunt Manufacturing, wore one of the gloomy faces that were just emerging from the conference room. "Wow, I knew it was bad, but not that bad," Claude thought to himself. "I don't look forward to sharing those numbers with shareholders."

The numbers he discussed with himself were fourth quarter losses which more than offset the profits of the first three quarters. Everyone had known for some time that poor sales forecasts and production delays had wreaked havoc on the bottom line, but most were caught off guard by the severity of damage.

Later that night he sat alone in his office, scanning and rescanning the preliminary financial statements on his computer monitor. Suddenly his mood brightened. "This may work," he said aloud, though no one could hear. Fifteen minutes later he congratulated himself, "Yes!"

The next day he eagerly explained his plan to Susan Barr, controller of Hunt for the last six years. The plan involved $300 million in convertible bonds issued three years earlier.

Meyer: By swapping stock for the bonds, we can eliminate a substantial liability from the balance sheet, wipe out most of our interest expense, and reduce our loss. In fact, the book value of the bonds is significantly more than the market value of the stock we'd issue. I think we can produce a profit.

Barr: But Claude, our bondholders are not inclined to convert the bonds.

Meyer: Right. But, the bonds are callable. As of this year, we can call the bonds at a call premium of 1%. Given the choice of accepting that redemption price or converting to stock, they'll all convert. We won't have to pay a cent. And, since no cash will be paid, we won't pay taxes either.

Required:

Do you perceive an ethical dilemma? What would be the impact of following up on Claude's plan? Who would benefit? Who would be injured?

Judgment Case 14–9
Analyzing financial statements; financial leverage; interest coverage
● LO1 LO4

AGF Foods Company is a large, primarily domestic, consumer foods company involved in the manufacture, distribution, and sale of a variety of food products. Industry averages are derived from Troy's *The Almanac of Business and Industrial Financial Ratios*. Following are the 2011 and 2010 comparative income statements and balance sheets for AGF. (The financial data we use are from actual financial statements of a well-known corporation, but the company name is fictitious and the numbers and dates have been modified slightly to disguise the company's identity.)

AGF FOODS COMPANY
Years Ended December 31, 2011 and 2010
($ in millions)

Comparative Income Statements	2011	2010
Net sales	$6,440	$5,800
Cost of goods sold	(3,667)	(3,389)
Gross profit	2,773	2,411
Operating expenses	(1,916)	(1,629)
Operating income	857	782
Interest expense	(54)	(53)
Income from operations before tax	803	729
Income taxes	(316)	(287)
Net income	$ 487	$ 442

Comparative Balance Sheets		
Assets		
Total current assets	$1,879	$1,490
Property, plant, and equipment (net)	2,592	2,291
Intangibles (net)	800	843
Other assets	74	60
Total assets	$5,345	$4,684
Liabilities and Shareholders' Equity		
Total current liabilities	$1,473	$ 941
Long-term debt	534	728
Deferred income taxes	407	344
Total liabilities	2,414	2,013
Shareholders' equity:		
Common stock	180	180
Additional paid-in capital	21	63
Retained earnings	2,730	2,428
Total shareholders' equity	2,931	2,671
Total liabilities and shareholders' equity	$5,345	$4,684

Long-term solvency refers to a company's ability to pay its long-term obligations. Financing ratios provide investors and creditors with an indication of this element of risk.

Required:

1. Calculate the debt to equity ratio for AGF for 2011. The average ratio for the stocks listed on the New York Stock Exchange in a comparable time period was 1.0. What information does your calculation provide an investor?

2. Is AGF experiencing favorable or unfavorable financial leverage?

3. Calculate AGF's times interest earned ratio for 2011. The coverage for the stocks listed on the New York Stock Exchange in a comparable time period was 5.1. What does your calculation indicate about AGF's risk?

Research Case 14–10
FASB codification research; researching the way long-term debt is reported; Macy's, Inc.
● LO1 through LO4
Real World Financials

EDGAR, the Electronic Data Gathering. Analysis, and Retrieval system, performs automated collection, validation, indexing, acceptance and forwarding of submissions by companies and others who are required by law to file forms with the U.S. Securities and Exchange Commission (SEC). All publicly traded domestic companies use EDGAR to make the majority of their filings. (Some foreign companies do so voluntarily.) Form 10-K, including the annual report, is required to be filed on EDGAR. The SEC makes this information available on the Internet.

Required:

1. Access EDGAR on the Internet at **www.sec.gov** or the **Macy's, Inc.,** website: **www.macys.com**.

2. Search for Macy's. Access its 10-K filing for the year ended January 31, 2009. Search or scroll to find the financial statements and related notes.

3. What is the total debt (including current liabilities and deferred taxes) reported in the balance sheet? How has that amount changed over the most recent two years?

4. Compare the total liabilities (including current liabilities and deferred taxes) with the shareholders' equity and calculate the debt to equity ratio for the most recent two years. Has the proportion of debt financing and equity financing changed recently?

5. Does Macy's obtain more financing through notes, bonds, or commercial paper? Are required debt payments increasing or decreasing over time? Is any short-term debt classified as long-term? Why?

6. Note 11: Financing includes the following statement: "On June 23, 2008, the Company issued $650 million aggregate principal amount of 7.875% senior notes due 2015. The net proceeds of the debt issuance were used for the repayment of amounts due on debt maturing in 2008." Under some circumstances, Macy's could have reported the amounts due in 2008 as long-term debt at the end of the previous year even though these amounts were due within the coming year. Obtain the relevant authoritative literature on classification of debt expected to be financed using the FASB's Codification Research System. You might gain access from the FASB website (**www.fasb.org**), from your school library, or some other source. Determine the criteria for reporting currently payable debt as long-term. What is the specific codification citation that Macy's would rely on in applying that accounting treatment?

Analysis
Case 14–11
Bonds; conversion; extinguishment
● LO5

On August 31, 2008, Chickasaw Industries issued $25 million of its 30-year, 6% convertible bonds dated August 31, priced to yield 5%. The bonds are convertible at the option of the investors into 1,500,000 shares of Chickasaw's common stock. Chickasaw records interest expense at the effective rate. On August 31, 2011, investors in Chickasaw's convertible bonds tendered 20% of the bonds for conversion into common stock that had a market value of $20 per share on the date of the conversion. On January 1, 2010, Chickasaw Industries issued $40 million of its 20-year, 7% bonds dated January 1 at a price to yield 8%. On December 31, 2011, the bonds were extinguished early through acquisition in the open market by Chickasaw for $40.5 million.

Required:

1. Using the book value method, would recording the conversion of the 6% convertible bonds into common stock affect earnings? If so, by how much? Would earnings be affected if the market value method is used? If so, by how much?

2. Were the 7% bonds issued at face value, at a discount, or at a premium? Explain.

3. Would the amount of interest expense for the 7% bonds be higher in the first year or second year of the term to maturity? Explain.

4. How should gain or loss on early extinguishment of debt be determined? Does the early extinguishment of the 7% bonds result in a gain or loss? Explain.

BRITISH AIRWAYS CASE

BRITISH AIRWAYS

● LO7

British Airways, Plc. (BA), a U.K. company, prepares its financial statements according to International Financial Reporting Standards. BA's annual report for the year ended March 31, 2009, which includes financial statements and disclosure notes, is included with all new textbooks and can be found at **www.britishairways.com**. When answering questions, focus on BA's "Group" financial information (which is equivalent to "Consolidated" under U.S. GAAP).

Required:

1. **Sealy Corporation** reported the following line items in its statement of cash flows for the nine months ended August 30, 2009:

Amortization of discount on secured notes	351,000
Amortization of debt issuance costs and other	2,925,000

In British Airways' financial statements, Note 28: "Long-term borrowings" describes the company's long-term debt. Neither of the two items above is reported in the financial statements of British Airways, and neither is likely to appear there in the future. Why?

2. Examine the long-term borrowings in BA's balance sheet and the related note. What, if any, convertible securities does the company have outstanding? Suppose BA issued £300 million fixed rate 8.75 percent Eurobonds, due 2031, at 101 in 2011 and that the bonds are convertible into shares of BA ordinary shares. Suppose, too, that the company simultaneously issued at 99, bonds similar in all respects except they are not convertible. Prepare the journal entry BA would use to record the issue of the convertible bonds. Prepare the journal entry BA would use to record the issue of the convertible bonds if BA used U.S. GAAP.

3. BA does not elect the fair value option (FVO) to report its financial liabilities. Examine Note 32: "Financial Instruments." If the company had elected the FVO for all of its fixed rate borrowings, what would be the balance at March 31, 2009, in the fair value adjustment account?

4. Is IFRS or U.S. GAAP more restrictive for determining when firms are allowed to elect the fair value option for financial assets and liabilities? Explain.

CPA SIMULATION 14–1

Ace Company
Long-Term Debt

CPA Review

Test your knowledge of the concepts discussed in this chapter, practice critical professional skills necessary for career success, and prepare for the computer-based CPA exam by accessing our CPA simulations at the text website: **www.mhhe.com/spiceland6e**.

The Ace Company simulation tests your knowledge of (a) the way we account for and report bonds from the perspective of both the issuer and investor, (b) reporting the cash flows related to bonds, and (c) capitalization of interest on funds provided by bonds and used to construct a building, as we studied in Chapter 10.

As on the CPA exam itself, you will be asked to use tools including a spreadsheet, a calculator, and generally accepted accounting principles, to conduct research, derive solutions, and communicate conclusions related to these issues in a simulated environment.

Specific tasks in the simulation include:

- Determining the selling price of bonds and analyzing the way an investor should report an investment in bonds.
- Applying judgment in the classification of cash flows from bond transactions on a statement of cash flows.
- Determining the amount of interest to be capitalized as part of the cost of an asset constructed with funding provided by bonds.
- Demonstrating an understanding of the way interest is calculated on debt.
- Communicating the way we account for convertible debt and debt with detachable warrants.
- Researching the way early extinguishments of debt is reported.

15

Leases

/// OVERVIEW

In the previous chapter, we saw how companies account for their long-term debt. The focus of that discussion was *bonds* and *notes.* In this chapter we continue our discussion of debt, but we now turn our attention to liabilities arising in connection with *leases.* Leases that produce such debtor/creditor relationships are referred to as *capital* leases by the lessee and as either *direct financing* or *sales-type* leases by the lessor. We also will see that some leases do not produce debtor/creditor relationships, but instead are accounted for as rental agreements. These are designated as *operating* leases.

/// LEARNING OBJECTIVES

After studying this chapter, you should be able to:

- **LO1** Identify and describe the operational, financial, and tax objectives that motivate leasing. (page 808)

- **LO2** Explain why some leases constitute rental agreements and some represent purchases/sales accompanied by debt financing. (page 809)

- **LO3** Explain the basis for each of the criteria and conditions used to classify leases. (page 811)

- **LO4** Record all transactions associated with operating leases by both the lessor and lessee. (page 815)

- **LO5** Describe and demonstrate how both the lessee and lessor account for a capital lease. (page 817)

- **LO6** Describe and demonstrate how the lessor accounts for a sales-type lease. (page 822)

- **LO7** Describe the way a bargain purchase option affects lease accounting. (page 824)

- **LO8** Explain how lease accounting is affected by the residual value of a leased asset. (page 827)

- **LO9** Explain the impact on lease accounting of executory costs, the discount rate, initial direct costs, and contingent rentals. (page 832)

- **LO10** Explain sale-leaseback agreements and other special leasing arrangements and their accounting treatment. (page 842)

- **LO11** Discuss the primary differences between U.S. GAAP and IFRS with respect to leases. (pages 814, 824, 834, 845, and 846)

FINANCIAL REPORTING CASE

It's a Hit!

"Don't get too comfortable with those big numbers," said Aaron Sanchez, controller for your new employer. "It's likely our revenues will take a hit over the next couple of years as more of our customers lease our machines rather than buy them."

You've just finished your first look at Higher Graphics' third quarter earnings report. Like most companies in your industry, HG leases its labeling machines to some customers and sells them to others. Eager to understand the implications of your new supervisor's concerns, you pull out your old intermediate accounting book and turn to the leases chapter.

By the time you finish this chapter, you should be able to respond appropriately to the questions posed in this case. Compare your response to the solution provided at the end of the chapter.

QUESTIONS ///

1. How would HG's revenues "take a hit" as a result of more customers leasing rather than buying labeling machines? (page 815)

2. Under what kind of leasing arrangements would the "hit" not occur? (page 822)

PART A

ACCOUNTING BY THE LESSOR AND LESSEE

An apartment lease is a typical rental agreement referred to as an *operating lease*.

If you ever have leased an apartment, you know that a lease is a contractual arrangement by which a **lessor** (owner) provides a **lessee** (user) the right to use an asset for a specified period of time. In return for this right, the lessee agrees to make stipulated, periodic cash payments during the term of the lease. An apartment lease is a typical rental agreement in which the fundamental rights and responsibilities of ownership are retained by the lessor; the lessee merely uses the asset temporarily. Businesses, too, lease assets under similar arrangements. These are referred to as **operating leases.** Many contracts, though, are formulated outwardly as leases, but in reality are installment purchases/sales. These are called **capital leases** (**direct financing** or **sales-type leases** to the lessor). Graphic 15–1 compares the classification possibilities.

GRAPHIC 15–1

Basic Lease Classifications

Lessee	Lessor
● Operating lease	● Operating lease
● Capital lease	● Capital lease:
	➡ Direct financing lease
	➡ Sales-type lease

After looking at some of the possible advantages of leasing assets rather than buying them in certain circumstances, we will explore differences in leases further.

DECISION MAKERS' PERSPECTIVE—Advantages of Leasing

● **LO1**

Leasing can facilitate asset acquisition.

The number one method of external financing by U.S. businesses is leasing.

When a young entrepreneur started a computer training center a few years ago, she had no idea how fast her business would grow. Now, while she knows she needs computers, she doesn't know how many. Just starting out, she also has little cash with which to buy them.

The U.S. Navy once leased a fleet of tankers to avoid asking Congress for appropriations.

The mutual funds department of a large investment firm often needs new computers and peripherals—fast. The department manager knows he can't afford to wait up to a year, the time it sometimes takes, to go through company channels to obtain purchase approval.

An established computer software publisher recently began developing a new line of business software. The senior programmer has to be certain he's testing the company's products on the latest versions of computer hardware. And yet he views large expenditures on equipment subject to rapid technological change and obsolescence as risky business.

Each of these individuals is faced with different predicaments and concerns. The entrepreneur is faced with uncertainty and cash flow problems, the department manager with time constraints and bureaucratic control systems, the programmer with fear of obsolescence. Though their specific concerns differ, these individuals have all met their firms' information technology needs with the same solution: each has decided to lease the computers rather than buy them.

Computers are by no means the only assets obtained through leasing arrangements. To the contrary, leasing has grown to be the most popular method of external financing of corporate assets in America. The airplane in which you last flew probably was leased, as was the gate from which it departed. Your favorite retail outlet at the local shopping mall likely leases the space it operates. Many companies actually exist for the sole purpose of acquiring assets and leasing them to others. And, leasing often is a primary method of "selling" a firm's products. **IBM** and **Boeing** are familiar examples.

In light of its popularity, you may be surprised that leasing usually is more expensive than buying. Of course, the higher apparent cost of leasing is because the lessor usually shoulders at least some of the financial and risk burdens that a purchaser normally would assume. So, why the popularity?

The lease decisions described above are motivated by operational incentives. Tax and market considerations also motivate firms to lease. Sometimes leasing offers tax saving advantages over outright purchases. For instance, a company with little or no taxable income—maybe a business just getting started, or one experiencing an economic downturn—will get little benefit from depreciation deductions. But the company can benefit *indirectly* by leasing assets rather than buying. By allowing the *lessor* to retain ownership and thus benefit from depreciation deductions, the lessee often can negotiate lower lease payments. Lessees with sufficient taxable income to take advantage of the depreciation deductions, but still in lower tax brackets than lessors, also can achieve similar indirect tax benefits.

The desire to obtain "off-balance-sheet financing" also is sometimes a leasing stimulus. When funds are borrowed to purchase an asset, the liability has a detrimental effect on the company's debt to equity ratio and other quantifiable indicators of riskiness. Similarly, the purchased asset increases total assets and correspondingly lowers calculations of the rate of return on assets. Despite research that indicates otherwise, management actions continue to reflect a belief that the financial market is naive and is fooled by off-balance-sheet financing. Managers continue to avoid reporting assets and liabilities by leasing rather than buying and by constructing lease agreements in such a way that capitalizing the assets and liabilities is not required.[1]

Whether or not there is any real effect on security prices, sometimes off-balance-sheet financing helps a firm avoid exceeding contractual limits on designated financial ratios (like the debt to equity ratio, for instance).[2] When the operational, tax, and financial market advantages are considered, the *net* cost of leasing often is less than the cost of purchasing. ●

Capital Leases and Installment Notes Compared

● LO2

You learned in the previous chapter how to account for an installment note. To a great extent, then, you already have learned how to account for a capital lease. To illustrate, let's recall the situation described in the previous chapter. We assumed that Skill Graphics purchased a package-labeling machine from Hughes–Barker Corporation by issuing a three-year installment note that required six semiannual installment payments of $139,857 each. That arrangement provided for the purchase of the $666,633 machine as well as interest at an annual rate of 14% (7% twice each year). Remember, too, that each installment payment consisted of part interest (7% times the outstanding balance) and part payment for the machine (the remainder of each payment).

Now let's suppose that Skill Graphics instead acquired the package-labeling machine from Hughes–Barker Corporation under a three-year *lease* that required six semiannual rental payments of $139,857 each. Obviously, the fundamental nature of the transaction remains the same regardless of whether it is negotiated as an installment purchase or as a lease. So, it would be inconsistent to account for this lease in a fundamentally different way than for an installment purchase:

Comparison of a Note and Capital Lease

At Inception (January 1)		
Installment Note		
Machinery	666,633	
Note payable		666,633
	(continued)	

Tax incentives often motivate leasing.

Leasing sometimes is used as a means of off-balance-sheet financing.

Operational, tax, and financial market incentives often make leasing an attractive alternative to purchasing.

[1]You will learn later in the chapter that accounting standards are designed to identify lease arrangements that, despite their outward appearance, are in reality purchases of assets. Assets acquired by these arrangements, *capital leases,* are required to be recorded as well as the related lease liability. Managers often structure lease terms so that capitalization requirements are avoided.

[2]It is common for debt agreements, particularly long-term ones, to include restrictions on the debtor as a way to provide some degree of protection to the creditor. Sometimes a minimum level is specified for current assets relative to current liabilities, net assets, debt as a ratio of equity, or many other financial ratios. Often a restriction is placed on dividend payments, share repurchases, or other activities that might impede the debtor's ability to repay the debt. Typically, the debt becomes due on demand when the debtor becomes in violation of such a debt covenant, often after a specified grace period.

(concluded)

Capital Lease

Leased machinery	666,633	
Lease payable		666,633

Consistent with the nature of the transaction, interest expense accrues each period at the effective rate times the outstanding balance:

At the First Semiannual Payment Date (June 30)		
Installment Note		
Interest expense (7% × $666,633)	46,664	
Note payable (difference)	93,193	
Cash (installment payment)		139,857
Capital Lease		
Interest expense (7% × $666,633)	46,664	
Lease payable (difference)	93,193	
Cash (rental payment)		139,857

Because the lease payable balance declines with each payment, the interest becomes less each period. An amortization schedule is convenient to track the changing amounts as shown in Graphic 15–2.

Date	Payments	Effective Interest	Decrease in Balance	Outstanding Balance
		(7% × Outstanding balance)		
				666,633
1	139,857	.07(666,633) = 46,664	93,193	573,440
2	139,857	.07(573,440) = 40,141	99,716	473,724
3	139,857	.07(473,724) = 33,161	106,696	367,028
4	139,857	.07(367,028) = 25,692	114,165	252,863
5	139,857	.07(252,863) = 17,700	122,157	130,706
6	139,857	.07(130,706) = 9,151*	130,706	0
	839,142	172,509	666,633	

*Rounded

You should recognize this as essentially the same amortization schedule we used in the previous chapter in connection with our installment note example. The reason for the similarity is that we view a capital lease as being, in substance, equivalent to an installment purchase. So naturally the accounting treatment of the two essentially identical transactions should be consistent.

Lease Classification

A lease is accounted for as either a rental agreement or a purchase/sale accompanied by debt financing. The choice of accounting method hinges on the nature of the leasing arrangement.

Capital leases are agreements that we identify as being formulated outwardly as leases, but which are in reality essentially installment purchases. Sometimes the true nature of an arrangement is obvious. For example, a 10-year noncancelable lease of a computer with a 10-year useful life, by which title passes to the lessee at the end of the lease term, obviously more nearly represents a purchase than a rental agreement. But what if the terms of the contract do not transfer title, and the lease term is for only seven years of the asset's 10-year life? Suppose contractual terms permit the lessee to obtain title under certain prearranged conditions? What if compensation provided by the lease contract is nearly equal to the value of the asset under lease? These situations are less clear-cut.

Professional judgment is needed to differentiate between leases that represent rental agreements and those that in essence are installment purchases/sales. It's important to note that from an accounting perspective legal ownership is irrelevant in the decision. The essential question is whether the usual risks and rewards of ownership have been transferred to the lessee. But judgment alone is likely to lead to inconsistencies in practice. The desire to encourage consistency in practice motivated the FASB to provide guidance for distinguishing between two fundamental types of leases: capital leases and operating leases.[3] As you study the classification criteria in the following paragraphs, keep in mind that some leases clearly fit the classifications we give them, but others fall in a gray area somewhere between the two extremes. For those, we end up forcing them into one category or the other by somewhat arbitrary criteria.

> Accounting for leases attempts to see through the legal form of the agreements to determine their economic substance.

Classification Criteria

A lessee should classify a lease transaction as a *capital lease* if it includes a noncancelable lease term and one or more of the four criteria listed in Graphic 15–3 are met.[4] Otherwise, it is an *operating lease*.

> ● LO3

1. The agreement specifies that ownership of the asset transfers to the lessee.
2. The agreement contains a bargain purchase option.
3. The noncancelable lease term is equal to 75% or more of the expected economic life of the asset.
4. The present value of the "minimum lease payments"[5] is equal to or greater than 90% of the fair value of the asset.

> **GRAPHIC 15–3**
> Criteria for Classification as a Capital Lease

Let's look closer at these criteria.

Since our objective is to determine when the risks and rewards of ownership have been transferred to the lessee, the first criterion is self-evident. If legal title passes to the lessee during, or at the end of, the lease term, obviously ownership attributes are transferred.

> Criterion 1: Transfer of ownership.

A **bargain purchase option (BPO)** is a provision in the lease contract that gives the lessee the option of purchasing the leased property at a bargain price. This is defined as a price sufficiently lower than the expected fair value of the property (when the option becomes exercisable) that the exercise of the option appears reasonably assured at the inception of the lease. Because exercise of the option appears reasonably assured, transfer of ownership is expected. So the logic of the second criterion is similar to that of the first. Applying criterion 2 in practice, though, often is more difficult because it is necessary to make a judgment now about whether a future option price will be a bargain.

> Criterion 2: Bargain purchase option.

If an asset is leased for most of its useful life, then most of the benefits and responsibilities of ownership are transferred to the lessee. We presume, quite arbitrarily, that 75% or more of the **expected economic life** of the asset is an appropriate threshold point for this purpose.

> Criterion 3: Lease term is 75% of economic life.

---

[3]FASB ASC 840–10–15: Leases–Overall–Recognition (previously "Accounting for Leases," *Statement of Financial Accounting Standards No. 13* (Stamford, Conn.: FASB, 1980), par. 7).

[4]Noncancelable in this context does not preclude the agreement from specifying that the lease is cancelable after a designated noncancelable lease term. Unless some portion of the lease term is noncancelable, it is an operating lease. Later in this section, we discuss treatment of any cancelable portion of the lease term.

[5]Minimum lease payments are defined on the next page.

Although the intent of this criterion is fairly straightforward, implementation some-times is troublesome. First, the lease term may be uncertain. It may be renewable beyond its initial term. Or the lease may be cancelable after a designated noncancelable period. When either is an issue, we ordinarily consider the lease term to be the noncancelable[6] term of the lease plus any periods covered by bargain renewal options.[7] A bargain renewal option gives the lessee the option to renew the lease at a bargain rate. That is, the rental payment is sufficiently lower than the expected fair rental of the property at the date the option becomes exercisable that exercise of the option appears reasonably assured.

ADDITIONAL CONSIDERATION

Periods covered by bargain renewal options are not included in the lease term if a **bargain purchase option** is present. This is because the lease term should not extend beyond the date a bargain purchase option becomes exercisable. For example, assume a BPO allows a lessee to buy a leased delivery truck at the end of the noncancelable five-year lease term. Even if an option to renew the lease beyond that date is considered to be a bargain renewal option, that extra period would not be included as part of the lease term. Remember, we presume the BPO will be exercised after the initial five-year term, making the renewal option irrelevant.

Another implementation issue is estimating the economic life of the leased property. This is the estimated remaining time the property is expected to be economically usable for its intended purpose, with normal maintenance and repairs, at the inception of the lease. Esti-mates of the economic life of leased property are subject to the same uncertainty limitations of most estimates. This uncertainty presents the opportunity to arrive at estimates that cause this third criterion not to be met.

Finally, if the inception of the lease occurs during the last 25% of an asset's economic life, this third criterion does not apply. This is consistent with the basic premise of this criterion that most of the risks and rewards of ownership occur during the first 75% of an asset's life.

Criterion 4: Present value of payments is 90% of fair value.

If the lease payments required by a lease contract substantially pay for a leased asset, it is logical to identify the arrangement as a lease equivalent to an installment purchase. This situation is considered to exist when the present value of the minimum lease payments is equal to or greater than 90% of the fair value of the asset at the inception of the lease. In general, minimum lease payments are payments the lessee is required to make in connection with the lease and consist of:

- the total of periodic rental payments
- any guaranteed residual value
- any bargain purchase option price

---

[6]Noncancelable in this context is a lease that is cancelable only by (a) the occurrence of some remote contingency, (b) permission of the lessor, (c) a new lease with the same lessor, or (d) payment by the lessee of a penalty in an amount such that continuation of the lease appears, at inception, reasonably assured. FASB ASC Master Glossary–Noncancelable Lease Term (previously "Accounting for Leases: Sale and Leaseback Transactions Involving Real Estate, Sales-Type Leases of Real Estate, Definition of the Lease Term, Initial Direct Costs of Direct Financing Leases," *Statement of Financial Accounting Standards No. 98* (Stamford, Conn.: FASB, 1988), par. 22).

[7]If applicable, the lease term also should include (a) periods for which failure to renew the lease imposes a penalty on the lessee in an amount such that renewal appears reasonably assured, (b) periods covered by ordinary renewal options during which a guarantee by the lessee of the lessor's debt directly or indirectly related to the leased property is expected to be in effect or a loan from the lessee to the lessor directly or indirectly related to the leased property is expected to be outstanding, (c) periods covered by ordinary renewal options preceding the date that a bargain purchase option is exercisable, or (d) periods representing renewals or extensions of the lease at the lessor's option. FASB ASC Master Glossary–Lease Term (previously "Accounting for Leases: Sale and Leaseback Transactions Involving Real Estate, Sales-Type Leases of Real Estate, Definition of the Lease Term, Initial Direct Costs of Direct Financing Leases," *Statement of Financial Accounting Standards No. 98* (Stamford, Conn.: FASB, 1988), par. 22).

We look closer at the make-up of minimum lease payments later in the chapter when we discuss residual values and bargain purchase options in more detail.

The 90% of fair value criterion often is the decisive one in identifying a capital lease. As mentioned earlier, lessees often try to avoid writing a lease agreement that will require recording an asset and liability. When this is an objective, it usually is relatively easy to avoid meeting the first three criteria. However, when the underlying motive for the lease agreement is that the lessee substantively acquire the asset, it is more difficult to avoid meeting the 90% recovery criterion without defeating that motive. New ways, though, continually are being devised to structure leases to avoid meeting this criterion. Later we will look at some popular devices that are used.

Again consistent with the basic premise that most of the risks and rewards of ownership occur during the first 75% of an asset's life, this fourth criterion does not apply if the inception of the lease occurs during the last 25% of an asset's economic life.

Additional Lessor Conditions

As we saw in the previous section, the lessee accounts for a capital lease as if an asset were purchased; that is, the lessee records both an asset and a liability at the inception of the lease. Consistency would suggest that the lessor in the same lease transaction should record the sale of an asset. Indeed, consistency is a goal of the FASB's lease accounting standards. The four classification criteria discussed in the previous section apply to both parties to the transaction, lessees and lessors. However, a fundamental difference is that for a lessor to record the sale side of the transaction, it is necessary also to satisfy the conditions of the realization principle we discussed in Chapter 5. In particular, the FASB specifies that for the lessor to record a lease as a direct financing lease or a sales-type lease, two conditions must be met in addition to one of the four classification criteria. These are listed in Graphic 15–4.

1. The collectibility of the lease payments must be reasonably predictable.
2. If any costs to the lessor have yet to be incurred, they are reasonably predictable. (Performance by the lessor is substantially complete.)

GRAPHIC 15–4
Additional Conditions for Classification as a Capital Lease by the Lessor

Additional lessor conditions for classification as a capital lease are consistent with criteria of the revenue realization principle.

In the case of a sales-type lease (discussed later in Part A of this chapter) in which the lessor recognizes sales revenue, the reason for these additional conditions is apparent; collectibility of payments and substantial completion of the earnings process are conditions of the revenue realization principle. This logic is extended to agreements classified as direct financing leases. Although sales revenue is not recorded in a direct financing lease, the leased asset is removed from the lessor's books and is replaced by a receivable.

Although uniformity of classification is a goal of lease accounting standards, it is obvious that the additional conditions allow inconsistencies.[8] Indeed, in lease negotiations an objective of the parties involved often is to devise terms that will result in a sale by the lessor but an operating lease by the lessee.[9]

In the remaining sections of Part A of this chapter we consider, in order, operating leases, direct financing leases (capital leases to the lessee), and sales-type leases (capital leases to the lessee).

---

[8]"FASB ASC 840–10–25–42: Leases–Overall–Recognition (previously "Accounting for Leases," *Statement of Financial Accounting Standards No. 13* (Stamford, Conn.: FASB, 1980)).
[9]Later in the chapter we discuss ways this is done.

● LO11

INTERNATIONAL FINANCIAL REPORTING STANDARDS

Lease Classification.

Lease accounting under U.S. GAAP and IFRS provides a good general comparison of **"rules-based accounting,"** as U.S. GAAP often is described, and **"principles-based accounting,"** which often is the description assigned to IFRS. We discussed four classification criteria used under U.S. GAAP to determine whether a lease is a capital lease. Under IFRS, we don't have such bright-line rules. Instead, a lease is deemed a capital lease (called a **finance lease** under *IAS No. 17*, "Leases"[10]), if substantially all risks and rewards of ownership are judged to have been transferred. Judgment is made based on a number of "indicators" including some similar to the specific criteria of U.S. GAAP. Here is a comparison:

IFRS ILLUSTRATION

IFRS Illustration	
IFRS	**U.S. GAAP**
Situations (individually or in combination) that ***normally would lead to*** classification as a finance lease are:	Situations that ***require*** classification as a capital lease if any one (or more) is met are:
• The agreement specifies that ownership of the asset transfers to the lessee.	Same as IFRS
• The agreement contains a bargain purchase option.	Same as IFRS
• The noncancelable lease term is for a "major portion" of the expected economic life of the asset.	"Major portion" is defined specifically as 75% or more.
• The present value of the minimum lease payments is equal to or greater than "substantially all" of the fair value of the asset.	"Substantially all" is defined specifically as 90%.
• The leased asset is of a specialized nature such that only the lessee can use it without major modifications being made.	No similar situation specified.
Other situations (individually or in combination) that ***might also lead to*** classification as a finance lease are:	
• The lessor's losses are borne by the lessee upon cancellation.	No similar situation specified.
• Gains or losses from changes in the fair value of the residual value go to the lessee (for instance, by means of a rebate of lease payments).	No similar situation specified.
• The lease contains a "bargain renewal option" whereby the lessee can continue the lease for substantially less than market rent.	No similar situation specified.

Ordinarily, it will not be a single indicator, but the combined implication of two or more indicators that will sway the classification decision under IFRS. Often the appropriate classification is obvious. At other times, careful consideration of all aspects of the agreement with reference to the classification indicators is needed. Substance over form is the goal. Professional judgment is key.

---

[10]"Leases," *International Accounting Standard No. 17* (IASCF), as amended effective January 1, 2009.

Operating Leases

If a lease does not meet any of the criteria for a capital lease it is considered to be more in the nature of a rental agreement and is referred to as an **operating lease.**[11] We assume that the fundamental rights and responsibilities of ownership are retained by the lessor and that the lessee merely is using the asset temporarily. In keeping with that presumption, a sale is not recorded by the lessor; a purchase is not recorded by the lessee. Instead, the periodic rental payments are accounted for merely as rent by both parties to the transaction—*rent revenue* by the lessor; *rent expense* by the lessee.

Let's look at an example that illustrates the relatively straightforward accounting for operating leases. The earlier example comparing a capital lease to an installment purchase assumed rental payments at the *end* of each period. A more typical leasing arrangement requires rental payments at the *beginning* of each period. This more realistic payment schedule is assumed in Illustration 15–1.

**FINANCIAL
Reporting Case**

Q1, p. 807

● **LO4**

On January 1, 2011, Sans Serif Publishers, Inc., a computer services and printing firm, leased a color copier from CompuDec Corporation.

The lease agreement specifies four annual payments of $100,000 beginning January 1, 2011, the inception of the lease, and at each January 1 thereafter through 2014. The useful life of the copier is estimated to be six years.

Before deciding to lease, Sans Serif considered purchasing the copier for its cash price of $479,079. If funds were borrowed to buy the copier, the interest rate would have been 10%. How should this lease be classified? We apply the four classification criteria:

1. Does the agreement specify that ownership of the asset transfers to the lessee?	No	
2. Does this agreement contain a bargain purchase option?	No	
3. Is the lease term equal to 75% or more of the expected economic life of the asset?	No	(4 yrs < 75% of 6 yrs)
4. Is the present value of the minimum lease payments equal to or greater than 90% of the fair value of the asset?	No	

($348,685 < 90% of $479,079)

$100,000 × 3.48685* = $348,685

Lease payments   Present value

Since none of the four classification criteria is met, this is an operating lease.

ILLUSTRATION 15–1

Application of Classification Criteria

Using Excel, enter:
=PV(.10,4,100000, 1)
Output: 348685.2

Using a calculator:
enter: BEG mode N 4 I 10
PMT −100000 FV
Output: PV 348685

---

*Present value of an annuity due of $1: *n* = 4, *i* = 10%. Recall from Chapter 6 that we refer to periodic payments at the beginning of each period as an *annuity due*.

Journal entries for Illustration 15–1 are shown in Illustration 15–1A on the next page.

In an operating lease, rent is recognized on a straight-line basis unless another systematic method more clearly reflects the benefits of the asset's use. So, if rental payments are uneven—for instance, if rent increases are scheduled—the total scheduled payments ordinarily would be expensed equally (straight-line basis) over the lease term.[12]

Advance Payments

Often lease agreements call for advance payments to be made at the inception of the lease that represent prepaid rent. For instance, it is common for a lessee to pay a bonus in return for negotiating more favorable lease terms. Such payments are recorded as prepaid rent and allocated (normally on a straight-line basis) to rent expense/rent revenue over the lease term. So the rent that is periodically reported in those cases consists of the periodic rent payments themselves plus an allocated portion of prepaid rent.

---

[11]The term *operating lease* got its name long ago when a lessee routinely received from the lessor an operator along with leased equipment.

[12]FASB ASC 840–20–25: Leases–Operating Leases–Recognition (previously "Accounting for Operating Leases with Scheduled Rent Increases," *FASB Technical Bulletin 85-3* (Stamford, Conn.: FASB, 1985), par. 1).

ILLUSTRATION 15–1A

Journal Entries for an Operating Lease

At the beginning of the year, the rent payments are prepaid rent to the lessee and unearned rent to the lessor.

The operating lease described in Illustration 15–1 is recorded as follows:

At Each of the Four Payment Dates

Sans Serif Publishers, Inc. (Lessee)

Prepaid rent	100,000	
Cash		100,000

CompuDec Corporation (Lessor)

Cash	100,000	
Unearned rent revenue		100,000

At the End of Each Year

Sans Serif Publishers, Inc. (Lessee)

Rent expense	100,000	
Prepaid rent		100,000

The lessor retains the asset on its books, and accordingly records depreciation on the asset.

CompuDec Corporation (Lessor)

Unearned rent revenue	100,000	
Rent revenue		100,000
Depreciation expense	x,xxx	
Accumulated depreciation		x,xxx

In the journal entries above and throughout the chapter, we look at the entries of the lessee and the lessor together. This way, we can be reminded that the entries for the lessor usually are essentially the mirror image of those for the lessee, the other side of the same coin.[13]

Sometimes advance payments include security deposits that are refundable at the expiration of the lease or prepayments of the last period's rent. A refundable security deposit is recorded as a long-term receivable (by the lessee) and liability (by the lessor) unless it is not expected to be returned. A prepayment of the last period's rent is recorded as prepaid rent and allocated to rent expense/rent revenue during the last period of the lease term.

At times, lease agreements call for uneven rent payments during the term of the lease. One way this can occur is when the initial payment (or maybe several payments) is waived. This is called a **rent abatement.** In any case, the total payments over the life of the lease are expensed on a straight-line basis.

Alternatively, rent payments may be scheduled to increase periodically over the lease term. In any event, the total rent over the term of the lease is allocated to individual periods on a straight-line basis. This means the (temporarily) unpaid portion of rent expense must be credited to deferred rent expense payable until later in the lease term when rent payments exceed rent expense.

Leasehold Improvements

The cost of a *leasehold improvement* is depreciated over its useful life to the lessee.

Sometimes a lessee will make improvements to leased property that reverts back to the lessor at the end of the lease. If a lessee constructs a new building or makes modifications to existing structures, that cost represents an asset just like any other capital expenditure. Like other assets, its cost is allocated as depreciation expense over its useful life to the lessee, which will be the shorter of the physical life of the asset or the lease term.[14] Theoretically, such assets can be recorded in accounts descriptive of their nature, such as buildings or plant. In practice, the traditional account title used is **leasehold improvements.**[15] In any case, the undepreciated cost usually is reported in the balance sheet under the caption *property, plant, and equipment.* Movable assets like office furniture and equipment that are not attached to the leased property are not considered leasehold improvements.

During 2005 hundreds of companies, particularly in the retail and restaurant industries, underwent one of the most widespread accounting correction events ever. Corrections were

---

[13]We see later in the chapter that sometimes this is not the case, particularly when the lease is a "sales-type" lease. Even when the two sides are not mirror images there are many similarities, so the comparison still is helpful.

[14]If the agreement contains an option to renew, and the likelihood of renewal is uncertain, the renewal period is ignored.

[15]Also, traditionally, depreciation sometimes is labeled amortization when in connection with leased assets and leasehold improvements. This is of little consequence. Remember, both depreciation and amortization refer to the process of allocating an asset's cost over its useful life.

in the way these companies, including **Pep Boys**, **Ann Taylor**, **Target**, and **Domino's Pizza**, had allocated the cost of leasehold improvements. Rather than expensing leasehold improvements properly over the lease terms, these firms for years had inappropriately expensed the cost over the longer estimated useful lives of the properties. Prompting the sweeping revisions was a Securities and Exchange Commission letter on February 7, 2005, urging companies to follow long-standing accounting standards in this area. A result of the improper practices was to defer expense, thereby accelerating earnings. For instance, **McDonald's Corp.** recorded a charge of $139 million in its 2004 fourth quarter to adjust for the difference.

Let's turn our attention now to accounting for leases that meet the criteria and conditions for classification as capital leases by both the lessee and the lessor.

> Hundreds of firms in 2005 corrected the way they accounted for leases.

Capital Leases—Lessee and Lessor

In the operating lease illustration, we assumed Sans Serif leased a copier directly from the manufacturer. Now, in Illustration 15–2, let's assume a financial intermediary provided financing by acquiring the copier and leasing it to the user.

● LO5

On January 1, 2011, Sans Serif Publishers, Inc., leased a copier from First LeaseCorp. First LeaseCorp purchased the equipment from CompuDec Corporation at a cost of $479,079.

The lease agreement specifies annual payments beginning January 1, 2011, the inception of the lease, and at each December 31 thereafter through 2015. The six-year lease term ending December 31, 2016, is equal to the estimated useful life of the copier.

First LeaseCorp routinely acquires electronic equipment for lease to other firms. The interest rate in these financing arrangements is 10%.

Since the lease term is equal to the expected useful life of the copier (>75%), the transaction must be recorded by the lessee as a **capital lease**.[16] If we assume also that collectibility of the lease payments and any costs to the lessor that are yet to be incurred are reasonably predictable, this qualifies also as a **direct financing lease** to First LeaseCorp. To achieve its objectives, First LeaseCorp must (a) recover its $479,079 investment as well as (b) earn interest revenue at a rate of 10%. So, the lessor determined that annual rental payments would be $100,000:

$$\$479,079 \div 4.79079^* = \$100,000$$

Lessor's cost	Rental payments

*Present value of an annuity due of $1: n = 6, i = 10%.

Of course, Sans Serif Publishers, Inc., views the transaction from the other side. The price the lessee pays for the copier is the present value of the rental payments:

$$\$100,000 \times 4.79079^* = \$479,079$$

Rental payments	Lessee's cost

*Present value of an annuity due of $1: n = 6, i = 10%.

Direct Financing Lease (January 1, 2011)

Sans Serif Publishers, Inc. (Lessee)

Leased equipment (present value of lease payments)	479,079	
Lease payable (present value of lease payments)		479,079

First LeaseCorp (Lessor)

Lease receivable (present value of lease payments)	479,079	
Inventory of equipment (lessor's cost)		479,079

First Lease Payment (January 1, 2011)*

Sans Serif Publishers, Inc. (Lessee)

Lease payable	100,000	
Cash		100,000

First LeaseCorp (Lessor)

Cash	100,000	
Lease receivable		100,000

*Of course, the entries to record the lease and the first payment could be combined into a single entry since they occur at the same time.

ILLUSTRATION 15–2

Capital Leases

Using Excel, enter:
=PMT(.10,6,479079, 1)
Output: 100000

Using a calculator:
enter: BEG mode [N] 6 [I] 10
[PV] −479079 [FV]
Output: [PMT] 100000

> Notice that the lessor's entries are the flip side or mirror image of the lessee's entries.

> The first lease payment reduces the balances in the lease payable and the lease receivable by $100,000 to $379,079.

---

[16]The fourth criterion also is met. The present value of lease payments ($479,079) is 100% (>90%) of the fair value of the copier ($479,079). Meeting any one of the four criteria is sufficient.

A leased asset is recorded by the lessee at the *present value of the minimum lease payments* or the asset's fair value, whichever is lower.

Interest is a function of time. It accrues at the effective rate on the balance outstanding during the period.

The amount recorded (capitalized) by the lessee is the present value of the minimum lease payments. However, if the fair value of the asset is lower than this amount, the recorded value of the asset should be limited to fair value. Unless the lessor is a manufacturer or dealer, the fair value typically will be the lessor's cost ($479,079 in this case). However, if considerable time has elapsed between the purchase of the property by the lessor and the inception of the lease, the fair value might be different. When the lessor is a manufacturer or dealer, the fair value of the property at the inception of the lease ordinarily will be its normal selling price (reduced by any volume or trade discounts). We study this situation (a sales-type lease) later. In unusual cases, market conditions may cause fair value to be less than the normal selling price.[17]

Be sure to note that the entire $100,000 first rental payment is applied to principal reduction.[18] Because it occurred at the inception of the lease, no interest had yet accrued. Subsequent rental payments include interest on the outstanding balance as well as a portion that reduces that outstanding balance. As of the second rental payment date, one year's interest has accrued on the $379,079 balance outstanding during 2012, recorded as in Illustration 15–2A. Notice that the outstanding balance is reduced by $62,092—the portion of the $100,000 payment remaining after interest is covered.

ILLUSTRATION 15–2A

Journal Entries for the Second Lease Payment

LESSEE
Lease Payable
$479,079
(100,000)
$379,079
(62,092)
$316,987

LESSOR
Lease Receivable
$479,079
(100,000)
$379,079
(62,092)
$316,987

Second Lease Payment (December 31, 2011)

Sans Serif Publishers, Inc. (Lessee)

Interest expense [10% × ($479,079 − 100,000)] 37,908
Lease payable (difference) 62,092
   Cash (lease payment) 100,000

First LeaseCorp (Lessor)

Cash (lease payment) 100,000
   Lease receivable 62,092
   Interest revenue [10% × ($479,079 − 100,000)] 37,908

ADDITIONAL CONSIDERATION

Some lessors use what's called the "gross method" to record the receivable in a capital lease. By this method, the lessor debits lease receivable for the gross sum of the lease payments and credits *unearned interest revenue* for the difference between the total of the payments and the present value of the payments since that's the amount that eventually will be recorded as interest revenue over the term of the lease. In Illustration 15–2, the lessor's entry by the gross method at the inception of the lease would be:

Lease receivable ($100,000 × 6) 600,000
   Unearned interest revenue (difference) 120,921
   Inventory of equipment (lessor's cost) 479,079

The same ultimate result is achieved either way. We use the net method in our illustrations to more easily demonstrate the lessee's entries and the lessor's entries being "two sides of the same coin." Whichever method is used, both the lessee and the lessor must report in the disclosure notes both the net and gross amounts of the lease.

---

[17]FASB ASC 840–10: Leases–Overall (previously "Accounting for Leases," *Statement of Financial Accounting Standards No. 13* (Stamford, Conn.: FASB, 1980)).

[18]Another way to view this is to think of the first $100,000 as a down payment with the remaining $379,079 financed by 5 (i.e., 6 − 1) *year-end* lease payments.

The amortization schedule in Graphic 15–5 shows how the lease balance and the effective interest change over the six-year lease term. Each rental payment after the first includes both an amount that represents interest and an amount that represents a reduction of principal. The periodic reduction of principal is sufficient that, at the end of the lease term, the outstanding balance is zero.

GRAPHIC 15–5

Lease Amortization Schedule

	Payments	Effective Interest	Decrease in Balance	Outstanding Balance
		(10% × Outstanding balance)		
1/1/11				479,079
1/1/11	100,000		100,000	379,079
12/31/11	100,000	.10 (379,079) = 37,908	62,092	316,987
12/31/12	100,000	.10 (316,987) = 31,699	68,301	248,686
12/31/13	100,000	.10 (248,686) = 24,869	75,131	173,555
12/31/14	100,000	.10 (173,555) = 17,355	82,645	90,910
12/31/15	100,000	.10 (90,910) = 9,090*	90,910	0
	600,000	120,921*	479,079	

The first rental payment includes no interest.

The total of the cash payments ($600,000) provides for:
1. Payment for the copier ($479,079).
2. Interest ($120,921) at an effective rate of 10%.

*Adjusted for rounding of other numbers in the schedule.

An interesting aspect of the amortization schedule that you may want to note at this point relates to a disclosure requirement that we discuss at the end of the chapter. Among other things, the lessee and lessor must report separately the current and noncurrent portions of the outstanding lease balance. Both amounts are provided by the amortization schedule. For example, if we want the amounts to report on the 2011 balance sheet, refer to the next row of the schedule. The portion of the 2012 payment that represents principal ($68,301) is the *current* (as of December 31, 2011) balance. The *noncurrent* amount is the balance outstanding after the 2012 reduction ($248,686). These amounts are the current and noncurrent lease liability for the lessee and the current and noncurrent net investment for the lessor.

Depreciation

Depreciation is recorded for leased assets in a manner consistent with the lessee's usual policy for depreciating its depreciable assets.

End of Each Year		
Sans Serif Publishers, Inc. (Lessee)		
Depreciation expense ($479,079 ÷ 6 years*)	79,847	
Accumulated depreciation		79,847

*If the lessee depreciates assets by the straight-line method.

Because a capital lease assumes the lessee purchased the asset, the lessee depreciates its cost.

DEPRECIATION PERIOD. The lessee normally should depreciate a leased asset over the term of the lease. However, if ownership transfers or a bargain purchase option is present (i.e., either of the first two classification criteria is met), the asset should be depreciated over its useful life. This means depreciation is recorded over the useful life of the asset *to the lessee* whether or not that useful life is limited by the term of the lease.

The depreciation period is restricted to the lease term unless the lease provides for transfer of title or a BPO.

A description of leased assets and related depreciation provided in a recent disclosure note (Graphic 15–6) of **Kroger Company** is representative of leased asset disclosures.

GRAPHIC 15–6

Disclosure of Leased Assets—Kroger Company

Real World Financials

3. PROPERTY, PLANT AND EQUIPMENT, NET
Property, plant and equipment, net consists of:

$ in millions	January 31, 2009	February 2, 2008
Land	$ 1,944	$ 1,779
Buildings and land improvements	6,457	5,875
Equipment	8,993	8,620
Leasehold improvements	5,076	4,626
Construction-in-progress	880	965
Leased property under capital leases	550	571
	23,900	22,436
Accumulated depreciation and amortization	(10,739)	(9,938)
Total	$ 13,161	$12,498

Accumulated depreciation for leased property under capital leases was $283 at January 31, 2009 and $286 at February 2, 2008.

Accrued Interest

At each financial statement date, any interest that has accrued since interest was last recorded must be accrued for all liabilities and receivables, including those relating to leases.

If a company's reporting period ends at any time between payment dates, it's necessary to record (as an adjusting entry) any interest that has accrued since interest was last recorded. We purposely avoided this step in the previous illustration by assuming that the lease agreement specified rental payments on December 31—the end of the reporting period. But if payments were made on another date, or if the company's fiscal year ended on a date other than December 31, accrued interest would be recorded prior to preparing financial statements. For example, if lease payments were made on January 1 of each year, the effective interest amounts shown in the lease amortization schedule still would be appropriate but would be recorded one day prior to the actual rental payment. For instance, the second cash payment of $100,000 would occur on January 1, 2012, but the interest component of that payment ($37,908) would be accrued a day earlier as shown in Illustration 15–2B.

ILLUSTRATION 15–2B

Journal Entries When Interest Is Accrued Prior to the Lease Payment

December 31, 2011 (to accrue interest)		
Sans Serif Publishers, Inc. (Lessee)		
Interest expense [10% × ($479,079 – 100,000)]	37,908	
Interest payable		37,908
First LeaseCorp (Lessor)		
Interest receivable	37,908	
Interest revenue [10% × ($479,079 – 100,000)]		37,908

Second Lease Payment (January 1, 2012)		
Sans Serif Publishers, Inc. (Lessee)		
Interest payable (from adjusting entry above)	37,908	
Lease payable (difference)	62,092	
Cash (lease payment)		100,000
First LeaseCorp (Lessor)		
Cash (lease payment)	100,000	
Lease receivable (difference)		62,092
Interest receivable (from adjusting entry above)		37,908

Notice that this is consistent with recording accrued interest on any debt, whether in the form of a note, a bond, or a lease.

We assumed in this illustration that First LeaseCorp bought the copier for $479,079 and then leased it for the same price. There was no profit on the "sale" itself. The only income derived by the lessor was interest revenue earned over the lease term. In effect, First LeaseCorp financed the purchase of the copier by Sans Serif Publishers. This type of lease is a direct financing lease. This kind of leasing is a thriving industry. It is a profitable part of operations for banks and other financial institutions (**Citicorp** is one of the largest). Some leasing companies do nothing else. Often leasing companies, like **IBM Credit Corporation**, are subsidiaries of larger corporations, formed for the sole purpose of conducting financing activities for their parent corporations.

CONCEPT REVIEW EXERCISE

United Cellular Systems leased a satellite transmission device from Pinnacle Leasing Services on January 1, 2012. Pinnacle paid $625,483 for the transmission device. Its fair value is $625,483.

DIRECT FINANCING LEASE

Terms of the Lease Agreement and Related Information:

Lease term	3 years (6 semiannual periods)
Semiannual rental payments	$120,000 at beginning of each period
Economic life of asset	3 years
Interest rate	12%

Required:

1. Prepare the appropriate entries for both United Cellular Systems and Pinnacle Leasing Services on January 1, the inception of the lease.
2. Prepare an amortization schedule that shows the pattern of interest expense for United Cellular Systems and interest revenue for Pinnacle Leasing Services over the lease term.
3. Prepare the appropriate entries to record the second lease payment on July 1, 2012, and adjusting entries on December 31, 2012 (the end of both companies' fiscal years).

1. Prepare the appropriate entries for both United Cellular Systems and Pinnacle Leasing Services on January 1, the inception of the lease.

SOLUTION

Present value of periodic rental payments:

$$($120,000 \times 5.21236^*) = $625,483$$

*Present value of an annuity due of $1: n = 6, i = 6%.

Calculation of the present value of minimum lease payments.

January 1, 2012		
United Cellular Systems (Lessee)		
Leased equipment (calculated above)	625,483	
Lease payable (calculated above)		625,483
Lease payable	120,000	
Cash (lease payment)		120,000
Pinnacle Leasing Services (Lessor)		
Lease receivable (calculated above)	625,483	
Inventory of equipment (lessor's cost)		625,483
Cash (lease payment)	120,000	
Lease receivable		120,000

2. Prepare an amortization schedule that shows the pattern of interest expense for United Cellular Systems and interest revenue for Pinnacle Leasing Services over the lease term.

Date	Payments	Effective Interest	Decrease in Balance	Outstanding Balance
		(6% × Outstanding balance)		
1/1/12				625,483
1/1/12	120,000		120,000	505,483
7/1/12	120,000	.06 (505,483) = 30,329	89,671	415,812
1/1/13	120,000	.06 (415,812) = 24,949	95,051	320,761
7/1/13	120,000	.06 (320,761) = 19,246	100,754	220,007
1/1/14	120,000	.06 (220,007) = 13,200	106,800	113,207
7/1/14	120,000	.06 (113,207) = 6,793*	113,207	0
	720,000		94,517	625,483

*Adjusted for rounding of other numbers in the schedule.

3. Prepare the appropriate entries to record the second lease payment on July 1, 2012, and adjusting entries on December 31, 2012 (the end of both companies' fiscal years).

July 1, 2012

United Cellular Systems (Lessee)

Interest expense [6% × ($625,483 − 120,000)]	30,329	
Lease payable (difference)	89,671	
Cash (lease payment)		120,000

Pinnacle Leasing Services (Lessor)

Cash (lease payment)	120,000	
Lease receivable (difference)		89,671
Interest revenue [6% × ($625,483 − 120,000)]		30,329

December 31, 2012

United Cellular Systems (Lessee)

Interest expense (6% × $415,812: from schedule)	24,949	
Interest payable		24,949
Depreciation expense ($625,483 ÷ 3 years)	208,494	
Accumulated depreciation		208,494

Pinnacle Leasing Services (Lessor)

Interest receivable	24,949	
Interest revenue (6% × $415,812: from schedule)		24,949

Let's turn our attention now to situations in which the lessors are manufacturers or retailers and use lease arrangements as a means of selling their products.

Sales-Type Leases

● LO6

FINANCIAL
Reporting Case

Q2, p. 807

A **sales-type lease** differs from a direct financing lease in only one respect. In addition to interest revenue earned over the lease term, the lessor receives a manufacturer's or dealer's profit on the "sale" of the asset.[19] This additional profit exists when the fair value of the asset (usually the present value of the minimum lease payments, or "selling price") exceeds the

---

[19]A lessor need not be a manufacturer or a dealer for the arrangement to qualify as a sales-type lease. The existence of a profit (or loss) on the sale is the distinguishing factor.

cost or carrying value of the asset sold. Accounting for a sales-type lease is the same as for a direct financing lease except for recognizing the profit at the inception of the lease.[20]

To illustrate, let's modify our previous illustration. Assume all facts are the same except Sans Serif Publishers leased the copier directly from CompuDec Corporation, rather than through the financing intermediary. Also assume CompuDec's cost of the copier was $300,000. If you recall that the lease payments (their present value) provide a selling price of $479,079, you see that CompuDec earns a gross profit on the sale of $479,079 − 300,000 = $179,079. This sales-type lease is demonstrated in Illustration 15–3.

On January 1, 2011, Sans Serif Publishers, Inc., leased a copier from CompuDec Corporation at a price of $479,079.

The lease agreement specifies annual payments of $100,000 beginning January 1, 2011, the inception of the lease, and at each December 31 thereafter through 2015. The six-year lease term ending December 31, 2016, is equal to the estimated useful life of the copier.

CompuDec manufactured the copier at a cost of $300,000.

CompuDec's interest rate for financing the transaction is 10%.

ILLUSTRATION 15–3
Sales-Type Lease

Sales revenue	$479,079
− COGS	300,000
Dealer's profit	$179,079

Remember, no interest has accrued when the first payment is made at the inception of the lease.

Sales-Type Lease*

CompuDec Corporation (Lessor)

Lease receivable (present value of lease payments)	479,079	
Cost of goods sold (lessor's cost)	300,000	
Sales revenue (present value of lease payments)		479,079
Inventory of equipment (lessor's cost)		300,000

First Lease Payment*

CompuDec Corporation (Lessor)

Cash	100,000	
Lease receivable		100,000

---

*Of course, the entries to record the lease and the first payment could be combined into a single entry:

Lease receivable ($479,079 − $100,000)	379,079	
Cost of goods sold	300,000	
Cash	100,000	
Sales revenue		479,079
Inventory of equipment		300,000

You should recognize the similarity between recording both the revenue and cost components of this sale by lease and recording the same components of other sales transactions. As in the sale of any product, gross profit is the difference between sales revenue and cost of goods sold. **Dell Inc.** "sells" some of its products using sales-type leases and disclosed the following in a recent annual report:

Recording a sales-type lease is similar to recording a sale of merchandise on account:

A/R .... {price}
  Sales rev ....   {price}
COGS .... {cost}
  Inventory ...   {cost}

Note 1 (in part)

Dell records revenue from the sale of equipment under sales-type leases as product revenue at the inception of the lease. Sales-type leases also produce financing income, which Dell recognizes at consistent rates of return over the lease term.

Real World Financials

All entries other than the entry at the inception of the lease, which includes the gross profit on the sale, are the same for a sales-type lease and a direct financing lease.

Accounting by the lessee is not affected by how the lessor classifies the lease. All lessee entries are precisely the same as in the previous illustration of a direct financing lease.

Graphic 15–7 shows the relationships among various lease components, using dollar amounts from the previous illustration.

---

[20]It is possible that the asset's carrying value will exceed its fair value, in which case a dealer's loss should be recorded.

GRAPHIC 15–7

Lease Payment Relationships

The difference between the total payments and their present value (selling price of the asset) represents interest.

If the price is higher than the cost to the lessor, the lessor realizes a profit on the sale.

Lessor:		Lessee:
SALES-TYPE LEASE		**CAPITAL LEASE**
Gross Investment in Lease*	**$600,000**	**Minimum Lease Payments**
	Less:	
	Interest during lease term	
	($120,921)	
	Equals:	
Selling Price	**$479,079**	**Purchase Price**
(present value of payments)		(present value of payments)
	Less:	
	Profit on sale[†]	
	($179,079)	
	Equals:	
Cost to Lessor	**$300,000**	**(irrelevant to lessee)**

*The lessor's gross investment in the lease also would include any *unguaranteed* residual value in addition to the minimum lease payments. Any residual value *guaranteed* by the lessee is included in the minimum lease payments (both companies). We address these issues later in the chapter.

[†]If profit is zero, this would be a direct financing lease.

● LO11

The FASB and IASB are working together on a standard that would dramatically impact the way we account for leases, perhaps eliminating the concept of operating leases.

IFRS ILLUSTRATION

WHERE WE'RE HEADED

The IASB and FASB are collaborating on a joint project for a revision of lease accounting standards. The Boards have agreed on a "right of use" model by which the lessee recognizes an asset representing the right to use the leased asset for the lease term and also recognizes a corresponding liability for the present value of the lease payments, regardless of the term of the lease. Many people expect the new standard to result in most, if not all, leases being recorded as an intangible asset for the right of use and a liability for the present value of the lease payments. Thus, the notion of operating leases might disappear.

For an example, let's revisit Sans Serif's operating lease in Illustration 15–1 on p. 815. None of the four criteria was met that would have caused it to be a capital lease, including Criterion 4:

Is the present value of the minimum lease payments
equal to or greater than 90% of the fair value of the asset: **NO**

($348,685 < 90% of $479,079)

$100,000 × 3.48685 = $348,685

Lease payments   Present value

Accordingly, under existing standards, we recorded no asset and no liability for this operating lease. Under the new standard, on the other hand, Sans Serif would be deemed to have received the "right of use" of the asset and would record an intangible asset for the right of use and a liability for the present value of the lease payments:

Leased equipment (intangible asset).. 348,685
    Lease payable (present value of lease payments).................... 348,685

The goal of the two Boards is to issue a final Standard by June of 2011. The focus of the project is *lessee* accounting. *Lessor* accounting will be considered at a later date. The impact of any changes will be significant; U.S. companies alone have over $1.25 *trillion* in operating lease obligations.[21]

PART B

BARGAIN PURCHASE OPTIONS AND RESIDUAL VALUE
Bargain Purchase Options

● LO7

We mentioned earlier that a **bargain purchase option (BPO)** is a provision of some lease contracts that gives the lessee the option of purchasing the leased property at a bargain price. We

---

[21]John Hepp, "Proposed Standard Would Eliminate Operating Lease Accounting," *Grant Thornton Marquee,* Winter 2009.

have discussed BPOs in the context of how they affect the classification of leases, but none of our earlier illustrations included a situation in which a BPO was present. You should have noted that a bargain price is defined in such a way that an additional cash payment is expected when a BPO is included in the agreement. Remember, a bargain price is one that is sufficiently below the property's expected fair value that the exercise of the option appears reasonably assured. Because exercise of the option appears at the inception of the lease to be reasonably assured, payment of the option price is expected to occur when the option becomes exercisable.

The expectation that the option price will be paid effectively adds an additional cash flow to the lease for both the lessee and the lessor. That additional payment is included as a component of minimum lease payments for both the lessor and the lessee. It therefore (a) is included in the computation of the amount to be capitalized (as an asset and a liability) by the *lessee* and (b) reduces the amount of the periodic rent payments the *lessor* will need to receive from the lessee to recover the desired "selling price." This is indicated in Graphic 15–8.

> When a BPO is present, both the lessee and the lessor view the option price as an additional cash payment.

- The **lessee** *adds* the present value of the BPO price to the present value of periodic rental payments when computing the amount to be recorded as a leased asset and a lease liability.
- The **lessor,** when computing periodic rental payments, *subtracts* the present value of the BPO price from the amount to be recovered (fair value) to determine the amount that must be recovered from the lessee through the periodic rental payments.

GRAPHIC 15–8

Effect of a Bargain Purchase Option

For demonstration, let's suppose the copier leased in Illustration 15–3 could be purchased by Sans Serif for an option price of $60,000 at the conclusion of the lease. To make this a "bargain" purchase option, assume the residual value at the conclusion of the lease is expected to be $75,000. This situation is assumed in Illustration 15–4.

ILLUSTRATION 15–4

Bargain Purchase Option

On January 1, 2011, Sans Serif Publishers, Inc., leased a color copier from CompuDec Corporation at a price of $479,079. The lease agreement specifies annual payments beginning January 1, 2011, the inception of the lease, and at each December 31 thereafter through 2015. The estimated useful life of the copier is seven years. On December 31, 2016, at the end of the six-year lease term, the copier is expected to be worth $75,000, and Sans Serif has the option to purchase it for $60,000 on that date. The residual value after seven years is zero.[22] CompuDec manufactured the copier at a cost of $300,000 and its interest rate for financing the transaction is 10%.

Lessee's calculation of PV of minimum lease payments:

Present value of periodic rental payments ($92,931 × 4.79079*)	$445,211
Plus: Present value of the BPO price ($60,000 × .56447†)	33,868
Present value of minimum lease payments (recorded as a leased asset and a lease liability)	$479,079

> The lessee *adds* the PV of the BPO price to determine its asset and liability.

Lessor's calculation of rental payments:

Amount to be recovered (fair value)	$479,079
Less: Present value of the BPO price ($60,000 × .56447†)	(33,868)
Amount to be recovered through periodic rental payments	$445,211
Rental payments at the beginning of each of the next six years: ($445,211 ÷ 4.79079*)	$ 92,931

> The lessor *subtracts* the PV of the BPO price to determine rental payments.

* Present value of an annuity due of $1: $n = 6$, $i = 10\%$.
† Present value of $1: $n = 6$, $i = 10\%$.

The lease amortization schedule for CompuDec and Sans Serif when a BPO is included in the lease agreement is shown in Graphic 15–9.

---

[22]Our discussion of the effect of a bargain purchase option would be precisely the same if our illustration were of a direct financing lease (for instance, if the lessor's cost were $479,079) except that, of course, neither sales revenue nor cost of goods sold would be recorded in a direct financing lease.

GRAPHIC 15-9

Amortization Schedule—with BPO

Date	Payments	Effective Interest	Decrease in Balance	Outstanding Balance
		(10% × Outstanding balance)		
1/1/11				479,079
1/1/11	92,931		92,931	386,148
12/31/11	92,931	.10 (386,148) = 38,615	54,316	331,832
12/31/12	92,931	.10 (331,832) = 33,183	59,748	272,084
12/31/13	92,931	.10 (272,084) = 27,208	65,723	206,361
12/31/14	92,931	.10 (206,361) = 20,636	72,295	134,066
12/31/15	92,931	.10 (134,066) = 13,407	79,524	54,542
12/31/16	60,000	.10 (54,542) = 5,458*	54,542	0
	617,586	138,507	479,079	

Both the lessor and lessee view the BPO price ($60,000) as an additional cash payment.

*Adjusted for rounding of other numbers in the schedule.

Be aware of several points the amortization schedule reveals. First, the six periodic cash payments are now $92,931 as we calculated previously. Notice also that we now include the $60,000 BPO price as an additional lease payment. Despite the different composition of the minimum lease payments, their present value ($479,079) is the same as when we assumed $100,000 periodic payments and no residual value. However, the effective interest that will be recorded over the lease term (as interest expense by the lessee and interest revenue by the lessor) now is more: $138,507. (It was $120,921 before.) The higher interest reflects the fact that payments are farther in the future, causing the outstanding lease balances (and interest on those balances) to be higher during the lease term. Also, note that the total of the lease payments now is more: $617,586. (It was $600,000 before.) This total is referred to as the lessor's **gross investment in the lease** and is disclosed in the lessor's lease footnote.

The lessor's *gross investment in the lease* is the total of periodic rental payments and any residual value.

Recording the exercise of the option is similar to recording the periodic rent payments. That is, a portion of the payment covers interest for the year, and the remaining portion reduces the outstanding liability/receivable balance (to zero with this last payment), as shown in Illustration 15–4A.

ILLUSTRATION 15–4A

Journal Entries—with BPO

The cash payment expected when the BPO is exercised represents part interest and part principal just like the other cash payments.

December 31, 2016

Sans Serif Publishers, Inc. (Lessee)

Depreciation expense ($479,079* ÷ 7 years)	68,440	
Accumulated depreciation		68,440
Interest expense (10% × $54,542)	5,458	
Lease payable (difference)	54,542	
Cash (BPO price)		60,000

CompuDec Corporation (Lessor)

Cash (BPO price)	60,000	
Lease receivable (account balance)		54,582
Interest revenue (10% × outstanding balance)		5,458

*The residual value is zero after the full seven-year useful life.

Note that depreciation also is affected by the BPO. As pointed out earlier, the lessee normally depreciates a leased asset over the term of the lease. But if ownership transfers by contract or by the expected exercise of a bargain purchase option, the asset should be depreciated over the asset's useful life. This reflects the fact that the lessee anticipates using the leased asset for its full useful life. In this illustration, the copier is expected to be useful for seven years, so depreciation is $68,440 ($479,079 ÷ 7 years).

When a BPO Is Exercisable Before the End of the Lease Term

In Illustration 15–4 we assumed that the BPO was exercisable on December 31, 2016—the end of the lease term. Sometimes, though, the lease contract specifies that a BPO becomes exercisable before the designated lease term ends. Since a BPO is expected to be exercised, the lease term ends for accounting purposes when the option becomes exercisable. For example, let's say the BPO in the illustration could be exercised a year earlier—at the end of the fifth year. The effect this would have on accounting for the lease is to change the lease term from six years to five. All calculations would be modified accordingly. Stated differently, minimum lease payments include only the periodic cash payments specified in the agreement that occur prior to the date a BPO becomes exercisable. (We assume the option is exercised at that time and the lease ends.)

> The length of the lease term is limited to the time up to when a bargain purchase option becomes exercisable.

ETHICAL DILEMMA

"I know we had discussed that they're supposed to be worth $24,000 when our purchase option becomes exercisable," Ferris insisted. "That's why we agreed to the lease terms. But, Jenkins, you know how fast computers become dated. We can make a good case that they'll be worth only $10,000 in three years."

The computers to which Ferris referred were acquired by lease. The lease meets none of the criteria for classification as a capital lease except that it would contain a bargain purchase option if the computers could be purchased for $10,000 after three years.

"We could avoid running up our debt that way," Jenkins agreed.

How could debt be avoided?

Do you perceive an ethical problem?

Residual Value

The **residual value** of leased property is an estimate of what its commercial value will be at the end of the lease term. In our previous examples of capital leases for which no BPOs were present, we assumed that the residual value was negligible. Now let's consider the economic effect of a leased asset that does have a material residual value and how that will affect the way both the lessee and the lessor account for the lease agreement.

Suppose the copier leased in Illustration 15–3 was expected to be worth $60,000 at the end of the six-year lease term. Should this influence the lessor's (CompuDec) calculation of periodic rental payments? Other than the possible influence on rental payments, should the lessee (Sans Serif Publishers) be concerned with the residual value of the leased assets? The answer to both questions is maybe. We'll use Illustration 15–5 to see why.

● LO8

On January 1, 2011, Sans Serif Publishers, Inc., leased a color copier from CompuDec Corporation at a price of $479,079. The lease agreement specifies annual payments beginning January 1, 2011, the inception of the lease, and at each December 31 thereafter through 2015. The estimated useful life of the copier is seven years. At the end of the six-year lease term, ending December 31, 2016, the copier is expected to be worth $60,000. CompuDec manufactured the copier at a cost of $300,000* and its interest rate for financing the transaction is 10%.

*This provision is for consistency with Illustration 15–3, which described a sales-type lease. However, our discussion of the effect of a residual value would be precisely the same if our illustration were of a direct financing lease (for instance, if the lessor's cost were $479,079). except that neither sales revenue nor cost of goods sold would be recorded in a direct financing lease.

ILLUSTRATION 15–5

Residual Value

We consider the lessee first.

Effect on the Lessee of a Residual Value

Should the lessee view the residual value as an additional "payment" by the lessee as it did for the BPO price in the previous section? That depends on whether the lessee *guarantees* the residual value to be a particular amount at the end of the lease term.

The guaranteed residual value is considered an additional lease payment that is to be paid in property, or cash, or both.

GUARANTEED RESIDUAL VALUE. Sometimes the lease agreement includes a guarantee by the lessee that the lessor will recover a specified residual value when custody of the asset reverts back to the lessor at the end of the lease term. This not only reduces the lessor's risk but also provides incentive for the lessee to exercise a higher degree of care in maintaining the leased asset to preserve the residual value. The lessee promises to return not only the property but also sufficient cash to provide the lessor with a minimum combined value. In effect, the guaranteed residual value is an additional lease payment that is to be paid in property, or cash, or both. As such, it is included in the minimum lease payments and affects the amount the lessee records as both a leased asset and a lease liability, as shown in Illustration 15–5A.

ILLUSTRATION 15–5A

Lessee's Calculation of the Present Value of Minimum Lease Payments Including a Guaranteed Residual Value

Present value of periodic rental payments ($92,931 × 4.79079*)	$445,211
Plus: Present value of the residual value ($60,000 × .56447†)	33,868
Present value of minimum lease payments (recorded as a leased asset and a lease liability)	$479,079

*Present value of an annuity due of $1: $n = 6$, $i = 10\%$.
†Present value of $1: $n = 6$, $i = 10\%$.

If the lessee obtains title, the lessor's computation of rental payments is unaffected by any residual value.

You should recognize this as the same calculation we used in the previous section when we had a BPO, and so the BPO price was considered an additional lease payment. In fact, the amortization schedule is precisely the same as in Graphic 15–9 on p. 826 when we had a BPO.

A question you might have at this point is: Why did we ignore the residual value earlier when we had a BPO? The reason is obvious when you recall an essential characteristic of a BPO—it's expected to be exercised. So, when it is exercised, title to the leased asset passes to the lessee and, with title, any residual value. When that happens, the residual value cannot be considered an additional lease payment to the lessor.

UNGUARANTEED RESIDUAL VALUE. The previous example demonstrates that when the residual value is guaranteed, the lessee views it as a component of minimum lease payments. But what if the lessee does *not* guarantee the residual value? In that case, the lessee is not obligated to make any payments other than the periodic rental payments. As a result, the present value of the minimum lease payments—recorded as a leased asset and a lease liability—is simply the present value of periodic rental payments ($445,211). The same is true when the residual value is guaranteed by a third-party guarantor. (Insurance companies sometimes assume this role.)

Effect on the Lessor of a Residual Value

GUARANTEED RESIDUAL VALUE. When the residual value is guaranteed, the lessor as well as the lessee views it as a component of minimum lease payments. In fact, even if it is not guaranteed, the lessor still expects to receive it in the form of property, or cash, or both. If CompuDec retains title to the asset at the end of the lease term, then it would anticipate receiving the $60,000 residual value at the conclusion of the lease term. That amount would contribute to the total amount to be recovered by the lessor and would reduce the amount needed to be recovered from the lessee through periodic rental payments. The amount of each payment would be reduced from $100,000 to $92,931, calculated in Illustration 15–5B.

The lessor *subtracts* the PV of the residual value to determine rental payments.

Amount to be recovered (fair value)		$479,079
Less: Present value of the residual value ($60,000 × .56447*)		(33,868)
Amount to be recovered through periodic rental payments		$445,211
Rental payments at the beginning of each of the next six years: ($445,211 ÷ 4.79079†)		$ 92,931

ILLUSTRATION 15–5B

Lessor's Calculation of Rental Payments When Lessor Retains Residual Value

*Present value of $1: $n = 6$, $i = 10\%$.
†Present value of an annuity due of $1: $n = 6$, $i = 10\%$.

You should notice that the lessor's calculation of periodic rental payments is precisely the same as when we had the $60,000 BPO price in a previous section. It also is precisely the reverse of the *lessee's* calculation of the amount to capitalize when the residual value is guaranteed. This is because when the residual value is guaranteed, both view it as an additional lease payment. In accordance with GAAP, the guaranteed residual value is a component of the minimum lease payments for both the lessor and lessee.[23] In fact, the amortization schedule is precisely the same as in Graphic 15–9 on p. 826 when we had a BPO.

If CompuDec had acquired the copier for the $479,079 "selling price," it would be a direct financing lease recorded as follows:

Lease receivable (present value of minimum lease payments)	479,079	
Inventory of equipment (lessor's cost)		479,079

Illustration 15–5, though, states that CompuDec manufactured it at a cost of $300,000, making it a sales-type lease. In Illustration 15–5C, we see the lessor's entries for this sales-type lease along with the lessee's entries for comparison. Only the lessor's initial entry on January 1, 2011, is different. All other entries in Illustration 15–5C are the same whether it's a sales-type lease or a direct financing lease.

Sales-Type Lease, January 1, 2011

ILLUSTRATION 15–5C

Sales-Type Lease with Guaranteed Residual Value

Sans Serif Publishers, Inc. (Lessee)

Leased equipment (present value of lease payments)	479,079	
Lease payable (present value of lease payments)		479,079

CompuDec Corporation (Lessor)

Lease receivable (present value of minimum lease payments*)	479,079	
Cost of goods sold (lessor's cost)	300,000	
Sales revenue (present value of minimum lease payments*)		479,079
Inventory of equipment (lessor's cost)		300,000

Sales revenue	$479,079
− COGS	300,000
Dealer's profit	$179,079

First Lease Payment, January 1, 2011

Sans Serif Publishers, Inc. (Lessee)

Lease payable	92,931	
Cash		92,931

CompuDec Corporation (Lessor)

Cash	92,931	
Lease receivable		92,931

The lessor's minimum lease payments include a residual value only if it is guaranteed (by either the lessee or a third-party guarantor).

*Minimum lease payments include the $60,000 residual value because it's guaranteed.

Notice, too, that the timing of the $60,000 payment is December 31, 2016, the end of the lease term. Remember, the final periodic cash payment on December 31, 2015, is at the beginning of the final year. The journal entries that accompany this final cash payment are shown in Illustration 15–5D.

---

[23]Later you will see that when the residual value is *not* guaranteed, it is *not* considered a component of minimum lease payments for either the lessor or the lessee; but it still affects the amount of periodic lease payments.

ILLUSTRATION 15–5D	December 31, 2015		
Entries to Accompany Final Periodic Payment	**Sans Serif Publishers, Inc. (Lessee)**		
	Depreciation expense [($479,079 − 60,000)* ÷ 6 years]	69,847	
The residual value reduces the asset's depreciable cost to $419,079.	Accumulated depreciation		69,847
	Interest expense (10% × outstanding balance)	13,407	
	Lease payable (difference)	79,524	
As the outstanding balance becomes less toward the end of the lease term, the portion of each payment that represents interest also becomes less.	Cash (lease payment)		92,931
	CompuDec Corporation (Lessor)		
	Cash (lease payment)	92,931	
	Lease receivable		79,524
	Interest revenue (10% × outstanding balance)		13,407

*The depreciable cost is reduced by the lessee-guaranteed residual value.

At December 31, 2016, the lessee's book value of the fully depreciated copier is its $60,000 estimated residual value. If we assume that the actual residual value also is at least $60,000, then the lessee is not obligated to pay cash in addition to returning the copier to the lessor (demonstrated in Illustration 15–5E).[24]

ILLUSTRATION 15–5E	December 31, 2016		
End of Lease Term— Actual Residual Value Equals the Guaranteed Amount	**Sans Serif Publishers, Inc. (Lessee)**		
	Depreciation expense [($479,079 − 60,000)* ÷ 6 years]	69,847	
	Accumulated depreciation		69,847
The sixth and final depreciation charge increases the balance in accumulated depreciation to $419,079.	Interest expense (10% × outstanding balance)	5,458	
	Lease payable (difference)	54,542	
	Accumulated depreciation (account balance)	419,079	
	Leased equipment (account balance)		479,079
The copier is reinstated on the books of the lessor at its fair value at the end of the lease term.	**CompuDec Corporation (Lessor)**		
	Inventory of equipment (residual value)	60,000	
	Lease receivable (account balance)		54,542
	Interest revenue (10% × outstanding balance)		5,458

*The depreciable cost is reduced by the lessee-guaranteed residual value.

However, if we assume that the actual residual value at December 31, 2016, is only $25,000, then the lessee is required to pay $35,000 cash to the lessor in addition to returning the copier. The lessee records this payment as a loss.[25]

UNGUARANTEED RESIDUAL VALUE.   The previous example demonstrates that when the residual value is guaranteed, both the lessor and lessee view it as a component of minimum lease payments. But what if the lessee does *not* guarantee the residual value? From the lessor's perspective, the residual value is a component of *minimum lease payments* only if it is guaranteed (by either the lessee or a third-party guarantor). Yet, even if it is not guaranteed, the lessor still expects to receive it. So, if we modify the previous illustration to assume the residual value is not guaranteed, the lessor's receivable still is $479,079, the

The lessor's minimum lease payments include a residual value only if it is guaranteed (by either the lessee or a third-party guarantor).

---

[24]If the actual value is *more* than the estimated residual value, the lessor may realize a gain if and when the asset subsequently is sold, but the potential gain does not affect the entries at the end of the lease term.

[25]Sometimes by mutual agreement the lessee will sell the leased asset at the end of the lease term and remit the proceeds (plus any deficiency under the guarantee) to the lessor.

present value of the lease payments, including the residual value, so a direct financing lease would be the same as if the residual value is guaranteed.

However, the sales revenue is only $445,211—the present value of the minimum lease payments *not* including the residual value. In other words, sales revenue includes the present value only of the periodic rental payments, not the unguaranteed residual value. Cost of goods sold is similarly reduced by the present value of the unguaranteed residual value, so the initial lessor entry would be modified as follows:

Lease receivable (PV of lease payments plus PV of $60,000 residual value) ...	479,079	
Cost of goods sold ($300,000 − 33,868)	266,132	
Sales revenue ($479,079 − 33,868)*		445,211
Inventory of equipment (lessor's cost)		300,000

*Also can be calculated as the present value of the lessor's minimum lease payments, which do not include the unguaranteed residual value.

> When the lessee doesn't guarantee the residual value, the lessee's net liability ($445,211) and the lessor's net receivable ($479,079) will differ because the former does not include the unguaranteed residual amount.

Sales revenue does not include the unguaranteed residual value because the revenue to be recovered from the lessee is lease payments only. The remainder of the lessor's investment is to be recovered—not from payment by the lessee (as is presumed when the residual value is guaranteed), but by selling, re-leasing, or otherwise obtaining value from the asset when it reverts back to the lessor. You might want to view the situation this way: The portion of the asset sold is the portion not represented by the unguaranteed residual value. So, both the asset's cost and its selling price are reduced by the present value of the portion not sold.

When the residual value is not guaranteed, the lessor bears any loss that results from the actual residual value of the leased asset being less than the original estimate.

Graphic 15–10 summarizes the effect of the residual value of a leased asset for each of the various possibilities regarding the nature of the residual value.

GRAPHIC 15–10

Effect of a Residual Value: A Summary

Is the residual value of a leased asset included in:

	the Lessor's		the Lessee's
	(a) Computation of Lease Payments	**(b)** Minimum Lease Payments	**(c)** Minimum Lease Payments
Lessee gets the residual value (by transfer of title or the expected exercise of a bargain purchase option)	No	No	No
Lessor gets the residual value (title does not transfer; no bargain purchase option)			
• Residual value is *not* guaranteed	Yes	No	No
• Residual value *is* guaranteed by the lessee.	Yes	Yes	Yes
• Residual value is guaranteed by a *third party* guarantor.	Yes	Yes	No

(a) The lessor, when computing periodic rental payments, subtracts the present value of the residual value from the amount to be recovered (fair value) to determine the amount that must be recovered from the lessee through the periodic rent payments.
(b) The present value of the lessor's minimum lease payments is the lease receivable and, in a sales-type lease, the sales revenue.
(c) The present value of the lessee's minimum lease payments is the amount to be capitalized as an asset and a liability.

We have seen how minimum lease payments are affected by a residual value and by a bargain purchase option. Let's now consider how maintenance, insurance, taxes, and other costs usually associated with ownership (called *executory costs*) affect minimum lease payments.

PART C OTHER LEASE ACCOUNTING ISSUES

Executory Costs

● LO9

One of the responsibilities of ownership that is transferred to the lessee in a capital lease is the responsibility to pay for maintenance, insurance, taxes, and any other costs usually associated with ownership. These are referred to as executory costs. Lease agreements usually are written in such a way that these costs are borne by the lessee. These expenditures simply are expensed by the lessee as incurred: repair expense, insurance expense, property tax expense, and so on. Let's return, for example, to Illustration 15–2. Now, suppose that a $2,000 per year maintenance agreement was arranged with an outside service for the leased copier. Sans Serif (the lessee) would expense this fee each year as incurred:

The lessee simply expenses executory costs as incurred.

Maintenance expense	2,000	
Cash (annual fee)		2,000

Any portion of rental payments that represents maintenance, insurance, taxes, or other executory costs is not considered part of minimum lease payments.

The lessor is unaffected by executory costs paid by the lessee.

Sometimes, as an expediency, a lease contract will specify that the lessor is to pay executory costs, but that the lessee will reimburse the lessor through higher rental payments. When rental payments are inflated for this reason, these executory costs are excluded in determining the minimum lease payments. They still are expensed by the lessee, even though paid through the lessor. For demonstration, let's modify Illustration 15–2 to assume the periodic rental payments were increased to $102,000 with the provision the lessor (First LeaseCorp) pays the maintenance fee. We do this in Illustration 15–6.

ILLUSTRATION 15–6

Rental Payments Including Executory Costs Paid by the Lessor

On January 1, 2011, Sans Serif Publishers, Inc., leased a copier from First LeaseCorp. First LeaseCorp purchased the equipment from CompuDec Corporation at a cost of $479,079.
- Six annual payments of $102,000 beginning January 1, 2011.
- Payments include $2,000 which First LeaseCorp will use to pay an annual maintenance fee.
- The interest rate in these financing arrangements is 10%.
- Capital lease to Sans Serif.
- Direct financing lease to First LeaseCorp.

Executory costs that are included in periodic rental payments to be paid by the lessor are, in effect, indirectly paid by the lessee—and expensed by the lessee.

First Payment (January 1, 2011)

Sans Serif Publishers, Inc. (Lessee)

Maintenance expense (2011 fee)	2,000	
Lease payable	100,000	
Cash (lease payment)		102,000

First LeaseCorp (Lessor)

Cash (rental payment)	102,000	
Lease receivable		100,000
Maintenance fee payable*		2,000

*This assumes the $2,000 maintenance fee has not yet been paid to the outside maintenance service.

Discount Rate

An important factor in the overall lease equation that we've glossed over until now is the discount rate used in present value calculations. Because lease payments occur in future periods, we must consider the time value of money when evaluating their present value. The rate is important because it influences virtually every amount reported by both the lessor and the lessee in connection with the lease.

One rate is implicit in the lease agreement. This is the effective interest rate the lease payments provide the lessor over and above the price at which the asset is sold under the lease. It is the desired rate of return the lessor has in mind when deciding the size of the lease payments. (Refer to our earlier calculations of the periodic rental payments.) Usually the lessee is aware of the lessor's implicit rate or can infer it from the asset's fair value.[26] When the lessor's implicit rate is unknown, the lessee should use its own incremental borrowing rate.

This is the rate the lessee would expect to pay a bank if funds were borrowed to buy the asset. When the lessor's implicit rate *is* known, the lessee should use the lower of the two rates.[27]

When the Lessee's Incremental Borrowing Rate is Less Than the Lessor's Implicit Rate

Instances are few in which the lessee actually would use its incremental borrowing rate. Here's why. We noted earlier that, like any other asset, a leased asset should not be recorded at more than its fair value. Look what happens to the present value payments if Sans Serif uses a discount rate less than the 10% rate implicit in Illustration 15–6 (let's say 9%):

$$\underset{\substack{\text{Rental} \\ \text{payments}}}{\$100,000} \times 4.88965^* = \underset{\substack{\text{Lessee's} \\ \text{cost}}}{\$488,965}$$

*Present value of an annuity due of $1: $n = 6$, $i = 9\%$.

But remember, the fair value of the copier was $479,079. The $100,000 amount for the rental payments was derived by the lessor, contemplating a fair value of $479,079 and a desired rate of return (implicit rate) of 10%. So, using a discount rate lower than the lessor's implicit rate usually would result in the present value of minimum lease payments being more than the fair value.

This conclusion does not hold when the leased asset has an unguaranteed residual value. You will recall that the lessor's determinations always include any residual value that accrues to the lessor; but when the lessee doesn't guarantee the residual value, it is *not* included in the lessee's present value calculations. Combining two previous examples, let's modify our demonstration of an unguaranteed residual value (Illustration 15–6) to assume the lessee's incremental borrowing rate was 9%. Because the residual value was expected to contribute to the lessor's recovery of the $479,079 fair value, the rental payments were only $92,931. But, the lessee would ignore the unguaranteed residual value and calculate its cost of the leased asset to be $454,400.

$$\underset{\substack{\text{Rental} \\ \text{payments}}}{\$92,931} \times 4.88965^* = \underset{\substack{\text{Lessee's} \\ \text{cost}}}{\$454,400}$$

*Present value of an annuity due of $1: $n = 6$, $i = 9\%$.

In this case, the present value of minimum lease payments would be *less than* the fair value even though a lower discount rate is used. But again, if there is no residual value, or if the lessee guarantees the residual value, or if the unguaranteed residual value is relatively small, a discount rate lower than the lessor's implicit rate will result in the present value of minimum lease payments being more than the fair value.

When the Lessor's Implicit Rate is Unknown

What if the lessee is unaware of the lessor's implicit rate? This is a logical question in light of the rule that says the lessee should use its own incremental borrowing rate when the lessor's implicit rate is unknown to the lessee. But in practice the lessor's implicit rate usually is known. Even if the lessor chooses not to explicitly disclose the rate, the lessee usually can deduce the rate using information he knows about the value of the leased asset and the lease payments. After all, in making the decision to lease rather than buy, the lessee typically becomes quite knowledgeable about the asset.

Even so, it is possible that a lessee might be unable to derive the lessor's implicit rate. This might happen, for example, if the leased asset has a relatively high residual value. Remember, a residual value (guaranteed or not) is an ingredient in the lessor's calculation of

---

[26]The corporation laws of some states, Florida for instance, actually require the interest rate to be expressly stated in the lease agreement.
[27]*Incremental borrowing rate* refers to the fact that lending institutions tend to view debt as being increasingly risky as the level of debt increases. Thus, additional (i.e., incremental) debt is likely to be loaned at a higher interest rate than existing debt, other things being equal.

the rental payments. Sometimes it may be hard for the lessee to identify the residual value estimated by the lessor if the lessor chooses not to make it known.[28] As the lease term and risk of obsolescence increase, the residual value typically is less of a factor.

ADDITIONAL CONSIDERATION

As pointed out earlier, the management of a lessee company sometimes will try to structure a lease to avoid the criteria that would cause the lease to be classified as a capital lease in order to gain the questionable advantages of off-balance-sheet financing. On the other hand, a lessor normally would prefer recording a capital lease, other things being equal. Two ways sometimes used to structure a lease to qualify as an operating lease by the lessee, but as a capital lease by the lessor are: (1) cause the two parties to use different interest rates and (2) avoid including the residual value in the lessee's minimum lease payments. Let's see how they work:

1. Cause the Two Parties to Use Different Interest Rates.

It was pointed out earlier that a lessee sometimes can claim to be unable to determine the lessor's implicit rate. Not knowing the lessor's implicit rate would permit the lessee to use its own incremental borrowing rate. If higher than the lessor's implicit rate, the present value it produces may cause the 90% of fair value criterion not to be met for the lessee (thus an operating lease) even though the criterion is met for the lessor (thus a capital lease).

2. Avoid Including the Residual Value in the Lessee's Minimum Lease Payments.

The residual value, if guaranteed by the lessee or by a third party guarantor, is included in the minimum lease payments by the lessor when applying the 90% of fair value criterion and thus increases the likelihood that a capital lease will be recorded. However, when the residual value is guaranteed by a third-party guarantor and not by the lessee, it is not included in the lessee's minimum lease payments. So, if a residual value is sufficiently large and guaranteed by a third-party guarantor, it may cause the 90% of fair value criterion to be met by the lessor, but not by the lessee.

Both schemes are unintentionally encouraged by lease accounting rules. As long as arbitrary cutoff points are used (90% of fair value in this case), maneuvers will be devised to circumvent them.

Lessor's Initial Direct Costs

The costs incurred by the lessor that are associated directly with originating a lease and are essential to acquire that lease are referred to as **initial direct costs.** They include legal fees, commissions, evaluating the prospective lessee's financial condition, and preparing and processing lease documents. The method of accounting for initial direct costs depends on the nature of the lease. Remember, a lessor can classify a lease as (1) an operating lease, (2) a direct financing lease, or (3) a sales-type lease. The accounting treatment for initial direct costs by each of the three possible lease types is summarized next.

● LO11

INTERNATIONAL FINANCIAL REPORTING STANDARDS

Present Value of Minimum Lease Payments. Under *IAS No. 17*, both parties to a lease generally use the rate implicit in the lease to discount minimum lease payments.[29] Under U.S. GAAP, lessors use the implicit rate and lessees use the incremental borrowing rate unless the implicit rate is known and is the lower rate.

---

[28]Disclosure requirements provide that the lessor company must disclose the components of its investments in nonoperating leases, which would include any estimated residual values. But the disclosures are aggregate amounts, not amounts of individual leased assets.
[29]"Leases," *International Accounting Standard No. 17* (IASCF), as amended effective January 1, 2009.

1. For *operating leases,* initial direct costs are recorded as assets and amortized over the term of the lease. Since the only revenue an operating lease produces is rental revenue, and that revenue is recognized over the lease term, initial direct costs also are automatically recognized over the lease term to match these costs with the rent revenues they help generate.

2. In *direct financing leases,* interest revenue is earned over the lease term, so initial direct costs are matched with the interest revenues they help generate. Therefore, initial direct costs are not expensed at the outset but are deferred and recognized over the lease term. This can be accomplished by increasing the lessor's *lease receivable* by the total of initial direct costs. Then, as interest revenue is recognized over the lease term at a constant effective rate, the initial direct costs are recognized at the same rate (that is, proportionally).

3. For *sales-type leases,* initial direct costs are expensed at the inception of the lease. Since the usual reason for a sales-type lease is for a manufacturer or a dealer to sell its product, it's reasonable to recognize the costs of creating the transaction as a selling expense in the period of the sale.

Contingent Rentals

Sometimes rental payments may be increased (or decreased) at some future time during the lease term, depending on whether or not some specified event occurs. Usually the contingency is related to revenues, profitability, or usage above some designated level. For example, a recent annual report of **Walmart Stores** included the note re-created in Graphic 15–11.

> **9 Commitments (in part)**
>
> Certain of the leases provide for the payment of contingent rentals based on percentage of sales. Such contingent rentals amounted to $21 million, $33 million and $41 million in 2009, 2008 and 2007, respectively.

GRAPHIC 15–11

Disclosure of Contingent Rentals— Walmart Stores

Real World Financials

Contingent rentals are *not* included in the minimum lease payments because they are not determinable at the inception of the lease. Instead, they are included as components of income when (and if) they occur. Increases or decreases in rental payments that are dependent only on the passage of time are not contingent rentals; these are part of minimum lease payments.

Although contingent rentals are not included in minimum lease payments, they are reported in disclosure notes by both the lessor and lessee.

A Brief Summary

Leasing arrangements often are complex. In studying this chapter you've encountered several features of lease agreements that alter the way we make several of the calculations needed to account for leases. Graphic 15–12 on the next page provides a concise review of the essential lease accounting components, using calculations from a hypothetical lease situation to provide a numerical perspective.

Lease Disclosures

Lease disclosure requirements are quite extensive for both the lessor and lessee. Virtually all aspects of the lease agreement must be disclosed. For *all* leases (a) a general description of the leasing arrangement is required as well as (b) minimum future payments, in the aggregate and for each of the five succeeding fiscal years. Other required disclosures are specific to the type of lease and include: residual values, contingent rentals, sublease rentals, and

The lessor's net investment in the lease is the present value of the gross investment, which is the total of the minimum lease payments (plus any unguaranteed residual value).

GRAPHIC 15–12 Lease Terms and Concepts: A Comprehensive Summary

Lease Situation for Calculations			
($ in 000s)			
Lease term (years)	4	Lessor's cost	$300
Asset's useful life (years)	5	Residual value (Total: $8 + 6 + 5 = $19):	
Lessor's implicit rate (known by lessee)	12%	Guaranteed by lessee	$8
Lessee's incremental borrowing rate	13%	Guaranteed by third party[a]	$6
Rental payments (including executory costs) at the beginning of each year	$102	Unguaranteed	$5
		Executory costs paid annually by lessor	$2
		Bargain purchase option	none

Amount	Description	Calculation
Lessee's:		
Minimum lease payments	Total of periodic rental payments[b] plus residual value guaranteed by lessee or plus BPO price[d]	($100 × 4) + $8 = $408
Leased asset	Present value of minimum lease payments (using lower of lessor's rate and lessee's incremental borrowing rate); cannot exceed fair value	($100 × 3.40183[e]) + ($8 × .63552[f]) = $345
Lease liability at inception	Same as leased asset	($100 × 3.40183[e]) + ($8 × .63552[f]) = $345
Lessor's:		
Minimum lease payments	Total of periodic rental payments[b] plus guaranteed[c] residual value or plus BPO price[d]	($100 × 4) + ($8 + 6) = $414
Lease receivable	Present value of minimum lease payments (using lessor's rate)	($100 × 3.40183[e]) + ($8 × .63552[f]) = $345
If sales-type lease:		
Sales revenue	Present value of lessor's minimum lease payments	($100 × 3.40183[e]) + ($14 × .63552[f]) = $349
Cost of goods sold	Lessor's cost – present value of unguaranteed residual value	$300 – ($5 × .63552[f]) = $297
Dealer's profit	Sales revenue – cost of goods sold	$349 – 297 = $52

[a]Beyond any amount guaranteed by the lessee ($8 + 6 minus any amount paid by the lessee).

[b]Any portion of rental payments that represents maintenance, insurance, taxes, or other executory costs is not considered part of minimum lease payments. In this case, rentals are reduced as follows: $102 – 2 = $100.

[c]By lessee and/or by third party.

[d]In this context, a residual value and a BPO price are mutually exclusive: if a BPO exists, any residual value is expected to remain with the lessee and is not considered an additional payment.

[e]Present value of annuity due of $1: $n = 4$, $i = 12\%$.

[f]Present value of $1: $n = 4$, $i = 12\%$.

executory costs. The lessor must disclose its **net investment in the lease.** This amount is the present value of the **gross investment in the lease,** which is the total of the minimum lease payments (plus any unguaranteed residual value). Some representative disclosure examples are shown in Graphics 15–13 (lessor) and 15–14 (lessee).

IBM is a manufacturer that relies heavily on leasing as a means of selling its products. Its disclosure of sales-type leases is shown in Graphic 15–13.

G Financing Receivables (in part)

(dollars in millions)

At December 31:	2008	2007
Current:		
Net investment in sales-type and direct financing leases	$ 4,226	$ 4,746
Commercial financing receivables	5,781	6,263
Customer loans receivable	4,861	4,652
Installment payment receivables	608	629
Total	$15,477	$16,289
Noncurrent:		
Net investment in sales-type and direct financing leases	$ 5,938	$ 6,805
Commercial financing receivables	94	113
Customer loans receivable	4,718	4,931
Installment payment receivables	433	474
Total	$11,183	$ 11,603

Net investment in sales-type and direct financing leases is for leases that relate principally to the company's equipment and are for terms ranging from two to seven years. Net investment in sales-type and direct financing leases includes unguaranteed residual values of $916 million and $915 million at December 31, 2008 and 2007, respectively, and is reflected net of unearned income of $1,049 million and $1,016 million and of allowance for uncollectible accounts receivable of $217 million and $127 million at those dates, respectively.

GRAPHIC 15–13

Lessor Disclosure of Sales-Type Leases—IBM Corporation

Real World Financials

Walmart Stores leases facilities under both operating and capital leases. Its long-term obligations under these lease agreements are disclosed in a note to its financial statements (see Graphic 15–14).

Note 9 Commitments (in part)

The Company and certain of its subsidiaries have long-term leases for stores and equipment. Rentals (including, for certain leases, amounts applicable to taxes, insurance, maintenance, other operating expenses and contingent rentals) under all operating leases were $1.8 billion, $1.6 billion, and $1.4 billion in 2009, 2008, and 2007, respectively. Aggregate minimum annual rentals at January 31, 2009, under non-cancelable leases are as follows (in millions):

Fiscal Year	Operating Leases	Capital Leases
2010	$ 1,161	$ 569
2011	1,138	556
2012	997	527
2013	888	492
2014	816	460
Thereafter	7,830	2,914
Total minimum rentals	$12,830	$5,518
Less estimated executory costs		47
Net minimum lease payments		5,471
Less imputed interest at rates ranging from 3.0% to 13.6%		1,956
Present value of minimum lease payments		$3,515

GRAPHIC 15–14

Lessee Disclosure of Leases—Walmart Stores

Real World Financials

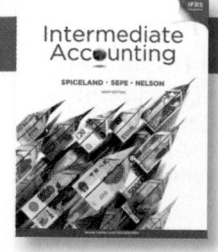

Leasing sometimes is used as a means of off-balance-sheet financing.

DECISION MAKERS' PERSPECTIVE—Financial Statement Impact

As indicated in the Decision Makers' Perspective at the beginning of the chapter, leasing can allow a firm to conserve assets, to avoid some risks of owning assets, and to obtain favorable tax benefits. These advantages are desirable. It also was pointed out earlier that some firms try to obscure the realities of their financial position through off-balance-sheet financing or by avoiding violating terms of contracts that limit the amount of debt a company can have. Accounting guidelines are designed to limit the ability of firms to hide financial realities. Nevertheless, investors and creditors should be alert to the impact leases can have on a company's financial position and on its risk. ●

Balance Sheet and Income Statement

Lease liabilities affect the debt to equity ratio and the rate of return on assets.

Capital lease transactions impact several of a firm's financial ratios. Because we record liabilities for capital leases, the debt-equity ratio (liabilities divided by shareholders' equity) is immediately impacted. Because we also record leased assets, the immediate impact on the rate of return on assets (net income divided by assets) is negative, but the lasting effect depends on how leased assets are utilized to enhance future net income. As illustrated in this chapter, the financial statement impact of a capital lease is no different from that of an installment purchase.

Do operating leases create long-term commitments equivalent to liabilities?

Operating lease commitments create problems during an economic downturn.

Even operating leases, though, can significantly affect risk. Operating leases represent long-term commitments that can become a problem if business declines and cash inflows drop off. For example, long-term lease commitments became a big problem for **Businessland** in the early 1990s. The company's revenues declined but it was saddled with lease commitments for numerous facilities the company no longer occupied. Additionally, the stock's market price declined from $11.88 to $.88 in one year. More recently, in 2009 the economic crisis caught many companies with a deadly combination of declining cash inflows and cash outflow commitments for lease agreements. Nearly four billion dollars in off-balance sheet obligations related to operating lease commitments was a major contributor to **Circuit City**'s demise after a 60-year history as a leader in the electronics industry.

The net income difference between treating a lease as a capital lease versus an operating lease generally is not significant.

Whether leases are capitalized or treated as operating leases affects the income statement as well as the balance sheet. However, the impact on the income statement generally is not significant. Over the life of a lease, total expenses are equal regardless of the accounting treatment of a lease. If the lease is capitalized, total expenses comprise interest and depreciation. The total of these equals the total amount of rental payments, which would constitute rent expense if not capitalized. There is, however, a timing difference between lease capitalization and operating lease treatment, but the timing difference usually isn't great.

The difference in impact on the balance sheet between capital leases and operating leases is significant.

The more significant difference between capital leases and operating leases is the impact on the balance sheet. As mentioned above, a capital lease adds to both the asset and liability side of the balance sheet; operating leases do not affect the balance sheet at all. How can external financial statement users adjust their analysis to incorporate the balance sheet differences between capital and operating leases? A frequently offered suggestion is to capitalize all noncancelable lease commitments, including those related to operating leases. Some financial analysts, in fact, do this on their own to get a better feel for a company's actual debt position.

To illustrate, refer to Graphic 15–14 on the previous page, which reveals the operating lease commitments disclosed by **Walmart Stores**. If these arrangements were considered capital leases, these payments would be capitalized (reported at the present value of all future payments). By making some reasonable assumptions, we can estimate the present value of all future payments to be made on existing operating leases. For example, the interest rates used by Walmart to discount rental payments on capital leases range from 3.0% to 13.6%. If we use the approximate average rate of 10%, and make certain other assumptions, we can determine the debt equivalent of the operating lease commitments as shown in Graphic 15–15.

GRAPHIC 15–15

Estimating the Debt Equivalent of Operating Lease Commitments; Walmart Stores

Real World Financials

Capitalized Value or Debt Equivalent of Walmart's Operating Leases

Fiscal Years	Operating Leases	PV Factor 10%	Present Value
2010	$ 1,161	.909	$1,055
2011	1,138	.826	940
2012	997	.751	749
2013	888	.683	607
2014	816	.621	507
Thereafter	7,830	.386*	3,022
Total minimum rentals	$12,830		$6,880

*This is the PV factor for $i = 10\%$, $n = 10$, which treats payments after 2014 as occurring in 2019, an assumption due to not knowing precise dates of specific payments after 2014.

If capitalized, these operating lease commitments would add $6,880 million to Walmart's liabilities and approximately $6,880 to the company's assets.[30] Let's look at the impact this would have on the company's debt to equity ratio and its return on assets ratio using selected financial statement information taken from Walmart's annual report for the fiscal year ending January 31, 2009, shown next:

	($ in millions)
Total assets	$163,429
Total liabilities	98,144
Total shareholders' equity	65,285
Net income	13,400

The debt to equity and return on assets ratios are calculated in Graphic 15–16 without considering the capitalization of operating leases and then again after adding $6,880 million to both total assets and total liabilities. In the calculation of return on assets, we use only the year-end total assets rather than the average total assets for the year. Also, we assume no impact on income.

GRAPHIC 15–16

Ratios with and without Capitalization of Operating Leases; Walmart Stores

	($ in millions)	
	Without Capitalization	**With Capitalization**
Debt to equity ratio	$\dfrac{\$98,144}{\$65,285} = 1.50$	$\dfrac{\$105,024}{\$65,285} = 1.61$
Return on assets	$\dfrac{\$13,400}{\$163,429} = 8.2\%$	$\dfrac{\$13,400}{\$170,309} = 7.9\%$

The debt to equity ratio rises from 1.50 to 1.61, and the return on assets ratio declines from 8.2% to 7.9%.

Statement of Cash Flow Impact

OPERATING LEASES.   Remember, lease payments for operating leases represent rent—expense to the lessee, revenue for the lessor. These amounts are included in net income, so both the lessee and lessor report cash payments for operating leases in a statement of cash flows as cash flows from operating activities.

Operating leases are not reported in a statement of cash flows at the lease's inception.

---

[30]If these operating leases were capitalized, both assets and liabilities would increase by the same amount at inception of the lease. However, in later years, the leased asset account balance and the lease liability account will, generally, not be equal. The leased asset account is reduced by depreciation and the lease liability account is reduced (amortized) to zero using the effective interest method.

The interest portion of a capital lease payment is a cash flow from operating activities and the principal portion is a cash flow from financing activities.

CAPITAL LEASES AND DIRECT FINANCING LEASES. You've learned in this chapter that capital leases are agreements that we identify as being formulated outwardly as leases, but which are in reality installment purchases, so we account for them as such. Each rental payment (except the first if paid at inception) includes both an amount that represents interest and an amount that represents a reduction of principal. In a statement of cash flows, then, the lessee reports the interest portion as a cash outflow from operating activities and the principal portion as a cash outflow from financing activities. On the other side of the transaction, the lessor in a direct financing lease reports the interest portion as a cash inflow from operating activities and the principal portion as a cash inflow from investing activities. Both the lessee and lessor report the lease at its inception as a noncash investing/financing activity.

Cash receipts from a sales-type lease are cash flows from operating activities.

SALES-TYPE LEASES. A sales-type lease differs from a direct-financing lease for the lessor in that we assume the lessor is actually selling its product. Consistent with reporting sales of products under installment sales agreements rather than lease agreements, the lessor reports cash receipts from a sales-type lease as cash inflows from operating activities.

CONCEPT REVIEW EXERCISE

VARIOUS LEASE ACCOUNTING ISSUES

(This is an extension of the previous Concept Review Exercise.)
United Cellular Systems leased a satellite transmission device from Satellite Technology Corporation on January 1, 2012. Satellite Technology paid $500,000 for the transmission device. Its retail value is $653,681.

Terms of the Lease Agreement and Related Information:

Lease term	3 years (6 semiannual periods)
Semiannual rental payments	$123,000 at the beginning of each period
Economic life of asset	4 years
Implicit interest rate	12%
(Also lessee's incremental borrowing rate)	
Unguaranteed residual value	$40,000
Regulatory fees paid by lessor	$3,000/twice each year (included in rentals)
Lessor's initial direct costs	$4,500
Contingent rental payments	Additional $4,000 if revenues exceed a specified base

Required:

1. Prepare an amortization schedule that describes the pattern of interest expense over the lease term for United Cellular Systems.
2. Prepare an amortization schedule that describes the pattern of interest revenue over the lease term for Satellite Technology.
3. Prepare the appropriate entries for both United Cellular Systems and Satellite Technology on January 1 and June 30, 2012.
4. Prepare the appropriate entries for both United Cellular Systems and Satellite Technology on December 31, 2014 (the end of the lease term), assuming the device is returned to the lessor and its actual residual value is $14,000 on that date.

SOLUTION

1. Prepare an amortization schedule that describes the pattern of interest expense over the lease term for United Cellular Systems.

Calculation of the Present Value of Minimum Lease Payments:

Present value of periodic rental payments excluding executory costs of $3,000:

$$(\$120,000 \times 5.21236^*) = \$625,483$$

*Present value of an annuity due of $1: $n = 6$, $i = 6\%$.
Note: The *unguaranteed* residual value is excluded from minimum lease payments for both the lessee and lessor.

Date	Payments	Effective Interest	Decrease in Balance	Outstanding Balance
		(6% × Outstanding balance)		
1/1/12				625,483
1/1/12	120,000		120,000	505,483
6/30/12	120,000	.06 (505,483) = 30,329	89,671	415,812
1/1/13	120,000	.06 (415,812) = 24,949	95,051	320,761
6/30/13	120,000	.06 (320,761) = 19,246	100,754	220,007
1/1/14	120,000	.06 (220,007) = 13,200	106,800	113,207
6/30/14	120,000	.06 (113,207) = 6,793*	113,207	0
	720,000		94,517	625,483

*Adjusted for rounding of other numbers in the schedule.

2. Prepare an amortization schedule that describes the pattern of interest revenue over the lease term for Satellite Technology.

Calculation of the Lessor's Net Investment:

Present value of periodic rental payments excluding executory costs of $3,000 ($120,000 × 5.21236*) $625,483

Plus: Present value of the unguaranteed residual value ($40,000 × .70496†) 28,198

Lessor's net investment in lease $653,681

*Present value of an annuity due of $1: $n = 6$, $i = 6\%$.
†Present value of $1: $n = 6$, $i = 6\%$.
Note: The *unguaranteed* residual value is excluded from minimum lease payments, but is part of the lessor's gross and net investment in the lease.

Date	Payments	Effective Interest	Decrease in Balance	Outstanding Balance
		(6% × Outstanding balance)		
1/1/12				653,681
1/1/12	120,000		120,000	533,681
6/30/12	120,000	.06 (533,681) = 32,021	87,979	445,702
1/1/13	120,000	.06 (445,702) = 26,742	93,258	352,444
6/30/13	120,000	.06 (352,444) = 21,147	98,853	253,591
1/1/14	120,000	.06 (253,591) = 15,215	104,785	148,806
6/30/14	120,000	.06 (148,806) = 8,928	111,072	37,734
12/31/14	40,000	.06 (37,734) = 2,266*	37,734	0
	760,000		106,319	653,681

*Adjusted for rounding of other numbers in the schedule.

3. Prepare the appropriate entries for both United Cellular Systems and Satellite Technology on January 1 and June 30, 2012.

January 1, 2012

United Cellular Systems (Lessee)

Leased equipment (calculated above) 625,483
  Lease payable (calculated above) 625,483

Lease payable (payment less executory costs) 120,000
Regulatory fees expense (executory costs) 3,000
  Cash (lease payment) 123,000

Satellite Technology (Lessor)

Lease receivable (PV of lease payments + PV $40,000 residual value)[a]	653,681	
Cost of goods sold [$500,000 − ($40,000[a] × .70496)]	471,802	
Sales revenue (present value of minimum lease payments[b])		625,483
Inventory of equipment (lessor's cost)		500,000
Selling expense	4,500	
Cash (initial direct costs)		4,500
Cash (lease payment)	123,000	
Regulatory fees payable (or cash)		3,000
Lease receivable (payment less executory costs)		120,000

[a]This is the unguaranteed residual value.
[b]Also, $653,681 − ($40,000[a] × .70496).

June 30, 2012

United Cellular Systems (Lessee)

Interest expense [6% × ($625,483 − 120,000)]	30,329	
Lease payable (difference)	89,671	
Regulatory fees expense (annual fee)	3,000	
Cash (lease payment)		123,000

Satellite Technology (Lessor)

Cash (lease payment)	123,000	
Regulatory fees payable (or cash)		3,000
Lease receivable (to balance)		87,979
Interest revenue [6% × ($653,681 − 120,000)]		32,021

4. Prepare the appropriate entries for both United Cellular Systems and Satellite Technology on December 31, 2014 (the end of the lease term), assuming the device is returned to the lessor and its actual residual value is $14,000 on that date.

December 31, 2014

United Cellular Systems (Lessee)

Depreciation expense ($625,483 ÷ 3 years)	208,494	
Accumulated depreciation		208,494
Accumulated depreciation (account balance)	625,483	
Leased equipment (account balance)		625,483

Satellite Technology (Lessor)

Inventory of equipment (actual residual value)	14,000	
Loss on leased assets ($40,000 − 14,000)	26,000	
Lease receivable (account balance)		37,734
Interest revenue (6% × $37,734: from schedule)		2,266

PART D SPECIAL LEASING ARRANGEMENTS

Sale-Leaseback Arrangements

● LO10

In a **sale-leaseback transaction,** the owner of an asset sells it and immediately leases it back from the new owner. Sound strange? Maybe, but this arrangement is common. In a sale-leaseback transaction two things happen:

1. The seller-lessee receives cash from the sale of the asset.
2. The seller-lessee pays periodic rent payments to the buyer-lessor to retain the use of the asset.

What motivates this kind of arrangement? The two most common reasons are: (1) If the asset had been financed originally with debt and interest rates have fallen, the sale-leaseback transaction can be used to effectively refinance at a lower rate. (2) The most likely motivation for a sale-leaseback transaction is to generate cash.

Capital Leases

Illustration 15–7 demonstrates a sale-leaseback involving a capital lease for warehouses. The sale and simultaneous leaseback of the warehouses should be viewed as a single borrowing transaction. Although there appear to be two separate transactions, look closer at the substance of the agreement. Teledyne still retains the use of the warehouses that it had prior to the sale and leaseback. What is different? Teledyne has $900,000 cash and a noncancelable obligation to make annual payments of $133,155. In substance, Teledyne simply has borrowed $900,000 to be repaid over 10 years along with 10% interest. From the perspective of substance over form, we do not immediately recognize the $300,000 gain on the sale of the warehouses but defer the gain to be recognized over the term of the lease (or the useful life of the asset if title is expected to transfer outright or by the exercise of a BPO).

Recording a sale-leaseback transaction follows the basic accounting concept of substance over form.

Teledyne Distribution Center was in need of cash. Its solution: sell its four warehouses for $900,000, then lease back the warehouses to obtain their continued use. The warehouses had a carrying value on Teledyne's books of $600,000 (original cost $950,000). Other information:

1. The sale date is December 31, 2011.
2. The noncancelable lease term is 10 years and requires annual payments of $133,155 beginning December 31, 2011. The estimated remaining useful life of the warehouses is 10 years.
3. The annual rental payments (present value $900,000) provides the lessor with a 10% rate of return on the financing arrangement.* Teledyne's incremental borrowing rate is 10%.
4. Teledyne depreciates its warehouses on a straight-line basis.

ILLUSTRATION 15–7

Sale-Leaseback

December 31, 2011

Cash	900,000	
Accumulated depreciation ($950,000 – 600,000)	350,000	
Warehouses (cost)		950,000
Deferred gain on sale-leaseback (difference)		300,000
Leased warehouses (present value of lease payments)	900,000	
Lease payable (present value of lease payments)		900,000
Lease payable	133,155	
Cash		133,155

The gain on sale-leaseback is deferred and recognized over the lease term as a reduction of depreciation expense.

December 31, 2012

Interest expense [10% × ($900,000 – 133,155)]	76,685	
Lease payable (difference)	56,470	
Cash (rental payment)		133,155
Depreciation expense ($900,000 ÷ 10 years)	90,000	
Accumulated depreciation		90,000
Deferred gain on sale-leaseback ($300,000 ÷ 10 years)	30,000	
Depreciation expense		30,000

*$133,155 × 6.75902 = $900,000 ($899,997.31 rounded)
  Rent   (from Table 6)   Present
payments $n = 10, i = 10\%$ value

Since the lease term is equal to the expected useful life of the warehouses (>75%), the leaseback must be recorded by the lessee as a capital lease.[31] There typically is interdependency between the lease terms and the price at which the asset is sold. The earnings process is not complete at the time of sale but is completed over the term of the lease. So, viewing the sale and the leaseback as a single transaction is consistent with the realization principle. Look closely at the 2012 entries to see the net effect of recording the sale-leaseback this way. Amortizing the deferred gain over the lease term as a reduction of depreciation expense decreases depreciation each year to $60,000.[32] Interest expense is $76,685. If Teledyne had *not* sold the warehouses ($600,000 carrying value) and had borrowed $900,000 cash by issuing an installment note, the 2012 effect would have been virtually identical:

<table>
<tr><td colspan="3" align="center">**December 31, 2012**</td></tr>
<tr><td>Interest expense [10% × ($900,000 − 133,155)]</td><td>76,685</td><td></td></tr>
<tr><td>Note payable (difference)</td><td>56,470</td><td></td></tr>
<tr><td>   Cash (installment payment)</td><td></td><td>133,155</td></tr>
<tr><td>Depreciation expense ($600,000 ÷ 10 years)</td><td>60,000</td><td></td></tr>
<tr><td>   Accumulated depreciation</td><td></td><td>60,000</td></tr>
</table>

Depreciating the carrying value of the warehouses over their remaining useful life produces depreciation equal to the net depreciation recorded in a sale-leaseback.

The deferred gain is reported in the balance sheet as a valuation (contra) account, offsetting the leased asset. The 2012 balance sheet effect of the sale-leaseback transaction and a $900,000 installment note are compared in Graphic 15–17. Once again, the effect is virtually identical.

GRAPHIC 15–17

Comparison of a Sale-Leaseback and a Purchase

	Sale-Leaseback	Retain Asset; Borrow Cash
Assets		
Leased asset	$900,000	$950,000
Less: Accumulated depreciation	(90,000)	(410,000)
Less: Deferred gain ($300,000 − 30,000)	(270,000)	
	$540,000	$540,000
Liabilities		
Lease payable ($900,000 − 133,155 − 56,470)	$710,375	
Note payable ($900,000 − 133,155 − 56,470)		$710,375

Accounting by the buyer/lessor is no different in a sale-leaseback transaction than another lease transaction. That is, it records a lease in accordance with the usual lease guidelines.

Operating Leases

If the leaseback portion of the previous sale-leaseback transaction were classified as an operating lease, the gain still would be deferred but would be recognized as a reduction of rent expense rather than depreciation. There is no leased asset to depreciate.[33]

<table>
<tr><td colspan="3" align="center">**December 31, 2012**</td></tr>
<tr><td>Deferred gain on sale-leaseback ($300,000 ÷ 10 years)</td><td>30,000</td><td></td></tr>
<tr><td>   Rent expense</td><td></td><td>30,000</td></tr>
</table>

Those of you with a healthy sense of skepticism will question whether the leaseback portion of our sale-leaseback situation could qualify as an operating lease. After all, the 10-year

---

[31]The fourth criterion also is met. The present value of lease payments ($900,000) is 100% (>90%) of the fair value of the warehouses ($900,000). Meeting any one of the four criteria is sufficient.
[32]If depreciation is over the useful life of the leased asset rather than the lease term because ownership is expected to transfer to the lessee, amortization of the deferred gain also would be over the useful life. If a leaseback of land is a capital lease, the amortization of the deferred gain is recorded as revenue.
[33]The deferred gain would be reported as a liability since it could not be offset against a leased asset.

lease term is equal to the 10-year remaining useful life. But when you remember that neither the third (75% of economic life) nor the fourth (90% recovery of fair value) capital lease classification criterion applies if the inception of the lease occurs during the last 25% of an asset's economic life, you see the possibility of an operating lease. Suppose, for instance, that the original useful life of the warehouses was 40 years. In that case, the current lease term would occur during the last 25% of an asset's economic life and we would have an operating lease.

Losses on Sale-Leasebacks

In a sale-leaseback, any gain on the sale of the asset is deferred and amortized. However, a real loss on the sale of the property is recognized immediately—not deferred. A real loss means the fair value is less than the carrying amount of the asset. On the other hand, if the fair value exceeds the carrying amount, but the asset is sold to the buyer/lessor for less than the carrying amount, an artificial loss is produced that is probably in substance a prepayment of rent and should be deferred and amortized.

INTERNATIONAL FINANCIAL REPORTING STANDARDS

Recognizing a Gain on a Sale and Leaseback Transaction.

Operating Lease:

● LO11

When the leaseback is an operating lease (as long as the lease payments and sales price are at fair value), under *IAS No. 17*, any gain on the sale is recognized immediately but is amortized over the lease term using U.S. GAAP.[34]

For example, suppose Madison Storage sold its warehouse to an insurance company on January 1, 2011, for $400,000 and immediately leased the building back. The operating lease calls for annual rental payments of $25,000 for 12 years of the building's estimated 50-year useful life. The building has a fair value of $400,000 and a carrying value of $325,000 (its original cost was $500,000). The rental payments of $25,000 are payable to the insurance company each December 31. Here's a comparison:

IFRS ILLUSTRATION

	U.S. GAAP		IFRS	
January 1, 2011				
Cash (given)	400,000		400,000	
Accumulated depreciation (cost minus carrying value)	175,000		175,000	
Building (original cost)		500,000		500,000
Deferred gain on sale-leaseback		75,000		
Gain on sale-leaseback (difference)				75,000
December 31, 2011				
Rent expense	25,000		25,000	
Cash (lease payment)		25,000		25,000
Deferred gain on sale-leaseback	6,250			
Rent expense ($75,000 ÷ 12 years)		6,250		

Finance (Capital) Lease:

When the leaseback is a finance (capital) lease, under *IAS No. 17*, the gain is recognized over the lease term, but is recognized over the useful life of the asset under U.S. GAAP. When debiting the deferred gain each period, by either set of standards, the credit is to depreciation expense.

---

[34]"Leases," *International Accounting Standard No. 17* (IASCF), as amended effective January 1, 2009.

Real Estate Leases

Some leases involve land—exclusively or in part. The concepts we discussed in the chapter also relate to **real estate leases.** But the fact that land has an unlimited life causes us to modify how we account for some leases involving real estate.

Leases of Land Only

Because the useful life of land is indefinite, the risks and rewards of ownership cannot be presumed transferred from the lessor to the lessee unless title to the land is expected to transfer—outright or by the expected exercise of a bargain purchase option (criterion 1 or criterion 2). Since the useful life is undefined, the third and fourth criteria are not applicable. Relatedly, because the leased asset is land, depreciation is inappropriate.

Leases of Land and Building

When the leased property includes both land and a building and the lease transfers ownership or is expected to by exercise of a BPO, the lessee should record each leased asset separately. The present value of the minimum lease payments is allocated between the leased land and leased building accounts on the basis of their relative fair values.

When neither of the first two capital lease criteria is met, the question arises as to whether the third and fourth criteria apply. Because they logically should apply to the building (because its life is limited) but not to the land (because its life is unlimited), the profession employs an arbitrary guideline. If the fair value of the land is less than 25% of the combined fair value, it is in effect ignored and both the lessee and the lessor treat the land and building as a single unit. The single leased asset is depreciated as if land were not involved. If the fair value of the land is 25% or more of the combined fair value, both the lessee and the lessor treat the land and building as two separate leases. Thus, the land lease is an operating lease, and the building lease is classified and accounted for in the manner described in the chapter.

Leases of Only Part of a Building

Some of the most common of leases involve leasing only part of a building. For instance, businesses frequently lease space in an office building or individual stores in a shopping mall. Practical difficulties arise when applying lease accounting procedures in these situations. What is the cost of the third shop from the entrance in a $14 million mall? What is the fair value of a sixth floor office suite in a 40-floor office complex? Despite practical difficulties, usual lease accounting treatment applies. It may, however, be necessary to employ real estate appraisals or replacement cost information to arrive at reasonable estimates of cost or fair value.

INTERNATIONAL FINANCIAL REPORTING STANDARDS

Leases of Land and Buildings. Under *IAS No. 17*, land and building elements are considered *separately* unless the land element is not material.[35] This often results in classification of the land component as an operating lease.

Under U.S. GAAP, land and building elements generally are accounted for as a single unit, unless land represents more than 25% of the total fair value of the leased property.

Leveraged Leases

In a **leveraged lease,** a third-party, long-term creditor provides nonrecourse financing for a lease agreement between a lessor and lessee. The term *leveraged* refers to the fact that the lessor acquires title to the asset after borrowing a large part of the investment.

---

[35]"Leases," *International Accounting Standard No. 17* (IASCF), as amended effective January 1, 2009.

From the lessee's perspective, accounting for a leveraged lease is not distinguishable from accounting for a nonleveraged lease. Accounting for leveraged leases by the lessor is similar to that for nonleveraged leases. A lessor records its investment (receivable) net of the nonrecourse debt. The lessor's liability to the lender is offset against its lease receivable from the lessee because its role is in substance that of a mortgage broker. That is, the lessor earns income by serving as an agent for a firm wishing to acquire property and a lender seeking an investment. The lessor borrows enough cash from the lender to acquire the property, which is in turn leased to the lessee under a capital lease. Payments from the lessee are applied to the note held by the lender. The note may be assumed by the lessee *without recourse* such that the lessor is absolved of responsibility for its payment. In order to qualify for favorable treatment under the tax code, the lessor must maintain at least a minimum percentage of equity position in the asset. Also, the lessor should report income from the lease only in those years when the receivable exceeds the liability.

> A lessor records its investment (receivable) net of the nonrecourse debt and reports income from the lease only in those years when the receivable exceeds the liability.

FINANCIAL REPORTING CASE SOLUTION

1. **How would HG's revenues "take a hit" as a result of more customers leasing than buying labeling machines?** *(p. 815)*   When HG leases machines under operating leases, it reports revenue as it collects "rent" over the lease term. When HG sells machines, on the other hand, it recognizes revenue "up front" in the year of sales. Actually, total revenues are not necessarily less with a lease, but are spread out over the several years of the lease term. This delays the recognition of revenues, creating the "hit" in the reporting periods in which a shift to leasing occurs.

2. **Under what kind of leasing arrangements would the "hit" not occur?** *(p. 822)*   The hit will not occur when HG leases its machines under sales-type leases. In those cases, despite the fact that the contract specifies a lease, in effect, HG actually sells its machines under the arrangement. Consequently, HG will recognize sales revenue (and cost of goods sold) at the inception of the lease. The amount recognized is roughly the same as if customers actually buy the machines. As a result, the income statement will not receive the hit created by the substitution of operating leases for outright sales. ●

THE BOTTOM LINE

- ● **LO1**   Leasing is used as a means of financing assets as well as achieving operational and tax objectives. (p. 808)
- ● **LO2**   In keeping with the concept of substance over form, a lease is accounted for as either a rental agreement or a purchase/sale accompanied by debt financing. (p. 809)
- ● **LO3**   A lessee should classify a lease transaction as a capital lease if it is noncancelable and if one or more of four classification criteria are met. Otherwise, it is an operating lease. A lessor records a lease as a direct financing lease or a sales-type lease only if two conditions relating to revenue realization are met in addition to one of the four classification criteria. (p. 811)
- ● **LO4**   In an operating lease a sale is not recorded by the lessor; a purchase is not recorded by the lessee. Instead, the periodic rental payments are accounted for as rent revenue by the lessor and rent expense by the lessee. (p. 815)
- ● **LO5**   In a capital lease the lessee records a leased asset at the present value of the minimum lease payments. A capital lease is recorded by the lessor as a sales-type lease or direct financing lease, depending on whether the lease provides the lessor a dealer's profit. (p. 817)
- ● **LO6**   A sales-type lease requires recording sales revenue and cost of goods sold by the lessor at the inception of the lease. All other entries are the same as in a direct financing lease. (p. 822)
- ● **LO7**   A bargain purchase option is included as a component of minimum lease payments for both the lessor and the lessee. The lease term effectively ends when the BPO is exercisable. (p. 824)

- **LO8**   A lessee-guaranteed residual value is included as a component of minimum lease payments for both the lessor and the lessee. An unguaranteed residual value is not (but is part of the lessor's gross investment in the lease). (p. 827)

- **LO9**   Executory costs (maintenance, insurance, taxes, and any other costs usually associated with ownership) are expenses of the lessee. Any costs incurred by the lessor that are associated directly with originating a lease and are essential to acquire that lease are called *initial direct costs* and are expensed in accordance with the matching principle. To find the present value of minimum lease payments to capitalize as an asset and liability, the lessee usually uses a discount rate equal to the lower of the rate implicit in the lease agreement and its own incremental borrowing rate. Contingent rentals are *not* included in the minimum lease payments because they are not determinable at the inception of the lease. (p. 832)

- **LO10**   A gain on the sale of an asset in a sale leaseback arrangement is deferred and amortized over the lease term (or asset life if title is expected to transfer to the lessee). The lease portion of the transaction is evaluated and accounted for like any lease. (p. 842)

- **LO11**   In general, IFRS is considered to be more principles-based while U.S. GAAP is more rules-based. This difference is evident in accounting for leases. To distinguish between a capital lease and an operating lease U.S. GAAP uses four specific classification criteria, whereas IFRS uses a variety of "indicators" of a capital (finance) lease. We also often see differences in the discount rate used and how we account for sale-leasebacks and leases of land and buildings. (pp. 814, 824, 834, 845 and 846) ●

QUESTIONS FOR REVIEW OF KEY TOPICS

Q 15–1   The basic concept of "substance over form" influences lease accounting. Explain.

Q 15–2   How is interest determined in a capital lease transaction? How does the approach compare to other forms of debt (say bonds payable or notes payable)?

Q 15–3   How are leases and installment notes the same? How do they differ?

● **IFRS**   **Q 15–4**   IASB chairman David Tweedie has noted that current GAAP allows airlines' balance sheets to appear as if the companies don't have airplanes. How can this be true?

Q 15–5   A lessee should classify a lease transaction as a capital lease if it is noncancelable and one or more of four classification criteria are met. Otherwise, it is an operating lease. What are these criteria?

Q 15–6   What is a bargain purchase option? How does it differ from other purchase options?

Q 15–7   Lukawitz Industries leased equipment to Seminole Corporation for a four-year period, at which time possession of the leased asset will revert back to Lukawitz. The equipment cost Lukawitz $4 million and has an expected useful life of six years. Its normal sales price is $5.6 million. The present value of the minimum lease payments for both the lessor and lessee is $5.2 million. The first payment was made at the inception of the lease. Collectibility of the remaining lease payments is reasonably assured, and Lukawitz has no material cost uncertainties. How should this lease be classified (a) by Lukawitz Industries (the lessor) and (b) by Seminole Corporation (the lessee)? Why?

Q 15–8   Can the present value of minimum lease payments differ between the lessor and lessee? If so, how?

Q 15–9   Compare the way a bargain purchase option and a residual value are treated by the lessee when determining minimum lease payments.

Q 15–10   What are executory costs? How are they accounted for by the lessee in a capital lease when paid by the lessee? When paid by the lessor? Explain.

Q 15–11   The discount rate influences virtually every amount reported in connection with a lease by both the lessor and the lessee. What is the lessor's discount rate when determining the present value of minimum lease payments? What is the lessee's discount rate?

Q 15–12   A lease might specify that rental payments may be increased (or decreased) at some future time during the lease term depending on whether or not some specified event occurs such as revenues or profits exceeding some designated level. Under what circumstances are contingent rentals included or excluded from minimum lease payments? If excluded, how are they recognized in income determination?

Q 15–13   The lessor's initial direct costs often are substantial. What are initial direct costs?

Q 15–14   When are initial direct costs recognized in an operating lease? In a direct financing lease? In a sales-type lease? Why?

Q 15–15   What are the required lease disclosures for the lessor and lessee?

Q 15–16   In a sale-leaseback transaction the owner of an asset sells it and immediately leases it back from the new owner. This dual transaction should be viewed as a single borrowing transaction. Why?

Q 15–17   Explain how the general classification criteria are applied to leases that involve land.

Q 15–18   What are the guidelines for determining when a material amount of land is involved in a lease?

Q 15–19   How does a leveraged lease differ from a nonleveraged lease?

IFRS   Q 15–20   Where can we find authoritative guidance for accounting for leases under IFRS?

IFRS   Q 15–21   Could a finance (capital) lease under IFRS be classified as an operating lease under U.S. GAAP? Explain.

IFRS   Q 15–22   Describe the primary differences between IFRS and U.S. GAAP in the way leases are classified as either operating or finance (capital) leases.

IFRS   Q 15–23   The IASB and FASB are collaborating on a joint project to revise accounting standards for leases. Briefly describe the direction the project is taking.

BRIEF EXERCISES

BE 15–1
Operating lease
● LO4

At the beginning of its fiscal year, Lakeside Inc. leased office space to LTT Corporation under a seven-year operating lease agreement. The contract calls for quarterly rent payments of $25,000 each. The office building was acquired by Lakeside at a cost of $2 million and was expected to have a useful life of 25 years with no residual value. What will be the effect of the lease on LTT's earnings for the first year (ignore taxes)?

BE 15–2
Operating lease
● LO4

In the situation described in BE 15-1, what will be the effect of the lease on Lakeside's earnings for the first year (ignore taxes)?

BE 15–3
Operating lease;
advance payment
● LO4

Ward Products leased office space under a 10-year operating lease agreement. The lease specified 120 monthly rent payments of $5,000 each, beginning at the inception of the lease. In addition to the first rent payment, Ward also paid a $100,000 advance payment at the lease's inception. What will be the effect of the lease on Ward's earnings for the first year (ignore taxes)?

BE 15–4
Lease classification
● LO3 LO5

Corinth Co. leased equipment to Athens Corporation for an eight-year period, at which time possession of the leased asset will revert back to Corinth. The equipment cost Corinth $16 million and has an expected useful life of 12 years. Its normal sales price is $22.4 million. The present value of the minimum lease payments for both the lessor and lessee is $20.4 million. The first payment was made at the inception of the lease. Collectibility of the remaining lease payments is reasonably assured, and Corinth has no material cost uncertainties. How should Athens classify this lease? Why?

BE 15–5
Lease classification
● LO3 LO5

In the situation described in BE 15-4, how should Corinth classify this lease? Why?

BE 15–6
Net investment in
leases
● LO5

The 2008 annual report of the **Sonic Corporation** reported minimum lease payments receivable of $3,292,000 and a net investment in direct financing leases of $2,500,000. What accounts for the difference between these two amounts? Explain.

BE 15–7
Capital lease;
calculate interest
● LO5

A lease agreement calls for quarterly lease payments of $5,376 over a 10-year lease term, with the first payment at July 1, the lease's inception. The interest rate is 8%. Both the fair value and the cost of the asset to the lessor are $150,000. What would be the amount of interest expense the lessee would record in conjunction with the second quarterly payment at October 1? What would be the amount of interest revenue the lessor would record in conjunction with the second quarterly payment at October 1?

BE 15–8
Capital lease; lessee;
balance sheet effects
● LO5

A lease agreement that qualifies as a capital lease calls for annual lease payments of $26,269 over a six-year lease term, with the first payment at January 1, the lease's inception. The interest rate is 5%. If lessee's fiscal year is the calendar year, what would be the amount of the lease liability that the lessee would report in its balance sheet at the end of the first year? What would be the interest payable?

BE 15–9
Capital lease;
lessee; income
statement effects
● LO5

In the situation described in BE 15–8, what would be the pretax amounts related to the lease that the lessee would report in its income statement for the year ended December 31?

BE 15–10
Sales-type lease;
lessor; income
statement effects
● LO6

In the situation described in BE 15–8, assume the asset being leased cost the lessor $125,000 to produce. Determine the price at which the lessor is "selling" the asset (present value of the lease payments). What would be the pretax amounts related to the lease that the lessor would report in its income statement for the year ended December 31?

BE 15–11

Sales-type lease; lessor; calculate lease payments

● LO6

Manning Imports is contemplating an agreement to lease equipment to a customer for five years. Manning normally sells the asset for a cash price of $100,000. Assuming that 8% is a reasonable rate of interest, what must be the amount of quarterly lease payments (beginning at the inception of the lease) in order for Manning to recover its normal selling price as well as be compensated for financing the asset over the lease term?

BE 15–12

Bargain purchase option; lessor; direct financing lease

● LO5 LO6 LO7

Ace Leasing acquires equipment and leases it to customers under long-term direct financing leases. Ace earns interest under these arrangements at a 6% annual rate. Ace leased a machine it purchased for $600,000 under an arrangement that specified annual payments beginning at the inception of the lease for five years. The lessee had the option to purchase the machine at the end of the lease term for $100,000 when it was expected to have a residual value of $160,000. Calculate the amount of the annual lease payments.

BE 15–13

Guaranteed residual value; direct financing lease

● LO5 through LO6 LO8

On January 1, James Industries leased equipment to a customer for a four-year period, at which time possession of the leased asset will revert back to James. The equipment cost James $700,000 and has an expected useful life of six years. Its normal sales price is $700,000. The residual value after four years, guaranteed by the lessee, is $100,000. Lease payments are due on December 31 of each year, beginning with the first payment at the end of the first year. Collectibility of the remaining lease payments is reasonably assured, and there are no material cost uncertainties. The interest rate is 5%. Calculate the amount of the annual lease payments.

BE 15–14

IFRS; lease classification

● LO3 LO11

Adams Storage and Appraisal leased equipment to OAC Corporation for an eight-year period, at which time possession of the leased asset will revert back to Adams. The equipment cost Adams $32 million and has an expected useful life of 11 years. Its normal sales price is $45 million. The present value of the minimum lease payments for both the lessor and lessee is $40 million. The first payment was made at the inception of the lease. How would OAC classify this lease if it prepares its financial statements using IFRS? Why?

EXERCISES

An alternate exercise and problem set is available on the text website: www.mhhe.com/spiceland6e

E 15–1

Operating lease

● LO4

On January 1, 2011, Nath-Langstrom Services, Inc., a computer software training firm, leased several computers from ComputerWorld Corporation under a two-year operating lease agreement. The contract calls for four rent payments of $10,000 each, payable semiannually on June 30 and December 31 each year. The computers were acquired by ComputerWorld at a cost of $90,000 and were expected to have a useful life of six years with no residual value.

Required:

Prepare the appropriate entries for both (a) the lessee and (b) the lessor from the inception of the lease through the end of 2011. (Use straight-line depreciation.)

E 15–2

Operating lease; advance payment; leasehold improvement

● LO4

On January 1, 2011, Winn Heat Transfer leased office space under a three-year operating lease agreement. The arrangement specified three annual rent payments of $80,000 each, beginning January 1, 2011, the inception of the lease, and at each January 1 through 2013. Winn also paid a $96,000 advance payment at the inception of the lease in addition to the first $80,000 rent payment. With permission of the owner, Winn made structural modifications to the building before occupying the space at a cost of $180,000. The useful life of the building and the structural modifications were estimated to be 30 years with no residual value.

Required:

Prepare the appropriate entries for Winn Heat Transfer from the inception of the lease through the end of 2011. Winn's fiscal year is the calendar year. Winn uses straight-line depreciation.

E 15–3

Capital lease; lessee

● LO5

(Note: Exercises 3, 4, and 5 are three variations of the same basic situation.)

Manufacturers Southern leased high-tech electronic equipment from Edison Leasing on January 1, 2011. Edison purchased the equipment from International Machines at a cost of $112,080.

Related Information:	
Lease term	2 years (8 quarterly periods)
Quarterly rental payments	$15,000 at the beginning of each period
Economic life of asset	2 years
Fair value of asset	$112,080
Implicit interest rate	8%
(Also lessee's incremental borrowing rate)	

Required:

Prepare a lease amortization schedule and appropriate entries for Manufacturers Southern from the inception of the lease through January 1, 2012. Depreciation is recorded at the end of each fiscal year (December 31) on a straight-line basis.

E 15–4
Direct financing
lease; lessor
● LO5

Edison Leasing leased high-tech electronic equipment to Manufacturers Southern on January 1, 2011. Edison purchased the equipment from International Machines at a cost of $112,080.

Related Information:

Lease term	2 years (8 quarterly periods)
Quarterly rental payments	$15,000 at the beginning of each period
Economic life of asset	2 years
Fair value of asset	$112,080
Implicit interest rate	8%
(Also lessee's incremental borrowing rate)	

Required:
Prepare a lease amortization schedule and appropriate entries for Edison Leasing from the inception of the lease through January 1, 2012. Edison's fiscal year ends December 31.

E 15–5
Sales-type lease;
lessor
● LO6

Manufacturers Southern leased high-tech electronic equipment from International Machines on January 1, 2011. International Machines manufactured the equipment at a cost of $85,000.

Related Information:

Lease term	2 years (8 quarterly periods)
Quarterly rental payments	$15,000 at the beginning of each period
Economic life of asset	2 years
Fair value of asset	$112,080
Implicit interest rate	8%
(Also lessee's incremental borrowing rate)	

Required:
1. Show how International Machines determined the $15,000 quarterly rental payments.
2. Prepare appropriate entries for International Machines to record the lease at its inception, January 1, 2011, and the second rental payment on April 1, 2011.

E 15–6
Lease classification
● LO3

Each of the four independent situations below describes a lease requiring annual lease payments of $10,000. For each situation, determine the appropriate lease classification by the lessee and indicate why.

	Situation			
	1	2	3	4
Lease term (years)	4	4	4	4
Asset's useful life (years)	6	5	6	6
Asset's fair value	$44,000	$43,000	$41,000	$39,000
Bargain purchase option?	No	Yes	No	No
Annual lease payments	Beg. of yr.	End of yr.	Beg. of yr.	End of yr.
Lessor's implicit rate (known by lessee)	5%	6%	5%	6%
Lessee's incremental borrowing rate	5%	5%	5%	5%

E 15–7
Capital lease
● LO5

American Food Services, Inc., leased a packaging machine from Barton and Barton Corporation. Barton and Barton completed construction of the machine on January 1, 2011. The lease agreement for the $4 million (fair value and present value of the lease payments) machine specified four equal payments at the end of each year. The useful life of the machine was expected to be four years with no residual value. Barton and Barton's implicit interest rate was 10% (also American Food Services' incremental borrowing rate).

Required:
1. Prepare the journal entry for American Food Services at the inception of the lease on January 1, 2011.
2. Prepare an amortization schedule for the four-year term of the lease.
3. Prepare the journal entry for the first lease payment on December 31, 2011.
4. Prepare the journal entry for the third lease payment on December 31, 2013.

(Note: You may wish to compare your solution to this exercise with that of Exercise 14–18 which deals with a parallel situation in which the packaging machine was acquired with an installment note.)

E 15–8
Capital lease;
lessee; balance
sheet and income
statement effects
● LO5

(Note: Exercises 8, 9, and 10 are three variations of the same situation.)
On June 30, 2011, Georgia-Atlantic, Inc., leased a warehouse facility from IC Leasing Corporation. The lease agreement calls for Georgia-Atlantic to make semiannual lease payments of $562,907 over a three-year lease term, payable each June 30 and December 31, with the first payment at June 30, 2011. Georgia-Atlantic's incremental borrowing rate is 10%, the same rate IC uses to calculate lease payment amounts. Depreciation is recorded on a straight-line basis at the end of each fiscal year. The fair value of the warehouse is $3 million.

Required:

1. Determine the present value of the lease payments at June 30, 2011 (to the nearest $000) that Georgia-Atlantic uses to record the leased asset and lease liability.
2. What pretax amounts related to the lease would Georgia-Atlantic report in its balance sheet at December 31, 2011?
3. What pretax amounts related to the lease would Georgia-Atlantic report in its income statement for the year ended December 31, 2011?

E 15–9
Direct financing lease; lessor; balance sheet and income statement effects
● LO5

On June 30, 2011, Georgia-Atlantic, Inc., leased a warehouse facility from IC Leasing Corporation. The lease agreement calls for Georgia-Atlantic to make semiannual lease payments of $562,907 over a three-year lease term, payable each June 30 and December 31, with the first payment at June 30, 2011. Georgia-Atlantic's incremental borrowing rate is 10%, the same rate IC used to calculate lease payment amounts. IC purchased the warehouse from Builders, Inc. at a cost of $3 million.

Required:

1. What pretax amounts related to the lease would IC report in its balance sheet at December 31, 2011?
2. What pretax amounts related to the lease would IC report in its income statement for the year ended December 31, 2011?

E 15–10
Sales-type lease; lessor; balance sheet and income statement effects
● LO6

On June 30, 2011, Georgia-Atlantic, Inc., leased a warehouse facility from Builders, Inc. The lease agreement calls for Georgia-Atlantic to make semiannual lease payments of $562,907 over a three-year lease term, payable each June 30 and December 31, with the first payment at June 30, 2011. Georgia-Atlantic's incremental borrowing rate is 10%, the same rate Builders used to calculate lease payment amounts. Builders constructed the warehouse at a cost of $2.5 million.

Required:

1. Determine the price at which Builders is "selling" the warehouse (present value of the lease payments) at June 30, 2011 (to the nearest $000).
2. What pretax amounts related to the lease would Builders report in its balance sheet at December 31, 2011?
3. What pretax amounts related to the lease would Builders report in its income statement for the year ended December 31, 2011?

E 15–11
IFRS; lease classification
● LO3 LO11

Airway Leasing entered into an agreement to lease aircraft to Ouachita Airlines. Consider each of the following, *a–e,* to be independent scenarios.

a. The agreement calls for ownership of the aircraft to be transferred to Ouachita Airlines at the end of the lease term.
b. The fair value of the aircraft is expected to be $500,000 at the end of the lease term. Ouachita has the option to purchase the aircraft at the end of the lease term for $90,000.
c. The aircraft has a useful life of 20 years, and the term of the lease is 14 years.
d. The present value of the lease payments is $8,900,000 and the fair value of the leased aircraft is $10,000,000.
e. The aircraft was manufactured to meet specifications provided by Ouachita to optimize the exclusively regional nature of its flights.

Required:

1. In each scenario, indicate whether Ouachita would classify the lease as an operating lease or capital lease under U.S. GAAP. Assume the lease agreement has not met any of the other criteria of a capital lease. Provide brief explanations.
2. In each scenario, indicate whether Ouachita would classify the lease as an operating lease or finance lease under *IAS 17.* Assume the lease agreement has not met any of the other indicators of a finance lease. Provide brief explanations.

E 15–12
Lessor calculation of annual lease payments; lessee calculation of asset and liability
● LO5

Each of the three independent situations below describes a capital lease in which annual lease payments are payable at the beginning of each year. The lessee is aware of the lessor's implicit rate of return.

| | Situation | | |
	1	2	3
Lease term (years)	10	20	4
Lessor's rate of return (known by lessee)	11%	9%	12%
Lessee's incremental borrowing rate	12%	10%	11%
Fair value of leased asset	$600,000	$980,000	$185,000

Required:

For each situation, determine:

a. The amount of the annual lease payments as calculated by the lessor.

b. The amount the lessee would record as a leased asset and a lease liability.

E 15–13
Lessor calculation
of annual lease
payments; lessee
calculation of asset
and liability
● LO5

(Note: This is a variation of the previous exercise modified to assume lease payments are at the end of each period.)

Each of the three independent situations below describes a capital lease in which annual lease payments are payable at the *end* of each year. The lessee is aware of the lessor's implicit rate of return.

	Situation		
	1	2	3
Lease term (years)	10	20	4
Lessor's rate of return	11%	9%	12%
Lessee's incremental borrowing rate	12%	10%	11%
Fair value of leased asset	$600,000	$980,000	$185,000

Required:

For each situation, determine:

a. The amount of the annual lease payments as calculated by the lessor.

b. The amount the lessee would record as a leased asset and a lease liability.

E 15–14
Calculation of
annual lease
payments; residual
value
● LO5 LO6 LO8

Each of the four independent situations below describes a capital lease in which annual lease payments are payable at the beginning of each year. Determine the annual lease payments for each:

	Situation			
	1	2	3	4
Lease term (years)	4	7	5	8
Lessor's rate of return	10%	11%	9%	12%
Fair value of leased asset	$50,000	$350,000	$75,000	$465,000
Lessor's cost of leased asset	$50,000	$350,000	$45,000	$465,000
Residual value:				
Guaranteed by lessee	0	$ 50,000	0	$ 30,000
Unguaranteed	0	0	$ 7,000	$ 15,000

E 15–15
Lease concepts;
direct financing
leases; guaranteed
and unguaranteed
residual value
● LO5 LO6 LO8

Each of the four independent situations below describes a direct financing lease in which annual lease payments of $100,000 are payable at the beginning of each year. Each is a capital lease for the lessee. Determine the following amounts at the inception of the lease:

A. The lessor's:
  1. Minimum lease payments
  2. Gross investment in the lease
  3. Net investment in the lease
B. The lessee's:
  4. Minimum lease payments
  5. Leased asset
  6. Lease liability

	Situation			
	1	2	3	4
Lease term (years)	7	7	8	8
Lessor's and lessee's discount rate	9%	11%	10%	12%
Residual value:				
Guaranteed by lessee	0	$50,000	0	$40,000
Unguaranteed	0	0	$50,000	$60,000

E 15–16
Calculation of
annual lease
payments; BPO
● LO5 LO6 LO7

For each of the three independent situations below determine the amount of the annual lease payments. Each describes a capital lease in which annual lease payments are payable at the beginning of each year. Each lease agreement contains an option that permits the lessee to acquire the leased asset at an option price that is sufficiently lower than the expected fair value that the exercise of the option appears reasonably certain.

	Situation		
	1	**2**	**3**
Lease term (years)	5	12	4
Lessor's rate of return	12%	11%	9%
Fair value of leased asset	$60,000	$420,000	$185,000
Lessor's cost of leased asset	$50,000	$420,000	$145,000
Bargain purchase option:			
Option price	$10,000	$ 50,000	$ 22,000
Exercisable at end of year:	5	5	3

E 15–17
Capital lease;
bargain purchase
options; lessee
● LO5 LO6 LO7

Federated Fabrications leased a tooling machine on January 1, 2011, for a three-year period ending December 31, 2013. The lease agreement specified annual payments of $36,000 beginning with the first payment at the inception of the lease, and each December 31 through 2012. The company had the option to purchase the machine on December 30, 2013, for $45,000 when its fair value was expected to be $60,000. The machine's estimated useful life was six years with no salvage value. Federated depreciates assets by the straight-line method. The company was aware that the lessor's implicit rate of return was 12%, which was less than Federated's incremental borrowing rate.

Required:

1. Calculate the amount Federated should record as a leased asset and lease liability for this capital lease.

2. Prepare an amortization schedule that describes the pattern of interest expense for Federated over the lease term.

3. Prepare the appropriate entries for Federated from the inception of the lease through the end of the lease term.

E 15–18
Bargain purchase
option; lessor;
direct financing
lease
● LO5 LO6 LO7

Universal Leasing leases electronic equipment to a variety of businesses. The company's primary service is providing alternate financing by acquiring equipment and leasing it to customers under long-term direct financing leases. Universal earns interest under these arrangements at a 10% annual rate.

The company leased an electronic typesetting machine it purchased for $30,900 to a local publisher, Desktop Inc., on December 31, 2010. The lease contract specified annual payments of $8,000 beginning January 1, 2011, the inception of the lease, and each December 31 through 2012 (three-year lease term). The publisher had the option to purchase the machine on December 30, 2013, the end of the lease term, for $12,000 when it was expected to have a residual value of $16,000.

Required:

1. Show how Universal calculated the $8,000 annual lease payments for this direct financing lease.

2. Prepare an amortization schedule that describes the pattern of interest revenue for Universal Leasing over the lease term.

3. Prepare the appropriate entries for Universal Leasing from the inception of the lease through the end of the lease term.

E 15–19
Executory costs;
lessor and lessee
● LO5 LO6 LO8
LO9

On January 1, 2011, NRC Credit Corporation leased equipment to Brand Services under a direct financing lease designed to earn NRC a 12% rate of return for providing long-term financing. The lease agreement specified:

a. Ten annual payments of $55,000 (including executory costs) beginning January 1, 2011, the inception of the lease and each December 31 thereafter through 2019.

b. The estimated useful life of the leased equipment is 10 years with no residual value. Its cost to NRC was $316,412.

c. The lease qualifies as a capital lease to Brand.

d. A 10-year service agreement with Quality Maintenance Company was negotiated to provide maintenance of the equipment as required. Payments of $5,000 per year are specified, beginning January 1, 2011. NRC was to pay this executory cost as incurred, but lease payments reflect this expenditure.

e. A partial amortization schedule, appropriate for both the lessee and lessor, follows:

	Payments	Effective Interest	Decrease in Balance	Outstanding Balance
		(12% × Outstanding balance)		
				316,412
1/1/11	50,000		50,000	266,412
12/31/11	50,000	.12 (266,412) = 31,969	18,031	248,381
12/31/12	50,000	.12 (248,381) = 29,806	20,194	228,187

Required:

Prepare the appropriate entries for both the lessee and lessor to record:

1. The lease at its inception.

2. The second lease payment and depreciation (straight line) on December 31, 2011.

E 15–20

Executory costs plus management fee; lessor and lessee

● LO5 LO6
  LO8 LO9

Refer to the lease agreement described in the previous exercise. Assume the contract specified that NRC (the lessor) was to pay, not only the $5,000 maintenance fees, but also insurance of $700 per year, and was to receive a $250 management fee for facilitating service and paying executory costs. The lessee's lease payments were increased to include an amount sufficient to reimburse executory costs plus NRC's fee.

Required:

Prepare the appropriate entries for both the lessee and lessor to record the **second** lease payment, executory costs, and depreciation (straight line) on December 31, 2011.

E 15–21

Lessor's initial direct costs; operating, direct financing and sales-type leases

● LO4 through
  LO6 LO9

Terms of a lease agreement and related facts were:
a. Leased asset had a retail cash selling price of $100,000. Its useful life was six years with no residual value (straight-line depreciation).
b. Annual lease payments at the beginning of each year were $20,873, beginning January 1.
c. Lessor's implicit rate when calculating annual rental payments was 10%.
d. Costs of negotiating and consummating the completed lease transaction incurred by the lessor were $2,062.
e. Collectibility of the lease payments by the lessor was reasonably predictable and there were no costs to the lessor that were yet to be incurred.

Required:

Prepare the appropriate entries for the lessor to record the lease, the initial payment at its inception, and at the December 31 fiscal year-end under each of the following three independent assumptions:
1. The lease term is three years and the lessor paid $100,000 to acquire the asset (operating lease).
2. The lease term is six years and the lessor paid $100,000 to acquire the asset (direct financing lease). Also assume that adjusting the net investment by initial direct costs reduces the effective rate of interest to 9%.
3. The lease term is six years and the lessor paid $85,000 to acquire the asset (sales-type lease).

E 15–22

Lessor's initial direct costs; operating lease

● LO9

The following relate to an operating lease agreement:
a. The lease term is 3 years, beginning January 1, 2011.
b. The leased asset cost the lessor $800,000 and had a useful life of eight years with no residual value. The lessor uses straight-line depreciation for its depreciable assets.
c. Annual lease payments at the beginning of each year were $137,000.
d. Costs of negotiating and consummating the completed lease transaction incurred by the lessor were $2,400.

Required:

Prepare the appropriate entries for the lessor from the inception of the lease through the end of the lease term.

E 15–23

Lessor's initial direct costs; direct financing lease

● LO9

Terms of a lease agreement and related facts were:
a. Costs of negotiating and consummating the completed lease transaction incurred by the lessor were $4,242.
b. The retail cash selling price of the leased asset was $500,000. Its useful life was three years with no residual value.
c. Collectibility of the lease payments by the lessor was reasonably predictable and there were no costs to the lessor that were yet to be incurred.
d. The lease term is three years and the lessor paid $500,000 to acquire the asset (direct financing lease).
e. Annual lease payments at the beginning of each year were $184,330.
f. Lessor's implicit rate when calculating annual rental payments was 11%.

Required:

1. Prepare the appropriate entries for the lessor to record the lease and related payments at its inception, January 1, 2011.
2. Calculate the effective rate of interest revenue after adjusting the net investment by initial direct costs.
3. Record any entry(s) necessary at December 31, 2011, the fiscal year-end.

E 15–24

Lessor's initial direct costs; sales-type lease

● LO9

The lease agreement and related facts indicate the following:
a. Leased equipment had a retail cash selling price of $300,000. Its useful life was five years with no residual value.
b. Collectibility of the lease payments by the lessor was reasonably predictable and there were no costs to the lessor that were yet to be incurred.
c. The lease term is five years and the lessor paid $265,000 to acquire the equipment (sales-type lease).
d. Lessor's implicit rate when calculating annual lease payments was 8%.
e. Annual lease payments beginning January 1, 2011, the inception of the lease, were $69,571.
f. Costs of negotiating and consummating the completed lease transaction incurred by the lessor were $7,500.

Required:

Prepare the appropriate entries for the lessor to record:
1. The lease and the initial payment at its inception.
2. Any entry(s) necessary at December 31, 2011, the fiscal year-end.

E 15–25
Concepts;
terminology

● LO3 through
LO9

Listed below are several terms and phrases associated with leases. Pair each item from List A with the item from List B (by letter) that is most appropriately associated with it.

	List A		List B
_____ 1.	Effective rate times balance.	a.	PV of BPO price.
_____ 2.	Realization principle.	b.	Lessor's net investment.
_____ 3.	Minimum lease payments plus unguaranteed residual value.	c.	Lessor's gross investment.
		d.	Operating lease.
_____ 4.	Periodic lease payments plus lessee-guaranteed residual value.	e.	Depreciable assets.
		f.	Loss to lessee.
_____ 5.	PV of minimum lease payments plus PV of unguaranteed residual value.	g.	Executory costs.
		h.	Depreciation longer than lease term.
_____ 6.	Initial direct costs.	i.	Disclosure only.
_____ 7.	Rent revenue.	j.	Interest expense.
_____ 8.	Bargain purchase option.	k.	Additional lessor conditions.
_____ 9.	Leasehold improvements.	l.	Lessee's minimum lease payments.
_____ 10.	Cash to satisfy residual value guarantee.	m.	Purchase price less than fair value.
_____ 11.	Capital lease expense.	n.	Sales-type lease selling expense.
_____ 12.	Deducted in lessor's computation of lease payments.	o.	Lessor's minimum lease payments.
_____ 13.	Title transfers to lessee.		
_____ 14.	Contingent rentals.		
_____ 15.	Lease payments plus lessee-guaranteed and third-party-guaranteed residual value.		

E 15–26
Sale-leaseback;
capital lease

● LO10

To raise operating funds, Signal Aviation sold an airplane on January 1, 2011, to a finance company for $770,000. Signal immediately leased the plane back for a 13-year period, at which time ownership of the airplane will transfer to Signal. The airplane has a fair value of $800,000. Its cost and its book value were $620,000. Its useful life is estimated to be 15 years. The lease requires Signal to make payments of $102,771 to the finance company each January 1. Signal depreciates assets on a straight-line basis. The lease has an implicit rate of 11%.

Required:

Prepare the appropriate entries for Signal on:
1. January 1, 2011, to record the sale-leaseback.
2. December 31, 2011, to record necessary adjustments.

E 15–27
IFRS; sale
leaseback; capital
lease

● LO10 LO11

Refer to the situation described in the previous exercise.

Required:

How might your solution differ if Signal Aviation prepares its financial statements according to International Financial Reporting Standards? Include any appropriate journal entries in your response.

E 15–28
Sale-leaseback;
operating lease

● LO10

To raise operating funds, National Distribution Center sold its office building to an insurance company on January 1, 2011, for $800,000 and immediately leased the building back. The operating lease is for the final 12 years of the building's estimated 50-year useful life. The building has a fair value of $800,000 and a book value of $650,000 (its original cost was $1 million). The rental payments of $100,000 are payable to the insurance company each December 31. The lease has an implicit rate of 9%.

Required:

Prepare the appropriate entries for National Distribution Center on:
1. January 1, 2011, to record the sale-leaseback.
2. December 31, 2011, to record necessary adjustments.

E 15–29
IFRS; sale
leaseback;
operating lease

● LO10 LO11

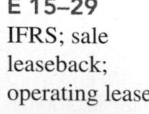

Refer to the situation described in the previous exercise.

Required:

How might your solution differ if National Distribution Center prepares its financial statements according to International Financial Reporting Standards? Include any appropriate journal entries in your response.

E 15–30
FASB codification
research; sale
leaseback

● LO10

In a sale-leaseback transaction, the owner of an asset sells it and immediately leases it back from the new owner. The *FASB Accounting Standards Codification* represents the single source of authoritative U.S. generally accepted accounting principles.

Required:

1. Obtain the relevant authoritative literature on disclosure requirements pertaining to a seller-lessee in a sale-leaseback transaction. Use your institution's Academic Accounting Access to the FASB's Codification Research System (**www.fasb.org**) or through your school library's subscription to a research database that includes the Codification. What is the specific citation that describes the guidelines for determining the disclosure requirements in the notes to the financial statements?

2. List the disclosure requirements.

E 15–31
Real estate lease;
land and building

● LO10

On January 1, 2011, Cook Textiles leased a building with two acres of land from Peck Development. The lease is for 10 years at which time Cook has an option to purchase the property for $100,000. The building has an estimated life of 20 years with a residual value of $150,000. The lease calls for Cook to assume all costs of ownership and to make annual payments of $200,000 due at the beginning of each year. On January 1, 2011, the estimated value of the land was $400,000. Cook uses the straight-line method of depreciation and pays 10% interest on borrowed money. Peck's implicit rate is unknown.

Required:

Prepare Cook Company's journal entries related to the lease in 2011.

E 15–32
FASB codification
research

● LO1 LO4 LO7

Access the FASB's Codification Research System at the FASB website (**www.fasb.org**). Determine the specific citation for accounting for each of the following items:

1. Definition of a bargain purchase option.

2. The calculation of the lessor's gross investment in a sales-type lease.

3. The disclosures required in the notes to the financial statements for an operating lease.

4. The additional disclosures necessary in the notes to the financial statements if the operating lease has a lease term greater than one year.

CPA AND CMA REVIEW QUESTIONS

**CPA Exam
Questions**

The following questions are used in the Kaplan CPA Review Course to study leases while preparing for the CPA examination. Determine the response that best completes the statements or questions.

● LO3

1. A company leases the following asset:
   • Fair value of $200,000.
   • Useful life of 5 years with no salvage value.
   • Lease term is 4 years.
   • Annual lease payment is $30,000 and the lease rate is 11%.
   • The company's overall borrowing rate is 9.5%.
   • The firm can purchase the equipment at the end of the lease period for $45,000.

   What type of lease is this?
   a. Operating.
   b. Capital.
   c. Financing.
   d. Long term.

● LO5

2. On January 1, 2011, Blaugh Co. signed a long-term lease for an office building. The terms of the lease required Blaugh to pay $10,000 annually, beginning December 30, 2011, and continuing each year for 30 years. The lease qualifies as a capital lease. On January 1, 2011, the present value of the lease payments is $112,500 at the 8% interest rate implicit in the lease. In Blaugh's December 31, 2011, balance sheet, the capital lease liability should be
   a. $102,500
   b. $111,500
   c. $112,500
   d. $290,000

● LO5

3. Glade Co. leases computer equipment to customers under direct-financing leases. The equipment has no residual value at the end of the lease and the leases do not contain bargain purchase options. Glade wishes to earn 8% interest on a five-year lease of equipment with a fair value of $323,400. The present value of an annuity due of $1 at 8% for five years is 4.312. What is the total amount of interest revenue that Glade will earn over the life of the lease?
   a. $ 51,600
   b. $ 75,000
   c. $129,360
   d. $139,450

● LO6

4. Peg Co. leased equipment from Howe Corp. on July 1, 2011, for an eight-year period expiring June 30, 2019. Equal payments under the lease are $600,000 and are due on July 1 of each year. The first payment was made on July 1, 2011. The rate of interest contemplated by Peg and Howe is 10%. The cash selling price of the equipment is $3,520,000, and the cost of the equipment on Howe's accounting records is $2,800,000. The lease is appropriately recorded as a sales-type lease. What is the amount of profit on the sale and interest revenue that Howe should record for the year ended December 31, 2011?

	Profit on Sale	Interest Revenue
a.	$ 45,000	$146,000
b.	$ 45,000	$176,000
c.	$720,000	$146,000
d.	$720,000	$176,000

● LO6

5. On January 2, 2011, Nori Mining Co. (lessee) entered into a 5-year lease for drilling equipment. Nori accounted for the acquisition as a capital lease for $240,000, which includes a $10,000 bargain purchase option. At the end of the lease, Nori expects to exercise the bargain purchase option. Nori estimates that the equipment's fair value will be $20,000 at the end of its 8-year life. Nori regularly uses straight-line depreciation on similar equipment. For the year ended December 31, 2011, what amount should Nori recognize as depreciation expense on the leased asset?
   a. $27,500
   b. $30,000
   c. $48,000
   d. $46,000

● LO8

6. At the inception of a capital lease, the guaranteed residual value should be
   a. Included as part of minimum lease payments at present value.
   b. Included as part of minimum lease payments at future value.
   c. Included as part of minimum lease payments only to the extent that guaranteed residual value is expected to exceed estimated residual value.
   d. Excluded from minimum lease payments.

● LO9

7. Neal Corp. entered into a nine-year capital lease on a warehouse on December 31, 2011. Lease payments of $52,000, which includes real estate taxes of $2,000, are due annually, beginning on December 31, 2012, and every December 31 thereafter. Neal does not know the interest rate implicit in the lease; Neal's incremental borrowing rate is 9%. The rounded present value of an ordinary annuity for nine years at 9% is 6.0. What amount should Neal report as capitalized lease liability at December 31, 2011?
   a. $300,000
   b. $312,000
   c. $450,000
   d. $468,000

● LO10

8. On December 31, 2011, Bain Corp. sold a machine to Ryan and simultaneously leased it back for one year. Pertinent information at this date follows:

Sales price	$360,000
Carrying amount	330,000
Present value of lease payments	34,100
($3,000 for 12 months at 12%)	
Estimated remaining useful life	12 years

In Bain's December 31, 2011, balance sheet, the deferred revenue from the sale of this machine should be
   a. $ 0
   b. $ 4,100
   c. $34,100
   d. $30,000

The following questions dealing with leases are adapted from questions that previously appeared on Certified Management Accountant (CMA) examinations. The CMA designation sponsored by the Institute of Management Accountants (**www.imanet.org**) provides members with an objective measure of knowledge and competence in the field of management accounting. Determine the response that best completes the statements or questions.

● LO5

1. For a direct-financing lease, the gross investment of the lessor is equal to the
   a. Present value of the minimum lease payments minus the unguaranteed residual value accruing to the lessor at the end of the lease term.
   b. Lower of 90% of the present value of the minimum lease payments or the fair value of the leased asset.
   c. Difference between the fair value of the leased asset and the unearned interest revenue.
   d. Minimum lease payments plus the unguaranteed residual value accruing to the lessor at the end of the lease term.

● LO7

2. Howell Corporation, a publicly traded corporation, is the lessee in a leasing agreement with Brandon Inc. to lease land and a building. If the lease contains a bargain purchase option, Howell should record the land and the building as a(n)
   a. Operating lease and capital lease, respectively.
   b. Capital lease and operating lease, respectively.
   c. Capital lease but recorded as a single unit.
   d. Capital lease but separately classified.

● LO9

3. Initial direct costs incurred by the lessor under a sales-type lease should be
   a. Deferred and allocated over the economic life of the leased property.
   b. Expensed in the period incurred.
   c. Deferred and allocated over the term of the lease in proportion to the recognition of rental income.
   d. Added to the gross investment in the lease and amortized over the term of the lease as a yield adjustment.

PROBLEMS

 |ACCOUNTING

An alternate exercise and problem set is available on the text website: www.mhhe.com/spiceland6e

P 15–1
Operating lease;
scheduled rent
increases

● LO4

On January 1, 2011, Sweetwater Furniture Company leased office space under a 21-year operating lease agreement. The contract calls for annual rent payments on December 31 of each year. The payments are $10,000 the first year and increase by $500 per year. Benefits expected from using the office space are expected to remain constant over the lease term.

Required:
Record Sweetwater's rent payment at December 31, 2015 (the fifth rent payment) and December 31, 2025 (the 15th rent payment).

P 15–2
Lease amortization
schedule

● LO5 LO8

On January 1, 2011, National Insulation Corporation (NIC) leased office space under a capital lease. Lease payments are made annually. Title does not transfer to the lessee and there is no bargain purchase option. Portions of the lessee's lease amortization schedule appear below:

Jan. 1	Payments	Effective Interest	Decrease in Balance	Outstanding Balance
2011				192,501
2011	20,000		20,000	172,501
2012	20,000	17,250	2,750	169,751
2013	20,000	16,975	3,025	166,726
2014	20,000	16,673	3,327	163,399
2015	20,000	16,340	3,660	159,739
2016	20,000	15,974	4,026	155,713
—	—	—	—	—
—	—	—	—	—
—	—	—	—	—
2028	20,000	7,364	12,636	61,006
2029	20,000	6,101	13,899	47,107
2030	20,000	4,711	15,289	31,818
2031	35,000	3,182	31,818	0

Required:

1. What is NIC's lease liability at the inception of the lease (after the first payment)?
2. What amount would NIC record as a leased asset?
3. What is the lease term in years?
4. What is the asset's residual value expected at the end of the lease term?
5. How much of the residual value is guaranteed by the lessee?
6. What is the effective annual interest rate?
7. What is the total amount of minimum lease payments?
8. What is the total effective interest expense recorded over the term of the lease?

P 15–3

Direct financing and sales-type lease; lessee and lessor

● LO3 LO5 LO6

Rand Medical manufactures lithotripters. Lithotripsy uses shock waves instead of surgery to eliminate kidney stones. Physicians' Leasing purchased a lithotripter from Rand for $2,000,000 and leased it to Mid-South Urologists Group, Inc., on January 1, 2011.

Lease Description:

Quarterly lease payments	$130,516—beginning of each period
Lease term	5 years (20 quarters)
No residual value; no BPO	
Economic life of lithotripter	5 years
Implicit interest rate and lessee's incremental borrowing rate	12%
Fair value of asset	$2,000,000

Collectibility of the lease payments is reasonably assured, and there are no lessor costs yet to be incurred.

Required:

1. How should this lease be classified by Mid-South Urologists Group and by Physicians' Leasing?
2. Prepare appropriate entries for both Mid-South Urologists Group and Physicians' Leasing from the inception of the lease through the second rental payment on April 1, 2011. Depreciation is recorded at the end of each fiscal year (December 31).
3. Assume Mid-South Urologists Group leased the lithotripter directly from the manufacturer, Rand Medical, which produced the machine at a cost of $1.7 million. Prepare appropriate entries for Rand Medical from the inception of the lease through the second lease payment on April 1, 2011.

P 15–4

Capital lease

● LO5

At the beginning of 2011, VHF Industries acquired a machine with a fair value of $6,074,700 by signing a four-year lease. The lease is payable in four annual payments of $2 million at the end of each year.

Required:

1. What is the effective rate of interest implicit in the agreement?
2. Prepare the lessee's journal entry at the inception of the lease.
3. Prepare the journal entry to record the first lease payment at December 31, 2011.
4. Prepare the journal entry to record the second lease payment at December 31, 2012.
5. Suppose the fair value of the machine and the lessor's implicit rate were unknown at the time of the lease, but that the lessee's incremental borrowing rate of interest for notes of similar risk was 11%. Prepare the lessee's entry at the inception of the lease.

(Note: You may wish to compare your solution to Problem 15–4 with that of Problem 14–12, which deals with a parallel situation in which the machine was acquired with an installment note.)

P 15–5

Capital lease; lessee; financial statement effects

● LO5

(Note: Problems 5, 6, and 7 are three variations of the same basic situation.)

Werner Chemical, Inc., leased a protein analyzer on September 30, 2011. The five-year lease agreement calls for Werner to make quarterly lease payments of $391,548, payable each September 30, December 31, March 31, June 30, with the first payment at September 30, 2011. Werner's incremental borrowing rate is 12%. Depreciation is recorded on a straight-line basis at the end of each fiscal year. The useful life of the equipment is five years.

Required:

1. Determine the present value of the lease payments at September 30, 2011 (to the nearest $000).
2. What pretax amounts related to the lease would Werner report in its balance sheet at December 31, 2011?
3. What pretax amounts related to the lease would Werner report in its income statement for the year ended December 31, 2011?
4. What pretax amounts related to the lease would Werner report in its statement of cash flows for the year ended December 31, 2011?

P 15–6
Direct financing lease; lessor; financial statement effects
● LO5

Abbott Equipment leased a protein analyzer to Werner Chemical, Inc., on September 30, 2011. Abbott purchased the machine from NutraLabs, Inc., at a cost of $6 million. The five-year lease agreement calls for Werner to make quarterly lease payments of $391,548, payable each September 30, December 31, March 31, June 30, with the first payment at September 30, 2011. Abbot's implicit interest rate is 12%.

Required:
1. What pretax amounts related to the lease would Abbott report in its balance sheet at December 31, 2011?
2. What pretax amounts related to the lease would Abbott report in its income statement for the year ended December 31, 2011?
3. What pretax amounts related to the lease would Abbott report in its statement of cash flows for the year ended December 31, 2011?

P 15–7
Sales-type lease; lessor; financial statement effects
● LO6

NutraLabs, Inc., leased a protein analyzer to Werner Chemical, Inc., on September 30, 2011. NutraLabs manufactured the machine at a cost of $5 million. The five-year lease agreement calls for Werner to make quarterly lease payments of $391,548, payable each September 30, December 31, March 31, June 30, with the first payment at September 30, 2011. NutraLabs' implicit interest rate is 12%.

Required:
1. Determine the price at which NutraLabs is "selling" the equipment (present value of the lease payments) at September 30, 2011 (to the nearest $000).
2. What pretax amounts related to the lease would NutraLabs report in its balance sheet at December 31, 2011?
3. What pretax amounts related to the lease would NutraLabs report in its income statement for the year ended December 31, 2011?
4. What pretax amounts related to the lease would NutraLabs report in its statement of cash flows for the year ended December 31, 2011?

P 15–8
Guaranteed residual value; direct financing lease
● LO3 LO5 LO8

(Note: Problems 8, 9, and 10 are three variations of the same basic situation.)
On December 31, 2011, Rhone-Metro Industries leased equipment to Western Soya Co. for a four-year period ending December 31, 2015, at which time possession of the leased asset will revert back to Rhone-Metro. The equipment cost Rhone-Metro $365,760 and has an expected useful life of six years. Its normal sales price is $365,760. The lessee-guaranteed residual value at December 31, 2015, is $25,000. Equal payments under the lease are $100,000 and are due on December 31 of each year. The first payment was made on December 31, 2011. Collectibility of the remaining lease payments is reasonably assured, and Rhone-Metro has no material cost uncertainties. Western Soya's incremental borrowing rate is 12%. Western Soya knows the interest rate implicit in the lease payments is 10%. Both companies use straight-line depreciation.

Required:
1. Show how Rhone-Metro calculated the $100,000 annual lease payments.
2. How should this lease be classified (a) by Western Soya Co. (the lessee) and (b) by Rhone-Metro Industries (the lessor)? Why?
3. Prepare the appropriate entries for both Western Soya Co. and Rhone-Metro on December 31, 2011.
4. Prepare an amortization schedule(s) describing the pattern of interest over the lease term for the lessee and the lessor.
5. Prepare all appropriate entries for both Western Soya and Rhone-Metro on December 31, 2012 (the second lease payment and depreciation).
6. Prepare the appropriate entries for both Western Soya and Rhone-Metro on December 31, 2015 assuming the equipment is returned to Rhone-Metro and the actual residual value on that date is $1,500.

P 15–9
Unguaranteed residual value; executory costs; sales-type lease
● LO6 LO8 LO9

Rhone-Metro Industries manufactures equipment that is sold or leased. On December 31, 2011, Rhone-Metro leased equipment to Western Soya Co. for a four-year period ending December 31, 2015, at which time possession of the leased asset will revert back to Rhone-Metro. The equipment cost $300,000 to manufacture and has an expected useful life of six years. Its normal sales price is $365,760. The expected residual value of $25,000 at December 31, 2015, is not guaranteed. Equal payments under the lease are $104,000 (including $4,000 executory costs) and are due on December 31 of each year. The first payment was made on December 31, 2011. Collectibility of the remaining lease payments is reasonably assured, and Rhone-Metro has no material cost uncertainties. Western Soya's incremental borrowing rate is 12%. Western Soya knows the interest rate implicit in the lease payments is 10%. Both companies use straight-line depreciation.

Required:
1. Show how Rhone-Metro calculated the $104,000 annual lease payments.
2. How should this lease be classified (a) by Western Soya Co. (the lessee) and (b) by Rhone-Metro Industries (the lessor)? Why?

3. Prepare the appropriate entries for both Western Soya Co. and Rhone-Metro on December 31, 2011.

4. Prepare an amortization schedule(s) describing the pattern of interest over the lease term for the lessee and the lessor.

5. Prepare the appropriate entries for both Western Soya and Rhone-Metro on December 31, 2012 (the second lease payment and depreciation).

6. Prepare the appropriate entries for both Western Soya and Rhone-Metro on December 31, 2015, assuming the equipment is returned to Rhone-Metro and the actual residual value on that date is $1,500.

P 15–10
Bargain purchase option exercisable before lease term ends; executor costs; sales-type lease

● LO3 LO6
LO7 LO9

Rhone-Metro Industries manufactures equipment that is sold or leased. On December 31, 2011, Rhone-Metro leased equipment to Western Soya Co. for a noncancelable stated lease term of four years ending December 31, 2015, at which time possession of the leased asset will revert back to Rhone-Metro. The equipment cost $300,000 to manufacture and has an expected useful life of six years. Its normal sales price is $365,760. The expected residual value of $25,000 at December 31, 2015, is not guaranteed. Western Soya Co. can exercise a bargain purchase option on December 30, 2014, at an option price of $10,000. Equal payments under the lease are $134,960 (including $4,000 annual executory costs) and are due on December 31 of each year. The first payment was made on December 31, 2011. Collectibility of the remaining lease payments is reasonably assured, and Rhone-Metro has no material cost uncertainties. Western Soya's incremental borrowing rate is 12%. Western Soya knows the interest rate implicit in the lease payments is 10%. Both companies use straight-line depreciation.

Hint: A lease term ends for accounting purposes when an option becomes exercisable if it's expected to be exercised (i.e., a BPO).

Required:

1. Show how Rhone-Metro calculated the $134,960 annual lease payments.

2. How should this lease be classified (a) by Western Soya Co. (the lessee) and (b) by Rhone-Metro Industries (the lessor)? Why?

3. Prepare the appropriate entries for both Western Soya Co. and Rhone-Metro on December 31, 2011.

4. Prepare an amortization schedule(s) describing the pattern of interest over the lease term for the lessee and the lessor.

5. Prepare the appropriate entries for both Western Soya and Rhone-Metro on December 31, 2012 (the second rent payment and depreciation).

6. Prepare the appropriate entries for both Western Soya and Rhone-Metro on December 30, 2014, assuming the BPO is exercised on that date.

P 15–11
Operating lease to lessee—capital lease to lessor

● LO3 LO4
LO5 LO8

Allied Industries manufactures high-performance conveyers that often are leased to industrial customers. On December 31, 2011, Allied leased a conveyer to Poole Carrier Corporation for a three-year period ending December 31, 2014, at which time possession of the leased asset will revert back to Allied. Equal payments under the lease are $200,000 and are due on December 31 of each year. The first payment was made on December 31, 2011. Collectibility of the remaining lease payments is reasonably assured, and Allied has no material cost uncertainties. The conveyer cost $450,000 to manufacture and has an expected useful life of six years. Its normal sales price is $659,805. The expected residual value of $150,000 at December 31, 2014, is guaranteed by United Assurance Group. Poole Carrier's incremental borrowing rate and the interest rate implicit in the lease payments are 10%.

Required:

1. Show how Allied Industries calculated the $200,000 annual lease payments.

2. How should this lease be classified (a) by Allied (the lessor) and (b) by Poole (the lessee)? Why?

3. Prepare the appropriate entries for both Poole and Allied on December 31, 2011.

4. Prepare an amortization schedule(s) describing the pattern of interest over the lease term.

5. Prepare the appropriate entries for both Poole and Allied on December 31, 2012, 2013, and 2014, assuming the conveyer is returned to Allied at the end of the lease and the actual residual value on that date is $105,000.

P 15–12
Lease concepts; direct financing leases; guaranteed and unguaranteed residual value

● LO3 LO5 LO8

Each of the four independent situations below describes a direct financing lease in which annual lease payments of $10,000 are payable at the beginning of each year. Each is a capital lease for the lessee. Determine the following amounts at the inception of the lease:

A. The lessor's:

1. Minimum lease payments
2. Gross investment in the lease
3. Net investment in the lease

B. The lessee's:

    4. Minimum lease payments

    5. Leased asset

    6. Lease liability

	Situation			
	1	**2**	**3**	**4**
Lease term (years)	4	4	4	4
Asset's useful life (years)	4	5	5	5
Lessor's implicit rate (known by lessee)	11%	11%	11%	11%
Lessee's incremental borrowing rate	11%	12%	11%	12%
Residual value:				
Guaranteed by lessee	0	$4,000	0	0
Guaranteed by third party	0	0	$4,000	0
Unguaranteed	0	0	0	$4,000

P 15–13

Lease concepts

● LO3 LO5 LO8

Four independent situations are described below. For each, annual lease payments of $100,000 (not including any executory costs paid by lessor) are payable at the beginning of each year. Each is a capital lease for both the lessor and lessee. Determine the following amounts at the inception of the lease:

A. The lessor's:

    1. Minimum lease payments

    2. Gross investment in the lease

    3. Net investment in the lease

    4. Sales revenue

    5. Cost of goods sold

    6. Dealer's profit

B. The lessee's:

    7. Minimum lease payments

    8. Leased asset

    9. Lease liability

	Situation			
	1	**2**	**3**	**4**
Lease term (years)	4	5	6	4
Lessor's cost	$369,175	$449,896	$500,000	$400,000
Asset's useful life (years)	6	7	7	5
Lessor's implicit rate (known by lessee)	10%	12%	9%	10%
Lessee's incremental borrowing rate	9%	10%	11%	12%
Residual value:				
Guaranteed by lessee	0	$ 53,000	$ 40,000	$ 60,000
Guaranteed by third party*	0	0	0	$ 50,000
Unguaranteed	$ 30,000	0	$ 35,000	$ 40,000
Executory costs paid annually by lessor	$ 1,000	$ 8,000	$ 5,000	$ 10,000

*Over and above any amount guaranteed by the lessee (after a deductible equal to any amount guaranteed by the lessee).

P 15–14

Executory costs; lessor and lessee

● LO3 LO5 LO9

Branif Leasing leases mechanical equipment to industrial consumers under direct financing leases that earn Branif a 10% rate of return for providing long-term financing. A lease agreement with Branson Construction specified 20 annual payments of $100,000 beginning December 31, 2011, the inception of the lease. The estimated useful life of the leased equipment is 20 years with no residual value. Its cost to Branif was $936,500. The lease qualifies as a capital lease to Branson. Maintenance of the equipment was contracted for through a 20-year service agreement with Midway Service Company requiring 20 annual payments of $3,000 beginning December 31, 2011. Both companies use straight-line depreciation.

Required:

Prepare the appropriate entries for both the lessee and lessor to record the second lease payment and depreciation on December 31, 2012, under each of three independent assumptions:

1. The lessee pays executory costs as incurred.

2. The contract specifies that the lessor pays executory costs as incurred. The lessee's lease payments were increased to $103,000 to include an amount sufficient to reimburse these costs.

3. The contract specifies that the lessor pays executory costs as incurred. The lessee's lease payments were increased to $103,300 to include an amount sufficient to reimburse these costs plus a 10% management fee for Branif.

P 15–15
Sales-type lease;
bargain purchase
option exercisable
before lease term
ends; lessor and
lessee

● LO3 LO5 LO6
   LO7 LO8

Mid-South Auto Leasing leases vehicles to consumers. The attraction to customers is that the company can offer competitive prices due to volume buying and requires an interest rate implicit in the lease that is one percent below alternate methods of financing. On September 30, 2011, the company leased a delivery truck to a local florist, Anything Grows.

The lease agreement specified quarterly payments of $3,000 beginning September 30, 2011, the inception of the lease, and each quarter (December 31, March 31, and June 30) through June 30, 2014 (three-year lease term). The florist had the option to purchase the truck on September 29, 2013, for $6,000 when it was expected to have a residual value of $10,000. The estimated useful life of the truck is four years. Mid-South Auto Leasing's quarterly interest rate for determining payments was 3% (approximately 12% annually). Mid-South paid $25,000 for the truck. Both companies use straight-line depreciation. Anything Grows' incremental interest rate is 12%.

Hint: A lease term ends for accounting purposes when an option becomes exercisable if it's expected to be exercised (i.e., a BPO).

Required:
1. Calculate the amount of dealer's profit that Mid-South would recognize in this sales-type lease. (Be careful to note that, although payments occur on the last calendar day of each quarter, since the first payment was at the inception of the lease, payments represent an annuity due.)
2. Prepare the appropriate entries for Anything Grows and Mid-South on September 30, 2011.
3. Prepare an amortization schedule(s) describing the pattern of interest expense for Anything Grows and interest revenue for Mid-South Auto Leasing over the lease term.
4. Prepare the appropriate entries for Anything Grows and Mid-South Auto Leasing on December 31, 2011.
5. Prepare the appropriate entries for Anything Grows and Mid-South on September 29, 2013, assuming the bargain purchase option was exercised on that date.

P 15–16
Lessee-guaranteed
residual value;
third-party-
guaranteed
residual value;
unguaranteed
residual value;
executory costs;
different interest
rates for lessor and
lessee

● LO3 LO5
   LO8 LO9

On December 31, 2011, Yard Art Landscaping leased a delivery truck from Branch Motors. Branch paid $40,000 for the truck. Its retail value is $45,114.

The lease agreement specified annual payments of $11,000 beginning December 31, 2011, the inception of the lease, and at each December 31 through 2014. Branch Motors' interest rate for determining payments was 10%. At the end of the four-year lease term (December 31, 2015) the truck was expected to be worth $15,000. The estimated useful life of the truck is five years with no salvage value. Both companies use straight-line depreciation.

Yard Art guaranteed a residual value of $6,000. Guarantor Assurance Corporation was engaged to guarantee a residual value of $11,000, but with a deductible equal to any amount paid by the lessee ($11,000 reduced by any amount paid by the lessee). Yard Art's incremental borrowing rate is 9%.

A $1,000 per year maintenance agreement was arranged for the truck with an outside service firm. As an expediency, Branch Motors agreed to pay this fee. It is, however, reflected in the $11,000 lease payments.

Collectibility of the lease payments by Yard Art is reasonably predictable and there are no costs to the lessor that are yet to be incurred.

Required:
1. How should this lease be classified by Yard Art Landscaping (the lessee)? Why?
2. Calculate the amount Yard Art Landscaping would record as a leased asset and a lease liability.
3. How should this lease be classified by Branch Motors (the lessor)? Why?
4. Show how Branch Motors calculated the $11,000 annual lease payments.
5. Calculate the amount Branch Motors would record as sales revenue.
6. Prepare the appropriate entries for both Yard Art and Branch Motors on December 31, 2011.
7. Prepare an amortization schedule that describes the pattern of interest expense over the lease term for Yard Art.
8. Prepare an amortization schedule that describes the pattern of interest revenue over the lease term for Branch Motors.
9. Prepare the appropriate entries for both Yard Art and Branch Motors on December 31, 2012.
10. Prepare the appropriate entries for both Yard Art and Branch Motors on December 31, 2014 (the final lease payment).
11. Prepare the appropriate entries for both Yard Art and Branch Motors on December 31, 2015 (the end of the lease term), assuming the truck is returned to the lessor and the actual residual value of the truck was $4,000 on that date.

P 15–17
Integrating
problem; bonds;
note; lease

● LO5

You are the new controller for Moonlight Bay Resorts. The company CFO has asked you to determine the company's interest expense for the year ended December 31, 2011. Your accounting group provided you the following information on the company's debt:
1. On July 1, 2011, Moonlight Bay issued bonds with a face amount of $2,000,000. The bonds mature in 20 years and interest of 9% is payable semiannually on June 30 and December 31. The bonds were issued at a price to yield investors 10%. Moonlight Bay records interest at the effective rate.

2. At December 31, 2010, Moonlight Bay had a 10% installment note payable to Third Mercantile Bank with a balance of $500,000. The annual payment is $60,000, payable each June 30.

3. On January 1, 2011, Moonlight Bay leased a building under a capital lease calling for four annual lease payments of $40,000 beginning January 1, 2011. Moonlight Bay's incremental borrowing rate on the date of the lease was 11% and the lessor's implicit rate, which was known by Moonlight Bay, was 10%.

Required:
Calculate interest expense for the year ended December 31, 2011.

P 15–18
Initial direct costs;
direct financing
lease

● LO3 LO5 LO9

Bidwell Leasing purchased a single-engine plane for its fair value of $645,526 and leased it to Red Baron Flying Club on January 1, 2011.

Terms of the lease agreement and related facts were:

a. Eight annual payments of $110,000 beginning January 1, 2011, the inception of the lease, and at each December 31 through 2017. Bidwell Leasing's implicit interest rate was 10%. The estimated useful life of the plane is eight years. Payments were calculated as follows:

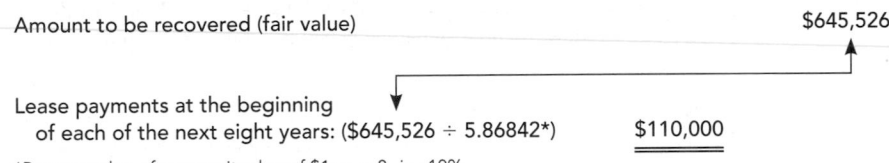

Amount to be recovered (fair value) $645,526

Lease payments at the beginning
   of each of the next eight years: ($645,526 ÷ 5.86842*) $110,000

*Present value of an annuity due of $1: $n = 8$, $i = 10\%$.

b. Red Baron's incremental borrowing rate is 11%.

c. Costs of negotiating and consummating the completed lease transaction incurred by Bidwell Leasing were $18,099.

d. Collectibility of the lease payments by Bidwell Leasing is reasonably predictable and there are no costs to the lessor that are yet to be incurred.

Required:
1. How should this lease be classified (a) by Bidwell Leasing (the lessor) and (b) by Red Baron (the lessee)?

2. Prepare the appropriate entries for both Red Baron Flying Club and Bidwell Leasing on January 1, 2011.

3. Prepare an amortization schedule that describes the pattern of interest expense over the lease term for Red Baron Flying Club.

4. Determine the effective rate of interest for Bidwell Leasing for the purpose of recognizing interest revenue over the lease term.

5. Prepare an amortization schedule that describes the pattern of interest revenue over the lease term for Bidwell Leasing.

6. Prepare the appropriate entries for both Red Baron and Bidwell Leasing on December 31, 2011 (the second lease payment). Both companies use straight-line depreciation.

7. Prepare the appropriate entries for both Red Baron and Bidwell Leasing on December 31, 2017 (the final lease payment).

P 15–19
Initial direct costs;
sales-type lease

● LO3 LO6 LO9

(Note: This problem is a variation of the preceding problem, modified to cause the lease to be a sales-type lease.)

Bidwell Leasing purchased a single-engine plane for $400,000 and leased it to Red Baron Flying Club for its fair value of $645,526 on January 1, 2011.

Terms of the lease agreement and related facts were:

a. Eight annual payments of $110,000 beginning January 1, 2011, the inception of the lease, and at each December 31 through 2017. Bidwell Leasing's implicit interest rate was 10%. The estimated useful life of the plane is eight years. Payments were calculated as follows:

Amount to be recovered (fair value) $645,526

Lease payments at the beginning
   of each of the next eight years: ($645,526 ÷ 5.86842*) $110,000

*Present value of an annuity due of $1: $n = 8$, $i = 10\%$.

b. Red Baron's incremental borrowing rate is 11%.

c. Costs of negotiating and consummating the completed lease transaction incurred by Bidwell Leasing were $18,099.

d. Collectibility of the lease payments by Bidwell Leasing is reasonably predictable and there are no costs to the lessor that are yet to be incurred.

Required:

1. How should this lease be classified (a) by Bidwell Leasing (the lessor) and (b) by Red Baron (the lessee)?
2. Prepare the appropriate entries for both Red Baron Flying Club and Bidwell Leasing on January 1, 2011.
3. Prepare an amortization schedule that describes the pattern of interest expense over the lease term for Red Baron Flying Club.
4. Prepare the appropriate entries for both Red Baron and Bidwell Leasing on December 31, 2011 (the second lease payment). Both companies use straight-line depreciation.
5. Prepare the appropriate entries for both Red Baron and Bidwell Leasing on December 31, 2017 (the final lease payment).

P 15–20
Sale-leaseback
● LO5 LO10

To raise operating funds, North American Courier Corporation sold its building on January 1, 2011, to an insurance company for $500,000 and immediately leased the building back. The lease is for a 10-year period ending December 31, 2020, at which time ownership of the building will revert to North American Courier. The building has a carrying amount of $400,000 (original cost $1,000,000). The lease requires North American to make payments of $88,492 to the insurance company each December 31. The building had a total original useful life of 30 years with no residual value and is being depreciated on a straight-line basis. The lease has an implicit rate of 12%.

Required:

1. Prepare the appropriate entries for North American on (a) January 1, 2011, to record the sale-leaseback and (b) December 31, 2011, to record necessary adjustments.
2. Show how North American's December 31, 2011, balance sheet and income statement would reflect the sale-leaseback.

P 15–21
Real estate lease;
land and building
● LO10

On January 1, 2011, Cook Textiles leased a building with two acres of land from Peck Development. The lease is for 10 years. No purchase option exists and the property will revert to Peck at the end of the lease. The building and land combined have a fair market value on January 1, 2011, of $1,450,000 and the building has an estimated life of 20 years with a residual value of $150,000. The lease calls for Cook to assume all costs of ownership and to make annual payments of $200,000 due at the beginning of each year. On January 1, 2011, the estimated value of the land was $400,000. Cook uses the straight-line method of depreciation and pays 10% interest on borrowed money. Peck's implicit rate is unknown.

Required:

1. Prepare journal entries for Cook Textiles for 2011. Assume the land could be leased without the building for $59,000 each year.
2. Assuming the land had a fair value on January 1, 2011, of $200,000 and could be leased alone for $30,000, prepare journal entries for Cook Textiles for 2011.

P 15–22
IFRS; real estate
lease; land and
building
● LO10 LO11

Refer to the situation described in Problem 15–21.

Required:

How might your solution differ if Cook Textiles prepares its financial statements according to International Financial Reporting Standards?

BROADEN YOUR PERSPECTIVE

Apply your critical-thinking ability to the knowledge you've gained. These cases will provide you an opportunity to develop your research, analysis, judgment, and communication skills. You also will work with other students, integrate what you've learned, apply it in real world situations, and consider its global and ethical ramifications. This practice will broaden your knowledge and further develop your decision-making abilities.

**Analysis
Case 15–1**
Reporting leases;
operating leases;
Walmart
● LO1 through
LO5

Real World Financials

Refer to the most recent financial statements and related disclosure notes of **Walmart Stores, Inc.** You can find these at the Walmart website, **walmartstores.com**, or by using Edgar at **www.sec.gov**. Management's Discussion and Analysis states that Walmart has $12,830,000,000 of "Unrecorded Contractual Obligations: Noncancelable operating leases."

Required:

1. What does Walmart's management mean when it says "Unrecorded Contractual Obligations" in this context?
2. See the note on "Commitments" in the disclosure notes. What is Walmart's capital lease liability?

3. If the operating leases were capitalized, approximately how much would that increase the capital lease liability?

4. What effect would that have on the company's debt-equity ratio? (Refer to the balance sheet.)

Research Case 15–2
FASB codification; locate and extract relevant information and authoritative support for a financial reporting issue; capital lease; sublease of a leased asset

● LO1 through LO5

"I don't see that in my intermediate accounting text I saved from college," you explain to another member of the accounting division of Dowell Chemical Corporation. "This will take some research." Your comments pertain to the appropriate accounting treatment of a proposed sublease of warehouses Dowell has used for product storage.

Dowell leased the warehouses one year ago on December 31. The five-year lease agreement called for Dowell to make quarterly lease payments of $2,398,303, payable each December 31, March 31, June 30, and September 30, with the first payment at the lease's inception. As a capital lease, Dowell had recorded the leased asset and liability at $40 million, the present value of the lease payments at 8%. Dowell records depreciation on a straight-line basis at the end of each fiscal year.

Today, Jason True, Dowell's controller, explained a proposal to sublease the underused warehouses to American Tankers, Inc. for the remaining four years of the lease term. American Tankers would be substituted as lessee under the original lease agreement. As the new lessee, it would become the primary obligor under the agreement, and Dowell would not be secondarily liable for fulfilling the obligations under the lease agreement. "Check on how we would need to account for this and get back to me," he had said.

Required:

1. After the first full year under the warehouse lease, what is the balance in Dowell's lease liability? An amortization schedule will be helpful in determining this amount.

2. After the first full year under the warehouse lease, what is the carrying amount (after accumulated depreciation) of Dowell's leased warehouses?

3. Obtain the relevant authoritative literature on accounting for derecognition of capital leases by lessees using the FASB's Codification Research System. You might gain access from the FASB website (**www.fasb.org**), from your school library, or some other source. Determine the appropriate accounting treatment for the proposed sublease. What is the specific Codification citation that Dowell would rely on to determine:

   a. if the proposal to sublease will qualify as a termination of a capital lease, and

   b. the appropriate accounting treatment for the sublease?

4. What, if any, journal entry would Dowell record in connection with the sublease?

Communication Case 15–3
Classification issues; lessee accounting; group interaction

● LO3 LO7 LO8

Interstate Automobiles Corporation leased 40 vans to VIP Transport under a four-year noncancelable lease on January 1, 2011. Information concerning the lease and the vans follows:

a. Equal annual lease payments of $300,000 are due on January 1, 2011, and thereafter on December 31 each year. The first payment was made January 1, 2011. Interstate's implicit interest rate is 10% and known by VIP.

b. VIP has the option to purchase all of the vans at the end of the lease for a total of $290,000. The vans' estimated residual value is $300,000 at the end of the lease term and $50,000 at the end of 7 years, the estimated life of each van.

c. VIP estimates the fair value of the vans to be $1,240,000. Interstate's cost was $1,050,000.

d. VIP's incremental borrowing rate is 11%.

e. VIP will pay the executory costs (maintenance, insurance, and other fees not included in the annual lease payments) of $1,000 per year. The depreciation method is straight-line.

f. The collectibility of the lease payments is reasonably predictable, and there are no important cost uncertainties.

Your instructor will divide the class into two to six groups depending on the size of the class. The mission of your group is to assess the proper recording and reporting of the lease described.

Required:

1. Each group member should deliberate the situation independently and draft a tentative argument prior to the class session for which the case is assigned.

2. In class, each group will meet for 10 to 15 minutes in different areas of the classroom. During that meeting, group members will take turns sharing their suggestions for the purpose of arriving at a single group treatment.

3. After the allotted time, a spokesperson for each group (selected during the group meetings) will share the group's solution with the class. The goal of the class is to incorporate the views of each group into a consensus approach to the situation.
   Specifically, you should address:

   a. Identify potential advantages to VIP of leasing the vans rather than purchasing them.

   b. How should the lease be classified by VIP? by Interstate?

   c. Regardless of your response to previous requirements, suppose VIP recorded the lease on January 1, 2011, as a capital lease in the amount of $1,100,000. What would be the appropriate journal entries related to the capital lease for the second lease payment on December 31, 2011?

Ethics Case 15–4
Leasehold improvements
● LO3

American Movieplex, a large movie theater chain, leases most of its theater facilities. In conjunction with recent operating leases, the company spent $28 million for seats and carpeting. The question being discussed over breakfast on Wednesday morning was the length of the depreciation period for these leasehold improvements. The company controller, Sarah Keene, was surprised by the suggestion of Larry Person, her new assistant.

> *Keene:* Why 25 years? We've never depreciated leasehold improvements for such a long period.
> *Person:* I noticed that in my review of back records. But during our expansion to the Midwest, we don't need expenses to be any higher than necessary.
> *Keene:* But isn't that a pretty rosy estimate of these assets' actual life? Trade publications show an average depreciation period of 12 years.

Required:

1. How would increasing the depreciation period affect American Movieplex's income?
2. Does revising the estimate pose an ethical dilemma?
3. Who would be affected if Person's suggestion is followed?

IFRS Case 15–5
Capitalizing operating leases; financial statement effects
● LO5 LO11

In concert with the International Accounting Standards Board, the FASB is rethinking accounting for leases. Because obligations to make operating lease payments contribute to a company's riskiness, some accountants speculate that new lease standards might require leases now considered to be operating leases to be capitalized the way we now record capital leases.

Refer to the financial statements and related disclosure notes of **Dell Inc.**, located in the company's 2009 financial statements and related disclosure notes in Appendix B located at the back of the text. You also can locate the 2009 report online at **www.dell.com**. Find disclosure note 10, "Commitments and Contingencies." Note the discussion of Dell's lease commitments for certain of its property and equipment, manufacturing facilities, and office space.

Required:

1. What is the total of Dell's operating lease commitments?
2. If the operating leases were capitalized, approximately how much would that increase Dell's debt? [Assume a 6% interest rate and state clearly any other assumptions you make in your calculations.]
3. Referring also to Dell's balance sheet, determine the effect that capitalizing the leases would have on the company's debt-equity ratio.

Real Word Case 15–6
Lease concepts; Walmart
● LO1 through LO6

Real World Financials

Walmart Stores, Inc., is the world's largest retailer. A large portion of the premises that the company occupies are leased. Its financial statements and disclosure notes revealed the following information:

Balance Sheet
($ in millions)

	2009	2008
Assets		
Property:		
Property under capital lease	$5,341	$5,736
Less: Accumulated amortization	(2,544)	(2,594)
Liabilities		
Current liabilities:		
Obligations under capital leases due within one year	315	316
Long-term debt:		
Long-term obligations under capital leases	3,200	3,603

Required:

1. Discuss some possible reasons why Walmart leases rather than purchases most of its premises.
2. The net asset "property under capital lease" has a 2009 balance of $2,797 million ($5,341 − 2,544). Liabilities for capital leases total $3,515 ($315 + 3,200). Why do the asset and liability amounts differ?
3. Prepare a 2009 summary entry to record Walmart's lease payments, which were $603 million.
4. What is the approximate average interest rate on Walmart's capital leases? (Hint: See Req. 3)

Real World Case 15–7
Sale-leaseback; FedEx
● LO10

Real World Financials

FedEx Corporation, the world's largest express transportation company, leases much of its aircraft, land, facilities, and equipment. A portion of those leases are part of sale and leaseback arrangements. An excerpt from FedEx's 2009 disclosure notes describes the company's handling of gains from those arrangements:

Deferred Gains

Gains on the sale and leaseback of aircraft and other property and equipment are deferred and amortized ratably over the life of the lease as a reduction of rent expense.

Required:

1. Why should companies defer gains from sale-leaseback arrangements?

2. Based on the information provided in the disclosure note, determine whether the leases in the leaseback portion of the arrangements are considered by FedEx to be capital leases or operating leases. Explain.

**Communication
Case 15–8**
Where's the gain?
● LO1 LO2
　LO3 LO10

General Tools is seeking ways to maintain and improve cash balances. As company controller, you have proposed the sale and leaseback of much of the company's equipment. As seller-lessee, General Tools would retain the right to essentially all of the remaining use of the equipment. The term of the lease would be six years. A gain would result on the sale portion of the transaction. The lease portion would be classified appropriately as a capital lease.

You previously convinced your CFO of the cash flow benefits of the arrangement, but now he doesn't understand the way you will account for the transaction. "I really had counted on that gain to bolster this period's earnings. What gives?" he wondered. "Put it in a memo, will you? I'm having trouble following what you're saying to me."

Required:

Write a memo to your CFO. Include discussion of each of these points:

1. How the sale portion of the sale-leaseback transaction should be accounted for at the lease's inception.

2. How the gain on the sale portion of the sale-leaseback transaction should be accounted for during the lease.

3. How the leaseback portion of the sale-leaseback transaction should be accounted for at the lease's inception.

4. The conceptual basis for capitalizing certain long-term leases.

**Trueblood
Case 15–9**
Lease inception
date issues
● LO3

The following Trueblood case is recommended for use with this chapter. The case provides an excellent opportunity for class discussion, group projects, and writing assignments. The case, along with Professor's Discussion Material, can be obtained by searching for "Trueblood Cases" on the Deloitte Foundation website: **www.deloitte.com**.

Case 07-7: Porky's Revenge

This case gives students the opportunity to extend their knowledge beyond chapter coverage by determining the lease commencement date. It focuses on a major issue in accounting for leases, but one which had often not been appropriately applied, resulting in incorrect accounting for many leases. It pertains to the situation described in the chapter in which over 200 companies in early 2005 accounted incorrectly for leases.

IFRS Case 15–10
Lease
classification; U.S.
GAAP
● LO1 LO2
　LO3 LO11

Security Devices Inc. (SDI) needs additional office space to accommodate expansion. SDI wants to avoid additional debt in its balance sheet.

Required:

1. What lease classification would management prefer? Explain.

2. If SDI follows U.S. GAAP, how might SDI structure the lease agreement to avoid the additional debt? Explain.

3. Would avoiding the additional debt be more or less difficult under IFRS? Explain.

BRITISH AIRWAYS CASE

BRITISH AIRWAYS
● LO11

British Airways, Plc. (BA), a U.K. company, prepares its financial statements according to International Financial Reporting Standards. BA's annual report for the year ended March 31, 2009, which includes financial statements and disclosure notes, is included with all new textbooks and can be found at **www.britishairways.com**. When answering questions, focus on BA's "Group" financial information (which is equivalent to "Consolidated" under U.S. GAAP).

Required:

1. In Note 2: Summary of significant accounting policies, part d: Leased and hire purchase assets, BA states that "Where assets are financed through finance leases or hire purchase arrangements, under which substantially all the risks and rewards of ownership are transferred to the Group, the assets are treated as if they had been purchased outright." Is this the policy companies using U.S. GAAP follow in accounting for capital leases? Explain.

2. Look at BA's Note 28: Long-term borrowings and Note 29: Operating lease commitments. Does BA obtain use of its aircraft more using operating leases or finance leases? Do lessees report operating and finance lease commitments the same way? Explain.

CPA SIMULATION 15–1

GA Company
Leases

CPA Review

Test your knowledge of the concepts discussed in this chapter, practice critical professional skills necessary for career success, and prepare for the computer-based CPA exam by accessing our CPA simulations at the text website: **www.mhhe.com/spiceland6e**.

The GA Company simulation tests your knowledge of (a) the way we account for and report leases from the perspective of both the lessor and lessee, (b) how lease accounting is influenced by bargain purchase options and guaranteed residual value, and (c) accounting for sale-leaseback arrangements.

As on the CPA exam itself, you will be asked to use tools including a spreadsheet, a calculator, and generally accepted accounting principles, to conduct research, derive solutions, and communicate conclusions related to these issues in a simulated environment.

Specific tasks in the simulation include:

- Completing a worksheet pertaining to interest revenue recognition on a sales-type lease.
- Demonstrating an understanding of the way a lessee accounts for a capital lease.
- Demonstrating an understanding of the way a lessor accounts for a sales-type lease.
- Applying judgment in deciding how bargain purchase options, residual value, and sale-leaseback arrangements affect lease accounting.
- Communicating the criteria applied when classifying leases.
- Researching whether sale-leaseback treatment is appropriate in a specific situation described.

16 Accounting for Income Taxes

|ı|ıı|ıııı|ıııı|ıııı|ıııı|ıııı|ıııı|ıııı|ıııı|

/// **OVERVIEW**

In this chapter we explore the financial accounting and reporting standards for the effects of income taxes. The discussion defines and illustrates temporary differences, which are the basis for recognizing deferred tax assets and deferred tax liabilities, as well as permanent differences, which have no deferred tax consequences. You will learn how to adjust deferred tax assets and deferred tax liabilities when tax laws or rates change. We also discuss accounting for operating loss carrybacks and carryforwards and intraperiod tax allocation.

/// **LEARNING OBJECTIVES**

After studying this chapter, you should be able to:

- **LO1** Describe the types of temporary differences that cause deferred tax liabilities and determine the amounts needed to record periodic income taxes. (page 875)

- **LO2** Identify and describe the types of temporary differences that cause deferred tax assets. (page 882)

- **LO3** Describe when and how a valuation allowance is recorded for deferred tax assets. (page 885)

- **LO4** Explain why permanent differences have no deferred tax consequences. (page 886)

- **LO5** Explain how a change in tax rates affects the measurement of deferred tax amounts. (page 890)

- **LO6** Determine income tax amounts when multiple temporary differences exist. (page 892)

- **LO7** Describe when and how an operating loss carryforward and an operating loss carryback are recognized in the financial statements. (page 894)

- **LO8** Explain how deferred tax assets and deferred tax liabilities are classified and reported in a classified balance sheet and describe related disclosures. (page 897)

- **LO9** Demonstrate how to account for uncertainty in income tax decisions. (page 900)

- **LO10** Explain intraperiod tax allocation. (page 902).

- **LO11** Discuss the primary differences between U.S. GAAP and IFRS with respect to accounting for income taxes. (pages 887 and 904).

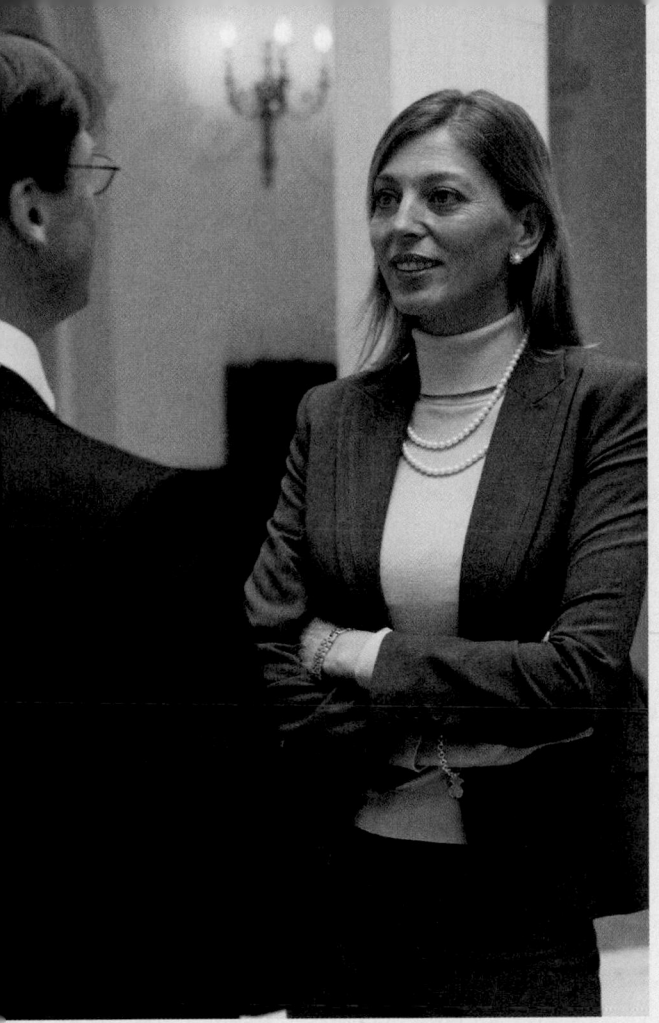

FINANCIAL REPORTING CASE

What's the Difference?

The board of directors for Times-Lehrer Industries is meeting for the first time since Laura Lynn was asked to join the board. Laura was the director of the regional office of United Charities. Although she has broad experience with the tax advantages of charitable giving and the vast array of investment vehicles available to donors, her 30 years of experience with not-for-profit organizations has not exposed her to the issues involved with corporate taxation. This gap in her considerable business knowledge causes her to turn to you, Times-Lehrer's CFO and long-time friend, who recommended Laura for appointment to the board.

"I must say," Laura confided, "I've looked long and hard at these statements, and I can't quite grasp why the amount reported for income tax expense is not the same as the amount of income taxes we paid. What's the difference?"

By the time you finish this chapter, you should be able to respond appropriately to the questions posed in this case. Compare your response to the solution provided at the end of the chapter.

QUESTIONS ///

1. What's the difference? Explain to Laura how differences between financial reporting standards and income tax rules might cause the income tax expense and the amount of income tax paid to differ. (page 874)

2. What is the conceptual advantage of determining income tax expense as we do? (page 874)

3. Are there differences between financial reporting standards and income tax rules that will not cause a difference between income tax expense and the amount of income taxes paid? (page 886)

PART **A**

DEFERRED TAX ASSETS AND DEFERRED TAX LIABILITIES

FINANCIAL
Reporting Case

Q1, p. 873

A manufacturer of leather accessories in the Midwest is obligated to pay the Internal Revenue Service $24 million in income taxes as determined by its 2011 income tax return. Another $9 million in income taxes also is attributable to 2011 activities. Conveniently, though, tax laws permit the company to defer paying the additional $9 million until subsequent tax years by reporting certain revenues and expenses on the tax return in years other than when reported in the income statement. Does the company have only a current income tax liability of $24 million? Or does it also have a deferred income tax liability for the other $9 million? To phrase the question differently: Should the company report a 2011 income tax expense of the $24 million tax payable for the current year, or $33 million to include the future tax effects of events already recognized? For perspective on this question, we should look closer at the circumstances that might create the situation. Such circumstances are called *temporary differences.*

Conceptual Underpinning

FINANCIAL
Reporting Case

Q2, p. 873

The goals of financial accounting and tax accounting are not the same.

Accounting for income taxes is consistent with the accrual concept of accounting.

Current GAAP focuses on the balance sheet and the recognition of liabilities and assets.

When a company prepares its tax return for a particular year, the revenues and expenses (and gains and losses) included on the return are, by and large, the same as those reported on the company's income statement for the same year. However, in some instances tax laws and financial accounting standards differ. The reason they differ is that the fundamental objectives of financial reporting and those of taxing authorities are not the same. Financial accounting standards are established to provide useful information to investors and creditors. Congress, through the Internal Revenue Service, on the other hand, is primarily concerned with raising public revenues in a socially acceptable manner and, frequently, with influencing the behavior of taxpayers. In pursuing the latter objective, Congress uses tax laws to encourage activities it deems desirable, such as investment in productive assets, and to discourage activities it deems undesirable, such as violations of law.

A consequence of differences between GAAP and tax rules is that tax payments frequently occur in years different from when the revenues and expenses that cause the taxes are generated. The financial reporting issue is *when* the tax expense should be recognized. In 1967, the profession embraced the concept of reporting income tax expense in the same period as events that give rise to the expense, regardless of when the tax actually is paid.[1] You may recognize this approach as being consistent with the accrual concept of accounting. The primary focus of that pronouncement was the matching principle. Income tax expense was calculated on the basis of pretax income reported in the income statement. Differences between the expense and the tax currently paid were reported on the balance sheet not as deferred tax liabilities (or assets) but as nebulous deferred credits (or debits).[2]

In 1987 the FASB issued a new standard that reiterated the objective of reporting deferred taxes but redirected the focus to an asset-liability approach.[3] This balance sheet focus emphasizes reporting the future tax sacrifice or benefit attributable to temporary differences between the reported amount of an asset or liability in the financial statements and its tax basis.[4] The objective of accounting for income taxes is to recognize a deferred tax liability or deferred tax asset for the tax consequences of amounts that will become taxable or deductible in future years as a result of transactions or events that already have occurred. Future taxable amounts and future deductible amounts arise as a result of temporary differences. We discuss those now.

---

[1]"Accounting for Income Taxes," *Accounting Principles Board Opinion No. 11* (New York: AICPA, 1967). This pronouncement is no longer GAAP.

[2]Some critics at the time referred to these amounts as "UGOs: Unidentified Growing Objects."

[3]"Accounting for Income Taxes," *Statement of Financial Accounting Standards No. 96* (Stamford, Conn.: FASB, 1987). This pronouncement is no longer GAAP.

[4]Research supports the notion that deferred tax liabilities are, in fact, viewed by investors as real liabilities.

Temporary Differences

The differences in the rules for computing taxable income and those for financial reporting often cause amounts to be included in taxable income in a year later—or earlier—than the year in which they are recognized for financial reporting purposes, or not to be included in taxable income at all. For example, you learned in Chapter 4 that income from selling properties on an installment basis is reported for financial reporting purposes in the year of the sale. But tax laws permit installment income to be reported on the tax return as it actually is received (by the installment method). This means taxable income might be less than accounting income in the year of an installment sale but higher than accounting income in later years when installment income is collected.

● **LO1**

The situation just described creates what's referred to as a **temporary difference** between pretax *accounting* income and *taxable* income and, consequently, between the reported amount of an asset or liability in the financial statements and its tax basis. In our example, the asset for which the temporary difference exists is the installment receivable that's recognized for financial reporting purposes, but not for tax purposes.

Deferred Tax Liabilities

It's important to understand that a temporary difference *originates* in one period and *reverses,* or turns around, in one or more subsequent periods. The temporary difference described above originates in the year the installment sales are made and are reported in the *income statement* and then reverses when the installments are collected and income is reported on the *tax return.* An example is provided in Illustration 16–1.

| Kent Land Management reported pretax accounting income in 2011, 2012, and 2013 of $100 million, plus additional 2011 income of $40 million from installment sales of property.[5] However, the installment sales income is reported on the tax return when collected, in 2012 ($10 million) and 2013 ($30 million).* The enacted tax rate is 40% each year.[†] | **ILLUSTRATION 16–1**
Revenue Reported on the Tax Return *after* the Income Statement |

($ in millions)	Temporary Difference				In 2011, taxable income is less than accounting income because income from installment sales is not reported on the tax return until 2012–2013.
	Originates	Reverses			
	2011	**2012**	**2013**	**Total**	
Pretax accounting income	$140	$100	$100	$340	
Installment sale income on the income statement	(40)	0	0	(40)	
Installment sale income on the tax return	0	10	30	40	
Taxable income (tax return)	$100	$110	$130	$340	

*The installment method is not available to accrual method taxpayers. H.R. 1180, sec. 536, 1999.
†The enacted rate refers to the tax rate indicated by currently enacted tax legislation (as distinguished from anticipated legislation). This is discussed later in the chapter.

Notice that pretax accounting income and taxable income total the same amount over the three-year period but are different in each individual year. In 2011, taxable income is $40 million *less* than accounting income because it does not include income from installment sales. The difference is temporary, though. That situation reverses over the next two years. In 2012 and 2013 taxable income is *more* than accounting income because income from the installment sales, reported in the income statement in 2011, becomes taxable during the next two years as installments are collected.

Because tax laws permit the company to delay reporting this income as part of taxable income, the company is able to defer paying the tax on that income. The tax is not avoided,

The 2011 tax liability is paid in the next two years.

---

[5]For simplicity, we consider the installment receivable to be the *net* amount of the installment receivable and the deferred gross profit in each of our illustrations involving installment sales.

just deferred. In the meantime, the company has a liability for the income tax deferred. The liability originates in 2011 and is paid over the next two years as follows:

Deferred Tax Liability

($ in millions)		16	2011 ($40 × 40%)
2012 ($10 × 40%)	4		
2013 ($30 × 40%)	12		
		0	Balance after 3 years

At the end of 2011, financial and taxable income for 2012 and 2013 are, of course, not yet known. We assumed knowledge of that information above so we could compare the three-year effect of the temporary difference, but seeing the future is unnecessary to determine amounts needed to record income taxes in 2011. This is demonstrated in Illustration 16–1A.

ILLUSTRATION 16–1A

Determining and Recording Income Taxes—2011

($ in millions)

	Current Year 2011	Future Taxable Amounts 2012	Future Taxable Amounts 2013	Future Taxable Amounts (total)
Pretax accounting income	$140			
Temporary difference:				
Installment income	(40)	$10	$30	$40
Taxable income (tax return)	100			
Enacted tax rate	40%	*Reported in the income statement, not on the tax return*		40%
Tax payable currently	40			
Deferred tax liability				$16

Deferred Tax Liability

		Future Taxable Amounts (total)
Desired ending balance		$16
Less: Beginning balance		0
Change in balance		$16

Deferred tax liability

0 beg. bal.	
16 change	
16 ending bal.	

Journal Entry at the End of 2011

Income tax expense (to balance)	56	
Income tax payable (determined above)		40
Deferred tax liability (determined above)		16

With **future taxable amounts** of $40 million, taxable at 40%, a $16 million **deferred tax liability** is indicated. Since no previous balance exists, we add this amount to the liability.

Each year, income tax expense comprises both the current and the deferred tax consequences of events and transactions already recognized. This means we:

Deferred tax liability

	16 beg. bal.
change 4	
	12 ending bal.

At the end of 2012, the deferred tax liability should have a balance of $12 million. Because the balance from 2011 is $16 million, we reduce it by $4 million.

1. Calculate the income tax that is payable currently.
2. Separately calculate the change in the deferred tax liability (or asset).
3. Combine the two to get the income tax expense.

Using the 2012 and 2013 income numbers, the journal entries to record income taxes for those years would be:

2012	($ in millions)
Income tax expense (to balance)	40
Deferred tax liability [($30 million × 40%) – 16 million]	4
Income tax payable ($110 million × 40%)	44

2013		
Income tax expense (to balance)	40	
Deferred tax liability ($0 million – 12 million)	12	
Income tax payable ($130 million × 40%)		52

At the end of 2013, the deferred tax liability should have a balance of zero. So, we eliminate the $12 million balance.

The FASB's Balance Sheet Approach

Our perspective in this example so far has centered around the income effects of the installment sales and thus on the changes in the deferred tax liability as the temporary difference reverses. Another perspective is to consider the balance sheet effect. From this viewpoint, we regard a deferred tax liability (or asset) to be the tax effect of the temporary difference between the *financial statement carrying amount* of an asset or liability and its *tax basis*. The tax basis of an asset or liability is its original value for tax purposes reduced by any amounts included to date on tax returns. In our example, a temporary book-tax difference exists for a receivable from installment sales that's recognized for financial reporting purposes but not for tax purposes. When a company sells something on an installment basis, it reports a receivable. From a tax perspective, though, there is no receivable because a "taxable sale" doesn't occur until installments are collected. This is shown in Illustration 16–1B.

Current GAAP focuses on the balance sheet and the recognition of liabilities and assets.

An installment receivable has no tax basis.

	December 31 ($ in millions)					
	2011		**2012**		**2013**	
Receivable from installment sales:						
Accounting basis	$40	$40	$(10)	$30	$(30)	$0
Tax basis	(0)	(0)	(0)	(0)	(0)	(0)
Temporary difference	$40	$40	$(10)	$30	$(30)	$0
Tax rate		× 40%		× 40%		× 40%
Deferred tax liability		$16		$12		$0
	Originating Difference		Reversing Differences			

ILLUSTRATION 16–1B

Balance Sheet Perspective

The deferred tax liability each year is the tax rate times the temporary difference between the financial statement carrying amount of the receivable and its tax basis.

Of course, the income statement view and the balance sheet view are two different perspectives on the very same event. In this example, we derive the same deferred tax liability whether we view it as a result of a temporary difference (a) between accounting and taxable income or (b) between the financial statement carrying amount of an installment receivable and its tax basis. Conceptually, though, the balance sheet approach strives to establish deferred tax assets and liabilities that meet the definitions of assets and liabilities provided by the FASB's conceptual framework. As specified by *SFAC 6,* assets represent "probable future economic benefits obtained or controlled by a particular entity as a result of past transactions or events," and liabilities are "probable future sacrifices of economic benefits as a result of past transactions or events."[6] In our example, the probable future sacrifices of economic benefits are the payments of $4 million in 2012 and $12 million in 2013. The past transactions or events resulting in the future tax payments are the installment sales in 2011.

This balance sheet approach, sometimes called the "asset/liability approach," is a perspective that extends beyond accounting for deferred taxes. In fact, the FASB and IASB increasingly appear to be moving to that perspective in their approach to accounting standards. The movement toward fair values we discussed in Chapters 12 (Investments) and 14 (Bonds and Long-term Notes) is consistent with that perspective. Measuring assets and liabilities at their fair values and then reporting changes in those fair values as holding gains and losses in the income statement is a fundamental departure from the "transactions approach," by which we report in the income statement the effects of external transactions such as gains and losses from the sale of assets and liabilities.

Recent accounting standards provide evidence that U.S. and international standard setters are embracing a "balance sheet approach" to accounting.

---

[6]"Elements of Financial Statements," *Statement of Financial Accounting Concepts No. 6* (Stamford, Conn.: FASB, 1985), par. 25, 35.

Types of Temporary Differences

Examples of temporary differences are provided in Graphic 16–1.

	Revenues (or gains)	**Expenses (or losses)**
Reported in the income statement now, but on the tax return later	• Installment sales of property (installment method for taxes) • Unrealized gain from recording investments at fair value (taxable when asset is sold)	• Estimated expenses and losses (tax-deductible when paid) • Unrealized loss from recording investments at fair value or inventory at LCM (tax-deductible when asset is sold)
Reported on the tax return now, but in the income statement later	• Rent collected in advance • Subscriptions collected in advance • Other revenue collected in advance	• Accelerated depreciation on the tax return in excess of straight-line depreciation in the income statement • Prepaid expenses (tax-deductible when paid)

- The temporary differences shown in the diagonal purple areas create *deferred tax liabilities* because they result in *taxable* amounts in some future year(s) when the related assets are recovered or the related liabilities are settled (when the temporary differences reverse).

- The temporary differences in the opposite diagonal blue areas create *deferred tax assets* because they result in *deductible* amounts in some future year(s) when the related assets are recovered or the related liabilities are settled (when the temporary differences reverse).

ADDITIONAL CONSIDERATION

Temporary differences between the reported amount of an asset or liability in the financial statements and its tax basis are primarily caused by revenues, expenses, gains, and losses being included in taxable income in a year other than the year in which they are recognized for financial reporting purposes as illustrated in Graphic 16–1. Other events also can cause temporary differences between the reported amount of an asset or liability in the financial statements and its tax basis. Three other such events that are beyond the scope of this textbook are briefly described in FASB ASC 740–10–25: Income Taxes–Overall–Recognition (previously "Accounting for Income Taxes," *Statement of Financial Accounting Standards No. 109* (Norwalk, Conn.: FASB, 1992), par. 11 e–h). Our discussions in this chapter focus on temporary differences caused by the timing of revenue and expense recognition, but it's important to realize that the concept of temporary differences embraces all differences that will result in taxable or deductible amounts in future years.

Be sure to notice that deferred tax liabilities can arise from either (a) a revenue being re-ported on the tax return after the income statement or (b) an expense being reported on the tax return before the income statement. Our previous illustration was of the first type. We look at the second type in Illustration 16–2.

Notice, too, that this temporary difference originates during more than a single year before it begins to reverse. This usually is true when depreciation is the cause of the temporary difference. Tax laws typically permit the cost of a depreciable asset to be deducted on the tax return sooner than it is reported as depreciation in the income statement.[7] This means

---

[7]Presently, the accelerated depreciation method prescribed by the tax code is the modified accelerated cost recovery system (MACRS). The method is described in the Chapter 11 appendix.

Courts Temporary Services reported pretax accounting income in 2011, 2012, 2013, and 2014 of $100 million. In 2011, an asset was acquired for $100 million. The asset is depreciated for financial reporting purposes over four years on a straight-line basis (no residual value). For tax purposes the asset's cost is deducted (by MACRS) over 2011–2014 as follows: $33 million, $44 million, $15 million, and $8 million. No other depreciable assets were acquired. The enacted tax rate is 40% each year.

($ in millions)	Originates		Reverses		
Temporary Difference					
	2011	**2012**	**2013**	**2014**	**Total**
Pretax accounting income	$100	$100	$100	$100	$400
Depreciation on the income statement	25	25	25	25	100
Depreciation on the tax return	(33)	(44)	(15)	(8)	(100)
Taxable income (tax return)	$ 92	$ 81	$110	$117	$400

ILLUSTRATION 16–2

Expense Reported on the Tax Return before the Income Statement

To determine taxable income, we add back to accounting income the actual depreciation taken in the income statement and then subtract the depreciation deduction allowed on the tax return.

taxable income will be less than pretax accounting income in the income statement during the years the tax deduction is higher than income statement depreciation, but higher than pretax accounting income in later years when the situation reverses.

2011 income taxes would be recorded as follows in Illustration 16–2A:

($ in millions)	Current Year 2011	Future Taxable Amounts			Future Taxable Amounts (total)
		2012	**2013**	**2014**	
Pretax accounting income	$ 100				
Temporary difference:					
Depreciation	(8)	$(19)	$10	$17	$8
Taxable income	$ 92				
Enacted tax rate	40%				40%
Tax payable currently	$36.8				
Deferred tax liability					$3.2
Deferred Tax Liability					
Ending balance needed					$3.2
Less: Beginning balance					0.0
Change in balance					$3.2

Tax depreciation is $8 million more than in the income statement.

ILLUSTRATION 16–2A

Determining and Recording Income Taxes—2011

Taxable income is $8 million less than accounting income because that much more depreciation is deducted on the 2011 tax return ($33 million) than is reported in the income statement ($25 million).

Income tax expense is comprised of two components: the amount payable currently and the amount deferred until later.

Journal Entry at the End of 2011

Income tax expense (to balance)	40	
Income tax payable (determined above)		36.8
Deferred tax liability (determined above)		3.2

Let's follow the determination of income taxes for this illustration all the way through the complete reversal of the temporary difference. We assume accounting income is $100 million each year and that the only difference between pretax accounting income and taxable income is caused by depreciation. 2012 income taxes would be determined as shown in Illustration 16–2B on the next page.

Notice that each year the appropriate balance is determined for the deferred tax liability. That amount is compared with any existing balance to determine whether the account must be either increased or decreased.

ILLUSTRATION 16–2B

Determining and Recording Income Taxes—2012

The cumulative temporary difference ($27 million) is both (a) the sum of the amounts originating in 2011 ($8 million) and in 2012 ($19 million) and (b) the sum of the amounts reversing in 2013 ($10 million) and in 2014 ($17 million).

Since a balance of $3.2 million already exists, **$7.6 million** must be added.

($ in millions)

	2011	Current Year 2012	Future Taxable Amounts 2013	Future Taxable Amounts 2014	Future Taxable Amounts (total)
Pretax accounting income		$ 100			
Temporary difference:					
Depreciation	$(8)	(19)	$10	$17	$ 27
Taxable income (tax return)		81			
Enacted tax rate		40%			40%
Tax payable currently		$32.4			
Deferred tax liability					$10.8

Deferred Tax Liability		
		3.2
Ending balance needed		7.6
Less: Beginning balance		10.8

	$10.8
	$10.8
Change in balance	(3.2)
	$ 7.6

Journal Entry at the End of 2012

Income tax expense (to balance)	40	
Income tax payable (determined above)		32.4
Deferred tax liability (determined above)		7.6

Income taxes for 2013 would be recorded as shown in Illustration 16–2C.

ILLUSTRATION 16–2C

Determining and Recording Income Taxes—2013

A credit balance of $6.8 million is needed in the deferred tax liability account.

Since a credit balance of $10.8 million already exists, **$4 million must be deducted (debited).**

A portion of the tax deferred from 2011 and 2012 is now being paid in 2013.

($ in millions)

	2011	2012	Current Year 2013	Future Taxable Amounts 2014	Future Taxable Amounts (total)
Pretax accounting income			$100		
Temporary difference:					
Depreciation	$(8)	$(19)	10	$17	$ 17
Taxable income (tax return)			$110		
Enacted tax rate			40%		40%
Tax payable currently			$ 44		
Deferred tax liability					$ 6.8

Deferred Tax Liability		
		10.8
Ending balance needed	4.0	
Less: Beginning balance		6.8

	$ 6.8
	$ 6.8
	(10.8)
Change in balance	$ (4.0)

Journal Entry at the End of 2013

Income tax expense (to balance)	40	
Deferred tax liability (determined above)	4	
Income tax payable (determined above)		44

Income taxes for 2014 would be recorded as shown in Illustration 16–2D:

($ in millions)	2011	2012	2013	Current Year 2014	Future Taxable Amounts (total)
Pretax accounting income				$100	
Temporary difference:					
Depreciation	$(8)	$(19)	$10	17	$ 0
Taxable income (tax return)				$117	
Enacted tax rate				40%	40%
Tax payable currently				$ 46.8	
Deferred tax liability					$ 0.0

Deferred Tax Liability

Ending balance needed		$ 0.0
Less: Beginning balance		(6.8)
Change in balance		$(6.8)

Journal Entry at the End of 2014

Income tax expense (to balance)	40.0	
Deferred tax liability (determined above)	6.8	
Income tax payable (determined above)		46.8

ILLUSTRATION 16–2D
Determining and Recording Income Taxes—2014

Because the entire temporary difference has now reversed, there is a zero cumulative temporary difference, and the balance in the deferred tax liability should be zero.

Since a credit balance of **$6.8** million exists, that amount must be deducted (debited).

The final portion of the tax deferred from 2011 and 2012 is paid in 2014.

Notice there that the deferred tax liability is increased in 2011–2012 and decreased in 2013–2014.

Deferred Tax Liability

($ in millions)			
		3.2	2011 ($ 8 × 40%)
2013 ($10 × 40%)	4.0	7.6	2012 ($19 × 40%)
2014 ($17 × 40%)	6.8		
		0	Balance after 4 years

The deferred tax liability increases the first two years and is paid over the next two years.

We can see this result from the alternate perspective of looking at the temporary book–tax difference that exists for the depreciable asset. Its carrying amount is its cost minus accumulated straight-line depreciation. Its tax basis is cost minus the accumulated cost recovery for tax purposes:

($ in millions)		2011		2012		2013		2014
Depreciable asset:								
Accounting basis	$100	$(25) $ 75	$(25)	$ 50	$(25)	$ 25	$(25)	$ 0
Tax basis	100	(33) 67	(44)	23	(15)	8	(8)	0
Temporary difference		$ 8 $ 8	$ 19	$ 27	$(10)	$ 17	$(17)	$ 0
Enacted tax rate		40%		40%		40%		40%
Deferred tax liability		$3.2		$10.8		$6.8		$ 0

Originating Differences   Reversing Differences

A balance sheet perspective focuses on the difference between the carrying amount and the tax basis.

Deferred Tax Assets

The temporary differences illustrated to this point produce future taxable amounts when the temporary differences reverse. Future taxable amounts mean taxable income will be increased relative to pretax accounting income in one or more future years. Sometimes, though, the future tax consequence of a temporary difference will be to decrease taxable income relative to accounting income. Such situations produce what's referred to as future deductible amounts. These have favorable future tax consequences that are recognized as deferred tax assets. Be sure to note, though, that unlike most assets, management views deferred tax assets to be undesirable relative to deferred tax liabilities. The reason is that deferred tax liabilities result from having lower taxable income (and thus lower tax) now. As we see in this section, deferred tax assets result from taxable income (and tax) being higher now than later. It's more desirable to delay paying taxes (any expense for that matter) as long as possible.

Two examples indicated in Graphic 16–1 are (1) estimated expenses that are recognized in income statements when incurred but deducted on tax returns in later years when actually paid and (2) revenues that are taxed when collected but recognized in income statements in later years when actually earned. An example of the first type is provided in Illustration 16–3.

ILLUSTRATION 16–3	RDP Networking reported pretax accounting income in 2011, 2012, and 2013 of $70 million, $100 million, and $100 million, respectively. The 2011 income statement includes a $30 million warranty expense that is deducted for tax purposes when paid in 2012 ($15 million) and 2013 ($15 million).* The income tax rate is 40% each year.

Expense Reported on the Tax Return after the Income Statement

In 2011, taxable income is more than pretax accounting income because the warranty expense is not deducted on the tax return until paid.

($ in millions)

| | Temporary Difference | | | |
| | Originates | Reverses | | |
	2011	2012	2013	Total
Pretax accounting income	$ 70	$100	$100	$270
Warranty expense on the income statement	30			30
Warranty expense on the tax return		(15)	(15)	(30)
Taxable income (tax return)	$100	$ 85	$ 85	$270

*Remember from Chapter 13 that warranty expense is estimated for the period the products are sold even though the actual cost isn't incurred until later periods.

At the end of 2011, the amounts needed to record income tax for 2011 would be determined as shown in Illustration 16–3A.

ILLUSTRATION 16–3A

Determining and Recording Income Taxes—2011

Because the warranty expense was subtracted in the 2011 income statement but isn't deductible on the 2011 tax return, it is added back to pretax accounting income to find taxable income.

The amounts deductible in 2012 and 2013 will produce tax benefits that are recognized now as a deferred tax asset.

($ in millions)

	Current Year 2011	Future Deductible Amounts 2012	Future Deductible Amounts 2013	Future Deductible Amounts (total)
Pretax accounting income	$ 70			
Temporary difference:				
Warranty expense	30	$(15)	$(15)	$(30)
Taxable income (tax return)	$100			
Enacted tax rate	40%			40%
Tax payable currently	$ 40			
Deferred tax asset				$(12)

Deferred Tax Asset

Ending balance needed		$ 12
Less: Beginning balance		0
Change in balance		$ 12

Journal Entry at the End of 2011

Income tax expense (to balance)	28	
Deferred tax asset (determined above)	12	
Income tax payable (determined above)		40

At the end of 2011 and 2012, the company reports a deferred tax asset for future income tax benefits.

Deferred Tax Asset			
			($ in millions)
2011 ($30 × 40%)	12		
		6	2012 ($15 × 40%)
		6	2013 ($15 × 40%)
Balance after 3 years	0		

Income taxes payable in 2012 and 2013 are less than otherwise payable because of the taxes prepaid in 2011.

If we continue the assumption of $85 million taxable income in each of 2012 and 2013, income tax those years would be recorded this way:

2012

Income tax expense (to balance)	40	
Deferred tax asset ($15 million × 40%)		6
Income tax payable ($85 million × 40%)		34

2013

Income tax expense (to balance)	40	
Deferred tax asset ($15 million × 40%)		6
Income tax payable ($85 million × 40%)		34

The deferred tax asset represents the future tax benefit from the reversal of a temporary difference between the financial statement carrying amount of the warranty liability and its tax basis.

($ in millions)		December 31				
		2011		**2012**		**2013**
Warranty liability:						
Accounting basis	$30	$30	$(15)	$15	$(15)	$0
Tax basis	(0)	(0)	(0)	(0)	(0)	(0)
Temporary difference	$30	$30	$(15)	$15	$(15)	$0
Tax rate		× 40%		× 40%		× 40%
Deferred tax asset		$12		$ 6		$0

Originating Difference · Reversing Differences

A liability is recognized for financial reporting purposes when the guaranteed product is sold:

2011 Warr. exp   30
    Liability   30

and reduced when the expense is paid:

2012 Liability   15
    Cash   15

2013 Liability   15
    Cash   15

The preceding is an illustration of an estimated expense that is reported in the income statement when incurred but deducted on tax returns in later years when actually paid. A second type of temporary difference that gives rise to a deferred tax asset is a *revenue* that is taxed when collected but recognized on income statements in later years when actually earned. Illustration 16–4 demonstrates this second type.

From a tax perspective, there is no liability.

Tomorrow Publications reported pretax accounting income in 2011, 2012, and 2013 of $80 million, $115 million, and $105 million, respectively. The 2011 income statement does *not* include $20 million of magazine subscriptions received that year for one- and two-year subscriptions. The subscription revenue is reported for tax purposes in 2011. The revenue will be earned in 2012 ($15 million) and 2013 ($5 million). The income tax rate is 40% each year.

($ in millions)	Temporary Difference			
	Originates	Reverses		
	2011	2012	2013	Total
Pretax accounting income	$ 80	$115	$105	$300
Subscription revenue on the income statement		(15)	(5)	(20)
Subscription revenue on the tax return	20	0	0	20
Taxable income (tax return)	$100	$100	$100	$300

ILLUSTRATION 16–4

Revenue Reported on the Tax Return *before* the Income Statement

In 2011, taxable income is more than accounting income because subscription revenue is not reported in the income statement until 2012 and 2013.

A deferred tax asset is recognized when an existing temporary difference will produce future deductible amounts.

Notice that this temporary difference produces future *deductible* amounts. In 2011, taxable income is $20 million *more* than pretax accounting income because it includes the unearned subscriptions revenue not yet reported in the income statement. However, in 2012 and 2013 taxable income is *less* than accounting income because the subscription revenue is earned and reported in the income statements but not on the tax returns of those two years.

In effect, tax laws require the company to prepay the income tax on this revenue, which is a sacrifice now but will benefit the company later when it avoids paying the taxes when the revenue is earned. In the meantime, the company has an asset representing this future income tax benefit.

At the end of 2011, the amounts needed to record income tax for 2011 would be determined as shown in Illustration 16–4A.

ILLUSTRATION 16–4A

Determining and Recording Income Taxes—2011

Deferred Tax Asset

beg. bal. 0	
change 8	
end. bal. 8	

($ in millions)

	2011	Future Deductible Amounts 2012	Future Deductible Amounts 2013	Future Deductible Amounts (total)
Pretax accounting income	$ 80			
Temporary difference:				
Subscription revenue	20	$(15)	$(5)	$(20)
Taxable income	$100			
Enacted tax rate	40%			40%
Tax payable currently	$ 40			
Deferred tax asset				$ (8)

$20 million is taxable now, but not yet in the income statement.

Deferred Tax Asset

Ending balance needed	$ 8
Less: Beginning balance	0
Change in balance	$ 8

Journal Entry at the End of 2011

Income tax expense (to balance)	32	
Deferred tax asset (determined above)	8	
Income tax payable (determined above)		40

At the end of 2011 and 2012, the company reports a deferred tax asset for future tax benefits.

Income taxes payable in 2012 and 2013 are less than otherwise payable because of the taxes prepaid in 2011.

Deferred Tax Asset

			($ in millions)
2011 ($20 × 40%)	8		
		6	2012 ($15 × 40%)
		2	2013 ($ 5 × 40%)
Balance after 3 years	0		

Again, we could also determine the deferred tax asset as the future tax benefit from the reversal of a temporary difference between the financial statement carrying amount of the subscription liability (an unearned revenue account) and its tax basis.[8]

---

[8]It is less intuitive to view an unearned revenue (Illustration 16–4) as producing future deductible amounts when the unearned revenue liability is settled than it is to view the future deductibility of an estimated expense (Illustration 16–3) as a future deductible amount. Nevertheless, the recognition of deferred tax assets for the future tax benefits of unearned revenue liability temporary differences is consistent with the asset/liability approach of current GAAP because these unearned revenue liabilities are reported as if they represent future refundable amounts and therefore future deductible amounts.

($ in millions)	December 31					
	2011		**2012**		**2013**	
Liability—subscriptions:						
Accounting basis	$20	$20	$(15)	$ 5	$(5)	$ 0
Tax basis	(0)	(0)	(0)	(0)	(0)	(0)
Temporary difference	$20	$20	$(15)	$ 5	$(5)	$ 0
Tax rate		× 40%		× 40%		× 40%
Deferred tax asset		$ 8		$ 2		$ 0

Originating Difference

Reversing Differences

Valuation Allowance

We recognize deferred tax assets for all deductible temporary differences.[9] However, we then reduce a deferred tax asset by a valuation allowance if it is "more likely than not" that some portion or all of the deferred tax asset will not be realized.[10] Remember, a future deductible amount reduces taxable income and saves taxes only if there is taxable income to be reduced when the future deduction is available. So, a **valuation allowance** is needed if taxable income is anticipated to be insufficient to realize the tax benefit.

For example, let's say that in the previous illustration management determines that it's more likely than not that $3 million of the deferred tax asset will not ultimately be realized. The deferred tax asset would be reduced by the creation of a valuation allowance as follows:

> A valuation allowance is needed if it is more likely than not that some portion or all of a deferred tax asset will not be realized.

	($ in millions)	
Income tax expense	3	
Valuation allowance—deferred tax asset		3

The effect is to increase the income tax expense as a result of reduced expectations of future tax savings. In the 2011 balance sheet, the deferred tax asset would be reported at its estimated net realizable value:

● LO3

Deferred tax asset	$8
Less: Valuation allowance—deferred tax asset	(3)
	$5

This is not a new concept for you. You've reduced assets before using a valuation allowance. Suppose, for example, that you have accounts receivable of $8 million but expect that $3 million of that amount will not ultimately be collected from your customers. You would reduce the asset indirectly using a valuation allowance:

Accounts receivable	$8
Less: Allowance for uncollectible accounts	(3)
	$5

ADDITIONAL CONSIDERATION

The decision as to whether a valuation allowance is needed should be based on the weight of all available evidence. The real question is whether or not there will be sufficient taxable income in future years for the anticipated tax benefit to be realized. The benefit of future deductible amounts can be realized only if future income is at least equal to the deferred deductions. After all, a deduction reduces taxes only if it reduces taxable income.

(continued)

---

[9]Unless the deductibility itself is uncertain. In that case, whether we recognize a deferred tax asset (and if so, its amount) is determined in accordance with FASB ASC 740–10–25: Income Taxes Overall–Recognition (previously *FIN 48*) discussed later in the chapter.
[10]"More likely than not" means a likelihood of more than 50%, FASB ASC 740–10–30: Income Taxes–Overall–Initial Measurement (previously "Accounting for Income Taxes," *Statement of Financial Accounting Standards No. 109* (Norwalk, Conn.: FASB, 1992), par. 17).

> (concluded)
>
> All evidence—both positive and negative—should be considered. For instance, operating losses in recent years or anticipated circumstances that would adversely affect future operations would constitute negative evidence. On the other hand, a strong history of profitable operations or sizable, existing contracts would constitute positive evidence of sufficient taxable income to be able to realize the deferred tax asset.
>
> Managerial actions that could be taken to reduce or eliminate a valuation allowance when deferred tax assets are not otherwise expected to be realized must be considered. These tax-planning strategies include any prudent and feasible actions management might take to realize a tax benefit while it is available.
>
> This having been said, it should be clear that the decision as to whether or not a valuation allowance is used, as well as how large the allowance should be, rests squarely on managerial judgment. Because that decision directly impacts the amount of income tax expense and therefore reported income, it has obvious implications for earnings quality assessment from an analyst's perspective.

At the end of each reporting period, the valuation allowance is reevaluated. The appropriate balance is decided on and the balance is adjusted—up or down—to create that balance. For instance, let's say that at the end of the following year, 2012, available evidence indicates that $500,000 of the deferred tax asset at the end of 2012 will not be realized. We would adjust the valuation allowance to reflect the indicated amount:

	($ in millions)	
Valuation allowance—deferred tax asset ($3 million – 0.5 million)...	2.5	
Income tax expense		2.5

The disclosure note shown in Graphic 16–2 accompanied the 2008 annual report of **Intel Corporation** indicating that some of its deferred tax assets were not expected to be realized:

GRAPHIC 16–2

Valuation Allowance—
Intel Corporation

Real World Financials

> The net deferred tax asset valuation allowance was $358 million as of December 27, 2008 compared to $133 million as of December 29, 2007. The valuation allowance is based on our assessment that it is more likely than not that certain deferred tax assets will not be realized in the foreseeable future.

Permanent Differences

● **LO4**

FINANCIAL
Reporting Case

Q3, p. 873

Permanent differences are disregarded when determining both the tax payable currently and the deferred tax asset or liability.

So far, we've dealt with temporary differences between the reported amount of an asset or liability in the financial statements and its tax basis. You learned that temporary differences result in future taxable or deductible amounts when the related asset or liability is recovered or settled. However, some differences are caused by transactions and events that under existing tax law will never affect taxable income or taxes payable. Interest received from investments in bonds issued by state and municipal governments, for instance, is exempt from taxation. Interest revenue of this type is, of course, reported as revenue on the recipient's income statement but not on its tax return—not now, not later. Pretax accounting income exceeds taxable income. This situation will not reverse in a later year. Taxable income in a later year will not exceed pretax accounting income because the tax-free income will never be reported on the tax return.

These permanent differences are disregarded when determining the tax payable currently, the deferred tax effect, and therefore the income tax expense. This is why we adjust accounting income in the illustrations that follow to eliminate any permanent differences from taxable income. Graphic 16–3 provides examples of differences with no deferred tax consequences.

INTERNATIONAL FINANCIAL REPORTING STANDARDS

Non-tax Differences Affect Taxes. Despite the similar approaches for accounting for taxation under *IAS No. 12*, "Income Tax,"[11] and U.S. GAAP, differences in reported amounts for deferred taxes are among the most frequent between the two reporting approaches. The reason is that a great many of the nontax differences between IFRS and U.S. GAAP affect deferred taxes as well.

For example, we noted in Chapter 13 that we accrue a loss contingency under U.S. GAAP if it's both probable and can be reasonably estimated and that IFRS guidelines are similar, but the threshold is "more likely than not." This is a lower threshold than "probable." In this chapter, we noted that accruing a loss contingency (like warranty expense) in the income statement leads to a deferred tax asset if it can't be deducted on the tax return until a later period. As a result, under the lower threshold of IFRS, we might record a loss contingency and thus a deferred tax asset, but under U.S. GAAP we might record neither. So, even though accounting for deferred taxes is the same, accounting for loss contingencies is different, causing a difference in the reported amounts of deferred taxes under IFRS and U.S. GAAP.

● LO11

● Interest received from investments in bonds issued by state and municipal governments (not taxable).
● Investment expenses incurred to obtain tax-exempt income (not tax deductible).
● Life insurance proceeds on the death of an insured executive (not taxable).
● Premiums paid for life insurance policies when the payer is the beneficiary (not tax deductible).
● Compensation expense pertaining to some employee stock option plans (not tax deductible).
● Expenses due to violations of the law (not tax deductible).
● Portion of dividends received from U.S. corporations that is not taxable due to the dividends received deduction.[12]
● Tax deduction for depletion of natural resources (percentage depletion) that permanently exceeds the income statement depletion expense (cost depletion).[13]

GRAPHIC 16–3

Differences without Deferred Tax Consequences

Provisions of the tax laws, in some instances, dictate that the amount of a revenue that is taxable or expense that is deductible permanently differs from the amount reported in the income statement.

To compare temporary and **permanent differences,** we can modify Illustration 16–1 to include nontaxable income in Kent Land Management's 2012 pretax accounting income. We do this in Illustration 16–5 on the next page. Note that the existence of an amount that causes a permanent difference has no effect on income taxes payable, deferred taxes, or income tax expense.

To this point, we've seen that our objective in accounting for income taxes is to recognize the tax consequences of amounts that will become taxable or deductible in future years as a result of transactions or events that already have occurred. To achieve the objective, we record a deferred tax liability or deferred tax asset for future taxable amounts or future deductible amounts that arise as a result of temporary differences. Permanent differences, on the other hand, do not create future taxable amounts and future deductible amounts and therefore have no tax consequences.

You might notice here that because of the permanent difference, Kent's "effective" tax rate is less than its 40% statutory rate. The effective rate is the total tax to be paid (eventually), $56 million, divided by accounting income, $145 million, or 38.6%. Without the

Permanent differences affect a company's effective tax rate.

---

[11]"Income Taxes," *International Accounting Standard No. 12* (IASCF), as amended effective January 1, 2009.

[12]When a corporation owns shares of another U.S. corporation, a percentage of the dividends from those shares is exempt from taxation due to the dividends received deduction. The percentage is 70% if the investor owns less than 20% of the investee's shares, 80% for 20% to 80% ownership, and 100% for more than 80% ownership.

[13]The cost of natural resources is reported as depletion expense over their extraction period for financial reporting purposes; but tax rules prescribe sometimes different percentages of cost to be deducted for tax purposes. There usually is a difference between the cost depletion and percentage depletion that doesn't eventually reverse.

ILLUSTRATION 16–5
Temporary and Permanent Differences

Because interest on municipal bonds is tax exempt, it is reported only in the income statement. This difference between pretax accounting income and taxable income does not reverse later.

Kent Land Management reported pretax accounting income in 2011 of $100 million except for additional income of $40 million from installment sales of property and $5 million interest from investments in municipal bonds in 2011. The installment sales income is reported for tax purposes in 2012 ($10 million) and 2013 ($30 million). The enacted tax rate is 40% each year.

($ in millions)	Current Year 2011	Future Taxable Amounts 2012	Future Taxable Amounts 2013	Future Taxable Amounts (total)
Pretax accounting income	$145			
Permanent difference:				
Municipal bond interest	(5)			
Temporary difference:				
Installment income	(40)	$10	$30	$40
Taxable income (tax return)	$100			
Enacted tax rate	40%			40%
Tax payable currently	$ 40			
Deferred tax liability				$16

Deferred Tax Liability

Ending balance needed	$16
Less: Beginning balance	0
Change in balance	$16

Journal Entry at the End of 2011

Income tax expense (to balance)	56	
Income tax payable (determined above)		40
Deferred tax liability (determined above)...................................		16

$5 million municipal bond interest, the effective rate would have been $56 million divided by $140 million, or 40%. Nontaxable revenues and gains, as we have for Kent, cause the effective rate to be *lower* than the statutory rate; whereas, nondeductible expenses and losses would cause the effective rate to be *higher* than the statutory rate. Companies report a comparison of their effective and statutory tax rates in disclosure notes, as in Graphic 16–4's example from **Walmart**'s 2009 financial statements.

GRAPHIC 16–4
Effective Tax Rate—Walmart

Real World Financials

Note 5: Income Taxes (in part)
Effective Tax Rate Reconciliation

A reconciliation of the significant differences between the effective income tax rate and the federal statutory rate on pre-tax income is as follows:

	Fiscal Year Ended January 31, 2009	2008
Statutory tax rate	35.00 %	35.00 %
State income taxes, net of federal income tax benefit	1.72 %	1.80 %
Income taxes outside the United States	−1.56 %	−1.90 %
Other	−0.98 %	−1.40 %
Effective income tax rate	34.18 %	33.50 %

CONCEPT REVIEW EXERCISE

Mid-South Cellular Systems began operations in 2011. That year the company reported pretax accounting income of $70 million, which included the following amounts:

1. Compensation expense of $3 million related to employee stock option plans granted to organizers was reported in the 2011 income statement. This expense is not deductible for tax purposes.
2. An asset with a four-year useful life was acquired last year. It is depreciated by the straight-line method in the income statement. MACRS is used on the tax return, causing deductions for depreciation to be more than straight-line depreciation the first two years but less than straight-line depreciation the next two years ($ in millions):

TEMPORARY AND PERMANENT DIFFERENCES

	Depreciation		
	Income Statement	**Tax Return**	**Difference**
2011	$150	$198	$ (48)
2012	150	264	(114)
2013	150	90	60
2014	150	48	102
	$600	$600	$ 0

The enacted tax rate is 40%.

Required:
Prepare the journal entry to record Mid-South Cellular's income taxes for 2011.

($ in millions)

		Future Taxable Amounts				
	Current Year 2011	**2012**	**2013**	**2014**	**Future Taxable Amounts (total)**	
Pretax accounting income	$70					
Permanent difference:						
Compensation expense	3					
Temporary difference:						
Depreciation	(48)	$(114)	$60	$102	$ 48	
Taxable income (tax return)	$25					
Enacted tax rate	40%				40%	
Tax payable currently	$10					
Deferred tax liability					$19.2	

SOLUTION

Because the compensation expense is not tax deductible, taxable income does not include the $3 million deduction and is higher by that amount than accounting income.

Deferred Tax Liability

Ending balance needed	$19.2
Less: Beginning balance	0.0
Change in balance	$19.2

Journal Entry at the End of 2011		
Income tax expense (to balance)	29.2	
Income tax payable (determined above)		10.0
Deferred tax liability (determined above)		19.2

Income tax expense is composed of: (1) the tax payable currently and (2) the tax deferred until later.

PART B   OTHER TAX ACCOUNTING ISSUES

Tax Rate Considerations

● LO5

To measure the deferred tax liability or asset, we multiply the temporary difference by the currently *enacted* tax rate that will be effective in the year(s) the temporary difference reverses.[14] We do not base calculations on *anticipated* legislation that would alter the company's tax rate. A conceptual case can be made that expected rate changes should be anticipated when measuring the deferred tax liability or asset. However, this is one of many examples of the frequent trade-off between relevance and reliability. In this case, the FASB chose to favor reliability by waiting until an anticipated change actually is enacted into law before recognizing its tax consequences.

When Enacted Tax Rates Differ

A deferred tax liability (or asset) is based on enacted tax rates and laws.

Existing tax laws may call for enacted tax rates to be different in two or more future years in which a temporary difference is expected to reverse. When a phased-in change in rates is scheduled to occur, the specific tax rates of each future year are multiplied by the amounts reversing in each of those years. The total is the deferred tax liability or asset.

To illustrate, let's again modify our Kent Land Management illustration, this time to assume a scheduled change in tax rates. See Illustration 16–6.

ILLUSTRATION 16–6
Scheduled Change in Tax Rates

Kent Land Management reported pretax accounting income in 2011 of $100 million except for additional income of $40 million from installment sales of property and $5 million interest from investments in municipal bonds in 2011. The installment sales income is reported for tax purposes in 2012 ($10 million) and 2013 ($30 million). The enacted tax rates are 40% for 2011 and 2012, and 35% for 2013.

($ in millions)	Current Year 2011	Future Taxable Amounts 2012	Future Taxable Amounts 2013	(total)
Pretax accounting income	$145			
Permanent difference:				
Municipal bond interest	(5)			
Temporary difference:				
Installment income	(40)	$10	$ 30	
Taxable income (tax return)	$100			
Enacted tax rate	40%	40%	35%	
Tax payable currently	$ 40			
Deferred tax liability		$ 4	$10.5	$14.5

The tax effects of the future taxable amounts depend on the tax rates at which those amounts will be taxed.

Deferred Tax Liability

Ending balance needed	$14.5
Less: Beginning balance	0.0
Change in balance	$14.5

Journal Entry at the End of 2011

Income tax expense (to balance)	54.5	
Income tax payable (determined above)		40.0
Deferred tax liability (determined above)		14.5

---

[14]The current U.S. corporate tax rate is 34%, or 35% for corporations with taxable income over $75,000. Most states tax corporate income at rates less than 10%. We use 40% in most of our illustrations to simplify calculations.

Be sure to note that the 2012 rate (40%) as well as the 2013 rate (35%) already is enacted into law as of 2011 when the deferred tax liability is established. In the next section we discuss how to handle a change resulting from new legislation.

Changes in Tax Laws or Rates

Tax laws sometimes change. If a change in a tax law or rate occurs, any existing tax liability

> As a result of a change [in tax law or rate] deferred tax consequences become larger or smaller.

or asset must be adjusted. Remember, the deferred tax liability or asset is meant to reflect the amount to be paid or recovered in the future. When legislation changes that amount, the deferred tax liability or asset also should change. The effect is reflected in operating income in the year of the enactment of the change in the tax law or rate.[15]

For clarification, reconsider the previous illustration. Without a change in tax rates and assuming that pretax accounting income reported in the income statement in 2012 is $100 million (with no additional temporary or permanent differences), the 2012 income tax amounts would be determined as shown in Illustration 16–6A.

ILLUSTRATION 16–6A
Reversal of Temporary Difference *without* a Tax Rate Change

($ in millions)

	2011	Current Year 2012	Future Taxable Amount 2013	
Pretax accounting income		$100		
Temporary difference:				
Installment income	(40)	10	$ 30	
Taxable income (tax return)		$110		
Enacted tax rate		40%	35%	
Tax payable currently		$ 44		
Deferred tax liability			$10.5	$10.5
	Deferred Tax Liability			↓
Ending balance needed				$10.5
Less: Beginning balance				(14.5)
Change in balance				$ (4.0)

The 40% 2012 rate and the 35% 2013 rate are established by previously enacted legislation.

Journal Entry at the End of 2012
Income tax expense (to balance)	40	
Deferred tax liability (determined above)	4	
Income tax payable (determined above)		44

Now assume Congress passed a new tax law in 2012 that will cause the 2013 tax rate to be 30% instead of the previously scheduled 35% rate. Because a deferred tax liability was established in 2011 with the expectation that the 2013 taxable amount would be taxed at 35%, it would now be adjusted to reflect taxation at 30%, instead. This is demonstrated in Illustration 16–6B on the next page.

Notice that the methods used to determine the deferred tax liability and the change in that balance are the same as without the rate change—the calculation merely uses the new rate (30%) rather than the old rate (35%). So recalculating the balance needed in the deferred tax liability each period and comparing that amount with any previously existing balance automatically takes into account tax rate changes.

Also notice that the income tax expense ($38.5 million) is $1.5 million less than it would have been without the tax rate change ($40 million). The effect of the change is included in income tax expense. In fact, this is highlighted if we separate the previous entry into

> When a tax rate changes, the deferred tax liability or asset should be adjusted with the effect reflected in operating income in the year of the change.

[15]FASD ASC 740–10–35; Income Taxes–Overall–Subsequent Measurement (previously "Accounting for Income Taxes," *Statement of Financial Accounting Standards No. 109* (Norwalk, Conn.: FASB, 1992)).

ILLUSTRATION 16–6B
Reversal of Temporary Difference with a Tax Rate Change

The deferred tax liability would have been $10.5 million (30 million × 35%) if the tax rate had not changed.

($ in millions)

	2011	Current Year 2012	Future Taxable Amount 2013	
Pretax accounting income		$100		
Temporary difference:				
Installment income	(40)	10	$ 30	
Taxable income (tax return)		$110		
Enacted tax rate		40%	30%*	
Tax payable currently		$ 44		
Deferred tax liability		$ 9	$ 9.0	

*2013 rate enacted into law in 2012.

Deferred Tax Liability

Ending balance needed		$ 9.0
Less: Beginning balance		(14.5)
Change in balance		$ (5.5)

Journal Entry at the End of 2012

Income tax expense (to balance)	38.5	
Deferred tax liability (determined above)	5.5	
Income tax payable (determined above)		44.0

its component parts: (1) record the income tax expense without the tax rate change and (2) separately record the adjustment of the deferred tax liability for the change:

Journal Entries at the End of 2012	($ in millions)	
Income tax expense	40	
Deferred tax liability	4	
Income tax payable		44
Deferred tax liability [$30 million × (35% − 30%)]	1.5	
Income tax expense		1.5

The tax consequence of a change in a tax law or rate is recognized in the period the change is enacted. In this case, the consequence of a lower tax rate is a reduced deferred tax liability, recognized as a reduction in income tax expense in 2012 when the change occurs.

Multiple Temporary Differences

● LO6

It would be unusual for any but a very small company to have only a single temporary difference in any given year. Having multiple temporary differences, though, doesn't change any of the principles you've learned so far in connection with single differences. All that's necessary is to categorize all temporary differences according to whether they create (a) future taxable amounts or (b) future deductible amounts. The total of the future taxable amounts is multiplied by the future tax rate to determine the appropriate balance for the deferred tax liability, and the total of the future deductible amounts is multiplied by the future tax rate to determine the appropriate balance for the deferred tax asset. This is demonstrated in Illustration 16–7 on the next page.

2011

During 2011, its first year of operations, Eli-Wallace Distributors reported pretax accounting income of $200 million which included the following amounts:

1. Income (net) from installment sales of warehouses in 2011 of $9 million to be reported for tax purposes in 2012 ($5 million) and 2013 ($4 million).
2. Depreciation is reported by the straight-line method on an asset with a four-year useful life. On the tax return, deductions for depreciation will be more than straight-line depreciation the first two years but less than straight-line depreciation the next two years ($ in millions):

	Income Statement	Tax Return	Difference
2011	$ 50	$ 66	$(16)
2012	50	88	(38)
2013	50	30	20
2014	50	16	34
	$200	$200	$ 0

3. Estimated warranty expense that will be deductible on the tax return when actually paid during the next two years. Estimated deductions are as follows ($ in millions):

	Income Statement	Tax Return	Difference
2011	$7		$7
2012		$4	(4)
2013		3	(3)
	$7	$7	$0

2012

During 2012, pretax accounting income of $200 million included an estimated loss of $1 million from having accrued a loss contingency. The loss is expected to be paid in 2014 at which time it will be tax deductible.

The enacted tax rate is 40% each year.

ILLUSTRATION 16–7

Multiple Temporary Differences

Look at Illustration 16–7A to see how Eli-Wallace determines the income tax amounts for 2011. Then turn to Illustration 16–7B on page 894 to see how those amounts are determined for 2012.

($ in millions)	Current Year 2011	Future Taxable (Deductible) Amounts			Future Taxable Amounts (total)	Future Deductible Amounts (total)
		2012	2013	2014		
Pretax accounting income	$ 200					
Temporary differences:						
Installment sales	(9)	$ 5	$ 4		$ 9	
Depreciation	(16)	(38)	20	$34	16	
Warranty expense	7	(4)	(3)			$ (7)
Taxable income (tax return)	$ 182				$25	(7)
Enacted tax rate	40%				40%	40%
Tax payable currently	$72.8					
Deferred tax liability					$10	
Deferred tax asset						$(2.8)
					Deferred Tax Liability	Deferred Tax Asset
Ending balances needed					$10	$ 2.8
Less: Beginning balances					0	(0.0)
Change in balances					$10	$ 2.8

Journal Entry at the End of 2011

Income tax expense (to balance)	80.0	
Deferred tax asset (determined above)	2.8	
Deferred tax liability (determined above)		10.0
Income tax payable (determined above)		72.8

ILLUSTRATION 16–7A

Multiple Temporary Differences—2011

Temporary differences are grouped according to whether they create future taxable amounts or future *deductible* amounts.

The balances needed in the deferred tax liability and the deferred tax asset are separately determined.

Income tax expense is composed of three components: (1) the tax payable currently plus (2) the tax deferred until later, reduced by (3) the deferred tax benefit.

ILLUSTRATION 16–7B

Multiple Temporary
Differences—2012

The future
taxable amount of
installment sales
($4 million) is equal
to the cumulative
temporary difference
($9 million − 5 million).

Similarly, the total of
other future taxable
and deductible
amounts is equal
to the cumulative
temporary differences
in the related assets
and liabilities.

Analysis indicates
that the deferred tax
liability should be
increased further and
the deferred tax asset
should be reduced.

($ millions)

	2011	Current Year 2012	Future Taxable (Deductible) Amounts		Future Taxable Amounts (total)*	Future Deductible Amounts (total)*
			2013	2014		
Pretax accounting income		$200				
Temporary differences:						
Installment sales	$ (9)	$ 5	$ 4		$ 4	
Depreciation	(16)	(38)	20	$34	54	
Warranty expense	7	(4)	(3)			$ (3)
Estimated loss		1		(1)		(1)
Taxable income (tax return)		$164			$58	$ (4)
Enacted tax rate		40%			40%	40%
Tax payable currently		$ 65.6				
Deferred tax liability					$23.2	
Deferred tax asset						$(1.6)
					↓	↓
					Deferred Tax Liability	Deferred Tax Asset
Ending balances needed					$23.2	$ 1.6
Less: Beginning balances					(10.0)	(2.8)
Change in balances					$13.2	$ (1.2)

Journal Entry at the End of 2012

Income tax expense (to balance)	80.0	
Deferred tax asset (determined above)		1.2
Deferred tax liability (determined above)		13.2
Deferred tax payable (determined above)		65.6

*Total future taxable and deductible amounts also are equal to the cumulative temporary differences in the related assets and liabilities.

After the journal entry at the end of 2012, the balances of both the deferred tax asset and the deferred tax liability reflect the required amounts as follows ($ in millions):

The deferred tax
asset declines and the
deferred tax liability
increases during 2012.

Deferred Tax Asset			Deferred Tax Liability
2.8		2011 balance	10.0
	1.2	Adjustment	13.2
1.6		2012 balance	23.2

Of course, if a phased-in change in rates is scheduled to occur, it would be necessary to determine the total of the future taxable amounts and the total of the future deductible amounts for each future year as outlined previously. Then the specific tax rates of each future year would be multiplied by the two totals in each of those years. Those annual tax effects would then be summed to find the balances for the deferred tax liability and the deferred tax asset.

Net Operating Losses

● LO7

A **net operating loss** is negative taxable income: tax-deductible expenses exceed taxable revenues. Of course, there is no tax payable for the year an operating loss occurs because there's no taxable income. In addition, tax laws permit the operating loss to be used to reduce taxable income in other, profitable years. Offsetting operating profits with operating losses is achieved by either a carryback of the loss to prior years or a carryforward of the loss to later years, or both. In essence, the tax deductible expenses that can't be deducted this year because they exceed taxable revenues can be deducted in other years. Specifically, the operating loss can be carried back 2 years and forward for up to 20 years:

Carryforward → Up to 20 Years

| 2009 | 2010 | LOSS | 2012 | 2013 | 2014 | → | 2030 | 2031 |

2 years ◄— Carryback

Tax laws permit a choice. A company can elect an operating loss carryback if taxable income was reported in either of the two previous years.[16] By reducing taxable income of a previous year, the company can receive an immediate refund of taxes paid that year.

If taxable income was not reported in either of the two previous years or higher tax rates are anticipated in the future, a company might elect to forgo the operating loss carryback and carry the loss forward for up to 20 years to offset taxable income of those years. Even if a loss carryback is used, any loss that remains after the two-year carryback can be carried forward. The carryforward election is a choice that must be made in the year of the operating loss and the choice is irrevocable. It usually is advantageous to carry back losses because by filing an amended tax return to get a refund, a company can realize the benefit much sooner than if the loss is carried forward.

The accounting question is: *When* should the tax benefit created by an operating loss be recognized in the income statement? The answer is: In the year the loss occurs.

Operating Loss Carryforward

First consider a loss carryforward. You have learned in this chapter that a deferred tax asset is recognized for the future tax benefit of temporary differences that create future deductible amounts. An operating loss carryforward also creates future deductible amounts. Logically, then, a deferred tax asset is recognized for an operating loss carryforward also. This is demonstrated in Illustration 16–8.

During 2011, its first year of operations, American Laminating Corporation reported an operating loss of $125 million for financial reporting and tax purposes. The enacted tax rate is 40%.			
($ in millions)	**Current Year 2011**	**Future Deductible Amounts (total)**	
Operating loss	$(125)		
Loss carryforward	125	$(125)	
	$ 0		
Enacted tax rate	40%	40%	
Tax payable	$ 0		
Deferred tax asset		$ (50)	
Deferred Tax Asset			
Ending balance needed			$50
Less. Beginning balance			0
Change in balance			$50
Journal Entry at the End of 2011			
Deferred tax asset (determined above)		50	
Income tax benefit—operating loss (to balance)			50

ILLUSTRATION 16–8

Operating Loss Carryforward

An operating loss carryforward can be deducted from taxable income in future years.

The tax benefit of being able to deduct amounts in the future represents a deferred tax asset.

The income tax benefit of an operating loss carryforward is recognized for accounting purposes in the year the operating loss occurs. The net after-tax operating loss reflects the future tax savings that the operating loss is expected to create:

Income Statement (partial)

	($ in millions)
Operating loss before income taxes	$125
Less: Income tax benefit—operating loss	(50)
Net operating loss	$ 75

The income tax benefit of an operating loss carryback, like a carryforward, is recognized in the year the operating loss occurs.

---

[16]Actually, a carryback is automatic unless a company elects to forego the carryback in favor of a carryforward.

VALUATION ALLOWANCE. Just as for all deductible temporary differences, deferred tax assets are recognized for any operating loss without regard to the likelihood of having taxable income in future years sufficient to absorb future deductible amounts. However, the deferred tax asset is then reduced by a valuation allowance if it is more likely than not that some portion or all of the deferred tax asset will not be realized. Remember, a valuation allowance both reduces the net deferred tax asset and increases the income tax expense just as if that portion of the deferred tax asset had not been recognized.

Operating Loss Carryback

An operating loss must be applied to the earlier year first and then brought forward to the next year.

To compare the treatment of an operating loss carryback, let's modify the illustration to assume that there was taxable income in the two years prior to the operating loss and that American Laminating will utilize the loss carryback (see Illustration 16–9). Note that the operating loss must be applied to the earlier year first and then brought forward to the next year. If any of the loss remains after reducing taxable income to zero in the two previous years, the remainder is carried forward to future years as an operating loss carryforward.

		($ in millions)
Operating loss before income taxes		$125
Less: Income tax benefit:		
Tax refund from loss carryback	$29	
Future tax savings from loss carryforward	20	49
Net operating loss		$ 76

ILLUSTRATION 16–9

Operating Loss Carryback and Carryforward

An *operating loss carryback* can be deducted from taxable income in the two prior years, creating a refund of taxes paid for those years.

The portion of an operating loss that remains after a carryback is carried forward.

The income tax benefit of an operating loss carryforward is recognized in the year the operating loss occurs.

During 2011, American Laminating Corporation reported an operating loss of $125 million for financial reporting and tax purposes. The enacted tax rate is 40% for 2011. Taxable income, tax rates, and income taxes paid in the two previous years were as follows:

	Taxable Income	Taxable Rates	Income Taxes Paid
2009	$20 million	35%	$ 7 million
2010	55 million	40%	22 million

Here's how the income tax benefit of the operating loss carryback and the operating loss carryforward is determined:

($ in millions)

	Prior Years		Current Year	Future Deductible Amounts
	2009	**2010**	**2011**	**(total)**
Operating loss			$(125)	
Loss carryback	$(20)	$(55)	75	
Loss carryforward			50	$(50)
			$ 0	
Enacted tax rate	35%	40%	40%	40%
Tax payable (refundable)	$ (7)	$(22)	$ 0	
Deferred tax asset				$(20)
Deferred Tax Asset				↓
Ending balance needed				$ 20
Less: Beginning balance				0
Change in balance				$ 20

Journal Entry at the End of 2011

Receivable—income tax refund ($7 + 22)	29
Deferred tax asset (determined above)	20
Income tax benefit—operating loss (to balance)	49

The income tax benefit of both an operating loss carryback and an operating loss carry forward is recognized for accounting purposes in the year the operating loss occurs. The net after-tax operating loss reflects the reduction of past taxes from the loss carryback and future tax savings that the loss carryforward is expected to create.

Notice that the income tax benefit ($49 million) is less than it was when we assumed a carryforward only ($50 million). This is because the tax rate in one of the carryback years (2009) was lower than the carryforward rate (40%).

Financial Statement Presentation

Balance Sheet Classification

In a classified balance sheet, deferred tax assets and deferred tax liabilities are classified as either current or noncurrent according to how the related assets or liabilities are classified for financial reporting. For instance, a deferred tax liability arising from different depreciation methods being used for tax and book purposes would be classified as noncurrent because depreciable assets are reported as noncurrent. A deferred tax asset or deferred tax liability is considered to be related to an asset or liability if reduction (including amortization) of that asset or liability will cause the temporary difference to reverse.

● LO8

Let's carry the illustration forward one year (see Illustration 16–9A) and assume a performance turnaround in 2012 resulted in pretax accounting income of $15 million.

($ in millions)	2011	Current Year 2012	Future Deductible Amounts (total)
Pretax accounting income		$15	
Temporary difference:			
Loss carryforward	$50	(15)	$(35)
Taxable income (tax return)		$ 0	
Enacted tax rate		40%	40%
Tax payable currently		$ 0	
Deferred tax asset			$(14)
Deferred Tax Asset			
Ending balance needed			$ 14.0
Less: Beginning balance			(20.0)
Change in balance			$ (6.0)
Journal Entry at the End of 2012			
Income tax expense (to balance)			6
Deferred tax asset (determined above)			6

ILLUSTRATION 16–9A

Determining and Recording Income Taxes—2012

$15 million of the carryforward can be used to offset 2012 income. The remaining $35 million is carried forward up to 19 more years.

The $20 million deferred tax asset is reduced to $14 million.

Most companies will have several different types of temporary differences that give rise to deferred tax amounts. The several deferred tax assets and liabilities should not be reported individually but combined instead into two summary amounts. Current deferred tax assets and liabilities should be offset (netted together). The resulting *net current* amount is then reported as either a current asset (if deferred tax assets exceed deferred tax liabilities) or current liability (if deferred tax liabilities exceed deferred tax assets). Similarly, a single *net noncurrent* amount should be reported as a net noncurrent asset or a net noncurrent liability. This is demonstrated in Illustration 16–10 on the next page.

A net current amount and a net noncurrent amount are reported as either an asset or a liability.

DEFERRED TAX AMOUNT NOT RELATED TO A SPECIFIC ASSET OR LIABILITY. Sometimes, a deferred tax asset or a deferred tax liability cannot be identified with a specific asset or liability. When that's the case, classification should be according to when the underlying temporary difference is expected to reverse. For instance, some

ILLUSTRATION 16–10

Balance Sheet Classification and Presentation

The current or noncurrent classification of deferred tax assets and deferred tax liabilities is the same as that of the related assets or liabilities.

Warren Properties, Inc., had future taxable amounts and future deductible amounts relating to temporary differences between the tax bases of the assets and liabilities indicated below and their financial reporting amounts:

($ in millions)

Related Balance Sheet Account	Classification Current—C Noncurrent—NC	Future Taxable (Deductible) Amounts	Tax Rate	Deferred Tax (Asset) Liability C	NC
Receivable—installment sales of land	C	$ 10	× 40%	$ 4	
Receivable—installment sales of land	NC	5	× 40%		$ 2
Depreciable assets	NC	105	× 40%		42
Allowance—uncollectible accounts	C	(15)	× 40%	(6)	
Liability—subscriptions received	C	(20)	× 40%	(8)	
Estimated warranty liability	C	(30)	× 40%	(12)	
Net current liability (asset)				$(22)	
Net noncurrent liability (asset)					$ 44

Balance Sheet Presentation

Current Assets:

  Deferred tax asset $22

Long-Term Liabilities:

  Deferred tax liability $44

Note: Before offsetting assets and liabilities within the current and noncurrent categories, the total of deferred tax assets is $26 ($6 + 8 + 12) and the **total** of deferred tax liabilities is $48 ($4 + 2 + 42).

A deferred tax asset or liability that is not related to a specific asset or liability should be classified according to when the underlying temporary difference is expected to reverse.

organization costs are recognized as expenses for financial reporting purposes when incurred, but are deducted for tax purposes in later years. When such expenditures are made, an expense is recorded, but no asset or liability is recognized on the balance sheet. The deferred tax asset recognized for the future deductible amounts is classified as a current asset for the tax effect of the deduction expected next year, and as a noncurrent asset for the tax effect of the deductions expected in later years.

Operating loss carryforwards also are unrelated to a specific asset or liability and so are classified as current or noncurrent according to when future income is expected to be sufficient to realize the benefit of the carryforward.

A valuation allowance is allocated between current and noncurrent on a pro rata basis.

VALUATION ALLOWANCE. Any valuation allowance for deferred tax assets should be allocated between the current and noncurrent amount in proportion to the amounts of deferred tax assets that are classified as current and noncurrent. In our illustration, all three deferred tax assets were classified as current, so any valuation allowance would be reported with the net current deferred tax asset.

Disclosure Notes

DEFERRED TAX ASSETS AND DEFERRED TAX LIABILITIES. Additional disclosures are required pertaining to amounts reported on the balance sheet. Disclosure notes should reveal the:

- Total of all deferred tax liabilities ($48 million in our Illustration 16–10 Note).
- Total of all deferred tax assets ($26 million in our Illustration 16–10 Note).
- Total valuation allowance recognized for deferred tax assets.
- Net change in the valuation allowance.
- Approximate tax effect of each type of temporary difference (and carryforward).

In its 2009 balance sheet, the **Walmart Stores, Inc.** reported the composition of its net deferred tax liabilities as shown in Graphic 16–5.

Note 5: Income Taxes (in part)

Items that give rise to significant portions of the deferred tax accounts are as follows:

GRAPHIC 16–5

Disclosure of Deferred Taxes—Walmart

Real World Financials

	January 31,	
(Amounts in millions)	**2009**	**2008**
Deferred tax assets:		
International operating and capital loss	$ 1,430	$ 1,073
Accrued liabilities	2,548	2,400
Equity compensation	206	324
Other	374	516
Total deferred tax assets	4,558	4,313
Valuation allowance	(1,852)	(1,589)
Deferred tax assets, net of valuation allowance	$ 2,706	$ 2,724
Deferred tax liabilities:		
Property and equipment	$ 3,257	$ 2,740
Inventories	1,079	705
Other	(25)	41
Total deferred tax liabilities	$ 4,311	$ 3,486
Net deferred tax liabilities	$ 1,605	$ 762

The deferred taxes noted above are classified as follows in the balance sheet:

	January 31,	
(Amounts in millions)	**2009**	**2008**
Balance Sheet Classification:		
Prepaid expenses and other	$1,293	$1,425
Other assets and deferred charges	202	327
Total assets	1,495	1,752
Accrued liabilities	24	165
Deferred income taxes and other	3,076	2,349
Total liabilities	3,100	2,514
Net deferred tax liabilities	$1,605	$ 762

OPERATING LOSS CARRYFORWARDS. In addition, the amounts and expiration dates should be revealed for any operating loss carryforwards. Remember, operating losses can be carried forward for reduction of future taxable income for 20 years. This potential tax benefit can foreshadow desirable cash savings for the company if earnings sufficient to absorb the loss carryforwards are anticipated before their expiration date. The presence of large operating loss carryforwards also can make an unprofitable company an attractive target for acquisition by a company that could use those loss carryforwards to shelter its own earnings from taxes with that loss deduction. If the IRS determines that an acquisition is made solely to obtain the tax benefits of operating loss carryforwards, the deductions will not be allowed. However, motivation is difficult to determine, so it is not uncommon for companies to purchase operating loss carryforwards.

INCOME TAX EXPENSE. Disclosures also are required pertaining to the income tax expense reported in the income statement. Disclosure notes should reveal the:

- Current portion of the tax expense (or tax benefit).
- Deferred portion of the tax expense (or tax benefit), with separate disclosure of amounts attributable to:
  - Portions that do not include the effect of separately disclosed amounts.
  - Operating loss carryforwards.

- Adjustments due to changes in tax laws or rates.
- Adjustments to the beginning-of-the-year valuation allowance due to revised estimates.
- Tax credits.

To relate this to the income tax journal entries we've seen in the chapter, remember that the current portion of the tax expense is the credit to the income tax payable; the deferred portion of the tax expense is the credit or debit to deferred tax assets and liabilities (and perhaps valuation allowance).

Coping with Uncertainty in Income Taxes

● LO9

Few expense items in the income statement rival the size of the income tax expense line, and few are subject to the complexities and differing interpretations inherent in reporting income tax expense. As you might imagine, most companies strive to legitimately reduce their overall tax burden and to reduce or delay cash outflows for taxes.

The IRS frequently disagrees with the position a company takes on its tax return.

Even without additional efforts to reduce taxes, most companies' tax returns will include many tax positions that are subject to multiple interpretations. That is, the position management takes with respect to an element of tax expense might differ from the position the IRS or the tax court might take on that same item. Despite good faith positions taken in preparing tax returns, those judgments may not ultimately prevail if challenged by the IRS. Managements' tax positions frequently are subjected to legal scrutiny before the uncertainty ultimately is resolved.

For example, assume that if Derrick Company claims on its tax return a particular deduction it believes is legitimate, that position will save the company $8 million in 2011 income taxes. Derrick knows that, historically, the IRS has challenged many deductions of this type. Since tax returns usually aren't examined for one, two, or more years, uncertainty exists.

TWO-STEP DECISION PROCESS. To deal with that uncertainty, companies are allowed to recognize in the financial statements the tax benefit of a position it takes, such as the reduction in tax expense from Derrick's decision to take the 2011 deduction, only if it is "more likely than not" (greater than 50% chance) to be sustained if challenged.[17] Guidance also prescribes how to *measure* the amount to be recognized. The decision, then, is a "two-step" process.

The identified tax position must have a "more-likely-than-not" probability—a more than 50 percent chance—of being sustained on examination.

Step 1. A tax benefit may be reflected in the financial statements only if it is "more likely than not" that the company will be able to sustain the tax return position, based on its technical merits.

Step 2. A tax benefit should be measured as the largest amount of benefit that is "cumulatively greater than 50 percent likely to be realized" (demonstrated later).

For the Step 1 decision as to whether the position can be sustained, companies must assume that the position will be reviewed by the IRS or other taxing authority and litigated to the "highest court possible," and that the taxing authority has knowledge of all relevant facts.

If there's a 50% chance or less of the company's position being sustained on examination, the tax expense can't reflect the tax benefit.

NOT "MORE LIKELY THAN NOT." Let's say that in the Step 1 decision, Derrick believes the more-likely-than-not criterion is *not* met. This means that none of the tax benefit (reduction in tax expense) can be recorded in 2011. The income tax expense must be recorded at the same amount as if the tax deduction is not available.

Suppose, for instance, that Derricks's current income tax payable is $24 million after being reduced by the full $8 million tax benefit.[18] However, if it's *more likely than not* that

---

[17]FASB ASC 740: Income Taxes–Overall (previously "Accounting for Uncertainty in Income Taxes, an Interpretation of FASB Statement No. 109," *FASB Interpretation No. 48* (Norwalk, Conn.: FASB, June 2006)), commonly called *FIN 48.*

[18]For illustration, if pretax accounting income is $80 million, the tax rate is 40%, and the questionable deduction is $20 million, income tax payable would be [$80 million − 20 million] × 40% = $24 million.

the tax benefit isn't allowable, the benefit can't be recognized as a reduction of tax expense. So, Derrick would record (a) tax expense as if there is no deduction (because that's the actual position taken), (b) income tax payable that reflects the benefit of the deduction, and (c) a liability that represents the potential obligation to pay the additional taxes if the deduction is not ultimately upheld:

	($ in millions)	
Income tax expense (without $8 tax benefit)	32	
Income tax payable (with $8 tax benefit)		24
Liability—potential additional tax		8

The $8 million liability can be viewed as a "reserve" to cover the possibility that tax officials might disallow the tax treatment the income tax payable presumes.

The $8 million difference is the tax not paid due to the deduction taken, but potentially due if the deduction is not upheld later. Because the ultimate outcome probably won't be determined within the upcoming year, the *Liability—potential additional tax* is reported as a long-term liability unless it's known to be current.

MEASURING THE TAX BENEFIT.   Now, let's say that even though Derrick is aware of the IRS's tendency to challenge deductions of this sort, management believes the more-likely-than-not criterion *is* met. Since we determine in Step 1 that—yes—a tax benefit can be recognized, we now need to decide how much. That's Step 2.

Suppose the following table represents management's estimates of the likelihood of various amounts of tax benefit that would be upheld:

Likelihood Table   ($ in millions)

Amount of the tax benefit that management expects to be upheld	$8	$7	$6	$5	$4
Percentage likelihood that the tax position will be upheld at this level	10%	20%	25%	25%	20%
Cumulative probability that the tax position will be upheld	10%	30%	55%	80%	100%

The largest amount that has a cumulative greater-than-50%-chance of being realized is **$6 million** (10% + 20% + 25% = **55%**).

The amount of tax benefit that Derrick can recognize in the financial statements (reduce tax expense) is $6 million because it represents the largest amount of benefit that is more than 50 percent likely to be the end result. So, Derrick would record (a) tax expense as if there is a $6 million benefit, (b) income tax payable that reflects the entire $8 million benefit of the deduction, and (c) a liability that represents the potential obligation to pay the additional taxes if the deduction is not ultimately upheld:

	($ in millions)	
Income tax expense (with $6 tax benefit)	26	
Income tax payable (with $8 tax benefit)		24
Liability—potential additional tax ($8 − 6)		2

Only **$6 million** of the tax benefit is recognized in income tax expense.

RESOLUTION OF THE UNCERTAINTY.   Now let's consider alternative possibilities for resolution of the uncertainty associated with the tax position. Note that, in each case, the "Liability—potential additional tax" gets reduced to zero with any offset to income tax expense of the period in which the uncertainty is resolved.

1. **Worst case scenario.** The entire deduction is disallowed, such that Derrick owes $8 million tax (plus interest and penalties, which we are ignoring)

	($ in millions)	
Income tax expense	6	
Liability—potential additional tax	2	
Income tax payable (or cash)		8

2. **Best case scenario.** The entire deduction is upheld, so Derrick owes no additional tax

	($ in millions)	
Liability—potential additional tax	2	
Income tax expense		2

3. **Intermediate scenario.** The $6 million position is allowed as expected, so Derrick owes the anticipated $2 million tax (plus interest and penalties, which we are ignoring)

	($ in millions)	
Liability—potential additional tax	2	
Income tax payable (or cash)		2

In its annual report for the year ended January 31, 2009, **Staples, Inc.** provided the disclosures shown in Graphic 16–6 regarding its tax uncertainties.

GRAPHIC 16–6

Disclosure of Deferred Taxes—Staples, Inc.

Real World Financials

NOTE A Summary of Significant Accounting Policies (In part)

Accounting for Income Taxes: In July 2006, the Financial Accounting Standards Board ("FASB") issued FASB Interpretation No. 48, "Accounting for Uncertainty in Income Taxes" ("FIN 48"). FIN 48 clarifies the accounting for uncertain income tax positions that are recognized in a company's financial statements in accordance with the provisions of FASB Statement No. 109, "Accounting for Income Taxes". FIN 48 also provides guidance on the derecognition of uncertain positions, financial statement classification, accounting for interest and penalties, accounting for interim periods, and new disclosure requirements.

The Company adopted FIN 48 as of February 4, 2007, the first day of the 2007 fiscal year. The adoption of FIN 48 did not result in any material adjustments to the Company's reserves for uncertain tax positions. At January 31, 2009, the Company had $217.0 million of gross unrecognized tax benefits, $84.1 million of which, if recognized would affect the Company's tax rate. At February 2, 2008, the Company had $87.7 million of gross unrecognized tax benefits, $66.1 million of which, if recognized would affect the Company's tax rate. At the beginning of fiscal 2007, the Company had $81.8 million of gross unrecognized tax benefits, $65.9 million of which, if recognized, would affect the Company's tax rate. The increase in unrecognized tax benefits at January 31, 2009 is primarily due to the acquisition of Corporate Express. The Company does not reasonably expect any material changes to the estimated amount of liability associated with its uncertain tax positions through fiscal 2009. A reconciliation of the beginning and ending amount of unrecognized tax benefits is as follows (in thousands):

	2008	2007
Balance at beginning of fiscal year	$ 87,688	$81,848
Additions for tax positions related to the current year	24,859	22,460
Additions for acquired business	107,699	—
Additions for tax positions of prior years	6,343	8,932
Reductions for tax positions of prior years	(7,597)	(18,430)
Settlements	(2,031)	(7,122)
Balance at end of fiscal year	$216,961	$87,688

Intraperiod Tax Allocation

● LO10

You should recall that an income statement reports certain items separately from income (or loss) from continuing operations when such items are present. Specifically, (a) discontinued operations and (b) extraordinary items are given a place of their own in the income statement to better allow the user of the statement to isolate irregular components of net income from those that represent ordinary, recurring business operations. Presumably, this permits the user to more accurately project future operations without neglecting events that affect current performance.[19] Following this logic, each component of net income should reflect the income tax effect directly associated with that component.

Consequently, the total income tax expense for a reporting period should be allocated among the income statement items that gave rise to it. Each of the following items should be reported net of its respective income tax effects:

- Income (or loss) from continuing operations.
- Discontinued operations.
- Extraordinary items.

The related tax effect can be either a tax expense or a tax benefit. For example, an extraordinary gain adds to a company's tax expense, while an extraordinary loss produces a tax reduction because it reduces taxable income and therefore reduces income taxes. So a company with a tax rate of 40% would report $100 million pretax income that includes a $10 million extraordinary gain this way:

	($ in millions)
Income before tax and extraordinary item ($100 − 10)	$ 90
Less: Income tax expense ($90 × 40%)	(36)
Income before extraordinary item	54
Extraordinary gain (net of $4 income tax expense)	6
Net income	$ 60

A gain causes an increase in taxes.

If the $100 million pretax income included a $10 million extraordinary loss rather than an extraordinary gain, the loss would be reported net of associated tax savings:

	($ in millions)
Income before tax and extraordinary item ($100 + 10)	$110
Less: Income tax expense ($110 × 40%)	(44)
Income before extraordinary item	66
Extraordinary loss (net of $4 income tax benefit)	(6)
Net income	$ 60

A loss causes a reduction in taxes.

ADDITIONAL CONSIDERATION

If the extraordinary gain in the earlier example had been of a type taxable at a capital gains tax rate of 30%, it would have been reported net of the specific tax associated with that gain:

Extraordinary gain (net of $3 income tax expense)	$7

Allocating income taxes among financial statement components in this way within a particular reporting period is referred to as *intraperiod tax allocation*. You should recognize the contrast with *inter*period tax allocation—terminology sometimes used to describe allocating income taxes between two or more reporting periods by recognizing deferred tax assets and liabilities. While interperiod tax allocation is challenging and controversial, intraperiod tax allocation is relatively straightforward and substantially free from controversy.

Allocating income taxes within a particular reporting period is intraperiod tax allocation.

OTHER COMPREHENSIVE INCOME. Allocating income tax expense or benefit also applies to components of comprehensive income reported separately from net income. You should recall from our discussions in Chapters 4 and 12 reveal that "comprehensive income" extends our view of income beyond conventional net income to include four

---

[19]We discussed this in Chapter 4.

types of gains and losses that traditionally haven't been included in income statements. The other comprehensive income (OCI) items relate to investments, postretirement benefit plans, derivatives, and foreign currency translation. When these OCI items are reported in a statement of comprehensive income and then accumulated in shareholders' equity, they are reported net of their respective income tax effects in the same way as for discontinued operations and extraordinary items.

● LO11

INTERNATIONAL FINANCIAL REPORTING STANDARDS

Extraordinary Items. Recall from Chapter 4 that extraordinary items are not reported separately under IFRS. *IAS No. 1,* "Presentation of Financial Statements," states that neither the income statement nor any notes may contain any items called "extraordinary."[20] As a result, according to IFRS the only income statement item reported separately net of tax is discontinued operations.

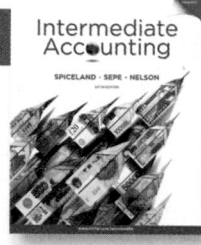

DECISION MAKERS' PERSPECTIVE

Income taxes represent one of the largest expenditures that many firms incur. When state, local, and foreign taxes are considered along with federal taxes, the total bite can easily consume 40% of income. A key factor, then, in any decision that managers make should be the impact on taxes. Decision makers must constantly be alert to options that minimize or delay taxes. During the course of this chapter, we encountered situations that avoid taxes (for example, interest on municipal bonds) and those that delay taxes (for example, using accelerated depreciation on the tax return). Astute managers make investment decisions that consider the tax effect of available alternatives. Similarly, outside analysts should consider how effectively management has managed its tax exposure and monitor the current and prospective impact of taxes on their interests in the company.

Investment patterns and other disclosures can indicate potential tax expenditures.

Consider an example. Large, capital-intensive companies with significant investments in buildings and equipment often have sizable deferred tax liabilities from temporary differences in depreciation. If new investments cause the level of depreciable assets to at least remain the same over time, the deferred tax liability can be effectively delayed indefinitely. Investors and creditors should be watchful for situations that might cause material paydowns of that deferred tax liability, such as impending plant closings or investment patterns that suggest declining levels of depreciable assets. Unexpected additional tax expenditures can severely diminish an otherwise attractive prospective rate of return.

Operating loss carryforwards can indicate significant future tax savings.

You also learned in the chapter that deferred tax assets represent future tax benefits. One such deferred tax asset that often reflects sizable future tax deductions is an operating loss carryforward. When a company has a large operating loss carryforward, a large amount of future income can be earned tax free. This tax shelter can be a huge advantage, not to be overlooked by careful analysts.

Deferred tax liabilities increase risk as measured by the debt to equity ratio.

Managers and outsiders are aware that increasing debt increases risk. Deferred tax liabilities increase reported debt. As discussed and demonstrated in the previous chapter, financial risk often is measured by the debt to equity ratio, total liabilities divided by shareholders' equity. Other things being equal, the higher the debt to equity ratio, the higher the risk. Should the deferred tax liability be included in the computation of this ratio? Some analysts will argue that it should be excluded, observing that in many cases the deferred tax liability account remains the same or continually grows larger. Their contention is that no future tax payment will be required. Others, though, contend that is no different from the common situation in which long-term borrowings tend to remain the same or continually grow larger.

---

[20]"Presentation of Financial Statements," *International Accounting Standard No. 1* (IASCF), as amended effective January 1, 2009.

Research supports the notion that deferred tax liabilities are, in fact, viewed by investors as real liabilities and they appear to discount them according to the timing and likelihood of the liabilities' settlement.[21]

Anytime managerial discretion can materially impact reported earnings, analysts should be wary of the implications for earnings quality assessment. We indicated earlier that the decision as to whether or not a valuation allowance is used, as well as the size of the allowance, is largely discretionary. Alert investors should not overlook the potential for "earnings management" here. In fact, recent empirical evidence indicates that some companies do use the deferred tax asset valuation allowance account to manage earnings upward to meet analyst forecasts.[22]

In short, managers who make decisions based on estimated pretax cash flows and outside investors and creditors who make decisions based on pretax income numbers are perilously ignoring one of the most important aspects of those decisions. Taxes should be a primary consideration in any business decision.

CONCEPT REVIEW EXERCISE

Mid-South Cellular Systems began operations in 2011. That year the company reported taxable income of $25 million. In 2012, its second year of operations, pretax accounting income was $88 million, which included the following amounts:

MULTIPLE DIFFERENCES AND OPERATING LOSS

1. Insurance expense of $14 million, representing one-third of a $42 million, three-year casualty and liability insurance policy that is deducted for tax purposes entirely in 2012.
2. Insurance expense for a $1 million premium on a life insurance policy for the company president. This is not deductible for tax purposes.
3. An asset with a four-year useful life was acquired last year. It is depreciated by the straight-line method in the income statement. MACRS is used on the tax return, causing deductions for depreciation to be more than straight-line depreciation the first two years but less than straight-line depreciation the next two years ($ in millions):

	Income Statement	Tax Return	Difference
2011	$150	$198	$ (48)
2012	150	264	(114)
2013	150	90	60
2014	150	48	102
	$600	$600	0

4. Equipment rental revenue of $80 million, which does not include an additional $20 million of advance payment for 2013 rent. $100 million of rental revenue is reported on the 2012 income tax return.

The enacted tax rate is 40%.

Required:

1. Prepare the journal entry to record Mid-South Cellular's income taxes for 2012.
2. What is Mid-South Cellular's 2012 net income?
3. Show how any deferred tax amount(s) should be reported in the 2012 balance sheet. Assume taxable income is expected in 2013 sufficient to absorb any deductible amounts carried forward from 2012.

---

[21]See Dan Givoly and Carla Hayn, "The Valuation of the Deferred Tax Liability: Evidence from the Stock Market," *The Accounting Review,* April 1992, pp. 394–410.
[22]Sonia O. Rego and Mary Margaret Frank, "Do Managers Use the Valuation Allowance Account to Manage Earnings Around Certain Earnings Targets?" April 16, 2004, Darden Business School Working Paper No. 03-09.

SOLUTION   1. Prepare the journal entry to record Mid-South Cellular's income taxes for 2012.

Differences in tax reporting and financial reporting of both the prepaid insurance and the depreciation create future taxable amounts.

Both the advance rent and the operating loss carryforward create future deductible amounts.

($ in millions)

	2011	Current Year 2012	Future Taxable (Deductible) Amounts		Future Taxable Amounts (total)	Future Deductible Amounts (total)
			2013	2014		
Pretax accounting income		$ 88				
Permanent difference:						
Life insurance premium		1				
Temporary differences:						
Prepaid insurance		(28)	$ 14	$ 14	$ 28	
Depreciation	$(48)	(114)	60	102	162	
Advance rent received		20	(20)			$(20)
Operating loss		$ (33)				
Loss carryback	(25)	25				
Loss carryforward		8				(8)
		$ 0			$190	$(28)
Enacted tax rate	40%	40%			40%	40%
Tax payable (refundable)	$(10)	$ 0				
Deferred tax liability					$ 76.0	
Deferred tax asset						$(11.2)

	Deferred Tax Liability	Deferred Tax Asset
Ending balances needed	$76.0	$11.2
Less: Beginning balance ($48* × 40%)	(19.2)	(0.0)
Change in balances	$56.8	$11.2

*2011's only temporary difference.

Income tax expense is composed of three components: (1) the tax deferred until later, reduced by (2) the deferred tax benefit and (3) the refund receivable of 2011 taxes paid.

Journal Entry at the End of 2012

Income tax expense (to balance)	35.6	
Receivable—income tax refund (determined above)	10.0	
Deferred tax asset (determined above)	11.2	
Deferred tax liability (determined above)		56.8

Note: Adjusting pretax accounting income by the permanent difference and the three temporary differences creates a negative taxable income, which is a net operating loss.

2. What is Mid-South Cellular's 2012 net income?

Pretax accounting income	$88.0
Income tax expense	(35.6)
Net income	$52.4

3. Show how any deferred tax amount(s) should be reported in the 2012 balance sheet. Assume taxable income is expected in 2013 sufficient to absorb any deductible amounts carried forward from 2012.

($ in millions)

Related balance sheet account	Classification Current—C Noncurrent— NC	Future Taxable (Deductible) Amounts	Tax Rate	Deferred Tax (Asset) Liability C	NC
Prepaid insurance	C	28	× 40%	11.2	
Depreciable assets	NC	162	× 40%		64.8
Liability—rent received in advance	C	(20)	× 40%	(8.0)	
Unrelated to any balance sheet account					
Operating loss carryforward	C*	(8)	× 40%	(3.2)	
Net current liability (asset)				0.0	
Net noncurrent liability (asset)					64.8

*Deferred tax asset classified entirely as current because 2013 income is expected to be sufficient to realize the benefit of the carryforward.

No net current amount
Long-term liabilities:

Deferred tax liability $64.8

Note: These net amounts ($0.0 + 64.8 = $64.8) sum to the net **total** deferred tax liabilities and deferred tax assets from requirement 1 ($76.0 − 11.2 = $64.8).

FINANCIAL REPORTING CASE SOLUTION

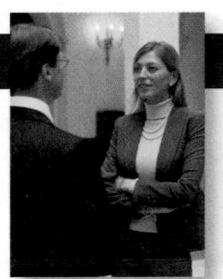

1. **What's the difference? Explain to Laura how differences between financial reporting standards and income tax rules might cause the income tax expense and the amount of income tax paid to differ.** (p. 874)   The differences in the rules for computing taxable income and those for financial reporting often cause amounts to be included in taxable income in a different year(s) from the year in which they are recognized for financial reporting purposes. Temporary differences result in future taxable or deductible amounts when the temporary differences reverse. As a result, tax payments frequently occur in years different from the years in which the revenues and expenses that cause the taxes are generated.

2. **What is the conceptual advantage of determining income tax expense as we do?** (p. 874)   Income tax expense is the combination of the current tax effect and the deferred tax consequences of the period's activities. Under the asset-liability approach, the objective of accounting for income taxes is to recognize a deferred tax liability or deferred tax asset for the tax consequences of amounts that will become taxable or deductible in future years as a result of transactions or events that already have occurred. A result is to recognize both the current and the deferred tax consequences of the operations of a reporting period.

3. **Are there differences between financial reporting standards and income tax rules that will not cause a difference between income tax expense and the amount of income taxes paid?** (p. 886)   Yes. Some differences between accounting income and taxable income are caused by transactions and events that will never affect taxable income or taxes payable. These differences between accounting income and taxable income do not reverse later. These are permanent differences that are disregarded when determining (a) the tax payable currently, (b) the deferred tax effect, and therefore (c) the income tax expense. ●

THE BOTTOM LINE

● **LO1** Temporary differences produce future taxable amounts when the taxable income will be increased relative to pretax accounting income in one or more future years. These produce deferred tax liabilities for the taxes to be paid on the future taxable amounts. Income tax expense for the year includes an amount for which payment (or receipt) is deferred in addition to the amount for which payment is due currently. The deferred amount is the change in the tax liability (or asset). (p. 875)

● **LO2** When the future tax consequence of a temporary difference will be to decrease taxable income relative to pretax accounting income, future deductible amounts are created. These have favorable tax consequences that are recognized as deferred tax assets. (p. 882)

● **LO3** Deferred tax assets are recognized for all deductible temporary differences. However, a deferred tax asset is then reduced by a valuation allowance if it is more likely than not that some portion or all of the deferred tax asset will not be realized. (p. 885)

● **LO4** Permanent differences between the reported amount of an asset or liability in the financial statements and its tax basis are those caused by transactions and events that under existing tax law will never affect taxable income or taxes payable. These are disregarded when determining both the tax payable currently and the deferred tax effect. (p. 886)

● **LO5** The deferred tax liability (or asset) for which payment (or receipt) is deferred is based on enacted tax rates applied to the taxable or deductible amounts. If a change in a tax law or rate occurs, the deferred tax liability or asset is adjusted to reflect the change in the amount to be paid or recovered. That effect is reflected in operating income in the year of the enactment of the change in the tax law or rate. (p. 890)

● **LO6** When multiple temporary differences exist, the total of the future **taxable** amounts is multiplied by the future tax rate to determine the appropriate balance for the deferred tax liability, and the total of the future **deductible** amounts is multiplied by the future tax rate to determine the appropriate balance for the deferred tax asset. (p. 892)

● **LO7** Tax laws permit an operating loss to be used to reduce taxable income in other, profitable years by either a carryback of the loss to prior years (2) or a carryforward of the loss to later years (up to 20). The tax benefit of an operating loss carryback or an operating loss carryforward is recognized in the year of the loss. (p. 894)

● **LO8** Deferred tax assets and deferred tax liabilities are classified as either current or noncurrent according to how the related assets or liabilities are classified for financial reporting. Disclosure notes should reveal additional relevant information needed for full disclosure pertaining to deferred tax amounts reported on the balance sheet, the components of income tax expense, and available operating loss carryforwards. (p. 897)

● **LO9** A tax benefit may be reflected in the financial statements only if it is "more likely than not" that the company will be able to sustain the tax return position, based on its technical merits. It should be measured as the largest amount of benefit that is cumulatively greater than 50 percent likely to be realized. (p. 900)

● **LO10** Through intraperiod tax allocation, the total income tax expense for a reporting period is allocated among the financial statement items that gave rise to it; specifically, income (or loss) from continuing operations, discontinued operations, extraordinary items, and prior period adjustments (to the beginning retained earnings balance). (p. 902)

● **LO11** Despite the similar approaches for accounting for taxation under IFRS and U.S. GAAP, differences in reported amounts for deferred taxes are among the most frequent between the two approaches because a great many of the *nontax* differences between IFRS and U.S. GAAP affect deferred taxes. (pp. 887 and 904) ●

QUESTIONS FOR REVIEW OF KEY TOPICS

Q 16–1 A member of the board of directors is concerned that the company's income statement reports income tax expense of $12.3 million, but the income tax obligation to the government for the year is only $7.9 million. How might the corporate controller explain this apparent discrepancy?

Q 16–2 A deferred tax liability (or asset) is described as the tax effect of the temporary difference between the financial statement carrying amount of an asset or liability and its tax basis. Explain this tax effect of the temporary difference. How might it produce a deferred tax liability? A deferred tax asset?

Q 16–3   Sometimes a temporary difference will produce future deductible amounts. Explain what is meant by future deductible amounts. Describe two general situations that have this effect. How are such situations recognized in the financial statements?

Q 16–4   The benefit of future deductible amounts can be achieved only if future income is sufficient to take advantage of the deferred deductions. For that reason, not all deferred tax assets will ultimately be realized. How is this possibility reflected in the way we recognize deferred tax assets?

Q 16–5   Temporary differences result in future taxable or deductible amounts when the related asset or liability is recovered or settled. Some differences, though, are not temporary. What events create permanent differences? What effect do these have on the determination of income taxes payable? Of deferred income taxes?

Q 16–6   Identify three examples of differences with no deferred tax consequences.

Q 16–7   The income tax rate for Hudson Refinery has been 35% for each of its 12 years of operation. Company forecasters expect a much-debated tax reform bill to be passed by Congress early next year. The new tax measure would increase Hudson's tax rate to 42%. When measuring this year's deferred tax liability, which rate should Hudson use?

Q 16–8   Suppose a tax reform bill is enacted that causes the corporate tax rate to change from 34% to 36%. How would this affect an existing deferred tax liability? How would the change be reflected in income?

Q 16–9   An operating loss occurs when tax-deductible expenses exceed taxable revenues. Tax laws permit the operating loss to be used to reduce taxable income in other, profitable years by either a carryback of the loss to prior years or a carryforward of the loss to later years. How are loss carrybacks and loss carryforwards recognized for financial reporting purposes?

Q 16–10   How are deferred tax assets and deferred tax liabilities reported in a classified balance sheet?

Q 16–11   Additional disclosures are required pertaining to deferred tax amounts reported on the balance sheet. What are the needed disclosures?

Q 16–12   Additional disclosures are required pertaining to the income tax expense reported in the income statement. What are the needed disclosures?

Q 16–13   The means of dealing with uncertainty in tax positions is prescribed by GAAP in FASB ASC 740–10: Income Taxes–Overall (previously *FASB Interpretation No. 48 (FIN 48)*). Describe the two-step process provided by *FIN 48*.

Q 16–14   What is intraperiod tax allocation?

● IFRS   Q 16–15   IFRS and U.S. GAAP follow similar approaches for accounting for taxation. Nevertheless, differences in reported amounts for deferred taxes are among the most frequent between IFRS and U.S. GAAP. Why?

BRIEF EXERCISES

BE 16–1
Temporary difference
● LO1

A company reports *pretax accounting income* of $10 million, but because of a single temporary difference, *taxable income* is only $7 million. No temporary differences existed at the beginning of the year, and the tax rate is 40%. Prepare the appropriate journal entry to record income taxes.

BE 16–2
Temporary difference; determine taxable income; determine prior year deferred tax amount
● LO1

Kara Fashions uses straight-line depreciation for financial statement reporting and MACRS for income tax reporting. Three years after its purchase, one of Kara's buildings has a carrying value of $400,000 and a tax basis of $300,000. There were no other temporary differences and no permanent differences. Taxable income was $4 million and Kara's tax rate is 40%. What is the deferred tax liability to be reported in the balance sheet? Assuming that the deferred tax liability balance was $32,000 the previous year, prepare the appropriate journal entry to record income taxes this year.

BE 16–3
Temporary difference
● LO2

A company reports *pretax accounting income* of $10 million, but because of a single temporary difference, *taxable income* is $12 million. No temporary differences existed at the beginning of the year, and the tax rate is 40%. Prepare the appropriate journal entry to record income taxes.

BE 16–4
Temporary difference; income tax payable given
● LO2

In 2011, Ryan Management collected rent revenue for 2012 tenant occupancy. For financial reporting, the rent is recognized as income in the period earned, but for income tax reporting it is taxed when collected. The unearned portion of the rent collected in 2011 was $50 million. Taxable income is $180 million. No temporary differences existed at the beginning of the year, and the tax rate is 40%. Prepare the appropriate journal entry to record income taxes.

BE 16–5
Temporary
difference; income
tax payable given
● LO2

Refer to the situation described in BE 16–4. Suppose the unearned portion of the rent collected was $40 million at the end of 2012. Taxable income is $200 million. Prepare the appropriate journal entry to record income taxes.

BE 16–6
Valuation
allowance
● LO2 LO3

At the end of the year, the deferred tax asset account had a balance of $12 million attributable to a cumulative temporary difference of $30 million in a liability for estimated expenses. Taxable income is $35 million. No temporary differences existed at the beginning of the year, and the tax rate is 40%. Prepare the journal entry(s) to record income taxes assuming it is more likely than not that one-fourth of the deferred tax asset will not ultimately be realized.

BE 16–7
Valuation
allowance
● LO2 LO3

Real World Financials

Hypercom Corporation is a provider of electronic card payment terminals, peripherals, network products, and software. In its 2008 annual report, it reported current and long-term deferred tax assets totaling about $61 million. The company also reported valuation allowances totaling about $61 million. What would motivate Hypercom to have a valuation allowance almost equal to its deferred tax assets?

BE 16–8
Temporary
and permanent
differences;
determine deferred
tax consequences
● LO1 LO4

Differences between financial statement and taxable income were as follows:

	($ in millions)
Pretax accounting income	$300
Permanent difference	(24)
	276
Temporary difference	(18)
Taxable income	$258

The cumulative temporary difference to date is $40 million (also the future taxable amount). The enacted tax rate is 40%. What is deferred tax asset or liability to be reported in the balance sheet?

BE 16–9
Calculate taxable
income
● LO1 LO4

Shannon Polymers uses straight-line depreciation for financial reporting purposes for equipment costing $800,000 and with an expected useful life of four years and no residual value. For tax purposes, the deduction is 40%, 30%, 20%, and 10% in those years. Pretax accounting income the first year the equipment was used was $900,000, which includes interest revenue of $20,000 from municipal bonds. Other than the two described, there are no differences between accounting income and taxable income. The enacted tax rate is 40%. Prepare the journal entry to record income taxes.

BE 16–10
Multiple tax rates
● LO5

J-Matt, Inc., had pretax accounting income of $291,000 and taxable income of $300,000 in 2011. The only difference between accounting and taxable income is estimated product warranty costs for sales this year. Warranty payments are expected to be in equal amounts over the next three years. Recent tax legislation will change the tax rate from the current 40% to 30% in 2013. Determine the amounts necessary to record J-Matt's income taxes for 2011 and prepare the appropriate journal entry.

BE 16–11
Change in tax rate
● LO5

Superior Developers sells lots for residential development. When lots are sold, Superior recognizes income for financial reporting purposes in the year of the sale. For some lots, Superior recognizes income for tax purposes when collected. In the *prior* year, income recognized for financial reporting purposes for lots sold this way was $20 million, which would be collected equally over the next two years. The enacted tax rate was 40%. This year, a new tax law was enacted, revising the tax rate from 40% to 35% beginning next year. Calculate the amount by which Superior should reduce its deferred tax liability this year.

BE 16–12
Operating loss
carryforward
● LO7

During its first year of operations, **Nile.com** reported an operating loss of $15 million for financial reporting and tax purposes. The enacted tax rate is 40%. Prepare the journal entry to recognize the income tax benefit of the operating loss.

BE 16–13
Operating loss
carryback
● LO7

AirParts Corporation reported an operating loss of $25 million for financial reporting and tax purposes. Taxable income last year and the previous year, respectively, was $20 million and $15 million. The enacted tax rate each year is 40%. Prepare the journal entry to recognize the income tax benefit of the operating loss. AirParts elects the carryback option.

BE 16–14
Tax uncertainty
● LO9

First Bank has some question as to the tax-free nature of $5 million of its municipal bond portfolio. This amount is excluded from First Bank's taxable income of $55 million. Management has determined that there is a 65% chance that the tax-free status of this interest can't withstand scrutiny of taxing authorities. Assuming a 40% tax rate, what amount of income tax expense should the bank report?

BE 16–15
Intraperiod tax allocation
● LO10

Southeast Airlines had pretax earnings of $65 million, including an extraordinary gain of $10 million. The company's tax rate is 40%. What is the amount of income tax expense that Southeast should report in its income statement? How should the extraordinary gain be reported?

BE 16–16
IFRS; Intraperiod tax allocation
● LO11

Refer to the situation described in BE 16–15. Suppose Southeast Airlines prepares its financial statements according to IFRS. What is the amount of income tax expense that Southeast should report in its income statement?

EXERCISES

An alternate exercise and problem set is available on the text website: www.mhhe.com/spiceland6e

E 16–1
Temporary difference; taxable income given
● LO1

Alvis Corporation reports *pretax accounting income* of $400,000, but due to a single temporary difference, *taxable income* is only $250,000. At the beginning of the year, no temporary differences existed.

Required:
1. Assuming a tax rate of 35%, what will be Alvis's net income?
2. What will Alvis report in the balance sheet pertaining to income taxes?

E 16–2
Determine taxable income; determine prior year deferred tax amount
● LO1

On January 1, 2008, Ameen Company purchased a building for $36 million. Ameen uses straight-line depreciation for financial statement reporting and MACRS for income tax reporting. At December 31, 2010, the carrying value of the building was $30 million and its tax basis was $20 million. At December 31, 2011, the carrying value of the building was $28 million and its tax basis was $13 million. There were no other temporary differences and no permanent differences. Pretax accounting income for 2011 was $45 million.

Required:
1. Prepare the appropriate journal entry to record Ameen's 2011 income taxes. Assume an income tax rate of 40%.
2. What is Ameen's 2011 net income?

E 16–3
Taxable income given; calculate deferred tax liability
● LO1

Ayres Services acquired an asset for $80 million in 2011. The asset is depreciated for financial reporting purposes over four years on a straight-line basis (no residual value). For tax purposes the asset's cost is depreciated by MACRS. The enacted tax rate is 40%. Amounts for pretax accounting income, depreciation, and taxable income in 2011, 2012, 2013, and 2014 are as follows:

	($ in millions)			
	2011	**2012**	**2013**	**2014**
Pretax accounting income	$330	$350	$365	$400
Depreciation on the income statement	20	20	20	20
Depreciation on the tax return	(25)	(33)	(15)	(7)
Taxable income	$325	$337	$370	$413

Required:
For December 31 of each year, determine (a) the temporary book–tax difference for the depreciable asset and (b) the balance to be reported in the deferred tax liability account.

E 16–4
Temporary difference; income tax payable given
● LO2

In 2011, DFS Medical Supply collected rent revenue for 2012 tenant occupancy. For income tax reporting, the rent is taxed when collected. For financial statement reporting, the rent is recognized as income in the period earned. The unearned portion of the rent collected in 2011 amounted to $300,000 at December 31, 2011. DFS had no temporary differences at the beginning of the year.

Required:
Assuming an income tax rate of 40% and 2011 income tax payable of $950,000, prepare the journal entry to record income taxes for 2011.

E 16–5
Temporary difference; future deductible amounts; taxable income given
● LO2

Lance Lawn Services reports bad debt expense using the allowance method. For tax purposes, the expense is deducted when accounts prove uncollectible (the direct write-off method). At December 31, 2011, Lance has accounts receivable and an allowance for uncollectible accounts of $20 million and $1 million, respectively, and taxable income of $75 million. At December 31, 2010, Lance reported a deferred tax asset of $435,000 related to this difference in reporting bad debts, its only temporary difference. The enacted tax rate is 40% each year.

Required:

Prepare the appropriate journal entry to record Lance's income tax provision for 2011.

E 16–6
Identify future taxable amounts and future deductible amounts
● LO1 LO2

Listed below are 10 causes of temporary differences. For each temporary difference, indicate (by letter) whether it will create future deductible amounts (D) or future taxable amounts (T).

Temporary Difference

_____ 1. Accrual of loss contingency, tax-deductible when paid.
_____ 2. Newspaper subscriptions; taxable when received, recognized for financial reporting when earned.
_____ 3. Prepaid rent, tax-deductible when paid.
_____ 4. Accrued bond interest expense, tax-deductible when paid.
_____ 5. Prepaid insurance, tax-deductible when paid.
_____ 6. Unrealized loss from recording investments available for sale at fair value (tax-deductible when investments are sold).
_____ 7. Bad debt expense; allowance method for financial reporting; direct write-off for tax purposes.
_____ 8. Advance rent receipts on an operating lease (as the lessor), taxable when received.
_____ 9. Straight-line depreciation for financial reporting; accelerated depreciation for tax purposes.
_____ 10. Accrued expense for employee postretirement benefits, tax-deductible when subsequent payments are made.

E 16–7
Identify future taxable amounts and future deductible amounts
● LO1 LO2

(This is a variation of the previous exercise, modified to focus on the balance sheet accounts related to the deferred tax amounts.)

Listed below are 10 causes of temporary differences. For each temporary difference indicate the balance sheet account for which the situation creates a temporary difference.

Temporary Difference

_____ 1. Accrual of loss contingency, tax-deductible when paid.
_____ 2. Newspaper subscriptions; taxable when received, recognized for financial reporting when earned.
_____ 3. Prepaid rent, tax-deductible when paid.
_____ 4. Accrued bond interest expense, tax-deductible when paid.
_____ 5. Prepaid insurance, tax-deductible when paid.
_____ 6. Unrealized loss from recording investments available for sale at fair value (tax-deductible when investments are sold).
_____ 7. Bad debt expense; allowance method for financial reporting; direct write-off for tax purposes.
_____ 8. Advance rent receipts on an operating lease (as the lessor), taxable when received.
_____ 9. Straight-line depreciation for financial reporting; accelerated depreciation for tax purposes.
_____ 10. Accrued expense for employee postretirement benefits, tax-deductible when subsequent payments are made.

E 16–8
Calculate income tax amounts under various circumstances
● LO1 LO2

Four independent situations are described below. Each involves future deductible amounts and/or future taxable amounts produced by temporary differences:

| | ($ in thousands) | | | |
| | Situation | | | |
	1	2	3	4
Taxable income	$85	$215	$195	$260
Future deductible amounts	15		20	20
Future taxable amounts		15	15	30
Balance(s) at beginning of the year:				
Deferred tax asset	2		9	4
Deferred tax liability		2	2	

The enacted tax rate is 40%.

Required:

For each situation, determine the:

a. Income tax payable currently.
b. Deferred tax asset—balance.
c. Deferred tax asset—change (dr) cr.
d. Deferred tax liability—balance.
e. Deferred tax liability—change (dr) cr.
f. Income tax expense.

E 16–9
Determine taxable income
● LO1 LO2 LO9

Eight independent situations are described below. Each involves future deductible amounts and/or future taxable amounts produced by:

($ in millions)
Temporary Differences Reported First on:

	The Income Statement		The Tax Return	
	Revenue	Expense	Revenue	Expense
1.		$20		
2.	$20			
3.			$20	
4.				$20
5.	15	20		
6.		20	15	
7.	15	20		10
8.	15	20	5	10

Required:

For each situation, determine taxable income assuming pretax accounting income is $100 million.

E 16–10
Deferred tax asset; taxable income given; valuation allowance
● LO3

At the end of 2010, Payne Industries had a deferred tax asset account with a balance of $30 million attributable to a temporary book–tax difference of $75 million in a liability for estimated expenses. At the end of 2011, the temporary difference is $70 million. Payne has no other temporary differences and no valuation allowance for the deferred tax asset. Taxable income for 2011 is $180 million and the tax rate is 40%.

Required:

1. Prepare the journal entry(s) to record Payne's income taxes for 2011, assuming it is more likely than not that the deferred tax asset will be realized.

2. Prepare the journal entry(s) to record Payne's income taxes for 2011, assuming it is more likely than not that one-half of the deferred tax asset will ultimately be realized.

E 16–11
Deferred tax asset; income tax payable given; previous balance in valuation allowance
● LO3

(This is a variation of Exercise 16–10, modified to assume a previous balance in the valuation allowance.)

At the end of 2010, Payne Industries had a deferred tax asset account with a balance of $30 million attributable to a temporary book-tax difference of $75 million in a liability for estimated expenses. At the end of 2011, the temporary difference is $70 million. Payne has no other temporary differences. Taxable income for 2011 is $180 million and the tax rate is 40%.

Payne has a valuation allowance of $10 million for the deferred tax asset at the beginning of 2011.

Required:

1. Prepare the journal entry(s) to record Payne's income taxes for 2011, assuming it is more likely than not that the deferred tax asset will be realized.

2. Prepare the journal entry(s) to record Payne's income taxes for 2011, assuming it is more likely than not that one-half of the deferred tax asset will ultimately be realized.

E 16–12
FASB codification research; valuation allowance
● LO3

When a company records a deferred tax asset, it may need to also report a valuation allowance if it is "more likely than not" that some portion or all of the deferred tax asset will not be realized. The *FASB Accounting Standards Codification* represents the single source of authoritative U.S. generally accepted accounting principles.

Required:

1. Obtain the relevant authoritative literature on disclosure requirements pertaining to how a firm should determine whether a valuation allowance for deferred tax assets is needed using the FASB's Codification Research System at the FASB website (**www.fasb.org**). What is the specific citation that describes the guidelines for determining the disclosure requirements?

2. What are the guidelines?

E 16–13
Multiple
differences;
calculate taxable
income
● LO1 LO4

Southern Atlantic Distributors began operations in January 2011 and purchased a delivery truck for $40,000. Southern Atlantic plans to use straight-line depreciation over a four-year expected useful life for financial reporting purposes. For tax purposes, the deduction is 50% of cost in 2011, 30% in 2012, and 20% in 2013. Pretax accounting income for 2011 was $300,000, which includes interest revenue of $40,000 from municipal bonds. The enacted tax rate is 40%.

Required:
Assuming no differences between accounting income and taxable income other than those described above:
1. Prepare the journal entry to record income taxes in 2011.
2. What is Southern Atlantic's 2011 net income?

E 16–14
Multiple
differences
● LO4 LO6

For the year ended December 31, 2011, Fidelity Engineering reported pretax accounting income of $977,000. Selected information for 2011 from Fidelity's records follows:

Interest income on municipal bonds	$32,000
Depreciation claimed on the 2011 tax return in excess of depreciation on the income statement	55,000
Carrying amount of depreciable assets in excess of their tax basis at year-end	85,000
Warranty expense reported on the income statement	26,000
Actual warranty expenditures in 2011	16,000

Fidelity's income tax rate is 40%. At January 1, 2011, Fidelity's records indicated balances of zero and $12,000 in its deferred tax asset and deferred tax liability accounts, respectively.

Required:
1. Determine the amounts necessary to record income taxes for 2011 and prepare the appropriate journal entry.
2. What is Fidelity's 2011 net income?

E 16–15
Multiple tax rates
● LO2 LO5

Allmond Corporation, organized on January 3, 2011, had pretax accounting income of $14 million and taxable income of $20 million for the year ended December 31, 2011. The 2011 tax rate is 35%. The only difference between accounting income and taxable income is estimated product warranty costs. Expected payments and scheduled tax rates (based on recent tax legislation) are as follows:

2012	$2 million	30%
2013	1 million	30%
2014	1 million	30%
2015	2 million	25%

Required:
1. Determine the amounts necessary to record Allmond's income taxes for 2011 and prepare the appropriate journal entry.
2. What is Allmond's 2011 net income?

E 16–16
Change in tax rates;
calculate taxable
income
● LO1 LO5

Arnold Industries has pretax accounting income of $33 million for the year ended December 31, 2011. The tax rate is 40%. The only difference between accounting income and taxable income relates to an operating lease in which Arnold is the lessee. The inception of the lease was December 28, 2011. An $8 million advance rent payment at the inception of the lease is tax-deductible in 2011 but, for financial reporting purposes, represents prepaid rent expense to be recognized equally over the four-year lease term.

Required:
1. Determine the amounts necessary to record Arnold's income taxes for 2011 and prepare the appropriate journal entry.
2. Determine the amounts necessary to record Arnold's income taxes for 2012 and prepare the appropriate journal entry. Pretax accounting income was $50 million for the year ended December 31, 2012.
3. Assume a new tax law is enacted in 2012 that causes the tax rate to change from 40% to 30% beginning in 2013. Determine the amounts necessary to record Arnold's income taxes for 2012 and prepare the appropriate journal entry.
4. Why is Arnold's 2012 income tax expense different when the tax rate change occurs from what it would be without the change?

E 16–17
Deferred taxes;
change in tax rates
● LO1 LO5

Bronson Industries reported a deferred tax liability of $8 million for the year ended December 31, 2010, related to a temporary difference of $20 million. The tax rate was 40%. The temporary difference is expected to reverse in 2012 at which time the deferred tax liability will become payable. There are no other temporary differences in 2010–2012. Assume a new tax law is enacted in 2011 that causes the tax rate to change from 40% to 30% beginning in 2012. (The rate remains 40% for 2011 taxes.) Taxable income in 2011 is $30 million.

Required:

Determine the effect of the change and prepare the appropriate journal entry to record Bronson's income tax expense in 2011. What adjustment, if any, is needed to revise retained earnings as a result of the change?

E 16–18
Multiple temporary differences; record income taxes
● **LO6**

The information that follows pertains to Esther Food Products:

a. At December 31, 2011, temporary differences were associated with the following future taxable (deductible) amounts:

Depreciation	$60,000
Prepaid expenses	17,000
Warranty expenses	(12,000)

b. No temporary differences existed at the beginning of 2011.

c. Pretax accounting income was $80,000 and taxable income was $15,000 for the year ended December 31, 2011.

d. The tax rate is 40%.

Required:

Determine the amounts necessary to record income taxes for 2011 and prepare the appropriate journal entry.

E 16–19
Multiple temporary differences; record income taxes
● **LO6**

The information that follows pertains to Richards Refrigeration, Inc.:

a. At December 31, 2011, temporary differences existed between the financial statement carrying amounts and the tax bases of the following:

	($ in millions)		
	Carrying Amount	**Tax Basis**	**Future Taxable (Deductible) Amount**
Buildings and equipment (net of accumulated depreciation)	$120	$90	$30
Prepaid insurance	50	0	50
Liability—loss contingency	25	0	(25)

b. No temporary differences existed at the beginning of 2011.

c. Pretax accounting income was $200 million and taxable income was $145 million for the year ended December 31, 2011. The tax rate is 40%.

Required:

1. Determine the amounts necessary to record income taxes for 2011 and prepare the appropriate journal entry.

2. What is the 2011 net income?

E 16–20
Operating loss carryforward
● **LO7**

During 2011, its first year of operations, Baginski Steel Corporation reported an operating loss of $375,000 for financial reporting and tax purposes. The enacted tax rate is 40%.

Required:

1. Prepare the journal entry to recognize the income tax benefit of the operating loss. Assume the weight of available evidence suggests future taxable income sufficient to benefit from future deductible amounts from the operating loss carryforward.

2. Show the lower portion of the 2011 income statement that reports the income tax benefit of the operating loss.

E 16–21
Operating loss carryback
● **LO7**

Wynn Sheet Metal reported an operating loss of $100,000 for financial reporting and tax purposes in 2011. The enacted tax rate is 40%. Taxable income, tax rates, and income taxes paid in Wynn's first four years of operation were as follows:

	Taxable Income	Tax Rates	Income Taxes Paid
2007	$60,000	30%	$18,000
2008	70,000	30	21,000
2009	80,000	40	32,000
2010	60,000	45	27,000

Required:

1. Prepare the journal entry to recognize the income tax benefit of the operating loss. Wynn elects the carryback option.

2. Show the lower portion of the 2011 income statement that reports the income tax benefit of the operating loss.

E 16–22
Operating loss
carryback and
carryforward
● LO7

(This exercise is based on the situation described in the previous exercise, modified to include a carryforward in addition to a carryback.)

Wynn Sheet Metal reported an operating loss of $160,000 for financial reporting and tax purposes in 2011. The enacted tax rate is 40%. Taxable income, tax rates, and income taxes paid in Wynn's first four years of operation were as follows:

	Taxable Income	Tax Rates	Income Taxes Paid
2007	$60,000	30%	$18,000
2008	70,000	30	21,000
2009	80,000	40	32,000
2010	60,000	45	27,000

Required:

1. Prepare the journal entry to recognize the income tax benefit of the operating loss. Wynn elects the carryback option.
2. Show the lower portion of the 2011 income statement that reports the income tax benefit of the operating loss.

E 16–23
Identifying income
tax deferrals
● LO1 LO2 LO4
   LO7

Listed below are ten independent situations. For each situation indicate (by letter) whether it will create a deferred tax asset (A), a deferred tax liability (L), or neither (N).

Situation

_____ 1. Advance payments on an operating lease; tax deductible when paid.
_____ 2. Estimated warranty costs, tax deductible when paid.
_____ 3. Rent revenue collected in advance; cash basis for tax purposes.
_____ 4. Interest received from investments in municipal bonds.
_____ 5. Prepaid expenses tax deductible when paid.
_____ 6. Operating loss carryforward.
_____ 7. Operating loss carryback.
_____ 8. Bad debt expense; allowance method for accounting; direct write-off for tax.
_____ 9. Organization costs expensed when incurred, tax deductible over 15 years.
_____ 10. Life insurance proceeds received upon the death of the company president.

E 16–24
Balance sheet
classification
● LO4 LO5 LO6
   LO8

At December 31, DePaul Corporation had a $16 million balance in its deferred tax asset account and a $68 million balance in its deferred tax liability account. The balances were due to the following cumulative temporary differences:

1. Estimated warranty expense, $15 million: expense recorded in the year of the sale; tax-deductible when paid (one-year warranty).
2. Depreciation expense, $120 million: straight-line in the income statement; MACRS on the tax return.
3. Income from installment sales of properties, $50 million: income recorded in the year of the sale; taxable when received equally over the next five years.
4. Bad debt expense, $25 million: allowance method for accounting; direct write-off for tax purposes.

Required:
Show how any deferred tax amounts should be classified and reported in the December 31 balance sheet. The tax rate is 40%.

E 16–25
Multiple tax rates;
balance sheet
classification
● LO1 LO4 LO5
   LO8

Case Development began operations in December 2011. When property is sold on an installment basis, Case recognizes installment income for financial reporting purposes in the year of the sale. For tax purposes, installment income is reported by the installment method. 2011 installment income was $600,000 and will be collected over the next three years. Scheduled collections and enacted tax rates for 2012–2014 are as follows:

2012	$150,000	30%
2013	250,000	40
2014	200,000	40

Pretax accounting income for 2011 was $810,000, which includes interest revenue of $10,000 from municipal bonds. The enacted tax rate for 2011 is 30%.

Required:

1. Assuming no differences between accounting income and taxable income other than those described above, prepare the appropriate journal entry to record Case's 2011 income taxes.
2. What is Case's 2011 net income?
3. How should the deferred tax amount be classified in a classified balance sheet?

E 16–26
Multiple
differences;
multiple tax rates;
balance sheet
classification

● LO1 LO2 LO4
  LO5 LO6 LO8

(This exercise is a variation of the previous exercise, modified to include a second temporary difference.)

Case Development began operations in December 2011. When property is sold on an installment basis, Case recognizes installment income for financial reporting purposes in the year of the sale. For tax purposes, installment income is reported by the installment method. 2011 installment income was $600,000 and will be collected over the next three years. Scheduled collections and enacted tax rates for 2012–2014 are as follows:

2012	$150,000	30%
2013	250,000	40
2014	200,000	40

Case also had product warranty costs of $80,000 expensed for financial reporting purposes in 2011. For tax purposes, only the $20,000 of warranty costs actually paid in 2011 was deducted. The remaining $60,000 will be deducted for tax purposes when paid over the next three years as follows:

2012	$20,000
2013	25,000
2014	15,000

Pretax *accounting* income for 2011 was $810,000, which includes interest revenue of $10,000 from municipal bonds. The enacted tax rate for 2011 is 30%.

Required:

1. Assuming no differences between accounting income and taxable income other than those described above, prepare the appropriate journal entry to record Case's 2011 income taxes.
2. What is Case's 2011 net income?
3. How should the deferred tax amounts be classified in a classified balance sheet?

E 16–27
Concepts;
terminology

● LO1 through
  LO8

Listed below are several terms and phrases associated with accounting for income taxes. Pair each item from List A with the item from List B (by letter) that is most appropriately associated with it.

List A	List B
___ 1. No tax consequences.	a. Deferred tax liability.
___ 2. Originates, then reverses.	b. Deferred tax asset.
___ 3. Revise deferred tax amounts.	c. 2 years.
___ 4. Operating loss.	d. Current and deferred tax consequence combined.
___ 5. Future tax effect of prepaid expenses tax deductible when paid.	e. Temporary difference.
	f. Specific tax rates times amounts reversing each year.
___ 6. Loss carryback.	g. Nontemporary differences.
___ 7. Future tax effect of estimated warranty expense.	h. When enacted tax rate changes.
	i. Same as related asset or liability.
___ 8. Valuation allowance.	j. "More likely than not" test.
___ 9. Phased-in change in rates.	k. Intraperiod tax allocation.
___ 10. Balance sheet classifications.	l. Negative taxable income.
___ 11. Individual tax consequences of financial statement components.	
___ 12. Income tax expense.	

E 16–28
Tax credit;
uncertainty
regarding
sustainability

● LO9

Delta Catfish Company has taken a position in its tax return to claim a tax credit of $10 million (direct reduction in taxes payable) and has determined that its sustainability is "more likely than not," based on its technical merits. Delta has developed the probability table shown below of all possible material outcomes:

Probability Table ($ in millions)					
Amount of the tax benefit that management expects to receive	$10	$ 8	$ 6	$ 4	$ 2
Percentage likelihood that the tax benefit will be sustained at this level	10%	20%	25%	20%	25%

Delta's taxable income is $85 million for the year. Its effective tax rate is 40%. The tax credit would be a direct reduction in current taxes payable.

Required:

1. At what amount would Delta measure the tax benefit in its income statement?
2. Prepare the appropriate journal entry for Delta to record its income taxes for the year.

E 16–29
Intraperiod tax
allocation
● LO10

The following income statement does not reflect intraperiod tax allocation.

Required:
Recast the income statement to reflect intraperiod tax allocation.

INCOME STATEMENT
For the Fiscal Year Ended March 31, 2011
($ in millions)

Revenues	$830
Cost of goods sold	(350)
Gross profit	480
Operating expenses	(180)
Income tax expense	(86)
Income before discontinued operations and extraordinary item	214
Loss from discontinued operations	(10)
Extraordinary casualty loss	(75)
Net income	$129

The company's tax rate is 40%.

E 16–30
FASB codification
research
● LO5 LO8 LO10

Access the FASB's Codification Research System at the FASB website (**www.fasb.org**). Determine the specific citation for accounting for each of the following items:
1. The specific items to which income tax expense is allocated for intraperiod tax allocation.
2. The tax rate used to calculate deferred tax assets and liabilities.
3. The required disclosures in the notes to financial statements for the components of income tax expense.

CPA AND CMA REVIEW QUESTIONS

CPA Exam
Questions

The following questions are used in the Kaplan CPA Review Course to study accounting for income taxes while preparing for the CPA examination. Determine the response that best completes the statements or questions.

● LO1

1. Scott Corp. received cash of $20,000 that was included in revenues in its 2011 financial statements, of which $12,000 will not be taxable until 2012. Scott's enacted tax rate is 30% for 2011, and 25% for 2012. What amount should Scott report in its 2011 balance sheet for deferred income tax liability?
   a. $2,000
   b. $2,400
   c. $3,000
   d. $3,600

● LO2

2. West Corp. leased a building and received the $36,000 annual rental payment on June 15, 2011. The beginning of the lease was July 1, 2011. Rental income is taxable when received. West's tax rates are 30% for 2011 and 40% thereafter. West had no other permanent or temporary differences. West determined that no valuation allowance was needed. What amount of deferred tax asset should West report in its December 31, 2011, balance sheet?
   a. $ 5,400
   b. $ 7,200
   c. $10,800
   d. $14,400

● LO3

3. In its December 31, 2011, balance sheet, Shin Co. had income taxes payable of $13,000 and a current deferred tax asset of $20,000 before determining the need for a valuation account. Shin had reported a current deferred tax asset of $15,000 at December 31, 2010. No estimated tax payments were made during 2011. At December 31,

2011, Shin determined that it was more likely than not that 10% of the deferred tax asset would not be realized. In its 2011 income statement, what amount should Shin report as total income tax expense?

a. $ 8,000
b. $ 8,500
c. $10,000
d. $13,000

● LO5

4. Stone Co. began operations in 2011 and reported $225,000 in income before income taxes for the year. Stone's 2011 tax depreciation exceeded its book depreciation by $25,000. Stone also had nondeductible book expenses of $10,000 related to permanent differences. Stone's tax rate for 2011 was 40%, and the enacted rate for years after 2011 is 35%. In its December 31, 2011, balance sheet, what amount of deferred income tax liability should Stone report?

a. $ 8,750
b. $10,000
c. $12,250
d. $14,000

● LO5

5. Black Co. organized on January 2, 2011, had pretax financial statement income of $500,000 and taxable income of $800,000 for the year ended December 31, 2011. The only temporary differences are accrued product warranty costs, which Black expects to pay as follows:

2012	$100,000
2013	$ 50,000
2014	$ 50,000
2015	$100,000

The enacted income tax rates are 25% for 2011, 30% for 2012 through 2014, and 35% for 2015. Black believes that future years' operations will produce profits. In its December 31, 2011, balance sheet, what amount should Black report as deferred tax asset?

a. $50,000
b. $75,000
c. $90,000
d. $95,000

● LO7

6. Dix, Inc., a calendar-year corporation, reported the following operating income (loss) before income tax for its first three years of operations:

2009	$100,000
2010	(200,000)
2011	400,000

There are no permanent or temporary differences between operating income (loss) for financial and income tax reporting purposes. When filing its 2010 tax return, Dix did not elect to forego the carryback of its loss for 2010. Assume a 40% tax rate for all years. What amount should Dix report as its income tax liability at December 31, 2011?

a. $ 60,000
b. $ 80,000
c. $120,000
d. $160,000

● LO10

7. An example of intraperiod income tax allocation is
a. Reporting an extraordinary item in the income statement, net of direct tax effects.
b. Interest income on municipal obligations.
c. Estimated expenses for major repairs accrued for financial statement purposes in one year, but deducted for income tax purposes when paid in a subsequent year.
d. Rental income included in income for income tax purposes when collected, but deferred for financial statement purposes until earned in a subsequent year.

CMA Exam Questions

The following questions dealing with accounting for income taxes are adapted from questions that previously appeared on Certified Management Accountant (CMA) examinations. The CMA designation sponsored by the Institute of Management Accountants (**www.imanet.org**) provides members with an objective measure of knowledge and competence in the field of management accounting. Determine the response that best completes the statements or questions.

● LO2

1. Which one of the following temporary differences will result in a deferred tax asset?

a. Use of the straight-line depreciation method for financial statement purposes and the modified Accelerated Cost Recovery System (MACRS) for income tax purposes.
b. Installment sale profits accounted for on the accrual basis for financial statement purposes and on a cash basis for income tax purposes.
c. Advance rental receipts accounted for on the accrual basis for financial statement purposes and on a cash basis for tax purposes.
d. Investment gains accounted for under the equity method for financial statement purposes and under the cost method for income tax purposes.

Questions 2 and 3 are based on the following information. Bearings Manufacturing Company Inc. purchased a new machine on January 1, 2012 for $100,000. The company uses the straight-line depreciation method with an estimated equipment life of 5 years and a zero salvage value for financial statement purposes, and uses the 3-year Modified Accelerated Cost Recovery System (MACRS) with an estimated equipment life of 3 years for income tax reporting purposes. Bearings is subject to a 35% marginal income tax rate. Assume that the deferred tax liability at the beginning of the year is zero and that Bearings has a positive earnings tax position. The MACRS depreciation rates for 3-year equipment are shown below.

Year	Rate
1	33.33%
2	44.45
3	14.81
4	7.41

● LO1

2. What is the deferred tax liability at December 31, 2012 (rounded to the nearest whole dollar)?
   a. $ 7,000
   b. $33,330
   c. $11,667
   d. $ 4,667

● LO5

3. For Bearings Manufacturing Company Inc., assume that the following new corporate income tax rates will go into effect:

2013–2015	40%
2016	45%

What is the amount of the deferred tax asset/liability at December 31, 2012 (rounded to the nearest whole dollar)?
   a. $0
   b. $9,000
   c. $2,668
   d. $6,332

PROBLEMS

 |ACCOUNTING

An alternate exercise and problem set is available on the text website: www.mhhe.com/spiceland6e

P 16–1
Single temporary difference originates each year for four years
● LO1

Alsup Consulting sometimes performs services for which it receives payment at the conclusion of the engagement, up to six months after services commence. Alsup recognizes service revenue for financial reporting purposes when the services are performed. For tax purposes, revenue is reported when fees are collected. Service revenue, collections, and pretax accounting income for 2010–2013 are as follows:

	Service Revenue	Collections	Pretax Accounting Income
2010	$650,000	$620,000	$186,000
2011	750,000	770,000	250,000
2012	715,000	700,000	220,000
2013	700,000	720,000	200,000

There are no differences between accounting income and taxable income other than the temporary difference described above. The enacted tax rate for each year is 40%.

Required:
1. Prepare the appropriate journal entry to record Alsup's 2011 income taxes.

2. Prepare the appropriate journal entry to record Alsup's 2012 income taxes.

3. Prepare the appropriate journal entry to record Alsup's 2013 income taxes.

(Hint: You may find it helpful to prepare a schedule that shows the balances in service revenue receivable at December 31, 2010–2013.)

P 16–2
Temporary difference; determine deferred tax amount for three years; balance sheet classification
● LO2 LO8

Times-Roman Publishing Company reports the following amounts in its first three years of operation:

($ in 000s)	**2011**	**2012**	**2013**
Pretax accounting income	$250	$240	$230
Taxable income	290	220	260

The difference between pretax accounting income and taxable income is due to subscription revenue for one-year magazine subscriptions being reported for tax purposes in the year received, but reported in the income statement in later years when earned. The income tax rate is 40% each year. Times-Roman anticipates profitable operations in the future.

Required:
1. What is the balance sheet account for which a temporary difference is created by this situation?
2. For each year, indicate the cumulative amount of the temporary difference at year-end.
3. Determine the balance in the related deferred tax account at the end of each year. Is it a deferred tax asset or a deferred tax liability?
4. How should the deferred tax amount be classified and reported in the balance sheet?

P 16–3
Change in tax rate; single temporary difference
● LO1 LO5

Dixon Development began operations in December 2011. When lots for industrial development are sold, Dixon recognizes income for financial reporting purposes in the year of the sale. For some lots, Dixon recognizes income for tax purposes when collected. Income recognized for financial reporting purposes in 2011 for lots sold this way was $12 million, which will be collected over the next three years. Scheduled collections for 2012–2014 are as follows:

2012	$ 4 million
2013	5 million
2014	3 million
	$12 million

Pretax accounting income for 2011 was $16 million. The enacted tax rate is 40%.

Required:
1. Assuming no differences between accounting income and taxable income other than those described above, prepare the journal entry to record income taxes in 2011.
2. Suppose a new tax law, revising the tax rate from 40% to 35%, beginning in 2013, is enacted in 2012, when pretax accounting income was $15 million. Prepare the appropriate journal entry to record income taxes in 2012.
3. If the new tax rate had not been enacted, what would have been the appropriate balance in the deferred tax liability account at the end of 2012? Why?

P 16–4
Change in tax rate; record taxes for four years
● LO1 LO5

Zekany Corporation would have had identical income before taxes on both its income tax returns and income statements for the years 2011 through 2014 except for differences in depreciation on an operational asset. The asset cost $120,000 and is depreciated for income tax purposes in the following amounts:

2011	$39,600
2012	52,800
2013	18,000
2014	9,600

The operational asset has a four-year life and no residual value. The straight-line method is used for financial reporting purposes.

Income amounts before depreciation expense and income taxes for each of the four years were as follows.

	2011	**2012**	**2013**	**2014**
Accounting income before taxes and depreciation	$60,000	$80,000	$70,000	$70,000

Assume the average and marginal income tax rate for 2011 and 2012 was 30%; however, during 2012 tax legislation was passed to raise the tax rate to 40% beginning in 2013. The 40% rate remained in effect through the years 2013 and 2014. Both the accounting and income tax periods end December 31.

Required:
Prepare the journal entries to record income taxes for the years 2011 through 2014.

P 16–5

Change in tax rate;
record taxes for
four years

● LO1 LO4 LO5

The DeVille Company reported pretax accounting income on its income statement as follows:

2011	$350,000
2012	270,000
2013	340,000
2014	380,000

Included in the income of 2011 was an installment sale of property in the amount of $50,000. However, for tax purposes, DeVille reported the income in the year cash was collected. Cash collected on the installment sale was $20,000 in 2012, $25,000 in 2013, and $5,000 in 2014.

Included in the 2013 income was $15,000 interest from investments in municipal bonds.

The enacted tax rate for 2011 and 2012 was 30%, but during 2012 new tax legislation was passed reducing the tax rate to 25% for the years 2013 and beyond.

Required:
Prepare the year-end journal entries to record income taxes for the years 2011–2014.

P 16–6

Multiple
differences;
temporary
difference yet
to originate;
multiple tax rates;
classification

● LO5 LO6 LO8

You are the new accounting manager at the Barry Transport Company. Your CFO has asked you to provide input on the company's income tax position based on the following:

1. Pretax accounting income was $41 million and taxable income was $8 million for the year ended December 31, 2011.

2. The difference was due to three items:

   a. Tax depreciation exceeds book depreciation by $30 million in 2011 for the business complex acquired that year. This amount is scheduled to be $60 million in 2012 and to reverse as ($50 million) and ($40 million) in 2013, and 2014, respectively.

   b. Insurance of $9 million was paid in 2011 for 2012 coverage.

   c. A $6 million loss contingency was accrued in 2011, to be paid in 2013.

3. No temporary differences existed at the beginning of 2011.

4. The tax rate is 40%.

Required:

1. Determine the amounts necessary to record income taxes for 2011 and prepare the appropriate journal entry.

2. How should the deferred tax amounts be classified in a classified balance sheet?

3. Assume the enacted federal income tax law specifies that the tax rate will change from 40% to 35% in 2013. When scheduling the reversal of the depreciation difference, you were uncertain as to how to deal with the fact that the difference will continue to originate in 2012 before reversing the next two years. Upon consulting **PricewaterhouseCoopers'** *Comperio* database, you found:

   .441 Depreciable and amortizable assets
   Only the reversals of the temporary difference at the balance sheet date would be scheduled. Future originations are not considered in determining the reversal pattern of temporary differences for depreciable assets. *FAS 109* [FASB ASC 740 – Income Taxes] is silent as to how the balance sheet date temporary differences are deemed to reverse, but the FIFO pattern is intended.

   You interpret that to mean that, when future taxable amounts are being scheduled, and a portion of a temporary difference has yet to originate, only the reversals of the *temporary difference at the balance sheet date* can be scheduled and multiplied by the tax rate that will be in effect when the difference reverses. Future originations (like the depreciation difference the second year) are not considered when determining the timing of the reversal. For the existing temporary difference, it is assumed that the difference will reverse the first year the difference begins reversing.
   Determine the amounts necessary to record income taxes for 2011 and prepare the appropriate journal entry.

P 16–7

Multiple
differences;
calculate taxable
income; balance
sheet classification

● LO4 LO6 LO8

Sherrod, Inc., reported pretax accounting income of $76 million for 2011. The following information relates to differences between pretax accounting income and taxable income:

a. Income from installment sales of properties included in pretax accounting income in 2011 exceeded that reported for tax purposes by $3 million. The installment receivable account at year-end had a balance of $4 million (representing portions of 2010 and 2011 installment sales), expected to be collected equally in 2012 and 2013.

b. Sherrod was assessed a penalty of $2 million by the Environmental Protection Agency for violation of a federal law in 2011. The fine is to be paid in equal amounts in 2011 and 2012.

c. Sherrod rents its operating facilities but owns one asset acquired in 2010 at a cost of $80 million. Depreciation is reported by the straight-line method assuming a four-year useful life. On the tax return, deductions for depreciation will be more than straight-line depreciation the first two years but less than straight-line depreciation the next two years ($ in millions):

	Income Statement	Tax Return	Difference
2010	$20	$26	$ (6)
2011	20	35	(15)
2012	20	12	8
2013	20	7	13
	$80	$80	$ 0

d. Bad debt expense of $3 million is reported using the allowance method in 2011. For tax purposes, the expense is deducted when accounts prove uncollectible (the direct write-off method): $2 million in 2011. At December 31, 2011, the allowance for uncollectible accounts was $2 million (after adjusting entries). The balance was $1 million at the end of 2010.

e. In 2011, Sherrod accrued an expense and related liability for estimated paid future absences of $7 million relating to the company's new paid vacation program. Future compensation will be deductible on the tax return when actually paid during the next two years ($4 million in 2012; $3 million in 2013).

f. During 2010, accounting income included an estimated loss of $2 million from having accrued a loss contingency. The loss is paid in 2011 at which time it is tax deductible.

Balances in the deferred tax asset and deferred tax liability accounts at January 1, 2011, were $1.2 million and $2.8 million, respectively. The enacted tax rate is 40% each year.

Required:
1. Determine the amounts necessary to record income taxes for 2011 and prepare the appropriate journal entry.
2. What is the 2011 net income?
3. Show how any deferred tax amounts should be classified and reported in the 2011 balance sheet.

P 16–8
Multiple differences; taxable income given; two years; balance sheet classification; change in tax rate
● LO4 LO6 LO8

Arndt, Inc., reported the following for 2011 and 2012 ($ in millions):

	2011	2012
Revenues	$888	$983
Expenses	760	800
Pretax accounting income (income statement)	$128	$183
Taxable income (tax return)	$120	$200
Tax rate: 40%		

a. Expenses each year include $30 million from a two-year casualty insurance policy purchased in 2011 for $60 million. The cost is tax-deductible in 2011.

b. Expenses include $2 million insurance premiums each year for life insurance on key executives.

c. Arndt sells one-year subscriptions to a weekly journal. Subscription sales collected and taxable in 2011 and 2012 were $33 million and $35 million, respectively. Subscriptions included in 2011 and 2012 financial reporting revenues were $25 million ($10 million collected in 2010 but not earned until 2011) and $33 million, respectively. Hint: View this as two temporary differences—one reversing in 2011; one originating in 2011.

d. 2011 expenses included a $17 million unrealized loss from reducing investments (classified as trading securities) to fair value. The investments were sold in 2012.

e. During 2010, accounting income included an estimated loss of $5 million from having accrued a loss contingency. The loss was paid in 2011 at which time it is tax deductible.

f. At January 1, 2011, Arndt had a deferred tax asset of $6 million and no deferred tax liability.

Required:
1. Which of the five differences described are temporary and which are permanent differences? Why?
2. Prepare a schedule that (a) reconciles the difference between pretax accounting income and taxable income and (b) determines the amounts necessary to record income taxes for 2011. Prepare the appropriate journal entry.
3. Show how any 2011 deferred tax amounts should be classified and reported on the 2011 balance sheet.
4. Prepare a schedule that (a) reconciles the difference between pretax accounting income and taxable income and (b) determines the amounts necessary to record income taxes for 2012. Prepare the appropriate journal entry.
5. Explain how any 2012 deferred tax amounts should be classified and reported on the 2012 balance sheet.
6. Suppose that during 2012, tax legislation was passed that will lower Arndt's effective tax rate to 35% beginning in 2013. Repeat requirement 4.

P 16–9
Determine deferred
tax assets and
liabilities
● LO6

Corning-Howell reported taxable income in 2011 of $120 million. At December 31, 2011, the reported amount of some assets and liabilities in the financial statements differed from their tax bases as indicated below:

	Carrying Amount	Tax Basis
Assets		
Current		
Accounts receivable (net of allowance)	$ 10 million	$ 12 million
Prepaid insurance	20 million	0
Prepaid rent expense (operating lease)	6 million	0
Noncurrent		
Buildings and equipment (net)	360 million	280 million
Liabilities		
Current		
Liability—subscriptions received	14 million	0
Long-term		
Liability—postretirement benefits	594 million	0
Shareholders' Equity		
Unrealized gain from recording investments available for sale at fair value*	4 million	0

*Taxable when investments are sold.

The total deferred tax asset and deferred tax liability amounts at January 1, 2011, were $250 million and $40 million, respectively. The enacted tax rate is 40% each year.

Required:
1. Determine the total deferred tax asset and deferred tax liability amounts at December 31, 2011.
2. Determine the increase (decrease) in the deferred tax asset and deferred tax liability accounts at December 31, 2011.
3. Determine the income tax payable currently for the year ended December 31, 2011.
4. Prepare the journal entry to record income taxes for 2011.
5. Show how the deferred tax amounts should be classified and reported in the 2011 balance sheet.

P 16–10
Operating loss
carryback and
carryforward;
multiple differences
● LO2 LO4 LO7

e**X**cel

Fores Construction Company reported a pretax operating loss of $135 million for financial reporting purposes in 2011. Contributing to the loss were (a) a penalty of $5 million assessed by the Environmental Protection Agency for violation of a federal law and paid in 2011 and (b) an estimated loss of $10 million from accruing a loss contingency. The loss will be tax deductible when paid in 2012.

The enacted tax rate is 40%. There were no temporary differences at the beginning of the year and none originating in 2011 other than those described above. Taxable income in Fores's two previous years of operation was as follows:

2009	$75 million
2010	30 million

Required:
1. Prepare the journal entry to recognize the income tax benefit of the operating loss in 2011. Fores elects the carryback option.
2. Show the lower portion of the 2011 income statement that reports the income tax benefit of the operating loss.
3. Prepare the journal entry to record income taxes in 2012 assuming pretax accounting income is $60 million. No additional temporary differences originate in 2012.

P 16–11
Valuation
allowance;
Sonic Solutions
● LO3 LO8

Real World Financials

Here's an excerpt from a press release by **Sonic Solutions** in January 2009 announcing a substantial deferred tax asset write-down:

Novato, California (February 5, 2009)—Sonic Solutions (NASDAQ: SNIC) today announced financial results for the third fiscal quarter ended December 31, 2008.

Valuation Allowance. During the third quarter, we established a valuation allowance of approximately $29.6 million for deferred tax assets in accordance with Statement of Financial Accounting Standards No. 109 "Accounting for Income Taxes" for deferred tax assets previously recorded. We had operating losses in fiscal 2008 and 2009.

The following is an excerpt from a disclosure note in Sonic Solutions' 2009 balance sheet:

	March 31,	
	2009	**2008**
Deferred tax assets:		
Accounts receivable	$ 83	$ 75
Inventories	215	399
Tax credit carryforwards	15,649	13,379
Net operating losses	17,532	8,581
Accrued vacation pay	729	922
Commissions and bonuses	24	38
Fixed assets	(349)	178
Intangible assets	23,750	—
Research and experimental expenses	115	—
Other reserves	4,381	5,072
Stock option compensation	3,645	5,384
Gross deferred tax assets	65,774	34,028
Valuation allowance	(65,712)	(3,113)
Total deferred tax assets, net of valuation allowance	62	30,915
Deferred tax liabilities:		
Intangible assets	—	(1,822)
State income taxes	—	(2,818)
Research and experimental expenses	—	68
Gross deferred tax assets	—	(4,572)
Total deferred tax liability	—	(4,572)
Net deferred taxes	$ 62	$ 26,343

Required:

1. As indicated in the note, Sonic Solutions had both deferred tax assets and deferred tax liabilities at the end of 2008. The balance sheets that year, though, reported only deferred tax assets. In fact, it reported both current and noncurrent deferred tax assets but no deferred tax liabilities. Explain why Sonic Solutions' deferred tax liabilities were not explicitly reported. Explain what the current and noncurrent deferred tax assets represent.

2. What is a valuation allowance against deferred tax assets? When must such an allowance be recorded? Use Sonic Solutions' situation to help illustrate your response. Assume an effective tax rate of 35%.

3. Is the write-down of deferred tax assets permanent? Under what circumstances might some or all of the $29.6 million be reclaimed?

P 16–12
Integrating problem—bonds, leases, taxes

● LO1 LO5 LO8

The long-term liabilities section of CPS Transportation's December 31, 2010, balance sheet included the following:

a. A capital lease liability with 15 remaining lease payments of $10,000 each, due annually on January 1:

Lease liability	$76,061
Less: current portion	2,394
	$73,667

The incremental borrowing rate at the inception of the lease was 11% and the lessor's implicit rate, which was known by CPS Transportation, was 10%.

b. A deferred income tax liability due to a single temporary difference. The only difference between CPS Transportation's taxable income and pretax accounting income is depreciation on a machine acquired on January 1, 2010, for $500,000. The machine's estimated useful life is five years, with no salvage value. Depreciation is computed using the straight-line method for financial reporting purposes and the MACRS method for tax purposes. Depreciation expense for tax and financial reporting purposes for 2011 through 2014 is as follows:

Year	MACRS Depreciation	Straight-line Depreciation	Difference
2011	$160,000	$100,000	$60,000
2012	80,000	100,000	(20,000)
2013	70,000	100,000	(30,000)
2014	60,000	100,000	(40,000)

The enacted federal income tax rates are 35% for 2010 and 40% for 2011 through 2014. For the year ended December 31, 2011, CPS's income before income taxes was $900,000.

On July 1, 2011, CPS Transportation issued $800,000 of 9% bonds. The bonds mature in 20 years and interest is payable each January 1 and July 1. The bonds were issued at a price to yield the investors 10%. CPS records interest at the effective interest rate.

Required:

1. Determine CPS Transportation's income tax expense and net income for the year ended December 31, 2011.
2. Determine CPS Transportation's interest expense for the year ended December 31, 2011.
3. Prepare the long-term liabilities section of CPS Transportation's December 31, 2011, balance sheet.

P 16–13
Multiple differences; uncertain tax position

● LO3 LO4 LO6 LO9

Tru Developers, Inc., sells plots of land for industrial development. Tru recognizes income for financial reporting purposes in the year it sells the plots. For some of the plots sold this year, Tru took the position that it could recognize the income for tax purposes when the installments are collected. Income that Tru recognized for financial reporting purposes in 2011 for plots in this category was $60 million. The company expected to collect 60% of each sale in 2012 and 40% in 2013. This amount over the next two years is as follows:

2012	$36 million
2013	24 million
	$60 million

Tru's pretax accounting income for 2011 was $90 million. In its income statement, Tru reported interest income of $15 million, unrelated to the land sales, for which the company's position is that the interest is not taxable. Accordingly, the interest was not reported on the tax return. There are no differences between accounting income and taxable income other than those described above. The enacted tax rate is 40 percent.

Management believes the tax position taken on the land sales has a greater than 50% chance of being upheld based on its technical merits, but the position taken on the interest has a less than 50% chance of being upheld. It is further believed that the following likelihood percentages apply to the tax treatment of the land sales ($ in millions):

Amount Qualifying for Installment Sales Treatment	Percentage Likelihood of Tax Treatment Being Sustained
$60	20%
50	20%
40	20%
30	20%
20	20%

Required:

1. What portion of the tax benefit of tax-free interest will Tru recognize on its 2011 tax return?
2. What portion of the tax benefit of tax-free interest will Tru recognize on its 2011 financial statements?
3. What portion of the tax on the $60 million income from the plots sold on an installment basis will Tru defer on its 2011 tax return? What portion of the tax on the $60 million income from the plots sold on an installment basis will Tru defer in its 2011 financial statements? How is the difference between these two amounts reported?
4. Prepare the journal entry to record income taxes in 2011 assuming full recognition of the tax benefits in the financial statements of both differences between pretax accounting income and taxable income.
5. Prepare the journal entry to record income taxes in 2011 assuming the recognition of the tax benefits in the financial statements you indicated in requirements 1–3.

BROADEN YOUR PERSPECTIVE

Apply your critical-thinking ability to the knowledge you've gained. These cases will provide you an opportunity to develop your research, analysis, judgment, and communication skills. You also will work with other students, integrate what you've learned, apply it in real world situations, and consider its global and ethical ramifications. This practice will broaden your knowledge and further develop your decision-making abilities.

Analysis
Case 16–1
Basic concepts

● LO1 through LO8

One of the longest debates in accounting history is the issue of deferred taxes. The controversy began in the 1940s and has continued, even after the FASB issued *Statement of Financial Accounting Standards No. 109* [FASB ASC 740: Income Taxes] in 1992. At issue is the appropriate treatment of tax consequences of economic events that occur in years other than that of the events themselves.

Required:

1. Distinguish between temporary differences and permanent differences. Provide an example of each.
2. Distinguish between *intraperiod* tax allocation and *interperiod* tax allocation (deferred tax accounting). Provide an example of each.
3. How are deferred tax assets and deferred tax liabilities classified and reported in the financial statements?

Integrating Case 16–2
Postretirement benefits
● LO2

FASB ASC 715–60: Compensation–Retirement Benefits–Defined Benefit Plans–Other Postretirement (previously *Statement of Financial Accounting Standards No. 106*) establishes accounting standards for postretirement benefits other than pensions, most notably postretirement health care benefits. Essentially, the standard requires companies to accrue compensation expense each year employees perform services, for the expected cost of providing future postretirement benefits that can be attributed to that service. Typically, companies do not prefund these costs for two reasons: (a) unlike pension liabilities, no federal law requires companies to fund nonpension postretirement benefits and (b) funding contributions, again unlike for pension liabilities, are not tax deductible. (The costs aren't tax deductible until paid to, or on behalf of, employees.)

Required:

1. As a result of being required to record the periodic postretirement expense and related liability, most companies now report lower earnings and higher liabilities. How might many companies also report higher assets as a result of GAAP for postretirement plans?
2. One objection to current GAAP as cited in the chapter is the omission of requirements to discount deferred tax amounts to their present values. This objection is inappropriate in the context of deferred tax amounts necessitated by accounting for postretirement benefits. Why?

Trueblood Accounting Case 16–3
Valuation allowance
● LO3

The following Trueblood case is recommended for use with this chapter. The case provides an excellent opportunity for class discussion, group projects, and writing assignments. The case, along with Professor's Discussion Material, can be obtained from the Deloitte Foundation at its website: **www.deloitte.com/us/truebloodcases.**

Case 07-6: *Graphic Inc.*

This case gives the students an opportunity to understand that judgment is involved in determining whether a valuation allowance should be recorded on deferred income tax assets. Students will identify and weigh positive and negative evidence to assess whether or how much of a valuation allowance should be recorded against an entity's deferred income tax assets.

Integrating Case 16–4
Income taxes and investment securities; Dominion Resources
● LO1 LO2 LO8

Real World Financials

Dominion Resources, Inc. is one of the nation's largest producers of energy. Corporate headquarters are in Richmond, Va. The following is an excerpt from a recent annual report.

INVESTMENT SECURITIES (IN PART)
Available-for-sale securities are reported at fair value with realized gains and losses and any other-than-temporary declines in fair value included in other income and unrealized gains and losses reported as a component of AOCI, net of tax.

Dominion's statement of comprehensive income reported an "Unrealized gain on investment securities, net of $83 million tax expense of $126 million."

Required:

1. Explain how investment securities classified as available for sale are accounted for.
2. What would have been Dominion's journal entry to reflect the fair value of the investments?

Integrating Case 16–5
Tax effects of accounting changes and error correction; six situations
● LO1 LO2 LO8

Williams-Santana, Inc. is a manufacturer of high-tech industrial parts that was started in 1997 by two talented engineers with little business training. In 2011, the company was acquired by one of its major customers. As part of an internal audit, the following facts were discovered. The audit occurred during 2011 before any adjusting entries or closing entries were prepared. The income tax rate is 40% for all years.

a. A five-year casualty insurance policy was purchased at the beginning of 2009 for $35,000. The full amount was debited to insurance expense at the time.
b. On December 31, 2010, merchandise inventory was overstated by $25,000 due to a mistake in the physical inventory count using the periodic inventory system.
c. The company changed inventory cost methods to FIFO from LIFO at the end of 2011 for both financial statement and income tax purposes. The change will cause a $960,000 increase in the beginning inventory at January 1, 2010.
d. At the end of 2010, the company failed to accrue $15,500 of sales commissions earned by employees during 2010. The expense was recorded when the commissions were paid in early 2011.
e. At the beginning of 2009, the company purchased a machine at a cost of $720,000. Its useful life was estimated to be 10 years with no salvage value. The machine has been depreciated by the double declining-balance method. Its carrying amount on December 31, 2010, was $460,800. On January 1, 2011, the company changed to the straight-line method.

f. Additional industrial robots were acquired at the beginning of 2008 and added to the company's assembly process. The $1,000,000 cost of the equipment was inadvertently recorded as repair expense. Robots have 10-year useful lives and no material salvage value. This class of equipment is depreciated by the straight-line method for both financial reporting and income tax reporting.

Required:

For each situation:

1. Identify whether it represents an accounting change or an error. If an accounting change, identify the type of change.

2. Prepare any journal entry necessary as a direct result of the change or error correction as well as any adjusting entry for 2011 related to the situation described. Any tax effects should be adjusted for through the deferred tax liability account.

3. Briefly describe any other steps that should be taken to appropriately report the situation.

Communication Case 16–6
Deferred taxes, changing rates; write a memo
● LO1 LO4 LO5

You are the new controller for Engineered Solutions. The company treasurer, Randy Patey, believes that as a result of pending legislation, the current 40% income tax rate will be decreased for 2012 to 35% and is uncertain which tax rate to apply in determining deferred taxes for 2011. Patey also is uncertain which differences should be included in that determination and has solicited your help. Your accounting group provided you the following information.

Two items are relevant to the decisions. One is the $50,000 insurance premium the company pays annually for the CEO's life insurance policy for which the company is the beneficiary. The second is that Engineered Solutions purchased a building on January 1, 2010, for $6,000,000. The building's estimated useful life is 30 years from the date of purchase, with no salvage value. Depreciation is computed using the straight-line method for financial reporting purposes and the MACRS method for tax purposes. As a result, the building's tax basis is $5,200,000 at December 31, 2011.

Required:

Write a memo to Patey that:
a. Identifies the objectives of accounting for income taxes.
b. Differentiates temporary differences and permanent differences.
c. Explains which tax rate to use.
d. Calculates the deferred tax liability at December 31, 2011.

Real World Case 16–7
Disclosure issues; balance sheet classifications; Walmart Stores
● LO1 LO2 LO8

Real World Financials

The income tax disclosure note accompanying the January 31, 2009, financial statements of **Walmart Stores** is reproduced below:

5 Income Taxes (in part)
Income Tax Provision

	Fiscal Year Ended January 31,		
(Amounts in millions)	2009	2008	2007
Current:			
Federal	$4,771	$5,145	$4,871
State and local	564	524	522
International	1,229	1,228	872
Total current tax provision	6,564	6,897	6,265
Deferred:			
Federal	614	12	(15)
State and local	41	6	4
International	(74)	(26)	100
Total deferred tax provision	581	(8)	89
Total provision for income taxes	$7,145	$6,889	$6,354

Deferred Taxes
Items that give rise to significant portions of the deferred tax accounts are as follows:

	January 31,	
(Amounts in millions)	2009	2008
Deferred tax assets:		
International operating and capital loss carryforwards	$1,430	$1,073
Accrued liabilities	2,548	2,400
Equity compensation	206	324
Other	374	516
Total deferred tax assets	4,558	4,313
Valuation allowance	(1,852)	(1,589)
Deferred tax assets, net of valuation allowance	$2,706	$2,724

(continued)

(concluded)

Deferred tax liabilities:		
Property and equipment	$3,257	$2,740
Inventories	1,079	705
Other	(25)	41
Total deferred tax liabilities	$4,311	$3,486
Net deferred tax liabilities	$1,605	$ 762

Required:

1. In its 2009 balance sheet, Walmart reported as a noncurrent liability, "Deferred income taxes" of $3,076 million. Why is this different from the $1,605 million "net deferred tax liability" reported in the disclosure note?

2. Re-create the journal entry that summarizes the entries Walmart used to record its 2009 income taxes.

Research Case 16–8
Researching the way tax deductions are reported on a corporation tax return; retrieving a tax form from the Internet
● LO1 LO2 LO3 LO8

The U.S. Treasury maintains an information site on the Internet. As part of this site the Internal Revenue Service provides tax information and services. Among those services is a server for publications and forms which allows a visitor to download a variety of IRS forms and publications.

Required:

1. Access the Treasury site on the Internet. The web address is **www.ustreas.gov**. After exploring the information available there, navigate to the IRS server for forms and publications via the IRS home page.

2. Download the corporation tax return, Form 1120.

3. Note the specific deductions listed that are deductible from total income to arrive at taxable income. Are any deductions listed that might not also be included among expenses in the income statement?

4. One of the deductions indicated is "net operating loss deduction." Under what circumstances might a company report an amount for this item?

5. Based on how taxable income is determined, how might temporary differences be created between taxable income and pretax income in the income statement?

Analysis Case 16–9
Reporting deferred taxes
● LO1 LO2 LO3 LO7 LO8

Real World Financials

Access the financial statements and related disclosure notes of **Google Inc.** from its website at **investor.google.com**. In Google's balance sheet, deferred income taxes in 2008 are reported as both an asset ($286,105 thousand) and a liability ($12,515 thousand).

Required:

1. Explain why deferred income taxes can be reported as both an asset and a liability. Why is the deferred tax asset reported as current and the deferred tax liability as long term in 2008? Is that also the situation in 2007?

2. Note 14 in the disclosure notes indicates that deferred tax assets are $650,634 thousand in 2008 and deferred tax liabilities are $377,044 thousand. How can that be explained in light of the two amounts reported in the balance sheet?

3. Does Google feel the need to record a valuation allowance for its deferred tax assets?

Analysis Case 16–10
Consult financial statements; analyze tax disclosures; recreate journal entry
● LO1 LO2 LO3 LO7 LO8

Real World Financials

Kroger Co. is one of the largest retail food companies in the United States as measured by total annual sales. The Kroger Co. operates supermarkets, convenience stores, and manufactures and processes food that its supermarkets sell. Kroger's stores operate under names such as Dillon Food Stores, City Market, Sav-Mor, Kwik Shop, and Ralph's.

Like most corporations, Kroger has significant deferred tax assets and liabilities. Using Edgar (**www.sec.gov**) or the company's website check the company's annual report for the year ended February 1, 2009.

Required:

1. From the income statement, determine the income tax expense for the most recent year. What is the current portion and the deferred portion of the expense? (See the "Taxes Based on Income" note in the Notes to Consolidated Financial Statements.) Why is the income tax expense from the income statement different from the "provision for income taxes in the disclosure note"?

2. How are the deferred taxes classified in Kroger's balance sheet? (See the "Taxes Based on Income" note in the Notes to Consolidated Financial Statements.) What amounts are reported among current assets or liabilities and among noncurrent assets or liabilities? Why?

Judgment Case 16–11
Analyzing the effect of deferred tax liabilities on firm risk; Macy's, Inc.
● LO8

The following is a portion of the January 31, 2009 and 2008, balance sheets of **Macy's, Inc.**:

Real World Financials

	January 31, 2009	January 31, 2008
LIABILITIES AND SHAREHOLDERS' EQUITY		
Current Liabilities:		
Short-term debt	$ 966	$ 666
Merchandise accounts payable	1,282	1,398
Accounts payable and accrued liabilities	2,628	2,729
Income taxes	28	344
Deferred income taxes	222	223
Total Current Liabilities	5,126	5,360
Long-Term Debt	8,733	9,087
Deferred Income Taxes	1,119	1,446
Other Liabilities	2,521	1,989
Shareholders' Equity:		
Common stock (420.1 and 419.7 shares outstanding)	5	5
Additional paid-in capital	5,663	5,609
Accumulated equity	2,008	7,032
Treasury stock	(2,544)	(2,557)
Accumulated other comprehensive loss	(486)	(182)
Total Shareholders' Equity	4,646	9,907
Total Liabilities and Shareholders' Equity	$ 22,145	$ 27,789

Macy's debt to equity ratio for the year ended January 31, 2009 was 3.8, calculated as $17,499 ÷ $4,646. Some analysts argue that long-term deferred tax liabilities should be excluded from liabilities when computing the debt to equity ratio.

Required:

1. What is the rationale for the argument that long-term deferred tax liabilities should be excluded from liabilities when computing the debt to equity ratio?

2. What would be the effect on Macy's debt to equity ratio of excluding deferred tax liabilities from its calculation? What would be the percentage change?

3. What might be the rationale for not excluding long-term deferred tax liabilities from liabilities when computing the debt to equity ratio?

Judgment Case 16–12
Intraperiod tax allocation
● LO10

Russell-James Corporation is a diversified consumer products company. During 2011, Russell-James discontinued its line of cosmetics, which constituted discontinued operations for financial reporting purposes. As vice president of the food products division, you are interested in the effect of the discontinuance on the company's profitability. One item of information you requested was an income statement. The income statement you received was labeled *preliminary* and *unaudited:*

RUSSELL-JAMES CORPORATION
Income Statement
For the Year Ended December 31, 2011
($ in millions, except per share amounts)

Revenues		$300
Cost of goods sold		90
Gross profit		210
Selling and administrative expenses		(60)
Income from continuing operations before income taxes		150
Income taxes		(22)
Income from continuing operations		128
Discontinued operations:		
Loss from operations of cosmetics division	$(100)	
Gain from disposal of cosmetics division	15	(85)
Income before extraordinary item		43
Extraordinary loss from earthquake		(10)
Net income		$ 33

(continued)

(concluded)

Per Share of Common Stock (100 million shares):	
Income from continuing operations	$1.28
Loss from operations of cosmetics division	(1.00)
Gain from disposal of cosmetics division	.15
Income before extraordinary item	.43
Extraordinary loss from earthquake	(.10)
Net income	$ .33

You are somewhat surprised at the magnitude of the loss incurred by the cosmetics division prior to its disposal. Another item that draws your attention is the apparently low tax rate indicated by the statement ($22 ÷ 150 = 15%). Upon further investigation you are told the company's tax rate is 40%.

Required:

1. Recast the income statement to reflect intraperiod tax allocation.

2. How would you reconcile the income tax expense shown on the statement above with the amount your recast statement reports?

BRITISH AIRWAYS CASE

BRITISH AIRWAYS

● LO11

British Airways, Plc. (BA), a U.K. company, prepares its financial statements according to International Financial Reporting Standards. BA's annual report for the year ended March 31, 2009, which includes financial statements and disclosure notes, is included with all new textbooks and can be found at **www.britishairways.com**. When answering questions, focus on BA's "Group" financial information (which is equivalent to "Consolidated" under U.S. GAAP).

Required:

1. Where in its March 31, 2009, balance sheet does BA report deferred taxes? How does this approach differ from the way deferred taxes are reported using U.S. GAAP? Using the Internet, determine how deferred taxes would be reported using IFRS at the time of your research. Explain why that approach might differ from the way BA reported deferred taxes at March 31, 2009.

2. Here's an excerpt from one of BA's notes to its financial statements:

> **Taxation (in part)**
> Current tax assets and liabilities are measured at the amount expected to be recovered from or paid to the taxation authorities, based on tax rates and laws that are enacted or substantively enacted at the balance sheet date.

Is this policy consistent with U.S. GAAP? Explain.

3. Here's an excerpt from one BA's notes to its financial statements:

> **Taxation (in part)**
> Deferred income tax assets are recognised only to the extent that it is probable that taxable profit will be available against which the deductible temporary differences, carried forward tax credits or tax losses can be utilised.

Is this policy consistent with U.S. GAAP? Explain.

CPA SIMULATION 16–1

Kerry Oil
Deferred Taxes

CPA Review

Test your knowledge of the concepts discussed in this chapter, practice critical professional skills necessary for career success, and prepare for the computer-based CPA exam by accessing our CPA simulations at the text website: **www.mhhe.com/spiceland6e**.

The Kerry Oil simulation tests your knowledge of the financial reporting implications of income taxes.

As on the CPA exam itself, you will be asked to use tools including a spreadsheet, a calculator, and generally accepted accounting principles, to conduct research, derive solutions, and communicate conclusions related to these issues in a simulated environment.

Specific tasks in the simulation include:

- Demonstrating an understanding of temporary and permanent differences.
- Analyzing transactions for their deferred tax reporting implications.
- Calculating the current and deferred tax components of income tax expense for multiple temporary differences.
- Applying judgment in deciding the deferred tax effects of a variety of transactions.
- Communicating the deferred tax effects of the two deferred tax reporting issues.
- Researching factors that might influence whether a valuation allowance might not be required in spite of evidence to the contrary.

17

Pensions and Other Postretirement Benefits

/// **OVERVIEW**

Employee compensation comes in many forms. Salaries and wages, of course, provide direct and current payment for services provided. However, it's commonplace for compensation also to include benefits payable after retirement. We discuss pension benefits and other postretirement benefits in this chapter. Accounting for pension benefits recognizes that they represent deferred compensation for current service. Accordingly, the cost of these benefits is recognized on an accrual basis during the years that employees earn the benefits.

/// **LEARNING OBJECTIVES**

After studying this chapter, you should be able to:

- **LO1** Explain the fundamental differences between a defined contribution pension plan and a defined benefit pension plan. (page 937)
- **LO2** Distinguish among the vested benefit obligation, the accumulated benefit obligation, and the projected benefit obligation. (page 941)
- **LO3** Describe the five events that might change the balance of the PBO. (page 942)
- **LO4** Explain how plan assets accumulate to provide retiree benefits and understand the role of the trustee in administering the fund. (page 947)
- **LO5** Describe the funded status of pension plans and how that amount is reported. (page 949)
- **LO6** Describe how pension expense is a composite of periodic changes that occur in both the pension obligation and the plan assets. (page 949)
- **LO7** Record for pension plans the periodic expense and funding as well as new gains and losses and new prior service cost as they occur. (page 955)
- **LO8** Understand the interrelationships among the elements that constitute a defined benefit pension plan. (page 962)
- **LO9** Describe the nature of postretirement benefit plans other than pensions and identify the similarities and differences in accounting for those plans and pensions. (page 966)
- **LO10** Explain how the obligation for postretirement benefits is measured and how the obligation changes. (page 969)
- **LO11** Determine the components of postretirement benefit expense. (page 970)
- **LO12** Discuss the primary differences between U.S. GAAP and IFRS with respect to accounting for postretirement benefit plans. (pages 955, 957, 961, and 965)

FINANCIAL REPORTING CASE

United Dynamics

You read yesterday that many companies in the United States have pension plans that are severely underfunded in the wake of the recent economic crisis. This caught your attention in part because you have your office interview tomorrow with United Dynamics. You hadn't really thought that much about the pension plan of your potential future employer, in part because your current employer has a defined contribution 401K plan, for which funding is not a concern. However, United Dynamics is an older firm with a defined benefit plan, for which funding is the employer's responsibility.

To prepare for your interview, you obtained a copy of United Dynamics' financial statements. Unfortunately, the financial statements themselves are of little help. You are unable to find any pension liability in the balance sheet, but the statement does report a relatively small "pension asset." The income statement reports pension expense for each of the years reported. For help, you search the disclosure notes. In part, the pension disclosure note reads as follows:

Note 7: Pension Plan

United Dynamics has a defined benefit pension plan covering substantially all of its employees. Plan benefits are based on years of service and the employee's compensation during the last three years of employment. The company's funding policy is consistent with the funding requirements of federal law and regulations. The net periodic pension expense for the company included the following components. The company's pension expense was as follows ($ in millions):

	2011	2010	2009
Current service costs	$ 43	$ 47	$ 42
Interest cost on projected benefit obligation	178	164	152
Return on assets	(213)	(194)	(187)
Amortization of prior service cost	43	43	43
Amortization of net gain	(2)	(1)	—
Net pension costs	$ 49	$ 59	$ 50

(continued)

By the time you finish this chapter, you should be able to respond appropriately to the questions posed in this case. Compare your response to the solution provided at the end of the chapter.

QUESTIONS ///

1. Why is pension plan underfunding not a concern in your present employment? (page 939)

2. Were you correct that pension assets are not reported in the balance sheet? What is the liability? (page 941)

3. What is the amount of the plan assets available to pay benefits? What are the factors that can cause that amount to change? (page 948)

4. What does the "pension asset" represent? Are you interviewing with a company whose pension plan is severely underfunded? (page 949)

5. How is the pension expense influenced by changes in the pension liability and plan assets? (page 950)

(concluded)

The following table describes the change in projected benefit obligation for the plan years ended December 31, 2011, and December 31, 2010 ($ in millions):

	2011	2010
Projected benefit obligation at beginning of year	$2,194	$2,121
Service cost	43	47
Interest cost	178	164
Actuarial (gain) loss	319	(40)
Benefits paid	(106)	(98)
Projected benefit obligation at end of year	$2,628	$2,194

The weighted-average discount rate and rate of increase in future compensation levels used in determining the actuarial present value of the projected benefit obligations in the above table were 8.1% and 4.3%, respectively, at December 31, 2011, and 7.73% and 4.7%, respectively, at December 31, 2010. The expected long-term rate of return on assets was 9.1% at December 31, 2011 and 2010.

The following table describes the change in the fair value of plan assets for the plan years ended December 31, 2011 and 2010 ($ in millions):

	2011	2010
Fair value of plan assets at beginning of year	$2,340	$2,133
Actual return on plan assets	215	178
Employer contributions	358	127
Benefits paid	(106)	(98)
Fair value of plan assets at end of year	$2,807	$2,340

"Ouch! I can't believe how much of my accounting I forgot," you complain to yourself. "I'd better get out my old intermediate accounting book."

PART A   THE NATURE OF PENSION PLANS

Over 125 million American workers are covered by pension plans. The United States' pension funds tripled in size during the previous two decades and now are roughly the size of Japan's gross national product. This powerful investment base now controls a sizable portion of the stock market. At the company level, the enormous size of pension funds is reflected in a periodic pension cost that constitutes one of the largest expenses many companies report. The corporate liability for providing pension benefits is huge. Obviously, then, the financial reporting responsibility for pensions has important social and economic implications.

Pension plans are designed to provide income to individuals during their retirement years. This is accomplished by setting aside funds during an employee's working years so that at retirement the accumulated funds plus earnings from investing those funds are available to replace wages. Actually, an individual who periodically invests in stocks, bonds, certificates of deposit (CDs), or other investments for the purpose of saving for retirement is establishing a personal pension fund. Often, such individual plans take the form of individual retirement accounts (IRAs) to take advantage of tax breaks offered by that arrangement. In employer plans, some or all of the periodic contributions to the retirement fund often are provided by the employer.

Corporations establish pension plans for a variety of reasons. Sponsorship of pension plans provides employees with a degree of retirement security and fulfills a moral obligation felt by many employers. This security also can induce a degree of job satisfaction and perhaps loyalty that might enhance productivity and reduce turnover. Motivation to sponsor a plan sometimes comes from union demands and often relates to being competitive in the labor market.

Pension plans often enhance productivity, reduce turnover, satisfy union demands, and allow employers to compete in the labor market.

ADDITIONAL CONSIDERATION

When established according to tight guidelines, a pension plan gains important tax advantages. Such arrangements are called *qualified plans* because they qualify for favorable tax treatment. In a qualified plan, the employer is permitted an immediate tax deduction for amounts paid into the pension fund (within specified limits). The employees, on the other hand, are not taxed at the time employer contributions are made—only when retirement benefits are received. Moreover, earnings on the funds set aside by the employer are not taxed while in the pension fund, so the earnings accumulate tax free. If you are familiar with the tax advantages of IRAs, you probably recognize the similarity between those individual plans and corporate pension arrangements.

> **Qualified pension plans offer important tax benefits.**

For a pension plan to be qualified for special tax treatment it must meet these general requirements.

1. It must cover at least 70% of employees.
2. It cannot discriminate in favor of highly compensated employees.
3. It must be funded in advance of retirement through contributions to an irrevocable trust fund.
4. Benefits must vest after a specified period of service, commonly five years. (We discuss this in more detail later.)
5. It complies with specific restrictions on the timing and amount of contributions and benefits.

Sometimes, employers agree to annually contribute a specific (defined) amount to a pension fund on behalf of employees but make no commitment regarding benefit amounts at retirement. In other arrangements, employers don't specify the amount of annual contributions but promise to provide determinable (defined) amounts at retirement. These two arrangements describe defined contribution pension plans and defined benefit pension plans, respectively:

> ● **LO1**

- **Defined contribution pension plans** promise fixed annual contributions to a pension fund (say, 5% of the employees' pay). Employees choose (from designated options) where funds are invested—usually stocks or fixed-income securities. Retirement pay depends on the size of the fund at retirement.

- **Defined benefit pension plans** promise fixed retirement benefits defined by a designated formula. Typically, the pension formula bases retirement pay on the employees' (a) years of service, (b) annual compensation (often final pay or an average for the last few years), and sometimes (c) age. Employers are responsible for ensuring that sufficient funds are available to provide promised benefits.

Today, approximately two-thirds of workers covered by pension plans are covered by defined contribution plans, roughly one-third by defined benefit plans. This represents a radical shift from previous years when the traditional defined benefit plan was far more common. However, very few new pension plans are of the defined benefit variety. In fact, many companies are terminating long-standing defined benefit plans and substituting defined contribution plans. Why the shift? There are three main reasons:

> **Virtually all new pension plans are defined contribution plans.**

1. Government regulations make defined benefit plans cumbersome and costly to administer.
2. Employers are increasingly unwilling to bear the risk of defined benefit plans; with defined contribution plans, the company's obligation ends when contributions are made.
3. There has been a shift among many employers from trying to "buy long-term loyalty" (with defined benefit plans) to trying to attract new talent (with more mobile defined contribution plans).

The two categories of pension plans are depicted in Graphic 17–1.

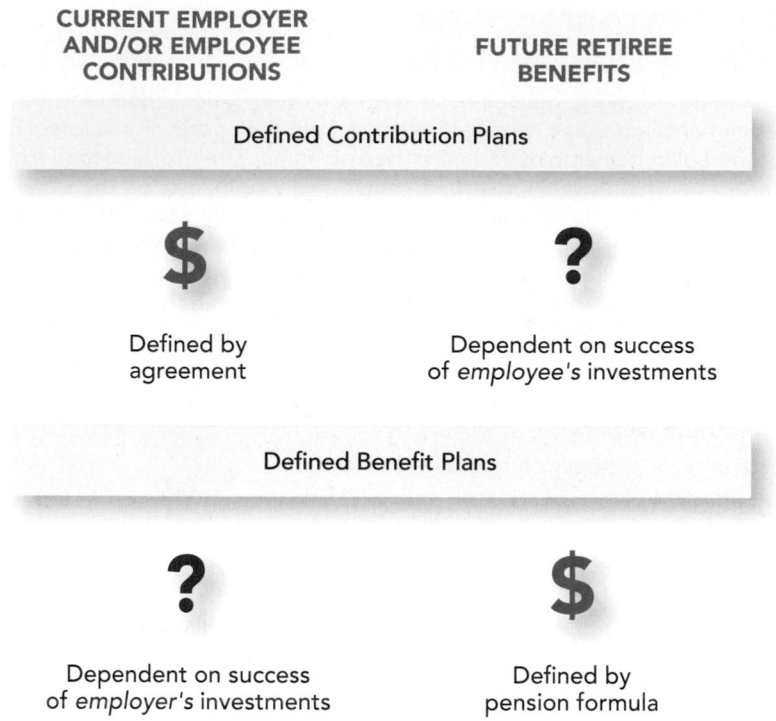

Both types of plans have a common goal: to provide income to employees during their retirement years. Still, the two types of plans differ regarding who bears the risk—the employer or the employees—for whether the retirement objectives are achieved. The two types of plans also have entirely different implications for accounting and financial reporting. Our discussion of defined contribution plans will be brief. Although these are now the most popular type of corporate pension plan, their relative simplicity permits a rather straightforward accounting treatment that requires little explanation. On the other hand, defined benefit plans require considerably more complex accounting treatment and constitute the primary focus of this chapter.

Defined Contribution Pension Plans

Defined contribution pension plans are becoming increasingly popular vehicles for employers to provide retirement income without the paperwork, cost, and risk generated by the more traditional defined benefit plans. Defined contribution plans promise fixed periodic contributions to a pension fund. Retirement income depends on the size of the fund at retirement. No further commitment is made by the employer regarding benefit amounts at retirement.

Defined contribution plans promise defined periodic contributions to a pension fund, without further commitment regarding benefit amounts at retirement.

These plans have several variations. In money purchase plans, employers contribute a fixed percentage of employees' salaries. Thrift plans, savings plans, and 401(k) plans (named after the Tax Code section that specifies the conditions for the favorable tax treatment of these plans) permit voluntary contributions by employees. These contributions typically are matched to a specified extent by employers. Approximately two-thirds of American workers participate in 401(k) plans. More than two trillion dollars are invested in these plans.

When plans link the amount of contributions to company performance, labels include profit-sharing plans, incentive savings plans, 401(k) profit-sharing plans, and similar titles. When employees make contributions to the plan in addition to employer contributions, it's called a *contributory* plan. Sometimes the amount the employer contributes is tied to the amount of the employee contribution.[1] Variations are seemingly endless. An example from a recent annual report of **Microsoft Corporation** is shown in Graphic 17–2.

---

[1]One popular way for employer companies to provide contributions is with shares of its own common stock. If so, the arrangements usually are designed to comply with government requirements to be designated an employee stock ownership plan (ESOP).

Note 20 (in part)
Savings Plan
We have a savings plan in the United States that qualifies under Section 401(k) of the Internal Revenue Code, and a number of savings plans in international locations. Participating U.S. employees may contribute up to 50% of their salary, but not more than statutory limits. We contribute fifty cents for each dollar a participant contributes in this plan, with a maximum contribution of 3% of a participant's earnings. Matching contributions for all plans were $262 million, $238 million, and $218 million in fiscal years 2009, 2008, and 2007, respectively, and were expensed as contributed.

Accounting for these plans is quite easy. Each year, the employer simply records pension expense equal to the amount of the annual contribution. Suppose a plan promises an annual contribution equal to 3% of an employee's salary. If an employee's salary is $110,000 in a particular year, the employer would simply recognize pension expense in the amount of the contribution:

**FINANCIAL
Reporting Case**

Q1, p. 935

For defined
contribution plans,
the employer simply
records pension
expense equal to the
cash contribution.

Pension expense	3,300	
Cash ($110,000 × 3%)		3,300

The employee's retirement benefits are totally dependent upon how well investments perform. Who bears the risk (or reward) of that uncertainty? The employee would bear the risk of uncertain investment returns and, potentially, settle for far less at retirement than at first expected.[2] On the other hand, the employer would be free of any further obligation. Because the actual investments are held by an independent investment firm, the employer is free of that recordkeeping responsibility as well.

Risk is reversed in a defined benefit plan. Because specific benefits are promised at retirement, the employer would be responsible for making up the difference when investment performance is less than expected. We look at defined benefit plans next.

Defined Benefit Pension Plans

When setting aside cash to fund a pension plan, the uncertainty surrounding the rate of return on plan assets is but one of several uncertainties inherent in a defined benefit plan. Employee turnover affects the number of employees who ultimately will become eligible for retirement benefits. The age at which employees will choose to retire as well as life expectancies will impact both the length of the retirement period and the amount of the benefits. Inflation, future compensation levels, and interest rates also have obvious influence on eventual benefits.

This is particularly true when pension benefits are defined by a pension formula, as usually is the case. A typical formula might specify that a retiree will receive annual retirement benefits based on the employee's years of service and annual pay at retirement (say, pay level in the final year, highest pay achieved, or average pay in the last two or more years). For example, a pension formula might define annual retirement benefits as:

*Defined benefit
plans* promise
fixed retirement
benefits defined by a
designated formula.

Uncertainties
complicate determining
how much to set aside
each year to ensure
that sufficient funds
are available to provide
promised benefits.

1½% × Years of service × Final year's salary

By this formula, the annual benefits to an employee who retires after 30 years of service, with a final salary of $100,000, would be:

1½% × 30 years × $100,000 = $45,000

---

[2]Of course, this is not entirely unappealing to the employee. Defined contribution plans allow an employee to select investments in line with his or her own risk preferences and often provide greater retirement benefits and flexibility than defined benefit plans.

A pension formula typically defines retirement pay based on the employees' (a) years of service, (b) annual compensation, and sometimes (c) age.

Pension gains and losses occur when the *pension obligation* is lower or higher than expected.

Pension gains and losses occur when the *return on plan assets* is higher or lower than expected.

Neither the pension obligation nor the plan assets are reported individually in the balance sheet.

The pension expense is a direct composite of periodic changes that occur in both the pension obligation and the plan assets.

Typically, a firm will hire an **actuary,** a professional trained in a particular branch of statistics and mathematics, to assess the various uncertainties (employee turnover, salary levels, mortality, etc.) and to estimate the company's obligation to employees in connection with its pension plan. Such estimates are inherently subjective, so regardless of the skill of the actuary, estimates invariably deviate from the actual outcome to one degree or another.[3] For instance, the return on assets can turn out to be more or less than expected. These deviations are referred to as *gains* and *losses* on pension assets. When it's necessary to revise estimates related to the pension obligation because it's determined to be more or less than previously thought, these revisions are referred to as *losses* and *gains,* respectively, on the pension liability. Later, we will discuss the accounting treatment of gains and losses from either source. The point here is that the risk of the pension obligation changing unexpectedly or the pension funds being inadequate to meet the obligation is borne by the employer with a defined benefit pension plan.

The key elements of a defined benefit pension plan are:

1. The *employer's obligation* to pay retirement benefits in the future.
2. The *plan assets* set aside by the employer from which to pay the retirement benefits in the future.
3. The *periodic expense* of having a pension plan.

As you will learn in this chapter, the first two of these elements are not reported individually in the employer's financial statements. This may seem confusing at first because it is inconsistent with the way you're accustomed to treating assets and liabilities. Even though they are not separately reported, it's critical that you understand the composition of both the pension obligation and the plan assets because (a) they are reported as a net amount in the balance sheet, and (b) their balances are reported in disclosure notes. And, importantly, the pension expense reported in the income statement is a direct composite of periodic changes that occur in both the pension obligation and the plan assets.

For this reason, we will devote a considerable portion of our early discussion to understanding the composition of the pension obligation and the plan assets before focusing on the derivation of pension expense and required financial statement disclosures. We will begin with a quick overview of how periodic changes that occur in both the pension obligation and the plan assets affect pension expense. Next we will explore how those changes occur, beginning with changes in the pension obligation followed by changes in plan assets. We'll then return to pension expense for a closer look at how those changes influence its calculation. After that, we will bring together the separate but related parts by using a simple spreadsheet to demonstrate how each element of the pension plan articulates with the other elements.

Current GAAP retains three fundamental aspects of past pension accounting: *delayed recognition* of certain events, reporting *net cost,* and *offsetting* liabilities and assets. Those three features of practice have shaped financial reporting for many years . . . and they conflict in some respects with accounting principles applied elsewhere.[4]

Pension Expense—An Overview

The annual pension expense reflects changes in both the pension obligation and the plan assets. Graphic 17–3 provides a brief overview of how these changes are included in pension expense. After the overview, we'll look closer at each of the components.

Next we explore each of these pension expense components in the context of its being a part of either (a) the pension obligation or (b) the plan assets. After you learn how the expense components relate to these elements of the pension plan, we'll return to explore further how they are included in the pension expense.

---

[3]We discuss changes in more detail in Chapter 20.
[4]FASB ASC 715: Compensation–Retirement Benefits (previously "Employers' Accounting for Pensions," *Statement of Financial Accounting Standards No. 87* (Stamford, Conn.: FASB, 1985)).

Components of Pension Expense	
+	**Service cost** ascribed to employee service during the period
+	**Interest** accrued on the pension liability
–	**Return** on the plan assets*
	Amortized portion of:
+	**Prior service cost** attributed to employee service before an amendment to the pension plan
+ or (–)	**Losses or (gains)** from revisions in the pension liability or from investing plan assets
=	**Pension expense**

*The actual return is adjusted for any difference between actual and expected return, resulting in the *expected* return being reflected in pension expense. This loss or gain from investing plan assets is combined with losses and gains from revisions in the pension liability for deferred inclusion in pension expense. (See the last component of pension expense.)

GRAPHIC 17–3

Components of Pension Expense—Overview (More Later)

Interest and investment return are financing aspects of the pension cost.

The recognition of some elements of the pension expense is delayed.

THE PENSION OBLIGATION AND PLAN ASSETS

The Pension Obligation

Now we consider more precisely what is meant by the pension obligation. Unfortunately, there's not just one definition, nor is there uniformity concerning which definition is most appropriate for pension accounting. Actually, three different ways to measure the pension obligation have meaning in pension accounting, as shown in Graphic 17–4.

1. **Accumulated benefit obligation (ABO)** The actuary's estimate of the total retirement benefits (at their discounted present value) earned so far by employees, applying the pension formula using existing compensation levels.
2. **Vested benefit obligation (VBO)** The portion of the accumulated benefit obligation that plan participants are entitled to receive regardless of their continued employment.
3. **Projected benefit obligation (PBO)** The actuary's estimate of the total retirement benefits (at their discounted present value) earned so far by employees, applying the pension formula using estimated future compensation levels. (If the pension formula does not include future compensation levels, the PBO and the ABO are the same.)

Later you will learn that the projected benefit obligation is the basis for some elements of the periodic pension expense. Remember, there is but one obligation; these are three ways to measure it. The relationship among the three is depicted in Graphic 17–5 on the next page.

Now let's look closer at how the obligation is measured in each of these three ways. Keep in mind, though, that it's not the accountant's responsibility to actually derive the measurement; a professional actuary provides these numbers. However, for the accountant to effectively use the numbers provided, she or he must understand their derivation.

Accumulated Benefit Obligation

The **accumulated benefit obligation (ABO)** is an estimate of the discounted present value of the retirement benefits earned so far by employees, applying the plan's pension formula using existing compensation levels. When we look at a detailed calculation of the projected benefit obligation later, keep in mind that simply substituting the employee's existing compensation in the pension formula for her projected salary at retirement would give us the accumulated benefit obligation.

Vested Benefit Obligation

Suppose an employee leaves the company to take another job. Will she still get earned benefits at retirement? The answer depends on whether the benefits are vested under the terms

PART B

FINANCIAL Reporting Case

Q2, p. 935

GRAPHIC 17–4

Ways to Measure the Pension Obligation

● LO2

The *accumulated benefit obligation* ignores possible pay increases in the future.

GRAPHIC 17–5
Alternative Measures
of the Pension
Obligation

of this particular pension plan. If benefits are fully vested—yes. **Vested benefits** are those that employees have the right to receive even if their employment were to cease today.

Pension plans typically require some minimum period of employment before benefits vest. Before the Employee Retirement Income Security Act (ERISA) was passed in 1974, horror stories relating to lost benefits were commonplace. It was possible, for example, for an employee to be dismissed a week before retirement and be left with no pension benefits. Vesting requirements were tightened drastically to protect employees. These requirements have been changed periodically since then. Today, benefits must vest (a) fully within five years or (b) 20% within three years with another 20% vesting each subsequent year until fully vested after seven years. Five-year vesting is most common. ERISA also established the Pension Benefit Guaranty Corporation (PBGC) to impose liens on corporate assets for unfunded pension liabilities in certain instances and to administer terminated pension plans. The PBGC provides a form of insurance for employees similar to the role of the FDIC for bank accounts and is financed by premiums from employers equal to specified amounts for each covered employee. It makes retirement payments for terminated plans and guarantees basic vested benefits when pension liabilities exceed assets. The vested benefit obligation is actually a subset of the ABO, the portion attributable to benefits that have vested.

> The benefits of most pension plans vest after five years.

Projected Benefit Obligation

● LO3

As described earlier, when the ABO is estimated, the most recent salary is included in the pension formula to estimate future benefits, even if the pension formula specifies the final year's salary. No attempt is made to forecast what that salary would be the year before retirement. Of course, the most recent salary certainly offers an objective number to measure the obligation, but is it realistic? Since it's unlikely that there will be no salary increases between now and retirement, a more meaningful measurement should include a projection of what the salary might be at retirement.[5] Measured this way, the liability is referred to as the **projected benefit obligation (PBO)**. The PBO measurement may be less reliable than the ABO but is more relevant and representationally faithful.

> The *PBO* estimates retirement benefits by applying the pension formula using projected future compensation levels.

To understand the concepts involved, it's helpful to look at a numerical example. We'll simplify the example (Illustration 17–1) by looking at how pension amounts would be determined for a single employee. Keep in mind though, that in actuality, calculations would be made (by the actuary) for the entire employee pool rather than on an individual-by-individual basis.

---

[5]To project future salaries for a group of employees, actuaries usually assume some percentage rate of increase in compensation levels in upcoming years. Recent estimates of the rate of compensation increase have ranged from 4.5% to 8.5% with 4.5% being the most commonly reported expectation (*Accounting Trends and Techniques—2009* (New York: AICPA, 2009), p. 372.)

Jessica Farrow was hired by Global Communications in 2000. The company has a defined benefit pension plan that specifies annual retirement benefits equal to:

1.5% × Service years × Final year's salary

Farrow is expected to retire in 2039 after 40 years service. Her retirement period is expected to be 20 years. At the end of 2009, 10 years after being hired, her salary is $100,000. The interest rate is 6%. The company's actuary projects Farrow's salary to be $400,000 at retirement.*

What is the company's projected benefit obligation with respect to Jessica Farrow?

Steps to calculate the projected benefit obligation:
1. Use the pension formula (including a projection of future salary levels) to determine the retirement benefits earned to date.
2. Find the present value of the retirement benefits as of the retirement date.
3. Find the present value of retirement benefits as of the current date.

3. Present value (n = 30, i = 6%) of retirement benefits at 2009 is
$688,195 × .17411 =
$119,822 (PBO)

1. Actuary estimates employee has earned (as of 2009) retirement benefits of
1.5% × 10 years × $400,000 =
$60,000 per year

2000   2009   2039   2059

10 years   30 years   20 years
Service period   **Retirement**

2. Present value (n = 20, i = 6%) of the retirement annuity at the retirement date is
$60,000 × 11.46992 =
$688,195

*This salary reflects an estimated compound rate of increase of about 5% and should take into account expectations concerning inflation, promotions, productivity gains, and other factors that might influence salary levels.

ILLUSTRATION 17–1

Projected Benefit Obligation

The actual includes projected salaries in the pension formula. The projected benefit obligation is the present value of those benefits.

Using Excel, enter:
=PV(.06,20,60000)
Output: 688195

Using a calculator:
enter: [N] 20 [I] 6
[PMT] −60000 [FV]
Output: [PV] 688195

If the actuary's estimate of the final salary hasn't changed, the PBO a year later at the end of 2010 would be $139,715 as demonstrated in Illustration 17–1A.

3. Present value (n = 29, i = 6%) of retirement benefits at 2010 is
$757,015 × .18456 =
$139,715 (PBO)

1. Actuary estimates employee has earned (as of 2010) retirement benefits of
1.5% × 11 years × $400,000 =
$66,000 per year

2000   2010   2039   2059

11 years   29 years   20 years
Service period   **Retirement**

2. Present value (n = 20, i = 6%) of the retirement annuity at the retirement date is
$66,000 × 11.46992 =
$757,015

ILLUSTRATION 17–1A

PBO in 2010

In 2010 the pension formula includes one more service year.

Also, 2010 is one year closer to the retirement date for the purpose of calculating the present value.

CHANGES IN THE PBO.   Notice that the PBO increased during 2010 (Illustration 17–1A) from $119,822 to $139,715 for two reasons:

1. One more service year is included in the pension formula calculation (service cost).
2. The employee is one year closer to retirement, causing the present value of benefits to increase due to the time value of future benefits (interest cost).

These represent two of the events that might possibly cause the balance of the PBO to change. Let's elaborate on these and the three other events that might change the balance of the PBO. The five events are (1) service cost, (2) interest cost, (3) prior service cost, (4) gains and losses, and (5) payments to retired employees.

1. Service cost.   As we just witnessed in the illustration, the PBO increases each year by the amount of that year's service cost. This represents the increase in the projected benefit obligation attributable to employee service performed during the period. As we explain later, it also is the primary component of the annual pension expense.

2. Interest cost.   The second reason the PBO increases is called the interest cost. Even though the projected benefit obligation is not formally recognized as a liability in the company's balance sheet, it is a liability nevertheless. And, as with other liabilities, interest accrues on its balance as time passes. The amount can be calculated directly as the assumed discount rate multiplied by the projected benefit obligation at the beginning of the year.[6]

ADDITIONAL CONSIDERATION

We can verify the increase in the PBO as being caused by the service cost and interest cost as follows:

PBO at the beginning of 2010 (end of 2009)	$119,822
Service cost: (1.5% × 1 yr. × $400,000) × 11.46992* × .18456†	12,701
Interest cost: $119,822 × 6%	7,189
PBO at the end of 2010	$139,712‡

Service cost annotations: "Annual retirement benefits from 2010 service", "To discount to 2039", "To discount to 2010".

*Present value of an ordinary annuity of $1: $n = 20$, $i = 6\%$.
†Present value of $1: $n = 29$, $i = 6\%$.
‡Differs from $139,715 due to rounding.

---

3. Prior service cost.   Another reason the PBO might change is when the pension plan itself is *amended* to revise the way benefits are determined. For example, Global Communications in our illustration might choose to revise the pension formula by which benefits are calculated. Let's back up and assume the formula's salary percentage is increased in 2010 from 1.5% to 1.7%:

$$\text{1.7\% × Service years × Final year's salary}$$
$$\text{(revised pension formula)}$$

Obviously, the annual service cost from this date forward will be higher than it would have been without the amendment. This will cause a more rapid future expansion of the PBO. But it also might cause an immediate increase in the PBO as well. Here's why.

Suppose the amendment becomes effective for future years' service only, without consideration of employee service to date. As you might imagine, the morale and dedication of long-time employees of the company could be expected to suffer. So, for economic as well as ethical reasons, most companies choose to make amendments retroactive to prior years. In other words, the more beneficial terms of the revised pension formula are not applied just to future service years, but benefits attributable to all prior service years also are recomputed under the more favorable terms. Obviously, this decision is not without cost to the company. Making the amendment retroactive to prior years adds an extra layer of retirement benefits, increasing the company's benefit obligation. The increase in the PBO attributable to making a plan amendment retroactive is referred to as prior service cost.[7] For instance, Graphic 17–6 presents an excerpt from an annual report of **Ecolab, Inc.** describing the increase in its PBO as a result of making an amendment retroactive:

---

[6]Assumed discount rates should reflect rates used currently in annuity contracts. Discount rates recently reported have ranged from 4.5% to 8.5%, with 6 % being the most commonly assumed rate (*Accounting Trends and Techniques—2009* (New York: AICPA, 2009), p. 371.)
[7]Prior service cost also is created if a defined benefit pension plan is initially adopted by a company that previously did not have one, and the plan itself is made retroactive to give credit for prior years' service. Prior service cost is created by plan amendments far more often than by plan adoptions because most companies already have pension plans, and new pension plans in recent years have predominantly been defined contribution plans.

Note 1: Retirement Plans (in part)
. . . The Company amended its U.S. pension plan to change the formula for pension benefits and to provide a more rapid vesting schedule. The plan amendments resulted in a $6 million increase in the projected benefits obligation.

GRAPHIC 17–6

Prior Service Cost—
Ecolab, Inc.

Real World Financials

Let's put prior service cost in the context of our illustration.

At the end of 2009, and therefore the beginning of 2010, the PBO is $119,822. If the plan is amended on January 3, 2010, the PBO could be recomputed as:

	PBO without Amendment		PBO with Amendment	
1.	1.5% × 10 yrs. × $400,000 = $ 60,000		1.7% × 10 yrs. × $400,000 = $ 68,000	
2.	$60,000 × 11.46992 = 688,195		$68,000 × 11.46992 = 779,955	
3.	$688,195 × .17411 = 119,822		$779,955 × .17411 = 135,798	

$15,976
Prior service cost

Retroactive benefits from an amendment add additional costs, increasing the company's PBO. This increase is the prior service cost.

The $15,976 increase in the PBO attributable to applying the more generous terms of the amendment to prior service years is the prior service cost. And, because we assumed the amendment occurred at the beginning of 2010, both the 2010 service cost and the 2010 interest cost would change as a result of the prior service cost. This is how:

PBO at the beginning of 2010 (end of 2009)	$119,822
Prior service cost (determined above)	15,976
PBO including prior service cost at the beginning of 2010	135,798
Service cost: (1.7% × 1 yr. × $400,000) × 11.46992* × .18456†	14,395
Interest cost: $135,798‡ × 6%	8,148
PBO at the end of 2010	$158,341

Annual retirement benefits from 2010 service / To discount to 2037 / To discount to 2010

Prior service cost increased the PBO at the beginning of the year.

*Present value of an ordinary annuity of $1: n = 20, i = 6%.
†Present value of $1: n = 29, i = 6%.
‡Includes the beginning balance plus the prior service cost because the amendment occurred at the beginning of the year.

ADDITIONAL CONSIDERATION

We can verify the PBO balance by calculating it directly:

The pension formula reflects the plan amendment.

*Adjusted by $2 to compensate for the rounding of present value factors

The plan amendment would affect not only the year in which it occurs, but also each subsequent year because the revised pension formula determines each year's service cost. Continuing our illustration to 2011 demonstrates this:

During 2011, the PBO increased as a result of service cost and interest cost.

PBO at the beginning of 2011 (end of 2010)	$158,341
Service cost: (1.7% × 1 yr. × $400,000) × 11.46992* × .19563†	15,258
Interest cost: $158,341 × 6%	9,500
PBO at the end of 2011	$183,099

Annual retirement benefits from 2011 service · To discount to 2039 · To discount to 2011

*Present value of an ordinary annuity of $1: n = 20, i = 6%.
†Present value of $1: n = 28, i = 6%.

Decreases and increases in estimates of the PBO because of periodic reevaluation of uncertainties are called gains and losses.

4. Gain or loss on the PBO.

We mentioned earlier that a number of estimates are necessary to derive the PBO. When one or more of these estimates requires revision, the estimate of the PBO also will require revision. The resulting decrease or increase in the PBO is referred to as a *gain* or *loss,* respectively. Let's modify our illustration to imitate the effect of revising one of the several possible estimates involved. Suppose, for instance, that new information at the end of 2011 about inflation and compensation trends suggests that the estimate of Farrow's final salary should be increased by 5% to $420,000. This would affect the estimate of the PBO as follows:

Changing the final salary estimate changes the PBO.

	PBO *without* Revised Estimate		PBO *with* Revised Estimate	
1.	1.7% × 12 yrs. × $400,000	= $ 81,600	1.7% × 12 yrs. × $420,000	= $ 85,680
2.	$81,600 × 11.46992	= 935,945	$85,680 × 11.46992	= 982,743
3.	$935,945 × .19563	= 183,099	$982,743 × .19563	= 192,254

$9,155
Loss on PBO

The difference of $9,155 represents a loss on the PBO because the obligation turned out to be higher than previously expected. Now there would be three elements of the increase in the PBO during 2011.[8]

The revised estimate caused the PBO to increase.

PBO at the beginning of 2011	$158,341
Service cost (calculated above)	15,258
Interest cost (calculated above)	9,500
Loss on PBO (calculated above)	9,155
PBO at the end of 2011	$192,254

If a revised estimate causes the PBO to be lower than previously expected, a gain would be indicated. Consider how a few of the other possible estimate changes would affect the PBO:

- A change in life expectancies might cause the retirement period to be estimated as 21 years rather than 20 years. Calculation of the present value of the retirement annuity would use $n = 21$, rather than $n = 20$. The estimate of the PBO would increase.
- The expectation that retirement will occur two years earlier than previously thought would cause the retirement period to be estimated as 22 years rather than 20 years and the service period to be estimated as 28 years rather than 30 years. The new expectation would probably also cause the final salary estimate to change. The net effect on the PBO would depend on the circumstances.
- A change in the assumed discount rate would affect the present value calculations. A lower rate would increase the estimate of the PBO. A higher rate would decrease the estimate of the PBO.

---

[8]The increase in the PBO due to amending the pension formula (prior service cost) occurred in 2010.

5. Payment of retirement benefits.   We've seen how the PBO will change due to the accumulation of service cost from year to year, the accrual of interest as time passes, making plan amendments retroactive to prior years, and periodic adjustments when estimates change. Another change in the PBO occurs when the obligation is reduced as benefits actually are paid to retired employees.

> Payment of retirement benefits reduces the PBO.

The payment of such benefits is not applicable in our present illustration because we've limited the situation to calculations concerning an individual employee who is several years from retirement. Remember, though, in reality the actuary would make these calculations for the entire pool of employees covered by the pension plan. But the concepts involved would be the same. Graphic 17–7 summarizes the five ways the PBO can change.

> **GRAPHIC 17–7**
> Components of Change in the PBO

The Projected Benefits Obligation Changes as a Result of:		
Cause	**Effect**	**Frequency**
Service cost	+	Each period
Interest cost	+	Each period (except the first period of the plan, when no obligation exists to accrue interest)
Prior service cost	+	Only if the plan is amended (or initiated) that period
Loss or gain on PBO	+ or −	Whenever revisions are made in the pension liability estimate
Retiree benefits paid	−	Each period (unless no employees have yet retired under the plan)

Illustration Expanded to Consider the Entire Employee Pool

For our single employee, the PBO at the end of 2011 is $192,254. Let's say now that Global Communications has 2,000 active employees covered by the pension plan and 100 retired employees receiving retirement benefits. Illustration 17–2 expands the numbers to represent all covered employees.

> The PBO is not formally recognized in the balance sheet.

> **ILLUSTRATION 17–2**
> The PBO Expanded to Include All Employees

The changes in the PBO for Global Communications during 2011 were as follows:

	($ in millions)*
PBO at the beginning of 2011† (amount assumed)	$400
Service cost, 2011 (amount assumed)	41
Interest cost: $400 × 6%	24
Loss (gain) on PBO (amount assumed)	23
Less: Retiree benefits paid (amount assumed)	(38)
PBO at the end of 2011	$450

*Of course, these expanded amounts are not simply the amounts for Jessica Farrow multiplied by 2,000 employees because her years of service, expected retirement date, and salary are not necessarily representative of other employees. Also, the expanded amounts take into account expected employee turnover and current retirees.
†Includes the prior service cost that increased the PBO when the plan was amended in 2010.

Pension Plan Assets

So far our focus has been on the employer's obligation to provide retirement benefits in the future. We turn our attention now to the resources with which the company will satisfy that obligation—the **pension plan assets.** Like the PBO, the pension plan assets are not reported separately in the employer's balance sheet but are netted together with the PBO to report either a net pension asset (debit balance) or a net pension liability (credit balance). Its separate balance, too, must be reported in the disclosure notes to the financial statements (as does the separate PBO balance), and as explained below, the return on these assets is included in the calculation of the periodic pension expense.

● LO4

FINANCIAL
Reporting Case

Q3, p. 935

A *trustee* manages pension plan assets.

We assumed in the previous section that Global Communications' obligation is $450 million for service performed to date. When employees retire, will there be sufficient funds to provide the anticipated benefits? To ensure sufficient funding, Global will contribute cash each year to a pension fund.

The assets of a pension fund must be held by a **trustee.** A trustee accepts employer contributions, invests the contributions, accumulates the earnings on the investments, and pays benefits from the plan assets to retired employees or their beneficiaries. The trustee can be an individual, a bank, or a trust company. Plan assets are invested in stocks, bonds, and other income-producing assets. The accumulated balance of the annual employer contributions plus the return on the investments (dividends, interest, market price appreciation) must be sufficient to pay benefits as they come due.

When an employer estimates how much it must set aside each year to accumulate sufficient funds to pay retirement benefits as they come due, it's necessary to estimate the return those investments will produce. This is the **expected return on plan assets.** The higher the return, the less the employer must actually contribute. On the other hand, a relatively low return means the difference must be made up by higher contributions. In practice, recent estimates of the rate of return have ranged from 4.5% to 9.5%, with 8% being the most commonly reported expectation.[9] In Illustration 17–3, we shift the focus of our numerical illustration to emphasize Global's pension plan assets.

ILLUSTRATION 17–3 How Plan Assets Change	Global Communications funds its defined benefit pension plan by contributing each year the year's service cost plus a portion of the prior service cost. Cash of $48 million was contributed to the pension fund at the end of 2011.

ILLUSTRATION 17–3

How Plan Assets Change

A trustee accepts employer contributions, invests the contributions, accumulates the earnings on the investments, and pays benefits from the plan assets.

Global Communications funds its defined benefit pension plan by contributing each year the year's service cost plus a portion of the prior service cost. Cash of $48 million was contributed to the pension fund at the end of 2011.

Plan assets at the beginning of 2011 were valued at $300 million. The expected rate of return on the investment of those assets was 9%, but the actual return in 2011 was 10%. Retirement benefits of $38 million were paid at the end of 2011 to retired employees.

What is the value of the company's pension plan assets at the end of 2011?

	($ in millions)
Plan assets at the beginning of 2011	$300
Return on plan assets (10% × $300)	30
Cash contributions	48
Less: Retiree benefits paid	(38)
Plan assets at the end of 2011	$340

An *underfunded* pension plan means the PBO exceeds plan assets.

Recall that Global's PBO at the end of 2011 is $450 million. Because the plan assets are only $340 million, the pension plan is said to be *underfunded*. One reason is that we assumed Global incurred a $60 million prior service cost from amending the pension plan at the beginning of 2010, and that cost is being funded over several years. Another factor is the loss from increasing the PBO due to the estimate revision, since funding has been based on the previous estimate. Later, we'll assume earlier revisions also have increased the PBO. Of course, actual performance of the investments also impacts a plan's funded status.

An *overfunded* pension plan means plan assets exceed the PBO.

It is not unusual for pension plans today to be underfunded. Historically the funded status of pension plans has varied considerably. Prior to the Employee Retirement Income Security Act (ERISA) in 1974, many plans were grossly underfunded. The new law established minimum funding standards among other matters designed to protect plan participants. The new standards brought most plans closer to full funding. Then the stock market boom of the 1980s caused the value of plan assets for many pension funds to swell to well over their projected benefit obligations. More than 80% of pension plans were overfunded. As a result, managers explored ways to divert funds to other areas of operations. Today a majority of plans again are underfunded. The economic crisis has taken its toll. Stock market declines

---

[9]*Accounting Trends and Techniques—2009* (New York: AICPA, 2009), p. 371.

reduced the funded status of pension plans from 108% at the end of 2007 to 79% at the end of 2008.[10] In 2009, pension plans of the country's 500 largest companies were underfunded by $200 billion. Partly in response to the severe underfunding and partly spurred by attractive stock prices, unusually high cash contributions to plan assets reduced the underfunded status from 79% at the end of 2008 to 87% at the end of 2009.[11] Many of the underfunded plans are with troubled companies, placing employees at risk. The PBGC guarantees are limited to about $3,400 per month, often less than promised pension benefits.

Reporting the Funded Status of the Pension Plan

● LO5

A company's PBO is not reported separately among liabilities in the balance sheet. Similarly, the plan assets a company sets aside to pay those benefits are not separately reported among assets in the balance sheet. However, firms do report the net difference between those two amounts, referred to as the "funded status" of the plan.[12] From our previous discussion, we see the funded status for Global to be the following at December 31, 2011, and December 31, 2010:

	($ in millions)	
	2011	**2010**
Projected benefit obligation (PBO)	$450	$400
Fair value of plan assets	340	300
Underfunded status	$110	$100

A company must report in its balance sheet a liability for the underfunded (or asset for the overfunded) status of its postretirement plans.

Because the plan is underfunded, Global reports a net pension liability of $110 million in its 2011 balance sheet and $100 million in 2010. Be sure to note that this is not an actual account balance. Instead, it's the PBO account balance and the Plan assets account balance simply reported in the balance sheet as a single net amount. If the plan becomes overfunded in the future, Global will report a net pension asset instead.

Now, let's look at all the ways that changes in the PBO and the pension plan assets affect pension expense.

DETERMINING PENSION EXPENSE

PART C

The Relationship between Pension Expense and Changes in the PBO and Plan Assets

● LO6

Like wages, salaries, commissions, and other forms of pay, pension expense is part of a company's compensation for employee services each year. Accordingly, the accounting objective is to achieve a matching of the costs of providing this form of compensation with the benefits of the services performed. However, the fact that this form of compensation actually is paid to employees many years after the service is performed means that other elements in addition to the annual service cost will affect the ultimate pension cost. These other elements are related to changes that occur over time in both the pension liability and the pension plan assets. Graphic 17–8 on the next page provides a summary of how some of these changes influence pension expense.

The matching principle and the time period assumption dictate that the costs be allocated to the periods the services are performed.

We've examined each of the components of pension expense from the viewpoint of its effect on the PBO or on plan assets, using the Global Communications illustration to demonstrate that effect. Now, let's expand the same illustration to see how these changes affect *pension expense*. Illustration 17–4 on the next page provides this expanded example.

[10]Goldman Sachs, "Global Markets Institute Accounting Policy Update: Pension review 2009 – Fallout from funded status decline just beginning," Global Markets Institute, June 4, 2009.
[11]Goldman Sachs, "Notable Contributions Boost Funded Levels," Global Markets Institute, December 15, 2009.
[12]FASB 715–30–25: Compensation–Retirement Benefits–Defined Benefit Plans–Pension–Recognition (previously "Employers' Accounting for Defined Benefit Pension and Other Postretirement Plans—an amendment of FASB Statements No. 87, 88, 106, and 132(R)," *Statement of Financial Accounting Standards No. 158* (Stamford, Conn.: FASB, 2006)).

GRAPHIC 17–8
Components of the Periodic Pension Expense

The pension expense reported in the income statement is a composite of periodic changes that occur in both the pension obligation and the plan assets.

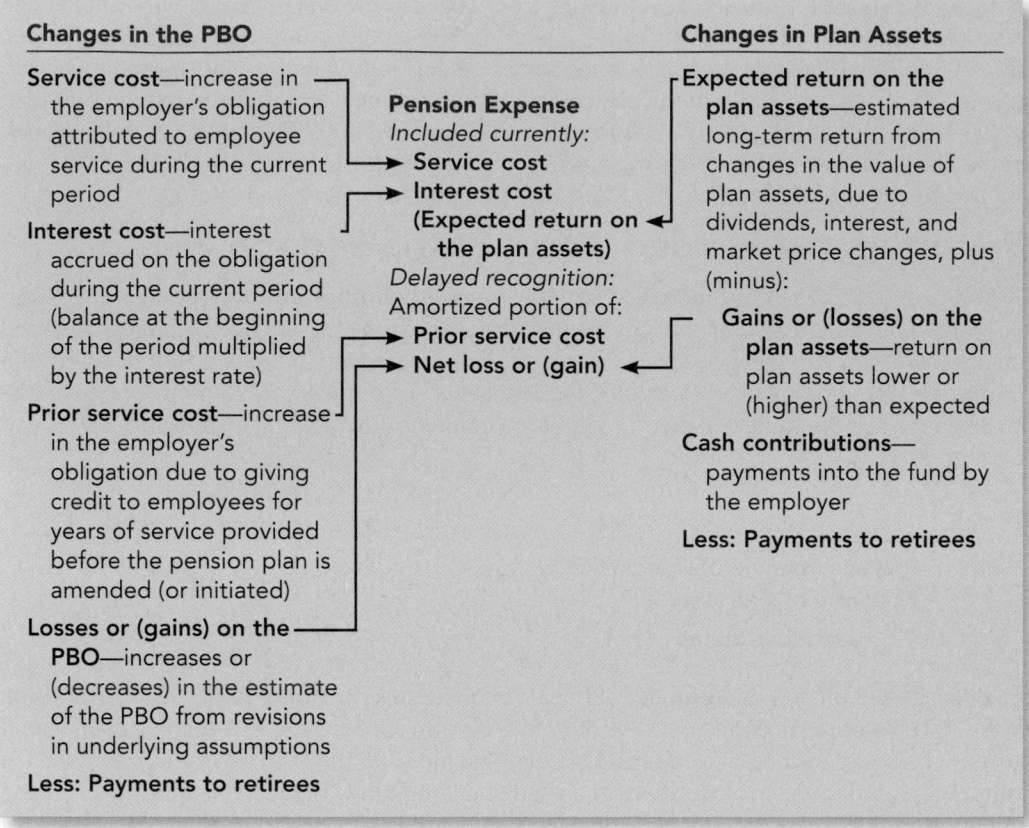

| **Changes in the PBO** | | **Changes in Plan Assets** |

Service cost—increase in the employer's obligation attributed to employee service during the current period

Interest cost—interest accrued on the obligation during the current period (balance at the beginning of the period multiplied by the interest rate)

Prior service cost—increase in the employer's obligation due to giving credit to employees for years of service provided before the pension plan is amended (or initiated)

Losses or (gains) on the PBO—increases or (decreases) in the estimate of the PBO from revisions in underlying assumptions

Less: Payments to retirees

Pension Expense
Included currently:
→ **Service cost**
→ **Interest cost**
   (Expected return on the plan assets)
Delayed recognition:
Amortized portion of:
→ **Prior service cost**
→ **Net loss or (gain)**

Expected return on the plan assets—estimated long-term return from changes in the value of plan assets, due to dividends, interest, and market price changes, plus (minus):

Gains or (losses) on the plan assets—return on plan assets lower or (higher) than expected

Cash contributions—payments into the fund by the employer

Less: Payments to retirees

ILLUSTRATION 17–4
Pension Expense

These are the changes in the PBO and in the plan assets we previously discussed (Illustration 17–2 and Illustration 17–3).

Reports from the actuary and the trustee of plan assets indicate the following changes during 2011 in the PBO and plan assets of Global Communications.

($ in millions)	**PBO**		**Plan Assets**
Beginning of 2011	$400	*Beginning* of 2011	$300
Service cost	41	Return on plan assets,*	30
Interest cost, 6%	24	10% (9% expected)	
Loss (gain) on PBO	23	Cash contributions	48
Less: Retiree benefits	(38)	Less: Retiree benefits	(38)
End of 2011	$450	*End* of 2011	$340

A *prior service cost* of $60 million was incurred at the beginning of the previous year (2010) due to a plan amendment increasing the PBO. At the beginning of 2011 Global had a *net loss* of $55 million (previous losses exceeded previous gains). The average remaining service life of employees is estimated at 15 years.

2011 Pension Expense

Global's 2011 Pension Expense Is Determined as Follows:	($ in millions)
Service cost	$41
Interest cost	24
Expected return on the plan assets ($30 actual, less $3 gain)	(27)
Amortization of prior service cost (calculated later)	4
Amortization of net loss (calculated later)	1
Pension expense	**$43**

*Expected rates of return anticipate the performance of various investments of plan assets. This is not necessarily the same as the discount rate used by the actuary to estimate the pension obligation. Assumed rates of return recently reported have ranged from 4.5% to 9.5%, with 8% being the most commonly assumed rate (AICPA, *Accounting Trends and Techniques*, 2009).

Components of Pension Expense

Illustration 17–4 demonstrates the relationship between some of the changes in the PBO and in plan assets and the components of pension expense: service cost, interest cost, the return on plan assets, prior service cost amortization, and net gain or loss amortization. Let's look at these five components of pension expense one at a time.

1. SERVICE COST.   The $41 million service cost represents the increase in the projected benefit obligation attributable to employee service performed during 2011 (benefits earned by employees during the year). Each year this is the first component of the pension expense.

2. INTEREST COST.   The interest cost is calculated as the interest rate (actuary's discount rate) multiplied by the projected benefit obligation at the beginning of the year. In 2011, this is 6% times $400 million, or $24 million.

> Interest cost is the discount rate times the PBO balance at the beginning of the year.

The PBO balance is not separately reported as a liability in the company's balance sheet,[13] but it is a liability nevertheless. The interest expense that accrues on its balance is not separately reported on the income statement but is instead combined with the service cost (and other amounts) as the second component of the annual pension expense.

3. RETURN ON PLAN ASSETS.   Remember, plan assets comprise funds invested in stocks, bonds, and other securities that presumably will generate dividends, interest, and capital gains. Each year these earnings represent the return on plan assets during that year. When accounting for the return, we need to differentiate between its two modes: the *expected* return and the *actual* return.

> The return earned on investment securities increases the plan asset balance.

Actual versus expected return.   We've assumed Global's expected rate of return is 9%, so its expected return on plan assets in 2011 was 9% times $300 million, or $27 million. But, as previously indicated, the actual rate of return in 2011 was 10%, producing an actual return on plan assets of 10% times $300 million, or $30 million.

> The interest and return-on-assets components are financial items created only because the compensation is delayed and the obligation is funded currently.

Obviously, investing plan assets in income-producing assets lessens the amounts employers must contribute to the fund. So, the return on plan assets reduces the net cost of having a pension plan. Accordingly, the return on plan assets each year *reduces* the amount recorded as pension expense. Just as the interest expense that accrues on the PBO is included as a component of pension expense rather than being separately reported, the investment revenue on plan assets is not separately reported either. In actuality, both the interest and return-on-assets components of pension expense do not directly represent employee compensation. Instead, they are financial items created only because the pension payment is delayed while the obligation is funded currently.

Adjustment for loss or gain.   A controversial question is *when* differences between the actual and expected return should be recognized in pension expense. It seems logical that since the net cost of having a pension plan is reduced by the actual return on plan assets, the charge to pension expense should be the actual return on plan assets. However, the FASB concluded that the actual return should first be adjusted by any difference between that return and what the return had been expected to be. So, it's actually the *expected* return that is included in the calculation of pension expense. In our illustration, Global's pension expense is reduced by the expected return of $27 million.

> The return on plan assets reduces the net *cost of having a* pension plan.

The difference between the actual and expected return is considered a loss or gain on plan assets. Although we don't include these losses and gains as part of pension expense when they occur, it's possible they will affect pension expense at a later time. On the next page, we will discuss how that might happen.

> Any loss or gain is not included in pension expense right away.

4. AMORTIZATION OF PRIOR SERVICE COST.   Recall that the $60 million increase in Global's PBO due to recalculating benefits employees earned in prior years as a result of a plan amendment is referred to as the prior service cost. Obviously, prior service cost adds to the cost of having a pension plan. But when should this cost be recognized as pension expense? An argument can be made that the cost should be recognized as expense in the

---

[13]As we discuss later, the PBO is combined with pension assets with the net difference reported in the balance sheet as either a net pension liability or a net pension asset.

year of the amendment when the cost increases the company's pension obligation. In fact, some members of the FASB have advocated this approach. At present, though, we amortize the cost gradually to pension expense. Here's the rationalization.

Amending a pension plan, and especially choosing to make that amendment retroactive, typically is done with the idea that future operations will benefit from those choices. For that reason, the cost is not recognized as pension expense in the year the plan is amended. Instead, it is recognized as pension expense over the time that the employees who benefited from the retroactive amendment will work for the company in the future. Presumably, this future service period is when the company will receive the benefits of its actions.

In our illustration, the amendment occurred in 2010, increasing the PBO at that time. For the individual employee, Jessica Farrow, the prior service cost was calculated to be $15,976. Our illustration assumes that, for *all* plan participants, the prior service cost was $60 million at the beginning of 2010. The prior service cost at the beginning of 2011 is $56 million. The following section explains how this amount was computed.

One assumption in our illustration is that the average remaining service life of the active employee group is 15 years. To recognize the $60 million prior service cost in equal annual amounts over this period, the amount amortized as an increase in pension expense each year is $4 million:[14]

Amortization of Prior Service Cost:	($ in millions)
Service cost	$41
Interest cost	24
Expected return on the plan assets	(27)
Amortization of prior service cost–AOCI	4
Amortization of net loss–AOCI	1
Pension expense	**$43**

Be sure to note that, even though we're amortizing it, the prior service cost is not an asset, but instead a part of *accumulated other comprehensive income* (AOCI), a shareholders' equity account. This is a result of the FASB's current disinclination to treat the cost as an expense as it is incurred. The Board, instead, prefers to ascribe it the off-the-income-statement designation as *other comprehensive income* (OCI) in the same manner as the handful of losses and gains also categorized the same way and not reported among the gains and losses in the traditional income statement. You first learned about comprehensive income in Chapter 4 and again in Chapter 12. We'll revisit it again later in this chapter.

The prior service cost declines by $4 million each year:

Prior Service Cost–AOCI	($ in millions)
Prior service cost at the beginning of 2011	$56
Less: 2011 amortization	(4)
Prior service cost at the end of 2011	$52

5. AMORTIZATION OF A NET LOSS OR NET GAIN. You learned previously that gains and losses can occur when expectations are revised concerning either the PBO or the return on plan assets. Graphic 17–9 summarizes the possibilities.

Like the prior service cost we just discussed, we don't include these gains and losses as part of pension expense in the income statement, but instead report them as OCI in the statement of comprehensive income as they occur. We then report the gains and losses on a cumulative basis as a net loss–AOCI or a net gain–AOCI, depending on whether we have greater losses or gains over time. We report this amount in the balance sheet as a part of *accumulated other comprehensive income* (AOCI), a shareholders' equity account.

There is no conceptual justification for not including losses and gains in earnings. After all, these increases and decreases in either the PBO or plan assets immediately impact the net cost of providing a pension plan and, conceptually, should be included in pension expense as they occur.

---

[14]An alternative to this straight-line approach, called the *service method*, attempts to allocate the prior service cost to each year in proportion to the fraction of the total remaining service years worked in each of those years. This method is described in the chapter appendix.

	Projected Benefit Obligation	Return on Plan Assets
Higher than expected	Loss	Gain
Lower than expected	Gain	Loss

GRAPHIC 17–9

Gains and Losses

Gains and losses occur when either the PBO or the return on plan assets turns out to be different than expected.

Nevertheless, the FASB requires that income statement recognition of gains and losses from either source be delayed. Why?—for practical reasons.

Income Smoothing

The FASB acknowledged the conceptual shortcoming of delaying the recognition of a gain or a loss while opting for this more politically acceptable approach. Delayed recognition was favored by a dominant segment of corporate America that was concerned with the effect of allowing gains and losses to immediately impact reported earnings. In 2008, the FASB decided to formally reconsider all aspects of accounting for postretirement benefit plans, including this treatment of gains and losses.[17] The project will consider overhauling the entire system for accounting for and reporting on postretirement benefits. This result might include immediately including gains and losses in pension expense, thereby eliminating income smoothing.

> The Board believes that it would be conceptually appropriate and preferable to [have] . . . no delay in recognition of gains and losses, or perhaps [to have] . . . gains and losses reported currently in comprehensive income but not in earnings. However, it concluded that those approaches would be too great a change from past practice to be adopted at the present time.[15]

> The Board acknowledges that the delayed recognition included in this Statement results in excluding the most current and most relevant information.[16]

The practical justification for delayed recognition is that, over time, gains and losses might cancel one another out. Given this possibility, why create unnecessary fluctuations in reported income by letting temporary gains and losses decrease and increase (respectively) pension expense? Of course, as years pass there may be more gains than losses, or vice versa, preventing their offsetting one another completely. So, if a net gain or a net loss gets "too large," pension expense must be adjusted.

The FASB defines too large rather arbitrarily as being when a net gain or a net loss at the beginning of a year exceeds an amount equal to 10% of the PBO, or 10% of plan assets, whichever is higher.[18] This threshold amount is referred to as the "corridor." When the corridor is exceeded, the excess is not charged to pension expense all at once. Instead, as a further concession to income smoothing, only a portion of the excess is included in pension expense. The minimum amount that should be included is the excess divided by the average remaining service period of active employees expected to receive benefits under the plan.[19]

A net gain or a net loss affects pension expense only if it exceeds an amount equal to 10% of the PBO, or 10% of plan assets, whichever is higher.

[15]FASB, "Employers' Accounting for Pension and Other Postretirement Benefits," *Preliminary Views,* November 1982, par. 107.

[16]Ibid., par. 88.

[17]FASB ASC 715: Compensation–Retirement Benefits (previously "Employers' Accounting for Defined Benefit Pension and Other Postretirement Plans—an amendment of FASB Statements No. 87, 88, 106, and 132(R)," *Statement of Financial Accounting Standards No. 158* (Stamford, Conn.: FASB, 2006), par. B16). This specific paragraph is not codified in the FASB Research System as it is reasoning and is therefore what codifiers consider "nonessential" material.

[18]For this purpose the FASB specifies the market-related value of plan assets. This can be either the fair value or a weighted-average fair value over a period not to exceed five years. We will uniformly assume fair value in this chapter.

[19]Companies are permitted to amortize the entire net loss (or gain) rather than just the excess, but few choose that option. (FASB ASC 715–30–35–25: Compensation–Retirement Benefits Defined Benefit Plans–Pension–Subsequent Measurement–Gains and Losses (previously "Employers' Accounting for Pensions," *Statement of Financial Accounting Standards No. 87* (Stamford, Conn.: FASB, 1985)).

In our illustration, we're assuming a net loss–AOCI of $55 million at the beginning of 2011. Also recall that the PBO and plan assets are $400 million and $300 million, respectively, at that time. The amount amortized to 2011 pension expense is $1 million, calculated as follows:

Because the net loss exceeds an amount equal to the greater of 10% of the PBO or 10% of plan assets, part of the excess is amortized to pension expense.

Determining Net Loss Amortization—2011	($ in millions)
Net loss (previous losses exceeded previous gains)	$55
10% of $400 ($400 is greater than $300): the "corridor"	(40)
Excess at the beginning of the year	$15
Average remaining service period	÷ 15 years
Amount amortized to 2011 pension expense	$ 1

The pension expense is increased because a net loss is being amortized. If a net *gain* were being amortized, the amount would be *deducted* from pension expense because a gain would indicate that the net cost of providing the pension plan had decreased.

Amortization of a net gain would decrease pension expense.

Amortization of a net loss increases pension expense.

Amortization of the Net Loss–AOCI:	($ in millions)
Service cost	$41
Interest cost	24
Expected return on the plan assets	(27)
Amortization of prior service cost–AOCI	4
Amortization of net loss–AOCI	1
Pension expense	**$43**

This amortization reduces the net loss–AOCI in 2011 by $1 million. Also recall that Global incurred (a) a $23 million loss in 2011 from revising estimates relating to the PBO and (b) a $3 million gain when the 2011 return on plan assets was higher than expected. These three changes affected the net loss–AOCI in 2011 as follows:

Net Loss–AOCI	($ in millions)
Net loss–AOCI at the beginning of 2011	$55
Less: 2011 amortization	(1)
Plus: 2011 loss on PBO	23
Less: 2011 gain on plan assets	(3)
Net loss–AOCI at the end of 2011	$74

New losses add to a net loss; new gains reduce a net loss.

ADDITIONAL CONSIDERATION

The $74 million balance at the end of 2011 would be the beginning balance in 2012. It would be compared with the 2012 beginning balances in the PBO and plan assets to determine whether amortization would be necessary in 2012. If you were to look back to our analyses of the changes in those two balances, you would see the 2012 beginning balances in the PBO and plan assets to be $450 million and $340 million, respectively. The amount amortized to 2012 pension expense will be $1.93 million, calculated as follows:

	($ in millions)
Net loss (previous losses exceeded previous gains)	$ 74
10% of $450 ($450 is greater than $340)	(45)
Excess at the beginning of the year	$ 29
Average remaining service period	÷ 15 years*
Amount amortized to 2012 pension expense	**$1.93**

*Assumes the average remaining service period of active employees is still 15 years in 2012 due to new employees joining the firm.

REPORTING ISSUES

Recording Gains and Losses

As we discussed earlier, gains and losses (either from changing assumptions regarding the PBO or from the return on assets being higher or lower than expected) are deferred and not immediately included in pension expense and net income. Instead, we report them as *other comprehensive income (OCI)* in the statement of comprehensive income. So Global records a *loss–OCI* for the $23 million loss that occurs in 2011 when it revises its estimate of future salary levels causing its PBO estimate to increase. Global also records a $3 million *gain–OCI* that occurred when the $30 million actual return on plan assets exceeded the $27 million expected return. Here's the entry:

● LO7

To Record Gains and Losses	($ in millions)	
Loss–OCI (from change in assumption)............	23	
PBO		23
Plan assets	3	
Gain–OCI ($30 actual return on assets – $27 expected return)...............		3

Losses and gains (as well as any new prior service cost should it occur) are reported as OCI.

The loss is an increase in the PBO due to a change in an assumption. In this entry, we are recording that increase in the PBO account balance. If the change in assumption had caused the PBO to be reduced instead, we would debit the PBO here and credit a gain–OCI.

Similarly, the gain due to the actual return on plan assets exceeding the expected return is an increase in plan assets. In the next section, we increase plan assets for the expected return (as a component of pension expense) so the two adjustments together cause the plan assets account balance to reflect the actual return (expected increase plus the additional increase represented by the gain). Of course, if the actual return had been less than expected, we would debit a loss–OCI and credit plan assets here.

ADDITIONAL CONSIDERATION

Just as we record new losses and gains as they occur, we also will record a change in the prior service cost account for any new prior service cost should it occur. For instance, if Global revised its pension formula again and recalculated its PBO using the more generous formula, causing a $40 million increase in the PBO, the company would record the new prior service cost this way:

To Record New Prior Service Cost	($ in millions)	
Prior service cost–OCI (increase in PBO due to plan amendment)	40	
PBO		40

If an amendment *reduces* rather than increases the PBO, the *negative prior service cost* would reduce both the prior service cost and pension liability.

INTERNATIONAL FINANCIAL REPORTING STANDARDS

Actuarial Gains and Losses. We've seen that U.S. GAAP requires that gains and losses be included among OCI items in the statement of comprehensive income, thus subsequently become part of AOCI. This is permitted under *IAS No. 19*, but not required. If this choice is made, under *IAS No. 19* the gains and losses are not subsequently amortized to expense and

● LO12

(continued)

IFRS ILLUSTRATION

(concluded)

recycled or reclassified from other comprehensive income as is required under U.S. GAAP (when the accumulated net gain or net loss exceeds the 10% threshold).[20]

A second alternative under IFRS is to expense gains and losses only when the accumulated net gain or net loss exceeds a specified corridor, or threshold, similar to U.S. GAAP. With this alternative we include gains and losses as they occur in the defined benefit obligation (DBO) or plan assets, but then report them as an offset or increase to the net pension liability (or net pension asset) using a valuation account called unrecognized net gain or loss. Let's compare using the numbers for the loss and gain in the chapter illustration:

To Record Gains and Losses ($ in millions)	U.S. GAAP	IFRS
Plan assets	3	3
Gain–OCI (from change in assumption)	3	
Unrecognized net gain or loss		3
Loss–OCI (from change in assumption)	23	
Unrecognized net gain or loss		23
PBO (DBO)	23	23

Using U.S. GAAP, the gain and the loss become part of AOCI in the shareholders' equity section of the balance sheet. Using IFRS, the gain and the loss become part of unrecognized net gain or loss reported as an offset or increase to the net pension liability (or net pension asset) in the liability (or asset) section of the balance sheet. We then amortize a portion of either the AOCI or unrecognized net gain or loss to expense when the accumulated net gain or net loss exceeds a specified corridor, or threshold, as demonstrated previously.

Another alternative under either U.S. GAAP or IFRS is to include the gains and losses in the income statement as they occur. Few companies choose this alternative.

Recording the Pension Expense

Recall from Illustration 17–4 that Global's 2011 pension expense is $43 million. The expense includes the $41 million service cost and the $24 million interest cost, both of which, as we learned earlier, add to Global's PBO. Similarly, the expense includes a $27 million expected return on plan assets, which adds to the plan assets.[21] These changes are reflected in the following entry:

Each component of the pension expense is recorded in the journal entry to record pension expense.

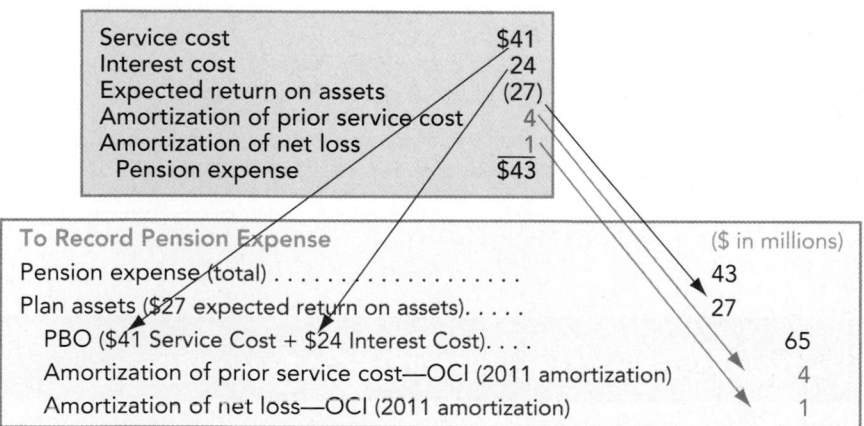

Service cost	$41
Interest cost	24
Expected return on assets	(27)
Amortization of prior service cost	4
Amortization of net loss	1
Pension expense	$43

Service cost and interest cost increase the PBO. The return on assets increases plan assets.

To Record Pension Expense	($ in millions)	
Pension expense (total)	43	
Plan assets ($27 expected return on assets).	27	
PBO ($41 Service Cost + $24 Interest Cost). . . .		65
Amortization of prior service cost—OCI (2011 amortization)		4
Amortization of net loss—OCI (2011 amortization)		1

The pension expense also includes the $4 million amortization of the prior service cost and the $1 million amortization of the net loss. As we discussed earlier, we report prior

---

[20]"Employee Benefits," *International Accounting Standard No. 17* (IASCF), as amended effective January 1, 2009.

[21]The increase in plan assets is the $30 million *actual* return, but the $27 million *expected* return is the component of pension expense because the $3 million gain isn't included in expense. We saw in the previous section that the $3 million gain also increases plan assets.

service cost when it arises as well as gains and losses as they occur as *other comprehensive income (OCI)* in the statement of comprehensive income. These OCI items accumulate as Prior service cost–AOCI and Net loss (or gain)–AOCI. So, when we amortize these AOCI accounts, we report the amortization amounts in the statement of comprehensive income as well. These amortized amounts are being "reclassified" from OCI to net income.

Amortization reduces the Prior service cost–AOCI and the Net loss–AOCI. Since these accounts have debit balances, we credit the amortization accounts. If we were amortizing a net gain, we would *debit* the account because a net gain has a credit balance.

Remember, we report the funded status of the plan in the balance sheet. That's the difference between the PBO and plan assets. In this case, it's a net pension liability since the plan is underfunded; that is, the PBO exceeds plan assets.

The pension expense is, of course, reported in the income statement. In addition, the composition of that amount must be reported in disclosure notes. For instance, **Macy's, Inc.** described the composition of its pension expense in the disclosure note in its annual report for the fiscal year ended January 1, 2009, shown in Graphic 17–10.

New gains and losses and prior service cost are reported as OCI. So is the amortization of their accumulated balances.

	2008	2007	2006
	(millions)		
Net Periodic Pension Cost			
Service cost	$ 97	$ 104	$119
Interest cost	159	157	163
Expected return on assets	(192)	(196)	(206)
Amortization of net actuarial loss	5	23	27
Amortization of prior service credit	—	(1)	—
	$ 69	$ 87	$103

GRAPHIC 17–10
Disclosure of Pension Expense—Macy's, Inc.

The components of pension expense are itemized in the disclosure note.

Real World Financials

INTERNATIONAL FINANCIAL REPORTING STANDARDS

Prior Service Cost. Under *IAS No. 19*, prior service cost (called past service cost under IFRS) is expensed immediately to the extent it relates to benefits that have vested.[22] The amount not yet expensed (nonvested portion) is reported as an offset or increase to the defined benefit obligation or DBO (called projected benefit obligation or PBO under U.S. GAAP).

Under U.S. GAAP, prior service cost is not expensed immediately, but is included among OCI items in the statement of comprehensive income and thus subsequently becomes part of AOCI where it is amortized over the average remaining service period. As an example, assume International Corporation has a defined benefit pension plan with these characteristics during 2011:

● LO12

IFRS ILLUSTRATION

	($ in millions)
DBO (PBO) balance, January 1	$120
Plan assets balance, January 1	70
Service cost	20
Interest cost	12
Loss from change in actuarial assumption	5
Benefits paid	(9)
Actual return on plan assets	9
Contributions 2011	20
Expected long-term rate of return on plan assets	10%

(continued)

[22]"Employee Benefits," *International Accounting Standard No. 17* (IASCF), as amended effective January 1, 2009.

(concluded)

There were no AOCI balances related to pensions on January 1, 2011, but at the end of 2011, the company amended the pension formula creating a prior (past) service cost of $8 million, three-fourths of which is related to employees whose pension benefits have vested. Let's compare accounting under the two approaches:

	U.S. GAAP	IFRS
Pension expense for 2011:		
Service cost	$ 20	$ 20
Interest cost	12	12
Expected return on the plan assets ($9 actual, less $2 gain)	(7)	(7)
Amortization of prior service cost	0*	
Expensing of past service cost		6**
Amortization of net gain or net loss–AOCI	0	0
Pension expense	$ 25	$31

* Since the amendment was at the end of the year, there is no amortization of prior service cost in 2011.
** ¾ of PSC that relates to benefits that have vested.

Journal entries to record pension expense, gains or losses, past (prior) service cost, funding, and benefits paid for 2011:	U.S. GAAP		IFRS	
Pension expense (calculated above).....................................	25		31	
Plan assets (expected return on assets: 10% × $70)	7		7	
PBO (DBO) ($20 service cost + $12 interest cost)...........		32		32
DBO (vested past service cost)		0		6
Unrecognized past service cost...			2	
DBO (unvested past service cost)				2
Prior service cost–OCI (from 2011 amendment)................	8			
PBO		8		
Loss–OCI...	5			
Unrecognized net gain or loss..			5	
PBO (DBO) (change in assumption)		5		5
Plan assets ($9 actual return– $8 expected return).............	1		1	
Gain–OCI		1		
Unrecognized net gain or loss.......................................				1
Plan assets	20		20	
Cash (given)...		20		20
PBO (DBO)...	9		9	
Plan assets (given)		9		9

Recording the Funding of Plan Assets

When Global adds its annual cash investment to its plan assets, the value of those plan assets increases by $48 million:

To Record Funding	($ in millions)	
Plan assets	48	
Cash (contribution to plan assets)		48

It's not unusual for the cash contribution to differ from that year's pension expense. After all, determining the periodic pension expense and the funding of the pension plan are two separate processes. Pension expense is an accounting decision. How much to contribute each year is a financing decision affected by cash flow and tax considerations, as well as minimum funding requirements. The Pension Protection Act of 2006 and the Employee Retirement Income Security Act of 1974 (ERISA) establish the pension funding requirements. Subject to these considerations, cash contributions are actuarially determined with the objective of accumulating (along with investment returns) sufficient funds to provide promised retirement benefits.

We saw earlier that when pension benefits are paid to retired employees, those payments reduce the plan assets established to pay the benefits and also reduce the obligation to pay the benefits, the PBO:

To Record Payment of Benefits	($ in millions)	
PBO	38	
Plan assets (payments to retired employees)		38

Now that we've recorded these entries for the funding of the pension plan and payment of benefits, we have recorded all the changes in the PBO and plan assets:

($ in millions)	**PBO**			**Plan Assets**		
		400	Balance	Balance	300	
		23	Loss	Gain	3	
		41	Service cost	Expected return	27	
		24	Interest cost	Funding	48	
Benefits paid	38					38 Benefits paid
		450	Balance	Balance	340	

Remember, though, we don't report either of these balances separately in the balance sheet. Instead, we combine the two and report a net pension liability of $450 - 340 = $110 million, the funded status of the pension plan.

ADDITIONAL CONSIDERATION

Rather than recording each of these changes in the PBO and Plan Asset accounts, we could have recorded them in a single Net pension (liability) asset account. For example, we could have recorded the gains and losses, pension expense, and funding as follows:

	($ in millions)	
Loss–OCI (from change in assumption)	23	
Net pension (liability) asset		23
Net pension (liability) asset	3	
Gain–OCI ($30 actual return on assets −$27 expected return)..........		3
Pension expense	43	
Net pension (liability) asset		38
Amortization of prior service cost-OCI		4
Amortization of net loss-OCI		1
Net pension (liability) asset	48	
Cash		48

In fact many companies use this abbreviated approach. However, recording the changes in the accounts they affect (PBO and Plan assets) and then combining the two accounts for balance sheet reporting as we do in our illustrations has two advantages. First, we need the separate balances for the required disclosure in the pension footnote. Second, it is a more logical approach. It's easier to see that the return on plan assets is an increase in plan assets than it is to see it as a reduction in Net pension (liability) asset.

Comprehensive Income

Comprehensive income, as you may recall from Chapter 4, is a more expansive view of income than traditional net income. In fact, it encompasses all changes in equity other than from transactions with owners.[23] So, in addition to net income, comprehensive income includes up to four other changes in equity. A statement of comprehensive income is demonstrated in Illustration 17–5, highlighting the presentation of the components of OCI pertaining to Global's pension plan.

ILLUSTRATION 17–5

Statement of Comprehensive Income

Gains and losses, as well as any new prior service cost should it arise, are among the OCI items reported in the period they occur.

	($ in millions)	
Net income		$xxx
Other comprehensive income:		
Unrealized holding gains (losses) on investments[24]	$ x	
Pension plan:		
Loss—due to revising a PBO estimate*	(23)	
Gain—return on plan assets exceeds expected*	3	
Amortization of net loss	1	
Amortization of prior service cost	4	
Deferred gains (losses) from derivatives	x	
Gains (losses) from foreign currency translation	x	xx
Comprehensive income		$xxx

*From Illustration 17–4 on p. 950.
Note: These amounts are shown without considering taxes. Actually each of the elements of comprehensive income should be reported net of tax. For instance, if the tax rate is 40%, the gain would be reported as $13.8 million: $23 million less a $9.2 million tax benefit.

Other comprehensive income (OCI) items are reported both (a) as they occur and (b) as an accumulated balance as shown in Illustrations 17–6 and 17–7.[25]

ILLUSTRATION 17–6

Reporting Comprehensive Income

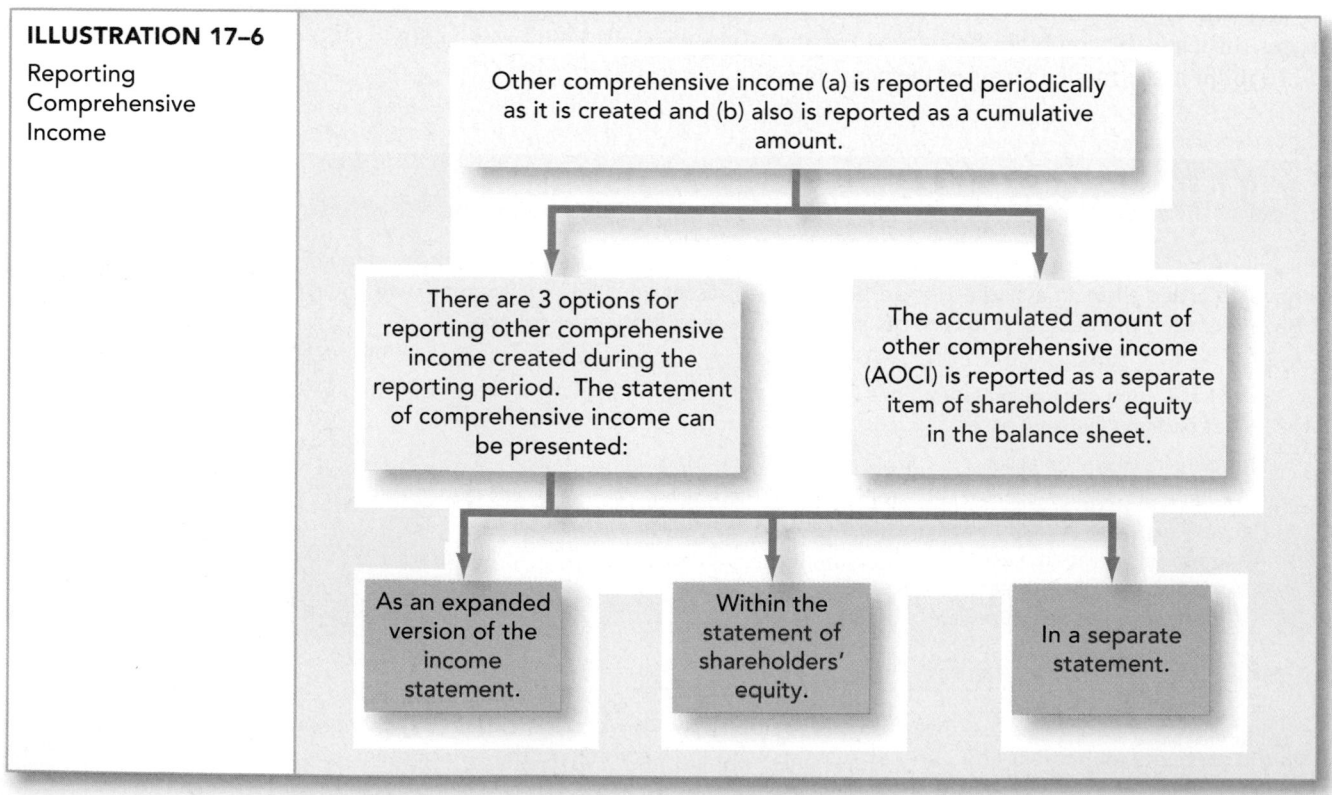

---

[23]Transactions with owners primarily include dividends and the sale or purchase of shares of the company's stock.

[24]An unrealized loss also might occur from recording an impairment of a debt security investment. As described in Chapter 12, if the fair value of a debt security investment falls below its amortized cost, and that decline is viewed as other than temporary, the current period credit loss is included in net income, but any amount that exceeds the current period credit loss is recorded as a loss in OCI.

[25]The statement of comprehensive income can be reported either (a) as an extension of the income statement, (b) in a disclosure note, or (c) as part of the statement of shareholders' equity.

Global Communication Balance Sheets For Years Ended December 31			ILLUSTRATION 17-7
	2011	**2010**	Balance Sheet Presentation of Pension Amounts
Assets			
Current assets	$xxx	$xxx	**If the plan had been overfunded, Global would have reported a pension asset among its assets rather than this pension liability.**
Property, plant, and equipment	xxx	xxx	
Liabilities			
Current Liabilities	$xxx	$xxx	
Net pension liability	110	100	
Other long-term liabilities	xxx	xxx	
Shareholders' Equity			
Common stock	$xxx	$xxx	
Retained earnings	xxx	xxx	
Accumulated other comprehensive income:			
Net unrealized holding gains and losses on investments—AOCI	xxx	xxx	**The net loss and prior service cost *reduce* shareholders' equity.**
Net loss–AOCI*	(74)	(55)	
Prior service cost—AOCI*	(52)	(56)	

*These are debit balances and therefore negative components of accumulated other comprehensive income; a net gain–AOCI would have a credit balance and be a positive component of accumulated other comprehensive income.

In addition to reporting the gains or losses (and other elements of comprehensive income) that occur in the current reporting period, we also report these amounts on a *cumulative* basis in the balance sheet. Comprehensive income includes (a) net income and (b) OCI. Notice that we report net income that occurs in the current reporting period in the income statement and also report accumulated net income (that hasn't been distributed as dividends) in the balance sheet as retained earnings. Similarly, we report OCI as it occurs in the current reporting period (see Illustration 17–5) and also report *accumulated other comprehensive income* in the balance sheet. In its 2011 balance sheet, Global will report the amounts as shown in Illustration 17–7.

> **Reporting OCI as it occurs and also as an accumulated balance is consistent with the way we report net income and its accumulated counterpart, retained earnings.**

Look back to the schedule on page 954 to see how the net loss–AOCI increased from $55 million to $74 million during 2011 and the schedule on page 952 to see how the prior service cost–AOCI decreased from $56 million to $52 million. The pension liability represents the underfunded status of Global's pension plan on the two dates.

INTERNATIONAL FINANCIAL REPORTING STANDARDS

Comprehensive Income. As part of a joint project with the FASB, the International Accounting Standards Board (IASB) in 2007 issued a revised version of *IAS No. 1*, "Presentation of Financial Statements," that revised the standard to bring international reporting of comprehensive income largely in line with U.S. standards.[26] It provides the option of presenting revenue and expense items and components of other comprehensive income either in (a) a single statement of comprehensive income or (b) in an income statement followed by a statement of comprehensive income. U.S. GAAP also allows reporting other comprehensive income in the statement of shareholders' equity, which is the way most U.S. companies report it.

● LO12

Income Tax Considerations

We have ignored the income tax effects of the amounts in order to focus on the core issues. Note, though, that as gains and losses occur, they are reported net of tax (tax expense for a gain, tax savings for a loss) in the statement of comprehensive income.[27] Likewise, AOCI in the balance sheet also is reported net of tax.

> **OCI items are reported net of tax, in both the (a) statement of comprehensive income and (b) AOCI.**

---

[26]"Presentation of Financial Statements," *International Accounting Standard No. 1* (IASCF), as amended effective January 1, 2009.
[27]Similarly, if any new prior service cost should arise due to a plan amendment, it too would be reported net of tax.

Putting the Pieces Together

● LO8

In preceding sections, we've discussed (1) the projected benefit obligation (including changes due to periodic service cost, accrued interest, revised estimates, plan amendments, and the payment of benefits); (2) the plan assets (including changes due to investment returns, employer contributions, and the payment of benefits); (3) prior service cost; (4) gains and losses; (5) the periodic pension expense (comprising components of each of these); and (6) the funded status of the plan. These elements of a pension plan are interrelated. It's helpful to see how each element relates to the others. One way is to bring each part together in a *pension spreadsheet*. We do this for our 2011 Global Communications Illustration in Graphic 17–11.

GRAPHIC 17–11

Pension Spreadsheet

When the PBO exceeds plan assets, we have net pension liability. If plan assets exceed the PBO we have a net pension asset.

The net pension liability (or net pension asset) is not recorded in a journal entry but is the amount reported in the balance sheet as the PBO and plan assets combined.

		Recorded in Accounts					Reported Only
	PBO	Plan Assets	Prior Service Cost –AOCI	Net Loss –AOCI	Pension Expense	Cash	Net Pension (Liability)/ Asset
Balance, Jan. 1, 2011	(400)	300	56	55			(100)
Service cost	(41)				41		(41)
Interest cost	(24)				24		(24)
Expected return on assets		27			(27)		27
Adjust for: Gain on assets		3		(3)			3
Amortization of:							
Prior service cost–AOCI			(4)		4		
Net loss–AOCI				(1)	1		
Loss on PBO	(23)			23			(23)
Prior service cost (new)*	0		0				0
Contributions to fund		48				(48)	48
Retiree benefits paid	38	(38)					0
Balance, Dec. 31, 2011	(450)	340	52	74	43		(110)

*This amount was $60 million in the 2009 pension spreadsheet.

You should spend several minutes studying this spreadsheet, focusing on the relationships among the elements that constitute a pension plan. Notice that the first numerical column simply repeats the actuary's report of how the PBO changed during the year, as explained previously (Illustration 17–2). Likewise, the second column reproduces the changes in plan assets we discussed earlier (Illustration 17–3). We've also previously noted the changes in the prior service cost–AOCI (page 952) and the net loss–AOCI (page 954) that are duplicated in the third and fourth columns. The fifth column repeats the calculation of the 2011 pension expense we determined earlier (page 950), and the cash contribution to the pension fund is the sole item in the next column.

Rather than report the PBO and plan asset balances separately, we combine those balances and report a single net pension liability or net pension asset in the balance sheet.

The last column shows the changes in the funded status of the plan. Be sure to notice that the funded status is the difference between the PBO (column 1) and the plan assets (column 2). That means that each of the changes we see in either of the first two columns also is reflected as a change in the funded status in the last column. The net pension liability (or net pension asset) balance is not carried in company records. Instead, we use this label to report the PBO and plan assets in the balance sheet as a single net amount.

Notice that each change in a formal account (light-shaded columns) is reflected in exactly two of those columns.

INTERNATIONAL FINANCIAL REPORTING STANDARDS

Reporting Pension Expense. Under IFRS there is no requirement to present the various components of pension expense as a single net amount. As a result, some companies using IFRS report interest cost, expected return on assets, and amortization of gains and losses as financing income and expense.

● LO12

DECISION MAKERS' PERSPECTIVE

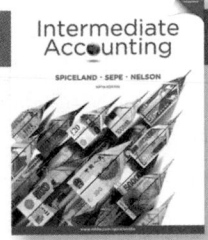

Although financial statement items are casualties of the political compromises of GAAP guidance, information provided in the disclosure notes fortunately makes up for some of the deficiencies.[28] Foremost among the useful disclosures are changes in the projected benefit obligation, changes in the fair value of plan assets, and a breakdown of the components of the annual pension expense. Other information also is made available to make it possible for interested analysts to reconstruct the financial statements with pension assets and liabilities included. We'll look at specific disclosures after we discuss postretirement benefits other than pensions because the two types of plans are reported together.

Investors and creditors must be cautious of the nontraditional treatment of pension information when developing financial ratios as part of an analysis of financial statements. The various elements of pensions that are not reported separately on the balance sheet and income statement (PBO, plan assets, gains and losses) can be included in ratios such as the debt to equity ratio or return on assets, but only by deliberately obtaining those numbers from the disclosure notes and adjusting the computation of the ratios. Similarly, without adjustment, profitability ratios and the times interest earned ratio will be distorted because pension expense includes the financial components of interest and return on assets.

Earnings quality (as defined in Chapter 4 and discussed in other chapters) also can be influenced by amounts reported in pension disclosures. Companies with relatively sizeable unrecognized pension costs (prior service cost, net gain or loss) can be expected to exhibit a relatively high "transitory" earnings component. Recall that transitory earnings are expected to be less predictive of future earnings than the "permanent" earnings component. ●

Pension amounts reported in the disclosure notes fill a reporting gap left by the minimal disclosures in the primary financial statements.

Settlement or Curtailment of Pension Plans

To cut down on cumbersome paperwork and lessen their exposure to the risk posed by defined benefit plans, many companies are providing defined contribution plans instead. When a plan is terminated, GAAP requires a gain or loss to be reported at that time.[29] For instance, **Melville Corporation** described the termination of its pension plan in the following disclosure note:

Companies sometimes terminate defined benefit plans to reduce costs and lessen risk.

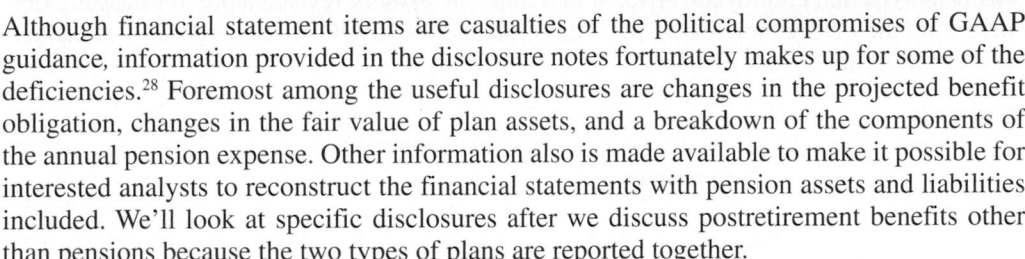

Retirement Plans (in part)
. . . As a result of the termination of the defined benefit plans, and after the settlement of the liability to plan participants through the purchase of nonparticipating annuity contracts or lump-sum rollovers into the new 401(k) Profit Sharing Plan, the Company recorded a nonrecurring gain of approximately $4,000,000 which was the amount of plan assets that reverted to the Company. This was accounted for in accordance with Statement of Financial Accounting Standards No. 88, "Employers' Accounting for Settlements and Curtailments of Defined Benefit Pension Plans and for Termination Benefits." [FASB ASC 715–30–35]

GRAPHIC 17–12

Gain on the Termination of a Defined Benefit Plan— Melville Corporation

Real World Financials

---

[28]FASB ASC 715–20–50: Compensation–Retirement Benefits–Defined Benefit Plans–General–Disclosure (previously "Employers' Disclosures about Pensions and Other Postretirement Benefits," *Statement of Financial Accounting Standards No. 132* (revised 2003), (Stamford, Conn.: FASB, 2003)).

[29]FASB ASC 715–30–35: Compensation–Retirement Benefits–Defined Benefit Plans–Pension–Subsequent Measurement (previously "Employers' Accounting for Settlements and Curtailments of Defined Benefit Pension Plans and for Termination Benefits," *Statement of Financial Accounting Standards No. 88* (Stamford, Conn.: FASB, 1985)).

CONCEPT REVIEW EXERCISE

PENSION PLANS

Allied Services, Inc., has a noncontributory, defined benefit pension plan. Pension plan assets had a fair market value of $900 million at December 31, 2010.

On January 3, 2011, Allied amended the pension formula to increase benefits for each service year. By making the amendment retroactive to prior years, Allied incurred a prior service cost of $75 million, adding to the previous projected benefit obligation of $875 million. The prior service cost is to be amortized (expensed) over 15 years. The service cost is $31 million for 2011. Both the actuary's discount rate and the expected rate of return on plan assets were 8%. The actual rate of return on plan assets was 10%.

At December 31, 2011, $16 million was contributed to the pension fund and $22 million was paid to retired employees. Also, at that time, the actuary revised a previous assumption, increasing the PBO estimate by $10 million. The net loss AOCI at the beginning of the year was $13 million.

Required:
Determine each of the following amounts as of December 31, 2011, the fiscal year-end for Allied: (1) projected benefit obligation; (2) plan assets; and (3) pension expense.

SOLUTION

($ in millions)	Projected Benefit Obligation	Plan Assets	Pension Expense
Balances at Jan. 1	$ 875	$900	$ 0
Prior service cost	75		
Service cost	31		31
Interest cost [($875 + 75)* × 8%]	76		76
Return on plan assets:			
Actual ($900 × 10%)		90	
Expected ($900 × 8%)			(72)
Amortization of prior service cost ($75 ÷ 15)			5
Amortization of net loss			0†
Loss on PBO	10		
Cash contribution		16	
Retirement payments	(22)	(22)	
Balance at Dec. 31	$1,045	$984	$40

Note: The $18 million gain on plan assets ($90 − 72 million) is not recognized yet; it is carried forward to be combined with previous and future gains and losses, which will be recognized only if the net gain or net loss exceeds 10% of the higher of the PBO or plan assets.
*Since the plan was amended at the beginning of the year, the prior service cost increased the PBO at that time.
†Since the net loss ($13) does not exceed 10% of $900 (higher than $875), no amortization is required for 2011.

WHERE WE'RE HEADED

The FASB and IASB are working together on a joint postretirement benefit standard.

We get a glimpse of the future, perhaps, from an Exposure Draft of a new postemployment benefit standard from the IASB. The document, issued in late 2009, indicates the direction of International Financial Reporting Standards for pensions and other postretirement plans. It proposes changes that "leapfrog" existing U.S. GAAP, and because the FASB and IASB are working together on a standard scheduled for completion by June 2011, this document may provide an indication of where both U.S. GAAP and IFRS are headed.

(continued)

(continued)

The major change proposed is that we would *report all changes in the obligation and the value of plan assets in net income.* The changes would be separated into (a) the cost of service (employment cost), (b) the cost of financing the deferred settlement of that cost, and (c) gains or losses from occasional remeasurement of the employment cost as assumptions change:

Employment cost includes:

● Past service costs (if any).

Finance cost includes:

● Interest cost.

● Remeasurements of the defined benefit obligation (called projected benefit obligation under U.S. GAAP) caused by changes in the discount rate return on plan assets.

Remeasurement cost includes:

● Remeasurements of service costs (in the DBO) caused by changes in assumptions other than the discount rate (i.e., assumptions like salary expectations, length of service, length of retirement, etc.).

Even though these three components of the total cost are reported in the income statement, we distinguish among them because the components are believed to have different predictive values. For instance, a decline in profit caused by an increase in pension cost due to rising employment costs might provide information of a different predictive value from an equivalent decline in profit arising from changes in the fair value of investments or interest rate changes. Investors' ability to make predictions is enhanced if income statement items with different predictive implications are reported as separate line items in the income statement.

Classifying the Components of the Total Pension Cost

Using the amounts from our Global Communications illustration, the changes would be classified as follows:

Pension employment cost	($ in millions)	
Service cost	$41	
Past service cost	0*	$41
Pension finance cost		
Interest cost	$24	
Loss (gain) on DBO—change in discount rate	3	
Return on plan assets	(30)	(3)
Pension remeasurement cost		
Loss (gain) on DBO—change in salary estimate	$25	
Loss (gain) on DBO—change in employee turnover estimate	(5)	20
Net periodic pension cost		$58

*Last year (2010) this amount was $60 million.

We would report the three components of the total pension cost in the income statement as follows:

Reporting the Components of the Total Pension Cost

Revenue	$xxx
Operating expenses (including pensions employment cost)	(xx)
Finance costs (including finance costs on pensions)	xx
Profit before tax	$xxx
Tax expense	(xx)
Profit from continuing operations	$xxx
Remeasurements arising from	
changes in pension assumptions (net of tax)	xx
Gains or losses on discontinued operations (net of tax)	xx
Net income	$xxx

(continued)

● LO12

IFRS ILLUSTRATION

We would report separately the three costs of having a defined benefit plan:
● employment cost
● finance costs
● remeasurement cost

(concluded)

Recording the Pension Costs

We would report the costs of service—employment, financing, remeasurement—in net income as a component of net periodic pension cost. Remember, each component is a change in either plan assets (the return on assets) or the defined benefit obligation (all others), so as we record each component we also would record its effect on plan assets and the defined benefit obligation, as follows:

To Record Net Periodic Pension Cost	($ in millions)	
Pension employment cost	41	
DBO (service cost)		41
Plan assets (return on plan assets)	30	
DBO (interest cost)		24
DBO (change in discount rate)		3
Pension financing cost (to balance)		3
Pension remeasurement cost	20	
DBO (change in employee turnover estimate)	5	
DBO (change in future salary estimate)		25

When Global adds its annual cash investment to its plan assets, the value of those plan assets increases by $48 million:

To Record Funding	($ in millions)	
Plan assets	48	
Cash (contribution to plan assets)		48

In our illustration, Global's retired employees were paid benefits of $38 million in 2011. Paying those benefits of course reduces the obligation to pay benefits (the DBO), and since the payments are made from the plan assets, that balance is reduced as well:

To Record Payment of Benefits	($ in millions)	
DBO	38	
Plan assets		38

PART E

POSTRETIREMENT BENEFITS OTHER THAN PENSIONS

As we just discussed, most companies have pension plans that provide for the future payments of retirement benefits to compensate employees for their current services. Many companies also furnish *other postretirement benefits* to their retired employees. These may include medical coverage, dental coverage, life insurance, group legal services, and other benefits. By far the most common is health care benefits. One of every three U.S. workers in medium- and large-size companies participates in health care plans that provide for coverage that continues into retirement. The aggregate impact is considerable; the total obligation for all U.S. corporations is about $500 billion.

Prior to 1993, employers accounted for postretirement benefit costs on a pay-as-you-go basis, meaning the expense each year was simply the amount of insurance premiums or medical claims paid, depending on the way the company provided health care benefits. The FASB revised GAAP to require a completely different approach. The expected future health care costs for retirees now must be recognized as an expense over the years necessary for employees to become entitled to the benefits.[30] This is the accrual basis that also is the basis for pension accounting.

● LO9

In fact, accounting for postretirement benefits is similar in most respects to accounting for pension benefits. This is because the two forms of benefits are fundamentally similar.

---

[30]FASB ASC 715–60: Compensation–Retirement Benefits–Defined Benefit Plans–Postretirement (previously "Employers' Accounting for Postretirement Benefits Other Than Pensions," *Statement of Financial Accounting Standards No. 106* (Norwalk, Conn.: FASB, 1990)). The Standard became effective (with some exceptions) in 1993.

Each is a form of deferred compensation earned during the employee's service life and each can be estimated as the present value of the cost of providing the expected future benefits. **General Motors** described its plan as shown in Graphic 17–13.

GRAPHIC 17–13

Disclosures—General Motors

Real World Financials

Note 5: Other Postretirement Benefits (in part)
The Corporation and certain of its domestic subsidiaries maintain hourly and salaried benefit plans that provide postretirement medical, dental, vision, and life insurance to retirees and eligible dependents. . . . . [GAAP] requires that the cost of such benefits be recognized in the financial statements during the period employees provide service to the Corporation.

Despite the similarities, though, there are a few differences in the characteristics of the benefits that necessitate differences in accounting treatment. Because accounting for the two types of retiree benefits is so nearly the same, our discussion in this portion of the chapter will emphasize the differences. This will allow you to use what you learned earlier in the chapter regarding pension accounting as a foundation for learning how to account for other postretirement benefits, supplementing that common base only when necessary. Focusing on the differences also will reinforce your understanding of pension accounting.

What Is a Postretirement Benefit Plan?

Before addressing the accounting ramifications, let's look at a typical retiree health care plan.[31] First, it's important to distinguish retiree health care benefits from health care benefits provided during an employee's working years. The annual cost of providing *preretirement* benefits is simply part of the annual compensation expense. However, many companies offer coverage that continues into retirement. It is the deferred aspect of these *postretirement* benefits that creates an accounting issue.

Usually a plan promises benefits in exchange for services performed over a designated number of years, or reaching a particular age, or both. For instance, a plan might specify that employees are eligible for postretirement benefits after both working 20 years and reaching age 62 while in service. Eligibility requirements and the nature of benefits usually are specified by a written plan, or sometimes only by company practice.

Eligibility usually is based on age and/or years of service.

Postretirement Health Benefits and Pension Benefits Compared

Keep in mind that retiree health benefits differ fundamentally from pension benefits in some important respects:

1. The amount of *pension* benefits generally is based on the number of years an employee works for the company so that the longer the employee works, the higher are the benefits. On the other hand, the amount of *postretirement health care* benefits typically is unrelated to service. It's usually an all-or-nothing plan in which a certain level of coverage is promised upon retirement, independent of the length of service beyond that necessary for eligibility.
2. Although coverage might be identical, the cost of providing the coverage might vary significantly from retiree to retiree and from year to year because of differing medical needs.
3. Postretirement health care plans often require the retiree to share in the cost of coverage through monthly contribution payments. For instance, a company might pay 80% of insurance premiums, with the retiree paying 20%. The net cost of providing coverage is reduced by these contributions as well as by any portion of the cost paid by Medicare or other insurance.
4. Coverage often is provided to spouses and eligible dependents.

---

[31]For convenience, our discussion focuses on health care benefits because these are by far the most common type of postretirement benefits other than pensions. But the concepts we discuss apply equally to other forms of postretirement benefits.

Determining the Net Cost of Benefits

To determine the postretirement benefit obligation and the postretirement benefit expense, the company's actuary first must make estimates of what the postretirement benefit costs will be for current employees. Then, as illustrated in Graphic 17–14, contributions to those costs by employees are deducted, as well as Medicare's share of the costs (for retirement years when the retiree will be 65 or older), to determine the estimated net cost of benefits to the employer:

GRAPHIC 17–14

Estimating the Net Cost of Benefits

Remember, postretirement health care benefits are anticipated actual costs of providing the promised health care, rather than an amount estimated by a defined benefit formula. This makes these estimates inherently more intricate, particularly because health care costs in general are notoriously difficult to forecast. And, since postretirement health care benefits are partially paid by the retiree and by Medicare, these cost-sharing amounts must be estimated as well.

On the other hand, estimating postretirement benefits costs is similar in many ways to estimating pension costs. Both estimates entail a variety of assumptions to be made by the company's actuary. Many of these assumptions are the same; for instance, both require estimates of:

Many of the assumptions needed to estimate postretirement health care benefits are the same as those needed to estimate pension benefits.

1. A discount rate.
2. Expected return on plan assets (if the plan is funded).
3. Employee turnover.
4. Expected retirement age.
5. Expected compensation increases (if the plan is pay-related).
6. Expected age of death.
7. Number and ages of beneficiaries and dependents.

Of course, the relative importance of some estimates is different from that for pension plans. Dependency status, turnover, and retirement age, for example, take on much greater significance. Also, additional assumptions become necessary as a result of differences between pension plans and other postretirement benefit plans. Specifically, it's necessary to estimate:

Some additional assumptions are needed to estimate postretirement health care benefits besides those needed to estimate pension benefits.

The postretirement benefit obligation is the discounted present value of the benefits during retirement.

1. The current cost of providing health care benefits at each age that participants might receive benefits.
2. Demographic characteristics of plan participants that might affect the amount and timing of benefits.
3. Benefit coverage provided by Medicare, other insurance, or other sources that will reduce the net cost of employer-provided benefits.
4. The expected health care cost trend rate.[32]

Taking these assumptions into account, the company's actuary estimates what the net cost of postretirement benefits will be for current employees in each year of their expected retirement. The discounted present value of those costs is the expected postretirement benefit obligation.

---

[32]Health care cost trend rates recently reported have ranged from 5.5% to 12.5%, with 9–9.5% being the most commonly assumed rate. *Accounting Trends and Techniques—2009* (New York: AICPA, 2009), p. 354.

Postretirement Benefit Obligation

There are two related obligation amounts. As indicated in Graphic 17–15, one measures the total obligation and the other refers to a specific portion of the total:

● LO10

1. **Expected postretirement benefit obligation (EPBO):** The actuary's estimate of the total postretirement benefits (at their discounted present value) expected to be received by plan participants.
2. **Accumulated postretirement benefit obligation (APBO):** The portion of the EPBO attributed to employee service to date.

GRAPHIC 17–15
Two Views of the Obligation for Postretirement Benefits Other Than Pensions

The accumulated postretirement benefit obligation (APBO) is analogous to the projected benefit obligation (PBO) for pensions. Like the PBO, the APBO is reported in the balance sheet only to the extent that it exceeds plan assets.

Measuring the Obligation

To illustrate, assume the actuary estimates that the net cost of providing health care benefits to Jessica Farrow (our illustration employee from earlier in the chapter) during her retirement years has a present value of $10,842 as of the end of 2009. This is the EPBO. If the benefits (and therefore the costs) relate to an estimated 35 years of service[33] and 10 of those years have been completed, the APBO would be:

$$\underset{\text{EPBO}}{\$10,842} \quad \times \quad \underset{\substack{\text{Fraction attributed} \\ \text{to service to date}}}{^{10}\!/_{35}} \quad = \quad \underset{\text{APBO}}{\$3,098}$$

$3,098 represents the portion of the EPBO related to the first 10 years of the 35-year service period.

If the assumed discount rate is 6%, a year later the EPBO will have grown to $11,493 simply because of a year's interest accruing at that rate ($10,842 × 1.06 = $11,493). Notice that there is no increase in the EPBO for service because, unlike the obligation in most pension plans, the total obligation is not increased by an additional year's service.

The APBO, however, is the portion of the EPBO related to service up to a particular date. Consequently, the APBO will have increased both because of interest and because the service fraction will be higher (service cost):

$$\underset{\text{EPBO}}{\$11,493} \quad \times \quad \underset{\substack{\text{Fraction attributed} \\ \text{to service to date}}}{^{11}\!/_{35}} \quad = \quad \underset{\text{APBO}}{\$3,612}$$

$3,612 represents the portion of the EPBO related to the first 11 years of the 35-year service period.

The two elements of the increase in 2010 can be separated as follows:

APBO at the beginning of the year	$3,098
Interest cost: $3,098 × 6%	186
Service cost: ($11,493 × $^1\!/_{35}$) portion of EPBO attributed to the year	328
APBO at the end of the year	$3,612

The APBO increases each year due to (a) interest accrued on the APBO and (b) the portion of the EPBO attributed to that year.

Attribution

Attribution is the process of assigning the cost of benefits to the years during which those benefits are assumed to be earned by employees. We accomplish this by assigning an equal fraction of the EPBO to each year of service from the employee's date of hire to the employee's

The cost of benefits is attributed to the years during which those benefits are assumed to be earned by employees.

---

[33]Assigning the costs to particular service years is referred to as the *attribution* of the costs to the years the benefits are assumed earned. We discuss attribution in the next section.

full eligibility date.[34] This is the date the employee has performed all the service necessary to have earned all the retiree benefits estimated to be received by the employee.[35] In our earlier example, we assumed the attribution period was 35 years and accordingly accrued ⅟₃₅ of the EPBO each year. The amount accrued each year increases both the APBO and the postretirement benefit expense. In Illustration 17–8 we see how the 35-year attribution (accrual) period was determined.

ILLUSTRATION 17–8

Determining the Attribution Period

The attribution period spans each year of service from the employee's date of hire to the employee's full eligibility date.

Jessica Farrow was hired by Global Communications at age 22 at the beginning of 2000 and is expected to retire at the end of 2039 at age 61. The retirement period is estimated to be 20 years.*

Global's employees are eligible for postretirement health care benefits after both reaching age 56 while in service and having worked 20 years.

Since Farrow becomes fully eligible at age 56 (the end of 2034), retiree benefits are attributed to the 35-year period from her date of hire through that date. Graphically, the situation can be described as follows:

*You probably recognize this as the situation used earlier in the chapter to illustrate pension accounting.

The attribution period does not include years of service beyond the full eligibility date even if the employee is expected to work after that date.

Some critics of this approach feel there is a fundamental inconsistency between the way we measure the benefits and the way we assign the benefits to specific service periods. The benefits (EPBO) are measured with the concession that the employee may work beyond the full eligibility date; however, the attribution period does not include years of service after that date. The counterargument is the fact that at the full eligibility date the employee will have earned the right to receive the full benefits expected under the plan and the amount of the benefits will not increase with service beyond that date.[36]

Accounting for Postretirement Benefit Plans Other Than Pensions

● LO11

We account for pensions and for other postretirement benefits essentially the same way.

As we just discussed, it's necessary to attribute a portion of the accumulated postretirement benefit obligation to each year as the service cost for that year as opposed to measuring the actual benefits employees earn during the year as we did for pension plans. That's due to the fundamental nature of these other postretirement plans under which employees are ineligible for benefits until specific eligibility criteria are met, at which time they become 100% eligible. This contrasts with pension plans under which employees earn additional benefits each year until they retire.

---

[34]If the plan specifically grants credit only for service from a date after employee's date of hire, the beginning of the attribution period is considered to be the beginning of that credited service period, rather than the employee's date of hire.

[35]Or any beneficiaries and covered dependents.

[36]FASB ASC 715–60: Compensation–Retirement Benefits–Defined Benefit Plans–Other Postretirement (previously "Employers' Accounting for Postretirement Benefits Other Than Pensions," *Statement of Financial Accounting Standards No. 106* (Norwalk, Conn.: FASB, 1990), par. 219–239. These specific paragraphs are not codified in the FASB Research System as they contain bases for conclusions and are therefore what codifiers consider "nonessential" material.

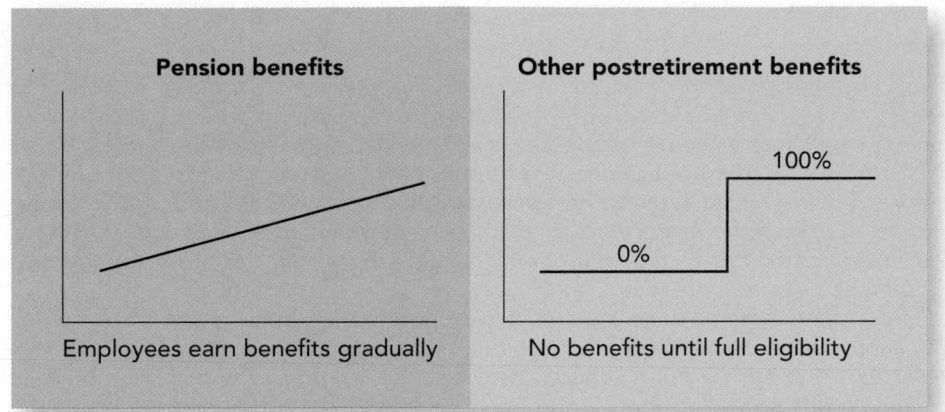

Measuring the service cost differs, though, due to a fundamental difference in the way employees acquire benefits under the two types of plans.

The way we measure service cost is the primary difference between accounting for pensions and for other postretirement benefits. Otherwise, though, accounting for the two is virtually identical. For example, a company with an underfunded postretirement benefit plan with existing prior service cost and net loss–AOCI would record the following journal entries annually:

To Record Postretirement Benefit Expense		
Postretirement benefit expense (total)	xx	
Plan assets (expected return on assets)	xx	
Amortization of net gain–OCI (current amortization)	xx	
APBO (service cost + interest cost)		xx
Amortization of net loss–OCI (current amortization)		xx
Amortization of prior service cost–OCI[37] (current amortization)		xx

We record the annual expense and funding for other postretirement benefit plans the same way we do for pensions.

To Record Cash Funding of Plan Assets		
Plan assets	xx	
Cash (contribution to plan assets)		xx

To Record Gains and Losses		
Loss–OCI (from change in assumption)	xx	
APBO		xx
or		
APBO	xx	
Gain–OCI (from change in assumption)		xx
Plan assets	xx	
Gain–OCI (actual return on assets – expected return)		xx
or		
Gain–OCI (expected return on assets – actual return)	xx	
Plan assets		xx

We record losses and gains (as well as any new prior service cost should it occur) the same way we do for pensions.

ETHICAL DILEMMA

Earlier this year, you were elected to the board of directors of Champion International, Inc. Champion has offered its employees postretirement health care benefits for 35 years. The practice of extending health care benefits to retirees began modestly. Most employees retired after age 65, when most benefits were covered by Medicare. Costs also were lower

(continued)

---

[37]The prior service cost for other postretirement benefits is amortized over the average remaining time until "full eligibility" for employees rather than until retirement as is the case for pension plans. This is consistent with recording "regular" service cost over the time to full eligibility.

(concluded)

because life expectancies were shorter and medical care was less expensive. Because costs were so low, little attention was paid to accounting for these benefits. The company simply recorded an expense when benefits were provided to retirees. The FASB changed all that. Now, the obligation for these benefits must be anticipated and reported in the annual report. Worse yet, the magnitude of the obligation has grown enormously, almost unnoticed. Health care costs have soared in recent years. Medical technology and other factors have extended life expectancies. Of course, the value to employees of this benefit has grown parallel to the growth of the burden to the company.

Without being required to anticipate future costs, many within Champion's management were caught by surprise at the enormity of the company's obligation. Equally disconcerting was the fact that such a huge liability now must be exposed to public view. Now you find that several board members are urging the dismantling of the postretirement plan altogether.

A Comprehensive Illustration

We assumed earlier that the EPBO at the end of 2009 was determined by the actuary to be $10,842. This was the present value on that date of all anticipated future benefits. Then we noted that the EPBO at the end of the next year would have grown by 6% to $11,493. This amount, too, would represent the present value of the same anticipated future benefits, but as of a year later. The APBO, remember, is the portion of the EPBO attributed to service performed to a particular date. So, we determined the APBO at the end of 2010 to be $11,493 \times \frac{11}{35}$, or $3,612. We determined the $328 service cost noted earlier for 2010 as the portion of the EPBO attributed to that year: $11,493 \times \frac{1}{35}$.

Now, let's review our previous discussion of how the EPBO, the APBO, and the postretirement benefit expense are determined by calculating those amounts a year later, at the end of 2011. Before doing so, however, we can anticipate (a) the EPBO to be $11,493 \times 1.06$, or $12,182, (b) the APBO to be $\frac{12}{35}$ of that amount, or $4,177, and (c) the 2009 service cost to be $\frac{1}{35}$ of that amount, or $348. In Illustration 17–9 we see if our expectations are borne out by direct calculation.

| **ILLUSTRATION 17–9** Determining the Postretirement Benefit Obligation

The EPBO is the discounted present value of the total benefits expected to be earned.

The fraction of the EPBO considered to be earned this year is the service cost.

The fraction of the EPBO considered to be earned so far is the APBO. | Assume the actuary has estimated the net cost of retiree benefits in each year of Jessica Farrow's 20-year expected retirement period to be the amounts shown in the calculation below. She is fully eligible for benefits at the end of 2034 and is expected to retire at the end of 2039.

Calculating the APBO and the postretirement benefit expense at the end of 2011, 12 years after being hired, begins with estimating the EPBO.

Steps to calculate (a) the EPBO, (b) the APBO, and (c) the annual service cost at the end of 2011, 12 years after being hired, are:

(a). 1. Estimate the cost of retiree benefits in each year of the expected retirement period and deduct anticipated Medicare reimbursements and retiree cost-sharing to derive the net cost to the employer in each year of the expected retirement period.
2. Find the present value of each year's net benefit cost as of the *retirement date*.
3. Find the present value of the total net benefit cost as of the *current date*. This is the EPBO.

(b). Multiply the EPBO by the attribution factor, (service to date/total attribution period). This is the APBO. The service cost in any year is simply one year's worth of the EPBO.

(c). Multiply the EPBO by $\frac{1}{\text{total attribution period}}$. |

The steps are demonstrated in Illustration 17–9A.

	(a.1). Actuary estimates the net cost of benefits paid during retirement years:			(a.2). Present value [n = 1, 2, 3, 4, . . . 19, 20: i = 6%] of the net benefits as of the retirement date:
Year	**Age**	**Net Benefit**		**Present Value at 2037**
2040	62	5,000		4,717
2041	63	5,600		4,984
2042	64	6,300		5,290
2043	65	3,000		2,376
~	~	~		~
2058	80	9,550		3,156
2059	81	10,300		3,212
				$62,269

Attribution Period
35 years

Retirement Period
20 years

12 years

2000   2011

2034   2039   2059

Retirement

Date hired

Full-eligibility date

(a.3). Present value (n = 28, i = 6%) of postretirement benefits at 2011 is
$62,269 × .19563 = $12,182 (EPBO)
(b). $12,182 × $\frac{12}{35}$ = $4,177 (APBO)
(c). $12,182 × $\frac{1}{35}$ = $348 (Service Cost)

ILLUSTRATION 17–9A

EPBO, APBO, and Service Cost in 2011

The actuary estimates the net cost to the employer in each year the retiree is expected to receive benefits.

As of the retirement date, the lump-sum equivalent of the expected yearly costs is $62,269.

The EPBO in 2011 is the present value of those benefits.

The APBO is the portion of the EPBO attributed to service to date.

The service cost is the portion of the EPBO attributed to a particular year's service.

DECISION MAKERS' PERSPECTIVE

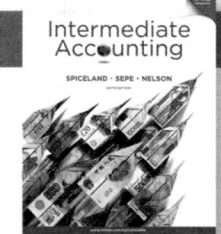

When they analyze financial statements, investors and creditors should be wary of the non-standard way companies report pension and other postretirement information. Recall that in the balance sheet, firms do not separately report the benefit obligation and the plan assets. Also, companies have considerable latitude in making the several assumptions needed to estimate the components of postretirement benefit plans. Fortunately, information provided in the disclosure notes makes up for some of the deficiency in balance sheet information and makes it possible for interested analysts to modify their analysis. As for pensions, the choices companies make for the discount rate, expected return on plan assets, and the compensation growth rate can greatly impact postretirement benefit expense and earnings quality. The disclosures required are very similar to pension disclosures. In fact, disclosures for the two types of retiree benefits typically are combined.[38] Disclosures include:

- Descriptions of the plans.
- Estimates of the obligations (PBO, ABO, vested benefit obligation, EPBO, and APBO).

Postretirement benefit amounts reported in the disclosure notes fill a reporting gap left by the minimal disclosures in the primary financial statements.

---

[38]FASB ASC 715–60–50: Compensation–Retirement Benefits–Defined Benefit Plans–Other Postretirement–Disclosure (previously "Employers' Disclosures about Pensions and Other Postretirement Benefits," *Statement of Financial Accounting Standards No. 132* (Stamford, Conn.: FASB, 1998)).

- The percentage of total plan assets for each major category of assets (equity securities, debt securities, real estate, other) as well as a description of investment strategies, including any target asset allocations and risk management practices.
- A breakdown of the components of the annual pension and postretirement benefit expenses for the years reported.
- The discount rates, the assumed rate of compensation increases used to measure the PBO, the expected long-term rate of return on plan assets, and the expected rate of increase in future medical and dental benefit costs.
- Estimated benefit payments presented separately for the next five years and in the aggregate for years 6–10.
- Estimate of expected contributions to fund the plan for the next year.
- Disclosures also include (a) any changes to the net gain or net loss and prior service cost arising during the period, (b) the accumulated amounts of these components of accumulated other comprehensive income, and (c) the amounts of those balances expected to be amortized in the next year.
- Other information to make it possible for interested analysts to reconstruct the financial statements with plan assets and liabilities included. ●

CONCEPT REVIEW EXERCISE

OTHER POSTRETIREMENT BENEFITS

Technology Group, Inc., has an unfunded retiree health care plan. The actuary estimates the net cost of providing health care benefits to a particular employee during his retirement years to have a present value of $24,000 as of the end of 2011 (the EPBO). The benefits and therefore the expected postretirement benefit obligation relate to an estimated 36 years of service and 12 of those years have been completed. The interest rate is 6%.

Required:
Pertaining to the one employee only:
1. What is the accumulated postretirement benefit obligation at the end of 2011?
2. What is the expected postretirement benefit obligation at the end of 2012?
3. What is the service cost to be included in 2012 postretirement benefit expense?
4. What is the interest cost to be included in 2012 postretirement benefit expense?
5. What is the accumulated postretirement benefit obligation at the end of 2012?
6. Show how the APBO changed during 2012 by reconciling the beginning and ending balances.
7. What is the 2012 postretirement benefit expense, assuming no net gains or losses and no prior service cost?

SOLUTION
1. What is the accumulated postretirement benefit obligation at the end of 2011?

$$\$24,000 \quad \times \quad {}^{12}\!/_{36} \quad = \quad \$8,000$$

EPBO 2011 / Fraction attributed to service to date / APBO 2011

2. What is the expected postretirement benefit obligation at the end of 2012?

$$\$24,000 \quad \times \quad 1.06 \quad = \quad \$25,440$$

EPBO 2011 / To accrue interest / EPBO 2012

3. What is the service cost to be included in 2012 postretirement benefit expense?

$$\$25,440 \quad \times \quad {}^{1}\!/_{36} \quad = \quad \$707$$

EPBO 2012 / Attributed to 2012 / Service cost

4. What is the interest cost to be included in 2012 postretirement benefit expense?

$$\$8,000 \text{ (beginning APBO)} \times 6\% = \$480$$

5. What is the accumulated postretirement benefit obligation at the end of 2012?

$\$25,440$	$\times$	$^{13}\!/_{36}$	$=$	$\$9,187$
EPBO		Fraction attributed		APBO
2012		to service to date		2012

6. Show how the APBO changed during 2012 by reconciling the beginning and ending balances.

APBO at the beginning of 2012 (from req. 1)	$8,000
Service cost: (from req. 3)	707
Interest cost: (from req. 4)	480
APBO at the end of 2012 (from req. 5)	$9,187

7. What is the 2012 postretirement benefit expense, assuming no net gains or losses and no prior service cost?

Service cost	$ 707
Interest cost	480
Actual return on the plan assets	(not funded)
Adjusted for: gain or loss on the plan assets	(not funded)
Amortization of prior service cost	none
Amortization of net gain or loss	none
Postretirement benefit expense	$1,187

FINANCIAL REPORTING CASE SOLUTION

1. **Why is pension plan underfunding not a concern in your present employment?** *(p. 939)*   In a defined contribution plan, the employer is not obliged to provide benefits beyond the annual contribution to the employees' plan. No liability is created. Unlike retirement benefits paid in a defined benefit plan, the employee's retirement benefits in a defined contribution plan are totally dependent on how well invested assets perform in the marketplace.

2. **Were you correct that the pension liability is not reported in the balance sheet? What is the liability?** *(p. 941)*   Yes and no. The pension liability is not reported separately in the balance sheet. It is, however, combined with pension assets with the net difference reported in the balance sheet. The separate balance is disclosed, though, in the notes. For United Dynamics, the PBO at the end of 2011 is $2,628 million.

3. **What is the amount of the plan assets available to pay benefits? What are the factors that can cause that amount to change?** *(p. 948)*   The plan assets at the end of 2011 total $2,807 million. A trustee accepts employer contributions, invests the contributions, accumulates the earnings on the investments, and pays benefits from the plan assets. So the amount is increased each year by employer cash contributions and (hopefully) a return on assets invested. It is decreased by amounts paid out to retired employees.

4. **What does the "pension asset" represent? Are you interviewing with a company whose pension plan is severely underfunded?** *(p. 949)*   The pension asset is not the plan assets available to pay pension benefits. Instead, it's the net difference between those assets and the pension obligation. United Dynamics' plan assets exceed the pension obligation in each year presented and therefore is one of the few companies whose pension plan is overfunded.

5. How is the pension expense influenced by changes in the pension liability and plan assets? *(p. 950)* The pension expense reported on the income statement is a composite of periodic changes that occur in both the pension obligation and the plan assets. For United Dynamics in 2011, the pension expense included the service cost and interest cost, which are changes in the PBO, and the return on plan assets. It also included an amortized portion of prior service costs (a previous change in the PBO) and of net gains (gains and losses result from changes in both the PBO and plan assets). ●

THE BOTTOM LINE

● **LO1** Pension plans are arrangements designed to provide income to individuals during their retirement years. *Defined contribution* plans promise fixed annual contributions to a pension fund, without further commitment regarding benefit amounts at retirement. *Defined benefit* plans promise fixed retirement benefits defined by a designated formula. The employer sets aside cash each year to provide sufficient funds to pay promised benefits. (p. 937)

● **LO2** The *accumulated benefit obligation* is an estimate of the discounted present value of the retirement benefits earned so far by employees, applying the plan's pension formula to *existing* compensation levels. The vested benefit obligation is the portion of the accumulated benefit obligation that plan participants are entitled to receive regardless of their continued employment. The *projected benefit obligation* estimates retirement benefits by applying the pension formula to *projected future* compensation levels. (p. 941)

● **LO3** The PBO can change due to the accumulation of *service cost* from year to year, the accrual of *interest* as time passes, making plan amendments retroactive to prior years (prior service cost), and periodic adjustments when estimates change (gains and losses). The obligation is reduced as benefits actually are paid to retired employees. (p. 942)

● **LO4** The plan assets consist of the accumulated balance of the annual employer contributions plus the return on the investments less benefits paid to retirees. (p. 947)

● **LO5** The difference between an employer's obligation (PBO for pensions, APBO for other postretirement benefit plans) and the resources available to satisfy that obligation (plan assets) is the funded status of the pension plan. The employer must report the "funded status" of the plan in the balance sheet as a net pension liability if the obligation exceeds the plan assets or as a net pension asset if the plan assets exceed the obligation. (p. 949)

● **LO6** The pension expense is a composite of periodic changes in both the pension obligation and the plan assets. Service cost is the increase in the PBO attributable to employee service and is the primary component of pension expense. The interest and return-on-assets components are financial items created only because the pension payment is delayed and the obligation is funded currently. Prior service cost is recognized over employees' future service period. Also, neither a loss (gain) on the PBO nor a loss (gain) on plan assets is immediately recognized in pension expense; they are recognized on a delayed basis to achieve income smoothing. (p. 949)

● **LO7** Recording pension expense causes the net pension liability/asset to change by the service cost, the interest cost, and the expected return on plan assets. Any amortization amounts included in the expense will reduce the *accumulated other comprehensive income* balances being amortized, e.g., net loss—AOCI and prior service cost–AOCI. Similarly, the plan assets are increased by the annual cash investment. New losses and gains (as well as any new prior service cost should it occur) are recognized as other comprehensive income. (p. 955)

● **LO8** The various elements of a pension plan—projected benefit obligation, plan assets, prior service cost, gains and losses, pension expense, and the funded status of the plan—are interrelated. One way to see how each element relates to the other is to bring each part together in a *pension spreadsheet.* (p. 962)

● **LO9** Accounting for postretirement benefits is similar in most respects to accounting for pension benefits. Like pensions, other postretirement benefits are a form of deferred compensation. Unlike pensions, their cost is attributed to the years from the employee's date of hire to the full eligibility date. (p. 966)

● **LO10** The expected postretirement benefit obligation (EPBO) is the actuary's estimate of the total postretirement benefits (at their discounted present value) expected to be received by plan participants. The accumulated postretirement benefit obligation (APBO) is the portion of the EPBO attributed to employee service to date. (p. 969)

● **LO11**   The components of postretirement benefit expense are essentially the same as those for pension expense. (p. 970)

● **LO12**   U.S. GAAP and IFRS are largely aligned with respect to accounting for postretirement benefit plans. Differences that remain include the option under IFRS to expense gains and losses, the requirement to expense prior service cost for benefits that have vested, and a difference in options regarding reporting comprehensive income. (pp. 955, 957, 961, and 965) ●

SERVICE METHOD OF ALLOCATING PRIOR SERVICE COST

APPENDIX 17

When amortizing prior service cost, our objective is to match the cost with employee service. The straight-line method described in this chapter allocates an equal amount of the prior service cost to each year of the 15-year average service period of affected employees. But consider this: fewer of the affected employees will be working for the company toward the end of that period than at the beginning. Some probably will retire or quit in each year following the amendment.

An allocation approach that reflects the declining service pattern is called the **service method.** This method allocates the prior service cost to each year in proportion to the fraction of the total remaining service years worked in each of those years. To do this, it's necessary to estimate how many of the 2,000 employees working at the beginning of 2010 when the amendment is made will still be employed in each year after the amendment.

Let's suppose, for example, that the actuary estimates that a declining number of these employees still will be employed in each of the next 28 years as indicated in the abbreviated schedule below. The portion of the prior service cost amortized to pension expense each year is $60 million times a declining fraction. Each year's fraction is that year's service divided by the 28-year total (30,000). This is demonstrated in Graphic 17A–1.

GRAPHIC 17A–1

Service Method of Amortizing Prior Service Cost

			($ in millions)		
Year	**Number of Employees Still Employed (assumed for the illustration)**	**Fraction of Total Service Years**		**Prior Service Cost**	**Amount Amortized**
2010	2,000	$^{2,000}/_{30,000}$	×	$60	=	$ 4.0
2011	2,000	$^{2,000}/_{30,000}$	×	60	=	4.0
2012	1,850	$^{1,850}/_{30,000}$	×	60	=	3.7
2013	1,700	$^{1,700}/_{30,000}$	×	60	=	3.4
2014	1,550	$^{1,550}/_{30,000}$	×	60	=	3.1
—	—	—	×	—		—
2035	400	$^{400}/_{30,000}$	×	60	=	.8
2036	250	$^{250}/_{30,000}$	×	60	=	.5
2037	100	$^{100}/_{30,000}$	×	60	=	.2
Totals	30,000	$^{30,000}/_{30,000}$				$60.0
	Total number of service years					Total amount amortized

By the service method, prior service cost is recognized each year in proportion to the fraction of the total remaining service years worked that year.

Conceptually, the service method achieves a better matching of the cost and benefits. In fact, this is the FASB's recommended approach. However, GAAP permits the consistent use of any method that amortizes the prior service cost at least as quickly.[39]

The service method amortized an equal amount *per employee* each year.

---

[39]FASB ASC 715–30–35–13: Compensation–Retirement Benefits–Defined Benefit Plans–Pension–Subsequent Measurement–Prior Service Costs (previously "Employers' Accounting for Pensions," *Statement of Financial Accounting Standards No. 87* (Stamford, Conn.: FASB, 1985), par. 26).

The straight-line method meets this condition and is the approach most often used in practice. In our illustration, the cost is completely amortized over 15 years rather than the 28 years required by the service method. The 15-year average service life is simply the total estimated service years divided by the total number of employees in the group:

$$\underset{\substack{\text{Total number} \\ \text{of service years}}}{30{,}000 \text{ years}} \quad \div \quad \underset{\substack{\text{Total number} \\ \text{of employees}}}{2{,}000} \quad = \quad \underset{\substack{\text{Average} \\ \text{service years}}}{15 \text{ years}}$$

QUESTIONS FOR REVIEW OF KEY TOPICS

Q 17–1 What is a pension plan? What motivates a corporation to offer a pension plan for its employees?

Q 17–2 Qualified pension plans offer important tax benefits. What is the special tax treatment and what qualifies a pension plan for these benefits?

Q 17–3 Lamont Corporation has a pension plan in which the corporation makes all contributions and employees receive benefits at retirement based on the balance in their accumulated pension fund. What type of pension plan does Lamont have?

Q 17–4 What is the vested benefit obligation?

Q 17–5 Differentiate between the accumulated benefit obligation and the projected benefit obligation.

Q 17–6 Name five events that might change the balance of the PBO.

Q 17–7 Name three events that might change the balance of the plan assets.

Q 17–8 What are the components that might be included in the calculation of net pension cost recognized for a period by an employer sponsoring a defined benefit pension plan?

Q 17–9 Define the service cost component of the periodic pension expense.

Q 17–10 Define the interest cost component of the periodic pension expense.

Q 17–11 The return on plan assets is the increase in plan assets (at fair value), adjusted for contributions to the plan and benefits paid during the period. How is the return included in the calculation of the periodic pension expense?

Q 17–12 Define prior service cost. How is it reported in the financial statements? How is it included in pension expense?

Q 17–13 How should gains or losses related to pension plan assets be recognized? How does this treatment compare to that for gains or losses related to the pension obligation?

Q 17–14 Is a company's PBO reported in the balance sheet? Its plan assets? Explain.

Q 17–15 What two components of pension expense may be negative (i.e., reduce pension expense)?

Q 17–16 Which are the components of pension expense that involve delayed recognition?

Q 17–17 Evaluate this statement: The excess of the actual return on plan assets over the expected return decreases the employer's pension cost.

Q 17–18 When accounting for pension costs, how should the payment into the pension fund be recorded? How does it affect the funded status of the plan?

Q 17–19 TFC Inc. revises its estimate of future salary levels, causing its PBO estimate to increase by $3 million. How is the $3 reflected in TFC's financial statements?

Q 17–20 A pension plan is underfunded when the employer's obligation (PBO) exceeds the resources available to satisfy that obligation (plan assets) and overfunded when the opposite is the case. How is this funded status reported on the balance sheet if plan assets exceed the PBO? If the PBO exceeds plan assets?

Q 17–21 What are two ways to measure the obligation for postretirement benefits other than pensions? Define these measurement approaches.

Q 17–22 How are the costs of providing postretirement benefits other than pensions expensed?

Q 17–23 The components of postretirement benefit expense are similar to the components of pension expense. In what fundamental way does the service cost component differ between these two expenses?

Q 17–24 The EPBO for Branch Industries at the end of 2011 was determined by the actuary to be $20,000 as it relates to employee Will Lawson. Lawson was hired at the beginning of 1997. He will be fully eligible to retire with health care benefits in 15 years but is expected to retire in 25 years. What is the APBO as it relates to Will Lawson?

IFRS **Q 17–25** The income statement of Mid-South Logistics includes $12 million for vested past service cost. Does Mid-South Logistics prepare its financial statements according to U.S. GAAP or IFRS? Explain.

IFRS **Q 17–26** How do U.S. GAAP and IFRS differ with regard to reporting gains and losses from changing assumptions used to measure the pension obligation?

BRIEF EXERCISES

BE 17–1
Changes in the projected benefit obligation
● LO3

The projected benefit obligation was $80 million at the beginning of the year. Service cost for the year was $10 million. At the end of the year, pension benefits paid by the trustee were $6 million and there were no pension-related other comprehensive income accounts requiring amortization. The actuary's discount rate was 5%. What was the amount of the projected benefit obligation at year-end?

BE 17–2
Changes in the projected benefit obligation
● LO3

The projected benefit obligation was $80 million at the beginning of the year and $85 million at the end of the year. At the end of the year, pension benefits paid by the trustee were $6 million and there were no pension-related other comprehensive income accounts requiring amortization. The actuary's discount rate was 5%. What was the amount of the service cost for the year?

BE 17–3
Changes in the projected benefit obligation
● LO3

The projected benefit obligation was $80 million at the beginning of the year and $85 million at the end of the year. Service cost for the year was $10 million. At the end of the year, there was no prior service cost and a negligible net loss–AOCI. The actuary's discount rate was 5%. What was the amount of the retiree benefits paid by the trustee?

BE 17–4
Changes in the projected benefit obligation
● LO3

The projected benefit obligation was $80 million at the beginning of the year and $85 million at the end of the year. Service cost for the year was $10 million. At the end of the year, pension benefits paid by the trustee were $6 million. The actuary's discount rate was 5%. At the end of the year, the actuary revised the estimate of the percentage rate of increase in compensation levels in upcoming years. What was the amount of the gain or loss the estimate change caused?

BE 17–5
Changes in pension plan assets
● LO4

Pension plan assets were $80 million at the beginning of the year. The return on plan assets was 5%. At the end of the year, retiree benefits paid by the trustee were $6 million and cash invested in the pension fund was $7 million. What was the amount of the pension plan assets at year-end?

BE 17–6
Changes in pension plan assets
● LO4

Pension plan assets were $80 million at the beginning of the year and $83 million at the end of the year. The return on plan assets was 5%. At the end of the year, cash invested in the pension fund was $7 million. What was the amount of the retiree benefits paid by the trustee?

BE 17–7
Changes in pension plan assets
● LO4

Pension plan assets were $100 million at the beginning of the year and $104 million at the end of the year. At the end of the year, retiree benefits paid by the trustee were $6 million and cash invested in the pension fund was $7 million. What was the percentage rate of return on plan assets?

BE 17–8
Reporting the funded status of pension plans
● LO5

JDS Foods' projected benefit obligation, accumulated benefit obligation, and plan assets were $40 million, $30 million, and $25 million, respectively, at the end of the year. What, if any, pension liability must be reported in the balance sheet? What would JDS report if the plan assets were $45 million instead?

BE 17–9
Pension expense
● LO6

The projected benefit obligation was $80 million at the beginning of the year. Service cost for the year was $10 million. At the end of the year, pension benefits paid by the trustee were $6 million and there were no pension-related other comprehensive income accounts requiring amortization. The actuary's discount rate was 5%. The actual return on plan assets was $5 million although it was expected to be only $4 million. What was the pension expense for the year?

BE 17–10
Pension expense; prior service cost
● LO6

The pension plan was amended last year, creating a prior service cost of $20 million. Service cost and interest cost for the year were $10 million and $4 million, respectively. At the end of the year, there was a negligible balance in the net gain–pensions account. The actual return on plan assets was $4 million although it was expected to be $6 million. On average, employees' remaining service life with the company is 10 years. What was the pension expense for the year?

BE 17–11
Net gain
● LO6

The projected benefit obligation and plan assets were $80 million and $100 million, respectively, at the beginning of the year. Due primarily to favorable stock market performance in recent years, there also was a net gain of $30 million. On average, employees' remaining service life with the company is 10 years. As a result of the net gain, what was the increase or decrease in pension expense for the year?

BE 17–12
Recording pension expense
● LO7

The Warren Group's pension expense is $67 million. This amount includes a $70 million service cost, a $50 million interest cost, a $55 million reduction for the expected return on plan assets, and a $2 million amortization of a prior service cost. How is the net pension liability affected when the pension expense is recorded?

BE 17–13
Recording pension expense
● LO7

Andrews Medical reported a net loss–AOCI in last year's balance sheet. This year, the company revised its estimate of future salary levels causing its PBO estimate to decline by $4 million. Also, the $8 million actual return on plan assets fell short of the $9 million expected return. How does this gain and loss affect Andrews' income statement, statement of comprehensive income, and balance sheet?

BE 17–14
Postretirement benefits; determine the APBO and service cost
● LO9 LO10

Prince Distribution Inc. has an unfunded postretirement benefit plan. Medical care and life insurance benefits are provided to employees who render 10 years service and attain age 55 while in service. At the end of 2011, Jim Lukawitz is 31. He was hired by Prince at age 25 (6 years ago) and is expected to retire at age 62. The expected postretirement benefit obligation for Lukawitz at the end of 2011 is $50,000 and $54,000 at the end of 2012. Calculate the accumulated postretirement benefit obligation at the end of 2011 and 2012 and the service cost for 2011 and 2012 as pertaining to Lukawitz.

BE 17–15
Postretirement benefits; changes in the APBO
● LO11

On January 1, 2011, Medical Transport Company's accumulated postretirement benefit obligation was $25 million. At the end of 2011, retiree benefits paid were $3 million. Service cost for 2011 is $7 million. Assumptions regarding the trend of future health care costs were revised at the end of 2011, causing the actuary to revise downward the estimate of the APBO by $1 million. The actuary's discount rate is 8%. Determine the amount of the accumulated postretirement benefit obligation at December 31, 2011.

EXERCISES

An alternate exercise and problem set is available on the text website: www.mhhe.com/spiceland6e

E 17–1
Changes in the PBO
● LO3

Indicate by letter whether each of the events listed below increases (**I**), decreases (**D**), or has no effect (**N**) on an employer's projected benefit obligation.

Events

_____ 1. Interest cost.
_____ 2. Amortization of prior service cost.
_____ 3. A decrease in the average life expectancy of employees.
_____ 4. An increase in the average life expectancy of employees.
_____ 5. A plan amendment that increases benefits is made retroactive to prior years.
_____ 6. An increase in the actuary's assumed discount rate.
_____ 7. Cash contributions to the pension fund by the employer.
_____ 8. Benefits are paid to retired employees.
_____ 9. Service cost.
_____ 10. Return on plan assets during the year is lower than expected.
_____ 11. Return on plan assets during the year is higher than expected.

E 17–2
Determine the projected benefit obligation
● LO3

On January 1, 2011, Burleson Corporation's projected benefit obligation was $30 million. During 2011 pension benefits paid by the trustee were $4 million. Service cost for 2011 is $12 million. Pension plan assets (at fair value) increased during 2011 by $6 million as expected. At the end of 2011, there was no prior service cost and a negligible balance in net loss–AOCI. The actuary's discount rate was 10%.

Required:

Determine the amount of the projected benefit obligation at December 31, 2011.

E 17–3
Components of pension expense
● LO6

Indicate by letter whether each of the events listed below increases (**I**), decreases (**D**), or has no effect (**N**) on an employer's periodic pension expense in the year the event occurs.

Events

_____ 1. Interest cost.
_____ 2. Amortization of prior service cost–AOCI.
_____ 3. Excess of the expected return on plan assets over the actual return.
_____ 4. Expected return on plan assets.
_____ 5. A plan amendment that increases benefits is made retroactive to prior years.

(continued)

(concluded)   _____ 6. Actuary's estimate of the PBO is increased.

_____ 7. Cash contributions to the pension fund by the employer.

_____ 8. Benefits are paid to retired employees.

_____ 9. Service cost.

_____ 10. Excess of the actual return on plan assets over the expected return.

_____ 11. Amortization of net loss–AOCI.

_____ 12. Amortization of net gain–AOCI.

E 17–4
Recording pension expense
● **LO6 LO7**

Harrison Forklift's pension expense includes a service cost of $10 million. Harrison began the year with a pension liability of $28 million (underfunded pension plan).

Required:

Prepare the appropriate general journal entries to record Harrison's pension expense in each of the following independent situations regarding the other components of pension expense ($ in millions):

1. Interest cost, $6; expected return on assets, $4; amortization of net loss, $2.

2. Interest cost, $6; expected return on assets, $4; amortization of net gain, $2.

3. Interest cost, $6; expected return on assets, $4; amortization of net loss, $2; amortization of prior service cost, $3 million.

E 17–5
Determine pension plan assets
● **LO4**

The following data relate to Voltaire Company's defined benefit pension plan:

	($ in millions)
Plan assets at fair value, January 1	$600
Expected return on plan assets	60
Actual return on plan assets	48
Contributions to the pension fund (end of year)	100
Amortization of net loss	10
Pension benefits paid (end of year)	11
Pension expense	72

Required:

Determine the amount of pension plan assets at fair value on December 31.

E 17–6
Changes in the pension obligation; determine service cost
● **LO3 LO6**

Pension data for Millington Enterprises include the following:

	($ in millions)
Discount rate, 10%	
Projected benefit obligation, January 1	$360
Projected benefit obligation, December 31	465
Accumulated benefit obligation, January 1	300
Accumulated benefit obligation, December 31	415
Cash contributions to pension fund, December 31	150
Benefit payments to retirees, December 31	54

Required:

Assuming no change in actuarial assumptions and estimates, determine the service cost component of pension expense for the year ended December 31.

E 17–7
Changes in plan assets; determine cash contributions
● **LO4**

Pension data for Fahy Transportation Inc. include the following:

	($ in millions)
Discount rate, 7%	
Expected return on plan assets, 10%	
Actual return on plan assets, 11%	
Projected benefit obligation, January 1	$730
Plan assets (fair value), January 1	700
Plan assets (fair value), December 31	750
Benefit payments to retirees, December 31	66

Required:

Assuming cash contributions were made at the end of the year, what was the amount of those contributions?

E 17–8
Components of
pension expense
● LO6

Pension data for Sterling Properties include the following:

	($ in 000s)
Service cost, 2011	$112
Projected benefit obligation, January 1, 2011	850
Plan assets (fair value), January 1, 2011	900
Prior service cost–AOCI (2011 amortization, $8)	80
Net loss–AOCI (2011 amortization, $1)	101
Discount rate, 6%	
Expected return on plan assets, 10%	
Actual return on plan assets, 11%	

Required:
Determine pension expense for 2011.

E 17–9
Components of
pension expense;
IFRS
● LO6 LO12

Refer to the situation described in Exercise 17–8.

Required:
How might your answer differ if we assume Sterling Properties prepares its financial statements according to International Financial Reporting Standards?

E 17–10
Determine pension
expense
● LO6 LO7

Abbott and Abbott has a noncontributory, defined benefit pension plan. At December 31, 2011, Abbott and Abbott received the following information:

	($ in millions)
Projected Benefit Obligation	
Balance, January 1	$120
Service cost	20
Interest cost	12
Benefits paid	(9)
Balance, December 31	$143
Plan Assets	
Balance, January 1	$ 80
Actual return on plan assets	9
Contributions 2011	20
Benefits paid	(9)
Balance, December 31	$100

The expected long-term rate of return on plan assets was 10%. There was no prior service cost and a negligible net loss–AOCI on January 1, 2011.

Required:
1. Determine Abbott and Abbott's pension expense for 2011.
2. Prepare the journal entries to record Abbott and Abbott's pension expense, funding, and payment for 2011.

E 17–11
Components of
pension expense;
journal entries
● LO6 LO7

Pension data for Barry Financial Services Inc. include the following:

	($ in 000s)
Discount rate, 7%	
Expected return on plan assets, 10%	
Actual return on plan assets, 9%	
Service cost, 2011	$ 310
January 1, 2011:	
Projected benefit obligation	2,300
Accumulated benefit obligation	2,000
Plan assets (fair value)	2,400
Prior service cost–AOCI (2011 amortization, $25)	325
Net gain–AOCI (2011 amortization, $6)	330
December 31, 2011:	
Cash contributions to pension fund, December 31, 2011	245
Benefit payments to retirees, December 31, 2011	270

Required:

1. Determine pension expense for 2011.
2. Prepare the journal entries to record pension expense, gains and losses (if any), funding, and retiree benefits for 2011.

E 17–12
PBO calculations;
ABO calculations;
present value
concepts
● LO1 LO2 LO3

e**X**cel

Clark Industries has a defined benefit pension plan that specifies annual retirement benefits equal to:

$$1.2\% \times \text{Service years} \times \text{Final year's salary}$$

Stanley Mills was hired by Clark at the beginning of 1992. Mills is expected to retire at the end of 2036 after 45 years of service. His retirement is expected to span 15 years. At the end of 2011, 20 years after being hired, his salary is $80,000. The company's actuary projects Mills's salary to be $270,000 at retirement. The actuary's discount rate is 7%.

Required:

1. Estimate the amount of Stanley Mills's annual retirement payments for the 15 retirement years earned as of the end of 2011.
2. Suppose Clark's pension plan permits a lump-sum payment at retirement in lieu of annuity payments. Determine the lump-sum equivalent as the present value as of the retirement date of annuity payments during the retirement period.
3. What is the company's projected benefit obligation at the end of 2011 with respect to Stanley Mills?
4. Even though pension accounting centers on the PBO calculation, the ABO still must be disclosed in the pension footnote. What is the company's accumulated benefit obligation at the end of 2011 with respect to Stanley Mills?
5. If we assume no estimates change in the meantime, what is the company's projected benefit obligation at the end of 2012 with respect to Stanley Mills?
6. What portion of the 2012 increase in the PBO is attributable to 2012 service (the service cost component of pension expense) and to accrued interest (the interest cost component of pension expense)?

E 17–13
Determining the
amortization of net
loss or net gain
● LO6

Hicks Cable Company has a defined benefit pension plan. Three alternative possibilities for pension-related data at January 1, 2011, are shown below:

	($ in 000s)		
	Case 1	**Case 2**	**Case 3**
Net loss (gain)–AOCI, Jan. 1	$ 320	$ (330)	$ 260
2011 loss (gain) on plan assets	(11)	(8)	2
2011 loss (gain) on PBO	(23)	16	(265)
Accumulated benefit obligation, Jan. 1	(2,950)	(2,550)	(1,450)
Projected benefit obligation, Jan. 1	(3,310)	(2,670)	(1,700)
Fair value of plan assets, Jan. 1	2,800	2,700	1,550
Average remaining service period of active employees (years)	12	15	10

Required:

1. For each independent case, calculate any amortization of the net loss or gain that should be included as a component of pension expense for 2011.
2. For each independent case, determine the net loss–AOCI or net gain–AOCI as of January 1, 2012.

E 17–14
Effect of
pension expense
components on
balance sheet
accounts
● LO7 LO8

e**X**cel

Warrick Boards calculated pension expense for its underfunded pension plan as follows:

	($ in 000s)
Service cost	$224
Interest cost	150
Expected return on the plan assets ($100 actual, less $10 gain)	(90)
Amortization of prior service cost	8
Amortization of net loss	2
Pension expense	$294

Required:

Which elements of Warrick's balance sheet are affected by the components of pension expense? What are the specific changes in these accounts?

E 17–15
Pension
spreadsheet
● LO8

A partially completed pension spreadsheet showing the relationships among the elements that comprise the defined benefit pension plan of Universal Products is given below. The actuary's discount rate is 5%. At the end of 2009, the pension formula was amended, creating a prior service cost of $120,000. The expected rate of return on assets was 8%, and the average remaining service life of the active employee group is 20 years in the current year as well as the previous two years.

Required:

Copy the incomplete spreadsheet and fill in the missing amounts.

( )s indicate credits; debits otherwise ($ in 000s)	PBO	Plan Assets	Prior Service Cost	Net Loss	Pension Expense	Cash	Net Pension (Liability)/ Asset
Balance, Jan. 1, 2011	(800)	600	114	80			(200)
Service cost					84		
Interest cost, 5%	(40)						
Expected return on assets					(48)		
Adjust for:							
Loss on assets				6			
Amortization: Prior service cost							
Amortization: Net loss							
Gain on PBO							12
Prior service cost	0						
Cash funding						(68)	
Retiree benefits							
Balance, Dec. 31, 2011	(862)		108				

E 17–16
Determine and
record pension
expense and gains
and losses; funding
and retiree benefits
● LO6 LO7

Actuary and trustee reports indicate the following changes in the PBO and plan assets of Douglas-Roberts Industries during 2011:

Prior service cost at Jan. 1, 2011, from plan amendment at the beginning of 2008 (amortization: $4 million per year)	$28 million
Net loss–AOCI at Jan.1, 2011 (previous losses exceeded previous gains)	$80 million
Average remaining service life of the active employee group	10 years
Actuary's discount rate	7%

($ in millions) PBO			Plan Assets
Beginning of 2011	$600	Beginning of 2011	$400
Service cost	80	Return on plan assets,	
Interest cost, 7%	42	8% (10% expected)	32
Loss (gain) on PBO	(14)	Cash contributions	90
Less: Retiree benefits	(38)	Less: Retiree benefits	(38)
End of 2011	$670	End of 2011	$484

Required:

1. Determine Douglas-Roberts' pension expense for 2011 and prepare the appropriate journal entries to record the expense.
2. Prepare the appropriate journal entry(s) to record any 2011 gains and losses.
3. Prepare the appropriate journal entry to record the cash contribution to plan assets.
4. Prepare the appropriate journal entry to record retiree benefits.

E 17–17
Concepts;
terminology
● LO2 through
LO8

Listed below are several terms and phrases associated with pensions. Pair each item from List A with the item from List B (by letter) that is most appropriately associated with it.

List A	List B
_____ 1. Future compensation levels estimated.	a. Actual return exceeds expected
_____ 2. All funding provided by the employer.	b. Net gain–AOCI
_____ 3. Credit to OCI and debit to plan assets.	c. Vested benefit obligation
_____ 4. Retirement benefits specified by formula.	d. Projected benefit obligation
_____ 5. Trade-off between relevance and reliability.	e. Choice between PBO and ABO

(continued)

(concluded)

_____ 6. Cumulative gains in excess of losses.
_____ 7. Current pay levels implicitly assumed.
_____ 8. Created by the passage of time.
_____ 9. Not contingent on future employment.
_____ 10. Risk borne by employee.
_____ 11. Increased by employer contributions.
_____ 12. Caused by plan amendment.
_____ 13. Loss on plan assets.
_____ 14. Excess over 10% of plan assets or PBO.

f. Noncontributory pension plan
g. Accumulated benefit obligation
h. Plan assets
i. Interest cost
j. Delayed recognition in earnings
k. Defined contribution plan
l. Defined benefit plan
m. Prior service cost
n. Amortize net loss–AOCI

E 17–18
IFRS; actuarial
gains and losses
● LO7 LO12

Patel Industries has a noncontributory, defined benefit pension plan. Since the inception of the plan, the actuary's discount rate has been 7%. During 2011, changing economic conditions caused the actuary to reassess the applicable discount rate. It was decided that 6% is the appropriate rate.

Required:

1. Does the change in discount rate create a gain or does it create a loss for Patel? Why?
2. Assume the magnitude of the change is $13 million. Prepare the appropriate journal entry to record any 2011 gain or loss. If Patel prepares its financial statements according to U.S. GAAP, how will the company report the gain or loss?
3. Would your response to requirement 2 differ if Patel prepares its financial statements according to International Financial Reporting Standards?

E 17–19
Record pension
expense, funding,
and gains and
losses; determine
account balances
● LO6 LO7 LO8

Beale Management has a noncontributory, defined benefit pension plan. On December 31, 2011 (the end of Beale's fiscal year), the following pension-related data were available:

Projected Benefit Obligation	($ in millions)
Balance, January 1, 2011	$480
Service cost	82
Interest cost, discount rate, 5%	24
Gain due to changes in actuarial assumptions in 2011	(10)
Pension benefits paid	(40)
Balance, December 31, 2011	$536
Plan Assets	
Balance, January 1, 2011	$500
Actual return on plan assets	40
(Expected return on plan assets, $45)	
Cash contributions	70
Pension benefits paid	(40)
Balance, December 31, 2011	$570
January 1, 2011, balances:	
Pension asset	$ 20
Prior service cost–AOCI (amortization $8 per year)	48
Net gain–AOCI (any amortization over 15 years)	80

Required:

1. Prepare the 2011 journal entry to record pension expense.
2. Prepare the journal entry(s) to record any 2011 gains and losses.
3. Prepare the 2011 journal entries to record the contribution to plan assets and benefit payments to retirees.
4. Determine the balances at December 31, 2011, in the PBO, plan assets, the net gain–AOCI, and prior service cost–AOCI and show how the balances changed during 2011. [Hint: You might find T-accounts useful.]
5. What amount will Beale report in its 2011 balance sheet as a net pension asset or net pension liability for the funded status of the plan?

E 17–20
Pension
spreadsheet
● LO8

Refer to the data provided in Exercise 17–19.

Required:

Prepare a pension spreadsheet to show the relationship among the PBO, plan assets, prior service cost, the net gain, pension expense, and the net pension asset.

E 17–21
Determine pension expense; prior service cost
● LO6 LO7

Lacy Construction has a noncontributory, defined benefit pension plan. At December 31, 2011, Lacy received the following information:

Projected Benefit Obligation	($ in millions)
Balance, January 1	$360
Service cost	60
Interest cost	36
Benefits paid	(27)
Balance, December 31	$429

Plan Assets	
Balance, January 1	$240
Actual return on plan assets	27
Contributions 2011	60
Benefits paid	(27)
Balance, December 31	$300

The expected long-term rate of return on plan assets was 10%. There were no AOCI balances related to pensions on January 1, 2011. At the end of 2011, Lacy amended the pension formula creating a prior service cost of $12 million, one-third of which is related to employees whose pension benefits have vested.

Required:

1. Determine Lacy's pension expense for 2011.
2. Prepare the journal entry(s) to record Lacy's pension expense, gains or losses, prior service cost, funding, and payment of retiree benefits for 2011.

E 17–22
IFRS; prior service cost
● LO7 LO12

Refer to the situation described in Exercise 17–21.

Required:

How might your solution differ if Lacy Construction prepares its financial statements according to International Accounting Standards? Include any appropriate journal entries in your response.

E 17–23
Classifying accounting changes and errors
● LO8

Indicate with the appropriate letter the nature of each adjustment described below:

Type of Adjustment
A. Change in principle
B. Change in estimate
C. Correction of an error
D. Neither an accounting change nor an error

_____ 1. Change in actuarial assumptions for a defined benefit pension plan.

_____ 2. Determination that the projected benefit obligation under a pension plan exceeded the fair value of plan assets at the end of the previous year by $17,000. The only pension-related amount on the balance sheet was a net pension liability of $30,000.

_____ 3. Pension plan assets for a defined benefit pension plan achieving a rate of return in excess of the amount anticipated.

_____ 4. Instituting a pension plan for the first time and adopting GAAP for employers' accounting for defined benefit pension and other postretirement plans.

E 17–24
Postretirement benefits; determine APBO, EPBO
● LO10

Classified Electronics has an unfunded retiree health care plan. Each of the company's three employees has been with the firm since its inception at the beginning of 2010. As of the end of 2011, the actuary estimates the total net cost of providing health care benefits to employees during their retirement years to have a present value of $72,000. Each of the employees will become fully eligible for benefits after 28 more years of service but aren't expected to retire for 35 more years. The interest rate is 6%.

Required:

1. What is the expected postretirement benefit obligation at the end of 2011?
2. What is the accumulated postretirement benefit obligation at the end of 2011?
3. What is the expected postretirement benefit obligation at the end of 2012?
4. What is the accumulated postretirement benefit obligation at the end of 2012?

E 17–25
Postretirement
benefits; determine
APBO, service
cost, interest cost;
prepare journal
entry
● LO10 LO11

The following data are available pertaining to Household Appliance Company's retiree health care plan for 2011:

Number of employees covered	2
Years employed as of January 1, 2011	3 [each]
Attribution period	25 years
Expected postretirement benefit obligation, Jan. 1	$50,000
Expected postretirement benefit obligation, Dec. 31	$53,000
Interest rate	6%
Funding	none

Required:
1. What is the accumulated postretirement benefit obligation at the beginning of 2011?
2. What is interest cost to be included in 2011 postretirement benefit expense?
3. What is service cost to be included in 2011 postretirement benefit expense?
4. Prepare the journal entry to record the postretirement benefit expense for 2011.

E 17–26
Postretirement
benefits; determine
EPBO; attribution
period
● LO10 LO11

Lorin Management Services has an unfunded postretirement benefit plan. On December 31, 2011, the following data were available concerning changes in the plan's accumulated postretirement benefit obligation with respect to one of Lorin's employees:

APBO at the beginning of 2011	$16,364
Interest cost: ($16,364 × 10%)	1,636
Service cost: ($44,000 × 1/22)	2,000
Portion of EPBO attributed to 2011	
APBO at the end of 2011	$20,000

Required:
1. Over how many years is the expected postretirement benefit obligation being expensed (attribution period)?
2. What is the expected postretirement benefit obligation at the *end* of 2011?
3. When was the employee hired by Lorin?
4. What is the expected postretirement benefit obligation at the *beginning* of 2011?

E 17–27
Postretirement
benefits;
components of
postretirement
benefit expense
● LO11

Data pertaining to the postretirement health care benefit plan of Sterling Properties include the following for 2011:

	($ in 000s)
Service cost	$124
Accumulated postretirement benefit obligation, January 1	700
Plan assets (fair market value), January 1	50
Prior service cost–AOCI	none
Net gain–AOCI (2011 amortization, $1)	91
Retiree benefits paid (end of year)	87
Contribution to health care benefit fund (end of year)	185
Discount rate, 7%	
Return on plan assets (actual and expected), 10%	

Required:
1. Determine the postretirement benefit expense for 2011.
2. Prepare the appropriate journal entries to record the postretirement benefit expense, funding, and retiree benefits for 2011.

E 17–28
Postretirement benefits; amortization of net loss
● LO11

Cahal-Michael Company has a postretirement health care benefit plan. On January 1, 2011, the following plan-related data were available:

	($ in 000s)
Net loss–AOCI	$ 336
Accumulated postretirement benefit obligation	2,800
Fair value of plan assets	500
Average remaining service period to retirement	14 years (same in previous 10 yrs.)

The rate of return on plan assets during 2011 was 10%, although it was expected to be 9%. The actuary revised assumptions regarding the APBO at the end of the year, resulting in a $39,000 increase in the estimate of that obligation.

Required:

1. Calculate any amortization of the net loss that should be included as a component of postretirement benefit expense for 2011.

2. Assume the postretirement benefit expense for 2011, not including the amortization of the net loss component, is $212,000. What is the expense for the year?

3. Determine the net loss or gain as of December 31, 2011.

E 17–29
Postretirement benefits; determine and record expense
● LO11

Gorky-Park Corporation provides postretirement health care benefits to employees who provide at least 12 years of service and reach age 62 while in service. On January 1, 2011, the following plan-related data were available:

	($ in millions)
Accumulated postretirement benefit obligation	$130
Fair value of plan assets	none
Average remaining service period to retirement	25 years (same in previous 10 yrs.)
Average remaining service period to full eligibility	20 years (same in previous 10 yrs.)

On January 1, 2011, Gorky-Park amends the plan to provide certain dental benefits in addition to previously provided medical benefits. The actuary determines that the cost of making the amendment retroactive increases the APBO by $20 million. Management chooses to amortize the prior service cost on a straight-line basis. The service cost for 2011 is $34 million. The interest rate is 8%.

Required:

1. Calculate the postretirement benefit expense for 2011.

2. Prepare the journal entry to record the expense.

E 17–30
Postretirement benefits; negative plan amendment
● LO11

Southeast Technology provides postretirement health care benefits to employees. On January 1, 2011, the following plan-related data were available:

	($ in 000s)
Prior service cost—originated in 2006	$ 50
Accumulated postretirement benefit obligation	530
Fair value of plan assets	none
Average remaining service period to retirement	20 years (same in previous 10 yrs.)
Average remaining service period to full eligibility	15 years (same in previous 10 yrs.)

On January 1, 2011, Southeast amends the plan in response to spiraling health care costs. The amendment establishes an annual maximum of $3,000 for medical benefits that the plan will provide. The actuary determines that the effect of this amendment is to decrease the APBO by $80,000. Management amortizes prior service cost on a straight-line basis. The interest rate is 8%. The service cost for 2011 is $114,000.

Required:

1. Calculate the prior service cost amortization for 2011.

2. Calculate the postretirement benefit expense for 2011.

E 17–31
Prior service cost; service method; straight-line method (Based on Appendix)

Frazier Refrigeration amended its defined benefit pension plan on December 31, 2011, to increase retirement benefits earned with each service year. The consulting actuary estimated the prior service cost incurred by making the amendment retroactive to prior years to be $110,000. Frazier's 100 present employees are expected to retire at the rate of approximately 10 each year at the end of each of the next 10 years.

Required:

1. Using the service method, calculate the amount of prior service cost to be amortized to pension expense in each of the next 10 years.

2. Using the straight-line method, calculate the amount of prior service cost to be amortized to pension expense in each of the next 10 years.

E 17–32
FASB codification research; postretirement benefit plan
● **LO11**

When a company sponsors a postretirement benefit plan other than a pension plan, benefits typically are not earned by employees on the basis of a formula, so assigning the service cost to specific periods is more difficult. The *FASB Accounting Standards Codification* represents the single source of authoritative U.S. generally accepted accounting principles.

Required:

1. Obtain the relevant authoritative literature on how a firm should attribute the expected postretirement benefit obligation to years of service using the FASB's Codification Research System at the FASB website (**www.fasb.org**). Find the specific citations that describe the guidelines for each of the following questions:
   a. What is the objective for attributing expected postretirement benefit obligations to years of service?
   b. When does the attribution period for expected postretirement benefits begin for an employee?
   c. When does the attribution period for expected postretirement benefits end for an employee?
2. What are the guidelines for each?

E 17–33
FASB codification research
● **LO1 LO2 LO5**

Access the FASB's Codification Research System at the FASB website (**www.fasb.org**). Determine the specific citation for accounting for each of the following items:
1. The disclosure required in the notes to the financial statements for pension plan assets.
2. Recognition of the net pension asset or net pension liability.
3. Disclosures required in the notes to the financial statements for pension cost for a defined contribution plan.

CPA AND CMA REVIEW QUESTIONS

CPA Exam Questions

The following questions are used in the Kaplan CPA Review Course to study pensions and other postretirement benefits while preparing for the CPA examination. Determine the response that best completes the statements or questions.

● **LO5**

1. Wolf Inc. began a defined benefit pension plan for its employees on January 1, 2011. The following data are provided for 2011 as of December 31, 2011:

Projected benefit obligation	$385,000
Accumulated benefit obligation	340,000
Plan assets at fair value	255,000
Pension expense	95,000
Employer's cash contribution (end of year)	255,000

What amount should Wolf report as a net pension liability at December 31, 2011?
   a. $ 0
   b. $ 45,000
   c. $ 85,000
   d. $130,000

● **LO7**

2. A statement of comprehensive income for a company with a defined benefit pension plan does *not* include
   a. net income.
   b. the return on plan assets.
   c. gains from the return on assets exceeding expectations.
   d. losses from changes in estimates regarding the pension obligation.

● **LO8**

3. JWS Corporation has a defined benefit pension plan. JWS reported a net pension liability in last year's balance sheet. This year, the company revised its estimate of future salary levels causing its projected benefit obligation estimate to decline by $8. Also, the $16 million actual return on plan assets was less than the $18 million expected return. As a result
   a. the net pension liability will decrease by $8 million.
   b. the statement of comprehensive income will report a $2 million gain and an $8 million loss.
   c. the net pension liability will increase by $6 million.
   d. accumulated other comprehensive income will increase by $6 million.

● LO8   4. Amortizing a net gain for pensions and other postretirement benefit plans will
   a. decrease retained earnings and decrease accumulated other comprehensive income.
   b. increase retained earnings and increase accumulated other comprehensive income.
   c. decrease retained earnings and increase accumulated other comprehensive income.
   d. increase retained earnings and decrease accumulated other comprehensive income.

● LO11   5. At December 31, 2010, Johnston and Johnston reported in its balance sheet as part of accumulated other comprehensive income a net loss of $37 million related to its postretirement benefit plan. The actuary for J&J increased her estimate of J&J's future health care costs at the end of 2011. J&J's entry to record the effect of this change will include
   a. a debit to other comprehensive income and a credit to postretirement benefit liability.
   b. a debit to postretirement benefit liability and a credit to other comprehensive income.
   c. a debit to pension expense and a credit to postretirement benefit liability.
   d. a debit to pension expense and a credit to other comprehensive income.

CMA Exam Questions

The following questions dealing with pensions and other postretirement benefits are adapted from questions that previously appeared on Certified Management Accountant (CMA) examinations. The CMA designation sponsored by the Institute of Management Accountants (**www.imanet.org**) provides members with an objective measure of knowledge and competence in the field of management accounting. Determine the response that best completes the statements or questions.

● LO3   1. The projected benefit obligation (PBO) is best described as the
   a. Present value of benefits accrued to date based on future salary levels.
   b. Present value of benefits accrued to date based on current salary levels.
   c. Increase in retroactive benefits at the date of the amendment of the plan.
   d. Amount of the adjustment necessary to reflect the difference between actual and estimated actuarial returns.

● LO6   2. On November 30, the Board of Directors of Baldwin Corporation amended its pension plan giving retroactive benefits to its employees. The information below is provided at November 30.

Accumulated benefit obligation (ABO)	$825,000
Projected benefit obligation (PBO)	900,000
Plan assets (fair value)	307,500
Market-related asset value	301,150
Prior service cost	190,000
Average remaining service life of employees	10 years
Useful life of pension goodwill	20 years

Using the straight-line method of amortization, the amount of prior service cost charged to expense during the year ended November 30 is
   a. $9,500
   b. $19,000
   c. $30,250
   d. $190,000

PROBLEMS

An alternate exercise and problem set is available on the text website: **www.mhhe.com/spiceland6e**

(Note: Problems 1–5 are variations of the same situation, designed to focus on different elements of the pension plan.)

P 17–1
ABO calculations; present value concepts
● LO2 LO3

Sachs Brands' defined benefit pension plan specifies annual retirement benefits equal to: 1.6% × service years × final year's salary, payable at the end of each year. Angela Davenport was hired by Sachs at the beginning of 1997 and is expected to retire at the end of 2031 after 35 years' service. Her retirement is expected to span 18 years. Davenport's salary is $90,000 at the end of 2011 and the company's actuary projects her salary to be $240,000 at retirement. The actuary's discount rate is 7%.

Required:
1. Draw a time line that depicts Davenport's expected service period, retirement period, and a 2011 measurement date for the pension obligation.
2. Estimate by the accumulated benefits approach the amount of Davenport's annual retirement payments earned as of the end of 2011.

3. What is the company's accumulated benefit obligation at the end of 2011 with respect to Davenport?

4. If no estimates are changed in the meantime, what will be the accumulated benefit obligation at the end of 2014 (three years later) when Davenport's salary is $100,000?

P 17–2
PBO calculations;
present value
concepts
● LO3

Sachs Brands' defined benefit pension plan specifies annual retirement benefits equal to: 1.6% × service years × final year's salary, payable at the end of each year. Angela Davenport was hired by Sachs at the beginning of 1997 and is expected to retire at the end of 2031 after 35 years' service. Her retirement is expected to span 18 years. Davenport's salary is $90,000 at the end of 2011 and the company's actuary projects her salary to be $240,000 at retirement. The actuary's discount rate is 7%.

Required:

1. Draw a time line that depicts Davenport's expected service period, retirement period, and a 2011 measurement date for the pension obligation.

2. Estimate by the projected benefits approach the amount of Davenport's annual retirement payments earned as of the end of 2011.

3. What is the company's projected benefit obligation at the end of 2011 with respect to Davenport?

4. If no estimates are changed in the meantime, what will be the company's projected benefit obligation at the end of 2014 (three years later) with respect to Davenport?

P 17–3
Service cost,
interest, and PBO
calculations;
present value
concepts
● LO3

Sachs Brands' defined benefit pension plan specifies annual retirement benefits equal to: 1.6% × service years × final year's salary, payable at the end of each year. Angela Davenport was hired by Sachs at the beginning of 1997 and is expected to retire at the end of 2031 after 35 years' service. Her retirement is expected to span 18 years. Davenport's salary is $90,000 at the end of 2011 and the company's actuary projects her salary to be $240,000 at retirement. The actuary's discount rate is 7%.

Required:

1. What is the company's projected benefit obligation at the beginning of 2011 (after 14 years' service) with respect to Davenport?

2. Estimate by the projected benefits approach the portion of Davenport's annual retirement payments attributable to 2011 service.

3. What is the company's service cost for 2011 with respect to Davenport?

4. What is the company's interest cost for 2011 with respect to Davenport?

5. Combine your answers to requirements 1, 3, and 4 to determine the company's projected benefit obligation at the end of 2011 (after 15 years' service) with respect to Davenport.

P 17–4
Prior service cost;
components of
pension expense;
present value
concepts
● LO3 LO6

Sachs Brands' defined benefit pension plan specifies annual retirement benefits equal to: 1.6% × service years × final year's salary, payable at the end of each year. Angela Davenport was hired by Sachs at the beginning of 1997 and is expected to retire at the end of 2031 after 35 years' service. Her retirement is expected to span 18 years. Davenport's salary is $90,000 at the end of 2011 and the company's actuary projects her salary to be $240,000 at retirement. The actuary's discount rate is 7%.

At the beginning of 2012, the pension formula was amended to:

$$1.75\% \times \text{Service years} \times \text{Final year's salary}$$

The amendment was made retroactive to apply the increased benefits to prior service years.

Required:

1. What is the company's prior service cost at the beginning of 2012 with respect to Davenport after the amendment described above?

2. Since the amendment occurred at the *beginning* of 2012, amortization of the prior service cost begins in 2012. What is the prior service cost amortization that would be included in pension expense?

3. What is the service cost for 2012 with respect to Davenport?

4. What is the interest cost for 2012 with respect to Davenport?

5. Calculate pension expense for 2012 with respect to Davenport, assuming plan assets attributable to her of $150,000 and a rate of return (actual and expected) of 10%.

P 17–5
Gain on PBO;
present value
concepts
● LO3 LO6

Sachs Brands' defined benefit pension plan specifies annual retirement benefits equal to: 1.6% × service years × final year's salary, payable at the end of each year. Angela Davenport was hired by Sachs at the beginning of 1997 and is expected to retire at the end of 2031 after 35 years' service. Her retirement is expected to span 18 years. Davenport's salary is $90,000 at the end of 2011 and the company's actuary projects her salary to be $240,000 at retirement. The actuary's discount rate is 7%.

At the beginning of 2012, changing economic conditions caused the actuary to reassess the applicable discount rate. It was decided that 8% is the appropriate rate.

Required:
Calculate the effect of the change in the assumed discount rate on the PBO at the beginning of 2012 with respect to Davenport.

P 17–6
Determine the PBO; plan assets; pension expense; two years
● LO3 LO4 LO6

Stanley-Morgan Industries adopted a defined benefit pension plan on April 12, 2011. The provisions of the plan were not made retroactive to prior years. A local bank, engaged as trustee for the plan assets, expects plan assets to earn a 10% rate of return. A consulting firm, engaged as actuary, recommends 6% as the appropriate discount rate. The service cost is $150,000 for 2011 and $200,000 for 2012. Year-end funding is $160,000 for 2011 and $170,000 for 2012. No assumptions or estimates were revised during 2011.

Required:
Calculate each of the following amounts as of both December 31, 2011, and December 31, 2012:
1. Projected benefit obligation
2. Plan assets
3. Pension expense
4. Net pension asset or net pension liability

P 17–7
Determining the amortization of net gain
● LO6

Herring Wholesale Company has a defined benefit pension plan. On January 1, 2011, the following pension-related data were available:

	($ in 000s)
Net gain–AOCI	$ 170
Accumulated benefit obligation	1,170
Projected benefit obligation	1,400
Fair value of plan assets	1,100
Average remaining service period of active employees (expected to remain constant for the next several years)	15 years

The rate of return on plan assets during 2011 was 9%, although it was expected to be 10%. The actuary revised assumptions regarding the PBO at the end of the year, resulting in a $23,000 decrease in the estimate of that obligation.

Required:
1. Calculate any amortization of the net gain that should be included as a component of net pension expense for 2011.
2. Assume the net pension expense for 2011, not including the amortization of the net gain component, is $325,000. What is pension expense for the year?
3. Determine the net loss—AOCI or net gain—AOCI as of January 1, 2012.

P 17–8
Pension spreadsheet; record pension expense and funding; new gains and losses
● LO7 LO8

A partially completed pension spreadsheet showing the relationships among the elements that constitute Carney, Inc.'s defined benefit pension plan follows. Six years earlier, Carney revised its pension formula and recalculated benefits earned by employees in prior years using the more generous formula. The prior service cost created by the recalculation is being amortized at the rate of $5 million per year. At the end of 2011, the pension formula was amended again, creating an additional prior service cost of $40 million. The expected rate of return on assets and the actuary's discount rate were 10%, and the average remaining service life of the active employee group is 10 years.

( )s indicate credits; debits otherwise ($ in millions)	PBO	Plan Assets	Prior Service Cost	Net Loss	Pension Expense	Cash	Net Pension (Liability) / Asset
Balance, Jan. 1, 2011	(830)	680	20	93			(150)
Service cost	?				74		?
Interest cost	?				?		?
Expected return on asset		?			?		?
Adjust for:							
Loss on assets		(7)		?			?
Amortization of:							
Prior service cost			?		?		
Net loss				?	?		
Loss on PBO	?			?			(13)
Prior service cost	?		?				?
Cash funding		?				?	84
Retiree benefits	?	?					
Balance, Dec. 31, 2011	?	775	?	?	?		?

Required:

1. Copy the incomplete spreadsheet and fill in the missing amounts.
2. Prepare the 2011 journal entry to record pension expense.
3. Prepare the journal entry(s) to record any 2011 gains and losses and new prior service cost in 2011.
4. Prepare the 2011 journal entries to record the cash contribution to plan assets and payment of retiree benefits.

P 17–9

Determine pension expense; PBO; plan assets; net pension asset or liability; journal entries

● LO3 through LO8

U.S. Metallurgical Inc. reported the following balances in its financial statements and disclosure notes at December 31, 2010.

Plan assets	$ 400,000
Projected benefit obligation	320,000

U.S.M.'s actuary determined that 2011 service cost is $60,000. Both the expected and actual rate of return on plan assets are 9%. The interest (discount) rate is 5%. U.S.M. contributed $120,000 to the pension fund at the end of 2011, and retirees were paid $44,000 from plan assets.

Required:
Determine the following amounts at the end of 2011.
1. Pension expense
2. Projected benefit obligation
3. Plan assets
4. Net pension asset or net pension liability
5. Prepare journal entries to record the pension expense, funding of plan assets, and retiree benefit payments.

P 17–10

Prior service cost; calculate pension expense; journal entries; determine net pension asset or liability

● LO5 through 7

Electronic Distribution has a defined benefit pension plan. Characteristics of the plan during 2011 are as follows:

	($ millions):
PBO balance, January 1	$480
Plan assets balance, January 1	300
Service cost	75
Interest cost	45
Gain from change in actuarial assumption	22
Benefits paid	(36)
Actual return on plan assets	20
Contributions 2011	60

The expected long-term rate of return on plan assets was 8%. There were no AOCI balances related to pensions on January 1, 2011, but at the end of 2011, the company amended the pension formula creating a prior service cost of $12 million, two-thirds of which is related to employees whose pension benefits have vested.

Required:
1. Calculate the pension expense for 2011.
2. Prepare the journal entry to record pension expense, gains or losses, prior service cost, funding, and payment of benefits for 2011.
3. What amount will Electronic Distribution report in its 2011 balance sheet as a net pension asset or net pension liability?

P 17–11

IFRS; calculate pension expense; journal entries; determine net pension asset or liability

● LO5 through 7
  LO12

Refer to the situation described in Problem 17–10. Assume Electronic Distribution prepares its financial statements according to International Accounting Standards.

Required:
1. Calculate the pension expense for 2011.
2. Prepare the journal entry to record pension expense, gains or losses, past service cost, funding, and payment of benefits for 2011.
3. What amount will Electronic Distribution report in its 2011 balance sheet as a net pension asset or net pension liability?

P 17–12

Determine pension expense; journal entries; two years

● LO3 through LO8

The Kollar Company has a defined benefit pension plan. Pension information concerning the fiscal years 2011 and 2012 are presented below ($ in millions):

Information Provided by Pension Plan Actuary:

a. Projected benefit obligation as of December 31, 2010 = $1,800.

b. Prior service cost from plan amendment on January 2, 2011 = $400 (straight-line amortization for 10-year average remaining service period).

c. Service cost for 2011 = $520.

d. Service cost for 2012 = $570.

e. Discount rate used by actuary on projected benefit obligation for 2011 and 2012 = 10%.

f. Payments to retirees in 2011 = $380.

g. Payments to retirees in 2012 = $450.

h. No changes in actuarial assumptions or estimates.

i. Net gain—AOCI on January 1, 2011 = $230.

j. Net gains and losses are amortized for 10 years in 2011 and 2012.

Information Provided by Pension Fund Trustee:

a. Plan asset balance at fair value on January 1, 2011 = $1,600.

b. 2011 contributions = $540.

c. 2012 contributions = $590.

d. Expected long-term rate of return on plan assets = 12%.

e. 2011 actual return on plan assets = $180.

f. 2012 actual return on plan assets = $210.

Required:

1. Calculate pension expense for 2011 and 2012.

2. Prepare the journal entries for 2011 and 2012 to record pension expense.

3. Prepare the journal entries for 2011 and 2012 to record any gains and losses and new prior service cost.

4. Prepare the journal entries for 2011 and 2012 to record the cash contribution to plan assets and benefit payments to retirees.

P 17–13

Determine the PBO, plan assets, pension expense; prior service cost

● LO3 LO4 LO6

Lewis Industries adopted a defined benefit pension plan on January 1, 2011. By making the provisions of the plan retroactive to prior years, Lewis incurred a prior service cost of $2 million. The prior service cost was funded immediately by a $2 million cash payment to the fund trustee on January 2, 2011. However, the cost is to be amortized (expensed) over 10 years. The service cost—$250,000 for 2011—is fully funded at the end of each year. Both the actuary's discount rate and the expected rate of return on plan assets were 9%. The actual rate of return on plan assets was 11%. At December 31, the trustee paid $16,000 to an employee who retired during 2011.

Required:

Determine each of the following amounts as of December 31, 2011, the fiscal year-end for Lewis:

1. Projected benefit obligation

2. Plan assets

3. Pension expense

P 17–14

Relationship among pension elements

● LO3 through LO8

The funded status of Hilton Paneling Inc.'s defined benefit pension plan and the balances in prior service cost and the net gain–pensions, are given below.

	($ in 000s)	
	2011 Beginning Balances	**2011 Ending Balances**
Projected benefit obligation	$2,300	$2,501
Plan assets	2,400	2,591
Funded status	100	90
Prior service cost–AOCI	325	300
Net gain–AOCI	330	300

Retirees were paid $270,000 and the employer contribution to the pension fund was $245,000 at the end of 2011. The expected rate of return on plan assets was 10%, and the actuary's discount rate is 7%. There were no changes in actuarial estimates and assumptions regarding the PBO.

Required:

Determine the following amounts for 2011:

1. Actual return on plan assets
2. Loss or gain on plan assets
3. Service cost
4. Pension expense
5. Average remaining service life of active employees (used to determine amortization of the net gain)

P 17–15

Comprehensive— pension elements; spreadsheet

● LO8

The following pension-related data pertain to Metro Recreation's noncontributory, defined benefit pension plan for 2011:

	($ in 000s)	
	Jan. 1	**Dec. 31**
Projected benefit obligation	$4,100	$4,380
Accumulated benefit obligation	3,715	3,950
Plan assets (fair value)	4,530	4,975
Interest (discount) rate, 7%		
Expected return on plan assets, 10%		
Prior service cost–AOCI (from Dec. 31, 2010, amendment)	840	
Net loss–AOCI	477	
Average remaining service life: 12 years		
Gain due to changes in actuarial assumptions		44
Contributions to pension fund (end of year)		340
Pension benefits paid (end of year)		295

Required:

Prepare a pension spreadsheet that shows the relationships among the various pension balances, shows the changes in those balances, and computes pension expense for 2011.

P 17–16

Comprehensive— reporting a pension plan; pension spreadsheet; determine changes in balances; two years

● LO3 through LO8

Actuary and trustee reports indicate the following changes in the PBO and plan assets of Lakeside Cable during 2011:

Prior service cost at Jan. 1, 2011, from plan amendment at the beginning of 2009 (amortization: $4 million per year)	$32 million
Net loss–pensions at Jan.1, 2011 (previous losses exceeded previous gains)	$40 million
Average remaining service life of the active employee group	10 years
Actuary's discount rate	8%

($ in millions)				Plan Assets
	PBO			
Beginning of 2011	$300	*Beginning* of 2011		$200
Service cost	48	Return on plan assets,		
Interest cost, 8%	24	7.5% (10% expected)		15
Loss (gain) on PBO	(2)	Cash contributions		45
Less: Retiree benefits	(20)	Less: Retiree benefits		(20)
End of 2011	$350	*End* of 2011		$240

Required:

1. Determine Lakeside's pension expense for 2011 and prepare the appropriate journal entries to record the expense as well as the cash contribution to plan assets and payment of benefits to retirees.
2. Determine the new gains and/or losses in 2011 and prepare the appropriate journal entry(s) to record them.
3. Prepare a pension spreadsheet to assist you in determining end of 2011 balances in the PBO, plan assets, prior service cost—AOCI, the net loss—AOCI, and the pension liability.

4. Assume the following actuary and trustee reports indicating changes in the PBO and plan assets of Lakeside Cable during 2012:

($ in millions)	PBO		Plan Assets
Beginning of 2012	$350	Beginning of 2012	$240
Service cost	38	Return on plan assets,	
Interest cost at 8%	28	15% (10% expected)	36
Loss (gain) on PBO	5	Cash contributions	30
Less: Retiree benefits	(16)	Less: Retiree benefits	(16)
End of 2012	$405	End of 2012	$290

Determine Lakeside's pension expense for 2012 and prepare the appropriate journal entries to record the expense, the cash funding of plan assets, and payment of benefits to retirees.

5. Determine the new gains and/or losses in 2012 and prepare the appropriate journal entry(s) to record them.

6. Using T-accounts, determine the balances at December 31, 2012, in the net loss–AOCI and prior service cost–AOCI.

7. Confirm the balances determined in Requirement 6 by preparing a pension spreadsheet.

P 17–17
Integrating Problem—Deferred tax effects of pension entries; integrate concepts learned in Chapter 16
● LO7

To focus on the core issues, we ignored the income tax effects of the pension amounts we recorded in the chapter. Reproduced below are the journal entries from the chapter that Global Communications used to record its pension expense and funding in 2011 and the new gain and loss that occurred that year.

	($ in millions)	
To Record Pension Expense		
Pension expense (total)	43	
Plan assets (expected return on plan assets)	27	
PBO ($41 service cost + $24 interest cost)		65
Amortization of prior service cost–OCI (2011 amortization)		4
Amortization of net loss–OCI (2011 amortization)		1
To Record Gains and Losses		
Loss–OCI (from change in assumption)	23	
PBO		23
Plan assets	3	
Gain–OCI (from actual return exceeding expected return)		3
To Record Funding and Payment of Benefits		
Plan assets	48	
Cash (contribution to plan assets)		48
PBO	38	
Plan assets (retiree benefits)		38

Required:

1. Recast these journal entries to include the income tax effects of the events being recorded. Assume that Global's tax rate is 40%. [Hint: Costs are incurred and recognized for financial reporting purposes now, but the tax impact comes much later—when these amounts are deducted for tax purposes as actual payments for retiree benefits occur in the future. As a result, the tax effects are deferred, creating the need to record deferred tax assets and deferred tax liabilities. So, you may want to refer back to Chapter 16 to refresh your memory on these concepts.]

2. Prepare a statement of comprehensive income for 2011 assuming Global's only other sources of comprehensive income were net income of $300 million and a $30 million unrealized holding gain on investments in securities available for sale.

P 17–18

Postretirement
benefits; EPBO
calculations;
APBO calculations;
components of
postretirement
benefit expense;
present value
concepts

● LO9 LO10

Century-Fox Corporation's employees are eligible for postretirement health care benefits after both being employed at the end of the year in which age 60 is attained and having worked 20 years. Jason Snyder was hired at the end of 1988 by Century-Fox at age 34 and is expected to retire at the end of 2016 (age 62). His retirement is expected to span five years (unrealistically short in order to simplify calculations). The company's actuary has estimated the net cost of retiree benefits in each retirement year as shown below. The discount rate is 6%. The plan is not prefunded.

Year	Expected Age	Net Cost
2017	63	$4,000
2018	64	4,400
2019	65	2,300
2020	66	2,500
2021	67	2,800

Assume costs are incurred at the end of each year.

Required:
1. Draw a time line that depicts Snyder's attribution period for retiree benefits and expected retirement period.
2. Calculate the present value of the net benefits as of the expected retirement date.
3. With respect to Snyder, what is the company's expected postretirement benefit obligation at the end of 2011?
4. With respect to Snyder, what is the company's accumulated postretirement benefit obligation at the end of 2011?
5. With respect to Snyder, what is the company's accumulated postretirement benefit obligation at the end of 2012?
6. What is the service cost to be included in 2012 postretirement benefit expense?
7. What is the interest cost to be included in 2012 postretirement benefit expense?
8. Show how the APBO changed during 2012 by reconciling the beginning and ending balances.

P 17–19

Postretirement
benefits; schedule
of postretirement
benefit costs

● LO9 through
LO11

Stockton Labeling Company has a retiree health care plan. Employees become fully eligible for benefits after working for the company eight years. Stockton hired Misty Newburn on January 1, 2011. As of the end of 2011, the actuary estimates the total net cost of providing health care benefits to Newburn during her retirement years to have a present value of $18,000. The actuary's discount rate is 10%.

Required:
Prepare a schedule that shows the EPBO, the APBO, the service cost, the interest cost, and the postretirement benefit expense for each of the years 2011–2018.

P 17–20

Postretirement
benefits;
relationship
among elements
of postretirement
benefit plan

● LO9 through
LO11

The information below pertains to the retiree health care plan of Thompson Technologies:

	($ in 000s)	
	2011 Beginning Balances	**2011 Ending Balances**
Accumulated postretirement benefit obligation	$460	$485
Plan assets	0	75
Funded status	(460)	(410)
Prior service cost–AOCI	120	110
Net gain–AOCI	(50)	(49)

Thompson began funding the plan in 2011 with a contribution of $127,000 to the benefit fund at the end of the year. Retirees were paid $52,000. The actuary's discount rate is 5%. There were no changes in actuarial estimates and assumptions.

Required:
Determine the following amounts for 2011:
1. Service cost.
2. Postretirement benefit expense.
3. Net postretirement benefit liability

P 17–21
Pension disclosure; amortization of actuarial gain or loss; Toys R Us, Inc.

● **LO3 through LO7**

Real World Financials

The **Toys R Us, Inc.**, is a leader in the retail toy industry. The following is an excerpt from a disclosure note in the company's annual report for the fiscal year ended January 31, 2009:

Note 14—Defined Benefit Pension Plans(in part)
($ in millions):

	Year Ended January 31,	
Change in projected benefit obligation:	**2009**	**2008**
Projected benefit obligation at beginning of year	$101	$ 91
Service cost	6	6
Interest cost	4	4
Employee contributions	1	1
Benefits, expenses paid	(2)	(3)
Actuarial gain	(11)	(1)
Foreign currency impact	(15)	3
Projected benefit obligation at end of year	$ 84	$101
Change in fair value of plan assets:		
Fair value of plan assets at beginning of year	$ 67	$ 59
Actual return on plan assets	(14)	(2)
Employer contributions	8	9
Employee contributions	1	1
Benefits, expenses paid	(2)	(3)
Foreign currency impact	(8)	3
Fair value of plan assets at end of year	$ 52	$ 67

Required:

1. What amount did Toys R Us report in its balance sheet related to the pension plan at January 31, 2009?

2. When calculating pension expense at January 31, 2009, what amount did Toys R Us include as the amortization of unrecognized net actuarial loss (net loss–AOCI), which was $20 million at the beginning of the year? The average remaining service life of employees was 10 years.

3. The expected return on plan assets was $2 million for the year ending January 31, 2009, and there was no unrecognized prior service cost. What was the pension expense?

4. What were the appropriate journal entries to record Toys R Us's pension expense and to record gains and/or losses related to the pension plan?

BROADEN YOUR PERSPECTIVE

Apply your critical-thinking ability to the knowledge you've gained. These cases will provide you an opportunity to develop your research, analysis, judgment, and communication skills. You also will work with other students, integrate what you've learned, apply it in real world situations, and consider its global and ethical ramifications. This practice will broaden your knowledge and further develop your decision-making abilities.

Judgment Case 17–1
Choose your retirement option

● **LO1 LO3 LO4 LO5**

"I only get one shot at this?" you wonder aloud. Mrs. Montgomery, human resources manager at Covington State University, has just explained that newly hired assistant professors must choose between two retirement plan options. "Yes, I'm afraid so," she concedes. "But you do have a week to decide."

Mrs. Montgomery's explanation was that your two alternatives are: (1) the state's defined benefit plan and (2) a defined contribution plan under which the university will contribute each year an amount equal to 8% of your salary. The defined benefit plan will provide annual retirement benefits determined by the following formula: 1.5% × years of service × salary at retirement.

"It's a good thing I studied pensions in my accounting program," you tell her. "Now let's see. You say the state is currently assuming our salaries will rise about 3% a year, and the interest rate they use in their calculations is 6%? And, for someone my age, you say they assume I'll retire after 40 years and draw retirement pay for 20 years. I'll do some research and get back to you."

Required:

1. You were hired at the beginning of 2011 at a salary of $100,000. If you choose the state's defined benefit plan and projections hold true, what will be your annual retirement pay? What is the present value of your retirement annuity as of the anticipated retirement date (end of 2050)?

2. Suppose instead that you choose the defined contribution plan. Assuming that the rate of increase in salary is the same as the state assumes and that the rate of return on your retirement plan assets will be 6% compounded annually, what will be the future value of your plan assets as of the anticipated retirement date (end of 2050)? What will be your annual retirement pay (assuming continuing investment of remaining assets at 6%)?

3. Based on this numerical comparison, which plan would you choose? What other factors must you also consider in making the choice?

Hint: The calculations are greatly simplified using an electronic spreadsheet such as Excel. There are many ways to set up the spreadsheet. One relatively easy way is to set up the first few rows with the formulas as shown below, then use the "fill down" function to fill in the remaining 38 rows, and use the Insert: Name: Define: function to name column B "n". Since contributions are assumed made at the end of each year, there are 39 years remaining to maturity at the end of 2011. Note that multiplying each contribution by $(1.06)^n$, where n equals the remaining number of years to retirement, calculates the future value of each contribution invested at 6% until retirement.

	A	B	C	D	E
1	End of	Years to			Future Value
2	Year:	Retirement	Salary	Contribution	at Retirement
3	2011	39	100,000	=C3*0.08	=D3*1.06^n
4	=A3+1	=B3−1	=C3*1.03	=C4*0.08	=D4*1.06^n

Communication Case 17–2

Pension concepts

● LO2 through LO8

Noel Zoeller is the newly hired assistant controller of Kemp Industries, a regional supplier of hardwood derivative products. The company sponsors a defined benefit pension plan that covers its 420 employees. On reviewing last year's financial statements, Zoeller was concerned about some items reported in the disclosure notes relating to the pension plan. Portions of the relevant note follow:

Note 8: Pensions

The company has a defined benefit pension plan covering substantially all of its employees. Pension benefits are based on employee service years and the employee's compensation during the last two years of employment. The company contributes annually the maximum amount permitted by the federal tax code. Plan contributions provide for benefits expected to be earned in the future as well as those earned to date. The following reconciles the plan's funded status and amount recognized in the balance sheet at December 31, 2011 ($ in 000s).

Actuarial Present Value Benefit Obligations:

Accumulated benefit obligation (including vested benefits of $318)	$(1,305)
Projected benefit obligation	(1,800)
Plan assets at fair value	1,575
Projected benefit obligation in excess of plan assets	$ (225)

Kemp's comparative income statements reported net periodic pension expense of $108,000 in 2011 and $86,520 in 2010. Since employment has remained fairly constant in recent years, Zoeller expressed concern over the increase in the pension expense. He expressed his concern to you, a three-year senior accountant at Kemp. "I'm also interested in the differences in these liability measurements," he mentioned.

Required:

Write a memo to Zoeller. In the memo:

1. Explain to Zoeller how the composition of the net periodic pension expense can create the situation he sees. Briefly describe the components of pension expense.

2. Briefly explain how pension gains and losses are recognized in earnings.

3. Describe for him the differences and similarities between the accumulated benefit obligation and the projected benefit obligation.

4. Explain how the "Projected benefit obligation in excess of plan assets" is reported in the financial statements.

**Judgment
Case 17–3**
Barlow's wife;
relationship among
pension elements
● LO8

LGD Consulting is a medium-sized provider of environmental engineering services. The corporation sponsors a noncontributory, defined benefit pension plan. Alan Barlow, a new employee and participant in the pension plan, obtained a copy of the 2011 financial statements, partly to obtain additional information about his new employer's obligation under the plan. In part, the pension footnote reads as follows:

Note 8: Retirement Benefits

The Company has a defined benefit pension plan covering substantially all of its employees. The benefits are based on years of service and the employee's compensation during the last two years of employment. The company's funding policy is consistent with the funding requirements of federal law and regulations. Generally, pension costs accrued are funded. Plan assets consist primarily of stocks, bonds, commingled trust funds, and cash.

The change in projected benefit obligation for the plan years ended December 31, 2011, and December 31, 2010:

($ in 000s)	2011	2010
Projected benefit obligation at beginning of year	$3,786	$3,715
Service cost	103	94
Interest cost	287	284
Actuarial (gain) loss	302	(23)
Benefits paid	(324)	(284)
Projected benefit obligation at end of year	$4,154	$3,786

The weighted average discount rate and rate of increase in future compensation levels used in determining the actuarial present value of the projected benefit obligations in the above table were 7.0% and 4.3%, respectively, at December 31, 2011, and 7.75% and 4.7%, respectively, at December 31, 2010. The expected long-term rate of return on assets was 10.0% at December 31, 2011 and 2010.

The change in the fair value of plan assets for the plan years ended December 31, 2011 and 2010:

($ in 000s)	2011	2010
Fair value of plan assets at beginning of year	$3,756	$3,616
Actual return on plan assets	1,100	372
Employer contributions	27	52
Benefits paid	(324)	(284)
Fair value of plan assets at end of year	$4,559	$3,756

Included in the Consolidated Balance Sheets are the following components of accumulated other comprehensive income:

($ in 000s)	2011	2010
Net actuarial gain	$(620)	$(165)
Prior service cost	44	46

Net periodic defined benefit pension cost for fiscal 2011, 2010, and 2009 included the following components:

($ in 000s)	2011	2010	2009
Service cost	$ 103	$ 94	$ 112
Interest cost	287	284	263
Expected return on plan assets	(342)	(326)	(296)
Amortization of prior service cost	2	2	1
Recognized net actuarial (gain) loss	(2)	2	4
Net periodic pension cost	$ 48	$ 56	$ 84

In attempting to reconcile amounts reported in the footnote with amounts reported in the income statement and balance sheet, Barlow became confused. He was able to find the pension expense on the income statement but was unable to make sense of the balance sheet amounts. Expressing his frustration to his wife, Barlow said, "It appears to me that the company has calculated pension expense as if they have the pension liability and pension assets they include in the footnote, but I can't seem to find those amounts in the balance sheet. In fact, there are several amounts here I can't seem to account for. They also say they've made some assumptions about interest rates, pay increases, and profits on invested assets. I wonder what difference it would make if they assumed other numbers,"

Barlow's wife took accounting courses in college and remembers most of what she learned about pension accounting. She attempts to clear up her husband's confusion.

Required:

Assume the role of Barlow's wife. Answer the following questions for your husband.

1. Is Barlow's observation correct that the company has calculated pension expense on the basis of amounts not reported in the balance sheet?
2. What amount would the company report as a pension liability in the balance sheet?
3. What amount would the company report as a pension asset in the balance sheet?
4. Which of the other amounts reported in the disclosure note would the company report in the balance sheet?
5. The disclosure note reports a net actuarial gain as well as an actuarial loss. How are these related? What do the amounts mean?
6. Which components of the pension expense represent deferred recognition? Where are these deferred amounts reported prior to amortization?

Communication Case 17–4
Barlow's wife; relationship among pension elements
● LO8

The focus of this case is question 1 in the previous case. Your instructor will divide the class into two to six groups, depending on the size of the class. The mission of your group is to assess the correctness of Barlow's observation and to suggest the appropriate treatment of the pension obligation. The suggested treatment need not be that required by GAAP.

Required:

1. Each group member should deliberate the situation independently and draft a tentative argument prior to the class session for which the case is assigned.
2. In class, each group will meet for 10 to 15 minutes in different areas of the classroom. During that meeting, group members will take turns sharing their suggestions for the purpose of arriving at a single group treatment.
3. After the allotted time, a spokesperson for each group (selected during the group meetings) will share the group's solution with the class. The goal of the class is to incorporate the views of each group into a consensus approach to the situation.

Real World Case 17–5
Types of pension plans; disclosures
● LO1

Real World Financials

Refer to the financial statements and related disclosure notes of **Dell Inc.** located in the company's financial statements and related disclosure notes in Appendix B located at the back of the text. The financial statements also can be found at the company's website: **www.dell.com** or via EDGAR at **www.sec.gov**.

Required:

1. What type of pension plan does Dell sponsor for its employees? Explain.
2. Who bears the "risk" of factors that might reduce retirement benefits in this type of plan? Explain.
3. Suppose a Dell employee contributes $10,000 to the pension plan during her first year of employment and directs investments to a municipal bond mutual fund. If she leaves Dell early in her second year, after the mutual fund's value has increased by 2%, how much will she be entitled to roll over into an Individual Retirement Account (IRA)?
4. How did Dell account for its participation in the pension plan in fiscal 2009?

Ethics Case 17–6
401(k) plan contributions
● LO1

You are in your third year as internal auditor with VXI International, manufacturer of parts and supplies for jet aircraft. VXI began a defined contribution pension plan three years ago. The plan is a so-called 401(k) plan (named after the Tax Code section that specifies the conditions for the favorable tax treatment of these plans) that permits voluntary contributions by employees. Employees' contributions are matched with one dollar of employer contribution for every two dollars of employee contribution. Approximately $500,000 of contributions is deducted from employee paychecks each month for investment in one of three employer-sponsored mutual funds.

While performing some preliminary audit tests, you happen to notice that employee contributions to these plans usually do not show up on mutual fund statements for up to two months following the end of pay periods from which the deductions are drawn. On further investigation, you discover that when the plan was first begun, contributions were invested within one week of receipt of the funds. When you question the firm's investment manager about the apparent change in the timing of investments, you are told, "Last year Mr. Maxwell (the CFO) directed me to initially deposit the contributions in the corporate investment account. At the close of each quarter, we add the employer matching contribution and deposit the combined amount in specific employee mutual funds."

Required:

1. What is Mr. Maxwell's apparent motivation for the change in the way contributions are handled?
2. Do you perceive an ethical dilemma?

Research Case 17–7
Codification research; researching pension disclosures; retrieving information from the Internet
● LO1 LO3 LO4

All publicly traded domestic companies use EDGAR, the Electronic Data Gathering, Analysis, and Retrieval system, to make the majority of their filings with the SEC. You can access EDGAR on the Internet at **www.sec.gov.**

Required:

1. Search for a company with which you are familiar and which you believe is likely to have a pension plan. (Older, established firms are good candidates.) Access the company's most recent 10-K filing. Search or scroll to find the financial statements and related notes.

2. From the disclosure notes, determine the type of pension plan(s) the company has.

3. For any defined contribution plans, determine the contributions the company made to the plans on behalf of employees during the most recent three years.

4. For any defined benefit plans, what interest (discount) rate was used in estimating the PBO? Access the FASB's Codification Research System at the FASB website (**www.fasb.org**). Determine the specific citation for accounting for the requirement to disclose the discount rate used to estimate the PBO.

5. Repeat steps 2 through 4 for a second firm. Compare and contrast the types of pension plans offered. Are actuarial assumptions the same for defined benefit plans?

Real World Case 17–8
Types of pension plans; reporting postretirement plans; disclosures
● LO5 LO8

Real World Financials

Refer to the most recent financial statements and related disclosure notes of **FedEx Corporation.** The financial statements can be found at the company's website: **www.fedex.com** or via EDGAR at **www.sec.gov.**

Required:

1. What pension and other postretirement benefit plans does FedEx sponsor for its employees? Explain.

2. What amount does FedEx report in its balance sheet for its pension and other postretirement benefit plans? Explain.

3. FedEx reports three actuarial assumptions used in its pension calculations. Did reported changes in those assumptions from the previous year increase or decrease the projected benefit obligation? Why?

Real World Case 17–9
Pension amendment
● LO5 LO8

Real World Financials

Charles Rubin is a 30-year employee of **General Motors.** Charles was pleased with recent negotiations between his employer and the United Auto Workers. Among other favorable provisions of the new agreement, the pact also includes a 13% increase in pension payments for workers under 62 with 30 years of service who retire during the agreement. Although the elimination of a cap on outside income earned by retirees has been generally viewed as an incentive for older workers to retire, Charles sees promise for his dream of becoming a part-time engineering consultant after retirement. What has caught Charles's attention is the following excerpt from an article in the financial press:

> **General Motors Corp.** will record a $170 million charge due to increases in retirement benefits for hourly United Auto Workers employees.
>
> The charge stems from GM's new tentative labor contract with the UAW. According to a filing with the Securities and Exchange Commission, the charge amounts to 22 cents a share and is tied to the earnings of GM's Hughes Electronics unit.
>
> The company warned that its "unfunded pension obligation and pension expense are expected to be unfavorably impacted as a result of the recently completed labor negotiations."

Taking advantage of an employee stock purchase plan, Charles has become an active GM stockholder as well as employee. His stockholder side is moderately concerned by the article's reference to the unfavorable impact of the recently completed labor negotiations.

Required:

1. When a company modifies its pension benefits the way General Motors did, what name do we give the added cost? How is it accounted for?

2. What does GM mean when it says its "unfunded pension obligation and pension expense are expected to be unfavorably impacted as a result of the recently completed labor negotiations"?

Analysis Case 17–10
Effect of pensions on earnings
● LO7

While doing some online research concerning a possible investment you come across an article that mentions in passing that a representative of **Morgan Stanley** had indicated that a company's pension plan had benefited its reported earnings. Curiosity piqued, you seek your old Intermediate Accounting text.

Required:

1. Can the net periodic pension "cost" cause a company's reported earnings to increase? Explain.

2. Companies must report the actuarial assumptions used to make estimates concerning pension plans. Which estimate influences the earnings effect in requirement 1? Can any of the other estimates influence earnings? Explain.

Research Case 17–11
Researching the way employee benefits are tested on the CPA Exam; retrieving information from the Internet
● LO9 LO10 LO11

The board of examiners of the American Institute of Certified Public Accountants (AICPA) is responsible for preparing the CPA examination. The boards of accountancy of all 50 states, the District of Columbia, Guam, Puerto Rico, the U.S. Virgin Islands, and the Mariana Islands use the examination as the primary way to measure the technical competence of CPA candidates. The content for each examination section is specified by the AICPA and described in outline form.

Required:

1. Access the AICPA website on the Internet. The web address is **www.aicpa.org**.
2. Access the CPA exam section within the site. Locate the exam content portion of the section.
3. In which of the four separately graded sections of the exam are postretirement benefits tested?
4. From the AICPA site, access the Board of Accountancy for your state. What are the education requirements in your state to sit for the CPA exam?

Analysis Case 17–12
Pensions and other postretirement benefit plans; analysis of disclosure notes
● LO6 LO11

Real World Financials

Clearwater Paper Corporation manufactures paperboard, consumer tissue, and wood products. Refer to the 2008 financial statements and related disclosure notes of the company. The financial statements can be found at the company's website: **www.clearwaterpaper.com** or via EDGAR at **www.sec.gov**.

Required:

1. From the information provided in various portions of Note 10, reconcile the beginning balance ($50,046) and ending balances for Net loss–AOCI associated with Clearwater's pension plan. Clearly label each reconciling amount.
2. Clearwater was required to amortize a portion of its Net loss–AOCI associated with its pension plan in 2008. Based on the calculation of that amount, determine the average remaining service life of the company's employees used in that calculation.
3. From the information provided in various portions of Note 10, reconcile the beginning balance ($35,442) and ending balances for Net loss–AOCI associated with Clearwater's Other postretirement employee benefit plan. Clearly label each reconciling amount.
4. Suppose you believe that Clearwater should have assumed a 1% lower healthcare cost trend during 2008. What would 2008 net income have been under that assumption? Assume a 35% income tax rate.

BRITISH AIRWAYS CASE

BRITISH AIRWAYS
● LO12

British Airways, Plc. (BA), a U.K. company, prepares its financial statements according to International Financial Reporting Standards. BA's annual report for the year ended March 31, 2009, which includes financial statements and disclosure notes, is included with all new textbooks and can be found at **www.britishairways.com**. When answering questions, focus on BA's "Group" financial information (which is equivalent to "Consolidated" under U.S. GAAP).

Required:

1. Look at Note 36, part c. What amount of past service cost (called prior service cost under U.S. GAAP) did BA recognize in earnings for the year ended March 31, 2009? The Employee Benefit section within Note 2: "Summary of significant accounting policies" in BA's financial statements states that "Past service costs are recognised when the benefit has been given." Is this policy consistent with U.S. GAAP? Explain.
2. The Employee Benefit section within Note 2: "Summary of significant accounting policies" in BA's financial statements states that:

   "The asset or liability recognised in the balance sheet in respect of defined benefit pension plans is the present value of the defined benefit obligation at the balance sheet date, less the fair value of plan assets, together with adjustments for unrecognised past service costs. Where plan assets exceed the defined benefit obligation, an asset is recognised to the extent that an economic benefit is available to the Group, in accordance with the terms of the plan and applicable statutory requirements." Is this the way pension plans are reported under U.S. GAAP? Explain.
3. U.S. GAAP requires that unrecognized actuarial gains and losses be included as part of Accumulated other comprehensive income (AOCI) in shareholders' equity. Under IFRS, AOCI often is referred to as a "reserve." Does BA report its unrecognized actuarial gains and losses this way? Explain. [Hint: see Note 35: Other reserves and minority interests.]
4. Locate Note 36: "Pension costs," part c "Amounts recognised in the income statement." Which components of pension expense does BA actually report in the operating profit (loss) section of its income statement? Where are the other components reported? Is this approach consistent with U.S. GAAP? Explain.

CPA SIMULATION 17–1

Schachter Company
Liabilities and Postretirement Benefits

CPA Review

Test your knowledge of the concepts discussed in this chapter, practice critical professional skills necessary for career success, and prepare for the computer-based CPA exam by accessing our CPA simulations at the text website: **www.mhhe.com/spiceland6e**.

The Schachter Company simulation tests your knowledge of contingencies, bonds, leases, deferred income taxes, transferring accounts receivables in a secured borrowing, and postretirement benefits.

As on the CPA exam itself, you will be asked to use tools including a spreadsheet, a calculator, and generally accepted accounting principles to conduct research, derive solutions, and communicate conclusions related to these issues in a simulated environment.

Specific tasks in the simulation include:

- Demonstrating an understanding of financial reporting effects of various contingencies.
- Applying judgment in deciding the deferred tax effects of a variety of transactions.
- Calculating interest and liabilities relating to bonds and leases.
- Communicating the way to calculate financial ratios related to liabilities and what they attempt to measure.
- Researching appropriate accounting for the transfer of accounts receivable to a third party.

18

Shareholders' Equity

|||||||||||||||||||||||||||||||||||||||||||||||||

We turn our attention from liabilities, which represent the creditors' interests in the assets of a corporation, to the shareholders' residual interest in those assets. The discussions distinguish between the two basic sources of shareholders' equity: (1) *invested capital* and (2) *earned* capital. We explore the expansion of corporate capital through the issuance of shares and the contraction caused by the retirement of shares or the purchase of treasury shares. In our discussions of retained earnings, we examine cash dividends, property dividends, stock dividends, and stock splits.

||| **LEARNING OBJECTIVES**

After studying this chapter, you should be able to:

- LO1 Describe the components of shareholders' equity and explain how they are reported in a statement of shareholders' equity. (page 1008)
- LO2 Describe comprehensive income and its components. (page 1010)
- LO3 Understand the corporate form of organization and the nature of stock. (page 1015)
- LO4 Record the issuance of shares when sold for cash and for noncash consideration. (page 1020)
- LO5 Distinguish between accounting for retired shares and for treasury shares. (page 1024)
- LO6 Describe retained earnings and distinguish it from paid-in capital. (page 1031)
- LO7 Explain the basis of corporate dividends, including the similarities and differences between cash and property dividends. (page 1031)
- LO8 Explain stock dividends and stock splits and how we account for them. (page 1033)
- LO9 Discuss the primary differences between U.S. GAAP and IFRS with respect to accounting for shareholders' equity. (pages 1012, 1013, 1014, and 1030)

FINANCIAL REPORTING CASE

Textron Inc.

Finally, you have some uninterrupted time to get back on the net. Earlier today you noticed on the Internet that the market price of Textron Inc.'s common stock was up almost 10%. You've been eager to look into why this happened, but have had one meeting after another all day.

Textron Inc. is a $14 billion multi-industry company operating in 32 countries known for its Bell Helicopter, Cessna Aircraft, and other brands. You've been a stockholder of Textron since the beginning of the year when your uncle bragged to you about his company's Cessna. The dividends of 19 cents a share that you receive quarterly are nice, but that's not why you bought the stock; you were convinced at the time that the stock price was poised to rise rapidly. A few well-placed clicks of the mouse and you come across the following news article:

World Financials

PROVIDENCE, RI–July 19–Textron Inc. today reported a 26% increase in earnings per share from continuing operations on a 15% revenue increase. The company also raised earnings and cash flow guidance for the year. "We experienced another strong quarter of solid revenue growth and improved profitability," said Textron Chairman, President and CEO Lewis B. Campbell.

The Board approved a two-for-one split of its Common Stock shares. The stock split will be effected through a 100% stock dividend, payable on August 24 to shareholders of record as of the close of business on August 3. Textron's Common Stock will begin trading at the split-adjusted price on August 27.

In addition, Textron's Board of Directors has approved a 19% increase in the company's annualized Common Stock dividend rate from $0.775 per share to $0.92 per share, stated on a post-split basis. Related to this action, Textron's Board of Directors declared a quarterly dividend of $0.23 per common share to holders of record as of the close of business on September 14.

Furthermore, the Board of Directors has authorized the repurchase of up to 24 million shares of Textron's Common Stock, stated on a post-split basis.

By the time you finish this chapter, you should be able to respond appropriately to the questions posed in this case. Compare your response to the solution provided at the end of the chapter.

QUESTIONS ///

1. Do you think the stock price increase is related to Textron's share repurchase plan? (page 1024)

2. What are Textron's choices in accounting for the share repurchases? (page 1025)

3. What effect does the quarterly cash dividend of 23 cents a share have on Textron's assets? Its liabilities? Its shareholders' equity? (page 1032)

4. What effect does the stock split have on Textron's assets? Its liabilities? Its shareholders' equity? (page 1035)

THE NATURE OF SHAREHOLDERS' EQUITY

A corporation raises money to fund its business operations by some mix of debt and equity financing. In earlier chapters, we examined debt financing in the form of notes, bonds, leases, and other liabilities. Amounts representing those liabilities denote *creditors' interest* in the company's assets. Now we focus on various forms of equity financing. Specifically, in this chapter we consider transactions that affect shareholders' equity—those accounts that represent the *ownership interests* of shareholders.

● LO1

In principle, shareholders' equity is a relatively straightforward concept. Shareholders' equity is a residual amount—what's left over after creditor claims have been subtracted from assets (in other words, net assets). You probably recall the residual nature of shareholders' equity from the basic accounting equation:

Net assets equal shareholders' equity.

$$\underbrace{\text{Assets} - \text{Liabilities}}_{\text{Net Assets}} = \text{Shareholders' equity}$$

Shareholders' equity accounts denote the ownership interests of shareholders.

Ownership interests of shareholders arise primarily from two sources: (1) amounts *invested* by shareholders in the corporation and (2) amounts *earned* by the corporation on behalf of its shareholders. These two sources are reported as (1) paid-in capital and (2) retained earnings.

Despite being a seemingly clear-cut concept, shareholders' equity and its component accounts often are misunderstood and misinterpreted. As we explore the transactions that affect shareholders' equity and its component accounts, try not to allow yourself to be overwhelmed by unfamiliar terminology or to be overly concerned with precise account titles. Terminology pertaining to shareholders' equity accounts is notoriously diverse. To give you one example—retained earnings is reported variously as *retained income* (**Smucker**), *reinvested earnings* (**Verizon**), *earnings reinvested* (**ExxonMobil**), *earnings retained in the business* (**Campbell Soup**), *retained earnings reinvested and employed in the business* (**L.S. Starret Company**), *accumulated* equity (**Federated Department Stores**), and *accumulated earnings* (**Intel**). Every shareholders' equity account has several aliases. Indeed, shareholders' equity itself is often referred to as *stockholders' equity, shareowners' equity, shareholders' investment,* and many other similar titles.

Complicating matters, transactions that affect shareholders' equity are influenced by corporation laws of individual states in which companies are located. And, as we see later, generally accepted accounting principles provide companies with considerable latitude when choosing accounting methods in this area.

Keeping this perspective in mind while you study the chapter should aid you in understanding the essential concepts. At a very basic level, each transaction we examine can be viewed simply as an increase or decrease in shareholders' equity, per se, without regard to specific shareholders' equity accounts. In fact, for a business organized as a single proprietorship, all capital changes are recorded in a single owner's equity account. The same concepts apply to a corporation. But for corporations, additional considerations make it desirable to separate owners' equity into several separate shareholders' equity accounts. These additional considerations—legal requirements and disclosure objectives—are discussed in later sections of this chapter. So, as you study the separate effects of transactions on retained earnings and specific paid-in capital accounts, you may find it helpful to ask yourself frequently "What is the net effect of this transaction on shareholders' equity?" or, equivalently, "By how much are net assets (assets minus liabilities) affected by this transaction?"

Legal requirements and disclosure objectives make it preferable to separate a corporation's capital into several separate shareholders' equity accounts.

Financial Reporting Overview

Before we examine the events that underlie specific shareholders' equity accounts, let's overview how individual accounts relate to each other. The condensed balance sheet in Graphic 18–1 of Exposition Corporation, a hypothetical company, provides that perspective.

Graphic 18–1 depicts a rather comprehensive situation. It's unlikely that any one company would have shareholders' equity from all of these sources at any one time. Remember that, at this point, our objective is only to get a general perspective of the items constituting shareholders' equity. You should, however, note a few aspects of the statement shown in Graphic 18–1. First, although company records would include separate accounts for each of these components of shareholders' equity, in the balance sheet, Exposition would report a more condensed version similar to that in Graphic 18–1A on the next page.

GRAPHIC 18–1
Detailed Shareholders' Equity Presentation

EXPOSITION CORPORATION
Balance Sheet
December 31, 2011

($ in millions)

Assets
$3,000
Liabilities
$1,000
Shareholders' Equity

Assets *minus* Liabilities equals Shareholders' Equity.

Paid-in capital:

Capital stock (par):		
Preferred stock, 10%, $10 par, cumulative, nonparticipating	$100	
Common stock, $1 par	55	
Common stock dividends distributable	5	
Additional paid-in capital:		
Paid-in capital—excess of par, preferred	50	
Paid-in capital—excess of par, common	260	
Paid-in capital—reacquired shares	8	
Paid-in capital—conversion of bonds	7	
Paid-in capital—stock options	9	
Paid-in capital—stock award plan	5	
Paid-in capital—lapse of stock options	1	
Total paid-in capital		$ 500
Retained earnings		1,670
Accumulated other comprehensive income:		
Net unrealized holding gains (losses) on investments	$ (85)	
Net unrecognized loss on pensions	(75)	
Deferred gains (losses) on derivatives*	(4)	
Gains (losses) from foreign currency translation**	-0-	(164)
Treasury stock (at cost)		(6)
Total shareholders' equity		$2,000

The primary source of paid-in capital is the investment made by shareholders when buying preferred and common stock.

Several other events also affect paid-in capital.

Retained earnings represents earned capital.

*When a derivative designated as a cash flow hedge is adjusted to fair value, the gain or loss is deferred as a component of other comprehensive income and included in earnings later, at the same time as earnings are affected by the hedged transaction (described in Appendix A at the end of the book).
**Gains or losses from changes in foreign currency exchange rates are discussed elsewhere in your accounting curriculum. The amount could be an addition to or reduction in shareholders' equity.

The four classifications within shareholders' equity are paid-in capital, retained earnings, accumulated other comprehensive income, and treasury stock. We discuss these now in the context of Exposition Corporation.

Paid-in Capital

Paid-in capital consists primarily of amounts invested by shareholders when they purchase shares of stock from the corporation. In addition, amounts sometimes are invested (or disinvested) by others on behalf of the shareholders. For Exposition Corporation, shareholders

Preferred stock, 10%	$ 100
Common stock	60
Additional paid-in capital	340
Retained earnings	1,670
Accumulated other comprehensive income (loss):	
Net unrealized holding losses on investments	(85)
Net unrealized loss on pensions	(75)
Deferred losses on derivatives	(4)
Treasury stock	(6)
Total shareholders' equity	$2,000

invested $470 million ($100 + 55 + 5 + 50 + 260). An additional $30 million ($8 + 7 + 9 + 5 + 1) of paid-in capital arose from financing activities, bringing the total to $500 million. Later in this chapter, we consider in more detail the events and transactions that affect paid-in capital.

Retained Earnings

Retained earnings is reported as a single amount, $1,670 million. We discuss retained earnings in Part C of this chapter.

Treasury Stock

We discuss the final component of shareholders' equity—treasury stock—later in the chapter. It indicates that some of the shares previously sold were bought back by the corporation from shareholders.

● LO2

Accumulated Other Comprehensive Income

Also notice that shareholders' equity of Exposition Corporation is adjusted for three events that are not included in net income and so don't affect retained earnings but are part of "other comprehensive income" and therefore are included as a separate component of shareholders' equity, accumulated comprehensive income.[1] Comprehensive income provides a more expansive view of the change in shareholders' equity than does traditional net income. It is the total *nonowner* change in equity for a reporting period. In fact, it encompasses all changes in equity other than those from transactions with *owners*. Transactions between the corporation and its shareholders primarily include dividends and the sale or purchase of shares of the company's stock. Most nonowner changes are reported in the income statement. So, the nonowner changes other than those that are part of traditional net income are the ones reported as "other comprehensive income."

Comprehensive income includes net income as well as other gains and losses that change shareholders' equity but are not included in traditional net income.

Comprehensive income extends our view of income beyond net income reported in an income statement to include four types of gains and losses that traditionally haven't been included in income statements:

1. Net holding gains (losses) on investments.
2. Gains (losses) from and amendments to postretirement benefit plans.
3. Deferred gains (losses) on derivatives.
4. Gains (losses) from foreign currency translation.

The first of these are the gains and losses on securities "available-for-sale" that occur when the fair values of these investments increase or decrease. As you learned in Chapter 12, these gains and losses aren't included in earnings until they are realized through the sale

---

[1]Comprehensive income was introduced in Chapter 4 and revisited in Chapters 12 and 17.

of the securities but are considered a component of *other comprehensive income* in the meantime. Similarly, as we discussed in Chapter 17, net gains and losses as well as "prior service cost" on pensions sometimes affect other comprehensive income but not net income. You have not yet studied the third and fourth potential components of other comprehensive income. As described in Appendix A, "Derivatives" at the back of this textbook, when a derivative designated as a *"cash flow hedge"* is adjusted to fair value, the gain or loss is deferred as a component of other comprehensive income and included in earnings later, at the same time as earnings are affected by the hedged transaction. Gains and losses from changes in foreign currency exchange rates are discussed elsewhere in your accounting curriculum, but also are included in other comprehensive income (OCI) but not net income.

OCI shares another trait with net income. Just as net income is reported periodically in the income statement and also on a cumulative basis as part of retained earnings, OCI too, is reported periodically in the statement of comprehensive income and also as accumulated other comprehensive income in the balance sheet along with retained earnings. In other words, we report two attributes of OCI: (1) components of comprehensive income *created during the reporting period* and (2) the comprehensive income *accumulated* over the current and prior periods.

> OCI is reported in the statement of comprehensive income.
>
> AOCI is reported in the balance sheet.

The first attribute—components of comprehensive income *created during the reporting period*—can be reported either as (a) an expanded version of the income statement, (b) part of the statement of shareholders' equity, or (c) a separate statement. Regardless of the placement a company chooses, the presentation is similar. It will report net income, other components of comprehensive income, and total comprehensive income, similar to the presentation in Graphic 18–2. Note that each component is reported net of its related income tax expense or income tax benefit.

GRAPHIC 18–2
Comprehensive Income

	($ in millions)	
Net income		$xxx
Other comprehensive income:		
Net unrealized holding gains (losses) on investments (net of tax)*	$ x	
Gains (losses) from and amendments to postretirement benefit plans (net of tax)†	(x)	
Deferred gains (losses) on derivatives (net of tax)‡	(x)	
Gains (losses) from foreign currency translation (net of tax)§	x	
Other than temporary impairment loss on investment in debt securities#	x	xx
Comprehensive income		$xxx

*Changes in the market value of securities available-for-sale (described in Chapter 12).
†Gains and losses due to revising assumptions or market returns differing from expectations and prior service cost from amending the plan (described in Chapter 17).
‡When a derivative designated as a cash flow hedge is adjusted to fair value, the gain or loss is deferred as a component of comprehensive income and included in earnings later, at the same time as earnings are affected by the hedged transaction (described in the Derivatives Appendix to the text).
§Gains or losses from changes in foreign currency exchange rates. The amount could be an addition to or reduction in shareholders' equity. (This item is discussed elsewhere in your accounting curriculum.)
#An unrealized loss also might occur from recording an "other than temporary" impairment in excess of a credit loss for a debt security that the company does not intend to sell, and for which it is more likely than not that the company will not be required to sell before the remaining amortized cost is anticipated to be recovered. This topic is discussed in Chapter 12.

The second measure—the comprehensive income *accumulated* over the current and prior periods—is reported as a separate component of shareholders' equity following retained earnings, similar to the presentation by Exposition Corporation in Graphic 18–1. Note that amounts reported here—accumulated other comprehensive income (AOCI)—represent the *cumulative* sum of the changes in each component created during each reporting period (Graphic 18–2) throughout all prior years.

Comprehensive Income. The International Accounting Standards Board (IASB) in 2007 issued a revised version of *IAS No.1*, "Presentation of Financial Statements," as part of a joint project with the FASB. It revised the standard to bring international reporting of comprehensive income largely in line with U.S. standards.[2] With regard to the presentation of comprehensive income, both sets of standards permit alternative formats, but IFRS provides one fewer choice. Here are options for reporting revenue and expense items and components of other comprehensive income:

IFRS	U.S. GAAP
1. single statement of comprehensive income	1. single statement of comprehensive income
2. two statements: a separate 'income statement' and 'statement of comprehensive income'	2. two statements: a separate 'income statement' and 'statement of comprehensive income'
	3. in the statement of shareholders' equity

The rationale behind the decision under IFRS not to allow the third presentation option is to clearly segregate changes in equity arising from transactions with owners in their capacity as owners (statement of shareholders' equity) from non-owner changes in equity (statement of comprehensive income).

IFRS ILLUSTRATION

When a company using IFRS chooses the two-statement option, the Statement of Comprehensive Income traditionally is referred to as the Statement of Recognized Income and Expense, or "SoRIE." Following is the SoRIE for **Sanofi-Aventis**, a global healthcare company based in France engaged in the research, development, manufacture and marketing of healthcare products:

Real World Financials

CONSOLIDATED STATEMENTS OF RECOGNIZED INCOME AND EXPENSE

(€ million)	6 mo. to June 30, 2009	6 mo. to June 30, 2008	12 mo. to Dec. 31, 2008
Net income for the period	2,869	2,555	4,292
Income/(expense) recognized directly in equity:			
Available-for-sale financial assets	16	(142)	(132)
Cash flow hedges	(140)	4	104
Revaluation reserve	130	—	—
Actuarial gains and (losses)	(69)	130	(829)
Currency translation differences	(167)	(1,654)	948
Tax effect on income and expense recognized directly in equity	50	(24)	132
Total income/(expense) recognized directly in equity	(180)	(1,686)	223
Total recognized income/(expense) for the period	2,689	869	4,515

Reporting Shareholders' Equity

You seldom if ever will see the degree of detail shown in Graphic 18–1 reported in the presentation of paid-in capital. Instead, companies keep track of individual additional paid-in capital accounts in company records but ordinarily report these amounts as a single subtotal—additional paid-in capital. Pertinent rights and privileges of various securities outstanding such as dividend and liquidation preferences, call and conversion information, and voting rights are summarized in disclosure notes.[3] The shareholders' equity portion of the balance sheet of **Southwest Airlines**, shown in Graphic 18–3, is a typical presentation format.

---

[2]"Presentation of Financial Statements," *International Accounting Standard No. 1* (IASCF), as amended effective January 1, 2009.
[3]FASB ACS 505–10–50: Equity–Overall–Disclosure (previously "Disclosure of Information about Capital Structure," *Statement of Financial Accounting Standards No. 129* (Norwalk, Conn.: FASB, 1997)).

SOUTHWEST AIRLINES, INC.
Balance Sheet
[Shareholders' Equity Section]
($ in millions)

	2008	2007
Stockholders' equity:		
Common stock, $1.00 par value: 2,000,000,000 shares authorized; 807,611,634 shares issued in 2008 and 2007	808	808
Capital in excess of par value	1,215	1,207
Retained earnings	4,919	4,788
Accumulated other comprehensive income	(984)	1,241
Treasury stock, at cost: 67,619,062 and 72,814,104 shares in 2008 and 2007, respectively	(1,005)	(1,103)
Total stockholders' equity	4,953	6,941

GRAPHIC 18–3

Typical Presentation Format—Southwest Airlines

Real World Financials

Details of each class of stock are reported on the face of the balance sheet or in disclosure notes.

INTERNATIONAL FINANCIAL REPORTING STANDARDS

Use of the term "reserves" and other terminology differences. Shareholders' equity is classified under IFRS into two categories: share capital and "reserves." The term reserves is considered misleading and thus is discouraged under U.S. GAAP. Here are some other differences in equity terminology:

● LO9

U.S. GAAP	IFRS
Capital stock:	Share capital:
Common stock	Ordinary shares
Preferred stock	Preference shares
Paid-in capital—excess of par, common	Share premium, ordinary shares
Paid-in capital—excess of par, preferred	Share premium, preference shares
Accumulated other comprehensive income:	Reserves:
Net gains (losses) on investments—AOCI	Investment revaluation reserve
Net gains (losses) foreign currency translation—AOCI	Translation reserve
{N/A: adjusting P,P, & E to fair value not permitted}	Revaluation reserve
Retained earnings	Retained earnings
Total shareholders' equity	**Total equity**
Presented after Liabilities	Often presented before Liabilities

The balance sheet reports annual balances of shareholders' equity accounts. However, companies also should disclose the sources of the changes in those accounts.[4] This is the purpose of the statement of shareholders' equity. To illustrate, Graphic 18–4 on the next page shows how **Southwest Airlines** reported the changes in its shareholders' equity balances (shown in Graphic 18–3).

The changes that Southwest Airlines' statements of shareholders' equity reveal are net income and two other items of comprehensive income, the purchase of treasury stock, the issuance of common stock, and dividends declared.

---

[4]FASB ASC 505–10–50–2: Equity–Overall–Disclosure (previously "Omnibus Opinion," *APB Opinion No. 12* (New York: AICPA, 1967)).

GRAPHIC 18–4 Changes in Stockholders' Equity—Southwest Airlines Real World Financials

SOUTHWEST AIRLINES
Consolidated Statements of Stockholders' Equity

(In millions, except per share amounts)	Common Stock	Capital in Excess of Par Value	Retained Earnings	Accumulated Other Comprehensive Income (Loss)	Treasury Stock	Total
Balance at December 31, 2005	$802	$ 963	$4,018	$ 892	$ —	$ 6,675
Purchase of shares of treasury stock	—	—	—	—	(800)	(800)
Issuance of common and treasury stock pursuant to employee stock plans	6	39	(196)	—	410	259
Tax benefit of options exercised	—	60	—	—	—	60
Share-based compensation	—	80	—	—	—	80
Cash dividends, $.018 per share	—	—	(14)	—	—	(14)
Comprehensive income (loss)						
Net income	—	—	499	—	—	499
Unrealized (loss) on derivative instruments	—	—	—	(306)	—	(306)
Other	—	—	—	(4)	—	(4)
Total comprehensive income						189
Balance at December 31, 2006	$808	$1,142	$4,307	$ 582	$ (390)	$ 6,449
Purchase of shares of treasury stock	—	—	—	—	(1,001)	(1,001)
Issuance of common and treasury stock pursuant to Employee stock plans	—	—	(150)	—	288	138
Tax benefit of options exercised	—	28	—	—	—	28
Share-based compensation	—	37	—	—	—	37
Cash dividends, $.018 per share	—	—	(14)	—	—	(14)
Comprehensive income (loss)						
Net income	—	—	645	—	—	645
Unrealized gain on derivative instruments	—	—	—	636	—	636
Other	—	—	—	23	—	23
Total comprehensive income						1,304
Balance at December 31, 2007	$808	$1,207	$4,788	$ 1,241	$(1,103)	$ 6,941
Purchase of shares of treasury stock	—	—	—	—	(54)	(54)
Issuance of common and treasury stock pursuant to Employee stock plans	—	—	(34)	—	152	118
Tax benefit of options exercised	—	(10)	—	—	—	(10)
Share-based compensation	—	18	—	—	—	18
Cash dividends, $.018 per share	—	—	(13)	—	—	(13)
Comprehensive income (loss)						
Net income	—	—	178	—	—	178
Unrealized (loss) on derivative instruments	—	—	—	(2,166)	—	(2,166)
Other	—	—	—	(59)	—	(59)
Total comprehensive income (loss)						(2,047)
Balance at December 31, 2008	$808	$1,215	$4,919	$ (984)	$(1,005)	$4,953

The Corporate Organization

A company may be organized in any of three ways: (1) a sole proprietorship, (2) a partnership, or (3) a corporation. In your introductory accounting course, you studied each form. In this course we focus exclusively on the corporate form of organization.

Most well-known companies, such as **Microsoft**, **IBM**, and **General Electric**, are corporations. Also, many smaller companies—even one-owner businesses—are corporations. Although fewer in number than proprietorships and partnerships, in terms of business volume, corporations are the predominant form of business organization.

In most respects, transactions are accounted for in the same way regardless of the form of business organization. Assets and liabilities are unaffected by the way a company is organized. The exception is the method of accounting for capital, the ownership interest in the company. Rather than recording all changes in ownership interests in a single capital account for each owner, as we do for sole proprietorships and partnerships, we use the several capital accounts overviewed in the previous section to record those changes for a corporation. Before discussing how we account for specific ownership changes, let's look at the characteristics of a corporation that make this form of organization distinctive and require special accounting treatment.

Limited Liability

The owners are not personally liable for debts of a corporation. Unlike a proprietorship or a partnership, a corporation is a separate legal entity, responsible for its own debts. Shareholders' liability is limited to the amounts they invest in the company when they purchase shares (unless the shareholder also is an officer of the corporation). The limited liability of shareholders is perhaps the single most important advantage of corporate organization. In other forms of business, creditors may look to the personal assets of owners for satisfaction of business debt.

Ease of Raising Capital

A corporation is better suited to raising capital than is a proprietorship or a partnership. All companies can raise funds by operating at a profit or by borrowing. However, attracting equity capital is easier for a corporation. Because corporations sell ownership interest in the form of shares of stock, ownership rights are easily transferred. An investor can sell his/her ownership interest at any time and without affecting the corporation or its operations.

From the viewpoint of a potential investor, another favorable aspect of investing in a corporation is the lack of mutual agency. Individual partners in a partnership have the power to bind the business to a contract. Therefore, an investor in a partnership must be careful regarding the character and business savvy of fellow co-owners. On the other hand, shareholders' participation in the affairs of a corporation is limited to voting at shareholders' meetings (unless the shareholder also is a member of management). Consequently, a shareholder needn't exercise the same degree of care that partners must in selecting co-owners.

Obviously, then, a corporation offers advantages over the other forms of organization, particularly in its ability to raise investment capital. As you might guess, though, these benefits do not come without a price.

Disadvantages

Paperwork! To protect the rights of those who buy a corporation's stock or who loan money to a corporation, the state in which the company is incorporated and the federal government impose expensive reporting requirements. Primarily the required paperwork is intended to ensure adequate disclosure of information needed by investors and creditors.

You read earlier that corporations are separate legal entities. As such, they also are separate taxable entities. Often this causes what is referred to as *double taxation*. Corporations first pay income taxes on their earnings. Then, when those earnings are distributed as cash dividends, shareholders pay personal income taxes on the previously taxed earnings. Proprietorships and partnerships are not taxed at the business level; each owner's share of profits is taxed only as personal income.

A statement of shareholders' equity reports the transactions that cause changes in its shareholders' equity account balances.

● **LO3**

Corporations are the dominant form of business organization.

Accounting for most transactions is the same regardless of the form of business organization.

A corporation is a separate legal entity—separate and distinct from its owners.

Ownership interest in a corporation is easily transferred.

Shareholders do not have a mutual agency relationship.

Corporations are subject to expensive government regulation.

Corporations create double taxation.

Types of Corporations

When referring to corporations in this text, we are referring to corporations formed by private individuals for the purpose of generating profits. These corporations raise capital by selling stock. There are, however, other types of corporations.

Some corporations such as churches, hospitals, universities, and charities do not sell stock and are not organized for profit. Also, some not-for-profit corporations are government-owned—the **Federal Deposit Insurance Corporation (FDIC)**, for instance. Accounting for not-for-profit corporations is discussed elsewhere in the accounting curriculum.

Corporations organized for profit may be publicly held or privately (or closely) held. The stock of publicly held corporations is available for purchase by the general public. You can buy shares of **General Electric**, **Ford Motor Company**, or **Walmart Stores** through a stockbroker. These shares are traded on the New York Stock Exchange. Other publicly held stock, like **Intel** and **Microsoft**, are available through Nasdaq (National Association of Securities Dealers Automated Quotations).

On the other hand, shares of privately held companies are owned by only a few individuals (perhaps a family) and are not available to the general public. Corporations whose stock is privately held do not need to register those shares with the Securities and Exchange Commission and are spared the voluminous, annual reporting requirements of the SEC. Of course, new sources of equity financing are limited when shares are privately held, as is the market for selling existing shares.

Frequently, companies begin as smaller, privately held corporations. Then as success broadens opportunities for expansion, the corporation goes public. For example, in 2008 **Visa** decided to take public the privately held company. The result was the largest technology initial public offering ever.

Margin notes

Not-for-profit corporations may be owned:
1. By the public sector.
2. By a governmental unit.

Corporations organized for profit may be:
1. Publicly held and traded:
   a. On an exchange.
   b. Over-the-counter.
2. Privately held.

Privately held companies' shares are held by only a few individuals and are not available to the general public.

Hybrid Organizations

A corporation can elect to comply with a special set of tax rules and be designated an **S corporation.** S corporations have characteristics of both regular corporations and partnerships. Owners have the limited liability protection of a corporation, but income and expenses are passed through to the owners as in a partnership, avoiding double taxation.

Two particular business structures have evolved in response to liability issues and tax treatment—limited liability companies and limited liability partnerships.

A **limited liability company** offers several advantages. Owners are not liable for the debts of the business, except to the extent of their investment. Unlike a limited partnership, all members of a limited liability company can be involved with managing the business without losing liability protection. Like an S corporation, income and expenses are passed through to the owners as in a partnership, avoiding double taxation, but there are no limitations on the number of owners as in an S corporation.

A **limited liability partnership** is similar to a limited liability company, except it doesn't offer all the liability protection available in the limited liability company structure. Partners are liable for their own actions but not entirely liable for the actions of other partners.

The Model Business Corporation Act

Corporations are formed in accordance with the corporation laws of individual states. State laws are not uniform, but share many similarities, thanks to the widespread adoption of the Model Business Corporation Act.[5] This act is designed to serve as a guide to states in the development of their corporation statutes. It presently serves as the model for the majority of states.

State laws regarding the nature of shares that can be authorized, the issuance and repurchase of those shares, and conditions for distributions to shareholders obviously influence actions of corporations. Naturally, differences among state laws affect how we account for many of the shareholders' equity transactions discussed in this chapter. For that reason, we will focus on

Margin note

The *Model Business Corporation Act* serves as the model for the corporation statutes of most states.

---

[5]*Model Business Corporation Act,* the American Bar Association, 2009.

the normal case, as described by the Model Business Corporation Act, and note situations where variations in state law might require different accounting. Your goal is not to learn diverse procedures caused by peculiarities of state laws, but to understand the broad concepts of accounting for shareholders' equity that can be applied to any specific circumstance.

The process of incorporating a business is similar in all states. The **articles of incorporation** (sometimes called the *corporate charter*) describe (a) the nature of the firm's business activities, (b) the shares to be issued, and (c) the composition of the initial **board of directors.** The board of directors establishes corporate policies and appoints officers who manage the corporation.

The number of shares authorized is the maximum number of shares that a corporation is legally permitted to issue, as specified in its articles of incorporation. The number of authorized shares is determined at the company's creation and can only be increased by a vote of the shareholders. At least some of the shares authorized by the articles of incorporation are sold (issued) at the inception of the corporation. Frequently, the initial shareholders include members of the board of directors or officers (who may be one and the same). Ultimately, it is the corporation's shareholders that control the company. Shareholders are the owners of the corporation. By voting their shares, it is they who determine the makeup of the board of directors—who in turn appoint officers, who in turn manage the company.

Shareholders' investment in a corporation ordinarily is referred to as paid-in capital. In the next section, we examine the methods normally used to maintain records of shareholders' investment and to report such paid-in capital in financial statements.

> **Variations among state laws influence GAAP pertaining to shareholders' equity transactions.**

PAID-IN CAPITAL

Fundamental Share Rights

In reading the previous paragraphs, you noted that corporations raise equity funds by selling shares of the corporation. Shareholders are the owners of a corporation. If a corporation has only one class of shares, no designation of the shares is necessary, but they typically are labeled *common shares.* Ownership rights held by common shareholders, unless specifically withheld by agreement with the shareholders, are:

- a. The right to vote on matters that come before the shareholders, including the election of corporate directors. Each share represents one vote.
- b. The right to share in profits when dividends are declared. The percentage of shares owned by a shareholder determines his/her share of dividends distributed.
- c. The right to share in the distribution of assets if the company is liquidated. The percentage of shares owned by a shareholder determines his/her share of assets after creditors and preferred shareholders are paid.

Another right sometimes given to common shareholders is the right to maintain one's percentage share of ownership when new shares are issued. This is referred to as a *preemptive right.* Each shareholder is offered the opportunity to buy a percentage of any new shares issued equal to the percentage of shares he/she owns at the time. In most states this right must be specifically granted; in others, it is presumed unless contractually excluded.

However, this right usually is not explicitly stated because of the inconvenience it causes corporations when they issue new shares. The exclusion of the preemptive right ordinarily is inconsequential because few shareholders own enough stock to be concerned about their ownership percentage.

Distinguishing Classes of Shares

It is not uncommon for a firm to have more than one, and perhaps several, classes of shares, each with different rights and limitations. To attract investors, companies have devised quite a variety of ownership securities.

If more than one class of shares is authorized by the articles of incorporation, the specific rights of each (for instance, the right to vote, residual interest in assets, and dividend rights) must be stated. Also, some designation must be given to distinguish each class.

Some of the distinguishing designations often used are:

1. Class A, class B, and so on (**Tyson Foods**).
2. Preferred stock, common stock, and class B stock (**Hershey Foods**).
3. Common and preferred (**Hewlett-Packard**).
4. Capital stock (**Reader's Digest**).
5. Common and serial preferred (**Smucker**).

Terminology varies in the way companies differentiate among share types.

In your introductory study of accounting, you probably became most familiar with the common stock–preferred stock distinction. That terminology has deep roots in tradition. Early English corporate charters provided for shares that were preferred over others as to dividends and liquidation rights. These provisions were reflected in early American corporation laws. But as our economy developed, corporations increasingly felt the need for innovative ways of attracting investment capital. The result has been a gradual development of a wide range of share classifications that cannot easily be identified by these historical designations.

It often is difficult to predict the rights and privileges of shares on the basis of whether they are labeled *common* or *preferred*.

To reflect the flexibility that now exists in the creation of equity shares, the Model Business Corporation Act, and thus many state statutes, no longer mention the words common and preferred. But the influence of tradition lingers. Most corporations still designate shares as common or preferred. For consistency with practice, the illustrations you study in this chapter use those designations. As you consider the examples, keep in mind that the same concepts apply regardless of the language used to distinguish shares.

Typical Rights of Preferred Shares

An issue of shares with certain preferences or features that distinguish it from the class of shares customarily called common shares may be assigned any of the several labels mentioned earlier. Very often the distinguishing designation is preferred shares. The special rights of preferred shareholders usually include one or both of the following:

a. Preferred shareholders typically have a preference to a specified amount of dividends (stated dollar amount per share or % of par value per share). That is, if the board of directors declares dividends, preferred shareholders will receive the designated dividend before any dividends are paid to common shareholders.
b. Preferred shareholders customarily have a preference (over common shareholders) as to the distribution of assets in the event the corporation is dissolved.

Shares may be:
1. *Convertible* into a specified number of another class of shares.
2. *Redeemable* at the option of:
  a. Shareholders.
  b. The corporation.

Preferred shareholders sometimes have the right of conversion which allows them to exchange shares of preferred stock for common stock at a specified conversion ratio. Alternatively, a redemption privilege might allow preferred shareholders the option, under specified conditions, to return their shares for a predetermined redemption price. For instance, in 2009, **Brookfield Homes Corporation** had outstanding 10 million shares of convertible preferred stock. Preferred shareholders have preference over common stockholders in dividends and liquidation rights. Each preferred share is convertible into 3.57 common shares. Similarly, shares may be redeemable at the option of the issuing corporation (sometimes referred to as *callable*).

Preferred shares may be cumulative or noncumulative. Typically, preferred shares are cumulative, which means that if the specified dividend is not paid in a given year, the unpaid dividends (called *dividends in arrears*) accumulate and must be made up in a later dividend year before any dividends are paid on common shares. Illustration 18–1 provides an example.

Preferred shares may be participating or nonparticipating. A participating feature allows preferred shareholders to receive additional dividends beyond the stated amount. If the preferred shares are fully participating, the distribution of dividends to common and preferred shareholders is a pro rata allocation based on the relative par value amounts of common and preferred stock outstanding. Participating preferred stock, previously quite common, is rare today.

Remember that the designations of common and preferred imply no necessary rights, privileges, or limitations of the shares so designated. Such relative rights must be specified by the contract with shareholders. A corporation can create classes of preferred shares that are indistinguishable from common shares in voting rights and/or the right to participate in assets (distributed as dividends or distributed upon liquidation). Likewise, it is possible to devise classes of common shares that possess preferential rights, superior to those of preferred shares.

ILLUSTRATION 18–1

Distribution
of Dividends
to Preferred
Shareholders

The shareholders' equity of Corbin Enterprises includes the items shown below. The board of directors declared cash dividends of $360,000, $500,000, and $700,000 in its first three years of operation—2010, 2011, and 2012, respectively.

Common stock	$3,000,000
Paid-in capital—excess of par, common	9,800,000
Preferred stock, 8%	6,000,000
Paid-in capital—excess of par, preferred	780,000

Determine the amount of dividends to be paid to preferred and common shareholders in each of the three years, assuming that the preferred stock is cumulative and nonparticipating.

	Preferred	Common
2010	$360,000*	$0
2011	500,000**	0
2012	580,000***	120,000 (remainder)

*   The preferred shareholders are entitled to dividends of $480,000 (8% × $6,000,000), but only $360,000 dividends are declared in 2010 so dividends in arrears are $120,000.
** $120,000 dividends in arrears plus $380,000 of the $480,000 current preference.
*** $100,000 dividends in arrears ($480,000 − 380,000) plus the $480,000 current preference.

If preferred shares are not cumulative, dividends not declared in any given year need never be paid.

Is It Equity or Is It Debt?

You probably also can imagine an issue of preferred shares that is almost indistinguishable from a bond issue. Let's say, for instance, that preferred shares call for annual cash dividends of 10% of the par value, dividends are cumulative, and the shares must be redeemed for cash in 10 years. Although the declaration of dividends rests in the discretion of the board of directors, the contract with preferred shareholders can be worded in such a way that directors are compelled to declare dividends each year the company is profitable. For a profitable company, it would be difficult to draw the line between this issue of preferred shares and a 10%, 10-year bond issue. Even in a more typical situation, preferred shares are somewhat hybrid securities—a cross between equity and debt.

The line between debt and equity is hard to draw.

INTERNATIONAL FINANCIAL REPORTING STANDARDS

● LO9

Distinction between Debt and Equity for Preferred Stock. Differences in the definitions and requirements can result in the same instrument being classified differently between debt and equity under IFRS and U.S. GAAP. Under U.S. GAAP, preferred stock normally is reported as equity, but is reported as debt with the dividends reported in the income statement as interest expense if it is "mandatorily redeemable" preferred stock. Under IFRS, most non-mandatorily redeemable preferred stock (preference shares) also is reported as debt as well as some preference shares that aren't redeemable. Under IFRS (*IAS No. 32*), the critical feature that distinguishes a liability is if the issuer is or can be required to deliver cash (or another financial instrument) to the holder.[6] Unilever describes such a difference in a disclosure note:

IFRS ILLUSTRATION

Additional Information for U.S. Investors [in part]
Preference Shares
Under *IAS 32*, Unilever recognises preference shares that provide a fixed preference dividend as borrowings with preference dividends recognised in the income statement. Under U.S. GAAP such preference shares are classified in shareholders' equity with dividends treated as a deduction to shareholder's equity.

The FASB and the IASB are cooperating on a project that addresses the distinction between liabilities and equity, which likely will eliminate many existing differences.

---

[6]"Financial Instruments: Presentation," *International Accounting Standard No. 32* (IASCF), as amended effective January 1, 2009.

Mandatorily
redeemable shares are
classified as liabilities.

Sometimes the similarity to debt is even more obvious. Suppose shares are mandatorily redeemable—the company is obligated to buy back the shares at a specified future date. The fact that the company is obligated to pay cash (or other assets) at a fixed or determinable date in the future makes this financial instrument tantamount to debt. A mandatorily redeemable financial instrument must be reported in the balance sheet as a liability, not as shareholders' equity.[7] **Six Flags**, for instance, reported its mandatorily redeemable preferred shares as a liability in its 2009 balance sheet.

The Concept of Par Value

We have inherited
the archaic concept of
par value from early
corporate law.

Another prevalent practice (besides labeling shares as common and preferred) that has little significance other than historical is assigning a par value to shares. The concept of par value dates back as far as the concept of owning shares of a business. Par value originally indicated the real value of shares. All shares were issued at that price.

During the late 19th and early 20th centuries, many cases of selling shares for less than par value—known as *watered shares*—received a great deal of attention and were the subject of a number of lawsuits. Investors and creditors contended that they relied on the par value as the permanent investment in the corporation and therefore net assets must always be at least that amount. Not only was par value assumed to be the amount invested by shareholders, but it also was defined by early corporation laws as the amount of net assets not available for distribution to shareholders (as dividends or otherwise).

Shares with nominal
par value became
common to dodge
elaborate statutory
rules pertaining to par
value shares.

Many companies began turning to par value shares with very low par values—often pennies—to escape the watered shares liability of issuing shares below an arbitrary par value and to limit the restrictions on distributions. This practice is common today.

Accountants and attorneys have been aware for decades that laws pertaining to par value and legal capital not only are bewildering but fail in their intent to safeguard creditors from payments to shareholders. Actually, to the extent that creditors are led to believe that they are afforded protection, they are misled. Like the designations of common and preferred shares, the concepts of par value and legal capital have been eliminated entirely from the Model Business Corporation Act.[8]

Most shares continue
to bear arbitrarily
designated par values.

Many states already have adopted these provisions of the Model Act. But most established corporations issued shares prior to changes in the state statutes. Consequently, most companies have par value shares outstanding and continue to issue previously authorized par value shares. The evolution will be gradual to the simpler, more meaningful provisions of the Model Act.

In the meantime, accountants must be familiar with the outdated concepts of par value and legal capital in order to properly record and report transactions related to par value shares. For that reason, most of the discussion in this chapter centers on par value shares. Largely, this means only that proceeds from shareholders' investment is allocated between stated capital and additional paid-in capital. Be aware, though, that in the absence of archaic laws that prompted the creation of par value shares, there is no theoretical reason to do so.

Accounting for the Issuance of Shares

Shares Issued For Cash

● LO4

When shares are sold for cash (see Illustration 18–2), the capital stock account (usually common or preferred) is credited for the amount representing stated capital. When shares have a designated par value, that amount denotes stated capital and is credited to the stock account. Proceeds in excess of this amount are credited to paid-in capital—excess of par (also called additional paid-in capital).

---

[7]"FASB ASC 480–10–25–4: Distinguishing Liabilities from Equity–Overall–Recognition (previously Accounting for Certain Financial Instruments with Characteristics of Both Liabilities and Equity," *Statement of Financial Accounting Standards No. 150* (Norwalk, Conn.: FASB, 2003)).

[8]*Model Business Corporation Act,* the American Bar Association, 2009, official comment to Section 6.21.

Dow Industrial sells 100,000 of its common shares, $1 par per share, for $10 per share:		**ILLUSTRATION 18–2**
	($ in 000s)	Shares Sold for Cash
Cash (100,000 shares at $10 price per share)	1,000	
Common stock (100,000 shares at $1 par per share)	100	
Paid-in capital—excess of par (remainder)	900	
The entire proceeds from the sale of no-par stock are deemed stated capital and recorded in the stock account. If the shares are no-par, the entry is as follows:		The total amount received from the sale of no-par shares is credited to the stock account.
Cash (100,000 shares at $10 price per share)	1,000	
Common stock	1,000	

Shares Issued for Noncash Consideration

Occasionally, a company might issue its shares for consideration other than cash. It is not uncommon for a new company, yet to establish a reliable cash flow, to pay for promotional and legal services with shares rather than with cash. Similarly, shares might be given in payment for land, or for equipment, or for some other noncash asset.

Shares should be issued at fair value.

Even without a receipt of cash to establish the fair value of the shares at the time of the exchange, the transaction still should be recorded at fair value. Best evidence of fair value might be:

- A quoted market price for the shares.
- A selling price established in a recent issue of shares for cash.
- The amount of cash that would have been paid in a cash purchase of the asset or service.
- An independent appraisal of the value of the asset received.
- Other available evidence.

Whichever evidence of fair value seems more clearly evident should be used.[9]

Illustration 18–3 demonstrates a situation where the quoted market price is the best evidence of fair value.

DuMont Chemicals issues 1 million of its common shares, $1 par per share, in exchange for a custom-built factory for which no cash price is available. Today's issue of *The Wall Street Journal* lists DuMont's stock at $10 per share:		**ILLUSTRATION 18–3**
	($ in millions)	Shares Sold for Noncash Consideration
Property, plant, and equipment (1 million shares at $10 per share)	10	The quoted market price for the shares issued might be the best evidence of fair value.
Common stock (1 million shares at $1 par per share)	1	
Paid-in capital—excess of par (remainder)	9	

More Than One Security Issued for a Single Price

Although uncommon, a company might sell more than one security—perhaps common shares and preferred shares—for a single price. As you might expect, the cash received usually is the sum of the separate market values of the two securities. Of course, each is then recorded at its market value. However, if only one security's value is known, the second security's market value is inferred from the total selling price as demonstrated in Illustration 18–4 on the next page.

Because the shares sell for a total of $100 million, and the market value of the common shares is known to be $40 million (4 million × $10), the preferred shares are inferred to have a market value of $60 million.

---

[9]Although stock issuances are not specifically mentioned in FASB ASC 845–10–30: Nonmonetary Transactions–Overall–Initial Measurement (previously *APB Opinion No. 29*), this treatment is consistent with the general rule for accounting for noncash transactions as described in that pronouncement, pars. 18 and 25.

ILLUSTRATION 18–4

More than One Security Sold for a Single Price

When only one security's value is known ($40 million), the second security's market value ($60 million) is assumed from the total selling price ($100 million).

AP&P issues 4 million of its common shares, $1 par per share, and 4 million of its preferred shares, $10 par, for $100 million. Today's issue of *The Wall Street Journal* lists AP&P's common at $10 per share. There is no established market for the preferred shares:

	($ in millions)	
Cash	100	
Common stock (4 million shares × $1 par)		4
Paid-in capital—excess of par common		36
Preferred stock (4 million shares × $10 par)		40
Paid-in capital—excess of par, preferred.....*(to balance)*......		20

ADDITIONAL CONSIDERATION

In the unlikely event that the total selling price is not equal to the sum of the two market prices (when both market values are known), the total selling price is allocated between the two securities, in proportion to their relative market values. You should note that this is the same approach we use (a) when more than one asset is purchased for a single purchase price to allocate the single price to the various assets acquired, (b) when detachable warrants and bonds are issued for a single price, and (c) in any other situation when more than one item is associated with a single purchase price or selling price.

Share Issue Costs

Share issue costs reduce the net cash proceeds from selling the shares and thus paid-in capital—excess of par.

Real World Financials

When a company sells shares, it obtains the legal, promotional, and accounting services necessary to effect the sale. The cost of these services reduces the net proceeds from selling the shares. Since paid-in capital—excess of par is credited for the excess of the proceeds over the par value of the shares sold, the effect of share issue costs is to reduce the amount credited to that account. For example, on completing a public offering of 825,000 shares at a price of $17.75 per share, the **Duriron Company, Inc.**, noted in its financial statements: "The proceeds of the offering, after deducting all associated costs, were $13,491,000 or $16.35 per newly issued share." Duriron's entry to record the sale was:

The cash proceeds is the net amount received after paying share issue costs.

	($ in millions)	
Cash (825,000 shares at $16.35 net price per share)	13.49	
Common stock (825,000 shares at $1.25 par per share)		1.03
Paid-in capital—excess of par (remainder)		12.46

You should notice that not separately reporting issue costs differs from how *debt* issue costs are recorded. In Chapter 14 you learned that the costs associated with a debt issue are recorded in a separate debt issue costs account and amortized to expense over the life of the debt.

Like dividends, share issue costs are not an expense.

It can be argued that share issue costs and debt issue costs are fundamentally different. That view would argue that a debt issue has a fixed maturity and, like interest expense, debt issue costs are part of the expense of borrowing funds for that period of time (even though it's reported in a separate expense account—debt issue expense—as it's amortized). Selling shares, on the other hand, represents a perpetual equity interest. Dividends paid on that capital investment are not an expense; neither are the costs of obtaining that capital investment (share issue costs).

Although expensing debt issue costs presently is required by GAAP, the FASB has suggested in *Concept Statement 6* that those costs should be treated the same way as share issue costs. That is, the recorded amount of the debt would be reduced by the debt issue costs instead of recording the costs separately as an asset. Remember, though, that concept statements do not constitute GAAP, so until a new FASB standard is issued to supersede FASB ASC 835–30–45:Interest–Imputation of Interest–Other Presentation Matters (previously *APB Opinion 21)*, the prescribed practice is to record debt issue costs as assets and expense the asset over the maturity of the debt.

CONCEPT REVIEW EXERCISE

Situation: The shareholders' equity section of the balance sheet of National Foods, Inc., included the following accounts at December 31, 2009:

EXPANSION OF CORPORATE CAPITAL

Shareholders' Equity	($ in millions)
Paid-in capital:	
Common stock, 120 million shares at $1 par	$ 120
Paid-in capital—excess of par	836
Retained earnings	2,449
Total shareholders' equity	$3,405

Required:

1. During 2010, several transactions affected the stock of National Foods. Prepare the appropriate entries for these events.

   a. On March 11, National Foods issued 10 million of its 9.2% preferred shares, $1 par per share, for $44 per share.

   b. On November 22, 1 million common shares, $1 par per share, were issued in exchange for eight labeling machines. Each machine was built to custom specifications so no cash price was available. National Food's stock was listed at $10 per share.

   c. On November 23, 1 million of the common shares and 1 million preferred shares were sold for $60 million. The preferred shares had not traded since March and their market value was uncertain.

2. Prepare the shareholders' equity section of the comparative balance sheets for National Foods at December 31, 2010 and 2009. Assume that net income for 2010 was $400 million and the only other transaction affecting shareholders' equity was the payment of the 9.2% dividend on the 11 million preferred shares ($1 million).

---

1. During 2010 several transactions affected the stock of National Foods. Prepare the appropriate entries for these events.

   a. On March 11, National Foods issued 10 million of its preferred shares, $1 par per share, for $44 per share.

SOLUTION

	($ in millions)	
Cash	440	
Preferred stock (10 million shares × $1 par per share)		10
Paid-in capital—excess of par, preferred		430

   b. On November 22, 1 million common shares, $1 par per share, were issued in exchange for 8 labeling machines:

Machinery (fair value of shares)	10	
Common stock (1 million shares × $1 par per share)		1
Paid-in capital—excess of par, common (1 million shares × $9)		9

The transaction was recorded at the fair value of the shares exchanged for the machinery.

   c. On November 23, 1 million of the common shares and 1 million preferred shares were sold for $60 million:

Cash	60	
Common stock (1 million shares × $1 par per share)		1
Paid-in capital—excess of par, common		9
Preferred stock (1 million shares × $1 par per share)		1
Paid-in capital—excess of par, preferred (to balance)		49

Since the value of only the common stock was known, the preferred stock's market value ($50/share) was inferred from the total selling price.

2. Prepare the shareholders' equity section of the comparative balance sheets for National Foods at December 31, 2010 and 2009.

NATIONAL FOODS, INC.
Balance Sheet
[Shareholders' Equity Section]

	($ in millions)	
	2010	**2009**
Shareholders' Equity		
Preferred stock, 9.2%, $1 par (2010: $10 million + 1 million)	$ 11	$ —
Common stock, $1 par (2010: $120 million + 1 million + 1 million)	122	120
Paid-in capital—excess of par, preferred (2010: $430 million + 49 million)	479	—
Paid-in capital—excess of par, common (2010: $836 million + 9 million + 9 million)	854	836
Retained earnings (2009: $2,449 million + 400 million − 1 million)	2,848	2,449
Total shareholders' equity	$4,314	$3,405

Note: This situation is continued in the next Concept Review Exercise on page 1028.

Share Buybacks

● LO5

In the previous section we examined various ways stock might be issued. In this section, we look at situations in which companies reacquire shares previously sold. Most medium- and large-size companies buy back their own shares. Many have formal share repurchase plans to buy back stock over a series of years.

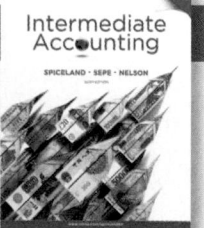

Intermediate Accounting
SPICELAND · SEPE · NELSON

Decreasing the supply of shares in the marketplace supports the price of remaining shares.

FINANCIAL
Reporting Case

Q1, p. 1007

Unlike an investment in another firm's shares, the acquisition of a company's own shares does not create an asset.

DECISION MAKER'S PERSPECTIVE

When a company's management feels the market price of its stock is undervalued, it may attempt to support the price by decreasing the supply of stock in the marketplace. A **Johnson & Johnson** announcement that it planned to buy back up to $5 billion of its outstanding shares triggered a buying spree that pushed the stock price up by more than 3 percent.

When announcing plans to repurchase up to $1 billion of its shares, **Bullion Monarch Mining** chairman and chief executive officer Don Morris explained, "We believe the current share price . . . represents an excellent investment opportunity for the company."[10] Although clearly a company may attempt to increase net assets by buying its shares at a low price and selling them back later at a higher price, that investment is not viewed as an asset. Similarly, increases and decreases in net assets from that activity are not reported as gains and losses in the company's income statement. Instead, buying and selling its shares are transactions between the corporation and its owners, analogous to retiring shares and then selling previously unissued shares. You should note the contrast between a company's purchasing of its own shares and its purchasing of shares in another corporation as an investment.

Though not considered an investment, the repurchase of shares often is a judicious use of a company's cash. By increasing per share earnings and supporting share price, shareholders benefit. When **Walmart** announced a $15 billion buyback of common stock in 2009, **Neil Currie**, an analyst with **UBS** Securities commented, "Walmart has taken a major step in attempting to improve returns on investment."[11]

---

[10]"Bullion Monarch Mining Announces Results of Stock Buyback Program for FY 2009," *Forbes.com*, July 6, 2009.
[11]"Walmart Plans to Buy Back $15 Billion in Shares," *Bloomberg.com*, June 1, 2009.

To the extent this strategy is effective, a share buyback can be viewed as a way to "distribute" company profits without paying dividends. Capital gains from any stock price increase are taxed at lower capital gains tax rates than ordinary income tax rates on dividends.

Perhaps the primary motivation for most stock repurchases is to offset the increase in shares that routinely are issued to employees under stock award and stock option compensation programs. **Microsoft** reported its stock buyback program designed to offset the effect of its stock option and stock purchase plans as shown in Graphic 18–5.

> **Note 11: Stockholders' Equity (in part)**
>
> Our board of directors has approved a program to repurchase shares of our common stock to reduce the dilutive effect of our stock option and stock purchase plans.

Similarly, shares might be reacquired to distribute in a stock dividend, a proposed merger, or as a defense against a hostile takeover.[12]

The usual pattern of stock buybacks was interrupted by the recent economic decline. With corporate profits down and cash in short supply, companies drastically reduced their share repurchases. Companies in the S&P 500 reduced their buybacks in the first quarter of 2009 a whopping 73% from the first quarter a year earlier.[13] For some companies, the decision was a choice between cutting buybacks or cutting dividends, and dividend reductions are more obvious and less palatable than curtailing a buyback program.

Whatever the reason shares are repurchased, a company has a choice of how to account for the buyback:

1. The shares can be formally retired.
2. The shares can be called treasury stock.

Unfortunately, the choice is not dictated by the nature of the buyback, but by practical motivations of the company. ●

Shares Formally Retired or Viewed as Treasury Stock

When a corporation retires its own shares, those shares assume the same status as authorized but unissued shares, just the same as if they never had been issued. We saw earlier in the chapter that when shares are sold, both cash (usually) and shareholders' equity are increased; the company becomes larger. Conversely, when cash is paid to retire stock, the effect is to decrease both cash and shareholders' equity; the size of the company literally is reduced.

Out of tradition and for practical reasons, companies usually reacquire shares of previously issued stock without formally retiring them.[14] Shares repurchased and not retired are referred to as treasury stock. Because reacquired shares are essentially the same as shares that never were issued at all, treasury shares have no voting rights nor do they receive cash dividends. As demonstrated in Illustration 18–5 on the next page, when shares are repurchased as treasury stock, we reduce shareholders' equity with a debit to a negative (or contra) shareholders' equity account labeled treasury stock. That entry is reversed later through a credit to treasury stock when the treasury stock is resold. Like the concepts of par value and legal capital, the concept of treasury shares no longer is recognized in most state statutes.[15] Some companies, in fact, are eliminating treasury shares from their financial statements as corporate statutes are modernized. **Microsoft** retires the shares it buys back rather than labeling them treasury stock. Still, you will see treasury shares reported in the balance sheets of many companies.

GRAPHIC 18–5

Disclosure of Share Repurchase Program—Microsoft

Real World Financials

FINANCIAL Reporting Case

Q2, p. 1007

Reacquired shares are equivalent to authorized but unissued shares.

---

[12]A corporate takeover occurs when an individual or group of individuals acquires a majority of a company's outstanding common stock from present shareholders. Corporations that are the object of a hostile takeover attempt—a public bid for control of a company's stock against the company's wishes—often take evasive action involving the reacquisition of shares.

[13]Ben Steverman, "The Incredible Shrinking Stock Buyback," *BusinessWeek,* June 19, 2009.

[14]The concept of treasury shares originated long ago when new companies found they could sell shares at an unrealistically low price equal to par value to incorporators, who then donated those shares back to the company. Since these shares already had been issued (though not outstanding), they could be sold at whatever the real market price was without adjusting stated capital.

Because treasury shares are already issued, different rules apply to their purchase and resale than to unissued shares. Companies can:
    a. Issue shares without regard to preemptive rights of shareholders.
    b. Distribute shares as a dividend to shareholders even without a balance in retained earnings.

[15]*The Revised Model Business Corporation Act* eliminated the concept of treasury shares in 1984 after 1980 revisions had eliminated the concepts of par value and legal capital. Most state laws have since followed suit.

American Semiconductor's balance sheet included the following:

Shareholders' Equity	($ in millions)
Common stock, 100 million shares at $1 par	$ 100
Paid-in capital—excess of par	900
Paid-in capital—share repurchase	2
Retained earnings	2,000

Retirement			**Treasury Stock**	

Reacquired 1 million of its common shares

Case 1: Shares repurchased at $7 per share

Common stock ($1 par × 1 million shares)	1		Treasury stock (cost)	7
Paid-in capital—excess of par ($9 per sh.)	9			
Paid-in capital—share repurchase (difference) ...		3		
Cash		7	Cash	7

OR
Case 2: Shares repurchased at $13 per share

Common stock ($1 par × 1 million shares)	1		Treasury stock (cost)	13
Paid-in capital—excess of par ($9 per sh.)	9			
Paid-in capital—share repurchase	2*			
Retained earnings (difference)	1			
Cash		13	Cash	13

*Because there is a $2 million credit balance.

Accounting for Retired Shares

When shares are formally retired, we should reduce precisely the same accounts that previously were increased when the shares were sold, namely, common (or preferred) stock and paid-in capital—excess of par. The first column of Illustration 18–5 demonstrates this. The paid-in capital—excess of par account for American Semiconductor shows a balance of $900 million while the common stock account shows a balance of $100 million. Thus the 100 million outstanding shares were originally sold for an average of $9 per share above par, or $10 per share. Consequently, when 1 million shares are retired (regardless of the retirement price), American Semiconductor should reduce its common stock account by $1 per share and its paid-in capital—excess of par by $9 per share. Another way to view the reduction is that because 1% of the shares are retired, both share account balances (common stock and paid-in capital—excess of par) are reduced by 1%.

How we treat the difference between the cash paid to buy the shares and the amount the shares originally sold for (amounts debited to common stock and paid-in capital—excess of par) depends on whether the cash paid is *less* than the original issue price (credit difference) or the cash paid is *more* than the original issue price (debit difference):

1. If a *credit* difference is created (as in Case 1 of Illustration 18–5), we credit paid-in capital—share repurchase.
2. If a *debit* difference is created (as in Case 2 of Illustration 18–5), we debit paid-in capital—share repurchase, but only if that account already has a credit balance. Otherwise, we debit retained earnings. (Reducing the account beyond its previous balance would create a negative balance.)

Why is paid-in capital credited in Case 1 and retained earnings debited in Case 2? The answer lies in the fact that the payments made by a corporation to repurchase its own shares are a distribution of corporate assets to shareholders.

In Case 1, only $7 million is distributed to shareholders to retire shares that originally provided $10 million of paid-in capital. Thus, some of the original investment ($3 million in this case) remains and is labeled *paid-in capital—share repurchase*.

In Case 2, more cash ($13 million) is distributed to shareholders to retire shares than originally was paid in. The amount paid in comprises the original investment of $10 million for the shares being retired plus $2 million of paid-in capital created by previous repurchase transactions—$12 million total. Thirteen million is returned to shareholders. The additional $1 million paid is viewed as a dividend on the shareholders' investment, and thus a reduction of retained earnings.[16]

Accounting for Treasury Stock

We view the purchase of treasury stock as a temporary reduction of shareholders' equity, to be reversed later when the treasury stock is resold. The cost of acquiring the shares is "temporarily" debited to the treasury stock account (second column of Illustration 18–5). At this point, the shares are considered to be *issued, but not outstanding.*

Recording the effects on specific shareholders' equity accounts is delayed until later when the shares are reissued. In the meantime, the shares assume the fictional status we discussed earlier of being neither unissued nor outstanding. Effectively, we consider the purchase of treasury stock and its subsequent resale to be a "single transaction."

When a share repurchase is viewed as treasury stock, recording the effects on specific shareholders' equity accounts is delayed until the shares are reissued.

ADDITIONAL CONSIDERATION

The approach to accounting for treasury stock we discuss in this chapter is referred to as the "cost method." Another permissible approach is the "par value method." It is essentially identical to formally retiring shares, which is why it sometimes is referred to as the *retirement method of accounting for treasury stock.* In fact, if we substitute Treasury stock for Common stock in each of the journal entries we used to account for retirement of shares in Illustrations 18–5 and 18–6, we have the par value method. Because the method has virtually disappeared from practice, we do not discuss it further in this chapter.

BALANCE SHEET EFFECT.   Formally retiring shares restores the balances in both the Common stock account and Paid-in capital—excess of par to what those balances would have been if the shares never had been issued at all. As discussed above, any net increase in assets resulting from the sale and subsequent repurchase is reflected as Paid-in capital—share repurchase. On the other hand, any net decrease in assets resulting from the sale and subsequent repurchase is reflected as a reduction in retained earnings.

In contrast, when a share repurchase is viewed as treasury stock, the cost of the treasury stock is simply reported as a reduction in total shareholders' equity. Reporting under the two approaches is compared in Graphic 18–6 using the situation described above for American Semiconductor after the purchase of treasury stock in Illustration 18–5 (Case 2) on page 1026. Notice that either way total shareholders' equity is the same.

	($ in millions)	
	Shares Retired	**Treasury Stock**
Shareholders' Equity		
Paid-in capital:		
Common stock, 100 million shares at $1 par	$ 99	$ 100
Paid-in capital—excess of par	891	900
Paid-in capital—reacquired shares		2
Retained earnings	1,999	2,000
Less: Treasury stock, 1 million shares (at cost)		(13)
Total shareholders' equity	$2,989	$2,989

GRAPHIC 18–6
Reporting Share Buyback in the Balance Sheet

Retirement reduces common stock and associated shareholders' equity accounts.

---

[16]In the next section of this chapter, you will be reminded that dividends reduce retained earnings. (You first learned this in your introductory accounting course.)

Resale of Shares

After shares are formally retired, any subsequent sale of shares is simply the sale of new, unissued shares and is accounted for accordingly. This is demonstrated in the first column of Illustration 18–6.

ILLUSTRATION 18–6	American Semiconductor sold 1 million shares after reacquiring shares at $13 per share (Case 2 in Illustration 18–5).

ILLUSTRATION 18–6

Comparison of Share Retirement and Treasury Stock Accounting— Subsequent Sale of Shares

After formally retiring shares, we record a subsequent sale of shares exactly like any sale of shares.

The resale of treasury shares is viewed as the consummation of the "single transaction" begun when the treasury shares were purchased.

American Semiconductor sold 1 million shares after reacquiring shares at $13 per share (Case 2 in Illustration 18–5).

	Retirement			**Treasury Stock**		
Sold 1 million shares						
Case A: Shares sold at $14 per share						
Cash	14			Cash	14	
Common stock (par)		1		Treasury stock (cost)		13
Paid-in capital—excess of par		13		Paid-in capital—share repurchase		1
OR						
Case B: Shares sold at $10 per share						
Cash	10			Cash	10	
Common stock (par)		1		Retained earnings (to balance)	1	
Paid-in capital—excess of par		9		Paid-in capital—share repurchase	2*	
				Treasury stock (cost)		13

*Because there is a $2 million credit balance.

Allocating the cost of treasury shares occurs when the shares are resold.

The resale of treasury shares is viewed as the consummation of the single transaction begun when the treasury shares were repurchased. The effect of the single transaction of purchasing treasury stock and reselling it for more than cost (Case 2 of Illustration 18–5 and Case A of Illustration 18–6) is to *increase* both cash and shareholders' equity (by $1 million). The effect of the single transaction of purchasing treasury stock and reselling it for less than cost (Case 2 of Illustration 18–5 and Case B of Illustration 18–6) is to *decrease* both cash and shareholders' equity (by $3 million).

Note that retained earnings may be debited in a treasury stock transaction, but not credited. Also notice that transactions involving treasury stock have no impact on the income statement. This follows the reasoning discussed earlier that a corporation's buying and selling of its own shares are transactions between the corporation and its owners and not part of the earnings process.

ADDITIONAL CONSIDERATION

Treasury Shares Acquired at Different Costs

Determining the cost of treasury stock sold is similar to determining the cost of goods sold.

Notice that the treasury stock account always is credited for the cost of the reissued shares ($13 million in Illustration 18–6). When shares are reissued, if treasury stock on hand has been purchased at different per share prices, the cost of the shares sold must be determined using a cost flow assumption—FIFO, LIFO, or weighted average—similar to determining the cost of goods sold when inventory items are acquired at different unit costs.

CONCEPT REVIEW EXERCISE

TREASURY STOCK

Situation: The shareholders' equity section of the balance sheet of National Foods, Inc., included the following accounts at December 31, 2010.

Shareholders' Equity	($ in millions)
Paid-in capital:	
Preferred stock, 11 million shares at $1 par	$ 11
Common stock, 122 million shares at $1 par	122
Paid-in capital—excess of par, preferred	479
Paid-in capital—excess of par, common	854
Retained earnings	2,848
Total shareholders' equity	$4,314

Required:

1. National Foods reacquired common shares during 2011 and sold shares in two separate transactions later that year. Prepare the entries for both the purchase and subsequent sale of shares during 2011 assuming that the shares were (a) retired and (b) considered to be treasury stock.

   a. National Foods purchased 6 million shares at $10 per share.
   b. National Foods sold 2 million shares at $12 per share.
   c. National Foods sold 2 million shares at $7 per share.

2. Prepare the shareholders' equity section of National Foods' balance sheet at December 31, 2011, assuming the shares were both (a) retired and (b) viewed as treasury stock. Net income for 2011 was $400 million, and preferred shareholders were paid $1 million cash dividends.

SOLUTION

1. National Foods reacquired common shares during 2011 and sold shares in two separate transactions later that year. Prepare the entries for both the purchase and subsequent sale of shares during 2011 assuming that the shares were (a) retired and (b) considered to be treasury stock.

   a. National Foods **purchased** 6 million shares at $10 per share:

Retirement ($ in millions)				**Treasury Stock** ($ in millions)		
Common stock (6 million shares × $1)	6			Treasury stock		
Paid-in capital—excess of par (6 million				(6 million shares × $10)	60	
shares × $7*)	42			Cash		60
Retained earnings (to balance)	12					
Cash		60				

*$854 million ÷ 122 million shares

   b. National Foods **sold** 2 million shares at $12 per share: ($ in millions)

Cash 24		Cash	24	
Common stock (2 million shares × $1)........	2	Treasury stock (2 million shares		
Paid-in capital—excess of par.......................	22	× $10)		20
		Paid-in capital—share		
		repurchase		4

   c. National Foods **sold** 2 million shares at $7 per share: ($ in millions)

Cash 14		Cash	14	
Common stock (2 million shares		Paid-in capital—share		
× $1 par)	2	repurchase	4	
Paid-in capital—excess of par	12	Retained earnings (to balance)	2	
		Treasury stock (2 million shares		
		× $10)		20

2. Prepare the shareholders' equity section of National Foods' balance sheet at December 31, 2011, assuming the shares were both (a) retired and (b) viewed as treasury stock.

NATIONAL FOODS, INC.
Balance Sheet
[Shareholders' Equity Section]
At December 31, 2011

($ in millions)

	Shares Retired	Treasury Stock
Shareholders' Equity		
Preferred stock, 11 million shares at $1 par	$ 11	$ 11
Common stock, 122 million shares at $1 par	120	122
Paid-in capital—excess of par, preferred	479	479
Paid-in capital—excess of par, common	846*	854
Retained earnings	3,235†	3,245†
Treasury stock, at cost; 2 million common shares	—	(20)
Total shareholders' equity	$4,691	$4,691

*$854 − 42 + 22 + 12
†$2,848 − 12 + 400 − 1
‡$2,848 − 2 + 400 − 1

Note: This situation is continued in the next Concept Review Exercise on page 1038.

WHERE WE'RE HEADED

The FASB and IASB are working together on a standard that would have a dramatic impact on the format of financial statements.

● LO9

The FASB and IASB are working together on a project, Financial Statement Presentation, to establish a common standard for presenting information in the financial statements, including classifying and displaying line items and aggregating line items into subtotals and totals. This standard will have a dramatic impact on the format of financial statements. An important part of the proposal involves the organization of elements of the balance sheet (statement of financial position), statement of comprehensive income (including the income statement), and statement of cash flows into a common set of classifications.

A key feature of the new format is that each of the financial statements will include classifications by operating, investing, and financing activities (similar to the current statement of cash flows), providing a "cohesive" financial picture that stresses the relationships among the financial statements.

Demonstrating the cohesiveness among the financial statements is a key objective of the Financial Statement Presentation project.

For each statement, though, operating and investing activities will be included within a new category, "business" activities. Each statement also will include three additional groupings: discontinued operations, income taxes, and equity (if needed). The new look for the financials will be:

Statement of Financial Position	Statement of Comprehensive Income	Statement of Cash Flows
Business • Operating assets and liabilities • Investing assets and liabilities	Business • Operating income and expenses • Investing income and expenses	Business • Operating cash flows • Investing cash flows
Financing • Financing assets • Financing liabilities	Financing • Financing asset income • Financing liability expense	Financing • Financing asset cash flows • Financing liability cash flows
Income Taxes	Income Taxes	Income Taxes
Discontinued Operations	Discontinued Operations (net of tax)	Discontinued Operations
Equity	Other Comprehensive Income (net of tax)	Equity

(continued)

(concluded)

Notice that we would have an equity section, not just in the balance sheet, but in the other statements as well. The proposal doesn't change the elements in the equity section of the balance sheet. Changes in equity items would be presented in the equity section of the statement of cash flows (for example cash dividends) and in the statement of changes in equity, which is essentially the same as the current statement of shareholders' equity described in this chapter. In a sense, the statement of comprehensive income also reports changes in equity because net income increases retained earnings and other comprehensive income changes accumulated OCI, both components of equity. The new format also standardizes the presentation of a separate statement of comprehensive income as opposed to the presentation choices available now.

Each statement is slated to have an equity section.

RETAINED EARNINGS

PART C

Characteristics of Retained Earnings

In the previous section we examined *invested* capital. Now we consider *earned* capital, that is, retained earnings. In general, retained earnings represents a corporation's accumulated, undistributed net income (or net loss). A more descriptive title used by some companies is reinvested earnings. A credit balance in this account indicates a dollar amount of assets previously earned by the firm but not distributed as dividends to shareholders. We refer to a debit balance in retained earnings as a **deficit**. **Microsoft** reported a deficit of $22.8 billion as of June 30, 2009.

● LO6

Real World Financials

You saw in the previous section that the buyback of shares (as well as the resale of treasury shares in some cases) can decrease retained earnings. We examine in this section the effect on retained earnings of dividends and stock splits.

Dividends

Shareholders' initial investments in a corporation are represented by amounts reported as paid-in capital. One way a corporation provides a return to its shareholders on their investments is to pay them a **dividend,** typically cash.[17]

● LO7

Dividends are distributions of assets the company has earned on behalf of its shareholders. If dividends are paid that exceed the amount of assets earned by the company, then management is, in effect, returning to shareholders a portion of their investments, rather than providing them a return on that investment. So most companies view retained earnings as the amount available for dividends.[18]

Liquidating Dividend

In unusual instances in which a dividend exceeds the balance in retained earnings, the excess is referred to as a **liquidating dividend** because some of the invested capital is being liquidated. This might occur when a corporation is being dissolved and assets (not subject to a superior claim by creditors) are distributed to shareholders. Any portion of a dividend not representing a distribution of earnings should be debited to additional paid-in capital rather than retained earnings.

Any dividend not representing a distribution of earnings should be debited to paid-in capital.

---

[17]Dividends are not the only return shareholders earn; when market prices of their shares rise, shareholders benefit also. Indeed, many companies have adopted policies of never paying dividends but reinvesting all assets they earn. The motivation is to accommodate more rapid expansion and thus, presumably, increases in the market price of the stock.

[18]Ordinarily, this is not the legal limitation. Most states permit a company to pay dividends so long as, after the dividend, its assets would not be "less than the sum of its total liabilities plus the amount that would be needed, if the corporation were to be dissolved at the time of the distribution, to satisfy the preferential rights upon dissolution of shareholders whose preferential rights are superior to those receiving the distribution." (Revised Model Business Corporation Act, American Bar Association, 1994.) Thus, legally, a corporation can distribute amounts equal to total shareholders' equity less dissolution preferences of senior equity securities (usually preferred stock). Note that Microsoft has recently paid cash dividends despite a deficit (negative retained earnings).

Retained Earnings Restrictions

Sometimes the amount available for dividends purposely is reduced by management. A restriction of retained earnings designates a portion of the balance in retained earnings as being *unavailable for dividends*. A company might restrict retained earnings to indicate management's intention to withhold for some specific purpose the assets represented by that portion of the retained earnings balance. For example, management might anticipate the need for a specific amount of assets in upcoming years to repay a maturing debt, to cover a contingent loss, or to finance expansion of the facilities. Be sure to understand that the restriction itself does not set aside cash for the designated event but merely communicates management's intention not to distribute the stated amount as a dividend.

A restriction of retained earnings normally is indicated by a disclosure note to the financial statements. Although instances are rare, a formal journal entry may be used to reclassify a portion of retained earnings to an "appropriated" retained earnings account.

Cash Dividends

You learned in Chapter 14 that paying interest to creditors is a contractual obligation. No such legal obligation exists for paying dividends to shareholders. A liability is not recorded until a company's board of directors votes to declare a dividend. In practice, though, corporations ordinarily try to maintain a stable dividend pattern over time.

When directors declare a cash dividend, we reduce retained earnings and record a liability. Before the payment actually can be made, a listing must be assembled of shareholders entitled to receive the dividend. A specific date is stated as to when the determination will be made of the recipients of the dividend. This date is called the **date of record.** Registered owners of shares of stock on this date are entitled to receive the dividend—even if they sell those shares prior to the actual cash payment. To be a registered owner of shares on the date of record, an investor must purchase the shares before the **ex-dividend date.** This date usually is two business days before the date of record. Shares purchased on or after that date are purchased ex dividend—without the right to receive the declared dividend. As a result, the market price of a share typically will decline by the amount of the dividend, other things being equal, on the ex-dividend date. Consider Illustration 18–7.

> **Microsoft Corp.** today announced that its Board of Directors declared a quarterly dividend of $0.13 per share. The dividend is payable Sept. 10, 2009, to shareholders of record on Aug. 20, 2009.[19]

ILLUSTRATION 18–7
Cash Dividends

At the declaration date, retained earnings is reduced and a liability is recorded.

Registered owners of shares on the date of record are entitled to receive the dividend.

On June 1, the board of directors of Craft Industries declares a cash dividend of $2 per share on its 100 million shares, payable to shareholders of record June 15, to be paid July 1:

	($ in millions)
June 1—Declaration Date	
Retained earnings	200
Cash dividends payable (100 million shares at $2/share)	200
June 13—Ex-Dividend Date	
No entry	
June 15—Date of Record	
No entry	
July 1—Payment Date	
Cash dividends payable	200
Cash	200

A sufficient balance in retained earnings permits a dividend to be declared. Remember, though, that retained earnings is a shareholders' equity account representing a dollar claim on assets in general, but not on any specific asset in particular. Sufficient retained earnings does not ensure sufficient cash to make payment. These are two separate accounts having no necessary connection with one another. When a dividend is "paid from retained earnings," this simply means that sufficient assets previously have been earned to pay the dividend without returning invested assets to shareholders.

Property Dividends

Because cash is the asset most easily divided and distributed to shareholders, most corporate dividends are cash dividends. In concept, though, any asset can be distributed to shareholders as a dividend. When a noncash asset is distributed, it is referred to as a **property dividend** (often called a *dividend in kind* or a *nonreciprocal transfer to owners*).

RFM Corporation recently declared to its shareholders a property dividend in shares of **Philipine Townships, Inc.**, stock that RFM was holding as an investment. Securities held as investments are the assets most often distributed in a property dividend due to the relative ease of dividing these assets among shareholders and determining their fair values.

A property dividend should be recorded at the fair value of the assets to be distributed, measured at the date of declaration. This may require revaluing the asset to fair value prior to recording the dividend. If so, a gain or loss is recognized for the difference between book value and fair value. This is demonstrated in Illustration 18–8.

> The *fair value* of the assets to be distributed is the amount recorded for a property dividend.
>
> **Real World Financials**

On October 1 the board of directors of Craft Industries declares a property dividend of 2 million shares of Beaman Corporation's preferred stock that Craft had purchased in March as an investment (book value: $9 million). The investment shares have a fair value of $5 per share, $10 million, and are payable to shareholders of record October 15, to be distributed November 1:

October 1—Declaration Date	($ in millions)	
Investment in Beaman Corporation preferred stock	1	
Gain on appreciation of investment ($10 – 9)		1
Retained earnings (2 million shares at $5 per share)	10	
Property dividends payable		10
October 15—Date of Record		
No entry		
November 1—Payment Date		
Property dividends payable	10	
Investment in Beaman Corporation preferred stock		10

ILLUSTRATION 18–8
Property Dividends

Before recording the property dividend, the asset first must be written up to fair value.

Stock Dividends and Splits

Stock Dividends

A **stock dividend** is the distribution of additional shares of stock to current shareholders of the corporation. Be sure to note the contrast between a stock dividend and either a cash or property dividend. A stock dividend affects neither the assets nor the liabilities of the firm. Also, because each shareholder receives the same percentage increase in shares, shareholders' proportional interest in (percentage ownership of) the firm remains unchanged.

● LO8

The prescribed accounting treatment of a stock dividend requires that shareholders' equity items be reclassified by reducing one or more shareholders' equity accounts and simultaneously increasing one or more paid-in capital accounts. The amount reclassified depends on the size of the stock dividend. For a small stock dividend, typically less than 25%, the fair market value of the additional shares distributed is transferred from retained earnings to paid-in capital as demonstrated in Illustration 18–9.[20]

---

[20]The Committee on Accounting Procedure prescribes this accounting treatment in FASB ASC 505–20: Equity–Stock Dividends and Stock Splits (previously "Restatement and Revision of Accounting Research Bulletins," *Accounting Research Bulletin No. 43* (New York: AICPA, 1961), Chap. 7, sec. B, pars. 10–14). In this pronouncement, a small stock dividend is defined as one 20 to 25% or less. For filings with that agency, the SEC has refined the definition to comprise stock distributions of less than 25%.

ILLUSTRATION 18–9

Stock Dividend

A small stock dividend requires reclassification to paid-in capital of retained earnings equal to the fair value of the additional shares distributed.

Craft declares and distributes a 10% common stock dividend (10 million shares) when the market value of the $1 par common stock is $12 per share.

	($ in millions)	
Retained earnings (10 million shares at $12 per share)	120	
Common stock (10 million shares at $1 par per share)		10
Paid-in capital—excess of par (remainder)..		110

ADDITIONAL CONSIDERATION

The entry above is recorded on the declaration date. Since the additional shares are not yet issued, some accountants would prefer to credit "common stock dividends issuable" at this point, instead of common stock. In that case, when the shares are issued, common stock dividends issuable is debited and common stock credited. The choice really is inconsequential; either way the $10 million amount would be reported as part of paid-in capital on a balance sheet prepared between the declaration and distribution of the shares.

STOCK MARKET REACTION TO STOCK DISTRIBUTIONS. As a Craft shareholder owning 10 shares at the time of the 10% stock dividend, you would receive an 11th share. Since each is worth $12, would you benefit by $12 when you receive the additional share from Craft? Of course not. If the value of each share were to remain $12 when the 10 million new shares are distributed, the total market value of the company would grow by $120 million (10 million shares × $12 per share).

The market price per share will decline in proportion to the increase in the number of shares distributed in a stock dividend.

A corporation cannot increase its market value simply by distributing additional stock certificates. Because all shareholders receive the same percentage increase in their respective holdings, you, and all other shareholders, still would own the same percentage of the company as before the distribution. Accordingly, the per share value of your shares should decline from $12 to $10.91 so that your 11 shares would be worth $120—precisely what your 10 shares were worth prior to the stock dividend. Any failure of the stock price to actually adjust in proportion to the additional shares issued probably would be due to information other than the distribution reaching shareholders at the same time.

Early rule-makers felt that per share market prices do not adjust in response to an increase in the number of shares.

Then, what justification is there for recording the additional shares at market value? In 1941 (and reaffirmed in 1953), accounting rule-makers felt that many shareholders are deceived by small stock dividends, believing they benefit by the market value of their additional shares. Furthermore they erroneously felt that these individual beliefs are collectively reflected in the stock market by per share prices that remain unchanged by stock dividends. Consequently, their prescribed accounting treatment is to reduce retained earnings by the same amount as if cash dividends were paid equal to the market value of the shares issued.[21]

This obsolete reasoning is inconsistent with our earlier conclusion that the market price per share will decline in approximate proportion to the increase in the number of shares distributed. Our intuitive conclusion is supported also by formal research.[22]

Capitalizing retained earnings for a stock dividend artificially reclassifies earned capital as invested capital.

Besides being based on fallacious reasoning, accounting for stock dividends by artificially reclassifying "earned" capital as "invested" capital conflicts with the reporting objective of reporting shareholders' equity by source. Despite these limitations, this outdated accounting standard still applies.

---

[21]FASB ASC 505–20–30–3: Equity–Stock Dividends and Stock Splits–Initial Measurement (previously "Restatement and Revision of Accounting Research Bulletins," *Accounting Research Bulletin No. 43* (New York: AICPA, 1961), chap. 7).

[22]Foster and Vickrey, "The Information Content of Stock Dividend Announcements," *Accounting Review* (April 1978), and Spiceland and Winters, "The Market Reaction to Stock Distributions: The Effect of Market Anticipation and Cash Returns," *Accounting and Business Research* (Summer 1986).

REASONS FOR STOCK DIVIDENDS.   Since neither the corporation nor its shareholders apparently benefits from stock dividends, why do companies declare them?[23] Occasionally, a company tries to give shareholders the illusion that they are receiving a real dividend.

Another reason is merely to enable the corporation to take advantage of the accepted accounting practice of capitalizing retained earnings. Specifically, a company might wish to reduce an existing balance in retained earnings—otherwise available for *cash* dividends—so it can reinvest the earned assets represented by that balance without carrying a large balance in retained earnings.

> **Companies sometimes declare a stock dividend in lieu of a real dividend.**
>
> **Companies sometimes declare a stock dividend so they can capitalize retained earnings.**

Stock Splits

A frequent reason for issuing a stock dividend is actually to induce the per share market price decline that follows. For instance, after a company declares a 100% stock dividend on 100 million shares of common stock, with a per share market price of $12, it then has 200 million shares, each with an approximate market value of $6. The motivation for reducing the per share market price is to increase the stock's *marketability* by making it attractive to a larger number of potential investors.

> **FINANCIAL**
> **Reporting Case**
>
> Q4, p. 1007

ADDITIONAL CONSIDERATION

No cash dividends are paid on treasury shares. Usually stock dividends aren't paid on treasury shares either. Treasury shares are essentially equivalent to shares that never have been issued. In some circumstances, though, the intended use of the repurchased shares will give reason for the treasury shares to participate in a stock dividend. For instance, if the treasury shares have been specifically designated for issuance to executives in a stock option plan or stock award plan it would be appropriate to adjust the number of shares by the stock distribution.

> Following on the heels of an enormous run up in price in shares, Apple Computer announced Friday a two-for-one stock split. Each share held on Feb. 18 gets an additional share. The company plans to start trading on a split-adjusted basis at the end of February. "It potentially makes it more attractive to individual investors," said Steve Lidberg, an analyst at Pacific Crest Securities, who doesn't own shares of Apple. "Outside of that, it doesn't impact at all the way I think of the company."[25]

A stock distribution of 25% or higher can be accounted for in one of two ways: (1) as a "large" stock dividend or (2) as a **stock split**.[24] Thus, a 100% stock dividend could be labeled a 2-for-1 stock split and accounted for as such. Conceptually, the proper accounting treatment of a stock distribution is to make no journal entry. This, in fact, is the prescribed accounting treatment for a stock split.

Since the same common stock account balance (total par) represents twice as many shares in a 2-for-1 stock split, the par value per share will be reduced by one-half. In the previous example, if the par were $1 per share before the stock distribution, then after the 2-for-1 stock split, the par would be $.50 per share.

As you might expect, having the par value per share change in this way is cumbersome and expensive. All records, printed or electronic, that refer to the previous amount must be changed to reflect the new amount. The practical solution is to account for the large stock distribution as a stock dividend rather than a stock split.

> **A large stock dividend is known as a stock split.**

Stock Splits Effected in the Form of Stock Dividends (Large Stock Dividends)

To avoid changing the per share par value of the shares, the stock distribution is referred to as a *stock split effected in the form of a stock dividend,* or simply a *stock dividend.* In that case,

---

[23]After hitting a high in the 1940s, the number of stock dividends has declined significantly. Currently, about 3% of companies declare stock dividends in any given year.

[24]FASB ASC 505–20–25–2: Equity–Stock Dividends and Stock Splits–Recognition (previously "Restatement and Revision of Accounting Research Bulletins," *Accounting Research Bulletin No. 43* (New York: AICPA, 1961), Chap. 7, sec. B, par. 11).

[25]"Apple's Share Price Surge Results in Stock Split," *CNN Money,* February 11, 2005.

a journal entry increases the common stock account by the par value of the additional shares. To avoid reducing retained earnings in these instances, most companies reduce (debit) paid-in capital—excess of par to offset the credit to common stock (Illustration 18–10).

ILLUSTRATION 18–10

Stock Split Effected in the Form of a Stock Dividend

If a *stock split* is effected in the form of a stock dividend, a journal entry prevents the par per share from changing.

Craft declares and distributes a 2-for-1 stock split effected in the form of a 100% stock dividend (100 million shares) when the market value of the $1 par common stock is $12 per share:

	($ in millions)	
Paid-in capital—excess of par	100	
Common stock (100 million shares at $1 par per share)		100

Notice that this entry does not reclassify earned capital as invested capital. Some companies, though, choose to debit retained earnings instead.[26]

Some companies capitalize retained earnings when recording a stock split effected in the form of a stock dividend.

	($ in millions)	
Retained earnings	100	
Common stock (10 million shares × $1 par per share)		100

Nike, Inc. described a stock split in its disclosure notes as shown in Graphic 18–7.

GRAPHIC 18–7

Stock Split Disclosure—Nike, Inc.

Real World Financials

Note 1—Summary of Significant Accounting Policies
Stock Split
On February 15the Board of Directors declared a two-for-one stock split of the Company's Class A and Class B common shares, which was effected in the form of a 100% common stock dividend distributed on April 2. All references to share and per share amounts in the consolidated financial statements and accompanying notes to the consolidated financial statements have been retroactively restated to reflect the two-for-one stock split.

ADDITIONAL CONSIDERATION

A company choosing to capitalize retained earnings when recording a stock split effected in the form of a stock dividend may elect to capitalize an amount other than par value. Accounting guidelines are vague in this regard, stating only that legal amounts are minimum requirements and do not prevent the capitalization of a larger amount per share.

Source: FASB ASC 505–20–30–4: Equity–Stock Dividends and Stock Splits–Initial Measurement (previously "Restatement and Revision of Accounting Research Bulletins," *Accounting Research Bulletin No. 43* (New York: AICPA, 1961), Chap. 7, sec. B, par. 14).

REVERSE STOCK SPLIT. A reverse stock split occurs when a company decreases, rather than increases, its outstanding shares. After a 1-for-4 reverse stock split, for example, 100 million shares, $1 par per share, would become 25 million shares, $4 par per share. No journal entry is necessary. Of course the market price per share theoretically would quadruple, which usually is the motivation for declaring a reverse stock split. Companies that reverse split their shares frequently are struggling companies trying to accomplish with the split what the market has been unwilling to do—increase the stock price. Often this is to prevent the stock's price from becoming so low that it is delisted from a market exchange. Reverse splits are not unusual occurrences, particularly during stock market downturns. **Time Warner Cable** was one of many in 2009, declaring a 1-for-3 reverse split.

---

[26]The 2009 *Accounting Trends & Techniques* (p. 508) reports that 10 of its 500 sample companies reported a stock split. Of those, none debited additional paid-in capital, 1 debited retained earnings, and 9 made no entry.

FRACTIONAL SHARES. Typically, a stock dividend or stock split results in some shareholders being entitled to fractions of whole shares. For example, if a company declares a 25% stock dividend, or equivalently a 5-for-4 stock split, a shareholder owning 10 shares would be entitled to 2½ shares. Another shareholder with 15 shares would be entitled to 3¾ shares.

Cash payments usually are made to shareholders for fractional shares and are called "cash in lieu of payments." In the situation described above, for instance, if the market price at declaration is $12 per share, the shareholder with 15 shares would receive 3 additional shares and $9 in cash ($12 × ¾).

> **Cash payments usually are made when shareholders are entitled to fractions of whole shares.**

DECISION MAKER'S PERSPECTIVE

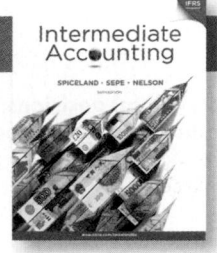

Profitability is the key to a company's long-run survival. A summary measure of profitability often used by investors and potential investors, particularly common shareholders, is the return on shareholders' equity. This ratio measures the ability of company management to generate net income from the resources that owners provide. The ratio is computed by dividing net income by average shareholders' equity. A variation of this ratio often is used when a company has both preferred and common stock outstanding. The return to common shareholders' equity is calculated by subtracting dividends to preferred shareholders from the numerator and using average common shareholders' equity as the denominator. The modified ratio focuses on the profits generated on the assets provided by common shareholders.

> **The return on shareholders' equity is a popular measure of profitability.**

Although the ratio is useful when evaluating the effectiveness of management in employing resources provided by owners, analysts must be careful not to view it in isolation or without considering how the ratio is derived. Keep in mind that shareholders' equity is a measure of the book value of equity, equivalent to the book value of net assets. Book value measures quickly become out of line with market values. An asset's book value usually equals its market value on the date it's purchased; the two aren't necessarily the same after that. Equivalently, the market value of a share of stock (or of total shareholders' equity) usually is different from its book value. As a result, to supplement the return on shareholders' equity ratio, analysts often relate earnings to the market value of equity, calculating the earnings-price ratio. This ratio is simply the earnings per share divided by the market price per share.

> **Book value measures have limited use in financial analysis.**

To better understand the differences between the book value ratio and the market value ratio, let's consider the following condensed information reported by Sharp-Novell Industries for 2011 and 2010:

($ in 000s except per share amounts)	2011	2010
Sales	$3,500	$3,100
Net income	125	114
Current assets	$ 750	$ 720
Property, plant, and equipment (net)	900	850
Total assets	$1,650	$1,570
Current liabilities	$ 550	$ 530
Long-term liabilities	540	520
Paid-in capital	210	210
Retained earnings	350	310
Liabilities and shareholders' equity	$1,650	$1,570
Shares outstanding	50,000	50,000
Stock price (average)	$42.50	$42.50

The 2011 return on shareholders' equity is computed by dividing net income by average shareholders' equity:

$$\$125 \div [(\$560 + 520)/2] = 23.1\%$$

The earnings-price ratio is the earnings per share divided by the market price per share:

$$\text{Earnings per share (2011)} = \$125 \div 50 = \$2.50$$
$$\text{Earnings-price ratio} = \$2.50 \div 42.50 = 5.9\%$$

Share retirement and treasury stock transactions can affect the return to owners.

Obviously, the return on the market value of equity is much lower than on the book value of equity. This points out the importance of looking at more than a single ratio when making decisions. While 23.1% may seem like a desirable return, 5.9% is not nearly so attractive. Companies often emphasize the return on shareholders' equity in their annual reports. Alert investors should not accept this measure of achievement at face value. For some companies this is a meaningful measure of performance; but for others, the market-based ratio means more, particularly for a mature firm whose book value and market value are more divergent.

Dividend decisions should be evaluated in light of prevailing circumstances.

Decisions managers make with regard to shareholders' equity transactions can significantly impact the return to shareholders. For example, when a company buys back shares of its own stock, the return on shareholders' equity goes up. Net income is divided by a smaller amount of shareholders' equity. On the other hand, the share buyback uses assets, reducing the resources available to earn net income in the future. So, managers as well as outside analysts must carefully consider the decision to reacquire shares in light of the current economic environment, the firm's investment opportunities, and cost of capital to decide whether such a transaction is in the long-term best interests of owners. Investors should be wary of buybacks during down times because the resulting decrease in shares and increase in earnings per share can be used to mask a slowdown in earnings growth.

The decision to pay dividends requires similar considerations. When earnings are high, are shareholders better off receiving substantial cash dividends or having management reinvest those funds to finance future growth (and future dividends)? The answer, of course, depends on the particular circumstances involved. Dividend decisions should reflect managerial strategy concerning the mix of internal versus external financing, alternative investment opportunities, and industry conditions. High dividends often are found in mature industries and low dividends in growth industries. ●

ETHICAL DILEMMA

Interworld Distributors has paid quarterly cash dividends since 1980. The dividends have steadily increased from $.25 per share to the latest dividend declaration of $2.00 per share. The board of directors is eager to continue this trend despite the fact that revenues fell significantly during recent months as a result of worsening economic conditions and increased competition. The company founder and member of the board proposes a solution. He suggests a 5% stock dividend in lieu of a cash dividend to be accompanied by the following press announcement:

"In lieu of our regular $2.00 per share cash dividend, Interworld will distribute a 5% stock dividend on its common shares, currently trading at $40 per share. Changing the form of the dividend will permit the Company to direct available cash resources to the modernization of physical facilities in preparation for competing in the 21st century."

What do you think?

CONCEPT REVIEW EXERCISE

CHANGES IN RETAINED EARNINGS

Situation: The shareholders' equity section of the balance sheet of National Foods, Inc., included the following accounts at December 31, 2011:

Shareholders' Equity	($ in millions)
Paid-in capital	
Preferred stock, 9.09%, 11 million shares at $1 par	$ 11
Common stock, 122 million shares at $1 par	122
Paid-in capital—excess of par, preferred	479
Paid-in capital—excess of par, common	854
Retained earnings	3,245
Treasury stock, at cost, 2 million common shares	(20)
Total shareholders' equity	$4,691

Required:

1. During 2012, several events and transactions affected the retained earnings of National Foods. Prepare the appropriate entries for these events.

   a. On March 1, the board of directors declared a cash dividend of $1 per share on its 120 million outstanding shares (122 million − 2 million treasury shares), payable on April 3 to shareholders of record March 11.

   b. On March 5, the board of directors declared a property dividend of 120 million shares of **Kroger** common stock that National Foods had purchased in February as an investment (book value: $900 million). The investment shares had a fair value of $8 per share and were distributed March 30 to shareholders of record March 15.

   c. On April 13, a 3-for-2 stock split was declared and distributed. The stock split was effected in the form of a 50% stock dividend. The market value of the $1 par common stock was $20 per share.

   d. On October 13, a 10% common stock dividend was declared and distributed when the market value of the $1 par common stock was $12 per share. Cash in lieu of payments was distributed for fractional shares equivalent to 1 million whole shares.

   e. On December 1, the board of directors declared the 9.09% cash dividend on the 11 million preferred shares, payable on December 23 to shareholders of record December 11.

2. Prepare a statement of shareholders' equity for National Foods reporting the changes in shareholders' equity accounts for 2010, 2011, and 2012. Refer to the previous two Concept Reviews in this chapter for the 2010 and 2011 changes. For 2011, assume that shares were reacquired as treasury stock. Also, look back to the statement of shareholders' equity in Graphic 18–4 on page 1014 for the format of the statement. Assume that net income for 2012 is $225 million.

1. During 2012, several events and transactions affected the retained earnings of National Foods. Prepare the appropriate entries for these events.

   a. Cash dividend of $1 per share on its 120 million *outstanding* common shares (122 million − 2 million treasury shares), payable on April 3 to shareholders of record March 11 (Note: Dividends aren't paid on treasury shares.):

SOLUTION

March 1—Declaration Date	($ in millions)	
Retained earnings	120	
Cash dividends payable (120 million shares at $1/share)		120
March 11—Date of Record		
No entry		
April 3—Payment Date		
Cash dividends payable	120	
Cash		120

The declaration of a dividend reduces retained earnings and creates a liability.

   b. Property dividend of 120 million shares of Kroger common stock:

March 5—Declaration Date	($ in millions)	
Investment in Kroger common stock	60	
Gain on appreciation of investment ($960 − 900)		60
Retained earnings (fair value of asset to be distributed)	960	
Property dividends payable		960
March 15—Date of Record		
No entry		
March 30—Payment Date		
Property dividends payable	960	
Investment in Kroger common stock		960

The investment first must be written up to the $960 million fair value ($8 × 120 million shares).

The liability is satisfied when the Kroger shares are distributed to shareholders.

c. 3-for-2 stock split effected in the form of a 50% stock dividend:

April 13		
Paid-in capital—excess of par*	60	
Common stock (60 million shares at $1 par per share)		60

*Alternatively, retained earnings may be debited.

d. 10% common stock dividend—with cash in lieu of payments for shares equivalent to 1 million whole shares:

October 13		
Retained earnings (18 million shares* at $12 per share)	216	
Common stock (17 million shares at $1 par per share)		17
Paid-in capital—excess of par		
(17 million shares at $11 per share above par)		187
Cash (1 million equivalent shares at $12 market price per share)		12

*(120 million + 60 million) × 10% = 18 million shares

e. 9.09% cash dividend on the 11 million preferred shares, payable on December 23 to shareholders of record December 11:

December 1—Declaration Date	($ in millions)	
Retained earnings	1	
Cash dividends payable ($11 million par × 9.09%)		1
December 11—Date of Record		
No entry		
December 23—Payment Date		
Cash dividends payable	1	
Cash		1

2. Prepare a statement of shareholders' equity for National Foods reporting the changes in shareholders' equity accounts for 2010, 2011, and 2012.

NATIONAL FOODS
Statement of Shareholders' Equity
For the Years Ended December 31, 2012, 2011, and 2010

($ in millions)

	Preferred Stock	Common Stock	Additional Paid-In Capital	Retained Earnings	Treasury Stock (at cost)	Total Share-holders' Equity
Balance at January 1, 2010		120	836	2,449		3,405
Sale of preferred shares	10		430			440
Issuance of common shares		1	9			10
Issuance of common and preferred shares	1	1	58			60
Net income				400		400
Cash dividends, preferred	—	—	——	——	——	(1)
Balance at December 31, 2010	11	122	1,333	2,848		4,314

(continued)

(concluded)

	Preferred Stock	Common Stock	Additional Paid-In Capital	Retained Earnings	Treasury Stock (at cost)	Total Share-holders' Equity	
Purchase of treasury shares					(60)	(60)	These are the transactions from Concept Review Exercise—Treasury Stock.
Sale of treasury shares			4		20	24	
Sale of treasury shares			(4)	(2)	20	14	
Net income				400		400	
Cash dividends, preferred	—	—	—	(1)	—	(1)	
Balance at December 31, 2011	**11**	**122**	**1,333**	**3,245**	**(20)**	**4,691**	
Cash dividends, common				(120)		(120)	These are the transactions from Concept Review Exercise—Changes in Retained Earnings.
Property dividends, common				(960)		(960)	
3-for-2 split effected in the form of a stock dividend		60	(60)				
10% stock dividend		17	187	(216)		(12)	
Preferred dividends				(1)		(1)	
Net income	—	—	—	225	—	225	
Balance at December 31, 2012	**11**	**199**	**1,460**	**2,173**	**(20)**	**3,823**	

FINANCIAL REPORTING CASE SOLUTION

1. **Do you think the stock price increase is related to Textron's share repurchase plan?** (p. 1024)   The stock price increase probably is related to Textron's buy-back plan. The marketplace realizes that decreasing the supply of shares supports the price of remaining shares. However, the repurchase of shares is not necessarily the best use of a company's cash. Whether it is in the shareholders' best interests depends on what other opportunities the company has for the cash available.

2. **What are Textron's choices in accounting for the share repurchases?** (p. 1025)   When a corporation reacquires its own shares, those shares assume the same status as authorized but unissued shares, just as if they never had been issued. However, for exactly the same transaction, companies can choose between two accounting alternatives: (a) formally retiring them or (b) accounting for the shares repurchased as treasury stock. In actuality, Textron's uses alternative (b).

3. **What effect does the quarterly cash dividend of 23 cents a share have on Textron's assets? Its liabilities? Its shareholders' equity?** (p. 1032)   Each quarter, when directors declare a cash dividend, retained earnings are reduced and a liability is recorded. The liability is paid with cash on the payment date. So, the net effect is a decrease in Textron's assets and its shareholders' equity. The effect on liabilities is temporary.

4. **What effect does the stock split have on Textron's assets? Its liabilities? Its shareholders' equity?** (p. 1035)   Conceptually, the proper accounting treatment of a stock split is to make no journal entry. However, since Textron refers to the stock distribution as a "stock split effected through a 100% stock dividend," a journal entry would increase the common stock account by the par value of the additional shares and would reduce paid-in capital—excess of par. This merely moves an amount from one part of shareholders' equity to another. Regardless of the accounting method, there is no change in Textron's assets, liabilities, or total shareholders' equity. ●

THE BOTTOM LINE

● **LO1** Shareholders' equity is the owners' residual interest in a corporation's assets. It arises primarily from (1) amounts invested by shareholders and (2) amounts earned by the corporation on behalf of its shareholders. These are reported as (1) paid-in capital and (2) retained earnings in a balance sheet. A statement of shareholders' equity reports the sources of the changes in individual shareholders' equity accounts. (p. 1008)

● **LO2** Comprehensive income encompasses all changes in equity except those caused by transactions with owners (like dividends and the sale or purchase of shares). It includes traditional net income as well as "other comprehensive income." (p. 1010)

● **LO3** A corporation is a separate legal entity—separate and distinct from its owners. A corporation is well suited to raising capital and has limited liability. However, it is subject to "double taxation." Common shareholders usually have voting rights; preferred shareholders usually have a preference to a specified amount of dividends and to assets in the event of liquidation. (p. 1015)

● **LO4** Shares sold for consideration other than cash (maybe services or a noncash asset) should be recorded at the fair value of the shares or the noncash consideration, whichever seems more clearly evident. (p. 1020)

● **LO5** When a corporation retires previously issued shares, those shares assume the same status as authorized but unissued shares—just the same as if they had never been issued. Payments made to retire shares are viewed as a distribution of corporate assets to shareholders. When reacquired shares are viewed as treasury stock, the cost of acquiring the shares is temporarily debited to the treasury stock account. Recording the effects on specific shareholders' equity accounts is delayed until later when the shares are reissued. (p. 1024)

● **LO6** Retained earnings represents, in general, a corporation's accumulated, undistributed or reinvested net income (or net loss). Distributions of earned assets are dividends. (p. 1031)

● **LO7** Most corporate dividends are paid in cash. When a noncash asset is distributed, it is referred to as a property dividend. The fair value of the assets to be distributed is the amount recorded for a property dividend. (p. 1031)

● **LO8** A stock dividend is the distribution of additional shares of stock to current shareholders. For a small stock dividend (25% or less), the fair value of the additional shares distributed is transferred from retained earnings to paid-in capital. For a stock distribution of 25% or higher, the par value of the additional shares is reclassified within shareholders' equity if referred to as a stock split effected in the form of a stock dividend, but if referred to merely as a stock split, no journal entry is recorded. (p. 1033)

● **LO9** U.S. GAAP and IFRS are generally compatible with respect to accounting for shareholders' equity. Some differences exist in presentation format and terminology and in choices regarding reporting comprehensive income. (pp. 1012, 1013, 1019, and 1030) ●

APPENDIX 18 QUASI REORGANIZATIONS

A firm undergoing financial difficulties, but with favorable future prospects, may use a quasi reorganization to write down inflated asset values and eliminate an accumulated deficit (debit balance in retained earnings). To effect the reorganization the following procedures are followed:

1. The firm's assets (and perhaps liabilities) are revalued (up or down) to reflect fair values, with corresponding credits or debits to retained earnings. This process typically increases the deficit.
2. The debit balance in retained earnings (deficit) is eliminated against additional paid-in capital. If additional paid-in capital is not sufficient to absorb the entire deficit, a reduction in stock may be necessary (with an appropriate restating of the par amount per share).
3. Retained earnings is dated. That is, disclosure is provided to indicate the date the deficit was eliminated and when the new accumulation of earnings began.

The procedure is demonstrated in Illustration 18A–1. The shareholders approved the quasi reorganization effective January 1, 2011. The plan was to be accomplished by a reduction of inventory by $75 million, a reduction in property, plant, and equipment (net) of $175 million, and appropriate adjustments to shareholders' equity.

The Emerson-Walsch Corporation has incurred operating losses for several years. A newly elected board of directors voted to implement a quasi reorganization, subject to shareholder approval. The balance sheet, on December 31, 2010, immediately prior to the restatement, includes the data shown below.

ILLUSTRATION 18A–1
Quasi Reorganization

	($ in millions)
Cash	$ 75
Receivables	200
Inventory	375
Property, plant, and equipment (net)	400
	$1,050
Liabilities	$ 400
Common stock (800 million shares at $1 par)	800
Additional paid-in capital	150
Retained earnings (deficit)	(300)
	$1,050

To Revalue Assets:

Retained earnings	75	
Inventory		75
Retained earnings	175	
Property, plant, and equipment		175

To Eliminate a Portion of the Deficit against Available Additional Paid-In Capital:

Additional paid-in capital	150	
Retained earnings		150

To Eliminate the Remainder of the Deficit against Common Stock:

Common stock	400	
Retained earnings		400

When assets are revalued to reflect fair values, the process often increases the deficit.

The deficit, $550 ($300 + 75 + 175), can be only partially absorbed by the balance of additional paid-in capital.

The remaining deficit, $400 ($300 + 75 + 175 − 150), must be absorbed by reducing the balance in common stock.

The balance sheet immediately after the restatement would include the following:

	($ in millions)
Cash	$ 75
Receivables	200
Inventory	300
Property, plant, and equipment (net)	225
	$800
Liabilities	$400
Common stock (800 million shares at $.50 par)	400
Additional paid-in capital	0
Retained earnings (deficit)	0
	$800

Assets and liabilities reflect current values.

Because a reduced balance represents the same 800 million shares, the par amount per share must be reduced.

The deficit is eliminated.

Note A: Upon the recommendation of the board of directors and approval by shareholders a quasi reorganization was implemented January 1, 2011. The plan was accomplished by a reduction of inventory by $75 million, a reduction in property, plant, and equipment (net) of $175 million, and appropriate adjustments to shareholders' equity. The balance in retained earnings reflects the elimination of a $300 million deficit on that date.

QUESTIONS FOR REVIEW OF KEY TOPICS

Q 18–1 Identify and briefly describe the two primary sources of shareholders' equity.

Q 18–2 Identify the three common forms of business organization and the primary difference between the way they are accounted for.

Q 18–3 Corporations offer the advantage of limited liability. Explain what is meant by that statement.

Q 18–4 Distinguish between not-for-profit and for-profit corporations.

Q 18–5 Distinguish between publicly held and privately (or closely) held corporations.

Q 18–6 How does the Model Business Corporation Act affect the way corporations operate?

Q 18–7 The owners of a corporation are its shareholders. If a corporation has only one class of shares, they typically are labeled common shares. Indicate the ownership rights held by common shareholders, unless specifically withheld by agreement.

Q 18–8 What is meant by a shareholder's preemptive right?

Q 18–9 Terminology varies in the way companies differentiate among share types. But many corporations designate shares as common or preferred. What are the two special rights usually given to preferred shareholders?

Q 18–10 Most preferred shares are cumulative. Explain what this means.

Q 18–11 The par value of shares historically indicated the real value of shares and all shares were issued at that price. The concept has changed with time. Describe the meaning of par value as it has evolved to today.

Q 18–12 What is comprehensive income? How does comprehensive income differ from net income? Where do companies report it in a balance sheet?

IFRS Q 18–13 Companies have a choice as to where in the financial statements to report comprehensive income. How does that choice differ between U.S. GAAP and IFRS?

Q 18–14 The balance sheet reports the balances of shareholders' equity accounts. What additional information is provided by the statement of shareholders' equity?

Q 18–15 At times, companies issue their shares for consideration other than cash. What is the measurement objective in those cases?

Q 18–16 Companies occasionally sell more than one security for a single price. How is the issue price allocated among the separate securities?

Q 18–17 The costs of legal, promotional, and accounting services necessary to effect the sale of shares are referred to as share issue costs. How are these costs recorded? Compare this approach to the way debt issue costs are recorded.

Q 18–18 When a corporation acquires its own shares, those shares assume the same status as authorized but unissued shares, as if they never had been issued. Explain how this is reflected in the accounting records if the shares are formally retired.

Q 18–19 Discuss the conceptual basis for accounting for a share buyback as treasury stock.

Q 18–20 The prescribed accounting treatment for stock dividends implicitly assumes that shareholders are fooled by small stock dividends and benefit by the market value of their additional shares. Explain this statement. Is it logical?

Q 18–21 Brandon Components declares a 2-for-1 stock split. What will be the effects of the split, and how should it be recorded?

Q 18–22 What is a reverse stock split? What would be the effect of a reverse stock split on one million $1 par shares? On the accounting records?

Q 18–23 Suppose you own 80 shares of **IBM** common stock when the company declares a 4% stock dividend. What will you receive as a result?

Q 18–24 (Based on Appendix 18) A quasi reorganization is sometimes employed by a firm undergoing financial difficulties, but with favorable future prospects. What are two objectives of this procedure? Briefly describe the procedural steps.

BRIEF EXERCISES

BE 18–1
Comprehensive
income
● LO2

Schaeffer Corporation reports $50 million accumulated other comprehensive income in its balance sheet as a component of shareholders' equity. In a related disclosure note reporting comprehensive income for the year, the company reveals net income of $400 million and other comprehensive income of $15 million. What was the balance in accumulated other comprehensive income in last year's balance sheet?

BE 18–2
Stock issued
● LO4

Penne Pharmaceuticals sold 8 million shares of its $1 par common stock to provide funds for research and development. If the issue price is $12 per share, what is the journal entry to record the sale of the shares?

BE 18–3
Stock issued
● LO4

Lewelling Company issued 100,000 shares of its $1 par common stock to the Michael Morgan law firm as compensation for 4,000 hours of legal services performed. Morgan's usual rate is $240 per hour. By what amount should Lewelling's paid-in capital—excess of par increase as a result of this transaction?

BE 18–4
Stock issued
● LO4

Hamilton Boats issued 175,000 shares of its no par common stock to Sudoku Motors in exchange for 1,000 four-stroke outboard motors that normally sell in quantity for $3,500 each. By what amount should Hamilton's shareholders' equity increase as a result of this transaction?

BE 18–5
Effect of preferred stock on dividends
● LO4

The shareholders' equity of MLS Enterprises includes $200 million of no par common stock and $400 million of 6% cumulative preferred stock. The board of directors of MLS declared cash dividends of $50 million in 2011 after paying $20 million cash dividends in both 2010 and 2009. What is the amount of dividends common shareholders will receive in 2011?

BE 18–6
Retirement of shares
● LO5

Horton Industries' shareholders' equity included 100 million shares of $1 par common stock and a balance in paid-in capital—excess of par of $900 million. Assuming that Horton retires shares it reacquires (restores their status to that of authorized but unissued shares), by what amount will Horton's total paid-in capital decline if it reacquires 2 million shares at $8.50 per share?

BE 18–7
Retirement of shares
● LO5

Agee Storage issued 35 million shares of its $1 par common stock at $16 per share several years ago. Last year, for the first time, Agee reacquired 1 million shares at $14 per share. Assuming that Agee retires shares it reacquires (restores their status to that of authorized but unissued shares), by what amount will Agee's total paid-in capital decline if it now reacquires 1 million shares at $19 per share?

BE 18–8
Treasury stock
● LO5

The Jennings Group reacquired 2 million of its shares at $70 per share as treasury stock. Last year, for the first time, Jennings sold 1 million treasury shares at $71 per share. By what amount will Jennings' retained earnings decline if it now sells the remaining 1 million treasury shares at $67 per share?

BE 18–9
Treasury stock
● LO5

In previous years, Cox Transport reacquired 2 million treasury shares at $20 per share and, later, 1 million treasury shares at $26 per share. By what amount will Cox's paid-in capital—share repurchase increase if it now sells 1 million treasury shares at $29 per share and determines cost as the weighted-average cost of treasury shares?

BE 18–10
Treasury stock
● LO5

Refer to the situation described in BE 18–9. By what amount will Cox's paid-in capital—share repurchase increase if it determines the cost of treasury shares by the FIFO method?

BE 18–11
Cash dividend
● LO7

Real World Financials

Following is a recent **Microsoft** press release:

REDMOND, Wash.—September 18, 2009— Microsoft Corp. today announced that its board of directors declared a quarterly dividend of $0.13 per share. The dividend is payable December 10, 2009 to shareholders of record on November 19, 2009.

Prepare the journal entries Microsoft used to record the declaration and payment of the cash dividend for its 8,908 million shares.

BE 18–12
Property dividend
● LO7

LaRoe Moving and Storage, a family-owned corporation, declared a property dividend of 1,000 shares of **GE** common stock that LaRoe had purchased in February for $37,000 as an investment. GE's shares had a market value of $35 per share on the declaration date. Prepare the journal entries to record the property dividend on the declaration and payment dates.

BE 18–13
Stock dividend
● LO8

On June 13, the board of directors of Siewert Inc. declared a 5% stock dividend on its 60 million, $1 par, common shares, to be distributed on July 1. The market price of Siewert common stock was $25 on June 13. Prepare the journal entry to record the stock dividend.

BE 18–14
Stock split
● LO8

Refer to the situation described in BE 18–13, but assume a 2-for-1 stock split instead of the 5% stock dividend. Prepare the journal entry to record the stock split if it is *not* to be effected in the form of a stock dividend. What is the par per share after the split?

BE 18–15
Stock split
● LO8

Refer to the situation described in BE 18–13, but assume a 2-for-1 stock split instead of the 5% stock dividend. Prepare the journal entry to record the stock split if it is to be effected in the form of a 100% stock dividend. What is the par per share after the split?

BE 18–16
IFRS; reporting shareholders' equity
● LO9

Nestlé S.A., the largest food and beverage company in the world, prepares its financial statements according to International Financial Reporting Standards. Its financial statements include ordinary share capital, translation reserve, and share premium. If Nestlé used U.S. GAAP, what would be the likely account titles for these accounts?

EXERCISES

An alternate exercise and problem set is available on the text website: www.mhhe.com/spiceland6e

E 18–1
Comprehensive income
● LO2

The following is an excerpt from a disclosure note from the 2011 annual report of Kaufman Chemicals, Inc.:

COMPREHENSIVE INCOME (LOSS)
The components of comprehensive income, net of tax, are as follows (in millions):

Years Ended December 31	2011	2010	2009
Net income	$856	$766	$594
Other comprehensive income:			
Change in net unrealized gains on available-for-sale investments, net of tax of $22, ($14), and $15 in 2011, 2010, and 2009, respectively	34	(21)	23
Other	(2)	(1)	1
Total comprehensive income	$888	$744	$618

Kaufman reports accumulated other comprehensive income in its balance sheet as a component of shareholders' equity as follows:

	($ in millions)	
	2011	**2010**
Shareholders' equity:		
Common stock	355	355
Additional paid-in capital	8,567	8,567
Retained earnings	6,544	5,988
Accumulated other comprehensive income	107	75
Total shareholders' equity	$15,573	$14,985

Required:

1. What is comprehensive income and how does it differ from net income?
2. How is comprehensive income reported in a balance sheet?
3. Why is Kaufman's 2011 balance sheet amount different from the 2011 amount reported in the disclosure note? Explain.
4. From the information provided, determine how Kaufman calculated the $107 million accumulated other comprehensive income in 2011.

E 18–2
FASB codification research; reporting other comprehensive income in shareholders' equity
● LO2

Companies are required to transfer "other comprehensive income" each period to shareholders' equity. The *FASB Accounting Standards Codification* represents the single source of authoritative U.S. generally accepted accounting principles.

Required:

1. Obtain the relevant authoritative literature on reporting other comprehensive income in shareholders' equity using the FASB's Codification Research System at the FASB website (**www.fasb.org**). What is the specific citation that describes the guidelines for reporting that component of shareholders' equity?
2. What is the specific citation that describes the guidelines for presenting accumulated other comprehensive income on the statement of shareholders' equity?

E 18–3
Earnings or OCI?
● LO2

Indicate by letter whether each of the items listed below most likely is reported in the income statement as Net Income (**NI**) or in the statement of comprehensive income as Other Comprehensive Income (**OCI**).

Items

_____ 1. Increase in the fair value of securities available-for-sale
_____ 2. Gain on sale of land
_____ 3. Loss on pension plan assets (actual return less than expected)
_____ 4. Gain from foreign currency translation
_____ 5. Increase in the fair value of trading securities
_____ 6. Loss from revising an assumption related to a pension plan
_____ 7. Loss on sale of patent
_____ 8. Prior service cost
_____ 9. Increase in the fair value of bonds outstanding; fair value option
_____ 10. Gain on postretirement plan assets (actual return more than expected)

E 18–4
Stock issued for cash; Wright Medical Group
● **LO4**

Real World Financials

The following is a news item reported by Reuters:

WASHINGTON, Jan 29 (Reuters)—**Wright Medical Group**, a maker of reconstructive implants for knees and hips, on Tuesday filed to sell 3 million shares of common stock.

In a filing with the U.S. Securities and Exchange Commission, it said it plans to use the proceeds from the offering for general corporate purposes, working capital, research and development, and acquisitions.

After the sale there will be about 31.5 million shares outstanding in the Arlington, Tennessee-based company, according to the SEC filing.

Wright shares closed at $17.15 on Nasdaq.

The common stock of Wright Medical Group has a par of $.01 per share.

Required:

Prepare the journal entry to record the sale of the shares assuming the price existing when the announcement was made and ignoring share issue costs.

E 18–5
Issuance of shares; noncash consideration
● **LO4**

During its first year of operations, Eastern Data Links Corporation entered into the following transactions relating to shareholders' equity. The articles of incorporation authorized the issue of 8 million common shares, $1 par per share, and 1 million preferred shares, $50 par per share.

Required:

Prepare the appropriate journal entries to record each transaction.

Feb. 12	Sold 2 million common shares, for $9 per share.
13	Issued 40,000 common shares to attorneys in exchange for legal services.
13	Sold 80,000 of its common shares and 4,000 preferred shares for a total of $945,000.
Nov. 15	Issued 380,000 of its common shares in exchange for equipment for which the cash price was known to be $3,688,000.

E 18–6
Redeemable shares
● **LO4**

Williams Industries has outstanding 30 million common shares, 20 million Class A shares, and 20 million Class B shares. Williams has the right but not the obligation to repurchase the Class A shares if a change in ownership of the voting common shares causes J. P. Williams, founder and CEO, to have less than 50% ownership. Williams has the unconditional obligation to repurchase the Class B shares upon the death of J. P. Williams.

Required:

Which, if any, of the shares should be reported in Williams' balance sheet as liabilities? Explain.

E 18–7
Share issue costs; issuance
● **LO4**

ICOT Industries issued 15 million of its $1 par common shares for $424 million on April 11. Legal, promotional, and accounting services necessary to effect the sale cost $2 million.

Required:

1. Prepare the journal entry to record the issuance of the shares.
2. Explain how recording the share issue costs differs from the way debt issue costs are recorded.

E 18–8
Reporting preferred shares
● **LO4**

Ozark Distributing Company is primarily engaged in the wholesale distribution of consumer products in the Ozark Mountain regions. The following disclosure note appeared in the company's 2011 annual report:

Note 5. CONVERTIBLE PREFERRED STOCK (in part):

The Company has the following Convertible Preferred Stock outstanding as of September 2011:

Date of issuance:	June 17, 2008
Optionally redeemable beginning	June 18, 2010
Par value (gross proceeds):	$2,500,000
Number of shares:	100,000
Liquidation preference per share:	$25.00
Conversion price per share:	$30.31
Number of common shares in which to be converted:	82,481
Dividend rate:	6.785%

(continued)

(concluded)

The Preferred Stock is convertible at any time by the holders into a number of shares of Ozark's common stock equal to the number of preferred shares being converted times a fraction equal to $25.00 divided by the conversion price. The conversion prices for the Preferred Stock are subject to customary adjustments in the event of stock splits, stock dividends and certain other distributions on the Common Stock. Cumulative dividends for the Preferred Stock are payable in arrears, when, as and if declared by the Board of Directors, on March 31, June 30, September 30 and December 31 of each year.

The Preferred Stock is optionally redeemable by the Company beginning on various dates, as listed above, at redemption prices equal to 112% of the liquidation preference. The redemption prices decrease 1% annually thereafter until the redemption price equals the liquidation preference after which date it remains the liquidation preference.

Required:

1. What amount of dividends is paid annually to a preferred shareholder owning 100 shares of the Series A preferred stock?
2. If dividends are not paid in 2012 and 2013, but are paid in 2014, what amount of dividends will the shareholder receive?
3. If the investor chooses to convert the shares in 2012, how many shares of common stock will the investor receive for his/her 100 shares?
4. If Ozark chooses to redeem the shares on June 18, 2012, what amount will the investor be paid for his/her 100 shares?

E 18–9
New equity
issues; offerings
announcements
● LO4

When companies offer new equity security issues, they publicize the offerings in the financial press and on Internet sites. Assume the following were among the equity offerings reported in December 2011:

NEW SECURITIES ISSUES

Equity

American Materials Transfer Corporation (AMTC)—7.5 million common shares, $.001 par, priced at $13.546 each through underwriters led by Second Tennessee Bank N.A. and Morgan, Dunavant & Co., according to a syndicate official.

Proactive Solutions Inc. (PSI)—Offering of nine million common shares, $.01 par, was priced at $15.20 a share via lead manager Stanley Brothers, Inc., according to a syndicate official.

Required:

Prepare the appropriate journal entries to record the sale of both issues to underwriters. Ignore share issue costs.

E 18–10
Effect of
cumulative,
nonparticipating
preferred stock on
dividends—3 years
● LO4

The shareholders' equity of WBL Industries includes the items shown below. The board of directors of WBL declared cash dividends of $8 million, $20 million, and $150 million in its first three years of operation—2011, 2012, and 2013, respectively.

	($ in millions)
Common stock	$100
Paid-in capital—excess of par, common	980
Preferred stock, 8%	200
Paid-in capital—excess of par, preferred	555

Required:

Determine the amount of dividends to be paid to preferred and common shareholders in each of the three years, assuming that the preferred stock is cumulative and nonparticipating.

	Preferred	**Common**
2011		
2012		
2013		

E 18–11
Retirement of
shares
● LO5

Borner Communications' articles of incorporation authorized the issuance of 130 million common shares. The transactions described below effected changes in Borner's outstanding shares. Prior to the transactions, Borner's shareholders' equity included the following:

Shareholders' Equity	($ in millions)
Common stock, 100 million shares at $1 par	$100
Paid-in capital—excess of par	300
Retained earnings	210

Required:

Assuming that Borner Communications retires shares it reacquires (restores their status to that of authorized but unissued shares), record the appropriate journal entry for each of the following transactions:

1. On January 7, 2011, Borner reacquired 2 million shares at $5.00 per share.
2. On August 23, 2011, Borner reacquired 4 million shares at $3.50 per share.
3. On July 25, 2012, Borner sold 3 million common shares at $6 per share.

E 18–12
Retirement of shares
● LO5

In 2011, Borland Semiconductors entered into the transactions described below. In 2008, Borland had issued 170 million shares of its $1 par common stock at $34 per share.

Required:

Assuming that Borland retires shares it reacquires, record the appropriate journal entry for each of the following transactions:

1. On January 2, 2011, Borland reacquired 10 million shares at $32.50 per share.
2. On March 3, 2011, Borland reacquired 10 million shares at $36 per share.
3. On August 13, 2011, Borland sold 1 million shares at $42 per share.
4. On December 15, 2011, Borland sold 2 million shares at $36 per share.

E 18–13
Treasury stock
● LO5

In 2011, Western Transport Company entered into the treasury stock transactions described below. In 2009, Western Transport had issued 140 million shares of its $1 par common stock at $17 per share.

Required:

Prepare the appropriate journal entry for each of the following transactions:

1. On January 23, 2011, Western Transport reacquired 10 million shares at $20 per share.
2. On September 3, 2011, Western Transport sold 1 million treasury shares at $21 per share.
3. On November 4, 2011, Western Transport sold 1 million treasury shares at $18 per share.

E 18–14
Treasury stock; weighted-average and FIFO cost
● LO5

At December 31, 2010, the balance sheet of Meca International included the following shareholders' equity accounts:

Shareholders' Equity	($ in millions)
Common stock, 60 million shares at $1 par	$ 60
Paid-in capital—excess of par	300
Retained earnings	410

Required:

Assuming that Meca International views its share buybacks as treasury stock, record the appropriate journal entry for each of the following transactions:

1. On February 12, 2011, Meca reacquired 1 million common shares at $13 per share.
2. On June 9, 2012, Meca reacquired 2 million common shares at $10 per share.
3. On May 25, 2013, Meca sold 2 million treasury shares at $15 per share—determine cost as the weighted-average cost of treasury shares.
4. For the previous transaction, assume Meca determines the cost of treasury shares by the FIFO method.

E 18–15
Reporting shareholders' equity after share repurchase
● LO5

On two previous occasions, the management of Dennison and Company, Inc., repurchased some of its common shares. Between buyback transactions, the corporation issued common shares under its management incentive plan. Shown below is shareholders' equity following these share transactions, as reported by two different methods of accounting for reacquired shares.

	($ in millions)	
	Method A	**Method B**
Shareholders' equity		
Paid-in capital:		
Preferred stock, $10 par	$ 150	$ 150
Common stock, $1 par	200	197
Additional paid-in capital	1,204	1,201
Retained earnings	2,994	2,979
Less: Treasury stock	(21)	
Total shareholders' equity	$4,527	$4,527

Required:

1. Infer from the presentation which method of accounting for reacquired shares is represented by each of the two columns.
2. Explain why presentation formats are different and why some account balances are different for the two methods.

E 18–16
Change from
treasury stock to
retired stock
● LO5

In keeping with a modernization of corporate statutes in its home state, UMC Corporation decided in 2011 to discontinue accounting for reacquired shares as treasury stock. Instead, shares repurchased will be viewed as having been retired, reassuming the status of unissued shares. As part of the change, treasury shares held were reclassified as retired stock. At December 31, 2010, UMC's balance sheet reported the following shareholders' equity:

	($ in millions)
Common stock, $1 par	$ 200
Paid-in capital—excess of par	800
Retained earnings	956
Treasury stock (4 million shares at cost)	(25)
Total shareholders' equity	$1,931

Required:

Identify the type of accounting change this decision represents, and prepare the journal entry to effect the reclassification of treasury shares as retired shares.

E 18–17
Stock buyback;
Adobe
Systems; press
announcement
● LO5

Real World Financials

The following excerpt is from an article reported in the April 9, 2009, online issue of *Reuters*.

Adobe Systems Incorporated (Nasdaq:ADBE)—April 9, 2009 announces its Board of Directors has approved a new stock repurchase program that authorizes the company to repurchase in aggregate up to 20 million shares of the company's common stock. The Board also authorized an additional $500 million in funds to repurchase shares under its existing stock repurchase program designed to offset dilution from stock issuances.

The par amount per share for Adobe's common stock is $.0001. Paid-in capital—excess of par is $40.48 per share on average. The market price was $43 on April 9, 2009.

Required:

1. Suppose Adobe reacquires the 20 million shares through repurchase on the open market at $43 per share. Prepare the appropriate journal entry to record the purchase. Adobe considers the shares it buys back to be treasury stock.
2. Suppose Adobe considers the shares it buys back to be retired rather than treated as treasury stock. Prepare the appropriate journal entry to record the purchase.
3. What does the company mean by saying that the buyback will serve "to offset dilution from stock issuances"?

E 18–18
Transactions
affecting retained
earnings
● LO6 LO7

Shown below in T-account format are the changes affecting the retained earnings of Brenner-Jude Corporation during 2011. At January 1, 2011, the corporation had outstanding 105 million common shares, $1 par per share.

Retained Earnings ($ in millions)

		90	Beginning balance
Retirement of 5 million common shares for $22 million	2		
		88	Net income for the year
Declaration and payment of a $.33 per share cash dividend	33		
Declaration and distribution of a 4% stock dividend	20		
		123	Ending balance

Required:

1. From the information provided by the account changes you should be able to recreate the transactions that affected Brenner-Jude's retained earnings during 2011. Prepare the journal entries that Brenner-Jude must have recorded during the year for these transactions.
2. Prepare a statement of retained earnings for Brenner-Jude for the year ended 2011.

E 18–19
Stock dividend
● LO8

The shareholders' equity of Core Technologies Company on June 30, 2010, included the following:

Common stock, $1 par; authorized, 8 million shares; issued and outstanding, 3 million shares	$ 3,000,000
Paid-in capital—excess of par	12,000,000
Retained earnings	14,000,000

On April 1, 2011, the board of directors of Core Technologies declared a 10% stock dividend on common shares, to be distributed on June 1. The market price of Core Technologies' common stock was $30 on April 1, 2011, and $40 on June 1, 2011.

Required:

Prepare the journal entry to record the distribution of the stock dividend on the declaration date.

E 18–20
Stock split;
Hanmi Financial
Corporation
● LO8

Real World Financials

Hanmi Financial Corporation is the parent company of Hanmi Bank. The company's stock split was announced in the following Business Wire:

LOS ANGELES (BUSINESS WIRE) Jan. 20—Hanmi Financial Corporation (Nasdaq), announced that the Board of Directors has approved a two-for-one stock split, to be effected in the form of a 100 percent common stock dividend. Hanmi Financial Corporation stockholders of record at the close of business on January 31 will receive one additional share of common stock for every share of common stock then held. Distribution of additional shares issued as a result of the split is expected to occur on or about February 15.

At the time of the stock split, 24.5 million shares of common stock, $.001 par per share, were outstanding.

Required:

1. Prepare the journal entry, if any, that Hanmi recorded at the time of the stock split.
2. What is the probable motivation for declaring the 2-for-1 stock split to be effected by a dividend payable in shares of common stock?
3. If Hanmi's stock price had been $36 at the time of the split, what would be its approximate value after the split (other things equal)?

E 18–21
Cash in lieu of
fractional share
rights
● LO8

Douglas McDonald Company's balance sheet included the following shareholders' equity accounts at December 31, 2010:

	($ in millions)
Paid-in capital:	
Common stock, 900 million shares at $1 par	$ 900
Paid-in capital—excess of par	15,800
Retained earnings	14,888
Total shareholders' equity	$31,588

On March 16, 2011, a 4% common stock dividend was declared and distributed. The market value of the common stock was $21 per share. Fractional share rights represented 2 million equivalent whole shares. Cash was paid in lieu of the fractional share rights.

Required:

1. What is a fractional share right?
2. Prepare the appropriate entries for the declaration and distribution of the stock dividend.

E 18–22
FASB codification
research
● LO1 LO5 LO8

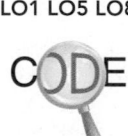

Access the FASB's Codification Research System at the FASB website (**www.fasb.org**). Determine the specific citation for accounting for each of the following items:

1. Requirements to disclose within the financial statements the pertinent rights and privileges of the various securities outstanding.
2. Requirement to record a "small" stock dividend at the fair value of the shares issued.
3. Requirement to exclude from the determination of net income gains and losses on transactions in a company's own stock.

E 18–23
Transactions
affecting retained
earnings
● LO6 through
LO8

The balance sheet of Consolidated Paper, Inc., included the following shareholders' equity accounts at December 31, 2010:

	($ in millions)
Paid-in capital:	
Preferred stock, 8.8%, 90,000 shares at $1 par	$ 90,000
Common stock, 364,000 shares at $1 par	364,000
Paid-in capital—excess of par, preferred	1,437,000
Paid-in capital—excess of par, common	2,574,000
Retained earnings	9,735,000
Treasury stock, at cost; 4,000 common shares	(44,000)
Total shareholders' equity	$14,156,000

During 2011, several events and transactions affected the retained earnings of Consolidated Paper.

Required:

1. Prepare the appropriate entries for these events:

   a. On March 3 the board of directors declared a property dividend of 240,000 shares of Leasco International common stock that Consolidated Paper had purchased in January as an investment (book value: $700,000). The investment shares had a fair value of $3 per share and were distributed March 31 to shareholders of record March 15.

   b. On May 3 a 5-for-4 stock split was declared and distributed. The stock split was effected in the form of a 25% stock dividend. The market value of the $1 par common stock was $11 per share.

   c. On July 5 a 2% common stock dividend was declared and distributed. The market value of the common stock was $11 per share.

   d. On December 1 the board of directors declared the 8.8% cash dividend on the 90,000 preferred shares, payable on December 28 to shareholders of record December 20.

   e. On December 1 the board of directors declared a cash dividend of $.50 per share on its common shares, payable on December 28 to shareholders of record December 20.

2. Prepare the shareholders' equity section of the balance sheet for Consolidated Paper, Inc., for the year ended at December 31, 2011. Net income for the year was $810,000.

E 18–24
Profitability ratio
● LO1

Comparative balance sheets for Softech Canvas Goods for 2011 and 2010 are shown below. Softech pays no dividends, and instead reinvests all earnings for future growth.

Comparative Balance Sheets
($ in 000s)

	December 31	
	2011	2010
Assets:		
Cash	$ 50	$ 40
Accounts receivable	100	120
Short-term investments	50	40
Inventory	200	140
Property, plant, and equipment (net)	600	550
	$1,000	$890
Liabilities and Shareholders' Equity:		
Current liabilities	$ 240	$210
Bonds payable	160	160
Paid-in capital	400	400
Retained earnings	200	120
	$1,000	$890

Required:

1. Determine the return on shareholders' equity for 2011.
2. What does the ratio measure?

E 18–25
IFRS; equity
terminology
● LO9

Indicate by letter whether each of the terms or phrases listed below is more associated with financial statements prepared in accordance with U.S. GAAP (**U**) or International Financial Reporting Standards (**I**).

Terms and phrases

_____ 1. Common stock
_____ 2. Preference shares
_____ 3. Liabilities often listed before equity in the balance sheet (statement of financial position)
_____ 4. Asset revaluation reserve
_____ 5. Accumulated other comprehensive income
_____ 6. Share premium
_____ 7. Equity often listed before liabilities in the balance sheet (statement of financial position)
_____ 8. Share premium
_____ 9. Ordinary shares
_____ 10. Paid-in capital—excess of par
_____ 11. Net gains (losses) on investments—AOCI
_____ 12. Investment revaluation reserve
_____ 13. Preferred stock

CPA AND CMA REVIEW QUESTIONS

CPA Exam
Questions

The following questions are used in the Kaplan CPA Review Course to study shareholders' equity while preparing for the CPA examination. Determine the response that best completes the statements or questions.

● LO5

1. In 2009, Fogg, Inc., issued $10 par value common stock for $25 per share. No other common stock transactions occurred until March 31, 2011, when Fogg acquired some of the issued shares for $20 per share and retired them. Which of the following statements correctly states an effect of this acquisition and retirement?
   a. 2011 net income is decreased.
   b. Additional paid-in capital is decreased.
   c. 2011 net income is increased.
   d. Retained earnings is increased.

● LO5

2. Copper, Inc., initially issued 100,000 shares of $1 par value stock for $500,000 in 2008. In 2010, the company repurchased 10,000 shares for $100,000. In 2011, 5,000 of the repurchased shares were resold for $80,000. In its balance sheet dated December 31, 2011, Copper, Inc.'s Treasury Stock account shows a balance of:
   a. $ 0
   b. $ 20,000
   c. $ 50,000
   d. $100,000

● LO7

3. On June 27, 2011, Brite Co. distributed to its common stockholders 100,000 outstanding common shares of its investment in Quik, Inc., an unrelated party. The carrying amount on Brite's books of Quik's $1 par common stock was $2 per share. Immediately after the distribution, the market price of Quik's stock was $2.50 per share. In its income statement for the year ended June 30, 2011, what amount should Brite report as gain before income taxes on disposal of the stock?
   a. $ 0
   b. $ 50,000
   c. $200,000
   d. $250,000

● LO7

4. Whipple Company has 1,000,000 shares of common stock authorized with a par value of $3 per share, of which 600,000 shares are outstanding. When the market value was $8 per share, Whipple issued a stock dividend whereby for each six shares held one share was issued as a stock dividend. The par value of the stock was not changed. What entry should Whipple make to record this transaction?

a. Retained earnings	$300,000	
Common stock		$300,000
b. Additional paid-in capital	300,000	
Common stock		300,000
c. Retained earnings	800,000	
Common stock		300,000
Additional paid-in capital		500,000
d. Additional paid-in capital	800,000	
Common stock		300,000
Retained earnings		500,000

● LO8

5. When a company issues a stock dividend which of the following would be affected?
   a. Earnings per share.
   b. Total assets.
   c. Total liabilities.
   d. Total stockholders' equity.

● LO8

6. Long Co. had 100,000 shares of common stock issued and outstanding at January 1, 2011. During 2011, Long took the following actions:

March 15	Declared a 2-for-1 stock split, when the fair value of the stock was $80 per share.
December 15	Declared a $0.50 per share cash dividend.

In Long's statement of shareholders' equity for 2011, what amount should Long report as dividends?
   a. $ 50,000
   b. $100,000
   c. $850,000
   d. $950,000

**CMA Exam
Questions**

The following questions dealing with shareholders' equity are adapted from questions that previously appeared on Certified Management Accountant (CMA) examinations. The CMA designation sponsored by the Institute of Management Accountants (**www.imanet.org**) provides members with an objective measure of knowledge and competence in the field of management accounting. Determine the response that best completes the statements or questions.

● LO1

1. The par value of common stock represents
   a. the estimated fair value of the stock when it was issued.
   b. the liability ceiling of a shareholder when a company undergoes bankruptcy proceedings.
   c. the total value of the stock that must be entered in the issuing corporation's records.
   d. the amount that must be recorded on the issuing corporation's record as paid-in capital.

● LO1

2. The equity section of Smith Corporation's statement of financial position is presented below.

Preferred stock, $100 par	$12,000,000
Common stock, $5 par	10,000,000
Paid-in capital in excess of par	18,000,000
Retained earnings	9,000,000
Shareholders' equity	$49,000,000

The common shareholders of Smith Corporation have preemptive rights. If Smith Corporation issues 400,000 additional share of common stock at $6 per share, a current holder of 20,000 shares of Smith Corporation's common stock must be given the option to buy
   a. 1,000 additional shares.
   b. 3,774 additional shares.
   c. 4,000 additional shares.
   d. 3,333 additional shares.

● LO8

3. A stock dividend
   a. increases the debt to equity ratio of a firm.
   b. decreases future earnings per share.
   c. decreases the size of the firm.
   d. increases shareholders' wealth.

PROBLEMS

An alternate exercise and problem set is available on the text website: www.mhhe.com/spiceland6e

P 18–1
Various stock
transactions;
correction of
journal entries
● LO4

Part A
During its first year of operations, the McCollum Corporation entered into the following transactions relating to shareholders' equity. The corporation was authorized to issue 100 million common shares, $1 par per share.

Required:
Prepare the appropriate journal entries to record each transaction.

Jan. 9   Issued 40 million common shares for $20 per share.

Mar. 11   Issued 5,000 shares in exchange for custom-made equipment. McCollum's shares have traded recently on the stock exchange at $20 per share.

Part B

A new staff accountant for the McCollum Corporation recorded the following journal entries during the second year of operations. McCollum retires shares that it reacquires (restores their status to that of authorized but unissued shares).

		($ in millions)	
Jan. 12	Land	2	
	Paid-in capital—donation of land		2
Sept. 1	Common stock	2	
	Retained earnings	48	
	Cash		50
Dec. 1	Cash	26	
	Common stock		1
	Gain on sale of previously issued shares		25

Required:

Prepare the journal entries that should have been recorded for each of the transactions.

P 18–2

Share buyback—comparison of retirement and treasury stock treatment

● LO5

The shareholders' equity section of the balance sheet of TNL Systems Inc. included the following accounts at December 31, 2010:

Shareholders' Equity	($ in millions)
Common stock, 240 million shares at $1 par	$ 240
Paid-in capital—excess of par	1,680
Paid-in capital—share repurchase	1
Retained earnings	1,100

Required:

1. During 2011, TNL Systems reacquired shares of its common stock and later sold shares in two separate transactions. Prepare the entries for both the purchase and subsequent resale of the shares assuming the shares are (a) retired and (b) viewed as treasury stock.

   a. On February 5, 2011, TNL Systems purchased 6 million shares at $10 per share.

   b. On July 9, 2011, the corporation sold 2 million shares at $12 per share.

   c. On November 14, 2013, the corporation sold 2 million shares at $7 per share.

2. Prepare the shareholders' equity section of TNL Systems' balance sheet at December 31, 2013, comparing the two approaches. Assume all net income earned in 2011–2013 was distributed to shareholders as cash dividends.

P 18–3

Reacquired shares—comparison of retired shares and treasury shares

● LO5

National Supply's shareholders' equity included the following accounts at December 31, 2010:

Shareholders' Equity	($ in millions)
Common stock, 6 million shares at $1 par	$ 6,000,000
Paid-in capital—excess of par	30,000,000
Retained earnings	86,500,000

Required:

1. National Supply reacquired shares of its common stock in two separate transactions and later sold shares. Prepare the entries for each of the transactions under each of two separate assumptions: the shares are (a) retired and (b) accounted for as treasury stock.

February 15, 2011	Reacquired 300,000 shares at $8 per share.
February 17, 2012	Reacquired 300,000 shares at $5.50 per share.
November 9, 2013	Sold 200,000 shares at $7 per share (assume FIFO cost).

2. Prepare the shareholders' equity section of National Supply's balance sheet at December 31, 2013, assuming the shares are (a) retired and (b) accounted for as treasury stock. Net income was $14 million in 2011, $15 million in 2012, and $16 million in 2013. No dividends were paid during the three-year period.

P 18–4
Statement of
retained earnings

● LO5 LO7

Comparative statements of retained earnings for Renn-Dever Corporation were reported in its 2011 annual report as follows.

RENN-DEVER CORPORATION
Statements of Retained Earnings

For the Years Ended December 31,	2011	2010	2009
Balance at beginning of year	$6,794,292	$5,464,052	$5,624,552
Net income (loss)	3,308,700	2,240,900	(160,500)
Deductions:			
Stock dividend (34,900 shares)	242,000		
Common shares retired (110,000 shares)		212,660	
Common stock cash dividends	889,950	698,000	0
Balance at end of year	$8,971,042	$6,794,292	$5,464,052

At December 31, 2008, common shares consisted of the following:

Common stock, 1,855,000 shares at $1 par	$1,855,000
Paid-in capital—excess of par	7,420,000

Required:
Infer from the reports the events and transactions that affected Renn-Dever Corporation's retained earnings during 2009, 2010, and 2011. Prepare the journal entries that reflect those events and transactions.

P 18–5
Shareholders'
equity transactions;
statement of
shareholders'
equity

● LO6 through
LO8

Listed below are the transactions that affected the shareholders' equity of Branch-Rickie Corporation during the period 2011–2013. At December 31, 2010, the corporation's accounts included:

	($ in 000s)
Common stock, 105 million shares at $1 par	$105,000
Paid-in capital—excess of par	630,000
Retained earnings	970,000

a. November 1, 2011, the board of directors declared a cash dividend of $.80 per share on its common shares, payable to shareholders of record November 15, to be paid December 1.

b. On March 1, 2012, the board of directors declared a property dividend consisting of corporate bonds of Warner Corporation that Branch-Rickie was holding as an investment. The bonds had a fair value of $1.6 million, but were purchased two years previously for $1.3 million. Because they were intended to be held to maturity, the bonds had not been previously written up. The property dividend was payable to shareholders of record March 13, to be distributed April 5.

c. On July 12, 2012, the corporation declared and distributed a 5% common stock dividend (when the market value of the common stock was $21 per share). Cash was paid in lieu of fractional shares representing 250,000 equivalent whole shares.

d. On November 1, 2012, the board of directors declared a cash dividend of $.80 per share on its common shares, payable to shareholders of record November 15, to be paid December 1.

e. On January 15, 2013, the board of directors declared and distributed a 3-for-2 stock split effected in the form of a 50% stock dividend when the market value of the common stock was $22 per share.

f. On November 1, 2013, the board of directors declared a cash dividend of $.65 per share on its common shares, payable to shareholders of record November 15, to be paid December 1.

Required:
1. Prepare the journal entries that Branch-Rickie recorded during the three-year period for these transactions.
2. Prepare comparative statements of shareholders' equity for Branch-Rickie for the three-year period ($ in 000s). Net income was $330 million, $395 million, and $455 million for 2011, 2012, and 2013, respectively.

P 18–6
Statement of
shareholders'
equity

● LO1 LO3
  through LO8

Comparative statements of shareholders' equity for Anaconda International Corporation were reported as follows for the fiscal years ending December 31, 2011, 2012, and 2013.

ANACONDA INTERNATIONAL CORPORATION
Statements of Shareholders' Equity
For the Years Ended Dec. 31, 2011, 2012, and 2013
($ in millions)

	Preferred Stock $10 par	Common Stock $1 par	Additional Paid-In Capital	Retained Earnings	Total Shareholders' Equity
Balance at January 1, 2011		55	495	1,878	2,428
Sale of preferred shares	10		470		480
Sale of common shares		7	63		70
Cash dividend, preferred				(1)	(1)
Cash dividend, common				(16)	(16)
Net income				290	290
Balance at December 31, 2011	10	62	1,028	2,151	3,251
Retirement of shares		(3)	(27)	(20)	(50)
Cash dividend, preferred				(1)	(1)
Cash dividend, common				(20)	(20)
3-for-2 split effected in the form of a dividend	5		(5)		
Net income				380	380
Balance at December 31, 2012	15	59	996	2,490	3,560
Common stock dividend		6	59	(65)	
Cash dividend, preferred				(1)	(1)
Cash dividend, common				(22)	(22)
Net income				412	412
Balance at December 31, 2013	15	65	1,055	2,814	3,949

Required:
1. Infer from the statements the events and transactions that affected Anaconda International Corporation's shareholders' equity during 2011, 2012, and 2013. Prepare the journal entries that reflect those events and transactions.
2. Prepare the shareholders' equity section of Anaconda's comparative balance sheets at December 31, 2013 and 2012.

P 18–7
Reporting shareholders' equity; comprehensive income; Cisco Systems

● LO1 through LO4

Real World Financials

The following is the 2009 Statement of Shareholders' Equity from **Cisco Systems**' 2009 annual report. Remember that for comparative purposes, three years are reported in these statements. The 2008 and 2007 portions of the statement are not shown here for brevity of presentation.

CISCO SYSTEMS, INC.
Consolidated Statements of Shareholders' Equity (in part)

($ in millions)	Shares of Common Stock	Common Stock and Additional Paid-In Capital	Retained Earnings	Accumulated Other Comprehensive Income	Total Shareholders' Equity
Balance at July 26, 2008	5,893	$33,505	$ 120	$728	$ 34,353
Net income	—	—	6,134	—	6,134
Change in unrealized gains and losses on investments	—	—	—	(3)	(3)
Change in derivative instruments	—	—	—	(49)	(49)
Change in cumulative translation adjustment and other	—	—	—	(192)	(192)
Comprehensive income					5,890
Cumulative effect of adopting FSP 115-2	—	—	49	(49)	—
Issuance of common stock	67	863	—	—	863
Repurchase of common stock	(202)	(1,188)	(2,435)	—	(3,623)

(continued)

(concluded)

Tax benefits from employee stock incentive plans, including transfer pricing adjustments	—	(582)	—	—	(582)
Purchase acquisitions	27	515	—	—	515
Employee share-based compensation expense	—	1,140	—	—	1,140
Share-based compensation expense related to acquisitions and investments	—	91	—	—	91
Balance at July 25, 2009	5,785	$34,344	$3,868	$435	$ 38,647

Required:

1. What is the purpose of the statement of shareholders' equity?

2. How does Cisco account for its share buybacks?

3. For its share buybacks in fiscal year 2009, was the price Cisco paid for the shares repurchased more or less than the average price at which Cisco had sold the shares previously? Reconstruct the journal entry Cisco used to record the buyback.

4. What is comprehensive income? What is other comprehensive income?

5. What caused the change in Cisco's comprehensive income in fiscal year 2009? What was the amount of Accumulated other comprehensive income (loss) that Cisco reported in its July 28, 2009 balance sheet? Be specific.

P 18–8
Share issue costs; issuance; dividends; early retirement
● LO3 LO4 LO7

During its first year of operations, Cupola Fan Corporation issued 30,000 of $1 par Class B shares for $385,000 on June 30, 2011. Share issue costs were $1,500. One year from the issue date (July 1, 2012), the corporation retired 10% of the shares for $39,500.

Required:

1. Prepare the journal entry to record the issuance of the shares.

2. Prepare the journal entry to record the declaration of a $2 per share dividend on December 1, 2011.

3. Prepare the journal entry to record the payment of the dividend on December 31, 2011.

4. Prepare the journal entry to record the retirement of the shares.

(Note: You may wish to compare your solution to this problem with that of Problem 14–16, which deals with parallel issues of debt issue costs and the retirement of debt.)

P 18–9
Effect of preferred stock characteristics on dividends
● LO7

The shareholders' equity of Kramer Industries includes the data shown below. During 2012, cash dividends of $150 million were declared. Dividends were not declared in 2010 or 2011.

	($ in millions)
Common stock	$200
Paid-in capital—excess of par, common	800
Preferred stock, 10%, nonparticipating	100
Paid-in capital—excess of par, preferred	270

Required:
Determine the amount of dividends payable to preferred shareholders and to common shareholders under each of the following two assumptions regarding the characteristics of the preferred stock.

Assumption A—The preferred stock is noncumulative.
Assumption B—The preferred stock is cumulative.

P 18–10
Transactions affecting retained earnings
● LO4 through LO8

Example

Indicate by letter whether each of the transactions listed below increases (**I**), decreases (**D**), or has no effect (**N**) on retained earnings. Assume the shareholders' equity of the transacting company includes only common stock, paid-in capital—excess of par, and retained earnings at the time of each transaction.

Transactions

__N__	1. Sale of common stock
_____	2. Purchase of treasury stock at a cost *less* than the original issue price
_____	3. Purchase of treasury stock at a cost *greater* than the original issue price
_____	4. Declaration of a property dividend
_____	5. Sale of treasury stock for *more* than cost

(continued)

(concluded)

_____ 6. Sale of treasury stock for *less* than cost

_____ 7. Net income for the year

_____ 8. Declaration of a cash dividend

_____ 9. Payment of a previously declared cash dividend

_____ 10. Issuance of convertible bonds for cash

_____ 11. Declaration and distribution of a 5% stock dividend

_____ 12. Retirement of common stock at a cost *less* than the original issue price

_____ 13. Retirement of common stock at a cost *greater* than the original issue price

_____ 14. A stock split effected in the form of a stock dividend

_____ 15. A stock split in which the par value per share is reduced (not effected in the form of a stock dividend)

_____ 16. A net loss for the year

P 18–11
Stock dividends
received on
investments;
integrative problem
● LO8

Ellis Transport Company acquired 1.2 million shares of stock in L&K Corporation at $44 per share. They are classified by Ellis as "available for sale." Ellis sold 200,000 shares at $46, received a 10% stock dividend, and then later in the year sold another 100,000 shares at $43.

Hint: There is no entry for the stock dividend, but a new investment per share must be calculated for use later when the shares are sold.

Required:
Prepare journal entries to record these transactions.

P 18–12
Various
shareholders'
equity topics;
comprehensive
● LO1 LO4
through LO8

Part A
In late 2010, the Nicklaus Corporation was formed. The corporate charter authorizes the issuance of 5,000,000 shares of common stock carrying a $1 par value, and 1,000,000 shares of $5 par value, noncumulative, nonparticipating preferred stock. On January 2, 2011, 3,000,000 shares of the common stock are issued in exchange for cash at an average price of $10 per share. Also on January 2, all 1,000,000 shares of preferred stock are issued at $20 per share.

Required:
1. Prepare journal entries to record these transactions.
2. Prepare the shareholders' equity section of the Nicklaus balance sheet as of March 31, 2011. (Assume net income for the first quarter 2011 was $1,000,000.)

Part B
During 2011, the Nicklaus Corporation participated in three treasury stock transactions:

    a. On June 30, 2011, the corporation reacquires 200,000 shares for the treasury at a price of $12 per share.

    b. On July 31, 2011, 50,000 treasury shares are reissued at $15 per share.

    c. On September 30, 2011, 50,000 treasury shares are reissued at $10 per share.

Required:
1. Prepare journal entries to record these transactions.
2. Prepare the Nicklaus Corporation shareholders' equity section as it would appear in a balance sheet prepared at September 30, 2011. (Assume net income for the second and third quarter was $3,000,000.)

Part C
On October 1, 2011, Nicklaus Corporation receives permission to replace its $1 par value common stock (5,000,000 shares authorized, 3,000,000 shares issued, and 2,900,000 shares outstanding) with a new common stock issue having a $.50 par value. Since the new par value is one-half the amount of the old, this represents a 2-for-1 stock split. That is, the shareholders will receive two shares of the $.50 par stock in exchange for each share of the $1 par stock they own. The $1 par stock will be collected and destroyed by the issuing corporation.

On November 1, 2011, the Nicklaus Corporation declares a $.05 per share cash dividend on common stock and a $.25 per share cash dividend on preferred stock. Payment is scheduled for December 1, 2011, to shareholders of record on November 15, 2011.

On December 2, 2011, the Nicklaus Corporation declares a 1% stock dividend payable on December 28, 2011, to shareholders of record on December 14. At the date of declaration, the common stock was selling in the open market at $10 per share. The dividend will result in 58,000 (.01 × 5,800,000) additional shares being issued to shareholders.

Required:
1. Prepare journal entries to record the declaration and payment of these stock and cash dividends.
2. Prepare the December 31, 2011, shareholders' equity section of the balance sheet for the Nicklaus Corporation. (Assume net income for the fourth quarter was $2,500,000.)
3. Prepare a statement of shareholders' equity for Nicklaus Corporation for 2011.

P 18–13
Quasi
reorganization
(based on
Appendix 18)
● **Appendix**

A new CEO was hired to revive the floundering Champion Chemical Corporation. The company had endured operating losses for several years, but confidence was emerging that better times were ahead. The board of directors and shareholders approved a quasi reorganization for the corporation. The reorganization included devaluing inventory for obsolescence by $105 million and increasing land by $5 million. Immediately prior to the restatement, at December 31, 2011, Champion Chemical Corporation's balance sheet appeared as follows (in condensed form):

CHAMPION CHEMICAL CORPORATION
Balance Sheet
At December 31, 2011
($ in millions)

Cash	$ 20
Receivables	40
Inventory	230
Land	40
Buildings and equipment (net)	90
	$420
Liabilities	$240
Common stock (320 million shares at $1 par)	320
Additional paid-in capital	60
Retained earnings (deficit)	(200)
	$420

Required:
1. Prepare the journal entries appropriate to record the quasi reorganization on January 1, 2012.
2. Prepare a balance sheet as it would appear immediately after the restatement.

BROADEN YOUR PERSPECTIVE

Apply your critical-thinking ability to the knowledge you've gained. These cases will provide you an opportunity to develop your research, analysis, judgment, and communication skills. You also will work with other students, integrate what you've learned, apply it in real world situations, and consider its global and ethical ramifications. This practice will broaden your knowledge and further develop your decision-making abilities.

**Real World
Case 18–1**
Initial public
offering of common
stock; Dolby
Laboratories
● **LO4**

Real World Financials

Ray Dolby started **Dolby Laboratories** nearly 40 years ago and since then has been a leader in the entertainment industry and consumer electronics. Closely held since its founding in 1965, Dolby decided to go public. Here's an AP news report:

DOLBY'S IPO EXPECTED TO PLAY SWEET MUSIC
The initial public offering market is hoping for a big bang this week from Dolby Laboratories Inc. The San Francisco company, whose sound systems and double-D logo are ubiquitous in the movie industry as well as in consumer electronics, plans to sell 27.5 million shares for $13.50 to $15.50 each. Founded by Cambridge-trained scientist Ray Dolby 39 years ago, the company started out manufacturing noise-reduction equipment for the music industry that eliminated the background "hiss" on recordings, and has since expanded to encompass everything from digital audio systems to Dolby Surround sound. The company's IPO, which is lead-managed by underwriters Morgan Stanley and Goldman Sachs Group Inc., is expected to do well not only because of its brand recognition, but also because of its strong financials. *(AP)*

Required:
1. Assuming the shares are issued at the midpoint of the price range indicated, how much capital did the IPO raise for Dolby Laboratories before any underwriting discount and offering expenses?
2. If the par amount is $.01 per share, what journal entry did Dolby use to record the sale?

Analysis
Case 18–2
Statement of
shareholders'
equity
● LO1 LO3 LO6
   LO7

The shareholders' equity portion of the balance sheet of Sessel's Department Stores, Inc., a large regional specialty retailer, is as follows:

SESSEL'S DEPARTMENT STORES, INC. **Comparative Balance Sheets** **Shareholders' Equity Section**		
($ in 000s, except per share amounts)	**Dec. 31, 2012**	**Dec. 31, 2011**
Shareholders' Equity		
Preferred stock—$1 par value; 20,000 total shares authorized,		
Series A—600 shares authorized, issued, and outstanding,	$ 57,700	$ —
$50 per share liquidation preference		
Series B—33 shares authorized, no shares outstanding		
Common stock—$.10 par; 200,000 shares authorized,		
19,940 and 18,580 shares issued and outstanding at		
Dec. 31, 2012, and Dec. 31, 2011, respectively	1,994	1,858
Additional paid-in capital	227,992	201,430
Retained income	73,666	44,798
Total shareholders' equity	**$361,352**	**$248,086**

Disclosures elsewhere in Sessel's annual report revealed the following changes in shareholders' equity accounts for 2012, 2011, 2010:

2012:

1. The only changes in retained earnings during 2012 were preferred dividends on preferred stock of $3,388,000 and net income.

2. The preferred stock is convertible. During the year, 6,592 shares were issued. All shares were converted into 320,000 shares of common stock. No gain or loss was recorded on the conversion.

3. Common shares were issued in a public offering and upon the exercise of stock options. On the statement of sharcholders' equity, Sessel's reports these two items on a single line entitled: "Issuance of shares."

2011:

1. Net income: $12,126,000.

2. Issuance of common stock: 5,580,000 shares at $112,706,000.

2010:

1. Net income: $13,494,000.

2. Issuance of common stock: 120,000 shares at $826,000.

Required:

From these disclosures, prepare comparative statements of shareholders' equity for 2012, 2011, and 2010.

Communication
Case 18–3
IFRS; Is preferred
stock debt or
equity? Group
interaction
● LO1 LO9

An unsettled question in accounting for stock is: Should preferred stock be recognized as a liability, or should it be considered equity? Under International Financial Reporting Standards, preferred stock (preference shares) often is reported as debt with the dividends reported in the income statement as interest expense. Under U.S. GAAP, that is the case only for "mandatorily redeemable" preferred stock.

Two opposing viewpoints are:

View 1: Preferred stock should be considered equity.

View 2: Preferred stock should be reported as a liability.

In considering this question, focus on conceptual issues regarding the practicable and theoretically appropriate treatment, unconstrained by GAAP.

Required:

1. Which view do you favor? Develop a list of arguments in support of your view prior to the class session for which the case is assigned.

2. In class, your instructor will pair you (and everyone else) with a classmate (who also has independently developed an argument).

    a. You will be given three minutes to argue your view to your partner. Your partner likewise will be given three minutes to argue his or her view to you. During these three-minute presentations, the listening partner is not permitted to speak.

b. Then after each person has had a turn attempting to convince his or her partner, the two partners will have a three-minute discussion in which they will decide which view is more convincing and arguments will be merged into a single view for each pair.

3. After the allotted time, a spokesperson for each of the two views will be selected by the instructor. Each spokesperson will field arguments from the class in support of that view's position and list the arguments on the board. The class then will discuss the merits of the two lists of arguments and attempt to reach a consensus view, though a consensus is not necessary.

Research Case 18–4

FASB codification; comprehensive income; locate and extract relevant information and authoritative support for a financial reporting issue; integrative; Cisco Systems

● LO2

Real World Financials

Titan Networking became a public company through an IPO (initial public offering) two weeks ago. You are looking forward to the challenges of being assistant controller for a publicly owned corporation. One such challenge came in the form of a memo in this morning's in-box. "We need to start reporting comprehensive income in our financials," the message from your boss said. "Do some research on that, will you? That concept didn't exist when I went to school." In response, you sought out the financial statements of **Cisco Systems**, the networking industry leader. The following are excerpts from disclosure notes from Cisco's 2009 annual report:

Comprehensive Income (Loss) (in part)

The components of comprehensive income (loss), net of tax, are as follows (in millions):

	Years Ended		
	July 25, 2009	July 26, 2008	July 28, 2007
Net income (loss)	$6,134	$8,052	$7,333
Other comprehensive income (loss):			
Change in unrealized gains and losses on investments net of tax benefit (expense) of $43, $13, and $43 in fiscal 2009, 2008, and 2007, respectively	(22)	(22)	128
Change in derivative instruments	(49)	—	5
Change in cumulative translation adjustment and other	(192)	227	166
Total comprehensive income	$5,890	$8,218	$7,623

Other-Than-Temporary Impairments (in part). Effective April 26, 2009, the Company adopted FSP 115-2, which amends other-than-temporary impairment guidance relating to debt securities. . . . Upon the adoption of FSP 115-2, the Company recorded a cumulative effect adjustment of $49 million, which resulted in an increase to the balance of retained earnings with a corresponding decrease to OCI.

Required:

1. Locate the financial statements of Cisco at **www.sec.gov** or Cisco's website. Search the 2009 annual report for information about how Cisco accounts for comprehensive income. What does Cisco report in its balance sheet regarding comprehensive income?

2. Obtain the relevant authoritative literature on reporting comprehensive income using the FASB's Codification Research System. You might gain access from the FASB website (**www.fasb.org**), from your school library, or some other source. Identify the specific citation from the authoritative literature that describes the three alternative formats for reporting comprehensive income.

3. What is comprehensive income? How does it differ from net income? Where is it reported in a balance sheet? Why does Cisco's 2009 other comprehensive income not reconcile with the beginning ($728 million) and ending ($435 million) balances of accumulated OCI? Explain.

4. One component of Other comprehensive income for Cisco is "Change in net unrealized gains on investments." What does this mean? From the information Cisco's financial statements provide, determine how the company calculated the $435 million accumulated other comprehensive income at the end of fiscal 2009.

5. What might be possible causes for the "Other" component of Cisco's Other comprehensive income?

Judgment Case 18–5
Treasury stock; stock split; cash dividends; Alcoa
● LO5 through LO8

Real World Financials

Alcoa is the world's leading producer of primary aluminum, fabricated aluminum, and alumina. The following is a press release from the company:

ALCOA ANNOUNCES 33% INCREASE IN BASE DIVIDEND, 2-FOR-1 STOCK SPLIT
PITTSBURGH—Alcoa today announced that its Board of Directors approved a base quarterly dividend increase of 33.3%, to 25 cents per common share from 18.75 cents per share. For a full year, base dividends will now total $1.00 compared with 75 cents before the increase.

2-FOR-1 STOCK SPLIT
The Board declared a two-for-one split of Alcoa's common stock. The stock split is subject to approval of Alcoa shareholders who must approve an amendment to the company's articles to increase the authorized shares of common stock at Alcoa's annual meeting. Shareholders of record on May 26 will receive an additional common share for each share held, which will be distributed on June 9.

COMMITMENT TO STOCK REPURCHASE PROGRAM
Alcoa restated its commitment to its previously authorized share repurchase program which it announced last year.

Required:

1. What are the two primary reporting alternatives Alcoa has in accounting for the repurchase of its shares? What would be the effect of the optional courses of action on total shareholders' equity? Explain. What would be the effect of the optional courses of action on how stock would be presented in Alcoa's balance sheet? If the shares are later resold for an amount greater than cost, how should Alcoa account for the sale?

2. What are the two primary courses of action Alcoa has in accounting for the stock split, and how would the choice affect Alcoa's shareholders' equity? Why?

3. How should Alcoa account for the cash dividend, and how would it affect Alcoa's balance sheet? Why?

Communication Case 18–6
Issuance of shares; share issue costs; prepare a report
● LO4

You are the newest member of the staff of Brinks & Company, a medium-size investment management firm. You are supervised by Les Kramer, an employee of two years. Les has a reputation as being technically sound but has a noticeable gap in his accounting education. Knowing you are knowledgeable about accounting issues, he requested you provide him with a synopsis of accounting for share issue costs.

"I thought the cost of issuing securities is recorded separately and expensed over time," he stated in a handwritten memo. "But I don't see that for IBR's underwriting expenses. What gives?"

He apparently was referring to a disclosure note on a page of IBR's annual report, photocopied and attached to his memo. To raise funds for expansion, the company sold additional shares of its $.10 par common stock. The following disclosure note appeared in the company's most recent annual report:

NOTES TO CONSOLIDATED FINANCIAL STATEMENTS
Note 10—Stock Transactions (in part)
In February and March, the Company sold 2,395,000 shares of Common Stock at $22.25 per share in a public offering. Net proceeds to the Company were approximately $50.2 million after the underwriting discount and offering expenses.

Required:

Write a formal memo to your supervisor. Briefly explain how share issue costs are accounted for and how that accounting differs from that of debt issue costs. To make sure your explanation is understood in context of the footnote, include in your memo the following:
a. At what total amount did the shares sell to the public? How is the difference between this amount and the $50.2 million net proceeds accounted for?
b. The appropriate journal entry to record the sale of the shares.

Analysis Case 18–7
Analyzing financial statements; price-earnings ratio; dividend payout ratio
● LO1

AGF Foods Company is a large, primarily domestic, consumer foods company involved in the manufacture, distribution, and sale of a variety of food products. Industry averages are derived from Troy's *The Almanac of Business and Industrial Financial Ratios* and Dun and Bradstreet's *Industry Norms and Key Business Ratios*. Following are the 2011 and 2010 comparative income statements and balance sheets for AGF. The market price of AGF's common stock is $47 during 2011. (The financial data we use are from actual financial statements of a well-known corporation, but the company name used in our illustration is fictitious and the numbers and dates have been modified slightly to disguise the company's identity.)

AGF FOODS COMPANY
Years Ended December 31, 2011 and 2010

($ in millions)	2011	2010
Comparative Income Statements		
Net sales	$6,440	$5,800
Cost of goods sold	(3,667)	(3,389)
Gross profit	2,773	2,411
Operating expenses	(1,916)	(1,629)
Operating income	857	782
Interest expense	(54)	(53)
Income from operations before tax	803	729
Income taxes	(316)	(287)
Net income	$ 487	$ 442
Net income per share	$ 2.69	$2.44
Average shares outstanding	181 million	181 million

Comparative Balance Sheets
Assets

	2011	2010
Current assets:		
Cash	$ 48	$ 142
Accounts receivable	347	320
Marketable securities	358	—
Inventories	914	874
Prepaid expenses	212	154
Total current assets	$1,879	$1,490
Property, plant, and equipment (net)	2,592	2,291
Intangibles (net)	800	843
Other assets	74	60
Total assets	$5,345	$4,684

Liabilities and Shareholders' Equity

	2011	2010
Current liabilities:		
Accounts payable	$ 254	$ 276
Accrued liabilities	493	496
Notes payable	518	115
Current portion of long-term debt	208	54
Total current liabilities	1,473	941
Long-term debt	534	728
Deferred income taxes	407	344
Total liabilities	2,414	2,013
Shareholders' equity:		
Common stock, $1 par	180	180
Additional paid-in capital	21	63
Retained earnings	2,730	2,428
Total shareholders' equity	2,931	2,671
Total liabilities and shareholders' equity	$5,345	$4,684

Profitability is the key to a company's long-run survival. Profitability measures focus on a company's ability to provide an adequate return relative to resources devoted to company operations.

Required:

1. Calculate the return on shareholders' equity for AGF. The average return for the stocks listed on the New York Stock Exchange in a comparable period was 18.8%. What information does your calculation provide an investor?

2. Calculate AGF's earnings per share and earnings-price ratio. The average return for the stocks listed on the New York Stock Exchange in a comparable time period was 5.4%. What does your calculation indicate about AGF's earnings?

**Ethics
Case 18–8**
The Swiss label maker; value of shares issued for equipment
● LO4

Bricker Graphics is a privately held company specializing in package labels. Representatives of the firm have just returned from Switzerland, where a Swiss firm is manufacturing a custom-made high speed, color labeling machine. Confidence is high that the new machine will help rescue Bricker from sharply declining profitability. Bricker's chief operating officer, Don Benson, has been under fire for not achieving the company's performance goals of achieving a rate of return on assets of at least 12%.

The afternoon of his return from Switzerland, Benson called Susan Sharp into his office. Susan is Bricker's Controller.

Benson:	I wish you had been able to go. We have some accounting issues to consider.
Sharp:	I wish I'd been there, too. I understand the food was marvelous. What are the accounting issues?
Benson:	They discussed accepting our notes at the going rate for a face amount of $12.5 million. We also discussed financing with stock.
Sharp:	I thought we agreed; debt is the way to go for us now.
Benson:	Yes, but I've been thinking. We can issue shares for a total of $10 million. The labeler is custom-made and doesn't have a quoted selling price, but the domestic labelers we considered went for around $10 million. It sure would help our rate of return if we keep the asset base as low as possible.

Required:

1. How will Benson's plan affect the return measure? What accounting issue is involved?

2. Is the proposal ethical?

3. Who would be affected if the proposal is implemented?

**Research
Case 18–9**
Researching the way shareholders' equity transactions are reported; retrieving financial statements from the Internet
● LO1 LO6

EDGAR, the Electronic Data Gathering, Analysis, and Retrieval system, performs automated collection, validation, indexing, and forwarding of submissions by companies and others who are required by law to file forms with the U.S. Securities and Exchange Commission (SEC). All publicly traded domestic companies use EDGAR to make the majority of their filings. (Filings by foreign companies are not required to be filed on EDGAR, but some of these companies do so voluntarily.) Form 10-K, which includes the annual report, is required to be filed on EDGAR. The SEC makes this information available on the Internet.

Required:

1. Access EDGAR on the Internet at **www.sec.gov**.

2. Search for a public company with which you are familiar. Access its most recent 10-K filing. Search or scroll to find the statement of shareholders' equity and related note(s). If a statement of shareholders' equity is not provided, try another company.

3. Determine from the statement the transactions that occurred during the most recent three years that affected retained earnings.

4. Determine from the statement the transactions that occurred during the most recent three years that affected common stock. Were any of these transactions identified in requirement 3 also?

5. Cross-reference your findings with amounts reported on the balance sheet. How do these two statements articulate with one another?

**Communication
Case 18–10**
Should the present two-category distinction between liabilities and equity be retained? Group interaction.
● LO1

The current conceptual distinction between liabilities and equity defines liabilities independently of assets and equity, with equity defined as a residual amount. The present proliferation of financial instruments that combine features of both debt and equity and the difficulty of drawing a distinction have led many to conclude that the present two-category distinction between liabilities and equity should be eliminated. Two opposing viewpoints are:

View 1: The distinction should be maintained.
View 2: The distinction should be eliminated and financial instruments should instead be reported in accordance with the priority of their claims to enterprise assets.

One type of security that often is mentioned in the debate is convertible bonds. Although stock in many ways, such a security also obligates the issuer to transfer assets at a specified price and redemption date. Thus it also has features of debt. In considering this question, focus on conceptual issues regarding the practicable and theoretically appropriate treatment, unconstrained by GAAP.

Required:

1. Which view do you favor? Develop a list of arguments in support of your view prior to the class session for which the case is assigned.

2. In class, your instructor will pair you (and everyone else) with a classmate (who also has independently developed an argument).

    a. You will be given three minutes to argue your view to your partner. Your partner likewise will be given three minutes to argue his or her view to you. During these three-minute presentations, the listening partner is not permitted to speak.

b. Then after each person has had a turn attempting to convince his or her partner, the two partners will have a three-minute discussion in which they will decide which view is more convincing and arguments will be merged into a single view for each pair.

3. After the allotted time, a spokesperson for each of the two views will be selected by the instructor. Each spokesperson will field arguments from the class in support of that view's position and list the arguments on the board. The class then will discuss the merits of the two lists of arguments and attempt to reach a consensus view, though a consensus is not necessary.

BRITISH AIRWAYS CASE

BRITISH AIRWAYS

● LO9

British Airways, Plc. (BA), a U.K. company, prepares its financial statements according to International Financial Reporting Standards. BA's annual report for the year ended March 31, 2009, which includes financial statements and disclosure notes, is included with all new textbooks and can be found at **www.britishairways.com**. When answering questions, focus on BA's "Group" financial information (which is equivalent to "Consolidated" under U.S. GAAP).

Required:

1. British Airways lists four items in the shareholders' equity section of its balance sheet. If British Airways used U.S. GAAP, what would be the likely account titles for the first three of those components?

2. Locate Note 35 in BA's financial statements. What three items comprise "Other reserves" as reported in the balance sheet? If British Airways used U.S. GAAP, what would be the likely account titles for the three items?

3. Describe the apparent differences in the order of presentation of the components of liabilities and shareholders' equity between IFRS as applied by BA and a typical balance sheet prepared in accordance with U.S. GAAP.

CPA SIMULATION 18–1

Hanson Corporation

Shareholders' Equity

CPA Review

Test your knowledge of the concepts discussed in this chapter, practice critical professional skills necessary for career success, and prepare for the computer-based CPA exam by accessing our CPA simulations at the text website: **www.mhhe.com/spiceland6e**.

The Hansen Corporation simulation tests your knowledge of a variety of shareholders' equity reporting issues.

As on the CPA exam itself, you will be asked to use tools including a spreadsheet, a calculator, and generally accepted accounting principles to conduct research, derive solutions, and communicate conclusions related to these issues in a simulated environment.

Specific tasks in the simulation include:

● Applying judgment in deciding the financial reporting implications of a variety of shareholders' equity transactions.

● Determining the financial statement effects of stock dividends and stock splits.

● Calculating dividends on preferred stock.

● Demonstrating an understanding of financial reporting effects of treasury stock transactions.

● Communicating the benefits of a stock buyback.

● Researching appropriate accounting for mandatorily redeemable preferred stock.

19 Share-Based Compensation and Earnings Per Share

/ /

/ / / **OVERVIEW**

We've discussed a variety of employee compensation plans in prior chapters, including pension and other postretirement benefits in Chapter 17. In this chapter we look at some common forms of compensation in which the amount of the compensation employees receive is tied to the market price of company stock. We will see that these *share-based* compensation plans—stock awards, stock options, and stock appreciation rights—create shareholders' equity, which was the topic of the previous chapter, and which also often affects the way we calculate earnings per share, the topic of the second part of the current chapter. Specifically, we view these as *potential common shares* along with convertible securities, and we calculate earnings per share as if the securities already had been exercised or converted into additional common shares.

/ / / **LEARNING OBJECTIVES**

After studying this chapter, you should be able to:

● **LO1** Explain and implement the accounting for stock award plans. (page 1070)
● **LO2** Explain and implement the accounting for stock options. (page 1071)
● **LO3** Explain and implement the accounting for employee share purchase plans. (page 1080)
● **LO4** Distinguish between a simple and a complex capital structure. (page 1083)
● **LO5** Describe what is meant by the weighted-average number of common shares. (page 1083)
● **LO6** Differentiate the effect on EPS of the sale of new shares, a stock dividend or stock split, and the reacquisition of shares. (page 1084)
● **LO7** Describe how preferred dividends affect the calculation of EPS. (page 1086)
● **LO8** Describe how options, rights, and warrants are incorporated in the calculation of EPS. (page 1087)
● **LO9** Describe how convertible securities are incorporated in the calculation of EPS. (page 1088)
● **LO10** Determine whether potential common shares are antidilutive. (page 1092)
● **LO11** Determine the three components of the proceeds used in the treasury stock method. (page 1096)
● **LO12** Explain the way contingently issuable shares are incorporated in the calculation of EPS. (page 1097)
● **LO13** Describe the way EPS information should be reported in an income statement. (page 1100)
● **LO14** Discuss the primary differences between U.S. GAAP and IFRS with respect to accounting for share-based compensation and earnings per share. (pages 1077, 1078, 1082, and 1102)

FINANCIAL REPORTING CASE

Proper Motivation?

The coffee room discussion Thursday morning was particularly lively. Yesterday's press release describing National Electronic Ventures' choice of Sandra Veres as its president and chief operating officer was today's hot topic in all the company's departments. The press release noted that Ms. Veres's compensation package includes elements beyond salary that are intended to not only motivate her to accept the offer, but also to remain with the company and work to increase shareholder value. Excerpts from the release follow:

> National Electronic Ventures, Inc., today announced it had attracted G. Sandra Veres, respected executive from the wireless communications industry, to succeed chairman Walter Kovac. Veres will assume the new role as CEO on Jan. 1, 2011. Ms. Veres will receive a compensation package at NEV of more than $1 million in salary, stock options to buy more than 800,000 shares of NEV stock and a grant of restricted stock.

By the time you finish this chapter, you should be able to respond appropriately to the questions posed in this case. Compare your response to the solution provided at the end of the chapter.

QUESTIONS ///

1. How can a compensation package such as this serve as an incentive to Ms. Veres? (page 1070)

2. Ms. Veres received a "grant of restricted stock." How should NEV account for the grant? (page 1070)

3. Included were stock options to buy more than 800,000 shares of NEV stock. How will the options affect NEV's compensation expense? (page 1072)

4. How will the presence of these and other similar stock options affect NEV's earnings per share? (page 1087)

SHARE-BASED COMPENSATION

Employee compensation plans frequently include share-based awards. These may be outright awards of shares, stock options, or cash payments tied to the market price of shares. Sometimes only key executives participate in a stock benefit plan. Typically, an executive compensation plan is tied to performance in a strategy that uses compensation to motivate its recipients. Some firms pay their directors entirely in shares. Actual compensation depends on the market value of the shares. Obviously, that's quite an incentive to act in the best interests of shareholders.

Although the variations of share-based compensation plans are seemingly endless, each shares common goals. Whether the plan is a stock award plan, a stock option plan, a stock appreciation rights (SARs) plan, or one of the several similar plans, the goals are to provide compensation to designated employees, while sometimes providing those employees with some sort of performance incentive. Likewise, our goals in accounting for each of these plans are the same for each: (1) to determine the fair value of the compensation and (2) to expense that compensation over the periods in which participants perform services. The issue is not trivial. Salary often is a minor portion of executive pay relative to stock awards and stock options, which, combined, averaged almost $4.5 million per chief executive in 2008.

Stock Award Plans

Executive compensation sometimes includes a grant of shares of stock. Usually, such shares are restricted in such a way as to provide some incentive to the recipient. Typically, restricted stock award plans are tied to continued employment. In a **restricted stock** plan, shares actually are awarded in the name of the employee, although the company might retain physical possession of the shares. The employee has all rights of a shareholder, subject to certain restrictions or forfeiture. Ordinarily, the shares are subject to forfeiture by the employee if employment is terminated within some specified number of years from the date of grant. The employee usually is not free to sell the shares during the restriction period and a statement to that effect often is inscribed on the stock certificates. These restrictions give the employee incentive to remain with the company until rights to the shares vest. Graphic 19–1 describes the restricted award plan for the **Sears Holdings Corporation**.

FINANCIAL Reporting Case

Q1, p. 1069

The accounting objective is to record compensation expense over the periods in which related services are performed.

Usually, restricted shares are subject to forfeiture if the employee doesn't remain with the company.

● LO1

GRAPHIC 19–1

Restricted Stock Award Plan—Sears Holdings

Real World Financials

> **Stock-based Compensation (in part)**
>
> The Company has granted restricted stock awards to certain associates. These restricted stock awards typically vest in full three years from the date of grant, provided the grantee remains employed by the Company as of the vesting date. The fair value of these awards is equal to the market price of the Company's common stock on the date of grant.

FINANCIAL Reporting Case

Q2, p. 1069

The compensation associated with a share of restricted stock (or nonvested stock) is the market price at the grant date of an unrestricted share of the same stock. This amount is accrued as compensation expense over the service period for which participants receive the shares, usually from the date of grant to when restrictions are lifted (the vesting date).[1] This is demonstrated in Illustration 19–1 on the next page.

Once the shares vest and the restrictions are lifted, paid-in capital—restricted stock is replaced by common stock and paid-in capital—excess of par.

The amount of the compensation is measured at the date of grant—at the market price on that date. Any market price changes that might occur after that don't affect the total compensation.

---

[1]Restricted stock plans usually are designed to comply with Tax Code Section 83 to allow employee compensation to be nontaxable to the employee until the year the shares become substantially vested, which is when the restrictions are lifted. Likewise, the employer gets no tax deduction until the compensation becomes taxable to the employee.

Under its restricted stock award plan, Universal Communications grants five million of its $1 par common shares to certain key executives at January 1, 2011. The shares are subject to forfeiture if employment is terminated within four years. Shares have a current market price of $12 per share.

January 1, 2011
No entry

Calculate total compensation expense:

$12	Fair value per share
× 5 million	Shares awarded
= $60 million	Total compensation

The total compensation is to be allocated to expense over the four-year service (vesting) period: 2011–2014

$$\$60 \text{ million} \div 4 \text{ years} = \$15 \text{ million per year}$$

December 31, 2011, 2012, 2013, 2014	($ in millions)	
Compensation expense ($60 million ÷ 4 years)	15	
Paid-in capital—restricted stock		15
December 31, 2014		
Paid-in capital—restricted stock (5 million shares at $12)	60	
Common stock (5 million shares at $1 par)		5
Paid-in capital—excess of par (difference)		55

ILLUSTRATION 19–1

Restricted Stock Award Plan

The total compensation is the market value of the shares ($12) times five million shares.

The **$60** million is accrued to compensation expense over the four-year service period.

When restrictions are lifted, paid-in capital—restricted stock, is replaced by common stock and paid-in capital— excess of par.

ADDITIONAL CONSIDERATION

An alternative way of accomplishing the same result is to debit deferred compensation for the full value of the restricted shares ($60 million in the illustration) on the date they are granted:

Deferred compensation (5 million shares at $12)	60	
Common stock (5 million shares at $1 par)		5
Paid-in capital—excess of par (difference)		55

If so, deferred compensation is reported as a reduction in shareholders' equity, resulting in a zero net effect on shareholders' equity. Then, deferred compensation is credited when compensation expense is debited over the service period. Just as in Illustration 19–1, the result is an increase in both compensation expense and shareholders' equity each year over the vesting period.

If restricted stock is forfeited because, say, the employee leaves the company, entries previously made related to that specific employee would simply be reversed. This would result in a decrease in compensation expense in the year of forfeiture. The total compensation, adjusted for the forfeited amount, is then allocated over the remaining service period.

Stock Option Plans

More commonly, employees aren't actually awarded shares, but rather are given the option to buy shares in the future. In fact, **stock options** have become an integral part of the total compensation package for key officers of most medium and large companies.[2] As with any compensation plan, the accounting objective is to report compensation expense during the period of service for which the compensation is given.

● LO2

---

[2]In a recent survey of 500 corporations, 489 companies disclosed the existence of stock option plans (AICPA, *Accounting Trends and Techniques*, 2009).

Expense—The Great Debate

Stock option plans give employees the option to purchase (a) a specified number of shares of the firm's stock, (b) at a specified price, (c) during a specified period of time. One of the most heated controversies in standard-setting history has been the debate over the amount of compensation to be recognized as expense for stock options. At issue is how the value of stock options is measured, which for most options determines whether any expense at all is recognized.

Historically, options have been measured at their intrinsic values—the simple difference between the market price of the shares and the option price at which they can be acquired. For instance, an option that permits an employee to buy $25 stock for $10 has an intrinsic value of $15. However, plans in which the exercise price equals the market value of the underlying stock at the date of grant (which describes most executive stock option plans) have no intrinsic value and therefore result in zero compensation when measured this way, even though the fair value of the options can be quite significant. In 2007, **eBay** CEO Meg Whitman exercised enough stock options to realize a pretax profit of $117 million from selling shares. To many, it seems counterintuitive to not recognize compensation expense for plans that routinely provide executives with a substantial part of their total compensation.

After lengthy debate, the FASB consented to encourage, rather than require, that the fair value of options be recognized as expense.

There were consistent criticisms of the FASB's requirement to expense option compensation.

FAILED ATTEMPT TO REQUIRE EXPENSING. This is where the controversy ensues. In 1993, the FASB issued an Exposure Draft of a new standard that would have required companies to measure options at their *fair values* at the time they are granted and to expense that amount over the appropriate service period. To jump straight to the punch line, the FASB bowed to public pressure and agreed to withdraw the requirement before it became a standard. The FASB consented to encourage, rather than require, that fair value compensation be recognized as expense. Companies were permitted to continue accounting under prior GAAP (the intrinsic value method referred to in the previous paragraph).[3] Before we discuss the details of accounting for stock options, it's helpful to look back at what led the FASB to first propose fair value accounting and later rescind that proposal.

As the 1990s began, the public was becoming increasingly aware of the enormity of executive compensation in general and compensation in the form of stock options in particular. The lack of accounting for this compensation was apparent, prompting the SEC to encourage the FASB to move forward on its stock option project. Even Congress got into the fray when, in 1992, a bill was introduced that would require firms to report compensation expense based on the fair value of options. Motivated by this encouragement, the FASB issued its exposure draft in 1993. The real disharmony began then. Opposition to the proposed standard was broad and vehement; and that perhaps is an understatement. Critics based their opposition on one or more of three objections:

1. *Options with no intrinsic value at issue have zero fair value and should not give rise to expense recognition.* The FASB, and even some critics of the proposal, were adamant that options provide valuable compensation at the grant date to recipients.
2. *It is impossible to measure the fair value of the compensation on the grant date.* The FASB argued vigorously that value can be approximated using one of several option pricing models. These are statistical models that use computers to incorporate information about a company's stock and the terms of the stock option to estimate the options' fair value. We might say the FASB position is that it's better to be approximately right than precisely wrong.
3. *The proposed standard would have unacceptable economic consequences.* Essentially, this argument asserted that requiring this popular means of compensation to be expensed would cause companies to discontinue the use of options.

The opposition included corporate executives, auditors, members of Congress, and the SEC.[4] Ironically, the very groups that provided the most impetus for the rule change

---

[3]"Accounting for Stock Issued to Employees," *Opinions of the Accounting Principles Board No. 25* (New York: AICPA, 1972). This pronouncement is superseded and therefore is not codified in the FASB Accounting Research System.

[4]All of the then "Big Six" CPA firms lobbied against the proposal. Senator Lieberman of Connecticut introduced a bill in Congress that if passed would have forbidden the FASB from passing a requirement to expense stock option compensation.

initially—the SEC and Congress—were among the most effective detractors in the end. The only group that offered much support at all was the academic community, and that was by-and-large nonvocal support. In reversing its decision, the FASB was not swayed by any of the specific arguments of any opposition group. Dennis Beresford, chair of the FASB at the time, indicated that it was fear of government control of the standard-setting process that prompted the Board to modify its position. The Board remained steadfast that the proposed change was appropriate.

VOLUNTARY EXPENSING.   Prior to 2002, only two companies—**Boeing** and **Winn-Dixie**—reported stock option compensation expense at fair value. However, in 2002 public outrage mounted amid high-profile accounting scandals at **Enron**, **WorldCom**, **Tyco**, and others. Some degree of consensus emerged that greed on the part of some corporate executives contributed to the fraudulent and misleading financial reporting at the time. In fact, many in the media were pointing to the proliferation of stock options as a primary form of compensation as a culprit in fueling that greed. An episode of the PBS series *Frontline* argued that not expensing the value of stock options contributed to the collapse of Enron. For these reasons, renewed interest surfaced in requiring stock option compensation to be reported in income statements.

> FRANK PARTNOY—
> AUTHOR, INFECTIOUS
> GREED
> . . . the increase in the use
> of stock options coincided
> with a massive increase in
> accounting fraud by corporate
> executives, who benefited
> from short-term increases in
> their stock prices.[5]

CURRENT REQUIREMENT TO EXPENSE.   Emerging from the rekindled debate was a GAAP revision that now requires fair value accounting for employee stock options, eliminating altogether the intrinsic value approach.[6] As you might expect, the proposal did not come without opposition. Many of the same groups that successfully blocked the FASB from enacting a similar requirement in 1995 led the opposition. Not surprisingly, at the forefront of the resistance were the high-tech companies that extensively use stock options as a primary form of compensating employees and thus are most susceptible to a reduction in reported earnings when that compensation is included in income statements. For example, consider **Apple Inc.**'s earnings for the 12 months ending March 27, 2004. Reported net income of $179 million would have been only $56 million, or 69% less, if the GAAP revision had been in effect then.[7]

Current GAAP now requires companies to record the value of options in their income statements.

It's important to note that the way we account for stock options has no effect whatsoever on cash flows, only on whether the value of stock options is included among expenses. This is not to say that companies haven't altered their compensation strategics. Already, we have seen a shift in the way some companies compensate their employees. Partly due to the negative connotation that has become associated with executive stock options, we've seen fewer options and more bonuses and restricted stock awards. Let's examine the way stock options are accounted for now.

We've witnessed a discernable shift in the way executives are compensated—fewer options, more stock awards and bonuses.

Recognizing the Fair Value of Options

Accounting for stock options parallels the accounting for restricted stock we discussed in the first part of this chapter. That is, we measure compensation as the fair value of the stock options at the grant date and then record that amount as compensation expense over the service period for which employees receive the options. Estimating the fair value requires the use of one of several option pricing models. These mathematical models assimilate a variety of information about a company's stock and the terms of the stock option to estimate the option's fair value. The model should take into account the:

The fair value of a stock option can be determined by employing a recognized option pricing model.

- Exercise price of the option.
- Expected term of the option.
- Current market price of the stock.

---

[5]Frank Partnoy, *Infectious Greed: How Deceit and Risk Corrupted the Financial Markets* (New York: Henry Holt/Times Books, Spring 2003), p. 159.
[6]FASB ASC 718–Compensation (previously "Share-Based Payment," *Statement of Financial Accounting Standards No. 123 (revised 2004),* (Norwalk, Conn.: FASB 2004)).
[7]Alex Salkever, "What Could Crunch Apple Shares," *BusinessWeek,* July 12, 2004, p. 11.

An option pricing model takes into account several variables.

- Expected dividends.
- Expected risk-free rate of return during the term of the option.
- Expected volatility of the stock.

The techniques for estimating fair value have been among the most controversial issues in the debate.

The current GAAP for accounting for employee stock options modified the way companies actually measure fair value. It calls for using models that permit greater flexibility in modeling the ways employees are expected to exercise options and their expected employment termination patterns after options vest.[8] Option-pricing theory, on which the pricing models are based, is a topic explored in depth in finance courses and is subject to active empirical investigation and development. A simplified discussion is provided in Appendix 19A.[9]

The total compensation as estimated by the options' fair value is reported as compensation expense over the period of service for which the options are given. Recipients normally are not allowed to exercise their options for a specified number of years. This delay provides added incentive to remain with the company. The time between the date options are granted and the first date they can be exercised is the vesting period and usually is considered to be the service period over which the compensation expense is reported. The process is demonstrated in Illustration 19–2.

ILLUSTRATION 19–2 Stock Options	At January 1, 2011, Universal Communications grants options that permit key executives to acquire 10 million of the company's $1 par common shares within the next eight years, but not before December 31, 2014 (the vesting date). The exercise price is the market price of the shares on the date of grant, $35 per share. The fair value of the options, estimated by an appropriate option pricing model, is $8 per option.
	January 1, 2011 No entry
Fair value is estimated at the date of grant.	Calculate total compensation expense:

$ 8	Estimated fair value per option
× 10 million	Options granted
= $80 million	Total compensation

The total compensation is to be allocated to expense over the four-year service (vesting) period: 2011–2012

$$\$80 \text{ million} \div 4 \text{ years} = \$20 \text{ million per year}$$

The value of the award is expensed over the service period for which the compensation is provided.

December 31, 2011, 2012, 2013, 2014   ($ in millions)

Compensation expense ($80 million ÷ 4 years)	20	
Paid-in capital—stock options		20

ESTIMATED FORFEITURES.   If previous experience indicates that a material number of the options will be forfeited before they vest (due to employee turnover or violation of other terms of the options), we adjust the fair value estimate made on the grant date to reflect that expectation. For instance, if a forfeiture rate of 5% is expected, Universal's estimated total compensation would be 95% of $80 million, or $76 million. In that case, the annual compensation expense in Illustration 19–2 would have been $19 million ($76/4) instead of $20 million. We see the effect of that possibility in Illustration 19–2A.

Option compensation expense is based on the number of options expected to vest.

When forfeiture estimates change, the cumulative effect on compensation is reflected in current earnings.

What if that expectation changes later? Universal should adjust the cumulative amount of compensation expense recorded to date in the year the estimate changes.[10] Suppose, for instance, that during 2013, the third year, Universal revises its estimate of forfeitures from 5% to 10%. The new estimate of total compensation would then be $80 million × 90%, or

---

[8]FASB ASC 718–10–55–30 to 32: Compensation–Stock Compensation–Overall–Implementation and Guidance Illustrations–Selecting or Estimating the Expected Term (previously "Share-Based Payment," *Statement of Financial Accounting Standards No. 123 (revised 2004),* (Norwalk, Conn.: FASB 2004), par. A27–A29)).

[9]An expanded discussion is provided in FASB ASC 718–10–55: Compensation–Stock Compensation–Overall–Implementation and Guidance Illustrations (previously *SFAS No. 123 (revised 2004)*).

[10]FASB ASC 718–10–35–3: Compensation–Stock Compensation–Overall–Subsequent Measurement (previously "Share-Based Payment," *Statement of Financial Accounting Standards No. 123 (revised 2004),* (Norwalk, Conn.: FASB 2004), par. 43).

2011	($ in millions)	
Compensation expense ($80 × 95% ÷ 4)	19	
Paid-in capital—stock options		19
2012		
Compensation expense ($80 × 95% ÷ 4)	19	
Paid-in capital—stock options		19
2013		
Compensation expense [($80 × 90% × 3/4) – ($19 + 19)]	16	
Paid-in capital—stock options		16
2014		
Compensation expense [($80 × 90% × 4/4) – ($19 + 19 + 16)]	18	
Paid-in capital—stock options		18

ILLUSTRATION 19–2A

Estimates with Revisions

The value of the compensation is originally estimated to be $76 million, or **$19** million per year.

The expense each year is the current estimate of total compensation that should have been recorded to date less the amount already recorded.

$72 million. For the first three years, the portion of the total compensation that should have been reported would be $72 million × 3/4, or $54 million, and since $38 million ($19 × 2) of that was recorded in 2011–2012 before the estimate changed, an additional $16 million would now be recorded in 2013. Then if the estimate isn't changed again, the remaining $18 million ($72 – 54) would be recorded in 2014.

ADDITIONAL CONSIDERATION

Notice that the $18 million in 2014 is the amount that would have been reported in each of the four years if Universal had assumed a 10% forfeiture rate from the beginning. Also be aware that this approach is contrary to the usual way companies account for changes in estimates. For instance, assume a company acquires a four-year depreciable asset having an estimated residual value of 5% of cost. The $76 million depreciable cost would be depreciated straight line at $19 million over the four-year useful life. If the estimated residual value changes after two years to 10%, the new estimated depreciable cost of $72 would be reduced by the $38 million depreciation recorded the first two years, and the remaining $34 million would be depreciated equally, $17 million per year, over the remaining two years.

When Options are Exercised

If half the options in Illustration 19–2 (five million shares) are exercised on July 11, 2017, when the market price is $50 per share, the following journal entry is recorded:

July 11, 2017	($ in millions)	
Cash ($35 exercise price × 5 million shares)	175	
Paid-in capital—stock options (½ account balance)	40	
Common stock (5 million shares at $1 par per share)		5
Paid-in capital—excess of par (to balance)		210

Recording the exercise of options is not affected by the market price on the exercise date.

Notice that the market price at exercise is irrelevant. Changes in the market price of underlying shares do not influence the previously measured fair value of options.

When Unexercised Options Expire

If options that have vested expire without being exercised, the following journal entry is made (assuming the remaining 5 million options in our illustration are allowed to expire):

	($ in millions)	
Paid-in capital—stock options (account balance)	40	
Paid-in capital—expiration of stock options		40

Paid-in capital—stock options becomes *paid-in capital—expiration of stock options*, when options expire without being exercised.

In effect, we rename the paid-in capital attributable to the stock option plan. Compensation expense for the four years' service, as of the measurement date, is not affected.

ADDITIONAL CONSIDERATION

Tax Consequences of Stock-Based Compensation Plans

In Illustration 19–2 we ignored the tax effect. To illustrate the effect of taxes, let's assume Universal Communications' income tax rate is 40%.

For tax purposes, plans can either qualify as "incentive stock option plans" under the Tax Code or be "nonqualified plans." Among the requirements of a qualified option plan is that the exercise price be equal to the market price at the grant date. Under a qualified incentive plan, the recipient pays no income tax until any shares acquired from exercise of stock options are subsequently sold. On the other hand, the company gets no tax deduction at all. With a nonqualified plan the employee can't delay paying income tax, but the employer is permitted to deduct the difference between the exercise price and the market price at the exercise date. Let's consider both.

> **Case 1.** With an incentive plan, the employer receives no tax deduction at all. If Universal's plan qualifies as an incentive plan, the company will receive no tax deduction upon exercise of the options and thus no tax consequences.
>
> **Case 2.** On the other hand, if we assume the plan does not qualify as an incentive plan, Universal will deduct from taxable income the difference between the exercise price and the market price at the exercise date. Recall from Chapter 16 that this creates a temporary difference between accounting income (for which compensation expense is recorded currently) and taxable income (for which the tax deduction is taken later upon the exercise of the options). We assume the temporary difference is the cumulative amount expensed for the options. The following entries would be recorded on the dates shown:

December 31, 2011, 2012, 2013, 2014	($ in millions)	
Compensation expense ($80 million ÷ 4 years)	20	
Paid-in capital—stock options		20
Deferred tax asset (40% × $20 million)	8	
Income tax expense (reduction in the expense)..		8

The after-tax effect on earnings is thus $12 million each year ($20 – 8).

If all of the options (ten million shares) are exercised on April 4, 2016:

Cash ($35 exercise price × 10 million shares)	350	
Paid-in capital—stock options (account balance)	80	
Common stock (10 million shares at $1 par per share)		10
Paid-in capital—excess of par (to balance)		420

a. Options exercised when the tax benefit *exceeds* the deferred tax asset:
If the market price on April 4, 2016, is $50 per share:

Income taxes payable [($50 – 35) × 10 million shares × 40%]	60	
Deferred tax asset (4 years × $8 million)		32
Paid-in capital—tax effect of stock options (remainder)*		28

b. Options exercised when the tax benefit is *less than* the deferred tax asset:
If the market price on April 4, 2016, is $40 per share:

Income taxes payable [($40 – 35) × 10 million shares × 40%]	20	
Income tax expense or paid-in capital—tax effect of stock options† (remainder)	12	
Deferred tax asset (4 years × $8 million)		32

The tax consequences of all nonqualifying stock options as well as restricted stock plans also are accounted for in the manner demonstrated above.

*This treatment is consistent with a provision of FASB ASC 740–20–45–11d: Income Taxes–Intraperiod Tax Allocation–Other Presentation Matters–Allocation to Items Other than Continuing Operations (previously *SFAS No. 109* (par. 36C)) that requires the tax effect of an increase or decrease in equity (paid-in capital—stock options, in this case) be allocated to equity.
†Paid-in capital—tax effect of stock options is debited only if that account has a sufficient credit balance from previous transactions in which the tax benefit exceeded the deferred tax asset.

Margin notes:

Tax treatment favors the employer in a nonqualified stock option plan.

Because an incentive plan provides no tax deduction, it has no deferred tax consequences.

A deferred tax asset is recognized now for the future tax savings from the tax deduction when the nonqualified stock options are exercised.

If the eventual tax savings exceed the deferred tax asset, the difference is recognized as equity.

INTERNATIONAL FINANCIAL REPORTING STANDARDS

Recognition of Deferred Tax Asset for Stock Options. Under U.S. GAAP, a deferred tax asset (DTA) is created for the cumulative amount of the fair value of the options the company has recorded for compensation expense. The DTA is the tax rate times the amount of compensation.

Under IFRS, the deferred tax asset isn't created until the award is "in the money;" that is, it has intrinsic value. When it is in the money, the addition to the DTA is the portion of the intrinsic value earned to date times the tax rate.

For illustration, refer to Case 2 in the Additional Consideration example on page 1076. Now assume the share price, which was equal to the $35 exercise price on January 1, 2011, was $35, $37, $37, and $37.50 on December 31, 2011, 2012, 2013, and 2014, respectively. We need this information to determine the intrinsic value for IFRS.

The addition to the DTA and reduction in the tax expense (tax benefit) is calculated in the following table for both U.S. GAAP and IFRS ($ in millions):

IFRS ILLUSTRATION

● **LO14**

Dec. 31	Comp- ensation expense	Addition to DTA and reduction in tax expense at 40% U.S. GAAP	Cumulative reduction in tax expense	Intrinsic value (price − $35) × 10M shares	Percent of services received	Percent × Intrinsic value	Addition to DTA and reduction in tax expense at 40%* IFRS
2011	$20	$ 8	$ 8	$ 0	25%	$ 0	$ 0
2012	20	8	16	20	50%	10	4
2013	20	8	24	20	75%	15	6
2014	20	8	32	25	100%	25	10

December 31, 2011, 2012, 2013, 2014 ($ in millions)	U.S. GAAP		IFRS	
Compensation expense ($80 million ÷ 4 years)	20		20	
Paid-in capital—stock options		20		20
Deferred tax asset	8		0	
Income tax expense		8		0
Deferred tax asset	8		4	
Income tax expense		8		4
Deferred tax asset	8		6	
Income tax expense		8		6
Deferred tax asset	8		10	
Income tax expense		8		10

*The tax benefit recorded in earnings (cumulative amount in this column) cannot exceed the cumulative tax effect of the compensation (4th column). Any tax benefit in excess of that amount is recorded in equity. In 2014, $20 ($0 + 4 + 6 + 10) does not exceed $32.

Plans with Graded Vesting

The stock option plans we've discussed so far vest (become exercisable) on one single date (e.g., four years from date of grant). This is referred to as *cliff vesting*. More frequently, though, awards specify that recipients gradually become eligible to exercise their options gradually rather than all at once. This is called *graded vesting*. For instance, a company might award stock options that vest 25% the first year, 25% the second year, and 50% the third year, or maybe 25% each year for four years.

In such a case, the company can choose to account for the options essentially the same as the cliff-vesting plans we've discussed to this point. It can estimate a single fair value for each of the options, even though they vest over different time periods, using a single weighted-average expected life of the options. The company then allocates that total compensation cost (fair value per option times number of options) over the entire vesting period.

Most companies, though, choose a slightly more complex method because it usually results in a lower expense.[11] In this approach, we view each vesting group (or tranche) separately, as if it were a separate award. See Illustration 19–3.

ILLUSTRATION 19–3 Stock Options; Graded Vesting; Separate Valuation Approach	Taggart Mobility issued 10 million executive stock options permitting executives to buy 10 million shares of stock for $25. The vesting schedule is 20% the first year, 30% the second year, and 50% the third year (graded vesting). The value of the options that vest over the 3-year period is estimated at January 1, 2011, by separating the total award into three groups (or tranches) according to the year in which they vest (because the expected life for each group differs). The fair value of the options is estimated as follows:

Vesting Date	Amount Vesting	Fair Value per Option
Dec. 31, 2011	20%	$3.50
Dec. 31, 2012	30%	$4.00
Dec. 31, 2013	50%	$6.00

The compensation expense related to the options to be recorded each year 2011–2013 is:

Vestingt Date	Amount Vesting (shares in millions)	Fair Value per Option	Compensation Cost ($ in millions)
Dec. 31, 2011	2	$3.50	$ 7
Dec. 31, 2012	3	$4.00	12
Dec. 31, 2013	5	$6.00	30
			$49

We allocate the compensation cost for each of the three groups (tranches) evenly over its individual vesting (service) period:

	Compensation Expense Recorded in: ($ in millions)			
Shares Vesting at:	**2011**	**2012**	**2013**	**Total**
Dec. 31, 2011	$ 7			$ 7
Dec. 31, 2012	6	$ 6		12
Dec. 31, 2013	10	10	$10	30
	$23	$16	$10	= $49

At any given date, a company must have recognized at least the amount vested by that date. The allocation in this instance meets that constraint:
- The $23 million recognized in 2011 exceeds the $7 million vested.
- The $39 million ($23 + $16) recognized by 2012 exceeds the $19 million ($7 + $12) vested by the same time.

Companies also can choose to use the straight-line method, which would allocate the $49 million total compensation cost equally to 2011, 2012, and 2013 at $16.333 million per year.

INTERNATIONAL FINANCIAL REPORTING STANDARDS

When options have graded vesting, U.S. GAAP permits companies to account for each vesting amount separately, for instance as if there were three separate awards as in the previous illustration, but also allows companies the option to account for the entire award on a straight-line basis over the entire vesting period. Either way, the company must recognize at least the amount of the award that has vested by that date.

Under IFRS, the straight-line choice is not permitted. Also, there's no requirement that the company must recognize at least the amount of the award that has vested by each reporting date.

● LO14

---

[11]The fair value of the options usually is higher when estimated using a single weighted-average expected life of the options rather than when estimated as the total of fair values of the multiple vesting groups.

Plans with Performance or Market Conditions

Stock option (and other share-based) plans often specify a performance condition or a market condition that must be satisfied before employees are allowed the benefits of the award. The objective is to provide employees with additional incentive for managerial achievement. For instance, an option might not be exercisable until a performance target is met. The target could be divisional revenue, earnings per share, sales growth, or rate of return on assets. The possibilities are limitless. On the other hand, the target might be market-related, perhaps a specified stock price or a stock price change exceeding a particular index. The way we account for such plans depends on whether the condition is performance-based or market-based.

> The terms of performance options vary with some measure of performance that ties rewards to productivity.

PLANS WITH PERFORMANCE CONDITIONS.   Whether we recognize compensation expense for performance-based options depends (a) initially on whether it's probable[12] that the performance target will be met and (b) ultimately on whether the performance target actually is met. Accounting is as described earlier for other stock options. Initial estimates of compensation cost as well as subsequent revisions of that estimate take into account the likelihood of both forfeitures and achieving performance targets. For example, in Illustration 19–2, if the options described also had included a condition that the options would become exercisable only if sales increase by 10% after four years, we would estimate the likelihood of that occurring; specifically, is it probable? Let's say we initially estimate that it is probable that sales will increase by 10% after four years. Then, our initial estimate of the total compensation would have been unchanged at:

> If compensation from a stock option depends on meeting a performance target, compensation is recorded only if we feel it's probable the target will be met.

$$\underset{\substack{\text{Options} \\ \text{expected} \\ \text{to vest}}}{\$10\text{ million}} \times \underset{\substack{\text{Fair value}}}{\$8} = \underset{\substack{\text{Estimated} \\ \text{total} \\ \text{compensation}}}{\$80\text{ million}}$$

Suppose, though, that after two years, we estimate that it is *not* probable that sales will increase by 10% after four years. Then, our new estimate of the total compensation would change to:

$$\underset{\substack{\text{Options} \\ \text{expected} \\ \text{to vest}}}{0} \times \underset{\substack{\text{Fair value}}}{\$8} = \underset{\substack{\text{Estimated} \\ \text{total} \\ \text{compensation}}}{0}$$

> If it later becomes probable that a performance target will not be met, we reverse any compensation expense already recorded.

In that case, we would reverse the $40 million expensed in 2011–2012. No compensation can be recognized for options that don't vest due to performance targets not being met, and that's our expectation.

Conversely, assume that our initial expectation is that it is *not* probable that sales will increase by 10% after four years and so we record no annual compensation expense. But then, in the third year, we estimate that it *is* probable that sales will increase by 10% after four years. At that point, our revised estimate of the total compensation would change to $80 million, and we would reflect the cumulative effect on compensation in 2013 earnings and record compensation thereafter:

> When we revise our estimate of total compensation because our expectation of probability changes, we record the effect of the change in the current period.

2013		
Compensation expense [($80 × ¾) – $0]	60	
Paid-in capital—stock options		60
2014		
Compensation expense [($80 × ¾) – $60]	20	
Paid-in capital—stock options		20

> If we had begun with our new estimate of total compensation, **$60 million would have been expensed in the first three years.**

---

[12]"Probable" means the same as it did in Chapter 13 when we were estimating the likelihood that payment would be made for a loss contingency and elsewhere when making accounting estimates. Probable is a matter of professional judgement (often 70–75%).

> If the target is based on changes in the market rather than on performance, we record compensation as if there were no target.

PLANS WITH MARKET CONDITIONS. If the award contains a market condition (e.g., a share option with an exercisability requirement based on the stock price reaching a specified level), then no special accounting is required. The fair value estimate of the share option already implicitly reflects market conditions due to the nature of share option pricing models. So, we recognize compensation expense regardless of when, if ever, the market condition is met.

DECLINE IN POPULARITY OF OPTIONS. Recent years have witnessed a steady shift in the way companies compensate their top executives. In the wake of recent accounting scandals, the image of stock options has been tarnished in the view of many who believe that the potential to garner millions in stock option gains created incentives for executives to boost company stock prices through risky or fraudulent behavior. That image has motivated many firms to move away from stock options in favor of other forms of share-based compensation, particularly restricted stock awards. Also contributing to the rise of restricted stock is the feeling by many that it better aligns pay with performance. As of 2009, the value of restricted stock awards given to top executives had surpassed the value of stock options awarded.

> In today's world, stock options are still important, but other equity compensation plans are rapidly assuming greater importance. Companies such as Amazon.com and Microsoft are moving from stock options to restricted stock.[13]

Employee Share Purchase Plans

● LO3

> Share purchase plans permit employees to buy shares directly from the corporation.

Employee share purchase plans often permit all employees to buy shares directly from their company at favorable terms. The primary intent of these plans is to encourage employee ownership of the company's shares. Presumably loyalty is enhanced among employee-shareholders. The employee also benefits because, typically, these plans allow employees to buy shares from their employer without brokerage fees and, perhaps, at a slight discount. Some companies even encourage participation by matching or partially matching employee purchases.

As long as (a) substantially all employees can participate, (b) employees have no longer than one month after the price is fixed to decide whether to participate, and (c) the discount is no greater than 5% (or can be justified as reasonable), accounting is straightforward. Simply record the sale of new shares as employees buy shares.

If these criteria for the plan being noncompensatory are not met, say the discount is 15%, accounting is similar to other share-based plans. The 15% discount to employees, then, is considered to be compensation, and that amount is recorded as expense.[14] Compensation expense replaces the cash debit for any employer-provided portion. Say an employee buys shares (no par) under the plan for $850 rather than the current market price of $1,000. The $150 discount is recorded as compensation expense:

Cash (discounted price)	850	
Compensation expense ($1,000 × 15%)	150	
Common stock (market value)		1,000

Intermediate Accounting
SPICELAND · SEPE · NELSON

DECISION MAKERS' PERSPECTIVE

In several previous chapters, we have revisited the concept of "earnings quality" (as first defined in Chapter 4). We also have noted that one rather common practice that negatively

---

[13]"Beyond Stock Options," *National Center for Employee Ownership,* 5th ed. (February 2007).
[14]FASB ASC 718–50–25–1 and 2: Compensation–Stock Compensation–Employee Share Purchase Plans–Recognition (previously "Share-Based Payment," *Statement of Financial Accounting Standards No. 123 (revised 2004),* (Norwalk, Conn.: FASB 2004), par. 12–13).

influences earnings quality is earnings management, which refers to companies' use of one or more of several techniques designed to artificially increase (or decrease) earnings. A frequent objective of earnings management is to meet analysts' expectations regarding projections of income. The share-based compensation plans we discuss in this chapter suggest another motive managers sometimes have to manipulate income. If a manager's personal compensation includes company stock, stock options, or other compensation based on the value of the firm's stock, it's not hard to imagine an increased desire to ensure that market expectations are met and that reported earnings have a positive effect on stock prices. In fact, as we discussed earlier, that is precisely the reaction these incentive compensation plans are designed to elicit. Investors and creditors, though, should be alert to indications of attempts to artificially manipulate income and realize that the likelihood of earnings management is probably higher for companies with generous share-based compensation plans.

> **Analysts should be aware of the possibility of earnings management as a way to increase managers' compensation.**

One way managers might manipulate numbers is to low-ball the data that go into the option-pricing models. The models used to estimate fair value are built largely around subjective assumptions. That possibility emphasizes the need for investors to look closely at the assumptions used as reported in the stock option footnote, and particularly at how those assumptions change from year to year. ●

CONCEPT REVIEW EXERCISE

Listed below are transactions dealing with various stock benefit plans of Fortune-Time Corporation during the period 2011–2013. The market price of the stock is $45 at January 1, 2011.

SHARE-BASED COMPENSATION PLANS

a. On January 1, 2011, the company issued 10 million common shares to divisional managers under its restricted stock award plan. The shares are subject to forfeiture if employment is terminated within three years.

b. On January 1, 2011, the company granted incentive stock options to its senior management exercisable for 1.5 million common shares. The options must be exercised within five years, but not before January 1, 2013. The exercise price of the stock options is equal to the fair value of the common stock on the date the options are granted. An option pricing model estimates the fair value of the options to be $4 per option. All recipients are expected to remain employed through the vesting date.

c. Recorded compensation expense on December 31, 2011.

d. A divisional manager holding 1 million of the restricted shares left the company to become CEO of a competitor on September 15, 2012, before the required service period ended.

e. Recorded compensation expense on December 31, 2012.

Required:
Prepare the journal entries that Fortune-Time recorded for each of these transactions. (Ignore any tax effects.)

January 1, 2011

SOLUTION

Restricted Stock Award Plan
No entry.
Total compensation is measured as 10 million shares × $45 = $450 million

Stock Options
No entry.
Total compensation is measured as 1.5 million shares × $4 = $6 million

December 31, 2011

	($ in millions)	
Restricted Stock		
Compensation expense ($450 million ÷ 3 years)	150	
Paid-in capital—restricted stock		150

Stock Options

Compensation expense ($6 million ÷ 2 years)	3	
Paid-in capital—stock options		3

September 15, 2012

$\frac{1\,\text{million}}{10\,\text{million}} \times 150$

Restricted Stock

Paid-in capital—restricted stock (10% × $150)	15	
Compensation expense		15

December 31, 2012

Restricted Stock

Compensation expense [$450 − (.10 × $450) − 150 + 15] ÷ 2 years ...	135	
Paid-in capital—restricted stock		135

Stock Options

Compensation expense ($6 million ÷ 2 years)	3	
Paid-in capital—stock options		3

PART B — EARNINGS PER SHARE

A typical corporate annual report contains four comparative financial statements, an extensive list of disclosure notes and schedules, and several pages of charts, tables, and textual descriptions. Of these myriad facts and figures, the single accounting number that is reported most frequently in the media and receives by far the most attention by investors and creditors is earnings per share (EPS). The reasons for the considerable attention paid to earnings per share certainly include the desire to find a way to summarize the performance of business enterprises into a single number.

Earnings per share is the single accounting number that receives the most media attention.

> The essence of decision making is choosing between alternatives. Thus, information about an entity is more useful if it can be compared with similar information about other entities and with similar information about the same entity for some other period or some other point in time.[15]

Summarizing performance in a way that permits comparisons is difficult because the companies that report the numbers are different from one another. And yet, the desire to condense performance to a single number has created a demand for EPS information. The profession has responded with rules designed to maximize the comparability of EPS numbers by minimizing the inconsistencies in their calculation from one company to the next.[16]

Comparability is an enhancing characteristic of relevant accounting information (Conceptual Framework).

Keep in mind as you study the requirements that a primary goal is comparability. As a result, many of the rules devised to achieve consistency are unavoidably arbitrary, meaning that other choices the FASB might have made in many instances would be equally adequate.

● LO14

INTERNATIONAL FINANCIAL REPORTING STANDARDS

Earnings per Share. The earnings per share requirements of U.S. GAAP, *FASB ASC 260: Earnings per Share*, are a result of the FASB's cooperation with the IASB to narrow the differences between IFRS and U.S. GAAP. A few differences remain. The differences that remain are the result of differences in the application of the treasury stock method, the treatment of contracts that may be settled in shares or cash, and contingently issuable shares.

---

[15]*Conceptual Framework for Financial Reporting: The Objective of Financial Reporting and Qualitative Characteristics and Constraints of Decision-Useful Financial Reporting Information,* FASB Exposure Draft (Norwalk, Conn.: FASB, 2009).

[16]FASB ASC 260: Earnings per Share (previously "Earnings per Share," *Statement of Financial Accounting Standards No. 128* (Norwalk, Conn.: FASB, 1997)).

Basic Earnings Per Share

A firm is said to have a simple capital structure if it has no outstanding securities that could potentially dilute earnings per share. In this context, to dilute means to *reduce* earnings per share. For instance, if a firm has convertible bonds outstanding and those bonds are converted, the resulting increase in common shares could decrease (or dilute) earnings per share. That is, the new shares replaced by the converted bonds might participate in future earnings. So convertible bonds are referred to as potential common shares. Other potential common shares are convertible preferred stock, stock options, and contingently issuable shares. We will see how the potentially dilutive effects of these securities are included in the calculation of EPS later in this chapter. Now, though, our focus is on the calculation of EPS for a simple capital structure—when no potential common shares are present. In these cases, the calculation is referred to as basic EPS, and is simply earnings available to common shareholders divided by the weighted-average number of common shares outstanding.

In the most elemental setting, earnings per share (or net loss per share) is merely a firm's net income (or net loss) divided by the number of shares of common stock outstanding throughout the year. The calculation becomes more demanding (a) when the number of shares has changed during the reporting period, (b) when the earnings available to common shareholders are diminished by dividends to preferred shareholders, or (c) when we attempt to take into account the impending effect of potential common shares (which we do in a later section of the chapter). To illustrate the calculation of EPS in each of its dimensions, we will use only one example in this chapter. We'll start with the most basic situation and then add one new element at a time until we have considered all the principal ways the calculation can be affected. In this way you can see the effect of each component of earnings per share, not just in isolation, but in relation to the effects of other components as well. The basic calculation is shown in Illustration 19–4.

> A firm has a simple capital structure if it has no *potential common shares.*

> ● LO4

> *Basic EPS* reflects no dilution, only shares now outstanding.

> EPS expresses a firm's profitability on a per share basis.

Sovran Financial Corporation reported net income of $154 million in 2011 (tax rate 40%). Its capital structure consisted of:

Common Stock

Jan. 1   60 million common shares were outstanding
                (amounts in millions, except per share amount)

Basic EPS:

$$\frac{\overset{\text{Net income}}{\$154}}{\underset{\substack{\text{Shares}\\\text{outstanding}}}{60}} = \$2.57$$

> **ILLUSTRATION 19–4**
> Fundamental Calculation

> In the most elemental setting, earnings per share is simply a company's earnings divided by the number of shares outstanding.

Issuance of New Shares

Because the shares discussed in Illustration 19–4 remained unchanged throughout the year, the denominator of the EPS calculation is simply the number of shares outstanding. But if the number of shares has changed, it's necessary to find the *weighted average* of the shares outstanding during the period the earnings were generated. For instance, if an additional 12 million shares had been issued on March 1 of the year just ended, we calculate the weighted-average number of shares to be 70 million as demonstrated in Illustration 19–5 on the next page.

Because the new shares were outstanding only 10 months, or $^{10}/_{12}$ of the year, we increase the 60 million shares already outstanding by the additional shares—weighted by the fraction of the year ($^{10}/_{12}$) they were outstanding. The weighted average is $60 + 12\,(^{10}/_{12}) = 60 + 10 = 70$ million shares. The reason for time-weighting the shares issued is that the resources the stock sale provides the company are available for generating income only after the date the shares are sold. So, weighting is necessary to make the shares in the fraction's denominator consistent with the income in its numerator.

> ● LO5

ILLUSTRATION 19–5 Weighted Average	Sovran Financial Corporation reported net income of $154 million for 2011 (tax rate 40%). Its capital structure included:

Common Stock

Jan. 1	60 million common shares were outstanding
Mar. 1	12 million new shares were sold

(amounts in millions, except per share amount)

Any new shares issued are time-weighted by the fraction of the period they were outstanding and then added to the number of shares outstanding for the entire period.

Basic EPS:

$$\frac{\overset{\text{Net income}}{\$154}}{\underset{\substack{\text{Shares} \\ \text{at Jan. 1}}}{60} + \underset{\substack{\text{New} \\ \text{shares}}}{12 \, (^{10}\!/_{12})}} = \frac{\$154}{70} = \$2.20$$

Stock Dividends and Stock Splits

● LO6

Recall that a stock dividend or a stock split is a distribution of additional shares to existing shareholders. But there's an important and fundamental difference between the increase in shares caused by a stock dividend and an increase from selling new shares. When new shares are sold, both assets and shareholders' equity are increased by an additional investment in the firm by shareholders. On the other hand, a stock dividend or stock split merely increases the number of shares without affecting the firm's assets. In effect, the same pie is divided into more pieces. The result is a larger number of less valuable shares. This fundamental change in the nature of the shares is reflected in a calculation of EPS by simply increasing the number of shares.

In Illustration 19–6, notice that the additional shares created by the stock dividend are *not* weighted for the time period they were outstanding. Instead, the increase is treated as if it occurred at the beginning of the year.

ILLUSTRATION 19–6 Stock Dividends and Stock Splits	Sovran Financial Corporation reported net income of $154 million in 2009 (tax rate 40%). Its capital structure included:

Common Stock

Jan. 1	60 million common shares were outstanding
Mar. 1	12 million new shares were sold
June 17	A 10% stock dividend was distributed

(amounts in millions, except per share amount)

Shares outstanding prior to the stock dividend are retroactively restated to reflect the 10% increase in shares—that is, treated as if the distribution occurred at the beginning of the period.

Basic EPS:

$$\frac{\overset{\text{Net income}}{\$154}}{\underset{\substack{\text{Shares} \\ \text{at Jan. 1}}}{60} \, (1.10) + \underset{\substack{\text{New} \\ \text{shares}}}{12 \, (^{10}\!/_{12}) \, (1.10)}} = \frac{\$154}{77} = \$2.00$$

Stock dividend adjustment

The number of shares outstanding after a 10% stock dividend is 1.10 times higher than before. This multiple is applied to both the beginning shares and the new shares sold before the stock distribution. If this had been a 25% stock dividend, the multiple would have been 1.25; a 2-for-1 stock split means a multiple of 2; and so on.

Notice that EPS without the 10% stock dividend ($2.20) is 10% more than it is with the stock distribution ($2). This is caused by the increase in the number of shares. But, unlike a sale of new shares, this should not be interpreted as a "dilution" of earnings per share. Shareholders' interests in their company's earnings have not been diluted. Instead, each shareholder's interest is represented by more—though less valuable—shares.

A simplistic but convenient way to view the effect is to think of the predistribution shares as having been "blue." After the stock dividend, the more valuable "blue" shares are gone, replaced by a larger number of, let's say, "green" shares. From now on, we compute the earnings per "green" share, whereas we previously calculated earnings per "blue" share. We restate the number of shares retroactively to reflect the stock dividend, as if the shares always had been "green." After all, our intent is to let the calculation reflect the fundamental change in the nature of the shares.

ADDITIONAL CONSIDERATION

When last year's EPS is reported in the current year's comparative income statements, it too should reflect the increased shares from the stock dividend. For instance, suppose EPS was $2.09 for 2011: $115 million net income divided by 55 million weighted-average shares. When reported again for comparison purposes in the 2011 comparative income statements, that figure would be restated to reflect the 10% stock dividend [$115 ÷ (55 × 1.10) = $1.90]:

Earnings per Share:	2011	2010
	$2.00	$1.90

The EPS numbers now are comparable—both reflect the stock dividend. Otherwise we would be comparing earnings per "green" share with earnings per "blue" share; this way both are earnings per "green" share.

Reacquired Shares

If shares were reacquired during the period (either retired or as treasury stock), the weighted-average number of shares is reduced. The number of reacquired shares is time-weighted for the *fraction of the year they were **not** outstanding,* prior to being *subtracted* from the number of shares outstanding during the period. Let's modify our continuing illustration to assume 8 million shares were reacquired on October 1 as treasury stock (Illustration 19–7).

ILLUSTRATION 19–7
Reacquired Shares

Sovran Financial Corporation reported net income of $154 million in 2011 (tax rate 40%). Its capital structure included:

Common Stock

Jan. 1	60 million common shares outstanding
Mar. 1	12 million new shares were sold
June 17	A 10% stock dividend was distributed
Oct. 1	8 million shares were reacquired as treasury stock

(amounts in millions, except per share amounts)

Basic EPS:

$$\frac{\text{Net income}}{60 \quad (1.10) + 12 \, (^{10}\!/_{12}) \, (1.10) - 8 \, (^{3}\!/_{12})} = \frac{\$154}{75} = \$2.05$$

$$\frac{\$154}{60 \quad (1.10) + 12 \, (^{10}\!/_{12}) \, (1.10) - 8 \, (^{3}\!/_{12})}$$

Shares at Jan. 1   New shares   Treasury shares

Stock dividend adjustment*

The **8 million shares reacquired as treasury stock are weighted by ($^{3}\!/_{12}$) to reflect the fact they were not outstanding the last three months of the year.**

*Not necessary for the treasury shares since they were reacquired after the stock dividend and thus already reflect the adjustment (that is, the shares repurchased are 8 million "new green" shares).

The adjustment for reacquired shares is the same as for new shares sold except the shares are deducted rather than added.

Any sales or purchases of shares that occur before, but not after, a stock dividend or split are affected by the distribution.

● LO7

Compare the adjustment for treasury shares with the adjustment for new shares sold. Each is time-weighted for the fraction of the year the shares were or were not outstanding. But also notice two differences. The new shares are added, while the reacquired shares are subtracted. The second difference is that the reacquired shares are not multiplied by 1.10 to adjust for the 10% stock dividend. The reason is the shares were repurchased after the June 17 stock dividend; the reacquired shares are 8 million of the new post-distribution shares. (To use our earlier representation, these are 8 million "green" shares.) To generalize, when a stock distribution occurs during the reporting period, any sales or purchases of shares that occur *before* the distribution are increased by the distribution. But the stock distribution does not increase the number of shares sold or purchased, if any, *after* the distribution.

Earnings Available to Common Shareholders

The denominator in an EPS calculation is the weighted-average number of common shares outstanding. Logically, the numerator should similarly represent earnings available to common shareholders. This was automatic in our illustrations to this point because the only shares outstanding were common shares. But when a senior class of shareholders (like preferred shareholders) is entitled to a specified allocation of earnings (like preferred dividends), those amounts are subtracted from earnings before calculating earnings per share.[17] This is demonstrated in Illustration 19–8.

ILLUSTRATION 19–8
Preferred Dividends

Sovran Financial Corporation reported net income of $154 million in 2011 (tax rate 40%). Its capital structure included:

Common Stock

January 1	60 million common shares were outstanding
March 1	12 million new shares were sold
June 17	A 10% stock dividend was distributed
October 1	8 million shares were reacquired as treasury stock

Preferred Stock, Nonconvertible

January 1–December 31   5 million 8%, $10 par, shares

(amounts in millions, except per share amount)

Preferred dividends are subtracted from net income so that "earnings available to common shareholders" is divided by the weighted-average number of common shares.

Basic EPS:

$$\frac{\overset{\text{Net income}}{\$154} \quad \overset{\text{Preferred dividends}}{-\$4^*}}{\underset{\substack{\text{Shares} \\ \text{at Jan. 1}}}{60}\ (1.10)\ +\ \underset{\substack{\text{New} \\ \text{shares}}}{12\ (^{10}\!/_{12})\ (1.10)}\ -\ \underset{\substack{\text{Treasury} \\ \text{shares}}}{8\ (^{3}\!/_{12})}} = \frac{\$150}{75} = \$2.00$$

Stock dividend adjustment*

*8% × $10 par × 5 million shares.

Preferred dividends reduce earnings available to common shareholders unless the preferred stock is noncumulative and no dividends were declared that year.

Suppose no dividends were declared for the year. Should we adjust for preferred dividends? Yes, if the preferred stock is cumulative—and most preferred stock is. This means that when dividends are not declared, the unpaid dividends accumulate to be paid in a future year when (if) dividends are subsequently declared. Obviously, the presumption is that, although the year's dividend preference isn't distributed this year, it eventually will be paid.

We have encountered no potential common shares to this point in our continuing illustration. As a result, we have what is referred to as a simple capital structure. (Although, at this point, you may question this label.) For a simple capital structure, a single presentation of basic earnings per common share is appropriate. We turn our attention now to situations described as complex capital structures. In these situations, two separate presentations are required: basic EPS and diluted EPS.

---

[17]You learned in Chapter 18 that when dividends are declared, preferred shareholders have a preference (over common shareholders) to a specified amount.

Diluted Earnings Per Share

Potential Common Shares

Imagine a situation in which convertible bonds are outstanding that will significantly increase the number of common shares if bondholders exercise their options to exchange their bonds for shares of common stock. Should these potential shares be ignored when earnings per share is calculated? After all, they haven't been converted as yet, so to assume an increase in shares for a conversion that may never occur might mislead investors and creditors. On the other hand, if conversion is imminent, not taking into account the dilutive effect of the share increase might mislead investors and creditors. The profession's solution to the dilemma is to calculate earnings per share twice.

Securities such as these convertible bonds, while not being common stock, may become common stock through their exercise or conversion. Therefore, they may dilute (reduce) earnings per share and are called potential common shares. A firm is said to have a complex capital structure if potential common shares are outstanding. Besides convertible bonds, other potential common shares are convertible preferred stock, stock options, and contingently issuable securities. (We'll discuss each of these shortly.) A firm with a complex capital structure reports two EPS calculations. Basic EPS ignores the dilutive effect of such securities, diluted EPS incorporates the dilutive effect of all potential common shares.

> In a complex capital structure, a second EPS computation takes into account the assumed effect of *potential common* shares, essentially a "worst case scenario."

Options, Rights, and Warrants

Stock options, stock rights, and stock warrants are similar. Each gives its holders the right to exercise their option to purchase common stock, usually at a specified exercise price. The dilution that would result from their exercise should be reflected in the calculation of diluted EPS, but not basic EPS.

● LO8

To include the dilutive effect of a security means to calculate EPS *as if* the potential increase in shares already has occurred (even though it hasn't yet). So, for stock options (or rights, or warrants), we pretend the options have been exercised. In fact, we assume the options were exercised at the beginning of the reporting period, or when the options were issued if that's later. We then assume the cash proceeds from selling the new shares at the exercise price are used to buy back as many shares as possible at the shares' average market price during the year. This is demonstrated in Illustration 19–9 on the next page.

> Stock options are assumed to have been exercised when calculating diluted EPS.

When we simulate the exercise of the stock options, we calculate EPS as if 15 million shares were sold at the beginning of the year. This obviously increases the number of shares in the denominator by 15 million shares. But it is insufficient to simply add the additional shares without considering the accompanying consequences. Remember, if this hypothetical scenario had occurred, the company would have had $300 million cash proceeds from the exercise of the options (15 million shares × $20 exercise price per share). What would have been the effect on earnings per share? This depends on what the company would have done with the $300 million cash proceeds. Would the proceeds have been used to buy more equipment? Increase the sales force? Expand facilities? Pay dividends?

> **FINANCIAL**
> **Reporting Case**
>
> Q4, p. 1069

Obviously, there are literally hundreds of choices, and it's unlikely that any two firms would spend the $300 million exactly the same way. But remember, our objective is to create some degree of uniformity in the way firms determine earnings per share so the resulting numbers are comparable. So, standard-setters decided on a single assumption for all firms to provide some degree of comparability.

For diluted EPS, we assume the proceeds from exercise of the options were used to reacquire shares as treasury stock at the average market price of the common stock during the reporting period. Consequently, the weighted-average number of shares is increased by the difference between the shares assumed issued and those assumed reacquired—in our illustration: 15 million shares issued minus 12 million shares reacquired ($300 million ÷ $25 per share) equals 3 million net increase in shares.

The way we take into account the dilutive effect of stock options is called the *treasury stock method* because of our assumption that treasury shares are purchased with the cash

ILLUSTRATION 19–9 Stock Options	Sovran Financial Corporation reported net income of $154 million in 2011 (tax rate 40%). Its capital structure included:

Common Stock

Jan. 1	60 million common shares outstanding
Mar. 1	12 million new shares were sold
June 17	A 10% stock dividend was distributed
Oct. 1	8 million shares were reacquired as treasury stock

(The average market price of the common shares during 2011 was $25 per share.)

Preferred Stock, Nonconvertible

January 1–December 31   5 million 8%, $10 par, shares

Incentive Stock Options

Executive stock options granted in 2006, exercisable after 2010 for 15 million common shares* at an exercise price of $20 per share

(amounts in millions, except per share amounts)

Stock options give their holders (company executives in this case) the right to purchase common stock at a specified exercise price ($20 in this case).

The stock options do not affect the calculation of *basic* EPS.

The calculation of diluted EPS assumes that the shares specified by stock options were issued at the exercise price and that the proceeds were used to buy back (as treasury stock) as many of those shares as can be purchased at the market price during the period.

Basic EPS (unchanged)

$$\frac{\overset{\text{Net income}}{\$154} \quad \overset{\text{Preferred dividends}}{-\$4}}{\underset{\text{Shares at Jan. 1}}{60} \quad (1.10) + \underset{\text{New shares}}{12\,(^{10}/_{12})}\,(1.10) - \underset{\text{Treasury shares}}{8\,(^{3}/_{12})}} = \frac{\$150}{75} = \$2$$

Stock dividend adjustment

Diluted EPS

$$\frac{\overset{\text{Net income}}{\$154} \qquad\qquad \overset{\text{Preferred dividends}}{-\$4}}{\underset{\text{Shares at Jan. 1}}{60}\,(1.10) + \underset{\text{New shares}}{12\,(^{10}/_{12})}\,(1.10) - \underset{\text{Treasury shares}}{8\,(^{3}/_{12})} + \underset{\text{Exercise of options}}{(15^* - 12^\dagger)}} = \frac{\$150}{78} = \$1.92$$

Stock dividend adjustment

*Adjusted for the stock dividend. Prior to the stock dividend, the options were exercisable for 13⁷⁄₁₁ million of the "old" shares. Upon the stock dividend, the new equivalent of 13⁷⁄₁₁ became 15 million (13⁷⁄₁₁ × 1.10) of the "new" shares.

†**Shares Reacquired for Diluted EPS**

15	million shares
× $ 20	(exercise price)
$300	million
÷ $ 25	(average market price)
12	million shares reacquired

proceeds of the exercise of the options. Besides providing comparability, this assumption actually is plausible because, if the options were exercised, more shares would be needed to issue to option-holders. And, as discussed in the previous chapter, many firms routinely buy back shares either to issue to option-holders or, equivalently, to offset the issuance of new shares.

● LO9

Convertible Securities

Sometimes corporations include a conversion feature as part of a bond offering, a note payable, or an issue of preferred stock. Convertible securities can be converted into (exchanged for) shares of stock at the option of the holder of the security. For that reason, convertible securities are potentially dilutive. EPS will be affected if and when such securities are converted and new shares of common stock are issued. In the previous section you learned that the potentially dilutive effect of stock options is reflected in diluted EPS calculations by assuming the options were exercised. Similarly, the potentially dilutive effect of convertible securities is reflected in diluted EPS calculations by assuming they were converted.

ADDITIONAL CONSIDERATION

In our diluted EPS calculation, we "pretend" the options are exercised at the end of the period *or at the time of actual exercise, if earlier, with shares repurchased at the average share price on that date.* Let's say the options in our illustration were exercised on October 1 and that the per-share price of the stock then was $24. In that case, we assume the proceeds (15 million shares × $20 = $300 million) are used to purchase shares at $24, or 12.5 million shares:

15	million shares
× $ 20	(exercise price)
$300	million
÷ $ 24	(market price at exercise)
12.5	million shares

The incremental number of shares to be included in the computation of diluted EPS, then, is weighted for the period the options were outstanding, the 9 months from January 1–October 1, or $\frac{9}{12}$ of a year. Thus, we would add to the denominator:

15 − 12.5 = 2.5 million shares
2.5 million shares × $\frac{9}{12}$ = 1.875 million shares,
rather than the 3 million shares we used in the illustration.

By the *if converted method* as it's called, we assume the conversion into common stock occurred at the beginning of the period (or at the time the convertible security is issued, if that's later). We increase the denominator of the EPS fraction by the additional common shares that would have been issued upon conversion. We increase the numerator by the interest (after-tax) on bonds or other debt or the preferred dividends that would have been avoided if the convertible securities had not been outstanding due to having been converted.

> When we assume conversion, the denominator of the EPS fraction is increased by the additional common shares that would have been issued upon conversion.

CONVERTIBLE BONDS.   Now, let's return to our continuing illustration and modify it to include the existence of convertible bonds (Illustration 19–10). We increase the denominator by the 12 million shares that would have been issued if the bonds had been converted. However, if that hypothetical conversion had occurred, the bonds would not have been outstanding during the year. What effect would the absence of the bonds have had on income? Obviously, the bond interest expense (10% × $300 million = $30 million) would have been saved, causing income to be higher. But saving the interest paid would also have meant losing a $30 million tax deduction on the income tax return. With a 40% tax rate that would mean paying $12 million more income taxes. So, to reflect in earnings the $18 million after-tax interest that would have been avoided in the event of conversion, we add back the $30 million of interest expense, but deduct 40% × $30 million for the higher tax expense.

> The numerator is increased by the after-tax interest that would have been avoided.

Sovran Financial Corporation reported net income of $154 million in 2011 (tax rate 40%). Its capital structure included:

Common Stock

Jan. 1	60 million common shares were outstanding
Mar. 1	12 million new shares were sold
June 17	A 10% stock dividend was distributed
Oct. 1	8 million shares were reacquired as treasury stock

(The average market price of the common shares during 2011 was $25 per share.)

Preferred Stock, Nonconvertible

January 1–December 31   5 million 8%, $10 par, shares

Incentive Stock Options

Executive stock options granted in 2006, exercisable after 2010 for 15 million common shares* at an exercise price of $20 per share

ILLUSTRATION 19–10
Convertible Bonds

(continued)

ILLUSTRATION 19–10
(concluded)

The convertible bonds do not affect the calculation of *basic* EPS.

If the bonds had been converted, 12 million more common shares would have been issued, and net income would have been higher by the interest saved (after tax) from not having the bonds outstanding.

Convertible Bonds

10%, $300 million face amount issued in 2010, convertible into 12 million common shares

(amounts in millions, except per share amounts)

Basic EPS (unchanged)

$$\frac{\overset{\text{Net income}}{\$154} \quad - \overset{\text{Preferred dividends}}{\$4}}{\underset{\substack{\text{Shares} \\ \text{at Jan. 1}}}{60} \; (1.10) \; + \; \underset{\substack{\text{New} \\ \text{shares}}}{12 \; (^{10}/_{12})} \; (1.10) \; - \; \underset{\substack{\text{Treasury} \\ \text{shares}}}{8 \; (^{3}/_{12})}} = \frac{\$150}{75} = \$2.00$$

Stock dividend adjustment

Diluted EPS

$$\frac{\overset{\text{Net income}}{\$154} \; - \overset{\text{Preferred dividends}}{\$4} \quad + \overset{\substack{\text{After-tax} \\ \text{interest savings}}}{\$30 - 40\% \,(30)}}{\underset{\substack{\text{Shares} \\ \text{at Jan. 1}}}{60} \,(1.10) + \underset{\substack{\text{New} \\ \text{shares}}}{12\,(^{10}/_{12})}\,(1.10) - \underset{\substack{\text{Treasury} \\ \text{shares}}}{8\,(^{3}/_{12})} + \underset{\substack{\text{Exercise} \\ \text{of options}}}{(15 - 12)} + \underset{\substack{\text{Conversion} \\ \text{of bonds}}}{12}} = \frac{\$168}{90} = \$1.87$$

Stock dividend adjustment

*Adjusted for the stock dividend. For example, prior to the stock dividend, the bonds were exercisable for $10^{10}/_{11}$ million of the "old" shares which became 12 million ($10^{10}/_{11} \times 1.10$) of the "new" shares after the stock dividend.

ADDITIONAL CONSIDERATION

The $300 million of convertible bonds in our illustration were issued at face value. Suppose the bonds had been issued for $282 million. In that case, the adjustment to earnings would be modified to include the amortization of the $18 million bond discount. Assuming straight-line amortization and a 10-year maturity, the adjustment to the diluted EPS calculation would have been:

$$\frac{+ \, [\$30 + (\$18 \div 10 \text{ years})] \times (1 - 40\%)^*}{+ \, 12}$$

to reflect the fact that the interest expense would include the $30 million stated interest plus one-tenth of the bond discount.[†]

*This is an alternative way to represent the after-tax adjustment to interest since subtracting 40% of the interest expense is the same as multiplying interest expense by 60%.

[†]See Chapter 14 if you need to refresh your memory about bond discount amortization.

Our illustration describes the treatment of convertible bonds. The same treatment pertains to other debt that is convertible into common shares such as convertible notes payable. Remember from our discussion of debt in earlier chapters that all debt is similar whether in the form of bonds, notes, or other configurations.

CONVERTIBLE PREFERRED STOCK. The potentially dilutive effect of convertible preferred stock is reflected in EPS calculations in much the same way as convertible debt. That is, we calculate EPS as if conversion already had occurred. Specifically, we add shares to the denominator of the EPS fraction. We do not subtract the preferred dividends in the numerator because those dividends would have been avoided if the preferred stock had been converted. In Illustration 19–11 we assume our preferred stock is convertible into 3 million shares of common stock.

ADDITIONAL CONSIDERATION

Notice that we assumed the bonds were converted at the beginning of the reporting period since they were outstanding all year. However, if the convertible bonds had been issued during the reporting period, we would assume their conversion occurred on the date of issue. It would be illogical to assume they were converted before they were issued. If the convertible bonds in our illustration had been sold on September 1, for instance, the adjustment to the EPS calculation would have been:

$$\frac{+ \ [\$30 - 40\% \ (\$30)] \ (^4/_{12})}{+ \ 12 \ (^4/_{12})}$$

to reflect the fact that the net increase in shares would have been effective for only nine months of the year.

> We assume convertible securities were converted (or options exercised) at the beginning of the reporting period or at the time the securities are issued, if later.

Sovran Financial Corporation reported net income of $154 million in 2011 (tax rate 40%). Its capital structure included:

Common Stock

Jan. 1	60 million common shares were outstanding
Mar. 1	12 million new shares were sold
June 17	A 10% stock dividend was distributed
Oct. 1	8 million shares were reacquired as treasury stock

(The average market price of the common shares during 2011 was $25 per share.)

Preferred Stock, Convertible into 3 million common shares*

January 1–December 31   5 million 8%, $10 par, shares

Incentive Stock Options

Executive stock options granted in 2006, exercisable after 2010 for 15 million common shares* at an exercise price of $20 per share

Convertible Bonds

10%, $300 million face amount issued in 2010, convertible into 12 million common shares

(amounts in millions, except per share amounts)

> **ILLUSTRATION 19–11**
> Convertible Preferred Stock

> Since diluted EPS is calculated as if the preferred shares had been converted, there are no dividends.

*Adjusted for the stock dividend. For example, prior to the stock dividend, the preferred shares were convertible into 2 $^8/_{11}$ million of the "old" shares which became 3 million (2 $^8/_{11}$ × 1.10) of the "new" shares after the stock dividend.

The adjustment for the conversion of the preferred stock is applied only to diluted EPS computations. Basic EPS is unaffected.

However, when diluted EPS is calculated, we hypothetically assume the convertible preferred stock was *not* outstanding. Accordingly, no preferred dividends on these shares would have been paid.

Antidilutive Securities

At times, the effect of the conversion or exercise of potential common shares would be to increase, rather than decrease, EPS. These we refer to as antidilutive securities. Such securities are ignored when calculating both basic and diluted EPS.

● LO10

Options, Warrants, Rights

For illustration, recall the way we treated the stock options in our continuing illustration. In applying the treasury stock method, the number of shares assumed repurchased is fewer than the number of shares assumed sold. This is the case any time the buyback (average market) price is higher than the exercise price. Consequently, there will be a net increase in the number of shares, so earnings per share will decline.

On the other hand, when the exercise price is *higher* than the market price, to assume shares are sold at the exercise price and repurchased at the market price would mean buying back *more* shares than were sold. This would produce a net decrease in the number of shares. EPS would increase, not decrease. These would have an antidilutive effect and would not be considered exercised. In fact, a rational investor would not exercise options at an exercise price higher than the current market price anyway. Let's look at the example provided by Illustration 19–12.

> Antidilutive securities are ignored when calculating both basic and diluted EPS.

ILLUSTRATION 19–12 Antidilutive Warrants	Sovran Financial Corporation reported net income of $154 million in 2011 (tax rate 40%). Its capital structure included: **Common Stock** Jan. 1 60 million common shares were outstanding Mar. 1 12 million new shares were sold June 17 A 10% stock dividend was distributed Oct. 1 8 million shares were reacquired as treasury stock (The average market price of the common shares during 2011 was $25 per share.) **Preferred Stock, Convertible into 3 million common shares.** January 1–December 31 5 million 8%, $10 par, shares **Incentive Stock Options** Executive stock options granted in 2006, exercisable after 2010 for 15 million common shares* at an exercise price of $20 per share **Convertible Bonds** 10%, $300 million face amount issued in 2010, convertible into 12 million common shares **Stock warrants** Warrants granted in 2010, exercisable for 4 million common shares* at an exercise price of $32.50 per share **Calculations:** The calculations of both basic and diluted EPS are unaffected by the warrants because the effect of exercising the warrants would be antidilutive. *Adjusted for the stock dividend. For example, prior to the stock dividend, the warrants were exercisable for 3⁷/₁₁ million of the "old" shares which became 4 million (3⁷/₁₁ 1.10) of the "new" shares after the stock dividend.

> The $32.50 exercise price is higher than the market price, $25, so to assume shares are sold at the exercise price and repurchased at the market price would mean reacquiring more shares than were sold.

To assume 4 million shares were sold at the $32.50 exercise price and repurchased at the lower market price ($25) would mean reacquiring 5.2 million shares. That's more shares than were assumed sold. Because the effect would be antidilutive, we would simply ignore the warrants in the calculations.

In our continuing illustration, only the stock warrants were antidilutive. The other potential common shares caused EPS to decline when we considered them exercised or converted. In the case of the executive stock options, it was readily apparent that their effect would be dilutive because the exercise price was less than the market price, indicating that fewer shares could be repurchased (at the average market price) than were assumed issued (at the exercise price). As a result, the denominator increased. When only the denominator of a fraction increases, the fraction itself decreases. On the other hand, in the case of the warrants, it was apparent that their effect would be antidilutive because the exercise price was higher than the market price, which would have decreased the denominator and therefore increased the fraction.

When a company has a net loss, rather than net income, it reports a loss per share. In that situation, stock options that otherwise are dilutive will be antidilutive. Here's why. Suppose we have a loss per share of $2.00 calculated as ($150 million) ÷ 75 million shares = ($2.00). Now suppose stock options are outstanding that, if exercised, will increase the number of shares by 5 million. If that increase is included in the calculation, the loss per share will be $1.88 calculated as ($150 million) ÷ 80 million shares = ($1.88). The *loss* per share *declines*. This represents an *increase* in performance—not a dilution of performance. The options would be considered antidilutive, then, and not included in the calculation of the net loss per share. Any potential common shares not included in dilutive EPS because they are antidilutive should be revealed in the disclosure notes.

Convertible Securities

For convertible securities, though, it's not immediately obvious whether the effect of their conversion would be dilutive or antidilutive because the assumed conversion would affect both the numerator and the denominator of the EPS fraction. We discovered each was dilutive only after including the effect in the calculation and observing the result—a decline in EPS. But there's an easier way.

To determine whether convertible securities are dilutive and should be included in a diluted EPS calculation, we can compare the "incremental effect" of the conversion (expressed as a fraction) with the EPS fraction before the effect of any convertible security is considered. This, of course is our basic EPS. Recall from Illustration 19–11 that basic EPS is $2.00.

For comparison, we determine the "earnings per incremental share" of the two convertible securities:

Conversion of bonds.

$$\frac{\underset{\text{interest savings}}{\overset{\text{After-tax}}{+\$30 - 40\% (\$30)}}}{\underset{\text{of bonds}}{\overset{+12}{\text{Conversion}}}} = \frac{\$18}{12} = \$1.50$$

The incremental effect (of conversion) of the bonds is the after-tax interest saved divided by the additional common shares from conversion.

Conversion of preferred stock.

$$\frac{\underset{\text{dividends}}{\overset{\text{Preferred}}{+\$4}}}{\underset{\text{preferred shares}}{\overset{+3}{\text{Conversion of}}}} = \$1.33$$

The incremental effect (of conversion) of the preferred stock is the dividends that wouldn't be paid divided by the additional common shares from conversion.

If the incremental effect of a security is *higher* than basic EPS, it is antidilutive. That's not the case in our illustration.

Order of Entry for Multiple Convertible Securities

A convertible security might seem to be dilutive when looked at individually but, in fact, may be antidilutive when included in combination with other convertible securities. This is because the *order of entry* for including their effects in the EPS calculation determines by how much, or even whether, EPS decreases as a result of their assumed conversion. Because our goal is to reveal the maximum potential dilution that might result, theoretically we should calculate diluted EPS using every possible combination of potential common shares to find the combination that yields the lowest EPS. But that's not necessary.

We can use the earnings per incremental share we calculated to determine the sequence of including securities' effects in the calculation. We include the securities in reverse order, beginning with the lowest incremental effect (that is, most dilutive), followed by the next lowest, and so on. This is, in fact, the order in which we included the securities in our continuing illustration.

ADDITIONAL CONSIDERATION

Actually, the order of inclusion made no difference in our example, but would in many instances. For example, suppose the preferred stock had been convertible into 2.1 million shares, rather than 3 million shares. The incremental effect of its conversion would have been:

Conversion of Preferred Stock

$$\frac{\text{Preferred dividends} + \$4}{+2.1 \text{ Conversion of preferred shares}} = \$1.90$$

On the surface, the effect would seem to be dilutive because $1.90 is less than $2.00, basic EPS. In fact, if this were the only convertible security, it would be dilutive. But, after the convertible bonds are assumed converted first, then the assumed conversion of the preferred stock would be *antidilutive*:

With Conversion of Bonds

$$\frac{\$154 - \$4 + \$30 - 40\%(\$30)}{60\ (1.10) + 12\ (^{10}\!/_{12})(1.10) - 8\ (^{3}\!/_{12}) + (15-12) + 12} = \frac{\$168}{90} = \$1.867$$

Net income / Preferred dividends / After-tax interest savings
Shares at Jan. 1 / New shares / Stock dividend adjustment / Treasury shares / Exercise of options / Conversion of bonds

With Conversion of Preferred Stock

$$\frac{\$154 - \$4 + \$30 - 40\%(\$30)}{60\ (1.10) + 12\ (^{10}\!/_{12})(1.10) - 8\ (^{3}\!/_{12}) + (15-12) + 12 + 2.1} = \frac{\$172}{92.1} = \$1.868$$

Net income / Preferred dividends / After-tax interest savings
Shares at Jan. 1 / New shares / Stock dividend adjustment / Treasury shares / Exercise of options / Conversion of bonds / Conversion of preferred shares

Although the incremental effect of the convertible preferred stock ($1.90) is lower than basic EPS ($2.00), when included in the calculation after the convertible bonds the effect is antidilutive (EPS increases).

Because the incremental effect of the convertible bonds ($1.50) is lower than the incremental effect of the convertible preferred stock ($1.90), it is included first.

A convertible security might seem to be dilutive when looked at individually but may be antidilutive when included in combination with other convertible securities.

CONCEPT REVIEW EXERCISE

At December 31, 2011, the financial statements of Clevenger Casting Corporation included the following:

BASIC AND DILUTED EPS

Net income for 2011	$500 million
Common stock, $1 par:	
Shares outstanding on January 1	150 million shares
Shares retired for cash on February 1	24 million shares
Shares sold for cash on September 1	18 million shares
2-for-1 split on July 23	
Preferred stock, 10%, $60 par, cumulative, nonconvertible	$ 70 million
Preferred stock, 8%, $50 par, cumulative, convertible into 4 million shares of common stock	$100 million
Incentive stock options outstanding, fully vested, for 4 million shares of common stock; the exercise price is $15	
Bonds payable, 12.5%, convertible into 20 million shares of common stock	$200 million

Additional data:

The market price of the common stock averaged $20 during 2011.

The convertible preferred stock and the bonds payable had been issued at par in 2009. The tax rate for the year was 40%.

Required:

Compute basic and diluted earnings per share for the year ended December 31, 2011.

(amounts in millions, except per share amounts)

SOLUTION

Basic EPS

Diluted EPS

[a]10% × $70 million = $7 million

[b]8% × $100 million = $8 million

[c]Exercise of warrants:

  4 million shares

× $15 (exercise price)

  $60 million

÷ $20 (average market price)

   3 million shares

[d]12.5% × $200 million = $25 million

Dilution:

Conversion of Bonds	Conversion of 8% Preferred Stock

$$\frac{\text{After-tax interest savings}}{\underset{\text{Conversion of bonds}}{+\ 20}} \quad \frac{+\ \$25\ -\ 40\%\ (\$25)}{} = \$0.75 \qquad \frac{\text{Preferred dividends}}{\underset{\text{Conversion of preferred shares}}{+\ 4}} \quad \frac{+\ \$8}{} = \$2.00^{*}$$

*Because the incremental effect of conversion of the preferred stock ($2) is higher than EPS without the conversion of the preferred stock, the conversion would be *antidilutive* and is *not* considered in the calculation of diluted EPS.

Additional EPS Issues

● LO11

Components of the "Proceeds" in the Treasury Stock Method

For the treasury stock method, "proceeds" include:

1. The amount, if any, received from the hypothetical exercise of options or vesting of restricted stock.

2. The total compensation from the award that's not yet expensed.

In calculating diluted EPS when stock options are outstanding, we assume the options have been exercised. That is, we pretend the company sold the shares specified by the options at the exercise price and that the "proceeds" were used to buy back (as treasury stock) as many shares as can be purchased at the average market price of the stock during the year. The proceeds for the calculation should include the amount received from the hypothetical exercise of the options ($300 million in Illustration 19–9 in the chapter). But that's only the first of three possible components.

The second component of the proceeds is the total compensation from the award that's not yet expensed. If the fair value of an option had been $4 at the grant date, the total compensation would have been 15 million shares times $4, or $60 million. In our illustration, though, we assumed the options were fully vested before 2011, so all $60 million already had been expensed and this second component of the proceeds was zero. If the options had been only half vested, half the compensation would have been unexpensed and $30 million would have been added to the $300 million proceeds.

The third component of the proceeds is what's called the *excess tax benefit.* We expense the fair value of stock options at the date of grant. If the options were nonqualified options, rather than incentive stock options, the corporation receives a tax deduction at exercise equal to the difference between the stock's market value and its exercise price. That amount usually is higher than the fair value of the options at the grant date, and the difference times the tax rate is the excess tax benefit. In our illustration, though, we assumed the options were incentive stock options, hence no tax benefit. Had they been nonqualified options, the proceeds also would have included a $6 million excess tax benefit:

$ 25	market price during 2011(and price at hypothetical exercise)
(20)	exercise price
$ 5	tax deduction at hypothetical exercise
(4)	fair value at grant date (and amount expensed over the vesting period)
$ 1	excess tax deduction per option
× 15	million options
$ 15	million excess tax deduction
× 40%	tax rate
$ 6	million excess tax benefit[18]

3. The difference between the eventual tax benefit and the amount recognized in expense.

Why do the proceeds include these three components? We might think of it like this. The "proceeds" include everything the firm will receive from the award: (1) cash, if any, at exercise, (2) services from the recipient (value of award given as compensation), and (3) tax savings. The reason we *exclude the expensed portion* is that, when it's expensed, earnings

---

[18]Journal entries for the tax benefit are described in the Additional Consideration on p. 1076.

are reduced, and that dilution is reflected in EPS. Excluding that expensed portion from the proceeds avoids the additional dilution that would occur if more proceeds are available in our hypothetical buyback of shares. Hence, we avoid double-counting the dilutive effect of the compensation.

RESTRICTED STOCK AWARDS IN EPS CALCULATIONS.   As we discussed earlier, restricted stock awards are quickly replacing stock options as the share-based compensation plan of choice. Like stock options, they represent potential common shares and their dilutive effect is included in diluted EPS. In fact, they too are included using the treasury stock method. That is, the shares are added to the denominator and then reduced by the number of shares that can be bought back with the "proceeds" at the average market price of the company's stock during the year. Unlike stock options, though, the first component of the proceeds usually is absent; employees don't pay to acquire their shares.

Also, only *unvested* restricted stock award shares are included in hypothetical EPS calculations; fully vested shares are actually distributed and thus outstanding. The proceeds for the EPS calculation include the total compensation from the unvested stock award that's not yet expensed, the second component. For an example, refer back to the restricted stock in Illustration 19–1 on page 1071. The total compensation for the award is $60 million ($12 market price per share $\times$ 5 million shares). Because the stock award vests over four years, it is expensed as $15 million each year for four years. At the end of 2011, the first year, $45 million remains unexpensed, so $45 million would be the assumed proceeds in an EPS calculation.[19] If we assume the market price remains at $12, the $45 million will buy back 3.75 million shares and we would add to the denominator of diluted EPS 1.25 million common shares:

$$\frac{\text{No adjustment to the numerator}}{\text{5 million} - \text{3.75* million} = \textbf{1.25 million}}$$

* Assumed purchase of treasury shares

$45	million
÷ $12	average market price
3.75	million shares

At the end of 2012, the *second* year, $30 million remains unexpensed, so assuming the average market price again is $12, we would add to the denominator of diluted EPS 2.5 million common shares:

$$\frac{\text{No adjustment to the numerator}}{\text{5 million} - \text{2.5* million} = \textbf{2.5 million}}$$

* Assumed purchase of treasury shares

$30	million
÷ $12	average market price
2.5	million shares

Contingently Issuable Shares

Sometimes an agreement specifies that additional shares of common stock will be issued, contingent on the occurrence of some future circumstance. For instance, in the disclosure note reproduced in Graphic 19–2, **Hunt Manufacturing Co.** reported contingent shares in connection with its acquisition of **Feeny Manufacturing Company**.

● LO12

At times, contingent shares are issuable to shareholders of an acquired company, certain key executives, or others in the event a certain level of performance is achieved. Contingent performance may be a desired level of income, a target stock price, or some other measurable activity level.

---

[19]The proceeds also must be increased (or decreased) by any tax benefits that would be added to (or deducted from) paid-in capital when the eventual tax deduction differs from the amount expensed as described for the stock options above and in the Additional Consideration on p. 1094. Because that occurs when the stock price at vesting differs from the stock price at the grant date, our assumption above that the market price remained at $12 avoided that complexity.

GRAPHIC 19–2

Contingently Issuable Shares—Hunt Manufacturing Company

Real World Financials

Note 12: Acquisitions (in part)

The Company acquired Feeny Manufacturing Company of Muncie, Indiana, for 135,000 shares of restricted common stock with a value of $7.71 per share. Feeny Manufacturing Company is a manufacturer of kitchen storage products. The acquisition was accounted for as a purchase. The purchase agreement calls for the issuance of up to 135,000 additional shares of common stock in the next fiscal year based on the earnings of Feeny Manufacturing Company. . . .

Contingently issuable shares are considered outstanding in the computation of diluted EPS.

When calculating EPS, contingently issuable shares are considered to be outstanding in the computation of diluted EPS if the target performance level already is being met (assumed to remain at existing levels until the end of the contingency period). For example, if shares will be issued at a future date if a certain level of income is achieved and that level of income or more was already earned this year, those additional shares are simply added to the denominator of the diluted EPS fraction.[20]

For clarification, refer to our continuing illustration of diluted EPS and assume 3 million additional shares will become issuable to certain executives in the following year (2012) if net income that year is $150 million or more. Recall that net income in 2011 was $154 million, so the additional shares would be considered outstanding in the computation of diluted EPS by simply adding 3 million additional shares to the denominator of the EPS fraction. Obviously, the 2012 condition ($150 million net income or more) has not been met yet since it's only year 2011. But because that level of income was achieved in 2011, the presumption is it's likely to be earned in 2012 as well.

If a level of income must be attained before the shares will be issued, and income already is that amount or more, the additional shares are simply added to the denominator.

Assumed Issuance of Contingently Issuable Shares (diluted EPS):

$$\frac{\text{No adjustment to the numerator}}{+3} \\ \text{Additional shares}$$

On the other hand, if the target income next year is $160 million, the contingent shares would simply be ignored in our calculation.

Summary of the Effect of Potential Common Shares on Earnings Per Share

You have seen that under certain circumstances, securities that have the potential of reducing earnings per share by becoming common stock are assumed already to have become common stock for the purpose of calculating EPS. The table in Graphic 19–3 summarizes the circumstances under which the dilutive effect of these securities is reflected in the calculation of basic and diluted EPS.

GRAPHIC 19–3

When Potential Common Shares Are Reflected in EPS

Potential Common Shares	Is the Dilutive Effect Reflected in the Calculation of EPS?*	
	Basic EPS	Diluted EPS
• Stock options (or warrants, rights)	no	yes
• Restricted stock	no	yes
• Convertible securities (bonds, notes, preferred stock)	no	yes
• Contingently issuable shares	no	yes[†]

*The effect is not included for any security if its effect is antidilutive.
†Unless shares are contingent upon some level of performance not yet achieved.

---

[20]The shares should be included in both basic and diluted EPS if all conditions have actually been met so that there is no *circumstance* under which those shares would not be issued. In essence, these *are no longer contingent shares.*

Graphic 19–4 summarizes the specific effects on the diluted EPS fraction when the dilutive effect of a potentially dilutive security is reflected in the calculation.

| Potential Common Shares | Modification to the Diluted EPS Fractions: | |
	Numerator	Denominator
• Stock options (or warrants, rights)	None	Add the shares that would be created by their exercise,* reduced by shares repurchased at the average share price.
• Restricted stock	None	Add shares that would be created by their vesting,* reduced by shares repurchased at the average share price.
• Convertible bonds (or notes)	Add the interest (after-tax) that would have been avoided if the debt had been converted.	Add shares that would be created by the conversion* of the bonds (or notes).
• Convertible preferred stock	Do not deduct the dividends that would have been avoided if the preferred stock had been converted.	Add shares that would have been created by the conversion* of the preferred stock.
• Contingently issuable shares: Issuable when specified conditions are met, and those conditions currently are being met	None	Add shares that are issuable.
• Contingently issuable shares: Issuable when specified conditions are met, and those conditions are **not** currently being met	None	None

*At the beginning of the year or when potential common shares were issued, whichever is later (time-weight the increase in shares if assumed exercised or converted in midyear).

Actual Conversions

When calculating EPS in our example, we "pretended" the convertible bonds had been converted at the beginning of the year. What if they actually had been converted, let's say on November 1? Interestingly, diluted EPS would be precisely the same. Here's why:

1. The actual conversion would cause an actual increase in shares of 12 million on November 1. These would be time-weighted so the denominator would increase by 12 ($\frac{2}{12}$) Also, the numerator would be higher because net income actually would be increased by the after-tax interest saved on the bonds for the last two months, [$30 − 40% ($30)] × ($\frac{2}{12}$). Be sure to note that this would not be an adjustment in the EPS calculation. Instead, net income would actually have been higher by [$30 − 40% ($30)] × ($\frac{2}{12}$) = $3. That is, reported net income would have been $157 rather than $154.

2. We would assume conversion for the period before November 1 because they were potentially dilutive during that period. The 12 million shares assumed outstanding from January 1 to November 1 would be time-weighted for that 10-month period: 12 ($\frac{10}{12}$). Also, the numerator would be increased by the after-tax interest assumed saved on the bonds for the first 10 months, [$30 − 40% ($30)] × ($\frac{10}{12}$).

Notice that the incremental effect on diluted EPS is the same either way:

EPS would be
precisely the same
whether convertible
securities were actually
converted or not.

Not Actually Converted: **Converted on November 1:**

$$\frac{+\ \$30 - 40\%\ (\$30)}{+\ 12} = \frac{+[\$30 - 40\%\ (\$30)] \times (^2\!/_{12}) - [\$30 - 40\%\ (\$30)] \times (^{10}\!/_{12})}{+\ 12\ (^2\!/_{12}) \qquad +\ 12\ (^{10}\!/_{12})}$$

Assumed after-tax interest savings / Assumed conversion of bonds = Actual after-tax interest savings / Actual conversion of bonds − Assumed after-tax interest savings / Assumed conversion of bonds

Graphic 19–5 shows the disclosure note **Clorox Company** reported after the conversion of convertible notes during the year.

GRAPHIC 19–5

Conversion of Notes—
The Clorox Company

Real World Financials

Note 1: Significant Accounting Policies—Earnings Per Common Share (in part)

A $9,000,000 note payable to Henkel Corporation was converted into 1,200,000 shares of common stock on August 1. . . . Earnings per common share and weighted-average shares outstanding reflect this conversion as if it were effective during all periods presented.

Financial Statement Presentation of Earnings Per Share Data

● LO13

Recall from Chapter 4 that the income statement sometimes includes items that require separate presentation within the statement as follows:

Income from Continuing Operations
Discontinued operations
Extraordinary items
Net income

When the income statement includes one or more of the separately reported items, EPS data (both basic and diluted) must also be reported separately for income from continuing operations and net income. Per share amounts for discontinued operations and extraordinary items would be disclosed either on the face of the income statement or in the notes to financial statements. Presentation on the face of the income statement is illustrated by the partial income statements of **The Bank of New York Mellon Corporation** from its 2008 annual report and exhibited in Graphic 19–6.

Basic and diluted EPS data should be reported on the face of the income statement for all reporting periods presented in the comparative statements. Businesses without potential common shares present basic EPS only. Disclosure notes should provide additional disclosures including:

1. A reconciliation of the numerator and denominator used in the basic EPS computations to the numerator and the denominator used in the diluted EPS computations. An example of this is presented in Graphic 19–7 using the situation described in Illustration 19–11.
2. Any adjustments to the numerator for preferred dividends.
3. Any potential common shares that weren't included because they were antidilutive.
4. Any transactions that occurred after the end of the most recent period that would materially affect earnings per share.

GRAPHIC 19–6

EPS Disclosure—Bank of New York Mellon

Real World Financials

Consolidated Income Statement (partial)

	($ in millions, except per share data)		
	2008	**2007**	**2006**
Income from continuing operations	$1,442	$2,227	$1,476
Income (loss) from discontinued operations, net of tax	3	(8)	1,371
Extraordinary loss on consolidation of CPC, net of tax	(26)	(180)	—
Net income	$1,419	$2,039	$ 2,847
Earnings per share			
Basic:			
Income from continuing operations	$ 1.23	$ 2.41	$ 2.07
Income (loss) from discontinued operations, net of tax	—	(0.01)	1.92
Extraordinary loss, net of tax	(0.02)	(0.19)	—
Net income	$ 1.21	$ 2.21	$ 3.99
Diluted:			
Income from continuing operations	$ 1.22	$ 2.38	$ 2.04
Income (loss) from discontinued operations, net of tax	—	(0.01)	1.90
Extraordinary loss, net of tax	(0.02)	(0.19)	—
Net income	$ 1.20	$ 2.18	$ 3.94

GRAPHIC 19–7

Reconciliation of Basic EPS Computations to Diluted EPS Computations

Earnings per Share Reconciliation:

	Income (Numerator)	Share (Denominator)	Per Share Amount
Net income	$154		
Preferred dividends	(4)		
Basic earnings per share	150	75	$2.00
Stock options	None	3*	
Convertible debt	18	12	
Convertible preferred stock	4	3	
Diluted earnings per share	$172	93	$1.85

Note: Stock warrants to purchase an additional 4 million shares at $32.50 per share were outstanding throughout the year but were not included in diluted EPS because the warrants' exercise price is greater than the average market price of the common shares.

*15 million − [(15 million × $20) ÷ $25] = 3 million net additional shares

---

ADDITIONAL CONSIDERATION

It is possible that potential common shares would have a dilutive effect on one component of net income but an antidilutive effect on another. When the inclusion of the potential common shares has a dilutive effect on "income from continuing operations," the effect should be included in all calculations of diluted EPS. In other words, the same number of potential common shares used in computing the diluted per-share amount for income from continuing operations is used in computing all other diluted per-share amounts, even when amounts are antidilutive to the individual per-share amounts.

WHERE WE'RE HEADED

● LO14

In 2008, the FASB issued an exposure draft of a proposed accounting standard on earnings per share. The proposal would amend GAAP for EPS with the intent to clarify and simplify EPS calculations, while at the same time promoting convergence with International Financial Reporting Standards (IFRS).[21] The exposure draft was issued concurrently with an International Accounting Standards Board (IASB) amendment to its own *IAS No. 33, Earnings Per Share.*

Among the changes proposed in the Exposure Drafts are:

1. We would *include* in the denominator of the EPS calculation (a) classes of common stock with dividend rates that differ from each other, (b) shares currently issuable for "little or no cost" to the holder (like fully vested restricted stock), (c) instruments currently exercisable for "little or no cost" to the holder, and (d) participating securities (say, an option that's entitled to receive $1 of dividends for every $2 paid to a share of common stock). Each of these inclusions is consistent with the objective of reporting per-share earnings for all financial instruments that have the right at the end of the period to share in current-period earnings.

2. We would *exclude* from the calculation of EPS any instrument that is measured at "fair value with changes in fair value reported in earnings." This would include, for instance, a convertible bond issue for which the company has elected the fair value option. If its fair value rises, the change in fair value is reported as a loss, decreasing earnings and earnings per share.[22] Reasoning that the dilutive effect of these bonds already is reflected in the EPS numerator, we exclude these and all other instruments measured at fair value with changes in fair value reported in earnings from the calculation of the EPS denominator. In other words, we would ignore the effect on the denominator of the exercise or conversion of these instruments since their dilutive effect already has been reflected in the numerator. The reasoning is that including them in the denominator of diluted EPS would "double-count" their dilutive impact on shareholders. Under current GAAP, we calculate diluted EPS as if convertible bonds such as these had been converted into shares of stock, increasing both the numerator and the denominator as demonstrated in this chapter.

3. When applying the "treasury stock method" to determine the shares that would be reacquired upon the hypothetical exercise of stock options in a diluted EPS calculation, we would assume shares are bought back at the **end-of-the-period** stock price rather than the **average** stock price as we use under current GAAP.

After the comment period for the exposure draft ended in 2009, both the FASB and the IASB decided to defer the project until other joint projects are completed and the underlying differences between U.S. GAAP and IFRS that still preclude comparability of EPS under the two sets of standards are resolved. Because the comments received lacked general consensus on individual changes proposed, it's likely that the ultimate joint standard will differ from the one described here. Presumably, though, the objectives of clarification and simplification will be achieved.

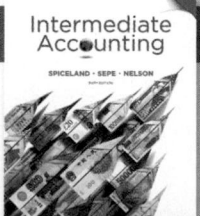

DECISION MAKERS' PERSPECTIVE

We noted earlier in the chapter that investors and creditors pay a great deal of attention to earnings per share information. Because of the importance analysts attach to earnings announcements, companies are particularly eager to meet earnings expectations. As we first noted in Chapter 4, this desire has contributed to a relatively recent trend, especially among technology

---

[21]Revised Exposure Draft: *Earnings per Share—an amendment of FASB Statement No. 128,* (Norwalk, Conn.: FASB, 2008).
[22]A decrease in fair value would be reported as a gain—increasing earnings and EPS. This is not a dilutive effect, in fact it's "antidilutive." Remember, we ignore antidilutive securities, just as we ignore the exercise or conversion of the bonds in this example.

Make sure you pay lots of attention to the man behind the curtain. If any earnings figure says pro forma, you should immediately look for a footnote or explanation telling you just what is and is not included in the calculation.[23]

firms, to report **pro forma** earnings per share. What exactly are pro forma earnings? Unfortunately there is no answer to that question. Essentially, pro forma earnings are actual (GAAP) earnings reduced by any expenses the reporting company feels are unusual and should be excluded. Always, though, the pro forma results of a company look better than the real results. **Broadcom Corporation**, a provider of broadband and network products, reported pro forma *earnings* of $0.49 per share. However on a GAAP basis, it actually had a *loss* of $3.29 per share. This is not an isolated example.

When companies report pro forma results, they argue they are trying to help investors by giving them numbers that more accurately reflect their normal business activities, because they exclude unusual expenses. Analysts should be skeptical, though. Because of the purely discretionary nature of pro forma reporting and several noted instances of abuse, analysts should, at a minimum, find out precisely what expenses are excluded and what the actual GAAP numbers are.

Another way management might enhance the appearance of EPS numbers is by massaging the denominator of the calculation. Reducing the number of shares increases earnings *per share*. Some companies judiciously use share buyback programs to manipulate the number of shares and therefore EPS. There is nothing inherently wrong with share buybacks and, as we noted in Chapter 18, they can benefit shareholders. The motivation for buybacks, though, can sometimes be detected in the year-to-year pattern. A *Fortune* article asserts that, "One way Big Blue has kept the fabulous EPS growth going has been by buying back shares of its own stock. Since 1995, **IBM** has spent a stunning $34.1 billion to shrink shares outstanding. Indeed, $34.1 billion is more than IBM reported in net income ($31.3 billion) over the same period."[24]

One way analysts use EPS data is in connection with the price-earnings ratio. This ratio is simply the market price per share divided by the earnings per share. It measures the market's perception of the quality of a company's earnings by indicating the price multiple the capital market is willing to pay for the company's earnings. Presumably, this ratio reflects the information provided by all financial information in that the market price reflects analysts' perceptions of the company's growth potential, stability, and relative risk. The price-earnings ratio relates these performance measures with the external judgment of the marketplace concerning the value of the firm.

The ratio measures the quality of earnings in the sense that it represents the market's expectation of future earnings as indicated by current earnings. Caution is called for in comparing price-earnings ratios. For instance, a ratio might be low, not because earnings expectations are low, but because of abnormally elevated current earnings. On the contrary, the ratio might be high, not because earnings expectations are high, but because the company's current earnings are temporarily depressed. Similarly, an analyst should be alert to differences among accounting methods used to measure earnings from company to company when making comparisons.

The price-earnings ratio measures the quality of a company's earnings.

Another ratio frequently calculated by shareholders and potential shareholders is the dividend payout ratio. This ratio expresses the percentage of earnings that is distributed to shareholders as dividends. The ratio is calculated by dividing dividends per common share by the earnings per share.

This ratio provides an indication of a firm's reinvestment strategy. A low payout ratio suggests that a company is retaining a large portion of earnings for reinvestment for new facilities and other operating needs. Low payouts often are found in growth industries and high payouts in mature industries. Often, though, the ratio is merely a reflection of managerial strategy concerning the mix of internal versus external financing. The ratio also is considered by investors who, for tax or other reasons, prefer current income over market price appreciation, or vice versa. ●

The dividend payout ratio indicates the percentage of earnings that is distributed to shareholders as dividends.

---

[23]Bill Mann, "Qualcomm's Globalstar Headache," *MotleyFool.com,* January 25, 2001.
[24]Bethany McLean, "Hocus-Pocus: How IBM Grew 27% a Year," *Fortune,* June 26, 2000.

CONCEPT REVIEW EXERCISE

**ADDITIONAL
EPS ISSUES**

At December 31, 2011, the financial statements of Bahnson General, Inc., included the following:

Net income for 2011 (including a net-of-tax extraordinary loss of $10 million) $180 million

Common stock, $1 par:

    Shares outstanding on January 1   44 million

    The share price was $25 and $28 at the beginning and end of the year, respectively.

Additional data:

- At January 1, 2011, $200 million of 10% convertible notes were outstanding. The notes were converted on April 1 into 16 million shares of common stock.
- An agreement with company executives calls for the issuance of up to 12 million additional shares of common stock in 2012 and 2013 based on Bahnson's net income in those years. Executives will receive 2 million shares at the end of each of those two years if the company's stock price is at least $26 and another 4 million shares each year if the stock price is at least $29.50.

The tax rate is 40%.

Required:
Compute basic and diluted earnings per share for the year ended December 31, 2011.

SOLUTION

(amounts in millions, except per share amounts)

Basic EPS

$$\underset{\substack{\text{Shares} \\ \text{at Jan. 1}}}{44} + \underset{\substack{\text{Actual} \\ \text{conversion} \\ \text{of notes}}}{16\ (\%_{12})} = \frac{\$180}{56} = \$3.21$$

where numerator is Net income $180.

Diluted EPS

$$\frac{\overset{\text{Net income}}{\$180} + \overset{\substack{\text{Assumed after-tax} \\ \text{interest savings}}}{[\$20 - 40\%\ (\$20)] \times (\%_{12})}}{\underset{\substack{\text{Shares} \\ \text{at Jan. 1}}}{44} + \underset{\substack{\text{Actual} \\ \text{conversion} \\ \text{of notes}}}{16\ (\%_{12})} + \underset{\substack{\text{Assumed} \\ \text{conversion} \\ \text{of notes}}}{16\ (\%_{12})} + \underset{\substack{\text{Contingent} \\ \text{shares}}}{(2 + 2)}} = \frac{\$183}{64} = \$2.86$$

Convertible Notes: Notice that the effect on diluted EPS would be precisely the same whether the convertible notes were actually converted or not.
Converted on April 1:

Converted on April 1:

$$\frac{\overset{\substack{\text{Net income including} \\ \text{actual after-tax} \\ \text{interest savings}}}{\$180} + \overset{\substack{\text{Assumed after-tax} \\ \text{interest savings}}}{[\$20 - 40\%\ (\$20)] \times (\%_{12})}}{\underset{\substack{\text{Shares} \\ \text{at Jan. 1}}}{44} + \underset{\substack{\text{Actual} \\ \text{conversion} \\ \text{of notes}}}{16\ (\%_{12})} + \underset{\substack{\text{Assumed} \\ \text{conversion} \\ \text{of notes}}}{16\ (\%_{12})}} = \frac{\$183}{60}$$

Not Actually Converted:

$$\frac{\underset{\substack{\text{actual after-tax} \\ \text{interest savings}}}{\overset{\text{Net income without}}{\$171^*}} + \overset{\substack{\text{Assumed after-tax} \\ \text{interest savings}}}{[\$20 - 40\%\,(\$20)]}}{\underset{\substack{\text{Shares} \\ \text{at Jan. 1}}}{44} + \underset{\substack{\text{Assumed} \\ \text{conversion} \\ \text{of notes}}}{16}} = \frac{\$183}{60}$$

*\$180 − {[\$20 − 40% (\$20)] × ($\frac{9}{12}$)} = \$171
After-tax interest from Apr. 1 to Dec. 31

Contingently Issuable Shares:
Because the conditions are met for issuing 4 million shares (2 million for each of two years), those shares are simply added to the denominator of diluted EPS. The current share price (\$28) is projected to remain the same throughout the contingency period, so the other 8 million shares (4 million for each of two years) are excluded.

Income Statement Presentation:
To determine the per share amounts for income before extraordinary items, we substitute that amount for net income in the numerator (in this case, that means adding back the \$10 million extraordinary loss):

Basic: $\dfrac{\$180 + 10}{56} = \$3.39$ Diluted: $\dfrac{\$183 + 10}{64} = \$3.02$

Earnings per Share:	Basic*	Diluted
Income before extraordinary items	\$3.39	\$3.02
Extraordinary loss	(.18)	(.16)
Net income	\$3.21	\$2.86

*Only diluted EPS is required on the face of the income statement. Basic EPS is reported in the EPS reconciliation shown in the disclosure note (below).

Disclosure Note:

Earnings per Share Reconciliation:

	Income (Numerator)	Shares (Denominator)	Per Share Amount
Basic Earnings per Share			
Income before extraordinary items	\$190	56	\$3.39
Extraordinary loss	(10)	56	(.18)
Net income	\$180	56	\$3.21
Convertible debt	3	4	
Contingently issuable shares	—	4	
Diluted Earnings per Share			
Income before extraordinary items	\$193	64	\$3.02
Extraordinary loss	(10)	64	(.16)
Net income	\$183	64	\$2.86

FINANCIAL REPORTING CASE SOLUTION

1. **How can a compensation package such as this serve as an incentive to Ms. Veres?** *(p. 1070)*   Stock-based plans like the restricted stock and stock options that Ms. Veres is receiving are designed to motivate recipients. If the shares awarded are restricted so that Ms. Veres is not free to sell the shares during the restriction period, she

has an incentive to remain with the company until rights to the shares vest. Likewise, stock options can be made exercisable only after a specified period of employment. An additional incentive of stock-based plans is that the recipient will be motivated to take actions that will maximize the value of the shares.

2. **Ms. Veres received a "grant of restricted stock." How should NEV account for the grant?** *(p. 1070)*   The compensation associated with restricted stock is the market price of unrestricted shares of the same stock. NEV will accrue this amount as compensation expense over the service period from the date of grant to when restrictions are lifted.

3. **Included were stock options to buy more than 800,000 shares of NEV stock. How will the options affect NEV's compensation expense?** *(p. 1072)*   Similar to the method used for restricted stock, the value of the options is recorded as compensation over the service period, usually the vesting period.

4. **How will the presence of these and other similar stock options affect NEV's earnings per share?** *(p. 1087)*   If outstanding stock options were exercised, the resulting increase in shares would reduce or dilute EPS. If we don't take into account the dilutive effect of the share increase, we might mislead investors and creditors. So, in addition to basic EPS, we also calculate diluted EPS to include the dilutive effect of options and other potential common shares. This means calculating EPS as if the potential increase in shares already has occurred (even though it hasn't yet). ●

THE BOTTOM LINE

● **LO1**   We measure the fair value of stock issued in a restricted stock award plan and expense it over the service period, usually from the date of grant to the vesting date. (p. 1070)

● **LO2**   Similarly, we estimate the fair value of stock options at the grant date and expense it over the service period, usually from the date of grant to the vesting date. Fair value is estimated at the grant date using an option-pricing model that considers the exercise price and expected term of the option, the current market price of the underlying stock and its expected volatility, expected dividends, and the expected risk-free rate of return. (p. 1071)

● **LO3**   Employee share purchase plans allow employees to buy company stock under convenient or favorable terms. Most such plans are considered compensatory and require any discount to be recorded as compensation expense. (p. 1080)

● **LO4**   A company has a simple capital structure if it has no outstanding securities that could potentially dilute earnings per share. For such a firm, EPS is simply earnings available to common shareholders divided by the weighted-average number of common shares outstanding. When potential common shares are outstanding, the company is said to have a complex capital structure. In that case, two EPS calculations are reported. Basic EPS assumes no dilution. Diluted EPS assumes maximum potential dilution. (p. 1083)

● **LO5**   EPS calculations are based on the weighted-average number of shares outstanding during the period. Any new shares issued during the period are time-weighted by the fraction of the period they were outstanding and then added to the number of shares outstanding for the period. (p. 1083)

● **LO6**   For a stock dividend or stock split, shares outstanding prior to the stock distribution are retroactively restated to reflect the increase in shares. When shares are reacquired, as treasury stock or to be retired, they are time-weighted for the fraction of the period they were not outstanding, prior to being subtracted from the number of shares outstanding during the reporting period. (p. 1084)

● **LO7**   The numerator in the EPS calculation should reflect earnings available to common shareholders. So, any dividends on preferred stock outstanding should be subtracted from reported net income. This adjustment is made for cumulative preferred stock whether or not dividends are declared that period. (p. 1086)

● **LO8**   For diluted EPS, it is assumed that stock options, rights, and warrants are exercised at the beginning of the period (or at the time the options are issued, if later) and the cash proceeds received are used to buy back (as treasury stock) as many of those shares as can be acquired at the average market price during the period. (p. 1087)

● **LO9**   To incorporate convertible securities into the calculation of diluted EPS, the conversion is assumed to have occurred at the beginning of the period (or at the time the convertible security is issued, if later).

The denominator of the EPS fraction is adjusted for the additional common shares assumed and the numerator is increased by the interest (after-tax) on bonds and not reduced by the preferred dividends that would have been avoided in the event of conversion. (p. 1088)

● **LO10**   If including potential common shares in the EPS calculation causes EPS to *increase* rather than decrease, then those potential common shares are considered *antidilutive* and are omitted from the calculation. (p. 1092)

● **LO11**   For the treasury stock method, "proceeds" include (1) the amount, if any, received from the hypothetical exercise of options or vesting of restricted stock, (2) the total compensation from the award that's not yet expensed, and (3) the difference between the eventual tax benefit and the amount recognized in expense. (p. 1096)

● **LO12**   Contingently issuable shares are considered outstanding in the computation of diluted EPS when they will later be issued upon the mere passage of time or because of conditions that currently are met. (p. 1097)

● **LO13**   EPS data (both basic and diluted) must be reported for (a) income before any separately reported items, (b) the separately reported items (discontinued operations and extraordinary gains and losses), and (c) net income. Disclosures also should include a reconciliation of the numerator and denominator used in the computations. (p. 1100)

● **LO14**   When options have graded vesting, unlike under U.S. GAAP, IFRS does not permit the straight-line method for allocating compensation or require that the company recognize at least the amount of the award that has vested by each reporting date. The earnings per share requirements of IFRS and U.S. GAAP are similar. The few differences that remain are the result of differences in the application of the treasury stock method, the treatment of contracts that may be settled in shares or cash, and contingently issuable shares. (pp. 1077, 1078, 1082, and 1102) ●

OPTION-PRICING THEORY

APPENDIX 19A

Option values have two essential components: (1) intrinsic value and (2) time value.

Intrinsic Value

Intrinsic value is the benefit the holder of an option would realize by exercising the option rather than buying the underlying stock directly. An option that permits an employee to buy $25 stock for $10 has an intrinsic value of $15. An option that has an exercise price equal to or exceeding the market price of the underlying stock has zero intrinsic value.

Time Value

In addition to their intrinsic value, options also have a time value due to the fact that (a) the holder of an option does not have to pay the exercise price until the option is exercised and (b) the market price of the underlying stock may yet rise and create additional intrinsic value. All options have time value so long as time remains before expiration. The longer the time until expiration, other things being equal, the greater the time value. For instance, the option described above with an intrinsic value of $15, might have a fair value of, say, $22 if time still remains until the option expires. The $7 difference represents the time value of the option. Time value can be subdivided into two components: (1) the effects of time value of money and (2) volatility value.

TIME VALUE OF MONEY

The time value of money component arises because the holder of an option does not have to pay the exercise price until the option is exercised. Instead, the holder can invest funds elsewhere while waiting to exercise the option. For measurement purposes, the time value of money component is assumed to be the rate of return available on risk-free U.S. Treasury Securities. The higher the time value of money, the higher the value of being able to delay payment of the exercise price.

An option's value is enhanced by the delay in paying cash for the shares.

When the underlying stock pays no dividends, the time value of money component is the difference between the exercise price (a future amount) and its discounted present value. Let's say the exercise price is $30. If the present value (discounted at the risk-free rate) is

The time value of
money component is
the difference between
the exercise price and
its discounted present
value minus the present
value of expected
dividends.

$24, the time value of money component is $6. On the other hand, if the stock pays a dividend (or is expected to during the life of the option), the time value of money component is lower. The value of being able to delay payment of the exercise price would be partially off-set by the cost of forgoing the dividend in the meantime. For instance, if the stock underlying the options just described were expected to pay dividends and the discounted present value of the expected dividends were $2, the time value of money component in that example would be reduced from $6 to $4.

VOLATILITY VALUE

The volatility value represents the possibility that the option holder might profit from market price appreciation of the underlying stock while being exposed to the loss of only the value of the option, rather than the full market value of the stock. For example, fair value of an option to buy a share at an exercise price of $30 might be measured as $7. The potential profit from market price appreciation is conceptually unlimited. And yet, the potential loss from the stock's value failing to appreciate is only $7.

Volatility enhances
the likelihood of stock
price appreciation.

A stock's volatility is the amount by which its price has fluctuated previously or is expected to fluctuate in the future. The greater a stock's volatility, the greater the potential profit. It usually is measured as one standard deviation of a statistical distribution. Statistically, if the expected annualized volatility is 25%, the probability is approximately 67% that the stock's year-end price will fall within roughly plus or minus 25% of its beginning-of-year price. Stated differently, the probability is approximately 33% that the year-end stock price will fall outside that range.

Option-pricing models make assumptions about the likelihood of various future stock prices by making assumptions about the statistical distribution of future stock prices that take into account the expected volatility of the stock price. One popular option pricing model, the Black–Scholes model, for instance, assumes a log-normal distribution. This assumption posits that the stock price is as likely to fall by half as it is to double and that large price movements are less likely than small price movements. The higher a stock's volatility, the higher the probability of large increases or decreases in market price. Because the cost of large decreases is limited to the option's current value, but the profitability from large increases is unlimited, an option on a highly volatile stock has a higher probability of a large profit than does an option on a less volatile stock.

Summary

In summary, the fair value of an option is (a) its intrinsic value plus (b) its time value of money component plus (c) its volatility component. The variables that affect an option's fair value and the effect of each are indicated in Graphic 19A–1.

GRAPHIC 19A–1

Effect of Variables on
an Option's Fair Value

All Other Factors Being Equal, If the:	The Option Value Will Be:
Exercise price is higher	Lower
Term of the option is longer	Higher
Market price of the stock is higher	Higher
Dividends are higher	Lower
Risk-free rate of return is higher	Higher
Volatility of the stock is higher	Higher

APPENDIX 19B STOCK APPRECIATION RIGHTS

Stock appreciation rights (SARs) overcome a major disadvantage of stock option plans that require employees to actually buy shares when the options are exercised. Even though the options' exercise price may be significantly lower than the market value of the shares, the employee still must come up with enough cash to take advantage of the bargain. This can be quite a burden if the award is sizable. In a nonqualified stock option plan, income taxes also would have to be paid when the options are exercised.[25]

SARs offer a solution. Unlike stock options, these awards enable an employee to benefit by the amount that the market price of the company's stock rises without having to buy shares. Instead, the employee is awarded the share appreciation, which is the amount by which the market price on the exercise date exceeds a prespecified price (usually the market price at the date of grant). For instance, if the share price rises from $35 to $50, the employee receives $15 cash for each SAR held. The share appreciation usually is payable in cash or the recipient has the choice between cash and shares. A plan of this type offered by **IBM** is described in Graphic 19B–1.

> In an SAR plan, the employer pays compensation equal to the increase in share price from a specified level.

Long-Term Performance Plan (in part)
SARs offer eligible optionees the alternative of electing not to exercise the related stock option, but to receive payment in cash and/or stock, equivalent to the difference between the option price and the average market price of IBM stock on the date of exercising the right.

GRAPHIC 19B–1

Stock Appreciation Rights—IBM Corporation

Real World Financials

IS IT DEBT OR IS IT EQUITY?

In some plans, the employer chooses whether to issue shares or cash at exercise. In other plans, the choice belongs to the employee.[26] Who has the choice determines the way it's accounted for. More specifically, the accounting treatment depends on whether the award is considered an equity instrument or a liability. If the employer can elect to settle in shares of stock rather than cash, the award is considered to be equity. On the other hand, if the employee will receive cash or can elect to receive cash, the award is considered to be a liability.

> If an employer can elect to settle in shares of stock rather than cash, the award is considered to be equity.

The distinction between share-based awards that are considered equity and those that are considered liabilities is based on whether the employer is obligated to transfer assets to the employee. A cash SAR requires the transfer of assets, and therefore is a liability. A stock option, on the other hand, is an equity instrument if it requires only the issuance of stock. This does not mean that a stock option whose issuer may later choose to settle in cash is not an equity instrument. Instead, cash settlement would be considered equivalent to repurchasing an equity instrument for cash.

> If an employee can elect to receive cash, the award is considered to be a liability.

SARS PAYABLE IN SHARES (EQUITY)

When an SAR is considered to be equity (because the employer can elect to settle in shares of stock rather than cash), we estimate the fair value of the SARs at the grant date and accrue that compensation to expense over the service period. Normally, the fair value of an SAR is the same as the fair value of a stock option with the same terms. The fair value is determined at the grant date and accrued to compensation expense over the service period the same way as for other share-based compensation plans. The total compensation is not revised for subsequent changes in the price of the underlying stock. This is demonstrated in Case 1 of Illustration 19B–1 on the next page.

> The cash settlement of an equity award is considered the repurchase of an equity instrument.

SARS PAYABLE IN CASH (LIABILITY)

When an SAR is considered to be a liability (because the employee can elect to receive cash upon settlement), we estimate the fair value of the SARs and recognize that amount as compensation expense over the requisite service period consistent with the way we account for options and other share-based compensation. However, because these plans are considered to be liabilities, it's necessary to periodically re-estimate the fair value in order to continually adjust the liability (and corresponding compensation) until it is paid. Be sure to note that this is consistent with the way we account for other liabilities. Recall from our

> Compensation expense reported to date is the estimated total compensation multiplied by the fraction of the service period that has expired.

---

[25]The tax treatment of share-based plans is discussed in an earlier Additional Consideration.

[26]Many such plans are called tandem plans and award an employee both a cash SAR and an SAR that calls for settlement in an equivalent amount of shares. The exercise of one cancels the other.

discussions in Chapter 16, for instance, that when a tax rate change causes a change in the eventual liability for deferred income taxes, we adjust that liability.

The periodic expense (and adjustment to the liability) is the fraction of the total compensation earned to date by recipients of the SARs (based on the elapsed fraction of the service period) reduced by any amounts expensed in prior periods. For example, if the fair value of SARs at the end of a period is $8, the total compensation would be $80 million if 10 million SARs are expected to vest. Let's say two years of a four-year service period have elapsed, and $21 million was expensed the first year. Then, compensation expense the second year would be $19 million, calculated as (2/4 of $80 million) minus $21. An example spanning several years is provided in Illustration 19B–1, case 2.

<table>
<tr><td>

ILLUSTRATION 19B–1

Stock Appreciation Rights

Case 1: Equity

Fair value is estimated at the date of grant.

The value of the award is expensed over the service period for which the compensation is provided.

Case 2: Liability

The value of the compensation is estimated each year at the fair value of the SARs.

The expense each year is the current estimate of total compensation that should have been recorded to date less the amount already recorded.

If the fair value falls below the amount expensed to date, both the liability and expense are reduced.

</td><td>

At January 1, 2011, Universal Communications issued SARs that, upon exercise, entitle key executives to receive compensation equal in value to the excess of the market price at exercise over the share price at the date of grant. The SARs vest at the end of 2014 (cannot be exercised until then) and expire at the end of 2018. The fair value of the SARs, estimated by an appropriate option pricing model, is $8 per SAR at January 1, 2011. The fair value re-estimated at December 31, 2011, 2012, 2013, 2014, and 2015, is $8.40, $8, $6, $4.30, and $5, respectively.

Case 1: SARs considered to be equity because Universal can elect to settle in shares of Universal stock at exercise

January 1, 2011
No entry
Calculate total compensation expense:

$$\begin{array}{ll} \$\ 8 & \text{Estimated fair value per SAR} \\ \times\ 10\text{ million} & \text{SARs granted} \\ \hline =\$80\text{ million} & \text{Total compensation} \end{array}$$

The total compensation is allocated to expense over the four-year service (vesting) period: 2011–2014

$$\$80\text{ million} \div 4\text{ years} = \$20\text{ million per year}$$

December 31, 2011, 2012, 2013, 2014 ($ in millions)
Compensation expense ($80 million ÷ 4 years) 20
   Paid-in capital—SAR plan 20

Case 2: SARs considered to be a liability because employees can elect to receive cash at exercise

January 1, 2011
No entry

December 31, 2011 ($ in millions)
Compensation expense ($8.40 × 10 million × 1/4) 21
   Liability—SAR plan 21

December 31, 2012
Compensation expense [($8 × 10 million × 2/4) − 21] 19
   Liability—SAR plan 19

December 31, 2013
Compensation expense [($6 × 10 million × 3/4) − 21 − 19] 5
   Liability—SAR plan 5

December 31, 2014
Liability—SAR plan 2
   Compensation expense [($4.30 × 10 million × 4/4) − 21 − 19 − 5] 2

</td></tr>
</table>

Note that the way we treat changes in compensation estimates entails a catch-up adjustment in the period of change, *inconsistent* with the usual treatment of a change in estimate.

Remember that for most changes in estimate, revisions are allocated over remaining periods, rather than all at once in the period of change. The treatment is, however, consistent with the way we treat changes in forfeiture rate estimates as we discussed earlier in the chapter.

The liability continues to be adjusted after the service period if the rights haven't been exercised yet.

December 31, 2015	($ in millions)	
Compensation expense [($5 × 10 million × all) − 21 − 19 − 5 + 2]	7	
Liability—SAR plan		7

Compensation expense and the liability continue to be adjusted until the SARs expire or are exercised.

It's necessary to continue to adjust both compensation expense and the liability until the SARs ultimately either are exercised or lapse.[27] Assume for example that the SARs are exercised on October 11, 2016, when their fair value is $4.50, and executives choose to receive the market price appreciation in cash:

Adjustment continues after the service period if the SARs have not yet been exercised.

October 11, 2016	($ in millions)	
Liability—SAR plan	5	
Compensation expense [($4.50 × 10 million × all) − 50]		5
Liability—SAR plan (balance)	45	
Cash		45

Let's look at the changes in the liability—SAR plan account during the 2011–2016 period:

Liability—SAR Plan

		($ in millions)	
		21	2011
		19	2012
		5	2013
2014	2		
		7	2015
2016	5		
2016	45		
		0	Balance after exercise

The liability is adjusted each period as changes in the fair value estimates cause changes in the liability.

QUESTIONS FOR REVIEW OF KEY TOPICS

Q 19–1   What is restricted stock? Describe how compensation expense is determined and recorded for a restricted stock award plan.

Q 19–2   Stock option plans provide employees the option to purchase: (a) a specified number of shares of the firm's stock, (b) at a specified price, (c) during a specified period of time. One of the most controversial aspects of accounting for stock-based compensation is how the fair value of stock options should be measured. Describe the general approach to measuring fair value.

Q 19–3   The Tax Code differentiates between qualified option plans, including incentive plans, and nonqualified plans. What are the major differences in tax treatment between incentive plans and nonqualified plans?

Q 19–4   Stock option (and other share-based) plans often specify a performance condition or a market condition that must be satisfied before employees are allowed the benefits of the award. Describe the general approach we use to account for performance-based options and options with market-related conditions.

Q 19–5   What is a simple capital structure? How is EPS determined for a company with a simple capital structure?

---

[27]Except that the cumulative compensation expense cannot be negative; that is, the liability cannot be reduced below zero.

Q 19–6   When calculating the weighted average number of common shares, how are stock dividends and stock splits treated? Compare this treatment with that of additional shares sold for cash in midyear.

Q 19–7   Blake Distributors had 100,000 common shares outstanding at the beginning of the year, January 1. On May 13, Blake distributed a 5% stock dividend. On August 1, 1,200 shares were retired. What is the weighted average number of shares for calculating EPS?

Q 19–8   Why are preferred dividends deducted from net income when calculating EPS? Are there circumstances when this deduction is not made?

Q 19–9   Distinguish between basic and diluted EPS.

Q 19–10   The treasury stock method is used to incorporate the dilutive effect of stock options, stock warrants, and similar securities. Describe this method as it applies to diluted EPS.

Q 19–11   The potentially dilutive effect of convertible securities is reflected in EPS calculations by the if-converted method. Describe this method as it relates to convertible bonds.

Q 19–12   How is the potentially dilutive effect of convertible preferred stock reflected in EPS calculations by the if-converted method? How is this different from the way convertible bonds are considered?

Q 19–13   A convertible security may appear to be dilutive when looked at individually but might be antidilutive when included in combination with other convertible securities. How should the order be determined for inclusion of convertible securities in an EPS calculation to avoid including an antidilutive security?

Q 19–14   If stock options and restricted stock are outstanding when calculating diluted EPS, what are the components of the "proceeds" available for the repurchase of shares under the treasury stock method?

Q 19–15   Wiseman Electronics has an agreement with certain of its division managers that 50,000 contingently issuable shares will be issued next year in the event operating income exceeds $2.1 million that year. In what way, if any, is the calculation of EPS affected by these contingently issuable shares assuming this year's operating income was $2.2 million? $2.0 million?

Q 19–16   Diluted EPS would be precisely the same whether convertible securities were actually converted or not. Why?

Q 19–17   When the income statement includes one or more of the separately reported items, such as discontinued operations or extraordinary items, which amounts require per share presentation?

Q 19–18   In addition to EPS numbers themselves, what additional disclosures should be provided concerning the EPS information?

Q 19–19   (Based on Appendix A) The fair value of stock options can be considered to comprise two main components. What are they?

Q 19–20   (Based on Appendix B) LTV Corporation grants SARs to key executives. Upon exercise, the SARs entitle executives to receive either cash or stock equal in value to the excess of the market price at exercise over the share price at the date of grant. How should LTV account for the awards?

BRIEF EXERCISES

BE 19–1
Restricted stock award
● LO1

First Link Services granted 8 million of its $1 par common shares to executives, subject to forfeiture if employment is terminated within three years. The common shares have a market price of $6 per share on the grant date. Ignoring taxes, what is the total compensation cost pertaining to the restricted shares? What is the effect on earnings in the year after the shares are granted to executives?

BE 19–2
Stock options
● LO2

Under its executive stock option plan, National Corporation granted options on January 1, 2011, that permit executives to purchase 12 million of the company's $1 par common shares within the next six years, but not before December 31, 2013 (the vesting date). The exercise price is the market price of the shares on the date of grant, $17 per share. The fair value of the options, estimated by an appropriate option pricing model, is $5 per option. No forfeitures are anticipated. Ignoring taxes, what is the total compensation cost pertaining to the stock options? What is the effect on earnings in the year after the options are granted to executives?

BE 19–3
Stock options; forfeiture
● LO2

Refer to the situation described in BE 19–2. Suppose that unexpected turnover during 2012 caused the forfeiture of 5% of the stock options. Ignoring taxes, what is the effect on earnings in 2012? In 2013?

BE 19–4
Stock options; exercise
● LO2

Refer to the situation described in BE 19–2. Suppose that the options are exercised on April 3, 2014, when the market price is $19 per share. Ignoring taxes, what journal entry will National record?

BE 19–5
Stock options;
expiration
● LO2

Refer to the situation described in BE 19–2. Suppose that the options expire without being exercised. Ignoring taxes, what journal entry will National record?

BE 19–6
Performance-based
options
● LO2

On October 1, 2011, Farmer Fabrication issued stock options for 100,000 shares to a division manager. The options have an estimated fair value of $6 each. To provide additional incentive for managerial achievement, the options are not exercisable unless divisional revenue increases by 5% in three years. Farmer initially estimates that it is probable the goal will be achieved. How much compensation will be recorded in each of the next three years?

BE 19–7
Performance-based
options
● LO2

Refer to the situation described in BE 19–6. Suppose that after one year, Farmer estimates that it is *not* probable that divisional revenue will increase by 5% in three years. What action will be taken to account for the options in 2012?

BE 19–8
Performance-based
options
● LO2

Refer to the situation described in BE 19–6. Suppose that Farmer initially estimates that it is *not* probable the goal will be achieved, but then after one year, Farmer estimates that it *is* probable that divisional revenue will increase by 5% by the end of 2013. What action will be taken to account for the options in 2012 and thereafter?

BE 19–9
Options with
market-based
conditions
● LO2

On October 1, 2011, Farmer Fabrication issued stock options for 100,000 shares to a division manager. The options have an estimated fair value of $6 each. To provide additional incentive for managerial achievement, the options are not exercisable unless Farmer Fabrication's stock price increases by 5% in three years. Farmer initially estimates that it is not probable the goal will be achieved. How much compensation will be recorded in each of the next three years?

BE 19–10
EPS; shares issued,
shares retired
● LO5 LO6

McDonnell-Myer Corporation reported net income of $741 million. The company had 544 million common shares outstanding at January 1 and sold 36 million shares on Feb. 28. As part of an annual share repurchase plan, 6 million shares were retired on April 30 for $47 per share. Calculate McDonnell-Myer's earnings per share for the year.

BE 19–11
EPS;
nonconvertible
preferred shares
● LO7

At December 31, 2010 and 2011, Funk & Noble Corporation had outstanding 820 million shares of common stock and 2 million shares of 8%, $100 par value cumulative preferred stock. No dividends were declared on either the preferred or common stock in 2010 or 2011. Net income for 2011 was $426 million. The income tax rate is 40%. Calculate earnings per share for the year ended December 31, 2011.

BE 19–12
EPS; stock options
● LO8

Fully vested incentive stock options exercisable at $50 per share to obtain 24,000 shares of common stock were outstanding during a period when the average market price of the common stock was $60 and the ending market price was $60. By how many shares will the assumed exercise of these options increase the weighted-average number of shares outstanding when calculating diluted earnings per share?

BE 19–13
EPS; convertible
preferred shares
● LO9

Ahnberg Corporation had 800,000 shares of common stock issued and outstanding at January 1. No common shares were issued during the year, but on January 1 Ahnberg issued 100,000 shares of convertible preferred stock. The preferred shares are convertible into 200,000 shares of common stock. During the year Ahnberg paid $60,000 cash dividends on the preferred stock. Net income was $1,500,000. What were Ahnberg's basic and diluted earnings per share for the year?

BE 19–14
EPS; restricted
stock award
● LO11

Niles Company granted 9 million of its no par common shares to executives, subject to forfeiture if employment is terminated within three years. The common shares have a market price of $5 per share on January 1, 2010, the grant date. When calculating diluted EPS at December 31, 2011, what will be the net increase in the denominator of the EPS fraction if the market price of the common shares averaged $5 per share during 2011?

EXERCISES

An alternate exercise and problem set is available on the text website: www.mhhe.com/spiceland6e

E 19–1
Restricted stock
award plan
● LO1

Allied Paper Products, Inc. offers a restricted stock award plan to its vice presidents. On January 1, 2011, the company granted 16 million of its $1 par common shares, subject to forfeiture if employment is terminated within two years. The common shares have a market price of $5 per share on the grant date.

Required:

1. Determine the total compensation cost pertaining to the restricted shares.
2. Prepare the appropriate journal entries related to the restricted stock through December 31, 2012.

E 19–2
Restricted stock
award plan
● LO1

On January 1, 2011, VKI Corporation awarded 12 million of its $1 par common shares to key personnel, subject to forfeiture if employment is terminated within three years. On the grant date, the shares have a market price of $2.50 per share.

Required:

1. Determine the total compensation cost pertaining to the restricted shares.
2. Prepare the appropriate journal entry to record the award of restricted shares on January 1, 2011.
3. Prepare the appropriate journal entry to record compensation expense on December 31, 2011.
4. Prepare the appropriate journal entry to record compensation expense on December 31, 2012.
5. Prepare the appropriate journal entry to record compensation expense on December 31, 2013.
6. Prepare the appropriate journal entry to record the lifting of restrictions on the shares at December 31, 2013.

E 19–3
Restricted stock
award; Kmart
● LO1

Real World Financials

Kmart Holding Co. included the following disclosure note in an annual report:

> **RESTRICTED STOCK (in part)**
> . . . , we issued 111,540 shares of restricted stock at market prices ranging from $23.00 to $29.65. . . . The restricted stock generally vests over three years, during which time we will recognize total compensation expense of approximately $3 million.

Required:

1. Based on the information provided in the disclosure note, determine the weighted average market price of the restricted stock issued.
2. How much compensation expense did Kmart report for the year following the year in which the restricted stock was issued?

E 19–4
Restricted stock
award plan;
forfeitures
anticipated
● LO1

Magnetic-Optical Corporation offers a variety of share-based compensation plans to employees. Under its restricted stock award plan, the company on January 1, 2011, granted 4 million of its $1 par common shares to various division managers. The shares are subject to forfeiture if employment is terminated within three years. The common shares have a market price of $22.50 per share on the grant date.

Required:

1. Determine the total compensation cost pertaining to the restricted shares.
2. Prepare the appropriate journal entry to record the award of restricted shares on January 1, 2011.
3. Prepare the appropriate journal entry to record compensation expense on December 31, 2011.
4. Suppose Magnetic-Optical expected a 10% forfeiture rate on the restricted shares prior to vesting. Determine the total compensation cost.

E 19–5
Stock options
● LO2

American Optical Corporation provides a variety of share-based compensation plans to its employees. Under its executive stock option plan, the company granted options on January 1, 2011, that permit executives to acquire 4 million of the company's $1 par common shares within the next five years, but not before December 31, 2012 (the vesting date). The exercise price is the market price of the shares on the date of grant, $14 per share. The fair value of the 4 million options, estimated by an appropriate option pricing model, is $3 per option. No forfeitures are anticipated. Ignore taxes.

Required:

1. Determine the total compensation cost pertaining to the options.
2. Prepare the appropriate journal entry to record the award of options on January 1, 2011.
3. Prepare the appropriate journal entry to record compensation expense on December 31, 2011.
4. Prepare the appropriate journal entry to record compensation expense on December 31, 2012.

E 19–6
Stock options;
forfeiture of
options
● LO2

On January 1, 2011, Adams-Meneke Corporation granted 25 million incentive stock options to division managers, each permitting holders to purchase one share of the company's $1 par common shares within the next six years, but not before December 31, 2013 (the vesting date). The exercise price is the market price of the shares on the date of grant, currently $10 per share. The fair value of the options, estimated by an appropriate option pricing model, is $3 per option.

Required:

1. Determine the total compensation cost pertaining to the options on January 1, 2011.
2. Prepare the appropriate journal entry to record compensation expense on December 31, 2011.
3. Unexpected turnover during 2012 caused the forfeiture of 6% of the stock options. Determine the adjusted compensation cost, and prepare the appropriate journal entry(s) on December 31, 2012 and 2013.

E 19–7
Stock options
exercise; forfeitures
● LO2

Walters Audio Visual Inc. offers an incentive stock option plan to its regional managers. On January 1, 2011, options were granted for 40 million $1 par common shares. The exercise price is the market price on the grant date—$8 per share. Options cannot be exercised prior to January 1, 2013, and expire December 31, 2017. The fair value of the 40 million options, estimated by an appropriate option pricing model, is $1 per option.

Required:

1. Determine the total compensation cost pertaining to the incentive stock option plan.
2. Prepare the appropriate journal entry to record compensation expense on December 31, 2011.
3. Prepare the appropriate journal entry to record compensation expense on December 31, 2012.
4. Prepare the appropriate journal entry to record the exercise of 75% of the options on March 12, 2013, when the market price is $9 per share.
5. Prepare the appropriate journal entry on December 31, 2017, when the remaining options that have vested expire without being exercised.

E 19–8
Stock options
● LO2

SSG Cycles manufactures and distributes motorcycle parts and supplies. Employees are offered a variety of share-based compensation plans. Under its nonqualified stock option plan, SSG granted options to key officers on January 1, 2011. The options permit holders to acquire 12 million of the company's $1 par common shares for $11 within the next six years, but not before January 1, 2014 (the vesting date). The market price of the shares on the date of grant is $13 per share. The fair value of the 12 million options, estimated by an appropriate option pricing model, is $3 per option.

Required:

1. Determine the total compensation cost pertaining to the incentive stock option plan.
2. Prepare the appropriate journal entries to record compensation expense on December 31, 2011, 2012, and 2013.
3. Record the exercise of the options if all of the options are exercised on May 11, 2015, when the market price is $14 per share.

E 19–9
Employee share
purchase plan
● LO3

In order to encourage employee ownership of the company's $1 par common shares, Washington Distribution permits any of its employees to buy shares directly from the company through payroll deduction. There are no brokerage fees and shares can be purchased at a 15% discount. During March, employees purchased 50,000 shares at a time when the market price of the shares on the New York Stock Exchange was $12 per share.

Required:

Prepare the appropriate journal entry to record the March purchases of shares under the employee share purchase plan.

E 19–10
EPS; shares issued;
stock dividend
● LO5 LO6

For the year ended December 31, 2011, Norstar Industries reported net income of $655,000. At January 1, 2011, the company had 900,000 common shares outstanding. The following changes in the number of shares occurred during 2011:

Apr. 30   Sold 60,000 shares in a public offering.
May 24   Declared and distributed a 5% stock dividend.
June 1   Issued 72,000 shares as part of the consideration for the purchase of assets from a subsidiary.

Required:

Compute Norstar's earnings per share for the year ended December 31, 2011.

E 19–11
EPS; treasury
stock; new shares;
stock dividends;
two years
● LO5 LO6

The Alford Group had 202,000 shares of common stock outstanding at January 1, 2011. The following activities affected common shares during the year. There are no potential common shares outstanding.

2011
Feb. 28   Purchased 6,000 shares of treasury stock.
Oct. 31   Sold the treasury shares purchased on February 28.
Nov. 30   Issued 24,000 new shares.
Dec. 31   Net income for 2011 is $400,000.

2012
Jan. 15   Declared and issued a 2-for-1 stock split.
Dec. 31   Net income for 2012 is $400,000.

Required:
1. Determine the 2011 EPS.
2. Determine the 2012 EPS.
3. At what amount will the 2011 EPS be presented in the 2012 comparative financial statements?

E 19–12
EPS; stock dividend; nonconvertible preferred stock
● LO5 LO6 LO7

Hardaway Fixtures' balance sheet at December 31, 2010, included the following:

Shares issued and outstanding:	
Common stock, $1 par	$800,000
Nonconvertible preferred stock, $50 par	20,000

On July 21, 2011, Hardaway issued a 25% stock dividend on its common stock. On December 12 it paid $50,000 cash dividends on the preferred stock. Net income for the year ended December 31, 2011, was $2,000,000.

Required:
Compute Hardaway's earnings per share for the year ended December 31, 2011.

E 19–13
EPS; net loss; nonconvertible preferred stock; shares sold
● LO5 LO6 LO7

At December 31, 2010, Albrecht Corporation had outstanding 373,000 shares of common stock and 8,000 shares of 9.5%, $100 par value cumulative, nonconvertible preferred stock. On May 31, 2011, Albrecht sold for cash 12,000 shares of its common stock. No cash dividends were declared for 2011. For the year ended December 31, 2011, Albrecht reported a net loss of $114,000.

Required:
Calculate Albrecht's net loss per share for the year ended December 31, 2011.

E 19–14
EPS; stock dividend; nonconvertible preferred stock; treasury shares; shares sold
● LO5 LO6 LO7

On December 31, 2010, Berclair Inc. had 200 million shares of common stock and 3 million shares of 9%, $100 par value cumulative preferred stock issued and outstanding. On March 1, 2011, Berclair purchased 24 million shares of its common stock as treasury stock. Berclair issued a 5% common stock dividend on July 1, 2011. Four million treasury shares were sold on October 1. Net income for the year ended December 31, 2011, was $150 million.

Required:
Compute Berclair's earnings per share for the year ended December 31, 2011.

E 19–15
EPS; stock dividend; nonconvertible preferred stock; treasury shares; shares sold; stock options
● LO5 through LO8

(Note: This is a variation of the previous exercise, modified to include stock options.) On December 31, 2010, Berclair Inc. had 200 million shares of common stock and 3 million shares of 9%, $100 par value cumulative preferred stock issued and outstanding. Berclair purchased 24 million shares of its common stock as treasury stock. Berclair issued a 5% common stock dividend on July 1, 2011. On March 1, 2011. Four million treasury shares were sold on October 1. Net income for the year ended December 31, 2011, was $150 million.

Also outstanding at December 31 were incentive stock options granted to key executives on September 13, 2006. The options are exercisable as of September 13, 2010, for 30 million common shares at an exercise price of $56 per share. During 2011, the market price of the common shares averaged $70 per share.

Required:
Compute Berclair's basic and diluted earnings per share for the year ended December 31, 2011.

E 19–16
EPS; stock dividend; nonconvertible preferred stock; treasury shares; shares sold; stock options exercised
● LO5 through LO8

(Note: This is a variation of the previous exercise, modified to include the exercise of stock options.)

On December 31, 2010, Berclair Inc. had 200 million shares of common stock and 3 million shares of 9%, $100 par value cumulative preferred stock issued and outstanding. Berclair purchased 24 million shares of its common stock as treasury stock. Berclair issued a 5% common stock dividend on July 1, 2011. On March 1, 2011. Four million treasury shares were sold on October 1. Net income for the year ended December 31, 2011, was $150 million.

Also outstanding at December 31 were incentive stock options granted to key executives on September 13, 2006. The options are exercisable as of September 13, 2010, for 30 million common shares at an exercise price of $56 per share. During 2011, the market price of the common shares averaged $70 per share.

The options were exercised on September 1, 2011.

Required:
Compute Berclair's basic and diluted earnings per share for the year ended December 31, 2011.

E 19–17
EPS; stock dividend; nonconvertible preferred stock; treasury shares; shares sold; stock options; convertible bonds
● **LO5 through LO9**

(Note: This is a variation of E 19–15 modified to include convertible bonds).

On December 31, 2010, Berclair Inc. had 200 million shares of common stock and 3 million shares of 9%, $100 par value cumulative preferred stock issued and outstanding. On March 1, 2011, Berclair purchased 24 million shares of its common stock as treasury stock. Berclair issued a 5% common stock dividend on July 1, 2011. Four million treasury shares were sold on October 1. Net income for the year ended December 31, 2011, was $150 million. The income tax rate is 40%.

Also outstanding at December 31 were incentive stock options granted to key executives on September 13, 2006. The options are exercisable as of September 13, 2010, for 30 million common shares at an exercise price of $56 per share. During 2011, the market price of the common shares averaged $70 per share.

$62.5 million of 8% bonds, convertible into 6 million common shares, were issued at face value in 2007.

Required:
Compute Berclair's basic and diluted earnings per share for the year ended December 31, 2011.

E 19–18
EPS; shares issued; stock options
● **LO6 through LO9**

Stanley Department Stores reported net income of $720,000 for the year ended December 31, 2011.

Additional Information:

Common shares outstanding at Jan. 1, 2011	80,000
Incentive stock options (vested in 2010) outstanding throughout 2011	24,000

(Each option is exercisable for one common share at an exercise price of $37.50)

During the year, the market price of Stanley's common stock averaged $45 per share.

On Aug. 30 Stanley sold 15,000 common shares.

Stanley's only debt consisted of $50,000 of 10% short term bank notes.

The company's income tax rate is 40%.

Required:
Compute Stanley's basic and diluted earnings per share for the year ended December 31, 2011.

E 19–19
EPS; convertible preferred stock; convertible bonds; order of entry
● **LO7 LO9**

Information from the financial statements of Ames Fabricators, Inc., included the following:

	December 31	
	2011	**2010**
Common shares	100,000	100,000
Convertible preferred shares (convertible into 32,000 shares of common)	12,000	12,000
10% convertible bonds (convertible into 30,000 shares of common)	$1,000,000	$1,000,000

Ames's net income for the year ended December 31, 2011, is $500,000. The income tax rate is 40%. Ames paid dividends of $5 per share on its preferred stock during 2011.

Required:
Compute basic and diluted earnings per share for the year ended December 31, 2011.

E 19–20
EPS; restricted stock
● **LO11**

As part of its executive compensation plan, Vertovec Inc. granted 54,000 of its no par common shares to executives, subject to forfeiture if employment is terminated within three years. Vertovec's common shares have a market price of $5 per share on January 1, 2010, the grant date, as well as on December 31, 2011. 800,000 shares were outstanding at January 1, 2011. Net income for 2011 was $120,000.

Required:
Compute Vertovec's basic and diluted earnings per share for the year ended December 31, 2011.

E 19–21
Record restricted stock; effect on EPS
● **LO1 LO11**

PHN Foods granted 18 million of its no par common shares to executives, subject to forfeiture if employment is terminated within three years. The common shares have a market price of $5 per share on January 1, 2010, the grant date.

Required:
1. What journal entry will PHN Foods prepare to record executive compensation regarding these shares at December 31, 2010 and December 31, 2011?
2. When calculating diluted EPS at December 31, 2011, what will be the net increase in the denominator of the EPS fraction if the market price of the common shares averages $5 per share during 2011?

E 19–22
New shares; contingently issuable shares
● LO6 LO12

During its first year of operations, McCollum Tool Works entered into the following transactions relating to shareholders' equity. The corporation was authorized to issue 100 million common shares, $1 par per share.

Jan. 2   Issued 35 million common shares for cash.

3   Entered an agreement with the company president to issue up to 2 million additional shares of common stock in 2012 based on the earnings of McCollum in 2012. If net income exceeds $140 million, the president will receive 1 million shares; 2 million shares if net income exceeds $150 million.

Mar. 31   Issued 4 million shares in exchange for plant facilities.

Net income for 2011 was $148 million.

Required:
Compute basic and diluted earnings per share for the year ended December 31, 2011.

E 19–23
EPS; new shares; contingent agreements
● LO6 LO12

Anderson Steel Company began 2011 with 600,000 shares of common stock outstanding. On March 31, 2011, 100,000 new shares were sold at a price of $45 per share. The market price has risen steadily since that time to a high of $50 per share at December 31. No other changes in shares occurred during 2011, and no securities are outstanding that can become common stock. However, there are two agreements with officers of the company for future issuance of common stock. Both agreements relate to compensation arrangements reached in 2010. The first agreement grants to the company president a right to 10,000 shares of stock each year the closing market price is at least $48. The agreement begins in 2012 and expires in 2015. The second agreement grants to the controller a right to 15,000 shares of stock if she is still with the firm at the end of 2019. Net income for 2011 was $2,000,000.

Required:
Compute Anderson Steel Company's basic and diluted EPS for the year ended December 31, 2011.

E 19–24
EPS; concepts; terminology
● LO5 through LO13

Listed below are several terms and phrases associated with earnings per share. Pair each item from List A with the item from List B (by letter) that is most appropriately associated with it.

List A	List B
____ 1. Subtract preferred dividends.	a. Options exercised.
____ 2. Time-weighted by $\frac{5}{12}$.	b. Simple capital structure.
____ 3. Time-weighted shares assumed issued plus time-weighted actual shares.	c. Basic EPS.
	d. Convertible preferred stock.
____ 4. Midyear event treated as if it occurred at the beginning of the reporting period.	e. Earnings available to common shareholders.
	f. Antidilutive.
____ 5. Preferred dividends do not reduce earnings.	g. Increased marketability.
____ 6. Single EPS presentation.	h. Extraordinary items.
____ 7. Stock split.	i. Stock dividend.
____ 8. Potential common shares.	j. Add after-tax interest to numerator.
____ 9. Exercise price exceeds market price.	k. Diluted EPS.
____ 10. No dilution assumed.	l. Noncumulative, undeclared preferred dividends.
____ 11. Convertible bonds.	m. Common shares retired at the beginning of August.
____ 12. Contingently issuable shares.	
____ 13. Maximum potential dilution.	n. Include in diluted EPS when conditions for issuance are met.
____ 14. Shown between per share amounts for net income and for income from continuing operations.	

E 19–25
FASB codification research
● LO2

The *FASB Accounting Standards Codification* represents the single source of authoritative U.S. generally accepted accounting principles.

Required:

1. Obtain the relevant authoritative literature on stock compensation using the FASB's Codification Research System at the FASB website (**www.fasb.org**). What is the specific citation that describes the information that companies must disclose about the exercise prices for their stock option plans?

2. List the disclosure requirements.

E 19–26
FASB codification research
● LO2 LO3 LO7 LO13

Access the FASB's Codification Research System at the FASB website (**www.fasb.org**). Determine the specific citation for accounting for each of the following items:

1. Initial measurement of stock options.

2. The measurement date for share-based payments classified as liabilities.

3. The formula to calculate diluted earnings per share.

4. The way stock dividends or stock splits in the current year affect the presentation of EPS in the income statement.

E 19–27
Stock appreciation rights; settlement in shares

● (Appendix B)

As part of its stock-based compensation package, International Electronics granted 24 million stock appreciation rights (SARs) to top officers on January 1, 2011. At exercise, holders of the SARs are entitled to receive stock equal in value to the excess of the market price at exercise over the share price at the date of grant. The SARs cannot be exercised until the end of 2014 (vesting date) and expire at the end of 2016. The $1 par common shares have a market price of $46 per share on the grant date. The fair value of the SARs, estimated by an appropriate option pricing model, is $3 per SAR at January 1, 2011. The fair value reestimated at December 31, 2011, 2012, 2013, 2014, and 2015, is $4, $3, $4, $2.50, and $3, respectively. All recipients are expected to remain employed through the vesting date.

Required:

1. Prepare the appropriate journal entry to record the award of SARs on January 1, 2011. Will the SARs be reported as debt or equity?

2. Prepare the appropriate journal entries pertaining to the SARs on December 31, 2011–December 31, 2014.

3. The SARs remain unexercised on December 31, 2015. Prepare the appropriate journal entry on that date.

4. The SARs are exercised on June 6, 2016, when the share price is $50. Prepare the appropriate journal entry(s) on that date.

E 19–28
Stock appreciation rights; cash settlement

● (Appendix B)

(Note: This is a variation of the previous exercise, modified to allow settlement in cash.)
As part of its stock-based compensation package, International Electronics granted 24 million stock appreciation rights (SARs) to top officers on January 1, 2011. At exercise, holders of the SARs are entitled to receive cash or stock equal in value to the excess of the market price at exercise over the share price at the date of grant. The SARs cannot be exercised until the end of 2014 (vesting date) and expire at the end of 2016. The $1 par common shares have a market price of $46 per share on the grant date. The fair value of the SARs, estimated by an appropriate option pricing model, is $3 per SAR at January 1, 2011. The fair value re-estimated at December 31, 2011, 2012, 2013, 2014, and 2015, is $4, $3, $4, $2.50, and $3, respectively. All recipients are expected to remain employed through the vesting date.

Required:

1. Prepare the appropriate journal entry to record the award of SARs on January 1, 2011.

2. Prepare the appropriate journal entries pertaining to the SARs on December 31, 2011–December 31, 2014.

3. The SARs remain unexercised on December 31, 2015. Prepare the appropriate journal entry on that date.

4. The SARs are exercised on June 6, 2016, when the share price is $50, and executives choose to receive the market price appreciation in cash. Prepare the appropriate journal entry(s) on that date.

CPA AND CMA REVIEW QUESTIONS

CPA Exam Questions

The following questions are used in the Kaplan CPA Review Course to study share-based compensation and earnings per share while preparing for the CPA examination. Determine the response that best completes the statements or questions.

● LO2

1. On January 1, 2011, Pall Corp. granted stock options to key employees for the purchase of 40,000 shares of the company's common stock at $25 per share. The options are intended to compensate employees for the next two years. The options are exercisable within a four-year period beginning January 1, 2013, by the grantees still in the employ of the company. No options were terminated during 2011, but the company does have an experience of 4% forfeitures over the life of the stock options. The market price of the common stock was $32 per share at the date of the grant. Pall Corp. used the binomial pricing model and estimated the fair value of each of the options at $10. What amount should Pall charge to compensation expense for the year ended December 31, 2011?
   a. $153,600
   b. $160,000
   c. $192,000
   d. $200,000

● LO2

2. On January 1, 2011, Doro Corp. granted an employee an option to purchase 3,000 shares of Doro's $5 par value common stock at $20 per share. The options became exercisable on December 31, 2012, after the employee completed two years of service. The options were exercised on January 10, 2013. The market prices of Doro's stock were as follows: January 1, 2011, $30; December 31, 2012, $50; and January 10, 2013, $45.

The Black-Scholes-Merton option pricing model estimated the value of the options at $8 each on the grant date. For 2011, Doro should recognize compensation expense of

a. $0
b. $12,000
c. $15,000
d. $45,000

● LO6

3. The following information pertains to Jet Corp.'s outstanding stock for 2011:

Common stock, $5 par value	
Shares outstanding, 1/1/11	20,000
2-for-1 stock split, 4/1/11	20,000
Shares issued, 7/1/11	10,000
Preferred stock, $10 par value, 5% cumulative	
Shares outstanding, 1/1/11	4,000

What is the number of shares Jet should use to calculate 2011 basic earnings per share?

a. 40,000
b. 45,000
c. 50,000
d. 54,000

● LO7

4. At December 31, 2011 and 2010, Gow Corp. had 100,000 shares of common stock and 10,000 shares of 5%, $100 par value cumulative preferred stock outstanding. No dividends were declared on either the preferred or common stock in 2011 or 2010. Net income for 2011 was $1,000,000. For 2011, basic earnings per common share amounted to

a. $ 5.00
b. $ 9.50
c. $ 9.00
d. $10.00

● LO8

5. January 1, 2011, Hage Corporation granted options to purchase 9,000 of its common shares at $7 each. The market price of common stock was $9 per share on March 31, 2011, and averaged $9 per share during the quarter then ended. There was no change in the 50,000 shares of outstanding common stock during the quarter ended March 31, 2011. Net income for the quarter was $8,268. The number of shares to be used in computing diluted earnings per share for the quarter is

a. 50,000
b. 52,000
c. 53,000
d. 59,000

● LO9

6. During 2011, Moore Corp. had the following two classes of stock issued and outstanding for the entire year:

- 100,000 shares of common stock, $1 par.
- 1,000 shares of 4% preferred stock, $100 par, convertible share for share into common stock.

Moore's 2011 net income was $900,000, and its income tax rate for the year was 30%. In the computation of diluted earnings per share for 2011, the amount to be used in the numerator is

a. $896,000
b. $898,800
c. $900,000
d. $901,200

● LO9

7. On January 2, 2011, Lang Co. issued at par $10,000 of 4% bonds convertible in total into 1,000 shares of Lang's common stock. No bonds were converted during 2011.

Throughout 2011, Lang had 1,000 shares of common stock outstanding. Lang's 2011 net income was $1,000. Lang's income tax rate is 50%.

No potential common shares other than the convertible bonds were outstanding during 2011.

Lang's diluted earnings per share for 2011 would be

a. $ .50
b. $ .60
c. $ .70
d. $1.00

**CMA Exam
Questions**

The following questions dealing with share-based compensation and earnings per share are adapted from questions that previously appeared on Certified Management Accountant (CMA) examinations. The CMA designation sponsored by the Institute of Management Accountants (**www.imanet.org**) provides members with an objective measure of knowledge and competence in the field of management accounting. Determine the response that best completes the statements or questions.

● LO2

1. Noncompensatory stock option plans have all of the following characteristics except
   a. participation by substantially all full-time employees who meet limited employment qualifications.
   b. equal offers of stock to all eligible employees.
   c. a limited amount of time permitted to exercise the option.
   d. a provision related to the achievement of certain performance criteria.

● LO2

2. A stock option plan may or may not be intended to compensate employees for their work. The compensation expense for compensatory stock option plans should be recognized in the periods the
   a. employees become eligible to exercise the options.
   b. employees perform services.
   c. stock is issued.
   d. options are granted.

PROBLEMS

An alternate exercise and problem set is available on the text website: www.mhhe.com/spiceland6e

P 19–1
Stock options;
forfeiture; exercise
● LO2

On October 15, 2010, the board of directors of Ensor Materials Corporation approved a stock option plan for key executives. On January 1, 2011, 20 million stock options were granted, exercisable for 20 million shares of Ensor's $1 par common stock. The options are exercisable between January 1, 2014, and December 31, 2016, at 80% of the quoted market price on January 1, 2011, which was $15. The fair value of the 20 million options, estimated by an appropriate option pricing model, is $6 per option.

   Two million options were forfeited when an executive resigned in 2012. All other options were exercised on July 12, 2015, when the stock's price jumped unexpectedly to $19 per share.

Required:
1. When is Ensor's stock option measurement date?
2. Determine the compensation expense for the stock option plan in 2011. (Ignore taxes.)
3. What is the effect of forfeiture of the stock options on Ensor's financial statements for 2012 and 2013?
4. Is this effect consistent with the general approach for accounting for changes in estimates? Explain.
5. How should Ensor account for the exercise of the options in 2015?

P 19–2
Stock options;
graded vesting
● LO2

Pastner Brands is a calendar-year firm with operations in several countries. As part of its executive compensation plan, at January 1, 2011, the company issued 400,000 executive stock options permitting executives to buy 400,000 shares of Pastner stock for $34 per share. One-fourth of the options vest in each of the next four years beginning at December 31, 2011 (graded vesting). Pastner elects to separate the total award into four groups (or tranches) according to the year in which they vest and measures the compensation cost for each vesting date as a separate award. The fair value of each tranche is estimated at January 1, 2011, as follows:

Vesting Date	Amount Vesting	Fair Value per Option
Dec. 31, 2011	25%	$3.50
Dec. 31, 2012	25%	$4.00
Dec. 31, 2013	25%	$4.50
Dec. 31, 2014	25%	$5.00

Required:
1. Determine the compensation expense related to the options to be recorded each year 2011–2014, assuming Pastner allocates the compensation cost for each of the four groups (tranches) separately.
2. Determine the compensation expense related to the options to be recorded each year 2011–2014, assuming Pastner uses the straight-line method to allocate the total compensation cost.

P 19–3
Stock options;
graded vesting;
measurement using
a single fair value
per option

● LO2

Refer to the situation described in Problem 19–2. Assume Pastner measures the fair value of all options on January 1, 2011, to be $4.50 per option using a single weighted-average expected life of the options assumption.

Required:

1. Determine the compensation expense related to the options to be recorded each year 2011–2014, assuming Pastner allocates the compensation cost for each of the four groups (tranches) separately.

2. Determine the compensation expense related to the options to be recorded each year 2011–2014, assuming Pastner uses the straight-line method to allocate the total compensation cost.

P 19–4
Stock options;
graded vesting;
IFRS

● LO2 LO14

Refer to the situation described in Problem 19–2. Assume Pastner prepares its financial statements using International Financial Reporting Standards.

Required:

How might your responses to requirement 1 and requirement 2 differ using IFRS? Explain.

P 19–5
Steve Jobs'
restricted stock; tax
effects

● LO2

Real World Financials

Apple Inc. provides its executives compensation under a variety of share-based compensation plans including restricted stock awards. The following disclosure note from Apple's 2007 annual report describes the plan created for the company's chief executive officer, Steve Jobs:

> ### CEO Restricted Stock Award
>
> On March 19, 2003, the Company's Board of Directors granted 10 million shares of restricted stock to the Company's CEO that vested on March 19, 2006. The amount of the restricted stock award expensed by the Company was based on the closing market price of the Company's common stock on the date of grant and was amortized ratably on a straight-line basis over the three-year requisite service period. Upon vesting during 2006, the 10 million shares of restricted stock had a fair value of $646.6 million and had grant-date fair value of $7.48 per share. The restricted stock award was net-share settled such that the Company withheld shares with value equivalent to the CEO's minimum statutory obligation for the applicable income and other employment taxes, and remitted the cash to the appropriate taxing authorities. The total shares withheld of 4.6 million were based on the value of the restricted stock award on the vesting date as determined by the Company's closing stock price of $64.66. The remaining shares net of those withheld were delivered to the Company's CEO. Total payments for the CEO's tax obligations to the taxing authorities were $296 million in 2006 and are reflected as a financing activity within the Consolidated Statements of Cash Flows. The net-share settlement had the effect of share repurchases by the Company as it reduced and retired the number of shares outstanding and did not represent an expense to the Company. The Company's CEO has no remaining shares of restricted stock.

Required:

1. How much compensation did Apple record for its CEO related to the restricted stock in its fiscal year ended September 24, 2005?

2. What was the CEO's combined income tax and employment tax rate that Apple used to determine the shares to be withheld at vesting?

3. From the information provided in the disclosure note, recreate the journal entries Apple used to record compensation expense and its related tax effects on September 24, 2005, the end of the 2005 fiscal year.

4. From the information provided in the disclosure note, recreate the journal entries Apple used to record the vesting of the restricted stock and its related tax effects on March 16, 2006, assuming the remaining compensation expense already has been recorded.

P 19–6
Stock option plan;
deferred tax effect
recognized

● LO2

Walters Audio Visual, Inc., offers a stock option plan to its regional managers. On January 1, 2011, options were granted for 40 million $1 par common shares. The exercise price is the market price on the grant date, $8 per share. Options cannot be exercised prior to January 1, 2013, and expire December 31, 2017. The fair value of the options, estimated by an appropriate option pricing model, is $2 per option. Because the plan does not qualify as an incentive plan, Walters will receive a tax deduction upon exercise of the options equal to the excess of the market price at exercise over the exercise price. The income tax rate is 40%.

Required:

1. Determine the total compensation cost pertaining to the stock option plan.

2. Prepare the appropriate journal entries to record compensation expense and its tax effect on December 31, 2011.

3. Prepare the appropriate journal entries to record compensation expense and its tax effect on December 31, 2012.

4. Record the exercise of the options and their tax effect if *all* of the options are exercised on March 20, 2016, when the market price is $12 per share.

5. Assume the option plan qualifies as an incentive plan. Prepare the appropriate journal entries to record compensation expense and its tax effect on December 31, 2011.

6. Assuming the option plan qualifies as an incentive plan, record the exercise of the options and their tax effect if *all* of the options are exercised on March 20, 2016, when the market price is $11 per share.

P 19–7

Stock option plan; deferred tax effect of a nonqualifying plan

● LO2

JBL Aircraft manufactures and distributes aircraft parts and supplies. Employees are offered a variety of share-based compensation plans. Under its nonqualified stock option plan, JBL granted options to key officers on January 1, 2011. The options permit holders to acquire six million of the company's $1 par common shares for $22 within the next six years, but not before January 1, 2014 (the vesting date). The market price of the shares on the date of grant is $26 per share. The fair value of the 6 million options, estimated by an appropriate option pricing model, is $6 per option. Because the plan does not qualify as an incentive plan, JBL will receive a tax deduction upon exercise of the options equal to the excess of the market price at exercise over the exercise price. The tax rate is 40%.

Required:

1. Determine the total compensation cost pertaining to the incentive stock option plan.

2. Prepare the appropriate journal entries to record compensation expense and its tax effect on December 31, 2011, 2012, and 2013.

3. Record the exercise of the options and their tax effect if *all* of the options are exercised on August 21, 2015, when the market price is $27 per share.

P 19–8

Performance option plan

● LO2

LCI Cable Company grants 1 million performance stock options to key executives at January 1, 2011. The options entitle executives to receive 1 million of LCI $1 par common shares, subject to the achievement of specific financial goals over the next four years. Attainment of these goals is considered probable initially and throughout the service period. The options have a current fair value of $12 per option.

Required:

1. Prepare the appropriate entry when the options are awarded on January 1, 2011.

2. Prepare the appropriate entries on December 31 of each year 2011–2014.

3. Suppose at the beginning of 2013, LCI decided it is not probable that the performance objectives will be met. Prepare the appropriate entries on December 31 of 2013 and 2014.

P 19–9

Net loss; stock dividend; nonconvertible preferred stock; treasury shares; shares sold; extraordinary loss

● LO5 through LO7 LO13

On December 31, 2010, Ainsworth, Inc., had 600 million shares of common stock outstanding. Twenty million shares of 8%, $100 par value cumulative, nonconvertible preferred stock were sold on January 2, 2011. On April 30, 2011, Ainsworth purchased 30 million shares of its common stock as treasury stock. Twelve million treasury shares were sold on August 31. Ainsworth issued a 5% common stock dividend on June 12, 2011. No cash dividends were declared in 2011. For the year ended December 31, 2011, Ainsworth reported a net loss of $140 million, including an after-tax extraordinary loss of $400 million from a litigation settlement.

Required:

1. Determine Ainsworth's net loss per share for the year ended December 31, 2011.

2. Determine the per share amount of income or loss from continuing operations for the year ended December 31, 2011.

3. Prepare an EPS presentation that would be appropriate to appear on Ainsworth's 2011 and 2010 comparative income statements. Assume EPS was reported in 2010 as $.75, based on net income (no extraordinary items) of $450 million and a weighted-average number of common shares of 600 million.

P 19–10

EPS from statement of retained earnings

● LO4 through LO6

(Note: Problem 19–10 is based on the same situation described in Problem 18–4 in Chapter 18, modified to focus on EPS rather than recording the events that affected retained earnings.)

Comparative Statements of Retained Earnings for Renn-Dever Corporation were reported as follows for the fiscal years ending December 31, 2009, 2010, and 2011.

RENN-DEVER CORPORATION
Statements of Retained Earnings

For the Years Ended December 31	2011	2010	2009
Balance at beginning of year	$6,794,292	$5,464,052	$5,624,552
Net income (loss)	3,308,700	2,240,900	(160,500)
Deductions:			
Stock dividend (34,900 shares)	242,000		
Common shares retired, September 30 (110,000 shares)		212,660	
Common stock cash dividends	889,950	698,000	0
Balance at end of year	$8,971,042	$6,794,292	$5,464,052

At December 31, 2008, paid-in capital consisted of the following:

Common stock, 1,855,000 shares at $1 par,	$1,855,000
Paid in capital—excess of par	7,420,000

No preferred stock or potential common shares were outstanding during any of the periods shown.

Required:
Compute Renn-Dever's earnings per share as it would have appeared in income statements for the years ended December 31, 2009, 2010, and 2011.

P 19–11
EPS from statement of shareholders' equity

● LO4 through LO6

Comparative Statements of Shareholders' Equity for Locke Intertechnology Corporation were reported as follows for the fiscal years ending December 31, 2009, 2010, and 2011.

LOCKE INTERTECHNOLOGY CORPORATION
Statements of Shareholders' Equity
For the Years Ended Dec. 31, 2009, 2010, and 2011
($ in millions)

	Preferred Stock, $10 par	Common Stock, $1 par	Additional Paid-In Capital	Retained Earnings	Total Shareholders' Equity
Balance at January 1, 2009		55	495	1,878	2,428
Sale of preferred shares	10		470		480
Sale of common shares, 7/1		9	81		90
Cash dividend, preferred				(1)	(1)
Cash dividend, common				(16)	(16)
Net income				290	290
Balance at December 31, 2009	10	64	1,046	2,151	3,271
Retirement of common shares, 4/1		(4)	(36)	(20)	(60)
Cash dividend, preferred				(1)	(1)
Cash dividend, common				(20)	(20)
3-for-2 split effected in the form of a common stock dividend, 8/12		30	(30)		
Net income				380	380
Balance at December 31, 2010	10	90	980	2,490	3,570
10% common stock dividend, 5/1		9	90	(99)	
Sale of common shares, 9/1		3	31		34
Cash dividend, preferred				(2)	(2)
Cash dividend, common				(22)	(22)
Net income				412	412
Balance at December 31, 2011	10	102	1,101	2,779	3,992

Required:
Infer from the statements the events and transactions that affected Locke Intertechnology Corporation's shareholders' equity and compute earnings per share as it would have appeared on the income statements for the years ended December 31, 2009, 2010, and 2011. No potential common shares were outstanding during any of the periods shown.

P 19–12
EPS; nonconvertible preferred stock; treasury shares; shares sold; stock dividend

● LO4 through LO7

On December 31, 2010, Dow Steel Corporation had 600,000 shares of common stock and 300,000 shares of 8%, noncumulative, nonconvertible preferred stock issued and outstanding. Dow issued a 4% common stock dividend on May 15 and paid cash dividends of $400,000 and $75,000 to common and preferred shareholders, respectively, on December 15, 2011.

On February 28, 2011, Dow sold 60,000 common shares. In keeping with its long-term share repurchase plan, 2,000 shares were retired on July 1. Dow's net income for the year ended December 31, 2011, was $2,100,000. The income tax rate is 40%.

Required:
Compute Dow's earnings per share for the year ended December 31, 2011.

P 19–13

EPS; nonconvertible preferred stock; treasury shares; shares sold; stock dividend; options

● LO4 through LO8 LO10

(Note: This is a variation of the previous problem, modified to include stock options.)

On December 31, 2010, Dow Steel Corporation had 600,000 shares of common stock and 300,000 shares of 8%, noncumulative, nonconvertible preferred stock issued and outstanding. Dow issued a 4% common stock dividend on May 15 and paid cash dividends of $400,000 and $75,000 to common and preferred shareholders, respectively, on December 15, 2011.

On February 28, 2011, Dow sold 60,000 common shares. In keeping with its long-term share repurchase plan, 2,000 shares were retired on July 1. Dow's net income for the year ended December 31, 2011, was $2,100,000. The income tax rate is 40%.

As part of an incentive compensation plan, Dow granted incentive stock options to division managers at December 31 of the current and each of the previous two years. Each option permits its holder to buy one share of common stock at an exercise price equal to market value at the date of grant and can be exercised one year from that date. Information concerning the number of options granted and common share prices follows:

Date Granted	Options Granted	Share Price
	(adjusted for the stock dividend)	
December 31, 2009	8,000	$24
December 31, 2010	3,000	$33
December 31, 2011	6,500	$32

The market price of the common stock averaged $32 per share during 2011.

Required:

Compute Dow's earnings per share for the year ended December 31, 2011.

P 19–14

EPS; nonconvertible preferred stock; treasury shares; shares sold; stock dividend; options; convertible bonds; contingently issuable shares

● LO4 through LO11

(Note: This is a variation of the previous problem, modified to include convertible bonds and contingently issuable shares.)

On December 31, 2010, Dow Steel Corporation had 600,000 shares of common stock and 300,000 shares of 8%, noncumulative, nonconvertible preferred stock issued and outstanding. Dow issued a 4% common stock dividend on May 15 and paid cash dividends of $400,000 and $75,000 to common and preferred shareholders, respectively, on December 15, 2011.

On February 28, 2011, Dow sold 60,000 common shares. Also, as a part of a 2010 agreement for the acquisition of Merrill Cable Company, another 23,000 shares (already adjusted for the stock dividend) are to be issued to former Merrill shareholders on December 31, 2012, if Merrill's 2012 net income is at least $500,000. In 2011, Merrill's net income was $630,000.

In keeping with its long-term share repurchase plan, 2,000 shares were retired on July 1. Dow's net income for the year ended December 31, 2011, was $2,100,000. The income tax rate is 40%.

As part of an incentive compensation plan, Dow granted incentive stock options to division managers at December 31 of the current and each of the previous two years. Each option permits its holder to buy one share of common stock at an exercise price equal to market value at the date of grant and can be exercised one year from that date. Information concerning the number of options granted and common share prices follows:

Date Granted	Options Granted	Share Price
	(adjusted for the stock dividend)	
December 31, 2009	8,000	$24
December 31, 2010	3,000	$33
December 31, 2011	6,500	$32

The market price of the common stock averaged $32 per share during 2011.

On July 12, 2009, Dow issued $800,000 of convertible 10% bonds at face value. Each $1,000 bond is convertible into 30 common shares (adjusted for the stock dividend).

Required:

Compute Dow's basic and diluted earnings per share for the year ended December 31, 2011.

P 19–15

EPS; convertible preferred stock; convertible bonds; order of entry

● LO7 LO9 LO10

Information from the financial statements of Henderson-Niles Industries included the following at December 31, 2011:

Common shares outstanding throughout the year	100 million
Convertible preferred shares (convertible into 32 million shares of common)	60 million
Convertible 10% bonds (convertible into 13.5 million shares of common)	$900 million

Henderson-Niles' net income for the year ended December 31, 2011, is $520 million. The income tax rate is 40%. Henderson-Niles paid dividends of $2 per share on its preferred stock during 2011.

Required:

Compute basic and diluted earnings per share for the year ended December 31, 2011.

P 19–16
EPS; antidilution
● **LO4 through LO10 LO13**

Alciatore Company earned a net income of $150,000 in 2011. The weighted-average number of common shares outstanding for 2011 was 40,000. The average stock price for 2011 was $33. Assume an income tax rate of 40%.

Required:

For each of the following independent situations, indicate whether the effect of the security is antidilutive for diluted EPS.

1. 10,000 shares of 7.7% of $100 par convertible, cumulative preferred stock. Each share may be converted into two common shares.

2. 8% convertible 10-year, $500,000 of bonds, issued at face value. The bonds are convertible to 5,000 shares of common stock.

3. Stock options exercisable at $30 per share after January 1, 2013.

4. Warrants for 1,000 common shares with an exercise price of $35 per share.

5. A contingent agreement to issue 5,000 shares of stock to the company president if net income is at least $125,000 in 2012.

P 19–17
EPS; convertible bonds; treasury shares
● **LO4 through LO6 LO9**

At December 31, 2011, the financial statements of Hollingsworth Industries included the following:

Net income for 2011	$560 million
Bonds payable, 10%, convertible into 36 million shares of common stock	$300 million
Common stock:	
Shares outstanding on January 1	400 million
Treasury shares purchased for cash on September 1	30 million
Additional data:	
The bonds payable were issued at par in 2009. The tax rate for 2011 was 40%.	

Required:

Compute basic and diluted EPS for the year ended December 31, 2011.

P 19–18
EPS; options; convertible preferred; additional shares
● **LO4 through LO9**

On January 1, 2011, Tonge Industries had outstanding 440,000 common shares (par $1) that originally sold for $20 per share, and 4,000 shares of 10% cumulative preferred stock (par $100), convertible into 40,000 common shares.

On October 1, 2011, Tonge sold and issued an additional 16,000 shares of common stock at $33. At December 31, 2011, there were incentive stock options outstanding, issued in 2010, and exercisable after one year for 20,000 shares of common stock at an exercise price of $30. The market price of the common stock at year-end was $48. During the year the price of the common shares had averaged $40.

Net income was $650,000. The tax rate for the year was 40%.

Required:

Compute basic and diluted EPS for the year ended December 31, 2011.

P 19–19
EPS; stock options; nonconvertible preferred; convertible bonds; shares sold
● **LO4 through LO9**

At January 1, 2011, Canaday Corporation had outstanding the following securities:

600 million common shares
20 million 6% cumulative preferred shares, $50 par
8% convertible bonds, $2,000 million face amount, convertible into 80 million common shares

The following additional information is available:

• On September 1, 2011, Canaday sold 72 million additional shares of common stock.

• Incentive stock options to purchase 60 million shares of common stock after July 1, 2010, at $12 per share were outstanding at the beginning and end of 2011. The average market price of Canaday's common stock was $18 per share during 2011.

• Canaday's net income for the year ended December 31, 2011, was $1,476 million. The effective income tax rate was 40%.

Required:

1. Calculate basic earnings per common share for the year ended December 31, 2011.

2. Calculate the diluted earnings per common share for the year ended December 31, 2011.

P 19–20

EPS; options;
restricted stock;
additional
components for
"proceeds" in
treasury stock
method

● LO1 LO2 LO4
LO8 LO11

Witter House is a calendar-year firm with 300 million common shares outstanding throughout 2011 and 2012. As part of its executive compensation plan, at January 1, 2010, the company had issued 30 million executive stock options permitting executives to buy 30 million shares of stock for $10 within the next eight years, but not prior to January 1, 2013. The fair value of the options was estimated on the grant date to be $3 per option.

In 2011, Witter House began granting employees stock awards rather than stock options as part of its equity compensation plans and granted 15 million restricted common shares to senior executives at January 1, 2011. The shares vest four years later. The fair value of the stock was $12 per share on the grant date. The average price of the common shares was $12 and $15 during 2011 and 2012, respectively.

The stock options qualify for tax purposes as an incentive plan. The restricted stock does not. The company's net income was $150 million and $160 million in 2011 and 2012, respectively. Its income tax rate is 40%.

Required:

1. Determine basic and diluted earnings per share for Witter House in 2011.
2. Determine basic and diluted earnings per share for Witter House in 2012.

BROADEN YOUR PERSPECTIVE

Apply your critical-thinking ability to the knowledge you've gained. These cases will provide you an opportunity to develop your research, analysis, judgment, and communication skills. You also will work with other students, integrate what you've learned, apply it in real world situations, and consider its global and ethical ramifications. This practice will broaden your knowledge and further develop your decision-making abilities.

Real World Case 19–1

Restricted stock plan; Microsoft

● LO1

Real World Financials

Microsoft provides compensation to executives in the form of a variety of incentive compensation plans including restricted stock award grants. The following is an excerpt from a disclosure note from Microsoft's 2009 annual report:

Note 20 Employee Stock and Savings Plans (in part)

Stock awards are grants that entitle the holder to shares of common stock as the award vests. Our stock awards generally vest over a five-year period. . . . During fiscal year 2009, the following activity occurred under our existing plans:

	Shares (in millions)	Weighted Average Grant-Date Fair Value
Stock awards:		
Nonvested balance, beginning of year	153	$26.12
Granted	91	24.95
Vested	(43)	25.56
Forfeited	(10)	26.08
Nonvested balance, end of year	**191**	**$25.69**

Required:

1. What is the "incentive" provided by Microsoft's restricted stock grants?
2. If all awards are granted, vested, and forfeited evenly throughout the year, what is the compensation expense in fiscal 2009 pertaining to the previous and current stock awards? Explain. Assume forfeited shares were granted evenly throughout the three previous years.

Communication Case 19–2

Stock options; basic concepts; prepare a memo

● LO2

You are Assistant Controller of Stamos & Company, a medium-size manufacturer of machine parts. On October 22, 2010, the board of directors approved a stock option plan for key executives. On January 1, 2011, a specific number of stock options were granted. The options were exercisable between January 1, 2013, and December 31, 2017, at 100% of the quoted market price at the grant date. The service period is for 2011 through 2013.

Your boss, the controller, is one of the executives to receive options. Neither he nor you have had occasion to deal with GAAP on accounting for stock options. He and you are aware of the traditional approach your company used years ago but do not know the newer method. Your boss understands how options might benefit him personally but wants to be aware also of how the options will be reported in the financial statements. He has asked you for a one-page synopsis of accounting for stock options under the fair value approach. He instructed you, "I don't care about the effect on taxes or earnings per share—just the basics, please."

Required:

Prepare such a report that includes the following:

1. At what point should the compensation cost be measured? How should it be measured?
2. How should compensation expense be measured for the stock option plan in 2011 and later?
3. If options are forfeited because an executive resigns before vesting, what is the effect of that forfeiture of the stock options on the financial statements?
4. If options are allowed to lapse after vesting, what is the effect on the financial statements?

Ethics Case 19–3
Stock options
● LO2

You are in your second year as an auditor with Dantly and Regis, a regional CPA firm. One of the firm's long-time clients is Mayberry-Cleaver Industries, a national company involved in the manufacturing, marketing, and sales of hydraulic devices used in specialized manufacturing applications. Early in this year's audit you discover that Mayberry-Cleaver has changed its method of determining inventory from LIFO to FIFO. Your client's explanation is that FIFO is consistent with the method used by some other companies in the industry. Upon further investigation, you discover an executive stock option plan whose terms call for a significant increase in the shares available to executives if net income this year exceeds $44 million. Some quick calculations convince you that without the change in inventory methods, the target will not be reached; with the change, it will.

Required:

Do you perceive an ethical dilemma? What would be the likely impact of following the controller's suggestions? Who would benefit? Who would be injured?

Trueblood Accounting Case 19–4
Modification of share-based awards
● LO1 LO2

The following Trueblood case is recommended for use with this chapter. The case provides an excellent opportunity for class discussion, group projects, and writing assignments. The case, along with Professor's Discussion Material, can be obtained from the Deloitte Foundation at its website: **www.deloitte.com/us/truebloodcases**.

Case 07-4: *Murray Compensation, Inc.*

This case gives students the opportunity to consider accounting for share-based compensation plans when a company modifies the existing award.

Real World Case 19–5
Share-based plans; Cisco Systems
● LO1 LO2
Appendix B

Real World Financials

Cisco Systems offers its employees a variety of share-based compensation plans including stock options, stock appreciation rights, and restricted stock. The following is an excerpt from a disclosure note from Cisco's 2009 financial statements:

Note 13 Employee Benefit Plans (in part)

Share-based compensation expense consists primarily of expenses for stock options, stock purchase rights, restricted stock, and restricted stock units granted to employees. The following table summarizes employee share-based compensation expense (in millions):

Years Ended	July 25, 2009	July 26, 2008	July 28, 2007
Cost of sales—product	$ 46	$ 40	$ 39
Cost of sales—service	128	108	104
Employee share-based compensation expense in cost of sales	174	148	143
Research and development	333	295	289
Sales and marketing	440	434	392
General and administrative	193	148	107
Employee share-based compensation expense in operating expenses	966	877	788
Total employee share-based compensation expense (1)	$ 1,140	$ 1,025	$ 931

Required:

1. Cisco's share-based compensation includes stock options, stock appreciation rights, restricted stock awards, and performance-based awards. What is the general financial reporting objective when recording compensation expense for these forms of compensation?
2. Cisco reported share-based expense of $1,140 million in 2009. Without referring to specific numbers and ignoring other forms of share-based compensation, describe how this amount reflects the value of stock options.

Real World Case 19–6
Employee stock purchase plan; Microsoft
● LO3

Real World Financials

Microsoft Corporation offers compensation to its employees and executives through a variety of compensation plans. One such plan is its employee stock purchase plan, which is described in the following disclosure note from its fiscal 2009 annual report:

Employee Stock Purchase Plan. We have an employee stock purchase plan for all eligible employees. Compensation expense for the employee stock purchase plan is recognized in accordance with *SFAS No. 123(R)*. Shares of our common stock may be purchased by employees at three-month intervals at 90% of the fair market value on the last day of each three-month period. Employees may purchase shares having a value not exceeding 15% of their gross compensation during an offering period. Employees purchased the following shares:

(Shares in millions)	2009	2008	2007
Shares purchased	24	18	17
Average price per share	$20.13	$26.78	$25.36

At June 30, 2009, 83 million shares were reserved for future issuance.

Required:

Describe the way "Compensation expense for the employee stock purchase plan is recognized" by Microsoft. Include in your explanation the journal entry that summarizes employee share purchases during 2009.

Ethics Case 19–7
International
Network Solutions
● LO6

International Network Solutions provides products and services related to remote access networking. The company has grown rapidly during its first 10 years of operations. As its segment of the industry has begun to mature, though, the fast growth of previous years has begun to slow. In fact, this year revenues and profits are roughly the same as last year.

One morning, nine weeks before the close of the fiscal year, Rob Mashburn, CFO, and Jessica Lane, controller, were sharing coffee and ideas in Lane's office.

Lane: About the Board meeting Thursday. You may be right. This may be the time to suggest a share buyback program.

Mashburn: To begin this year, you mean?

Lane: Right! I know Barber will be lobbying to use the funds for our European expansion. She's probably right about the best use of our funds, but we can always issue more notes next year. Right now, we need a quick fix for our EPS numbers.

Mashburn: Our shareholders are accustomed to increases every year.

Required:

1. How will a buyback of shares provide a "quick fix" for EPS?
2. Is the proposal ethical?
3. Who would be affected if the proposal is implemented?

**Real World
Case 19–8**
Per share data;
stock options;
antidilutive
securities; Sun
Microsystems
● LO8

Real World Financials

Sun Microsystems, Inc., headquartered in Santa Clara, California, is a prominent provider of products and services for network computing. Sun's 2009 annual report included the following disclosure note:

Computation of Net Income (Loss) per Common Share (in part)
Basic net income (loss) per common share is computed using the weighted-average number of common shares outstanding (adjusted for treasury stock and common stock subject to repurchase activity) during the period. Diluted net income (loss) per common share is computed using the weighted-average number of common and dilutive common equivalent shares outstanding during the period. Common equivalent shares are anti-dilutive when their conversion would increase earnings per share. Dilutive common equivalent shares consist primarily of stock options and restricted stock awards (restricted stock and restricted stock units that are settled in stock).

The following table sets forth the computation of basic and diluted income (loss) per share for each of the past three fiscal years (in millions, except per share amounts):

	Fiscal Years Ended June 30,		
	2009	2008	2007
Basic earnings per share			
Net income (loss)	$(2,234)	$ 403	$ 473
Basic weighted average shares outstanding	747	809	883
Net income (loss) per common share—basic	$ (2.99)	$ 0.50	$ 0.54
Diluted earnings per share			
Net income (loss)	$(2,234)	$ 403	$ 473
Diluted weighted average shares outstanding	747	822	902
Net income (loss) per common share—diluted	$ (2.99)	$ 0.49	$ 0.52

As a result of our net loss for the fiscal year ended June 30, 2009, all potentially dilutive shares were antidilutive and therefore excluded from the computation of diluted net loss per share.

For the fiscal years ended June 30, 2008 and 2007, we added 13 million and 19 million common equivalent shares, respectively, to our basic weighted-average shares outstanding to compute the diluted weighted-average shares outstanding. We are required to include these dilutive shares in our calculations of net income per share for fiscal 2008 because we earned a profit.

Required:

1. The note indicates that "diluted net income (loss) per common share is computed using the weighted-average number of common and dilutive common equivalent shares outstanding during the period." What are dilutive common equivalent shares?

2. The note indicates that "For the fiscal years ended June 30, 2008 and 2007, we added 13 million and 19 million common equivalent shares, respectively, to our basic weighted-average shares outstanding to compute the diluted weighted-average shares outstanding." Does that mean Sun had outstanding a total of 13 million and 19 million stock options and restricted shares in 2008 and 2007? Explain.

3. Sun does not include potentially dilutive shares when calculating EPS for fiscal 2009. Why not? Assume Sun had 20 million common equivalent shares in fiscal 2009 and included them in the calculation, what would have been the amount of diluted loss per share for fiscal 2009?

Analysis Case 19–9

EPS concepts

● LO4 through LO8

The shareholders' equity of Proactive Solutions, Inc., included the following at December 31, 2011:

Common stock, $1 par
Paid-in capital—excess of par on common stock
7% cumulative convertible preferred stock, $100 par value
Paid-in capital—excess of par on preferred stock
Retained earnings

Additional information:

- Proactive had 7 million shares of preferred stock authorized of which 2 million were outstanding. All 2 million shares outstanding were issued in 2005 for $112 a share. The preferred stock is convertible into common stock on a two-for-one basis until December 31, 2013, after which the preferred stock no longer is convertible. None of the preferred stock has been converted into common stock at December 31, 2011. There were no dividends in arrears.

- Of the 13 million common shares authorized, there were 8 million shares outstanding at January 1, 2011. Proactive also sold 3 million shares at the beginning of September 2011 at a price of $52 a share.

- The company has an employee stock option plan in which certain key employees and officers may purchase shares of common stock at the market price at the date of the option grant. All options are exercisable beginning one year after the date of the grant and expire if not exercised within five years of the grant date. On January 1, 2011, options for 2 million shares were outstanding at prices ranging from $45 to $53 a share. Options for 1 million shares were exercised at $49 a share at the end of June 2011. No options expired during 2011. Additional options for 1.5 million shares were granted at $55 a share during the year. The 2.5 million options outstanding at December 31, 2011, were exercisable at $45 to $55 a share.

The only changes in the shareholders' equity for 2011 were those described above, 2011 net income, and cash dividends paid.

Required:

Explain how each of the following amounts should be determined when computing earnings per share for presentation in the income statements. For each, be specific as to the treatment of each item.

1. Numerator for basic EPS.

2. Denominator for basic EPS.

3. Numerator for diluted EPS.

4. Denominator for diluted EPS.

Analysis Case 19–10

EPS; AIG

● LO5 through LO8

Real World Financials

"I guess I'll win that bet!" you announced to no one in particular.

"What bet?" Renee asked. Renee Patey was close enough to overhear you.

"When I bought my **AIG** stock last year Randy insisted it was a mistake, that they were going to collapse. I bet him a Coke he was wrong. This press release says they have positive earnings," you bragged. Renee was looking over your shoulder now at the article you were pointing at:

August 7, 2009 (Business Wire) American International Group, Inc. (AIG) today reported its first quarterly profit since the third quarter of 2007, as certain of its businesses stabilized and the company's results reflected positive valuation changes. . . . For the second quarter ended June 30, 2009, AIG reported net income attributable to AIG of $1.8 billion, including net income attributable to AIG common shareholders of $311 million or $2.30 per diluted common share, compared with a net loss of $5.4 billion or $41.13 per diluted share in the second quarter of 2008.

(a) Share and per share amounts prior to the second quarter of 2009 have been restated to reflect the 1 for 20 reverse stock split effective June 30, 2009.

Excerpt from: "AIG Reports Second Quarter 2009 Results," August 7, 2009.

"Two dollars and thirty cents a share, huh?" Renee asked. "How many shares do you have? When do you get the check?"

Required:

1. Renee's questions imply that she thinks you will get cash dividends of $2.30 a share. What does earnings per share really tell you?
2. The press release says that "Share and per share amounts prior to the second quarter of 2009 have been restated to reflect the 1-for-20 reverse stock split effective June 30, 2009." What does that mean?
3. At February 18, 2009, AIG had board of director authorization for repurchasing up to $9 billion of its own stock, but pursuant to the Fed Credit Agreement, AIG is restricted from repurchasing shares of its common stock. Would the reduction in shares from a stock repurchase be taken into account when EPS is calculated? How?
4. You know from statements AIG mailed you that AIG grants stock options to company executives. If those options are exercised, you know the resulting increase in shares might reduce earnings per share. Is that possibility taken into account when EPS is calculated? Explain.

Judgment Case 19–11
Where are the profits?
● LO4 through LO7 LO9

Del Conte Construction Company has experienced generally steady growth since its inception in 1953. Management is proud of its record of having maintained or increased its earnings per share in each year of its existence.

The economic downturn has led to disturbing dips in revenues the past two years. Despite concerted cost-cutting efforts, profits have declined in each of the two previous years. Net income in 2009, 2010, and 2011 was as follows:

2009	$145 million
2010	$134 million
2011	$ 95 million

A major shareholder has hired you to provide advice on whether to continue her present investment position or to curtail that position. Of particular concern is the declining profitability, despite the fact that earnings per share has continued a pattern of growth:

	Basic	Diluted
2009	$2.15	$1.91
2010	$2.44	$2.12
2011	$2.50	$2.50

She specifically asks you to explain this apparent paradox. During the course of your investigation you discover the following events:

- For the decade ending December 31, 2008, Del Conte had 60 million common shares and 20 million shares of 8%, $10 par nonconvertible preferred stock outstanding. Cash dividends have been paid quarterly on both.
- On July 1, 2010, half the preferred shares were retired in the open market. The remaining shares were retired on December 30, 2010.
- $55 million of 8% nonconvertible bonds were issued at the beginning of 2011 and a portion of the proceeds were used to call and retire $50 million of 10% debentures (outstanding since 2006) that were convertible into 9 million common shares.
- In 2009 management announced a share repurchase plan by which up to 24 million common shares would be retired. 12 million shares were retired on March 1 of both 2009 and 2010.
- Del Conte's income tax rate is 40% and has been for the last several years.

Required:

Explain the apparent paradox to which your client refers. Include calculations that demonstrate your explanation.

Communication Case 19–12
Dilution
● LO9

"I thought I understood earnings per share," lamented Brad Dawson, "but you're telling me we need to pretend our convertible bonds have been converted! Or maybe not?"

Dawson, your boss, is the new manager of the Fabricating division of BVT Corporation. His background is engineering and he has only a basic understanding of earnings per share. Knowing you are an accounting graduate, he asks you to explain the questions he has about the calculation of the company's EPS. His reaction is to your explanation that the company's convertible bonds might be included in this year's calculation.

"Put it in a memo!" he grumbled as he left your office.

Required:

Write a memo to Dawson. Explain the effect on earnings per share of each of the following:

1. Convertible securities.
2. Antidilutive securities.

The Alberto-Culver Company develops, manufactures, distributes, and markets branded beauty care products as well as branded food and household products in the United States and more than 100 other countries. The following is an excerpt from the comparative income statements (beginning with earnings from continuing operations) from Alberto-Culver's 2008 annual report ($ in thousands):

	2008	2007	2006
Earnings from continuing operations	$106,039	$72,564	$ 65,845
Earnings (loss) from discontinued operations, net of income taxes	122,115	5,700	139,476
Net earnings	$228,154	$78,264	$205,321

An income statement sometimes includes items that require separate presentation (net of income taxes) within the statement. The two possible "separately reported items" are discontinued operations and extraordinary items. Alberto-Culver reports one of these items.

A disclosure note from Alberto-Culver's 2008 annual report is shown below:

Weighted Average Shares Outstanding

The following table provides information about basic and diluted weighted average shares outstanding:

(shares in thousands)	2008	2007	2006
Basic weighted average shares outstanding	98,424	95,896	92,426
Effect of dilutive securities:			
Assumed exercise of stock options	2,254	2,443	1,110
Assumed vesting of restricted stock	390	237	199
Effect of unrecognized stock-based compensation related to future services	(424)	(218)	(250)
Diluted weighted average shares outstanding	100,644	98,358	93,485

The computations of diluted weighted average shares outstanding exclude 1.4 million shares in fiscal years 2008 and 2007, and 2.1 million shares in fiscal year 2006 since the options were antidilutive.

Required:

1. The disclosure note shows adjustments for "assumed exercise of stock options and assumed vesting of restricted stock." What other adjustments might be needed? Explain why and how these adjustments are made to the weighted-average shares outstanding.
2. The disclosure note indicates that the effect of some of the stock options were not included because they would be antidilutive. What does that mean? Why not include antidilutive securities?
3. Based on the information provided, prepare the presentation of basic and diluted earnings per share for 2008, 2007, and 2006 that Alberto-Culver reports in its 2008 annual report.

IGF Foods Company is a large, primarily domestic, consumer foods company involved in the manufacture, distribution and sale of a variety of food products. Industry averages are derived from Troy's *The Almanac of Business and Industrial Financial Ratios* and Dun and Bradstreet's *Industry Norms and Key Business Ratios.* Following are the 2011 and 2010 comparative income statements and balance sheets for IGF. The market price of IGF's common stock is $47 during 2011. (The financial data we use are from actual financial statements of a well-known corporation, but the company name used in our illustration is fictitious and the numbers and dates have been modified slightly to disguise the company's identity.)

IGF FOODS COMPANY
Years Ended December 31, 2011 and 2010

($ in millions)	2011	2010
Comparative Income Statements		
Net sales	$6,440	$5,800
Cost of goods sold	(3,667)	(3,389)
Gross profit	2,773	2,411
Operating expenses	(1,916)	(1,629)
Operating income	857	782
Interest expense	(54)	(53)
Income from operations before tax	803	729
Income taxes	(316)	(287)
Net income	$ 487	$ 442
Net income per share	$ 2.69	$2.44
Average shares outstanding	181 million	181 million

(continued)

(concluded)

Comparative Balance Sheets
Assets

Total current assets	$1,879	$1,490
Property, plant, and equipment (net)	2,592	2,291
Intangibles (net)	800	843
Other assets	74	60
Total assets	$5,345	$4,684

Liabilities and Shareholders' Equity

Total current liabilities	$1,473	$ 941
Long term debt	534	728
Deferred income taxes	407	344
Total liabilities	2,414	2,013
Shareholders' equity:		
Common stock	180	180
Additional paid-in capital	21	63
Retained earnings	2,730	2,428
Total shareholders' equity	2,931	2,671
Total liabilities and shareholders' equity	$5,345	$4,684

Some ratios express income, dividends, and market prices on a per share basis. As such, these ratios appeal primarily to common shareholders, particularly when weighing investment possibilities. These ratios focus less on the fundamental soundness of a company and more on its investment characteristics.

Required:

1. Earnings per share expresses a firm's profitability on a per share basis. Calculate 2011 earnings per share for IGF.

2. Calculate IGF's 2011 price-earnings ratio. The average price-earnings ratio for the stocks listed on the New York Stock Exchange in a comparable time period was 18.5. What does your calculation indicate about IGF's earnings?

3. Calculate IGF's 2011 dividend payout ratio. What information does the calculation provide an investor?

Research Case 19–15
Determining and comparing price-earnings ratios; retrieving stock prices and earnings per share numbers from the Internet
● LO13

Many sites on the Internet allow the retrieval of current stock price information. Among those sites are Market-watch (**cbs.marketwatch.com**) and Quicken (**www.quicken.com**).

Required:

1. Access any site on the Internet that permits you to get a current stock quote. Determine the current price of **Microsoft Corporation**'s common stock (MSFT) and that of **Intel Corporation** (INTC).

2. Access EDGAR on the Internet at **www.sec.gov.** Search for Microsoft and access its most recent 10-K filing. Search or scroll to find the income statement and related note(s). Determine the most recent earnings per share. Repeat this step for Intel.

3. Calculate the price-earnings ratio for each company.

4. Compare the PE ratios of Microsoft and Intel. What information might be gleaned from your comparison?

Analysis Case 19–16
Kellogg's EPS; PE ratio; dividend payout
● LO13

Real World Financials

While eating his **Kellogg's** Frosted Flakes one January morning, Tony noticed the following article in his local paper:

Kellogg Announces Strong 2008 Performance

BATTLE CREEK, Mich., Feb. 5, 2009 (Globe Newswire via COMTEX News Network)—Kellogg Company (NYSE:K) today reported strong 2008 sales and earnings growth. Fourth quarter earnings per diluted share grew 7% to $0.47, bringing the 2008 full-year earnings per share to $2.99.

As a shareholder, Tony is well aware that Kellogg pays a regular cash dividend of $.34 per share quarterly. A quick click on a price quote service indicated that Kellogg's shares closed at $43.85 on December 31. That web page also reported Kellogg's previous year's EPS as $2.76.

Required:

1. Using the numbers provided, determine the price/earnings ratio for Kellogg Company for 2008. What information does this ratio impart?

2. What is the dividend payout ratio for Kellogg? What does it indicate?

Research Case 19–17
FASB codification; locate and extract relevant information and cite authoritative support for a financial reporting issue; change in classification of a share-based compensation instrument
● **LO13**

"Now what do I do?" moaned your colleague, Matt. "This is a first for me," he confided. You and Matt are recent hires in the Accounting Division of National Paper. A top executive in the company has been given share-based incentive instruments that permit her to receive shares of National Paper equal in value to the amount the company shares rise above the shares' value two years ago when the instruments were issued to her as compensation. The instruments vest in three years. A clause was included in the compensation agreement that would permit her to receive cash rather than shares upon exercise if sales revenue in her division were to double by that time. Because that contingency was considered unlikely, the instruments have been accounted for as equity, with the grant date fair value being expensed over the five-year vesting period.

Now, though, surging sales of her division indicate that the contingent event has become probable, and the instruments should be accounted for as a liability rather than equity. The fair value of the award was estimated at $5 million on the grant date, but now is $8 million. Matt has asked your help in deciding what to recommend to your controller as the appropriate action to take at this point.

Required:

1. Obtain the relevant authoritative literature on accounting for a change in classification due to a change in probable settlement outcome using the FASB's Codification Research System. You might gain access at the FASB website (**www.fasb.org**). Explain to Matt the basic treatment of the situation described. What is the specific citation that you would rely on in applying that accounting treatment?

2. Prepare the journal entry to record the change in circumstance.

BRITISH AIRWAYS CASE

● **LO14**

British Airways, Plc. (BA), a U.K. company, prepares its financial statements according to International Financial Reporting Standards. BA's annual report for the year ended March 31, 2009, which includes financial statements and disclosure notes, is included with all new textbooks and can be found at **www.britishairways.com**. When answering questions, focus on BA's "Group" financial information (which is equivalent to "Consolidated" under U.S. GAAP).

Required:

What is the amount that BA reports in its income statement for its stock options and other share-based compensation plans for the year ended March 31, 2009? [Hint: See Note 34: "Share options."] Are BA's share options cliff vesting or graded vesting? How does accounting differ between U.S. GAAP and IFRS for graded-vesting plans?

CPA SIMULATION 19–1

Houston County Energy
EPS and Share-Based Compensation

CPA Review

Test your knowledge of the concepts discussed in this chapter, practice critical professional skills necessary for career success, and prepare for the computer-based CPA exam by accessing our CPA simulations at the text website: **www.mhhe.com/spiceland6e**.

The Houston County Energy simulation tests your knowledge of a variety of earnings per share and share-based compensation reporting issues.

As on the CPA exam itself, you will be asked to use tools including a spreadsheet, a calculator, and professional accounting standards, to conduct research, derive solutions, and communicate conclusions related to these issues in a simulated environment.

Specific tasks in the simulation include:

● Calculating basic and diluted earnings per share.
● Applying judgment in deciding the financial reporting implications of the issuance, exercise, and expiration of stock rights and the conversion of preferred shares.
● Demonstrating an understanding of appropriate financial statement reporting of earnings per share.
● Analyzing the financial statement effects of treasury stock transactions.
● Communicating the financial reporting implications of stock options.
● Researching the purpose of and procedures for a quasi-reorganization.

20 Accounting Changes and Error Corrections

| | | | | | | | | | | | | | | | | | | | | | | | | | | | | | | | | | | | | | | | | |

/// **OVERVIEW**

Chapter 4 provided an overview of accounting changes and error correction. Later, we discussed changes encountered in connection with specific assets and liabilities as we dealt with those topics in subsequent chapters.

Here we revisit accounting changes and error correction to synthesize the way these are handled in a variety of situations that might be encountered in practice. We see that most changes in accounting principle are reported retrospectively. Changes in estimates are accounted for prospectively. A change in depreciation methods is considered a change in estimate resulting from a change in principle. Both changes in reporting entities and the correction of errors are reported retrospectively.

/// **LEARNING OBJECTIVES**

After studying this chapter, you should be able to:

- **LO1** Differentiate among the three types of accounting changes and distinguish between the retrospective and prospective approaches to accounting for and reporting accounting changes. (page 1138)

- **LO2** Describe how changes in accounting principle typically are reported. (page 1141)

- **LO3** Explain how and why some changes in accounting principle are reported prospectively. (page 1144)

- **LO4** Explain how and why changes in estimates are reported prospectively. (page 1146)

- **LO5** Describe the situations that constitute a change in reporting entity. (page 1148)

- **LO6** Understand and apply the four-step process of correcting and reporting errors, regardless of the type of error or the timing of its discovery. (page 1152)

- **LO7** Discuss the primary differences between U.S. GAAP and IFRS with respect to accounting changes and error corrections. (pages 1145, 1151, and 1158)

FINANCIAL REPORTING CASE

In a Jam

"What the heck!" Martin yelped as he handed you the annual report of **J.M. Smucker** he'd received in the mail today. "It looks like Smucker found a bunch of lost jelly. It says here that their inventory was $54 million last year. I distinctly remember them reporting that number last year as $52 million because my dad was born in '52, and I did a little wordplay in my mind about him 'taking inventory' of his life when he bought the red Mustang." He had circled the number in the comparative balance sheets. "When I bought Smucker shares last year, I promised myself I would monitor things pretty closely, but it's not as easy as I thought it would be."

As an accounting graduate, you can understand Martin's confusion. Flipping to the footnote on accounting changes, you proceed to clear things up for him.

By the time you finish this chapter, you should be able to respond appropriately to the questions posed in this case. Compare your response to the solution provided at the end of the chapter.

QUESTIONS ///

1. How can an accounting change cause a company to increase a previously reported inventory amount? (page 1141)

2. Are all accounting changes reported this way? (page 1147)

You learned early in your study of accounting that two of the qualitative characteristics of accounting information that contribute to its relevance and reliability are *consistency* and *comparability*. Though we strive to achieve and maintain these financial reporting attributes, we cannot ignore the forces of change. Ours is a dynamic business environment. The economy is increasingly a global one. Technological advances constantly transform both day-to-day operations and the flow of information about those operations. The accounting profession's response to the fluid environment often means issuing new standards that require companies to change accounting methods. Often, developments within an industry or the economy will prompt a company to voluntarily switch methods of accounting or to revise estimates or expectations. In short, change is inevitable. The question then becomes a matter of how best to address change when reporting financial information from year to year.

In the first part of this chapter, we differentiate among the various types of accounting changes that businesses face, with a focus on the most meaningful and least disruptive ways to report those changes. Then, in the second part of the chapter, we direct our attention to a closely related circumstance—the correction of errors.

PART A

ACCOUNTING CHANGES

Accounting changes fall into one of the three categories listed in Graphic 20–1.[1]

GRAPHIC 20–1

Types of Accounting Changes

● LO1

Type of Change	Description	Examples
Change in accounting principle	Change from one generally accepted accounting principle to another.	• Adopt a new FASB standard. • Change methods of inventory costing. • Change from cost method to equity method, or vice versa. • Change from completed contract to percentage-of-completion, or vice versa.
Change in accounting estimate	Revision of an estimate because of new information or new experience.	• Change depreciation methods.* • Change estimate of useful life of depreciable asset. • Change estimate of residual value of depreciable asset. • Change estimate of bad debt percentage. • Change estimate of periods benefited by intangible assets. • Change actuarial estimates pertaining to a pension plan.
Change in reporting entity	Change from reporting as one type of entity to another type of entity.	• Consolidate a subsidiary not previously included in consolidated financial statements. • Report consolidated financial statements in place of individual statements.

*A change in depreciation methods is a change in estimate that is achieved by a change in accounting principle.

The correction of an error is another adjustment sometimes made to financial statements that is not actually an accounting change but is accounted for similarly. Errors occur when transactions are either recorded incorrectly or not recorded at all as shown in Graphic 20–2.

GRAPHIC 20–2

Correction of Errors

Type of Change	Description	Examples
Error correction	Correction of an error caused by a transaction being recorded incorrectly or not at all.	• Mathematical mistakes. • Inaccurate physical count of inventory. • Change from the cash basis of accounting to the accrual basis. • Failure to record an adjusting entry. • Recording an asset as an expense, or vice versa. • Fraud or gross negligence.

Two approaches to reporting accounting changes and error corrections are used, depending on the situation.

The retrospective approach offers consistency and comparability.

1. Using the **retrospective approach,** financial statements issued in previous years are revised to reflect the impact of the change whenever those statements are presented again for comparative purposes. An advantage of this approach is that it achieves

[1]FASB ASC 250: Accounting Changes and Error Corrections (previously "Accounting Changes and Error Corrections—A Replacement of APB Opinion No. 20 and FASB Statement No. 3," *Statement of Financial Accounting Standards No. 154,* (Norwalk, Conn: FASB, 2005)).

comparability among financial statements. All financial statements presented are prepared on the same basis. However, some argue that public confidence in the integrity of financial data suffers when numbers previously reported as correct are later superseded. On the other hand, proponents argue the opposite—that it's impossible to maintain public confidence unless the financial statements are comparable.

For each year reported in the comparative statements reported, the balance of each account affected is revised. In other words, those statements are made to appear as if the newly adopted accounting method had been applied all along or that the error had never occurred. Then, a journal entry is created to adjust all account balances affected to what those amounts would have been. In addition, if retained earnings is one of the accounts that requires adjustment, that adjustment is made to the beginning balance of retained earnings for the earliest period reported in the comparative statements of shareholders' equity.

2. The **prospective approach** requires neither a modification of prior years' financial statements nor a journal entry to adjust account balances. Instead, the change is simply implemented now, and its effects are reflected in the financial statements of the current and future years only.

The effects of a change are reflected in the financial statements of only the current and future years under the prospective approach.

Now, let's look at each type of accounting change, one at a time, focusing on the selective application of these approaches.

Change in Accounting Principle

Accounting is not an exact science. Professional judgment is required to apply a set of principles, concepts, and objectives to specific sets of circumstances. This means choices must be made. In your study of accounting to date, you've encountered many areas where choices are necessary. For example, management must choose whether to use accelerated or straight-line depreciation. Is FIFO, LIFO, or average cost most appropriate to measure inventories? Would the completed contract or percentage-of-completion method best reflect the performance of our construction operations? Should we adopt a new FASB pronouncement early or wait until it's mandatory? These are but a few of the accounting choices management makes.

You also probably recall that consistency and comparability are two fundamental qualitative characteristics of accounting information. To achieve these attributes of information, accounting choices, once made, should be consistently followed from year to year. This doesn't mean, though, that methods can never be changed. Changing circumstances might make a new method more appropriate. A change in economic conditions, for instance, might prompt a company to change accounting methods. The most extensive voluntary accounting change ever—a switch by hundreds of companies from FIFO to LIFO in the mid-1970s, for example—was a result of heightened inflation. Changes within a specific industry, too, can lead a company to switch methods, often to adapt to new technology or to be consistent with others in the industry. And, of course, a change might be mandated when the FASB issues a new accounting standard. For these reasons, it's not uncommon for a company to switch from one accounting method to another. This is called a **change in accounting principle.**

Although consistency and comparability are desirable, changing to a new method sometimes is appropriate.

DECISION MAKERS' PERSPECTIVE—Motivation for Accounting Choices

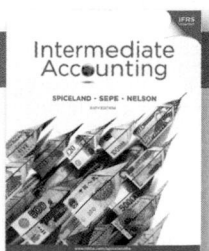

It would be nice to think that all accounting choices are made by management in the best interest of fair and consistent financial reporting. Unfortunately, other motives influence the choices among accounting methods and whether to change methods. It has been suggested that the effect of choices on management compensation, on existing debt agreements, and on union negotiations each can affect management's selection of accounting methods.[2] For

---

[2]R. L. Watts and J. L. Zimmerman, "Towards a Positive Theory of the Determination of Accounting Standards," *The Accounting Review,* January 1978, and "Positive Accounting Theory: A Ten Year Perspective," *The Accounting Review,* January 1990.

instance, research has suggested that managers of companies with bonus plans are more likely to choose accounting methods that maximize their bonuses (often those that increase net income).[3] Other research has indicated that the existence and nature of debt agreements and other aspects of a firm's capital structure can influence accounting choices.[4] Whether a company is forbidden from paying dividends if retained earnings fall below a certain level, for example, can affect the choice of accounting methods.

A financial analyst must be aware that different accounting methods used by different firms and by the same firm in different years complicate comparisons. Financial ratios, for example, will differ when different accounting methods are used, even when there are no differences in attributes being compared.

Investors and creditors also should be alert to instances in which companies change accounting methods. They must consider not only the effect on comparability but also possible hidden motivations for making the changes. Are managers trying to compensate for a downturn in actual performance with a switch to methods that artificially inflate reported earnings? Is the firm in danger of violating debt covenants or other contractual agreements regarding financial position? Are executive compensation plans tied to reported performance measures? Fortunately, the nature and effect of changes are reported in the financial statements. Although a justification for a change is provided by management, analysts should be wary of accepting the reported justification at face value without considering a possible hidden agenda.

Choices are not always those that tend to increase income. As you learned in Chapter 8, many companies use the LIFO inventory method because it reduces income and therefore reduces the amount of income taxes that must be paid currently. Also, some very large and visible companies might be reluctant to report high income that might render them vulnerable to union demands, government regulations, or higher taxes.[5]

Another reason managers sometimes choose accounting methods that don't necessarily increase earnings was mentioned earlier. Most managers tend to prefer to report earnings that follow a regular, smooth trend from year to year. The desire to "smooth" earnings means that any attempt to manipulate earnings by choosing accounting methods is not always in the direction of higher income. Instead, the choice might be to avoid irregular earnings, particularly those with wide variations from year to year, a pattern that might be interpreted by analysts as denoting a risky situation.

Obviously, any time managers make accounting choices for any of the reasons discussed here, when the motivation is an objective other than to provide useful information, earnings quality suffers. As mentioned frequently throughout this text, earnings quality refers to the ability of reported earnings (income) to predict a company's future earnings.

A notable example of alleged "cooking the books" involved **General Electric**. The company was often suspected of using "cookie jar accounting," the practice of using unrealistic estimates and strategic choices of accounting methods to smooth out its earnings. In 2009 GE appeared to get its hand caught in the cookie jar for going beyond acceptable limits. GE paid a $50 million civil penalty to settle charges by the Securities and Exchange Commission accusing the company of violating U.S. securities laws four times between 2002 and 2003 to help it maintain a succession of earnings reports that beat Wall Street expectations each quarter from 1995 through 2004.

Let's turn our attention now to situations involving changes in methods and how we account for those changes. ●

---

[3]For example, see P. M. Healy, "The Effect of Bonus Schemes on Accounting Decisions," *Journal of Accounting and Economics,* April 1985, and D. Dhaliwal, G. Salamon, and E. Smith, "The Effect of Owner versus Management Control on the Choice of Accounting Methods," *Journal of Accounting and Economics,* July 1992.

[4]R. M. Bowen, E. W. Noreen, and J. M. Lacy, "Determinants of the Corporate Decision to Capitalize Interest," *Journal of Accounting and Economics,* August 1981.

[5]This political cost motive is suggested by R. L. Watts and J. L. Zimmerman, "Positive Accounting Theory: A Ten Year Perspective," *The Accounting Review,* January 1990, and M. Zmijewski and R. Hagerman, "An Income Strategy Approach to the Positive Theory of Accounting Standard Setting/Choice," *Journal of Accounting and Economics,* August 1981.

The Retrospective Approach: Most Changes in Accounting Principle

We report most voluntary changes in accounting principles retrospectively.[6] This means reporting all previous period's financial statements as if the new method had been used in all prior periods. An example is provided in Illustration 20–1.

● LO2

	2011	2010	2009	Previous Years
Cost of goods sold (LIFO)	$430	$420	$405	$2,000
Cost of goods sold (FIFO)	370	365	360	1,700
Difference	$ 60	$ 55	$ 45	$ 300
Revenues	$950	$900	$875	$4,500
Operating expenses	230	210	205	1,000

Air Parts Corporation used the LIFO inventory costing method. At the beginning of 2011, Air Parts decided to change to the FIFO method. Income components for 2011 and prior years were as follows ($ in millions):

Air Parts has paid dividends of $40 million each year beginning in 2004. Its income tax rate is 40%. Retained earnings on January 1, 2009, was $700 million; inventory was $500 million.

ILLUSTRATION 20–1
Change in Accounting Principle

LIFO usually produces higher cost of goods sold than does FIFO because more recently purchased goods (usually higher priced) are assumed sold first.

1. REVISE COMPARATIVE FINANCIAL STATEMENTS. For each year reported in the comparative statements, Air Parts makes those statements appear as if the newly adopted accounting method (FIFO) had been applied all along. As you learned in Chapter 1, consistency is one of the important qualitative characteristics of accounting information.

When accounting changes occur, the usefulness of the comparative financial statements is enhanced with retrospective application of those changes.

FINANCIAL Reporting Case

Q1, p. 1137

Income statements.

($ in millions)	2011	2010	2009
Revenues	$950	$900	$875
Cost of goods sold (FIFO)	(370)	(365)	(360)
Operating expenses	(230)	(210)	(205)
Income before tax	$350	$325	$310
Income tax expense (40%)	(140)	(130)	(124)
Net income	$210	$195	$186

The company recasts the comparative statements to appear as if the accounting method adopted in 2011 (FIFO) had been used in 2010 and 2009 as well.

Earnings per share each year, of course, also will be based on the revised net income numbers.

Balance sheets.

Inventory. In its comparative balance sheets, Air Parts will report 2011 inventory by its newly adopted method, FIFO, and also will revise the amounts it reported last year for its 2010 and 2009 inventory. Each year, inventory will be higher than it would have been by LIFO. Here's why:

Since the cost of goods *available for sale* each period is the sum of the cost of goods *sold* and the cost of goods *unsold* (inventory), a difference in cost of goods sold resulting from having used LIFO rather than FIFO means there also is an opposite difference in inventory. Because cost of goods sold by the FIFO method is *less* than by LIFO, inventory by FIFO is

FIFO usually produces *lower* cost of goods sold and thus *higher* inventory than does LIFO.

[6]FASB ASC 250–10–45: Accounting Changes and Error Corrections–Overall–Other Presentation Matters (previously "Accounting Changes and Error Corrections—A Replacement of APB Opinion No. 20 and FASB Statement No. 3," *Statement of Financial Accounting Standards No. 154,* (Norwalk, Conn: FASB, 2005)).

greater than by LIFO. The amounts of the differences and also the cumulative differences over the years are calculated in Illustration 20–1A.

	Years Ending Dec. 31:			
($ in millions)	**2011**	**2010**	**2009**	**Previous Years**
Cost of goods sold (LIFO)	$430	$420	$405	$2,000
Cost of goods sold (FIFO)	370	365	360	1,700
Differences	$ 60	$ 55	$ 45	$ 300
Cumulative differences:				
Cost of goods sold	$460	$400	$345	$ 300
Income taxes (40%)	184	160	138	120
Net income and retained earnings	$276	$240	$207	$ 180

ILLUSTRATION 20–1A

Effects of Switch to FIFO

By FIFO, cost of goods sold is lower.

The cumulative income effect increases each year by the annual after-tax difference in COGS.

Inventory, pretax income, income taxes, net income, and retained earnings all are higher.

Comparative balance sheets, then, will report 2009 inventory $345 million higher than it was reported in last year's statements. Likewise, 2010 inventory will be increased by $400 million. Inventory for 2011, being reported for the first time without restatement, is $460 million higher than it would have been if the switch from LIFO had not occurred.

When costs are rising, FIFO produces *lower* cost of goods sold than does LIFO and thus *higher* net income and retained earnings.

Retained earnings is revised each year to reflect FIFO.

Retained earnings.   Similarly, Air Parts will report retained earnings by FIFO each year as well. Retained earnings is different because the two inventory methods affect income differently. Because cost of goods sold by FIFO is *less* than by LIFO, income and therefore retained earnings by FIFO are *greater* than by LIFO.

Comparative balance sheets, then, will report retained earnings for 2011, 2010, and 2009 at amounts $276, $240, and $207 million higher than would have been reported if the switch from LIFO had not occurred. These are the cumulative net income differences shown in Illustration 20–1A.

Statements of shareholders' equity.

Recall that a statement of shareholders' equity reports changes that occur in each shareholders' equity account starting with the beginning balances in the earliest year reported.

Because it's the earliest year reported, 2009's beginning retained earnings is increased by the **$180** million cumulative income effect of the difference in inventory methods that occurred before 2009.

So, if retained earnings is one of the accounts whose balance requires adjustment due to a change in accounting principle (and it usually is), we must adjust the beginning balance of retained earnings for the earliest period reported in the comparative statements of shareholders' equity. The amount of the revision is the cumulative effect of the change on years prior to that date. Air Parts will revise its 2009 beginning retained earnings since that's the earliest year in its comparative statements. That balance had been reported in prior statements as $700 million. If FIFO had been used for inventory rather than LIFO, that amount would have been higher by **$180** million as calculated in Illustration 20–1A. The disclosure note pertaining to the inventory change should point out the amount of the adjustment. The January 1, 2009, retained earnings balance reported in the comparative statements of shareholders' equity below has been adjusted from $700 million to **$880** million.

ILLUSTRATION 20–1B

Comparative Statements of Shareholders' Equity

A footnote should indicate that the beginning retained earnings balance has been increased by **$180** million from $700 million to **$880** million.

($ in millions)	Common Stock	Additional Paid-In Capital	Retained Earnings	Total Shareholders' Equity
Jan. 1, 2009			$ 880	
Net income (revised to FIFO)			186	
Dividends			(40)	
Dec. 31, 2009			$1,026	
Net income (revised to FIFO)			195	
Dividends			(40)	
Dec. 31, 2010			$1,181	
Net income (using FIFO)			210	
Dividends			(40)	
Dec. 31, 2011			$1,351	

2. ADJUST ACCOUNTS FOR THE CHANGE.   Besides reporting revised amounts in the comparative financial statements, Air Parts must also adjust the book balances of affected accounts. It does so by creating a journal entry to change those balances from their current amounts (from using LIFO) to what those balances would have been using the newly adopted method (FIFO). As discussed in the previous section, differences in cost of goods sold and income are reflected in retained earnings, as are the income tax effects of changes in income. So, the journal entry updates inventory, retained earnings, and the income tax liability for revisions resulting from differences in the LIFO and FIFO methods prior to the switch, pre-2011. Repeating a portion of the calculation we made in Illustration 20–1A, we determine the difference in cost of goods sold and therefore in inventory.

	($ in millions)			
	2010	**2009**	**Cumulative Difference pre-2009**	**Cumulative Difference pre-2011**
Cost of goods sold (LIFO)	$420	$405	$2,000	
Cost of goods sold (FIFO)	365	360	1,700	
Difference	$ 55	$ 45	$ 300	$400

Cost of goods sold would have been **$400** million *less* if FIFO rather than LIFO had been used in years before the change.

The $400 million cumulative difference in cost of goods sold also is the difference between the balance in inventory and what that balance would have been if the FIFO method, rather than LIFO, had been used before 2011. Inventory must be increased by that amount. Retained earnings must be increased also, but by only 60% of that amount because income taxes would have been higher by 40% of the change in pretax income.

Journal entry to record the change in principle.		
January 1, 2011		
Inventory (additional inventory if FIFO had been used)	400	
Retained earnings (additional net income if FIFO had been used)		240
Income tax payable ($400 × 40%)		160

Inventory would have been **$400** million more and cumulative prior earnings $240 more if FIFO rather than LIFO had been used.

Notice that the income tax effect is reflected in the income tax payable account. The reason is that an accounting method used for tax purposes cannot be changed retrospectively for prior years. The Internal Revenue Code requires that taxes saved previously ($160 million in this case) from having used another inventory method must now be repaid (over no longer than six years). As a result, this liability has both current (portion payable within one year) and noncurrent (payable after one year), but is not a deferred tax liability.

ADDITIONAL CONSIDERATION

What if the tax law did not require a recapture of the tax difference? Then there would be a credit to a deferred tax liability. That's because retrospectively increasing accounting income, but not taxable income, creates a temporary difference between the two that will reverse over time as the unsold inventory becomes cost of goods sold. Recall from Chapter 16 that in the meantime, there is a temporary difference, reflected in the deferred tax liability.

If we were switching from FIFO to, say, the average method, we would record a deferred tax asset instead. For financial reporting purposes, but not for tax, we would be retrospectively decreasing accounting income, but not taxable income. This creates a temporary difference between the two that will reverse over time as the unsold inventory becomes cost of goods sold. When that happens, taxable income will be less than accounting income. When taxable income will be less than accounting income as a temporary difference reverses, we have a "future deductible amount" and record a deferred tax asset.

Footnote disclosure explains why the change was needed as well as its effects on items not reported on the face of the primary statements.

3. DISCLOSURE NOTES.   To achieve consistency and comparability, accounting choices once made should be consistently followed from year to year. Any change, then, requires that the new method be justified as clearly more appropriate. In the first set of financial statements after the change, a disclosure note is needed to provide that justification. The note also should point out that comparative information has been revised, or that retrospective revision has not been made because it is impracticable, and report any per share amounts affected for the current period and all prior periods presented. Disclosure of a recent change by **IDEX Corporation** in its June 30, 2009 quarterly report provides us the example shown in Graphic 20–3.

GRAPHIC 20–3

Disclosure of a Change in Inventory Method— IDEX Corporation

Real World Financials

5. Inventories

Inventories are stated at the lower of cost or market. Cost, which includes material, labor, and factory overhead, is determined on a FIFO basis. Prior to 2009, we valued certain inventories under the LIFO cost method. As of January 1, 2009, we changed our method of accounting for these inventories from the LIFO method to the FIFO method. As of December 31, 2008, the inventories for which the LIFO method of accounting was applied represented approximately 85% of total net inventories. We believe that this change is to a preferable method which better reflects the current cost of inventory on our consolidated balance sheets. Additionally, this change conforms all of our worldwide inventories to a consistent inventory costing method and provides better comparability to our peers. We applied this change in accounting principle retrospectively to all prior periods presented herein in accordance with SFAS No. 154, "Accounting Changes and Error Corrections." [FASB ASC 250–10–45] As a result of this accounting change, our retained earnings as of January 1, 2009, decreased to $822.3 million using the FIFO method from $845.4 million as originally reported using the LIFO method. The following tables summarize the effect of the accounting change on our consolidated financial statements.

The Prospective Approach

Although we usually report voluntary changes in accounting principles retrospectively, it's not always practicable or appropriate to do so.

● LO3

Sometimes a lack of information makes it impracticable to report a change retrospectively so the new method is simply applied prospectively.

THE PROSPECTIVE APPROACH: WHEN RETROSPECTIVE APPLICATION IS IMPRACTICABLE.   For some changes in principle, insufficient information is available for retrospective application to be practicable. Revising balances in prior years means knowing what those balances should be. But suppose we're switching from the FIFO method of inventory costing to the LIFO method. Recall from your study of inventory costing methods that LIFO inventory consists of "layers" added in prior years at costs existing in those years. If another method has been used, though, the company likely hasn't kept track of those costs. So, accounting records of prior years usually are inadequate to report the change retrospectively. In that case, a company changing *to* LIFO usually reports the change prospectively, and the beginning inventory in the year the LIFO method is adopted becomes the base year inventory for all future LIFO calculations. Footnote disclosure should indicate reasons why retrospective application was impracticable. Prospective changes usually are accounted for as of the beginning of the year of change.

When **Books A Million, Inc.**, adopted the LIFO cost flow assumption for valuing its inventories, the change was reported in a disclosure note as shown in Graphic 20–4.

If it's impracticable to adjust each year reported, the change is applied retrospectively as of the earliest year practicable.

When it is impracticable to determine some period-specific effects.   A company may have some, but not all, the information it needs to account for a change retrospectively. For instance, let's say a company changes to the LIFO inventory method effective as of the beginning of 2011. It has information that would allow it to revise all assets and liabilities on the basis of the newly adopted method for 2010 in its comparative statements, but not for 2009. In that case, the company should report 2010 statement amounts (revised) and

2011 statement amounts (reported without restatement for the first time) based on LIFO, but not revise 2009 numbers. Then, account balances should be retrospectively adjusted at the beginning of 2010 since that's the earliest date it's practicable to do so.

> **Inventories (in part)**
>
> . . . the Company changed from the first-in, first-out (FIFO) method of accounting for inventories to the last-in, first-out (LIFO) method. Management believes this change was preferable in that it achieves a more appropriate matching of revenues and expenses. The impact of this accounting change was to increase "Costs of Products Sold" in the consolidated statements of operations by $0.7 million for the fiscal year. . . . The cumulative effect of a change in accounting principle from the FIFO method to LIFO method is not determinable. Accordingly, such change has been accounted for prospectively.

When it is impracticable to determine the cumulative effect of prior years. Another possibility is that the company doesn't have the information necessary to retrospectively adjust retained earnings, but does have information that would allow it to revise all assets and liabilities for one or more specific years. Let's say the records of inventory purchases and sales are not available for some previous years, which would have allowed it to determine the cumulative effect of applying this change to LIFO retrospectively. However, it does have all of the information necessary to apply the LIFO method on a prospective basis beginning in, say, 2009. In that case, the company should report numbers for years beginning in 2009 as if it had carried forward the 2008 ending balance in inventory (measured on the previous inventory costing basis) and then had begun applying LIFO as of January 1, 2009. Of course there would be no adjustment to retained earnings for the cumulative income effect of not using LIFO prior to that.

> If full retrospective application isn't possible, the new method is applied prospectively beginning in the earliest year practicable.

THE PROSPECTIVE APPROACH: WHEN MANDATED BY AUTHORITATIVE PRONOUNCEMENTS. Another exception to retrospective application of voluntary changes in accounting principle is when authoritative literature requires prospective application for specific changes in accounting methods. For instance, for a change from the equity method to another method of accounting for long-term investments, GAAP requires the prospective application of the new method.[7] Recall from Chapter 12 that when an investor's level of influence changes, it may be necessary to change from the equity method to another method. This could happen, for instance, if a sale of shares causes the investor's ownership interest to fall from, say, 25% to 15%, resulting in the equity method no longer being appropriate. When this situation happens, no adjustment is made to the remaining carrying amount of the investment. Instead, the equity method is simply discontinued and the new method applied from then on. The balance in the investment account when the equity method is discontinued would serve as the new "cost" basis for writing the investment up or down to fair value on the next set of financial statements.

> If an authoritative pronouncement specifically requires prospective accounting, that requirement is followed.

INTERNATIONAL FINANCIAL REPORTING STANDARDS

The changes to and from the LIFO method we've discussed would not occur if International standards were being applied. Why? Remember from Chapter 7 that LIFO is not a permissible method for accounting for inventory under IFRS.

● LO7

---

[7]FASB ACS 323–10–35–35: Investments–Equity Method and Joint Ventures–Overall–Subsequent Measurement–Decrease in Level of Ownership or Degree of Influence (previously "The Equity Method of Accounting for Investments in Common Stock," *Accounting Principles Board Opinion No. 18* (New York: AICPA, 1971)).

THE PROSPECTIVE APPROACH: CHANGING DEPRECIATION, AMORTIZATION, AND DEPLETION METHODS.   A change in depreciation methods is considered to be a change in accounting estimate that is achieved by a change in accounting principle. As a result, we account for such a change prospectively—precisely the way we account for changes in estimates. We discuss that approach in the next section.

Change in Accounting Estimate

● LO4

You've encountered many instances during your study of accounting in which it's necessary to make estimates of uncertain future events. Depreciation, for example, entails estimates not only of the useful lives of depreciable assets, but their anticipated residual values as well. Anticipating uncollectible accounts receivable, predicting warranty expenses, amortizing intangible assets, and making actuarial assumptions for pension benefits are but a few of the accounting tasks that require estimates.

Revisions are viewed as a natural consequence of making estimates.

Accordingly, estimates are an inherent aspect of accounting. Unfortunately, though, estimates routinely turn out to be wrong. No matter how carefully known facts are considered and forecasts are prepared, new information and experience frequently force the revision of estimates. Of course, if the original estimate was based on erroneous information or calculations or was not made in good faith, the revision of that estimate constitutes the correction of an error.

A change in estimate is reflected in the financial statements of the current period and future periods.

Changes in accounting estimates are accounted for prospectively. When a company revises a previous estimate, prior financial statements are *not* revised. Instead, the company merely incorporates the new estimate in any related accounting determinations from then on. So, it usually will affect some aspects of both the balance sheet and the income statement in the current period and future periods. A disclosure note should describe the effect of a change in estimate on income before extraordinary items, net income, and related per share amounts for the current period.

When **Owens-Corning Fiberglass** revised estimates of the useful lives of some of its depreciable assets, the change was disclosed in its annual report as shown in Graphic 20–5.

GRAPHIC 20–5

Change in Estimate— Owens-Corning Fiberglass Corporation

Real World Financials

> **Note 6: Depreciation of Plant and Equipment (in part)**
>
> . . . the Company completed a review of its fixed asset lives. The Company determined that as a result of actions taken to increase its preventative maintenance and programs initiated with its equipment suppliers to increase the quality of their products, actual lives for certain asset categories were generally longer than the useful lives for depreciation purposes. Therefore, the Company extended the estimated useful lives of certain categories of plant and equipment, effective . . . The effect of this change in estimate reduced depreciation expense for the year ended . . ., by $14 million and increased income before cumulative effect of accounting change by $8 million ($.19 per share).

An example of another change in estimate is provided in Illustration 20–2.

ILLUSTRATION 20–2

Change in Accounting Estimate

> Universal Semiconductors estimates bad debt expense as 2% of credit sales. After a review during 2011, Universal determined that 3% of credit sales is a more realistic estimate of its collection experience. Credit sales in 2011 are $300 million. The effective income tax rate is 40%.
>
> Neither bad debt expense nor the allowance for uncollectible accounts reported in prior years is restated. No account balances are adjusted. The cumulative effect of the estimate change is not reported in current income. Rather, in 2011 and later years, the adjusting entry to record bad debt expense simply will reflect the new percentage. In 2011, the entry would be:
>
> ($ in millions)
>
> Bad debt expense (3% × $300 million)   9
>   Allowance for uncollectible accounts   9

The after-tax effect of the change in estimate is $1.8 million [$300 million $\times$ (3% − 2%) = $3 million, less 40% of $3 million]. Assuming 100 million outstanding shares of common stock, the effect is described in a disclosure note to the financial statements as follows:

Note A: Accounts Receivable

In 2011, the company revised the percentage used to estimate bad debts. The change provides a better indication of collection experience. The effect of the change was to decrease 2011 net income by $1.8 million, or $.018 per share.

Changing Depreciation, Amortization, and Depletion Methods

When a company acquires an asset that will provide benefits for several years, it allocates the cost of the asset over the asset's useful life. If the asset is a building, equipment, or other tangible asset, the allocation process is called *depreciation*. It's referred to as *amortization* if an intangible asset or *depletion* if a natural resource. In each case, estimates are essential to the allocation process. How long will benefits accrue? What will be the value of the asset when its use is discontinued? Will the benefits be realized evenly over the asset's life or will they be higher in some years than in others?

The choice of depreciation method and application reflects these estimates. Likewise, when a company changes the way it depreciates an asset in midstream, the change would be made to reflect a change in (a) estimated future benefits from the asset, (b) the pattern of receiving those benefits, or (c) the company's knowledge about those benefits. For instance, suppose Universal Semiconductors originally chose an accelerated depreciation method because it expected greater benefits in the earlier years of an asset's life. Then, two years later, when it became apparent that remaining benefits would be realized approximately evenly over the remaining useful life, Universal Semiconductor switched to straight-line depreciation. Even though the company is changing its depreciation method, it is doing so to reflect changes in its estimates of future benefits. As a result, we report a change in depreciation method as a change in estimate, rather than as a change in accounting principle.

For this reason, a company reports a change in depreciation method (say to straight-line) prospectively; previous financial statements are not revised. Instead, the company simply employs the straight-line method from then on. The undepreciated cost remaining at the time of the change would be depreciated straight-line over the remaining useful life. Illustration 20–3 on the next page provides an example.

Is a change in depreciation method a change in accounting principle, or is it a change in estimate? As we've seen, it's both. Even though it's considered to reflect a change in estimate and is accounted for as such, a change to a new depreciation method requires the company to justify the new method as being preferable to the previous method, just as for any other change in principle. A disclosure note should justify that the change is preferable and describe the effect of a change on any financial statement line items and per share amounts affected for all periods reported.

In practice, the situation arises infrequently. Most companies changing depreciation methods do not apply the change to existing assets, but instead to assets placed in service after that date. In those cases, of course, the new method is simply applied prospectively (see Graphic 20–6).

Note 12: Land, Buildings, and Equipment, Net (in part)

. . . the company changed its method of depreciation for newly acquired buildings and equipment to the straight-line method. The change had no cumulative effect on prior years' earnings but did increase [current year] net earnings by $9 million, or $.14 per share . . .

FINANCIAL Reporting Case

Q2, p. 1137

An exception to retrospective application of a change in accounting principle is a change in the method of depreciation (or amortization or depletion).

Companies report a change in depreciation prospectively.

A company must justify any change in principle as preferable to the previous method.

GRAPHIC 20–6

Change in Depreciation Method for Newly Acquired Assets—Rohm and Haas Company

Real World Financials

ILLUSTRATION 20–3
Change in depreciation methods

Universal Semiconductors switched from the SYD depreciation method to straight-line depreciation in 2011. The change affects its precision equipment purchased at the beginning of 2009 at a cost of $63 million. The machinery has an expected useful life of five years and an estimated residual value of $3 million.

The depreciation prior to the change is as follows ($ in millions):

Sum-of-the-Years'-Digits Depreciation:

2009 depreciation	$20 ($60 × 5/15)
2010 depreciation	16 ($60 × 4/15)
Accumulated depreciation	$36

A change in depreciation method is considered a change in accounting estimate resulting from a change in accounting principle. So, Universal Semiconductors reports the change prospectively; previous financial statements are not revised. Instead, the company simply employs the straight-line method from 2011 on. The undepreciated cost remaining at the time of the change is depreciated straight-line over the remaining useful life.

The $24 million depreciable cost not yet depreciated is spread over the asset's remaining three years.

Calculation of Straight-Line Depreciation:	($ in millions)
Asset's cost	$63
Accumulated depreciation to date (calculated above)	(36)
Undepreciated cost, Jan. 1, 2011	$27
Estimated residual value	(3)
To be depreciated over remaining 3 years	$24
	÷ 3 years
Annual straight-line depreciation 2011–2013	$ 8

Adjusting entry (2011, 2012, and 2013 depreciation):	($ in millions)	
Depreciation expense (calculated above)	8	
Accumulated depreciation		8

When it's not possible to distinguish between a change in principle and a change in estimate, the change should be treated as a change in estimate.

Sometimes, it's not easy to distinguish between a change in principle and a change in estimate. For example, if a company begins to capitalize rather than expense the cost of tools because their benefits beyond one year become apparent, the change could be construed as either a change in principle or a change in the estimated life of the asset. When the distinction is not possible, the change should be treated as a change in estimate. This treatment also is appropriate when both a change in principle and a change in estimate occur simultaneously.

Change in Reporting Entity

● LO5

A reporting entity can be a single company, or it can be a group of companies that reports a single set of financial statements. For example, the consolidated financial statements of **PepsiCo Inc.** report the financial position and results of operations not only for the parent company but also for its subsidiaries which include **Frito-Lay** and **Gatorade**. A change in reporting entity occurs as a result of (1) presenting consolidated financial statements in place of statements of individual companies or (2) changing specific companies that constitute the group for which consolidated or combined statements are prepared.[8]

Some changes in reporting entity are a result of changes in accounting rules. For example, companies like **Ford**, **General Motors**, and **General Electric** must consolidate their manufacturing operations with their financial subsidiaries, creating a new entity that includes them both.[9] For those changes in entity, the prior-period financial statements that are presented for comparative purposes must be restated to appear as if the new entity existed in those periods.

However, the more frequent change in entity occurs when one company acquires another one. In those circumstances, the financial statements of the acquirer include the acquiree

---

[8]FASB ASC 810: Consolidation and 840: Leases (previously "Consolidation of All Majority-Owned Subsidiaries," *Statement of Financial Accounting Standards No. 94* (Stamford, Conn.: FASB, 1987)).

[9]The issuance of *SFAS No. 94*, "Consolidation of All Majority-Owned Subsidiaries," [FASB ASC 810: Consolidation and 840: Leases] resulted in hundreds of entities consolidating previously unconsolidated finance subsidiaries.

as of the date of acquisition, and the acquirer's prior-period financial statements that are presented for comparative purposes are not restated. This makes it difficult to make year-to-year comparisons for a company that frequently acquires other companies. Acquiring companies are required to provide a footnote that presents key financial statement information as if the acquisition had occurred before the beginning of the previous year. At a minimum, the supplemental pro forma information should display revenue, income before extraordinary items, net income, and earnings per share.

A change in reporting entity is reported by recasting all previous periods' financial statements as if the new reporting entity existed in those periods.[10] In the first set of financial statements after the change, a disclosure note should describe the nature of the change and the reason it occurred. Also, the effect of the change on net income, income before extraordinary items, and related per share amounts should be indicated for all periods presented. These disclosures aren't necessary in subsequent financial statements. **Hartford Life Insurance Company**, a financial services company, changed the composition of its reporting entity and described it this way:

> ### 1. Basis of Presentation and Accounting Policies (in part)
> Effective March 31, 2009, Hartford Life changed its reporting entity structure to contribute certain wholly owned subsidiaries, including Hartford Life's European insurance operations, several broker dealer entities and investment advisory and service entities from Hartford Life and Accident to the Company. The contribution of subsidiaries was effected to more closely align servicing entities with the writing company issuing the business they service as well as to more efficiently deploy capital across the organization. The change in reporting entity was retrospectively applied to the financial statements of the Company for all periods presented. The contributed subsidiaries resulted in an increase in stockholder's equity of approximately $1.3 billion as of March 31, 2009.

A change in reporting entity requires that financial statements of prior periods be retrospectively revised to report the financial information for the new reporting entity in all periods.

GRAPHIC 20–7

Change in Reporting Entity—Hartford Life Insurance

Real World Financials

Error Correction

The correction of an error is not actually an accounting change but is accounted for similarly. In fact, it's accounted for retrospectively like a change in reporting entity and like most changes in accounting principle.

More specifically, previous years' financial statements that were incorrect as a result of the error are retrospectively restated to reflect the correction. And, of course, any account balances that are incorrect as a result of the error are corrected by a journal entry. If retained earnings is one of the incorrect accounts, the correction is reported as a prior period adjustment to the beginning balance in a statement of shareholders' equity (or statement of retained earnings if that's presented instead).[11] And, as for accounting changes, a disclosure note is needed to describe the nature of the error and the impact of its correction on operations. We discuss the correction of errors in more detail in Part B of this chapter. But first, let's compare the two approaches for reporting accounting changes and error corrections (Graphic 20–8).

Previous years' financial statements are retrospectively restated to reflect the correction of an error.

GRAPHIC 20–8

Approaches to Reporting Accounting Changes and Error Corrections

Previous Years	Current Year	Later Years

◄─────────────── Retrospective: ────────
Most changes in accounting principle
Change in reporting entity
Corrections of errors

──────── Prospective ──────────────────►
Changes in estimate including changes in depreciation method
Changes in accounting principle when retrospective application is impractical
Changes in accounting principle when prospective application is mandated

---

[10]Any prior periods' statements are recast when those statements are presented again for comparative purposes.

[11]"FASB ASC 250–10–45: Accounting Changes and Error Corrections–Overall–Other Presentation Matters (previously "Prior Period Adjustments," *Statement of Financial Accounting Standards No. 16* (Stamford, CT: FASB, 1977)).

A comparison of accounting treatments is provided by Graphic 20–9.

GRAPHIC 20–9 Accounting Changes and Errors: A Summary

	Change in Accounting Principle		Change in Estimate (including depreciation changes)	Change in Reporting Entity	Error
	Most Changes*	**Exceptions†**			
Method of accounting:	Retrospective	Prospective	Prospective	Retrospective	Retrospective
• Restate prior years' statements?	Yes	No	No	Yes	Yes
• Cumulative effect on prior years' income reported:	As adjustment to retained earnings of earliest year reported.‡	Not reported.	Not reported.	Not reported.	As adjustment to retained earnings of earliest year reported.‡
• Journal entry:	To adjust affected balances to new method.	None, but subsequent accounting is affected by the change.	None, but subsequent accounting is affected by the new estimate.	Involves consolidated financial statements discussed in other courses.	To correct any balances that are incorrect as a result of the error.
• Disclosure note?	Yes	Yes	Yes	Yes	Yes

*Changes in depreciation, amortization, and depletion methods are considered changes in estimates.
†When retrospective application is impracticable such as most changes to LIFO and certain mandated changes.
‡In the statement of shareholders' equity or statement of retained earnings.

CONCEPT REVIEW EXERCISE

ACCOUNTING CHANGES

Modern Business Machines recently conducted an extensive review of its accounting and reporting policies. The following accounting changes are an outgrowth of that review:

1. MBM has a patent on a copier design. The patent has been amortized on a straight-line basis since it was acquired at a cost of $400,000 in 2008. During 2011, MBM decided that the benefits from the patent would be experienced over a total of 13 years rather than the 20-year legal life now being used to amortize its cost.
2. At the beginning of 2011, MBM changed its method of valuing inventory from the FIFO cost method to the average cost method. At December 31, 2010 and 2009, MBM's inventories were $560 and $540 million, respectively, on a FIFO cost basis but would have totaled $500 and $490 million, respectively, if determined on an average cost basis. MBM's income tax rate is 40%.

Required:
Prepare all journal entries needed in 2011 related to each change. Also, briefly describe any other measures MBM would take in connection with reporting the changes.

SOLUTION **1. Change in estimate**

	($ in 000s)	
Patent amortization expense (determined below)	34	
Patent		34

Calculation of Annual Amortization after the Estimate Change

	$400,000	Cost
$20,000		Old annual amortization ($400,000 ÷ 20 years)
× 3 years	(60,000)	Amortization to date (2008, 2009, 2010)
	340,000	Unamortized cost
	÷ 10	Estimated remaining life (13 years revised life – 3 years used)
	$ 34,000	New annual amortization

A disclosure note should describe the effect of a change in estimate on income before extraordinary items, net income, and related per-share amounts for the current period.

2. Change in principle

MBM creates a journal entry to bring up to date all account balances affected.

	($ in millions)	
Retained earnings (reduction in net income if average method had been used)	36	
Deferred tax asset ($60 million × 40%)	24	
Inventory ($560 million – 500 million)		60

For financial reporting purposes, but not for tax, MBM is retrospectively *decreasing* accounting income, but not taxable income. This creates a temporary difference between the two that will reverse over time as the unsold inventory becomes cost of goods sold. When that happens, taxable income will be less than accounting income. When taxable income will be less than accounting income as a temporary difference reverses, we have a "future deductible amount" and record a deferred tax asset.

Prior years' financial statements are revised to reflect the use of the new accounting method.

Also, MBM will revise all previous periods' financial statements (in this case 2010) as if the new method (average cost) were used in those periods. In other words, for each year in the comparative statements reported, the balance of each account affected will be revised to appear as if the average method had been applied all along.

Since retained earnings is one of the accounts whose balance requires adjustment (and it usually is), MBM makes an adjustment to the beginning balance of retained earnings for the earliest period (2010) reported in the comparative statements of shareholders' equity. Also, in the first set of financial statements after the change, a *disclosure note* describes the nature of the change, justifies management's decision to make the change, and indicates its effect on each item affected in the financial statements.

Since it's the earliest year reported, 2010's beginning retained earnings is adjusted for the portion of the cumulative income effect of the change attributable to prior years.

INTERNATIONAL FINANCIAL REPORTING STANDARDS

The FASB and the International Accounting Standards Board have a continuing commitment to converge their accounting standards. As part of their short-term convergence effort, they identified how companies report accounting changes as an area in which the FASB could improve its guidance by converging it with the provisions of *IAS No. 8*, "Accounting Policies, Changes in Accounting Estimates and Errors."[12] The product of this effort was new FASB guidance issued in 2005.[13] Few differences remain, so it's unlikely we will see much change in this area.

● LO7

[12]"Accounting Policies, Changes in Accounting Estimates and Errors, "*International Accounting Standard No. 8* (IASCF), as amended effective January 1, 2009

[13]FASB ASC 250: Accounting Changes and Error Corrections (previously "Accounting Changes and Error Corrections—A Replacement of APB Opinion No. 20 and FASB Statement No. 3," *Statement of Financial Accounting Standards No. 154*, (Norwalk, Conn: FASB, 2005)).

PART B

CORRECTION OF ACCOUNTING ERRORS

● LO6

Nobody's perfect. People make mistakes, even accountants. When errors are discovered, they should be corrected.[14] Graphic 20–10 describes the steps to be taken to correct an error, if the effect of the error is material.[15]

GRAPHIC 20–10

Steps to Correct an Error

The retrospective approach is used for the correction of errors.

The correction of an error is treated as a prior period adjustment.

> **Step 1.** A journal entry is made to correct any account balances that are incorrect as a result of the error.
> **Step 2.** Previous years' financial statements that were incorrect as a result of the error are retrospectively restated to reflect the correction (for all years reported for comparative purposes).
> **Step 3.** If retained earnings is one of the accounts incorrect as a result of the error, the correction is reported as a prior period adjustment to the beginning balance in a statement of shareholders' equity (or statement of retained earnings if that's presented instead).
> **Step 4.** A disclosure note should describe the nature of the error and the impact of its correction on net income.

Prior Period Adjustments

Before we see these steps applied to the **correction of an error,** one of the steps requires elaboration. As discussed in Chapter 4, the correction of errors is the situation that creates prior period adjustments. A **prior period adjustment** refers to an addition to or reduction in the beginning retained earnings balance in a statement of shareholders' equity (or statement of retained earnings if that's presented instead).

In an earlier chapter we saw that a statement of shareholders' equity is the most commonly used way to report the events that cause components of shareholders' equity to change during a particular reporting period. Some companies, though, choose to report the changes that occur in the balance of retained earnings separately in a statement of retained earnings. When it's discovered that the ending balance of retained earnings in the period prior to the discovery of an error was incorrect as a result of that error, the balance must be corrected when it appears as the beginning balance the following year. However, simply reporting a corrected amount might cause misunderstanding for someone familiar with the previously reported amount. Explicitly reporting a prior period adjustment on the statement itself avoids this confusion. Assume, for example, the following comparative statements of retained earnings:

A statement of retained earnings reports the events that cause changes in retained earnings.

STATEMENTS OF RETAINED EARNINGS
For the Years Ended December 31, 2010 and 2009

	2010	2009
Balance at beginning of year	$600,000	$450,000
Net income	400,000	350,000
Less: Dividends	(200,000)	(200,000)
Balance at end of year	$800,000	$600,000

Now suppose that in 2011 it's discovered that an error in 2009 caused that year's net income to be overstated by $20,000 (it should have been $330,000). This means retained

---

[14]Interestingly, it appears that not all accounting errors are unintentional. Research has shown that firms with errors that overstate income are more likely "to have diffuse ownership, lower growth in earnings and fewer income-increasing GAAP alternatives available, and are less likely to have audit committees," suggesting that "overstatement errors are the result of managers responding to economic incentives." M. L. DeFond and J. Jiambaolvo, "Incidence and Circumstances of Accounting Errors," *The Accounting Review,* July, 1991.

[15]In practice, the vast majority of errors are not material with respect to their effect on the financial statements and are, therefore, simply corrected in the year discovered (step 1 only).

earnings in both prior years were overstated. Because comparative financial statements are presented and the current year is the year in which the error was discovered, the prior year would include a prior period adjustment as shown below:

STATEMENTS OF RETAINED EARNINGS
For the Years Ended December 31, 2011 and 2010

	2011	2010
Balance at beginning of year	$ 780,000	$600,000
Prior period adjustment		(20,000)
Corrected balance		$580,000
Net Income	500,000	400,000
Less: Dividends	(200,000)	(200,000)
Balance at end of year	$1,080,000	$780,000

The incorrect balance as previously reported is corrected by the prior period adjustment.

At least two years' (as in our example) and often three years' statements are reported in comparative financial statements. The prior period adjustment is applied to beginning retained earnings for the year following the error, or for the earliest year being reported in the comparative financial statements when the error occurs prior to the earliest year presented.[16]

Error Correction Illustrated

Now, let's discuss these procedures to correct errors in the context of a variety of the most common types of errors. Since there are literally thousands of possibilities, it's not practical to describe every error in every stage of its discovery. However, by applying the process to the situations described below, you should become sufficiently comfortable with the *process* that you could apply it to whatever situation you might encounter.

You shouldn't try to memorize how specific errors are corrected; you should learn the process needed to analyze whatever errors you might encounter.

As you study these examples, be sure to notice that it's significantly more complicated to deal with an error if (a) it affected net income in the reporting period in which it occurred and (b) it is not discovered until a later period.

Error Discovered in the Same Reporting Period That It Occurred

If an accounting error is made and discovered in the same accounting period, the original erroneous entry should simply be reversed and the appropriate entry recorded. The possibilities are limitless. Let's look at the one in Illustration 20–4.

G. H. Little, Inc. paid $3 million for replacement computers and recorded the expenditure as maintenance expense. The error was discovered a week later.		**ILLUSTRATION 20–4** Error Discovered in the Same Reporting Period That It Occurred
To Reverse Erroneous Entry	($ in millions)	
Cash	3	
Maintenance expense	3	
To Record Correct Entry		
Equipment	3	
Cash	3	

Note: These entries can, of course, be combined.

---

[16]The retained earnings balances in years after the first year also are adjusted to what those balances would be if the error had not occurred, but a company may choose not to explicitly report those adjustments as separate line items.

Error Affecting Previous Financial Statements, but Not Net Income

If an error did *not* affect net income in the year it occurred, it's relatively easy to correct. Examples are incorrectly recording salaries payable as accounts payable, recording a loss as an expense, or classifying a cash flow as an investing activity rather than a financing activity on the statement of cash flows. A 2009 restatement by **Skilled Healthcare Group, Inc.**, operator of long-term care facilities, reproduced in Graphic 20–11 provides an example. Illustration 20–5 provides another.

GRAPHIC 20–11

Error Correction; Skilled Healthcare Group, Inc.

Real World Financials

> **2. Restatement (in part)**
>
> On June 29, 2009, the Company restated its consolidated financial statements for the annual periods in fiscal years 2006 through 2008. . . . The restatement related to an understatement of accounts receivable allowance for doubtful accounts for the Company's long-term care ("LTC") operating segment, which was caused by improper dating of accounts receivable for that segment by a former senior officer of the LTC segment (the "former employee").
>
> The following tables show the previously reported restatement adjustments and restated amounts for those accounts in the Statements of Condensed Consolidated Statement of Operations for the three and six months ended June 30, 2008, and the Statement of Condensed Consolidated Cash Flows for the six months ended June 30, 2008, affected by the restatements. [Tables intentionally omitted.]

ILLUSTRATION 20–5

Error Affecting Previous Financial Statements, but Not Net Income

Step 1

Step 2

Step 3

Step 4

> MDS Transportation incorrectly recorded a $2 million note receivable as accounts receivable. The error was discovered a year later.
>
> | **To Correct Incorrect Accounts** | ($ in millions) | |
> |---|---|---|
> | Note receivable .... | 2 | |
> | Accounts receivable .... | | 2 |
>
> When reported for comparative purposes in the current year's annual report, last year's balance sheet would be restated to report the note as it should have been reported last year.
>
> Since last year's net income was not affected by the error, the balance in retained earnings was not incorrect. So no prior period adjustment to that account is necessary.
>
> A disclosure note would describe the nature of the error, but there would be no impact on net income, income before extraordinary items, and earnings per share to report.

Error Affecting a Prior Year's Net Income

Most errors affect net income in some way. When they do, they affect the balance sheet as well. Both statements must be retrospectively restated; the statement of cash flows sometimes is affected, too. As with any error, all incorrect account balances must be corrected. Because these errors affect income, one of the balances that will require correction is retained earnings. Complicating matters, income taxes often are affected by income errors. In those cases, amended tax returns are prepared either to pay additional taxes or to claim a tax refund for taxes overpaid.

In Illustration 20–6 (except as indicated), we ignore the tax effects of the errors and their correction to allow us to focus on the errors themselves rather than their tax aspects.

The effect of most errors is different, depending on *when* the error is discovered. For example, if the error in Illustration 20–6 is not discovered until 2012, rather than 2011, accumulated depreciation would be understated by another $1.4 million, or a total of $4.2 million. If not discovered until 2015 or after, no correcting entry at all would be needed. By then, the sum of the omitted depreciation amounts ($1.4 million $\times$ 5 years) would equal the expense incorrectly recorded in 2009 ($7 million), so the retained earnings balance would

In 2011, internal auditors discovered that Seidman Distribution, Inc., had debited an expense account for the $7 million cost of sorting equipment purchased at the beginning of 2009. The equipment's useful life was expected to be five years with no residual value. Straight-line depreciation is used by Seidman.

ILLUSTRATION 20–6

Error Affecting Net Income: Recording an Asset as an Expense

Analysis:

($ in millions)

	Correct			Incorrect	
	(Should have been recorded)			(As recorded)	
2009	Equipment	7.0		Expense	7.0
	Cash		7.0	Cash	7.0
2009	Expense	1.4		Depreciation entry omitted	
	Accum. deprec.		1.4		
2010	Expense	1.4		Depreciation entry omitted	
	Accum. deprec.		1.4		

Sometimes, the analysis is easier if you re-create the entries actually recorded incorrectly and those that would have been recorded if the error hadn't occurred and then compare them.

During the two-year period, depreciation expense was understated by $2.8 million, but other expenses were overstated by $7 million, so net income during the period was understated by $4.2 million. This means retained earnings is currently understated by that amount.

Accumulated depreciation is understated by $2.8 million.

To Correct Incorrect Accounts	($ in millions)
Equipment	7.0
Accumulated depreciation	2.8
Retained earnings	4.2

Step 1

The 2009 and 2010 financial statements that were incorrect as a result of the error are retrospectively restated to report the equipment acquired and to reflect the correct amount of depreciation expense and accumulated depreciation, assuming both statements are reported again for comparative purposes in the 2011 annual report.

Step 2
Restate previous years' financial statements

Because retained earnings is one of the accounts that is incorrect as a result of the error, a correction to that account of $4.2 million is reported as a prior period adjustment to the 2011 beginning retained earnings balance in Seidman's comparative statements of shareholders' equity. A correction would be made also to the 2010 beginning retained earnings balance. That prior period adjustment, though, would be for the pre-2010 difference: $7 million − 1.4 million = $5.6 million. If 2009 statements also are included in the comparative report, no adjustment would be necessary for that period because the error didn't occur until after the beginning of 2009.

Step 3

Prior period adjustment

Also, a disclosure note accompanying Seidman's 2011 financial statements should describe the nature of the error and the impact of its correction on each year's net income (understated by $5.6 million in 2009 and overstated by $1.4 million in 2010), income before extraordinary items (same as net income), and earnings per share.

Step 4 Disclosure note

be the same as if the error never had occurred. Also, the asset may have been disposed of—if the useful life estimate was correct—so neither the equipment nor accumulated depreciation would need to be recorded. Of course, any statements of prior years that were affected and are reported again in comparative statements still would be restated, and a footnote would describe the error.

Most errors, in fact, eventually self-correct. An example of an uncommon instance in which an error never self-corrects would be an expense account debited for the cost of land. Because land doesn't depreciate, the error would continue until the land is sold.

Some errors correct themselves the following year. For instance, if a company's ending inventory is incorrectly counted or otherwise misstated, the income statement would be in error for the year of the error and the following year, but the balance sheet would be incorrect only for the year the error occurs. After that, all account balances will be correct. This is demonstrated in Illustration 20–7 on the next page.

Even errors that eventually correct themselves cause financial statements to be misstated in the meantime.

ADDITIONAL CONSIDERATION

We ignored the tax impact of the error and its correction in Illustration 20–6. To consider taxes, we need to know whether depreciation was also omitted from the tax return and the depreciation methods used for tax reporting. Let's say that depreciation was omitted from the tax return also, and that straight-line depreciation is used by Seidman for both tax and financial reporting. The tax rate is 40%.

Total operating expenses (nontax) still would have been overstated by $4.2 million over the two-year period. But that would have caused taxable income to be understated and the tax liability and income tax expense to be understated by 40% of $4.2 million, or $1.68 million. So net income and retained earnings would have been understated by only $2.52 million:

Operating expenses *overstated*	$4.20 million
Income tax expense *understated*	(1.68) million
Net income (and retained earnings) *understated*	$2.52 million

To Correct Incorrect Accounts:	($ in millions)	
Equipment	7.00	
Accumulated depreciation		2.80
Income tax payable (40% × $4.2 million)		1.68
Retained earnings		2.52

If depreciation had been omitted from the income statement but not from the tax return, or if accelerated depreciation was used for tax reporting but straight-line depreciation for financial reporting, the credit to income tax payable in the correcting entry would be replaced by a credit to deferred tax liability.

ILLUSTRATION 20–7

Error Affecting Net Income: Inventory Misstated

When analyzing inventory errors or other errors that affect cost of goods sold, you may find it helpful to visualize the determination of cost of goods sold, net income, and retained earnings.

In early 2011, Overseas Wholesale Supply discovered that $1 million of inventory had been inadvertently excluded from its 2009 ending inventory count.

Analysis:
U = Understated   O = Overstated

2009		2010	
Beginning inventory		Beginning inventory	U
Plus: Net purchases		Plus: Net purchases	
Less: Ending inventory	U	Less: Ending inventory	
Cost of goods sold	O	Cost of goods sold	U
Revenues		Revenues	
Less: Cost of goods sold	O	Less: Cost of goods sold	U
Less: Other expenses		Less: Other expenses	
Net income	U	Net income	O
Retained earnings	U	Retained earnings	*corrected*

Step 1

If Error Is Discovered in 2010 (before closing):	($ in millions)	
Inventory	1	
Retained earnings		1

If Error Discovered in 2011 or Later:
No correcting entry needed

Step 2

If the error is discovered in 2010, the 2009 financial statements that were incorrect as a result of the error are retrospectively restated to reflect the correct inventory amounts, cost of goods sold, and retained earnings when those statements are reported again for comparative purposes in the 2010 annual report. If the error is discovered in 2011, the

(continued)

2010 financial statements also are retrospectively restated to reflect the correct inventory amounts and cost of goods sold (retained earnings would not require adjustment), even though no correcting entry would be needed at that point. Because retained earnings is one of the accounts incorrect if the error is discovered in 2010, the correction to that account is reported as a prior period adjustment to the 2010 beginning retained earnings balance in Overseas' statement of shareholders' equity. Of course, no prior period adjustment is needed if the error isn't discovered until 2011 or later. Also, a disclosure note in Overseas' annual report should describe the nature of the error and the impact of its correction on each year's net income (understated by $1 million in 2009, overstated by $1 million in 2010), income before extraordinary items (same as net income), and earnings per share.	**ILLUSTRATION 20–7** (concluded) Step 3 Step 4

Other error corrections that benefit from a similar analysis are the overstatement of ending inventory, the overstatement or understatement of beginning inventory, and errors in recording merchandise purchases (or returns).

An error also would occur if a revenue or an expense is recorded in the wrong accounting period. Illustration 20–8 offers an example.

In 2011, General Paper Company discovered that $3,000 of merchandise (credit) sales the last week of 2010 were not recorded until the first week of 2011. The merchandise sold was appropriately excluded from 2010 ending inventory.	**ILLUSTRATION 20–8** Error Affecting Net Income: Failure to Record Sales Revenue

Analysis:

($ in 000s)

	Correct (Should have been recorded)			Incorrect (As recorded)	
2010	Accounts receivable	3		No entry	
	Sales revenue		3		
2011	No entry			Accounts receivable	3
				Sales revenue	3

2010 sales revenue was incorrectly recorded in 2011, so 2010 net income was understated. Beginning retained earnings is understated in 2011. 2011 sales revenue is overstated.

To Correct Incorrect Accounts	($ in 000s)	
Sales revenue	3	
Retained earnings		3

Step 1

Note: If the sales revenue had not been recorded at all, the correcting entry would include a debit to accounts receivable rather than sales revenue.

The 2010 financial statements that were incorrect as a result of the error are retroactively restated to reflect the correct amount of sales revenue and accounts receivable when those statements are reported again for comparative purposes in the 2011 annual report.

Step 2

Because retained earnings is one of the accounts incorrect as a result of the error, the correction to that account is reported as a prior period adjustment to the 2011 beginning retained earnings balance in General Paper's comparative statements of shareholders' equity.

Step 3

Also, a disclosure note in General Paper's 2011 annual report should describe the nature of the error and the impact of its correction on each year's net income ($3,000 in 2010), income before extraordinary items ($3,000 in 2010), and earnings per share.

Step 4

ETHICAL DILEMMA

As a second-year accountant for McCormack Chemical Company, you were excited to be named assistant manager of the Agricultural Chemicals Division. After two weeks in your new position, you were supervising the year-end inventory count when the senior manager

(continued)

> (concluded)
>
> mentioned that two carloads of herbicides were omitted from the count and should be added. Upon checking, you confirm your understanding that the inventory in question had been deemed to be unsalable. "Yes," your manager agreed, "but we'll write that off next year when our bottom line won't be so critical to the continued existence of the Agricultural Chemicals Division. Jobs and families depend on our division showing well this year."

Graphic 20–12 illustrates how **Benihana, Inc.**, corrected its financial statements for having incorrectly expensed leasehold improvements and assets on leased properties in past years. Benihana was one of hundreds of firms making similar correction in 2007 following a Securities and Exchange Commission letter on February 7, 2007, urging companies to follow long-standing accounting standards in this area. As the note indicates, Benihana's previous earnings had been overstated by $2.2 million as a result of the error and the balance in retained earnings was accordingly decreased in the correcting journal entry. At about the same time, **McDonald's Corp.** recorded a similar charge of $139 million.

GRAPHIC 20–12

Error Correction;
Benihana, Inc.

Real World Financials

2. Restatement of Previously Issued Financial Statements (in part)

Following a February 2005 review . . . we have restated our consolidated financial statements for the fiscal years through 2004 and for the third quarter of fiscal 2004 included herein. Previously, when accounting for leases with renewal options, we recorded rent expense on a straight-line basis over the initial noncancelable lease term, with the term commencing when actual rent payments began. We depreciate our buildings, leasehold improvements and other long-lived assets on those properties over a period that includes both the initial noncancelable lease term and all option periods provided for in the lease (or the useful life of the assets if shorter). We previously believed that these long-standing accounting treatments were appropriate under generally accepted accounting principles. We now have restated our financial statements to recognize rent expense on a straight-line basis over the expected lease term, including cancelable option periods where failure to exercise such options would result in an economic penalty and including the period that commences when the underlying property is made available to us for construction.

The cumulative effect of the Restatement through fiscal 2004 is an increase in deferred rent liability of $3.6 million and a decrease in deferred income tax liability of $1.4 million. As a result, retained earnings at the end of fiscal 2004 decreased by $2.2 million. Rent expense for fiscal year ended 2004 and for the three and ten periods ended January 4, 2004 increased by $0.4 million, and $0.1 million and $0.3, respectively. The Restatement decreased reported diluted net earnings per share $0.01 and $0.03 for the three and ten periods ended January 4, 2004, respectively.

As mentioned at the outset, we've made no attempt to demonstrate the correction process for every kind of error in every stage of its discovery. However, after seeing the process applied to the few situations described, you should feel comfortable that the process is the same regardless of the specific situation you might encounter.

● **LO7**

INTERNATIONAL FINANCIAL REPORTING STANDARDS

Accounting Changes and Error Corrections. U.S. GAAP and International standards are largely converged regarding accounting changes and error corrections, but one difference concerns error corrections. When correcting errors in previously issued financial statements, IFRS (IAS No. 8[17]) permits the effect of the error to be reported in the current period if it's not considered practicable to report it retrospectively as is required by U.S. GAAP.

---

[17]"Accounting Policies, Changes in Accounting Estimates and Errors, "*International Accounting Standard No. 8* (IASCF), as amended effective January 1, 2009.

CONCEPT REVIEW EXERCISE

In 2011, the following errors were discovered by the internal auditors of Development Technologies, Inc.

1. 2010 accrued wages of $2 million were not recognized until they were paid in 2011.
2. A $3 million purchase of merchandise in 2011 was recorded in 2010 instead. The physical inventory count at the end of 2010 was correct.

Required:
Prepare the journal entries needed in 2011 to correct each error. Also, briefly describe any other measures Development Technologies would take in connection with correcting the errors. (Ignore income taxes.)

Step 1:

1. To reduce 2011 wages expense and reduce retained earnings to what it would have been if the expense had reduced net income in 2010.

	($ in millions)	
Retained earnings	2	
Wages expense		2

2. To include the $3 million in 2011 purchases and increase retained earnings to what it would have been if 2010 cost of goods sold had not included the $3 million purchases.

Analysis
U = Understated   O = Overstated

2010		**2011**	
Beginning inventory		Beginning inventory	
Purchases	O	Purchases	U
Less: Ending inventory			
Cost of goods sold	O ⌐		
	=		
Revenues			
Less: Cost of goods sold	O ◄─┘		
Less: Other expenses			
Net income	U		
↓			
Retained earnings	U		

	($ in millions)	
Purchases	3	
Retained earnings		3

Step 2:
The 2010 financial statements that were incorrect as a result of the errors would be *retrospectively restated* to reflect the correct wages expense, cost of goods sold (income tax expense if taxes are considered), net income, and retained earnings when those statements are reported again for comparative purposes in the 2011 annual report.

Step 3:
Because retained earnings is one of the accounts that is incorrect, the correction to that account is reported as a *"prior period adjustment"* to the 2011 beginning retained earnings balance in the comparative Statements of Shareholders' Equity.

Step 4:
Also, a *disclosure note* should describe the nature of the error and the impact of its correction on each year's net income, income before extraordinary items, and earnings per share.

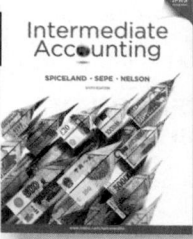

FINANCIAL REPORTING CASE SOLUTION

1. **How can an accounting change cause a company to increase a previously reported inventory amount?** *(page 1141)* Smucker didn't find any lost jelly. The company increased last year's inventory number by $2 million to reflect its change from **LIFO** to **FIFO** this year. If it had not revised the number, last year's inventory would be based on **LIFO** and this year's inventory on **FIFO**. Analysts would be comparing apples and oranges (or apple jelly and orange jelly). Retrospective application of an accounting change provides better comparability in accounting information.

2. **Are all accounting changes reported this way?** *(page 1147)* Not all accounting changes are reported retrospectively. Besides most changes in accounting principle, changes in reporting entity and the correction of errors are reported that way, but some changes are reported prospectively instead. Changes in depreciation method, changes in accounting estimate, and some changes for which retrospective application is either impracticable or prohibited are reported prospectively in current and future periods only. ●

THE BOTTOM LINE

● **LO1** Accounting changes are categorized as:

a. Changes in *principle,*
b. Changes in *estimates,* or
c. Changes in *reporting entity.*

Accounting changes can be accounted for retrospectively (prior years revised) or prospectively (only current and future years affected). (p. 1138)

● **LO2** Most voluntary changes in accounting principles are reported retrospectively. This means revising all previous periods' financial statements to appear as if the newly adopted accounting method had been applied all along. A journal entry is created to adjust all account balances affected as of the date of the change. In the first set of financial statements after the change, a disclosure note describes the change and justifies the new method as preferable. It also describes the effects of the change on all items affected, including the fact that the retained earnings balance was revised in the statement of shareholders' equity. (p. 1141)

● **LO3** Some changes are reported prospectively. These include (a) changes in the method of depreciation, amortization, or depletion, (b) some changes in principle for which retrospective application is impracticable, and (c) a few changes for which an authoritative pronouncement requires prospective application. (p. 1144)

● **LO4** Changes in estimates are accounted for prospectively. When a company revises a previous estimate, prior financial statements are not revised. Instead, the company merely incorporates the new estimate in any related accounting determinations from then on. (p. 1146)

● **LO5** A change in reporting entity requires that financial statements of prior periods be retrospectively revised to report the financial information for the new reporting entity in all periods. (p. 1148)

● **LO6** When errors are discovered, they should be corrected and accounted for retrospectively. Previous years' financial statements that were incorrect as a result of an error are retrospectively restated, and any account balances that are incorrect are corrected by a journal entry. If retained earnings is one of the incorrect accounts, the correction is reported as a prior period adjustment to the beginning balance in a statement of shareholders' equity. And, a disclosure note should describe the nature of the error and the impact of its correction on operations. (p. 1152)

● **LO7** U.S. GAAP and International standards are largely converged with respect to accounting changes and error corrections. One remaining difference is that when correcting errors in previously issued financial statements, IFRS permits the effect of the error to be reported in the current period if it's not considered practicable to report it retrospectively as is required by U.S. GAAP. (pp. 1145, 1151, and 1158) ●

QUESTIONS FOR REVIEW OF KEY TOPICS

Q 20–1   For accounting purposes, we classify accounting changes into three categories. What are they? Provide a short description of each.

Q 20–2   There are two basic accounting approaches to reporting accounting changes. What are they?

Q 20–3   We report most changes in accounting principle retrospectively. Describe this general way of recording and reporting changes in accounting principle.

Q 20–4   Lynch Corporation changes from the sum-of-the-years'-digits method of depreciation for existing assets to the straight-line method. How should the change be reported? Explain.

Q 20–5   Sugarbaker Designs, Inc., changed from the FIFO inventory costing method to the average cost method during 2011. Which items from the 2010 financial statements should be restated on the basis of the average cost method when reported in the 2011 comparative financial statements?

Q 20–6   Most accounting principles are recorded and reported retrospectively. In a few situations, though, the changes should be reported prospectively. When is prospective application appropriate? Provide examples.

Q 20–7   Southeast Steel, Inc., changed from the FIFO inventory costing method to the LIFO method during 2010. How would this change likely be reported in the 2011 comparative financial statements?

Q 20–8   Direct Assurance Company revised the estimates of the useful life of a trademark it had acquired three years earlier. How should Direct account for the change?

Q 20–9   It's not easy sometimes to distinguish between a change in principle and a change in estimate. In these cases, how should the change be accounted for?

Q 20–10   For financial reporting, a reporting entity can be a single company, or it can be a group of companies that reports a single set of financial statements. When changes occur that cause the financial statements to be those of a different reporting entity, we account for the situation as a change in reporting entity. What are the situations deemed to constitute a change in reporting entity?

Q 20–11   The issuance of FASB guidance regarding consolidation of all majority-owned subsidiaries required **Ford Motors** to include a previously unconsolidated finance subsidiary as part of the reporting entity. How did Ford report the change?

Q 20–12   Describe the process of correcting an error when it's discovered in a subsequent reporting period.

Q 20–13   If merchandise inventory is understated at the end of 2010, and the error is not discovered, how will net income be affected in 2011?

Q 20–14   If it is discovered that an extraordinary repair in the previous year was incorrectly debited to repair expense, how will retained earnings be reported in the current year's statement of shareholders' equity?

Q 20–15   What action is required when it is discovered that a five-year insurance premium payment of $50,000 two years ago was debited to insurance expense? (Ignore taxes.)

Q 20–16   Suppose the error described in the previous question is not discovered until six years later. What action will the discovery of this error require?

IFRS   Q 20–17   With regard to the correction of accounting errors, what is the difference between U.S. GAAP and IFRS?

BRIEF EXERCISES

BE 20–1
Change in inventory methods
● LO2

In 2011, the Carney Company changed its method of valuing inventory from the FIFO method to the average cost method. At December 31, 2010, Carney's inventories were $32 million (FIFO). Carney's records indicated that the inventories would have totaled $23.8 million at December 31, 2010, if determined on an average cost basis. Ignoring income taxes, what journal entry will Carney use to record the adjustment in 2011? Briefly describe other steps Carney should take to report the change.

BE 20–2
Change in inventory methods
● LO2

In 2011, DeWash Industries changed its method of valuing inventory from the average cost method to the FIFO method. At December 31, 2010, DeWash's inventories were $47.6 million (average cost). DeWash's records indicated that the inventories would have totaled $64 million at December 31, 2010, if determined on a FIFO basis. Ignoring income taxes, what journal entry will DeWash use to record the adjustment in 2011?

BE 20–3
Change in inventory methods
● LO3

In 2011, Dorsey Markets changed its method of valuing inventory from the FIFO method to the LIFO method. At December 31, 2010, Dorsey's inventories were $96 million (FIFO). Dorsey's records were insufficient to determine what inventories would have totaled if determined on a LIFO cost basis. Briefly describe the steps Dorsey should take to report the change.

BE 20–4
Change in depreciation methods
● LO3

Irwin, Inc., constructed a machine at a total cost of $35 million. Construction was completed at the end of 2007 and the machine was placed in service at the beginning of 2008. The machine was being depreciated over a 10-year life using the sum-of-the-years'-digits method. The residual value is expected to be $2 million. At the beginning of 2011, Irwin decided to change to the straight-line method. Ignoring income taxes, what journal entry(s) should Irwin record relating to the machine for 2011?

BE 20–5
Change in depreciation methods
● LO3

Refer to the situation described in BE 20–4. Suppose Irwin has been using the straight-line method and switches to the sum-of-the-years'-digits method. Ignoring income taxes, what journal entry(s) should Irwin record relating to the machine for 2011?

BE 20–6
Book royalties
● LO4

Three programmers at Feenix Computer Storage, Inc., write an operating systems control manual for Hill-McGraw Publishing, Inc., for which Feenix receives royalties equal to 12% of net sales. Royalties are payable annually on February 1 for sales the previous year. The editor indicated to Feenix on December 31, 2011, that book sales subject to royalties for the year just ended are expected to be $300,000. Accordingly, Feenix accrued royalty revenue of $36,000 at December 31 and received royalties of $36,500 on February 1, 2012. What adjustments, if any, should be made to retained earnings or to the 2011 financial statements? Explain.

BE 20–7
Warranty expense
● LO4

In 2010, Quapau Products introduced a new line of hot water heaters that carry a one-year warranty against manufacturer's defects. Based on industry experience, warranty costs were expected to approximate 5% of sales revenue. First-year sales of the heaters were $300,000. An evaluation of the company's claims experience in late 2011 indicated that actual claims were less than expected—4% of sales rather than 5%. Assuming sales of the heaters in 2011 were $350,000 and warranty expenditures in 2011 totaled $12,000, what is the 2011 warranty expense?

BE 20–8
Change in estimate; useful life of patent
● LO4

Van Frank Telecommunications has a patent on a cellular transmission process. The company has amortized the $18 million cost of the patent on a straight-line basis since it was acquired at the beginning of 2007. Due to rapid technological advances in the industry, management decided that the patent would benefit the company over a total of six years rather than the nine-year life being used to amortize its cost. The decision was made at the end of 2011 (before adjusting and closing entries). What is the appropriate adjusting entry for patent amortization in 2011 to reflect the revised estimate?

BE 20–9
Error correction
● LO6

When DeSoto Water Works purchased a machine at the end of 2010 at a cost of $65,000, the company debited Buildings and credited Cash $65,000. The error was discovered in 2011. What journal entry will DeSoto use to correct the error? What other step(s) would be taken in connection with the error?

BE 20–10
Error correction
● LO6

In 2011, internal auditors discovered that PKE Displays, Inc., had debited an expense account for the $350,000 cost of a machine purchased on January 1, 2008. The machine's useful life was expected to be five years with no residual value. Straight-line depreciation is used by PKE. Ignoring income taxes, what journal entry will PKE use to correct the error?

BE 20–11
Error correction
● LO6

Refer to the situation described in BE 20–10. Assume the error was discovered in 2013 after the 2012 financial statements are issued. Ignoring income taxes, what journal entry will PKE use to correct the error?

BE 20–12
Error correction
● LO6

In 2011, the internal auditors of Development Technologies, Inc., discovered that (a) 2010 accrued wages of $2 million were not recognized until they were paid in 2011 and (b) a $3 million purchase of merchandise in 2011 was recorded in 2010 instead. The physical inventory count at the end of 2010 was correct. Ignoring income taxes, what journal entries are needed in 2011 to correct each error? Also, briefly describe any other measures Development Technologies would take in connection with correcting the errors.

EXERCISES

An alternate exercise and problem set is available on the text website: www.mhhe.com/spiceland6e

E 20–1
Change in principle; change in inventory methods
● LO2

During 2009 (its first year of operations) and 2010, Batali Foods used the FIFO inventory costing method for both financial reporting and tax purposes. At the beginning of 2011, Batali decided to change to the average method for both financial reporting and tax purposes.

Income components before income tax for 2011, 2010, and 2009 were as follows ($ in millions):

	2011	2010	2009
Revenues	$420	$390	$380
Cost of goods sold (FIFO)	(46)	(40)	(38)
Cost of goods sold (average)	(62)	(56)	(52)
Operating expenses	(254)	(250)	(242)

Dividends of $20 million were paid each year. Batali's fiscal year ends December 31.

Required:

1. Prepare the journal entry at the beginning of 2011 to record the change in accounting principle. (Ignore income taxes.)
2. Prepare the 2011–2010 comparative income statements.
3. Determine the balance in retained earnings at January 1, 2010, as Batali reported previously using the FIFO method.
4. Determine the adjustment to the January 1, 2010, balance in retained earnings that Batali would include in the 2011–2010 comparative statements of retained earnings or retained earnings column of the statements of shareholders' equity to revise it to the amount it would have been if Batali had used the average method.

E 20–2
Change in principle; change in inventory methods
● LO2

Aquatic Equipment Corporation decided to switch from the LIFO method of costing inventories to the FIFO method at the beginning of 2011. The inventory as reported at the end of 2010 using LIFO would have been $60,000 higher using FIFO. Retained earnings at the end of 2010 was reported as $780,000 (reflecting the LIFO method). The tax rate is 40%.

Required:

1. Calculate the balance in retained earnings at the time of the change (beginning of 2011) as it would have been reported if FIFO had been used in prior years.
2. Prepare the journal entry at the beginning of 2011 to record the change in accounting principle.

E 20–3
Change from the treasury stock method to retired stock
● LO2

In keeping with a modernization of corporate statutes in its home state, UMC Corporation decided in 2011 to discontinue accounting for reacquired shares as treasury stock. Instead, shares repurchased will be viewed as having been retired, reassuming the status of unissued shares. As part of the change, treasury shares held were reclassified as retired stock. At December 31, 2010, UMC's balance sheet reported the following shareholders' equity:

	($ in millions)
Common stock, $1 par	$ 200
Paid-in capital—excess of par	800
Retained earnings	956
Treasury stock (4 million shares at cost)	(25)
Total shareholders' equity	$1,931

Required:

Identify the type of accounting change this decision represents and prepare the journal entry to effect the reclassification of treasury shares as retired shares.

E 20–4
Change in principle; change to the equity method
● LO2

The Trump Companies, Inc., has ownership interests in several public companies. At the beginning of 2011, the company's ownership interest in the common stock of Milken Properties increased to the point that it became appropriate to begin using the equity method of accounting for the investment. The balance in the investment account was $31 million at the time of the change. Accountants working with company records determined that the balance would have been $48 million if the account had been adjusted to reflect the equity method.

Required:

1. Prepare the journal entry to record the change in accounting principle. (Ignore income taxes.)
2. Briefly describe other steps Trump should take to report the change.
3. Suppose Trump is changing *from* the equity method rather than *to* the equity method. How would your answers to requirements 1 and 2 differ?

E 20–5
FASB codification research; change in accounting for investments
● LO2

Companies often invest in the common stock of other corporations. The way we report these investments depends on the nature of the investment and the investor's motivation for the investment. The *FASB Accounting Standards Codification* represents the single source of authoritative U.S. generally accepted accounting principles.

Required:

1. Obtain the relevant authoritative literature on accounting for a change from the cost method to the equity method for investments in common stock using the FASB's Codification Research System at the FASB website (**www.fasb.org**).
2. What is the specific citation that describes how to account for a change from the cost method to the equity method for investments in common stock?
3. What are the specific requirements?

E 20–6
FASB codification research
● LO2

Access the FASB's Codification Research System at the FASB website (**www.fasb.org**). Determine the specific citation for accounting for each of the following items:

1. Reporting most changes in accounting principle.
2. Disclosure requirements for a change in accounting principle.
3. Illustration of the application of a retrospective change in the method of accounting for inventory.

E 20–7
Change in principle; change to the percentage-of completion method
● LO2

The Long Island Construction Company has used the completed contract method of accounting for construction contracts. At the beginning of 2011, the company decides to change to the percentage-of-completion method for financial reporting purposes, but will continue to use the completed contract method for tax reporting. The following table presents information concerning the change. The income tax rate for all years is 40%.

| | Income before Income Tax | | |
	Percentage of Completion Method	Completed Contract Method	Difference
Before 2010	$15 million	$8 million	$7 million
2010	8 million	5 million	3 million
2011	10 million	9 million	1 million

Required:

1. Prepare the journal entry to record the change in accounting principle. (All tax effects should be reflected in the deferred tax liability account.)

2. Determine the net income to be reported in the 2011–2010 comparative income statements.

3. Which other 2010 amounts would be reported differently in the 2011–2010 comparative income statements and 2011–2010 comparative balance sheets than they were reported the previous year?

4. How would the change be reflected in the 2011–2010 comparative statements of shareholders' equity? Cash dividends were $1 million each year.

E 20–8
Change in inventory methods; incomplete information
● LO3

Moulton Foods has always used the FIFO inventory costing method for both financial reporting and tax purposes. At the beginning of 2011, Moulton decided to change to the LIFO method. As a result of the change, net income in 2011 was $80 million. If the company had used LIFO in 2010, its cost of goods sold would have been higher by $6 million that year. Moulton's records of inventory purchases and sales are not available for 2009 and several previous years. Last year, Moulton reported the following net income amounts in its comparative income statements:

($ in millions)	2010	2009	2008
Net income	$84	$82	$80

Required:

1. Prepare the journal entry at the beginning of 2011 to record the change in accounting principle. (Ignore income taxes.)

2. Briefly describe other steps Moulton will take to report the change.

3. What amounts will Moulton report for net income in its 2011–2009 comparative income statements?

E 20–9
Change in inventory methods; incomplete information
● LO3

Wolfgang Kitchens has always used the FIFO inventory costing method for both financial reporting and tax purposes. At the beginning of 2011, Wolfgang decided to change to the LIFO method. Net income in 2011 was correctly stated as $90 million. If the company had used LIFO in 2010, its cost of goods sold would have been higher by $7 million that year. Company accountants are able to determine that the cumulative net income for all years prior to 2010 would have been lower by $23 million if LIFO had been used all along, but have insufficient information to determine specific effects of using LIFO in 2009. Last year, Wolfgang reported the following net income amounts in its comparative income statements:

($ in millions)	2010	2009	2008
Net income	$94	$92	$90

Required:

1. Prepare the journal entry at the beginning of 2011 to record the change in accounting principle. (Ignore income taxes.)

2. Briefly describe other steps Wolfgang will take to report the change.

3. What amounts will Wolfgang report for net income in its 2011–2009 comparative income statements?

E 20–10
Change in depreciation methods
● LO3

For financial reporting, Clinton Poultry Farms has used the declining-balance method of depreciation for conveyor equipment acquired at the beginning of 2008 for $2,560,000. Its useful life was estimated to be six years with a $160,000 residual value. At the beginning of 2011, Clinton decides to change to the straight-line method. The effect of this change on depreciation for each year is as follows ($ in 000s):

Year	Straight-Line	Declining Balance	Difference
2008	$ 400	$ 853	$453
2009	400	569	169
2010	400	379	(21)
	$1,200	$1,801	$601

Required:

1. Briefly describe the way Clinton should report this accounting change in the 2010–2011 comparative financial statements.
2. Prepare any 2011 journal entry related to the change.

E 20–11
Change in depreciation methods
● LO3

The Canliss Milling Company purchased machinery on January 2, 2009, for $800,000. A five-year life was estimated and no residual value was anticipated. Canliss decided to use the straight-line depreciation method and recorded $160,000 in depreciation in 2009 and 2010. Early in 2011, the company changed its depreciation method to the sum-of-the-years'-digits (SYD) method.

Required:

1. Briefly describe the way Canliss should report this accounting change in the 2010–2011 comparative financial statements.
2. Prepare any 2011 journal entry related to the change.

E 20–12
Book royalties
● LO4

Dreighton Engineering Group receives royalties on a technical manual written by two of its engineers and sold to William B. Irving Publishing, Inc. Royalties are 10% of net sales, receivable on October 1 for sales in January through June and on April 1 for sales in July through December of the prior year. Sales of the manual began in July 2010, and Dreighton accrued royalty revenue of $31,000 at December 31, 2010, as follows:

Receivable—royalty revenue	31,000	
Royalty revenue		31,000

Dreighton received royalties of $36,000 on April 1, 2011, and $40,000 on October 1, 2011. Irving indicated to Dreighton on December 31 that book sales subject to royalties for the second half of 2011 are expected to be $500,000.

Required:

1. Prepare any journal entries Dreighton should record during 2011 related to the royalty revenue.
2. What adjustments, if any, should be made to retained earnings or to the 2010 financial statements? Explain.

E 20–13
Loss contingency
● LO4

The Commonwealth of Virginia filed suit in October 2009, against Northern Timber Corporation seeking civil penalties and injunctive relief for violations of environmental laws regulating forest conservation. When the financial statements were issued in 2010, Northern had not reached a settlement with state authorities, but legal counsel advised Northern Timber that it was probable the ultimate settlement would be $1,000,000 in penalties. The following entry was recorded:

Loss—litigation	1,000,000	
Liability—litigation		1,000,000

Late in 2011, a settlement was reached with state authorities to pay a total of $600,000 to cover the cost of violations.

Required:

1. Prepare any journal entries related to the change.
2. Briefly describe other steps Northern should take to report the change.

E 20–14
Warranty expense
● LO4

Woodmier Lawn Products introduced a new line of commercial sprinklers in 2010 that carry a one-year warranty against manufacturer's defects. Because this was the first product for which the company offered a warranty, trade publications were consulted to determine the experience of others in the industry. Based on that experience, warranty costs were expected to approximate 2% of sales. Sales of the sprinklers in 2010 were $2,500,000. Accordingly, the following entries relating to the contingency for warranty costs were recorded during the first year of selling the product:

Accrued liability and expense

Warranty expense (2% × $2,500,000)	50,000	
Estimated warranty liability		50,000

Actual expenditures (summary entry)

Estimated warranty liability	23,000	
Cash, wages payable, parts and supplies, etc		23,000

In late 2011, the company's claims experience was evaluated and it was determined that claims were far more than expected—3% of sales rather than 2%.

Required:

1. Assuming sales of the sprinklers in 2011 were $3,600,000 and warranty expenditures in 2011 totaled $88,000, prepare any journal entries related to the warranty.

2. Assuming sales of the sprinklers were discontinued after 2010, prepare any journal entry(s) in 2011 related to the warranty.

E 20–15
Deferred taxes;
change in tax rates
● **LO4**

Bronson Industries reported a deferred tax liability of $8 million for the year ended December 31, 2010, related to a temporary difference of $20 million. The tax rate was 40%. The temporary difference is expected to reverse in 2012 at which time the deferred tax liability will become payable. There are no other temporary differences in 2010–2012. Assume a new tax law is enacted in 2011 that causes the tax rate to change from 40% to 30% beginning in 2012. (The rate remains 40% for 2011 taxes.) Taxable income in 2011 is $30 million.

Required:

1. Determine the effect of the change and prepare the appropriate journal entry to record Bronson's income tax expense in 2011.

2. What adjustment, if any, is needed to revise retained earnings as a result of the change?

E 20–16
Accounting change
● **LO4**

The Peridot Company purchased machinery on January 2, 2009, for $800,000. A five-year life was estimated and no residual value was anticipated. Peridot decided to use the straight-line depreciation method and recorded $160,000 in depreciation in 2009 and 2010. Early in 2011, the company revised the total estimated life of the machinery to eight years.

Required:

1. What type of change is this?

2. Briefly describe the accounting treatment for this change.

3. Determine depreciation for 2011.

E 20–17
Change in estimate;
useful life and
residual value of
equipment
● **LO4**

Wardell Company purchased a mini computer on January 1, 2009, at a cost of $40,000. The computer has been depreciated using the straight-line method over an estimated five-year useful life with an estimated residual value of $4,000. On January 1, 2011, the estimate of useful life was changed to a total of 10 years, and the estimate of residual value was changed to $900.

Required:

1. Prepare the appropriate adjusting entry for depreciation in 2011 to reflect the revised estimate.

2. Repeat requirement 1 assuming that the company uses the sum-of-the-years'-digits method instead of the straight-line method.

E 20–18
Classifying
accounting changes
● **LO1 through**
  LO5

Indicate with the appropriate letter the nature of each situation described below:

Type of Change

PR	Change in principle reported retrospectively
PP	Change in principle reported prospectively
E	Change in estimate
EP	Change in estimate resulting from a change in principle
R	Change in reporting entity
N	Not an accounting change

_____ 1. Change from declining balance depreciation to straight-line.

_____ 2. Change in the estimated useful life of office equipment.

_____ 3. Technological advance that renders worthless a patent with an unamortized cost of $45,000.

_____ 4. Change from determining lower of cost or market for the inventories by the individual item approach to the aggregate approach.

_____ 5. Change from LIFO inventory costing to the weighted-average inventory costing.

_____ 6. Settling a lawsuit for less than the amount accrued previously as a loss contingency.

_____ 7. Including in the consolidated financial statements a subsidiary acquired several years earlier that was appropriately not included in previous years.

_____ 8. Change by a retail store from reporting bad debt expense on a pay-as-you-go basis to the allowance method.

_____ 9. A shift of certain manufacturing overhead costs to inventory that previously were expensed as incurred to more accurately measure cost of goods sold. (Either method is generally acceptable.)

_____ 10. Pension plan assets for a defined benefit pension plan achieving a rate of return in excess of the amount anticipated.

E 20–19
Error correction;
inventory error
● LO6

During 2011, WMC Corporation discovered that its ending inventories reported on its financial statements were misstated by the following amounts:

2009	understated by	$120,000
2010	overstated by	150,000

WMC uses the periodic inventory system and the FIFO cost method.

Required:
1. Determine the effect of these errors on retained earnings at January 1, 2011, before any adjustments. Explain your answer. (Ignore income taxes.)
2. Prepare a journal entry to correct the error.
3. What other step(s) would be taken in connection with the error?

E 20–20
Error corrections;
investment
● LO6

On December 12, 2011, an investment costing $80,000 was sold for $100,000. The total of the sale proceeds was credited to the investment account.

Required:
1. Prepare the journal entry to correct the error assuming it is discovered before the books are adjusted or closed in 2011. (Ignore income taxes.)
2. Prepare the journal entry to correct the error assuming it is not discovered until early 2012. (Ignore income taxes.)

E 20–21
Error in
amortization
schedule
● LO6

Wilkins Food Products, Inc. acquired a packaging machine from Lawrence Specialists Corporation. Lawrence completed construction of the machine on January 1, 2009. In payment for the machine Wilkins issued a three-year installment note to be paid in three equal payments at the end of each year. The payments include interest at the rate of 10%. Lawrence made a conceptual error in preparing the amortization schedule which Wilkins failed to discover until 2011. As a result of the error, Wilkins understated interest expense by $45,000 in 2009 and $40,000 in 2010.

Required:
1. Determine which accounts are incorrect as a result of these errors at January 1, 2011, before any adjustments. Explain your answer. (Ignore income taxes.)
2. Prepare a journal entry to correct the error.
3. What other step(s) would be taken in connection with the error?

E 20–22
Error correction;
accrued interest on
bonds
● LO6

At the end of 2010, Majors Furniture Company failed to accrue $61,000 of interest expense that accrued during the last five months of 2010 on bonds payable. The bonds mature in 2024. The discount on the bonds is amortized by the straight-line method. The following entry was recorded on February 1, 2011, when the semiannual interest was paid:

Interest expense	73,200	
Discount on bonds payable		1,200
Cash		72,000

Required:
Prepare any journal entry necessary to correct the error as well as any adjusting entry for 2011 related to the situation described. (Ignore income taxes.)

E 20–23
Error correction;
three errors
● LO6

Below are three independent and unrelated errors.
a. On December 31, 2010, Wolfe-Bache Corporation failed to accrue office supplies expense of $1,800. In January 2011, when it received the bill from its supplier, Wolfe-Bache made the following entry:

Office supplies expense	1,800	
Cash		1,800

b. On the last day of 2010, Midwest Importers received a $90,000 prepayment from a tenant for 2011 rent of a building. Midwest recorded the receipt as rent revenue.
c. At the end of 2010, Dinkins-Lowery Corporation failed to accrue interest of $8,000 on a note receivable. At the beginning of 2011, when the company received the cash, it was recorded as interest revenue.

Required:

For each error:

1. What would be the effect of each error on the income statement and the balance sheet in the 2010 financial statements?
2. Prepare any journal entries each company should record in 2011 to correct the errors.

E 20–24
Inventory errors
● LO6

For each of the following inventory errors occurring in 2011, determine the effect of the error on 2011's cost of goods sold, net income, and retained earnings. Assume that the error is not discovered until 2012 and that a periodic inventory system is used. Ignore income taxes.

U = Understated   O = Overstated   NE = No effect

	Cost of Goods Sold	Net Income	Retained Earnings
(Example) 1. Overstatement of ending inventory	U	O	O
2. Overstatement of purchases			
3. UnderStatement of beginning inventory			
4. Freight-in charges are understated			
5. Understatement of ending inventory			
6. Understatement of purchases			
7. Overstatement of beginning inventory			
8. Understatement of purchases and understatement of ending inventory, by the same amount			

E 20–25
Classifying accounting changes and errors
● LO1 through LO6

Indicate with the appropriate letter the nature of each adjustment described below:

Type of Adjustment

A.   Change in accounting principle (reported retrospectively)
B.   Change in accounting principle (exception reported prospectively)
C.   Change in estimate
D.   Change in estimate resulting from a change in accounting principle
E.   Change in reporting entity
F.   Correction of an error

_____ 1. Change from expensing extraordinary repairs to capitalizing the expenditures.
_____ 2. Change in the residual value of machinery.
_____ 3. Change from FIFO inventory costing to LIFO inventory costing.
_____ 4. Change in the percentage used to determine bad debts.
_____ 5. Change from LIFO inventory costing to FIFO inventory costing.
_____ 6. Change from reporting an investment by the equity method due to a reduction in the percentage of shares owned.
_____ 7. Change in the composition of a group of firms reporting on a consolidated basis.
_____ 8. Change from sum-of-the-years'-digits depreciation to straight-line depreciation.
_____ 9. Change from the percentage-of-completion method by a company in the long-term construction industry.
_____10. Change in actuarial assumptions for a defined benefit pension plan.

CPA AND CMA REVIEW QUESTIONS

CPA Exam Questions

● LO3

The following questions are used in the Kaplan CPA Review Course to study accounting changes and errors while preparing for the CPA examination. Determine the response that best completes the statements or questions.

1. Kap Company switched from the sum-of-the-years-digits depreciation method to straight-line depreciation in 2011. The change affects machinery purchased at the beginning of 2009 at a cost of $36,000. The

machinery has an estimated life of five years and an estimated residual value of $1,800. What is Kap's 2011 depreciation expense?

a. $4,200
b. $4,560
c. $4,800
d. $7,920

● LO4

2. Retrospective restatement usually is appropriate for a change in:

	Accounting Principle	**Accounting Estimate**
a.	Yes	Yes
b.	Yes	No
c.	No	Yes
d.	No	No

● LO4

3. For 2010, Pac Co. estimated its two-year equipment warranty costs based on $100 per unit sold in 2010. Experience during 2011 indicated that the estimate should have been based on $110 per unit. The effect of this $10 difference from the estimate is reported

a. In 2011 income from continuing operations.
b. As an accounting change, net of tax, below 2011 income from continuing operations.
c. As an accounting change requiring 2010 financial statements to be restated.
d. As a correction of an error requiring 2010 financial statements to be restated.

● LO5

4. A company has included in its consolidated financial statements this year a subsidiary acquired several years ago that was appropriately excluded from consolidation last year. This results in

a. An accounting change that should be reported prospectively.
b. An accounting change that should be reported by restating the financial statements of all prior periods presented.
c. A correction of an error.
d. Neither an accounting change nor a correction of an error.

● LO6

5. Conn Co. reported a retained earnings balance of $400,000 at December 31, 2010. In August 2011, Conn determined that insurance premiums of $60,000 for the three-year period beginning January 1, 2010, had been paid and fully expensed in 2010. Conn has a 30% income tax rate. What amount should Conn report as adjusted beginning retained earnings in its 2011 statement of retained earnings?

a. $420,000
b. $428,000
c. $440,000
d. $442,000

● LO6

6. During 2012, Paul Company discovered that the ending inventories reported on its financial statements were incorrect by the following amounts:

2010	$ 60,000 understated
2011	75,000 overstated

Paul uses the periodic inventory system to ascertain year-end quantities that are converted to dollar amounts using the FIFO cost method. Prior to any adjustments for these errors and ignoring income taxes, Paul's retained earnings at January 1, 2012, would be

a. Correct.
b. $15,000 overstated.
c. $75,000 overstated.
d. $135,000 overstated.

CMA Exam Questions

The following questions dealing with accounting changes and errors are adapted from questions that previously appeared on Certified Management Accountant (CMA) examinations. The CMA designation sponsored by the Institute of Management Accountants (**www.imanet.org**) provides members with an objective measure of knowledge and competence in the field of management accounting. Determine the response that best completes the statements or questions.

● LO4

1. A change in the liability for warranty costs requires

a. presenting prior-period financial statements as previously reported.
b. presenting the effect of pro forma data on income and earnings per share for all prior periods presented.
c. reporting an adjustment to the beginning retained earnings balance in the statement of retained earnings.
d. reporting current and future financial statements on the new basis.

● **LO6**

2. In a review of the May 31, 2011, financial statements during the normal year-end closing process, it was discovered that the interest income accrual on Simpson Company's notes receivable was omitted. The amounts omitted were calculated as follows:

May 31, 2010	$ 91,800
May 31, 2011	100,200

The May 31, 2011, entry to correct for these errors, ignoring the effect of income taxes, includes a
   a. credit to retained earnings for $91,800.
   b. credit to interest revenue for $91,800.
   c. debit to interest revenue for $100,200.
   d. credit to interest receivable for $100,200.

● **LO6**

3. An example of an item that should be reported as a prior-period adjustment in a company's annual financial statements is
   a. a settlement resulting from litigation.
   b. an adjustment of income taxes.
   c. a correction of an error that occurred in a prior period.
   d. an adjustment of utility revenue because of rate revisions ordered by a regulatory commission.

PROBLEMS

An alternate exercise and problem set is available on the text website: www.mhhe.com/spiceland6e

P 20–1
Change in inventory costing methods; comparative income statements
● **LO2**

The Cecil-Booker Vending Company changed its method of valuing inventory from the average cost method to the FIFO cost method at the beginning of 2011. At December 31, 2010, inventories were $120,000 (average cost basis) and were $124,000 a year earlier. Cecil-Booker's accountants determined that the inventories would have totaled $155,000 at December 31, 2010, and $160,000 at December 31, 2009, if determined on a FIFO basis. A tax rate of 40% is in effect for all years.

One hundred thousand common shares were outstanding each year. Income from continuing operations was $400,000 in 2010 and $525,000 in 2011. There were no extraordinary items either year.

Required:
1. Prepare the journal entry to record the change in accounting principle. (All tax effects should be reflected in the deferred tax liability account.)
2. Prepare the 2011–2010 comparative income statements beginning with income from continuing operations. Include per share amounts.

P 20–2
Change in principle; change in method of accounting for long-term construction
● **LO2**

The Pyramid Construction Company has used the completed-contract method of accounting for construction contracts during its first two years of operation, 2009 and 2010. At the beginning of 2011, Pyramid decided to change to the percentage-of-completion method for both tax and financial reporting purposes. The following table presents information concerning the change for 2009–2011. The income tax rate for all years is 40%.

	Income before Income Tax				
	Percentage of Completion Method	Completed Contract Method	Difference	Income Tax Effect	Difference after Tax
2009	$ 90,000	$60,000	$30,000	$12,000	$18,000
2010	45,000	36,000	9,000	3,600	5,400
Total	$135,000	$96,000	$39,000	$15,600	$23,400
2011	$ 51,000	$46,000	$ 5,000	$ 2,000	$ 3,000

Pyramid issued 50,000 $1 par, common shares for $230,000 when the business began, and there have been no changes in paid-in capital since then. Dividends were not paid the first year, but $10,000 cash dividends were paid in both 2010 and 2011.

Required:
1. Prepare the journal entry to record the change in accounting principle. (All tax effects should be reflected in the deferred tax liability account.)
2. Prepare the 2011–2010 comparative income statements beginning with income before income taxes.
3. Prepare the 2011–2010 comparative statements of shareholders' equity. (Hint: The 2009 statements reported retained earnings of $36,000. This is $60,000 − [$60,000 × 40%].

P 20–3
Change in inventory costing methods; comparative income statements
● LO2 LO3

Shown below are net income amounts as they would be determined by Weihrich Steel Company by each of three different inventory costing methods ($ in 000s).

	FIFO	Average Cost	LIFO
Pre-2010	$2,800	$2,540	$2,280
2010	750	600	540
	$3,550	$3,140	$2,820

Required:
1. Assume that Weihrich used FIFO before 2011, and then in 2011 decided to switch to average cost. Prepare the journal entry to record the change in accounting principle and briefly describe any other steps Weihrich should take to appropriately report the situation. (Ignore income tax effects.)
2. Assume that Weihrich used FIFO before 2011, and then in 2011 decided to switch to LIFO. Assume accounting records are inadequate to determine LIFO information prior to 2011. Therefore, the 2010 ($540) and pre-2010 ($2,280) data are not available. Prepare the journal entry to record the change in accounting principle and briefly describe any other steps Weihrich should take to appropriately report the situation. (Ignore income tax effects.)
3. Assume that Weihrich used FIFO before 2011, and then in 2011 decided to switch to LIFO cost. Weihrich's records of inventory purchases and sales are not available for several previous years. Therefore, the pre-2010 LIFO information ($2,280) is not available. However, Weihrich does have the information needed to apply LIFO on a prospective basis beginning in 2010. Prepare the journal entry to record the change in accounting principle and briefly describe any other steps Weihrich should take to appropriately report the situation. (Ignore income tax effects.)

P 20–4
Change in inventory methods
● LO2

The Rockwell Corporation uses a periodic inventory system and has used the FIFO cost method since inception of the company in 1974. In 2011, the company decided to change to the average cost method. Data for 2011 are as follows:

Beginning inventory, FIFO (5,000 units @ $30.00)		$150,000
Purchases:		
5,000 units @ $36.00	$180,000	
5,000 units @ $40.00	200,000	380,000
Cost of goods available for sale		$530,000
Sales for 2011 (8,000 units @ $70.00)		$560,000

Additional information:
1. The company's effective income tax rate is 40% for all years.
2. If the company had used the average cost method prior to 2011, ending inventory for 2010 would have been $130,000.
3. 7,000 units remained in inventory at the end of 2011.

Required:
1. Prepare the journal entry at the beginning of 2011 to record the change in principle.
2. In the 2011–2009 comparative financial statements, what will be the amounts of cost of goods sold and inventory reported for 2011?

P 20–5
Change in inventory methods
● LO2

Fantasy Fashions had used the LIFO method of costing inventories, but at the beginning of 2011 decided to change to the FIFO method. The inventory as reported at the end of 2010 using LIFO would have been $20 million higher using FIFO.
   Retained earnings reported at the end of 2009 and 2010 was $240 million and $260 million, respectively (reflecting the LIFO method). Those amounts reflecting the FIFO method would have been $250 million and $272 million, respectively. 2010 net income reported at the end of 2010 was $28 million (LIFO method) but would have been $30 million using FIFO. After changing to FIFO, 2011 net income was $36 million. Dividends of $8 million were paid each year. The tax rate is 40%.

Required:
1. Prepare the journal entry at the beginning of 2011 to record the change in accounting principle.
2. In the 2011–2010 comparative income statements, what will be the amounts of net income reported for 2010 and 2011?
3. Prepare the 2011–2010 retained earnings column of the comparative statements of shareholders' equity.

P 20–6
Change in
principle; change
in depreciation
methods
● LO3

During 2009 and 2010, Faulkner Manufacturing used the sum-of-the-years'-digits (SYD) method of depreciation for its depreciable assets, for both financial reporting and tax purposes. At the beginning of 2011, Faulkner decided to change to the straight-line method for both financial reporting and tax purposes. A tax rate of 40% is in effect for all years.

For an asset that cost $21,000 with an estimated residual value of $1,000 and an estimated useful life of 10 years, the depreciation under different methods is as follows:

Year	Straight Line	SYD	Difference
2009	$2,000	$3,636	$1,636
2010	2,000	3,273	1,273
	$4,000	$6,909	$2,909

Required:
1. Describe the way Faulkner should account for the change described. Include in your answer any journal entry Faulkner will record in 2011 related to the change and any required footnote disclosures.

2. Suppose instead that Faulkner previously used straight-line depreciation and changed to sum-of-the-years'-digits in 2011. Describe the way Faulkner should account for the change. Include in your answer any journal entry Faulkner will record in 2011 related to the change and any required footnote disclosures.

P 20–7
Depletion; change
in estimate
● LO4

In 2011, the Marion Company purchased land containing a mineral mine for $1,600,000. Additional costs of $600,000 were incurred to develop the mine. Geologists estimated that 400,000 tons of ore would be extracted. After the ore is removed, the land will have a resale value of $100,000.

To aid in the extraction, Marion built various structures and small storage buildings on the site at a cost of $150,000. These structures have a useful life of 10 years. The structures cannot be moved after the ore has been removed and will be left at the site. In addition, new equipment costing $80,000 was purchased and installed at the site. Marion does not plan to move the equipment to another site, but estimates that it can be sold at auction for $4,000 after the mining project is completed.

In 2011, 50,000 tons of ore were extracted and sold. In 2012, the estimate of total tons of ore in the mine was revised from 400,000 to 487,500. During 2012, 80,000 tons were extracted.

Required:
1. Compute depletion and depreciation of the mine and the mining facilities and equipment for 2011 and 2012. Marion uses the units-of-production method to determine depreciation on mining facilities and equipment.

2. Compute the book value of the mineral mine, structures, and equipment as of December 31, 2012.

P 20–8
Accounting
changes; six
situations
● LO1 LO3 LO4

Described below are six independent and unrelated situations involving accounting changes. Each change occurs during 2011 before any adjusting entries or closing entries were prepared. Assume the tax rate for each company is 40% in all years. Any tax effects should be adjusted through the deferred tax liability account.

a. Fleming Home Products introduced a new line of commercial awnings in 2010 that carry a one-year warranty against manufacturer's defects. Based on industry experience, warranty costs were expected to approximate 3% of sales. Sales of the awnings in 2010 were $3,500,000. Accordingly, warranty expense and a warranty liability of $105,000 were recorded in 2010. In late 2011, the company's claims experience was evaluated and it was determined that claims were far fewer than expected: 2% of sales rather than 3%. Sales of the awnings in 2011 were $4,000,000 and warranty expenditures in 2011 totaled $91,000.

b. On December 30, 2007, Rival Industries acquired its office building at a cost of $1,000,000. It was depreciated on a straight-line basis assuming a useful life of 40 years and no salvage value. However, plans were finalized in 2011 to relocate the company headquarters at the end of 2015. The vacated office building will have a salvage value at that time of $700,000.

c. Hobbs-Barto Merchandising, Inc., changed inventory cost methods to LIFO from FIFO at the end of 2011 for both financial statement and income tax purposes. Under FIFO, the inventory at January 1, 2012, is $690,000.

d. At the beginning of 2008, the Hoffman Group purchased office equipment at a cost of $330,000. Its useful life was estimated to be 10 years with no salvage value. The equipment was depreciated by the sum-of-the-years'-digits method. On January 1, 2011, the company changed to the straight-line method.

e. In November 2009, the State of Minnesota filed suit against Huggins Manufacturing Company, seeking penalties for violations of clean air laws. When the financial statements were issued in 2010, Huggins had not reached a settlement with state authorities, but legal counsel advised Huggins that it was probable the company would have to pay $200,000 in penalties. Accordingly, the following entry was recorded:

Loss—litigation 200,000
Liability—litigation 200,000

Late in 2011, a settlement was reached with state authorities to pay a total of $350,000 in penalties.

f. At the beginning of 2011, Jantzen Specialties, which uses the sum-of-the-years'-digits method, changed to the straight-line method for newly acquired buildings and equipment. The change increased current year net earnings by $445,000.

Required:

For each situation:

1. Identify the type of change.

2. Prepare any journal entry necessary as a direct result of the change as well as any adjusting entry for 2011 related to the situation described.

3. Briefly describe any other steps that should be taken to appropriately report the situation.

P 20–9
Accounting changes; identify type and reporting approach

● **LO1 through LO4**

At the beginning of 2011, Wagner Implements undertook a variety of changes in accounting methods, corrected several errors, and instituted new accounting policies.

Required:

On a sheet of paper numbered from 1 to 10, indicate for each item below the type of change and the reporting approach Wagner would use.

Type of Change (choose one)	Reporting Approach (choose one)
P. Change in accounting principle	R. Retrospective approach
E. Change in accounting estimate	P. Prospective approach
EP. Change in estimate resulting from a change in principle	
X. Correction of an error	
N. Neither an accounting change nor an accounting error.	

Change:

1. By acquiring additional stock, Wagner increased its investment in Wise, Inc., from a 12% interest to 25% and changed its method of accounting for the investment from an available-for-sale investment to the equity method.

2. Wagner instituted a postretirement benefit plan for its employees in 2011. Wagner did not previously have such a plan.

3. Wagner changed its method of depreciating computer equipment from the SYD method to the straight-line method.

4. Wagner determined that a liability insurance premium it both paid and expensed in 2010 covered the 2010–2012 period.

5. Wagner custom-manufactures farming equipment on a contract basis. Wagner switched its accounting for these long-term contracts from the completed-contract method to the percentage-of-completion method.

6. Due to an unexpected relocation, Wagner determined that its office building, previously depreciated using a 45-year life, should be depreciated using an 18-year life.

7. Wagner offers a three-year warranty on the farming equipment it sells. Manufacturing efficiencies caused Wagner to reduce its expectation of warranty costs from 2% of sales to 1% of sales.

8. Wagner changed from LIFO to FIFO to account for its materials and work-in-process inventories.

9. Wagner changed from FIFO to average cost to account for its equipment inventory.

10. Wagner sells extended service contracts on some of its equipment sold. Wagner performs services related to these contracts over several years, so in 2011 Wagner changed from recognizing revenue from these service contracts on a cash basis to the accrual basis.

P 20–10
Inventory errors

● **LO6**

You have been hired as the new controller for the Ralston Company. Shortly after joining the company in 2011, you discover the following errors related to the 2009 and 2010 financial statements:

a. Inventory at 12/31/09 was understated by $6,000.

b. Inventory at 12/31/10 was overstated by $9,000.

c. On 12/31/10, inventory was purchased for $3,000. The company did not record the purchase until the inventory was paid for early in 2011. At that time, the purchase was recorded by a debit to purchases and a credit to cash.

The company uses a periodic inventory system.

Required:

1. Assuming that the errors were discovered after the 2010 financial statements were issued, analyze the effect of the errors on 2010 and 2009 cost of goods sold, net income, and retained earnings. (Ignore income taxes.)

2. Prepare a journal entry to correct the errors.

3. What other step(s) would be taken in connection with the error?

P 20–11
Error correction;
change in
depreciation
method

● LO6

The Collins Corporation purchased office equipment at the beginning of 2009 and capitalized a cost of $2,000,000. This cost included the following expenditures:

Purchase price	$1,850,000
Freight charges	30,000
Installation charges	20,000
Annual maintenance charge	100,000
Total	$2,000,000

The company estimated an eight-year useful life for the equipment. No residual value is anticipated. The double-declining-balance method was used to determine depreciation expense for 2009 and 2010.

In 2011, after the 2010 financial statements were issued, the company decided to switch to the straight-line depreciation method for this equipment. At that time, the company's controller discovered that the original cost of the equipment incorrectly included one year of annual maintenance charges for the equipment.

Required:

1. Ignoring income taxes, prepare the appropriate correcting entry for the equipment capitalization error discovered in 2011.

2. Ignoring income taxes, prepare any 2011 journal entry(s) related to the change in depreciation methods.

P 20–12
Accounting
changes and error
correction; eight
situations; tax
effects ignored

● LO1 through
LO4 LO6

Williams-Santana, Inc., is a manufacturer of high-tech industrial parts that was started in 1999 by two talented engineers with little business training. In 2011, the company was acquired by one of its major customers. As part of an internal audit, the following facts were discovered. The audit occurred during 2011 before any adjusting entries or closing entries were prepared.

a. A five-year casualty insurance policy was purchased at the beginning of 2009 for $35,000. The full amount was debited to insurance expense at the time.

b. Effective January 1, 2011, the company changed the salvage value used in calculating depreciation for its office building. The building cost $600,000 on December 29, 2000, and has been depreciated on a straight-line basis assuming a useful life of 40 years and a salvage value of $100,000. Declining real estate values in the area indicate that the salvage value will be no more than $25,000.

c. On December 31, 2010, merchandise inventory was overstated by $25,000 due to a mistake in the physical inventory count using the periodic inventory system.

d. The company changed inventory cost methods to FIFO from LIFO at the end of 2011 for both financial statement and income tax purposes. The change will cause a $960,000 increase in the beginning inventory at January 1, 2012.

e. At the end of 2010, the company failed to accrue $15,500 of sales commissions earned by employees during 2010. The expense was recorded when the commissions were paid in early 2011.

f. At the beginning of 2009, the company purchased a machine at a cost of $720,000. Its useful life was estimated to be 10 years with no salvage value. The machine has been depreciated by the double-declining balance method. Its carrying amount on December 31, 2010, was $460,800. On January 1, 2011, the company changed to the straight-line method.

g. Bad debt expense is determined each year as 1% of credit sales. Actual collection experience of recent years indicates that 0.75% is a better indication of uncollectible accounts. Management effects the change in 2011. Credit sales for 2011 are $4,000,000; in 2010 they were $3,700,000.

Required:
For each situation:

1. Identify whether it represents an accounting change or an error. If an accounting change, identify the type of change.

2. Prepare any journal entry necessary as a direct result of the change or error correction as well as any adjusting entry for 2011 related to the situation described. (Ignore tax effects.)

3. Briefly describe any other steps that should be taken to appropriately report the situation.

P 20–13
Accounting
changes and error
correction; eight
situations; tax
effects considered

● LO1 through
LO4 LO6

(Note: This problem is a variation of the previous problem, modified to consider income tax effects.)

Williams-Santana, Inc., is a manufacturer of high-tech industrial parts that was started in 1999 by two talented engineers with little business training. In 2011, the company was acquired by one of its major customers. As part of an internal audit, the following facts were discovered. The audit occurred during 2011 before any adjusting entries or closing entries were prepared. The income tax rate is 40% for all years.

a. A five-year casualty insurance policy was purchased at the beginning of 2009 for $35,000. The full amount was debited to insurance expense at the time.

b. Effective January 1, 2011, the company changed the salvage values used in calculating depreciation for its office building. The building cost $600,000 on December 29, 2000, and has been depreciated on a straight-line basis assuming a useful life of 40 years and a salvage value of $100,000. Declining real estate values in the area indicate that the salvage value will be no more than $25,000.

c. On December 31, 2010, merchandise inventory was overstated by $25,000 due to a mistake in the physical inventory count using the periodic inventory system.

d. The company changed inventory cost methods to FIFO from LIFO at the end of 2011 for both financial statement and income tax purposes. The change will cause a $960,000 increase in the beginning inventory at January 1, 2012.

e. At the end of 2010, the company failed to accrue $15,500 of sales commissions earned by employees during 2010. The expense was recorded when the commissions were paid in early 2011.

f. At the beginning of 2009, the company purchased a machine at a cost of $720,000. Its useful life was estimated to be ten years with no salvage value. The machine has been depreciated by the double-declining balance method. Its carrying amount on December 31, 2010, was $460,800. On January 1, 2011, the company changed to the straight-line method.

g. Bad debt expense is determined each year as 1% of credit sales. Actual collection experience of recent years indicates that 0.75% is a better indication of uncollectible accounts. Management effects the change in 2011. Credit sales for 2011 are $4,000,000; in 2010 they were $3,700,000.

Required:

For each situation:

1. Identify whether it represents an accounting change or an error. If an accounting change, identify the type of change.

2. Prepare any journal entry necessary as a direct result of the change or error correction as well as any adjusting entry for 2011 related to the situation described. Any tax effects should be adjusted for through the deferred tax liability account.

3. Briefly describe any other steps that should be taken to appropriately report the situation.

P 20–14

Errors; change in estimate; change in principle; restatement of previous financial statements

● LO1 LO3 LO4 LO6

Whaley Distributors is a wholesale distributor of electronic components. Financial statements for the years ended December 31, 2009 and 2010, reported the following amounts and subtotals ($ in millions):

	Assets	Liabilities	Shareholders' Equity	Net Income	Expenses
2009	$740	$330	$410	$210	$150
2010	820	400	420	230	175

In 2011 the following situations occurred or came to light:

a. Internal auditors discovered that ending inventories reported on the financial statements the two previous years were misstated due to faulty internal controls. The errors were in the following amounts:

2009 inventory	Overstated by $12 million
2010 inventory	Understated by $10 million

b. A liability was accrued in 2009 for a probable payment of $7 million in connection with a lawsuit ultimately settled in December 2011 for $4 million.

c. A patent costing $18 million at the beginning of 2009, expected to benefit operations for a total of six years, has not been amortized since acquired.

d. Whaley's conveyer equipment was depreciated by the sum-of-the-years'-digits (SYD) basis since it was acquired at the beginning of 2009 at a cost of $30 million. It has an expected useful life of five years and no expected residual value. At the beginning of 2011, Whaley decided to switch to straight-line depreciation.

Required:

For each situation:

1. Prepare any journal entry necessary as a direct result of the change or error correction as well as any adjusting entry for 2011 related to the situation described. (Ignore tax effects.)

2. Determine the amounts to be reported for each of the five items shown above from the 2009 and 2010 financial statements when those amounts are reported again in the 2009–2011 comparative financial statements.

P 20–15

Correction of errors; six errors

● LO6

Conrad Playground Supply underwent a restructuring in 2011. The company conducted a thorough internal audit, during which the following facts were discovered. The audit occurred during 2011 before any adjusting entries or closing entries are prepared.

a. Additional computers were acquired at the beginning of 2009 and added to the company's office network. The $45,000 cost of the computers was inadvertently recorded as maintenance expense. Computers have five-year useful lives and no material salvage value. This class of equipment is depreciated by the straight-line method.

b. Two weeks prior to the audit, the company paid $17,000 for assembly tools and recorded the expenditure as office supplies. The error was discovered a week later.

c. On December 31, 2010, merchandise inventory was understated by $78,000 due to a mistake in the physical inventory count. The company uses the periodic inventory system.

d. Two years earlier, the company recorded a 4% stock dividend (2,000 common shares, $1 par) as follows:

Retained earnings	2,000	
Common stock		2,000

The shares had a market price at the time of $12 per share.

e. At the end of 2010, the company failed to accrue $104,000 of interest expense that accrued during the last four months of 2010 on bonds payable. The bonds, which were issued at face value, mature in 2015. The following entry was recorded on March 1, 2011, when the semiannual interest was paid:

Interest expense	156,000	
Cash		156,000

f. A three-year liability insurance policy was purchased at the beginning of 2010 for $72,000. The full premium was debited to insurance expense at the time.

Required:
For each error, prepare any journal entry necessary to correct the error as well as any year-end adjusting entry for 2011 related to the situation described. (Ignore income taxes.)

P 20–16
Integrating problem; errors; deferred taxes; contingency; change in tax rates
● LO6

You are internal auditor for Shannon Supplies, Inc., and are reviewing the company's preliminary financial statements. The statements, prepared after making the adjusting entries, but before closing entries for the year ended December 31, 2011, are as follows:

SHANNON SUPPLIES, INC.
Balance Sheet
December 31, 2011

Assets	($ in 000s)
Cash	$2,400
Investments	250
Accounts receivable, net	810
Inventory	1,060
Property, plant, and equipment	1,240
Less: Accumulated depreciation	(560)
Total assets	$5,200

Liabilities and Stockholders' Equity	
Accounts payable and accrued expenses	$3,320
Income tax payable	220
Common stock, $1 par	200
Additional paid-in capital	750
Retained earnings	710
Total liabilities and shareholders' equity	$5,200

SHANNON SUPPLIES, INC.
Income Statement
For the Year Ended December 31, 2011

Sales revenue		$3,400
Operating expenses:		
Cost of goods sold	$1,140	
Selling and administrative	896	
Depreciation	84	2,120
Income before income tax		$1,280
Income tax expense		(512)
Net income		$ 768

Shannon's income tax rate was 40% in 2011 and previous years. During the course of the audit, the following additional information (not considered when the above statements were prepared) was obtained:

a. Shannon's investment portfolio consists of blue chip stocks held for long-term appreciation. To raise working capital, some of the shares with an original cost of $180,000 were sold in May 2011. Shannon accountants debited cash and credited investments for the $220,000 proceeds of the sale.

b. At December 31, 2011, the fair value of the remaining securities in the portfolio was $274,000.

c. The state of Alabama filed suit against Shannon in October 2009 seeking civil penalties and injunctive relief for violations of environmental regulations regulating emissions. Shannon's legal counsel previously believed that an unfavorable outcome was not probable, but based on negotiations with state attorneys in 2011, now believe eventual payment to the state of $130,000 is probable, most likely to be paid in 2014.

d. The $1,060,000 inventory total, which was based on a physical count at December 31, 2011, was priced at cost. Based on your conversations with company accountants, you determined that the inventory cost was overstated by $132,000.

e. Electronic counters costing $80,000 were added to the equipment on December 29, 2010. The cost was charged to repairs.

f. Shannon's equipment on which the counters were installed had a remaining useful life of four years on December 29, 2010, and is being depreciated by the straight-line method for both financial and tax reporting.

g. A new tax law was enacted in 2011 which will cause Shannon's income tax rate to change from 40% to 35% beginning in 2012.

Required:
Prepare journal entries to record the effects on Shannon's accounting records at December 31, 2011, for each of the items described above. Show all calculations.

P 20–17
Integrating problem; error; depreciation; deferred taxes
● LO6

George Young Industries (GYI) acquired industrial robots at the beginning of 2008 and added them to the company's assembly process. During 2011, management became aware that the $1 million cost of the machinery was inadvertently recorded as repair expense on GYI's books and on its income tax return. The industrial robots have 10-year useful lives and no material salvage value. This class of equipment is depreciated by the straight-line method for financial reporting purposes and for tax purposes it is considered to be MACRS 7-year property (cost deducted over 7 years by the modified accelerated recovery system as follows):

Year	MACRS Deductions
2008	$ 142,900
2009	244,900
2010	174,900
2011	124,900
2012	89,300
2013	89,200
2014	89,300
2015	44,600
Totals	$ 1,000,000

The tax rate is 40% for all years involved.

Required:
1. Prepare any journal entry necessary as a direct result of the error described.
2. Briefly describe any other steps GYI would take to appropriately report the situation.
3. Prepare the adjusting entry for 2011 depreciation.

BROADEN YOUR PERSPECTIVE

Apply your critical-thinking ability to the knowledge you've gained. These cases will provide you an opportunity to develop your research, analysis, judgment, and communication skills. You also will work with other students, integrate what you've learned, apply it in real world situations, and consider its global and ethical ramifications. This practice will broaden your knowledge and further develop your decision-making abilities.

Integrating Case 20–1
Change to dollar-value LIFO
● LO3

Webster Products, Inc., adopted the dollar-value LIFO method of determining inventory costs for financial and income tax reporting on January 1, 2011. Webster continues to use the FIFO method for internal decision-making purposes. Webster's FIFO inventories at December 31, 2011, 2012, and 2013, were $300,000, $412,500, and

$585,000, respectively. Internally generated cost indexes are used to convert FIFO inventory amounts to dollar-value LIFO amounts. Webster estimated these indexes as follows:

2011	1.00
2012	1.25
2013	1.50

Required:

1. Determine Webster's dollar-value LIFO inventory at December 31, 2012 and 2013.

2. Describe how the change should have been reported in Webster's 2011 financial statements.

Real World Case 20–2
Change in inventory method
● LO2

Real World Financials

On November 8, 2007, **AMCON Distributing Company** ("AMCON" or "Company") issued a press release announcing its financial results for the fiscal year ended September 30, 2007. Included was the following information regarding a change in inventory method (in part):

In the fourth quarter of fiscal 2007, the Company changed its inventory valuation method from the Last-In First-Out (LIFO) method to the First-In First-Out (FIFO) method. The change is preferable as it provides a more meaningful presentation of the Company's financial position as it values inventory in a manner which more closely approximates current cost; better represents the underlying commercial substance of selling the oldest products first; and more accurately reflects the Company's realized periodic income.

As required by U.S. generally accepted accounting principles, this change in accounting principle has been reflected in the consolidated statements of financial position, consolidated statements of operations, and consolidated statements of cash flows through retroactive application of the FIFO method. Previously reported net income (loss) available to common shareholders' for the fiscal years 2006 and 2005 were increased by $0.1 million and $0.5 million after income taxes, respectively.

Required:

1. Why does GAAP require AMCON to retrospectively adjust prior years' financial statements for this type of accounting change?

2. Assuming that the quantity of inventory remained stable during the previous two years, did the cost of AMCON's inventory move up or down during that year?

Communication Case 20–3
Change in inventory method; disclosure note
● LO2

Mayfair Department Stores, Inc., operates over 30 retail stores in the Pacific Northwest. Prior to 2011, the company used the FIFO method to value its inventory. In 2011, Mayfair decided to switch to the dollar-value LIFO retail inventory method. One of your responsibilities as assistant controller is to prepare the disclosure note describing the change in method that will be included in the company's 2011 financial statements. Kenneth Meier, the controller, provided the following information:

- Internally developed retail price indexes are used to adjust for the effects of changing prices.

- If the change had not been made, cost of goods sold for the year would have been $22 million lower. The company's income tax rate is 40% and there were 100 million shares of common stock outstanding during 2011.

- The cumulative effect of the change on prior years' income is not determinable.

- The reasons for the change were (a) to provide a more consistent matching of merchandise costs with sales revenue, and (b) the new method provides a more comparable basis of accounting with competitors that also use the LIFO method.

Required:

1. Prepare for Kenneth Meier the disclosure note that will be included in the 2011 financial statements.

2. Explain why the "cumulative effect of the change on prior years' income is not determinable."

Trueblood Case 20–4
Preferability of accounting changes
● LO2

The following Trueblood case is recommended for use with this chapter. The case provides an excellent opportunity for class discussion, group projects, and writing assignments. The case, along with Professor's Discussion Material, can be obtained from the Deloitte Foundation at its website: **www.deloitte.com/us/truebloodcases**.

Case 07-2: *Western Aluminum*
This case gives students the opportunity to consider the treatment of changes in accounting principle. It requires a judgment as to the preferability of one accounting method over another when making a change. Assuming that the change is preferable, it requires calculating the financial statement impact of the change.

Ethics Case 20–5
Softening the blow
● LO1 LO2 LO3

Late one Thursday afternoon, Joy Martin, a veteran audit manager with a regional CPA firm, was reviewing documents for a long-time client of the firm, AMT Transport. The year-end audit was scheduled to begin Monday.

For three months, the economy had been in a down cycle and the transportation industry was particularly hard hit. As a result, Joy expected AMT's financial results would not be pleasant news to shareholders. However, what Joy saw in the preliminary statements made her sigh aloud. Results were much worse than she feared.

"Larry (the company president) already is in the doghouse with shareholders," Joy thought to herself. "When they see these numbers, they'll hang him out to dry."

"I wonder if he's considered some strategic accounting changes," she thought, after reflecting on the situation. "The bad news could be softened quite a bit by changing inventory methods from LIFO to FIFO or reconsidering some of the estimates used in other areas."

Required:

1. How would the actions contemplated contribute toward "softening" the bad news?

2. Do you perceive an ethical dilemma? What would be the likely impact of following up on Joy's thoughts? Who would benefit? Who would be injured?

Analysis Case 20–6
Change in inventory methods; concepts
● LO2 LO3

Generally accepted accounting principles should be applied consistently from period to period. However, changes within a company, as well as changes in the external economic environment, may force a company to change an accounting method. The specific reporting requirements when a company changes from one generally accepted inventory method to another depend on the methods involved.

Required:

Explain the accounting treatment for a change in inventory method (a) not involving LIFO, (b) from the LIFO method, and (c) to the LIFO method. Explain the logic underlying those treatments. Also, describe how disclosure requirements are designed to address the departure from consistency and comparability of changes in accounting principle.

Communication Case 20–7
Change in loss contingency; write a memo
● LO4

Late in 2011, you and two other officers of Curbo Fabrications Corporation just returned from a meeting with officials of The City of Jackson. The meeting was unexpectedly favorable even though it culminated in a settlement with city authorities that your company pay a total of $475,000 to cover the cost of violations of city construction codes. Jackson filed suit in November 2009 against Curbo Fabrications Corporation, seeking civil penalties and injunctive relief for violations of city construction codes regulating earthquake damage standards. Alleged violations involved several construction projects completed during the previous three years. When the financial statements were issued in 2010, Curbo had not reached a settlement with state authorities, but legal counsel had advised the company that it was probable the ultimate settlement would be $750,000 in penalties. The following entry was recorded:

Loss—litigation	750,000	
Liability—litigation		750,000

The final settlement, therefore, was a pleasant surprise. While returning from the meeting, conversation turned to reporting the settlement in the 2011 financial statements. You drew the short straw and were selected to write a memo to Janet Zeno, the financial vice president, advising the proper course of action.

Required:

Write the memo. Include descriptions of any journal entries related to the change in amounts. Briefly describe other steps Curbo should take to report the settlement.

Analysis Case 20–8
Two wrongs make a right?
● LO4

Early one Wednesday afternoon, Ken and Larry studied in the dormitory room they shared at Fogelman College. Ken, an accounting major, was advising Larry, a management major, regarding a project for Larry's Business Policy class. One aspect of the project involved analyzing the 2010 annual report of Craft Paper Company. Though not central to his business policy case, a footnote had caught Larry's attention.

Depreciation and Cost of Timber Harvested (in part)

($ in millions)

	2010	2009	2008
Depreciation of buildings, machinery and equipment	$260.9	$329.8	$322.5
Cost of timber harvested and amortization of logging roads	4.9	4.9	4.9
	$265.8	$334.7	$327.4

Beginning in 2010, the Company revised the estimated average useful lives used to compute depreciation for most of its pulp and paper mill equipment from 16 years to 20 years and for most of its finishing and converting equipment from 12 years to 15 years. These revisions were made to more properly reflect the true economic lives of the assets and to better align the Company's depreciable lives with the predominant practice in the industry. The change had the effect of increasing net income by approximately $55 million.

"If I understand this right, Ken, the company is not going back and recalculating a lower depreciation for earlier years. Instead they seem to be leaving depreciation overstated in earlier years and making up for that by understating it in current and future years," Larry mused. "Is that the way it is in accounting? Two wrongs make a right?"

Required:

What are the two wrongs to which Larry refers? Is he right?

Research Case 20–9

FASB codification; researching the way changes in postretirement benefit estimates are reported; retrieving disclosures from the Internet

● LO4

It's financial statements preparation time at Center Industries where you have been assistant controller for two months. Ben Huddler, the controller, seems to be pleasant but unpredictable. Today, although your schedule is filled with meetings with internal and outside auditors and two members of the board of directors, Ben made a request. "As you know, we're decreasing the rate at which we assume health care costs will rise when measuring our postretirement benefit obligation. I'd like to know how others have reported similar changes. Can you find me an example?" he asked. "I'd bet you could get one off the Internet." As a matter of fact, you often use EDGAR, the Electronic Data Gathering, Analysis, and Retrieval system (**www.sec.gov**) to access financial statements filed with the U.S. Securities and Exchange Commission (SEC).

Required:

1. Access EDGAR on the Internet. Access a recent 10-K filing of a firm you think might have a postretirement health care plan. You may need to look up several companies before you find what you're looking for. Older, established companies are most likely to have such benefit plans.

   (Note: You may be able to focus your search by searching with key words and phrases in Google on the Internet.)

2. Find the portion of the disclosures that reports the effect of a change in health care cost trends.

3. What information is provided about the effect of the change on the company's estimated benefit obligation?

4. Obtain the relevant authoritative literature on disclosure requirements for health care cost trends using the FASB's Codification Research System. You might gain access from the FASB website (**www.fasb.org**), from your school library, or some other source. What authoritative literature do companies rely on when disclosing the effect of a change in health care cost trends?

Analysis Case 20–10

Various changes

● LO1 through LO4

DRS Corporation changed the way it depreciates its computers from the sum-of-the-year's-digits method to the straight-line method beginning January 1, 2011. DRS also changed its estimated residual value used in computing depreciation for its office building. At the end of 2011, DRS changed the specific subsidiaries constituting the group of companies for which its consolidated financial statements are prepared.

Required:

1. For each accounting change DRS undertook, indicate the type of change and how DRS should report the change. Be specific.

2. Why should companies disclose changes in accounting principles?

Analysis Case 20–11

Various changes

● LO1 through LO4

Ray Solutions decided to make the following changes in its accounting policies on January 1, 2011:

a. Changed from the cash to the accrual basis of accounting for recognizing revenue on its service contracts.

b. Adopted straight-line depreciation for all future equipment purchases, but continued to use accelerated depreciation for all equipment acquired before 2011.

c. Changed from the LIFO inventory method to the FIFO inventory method.

Required:

For each accounting change Ray undertook, indicate the type of change and how Ray should report the change. Be specific.

Judgment Case 20–12

Accounting changes; independent situations

● LO1 through LO5

Sometimes a business entity will change its method of accounting for certain items. The change may be classified as a change in accounting principle, a change in accounting estimate, or a change in reporting entity.

   Listed below are three independent, unrelated sets of facts relating to accounting changes.

Situation I: A company determined that the depreciable lives of its fixed assets are presently too long to fairly match the cost of the fixed assets with the revenue produced. The company decided at the beginning of the current year to reduce the depreciable lives of all of its existing fixed assets by five years.

Situation II: On December 31, 2010, Gary Company owned 51% of Allen Company, at which time Gary reported its investment on a nonconsolidated basis due to political uncertainties in the country in which Allen was located. On January 2, 2011, the management of Gary Company was satisfied that the political uncertainties were resolved and the assets of the company were in no danger of nationalization. Accordingly, Gary will prepare consolidated financial statements for Gary and Allen for the year ended December 31, 2011.

Situation III: A company decides in January 2011 to adopt the straight-line method of depreciation for plant equipment. The straight-line method will be used for new acquisitions as well as for previously acquired plant equipment for which depreciation had been provided on an accelerated basis.

Required:

For each of the situations described above, provide the information indicated below. Complete your discussion of each situation before going on to the next situation.

1. Type of accounting change.
2. Manner of reporting the change under current generally accepted accounting principles including a discussion, where applicable, of how amounts are computed.
3. Effect of the change on the balance sheet and income statement.
4. Footnote disclosures that would be necessary.

Judgment Case 20–13
Inventory errors
● LO6

Some inventory errors are said to be "self-correcting" in that the error has the opposite financial statement effect in the period following the error, thereby "correcting" the original account balance errors.

Required:

Despite this self-correcting feature, discuss why these errors should not be ignored and describe the steps required to account for the error correction.

Ethics Case 20–14
Overstatement of ending inventory
● LO6

Danville Bottlers is a wholesale beverage company. Danville uses the FIFO inventory method to determine the cost of its ending inventory. Ending inventory quantities are determined by a physical count. For the fiscal year-end June 30, 2011, ending inventory was originally determined to be $3,265,000. However, on July 17, 2011, John Howard, the company's controller, discovered an error in the ending inventory count. He determined that the correct ending inventory amount should be $2,600,000.

Danville is a privately owned corporation with significant financing provided by a local bank. The bank requires annual audited financial statements as a condition of the loan. By July 17, the auditors had completed their review of the financial statements which are scheduled to be issued on July 25. They did not discover the inventory error.

John's first reaction was to communicate his finding to the auditors and to revise the financial statements before they are issued. However, he knows that his and his fellow workers' profit-sharing plans are based on annual pretax earnings and that if he revises the statements, everyone's profit sharing bonus will be significantly reduced.

Required:

1. Why will bonuses be negatively affected? What is the effect on pretax earnings?
2. If the error is not corrected in the current year and is discovered by the auditors during the following year's audit, how will the error be reported in the company's financial statements?
3. Discuss the ethical dilemma Howard faces.

21

The Statement of Cash Flows Revisited

/// **OVERVIEW**

The objective of financial reporting is to provide investors and creditors with useful information, primarily in the form of financial statements. The balance sheet and the income statement—the focus of your study in earlier chapters—do not provide all the information needed by these decision makers. Here you will learn how the statement of cash flows fills the information gap left by the other financial statements.

The statement lists all cash inflows and cash outflows, and classifies them as cash flows from (a) operating, (b) investing, or (c) financing activities. Investing and financing activities that do not directly affect cash also are reported.

/// **LEARNING OBJECTIVES**

After studying this chapter, you should be able to:

● **LO1** Explain the usefulness of the statement of cash flows. (page 1184)

● **LO2** Define cash equivalents. (page 1187)

● **LO3** Determine cash flows from operating activities by the direct method. (page 1188)

● **LO4** Determine cash flows from operating activities by the indirect method. (page 1190)

● **LO5** Identify transactions that are classified as investing activities. (page 1192)

● **LO6** Identify transactions that are classified as financing activities. (page 1193)

● **LO7** Identify transactions that represent noncash investing and financing activities. (page 1194)

● **LO8** Prepare a statement of cash flows with the aid of a spreadsheet or T-accounts. (page 1194)

● **LO9** Discuss the primary differences between U.S. GAAP and IFRS with respect to the statement of cash flows. (pages 1191 and 1212)

FINANCIAL REPORTING CASE

Where's the Cash?

"What do you mean you can't afford a wage increase?" union negotiator Vince Barr insisted. "We've all seen your income statement. You had record earnings this year."

This is the first day of negotiations with the company's union representatives. As company controller, you know it's going to be up to you to explain the company's position on the financial aspects of the negotiations. In fact, you've known for some time that a critical point of contention would be the moderate increase in this year's profits after three years of level or slightly declining earnings. Not helping the situation is that the company has always used accelerated depreciation on its equipment which it began replacing this year at considerably higher prices than it cost several years back.

By the time you finish this chapter, you should be able to respond appropriately to the questions posed in this case. Compare your response to the solution provided at the end of the chapter.

QUESTIONS ///

1. What are the cash flow aspects of the situation that Mr. Barr may be overlooking in making his case for a wage increase? How can a company's operations generate a healthy profit and yet produce meager or even negative cash flows? (page 1188)

2. What information can a statement of cash flows provide about a company's investing activities that can be useful in decisions such as this? (page 1192)

3. What information can a statement of cash flows provide about a company's financing activities that can be useful in decisions such as this? (page 1193)

PART **A**

THE CONTENT AND VALUE OF THE STATEMENT OF CASH FLOWS

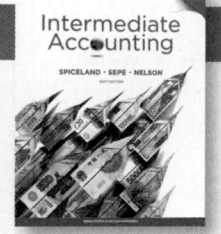

● **LO1**

Investors and creditors require cash flows from the corporation.

Cash flows to investors and creditors depend on the corporation generating cash flows to itself.

Many decisions benefit from information about the company's underlying cash flow process.

DECISION MAKERS' PERSPECTIVE—Usefulness Of Cash Flow Information

A fund manager of a major insurance company, considering investing $8,000,000 in the common stock of **The Coca-Cola Company**, asks herself: "What are the prospects of future dividends and market-price appreciation? Will we get a return commensurate with the cost and risk of our investment?" A bank officer, examining an application for a business loan, asks himself: "If I approve this loan, what is the likelihood of the borrower making interest payments on time and repaying the loan when due?" Investors and creditors continually face these and similar decisions that require projections of the relative ability of a business to generate future cash flows and of the risk associated with those forecasts.

To make these projections, decision makers rely heavily on the information reported in periodic financial statements. In the final analysis, cash flows into and out of a business enterprise are the most fundamental events on which investors and creditors base their decisions. Naturally, these decisions focus on the prospects of the decision makers receiving cash returns from their dealings with the firm. However, it is the ability of the firm to generate cash flows to itself that ultimately determines the potential for cash flows from the firm to investors and creditors.

The financial statements that have been the focus of your study in earlier chapters— the income statement and the balance sheet—offer information helpful in forecasting future cash-generating ability. Some important questions, however, are not easily answered from the information these statements provide. For example, meaningful projections of a company's future profitability and risk depend on answers to such questions as:

- In what types of activities is the company investing?
- Are these activities being financed with debt? with equity? by cash generated from operations?
- Are facilities being acquired to accommodate future expansion?
- How does the amount of cash generated from operations compare with net income over time?
- Why isn't the increase in retained earnings reflected as an increase in dividends?
- What happens to the cash received from the sale of assets?
- By what means is debt being retired?

The information needed to answer these and similar questions is found in the continuous series of cash flows that the income statement and the balance sheet describe only indirectly. This underlying cash flow process is considered next. ●

Cash Inflows and Outflows

Cash continually flows into and out of an active business. Businesses disburse cash to acquire property and equipment to maintain or expand productive capacity. When no longer needed, these assets may be sold for cash. Cash is paid to produce or purchase inventory for resale, as well as to pay for the expenses of selling these goods. The ultimate outcome of these selling activities is an inflow of cash. Cash might be invested in securities of other firms. These investments provide cash inflows during the investment period in the form of dividends or interest and at the end of the investment period when the securities are sold. To raise cash to finance their operations, firms sell stock and/or acquire debt. Cash payments are made as dividends to shareholders and interest to creditors. When debt is repaid or stock repurchased, cash flows out of the firm. To help you visualize the continual process of cash receipts and cash payments, that process is diagrammed in Graphic 21–1. The diagram also previews the way we will later classify the cash flows in a statement of cash flows.

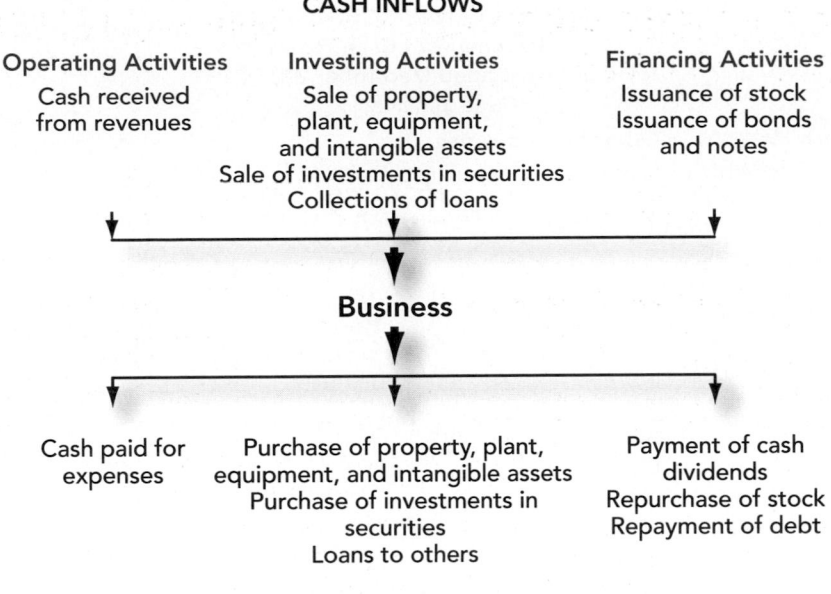

Embodied in this assortment of cash flows is a wealth of information that investors and creditors require to make educated decisions. Much of the value of the underlying information provided by the cash flows is lost when reported only indirectly by the balance sheet and the income statement. Each cash flow eventually impacts decision makers by affecting the balances of various accounts in the balance sheet. Also, many of the cash flows—those related to income-producing activities—are represented in the income statement. However, they are not necessarily reported in the period the cash flows occur because the income statement measures activities on an accrual basis. The statement of cash flows fills the information gap by reporting the cash flows directly.

Role of the Statement of Cash Flows

A statement of cash flows is shown in Graphic 21–2 on the next page. The statement lists all cash inflows and cash outflows during the reporting period. To enhance the informational value of the presentation, the cash flows are classified according to the nature of the activities that bring about the cash flows. The three primary categories of cash flows are (1) cash flows from operating activities, (2) cash flows from investing activities, and (3) cash flows from financing activities. Classifying each cash flow by source (operating, investing, or financing activities) is more informative than simply listing the various cash flows. Notice, too, that the noncash investing and financing activities— investing and financing activities that do not directly increase or decrease cash—also are reported. The GAAP requirement for the statement of cash flows was issued in direct response to *FASB Concept Statement 1,* which states that the primary objective of financial reporting is to "provide information to help investors and creditors, and others assess the amounts, timing, and uncertainty of prospective net cash inflows to the related enterprise."[1]

Many companies have experienced bankruptcy because they were unable to generate sufficient cash to satisfy their obligations. Doubtless, many investors in the stock of these firms would have been spared substantial losses if the financial statements had been designed to foresee the cash flow problems the companies were experiencing. A noted illustration is the demise of **W. T. Grant** during the 1970s. Grant, a general retailer in the days before malls, was a blue chip stock of its time. Grant's statement of changes in financial position (the predecessor of the statement of cash flows) reported working capital from operations of $46 million in 1972. Yet, if presented, a statement of cash flows would have reported cash flows from operating activities of negative $10 million. In fact, the unreported cash flow

The statement of cash flows provides information about cash flows that is lost when reported only indirectly by the balance sheet and the income statement.

---

[1]"Objectives of Financial Reporting by Business Enterprises," *FASB Statement of Financial Accounting Concepts* No. 1, par 37.

GRAPHIC 21–2

Statement of Cash Flows

UNITED BRANDS CORPORATION
Statement of Cash Flows
For Year Ended December 31, 2011
($ in millions)

Cash Flows from Operating Activities

Cash inflows:

From customers	$98	
From investment revenue	3	
Cash outflows:		
To suppliers of goods	(50)	
To employees	(11)	
For interest	(3)	
For insurance	(4)	
For income taxes	(11)	
Net cash flows from operating activities		$22
Cash Flows from Investing Activities		
Purchase of land	(30)	
Purchase of short-term investment	(12)	
Sale of land	18	
Sale of equipment	5	
Net cash flows from investing activities		(19)
Cash Flows from Financing Activities		
Sale of common shares	26	
Retirement of bonds payable	(15)	
Payment of cash dividends	(5)	
Net cash flows from financing activities		6
Net increase in cash		9
Cash balance, January 1		20
Cash balance, December 31		$29

- -

Note X:

Noncash Investing and Financing Activities

Acquired $20 million of equipment by issuing a 12%, 5-year note.	$20

Reconciliation of Net Income to Cash Flows from Operating Activities:

Net income	$12
Adjustments for noncash effects:	
Gain on sale of land	(8)
Depreciation expense	3
Loss on sale of equipment	2
Changes in operating assets and liabilities:	
Increase in accounts receivable	(2)
Decrease in inventory	4
Increase in accounts payable	6
Increase in salaries payable	2
Discount on bonds payable	2
Decrease in prepaid insurance	3
Decrease in income tax payable	(2)
Net cash flows from operating activities	$22

deficiency grew to $114 million in 1973, while working capital from operations was reported as having increased by $1 million. That year, without the benefit of cash flow information, investors were buying Grant's stock at prices that represented up to 20 times its earnings.[2]

---

[2]Cheryl A. Zega, "The New Statement of Cash Flows," *Management Accounting*, September 1988.

More recently, even with cash flow information available, cash flow problems can go un-noticed. An example is the rapid growth and subsequent bankruptcy of the **Wicks 'N' Sticks** franchise. The company's drive for rapid growth led to a dependence on the sale of new franchises in order to generate cash flow instead of doing so in a more healthy way through its operations. As we see shortly, a statement of cash flows can indicate not just the amount of cash flows, but also whether those cash flows are coming from operations or from outside sources. Wicks 'N' Sticks was able to emerge from bankruptcy through restructuring and a new perspective on cash flow management.

Realize, too, that an unprofitable company with good cash flow can survive. **Amazon.com** provides an excellent example. Founded as an online seller of books in 1995, Amazon.com didn't actually make a profit for a decade, but it did raise huge amounts of cash by selling stock, so much so that it was able to weather 10 years of sizable losses. The financing cash inflows funded expansion into many new lines of business and made up for the continual losses. Amazon now has good operating cash flows and is profitable.

The Importance of Cash Flows in an Economic Decline

The near-collapse of **Bear Stearns** in the Spring of 2008 likely will be remembered as the single most dramatic event in exposing the fragility of Wall Street and precipitating the most severe financial crisis since the Great Depression. At the heart of Bear's calamity and the subsequent worldwide economic decline was a shortage of cash flows. First Bear Stearns; then **Lehman Brothers**; then **AIG**, **Citigroup**, **Fannie Mae**, and **Freddie Mac**. As we know, it didn't stop there. Each of these meltdowns involved a lack of measuring and monitoring the ebb and flow of cash.

When the financial industry is burdened with enormous amounts of uncollectible debt, as during the recent credit crisis, banks and others are reluctant to lend money. Cash becomes scarce. It's critical for companies to monitor their cash flows.

Let's say Lucky Strike Lures, Inc., manufactures fishing lures and sells them to a dis-tributor. The distributor warehouses them before selling them to Bubba's Bait Shop, where they are put on display awaiting customers to buy them. During an economic downturn, the customers may delay buying the lures or not buy them at all. So, the lures stay in the store gathering dust, and Bubba's Bait can't pay for the lures that haven't sold. The distributor is then slow to pay Lucky Strike. Lucky Strike has bills to pay but no cash. In normal times, the company would go to the bank and borrow money. But in hard times, the bank is reluctant to lend. There is no quick fix as normal financing options are closed. Lucky Strike has cash flowing out, but not flowing in.

The survival and success of every business depends on its ability to create or otherwise attain cash. You can be profitable and still go broke. Companies must closely plan and mon-itor their cash flows to stay in business. During the recent economic decline, even some of the most well-known companies suffered the consequences of not following this principle.

Cash is king! Especially during an economic downturn.

The statement of cash flows for United Brands Corporation (UBC), shown in Graphic 21–2, is intended at this point in the discussion to illustrate the basic structure and composition of the statement. Later we will see how the statement of cash flows for UBC is prepared from the information typically available for this purpose. We will refer to UBC's statement of cash flows frequently throughout the chapter as the discussion becomes more specific regarding the criteria for classifying cash flows in the three pri-mary categories and as we identify the specific cash flows to be reported on the statement. We will examine the content of the statement in more detail following a look at how this relatively recent financial statement has evolved to its present form over the course of the last several decades.

● LO2

Cash and Cash Equivalents

Skilled cash managers will invest temporarily idle cash in short-term investments to earn interest on those funds, rather than maintain an unnecessarily large balance in a checking account. The FASB views short-term, highly liquid investments that can be readily con-verted to cash, with little risk of loss, as **cash equivalents.** Amounts held as investments

There is no differentiation between amounts held as cash and amounts held in cash equivalent investments.

of this type are essentially equivalent to cash because they are quickly available for use as cash. Therefore, on the statement of cash flows there is no differentiation between amounts held as cash (e.g., currency and checking accounts) and amounts held in cash equivalent investments. So, when we refer in this chapter to cash, we are referring to the total of cash and cash equivalents.

Examples of cash equivalents are money market funds, Treasury bills, and commercial paper. To be classified as cash equivalents, these investments must have a maturity date not longer than three months from the date of purchase. Flexibility is permitted in designating cash equivalents. Each company must establish a policy regarding which short-term, highly liquid investments it classifies as cash equivalents. The policy should be consistent with the company's customary motivation for acquiring various investments and should be disclosed in the notes to the statement.[3] A recent annual report of **ExxonMobil Corporation** provides this description of its cash equivalents (Graphic 21–3):

GRAPHIC 21–3

Disclosure of Cash Equivalents— ExxonMobil Corporation

> **Note 4: Cash Flow Information (in part)**
>
> The consolidated statement of cash flows provides information about changes in cash and cash equivalents. Highly liquid investments with maturities of three months or less when acquired are classified as cash equivalents.

Transactions that involve merely transfers from cash to cash equivalents (such as the purchase of a three-month Treasury bill), or from cash equivalents to cash (such as the sale of a Treasury bill), should not be reported on the statement of cash flows. The total of cash and cash equivalents is not altered by such transactions.[4] The cash balance reported in the balance sheet also represents the total of cash and cash equivalents, which allows us to compare the change in that balance with the net increase or decrease in the cash flows reported on the statement of cash flows.

Primary Elements of the Statement of Cash Flows

This section describes the three primary activity classifications: (1) operating activities, (2) investing activities, and (3) financing activities; and two other requirements of the statement of cash flows: (4) the reconciliation of the net increase or decrease in cash with the change in the balance of the cash account and (5) noncash investing and financing activities.

FINANCIAL Reporting Case

Q1, p. 1183

● LO3

The cash effects of the elements of net income are reported as cash flows from operating activities.

CASH FLOWS FROM OPERATING ACTIVITIES.   The income statement reports the success of a business in generating a profit from its operations. Net income (or loss) is the result of netting together the revenues earned during the reporting period, regardless of when cash is received, and the expenses incurred in generating those revenues, regardless of when cash is paid. This is the accrual concept of accounting that has been emphasized throughout your study of accounting. Information about net income and its components, measured by the accrual concept, generally provides a better indication of current operating performance than does information about current cash receipts and payments.[5] Nevertheless, as indicated earlier, the cash effects of earning activities also provide useful information that is not directly accessible from the income statement. The first cash flow classification in the statement of cash flows reports that information.

Cash flows from operating activities are both inflows and outflows of cash that result from activities reported in the income statement. In other words, this classification of cash flows includes the elements of net income, but reported on a cash basis. The components of this section of the statement of cash flows, and their relationship with the elements of the income statement, are illustrated in Graphic 21–4.

---

[3]A change in that policy is treated as a change in accounting principle.
[4]An exception is the sale of a cash equivalent at a gain or loss. This exception is described in more detail later in the chapter.
[5]*FASB Statement of Financial Accounting Concepts No. 1*, par. 44.

Income Statement	Cash Flows from Operating Activities
Revenues:	Cash inflows:
Sales and service revenue	Cash received from customers
Investment revenue	Cash revenue received (e.g., dividends,
Noncash revenues and gains (e.g., gain	interest)
on sale of assets)	(Not reported)
Less: Expenses:	Less: Cash outflows:
Cost of goods sold	Cash paid to suppliers of inventory
Salaries expense	Cash paid to employees
Noncash expenses and losses (e.g.,	
depreciation, amortization, bad debts,	
loss on sale of assets)	(Not reported)
Interest expense	Cash paid to creditors
Other operating expenses	Cash paid to insurance companies/others
Income tax expense	Cash paid to the government
Net income	*Net cash flows from operating activities*

GRAPHIC 21–4

Relationship between the Income Statement and Cash Flows from Operating Activities (Direct Method)

To see the concept applied, let's look again at the cash flows from operating activities reported by United Brands Corporation. That section of the statement of cash flows is extracted from Graphic 21–2 and reproduced in Graphic 21–5.

Cash Flows from Operating Activities:	
Cash inflows:	
From customers	$98
From investment revenue	3
Cash outflows:	
To suppliers of goods	(50)
To employees	(11)
For interest	(3)
For insurance	(4)
For income taxes	(11)
Net cash flows from operating activities	$22

GRAPHIC 21–5

Cash Flows from Operating Activities (Direct Method)

Cash flows from operating activities are the elements of net income, but reported on a cash basis.

Cash inflows from operating activities exceeded cash outflows for expenses by $22 million. We'll see later (in Illustration 21–1) that UBC's net income from the same operating activities was only $12 million. Why did operating activities produce net cash inflows greater than net income? The reason will become apparent when we determine, in a later section, the specific amounts of these cash flows.

You also should be aware that the generalization stated earlier that cash flows from operating activities include the elements of net income reported on a cash basis is not strictly true for all elements of the income statement. Notice in Graphic 21–5 that no cash effects are reported for depreciation and amortization of property, plant, and equipment, and intangibles, nor for gains and losses from the sale of those assets. Cash outflows occur when these assets are acquired, and cash inflows occur when the assets are sold. However, as described later, the acquisition and subsequent resale of these assets are classified as investing activities, rather than as operating activities.

Quite the opposite, the purchase and the sale of inventory are considered operating activities. The cash effects of these transactions—namely, (1) cash payments to suppliers and (2) cash receipts from customers—are included in the determination of cash flows from operating activities. Why are inventories and noncurrent assets treated differently when classifying their cash effects if both are acquired for the purpose of producing revenues? The essential difference is that inventory typically is purchased for the purpose of being sold as part of the firm's current operations, while a noncurrent asset is purchased as an investment to benefit the business over a relatively long period of time.

DIRECT METHOD OR INDIRECT METHOD OF REPORTING CASH FLOWS FROM OPERATING ACTIVITIES. The presentation by UBC of cash flows from operating activities illustrated in Graphic 21–2 and reproduced in Graphic 21–5 is referred to as the **direct method.** The method is named for the fact that the cash effect of each operating activity (i.e., income statement item) is reported *directly* on the statement of cash flows. For instance, UBC reports "cash received from customers" as the cash effect of sales activities, "cash paid to suppliers" as the cash effect of cost of goods sold, and so on. Then, UBC simply omits from the presentation any income statement items that do not affect cash at all, such as depreciation expense.

● LO4

Another way UBC might have reported cash flows from operating activities is by the **indirect method.** By this approach, the net cash increase or decrease from operating activities ($22 million in our example) would be derived *indirectly* by starting with reported net income and working backwards to convert that amount to a cash basis. As we see later in the chapter, UBC's net income is $12 million. Using the indirect method, UBC would replace the previous presentation of net cash flows from operating activities with the one shown in Graphic 21–6.

GRAPHIC 21–6

Indirect Method

By the indirect method, UBC derives the net cash increase or decrease from operating activities *indirectly,* by starting with reported net income and working backwards to convert that amount to a cash basis.

Cash Flows from Operating Activities:	
Net income	$12
Adjustments for noncash effects:	
Gain on sale of land	(8)
Depreciation expense	3
Loss on sale of equipment	2
Changes in operating assets and liabilities:	
Increase in accounts receivable	(2)
Decrease in inventory	4
Increase in accounts payable	6
Increase in salaries payable	2
Discount on bonds payable	2
Decrease in prepaid insurance	3
Decrease in income tax payable	(2)
Net cash flows from operating activities	$22

Be sure to note that the indirect method generates the same $22 million net cash flows from operating activities as did the direct method. Rather than directly reporting only the components of the income statement that *do* represent increases or decreases in cash, by the indirect method we begin with net income—which includes both cash and noncash components—and back out all amounts that *don't* reflect increases or decreases in cash. Later in the chapter, we explore the specific adjustments made to net income to achieve this result. At this point it is sufficient to realize that two alternative methods are permitted for reporting net cash flows from operating activities. Either way, we convert accrual-based income to cash flows produced by those same operating activities.

Notice also that the indirect method presentation is identical to what UBC reported earlier as the "Reconciliation of Net Income to Cash Flows from Operating Activities" in Note X of Graphic 21–2. Whether cash flows from operating activities are reported by the direct method or by the indirect method, the financial statements must reconcile the difference between net income and cash flows from operating activities. When a company uses the *direct method,* the company presents the reconciliation in a separate schedule as UBC did. That presentation is precisely the same as the presentation of net cash flows from operating activities by the indirect method. On the other hand, a company choosing to use the indirect method is not required to provide a separate reconciliation schedule because the "cash flows from operating activities" section of the statement of cash flows serves that purpose.

Most companies use the indirect method.[6] This is slated to change. A joint project of the FASB and IASB is under way that would require the direct method and disallow the indirect method.[7]

WHERE WE'RE HEADED

The FASB and IASB are working together on a project, Financial Statement Presentation, to establish a common standard for presenting information in the financial statements, including classifying and displaying line items and aggregating line items into subtotals and totals. This standard will have a dramatic impact on the format of financial statements. An important part of the proposal involves the organization of elements of the balance sheet (statement of financial position), statement of comprehensive income (including the income statement), and statement of cash flows into a common set of classifications.

The statement of cash flows is slated to change in several ways. First, though, we should note that the three major classifications of cash flows are retained. In fact, each of the other financial statements also will include classifications by operating, investing, and financing activities, providing a "cohesive" financial picture that stresses the relationships among the financial statements.

For each statement, though, operating and investing activities will be included within a new category, "business" activities. Each statement also will include three additional groupings: discontinued operations, income taxes, and equity (if needed). The new look for the financials would be:

Statement of Financial Position	Statement of Comprehensive Income	Statement of Cash Flows
Business • Operating assets and liabilities • Investing assets and liabilities	Business • Operating income and expenses • Investing income and expenses	Business • Operating cash flows • Investing cash flows
Financing • Financing assets • Financing liabilities	Financing • Financing asset income • Financing liability expense	Financing • Financing asset cash flows • Financing liability cash flows
Income Taxes	Income Taxes	Income Taxes
Discontinued Operations	Discontinued Operations (net of tax)	Discontinued Operations
Equity	Other Comprehensive Income (net of tax)	Equity

One change planned for the statement of cash flows is to no longer permit a choice between the direct method and the indirect method, but to require the direct method, reasoning that it provides more useful information to investors. Another change is to eliminate the concept of cash equivalents in favor of cash only. Also, while we still will have operating, investing, and financing activities, some cash flows will switch categories. Under the new "management approach," cash flows will be classified based on how related assets and liabilities are used by management. For instance, expenditures for property, plant and equipment likely would be classified as operating, because those assets are used in the "core" business. Investing activities would be limited primarily to investments in stock, bonds, and other securities.

The FASB and IASB are working together on a standard that would have a dramatic impact on the format of financial statements.

● LO9

Demonstrating the cohesiveness among the financial statements is a key objective of the Financial Statement Presentation project.

The proposed new Standard would require the direct method.

---

[6]According to the *AICPA, Accounting Trends and Techniques,* 2008, a recent survey of 600 companies showed that 594 companies chose to use the indirect method, only 6 the direct method.

[7]Discussion Paper, *Preliminary Views on Financial Statement Presentation,* FASB/IASB, October 16, 2008.

It's important to understand, too, that regardless of which method a company chooses to report *operating* activities, that choice has no effect on the way it identifies and reports cash flows from *investing* and *financing* activities. We turn our attention now to those two sections of the statement of cash flows. Later in Part C, we'll return for a more thorough discussion of the alternative methods of reporting the operating activities section.

CASH FLOWS FROM INVESTING ACTIVITIES. Companies periodically invest cash to replace or expand productive facilities such as property, plant, and equipment. Investments might also be made in other assets, such as securities of other firms, with the expectation of a return on those investments. Information concerning these investing activities can provide valuable insight to decision makers regarding the nature and magnitude of assets being acquired for future use, as well as provide clues concerning the company's ambitions for the future.

Cash flows from investing activities are both outflows and inflows of cash caused by the acquisition and disposition of assets. Included in this classification are cash payments to acquire (1) property, plant, and equipment and other productive assets (except inventories), (2) investments in securities (except cash equivalents and trading securities[8]), and (3) non-trade receivables.[9] When these assets later are liquidated, any cash receipts from their disposition also are classified as investing activities. For instance, cash received from the sale of the assets or from the collection of a note receivable (principal amount only) represents cash inflows from investing activities. Be sure to realize that, unlike the label might imply, any investment revenue like interest, dividends, or other cash return from these investments is not an investing activity. The reason, remember, is that investment revenue is an income statement item and therefore is an operating activity.

For illustration, notice the cash flows reported as investing activities by UBC. That section of the statement of cash flows is extracted from the complete statement in Graphic 21–2 and reproduced in Graphic 21–7.

FINANCIAL
Reporting Case

Q2, p. 1183

● LO5

Cash outflows and cash inflows due to the acquisition and disposition of assets (other than inventory and assets classified as cash equivalents) are reported as cash flows from investing activities.

GRAPHIC 21–7

Cash Flows from Investing Activities

Cash flows from investing activities include investments in assets and their subsequent sale.

Cash Flows from Investing Activities:		
Purchase of land	(30)	
Purchase of short-term investment	(12)	
Sale of land	18	
Sale of equipment	5	
Net cash flows from investing activities		(19)

UBC reports as investing activities the cash paid to purchase both land and a short-term investment. The other two investing activities reported are cash receipts for the sale of assets—equipment and land—that were acquired in earlier years. The specific transactions creating these cash flows are described in a later section of this chapter.

The purchase and sale of inventories are not considered investing activities. Inventories are purchased for the purpose of being sold as part of the firm's primary operations, so their purchase and sale are classified as operating activities.

Also, the purchase and sale of assets classified as cash equivalents are not reported as investing activities. In fact, these activities usually are not reported on the statement of cash flows. For example, when temporarily idle cash is invested in a money market fund considered to be a cash equivalent, the total of cash and cash equivalents does not change. Likewise, when the cash is later withdrawn from the money market fund, the total remains unchanged. The exception is when cash equivalents are sold at a gain or a loss. In that case, the total of cash and cash equivalents actually increases or decreases in the process of transferring from

---

[8]Inflows and outflows of cash from buying and selling trading securities typically are considered operating activities because financial institutions that routinely transact in trading securities consider them an appropriate part of their normal operations.

[9]A nontrade receivable differs from a trade receivable in that it is not one associated with the company's normal trade; that is, it's not received from a customer. A trade receivable, or accounts receivable, is an *operating asset.* A nontrade receivable, on the other hand, might be a loan to an affiliate company or to an officer of the firm. To understand how the creation of a nontrade receivable is an *investing* activity, you might view such a loan as an investment in the receivable.

one cash equivalent account to another cash equivalent account. As a result, the change in cash would be reported as a cash flow from operating activities. This is illustrated later in the chapter.

CASH FLOWS FROM FINANCING ACTIVITIES.
Not only is it important for investors and creditors to be informed about how a company is investing its funds, but also how its investing activities are being financed. Hopefully, the primary operations of the firm provide a source of internal financing. Information revealed in the cash flows from operating activities section of the statement of cash flows lets statement users know the extent of available internal financing. However, a major portion of financing for many companies is provided by external sources, specifically by shareholders and creditors.

Cash flows from financing activities are both inflows and outflows of cash resulting from the external financing of a business. We include in this classification cash inflows from (a) the sale of common and preferred stock and (b) the issuance of bonds and other debt securities. Subsequent transactions related to these financing transactions, such as a buyback of stock (to retire the stock or as treasury stock), the repayment of debt, and the payment of cash dividends to shareholders, also are classified as financing activities.

For illustration, refer to Graphic 21–8 excerpted from the complete statement of cash flows of UBC in Graphic 21–2.

FINANCIAL
Reporting Case

Q3, p. 1183

● LO6

Cash inflows and cash outflows due to the external financing of a business are reported as cash flows from financing activities.

Cash Flows from Financing Activities		
Sale of common shares	26	
Retirement of bonds payable	(15)	
Payment of cash dividends	(5)	
Net cash flows from financing activities		6

GRAPHIC 21–8
Cash Flows from Financing Activities

Cash flows from financing activities include the sale or repurchase of shares, the issuance or repayment of debt securities, and the payment of cash dividends.

The cash received from the sale of common stock is reported as a financing activity. Since the sale of common stock is a financing activity, providing a cash return (dividend) to common shareholders also is a financing activity. Similarly, when the bonds being retired were issued in a prior year, that cash inflow was reported as a financing activity. In the current year, when the bonds are retired, the resulting cash outflow is likewise classified as a financing activity.

At first glance, it may appear inconsistent to classify the payment of cash dividends to shareholders as a financing activity when, as stated earlier, paying interest to creditors is classified as an operating activity. But remember, cash flows from operating activities should reflect the cash effects of items that enter into the determination of net income. Interest expense is a determinant of net income. A dividend, on the other hand, is a distribution of net income and not an expense.

Interest, unlike dividends, is a determinant of net income and therefore an operating activity.

RECONCILIATION WITH CHANGE IN CASH BALANCE.
One of the first items you may have noticed about UBC's statement of cash flows is that there is a net change in cash of $9 million. Is this a significant item of information provided by the statement? The primary objective of the statement of cash flows is not to tell us that cash increased by $9 million. We can readily see the increase or decrease in cash by comparing the beginning and ending balances in the cash account in comparative balance sheets. Instead, the purpose of the statement of cash flows is to explain *why* cash increased by $9 million.

To reinforce the fact that the net amount of cash inflows and outflows explains the change in the cash balance, the statement of cash flows includes a reconciliation of the net increase (or decrease) in cash with the company's beginning and ending cash balances. Notice, for instance, that on UBC's statement of cash flows, the reconciliation appears as:

The net amount of cash inflows and outflows reconciles the change in the company's beginning and ending cash balances.

Net Increase in Cash	$ 9
Cash balance, January 1	20
Cash balance, December 31	$29

NONCASH INVESTING AND FINANCING ACTIVITIES. Suppose UBC were to borrow $20 million cash from a bank, issuing a long-term note payable for that amount. This transaction would be reported on a statement of cash flows as a financing activity. Now suppose UBC used that $20 million cash to purchase new equipment. This second transaction would be reported as an investing activity.

● LO7

Instead of two separate transactions, as indicated by Graphic 21–2, UBC acquired $20 million of new equipment by issuing a $20 million long-term note payable in a single transaction. Undertaking a significant investing activity and a significant financing activity as two parts of a single transaction does not diminish the value of reporting these activities. For that reason, transactions that do not increase or decrease cash, but which result in significant investing and financing activities, must be reported in related disclosures.

These **noncash investing and financing activities,** such as UBC's acquiring equipment (an investing activity) by issuing a long-term note payable (a financing activity), are reported in a separate disclosure schedule or note. UBC reported this transaction in the following manner:

Noncash investing and financing activities are reported also.

Noncash Investing and Financing Activities:
Acquired $20 million of equipment by issuing a 12%, 5-year note.

It's convenient to report noncash investing and financing activities on the same page as the statement of cash flows as did UBC only if there are few such transactions. Otherwise, precisely the same information would be reported in disclosure notes to the financial statements.[10]

Examples of noncash transactions that would be reported in this manner are:

1. Acquiring an asset by incurring a debt payable to the seller.
2. Acquiring an asset by entering into a capital lease.
3. Converting debt into common stock or other equity securities.
4. Exchanging noncash assets or liabilities for other noncash assets or liabilities.

Noncash transactions that do not affect a company's assets or liabilities, such as the distribution of stock dividends, are not considered investing or financing activities and are not reported. Recall from Chapter 18 that stock dividends merely increase the number of shares of stock owned by existing shareholders. From an accounting standpoint, the stock dividend causes a dollar amount to be transferred from one part of shareholders' equity (retained earnings) to another part of shareholders' equity (paid-in capital). Neither assets nor liabilities are affected; therefore, no investing or financing activity has occurred.

● LO8

Preparation of the Statement of Cash Flows

The objective in preparing the statement of cash flows is to identify all transactions and events that represent operating, investing, or financing activities and to list and classify those activities in proper statement format. A difficulty in preparing a statement of cash flows is that typical accounting systems are not designed to produce the specific information we need for the statement. At the end of a reporting cycle, balances exist in accounts reported in the income statement (sales revenue, cost of goods sold, etc.) and the balance sheet (accounts receivable, common stock, etc.). However, the ledger contains no balances for cash paid to acquire equipment, or cash received from sale of land, or any other cash flow needed for the statement. As a result, it's necessary to find a way of using available information to reconstruct the various cash flows that occurred during the reporting period. Typically, the information available to assist the statement preparer includes an income statement for the year and balance sheets for both the current and preceding years (comparative statements). The accounting records also can provide additional information about transactions that caused changes in account balances during the year.

---

[10]FASB ASC 230–10–50–6: Statement of Cash Flows–Overall–Disclosure–Noncash Investing and Financing Activities (previously "Statement of Cash Flows," *Statement of Financial Accounting Standards No. 95* (Stamford, Conn.: FASB, 1987), par. 74).

ADDITIONAL CONSIDERATION

A transaction involving an investing and financing activity may be part cash and part noncash. For example, a company might pay cash for a part of the purchase price of new equipment and issue a long-term note for the remaining amount. In our previous illustration, UBC issued a note payable for the $20 million cost of the equipment it acquired. Suppose the equipment were purchased in the following manner:

Equipment	20	
Cash		6
Note payable		14

In that case, $6 million would be reported under the caption "Cash flows from investing activities," and the noncash portion of the transaction—issuing a $14 million note payable for $14 million of equipment—would be reported as a "noncash investing and financing activity." UBC's statement of cash flows, if modified by the assumption of a part cash/part noncash transaction, would report these two elements of the transaction as follows:

Cash Flows from Investing Activities:

Purchase of land	$(30)
Purchase of short-term investments	(12)
Sale of land	18
Sale of equipment	5
Purchase of equipment	(6)
Net cash flows from investing activities	(25)

Noncash Investing and Financing Activities:

Acquired $20 million of equipment by paying cash and issuing a 12%, 5-year note as follows:

Cost of equipment	$20 million
Cash paid	6 million
Note issued	$14 million

The typical year-end data is provided for UBC in Illustration 21–1 on the next page. We have referred frequently to the statement of cash flows of UBC to illustrate the nature of the activities the statement reports. Now we will see how that statement is developed from the data provided in that illustration.

In situations involving relatively few transactions, it is possible to prepare the statement of cash flows by merely inspecting the available data and logically determining the reportable activities. Few real-life situations are sufficiently simple to be solved this way. Usually, it is more practical to use some systematic method of analyzing the available data to ensure that all operating, investing, and financing activities are detected. A common approach is to use either a manual or electronic spreadsheet to organize and analyze the information used to prepare the statement.[11]

Whether the statement of cash flows is prepared by an unaided inspection and analysis or with the aid of a systematic technique such as spreadsheet analysis, the analytical process is the same. To identify the activities to be reported on the statement, we use available data to reconstruct the events and transactions that involved operating, investing, and financing activities during the year. It is helpful to reproduce the journal entries that were recorded at the time of the transaction. Examining reconstructed journal entries makes it easier to visualize whether a reportable activity is involved and how that activity is to be classified.

Reconstructing the events and transactions that occurred during the period helps identify the operating, investing, and financing activities to be reported.

---

[11]The T-account method is a second systematic approach to the preparation of the statement of cash flows. This method is identical in concept and similar in application to the spreadsheet method. The T-account method is used to prepare the statement of cash flows for UBC in Appendix 21B.

ILLUSTRATION 21–1

Comparative
Balance Sheets and
Income Statement

UNITED BRANDS CORPORATION
Comparative Balance Sheets
December 31, 2011 and 2010
($ in millions)

Assets	2011	2010
Cash	$ 29	$ 20
Accounts receivable	32	30
Short-term investments	12	0
Inventory	46	50
Prepaid insurance	3	6
Land	80	60
Buildings and equipment	81	75
Less: Accumulated depreciation	(16)	(20)
	$267	$221
Liabilities		
Accounts payable	$ 26	$ 20
Salaries payable	3	1
Income tax payable	6	8
Notes payable	20	0
Bonds payable	35	50
Less: Discount on bonds	(1)	(3)
Shareholders' Equity		
Common stock	130	100
Paid-in capital—excess of par	29	20
Retained earnings	19	25
	$267	$221

Revenues		
Sales revenue	$100	
Investment revenue	3	
Gain on sale of land	8	$111
Expenses		
Cost of goods sold	60	
Salaries expense	13	
Depreciation expense	3	
Bond interest expense	5	
Insurance expense	7	
Loss on sale of equipment	2	
Income tax expense	9	99
Net income		$ 12

Additional Information from the Accounting Records

a. A portion of company land, purchased in a previous year for $10 million, was sold for $18 million.

b. Equipment that originally cost $14 million, and which was one-half depreciated, was sold for $5 million cash.

c. The common shares of Mazuma Corporation were purchased for $12 million as a short-term investment.

d. Property was purchased for $30 million cash for use as a parking lot.

e. On December 30, 2011, new equipment was acquired by issuing a 12%, five-year, $20 million note payable to the seller.

f. On January 1, 2011, $15 million of bonds were retired at maturity.

g. The increase in the common stock account is attributable to the issuance of a 10% stock dividend (1 million shares) and the subsequent sale of 2 million shares of common stock. The market price of the $10 par value common stock was $13 per share on the dates of both transactions.

h. Cash dividends of $5 million were paid to shareholders.

Next, in Part B, we see how a spreadsheet simplifies the process of preparing a statement of cash flows. Even if you choose not to use a spreadsheet, the summary entries described can be used to help you find the cash inflows and outflows you need to prepare a statement of cash flows. For this demonstration, we assume the direct method is used to determine and report cash flows from operating activities. Appreciation of the direct method provides the backdrop for a thorough understanding of the indirect method that we explore in Part C.

PREPARING AN SCF: THE DIRECT METHOD OF REPORTING CASH FLOWS FROM OPERATING ACTIVITIES

PART B

Using a Spreadsheet

An important advantage gained by using a spreadsheet is that it ensures that no reportable activities are inadvertently overlooked. Spreadsheet analysis relies on the fact that, in order for cash to increase or decrease, there must be a corresponding change in a noncash account. Therefore, if we can identify the events and transactions that caused the change in each noncash account during the year, we will have identified all the operating, investing, and financing activities that are to be included in the statement of cash flows.

> There can be no cash inflow or cash outflow without a corresponding change in a noncash account.

The beginning and ending balances of each account are entered on the spreadsheet. Then, as journal entries are reconstructed in our analysis of the data, those entries are recorded on the spreadsheet so that the debits and credits of the spreadsheet entries explain the changes in the account balances. Only after spreadsheet entries have explained the changes in all account balances, can we feel confident that all operating, investing, and financing activities have been identified. The spreadsheet is designed in such a way that, as we record spreadsheet entries that explain account balance changes, we are simultaneously identifying and classifying the activities to be reported on the statement of cash flows.

> Recording spreadsheet entries that explain account balance changes simultaneously identifies and classifies the activities to be reported on the statement of cash flows.

We begin by transferring the comparative balance sheets and income statement to a blank spreadsheet. For illustration, refer to the 2011 and 2010 balances in the completed spreadsheet for UBC, shown in Illustration 21–1A on the next two pages. Notice that the amounts for elements of the income statement are ending balances resulting from accumulations during the year. Beginning balances in each of these accounts are always zero.

Following the balance sheets and income statement, we allocate space on the spreadsheet for the statement of cash flows. Although at this point we have not yet identified the specific cash flow activities shown in the completed spreadsheet, we can include headings for the major categories of activities: cash flows from operating activities, cash flows from investing activities, and cash flows from financing activities. Leaving several lines between headings allows adequate space to include the specific cash flows identified in subsequent analysis.

The spreadsheet entries shown in the two changes columns, which separate the beginning and ending balances, explain the increase or decrease in each account balance. You will see in the next section how these entries were reconstructed. Although spreadsheet entries are in the form of debits and credits like journal entries, they are entered on the spreadsheet only. They are not recorded in the formal accounting records. In effect, these entries duplicate, frequently in summary form, the actual journal entries used to record the transactions as they occurred during the year.

> Spreadsheet entries duplicate the actual journal entries used to record the transactions as they occurred during the year.

To reconstruct the journal entries, we analyze each account, one at a time, deciding at each step what transaction or event caused the change in that account. Often, the reason for the change in an account balance is readily apparent from viewing the change in conjunction with that of a related account elsewhere in the financial statements. Sometimes it is necessary to consult the accounting records for additional information to help explain the transaction that resulted in the change.

ILLUSTRATION 21–1A

Spreadsheet— Direct method

UNITED BRANDS CORPORATION
Spreadsheet for the Statement of Cash Flows

	Dec. 31 2010	Changes Debits		Changes Credits		Dec. 31 2011
Balance Sheet						
Assets:						
Cash	20	(19)	9			29
Accounts receivable	30	(1)	2			32
Short-term investments	0	(12)	12			12
Inventory	50			(4)	4	46
Prepaid insurance	6			(8)	3	3
Land	60	(13)	30	(3)	10	80
Buildings and equipment	75	(14)	20X	(9)	14	81
Less: Accumulated depreciation	(20)	(9)	7	(6)	3	(16)
	221					267
Liabilities:						
Accounts payable	20			(4)	6	26
Salaries payable	1			(5)	2	3
Income tax payable	8	(10)	2			6
Notes payable	0			(14)	20X	20
Bonds payable	50	(15)	15			35
Less: Discount on bonds	(3)			(7)	2	(1)
Shareholders' Equity:						
Common stock	100			(16)	10	
				(17)	20	130
Paid-in capital—excess of par	20			(16)	3	
				(17)	6	29
Retained earnings	25	(16)	13			
		(18)	5	(11)	12	19
	221					267
Income Statement						
Revenues:						
Sales revenue				(1)	100	100
Investment revenue				(2)	3	3
Gain on sale of land				(3)	8	8
Expenses:						
Cost of goods sold		(4)	60			(60)
Salaries expense		(5)	13			(13)
Depreciation expense		(6)	3			(3)
Bond interest expense		(7)	5			(5)
Insurance expense		(8)	7			(7)
Loss on sale of equipment		(9)	2			(2)
Income tax expense		(10)	9			(9)
Net income		(11)	**12**			**12**
Statement of Cash Flows						
Operating Activities:						
Cash inflows:						
From customers		(1)	98			
From investment revenue		(2)	3			
Cash outflows:						
To suppliers of goods				(4)	50	
To employees				(5)	11	
To bondholders				(7)	3	
For insurance expense				(8)	4	
For income taxes				(10)	11	
Net cash flows						22

(continued)

	Dec. 31 2010	Changes		Dec. 31 2011	ILLUSTRATION 21–1A
		Debits	Credits		(concluded)
Investing Activities:					
Sale of land		(3) 18			
Sale of equipment		(9) 5			
Purchase of S-T investment			(12) 12		
Purchase of land			(13) 30		
Net cash flows				(19)	
Financing Activities:					
Retirement of bonds payable			(15) 15		
Sale of common shares		(17) 26			
Payment of cash dividends			(18) 5		
Net cash flows				6	
Net increase in cash			(19) 9	9	
Totals		376	376		

X—As explained later, the X's serve as a reminder to report this noncash transaction.

You may find it helpful to diagram in T-account format the relationship between accounts to better visualize certain changes, particularly in your initial study of the chapter. The analysis that follows is occasionally supplemented with such diagrams to emphasize *why,* rather than merely *how,* specific cash flow amounts emerge from the analysis.

Although there is no mandatory order in which to analyze the accounts, it is convenient to begin with the income statement accounts, followed by the balance sheet accounts. We analyze the accounts of UBC in that order below. Although our analysis of each account culminates in a spreadsheet entry, keep in mind that the analysis described also is appropriate to identify reportable activities when a spreadsheet is not used.[12]

Income Statement Accounts

As described in an earlier section, cash flows from operating activities are inflows and outflows of cash that result from activities reported in the income statement. Thus, to identify those cash inflows and outflows, we begin by analyzing the components of the income statement. It is important to keep in mind that the amounts reported in the income statement usually do not represent the cash effects of the items reported. For example, UBC reports sales revenue of $100 million. This does not mean, however, that it collected $100 million cash from customers during the year. In fact, by referring to the beginning and ending balances in accounts receivable, we see that cash received from customers could not have been $100 million. Since accounts receivable increased during the year, some of the sales revenue earned must not yet have been collected. This is explained further in the next section.

Amounts reported in the income statement usually are not the same as the cash effects of the items reported.

The cash effects of other income statement elements can be similarly discerned by referring to changes in the balances of the balance sheet accounts that are directly related to those elements. So, to identify cash flows from operating activities we examine, one at a time, the elements of the income statement in conjunction with any balance sheet accounts affected by each element.

1. SALES REVENUE.   Accounts receivable is the balance sheet account that is affected by sales revenue. Specifically, accounts receivable is increased by credit sales and is decreased as cash is received from customers. We can compare sales and the change in accounts

---

[12]The spreadsheet entries also are used to record the same transactions when the T-account method is used. We refer again to these entries when that method is described in Appendix 21B.

receivable during the year to determine the amount of cash received from customers. This relationship can be viewed in T-account format as follows:

Accounts Receivable

Beginning balance	30		
Credit sales	100	?	Cash received
(increases A/R)			*(decreases A/R)*
Ending balance	32		

We see from this analysis that cash received from customers must have been $98 million. Note that even if some of the year's sales were cash sales, say $40 million cash sales and $60 million credit sales, the result is the same:

Accounts Receivable

Beginning balance	30		Cash sales	$40
Credit sales	60	58 ⟶	Received on account	58
Ending balance	32		Cash received	$98

Thus, cash flows from operating activities should include cash received from customers of $98 million. The net effect of sales revenue activity during the year can be summarized in the following entry.

	($ in millions)	
Entry (1) Cash (received from customers)	98	
Accounts receivable (given)	2	
Sales revenue ($100 − 0)		100

The entry above appears as entry (1) in the completed spreadsheet for UBC, shown in Illustration 21–1A. The entry explains the changes in two account balances—accounts receivable and sales revenue. Since the entry affects cash, it also identifies a cash flow to be reported on the statement of cash flows. The $98 million debit to cash is therefore entered in the statement of cash flows section of the spreadsheet under the heading of cash flows from operating activities.

ADDITIONAL CONSIDERATION

The preceding discussion describes the most common situation—companies earn revenue by selling goods and services, increase accounts receivable, and then collect the cash and decrease accounts receivable later. Some companies, though, often collect the cash in advance of earning it, record unearned revenue, and then later record revenue and decrease unearned revenue. In those cases, we need to analyze any changes in the unearned revenue account for differences between revenue reported and cash collected. For instance, if UBC also had a $1 million increase in unearned revenue, the summary entry would be modified as follows:

	($ in millions)	
Entry (1) Cash (received from customers)	99	
Accounts receivable (given)	2	
Unearned revenue (given)		1
Sales revenue ($100 − 0)		100

Notice that we enter the cash portion of entry (1) as one of several cash flows on the statement of cash flows rather than as a debit to the cash account. Only after all cash inflows and outflows have been identified will the net change in cash be entered as a debit to the cash account. In fact, the entry to reconcile the $9 million increase in the cash account and the $9 million net increase in cash on the statement of cash flows will serve as a final check of the accuracy of our spreadsheet analysis.

ADDITIONAL CONSIDERATION

Notice that bad debt expense does not appear in the income statement and allowance for uncollectible accounts does not appear in the balance sheet. We have assumed that bad debts are immaterial for UBC. When this is not the case, it's necessary to consider the write-off of bad debts as we determine cash received from customers. Here's why.

When using the allowance method to account for bad debts, a company estimates the dollar amount of customer accounts that will ultimately prove uncollectible and records both bad debt expense and allowance for uncollectible accounts for that estimate.

Bad debt expense	xxx	
Allowance for uncollectible accounts		xxx

Then, when accounts actually prove uncollectible, accounts receivable and the allowance are reduced.

Allowance for uncollectible accounts	xxx	
Accounts receivable		xxx

In our illustration, we concluded that UBC received $2 million less cash ($98 million) than sales for the year ($100 million) because accounts receivable increased by that amount. However, if a portion of the change in accounts receivable had been due to write-offs of bad debts, that conclusion would be incorrect. Let's say, for instance, that UBC had bad debt expense of $2 million and its allowance for uncollectible accounts had increased by $1 million. Because the allowance for uncollectible accounts would be credited by $2 million in the adjusting entry for bad debts expense, necessarily there also would have been a $1 million debit to the account in order for there to have been a net increase (credit) in its balance of only $1 million. That debit would occur due to write-offs of bad debts totaling $1 million.

	($ in millions)
Allowance for uncollectible accounts	1
Accounts receivable	1

This would indicate that a portion ($1 million credit) of the total change in accounts receivable ($2 million debit) would have been due to write-offs of bad debts, and the remaining change ($3 million debit) would have been due to cash collections being less than sales revenue. Cash received from customers would have been only $97 million in that case. We can view this in the framework of our T-account analysis as follows:

Accounts Receivable

Beginning balance	30		
Credit sales	100	97	Cash received
		1	Bad Debt write-offs
Ending balance	32		

The effect of write-offs of bad debts can be explicitly considered by combining all the accounts related to sales and collection activities into a single summary entry:

	($ in millions)	
Entry (1) Cash (received from customers)	97	
Accounts receivable ($32 – 30)	2	
Bad debt expense (from income statement)	2	
Allowance for uncollectible accounts ($3 – 2)		1
Sales revenue ($100 – 0)		100

This single entry summarizes all transactions related to sales, bad debts expense, write-offs of accounts receivable, and cash collections from sales.

The remaining summary entries are described in subsections 2 through 19. When including the entries on the spreadsheet, it is helpful to number the entries sequentially to provide a means of retracing the steps taken in the analysis if the need arises. You also may find it helpful to put a check mark (✔) to the right of the ending balance when the change in that balance has been explained. Then, once you have check marks next to every noncash account, you will know you are finished.

2. INVESTMENT REVENUE. The income statement reports investment revenue of $3 million. Before concluding that this amount was received in cash, we first refer to the balance sheets to see whether a change in an account there indicates otherwise. A change in either of two balance sheet accounts, (a) investment revenue receivable or (b) long-term investments, might indicate that cash received from investment revenue differs from the amount reported in the income statement.

> Changes in related accounts might indicate that investment revenue reported in the income statement is a different amount from cash received from the investment.

a. If we observe either an increase or a decrease in an *investment revenue receivable* account (e.g., interest receivable, dividends receivable), we would conclude that the amount of cash received during the year was less than (if an increase) or more than (if a decrease) the amount of revenue reported. The analysis would be identical to that of sales revenue and accounts receivable.

b. Also, an unexplained increase in a *long-term investment* account might indicate that a portion of investment revenue has not yet been received in cash. Recall from Chapter 12 that when using the equity method to account for investments in the stock of another corporation, investment revenue is recognized as the investor's percentage share of the investee's income, whether or not the revenue is received currently as cash dividends. For example, assume the investor owns 25% of the common stock of a corporation that reports net income of $12 million and pays dividends of $4 million. This situation would have produced a $2 million increase in long-term investments, which can be demonstrated by reconstructing the journal entries for the recognition of investment and the receipt of cash dividends:

		($ in millions)
Long-term investments	3	
Investment revenue ($12 × 25%)		3
Cash ($4 × 25%)	1	
Long-term investments		1

A combined entry would produce the same results:

		($ in millions)
Long-term investments	2	
Cash ($4 × 25%)	1	
Investment revenue ($12 × 25%)		3

The $2 million net increase in long-term investments would represent the investment revenue not received in cash. This would also explain why there is a $3 million increase (credit) in investment revenue. If these events had occurred, we would prepare a spreadsheet entry identical to the combined entry above. The spreadsheet entry would (a) explain the $2 million increase in long-term investments, (b) explain the $3 million increase in investment revenue, and (c) identify a $1 million cash inflow from operating activities.

However, because neither an investment revenue receivable account nor a long-term investment account appears on the comparative balance sheets, we can conclude that $3 million of investment revenue was collected in cash. Entry (2) on the spreadsheet is:

> Because no other transactions are apparent that would have caused a change in investment revenue, we can conclude that $3 million of investment revenue was collected in cash.

		($ in millions)
Entry (2) Cash (received from investment revenue)	3	
Investment revenue ($3 − 0)		3

3. GAIN ON SALE OF LAND. The third item reported in the income statement is an $8 million gain on the sale of land. Recall that our objective in analyzing each element of the statement is to determine the cash effect of that element. To do so, we need additional information about the transaction that caused this gain. The accounting records—item (a) in Illustration 21–1—indicate that land that originally cost $10 million was sold for $18 million. The entry recorded in the journal when the land was sold also serves as our summary entry:

	($ in millions)	
Entry (3) Cash (received from sale of land)	18	
Land (given)		10
Gain on sale of land ($8 − 0)		8

> A gain (or loss) is simply the difference between cash received in the sale of an asset and the book value of the asset—not a cash flow.

The cash effect of this transaction is a cash increase of $18 million. We therefore include the debit as a cash inflow in the statement of cash flows section of the spreadsheet. However, unlike the cash effect of the previous two spreadsheet entries, it is not reported as an operating activity. The sale of land is an *investing* activity, so this cash inflow is listed under that heading of the spreadsheet. The entry also accounts for the $8 million gain on sale of land. The $10 million credit to land does not, by itself, explain the $20 million increase in that account. As we will later discover, another transaction also affected the land account.

It is important to understand that the gain is simply the difference between cash received in the sale of land (reported as an investing activity) and the book value of the land. To report the $8 million gain as a cash flow from operating activities, in addition to reporting $18 million as a cash flow from investing activities, would be to report the $8 million twice.

4. COST OF GOODS SOLD.   During the year UBC sold goods that had cost $60 million. This does not necessarily indicate that $60 million cash was paid to suppliers of those goods. To determine the amount of cash paid to suppliers, we look to the two current accounts affected by merchandise purchases—inventory and accounts payable. The analysis can be viewed as a two-step process.

First, we compare cost of goods sold with the change in inventory to determine the cost of goods *purchased* (not necessarily cash paid) during the year. To facilitate our analysis, we can examine the relationship in T-account format:

Inventory			
Beginning balance	50		
Cost of goods **purchased** (increases inventory)	?	60	Cost of goods **sold** (decreases inventory)
Ending balance	46		

From this analysis, we see that $56 million of goods were *purchased* during the year. It is not necessarily true, though, that $56 million cash was paid to suppliers of these goods. By looking in accounts payable, we can determine the cash paid to suppliers:

> Determining the amount of cash paid to suppliers means looking at not only the cost of goods sold, but also the changes in both inventory and accounts payable.

Accounts Payable			
		20	Beginning balance
Cash paid to suppliers (decreases A/P)	?	56	Cost of goods *purchased* (increases A/P)
		26	Ending Balance

We now see that cash paid to suppliers was $50 million. The entry that summarizes merchandise acquisitions is:

	($ in millions)	
Entry (4) Cost of goods sold ($60 − 0)	60	
Inventory ($46 − 50)		4
Accounts payable ($26 − 20)		6
Cash (paid to suppliers of goods)		50

> Although $60 million of goods were sold during the year, only $50 million cash was paid to suppliers of these goods.

5. SALARIES EXPENSE. The balance sheet account affected by salaries expense is salaries payable. By analyzing salaries expense in relation to the change in salaries payable, we can determine the amount of cash paid to employees:

Salaries Payable

Cash paid to employees ? *(decreases salaries payable)*	1 13	Beginning balance Salaries expense *(increases salaries payable)*
	3	Ending Balance

This analysis indicates that only $11 million cash was paid to employees; the remaining $2 million of salaries expense is reflected as an increase in salaries payable.

Viewing the relationship in journal entry format provides the same conclusion and also gives us the entry in our spreadsheet analysis:

Although salaries expense was $13 million, only $11 million cash was paid to employees.

	($ in millions)
Entry (5) Salaries expense ($13 – 0)	13
Salaries payable ($3 – 1)	2
Cash (paid to employees)	11

6. DEPRECIATION EXPENSE. The income statement reports depreciation expense of $3 million. The entry used to record depreciation, which also serves as our summary entry, is:

Depreciation expense does not require a current cash expenditure.

	($ in millions)
Entry (6) Depreciation expense ($3 – 0)	3
Accumulated depreciation	3

Depreciation is a noncash expense. It is merely an allocation in the current period of a prior cash expenditure (for the depreciable asset). Therefore, unlike the other entries to this point, the depreciation entry has no effect on the statement of cash flows. However, it does explain the change in the depreciation expense account and a portion of the change in accumulated depreciation.

7. INTEREST EXPENSE. Recall from Chapter 14 that bond interest expense differs from the amount of cash paid to bondholders when bonds are issued at either a premium or a discount. The difference between the two amounts is the reduction of the premium or discount. By referring to the balance sheet, we see that UBC's bonds were issued at a discount. Since we know that bond interest expense is $5 million and that $2 million of the discount was reduced in 2011, we can determine that $3 million cash was paid to bondholders by recreating the entry that summarizes the recording of bond interest expense.

Bond interest expense is not the same as the amount of cash paid to bondholders when bonds are issued at either a premium or a discount.

	($ in millions)
Entry (7) Interest expense ($5 – 0)	5
Discount on bonds payable ($1 – 3)	2
Cash (paid to bondholders)	3

Recording this entry on the spreadsheet explains the change in both the bond interest expense and discount on bonds payable accounts. It also provides us with another cash outflow from operating activities. Of course, if a premium were being reduced, rather than a discount, the cash outflow would be *greater* than the expense.

8. INSURANCE EXPENSE. A decrease of $3 million in the prepaid insurance account indicates that cash paid for insurance coverage was $3 million less than the $7 million insurance expense for the year. Viewing prepaid insurance in T-account format clarifies this point.

ADDITIONAL CONSIDERATION

If the balance sheet had revealed an increase or decrease in an accrued bond interest payable account, the entry calculating cash paid to bondholders would require modification. For example, if UBC had a bond interest payable account, and that account had increased (a credit) by $1 million, the entry would have been:

		($ in millions)	
Entry (7)	Interest expense	5	
(revised)	Discount on bonds payable		2
	Interest payable		1
	Cash (paid to bondholders)		2

If the amount owed to bondholders increased by $1 million, they obviously were paid $1 million less cash than if there had been no change in the amount owed them. Similarly, if bond interest payable decreased by $1 million, the opposite would be true; that is, cash paid to them would have been $1 million more.

Prepaid Insurance

Beginning balance	6		
Cash paid for insurance	?	7	Insurance expense
(increases prepaid insurance)			*(decreases prepaid insurance)*
Ending balance	3		

From this analysis, we can conclude that $4 million was paid for insurance. We reach the same conclusion by preparing the following summary entry:

	($ in millions)	
Entry (8) Insurance expense ($7 – 0)	7	
Prepaid insurance ($3 – 6)		3
Cash (paid for insurance)		4

Since $3 million of prepaid insurance was allocated to insurance expense, only **$4 million** of the expense was paid in cash during the period.

The entry accounts for the change in both the insurance expense and prepaid insurance accounts and also identifies a cash outflow from operating activities.

9. LOSS ON SALE OF EQUIPMENT.

A $2 million loss on the sale of equipment is the next item reported in the income statement. To determine the cash effect of the sale of equipment, we need additional information about the transaction. The information we need is provided in item (b) of Illustration 21–1. Recreating the journal entry for the transaction described gives us the following entry:

	($ in millions)	
Entry (9) Cash (from the sale of equipment)	5	
Loss on sale of equipment ($2 – 0)	2	
Accumulated depreciation ($14 × 50%)	7	
Buildings and equipment (given)..................................		14

Recreating the journal entry for the sale of equipment reveals a **$5 million** cash inflow from investing activities.

The $5 million cash inflow is entered in the statement of cash flows section of the spreadsheet as an investing activity. The $2 million debit to the loss on sale of equipment explains the change in that account balance. Referring to the spreadsheet, we see that a portion of the change in accumulated depreciation was accounted for in entry (6). The debit to accumulated depreciation in the entry above completes the explanation for the change in that account. However, the credit to buildings and equipment only partially justifies the change in that account. We must assume that the analysis of a subsequent transaction will account for the unexplained portion of the change.

Recognize too that the loss, like the gain in entry (3), has no cash effect in the current period. Therefore, it is not reported in the statement of cash flows when using the direct method.

10. INCOME TAX EXPENSE. The final expense reported in the income statement is income tax expense. Since income taxes payable is the balance sheet account affected by this expense, we look to the change in that account to help determine the cash paid for income taxes. A T-account analysis can be used to find the cash effect as follows:

Income Tax Payable

	8	Beginning balance
Cash paid for income tax **?**	9	Income tax expense
(decreases the liability)		
	6	Ending Balance

This analysis reveals that $11 million cash was paid for income taxes, $2 million more than the year's expense. The overpayment explains why the liability for income taxes decreased by $2 million.

The same conclusion can be reached from the following summary entry, which represents the net effect of income taxes on UBC's accounts.

	($ in millions)	
Entry (10) Income tax expense ($9 – 0)	9	
Income tax payable ($6 – 8)	2	
Cash (paid for income taxes)		11

ADDITIONAL CONSIDERATION

Entry (10) would require modification in either of the two independent situations described below.

1. Note that UBC does not have a deferred income tax account. Recall from Chapter 16 that temporary differences between taxable income and pretax accounting income give rise to deferred taxes. If temporary differences had been present, which would be evidenced by a change in a deferred income taxes account, the calculation of cash paid for income taxes would require modification. Assume, for example, that a deferred income tax liability account had experienced a credit change of $1 million for the year. In that case, the previous summary entry would be revised as follows:

	($ in millions)	
Entry (10) Income tax expense	9	
(revised) Income tax payable..	2	
Deferred income tax liability		1
Cash (paid for income taxes)...		10

As the revised entry indicates, only $10 million cash would have been paid in this situation, rather than $11 million. The $1 million difference represents the portion of the income tax expense whose payment is deferred to a later year.

2. The summary entry also would be affected if the income statement includes either an extraordinary gain or an extraordinary loss. Recall from Chapter 3 and Chapter 16 that the income tax effect of an extraordinary item is not reflected in income tax expense, but instead is separately reported as a reduction in the extraordinary item. For example, if UBC's loss on the sale of equipment had been due to an extraordinary event, the tax savings from that loss would be reported as a reduction in the extraordinary loss rather than as a reduction in income tax expense. (Since the loss reduces taxable income by $2 million, assuming a marginal tax rate of 50%, taxes would be reduced by $1 million.) The lower portion of the income statement would have appeared as shown on the next page, in comparison with the presentation in Illustration 21–1:

(continued)

(concluded)

Ordinary Loss		**Extraordinary Loss**		
(from Illustration 21–1)				
		Income tax expense		(10)
		Income before extraordinary items		$13
Loss on sale of equipment	(2)	Extraordinary loss—sale of equipment	$2	
Income tax expense	(9)	Less: Tax savings	(1)	(1)
Net income	$12	Net income		$12

Without the tax savings produced by the loss, income tax expense would have been $10 million, rather than $9 million. But the tax savings still reduces the amount of cash paid for income taxes, even though it is reported separately from the income tax expense. Therefore, whether the loss is extraordinary or not, the amount of cash paid for income taxes is the same. If the loss is extraordinary, entry (10) would be modified as follows:

	($ in millions)	
Entry (10) Income tax expense (on ordinary income)	10	
(revised) Income tax payable	2	
Income tax expense		
(savings from extraordinary loss)		1
Cash (paid for income taxes)		11

Entry (9) would be unaffected. Whether or not the loss is extraordinary, it is not reported in the statement of cash flows, and the cash inflow from the sale is reported as an investing activity.

11. NET INCOME.
The balance in the retained earnings account at the end of the year includes an increase due to net income. If we are to account for all changes in each of the accounts, we must include the following entry on the spreadsheet, which represents the closing of net income to retained earnings.

	($ in millions)	
Entry (11) Net income	12	
Retained earnings		12

This entry partially explains the change in the retained earnings account.

This entry does not affect amounts reported on the statement of cash flows. We include the entry in the spreadsheet analysis only to help explain account balance changes.

Balance Sheet Accounts

To identify all the operating, investing, and financing activities when using a spreadsheet, we must account for the changes in each account on both the income statement and the balance sheet. Thus far, we have explained the change in each income statement account. Since the transactions that gave rise to some of those changes involved balance sheet accounts as well, some changes in balance sheet accounts have already been explained. We now reconstruct the transactions that caused changes in the remaining balances.

With the exception of the cash account, the accounts are analyzed in the order of their presentation in the balance sheet. As noted earlier, we save the entry that reconciles the change in the cash account with the net change in cash from the statement of cash flows as a final check on the accuracy of the spreadsheet.

12. SHORT-TERM INVESTMENTS.
Since the change in accounts receivable was explained previously [in entry (1)], we proceed to the next asset in the balance sheet. The balance in short-term investments increased from zero to $12 million. In the absence of evidence to the contrary, we could assume that the increase is due to the purchase of short-term investments during the year. This assumption is confirmed by item (c) of Illustration 21–1.

The entry to record the investment and our summary entry is:

	($ in millions)	
Entry (12) Short-term investment ($12 − 0)	12	
Cash (purchase of short-term investment)		12

The $12 million cash outflow is entered in the statement of cash flows section of the spreadsheet as an investing activity. An exception is when an investment is classified as a "trading security," in which case the cash outflow is reported as an operating activity.

ADDITIONAL CONSIDERATION

Recall that some highly liquid, short-term investments such as money market funds, Treasury bills, or commercial paper might be classified as cash equivalents. If the short-term investment above were classified as a cash equivalent, its purchase would have no effect on the total of cash and cash equivalents. In other words, since cash would include this investment, its purchase would constitute both a debit and a credit to cash. We would neither prepare a spreadsheet entry nor report the transaction on the statement of cash flows.

Likewise, a sale of a cash equivalent would not affect the total of cash and cash equivalents and would not be reported.

An exception would be if the cash equivalent investment were sold for either more or less than its acquisition cost. For example, assume a Treasury bill classified as a cash equivalent were sold for $1 million more than its $2 million cost. The sale would constitute both a $3 million increase and a $2 million decrease in cash. We see the effect more clearly if we reconstruct the transaction in journal entry format:

	($ in millions)	
Cash	3	
Gain on sale of cash equivalent		1
Cash (cash equivalent investment)		2

The summary entry to reflect the net increase in cash would be:

Entry (X) Cash (from sale of cash equivalents)	1	
Gain on sale of cash equivalent		1

The $1 million net increase in cash and cash equivalents would be reported as a cash inflow from *operating* activities.

---

13. LAND.
The changes in the balances of both inventory and prepaid insurance were accounted for in previous summary entries: (4) and (8). Land is the next account whose change has yet to be fully explained. We discovered in a previous transaction that a sale of land caused a $10 million reduction in the account. Yet, the account shows a net *increase* of $20 million. It would be logical to assume that the unexplained increase of $30 million was due to a purchase of land. The transaction described in item (d) of Illustration 21–1 supports that assumption and is portrayed in the following summary entry:

	($ in millions)	
Entry (13) Land (given)	30	
Cash (purchase of land)		30

The $30 million payment is reported as a cash outflow from investing activities.

14. BUILDINGS AND EQUIPMENT.
When examining a previous transaction [entry (9)], we determined that the buildings and equipment account was reduced by $14 million from the sale of used equipment. And yet the account shows a net *increase* of $6 million for the

year. The accounting records [item (e) of Illustration 21–1] reveal the remaining unexplained cause of the net increase. New equipment costing $20 million was purchased by issuing a $20 million note payable. Recall from the discussion in a previous section of this chapter that, although this is a noncash transaction, it represents both a significant investing activity (investing in new equipment) and a significant financing activity (financing the acquisition with long-term debt).

The journal entry used to record the transaction when the equipment was acquired also serves as our summary entry:

Investing in new equipment is a significant investing activity and financing the acquisition with long-term debt is a significant financing activity.

	($ in millions)	
Entry (14) Buildings and equipment (given)	20	
Note payable (given)		20

Remember that the statement of cash flows section of the spreadsheet will serve as the basis for our preparation of the formal statement. But the noncash entry above will not affect the cash flows section of the spreadsheet. Because we want to report this non-cash investing and financing activity when we prepare the statement of cash flows, it is helpful to "mark" the spreadsheet entry as a reminder not to overlook this transaction when the statement is prepared. Crosses (X) serve this purpose on the spreadsheet in Illustration 21–1A.

ADDITIONAL CONSIDERATION

Payments on Debt

When a debt, such as the note payable above, is paid, the payment is reported in a statement of cash flows as a financing activity. However, any interest paid on the debt is reported as a cash outflow from operating activities. The reason is that interest expense is a component of net income, and the cash effects of income statement elements are reported as cash flows from operating activities. If the note is an installment note, each installment payment includes both an amount that represents interest and an amount that represents a reduction of principal. In a statement of cash flows, then, the interest portion is reported as a cash outflow from operating activities and the principal portion as a cash outflow from financing activities.

Leases

As we discussed in Chapter 15, lease arrangements vary greatly, in both their purpose and the ways we account for them. Consistent with those differences, we also report leases differently in a statement of cash flows depending on their type. Lease payments for **operating leases,** for instance, represent rent—expense to the lessee, revenue for the lessor. These amounts are included in net income, so both the lessee and lessor report cash payments for operating leases in a statement of cash flows as cash flows from operating activities. **Capital leases,** on the other hand, are agreements that we identify as being formulated outwardly as leases, but which are in reality installment purchases, so we account for them as such. Each rental payment (except the first if paid at inception) includes both an amount that represents interest and an amount that represents a reduction of principal. In a statement of cash flows, then, the lessee reports the interest portion as a cash outflow from operating activities and the principal portion as a cash outflow from financing activities. On the other side of the transaction, the lessor in a **direct financing lease** reports the interest portion as a cash inflow from operating activities and the principal portion as a cash inflow from investing activities. Both the lessee and lessor report the lease at its inception as a noncash investing/financing activity. Remember, though, that a **sales-type lease** differs from a direct financing lease for the lessor in that we assume the lessor is actually selling its product. Consistent with reporting sales of products under installment sales agreements rather than lease agreements, the lessor reports cash receipts from a sales-type lease as cash inflows from operating activities.

15. BONDS PAYABLE.   The balance in the bonds payable account decreased during the year by $15 million. Illustration 21–1, item (f), reveals the cause. Cash was paid to retire $15 million face value of bonds. The spreadsheet entry that duplicates the journal entry that was recorded when the bonds were retired is:

		($ in millions)
Entry (15) Bonds payable ($35 – 50)	15	
Cash (retirement of bonds payable)		15

The cash outflow is reported as a financing activity.

ADDITIONAL CONSIDERATION

The description of the transaction stipulated that $15 million of bonds were retired at their maturity on the first day of the year. Thus, any discount or premium on the bonds would have been completely amortized before the start of the year. If bonds are retired prior to their scheduled maturity, any unamortized discount or premium would be removed from the accounts at that time. For instance, assume that the bonds above were callable at $16 million and that $1 million of unamortized discount remained when they were retired by a call at that price. The summary entry would be revised as follows:

		($ in millions)
Entry (15) Bonds payable	15	
(revised) Loss on early extinguishment of bonds	2	
Discount on bonds payable		1
Cash (retirement of bonds payable)		16

The loss, of course, would not be reported in the statement of cash flows. The amortization of the discount, however, would affect a previous summary entry. In entry (7) we concluded that the decrease in discount on bonds payable was due to the amortization of $2 million of the discount when recording bond interest expense. However, if the early retirement assumed above had occurred, that transaction would have accounted for $1 million of the $2 million decrease in the discount. Entry (7) would be modified as follows:

		($ in millions)
Entry (7) Interest expense...	5	
(revised) Discount on bonds payable		1
Cash (paid to bondholders)		4

16–17. COMMON STOCK.   The comparative balance sheets indicate that the common stock account balance increased by $30 million. We look to the accounting records—Illustration 21–1, item (g)—for an explanation. Two transactions, a stock dividend and a sale of new shares of common stock, combined to cause the increase. To create the summary entries for our analysis, we replicate the journal entries for the two transactions as described below.

Remember from Chapter 18 that to record a small stock dividend, we capitalize retained earnings for the market value of the shares distributed—in this case, 1 million shares times $13 per share, or $13 million. The entry is:

Although this transaction does not identify a cash flow, nor does it represent an investing or financing activity, we include the summary entry to help explain changes in the three account balances affected.

		($ in millions)
Entry (16) Retained earnings (1 million shares × $13)	13	
Common stock (1 million shares × $10 par)		10
Paid-in capital—excess of par (difference)		3

Also recall from the discussion of noncash investing and financing activities earlier in the chapter, that stock dividends do not represent a significant investing or financing activity. Therefore, this transaction is not reported in the statement of cash flows. We include the entry in our spreadsheet analysis only to help explain changes in the account balances affected.

The sale of 2 million shares of common stock at $13 per share is represented by the following spreadsheet entry:

		($ in millions)	
Entry (17) Cash (from sale of common stock)		26	
Common stock ([$130 – 100] – 10)			20
Paid-in capital—excess of par ([$29 – 20] – 3)			6

> The sale of common shares explains the remaining increase in the common stock account and the remaining increase in paid-in capital—excess of par.

The cash inflow is reported in the statement of cash flows as a financing activity.

ADDITIONAL CONSIDERATION

If cash is paid to retire outstanding shares of stock or to purchase those shares as treasury stock, the cash outflow would be reported in a statement of cash flows as a financing activity.

Together, the two entries above account for both the $30 million increase in the common stock account and the $9 million increase in paid-in capital—excess of par.

18. RETAINED EARNINGS.   The stock dividend in entry (16) above includes a $13 million reduction of retained earnings. Previously, we saw in entry (11) that net income increased retained earnings by $12 million. The net reduction of $1 million accounted for by these two entries leaves $5 million of the $6 million net decrease in the account unexplained.

Retained Earnings

		25	Beginning balance
(16) Stock dividend	13	12	Net income (11)
(18) ?	?		
		19	Ending balance

Without additional information about the $5 million decrease in retained earnings, we might assume it was due to a $5 million cash dividend. This assumption is unnecessary, though, because the cash dividend is described in Illustration 21–1, item (h).

Retained Earnings

		25	Beginning balance
(16) Stock dividend	13	12	Net income (11)
(18) Cash dividend	5		
		19	Ending balance

The summary entry for the spreadsheet is:

		($ in millions)	
Entry (18) Retained earnings		5	
Cash (payment of cash dividends)			5

> The cash dividend accounts for the previously unexplained change in retained earnings.

19. COMPLETING THE SPREADSHEET.   In preparing the spreadsheet to this point, we have analyzed each noncash account on both the income statement and the balance sheet. Our purpose was to identify the transactions that, during the year, had affected each account. By recreating each transaction in the form of a summary entry—in effect, duplicating the journal entry that had been used to record the transaction—we were able to explain the change in the balance of each account. That is, the debits and credits in the changes columns of the spreadsheet account for the increase or decrease in each noncash account. When a transaction being entered on the spreadsheet included an operating, investing, or financing activity, we entered that portion of the entry under the corresponding heading of the statement of cash flows section of the spreadsheet. Since, as noted earlier, there can be no operating, investing, or financing activity without a corresponding change in one or more of the noncash accounts, we should feel confident at this point that we have identified all of the activities that should be reported on the statement of cash flows.

To check the accuracy of the analysis, we compare the change in the balance of the cash account with the net change in cash flows produced by the activities listed in the statement of cash flows section of the spreadsheet. The net increase or decrease in cash flows from each of the statement of cash flows categories is extended to the extreme right column of the spreadsheet. By reference to Illustration 21–1A, we see that net cash flows from operating, investing, and financing activities are: $22 million; ($19 million); and $6 million, respectively. Together these activities provide a net increase in cash of $9 million. This amount corresponds to the increase in the balance of the cash account from $20 million to $29 million. To complete the spreadsheet, we include the final summary entry:

	($ in millions)
Entry (19) Cash	9
Net increase in cash	
(from statement of cash flows activities)	9

As a final check of accuracy, we can confirm that the total of the debits is equal to the total of the credits in the changes columns of the spreadsheet.[13]

ETHICAL DILEMMA

"We must get it," Courtney Lowell, president of Industrial Fasteners, roared. "Without it we're in big trouble." The "it" Mr. Lowell referred to is the renewal of a $14 million loan with Community First Bank. The big trouble he fears is the lack of funds necessary to repay the existing debt and few, if any, prospects for raising the funds elsewhere.

Mr. Lowell had just hung up the phone after a conversation with a bank vice president in which it was made clear that this year's statement of cash flows must look better than last year's. Mr. Lowell knows that improvements are not on course to happen. In fact, cash flow projections were dismal.

Later that day, Tim Cratchet, assistant controller, was summoned to Mr. Lowell's office. "Cratchet," Lowell barked, "I've looked at our accounts receivable. I think we can generate quite a bit of cash by selling or factoring most of those receivables. I know it will cost us more than if we collect them ourselves, but it sure will make our cash flow picture look better."

Is there an ethical question facing Cratchet?

● LO9

INTERNATIONAL FINANCIAL REPORTING STANDARDS

Classification of Cash Flows. Like U.S. GAAP, international standards also require a statement of cash flows. Consistent with U.S. GAAP, cash flows are classified as operating, investing, or financing. However, the U.S. standard designates cash outflows for interest payments and cash inflows from interest and dividends received as operating cash flows. Dividends paid to shareholders are classified as financing cash flows.

IAS No. 7, on the other hand, allows more flexibility. Companies can report interest and dividends paid as either operating or financing cash flows and interest and dividends received as either operating or investing cash flows. Interest and dividend payments usually are reported as financing activities. Interest and dividends received normally are classified as investing activities.

(continued)

---

[13]The mechanical and computational aspects of the spreadsheet analysis are simplified greatly when performed on an electronic spreadsheet such as Microsoft Excel.

(concluded)

Typical Classification of Cash Flows from Interest and Dividends	**IFRS ILLUSTRATION**

U.S. GAAP	**IFRS**
Operating Activities	*Operating Activities*
Dividends received	
Interest received	
Interest paid	
Investing Activities	*Investing Activities*
	Dividends received
	Interest received
Financing Activities	*Financing Activities*
Dividends paid	Dividends paid
	Interest paid

The spreadsheet is now complete. The statement of cash flows can now be prepared directly from the spreadsheet simply by presenting the items included in the statement of cash flows section of the spreadsheet in the appropriate format of the statement.

The statements of cash flows from an annual report of **Hooker Furniture Corporation** are shown in Graphic 21–9. Notice that the reconciliation schedule was reported by Hooker Furniture in the statement of cash flows itself. Many companies report the schedule separately in the disclosure notes.

GRAPHIC 21–9

Statement of Cash Flows—Hooker Furniture Corporation*

HOOKER FURNITURE CORPORATION AND SUBSIDIARIES
Consolidated Statements of Cash Flows
(In thousands)

For the Years Ended	Feb. 1, 2009	Feb. 3, 2008
Cash flows from operating activities		
Cash received from customers	$269,483	$ 321,189
Cash paid to suppliers and employees	(258,701)	(265,842)
Income taxes paid, net	(7,219)	(12,717)
Interest received (paid), net	167	1,195
Net cash provided by operating activities	3,730	43,825
Cash flows from investing activities		
Acquisitions, net of cash required	(181)	(15,826)
Purchase of property, plant and equipment	(2,271)	(1,942)
Proceeds from the sale of property and equipment	28	3,668
Premiums paid on life insurance policies	(1,328)	(1,411)
Proceeds received on life insurance policies		1,244
Net cash used in investing activities	(3,752)	(14,267)
Cash flows from financing activities		
Purchase and retirement of common stock	(14,097)	(36,028)
Cash dividends paid	(4,459)	(5,036)
Payments on long-term debt	(2,694)	(2,503)
Net cash used in financing activities	(21,250)	(43,567)
Net (decrease) increase in cash and cash equivalents	(21,272)	(14,009)
Cash and cash equivalents at beginning of year	33,076	47,085
Cash and cash equivalents at end of year	$ 11,804	$ 33,076

*Typically, statements for three years are reported for comparative purposes. Hooker changed its fiscal year ending date from November to February in 2008, so its 2007 statements were for two months.

(continued)

GRAPHIC 21–9
(concluded)

For the Years Ended	Feb 1, 2009	Feb. 3, 2008
Reconciliation of net income (loss) to net cash provided by operating activities		
Net income (loss)	$ 6,910	$ 19,655
Depreciation and amortization	2,912	3,352
Noncash ESOP cost		
Restricted stock compensation cost	74	47
Impairment of goodwill and intangibles	4,914	
Restructuring and related asset impairment charges	(951)	309
Loss (gain) on disposal of property	154	(100)
Donation of showroom facilities		1,082
Provision (credit) for doubtful accounts	2,245	1,313
Loss (gain) on life insurance policies	95	(788)
Deferred income tax expense (benefit)	(2,005)	2,624
Changes in assets and liabilities, net of effect from acquisitions:		
Trade accounts receivable	5,767	2,972
Inventories	(9,629)	18,757
Prepaid expenses and other assets	(730)	(186)
Trade accounts payable	(4,633)	2,063
Accrued salaries, wages and benefits	(669)	(3,256)
Accrued income taxes	(1,274)	(3,826)
Other accrued expenses	79	(1,198)
Other long-term liabilities	471	1,005
Net cash provided by operating activities	$ 3,730	$ 43,825

CONCEPT REVIEW EXERCISE

COMPREHENSIVE REVIEW

The comparative balance sheets for 2011 and 2010 and the income statement for 2011 are given below for Beneficial Drill Company. Additional information from Beneficial Drill's accounting records is provided also.

Required:
Prepare the statement of cash flows of Beneficial Drill Company for the year ended December 31, 2011. Present cash flows from operating activities by the direct method and use a spreadsheet to assist in your analysis.

BENEFICIAL DRILL COMPANY
Comparative Balance Sheets
December 31, 2011 and 2010
($ in millions)

Assets	2011	2010
Cash	$ 20	$ 40
Accounts receivable	99	100
Less: Allowance for uncollectible accounts	(5)	(4)
Investment revenue receivable	3	2
Inventory	115	110
Prepaid insurance	2	3
Long-term investments	77	60
Land	110	80
Buildings and equipment	220	240
Less: Accumulated depreciation	(35)	(60)
Patent	15	16
	$621	$587

(continued)

(concluded)

Liabilities		
Accounts payable	$ 23	$ 30
Salaries payable	2	5
Bond interest payable	4	2
Income tax payable	6	7
Deferred income tax liability	5	4
Notes payable	15	0
Bonds payable	150	130
Less: Discount on bonds	(9)	(10)
Shareholders' Equity		
Common stock	210	200
Paid-in capital—excess of par	44	40
Retained earnings	178	179
Less: Treasury stock (at cost)	(7)	0
	$621	$587

BENEFICIAL DRILL COMPANY
Income Statement
For Year Ended December 31, 2011
($ in millions)

Revenues			
Sales revenue		$200	
Investment revenue		6	
Investment revenue—sale of treasury bills		1	$207
Expenses			
Cost of goods sold		110	
Salaries expense		30	
Depreciation expense		5	
Patent amortization expense		1	
Bad debts expense		4	
Insurance expense		3	
Bond interest expense		14	
Extraordinary loss on destruction of equipment	$ 10		
Less: Tax savings	(5)	5	
Income tax expense		12	(184)
Net income			$ 23

Additional information from the accounting records:

a. During 2011, $3 million of customer accounts were written off as uncollectible.
b. Investment revenue includes Beneficial Drill Company's $3 million share of the net income of Hammer Company, an equity method investee.
c. Treasury bills were sold during 2011 at a gain of $1 million. Beneficial Drill Company classifies its investments in Treasury bills as cash equivalents.
d. A machine that originally cost $60 million and was one-half depreciated was rendered unusable by a freak bolt of lightning. Most major components of the machine were unharmed and were sold for $20 million.
e. Temporary differences between pretax accounting income and taxable income caused the deferred income tax liability to increase by $1 million.
f. The common stock of Wrench Corporation was purchased for $14 million as a long-term investment.
g. Land costing $30 million was acquired by paying $15 million cash and issuing a 13%, seven-year, $15 million note payable to the seller.
h. New equipment was purchased for $40 million cash.
i. $20 million of bonds were sold at face value.

j. On January 19, Beneficial issued a 5% stock dividend (1 million shares). The market price of the $10 par value common stock was $14 per share at that time.

k. Cash dividends of $10 million were paid to shareholders.

l. In November, 500,000 common shares were repurchased as treasury stock at a cost of $7 million.

SOLUTION

BENEFICIAL DRILL COMPANY
Spreadsheet for the Statement of Cash Flows

	Dec. 31 2010	Changes Debits		Changes Credits		Dec. 31 2011
Balance Sheet						
Assets						
Cash	40			(20)	20	20
Accounts receivable	100			(1)	1	99
Less: Allowance for uncollectible accounts	(4)			(1)	1	(5)
Investment revenue receivable	2	(2)	1			3
Inventory	110	(4)	5			115
Prepaid insurance	3			(8)	1	2
Long-term investments	60	(2)	3			
		(13)	14			77
Land	80	(14)	30X			110
Buildings and equipment	240	(15)	40	(10)	60	220
Less: Accumulated depreciation	(60)	(10)	30	(6)	5	(35)
Patent	16			(7)	1	15
	587					621
Liabilities						
Accounts payable	30	(4)	7			23
Salaries payable	5	(5)	3			2
Bond interest payable	2			(9)	2	4
Income tax payable	7	(11)	1			6
Deferred income tax liability	4			(11)	1	5
Notes payable	0			(14)	15X	15
Bonds payable	130			(16)	20	150
Less: Discount on bonds	(10)			(9)	1	(9)
Shareholders' Equity						
Common stock	200			(17)	10	210
Paid-in capital—excess of par	40			(17)	4	44
Retained earnings	179	(17)	14			
		(18)	10	(12)	23	178
Less: Treasury stock	0	(19)	7			(7)
	587					621
Income Statement						
Revenues:						
Sales revenue				(1)	200	200
Investment revenue				(2)	6	6
Investment revenue—sale of Treasury bills				(3)	1	1
Expenses:						
Cost of goods sold		(4)	110			(110)
Salaries expense		(5)	30			(30)
Depreciation expense		(6)	5			(5)
Patent amortization expense		(7)	1			(1)
Bad debts expense		(1)	4			(4)
Insurance expense		(8)	3			(3)
Bond interest expense		(9)	14			(14)
Extraordinary loss		(10)	10			(10)
Less: Tax savings				(11)	5	5
Income tax expense		(11)	12			(12)
Net income		(12)	23			23

(continued)

(concluded)

Statement of Cash Flows
Operating Activities:

Cash inflows:				
From customers	(1)	198		
From investment revenue	(2)	2		
From sale of Treasury bills	(3)	1		
Cash outflows:				
To suppliers of goods			(4)	122
To employees			(5)	33
For insurance expense			(8)	2
For bond interest expense			(9)	11
For income taxes			(11)	7
Net cash flows				26
Investing Activities:				
Sale of equipment	(10)	20		
Purchase of LT investments			(13)	14
Purchase of land			(14)	15
Purchase of equipment			(15)	40
Net cash flows				(49)
Financing Activities:				
Sale of bonds payable	(16)	20		
Payment of cash dividends			(18)	10
Purchase of treasury stock			(19)	7
Net cash flows				3
Net decrease in cash	(20)	20		(20)
Totals		638		638

BENEFICIAL DRILL COMPANY
Statement of Cash Flows
For Year Ended December 31, 2011
(\$ in millions)

Cash Flows from Operating Activities

Cash inflows:		
From customers	\$198	
From investment revenue	2	
From sale of Treasury bills	1	
Cash outflows:		
To suppliers of goods	(122)	
To employees	(33)	
For insurance expense	(2)	
For bond interest expense	(11)	
For income taxes	(7)	
Net cash flows from operating activities		\$26
Cash Flows from Investing Activities		
Sale of equipment	\$ 20	
Purchase of long-term investments	(14)	
Purchase of land	(15)	
Purchase of equipment	(40)	
Net cash flows from investing activities		(49)
Cash Flows from Financing Activities		
Sale of bonds payable	\$ 20	
Payment of cash dividends	(10)	
Purchase of treasury stock	(7)	
Net cash flows from financing activities		3
Net decrease in cash		(\$20)
Cash balance, January 1		40
Cash balance, December 31		\$20

(continued)

(concluded)

Noncash Investing and Financing Activities
Acquired $30 million of land by paying cash and issuing a 13%, 7-year note as follows:

Cost of land	$ 30
Cash paid	15
Note issued	$ 15

PART C   PREPARING AN SCF: THE INDIRECT METHOD OF REPORTING CASH FLOWS FROM OPERATING ACTIVITIES

Getting There through the Back Door

The presentation of cash flows from operating activities illustrated in Part B is referred to as the *direct method.* By this method, the cash effect of each operating activity (i.e., income statement item) is reported directly on the statement of cash flows. For instance, cash received from customers is reported as the cash effect of sales activities, and cash paid to suppliers is reported as the cash effect of cost of goods sold. Income statement items that have *no* cash effect, such as depreciation expense, bad debt expense, gains, and losses, are simply not reported.

As pointed out previously, a permissible alternative is the *indirect method,* by which the net cash increase or decrease from operating activities is derived indirectly by starting with reported net income and working backwards to convert that amount to a cash basis. The derivation by the indirect method of net cash flows from operating activities for UBC is shown in Illustration 21–1B. For the adjustment amounts, you may wish to refer back to UBC's balance sheets and income statement presented in Illustration 21–1.

ILLUSTRATION 21–1B Indirect Method	**Cash Flows from Operating Activities—Indirect Method** ***and*** **Reconciliation of Net Income to** **Net Cash Flows from Operating Activities**	
	Net Income	$12
	Adjustments for noncash effects:	
	Gain on sale of land	(8)
The indirect method derives the net cash increase or decrease from operating activities indirectly, by starting with reported net income and "working backwards" to convert that amount to a cash basis.	Depreciation expense	3
	Loss on sale of equipment	2
	Changes in operating assets and liabilities:	
	Increase in accounts receivable	(2)
	Decrease in inventory	4
	Increase in accounts payable	6
	Increase in salaries payable	2
	Discount on bonds payable	2
	Decrease in prepaid insurance	3
	Decrease in income tax payable	(2)
	Net cash flows from operating activities	$22

Notice that the indirect method yields the same $22 million net cash flows from operating activities as does the direct method. This is understandable when you consider that the indirect method simply reverses the differences between the accrual-based income statement and cash flows from operating activities. We accomplish this as described in the next two sections.

Components of Net Income That Do Not Increase or Decrease Cash

Amounts that were subtracted in determining net income but did not reduce cash are *added back* to net income to reverse the effect of their having been subtracted. For example, depreciation expense and the loss on sale of equipment are added back to net income. Other things being equal, this restores net income to what it would have been had depreciation and the loss not been subtracted at all.

Similarly, amounts that were added in determining net income but did not increase cash are subtracted from net income to reverse the effect of their having been added. For example, UBC's gain on sale of land is deducted from net income. Here's why. UBC sold for $18 million land that originally cost $10 million. Recording the sale produced a gain of $8 million, which UBC appropriately included in its income statement. But did this gain increase UBC's cash? No. Certainly selling the land increased cash—by $18 million. We therefore include the $18 million as a cash inflow in the statement of cash flows. However, the sale of land is an investing activity. The gain itself, though, is simply the difference between cash received in the sale of land (reported as an investing activity) and the original cost of the land. If UBC also reported the $8 million gain as a cash flow from operating activities, in addition to reporting $18 million as a cash flow from investing activities, UBC would report the $8 million twice. So, because UBC added the gain in determining its net income but the gain had no effect on cash, the gain must now be subtracted from net income to reverse the effect of its having been added.

Components of Net Income That Do Increase or Decrease Cash

For components of net income that increase or decrease cash, but by an amount different from that reported in the income statement, net income is adjusted for changes in the balances of related balance sheet accounts to *convert the effects of those items to a cash basis.* For example, sales of $100 million are included in the income statement as a component of net income, and yet, since accounts receivable increased by $2 million, only $98 million cash was collected from customers during the reporting period. Sales are converted to a cash basis by subtracting the $2 million increase in accounts receivable. Here's another example:

The income statement reports salaries expense as $13 million. Just because employees earned $13 million during the reporting period, though, doesn't necessarily mean UBC paid those employees $13 million in cash during the same period. In fact, we see in the comparative balance sheets that salaries payable increased from $1 million to $3 million; UBC owes its employees $2 million more than before the year started. The company must not have paid the entire $13 million expense. By analyzing salaries expense in relation to the change in salaries payable, we can determine the amount of cash paid to employees:

Salaries Payable

		1	Beginning balance
Cash paid to employees	?	13	Salaries expense
(decreases salaries payable)			*(increases salaries payable)*
		3	Ending balance

This inspection indicates that UBC paid only $11 million cash to its employees; the remaining $2 million of salaries expense is reflected as an increase in salaries payable. From a cash perspective, then, by subtracting $13 million for salaries in the income statement, UBC has subtracted $2 million more than the reduction in cash. Adding back the $2 million leaves UBC in the same position as if it had deducted only the $11 million cash paid to employees.

Following a similar analysis of the cash effects of the remaining components of net income, those items are likewise converted to a cash basis by adjusting net income for increases and decreases in related accounts.

For components of net income that increase or decrease cash by an amount exactly the same as that reported in the income statement, no adjustment of net income is required. For example, investment revenue of $3 million is included in UBC's $12 million net income amount. Because $3 million also is the amount of cash received from that activity, this element of net income already represents its cash effect and needs no adjustment.[14]

Comparison with the Direct Method

The indirect method is compared with the direct method in Graphic 21–10, using the data of UBC. To better illustrate the relationship between the two methods, the adjustments to net income using the indirect method are presented parallel to the related cash inflows and cash outflows of the direct method. The income statement is included in the graphic to demonstrate that the indirect method also serves to reconcile differences between the elements of that statement and the cash flows reported by the direct method.

GRAPHIC 21–10 Comparison of the Indirect Method and the Direct Method of Determining Cash Flows from Operating Activities

Income Statement		Cash Flows from Operating Activities			
		Indirect Method		**Direct Method**	
		Net income	$12		
		Adjustments:			
Sales	$100	Increase in accounts receivable	(2)	Cash received from customers	$98
Investment revenue	3	(No adjustment—no investment revenue receivable or long-term investments)			
				Cash received from investments	3
Gain on sale of land	8	Gain on sale of land	(8)	(Not reported—no cash effect)	
Cost of goods sold	(60)	Decrease in inventory	4		
		Increase in accounts payable	6	Cash paid to suppliers	(50)
Salaries expense	(13)	Increase in salaries payable	2	Cash paid to employees	(11)
Depreciation expense	(3)	Depreciation expense	3	(Not reported—no cash effect)	
Interest expense	(5)	Decrease in bond discount	2	Cash paid for interest	(3)
Insurance expense	(7)	Decrease in prepaid insurance	3	Cash paid for insurance	(4)
Loss on sale of equipment	(2)	Loss on sale of equipment	2	(Not reported—no cash effect)	
Income tax expense	(9)	Decrease in income tax payable	(2)	Cash paid for income taxes	(11)
Net Income	$ 12	Net cash flows from operating activities	$22	Net cash flows from operating activities	$22

As a practical consideration, you might notice that the adjustments to net income using the indirect method follow a convenient pattern. *Increases* in related assets are deducted from net income (i.e., the increase in accounts receivable) when converting to cash from operating activities. Conversely, *decreases* in assets are added (inventory and prepaid insurance in this case). Changes in related liabilities are handled in just the opposite way. Increases in related liabilities are *added* to net income (i.e., the increases in accounts payable and salaries payable) while decreases in liabilities are subtracted (i.e., decrease in income tax payable).[15]

Of course, these are adjustments to net income that effectively convert components of income from reported accrual amounts to a cash basis. The other adjustments to net income (gain, depreciation, loss) as pointed out earlier are to get rid of the three income statement components that have no effect at all on cash. This pattern is summarized in Graphic 21–11 on the next page.

---

[14]We determined in Part B (subsection 2) that there is no evidence that cash received from investments differs from investment revenue.
[15]The adjustment for the decrease in bond discount is logically consistent with this pattern as well. Bond discount is a contra liability. It's logical, then, that an adjustment for a decrease in this account be added—the opposite of the way a decrease in a liability is treated.

GRAPHIC 21–11

Adjustments to
Convert Net Income to
a Cash Basis—Indirect
Method

Type of Adjustment	To Adjust for Noncash Effect
Adjustments for Noncash Effects:	
Income statement components that have *no effect* at all on cash but are *additions* to income	Deduct from net income
Income statement components that have *no effect* at all on cash but are *deductions* from income	Add to net income
Changes in Operating Assets and Liabilities:	
Increases in assets related to an income statement component	Deduct from net income
Decreases in assets related to an income statement component	Add to net income
Increases in liabilities related to an income statement component	Add to net income
Decreases in liabilities related to an income statement component	Deduct from net income

Although either the direct method or the indirect method is permitted, the FASB strongly encourages companies to report cash flows from operating activities by the direct method. The obvious appeal of this approach is that it reports specific operating cash receipts and operating cash payments, which is consistent with the primary objective of the statement of cash flows. Investors and creditors gain additional insight into the specific sources of cash receipts and payments from operating activities revealed by this reporting method. Also, statement users can more readily interpret and understand the information presented because the direct method avoids the confusion caused by reporting noncash items and other reconciling adjustments under the caption *cash flows from operating activities*. Nonetheless, the vast majority of companies choose to use the indirect method. Reasons for this choice range from longstanding tradition to the desire to withhold as much information as possible from competitors.[16]

Reconciliation of Net Income to Cash Flows from Operating Activities

As we discussed earlier, whether cash flows from operating activities are reported by the direct method or by the indirect method, the financial statements must report a reconciliation of net income to net cash flows from operating activities. When the direct method is used, the reconciliation is presented in a separate schedule and is identical to the presentation of net cash flows from operating activities by the indirect method. In other words, Illustration 21–1B also serves as the reconciliation schedule to accompany a statement of cash flows using the direct method. Obviously, a separate reconciliation schedule is not required when using the indirect method because the cash flows from operating activities section of the statement of cash flows *is* a reconciliation of net income to net cash flows from operating activities.[17]

Remember that the direct and indirect methods are alternative approaches to deriving net cash flows from *operating* activities only. The choice of which method is used for that purpose does not affect the way cash flows from *investing* and *financing* activities are identified and reported.

The statements of cash flows from the annual report of **Walmart Stores, Inc.**, which uses the indirect method, are shown in Graphic 21–12 on the next page.

---

[16]As indicated earlier, a recent Discussion Paper from the IASB and FASB advocates requiring the direct method and dissallowing the indirect method, for the proposed new Financial Statement Presentation format.

[17]It is permissible to present the reconciliation in a separate schedule and to report the net cash flows from operating activities as a single line item on the statement of cash flows.

GRAPHIC 21–12   Statement of Cash Flows—Indirect Method; Walmart

WALMART STORES, INC.
Consolidated Statements of Cash Flows

(Amounts in millions)

Fiscal Year Ended January 31,	2009	2008	2007
Cash flows from operating activities:			
Net income	$13,400	$12,731	$11,284
(Income) loss from discontinued operations, net of tax	(146)	132	905
Income from continuing operations	13,254	12,863	12,189
Adjustments to reconcile income from continuing operations to net cash provided by operating activities:			
Depreciation and amortization	6,739	6,317	5,459
Deferred income taxes	581	(8)	89
Other operating activities	1,268	910	1,311
Changes in certain assets and liabilities, net of effects of acquisitions:			
(Increase) in accounts receivable	(101)	(564)	(214)
(Increase) in inventories	(220)	(775)	(1,274)
(Decrease) increase in accounts payable	(410)	865	2,132
Increase in accrued liabilities	2,036	1,034	588
Net cash provided by continuing operating activities	23,147	20,642	20,280
Net cash used in operating activities of discontinued	—	—	(45)
Net cash provided by operating activities	23,147	20,642	20,235
Cash flows from investing activities:			
Payments for property and equipment	(11,499)	(14,937)	(15,666)
Proceeds from disposal of property and equipment	714	957	394
Proceeds from (payments for) disposal of certain international operations, net	838	(257)	610
Investment in international operations	(1,576)	(1,338)	(68)
Other investing activities	781	(95)	223
Net cash used in continuing investing activities	(10,742)	(15,670)	(14,507)
Net cash provided by discontinued investing activities	—	—	44
Net cash used in investing activities	(10,742)	(15,670)	(14,463)
Cash flows from financing activities:			
(Decrease) increase in commercial paper	(3,745)	2,376	(1,193)
Proceeds from issuance of long-term debt	6,566	11,167	7,199
Payment of long-term debt	(5,387)	(8,723)	(5,758)
Dividends paid	(3,746)	(3,586)	(2,802)
Purchase of Company stock	(3,521)	(7,691)	(1,718)
Payment of capital lease obligations	(352)	(343)	(340)
Other financing activities	267	(622)	(510)
Net cash used in financing activities	(9,918)	(7,422)	(5,122)
Effect of exchange rates on cash	(781)	252	97
Net increase (decrease) in cash and cash equivalents	1,706	(2,198)	747
Cash and cash equivalents at beginning of year	5,569	7,767	7,020
Cash and cash equivalents at end of year	$ 7,275	$ 5,569	$ 7,767
Supplemental disclosure of cash flow information			
Income tax paid	$ 6,596	$ 6,299	$ 6,665
Interest paid	1,787	1,622	1,553
Capital lease obligations incurred	284	447	159

For most companies, expenditures for interest and for taxes are significant. Cash payments for interest and for taxes usually are specifically indicated when the direct method is employed as is the case for **Hooker Furniture Corporation** reported earlier in Graphic 21–9. When the indirect method is used, those amounts aren't readily apparent and must be *separately reported* either on the face of the statement or in an accompanying disclosure note as Hewlett-Packard does.

We use a spreadsheet to help prepare a statement of cash flows by the indirect method in Appendix 21A.

DECISION MAKERS' PERSPECTIVE—Cash Flow Ratios

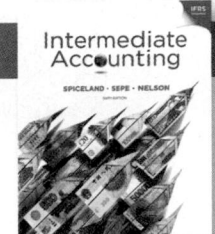

We have emphasized the analysis of financial statements from a decision maker's perspective throughout this text. Often that analysis included the development and comparison of financial ratios. Ratios based on income statement and balance sheet amounts enjoy a long tradition of acceptance from which several standard ratios, including those described in earlier chapters, have evolved. To gain another viewpoint, some analysts supplement their investigation with cash flow ratios. Some cash flow ratios are derived by simply substituting cash flow from operations (CFFO) from the statement of cash flows in place of net income in many ratios, not to replace those ratios but to complement them. For example, the times interest earned ratio can be modified to reflect the number of times the cash outflow for interest is provided by cash inflow from operations and any of the profitability ratios can be modified to determine the cash generated from assets, shareholders' equity, sales, etc. Graphic 21–13 summarizes the calculation and usefulness of several representative cash flow ratios.

GRAPHIC 21–13
Cash Flow Ratios

	Calculation	Measures
Performance Ratios		
Cash flow to sales	$\dfrac{\text{CFFO}}{\text{Net sales}}$	Cash generated by each sales dollar
Cash return on assets	$\dfrac{\text{CFFO}}{\text{Average total assets}}$	Cash generated from all resources
Cash return on shareholders' equity	$\dfrac{\text{CFFO}}{\text{Average shareholders' equity}}$	Cash generated from owner-provided resources
Cash to income	$\dfrac{\text{CFFO}}{\text{Income from continuing operations}}$	Cash-generating ability of continuing operations
Cash flow per share	$\dfrac{\text{CFFO} - \text{preferred dividends}}{\text{Weighted-average shares}}$	Operating cash flow on a per share basis
Sufficiency Ratios		
Debt coverage	$\dfrac{\text{Total liabilities}}{\text{CFFO}}$	Financial risk and financial leverage
Interest coverage	$\dfrac{\text{CFFO} + \text{interest} + \text{taxes}}{\text{Interest}}$	Ability to satisfy fixed obligations
Reinvestment	$\dfrac{\text{CFFO}}{\text{Cash outflow for noncurrent assets}}$	Ability to acquire assets with operating cash flows
Debt payment	$\dfrac{\text{CFFO}}{\text{Cash outflow for LT debt repayment}}$	Ability to pay debts with operating cash flows
Dividend payment	$\dfrac{\text{CFFO}}{\text{Cash outflow for dividends}}$	Ability to pay dividends with operating cash flows
Investing and financing activity	$\dfrac{\text{CFFO}}{\text{Cash outflows for investing and financing activities}}$	Ability to acquire assets, pay debts, and make distributions to owners

Cash flow ratios have received limited acceptance to date, due in large part to the long tradition of accrual-based ratios coupled with the relatively brief time that all companies have published statements of cash flows. A lack of consensus on cash flow ratios by which to make comparisons also has slowed their acceptance. In fact, companies are prohibited from reporting cash flow per share in the statement of cash flows. Nevertheless, cash flow ratios offer insight in the evaluation of a company's profitability and financial strength.[18] ●

FINANCIAL REPORTING CASE SOLUTION

1. **What are the cash flow aspects of the situation that Mr. Barr may be overlooking in making his case for a wage increase? How can a company's operations generate a healthy profit and yet produce meager or even negative cash flows?** *(p. 1188)*   Positive net income does not necessarily indicate a healthy cash position. A statement of cash flows provides information about cash flows not seen when looking only at the balance sheet and the income statement. Although cash flows from operating activities result from the same activities that are reported in the income statement, the income statement reports the activities on an accrual basis. That is, revenues reported are those earned during the reporting period, regardless of when cash is received, and the expenses incurred in generating those revenues, regardless of when cash is paid. Thus, the very same operations can generate a healthy profit and yet produce meager or even negative cash flows.

2. **What information can a statement of cash flows provide about a company's investing activities that can be useful in decisions such as this?** *(p. 1192)*   Cash flows from investing activities result from the acquisition and disposition of assets. Information about investing activities is useful to decision makers regarding the nature and magnitude of productive assets being acquired for future use. In the union negotiations, for instance, Mr. Barr may not be aware of the substantial investments under way to replace and update equipment and the cash requirements of those investments. Relatedly, the relatively low depreciation charges accelerated depreciation provides in the later years of assets' lives may cause profits to seem artificially high given the necessity to replace those assets at higher prices.

3. **What information can a statement of cash flows provide about a company's financing activities that can be useful in decisions such as this?** *(p. 1193)*   Information about financing activities provides insights into sources of a company's external financing. Recent debt issues, for instance, might indicate a need for higher cash flows to maintain higher interest charges. Similarly, recent external financing activity may suggest that a company might be near its practical limits from external sources and, therefore, may need a greater reliance on internal financing through operations. ●

THE BOTTOM LINE

● **LO1**   Decision makers focus on the prospects of receiving a cash return from their dealings with a firm. But it is the ability of the firm to generate cash flows to itself that ultimately determines the potential for cash flows to investors and creditors. The statement of cash flows fills an information gap left by the balance sheet and the income statement by presenting information about cash flows that the other statements either do not provide or provide only indirectly. The stipulation that companies present the statement of cash flows is a relatively recent requirement. (p. 1184)

---

[18]Proposals for informative sets of cash flow ratios are offered by Charles Carslaw and John Mills, "Developing Ratios for Effective Cash Flow Analysis," *Journal of Accountancy*, November 1991; Don Giacomino and David Mielke, "Cash Flows: Another Approach to Ratio Analysis," *Journal of Accountancy*, March 1993; and John Mills and Jeanne Yamamura, "The Power of Cash Flows Ratios," *Journal of Accountancy*, October 1998.

● **LO2**   Cash includes cash equivalents. These are short-term, highly liquid investments that can readily be converted to cash with little risk of loss. (p. 1187)

● **LO3**   Cash flows from operating activities are both inflows and outflows of cash that result from activities reported in the income statement. (p. 1188)

● **LO4**   Unlike the direct method, which directly lists cash inflows and outflows, the indirect method derives cash flows indirectly, by starting with reported net income and working backwards to convert that amount to a cash basis. (p. 1190)

● **LO5**   Cash flows from investing activities are related to the acquisition and disposition of assets, other than inventory and assets classified as cash equivalents. (p. 1192)

● **LO6**   Cash flows from financing activities result from the external financing of a business. (p. 1193)

● **LO7**   Noncash investing and financing activities, such as acquiring equipment (an investing activity) by issuing a long-term note payable (a financing activity), are reported in a related disclosure schedule or note. (p. 1194)

● **LO8**   A spreadsheet provides a systematic method of preparing a statement of cash flows by analyzing available data to insure that all operating, investing, and financing activities are detected. Recording spreadsheet entries that explain account balance changes simultaneously identifies and classifies the activities to be reported on the statement of cash flows. (p. 1194)

● **LO9**   IFRS allows more flexibility than U.S. GAAP in the classification of cash flows. Companies can report interest and dividends paid as either operating or financing cash flows and interest and dividends received as either operating or investing cash flows. (pp. 1191 and 1212) ●

SPREADSHEET FOR THE INDIRECT METHOD

APPENDIX **21A**

A spreadsheet is equally useful in preparing a statement of cash flows whether we use the direct or the indirect method of determining cash flows from operating activities. The format of the spreadsheet differs only with respect to operating activities. The analysis of transactions for the purpose of identifying cash flows to be reported is the same. To illustrate, Illustration 21A–1 on the next page provides a spreadsheet analysis of the data for UBC.

Two differences should be noted between the spreadsheet in Illustration 21A–1 and the spreadsheet we used earlier for the direct method. First, in the statement of cash flows section of the spreadsheet, under the heading of "cash flows from operating activities," specific cash inflows and cash outflows are replaced by net income and the required adjustments for noncash effects. Second, we do not include an income statement section. This section is unnecessary because, using the indirect method, we are not interested in identifying specific operating activities that cause increases and decreases in cash. Instead, we need from the income statement only the amount of net income, which is converted to a cash basis by adjusting for any noncash amounts included in net income. The spreadsheet entries in journal entry form for the indirect method are illustrated in Illustration 21A–2 on page 1227.

Remember that there is no mandatory order in which the account changes must be analyzed. However, since we determine net cash flows from operating activities by working backwards from net income when using the indirect method, it is convenient to start with the spreadsheet entry that represents the credit to retained earnings due to net income. This entry corresponds to summary entry (11) using the direct method. By entering the debit portion of the entry as the first item under the cash flows from operating activities (CFOA), we establish net income as the initial amount of cash flows from operating activities, which is then adjusted to a cash basis by subsequent entries. Entries (2)–(4) duplicate the transactions that involve noncash components of net income. Changes in current assets and current liabilities that represent differences between revenues and expenses and the cash effects of those revenues and expenses are accounted for by entries (5)–(11). Summary entries (12)–(19) explain the changes in the balance sheet not already accounted for by previous entries, and are identical to entries (12)–(19) recorded using the direct method.

ILLUSTRATION 21A–1

Indirect Method

UNITED BRANDS CORPORATION
Spreadsheet for the Statement of Cash Flows

	Dec. 31 2010	Changes Debits		Changes Credits		Dec. 31 2011
Balance Sheet						
Assets						
Cash	20	(19)	9			29
Accounts receivable	30	(5)	2			32
Short-term investments	0	(12)	12			12
Inventory	50			(6)	4	46
Prepaid insurance	6			(8)	3	3
Land	60	(13)	30	(2)	10	80
Buildings and equipment	75	(14)	20X	(3)	14	81
Less: Accumulated depreciation	(20)	(3)	7	(4)	3	(16)
	221					267
Liabilities						
Accounts payable	20			(7)	6	26
Salaries payable	1			(9)	2	3
Income tax payable	8	(11)	2			6
Notes payable	0			(14)	20X	20
Bonds payable	50	(15)	15			35
Less: Discount on bonds	(3)			(10)	2	(1)
Shareholders' Equity						
Common stock	100			(16)	10	
				(17)	20	130
Paid-in capital—excess of par	20			(16)	3	
				(17)	6	29
Retained earnings	25	(16)	13			
		(18)	5	(1)	12	19
	221					267
Statement of Cash Flows						
Operating activities:						
Net income		(1)	12			
Adjustments for noncash effects:						
Gain on sale of land				(2)	8	
Depreciation expense		(4)	3			
Loss on sale of equipment		(3)	2			
Increase in accounts receivable				(5)	2	
Decrease in inventory		(6)	4			
Decrease in prepaid insurance		(8)	3			
Increase in accounts payable		(7)	6			
Increase in salaries payable		(9)	2			
Decrease in income tax payable				(11)	2	
Amortization of discount		(10)	2			
Net cash flows						22
Investing activities:						
Purchase of land				(13)	30	
Purchase of S-T investment				(12)	12	
Sale of land		(2)	18			
Sale of equipment		(3)	5			
Net cash flows						(19)
Financing activities:						
Sale of common shares		(17)	26			
Retirement of bonds payable				(15)	15	
Payment of cash dividends				(18)	5	
Net cash flows						6
Net increase in cash				(19)	9	9
Totals			198		198	

Entry (1)   Net income—CFOA 12
        Retained earnings 12
        Establishes net income as the initial amount of cash flows from operating
        activities, to be adjusted to a cash basis by subsequent entries.

Entry (2)   Cash (received from sale of land) 18
        Land 10
        Gain on sale of land—CFOA 8
        Deducts the noncash gain added in determining net income, explains a portion
        of the change in land, and identifies a cash inflow from investing activities.

Entry (3)   Cash (received from sale of equipment) 5
        Loss on sale of equipment—CFOA 2
        Accumulated depreciation 7
        Buildings and equipment 14
        Adds back the noncash loss subtracted in determining net income, explains
        portions of the changes in accumulated depreciation and buildings and
        equipment, and identifies a cash inflow from investing activities.

Entry (4)   Depreciation expense—CFOA 3
        Accumulated depreciation 3
        Adds back the noncash expense subtracted in determining net income.

Entry (5)   Accounts receivable 2
        Increase in accounts receivable—CFOA 2
        Reduces net income to reflect $98 million cash received from customers rather
        than $100 million sales.

Entry (6)   Decrease in inventory—CFOA 4
        Inventory 4
        Increases net income to reflect a deduction of $56 million cost of goods
        purchased rather than $60 million cost of goods sold.

Entry (7)   Increase in accounts payable—CFOA 6
        Accounts payable 6
        Increases net income to reflect a deduction of $50 million cash paid to
        suppliers rather than $56 million cost of goods purchased.

Entry (8)   Decrease in prepaid insurance—CFOA 3
        Prepaid insurance 3
        Increases net income to reflect a deduction of $4 million cash paid for
        insurance rather than $7 million insurance expense.

Entry (9)   Increase in salaries payable—CFOA 2
        Salaries payable 2
        Increases net income to reflect a deduction of $11 million cash paid to
        employees rather than $13 million salaries expense.

Entry (10) Amortization of discount on bonds—CFOA 2
        Discount on bonds 2
        Increases net income to reflect a deduction of $3 million cash paid for bond
        interest rather than $5 million bond interest expense.

Entry (11) Income taxes payable 2
        Decrease in income taxes payable—CFOA 2
        Reduces net income to reflect a deduction of $11 million cash paid for income
        taxes rather than $9 million income tax expense.

Entry (12) Short-term investment 12
        Cash (purchase of short-term investment) 12
        Explains the increase in the short-term investment account and identifies a cash
        outflow from investing activities.

Entry (13) Land 30
        Cash (purchase of land) 30
        Explains a portion of the change in the land account and identifies a cash
        outflow from investing activities.

(continued)

ILLUSTRATION 21A–2

Summary Entries for
the Indirect Method
Spreadsheet

ILLUSTRATION 21A–2
(concluded)

Entry (14) Buildings and equipment 20
        Note payable 20
Partially explains the changes in the buildings and equipment and notes payable accounts and identifies a noncash investing and financing activity.

Entry (15) Bonds payable 15
        Cash (retirement of bonds payable) 15
Explains the decrease in the bonds payable account and identifies a cash outflow from financing activities.

Entry (16) Retained earnings 13
        Common stock 10
        Paid-in capital—excess of par 3
Partially explains the changes in the retained earnings, common stock, and paid-in capital—excess of par accounts.

Entry (17) Cash (from sale of common stock) 26
        Common stock 20
        Paid-in capital—excess of par 6
Partially explains the changes in the common stock and paid-in capital—excess of par accounts and identifies a cash inflow from financing activities.

Entry (18) Retained earnings 5
        Cash (payment of cash dividends) 5
Partially explains the change in the retained earnings account and identifies a cash outflow from financing activities.

Entry (19) Cash 9
        Net increase in cash (from statement of cash flows activities) 9
Reconciles the net increase in cash from operating, investing, and financing activities to the increase in the cash balance.

The statement of cash flows presenting net cash flows from operating activities by the indirect method is illustrated in Illustration 21A–3.

ILLUSTRATION 21A–3
Statement of Cash Flows—Indirect Method

All parts of the statement of cash flows except operating activities are precisely the same as in the direct method.

UNITED BRANDS CORPORATION
Statement of Cash Flows
For Year Ended December 31, 2011
($ in millions)

Cash Flows from Operating Activities
Net income $12
Adjustments for noncash effects:
  Gain on sale of land ..... (8)
  Depreciation expense 3
  Loss on sale of equipment 2
  Increase in accounts receivable ..... (2)
  Decrease in inventory 4
  Decrease in prepaid insurance 3
  Increase in accounts payable 6
  Increase in salaries payable 2
  Decrease in income tax payable ..... (2)
  Amortization of discount on bonds 2
Net cash flows from operating activities $22
Cash Flows from Investing Activities
Purchase of land ..... (30)
Purchase of short-term investment ..... (12)
Sale of land 18
Sale of equipment 5
Net cash from investing activities ..... (19)

(continued)

Cash Flows from Financing Activities		
Sale of common shares	26	
Retirement of bonds payable	(15)	
Payment of cash dividends	(5)	
Net cash flows from financing activities		6
Net increase in cash		9
Cash balance, January 1		20
Cash balance, December 31		$29
Note X:		
Noncash Investing and Financing Activities		
Acquired $20 million of equipment		
by issuing a 12%, 5-year note		$20

ILLUSTRATION 21A–3
(concluded)

THE T-ACCOUNT METHOD OF PREPARING THE STATEMENT OF CASH FLOWS

APPENDIX 21B

The T-account method serves the same purpose as a spreadsheet in assisting in the preparation of a statement of cash flows.

This chapter demonstrates the use of a spreadsheet to prepare the statement of cash flows. A second systematic approach to the preparation of the statement is referred to as the T-account method. The two methods are identical in concept. Both approaches reconstruct the transactions that caused changes in each account balance during the year, simultaneously identifying the operating, investing, and financing activities to be reported on the statement of cash flows. The form of the two methods differs only by whether the entries for those transactions are recorded on a spreadsheet or in T-accounts. In both cases, entries are recorded until the net change in each account balance has been explained.

Some accountants feel that the T-account method is less time-consuming than preparing a spreadsheet but accomplishes precisely the same goal. Since both methods are simply analytical techniques to assist in statement preparation, the choice is a matter of personal preference. The following five steps outline the T-account method:

1. Draw T-accounts for each income statement and balance sheet account.
2. The T-account for cash should be drawn considerably larger than other T-accounts because more space is required to accommodate the numerous debits and credits to cash. Also, the cash T-account will serve the same purpose as the statement of cash flows section of the spreadsheet in that the formal statement of cash flows is developed from the cash flows reported there. Therefore, it is convenient to partition the cash T account with headings for "Operating Activities," "Investing Activities," and "Financing Activities" before entries are recorded.
3. Enter each account's net change on the appropriate side (debit or credit) of the uppermost portion of each T-account. These changes will serve as individual check figures for determining whether the increase or decrease in each account balance has been explained. These first three steps establish the basic work form for the T-account method.
4. Reconstruct the transactions that caused changes in each account balance during the year and record the entries for those transactions directly in the T-accounts. Again using UBC as an example, the entries we record in the T-accounts are exactly the same as the spreadsheet entries we created in the chapter when using the spreadsheet method. The analysis we used in creating those spreadsheet entries is equally applicable to the T-account method. For that reason, that analysis is not repeated here. The complete T-account work form for UBC is presented below. Account balance changes are provided by Illustration 21–1.

BALANCE SHEET ACCOUNTS
Cash (statement of cash flows)

		9				
Operating Activities:						
From customers	(1)	98	50	(4)	To suppliers of goods	
From investment revenue	(2)	3	11	(5)	To employees	
			3	(7)	For interest	
			4	(8)	For insurance	
			11	(10)	For income taxes	
Investing Activities:						
Sale of land	(3)	18	12	(12)	Purchase of short-term investment	
Sale of equipment	(9)	5	30	(13)	Purchase of land	
Financing Activities:						
Sale of common stock	(17)	26	15	(15)	Retirement of bonds payable	
			5	(18)	Payment of cash dividends	

Accounts Receivable

	2		
(1)	2		

Short-Term Investments

	12		
(12)	12		

Inventory

	4		
	4	(4)	

Prepaid Insurance

	3		
	3	(8)	

Land

		20		
(13)		30	10	(3)

Buildings and Equipment

	6		
X(14)	20	14	(9)

Accumulated Depreciation

		4	
(9)		7	3	(6)

Accounts Payable

		6	
		6	(4)

Salaries Payable

		2	
		2	(5)

Income Tax Payable

		2	
(10)		2	

Notes Payable

		20	
		20	(14)X

Bonds Payable

	15		
(15)	15		

Discount on Bonds

	2		
	2	(7)	

Common Stock

		30	
		10	(16)
		20	(17)

Paid-in Capital— excess of par

		9	
		3	(16)
		6	(17)

Retained Earnings

		6	
(16)	13		
(18)	5	12	(11)

X Noncash Investing and Financing Activity

(continued)

(concluded)

INCOME STATEMENT ACCOUNTS

Sales Revenue			Investment Revenue			Gain on Sale of Land		
	100			3			8	
	100	(1)		3	(2)		8	(3)

	Cost of Goods Sold				Salaries Expense				Depreciation Expense	
	60				13				3	
(4)	60		(5)		13		(6)		3	

	Interest Expense				Insurance Expense				Loss on Sale of Equipment	
	5				7				2	
(7)	5		(8)		7		(9)		2	

	Income Tax Expense				Net Income (Income Summary)	
	9				12	
(10)	9		(11)		12	

5. After all account balances have been explained by T-account entries, prepare the statement of cash flows from the cash T-account, being careful also to report noncash investing and financing activities. The statement of cash flows for UBC appears in Graphic 21–2 on page 1186. ●

QUESTIONS FOR REVIEW OF KEY TOPICS

Q 21–1 Effects of all cash flows affect the balances of various accounts reported in the balance sheet. Also, the activities that cause some of these cash flows are reported in the income statement. What, then, is the need for an additional financial statement that reports cash flows?

Q 21–2 The statement of cash flows provides a list of all the cash inflows and cash outflows during the reporting period. To make the list more informative, the cash flows are classified according to the nature of the activities that create the cash flows. What are the three primary classifications?

Q 21–3 Is an investment in Treasury bills always classified as a cash equivalent? Explain.

Q 21–4 Transactions that involve merely purchases or sales of cash equivalents generally are not reported in a statement of cash flows. Describe an exception to this generalization. What is the essential characteristic of the transaction that qualifies as an exception?

Q 21–5 What are the differences between cash flows from operating activities and the elements of an income statement?

Q 21–6 Do cash flows from operating activities report all the elements of the income statement on a cash basis? Explain.

Q 21–7 Investing activities include the acquisition and disposition of assets. Provide four specific examples. Identify two exceptions.

Q 21–8 The sale of stock and the sale of bonds are reported as financing activities. Are payments of dividends to shareholders and payments of interest to bondholders also reported as financing activities? Explain.

Q 21–9 Does the statement of cash flows report only transactions that cause an increase or a decrease in cash? Explain.

Q 21–10 How would the acquisition of a building be reported on a statement of cash flows if purchased by issuing a mortgage note payable in addition to a significant cash down payment?

Q 21–11 Perhaps the most noteworthy item reported on an income statement is net income—the amount by which revenues exceed expenses. The most noteworthy item reported on a statement of cash flows is *not* the amount of net cash flows. Explain.

Q 21–12 What is the purpose of the "changes" columns of a spreadsheet to prepare a statement of cash flows?

Q 21–13 Given sales revenue of $200,000, how can it be determined whether or not $200,000 cash was received from customers?

Q 21–14 When an asset is sold at a gain, why is the gain not reported as a cash inflow from operating activities?

Q 21–15 Are ordinary losses and extraordinary losses treated alike in preparing a statement of cash flows? Explain.

Q 21–16 When determining the amount of cash paid for income taxes, what would be indicated by an increase in the deferred income tax liability account?

Q 21–17 When using the indirect method of determining net cash flows from operating activities, how is bad debt expense reported? Why? What other expenses are reported in a like manner?

Q 21–18 When using the indirect method of determining net cash flows from operating activities, how are revenues and expenses reported on the statement of cash flows if their cash effects are identical to the amounts reported in the income statement?

Q 21–19 Why does the FASB recommend the direct method over the indirect method?

Q 21–20 Compare the manner in which investing activities are reported on a statement of cash flows prepared by the direct method and by the indirect method.

● IFRS Q 21–21 Where can we find authoritative guidance for the statement of cash flows under IFRS?

● IFRS Q 21–22 U.S. GAAP designates cash outflows for interest payments and cash inflows from interest and dividends received as operating cash flows. Dividends paid to shareholders are classified as financing cash flows. How are these cash flows reported under IFRS?

BRIEF EXERCISES

BE 21–1
Determine cash received from customers
● LO3

Horton Housewares' accounts receivable decreased during the year by $5 million. What is the amount of cash Horton received from customers during the reporting period if its sales were $33 million? Prepare a summary entry that represents the net effect of the selling and collection activities during the reporting period.

BE 21–2
Determine cash received from customers
● LO3

April Wood Products' accounts receivable increased during the year by $4 million. Its bad debt expense was $2 million, and its allowance for uncollectible accounts increased by $1 million. What is the amount of cash April Wood Products received from customers during the reporting period if its sales were $44 million? Prepare a summary entry that represents the net effect of the selling and collection activities during the reporting period.

BE 21–3
Determine cash paid to suppliers
● LO3

LaRoe Lawns' inventory increased during the year by $6 million. Its accounts payable increased by $5 million during the same period. What is the amount of cash LaRoe paid to suppliers of merchandise during the reporting period if its cost of goods sold was $25 million? Prepare a summary entry that represents the net effect of merchandise purchases during the reporting period.

BE 21–4
Determine cash paid to employees
● LO3

Sherriane Baby Products' salaries expense was $17 million. What is the amount of cash Sherriane paid to employees during the reporting period if its salaries payable increased by $3 million? Prepare a summary entry that represents the net effect of salaries expense incurred and paid during the reporting period.

BE 21–5
Bond interest and discount
● LO3 LO6

Agee Technology, Inc., issued 9% bonds, dated January 1, with a face amount of $400 million on July 1, 2011, at a price of $380 million. For bonds of similar risk and maturity, the market yield is 10%. Interest is paid semiannually on June 30 and December 31. Prepare the journal entry to record interest at December 31. What would be the amount(s) related to the bonds that Agee would report in its statement of cash flows for the year ended December 31, 2011, if it uses the direct method?

BE 21–6
Bond interest and discount
● LO4 LO6

Refer to the situation described in BE 21–5. What would be the amount(s) related to the bonds that Agee would report in its statement of cash flows for the year ended December 31, 2011, if it uses the indirect method?

BE 21–7
Installment note
● LO3 LO6

On January 1, 2011, the Merit Group issued to its bank a $41 million, five-year installment note to be paid in five equal payments at the end of each year. Installment payments of $10 million annually include interest at the rate of 7%. What would be the amount(s) related to the note that Merit would report in its statement of cash flows for the year ended December 31, 2011?

BE 21–8
Sale of land
● LO3 LO4 LO5

On July 15, 2011, M.W. Morgan Distribution sold land for $35 million that it had purchased in 2006 for $22 million. What would be the amount(s) related to the sale that Morgan would report in its statement of cash flows for the year ended December 31, 2011, using the direct method? The indirect method?

BE 21–9
Investing activities
● LO5

Carter Containers sold marketable securities, land, and common stock for $30 million, $15 million, and $40 million, respectively. Carter also purchased treasury stock, equipment, and a patent for $21 million, $25 million, and $12 million, respectively. What amount should Carter report as net cash from investing activities?

BE 21–10
Financing activities
● LO6

Refer to the situation described in BE 21–9. What amount should Carter report as net cash from financing activities?

BE 21–11
Indirect method
● LO4

Sheen Awnings reported net income of $90 million. Included in that number were depreciation expense of $3 million and a loss on the sale of equipment of $2 million. Records reveal increases in accounts receivable, accounts payable, and inventory of $1 million, $4 million, and $3 million, respectively. What were Sheen's cash flows from operating activities?

BE 21–12
Indirect method
● LO4

Sunset Acres reported net income of $60 million. Included in that number were trademark amortization expense of $2 million and a gain on the sale of land of $1 million. Records reveal decreases in accounts receivable, accounts payable, and inventory of $2 million, $5 million, and $4 million, respectively. What were Sunset's cash flows from operating activities?

EXERCISES

An alternate exercise and problem set is available on the text website: www.mhhe.com/spiceland6e

E 21–1
Classification of cash flows
● LO3 through LO6

Listed below are several transactions that typically produce either an increase or a decrease in cash. Indicate by letter whether the cash effect of each transaction is reported on a statement of cash flows as an operating (**O**), investing (**I**), or financing (**F**) activity.

Transactions

_F_   1. Sale of common stock
____ 2. Sale of land
____ 3. Purchase of treasury stock
____ 4. Merchandise sales
____ 5. Issuance of a long-term note payable
____ 6. Purchase of merchandise
____ 7. Repayment of note payable
____ 8. Employee salaries
____ 9. Sale of equipment at a gain
____ 10. Issuance of bonds
____ 11. Acquisition of bonds of another corporation
____ 12. Payment of semiannual interest on bonds payable
____ 13. Payment of a cash dividend
____ 14. Purchase of a building
____ 15. Collection of nontrade note receivable (principal amount)
____ 16. Loan to another firm
____ 17. Retirement of common stock
____ 18. Income taxes
____ 19. Issuance of a short-term note payable
____ 20. Sale of a copyright

E 21–2
Determine cash paid to suppliers of merchandise
● LO3

Shown below in T-account format are the beginning and ending balances ($ in millions) of both inventory and accounts payable.

Inventory	
Beginning balance	90
Ending balance	93

Accounts Payable	
14	Beginning balance
16	Ending balance

Required:

1. Use a T-account analysis to determine the amount of cash paid to suppliers of merchandise during the reporting period if cost of goods sold was $300 million.

2. Prepare a summary entry that represents the net effect of merchandise purchases during the reporting period.

E 21–3
Determine cash received from customers
● LO3

Determine the amount of cash received from customers for each of the six independent situations below. All dollars are in millions.

Situation	Sales Revenue	Accounts Receivable Increase (Decrease)	Bad Debt Expense	Allowance for Uncollectible Accounts Increase (Decrease)	Cash Received from Customers
1	100	–0–	–0–	–0–	?
2	100	5	–0–	–0–	?
3	100	(5)	–0–	–0–	?
4	100	5	2	2	?
5	100	(5)	2	1	?
6	100	5	2	(1)	?

E 21–4

Summary entries for cash received from customers

● LO3

For each of the four independent situations below, prepare journal entries that summarize the selling and collection activities for the reporting period in order to determine the amount of cash received from customers and to explain the change in each account shown. All dollars are in millions.

Situation	Sales Revenue	Accounts Receivable Increase (Decrease)	Bad Debt Expense	Allowance for Uncollectible Accounts Increase (Decrease)	Cash Received from Customers
1	200	–0–	–0–	–0–	?
2	200	10	–0–	–0–	?
3	200	10	4	4	?
4	200	10	4	(2)	?

E 21–5

Determine cash paid to suppliers of merchandise

● LO3

Determine the amount of cash paid to suppliers of merchandise for each of the nine independent situations below. All dollars are in millions.

Situation	Cost of Goods Sold	Inventory Increase (Decrease)	Accounts Payable Increase (Decrease)	Cash Paid to Suppliers
1	100	0	0	?
2	100	3	0	?
3	100	(3)	0	?
4	100	0	7	?
5	100	0	(7)	?
6	100	3	7	?
7	100	3	(7)	?
8	100	(3)	(7)	?
9	100	(3)	7	?

E 21–6

Summary entries for cash paid to suppliers of merchandise

● LO3

For each of the five independent situations below, prepare a journal entry that summarizes the purchases, sales, and payments related to inventories in order to determine the amount of cash paid to suppliers and explain the change in each account shown. All dollars are in millions.

Situation	Cost of Goods Sold	Inventory Increase (Decrease)	Accounts Payable Increase (Decrease)	Cash Paid to Suppliers
1	200	0	0	?
2	200	6	0	?
3	200	0	14	?
4	200	6	14	?
5	200	(6)	(14)	?

E 21–7

Determine cash paid for bond interest

● LO3

Determine the amount of cash paid to bondholders for bond interest for each of the six independent situations below. All dollars are in millions.

Situation	Bond Interest Expense	Bond Interest Payable Increase (Decrease)	Unamortized Discount Increase (Decrease)	Cash Paid for Interest
1	10	0	0	?
2	10	2	0	?
3	10	(2)	0	?
4	10	0	(3)	?
5	10	2	(3)	?
6	10	(2)	(3)	?

E 21–8

Determine cash paid for bond interest

For each of the four independent situations below, prepare a single journal entry that summarizes the recording and payment of interest in order to determine the amount of cash paid for bond interest and explain the change (if any) in each of the accounts shown. All dollars are in millions.

● LO3

Situation	Bond Interest Expense	Bond Interest Payable Increase (Decrease)	Unamortized Discount Increase (Decrease)	Cash Paid for Interest
1	20	0	0	?
2	20	4	0	?
3	20	0	(6)	?
4	20	(4)	(6)	?

E 21–9
Determine cash paid for income taxes
● LO3

Determine the amount of cash paid for income taxes in each of the nine independent situations below. All dollars are in millions.

Situation	Income Tax Expense	Income Tax Payable Increase (Decrease)	Deferred Tax Liability Increase (Decrease)	Cash Paid for Taxes
1	10	0	0	?
2	10	3	0	?
3	10	(3)	0	?
4	10	0	2	?
5	10	0	(2)	?
6	10	3	2	?
7	10	3	(2)	?
8	10	(3)	(2)	?
9	10	(3)	2	?

E 21–10
Summary entries for cash paid for income taxes
● LO3

For each of the five independent situations below, prepare a single journal entry that summarizes the recording and payment of income taxes in order to determine the amount of cash paid for income taxes and explain the change (if any) in each of the accounts shown. All dollars are in millions.

Situation	Income Tax Expense	Income Tax Payable Increase (Decrease)	Deferred Tax Liability Increase (Decrease)	Cash Paid for Taxes
1	10	0	0	?
2	10	3	0	?
3	10	0	(2)	?
4	10	3	2	?
5	10	(3)	(2)	?

E 21–11
Bonds; statement of cash flow effects
● LO3

Most Solutions, Inc., issued 10% bonds, dated January 1, with a face amount of $640 million on January 1, 2011. The bonds mature in 2021 (10 years). For bonds of similar risk and maturity the market yield is 12%. Interest is paid semiannually on June 30 and December 31. Most recorded the sale as follows:

January 1, 2011

Cash (price)	566,589,440	
Discount on bonds (difference)	73,410,560	
Bonds payable (face amount)		640,000,000

Required:

What would be the amount(s) related to the bonds that Most would report in its statement of cash flows for the year ended December 31, 2011?

E 21–12
Installment note; statement of cash flow effects
● LO3 LO6

National Food Services, Inc., borrowed $4 million from its local bank on January 1, 2011, and issued a 4-year installment note to be paid in four equal payments at the end of each year. The payments include interest at the rate of 10%. Installment payments are $1,261,881 annually.

Required:

What would be the amount(s) related to the note that National would report in its statement of cash flows for the year ended December 31, 2011?

E 21–13
Identifying cash flows from investing activities and financing activities
● LO5 LO6

In preparation for developing its statement of cash flows for the year ended December 31, 2011, Rapid Pac, Inc., collected the following information:

	($ in millions)
Fair value of shares issued in a stock dividend	$ 65
Payment for the early extinguishment of	
long-term bonds (carrying amount: $97 million)	102
Proceeds from the sale of treasury stock (cost: $17 million)	22
Gain on sale of land	4

(continued)

(concluded)

Proceeds from sale of land	12
Purchase of Microsoft common stock	160
Declaration of cash dividends	44
Distribution of cash dividends declared in 2010	40

Required:

1. In Rapid Pac's statement of cash flows, what were net cash inflows (or outflows) from investing activities for 2011?
2. In Rapid Pac's statement of cash flows, what were net cash inflows (or outflows) from financing activities for 2011?

E 21–14
Identifying
cash flows from
investing activities
and financing
activities

● LO5 LO6

In preparation for developing its statement of cash flows for the year ended December 31, 2011, Millennium Solutions, Inc., collected the following information ($ in millions):

Payment for the early extinguishments of long-term notes (book value: $50 million)	$ 54
Sale of common shares	176
Retirement of common shares	122
Loss on sale of equipment	2
Proceeds from sale of equipment	8
Issuance of short-term note payable for cash	10
Acquisition of building for cash	7
Purchase of marketable securities (not a cash equivalent)	5
Purchase of marketable securities (considered a cash equivalent)	1
Cash payment for 3-year insurance policy	3
Collection of note receivable with interest (principal amount, $11)	13
Declaration of cash dividends	33
Distribution of cash dividends declared in 2010	30

Required:

1. In Millennium's statement of cash flows, what were net cash inflows (or outflows) from investing activities for 2011?
2. In Millennium's statement of cash flows, what were net cash inflows (or outflows) from financing activities for 2011?

E 21–15
Capital lease;
lessee; statement of
cash flows effects

● LO3 LO5 LO6

Wilson Foods Corporation leased a commercial food processor on September 30, 2011. The five-year lease agreement calls for Wilson to make quarterly lease payments of $195,774, payable each September 30, December 31, March 31, June 30, with the first payment at September 30, 2011. Wilson's incremental borrowing rate is 12%. Wilson records depreciation on a straight-line basis at the end of each fiscal year. Wilson recorded the lease as follows:

September 30, 2011		
Leased equipment (calculated below)	3,000,000	
Lease payable (calculated below)		3,000,000
Lease payable	195,774	
Cash (rental payment)		195,774

Calculation of the present value of lease payments
$195,774 \times 15.32380^* = \$3,000,000$
(rounded)
*Present value of an annuity due of $1: n = 20, i = 3% (from Table 6)

Required:

What would be the pretax amounts related to the lease that Wilson would report in its statement of cash flows for the year ended December 31, 2011?

E 21–16
Equity method
investment;
statement of cash
flow effects

● LO3 LO5

On January 1, 2011, Beilich Enterprises bought 20% of the outstanding common stock of Wolfe Construction Company for $600 million cash. Wolfe's net income for the year ended December 31, 2011, was $300 million. During 2011, Wolfe declared and paid cash dividends of $60 million. Beilich recorded the investment as follows:

Purchase	($ in millions)	
Investment in Wolfe Construction shares	600	
Cash		600
Net income		
Investment in Wolfe Construction shares (20% × $300 million)	60	
Investment revenue		60
Dividends		
Cash (20% × $60 million)	12	
Investment in Wolfe Construction shares		12

Required:

What would be the pretax amounts related to the investment that Beilich would report in its statement of cash flows for the year ended December 31, 2011?

E 21–17
Indirect method; reconciliation of net income to net cash flows from operating activities
● LO4

The accounting records of EZ Company provided the data below. Prepare a reconciliation of net income to net cash flows from operating activities.

Net income	$50,000
Depreciation expense	7,000
Increase in inventory	1,500
Decrease in salaries payable	800
Decrease in accounts receivable	2,000
Amortization of patent	500
Amortization of premium on bonds	1,000
Increase in accounts payable	4,000
Cash dividends	12,000

E 21–18
Spreadsheet entries from statement of retained earnings
● LO3 through LO8

The statement of retained earnings of Gary Larson Publishers is presented below.

GARY LARSON PUBLISHERS
Statement of Retained Earnings
For the Year Ended December 31, 2011
($ in millions)

Retained earnings, January 1		$200
Add:	Net income	75
Deduct:	Cash dividend	(25)
	Stock dividend (1 million shares of $1 par common stock)	(16)
	Property dividend (Garfield Company preferred stock held as a short-term investment)	(12)
	Sale of treasury stock (cost $53 million)	(10)
Retained earnings, December 31		$212

Required:

For the transactions that affected Larson's retained earnings, reconstruct the journal entries for the transactions that affected retained earnings and that can be used to determine cash flows to be reported in a statement of cash flows. Also indicate any investing and financing activities you identify from this analysis that should be reported on the statement of cash flows.

E 21–19
Relationship between the income statement and cash flows from operating activities (direct method and indirect method)
● LO3 LO4

The following schedule relates the income statement with cash flows from operating activities, derived by both the direct and indirect methods, in the format illustrated by Graphic 21–10 in the chapter. The amounts for income statement elements are missing.

Cash Flows from Operating Activities

Income Statement		Indirect Method		Direct Method	
		Net income	$?		
		Adjustments:			
Sales	$?	Decrease in accounts receivable	12	Cash received from customers	$612
Cost of goods sold	?	Increase in inventory	(24)		
		Decrease in accounts payable	(36)	Cash paid to suppliers	(420)
Salaries expense	?	Increase in salaries payable	12	Cash paid to employees	(66)
Depreciation expense	?	Depreciation expense	18	(Not reported—no cash effect)	
Insurance expense	?	Decrease in prepaid insurance	18	Cash paid for insurance	(24)
Loss on sale of land	?	Loss on sale of land	12	(Not reported—no cash effect)	
Income tax expense	?	Increase in income tax payable	12	Cash paid for income taxes	(42)
Net income	$?	Net cash flows from operating activities	$60	Net cash flows from operating activities	$ 60

Required:

Deduce the missing amounts and prepare the income statement.

E 21–20
Reconciliation of net cash flows from operating activities to net income

● LO3 LO4

The income statement and the cash flows from the operating activities section of the statement of cash flows are provided below for Syntric Company. The merchandise inventory account balance neither increased nor decreased during the reporting period. Syntric had no liability for either insurance, deferred income taxes, or interest at any time during the period.

SYNTRIC COMPANY
Income Statement
For the Year Ended December 31, 2011
($ in 000s)

Sales		$312
Cost of goods sold		(188)
Gross margin		124
Salaries expense	$41	
Insurance expense	22	
Depreciation expense	11	
Depletion expense	5	
Bond interest expense	10	(89)
Gains and losses:		
Gain on sale of equipment		25
Loss on sale of land		(8)
Income before tax		52
Income tax expense		(26)
Net income		**$ 26**
Cash Flows from Operating Activities:		
Cash received from customers		$258
Cash paid to suppliers		(175)
Cash paid to employees		(37)
Cash paid for interest		(9)
Cash paid for insurance		(16)
Cash paid for income taxes		(14)
Net cash flows from operating activities		**$ 7**

Required:
Prepare a schedule to reconcile net income to net cash flows from operating activities.

E 21–21
Cash flows from operating activities (direct method) derived from an income statement and cash flows from operating activities (indirect method)

● LO3 LO4

The income statement and a schedule reconciling cash flows from operating activities to net income are provided below ($ in 000s) for Peach Computers.

PEACH COMPUTERS
Income Statement
For the Year Ended December 31, 2011

Sales		$305
Cost of goods sold		(185)
Gross margin		120
Salaries expense	$41	
Insurance expense	19	
Depreciation expense	11	
Loss on sale of land	5	76
Income before tax		44
Income tax expense		(22)
Net income		**$ 22**

Reconciliation of Net Income
To Net Cash Flows from Operating Activities

Net income	$22
Adjustments for Noncash Effects	
Depreciation expense	11
Loss on sale of land	5
Changes in operating assets and liabilities:	
Decrease in accounts receivable	6
Increase in inventory	(13)
Decrease in accounts payable	(8)
Increase in salaries payable	5
Decrease in prepaid insurance	9
Increase in income tax payable	20
Net cash flows from operating activities	**$57**

Required:
1. Calculate each of the following amounts for Peach Computers:
   a. Cash received from customers during the reporting period.
   b. Cash paid to suppliers of goods during the reporting period.
   c. Cash paid to employees during the reporting period.

d. Cash paid for insurance during the reporting period.

e. Cash paid for income taxes during the reporting period.

2. Prepare the cash flows from operating activities section of the statement of cash flows (direct method).

E 21–22
Indirect method; reconciliation of net income to net cash flows from operating activities
● LO4

The accounting records of Baddour Company provided the data below. Prepare a reconciliation of net income to net cash flows from operating activities.

Net loss	$5,000
Depreciation expense	6,000
Increase in salaries payable	500
Decrease in accounts receivable	2,000
Increase in inventory	2,300
Amortization of patent	300
Reduction in discount on bonds	200

E 21–23
Cash flows from operating activities (direct method)—includes extraordinary loss
● LO3

Portions of the financial statements for Myriad Products are provided below.

MYRIAD PRODUCTS COMPANY
Income Statement
For the Year Ended December 31, 2011
($ in millions)

Sales		$ 660
Cost of goods sold		(250)
Gross margin		410
Salaries expense	$110	
Depreciation expense	90	
Patent amortization expense	5	
Interest expense	20	
Loss on sale of investments	3	(228)
Income before taxes and extraordinary loss		182
Income tax expense		(91)
Income before extraordinary loss		91
Extraordinary loss (earthquake)	10	
Less: Tax savings	(5)	(5)
Net Income		$ 86

MYRIAD PRODUCTS COMPANY
Selected Accounts from Comparative Balance Sheets
December 31, 2011 and 2010
($ in millions)

	Year 2011	2010	Change
Cash	$102	$100	$ 2
Accounts receivable	220	232	(12)
Inventory	440	450	(10)
Accounts payable	140	134	6
Salaries payable	80	86	(6)
Interest payable	25	20	5
Income taxes payable	15	10	5

Required:
Prepare the cash flows from operating activities section of the statement of cash flows for Myriad Products Company using the *direct method.*

E 21–24
Cash flows from operating activities (indirect method)—includes extraordinary loss
● LO4

Refer to the data provided in the previous exercise for Myriad Products Company.

Required:
Prepare the cash flows from operating activities section of the statement of cash flows for Myriad Products Company using the *indirect method.*

E 21–25
Cash flows
from operating
activities (direct
method)—includes
extraordinary gain

● LO3

Portions of the financial statements for Clear Transmissions Company are provided below.

CLEAR TRANSMISSIONS COMPANY
Income Statement
For the Year Ended December 31, 2011 ($ in 000s)

Sales		$1,320
Cost of goods sold		(500)
Gross margin		820
Salaries expense	$220	
Depreciation expense	180	
Patent amortization expense	10	
Interest expense	40	
Loss on sale of investment	6	(456)
Income before taxes and extraordinary gain		364
Income tax expense		(182)
Income before extraordinary gain		182
Extraordinary gain (sale of subsidiary)	20	
Less: Tax on gain	(10)	10
Net Income		$ 192

CLEAR TRANSMISSIONS COMPANY
Selected Accounts from Comparative Balance Sheets
December 31, 2011 and 2010 ($ in 000s)

	Year		
	2011	**2010**	**Change**
Cash	$102	$100	$ 2
Accounts receivable	220	232	(12)
Inventory	440	450	(10)
Accounts payable	140	134	6
Salaries payable	80	86	(6)
Interest payable	25	20	5
Income taxes payable	15	10	5

Required:
Prepare the cash flows from operating activities section of the statement of cash flows for Clear Transmissions Company using the *direct method.*

E 21–26
Cash flows
from operating
activities (indirect
method)—includes
extraordinary gain

● LO4

Refer to the data provided in the previous exercise for Clear Transmissions Company.

Required:
Prepare the cash flows from operating activities section of the statement of cash flows for Clear Transmissions Company using the *indirect method.*

E 21–27
Statement of
cash flows; direct
method

● LO3 LO5 LO6
LO8

Comparative balance sheets for 2011 and 2010, a statement of income for 2011, and additional information from the accounting records of Red, Inc., are provided below.

RED, INC.
Comparative Balance Sheets
December 31, 2011 and 2010 ($ in millions)

	2011	2010
Assets		
Cash	$ 24	$110
Accounts receivable	178	132
Prepaid insurance	7	3
Inventory	285	175
Buildings and equipment	400	350
Less: Accumulated depreciation	(119)	(240)
	$775	$530
Liabilities		
Accounts payable	$ 87	$100
Accrued expenses payable	6	11
Notes payable	50	0
Bonds payable	160	0

(continued)

(concluded)

Shareholders' Equity

Common stock	400	400
Retained earnings	72	19
	$775	$530

RED, INC.
Statement of Income
For Year Ended December 31, 2011 ($ in millions)

Revenues		
Sales revenue		$2,000
Expenses		
Cost of goods sold	$1,400	
Depreciation expense	50	
Operating expenses	447	1,897
Net income		$ 103

Additional information from the accounting records:

a. During 2011, $230 million of equipment was purchased to replace $180 million of equipment (95% depreciated) sold at book value.

b. In order to maintain the usual policy of paying cash dividends of $50 million, it was necessary for Red to borrow $50 million from its bank.

Required:

Prepare the statement of cash flows of Red, Inc., for the year ended December 31, 2011. Present cash flows from operating activities by the direct method. (You may omit the schedule to reconcile net income to cash flows from operating activities.)

E 21–28
Pension plan funding
● **LO3**

Mayer Corporation has a defined benefit pension plan. Mayer's policy is to fund the plan annually, cash payments being made at the end of each year. Data relating to the pension plan for 2011 are as follows:

	December 31 ($ in millions)	
	2011	**2010**
Plan assets	$1,080	$900
Net Pension Expense for 2011:		
Service cost	$ 112	
Interest cost (6% × $850)	51	
Actual return on the plan assets (11% × $900 = $99)		
Adjusted for: $9 gain on the plan assets*	(90)	
Amortization of prior service cost	8	
Amortization of net loss	1	
	$ 82	

*(11% × $900) – (10% × $900)

Required:

Recreate the journal entries used to record Mayer's 2011 pension expense, gain on plan assets, and funding of plan assets in order to determine the cash paid to the pension trustee as reported in the statement of cash flows.

E 21–29
FASB codification research
● **LO2**

The statement of cash flows (as well as the balance sheet) includes within cash the notion of cash equivalents. The *FASB Accounting Standards Codification* represents the single source of authoritative U.S. generally accepted accounting principles.

Required:

1. Obtain the relevant authoritative literature on cash equivalents using the FASB's Codification Research System at the FASB website (**www.fasb.org**). What is the specific citation that describes the guidelines for determining what items should be deemed cash equivalents?

2. List the guidelines.

E 21–30
FASB codification research
● **LO1 LO4 LO7**

Access the FASB's Codification Research System at the FASB website (**www.fasb.org**). Determine the specific citation for accounting for each of the following items:

1. Disclosure of interest and income taxes paid if the indirect method is used.

2. Primary objectives of a statement of cash flows.

3. Disclosure of noncash investing and financing activities.

E 21–31
Statement of cash
flows; indirect
method
● LO4 LO5 LO6
LO8 Appendix A

Refer to the data provided in Exercise 21–27 for Red, Inc.

Required:
Prepare the statement of cash flows for Red, Inc., using the indirect method to report operating activities.

E 21–32
Statement of cash
flows; T-account
method
● LO8 Appendix B

Refer to the data provided in Exercise 21–27 for Red, Inc.

Required:
Prepare the statement of cash flows (direct method) for Red, Inc. Use the T-account method to assist in your analysis.

CPA AND CMA REVIEW QUESTIONS

**CPA Exam
Questions**

The following questions are used in the Kaplan CPA Review Course to study the statement of cash flows while preparing for the CPA examination. Determine the response that best completes the statements or questions.

● LO3

1. In a statement of cash flows in which operating activities are reported by the direct method, which of the following would increase reported cash flows from operating activities?
    a. Gain on sale of land.
    b. Interest revenue.
    c. Gain on early extinguishment of bonds.
    d. Proceeds from sale of equipment.

● LO6

2. During 2011, TEL Company engaged in the following activities:

Distribution of cash dividends declared in 2010	$ 24
Fair value of shares issued in a stock dividend	110
Payment to retire bonds	226
Proceeds from the sale of treasury stock (cost: $26)	30

In TEL's statement of cash flows, what were net cash outflows from financing activities for 2011?
    a. $196
    b. $220
    c. $280
    d. $366

● LO4

3. SOL Company reported net income for 2011 in the amount of $200,000. The company's financial statements also included the following:

Increase in accounts receivable	$ 40,000
Decrease in inventory	30,000
Increase in accounts payable	100,000
Depreciation expense	52,000
Gain on sale of land	74,000

What is net cash provided by operating activities under the indirect method?
    a. $216,000
    b. $268,000
    c. $290,000
    d. $416,000

● LO3

4. Which of the following does *not* represent a cash flow relating to operating activities?
    a. Dividends paid to stockholders.
    b. Cash received from customers.
    c. Interest paid to bondholders.
    d. Cash paid for salaries.

● LO5

5. Which of the following would *not* be a component of cash flows from investing activities?
    a. Sale of land.
    b. Purchase of securities.

    c. Purchase of equipment.

    d. Dividends paid.

● LO4

6. An analyst compiled the following information for Universe, Inc., for the year ended December 31, 2011:
   - Net income was $850,000.
   - Depreciation expense was $200,000.
   - Interest paid was $100,000.
   - Income taxes paid were $50,000.
   - Common stock was sold for $100,000.
   - Preferred stock (8% annual dividend) was sold at par value of $125,000.
   - Common stock dividends of $25,000 were paid.
   - Preferred stock dividends of $10,000 were paid.
   - Equipment with a book value of $50,000 was sold for $100,000.

   Using the indirect method, what was Universe, Inc.'s net cash flow from operating activities for the year ended December 31, 2011?

   a. $1,000,000

   b. $1,015,000

   c. $1,040,000

   d. $1,050,000

CMA Exam Questions

The following questions dealing with the statement of cash flows are adapted from questions that previously appeared on Certified Management Accountant (CMA) examinations. The CMA designation sponsored by the Institute of Management Accountants (**www.imanet.org**) provides members with an objective measure of knowledge and competence in the field of management accounting. Determine the response that best completes the statements or questions.

● LO3

1. When preparing the statement of cash flows, companies are required to report separately as operating cash flows all of the following except

   a. interest received on investments in bonds.

   b. interest paid on the company's bonds.

   c. cash collected from customers.

   d. cash dividends paid on the company's stock.

● LO5 LO6

2. The following information was taken from the accounting records of Oak Corporation for the year ended December 31:

Proceeds from issuance of preferred stock	$4,000,000
Dividends paid on preferred stock	400,000
Bonds payable converted to common stock	2,000,000
Payment for purchase of machinery	500,000
Proceeds from sale of plant building	1,200,000
2% stock dividend on common stock	300,000
Gain on sale of plant building	200,000

   The net cash flows from investing and financing activities that should be presented on Oak's statement of cash flows for the year ended December 31 are, respectively

   a. $700,000 and $3,600,000.

   b. $700,000 and $3,900,000.

   c. $900,000 and $3,900,000.

   d. $900,000 and $3,600,000.

● LO4

3. The net income for Cypress Inc. was $3,000,000 for the year ended December 31. Additional information is as follows:

Depreciation on fixed assets	$1,500,000
Gain from cash sale of land	200,000
Increase in accounts payable	300,000
Dividends paid on preferred stock	400,000

   The net cash provided by operating activities in the statement of cash flows for the year ended December 31 should be

   a. $4,200,000.

   b. $4,500,000.

   c. $4,600,000.

   d. $4,800,000.

PROBLEMS

An alternate exercise and problem set is available on the text website: www.mhhe.com/spiceland6e

P 21–1
Classification of cash flows from investing and financing activities

● LO2 LO5
   through LO7

Listed below are transactions that might be reported as investing and/or financing activities on a statement of cash flows. Possible reporting classifications of those transactions are provided also.

Required:
Indicate the reporting classification of each transaction by entering the appropriate classification code.

	Classifications
+I	Investing activity (cash inflow)
−I	Investing activity (cash outflow)
+F	Financing activity (cash inflow)
−F	Financing activity (cash outflow)
N	Noncash investing and financing activity
X	Not reported as an investing and/or a financing activity

Transactions

Example   +I   1. Sale of land.

_____ 2. Issuance of common stock for cash.
_____ 3. Purchase of treasury stock.
_____ 4. Conversion of bonds payable to common stock.
_____ 5. Lease of equipment by capital lease.
_____ 6. Sale of patent.
_____ 7. Acquisition of building for cash.
_____ 8. Issuance of common stock for land.
_____ 9. Collection of note receivable (principal amount).
_____ 10. Issuance of bonds.
_____ 11. Issuance of stock dividend.
_____ 12. Payment of property dividend.
_____ 13. Payment of cash dividends.
_____ 14. Issuance of short-term note payable for cash.
_____ 15. Issuance of long-term note payable for cash.
_____ 16. Purchase of marketable securities ("avaible for sale").
_____ 17. Payment of note payable.
_____ 18. Cash payment for 5-year insurance policy.
_____ 19. Sale of equipment.
_____ 20. Issuance of note payable for equipment.
_____ 21. Acquisition of common stock of another corporation.
_____ 22. Repayment of long-term debt by issuing common stock.
_____ 23. Payment of semiannual interest on bonds payable.
_____ 24. Retirement of preferred stock.
_____ 25. Loan to another firm.
_____ 26. Sale of inventory to customers.
_____ 27. Purchase of marketable securities (cash equivalents).

P 21–2
Statement of cash flows; direct method

● LO3 LO8

The comparative balance sheets for 2011 and 2010 and the statement of income for 2011 are given below for Wright Company. Additional information from Wright's accounting records is provided also.

WRIGHT COMPANY
Comparative Balance Sheets
December 31, 2011 and 2010
($ in 000s)

	2011	2010
Assets		
Cash	$ 42	$ 30
Accounts receivable	73	75
Short-term investment	40	15
Inventory	75	70
Land	50	60
Buildings and equipment	550	400
Less: Accumulated depreciation	(115)	(75)
	$ 715	$575

(continued)

(concluded)

Liabilities

Accounts payable	$ 28	$ 35
Salaries payable	2	5
Interest payable	5	3
Income tax payable	9	12
Notes payable	0	30
Bonds payable	160	100

Shareholders' Equity

Common stock	250	200
Paid-in capital—excess of par	126	100
Retained earnings	135	90
	$ 715	$575

WRIGHT COMPANY
Income Statement
For Year Ended December 31, 2011
($ in 000s)

Revenues		
Sales revenue		$380
Expenses		
Cost of goods sold	$130	
Salaries expense	45	
Depreciation expense	40	
Interest expense	12	
Loss on sale of land	3	
Income tax expense	70	300
Net income		$ 80

Additional information from the accounting records:

a. Land that originally cost $10,000 was sold for $7,000.

b. The common stock of Microsoft Corporation was purchased for $25,000 as a short term investment not classified as a cash equivalent.

c. New equipment was purchased for $150,000 cash.

d. A $30,000 note was paid at maturity on January 1.

e. On January 1, 2011, $60,000 of bonds were sold at face value.

f. Common stock ($50,000 par) was sold for $76,000.

g. Net income was $80,000 and cash dividends of $35,000 were paid to shareholders.

Required:
Prepare the statement of cash flows of Wright Company for the year ended December 31, 2011. Present cash flows from operating activities by the direct method. (You may omit the schedule to reconcile net income to cash flows from operating activities.)

P 21–3
Statement of
cash flows; direct
method
● LO3 LO8

The comparative balance sheets for 2011 and 2010 and the statement of income for 2011 are given below for National Intercable Company. Additional information from NIC's accounting records is provided also.

NATIONAL INTERCABLE COMPANY
Comparative Balance Sheets
December 31, 2011 and 2010
($ in millions)

	2011	2010
Assets		
Cash	$ 72	$ 55
Accounts receivable	181	170
Less: Allowance for uncollectible accounts	(8)	(6)
Prepaid insurance	7	12
Inventory	170	165
Long-term investment	66	90
Land	150	150
Buildings and equipment	290	270
Less: Accumulated depreciation	(85)	(75)
Trademark	24	25
	$867	$856

(continued)

(concluded)

Liabilities		
Accounts payable	$ 30	$ 45
Salaries payable	3	8
Deferred income tax liability	18	15
Lease liability	80	0
Bonds payable	145	275
Less: Discount on bonds	(22)	(25)
Shareholders' Equity		
Common stock	310	290
Paid-in capital—excess of par	95	85
Preferred stock	50	0
Retained earnings	158	163
	$867	$856

NATIONAL INTERCABLE COMPANY
Income Statement
For Year Ended December 31, 2011
($ in millions)

Revenues		
Sales revenue	$320	
Investment revenue	15	
Gain on sale of investments	5	$ 340
Expenses		
Cost of goods sold	125	
Salaries expense	55	
Depreciation expense	25	
Trademark amortization expense	1	
Bad debt expense	7	
Insurance expense	13	
Bond interest expense	30	(256)
Income before tax and extraordinary items		84
Income tax expense		(38)
Income before extraordinary items		46
Extraordinary loss (tornado)	42	
Less: Tax savings	(21)	(21)
Net income		$ 25

Additional information from the accounting records:

a. During 2011, $5 million of customer accounts were written off as uncollectible.

b. Investment revenue includes National Intercable Company's $6 million share of the net income of Central Fiber Optics Corporation, an equity method investee.

c. A long-term investment in bonds, originally purchased for $30 million, was sold for $35 million.

d. Pretax accounting income exceeded taxable income causing the deferred income tax liability to increase by $3 million.

e. A building that originally cost $60 million, and which was one-fourth depreciated, was destroyed by a tornado. Some undamaged parts were sold for $3 million.

f. A building was acquired by a seven-year capital lease; present value of lease payments, $80 million.

g. $130 million of bonds were retired at maturity.

h. $20 million par value of common stock was sold for $30 million, and $50 million of preferred stock was sold at par.

i. Shareholders were paid cash dividends of $30 million.

Required:

1. Prepare a spreadsheet for preparation of the statement of cash flows (direct method) of National Intercable Company for the year ended December 31, 2011.

2. Prepare the statement of cash flows. (A reconciliation schedule is not required.)

P 21–4

Statement of
cash flows; direct
method

● LO3 LO8

The comparative balance sheets for 2011 and 2010 and the statement of income for 2011 are given below for Dux Company. Additional information from Dux's accounting records is provided also.

DUX COMPANY
Comparative Balance Sheets
December 31, 2011 and 2010
($ in 000s)

	2011	2010
Assets		
Cash	$ 33	$ 20
Accounts receivable	48	50
Less: Allowance for uncollectible accounts	(4)	(3)
Dividends receivable	3	2
Inventory	55	50
Long-term investment	15	10
Land	70	40
Buildings and equipment	225	250
Less: Accumulated depreciation	(25)	(50)
	$420	$369
Liabilities		
Accounts payable	$ 13	$ 20
Salaries payable	2	5
Interest payable	4	2
Income tax payable	7	8
Notes payable	30	0
Bonds payable	95	70
Less: Discount on bonds	(2)	(3)
Shareholders' Equity		
Common stock	210	200
Paid-in capital—excess of par	24	20
Retained earnings	45	17
Less: Treasury stock	(8)	0
	$420	$369

DUX COMPANY
Income Statement
For the Year Ended December 31, 2011
($ in 000s)

Revenues		
Sales revenue	$200	
Dividend revenue	3	$203
Expenses		
Cost of goods sold	120	
Salaries expense	25	
Depreciation expense	5	
Bad debt expense	1	
Interest expense	8	
Loss on sale of building	3	
Income tax expense	16	178
Net income		$ 25

Additional information from the accounting records:

a. A building that originally cost $40,000, and which was three-fourths depreciated, was sold for $7,000.

b. The common stock of Byrd Corporation was purchased for $5,000 as a long-term investment.

c. Property was acquired by issuing a 13%, seven-year, $30,000 note payable to the seller.

d. New equipment was purchased for $15,000 cash.

e. On January 1, 2011, $25,000 of bonds were sold at face value.

f. On January 19, Dux issued a 5% stock dividend (1,000 shares). The market price of the $10 par value common stock was $14 per share at that time.

g. Cash dividends of $13,000 were paid to shareholders.

h. On November 12, 500 shares of common stock were repurchased as treasury stock at a cost of $8,000.

Required:

Prepare the statement of cash flows of Dux Company for the year ended December 31, 2011. Present cash flows from operating activities by the direct method. (You may omit the schedule to reconcile net income to cash flows from operating activities.)

P 21–5

Statement of cash flows; direct method

● LO3 LO8

Comparative balance sheets for 2011 and 2010 and a statement of income for 2011 are given below for Metagrobolize Industries. Additional information from the accounting records of Metagrobolize also is provided.

METAGROBOLIZE INDUSTRIES
Comparative Balance Sheets
December 31, 2011 and 2010
($ in 000s)

	2011	2010
Assets		
Cash	$ 600	$ 375
Accounts receivable	600	450
Inventory	900	525
Land	675	600
Building	900	900
Less: Accumulated depreciation	(300)	(270)
Equipment	2,850	2,250
Less: Accumulated depreciation	(525)	(480)
Patent	1,200	1,500
	$6,900	$5,850
Liabilities		
Accounts payable	$ 750	$ 450
Accrued expenses payable	300	225
Lease liability—land	150	0
Shareholders' Equity		
Common stock	3,150	3,000
Paid-in capital—excess of par	750	675
Retained earnings	1,800	1,500
	$6,900	$5,850

METAGROBOLIZE INDUSTRIES
Income Statement
For the Year Ended December 31, 2011
($ in 000s)

Revenues		
Sales revenue	$2,645	
Gain on sale of land	90	$2,735
Expenses		
Cost of goods sold	$ 600	
Depreciation expense—building	30	
Depreciation expense—equipment	315	
Loss on sale of equipment	15	
Amortization of patent	300	
Operating expenses	500	1,760
Net income		$ 975

Additional information from the accounting records:

a. During 2011, equipment with a cost of $300,000 (90% depreciated) was sold.

b. The statement of shareholders' equity reveals reductions of $225,000 and $450,000 for stock dividends and cash dividends, respectively.

Required:

Prepare the statement of cash flows of Metagrobolize for the year ended December 31, 2011. Present cash flows from operating activities by the direct method. (You may omit the schedule to reconcile net income to cash flows from operating activities.)

P 21–6

Cash flows from operating activities (direct method) derived from an income statement and cash flows from operating activities (indirect method)

● LO3 LO4

The income statement and a schedule reconciling cash flows from operating activities to net income are provided below ($ in millions) for Mike Roe Computers.

MIKE ROE COMPUTERS Income Statement For the Year Ended December 31, 2011		
Sales		$150
Cost of goods sold		(90)
Gross margin		60
Salaries expense	$20	
Insurance expense	10	
Depreciation expense	5	
Bad debt expense	2	
Interest expense	6	(43)
Gains and losses:		
Gain on sale of equipment	12	
Loss on sale of land	(3)	
Income before tax		26
Income tax expense		(13)
Net income		$ 13

Reconciliation of Net Income to Net Cash Flows from Operating Activities	
Net income	$13
Adjustments for noncash effects:	
Decrease in accounts receivable	3
Gain on sale of equipment	(12)
Increase in inventory	(6)
Increase in accounts payable	9
Increase in salaries payable	3
Depreciation expense	5
Increase in allowance for uncoll.	2
Decrease in bond discount	3
Decrease in prepaid insurance	2
Loss on sale of land	3
Increase in income tax payable	6
Net cash flows from operating activities	$31

Required:
1. Calculate each of the following amounts for Mike Roe Computers:
   a. Cash received from customers during the reporting period.
   b. Cash paid to suppliers of goods during the reporting period.
   c. Cash paid to employees during the reporting period.
   d. Cash paid for interest during the reporting period.
   e. Cash paid for insurance during the reporting period.
   f. Cash paid for income taxes during the reporting period.
2. Prepare the cash flows from operating activities section of the statement of cash flows (direct method).

P 21–7

Cash flows from operating activities (direct method) derived from an income statement and cash flows from operating activities (indirect method)

● LO3 LO4

The income statement and a schedule reconciling cash flows from operating activities to net income are provided below for Macrosoft Corporation.

MACROSOFT CORPORATION Income Statement For the Year Ended December 31, 2011 ($ in millions)		
Sales		$310
Cost of goods sold		(120)
Gross margin		$190
Salaries expense	$40	
Insurance expense	20	
Depreciation expense	10	
Patent amortization expense	4	
Interest expense	12	(86)
Loss on sale of land		(4)
Income before taxes and extraordinary gain		100
Income tax expense		(50)
Income before extraordinary gain		50
Extraordinary gain (sale of subsidiary)	24	
Less: Tax on gain	(12)	12
Net income		$ 62

Reconciliation of Net Income to Net Cash Flows from Operating Activities	
Net income	$62
Adjustments for noncash effects:	
Depreciation expense	10
Patent amortization expense	4
Loss on sale of land	6
Extraordinary gain (sale of subsidiary)	(24)
Changes in operating assets and liabilities:	
Decrease in accounts receivable	6
Increase in inventory	(12)
Increase in accounts payable	18
Decrease in bond discount	1
Increase in salaries payable	6
Decrease in prepaid insurance	4
Increase in income tax payable	10
Net cash flows from operating activities	$91

Required:
Prepare the cash flows from operating activities section of the statement of cash flows (direct method).

P 21–8
Cash flows from
operating activities
(direct method
and indirect
method)—deferred
income tax liability
and amortization of
bond discount

● LO3 LO4

Portions of the financial statements for Parnell Company are provided below.

PARNELL COMPANY
Income Statement
For the Year Ended December 31, 2011
($ in 000s)

Sales		$ 800
Cost of goods sold		(300)
Gross margin		500
Salaries expense	$120	
Insurance expense	40	
Depreciation expense	123	
Interest expense	50	(333)
Gains and losses:		
Gain on sale of buildings		11
Loss on sale of machinery		(12)
Income before tax		166
Income tax expense		(78)
Net income		$ 88

PARNELL COMPANY
Selected Accounts from Comparative Balance Sheets
December 31, 2011 and 2010
($ in 000s)

	Year 2011	2010	Change
Cash	$134	$100	$ 34
Accounts receivable	324	216	108
Inventory	321	425	(104)
Prepaid insurance	66	88	(22)
Accounts payable	210	117	93
Salaries payable	102	93	9
Deferred income tax liability	60	52	8
Bond discount	190	200	(10)

Required:
1. Prepare the cash flows from operating activities section of the statement of cash flows for Parnell Company using the direct method.
2. Prepare the cash flows from operating activities section of the statement of cash flows for Parnell Company using the indirect method.

P 21–9
Cash flows from
operating activities
(direct method and
indirect method)—
extraordinary loss

● LO3 LO4

Portions of the financial statements for Hawkeye Company are provided below.

HAWKEYE COMPANY
Income Statement
For the Year Ended December 31, 2011

Sales		$900
Cost of goods sold		(350)
Gross margin		550
Salaries expense	$220	
Depreciation expense	190	
Bad debt expense	12	
Interest expense	36	(458)
Income before taxes and extraordinary loss		92
Income tax expense		(46)
Income before extraordinary loss		46
Extraordinary loss (flood damage)	12	
Less: Tax savings	(6)	(6)
Net Income		$ 40

(continued)

(concluded)

HAWKEYE COMPANY
Selected Accounts from Comparative Balance Sheets
December 31, 2011 and 2010

	Year		
	2011	**2010**	**Change**
Cash	$212	$200	$ 12
Accounts receivable	418	432	(14)
Allowance for uncollectibles	23	11	12
Inventory	860	850	10
Accounts payable	210	234	(24)
Salaries payable	180	188	(8)
Interest payable	55	50	5
Income taxes payable	90	104	(14)

Required:

1. Prepare the cash flows from operating activities section of the statement of cash flows for Hawkeye Company using the direct method.

2. Prepare the cash flows from operating activities section of the statement of cash flows for Hawkeye Company using the indirect method.

P 21–10
Relationship between the income statement and cash flows from operating activities (direct method and indirect method)
● LO3 LO4

The following schedule relates the income statement with cash flows from operating activities, derived by both the direct and indirect methods, in the format illustrated by Graphic 21–10 in the chapter. Some elements necessary to complete the schedule are missing.

Cash Flows from Operating Activities

Income Statement		Indirect Method		Direct Method	
		Net income	$?		
		Adjustments:			
Sales	$300	Decrease in accounts receivable	6	Cash received from customers	$?
Gain on sale of equipment	24	Gain on sale of equipment	(24)	(Not reported—no cash effect)	
		Increase in inventory	(12)		
Cost of goods sold	(?)	Increase in accounts payable	18	Cash paid to suppliers	(174)
Salaries expense	(39)	? in salaries payable	6	Cash paid to employees	(33)
Depreciation expense	(9)	Depreciation expense	9	Cash paid for depreciation	?
Bad debt expense	(3)	Bad debt expense	3	(Not reported—no cash effect)	
Interest expense	(?)	Decrease in bond discount	3	Cash paid for interest	(9)
Insurance expense	(21)	Decrease in prepaid insurance	9	Cash paid for insurance	(?)
Loss on sale of land	(6)	Loss on sale of land	6	(Not reported—no cash effect)	
Income tax expense	(27)	Increase in income tax payable	?	Cash paid for income taxes	(21)
Net Income	**$?**	**Net cash flows from operating activities**	**$ 57**	**Net cash flows from operating activities**	**$ 57**

Required:
Complete the schedule by determining each of the following missing elements:

1. Cash received from customers
2. Cost of goods sold
3. ? in salaries payable (Increase? or decrease?)
4. Cash paid for depreciation
5. Interest expense
6. Cash paid for insurance
7. Increase in income tax payable
8. Net income

P 21–11

Prepare a statement
of cash flows;
direct method

● LO3 LO8

The comparative balance sheets for 2011 and 2010 and the income statement for 2011 are given below for Arduous Company. Additional information from Arduous's accounting records is provided also.

ARDUOUS COMPANY
Comparative Balance Sheets
December 31, 2011 and 2010
($ in millions)

	2011	2010
Assets		
Cash	$ 116	$ 81
Accounts receivable	200	202
Less: Allowance for uncollectible accounts	(10)	(8)
Investment revenue receivable	6	4
Inventory	205	200
Prepaid insurance	4	8
Long-term investment	156	125
Land	196	150
Buildings and equipment	412	400
Less: Accumulated depreciation	(97)	(120)
Patent	30	32
	$1,218	$1,074
Liabilities		
Accounts payable	$ 50	$ 65
Salaries payable	6	11
Bond interest payable	8	4
Income tax payable	12	14
Deferred income tax liability	11	8
Notes payable	23	0
Lease liability	82	0
Bonds payable	215	275
Less: Discount on bonds	(22)	(25)
Shareholders' Equity		
Common stock	430	410
Paid-in capital—excess of par	95	85
Preferred stock	75	0
Retained earnings	242	227
Less: Treasury stock	(9)	0
	$1,218	$1,074

ARDUOUS COMPANY
Income Statement
For Year Ended December 31, 2011
($ in millions)

Revenues		
Sales revenue	$410	
Investment revenue	11	
Gain on sale of treasury bills	2	$423
Expenses		
Cost of goods sold	180	
Salaries expense	65	
Depreciation expense	12	
Patent amortization expense	2	
Bad debt expense	8	
Insurance expense	7	
Bond interest expense	28	
Extraordinary loss (flood)	$18	
Less: Tax savings	(9)	9
Income tax expense	45	356
Net income		$ 67

Additional information from the accounting records:

a. During 2011, $6 million of customer accounts were written off as uncollectible.

b. Investment revenue includes Arduous Company's $6 million share of the net income of Demur Company, an equity method investee.

c. Treasury bills were sold during 2011 at a gain of $2 million. Arduous Company classifies its investments in Treasury bills as cash equivalents.

d. A machine originally costing $70 million that was one-half depreciated was rendered unusable by a rare flood. Most major components of the machine were unharmed and were sold for $17 million.

e. Temporary differences between pretax accounting income and taxable income caused the deferred income tax liability to increase by $3 million.

f. The preferred stock of Tory Corporation was purchased for $25 million as a long-term investment.

g. Land costing $46 million was acquired by issuing $23 million cash and a 15%, four-year, $23 million note payable to the seller.

h. A building was acquired by a 15-year capital lease; present value of lease payments, $82 million.

i. $60 million of bonds were retired at maturity.

j. In February, Arduous issued a 4% stock dividend (4 million shares). The market price of the $5 par value common stock was $7.50 per share at that time.

k. In April, 1 million shares of common stock were repurchased as treasury stock at a cost of $9 million.

Required:

Prepare the statement of cash flows of Arduous Company for the year ended December 31, 2011. Present cash flows from operating activities by the direct method. (A reconciliation schedule is not required.)

P 21–12
Transactions affecting retained earnings
● LO5 LO6 LO8

Shown below in T-account format are the changes affecting the retained earnings of Brenner-Jude Corporation during 2011. At January 1, 2011, the corporation had outstanding 105 million common shares, $1 par per share.

Retained Earnings ($ in millions)

		90	Beginning balance
Retirement of 5 million common shares for $22 million	2		
		88	Net income for the year
Declaration and payment of a $.33 per share cash dividend	33		
Declaration and distribution of a 4% stock dividend	20		
		123	Ending balance

Required:

1. From the information provided by the account changes you should be able to re-create the transactions that affected Brenner-Jude's retained earnings during 2011. Reconstruct the journal entries which can be used as spreadsheet entries in the preparation of a statement of cash flows. Also indicate any investing and financing activities you identify from this analysis that should be reported on the statement of cash flows.

2. Prepare a statement of retained earnings for Brenner-Jude for the year ended 2011. (You may wish to compare your solution to this problem with the parallel situation described in Exercise 18–18.)

P 21–13
Various cash flows
● LO3 through LO8

Following are selected balance sheet accounts of Del Conte Corp. at December 31, 2011 and 2010, and the increases or decreases in each account from 2010 to 2011. Also presented is selected income statement information for the year ended December 31, 2011, and additional information.

Selected Balance Sheet Accounts	2011	2010	Increase (Decrease)
Assets			
Accounts receivable	$ 34,000	$ 24,000	$ 10,000
Property, plant, and equipment	277,000	247,000	30,000
Accumulated depreciation	(178,000)	(167,000)	11,000
Liabilities and Stockholders' Equity			
Bonds payable	49,000	46,000	3,000
Dividends payable	8,000	5,000	3,000
Common stock, $1 par	22,000	19,000	3,000
Additional paid-in capital	9,000	3,000	6,000
Retained earnings	104,000	91,000	13,000

Selected Income Statement Information for the Year Ended December 31, 2011	
Sales revenue	$ 155,000
Depreciation	33,000
Gain on sale of equipment	13,000
Net income	28,000

Additional information:

a. Accounts receivable relate to sales of merchandise.

b. During 2011, equipment costing $40,000 was sold for cash.

c. During 2011, $20,000 of bonds payable were issued in exchange for property, plant, and equipment. There was no amortization of bond discount or premium.

Required:

Items 1 through 5 represent activities that will be reported in Del Conte's statement of cash flows for the year ended December 31, 2011. The following two responses are required for each item:

• Determine the amount that should be reported in Del Conte's 2011 statement of cash flows.

• Using the list below, determine the category in which the amount should be reported in the statement of cash flows.

    O. Operating activity

     I. Investing activity

    F. Financing activity

	Amount	Category
1. Cash collections from customers (direct method).	____	____
2. Payments for purchase of property, plant, and equipment.	____	____
3. Proceeds from sale of equipment.	____	____
4. Cash dividends paid.	____	____
5. Redemption of bonds payable.	____	____

(AICPA adapted)

P 21–14
Statement of cash flows; indirect method; limited information
● LO4 LO8

The comparative balance sheets for 2011 and 2010 are given below for Surmise Company. Net income for 2011 was $50 million.

SURMISE COMPANY
Comparative Balance Sheets
December 31, 2011 and 2010
($ in millions)

	2011	2010
Assets		
Cash	$ 45	$ 40
Accounts receivable	92	96
Less: Allowance for uncollectible accounts	(12)	(4)
Prepaid expenses	8	5
Inventory	145	130
Long-term investment	80	40
Land	100	100
Buildings and equipment	411	300
Less: Accumulated depreciation	(142)	(120)
Patent	16	17
	$ 743	$ 604
Liabilities		
Accounts payable	$ 17	$ 32
Accrued liabilities	(2)	10
Notes payable	35	0
Lease liability	111	0
Bonds payable	65	125
Shareholders' Equity		
Common stock	60	50
Paid-in capital—excess of par	245	205
Retained earnings	212	182
	$ 743	$ 604

Required:

Prepare the statement of cash flows of Surmise Company for the year ended December 31, 2011. Use the indirect method to present cash flows from operating activities because you do not have sufficient information to use the direct method. You will need to make reasonable assumptions concerning the reasons for changes in some account balances. A spreadsheet or T-account analysis will be helpful.

P 21–15

Integrating
problem; bonds;
lease transactions;
lessee and lessor;
statement of cash
flow effects

● LO3 LO5 LO6

Digital Telephony issued 10% bonds, dated January 1, with a face amount of $32 million on January 1, 2011. The bonds mature in 2021 (10 years). For bonds of similar risk and maturity the market yield is 12%. Interest is paid semiannually on June 30 and December 31. Digital recorded the issue as follows:

Cash	28,329,472	
Discount on bonds	3,670,528	
Bonds payable		32,000,000

Digital also leased switching equipment to Midsouth Communications, Inc., on September 30, 2011. Digital purchased the equipment from MDS Corp. at a cost of $6 million. The five-year lease agreement calls for Midsouth to make quarterly lease payments of $391,548, payable each September 30, December 31, March 31, and June 30, with the first payment on September 30, 2011. Digital's implicit interest rate is 12%.

Required:

1. What would be the amount(s) related to the bonds that Digital would report in its statement of cash flows for the year ended December 31, 2011, if Digital uses the direct method? The indirect method?

2. What would be the amounts related to the lease that *Midsouth* would report in its statement of cash flows for the year ended December 31, 2011?

3. What would be the amounts related to the lease that *Digital* would report in its statement of cash flows for the year ended December 31, 2011?

4. Assume MDS manufactured the equipment at a cost of $5 million and that Midsouth leased the equipment directly from MDS. What would be the amounts related to the lease that *MDS* would report in its statement of cash flows for the year ended December 31, 2011?

P 21–16

Statement of cash
flows; indirect
method

● LO4 LO8

Refer to the data provided in Problem 21–4 for Dux Company.

Required:
Prepare the statement of cash flows for Dux Company using the *indirect method.*

P 21–17

Statement of cash
flows; indirect
method

● LO4 LO8

Refer to the data provided in Problem 21–5 for Metagrobolize Industries.

Required:
Prepare the statement of cash flows for Metagrobolize Industries using the *indirect method.*

P 21–18

Statement of cash
flows; indirect
method

● LO4 LO8

Refer to the data provided in Problem 21–11 for Arduous Company.

Required:
Prepare the statement of cash flows for Arduous Company using the *indirect method.*

(Note: The following problems use the technique learned in Appendix 21B.)

P 21–19

Statement of cash
flows; T-account
method

● LO3 LO8

Refer to the data provided in Problem 21–4 for Dux Company.

Required:
Prepare the statement of cash flows for Dux Company. Use the T-account method to assist in your analysis.

P 21–20

Statement of cash
flows; T-account
method

● LO3 LO8

Refer to the data provided in Problem 21–5 for Metagrobolize Industries.

Required:
Prepare the statement of cash flows for Metagrobolize Industries. Use the T-account method to assist in your analysis.

P 21–21
Statement of cash
flows; T-account
method

● LO3 LO8

Refer to the data provided in Problem 21–11 for Arduous Company.

Required:

Prepare the statement of cash flows for Arduous Company. Use the T-account method to assist in your analysis.

BROADEN YOUR PERSPECTIVE

Apply your critical-thinking ability to the knowledge you've gained. These cases will provide you an opportunity to develop your research, analysis, judgment, and communication skills. You also will work with other students, integrate what you've learned, apply it in real world situations, and consider its global and ethical ramifications. This practice will broaden your knowledge and further develop your decision-making abilities.

**Communication
Case 21–1**
Distinguish income
and cash flows

● LO1 LO3 LO4

"Why can't we pay our shareholders a dividend?" shouted your new boss. "This income statement you prepared for me says we earned $5 million in our first half-year!"

You were hired last month as the chief accountant for Enigma Corporation which was organized on July 1 of the year just ended. You recently prepared the financial statements below:

ENIGMA CORPORATION
Income Statement
For the Six Months Ended December 31, 2011
($ in millions)

Sales revenue	$ 75
Cost of goods sold	(30)
Depreciation expense	(5)
Remaining expenses	(35)
Net income	$ 5

ENIGMA CORPORATION
Balance Sheet
December 31, 2011 ($ in millions)

Cash	$ 1
Accounts receivable (net)	20
Merchandise inventory	15
Machinery (net)	44
Total	$80
Accounts payable	$ 2
Accrued expenses payable	7
Notes payable	36
Common stock	30
Retained earnings	5
Total	$80

You have just explained to your boss, Robert James, that although net income was $5 million, operating activities produced a net decrease in cash. Unable to understand your verbal explanation, he has asked you to prepare a written report.

Required:

Prepare a report explaining the apparent discrepancy between Enigma's profitability and its cash flows. To increase the chances of your boss's understanding the situation, include in your report a determination of net cash flows from operating activities by both the direct and indirect methods. Your report should also include a narrative explanation of how it is possible for operating activities to simultaneously produce a positive net income and negative net cash flows.

Judgment Case 21–2

Distinguish income and cash flows

● LO3 LO8

You are a loan officer for First Benevolent Bank. You have an uneasy feeling as you examine a loan application from Daring Corporation. The application included the following financial statements.

DARING CORPORATION
Income Statement
For the Year Ended December 31, 2011

Sales revenue	$100,000
Cost of goods sold	(50,000)
Depreciation expense	(5,000)
Remaining expenses	(25,000)
Net income	$ 20,000

DARING CORPORATION
Balance Sheet
December 31, 2011

Cash	$ 5,000
Accounts receivable	25,000
Inventory	20,000
Depreciable assets	55,000
Accumulated depreciation	(5,000)
Total	$100,000
Accounts payable	$ 10,000
Interest payable	5,000
Note payable	45,000
Common stock	20,000
Retained earnings	20,000
Total	$100,000

It is not Daring's profitability that worries you. The income statement submitted with the application shows net income of $20,000 in Daring's first year of operations. By referring to the balance sheet, you see that this net income represents a 20% rate of return on assets of $100,000. Your concern stems from the recollection that the note payable reported on Daring's balance sheet is a two-year loan you approved earlier in the year.

You also recall another promising new company that, just last year, defaulted on another of your bank's loans when it failed due to its inability to generate sufficient cash flows to meet its obligations. Before requesting additional information from Daring, you decide to test your memory of the intermediate accounting class you took in night school by attempting to prepare a statement of cash flows from the information available in the loan application.

Research Case 21–3

Information from cash flow activities; FedEx

● LO3 through LO8

Real World Financials

Locate the most recent financial statements and related disclosure notes of **FedEx Corporation**. You can locate the report online at **www.fedex.com** or by accessing EDGAR at **www.sec.gov**.

Required:

1. From the information provided in the statement of cash flows, explain what allows FedEx Corporation to expand its business as evidenced by the investing activities, while at the same time not raising as much cash through financing activities.

2. Describe the activities listed under financing activities for the most recent fiscal year. [*Hint:* FedEx's Statement of Changes in Common Stockholders' Investment (statement of shareholders' equity) will help you determine the nature of the stock activity.] What is the most notable financing activity reported?

3. What are the cash payments FedEx made for interest and for income taxes in the three years reported? (*Hint:* See the disclosure notes.)

4. Obtain the relevant authoritative literature on disclosure of interest and income taxes using the FASB's Codification Research System. You might gain access at the FASB website (**www.fasb.org**). What is the specific citation that specifies the way FedEx reports interest and income taxes separately that enabled you to answer requirement 3?

Research Case 21–4

Locate and extract relevant information for a financial reporting issue; integrative; Microsoft Corporation

● LO4

A meeting of your accounting department is scheduled for early tomorrow morning. One topic of discussion is certain to be the appropriate adjustments to net income in your company's statement of cash flows using the indirect method of reporting operating activities. Hallway discussions have suggested some degree of uncertainty, particularly regarding unearned revenues, which are substantial for the company. Because your firm went public only seven months ago, this reporting issue is a new one for you and most other members of the department. In preparation for the meeting, you sought out the financial statements of **Microsoft Corporation**, knowing that it too had substantial unearned revenues. The operating activities section of the comparative statements of cash flows for Microsoft is presented below.

Cash Flows Statements (in millions)

Year Ended June 30,	2009	2008	2007
Operations			
Net income	$ 14,569	$ 17,681	$ 14,065
Adjustments to reconcile net income to net cash from operations:			
Depreciation, amortization, and other noncash items	2,562	2,056	1,440
Stock-based compensation	1,708	1,479	1,550
Net recognized losses (gains) on investments and derivatives	683	(572)	(292)
Excess tax benefits from stock-based compensation	(52)	(120)	(77)
Deferred income taxes	762	935	421
Deferral of unearned revenue	24,409	24,532	21,032
Recognition of unearned revenue	(25,426)	(21,944)	(19,382)
Changes in operating assets and liabilities:			
Accounts receivable	2,215	(1,569)	(1,764)
Other current assets	(422)	153	232
Other long-term assets	(273)	(98)	(435)
Other current liabilities	(3,371)	(748)	(552)
Other long-term liabilities	1,673	(173)	1,558
Net cash from operations	19,037	21,612	17,796

Real World Financials

Required:

1. Locate the financial statements of Microsoft Corporation on the Internet. Search the disclosure notes for information about how Microsoft accounts for its unearned revenues. How is the undelivered portion of Microsoft's sales of Windows XP Professional recorded initially?

2. Why does the statement of cash flows include "unearned revenue" as an addition to net income in the operations section? Why is "recognition of unearned revenue" included as a deduction from net income? Why do you think Microsoft reported these two items separately rather than just adjusting net income for the change in the unearned revenue account balance?

3. Why is stock-based compensation added to net income?

Analysis Case 21–5
Smudged ink; find missing amounts
● LO3 LO4

"Be careful with that coffee!" Your roommate is staring in disbelief at the papers in front of her. "This was my contribution to our team project," she moaned. "When you spilled your coffee, it splashed on this page. Now I can't recognize some of these numbers, and Craig has my source documents."

Knowing how important this afternoon's presentation is to your roommate, you're eager to see what can be done. "Let me see that," you offer. "I think we can figure this out." The statement of cash flows and income statement are intact. The reconciliation schedule and the comparative balance sheets are coffee casualties.

DISTINCTIVE INDUSTRIES
Statement of Cash Flows
For the Year Ended December 31, 2011
($ in millions)

Cash Flows from Operating Activities:		
Collections from customers	$213	
Payment to suppliers	(90)	
Payment of general & administrative expenses	(54)	
Payment of income taxes	(27)	
Net cash flows from operating activities		$ 42
Cash Flows from Investing Activities:		
Sale of equipment		120
Cash Flows from Financing Activities:		
Issuance of common stock	30	
Payment of dividends	(9)	
Net cash flows from financing activities		21
Net increase in cash		$183
Reconciliation of net income to cash flows from operating activities:		
Net income	$ 84	
Adjustments for noncash items:		
Depreciation expense	☐	
▭	☐	
▭	☐	
▭	☐	
▭	☐	
▭	☐	
Net cash flows from operating activities	☐	(continued)

(concluded)

DISTINCTIVE INDUSTRIES
Income Statement
For the Year Ended December 31, 2011

Sales revenue		$240
Cost of goods sold		96
Gross profit		144
Operating expenses:		
General and administrative	$54	
Depreciation	30	
Total operating expenses		84
Operating income		60
Other income:		
Gain on sale of equipment		45
Income before income taxes		105
Income tax expense		21
Net income		$ 84

DISTINCTIVE INDUSTRIES
Comparative Balance Sheets
At December 31

	2011	2010
Assets:		
Cash	$360	☐
Accounts receivable (net)	☐	252
Inventory	180	☐
Property, plant, & equipment	450	600
Less: Accumulated depreciation	(120)	☐
Total assets	☐	☐
Liabilities and shareholders' equity:		
Accounts payable	$120	$ 90
General and administrative expenses payable	27	27
Income taxes payable	66	☐
Common stock	720	690
Retained earnings	☐	141
Total liabilities and shareholders' equity	☐	☐

Required:

1. Determine the missing amounts.

2. Reconstruct the reconciliation of net income to cash flows from operating activities (operating cash flows using the indirect method).

Real World Case 21–6

Analyze cash flow activities; Procter & Gamble

● LO1 through LO8

Real World Financials

Procter & Gamble Company is a multinational manufacturer of products including personal care, household cleaning, laundry detergents, prescription drugs, and disposable nappies. Here are the company's statements of cash flows from its 2009 annual report:

Amounts in millions; Years ended June 30	2009	2008	2007
Cash and Cash Equivalents, Beginning of Year	$ 3,313	$ 5,354	$ 6,693
Operating Activities			
Net earnings	13,436	12,075	10,340
Depreciation and amortization	3,082	3,166	3,130
Share-based compensation expense	516	555	668
Deferred income taxes	596	1,214	253
Gain on sale of businesses	(2,377)	(284)	(153)
Change in accounts receivable	415	432	(729)
Change in inventories	721	(1,050)	(389)
Change in accounts payable, accrued and other liabilities	(742)	297	(278)
Change in other operating assets and liabilities	(758)	(1,270)	(151)
Other	30	(127)	719
Total Operating Activities	14,919	15,008	13,410

(continued)

(concluded)

Investing Activities

Capital expenditures	(3,238)	(3,046)	(2,945)
Proceeds from asset sales	1,087	928	281
Acquisitions, net of cash acquired	(368)	(381)	(492)
Change in investments	166	(50)	673
Total Investing Activities	(2,353)	(2,549)	(2,483)
Financing Activities			
Dividends to shareholders	(5,044)	(4,655)	(4,209)
Change in short-term debt	(2,420)	2,650	9,006
Additions to long-term debt	4,926	7,088	4,758
Reductions of long-term debt	(2,587)	(11,747)	(17,929)
Treasury stock purchases	(6,370)	(10,047)	(5,578)
Impact of stock options and other	681	1,867	1,499
Total Financing Activities	(10,814)	(14,844)	(12,453)
Effect of Exchange Rate Changes on Cash and Cash Equivalents	(284)	344	187
Change in Cash and Cash Equivalents	1,468	(2,041)	(1,339)
Cash and Cash Equivalents, End of Year	$ 4,781	$ 3,313	$ 5,354

Required:

1. In the three years reported, what were P&G's primary investing activities? How were these activities financed? Be specific.

2. During the most recent fiscal year, P&G purchased certificates of deposit. How were these purchases reported in the statement of cash flows? (Note: This is not an investing activity.)

3. How are issuances of debt securities and issuances of equity securities classified in a statement of cash flows?

4. How are payments to investors in debt securities (interest) and payments to investors in equity securities (dividends) classified in a statement of cash flows? Is this a conceptual inconsistency? Explain.

5. P&G's statement of cash flows reports expenditures for acquisition of businesses. It also reports additions to long-term debt. Suppose the businesses had been acquired, not with cash, but by exchange for debt securities. Would such a transaction be reported? Explain.

Ethics Case 21–7
Where's the cash?
● LO1 LO3

After graduating near the top of his class, Ben Naegle was hired by the local office of a Big 4 CPA firm in his hometown. Two years later, impressed with his technical skills and experience, Park Electronics, a large regional consumer electronics chain, hired Ben as assistant controller. This was last week. Now Ben's initial excitement has turned to distress.

The cause of Ben's distress is the set of financial statements he's stared at for the last four hours. For some time prior to his recruitment, he had been aware of the long trend of moderate profitability of his new employer. The reports on his desk confirm the slight, but steady, improvements in net income in recent years. The trend he was just now becoming aware of, though, was the decline in cash flows from operations.

Ben had sketched out the following comparison ($ in millions):

	2011	2010	2009	2008
Income from operations	$140.0	$132.0	$127.5	$127.0
Net income	38.5	35.0	34.5	29.5
Cash flow from operations	1.6	17.0	12.0	15.5

Profits? Yes. Increasing profits? Yes. The cause of his distress? The ominous trend in cash flow which is consistently lower than net income.

Upon closer review, Ben noticed three events in the last two years that, unfortunately, seemed related:

a. Park's credit policy had been loosened; credit terms were relaxed and payment periods were lengthened.

b. Accounts receivable balances had increased dramatically.

c. Several of the company's compensation arrangements, including that of the controller and the company president, were based on reported net income.

Required:

1. What is so ominous about the combination of events Ben sees?

2. What course of action, if any, should Ben take?

Real World Case 21–8
Cash flow despite losses; Dell Inc.
● LO3 LO4

"I've been reading that the computer industry is having money problems along with the rest of the economy," said Bee Del Conte as you walked with her to the library. "How is it, then, that I hear on the radio this morning that although **Dell's** cash flows from its operations last year were down significantly from prior years, its net income was not much lower than the year before?" Curious, the two of you stop by a computer terminal on the way to the reference section and do a quick search. A few clicks later you're looking at Dell's income statements and cash flow statements for the fiscal year ended January 30, 2009. These are reproduced in the financial statements and related disclosure notes of **Dell** in Appendix B located at the back of the text. They also can be found at **www.Dell.com**.

Required:

1. Without regard to Dell specifically, explain to Bee the difference between net income or net loss and the cash flows from operating activities.
2. Why did Dell add $769 million in the determination of cash flows from operating activities for depreciation and amortization?
3. The major contributor to Dell's having lower cash flows from operating activities than net income in fiscal 2009 is a sizable reduction in the amount Dell owes its suppliers. If Dell had used the direct rather than the indirect method of reporting operating activities, how would this reduction in accounts payable have affected cash from operating activities? Specifically, what is the dollar amount of the line item in the operating cash flows section of the statement (using the direct method) that would encompass the reduction in accounts payable?
4. Cash used in financing activities during fiscal 2009 was $1.4 billion, as compared to $4.1 billion in fiscal 2008 and $2.6 billion in fiscal 2007. What is the major contributor from year to year in the amount of cash used in financing activities? What other activity contributed to that reduction in cash used in financing activities during fiscal 2009?

**Research
Case 21–9**
Researching the way cash flows are reported; retrieving information from the Internet

● LO3 through
  LO8

EDGAR, the Electronic Data Gathering, Analysis, and Retrieval system, performs automated collection, valida- tion, indexing, acceptance, and forwarding of submissions by companies and others who are required by law to file forms with the U.S. Securities and Exchange Commission (SEC). All publicly traded domestic companies use EDGAR to make the majority of their filings. (Filings by foreign companies are not required to be filed on EDGAR, but some of these companies do so voluntarily.) Form 10-K, which includes the annual report, is required to be filed on EDGAR. The SEC makes this information available on the Internet.

Required:

1. Access EDGAR on the Internet. The web address is **www.sec.gov**.
2. Search for a public company with which you are familiar. Access its most recent 10-K filing. Search or scroll to find the statement of cash flows and related note(s).
3. Is the direct or indirect method used to report operating activities? What is the largest adjustment to net income in reconciling net income and cash flows from operations in the most recent year?
4. What are the cash payments for interest and for taxes?
5. What has been the most significant investing activity for the company in the most recent three years?
6. What has been the most significant financing activity for the company in requirements 2–6 for another company?

**Analysis
Case 21–10**
Information from cash flow activities; Dell

● LO3 through
  LO8

Refer to the financial statements and related disclosure notes of **Dell Inc.** located in the company's annual report for the fiscal year ending January 30, 2009, included with all new copies of the text. You also can locate the report online at **www.dell.com**.

Notice that Dell's net income has steadily increased over the three years reported. To supplement their analysis of profitability, many analysts like to look at "free cash flow." A popular way to measure this metric is "structural free cash flow" (or as Warren Buffett calls it "owner's earnings"), which is calculated as net income from opera- tions plus depreciation and amortization minus capital expenditures.

Required:

Determine free cash flows for Dell in each of the three years reported. Compare that amount with net income each year. What pattern do you detect?

**Research
Case 21–11**
FASB codification; locate and extract relevant information and cite authoritative support for a financial reporting issue; cash flow classification

● LO4 through
  LO6

"This one's got me stumped," you say to no one in particular. "First day on the job; I'd better get it right." It's the classification of notes payable in the statement of cash flows that has you in doubt. Having received an "A" in Intermediate Accounting, you know that a note payable representing a bank loan is a financing activity, but this one is a note payable to your employer's primary merchandise supplier. "I wonder if the accounting is the same."

Required:

1. Obtain the relevant authoritative literature on cash flow classification using the FASB's Codification Research System. You might gain access at the FASB website (**www.fasb.org**). What is the specific citation that speci- fies the classification of notes payable to suppliers?
2. Is accounting the same as for notes payable to banks? Explain.
3. Is accounting the same for both short-term and long-term notes payable to suppliers?

CODE

IFRS Case 21–12
Statement of
cash flows
presentation, British
Telecommunications

● LO3 through
  LO6 LO9

British Telecommunications Plc (BT), a U.K. company, is the world's oldest communications company. The company prepares its financial statements in accordance with International Financial Reporting Standards. Below are partial cash flow statements included in a recent annual report:

GROUP CASH FLOW STATEMENT

Year ended 31 March	2009 £m	2008 £m	2007 £m
Cash flow from operating activities			
(Loss) profit before taxation	(134)	1,976	2,484
Depreciation and amortisation	2,890	2,889	2,920
Loss (profit) on sale of associates and noncurrent asset investments	13	1	(19)
Net finance expense	620	378	94
Other noncash charges	486	60	50
Share of (profits) losses of associates and joint ventures	(75)	11	(15)
Decrease (increase) in inventories	11	23	(6)
Decrease (increase) in trade and other receivables	1,063	(498)	(373)
(Decrease) increase in trade and other payables	(379)	451	282
Increase (decrease) in provisions and other liabilities	439	(104)	(172)
Cash generated from operations	**4,934**	**5,187**	**5,245**
Income taxes paid	(232)	(222)	(411)
Income tax repayment for prior years	4	521	376
Net cash inflow from operating activities	**4,706**	**5,486**	**5,210**
Cash flow from investing activities			
Interest received	19	111	147
Dividends received from associates and joint ventures	6	2	6
Proceeds on disposal of group undertakings	—	—	27
Proceeds on disposal of property, plant and equipment	44	62	89
Proceeds on disposal of associates and joint ventures	—	13	27
Proceeds on disposal of noncurrent financial assets	—	1	4
Proceeds on disposal of current financial assets	6,316	4,779	8,525
Acquisition of subsidiaries, net of cash acquired	(227)	(377)	(284)
Purchases of property, plant and equipment and computer software	(3,082)	(3,315)	(3,298)
Investment in associates and joint ventures	—	—	(7)
Purchases of noncurrent financial assets	—	(2)	(7)
Purchases of current financial assets	(6,030)	(4,938)	(8,007)
Net cash outflow from investing activities	**(2,954)**	**(3,664)**	**(2,778)**
Cash flow from financing activities			
Equity dividends paid	(1,221)	(1,236)	(1,054)
Dividends paid to minority interests	(1)	—	(3)
Interest paid	(956)	(842)	(797)
Repayments of borrowings	(863)	(913)	(809)
Repayment of finance lease liabilities	(16)	(284)	(276)
Net proceeds on issue of (purchase of) commercial paper	606	(681)	309
New bank loans raised	795	3,939	11
Repurchase of ordinary shares	(334)	(1,498)	(400)
Proceeds on issue of treasury shares	125	85	123
Repurchase of ordinary shares by subsidiary	—	—	(2)
Net cash used in financing activities	**(1,865)**	**(1,430)**	**(2,898)**
Effect of exchange rate changes on cash and cash equivalents	54	25	(35)
Net (decrease) increase in cash and cash equivalents	**(59)**	**417**	**(501)**
Cash and cash equivalents at the start of the year	1,174	757	1,258
Cash and cash equivalents at the end of the year	**1,115**	**1,174**	**757**

Required:

1. What are the primary classifications into which BT's cash inflows and cash outflows are separated? Is this classification the same as or different from cash flow statements prepared in accordance with U.S. GAAP?

2. How are cash inflows from dividends and interest and cash outflows for dividends and interest classified in BT's cash flow statements? Is this classification the same as or different from cash flow statements prepared in accordance with U.S. GAAP?

BRITISH AIRWAYS CASE

BRITISH AIRWAYS

● LO9

British Airways, Plc. (BA), a U.K. company, prepares its financial statements according to International Financial Reporting Standards. BA's annual report for the year ended March 31, 2009, which includes financial statements and disclosure notes, is included with all new textbooks and can be found at **www.britishairways.com**. When answering questions, focus on BA's "Group" financial information (which is equivalent to "Consolidated" under U.S. GAAP).

Required:

1. What are the primary classifications into which BA's cash inflows and cash outflows are separated? Is this classification the same as or different from cash flow statements prepared in accordance with U.S. GAAP?

2. How are cash inflows from dividends and interest and cash outflows for dividends and interest classified in BA's cash flow statements? Is this classification the same as or different from cash flow statements prepared in accordance with U.S. GAAP?

CPA SIMULATION 21–1

Ark Company
Statement of Cash
Flows

CPA Review

Test your knowledge of the concepts discussed in this chapter, practice critical professional skills necessary for career success, and prepare for the computer-based CPA exam by accessing our CPA simulations at the text website: **www.mhhe.com/spiceland6e**.

The Ark Company simulation tests your knowledge of a variety of statement of cash flows reporting issues.

As on the CPA exam itself, you will be asked to use tools including a spreadsheet, a calculator, and professional accounting standards, to conduct research, derive solutions, and communicate conclusions related to these issues in a simulated environment.

Specific tasks in the simulation include:

● Analyzing accrual transactions to determine their related cash flows.

● Applying judgment in deciding the appropriate financial statement classification of various cash flows.

● Calculating cash flows from operations.

● Determining cash flows from a trial balance.

● Communicating the definition and role of cash equivalents.

● Researching the disclosure requirements for the direct and indirect method of reporting operating activities.

Derivatives

"... derivatives are financial weapons of mass destruction ..."
— Warren Buffett, Berkshire Hathaway CEO

"... the growing use of complex financial instruments known as derivatives does not pose a threat to the country's financial system ..."
— Alan Greenspan, Federal Reserve Chairman

"Total world derivatives are $1000 trillion or 19 times the total world GDP of $54 trillion."
— Chuck Burr, *Culture Change*

In today's global economy and evolving financial markets, businesses are increasingly exposed to a variety of risks, which, unmanaged, can have major impacts on earnings or even threaten a company's very existence. Risk management, then, has become critical. Derivative financial instruments have become the key tools of risk management.[1]

Derivatives are financial instruments that "derive" their values or contractually required cash flows from some other security or index. For instance, a contract allowing a company to buy a particular asset (say steel, gold, or flour) at a designated future date at a predetermined price is a financial instrument that derives its value from expected and actual changes in the price of the underlying asset. Financial futures, forward contracts, options, and interest rate swaps are the most frequently used derivatives. Derivatives are valued as tools to manage or hedge companies' increasing exposures to risk, including interest rate risk, price risk, and foreign exchange risk. The variety, complexity, and magnitude of derivatives have grown rapidly in recent years. Accounting standard-setters have scrambled to keep pace.

A persistent stream of headline stories has alerted us to multimillion-dollar losses by many companies and the financial collapse of Bear Stearns and AIG. Focusing on these headlines, it would be tempting to conclude that derivatives are risky business indeed. Certainly they can be quite risky, if misused, but the fact is, these financial instruments exist to lessen, not increase, risk. Properly used, they serve as a form of "insurance" against risk. In fact, if a company is exposed to a substantial risk and does not hedge that risk, it is taking a gamble. On the other hand, if a derivative is used improperly, it can be a huge gamble itself. Total world derivatives are $1,000 trillion or 19 times the total world GDP of $54 trillion.

Derivatives Used to Hedge Risk

Hedging means taking an action that is expected to produce exposure to a particular type of risk that is precisely the *opposite* of an actual risk to which the company already is exposed. For instance, the volatility of interest rates creates exposure to interest-rate risk for companies that issue debt—which, of course, includes most companies. So, a company that frequently arranges short-term loans from its bank under a floating (variable) interest rate agreement is exposed to the risk that interest rates might increase and adversely affect borrowing costs. Similarly, a company that regularly reissues commercial paper as it matures faces the possibility that new rates will be higher and cut into forecasted income. When borrowings are large, the potential cost can be substantial. So, the firm might choose to hedge its position by entering into a transaction that would produce a *gain* of roughly the same amount as the potential loss if interest rates do, in fact, increase.

Hedging is used to deal with three areas of risk exposure: fair value risk, cash flow risk, and foreign currency risk. Let's look at some of the more common derivatives.

---
[1] Almost all financial institutions and over half of all nonfinancial companies use derivatives.

Derivatives are financial instruments that "derive" their values from some other security or *index*.

Derivatives serve as a form of "insurance" against risk.

Hedging means taking a risk position that is opposite to an actual position that is exposed to risk.

Financial Futures

A futures contract is an agreement between a seller and a buyer that requires the seller to deliver a particular commodity (say corn, gold, or pork bellies) at a designated future date, at a *predetermined* price. These contracts are actively traded on regulated futures exchanges. When the "commodity" is a *financial instrument,* such as a Treasury bond, Treasury bill, commercial paper, or a certificate of deposit, the agreement is referred to as a *financial futures contract.*[2]

> A *futures contract* allows a firm to sell (or buy) a financial instrument at a designated future date, at today's price.

To appreciate the way these hedges work, you need to remember that when interest rates rise, the market price of interest-bearing securities goes down. For instance, if you have an investment in a 10% bond and market interest rates go up to, say, 12%, your 10% bond is less valuable relative to other bonds paying the higher rate. Conversely, when interest rates decline, the market price of interest-bearing securities goes up. This risk that the investment's value might change is referred to as *fair value risk.* The company that issued the securities is faced with fair value risk also. If interest rates decline, the fair value of that company's debt would rise, a risk the borrower may want to hedge against. Later in this section, we'll look at an illustration of how the borrower would account for and report such a hedge.

Now let's look at the effect on a contract to sell or buy securities (or any asset for that matter) at preset prices. One who is contracted to *sell* securities at a *preset* price after their market price has fallen benefits from the rise in interest rates. Consequently, the value of the *contract* that gives one the right to sell securities at a preset price goes up as the market price declines. The seller in a futures contract derives a gain (loss) when interest rates rise (decline).[3] Conversely, the one obligated to *buy* securities at a preset price experiences a loss. This risk of having to pay more cash or receive less cash is referred to as *cash flow risk.*

> The seller in a financial futures contract realizes a gain (loss) when interest rates rise (decline).

Another example of cash flow risk would be borrowing money by issuing a variable (floating) rate note. If market interest rates rise, the borrower would have to pay more interest. Similarly, the lender (investor) in the variable (floating) rate note transaction would face cash flow risk that interest rates would decline, resulting in lower cash interest receipts.

Let's look closer at how a futures contract can mitigate cash flow risk. Consider a company in April that will replace its $10 million of 8.5% bank notes when they mature in June. The company is exposed to the risk that interest rates in June will have risen, increasing borrowing costs. To counteract that possibility, the firm might enter a contract in April to deliver (sell) bonds in June at their *current* price. Since there are no corporate bond futures contracts, the company buys Treasury bond futures, which will accomplish essentially the same purpose. In essence, the firm agrees to sell Treasury bonds in June at a price established now (April). Let's say it's April 6 and the price of Treasury bond futures on the International Monetary Market of the Chicago Mercantile Exchange is quoted as 95.24.[4] Since the trading unit of Treasury bond futures is a 15-year, $100,000, 8% Treasury bond, the company might sell 105 Treasury bond futures to hedge the June issuance of debt. This would effectively provide a hedge of 105 × $100,000 × 95.24% = $10,000,200.[5]

Here's what happens then. If interest rates rise, borrowing costs will go up for our example company because it will have to sell debt securities at a higher interest cost (or lower price). But that loss will be offset (approximately) by the gain produced by being in the opposite position on Treasury bond futures. Take note, though, this works both ways. If interest rates go down causing debt security prices to rise, the potential benefit of being able to issue debt at that lower interest rate (higher price) will be offset by a loss on the futures position.

A very important point about futures contracts is that the seller does not need to have actual possession of the commodity (the Treasury bonds, in this case), nor is the purchaser of the contract required to take possession of the commodity. In fact, virtually all financial futures contracts are "netted out" before the actual transaction is to take place. This is

---

[2]Note that a financial futures contract meets the definition of a financial instrument because it entails the exchange of financial instruments (cash for Treasury bonds, for instance). But, a futures contract for the sale or purchase of a nonfinancial commodity like corn or gold does not meet the definition because one of the items to be exchanged is not a financial instrument.

[3]The seller of a futures contract is obligated to sell the bonds at a future date. The buyer of a futures contract is obligated to buy the bonds at a future date. The company in our example, then, is the seller of the futures contract.

[4]Price quotes are expressed as a percentage of par.

[5]This is a simplification of the more sophisticated way financial managers determine the optimal number of futures.

simply a matter of reversing the original position. A seller closes out his transaction with a purchase. Likewise, a purchaser would close out her transaction with a sale. After all, the objective is not to actually buy or sell Treasury bonds (or whatever the commodity might be), but to incur the financial impact of movements in interest rates as reflected in changes in Treasury bond prices. Specifically, it will buy at the lower price (to reverse the original seller position) at the same time it's selling its new bond issue at that same lower price. The financial futures market is an "artificial" exchange in that its reason for existing is to provide a mechanism to transfer risk from those exposed to it to those willing to accept the risk, not to actually buy and sell the underlying financial instruments.

The effectiveness of a hedge is influenced by the closeness of the match between the item being hedged and the financial instrument chosen as a hedge.

If the impending debt issue being hedged is a short-term issue, the company may attain a more effective hedge by selling Treasury *bill* futures since Treasury bills are 90-day securities, or maybe certificate of deposit (CD) futures that also are traded in futures markets. The object is to get the closest association between the financial effects of interest rate movements on the actual transaction and the effects on the financial instrument used as a hedge.

Financial Forward Contracts

A forward contract is similar to a futures contract but differs in three ways:

1. A forward contract calls for delivery on a specific date, whereas a futures contract permits the seller to decide later which specific day within the specified month will be the delivery date (if it gets as far as actual delivery before it is closed out).
2. Unlike a futures contract, a forward contract usually is not traded on a market exchange.
3. Unlike a futures contract, a forward contract does not call for a daily cash settlement for price changes in the underlying contract. Gains and losses on forward contracts are paid only when they are closed out.

Options

Options frequently are purchased to hedge exposure to the effects of changing interest rates. Options serve the same purpose as futures in that respect but are fundamentally different. An option on a financial instrument—say a Treasury bill—gives its holder the right either to buy or to sell the Treasury bill at a specified price and within a given time period. Importantly, though, the option holder has no obligation to exercise the option. On the other hand, the holder of a futures contract must buy or sell within a specified period unless the contract is closed out before delivery comes due.

Foreign Currency Futures

Foreign loans frequently are denominated in the currency of the lender (Japanese yen, Swiss franc, Euro, and so on). When loans must be repaid in foreign currencies, a new element of risk is introduced. This is because if exchange rates change, the dollar equivalent of the foreign currency that must be repaid differs from the dollar equivalent of the foreign currency borrowed.

Foreign exchange risk often is hedged in the same manner as interest rate risk.

To hedge against "foreign exchange risk" exposure, some firms buy or sell foreign currency futures contracts. These are similar to financial futures except specific foreign currencies are specified in the futures contracts rather than specific debt instruments. They work the same way to protect against foreign exchange risk as financial futures protect against fair value or cash flow risk.

Interest Rate Swaps

Over 65% of derivatives are interest rate swaps. These contracts exchange fixed interest payments for floating rate payments, or vice versa, without exchanging the underlying principal amounts. For example, suppose you owe $100,000 on a 10% fixed rate home loan. You envy your neighbor who also is paying 10% on her $100,000 mortgage, but hers is a floating rate loan, so if market rates fall, so will her loan rate. To the contrary, she is envious of your fixed rate, fearful that rates will rise, increasing her payments. A solution would be for the two of you to effectively swap interest payments using an interest rate swap agreement. The way a swap works, you both would continue to actually make your own interest payments, but would exchange the net cash difference between payments at specified intervals. So, in this case, if market rates (and thus floating payments) increase, you would pay your neighbor; if rates fall, she pays you. The net effect is to exchange the consequences of rate changes. In other words, you have effectively converted your fixed-rate debt to floating-rate debt; your neighbor has done the opposite.

Interest rate swaps exchange fixed interest payments for floating rate payments, or vice versa, without exchanging the underlying notional amounts.

Of course, this technique is not dependent on happening into such a fortuitous pairing of two borrowers with opposite philosophies on interest rate risk. Instead, banks or other intermediaries offer, for a fee, one-sided swap agreements to companies desiring to be either fixed-rate payers or variable-rate payers. Intermediaries usually strive to maintain a balanced portfolio of matched, offsetting swap agreements.

Theoretically, the two parties to such a transaction exchange principal amounts, say the $100,000 amount above, in addition to the interest on those amounts. It makes no practical sense, though, for the companies to send each other $100,000. So, instead, the principal amount is not actually exchanged, but serves merely as the computational base for interest calculations and is called the *notional amount*. Similarly, the fixed-rate payer doesn't usually send the entire fixed interest amount (say 10% × $100,000 = $10,000) and receive the entire variable interest amount (say 9% × $100,000 = $9,000). Generally, only the net amount ($1,000 in this case) is exchanged. This is illustrated in Graphic A–1.

Swap of annual payments on $100,000 notional amount; fixed interest rate: 10% ($10,000)

Company A —— Fixed 10% ——▶ Company B
Company A ◀—— Floating % —— Company B

Floating rate: 9% at time of first payment ($9,000); Company A pays Company B $1,000

GRAPHIC A–1
Interest Rate Swap—
Shortcut Method

From an accounting standpoint, the central issue is not the operational differences among various hedge instruments, but their similarities in functioning as hedges against risk.

Accounting for Derivatives

A key to accounting for derivatives is knowing the purpose for which a company holds them and whether the company is effective in serving that purpose. Derivatives, for instance, may be held for risk management (hedging activities). The desired effect, and often the real effect, is a reduction in risk. On the other hand, derivatives sometimes are held for speculative position taking, hoping for large profits. The effect of this activity usually is to *increase* risk. Perhaps more important, derivatives acquired as hedges and intended to reduce risk may, in fact, unintentionally increase risk instead.

It's important to understand that, serving as investments rather than as hedges, derivatives are extremely speculative. This is due to the high leverage inherent in derivatives. Here's why. The investment outlay usually is negligible, but, the potential gain or loss on the investment usually is quite high. A small change in interest rates or another underlying event can trigger a large change in the fair value of the derivative. Because the initial investment was minimal, the change in value relative to the investment itself represents a huge percentage gain or loss. Their extraordinarily risky nature prompted Warren Buffett, one of the country's most celebrated financiers, to refer to derivatives as "financial weapons of mass destruction." Accounting for derivatives is designed to treat differently (a) derivatives designated as hedges and those not designated as hedges as well as (b) the effective portion and the ineffective portion of gains and losses from intended hedges.

Derivatives not serving as hedges are extremely speculative due to the high leverage inherent in such investments.

The basic approach to accounting for derivatives is fairly straightforward, although implementation can be quite cumbersome. All derivatives, no exceptions, are carried on the

Each derivative contract has a "fair value," which is an amount that one side owes the other at a particular moment.

balance sheet as either assets or liabilities at fair (or market) value.[6] The reasoning is that (a) derivatives create either rights or obligations that meet the definition of assets or liabilities, and (b) fair value is the most meaningful measurement.

Accounting for the gain or loss on a derivative depends on how it is used. Specifically, if the derivative is not designated as a hedging instrument, or doesn't qualify as one, any gain or loss from fair value changes is recognized immediately in earnings. On the other hand, if a derivative is used to hedge against exposure to risk, any gain or loss from fair value changes is either (a) recognized immediately in earnings along with an offsetting loss or gain on the item being hedged or (b) deferred in comprehensive income until it can be recognized in earnings at the same time as earnings are affected by a hedged transaction. Which way depends on whether the derivative is designated as a (a) fair value hedge, (b) cash flow hedge, or (c) foreign currency hedge. Let's look now at each of the three hedge designations.

Fair Value Hedges

A gain or loss from a *fair value hedge* is recognized immediately in earnings along with the loss or gain from the item being hedged.

A company can be adversely affected when a change in either prices or interest rates causes a change in the fair value of one of its assets, its liabilities, or a commitment to buy or sell assets or liabilities. If a derivative is used to hedge against the exposure to changes in the fair value of an asset or liability or a firm commitment, it can be designated as a fair value hedge. In that case, when the derivative is adjusted to reflect changes in fair value, the other side of the entry recognizes a gain or loss to be included *currently* in earnings. At the same time, though, the loss or gain from changes in the fair value (due to the risk being hedged)[7] of the item being hedged also is included currently in earnings. This means that, to the extent the hedge is effective in serving its purpose, the gain or loss on the derivative will be offset by the loss or gain on the item being hedged. In fact, this is precisely the concept behind the procedure.

The income effects of the hedge instrument and the income effects of the item being hedged should affect earnings at the same time.

The reasoning is that as interest rates or other underlying events change, a hedge instrument will produce a gain approximately equal to a loss on the item being hedged (or vice versa). These income effects are interrelated and offsetting, so it would be improper to report the income effects in different periods. More critically, the intent and effect of having the hedge instrument is to *lessen* risk. And yet, recognizing gains in one period and counterbalancing losses in another period would tend to cause fluctuations in income that convey an *increase* in risk. However, to the extent that a hedge is ineffective and produces gains or losses different from the losses or gains being hedged, the ineffective portion is recognized in earnings immediately.

Some of the more common fair value hedges use:

- An interest rate swap to synthetically convert fixed-rate debt (for which interest rate changes could change the fair value of the debt) into floating-rate debt.
- A futures contract to hedge changes in the fair value (due to price changes) of aluminum, sugar, or some other type of inventory.
- A futures contract to hedge the fair value (due to price changes) of a firm commitment to sell natural gas or some other asset.

Illustration

Because interest rate swaps comprise over 65% of derivatives in use, we will use swaps to illustrate accounting for derivatives. Let's look at the example in Illustration A–1 on the next page.

When the floating rate declined from 10% to 9%, the fair values of both the derivative (swap) and the note increased. This created an offsetting gain on the derivative and holding loss on the note. Both are recognized in earnings at the same time (at June 30, 2011).

---

[6]FASB ASC 815–10: Derivatives and Hedging–Overall (previously "Accounting for Derivative Instruments and Hedging Activities," *Statement of Financial Accounting Standards No. 133* (Norwalk, Conn.: FASB, 1998)).

[7]The fair value of a hedged item might also change for reasons other than from effects of the risk being hedged. For instance, the hedged risk may be that a change in interest rates will cause the fair value of a bond to change. The bond price might also change, though, if the market perceives that the bond's default risk has changed.

Wintel Semiconductors issued $1 million of 18-month, 10% bank notes on January 1, 2011. Wintel is exposed to the risk that general interest rates will decline, causing the fair value of its debt to rise. (If the fair value of Wintel's debt increases, its effective borrowing cost is higher relative to the market.) To hedge against this fair value risk, the firm entered into an 18-month interest rate swap agreement on January 1 and designated the swap as a hedge against changes in the fair value of the note. The swap calls for the company to *receive payment* based on a 10% fixed interest rate on a notional amount of $1 million and to *make payment* based on a floating interest rate tied to changes in general rates.[8] As the Illustration will show, this effectively converts Wintel's fixed-rate debt to floating-rate debt. Cash settlement of the net interest amount is made semiannually at June 30 and December 31 of each year with the net interest being the difference between the $50,000 fixed interest [$1 million × (10% × ½)] and the floating interest rate times $1 million at those dates.

Floating (market) settlement rates were 9% at June 30, 2011, 8% at December 31, 2011, and 9% at June 30, 2012. Net interest receipts can be calculated as shown below. Fair values of both the derivative and the note resulting from those market rate changes are assumed to be quotes obtained from securities dealers.

	1/1/11	6/30/11	12/31/11	6/30/12
Fixed rate	10%	10%	10%	10%
Floating rate	10%	9%	8%	9%
Fixed payments ($1 million × [10% × ½])		$ 50,000	$ 50,000	$ 50,000
Floating payments ($1 million × ½ floating rate)		45,000	40,000	45,000
Net interest receipts		$ 5,000	$ 10,000	$ 5,000
Fair value of interest rate swap	0	$ 9,363	$ 9,615	0
Fair value of note payable	$1,000,000	$1,009,363	$1,009,615	$1,000,000

ILLUSTRATION A–1

Interest Rate Swap—Shortcut Method

January 1, 2011

Cash	1,000,000	
Notes payable		1,000,000

To record the issuance of the note.

The interest rate swap is designated as a fair value hedge on this note at issuance.

June 30, 2011

Interest expense (10% × ½ × $1 million)	50,000	
Cash		50,000

To record interest.

Cash ($50,000 – [9% × ½ × $1 million])	5,000	
Interest expense		5,000

To record the net cash settlement.

The swap settlement is the difference between the fixed interest (**5%**) and variable interest (**4.5%**).

Interest rate swap[9] ($9,363 – 0)	9,363	
Holding gain—interest rate swap		9,363

To record change in fair value of the derivative.

The fair value of derivatives is recognized in the balance sheet.

Holding loss—hedged note	9,363	
Note payable ($1,009,363 – 1,000,000)		9,363

To record change in fair value of the note due to interest rate changes.

The hedged liability (or asset) is adjusted to fair value as well.

The net interest settlement on June 30, 2011, is $5,000 because the fixed rate is 5% (half of the 10% annual rate) and the floating rate is 4.5% (half of the 9% annual rate).

---

[8]A common measure for benchmarking variable interest rates is LIBOR, the London Interbank Offered Rate, a base rate at which large international banks lend funds to each other.

[9]This would be a liability rather than an investment (asset) if the fair value had declined.

As with any debt, interest expense is the effective rate times the outstanding balance.

The settlement is the difference between the fixed interest (5%) and variable interest (4%).

The derivative is increased by the change in fair value. The note is increased by the change in fair value.

December 31, 2011

Interest expense	50,000	
Cash (10% × ½ × $1,000,000)		50,000
To record interest.		
Cash ($50,000 – [8% × ½ × $1 million])	10,000	
Interest expense		10,000
To record the net cash settlement.		
Interest rate swap ($9,615 – 9,363)	252	
Holding gain—interest rate swap		252
To record the change in fair value of the derivative.		
Holding loss—hedged note	252	
Note payable ($1,009,615 – 1,009,363)		252
To record the change in fair value of the note due to interest rate changes.		

The fair value of the swap increased by $252 (from $9,363 to $9,615). Similarly, we adjust the note's carrying value by the amount necessary to increase it to fair value. This produces a holding loss on the note that exactly offsets the gain on the swap. This result is the hedging effect that motivated Wintel to enter the fair value hedging arrangement in the first place.

At June 30, 2012, Wintel repeats the process of adjusting to fair value both the derivative investment and the note being hedged.

The net interest received is the difference between the fixed interest (5%) and floating interest (4.5%).

The swap's fair value now is zero.

June 30, 2012

Interest expense	50,000	
Cash (10% × ½ × $1,000,000)		50,000
To record interest.		
Cash [$50,000 – (9% × ½ × $1 million)]	5,000	
Interest expense		5,000
To record the net cash settlement.		
Holding loss—interest rate swap	9,615	
Interest rate swap ($0 – 9,615)		9,615
To record the change in fair value of the derivative.		
Note payable ($1,000,000 – 1,009,615)	9,615	
Holding gain—hedged note		9,615
To record the change in fair value of the note due to interest rate changes.		
Note payable	1,000,000	
Cash		1,000,000
To repay the loan.		

The net interest received is the difference between the fixed rate (5%) and floating rate (4.5%) times $1 million. The fair value of the swap decreased by $9,615 (from $9,615 to zero).[10] That decline represents a holding *loss* that we recognize in earnings. Similarly, we record an offsetting holding *gain* on the note for the change in its fair value.

Now let's see how the carrying values changed for the swap account and the note:

	Swap			Note	
Jan. 1, 2011					1,000,000
June 30, 2011	9,363				9,363
Dec. 31, 2011	252				252
June 30, 2012		9,615		9,615	
				1,000,000	
	0				0

---

[10]Because there are no future cash receipts from the swap arrangement at this point, the fair value of the swap is zero.

The income statement is affected as follows:

Income Statement + (−)

June 30, 2011	(50,000)	Interest expense—fixed payment
	5,000	Interest expense—net cash settlement
	9,363	Holding gain—interest rate swap
	(9,363)	Holding loss—hedged note
	(45,000)	Net effect—same as floating interest payment
Dec. 31, 2011	(50,000)	Interest expense—fixed payment
	10,000	Interest expense—net cash settlement
	252	Holding gain—interest rate swap
	(252)	Holding loss—hedged note
	(40,000)	Net effect—same as floating interest payment
June 30, 2012	(50,000)	Interest expense—fixed payment
	5,000	Interest expense—net cash settlement
	9,615	Holding gain—interest rate swap
	(9,615)	Holding loss—hedged note
	(45,000)	Net effect—same as floating interest payment

As this demonstrates, the swap effectively converts fixed-interest debt to floating-interest debt.

ADDITIONAL CONSIDERATION

Fair Value of the Swap

The fair value of a derivative typically is based on a quote obtained from a derivatives dealer. That fair value will approximate the present value of the expected net interest settlement receipts for the remaining term of the swap. In fact, we can actually calculate the fair value of the swap that we accepted as given in our illustration.

Since the June 30, 2011, floating rate of 9% caused the cash settlement on that date to be $5,000, it's reasonable to look at 9% as the best estimate of future floating rates and therefore assume the remaining two cash settlements also will be $5,000 each. We can then calculate at June 30, 2011, the present value of those expected net interest settlement receipts for the remaining term of the swap:

Fixed interest	10% × ½ × $1 million	$ 50,000
Expected floating interest	9% × ½ × $1 million	45,000
Expected cash receipts for both Dec. 31, 2011 and June 30, 2012		$ 5,000
		× 1.87267*
Present value		$ 9,363

*Present value of an ordinary annuity of $1: $n = 2$, $i = 4.5\%$ (½ of 9%) (from Table 4)

Fair Value of the Notes

The fair value of the note payable will be the present value of principal and remaining interest payments discounted at the *market rate*. The market rate will vary with the designated floating rate but might differ due to changes in default (credit) risk and the term structure of interest rates. Assuming it's 9% at June 30, 2011, we can calculate the fair value (present value) of the notes:

Interest	$50,000* × 1.87267[†] =	$ 93,633
Principal	$1,000,000 × .91573[‡] =	915,730
		$1,009,363

*½ of 10% × $1,000,000
[†]Present value of an ordinary annuity of $1: $n = 2$, $i = 4.5\%$ (from Table 4)
[‡]Present value of $1: $n = 2$, $i = 4.5\%$ (from Table 2)

(continued)

> (concluded)
>
> Note: Often the cash settlement rate is "reset" as of each cash settlement date (thus the floating rate actually used at the end of each period to determine the payment is the floating market rate as of the *beginning* of the same period). In our illustration, for instance, there would have been no cash settlement at June 30, 2011, since we would use the beginning floating rate of 10% to determine payment. Similarly, we would have used the 9% floating rate at June 30, 2011, to determine the cash settlement six months later at December 31. In effect, each cash settlement would be delayed six months. Had this arrangement been in effect in the current illustration, there would have been one fewer cash settlement payments (two rather than three), but would not have affected the fair value calculations above because, either way, our expectation would be cash receipts of $5,000 for both Dec. 31, 2011, and June 30, 2012.

Cash Flow Hedges

The risk in some transactions or events is the risk of a change in cash flows, rather than a change in fair values. We noted earlier, for instance, that *fixed-rate* debt subjects a company to the risk that interest rate changes could change the fair value of the debt. On the other hand, if the obligation is *floating-rate* debt, the fair value of the debt will not change when interest rates do, but cash flows will. If a derivative is used to hedge against the exposure to changes in cash inflows or cash outflows of an asset or liability or a forecasted transaction (like a future purchase or sale), it can be designated as a cash flow hedge. In that case, when the derivative is adjusted to reflect changes in fair value, the other side of the entry is a gain or loss to be deferred as a component of other comprehensive income and included in earnings later, at the same time as earnings are affected by the hedged transaction. Once again, the effect is matching the earnings effect of the derivative with the earnings effect of the item being hedged, precisely the concept behind hedge accounting.

To understand the deferral of the gain or loss, we need to revisit the concept of comprehensive income. Comprehensive income, as you may recall from Chapters 4, 12, 17, and 18, is a more expansive view of the change in shareholders' equity than traditional net income. In fact, it encompasses all changes in equity other than from transactions with owners.[11] So, in addition to net income itself, comprehensive income includes up to four other changes in equity that don't (yet) belong in net income, namely, net holding gains (losses) on investments (Chapter 12), gains (losses) from and amendments to postretirement benefit plans (Chapter 17), gains (losses) from foreign currency translation, and deferred gains (losses) from derivatives designated as cash flow hedges.[12]

Some of the more commonly used cash flow hedges are:

- An interest rate swap to synthetically convert floating rate debt (for which interest rate changes could change the cash interest payments) into fixed rate debt.
- A futures contract to hedge a forecasted sale (for which price changes could change the cash receipts) of natural gas, crude oil, or some other asset.

Foreign Currency Hedges

Today's economy is increasingly a global one. The majority of large "U.S." companies are, in truth, multinational companies that may receive only a fraction of their revenues from U.S. operations. Many operations of those companies are located abroad. Foreign operations often are denominated in the currency of the foreign country (the Euro, Japanese yen, Russian rubles, and so on). Even companies without foreign operations sometimes hold investments, issue debt, or conduct other transactions denominated in foreign currencies. As exchange rates change, the dollar equivalent of the foreign currency changes. The possibility

A gain or loss from a *cash flow hedge* is deferred as other comprehensive income until it can be recognized in earnings along with the earnings effect of the item being hedged.

The possibility that foreign currency exchange rates might change exposes many companies to foreign currency risk.

---

[11]Transactions with owners primarily include dividends and the sale or purchase of shares of the company's stock.

[12]FASB ASC 220–10–55–2: Comprehensive Income–Overall–Implementation Guidance and Illustrations (previously "Reporting Comprehensive Income," *Statement of Financial Accounting Standards No. 130* (Norwalk, Conn.: FASB, 1997)).

of currency rate changes exposes these companies to the risk that some transactions require settlement in a currency other than the entities' functional currency or that foreign operations will require translation adjustments to reported amounts.

A **foreign currency hedge** can be a hedge of foreign currency exposure of:

- A firm commitment—treated as a fair value hedge.
- An available-for-sale security—treated as a fair value hedge.
- A forecasted transaction—treated as a cash flow hedge.
- A company's net investment in a foreign operation—the gain or loss is reported in *other comprehensive income* as part of unrealized gains and losses from foreign currency translation.[13]

Hedge Effectiveness

When a company elects to apply hedge accounting, it must establish at the inception of the hedge the method it will use to assess the effectiveness of the hedging derivative as well as the measurement approach it will use to determine the ineffective portion of the hedge.[14] The key criterion for qualifying as a hedge is that the hedging relationship must be "highly effective" in achieving offsetting changes in fair values or cash flows based on the hedging company's specified risk management objective and strategy.

An assessment of this effectiveness must be made at least every three months and whenever financial statements are issued. There are no precise guidelines for assessing effectiveness, but it generally means a high correlation between changes in the fair value or cash flows of the derivative and of the item being hedged, not necessarily a specific reduction in risk. Hedge accounting must be terminated for hedging relationships that no longer are highly effective.

> To qualify as a hedge, the hedging relationship must be highly effective in achieving offsetting changes in fair values or cash flows.

Hedge Ineffectiveness

In Illustration A–1, the loss on the hedged note exactly offset the gain on the swap. This is because the swap in this instance was highly effective in hedging the risk due to interest rate changes. However, the loss and gain would not have exactly offset each other if the hedging arrangement had been ineffective. For instance, suppose the swap's term had been different from that of the note (say a three-year swap term compared with the 18-month term of the note) or if the notional amount of the swap differed from that of the note (say $500,000 rather than $1 million). In that case, changes in the fair value of the swap and changes in the fair value of the note would not be the same. The result would be a greater (or lesser) amount recognized in earnings for the swap than for the note. Because there would not be an exact offset, earnings would be affected, an effect resulting from hedge ineffectiveness. That is a desired effect of hedge accounting; to the extent that a hedge is effective, the earnings effect of a derivative cancels out the earnings effect of the item being hedged. However, even if a hedge is highly effective, all ineffectiveness is recognized currently in earnings.

> Imperfect hedges result in part of the derivative gain or loss being included in current earnings.

Fair Value Changes Unrelated to the Risk Being Hedged

In Illustration A–1, the fair value of the hedged note and the fair value of the swap changed by the same amounts each year because we assumed the fair values changed only due to interest rate changes. It's also possible, though, that the note's fair value would change by an amount different from that of the swap for reasons unrelated to interest rates. Remember from our earlier discussion that the market's perception of a company's creditworthiness, and thus its ability to pay interest and principal when due, also can affect the value of debt,

---

[13]This is the same treatment previously prescribed for these translation adjustments by *Statement of Financial Accounting Standards No. 52* [FASB ASC 830: Foreign Currency Matters].

[14]Remember, if a derivative is not designated as a hedge, any gains or losses from changes in its fair value are recognized immediately in earnings.

whether interest rates change or not. In hedge accounting, we ignore those changes. We recognize only the fair value changes in the hedged item that we can attribute to the risk being hedged (interest rate risk in this case). For example, if a changing perception of default risk had caused the note's fair value to increase by an additional, say $5,000, our journal entries in Illustration A–1 would have been unaffected. Notice, then, that although we always mark a *derivative* to fair value, the reported amount of the *item being hedged* may not be its fair value. We mark a hedged item to fair value only to the extent that its fair value changed due to the risk being hedged.

Fair value changes unrelated to the risk being hedged are ignored.

Disclosure of Derivatives and Risk

To be adequately informed about the effectiveness of a company's risk management, investors and creditors need information about strategies for holding derivatives and specific hedging activities. Toward that end, extensive disclosure requirements provide information that includes:

- Objectives and strategies for holding and issuing derivatives.
- A description of the items for which risks are being hedged.
- For forecasted transactions: a description, time before the transaction is expected to occur, the gains and losses accumulated in other comprehensive income, and the events that will trigger their recognition in earnings.
- Beginning balance of, changes in, and ending balance of the derivative component of other comprehensive income.
- The net amount of gain or loss reported in earnings (representing aggregate hedge ineffectiveness).
- Qualitative and quantitative information about failed hedges: canceled commitments or previously hedged forecasted transactions no longer expected to occur.

The intent is to provide information about the company's success in reducing risks and consequently about risks not managed successfully. Remember, too, that when derivatives are employed ineffectively, risks can escalate. Ample disclosures about derivatives are essential to maintain awareness of potential opportunities and problems with risk management.

In addition, newly issued GAAP requires companies to provide enhanced disclosures indicating (a) how and why the company uses derivative instruments, (b) how the company accounts for derivative instruments and related hedged items, and (c) how derivative instruments and related hedged items affect the company's balance sheet, income statement, and cash flows.[15] The required disclosures includes two tables, one that highlights the location and fair values of derivative instruments in the balance sheet, and another that indicates the location and amounts of gains and losses on derivative instruments in the income statement. The two tables distinguish between derivative instruments that are designated as hedging instruments and those that are not. The tables also categorize derivative instruments by each major type—interest rate contracts, foreign exchange contracts, equity contracts, commodity contracts, credit contracts and other types of contracts.

Even for some traditional liabilities, the amounts reported on the face of the financial statements provide inadequate disclosure about the degree to which a company is exposed to risk of loss. To provide adequate disclosure about a company's exposure to risk, additional information must be provided about (a) concentrations of credit risk and (b) the fair value of all financial instruments.[16]

---

[15]FASB ASC 815: Derivatives and Hedging (previously "Disclosures about Derivative Instruments and Hedging Activities—an amendment of FASB Statement No. 133)," *Statement of Financial Accounting Standards No. 161* (Stamford, Conn.: FASB, 2008)).

[16]FASB ASC 825–10–50–1: Financial Instruments–Overall–Disclosure (previously "Disclosures About Fair Values of Financial Instruments," *Statement of Financial Accounting Standards No. 107* (Norwalk, Conn.: FASB, 1991) as amended by *Statement of Financial Accounting Standards No. 133,* "Accounting for Derivative Instruments and Hedging Activities" (Norwalk, Conn.: FASB, 1998)).

Extended Method for Interest Rate Swap Accounting

A shortcut method for accounting for an interest rate swap is permitted when a hedge meets certain criteria. In general, the criteria are designed to see if the hedge supports the assumption of "no ineffectiveness." Illustration A–1 of a fair value hedge met those criteria, in particular, (a) the swap's notional amount matches the note's principal amount, (b) the swap's expiration date matches the note's maturity date, (c) the fair value of the swap is zero at inception, and (d) the floating payment is at the market rate.[17] Because Wintel can conclude that the swap will be highly effective in offsetting changes in the fair value of the debt, it can use the changes in the fair value of the swap to measure the offsetting changes in the fair value of the debt. That's the essence of the shortcut method used in Illustration A–1. The extended method required when the criteria are *not* met for the short-cut method is described in this section (Illustration A–2). It produces the same effect on earnings and in the balance sheet as does the procedure shown in Illustration A–1.

	ILLUSTRATION A–2

Wintel Semiconductors issued $1 million of 18-month, 10% bank notes on January 1, 2011. Wintel is exposed to the risk that general interest rates will decline, causing the fair value of its debt to rise. (If the fair value of Wintel's debt increases, its effective borrowing cost is higher relative to the market.) To hedge against this fair value risk, the firm entered into an 18-month interest rate swap agreement on January 1 and designated the swap as a hedge against changes in the fair value of the note. The swap calls for the company to *receive payment* based on a 10% fixed interest rate on a notional amount of $1 million and to *make payment* based on a floating interest rate tied to changes in general rates. Cash settlement of the net interest amount is made semiannually at June 30 and December 31 of each year with the net interest being the difference between the $50,000 fixed interest [$1 million × (10% × ½)] and the floating interest rate times $1 million at those dates.

ILLUSTRATION A–2
Interest Rate Swap—Extended Method

Floating (market) settlement rates were 9% at June 30, 2011, 8% at December 31, 2011, and 8% at June 30, 2012. Net interest receipts can be calculated as shown below. Fair values of both the derivative and the note resulting from those market rate changes are assumed to be quotes obtained from securities dealers.

	1/1/11	6/30/11	12/31/11	6/30/12
Fixed rate	10%	10%	10%	10%
Floating rate	10%	9%	8%	9%
Fixed payments				
[$1 million × (10% × ½)]		$ 50,000	$ 50,000	$ 50,000
Floating payments				
($1 million × ½ floating rate)		45,000	40,000	45,000
Net interest receipts		$ 5,000	$ 10,000	$ 5,000
Fair value of interest rate swap	0	$ 9,363	$ 9,615	0
Fair value of note payable	$1,000,000	$1,009,363	$1,009,615	$1,000,000

When the floating rate declined in Illustration A–2 from 10% to 9%, the fair values of both the derivative (swap) and the note increased. This created an offsetting gain on the derivative and holding loss on the note. Both are recognized in earnings the same period (June 30, 2011).

January 1, 2011		
Cash	1,000,000	
Notes payable		1,000,000
To record the issuance of the note.		

The interest rate swap is designated as a fair value hedge on this note at issuance.

The swap settlement is the difference between the fixed interest (5%) and variable interest (4.5%).

June 30, 2011

Interest expense (10% × ½ × $1 million)	50,000	
Cash		50,000
To record interest.		
Cash ($50,000 − [9% × ½ × $1 million])	5,000	
Interest rate swap ($9,363 − 0)	9,363	
Interest revenue (10% × ½ × $0)		0
Holding gain—interest rate swap (to balance)		14,363
To record the net cash settlement, accrued interest on the swap,		
and change in the fair value of the derivative.		
Holding loss—hedged note	9,363	
Notes payable ($1,009,363 − 1,000,000)		9,363
To record change in fair value of the note due to interest rate changes.		

The fair value of derivatives is recognized in the balance sheet.

The hedged liability (or asset) is adjusted to fair value as well.

The net interest settlement on June 30, 2011, is $5,000 because the fixed rate is 5% (half of the 10% annual rate) and the floating rate is 4.5% (half of the 9% annual rate). A holding gain ($14,363) is produced by holding the derivative security during a time when an interest rate decline caused an increase in the value of that asset. A portion ($5,000) of the gain was received in cash and another portion ($9,363) is reflected as an increase in the value of the asset.

We also have holding loss of the same amount. This is because we also held a liability during the same time period, and the interest rate change caused its fair value to increase as well.

As with any debt, interest expense is the effective rate times the outstanding balance.

December 31, 2011

Interest expense (9% × ½ × $1,009,363)	45,421	
Notes payable (difference)*	4,579	
Cash (10% × ½ × $1,000,000)		50,000
To record interest.		
Cash [$50,000 − (8% × ½ × $1 million)]	10,000	
Interest rate swap ($9,615 − 9,363)	252	
Interest revenue (9% × ½ × $9,363)		421
Holding gain—interest rate swap (to balance)		9,831
To record the net cash settlement, accrued interest on the swap,		
and change in the fair value of the derivative.		
Holding loss—hedged note	4,831	
Notes payable ($1,009,615 − 1,009,363 + 4,579)		4,831
To record the change in fair value of the note due to interest rate changes.		

*We could use a premium on the note to adjust its carrying amount.

The cash settlement is the difference between the fixed interest (5%) and variable interest (4%).

Interest ($421) accrues on the asset.

The note is increased by the change in fair value.

We determine interest on the note the same way we do for any liability, as you learned earlier—at the effective rate (9% × ½) times the outstanding balance ($1,009,363). This results in reducing the note's carrying amount for the cash interest paid in excess of the interest expense.

The fair value of the swap increased due to the interest rate decline by $252 (from $9,363 to $9,615). The holding gain we recognize in earnings consists of that increase (a) plus the $10,000 cash settlement also created by the interest rate decline and (b) minus the $421 increase that results not from the interest rate decline, but from interest accruing on the asset.[18] Similarly, we adjust the note's carrying value by the amount necessary to increase it to fair value, allowing for the $4,579 reduction in the note in the earlier entry to record interest.

At June 30, 2012, Wintel repeats the process of adjusting to fair value both the derivative investment and the note being hedged.

---

[18]The investment in the interest rate swap represents the present value of expected future net interest receipts. As with other such assets, interest accrues at the effective rate times the outstanding balance. You also can think of the accrued interest mathematically as the increase in present value of the future cash flows as we get one period nearer to the dates when the cash will be received.

June 30, 2012		
Interest expense (8% × ½ × $1,009,615)	40,385	
Notes payable (difference)	9,615	
Cash (10% × ½ × $1,000,000)		50,000
To record interest.		
Cash [$50,000 − (9% × ½ × $1 million)]..	5,000	
Holding loss—interest rate swap (to balance)	5,000	
Interest rate swap ($0 − $9,615)		9,615
Interest revenue (8% × ½ × $9,615)		385
To record the net cash settlement, accrued interest on the swap,		
and change in the fair value of the derivative.		
Notes payable ($1,000,000 − 1,009,615 + 9,615).............................	0	
Holding gain—hedged note		0
To record the change in fair value of the note due to interest rate changes.		
Note payable	1,000,000	
Cash		1,000,000
To repay the loan		

Sidebar notes:
- Interest expense is the effective rate times the outstanding balance.
- The net interest received is the difference between the fixed interest (5%) and floating interest (4.5%).
- The swap's fair value now is zero.

The net interest received is the difference between the fixed rate (5%) and floating rate (4.5%) times $1 million. The fair value of the swap decreased by $9,615 (from $9,615 to zero).[19] The holding loss we recognize in earnings consists of that decline (a) minus the $5,000 portion of the decline resulting from it being realized in cash settlement and (b) plus the $385 increase that results not from the interest rate change, but from interest accruing on the asset.

Now let's see how the carrying values changed for the swap account and the note:

	Swap		**Note**	
Jan. 1, 2011				1,000,000
June 30, 2011	9,363			9,363
Dec. 31, 2011	252		4,579	4,831
June 30, 2012		9,615	9,615	
			1,000,000	
	0			0

The income statement is affected as follows:

	Income Statement + (−)	
June 30, 2011	(50,000)	Interest expense
	0	Interest revenue (no time has passed)
	14,363	Holding gain interest rate swap
	(9,363)	Holding loss—hedged note
	(45,000)	Net effect—same as floating interest payment
Dec. 31, 2011	(45,421)	Interest expense
	421	Interest revenue
	9,831	Holding gain—interest rate swap
	(4,831)	Holding loss—hedged note
	(40,000)	Net effect—same as floating interest payment
June 30, 2012	(40,385)	Interest expense
	385	Interest revenue
	(5,000)	Holding gain—interest rate swap
	0	Holding loss—hedged note
	(45,000)	Net effect—same as floating interest payment

---

[19]Because there are no future cash receipts or payments from the swap arrangement at this point, the fair value of the swap is zero.

As this demonstrates, the swap effectively converts Wintel's fixed-interest debt to floating-interest debt.

INTERNATIONAL FINANCIAL REPORTING STANDARDS

Accounting for Derivatives.

"With IAS 39, if you understand it, you haven't read it properly," said International Accounting Standards Board Chairman, Sir David Tweedie.[20]

As with U.S. GAAP, accounting for derivatives under IFRS is quite complex. In fact, *IAS No. 39* provides an example of international accounting that defies the usual characterization of IFRS as being "principles-based accounting" in comparison with "rules-based" U.S. GAAP. Like U.S. GAAP, all freestanding derivatives are recognized in the balance sheet and measured at fair value under IFRS. And, unless they qualify as hedging instruments in a cash flow hedge or net investment in a foreign operation, all changes in fair value are recognized immediately in net income, as under U.S. GAAP. Although the hedging models under U.S. GAAP and IFRS are similar, several differences exist. Here are a few significant ones:

- The short-cut method for interest rate swaps described in this Appendix is not permitted under IFRS.
- The key criterion for qualifying as a hedge is that the hedging relationship must be "highly effective" in achieving offsetting changes in fair values or cash flows, which under U.S. GAAP generally means a high correlation between changes in the fair value or cash flows of the derivative and the item being hedged. Highly effective is more precisely defined under IFRS: the hedge must be within the range of 80-120 percent effective.
- U.S. GAAP does not permit a single hedging instrument to hedge more than one risk in two or more hedged items. However, IFRS allows a single hedging instrument to be designated as a hedge of more than one type of risk if the risks being hedged can be clearly identified, the hedge effectiveness can be demonstrated, and specific designation to different risk positions can be ensured.

WHERE WE'RE HEADED

Both the FASB and IASB have ongoing projects to amend the accounting for derivatives and hedge accounting in particular. Exposure drafts issued by each Board have the potential to create differences between U.S. GAAP and IFRS in these areas. Fortunately, though, both the FASB and IASB have mandates to simplify hedge accounting and are coordinating efforts to make the rules and disclosures more useful and easier for users to understand. Whether or not the standards become fully converged before the U.S. adopts IFRS, the complexity of the standards likely will be reduced.

THE BOTTOM LINE

1.   All derivatives are reported in the balance sheet at fair value.
2.   *Hedging* means taking a risk position that is opposite to an actual position that is exposed to risk. For a derivative used to hedge against exposure to risk, treatment of any gain or loss from fair value changes depends on whether the derivative is designated as (a) a fair value hedge, (b) a cash flow hedge, or (c) a foreign currency hedge.

---

[20]Michael Cohn, "Tweedie Says FASB Will Always Play a Role," WebCPA, December 11, 2008.

3.   We recognize a gain or loss from a *fair value hedge* immediately in earnings along with the loss or gain from the item being hedged. This is so the income effects of the hedge instrument and the income effects of the item being hedged will affect earnings at the same time.

4.   We defer a gain or loss from a *cash flow hedge* as part of other comprehensive income until it can be recognized in earnings along with the earnings effect of the item being hedged.

5.   Imperfect hedges result in part of the derivative gain or loss being included in current earnings. We ignore market value changes unrelated to the risk being hedged.

6.   Extensive disclosure requirements about derivatives are designed to provide investors and creditors information about the adequacy of a company's risk management and the company's success in reducing risks, including risks not managed successfully. ●

QUESTIONS FOR REVIEW OF KEY TOPICS

Q A–1   Some financial instruments are called derivatives. Why?

Q A–2   Should gains and losses on a fair value hedge be recorded as they occur, or should they be recorded to coincide with losses and gains on the item being hedged?

Q A–3   Hines Moving Company held a fixed-rate debt of $2 million. The company wanted to hedge its fair value exposure with an interest rate swap. However, the only notional available at the time, on the type of swap it desired, was $2.5 million. What will be the effect of any gain or loss on the $500,000 notional difference?

Q A–4   What is a futures contract?

Q A–5   What is the effect on interest of an interest rate swap?

Q A–6   How are derivatives reported on the balance sheet? Why?

Q A–7   When is a gain or a loss from a cash flow hedge reported in earnings?

EXERCISES

E A–1
Derivatives-hedge classification

Indicate (by abbreviation) the type of hedge each activity described below would represent.

Hedge Type

    FV   Fair value hedge
    CF   Cash flow hedge
    FC   Foreign currency hedge
    N   Would not qualify as a hedge

Activity

_____ 1. An options contract to hedge possible future price changes of inventory.
_____ 2. A futures contract to hedge exposure to interest rate changes prior to replacing bank notes when they mature.
_____ 3. An interest rate swap to synthetically convert floating rate debt into fixed rate debt.
_____ 4. An interest rate swap to synthetically convert fixed rate debt into floating rate debt.
_____ 5. A futures contract to hedge possible future price changes of timber covered by a firm commitment to sell.
_____ 6. A futures contract to hedge possible future price changes of a forecasted sale of tin.
_____ 7. ExxonMobil's net investment in a Kuwait oil field.
_____ 8. An interest rate swap to synthetically convert floating rate interest on a stock investment into fixed rate interest.
_____ 9. An interest rate swap to synthetically convert fixed rate interest on a held-to-maturity debt investment into floating rate interest.
_____ 10. An interest rate swap to synthetically convert floating rate interest on a held-to-maturity debt investment into fixed rate interest.
_____ 11. An interest rate swap to synthetically convert fixed rate interest on a stock investment into floating rate interest.

E A–2
Derivatives; interest rate swap; fixed rate debt

On January 1, 2011, LLB Industries borrowed $200,000 from Trust Bank by issuing a two-year, 10% note, with interest payable quarterly. LLB entered into a two-year interest rate swap agreement on January 1, 2011, and designated the swap as a fair value hedge. Its intent was to hedge the risk that general interest rates will decline, causing the fair value of its debt to increase. The agreement called for the company to receive payment based on a 10%

fixed interest rate on a notional amount of $200,000 and to pay interest based on a floating interest rate. The contract called for cash settlement of the net interest amount quarterly.

Floating (LIBOR) settlement rates were 10% at January 1, 8% at March 31, and 6% June 30, 2011. The fair values of the swap are quotes obtained from a derivatives dealer. Those quotes and the fair values of the note are as indicated below.

	January 1	March 31	June 30
Fair value of interest rate swap	0	$ 6,472	$ 11,394
Fair value of note payable	$200,000	$206,472	$211,394

Required:

1. Calculate the net cash settlement at March 31 and June 30, 2011.

2. Prepare the journal entries through June 30, 2011, to record the issuance of the note, interest, and necessary adjustments for changes in fair value.

E A–3
Derivatives; interest rate swap; fixed rate investment

(This is a variation of Exercise A–2, modified to consider an investment in debt securities.)

On January 1, 2011, S&S Corporation invested in LLB Industries' negotiable two-year, 10% notes, with interest receivable quarterly. The company classified the investment as available-for-sale. S&S entered into a two-year interest rate swap agreement on January 1, 2011, and designated the swap as a fair value hedge. Its intent was to hedge the risk that general interest rates will decline, causing the fair value of its investment to increase. The agreement called for the company to make payment based on a 10% fixed interest rate on a notional amount of $200,000 and to receive interest based on a floating interest rate. The contract called for cash settlement of the net interest amount quarterly.

Floating (LIBOR) settlement rates were 10% at January 1, 8% at March 31, and 6% June 30, 2011. The fair values of the swap are quotes obtained from a derivatives dealer. Those quotes and the fair values of the investment in notes are as follows:

	January 1	March 31	June 30
Fair value of interest rate swap	0	$ 6,472	$ 11,394
Fair value of the investment in notes	$200,000	$206,472	$211,394

Required:

1. Calculate the net cash settlement at March 31 and June 30, 2011

2. Prepare the journal entries through June 30, 2011, to record the investment in notes, interest, and necessary adjustments for changes in fair value.

E A–4
Derivatives; interest rate swap; fixed rate debt; fair value change unrelated to hedged risk

(This is a variation of Exercise A–2, modified to consider fair value change unrelated to hedged risk.)

LLB Industries borrowed $200,000 from Trust Bank by issuing a two-year, 10% note, with interest payable quarterly. LLB entered into a two-year interest rate swap agreement on January 1, 2011 and designated the swap as a fair value hedge. Its intent was to hedge the risk that general interest rates will decline, causing the fair value of its debt to increase. The agreement called for the company to receive payment based on a 10% fixed interest rate on a notional amount of $200,000 and to pay interest based on a floating interest rate.

Floating (LIBOR) settlement rates were 10% at January 1, 8% at March 31, and 6% at June 30, 2011. The fair values of the swap are quotes obtained from a derivatives dealer. Those quotes and the fair values of the note are as indicated below. The additional rise in the fair value of the note (higher than that of the swap) on June 30 was due to investors' perceptions that the creditworthiness of LLB was improving.

	January 1	March 31	June 30
Fair value of interest rate swap	0	$ 6,472	$ 11,394
Fair value of note payable	$200,000	$206,472	$220,000

Required:

1. Calculate the net cash settlement at June 30, 2011

2. Prepare the journal entries on June 30, 2011, to record the interest and necessary adjustments for changes in fair value.

E A–5
Derivatives; interest rate swap; fixed rate debt; extended method

(This is a variation of Exercise A–2, modified to consider the extended method.)

On January 1, 2011, LLB Industries borrowed $200,000 from Trust Bank by issuing a two-year, 10% note, with interest payable quarterly. LLB entered into a two-year interest rate swap agreement on January 1, 2011, and designated the swap as a fair value hedge. Its intent was to hedge the risk that general interest rates will decline, causing the fair value of its debt to increase. The agreement called for the company to receive payment based on a

10% fixed interest rate on a notional amount of $200,000 and to pay interest based on a floating interest rate. The contract called for cash settlement of the net interest amount quarterly.

Floating (LIBOR) settlement rates were 10% at January 1, 8% at March 31, and 6% at June 30, 2011. The fair values of the swap are quotes obtained from a derivatives dealer. Those quotes and the fair values of the note are as follows:

	January 1	March 31	June 30
Fair value of interest rate swap	0	$ 6,472	$ 11,394
Fair value of note payable	$200,000	$206,472	$211,394

Required:

Prepare the journal entries through June 30, 2011, to record the issuance of the note, interest, and necessary adjustments for changes in fair value. Use the extended method demonstrated in Illustration A–2.

E A–6
Derivatives; interest
rate swap; fixed-
rate debt; fair value
change unrelated
to hedged risk;
extended method

(Note: This is a variation of Exercise A–5, modified to consider fair value change unrelated to hedged risk.)

On January 1, 2011, LLB Industries borrowed $200,000 from trust Bank by issuing a two-year, 10% note, with interest payable quarterly. LLB entered into a two-year interest rate swap agreement on January 1, 2011, and designated the swap as a fair value hedge. Its intent was to hedge the risk that general interest rates will decline, causing the fair value of its debt to increase. The agreement called for the company to receive payment based on a 10% fixed interest rate on a notional amount of $200,000 and to pay interest based on a floating interest rate. The contract called for cash settlement of the net interest amount quarterly.

Floating (LIBOR) settlement rates were 10% at January 1, 8% at March 31, and 6% June 30, 2011. The fair values of the swap are quotes obtained from a derivatives dealer. Those quotes and the fair values of the note are as indicated below. The additional rise in the fair value of the note (higher than that of the swap) on June 30 was due to investors' perceptions that the creditworthiness of LLB was improving.

	January 1	March 31	June 30
Fair value of interest rate swap	0	$ 6,472	$ 11,394
Fair value of note payable	$200,000	206,472	220,000

Required:

1. Calculate the net cash settlement at June 30, 2011.
2. Prepare the journal entries on June 30, 2011, to record the interest and necessary adjustments for changes in fair value. Use the extended method demonstrated in Illustration A–2.

PROBLEMS

P A–1
Derivatives—
interest rate swap

On January 1, 2011, Labtech Circuits borrowed $100,000 from First Bank by issuing a three-year, 8% note, payable on December 31, 2013. Labtech wanted to hedge the risk that general interest rates will decline, causing the fair value of its debt to increase. Therefore, Labtech entered into a three-year interest rate swap agreement on January 1, 2011, and designated the swap as a fair value hedge. The agreement called for the company to receive payment based on an 8% fixed interest rate on a notional amount of $100,000 and to pay interest based on a floating interest rate tied to LIBOR. The contract called for cash settlement of the net interest amount on December 31 of each year.

Floating (LIBOR) settlement rates were 8% at inception and 9%, 7%, and 7% at the end of 2011, 2012, and 2013, respectively. The fair values of the swap are quotes obtained from a derivatives dealer. These quotes and the fair values of the note are as follows:

	January 1	December 31		
	2011	2011	2012	2013
Fair value of interest rate swap	0	$ (1,759)	$ 935	0
Fair value of note payable	$100,000	$98,241	$100,935	$100,000

Required:

1. Calculate the net cash settlement at the end of 2011, 2012, and 2013.
2. Prepare the journal entries during 2011 to record the issuance of the note, interest, and necessary adjustments for changes in fair value.
3. Prepare the journal entries during 2012 to record interest, net cash interest settlement for the interest rate swap, and necessary adjustments for changes in fair value.

4. Prepare the journal entries during 2013 to record interest, net cash interest settlement for the interest rate swap, necessary adjustments for changes in fair value, and repayment of the debt.

5. Calculate the carrying values of both the swap account and the note in each of the three years.

6. Calculate the net effect on earnings of the hedging arrangement in each of the three years. (Ignore income taxes.)

7. Suppose the fair value of the note at December 31, 2011, had been $97,000 rather than $98,241 with the additional decline in fair value due to investors' perceptions that the creditworthiness of Labtech was worsening. How would that affect your entries to record changes in the fair values?

P A–2
Derivatives;
interest rate swap;
comprehensive

CMOS Chips is hedging a 20-year, $10 million, 7% bond payable with a 20-year interest rate swap and has designated the swap as a fair value hedge. The agreement called for CMOS to receive payment based on a 7% fixed interest rate on a notional amount of $10 million and to pay interest based on a floating interest rate tied to LIBOR. The contract calls for cash settlement of the net interest amount on December 31 of each year.

At December 31, 2011, the fair value of the derivative and of the hedged bonds has increased by $100,000 because interest rates declined during the reporting period.

Required:

1. Does CMOS have an unrealized gain or loss on the derivative for the period? On the bonds? Will earnings increase or decrease due to the hedging arrangement? Why?

2. Suppose interest rates increased, rather than decreased, causing the fair value of both the derivative and of the hedged bonds to decrease by $100,000. Would CMOS have an unrealized gain or loss on the derivative for the period? On the bonds? Would earnings increase or decrease due to the hedging arrangement? Why?

3. Suppose the fair value of the bonds at December 31, 2011, had increased by $110,000 rather than $100,000, with the additional increase in fair value due to investors' perceptions that the creditworthiness of CMOS was improving. Would CMOS have an unrealized gain or loss on the derivative for the period? On the bonds? Would earnings increase or decrease due to the hedging arrangement? Why?

4. Suppose the notional amount of the swap had been $12 million, rather than the $10 million principal amount of the bonds. As a result, at December 31, 2011, the swap's fair value had increased by $120,000 rather than $100,000. Would CMOS have an unrealized gain or loss on the derivative for the period? On the bonds? Would earnings increase or decrease due to the hedging arrangement? Why?

5. Suppose BIOS Corporation is an investor having purchased all $10 million of the bonds issued by CMOS as described in the original situation above. BIOS is hedging its investment, classified as available-for-sale, with a 20-year interest rate swap and has designated the swap as a fair value hedge. The agreement called for BIOS to make *payment* based on a 7% fixed interest rate on a notional amount of $10 million and to *receive* interest based on a floating interest rate tied to LIBOR. Would BIOS have an unrealized gain or loss on the derivative for the period due to interest rates having declined? On the bonds? Would earnings increase or decrease due to the hedging arrangement? Why?

P A–3
Derivatives; interest
rate swap; fixed
rate debt; extended
method

(Note: This is a variation of Problem A–1, modified to consider the extended method demonstrated in Illustration A–2.)

On January 1, 2011, Labtech Circuits borrowed $100,000 from First Bank by issuing a three-year, 8% note, payable on December 31, 2013. Labtech wanted to hedge the risk that general interest rates will decline, causing the fair value of its debt to increase. Therefore, Labtech entered into a three-year interest rate swap agreement on January 1, 2011, and designated the swap as a fair value hedge. The agreement called for the company to receive payment based on an 8% fixed interest rate on a notional amount of $100,000 and to pay interest based on a floating interest rate tied to LIBOR. The contract called for cash settlement of the net interest amount on December 31 of each year.

Floating (LIBOR) settlement rates were 8% at inception and 9%, 7%, and 7% at the end of 2011, 2012, and 2013, respectively. The fair values of the swap are quotes obtained from a derivatives dealer. Those quotes and the fair values of the note are as follows:

| | January 1 | December 31 | | |
	2011	2011	2012	2013
Fair value of interest rate swap	0	$ (1,759)	$ 935	0
Fair value of note payable	$100,000	$ 98,241	100,935	$100,000

Required:

Use the extended method demonstrated in Illustration A–2.

1. Calculate the net cash settlement at the end of 2011, 2012, and 2013.

2. Prepare the journal entries during 2011 to record the issuance of the note, interest, and necessary adjustments for changes in fair value.

3. Prepare the journal entries during 2012 to record interest, net cash interest settlement for the interest rate swap, and necessary adjustments for changes in fair value.

4. Prepare the journal entries during 2013 to record interest, net cash interest settlement for the interest rate swap, necessary adjustments for changes in fair value, and repayment of the debt.

5. Calculate the carrying values of both the swap account and the note in each of the three years.

6. Calculate the net effect on earnings of the hedging arrangement in each of the three years. (Ignore income taxes.)

7. Suppose the fair value of the note at December 31, 2011, had been $97,000 rather than $98,241 with the additional decline in fair value due to investors' perceptions that the creditworthiness of Labtech was worsening. How would that affect your entries to record changes in the fair values?

BROADEN YOUR PERSPECTIVE

Apply your critical-thinking ability to the knowledge you've gained. These cases will provide you an opportunity to develop your research, analysis, judgment, and communication skills. You also will work with other students, integrate what you've learned, apply it in real world situations, and consider its global and ethical ramifications. This practice will broaden your knowledge and further develop your decision-making abilities.

Real World Case A–1
Derivative losses; recognition in earnings

The following is an excerpt from a disclosure note of **Johnson & Johnson**:

15. Financial Instruments (in part)
As of December 28, 2008, the balance of deferred net gains on derivatives included in accumulated other comprehensive income was $121 million after-tax. The Company expects that substantially all of this amount will be reclassified into earnings over the next 12 months as a result of transactions that are expected to occur over that period.

Required:

1. Johnson & Johnson indicates that it expects that substantially all of the balance of deferred net gains on derivatives will be reclassified into earnings over the next 12 months as a result of transactions that are expected to occur over that period. What is meant by "reclassified into earnings"?

2. What type(s) of hedging transaction might be accounted for in this way?

Communication Case A–2
Derivatives; hedge accounting

A conceptual question in accounting for derivatives is: Should gains and losses on a hedge instrument be recorded as they occur, or should they be recorded to coincide (match) with income effects of the item being hedged?

ABI Wholesalers plans to issue long-term notes in May that will replace its $20 million of 9.5% bonds when they mature in July. ABI is exposed to the risk that interest rates in July will have risen, increasing borrowing costs (reducing the selling price of its notes). To hedge that possibility, ABI entered a (Treasury bond) futures contract in May to deliver (sell) bonds in July at their *current* price.

As a result, if interest rates rise, borrowing costs will go up for ABI because it will sell notes at a higher interest cost (or lower price). But that loss will be offset (approximately) by the gain produced by being in the opposite position on Treasury bond futures.

Two opposing viewpoints are:

View 1: Gains and losses on instruments designed to hedge anticipated transactions should be recorded as they occur.

View 2: Gains and losses on instruments designed to hedge anticipated transactions should be recorded to coincide (match) with income effects of the item being hedged.

In considering this question, focus on conceptual issues regarding the practicable and theoretically appropriate treatment, unconstrained by GAAP. Your instructor will divide the class into two to six groups depending on the size of the class. The mission of your group is to reach consensus on the appropriate accounting for the gains and losses on instruments designed to hedge anticipated transactions.

Required:

1. Each group member should deliberate the situation independently and draft a tentative argument prior to the class session for which the case is assigned.

2. In class, each group will meet for 10 to 15 minutes in different areas of the classroom. During that meeting, group members will take turns sharing their suggestions for the purpose of arriving at a single group treatment.

3. After the allotted time, a spokesperson for each group (selected during the group meetings) will share the group's solution with the class. The goal of the class is to incorporate the views of each group into a consensus approach to the situation.

Real World Case A–3
Researching the way interest rate futures prices are quoted on the Chicago Mercantile Exchange; retrieving information from the Internet

The **Chicago Mercantile Exchange**, or Merc, at 30 S. Wacker Drive in Chicago, is the world's largest financial exchange, an international marketplace enabling institutions and businesses to trade futures and options contracts including currencies, interest rates, stock indices, and agricultural commodities.

Required:

1. Access the Merc on the Internet. The web address is **www.cme.com**.

2. Access the daily settlement prices within the site. Scroll to find the 13-week Treasury bill futures.

3. What are the settlement prices for September futures contracts?

Research Case A–4
Issue related to the derivatives standard; research an article

In an effort to keep up with the rapidly changing global financial markets, the FASB issued standards on accounting for and disclosure of derivative financial instruments. A *Journal of Accountancy* article that discusses this standard is "The Decision on Derivatives," by Arlette C. Wilson, Gary Waters and Barry J. Bryan, November 1998.

Required:

On the Internet, go to the AICPA site at **www.aicpa.org** and find the article mentioned.

1. What are the primary problems or issues the FASB attempts to address regarding accounting for derivative financial instruments?

2. In considering the issues, the FASB made four fundamental decisions that became the cornerstones of the statement issued in 1998. What are those fundamental decisions? Which do you think is most critical to fair financial reporting?

UNITED STATES
SECURITIES AND EXCHANGE COMMISSION
Washington, D.C. 20549

Form 10-K

(Mark One)

☒ **ANNUAL REPORT PURSUANT TO SECTION 13 OR 15(d) OF THE SECURITIES EXCHANGE ACT OF 1934**

For the fiscal year ended: January 30, 2009

or

☐ **TRANSITION REPORT PURSUANT TO SECTION 13 OR 15(d) OF THE SECURITIES EXCHANGE ACT OF 1934**

For the transition period from _____ to _____

Commission file number: 0-17017

Dell Inc.
(Exact name of registrant as specified in its charter)

Delaware	**74-2487834**
(State or other jurisdiction of incorporation or organization)	(I.R.S. Employer Identification No.)

One Dell Way, Round Rock, Texas 78682
(Address of principal executive offices) (Zip Code)

Registrant's telephone number, including area code: **(512) 338-4400**

Securities registered pursuant to Section 12(b) of the Act:

Title of each class	Name of each exchange on which registered
Common Stock, par value $.01 per share	The NASDAQ Stock Market LLC

Securities Registered Pursuant to Section 12(g) of the Act: None

Indicate by check mark if the registrant is a well-known seasoned issuer, as defined in Rule 405 of the Securities Act.   Yes ☑   No ☐

Indicate by check mark if the registrant is not required to file reports pursuant to Section 13 or Section 15(d) of the Act.   Yes ☐   No ☑

Indicate by check mark whether the registrant (1) has filed all reports required to be filed by Section 13 or 15(d) of the Securities Exchange Act of 1934 during the preceding 12 months (or for such shorter period that the registrant was required to file such reports), and (2) has been subject to such filing requirements for the past 90 days.   Yes ☑ No ☐

Indicate by check mark if disclosure of delinquent filers pursuant to Item 405 of Regulation S-K is not contained herein, and will not be contained, to the best of registrant's knowledge, in definitive proxy or information statements incorporated by reference in Part III of this Form 10-K or any amendment to this Form 10-K.   ☐

Indicate by check mark whether the registrant is a large accelerated filer, an accelerated filer, a non-accelerated filer, or a smaller reporting company. See the definitions of "large accelerated filer", "accelerated filer", and "smaller reporting company" in Rule 12b-2 of the Exchange Act. (Check One):

Large accelerated filer ☑   Accelerated filer ☐

Non-accelerated filer ☐ (do not check if smaller reporting company)   Smaller reporting company ☐

Indicate by check mark whether the registrant is a shell company (as defined in Rule 12b-2 of the Act).   Yes ☐   No ☑

Approximate aggregate market value of the registrant's common stock held by non-affiliates as of August 1, 2008, based upon the closing price reported for such date on The NASDAQ Stock Market . . . . **$41.8 billion**

Number of shares of common stock outstanding as of March 13, 2009 . . . . **1,951,045,734**

Report of Independent Registered Public Accounting Firm

To the Board of Directors and
Shareholders of Dell Inc.:

In our opinion, the consolidated financial statements listed in the accompanying index present fairly, in all material respects, the financial position of Dell Inc. and its subsidiaries ("Company") at January 30, 2009 and February 1, 2008, and the results of their operations and their cash flows for each of the three years in the period ended January 30, 2009 in conformity with accounting principles generally accepted in the United States of America. In addition, in our opinion, the financial statement schedule listed in the accompanying index presents fairly, in all material respects, the information set forth therein when read in conjunction with the related consolidated financial statements. Also in our opinion, the Company maintained, in all material respects, effective internal control over financial reporting as of January 30, 2009, based on criteria established in *Internal Control — Integrated Framework* issued by the Committee of Sponsoring Organizations of the Treadway Commission (COSO). The Company's management is responsible for these financial statements and the financial statement schedule, for maintaining effective internal control over financial reporting, and for its assessment of the effectiveness of internal control over financial reporting included in Management's Report on Internal Control Over Financial Reporting appearing under Item 9A. Our responsibility is to express opinions on these financial statements, on the financial statement schedule, and on the Company's internal control over financial reporting based on our integrated audits. We conducted our audits in accordance with the standards of the Public Company Accounting Oversight Board (United States). Those standards require that we plan and perform the audits to obtain reasonable assurance about whether the financial statements are free of material misstatement and whether effective internal control over financial reporting was maintained in all material respects. Our audits of the financial statements included examining, on a test basis, evidence supporting the amounts and disclosures in the financial statements, assessing the accounting principles used and significant estimates made by management, and evaluating the overall financial statement presentation. Our audit of internal control over financial reporting included obtaining an understanding of internal control over financial reporting, assessing the risk that a material weakness exists, and testing and evaluating the design and operating effectiveness of internal control based on the assessed risk. Our audits also included performing such other procedures as we considered necessary in the circumstances. We believe that our audits provide a reasonable basis for our opinions.

In Fiscal 2008, the Company adopted new accounting standards which changed the manner in which it accounts for uncertain tax positions (Note 3) and certain hybrid financial instruments (Note 1).

A company's internal control over financial reporting is a process designed to provide reasonable assurance regarding the reliability of financial reporting and the preparation of financial statements for external purposes in accordance with generally accepted accounting principles. A company's internal control over financial reporting includes those policies and procedures that (i) pertain to the maintenance of records that, in reasonable detail, accurately and fairly reflect the transactions and dispositions of the assets of the company; (ii) provide reasonable assurance that transactions are recorded as necessary to permit preparation of financial statements in accordance with generally accepted accounting principles, and that receipts and expenditures of the company are being made only in accordance with authorizations of management and directors of the company; and (iii) provide reasonable assurance regarding prevention or timely detection of unauthorized acquisition, use, or disposition of the company's assets that could have a material effect on the financial statements.

Because of its inherent limitations, internal control over financial reporting may not prevent or detect misstatements. Also, projections of any evaluation of effectiveness to future periods are subject to the risk that controls may become inadequate because of changes in conditions, or that the degree of compliance with the policies or procedures may deteriorate.

/s/ PRICEWATERHOUSECOOPERS LLP

Austin, Texas
March 26, 2009

DELL INC.
CONSOLIDATED STATEMENTS OF FINANCIAL POSITION
(in millions)

	January 30, 2009	February 1, 2008
ASSETS		
Current assets:		
Cash and cash equivalents	$ 8,352	$ 7,764
Short-term investments	740	208
Accounts receivable, net	4,731	5,961
Financing receivables, net	1,712	1,732
Inventories, net	867	1,180
Other current assets	3,749	3,035
Total current assets	20,151	19,880
Property, plant, and equipment, net	2,277	2,668
Investments	454	1,560
Long-term financing receivables, net	500	407
Goodwill	1,737	1,648
Purchased intangible assets, net	724	780
Other non-current assets	657	618
Total assets	$ 26,500	$ 27,561
LIABILITIES AND EQUITY		
Current liabilities:		
Short-term debt	$ 113	$ 225
Accounts payable	8,309	11,492
Accrued and other	3,788	4,323
Short-term deferred service revenue	2,649	2,486
Total current liabilities	14,859	18,526
Long-term debt	1,898	362
Long-term deferred service revenue	3,000	2,774
Other non-current liabilities	2,472	2,070
Total liabilities	22,229	23,732
Commitments and contingencies (Note 10)		
Redeemable common stock and capital in excess of $.01 par value; shares issued and outstanding: 0 and 4, respectively (Note 4)	-	94
Stockholders' equity:		
Preferred stock and capital in excess of $.01 par value; shares authorized: 5,000; shares issued and outstanding: none	-	-
Common stock and capital in excess of $.01 par value; shares authorized: 7,000; shares issued: 3,338 and 3,320, respectively; shares outstanding: 1,944 and 2,060, respectively	11,189	10,589
Treasury stock at cost: 919 and 785 shares, respectively	(27,904)	(25,037)
Retained earnings	20,677	18,199
Accumulated other comprehensive income (loss)	309	(16)
Total stockholders' equity	4,271	3,735
Total liabilities and equity	$ 26,500	$ 27,561

The accompanying notes are an integral part of these consolidated financial statements.

DELL INC.
CONSOLIDATED STATEMENTS OF INCOME
(in millions, except per share amounts)

	Fiscal Year Ended		
	January 30, 2009	February 1, 2008	February 2, 2007
Net revenue	$ 61,101	$ 61,133	$ 57,420
Cost of net revenue	50,144	49,462	47,904
Gross margin	10,957	11,671	9,516
Operating expenses:			
Selling, general, and administrative	7,102	7,538	5,948
In-process research and development	2	83	-
Research, development, and engineering	663	610	498
Total operating expenses	7,767	8,231	6,446
Operating income	3,190	3,440	3,070
Investment and other income, net	134	387	275
Income before income taxes	3,324	3,827	3,345
Income tax provision	846	880	762
Net income	$ 2,478	$ 2,947	$ 2,583
Earnings per common share:			
Basic	$ 1.25	$ 1.33	$ 1.15
Diluted	$ 1.25	$ 1.31	$ 1.14
Weighted-average shares outstanding:			
Basic	1,980	2,223	2,255
Diluted	1,986	2,247	2,271

The accompanying notes are an integral part of these consolidated financial statements.

DELL INC.
CONSOLIDATED STATEMENTS OF CASH FLOWS
(in millions)

	Fiscal Year Ended		
	January 30, 2009	February 1, 2008	February 2, 2007
Cash flows from operating activities:			
Net income	$ 2,478	$ 2,947	$ 2,583
Adjustments to reconcile net income to net cash provided by operating activities:			
Depreciation and amortization	769	607	471
Stock-based compensation	418	329	368
In-process research and development charges	2	83	-
Effects of exchange rate changes on monetary assets and liabilities denominated in foreign currencies	(115)	30	37
Deferred income taxes	86	(308)	(262)
Other	231	121	(19)
Changes in operating assets and liabilities, net of effects from acquisitions:			
Accounts receivable	591	(990)	(542)
Financing receivables	(302)	(394)	(163)
Inventories	309	(498)	(72)
Other assets	(106)	(121)	(286)
Accounts payable	(3,117)	837	505
Deferred service revenue	611	1,032	516
Accrued and other liabilities	39	274	833
Change in cash from operating activities	1,894	3,949	3,969
Cash flows from investing activities:			
Investments:			
Purchases	(1,584)	(2,394)	(8,343)
Maturities and sales	2,333	3,679	10,320
Capital expenditures	(440)	(831)	(896)
Proceeds from sale of facility and land	44	-	40
Acquisition of business, net of cash received	(176)	(2,217)	(118)
Change in cash from investing activities	177	(1,763)	1,003
Cash flows from financing activities:			
Repurchase of common stock	(2,867)	(4,004)	(3,026)
Issuance of common stock under employee plans	79	136	314
Issuance (payment) of commercial paper, net	100	(100)	100
Proceeds from issuance of debt	1,519	66	52
Repayments of debt	(237)	(165)	(63)
Other	-	(53)	72
Change in cash from financing activities	(1,406)	(4,120)	(2,551)
Effect of exchange rate changes on cash and cash equivalents	(77)	152	71
Change in cash and cash equivalents	588	(1,782)	2,492
Cash and cash equivalents at beginning of the year	7,764	9,546	7,054
Cash and cash equivalents at end of the year	$ 8,352	$ 7,764	$ 9,546
Income tax paid	$ 800	$ 767	$ 652
Interest paid	$ 74	$ 54	$ 57

The accompanying notes are an integral part of these consolidated financial statements.

DELL INC.

CONSOLIDATED STATEMENTS OF STOCKHOLDERS' EQUITY
(in millions)

	Common Stock and Capital in Excess of Par Value		Treasury Stock		Retained Earnings	Accumulated Other Comprehensive Income/(Loss)	Other	Total
	Issued Shares	Amount	Shares	Amount				
Balances at February 3, 2006	2,818	$ 9,503	488	$ (18,007)	$ 12,699	$ (101)	$ (47)	$ 4,047
Net income	-	-	-	-	2,583	-	-	2,583
Change in net unrealized gain on investments, net of taxes	-	-	-	-	-	31	-	31
Foreign currency translation adjustments	-	-	-	-	-	(11)	-	(11)
Change in net unrealized gain on derivative instruments, net of taxes	-	-	-	-	-	30	-	30
Valuation of retained interests in securitized assets, net of taxes	-	-	-	-	-	23	-	23
Total comprehensive income	-	-	-	-	-	-	-	2,656
Stock issuances under employee plans	14	196	-	-	-	-	-	196
Repurchases	-	-	118	(3,026)	-	-	-	(3,026)
Stock-based compensation expense under SFAS 123(R)	-	368	-	-	-	-	-	368
Tax benefit from employee stock plans	-	56	-	-	-	-	-	56
Other and shares issued to subsidiaries	475	(16)	-	-	-	-	47	31
Balances at February 2, 2007	3,307	10,107	606	(21,033)	15,282	(28)	-	4,328
Net income	-	-	-	-	2,947	-	-	2,947
Impact of adoption of SFAS 155	-	-	-	-	29	(23)	-	6
Change in net unrealized gain on investments, net of taxes	-	-	-	-	-	56	-	56
Foreign currency translation adjustments	-	-	-	-	-	17	-	17
Change in net unrealized loss on derivative instruments, net of taxes	-	-	-	-	-	(38)	-	(38)
Total comprehensive income	-	-	-	-	-	-	-	2,988
Impact of adoption of FIN 48	-	(3)	-	-	(59)	-	-	(62)
Stock issuances under employee plans[a]	13	153	-	-	-	-	-	153
Repurchases	-	-	179	(4,004)	-	-	-	(4,004)
Stock-based compensation expense under SFAS 123(R)	-	329	-	-	-	-	-	329
Tax benefit from employee stock plans	-	3	-	-	-	-	-	3
Balances at February 1, 2008	3,320	10,589	785	(25,037)	18,199	(16)	-	3,735
Net income	-	-	-	-	2,478	-	-	2,478
Change in net unrealized loss on investments, net of taxes	-	-	-	-	-	(29)	-	(29)
Foreign currency translation adjustments	-	-	-	-	-	5	-	5
Change in net unrealized gain on derivative instruments, net of taxes	-	-	-	-	-	349	-	349
Total comprehensive income	-	-	-	-	-	-	-	2,803
Stock issuances under employee plans	18	173	-	-	-	-	-	173
Repurchases	-	-	134	(2,867)	-	-	-	(2,867)
Stock-based compensation expense under SFAS 123(R)	-	419	-	-	-	-	-	419
Tax benefit from employee stock plans	-	8	-	-	-	-	-	8
Balances at January 30, 2009	3,338	$ 11,189	919	$ (27,904)	$ 20,677	$ 309	$ -	$ 4,271

(a) Includes 1 million shares and $17 million related to redeemable common stock.

The accompanying notes are an integral part of these consolidated financial statements.

DELL INC.
NOTES TO CONSOLIDATED FINANCIAL STATEMENTS

NOTE 1 — DESCRIPTION OF BUSINESS AND SUMMARY OF SIGNIFICANT ACCOUNTING POLICIES

Description of Business — Dell Inc., a Delaware corporation (both individually and together with its consolidated subsidiaries, "Dell"), offers a broad range of technology product categories, including mobility products, desktop PCs, software and peripherals, servers and networking products, services, and storage. Dell sells its products and services directly to customers through dedicated sales representatives, telephone-based sales, and online at www.dell.com, and through a variety of indirect sales channels. Dell's customers include large corporate, government, healthcare, and education accounts, as well as small and medium businesses and individual consumers.

Fiscal Year — Dell's fiscal year is the 52- or 53-week period ending on the Friday nearest January 31. The fiscal years ending January 30, 2009, February 1, 2008, and February 2, 2007 included 52 weeks.

Principles of Consolidation — The accompanying consolidated financial statements include the accounts of Dell Inc. and its wholly-owned subsidiaries and have been prepared in accordance with accounting principles generally accepted in the United States of America ("GAAP"). All significant intercompany transactions and balances have been eliminated.

Dell was formerly a partner in Dell Financial Services L.L.C. ("DFS"), a joint venture with CIT Group Inc. ("CIT"). Dell purchased the remaining 30% interest in DFS from CIT effective December 31, 2007; therefore, DFS is a wholly-owned subsidiary at February 1, 2008. DFS' financial results have previously been consolidated by Dell in accordance with Financial Accounting Standards Board ("FASB") Interpretation No. 46R ("FIN 46R"), as Dell was the primary beneficiary. DFS allows Dell to provide its customers with various financing alternatives. See Note 6 of Notes to Consolidated Financial Statements for additional information.

Use of Estimates — The preparation of financial statements in accordance with GAAP requires the use of management's estimates. These estimates are subjective in nature and involve judgments that affect the reported amounts of assets and liabilities, the disclosure of contingent assets and liabilities at fiscal year-end, and the reported amounts of revenues and expenses during the fiscal year. Actual results could differ from those estimates.

Cash and Cash Equivalents — All highly liquid investments, including credit card receivables due from banks, with original maturities of three months or less at date of purchase are carried at cost and are considered to be cash equivalents. All other investments not considered to be cash equivalents are separately categorized as investments.

Investments — Dell's investments in debt securities are classified as available-for-sale and are reported at fair value (based on quoted prices and market observable inputs) using the specific identification method. Unrealized gains and losses, net of taxes, are reported as a component of stockholders' equity. Publicly traded equity securities are classified as trading and are reported at fair value (based on quoted prices and market observable inputs) using the specific identification method. Unrealized gains and losses are reported in investment and other income, net. Realized gains and losses on investments are included in investment and other income, net when realized. All other investments are initially recorded at cost. Any impairment loss to reduce an investment's carrying amount to its fair market value is recognized in income when a decline in the fair market value of an individual security below its cost or carrying value is determined to be other than temporary.

Financing Receivables — Financing receivables consist of customer receivables, residual interest and retained interest in securitized receivables. Customer receivables include revolving loans and fixed-term leases and loans resulting from the sale of Dell products and services. Financing receivables are presented net of the allowance for losses. See Note 6 of Notes to Consolidated Financial Statements for additional information.

Asset Securitization — Dell transfers certain financing receivables to unconsolidated qualifying special purpose entities in securitization transactions. These receivables are removed from the Consolidated Statement of Financial Position at the time they are sold in accordance with Statement of Financial Accounting Standards ("SFAS") No. 140, *Accounting for Transfers and Servicing of Financial Assets and Extinguishment of Liabilities — a Replacement of SFAS No. 125*. Receivables are considered sold when the receivables are transferred beyond the reach of Dell's creditors, the transferee has the right to pledge or exchange the assets, and Dell has surrendered control over the rights and obligations of the receivables. Gains and losses from the sale of revolving loans and fixed-term leases and loans are recognized in the period the sale occurs, based upon the relative fair value of the assets sold and the remaining retained interest. Subsequent to the sale, retained interest estimates are periodically updated based upon current information and events to determine the current fair value, with any changes in fair value recorded in earnings. In estimating the value of retained interest, Dell makes a variety of

DELL INC.

NOTES TO CONSOLIDATED FINANCIAL STATEMENTS (Continued)

financial assumptions, including pool credit losses, payment rates, and discount rates. These assumptions are supported by both Dell's historical experience and anticipated trends relative to the particular receivable pool. See Note 6 of Notes to Consolidated Financial Statements for additional information.

Allowance for Doubtful Accounts — Dell recognizes an allowance for losses on accounts receivable in an amount equal to the estimated probable future losses. The allowance is based on an analysis of historical bad debt experience, current receivables aging, expected future write-offs, as well as an assessment of specific identifiable customer accounts considered at risk or uncollectible. The expense associated with the allowance for doubtful accounts is recognized as selling, general, and administrative expense.

Allowance for Financing Receivables Losses — Dell recognizes an allowance for losses on financing receivables in an amount equal to the probable future losses net of recoveries. The allowance for losses is determined based on a variety of factors, including historical experience, past due receivables, receivable type, and risk composition. Financing receivables are charged to the allowance at the earlier of when an account is deemed to be uncollectible or when the account is 180 days delinquent. Recoveries on receivables previously charged off as uncollectible are recorded to the allowance for losses on financing receivables. The expense associated with the allowance for financing receivables losses is recognized as cost of net revenue. See Note 6 of Notes to Consolidated Financial Statements for additional information.

Inventories — Inventories are stated at the lower of cost or market with cost being determined on a first-in, first-out basis.

Property, Plant, and Equipment — Property, plant, and equipment are carried at depreciated cost. Depreciation is provided using the straight-line method over the estimated economic lives of the assets, which range from ten to thirty years for buildings and two to five years for all other assets. Leasehold improvements are amortized over the shorter of five years or the lease term. Gains or losses related to retirements or disposition of fixed assets are recognized in the period incurred. Dell capitalizes eligible internal-use software development costs incurred subsequent to the completion of the preliminary project stage. Development costs are amortized over the shorter of the expected useful life of the software or five years.

Impairment of Long-Lived Assets — In accordance with the provisions SFAS No. 144, "*Accounting for the Impairment or Disposal of Long-Lived Assets,*" Dell reviews long-lived assets for impairment when circumstances indicate the carrying amount of an asset may not be recoverable based on the undiscounted future cash flows of the asset. If the carrying amount of the asset is determined not to be recoverable, a write-down to fair value is recorded. Fair values are determined based on quoted market values, discounted cash flows, or external appraisals, as applicable. Dell reviews long-lived assets for impairment at the individual asset or the asset group level for which the lowest level of independent cash flows can be identified.

Business Combinations and Intangible Assets Including Goodwill — Dell accounts for business combinations using the purchase method of accounting and accordingly, the assets and liabilities of the acquired entities are recorded at their estimated fair values at the acquisition date. Goodwill represents the excess of the purchase price over the fair value of net assets, including the amount assigned to identifiable intangible assets. Given the time it takes to obtain pertinent information to finalize the fair value of the acquired assets and liabilities, it may be several quarters before Dell is able to finalize those initial fair value estimates. Accordingly, it is common for the initial estimates to be subsequently revised. The results of operations of acquired businesses are included in the Consolidated Financial Statements from the acquisition date.

Identifiable intangible assets with finite lives are amortized over their estimated useful lives. They are generally amortized on a non-straight line approach based on the associated projected cash flows in order to match the amortization pattern to the pattern in which the economic benefits of the assets are expected to be consumed. They are reviewed for impairment if indicators of potential impairment exist. Goodwill and indefinite lived intangible assets are tested for impairment on an annual basis in the second fiscal quarter, or sooner if an indicator of impairment occurs.

Foreign Currency Translation — The majority of Dell's international sales are made by international subsidiaries, most of which have the U.S. dollar as their functional currency. Dell's subsidiaries that do not have the U.S. dollar as their functional currency translate assets and liabilities at current rates of exchange in effect at the balance sheet date. Revenue and expenses from these international subsidiaries are translated using the monthly average exchange rates in effect for the period in which the items occur. Cumulative foreign currency translation adjustments totaled an $11 million loss, $16 million loss, and $33 million loss at January 30, 2009, February 1, 2008, and

DELL INC.

NOTES TO CONSOLIDATED FINANCIAL STATEMENTS (Continued)

February 2, 2007, respectively, and are included as a component of accumulated other comprehensive income (loss) in stockholders' equity.

Local currency transactions of international subsidiaries that have the U.S. dollar as the functional currency are remeasured into U.S. dollars using current rates of exchange for monetary assets and liabilities and historical rates of exchange for nonmonetary assets and liabilities. Gains and losses from remeasurement of monetary assets and liabilities are included in investment and other income, net. See Note 12 of Notes to Consolidated Financial Statements for additional information.

Hedging Instruments — Dell uses derivative financial instruments, primarily forwards, options, and swaps to hedge certain foreign currency and interest rate exposures. Dell also uses other derivative instruments not designated as hedges such as forwards to hedge foreign currency balance sheet exposures. Dell does not use derivatives for speculative purposes.

Dell applies SFAS No. 133, *Accounting for Derivative Instruments and Hedging Activities*, ("SFAS 133") as amended, which establishes accounting and reporting standards for derivative instruments and hedging activities. SFAS 133 requires Dell to recognize all derivatives as either assets or liabilities in its Consolidated Statements of Financial Position and measure those instruments at fair value. See Note 2 of Notes to Consolidated Financial Statements for a full description of Dell's derivative financial instrument activities and related accounting policies.

Treasury Stock — Dell accounts for treasury stock under the cost method and includes treasury stock as a component of stockholders' equity.

Revenue Recognition — Dell's revenue recognition policy is in accordance with the requirements of Staff Accounting Bulletin ("SAB") No. 104, *Revenue Recognition,* Emerging Issues Task Force ("EITF") 00-21, *Accounting for Revenue Arrangements with Multiple Deliverables*, AICPA Statement of Position ("SOP") No. 97-2, *Software Revenue Recognition,* EITF 01-09, *Accounting for Consideration Given by a Vendor to a Customer (Including a Reseller of the Vendor's Products)* ("EITF 01-09") and other applicable revenue recognition guidance and interpretations. Net revenues include sales of hardware, software and peripherals, and services (including extended service contracts and professional services). Dell recognizes revenue for these products when it is realized or realizable and earned. Revenue is considered realized and earned when:

- persuasive evidence of an arrangement exists;
- delivery has occurred or services have been rendered;
- Dell's fee to its customer is fixed or determinable; and
- collection of the resulting receivable is reasonably assured.

Revenue from the sale of products are recognized when title and risk of loss passes to the customer. Delivery is considered complete when products have been shipped to Dell's customer or services have been rendered, title and risk of loss has transferred to the customer, and customer acceptance has been satisfied through obtaining acceptance from the customer, the acceptance provision lapses, or Dell has evidence that the acceptance provisions have been satisfied.

Dell sells its products and services either separately or as part of a multiple-element arrangement. Dell allocates revenue from multiple-element arrangements to the elements based on the relative fair value of each element, which is generally based on the relative sales price of each element when sold separately. The allocation of fair value for a multiple-element arrangement involving software is based on vendor specific objective evidence ("VSOE"), or in the absence of VSOE for delivered elements, the residual method. Under the residual method, Dell allocates the residual amount of revenue from the arrangement to software licenses at the inception of the license term when VSOE for all undelivered elements, such as Post Contract Customer Support ("PCS"), exists and all other revenue recognition criteria have been satisfied. In the absence of VSOE for undelivered elements, revenue is deferred and subsequently recognized over the term of the arrangement. For sales of extended warranties with a separate contract price, Dell defers revenue equal to the separately stated price. Revenue associated with undelivered elements is deferred and recorded when delivery occurs or services are provided. Product revenue is recognized, net of an allowance for estimated returns, when both title and risk of loss transfer to the customer, provided that no significant obligations remain. Revenue from extended warranty and service contracts, for which Dell is obligated to perform, is recorded as deferred revenue and subsequently recognized over the term of the contract or when the service is completed. Revenue from sales of third-party extended warranty and service contracts or other products or software PCS, for which Dell is not obligated to perform, and for

DELL INC.

NOTES TO CONSOLIDATED FINANCIAL STATEMENTS (Continued)

which Dell does not meet the criteria for gross revenue recognition under EITF 99-19, *Reporting Revenue Gross as a Principal versus Net as an Agent*, is recognized on a net basis. All other revenue is recognized on a gross basis.

Dell records reductions to revenue for estimated customer sales returns, rebates, and certain other customer incentive programs. These reductions to revenue are made based upon reasonable and reliable estimates that are determined by historical experience, contractual terms, and current conditions. The primary factors affecting our accrual for estimated customer returns include estimated return rates as well as the number of units shipped that have a right of return that has not expired as of the balance sheet date. If returns cannot be reliably estimated, revenue is not recognized until a reliable estimate can be made or the return right lapses.

During Fiscal 2008, Dell began selling its products through retailers. Sales to Dell's retail customers are generally made under agreements allowing for limited rights of return, price protection, rebates, and marketing development funds. Dell has generally limited the return rights through contractual caps. Dell's policy for sales to retailers is to defer the full amount of revenue relative to sales for which the rights of return apply as Dell does not currently have sufficient historical data to establish reasonable and reliable estimates of returns, although Dell is in the process of accumulating the data necessary to develop reliable estimates in the future. All other sales for which the rights of return do not apply are recognized upon shipment when all applicable revenue recognition criteria have been met. To the extent price protection and return rights are not limited, all of the revenue and related cost are deferred until the product has been sold by the retailer, the rights expire, or a reliable estimate of such amounts can be made. Generally, Dell records estimated reductions to revenue or an expense for retail customer programs at the later of the offer or the time revenue is recognized in accordance with EITF 01-09. Dell's customer programs primarily involve rebates, which are designed to serve as sales incentives to resellers of Dell products and marketing funds.

Dell defers the cost of shipped products awaiting revenue recognition until revenue is recognized. These deferred costs totaled $556 million and $519 million at January 30, 2009, and February 1, 2008, respectively, and are included in other current assets on Dell's Consolidated Statement of Financial Position.

Dell records revenue from the sale of equipment under sales-type leases as product revenue at the inception of the lease. Sales-type leases also produce financing income, which Dell recognizes at consistent rates of return over the lease term. Customer revolving loan financing income is recognized when billed to the customer.

Dell reports revenue net of any revenue-based taxes assessed by governmental authorities that are imposed on and concurrent with specific revenue-producing transactions.

Warranty — Dell records warranty liabilities at the time of sale for the estimated costs that may be incurred under its limited warranty. The specific warranty terms and conditions vary depending upon the product sold and country in which Dell does business, but generally includes technical support, parts, and labor over a period ranging from one to three years. Factors that affect Dell's warranty liability include the number of installed units currently under warranty, historical and anticipated rates of warranty claims on those units, and cost per claim to satisfy Dell's warranty obligation. The anticipated rate of warranty claims is the primary factor impacting the estimated warranty obligation. The other factors are less significant due to the fact that the average remaining aggregate warranty period of the covered installed base is approximately 20 months, repair parts are generally already in stock or available at pre-determined prices, and labor rates are generally arranged at pre-established amounts with service providers. Warranty claims are relatively predictable based on historical experience of failure rates. If actual results differ from the estimates, Dell revises its estimated warranty liability. Each quarter, Dell reevaluates its estimates to assess the adequacy of its recorded warranty liabilities and adjusts the amounts as necessary.

Vendor Rebates — Dell may receive consideration from vendors in the normal course of business. Certain of these funds are rebates of purchase price paid and others are related to reimbursement of costs incurred by Dell to sell the vendor's products. Dell's policy for accounting for these funds is in accordance with EITF 02-16, *Accounting by a Customer (Including a Reseller) for Certain Consideration Received from a Vendor*. The funds are recognized as a reduction of cost of goods sold and inventory if the funds are a reduction of the price of the vendor's products. If the consideration is a reimbursement of costs incurred by Dell to sell or develop the vendor's products, then the consideration is classified as a reduction of that cost in the income statement, most often operating expenses. In order to be recognized as a reduction of operating expenses, the reimbursement must be for a specific, incremental, identifiable cost incurred by Dell in selling the vendor's products or services.

DELL INC.

NOTES TO CONSOLIDATED FINANCIAL STATEMENTS (Continued)

Loss Contingencies — Dell is subject to the possibility of various losses arising in the ordinary course of business. Dell considers the likelihood of loss or impairment of an asset or the incurrence of a liability, as well as Dell's ability to reasonably estimate the amount of loss, in determining loss contingencies. An estimated loss contingency is accrued when it is probable that an asset has been impaired or a liability has been incurred and the amount of loss can be reasonably estimated. Dell regularly evaluates current information available to determine whether such accruals should be adjusted and whether new accruals are required. Third parties have in the past and may in the future assert claims or initiate litigation related to exclusive patent, copyright, and other intellectual property rights to technologies and related standards that are relevant to Dell.

Shipping Costs — Dell's shipping and handling costs are included in cost of sales in the accompanying Consolidated Statements of Income for all periods presented.

Selling, General, and Administrative — Selling expenses include items such as sales salaries and commissions, marketing and advertising costs, and contractor services. Advertising costs are expensed as incurred and were $811 million, $943 million, and $836 million, during Fiscal 2009, 2008, and 2007, respectively. General and administrative expenses include items for Dell's administrative functions, such as Finance, Legal, Human Resources, and Information Technology support. These functions include costs for items such as salaries, maintenance and supplies, insurance, depreciation expense, and allowance for doubtful accounts.

Research, Development, and Engineering Costs — Research, development, and engineering costs are expensed as incurred, in accordance with SFAS No. 2, *Accounting for Research and Development Costs*. Research, development, and engineering expenses primarily include payroll and headcount related costs, contractor fees, infrastructure costs, and administrative expenses directly related to research and development support.

In Process Research and Development ("IPR&D") — IPR&D represents the fair value of the technology acquired in a business combination where technological feasibility has not been established and no future alternative uses exist. IPR&D is expensed immediately upon completion of the associated acquisition.

Website Development Costs — Dell expenses, as incurred, the costs of maintenance and minor enhancements to the features and functionality of its websites.

Income Taxes — Deferred tax assets and liabilities are recorded based on the difference between the financial statement and tax basis of assets and liabilities using enacted tax rates in effect for the year in which the differences are expected to reverse. Dell calculates a provision for income taxes using the asset and liability method, under which deferred tax assets and liabilities are recognized by identifying the temporary differences arising from the different treatment of items for tax and accounting purposes. In determining the future tax consequences of events that have been recognized in the financial statements or tax returns, judgment and interpretation of statutes is required. Additionally, Dell uses tax planning strategies as a part of its global tax compliance program. Judgments and interpretation of statutes are inherent in this process.

Comprehensive Income — Dell's comprehensive income is comprised of net income, unrealized gains and losses on marketable securities classified as available-for-sale, unrealized gains and losses related to the change in valuation of retained interest in securitized assets, foreign currency translation adjustments, and unrealized gains and losses on derivative financial instruments related to foreign currency hedging. Upon the adoption of SFAS No. 155, *Accounting for Certain Hybrid Financial Instruments — an amendment of FASB Statements No. 133 and 140*, beginning the first quarter of Fiscal 2008, all gains and losses in valuation of retained interest in securitized assets are recognized in income immediately and no longer included as a component of accumulated other comprehensive income (loss).

Earnings Per Common Share — Basic earnings per share is based on the weighted-average effect of all common shares issued and outstanding, and is calculated by dividing net income by the weighted-average shares outstanding during the period. Diluted earnings per share is calculated by dividing net income by the weighted-average number of common shares used in the basic earnings per share calculation plus the number of common shares that would be issued assuming exercise or conversion of all potentially dilutive common shares outstanding. Dell excludes equity instruments from the calculation of diluted earnings per share if the effect of including such instruments is antidilutive. Accordingly, certain stock-based incentive awards have been excluded from the calculation of diluted earnings per share totaling 252 million, 230 million, and 268 million shares during Fiscal 2009, 2008, and 2007, respectively.

DELL INC.

NOTES TO CONSOLIDATED FINANCIAL STATEMENTS (Continued)

The following table sets forth the computation of basic and diluted earnings per share for each of the past three fiscal years:

	Fiscal Year Ended		
	January 30, 2009	February 1, 2008	February 2, 2007
	(in millions, except per share amounts)		
Numerator:			
Net income	$ 2,478	$ 2,947	$ 2,583
Denominator:			
Weighted-average shares outstanding:			
Basic	1,980	2,223	2,255
Effect of dilutive options, restricted stock units, restricted stock, and other	6	24	16
Diluted	1,986	2,247	2,271
Earnings per common share:			
Basic	$ 1.25	$ 1.33	$ 1.15
Diluted	$ 1.25	$ 1.31	$ 1.14

Stock-Based Compensation — Effective February 4, 2006, stock-based compensation expense is recorded based on the grant date fair value estimate in accordance with the provisions of SFAS No. 123 (revised 2004), *Share-Based Payment* ("SFAS 123(R)"). In March 2005, the SEC issued SAB No. 107 ("SAB 107") regarding the SEC's interpretation of SFAS 123(R) and the valuation of share-based payments for public companies. We have applied the provisions of SAB 107 in our adoption of SFAS 123(R). See Note 5 of Notes to Consolidated Financial Statements included for further discussion of stock-based compensation.

Recently Issued and Adopted Accounting Pronouncements — In September 2006, the FASB issued SFAS No. 157, *Fair Value Measurements* ("SFAS 157"), which defines fair value, provides a framework for measuring fair value, and expands the disclosures required for assets and liabilities measured at fair value. SFAS 157 applies to existing accounting pronouncements that require fair value measurements; it does not require any new fair value measurements. Dell adopted the effective portions of SFAS 157 beginning the first quarter of Fiscal 2009, and it did not have a material impact to Dell's consolidated financial statements. In February 2008, FASB issued FASB Staff Position ("FSP") 157-2, *Effective Date of FASB Statement No. 157* ("FSP 157-2"), which delays the effective date of SFAS 157 for all nonfinancial assets and nonfinancial liabilities, except for items that are recognized or disclosed at fair value in the financial statements on a recurring basis (at least annually), until the beginning of the first quarter of Fiscal 2010. Dell is currently evaluating the inputs and techniques used in these measurements, including items such as impairment assessments of fixed assets and goodwill impairment testing. Management does not expect the adoption of FSP 157-2 to have a material impact on Dell's results of operations, financial position, and cash flows. See Note 2 of Notes to Consolidated Financial Statements for the impact of the adoption SFAS 157.

On October 10, 2008, the FASB issued FSP No. FAS 157-3 "*Determining the Fair Value of a Financial Asset When the Market for that Asset is Not Active*" ("FSP FAS 157-3"), which clarifies the application of SFAS 157 in a market that is not active. Additional guidance is provided regarding how the reporting entity's own assumptions should be considered when relevant observable inputs do not exist, how available observable inputs in a market that is not active should be considered when measuring fair value, and how the use of market quotes should be considered when assessing the relevance of inputs available to measure fair value. FSP FAS 157-3 became effective immediately upon issuance. Dell considered the additional guidance with respect to the valuation of its financial assets and liabilities and their corresponding designation within the fair value hierarchy. Its adoption did not have a material effect on Dell's consolidated financial statements.

In February 2007, the FASB issued SFAS No. 159, *The Fair Value Option for Financial Assets and Financial Liabilities* ("SFAS 159"), which provides companies with an option to report selected financial assets and liabilities at fair value with the changes in fair value recognized in earnings at each subsequent reporting date. SFAS 159 provides an opportunity to mitigate potential volatility in earnings

DELL INC.

NOTES TO CONSOLIDATED FINANCIAL STATEMENTS (Continued)

caused by measuring related assets and liabilities differently, and it may reduce the need for applying complex hedge accounting provisions. While SFAS 159 became effective for Dell's 2009 fiscal year, Dell did not elect the fair value measurement option for any of its financial assets or liabilities.

Recently Issued Accounting Pronouncements — In December 2007, the FASB issued SFAS No. 141(R), *Business Combinations* ("SFAS 141(R)"). SFAS 141(R) requires that the acquisition method of accounting be applied to a broader set of business combinations and establishes principles and requirements for how an acquirer recognizes and measures in its financial statements the identifiable assets acquired, liabilities assumed, any noncontrolling interest in the acquiree, and the goodwill acquired. SFAS 141(R) also establishes the disclosure requirements to enable the evaluation of the nature and financial effects of the business combination. SFAS 141(R) is effective for fiscal years beginning after December 15, 2008, and is required to be adopted by Dell beginning in the first quarter of Fiscal 2010. Management believes the adoption of SFAS 141(R) will not have an impact on Dell's results of operations, financial position, and cash flows for acquisitions completed prior to Fiscal 2010. The impact of SFAS 141 (R) on Dell's future consolidated results of operations and financial condition will be dependent on the size and nature of future combinations.

In December 2007, the FASB issued SFAS No. 160, *Noncontrolling Interests in Consolidated Financial Statements — an amendment of ARB No. 51* ("SFAS 160"). SFAS 160 requires that the noncontrolling interest in the equity of a subsidiary be accounted for and reported as equity, provides revised guidance on the treatment of net income and losses attributable to the noncontrolling interest and changes in ownership interests in a subsidiary and requires additional disclosures that identify and distinguish between the interests of the controlling and noncontrolling owners. SFAS 160 also establishes disclosure requirements that clearly identify and distinguish between the interests of the parent and the interests of the noncontrolling owners. SFAS 160 is effective for fiscal years beginning after December 15, 2008 and is required to be adopted by Dell beginning in the first quarter of Fiscal 2010. Management does not expect the adoption of SFAS 160 to have a material impact on Dell's results of operations, financial position, and cash flows.

In March 2008, the FASB issued SFAS No. 161, *Disclosures about Derivative Instruments and Hedging Activities, an amendment of FASB Statement No. 133* ("SFAS 161"), which requires additional disclosures about the objectives of derivative instruments and hedging activities, the method of accounting for such instruments under SFAS 133 and its related interpretations, and a tabular disclosure of the effects of such instruments and related hedged items on a company's financial position, financial performance, and cash flows. SFAS 161 does not change the accounting treatment for derivative instruments and is effective for Dell beginning Fiscal 2010.

Reclassifications — To maintain comparability among the periods presented, Dell has revised the presentation of certain prior period amounts reported within cash flow from operations presented in the Consolidated Statements of Cash Flows. The revision had no impact to the total change in cash from operating activities. Dell has also revised the classification of certain prior period amounts within the Notes to Consolidated Financial Statements. For further discussion regarding the reclassification of deferred service revenue and warranty liability, see Note 9 of Notes to Consolidated Financial Statements.

NOTE 2 — FINANCIAL INSTRUMENTS

Fair Value Measurements

On February 2, 2008, Dell adopted the effective portions of SFAS 157. In February 2008, the FASB issued FSP 157-2, which provides a one year deferral of the effective date of SFAS 157 for all nonfinancial assets and nonfinancial liabilities, except those that are recognized or disclosed at fair value in the financial statements on a recurring basis (at least annually). Therefore, Dell adopted the provisions of SFAS 157 with respect to only financial assets and liabilities. SFAS 157 defines fair value, establishes a framework for measuring fair value, and enhances disclosure requirements for fair value measurements. This statement does not require any new fair value measurements. SFAS 157 defines fair value as the price that would be received to sell an asset or paid to transfer a liability in an orderly transaction between market participants at the measurement date. In determining fair value, Dell uses various methods including market, income, and cost approaches. Dell utilizes valuation techniques that maximize the use of observable inputs and minimizes the use of unobservable inputs. The adoption of this statement did not have a material effect on the consolidated financial statements.

As a basis for categorizing these inputs, SFAS 157 establishes the following hierarchy, which prioritizes the inputs used to measure fair value from market based assumptions to entity specific assumptions:

• Level 1: Inputs based on quoted market prices for identical assets or liabilities in active markets at the measurement date.

DELL INC.

NOTES TO CONSOLIDATED FINANCIAL STATEMENTS (Continued)

- Level 2: Observable inputs other than quoted prices included in Level 1, such as quoted prices for similar assets and liabilities in active markets; quoted prices for identical or similar assets and liabilities in markets that are not active; or other inputs that are observable or can be corroborated by observable market data.

- Level 3: Inputs reflect management's best estimate of what market participants would use in pricing the asset or liability at the measurement date. The inputs are unobservable in the market and significant to the instrument's valuation.

The following table presents Dell's hierarchy for its assets and liabilities measured at fair value on a recurring basis as of January 30, 2009:

	Level 1 Quoted Prices in Active Markets for Identical Assets	Level 2 Significant Other Observable Inputs	Level 3 Significant Unobservable Inputs	Total
	(in millions)			
Investments — available for sale securities	$ -	$ 1,135	$ 27	$ 1,162
Investments — trading securities	1	73	-	74
Retained interest	-	-	396	396
Derivative instruments	-	627	-	627
Total assets measured at fair value on recurring basis	$ 1	$ 1,835	$ 423	$ 2,259
Derivative instruments	$ -	$ 131	$ -	$ 131
Total liabilities measured at fair value on recurring basis	$ -	$ 131	$ -	$ 131

The following section describes the valuation methodologies Dell uses to measure financial instruments at fair value:

Investments Available for Sale — The majority of Dell's investment portfolio consists of various fixed income securities such as U.S. government and agencies, U.S. and international corporate, and state and municipal bonds. This portfolio of investments, at January 30, 2009, is valued based on model driven valuations whereby all significant inputs are observable or can be derived from or corroborated by observable market data for substantially the full term of the asset. Dell utilizes a pricing service to obtain fair value pricing for the majority of the investment portfolio. Pricing for securities is based on proprietary models and inputs are documented in accordance with the SFAS 157 hierarchy. Dell conducts reviews on a quarterly basis to verify pricing, assess liquidity and determine if significant inputs have changed that would impact the SFAS 157 hierarchy disclosure.

Investments Trading Securities — The majority of Dell's trading portfolio consists of various mutual funds and a small amount of equity securities. The Level 1 securities are valued using quoted prices for identical assets in active markets. The Level 2 securities include various mutual funds that are not exchange-traded and valued at their net asset value, which can be market corroborated.

Retained Interest — The fair value of the retained interest in securitized receivables is determined using a discounted cash flow model. Significant assumptions to the model include pool credit losses, payment rates, and discount rates. These assumptions are supported by both historical experience and anticipated trends relative to the particular receivable pool. Retained interest in securitized receivables is included in financing receivables, current and long-term, on the Consolidated Statement of Financial Position. See Note 6 of Notes to Consolidated Financial Statements for additional information about retained interest.

Derivative Instruments — Dell's derivative financial instruments consist of foreign currency forward and purchased option contracts. The portfolio is valued using internal models based on market observable inputs, including forward and spot prices for currencies, and implied volatilities. Upon adoption of SFAS 157 in the first quarter of Fiscal 2009, Dell began factoring credit risk into the fair value

DELL INC.

NOTES TO CONSOLIDATED FINANCIAL STATEMENTS (Continued)

calculation of its derivative instrument portfolio. Credit risk is quantified through the use of Credit Default Swaps spreads based on a composite of Dell's counterparties, which represents the cost of protection in the event the counterparty or Dell were to default on the obligation.

The following table shows a reconciliation of the beginning and ending balances for fair value measurements using significant unobservable inputs (Level 3) for the fiscal year ended January 30, 2009:

Fiscal Year Ended January 30, 2009	Retained Interest	Investments Available for Sale	Total
	(in millions)		
Balance at February 1, 2008	$ 223	$ -	$ 223
Net unrealized (losses) gains included in earnings[a]	(8)	2	(6)
Issuances and settlements, net	181	-	181
Purchases	-	25	25
Balance at January 30, 2009	$ 396	$ 27	$ 423

(a) The unrealized gains on investments available for sale represent accrued interest.

Unrealized losses for the fiscal year ended January 30, 2009, related to the Level 3 retained interest asset and convertible debt security asset still held at the reporting date, are reported in income.

Items Measured at Fair Value on a Nonrecurring Basis — Certain financial assets and liabilities are measured at fair value on a nonrecurring basis and therefore not included in the recurring fair value table. The balances are not material relative to Dell's balance sheet, and there were no material non-recurring adjustments to disclose under the provisions of SFAS 157 for the fiscal year ended January 30, 2009.

Investments

The following table summarizes, by major security type, the fair value and cost of Dell's investments. All investments with remaining maturities in excess of one year are recorded as long-term investments in the Consolidated Statements of Financial Position.

	January 30, 2009				February 1, 2008			
	Fair Value	Cost	Unrealized Gain	Unrealized (Loss)	Fair Value	Cost	Unrealized Gain	Unrealized (Loss)
	(in millions)							
Debt securities:								
U.S. government and agencies	$ 539	$ 537	$ 3	$ (1)	$ 1,013	$ 991	$ 23	$ (1)
U.S. corporate	457	464	2	(9)	571	569	10	(8)
International corporate	78	77	1	(0)	68	67	1	-
State and municipal governments	5	5	0	-	5	5	-	-
Subtotal	1,079	1,083	6	(10)	1,657	1,632	34	(9)
Equity and other securities	115	115	-	-	111	111	-	-
Investments	$ 1,194	$ 1,198	$ 6	$ (10)	$ 1,768	$ 1,743	$ 34	$ (9)
Short-term	$ 740	$ 737	$ 4	$ (1)	$ 208	$ 206	$ 2	$ -
Long-term	454	461	2	(9)	1,560	1,537	32	(9)
Investments	$ 1,194	$ 1,198	$ 6	$ (10)	$ 1,768	$ 1,743	$ 34	$ (9)

DELL INC.

NOTES TO CONSOLIDATED FINANCIAL STATEMENTS (Continued)

The fair value of Dell's portfolio is affected primarily by interest rates more than the credit and liquidity issues currently facing the capital markets. Dell believes that its investments can be liquidated for cash on short notice. Dell's exposure to asset and mortgage backed securities was less than 1% of the value of the portfolio at January 30, 2009. Dell attempts to mitigate these risks by investing primarily in high credit quality securities with AAA and AA ratings and short-term securities with an A-1 rating, limiting the amount that can be invested in any single issuer, and by investing in short to intermediate term investments whose market value is less sensitive to interest rate changes. As part of its cash and risk management processes, Dell performs periodic evaluations of the credit standing of the institutions in accordance with its investment policy. Dell's investments in debt securities have effective maturities of less than five years. Management believes that no significant concentration of credit risk for investments exists for Dell.

At January 30, 2009, and February 1, 2008, Dell did not hold any auction rate securities. At January 30, 2009, and February 1, 2008, the total carrying value of investments in asset-backed and mortgage-backed debt securities was approximately $54 million and $550 million, respectively.

The following table summarizes Dell's debt securities that had unrealized losses at January 30, 2009, and their duration:

	Less Than 12 Months		12 Months or Greater		Total	
	Fair Value	Unrealized Loss	Fair Value	Unrealized Loss	Fair Value	Unrealized Loss
	(in millions)					
U.S. government and agencies	$ 158	$ (0)	$ 1	$ (1)	$ 159	$ (1)
U.S. corporate	197	(6)	13	(3)	210	(9)
International corporate	51	(0)	-	-	51	(0)
State and municipal governments	-	-	-	-	-	-
Total	$ 406	$ (6)	$ 14	$ (4)	$ 420	$ (10)

At January 30, 2009, Dell held investments in 160 debt securities that had fair values below their carrying values for a period of less than 12 months and 11 debt securities that had fair values below their carrying values for a period of 12 months or more. The unrealized losses are due to changes in interest rates and are expected to be recovered over the contractual term of the instruments. The unrealized loss of $10 million has been recorded in other comprehensive income (loss) as Dell believes that the investments are not other-than-temporarily impaired.

Dell periodically reviews its investment portfolio to determine if any investment is other-than-temporarily impaired due to changes in credit risk or other potential valuation concerns. During Fiscal 2009 Dell recorded an $11 million other-than-temporary impairment loss. Factors considered in determining whether a loss is other-than-temporary include the length of time and extent to which fair value has been less than the cost basis, the financial condition and near-term prospects of the investee, previous other-than-temporary impairment, and our intent and ability to hold the investment for a period of time sufficient to allow for any anticipated recovery in market value. The investments other-than-temporarily impaired during Fiscal 2009 were asset-backed securities and were impaired due to severe price degradation or price degradation over an extended period of time, rise in delinquency rates and general credit enhancement declines.

The following table summarizes Dell's gains and losses on investments recorded in investment and other income:

	Fiscal Year Ended		
	January 30, 2009	February 1, 2008	February 2, 2007
	(in millions)		
Gains	$ 14	$ 17	$ 9
Losses	(24)	(3)	(14)
Net realized (losses) gains	$ (10)	$ 14	$ (5)

DELL INC.

NOTES TO CONSOLIDATED FINANCIAL STATEMENTS (Continued)

Foreign Currency Instruments

As part of its risk management strategy, Dell uses derivative instruments, primarily forward contracts and options, to hedge certain foreign currency exposures. Dell's objective is to offset gains and losses resulting from these exposures with gains and losses on the derivative contracts used to hedge them, thereby reducing volatility of earnings and protecting fair values of assets and liabilities. Dell applies hedge accounting based upon the criteria established by SFAS 133, whereby Dell designates its derivatives as fair value hedges or cash flow hedges. Dell estimates the fair values of derivatives based on quoted market prices or pricing models using current market rates and records all derivatives in the Consolidated Statements of Financial Position at fair value.

Cash Flow Hedges

Dell uses a combination of forward contracts and options designated as cash flow hedges to protect against the foreign currency exchange rate risks inherent in its forecasted transactions denominated in currencies other than the U.S. dollar. The risk of loss associated with purchased options is limited to premium amounts paid for the option contracts. The risk of loss associated with forward contracts is equal to the exchange rate differential from the time the contract is entered into until the time it is settled. These contracts typically expire in 12 months or less. For derivative instruments that are designated and qualify as cash flow hedges, Dell records the effective portion of the gain or loss on the derivative instrument in accumulated other comprehensive income (loss) as a separate component of stockholders' equity and reclassifies these amounts into earnings in the period during which the hedged transaction is recognized in earnings. Dell reports the effective portion of cash flow hedges in the same financial statement line item, within earnings, as the changes in value of the hedged item.

For foreign currency option and forward contracts designated as cash flow hedges, Dell assesses hedge effectiveness both at the onset of the hedge as well as at the end of each fiscal quarter throughout the life of the derivative. Dell measures hedge ineffectiveness by comparing the cumulative change in the fair value of the hedge contract with the cumulative change in the fair value of the hedged item, both of which are based on forward rates. Dell recognizes any ineffective portion of the hedge, as well as amounts not included in the assessment of effectiveness, currently in earnings as a component of investment and other income, net. Hedge ineffectiveness for cash flow hedges was not material for Fiscal 2009, 2008, and 2007. During Fiscal 2009, 2008, and 2007, Dell did not discontinue any cash flow hedges that had a material impact on Dell's results of operations as substantially all forecasted foreign currency transactions were realized in Dell's actual results.

Changes in the aggregate unrealized net gain (loss) of Dell's cash flow hedges that are recorded as a component of comprehensive income (loss), net of tax, are presented in the table below. Dell expects to reclassify substantially all of the unrealized net gain recorded in accumulated other comprehensive income (loss) at January 30, 2009, into earnings during the next fiscal year, providing an offsetting economic impact against the settlement of the underlying transactions.

	Fiscal Year Ended		
	January 30, 2009	February 1, 2008	February 2, 2007
	(in millions)		
Aggregate unrealized net (losses) gains at beginning of year	$ (25)	$ 13	$ (17)
Net gains (losses) reclassified to earnings	603	(392)	(260)
Change in fair value of cash flow hedges	(254)	354	290
Aggregate unrealized net gains (losses) at end of year	$ 324	$ (25)	$ 13

Other Foreign Currency Derivative Instruments

Dell uses forward contracts to hedge monetary assets and liabilities, primarily receivables and payables, denominated in a foreign currency. The change in the fair value of these instruments represents a natural hedge as their gains and losses offset the changes in the underlying fair value of the monetary assets and liabilities due to movements in currency exchange rates. These contracts generally

DELL INC.

NOTES TO CONSOLIDATED FINANCIAL STATEMENTS (Continued)

expire in three months or less. These contracts are not designated as hedges under SFAS 133, and therefore, the change in the instrument's fair value is recognized currently in earnings as a component of investment and other income, net.

The gross notional value of foreign currency derivative financial instruments and the related net asset or liability was as follows:

	January 30, 2009		February 1, 2008	
	Gross Notional	Net Asset (Liability)	Gross Notional	Net Asset (Liability)
	(in millions)			
Cash flow hedges	$ 6,581	$ 542	$ 7,772	$ (9)
Other derivatives	581	(46)	(1,338)	8
	$ 7,162	$ 496	$ 6,434	$ (1)

Commercial Paper

Dell has a commercial paper program with a supporting senior unsecured revolving credit facility that allows Dell to obtain favorable short-term borrowing rates. The commercial paper program and related revolving credit facility were increased from $1.0 billion to $1.5 billion on April 4, 2008. Dell pays facility commitment fees at rates based upon Dell's credit rating. Unless extended, $500 million expires on April 3, 2009, and $1.0 billion expires on June 1, 2011. The credit facility requires compliance with conditions that must be satisfied prior to any borrowing, as well as ongoing compliance with specified affirmative and negative covenants, including maintenance of a minimum interest coverage ratio. Amounts outstanding under the facility may be accelerated for typical defaults, including failure to pay principal or interest, breaches of covenants, non-payment of judgments or debt obligations in excess of $200 million, occurrence of a change of control, and certain bankruptcy events. There were no events of default as of January 30, 2009.

At January 30, 2009, there was $100 million outstanding under the commercial paper program and no outstanding advances under the related revolving credit facilities. The weighted-average interest rate on these outstanding short-term borrowings was 0.19%. At February 1, 2008, there were no outstanding advances under the commercial paper program or the related credit facility. Dell uses the proceeds of the program for short-term liquidity needs.

India Credit Facilities

Dell India Pvt Ltd. ("Dell India"), Dell's wholly-owned subsidiary, maintains unsecured short-term credit facilities with Citibank N.A. Bangalore Branch India ("Citibank India") that provide a maximum capacity of $30 million to fund Dell India's working capital and import buyers' credit needs. The capacity increased from $30 million to $55 million on August 6, 2008. The incremental $25 million line of credit expired on December 31, 2008, and was not renewed. Financing is available in both Indian Rupees and foreign currencies. The borrowings are extended on an unsecured basis based on Dell's guarantee to Citibank N.A. Citibank India can cancel the facilities in whole or in part without prior notice, at which time any amounts owed under the facilities will become immediately due and payable. Interest on the outstanding loans is charged monthly and is calculated based on Citibank India's internal cost of funds plus 0.25%. At January 30, 2009, and February 1, 2008, outstanding advances from Citibank India totaled $12 million and $23 million, respectively, and are included in short-term debt on Dell's Consolidated Statement of Financial Position. There have been no events of default.

DELL INC.

NOTES TO CONSOLIDATED FINANCIAL STATEMENTS (Continued)

Long-Term Debt and Interest Rate Risk Management

The following table summarizes our long-term debt at:

	January 30, 2009	February 1, 2008
	(in millions)	
Long-term debt:		
Indenture:		
$600 million issued on April 17, 2008 at 4.70% due April 2013 with interest payable April 15 and October 15	$ 599	$ -
$500 million issued on April 17, 2008 at 5.65% due April 2018 with interest payable April 15 and October 15	499	-
$400 million issued on April 17, 2008 at 6.50% due April 2038 with interest payable April 15 and October 15	400	-
Senior Debentures		
$300 million issued on April 1998 at 7.10% due April 2028 with interest payable April 15 and October 15 (includes the impact of interest rate swaps)	400	359
Senior Notes		
$200 million issued on April 1998 at 6.55% due April 2008 with interest payable April 15 and October 15 (includes fair value adjustment related to SFAS 133)	-	201
	1,898	560
Other	-	2
Less current portion	-	(200)
Total long-term debt	$ 1,898	$ 362

During Fiscal 2009, Dell Inc. issued and sold debt comprising $600 million aggregate principal amount due 2013 with a fixed interest rate of 4.70% ("2013 Notes"), $500 million aggregate principal amount due 2018 with a fixed interest rate of 5.65% ("2018 Notes"), and $400 million aggregate principal amount due 2038 with a fixed interest rate of 6.50% Notes ("2038 Notes"), and together with the 2013 Notes and the 2018 Notes, ("Notes"). The Notes are unsecured obligations and rank equally with Dell's existing and future unsecured senior indebtedness. The Notes effectively rank junior to all indebtedness and other liabilities, including trade payables, of Dell's subsidiaries. The net proceeds from the offering of the Notes were approximately $1.5 billion after payment of expenses of the offering. The estimated fair value of the long-term debt was approximately $1.5 billion at January 30, 2009, compared to a carrying value of $1.5 billion at that date.

The Notes were issued pursuant to an Indenture dated as of April 17, 2008 ("Indenture"), between Dell and a trustee. The Indenture contains customary events of default with respect to the Notes, including failure to make required payments, failure to comply with certain agreements or covenants and certain events of bankruptcy and insolvency. The Indenture also contains covenants limiting Dell's ability to create certain liens, enter into sale-and-leaseback transactions and consolidate or merge with, or convey, transfer or lease all or substantially all of Dell's assets to, another person. The Notes will be redeemable, in whole or in part at any time, at Dell's option, at a "make-whole premium" redemption price calculated by Dell equal to the greater of (i) 100% of the principal amount of the Notes to be redeemed; and (ii) the sum of the present values of the remaining scheduled payments of principal and interest thereon (not including any portion of such payments of interest accrued as of the date of redemption) discounted to the date of redemption on a semi-annual basis (assuming a 360-day year consisting of twelve 30-day months) at the Treasury Rate (as defined in the Indenture) plus 35 basis points, plus accrued interest thereon to the date of redemption.

The Senior Debentures generally contain no restrictive covenants, other than a limitation on liens on Dell's assets and a limitation on sale-and-leaseback transactions involving Dell property. Interest rate swap agreements were entered into concurrently with the issuance of the Senior Debentures to convert the fixed rate to a floating rate for a notional amount of $300 million and were set to mature April 15, 2028.

DELL INC.

NOTES TO CONSOLIDATED FINANCIAL STATEMENTS (Continued)

The floating rates were based on three-month London Interbank Offered Rates plus 0.79%. In January 2009, Dell terminated its interest rate swap contracts with notional amounts totaling $300 million. Dell received $103 million in cash proceeds from the swap terminations, which included $1 million in accrued interest. These swaps had effectively converted its $300 million, 7.10% fixed rate Senior Debentures due 2028 to variable rate debt. As a result of the swap terminations, the fair value of the terminated swaps are reported as part of the carrying value of the Senior Debentures and are amortized as a reduction of interest expense over the remaining life of the debt. The cash flows from the terminated swap contracts are reported as operating activities in the Consolidated Statement of Cash Flows.

As of January 30, 2009, there were no events of default for the Indenture and the Senior Debentures.

Dell's effective interest rate for the Senior Debentures was 4.57% for Fiscal 2009. The principal amount of the debt was $300 million at January 30, 2009. The estimated fair value of the long-term debt was approximately $294 million at January 30, 2009, compared to a carrying value of $400 million at that date as a result of the termination of the interest rate swap agreements.

Prior to the termination of the interest rate swap contracts, the interest rate swaps qualified for hedge accounting treatment pursuant to SFAS No. 133, *Accounting for Derivative Instruments and Hedging Activities, as amended*. Dell designated the issuance of the Senior Debentures and the related interest rate swap agreements as an integrated transaction. The changes in the fair value of the interest rate swaps were reflected in the carrying value of the interest rate swaps on the balance sheet. The carrying value of the debt on the balance sheet was adjusted by an equal and offsetting amount. The differential to be paid or received on the interest rate swap agreements was accrued and recognized as an adjustment to interest expense as interest rates changed.

On April 15, 2008, Dell repaid the principal balance of the 1998 $200 million 6.55% fixed rate senior notes (the "Senior Notes") upon their maturity. Interest rate swap agreement related to the Senior Notes had a notional amount of $200 million and also matured April 15, 2008. Dell's effective interest rate for the Senior Notes, prior to repayment, was 4.03% for the first quarter of Fiscal 2009.

In November 2008, Dell filed a shelf registration statement with the SEC, which provides Dell with the ability to issue additional term debt up to $1.5 billion, subject to market conditions.

NOTE 3 — INCOME TAXES

Income before income taxes included approximately $2.6 billion, $3.2 billion, and $2.6 billion related to foreign operations in Fiscal 2009, 2008 and 2007 respectively.

The provision for income taxes consisted of the following:

	Fiscal Year Ended		
	January 30, 2009	February 1, 2008	February 2, 2007
	(in millions)		
Current:			
Domestic	$ 465	$ 901	$ 846
Foreign	295	287	178
Deferred	86	(308)	(262)
Provision for income taxes	$ 846	$ 880	$ 762

Deferred tax assets and liabilities for the estimated tax impact of temporary differences between the tax and book basis of assets and liabilities are recognized based on the enacted statutory tax rates for the year in which Dell expects the differences to reverse. A valuation allowance is established against a deferred tax asset when it is more likely than not that the asset or any portion thereof will not be realized. Based upon all the available evidence including expectation of future taxable income, Dell has provided a valuation allowance of $31 million related to state credit carryforwards, but determined that it will be able to realize the remainder of its deferred tax assets.

DELL INC.

NOTES TO CONSOLIDATED FINANCIAL STATEMENTS (Continued)

The components of Dell's net deferred tax asset are as follows:

	January 30, 2009	February 1, 2008
	(in millions)	
Deferred tax assets:		
Deferred revenue	$ 633	$ 597
Inventory and warranty provisions	36	46
Investment impairments and unrealized losses	5	10
Provisions for product returns and doubtful accounts	53	61
Capital loss	1	7
Leasing and financing	242	302
Credit carryforwards	47	3
Loss carryforwards	88	16
Stock-based and deferred compensation	233	188
Operating accruals	33	58
Compensation related accruals	48	40
Other	116	78
Deferred tax assets	1,535	1,406
Deferred tax liabilities:		
Property and equipment	(160)	(105)
Acquired intangibles	(204)	(199)
Unrealized gains	(14)	-
Other	(59)	(21)
Deferred tax liabilities	(437)	(325)
Valuation allowance	(31)	-
Net deferred tax asset	$ 1,067	$ 1,081
Current portion (included in other current assets)	$ 499	$ 596
Non-current portion (included in other non-current assets)	568	485
Net deferred tax asset	$ 1,067	$ 1,081

As of January 30, 2009, Dell has recorded $76 million of deferred tax assets related to acquired net operating loss and credit carryforwards. The offset for recording the acquired net operating loss and credit carryforwards was $56 million to goodwill and $20 million to additional-paid-in-capital. Utilization of the acquired carryforwards is subject to limitations due to ownership changes, which may delay the utilization of a portion of the acquired carryforwards. The carryforwards for significant taxing jurisdictions expire beginning Fiscal 2017.

Deferred taxes have not been recorded on the excess book basis in the shares of certain foreign subsidiaries because these basis differences are not expected to reverse in the foreseeable future and are expected to be permanent in duration. These basis differences in the amount of approximately $9.9 billion arose primarily from the undistributed book earnings of substantially all of the subsidiaries in which Dell intends to reinvest indefinitely. The basis differences could reverse through a sale of the subsidiaries or the receipt of dividends from the subsidiaries, as well as various other events. Net of available foreign tax credits, residual income tax of approximately $3.2 billion would be due upon reversal of this excess book basis as of January 30, 2009.

DELL INC.

NOTES TO CONSOLIDATED FINANCIAL STATEMENTS (Continued)

A portion of Dell's operations is subject to a reduced tax rate or is free of tax under various tax holidays that expire in whole or in part during Fiscal 2010 through 2018. Many of these tax holidays and reduced tax rates may be extended when certain conditions are met or may be terminated early if certain conditions are not met. The income tax benefits attributable to the tax status of these subsidiaries were estimated to be approximately $338 million ($0.17 per share) in Fiscal 2009, $502 million ($0.23 per share) in Fiscal 2008, and $282 million ($0.13 per share) in Fiscal 2007.

In March 2007, China announced a broad program to reform tax rates and incentives, effective January 1, 2008, including the introduction of phased-in transition rules that could significantly alter the Chinese tax structure for U.S. companies operating in China. Clarification of the rules, which phase in higher statutory tax rates over a five year period, was issued in late Fiscal 2008. As a result, Dell increased the relevant deferred tax assets to reflect the enacted statutory rates for the year in which it expects the differences to reverse, which resulted in an additional tax benefit of $27 million in Fiscal 2008.

The effective tax rate differed from the statutory U.S. federal income tax rate as follows:

	Fiscal Year Ended		
	January 30, 2009	February 1, 2008	February 2, 2007
U.S. federal statutory rate.....................................	35.0%	35.0%	35.0%
Foreign income taxed at different rates...........................	(11.2)	(13.6)	(14.9)
Imputed intercompany charges..................................	-	-	2.0
In-process research and development	-	0.8	-
Other..	1.6	0.8	0.7
Total	25.4%	23.0%	22.8%

The increase in Dell's Fiscal 2009 effective tax rate, compared to Fiscal 2008, is due primarily to an increased profitability mix in higher tax jurisdictions during Fiscal 2009 as compared to Fiscal 2008. The increase in Dell's Fiscal 2008 effective tax rate, compared to Fiscal 2007, is due to the tax related to accessing foreign cash and the nondeductibility of acquisition-related IPR&D charges offset primarily by the increase of consolidated profitability in lower foreign tax jurisdictions during Fiscal 2008 as compared to Fiscal 2007.

Dell adopted FIN No. 48, *Accounting for Uncertainty in Income Taxes — an interpretation of FASB Statement No. 109* ("FIN 48") effective February 3, 2007. FIN 48 provides that a tax benefit from an uncertain tax position may be recognized in the financial statements only when it is more likely than not that the position will be sustained upon examination, including resolution of any related appeals or litigation processes, based on the technical merits and a consideration of the relevant taxing authority's widely understood administrative practices and precedents. Once the recognition threshold is met, the portion of the tax benefit that is recorded represents the largest amount of tax benefit that is greater than 50 percent likely to be realized upon settlement with a taxing authority. The cumulative effect of adopting FIN 48 was a $62 million increase in tax liabilities and a corresponding decrease to the February 2, 2007 stockholders' equity balance of which $59 million related to retained earnings and $3 million related to additional-paid-in-capital. In addition, consistent with the provisions of FIN 48, Dell changed the classification of $1.1 billion of income tax liabilities from current to non-current because payment of cash is not anticipated within one year of the balance sheet date. These non-current income tax liabilities are recorded in other

DELL INC.

NOTES TO CONSOLIDATED FINANCIAL STATEMENTS (Continued)

non-current liabilities in the Consolidated Statements of Financial Position. A reconciliation of the beginning and ending amount of unrecognized tax benefits is as follows:

	Total
	(in millions)
Balance at February 3, 2007 (adoption)	$ 1,096
Increases related to tax positions of the current year	390
Increases related to tax positions of prior years	34
Reductions for tax positions of prior years	(13)
Lapse of statute of limitations	(6)
Settlements	(18)
Balance at February 1, 2008	$ 1,483
Increases related to tax positions of the current year	298
Increases related to tax positions of prior years	19
Reductions for tax positions of prior years	(217)
Lapse of statute of limitations	(7)
Settlements	(38)
Balance at January 30, 2009	$ 1,538

Fiscal 2009 reductions for tax positions of prior years in the table above include $163 million of items that did not impact Dell's effective tax rate for Fiscal 2009. These items include foreign currency translation, withdrawal of positions expected to be taken for prior year tax filings, and a reduction that is included in the deferred tax asset valuation allowance at January 30, 2009.

Associated with the unrecognized tax benefits of $1.5 billion at January 30, 2009, are interest and penalties as well as $166 million of offsetting tax benefits associated with estimated transfer pricing, the benefit of interest deductions, and state income tax benefits. The net amount of $1.8 billion, if recognized, would favorably affect Dell's effective tax rate.

Interest and penalties related to income tax liabilities are included in income tax expense. The balance of gross accrued interest and penalties recorded in the Consolidated Statements of Financial Position at January 30, 2009 and February 1, 2008, was $400 million and $288 million, respectively. During Fiscal 2009 and Fiscal 2008, $112 million and $88 million, respectively, related to interest and penalties were included in income tax expense.

Dell is currently under income tax audits in various jurisdictions, including the U.S. The tax periods open to examination by the major taxing jurisdictions to which Dell is subject include fiscal years 1997 through 2009. As a result of these audits, Dell maintains ongoing discussions and negotiations relating to tax matters with the taxing authorities in these various jurisdictions. Dell's U.S. Federal income tax returns for fiscal years 2004 through 2006 are under examination, and the Internal Revenue Service has proposed certain preliminary assessments primarily related to transfer pricing matters. Dell anticipates this audit will take several years to resolve and continues to believe that it has provided adequate reserves related to the matters under audit. However, should Dell experience an unfavorable outcome in this matter, it could have a material impact on its results of operations, financial position, or cash flows. Although the timing of income tax audit resolution and negotiations with taxing authorities are highly uncertain, Dell does not anticipate a significant change to the total amount of unrecognized income tax benefits within the next 12 months.

Dell takes certain non-income tax positions in the jurisdictions in which it operates and has received certain non-income tax assessments in various jurisdictions. Dell is also involved in related non-income tax litigation matters in various jurisdictions. Dell believes its positions are supportable, a liability is not probable, and that it will ultimately prevail. However, significant judgment is required in determining the ultimate outcome of these matters. In the normal course of business, Dell's positions and conclusions related to its non-income taxes could be challenged and assessments may be made. To the extent new information is obtained and Dell's views on its positions, probable outcomes of assessments, or litigation changes, changes in estimates to Dell's accrued liabilities would be recorded in the period in which the determination is made.

DELL INC.

NOTES TO CONSOLIDATED FINANCIAL STATEMENTS (Continued)

NOTE 4 — CAPITALIZATION

Preferred Stock

Authorized Shares — Dell has the authority to issue five million shares of preferred stock, par value $.01 per share. At January 30, 2009, and February 1, 2008, no shares of preferred stock were issued or outstanding.

Redeemable Common Stock

In prior years, Dell inadvertently failed to register with the SEC the issuance of some shares under certain employee benefit plans. These shares were purchased by participants between March 31, 2006, and April 3, 2007. As a result, certain purchasers of securities pursuant to those plans may have had the right to rescind their purchases for an amount equal to the purchase price paid for the securities, plus interest from the date of purchase. Dell made a registered rescission offer to eligible plan participants effective as of August 12, 2008. At February 1, 2008, and February 2, 2007, approximately 4 million shares ($94 million) and 5 million shares ($111 million), respectively, were classified outside stockholders' equity because the redemption features were not within Dell's control. Prior to the effective date of the rescission offer, as participants sold shares in the open market, the shares held outside of stockholders' equity were reclassified to common stock and capital in excess of $0.01 par value, accordingly. These shares were treated as outstanding for financial reporting purposes. The registered rescission offer expired on September 26, 2008, and payments of $29 million under the offer have been substantially completed. Upon expiration of the rescission offer, all remaining redeemable shares were reclassified to within stockholders' equity.

Common Stock

Authorized Shares — At January 30, 2009, Dell is authorized to issue 7.0 billion shares of common stock, par value $.01 per share.

Share Repurchase Program — Dell has a share repurchase program that authorizes it to purchase shares of common stock in order to increase shareholder value and manage dilution resulting from shares issued under Dell's equity compensation plans. However, Dell does not currently have a policy that requires the repurchase of common stock in conjunction with stock-based payment arrangements. During Fiscal 2009, Dell repurchased approximately 134 million shares for an aggregate cost of approximately $2.9 billion. At January 30, 2009, Dell's remaining authorized amount for share repurchases was $4.5 billion.

NOTE 5 — BENEFIT PLANS

Description of the Plans

Employee Stock Plans — Dell is currently issuing stock grants under the Dell Amended and Restated 2002 Long-Term Incentive Plan ("the 2002 Incentive Plan"), which was approved by shareholders on December 4, 2007. There are previous plans that have been terminated except for options previously granted under those plans that are still outstanding. These are all collectively referred to as the "Stock Plans".

The 2002 Incentive Plan provides for the granting of stock-based incentive awards to Dell's employees and non-employee directors. Awards may be incentive stock options within the meaning of Section 422 of the Internal Revenue Code, nonqualified stock options, restricted stock, or restricted stock units. There were approximately 313 million, 292 million, and 271 million shares of Dell's common stock available for future grants under the Stock Plans at January 30, 2009, February 1, 2008, and February 2, 2007, respectively. To satisfy stock option exercises, Dell has a policy of issuing new shares as opposed to repurchasing shares on the open market.

Stock Option Agreements — The right to purchase shares pursuant to existing stock option agreements typically vests pro-rata at each option anniversary date over a three- to five-year period. The options, which are granted with option exercise prices equal to the fair market value of Dell's common stock on the date of grant, generally expire within ten to twelve years from the date of grant.

Restricted Stock Awards — Awards of restricted stock may be either grants of restricted stock, restricted stock units, or performance-based stock units that are issued at no cost to the recipient. For restricted stock grants, at the date of grant, the recipient has all rights of a stockholder, subject to certain restrictions on transferability and a risk of forfeiture. Restricted stock grants typically vest over a three- to seven-year period beginning on the date of grant. For restricted stock units, legal ownership of the shares is not transferred to the

DELL INC.

NOTES TO CONSOLIDATED FINANCIAL STATEMENTS (Continued)

employee until the unit vests, which is generally over a three- to five-year period. Dell also grants performance-based restricted stock units as a long-term incentive in which an award recipient receives shares contingent upon Dell achieving performance objectives and the employees' continuing employment through the vesting period, which is generally over a three- to five-year period. Compensation expense recorded in connection with these performance-based restricted stock units is based on Dell's best estimate of the number of shares that will eventually be issued upon achievement of the specified performance criteria and when it becomes probable that certain performance goals will be achieved. The cost of these awards is determined using the fair market value of Dell's common stock on the date of the grant. Compensation expense for restricted stock awards with a service condition is recognized on a straight-line basis over the vesting term. Compensation expense for performance-based restricted stock awards is recognized on an accelerated multiple-award approach based on the most probable outcome of the performance condition.

Acceleration of Vesting of Options — On January 23, 2009, Dell's Board of Directors approved the acceleration of the vesting of unvested "out-of-the-money" stock options (options that have an exercise price greater than the current market stock price) with exercise prices equal to or greater than $10.14 per share for approximately 2,800 employees holding options to purchase approximately 21 million shares of common stock. Dell concluded the modification to the stated vesting provisions was substantive after Dell considered the volatility of its share price and the exercise price of the amended options in relation to recent share values. Because the modification was considered substantive, the remaining unearned compensation expense of $104 million was recorded as an expense in Fiscal 2009. The weighted-average exercise price of the options that were accelerated was $21.90.

Temporary Suspension of Option Exercises, Vesting of Restricted Stock Units, and Employee Stock Purchase Plan ("ESPP") Purchases — As a result of Dell's inability to timely file its Annual Report on Form 10-K for Fiscal 2007, Dell suspended the exercise of employee stock options, the settlement of restricted stock units, and the purchase of shares under the ESPP on April 4, 2007. Dell resumed allowing the exercise of employee stock options by employees and the settlement of restricted stock units on October 31, 2007. The purchase of shares under the ESPP was not resumed as the plan was discontinued during the first quarter of Fiscal 2009.

Dell decided to pay cash to current and former employees who held "in-the-money" stock options (options that have an exercise price less than the current market stock price) that expired during the period of unexercisability due to Dell's inability to timely file its Annual Report on Form 10-K for Fiscal 2007. During Fiscal 2008, Dell made payments of approximately $107 million, which were expensed, relating to in-the-money stock options that expired in the second and third quarters of Fiscal 2008.

General Information

Stock Option Activity — The following table summarizes stock option activity for the Stock Plans during Fiscal 2009:

	Number of Options (in millions)	Weighted-Average Exercise Price (per share)	Weighted-Average Remaining Contractual Term (in years)	Aggregate Intrinsic Value (in millions)
Options outstanding — February 1, 2008	264	$ 32.30		
Granted	13	19.71		
Exercised	(4)	19.08		
Forfeited	(4)	23.97		
Cancelled/expired	(39)	33.14		
Options outstanding — January 30, 2009	230	$ 31.85		
Vested and expected to vest (net of estimated forfeitures) — January 30, 2009[(a)(b)]	230	$ 31.86	3.9	$ -
Exercisable — January 30, 2009[(a)(b)]	230	$ 31.86	3.9	$ -

(a) For options vested and expected to vest and options exercisable, the aggregate intrinsic value in the table above represents the total pre-tax intrinsic value (the difference between Dell's closing stock price on January 30, 2009, and the exercise price multiplied by the number of in-the-money options) that would have been received by the option holders had the holders exercised their options on January 30, 2009. The intrinsic value changes based on changes in the fair market value of Dell's common stock.

(b) No options were in-the-money at January 30, 2009.

DELL INC.

NOTES TO CONSOLIDATED FINANCIAL STATEMENTS (Continued)

The following table summarizes stock option activity for the Stock Plans during Fiscal 2008:

	Number of Options (in millions)	Weighted-Average Exercise Price (per share)	Weighted-Average Remaining Contractual Term (in years)	Aggregate Intrinsic Value (in millions)
Options outstanding — February 2, 2007	314	$ 32.16		
Granted	12	24.45		
Exercised	(7)	18.99		
Forfeited.	(5)	26.80		
Cancelled/expired	(50)	32.01		
Options outstanding — February 1, 2008	264	$ 32.30		
Vested and expected to vest (net of estimated forfeitures) — February 1, 2008[a]	259	$ 32.43	4.5	$ 13
Exercisable — February 1, 2008[a]	242	$ 32.89	4.2	$ 12

The following table summarizes stock option activity for the Stock Plans during Fiscal 2007:

	Number of Options (in millions)	Weighted-Average Exercise Price (per share)	Weighted-Average Remaining Contractual Term (in years)	Aggregate Intrinsic Value (in millions)
Options outstanding — February 3, 2006	343	$ 31.86		
Granted	10	25.97		
Exercised	(13)	14.09		
Forfeited.	(4)	25.84		
Cancelled/expired	(22)	36.43		
Options outstanding — February 2, 2007	314	$ 32.16		
Vested and expected to vest (net of estimated forfeitures) — February 2, 2007[a]	309	$ 32.26	5.2	$ 148
Exercisable — February 2, 2007[a]	284	$ 32.74	5.1	$ 145

(a) For options vested and expected to vest and options exercisable, the aggregate intrinsic value in the table above represents the total pre-tax intrinsic value (the difference between Dell's closing stock price on February 1, 2008, and February 2, 2007, respectively, and the exercise price multiplied by the number of in-the-money options) that would have been received by the option holders had the holders exercised their options on February 1, 2008, and February 2, 2007, respectively. The intrinsic value changes based on changes in the fair market value of Dell's common stock.

DELL INC.

NOTES TO CONSOLIDATED FINANCIAL STATEMENTS (Continued)

Other information pertaining to stock options for the Stock Plans is as follows:

	Fiscal Years Ended		
	January 30, 2009	February 1, 2008	February 2, 2007
	(in millions, except per option data)		
Weighted-average grant date fair value of stock options granted per option	$ 5.87	$ 6.29	$ 6.90
Total fair value of options vested[a]	$ 187	$ 208	$ 415
Total intrinsic value of options exercised[b]	$ 15	$ 64	$ 171

(a) Includes the $104 million charge for the Fiscal 2009 acceleration of vesting of certain unvested and "out-of-the-money" stock options with exercise prices equal to or greater than $10.14 per share previously awarded under equity compensation plans.

(b) The total intrinsic value of options exercised represents the total pre-tax intrinsic value (the difference between the stock price at exercise and the exercise price multiplied by the number of options exercised) that was received by the option holders who exercised their options during the fiscal year.

At January 30, 2009, approximately $1 million of total unrecognized stock-based compensation expense, net of estimated forfeitures, related to stock options is expected to be recognized over a weighted-average period of approximately 2.3 years.

Non-vested Restricted Stock Activity — Non-vested restricted stock awards and activities were as follows:

	Fiscal 2009		Fiscal 2008		Fiscal 2007	
	Number of Shares	Weighted-Average Grant Date Fair Value	Number of Shares	Weighted-Average Grant Date Fair Value	Number of Shares	Weighted-Average Grant Date Fair Value
	(in millions)	(per share)	(in millions)	(per share)	(in millions)	(per share)
Non-vested restricted stock beginning balance ...	36	$ 24.90	17	$ 28.76	2	$ 34.66
Granted	18	19.11	26	22.85	21	28.36
Vested	(10)	24.64	(3)	28.79	(1)	28.84
Forfeited	(8)	23.15	(4)	24.71	(5)	29.29
Non-vested restricted stock ending balance	36	$ 22.45	36	$ 24.90	17	$ 28.76

	Fiscal Years Ended		
	January 30, 2009	February 1, 2008	February 2, 2007
	(in millions, except per option data)		
Weighted-average grant date fair value of restricted stock awards granted	$ 19.11	$ 22.85	$ 28.36
Total estimated grant date fair value of restricted stock awards vested	$ 252	$ 103	$ 16

At January 30, 2009, $507 million of unrecognized stock-based compensation expense, net of estimated forfeitures, related to non-vested restricted stock awards is expected to be recognized over a weighted-average period of approximately 2.0 years.

DELL INC.

NOTES TO CONSOLIDATED FINANCIAL STATEMENTS (Continued)

Expense Information under SFAS 123(R)

Stock-based compensation expense was allocated as follows:

	Fiscal Year Ended		
	January 30, 2009	February 1, 2008	February 2, 2007
	(in millions)		
Cost of net revenue	$ 62	$ 62	$ 59
Operating expenses	356	374	309
Stock-based compensation expense before taxes	418	436	368
Income tax benefit.	(131)	(127)	(110)
Stock-based compensation expense, net of income taxes	$ 287	$ 309	$ 258

Stock-based compensation in the table above includes $104 million of expense for accelerated options and a reduction of $1 million for the release of the accrual for expired stock options in Fiscal 2009 and $107 million of cash expense in Fiscal 2008 for expired stock options, as previously discussed.

Stock-based compensation expense is based on awards expected to vest, reduced for estimated forfeitures. SFAS 123(R) requires forfeitures to be estimated at the time of grant and revised, if necessary, in subsequent periods if actual forfeitures differ from those estimates.

Valuation Information

SFAS 123(R) requires the use of a valuation model to calculate the fair value of stock option awards. Dell has elected to use the Black-Scholes option pricing model, which incorporates various assumptions, including volatility, expected term, and risk-free interest rates. The volatility is based on a blend of implied and historical volatility of Dell's common stock over the most recent period commensurate with the estimated expected term of Dell's stock options. Dell uses this blend of implied and historical volatility, as well as other economic data, because management believes such volatility is more representative of prospective trends. The expected term of an award is based on historical experience and on the terms and conditions of the stock awards granted to employees. The dividend yield of zero is based on the fact that Dell has never paid cash dividends and has no present intention to pay cash dividends.

The weighted-average fair value of stock options and purchase rights under the employee stock purchase plan was determined based on the Black-Scholes option pricing model weighted for all grants utilizing the assumptions in the following table:

	Fiscal Years Ended		
	January 30, 2009	February 1, 2008	February 2, 2007
Expected term:			
Stock options	3.6 years	3.5 years	3.6 years
Employee stock purchase plan	N/A(a)	N/A(a)	3 months
Risk-free interest rate (U.S. Government Treasury Note)	2.3%	4.4%	4.8%
Volatility	37%	27%	26%
Dividends	0%	0%	0%

(a) No purchase rights were granted under the ESPP in Fiscal 2009 and Fiscal 2008 due to Dell suspending the ESPP on April 4, 2007, and subsequently discontinuing the plan effective the first quarter of Fiscal 2009 as a part of an overall assessment of its benefits strategy.

401(k) Plan — Dell has a defined contribution retirement plan (the "401(k) Plan") that complies with Section 401(k) of the Internal Revenue Code. Substantially all employees in the U.S. are eligible to participate in the 401(k) Plan. Effective January 1, 2008, Dell

DELL INC.

NOTES TO CONSOLIDATED FINANCIAL STATEMENTS (Continued)

matches 100% of each participant's voluntary contributions, subject to a maximum contribution of 5% of the participant's compensation, and participants vest immediately in all Dell contributions to the 401(k) Plan. From January 1, 2005, to December 31, 2007, Dell matched 100% of each participant's voluntary contributions, subject to a maximum contribution of 4% of the participant's compensation. Prior to January 1, 2005, Dell matched 100% of each participant's voluntary contributions, subject to a maximum contribution of 3% of the participant's compensation. Dell's contributions during Fiscal 2009, 2008, and 2007 were $93 million, $76 million, and $70 million, respectively. Dell's contributions are invested according to each participant's elections in the investment options provided under the Plan. Investment options include Dell stock, but neither participant nor Dell contributions are required to be invested in Dell stock.

Deferred Compensation Plan — Dell has a nonqualified deferred compensation plan (the "Deferred Compensation Plan") for the benefit of certain management employees and non-employee directors. The Deferred Compensation Plan permits the deferral of base salary and annual incentive bonus. The deferrals are held in a separate trust, which has been established by Dell to administer the Plan. The assets of the trust are subject to the claims of Dell's creditors in the event that Dell becomes insolvent. Consequently, the trust qualifies as a grantor trust for income tax purposes (i.e. a "Rabbi Trust"). In accordance with the provisions of EITF No. 97-14, *Accounting for Deferred Compensation Arrangements Where Amounts Earned are Held in a Rabbi Trust and Invested*, the assets and liabilities of the Deferred Compensation Plan are presented in long-term investments and accrued and other liabilities in the Consolidated Statements of Financial Position, respectively. The assets held by the trust are classified as trading securities with changes recorded to investment and other income, net. These assets are valued at $73 million and are disclosed in Note 2 of Notes to Consolidated Financial Statements. Changes in the deferred compensation liability are recorded to compensation expense.

Employee Stock Purchase Plan — Dell discontinued its shareholder approved employee stock purchase plan during the first quarter of Fiscal 2009. Prior to discontinuance, the ESPP allowed participating employees to purchase common stock through payroll deductions at the end of each three-month participation period at a purchase price equal to 85% of the fair market value of the common stock at the end of the participation period. Upon adoption of SFAS 123(R) in Fiscal 2007, Dell began recognizing compensation expense for the 15% discount received by the participating employees. No common stock was issued under this plan in Fiscal 2009 or Fiscal 2008 due to Dell suspending the ESPP on April 4, 2007, and subsequently discontinuing the ESPP as part of an overall assessment of its benefits strategy. Common stock issued under ESPP totaled 6 million shares in Fiscal 2007, and the weighted-average fair value of the purchase rights under the ESPP during Fiscal 2007 was $3.89.

NOTE 6 — FINANCIAL SERVICES

Dell Financial Services L.L.C.

Dell offers or arranges various financing options and services for its business and consumer customers in the U.S. through DFS. a wholly-owned subsidiary of Dell. DFS's key activities include the origination, collection, and servicing of customer receivables related to the purchase of Dell products.

Dell utilizes DFS to facilitate financing for customers who elect to finance products sold by Dell. New financing originations, which represent the amounts of financing provided to customers for equipment and related software and services through DFS, were $4.5 billion, $5.7 billion, and $6.1 billion, during the fiscal years ended January 30, 2009, February 1, 2008, and February 2, 2007, respectively.

CIT, formerly a joint venture partner of DFS, continues to have the right to purchase a percentage of new customer receivables facilitated by DFS until January 29, 2010 ("Fiscal 2010"). CIT's contractual funding right is up to 35% in Fiscal 2009 and up to 25% in Fiscal 2010. During Fiscal 2009 CIT's funding percentage was approximately 34%. DFS services the receivables purchased by CIT. However, Dell's obligation related to the performance of the DFS originated receivables purchased by CIT is limited to the cash funded credit reserves established at the time of funding.

DELL INC.

NOTES TO CONSOLIDATED FINANCIAL STATEMENTS (Continued)

Financing Receivables

The following table summarizes the components of Dell's financing receivables, net of the allowance for financing receivables losses:

	January 30, 2009	February 1, 2008
	(in millions)	
Customer receivables:		
Revolving loans, gross	$ 963	$ 1,063
Fixed-term leases and loans, gross	723	654
Customer receivables, gross	1,686	1,717
Customer receivables allowance	(149)	(96)
Customer receivables, net	1,537	1,621
Residual interest	279	295
Retained interest	396	223
Financing receivables, net	$ 2,212	$ 2,139
Short-term	$ 1,712	$ 1,732
Long-term	500	407
Financing receivables, net	$ 2,212	$ 2,139

Of the gross customer receivable balance at January 30, 2009, and February 1, 2008, $45 million and $444 million, respectively, represent balances which are due from CIT in connection with specified promotional programs.

Customer Receivables — The composition and credit quality of customer receivables vary from investment grade commercial customers to subprime consumers. Dell's estimate of subprime customer receivables was approximately 20% of the gross customer receivable balance at January 30, 2009, and February 1, 2008.

As of January 30, 2009, and February 1, 2008, customer financing receivables 60 days or more delinquent was $58 million and $34 million, respectively. These amounts represent 3.7% and 2.1% of the ending customer financing receivables balances for the respective years.

Net principal charge-offs for Fiscal 2009 and Fiscal 2008 were $86 million and $40 million, respectively. These amounts represent 5.5% and 2.7% of the average outstanding customer financing receivable balance (including accrued interest) for the respective years.

The following is a description of the components of customer receivables.

- Revolving loans offered under private label credit financing programs provide qualified customers with a revolving credit line for the purchase of products and services offered by Dell. Revolving loans bear interest at a variable annual percentage rate that is tied to the prime rate. Based on historical payment patterns, revolving loan transactions are typically repaid on average within 12 months. Revolving loans are included in short-term financing receivables in the table above. From time to time, account holders may have the opportunity to finance their Dell purchases with special programs during which, if the outstanding balance is paid in full, no interest is charged. These special programs generally range from 3 to 12 months. At January 30, 2009, and February 1, 2008, $352 million and $668 million, respectively, were receivable under these special programs.

- Dell enters into sales-type lease arrangements with customers who desire lease financing. Leases with business customers have fixed terms of two to five years. Future maturities of minimum lease payments at January 30, 2009 for future fiscal years are as follows: 2010: $219 million; 2011: $144 million; 2012: $67 million; 2013: $7 million and 2014: $0.1 million. Fixed-term loans are also offered to qualified small businesses, large commercial accounts, governmental organizations and educational entities.

DELL INC.

NOTES TO CONSOLIDATED FINANCIAL STATEMENTS (Continued)

Residual Interest — Dell retains a residual interest in the leased equipment. The amount of the residual interest is established at the inception of the lease based upon estimates of the value of the equipment at the end of the lease term using historical studies, industry data, and future value-at-risk demand valuation methods. On a quarterly basis, Dell assesses the carrying amount of its recorded residual values for impairment. Anticipated declines in specific future residual values that are considered to be other-than-temporary are recorded in current earnings.

Retained Interest — Retained interest represents the residual beneficial interest Dell retains in certain pools of securitized financing receivables. Retained interest is stated at the present value of the estimated net beneficial cash flows after payment of all senior interests. Dell values the retained interest at the time of each receivable transfer and at the end of each reporting period. The fair value of the retained interest is determined using a discounted cash flow model with various key assumptions, including payment rates, credit losses, discount rates, and remaining life of the receivables sold. These assumptions are supported by both Dell's historical experience and anticipated trends relative to the particular receivable pool. The weighted average assumptions for retained interest can be affected by the many factors, including asset type (revolving versus fixed), repayment terms, and the credit quality of assets being securitized.

The implementation of SFAS 157 did not result in material changes to the models or processes used to value retained interest. See Note 2 of Notes to Consolidated Financial Statements for the impact of the implementation of SFAS 157.

The following table summarizes the activity in retained interest balances and related cash flows:

	Fiscal Year Ended		
	January 30, 2009	February 1, 2008	February 2, 2007
	(in millions)		
Retained interest:			
Retained interest at beginning of year	$ 223	$ 159	$ 90
Issuances	427	173	167
Distributions from conduits	(246)	(132)	(142)
Net accretion	16	31	17
Change in fair value for the period	(24)	(8)	27
Retained interest at end of year	$ 396	$ 223	$ 159
Cash flows during the periods:			
Proceeds from new securitizations	$ 350	$ 538	$ 607
Distributions from conduits	246	132	142
Servicing and administration fees received	19	15	9
Repurchases of ineligible contracts	(5)	(11)	(7)
Cash flows during the period	$ 610	$ 674	$ 751

The table below summarizes the key assumptions used to measure the fair value of the retained interest as of January 30, 2009.

	Weighted Average Key Assumptions			
	Monthly Payment Rates	Credit Losses	Discount Rates	Life
		(lifetime)	(annualized)	(months)
Time of sale valuation of retained interest	12%	8%	14%	14
Valuation of retained interest	8%	12%	11%	11

DELL INC.

NOTES TO CONSOLIDATED FINANCIAL STATEMENTS (Continued)

The impact of adverse changes to the key valuation assumptions to the fair value of retained interest at January 30, 2009 is shown in the following table (in millions):

Expected prepayment speed: 10%	$ (9)
Expected prepayment speed: 20%	$ (17)
Expected credit losses: 10%	$ (13)
Expected credit losses: 20%	$ (21)
Discount rate: 10%	$ (5)
Discount rate: 20%	$ (10)

The analyses above utilized 10% and 20% adverse variation in assumptions to assess the sensitivities in fair value of the retained interest. However, these changes generally cannot be extrapolated because the relationship between a change in one assumption to the resulting change in fair value may not be linear. For the above sensitivity analyses, each key assumption was isolated and evaluated separately. Each assumption was adjusted by 10% and 20% while holding the other key assumptions constant. Assumptions may be interrelated, and changes to one assumption may impact others and the resulting fair value of the retained interest. For example, increases in market interest rates may result in lower prepayments and increased credit losses. The effect of multiple assumption changes were not considered in the analyses.

Asset Securitization

During Fiscal 2009 and Fiscal 2008, Dell transferred $1.4 billion and $1.2 billion respectively, of fixed-term leases and loans and revolving loans to unconsolidated qualifying special purpose entities. The qualifying special purpose entities are bankruptcy remote legal entities with assets and liabilities separate from those of Dell. The purpose of the qualifying special purpose entities is to facilitate the funding of financing receivables in the capital markets. The qualifying special purpose entities have entered into financing arrangements with three multi-seller conduits that, in turn, issue asset-backed debt securities in the capital markets. Two of the three conduits fund fixed-term leases and loans, and one conduit funds revolving loans. The principal balance of the securitized receivables at the end of Fiscal 2009 and Fiscal 2008 was $1.4 billion and $1.2 billion, respectively.

Dell services securitized contracts and earns a servicing fee. Dell's securitization transactions generally do not result in servicing assets and liabilities as the contractual fees are adequate compensation in relation to the associated servicing cost.

During Fiscal 2009, the disruption in the debt and capital markets resulted in reduced liquidity and increased costs for funding of financial assets. Due to a proposed increase to the cost structure in Dell's revolving securitization arrangement, Dell elected not to extend the terms of the agreement. This resulted in a scheduled amortization of the transaction. During this scheduled amortization period, all principal collections will be used to pay down the outstanding debt amount related to the securitized assets. The right to receive cash collections is delayed until the debt is fully paid.

During the scheduled amortization, no transfers of new revolving loans will occur. Additional purchases made on existing securitized revolving loans (repeat purchases) will continue to be transferred to the qualified special purpose entity and will increase the retained interest in securitized assets on the balance sheet.

Dell's securitization programs contain standard structural features related to the performance of the securitized receivables. These structural features include defined credit losses, delinquencies, average credit scores, and excess collections above or below specified levels. In the event one or more of these features are met and Dell is unable to restructure the program, no further funding of receivables will be permitted and the timing of expected retained interest cash flows will be delayed, which would impact the valuation of the retained interest. For the revolving transaction currently under scheduled amortization, performance features have been suspended.

As of January 30, 2009, and February 1, 2008, securitized financing receivables 60 days or more delinquent were $63 million and $54 million, respectively. These amounts represent 4.6% and 4.4% of the ending securitized financing receivables balances for the respective years.

Net principal charge-offs for Fiscal 2009 and Fiscal 2008, were $114 million and $81 million, respectively. These amounts represent 8.2% and 7.0% of the average outstanding securitized financing receivable balance for the respective years.

DELL INC.

NOTES TO CONSOLIDATED FINANCIAL STATEMENTS (Continued)

NOTE 7 — ACQUISITIONS

Dell has recorded all of its acquisitions using the purchase method of accounting in accordance with SFAS No. 141, *Business Combinations*. Accordingly, the results of operations of the acquired companies have been included in Dell's consolidated results since the date of each acquisition. Dell allocates the purchase price of its acquisitions to the tangible assets, liabilities, and intangible assets acquired, which include IPR&D charges, based on their estimated fair values. The excess of the purchase price over the fair value of the identified assets and liabilities has been recorded as goodwill. The fair value assigned to the assets acquired is based on valuations using management's estimates and assumptions. Dell does not expect the majority of goodwill related to these acquisitions to be deductible for tax purposes. In compliance with SFAS No. 142, *Goodwill and Other Intangible Assets*, Dell defines its reporting units as its reportable business segments. Dell has not presented pro forma results of operations because these acquisitions are not material to Dell's consolidated results of operations, financial position or cash flows on either an individual or an aggregate basis. Dell has included the results of operations of these transactions prospectively from the respective date of the transaction.

The purchase price allocations for these acquisitions are preliminary and subject to revision as more detailed analyses are completed and additional information about the fair value of assets and liabilities becomes available. Any change in the estimated fair value of the net assets, within one year of acquisition of the acquired companies, will change the amount of the purchase price allocable to goodwill.

Fiscal 2009 Acquisitions

Dell completed three acquisitions, The Networked Storage Company, MessageOne, Inc. ("MessageOne"), and Allin Corporation ("Allin") during Fiscal 2009 for approximately $197 million in cash. Dell recorded approximately $136 million of goodwill and approximately $64 million of purchased intangible assets related to these acquisitions. Dell also expensed approximately $2 million of IPR&D related to these acquisitions in Fiscal 2009. The larger of these transactions was the purchase of MessageOne for approximately $164 million in cash plus an additional $10 million to be used for management retention. MessageOne and Allin have been integrated into Dell's Global Services organization, which supports Dell's Americas Commercial; Europe, Middle East, and Africa ("EMEA") Commercial; and Asia Pacific-Japan ("APJ") Commercial segments, and The Networked Storage Company has been integrated into Dell's EMEA Commercial segment.

The acquisition of MessageOne was identified and acknowledged by Dell's Board of Directors as a related party transaction because Michael Dell and his family held indirect ownership interests in MessageOne. Consequently, Dell's Board directed management to implement a series of measures designed to ensure that the transaction was considered, analyzed, negotiated, and approved objectively and independent of any control or influence from the related parties.

Fiscal 2008 Acquisitions

EqualLogic Acquisition

On January 25, 2008, Dell completed its acquisition of EqualLogic Inc. ("EqualLogic"), a provider of high performance Internet Protocol (IP) iSCSI storage area network (SAN) solutions uniquely designed for virtualization and ease-of-use. Dell acquired 100% of the common shares of EqualLogic for approximately $1.4 billion in cash. Dell originally recorded approximately $969 million of goodwill and $486 million of amortizable intangible assets. This acquisition will strengthen Dell's product and channel position and assist Dell in its strategic efforts to simplify and virtualize IT for its customers globally. Dell also expensed IPR&D of $75 million resulting from the EqualLogic acquisition. Dell has included EqualLogic in its storage line of business for product revenue reporting purposes. Goodwill, which represents the excess of the purchase price over the net tangible and intangible assets acquired, is not deductible for tax purposes.

ASAP Software Acquisition

On November 9, 2007, Dell completed its acquisition of ASAP Software Express, Inc., ("ASAP"), a provider of software solutions and licensing services for approximately $353 million in cash. This acquisition will help Dell to simplify information technology by combining Dell's reach as a leading supplier of commercial technology and services and ASAP's expertise in software licensing and license management. In connection with the acquisition, Dell originally recorded approximately $130 million of goodwill and $171 million of amortizable intangible assets. Dell did not record any IPR&D in connection with the ASAP acquisition. Dell has

DELL INC.

NOTES TO CONSOLIDATED FINANCIAL STATEMENTS (Continued)

included ASAP in its software and peripherals line of business for product revenue reporting purposes. Goodwill, which represents the excess of the purchase price over the net tangible and intangible assets acquired, is expected to be deductible for tax purposes.

Other Acquisitions in Fiscal 2008

Dell acquired three other companies in Fiscal 2008, Everdream Corporation, Silverback Technologies Inc., and Zing Systems Inc. Dell also purchased CIT Group Inc.'s remaining 30% interest in DFS during Fiscal 2008. Total consideration for these purchases was approximately $553 million, which included direct transaction costs and certain liabilities recorded in connection with these acquisitions. The largest of these transactions was the purchase of CIT's 30% minority interest in DFS for approximately $306 million, which resulted in recognition of $245 million of goodwill and gave Dell 100% ownership of DFS. With these acquisitions Dell expects to be able to broaden its services and financing offerings to customers while simplifying IT. Dell originally recorded approximately $438 million of goodwill and $78 million of amortizable intangible assets in connection with these other acquisitions. Dell also expensed approximately $8 million of IPR&D related to these acquisitions in Fiscal 2008.

The following table summarizes the purchase price allocations of all Fiscal 2008 acquisitions, including original estimates and adjusted allocations:

	Original Allocations	Adjusted Allocations
	(in millions)	
Cash, cash equivalents, and short-term investments..............................	$ 31	$ 31
Other tangible assets	239	358
Liabilities..	(382)	(455)
Total net liabilities assumed	(112)	(66)
Amortizable intangible assets	735	725
Indefinite lived intangible assets	27	25
Total purchased intangibles	762	750
Goodwill	1,538	1,510
IPR&D	83	83
Total purchase price	$ 2,271	$ 2,277

The amortizable intangible assets are being amortized over their estimated useful lives based upon their expected future cash flows. The following table summarizes the original and adjusted cost of amortizable intangible assets related to Fiscal 2008 acquisitions and their weighted-average useful lives:

	Original Estimated Cost	Original Weighted-Average Useful Life	Adjusted Cost	Adjusted Weighted-Average Useful Life
	(in millions)	(years)	(in millions)	(years)
Technology	$ 484	5.8	$ 480	5.7
Customer relationships........................	220	9.4	212	9.0
Covenants not-to-compete	22	3.9	22	4.9
Tradenames.................................	8	5.3	10	5.3
Other	1	3.4	1	3.4
Total amortizable intangible assets	$ 735	6.8	$ 725	6.6

DELL INC.

NOTES TO CONSOLIDATED FINANCIAL STATEMENTS (Continued)

NOTE 8 — GOODWILL AND INTANGIBLE ASSETS

Goodwill

Goodwill allocated to Dell's business segments as of January 30, 2009, and February 1, 2008, and changes in the carrying amount of goodwill for the fiscal year ended January 30, 2009, were as follows:

	Americas Commercial	EMEA Commercial	APJ Commercial	Global Consumer	Total
	(in millions)				
Balance at February 1, 2008	$ 822	$ 412	$ 127	$ 287	$ 1,648
Goodwill acquired	78	37	21	-	136
Adjustments to goodwill	(31)	(14)	(10)	8	(47)
Balance at January 30, 2009	$ 869	$ 435	$ 138	$ 295	$ 1,737

	January 30, 2009	February 1, 2008
	(in millions)	
Balance at beginning of the year	$ 1,648	$ 110
Goodwill acquired during the year	136	1,538
Adjustments to goodwill	(47)	-
Balance at end of the year	$ 1,737	$ 1,648

Goodwill is tested annually during the second fiscal quarter and whenever events or circumstances indicate an impairment may have occurred. If the carrying amount of goodwill exceeds its fair value, estimated based on discounted cash flow analyses, an impairment charge would be recorded. Based on the results of its annual impairment tests, Dell determined that no impairment of goodwill existed at August 1, 2008, and for the fiscal years ended January 30, 2009, and February 1, 2008. The goodwill adjustments are primarily the result of purchase price allocation adjustments related to the finalization of deferred tax calculations and the effects of foreign currency adjustments where the purchase price was recorded in entities where the local currency is the functional currency. In the fourth quarter of Fiscal 2009, Dell updated its annual analysis of potential triggering events for goodwill and indefinite lived intangible asset impairments. Based on this analysis, Dell concluded that there was no evidence that would indicate an impairment of goodwill or indefinite lived intangible assets.

Intangible Assets

Dell's intangible assets associated with completed acquisitions at January 30, 2009, and February 1, 2008, are as follows:

	January 30, 2009			February 1, 2008		
	Gross	Accumulated Amortization	Net	Gross	Accumulated Amortization	Net
	(in millions)					
Technology	$ 524	$ (82)	$ 442	$ 492	$ (16)	$ 476
Customer relationships	243	(38)	205	231	(9)	222
Tradenames	41	(9)	32	39	(6)	33
Covenants not-to-compete	26	(6)	20	23	(1)	22
Amortizable intangible assets	$ 834	$ (135)	$ 699	$ 785	$ (32)	$ 753
Indefinite lived intangible assets	25	-	25	27	-	27
Total intangible assets	$ 859	$ (135)	$ 724	$ 812	$ (32)	$ 780

DELL INC.

NOTES TO CONSOLIDATED FINANCIAL STATEMENTS (Continued)

During Fiscal 2009 and Fiscal 2008, Dell recorded additions to intangible assets of $64 million and $762 million, respectively. Amortization expense related to finite-lived intangible assets was approximately $103 million and $27 million in Fiscal 2009 and in Fiscal 2008. During the year ended January 30, 2009, Dell did not record any impairment charges as a result of its analysis of its intangible assets.

Estimated future annual pre-tax amortization expense of finite-lived intangible assets as of January 30, 2009, over the next five fiscal years and thereafter is as follows:

Fiscal Years	(in millions)
2010.	$ 159
2011.	144
2012.	124
2013.	100
2014.	69
Thereafter.	103
Total.	$ 699

NOTE 9 — WARRANTY LIABILITY AND RELATED DEFERRED SERVICE REVENUE

Revenue from extended warranty and service contracts, for which Dell is obligated to perform, is recorded as deferred revenue and subsequently recognized over the term of the contract or when the service is completed. Dell records warranty liabilities at the time of sale for the estimated costs that may be incurred under its standard warranty. Changes in Dell's deferred revenue for extended warranties, and warranty liability for standard warranties which are included in other current and non-current liabilities on Dell's Consolidated Statements of Financial Position, are presented in the following tables:

	Fiscal Year Ended		
	January 30, 2009	February 1, 2008	February 2, 2007
	(in millions)		
Deferred service revenue:			
Deferred service revenue at beginning of year.	$ 5,260	$ 4,221	$ 3,707
Revenue deferred for new extended warranty and service contracts sold[b]	3,545	3,806	3,188
Revenue recognized[c]	(3,156)	(2,767)	(2,674)
Deferred service revenue at end of year	$ 5,649	$ 5,260	$ 4,221
Current portion	$ 2,649	$ 2,486	$ 2,032
Non-current portion	3,000	2,774	2,189
Deferred service revenue at end of year	$ 5,649	$ 5,260	$ 4,221

DELL INC.

NOTES TO CONSOLIDATED FINANCIAL STATEMENTS (Continued)

	Fiscal Year Ended		
	January 30, 2009	February 1, 2008	February 2, 2007
	(in millions)		
Warranty liability:			
Warranty liability at beginning of year	$ 929	$ 958	$ 951
Costs accrued for new warranty contracts and changes in estimates for pre-existing warranties[(a)(b)]	1,180	1,176	1,255
Service obligations honored[(c)]	(1,074)	(1,205)	(1,248)
Warranty liability at end of year	$ 1,035	$ 929	$ 958
Current portion	$ 721	$ 690	$ 768
Non-current portion	314	239	190
Warranty liability at end of year	$ 1,035	$ 929	$ 958

(a) Changes in cost estimates related to pre-existing warranties are aggregated with accruals for new standard warranty contracts. Dell's warranty liability process does not differentiate between estimates made for pre-existing warranties and new warranty obligations.

(b) Includes the impact of foreign currency exchange rate fluctuations.

(c) Fiscal 2008 and Fiscal 2007 amounts have been revised to include foreign currency exchange rate fluctuations in revenue deferred for new extended warranty and service contracts sold and costs accrued for new warranty contracts and changes in estimates for pre-existing warranties to conform to the current period presentation.

NOTE 10 — COMMITMENTS AND CONTINGENCIES

Severance Costs and Facility Closures — In Fiscal 2008, Dell announced a comprehensive review of costs that is currently ongoing. Since this announcement and through the end of Fiscal 2009, Dell reduced headcount and closed certain Dell facilities. Results of operations for Fiscal 2009 include net pre-tax charges of $282 million for these actions, which is comprised of $235 million related to headcount and a net $47 million related to facilities actions, including accelerated depreciation. Additionally, the sales of three facilities were finalized during Fiscal 2009 resulting in $44 million of proceeds reflected in cash from investing activities in the Consolidated Statements of Cash Flows. As of January 30, 2009, and February 1, 2008, the accrual related to these cost reductions and efficiency actions was $98 million and $35 million, respectively, which is included in accrued and other liabilities in the Consolidated Statements of Financial Position.

Lease Commitments — Dell leases property and equipment, manufacturing facilities, and office space under non-cancelable leases. Certain of these leases obligate Dell to pay taxes, maintenance, and repair costs. At January 30, 2009, future minimum lease payments under these non-cancelable leases are as follows: $89 million in Fiscal 2010; $77 million in Fiscal 2011; $63 million in Fiscal 2012; $42 million in Fiscal 2013; $34 million in Fiscal 2014; and $153 million thereafter.

Rent expense under all leases totaled $116 million, $118 million, and $78 million for Fiscal 2009, 2008, and 2007 respectively.

Restricted Cash — Pursuant to an agreement between DFS and CIT, Dell is required to maintain escrow cash accounts that are held as recourse reserves for credit losses, performance fee deposits related to Dell's private label credit card, and deferred servicing revenue. Restricted cash in the amount of $213 million and $294 million is included in other current assets on Dell's Consolidated Statements of Financial Position at January 30, 2009, and February 1, 2008, respectively.

Legal Matters — Dell is involved in various claims, suits, investigations, and legal proceedings. As required by SFAS No. 5, *Accounting for Contingencies*, Dell accrues a liability when it believes that it is both probable that a liability has been incurred and that it can reasonably estimate the amount of the loss. Dell reviews these accruals at least quarterly and adjusts them to reflect ongoing negotiations, settlements, rulings, advice of legal counsel, and other relevant information. However, litigation is inherently unpredictable. Therefore, Dell could incur judgments or enter into settlements of claims that could adversely affect its operating results or cash flows in a particular period.

DELL INC.

NOTES TO CONSOLIDATED FINANCIAL STATEMENTS (Continued)

The following is a discussion of Dell's significant legal matters.

• *Investigations and Related Litigation* — In August 2005, the SEC initiated an inquiry into certain of Dell's accounting and financial reporting matters and requested that Dell provide certain documents. The SEC expanded that inquiry in June 2006 and entered a formal order of investigation in October 2006. The SEC's requests for information were joined by a similar request from the United States Attorney for the Southern District of New York ("SDNY"), who subpoenaed documents related to Dell's financial reporting from and after Fiscal 2002. In August 2006, because of potential issues identified in the course of responding to the SEC's requests for information, Dell's Audit Committee, on the recommendation of management and in consultation with PricewaterhouseCoopers LLP, Dell's independent registered public accounting firm, initiated an independent investigation, which was completed in the third quarter of Fiscal 2008. Although the Audit Committee investigation has been completed, the investigations being conducted by the SEC and the SDNY are ongoing. Dell continues to cooperate with the SEC and the SDNY.

Dell and several of its current and former directors and officers were named as parties to securities, Employee Retirement Income Security Act of 1974 ("ERISA"), and shareholder derivative lawsuits all arising out of the same events and facts.

Four putative securities class actions filed between September 13, 2006 and January 31, 2007, in the Western District of Texas, Austin Division, against Dell and certain of its current and former officers were consolidated as *In re Dell Securities Litigation*, and a lead plaintiff was appointed by the court. The lead plaintiff asserted claims under sections 10(b), 20(a), and 20A of the Securities Exchange Act of 1934 based on alleged false and misleading disclosures or omissions regarding Dell's financial statements, governmental investigations, internal controls, known battery problems and business model, and based on insiders' sales of Dell securities. This action also included Dell's independent registered public accounting firm, PricewaterhouseCoopers LLP, as a defendant. On October 6, 2008, the court dismissed all of the plaintiff's claims with prejudice and without leave to amend. On November 3, 2008, the plaintiff filed a notice of appeal to the Fifth Circuit Court of Appeals with respect to the dismissal of Dell and the officer defendants.

Four other putative class actions filed between September 25, 2006 and October 5, 2006, in the Western District, Austin Division, by purported participants in the Dell 401(k) Plan were consolidated as *In re Dell ERISA Litigation*, and lead plaintiffs were appointed by the court. The lead plaintiffs asserted claims under ERISA based on allegations that Dell and certain current and former directors and officers imprudently invested and managed participants' funds and failed to disclose information regarding its stock held in the 401(k) Plan. On June 23, 2008, the court granted the defendants' motion to dismiss as to the plaintiffs' claims under ERISA based on allegations of imprudence, but the court denied the motion to dismiss as to the claims under ERISA based on allegations of a failure to accurately disclose information. On October 29, 2008, the court dismissed all of the individual plaintiffs' claims with prejudice.

In addition, seven shareholder derivative lawsuits filed between September 29, 2006 and January 22, 2007, in three separate jurisdictions were consolidated as *In re Dell Derivative Litigation* into three actions. One of those consolidated actions was pending in the Western District of Texas, Austin Division, but was dismissed without prejudice by an order filed October 9, 2007. The second consolidated shareholder derivative action was pending in Delaware Chancery Court. On October 16, 2008, the Delaware court granted the parties' stipulation to dismiss all of the plaintiffs' claims in the Delaware lawsuit without prejudice. The third consolidated shareholder derivative action is pending in state district court in Williamson County, Texas. These shareholder derivative lawsuits named various current and former officers and directors as defendants and Dell as a nominal defendant, and asserted various claims derivatively on behalf of Dell under state law, including breaches of fiduciary duties.

The Board of Directors received a shareholder demand letter, dated November 12, 2008, asserting allegations similar to those made in the securities and derivative lawsuits against various current and former officers and directors and PricewaterhouseCoopers LLP, and requesting that the Board of Directors investigate and assert claims relating to those allegations on behalf of Dell. The Board of Directors will consider and address the demand.

• *Copyright Levies* — Proceedings against the IT industry in Germany seek to impose levies on equipment such as personal computers and multifunction devices that facilitate making private copies of copyrighted materials. The total levies due, if imposed, would be based on the number of products sold and the per-product amounts of the levies, which vary. Dell, along with other companies and various industry associations, are opposing these levies and instead are advocating compensation to rights holders through digital rights management systems.

DELL INC.

NOTES TO CONSOLIDATED FINANCIAL STATEMENTS (Continued)

On December 29, 2005, Zentralstelle Für private Überspielungrechte ("ZPÜ"), a joint association of various German collection societies, instituted arbitration proceedings against Dell's German subsidiary before the Arbitration Body in Munich. ZPÜ claims a levy of €18.4 per PC that Dell sold in Germany from January 1, 2002, through December 31, 2005. On July 31, 2007, the Arbitration Body recommended a levy of €15 on each PC sold during that period for audio and visual copying capabilities. Dell and ZPÜ rejected the recommendation, and on February 21, 2008, ZPÜ filed a lawsuit in the German Regional Court in Munich. Dell plans to continue to defend this claim vigorously and does not expect the outcome to have a material adverse effect on its financial condition or results of operations.

Dell is involved in various other claims, suits, investigations, and legal proceedings that arise from time to time in the ordinary course of its business. Dell does not expect that the outcome in any of these other legal proceedings, individually or collectively, will have a material adverse effect on its financial condition or results of operations.

Certain Concentrations — All of Dell's foreign currency exchange and interest rate derivative instruments could involve elements of market and credit risk in excess of the amounts recognized in the consolidated financial statements. The counterparties to the financial instruments consist of a number of major financial institutions rated AA and A. In addition to limiting the amount of agreements and contracts it enters into with any one party, Dell monitors its positions with, and the credit quality of the counterparties to, these financial instruments. Dell does not anticipate nonperformance by any of the counterparties.

Dell's investments in debt securities are in high quality financial institutions and companies. As part of its cash and risk management processes, Dell performs periodic evaluations of the credit standing of the institutions in accordance with its investment policy. Dell's investments in debt securities have effective maturities of less than five years. Management believes that no significant concentration of credit risk for investments exists for Dell.

As of January 30, 2009, approximately 25% of Dell's cash and cash equivalents were deposited with two large financial institutions.

Dell markets and sells its products and services to large corporate clients, governments, healthcare and education accounts, as well as small and medium businesses and individuals. No single customer accounted for more than 10% of Dell's consolidated net revenue during Fiscal 2009, 2008, and 2007.

Dell purchases a number of components from single or limited sources. In some cases, alternative sources of supply are not available. In other cases, Dell may establish a working relationship with a single source or a limited number of sources if Dell believes it is advantageous due to performance, quality, support, delivery, capacity, or price considerations.

NOTE 11 — SEGMENT INFORMATION

Dell conducts operations worldwide. Effective the first quarter of Fiscal 2009, Dell combined the consumer business of EMEA, APJ, and Americas International (formerly reported through Americas Commercial) with the U.S. Consumer business and re-aligned its management and financial reporting structure. As a result, effective May 2, 2008, Dell's operating segments consisted of the following four segments: Americas Commercial, EMEA Commercial, APJ Commercial, and Global Consumer. Dell's commercial business includes sales to corporate, government, healthcare, education, small and medium business customers, and value-added resellers and is managed through the Americas Commercial, EMEA Commercial, and APJ Commercial segments. The Americas Commercial segment, which is based in Round Rock, Texas, encompasses the U.S., Canada, and Latin America. The EMEA Commercial segment, based in Bracknell, England, covers Europe, the Middle East, and Africa; and the APJ Commercial segment, based in Singapore, encompasses the Asian countries of the Pacific Rim as well as Australia, New Zealand, and India. The Global Consumer segment, which is based in Round Rock, Texas, includes global sales and product development for individual consumers and retailers around the world. Dell revised previously reported operating segment information to conform to its new operating segments in effect as of May 2, 2008.

On December 31, 2008, Dell announced its intent during Fiscal 2010 to move from geographic commercial segments to global business units reflecting the impact of globalization on its customer base. Customer requirements now share more commonality based on their sector rather than physical location. Dell expects to combine its current Americas Commercial, EMEA Commercial, and APJ Commercial segments and realign its management structure. After this realignment, Dell's operating structure will consist of the following segments: Global Large Enterprise, Global Public, Global Small and Medium Business, and its existing Global Consumer

DELL INC.

NOTES TO CONSOLIDATED FINANCIAL STATEMENTS (Continued)

segment. Dell will begin reporting these four global businesses once it completes the realignment of its management and financial reporting structure which is expected to be in the first half of Fiscal 2010.

Corporate expenses are included in Dell's measure of segment operating income for management reporting purposes; however, with the adoption of SFAS 123(R), stock-based compensation expense is not allocated to Dell's operating segments. Beginning in the fourth quarter of Fiscal 2008, acquisition-related charges such as in-process research and development and amortization of intangibles are not allocated to Dell's operating segments. The asset totals disclosed by geography are directly managed by those regions and include accounts receivable, inventory, certain fixed assets, and certain other assets. Corporate assets primarily include cash and cash equivalents, investments, deferred tax assets, goodwill, intangible assets, and other assets.

The following tables present net revenue by Dell's reportable segments as well as a reconciliation of consolidated segment operating income to Dell's consolidated operating income:

	Fiscal Year Ended		
	January 30, 2009	February 1, 2008	February 2, 2007
	(in millions)		
Net revenue			
Americas Commercial	$ 28,614	$ 29,981	$ 28,289
EMEA Commercial	13,617	13,607	11,842
APJ Commercial	7,341	7,167	6,223
Global Consumer	11,529	10,378	11,066
Net revenue	$ 61,101	$ 61,133	$ 57,420
Consolidated operating income			
Americas Commercial	$ 2,568	$ 2,566	$ 2,351
EMEA Commercial	544	978	622
APJ Commercial	458	424	335
Global Consumer	143	2	130
Consolidated segment operating income	$ 3,713	$ 3,970	$ 3,438
Stock-based compensation expense[a]	(418)	(436)	(368)
In-process research and development[b]	(2)	(83)	-
Amortization of intangible assets[b]	(103)	(11)	-
Consolidated operating income	$ 3,190	$ 3,440	$ 3,070

(a) Stock-based compensation expense includes $104 million of expense for accelerated options in Fiscal 2009 and $107 million of cash expense for expired stock options in Fiscal 2008. See Note 5 of Notes to Consolidated Financial Statements for additional information.

(b) Prior to the fourth quarter of Fiscal 2008, amortization of intangibles and IPR&D expenses of $16 million and $5 million are included in total consolidated segment operating income in Fiscal 2008 and 2007, respectively.

DELL INC.

NOTES TO CONSOLIDATED FINANCIAL STATEMENTS (Continued)

The following tables present depreciation expense and capital expenditures by Dell's reportable segments and assets by region:

	Fiscal Year Ended		
	January 30, 2009	February 1, 2008	February 2, 2007
	(in millions)		
Depreciation expense:			
Americas Commercial	$ 355	$ 286	$ 214
EMEA Commercial	101	124	95
APJ Commercial	80	86	71
Global Consumer	130	103	91
Total	$ 666	$ 599	$ 471
Capital expenditures:			
Americas Commercial	$ 242	$ 387	$ 490
EMEA Commercial	54	179	125
APJ Commercial	56	125	103
Global Consumer	88	140	178
Total	$ 440	$ 831	$ 896

	January 30, 2009	February 1, 2008
	(in millions)	
Assets:		
Corporate	$ 12,664	$ 15,336
Americas	8,781	6,524
EMEA	3,026	3,597
APJ	2,029	2,104
Total	$ 26,500	$ 27,561

The following tables present net revenue and long-lived asset information allocated between the U.S. and foreign countries:

	Fiscal Year Ended		
	January 30, 2009	February 1, 2008	February 2, 2007
	(in millions)		
Net revenue:			
United States	$ 31,569	$ 32,687	$ 32,361
Foreign countries	29,532	28,446	25,059
Net revenue	$ 61,101	$ 61,133	$ 57,420

DELL INC.

NOTES TO CONSOLIDATED FINANCIAL STATEMENTS (Continued)

	January 30, 2009	February 1, 2008	February 2, 2007
	(in millions)		
Long-lived assets:			
United States	$ 1,495	$ 1,622	$ 1,538
Foreign countries	782	1,046	871
Long-lived assets	$ 2,277	$ 2,668	$ 2,409

The allocation between domestic and foreign net revenue is based on the location of the customers. Net revenue and long-lived assets from any single foreign country did not comprise more than 10% of Dell's consolidated net revenues or long-lived assets during Fiscal 2009, 2008, and 2007. No single customer accounted for more than 10% of Dell's consolidated net revenue during Fiscal 2009, 2008, and 2007.

The following table presents net revenue by product groups:

	Fiscal Year Ended		
	January 30, 2009	February 1, 2008	February 2, 2007
	(in millions)		
Net revenue:			
Mobility	$ 18,638	$ 17,423	$ 15,480
Desktop PCs	17,244	19,573	19,815
Software and peripherals	10,603	9,908	9,001
Servers and networking	6,275	6,474	5,805
Enhanced services	5,715	5,320	5,063
Storage	2,626	2,435	2,256
Net revenue	$ 61,101	$ 61,133	$ 57,420

DELL INC.

NOTES TO CONSOLIDATED FINANCIAL STATEMENTS (Continued)

NOTE 12 — SUPPLEMENTAL CONSOLIDATED FINANCIAL INFORMATION

Supplemental Consolidated Statements of Financial Position Information:	January 30, 2009	February 1, 2008
	(in millions)	
Accounts receivable, net:		
Gross accounts receivable	$ 4,843	$ 6,064
Allowance for doubtful accounts	(112)	(103)
Total	$ 4,731	$ 5,961
Inventories, net:		
Production materials[a]	$ 454	$ 714
Work-in-process[a]	150	144
Finished goods[a]	263	322
Total	$ 867	$ 1,180
Prepaid expenses[b]	$ 447	$ 370
Property, plant, and equipment, net:		
Computer equipment	$ 1,967	$ 1,968
Land and buildings	1,544	1,635
Machinery and other equipment	999	1,011
Total property, plant, and equipment	4,510	4,614
Accumulated depreciation and amortization	(2,233)	(1,946)
Total	$ 2,277	$ 2,668
Accrued and other current liabilities:		
Warranty liability	$ 721	$ 690
Income taxes	6	99
Compensation	817	1,131
Other	2,244	2,403
Total	$ 3,788	$ 4,323
Other non-current liabilities:		
Warranty liability	$ 314	$ 239
Income taxes	1,738	1,463
Other	420	368
Total	$ 2,472	$ 2,070

(a) Certain prior period amounts have been changed to conform to the current year presentation. There is no impact to the consolidated financial statements as a result of this change.

(b) Prepaid expenses are included in other current assets on the Consolidated Statement of Financial Position.

DELL INC.

NOTES TO CONSOLIDATED FINANCIAL STATEMENTS (Continued)

The table below provides a detailed presentation of investment and other income, net for Fiscal 2009, Fiscal 2008, and Fiscal 2007:

	Fiscal Year Ended		
	January 30, 2009	February 1, 2008	February 2, 2007
	(in millions)		
Investment and other income, net:			
Investment income, primarily interest	$ 180	$ 496	$ 368
(Losses) gains on investments, net	(10)	14	(5)
Interest expense	(93)	(45)	(45)
CIT minority interest	-	(29)	(23)
Foreign exchange	115	(30)	(37)
Gain on sale of building	-	-	36
Other	(58)	(19)	(19)
Investment and other income, net	$ 134	$ 387	$ 275

NOTE 13 — UNAUDITED QUARTERLY RESULTS AND STOCK PRICES

Unaudited Quarterly Results — The following tables present selected unaudited Consolidated Statements of Income and stock sales price data for each quarter of Fiscal 2009 and Fiscal 2008:

	Fiscal Year 2009			
	First Quarter	Second Quarter	Third Quarter	Fourth Quarter
	(in millions, except per share data)			
Net revenue	$ 16,077	$ 16,434	$ 15,162	$ 13,428
Gross margin	$ 2,965	$ 2,827	$ 2,853	$ 2,312
Net income	$ 784	$ 616	$ 727	$ 351
Earnings per common share:				
Basic	$ 0.39	$ 0.31	$ 0.37	$ 0.18
Diluted	$ 0.38	$ 0.31	$ 0.37	$ 0.18
Weighted-average shares outstanding:				
Basic	2,036	1,991	1,953	1,944
Diluted	2,040	1,999	1,957	1,948
Stock sales price per share:				
High	$ 21.18	$ 25.26	$ 26.04	$ 13.32
Low	$ 18.13	$ 18.66	$ 10.59	$ 8.72

DELL INC.

NOTES TO CONSOLIDATED FINANCIAL STATEMENTS (Continued)

	Fiscal Year 2008			
	First Quarter	Second Quarter	Third Quarter	Fourth Quarter
	(in millions, except per share data)			
Net revenue	$ 14,722	$ 14,776	$ 15,646	$ 15,989
Gross margin	$ 2,838	$ 2,951	$ 2,888	$ 2,994
Net income	$ 756	$ 746	$ 766	$ 679
Earnings per common share:				
Basic	$ 0.34	$ 0.33	$ 0.34	$ 0.31
Diluted	$ 0.34	$ 0.33	$ 0.34	$ 0.31
Weighted-average shares outstanding:				
Basic	2,234	2,237	2,236	2,184
Diluted	2,254	2,264	2,266	2,201
Stock sales price per share:				
High	$ 25.95	$ 29.61	$ 30.77	$ 30.37
Low	$ 21.61	$ 24.64	$ 24.96	$ 18.87

IFRS Comprehensive Case

BRITISH AIRWAYS

British Airways, Plc. (BA), a U.K. company, prepares its financial statements according to International Financial Reporting Standards. BA's annual report for the year ended March 31, 2009, which includes financial statements and disclosure notes, is included with all new textbooks and can be found at **www.britishairways.com**. This case addresses a variety of characteristics of financial statements prepared using IFRS often comparing and contrasting those attributes of statements prepared under U.S. GAAP. Questions are grouped in parts according to various sections of the textbook. When answering questions, focus on BA's "Group" financial information (which is equivalent to "Consolidated" under U.S. GAAP).

Part A: Financial Statements, Income Measurement, and Current Assets

A1. Describe the apparent differences in the order of presentation of the components of the balance sheet between IFRS as applied by British Airways (BA) and a typical balance sheet prepared in accordance with U.S. GAAP.

A2. How does BA classify operating expenses in its income statement? How are these expenses typically classified in an income statement prepared in accordance with U.S. GAAP?

A3. How does BA classify interest paid, interest received, and dividends received in its statement of cash flows? What other alternatives, if any, does the company have for the classification of these items? How are these items classified under U.S. GAAP?

A4. BA changed how it accounts for BA miles that are earned by members of their "Executive Club." How does BA account for that revenue? Is this accounting approach consistent with how U.S. GAAP accounts for multiple-deliverable contracts? Explain. Based on your reading of the notes to the accounts, how important do you think this revenue is for BA?

A5. Examine BA's note 23, dealing with trade receivables. Do any aspects of that note appear unusual to you from the perspective of U.S. GAAP? Explain.

A6. What method does the company use to value its inventory? What other alternatives are available under IFRS? Under U.S. GAAP?

A7. BA's inventories are valued at the lower of cost and net realizable value. How does this approach differ from U.S. GAAP?

Part B: Property, Plant, and Equipment and Intangible Assets

B1. What method does BA use to amortize the cost of computer software development costs? How does this approach differ from U.S. GAAP?

B2. BA's property, plant and equipment is reported at cost. The Group has a policy of not revaluing property, plant and equipment. Suppose BA decided to revalue its equipment on March 31, 2009 and that the fair value of the equipment on that date was $280 million. Prepare the journal entry to record the revaluation assuming that the journal entry to record annual depreciation had already been recorded. (Hint: you will need to locate the original cost and accumulated depreciation of the equipment at the end of the year in the appropriate disclosure note.)

B3. Under U.S. GAAP, what alternatives do companies have to value their property, plant, and equipment?

B4. BA calculates depreciation of plant and equipment on a straight-line basis, over the useful life of the asset. Describe any differences between IFRS and U.S. GAAP in the calculation of depreciation.

B5. How often does BA review the residual values of its depreciable assets? How does this approach differ from U.S. GAAP?

B6. When does BA test for the possible impairment of goodwill and for other non-financial assets? How do these approaches differ from U.S. GAAP?

B7. Describe the approach BA uses to determine goodwill impairment losses. (Hint: see Note 19). How does this approach differ from U.S. GAAP?

B8. BA does not report any research and development expenses in its income statement. If it did, its approach to accounting for research and development would be significantly different from U.S. GAAP. Describe the differences between IFRS and U.S. GAAP in accounting for research and development expenditures.

B9. The following is included in BA's summary of significant accounting policies disclosure note. "Intangible assets are held at cost and are either amortised on a straight-line basis over their economic life, or they are deemed to have an indefinite economic life and are not amortised, but tested annually for impairment." Assume that on March 31, 2009, BA decided to revalue its Landing rights intangible assets and that the fair value on that date was determined to be $190 million. Amortization expense for the year already has been recorded. Prepare the journal entry to record the revaluation.

Part C: Investments

C1. How does BA account for "other current interest-bearing deposits"? Is that consistent with U.S. GAAP? What is the amount of those investments that are maturing after three months, as of March 31, 2009?

C2. How does BA account for "available-for-sale assets"? Is that approach consistent with U.S. GAAP? What is the amount of those investments as of March 31, 2009?

C3. How does BA account for its investments in associates? Is that accounting approach consistent with U.S. GAAP? Explain.

C4. BA accounts for its investment in Iberia airline using the equity method, even though it holds only 13.15% of Iberia's equity. Is that approach consistent with U.S. GAAP? Explain.

C5. BA indicates that it sometimes recognizes impairments on held-to-maturity and available-for-sale investments. Describe how recognition of impairments could differ for IFRS and U.S. GAAP. (Appendix 12B)

C6. BA recognized a £13 million impairment of their investment in Flybe for the year ended March 31, 2009. On what criteria did BA base their determination that the investment was impaired? Would that be handled similarly in U.S. GAAP? (Appendix 12B)

Part D: Liabilities

D1. BA has an account entitled "sales in advance of carriage." Explain the purpose of that account. Would transactions of this type be handled similarly under U.S. GAAP? What is the amount of "sales in advance of carriage," as of March 31, 2009?

D2. Note 30 lists "provisions for liabilities and charges." Is the threshold for recognizing a liability associated with these items any different under IFRS than it is under U.S. GAAP? Explain. By how much has the total amount of the BA Group's "provisions for liabilities and charges" increased or decreased during fiscal 2009?

D3. BA's note 37 lists contingent liabilities. Explain how the use of that term differs between IFRS and U.S. GAAP.

D4. **Sealy Corporation** reported the following line items in its statement of cash flows for the nine months ended August 30, 2009:

Amortization of discount on secured notes...	351,000
Amortization of debt issuance costs and other...	2,925,000

In British Airways' financial statements, Note 28: "Long-term borrowings" describes the company's long-term debt. Neither of the two items above is reported in the financial statements of British Airways, and neither is likely to appear there in the future. Why?

D5. Examine the long-term borrowings in BA's balance sheet and the related note. What, if any, convertible securities does the company have outstanding? Suppose BA issued £300 million fixed rate 8.75 per cent Eurobonds, due 2031, at 101 in 2011 and that the bonds are convertible into shares of BA ordinary shares. Suppose, too, that the company simultaneously issued at 99, bonds similar in all respects except they are not convertible. Prepare the journal entry BA would use to record the issue of the convertible bonds. Prepare the journal entry BA would use to record the issue of the convertible bonds if BA used U.S. GAAP.

D6. BA does not elect the fair value option (FVO) to report its financial liabilities. Examine Note 32: "Financial Instruments." If the company had elected the FVO for all of its fixed rate borrowings, what would be the balance at March 31, 2009 in the Fair value adjustment account?

D7. Is IFRS or U.S. GAAP more restrictive for determining when firms are allowed to elect the fair value option for financial assets and liabilities? Explain.

Part E: Leases, Income Taxes, and Pensions

E1. In Note 2: Summary of significant accounting policies, part d: Leased and hire purchase assets, BA states that "Where assets are financed through finance leases or hire purchase arrangements, under which substantially all the risks and rewards of ownership are transferred to the Group, the assets are treated as if they had been purchased outright." Is this the policy companies using U.S. GAAP follow in accounting for capital leases? Explain.

E2. Look at BA's Note 28: Long-term borrowings and Note 29: Operating lease commitments. Does BA obtain use of its aircraft more using operating leases or finance leases? Do lessees report operating and finance lease commitments the same way? Explain.

E3. Where in its March 31, 2009 balance sheet does BA report deferred taxes? How does this approach differ from the way deferred taxes are reported using U.S. GAAP? Using the Internet, determine how deferred taxes would be reported using IFRS at the time of your research. Explain why that approach might differ from the way BA reported deferred taxes at March 31, 2009.

E4. Here's an excerpt from one of BA's notes to its financial statements:

Taxation (in part)

Current tax assets and liabilities are measured at the amount expected to be recovered from or paid to the taxation authorities, based on tax rates and laws that are enacted or substantively enacted at the balance sheet date.

Is this policy consistent with U.S. GAAP? Explain.

E5. Here's an excerpt from one of BA's notes to its financial statements:

Taxation (in part)

Deferred income tax assets are recognised only to the extent that it is probable that taxable profit will be available against which the deductible temporary differences, carried forward tax credits or tax losses can be utilised.

Is this policy consistent with U.S. GAAP? Explain.

E6. Look at Note 36, part c. What amount of past service cost (called prior service cost under U.S. GAAP) did BA recognize in earnings for the year ended March 31, 2009? The Employee Benefit section within Note 2: "Summary of significant accounting policies" in BA's financial statements states that "Past service costs are recognised when the benefit has been given." Is this policy consistent with U.S. GAAP? Explain.

E7. The Employee Benefit section within Note 2: "Summary of significant accounting policies" in BA's financial statements states that:

"The asset or liability recognised in the balance sheet in respect of defined benefit pension plans is the present value of the defined benefit obligation at the balance sheet date, less the fair value of plan assets, together with adjustments for unrecognised past service costs. Where plan assets exceed the defined benefit obligation, an asset is recognised to the extent that an economic benefit is available to the Group, in accordance with the terms of the plan and applicable statutory requirements." Is this the way pension plans are reported under U.S. GAAP? Explain.

E8. U.S. GAAP requires that unrecognized actuarial gains and losses be included as part of Accumulated other comprehensive income (AOCI) in shareholders' equity. Under IFRS, AOCI often is referred to as a "reserve." Does BA report its unrecognized actuarial gains and losses this way? Explain. [Hint: see Note 35: Other reserves and minority interests.]

E9. Locate Note 36: "Pension costs," part c: "Amounts recognised in the income statement." Which components of pension expense does BA actually report in the operating profit (loss) section of its income statement? Where are the other components reported? Is this approach consistent with U.S. GAAP? Explain.

Part F: Shareholders' Equity and Additional Financial Reporting Issues

F1. British Airways lists four items in the shareholders' equity section of its balance sheet. If British Airways used U.S. GAAP, what would be the likely account titles for the first three of those components?

F2. Locate Note 35 in BA's financial statements. What three items comprise "Other reserves" as reported in the balance sheet? If British Airways used U.S. GAAP, what would be the likely account titles for the three items?

F3. Describe the apparent differences in the order of presentation of the components of liabilities and shareholders' equity between IFRS as applied by BA and a typical balance sheet prepared in accordance with U.S. GAAP.

F4. What is the amount that BA reports in its income statement for its stock options and other share-based compensation plans for the year ended March 31, 2009? [Hint: See Note 34: "Share options."] Are BA's share options cliff-vesting or graded-vesting? How does accounting differ between U.S. GAAP and IFRS for graded-vesting plans?

F5. What are the primary classifications into which BA's cash inflows and cash outflows are separated? Is this classification the same as or different from cash flow statements prepared in accordance with U.S. GAAP?

F6. How are cash inflows from dividends and interest and cash outflows for dividends and interest classified in BA's cash flow statements? Is this classification the same as or different from cash flow statements prepared in accordance with U.S. GAAP?

Glossary

Accounting equation the process used to capture the effect of economic events; Assets = Liabilities + Owner's Equity.

Accounting Principles Board (APB) the second private sector body delegated the task of setting accounting standards.

Accounts storage areas to keep track of the increases and decreases in financial position elements.

Accounts payable obligations to suppliers of merchandise or of services purchased on open account.

Accounts receivable receivables resulting from the sale of goods or services on account.

Accounts receivable aging schedule applying different percentages to accounts receivable balances depending on the length of time outstanding.

Accrual accounting measurement of the entity's accomplishments and resource sacrifices during the period, regardless of when cash is received or paid.

Accruals when the cash flow comes after either expense or revenue recognition.

Accrued interest interest that has accrued since the last interest date.

Accrued liabilities expenses already incurred but not yet paid (accrued expenses).

Accrued receivables the recognition of revenue earned before cash is received.

Accumulated benefit obligation (ABO) the discounted present value of estimated retirement benefits earned so far by employees, applying the plan's pension formula using existing compensation levels.

Accumulated other comprehensive income amount of other comprehensive income (nonowner changes in equity other than net income) accumulated over the current and prior periods.

Accumulated postretirement benefit obligation (APBO) portion of the EPBO attributed to employee service up to a particular date.

Acid-test ratio current assets, excluding inventories and prepaid items, divided by current liabilities.

Acquisition costs the amounts paid to acquire the rights to explore for undiscovered natural resources or to extract proven natural resources.

Activity-based method allocation of an asset's cost base using a measure of the asset's input or output.

Actuary a professional trained in a particular branch of statistics and mathematics to assess the various uncertainties and to estimate the company's obligation to employees in connection with its pension plan.

Additions the adding of a new major component to an existing asset.

Adjusted trial balance trial balance after adjusting entries have been recorded.

Adjusting entries internal transactions recorded at the end of any period when financial statements are prepared.

Allocation base the value of the usefulness that is expected to be consumed.

Allocation method the pattern in which the usefulness is expected to be consumed.

Allowance method recording bad debt expense and reducing accounts receivable indirectly by crediting a contra account (allowance for uncollectible accounts) to accounts receivable for an estimate of the amount that eventually will prove uncollectible.

American Institute of Accountants (AIA)/American Institute of Certified Public Accountants (AICPA) national organization of professional public accountants.

Amortization cost allocation for intangibles.

Amortization schedule schedule that reflects the changes in the debt over its term to maturity.

Annuity cash flows received or paid in the same amount each period.

Annuity due cash flows occurring at the beginning of each period.

Antidilutive securities the effect of the conversion or exercise of potential common shares would be to increase rather than decrease, EPS.

Articles of incorporation statement of the nature of the firm's business activities, the shares to be issued, and the composition of the initial board of directors.

Asset retirement obligations (AROs) obligations associated with the disposition of an operational asset.

Assets probable future economic benefits obtained or controlled by a particular entity as a result of past transactions or events.

Asset turnover ratio measure of a company's efficiency in using assets to generate revenue.

Assigning using receivables as collateral for loans; nonpayment of a debt will require the proceeds from collecting the assigned receivables to go directly toward repayment of the debt.

Attribution process of assigning the cost of benefits to the years during which those benefits are assumed to be earned by employees.

Auditors independent intermediaries who help ensure that management has appropriately applied GAAP in preparing the company's financial statements.

Auditor's report report issued by CPAs who audit the financial statements that informs users of the audit findings.

Average collection period indication of the average age of accounts receivable.

Average cost method assumes cost of goods sold and ending inventory consist of a mixture of all the goods available for sale.

Average days in inventory indicates the average number of days it normally takes to sell inventory.

Bad debt expense an operating expense incurred to boost sales; inherent cost of granting credit.

Balance sheet a position statement that presents an organized list of assets, liabilities, and equity at a particular point in time.

Balance sheet approach determination of bad debt expense by estimating the net realizable value of accounts receivable to be reported in the balance sheet.

Bank reconciliation comparison of the bank balance with the balance in the company's own records.

Bargain purchase option (BPO) provision in the lease contract that gives the lessee the option of purchasing the leased property at a bargain price.

Bargain renewal option gives the lessee the option to renew the lease at a bargain rate.

Basic EPS computed by dividing income available to common stockholders (net income less any preferred stock dividends) by the weighted-average number of common shares outstanding for the period.

Billings of construction contract contra account to the asset construction in progress; subtracted from construction in progress to determine balance sheet presentation.

Board of directors establishes corporate policies and appoints officers who manage the corporation.

Bond indenture document that describes specific promises made to bondholders.

Bonds A form of debt consisting of separable units (bonds) that obligates the issuing corporation to repay a stated amount at a specified maturity date and to pay interest to bondholders between the issue date and maturity.

Book value assets minus liabilities as shown in the balance sheet.

Callable allows the issuing company to buy back, or call, outstanding bonds from the bondholders before their scheduled maturity date.

Capital budgeting The process of evaluating the purchase of operational assets.

Capital leases installment purchases/sales that are formulated outwardly as leases.

Capital markets mechanisms that foster the allocation of resources efficiently.

Cash currency and coins, balances in checking accounts, and items acceptable for deposit in these accounts, such as checks and money orders received from customers.

Cash basis accounting/net operating cash flow difference between cash receipts and cash disbursements during a reporting period from transactions related to providing goods and services to customers.

Cash disbursements journal record of cash disbursements.

Cash discounts sales discounts; represent reductions not in the selling price of a good or service but in the amount to be paid by a credit customer if paid within a specific period of time.

Cash equivalents certain negotiable items such as commercial paper, money market funds, and U.S. Treasury bills that are highly liquid investments quickly convertible to cash.

Cash equivalents short-term, highly liquid investments that can be readily converted to cash with little risk of loss.

Cash flow hedge a derivative used to hedge against the exposure to changes in cash inflows or cash outflows of an asset or liability or a forecasted transaction (like a future purchase or sale).

Cash flows from financing activities both inflows and outflows of cash resulting from the external financing of a business.

Cash flows from investing activities both outflows and inflows of cash caused by the acquisition and disposition of assets.

Cash flows from operating activities both inflows and outflows of cash that result from activities reported on the income statement.

Cash receipts journal record of cash receipts.

Certified Public Accountants (CPAs) licensed individuals who can represent that the financial statements have been audited in accordance with generally accepted auditing standards.

Change in accounting estimate a change in an estimate when new information comes to light.

Change in accounting principle switch by a company from one accounting method to another.

Change in reporting entity presentation of consolidated financial statements in place of statements of individual companies, or a change in the specific companies that constitute the group for which consolidated or combined statements are prepared.

Closing process the temporary accounts are reduced to zero balances, and these temporary account balances are closed (transferred) to retained earnings to reflect the changes that have occurred in that account during the period.

Commercial paper unsecured notes sold in minimum denominations of $25,000 with maturities ranging from 30 to 270 days.

Committee on Accounting Procedure (CAP) the first private sector body that was delegated the task of setting accounting standards.

Comparability the ability to help users see similarities and differences among events and conditions.

Comparative financial statements corresponding financial statements from the previous years accompanying the issued financial statements.

Compensating balance a specified balance (usually some percentage of the committee amount) a borrower of a loan is asked to maintain in a low-interest or noninterest-bearing account at the bank.

Completed contract method recognition of revenue for a long-term contract when the project is complete.

Complex capital structure potential common shares are outstanding.

Composite depreciation method physically dissimilar assets are aggregated to gain the convenience of group depreciation.

Compound interest interest computed not only on the initial investment but also on the accumulated interest in previous periods.

Comprehensive income traditional net income plus other nonowner changes in equity.

Conceptual framework deals with theoretical and conceptual issues and provides an underlying structure for current and future accounting and reporting standards.

Conservatism practice followed in an attempt to ensure that uncertainties and risks inherent in business situations are adequately considered.

Consignment the consignor physically transfers the goods to the other company (the consignee), but the consignor retains legal title.

Consistency permits valid comparisons between different periods.

Consolidated financial statements combination of the separate financial statements of the parent and subsidiary each period into a single aggregate set of financial statements as if there were only one company.

Construction in progress asset account equivalent to the asset work-in-progress inventory in a manufacturing company.

Contingently issuable shares additional shares of common stock to be issued, contingent on the occurrence of some future circumstance.

Conventional retail method applying the retail inventory method in such a way that LCM is approximated.

Convertible bonds bonds for which bondholders have the option to convert the bonds into shares of stock.

Copyright exclusive right of protection given to a creator of a published work, such as a song, painting, photograph, or book.

Corporation the dominant form of business organization that acquires capital from investors in exchange for ownership interest and from creditors by borrowing.

Correction of an error an adjustment a company makes due to an error made.

Cost effectiveness the perceived benefit of increased decision usefulness exceeds the anticipated cost of providing that information.

Cost of goods sold cost of the inventory sold during the period.

Cost recovery method deferral of all gross profit recognition until the cost of the item sold has been recovered.

Cost-to-retail percentage ratio found by dividing goods available for sale at cost by goods available for sale at retail.

Coupons bonds name of the owner was not registered; the holder actually clipped an attached coupon and redeemed it in accordance with instructions on the indenture.

Credits represent the right side of the account.

Cumulative if the specified dividend is not paid in a given year, the unpaid dividends accumulate and must be made up in a later dividend year before any dividends are paid on common shares.

Current assets includes assets that are cash, will be converted into cash, or will be used up within one year or the operating cycle, whichever is longer.

Current liabilities expected to require current assets and usually are payable within one year.

Current maturities of long-term debt the current installment due on long-term debt, reported as a current liability.

Current ratio current assets divided by current liabilities.

Date of record specific date stated as to when the determination will be made of the recipient of the dividend.

Debenture bond secured only by the "full faith and credit" of the issuing corporation.

Debits represent the left side of the account.

Debt issue cost with either publicly or privately sold debt, the issuing company will incur costs in connection with issuing bonds or notes, such as legal and accounting fees and printing costs, in addition to registration and underwriting fees.

Debt to equity ratio compares resources provided by creditors with resources provided by owners.

Decision usefulness the quality of being useful to decision making.

Default risk a company's ability to pay its obligations when they come due.

Deferred annuity the first cash flow occurs more than the one period after the date the agreement begins.

Deferred tax asset taxes to be saved in the future when future deductible amounts reduce taxable income (when the temporary differences reverse).

Deferred tax liability taxes to be paid in the future when future taxable amounts become taxable (when the temporary differences reverse).

Deficit debit balance in retained earnings.

Defined benefit pension plans fixed retirement benefits defined by a designated formula, based on employees' years of service and annual compensation.

Defined contribution pension plans fixed annual contributions to a pension fund; employees choose where funds are invested—usually stocks or fixed-income securities.

Depletion allocation of the cost of natural resources.

Depreciation cost allocation for plant and equipment.

Derivatives financial instruments usually created to hedge against risks created by other financial instruments or by transactions that have yet to occur but are anticipated and that "derive" their values or contractually required cash flows from some other security or index.

Detachable stock purchase warrants the investor has the option to purchase a stated number of shares of common stock at a specified option price, within a given period of time.

Development costs for natural resources, costs incurred after the resource has been discovered but before production begins.

Diluted EPS incorporates the dilutive effect of all potential common shares.

Direct financing lease lease in which the lessor finances the asset for the lessee and earns interest revenue over the lease term.

Direct method the cash effect of each operating activity (i.e., income statement item) is reported directly on the statement of cash flows.

Direct write-off method an allowance for uncollectible accounts is not used; instead bad debts that do arise are written off as bad debt expense.

Disclosure notes additional insights about company operations, accounting principles, contractual agreements, and pending litigation.

Discontinued operations the discontinuance of a component of an entity whose operations and cash flows can be clearly distinguished from the rest of the entity.

Discount arises when bonds are sold for less than face amount.

Discounting the transfer of a note receivable to a financial institution.

Distributions to owners decreases in equity resulting from transfers to owners.

Dividend distribution to shareholders of a portion of assets earned.

Dollar-value LIFO (DVL) Inventory is viewed as a quantity of value instead of a physical quantity of goods. Instead of layers of units from different purchases, the DVL inventory pool is viewed as comprising layers of dollar value from different years.

Dollar-value LIFO retail method LIFO retail method combined with dollar-value LIFO.

Double-declining-balance (DDB) method 200% of the straight-line rate is multiplied by book value.

Double-entry system dual effect that each transaction has on the accounting equation when recorded.

DuPont framework depict return on equity as determined by profit margin (representing profitability), asset turnover (representing efficiency), and the equity multiplier (representing leverage).

Early extinguishment of debt debt is retired prior to its scheduled maturity date.

Earnings per share (EPS) the amount of income earned by a company expressed on a per share basis.

Earnings quality refers to the ability of reported earnings (income) to predict a company's future earnings.

Economic events any event that directly affects the financial position of the company.

Effective interest method recording interest each period as the effective rate of interest multiplied by the outstanding balance of the debt.

Effective rate the actual rate at which money grows per year.

Emerging Issues Task Force (EITF) responsible for providing more timely responses to emerging financial reporting issues.

Employee share purchase plans permit all employees to buy shares directly from their company, often at favorable terms.

Equity method used when an investor can't control, but can significantly influence, the investee.

Equity multiplier depicts leverage as total assets divided by total equity.

Equity/net assets called shareholders' equity or stockholders' equity for a corporation; the residual interest in the assets of an entity that remains after deducting liabilities.

Estimates prediction of future events.

Ethics a code or moral system that provides criteria for evaluating right and wrong.

Ex-dividend date date usually two business days before the date of the record and is the first day the stock trades without the right to receive the declared dividend.

Executory costs maintenance, insurance, taxes, and any other costs usually associated with ownership.

Expected cash flow approach adjusts the cash flows, not the discount rate, for the uncertainty or risk of those cash flows.

Expected economic life useful life of an asset.

Expected postretirement benefit obligation (EPBO) discounted present value of the total net cost to the employer of postretirement benefits.

Expected return on plan assets estimated long-term return on invested assets.

Expenses outflows or other using up of assets or incurrences of liabilities during a period from delivering or producing good, rendering services, or other activities that constitute the entity's ongoing major, or central, operations.

Exploration costs for natural resources, expenditures such as drilling a well, or excavating a mine, or any other costs of searching for natural resources.

External events exchange between the company and a separate economic entity.

Extraordinary items material events and transactions that are both unusual in nature and infrequent in occurrence.

F.O.B. (free on board) shipping point legal title to the goods changes hands at the point of shipment when the seller delivers the goods to the common carrier, and the purchaser is responsible for shipping costs and transit insurance.

F.O.B. destination the seller is responsible for shipping and the legal title does not pass until the goods arrive at their destination.

Factor financial institution that buys receivables for cash, handles the billing and collection of the receivables, and charges a fee for this service.

Fair value hedge a derivative is used to hedge against the exposure to changes in the fair value of an asset or liability or a firm commitment.

Fair value hierarchy prioritizes the inputs companies should use when determinig fair value.

Fair value option allows companies to report their financial assets and liabilities at fair value.

Faithful representation exists when there is agreement between a measure or description and the phenomenon it purports to represent.

Financial accounting provides relevant financial information to various external users.

Financial Accounting Foundation (FAF) responsible for selecting the members of the FASB and its Advisory Council, ensuring adequate funding of FASB activities, and exercising general oversight of the FASB's activities.

Financial Accounting Standards Board (FASB) the current private sector body that has been delegated the task of setting accounting standards.

Financial activities cash inflows and outflows from transactions with creditors and owners.

Financial instrument cash; evidence of an ownership interest in an entity; a contract that imposes on one entity an obligation to deliver cash or another financial instrument, and conveys to the second entity a right to receive cash or another financial instrument; and a contract that imposes on one entity an obligation to exchange financial instruments on potentially unfavorable terms and conveys to a second entity a right to exchange other financial instruments on potentially favorable terms.

Financial leverage by earning a return on borrowed funds that exceeds the cost of borrowing the funds, a company can provide its shareholders with a total return higher than it could achieve by employing equity funds alone.

Financial reporting process of providing financial statement information to external users.

Financial statements primary means of communicating financial information to external parties.

Finished goods costs that have accumulated in work in process are transferred to finished goods once the manufacturing process is completed.

Fiscal year the annual time period used to report to external users.

Fixed-asset turnover ratio used to measure how effectively managers used PP&E.

$$\frac{\text{Fixed-asset}}{\text{turnover ratio}} = \frac{\text{Net sales}}{\text{Average-fixed assets}}$$

Foreign currency futures contract agreement that requires the seller to deliver a specific foreign currency at a designated future date at a specific price.

Foreign currency hedge if a derivative is used to hedge the risk that some transactions require settlement in a currency other than the entities' functional currency or that foreign operations will require translation adjustments to reported amounts.

Forward contract calls for delivery on a specific date; is not traded on a market exchange; does not call for a daily cash settlement for price changes in the underlying contract.

Fractional shares a stock dividend or stock split results in some shareholders being entitled to fractions of whole shares.

Franchise contractual arrangement under which the franchisor grants the franchisee the exclusive right to use the franchisor's trademark or tradename within a geographical area, usually for specified period of time.

Franchisee individual or corporation given the right to sell the franchisor's products and use its name for a specified period of time.

Franchisor grants to the franchisee the right to sell the franchisor's products and use its name for a specific period of time.

Freight-in transportation-in; in a periodic system, freight costs generally are added to this temporary account, which is added to purchases in determining net purchases.

Full-cost method allows costs incurred in searching for oil and gas within a large geographical area to be capitalized as assets and expensed in the future as oil and gas from the successful wells are removed from that area.

Full-disclosure principle the financial reports should include any information that could affect the decisions made by external users.

Funded status difference between the employer's obligation (PBO) and the resources available to satisfy that obligation (plan assets).

Future deductible amounts the future tax consequence of a temporary difference will be to decrease taxable income relative to accounting income.

Futures contract agreement that requires the seller to deliver a particular commodity at a designated future date at a specified price.

Future taxable amounts the future tax consequence of temporary difference will be to increase taxable income relative to accounting income.

Future value amount of money that a dollar will grow to at some point in the future.

Gain or loss on the PBO the decrease or increase in the PBO when one or more estimates used in determining the PBO require revision.

Gains increases in equity from peripheral, or incidental, transactions of an entity.

General journal used to record any type of transaction.

General ledger collection of accounts.

Generally Accepted Accounting Principles (GAAP) set of both broad and specific guidelines that companies should follow when measuring and reporting the information in their financial statements and related notes.

Going concern assumption in the absence of information to the contrary, it is anticipated that a business entity will continue to operate indefinitely.

Goodwill unique intangible asset in that its cost can't be directly associated with any specifically identifiable right and it is not separable from the company itself.

Government Accounting Standards Board (GASB) responsible for developing accounting standards for governmental units such as states and cities.

Gross investment in the lease total of periodic rental payments and residual value.

Gross method For the buyer, views a discount not taken as part of the cost of inventory. For the seller, views a discount not taken by the customer as part of sales of revenue.

Gross profit method (gross margin method) estimates cost of goods sold which is then subtracted from cost of goods available for sale to estimate ending inventory.

Gross profit/ratio highlights the important relationship between net sales revenue and cost of goods sold.

$$\text{Gross profit ratio} = \frac{\text{Gross profit}}{\text{Net sales}}$$

Group depreciation method collection of assets defined as depreciable assets that share similar service lives and other attributes.

Half-year convention record one-half of a full year's depreciation in the year of acquisition and another half year in the year of disposal.

Hedging taking an action that is expected to produce exposure to a particular type of risk that is precisely the opposite of an actual risk to which the company already is exposed.

Historical costs original transaction value.

Horizontal analysis comparison by expressing each item as a percentage of that same item in the financial statements of another year (base amount) in order to more easily see year-to-year changes.

Illegal acts violations of the law, such as bribes, kickbacks, and illegal contributions to political candidates.

Impairment of value operational assets should be written down if there has been a significant impairment (fair value less than book value) of value.

Implicit rate of interest rate implicit in the agreement.

Improvements replacement of a major component of an operational asset.

Income from continuing operations revenues, expenses (including income taxes), gain, and losses, excluding those related to discontinued operations and extraordinary items.

Income statement statement of operations or statement of earnings is used to summarize the profit-generating activities that occurred during a particular reporting period.

Income statement approach estimating bad debt expense as a percentage of each period's net credit sales; usually determined by reviewing the company's recent history of the relationship between credit sales and actual bad debts.

Income summary account that is a bookkeeping convenience used in the closing process that provides a check that all temporary accounts have been properly closed.

Income tax expense provision for income taxes; reported as a separate expense in corporate income statements.

Indirect method the net cash increase or decrease from operating activities is derived indirectly by starting with reported net income and working backwards to convert that amount to a cash basis.

Initial direct costs costs incurred by the lessor that are associated directly with originating a lease and are essential to acquire the lease.

In-process research and development the amount of the purchase price in a business acquisition that is allocated to projects that have not yet reached technological feasibility.

Installment notes notes payable for which equal installment payments include both an amount that represents interest and an amount that represents a reduction of the outstanding balance so that at maturity the note is completely paid.

Installment sales method recognizes revenue and costs only when cash payments are received.

Institute of Internal Auditors national organization of accountants providing internal auditing services for their own organizations.

Institute of Management Accountants (IMA) primary national organization of accountants working in industry and government.

Intangible assets operational assets that lack physical substance; examples include patents, copyrights, franchises, and goodwill.

Interest "rent" paid for the use of money for some period of time.

Interest cost interest accrued on the projected benefit obligation calculated as the discount rate multiplied by the projected benefit obligation at the beginning of the year.

Interest rate swap agreement to exchange fixed interest payments for floating rate payments, or vice versa, without exchanging the underlying principal amounts.

Internal control a company's plan to encourage adherence to company policies and procedures, promote operational efficiency, minimize errors and theft, and enhance the reliability and accuracy of accounting data.

Internal events events that directly affect the financial position of the company but don't involve an exchange transaction with another entity.

International Accounting Standards Board (IASB) objectives are to develop a single set of high-quality, understandable global accounting standards, to promote the use of those standards, and to bring about the convergence of national accounting standards and International Accounting Standards.

International Accounting Standards Committee (IASC) umbrella organization formed to develop global accounting standards.

International Financial Reporting Standards developed by the IASB and used by more than 100 countries.

Intraperiod tax allocation associates (allocates) income tax expense (or income tax Gross profit Net sales benefit if there is a loss) with each major component of income that causes it.

Intrinsic value the difference between the market price of the shares and the option price at which they can be acquired.

Inventories goods awaiting sale (finished goods), goods in the course of production (work in process), and goods to be consumed directly or indirectly in production (raw materials).

Inventory goods acquired, manufactured, or in the process of being manufactured for sale.

Inventory turnover ratio measures a company's efficiency in managing its investment in inventory.

Investing activities involve the acquisition and sale of long-term assets used in the business and non-operating investment assets.

Investments by owners increases in equity resulting from transfers of resources (usually cash) to a company in exchange for ownership interest.

Irregularities intentional distortions of financial statements.

Journal a chronological record of all economic events affecting financial position.

Journal entry captures the effect of a transaction on financial position in debit/credit form.

Just-in-time (JIT) system a system used by a manufacturer to coordinate production with suppliers so that raw materials or components arrive just as they are needed in the production process.

Land improvements the cost of parking lots, driveways, and private roads and the costs of fences and lawn and garden sprinkler systems.

Last-in, first-out (LIFO) method assumes units sold are the most recent units purchased.

Leasehold improvements account title when a lessee makes improvements to leased property that reverts back to the lessor at the end of the lease.

Lessee user of a leased asset.

Lessor owner of a leased asset.

Leveraged lease a third-party, long-term creditor provides nonrecourse financing for a lease agreement between a lessor and a lessee.

Liabilities probable future sacrifices of economic benefits arising from present obligations of a particular entity to transfer assets or provide services to other entities in the future as a result of past transactions or events.

LIFO conformity rule if a company uses LIFO to measure taxable income, the company also must use LIFO for external financial reporting.

LIFO inventory pools simplifies recordkeeping and reduces the risk of LIFO liquidation by grouping inventory units into pools based on physical similarities of the individual units.

LIFO liquidation the decline in inventory quantity during the period.

Limited liability company owners are not liable for the debts of the business, except to the extent of their investment; all members can be involved with managing the business without losing liability protection; no limitations on the number of owners.

Limited liability partnership similar to a limited liability company, except it doesn't offer all the liability protection available in the limited liability company structure.

Line of credit allows a company to borrow cash without having to follow formal loan procedures and paperwork.

Liquidating dividend when a dividend exceeds the balance in retained earnings.

Liquidity period of time before an asset is converted to cash or until a liability is paid.

Long-term solvency the riskiness of a company with regard to the amount of liabilities in its capital structure.

Loss contingency existing, uncertain situation involving potential loss depending on whether some future event occurs.

Losses decreases in equity arising from peripheral, or incidental, transactions of the entity.

Lower-of-cost-or-market (LCM) recognizes losses in the period that the value of inventory declines below its cost.

Management discussion and analysis (MDA) provides a biased but informed perspective of a company's operations, liquidity, and capital resources.

Managerial accounting deals with the concepts and methods used to provide information to an organization's internal users (i.e., its managers).

Matching principle expenses are recognized in the same period as the related revenues.

Materiality if a more costly way of providing information is not expected to have a material effect on decisions made by those using the information, the less costly method may be acceptable.

Measurement process of associating numerical amounts to the elements.

Minimum lease payments payments the lessee is required to make in connection with the lease.

Minimum pension liability an employer must report a pension liability at least equal to the amount by which its ABO exceeds its plan assets.

Model Business Corporation Act designed to serve as a guide to states in the development of their corporation statutes.

Modified accelerated cost recovery system (MACRS) The federal income tax code allows taxpayers to compute depreciation for their tax returns using this method.

Monetary assets money and claims to receive money, the amount of which is fixed or determinable.

Monetary liabilities obligations to pay amounts of cash, the amount of which is fixed or determinable.

Mortgage bond backed by a lien on specified real estate owned by the issuer.

Multiple-deliverable arrangements require allocation of revenue to multiple elements that qualify for separate revenue recognition.

Multiple-step income statement format that includes a number of intermediate subtotals before arriving at income from continuing operations.

Natural resources oil and gas deposits, timber tracts, and mineral deposits.

Net income/net loss revenue + gains − (expenses and losses for a period) income statement bottom line.

Net markdown net effect of the change in selling price (increase, decrease, increase).

Net markup net effect of the change in selling price (increase, increase, decrease).

Net method For the buyer, considers the cost of inventory to include the net, after-discount amount, and any discounts not taken are reported as interest expense. For the seller, considers sales revenue to be the net amount, after discount, and any discounts not taken by the customer as interest revenue.

Net operating loss negative taxable income because tax-deductible expenses exceed taxable revenues.

Net realizable less a normal profit margin (NRV − NP) lower limit of market.

Net realizable value the amount of cash the company expects to actually collect from customers.

Net realizable value (NRV) upper limit of market.

Neutrality neutral with respect to parties potentially affected.

Noncash investing and financing activities transactions that do not increase or decrease cash but that result in significant investing and financing activities.

Noninterest-bearing note notes that bear interest, but the interest is deducted (or discounted) from the face amount to determine the cash proceeds made available to the borrower at the outset.

Nonoperating income includes gains and losses and revenues and expenses related to peripheral or incidental activities of the company.

Note payable promissory note (essentially an IOU) that obligates the issuing corporation to repay a stated amount at or by a specified maturity date and to pay interest to the lender between the issue date and maturity.

Notes receivable receivables supported by a formal agreement or note that specifies payment terms.

Objectives-oriented/principles-based accounting standards approach to standard setting stresses professional judgment, as opposed to following a list of rules.

Operating activities inflows and outflows of cash related to transactions entering into the determination of net income.

Operating cycle period of time necessary to convert cash to raw materials, raw materials to finished product, the finished product to receivables, and then finally receivables back to cash.

Operating income includes revenues and expenses directly related to the principal revenue-generating activities of the company.

Operating leases fundamental rights and responsibilities of ownership are retained by the lessor and that the lessee merely is using the asset temporarily.

Operating loss carryback reduction of prior (up to two) years' taxable income by a current net operating loss.

Operating loss forward reduction of future (up to 20) years' taxable income by a current net operating loss.

Operating segment a component of an enterprise that engages in business activities from which it may earn revenues and incur expenses (including revenues and expenses relating to transactions with other companies of the same enterprise); whose operating results are regularly reviewed by the enterprise's chief operating decision maker to make decisions about resources to be allocated to the segment and assess its performance; for which discrete financial information is available.

Operational assets property, plant, and equipment, along with intangible assets.

Operational risk how adept a company is at withstanding various events and circumstances that might impair its ability to earn profits.

Option gives the holder the right either to buy or sell a financial instrument at a specified price.

Option pricing models statistical models that incorporate information about a company's stock and the terms of the stock option to estimate the option's fair value.

Ordinary annuity cash flows occur at the end of each period.

Other comprehensive income certain gains and losses that are excluded from the calculation of net income, but included in the calculation of comprehensive income.

Paid-in capital invested capital consisting primarily of amounts invested by shareholders when they purchase shares of stock from the corporation.

Parenthetical comments/modifying comments supplemental information disclosed on the face of financial statements.

Participating preferred shareholders are allowed to receive additional dividends beyond the stated amount.

Patent exclusive right to manufacture a product or to use a process.

Pension plan assets employer contributions and accumulated earnings on the investment of those contributions to be used to pay retirement benefits to retired employees.

Percentage-of-completion method allocation of a share of a project's revenues and expenses to each reporting period during the contract period.

Periodic inventory system the merchandise inventory account balance is not adjusted as purchases and sales are made but only periodically at the end of a reporting period when a physical count of the period's ending inventory is made and costs are assigned to the quantities determined.

Periodicity assumption allows the life of a company to be divided into artificial time periods to provide timely information.

Permanent accounts represent assets, liabilities, and shareholders' equity at a point in time.

Permanent difference difference between pretax accounting income and taxable income and, consequently, between the reported amount of an asset or liability in the financial statements and its tax basis that will not "reverse" resulting from transactions and events that under existing tax law will never affect taxable income or taxes payable.

Perpetual inventory system account inventory is continually adjusted for each change in inventory, whether it's caused by a purchase, a sale, or a return of merchandise by the company to its supplier.

Pledging trade receivables in general rather than specific receivables are pledged as collateral; the responsibility for collection of the receivables remains solely with the company.

Point-of-sale the goods or services sold to the buyer are delivered (the title is transferred).

Post-closing trial balance verifies that the closing entries were prepared and posted correctly and that the accounts are now ready for next year's transactions.

Posting transferring debits and credits recorded in individual journal entries to the specific accounts affected.

Postretirement benefits all types of retiree benefits; may include medical coverage, dental coverage, life insurance, group legal services, and other benefits.

Potential common shares Securities that, while not being common stock may become common stock through their exercise, conversion, or issuance and therefore dilute (reduce) earnings per share.

Predictive value/confirmatory value confirmation of investor expectations about future cash-generating ability.

Preferred stock typically has a preference (a) to specified amount of dividends (stated dollar amount per share or percentage of par value per share) and (b) to distribution of assets in the event the corporation is dissolved.

Premium arises when bonds are sold for more than face amount.

Prepaid expense represents an asset recorded when an expense is paid in advance, creating benefits beyond the current period.

Prepayments/deferrals the cash flow precedes either expense or revenue recognition.

Present value today's equivalent to a particular amount in the future.

Prior period adjustment addition to or reduction in the beginning retained earnings balance in a statement of shareholders' equity due to a correction of an error.

Prior service cost the cost of credit given for an amendment to a pension plan to employee service rendered in prior years.

Product costs costs associated with products and expensed as cost of goods sold only when the related products are sold.

Profit margin on sales net income divided by net sales; measures the amount of net income achieved per sales dollar.

Pro forma earnings actual (GAAP) earnings reduced by any expenses the reporting company feels are unusual and should be excluded.

Projected benefit obligation (PBO) the discounted present value of estimated retirement benefits earned so far by employees, applying the plan's pension formula using projected future compensation levels.

Property dividend when a noncash asset is distributed.

Property, plant, and equipment land, buildings, equipment, machinery, autos, and trucks.

Prospective approach the accounting change is implemented in the present, and its effects are reflected in the financial statements of the current and future years only.

Proxy statement contains disclosures on compensation to directors and executives; sent to all shareholders each year.

Purchase commitments contracts that obligate a company to purchase a specified amount of merchandise or raw materials at specified prices on or before specified dates.

Purchase discounts reductions in the amount to be paid if remittance is made within a designated period of time.

Purchase return a reduction in both inventory and accounts payable (if the account has not yet been paid) at the time of the return.

Purchases journal records the purchase of merchandise on account.

Quasi reorganization a firm undergoing financial difficulties, but with favorable future prospects, may use a quasi reorganization to write down inflated asset values and eliminate an accumulated deficit.

Rate of return on stock investment

$$\frac{\text{Dividends + Share price appreciation}}{\text{Initial investment}}$$

Ratio analysis comparison of accounting numbers to evaluate the performance and risk of a firm.

Raw materials cost of components purchased from other manufacturers that will become part of the finished product.

Real estate lease involves land—exclusively or in part.

Realization principle requires that the earnings process is judged to be complete or virtually complete, and there is reasonable certainty as to the collectibility of the asset to be received (usually cash) before revenue can be recognized.

Rearrangements expenditures made to restructure an asset without addition, replacement, or improvement.

Receivables a company's claims to the future collection of cash, other assets, or services.

Receivables turnover ratio indicates how quickly a company is able to collect its accounts receivable.

Recognition process of admitting information into the basic financial statements.

Redemption privilege might allow preferred shareholders the option, under specified conditions, to return their shares for a predetermined redemption price.

Related-party transactions transactions with owners, management, families of owners or management, affiliated companies, and other parties that can significantly influence or be influenced by the company.

Relevance one of the primary decision-specific qualities that make accounting information useful; made up of predictive value and/or feedback value, and timeliness.

Reliability the extent to which information is verifiable, representationally faithful, and neutral.

Rent abatement lease agreements may call for uneven rent payments during the term of the lease, e.g., when the initial payment (or maybe several payments) is waived.

Replacement cost (RC) the cost to replace the item by purchase or manufacture.

Replacement depreciation method depreciation is recorded when assets are replaced.

Representational faithfulness agreement between a measure or description and the phenomenon it purports to represent.

Residual value or salvage value, the amount the company expects to receive for the asset at the end of its service life less any anticipated disposal costs.

Restoration costs costs to restore land or other property to its original condition after extraction of the natural resource ends.

Restricted stock shares subject to forfeiture by the employee if employment is terminated within some specified number of years from the date of grant.

Retail inventory method relies on the relationship between cost and selling price to estimate ending inventory and cost of goods sold; provides a more accurate estimate than the gross profit method.

Retained earnings amounts earned by the corporation on behalf of its shareholders and not (yet) distributed to them as dividends.

Retired stock shares repurchased and not designated as treasury stock.

Retirement depreciation method records depreciation when assets are disposed of and measures depreciation as the difference between the proceeds received and cost.

Retrospective approach financial statements issued in previous years are revised to reflect the impact of an accounting change whenever those statements are presented again for comparative purpose.

Return on assets (ROA) indicates a company's overall profitability.

Return on shareholders' equity amount of profit management can generate from the assets that owners provide.

Revenues inflows or other enhancements of assets or settlements of liabilities from delivering or producing goods, rendering services, or other activities that constitute the entity's ongoing major, or central, operations.

Reverse stock split when a company decreases, rather than increases, its outstanding shares.

Reversing entries optional entries that remove the effects of some of the adjusting entries made at the end of the previous reporting period for the sole purpose of simplifying journal entries made during the new period.

Right of conversion shareholders' right to exchange shares of preferred stock for common stock at specified conversion ratio.

Right of return customers' right to return merchandise to retailers if they are not satisfied.

Rules-based accounting standards a list of rules for choosing the appropriate accounting treatment for a transaction.

S corporation characteristics of both regular corporations and partnerships.

SAB No. 101 *Staff Accounting Bulletin 101* summarizes the SEC's views on revenue recognition.

Sale-leaseback transaction the owner of an asset sells it and immediately leases it back from the new owner.

Sales journal records credit sales.

Sales return the return of merchandise for a refund or for credit to be applied to other purchases.

Sales-type lease in addition to interest revenue earned over the lease term, the lessor receives a manufacturer's or dealer's profit on the sale of the asset.

Sarbanes-Oxley Act law provides for the regulation of the key players in the financial reporting process.

Secondary market transactions provide for the transfer of stocks and bonds among individuals and institutions.

Securities and Exchange Commission (SEC) responsible for setting accounting and reporting standards for companies whose securities are publicly traded.

Securities available-for-sale equity or debt securities the investor acquires, not for an active trading account or to be held to maturity.

Securities to be held-to-maturity debt securities for which the investor has the "positive intent and ability" to hold the securities to maturity.

Securitization the company creates a special purpose entity (SPE), usually a trust or a subsidiary; the SPE buys a pool of trade receivables, credit card receivables, or loans from the company and then sells related securities.

Serial bonds more structured (and less popular) way to retire bonds on a piecemeal basis.

Service cost increase in the projected benefit obligation attributable to employee service performed during the period.

Service life (useful life) the estimated use that the company expects to receive from the asset.

Service method allocation approach that reflects the declining service pattern of the prior service cost.

Share purchase contract shares ordinarily are sold in exchange for a promissory note from the subscriber—in essence, shares are sold on credit.

Short-term investments investments not classified as cash equivalents that will be liquidated in the coming year or operating cycle, whichever is longer.

Significant influence effective control is absent but the investor is able to exercise significant influence over the operating and financial policies of the investee (usually between 20% and 50% of the investee's voting shares are held).

Simple capital structure a firm that has no potential common shares (outstanding securities that could potentially dilute earnings per share).

Simple interest computed by multiplying an initial investment times both the applicable interest rate and the period of time for which the money is used.

Single-step income statement format that groups all revenues and gains together and all expenses and losses together.

Sinking fund debentures bonds that must be redeemed on a prespecified year-by-year basis; administered by a trustee who repurchases bonds in the open market.

Source documents relay essential information about each transaction to the accountant, e.g., sales invoices, bills from suppliers, cash register tapes.

Special journal record of a repetitive type of transaction, e.g., a sales journal.

Specific identification method each unit sold during the period or each unit on hand at the end of the period to be matched with its actual cost.

Specific interest method for interest capitalization, rates from specific construction loans to the extent of specific borrowings are used before using the average rate of other debt.

Start-up costs whenever a company introduces a new product or service, or commences business in a new territory or with a new customer, it incurs one-time costs that are expensed in the period incurred.

Statement of cash flows change statement summarizing the transactions that caused cash to change during the period.

Statement of shareholders' equity statement disclosing the source of changes in the shareholders' equity accounts.

Stock appreciation rights (SARs) awards that enable an employee to benefit by the amount that the market price of the company's stock rises above a specified amount without having to buy shares.

Stock dividend distribution of additional shares of stock to current shareholders of the corporation.

Stock options employees aren't actually awarded shares, but rather are given the option to buy shares at a specified exercise price within some specified number of years from the date of grant.

Stock split stock distribution of 25% or higher, sometimes called a *large* stock dividend.

Straight line an equal amount of depreciable base is allocated to each year of the asset's service life.

Straight-line method recording interest each period at the same dollar amount.

Subordinated debenture the holder is not entitled to receive any liquidation payments until the claims of other specified debt issues are satisfied.

Subsequent event a significant development that takes place after the company's fiscal year-end but before the financial statements are issued.

Subsidiary ledger record of a group of subsidiary accounts associated with a particular general ledger control account.

Successful efforts method requires that exploration costs that are known not to have resulted in the discovery of oil or gas be included as expense in the period the expenditures are made.

Sum-of-the-years'-digits (SYD) method systematic acceleration of depreciation by multiplying the depreciable base by a fraction that declines each year.

Supplemental financial statements reports containing more detailed information than is shown in the primary financial statements.

T-account account with space at the top for the account title and two sides for recording increases and decreases.

Taxable income comprises revenues, expenses, gains, and losses as measured according to the regulations of the appropriate taxing authority.

Technological feasibility established when the enterprise has completed all planning, designing, coding, and testing activities that are necessary to establish that the product can be produced to meet its design specifications including functions, features, and technical performance requirements.

Temporary accounts represent changes in the retained earnings component of shareholders' equity for a corporation caused by revenue, expense, gain, and loss transactions.

Temporary difference difference between pretax accounting income and taxable income and, consequently, between the reported amount of an asset or liability in the financial statements and its tax basis which will "reverse" in later years.

Time-based methods allocates the cost base according to the passage of time.

Timeliness information that is available to users early enough to allow its use in the decision process.

Times interest earned ratio a way to gauge the ability of a company to satisfy its fixed debt obligations by comparing interest charges with the income available to pay those charges.

Time value of money money can be invested today to earn interest and grow to a larger dollar amount in the future.

Trade discounts percentage reduction from the list price.

Trademark (tradename) exclusive right to display a word, a slogan, a symbol, or an emblem that distinctively identifies a company, a product, or a service.

Trade notes payable formally recognized by a written promissory note.

Trading securities equity or debt securities the investor (usually a financial institution) acquires principally for the purpose of selling in the near term.

Transaction analysis process of reviewing the source documents to determine the dual effect on the accounting equation and the specific elements involved.

Transaction obligation the unfunded accumulated postretirement benefit obligation existing when *SFAS 106* was adopted.

Transactions economic events.

Treasury stock shares repurchased and not retired.

Troubled debt restructuring the original terms of a debt agreement are changed as a result of financial difficulties experienced by the debtor (borrower).

Trustee person who accepts employer contributions, invests the contributions, accumulates the earnings on the investments, and pays benefits from the plan assets to retired employees or their beneficiaries.

Unadjusted trial balance a list of the general ledger accounts and their balances at a particular date.

Understandability users must understand the information within the context of the decision being made.

Unearned revenues cash received from a customer in one period for goods or services that are to be provided in a future period.

Units-of-production method computes a depreciation rate per measure of activity and then multiplies this rate by actual activity to determine periodic depreciation.

Unqualified opinion auditors are satisfied that the financial statements present fairly the company's financial position, results of operations, and cash flows and are in conformity with generally accepted accounting principles.

Valuation allowance indirect reduction (contra account) in a deferred tax asset when it is more likely than not that some portion or all of the deferred tax asset will not be realized.

Verifiability implies a consensus among different measurers.

Vertical analysis expression of each item in the financial statements as a percentage of an appropriate corresponding total, or base amount, but within the same year.

Vested benefits benefits that employees have the right to receive even if their employment were to cease today.

Weighted-average interest method for interest capitalization, weighted-average rate on all interest-bearing debt, including all construction loans, is used.

Without recourse the buyer assumes the risk of bad debts.

With recourse the seller retains the risk of uncollectibility.

Working capital differences between current assets and current liabilities.

Work-in-process inventory products that are not yet complete.

Worksheet used to organize the accounting information needed to prepare adjusting and closing entries and the financial statements.

Credits

3   BananaStock/JupiterImages
51   Digital Vision/Getty Images
113   AP Wide World Images
169   Goodshoot/Punchstock
233   Ken Reid/Photographers Choice/Getty Images
299   Michael Newman/Photoedit
337   IT Stock/PunchStock
395   BananaStock/JupiterImages
447   The McGraw-Hill Companies/John Flournoy, photographer
501   Steve Vidler/eStock Photo
557   fstop/Getty Images
619   Nasha Lee/Bloomberg News/Landov
691   LWA-Stephen Welstead/Corbis
747   David De Lossy/Photodisc/Getty Images
807   John F. Rizzo/Photodisc/Getty Images
873   Allan Danahar/Getty Images
935   Getty Images/Photodisc
1007 Courtesy of Cessna Corp./Newsmakers/Getty Images
1069 Will Woods/Digital Vision/Getty Images
1137 Lisa Poole/AP Images
1183 Corbis

Subject Index

Note: Page numbers followed by *n* indicate material in footnotes. All specifically named accounting standards may be found in the *Accounting Standards Index.*

A

Abnormal shortages, 463
ABO (accumulated benefit obligation), 941, 942, 976
Accelerated depreciation methods, 561–562
  declining balance methods, 561–562
  deferred tax liabilities, 878
  sum-of-the-years' digits (SYD), 561, 561*n*, 566
  switch to straight-line, 562
Account(s), 54
Accountants, 16, 133
Accounting changes, 188–192, 1137, 1138–1151, 1160
  in accounting estimate. *See* Change in accounting estimate
  in accounting method. *See* Change in accounting method
  in accounting principle. *See* Change in accounting principle
  decision makers' perspective of, 1139*n*, 1139–1140, 1140*n*
  in depreciation, amortization, or depletion method, 189, 1147
  error correction. *See* Accounting error correction
  global perspective, 1151, 1151*n*, 1160
  interim reporting, 272
  inventory method. *See* Change in inventory method
  in reporting entity, 191–192, 1148–1149
  review, 1150–1151
Accounting choices
  justification for (disclosures), 1144
  materiality and, 595
  motivation for, 1139*n*, 1139–1140, 1140*n*
Accounting equation, 52–54, 86
Accounting error(s)
  correction of. *See* Accounting error correction
  intentional, 1153*n*
  inventory errors. *See* Inventory(ies)
  irregularities distinguished from, 127, 127*n*
  material error, 24, 578–579, 1152*n*
  self-correcting, 473, 1155
Accounting error correction, 192, 1152*n*, 1152–1159, 1160
  asset recorded as expense, 1155
  bank reconciliations, 368, 369
  in cost allocation, 578–580, 593
  disclosures, 474, 580, 1154, 1158, 1159
  ethical dilemma, 1157
  global perspective, 1158, 1160
  illustrated, 1153–1158
    error affecting previous financial statements, 1154
    error affecting prior year's net income, 1154–1158
    error discovered in same reporting period, 1153
    tax impact of errors, 1156
  prior period adjustments
    disclosures, 1158, 1159
    income statement, 192, 192*n*
    inventory errors, 472, 472*n*
    retained earnings, 579, 579*n*
    statement of retained earnings, 1152–1153, 1153*n*
  retrospective reporting of, 192, 579, 1138, 1149–1150, 1159

review, 1159
self-correcting errors, 473, 1155
Accounting estimates
  adjusting entries for, 72–74
  changes in. *See* Change in accounting estimate
  expenses and losses, 878
  potentially inaccurate, 657
  stock options forfeitures, 1074–1075
  of warranty costs, 708
Accounting information. *See* Financial information
Accounting information systems
  basic model of, 52–55
    accounting equation, 52–53
    account relationships, 53–55
  computerized, 52, 56, 58, 92
  manual, 52
Accounting principles, 9, 9*n*, 29–32
  changes in. *See* Change in accounting principle
  evolution of, 33–36
    asset/liability approach, 33
    fair value approach to, 34–36
  full-disclosure principle, 31–32
  GAAP. *See* Generally accepted accounting principles
  historical cost principle, 29–30, 32, 522
  matching principle. *See* Matching principle
  realization principle. *See* Realization principle
  summary of, 32, 37
Accounting Principles Board (APB), 9–10
  Accounting Principles Board Opinions (APBOs). See Accounting Standards Index
  APB Interpretations. See Accounting Standards Index
  APB Statements. See Accounting Standards Index
Accounting process, 50–87
  adjusting entries. *See* Adjusting entries
  basic model of, 52–55
    accounting equation, 52–53
    account relationships, 53–55
  closing process
    illustrated, 79–81
    purposes of, 79, 87
    review of, 82–83
  financial statement preparation.
    See Financial statement(s)
  processing cycle, 55–64
  reversing entries used in, 88–90
  review of, 64–66
  special journals used in, 91–92
  subsidiary ledgers used in, 90
  worksheet used in, 87–88
Accounting standards, 3–36, 9, 9*n*, 37
Accounts payable, 61, 694
Accounts receivable, 247, 342–352
  balance sheet classification, 118, 351
  effects of sales revenue on, 1199–1200
  global perspective, 356, 356*n*, 369

initial valuation of, 342–344, 351
  cash discounts, 343–344
  trade discounts, 343
subsequent valuation of, 344–351
  sales returns, 344–346, 345*n*, 346*n*
  uncollectible accounts. *See* Uncollectible accounts
trade receivables, 118, 357
unearned revenue effects, 1200
Accounts receivable aging schedule, 348–349
Account titles, in worksheet, 88
Accrual basis accounting, 7, 8, 26, 28, 87
  adjusting entries required in, 67–68
  cash basis accounting compared, 7–8
  conversion from cash basis, 83–84
  conversion to cash basis, 84–85
  required by GAAP, 84*n*
Accrual concept, 1188
Accruals
  adjusting entries for, 70–72
    bad debts, 352
    estimates, 72–74
    liabilities, 70–71
    receivables, 71, 72
  discretionary, 367, 367*n*
  reversing entries used with, 88–89
Accrued interest
  on bonds, 756, 779–780
  on capital leases, 820–821
  interest payable, 698
  on interest rate swaps, A-12, A-12*n*
Accrued liabilities, 697–700, 720, 721
  adjusting entries for, 70–71
  balance sheet classifications, 120
  current, 697–700
    interest payable, 698
    salaries, commissions, and bonuses, 70, 71, 698–700, 700*n*
  interest payable, 698
  salaries, commissions, and bonuses
    annual bonuses, 700, 700*n*, 1140, 1140*n*
    current or accrued liability for, 70, 71, 698–700, 700*n*
    paid future absences, 698–700
Accrued receivables, 71, 72
Accumulated benefit obligation (ABO), 941, 942, 976
Accumulated depreciation, 68, 567, 590, 1205
Accumulated other comprehensive income (AOCI), 121
  balance sheet classification, 139, 961
  OCI accumulated in, 630
  pensions, 961, 976
    net loss or gain on PBO, 952–953, 954
    prior service cost as, 952
  reported in balance sheet, 1011
  shown in income statement, 196–197
Accumulated postretirement benefit obligation (APBO), 969, 969*n*
  comprehensive illustration, 972, 973
  review, 974, 975
Acid-test (quick) ratio, 134–135, 341, 719

Acquired contingencies, 714
Acquisition costs (natural resources), 506, 533
Acquisition of companies
    change in reporting entity, 192
    consolidated financial statements, 645, 645n
    goodwill acquired in, 510–511
    R&D purchased with, 531–532
Active trading portfolio, 626
Activity, in DuPont framework, 266
Activity-based depreciation methods, 560, 562–563
Activity ratios, 263–264, 267, 268, 270
    asset turnover ratio, 263, 265, 267, 268, 269
    average collection period, 264, 267, 268, 366
    average days in inventory, 264, 267, 268, 269, 419, 425
    fixed-asset turnover ratio, 516–517, 517n, 534
    inventory turnover ratio, 263, 264, 264n, 267, 268, 419, 425
    receivables turnover ratio, 263, 264, 264n, 342, 366
Actual interest limitation, 526
Actuarial gains (losses), 946, 955–956, 956n
Actuary, 940, 942, 977
Additional markup, 459
Additions, 590, 591, 593
Adelphia Communications, 16
ADESA, Inc., 713
Adjusted trial balance, 73, 74, 75, 86
Adjusting entries, 66–76, 86
    for accruals, 70–72
        of bad debts, 352
        estimates, 72–74
        of interest on bonds, 756
        liabilities, 70–71, 71n
        receivables, 71, 72
    for bad debt expense, 72–73, 73n, 75
    for bank reconciliations, 369
    as conversion to accrual basis accounting, 83–84
    facilitated by trial balance, 64
    in general journal, 73
    for inventories, 415–416
    for prepayments, 67–70, 72
        alternative recording of, 69–70
        prepaid expenses, 67–68
        unearned revenues, 68–69
    purpose of, 51, 85
    recording transactions, 69–70, 86
    in reporting cash flows, 200–201
    in retrospective reporting, 188–189, 189n, 470
    review, 74–76
    worksheet used in preparing, 87–88
    year-end adjustments, 51, 86, 88
Adjustments
    fair value adjustment
        AFS securities, 631n, 631–634, 632n
        interest rate swaps, A-5–A-6
        trading securities, 627, 627n, 628–629
    foreign currency translation, 194, A-9
    to investment accounts, 647–649
        for additional depreciation, 648–649
        deferred income taxes, 649
        not for land or goodwill, 649
        for other assets and liabilities, 649
    loss or gain on plan assets, 951

to net income. See Net income
prior period adjustments. See Prior period adjustments
Adobe Systems, 530
Advance collections, 700–702
    collections for third parties, 702
    deferred tax assets
        rent revenue, 878
        subscription revenue, 878, 884, 884n
    deposits and advances, 700–701
        advances from customers, 701
        refundable deposits, 700
    gift cards, 701–702
Advance payments, 720, 720n, 815–816
Adverse opinions, in auditors' reports, 130–131
Advertising expenditures, 31
Advertising expenses, 20, 67–68
Affiliated Computer Services, 259, 260
AFS. See Available-for-sale securities
AIA (American Institute of Accountants), 9
AICPA. See American Institute of Certified Public Accountants
AIG, 1187, A-0
Alabama Gas Corporation (Alagasco), 707
Alberto-Culver Company, 169
Allied Construction Products Corporation, 246
Allocation base, 559–560
Allocation methods, 560
    in amortization, 571–572
    cost allocation. See Cost allocation; specific allocation methods
    effective interest method. See Effective interest method
    income tax allocation. See Income tax(es)
    for prior service cost
        service method, 952n, 977–978
        straight-line method, 952, 952n, 978
Allowance for sales returns, 368
Allowance for uncollectible accounts, 72–73, 73n, 75
Allowance method of accounting for bad debts, 25, 337, 347, 368, 1201
Amazon.com, 1080, 1187
Amended tax returns, 1154
American Accounting Association, 19n, 339n
American Airlines, 580, 781
American Institute of Accountants (AIA), 9
American Institute of Certified Public Accountants (AICPA), 9, 17
    Code of Professional Conduct, 19
    on multiple-deliverable arrangements, 259
    sponsorship of COSO, 339n
Amortization, 502, 557, 558, 592, 593
    accounting changes
        accounting estimate, 1147–1148
        accounting principle, 1146
        amortization method, 189, 190, 577–578, 593, 1146
    of bond discount, 1090, 1210
    intangible assets not subject to, 511, 572–573
    intangible assets subject to
        allocation method, 571–572
        residual value, 571
        useful life, 571
    no cash effects reported for, 1189
    pension expense, 941
        net loss or net gain, 941, 952–953
        prior service cost, 951–952, 952n, 977

premium and discount amortization compared, 755
of product costs, 558, 572
review of, 576
Amortization schedules
    bonds
        discount bonds, 624, 753
        interest on bonds (review), 758
        premium bonds, 755
        straight-line method, 757
    installment notes, 763
    leases, 810
        with BPO, 826
        capital leases, 818–819
        direct financing leases, 821
        lessee's interest expense, 840–841
        lessor's interest revenue, 841
    notes, 762, 762n, 763, 768
    in troubled debt restructuring, 783
Amortized cost of investment, 627, 627n
"Amortizing the differential," 647
Analytical model, 19n, 19–20
Anderson, Bradbury H., 132
Anheuser-Busch, 620
Ann Taylor, 817
Annual bonuses. See also Accrued liabilities
    accounting choices and, 1140, 1140n
    as current liability, 700, 700n
Annual reports, 128, 139
Annuity(ies), 309–323, 324
    future value of, 310–312, 324
        annuity due, 311–312
        ordinary annuity, 310–311
    present value of, 312–316, 323
        annuity due, 313–314
        deferred annuity, 314n, 314–316
        ordinary annuity, 312–313, 324
        solving for unknown values, 316–319
    present value techniques, 320–322
        long-term bonds, 320–321, 324
        long-term leases, 321
        pension obligations, 321–322
    review of, 319–320
    time diagrams, 309–311, 313–315, 317, 318, 322
Annuity due, 309–310
    future value of, 311–312
    present value of, 313–314
Antidilutive securities, 1092–1096, 1107
    convertible securities, 1093, 1107
    options, rights, and warrants, 1092–1093
    order of entry for multiple convertible securities, 1093–1094
    potential common shares, 1101
AOCI. See Accumulated other comprehensive income
AOL Time Warner, 586
APB. See Accounting Principles Board
APBO. See Accumulated postretirement benefit obligation
Apple Inc., 396, 1035, 1073
ARO. See Asset retirement obligations
Arthur Andersen, 16
Articles of incorporation, 1017
Assessments, unasserted, 715, 721
Asset(s), 27
    in accounting equation, 54
    acquisition of. See Asset acquisition
    balance sheet classifications, 116–120
        current assets, 116–118, 138, 351
        intangible assets, 119, 138

Asset(s)—*Cont.*
  balance sheet classifications—*Cont.*
    investments, 119
    other assets, 119
    property, plant, and equipment,
      119, 138
  biological assets, 571, 571*n*
  book value of, 561, 568*n*, 568–569
  carrying value of, 561, 881, A-13
  control of, 361–362, 362*n*
  cost allocation. *See* Cost allocation;
    specific allocation methods
  creditors' interest in, 1008
  current. *See* Current assets
  derecognition of, 364, 364*n*
  disposition of. *See* Disposition of assets
  expected economic life of, 811–812
  fair value of
    asset retirement obligations, 711
    in capital leases, 817
    exchanges, 519, 534
    goodwill, 512, 512*n*, 585
    implicit rate of interest, 733*n*, 833
    reporting, 568*n*, 568–569
  "held for sale" assets, 518, 518*n*
  impairment of value. *See* Impairment of
    asset value
  intangible. *See* Intangible assets
  long-lived, 142, 142*n*, 178
  monetary, 306
  movable, 817
  net assets, 27
  net realizable value of, 30
  noncurrent, 78, 118, 119
  nonearning asset (cash), 341
  note exchanged for, 760–762, 760*n*–762*n*
  ownership of
    lease classification and, 811, 811*n*
    risks and rewards, 812
  pension plans. *See* Pension plan assets
  physical v. financial, 247
  plant assets. *See* Property, plant, and
    equipment
  residual value of, 559–560, 571, 593
    change in accounting estimate and, 576
    global perspective, 565
    leases. *See* Residual value of asset
      (leases)
  revalued in quasi reorganization, 1042
  self-constructed. *See* Self-constructed
    assets
  service life of. *See* Useful life of asset
  shown in balance sheet, 116
  subsequent expenditures for, 589–592
    additions, 590
    costs of defending intangible rights,
      591–592, 592*n*
    improvements, 590, 591
    rearrangements, 590–591
    repairs and maintenance, 589, 590
  valuation of. *See* Asset valuation
  working definitions of, 32
Asset acquisition
  natural resources, 506, 533
  subsequent expenditures for, 589–592
    additions, 590
    costs of defending intangible rights,
      591–592, 592*n*
    improvements, 590, 591, 593
    rearrangements, 590–591, 593
    repairs and maintenance, 589, 590,
      591, 593

  valuation at acquisition, 502–517
    costs to be capitalized, 504–512
    noncash acquisitions, 512–516, 533
    types of assets, 502–503
Asset distribution rights, 1017
Asset/liability approach
  to accounting principles, 33
  to deferred tax asset, 884, 884*n*
  to deferred tax liability, 877
Asset retirement obligations (AROs)
  capitalization of costs, 506–509
    measurement, 507
    present value calculations, 507, 507*n*,
      508
    recognition, 507
    scope, 507
  fair value approaches to, 711
  restoration costs for natural resources, 506
Asset turnover ratio, 263, 265, 267, 268, 269
Asset valuation
  at acquisition, 502–517
    costs to be capitalized, 504–512
    types of assets, 502–503
  at disposal, 517–521
    exchanges, 518–520, 521
    sale or retirement of asset, 517–518
  impairment. *See* Impairment of asset value
Assignee (lender), 357
Assignment of receivables, 356–357
Assignor (borrower), 357
Association of Investment Management
    and Research, 10*n*
Astro-Med Inc., 195, 196
AT&T, 651
Audit(s), 129, 139
Auditor(s), 6, 17
Auditors' report, 129*n*, 129–131
Authorization of expenditures, 339
Autodesk, 366
Available-for-sale (AFS) securities, 118,
    629–637, 659
  comprehensive income, 630, 630*n*
  disclosures, 642*n*, 642–643
  as fair value hedges, A-9
  financial statement presentation, 634*n*,
    634–635
  income taxes and, 636
  lack of significant influence and, 646, 646*n*
  other approaches compared
    equity method and TS, 656
    HTM and TS approaches, 635–636
    OTT impairment, 639
    debt investments, 661, 663–665
    equity investments, 661, 662–663
  purchase of, 631
  receivables, 356, 356*n*
  revenue recognition, 631
  selling, 632
  transfers between reporting categories,
    637–638
  unrealized holding gains and losses, 30*n*,
    619–620, 630–631, 634, 658
Average accumulated expenditures, 522–523
Average collection period (ratio), 264, 267,
    268, 366
Average cost method (inventories), 405–407,
    425
  adjusting entries for, 415–416
  approximating, 460
  FIFO and LIFO compared to, 410–411
  income reported under, 418

  periodic average cost, 406
  perpetual average cost, 406–407
  review of, 464
Average days in inventory (ratio), 264, 267,
    268, 269, 419, 425
AVX Corporation, 346

B

Bad debt(s). *See also* Uncollectible accounts
  accounting for
    adjusting entries for accruals, 352
    allowance method, 25, 337, 347, 368,
      1201
    direct write-off method, 25, 350–351,
      368, 1201
    installment sales method, 242
  provision for, 337, 368
Bad debt expense
  adjusting entries for, 72–73, 73*n*, 75
  income statement approach, 347,
    351, 352
Balance per bank, 370–371
Balance per books, 370–371
Balance sheet, 4, 78, 114, 115–124, 139
  affected by accounting errors, 1154
  "business activities" category,
    122–123, 205, 1030
  cash flow information, 1184
  classifications, 77–78, 113, 116–121,
    138–139
    accumulated other comprehensive
      income, 139, 961
    assets, 116–120, 138, 351
    income taxes, 897–898
    liabilities, 120–121, 138–139
    review of, 123–124
    shareholders' equity, 121, 139
  classified
    deferred tax assets and liabilities,
      897–898
    preparation of, 123–124
  current liabilities recorded in, 693
  equity method investments, 655
  function of, 113, 138
  impact of leases, 838–839
  long-term construction contracts, 248,
    252, 253
  organization of elements in, 1191
  pension liability reporting, 935, 975
  pension plans reported in, 940
  preparation of, 77–78, 81, 86
    in preparation of SCF, 1194, 1196
  presentation of items in. *See* Balance sheet
    presentation
  quasi reorganization and, 1043
  reporting share buyback, 1027, 1030
  revising due to change in accounting
      principle
    inventory, 1141–1142
    retained earnings, 1142
  spreadsheet preparation of SCF, 1207–
    1214
    bonds payable, 1210
    buildings and equipment, 1208–1209
    common shares, 1210–1211
    land, 1208
    retained earnings, 1211
    short-term investments,
      1207–1208
  usefulness and limitations of, 115–116
Balance sheet approach
  to deferred tax liability, 877, 877*n*

to temporary differences, 874
to uncollectible accounts, 348–349, 349n, 369
Balance sheet effects
  of accounting for treasury stock, 1027
  of discontinued operations, 185
  of treasury stock, 1027
Balance sheet presentation
  AFS securities, 634
  FASB/IASB project on, 122–123
  GAAP on, 139, 141
  global perspective, 122, 139
  income taxes
    deferred tax amount, 897–898
    valuation allowance, 898
  pension amounts, 961
  shareholders' equity, 1009
  trading securities, 629
Ballard, Shari L., 132
Bank accounts, 54
Bankers Mutual Capital Corporation, 358
Bank loans. See Short-term notes payable
Bank of America, 115, 622
The Bank of New York Mellon Corporation, 1100, 1101
Bank of Tokyo-Mitsubishi UFJ, 651
Bank overdrafts, 341
Bank reconciliation, 340, 369–371
Bankruptcy, 1185–1187
Bargain purchase option (BPO), 824–827, 825n, 847
  in capital leases, 811, 812, 812n
  ethical dilemma, 827
  exercisable before end of lease term, 827
  guaranteed residual value and, 828
"Bargain purchase" situation, 512
Bargain renewal options, 812, 812n
Barnes & Noble Inc., 529
Basic EPS. See Earnings per share (EPS)
Bear Stearns, 693, 1187, A-0
Beneficial conversion feature, 770, 770n
Benihana, Inc., 1158
Beresford, Dennis, 1073
Berkshire Hathaway, A-0
Best Buy Co. Inc., 131, 132, 701
"Big bath" accounting, 176, 474–475, 588
"Big Six" CPA firms, 1072n
"Bill and hold" strategy, 235, 367
Billings on construction in progress, 247, 247n, 252
Biological assets, 571, 571n
Black-Scholes model, 1108
Blake, Francis S., 128, 129
Blockbuster Inc., 585, 586
Board of directors, 1017, 1032
Boeing, 808, 1073
Bond(s), 748–759, 779
  amortization schedules
    discount bonds, 624, 753
    interest on bonds (review), 758
    premium bonds, 755
    straight-line method, 757
  bond indenture, 748–749
  callable, 747, 749, 772, 778
  cash flows from bond issue, 751
  convertible. See Convertible securities
  coupon bonds, 749
  debenture bonds, 748–749
  debt issue costs, 758–759
  with detachable warrants, 772–774
  face amount of, 748, 751, 756
  holding gains and losses, 753

interest on
  accrued interest, 756, 779–780
  coupon rate of interest, 748, 749
  effective interest method. See Effective interest method
  interest expense, 1204, 1205
  market rate, 750
  review, 758
  straight-line method, 756–757
  tax exempt government bonds, 886
issuance between interest dates, 750, 779–780
long-term bond valuation, 320–321, 324
mortgage bonds, 747, 749, 778
par value of, 748
private placement of, 759, 759n
recording at issuance, 749n, 749–751
  determining selling price, 750–751
  review, 757–758
retirement at maturity, 1210
serial bonds, 749
subordinated debentures, 749
tax-exempt government bonds, 886, 887
treasury bonds, A-1
zero-coupon bonds, 753, 753n, 754
Bond indenture, 748–749
Bond ratings, 750
Bonds payable, 1210
Books a Million, Inc., 1144, 1145
Book value
  of asset, 561, 568n, 568–569
  of company, 115
  market to book ratio, 115
  of shareholders' equity, 1038
Book value method, 771, 772
Borrower (assignor), 357
Bowen, R. M., 1140n
BPO. See Bargain purchase option
Bridgestone Americas Holding, 14
Brigham, Eugene, 417n
Broadcom Corporation, 1103
Brookfield Homes Corporation, 1018
Brown, F. Donaldson, 266n
Brown, K. L., 249n
Brown, Robert Moren, 412n
Brown & Sharpe Manufacturing Company, 235, 244
Buffett, Warren, A-0, A-3
Buffini, Fiona, 448n
Buildings
  acquisition costs, 503, 506
  land-and-building leases, 846, 846n
  real estate leases, 846
  spreadsheet preparation of SCF, 1208–1209
Bullion Monarch Mining, 1024
Burr, Chuck, 949n, A-0
Business, defined, 183, 183n
"Business activities" category, 122–123, 205, 1030, 1191
Business environment, 186
Businessland, 838
BusinessWeek magazine, 175

C

Cadbury Schweppes, Plc., 454, 583
CA Inc., 366–367
Callable bonds, 747, 749, 778
Callable obligations, 702–703
Callable preferred shares, 1018
Call provision, 772
Campbell, Lewis B., 1007

Campbell Soup Company, 29, 1008
CANTV, 187
CAP (Committee on Accounting Procedure), 9, 1033n
Capital
  ease of raising by corporations, 1015
  paid-in. See Paid-in capital
  working capital, 134
Capital budgeting, 516–517
Capitalization, 501, 504–512, 533
  asset retirement obligations, 506–509, 711
    measurement, 507
    present value calculations, 507, 507n, 508
    recognition, 507
    scope, 507
  intangible assets, 503, 509–512
    copyrights, 510
    franchises, 510
    goodwill, 510–512
    patents, 509, 527
    trademarks, 510
  lump-sum purchases, 512, 533
  of new cost, 590
  noncash acquisitions, 512–516
    deferred payments, 513–515, 533
    donated assets, 515–516
    issuance of equity securities, 515
  oil and gas accounting, 534–535, 535n
  property, plant, and equipment, 503, 504–509
    asset retirement obligations, 506–509, 711
    cost of buildings, 506
    equipment costs, 504, 505
    land costs, 504–505
    land improvements, 505
    natural resources costs, 506
  of R&D costs. See Research and development
  of self-constructed assets. See Self-constructed assets
Capital leases, 18, 808, 817–821, 847
  accrued interest, 820–821
  additional lessor conditions, 813
  amortization schedule, 818–819
  classification by lessee, 818, 818n
  criteria for classification as, 811n, 811–813, 812n, 834
  debt-to-equity ratio and, 838
  depreciation, 819–820
  equivalent to installment notes, 764
  financial statement impact of, 840
  global perspective, 845, 845n
  gross method of recording receivable, 817
  installment notes compared, 764, 809–810
  "off-balance-sheet" financing and, 809, 809n
  operating leases compared, 811, 811n
  reported in SCF, 1209
  sale-leaseback arrangements, 843–844, 844n
  sales-type leases compared, 824
Capital market efficiency, 412n
Capital structure
  accounting choices and, 1140, 1140n
  complex, 1087, 1106
  simple, 1083, 1086, 1106
Carrying costs, 781
  cash payments exceed carrying amount, 782–784

Carrying costs—*Cont.*
  cash payments less than carrying amount, 781–782
Carrying value of asset, 561, 881, A-13
Carslaw, Charles, 1224n
Carter, Larry, 448
Cash, 338–342. *See also* Liquidity
  balance sheet classification, 117, 117n
  cash equivalents and. *See* Cash equivalents
  common shares issued for, 1020, 1021
  decision makers' perspective of, 341–342
  global perspective, 341, 341n
  importance in economic decline, 1187
  internal control over, 338–340, 369–372
    bank reconciliation, 369–371
    cash disbursements, 339–340
    cash receipts, 339
    restrictions and compensating balances, 340, 368
  as nonearning asset, 341
  notes issued for
    long-term notes, 760
    noninterest-bearing notes, 354n, 354–355
  pension fund contributions, 950
  received in exchanges, 520, 520n
  restricted, 340, 368
  SARs payable in, 1109–1111, 1111n
Cash balance, 1193
Cash basis accounting, 8n, 37, 87
  accrual basis accounting compared, 7–8
  conversion to accrual basis, 83–84
Cash disbursements, 339–340
Cash disbursements journal, 91
Cash discounts, 343–344
Cash dividends, 1007, 1032–1033, 1041
  alternative recording of, 80
  not paid on treasury stock, 1035
  payment of, 1193
  recording in journal, 61, 66n
Cash equivalents, 198, 338–342, 1225
  balance sheet classification, 117, 117n
  decision makers' perspective of, 341–342
  disclosure notes, 117, 338, 1188
  global perspective, 341, 341n
  kinds of, 1188, 1208
  purchase and sale of, 1192–1193, 1208
  reported in SCF, 1187–1188, 1188n
Cash flow(s)
  ability to generate, 1224
  bankruptcy and, 1185–1187
  from bond issue, 751
  classification of, 199–205, 1185
    financing activities, 203–204
    global perspective, 199–200, 200n, 1212–1213
    investing activities. *See* Investing activities
    noncash investing and financing activities, 204, 1194, 1195, 1225
    operating activities, 199–203
  expected cash flow approach, 308–309
  from financing activities. *See* Financing activities
  future cash flows, 115
  importance in economic decline, 1187
  from investing activities. *See* Investing activities
  negative, 8n
  net cash inflows/outflows, 1193
  net operating cash flow, 8, 8n, 199, 203

from operating activities. *See* Operating activities
  reporting. *See* Statement of cash flows (SCF)
  usefulness of cash flow information, 1184
Cash flow hedges, 1009, A-15
  deferred gains, A-8, A-8n
  forecasted transactions, A-9
  other comprehensive income, 1010
Cash flow per share ratio, 1223
Cash flow perspective, 6–7
Cash flow ratios, 1223–1224
Cash flow risk, A-0, A-1, A-1n
Cash flow to sales ratio, 1223
Cash-generating unit (CGU), 586
Cash inflows, 1184–1185, 1193
Cash outflows, 1184–1185, 1193
Cash rebates, 710
Cash receipts, 61, 339
Cash receipts journal, 91, 92
Cash return on assets ratio, 1223
Cash return on shareholders' equity ratio, 1223
Cash sales, 59–60
Cash surrender value, 660
Cash to income ratio, 1223
Caterpillar, 521
Cause-and-effect relationships, 30–31
Cents-off coupons, 712
Certificates of deposit, A-1
Certified public accountants (CPAs), 16
CGU (cash-generating unit), 586
Change in accounting estimate, 190–191, 208, 1138, 1160
  changes in compensation estimates and, 1110–1111
  cost allocation (assets), 576–577
  depreciation, amortization, and depletion methods, 1147–1148
  disclosure notes, 190–191, 576, 577, 1146, 1147
  estimated forfeitures of stock options, 1074–1075
  long-term construction projects, 253
  prospective reporting, 190, 1146–1148, 1150
  review, 1150–1151
Change in accounting method
  amortization, depreciation, or depletion, 189, 190, 577–578, 593, 1146
  cautions regarding, 1140, 1140n
  income smoothing and, 1149
  for OTT impairment, 665
Change in accounting policy, 569
Change in accounting principle, 188–189, 190, 208, 1138, 1160
  cumulative effect of, 180, 188, 1145
  disclosure notes, 189, 190, 1144
  mandated changes, 189, 190, 1145
  prospective approach, 1139, 1144–1146, 1150, 1160
    changing depreciation, depletion, and amortization methods, 1146
    when mandated, 1145
    when retrospective approach is impracticable, 1144–1145
  retrospective approach, 1141–1144, 1150, 1160
    adjusting accounts for change, 1143
    impracticable: prospective approach, 1144–1145

revising comparative financial statements, 1141–1143
    voluntary changes, 188n, 188–189, 189n, 208, 469, 476
  review, 1151
  voluntary changes, 188n, 188–189, 189n, 208
Change in inventory method, 469–472
  change to FIFO method, 1143
  change to LIFO method, 471n, 471–472, 1139
  deferred tax liabilities and, 1143
  disclosure notes, 470, 471, 1144, 1145
  global perspective, 1145
  inventory layers, 1144
  revised reporting
    balance sheets, 1141–1142
    comparative financial statements, 189, 470
    to IRS, 472
Change in reporting entity, 1138, 1160
  consolidation of subsidiaries, 191–192, 192n
  disclosure notes, 1149
  retrospective approach, 1148–1149, 1150
Changes in fair value of derivatives, 194
Changes in revaluation surplus, 195, 195n
Change statements, 76, 78, 79
  income statement. *See* Income statement
  statement of cash flows. *See* Statement of cash flows
"Channel stuffing," 176
Charming Shoppes, Inc., 193
Checks outstanding, 370
Chevron Corp., 535
Chicago Board of Trade, 658n
Chicago Mercantile Exchange, A-1, A-1n
Choice Hotels, Inc., 354
Chromcraft Revington, Inc., 470–471
CIP (construction in progress) account, 247, 252
Circuit City, 838
Cisco Systems, Inc., 13, 337, 368, 448, 452–453, 475, 532, 635
Citicorp, 821
Citigroup, 115, 1187
Claims, unasserted, 715
Classifications
  for balance sheet. *See* Balance sheet
  of cash flows, 199–205, 1185
    financing activities, 203–204
    global perspective, 199–200, 200n
    investing activities. *See* Investing activities
    noncash investing and financing activities, 204, 1194, 1195, 1225
    operating activities, 199–203
  of expenses by function, 174
  of extraordinary gains/losses, 118, 636, 637
  FASB/IASB project on, 204–205
  for income statement, 76–77, 176
  leases, 810–814
    additional lessor conditions, 813
    application to operating leases, 815
    criteria for, 811n, 811–813, 812n, 815, 818
    global perspective, 814, 814n
    by lessee, 818, 818n
  of securities, 118, 636, 637
  total cost of pension plans, 965

Classified balance sheet, 123–124, 897–898
Clean opinion, 16
Cliff vesting, 1077
Clorox Company, 29, 1100
Closing entries, 87–88
Closing process
    illustrated, 79–81
    purposes of, 79, 87
    review of, 82–83
CNB Financial Services, Inc., 340
Coca-Cola Company, 13, 448, 509, 509n, 510, 619, 629, 658, 765–767, 1184
Cohan, William D., 693n
Cohn, Michael, A-14n
Colgate-Palmolive, 13
Collateral, 356–358
Collectibility of payments, 813
Collections
    in advance. See Advance collections
    by bank, 369
    for third parties, 702
    uncertainty of, 239–240
Collins Industries, Inc., 696, 697
Comiskey, E. E., 657n
Commercial paper, 697, 720, 1188, 1208, A-1
Commercial production, start of, 527–528
Commercial substance, 519–520, 520n
Committed line of credit, 695
Committee of Sponsoring Organizations (COSO) of Treadway Commission, 129, 339, 339n
Committee on Accounting Procedure (CAP), 9, 1033n
Common shares, 645n. See also Earnings per share (EPS); Preferred shares
    balance sheet classification, 139
    fundamental share rights, 1017
    issuance of, 1020–1024
        basic EPS, 1083, 1084
        for cash, 1020, 1021
        issue costs, 1022
        multiple securities at single price, 1021, 1022
        for noncash consideration, 1021, 1021n, 1042
        recording, 58
        review, 1023–1024
    other classes of shares distinguished, 1017–1020
    potential
        antidilutive securities, 1101
        convertible bonds as, 1083
        diluted EPS and, 1087
        effect on EPS, 1098, 1099, 1101
    sale of, 1193
    spreadsheet preparation of SCF, 1210–1211
    variables in valuation of, 367, 367n
Company policy, on paid absences, 699
Compaq Computer Corporation, 510, 572
Comparability of financial information, 24, 1082, 1137, 1139
Comparative financial statements, 132
    accounting errors reported in, 1153
    in preparation of SCF, 1194, 1196
    revision of
        change in accounting principle, 1141–1143
        change in inventory method, 189, 470
Comparison, 9
Compensating balances, 340, 340n, 695, 695n

Competitive disadvantage costs, 25
Completed contract method, 236, 237, 245, 246
    costs of construction, 247
    percentage-of-completion method compared, 246, 251–256
        balance sheet recognition, 252, 253
        income recognition, 251–252, 252n
        long-term contract losses, 253–256
    review of, 257–258
    timing of gross profit recognition, 248, 249
Complete information, 23–24
Complex capital structure, 1087, 1106
Components of other comprehensive income, A-8
Composite depreciation methods, 566–568
Compounding, effects of, 300–301, 302n
Compound interest, 300–301
Comprehensive income, 27, 208, 1042
    AOCI. See Accumulated other comprehensive income
    composition of, 630, 630n, 1010
    effects of investments on, 642
    flexibility in reporting, 194–195, 195n
    global perspective, 194, 195n, 961, 961n, 1012, 1012n
    IASB on, 195, 195n, 1012, 1012n
    OCI. See Other comprehensive income
    pension plan issues, 960n, 960–961
    reporting. See Statement of comprehensive income
    shareholders' equity and, 1010n, 1010–1011
    shown in income statement, 194–197
Computer Associates, Inc., 366–367
Computer software
    costs to develop. See Software development costs
    technological feasibility of, 530, 530n
    useful life of asset, 531
Computer spreadsheet programs. See Spreadsheet(s)
Conceptual framework, 3, 10, 20–26, 37
    efforts to merge GAAP and IFRS, 15, 21
    elements of financial statements, 26–27
    financial reporting. See Financial reporting
    objective of financial reporting, 21, 22
    qualitative characteristics, 22–24
    recognition and measurement, 27–32
Condor Capital Management, 175
Confirmatory value of information, 23
ConocoPhillips, 395, 410, 424, 570
Conservatism, 26, 26n, 450
Consignee, 401
Consignment, 401
Consignment Sales, 245
Consignor, 401
Consistency
    of financial information, 24, 24n, 1137, 1139
    lacking in auditors' reports, 130
Consolidated financial statements, 645, 645n, 647–648
    change in reporting entity, 1148–1149
    equity method and, 644–645, 645n
Consolidation method (securities), 621, 659
Constraints on financial reporting
    conservatism, 26
    cost effectiveness, 25
    materiality, 25–26

Construction in progress (CIP) account, 247, 252
Consumer Price Index, 422
Contingencies, 705–720
    acquired, 714
    fair value of, 714
    gain contingencies, 716–717, 721
    global perspective, 716, 716n
    IASB on, 716, 721
    income taxes, 706n
    litigation contingencies, 712, 713
    loss contingencies. See Loss contingencies
    review of, 717–718
Contingently issuable shares, 1097–1098, 1107
    effect on diluted EPS, 1105
    as potential common shares, 1098, 1099
Contingent rentals, 835
Continuing franchise fees, 260, 262, 510
Continuing operations, income from, 170–174, 208
    discontinued operations reported separately, 183, 183n
    income statement formats, 172–174
    income tax effects, 903
    income tax expense, 172
    net income, 172, 172n
    operating v. nonoperating income, 172
    presentation order of reporting, 180, 180n
    revenues, expenses, gains, and losses, 170–171
Contra accounts
    allowance for uncollectible accounts, 72–73, 73n, 75
    contra asset accounts, 68
    deferred gross profit, 241, 241n
    discount on note receivable, 354
    sales discounts, 343
    sales returns, 345, 345n
    used in depletion, 570
Contracts
    in construction. See Long-term construction contracts
    debt covenants, 809, 809n
    derivatives
        forward contracts, A-0, A-2
        futures contracts, A-1, A-1n, A-4, A-8
    extended warranties, 710
    in financial instruments, 657
    inventory purchase commitments
        contract beyond fiscal year, 477–478
        contract within fiscal year, 477, 477n
    to perform R&D for others, 529
    share rights specified by, 1018, 1019
Contractual life of intangible asset, 559, 571
Contributory (pension) plans, 938, 938n
Control accounts, 55, 90
Controlling interest, 644–645
Control of asset, 361–362, 362n
Conventional retail method, 461, 464, 475–476
Conversion option, 747, 778
    diluted EPS and, 1088
    exercise of, 771–772
    monetary value of, 770
Convertible securities, 1088–1092, 1106–1107
    antidilutive, 1093, 1107
    bonds, 749, 769–772
        actual conversion, 1099–1100
        beneficial conversion feature, 770, 770n

Convertible securities—*Cont.*
  bonds—*Cont.*
    conversion of, 1093, 1094
    diluted EPS and, 1087,
      1089–1090
    global perspective, 771, 771*n*
    induced conversion, 772
    as potential common shares, 1083
    when conversion option is exercised,
      771–772
  convertible preferred stock,
    1090–1092
  effect on diluted EPS, 1104–1105
  multiple, order of entry for,
    1093–1094
  as potential common shares, 1098, 1099
  potential dilutive effect of, 1088
Con-way Inc., 576, 577
"Cookie jar accounting," 1140
"Cooking the books," 1140
Copyrights, 503, 510
Corporate charter, 1017
Corporate executives
  accountability under Sarbanes-Oxley, 17
  compensation of
    disclosure, 131, 132
    share-based. *See* Share-based
      compensation
Corporate form of organization,
    1015–1017, 1042
  complex capital structure, 1087, 1106
  disadvantages, 1015
  ease of raising capital, 1015
  hybrid organizations, 1016
  limited liability, 1015
  Model Business Corporation Act (2009),
    1016–1017
  simple capital structure, 1083, 1086, 1106
  types of corporations, 1016
Corporation(s), 5
  double taxation of, 1015
  ease of raising capital, 1015
  government-owned, 1016
  kinds of, 1016
  multinational, 13–14
  shareholders' equity in, 53
"Corridor," 953, 954, 956
COSO (Committee of Sponsoring
    Organizations) of Treadway
    Commission, 129, 339, 339*n*
Cost(s)
  amortization of investment costs, 627,
    627*n*
  capitalization of. *See* Capitalization
  competitive disadvantage costs, 25
  of compliance with Sarbanes-Oxley, 17*n*,
    17–18
  of construction. *See* Long-term
    construction contracts
  of copyrights, 503, 510
  debt issue costs, 758–759, 1022
  of defending intangible rights, 591–592,
    592*n*
  development costs, 506, 509, 511, 530, 531
  employment cost (pensions), 965
  of equipment, 501, 503
  historical costs, 29, 29*n*
  inventory costs. *See* Inventory(ies)
  land costs, 505
  leases
    costs to lessor, 813, 834–835, 848
    executory costs, 831, 832, 848

    initial direct costs of, 835
    markup on cost, 457
    natural resources
      acquisition costs, 506, 533
      restoration costs of, 506
    net periodic pension cost, 966
    organization costs, 529, 529*n*
    period costs, 401*n*, 558, 572
    prior service cost. *See* Prior service cost
    product costs. *See* Product costs
    replacement cost (RC), 449–450, 475
    research and development (R&D)
      determining costs, 527–529
      start-up costs, 529
    restructuring costs, 169, 177–178, 207
    service cost. *See* Service cost
    share issue costs, 1022
    warranty costs, 708
Cost allocation (assets), 503, 558–573
  accounting error correction in, 578–580,
    593
  amortization of intangible assets. *See*
    Amortization
  change in depreciation, amortization, or
    depletion method, 577–578
  changes in estimates, 576–577
  depletion of natural resources. *See*
    Depletion (natural resources)
  depreciation. *See* Depreciation
  error correction, 578–580, 593
  impairment of value. *See* Impairment of
    asset value
  matching principle in, 558
  measurement of
    allocation base, 559–560
    allocation method, 560
    useful life of asset, 559
  overview, 558
  partial periods, 574*n*, 574–575
  revaluation option, 568*n*, 568–569
    changes in revaluation surplus, 195,
      195*n*
    global perspective, 573, 573*n*
Cost approaches to fair value, 34
Cost depletion, 887, 887*n*
Cost effectiveness, 25
Cost flow assumptions
  in inventory measurement. *See* Inventory
    measurement
  reissued treasury stock, 1028
Cost flow methods, 460–462
  approximating average cost, 460
  approximating average LCM, 461
  LIFO retail method, 461–462, 462*n*, 465,
    475–476
Cost indexes
  for dollar-value LIFO, 422, 447, 475
  for dollar-value LIFO retail, 466, 467
Cost method, 639, 640, 1027
Cost of ending inventory, 416, 423, 459
Cost of goods available for sale, 425, 456
  allocation of, 404–405, 458
  change in accounting principle, 1141
Cost of goods sold
  adjusting cost to market, 452–453
  calculation of, 417, 456, 472–473
  change in inventory method, 1141–1142
  inventory measurement and, 396, 398–399
  product costs, 401*n*, 401–403
  revenue-expense relationship in, 31
  spreadsheet preparation of SCF, 1203
Cost recovery, 240–242

Cost recovery method
  in installment sales, 236, 237, 240,
    242–243
  in long-term construction, 256, 256*n*
"Cost-to-cost ratio," 249, 249*n*
Cost-to-retail percentage, 458, 461, 462, 463
Coupon bonds, 749
Coupon rate of interest, 748, 749
CPA Journal, 175–176
CPAs (certified public accountants), 16
Credit(s), 54
Credit-adjusted risk free rate of interest, 507
Credit losses, 663–664, 665
Creditors, 5, 341
  interest in company assets, 1008
  liquidation forced by, 780
  obligations callable by, 702–703
Credit policies, 365
Credit sales, 60, 91
Cumulative effect of change in accounting
    principle, 180, 188, 1145
Cumulative preferred shares, 1018
Current assets, 77, 139
  accounts receivable. *See* Accounts
    receivable
  balance sheet classifications,
    116–118, 138
    accounts receivable, 118, 351
    cash and cash equivalents, 117, 117*n*
    inventories, 118
    prepaid expenses, 118, 118*n*
    short-term investments, 117–118
  current liabilities satisfied with, 693
  net current tax assets, 897–898, 908
Current liabilities, 77, 139, 692–705, 720. *See
    also* Accrued liabilities; Liabilities
  accrued liabilities, 697–700
    interest payable, 698
    salaries, commissions, and bonuses, 70,
      71, 698–700, 700*n*
  from advance collections, 700–702
    collections from third parties, 702
    deposits and advances from customers,
      700–701
    gift cards, 701–702
  balance sheet classifications, 120, 138–139
  callable obligations, 702–703
  characteristics of, 692*n*, 692–693
  contingencies. *See* Contingencies
  decision makers' perspective of, 719–720
  journal entries for, 704–705
  long-term liabilities compared, 702–704
    current maturities of long-term debt,
      120, 702, 720
    obligations callable by creditor,
      702–703
    refinancing short-term obligations,
      703–704
  nature of, 693
  net current tax liabilities, 897–898, 908
  open accounts and notes, 693–697
    accounts payable, 694
    commercial paper, 697
    short-term notes payable, 694–697
    trade notes payable, 694
  payroll-related liabilities, 721–722
    employee withholding taxes, 721
    employer payroll taxes, 721
    fringe benefits, 722
    voluntary deductions, 721
  recorded at maturity amounts, 693, 693*n*
  recorded at present values, 693, 693*n*

review of, 704–705
short-term borrowings. *See* Short-term
    notes payable
uncertainty (risk) of, 691–692, 720
Current maturities of long-term debt, 120,
    702, 720
Current ratio, 134, 341, 719
Current receivables, 337, 342–368. *See also*
    Receivables
    accounts receivable. *See* Accounts
        receivable
    decision makers' perspective,
        365–368, 367–368
    financing with, 356–365, 366, 369
        "gain-on-sale" accounting, 360
        "participating interests," 362
        required disclosures, 362–363
        review of, 365
        sale and borrowing compared, 361–362
        sale of receivables, 358–360
        secured borrowing, 356–358
        transfers of notes receivable, 361
    notes receivable. *See* Notes receivable
Currie, Neil, 1024
Customary practice, 699
Customers, 142–143, 710

D
Date of record, 1032
DDB (double-declining-balance)
    depreciation, 562, 566
Debenture bonds, 748–749
Debits, 54
Debt, 769–774
    asset acquired with, 513–515, 514n
    bad debts. *See* Bad debt(s); Uncollectible
        accounts
    convertible bonds. *See* Convertible
        securities
    decision makers' perspective of, 765–767
    early extinguishment of, 769, 769n, 774
    payments shown in SCF, 1209
    review, 774
    troubled debt restructuring, 780n, 780–784
        debt is continued, modified, 781–784
        debt is settled, 781
Debt covenants, 809, 809n
Debt coverage ratio, 1223
Debt financing, with receivables,
    356–365, 366, 369
    "gain-on-sale" accounting, 360
    "participating interests," 362
    required disclosures, 362–363
    review of, 365
    sale and borrowing compared, 361–362
    sale of receivables, 358–360
    secured borrowing, 356–358
    transfers of notes receivable, 361
Debt instruments, 340, 368
Debt investments, 661, 663–665
Debt issue costs, 758–759, 1022
Debt payment ratio, 1223
Debt securities, 636, 639, 659, 661
Debt-to-equity ratio, 135n, 135–137, 765
    avoiding limits on, 809, 809n
    capitalization of operating leases, 839
    deferred tax liability and, 904–905
    impact of capital lease transactions, 838
    pension disclosures and, 963
Debt v. equity issue (SARS), 1109, 1109n
DeChow, Patricia M., 8n, 367n
Decision makers' perspective

of accounting for securities, 656n, 656–657
of capital budgeting decisions, 516–517
of cash and cash equivalents, 341–342
of current liabilities, 719–720
of current receivables, 365–368
    earnings quality, 367–368
    receivables management, 365–367
of debt, 765–767
of depreciation methods, 563–564
of earnings per share, 1102–1103
of income taxes, 412, 904–905
inventory measurement
    cost flow assumptions, 411–414
    earnings quality, 420
    inventory management, 417n, 417–419
of leases, 808–809, 838
of motivation for accounting choices,
    1139n, 1139–1140, 1140n
of net income, 412
of pension disclosures, 963, 963n, 973–974
of postretirement benefits, 973–974
ratio analysis
    cash flow ratios, 1223–1224
    return on equity ratios, 766–767, 1037
of share-based compensation, 1080–1081
of share buybacks, 1024–1025
of shareholders' equity, 1037–1038
usefulness of cash flow information, 1184
Decision making
    investment-credit decision, 6–7
    ratio analysis used in. *See* Ratio analysis;
        specific ratios
    two-step process, 900, 900n
    using financial statement information,
        132–133
Decision usefulness, 22, 25
Declaration date, 1034
Declining balance depreciation methods,
    561–562, 566n
Default risk, 133, 765
Deferrals. *See also* Prepayments
    deferred compensation, 1071
    of revenue recognition. *See* Revenue
        recognition
Deferred annuity, 314n, 314–316
Deferred charges, 119
Deferred gross profit account, 241, 241n
Deferred revenue, 701
Deferred tax assets and liabilities, 874–889,
    908
    in classified balance sheet, 897–898
    conceptual underpinning, 847n, 873,
        874, 907
    deferred tax assets, 878, 882–885
        advance collections, 878, 884, 884n
        global perspective, 1077
        valuation allowance on, 885n, 885–886,
            896
    deferred tax liabilities, 875–881
        balance sheet approach (FASB), 877,
            877n
        change in inventory method, 1143
        debt-to-equity ratio and, 904–905
        types of temporary differences, 878–881
    disclosure notes, 898–899
    multiple temporary differences, 892–894,
        905–907
    permanent differences, 886–888, 889, 908
    review, 889
    temporary differences. *See* Temporary
        differences
    valuation allowance, 885n, 885–886, 898

Deficit, 1031
Defined benefit pension plans, 937, 939–940,
    976
Defined contribution pension plans, 937,
    938–939, 976
DeFond, M. L., 1152n
Dell, Michael S., 4
Dell Inc., 4, 5, 16, 24, 29, 31, 32, 117, 118,
    119, 120, 121, 134, 135, 136, 137,
    138, 142, 172, 173, 193, 195, 271,
    347, 367, 397, 417–418, 823
Deloitte & Touche LLP, 129, 130
Demographics, 968
Depletion (natural resources), 502, 557, 558,
    569–571, 592
    biological assets, 571, 571n
    change in depletion method, 189, 190, 577,
        593, 1146
    percentage depletion, 570, 887, 887n
    present value calculations, 507
    review of, 575–576
    tax deduction for, 887, 887n
    units-of-production method, 557, 570, 592
Depletion methods, 189, 570, 1147
Deposits outstanding, 370
Depreciation, 502, 557, 558, 592, 593
    accumulated, 68, 567, 590, 1205
    adjustments for, 648–649
    affected by accounting errors, 1156
    affected by BPO, 826
    capital leases, 819–820
    of leased assets, 819
    no cash effects reported for, 1189
    partial-year, 574n, 574–575
    present value calculations, 507
    temporary differences due to, 878n,
        878–879
Depreciation expense, 68, 1204
Depreciation methods, 560–566
    accelerated. *See* Accelerated depreciation
        methods
    activity-based, 560, 562–563
    change in, 189, 593
        disclosure notes, 577, 578, 1147
        justification for, 190, 191, 577–578
        prospective approach, 1146
    change in accounting estimate, 1147–1148
    comparison of
        decision makers' perspective, 563–564
        with MACRS, 564, 594, 594n, 878n
    disclosure notes, 564, 565, 567
    double-declining-balance, 562, 566
    global perspective, 565, 565n, 568n,
        568–569
    group and composite, 566–568
    replacement method, 594, 595
    retirement method, 594, 595
    review of, 565–566
    straight-line, 560–561
        popularity of, 564
        switch from accelerated, 562
    sum-of-the-years' digits, 561, 561n, 566
    time-based, 560–562
        accelerated methods, 561–562
        straight-line method, 560–561
Depreciation period, 819–820
Derecognition of assets and liabilities, 364,
    364n
Derivative mark-to-market adjustments, 194
Derivatives, 657–658, A-0–A-15. *See also*
    Hedging
    accounting for, A-3–A-10

Derivatives—*Cont.*
  cash flow hedges, 1009, A-8, A-8n, A-15
    fair value. *See* Fair value
    foreign currency hedges, A-8–A-9, A-9n
    hedge effectiveness, A-9, A-9n
    hedge ineffectiveness, A-9
    interest rate swaps. *See* Interest rate swaps
  cash flow hedges, 1009, A-8, A-8n
  disclosure requirements, A-10, A-10n, A-15
  equity method (securities), 657–658
  extended method: interest rate swaps, A-11n–A-13n, A-11–A-14
  global perspective, A-14, A-14n
  interest rate swaps. *See* Interest rate swaps
  losses on, 658
  market value of, A-3–A-4, A-4n, A-15
  other comprehensive income, 194, 1010, 1011
  speculation in, A-3
  used to hedge risk, A-0–A-3
    financial futures, A-1n, A-1–A-2
    foreign currency futures, A-2
    forward contracts, A-0, A-2
    futures contracts, A-1, A-1n, A-4, A-8
    interest rate swaps, A-2–A-3
    options, A-2
Detachable stock purchase warrants, 772–774
Development costs
  of goodwill, 511
  of intangible assets, 509
  of natural resources, 506
  software development. *See* Software development costs
Development stage enterprises, 529, 529n
Dhaliwal, D., 412n, 1140n
Diluted earnings per share. *See* Earnings per share (EPS)
"Dilution" of EPS, 1083, 1085
Direct financing leases, 808, 821, 847
  bargain purchase option and, 825n
  classification by lessor, 818
  financial statement impact of, 840
  initial direct costs, 835
  reported in SCF, 1209
  review, 821–822
Direct reporting method (SCF), 1225
  comprehensive review, 1214–1218
  indirect reporting contrasted, 200–201, 1190–1192
  as proposed requirement, 205
  spreadsheet used in, 1197–1214, 1199n
    balance sheet accounts, 1207–1214
    completion of spreadsheet, 1211–1214
    comprehensive review, 1214–1218
    illustrated, 1198–1199
    income statement accounts, 1199–1207
  in statement of cash flows, 200, 206
Direct write-off method, 25, 350–351, 368, 1201
Disasters (unexpected events)
  destruction of plant assets, 580
  Hurricane Katrina (2005), 187
  involuntary conversion due to, 518
Disclaimers, 131
Disclosure(s). *See* Financial disclosures
Disclosure notes, 4, 31, 125–127
  accounting changes

accounting estimate, 190–191, 576, 577, 1146, 1147
  accounting policy, 569
  accounting principle, 189, 190, 1144
  depreciation method, 577, 578, 1147
  error correction, 474, 580, 1154, 1158, 1159
  reporting entity, 1149
acquisitions, 192
allowance for loan losses, 355
assets
  asset retirement obligations, 508
  financial, reclassification of, 638
  impairment losses, 582, 583, 585, 586, 664
  indefinite-life assets, 572
  leased assets, 820
  property, plant, and equipment, 502
  self-constructed assets, 526
  service life of, 559
callable bonds, 749
cash equivalents, 117, 338, 1188
commercial paper, 697
compensating balances, 340
contingencies
  litigation contingencies, 712, 713
  loss contingencies, 707
  pending litigation, 706
contingent rentals, 835
conversion of notes, 1100
debt, 764
defined contribution plans, 939
depletion method, 570
depreciation methods, 564, 565, 567
discontinued components, 184, 185
election of fair value option, 777
extraordinary loss, 187, 187n
factoring arrangements, 362
fair value hierarchy in, 643
gift cards, 701
impairment of value
  goodwill, 585, 586
  losses, 582
  loss policy, 583
  OTT impairment, 664
income taxes, 898–900
  deferred, 902
  deferred tax assets and liabilities, 898–899
  effective tax rates, 888
  income tax expense, 899–900
  operating loss carryforwards, 899
as information source for ratio analysis, 963
intangible assets, 502, 503
  indefinite-life assets, 572
  useful life of, 571
inventories, 118, 397
  change in inventory method, 470, 471, 1144, 1145
  cost flow assumptions, 411
  inventory method, 448, 467
  LIFO liquidation, 414
  policies, 413
  valuation, 454
  write-downs, 453
investments, 622
  financial statement presentation of, 642–643
  HTM securities, 625, 625n
  noncash investing and financing, 204

leases
  leased assets, 820
  operating leases, 837, 838
  sales-type leases, 823, 836, 837
lines of credit, 693, 694, 695
material events reported in, 273
maturity date of debt securities, 643
noteworthy events and transactions, 126–127
oil and gas accounting, 535
pensions
  gain on termination of plan, 963
  pension expense, 957
  pension plans, 935–936, 957, 963
pledging of receivables, 357, 358
postretirement benefits, 967
prior service cost, 945
on R&D expenditures, 532
related-party transactions, 127
reporting liabilities at fair value, 777
revenue recognition policy, 235, 239, 240, 244, 245, 260, 354
sales returns policy, 346
secured loans, 696, 697
securitizations, 358–359
segment information, 141, 142, 143
shareholders' equity
  contingently issuable shares, 1098
  earnings per share data, 1100, 1101, 1105, 1107
  restricted stock award plans, 1070
  share repurchase program, 1025
  stock appreciation rights, 1109
  stock splits, 1036
software development costs, 530, 531
subsequent events, 125–126, 126n, 714
summary of significant accounting policies, 125, 125n, 252, 253
unasserted claims, 715
valuation allowances, 886
Disclosure requirements. *See* Financial disclosures
Discontinued operations, 169, 207, 208
  nature of operations, 182–183
  separately reported in income statement, 180n, 182–186, 902
  interim reporting, 186
  when component has been sold, 183–184
  when component is held for sale, 184–186
  tax effects of, 188n
Discounting notes receivable, 361
Discount on bonds, 747, 750, 751, 778
  adjustment in preparing SCF, 1220n
  amortization of, 1090, 1210
  amortization schedule, 624, 753
Discount on note payable, 514
Discount on securities, 622
Discount (interest) rate
  actuary's discount rate, 951
  leases
    incremental borrowing rate, 833, 833n
    lessor's implicit rate, 833–834
    lessor's initial direct costs, 834–835, 848
Discretionary accruals, 367, 367n
Disposition of assets, 517–521
  exchanges. *See* Exchanges
  involuntary conversion, 518
  by sale or retirement, 517–518
Distributions to owners, 27

Dividend(s), 1031*n*, 1031–1033
  cash dividends. *See* Cash dividends
  cautions about, 1038
  declaration of, 1032
  distribution to preferred shareholders, 1019, 1086, 1086*n*
  liquidating dividend, 1031
  payment of, 1193
  property dividends, 1033
  receiving, 647
  restrictions on, 1032
  share retirement and, 1027, 1027*n*
  stock dividends. *See* Stock dividends
  stock splits, 1035
Dividend in kind, 1033
Dividend payment ratio, 1223
Dividend payout ratio, 1103
Dividend rights of common shares, 1017
Dividends in arrears, 1018
Dividends received deduction, 887, 887*n*
Dollar-value LIFO (DVL), 421–423
  advantages of, 422
  cost indexes for, 422, 447, 475
  DVL pools, 421–422
  inventory estimation technique, 422–423, 423*n*
  price indices used in, 475
  review of, 423–424
Dollar-value LIFO retail, 465–467, 476
  cost indexes for, 466, 467
  inventory layers in, 466
  review of, 468–469
Domino's Pizza, 817
Donated assets, 515–516, 516*n*
Dot-com companies, 448
Double counting, 645*n*
Double-declining-balance (DDB) depreciation, 562, 566
Double-entry system, 53
Double-extension method, 422
Double taxation of corporations, 1015
Dow Chemical Company, 507
Dow Jones Industrial Average, 115
Dow Jones Industrial companies, 177–178
Dunn, Brian J., 132
DuPont framework, 266, 266*n*, 267, 268
Duriron Company, Inc., 1022
DVL. *See* Dollar-value LIFO
DVL pools, 421–422

E

Early extinguishment of debt, 769, 769*n*, 774, 779
"Earnings management," 1080–1081
Earnings per share (EPS), 208, 1082–1105
  additional issues, 1096–1105
    actual conversions, 1099–1100
    contingently issuable shares, 1097–1098
    effect of potential common shares, 1098, 1099, 1101
    financial statement presentation, 1100, 1101
    "proceeds" in treasury stock method, 1096–1097
    restricted stock awards, 1097, 1097*n*
    review, 1104–1105
  antidilutive securities, 1092–1096
    convertible securities, 1093, 1107
    options, rights, and warrants, 1092–1093
    order of entry for multiple convertible securities, 1093–1094
    potential common shares, 1101

  basic, 1083–1086
    diluted EPS compared, 169, 208, 1087
    earnings available to common shareholders, 1086
    issuance of new shares, 1083, 1084
    reacquired shares, 1085–1086
    reconciliation to diluted EPS, 1101, 1105
    review, 1095, 1104
    stock dividends and stock splits, 1084–1085, 1106
  decision makers' perspective of, 1102–1103
  diluted, 169, 193, 208, 1087–1092
    basic EPS compared, 169, 208, 1087
    convertible bonds, 1087, 1089–1090
    convertible securities, 1104–1105
    end-of-period stock price, 1102
    maximum potential dilution, 1093–1094
    options, rights, and warrants, 1087–1088, 1106
    potential common shares, 1087
    reconciliation to basic EPS, 1101, 1105
    review, 1095–1096, 1104–1105
    treasury stock method, 1102
  disclosure notes, 1100, 1101, 1105, 1107
  disclosures, 192–193, 198
  FASB on, 1102
  global perspective, 1082, 1102, 1102*n*, 1107
  IASB on, 1082, 1102, 1102*n*
  interim reporting, 272
  per incremental share, 1094
  pro forma, 1102–1103
  pro forma EPS, 1102–1103
  ratio analysis, 192–193
  review, 1095–1096
Earnings-price ratio, 1037
Earnings quality, 175–179, 208
  current receivables, 367–368
  EPS data and, 1103
  impact of revenues on, 177–178
  impairment losses and, 588
  income manipulation and income smoothing, 175–176
  inventories and, 474–475
  inventory management and, 420
  nonoperating income and, 179
  operating income and, 176–178
  pension disclosures and, 963
  predictive value of information and, 23
  share-based compensation and, 1080–1081
Earthlink, 651
eBay, 1072
Ecolab, Inc., 944, 945
Economic entity assumption, 28, 32
Economic events, 52, 52*n*
The Economist, 627, 627*n*
Eddie Bauer Holdings, Inc., 572
EDS, 246
Effective interest method
  bonds, 752–756, 779
    financial statements between interest dates, 756
    journal entries, 762
    market rate of interest, 753
    sold at face amount, 756
    sold at premium, 754–755
    zero-coupon bonds, 753, 754
  securities, 623
Effective (annual) interest rate, 300–301, 354
  investments, 623–624

  on noninterest-bearing notes, 696, 696*n*
  in troubled debt restructuring, 782, 783
Effective tax rate, 887, 888
Electronic Arts, 113
Eligibility for postretirement benefits, 970–971
El Paso Natural Gas Company (EPNG), 567
Emhart Corporation, 749
Emphasis noted in auditors' reports, 130
Employee compensation
  changes in compensation estimates, 1110–1111
  as current liability, 698
  as employee incentive, 1069, 1105–1106
  pension plans. *See* Pension plan(s)
  postretirement benefits, 966–967
  salaries, commissions, and bonuses
    annual bonuses, 700, 700*n*, 1140, 1140*n*
    current or accrued liability for, 70, 71, 698–700, 700*n*
    paid future absences, 698–700
  share-based. *See* Share-based compensation
Employee discounts, 463
Employee pool, 942, 947
Employee Retirement Income Security Act (ERISA) of 1974, 942, 948, 959
Employee share purchase plans, 1080, 1106
Employee stock option plans. *See* Stock option plans
Employee stock ownership plan (ESOP), 938*n*
Employee withholding taxes, 721
Employer payroll taxes, 721
Employment cost (pensions), 965
End-of-period stock price, 1102
Enron Corporation, 4, 16, 17, 19, 658, 1073
Enterprise Resource Planning (ERP) systems, 52
EPBO. *See* Expected postretirement benefit obligation
EPNG (El Paso Natural Gas Company), 567
EPS. *See* Earnings per share
Equipment
  acquisition costs, 501, 503
  capitalization of costs, 504, 505
  initial costs of, 501, 533
  loss on sale of, 1205
  spreadsheet preparation of SCF, 1208–1209
Equity. *See* Shareholders' equity
Equity investments, 639
Equity method (securities), 619–620, 621, 644–658, 659
  change in conditions, 651–653
    from another method to equity method, 651–652
    equity method investment is sold, 652
    from equity method to another method, 651, 1145, 1145*n*
    fair value and equity methods compared, 652–653
    fair value option, 653
  consolidated statements and, 644–645, 645*n*
  decision makers' perspective of, 656*n*, 656–657
  effect on deferred income taxes, 649
  financial instruments and derivatives, 657–658
  further adjustments, 647–649
    for additional depreciation, 648–649
    deferred income taxes, 649

Equity method (securities)—*Cont.*
  further adjustments—*Cont.*
    land or goodwill not adjusted, 649
    other assets and liabilities, 649
  IFRS requirements for, 653n, 653–654, 654n, 659
  inappropriate with lack of significant influence, 646, 646n
  indications of lack of influence, 646, 646n
  nature of significant influence, 645
  reporting investments, 649–651, 650n
    in financial statements, 644–645, 645n, 655
    investee reports net loss, 650
    investment acquired mid-year, 650–651
    when to discontinue equity method, 650
  review, 654–656
  single entity concept, 645–647
Equity multiplier (ratio), 266, 267, 268
Equity securities, 659
  asset acquired by issuance of, 515, 533
  IFRS classification, 637
  recognizing OTT loss, 661
ERISA (Employee Retirement Income Security Act) of 1974, 942, 948, 959
ERP (Enterprise Resource Planning) systems, 52
ESOP (employee stock ownership plan), 938n
Estimated forfeitures (stock options), 1074–1075
Ethical dilemmas, 19
  accounting error correction, 1157
  bargain purchase options, 827
  current ratio, 134
  expense manipulation, 20
  inventory write-downs, 451
  lump-sum purchases, 513
  postretirement health benefits, 971–972
  revenue recognition, 236
  statement of cash flows, 1212
  stock dividends, 1038
  uncollectible accounts, 350
Ethics
  analytical decision model, 19n, 19–20
  changes in PBO and, 944
  professionalism and, 19
Excess tax benefit, 1096
Exchanges, 518–520, 521
  fair value of, 519, 534
  lacking commercial substance, 519–520, 520n
    cash received, 520, 520n
    gain situation, 520
    loss situation, 520, 534
  nonmonetary, 518n, 518–519
  review of, 521
Ex-dividend date, 1032
Executive compensation
  disclosure of, 131, 132
  share-based. *See* Share-based compensation
Executory costs (leases), 831, 832, 848
Exercise of options
  conversion option, 771–772
  stock options, 1075–1076
Existing violation of debt provision, 702
Expected cash flow approach
  to asset retirement obligations, 507, 507n, 508
  to contingent liabilities, 711
  present value and, 308n, 308–309

product warranties and guarantees, 709, 709n
Expected economic life of asset, 811–812
Expected postretirement benefit obligation (EPBO), 969–970, 976
  attribution of, 969–970, 970n
  comprehensive illustration, 972, 973
  measuring, 969, 969n
  review, 974
Expected rate of return, 6
Expenditures
  for advertising, 31
  authorization of, 339
  capitalization of, 589
  improper capitalization of, 504
  included in inventories, 401n, 401–403
    freight-in on purchases, 401–402
    purchase discounts, 402–403
    purchase returns, 402
    sales returns, 401
  in interest capitalization, 522–523, 525
  R&D expenditures, 532, 532n, 534
  subsequent to asset acquisition, 589–592
    additions, 590
    costs of defending intangible rights, 591–592, 592n
    improvements, 590, 591, 593
    rearrangements, 590–591, 593
    repairs and maintenance, 589, 590, 591, 593
Expense accounts, 79, 80
Expenses, 8, 27, 170
  abnormal product costs, 401, 401n
  classification by function, 174
  closing account to income summary, 79–80
  from continuing operations, 170–171
  deferred tax assets and liabilities, 878, 882–883
  due to illegal acts, 887
  of having pension plan, 940
  income tax expense, 172
  interim reporting, 271–272
  manipulation of (ethical dilemma), 20
  prepaid
    adjusting entries for, 67–68
    balance sheet classifications, 118, 118n
    deferred tax liabilities, 878
    future deductible amounts, 883–884, 884n
    recording in journal, 59
Explanatory paragraphs, 130, 131
Exploration costs, 506
Extended warranty contracts, 710
External transactions, 52, 55–64, 86
External users of financial information, 4, 5
Extraordinary gains (losses)
  classification of, 180n
  forced sale, 186–187, 187n
  income statement presentation, 180n, 180–182
  SCF summary entry affected by, 1206–1207
Extraordinary items, 169, 207, 208
  criteria for, 769n
  global perspective, 180n, 904, 904n
  income tax effects of
    global perspective, 904, 904n
    reporting, 902–903
  separately reported in income statement, 174, 180n, 186n, 186–187, 187n
ExxonMobil Corporation, 411, 1008, 1188

F
Face amount
  of bonds, 748, 751, 756
  of convertible bonds, 1090
  of securities, 622, 623
Factor, 358, 360n
Factoring, 358, 360n
Factoring receivables, 697, 697n
FAF (Financial Accounting Foundation), 10, 10n, 12
Fair value, 34–36
  of assets
    asset retirement obligations, 711
    in capital leases, 817
    exchanges, 519, 534
    goodwill, 512, 512n, 585
    implicit rate of interest inferred from, 733n, 833
    reporting, 568n, 568–569
  of contingencies, 714
  of derivatives, A-3–A-4, A-4n, A-7–A-8, A-14
    changes in, 194
    changes not related to risk, A-9–A-10
    fair value hedges. *See* Fair value hedges
    interest rate swaps, A-11, A-11n, A-12
  determination of, 624, 625
  estimation of, 581
  of financial instruments, 764, 764n
  GAAP on, 34, 34n, 35, 355
  of in-process R&D, 531–532
  inputs, 34, 35
  of lump-sum purchases, 512, 513
  in measuring liabilities, 177
  movement toward, 34n, 34–36
    asset/liability approach and, 877
    fair value defined, 34, 35
    fair value option, 35n, 35–36
  in multiple-deliverable arrangements, 260
  90% criterion in capital leases, 811, 812–813, 834
  of noncash acquisitions, 512
  noncash transactions, 781
  of notes payable, 514n, 514–515
  of notes receivable, 355
  reporting changes in, 775–777
  of securities
    AFS securities, 629
    HTM securities, 622
    not readily determinable, 639, 639n, 640
    trading securities, 625–626, 628, 628n
  of stock options
    attempt to require, 1072, 1072n
    estimated forfeitures, 1074–1075
    recognizing, 1073–1075
    restricted stock award plans, 1106
    vendor-specific objective evidence (VSOE), 259, 259n, 260
Fair value adjustment
  AFS securities, 631n, 631–634, 632n
    new changes, 633
    reclassification adjustment, 633n, 633–634
  interest rate swaps, A-5–A-6
  trading securities, 627, 627n, 628–629
Fair value approaches, 34–36, 711
Fair value hedges, A-4, A-4n, A-15
  available-for-sale securities, A-9
  firm commitments, A-9
  futures contracts, A-4

interest rate swaps, A-4
against risk, A-0
Fair value hierarchy, 35, 624, 643
Fair value method (securities)
AFS securities. *See* Available-for-sale
securities
equity method compared, 652–653
potentially inaccurate estimates, 657
trading securities. *See* Trading securities
Fair value option, 644, 653, 659
for financial instruments, 35*n*, 35–36, 36*n*,
355, 355*n*
global perspective, 638, 638*n*, 639
in hedging, 638
for investments
change in conditions, 653
disclosure requirements, 643
global perspective, 638, 638*n*
HTM securities, 621, 625, 625*n*
transfers between reporting categories,
637–638, 638*n*
for liabilities, 775–778, 779
determining fair value, 775
global perspective, 777–778, 778*n*
mix and match, 777
reporting changes in fair value, 775–777
Fair value standard, 13
Fair Value through Other Comprehensive
Income (FVTOCI), 637, 644
Fair Value through Profit & Loss (FVTPL),
636, 637, 638, 638*n*
Faithful representation, 23–24
Fannie Mae, 1187
FASAC. *See* Financial Accounting Standards
Advisory Council
FASAC (Financial Accounting Standards
Advisory Council), 10*n*
FASB. *See* Financial Accounting Standards
Board
FASB/IASB joint projects
accounting for financial instruments, 644,
644*n*
on derivatives and hedge accounting, A-14
Financial Statement Presentation,
1030–1031, 1191
balance sheet presentation, 122–123
new classification system, 204–205
hybrid securities, 771, 771*n*
Memorandum of Understanding (2006),
589
other comprehensive income, 195, 195*n*
on performance reporting, 704, 704*n*
postretirement benefit standard, 964–966
on revenue recognition, 236*n*, 262*n*,
262–263
right-of-use model for leases, 824, 824*n*
Favorable financial leverage, 765
FDA (Food and Drug Administration), 531
FDIC (Federal Deposit Insurance
Corporation), 1016
Federal Deposit Insurance Corporation
(FDIC), 1016
Federal Insurance Contributions Act
(FICA), 721
Federal Reserve, A-0
Federal Unemployment Tax Act (FUTA), 721
Federated Department Stores, 1008
FedEx, 170, 239
Feeny Manufacturing Company, 1097, 1098
FICA (Federal Insurance Contributions Act),
721

FIFO. *See* First-in, first-out (FIFO) inventory
method
Finance cost (pensions), 965
Financial accounting, 2–37
conceptual framework of, 20–36
development of standards for. *See*
Financial accounting and reporting
standards
environment of. *See* Financial accounting
environment
ethics in. *See* Ethics
Financial accounting and reporting standards,
9–19
financial reporting reform, 16–18
global issues in, 13–16
historical perspective, 9–12
current standard setting, 10–12
early standard setting, 9–10
global standard setting, 14–16
government standard setting, 12
objectives-oriented v. rules-based
approach, 18–19
political process of setting, 3, 12–13,
36–37
role of auditor in, 16
Financial accounting environment, 4–20
development of standards, 9–19
current standard setting, 10–12
early standard setting, 9–10
ethics, 19*n*, 19–20
financial reporting reform, 16–18
global standard setting, 14–16
government standard setting, 12
economic environment, 5–8
cash accounting v. accrual accounting,
7–8
investment-credit decision, 6–7
of standard setting, 3, 36–37
Financial Accounting Foundation (FAF), 10,
10*n*, 12
Financial Accounting Standards Advisory
Council (FASAC), 10*n*
Financial Accounting Standards Board
(FASB), 7, 37
on accounting for financial instruments,
644, 644*n*
Accounting Standards Codification project,
11, 11*n*
approach to deferred tax liability, 877,
877*n*
attempt to require fair value of stock
options, 1072, 1072*n*
change in accounting principle mandated
by, 189, 190
on change in tax laws, 890
creation of (1973), 10
on disclosure of contingencies, 716
Discussion Memoranda (DM), 14
on earnings per share, 1102
efforts to merge GAAP and IFRS, 15, 21,
32–33
Emerging Issues Task Force (EITF)
*EITF Issues. See Accounting Standards
Index*
formation of, 10
on multiple deliverables, 259, 259*n*
role in standard setting, 14
Exposure Drafts (ED), 14. *See also
Accounting Standards Index*
*Interpretations. See Accounting Standards
Index*

joint projects with IASB. *See* FASB/IASB
joint projects
management approach to reportable
segments, 140
Norwalk Agreement (2002), 15
operating segments defined, 182–183,
183*n*
on pension plans
income smoothing, 953, 953*n*
net loss or gain on PBO, 952–953, 954
prior service cost as OCI, 952
on principles-based accounting, 18
project on off-balance-sheet financing, 658
on reporting cash flows, 202
role in standard setting, 12
on special purpose entities, 359, 359*n*
*Staff Positions. See Accounting Standards
Index*
standards-setting process, 13, 14
*Statements of Financial Accounting
Concepts (SFACs)*
as conceptual framework, 20–21
individual statements. *See Accounting
Standards Index*
*Statements of Financial Accounting
Standards (SFASs)*
individual statements. *See Accounting
Standards Index*
issuance of, 14
*Technical Bulletins. See Accounting
Standards Index*
Financial Analysts Federation, 10*n*
Financial calculators, 302, 316
Financial crises
crisis of 2008-2009, 13, 36, 115, 697,
697*n*, 1187
stock market crash of 1929, 9
Financial disclosures, 114, 124–132, 139.
See also Disclosure notes
accounting error correction, 474, 580,
1154, 1158, 1159
auditor's report, 129–131
disclosure notes. *See* Disclosure notes
earnings per share, 192–193, 198
enhanced disclosure of derivatives, A-10,
A-10*n*
executive compensation, 131, 132
fair value disclosures, 643, 643*n*, 777
investment in securities, 642*n*, 642–643
justification for accounting choices, 1144
management discussion and analysis,
128, 139
management's responsibilities, 128, 129
notes receivable, 355
operating loss carryforwards, 899
pension-related disclosures, 940, 963,
963*n*, 973–974
prior period adjustments, 1158, 1159
required
accounting errors, 1149, 1157, 1158,
1159
amortization of capital leases, 818
derivatives and risk, A-10, A-10*n*, A-15
executive compensation, 131, 132
fair value option (investments), 643
financing with receivables, 362–363
for interim reporting, 272*n*, 272–273,
643, 643*n*
lease disclosures, 818, 834*n*, 835–837
long-term debt, 763–764, 779
Financial Executives International, 10*n*, 339*n*

Financial flexibility, 116
Financial futures, A-0, A-1n, A-1–A-2
Financial information
  about major customers, 142–143
  cash flow information, 115, 1184
  constraints on
    conservatism, 26, 26n
    cost effectiveness, 25
    materiality, 25–26
  in decision making, 25, 132–133
  hierarchy of, 23, 26n
  internal and external users of, 4, 5
  operating segment information. See
      Operating segments
  qualitative characteristics of, 22–24, 37
    comparability, 24, 1082, 1137, 1139
    confirmatory value, 23
    consistency, 24, 24n, 1137, 1139
    enhancing, 24
    faithful representation, 23–24
    neutrality/objectivity, 24
    predictive value, 23, 175
    relevance, 23, 27
    reliability, 27, 890
    timeliness, 24, 29, 271–273
    understandability, 24
    verifiability, 24, 29
  use in risk analysis, 132–133
Financial institutions, 642–643
Financial instruments
  defined, 657
  derivatives. See Derivatives
  fair value option for, 35, 35n, 36, 36n, 355,
      355n
Financial leverage, 136n, 136–137, 137n
  in DuPont framework, 266
  favorable, 765
Financial reporting, 5, 20–26
  constraints on
    conservatism, 26
    cost effectiveness, 25
    materiality, 25–26
  elements of financial statements.
      See Financial statement(s)
  flexibility in reporting comprehensive
      income, 194–195, 195n
  interim reporting, 271–273
    accounting changes, 272
    discontinued operations, 186
    earnings per share, 272
    inventory estimation techniques and,
        400, 400n
    minimum disclosures, 272n, 272–273,
        643, 643n
    revenues and expenses, 271–272
    unusual items, 272
  internal control over, 128, 129
  inventory reporting. See Inventory(ies)
  objective of, 21, 22
  pensions. See Pension plan(s)
  qualitative characteristics of information.
      See Financial information
  reform of, 16–18
  requirements
    for auditors' reports (PCAOB), 129,
        129n, 130
    changes in accounting principle, 1145
    disclosures. See Financial disclosures
    by GAAP. See Generally accepted
        accounting principles
    of Sarbanes-Oxley, 17

of SEC. See Securities and Exchange
    Commission
  segment information, 25, 25n
segment information. See Operating
    segments
shareholders' equity, 1008–1014
  accumulated other comprehensive
      income, 1010n, 1010–1011
  equity reporting, 1012–1013, 1014
  global perspective, 1012, 1012n, 1013
  paid-in capital, 1009–1010
  retained earnings, 1010
  treasury stock, 1010
Financial statement(s)
  available to be issued, 713, 713n
  comparative. See Comparative financial
      statements
  consolidated, 645, 645n, 647–648
    change in reporting entity, 1148–1149
    equity method and, 644–645, 645n
  distribution of, 126n
  elements of, 26–27
  error affecting previous statements, 1154
  impact of leases, 838–840
    balance sheet and income statement,
        838–839
    statement of cash flows, 839–840, 1209
  inventories, 400
  management responsibilities for, 128, 129
  new "business activities" category in,
      122–123, 205, 1030, 1191
  preparation of, 76–79, 86
    balance sheet, 77–78, 81, 86
    income statement, 76–77
    between interest dates, 756
    review of, 81–82
    statement of cash flows, 78–79
    statement of shareholders' equity, 79, 79n
    worksheet used in, 87–88
  recognition and measurement concepts,
      27–32
    broad principles of GAAP, 29–32
    measurement, 28
    recognition, 27–28
    underlying assumptions of GAAP,
        28–29
  supplemental, 31
Financial statement carrying amount, 877
Financial statement presentation
  of earnings per share, 1100, 1101
  fair presentation, 3, 37
  FASB/IASB joint project on, 1030–1031,
      1191
    balance sheet presentation, 122–123
    new classification system, 204–205
  GAAP on income statement, 174
  gains and losses from extraordinary items,
      180n, 180–182
  global issues, 122–123
  of income taxes, 897–900
    balance sheet classification, 897–898
    disclosure notes, 898–900
  investments
    AFS securities, 634n, 634–635
    disclosures, 642–643
    trading securities, 629, 629n
Financing
  "off-balance-sheet," 658, 767, 809,
      809n, 834
  with receivables, 356–365, 366, 369
    "gain-on-sale" accounting, 360

"participating interests," 363, 363n
    required disclosures, 362–363
    review of, 365
    sale and borrowing compared, 361–362
    sale of receivables, 358–360
    secured borrowing, 356–358
    transfers of notes receivable, 361
Financing activities, 78
  cash flows from, 1185, 1225
    commercial paper, 697
    noncash financing activities, 204, 1194,
        1195, 1225
    payment of dividends, 1193
    share retirement, 1211
    in statement of cash flows, 203–204,
        1193
  cash/noncash transactions, 1195
  information from SCF, 1183, 1224
  investing and financing activity ratio, 1223
Financing ratios, 135–138
  debt-to-equity ratio. See Debt-to-equity
      ratio
  times interest earned ratio, 137–138, 138n,
      765, 767
Finished goods inventory, 118, 396
Firm commitments, A-9
First-in, first-out (FIFO) inventory method,
    407–408, 425
  adjusting entries for, 416
  average cost and LIFO compared to,
      410–411
  income reported under, 418
  income tax issues, 412, 412n
  periodic FIFO, 407
  perpetual FIFO, 408
  physical flow of inventory and, 411
  switch from LIFO
    adjusting accounts for change, 1143
    retrospective reporting of, 189, 1137,
        1141–1142, 1160
  switch to LIFO, 1139
    disclosure of, 471n, 471–472
    LIFO reserve account and, 413
Fiscal year, 29
Fixed assets. See Property, plant, and
    equipment
Fixed-asset turnover ratio, 516–517,
    517n, 534
Flextronics International Limited, 358–359,
    706, 711
Floating payment, A-11, A-11n
Fluor Corporation, 252, 253
f.o.b. (free on board) destination, 238,
    238n, 401
f.o.b. (free on board) shipping point, 238,
    238n, 400
Food and Drug Administration (FDA), 531
"Forced sale" acquisition, 512
Ford Motor Company, 1016, 1148
Forecasted transactions, A-9
Foreign Corrupt Practices Act of 1977, 127
Foreign currency futures, A-2
Foreign currency hedges, A-8–A-9, A-9n
Foreign currency risk, A-0
Foreign currency translation, 1009
  adjustments, 194, A-9
  gains (losses) from, 1010, 1011
Foreign exchange risk, A-0, A-2
Form 10-K (SEC), 9n, 29n, 271n
Form 10-Q (SEC), 9n, 29n, 271n
Fortune magazine, 175, 1103

Forward contracts, A-0, A-2
Foster, Taylor W., 1034n
Foster Wheeler Corporation, 246
401(k) plans, 938
Fractional shares, 1037
Franchise(s)
   acquisition costs, 503
   capitalization of costs, 510
   revenue recognition, 260–262, 270
      continuing franchise fees, 260, 262, 510
      initial franchise fee, 260, 261, 261n, 510
      substantial performance concept, 261
Franchisee, 260
Franchisor, 260
Frank, Mary Margaret, 905n
Freddie Mac, 1187
Freight-in, 401–402, 462, 463
Fringe benefits, 722
Frito-Lay, 1148
Frontline (PBS series), 1073
Full-cost method, 522, 534–535
Full-disclosure principle, 31–32
Fundamental share rights, 1017
"Funded status" of pension plan, 949, 949n, 976
FUTA (Federal Unemployment Tax Act), 721
Future deductible amounts
   adjusting accounts for, 1143
   caused by temporary differences, 882–884, 884n, 892, 908
Futures contracts, A-1, A-1n
   as cash flow hedges, A-8
   as fair value hedges, A-4
Future taxable amounts, 876, 892, 908
Future value (FV)
   of annuities, 310–312, 323
      annuity due (FVAD), 311–312
      ordinary annuity (FVA), 310–311, 324
   compound interest included, 304
   of single cash flow amount, 301–302, 323, 324
   solving for unknown values, 304–305
   summary of concepts, 322–323
   using financial calculators and spreadsheets, 302, 316
Future value tables
   Future Value of $1, 301–302, 305, 310, 324
   Future Value of Annuity Due, 312
   Future Value of Ordinary Annuity, 310–311
FV. See Future value
"FV through net income" category, 644
FVTOCI (Fair Value through Other Comprehensive Income), 637
FVTPL (Fair Value through Profit & Loss), 636, 637, 638, 638n

G

GAAP. See Generally accepted accounting principles
Gain(s), 27, 171
   deferred
      in cash flow hedges, A-8, A-8n
      in sale-leaseback transactions, 844, 844n, 848
   delayed, justification for, 953, 953n
   on disposal of discontinued operation, 183, 184
   on exchange of assets. See Exchanges
   extraordinary. See Extraordinary gains (losses)

from foreign currency translation, 1010, 1011
   holding gains. See Holding gains (losses)
   on nonmonetary exchange, 520, 534
   on PBO, 946, 950
   pensions
      actuarial gains (losses), 946, 955–956, 956n
      gain on pension plan assets, 940, 950, 951
      net loss or gain on PBO, 952–953, 954
   on sale of land, 1202–1203
   unrealized. See Unrealized gain (loss)
Gain contingencies, 716–717, 721
"Gain-on-sale accounting," 360
The Gap, Inc., 517
GASB (Government Accounting Standards Board), 10n, 12
Gatorade, 1148
General Electric, 1015, 1016, 1140, 1148
General journal, 56, 91, 91n
   adjusting entries in, 73
   transactions recorded in, 62
General ledger, 54
   control accounts in, 55, 90
   transactions posted in, 63
Generally accepted accounting principles (GAAP), 9, 9n, 37
   on accounts receivable valuation, 342–343
   accrual basis accounting required by, 84n
   on asset retirement obligations, 506, 506n
   on balance sheet presentation, 139, 141
   on classification of cash flows, 199, 200, 209
   differences with tax rules. See Temporary differences
   efforts to merge with IFRS, 15, 21, 32–33
   enhanced disclosures of derivatives, A-10, A-10n
   on fair value, 34, 34n, 35, 355
   income statement presentation, 174
   on initial franchise fees, 261
   installment sales method required by, 240, 240n
   on lease classifications, 814, 814n
   materiality constraint and, 25
   move toward fair value, 34, 34n, 35
   offsetting not permitted by, 357
   on operating segment information, 141, 142
   on past pension accounting, 940, 940n
   percentage-of-completion method required by, 246, 246n
   on recording prior service cost, 957–958
   on sale of receivables, 360, 361–362
   on statement of cash flows, 202
   tax rules different from, 172, 873, 907
   terminology differences with IFRS, 1013, 1042
   underlying assumptions of
      economic entity assumption, 28, 32
      going concern assumption, 28–29
      monetary unit assumption, 29
      periodicity assumption, 29
      summary of, 32, 37
   on voluntary accounting changes, 188, 188n
General Mills, Inc., 366, 411, 693, 694, 695, 702, 753, 754
General Motors Corporation, 131, 501, 775, 967, 1148

Geographic area reporting, 142
Giacomino, Don, 1224n
Gibson Greetings, 658
Gift cards, 701–702
Givoly, Dan, 905n
Global economy, 13–16
   multinational corporations in, 13–14
   standard-setting in, 14–16
Global issues, 15
   accounting error correction, 1158, 1160
   accounts receivable, 356, 356n, 369
   balance sheet presentation, 122, 139
   biological assets, 571, 571n
   cash and cash equivalents, 341, 341n
   change in inventory method, 1145
   classification of cash flows, 199–200, 200n, 209, 1212–1213, 1225
   comprehensive income, 194, 195, 195n, 961, 961n, 1012, 1012n
   contingencies, 716, 716n
   convertible bonds, 771, 771n
   cost method for equity investments, 640
   cost of defending intangible rights, 592, 592n
   debt-equity distinction in preferred shares, 1019, 1019n
   debt issue costs, 759
   deferred taxes, 887, 887n, 908
   depreciation methods, 565, 565n, 568n, 568–569
   derivatives, A-14, A-14n
   earnings per share, 1082, 1102, 1102n, 1107
   extraordinary items, 187, 187n
   fair value option, 638, 638n, 639, 777–778, 778n
   financial statement presentation, 122–123
   impairment of asset value
      goodwill, 586n, 586–587
      indefinite-life intangibles, 584, 584n
      other-than-temporary impairment, 665–666
      property, plant, and equipment, 583, 583n
   income statement presentation, 174
   inventory cost flow assumption, 411, 411n
   investments without significant influence, 636n, 636–637
   land-and-building leases, 846, 846n
   liabilities to be refinanced, 704
   long-term construction contracts, 256, 256n, 260, 260n, 270
   lower of cost or market (LCM), 453n, 453, 454, 476
   multiple deliverable arrangements, 260, 260n, 270
   pension plan issues, 977
      actuarial gains and losses, 955–956, 956n
      pensions and postretirement benefits, 964–966
      prior service cost, 957n, 957–958
      reporting pension expense, 963
   R&D expenditures, 532, 532n, 534
   refinancing current liabilities, 704
   reporting accounting changes, 1151, 1151n, 1160
   retail inventory method, 459n
   revenue recognition, 237, 237n
   sale-leaseback transactions, 845, 845n
   segment reporting, 141
   software development costs, 532

Global issues—*Cont.*
  stock option plans, 1077, 1078, 1107
  terminology differences with GAAP, 1013, 1042
  transfers between reporting categories, 638, 638*n*
  transfers of receivables, 364, 364*n*
  valuation of intangible assets, 573, 573*n*
GMAC Financial Services, 697
Going concern assumption, 28–29, 32
Going concern paragraph, 131
Goldman Sachs, 758, 949*n*
Gold's Gym, 239
Goods available for sale, 404
Goods in transit, 400–401
Goods on consignment, 401
Goodwill, 501, 645, 645*n*
  accounting for, 12–13
  acquired with companies, 510–511
  acquisition costs, 503
  balance sheet classification, 138
  capitalization of costs, 501, 510–512, 533
  fair value of, 512, 512*n*, 585
  impairment of asset value, 178, 584*n*, 584–587
  lack of income effect, 648, 648*n*
  negative, 512, 512*n*
  no depreciation adjustments for, 649
  not subject to amortization, 572–573
  shown in consolidated financial statements, 645, 645*n*
Google Inc., 28, 179
Government Accounting Standards Board (GASB), 10*n*, 12
Governmental Accounting Standards Advisory Council, 12
Government-owned corporations, 1016
Graded vesting, 1077–1078
The Great Atlantic & Pacific Tea Company, Inc., 412, 412*n*, 413, 418, 419
Greenspan, Alan, 697*n*, A-0
Gross investment in lease, 826, 836
Gross margin method, 456–457
Gross method
  of discounting noninterest-bearing notes, 353
  of imputing interest rate, 761, 761*n*
  of recording transactions
    cash discounts, 343–344, 368
    interest on notes, 696, 696*n*
    purchase discounts, 402*n*, 402–403
    receivable in capital leases, 817
Gross profit (loss), 77
  recognition of
    in completed contract method, 248, 249
    in cost recovery method, 242–243
    deferred gross profit account, 241, 241*n*
    input and output measures in, 249, 249*n*
    in installment sales method, 270
    in long-term construction contracts, 247–249
    in percentage-of-completion method, 233, 248, 249–251, 269
    reported in income statement, 250–251
Gross profit method, 456–457, 475
Gross profit (gross margin) ratio, 419, 425, 457
Group depreciation methods, 566–568
Guaranteed residual value (leases), 828–830, 830*n*
Guarantees, 711
The Gymboree Corporation, 517

H

Hagerman, R., 1140*n*
Half-year convention, 574, 574*n*
Halliburton, 246
Harley-Davidson, 358
Hartford Life Insurance Company, 1149
Hayn, Carla, 905*n*
Health care cost trend rates, 968, 968*n*
Healy, P. M., 412*n*, 1140*n*
Hecla Mining, 179
Hedging, 630, A-0–A-3, A-14. *See also* Derivatives
  accounting for, A-4
  fair value hedges. *See* Fair value hedges
  fair value option in, 638
  against foreign currency risk, A-0
  hedge effectiveness, A-9, A-9*n*
  hedge ineffectiveness, A-9
  "highly effective" criterion in, A-14
Heineken, 532
"Held for sale" assets, 518, 518*n*
Held for sale components, 184*n*, 184–186
Held-to-maturity bonds, 749, 749*n*
Held-to-maturity (HTM) securities, 118, 619–620, 658, 658*n*, 659
  AFS and TS approaches compared, 635–636
  disclosures, 625, 625*n*, 642*n*, 642–643
  impairment of value, 194*n*
  investor lacks significant influence, 621, 622–625
    fair value, 622
    fair value hierarchy, 624
    fair value option, 621, 625, 625*n*
    purchase of, 623
    revenue recognition, 623–624
    selling, 625, 625*n*
    unrealized holding gains and losses, 194*n*, 621, 624*n*, 624–625, 625*n*
  OTT impairment, 639, 665, 666
  transfers between reporting categories, 637–638
Helicos Biosciences Corporation, 244, 245
Henry, David, 780*n*
Hepp, John, 824*n*
Hershey Foods, 366, 1018
Herz, Robert, 14, 18
Hewlett-Packard Company (HP), 136, 418, 510, 572, 1018, 1223
"Highly effective" criterion, A-14
Historical cost principle, 29–30, 32, 522
Historical costs, 29, 29*n*
Holding gains (losses)
  on bonds, 753
  as component of comprehensive income, 1010
  on interest rate swaps, A-6, A-12
  unrealized
    on AFS securities, 619–620, 630–631, 658
    on HTM securities, 194*n*, 621, 624*n*, 624–625, 625*n*
Home Depot, Inc., 128, 129
Hooker Furniture Corporation, 1213–1214, 1223
Horizontal analysis, 132, 139
Hostile takeover, 1025, 1025*n*
Houston, Joel, 417*n*
H&R Block, Inc., 182, 183
HTM. *See* Held-to-maturity securities

http://www.fasb.org/revenue_recognition. shtml, 236*n*, 262*n*
Humphrey, Joseph, 187*n*
Hunt Manufacturing Co., 1097, 1098
Hurricane Katrina (2005), 187
Hybrid organizations, 1016
Hybrid securities
  convertible bonds. *See* Convertible securities
  preferred shares as, 1019

I

IASB. *See* International Accounting Standards Board
IASC. *See* International Accounting Standards Committee
IBM Corporation, 13, 115, 118, 175, 366, 516, 530, 559, 695, 808, 836, 837, 1015, 1103, 1109
IBM Credit Corporation, 821
IDEX Corporation, 1144
"If converted method," 1089
IFRS (International Financial Reporting Standards). See Accounting Standards Index
Illegal acts, 127, 127*n*. *See also* Income manipulation
  expenses due to, 887
  fraud
    improper capitalization of expenditures, 504
    securities fraud, 178, 178*n*
    stock option plans and, 1080, 1080*n*
    submission of false statements, 128
IMA (Institute of Management Accountants), 19, 339*n*
Impairment of asset value, 557, 580–589, 592
  annual impairment testing, 584, 585
  assets to be held and used, 580–587
  assets to be sold, 587–588, 588*n*
  earnings quality and, 588
  goodwill, 584–587
  held-to-maturity (HTM) investments, 194*n*
  impairment losses, 593
    as "big bath" accounting, 588
    disclosure notes, 582, 583, 585, 586, 664
    earnings quality and, 588
    measurement of, 581
    from OTT impairment, 661, 661*n*, 663, 664, 665
    recoverability test for, 581
    reversal of loss, 583, 583*n*
    unrealized loss, 960*n*
  indefinite-life intangibles other than goodwill, 584, 584*n*
  intangible assets, 581–583
    goodwill, 178, 584*n*, 584–587
    indefinite-life assets, 584, 584*n*
    measurement, 581–582
    shareholders' equity, 583, 583*n*
    testing for impairment, 581, 581*n*
  investments, 660–666
    debt investments, 661, 663–665
    equity investments, 661, 662–663
    OTT impairments, 665–666
  noncash assets, 707
  OTT impairment. *See* Other-than-temporary (OTT) impairment
  receivables. *See* Impairment of receivables
  shown in income statement, 178
  summary of guidelines for, 588

Impairment of receivables, 355
    troubled debt restructuring, 372*n*, 372–374
        global perspective, 374
        receivable is continued (modified), 373
        receivable is settled outright, 374
Implicit rate of interest, 515, 760*n*, 760–761
    in accounting for leases, 832–833, 833*n*
    unknown, deducing, 833–834
Implied fair value of goodwill, 585
Improvements, 590, 591, 593
InBev, 620
"Incentive plans" (stock options), 1076
Incentive savings (pension) plans, 938
Income
    AOCI. *See* Accumulated other
        comprehensive income
    comprehensive. *See* Comprehensive
        income
    from continuing operations. *See*
        Continuing operations
    net. *See* Net income
    OCI. *See* Other comprehensive income
Income approaches to fair value, 34
Income effects
    of consolidation, 648
    of discontinued operations, 185, 185*n*
Income manipulation, 175–176
    avoided by equity method, 657, 657*n*
    "cooking the books," 1140
    deferred tax valuation allowance, 905,
        905*n*
    discretionary accruals, 367, 367*n*
    "earnings management," 1080–1081
    inventory management and, 420
    "massaging" EPS calculations, 1103
    securitizations, 367*n*, 367–368, 368*n*
    unearned revenue, 720, 720*n*
Income recognition
    long-term construction contracts, 251–252,
        252*n*
    net income, 653
    SoRIE, 1012
Income shifting, 176
Income smoothing
    alertness to evidence of, 719
    change in accounting method and, 1149
    earnings quality and, 175–176
    pension expense, 953*n*, 953–954
    timing sale of investments, 647
Income statement, 4, 170–198
    accounting changes, 188–192
        in accounting estimate, 190–191
        change in accounting principle, 188–
            189, 190, 1141
        in depreciation, amortization, or
            depletion method, 189
        in reporting entity, 191–192
    affected by accounting errors, 192, 1154
    cash flow information, 1184
    classification schemes for, 76–77, 176
    comprehensive income shown in, 194–197
        accumulated other comprehensive
            income, 196–197
        flexibility in reporting, 194–195, 195*n*
        other comprehensive income, 194, 194*n*
    diluted EPS, 1105
    earnings per share disclosures, 192–193,
        198
    earnings quality, 175–179
        income manipulation and income
            smoothing, 175–176

    nonoperating income and, 179
    operating income and, 176–178
equity method investments, 655
extraordinary gains and losses, 180*n*,
    180–182
formats for, 172–174
    multiple-step, 173, 174
    single-step, 173, 174, 180, 180*n*
GAAP on, 174
global perspective, 174
gross profit reported in, 250–251
impact of leases, 838–839
income from continuing operations,
    170–174, 208
    discontinued operations reported
        separately, 183, 183*n*
    income statement formats, 172–174
    income tax effects, 903
    income tax expense, 172
    operating v. nonoperating income, 172
    presentation order, 180, 180*n*
    revenues, expenses, gains, and losses,
        170–171
income from investments, 629, 634
misleading effects of liabilities, 767
OTT impairment shown in, 664
preparation of, 76–77, 80, 86
    in preparation of SCF, 1194
prior period adjustments, 192, 192*n*
purpose of, 170
reporting components of total pension
    cost, 965
review of, 197–198
separately reported items, 180*n*, 180–188
    discontinued operations, 180*n*,
        182–186, 902
    extraordinary items, 174, 180*n*, 186*n*,
        186–187, 187*n*, 902
    income tax effects of, 902–904
    intraperiod income tax allocation, 180*n*,
        180–182, 902–904
    unusual or infrequent items, 187–188
spreadsheet preparation of SCF, 1199–
    1207
    cost of goods sold, 1203
    depreciation expense, 1204
    gain on sale of land, 1202–1203
    income tax expense, 1206–1207, 1223
    insurance expense, 1204–1205
    interest expense, 1204, 1223
    investment revenue, 1202
    loss on sale of equipment, 1205
    net income, 1207
    salaries expense, 1204
    sales revenue, 1199–1202
    temporary differences, 875
Income statement approach, 347–348, 369
Income statement classification, 176
Income statement effects, A-7, A-13
Income summary, 86
    closing expenses and revenues to, 79–80
    closing to retained earnings, 80
Income tax(es), 872–908
    adjusting entries for, 71*n*
    affected by accounting errors, 1154, 1156
    AFS securities and, 636
    contingencies, 706*n*
    coping with uncertainty in, 900–902
        more-likely-than-not criterion, 900–901
        resolution of uncertainty, 901–902
        tax benefit measurement, 901

    two-step decision process, 900
    decision makers' perspective of, 904–905
    deferred, 138, 649
    deferred assets and liabilities. *See* Deferred
        tax assets and liabilities
    depreciation using MACRS, 564, 594,
        594*n*, 878*n*
    employee withholdings, 721
    excess tax benefit, 1096
    extraordinary items, 904, 904*n*
    financial statement presentation, 897–900
        balance sheet classification, 897–898
        disclosure notes, 898–900
    incentives for leasing, 809
    intraperiod tax allocation, 902–904, 908
    inventory methods and, 412, 412*n*
    LIFO conformity rule, 412
    net income and, 412
    net operating losses and, 894–897
        operating loss carryback, 894, 895,
            895*n*, 896–897
        operating loss carryforward, 894,
            895–896, 899
    pension plans, 961, 961*n*
    review, 905–907
    tax law requirements
        changes in laws or rates, 891–892
        differences with GAAP. *See* Temporary
            differences
        installment sales method, 240*n*
        on operating losses, 908
    tax rate considerations, 890–892
    zero-coupon bonds and, 753
Income tax effects
    of equity method (securities), 649
    of extraordinary items
        global perspective, 904, 904*n*
        reporting, 902–903
    income from continuing operations, 903
    of separately reported items, 902–904
Income tax expense, 172
    current and deferred, 876–877
    disclosure note, 899–900
    spreadsheet preparation of SCF,
        1206–1207, 1223
    temporary differences, 1206
Incremental borrowing rate, 833, 833*n*
Incremental-cost approach, 522
Indirect manufacturing costs, 521, 522
Indirect method of reporting operating
    activities
    direct reporting contrasted, 200–201
    in statement of cash flows, 200, 207
Indirect reporting method (SCF), 1218–1224,
    1225
    cash increased or decreased, 1219–1220,
        1220*n*
    cash not increased or decreased, 1219
    comparison with direct method, 1220*n*,
        1220–1221, 1221*n*
    direct reporting contrasted, 1190–1192
    overview, 1218
    reconciliation of net income, 1221*n*,
        1221–1223
    spreadsheet for, 1225–1229
        illustrated, 1226
        order of entries, 1225
        SCF illustrated, 1228–1229
        summary entries, 1227–1228
Individual retirement accounts (IRAs), 936
Induced conversion (bonds), 772

Industry averages, 135, 136
Industry-specific guidance, 237
Industry-specific revenue issues, 258–263
    adequacy of ratio analysis, 341–342
    franchise sales. *See* Franchise(s)
    production basis, 262, 262*n*
    sales returns, 346
    software and other multiple deliverables, 259, 260
Inflation rate, 300
Initial direct costs to lessor, 834–835, 848
Initial franchise fee, 260, 261, 261*n*, 510
Initial markup, 459
Initial public offering, 1016
Initial valuation
    of accounts receivable, 342–344, 351
        cash discounts, 343–344
        trade discounts, 343
    of operational assets, 504
Input measures
    in activity-based depreciation, 562
    in gross profit recognition, 249, 249*n*
Inputs, 34, 35
Installment notes
    capital leases compared, 764, 809–810
    long-term notes, 762–763
Installment sales, 239–243
    cost recovery method, 236, 237, 240, 242–243
    deferred tax liabilities, 875–881
    installment sales method. *See* Installment sales method
    review, 243
    uncertainty of collection, 239–240
Installment sales method, 236, 237, 243
    accounting for bad debts, 242
    calculations, 240*n*, 240–242, 241*n*
    cost recovery in, 240–242
    gross profit recognition, 270
    tax laws regarding, 875
Institute of Internal Auditors, 19, 339*n*
Institute of Management Accountants (IMA), 19, 339*n*
Insurance expense, 83, 1204–1205
Intangible assets, 500, 502
    acquisition costs, 503
    amortization of. *See* Amortization
    capitalization of costs, 503, 509–512
        copyrights, 510
        franchises, 510
        goodwill, 501, 510–512, 533
        patents, 509, 527
        trademarks, 510
    contractual or legal life of, 559, 571
    disclosure notes, 502, 503, 571
    goodwill. *See* Goodwill
    impairment of value, 581–583
        global perspective, 583, 583*n*
        goodwill, 178, 584*n*, 584–587
        indefinite-life assets, 584, 584*n*
        measurement, 581–582
        shareholders' equity, 583, 583*n*
        testing for impairment, 581, 581*n*
    indefinite-life assets
        disclosure notes, 572
        impairment of value, 584, 584*n*
        in-process R&D, 531–532, 532*n*
    not subject to amortization, 572–573
    subject to amortization, 571–572
    valuation of, 573, 573*n*
    workforce as, 512*n*

Intangible rights, 591–592, 592*n*
Intel Corporation, 13, 179, 244, 521, 571, 656*n*, 886, 1008, 1016
Interbrand Samson, 509
Interest
    accrued
        on bonds, 756, 779–780
        on capital leases, 820–821
        interest payable, 698
        on interest rate swaps, A-12, A-12*n*
    on bonds. *See* Bond(s)
    effective interest method. *See* Effective interest method
    explicit, 307
    installment notes v. capital leases, 810
    on notes, 352–353, 695–696
    simple v. compound, 300–301
Interest-bearing notes, 352–353
Interest capitalization, 501, 521, 522–526, 533
    actual interest limitation, 526
    average accumulated expenditures, 522–523
    calculation of, 524–526
    capitalization period, 522
    disclosure, 526
    interest rates, 523–524
    qualifying assets, 522
Interest costs
    changes in PBO, 944, 944*n*
    as component of pension expense, 950, 951
    review, 975
Interest coverage ratio, 1223
Interest dates, 750, 756, 779–780
Interest expense
    lessee's interest expense, 840–841
    purchase discounts not taken, 402, 402*n*
    recording accrued liability, 71
    spreadsheet preparation of SCF, 1204, 1223
Interest payable, accrued, 698
Interest rate(s)
    actuary's discount rate, 951
    on bonds, 748, 749, 750
    credit-adjusted risk-free rate, 308, 507
    discount rate. *See* Discount (interest) rate
    effective rate. *See* Effective (annual) interest rate
    financial futures, A-1
    imputing, 760*n*, 760–761
    incremental borrowing rate and, 833, 833*n*
    in interest capitalization, 523–524
    stated as annual rate, 71
    unknown, solving for, 299, 304, 304*n*, 323
    unrealistic rate on notes, 761, 767–768
    variable, A-5, A-5*n*
    weighted-average rate, 524, 524*n*
Interest rate futures, 658*n*
Interest rate risk, A-0
Interest rate swaps, 658*n*, A-0, A-2–A-3
    adjustment to fair value, A-5–A-6
    calculating fair value, A-7, A-8
    as cash flow hedges, A-8
    extended method, A-11*n*–A-13*n*, A-11–A-14
    as fair value hedges, A-4
    holding gains (losses), A-6, A-12
    illustration, A-4–A-7, A-5*n*, A-6*n*
    income statement effects, A-7, A-13
    net interest, A-12, A-13
    "no ineffectiveness" criterion, A-11, A-11*n*
    notional amount, A-3, A-11
    shortcut method, A-5, A-5*n*, A-14

Interest revenue, 623
Interim financial statements, 234*n*, 643, 643*n*
Interim reporting, 271–273
    accounting changes, 272
    discontinued operations, 186
    earnings per share, 272
    inventory estimation techniques and, 400, 400*n*
    minimum disclosures, 272*n*, 272–273, 643, 643*n*
    revenues and expenses, 271–272
    unusual items, 272
Intermediaries, A-3
Internal control
    cash controls, 338–340, 368, 369–372
        bank reconciliation, 369–371
        cash disbursements, 339–340
        cash receipts, 339
        petty cash, 371–372
    over financial reporting, 128, 129
    Sarbanes-Oxley requirements, 17, 338–339
Internal events, 52, 86
Internal Revenue Service (IRS), 721, 874
    inventory measurement issues, 412, 412*n*
    prescribed depreciation method (MACRS), 564, 594, 594*n*, 878*n*
    reporting change in inventory method, 472
    on retail inventory method, 458, 458*n*
    Tax Code, 1070*n*, 1076, 1143
    uncertainty in income taxes, 900
Internal users of financial information, 4
International Accounting Standards Board (IASB), 14, 14*n*, 15, 37
    on accounting for financial instruments, 644, 644*n*
    on comprehensive income, 195, 195*n*, 1012, 1012*n*
    on contingencies, 716, 721
    on earnings per share, 1082, 1102, 1102*n*
    efforts to merge GAAP and IFRS, 15, 21, 32–33
    International Accounting Standards (IASs). *See Accounting Standards Index*
    International Financial Reporting Standards (IFRS). See Accounting Standards Index
    joint projects with FASB. *See* FASB/IASB joint projects
    on matching, 30*n*
    Norwalk Agreement (2002), 15
    principles-based approach of, 18
International Accounting Standards Committee (IASC), 14, 15
International Accounting Standards (IASs) of IASC, 15
International Financial Reporting Standards (IFRS). See Accounting Standards Index
International Monetary Market, A-1, A-1*n*
International Organization of Securities Commissions (IOSCO), 15
International Paper Company, 410, 501, 564
International Rectifier Corporation, 178
Interperiod tax allocation, 180*n*
Intraperiod tax allocation
    income taxes, 902–904, 908
    separately reported, 180*n*, 180–182
Intrinsic value
    of conversion option, 770
    in option-pricing theory, 1107
    of stock options, 1072, 1073, 1073*n*, 1077

Inventory(ies), 446–476
  activity ratios
    average days in inventory, 264, 267, 268, 269, 419, 425
    inventory turnover ratio, 263, 264, 264n, 267, 268, 419, 425
  adjustments for, 649
  balance sheet classification, 118
  change in inventory method. See Change in inventory method
  cost of ending inventory, 416, 423, 459
  damaged or defective items, 346, 399
  disclosure notes. See Disclosure notes
  earnings quality and, 474–475
  estimation techniques. See Inventory estimation techniques
  expenditures included in, 401n, 401–403
    freight-in on purchases, 401–402
    purchase discounts, 402–403
    purchase returns, 402
    sales returns, 401
  inventory errors, 472n, 472–474
    correcting error affecting net income, 1156–1157
    discovered after following year, 473–474
    discovered in following year, 473
    review of, 474
  inventory management, 417n, 417–419
  measuring. See Inventory measurement
  not considered investing activities, 203
  periodic system. See Periodic inventory system
  perpetual system. See Perpetual inventory system
  physical quantities included in
    goods in transit, 400–401
    goods on consignment, 401
  purchase commitments, 476–478
    contract beyond fiscal year, 477–478
    contract within fiscal year, 477, 477n
  reporting at LCM. See Lower of cost or market
  revised reporting, 1141–1142
  valuation of
    by LCM. See Lower of cost or market
    reversal of write-downs, 453, 453n, 454
Inventory errors, 472n, 472–474, 476
  discovered after following year, 473–474
  discovered in following year, 473
  review of, 474
Inventory estimation techniques, 455–465
  DVL technique, 422–423, 423n
  gross profit method, 456–457
  interim reporting and, 400, 400n
  retail inventory method, 458–463
    other issues, 462–463
    retail terminology and, 459, 460
    review of, 463–465
Inventory layers, 461–462, 462n
  change in inventory method, 1144
  in dollar-value LIFO retail, 466
Inventory measurement, 396–420
  capital market efficiency and, 412n
  cost flow assumptions, 404–417
    average cost method. See Average cost method
    comparison of methods, 410–411
    decision makers' perspective of, 411–414
    in estimating gross profit ratio, 457
    FIFO method. See First-in, first-out (FIFO) inventory method

    global perspective, 411, 425
    LIFO method. See Last-in, first-out (LIFO) inventory method
    review of, 414–417
    specific identification, 405, 458
  cost of goods sold and, 396, 398–399
  decision makers' perspective
    cost flow assumptions, 411–414
    earnings quality, 420
    inventory management, 417n, 417–419
  IRS issues, 412, 412n
  items included in, 400–403
    expenditures, 401n, 401–403
    physical quantities, 400–401
  net income and, 412, 412n
  periodic system. See Periodic inventory system
  perpetual system. See Perpetual inventory system
  physical count, 399
  simplification of LIFO, 420–424
  types of inventory
    manufacturing inventories, 396–397
    merchandising inventory, 396
Inventory shortages, 463
Inventory turnover ratio, 263, 264, 264n, 267, 268, 419, 425
Investcorp, 569
Investee "associates," 653, 653n
Investing activities, 78
  buying and selling securities, 643
  cash flows from, 1185, 1192n, 1192–1193, 1225
    in AFS securities, 634
    net cash flows, 203
    noncash investing activities, 204
    sale of land, 1203
    in statement of cash flows, 199n, 203
  cash/noncash transactions, 1195
  information from SCF, 1183, 1224
  investing and financing activity ratio, 1223
Investing and financing activity ratio, 1223
Investment(s), 618–659
  balance sheet classifications, 119
  diversity in objectives, 620
  in foreign operations, A-9, A-9n
  impairment of value, 660–666
    debt investments, 661, 663–665
    equity investments, 661, 662–663
    OTT impairments, 665–666
  investor has significant influence, 644–658
  investor lacks significant influence, 620–644
    AFS securities. See Available-for-sale (AFS) securities
    change in level of influence, 651, 651n
    comparison of HTM, TS, and AFS approaches, 635–636
    financial statement presentation and disclosure, 642–643
    global perspective, 636n, 636–637
    held-to-maturity securities, 621, 622–625
    impairment of investment, 639, 639n
    income taxes and, 636
    review of, 640–642
    trading securities, 625–629
    transfers between reporting categories, 637–638
  in life insurance policies, 660
  other investments

    life insurance policies, 660
    special purpose funds, 659–660
  by owner, 27, 53, 57
  reporting (equity method), 649–651, 650n
    in financial statements, 644–645, 645n, 655
    investee reports net loss, 650
    investment acquired mid-year, 650–651
    when to discontinue equity method, 650
  securities. See Securities
  special purpose funds, 659–660
Investment-credit decision, 6–7
Investment revenue, 1202
Investment revenue receivable account, 1202
Investors, 5, 341
Involuntary conversions, 518
IOSCO (International Organization of Securities Commissions), 15
IRAs (individual retirement accounts), 936
Irregularities, 127, 127n
IRS. See Internal Revenue Service
Ittner, C. D., 700n

J

J. Jill, 185–186
Jaces Co., 651
J.C. Penney Company, Inc., 239, 458, 467
JDS Uniphase Corporation, 176, 177, 178, 475, 586
Jiambalvo, J., 1152n
JIT (just-in-time) system, 417–418
J.M. Smucker, 1008, 1018, 1137, 1160
Johnson, Sarah, 627n
Johnson & Johnson, 1024
Joint ventures, 654, 654n, 659
Journal(s), 86
  cash disbursements journal, 91
  general journal, 56, 91, 91n
    adjusting entries in, 73
    transactions recorded in, 62
  recording transactions, 56
  special journals, 56, 91, 91n
    cash receipts journal, 91, 92
    sales journal, 91–92
Journal entries, 56, 73
  adjusting entries. See Adjusting entries
  bonds sold at premium, 754
  current liabilities, 704–705
  detachable warrants, 773
  early extinguishment of debt, 774
  effective interest method, 762
  installment notes, 763
  inventories, 399, 415, 416
  investment securities, 640–642
  leases
    capital leases, 819, 820
    direct financing leases, 821, 822
    operating leases, 816
    review, 841–842
    sales-type leases, 816n
  reconstructed, 1195, 1197
  recording transactions, 56–64
  review of, 64–66
J.P. Morgan, 638, 638n
JPMorgan Chase, 758
Justification
  for accounting choices (disclosures), 1144
  for change in depreciation methods, 190, 191, 577–578
  for delayed gains (losses), 953, 953n
Just-in-time (JIT) system, 417–418

K

Kaufman & Broad Home Corporation, 246
KPMG LLP, 129
Krispy Kreme Doughnuts, 234
Kroger Company, 820, 1039
Kuhnhenn, James, 16*n*

L

Lacy, J. M., 1140*n*
Land
  acquisition costs, 503
  capitalization of costs, 504*n*, 504–505
  indefinite useful life of, 846
  land-and-building leases, 846, 846*n*
  land-only leases, 846
  no depreciation adjustments for, 649
  spreadsheet preparation of SCF
    balance sheet, 1208
    income statement, 1202–1203
Land improvements, 503, 505
Landsman, W. R., 368*n*
Langenderfer, Harold Q., 19*n*
Large stock dividends, 1035–1037, 1036*n*
  fractional shares, 1037
  reverse stock split, 1036
Larker, D. F., 700*n*
Larson, R. K., 249*n*
Last-in, first-out (LIFO) inventory method,
    395, 408–410, 424, 425
  adjusting entries for, 416
  average cost and FIFO compared to,
    410–411
  dollar-value LIFO retail. See Dollar-value
    LIFO retail
  income reported under, 418, 1140
  income tax issues, 412, 412*n*
  periodic LIFO, 408–409
  perpetual LIFO, 409–410
  simplification methods, 420–424
    dollar-value LIFO. See Dollar-value
      LIFO
    LIFO inventory pools, 420–421
    review of, 423–424
  switch from FIFO
    disclosure of, 471*n*, 471–472, 1139
    LIFO reserve account and, 413
  switch to FIFO
    adjusting accounts for change, 1143
    retrospective reporting of, 189, 1137,
      1141–1142, 1160
Las Vegas Sands Corporation, 713
Layne Christensen Company, 246, 502, 503
LCM. See Lower of cost or market
Lease(s), 806–848
  accounting by lessor and lessee, 808–824
  advantages of, 808–809
  amortization schedules, 810
    with BPO, 826
    capital leases, 818–819
    direct financing leases, 821
    lessee's interest expense, 840–841
    lessor's interest revenue, 841
  bargain purchase options. See Bargain
    purchase option
  capital leases. See Capital leases
  classification of, 810–814
    additional lessor conditions, 813
    application to operating leases, 815
    criteria for, 811*n*, 811–813, 812*n*, 815,
      818
    IFRS v. GAAP on, 814, 814*n*
    by lessee, 818, 818*n*
  contingent rentals, 835
  decision makers' perspective of, 808–809,
    838
  direct financing lease. See Direct financing
    leases
  disclosures, 835–837

discount rate, 832–835, 833*n*
  incremental borrowing rate, 833, 833*n*
  lessor's implicit rate, 833–834
  lessor's initial direct costs, 834–835,
    848
essential lease components (summary),
    835, 836
executory costs, 832
financial statement impact of, 838–840
  balance sheet and income statement,
    838–839
  statement of cash flows, 839–840, 1209
global perspective, 834, 834*n*
long-term leases, 321, 324
off-balance-sheet financing, 834
operating leases. See Operating leases
reported in SCF, 1209
residual value, 827–831
  effect on lessee, 828, 831
  effect on lessor, 828–831
review of accounting issues, 840–842
"right of use" model, 824, 824*n*
sales-type. See Sales-type leases
special arrangements, 842–847
  global perspective, 846, 846*n*
  leveraged leases, 846–847
  real estate leases, 846
  sale-leasebacks, 842–845
Leased assets
  depreciation of, 819
  disclosure notes, 820
  expected economic life of, 811–812
  fair value of, 817
  ownership of asset, 811, 811*n*
  residual value of, 827–831, 848
    avoiding use of, 834
    effect on lessee, 828, 831
    effect on lessor, 828–831
    guaranteed residual value,
      828–830, 830*n*
    implicit rate of interest and, 833–834
    unguaranteed residual value, 830–831
Leasehold improvements, 816*n*, 816–817
Lease payments
  advance payments on operating leases,
    815–816
  expected cash flow approach, 308
  minimum payments
    on capital leases, 811, 812–813
    global perspective, 834, 834*n*
    guaranteed residual value and, 829, 829*n*
    present value of, 817, 825, 834, 834*n*, 840
    summary, 836
    unguaranteed residual value and,
      830–831
  rental payments
    bargain purchase option and, 825
    first payment applied to principal,
      817, 818
    operating leases, 815, 816
Lease receivable, 835
Leasing
  incentives for, 809, 809*n*
  present value in
    guaranteed residual value, 828
    minimum lease payments, 817, 825,
      834, 834*n*, 840
  rules-based accounting and, 18
Legal capital concept, 1020, 1025*n*
Legal life of intangible asset, 559, 571
Legal title. See also Ownership

to inventories, 400
profit recognition and, 248
Lehman Brothers, 1187
Lender (assignee), 357
Lessee, 808
  accounting for leases, 824, 824*n*
  amortization of interest expense, 840–841
  capital leases. See Capital leases
  classification of leases by, 818, 818*n*
  disclosure of leases, 837
  effect of BPO, 825
  effect of residual value, 828, 831
  leasehold improvements, 816, 816*n*
  lease terms and concepts, 836
  lessor's interest rate different from, 834
  operating leases. See Operating leases
  penalty for failure to renew lease, 812*n*
  perspective of leveraged leases, 847
  rent expense on operating leases, 815
Lessor, 808
  amortization of interest revenue, 841
  capital leases. See Capital leases
  collectibility of payments, 813
  costs of leases to, 813, 834–835, 848
  direct financing leases. See Direct
    financing leases
  disclosure of sales-type leases, 837
  discount (interest) rate
    implicit rate, 833–834
    initial direct costs, 834–835, 848
  effect of BPO, 825
  effect of residual value, 828–831
    guaranteed value, 828–830, 830*n*
    unguaranteed value, 830–831
  gross investment in lease, 826
  lease terms and concepts, 836
  lessee's interest rate different from, 834
  operating leases. See Operating leases
  sales-type leases. See Sales-type leases
  unaffected by executory costs, 832
Lester, W. Howard, 127
Lev, B., 367, 367*n*, 419, 419*n*
Leverage. See Financial leverage
Leveraged leases, 846–847
Leverage ratios, 266, 267
Levitt, Arthur, Jr., 175*n*, 175–176, 178, 178*n*,
    234, 234*n*, 367, 367*n*
Liabilities, 27, 779. See also Deferred tax
    assets and liabilities
  in accounting equation, 54
  accounting for, 748
  accrued. See Accrued liabilities
  associated with capital leases, 764
  balance sheet classifications, 120–121,
    138–139
    current liabilities, 120
    long-term liabilities, 120, 120*n*,
      121, 139
  bonds. See Bonds
  current. See Current liabilities
  fair value option for, 775–778, 779
    determining fair value, 775
    global perspective, 777–778, 778*n*
    mix and match, 777
    reporting changes in fair value, 775–777
  long-term. See Long-term liabilities
  long-term notes. See Long-term notes
  potential liabilities. See Contingencies
  SARs payable in cash, 1109–1111, 1111*n*
  shown in balance sheet, 116
  working definitions of, 32

LIBOR (London Interbank Offered Rate), A-5n
Lidberg, Steve, 1035
Lieberman, Joe, 1072n
Life insurance, 660, 887
LIFO. See Last-in, first-out (LIFO) inventory method
LIFO conformity rule, 411, 412, 418, 425, 564
LIFO inventory pools
  average costs for, 420–421
  DVL pool, 421
LIFO liquidations, 425
  decision makers' perspective, 413–414
  disclosure of, 414
  dollar-value LIFO and, 422
LIFO reserve (allowance), 412–413
LIFO retail method, 461–462, 462n, 465, 475–476
Limited liability companies, 1016
Limited liability of corporation, 1015
Limited liability partnerships, 1016
Lines of credit, 695, 720
Link-chain method, 422
Liquidating dividend, 1031
Liquidation, 780
Liquidity, 133, 341–342, 719–720
Liquidity ratios, 133–135
  acid-test (quick) ratio, 134–135, 341, 719
  current ratio, 134, 341, 719
  inventory measurement and, 418
Litigation
  cost of defending intangible rights, 591–592
  loss contingencies
    claims as, 711–713
    disclosure notes, 712, 713
  pending litigation, 706, 712–713
Lloyds Banking Group, 638
Loans
  allowance for loan losses, 355
  assignee (lender), 357
  bank loans. See Short-term notes payable
  compensating balances, 340, 340n, 695, 695n
  secured loans, 696–697
  specific construction loan, 524
Lockheed Martin Corporation, 233, 246
London Interbank Offered Rate (LIBOR), A-5n
London Stock Exchange, 14
Long-lived assets, 142, 142n, 178
Long-term bonds, 320–321, 324
Long term construction contracts, 245–256, 270
  completed contract method. See Completed contract method
  cost of construction and accounts receivable, 247
  costs of construction, 247, 251, 251n
  global perspective, 256, 256n, 260, 260n, 270
  gross profit recognition, 247–249
  losses on, 253–256
    loss on entire project, 254–256
    periodic loss for profitable project, 253–254
  percentage-of-completion method. See Percentage-of-completion method
  revenue recognition methods compared, 251–256
  review of, 257–258

shown in balance sheet, 248, 252, 253
Long-term debt
  current maturities of, 120, 702, 720
  financial disclosures, 763–764, 779
  nature of, 747–748
Long-term leases, 321
Long-term liabilities. See also Liabilities
  balance sheet classifications, 120, 120n, 121, 139
  current liabilities compared, 702–704
    current maturities of long-term debt, 120, 702, 720
    obligations callable by creditor, 702–703
    refinancing short-term obligations, 703–704
Long-term notes, 759–768, 779
  exchanged for assets or services, 760–762, 760n–762n
  financial statement disclosures, 763–764
  installment notes, 762–763
  issued for cash, 760
  with unrealistic interest rate (review), 767–768
Long-term solvency, 116, 133
Loss(es), 27, 171
  deferred, A-8, A-8n
  delayed, 953, 953n
  impairment loss
    on component held for sale, 184, 185
    on disposal of discontinued operation, 183, 184
  on long-term construction contracts, 253–256
    loss on entire project, 254–256
    periodic loss for profitable project, 253–254
  on nonmonetary exchange, 520, 534
  operating losses
    carrybacks, 894, 895, 895n, 896–897
    carryforwards, 894, 895–896, 899
    review, 905–907
    tax laws on, 908
  on PBO, 946, 950
  on pension assets, 940, 950, 951
  per share, 1093
  on purchase commitments, 477–478
  on sale-leaseback transactions, 845
  on sale of equipment, 1205
Loss contingencies, 706–716, 721
  acquired contingencies, 714
  cents-off coupons, 712
  disclosure notes, 707
  fair value approaches, 711
  FASB project on, 716
  global perspective, 716, 887, 887n
  impairment of noncash asset value, 707
  litigation claims, 711–713
  premiums, 710–711
  product warranties and guarantees, 708–710
    expected cash flow approach, 709, 709n
    extended warranty contracts, 710
    manufacturer's original warranty, 708
  subsequent events, 713–714
  unasserted claims and assessments, 715, 721
Lotteries, 299, 323
Lower of cost or market (LCM), 447, 448–455, 475
  applied to purchase commitments, 476

conventional retail method, 461
determining market value, 449–453
  adjusting cost to market, 452n, 452–453
  application of, 451, 451n, 452
  global perspective, 453n, 453–454, 476
  production basis recognition, 454, 454n
  theoretical merits of, 449–451
review of, 454–455
L.S. Starret Company, 1008
Lucent Technologies, 178, 475, 586
Lump-sum purchases, 512, 513, 533

M

MACRS (modified accelerated cost recovery system), 564, 594, 594n, 878n
Macy's, Inc., 458, 957
Management
  intent of, 559
  managerial judgment, 885–886
  responsibilities of, 128, 129
Management approach, 140, 205, 1191
Management discussion and analysis (MD&A), 128, 139
Managerial accounting, 4
Mandatorily redeemable shares, 1020
Mann, Bill, 1103n
Mannatech Incorporated, 338
Manufacturing companies, 77–78, 397
Manufacturing inventories, 396–397
Manufacturing overhead, 396
Markdown(s)
  in conventional retail method, 461
  markdown cancellation, 459
  net markdown, 459, 460
Market(s)
  capital market efficiency, 412n
  market conditions on stock option plans, 1080
  participants as focus in fair value, 34
  primary and secondary transactions, 6
  stock market. See Stock market
Market approaches to fair value, 34
Market prices, 35, 1022, 1075
Market rate of interest
  bonds priced to yield, 750
  established by value of asset exchanged, 760n, 760–761
  holding gains and losses, 753
Market to book ratio, 115
Market value(s)
  of bonds, relative, 772–774
  of company, 115
  of derivatives, A-3–A-4, A-4n, A-15
  determining by LCM. See Lower of cost or market
  market to book ratio, 115
  replacement cost as meaning of, 449–450
  of shareholders' equity, 1038
Market value method, 772
Markup, 457
  cancellation, 459
  net markup, 459, 460
Marshall, Jeffrey, 178n
Massoud, Marcos, 187n
Matching principle, 30n, 30–31, 32, 33
  adjusting entries required for, 67–68
  in cost allocation, 558
  in interest capitalization, 522
  measurement of expenses and, 170
Material error, 24, 578–579, 1152n
Material events, 273

Materiality
  accounting choices and, 595
  capitalization of expenditures and, 589
  as constraint on financial information,
    25–26
  of illegal acts, 127, 127n
  of income statement effects, 180, 180n
  of sales returns, 345, 345n
Maturity amounts, 693, 693n
Maturity date, 338, 643, 1210
Maturity value, 748
McAfee, Inc., 195
McDonald's Corporation, 260, 510, 817, 1158
McDonough, William J., 17
McKesson Corporation, 469–470
McLean, Bethany, 175n, 1103n
MD&A (management discussion and
    analysis), 128, 139
Measurability of information, 27
Measurement
  conceptual framework, 27–32
  in cost allocation, 559–560
  of inventories. See Inventory measurement
  matching principle and, 170
  of PBO, 969
  present value measurements, 28, 28n
  of tax benefit, 901
Measurement concepts, 28, 33
  asset retirement obligations, 507
  measurement of impairment loss,
    581–582
Medicare taxes, 721
Medtronic, 366
Melville Corporation, 963
Memorandum of Understanding (2006), 589
Merchandise inventory. See also
    Inventory(ies); Inventory
    measurement
  recording in journal, 59
  types of, 396
Merck & Co., 16, 564
Microsoft Corporation, 129, 130, 501, 529,
    530, 643, 938, 939, 1015, 1016,
    1025, 1031, 1031n, 1032, 1032n,
    1080
Microsoft Excel, 762n, 1212n
Mielke, David, 1224n
Mills, John, 1224n
Minimum lease payments
  on capital leases, 811, 812–813
  global perspective, 834, 834n
  present value of, 817, 825, 834, 834n, 840
  residual value and
    guaranteed, 829, 829n
    unguaranteed, 830–831
  summary, 836
Model Business Corporation Act (2009),
    1016–1017, 1018, 1020
Modified accelerated cost recovery system
    (MACRS), 564, 594, 594n, 878n
Modifying comments, 31, 32
Momentive Performance Materials Inc., 769
Monetary assets, 306
Monetary liabilities, 306
Monetary unit assumption, 29, 32
Money market funds, 1188, 1208
Money purchase (pension) plans, 938
Monsanto, 29
Moody's Investors Service, Inc., 750
"More likely than not" criterion, 908
  managerial judgment and, 885, 885n

uncertainty in income taxes, 900n,
    900–901
Morris, Don, 1024
Morrish, David J., 132
Mortgage bonds, 747, 749, 778
Motivation
  for accounting choices, 1139n, 1139–1140,
    1140n
  for offering pension plans, 936
Motorola Corporation, 244
Muehlbauer, James L., 132
Mulford, C. W., 657n
Multiple convertible securities, 1093–1094
Multiple deliverable arrangements
  global perspective, 260, 260n, 270
  industry guidelines, 270
  revenue recognition for, 259, 260
Multiple-step format, 173, 174, 180, 180n
Multiple temporary differences,
    892–894, 905–907
Myers, L. A., 367n

N

NASDAQ (National Association of Securities
    Dealers Automated Quotations), 5,
    1016
National Penn Bank Shares, 777
Natural resources, 110, 502
  acquisition costs, 503, 533
  asset retirement obligations, 506
  capitalization of costs, 506, 506n
  depletion of. See Depletion (natural
    resources)
Negative goodwill, 512, 512n
Net assets, 27
Net cash flows, 203, 204, 1193
Net gain (loss)
  amortization of, 941, 952–953
  on investments, 650
  on PBO, 952–953, 954
Net income, 8, 8n, 37
  accounting errors
    affecting prior year's net income,
      1154–1158
    inventory errors, 1156–1157
    not affecting net income, 1154
  accumulated other comprehensive income
    and, 196
  adjustments for SCF (indirect method)
    direct method compared, 1220n,
      1220–1221, 1221n
    discount on bonds, 1220n
    increase/decrease in cash, 1219–1220,
      1220n
    no increase/decrease in cash, 1219
    reconciliation to cash flows, 1221n,
      1221–1223
  cash flows and, 1183, 1224
  from continuing operations, 172, 172n
  decision makers' perspective of, 412
  effects of investments on, 642
  income statement format and, 174, 174n
  inventory measurement issues, 412, 412n
  recognition of, 653
  reconciled with operating cash flows, 1190
  spreadsheet preparation of SCF, 1207
Net interest, interest rate swaps, A-12, A-13
Net investment in lease, 836
Net markdown, 459, 460
Net markup, 459, 460
Net method

of discounting noninterest-bearing notes,
    353n
  of imputing interest rate, 761n
  of recording transactions
    cash discounts, 343–344, 368
    interest on notes, 696n
    purchase discounts, 402–403
    receivable in capital leases, 817
Net operating cash flows, 7, 8, 8n, 37
  in cash basis accounting, 83, 86
  classification of, 199, 203
Net operating losses, 894–897
  operating loss carryback, 894, 895, 895n,
    896–897
  operating loss carryforward, 894,
    895–896, 899
Net periodic pension cost, 966
Net present value model, 516
Net realizable value (NRV), 475
  of assets, 30
  inventory valuation, 449, 453n, 453–454
  uncollectible accounts and, 347, 350
Net realizable value less normal profit margin
    (NRV – NP), 449, 455, 475
"Netting out" financial futures, A-1–A-2
Neutrality of financial information, 24
New York Stock Exchange (NYSE), 5, 14
Nike, Inc., 1036
90% criterion, 811, 812–813, 834
"No call" provisions, 749
"No ineffectiveness" criterion, A-11, A-11n
Nominal rate of interest, 748
Nonaudit services, prohibited, 17
Noncancelable lease term
  of capital leases, 811–812, 812n
  lacking in operating leases, 811, 811n
Noncash acquisitions
  capitalization of, 512–516
    deferred payments, 513–515, 533
    donated assets, 515–516
    issuance of equity securities, 515
    notes payable for, 513–515, 514n, 1209
    property, plant, and equipment. See
      Property, plant, and equipment
    shown in SCF, 1208–1209
Noncash assets, 781
Noncash investing and financing, 204, 1194,
    1195, 1225
Noncash transactions
  issuance of common shares, 1021, 1021n,
    1042
  recorded at fair value, 781
Noncommitted line of credit, 695, 695n
Noncredit losses, 663, 664, 665
Noncumulative preferred shares, 1018
Noncurrent assets, 78, 118, 119
Nonearning asset (cash), 341
Noninterest-bearing notes, 353n, 353–355
  effective (annual) rate on, 696, 696n
  received solely for cash, 354n, 354–355
Nonmonetary exchanges, 518n, 518–519
Nonoperating income, 172, 179
Nonparticipating preferred shares, 1018
"Nonqualified plans" (stock options), 1076
Nonreciprocal transfer to owners, 1033
Nonsufficient funds (NSF) checks, 369
Nontrade receivables, 118, 342
Nordstrom, 521
Noreen, E. W., 1140n
Normal shortages, 463
Nortel Networks Corporation, 246, 586

Northrop Grumman Newport News, 246
Norwalk Agreement (2002), 15
Notational amount, A-3, A-11
Notes
    amortization schedules, 762, 762n, 763, 768
    exchanged for assets, 760–762, 760n–762n
    installment notes
        capital leases compared, 764, 809–810
        long-term notes, 762–763
    interest-bearing, 352–353
    interest on, 307, 695–696
    issuance reported in SCF, 764
    issued for cash
        long-term notes, 760
        noninterest-bearing notes, 354n, 354–355
    long-term notes. See Long-term notes
    noninterest-bearing. See Noninterest-bearing notes
    promissory notes, 748
    with unrealistic interest rate, 761, 767–768
Notes payable
    balance sheet classifications, 120
    commercial paper, 697
    fair value of
        in interest rate swaps, A-7–A-8
        noncash acquisitions, 514n, 514–515
    for noncash acquisitions, 513–515, 514n, 1209
    recording accrued liability, 71
    recording in journal, 58–59
    short-term notes payable, 694–697
        credit lines, 695
        interest, 695–696
        secured loans, 696–697
    trade notes payable, 694
    transaction analysis, 53, 57
Notes receivable, 118, 352–355, 369
    balance sheet classification, 118
    disclosures, 355
    financing with, 361
    interest-bearing notes, 352–353
    noninterest-bearing notes, 353n, 353–355
    transfers of (discounting), 361
    valuation of
        present value techniques, 307, 324
        subsequent valuation, 355
Noteworthy events and transactions, 126–127
Not-for-profit corporations, 1016
NRV. See Net realizable value
NRV – NP (net realizable value less normal profit margin), 449, 455, 475
NSF (nonsufficient funds) checks, 369
NYSE New York Stock Exchange, 5, 14

O

Objectives-oriented accounting. See Principles-based accounting
Objectivity of financial information, 24
Observable inputs, 35
Obsolescence, 559
OCI. See Other comprehensive income
"Off-balance-sheet" financing, 834
    FASB project on, 658
    as leasing stimulus, 809, 809n
    risks of, 767
Offsetting, not permitted by GAAP, 357
Oil and gas accounting, 534–535, 535n
    full-cost method, 534–535
    successful efforts method, 534, 535, 535n

"One-line consolidation," 645
Open accounts and notes, 693–697
    accounts payable, 694
    commercial paper, 697
    short-term notes payable, 694–697
    trade notes payable, 694
Operating activities, 78, 1208
    cash flows from, 1185, 1188n, 1188–1189, 1225
    direct reporting method (SCF). See Direct reporting method
    of financial institutions, 642–643
    indirect reporting method (SCF). See Indirect reporting method
    purchase and sale of inventory, 1189
    in statement of cash flows, 199–203, 1177–1178, 1188n
        direct and indirect reporting contrasted, 200–201, 1190–1192
        direct reporting method, 200, 206
        indirect reporting method, 200, 207
        reconciled with net income, 1190
        use in cash flow ratios, 1223
Operating cycle, 77–78, 116
Operating efficiency, 589
Operating income
    earnings quality and, 176–178
    impact of restructuring costs on, 177–178
    nonoperating income distinguished, 172
Operating leases, 18, 808, 815n, 815–817, 847
    advance payments, 815–816
    capital leases compared, 811, 811n
    criteria for classification as, 811, 815
    disclosure note, 837, 838
    estimating debt equivalent, 839, 839n
    financial statement impact of, 838, 839
    global perspective, 845, 845n
    initial direct costs, 835
    land lease, 846
    leasehold improvements, 816n, 816–817
    noncancelable lease term lacking in, 811, 811n
    rent revenue on, 807, 815, 847
    reported in SCF, 1209
    "right of use" model and, 824, 824n
    sale-leaseback arrangements, 844n, 844–845
Operating losses
    carrybacks, 894, 895, 895n, 896–897
    carryforwards, 894, 895–896, 899
    review, 905–907
    tax laws on, 908
Operating segments, 140, 140n
    defined, 182–183, 183n
    reporting segment information, 140–143
        amounts reported, 140–141, 141n
        GAAP on, 141, 142
        geographic area reporting, 142
        major customer information, 142–143
        reportable segments, 140
        requirements, 25, 25n
Operation(s), defined, 182
Operational assets
    intangibles. See Intangible assets
    property, plant, and equipment. See Property, plant, and equipment
Operational risk, 133
Option(s), A-0, A-2
    bargain purchase option. See Bargain purchase option

bargain renewal options, 812, 812n
conversion option, 747, 770, 771–772, 778, 1088
fair value option. See Fair value option
stock options. See Stock option(s); Stock option plans
Option price, 772
Option pricing models, 1072
Option-pricing theory, 1074, 1074n
    intrinsic value, 1107
    summary, 1108
    time value of money, 1107–1108
    volatility value, 1108
Oracle Corporation, 246
Orange County (Calif.), 658
Order of entry, 1093–1094
Ordinary annuity, 309
    future value of, 310–311, 324
    present value of, 312–313, 324
    solving for unknown values, 317
Organization costs, 529, 529n
Other asset classifications, 119, 138
Other comprehensive income (OCI), 194, 194n, 630
    accumulated over current and prior periods, 1011
    actuarial gains and losses, 955–956, 956n
    components of, 1010, A-8
    created during reporting period, 1011
    derivatives, 194, 1010, 1011
    effects of investments on, 642
    FASB/IASB joint project on, 195, 195n
    FVTOCI, 637
    prior service cost as, 952
    reporting, 960n, 960–961
        gains and losses, 955
        income tax effects, 903–904
    for trading securities, 630, 631, 631n
Other income (expense), 172
Other-than-temporary (OTT) impairment, 624n, 639, 639n
    "available for sale" investments, 639
        debt investments, 661, 663–665
        equity investments, 661, 662–663
    changes in accounting for, 665
    global perspective, 665–666
    recognizing loss from, 661, 661n
OTT. See Other-than-temporary impairment
Output measures
    in activity-based depreciation, 562
    in gross profit recognition, 249, 249n
Overhead allocation, 521, 522
Owens-Corning Fiberglass, 1146, 1147
Ownership. See also Legal title
    of asset, 811, 811n, 812
    ownership interests, 657, 657n, 1008

P

Pacific Crest Securities, 1035
Paid absences, 698–700
Paid-in capital, 53, 1017–1031
    accounting for share issuance, 1020–1024
    accounting for share retirement, 1026–1027
    balance sheet classification, 139
    classes of shares distinguished, 1017–1020
        debt-equity distinction, 1019–1020
        preferred share rights, 1018, 1019
    par value concept, 1020
    share buybacks, 1024–1028
    shareholders' equity and, 1009–1010

Paid-in capital—*Cont.*
  shareholders' equity reported as, 121
  shown in balance sheet, 78
  unexercised stock options, 1075–1076
PaineWebber Inc., 367
Palacky, Georgene, 627
Parent (investor), 645
Parenthetical comments, 31, 32
Partial periods
  depreciation, 574n, 574–575
  investment acquired mid-year, 650–651
"Participating interests," 363, 363n
Participating preferred shares, 1018
Partnerships, 5, 1015
Partnoy, Frank, 1073, 1073n
Par value concept, 1020, 1025n
Par value method, 1027
Par value of bonds, 748
Patents, 503, 509, 527, 529
Payments. *See also* Troubled debt
    restructuring
  on account, 53, 57
  of cash dividends, 1193
  on debt, 1209
  deferred (noncash acquisitions),
    513–515, 533
  floating, A-11, A-11n
  lease payments. *See* Lease payments
  pensions. *See* Pension benefits
  prepayment. *See* Prepayments
  rent. *See* Rental payments
  of salaries, 53, 57, 61
Payroll-related deductions, 702
Payroll-related liabilities, 721–722
  employee withholding taxes, 721
  employer payroll taxes, 721
  fringe benefits, 722
  voluntary deductions, 721
PBGC (Pension Benefit Guaranty Company),
    942, 949
PBO. *See* Projected benefit obligation
PBS, 1073
PCAOB. *See* Public Company Accounting
    Oversight Board
PC's Limited, 4
Peachtree Accounting Software, 52
Peasnell, K., 368n
Pension Benefit Guaranty Company (PBGC),
    942, 949
Pension benefits
  payment of
    amount of assets available for, 935, 975
    changes in PBO, 947
    recording, 966
  postretirement health benefits compared, 967
  vested benefits, 942
Pension expense
  changes in PBO and plan assets, 935,
    949–954, 976
  components of, 941, 951–953, 976
    interest cost, 950, 951
    net loss or gain amortization, 941,
      952–953
    prior service cost amortization, 941,
      951–952, 952n, 977
    return on plan assets, 941, 950, 951
    service cost, 941, 950, 951
  disclosure notes, 957
  income smoothing and, 953n, 953–954
  overview, 940–941
  recording, 956n, 956–957, 976
  reporting (global issue), 963

Pension formula, 939, 945, 946n
Pension obligation, 940, 941–947
  accumulated benefit obligation, 941,
    942, 976
  for entire employee pool, 942, 947
  present value techniques in, 321–322
  projected benefit obligation, 941, 942n,
    942–947
    calculating balance, 945
    changes in, 943–947, 959
    as liability, 951, 951n
  reporting changes in, 965
  valuation of, 321–322
  vested benefit obligation, 941–942
Pension plan(s), 936–941
  assets of. *See* Pension plan assets
  classifying total cost of, 965
  defined benefit plans, 937, 939–940, 976
  defined contribution plans, 937, 938–939,
    976
  disclosure notes, 935–936, 957, 963
  FASB on
    income smoothing, 953, 953n
    net loss or gain on PBO,
      952–953, 954
    prior service cost as OCI, 952
  money purchase plans, 938
  pension expense. *See* Pension expense
  pension obligation. *See* Pension obligation
  profit-sharing plans, 938
  qualified plans, 937
  reporting issues, 955–966
    actuarial gains and losses, 955–956,
      956n
    comprehensive income, 960n, 960–961
    decision makers' perspective of, 963,
      963n
    "funded status" of plan, 949, 949n, 976
    income tax considerations, 961
    pension expense, 963
    pension spreadsheets, 962, 976
    prior service cost, 957n, 957–958
    recording funding of plan assets,
      958–959, 966
    recording pension expense, 956n,
      956–957
    settlement or curtailment, 963
    using net pension (liability) asset
      account, 959
  review, 964
  savings or thrift plans, 938
  uncertainty (risk) of, 938, 939, 939n
  underfunding, 935, 948–949, 949n, 975
Pension plan assets, 947–949, 976
  amount available to pay benefits, 935, 975
  changes in PBO and pension expense, 935,
    949–954, 976
  defined benefit pension plans, 940
  expected return on, 948, 948n
  recording funding of, 958–959, 966
  reporting funded status, 949
  return on, 941, 950, 951
Pension Protection Act of 2006, 959
Pension spreadsheets, 962, 976
Pep Boys, 817
PepsiCo Inc., 765–767, 1148
Percentage depletion, 570, 887, 887n
Percentage-of-completion method, 236, 237,
    246, 246n
  completed contract method compared,
    246, 251–256
    balance sheet recognition, 252, 253

    income recognition, 251–252, 252n
    long-term contract losses, 253–256
  costs of construction, 247
  review of, 257
  timing of gross profit recognition, 233,
    248, 249–251, 269
Performance conditions, 1079, 1079n
Performance obligations, 263
Performance ratios, 1223
Performed Line Products (PLP), 577, 578
Period costs, 401n, 558, 572
Periodic average cost (inventories), 406
Periodic inventory system, 398–399, 425
  allocation of cost of goods available for
    sale, 404–405
  comparison of cost flow methods, 410–411
  FIFO in, 407
  LIFO in, 408–409
  perpetual system compared, 399–400
  purchase commitments, 477n
  purchase discounts in (net method), 403
  recording transactions, 60, 415
Periodicity assumption, 29, 32
Period-specific effects, 1144–1145
Permanent accounts, 55, 88
Permanent differences, 886–888, 889, 908
Permanent earnings, 175, 179, 208, 265
Perpetual average cost (inventories), 406–407
Perpetual inventory system, 397–398, 425
  comparison of cost flow methods, 410–411
  FIFO in, 408
  LIFO in, 409–410
  periodic system compared, 399–400
  purchase discounts in (net method), 403
  purchase returns in, 397–398, 402
  recording transactions, 59
  sales returns in, 345, 397–398
PetSmart, Inc., 128
Petty cash fund, 371–372, 659
Petty cash system, 340
Pfizer, 178, 620, 711, 712, 714
Philippine Townships, Inc., 1033
Physical count of inventory, 399, 425
Physical flow of inventory, 411
Piper Jaffrey, 658
Plant assets. *See* Property, plant, and
    equipment
Pledging of receivables, 356, 357
PLP (Performed Line Products), 577, 578
Point of sale, 30
Pooling of interests method, 12–13
Post-closing trial balance, 80, 81, 83, 123
Posting, 56, 58, 86
Posting reference, 61–62
PostPath, Inc., 532
Postretirement benefits, 966–975, 976, 977
  accounting for, 970–973
  APBO. *See* Accumulated postretirement
    benefit obligation (APBO)
  benefit plans, 967–968
    determining net cost of, 968
    health and pension benefits compared,
      967
  comprehensive illustration of, 972, 973
  decision makers' perspective of, 973–974
  eligibility for, 970–971
  EPBO. *See* Expected postretirement
    benefit obligation
  ethical dilemma, 971–972
  FASB/IASB project on, 964–966
  gains (losses) from amendments to, 1010
  health benefits, 966

determining net cost of, 968
ethical dilemma, 971–972
pension benefits compared, 967
pensions. *See* Pension plan(s)
postretirement benefit obligation, 969–970
attribution of, 969–970, 970n
comprehensive illustration, 972, 973
measurement of, 969
review, 974–975
Potential common shares
antidilutive securities, 1101
convertible bonds as, 1083
diluted EPS, 1087
effect on EPS, 1098, 1099, 1101
Powell, Dennis, 13
Predictive value, 23, 175
Preemptive rights, 1017
Preferred share(s), 1017
convertible, 1090–1092, 1093, 1094
debt-equity distinction, 1019–1020
excluded from calculation of ROE, 267
global perspective, 1019, 1019n
as hybrid securities, 1019
kinds of, 1018
typical rights of, 1018, 1019
with voting rights, 645n
Preferred shareholders, 1019, 1086, 1086n
Premium on bonds, 750
amortization schedule, 755
effective interest method, 754–755
Premium on securities, 622
Premiums, 710–711
Prepaid expenses. *See* Expenses
Prepayments
adjusting entries for, 67–70, 72
alternative recording of, 69–70
prepaid expenses, 67–68
unearned revenues, 68–69
reversing entries used with, 89–90
Present value (PV)
accounting applications of, 306–308
of annuities, 312–316, 323
annuity due (PVAD), 313–314
deferred annuity, 314n, 314–316
ordinary annuity (PVA), 312–313
solving for unknown values, 316–319
compound interest excluded, 304
expected cash flow approach, 308n,
308–309
in leasing
guaranteed residual value and, 828
PV of minimum lease payments, 817,
825, 834, 834n, 840
of single cash flow amount, 302–304,
323, 324
solving for unknown values, 304–305
using financial calculators and
spreadsheets, 316
Present value measurements, 28, 28n
Present values, 693, 693n
Present value tables
Present Value of $1, 303, 303n, 304, 305,
314, 324
Present Value of Annuity Due, 314, 323
Present Value of Ordinary Annuity of $1,
312–313, 316, 318
Present value techniques, 320–322
long-term bonds, 320–321, 324
long-term leases, 321
notes receivable, 354
pension obligations, 321–322
Price-earnings ratio, 1103

Price risk, A-0
PricewaterhouseCoopers LLP, 16
Primary market transactions, 6
Principal
of bonds, 748
of capital lease, 817, 818
of note receivable, 352
Principles-based accounting, 18–19, 814
Prior period adjustments
accounting errors
disclosures, 1158, 1159
income statement, 192, 192n
retained earnings, 579, 579n
statement of retained earnings,
1152–1153, 1153n
inventory errors, 472, 472n
Prior service cost
allocation of
service method, 952n, 977–978
straight-line method, 952, 952n, 978
amortization of, 941, 951–952, 952n, 977
change in account, 955
changes in PBO and, 944n, 944–946
as component of pension expense, 950
global perspective, 957n, 957–958
for other postretirement benefits, 971, 971n
Privately held corporations, 1016
Private placement of bonds, 759, 759n
"Proceeds," 1096–1097, 1107
Procter & Gamble Company, 143, 658
Producer Price Index, 422
Product costs, 401n, 401–403
amortization, 558, 572
freight-in on purchases, 401–402
purchase discounts, 402–403
purchase returns, 402
sales returns, 401
Production basis of revenue recognition,
262, 262n
Product quality, 589
Product revenue, 238
Product warranties and guarantees,
708–710
expected cash flow approach, 709, 709n
extended warranty contracts, 710
manufacturer's original warranty, 708
Professionalism, 19
Profitability, 136–137, 266
Profitability analysis, 263–269
activity ratios. *See* Activity ratios
DuPont framework, 266, 266n, 267, 268
illustrated, 267–269
leverage ratio, 266, 267
profitability ratios. *See* Profitability ratios
Profitability ratios, 265–266, 267, 270
gross profit (gross margin), 419, 425, 457
inventory measurement and, 418–419
profit margin on sales, 265, 267, 268
return on assets. *See* Return on assets
(ROA) ratio
return on shareholders' equity,
265–266, 267
Profit margin, 265
Profit margin on sales ratio, 265, 267, 268
Profit-sharing (pension) plans, 938
Pro forma earnings, 179
Pro forma EPS, 1102–1103
Projected benefit obligation (PBO), 941,
942n, 942–947, 976
calculating PBO balance, 945
changes in, 943–947
gain or loss on, 946

interest cost, 944, 944n
payment of benefits, 947
pension expense and plan assets, 935,
949–954, 976
prior service cost, 944n, 944–946
recording, 959
service cost, 944
summary of, 947
as liability, 951, 951n
Promissory notes, 748
Property, plant, and equipment, 500, 502
acquisition costs, 503, 533
balance sheet classifications, 119, 138
capitalization of acquisition costs, 504n,
504–509
asset retirement obligations, 506–509
cost of buildings, 506
equipment costs, 504, 505
land costs, 504n, 504–505
land improvements, 505
natural resources costs, 506
depreciation of, 502
fixed-asset turnover ratio, 516–517
impairment of value, 581–583
global perspective, 583, 583n
measurement, 581–582
testing for impairment, 581, 581n
initial valuation of, 504
leasehold improvements, 816
sale of, 517–518, 518n
used in development of natural
resources, 506
Property dividends, 1033
Proportionate consolidation, 654, 654n, 659
Prospective reporting, 1144–1146, 1160
change in accounting estimate, 190,
1146–1148, 1150
change in accounting principle, 1139,
1144–1146, 1150, 1160
depreciation, depletion, and
amortization methods, 1146
when mandated, 1145
when retrospective approach is
impracticable, 1144–1145
Provision for income taxes. *See* Income tax
expense
"Provisions," 716
Public Company Accounting Oversight
Board (PCAOB), 17–18
*Auditing Standards of. See Accounting
Standards Index*
requirements for auditors' reports, 129,
129n, 130
Public Company Accounting Reform and
Investor Protection Act of 2002.
See Sarbanes-Oxley Act of 2002
Publicly held corporations, 1016
Purchase(s)
adjusting entries for, 68
freight-in on, 401–402
intangible assets, 509
investments
AFS securities, 631
HTM securities, 623
recording, 646
trading securities, 626
lump-sum purchases, 512, 513, 533
recording in journal, 59
transaction analysis, 53, 57
Purchase commitments, 476–478
contract beyond fiscal year, 477–478
contract within fiscal year, 477, 477n

Purchase discounts
    included in inventories, 402n, 402–403
    in retail inventory method, 462, 463
Purchase discounts lost account, 402, 402n
Purchase method, 12–13, 13n
Purchase returns
    included in inventories, 402
    perpetual inventory system,
        397–398, 402
    in retail inventory method, 462, 463
Purchases journal, 91
PV. See Present value

Q

QSPE (qualifying SPE), 359, 359n
Qualified opinions, 130
Qualified pension plans, 937
Qualifying SPE (QSPE), 359, 359n
Qualitative characteristics of financial
        information. See Financial
        information
Quasi reorganizations, 1042–1043
QuickBooks, 52
Quick (acid-test) ratio, 134–135, 341, 719

R

Raiborn, Cecily, 187n
Rajan, M. V., 700n
Rate of return, 6
Ratio analysis, 133–138, 139. See also
        specific ratios
    activity ratios. See Activity ratios
    cash flow ratios
        decision makers' perspective,
            1223–1224
        performance ratios, 1223
        sufficiency ratios, 1223
    disclosure notes as information source, 963
    earnings per share (EPS), 192–193
    financing ratios, 135–138
        debt-to-equity ratio. See Debt-to-equity
            ratio
        times interest earned ratio, 137–138,
            138n, 765, 767
    liquidity ratios, 133–135
        acid-test (quick) ratio, 134–135,
            341, 719
        current ratio, 134, 341, 719
        inventory measurement and, 418
    profitability ratios. See Profitability ratios
Raw materials, 118, 396
Raytheon Company, 246, 358
RC (replacement cost), 449–450, 475
R&D. See Research and development
Reacquired shares
    basic EPS, 1085–1086
    retired shares. See Retired shares
    treasury stock. See Treasury stock
Reader's Digest Association, Inc., 701, 1018
Realization principle, 26, 30, 31, 32, 33
    adjusting entries required for, 67–68
    in capital leases, 813
    in LCM method, 450–451
    revenue recognition and, 270
        completed contract method, 245
        cost recovery method, 243
        recognition criteria, 234, 234n, 235
Rearrangements, 590–591, 593
Receivables
    accounts receivable. See Accounts
        receivable
    accrued, 71, 72
    assignment of, 356–357

current. See Current receivables
factoring, 697, 697n
impairment of, 355, 372n, 372–374
    notes receivable, 355
    troubled debt restructuring, 372n,
        372–374
lease receivable, 835
nontrade receivables, 118, 342
notes receivable. See Notes receivable
pledging of, 357, 358
sale of, 358–360
    GAAP on, 360, 361–362
    income manipulation through, 367–368
    with recourse, 359–360
    without recourse, 359, 360, 360n
    secured borrowing compared, 361–362
transfers of, 364, 364n
used as collateral, 356–358
Receivables management, 365–367
Receivables turnover ratio, 263, 264, 264n,
        268, 342, 366
Reclassification adjustment, 633n, 633–634
Recognition
    of asset retirement obligations, 507
    "derecognition" of assets/liabilities, 364, 364n
    of gross profit (loss)
        in completed contract method, 248, 249
        in cost recovery method, 242–243
        deferred gross profit account, 241, 241n
        input and output measures in, 249, 249n
        in installment sales method, 270
        in long-term construction contracts,
            247–249
        in percentage-of-completion method,
            233, 248, 249–251, 269
    income recognition, 251–252, 252n,
        653, 1012
    of revenues. See Revenue recognition
Recognition and measurement concepts,
        27–32
    broad principles, 29–32
    measurement, 28
    recognition, 27–28
    summary of, 32
    underlying assumptions, 28–29
Recording transactions
    adjusting entries, 69–70, 86
    alternative recording of adjusting entries,
        69–70
    changes in PBO, 959
    funding of pension plan assets, 958–959, 966
    gross method. See Gross method
    indirect, of retained earnings, 54–55
    in journals, 56, 58–62
    net method. See Net method
    pensions
        payment of benefits, 966
        pension expense, 956n, 956–957, 976
    periodic inventory system, 60, 415
    perpetual inventory system, 59
    recording bonds at issuance, 749n, 749–751
        determining selling price, 750–751
        held-to-maturity bonds, 749, 749n
    revenue from investments, 646–648
Recoverability test, 581
Redemption privilege, 1018
Reduction of accumulated depreciation, 590
Refinancing short-term obligations, 691,
        703–704, 720
Refundable deposits, 700
Rego, Sonia O., 905n
Reinvestment ratio, 1223
Reinvestment strategy, 1103

Related-party transactions, 126–127, 127n
Relative market values, 772–774
Relevance of financial information, 23, 27
Reliability of information, 27, 890
Remeasurement costs (pensions), 965
Rent
    on operating leases, 807, 815, 847
    prepaid, 59, 68
    received in advance, 878
    unearned revenues from, 69, 70
Rent abatement, 816
Rental payments
    including executory costs, 832
    on leases
        bargain purchase option and, 825
        first payment applied to principal, 817,
            818
        operating leases, 815, 816
Repairs and maintenance, 589, 590, 591, 593
Replacement cost (RC), 449–450, 475
Replacement method of depreciation, 594, 595
Reporting entity
    change in, 1138, 1160
        consolidation of subsidiaries, 191–192, 192n
        disclosure notes, 1149
        retrospective approach, 1148–1149, 1150
    component of entity, 182
    definition of term, 33
    goodwill inseparable from, 584, 586
Reporting segment information, 140–143
    amounts reported, 140–141, 141n
    GAAP on, 141, 142
    geographic area reporting, 142
    major customer information, 142–143
    reportable segments, 140
    requirements, 25, 25n
Research and development (R&D), 526–532,
        527n, 534
    determining costs, 527–529
    development stage enterprises, 529
    global perspective, 532, 532n
    performed for others, 529
    purchased R&D, 531–532
    software development costs, 529, 530n,
        530–531, 532, 571
    start-up costs, 529
Residual value of asset, 559–560, 571, 593
    change in accounting estimate and, 576
    IFRS requirements, 565
Residual value of asset (leases), 827–831, 848
    avoiding use of, 834
    effect on lessee, 828, 831
    effect on lessor, 828–831
        guaranteed residual value, 828–830, 830n
        unguaranteed residual value, 830–831
    implicit rate of interest and, 833–834
Restoration costs, 506
Restricted cash, 340, 368
Restricted stock, 1098, 1099
Restricted stock awards, 1070n, 1070–1071
    accounting for, 1069, 1106
    in EPS calculations, 1097, 1097n
    fair value of, 1106
Restructuring costs, 169, 177–178, 207
Retail information, 458
Retail inventory method, 458–463, 475
    cost flow methods, 460–462
        approximating average cost, 460, 460n
        conventional retail method, 461
        LIFO retail method, 461–462, 462n,
            465, 475–476
    cost of ending inventory in, 459
    other issues, 462–463

retail terminology and, 459, 460
review of, 463–465
Retail terminology, 459, 460
Retained earnings, 53, 87, 1031–1041, 1042
AFS investments, 636
balance sheet, 139, 1142, 1211
changes in (review), 1038–1041
characteristics of, 1031
closing temporary accounts to, 78, 79, 87
dividends, 1031n, 1031–1033
cash dividends, 1032–1033
liquidating dividend, 1031
property dividends, 1033
restrictions on, 1032
indirect recording of, 54–55
large stock dividends, 1035–1037, 1036n
fractional shares, 1037
reverse stock split, 1036
prior period adjustments, 579, 579n
quasi reorganization and, 1042
revising due to change in accounting
principle, 1142
shareholders' equity and, 121, 1010
shown in balance sheet, 78
spreadsheet preparation of SCF, 1211
stock dividends, 1033–1035
ethical dilemma, 1038
reasons for, 1035, 1035n
stock market reaction to, 1034
stock splits, 1035
terminology for, 1008
Retired shares, 1025, 1025n, 1026, 1042
accounting for, 1026–1027
basic EPS and, 1085–1086
as financing activity in SCF, 1211
reselling, 1028
Retirement method, 1027
Retirement method of depreciation, 594, 595
Retrospective reporting
change in accounting principle, 180,
1138–1139, 1141–1144, 1160
adjusting accounts for change, 1143
disclosure notes, 1144
mandated changes, 189, 190
revising comparative financial
statements, 1141–1143
voluntary changes, 188n, 188–189,
189n, 208, 469, 476
when to use prospective approach,
1144–1145
correction of accounting errors, 192, 579,
1138, 1149–1150, 1159
Return on assets (ROA) ratio, 265, 266, 267,
766, 766n
capitalization of operating leases, 839
illustration, 268
pension disclosures and, 963
Return on pension plan assets, 941, 950, 951
actual v. expected return, 951
adjustment for loss or gain, 951
Return on shareholders' equity (ROE) ratio,
265–267, 268, 269
decision makers' perspective of, 766–767,
1037
leverage and, 136n, 136–137, 137n
Revaluation option
changes in revaluation surplus, 195, 195n
global perspective, 573, 573n, 593
Revenue(s), 8, 27, 170
collected in advance, 878, 884, 884n
as defined by FASB, 234
donated assets recorded as, 516, 516n
future deductible amounts, 883–884, 884n

geographic area reporting, 142
impact on earnings quality, 177–178
interim reporting, 271–272
from investment, 646–648, 649
product revenue, 238
service revenue, 238–239
unearned. See Unearned revenues
Revenue accounts, 79, 80
Revenue/expense approach, 33
Revenue recognition, 234–263, 270
accounts receivable, 351
after delivery, 233, 236, 237,
239–245, 269
consignment sales, 245
installment sales. See Installment sales
right of return, 243–245, 244n, 270
at delivery, 236, 237
product revenue, 238
service revenue, 238–239
ethical dilemma, 236
FASB/IASB joint project on, 236n, 262n,
262–263
global perspective, 237
impact on earnings quality, 178
industry-specific issues, 258–263
adequacy of ratio analysis, 341–342
franchise sales. See Franchise(s)
production basis, 262, 262n
sales returns, 346
software and other multiple
deliverables, 259, 260
investment revenue
AFS securities, 631
HTM securities, 623–624
trading securities, 626–627
prior to delivery, 236, 237, 245–256
comparison of methods, 251–256
completed contract method. See
Completed contract method
cost of construction and accounts
receivable, 247
gross profit recognition, 247–249
percentage-of-completion method.
See Percentage-of-completion
method
production basis of, 262, 262n, 454, 454n
realization principle and, 270
completed contract method, 245
cost recovery method, 243
recognition criteria, 234, 234n, 235
unearned revenue, 720, 720n
Revenue recognition criteria
general criteria, 233, 269
realization principle and, 234, 234n, 235
Revenue recognition principle. See
Realization principle
Reversal of loss, 583, 583n
Reverse stock split, 1036
Reversing entries, 88–90
The Revised Model Business Corporation
Act (1994), 1025n, 1031n
RFM Corporation, 1033
Ricks, William E., 412n
Right of conversion, 1018
Right of return, 243–245, 244n, 270
Risk (uncertainty), 6
amounts and timing of cash flows, 709
as to collectibility of asset, 238, 451
of current liabilities, 691–692, 720
default risk, 133, 765
enhanced disclosure of, A-10, A-10n
in income taxes, 900–902
more-likely-than-not criterion, 900–901

resolution of uncertainty, 901–902
tax benefit measurement, 901
two-step decision process, 900
in installment sales, 240
measuring residual value of asset, 560
noted in auditors' reports, 130
of "off-balance-sheet" financing, 767
operational risk, 133
outcome of pending litigation, 712–713
of pension plans, 938, 939, 939n
R&D costs, 527
relationship to profitability, 136–137
Risk analysis, 132–138, 139
ratio analysis. See Ratio analysis
using financial statement information,
132–133
Risk.com, 36n
Risk management. See Derivatives
ROA. See Return on assets (ROA) ratio
Rockness, Joanne W., 19n
ROE. See Return on shareholders' equity
(ROE) ratio
Rohm and Haas Company, 1147
Rouse Company, 240
Rules-based accounting, 18–19, 814

S
Saga, Inc., 190, 191
Saks, 458
Salamon, G., 412n, 1140n
Salaries
as current liability, 698
payment of, 53, 57, 61
recording accrued liability, 70, 71
salaries expense, 84, 1204, 1219
Sale-leaseback transactions, 842–845
capital leases, 843–844, 844n
deferred gains on, 844, 844n, 848
global perspective, 845, 845n
losses on, 845
operating leases, 844n, 844–845
purchase compared, 844
Sale of receivables, 356, 358–360
with recourse, 359–360
without recourse, 359, 360, 360n
Sales allowances, 344, 344n
Sales discounts, 462
Sales discounts account, 343
Sales journal, 91–92
Sales returns, 344–346, 345n, 346n, 368
included in inventories, 401
perpetual inventory system, 345, 397–398
in retail inventory method, 462
Sales revenue
accounting error: failure to record,
1157–1158
conversion from cash to accrual basis
accounting, 84
spreadsheet preparation of SCF, 1199–1202
Sales taxes, 702
Sales-type leases, 808, 817, 822n, 822–823,
823n, 824, 847
additional lessor conditions, 813
capital leases compared, 824
disclosure notes, 823
disclosure of, by lessor, 837
effect of residual value on, 829
financial statement impact of, 840
initial direct costs, 835
journal entries for, 816n
lease terms and concepts, 836
reported in SCF, 1209
revenue from, 806, 847

Salkever, Alex, 1073*n*
Salvaged materials, 505
Salvage value of asset, 559–560
Sanofi-Aventis, 122, 565, 1012
Sara Lee Corporation, 396, 397
Sarbanes, Paul, 16
Sarbanes-Oxley Act of 2002, 16–17
   costs of compliance with, 17*n*, 17–18
   internal control requirements, 17, 338–339
   key provisions of, 17, 18
   on management responsibilities, 128
   on pro forma earnings, 179, 179*n*
SARS. *See* Stock appreciation rights
Savings (pension) plans, 938
SBA Communications Corporation, 246
SCF. *See* Statement of cash flows
Schaff, William, 474, 474*n*
Schapiro, Ken, 175
Schwinn, Elizabeth, 4*n*
S corporations, 1016
Sears Holdings, 458, 1070
Sears Roebuck & Co., 239, 447, 475, 521
SEC. *See* Securities and Exchange
   Commission
Secondary market transactions, 6
Secured borrowing, 356–358, 361–362
Secured loans, 696–697
Securities
   antidilutive. *See* Antidilutive securities
   classification of, 118
   convertible. *See* Convertible securities
   equity method of reporting. *See* Equity
      method
   fair value of. *See* Fair value
   hybrid. *See* Convertible securities
   investor has significant influence, 644–658
   investor lacks significant influence,
      620–644
      change in level of influence, 651, 651*n*
      comparison of HTM, TS, and AFS
         approaches, 635–636
      financial statement presentation and
         disclosure, 642–643
      global perspective, 636*n*, 636–637
      held to maturity securities. *See* Held-to-
         maturity securities
      impairment of investment, 639, 639*n*
      income taxes and, 636
      review of, 640–642
      securities available for sale. *See*
         Available-for-sale (AFS) securities
      trading securities. *See* Trading securities
      transfers between reporting categories,
         637–638
Securities Act of 1933, 9, 759*n*
Securities and Exchange Commission (SEC),
      17, 37, 1016, 1072, 1140
   disclosure requirements
      executive compensation, 131, 132
      regulation FD (Fair Disclosure), 9*n*
   Financial Reporting Releases (FRRs).
      See Accounting Standards Index
   on illegal activities
      income manipulation, 367
      securities fraud, 178
   on materiality, 26
   reporting requirements of, 9, 15, 24
      classification of expenses by function,
         174
      Form 10-K (annual), 9*n*, 29*n*, 271*n*
      Form 10-Q (quarterly), 9*n*, 29*n*, 271*n*
      interim financial statements, 186, 234*n*
      timeliness of information and, 29

Roadmap (proposed), 15
Staff Accounting Bulletins. See Accounting
   Standards Index
Securities Exchange Act of 1934, 9
Securities fraud, 178
Securitizations, 357*n*, 358–359, 367*n*,
   367–368, 368*n*
Segment information, 141, 142, 143
Selective disclosure, prohibited, 9*n*
Self-constructed assets, 521–526, 534
   interest capitalization, 522–526
      actual interest limitation, 526
      average accumulated expenditures,
         522–523
      calculation of, 524–526
      disclosure, 526
      interest rates, 523–526
      period of capitalization, 522
      qualifying assets, 522, 522*n*
   overhead allocation, 522
Seneca Foods Corporation, 471
Separately reported items (income statement),
   180*n*, 180–188
   discontinued operations, 180*n*, 182–186,
      902
   extraordinary items, 174, 180*n*, 186*n*,
      186–187, 187*n*
   intraperiod income tax allocation, 180*n*,
      180–182
   unusual or infrequent items, 187–188
Separation of duties, 339
Serial bonds, 749
Service charges by bank, 369
Service cost
   changes in PBO, 944, 976
   as component of pension expense,
      941, 950, 951
   postretirement benefits, 972, 973
   review, 974
Service life. *See* Useful life of asset
Service method, 952*n*, 977–978
Service revenue, 238–239
Services
   note exchanged for, 760–762, 760*n*–762*n*
   revenue from, 53, 57
Shakespeare, C., 367*n*, 368*n*
Share-based compensation, 1070–1082
   decision makers' perspective of, 1080–1081
   deferred, 1071
   employee share purchase plans, 1080
   review, 1081–1082
   stock award plans, 1070–1071
   stock option plans. *See* Stock option plans
Share buybacks, 1024–1028
   accounting for retired shares, 1026–1027
   accounting for treasury stock, 1027
   cautions about, 1038
   decision makers' perspective of, 1024–1025
   resale of shares, 1028
   retired stock and treasury stock, 1025,
      1026
   review, 1028–1030
Shareholders
   control of company, 1017
   earnings available to, 1086, 1086*n*
   preferred shareholders, 1019, 1086, 1086*n*
Shareholders' equity, 27, 53, 1006–1042
   in accounting equation, 54
   balance sheet classifications, 121, 139
   corporate organization and, 1015–1017
      disadvantages, 1015
      ease of raising capital, 1015
      hybrid organizations, 1016

      limited liability, 1015
      Model Business Corporation Act
         (2009), 1016–1017
      types of corporations, 1016
   decision makers' perspective of, 1037–1038
   financial reporting overview, 1008–1014
      accumulated other comprehensive
         income, 1010*n*, 1010–1011
      equity reporting, 1012–1013, 1014
      global perspective, 1012, 1012*n*, 1013
      paid-in capital, 1009–1010
      retained earnings, 1010
      treasury stock, 1010
   market v. book value of, 1038
   nature of, 1008–1017
   paid-in capital. *See* Paid-in capital
   quasi reorganizations and, 1042–1043
   retained earnings. *See* Retained earnings
   return on shareholders' equity, 136*n*,
      136–137, 137*n*
   review, 1023–1024
   SARS payable in shares, 1109, 1110
   shown in balance sheet, 78, 116, 1024
   typical presentation format, 1012, 1013
Share repurchase plans, 1007, 1041
Share retirement, 1025, 1025*n*, 1026
Shipping charges, 401–402
Shortcut method, A-5, A-5*n*, A-14
Short-term investments
   balance sheet classification, 117–118
   spreadsheet preparation of SCF, 1207–1208
Short-term notes payable, 691, 694–697,
      720, 721
   credit lines, 695
   interest, 695–696
   secured loans, 696–697
Short-term obligations, 691, 703–704, 720
Sick days, 698–700
Sick pay, 699–700
Siemens AG, 200
Significant influence, 658
   defined, 645, 645*n*
   inability to exercise, 646, 646*n*
   investor has significant influence, 621,
      644–658, 659
   investor lacks significant influence,
      620–644, 659
   reporting categories and, 621
Simple capital structure, 1083, 1086, 1106
Simple interest, 300–301
Single cash flow amount
   present value techniques, 306–308
   valuation of, 301–305
      future value, 301–302, 323, 324
      present value, 302–304
      review of, 305–306
Single entity concept, 645–647
   in equity method, 645–647
      purchase of investment, 646
      receiving dividends, 647
      recording investment revenue, 646–647
   purchase of investment, 646
   receipt of dividends, 647
   recording investment revenue, 646–647
Single-step format
   for income statement, 173, 174
   separately reported items, 180, 180*n*
Sinking fund, 749
Sinking fund debentures, 749
Six Flags, 781, 1020
Skilled Healthcare Group, Inc., 1154
Small stock dividend, 1033, 1033*n*, 1034, 1210
Smith, E., 412*n*, 1140*n*

Smucker Company, 1008, 1018, 1137, 1160
Social Security taxes, 721
Software development costs, 529, 571
    capitalization of, 530n, 530–531
    global perspective, 532
Software industry
    R&D costs, 529, 530n, 530–531
    revenue recognition in, 259, 260
    sales guidelines, 270
Sole proprietorships, 5, 1015
Sonic Solutions, 245
SoRIE (Statement of Recognized Income
        and Expense), 1012
Source documents, 55–56, 58
Southwest Airlines, 1012, 1013, 1014
SPE (special purpose entity), 358, 358n,
        359, 359n
"Special charge" categories, 176
Special journals, 56, 91, 91n
    cash receipts journal, 91, 92
    sales journal, 91–92
Special purpose entity (SPE), 358, 358n,
        359, 359n
Special purpose funds, 659–660
Specific construction loan, 524
Specific goods LIFO, 420, 420n
Specific identification, 510
Specific identification method, 405, 458
Specific interest method, 523–526
Speculation, in derivatives, A-3
Spiceland, David J., 1034n
Sport Chalet Inc., 582
Spreadsheet(s)
    future value calculations, 302, 316
    pension spreadsheets, 962, 976
Spreadsheet preparation of SCF,
        1197–1214, 1199n, 1225
    balance sheet accounts, 1207–1214
        bonds payable, 1210
        buildings and equipment, 1208–1209
        common stock, 1210–1211
        land, 1208
        retained earnings, 1211
        short-term investments, 1207–1208
    completion of spreadsheet, 1211–1214
    comprehensive review, 1214–1218
    income statement accounts,
            1199–1207
        cost of goods sold, 1203
        depreciation expense, 1204
        gain on sale of land, 1202–1203
        income tax expense, 1206–1207, 1223
        insurance expense, 1204–1205
        interest expense, 1204, 1223
        investment revenue, 1202
        loss on sale of equipment, 1205
        net income, 1207
        salaries expense, 1204
        sales revenue, 1199–1202
    for indirect reporting method, 1225–1229
Sprint, 651
St. Mary Land & Exploration Company, 507,
        508
Standard & Poor's Corporation, 750
The Standard Register Company, 195
"Stand ready obligation," 711
Staples, Inc., 902
Starbucks Corporation, 125, 126
Start-up costs, 529, 529n
Stated rate of interest, 622, 623, 748
State Farm Insurance, 170
Statement of cash flows (SCF), 4, 8, 198–207,
        209, 1182–1225

cash inflows and outflows, 1184–1185
classification of cash flows, 199–205, 209
    financing activities, 203–204, 1193
    investing activities. See Investing
        activities
    noncash investing and financing, 204,
        1194, 1195, 1225
    operating activities, 199–203,
        1177–1178, 1188n
comprehensive review, 1214–1218
content and value of, 1184–1197
decision makers' perspective of, 1184
direct method investments, 655
ethical dilemma, 1212
from financing activities. See Financing
    activities
illustration of, 1213–1214
impact of leases, 839–840, 1209
    capital and direct financing leases, 840
    operating leases, 839
    sales-type leases, 840
from investing activities. See Investing
    activities
investments reported in, 650, 650n
issuance of bonds or notes reported in, 764
from operating activities. See Operating
    activities
payments of debt reported in, 1209
preparation of, 78–79, 86, 1194–1197,
        1195n
    indirect method, 1218–1224
    T-account method, 1195n, 1229–1231
    using spreadsheet. See Spreadsheet
        preparation of SCF
presentation of securities
    AFS securities, 634
    trading securities, 629, 629n
primary elements of, 1188–1194, 1195
purpose of, 170
review of, 205–207
role of, 1185–1194
    cash and cash equivalents, 1187–1188,
        1188n
    importance of cash flows in economic
        decline, 1187
    primary elements of, 1188–1194
usefulness of, 198–199
Statement of comprehensive income, 960n
    organization of elements in, 1191
    presentation of securities
        AFS securities, 629, 634, 634n
        trading securities, 629
    recording pension expense, 956–957
Statement of earnings. See Income statement
Statement of financial position. See Balance
    sheet
Statement of operations. See Income
    statement
Statement of Recognized Income and
        Expense (SoRIE), 1012
Statement of retained earnings,
        1152–1153, 1153n
Statement of shareholders' equity, 4
    illustrated, 1013, 1014
    preparation of, 79, 79n, 81, 86
    prior period adjustments, 192
    revising due to change in accounting
        principle, 1142–1143
State unemployment taxes, 721, 721n
Statutory depletion, 570
Steverman, Ben, 1025n
Stock(s)
    classes of shares, 1017–1020

debt-equity distinction, 1019–1020
    preferred share rights, 1018, 1019
common. See Common shares
EPS. See Earnings per share
issuance of. See Common shares
par value concept, 1020
preferred. See Preferred shares
retained earnings. See Retained earnings
retired shares. See Retired shares
share-based compensation, 1070–1082
share buybacks (repurchases), 1024–1028
    accounting for retired shares, 1026–1027
    accounting for treasury stock, 1027
    cautions about, 1038
    decision makers' perspective of,
        1024–1025
    resale of shares, 1028
    retired stock and treasury stock,
        1025, 1026
    review, 1028–1030
share rights, 1017–1019
treasury stock. See Treasury stock
watered shares, 1020
weighted average of shares outstanding,
        1083, 1084, 1087, 1106
Stock appreciation rights (SARS), 1108–1111
    debt v. equity issue, 1109, 1109n
    payable in cash (liability), 1109–1111,
        1111n
    payable in shares (equity), 1109, 1110
Stock award plans, 1070–1071
Stock distributions, 1034, 1034n
Stock dividends, 1033–1035, 1042
    basic EPS and, 1084–1085, 1106
    ethical dilemma, 1038
    large stock dividends, 1035–1037, 1036n
        fractional shares, 1037
        reverse stock split, 1036
    not reported in SCF, 1194, 1210
    reasons for, 1035, 1035n
    stock market reaction to, 1034
Stockholders' equity. See Shareholders' equity
Stock market, 9, 1034, 1034n
Stock option(s)
    accounting for, 1069, 1106
    antidilutive securities, 1092–1093
    diluted EPS and, 1087–1088, 1106
    exercise of options, 1075–1076
    fair value of
        attempt to require, 1072, 1072n
        estimated forfeitures, 1074–1075
        recognizing, 1073–1075
    intrinsic value of, 1072, 1073, 1073n, 1077
    as potential common shares, 1098, 1099
    SEC disclosure requirements, 131, 132
    treasury stock method, 1087–1088, 1092
    voluntary expensing, 1073
Stock option plans, 1071–1080
    accounting for, 12
    decline in popularity of, 1080
    expensing
        attempt to require, 1072–1073
        current requirement, 1073, 1073n
        exclusions in treasury stock method,
            1097–1098
        voluntary, 1073
    fair value of options, 1072, 1072n
        estimated forfeitures, 1074–1075
        expensing, 1106
        recognizing, 1073–1075
    global perspective, 1077, 1078, 1107
    with graded vesting, 1077–1078
    not tax deductible, 887

Stock option plans,—*Cont.*
with performance or market conditions, 1079–1080
decline in popularity of options, 1080
market conditions, 1080
performance conditions, 1079, 1079*n*
SARs and, 1108–1109
tax consequences of, 1076, 1076*n*
when options are exercised, 1075
when unexercised options expire, 1075–1076
Stock rights
antidilutive securities, 1092–1093
diluted EPS and, 1087–1088, 1106
Stock splits, 1007, 1035, 1041
basic EPS and, 1084–1085, 1106
reverse stock split, 1036
Stock warrants
antidilutive securities, 1092–1093
diluted EPS and, 1087–1088, 1106
Straight-line method, 560–561
of allocating prior service cost, 952, 952*n*, 978
amortization schedule, 757
determining bond interest, 756–757
popularity of, 564
for rental on operating leases, 816
switch from accelerated, 562
Subscription revenue
adjusting entries for, 68–69
as deferred tax asset, 878, 884, 884*n*
Subsequent events
disclosure notes, 125–126, 126*n*, 714
as loss contingencies, 713–714
Subsequent valuation
of accounts receivable, 344–351
sales returns, 344–346, 345*n*, 346*n*
uncollectible accounts. *See* Uncollectible accounts
of notes receivable, 355
Subsidiary(ies), 191–192, 192*n*, 645
Subsidiary (investee), 645
Subsidiary ledgers, 90
Substance of transaction, 761, 811, 843, 847
Substantial performance concept, 261
Substitution method, 590
Successful efforts method, 534, 535, 535*n*
Sufficiency ratios, 1223
Summary entries (SCF)
affected by extraordinary items, 1206–1207
completing spreadsheet, 1211–1212
Summary of significant accounting policies, 125, 125*n*, 252, 253
Summary transactions, 59–60
Sum-of-the-years' digits (SYD) depreciation, 561, 561*n*, 566
Sunbeam, Inc., 367
SuperValue Inc., 414
Supplemental financial statements, 31
Supplies, 53, 57, 67–68
Sycamore Networks, 475
SYD (sum-of-the-years' digits) depreciation, 561, 561*n*, 566
Symantec Corp., 366–367
Systematic and rational allocation, 31, 68
"Systematic and rational manner," 560, 560*n*

T

T-account method (SCF), 1195*n*, 1199, 1199*n*, 1229–1231
balance sheet accounts, 1230
cost of goods sold, 1203

income statement accounts, 1231
sales revenue, 1200
steps in, 1229
T-accounts, 54, 63, 89
Talbots, Inc., 185–186
Tandem plans, 1109*n*
Target Corporation, 267*n*, 267–269, 458, 817
Taxable income, 172
Tax effects, 181, 183–186, 188*n*, 196–197
Taxes
income taxes. *See* Income tax(es)
tax basis of asset or liability, 877
tax benefits, 181, 184, 901
tax exempt interest, 886
tax-exempt (-deferred) status, 753
Tax-exempt income, 887, 937
Tax laws
changes in, 890–892
different from GAAP, 172, 873, 907
installment sales method, 240*n*
on operating losses, 908
Tax rates, 890–892
changes in tax laws or rates, 891–892
differing enacted rates, 890–891
effective tax rate, 887, 888
Technological change, 559, 580
Technological feasibility
purchased R&D, 531–532
of software, 530, 530*n*
Technology, 398
Temporary accounts, 55, 60
alternative recording of dividends, 61
closing to retained earnings, 78, 79, 87
in worksheet, 88
Temporary differences, 873, 874, 875, 889, 907, 908
deferred tax liabilities, 875–881
financial statement presentation of income taxes, 897–900
future deductible amounts, 882–884, 884*n*, 892, 908
future taxable amounts, 876, 892, 908
income tax expense, 1206
multiple differences, 892–894, 905–907
permanent differences compared, 887–888
reversal of, 879–881
with tax rate change, 892
without tax rate change, 891
review, 889
types of, 878–881, 892
Temporary investments. *See* Short-term investments
Terrorist attacks of September 11, 2001, 187
Textron Inc., 1007, 1041
TheStreet.com, 337
Thiagarajan, S. R., 367, 367*n*, 419, 419*n*
3M Co., 141, 142
Thrift (pension) plans, 938
Time-based depreciation methods, 560–562
accelerated methods, 561–562
straight-line method, 560–561
Time diagrams
annuities, 309–311, 313–315, 317, 318, 322
future value of single amount, 301
present value of single amount, 303, 307
solving for unknown values, 304, 305
Timeliness of financial information, 24, 29, 271–273
Times interest earned ratio, 137–138, 138*n*, 765, 767
Time value, 1107–1108
Time value of money, 298–324
annuities. *See* Annuity(ies)

expected cash flow approach, 308*n*, 308–309
financial calculators and Excel, 316
present value situations
annuities. *See* Annuity(ies)
solving for unknown values, 316–319
present value techniques, 306–308
simple v. compound interest, 300–301
single amount valuation, 301–305
future value, 301–302, 323, 324
present value, 302–304
review of, 305–306
solving for unknown values, 304–305
summary of concepts, 322–323
Time Warner, Inc., 182, 183, 183*n*, 1036
Time-weighting common shares, 1083, 1099, 1106
Timing of revenue recognition, 30, 234, 234*n*, 369, 370
Tomé, Carol B., 128, 129
Toyota, 358
Toys R Us, Inc., 764
Trade discounts, 343
Trademarks (tradenames), 503, 510
Trade notes payable, 694
Trade receivables. *See* Accounts receivable
Trading securities (TS), 118, 621, 625–629, 659
adjustment to fair value
in 2011, 627, 627*n*
in 2012, 628–629
disclosures, 642*n*, 642–643
fair value accounting for, 625–626
fair value controversy, 628, 628*n*
financial statement presentation, 629, 629*n*
other approaches compared
AFS and equity method, 656
AFS and HTM approaches, 635–636
purchase of, 626
reporting
as operating activity, 1208
unrealized gain (loss), 626
revenue recognition, 626–627
selling, 628, 628*n*
transfers between reporting categories, 637–638
unrealized gain (loss) on, 619–620, 626, 658
Tranches (vesting groups), 1078
Transaction(s), 53
with owners
cash flow hedges not included, A-8, A-8*n*
distributions, 27
investment by owner, 27, 53, 57
reported in OCI, 960*n*
recording. *See* Recording transactions
sale-leasebacks, 842–845, 848
Transaction analysis, 53, 56, 57
Transactions approach, 877
Transferee, 356
Transferor, 356
Transitory earnings, 175, 208, 265
Transportation-in, 401–402
Treadway Commission, 129, 339, 339*n*
Treasury bill futures, A-2
Treasury bills, 1188, 1208, A-1
Treasury bonds, A-1
Treasury stock, 1025, 1025*n*, 1026, 1042
accounting for, 1027
acquired at different costs, 1028
basic EPS and, 1085–1086
dividends not paid on, 1035

no cash dividends paid on, 1035
resale of shares, 1028
reselling, 1028
review, 1028–1030
shareholders' equity and, 1010
Treasury stock method
components of "proceeds" in,
1096–1097, 1107
diluted EPS calculation, 1102
dilutive effect of stock options,
1087–1088
options, rights, and warrants, 1092
Trial balance
adjusted, 73, 74, 75
post-closing, 80, 81, 83, 123
unadjusted, 64, 67
Troubled debt restructuring, 780n,
780–784
amortization schedule in, 783
debt is continued, modified, 781–784
cash payments exceed carrying
amount, 782–784
cash payments less than carrying
amount, 781–782
debt is settled, 781
impairment of receivables, 372n,
372–374
global perspective, 374
receivable is continued (modified), 373
receivable is settled outright, 374
Trustee, 948
TS. *See* Trading securities
Turnover ratios, 135
efficiency of asset management and, 719
fixed-asset turnover ratio, 516–517,
517n, 534
TWA, 781
Tweedie, (Sir) David, A-14
Tyco International, 1073
Tyson Foods, Inc., 502, 1018

U

UBS, 1024
UCI (United Components Inc.), 362
Unadjusted trial balance, 64, 67
Unasserted claims and assessments, 715, 721
Uncertainty. *See* Risk
Uncollectible accounts, 347–351, 369. *See
also* Bad debt(s)
actual write-offs of, 349–350
allowance for (contra account), 72–73,
73n, 75
balance sheet approach to, 348–349,
349n, 369
collection of previously written-off
accounts, 350
direct write-off method, 25, 350–351,
368, 1201
ethical dilemma, 350
income statement approach to,
347–348, 369
net realizable value and, 347, 350
review of, 351–352
Underfunded pension plans, 935,
948–949, 949n, 975
Understandability of financial
information, 24
Underwriting fees, 759, 759n
"Undistributed earnings of investee," 650n
Unearned revenues, 84, 1200
adjusting entries for, 68–69
from advance payments, 720, 720n
balance sheet classifications, 120

customer advances, 701
franchise fees, 261, 261n
income manipulation, 720, 720n
interest revenue, 817
recording in journal, 60–61
from rent, 69, 70
reversing entries used with, 89–90
Unexpected events, 186, 186n
Unguaranteed residual value (leases),
830–831, 833
Uniform CPA Examination, 16
Union Pacific Corporation, 715
United Components Inc. (UCI), 362
Unit LIFO, 420, 420n
Units-of-production method
depletion, 557, 570, 592
depreciation, 562–563, 566
Unobservable inputs, 34, 35
Unrealistic interest rate, 761, 767–768
Unrealized gain (loss), 620
available-for-sale securities, 30n,
619–620, 630–631, 634, 658
deferred tax assets/liabilities, 878
different treatments of, 622, 637
held-to-maturity (HTM) securities, 194n,
621, 624n, 624–625, 625n
investor lacks significant influence, 621
from recording impairment of
investment, 960n
on trading or AFS securities, 619–620, 658
trading securities, 619–620, 627, 658
Unusual or infrequent items, 187–188, 272
Unvested restricted stock awards, 1097, 1097n
U.S. Patent Office, 509
Useful life of asset, 559, 593, 877
depreciation of leased asset, 819
expected economic life (leases),
811–812
extending, 589
land, 846
limitations on, 571
software, 531

V

Vacations, 698–700
Valuation allowance
on deferred tax assets, 885n, 885–886, 898
disclosure notes, 886
income manipulation and, 905, 905n
Varian Medical Systems, Inc., 707
VBO (vested benefit obligation),
941–942
Vendor-specific objective evidence (VSOE)
of fair value, 259, 259n, 260
Verifiability of financial information,
24, 29
Verizon Communications, Inc., 187, 1008
Vertical analysis, 132–133, 139
Vested benefit obligation (VBO), 941–942
Vested (pension) benefits, 942
Vesting
cliff vesting, 1077
graded vesting, 1077–1078
Vesting groups (tranches), 1078
Vickrey, Don W., 1034n
Virco Mfg. Corporation, 357, 358
Visa, 1016
Vivendi Universal SA, 586
Vodafone, 716
Volatility value, 1108
Voluntary deductions, 721
Voluntary expensing, 1073
Voting rights of common shares, 1017

VSOE (vendor-specific objective evidence)
of fair value, 259, 259n, 260

W

W. T. Grant, 1185–1186
The Wall Street Journal, 624, 747, 775
Walmart Stores, Inc., 29, 126, 143, 170,
267n, 267–269, 458, 526, 835, 837,
838, 839, 888, 898, 899, 1016, 1024,
1221, 1222
Walt Disney Company, 239, 501, 521, 533
Watered shares, 1020
Watts, R. L., 36n, 1139n, 1140n
Weighted-average accumulated expenditures,
523, 525
Weighted-average interest rate, 524, 524n
Weighted-average method, 526
Weighted average of shares outstanding,
1083, 1084, 1087, 1106
Weighted-average unit cost of inventory,
405, 406
Weil, Jonathan, 13n
Wells Fargo & Company, 355, 664, 665
Weyerhaeuser Company, 557, 592
Whirlpool, 358
Whitmore, Meg, 1072
Wicks 'N' Sticks, 1187
Willett, Robert A., 132
Williams-Sonoma, Inc., 127
Winn-Dixie, 1073
Winnebago Industries, Inc., 413
Winstar Communications, 178
Workforce, 512n
Working capital, 134
Work-in-process inventory, 118, 396
Work papers, retention of, 17
Worksheet, 87–88
WorldCom, Inc., 16, 19, 504, 1073
Worthy, Ford S., 175n
Write-downs of inventory
adjusting cost to market, 452–453
as "big bath" accounting, 474–475
ethical dilemma, 451
obsolete inventory, 417n
review of, 455
Write-offs
direct write-off method of accounting
for, 25, 350–351, 368, 1201
when account is deemed uncollectible,
349–350
www.coso.org, 339n
www.dell.com, 5
www.FASB.org, 10n, 11, 236n, 262n, 644n
www.fundinguniverse.com, 4n
www.iasb.org, 14n
www.iasplus.com/country/useias.htm, 15n
Wyeth, 620

X

Xerox, 16

Y

Yahoo! Inc., 28
Yamamura, Jeanne, 1224n

Z

Zega, Cheryl A., 1186n
Zero balances, 79
Zero-coupon bonds, 753, 753n, 754
"Zero-profit method," 256
Zhan, Yuan, 720n
Zimmerman, J. L., 1139n, 1140n
Zmijewski, M., 1140n

Accounting Standards Index

Note: Page numbers followed by *n* indicate material in footnotes. Unless otherwise noted, standards are listed under the name of the issuing organization.

Accounting Principles Board (APB)

Interpretations, 10

Opinions (APBOs), 10

No. 11: "Accounting for Income Taxes," 874*n*

No. 12: "Omnibus Opinion," 1013*n*

No. 14: "Accounting for Convertible Debt and Debt Issued with Stock Purchase Warrants," 770*n*

No. 18: "The Equity Method of Accounting for Investments in Common Stock," 1145*n*

No. 21: "Interest on Receivables and Payables," 306*n*, 342*n*, 693*n*, 1022

No. 22: "Disclosure of Accounting Policies," 125*n*

No. 25: "Accounting for Stock Issued to Employees," 1072*n*

No. 28: "Interim Financial Reporting," 272*n*

No. 29: "Accounting for Nonmonetary Transactions," 1021*n*

No. 30: "Reporting Results of Operations," 180*n*

Statements, 10

No. 4: "Basic Concepts and Accounting Principles Underlying Financial Statements of Business Enterprises," 10

Accounting Standards Codification System (ASC) of FASB

Master Glossary, 693*n*

Financial Instrument(s), 657*n*

Noncancelable Lease Term, 812*n*

No. 105-10: Generally Accepted Accounting Principles–Overall, 11*n*

No. 205-20-45: Presentation of Financial Statement–Discontinued Operations–Other Presentation Matters, 180*n*

No. 210-10-S99-2: Balance Sheet–Overall–SEC Materials–SAB Topic 6.H, Accounting Series Release 148, Disclosures of Compensating Balances and Short-Term Borrowing Arrangements, 340*n*

No. 220-10: Comprehensive Income–Overall

45: Other Presentation Matters, 194*n*

55-2: Implementation Guidance and Illustrations, 1272*n*

No. 225-20-45: Income Statement–Extraordinary and Unusual Items–Other Presentation Matters, 180*n*, 186*n*

No. 230-10: Statement of Cash Flows–Overall

45: Other Presentation Matters, 198*n*

50-6: Disclosure–Noncash Investing and Financing Activities, 1194*n*

No. 235-10-50: Notes to Financial Statements–Overall–Disclosure, 125*n*

No. 250-10: Accounting Changes and Error Corrections–Overall, 1138*n*, 1151*n*

45: Other Presentation Matters, 1141*n*, 1149*n*

45-5: Other Presentation Matters–Change in Accounting Principle, 188*n*

45-23: Other Presentation Matters–Correction of an Error in Previously Issued Financial Statements, 192*n*

S99-1: SEC Materials, SAB Topic 1.M, Assessing Materiality, 26*n*, 127*n*

No. 260: Earnings Per Share, 1082, 1082*n*

No. 270-10-50: Interim Reporting–Overall–Disclosure, 272*n*

No. 280: Segment Reporting, 25*n*

10-50-1: Overall–Disclosure–Operating Segments, 140*n*, 183*n*

10-50-20 through 32: Overall–Disclosure–Disclosure Requirements, 141*n*

No. 310-10-35: Receivables–Overall–Subsequent Measurement, 372*n*

No. 320: Investments–Debt and Equity Securities, 629*n*

10-20: Overall–Glossary–Readily Determinable Fair Value, 639*n*

10-25: Overall–Recognition, 622*n*, 625*n*

10-35: Overall–Subsequent Measurement, 639*n*, 661*n*, 663*n*

10-45-13: Overall–Other Presentation Matters–Cash Flow Presentation, 642*n*

10-50: Overall–Disclosure, 643*n*

10-S99: Overall–SEC Materials, 643*n*

No. 323-10: Investments–Equity Method and Joint Ventures–Overall

15-10: Scope and Scope Exceptions–Significant Influence, 646*n*

35-35: Subsequent Measurement–Decrease in Level of Ownership or Degree of Influence, 1145*n*

No. 330: Inventory–Overall

30: Initial Measurement, 401*n*

35-16: Subsequent Measurement–Stating Inventories Above Cost, 262*n*, 454*n*

50-2: Disclosure–Losses from Application of Lower of Cost or Market, 452*n*

35-9 and 10: Subsequent Measurement–Adjustments to Lower of Cost or Market, 451*n*

35-S35-1: Subsequent Measurement–Restoration of Previously Written-Down Inventory Value (SAB Topic 5.BB), 453*n*

No. 350: Intangibles–Goodwill and Other, 593

20-35: Goodwill–Subsequent Measurement, 584*n*, 648*n*

30: General Intangibles Other Than Goodwill, 13*n*

30-35: General Intangibles Other Than Goodwill–Subsequent Measurement, 509*n*, 572*n*

40-25: Internal-Use Software–Recognition, 530*n*

No. 360: Property, Plant, and Equipment, 593

10-35-4: Overall–Subsequent Measurement–Depreciation, 560*n*

10-35-15: Overall–Subsequent Measurement–Impairment or Disposal of Long-Lived Assets, 518*n*, 581*n*

10-35-21: Overall–Subsequent Measurement–Impairment or Disposal of Long-Lived Assets, 581*n*

10-45-5: Overall–Other Presentation Matters–Presentation of Disposal Gains or Losses in Discontinued Operations, 172*n*

10-45-9: Overall–Other Presentation Matters–Long-Lived Assets Classified as Held for Sale, 184*n*

20: Real Estate Sales, 240*n*

No. 410: Asset Retirement and Environmental Obligations

20-25: Asset retirement Obligations–Recognition, 506*n*

30-35-12: Environmental Obligations–Subsequent Measurement–Impact of Potential Recoveries, 716*n*

No. 450: Contingencies, 714*n*

10: Overall, 706*n*

20-30: Loss Contingencies–Initial Measurement, 707*n*

20-50: Loss Contingencies–Disclosure, 714*n*

30-50: Gain Contingencies–Disclosure, 717*n*

No. 460-10-25: Guarantees–Overall–Recognition, 711*n*

No. 470: Debt

10-45: Overall–Other Presentation Matters, 703*n*

10-45-14: Overall–Other Presentation Matters–Intent and Ability to Refinance on a Long-Term Basis, 703*n*

20-25: Debt with Conversion and Other Options–Recognition, 770*n*

20-25-5: Debt with Conversion and Other Options–Recognition–Beneficial Conversion Features, 770*n*

20-40: Debt with Conversion and Other Options–Derecognition, 772*n*

50-45: Modifications and Extinguishments–Other Presentation Matters, 769*n*

No. 480-10-25: Distinguishing Liabilities from Equity–Overall–Recognition, 1020*n*

No. 505: Equity, 190

10-50: Overall–Disclosure, 1012*n*

20: Stock Dividends and Stock Splits, 1033*n*

20-25-2: Stock Dividends and Stock Splits–Recognition–Stock Dividend in Form, 1034*n*

20-30-3: Stock Dividends and Stock Splits–Initial Measurement–Stock Dividend, 1034*n*

No. 605: Revenue Recognition

10-S99: Overall–SEC Materials, 235*n*

15-25: Products–Recognition, 244*n*

20-25: Services–Recognition, 710*n*

25-25: Multiple-Element Arrangements–Recognition, 259*n*

35-25: Construction-Type and Production-Type Contracts–Recognition, 246*n*

35-25-71: Construction-Type and Production-Type Contracts–Recognition–Input and Output Measures, 249*n*

45-50-2: Principal Agent Considerations–Disclosure–Shipping and Handling Fees and Costs, 401*n*

No. 710-10-25: Compensation–General–Overall–Recognition, 699*n*

No. 715: Compensation–Retirement Benefits, 940*n*, 953*n*

20-50: Defined Benefit Plans–General–Disclosure, 963*n*

30-25: Defined Benefit Plans–Pension–Recognition, 949*n*

30-35: Defined Benefit Plans–Pension–Subsequent Measurement, 963*n*

30-35-13: Defined Benefit Plans–Pension–Subsequent Measurement–Prior Service Costs, 977*n*

30-35-25: Defined Benefit Plans–Pension–Subsequent Measurement–Gains and Losses, 949*n*

60: Defined Benefit Plans–Other Postretirement, 966*n*, 970*n*

60-50: Defined Benefit Plans–Other Postretirement–Disclosure, 973*n*

No. 718: Compensation– Stock Compensation, 190, 1073*n*

10-35-3: Overall–Subsequent Measurement–Recognition of Compensation Costs Over the Requisite Service Period, 1074*n*

10-55: Overall–Implementation and Guidance Illustrations, 1074*n*

50-25: Employee Share Purchase Plans–Recognition, 1080*n*

10-55-30 through 32: Overall–Implementation and Guidance Illustrations–Selecting or Estimating the Expected Term, 1074*n*

No. 720-15-25-1: Other Expenses–Start-Up Costs–Recognition, 529*n*

No. 730-10-25-1: Research and Development–Overall–Recognition, 527*n*

No. 740: Income Taxes

10: Overall, 900*n*

10-25: Overall–Recognition, 706*n*, 878, 885*n*

10-30: Overall–Initial Measurement, 885n
10-35: Overall–Subsequent Measurement, 891n
20-45: Intraperiod Tax Allocation–Other Presentation Matters–Allocation to Items Other than Continuing Operations, 1076n
No. 805: Business Combinations, 13n, 512n, 532n
10-20: Overall–Disclosure, 183n
20-15: Identifiable Assets and Liabilities, and Any Noncontrolling Interest–Recognition, 714n
No. 810: Consolidation, 192n, 1148n
No. 815: Derivatives and Hedging, 1274n
10: Overall, 1268n
20-25-104: Hedging-General–Recognition–Shortcut Method, 1275n
No. 820: Fair Value Measurements and Disclosures, 34n
No. 825: Financial Instruments
10-25: Overall–Recognition, 638n
10-25-1: Overall–Recognition–Fair Value Option, 34n, 355n, 775n
10-50-1: Overall–Disclosure, 1274n
10-50-10: Overall–Disclosure–Fair Value of Financial Instruments, 355n, 764n
10-50-28: Overall–Disclosure–Fair Value Option, 653n
No. 830: Foreign Currency Matters, 1273n
No. 835: Interest
20-25: Capitalization of Interest–Recognition, 522n
30: Imputation of Interest, 306n
30-15-3: Imputation of Interest–Scope and Scope Exceptions–Instruments, 342n, 693n
30-45: Imputation of Interest–Other Presentation Matters, 1022
No. 840: Leases, 192n, 1148n
10: Overall, 817n
10-25: Overall–Recognition, 811n
10-25-42: Overall–Recognition–Lessor Application of Lease Classification Criteria, 813n
20-25: Operating Leases–Recognition, 815n
No. 845: Nonmonetary Transactions, 518n
10-25-6: Overall–Recognition–Exchanges Involving Monetary Consideration, 520n
10-30: Overall–Initial Measurement, 1021n
No. 850-10-50: Related Party Disclosures–Overall–Disclosure, 127n
No. 855: Subsequent Events, 126n, 713n
No. 860: Transfers and Servicing, 364, 364n
10-40: Overall–Derecognition, 362n, 363n
No. 915: Development Stage Entities, 529n
No. 922: Entertainment–Cable Television, 262n
No. 926: Entertainment–Films, 262n
No. 928: Entertainment–Music, 262n
No. 932: Extractive Activities–Oil and Gas, 535n
No. 944: Financial Services–Insurance, 262n
No. 952-605-25: Franchisors–Revenue Recognition–Recognition, 260, 260n
No. 958-605-15-2 and 4: Not-for-Profit Entities–Revenue Recognition–Scope and Scope Exceptions–Contributions Received, 516n
No. 985: Software
20-25-1: Costs of Software to be Sold, Leased, or Marketed–Recognition–Research and Development Costs of Computer Software, 530n
605-25: Revenue Recognition–Recognition, 259n
American Institute of Certified Public Accountants (AICPA)
Accounting Research and Terminology Bulletin, 693n
Accounting Research Bulletin No. 43: "Restatement and Revision of Accounting Research Bulletins," 262n, 451n, 452n, 454n, 560n, 1033n, 1034n, 1035n
Accounting Trends and Techniques
2008 Edition, 174n, 177n, 187n, 410n, 564n, 968n, 1036n, 1191n
2009 Edition, 942n, 944n, 948n, 950n, 1071n
Statements of Position
No. 00-2: "Accounting by Producers or Distributors of Films," 262n
No. 81-1: "Accounting for Performance of Construction-Type and Certain Production-Type Contracts," 246n, 249n
No. 97-2: "Software Revenue Recognition," 259n
No. 98-1: "Accounting for the Costs of Computer Software Developed or Obtained for Internal Use," 530n
No. 98-5: "Reporting on the Costs of Start-Up Activities," 529n
Statements on Auditing Standards
No. 53: "The Auditor's Responsibility to Detect and Report Errors and Irregularities," 127n
No. 54: "Illegal Acts by Clients," 127n
No. 59: "The Auditor's Consideration of an Entity's Ability to Continue as a Going Concern," 131n
Committee on Accounting Procedure (CAP)
Accounting Research Bulletins (ARBs), 9
Financial Accounting Standards Board (FASB)
Accounting Standards Codification System (ASC); See Accounting Standards Codification System

Discussion Memorandum (DM) "Conceptual Framework for Financial Accounting and Reporting: Elements of Financial Statements and Their Measurement," 20n
Discussion Papers (with IASB), "Preliminary Views on Financial Statement Presentation," 704, 704n, 1191n
Emerging Issues Task Force (EITF) Abstracts
No. 98-5: "Accounting for Convertible Securities with Beneficial Conversion Features or Contingently Adjustable Conversion Ratios," 770n
No. 00-10: "Accounting for Shipping and Handling Fees and Costs," 401n
No. 01-02: "Interpretations of APB Opinion No. 29," 520n
No. 06-2: "Accounting for Sabbatical Leave and Other Similar Benefits Pursuant to FASB Statement No. 43," 130
No. 08-1: "Revenue Arrangements with Multiple Deliverables," 259n
No. 09-3: "Applicability of AICPA Statement of Position 97-2 to Certain Arrangements That Include Software Elements," 259n
Exposure Drafts
"Conceptual Framework for Financial Reporting: The Objective of Financial Reporting and Qualitative Characteristics and Constraints of Decision-Useful Financial Reporting Information," 20n, 22n, 24n, 1082n
"Earnings per Share–an amendment of FASB Statement No. 128" (Revised), 1102, 1102n
Interpretations
No. 35: "Criteria for Applying the Equity Method of Accounting for Investments in Common Stock," 646n
No. 45: "Guarantor's Accounting and Disclosure Requirements for Guarantees, Including Indirect Guarantees of Indebtedness of Others," 711n
No. 48: "Accounting for Uncertainty in Income Taxes–an interpretation of FASB Statement No. 109," 130, 706n, 885n, 900n
Preliminary View: "Accounting for Pension and Other Postretirement Benefits," 953n
Proposal: "Principles-Based Approach to U.S. Standard Setting," 18, 18n
Staff Positions
No. 14-1: "Accounting for Convertible Debt Instruments That May Be Settled in Cash upon Conversion (Including Partial Cash Settlement)," 771
No. 115-1 and 124-1: "The Meaning of Other-Than-Temporary Impairment and Its Application to Certain Investments," 661n
No. 115-2 and 124-2: "Recognition and Presentation of Other-Than-Temporary Impairments," 639n, 663n
No. 107-1 and APB 28-1: "Interim Disclosures about Fair Value of Financial Instruments," 643n
No. 144-d (proposed): "Amending the Criteria for Reporting a Discontinued Operation," 182n
Statements of Financial Accounting Concepts; See Statements of Financial Accounting Concepts (SFAC)
Statements of Financial Accounting Standards; See Statements of Financial Accounting Standards (SFAS)
Technical Bulletin 85-3: "Accounting for Operating Leases with Scheduled Rent Increases," 815n
Internal Control–Integrated Framework (COSO), 129
International Accounting Standards Board (IASB)
Exposure Drafts (EDs)
No. 9: "Joint Arrangements," 654, 654n
Proposed Amendments to IAS 37 and IAS 19, 716n
International Accounting Standards (IAS)
No. 1: "Presentation of Financial Statements," 122, 122n, 187n, 195, 195n, 704n, 904, 904n, 961, 961n, 1012, 1012n
No. 2: "Inventories," 411, 411n, 453, 453n, 459n, 476
No. 7: "Statement of Cash Flows," 200, 200n, 341, 341n, 1212
No. 8: "Accounting Policies, Changes in Accounting Estimates and Errors," 1151, 1151n
No. 11: "Construction Contracts," 256, 256n, 262, 262n
No. 12: "Income Taxes," 887, 887n
No. 16: "Property, Plant, and Equipment," 195, 195n, 565, 565n, 568, 568n
No. 17: "Leases," 18, 814, 814n, 834, 834n, 845, 845n, 846, 846n
No. 18: "Revenue," 237, 237n, 260, 260n, 262, 262n
No. 19: "Employee Benefits," 716n, 955–956, 956n, 957, 957n
No. 28: "Investments in Associates," 653, 653n
No. 31: "Interests in Joint Ventures," 654, 654n
No. 32: "Financial Instruments: Presentation," 771, 771n, 1019, 1019n
No. 33: "Earnings Per Share," 1102
No. 36: "Impairment of Assets," 583, 583n, 586, 586n, 587
No. 37: "Provisions, Contingent Liabilities and Contingent Assets," 716, 716n
No. 38: "Intangible Assets," 195, 195n, 532, 532n, 534, 573, 573n, 592n
No. 39: "Financial Instruments: Recognition and Measurement," 356, 356n, 364, 364n, 636, 636n, 638, 638n, 639, 640, 659, 665, 777, 778, 778n, 1278
No. 41: "Agriculture," 571n
"Reclassification of Financial Assets" (Amendments to IAS 39 Financial Instruments: Recognition and Measurement and IFRS 7 Financial Instruments: Disclosures), 638, 638n

International Financial Reporting Standards (IFRS)

No. 5: "Non-Current Assets Held for Sale and Discontinued Operations," 182*n*

No. 7: "Financial Instruments: Disclosures," 638*n*

No. 8: "Operating Segments," 141*n*

No. 9: "Financial Instruments," 356, 356*n*, 636*n*, 636–637, 638, 639, 640, 644, 659

International Accounting Standards Committee Foundation (IASCF)

Exposure Draft: Derecognition, Proposed Amendments to IAS 39 and IFRS 7, 364N

Public Company Accounting Oversight Board (PCAOB)

Accounting Standards

No. 2: "An Audit of Internal Control Over Financial Reporting Performed in Conjunction with an Audit of Financial Statements," 338, 339*n*

No. 5: "An Audit of Internal Control Over Financial Reporting That Is Integrated with an Audit of Financial Statements," 339*n*

Auditing Standards

No. 2: "An Audit of Internal Control over Financial Reporting Performed in Conjunction with an Audit of Financial Statements," 17, 17*n*

No. 5: "An Audit of Internal Control Over Financial Reporting that is Integrated with an Audit of Financial Statements," 17, 18, 18*n*

Securities and Exchange Commission (SEC)

Accounting Series Releases

No. 148: "Amendments to Regulations S-X and Related Interpretations and Guidelines Regarding the Disclosure of Compensating Balances and Short-Term Borrowing Arrangements," 340*n*

Financial Reporting Releases (FRR), 9

Staff Accounting Bulletins, 9

No. 99: "Materiality," 26, 26*n*, 127*n*

No. 100: "Restructuring and Impairment Charges," 453*n*

No. 101: "Revenue Recognition in Financial Statements," 235, 235*n*, 239

No. 104: "Revenue Recognition," 235*n*

Topic 5.M: "Other-Than-Temporary Impairment of Certain Investments in Equity Securities," 662*n*

Statements of Financial Accounting Concepts (SFAC) of FASB

No. 1: "Objectives of Financial Reporting by Business Enterprises," 20–21, 1185, 1185*n*, 1188*n*

No. 2: "Qualitative Characteristics of Accounting Information," 20–21

No. 3: "Elements of Financial Statements of Business Enterprises," 21

No. 4: "Objectives of Financial Reporting by Nonbusiness Organizations," 21

No. 5: "Recognition and Measurement in Financial Statements of Business Enterprises," 21, 27, 27*n*, 28, 29, 234*n*

No. 6: "Elements of Financial Statements–a replacement of FASB Concepts Statement No. 3 (incorporating an amendment of FASB Concepts Statement No. 2)", 21, 26, 26*n*, 30*n*, 32–33, 692*n*, 700*n*, 715*n*, 877, 877*n*, 1022

No. 7: "Using Cash Flow Information and Present Value in Accounting Measurements," 21, 28, 28*n*, 308*n*, 308–309, 507, 507*n*, 709, 709*n*

Statements of Financial Accounting Standards (SFAS) of FASB

No. 5: "Accounting for Contingencies," 706*n*, 714*n*, 717*n*

No. 6: "Classification of Short-Term Obligations Expected to Be Refinanced," 703*n*

No. 7: "Accounting and Reporting by Development Stage Enterprises," 529*n*

No. 13: "Accounting for Leases," 811*n*, 813*n*, 817*n*

No. 16: "Prior Period Adjustments," 192*n*, 1149*n*

No. 19: "Financial Accounting and Reporting by Oil and Gas Producing Companies," 535*n*

No. 34: "Capitalization of Interest Cost," 522*n*

No. 43: "Accounting for Compensated Absences," 699*n*

No. 48: "Revenue Recognition When Right of Return Exists," 244*n*

No. 50: "Financial Reporting in the Record and Music Industry," 262*n*

No. 51: "Financial Reporting by Cable Television Companies," 262*n*

No. 52: "Foreign Currency Translation," 1273*n*

No. 57: "Related Party Disclosures," 127*n*

No. 60: "Accounting and Reporting by Insurance Enterprises," 262*n*

No. 66: "Accounting for Sales of Real Estate," 240*n*

No. 78: "Classification of Obligations That Are Callable by the Creditor," 703*n*

No. 86: "Accounting for the Costs of Computer Software to be Sold, Leased, or Otherwise Marketed," 530*n*

No. 87: "Employers' Accounting for Pensions," 940*n*, 953*n*, 977*n*

No. 88: "Employers' Accounting for Settlements and Curtailments of Defined Benefit Pension Plans and For Termination Benefits," 963*n*

No. 94: "Consolidation of All Majority-Owned Subsidiaries," 192*n*, 1148*n*

No. 95: "Statement of Cash Flows," 198*n*, 1194*n*

No. 96: "Accounting for Income Taxes," 874*n*

No. 98: "Accounting for Leases: Sale-Leaseback Transactions Involving Real Estate, Sales-Type Leases of Real Estate, Definition of the Lease Term, and Initial Direct Costs of Direct Financing Leases," 812*n*

No. 105: "Disclosure of Information about Financial Instruments with Off-Balance-Sheet Risk and Financial Instruments with Concentrations of Credit Risk," 657*n*

No. 106: "Employers' Accounting for Postretirement Benefits Other Than Pensions," 966*n*, 970*n*

No. 107: "Disclosures About Fair Value of Financial Instruments," 355*n*, 764*n*, 1274*n*

No. 109: "Accounting for Income Taxes," 878, 885*n*, 1076*n*

No. 114: "Accounting by Creditors for Impairment of a Loan–an amendment of FASB Statements No. 5 and 15," 372*n*, 784*n*

No. 115: "Accounting for Certain Investments in Debt and Equity Securities," 622*n*, 625*n*, 630*n*, 642*n*

No. 116: "Accounting for Contributions Received and Contributions Made," 516*n*

No. 123: "Accounting for Stock-Based Compensation," 1073*n*, 1074*n*, 1080*n*

No. 123R: "Share-Based Payment," 190

No. 128: "Earnings per Share," 1082*n*

No. 129: "Disclosure of Information about Capital Structure," 1012*n*

No. 130: "Reporting Comprehensive Income," 194*n*, 1272*n*

No. 131: "Disclosures about Segments of an Enterprise and Related Information," 25*n*, 141*n*, 183*n*

No. 132: "Employers' Disclosures about Pensions and Other Postretirement Benefits," 963*n*

No. 133: "Accounting for Derivative Instruments and Hedging Activities," 1268*n*, 1274*n*, 1275*n*

No. 140: "Accounting for Transfers and Servicing of Financial Assets and Extinguishments of Liabilities," 362*n*, 363*n*, 364m

No. 141: "Business Combinations," 13*n*, 183*n*, 512*n*, 532*n*

No. 141R: "Business Combinations," 714*n*

No. 142: "Goodwill and Other Intangible Assets," 13*n*, 509*n*, 572*n*, 648*n*

No. 143: "Accounting for Asset Retirement Obligations," 506*n*

No. 144: "Accounting for the Impairment or Disposal of Long-Lived Assets," 172*n*, 184*n*, 518*n*, 581*n*

No. 145: "Recission of FASB Statements No. 4, 44, and 64, Amendment of FASB Statement No. 13, and Technical Corrections," 769*n*

No. 150: "Accounting for Certain Financial Instruments with Characteristics of Both Liabilities and Equity," 1020*n*

No. 151: "Inventory Costs–An Amendment of *ARB No. 43*, Chapter 4," 401*n*

No. 153: "Exchanges of Nonmonetary Assets–an amendment of APB Opinion No. 29," 518*n*

No. 154: "Accounting Changes and Error Corrections–A Replacement of APB Opinion No. 20 and FASB Statement No. 3," 1138*n*, 1141*n*, 1151*n*

No. 157: "Fair Value Measurements," 34*n*

No. 158: "Employers' Accounting for Defined Benefit Pension and Other Postretirement Plans–an amendment of FASB Statements No. 87, 88, 106, and 132(R)," 949*n*, 953*n*

No. 159: "The Fair Value Option for Financial Assets and Financial Liabilities–including an amendment of FASB Statement No. 115," 34*n*, 36*n*, 355*n*, 629*n*, 775*n*

No. 161: "Disclosures about Derivative Instruments and Hedging Activities–an amendment of FASB Statement No. 133," 1274*n*

No. 165: "Subsequent Events," 126*n*, 713*n*

No. 166: "Accounting for Transfers of Financial Assets–an amendment of FASB Statement No. 140," 362*n*, 363*n*, 364m

No. 168: "The FASB Accounting Standards Codification™ and the Hierarchy of Generally Accepted Accounting Principles–a replacement of FASB Statement No. 162," 11*n*

This page is intentionally blank

This page is intentionally blank

This page is intentionally blank

This page is intentionally blank

Present and Future Value Tables

This table shows the future value of $1 at various interest rates (i) and time periods (n). It is used to calculate the future value of any single amount.

TABLE 1   Future Value of $1

$$FV = \$1\,(1 + i)^n$$

n/i	1.0%	1.5%	2.0%	2.5%	3.0%	3.5%	4.0%	4.5%	5.0%	5.5%	6.0%	7.0%	8.0%	9.0%	10.0%	11.0%	12.0%	20.0%
1	1.01000	1.01500	1.02000	1.02500	1.03000	1.03500	1.04000	1.04500	1.05000	1.05500	1.06000	1.07000	1.08000	1.09000	1.10000	1.11000	1.12000	1.20000
2	1.02010	1.03022	1.04040	1.05063	1.06090	1.07123	1.08160	1.09203	1.10250	1.11303	1.12360	1.14490	1.16640	1.18810	1.21000	1.23210	1.25440	1.44000
3	1.03030	1.04568	1.06121	1.07689	1.09273	1.10872	1.12486	1.14117	1.15763	1.17424	1.19102	1.22504	1.25971	1.29503	1.33100	1.36763	1.40493	1.72800
4	1.04060	1.06136	1.08243	1.10381	1.12551	1.14752	1.16986	1.19252	1.21551	1.23882	1.26248	1.31080	1.36049	1.41158	1.46410	1.51807	1.57352	2.07360
5	1.05101	1.07728	1.10408	1.13141	1.15927	1.18769	1.21665	1.24618	1.27628	1.30696	1.33823	1.40255	1.46933	1.53862	1.61051	1.68506	1.76234	2.48832
6	1.06152	1.09344	1.12616	1.15969	1.19405	1.22926	1.26532	1.30226	1.34010	1.37884	1.41852	1.50073	1.58687	1.67710	1.77156	1.87041	1.97382	2.98598
7	1.07214	1.10984	1.14869	1.18869	1.22987	1.27228	1.31593	1.36086	1.40710	1.45468	1.50363	1.60578	1.71382	1.82804	1.94872	2.07616	2.21068	3.58318
8	1.08286	1.12649	1.17166	1.21840	1.26677	1.31681	1.36857	1.42210	1.47746	1.53469	1.59385	1.71819	1.85093	1.99256	2.14359	2.30454	2.47596	4.29982
9	1.09369	1.14339	1.19509	1.24886	1.30477	1.36290	1.42331	1.48610	1.55133	1.61909	1.68948	1.83846	1.99900	2.17189	2.35795	2.55804	2.77308	5.15978
10	1.10462	1.16054	1.21899	1.28008	1.34392	1.41060	1.48024	1.55297	1.62889	1.70814	1.79085	1.96715	2.15892	2.36736	2.59374	2.83942	3.10585	6.19174
11	1.11567	1.17795	1.24337	1.31209	1.38423	1.45997	1.53945	1.62285	1.71034	1.80209	1.89830	2.10485	2.33164	2.58043	2.85312	3.15176	3.47855	7.43008
12	1.12683	1.19562	1.26824	1.34489	1.42576	1.51107	1.60103	1.69588	1.79586	1.90121	2.01220	2.25219	2.51817	2.81266	3.13843	3.49845	3.89598	8.91610
13	1.13809	1.21355	1.29361	1.37851	1.46853	1.56396	1.66507	1.77220	1.88565	2.00577	2.13293	2.40985	2.71962	3.06580	3.45227	3.88328	4.36349	10.69932
14	1.14947	1.23176	1.31948	1.41297	1.51259	1.61869	1.73168	1.85194	1.97993	2.11609	2.26090	2.57853	2.93719	3.34173	3.79750	4.31044	4.88711	12.83918
15	1.16097	1.25023	1.34587	1.44830	1.55797	1.67535	1.80094	1.93528	2.07893	2.23248	2.39656	2.75903	3.17217	3.64248	4.17725	4.78459	5.47357	15.40702
16	1.17258	1.26899	1.37279	1.48451	1.60471	1.73399	1.87298	2.02237	2.18287	2.35526	2.54035	2.95216	3.42594	3.97031	4.59497	5.31089	6.13039	18.48843
17	1.18430	1.28802	1.40024	1.52162	1.65285	1.79468	1.94790	2.11338	2.29202	2.48480	2.69277	3.15882	3.70002	4.32763	5.05447	5.89509	6.86604	22.18611
18	1.19615	1.30734	1.42825	1.55966	1.70243	1.85749	2.02582	2.20848	2.40662	2.62147	2.85434	3.37993	3.99602	4.71712	5.55992	6.54355	7.68997	26.62333
19	1.20811	1.32695	1.45681	1.59865	1.75351	1.92250	2.10685	2.30786	2.52695	2.76565	3.02560	3.61653	4.31570	5.14166	6.11591	7.26334	8.61276	31.94800
20	1.22019	1.34686	1.48595	1.63862	1.80611	1.98979	2.19112	2.41171	2.65330	2.91776	3.20714	3.86968	4.66096	5.60441	6.72750	8.06231	9.64629	38.33760
21	1.23239	1.36706	1.51567	1.67958	1.86029	2.05943	2.27877	2.52024	2.78596	3.07823	3.39956	4.14056	5.03383	6.10881	7.40025	8.94917	10.80385	46.00512
25	1.28243	1.45095	1.64061	1.85394	2.09378	2.36324	2.66584	3.00543	3.38635	3.81339	4.29187	5.42743	6.84848	8.62308	10.83471	13.58546	17.00006	95.39622
30	1.34785	1.56308	1.81136	2.09757	2.42726	2.80679	3.24340	3.74532	4.32194	4.98395	5.74349	7.61226	10.06266	13.26768	17.44940	22.89230	29.95992	237.37631
40	1.48886	1.81402	2.20804	2.68506	3.26204	3.95926	4.80102	5.81636	7.03999	8.51331	10.28572	14.97446	21.72452	31.40942	45.25926	65.00087	93.05097	1469.77160

This table shows the present value of $1 at various interest rates (i) and time periods (n). It is used to calculate the present value of any single amount.

TABLE 2 Present Value of $1

$$PV = \frac{\$1}{(1+i)^n}$$

n/i	1.0%	1.5%	2.0%	2.5%	3.0%	3.5%	4.0%	4.5%	5.0%	5.5%	6.0%	7.0%	8.0%	9.0%	10.0%	11.0%	12.0%	20.0%
1	0.99010	0.98522	0.98039	0.97561	0.97087	0.96618	0.96154	0.95694	0.95238	0.94787	0.94340	0.93458	0.92593	0.91743	0.90909	0.90090	0.89286	0.83333
2	0.98030	0.97066	0.96117	0.95181	0.94260	0.93351	0.92456	0.91573	0.90703	0.89845	0.89000	0.87344	0.85734	0.84168	0.82645	0.81162	0.79719	0.69444
3	0.97059	0.95632	0.94232	0.92860	0.91514	0.90194	0.88900	0.87630	0.86384	0.85161	0.83962	0.81630	0.79383	0.77218	0.75131	0.73119	0.71178	0.57870
4	0.96098	0.94218	0.92385	0.90595	0.88849	0.87144	0.85480	0.83856	0.82270	0.80722	0.79209	0.76290	0.73503	0.70843	0.68301	0.65873	0.63552	0.48225
5	0.95147	0.92826	0.90573	0.88385	0.86261	0.84197	0.82193	0.80245	0.78353	0.76513	0.74726	0.71299	0.68058	0.64993	0.62092	0.59345	0.56743	0.40188
6	0.94205	0.91454	0.88797	0.86230	0.83748	0.81350	0.79031	0.76790	0.74622	0.72525	0.70496	0.66634	0.63017	0.59627	0.56447	0.53464	0.50663	0.33490
7	0.93272	0.90103	0.87056	0.84127	0.81309	0.78599	0.75992	0.73483	0.71068	0.68744	0.66506	0.62275	0.58349	0.54703	0.51316	0.48166	0.45235	0.27908
8	0.92348	0.88771	0.85349	0.82075	0.78941	0.75941	0.73069	0.70319	0.67684	0.65160	0.62741	0.58201	0.54027	0.50187	0.46651	0.43393	0.40388	0.23257
9	0.91434	0.87459	0.83676	0.80073	0.76642	0.73373	0.70259	0.67290	0.64461	0.61763	0.59190	0.54393	0.50025	0.46043	0.42410	0.39092	0.36061	0.19381
10	0.90529	0.86167	0.82035	0.78120	0.74409	0.70892	0.67556	0.64393	0.61391	0.58543	0.55839	0.50835	0.46319	0.42241	0.38554	0.35218	0.32197	0.16151
11	0.89632	0.84893	0.80426	0.76214	0.72242	0.68495	0.64958	0.61620	0.58468	0.55491	0.52679	0.47509	0.42888	0.38753	0.35049	0.31728	0.28748	0.13459
12	0.88745	0.83639	0.78849	0.74356	0.70138	0.66178	0.62460	0.58966	0.55684	0.52598	0.49697	0.44401	0.39711	0.35553	0.31863	0.28584	0.25668	0.11216
13	0.87866	0.82403	0.77303	0.72542	0.68095	0.63940	0.60057	0.56427	0.53032	0.49856	0.46884	0.41496	0.36770	0.32618	0.28966	0.25751	0.22917	0.09346
14	0.86996	0.81185	0.75788	0.70773	0.66112	0.61778	0.57748	0.53997	0.50507	0.47257	0.44230	0.38782	0.34046	0.29925	0.26333	0.23199	0.20462	0.07789
15	0.86135	0.79985	0.74301	0.69047	0.64186	0.59689	0.55526	0.51672	0.48102	0.44793	0.41727	0.36245	0.31524	0.27454	0.23939	0.20900	0.18270	0.06491
16	0.85282	0.78803	0.72845	0.67362	0.62317	0.57671	0.53391	0.49447	0.45811	0.42458	0.39365	0.33873	0.29189	0.25187	0.21763	0.18829	0.16312	0.05409
17	0.84438	0.77639	0.71416	0.65720	0.60502	0.55720	0.51337	0.47318	0.43630	0.40245	0.37136	0.31657	0.27027	0.23107	0.19784	0.16963	0.14564	0.04507
18	0.83602	0.76491	0.70016	0.64117	0.58739	0.53836	0.49363	0.45280	0.41552	0.38147	0.35034	0.29586	0.25025	0.21199	0.17986	0.15282	0.13004	0.03756
19	0.82774	0.75361	0.68643	0.62553	0.57029	0.52016	0.47464	0.43330	0.39573	0.36158	0.33051	0.27651	0.23171	0.19449	0.16351	0.13768	0.11611	0.03130
20	0.81954	0.74247	0.67297	0.61027	0.55368	0.50257	0.45639	0.41464	0.37689	0.34273	0.31180	0.25842	0.21455	0.17843	0.14864	0.12403	0.10367	0.02608
21	0.81143	0.73150	0.65978	0.59539	0.53755	0.48557	0.43883	0.39679	0.35894	0.32486	0.29416	0.24151	0.19866	0.16370	0.13513	0.11174	0.09256	0.02174
24	0.78757	0.69954	0.62172	0.55288	0.49193	0.43796	0.39012	0.34770	0.31007	0.27666	0.24698	0.19715	0.15770	0.12640	0.10153	0.08170	0.06588	0.01258
25	0.77977	0.68921	0.60953	0.53939	0.47761	0.42315	0.37512	0.33273	0.29530	0.26223	0.23300	0.18425	0.14602	0.11597	0.09230	0.07361	0.05882	0.01048
28	0.75684	0.65910	0.57437	0.50088	0.43708	0.38165	0.33348	0.29157	0.25509	0.22332	0.19563	0.15040	0.11591	0.08955	0.06934	0.05382	0.04187	0.00607
29	0.74934	0.64936	0.56311	0.48866	0.42435	0.36875	0.32065	0.27902	0.24295	0.21168	0.18456	0.14056	0.10733	0.08215	0.06304	0.04849	0.03738	0.00506
30	0.74192	0.63976	0.55207	0.47674	0.41199	0.35628	0.30832	0.26700	0.23138	0.20064	0.17411	0.13137	0.09938	0.07537	0.05731	0.04368	0.03338	0.00421
31	0.73458	0.63031	0.54125	0.46511	0.39999	0.34423	0.29646	0.25550	0.22036	0.19018	0.16425	0.12277	0.09202	0.06915	0.05210	0.03935	0.02980	0.00351
40	0.67165	0.55126	0.45289	0.37243	0.30656	0.25257	0.20829	0.17193	0.14205	0.11746	0.09722	0.06678	0.04603	0.03184	0.02209	0.01538	0.01075	0.00068

This table shows the future value of an ordinary annuity of $1 at various interest rates (i) and time periods (n). It is used to calculate the future value of any series of equal payments made at the *end* of each compounding period.

TABLE 3 Future Value of an Ordinary Annuity of $1

$$FVA = \frac{(1 + i)^n - 1}{i}$$

n/i	1.0%	1.5%	2.0%	2.5%	3.0%	3.5%	4.0%	4.5%	5.0%	5.5%	6.0%	7.0%	8.0%	9.0%	10.0%	11.0%	12.0%	20.0%
1	1.0000	1.0000	1.0000	1.0000	1.0000	1.0000	1.0000	1.0000	1.0000	1.0000	1.0000	1.0000	1.0000	1.0000	1.0000	1.0000	1.0000	1.0000
2	2.0100	2.0150	2.0200	2.0250	2.0300	2.0350	2.0400	2.0450	2.0500	2.0550	2.0600	2.0700	2.0800	2.0900	2.1000	2.1100	2.1200	2.2000
3	3.0301	3.0452	3.0604	3.0756	3.0909	3.1062	3.1216	3.1370	3.1525	3.1680	3.1836	3.2149	3.2464	3.2781	3.3100	3.3421	3.3744	3.6400
4	4.0604	4.0909	4.1216	4.1525	4.1836	4.2149	4.2465	4.2782	4.3101	4.3423	4.3746	4.4399	4.5061	4.5731	4.6410	4.7097	4.7793	5.3680
5	5.1010	5.1523	5.2040	5.2563	5.3091	5.3625	5.4163	5.4707	5.5256	5.5811	5.6371	5.7507	5.8666	5.9847	6.1051	6.2278	6.3528	7.4416
6	6.1520	6.2296	6.3081	6.3877	6.4684	6.5502	6.6330	6.7169	6.8019	6.8881	6.9753	7.1533	7.3359	7.5233	7.7156	7.9129	8.1152	9.9299
7	7.2135	7.3230	7.4343	7.5474	7.6625	7.7794	7.8983	8.0192	8.1420	8.2669	8.3938	8.6540	8.9228	9.2004	9.4872	9.7833	10.0890	12.9159
8	8.2857	8.4328	8.5830	8.7361	8.8923	9.0517	9.2142	9.3800	9.5491	9.7216	9.8975	10.2598	10.6366	11.0285	11.4359	11.8594	12.2997	16.4991
9	9.3685	9.5593	9.7546	9.9545	10.1591	10.3685	10.5828	10.8021	11.0266	11.2563	11.4913	11.9780	12.4876	13.0210	13.5795	14.1640	14.7757	20.7989
10	10.4622	10.7027	10.9497	11.2034	11.4639	11.7314	12.0061	12.2882	12.5779	12.8754	13.1808	13.8164	14.4866	15.1929	15.9374	16.7220	17.5487	25.9587
11	11.5668	11.8633	12.1687	12.4835	12.8078	13.1420	13.4864	13.8412	14.2068	14.5835	14.9716	15.7836	16.6455	17.5603	18.5312	19.5614	20.6546	32.1504
12	12.6825	13.0412	13.4121	13.7956	14.1920	14.6020	15.0258	15.4640	15.9171	16.3856	16.8699	17.8885	18.9771	20.1407	21.3843	22.7132	24.1331	39.5805
13	13.8093	14.2368	14.6803	15.1404	15.6178	16.1130	16.6268	17.1599	17.7130	18.2868	18.8821	20.1406	21.4953	22.9534	24.5227	26.2116	28.0291	48.4966
14	14.9474	15.4504	15.9739	16.5190	17.0863	17.6770	18.2919	18.9321	19.5986	20.2926	21.0151	22.5505	24.2149	26.0192	27.9750	30.0949	32.3926	59.1959
15	16.0969	16.6821	17.2934	17.9319	18.5989	19.2957	20.0236	20.7841	21.5786	22.4087	23.2760	25.1290	27.1521	29.3609	31.7725	34.4054	37.2797	72.0351
16	17.2579	17.9324	18.6393	19.3802	20.1569	20.9710	21.8245	22.7193	23.6575	24.6411	25.6725	27.8881	30.3243	33.0034	35.9497	39.1899	42.7533	87.4421
17	18.4304	19.2014	20.0121	20.8647	21.7616	22.7050	23.6975	24.7417	25.8404	26.9964	28.2129	30.8402	33.7502	36.9737	40.5447	44.5008	48.8837	105.9306
18	19.6147	20.4894	21.4123	22.3863	23.4144	24.4997	25.6454	26.8551	28.1324	29.4812	30.9057	33.9990	37.4502	41.3013	45.5992	50.3959	55.7497	128.1167
19	20.8109	21.7967	22.8406	23.9460	25.1169	26.3572	27.6712	29.0636	30.5390	32.1027	33.7600	37.3790	41.4463	46.0185	51.1591	56.9395	63.4397	154.7400
20	22.0190	23.1237	24.2974	25.5447	26.8704	28.2797	29.7781	31.3714	33.0660	34.8683	36.7856	40.9955	45.7620	51.1601	57.2750	64.2028	72.0524	186.6880
21	23.2392	24.4705	25.7833	27.1833	28.6765	30.2695	31.9692	33.7831	35.7193	37.7861	39.9927	44.8652	50.4229	56.7645	64.0025	72.2651	81.6987	225.0256
30	34.7849	37.5387	40.5681	43.9027	47.5754	51.6227	56.0849	61.0071	66.4388	72.4355	79.0582	94.4608	113.2832	136.3075	164.4940	199.0209	241.3327	1181.8816
40	48.8864	54.2679	60.4020	67.4026	75.4013	84.5503	95.0255	107.0303	120.7998	136.6056	154.7620	199.6351	259.0565	337.8824	442.5926	581.8261	767.0914	7343.8578

This table shows the present value of an ordinary annuity of $1 at various interest rates (*i*) and time periods (*n*). It is used to calculate the present value of any series of equal payments made at the *end* of each compounding period.

TABLE 4 Present Value of an Ordinary Annuity of $1

$$PVA = \frac{1 - \frac{1}{(1+i)^n}}{i}$$

n/i	1.0%	1.5%	2.0%	2.5%	3.0%	3.5%	4.0%	4.5%	5.0%	5.5%	6.0%	7.0%	8.0%	9.0%	10.0%	11.0%	12.0%	20.0%
1	0.99010	0.98522	0.98039	0.97561	0.97087	0.96618	0.96154	0.95694	0.95238	0.94787	0.94340	0.93458	0.92593	0.91743	0.90909	0.90090	0.89286	0.83333
2	1.97040	1.95588	1.94156	1.92742	1.91347	1.89969	1.88609	1.87267	1.85941	1.84632	1.83339	1.80802	1.78326	1.75911	1.73554	1.71252	1.69005	1.52778
3	2.94099	2.91220	2.88388	2.85602	2.82861	2.80164	2.77509	2.74896	2.72325	2.69793	2.67301	2.62432	2.57710	2.53129	2.48685	2.44371	2.40183	2.10648
4	3.90197	3.85438	3.80773	3.76197	3.71710	3.67308	3.62990	3.58753	3.54595	3.50515	3.46511	3.38721	3.31213	3.23972	3.16987	3.10245	3.03735	2.58873
5	4.85343	4.78264	4.71346	4.64583	4.57971	4.51505	4.45182	4.38998	4.32948	4.27028	4.21236	4.10020	3.99271	3.88965	3.79079	3.69590	3.60478	2.99061
6	5.79548	5.69719	5.60143	5.50813	5.41719	5.32855	5.24214	5.15787	5.07569	4.99553	4.91732	4.76654	4.62288	4.48592	4.35526	4.23054	4.11141	3.32551
7	6.72819	6.59821	6.47199	6.34939	6.23028	6.11454	6.00205	5.89270	5.78637	5.68297	5.58238	5.38929	5.20637	5.03295	4.86842	4.71220	4.56376	3.60459
8	7.65168	7.48593	7.32548	7.17014	7.01969	6.87396	6.73274	6.59589	6.46321	6.33457	6.20979	5.97130	5.74664	5.53482	5.33493	5.14612	4.96764	3.83716
9	8.56602	8.36052	8.16224	7.97087	7.78611	7.60769	7.43533	7.26879	7.10782	6.95202	6.80169	6.51523	6.24689	5.99525	5.75902	5.53705	5.32825	4.03097
10	9.47130	9.22218	8.98259	8.75206	8.53020	8.31661	8.11090	7.91272	7.72173	7.53763	7.36009	7.02358	6.71008	6.41766	6.14457	5.88923	5.65022	4.19247
11	10.36763	10.07112	9.78685	9.51421	9.25262	9.00155	8.76048	8.52892	8.30641	8.09254	7.88687	7.49867	7.13896	6.80519	6.49506	6.20652	5.93770	4.32706
12	11.25508	10.90751	10.57534	10.25776	9.95400	9.66333	9.38507	9.11858	8.86325	8.61852	8.38384	7.94269	7.53608	7.16073	6.81369	6.49236	6.19437	4.43922
13	12.13374	11.73153	11.34837	10.98319	10.63496	10.30274	9.98565	9.68285	9.39357	9.11708	8.85268	8.35765	7.90378	7.48690	7.10336	6.74987	6.42355	4.53268
14	13.00370	12.54338	12.10625	11.69091	11.29607	10.92052	10.56312	10.22283	9.89864	9.58965	9.29498	8.74547	8.24424	7.78615	7.36669	6.98187	6.62817	4.61057
15	13.86505	13.34323	12.84926	12.38138	11.93794	11.51741	11.11839	10.73955	10.37966	10.03758	9.71225	9.10791	8.55948	8.06069	7.60608	7.19087	6.81086	4.67547
16	14.71787	14.13126	13.57771	13.05500	12.56110	12.09412	11.65230	11.23402	10.83777	10.46216	10.10590	9.44665	8.85137	8.31256	7.82371	7.37916	6.97399	4.72956
17	15.56225	14.90765	14.29187	13.71220	13.16612	12.65132	12.16567	11.70719	11.27407	10.86461	10.47726	9.76322	9.12164	8.54363	8.02155	7.54879	7.11963	4.77463
18	16.39827	15.67256	14.99203	14.35336	13.75351	13.18968	12.65930	12.15999	11.68959	11.24607	10.82760	10.05909	9.37189	8.75563	8.20141	7.70162	7.24967	4.81219
19	17.22601	16.42617	15.67846	14.97889	14.32380	13.70984	13.13394	12.59329	12.08532	11.60765	11.15812	10.33560	9.60360	8.95011	8.36492	7.83929	7.36578	4.84350
20	18.04555	17.16864	16.35143	15.58916	14.87747	14.21240	13.59033	13.00794	12.46221	11.95038	11.46992	10.59401	9.81815	9.12855	8.51356	7.96333	7.46944	4.86958
21	18.85698	17.90014	17.01121	16.18455	15.41502	14.69797	14.02916	13.40472	12.82115	12.27524	11.76408	10.83553	10.01680	9.29224	8.64869	8.07507	7.56200	4.89132
25	22.02316	20.71961	19.52346	18.42438	17.41315	16.48151	15.62208	14.82821	14.09394	13.41393	12.78336	11.65358	10.67478	9.82258	9.07704	8.42174	7.84314	4.94759
30	25.80771	24.01584	22.39646	20.93029	19.60044	18.39205	17.29203	16.28889	15.37245	14.53375	13.76483	12.40904	11.25778	10.27365	9.42691	8.69379	8.05518	4.97894
40	32.83469	29.91585	27.35548	25.10278	23.11477	21.35507	19.79277	18.40158	17.15909	16.04612	15.04630	13.33171	11.92461	10.75736	9.77905	8.95105	8.24378	4.99660

This table shows the future value of an annuity due of $1 at various interest rates (i) and time periods (n). It is used to calculate the future value of any series of equal payments made at the *beginning* of each compounding period.

TABLE 5 Future Value of an Annuity Due of $1

$$FVAD = \left[\frac{(1+i)^n - 1}{i}\right] \times (1+i)$$

n/i	1.0%	1.5%	2.0%	2.5%	3.0%	3.5%	4.0%	4.5%	5.0%	5.5%	6.0%	7.0%	8.0%	9.0%	10.0%	11.0%	12.0%	20.0%
1	1.0100	1.0150	1.0200	1.0250	1.0300	1.0350	1.0400	1.0450	1.0500	1.0550	1.0600	1.0700	1.0800	1.0900	1.1000	1.1100	1.1200	1.2000
2	2.0301	2.0452	2.0604	2.0756	2.0909	2.1062	2.1216	2.1370	2.1525	2.1680	2.1836	2.2149	2.2464	2.2781	2.3100	2.3421	2.3744	2.6400
3	3.0604	3.0909	3.1216	3.1525	3.1836	3.2149	3.2465	3.2782	3.3101	3.3423	3.3746	3.4399	3.5061	3.5731	3.6410	3.7097	3.7793	4.3680
4	4.1010	4.1523	4.2040	4.2563	4.3091	4.3625	4.4163	4.4707	4.5256	4.5811	4.6371	4.7507	4.8666	4.9847	5.1051	5.2278	5.3528	6.4416
5	5.1520	5.2296	5.3081	5.3877	5.4684	5.5502	5.6330	5.7169	5.8019	5.8881	5.9753	6.1533	6.3359	6.5233	6.7156	6.9129	7.1152	8.9299
6	6.2135	6.3230	6.4343	6.5474	6.6625	6.7794	6.8983	7.0192	7.1420	7.2669	7.3938	7.6540	7.9228	8.2004	8.4872	8.7833	9.0890	11.9159
7	7.2857	7.4328	7.5830	7.7361	7.8923	8.0517	8.2142	8.3800	8.5491	8.7216	8.8975	9.2598	9.6366	10.0285	10.4359	10.8594	11.2997	15.4991
8	8.3685	8.5593	8.7546	8.9545	9.1591	9.3685	9.5828	9.8021	10.0266	10.2563	10.4913	10.9780	11.4876	12.0210	12.5795	13.1640	13.7757	19.7989
9	9.4622	9.7027	9.9497	10.2034	10.4639	10.7314	11.0061	11.2882	11.5779	11.8754	12.1808	12.8164	13.4866	14.1929	14.9374	15.7220	16.5487	24.9587
10	10.5668	10.8633	11.1687	11.4835	11.8078	12.1420	12.4864	12.8412	13.2068	13.5835	13.9716	14.7836	15.6455	16.5603	17.5312	18.5614	19.6546	31.1504
11	11.6825	12.0412	12.4121	12.7956	13.1920	13.6020	14.0258	14.4640	14.9171	15.3856	15.8699	16.8885	17.9771	19.1407	20.3843	21.7132	23.1331	38.5805
12	12.8093	13.2368	13.6803	14.1404	14.6178	15.1130	15.6268	16.1599	16.7130	17.2868	17.8821	19.1406	20.4953	21.9534	23.5227	25.2116	27.0291	47.4966
13	13.9474	14.4504	14.9739	15.5190	16.0863	16.6770	17.2919	17.9321	18.5986	19.2926	20.0151	21.5505	23.2149	25.0192	26.9750	29.0949	31.3926	58.1959
14	15.0969	15.6821	16.2934	16.9319	17.5989	18.2957	19.0236	19.7841	20.5786	21.4087	22.2760	24.1290	26.1521	28.3609	30.7725	33.4054	36.2797	71.0351
15	16.2579	16.9324	17.6393	18.3802	19.1569	19.9710	20.8245	21.7193	22.6575	23.6411	24.6725	26.8881	29.3243	32.0034	34.9497	38.1899	41.7533	86.4421
16	17.4304	18.2014	19.0121	19.8647	20.7616	21.7050	22.6975	23.7417	24.8404	25.9964	27.2129	29.8402	32.7502	35.9737	39.5447	43.5008	47.8837	104.9306
17	18.6147	19.4894	20.4123	21.3863	22.4144	23.4997	24.6454	25.8551	27.1324	28.4812	29.9057	32.9990	36.4502	40.3013	44.5992	49.3959	54.7497	127.1167
18	19.8109	20.7967	21.8406	22.9460	24.1169	25.3572	26.6712	28.0636	29.5390	31.1027	32.7600	36.3790	40.4463	45.0185	50.1591	55.9395	62.4397	153.7400
19	21.0190	22.1237	23.2974	24.5447	25.8704	27.2797	28.7781	30.3714	32.0660	33.8683	35.7856	39.9955	44.7620	50.1601	56.2750	63.2028	71.0524	185.6880
20	22.2392	23.4705	24.7833	26.1833	27.6765	29.2695	30.9692	32.7831	34.7193	36.7861	38.9927	43.8652	49.4229	55.7645	63.0025	71.2651	80.6987	224.0256
21	23.4716	24.8376	26.2990	27.8629	29.5368	31.3289	33.2480	35.3034	37.5052	39.8643	42.3923	48.0057	54.4568	61.8733	70.4027	80.2143	91.5026	270.0307
25	28.5256	30.5140	32.6709	35.0117	37.5530	40.3131	43.3117	46.5706	50.1135	53.9660	58.1564	67.6765	78.9544	92.3240	108.1818	126.9988	149.3339	566.3773
30	35.1327	38.1018	41.3794	45.0003	49.0027	53.4295	58.3283	63.7524	69.7608	76.4194	83.8017	101.0730	122.3459	148.5752	180.9434	220.9132	270.2926	1418.2579
40	49.3752	55.0819	61.6100	69.0876	77.6633	87.5095	98.8265	111.8467	126.8398	144.1189	164.0477	213.6096	279.7810	368.2919	486.8518	645.8269	859.1424	8812.6294

This table shows the present value of an annuity due of $1 at various interest rates (*i*) and time periods (*n*). It is used to calculate the present value of any series of equal payments made at the *beginning* of each compounding period.

TABLE 6 Present Value of an Annuity Due of $1

$$PVAD = \left[\frac{1 - \frac{1}{(1+i)^n}}{i}\right] \times (1 + i)$$

n/i	1.0%	1.5%	2.0%	2.5%	3.0%	3.5%	4.0%	4.5%	5.0%	5.5%	6.0%	7.0%	8.0%	9.0%	10.0%	11.0%	12.0%	20.0%
1	1.00000	1.00000	1.00000	1.00000	1.00000	1.00000	1.00000	1.00000	1.00000	1.00000	1.00000	1.00000	1.00000	1.00000	1.00000	1.00000	1.00000	1.00000
2	1.99010	1.98522	1.98039	1.97561	1.97087	1.96618	1.96154	1.95694	1.95238	1.94787	1.94340	1.93458	1.92593	1.91743	1.90909	1.90090	1.89286	1.83333
3	2.97040	2.95588	2.94156	2.92742	2.91347	2.89969	2.88609	2.87267	2.85941	2.84632	2.83339	2.80802	2.78326	2.75911	2.73554	2.71252	2.69005	2.52778
4	3.94099	3.91220	3.88388	3.85602	3.82861	3.80164	3.77509	3.74896	3.72325	3.69793	3.67301	3.62432	3.57710	3.53129	3.48685	3.44371	3.40183	3.10648
5	4.90197	4.85438	4.80773	4.76197	4.71710	4.67308	4.62990	4.58753	4.54595	4.50515	4.46511	4.38721	4.31213	4.23972	4.16987	4.10245	4.03735	3.58873
6	5.85343	5.78264	5.71346	5.64583	5.57971	5.51505	5.45182	5.38998	5.32948	5.27028	5.21236	5.10020	4.99271	4.88965	4.79079	4.69590	4.60478	3.99061
7	6.79548	6.69719	6.60143	6.50813	6.41719	6.32855	6.24214	6.15787	6.07569	5.99553	5.91732	5.76654	5.62288	5.48592	5.35526	5.23054	5.11141	4.32551
8	7.72819	7.59821	7.47199	7.34939	7.23028	7.11454	7.00205	6.89270	6.78637	6.68297	6.58238	6.38929	6.20637	6.03295	5.86842	5.71220	5.56376	4.60459
9	8.65168	8.48593	8.32548	8.17014	8.01969	7.87396	7.73274	7.59589	7.46321	7.33457	7.20979	6.97130	6.74664	6.53482	6.33493	6.14612	5.96764	4.83716
10	9.56602	9.36052	9.16224	8.97087	8.78611	8.60769	8.43533	8.26879	8.10782	7.95220	7.80169	7.51523	7.24689	6.99525	6.75902	6.53705	6.32825	5.03097
11	10.47130	10.22218	9.98259	9.75206	9.53020	9.31661	9.11090	8.91272	8.72173	8.53763	8.36009	8.02358	7.71008	7.41766	7.14457	6.88923	6.65022	5.19247
12	11.36763	11.07112	10.78685	10.51421	10.25262	10.00155	9.76048	9.52892	9.30641	9.09254	8.88687	8.49867	8.13896	7.80519	7.49506	7.20652	6.93770	5.32706
13	12.25508	11.90751	11.57534	11.25776	10.95400	10.66333	10.38507	10.11858	9.86325	9.61852	9.38384	8.94269	8.53608	8.16073	7.81369	7.49236	7.19437	5.43922
14	13.13374	12.73153	12.34837	11.98318	11.63496	11.30274	10.98565	10.68285	10.39357	10.11708	9.85268	9.35765	8.90378	8.48690	8.10336	7.74987	7.42355	5.53268
15	14.00370	13.54338	13.10625	12.69091	12.29607	11.92052	11.56312	11.22283	10.89864	10.58965	10.29498	9.74547	9.24424	8.78615	8.36669	7.98187	7.62817	5.61057
16	14.86505	14.34323	13.84926	13.38138	12.93794	12.51741	12.11839	11.73955	11.37966	11.03758	10.71225	10.10791	9.55948	9.06069	8.60608	8.19087	7.81086	5.67547
17	15.71787	15.13126	14.57771	14.05500	13.56110	13.09412	12.65230	12.23402	11.83777	11.46216	11.10590	10.44665	9.85137	9.31256	8.82371	8.37916	7.97399	5.72956
18	16.56225	15.90765	15.29187	14.71220	14.16612	13.65132	13.16567	12.70719	12.27407	11.86461	11.47726	10.76322	10.12164	9.54363	9.02155	8.54879	8.11963	5.77463
19	17.39827	16.67256	15.99203	15.35336	14.75351	14.18968	13.65930	13.15999	12.68959	12.24607	11.82760	11.05909	10.37189	9.75563	9.20141	8.70162	8.24967	5.81219
20	18.22601	17.42617	16.67846	15.97889	15.32380	14.70984	14.13394	13.59329	13.08532	12.60765	12.15812	11.33560	10.60360	9.95011	9.36492	8.83929	8.36578	5.84350
21	19.04555	18.16864	17.35143	16.58916	15.87747	15.21240	14.59033	14.00794	13.46221	12.95038	12.46992	11.59401	10.81815	10.12855	9.51356	8.96333	8.46944	5.86958
25	22.24339	21.03041	19.91393	18.88499	17.93554	17.05837	16.24696	15.49548	14.79864	14.15170	13.55036	12.46933	11.52876	10.70661	9.98474	9.34814	8.78432	5.93710
30	26.06579	24.37608	22.84438	21.45355	20.18845	19.03577	17.98371	17.02189	16.14107	15.33310	14.59072	13.27767	12.15841	11.19828	10.36961	9.65011	9.02181	5.97472
40	33.16303	30.36458	27.90259	25.73034	23.80822	22.10250	20.58448	19.22966	18.01704	16.92866	15.94907	14.26493	12.87858	11.72552	10.75696	9.93567	9.23303	5.99592

IFRS Standards	FASB Accounting Standards Codification	Textbook Chapters
	Corresponding content found primarily in:	
Conceptual Framework		
Framework for the Preparation and Presentation of Financial Statements	Not codified	1
International Financial Reporting Standards		
IFRS 1 First-time Adoption of International Financial Reporting Standards	N/A	
IFRS 2 Share-based Payment	505, 718	19
IFRS 3 Business Combinations	805	
IFRS 4 Insurance Contracts	944	
IFRS 5 Non-current Assets Held for Sale and Discontinued Operations	205, 280, 360	4
IFRS 6 Exploration for and Evaluation of Mineral Assets	932	
IFRS 7 Financial Instruments: Disclosures	815	14, 18
IFRS 8 Operating Segments	280	3
IFRS 9 Financial Instruments	450, 470	7, 12, 14
International Accounting Standards		
IAS 1 Presentation of Financial Statements	220, 225, 250, 505, 835	3, 4, 13, 18, 21
IAS 2 Inventories	330	8, 9
IAS 7 Statement of Cash Flows	230, 962	4, 7, 21
IAS 8 Accounting Policies, Changes in Accounting Estimates and Errors	250	3, 4, 9, 11, 20
IAS 10 Events After the Reporting Period	855	3, 13
IAS 11 Construction Contracts	605	5
IAS 12 Income Taxes	740	16
IAS 14 Segment Reporting	280	3
IAS 16 Property, Plant and Equipment	410, 420, 845	4, 10, 11
IAS 17 Leases	840	15
IAS 18 Revenue	360, 470, 605, 952	5
IAS 19 Employee Benefits	715	17
IAS 20 Accounting for Government Grants and Disclosure of Government Assistance	912	
IAS 21 The Effects of Changes in Foreign Exchange Rates	830	4, 12, 17, 18
IAS 23 Borrowing Costs	835	10
IAS 24 Related Party Disclosures	850	3
IAS 26 Accounting and Reporting by Retirement Benefit Plans	960	
IAS 27 Consolidated and Separate Financial Statements	810, 840	12
IAS 28 Investments in Associates	323, 325	12
IAS 29 Financial Reporting in Hyperinflationary Economies	830	
IAS 31 Interests In Joint Ventures	323, 325	12
IAS 32 Financial Instruments: Presentation and Disclosure	450, 470, 820, 825	7, 12, 14
IAS 33 Earnings Per Share	260	4, 19
IAS 34 Interim Financial Reporting	270, 740	5
IAS 36 Impairment of Assets	205, 360	11
IAS 37 Provisions, Contingent Liabilities and Contingent Assets	410, 420, 450	13
IAS 38 Intangible Assets	350, 805, 985	4, 38
IAS 39 Financial Instruments: Recognition and Measurement	310, 450, 470, 820, 825	7, 12, 14, A
IAS 40 Investment Property	845	
IAS 41 Agriculture	205, 350, 820	11

Note: Superseded and withdrawn standards are not included in the listing above.